New Richmond Surplus Electric
1930's

Bymaster Homstead

Shades State Park Hotel

Waterworks, Crawfordsville, Indiana

Compiled By The
Genealogy Section Of The
Montgomery County Historical Society

The materials were compiled and produced using available information; Turner Publishing Company regrets they cannot assume liability for errors or omissions.

Library of Congress
Catalog Card No.: 89-051787

ISBN: 978-1-68162-496-9

Created and Designed by: Mark A. Thompson, Independent Publishing Consultant for Turner Publishing Company

Book Design: Elizabeth Dennis
Paula Borman

Copyright 1989 by Genealogy Section of the Montgomery County Historical Society

Author: Genealogy Section of the Montgomery County Historical Society

This book or any part thereof may not be reproduced without the written consent of the Author and Publisher

Limited edition of 1,000 copies of which this copy is number _____

Haywood-Detchen Union Elevator built 1903, burned 1950.

TABLE OF CONTENTS

Genealogy Section of The Historical Society 4
Montgomery County Historical Society 6
Introduction 8
County History 9
    Brown Township 10
    Clark Township 14
    Coal Creek Township 16
    Franklin Township 17
    Madison Township 18
    Ripley Township 20
    Scott Township 21
    Sugar Creek Township 22
    Union Township 22
    Walnut Township 25
    Waynetown-Wayne Township 26
Feature Stories 27
Church History 47
Family History 77
Club History 363
Business History 367
Index 385

Alamo Post Office

GENEALOGY SECTION OF THE MONTGOMERY COUNTY HISTORICAL SOCIETY

In August of 1981, the Montgomery County Historical Society expanded its horizons to include interest groups: the first being their Genealogy Section. First officers in the group were: Eulalia Mason, Chair; Ralph Barker, Vice; Barbara Taylor, Secretary; Pat Ferguson, Treasurer; Al Boone, Historian and Karen Zach, Representative to the Historical Society.

Throughout the years, the members of the section have helped sponsor various genealogy-related endeavors, such as: how-to-seminars, workshops on history of the county; indexing projects (1860 Fountain County census, 1900-1936 newspapers); restoration work (helped save the early school class negatives, worked with the Courthouse clean-up); a family cookbook (collected and published old family recipes); Eagle Scout projects (helped with the cemetery update for the county, 1880 census index, 1969 newspaper index and cemeteries of townships of other counties which touch Montgomery); creation of new organizations (such as the nation-wide Orphans' Train Society).

Volunteers from the society have totalled thousands of hours of work in the Local History Room of the Crawfordville District Public Library helping historians of all walks of life research their given topic. Hundreds of books and much genealogical materials have also been donated.

The club sponsors are the *Balhinch Gazette*, a newsletter which comes out three times a year and is chocked-full of Montgomery County tidbits. It is edited by Barbara Taylor.

The Genealogy Section honors an individual for promoting genealogy by giving a Genealogists of the Year Award. Barbara Taylor, Al Boone, Ralph Barker, Pat Ferguson and Karen Zach have received the honor.

1989 Officers are: Norm Cramer, President; Mary Cramer, Vice; Karen Zach, Secretary; Barbara Taylor, Treasurer and Pat Ferguson, Historian. Ralph Barker serves as Montgomery County Historical Society Representative.

This year, 1989, we would like to thank the following for their aide in making the Montgomery County Family History Book a success.

HISTORY BOOK REPRESENTATIVES

BROWN TOWNSHIP
Terry Fullenwider
Sam Tom Patton
Lillian Presslor

CLARK TOWNSHIP
Corky Brewer
JoAnne Van Cleave

COAL CREEK TOWNSHIP
Frances Beardsley
Irene McCorkle
Joan Oppy

FRANKLIN TOWNSHIP
Ramona Ainsworth
Geneva Fugate

MADISON TOWNSHIP
Linda Burkle
Mary Wilkins

RIPLEY TOWNSHIP
Helen Rush
Joann Spragg

SCOTT TOWNSHIP
Imogene DeBusk
Larry Gentry

SUGAR CREEK TOWNSHIP
Phyllis Boots

UNION TOWNSHIP
Barbara Taylor
Karen Zach
Carolyn Ellis

(CRAWFORDSVILLE)
Gwen Frees
Becky Neideffer

WALNUT TOWNSHIP
Pauline Walters
Mr. & Mrs. Denver Feltner

WAYNE TOWNSHIP
Katherine Grimble
Maxine Rush
Businesses: Norm Cramer
Churches: Ralph Barker

"The Waveland Bandits" Participating in the Re-enactment of the 1932 attempted bank heist are from left to right: Dick Hockett, Les Shelton and Terry Fullenwider. All Waveland residents

THE MONTGOMERY COUNTY HISTORICAL SOCIETY AND LANE PLACE

Fascination with this county's past has a long history. Soon after the county was settled the first frontiersmen began creating an oral tradition about their experiences. The tradition was continued when the Old Settlers organized to hold annual meetings at which families met in wooded areas all over the county. These social outings, a day-long mix of storytelling, basket dinners and general hilarity, became the format for Montgomery County's first historic record keeping.

After the Civil War Peter Kennedy and Lew Wallace, both attorneys of Crawfordsville, advised that the records should be written down in order to preserve them. Wallace recommended that each township collect its own record. Kennedy wrote for Beckwith's county history published in 1881. Although he was not a resident until after the Civil War, he wrote about one dramatic experience of 1845. On June 16 county families gathered on the lawn at Lane Place to send their men folk off to the War with Mexico. This county formed the first volunteer regiment in the state. The women folk had made a silk banner for the men to take into battle—and Joanna Elston Lane, a 19-year old bride of the commander, made a patriotic speech from the west portico of the newly built house. Surely Kennedy had heard about this event from an Old Settler.

The seeds for organizing a formal group to preserve heritage germinated in late 1911 when the Dorothy Q Chapter of the Daughters of the American Revolution succeeded in influencing Dumont Kennedy, Peter K.'s son, and seven other incorporators. These organizers were: Kennedy; Alice and Claude Thompson (wife and son of author Maurice Thompson); Charles A. Tuttle; Julia Davidson Waugh; Addie Harding; Josephine Tuttle Thomas; and Theodore H. Ristine. Kennedy was chosen as president and served for fifteen years. Members of the DAR were given honorary memberships for 1912.

This small group was keenly aware of the importance of keeping the lives of Lew Wallace and Henry Smith Lane before the public for they had brought fame to this county, state and nation. The young historical society had another priority, however. The major effort was to be expended in collecting pioneer artifacts and locating all county log cabin sites. Residents of each township were urged to join in this project.

Storage and exhibit space became necessary after the collection mushroomed into more than members' homes and sheds could contain. So large show cases were purchased from local merchants and the relics were moved into the basement rooms of the Public Library.

Early minutes reveal that formal meetings were rare and were held anywhere from law offices to the Community House and finally at the DAR House. Open meetings were scheduled for the High School auditorium and consisted of lectures about the county's heritage. These latter meetings were well-reported the following day on the front page of the *Crawfordsville Review*. Thus was posterity served.

The Society supported and acted in the 1916 pageant staged in the Crawford Woods, the county's observance of Indiana's Centennial. In 1922 Kennedy proposed a re-dedication of the Offield monument. Hundreds motored out to the site and heard speeches and an original poem given by Mary Hannah Krout.

In 1930 Miss Helen Elston Smith, niece of Joanna Elston Lane, who had inherited the Lane Place property in 1914, offered a room at Lane Place for the Society's meetings. Then in 1931 Miss Smith, with her cousin and guardian Blair Taylor, offered the property to the Historical Society. Lane Place, built by the man who had secured Abraham Lincoln's nomination for president, was deeded to become the museum to perpetuate Henry Smith Lane's life and display the county's relics.

The following decade proved to be very difficult for the Society's thirty members paying $.50 dues per year. The property had a lien and it was the Depression era. Due to Shirl Herr's determination to save Lane Place and T.H. Ristine's legal guidance a lease agreement was made with the City Administration. The City would pay the debt and care for the exterior of the house and the grounds for 25 years, and the Historical Society would take care of the interior of the house and its collection. No doubt the struggle to achieve these goals was the greatest challenge the Society has faced in its 75-year history.

The care-taking proved to be necessarily minimal for decades, but thousands of visitors came and marveled at what they saw. The goals of preservation and education were being met, but other projects were done as well. The Speed cabin was preserved and resurrected at Milligan Park (1935). Members influenced the preservation of the covered bridges at Deer's Mill and Darlington. When the Civil Band played on the grounds at Lane Place, Lane Place had Open House—a popular program during Helen and John Remley's residency. In 1965 the Society earned recognition for Lane Place and Yount's Mill when the Civil War Commission erected historic markers at both sites.

With the 1970s came expanded educational programs. Oral histories were taped, transcribed and placed in the Library; various kinds of historic reviews were published in the *Journal-Review*; *Montgomery Magazine* became a monthly publication which was placed in all county libraries by the Historical Society. In 1978 the Society's first annual publication was printed for its membership. In 1979 the first annual Christmas Candlelight Tour of Historic Homes was introduced.

All of these visible projects presented an active organization at work. Membership increased by the hundreds with many more of them involved in all phases of the growth. The nation's focus on historic house preservation made local residents aware of the deteriorating condition of Lane Place.

The house of Greek-Revival design had been built in 1845 and remodeled in 1875, 1884, 1916 and 1922. The society's Board of Directors sought advice about feasibility of restoration by hiring an architectural-engineering consultant (1982). One year later work was begun.

Five years later two porches, and eight rooms had been repaired and decorated; a climate-control system had been installed; electrical system initiated; and a copper standing seam roof built to replace a badly deteriorating one. Some of the extensive exterior work was done by professionals, but almost all of the interior repair and decorating was the work of volunteer members. This restoration effort has been the largest project of preservation and education the Historical

Society has ever undertaken—and no doubt has created the greatest amount of publicity since the Society's founding in 1911.

Preservation of the 150-year-old historic home of Henry and Joanna Lane was not the only undertaking, however. During these same years society members helped plan the Ben-Hur Centennial observance. They staged countywide Bus Tours in June and October of 1983. During 1986 and '87 oral histories were taped and many of local resident's memories were incorporated in the documentary of the Lane Place Restoration. *Indians of Montgomery County, Henry Smith Lane: The Old War-Horse, Lew Wallace: Father of Ben-Hur,* and *Montgomery County Legend and Lore* were added to the list of publications written and financed by the Society. A Genealogy Section was organized, but is autonomous. A Preservation Section is presently being planned. Perhaps the greatest historical even to occur was the City's deeding of the Lane Place property to the Montgomery County Historical Society in 1988. The change was made possible by the gifts of many members and particularly that of Max Tannenbaum.

The development of this organization has been dynamic with every indication that its impact within the community will continue to help make Montgomery County a richly endowed place in which to live. Preserving the heritage and informing the community about it is one of the most vital programs its membership can pursue.

*Pictured here (l. to r. facing pic)
Front row: Barb Taylor, Karen Zach, Pat Ferguson, Mary Cramer, Mary Wilkins, Marcella Feltner. Back Row: Norm Cramer, Ralph Barker, Terry Fullenwider, Ramona Ainsworth, Geneva Fugate, Deb Nykamp, Denver Feltner, Dave Reed*

INTRODUCTION

Seventy-five years of silence concerning Montgomery County biographical information had just passed. Several excellent works on our county's history ("Some" of which are: *Sugar Creek Saga; Indians of Montgomery County; Montgomery County Legend & Lore*) have been published and Pat Cline and her Montgomery *County Magazine* staff continue to spread our county's rich history worldwide. Some of these works have biographical information included, but the compilation of a major biographical collection for the county has not been tackled; therefore, the Genealogy Section of the Montgomery County Historical Society decided it was high time to do something about it. A vote was taken, and under the leadership of President, Norm Cramer, it was (almost) unanimously agreed upon to celebrate the 75 years with a new biographical publication.

In the fall of 1988, the Genealogy group, as well as many interested individuals, met in the Meeting Room of the Crawfordsville District Public Library, formed committees and appointed representatives for each township.

Although these were the original interested parties, word soon spread and many others in our group, as well as the whole county. became involved in gathering biographical information, writing sketches, doing research, typing and telling the "good news." We thank you all!

Those working on the book met regularly in the public libraries for progress reports. Pat Ferguson,. historian for the club, absorbed the major brunt of the work collecting the biographies and we'd like to thank the staff of the library as many of these biographical sketches also travelled through their hands.

Considerable advertising of the book was done through the Crawfordsville *Journal Review, Montgomery County Magazine; Messenger Crier; WCVL*, all state genealogy columns excellent brochures *graciously* furnished by Turner Publishing Company, our club's newsletter (BAL-Hinch Gazette, Barb Taylor, editor), the Crawfordsville District Public Library's newsletter, a family history exhibit at the library, talks to local clubs and schools, sample books displayed in all county libraries, and of course, the thousands of hours of personal contacts logged by our area representative and other friends.

Over 900 biographies were collected,; 20 businesses, 31 churches, and seven organizations, also.

Many thanks are given to Mark Thompson, representative of Turner Publishing, without whose kindness, understanding and expertise, this book would not have been possible. Special thanks is given to each individual who took the time to compile his biography—future generations will commend you. Kudos to all of you who helped in ANY way!!

COUNTY HISTORY

Walter Kiley in 1904 Buick, one of the first "horseless carriages" in Clark Township.

BROWN TOWNSHIP

"WAVELAND"

Waveland is the oldest town in Brown Township and occupies the very southwest corner of both the township and Montgomery County, lying only two miles from the west line and one half mile from the south line. In the early period of settlement four towns were platted in Brown Twp. Waveland was the first, Browns Valley, Fairview and Deerford. The latter two have completely vanished as far as definite location is concerned. The name of Waveland was chosen because many of the early settlers came from Kentucky, near the Waveland Plantation. This plantation is five miles out of Lexington, Ky. and at this writing the beautiful old home and slave quarters are still standing and in excellent condition. This can be visited by tourist.

Probably the most outstanding gift to Waveland was the Andrew Carnegie Library, which was procured through the efforts of the Priscilla Circle of the Women's Club and Mr. and Mrs. Tom Huston who ran the Waveland Independent at that time. The library was completed and opened to the public in 1915, with over 1,000 books available. In 1989 there were well over 13,000 books plus magazines and video tapes, which were added in 1988.

In the early 1880s two railroad systems arrived at Waveland, with passenger and freight service. With the coming of semi-trucks, the railway service was soon gone and with it the railroads. The last of the railroad on the north side of town was removed in 1965.

In 1923 the Good brothers started a bus service and operated it for some 20 years or more.

After years of paths through the wilderness and dirt roads, the first State road to go through Waveland in 1919 was State Road 47, which followed the old Ben Hur Trail from Crawfordsville to Terre Haute. In the 1930s the road was resurveyed and rerouted with a concrete surface. The second State road was SR 59, intersecting with SR 47 on the north side of Waveland.

For several years a lime and stone quarry operated southwest of town on the railroad and a county road. This area was later used by the Conservation-Club for a recreation area, and east of that the Saddle Club has many of their meetings.

After a tragic fire in 1873 the citizens realized better fire equipment than a bucket brigade was needed. In 1896 the first horse-drawn engine was purchased for $585.00. In 1920 the first modernized truck was purchased; the present fire engine was purchased in 1986 at the cost of around $60,000.00.

In the 1800s there were four churches: the Baptist, Christian, Methodist and Presbyterian. In 1989 the Christian Church remains on west Main St. The Methodist and Presbyterian consolidated into the Methodist on East Green St.

Through the years Waveland and the surrounding community has seen many types of businesses. The first grist mill was built by Joel Deer in 1829. Thomas Armstrong built a carding mill in 1840. The first steam powered sawmill was operated in 1850. The boiler for it was brought from Indianapolis on two lumber wagons drawn by six horses, taking a week for the trip. In 1875 S.J. Milligan built the building on the northeast corner of Main and Cross. This housed a grocery and bakery, later a post office, to a beauty shop and at present a Pizza restaurant. The second floor was the Opera House, used for Opera, hometown programs and later on movies. A sawmill and Auctioneer business.

In the late 1920s a large building across from the library was destroyed by fire, taking with it several cars that were stored there. In years past this was the livery stable.

On February 5, 1932 a burglary was attempted at the bank, but with the Vigilante Organization in town the robbers were kept from blowing the safe open. Many others helped in getting word to other towns asking for help, as the telephone lines had been cut leading out of town. In 1985 (see pic) a re-enactment of the event was held.

In the 1930s the street movies and band concerts were quite popular, with large attendance and the business men extended their hours during the evening.

The Waveland Park was purchased by the Lion's Club, and with the help of the American Legion, Department Club and other organizations of the town improvements were made. Playground equipment was added. Yearly fish fries and carnivals were a tradition and in 1985 the expansion of a shelter house was added to the Park.

The construction of Lake Waveland, just west of Waveland on SR 47, by the Conservancy District has been an added attraction for the Waveland Community and brings business to the town. Visitors enjoy camping, boating and fishing. Also an added attraction is the Turkey Run Golf Club just west of the Lake entrance.

Waveland has had many gifted people who have lived or been raised in the town and community. The artist, T.C. Steele came here at a young age with his family in 1850. He attended public school and was later a secondary teacher at the Academy. After leaving he studied art in Cincinnati, then on to Munich, Germany and in 1900 his paintings were exhibited in Paris, France. His later years

East side of Cross Street in 1913

were spent near Nashville, Indiana, where his studio and home are open for public visits. His paintings are exhibited there and also at the Museum of Art in Indianapolis, as well as other locations. Another citizen, Mark Moore, invented the railroad signal. Barnett Harris invented the tranquilizer gun used in capturing wild animals. C.F. Crowder invented a combined typewriter and cash register. Waveland has also been the home of many State officials.

In 1834 John Milligan signed a deed to the Town of Waveland, however with transportation of the times the deed was not recorded at Crawfordsville until January 1835. The first lot was sold on Christmas Day 1835. In 1985 Waveland celebrated its sesquicentennial with a three-day celebration. It was a huge success. The last day a large parade was held with people from all over the county, participating. Food for the three days was served by all the organizations of the town, and everyone enjoyed the fellowship of the community. Waveland was incorporated in 1866 and August of that year the first election was held with 110 votes cast. At one time the town had a population of around 800 citizens. In 1989 there are approximately 600 citizens.

During the years a number of social circles existed; namely the Women's Club which started with the Coterie in 1906, later there were the REG studying books, art, history, plays and music. The Priscilla Club, a sewing Club. Several quilts were made by this group and sold during the years. The Current Events Club, The Mother's Circle, Flower and Garden Club with flower shows. In 1919 the REG and Priscilla were combined as the Department Club. In 1988 the name was changed to the Waveland Women's Club with one group membership. The younger groups had Rainbow and Girl Scouts. Men's organizations consisted of Mason's, Gun Club, Detective Association organized in 1915, Conservation Club for recreation and fishing, Eastern Star for men and women, I.O.O.F., Ancient Order of Workmen and K of P.

After World War I the American Legion was organized and the Waveland Raymond Todd Post #323 was chartered November 15, 1921, and later the Women's Legion Auxiliary was chartered in 1934. In 1989 the American Legion building was sold and the flags, etc. were moved to the Community Building.

In 1983 the Waveland Community Economic Development Corp was organized to promote, aid and control growth of the town. This organization helps with spring cleanup and any other projects needed. Money making projects were conducted and by 1986 the organization purchased the old Methodist Church building and deeded it to the town of Waveland to be used as a Community Center. Any group can use it for a nominal fee; Scout groups and other meetings for the Community organizations are free of charge. Family dinners, parties and weddings have been held from time to time.

The Urban Renewal Development purchased the Armory Building and it is an asset to the community.

In 1935 the State Fire Marshall condemned the gymnasium in the school constructed in 1912, and ordered it closed to the public because of fire exits. A new gymnasium was built in 1937, just west of the school. Later with the coming of more modern school systems on consolidation, Waveland was faced with the possibility of losing their school to a new area. With the aid of the members of the Waveland Community Economic Development, and much work on the part of the citizens of the community, ground was broken in March of 1985 for a new school building to be placed in front of the one built in 1912 (see picture), the new school to be for grades one through six. Due to consolidation with other schools of the south unit of Montgomery County a new school was built near New Market for Jr. and Sr. High School students. This school was called South Montgomery Jr./Sr. High School, but it is known as Southmont. The class of 1971 was the last graduating class of Waveland High School.

Basketball was always a great sport in the schools, and many times the team at Waveland went on to Sectional and Regional tournaments, one team going to State before being defeated.

Many incidents and much history has built the town and it would be hard to write anything about Waveland and get everyone and everything mentioned. Many names and many stories are naturally missed and not told, but a small town through years has many happy and sad times. Memories would write a book that would never end. Wishing Waveland a happy and prosperous future.

Assembled from Virginia Sharpe's book published in 1958 and material assembled by Lillian Presslor for the 1985 Sesquicentennial. Submitted by Lillian Presslor, Waveland, Indiana 1989

Much has been written about the Shades State Park in *Outdoor Indiana, Montgomery County Magazine* and various local newspapers (see also Joseph Frisz and Clay Overpeck biographies in this book), but this history would not be complete without at least the mention of the beauty of the park and the Pine Hills area in Brown Township, Montgomery County, Indiana. The Civilian Conservation Corps Camp located at the Shades played a prominent role in Brown Township's history, also, and much information about the CCC Camp can be gleaned from the Waveland newspaper (located in the Waveland Library) and from the Shady News newsletter for the camp (located in the Indiana Room, Indiana State Library).

"BROWNS VALLEY SINCE 1900"

Browns Valley (or, Brownsvalley) is an old town, having been platted on Dec. 17, 1836 by Matthias Vancleave. It is situated in roughly the middle of the township, and was on the old state road. It has been a trading center, has had stock yards and steam saw mills, which helped the town considerably when the railroad came through in the 1870's. For most of its existence, though, Browns Valley has remained small in size and population.

Previous histories of the county have roughly covered the early days of Browns Valley. I am going to pick it up around the turn of the century.

In 1900, the Missionary Baptist Church was about 26 years old, and the Christian Church was about two. The following were in business: Richard D. Allen, dry goods; Alex A. Mayhall, general store; J.W. Patton, grocer; Thomas (or T.F.) Patton, postmaster and T.F. Patton & Son, grocers; Patton & Bayless, livery; Lewis W. Reynolds, grocer and hardware; W.A. Servis, general store; and John Sharpe, blacksmith.

In 1903, J.C. Allen had a poultry wagon; William W. Bayless was a farmer and stock buyer; Jessie V. Boyland was a teacher; S.N. Boyland was assessor and carpenter; Michael Dailey was the section foreman of the Vandalia Railroad; T.J. Davis was a carpenter; S.T. Hicks was a barber; Bert A. Hill was a section hand on the Vandalia Railroad; A.W. Johnson was the agent for the Vandalia Railroad; James Lane was a painter; D.P. Liston was minister of the Baptist Church; W.S. Muck was a general merchant; Ida Owens was a telephone operator; J.W. Patton was a general merchant and postmaster; O.E. Servies was a blacksmith; W.A. Servies was a huckster; Clifford Whittington was an electrician; Charles Williams, Henry Williams, and W.T. Williams were carpenters; and G.T. Williams was a physician and surgeon.

The businesses in 1912 were: Adams Express Co., George F. Sensabaugh, agent; John C. Allen, livery, feed barn, and stock buyer; John W. Bayless, rural mail carrier; William W. Bayless, vice president of Browns Valley Bank and stock buyer; Jessie Boyland, school teacher; Browns Valley Bank—J.W. Todd, president, W.W. Bayless, vice president, L.M. McLeod, cashier; Browns Valley Telephone Co., F. Mason, president and manager; Jess Carrington, painter; Christian Church; James J. Clements, Clements and Moody, general merchandise; Thomas J. Davis, carpenter; Nellie Galey, school teacher; Robert Goff, painter; Birdie Hoss, school teacher; Walter and Iva Layne, telephone operators; Clem Ludlow, telegraph operator; Leslie M. McLeod, cashier Browns Valley Bank; Frank Mason, president and manager of Browns Valley Telephone Co.; Methodist Episcopal Church (built between 1907-09); Missionary Baptist Church; Charles W. Moody, Clements & Moody, general merchandise; James W. Patton, general merchandise and postmaster; post office; George F. Sensabaugh, agent Vandalia Railroad Co. and Adams Express Co.; Orville E. Servies, proprietor blacksmith shop; William A. Servies, huckster; John W. Todd, president of Browns Valley Bank; Spencer H. Wood, pastor of Missionary Baptist Church.

My father told me that he was told that the west room of Nellie Canine's house once sat behind the house across the alley and that Tom Patton (who built and lived in the house) had his postoffice there. His son, Jim Patton, later served as postmaster. Jim apparently had the postoffice in his store. Also, William Muck served as postmaster in the Knights of Pythias lodge building. Later, Clyde Patton (son of Tom and brother of Jim) ran a barber shop and postoffice in the K. of P. building. When the bank went out of the K. of P. up to the north end of town, Clyde rented the front as a restaurant, moving the barber shop and postoffice to the little building north of Steve Deer's store in the late 1920's. In the early 1940's Clyde moved the barber shop and postoffice in the Charlie Moody store building. Clyde and his wife Lottie died about 1945-46, and their daughter Mayme was postmistress when the postoffice closed in 1946.

The two-story brick K. of P. building was built between 1904 and 1905, as the bank was organized in 1905. The building housed on the first floor, Charlie Moody's store (on the east side), and the bank, barbershop, and postoffice (on the west side). On the second floor was the telephone exchange and an apartment for Walter Vancleave (lineman who took care of the telephone exchange), storage rooms for the Knights of Pythias and the Modern Woodmen lodges, and the main room, the lodge hall. In 1917 the building was sold to Preston Layne and then in 1923 to Doc Beeson, who eventually had it demolished by 1938.

The bank (started 1905) was moved to the north end of town in the early 1920's, when a new brick building was constructed. Officers of the bank included John Foster, Tude Canine, and Edgar Pitts. It was a class A bank and was closed about 1932 or 33. It was said that in the late 1920's some men tried to rob the Browns Valley Bank. They managed to cut through the vault door but were unable to break into the safe. That old safe wound up in the elevator office after the bank closed. As my grandfather, Ben Cornell, Sr., fixed the vault door, I've seen a part of that old vault door.

Charlie Moody built a new store building across from the K. of P. about 1933 or 34, and ran it until he died in 1940. Roy and Zella Clark had a store there in 1940 or 41, but then they moved up to the gas station by the elevator and had a lunch room and small grocery. They left in about 1942 and tried it again about 1948, 49. The Moody store building was Clyde Patton's barber shop and postoffice, and then after 1946 became a dwelling. My father lives there now.

Jim Patton had his store at one time on my father's property (just west of my father's house), and according to Lester Bayless, Reuben Miles had a small store there too. Dad said that there was an ice house out back, too. Eventually Jim Patton had his store in the north end of the frame building, until about 1912, and then he sold to Mr. Labaw. He sold out to Steve Deer between 1912-15, then Steve and Fannie ran it until Steve's death, and then Fannie ran it about five years more in the frame building, and then ten more years in the old bank building across the street. Fannie sold out to Edna Taylor in 1945, and Edna and Betty ran the store until 1975, when they sold it to Willard Ventro. Attempts were made to keep a store going, but to no avail. The old frame building was demolished, and the old bank/store is now a dwelling. At one time Bill "Hump" Vancleave had a store in a frame building that used to stand on my father's property. The only store in town presently is Asher's Produce, in the old gas station on the east side of town.

The telephone exchange had a variety of locations. Jess Carrington ran it for a while in one room of my parents' old house. Walter Vancleave bought it and ran it in about 1920. In the fall of 1921, Boss Bayless worked on a farm and Margaret was the switchboard operator, and when she got supper, Boss ran the switchboard. In 1932, the telephone company was moved to the Johnny Allen house (now belonging to the Bonebrake's).

The railroad came through in the 1870's and by 1878 there was a depot building. Agents since 1900 include: A.W. Johnson, George F. Sensabaugh; Roy Hardee (when laid off worked at Barney Brooks' garage); Orrin and Blanche Hooker; Mr. Turner; Mr. Abbott; a lady from Waveland who was agent for Waveland, Browns Valley, and New Market; and finally Herman Rouk who sold tickets out of the west side of the section crew's car house after the depot no longer was used. Dad said that the depot was used for storage and then was demolished between 1943 and 1946. The railroad was closed and the rails removed around 1981-82.

There was once a steam saw mill and a stock yard (perhaps the one run by Will Bayless, Johnny Allen, and Albert Rice). Harold Taylor recalled that when he was young he helped to run livestock to the stock yard. Both businesses were located west of the old elevator, between the railroad and the north side of the highway. The old elevator, which was once powered by steam, was built about 1904 and was run by William Bayless. It was called the Browns Valley Grain Co., after Will Bayless, the following were managers: Guy Haas (1915-19), Harry Hocker (1919-24), Frank Wilkinson (1924-29). Farm Bureau Coop bought out the elevator in 1929 and then the managers were: Fred Rice (1930-40), Nelson G. "Boss" Bayless (1940-50), followed by Earl French, Burley Grimes, and Don Myers. The operation was eventually rebuilt and finally moved to the Petty 7 acres across the tracks. The old elevator was closed and demolished in 1982, as the lease from the railroad ran out and they wanted too much for the property.

Blacksmiths were important to the town early on. Some of this century's blacksmiths included: Orville Servies, Mr. Wilson, Eldon and Verne Starnes (who also had an implement business), and finally my grandfather, Ben Cornell, Sr. Grandpa started in 1923 in a shop south of John Bayless' garage. He was there until it was torn down in about 1930, then he moved the operation down to his house until he quit in 1936 and went into carpentry and farming.

Browns Valley had two doctors after 1900. Dr. G.T. Williams was here until about 1904. Dr. H.H. Elmore, who started in 1903, was the last doctor, and he eventually left the practice and took up the ministry for the Freedom Baptist Church. Dad thought part of the house which used to stand behind Taylor's Grocery was used as the doctor's office. Jude Starnes had an ice cream stand in the old doctor's office before the bank was built.

S.N. Boyland once had a sawmill on his place—the Lester Bayless property. Lester told me that Mr. Boyland brought a piano all the way from Oregon to Browns Valley.

Bob Shamness had a shoe store and harness repair in the north end of the old frame store in the late teens. Also Johnny Allen had a livery barn and stud service from 1910-20. Andy Stillwell once lived in Maud Delp's house and he ran a dray line and stud service. Andy traded his house to Harry Thompson (bank manager) for forty acres north of Browns Valley.

At one time Browns Valley had a band (Fisher Galey, father of Nellie Canine and Marjorie Shanks, was in it). There was a community hall on the old school lot on the north end of town (now property of Greg Norman). Browns Valley also had a baseball club, and it even had movies shown for a time on the street by the frame store. Ed Armstrong told Dad that there was a log schoolhouse north of the John Bayless house during the last century, and later a frame school was eventually built in Norman's lot. The big brick school on the south end of town replaced the old school in 1904. It housed grades 1-8 and sometimes two more years of high school. The school was closed in 1938-39. Afterwards it was used for poultry, hogs, and then it was demolished about 1987.

John Bayless drove two ponies on the mail route in 1910 until he retired in 1919 or 20 to build his garage (now owned by the Graham's) and trucking business (it was used many years as a polling place, as was Mason's garage). Roy Bayless took over the route until his death in 1930.

In 1922 the Christian Church purchased the Methodist Church building and sold the old building to the Primitive Baptists. When that old building burned in 1936 the Primitive Baptists built a smaller frame building, which stands to this day. The tiny church disbanded in the 1960's or 70's, leaving only the Christian Church and the Missionary Baptist Church. The book *Three Steeples* is based on the three churches in Browns Valley.

In 1936 there was a terrible fire which started in the old Missionary Baptist parsonage garage (north of the church), and burnt the old Christian Church building, a barn, and skipped over to the Mary Todd house. Many people came to help put out the fire. Due to the volunteers efforts (and maybe some luck), the store and barber shop, John Bayless' house and garage, avoided being destroyed.

The highway came through in about 1930-32. After that, gas stations were built. Nig and Jamie Baldwin built one in about 1933 and then rented it and sold it to Bill and Lucille Redden in 1934. After Bill's death in the 1960's, Lucille ran it for a while and then sold it to Loren "Dutch" Hunt, who ran the station a number of years. Afterwards others tried to run it until the Norman's bought it. Finally the station was closed. Asher's Produce now occupies the building.

The other gas station was built by Dan and Tug Goodin for Barney Brooks in 1934. He ran it about 3 years and sold it to Paul Rhoads. Various people had businesses there including Roy and Zella Clark in 1948 or 49, and Bob Lewellen who worked in the garage. It eventually belonged to Texaco/DX/Sunoco, then it was sold to the Farm Bureau. Boss Bayless told me that when the station was being built, an old tramp passing by told Fred Rice that the station would never do well because it was on a "flatiron road"—hidden by the elevator and not easily seen from the road. Harold Kern also had the old veterinary office built originally as a garage.

Joe and Nellie Canine had a restaurant in their home in 1949-50, called the "Weatherill." Zella Clark helped them briefly. Afterwards, Doc Canine opened his chiropractic practice in his home.

Boss Bayless told me that he was in the vigilantes (the Horsethief Detectives Association), along with Steve Deer and Edgar Pitts. They were out with guns after the robbery at the Waveland bank (Dad added that Jess Carrington and Claude Wilson both were out with shotguns on the south end of town). Boss said that the robbers came through in a car and Edgar Pitts called, "Halt!" The car didn't stop, and the men didn't want to shoot because they weren't positive that it was the robbers. Boss thought the man in the back had a gun. There was a dispute about which way the car went. Steve and Edgar thought it headed up the state road, but Boss thought it went up the north road. Shortly afterwards the sheriff arrived (delayed by a flat tire) and said that the car didn't go up the state road.

There was once a veterinarian in town, across from the east gas station. Also, Bob Watson had a fertilizer plant in the 1970's. *Written By Bob Cornell*

CIRR Round House Waveland, Indiana

CLARK TOWNSHIP

Ladoga, with its shaded trees and stately old homes is the only existing town in Clark Township, Montgomery County, Indiana. The community claims "approximately 1,000" in population. It is ideally located on State Road 234 on a direct line from Indianapolis to the Shades State Park. On a flier from the Ladoga Jaycees, it is stated, "We believe you will like Ladoga and its friendly people ... its modern water plant, sanitary sewage disposal plant and adequate supply of electricity provide an atmosphere conducive to gracious COUNTRY living with CITY conveniences."

Ladoga today can boast of the above, as well as other added attractions, such as a fine post office (Mary Lou Zimmerman, current postmistress); shown is Frederick M. Long, 1st Rural Mail Carrier, a trained volunteer fire department, a beautiful school, a fine library, and an impressive park.

Town improvements in the last seventy-five years have included: 1937 — a "new" sewage system was completed. Total length of the system was 25,571 feet. Total cost of the system was about $77,000. The town provided about $36,000 and the Federal Government about $41,000.

Telephone services began in the early 1900's. Sometime in the late 30's or early 40's the Telephone Company was sold to the Detchon Company of New Richmond and moved the office from the upstairs over the Harris Grocery on the corner of Main and Washington to the downstairs rooms. Indiana Bell is today's telephone system.

1942-43—the old White Covered Bridge (originally built 1881 for $325) over Raccoon was replaced with a modern cement structure, at a cost of $4,000.

1946—an underground street lighting system was completed with 32 lights placed on metal posts.

1957—new 75,000 gallon water storage tanks was erected.

1967—New library built.

1972—Widened Washington Street by three feet on each side.

1972—Earl Anderson Public Park—now has a baseball field, basketball courts, football field, tennis courts, two shelter houses and nice playground equipment.

May 8, 1976—Ladoga Alumni Banquet—last chance to view old school.

1985-86—Main Street reworkings—new curbs, gutters installed. $211,688.00 cost of project.

Railroads have played an important role in Ladoga's development (as in many towns) in the last seventy-five years. The Central Indiana Railroad was built through Ladoga about 1888, but abandoned in 1930. The Monon had but four small diesel engines in 1947 and John W. Barriger, President, felt diesel power was more economical. Between 1946-49, 54 units were delivered. Three were lost within the first three months due to loss of wreckage at Ash Grove. On May 14, 1949, Ladoga had a big wreck, derailing 15 cars. In January, the following year there was another wreck near the same area. Passenger service was discontinued in 1967, and in September of 1968, the Monon and the L&N merged (final approval July 31, 1971). In July, 1947, one of the great events of Ladoga, as well as for the whole of Clark Township, occurred. This was, of course, the Monon Centennial. Wabash doesn't have the only Monon bell — Mary Etta Ronk, daughter of Mr. and Mrs. Paul Ronk was the "Monon Belle" who met the Centennial Train that year. Sadly, on January 8, 1986, the old Monon bridge, just south of Ladoga, toppled into the creek bed of Raccoon Creek and a new bridge eased into place — thus, another era passed! The CSX goes through Ladoga today.

One can hardly think of the Ladoga-Clark Township library without it being synonymous with the Peffley family name. Three sisters, daughter of Chester and Bertha (Overman) Peffley, have served as librarians—Betty Carmichael, Bertha Boone and present librarian, Carolyn Cross. Carolyn's assistants are JoAnne Vancleave, clerk and her son, Russell Cross, janitor. Library board members are: M/M Louis Goshorn, Joe Seale, Quentin Carney, Mark Kessler, Rosemary Duncan and Frances Sanders. The original library was in the same home where the Cross sisters' grandparents—M/M B.F. Overman lived. The present library building was completed in 1967 and the doors were opened to a real mess for several months as there were no book shelves, therefore, books were piled on the floor and in boxes — people crawled around on the floor and checked out books, anyway!

The Old Ladoga Normal School House (last used for the American Legion Post), over 100 years old still stands. In 1917, a high school building was erected to serve Clark Township. In 1940, a gym was added. In 1976-77, the present grade school was built. This year, 1989, Ladoga elementary (K-6) expects a 204 student enrollment and will employ 15 teachers. Charlie Coffman is principal.

Throughout the years, financial needs of the community have been taken care of by a Citizens Building and Loan (still in existence 1936), Citizens State Bank (closed 1926), Ladoga State Bank and Ladoga Federal Savings and Loan. Today, 1989, the Ladoga Branch of Bank One serves the community.

Some of the prominent businesses throughout the 20th century have been: Ladoga Canning Company (1903-50) "at the peak of the Pack they employed 300 people"; Ladoga Lumber and Coal Company, VanMeter Hardware, Ladoga Theatre (showed Shirley Temple's "Captain January" July 24-26 during Ladoga's Centennial Celebration in 1936), National Refining Company, McMurtrey Grocery, American Theatre, Hoosier Mineral Products, John B. Rogers Productions, Walter Riddlebarger Blacksmith, W.P. McIntire Dodge, Etter and Reeves Ford, Highpoint Oil, Young Metal Production; Myers & Myers Lumber, Bouse Pharmacy, Knox Hardware, Snyder Drugs, Ladoga Light Company, Quality Printers, Harshbarger Garage, Barnes Brothers Grocery (Sugar Creek Creamery located there), Henry Ragsdale Dead Animal Removal, Ladoga Laundromat, Golden Rule Garage, Charles Galloway Meat Market, People's Furniture, Perkins Funeral Home, Twin Rake Manufacturer, Indiana Vault, Hartman Elevator, Hotschier Photo Studio, White Lily Flour, Carney-Stewart Ford, Cottage Hotel, Branch Library at Parkersburg, Hicks Bakery, Ladoga Feed Store, Shelton Gas, Herman Davis Chevrolet, Little Motor Shop, Hillis and Oliver Machine Shop, McClellan, Hubble, Featherstone, Himes, and Graybill Truckers, Rainier Drug Store, Carrie Robbins Style Shoppe, Harshbarger Cement, Maple Hill Greenhouse, Gottschall Funeral Home, Hueston Clothing, Blaydes Store, Gates Tin Shop, Gibson Barber Shop, Harrison Gravel, Coffee Cup, Boone's Mill, Horn's Photography, Brookshire Hatchery, Bindhammer Shoes, Ladoga Journal (later Ladoga Leader), Ladoga Meat Market, The Berrys, Brunst Meat, Rapp

& Sons, Ullmayer Baker, Young Brothers Meat, Carriage Manufacturer, Cummings & Patterson Chevrolet, Good Brothers Bus Co., Redlines Bus, Elliott's Marathon, Barker Excavating, Hedge Monuments, Craig's, Hostetter's and Gray's Flower Shops, Sidener, Vergon, Foxworthy, Jackson, Brown, Flick and Cox Variety Stores, Havens Brothers, Werts Radio, Roy Stover's Store, Polar Ice and Fuel, Farmer's Supply Co., and several barbers, dentists, doctors and lawyers. Current merchants: Brewer's Furniture Store, Bank 1, Bob Aliff Auto Repair, Larry Burnett Grocery, Wilson's Meat, Kenny Vice Ford, Wright's Alignment, Lowe's Frozen Locker, Garlock & Gibson's Hardware, Crestline, Autumn Care, Bryan's Ladoga Tire Service, The Culvert, J&D Steele's Tree Surgery, J&M Gas Station, Lowe's Video, Byrd's Pizza, Wethington Family Restaurant, Prosser's Body Shop, Wethington All-American Homes, Chris Todd's Clip & Curl, Janet Moore's Hair Care, Service Lumber, Servies and Morgan Funeral Home, Stull's Body Shop; Bradley Styles-R-Us, Barnard Home Comfort Shop; McClure Grocery & Gas, Anderson's King Kone, L&M Lounge, John's Package Liquor, Brook's Cabinet Magician, Porter Insurance (also Byrd's), Heart Land Co-Op (Louis Himes, Agent) and possibly others.

Clubs are usually organized for good fellowship or mutual interest—some of these clubs and organizations active since 1913 were: Alpha Pi Omega, Bachelor Maids Culture Club, Calico Kitchen Cuties, Clark Township Home Ec Club, Detective Association #22 (1880-1932), Eastern Star, Agriculture Society, Ladoga National Guard (1921-26), Modern Woodmen, American Legion #82, G.A.R., United Confederate Vets, Order of Owls, Redman's Lodge, Chamber of Commerce, Boy Scouts, Girl Scouts, Ladoga Court #79 Tribe of Ben Hur, Friends of the Library, Get-Together, Good Humor, Happy Homemaker, IOOF, Job's Daughters, Hook & Needle Club, K of P, Ladoga Jaycees, Ladoga Music Club, Lions, Masons, Rebekahs, Tri-Kappa and Willing War Workers.

In 1961, the Indiana Children's Christian Home (then called "Ladoga Children's Home") was built. 219 young people were provided homes in the first 16 years of its existence and many are Montgomery County citizens today. In 1980, the home became a residential treatment center for delinquent youth. It features a new school and hard-working teachers for the troubled young.

Current churches in Clark Township include the Christian, Presbyterian, Nazarene, Church of Christ, Baptist and Haw Creek. Others having been active in the area in the last 75 years were: Lutheran, Catholic, German Baptist, Methodist Episcopal, Bethel, Wesley Chapel, and Brethern. Some of these churches had adjoining cemeteries (13 known graveyards in the township, three of which are still accepting burials). Many of the town's pioneers are buried in the Poplar Grove (now Ladoga) cemetery. Chet Vice is current care taker. The War Memorial Monument was erected by the Bachelor Maid's Culture Club in 1927 and placed in the middle of the street of Washington and Main in Ladoga, but when Main Street became 234, the monument was moved to the cemetery (1938).

Town board members today are: Chet Vice, Jim Harris and Bob Sandusky. Township Trustee is Donald Rhoads. Ladoga continues as a thriving community and is the heartthrob of Clark Township, Montgomery County, Indiana.

Also pictured here is Walter Kiley in his 1904 Buick, probably the first "horseless carriage" in Clark Township.

Submitted by: Karen Zach

Much information was taken from the Ladoga Sesquicentennial History and Librarians, Carolyn Cross and Joanne Vancleave. Thanks also to Keith Houk for his expertise. Pictures contributed by: Mildred Leckrone and Mary McAllister

Fredick M. Long, first rural mail carrier, R.R. #1 Lodoga, Indiana-Clark Township 1909

COAL CREEK TOWNSHIP

Many changes have taken place in the last three-quarters of a century in the Hoosier State. Coal Creek Township, in the extreme northwest portion of Montgomery County and named for the stream that originates there, is no exception.

New Richmond and Wingate, the township's two incorporated towns, still exist but now have smaller populations. The 1910 census of New Richmond listed 464; Wingate listed 446. By 1980 New Richmond had decreased to 402 and Wingate to 372. Elmdale, once a thriving village but never incorporated, now has one church and a few houses. The entire township had 2290 people in 1910; by 1980 the population decreased to 1529. The assessed valuation of the township has increased from $1,909,470 in 1912 to $8,858,180 in 1988.

The school system has made great changes, decreasing in number of schools, consolidating and putting more students into larger, state of the art, facilities. In the early 1900's as many as 14 schools were listed in the township. In 1913, Center, the last one-room school, closed. Elmdale's high school was discontinued in 1912, its elementary school in 1932. The New Richmond and Wingate schools consolidated in 1953 in a new educational complex located between the two towns and called Coal Creek Central. All township children attended grades 1 through 12 there until North Montgomery High School located at 575N on Route 231 opened its doors in 1971. Northridge Middle School, grades 6-8, was built west of the high school and opened in 1987. Coal Creek Central closed when the new grade school, Pleasant Hill, opened in the fall of 1988. This grade school, which is the last remaining school in Coal Creek Township, is located in the southeastern corner of the township. All Coal Creek children from kindergarten-5 grades, and many from adjourning townships, attend this school.

While churches have changed in many ways in the past three-quarters of a century, most that were active then are still in existence and hold services. Two have disappeared. Round Hill Methodist, located approximately four miles south of New Richmond, closed and was razed in the 1930's. Bethel Baptist at Elmdale discontinued services in 1940, and the building was converted into a residence. Wingate Methodist is now known as New Hope Chapel, while Elmdale Methodist is Elmdale Community Church. New Richmond United Methodist is presently the only Methodist church in the township. Wingate Christian is now called United Church of Christ. Only New Richmond Christian and Center Congregational now have active Christian Church lineage.

The railroad built through Coal Creek Township in the 1880's was a very important addition to both towns and contributed greatly to the growth of the whole community. It served the area for over a century hauling freight and, much of the time, providing passenger service. Economic factors forced discontinuance of the trains, and in 1988 the rail company started pulling up the tracks.

During times of war and conflict, many people of Coal Creek Township served their country bravely. Shortly after World War II veterans formed American Legion Posts and Auxiliaries. Still remaining are The New Richmond Todd Post #458 and the Wingate Post #174 and its Auxiliary. Of the several fraternal organizations that were active in the township, only Mercer Masonic Lodge #633 of Wingate and New Richmond Masonic Lodge #604 and New Richmond Chapter #377 Order of the Eastern Star are still chartered.

In 1913 and 1914 Wingate entered Indiana's high school basketball championship's list when their boys won consecutive state championships. It was a remarkable feat in view of the fact Wingate had no gymnasium. The team traveled by horse and buggy to New Richmond once a week to practice and other nights they ran 20 minutes in their own high school auditorium. Word of their victories made hearts leap in Wingate, and great bonfires blazed in celebration to honor the champions. At that time there were only about 60 students in Wingate High School. Members of Wingate's famous teams were: John Blacker, Forest Crane, Jesse Graves, McKinley Murdock, Leland Olin, Lee Sinclair, Homer Stonebraker, Paul Swank and Lee Thorne. The 1913 coach was Jesse Wood; the 1914 coach was Leonard Lehman.

In the autumn of 1985 there was great excitement in New Richmond when a movie company shot scenes in the town. The film was **Hoosiers,** starring Gene Hackman as a coach who took a small school's team to the state championship game and won. The story was based on the victory of Milan in 1952. Clothes of the 50's came out of closets, New Richmond was renamed Hickory and a wildfire of excitement filled the town. A richly nostalgic film was produced which won hearts nationwide.

The business picture of the township over the past 75 years has been fluid, businesses and professional people coming and going as needs demanded. In 1988 the existing businesses are:

New Richmond—Hometown Furniture (formerly Alexander's), Altra (pre-cut sewing kits), Barnes' Crafts & Critters, Elpha's Pinch & Curl Beauty Shop, Heartland Co-op Elevator, Hickory Cafe, Kelp Shell Oil Distributor, Kunkel Plumbing and Heating, New Richmond Bar & Grill, New Richmond Branch Linden State Bank, Snellenbarger Oil Company, Thayer's Service Station, Tri-County Telephone Company, Waltz Trucking.

Wingate—Advance Electronics (Foster's Repair Service), B. & B. Lumber Company (Bane Building Contractor), Bank One, Dazey's Garage, Elsie's Place (convenience store), Gross Lime & Stone Hauling, Haase Trucking, Heartland Co-Op Elevator, Jones Machine Shop, Keil Bros. Oil Co., Lawson Gun Shop, Lidester Horse Training and Boarding, M.H. Bookkeeping & Tax Service, Lindley-Johnson Insurance (formerly Oxley Agency), Pipher's Radiator Repair Service, The Old Drugstore Restaurant, Priscilla's Beauty Salon, The Paper Shop, Roger's Tree Trimming Spray Painting, Stephens Apiaries, Stone's Upholstery, VanHook Trucking, Wilson's Wingate Fertilizer, and Wingate Bar & Grill.

Coal Creek Township—Bane Equipment Sales, Bane Saw Mill, Country Corner Beauty Shop, Dave Brown's Repair Service, Emerald Acres Alfalfa Cubes, Horton's New Horizons Greenhouse, Keith's Blacksmith & Ferrier Service, Larry's Taxidermy, Meharry Ag Service, Meharry's Farm Service Center, Meritt Auction Service, Padgett Remodeling and Construction, Snellenbarger's Wingate Garage, United Farm Tools, Verhey Erection Inc., Weaver's Popcorn Research Facility, and several commercial hog farms.

Many names of the early settlers are still in Coal Creek Township. Among them are the names Alexander, Brown,

Oppy home near New Richmond, built in 1863 Sarah Oppy at gate, George Oppy behind fence, Ernest Oppy their son in front of fence, Jack Oppy never married, Ed Oppy sitting in photographer's 1908 Maxwell.

Clark, Cook, Coon, Dazey, Grenard, Meharry, Oppy, Patton, Smith, and Thompson. Some of these are descendants of original settlers. It is regrettable space does not permit the mention of all the other important names. Coal Creek residents work and hope for prosperity and good living conditions for future generations.

Written by: Coal Creek Township Resident

FRANKLIN TOWNSHIP

LANDMARKS

Franklin Township history begins with landmarks and milestones in and about Darlington, now more than 150 years old, in the heart of the farming community.

Sugar Creek has supplied power for mills; holes for fishing and swimming; boating pleasures; the bayou for skating—all in turn as the season allows. Vivid are the scenes of the 1913 flood and the ice jam of the 1930's.

Today, canoe enthusiasts crowd the banks to watch the annual canoe races, in mid-April.

Honey Creek lends picturesqueness as its course cuts behind the toll house. This old shelter, restored and furnished, now is open to local groups as a community center.

At the west extension of Main St. stands the covered bridge spanning Sugar Creek, closed to traffic in 1976—a project of restoration under the park board, today. A new bridge carries traffic.

The grain elevator marks the site where farmers weighed in the harvest in exchange for wealth.

Gone from the landscape are: Franklin Mills, with its overshot wheel; the Vandalia Depot; the Pennsylvania overpass of the late 1970's; and the iron bridge over Sugar Creek, in the late 1960's.

CULTURAL INFLUENCES

Churches of Franklin Township, in spite of somber chapters in latter history remain a spiritual force in the life of the residents. In the first three decades, five denominations in town held regular worship services-Christian, Congregational, Presbyterian, Friends, and Methodist. About as many rural neighborhoods remained active—Gravelly Run, Lutheran, Shannondale (Bethel), and Center Grove.

Changes have taken place over the years: about 1921, the Congregational Church welcomed the remnant of Center Grove in fellowship. The Presbyterians in 1937, the Friends in 1927, closed their doors, occasioned by old age and death.

Gravelly Run holds Bible study in the church built in 1880. Lutheran closed in 1966, razed the building and erected a memorial on the site, holding the original bell. Shannondale (Bethel) has been serving the farm community for over 150 years.

The Christian Church keeps a strong focus on missions; has built an educational unit and installed a stained glass window. The Darlington United Methodist Church has added an educational unit; and built a new parsonage in the 1970's.

The Darlington Area Fellowship of Churches is a thriving expression of unity and faith, which sponsors Vacation Bible School.

The community supported a local small-town newspaper for many years. One publisher, starting in 1913, issued *The Herald* for thirty-one years. After 1944 another publisher-printer continued until 1951, when *The Herald* was suspended.

The Sunshine Theater afforded entertainment and enlightenment for all in the 1920's throughout the 1950's.

The studious and those seeking quiet absorption retired to the public library.

A variety of adult and youth organizations has served civic cultural interests-Scouts-Boy, Girl; 4-H-Boys, Girls; Jaycees; Conservation; Garden Club; Farm Bureau; Homemakers Extension Club—still active. No longer active, today, are Home Art Club; Fortnightly Needle; Lions; Thursday Afternoon; and several lodges. The Booklovers, more than eighty years old, still meets every two weeks.

Organizations serving military interests include the American Legion Post #302, chartered in 1945, meeting in its own clubhouse since 1964, and its auxiliary unit. The Armory Club promoting pride in the new National Guard Armory, dedicated in 1936, sponsored community functions, several years.

HEALTH AND RECREATION

In the interest of public health, the town under the supervision of the EPA, installed a sewage system and a sanitation plant in the 1980's. In late 1988, old buried gasoline tanks at service stations were ordered removed to avoid pollution.

Formerly, two or three resident doctors and a dentist served the community. Currently, doctors from Crawfordsville keep office hours on a part-time basis. County ambulance service, assisted by the local EMP, bring prompt response to emergency calls.

Since 1971, a lady veterinarian specializing in small animals, replaces the full scale vets of 20's-60's.

For many, recreation has centered around the school sports program. Summer League activities involved whole families. Facilities within driving distance offer rendezvous for skaters, bowlers, golfers, square dancers, and movie goers. Coon hunters revel in the chase. Horse race enthusiasts raised, trained, and raced their own for ribbons.

GOVERNMENT

Headquarters for civic authority and town business is the Darlington Town Office dedicated in 1966, located on S. Franklin, off Main St. A town board, clerk-treasurer, and utility clerk represent local government. A township trustee administers township funds.

Law enforcement rests with the town marshal and his deputy, provided with a portable oxygen unit. A pager system is in use.

BUSINESS AND SERVICES

Vacant store rooms bear witness to the passing of former merchants from Main St. Householders welcome new ventures, such as the Toll-Bridge Grocery, True Value Hardware, Spi-Binding Co., the monument shop, a restaurant, Dar-Ray Battery, the Hair Den ...

Today, the former Farmers and Merchants State Bank, under new management, has adopted the name, The Heritage Bank and Trust Company, has added more working area, and has computerized bookkeeping.

Postal service to the community is dispatched through a new brick office dedicated in 1945, equipped with lock boxes and air conditioning. Rural delivery is limited to one route.

Mortuary services are rendered by local proprietorship at a beautiful chapel on W. Main. Local memorial grounds under prudent boards of directors evoke civic pride and support.

The Darlington Telephone Company passed from private ownership to Indiana Bell in 1954. Cables were buried. New equipment and a modern dial system were introduced in 1957.

A twelve-member volunteer fire department has provided protection to both Franklin and Sugar Creek Townships since 1961. Upgraded equipment enables the force to meet emergencies.

Electric Light and Power, owned by the town, supplies current at monthly rates. For rural areas, Tipmont R.E.M.C. is the supplier since 1940.

The Darlington Water Works, under private ownership over the years, supplies water from driven wells. An electric pumping station and an elevated water tower have been installed to meet needs of the townspeople. Beauty shops encourage personal grooming.

CHANGES

Old SR 47, a concrete surface, laid about 1920, entered Darlington over Madison on its way between Crawfordsville and Thorntown. In 1960 an altered course of blacktop skirted the town on the south. Street lights and paved streets have for many decades spoken for the progressive spirit of the citizens. New apartment buildings add appeal.

Main Street has changed, but community spirit is alive. Natives take pride in our town and community, which once made the celebrated Ripley Column-Believe It or Not: "Darlington, on the banks of Honey Creek and Sugar Creek, the sweetest town on earth".

Signposts spelling out welcome and civic pride mark entrances to Darlington, just off SR 47-e.g. "The Good Life".
Submitted by: Ramona Ainsworth

MADISON TOWNSHIP

The story of Madison Township is the story of two communities: Linden and Kirkpatrick.

Linden, 1850, was located on the old stage road connecting Crawfordsville and Lafayette. The last half of the nineteenth century saw great areas of swamp drained, population increase and factories locate; broom and chair manufacturing and the Marsden Company; a complex of eleven buildings producing primarily cellulose from the pith of corn stalks. In peak season employing 100 men.

Kirkpatrick, growing rapidly, had two large grain elevators and a dozen of so businesses including a saw mill and a bank. In 1900 a school was built for grades 1-8 and the population numbered nearly 150.

The hub of each town was the railroad. The Monon running north and south and the Cloverleaf of Nickle Plate intersecting at Linden, going on east through Kirkpatrick.

In the early 1900's the depot was a hive of commercial and social activity. Because two rail-lines crossed at Linden the depot was unique: although both lines shared a common waiting room each had separate ticket and baggage areas. The Monon ran eight trains a day while the Cloverleaf ran four. Linden became the second largest grain shipping point in the county. Interurban trains for shopping or visiting trips were popular and so much freight was handled that a large warehouse was built north of the tracks and dray and taxi services began. Drummers arriving by rail made one of Linden's two hotels their headquarters while making their business calls in the area by rented rig from the livery.

Opening the door of the world to these two communities the railroad took our students away to college and took our sons to the Civil War and to too many wars after, and sorrowfully, it didn't bring all of them home again.

The new century had disastrous setbacks in store for these two burgeoning towns.

In 1908 the Marsden Company exploded and burned, never to be rebuilt; taking with it jobs and a great corn byproduct market.

June 1917, the giver of life to Kirkpatrick was involved in the "beginning of the end" for this town. Seven rail cars filled with gasoline derailed and burned taking out an elevator and several businesses and homes. The heat was so intense that 150' of rail was melted. The fire and the "shrinking" of the township due to motorized vehicles soon made the consolidation with Linden of church, school and bank an economic necessity. Today there is an elevator, a few homes, a long abandoned store and about 20 people in Kirkpatrick. In the Spring of 1989 the rails of the old Nickle Plate were taken up, severing the once vital artery.

Linden survived the Marsden disaster and supported by the lifeblood of the township, the family farm moved forward. Hard work was the way of life. The land didn't give of its fruits easily-long hard hours produced a living from the farm. In town, shops, the railroad and later the utility companies were major employers.

Until the late teens the gravel streets were maintained by the able bodied men between the ages of 21 and 50 who were required by law to give four days work on the streets annually. When the automobile became widely used it became necessary to oil and later pave the streets to keep the dust down.

Dust——the ever present plague to women and their homes. From roads, fields and heating fuels DUST got everywhere. AND THE DREADED SPRING CLEANING RITUAL WAS BORN!!!! Since in those days the upkeep of her home, the appearance of her laundry on the line, and possibly, the way her children turned out were the marks of a woman's worth, so each Spring the house was attacked. Rugs were rolled up and taken outside to be beaten with a vengeance; every drawer and cupboard was emptied and scrubbed, all draperies and curtains washed and in some cases starched and hung on stretchers to dry as stiff as a board; featherbeds and pillows drug outside by grumbling husbands and sons to be filled with new goose down, which she had plucked from her own geese, or at least to be aired and fluffed. Windows were rubbed to a sparkle and every inch of interior wood scrubbed, waxed and polished to a glistening shine; wallpaper and paint either cleaned or replaced. Once all of this was done she could resume her normal routine of working 12-14 hours a day completing her everyday chores: three big meals a day, doing laundry etc. without running water, much less hot water, no appliances and a wood burning cook stove. During the summer she also raised, canned, preserved, pickled and dried everything from the garden. Well so much for the "good old days before women worked".

School and chores were a part of every child's life but what a time to be a kid. Freedom to explore the area and themselves. Not much traffic—and crime was something read about in detective magazines or the theme of the show at the local movie house.

Seemingly endless days of sunshine, bike riding, playing made up games or ball or just plain loafing, ah! what a luxury; loafing without guilt.

As life became a little easier people began to have time for leisure activities. In 1915 the Will of Jane M. Stoddard left the town an area "to be beautified, occupied and used as a park". Over the years trees have been planted, a pavilion built and a stone memorial arch erected. For the past 75 years the community has indeed "occupied, used" and enjoyed Mrs. Stoddard's gift.

Sports became a preoccupation if not an obsession. Kirkpatrick had a men's baseball team and in the 1920's Linden had a 15 man football team. Each player played both offense and defense; they had uniforms with thin leather helmets but no pads. There was no passing just bone crushing line contact. Some games were played in a field across from the cemetery, an appropriate location, and had a following of 3-400 fans for a Sunday afternoon game.

The school was a focal point of the community and basketball the primary passion. Between 1932 and 1971 when the high school was closed, the Linden Bulldogs won six County championships. After a ballgame everyone crowded into the restaurant, parents, kids and all to rehash the game and visit over hamburgers, fries and a coke.

Summer baseball and girls softball have long been popular. Ralph Waltz was a great supporter of sports and kids. From his own pocket he financed the lighting of the ball diamond, and any kid who needed it was given a glove.

In the 30's, 40's and 50's the town was full of people every Saturday night. The stores were open and, when a novelty, a TV was played at the Square Corner Hardware for all to see. Free movies were shown on makeshift screens stretched across a street or at the ball diamond. The Linden Orchestra sometimes gave openair concerts; there were traveling stage shows and circuses arriving by train. Every kid in town witnessed the unloading of the circus train.

A roller skating rink above the hardware was a great courting spot. Around and around they glided to the recorded music but since people from all over the county attended, the main activity was "seeing and being seen".

Harvest time was always special, capped off with Halloween pranks that kept some kids in trouble nearly to Thanksgiving. Caroling parties, sledding and just gathering at the drug store, barbershop or restaurant to catch up on the news" were favorite winter activities—hometown entertainment by hometown people. There was some "keeping up with the Joneses" but at least then we knew who the "Joneses" were.

The small town telephone system, before dial, was a novel tool. An operator (Tannie Blair comes to mind) had the switchboard in her home; the upstairs of a downtown building which had a large balcony overlooking main street. When you made a call Tannie answered, "Central" and after a little conversation with her about this and that you told her who you wished to speak with, by name; no numbers needed. Tannie would hook you up or she might say, "she's not at home, I just saw her go into the drug store, etc." "Central" was called often to see if an absent husband or child could be seen downtown around meal time. She was an ever-present emergency squad.

Dotted along country roads are squares of green where a home once stood. Overgrown fruit trees and lilacs still bloom, and gray weathered crib or barn house, rusty, castoff machinery. The drive nearly reclaimed by the grasses and weeds; Iris and Peony bushes stretch for the sun near where the house once stood. Giant old trees dance their slow patient dance in the Spring wind as an ancient cedar silently stands watch for those who will return no more. These victims of

Town of Linden, early 1960's

"more land in fewer hands" may soon be joined by others of our township. The family farm is in the last battle for survival.

The last three decades have been very traumatic. We have survived war, Depression, blizzard and drought, but now we face an even more dangerous enemy; apathy. Linden has changed a lot over the past few years, the hardware building burnt and a vacant lot now holds that spot on main street. Business after business has closed; the buildings fallen into disrepair. There are still many businesses in town but for the most part they are not "people" businesses or services but rather wholesale and storage. Tipmont REMC, celebrating its 50th anniversary, continues to be a bright spot as does the Linden State Bank, opening a branch in Crawfordsville in June of 1989, but for the most part our citizens work and shop elsewhere.

Change is not always bad, but we have lost so much "flavor" from our lives; there are things we just simply miss. The chugging of a steam engine with its shrill whistle and the great hiss and cloud of steam as the brakes slowed her to a stop at the depot. No train stops here at all and the east/west tracks have been ripped up. We miss a town full of friends and neighbors on a warm, sultry Saturday night, or just quietly relaxing on the porch after supper and knowing everyone in town—people you loved or hated, celebrated and cried with.

For the first time in over a century there is no school in Madison township. This is perhaps the deadliest blow of all because the school departure stole the town's identity and lifeblood. There are no young people coming on to replenish the town's soul; they will not care about what they do not truly feel or know. We are cheated, but, oh, so are they; for they will never know the joy of a "hometown" that we so cherish.

According to the dictionary, a "community" is the people of the same area sharing like needs; while a "town" is a concentration of houses and buildings. Madison Township faces the toughest challenge of her history: to prevent our "community" from becoming—just a "town".

Dedicated to three people, recently lost, who personified Linden; Ike and Hallie McBee and Ruth I. White. By: Rebecca L. Royer

RIPLEY TOWNSHIP

Today, Alamo is the only incorporated town in Ripley Township, Montgomery County, Indiana. The purpose of the town was to be a small trading center for nearby farmers. It was named for the famous Alamo Mission where the great struggle and massacre occurred, which was the foremost topic of discussion when the *Crawfordsville Record* (January 11, 1837) advertised the selling of lots in the newly formed village. In 1840, the first store was built by Noah Grimes. By 1881, there were three stores, one harness shop, three blacksmiths, two wagon shops, copper shop, tile mill, saw mill and undertaker. In the early 1900s, Tilman Gass had a horsedrawn hack (complete with curtains for bad weather) that ran from Alamo to Crawfordsville. 1918 was a bad year as three buildings in the town area were burned down. In the 1920s, a hotel, millinery, woodworking shop, coffin maker, pottery, barber, livery stable, billiard parlor and creamery (with ice cream for the youngsters) were added. There was also three churches. Until about 1930, Alamo was quite fortunate to have some excellent doctors.

In the 1930's - 50's, an especially favorite time of year was summer when picture shows were shown on the streets, dances were held in Etter's upstairs store room, Vacation Bible School was enjoyed, 4-H workers were active and yearly homecomings under the Big Tent were held on the school grounds (later moved to the church yard). Likely the most exciting of the homecomings was held in August of 1937 when the Centennial of Alamo was celebrated. A display of Alamo memorabilia was enjoyed by a large crowd. A loud speaker enabled all to hear the 2 o'clock program which began by the singing of "America." More information on the event can be found in the July 1979 *Montgomery County Magazine*.

An interesting memory to many old Alamo residents (as well as descendants of theirs) is the town pump. It was located in the public square and was encased in a cement trough. It was built August 30, 1906. About 1913, a major event was when the circus came to the community - the elephants and other animals drank from the town pump, along with the Alamo citizens.

In the teens, like many towns, Alamo had sidewalks made of saw dust. The street lights were coal oil lamps and yes, there truly was an "old lamp lighter of long, long ago!"

Improvements in the town have included a telephone system (the first one being owned by Dan McSpadden and operated from his home) - later a telephone company was organized with a manual system and in 1965 with Indiana Bell, Alamo residents could dial! About 1924, the townsfolk could blow out the candles and turn on their lights which were furnished by Crawfordsville Electric Light and Power — Public Service took over later. In the early days, there were many fires since most homes were wood framed, had wooden shingled roofs and were heated by wood. Men, women and children came out to help fight a fire with wooden and metal buckets. Today a trained Volunteer Fire Department of 21 men is led by Fire Chief Max Nichols. Law enforcement has mainly consisted of those men who belonged to the Horse Thief Detective Association and a Town Marshall.

Alamo today is not the thriving metropolis Samuel Truax hoped it would become when he gave 40 acres of his own land for its growth; however, it is a happy little community with a Post Office (Lottie White, Postmistress), Harvey's Machine Shop, Masonic Lodge/ Eastern Star, and a saw mill. Alamo's only church is the Christian Church with 274 members and Rev. James Daniel as its Pastor. The town has 175 people (1,023 in Ripley Township), and remains a quiet little village in the Southwest part of Montgomery County, one perhaps old Sam would love.

In 1975, Scott Selby, then 86 years old had lived 80 of those years in or near Alamo. He wrote of Old Sam Truax's village, "It is altogether a rather happy little town - we're all one big happy family!" Now, 13 years later, it seems very much the same!

Hibernia, meaning "Winter Quarters" was never much of a town. At one time, there was a small community with an excellent mill (Gilkey's) and a school (which became defunct in 1913). There were other Ripley Township schools in existence that year but the two main ones were at Yountsville (until 1938) and Alamo (until 1967 when the last four

Ripley Township Float 1925. Every Fall Montgomery County had a Fall Festival. Each township had a float in the parade, this float won second place. Queen-Reba (Fink) Swearingen, twins left-Edith (Elmore) Hauser and right-Ethel (Elmore) Boyle.

pupils graduated). With all the Ripley Township youngsters attending Alamo, Coach Tom Bowerman saw some mighty good players which held County Basketball Championships in 1946 and 57 with 1934 and 1938 Championships prior to his arrival. His baseball Championships were in 40, 41, 42 and 47 with 1936 and 1937 prior. Overall, under Tom's coachmanship, the Alamo Warriors totalled 65 wins and 54 losses in baseball and 217 wins and 210 losses in basketball from 1939 to 1961; a mighty fine record!

Alamo school still holds get-togethers for past classes (in the Fire Department) and had 119 attend in 1989. An excellent source of interest on area education is Ruth and Harold McCormick's *Ripley Township Schools - Montgomery County, Indiana* found in the Crawfordsville District Public Library.

In Yountsville, the other major town Ripley has owned, the prominent business was, of course, the woolen mill which has recently been renovated by (Bless Them) Mr. and Mr. John Hardwick. See the July 1979 *Montgomery County Magazine* for information on Yountsville Mill. The town also had a Post Office, Church, School, Factory and Stores earlier.

Ripley Township residents seek, record and enjoy history. A parade, Pony Express rider, antique exhibits, food and period dress highlighted a Sesquicentennial celebration on October 27, 1984. In 1987, Helen Rush, Edith Hauser (and son, Bill) discovered an unindexed cemetery with four stones and copied the information. Impressive well-kept cemeteries under Twp. Trustee, Max Tucker, are abundant in Ripley Township, the major ones being McCormick, Sparks, Stonebraker, Vaughn, Denman, Moore, Wright and Texas. The body of the controversial Revolutionary War Soldier George Fruits (his biography is in this book) is buried in the Bunker Hill Cemetery and the tallest tombstone (60 ton granite stone, 9' 3" square on a 5' cement slab), in Montgomery County belongs to Joe Willis, patent medicine (Pansy Compound) maker, who is buried in Alamo.

The most impressive thing about Ripley Township, however, is the scenery — thick forests, wild flowers and wild animals still exist in one of the most beautiful areas in our state! *Written by: Karen Zach, with help from Helen Rush, Pat Ferguson, Tom Bowerman, Max Nichols and Debbie Barry.*

Special thanks to Bob Elmore for his pictures.

SCOTT TOWNSHIP

Scott Township is located in the south central portion of Montgomery County. It is bordered by Putnam County on the south, Brown Township on the west and Clark Township on the east. The population of Scott Township in the 1980 United States census was 824 people. It comprises all of the congressional township number 17, Range 4 west and contains 36 square miles.

The town of Parkersburg and a portion of the town of New Market are the only towns in Scott Township at this time.

Parkersburg, a small town in the southwest corner, has long been identified with the Spring Water. A Spring in the center of town provided water for the people. In early days, many people came from miles around to fill their containers with water for their homes. Highway U.S. 231 runs through town and is the only street in town.

New Market is a unique town. It is set in the corners of three townships. Scott township on the south and east side of town; Brown on the south and west side, and Union on the north. There is no tavern in New Market. This has been attributed to the women of the town. The legend is: every time a tavern was built, the women would band together and burn it down. The railroad ran through the center of the town and an elevator was built near the railroad to handle the grain from the farms in Scott, Brown and Union Townships. This elevator is still operational today, however, there is no longer a Railroad running through the town. In 1872 New Market was established as a town and in 1972 a celebration was held in honor of its 100th birthday.

As a result of the Indiana School Reorganization Act of 1959, three school units were created in Montgomery County. The South Montgomery School Corporation was established. The new Junior-Senior High School consolidation, Southmont, was constructed one mile east and one-fourth a mile south of New Market on Highway U.S. 231 and was nicknamed the Southmont Mounties. This school was to accommodate students from Ladoga, New Market, New Ross, and Waveland schools. The new building opened in the fall of 1971 with an enrollment in excess of 1000 Junior-Senior high students. The first elected school board for the South Montgomery Corporation was Bob Tandy, Superintendent; Larry Williams, Assistant Superintendent; Warner Kessler, President; Lewis

Goshorn, Vice President; Bill Etter, Secretary; Clifford Davis; Damon Crumm; Lawrence Hazlett; and Lee O. Servies, members. There are elementary schools in Walnut Township, Ladoga, Waveland and New Market.

Scott Township, Montgomery County became nationally known on September 25, 26, and 27, 1979, when Lincoln Priebe hosted the Farm Progress Show on his farm on highway U.S. 231. Sheriff, Charlie Stewart estimated the number of people in attendance on the first day was 100,000 to 125,000. They came from all over the world to compare methods of farming and to increase their knowledge of machinery and products. 500 to 600 small planes landed on the Priebe farm in Scott Township on the first day. This event filled the radio airways and newspapers for days. It was a farmer's dream come true, to be able to see all that farming had to offer in one spot, not for just one day, but three.

Scott Township is home to many descendants of the original settlers of this township. Some of the names of the early settlers were Armstrong, Morrison, Miller, Paxton, Quinley, Rock, Hyten, Howard, Hulse, James, Johnson, Wasson, Welch, White, Frame, Foster, Freeman, Akers, Busenbark, Cramer, Cleveland, Goodbar, Galey, Hampton, Higen, Hendricks, Sutherlin, Shannon, Vancleave, Taylor, and Shuck. *Submitted by: Barbara (House) Taylor*

SUGAR CREEK TOWNSHIP

Sugar Creek Township has primarily been known for agriculture since it was first settled in 1828, and so it continues today. Some farms are worked by second, third, fourth, and even a few fifth generation families. A few newcomers have been welcomed to the areas in recent years, but most families have been here some time.

Some of the parcels of land are owned by large corporations, some by family corporations, but most are just family farms.

The small businesses located at Bowers, the township's only village, have been gone for many years. A few homes remain there.

There are some businesses scattered around in the township, such as trucking firms, a monument company, two strawberry truck farms, and a greenhouse. The people not involved in these businesses or in agriculture drive to Crawfordsville, Lafayette, Thorntown, or Clinton County to work.

The children have attended schools out of the township since the late 1950s, and presently go to Sugar Creek Elementary, Northridge Middle School, or North Montgomery High School. No longer are one's classmates necessarily your nearby neighbor, but may come from several miles away in the school district. Distance however, is no barrier to friendship in a classroom or on the playground.

The bells that rang from the churches in the township have been silent for many years. The faithful that worshipped in these buildings are driving to various neighboring towns, or have gone on to their just rewards. But for the living, the memories of being at worship with family and close neighbors will never be forgotten.

The old Boots one room school located on 700E about 950N is one of the few landmarks remaining in the township. The Jackson house, located on 600E, and the Turnipseed house at the crossroads of 1000N and 700E are interesting forms of architecture.

Along with their fellow citizens of Montgomery County, the young men, and later young women, have answered the call to duty in the armed forces. Three such men, Delbert Phebus, Charles Gilmore, and Roach Bowers lost their lives while serving in World War II. Ted Alexander lost his life in the Vietnam Conflict.

For a more detailed history of Sugar Creek Township, please read *Montgomery County Magazine*, Sept. 1979 issue, found in the public libraries of the county. You will find excellent articles by James Leas, Lewis Dunbar, Donnis Widener, and Pat Cline.

In 1989 the people of Sugar Creek Township give thanks to the many people who lived, loved, worked, and served here before us. The elected officials, the merchants (though few in number) the school teachers and bus drivers, and mostly our thanks go to the ordinary farm people who cleared the land, then worked it, raised their families, cared about their friends and neighbors, and left the love of the land to generations to come. May we do as well. *Submitted by: Phyllis Boots*

UNION TOWNSHIP

Union Township is the largest township east of the Mississippi with an area covering about ten miles from east to west and twelve miles from north to south. It is located in the center of the county with the city of Crawfordsville at its center. Union township is a part of the 7th Congressional District, the 23rd Senate District and the 41st Representative District and is divided into ten voting precincts for the city of Crawfordsville and five precincts for the remainder of the township. Union township including the city of Crawfordsville has over half of the county's 35,500 population and is growing each year.

In catching up the history of Union township and Crawfordsville for the past 75 years, I read the following in the 1913 History by Bowen. "In the autumn of 1907, the following was advertised as the advantages of the city of Crawfordsville: a country club, machine shop, iron foundry, match factory, bottling works, casket factory, ten rural delivery routes, mitten factory, good newspapers, an orphan's home, a modern abattoir, business college, a cresting factory, commercial club, stone courthouse, first class theater, four cigar factories, an ice plant, two interurban lines, two first class hotels, pressed brick factory, a paving brick plant, excellent greenhouses, wire and nail mills, box making factory, modern city hospital, two express com-

Montgomery County Fall Festival at Crawfordsville. Left to right: Mildred and Marian Perkins, Otis and Oakle Bayless, Edith and Ethel Elmore

panies, a sixty-five thousand dollar federal building, modern fire department, a corrugated iron sewer factory, two large department stores, twelve churches, an acetylene gas plant factory, galvanized tank works, municipal lighting plant, the Gamewell system of fire alarm, three steam railroads, the best county fair in the West, private water and gas plant, the home for the Elks, the best Masonic temple in the section, three large loan companies, four banks, a beautiful soldiers monument, a splendid Carnegie library, head offices of the Tribe of Ben-Hur, five public school buildings, Wabash College, a forty thousand dollar Young Men's Christian Association building, hall of Knights of Pythias, Gen. Lew Wallace's study, a system of excellent water works, two telephone companies, twenty-four daily steam railroad trains, the same number of interurban cars, and fifty miles of cement side walks, with five miles of paved streets."

As you have read, many of the businesses are not in existence today, but to the credit of this community, many of the businesses and organizations are still thriving in 1989.

The Crawfordsville Electric Company was organized April 15, 1903 and still supplies a part of the electricity for the township. Additional electric needs are serviced by Public Service of Indiana. Crawfordsville also boasts of a Wastewater Treatment Plant, Solid Waste management for trash pick-up for residences once a week free of charge, Indiana Cities Water Corporation, a private company, provides water within city limits and Indiana Gas Company supplies natural gas.

In 1984 the following was advertised as the Manufacturing Economy of Union Township:

Ag Services includes Dekalb Pfizer (seed grain) which has 20 employees with an additional 175 seasonal employees and Pace Dairy Foods (cheese) with 190 employees.

Plastics, Fillers and Containers are Ingress Manufacturing Co. (injection moldings) with 230 employees, W & M Plastics (injection moldings) with 40 employees, Inland Container (corrugated boxes) with 115 employees, and Grefco (insulating and finishing cement, perlite filters and fillers) with 22 employees.

Equipment manufacturers are Puritan Water Conditioning Co. with 8 employees and Hi-Tek Lighting (high intensity discharge lighting fixtures) with 425 employees; H-C Industries and Crown, Cork and Seal.

Metal Fabrication includes Raymark (sintered metal, brake friction materials/wet clutch) with 545 employees, Impex Lock Corporation (semi-conductor heat sinks, brake pistons, electrical contacts for vehicles, shoe horns, wrist pins) with 130 employees, Midstates Wire (welding, industrial & specialty wire) with 261 employees and Sommer Metal Craft (specialty OEM wire products) with 280 employees; Nu-Cor (hot sheet strip metal) with 500 employees.

General Machinery, Mill Pars, Dies, etc. are B & L Engineering (job shop) with 11 employees, California Pellet Mill (mill parts, roller sheets) with 110 employees, Hudson Machine & Tool with 14 employees, Terra-Products (ball valves, pumps) with 40 employees and Vista Equipment (portable air compressors, production parts, pipe fittings) with 4 employees.

Commercial Printing and Binding companies are Allco Corporation (newspaper printing) with 10 employees, R.R. Donnelley & Sons (commercial printing & binding) with 2200 employees, Nor-Cote Chemical Company (ultra-violet light curable inks and coatings) with 20 employees, Spi-Binding Company (spiral book binding) with 9 employees, Crawford Industries (polyethylene sheet, plastic covers, binders) with 164 employees and Indiana Printing (commercial printing) with 19 employees.

Local Suppliers are Athens Press (commercial printing) with 4 employees, Bower Printing (personalized offset) with 4 employees, Journal Review (printing & publication) with 40 employees, Crawfordsville Burial Vault with 2 employees, Gibbs Industries (pallets and skids) with 2 employees, Kyger Inc. (sheet metal fabrication) with 8 employees and IMI (ready mix concrete) with 6 employees.

Transportation Equipment manufacturers are Fleetwood Travel Trailers (fifth wheel & travel trailers) with 150-200 employees and No-Sail Splash (mud flaps etc.) with 4 employees.

Non-manufacturing employers of Crawfordsville with 90 plus employees are Houston: Williamsburg Health Care,

Houston Companies, Houston Home Health Agency, Ben Hur Home, Houston Group Homes, Houston Health Care, Transportation Company, Coast to Coast and Target Stores.

The personal and business financial needs are met by a variety of institutions in Union township. The deposits of all banks are insured by the Federal Deposit Insurance Corporation and include Elston Bank and Trust Company, Bank One (previously First National Bank and Trust Company of Crawfordsville), Linden State Bank and Tri-County Bank and Trust. Savings and loan institutions are insured by the Federal Savings and Loan Insurance Corporation and include Lincoln Federal Savings Bank, the Montgomery Savings Association and Union Federal Savings and Loan Association. Other financial institutions are Ben Hur Life Association, Leavell & Bates, Household Finance Corporation, Production Credit Association of Montgomery County and the Federal Land Bank Association.

In the communication field the township offers the U.S. Postal Service and Express Mail, United Parcel Service (UPS), Federal Express drop box in City Building and Western Union. The Journal Review is a daily except Sunday newspaper and the Messenger-Crier a weekly delivered free of charge to every household in the county. The county is serviced by two radio stations, WCVL AM-WLFQ FM and WNDY FM (Wabash College). The local television station is the Crawfordsville Community Cable.

In transportation, Crawfordsville has two accesses to I-74 interstate, one at the northern city limits, the other four miles to the east of the city on SR 32. Conrail and Seaboard systems provide freight train service to local industries. The Crawfordsville Municipal Airport is located four miles south of the downtown on US 231 in Union township. There is a 4000 feet long, 75 foot wide, hard surfaced main runway with a 900 foot long overrun. The runway will accommodate a DC-3 or Sideley Hawker Jet. There is a non-directional beacon landing system with runway lights and strobe lights at each threshold.

Union township government consists of a township assessor, trustee and township board of three persons. Crawfordsville is a third class city with a full-time Mayor, a seven-member common council and a clerk-treasurer. The following people have served as Mayor of Crawfordsville since the last publication of the history of Montgomery County. William C. Murphy 1913-18, Dumont Kennedy 1918-22, Earl Berry 1922-26, Dumont Kennedy 1926-30, Thomas L. Cooksey 1930-35, Bert E. May 1935-41, Thomas L. Cooksey, 1941-49, Clark Jones 1949-53, Carroll Beeson 1953-57, Paul Stump 1957-61, Carl Henthron 1961-65, Will Hays 1965-72, David Gerard 1972-76, Glenn Knecht 1976-88 and Philip Michal 1988 (currently serving). The Crawfordsville Police Department has approximately 25 professional officers, including the Chief and Captain. The Fire & Ambulance force give professional service to the city and surrounding Union township. There is one main station and one sub-station on the east side of the city and the intersection of Wabash St. and Main St. There is a land use plan and a Zoning Ordinance for the city and the area two miles outside the city limits in Union township.

Many services are available for the residents of both the city and township and many are available for the entire county. They include Adult Health Clinic, AA, Alanon, Alateen, American Red Cross, CARA (Crawfordsville Adult Reading Association), Christian Counseling Center, Christian Nursing Services, Community Action Program, Crawfordsville Chemical Dependency Service, Crawfordsville Commission on the Status of Women, Crawfordsville Counseling Associates, Crawfordsville Housing Authority, Chamber of Commerce, Day Care, Disability Services, Inc., Family Crisis Shelter, Fish, Headstart, Homemaker Service, Indiana Children's Christian Home, Kiwanis, Lions Club, Meals on Wheels, Montgomery County Association for Retarded Citizens, Montgomery County Court Referral Program, Montgomery County Council on Aging, Montgomery County Department of Public Welfare, Montgomery County Educational Services, Montgomery County Extension Service, Montgomery County Health Department, Montgomery County Legal Aid Society, Montgomery County Mental Health Center, Montgomery County Shrine Club, Montgomery County Youth Service Bureau, Muffy (Montgomery United Fund For You), Planned Parenthood, Pre-Schools for Educationally Deprived, PSI IOTA Speech and Hearing Clinic, Social Security Administration, Sunshine Van (for elderly), Telecheck, Township House, Visiting Nurse Home Health Service, Volunteers for Mental Health in Montgomery Co., Well Baby Clinic, and WIC Nutrition Program. Children's Recreational Groups include Boy's Club, Boy Scouts, Campfire, Inc., Crawfordsville Park & Recreation Dept., 4-H Inc., Girl Scouts, Junior Achievement, Montgomery County Youth Camps, Inc., Special Olympics and Sugar Creek Swim Club.

The Crawfordsville Park & Recreation Dept. is not only a service to the children of the area, but has adult services as well, such as organized softball leagues, volleyball, aerobics, and many other services for both men and women. There are five lighted softball diamonds, a 50m outdoor swimming pool and water slide and an 18 hole public golf course under this department.

In 1965 Montgomery County was divided into three school districts: Crawfordsville Community Schools, North Montgomery Community Schools and South Montgomery Community Schools. Both North and South built new facilities which opened for use in the fall of 1971. Each facility was equipped with the latest in athletic and educational equipment. Crawfordsville voted this year to build a new facility on the southwest edge of town which should be completed by 1991.

Wabash College founded in 1832 is a liberal arts college for men with an enrollment of 850 and supports a varied curriculum consisting of courses in the sciences, the humanities, and the social sciences leading to the Bachelor of Arts Degree. Eighty percent of the alumni are admitted to graduate and professional schools.

There are 38 churches in the Crawfordsville area nd many sponsor activities and services for the community.

Many buildings of the 19th century in Union township are listed on the National Register of Historic Places. They include the Major Isaac C. Elston House, home of the President of Wabash College; the Henry S. Lane Place, home and museum; Colonel Isaac Elston, home of Dorothy Q Chapter DAR; St. John's Episcopal Church; the Otto Schlemmer Building; the General Lew Wallace Study, museum and park. The old county jail with its rotating circular cell blocks has been preserved as a museum of great interest. The Cultural Foundation is in charge of the museum and its operation. The new jail was built on Covington Street in 1971.

In 1984 the new Culver Hospital was completed on north US 231. The old hospital sold by the County and then rented by the County to house the Government offices during the renovation of the Courthouse in 1986. The new hospital has 120 beds and includes special care units and diagnostic services. There is a helicopter life line service to Methodist Hospital in Indianapolis. *Submitted by: Becky Neideffer, Montgomery County Clerk. Photos contributed by: Suzie Zach*

WALNUT TOWNSHIP

Both H.W. Beckwith in 1881 and A.W. Bowen in 1913 compiled great histories of Montgomery County. Each account deals in detail with the origin, development, early settlers, terrain, schools, churches, and civic leaders of each of the townships. This account will attempt to offer the reader an "over-view" of events in one particular township, namely, Walnut, since 1913. And as that is the year this writer was born, it is not hard to identify with the intervening years!

Walnut Township is located in the southeastern part of the county and is bordered on the east by Boone County, by Clark Township on the south, by Franklin on the north, and by Union on the west. Only a few wooded areas remain to remind one of the great stands of timber which greeted the early settlers. Walnut trees were in abundance, thus the name of the township and Walnut Fork Creek, which meanders through the area. Cornstalk Creek and Big Raccoon Creek still flow, but they have altered their courses in some degree over the years. Walnut Township is a fine farming community with good corn and other crop lands, and much livestock is raised in its confines — both cattle and hogs. Lands once owned by many families are now in the possession of a few. Fences have been removed, and old houses torn down. The west end of the township is feeling the effects of the new steel plant, Nucor, which has been built in the Whitesville area. While no Walnut land is involved, the impact of such activity is felt in the quiet farming community.

Some gravel roads remain, but the roads carrying the major flow of traffic are "black-topped". The old, tall iron bridges are abandoned or replaced by concrete structures. The old State Road, known as "The Dixie Highway" after 1916, running from Indianapolis through New Ross, Mace, and Crawfordsville, was designated as #34 for a time; later it became State Road #136 and remains so today. "I-74", a four-lane super highway, was built in the sixties. It crosses Indiana in a northwesterly direction from the Cincinnati, Ohio area to the Illinois State line near Danville. It intersects Walnut Township about two miles north of New Ross and of Mace. Many acres of good farm land were taken to create this highway.

Of the three railroad tracks which carried people and freight through this area, only one, the "Big Four", now known as Conrail and the Amtrack train, remains. Once running from Indianapolis to Peoria, it now switches at Crawfordsville to continue its route to Chicago. One passenger train, the Amtrack, makes a round-trip from Indianapolis to Chicago daily, passing through this township. Freight service is offered. The Interurban, an electric line running from Crawfordsville to Indianapolis was a "life line" for persons in the rural areas and small towns who commuted to work in the cities. This service began in 1907 and ended in 1930. There were stations at Linnsburg and New Ross. The Midland Railroad, which had its origin at Anderson and had aspired to reach St. Louis, fell on hard times in the twenties, and the section between Advance in Boone County, and Ladoga was abandoned. It provided transportation between New Ross and Ladoga.

Walnut Township boasted of four towns, each having stores and other businesses. They were Linnsburg and Mace near the western boundary, and Beckville and New Ross in the eastern section. Beckville, (its post office once named "Orth") was a thriving little village with several businesses and its own doctors, but is now a crossroads community with a few families living there. The Providence Christian Church is still a beacon to the area. The school was abandoned in the early twenties, and the students enrolled at New Ross. Linnsburg had a bank, a grocery, and a grain company, among other enterprises, but no businesses exist now. Children from that area attended the Mace School. The Mace High School consolidated with New Ross in 1925, the Junior High in 1938. All of the township's elementary students attended Mace School from 1937 until the new Walnut Elementary was built in 1963. At that time the Mace School closed. It still stands and has been used as a store and apartments. New Ross High School became a part of the consolidation of schools in the South Montgomery system in 1971. That building was dismantled.

Mace, located on State Road #136, is a well-kept community of homes. The Mace United Methodist Church is located there, as well as a Standard Service Station and Restaurant owned and operated by Don and Jean Edwards, and a Country Store which carries women's clothing and is owned and operated by Vivian and Charles Norman. Mr. and Mrs. Kenneth Gass operate a sawmill business south of the highway on the Linnsburg road. "The Ole Cow Shed" is a delightful craft and antique shop owned by Don and Pat Paddack, also located on 136 between Mace and New Ross.

Two churches, the New Ross Christian and the New Ross United Methodist, have served the area continuously for well over a hundred years. No physicians have practiced in the township since the thirties. There were active lodges and other organizations in the township for many years, but none are in existence at

Bert Zuck, Huckster

this time. Both Mace and New Ross had Knights of Pythias Lodges with the accompanying Pythian Sister Temples. The Independent Order of Odd Fellows with its affiliated Rebeckah Lodge for women was active. The town still has its Conservation Club and a Community Club.

More than three hundred men from Walnut Township served in the four wars of this century. Those who did not return were: Floyd Bowman, WW I; Wayne Feather, Robert Turner, Eugene Chadwick, Carroll Canine, and Okel Cline, WW II; Kenneth Teague, Korean War; Samuel Benge, Vietnam War. The Robert Turner Post of the American Legion has recently made improvements to its headquarters in the old Bronaugh building in New Ross. Damon Crumm is Post Commander. The active Auxiliary Unit is headed by Beth Baer Bamish. A Fish Fry is held each June to keep interest alive and bring friends back to town. An annual Memorial Day Service is conducted by the Post alternately at the Mace and New Ross Cemeteries.

The schools of Walnut are discussed in another section of this book. However, the one-room grade schools at Greenwood and at Beckville were closed in the early twenties. Ruth Nees and Helen Hayes Evans are teachers still living in the area who taught their first schools at Greenwood.

The population figures for New Ross have not varied much in the past century, averaging about 350 people. One bank existed in 1913, having been organized as the Citizens Bank in 1902. It was closed by its own directors in 1928. The Farmers State Bank was organized in 1920 and still serves the community. Cashiers are William E. Etcheson, III, and Betty Kinnett. Dorman Harris is president of the board of directors. Milton L. Nees was the first cashier, and he was succeeded by Karl Dickerson and James Iverson. Once a thriving town with many businesses, it now has a Post Office, (Mary Ellen Needham is Post Master), Clark's Grocery, Rice Tire Service, New Ross Grain, Rusty Carter, owner, Wrede's Service Station, Simms' Garage, Smith's Welding, a Steak House, Frederick's Bicycle Repair, Carolyn Norris' Hair Plus Shop, Harris Electric, Dale and Gayle Canada's Green House. The Farm Bureau's "Heartland Coop" is located west of town on 136. Larry Walters' Feed Service north of town. The Town Hall and Fire Station is located at State and Green Streets. Well-trained volunteers man the fire equipment, and EMTs provide good ambulance service. Rebecca Patton Lowe is Town Clerk.

The New Ross Community celebrated its Centennial year of incorporation as a town July 10-13, 1975. While early settlers had come as early as 1825 to the area, no steps were taken to incorporate until 1875. The town was platted as Valley City in 1855 and changed to New Ross in 1872. The whole community united to make the Centennial Celebration a huge success. A pageant with twelve episodes and local players portrayed the early history of the area, before a sell-out audience for three nights. A magnificent parade was viewed by an estimated crowd of 10,000. Memorabilia was collected and placed in a sealed vault on the Town Hall lawn. The marker is inscribed: "To be Opened in 2025". Hopefully the Centennial Queen, Maggie Feltner (Rosen), who placed her cherished crown in the vault, will be around to place it on the head of the Sesquicentennial Queen when the New Ross community again celebrates!

Submitted by: Marcella N. Feltner. Source: Beckwith, Bowen, & Ruth Nees in "Centennial History of the New Ross Community" Vols. I and II

WAYNETOWN - WAYNE TOWNSHIP

The Sesquicentennial Book is a fine history of this community. There are very few errors to be found. The Sesquicentennial Book tells much of the beginning of this city and township. It then brings the history up to date from 1930 to 1980. Very few changes have been made since then except for the High School burning. Because of consolidation the school and the gym were to be torn down. Some youths were smoking in the school building which later caused the school to go down in flames (March 4, 1989).

Submitted by: Norm Cramer

FEATURE STORIES

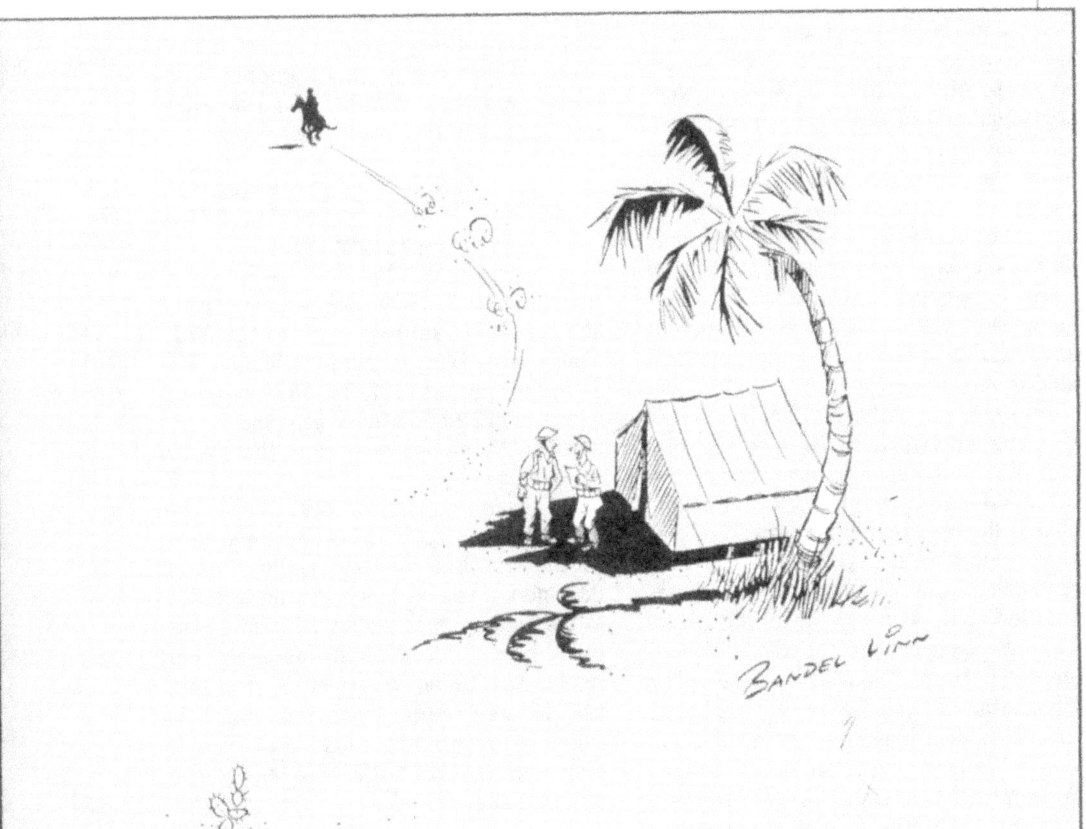

"My request for a day's furlough has finally been okayed!"

Bandel Linn, born in Montgomery County became a well known artist.

BEN HUR HOME FOR AGED

This was a home for aged, but well persons, and not a nursing home. People, who were eligible were in good health, but, aged, and had a Ben Hur Insurance Policy. They had to turn over their assets to the Ben Hur Insurance Company, but they were treated exceptionally well at the home. Had the best of food, nicely furnished bedrooms, carpeted, downstairs was a card game room, lounge, large living room, and a large dining room, with French windows on south side of dining room. Staff consisted of two cooks, practical nurse, a housekeeper, and the Host and Hostess, as those who ran it were called.

They were taken to town whenever they wanted to go. Men were taken to the barbershop every Wednesday, and all those who wanted to go to a movie were taken to a matinee.

One of the men had been a good gardener, and he kept himself busy raising flowers, etc., and he enjoyed it. The women made quilts, crocheted afghans, and did other crochet work. One woman made an afghan for the Hostess, very pretty, but one of the other women guest, said she could do a better job, so she made the Hostess one. The Home and guests, as the aged people were called had to be ready for visitors at any time during the day. Visitors came from other states to see just how the Home operated. This was a wonderful Home for aged healthy people, and they appreciated it very much.

In 1926, the Tribe of Ben Hur, or as it is now known, Ben Hur Life Association, was authorized to have a home for the aged policy holders, so they purchased the old Ristine homestead of 100 acres, South Grant Avenue, which they remodeled so as to not look like an institution, but, a private dwelling place. The first aged person, called a guest entered the Home on May 5, 1927. The Home was dedicated May 29, 1927. The first Host and Hostesses were James and Cretta Wallace, then Harold and Pauline Walters and son Robert, 1931 to 1942, then Fred Utterback and Power; they started the Home. They also started a modern dairy, raising purebred guernseys, and they had plenty of milk, cream, cottage cheese, etc., and they had a dairy route in Crawfordsville. They built a modern milk house. They had many chickens and always had fresh eggs. They later bought the brick house across the road, and those who lived there were able to walk to the white house 3 times a day for their meals. The Host of the home was called superintendent of farm and dairy. North of the white house was a large expanse of beautiful landscaping, there was always a green field of alfalfa beyond the lawn. Now that's all residential and a nursing home, since 1950's, John Snyder, president of Ben Hur, Ed Mason, Secretary. As soon as the aged began to get social security checks, they didn't make applications to come to the Home for the aged, and so the Ben Hur Life Association sold the White House to Martha Vancleave Cowan Williams, and she started a nursing home, and the 3 or 4 who were still at the Home for the Aged, became patients in the nursing home. It is called Ben Hur Nursing Home, but the brick house was never called after Ben Hur Home for the Aged.

The ones in the Home for the Aged came from all over the United States as Ben Hur Life Association sold insurance everywhere, and many policies were purchased because they knew when they became old, they'd have a beautiful home to come to. Most of them had come to visit the Home, and they knew how wonderfully it was run, more like a real home. There are a lot of people who never knew about the Ben Hur Home for the Aged, and how well it was run.

DANIEL BOONE TURTLE

On March 1, 1929, Oasey Laurel Hershberger and family moved to the W.J. Haney farm West of New Richmond, Indiana. In the fall of 1928, he had sowed wheat on E. Ogle's land near the Fountain and Montgomery County line, West of Wingate.

In the Spring of 1929, Mr. Hershberger and his crew of men returned to harvest his wheat. His wife and daughters prepared lunch and delivered it to the tenant house where William Lyons lived. Fauneil Hershberger ran to tell her father that lunch was waiting for him and the crew. But Fauneil found a turtle jogging toward the shade of a young walnut tree. The turtle was strong and healthy. Fauneil put it in a portable chicken wire circle on fresh grass; fed it fruit and mushrooms.

Mr. Hershberger took the turtle to the zoology department at Purdue. They sent it to the State Entomologist at Indianapolis. In the course of movement, it was decided that the famous scout had indeed carved his name on the turtle. It may have walked a circle of 100 miles before Fauneil found it!

Fauneil's Uncle Ralph Lyons said that he found it and took it away from Fauneil. Fauneil flew from Florida to her Uncle Ralph on his death bed and asked for her turtle back. He could not remember where he got it and refused to give her the turtle shell. He had kept the turtle in a tub and had given it hard boiled eggs and it died.

In 1979, the 50th anniversary of the shell finding, Fauneil and Mary went back to where Fauneil had found the turtle. The walnut tree was showing its age, too!

BREAKS SCHOOL

Breaks School, located on road 400N, two and one-half miles west of its intersection with US 231N, was built on land donated by John Beard Breaks; son of Richard Breeks (later Breaks), an immigrant from England who settled in the area.

The school was first built in 1901. In the early morning hours of May 26, 1906 fire destroyed a major portion of the building, necessitating the removal of the remainder of the building. Almost immediately the community began rebuilding the school and by Nov. 12, 1906 a nearly identical school building was opened.

All twelve grades were taught until 1916. High school students then attended Crawfordsville High School or nearby township schools. The eight grades were taught until 1949. At that time the school was closed and students attended either Mount Zion or East Union Schools.

The building is now being used as a private residence. *Submitted by John Breaks Lofland*

CARRY NATION IN CRAWFORDSVILLE

John T. Frye wrote an article in 1970 in the *Indianapolis Star Magazine* about Carry Nation being in Crawfordsville, excerpts given below.

He said the Crawfordsville Elks and Carry Nation teamed up to produce a colorful Fourth of July, 1901. At the beginning of the 20th century, Mrs. Nation was probably the most famous or infamous woman in the United States. She was half reformer, half showman. In the 1890's she had been in Medicine Lodge, Kansas with her hatchet battling saloons. She had hit her peak in 1900's. In her mid-50's she went all over the United States chopping artistic mahogany bars, cut glass chandeliers, and bottle laden back bars, shouting hymns, and thundered at the rum consumers. She was 6 ft. tall and weighed 190 pounds.

J.J. Insley of the Elks, sent her an invitation to come to Crawfordsville on July 1901 for their fourth of July celebration for the Elks. In her magazine, *The Smashers Mail*, she said she would attend to give a temperance lecture. She said the "poor, lost Elks needed her service, and that she'd not object to $50 and expenses for her trouble." On May 29th, 1901, W.W. Morgan, received a letter saying she would be here the Fourth. Said it was God's will. *The Crawfordsville Weekly Journal* said she was coming here. She wore a black bonnet, linen duster, had a large umbrella, and with a large hatchet, came to Crawfordsville on July 3rd, with piles of luggage. She was met by the Elks and some yelping boys, and she was taken to the Crawford Hotel. She asked a newspaper reporter about the Elks, why they were called after an animal with big horns. She wanted to go to some bars on July 3rd, but Mr. Insley talked her out of it. They had a parade and about 6,000

CONFEDERATE CIVIL WAR VETERANS WHO SETTLED IN MONTGOMERY COUNTY, INDIANA

James M. Anderson, Private, Tennessee, C.S.A., Confederate P.O.W.
William B. Ashwell, Co. B, 14th Virginia Infantry, C.S.A.
William H. Boger
John Booker
Noah Monroe Brock, Co. B, 10th Virginia Cavalry, C.S.A.
Valentine Byrum
William P. Camden
Braxton Cash
William A. Clark
Lewellyn J. Coppage
John A. Fullwider
Andrew Gayhart
Jonas T. Gish, Co. K, 28th Virginia Infantry, C.S.A.
Clifton Hill
Charles A. Howell
James Isaacs
David A. Kennedy
Madison Linkinhoker, Co. K, 28th Virginia Infantry, C.S.A.
William E. Lollis
Thomas Luster
William Luster
William R. Lynch
William Manger
John Mangus, 42nd Virginia Infantry, C.S.A.

Broyles Milligan
William "Billy" Mitchell, Co. M, 2nd North Carolina Infantry, C.S.A.
Joseph Moody
Richard L. Moore, Co. C, 1st Virginia Cavalry, C.S.A.
David F. Olinger, M.D.
James L. Patterson
James W. Patterson Co. A, 14th Va. Cavalry
Frank Rayner
James Q. Shannon
Andrew Smiley 14th Va. Inf. C.S.A.
Isaac F. Sperry
Wm. Snodgrass
Thomas B. Terry, Virginia Cavalry, C.S.A.
Mathew Grigg Thompson, Chaplain, 46th Georgia, C.S.A.
Maurice J. Thompson
Will H. Thompson
James M. Walker
Jacob Wingert, Co. A, 28th Virginia Infantry, C.S.A.
William H. Wolfe, Co. E, 5th Virginia Infantry, C.S.A.
George Washington Zimmerman
Jacob Zimmerman
John M. Zimmerman
William H. Zimmerman, Co. D, 5th Virginia Infantry, C.S.A.

This list was compiled while doing research for an upcoming book on Montgomery County Confederate Civil War Veterans. We wish to express a special thank you to Karen Zach, of the Crawfordsville Public Library, Pauline Walters, Crawfordsville and Carolyn Cross of Ladoga Public Library for their help in this project. *Submitted by: Andrew Keith Houk, Jr., Jamestown, Indiana; Jay Wilson, Jr., Oolitic, Indiana* people attended the affair. Mayor Elmore introduced Carry Nation. The Elks cleared $500. The stand they had prepared for her and other speakers collapsed, and she fell about 4 feet to the ground. Her fall was broken by Charley Gilbert. She got up at 4 A.M. on July 4, washed some clothes and hung them in the window, then went downstairs at the hotel and tried to get into the bar, arguing with the night clerk about his smoking, then went outside and argued with a group of loafers about spitting on the sidewalks. She didn't do much damage here, although she gathered a group of boys and had them downtown in minor forays. Carry did well on selling hatchets, her magazine, *The Smasher's Mail* and pictures. Her story about being here got more coverage in all newspapers than a lynching and a race riot in Ohio.

FRANKLIN TOWNSHIP SCHOOLS

From the beginning, residents of Franklin Township considered adequate school facilities and instruction a prime responsibility. As school enrollments in Darlington increased, about 1928, school officials and patrons saw to the addition of more grade rooms to the fourteen-year-old brick structure of 1914. A complete renovation of old furnishings followed, under strong trusteeship.

In 1937 Shannondale grade school closed, and the children were sent to Darlington School.

To accommodate increased enrollments and to meet state standards, in 1954-5 additional acreage was acquired for the extended building and enlargement program planned — classrooms, shops, cafeteria, gymnasium, playgrounds, and sports activities.

In 1956 high school pupils were transferred from Sugar Creek Township (Bowers). In 1959 Bowers School closed, moving the elementary pupils to town. Thus came about Darlington Consolidated School.

Wider curricula were offered. Band became an integral part of the curriculum, with grades 5 to 12 participating. Vocational agriculture was added. An accelerated health program included a school nurse; dental unit visits; a hot lunch program; special education and speech therapy—all beneficial to many pupils.

Extra-curricular activities provide a showcase for the display of skills, talents, and interests of young people. The Dar-

Darlington Academy Track Team, 1905 Top row, left to right: Will Holloway, Ellis Booker. Front row, left to right: Roy Conrad, Owen Booker, Ernest Francis, Earl Pickering, and J. Leon LePage

lington Indians, cheered on to victory by loyal fans sharing in "Hoosier hysteria", made a strong bid to be county champs, season after season. Thinly-clads cleared the hurdles and set new records in track events.

Choral groups under the skillful direction of inspiring teachers developed talents and produced colorful musicals and operettas. The county music festival was a delight to performers and to the audience.

Four more classrooms added in 1961 allowed for a long-awaited kindergarten. The school system was updated as to enriched curricula, professional dedicated teachers. The old assembly room was converted into a library-study hall, with a growing collection of books and magazines; films and projectors available. Appropriate book collections in every grade room furthered emphasis on reading and reference. The trend was carried out under a licensed library administrator.

At the mandate of the State Department of Public Instruction, reorganization and consolidation became paramount. After much controversy, North Montgomery School Corporation evolved as one of three units in the county, under the administration of a superintendent of schools and a school board.

The last class to graduate from Darlington was the class of 1971. All the high school pupils of the north unit were bused to NMHS, the newly - built school near Cherry Grove on 231. Pupils from East Union ready for grades 7 and 8 were sent to Darlington during the years 1972-87. Darlington continued to serve middle and elementary grades until 1987.

Teacher training requirements were increased; teacher salaries were improved; benefits, enhanced.

In 1987 North Ridge Middle School built near NMHS opened its doors to grades 6 to 8. In 1988 grades K - 5 boarded buses to Sugar Creek, one of the three new elementary schools in the north unit.

Darlington no longer has a school to rally around, for the first time in 147 years. There remains an abandoned building and nostalgic memories. *Contributed by: Ramona Ainsworth*

FREDRICKSBURG SCHOOL

This school was no. 4 in Walnut Township. In 1873 Jennie B. Hall taught a school in Mace. Where this building was, I don't know, but, Douglas Grigg said in 1874, land where the 1913 building stood was deeded to Curtis Edwards, trustee. So a frame, two story building was built on this site, and before they built the 1913 building, this frame building was moved near to Linnsburg, and Meredith Keffer can remember playing ball in the second story, a large room.

From 1854 to 1860, three trustees served at one time, Jonathan Martin, James Youell, Smith Conners, then J.F. Porter, Jesse Routh, J.L. Lockridge, Isaac Miller, Thomas Wilson, J.J. Johnson, Andrew Loop, William Walkup, Elijah Mount, W.W. Ward, R.F. King, G.W. Powell, Curtis Edwards, Oscar Eddingfield, John Foster, Orph Bratton, George G. Brown, John Miller, C.L. Lauthers,

Joseph A. Linn, Ed Mount (served twice), Harry Shervey, Lawrence Foster, Joseph Grimes, Chalmer Miller, William Shervey, Ralph Miller, Robert L. Walters, and Meredith Keffer.

In 1913 the two story brick building, with basement was erected on same lot as the two story frame building was located, across from the old cemetery, on the south edge of Mace.

The first graduates at the Mace school of whom we have record in 1906. Last graduation in the Mace building was in 1925. After that high school students went to New Ross.

Back then they had a superintendent for each township, now they have a superintendent in each of the three units in Montgomery County.

The 1913 building was sold to Kenneth Steele, after school was disbanded in 1963. The last teachers at Mace school, who continued teaching in the new consolidated school were Denver Feltner, Mrs. Earl Meek, Thelma Parnell, Mrs. Jean Hostetter, and Mrs. Mary Duncan.

The 1878 Atlas shows the site of the school across from the old cemetery, but I don't know where the 1873 building stood.

The teachers in 1906 at Mace School were Charles Lockhart, Charles Lauthers, Mary G. Smith, and Bertha Peterson.
Submitted by Pauline Walters

GREENWOOD SCHOOL

On February 11, 1836, the United States sold to Caleb and Jane Brown land, and they in turn sold it to William and Effie Beck, and they sold it to Robert and Margaret McCoy Lytle on July 23, 1857. In the abstract it says one acre of this land is to be used for school purposes. In 1916 issue of the *Crawfordsville Journal* it said Greenwood School began in 1859, Wesley Beck, was the first teacher. This was on Section 33 Township 18 Range 3, Walnut Township, Montgomery County, Indiana, two miles west of New Ross. This school operated until 1925. In 1928, Kenneth Davidson bought the building, used it as part of a barn, but it was destroyed by a tornado in 1954.

This was a one room, one door, six window, white frame building. First school built in 1857, then second building built in 1873. There were 8 grades in this one room. In 1881 there were 39 enrolled. Curriculum was reading, writing, spelling, geography, grammar, history, physiology, etc. An inspection of the school said there was no whispering, recitations were good, discipline and method of instruction good. In 1881 it was also used as a church, Martin Hosier, Minister.

My maternal grandfather, my mother, and me, all attended Greenwood School. I was a pupil there from 1914 to 1918. All students walked to school. I was only a half a mile from the school. I attended 4 years.

In January 1915, Opal (Rhoades) Shewey, the teacher was assigning a lesson to my class near the stove, and a cartridge which had been put on the stove by an older student, exploded, hitting her in the eye. She lost the sight of the eye. Substitutes were Forest Baber and Homer Miller, finished the term.

Teachers in the 1857 building were Wesley Beck, Enoch Barnett, who named the school, Greenwood, Jennie Britts, Charles Ruggs, Mary Kirk, Melissa Powers, Madison Kelsey, Garrett Vanhorn, James Barnett, Taylor Patterson, Hickman Hall, Alice (Shaver) Foxworthy, Dorsey Martin, William T. Eddingfield, J.W. Miller and George Buell.

Teachers in the building built in 1873 were Tilghman Brown, W.B. Walkup, James C. Eddingfield, Frank Hobson, Johnnie Miller, Clarence Burroughs, Aubrey Bowers, Charles Johnson, Jennie Clahan, Josephine Imel, Edith (Lindley) Hendricks, Minnie Marshall, Maud (Moss) Sperry, Vinnie (Hostetter) Bradley, Carl Smith, Romerlus D. Minnich, Walter D. Vanscoyce, Mary Alexander, M.C. Clodfelter, Lola (Ward) Bortz Scott, Mabel (Bushong) Glover, Opal (Rhoads) Shewey, Letha (Elliot) Proctor,

Greenwood School built 1873, all that remains is the two trees 1967.

Georgia (Shannon) Jones, Clifford Davis, Lawrence Surface, Beulah Wingert, Ruth Nees, Mabel (Linn) Myers, and Frances Minnick. Helen (Hays) Hughes Evans was substitute.

Before the school disbanded in 1925, they started music and manual training. Jean (Springer) Spencer had music and Tom Ricketts was manual training teacher.

In 1874, the school was a 7 month term, then in 1918 they had an 8 month term. After the school closed in 1925, they continued having reunions, last one was in 1927, with 56 former pupils in attendance. *By C. Pauline Walters*

HORSE THIEF DETECTIVE ASSOCIATION

The first Horse Thief Detective Association organized in Montgomery County was in Coal Creek Township in 1844. In 1854 Mace organized an association. This one must have been disbanded some time later, for in 1911 they reorganized another one. Back in those days everyone had horses, and many times horses were stolen. The 1911 one was called Fredericksburg (original name of Mace) Detectives No. 36. Clyde Loop was President; Brent Engle, Vice President; Mark Dice, Secretary; Pearlie Patterson, Assistant Secretary; Charles Minnich, Sr. Chaplain; John H. Finch, Doorkeeper; Trustees were Orph Bratton, John W. Ward, Sr., and William A. Stafford; Captains and Minutemen were Newt

Everson; Captain East; Fred Welliver; W. Harney Morris; John H. West; Odis Stafford; Joe E. Pattison; John Fletcher, Sr.; Charles Ward; William Rhoads. Committees on by-laws Brent Engle, Odis Strafford and Homer Chambers.

Members had to live within a 5-mile radius of Fredericksburg. Each meeting was at 1:30 P.M. Captains and minutemen had to be mounted and ready to ride in search of criminals. They received $1.50 a day—double if they had to search night and day. Members had to "work" their way into meeting. Password had to be whispered, for it was secret too. Each member became a constable as soon as he was received into membership. There were 34 charter members in 1911, and many others joined later. When it disbanded is not known — but I presume in early 1920's, for horse stealing wasn't as prevalent then. *By C. Pauline Walters*

THE INDIANAPOLIS, CRAWFORDSVILLE AND WESTERN TRACTION COMPANY

The idea of an electric railroad connecting Crawfordsville and Indianapolis was started in early 1903 with the building of the Indianapolis and Northwestern Traction Company.

The company obtained an ordinance in Crawfordsville in September of 1905 and was incorporated on September 19, 1905.

This electric railroad or interurban was to start in Crawfordsville and go southeasterly, passing through the towns of Linnsburg, New Ross, Jamestown, Lizton, Raintown, Pittsboro, Brownsburg, Clermont, Speedway and end in Indianapolis. The railroad took two years to build and was considered to be one of the finest lines ever built.

The roadbed was designed for speed of 60 miles per hour, with a maximum grade of 1-1/4 percent. The 70-pound rails were laid on oak ties and ballasted with gravel. The bridges were constructed of concrete and steel. There were three substation powerhouses built, with one located one mile east of New Ross on old State Road 34. Another was 3/4 miles west of Pittsboro and the last was at the west edge of Speedway. The main powerhouse was constructed on Lafayette Avenue and it still exists in Elston Park. In later years, this building was the Coca Cola plant. There were depots built in Linnsburg and New Ross. The New Ross depot still exists today and is the town hall and fire station. The interurbans were of steel and wood construction and were just over 57 feet long and 9 feet high and were designed for comfort and speed.

The first interurban ran on July 4, 1907 from Crawfordsville to New Ross and back. Regular service began on July 7, 1907.

During the next 13 years the interurbans enjoyed good revenues and ridership, but with better roads and automobiles, the decline of the electric railroads began. The 1920's were had years for Indiana's interurbans. By 1930, the end was in sight for the Ben Hur (Crawfordsville) division. The cars were old and in poor condition and the roadbed was in need of repair.

In the last summer of 1930, the Terre Haute, Indianapolis and Eastern Company asked for permission to abandon the Ben Hur Line. The last day of operation was on October 31, 1930 with the last car coming into Crawfordsville shortly after midnight on November 1st. The Crawfordsville Streetcar Line also ended on October 31, thus ending over 27 years of electric railway service to Crawfordsville. The line was dismantled over the next two years and all that remains of the interurbans are old bridges and old roadbeds through the countryside. *Submitted by: Andrew Keith Houk, Jr., Jamestown, Indiana*

THE INTERURBANS

Montgomery County, was in a way, the birthplace of the idea for electric railways to go from town to town and city to city. Noah J. Clodfelter born December 14, 1853, reared near Alamo, originated the idea. He had been to many cities that had electric cars that only ran in the city. He enlisted the aid of men with money, and with $500,000, he and Charles L. Henry, a lawyer from Anderson, were pioneer promoters to develop his theory.

The first interurban line in Crawfordsville was a branch called the Northwestern from Lebanon to Crawfordsville, 26 miles, and started in 1903. There was supposed to be another line granted by ordinance of city council, I.C. Elston, Crawford Fairbank, J.R. Bounnell, Floyd A. Wood, and H.C. Brubaker, Jr., but this never materialized. The Northwestern obtained franchise on February 1903. They submitted bond on July 25, 1904. First franchise signed by Mayor on August 6, 1902. Then they revoked their franchise, and there was quite a fracas developed over this. Then they were granted another franchise on March 1903, and they were to enter Crawfordsville on what is now Traction Line Road to Wabash Avenue. Cars were to run every 3 hours. The first car ran on October 1903, and took 70 minutes to make the trip of 26 miles. This line came from Lebanon through Shannondale to here. They built a viaduct over the Vandalia railroad here. They crossed the Monon over a bridge on Wabash Avenue. There was a city car here called "Back & Forth" or "Yellow Peril". On September 18, 1905, an ordinance gave Indianapolis, Crawfordsville, and Western Traction Company permission to operate an interurban, from Indianapolis to Crawfordsville, through, Linnsburg, New Ross, Jamestown, Pittsboro and Brownsburg. Both interurbans stopped at every road crossing, and each crossing had a name. At many stops they had a little covered place with a bench for people to sit on while waiting for an interurban. It was parallel to the Big Four tracks. They used the viaduct over the Vandalia railroad, just as Northwestern did.

This writer can remember, when going over viaduct, she became almost sick. It was after 1912 when both interurbans used viaducts.

There was no extra fee for baggage if one kept it in their lap. Children under 5 rode free. This Indianapolis line was called "Ben Hur Line". They had a power house east of New Ross. New Ross and Linnsburg had a passenger and freight depot. Ben Hur interurban could travel 60 miles per hour. A trip could be made to Indianapolis in one hour and 25 minutes. Each car had a telephone. At Crawfordsville, at 117 West Main, in building Mr. Durham had given to YMCA in 1889.

First run of the "Ben Hur Line", Omer Glover was the motorman, and he was on the last car that ran on October 31, 1930. Both interurban lines had ceased by 1931. In 4 years, 1907-1911, 662 and 927 passengers had ridden the Ben Hur Line. Some of the men who worked on interurban besides Glover, was Nevitt, Hall, Clark, Houlehan, Denny, Jones, Aber, Arnold, Elliot, and Mills. *Submitted by Pauline Walters*

LINNSBURG STATE BANK

In 1879's Susanna Fenders Linn Mullen had platted the town of Linnsburg on

55 acres owned by her first husband, John Linn. The area had been called Mace Station until 1873, it became Linnsburg. The town began to do very good: had two grocery stores, elevator, blacksmith, stockyards, and the Big Four Railroad went through there. There was also a barber shop, two churches, and Linn Hall for gatherings. A big dairy was at the north edge of Linnsburg and they sold milk to the Claypool Hotel in Indianapolis.

As business prospered so well, they decided they needed a bank, and on June 1913, a bank was organized in Linnsburg, with a capital stock of $25,000. Orph W. Bratton was named president, Charles F. Linn, Cashier, Charles Minnich, Vice President and the directors were: Orph Bratton; Charles Minnich, Sr.; Harvey A. Bratton; Odis Stafford; William A. Collings; and Walter Linn were the bank's attorneys.

The Bank opened on September 1, 1913 under tutelage of American National Bank Equipment bought from the First National Bank in Crawfordsville. It had a burglar proof safe, encased in brick. Linnsburg State Bank in large gold letters decorated the large front window. The building was made of oriental brick. Lower walls inside were white tiling at bottom and tinted colors for the ceiling.

In 1923, May 2, a couple of armed men robbed the bank when Charles Linn was there alone, taking $1,900.

The Department of Financial Institutions of Indiana said the bank closed its doors April 9, 1925. The building still stands, as a reminder of better days in Linnsburg. *By Pauline Walters*

THE LADOGA CANNING COMPANY

John Foxworthy had a small article taken from the *Ladoga Leader* about the Ladoga Canning Company, but it did not give any history of the company.

In 1901, John P. Servies from Advance opened a factory for canning tomatoes north east of Ladoga. In 1903, the Ladoga Canning Company was organized. Muter Bachelder and Foster Shroudt were the promoters. The organizers were Eugene Ashby, George Havens, Harry Daugherty, James Knox and Alex Scott. Mr. Shroudt was manager until 1913, followed by Edgar Ashby as manager and president. I don't know when the large canning factory was built, but it was a large place.

In 1905 Mrs. Emma Knox, Edgar Ashby, Muter Bachelder or his sons Clay and Harold, owned or controlled the company.

In 1936, at the time of the Ladoga Centennial, Mrs. Denny said the canning company was doing a $2 or $3 million dollar business yearly. Their weekly payroll was $4,500. (wages were very low then). They sent canned goods to every state and in W.W.I they sent canned goods to the English government, about $2,000,000 worth.

They opened plants at Lebanon, Brownsburg, Clay City, Brookston, Edinburg, all in Indiana. Also plants in Chilicothe and Circleville, Ohio; and Mound City, Illinois.

Every fall women worked at the factory, during the tomato season. Each woman was paid for how many buckets of tomatoes she could peel. Slow peelers, received a small wage. My mother and a friend of hers worked there, and for years afterwards she couldn't buy canned tomatoes for back then sanitary conditions weren't maintained, as they are today.

In later years Ralph Strickler was superintendent of the plant. After it closed, he and his wife Esther, opened up a room downtown, a home canning place. Women prepared peas, tomatoes, corn, etc. ready to can brought them to Stricklers, and they canned them. They canned fruits, too. This operated for several years. *By Pauline Walters*

THE MIDLAND RAILWAY COMPANY

The Midland Railway Company was incorporated on July 7, 1885. The Midland was started in 1871 as the "Anderson, Lebanon and St. Louis Railway Company." The railroad started at Muncie and went west toward Anderson and

Ladoga Canning Company, Lodoga Plant

BLACK CIVIL WAR SOLDIERS
Company D, 28th U.S. Colored Troops

Corporal Abraham Richy　　　　Crawfordsville　　　　Jan. 15, 1864 - Nov. 8, 1865

Unassigned Recruits
28th U.S. Colored Troops

Charles Thompson　　　　Montgomery County　　　　April 4, 1865 - May 24, 1865

Recruits
8th Reg. Infantry U.S. Colored Troops

Bartlett Bridges　　　　Montgomery County　　　　October 19, 1864
William Cook　　　　Montgomery County　　　　March 24, 1865

Various Regiments

Jere Bias	Co. B, 124th U.S.C.T.	William H. Jordan	Co. D, 28th U.S.C.T.
John Bias	U.S.C.T.	James Upton Keene	Co. H, 124th U.S.C.T.
Daniel Boone	Co. C, 28th U.S.C.T.	Aaron McCrea	Co. E, 14th U.S.C.T.
Samuel Calloway (alias Fred Stewart)	28th U.S.C.T.	Jackson Newkirk	2nd Colored Cavalry
Austin Carpenter	Co. D, 28th U.S.C.T.	Nelson Patterson	Co. G, 28th U.S.C.T.
Harmon Churchill	U.S.C.T.	William Walker Robb	U.S.C.T.
Benjamin Cline	Co. C, 28th U.S.C.T.	Harvey Smith	Co. E, 109th U.S.C.T.
Wesley Foster	Co. C, 28th U.S.C.T.	William D. Taylor	Co. D, 28th U.S.C.T.
Robert T. Hopkins	Co. C, 118th U.S.C.T.	Monroe Vick	8th U.S.C.V.
George Johnson	Co. B, 47th U.S.C.T.	Henry Warren	Co. C, 28th U.S.C.T.
Isaac A. Jones	Mass. Inf. U.S.C.T.	Charles Wickliffe	Co. D, 28th U.S.C.T.
Joseph Jones	U.S.C.T.	Zack Williams	U.S.C.T.

This list was compiled by using Adjutant General Terrell's report of the State of Indiana during the Civil War, Volume 7, printed in 1867. Also used were:
Montgomery County Soldier and Sailor Dead, 9154 Memorial Edition.
Montgomery County Grave Registration Cards located in the Indiana State Archives in Indianapolis. Enlistment records of the 28th U.S Colored Troops. *Submitted by: Andrew Keith Houk, Jr., Jamestown, Indiana*

---

reached Noblesville in 1876. The Midland opened the stretch of track between Noblesville and Westfield in October, 1885. The Westfield to Eagletown section opened in September, 1886. The Midland opened the 35-mile section of track from Eagletown to Ladoga and opened for business on July 4, 1887. The first train into Ladoga brought a large celebration with an oxen and mutton roast, speeches and singing. The Midland continued on southwest to Browns Valley in 1888 and to Waveland in May of 1890. At Waveland the Midland used the Vandalia Railroad (Pennsylvania Railroad) to Sand Creek in Parke County and the railroad ended in Brazil.

The Midland became the Chicago and Southeastern Railway on October 9, 1891 and was owned by Henry Crawford of Chicago, Illinois. On March 16, 1903 the Midland became the Central Indiana Railway Company and was jointly operated by the Pennsylvania Railroad and the Big Four Railroad. The Central Indiana operated six daily passenger trains between Anderson and Waveland, and two trains a day between Brazil and Waveland.

In the early 1920's, the Central Indiana had labor and financial problems. On September 14, 1928, the Interstate Commerce Commission granted permission to abandon the Central Indiana Railroad from Advance to Brazil. In Montgomery County, the Central Indiana went from New Ross to Ladoga to Pawnee to Lapland to Penobscot to Browns Valley to Waveland. The Ladoga to Brazil section was abandoned on November 30, 1928. The Advance to New Ross to Ladoga section was abandoned on February 8, 1929. The Advance to Lebanon section was abandoned on December 18, 1943. The Lebanon to Anderson section was abandoned in 1978. On May 16, 1989, the last of the tracks were removed from Superior Street in Lebanon, thus ending the old Midland Railroad. *Submitted by: Andrew Keith Houk, Jr., Jamestown, Indiana*

ORPHAN TRAIN

It was a crisp fall day, the smoke puffed from the engine of the train as it pulled into the station in Montgomery County, Indiana. The year was 1894, and this was a very special train. The "Orphan Train." It carried homeless children on board to the heartland of our country. The children ranged from infants to 16 years of age.

People with their horses and buggies waited at the station to take their turn in picking out a child to live with them. Through a pre-arrangement with the families in the area a child would be taken into their homes. The new family was to provide food, clothing, religious training, and schooling in return for the child's labor.

This placing-out system started in New York in 1854, to help the children, waifs, orphans; yes, even thieves, as they were called, to escape the poverty, slums, famine, filth, disease, and rodents. Emigrants had flocked to the shores of the United States in search of religious freedom and wealth. Instead they found no jobs, or jobs that paid so little they could not live adequately. Long hours and rapid spread of diseases such as cholera, measles, and influenza caused the death

Orphan Train

of the family provider, leaving the children homeless and requiring them to care for themselves. They lived in gunnysacks, didn't have clothing, or food, sometimes for days.

In 1853, Rev. Charles Loring Brace, a pioneering social worker, age 26, established the Children's Aid Society in New York City, New York. Convinced that the West had "many spare places at the table of life," he initiated the orphan train concept. The first children were sent out into the country in the state of New York. From 1854 to 1929 one hundred fifty thousand children were placed in homes throughout the United States and Canada. A report from the Children's Aid Society in 1910 states that there were children in every state in the Union. It listed Indiana had taken 3,955 children through this placing-out system.

Many of the children became happy with their new lives, but, they were always separated from their siblings and other members of their original family. Some have been able to establish some link with their past, while others were not fortunate enough to even find out their real family name. Most of the children were taken as cheap farm labor, but there were some very Christian people who took them because they just loved children. In 1929, a law was passed which did not permit the system of placing-out to continue. The Children's Aid Society is still in business today helping the orphan in New York.

Yes, even Montgomery County provided homes for some of these children. The train I spoke of in the first paragraph did indeed stop in Montgomery County. My great Aunt was on that train and she remained in Montgomery County living with the family in Ladoga who took her in. Her new family said they "collected her from the Orphan Train." She married their son and gave them 5 grandchildren.

There is evidence that others here in Montgomery County are descendents of an "Orphan Train Rider".

Submitted by Barbara J. Taylor

MONON PASSENGER TRAIN, LAST

The Monon Railroad, now the CSX System, offered passenger train service from Louisville, Kentucky to Chicago, Illinois, and it also offered passenger service from Lafayette, Indiana to Indianapolis, Indiana and Lafayette, Indiana to Michigan City, Indiana.

The Monon Railroad offered as many as 10 passenger trains a day, but by 1967, the Monon was down to one passenger train in each direction a day. The last passenger train was numbered 5 and 6 and was called The Thoroughbred. The Monon Railroad in the summer of 1967 still served the cities of Chicago, Illinois, Hammond, Rensselaer, Monon, Lafayette, Crawfordsville, Greencastle, Bloomington, Bedford, Mitchell, Orleans, Salem, New Albany, Indiana and Louisville, Kentucky.

In the summer of 1967, the Monon Railroad filed with the Interstate Commerce Commission to discontinue passenger service. On September 7, 1967 the Interstate Commerce Commission approved the end of the Chicago to Louisville passenger service. The last southbound train from Chicago to Louisville left Chicago's Dearborn Station at 5:25 p.m. on September 29, 1967 and arrived in Louisville at 3:15 a.m. the following morning. The last northbound train left Louisville at 6:30 a.m. on September 30, 1967. Many railfans and passengers made the last run. The last Monon Railroad passenger train arrived in Crawfordsville at 10:10 a.m.

The station platform was crowded with several hundred people who were there to bid a sad farewell to The Thoroughbred. I was a 17-year-old railfan that day taking pictures of my favorite train when my parents handed me a ticket on the last train and said they would pick me up in Hammond, Indiana. I was overjoyed to say the least. I stood in the doorway the entire trip to Hammond taking pictures. There were people along the tracks waving and taking pictures. At each stop, people would disembark and more would board to take a trip into railroad history. At several stops, there were high school bands and short speeches. It was a day that a 17-year-old railfan would remember for the rest of his life.

During the 1970's, the Chicago to

Louisville line was used by Amtrak for passenger service and on October 1, 1980, Amtrak started The Hoosier State with service from Chicago to Indianapolis. Crawfordsville in 1989 is served by two Amtrak passenger trains.
Submitted by: Andrew Keith Houk, Jr., Jamestown, Indiana

MAPLE GROVE SCHOOL

This school was 2 miles north of Ladoga, 1/2 mile east, and 1/2 mile north. The land was sold by the United States to John and Nancy Barnett Pottinger, original entry Sept. 19, 1831. John Pottinger to John Barnett, his heirs, etc., warranty deed February 24, 1826 recorded August 10, 1836. Deed record 47, John Barnett and wife to Silas Kyle, trustees for school district, Clark Township to John N. Brown October 21, 1919(?), Ed Barnes Trustee 1880. This school was built in 1880, and closed in 1911. In 1928, John N. Brown's daughter, Lucille Wine sold the school building and lot to Robert Hoagland, and he in turn sold it to Norman Burkett, and he in turn sold it to James Stadler, and he remodeled inside—made 4 rooms out of it, then in 1962 Harold and Pauline Walters; Robert and Mary Walters bought it, and their son Jeffrey bought 3/4 of it, and they completely modernized the building inside, then he sold it back to Robert Walters, and it was rented out, then a big fire occurred and Maple Grove School was almost damaged beyond repair. This school building was built very strong and good. As lights and water are still available there, the grounds have been used for trailer living.

(OLD) SOAP FACTORY SCHOOLHOUSE

How this school received its name was a favorite story of this writer since he attended school there. Schools throughout the county were known officially by numbers. This particular one was Union Township School 6. Many schools were named unofficially for their location or some incident that occurred in the neighborhood. The latter being the case of this school.

This school was located in the general area of the present state highway garage—north and west of the I-74 and US 231 Interchange.

In the neighborhood at the time this school was newly-built there lived a family of Dutch descent. One of their cows wandered onto the tracks and was killed by an oncoming train. The family tried in vain to receive payment from the railroad company. Angered by such utter disregard for the common man from such a huge railroad company the housewife took matters into her own hands.

One night she took a large supply of her homemade laundry soap and proceeded to liberally coat the tracks for about half a mile. Since there was a slight upgrade into town the trains lost traction and were stalled; "Pioneer justice" was done.

The school quickly became known as the "Soap Factory Schoolhouse". *Submitted by John Breaks Lofland*

PISGAH CHURCH

"The 4th Book of the Regular Predestinarian Baptist Church of Jesus Christ called Pisgah located near Beckville in Montgomery County and State of Indiana" and the Pisgah Cemetery is all that is materially left of this church. The building has deteriorated and disappeared from the view, but not from the memory and cultural background of many of the Montgomery County residents. This Baptist church was one of the several community churches that has influenced the spiritual beliefs and lives of some who live today in Montgomery County.

The church was organized October the 22nd, 1831 and those who are recorded to have participated in its organization are: Johnathan Clark, Paul Burk, Jeramiah West, Jesse Routh, Isaac Jones, Usual Lafolette, William D. Bruce, Noah Ferguson, John Watts, Ruth Watts, Elizabeth Beck, Anthony Beck, John Ferguson, Mary Ferguson, Solomon Beck, and Joseph Betts Sr. There are nineteen rules of decorum listed and eight articles of faith. The members listed on Saturday before the first Sunday in January of the year 1900 came to a total of 27.

The last recorded meeting of the church in Walnut Township was moderated by Elder George S. Joseph, with George S. Threkeld, as county clerk. Further records dated 31 August 1925, and concerned the disposition of the church and cemetery.

The church has disappeared, but the spirit of its members is still alive in their posterity. This church was one of the rich cultural influences in Montgomery county.

This 4th book was handed down to the keeping of Judy K. Spurgeon and kept in the family by request of Anna Dickson, daughter of George S. Joseph. A copy has been placed in the Crawfordsville Public Library, Local History Section for public access. *by Roger G. Spurgeon, Sr.*

QUAKERS IN MONTGOMERY COUNTY

The first Quaker group to erect a Meeting house was the Sugar River Monthly Meeting. This site stood on Peter Binford's land in Section 23 of North Union Township. The location is now located on County Road 300 North, 1/2 Mile west of Garfield. The Meeting House is gone but the cemetery is still there. It has been recently cleared of undergrowth and is visible on the south side of the road. On May 13, 1989 the historic marker pictured here was erected by a group interested in restoring this vital link to the pioneer days in Montgomery County. Sixteen graves occupy this site but several tomb stones are now missing. A record of the Quakers buried here may be found in the Local History Room of the Crawfordsville District Public library. The record is given under "Binford Cemetery" as well as its original name "Sugar River Cemetery." The cemetery was abandoned in 1878 because the land was too low and wet.

Willard Heiss, eminent genealogist of Indiana, states that the Sugar River Monthly Meeting was first held on the "the 25th of Twelfth Month 1830," but it was "set-off from White Lick Monthly" before that date. Two other Meetings were established in Montgomery County: Center in 1841 and Gravelly Run in 1844. Center Meeting was in Section 9 of Franklin Township and was located on the present site of the Greenlawn Cemetery east of Darlington. The Gravelly Run Meeting was established in Section 30 of Franklin Twp. and the Meeting House was built on Butler ground. (Louise Butler Kuonen wrote "A Quaker History as I Have Heard It" which is also on file in the Local History Room.)

Of the three Meetings only Gravelly Run Meeting is still functioning. Their Meeting House stands on the south side of County Road 150 North just 1/4 mile from where 550 East joins with 150 North. The Gravelly Run Meeting provided assistance for reclamation of the Sugar River Cemetery in May of 1989.

Each of these three sites represent a significant heritage for Montgomery County and more history of the people who brought the Quaker faith to this area should be recorded.

SPEECH GIVEN BY THOMAS NEWTON RICE TO OLD SETTLERS WAVELAND, INDIANA

The generations of men come and go intermingling and lapping over each other like the waves of the sea. From thirty to fifty years fixes the limit to a wave of human life or generation. Thirty-three years have been the limit heretofore, but that limit is being extended by the better care bestowed on the weaker members of the race, as a result of the benign teachings and life of the Savior of men. All the lives which start in with the wave, do not continue until it has spent its force; more than half die in infancy, a large number before the age of majority, while but a few hold on and lap over on the succeeding wave; but still the rhythmic click of the heart of infant life, the bounding throb of youth, the majestic pulse of manhood and the decreasing pulsation of old age are heard along the wave and die as the though beat on the verge of that mysterious ocean which receives us all.

The life wave of the Fathers broke on a majestic forest, whose towering branches benignly down and caring for his own.

There were clustered all the homely virtues honesty, humility, charity, industry and thrift freedom from guild, with a generous open hearted hospitality, which absolutely bubbled up and ran over toward any stranger who might happen to be jorneying through the wilderness or neighbor who might call and spend the day. The fare was not elaborate, but it was substantial. It beat the fare of the Prophet Elijah when the Ravens called. And was as good as that set at the boarding house at Saripta. I am not an old settler (I am a native to the manner born) but my Father was, and when I remember what the men of his generation encountered to my personal knowledge, in felling trees, rolling logs, burning the brush, plowing the ground, matted as it was with green roots, building houses, splitting rails, making fence, making roads and the thousand other labors devolved upon them. I stand in admiration of their splendid courage and endurance and reverently lift my hat as the procession passes in review.

My earliest recollections are of a log house with two rooms, an outside door and one window to each room with four acres of cleared land in front from which the timber has been out in the green. There were no public roads, but wagon ways through the woods and paths blazed through the woods to the school house and the neighbors-who were transient, and did not tarry long in the neighborhood.

They were men who lived by the chase, they did not like to be crowded, they wanted elbow room, and as soon as the deer and wild turkey and other game became scarce and small farms began to intrude upon the forest, were up and off with wife, children, dogs and household plunder to forests dense and hunting fields new. They were the scud preceeding the rain cloud. The advanced couriers of civilization, yet they were a part of that wave of human life, which was bearing down upon the forest, the spray of the advancing wave. One picture of this class is hung up in memories hall. Twas autumn, the sun had tinged the forest leaves with natures dyes of gold, yellow and russet brown, the hens had ceased cackling and nothing but the mournful cooing of the wood dove was heard. The winds had gone to sleep and all nature had lapsed into that lazy lazy dream life so delightful in the life of a boy. Three or four bareheaded and barefooted children were enjoying the quiet of the scene when the attention was arrested by the distant baying of dogs and the sound of the hunters horse.

The sound came from the north, and was nearing us, and becoming more distinct. The little company was standing in the yard with mouths open, hands locked behind their backs, with heads up and eyes and ears alert, and mother in the back ground, all facing the sound, when sure enough the expected did happen, emerging through the brush across the branch, on came the deer. She cleared the branch at a bound, shunned the quagmire to the right, strained up the bank, passed the spring within fifty feet of us, bounded along the west side of the four acre field and out of sight before we could realize what was transpiring. "Oh" it was a race for life, for turning again to the sound of dogs and men we saw the leader of the chase, a noble hound with head down, whimpering cry with now and then a deep mouthed bawl, full fifty yards ahead of the pack, he came down the slope, crossed the branch shunned the quagmire, up the bank, past the spring, around the corner of the fence and gone; after him came the pack in full cry, while further down the branch up the hill appears a horseman, and directly after him came another, cheering on the dogs, and last of all came boys and men on foot, following the trail with whoop and shout and hollow which made the welkin ring. The rout past, the sound died away in the distance and was lost in Cumming gore and Richey woods to the west of Waveland, and silence settled down again on forest, brake and field.

The quarry was started on Sugar Creek near the shades, had turned to the south, past by our place and to the west of where Waveland now stands, and on south through the Wymore settlement and was lost or caught to the south of Portland Mills. Along with this restless moving class of settlers came others who came to stay, bringing with them the sober steady habits of the older communities from which they came.

The early settlers of Parke and Montgomery Counties were mostly from the States of Kentucky, Virginia and North

VETERANS WHO MADE THE SUPREME SACRIFICE IN VIETNAM 1961 - 1975

Richard E. Lynch, died October 8, 1965

Delbert W. Haase, died October 18, 1967

Samuel H. Howard, died December 2, 1967

William K. Clawson, died December 14, 1967

Leonard A. Stalnaker, died February 8, 1968

Harold W. Abbott, died February 17, 1968

Lloyd Tribbett, died May 8, 1968

Carl T. Alexander, died January 10, 1969

John J. Corwin, II, died April 17, 1969

Samuel E. Benge, died June 3, 1969

Submitted by: Andrew Keith Houk, Jr.,

Vietnam Veteran, Jamestown, Indiana

Carolina. Men and women of strong moral, religions, and political, convictions, and had quietly moved away from the contaminating influence of human slavery and sought a home in the wilderness, wherever they settled. They impressed their character upon the community, which remains to this day. The church and school house were built and along with the material development of the neighborhood came the moral religious and intellectual development pari passu, being men and women of conviction and conscience, they held to them with tenacity. The political contests of 1836-40 and 44 were marked with an enthusiasm, and at the same time with a bitterness and acrimony which I have not known since.

In matters of religious faith the war was waged against sin and the Devil with as much zeal as now. But it was waged along denominational lines. The age of controversy had not passed and denominational fences were all up and the assault was made by divisions, which often fired into each other, but on the whole it was against the enemy and if he was routed by the Baptist he might fall under the fire of the Presbyterian battery, and if that failed to make him surrender, he was sure to be blown sky high by Methodist dynamite where he was held hair hung and breeze shaken over the infernal regions until he capitulated; or escaping that, he would be brought down by the gatling gun of the Reformers. This kind of warfare had this advantage, it made every professor wide awake and alert to lengthen the cords and strengthen the stakes of his part of Zion. And produced a type of robust Christians, who were ever ready to do battle for the cause. My memory is full of saintly men and women in all denominations whose lives were an inspiration, a letter known and read of all men, and redolent with the spirit of the Master.

I now see a typical family of the neighbor-hood. The same courage which brought the loving wife and her little brood with the husband and father into the wilderness sustains and supports her in the discharge of the multifarious duties of her life. Her busy hands prepare the food and care for the children, teaching, cheering and encouraging them and by precept and example impressing her very life upon their susceptible natures. While to cloth their bodies the spindle hums and the shuttle flies literally weaving her own life into the web of the life of her children. At home, at the log rolling and quilting, at the wedding, at church, though clothed in humble garb, she walked a goddess and looked a queen, heaven was in her eye in every motion grace and dignity.

While to clear the land and supply the food the father leaves the humble home at early dawn and soon the sound of the ax is heard in forest or clearing; how distinctly it falls on the ear; every stroke is heard and the sound discloses the progress the axman is making in felling the trees. Or were the oxen needed they were yoked and hitched to the home made wagon with wheels made from 6 or 8 inch rings cut from the body of the black gum; the rails were hauled and the fence built or with log chain dulled around a log with many a whoop and crack of the whip, with divers encouraging words such as Gee Buck get up Bright, get right along. The log is moved into position; or hitched to the plow with wooden mould board; the hired hand driving the owner hold of the plow, all goes well until the plow snaps a green root which in its back action whacks the owner on the shin; or the point of the plow strikes an obstruction and stops suddenly thus lifting the handle so as to strike the plower under the first rib, greatly to the disturbance of his pleura or whatever is under the aforesaid rib. Thus the day wares on; the blessed dinner horn sounds, the dinner is eaten with such conversation as the incidents of the morning furnish, and the answering of such questions as the children may ask, and the afternoons work both in and out of the house is resumed and continued until the shades of night settle down upon cabin, forest and field.

The simple supper is eaten, the children put in their beds the latch string pulled inside and sleep the innocent sleep "Sleep that knits up the raveled sleave of care. The death of each days life, sore labors bath."

Balm of hurt minds, great natures second course chief nourishes in life feast, seals up the eyelids of the tired sleepers, until the cocks shrill clarion awakes the echoing morn-thus the days pass and summer glides into autumn and autumn into winter.

The long evenings are here and the social life of the neighborhood begins; social visits are received and returned-the capacious fire place is filled to its utmost capacity with blazing logs and light wood which casts a ruddy glow cuts every crack and cranny in the room. A rap is heard on the door, which is opened and Mrs. and Mr. B. our nearest neighbors are ushered into the warm room, a couple of say 40 summers, they were here before my father. I speak of Mrs. B. first - she was in her prime, the mother of three or four children and full of robust life, she had a cherry lip, a bonny eye and a passing, pleasing tongue. And her rippling laughter and the rich mellow cadence of her voice are beating now on the tympanum of my ear and have been since boyhood. She had a ready wit, which at times cut like a knife but with all a kind generous Irish heart.

In a few minutes Mr. and Mrs. C. dropped in and an evening of rare enjoyment began which was kept up with conversation light and grave joke and laughter until bed time when the table was cleared away and bible and hymn book was brought out and a portion of Gods word was read and a song was sung.

"Then kneeling down to Heavens eternal King

The saint the father and the Husband prays;

Hope springs exulting on triumphant wing

That thus they all shall meet in future days

There even to bask in uncreated rays;

No more to sigh or shed the bitter tear

Together hymning there Creators praise,

In such society: yet still more dear

While circling time moves round in an eternal sphere.

The worship over, the neighbors go off their separate ways home."

RIDGE FARM SCHOOL & CHURCH

One of the most historic areas in Montgomery County is the area adjoining the intersection of Indiana 32 and State Road 25 in Ripley Township. This is commonly known as Myers Corner.

James D. Herron and his wife Rebecca entered land here in October 1825. They came from Ohio by wagon entering into Indian territory. A short distance from the Myers Corner and west on the south side of the highway the Ridge Farm School and the Ridge Farm Church of Christ was built. In later years the land for the school building was deeded to the township. In February 1881 about one third of an acre was used for the school. School was held there until 1917. One of the teachers is still living, Stella Smith Myers. A few students remain. Harold McCormick and his wife Ruth did so much in the recording of history in this county. Harold was an alumni of Ridge Farm School. They both died in 1988.

The school building was used as a gathering place for church services until 1904 when the Ridge Farm Church was built.

The vacant school building was sold to Charley Myers in 1919 who at that time owned the adjoining farm. The school children were transferred to school at Alamo, Indiana. On September 19, 1903 Andrew W. Herron deeded to the trustees of the Ridge Farm Church the sum of $50.00 about one half acre adjoining the school ground. This made it possible for any denomination to have services in the building.

In November 1926 Evangelist Emanuel Eckerly from the White River Conference United Brethern in Christ of Indianapolis, Indiana came to the Ridge Farm Community. He organized the Church as United Brethern in Christ. He held two weeks of evangelistic meetings filling the church with neighboring friends. The following families were loyal workers in the church Fred Fruits, Charley Ceders, Frank "Doc" Herron Vol. Norman, Fred Norman, Elam Reath, Mary Mullen, Carol Myers, Sybil Myers. Sybil Myers who is ninety one years of age and lives in Waynetown, Indiana remembers lots of enjoyable times with the different pastors that served the church and community from 1926 to 1934. Rev. Lucy Sharp, Veedersburg Circuit was pastor of Centennial Church near Kingman, Indiana years prior to Ridge Farm Church. Rev. Heedlie Cobb of Muncie, Indiana was a college student when he came to Ridge Farm Church studying to be an evangelist. Rev. Cobb ministered at the funeral of a loyal member of the church Fred Norman September 13, 1988. Fred was the janitor and kept those pot bellied stoves burning on those cold winter Sunday mornings. Rev. Cobb reminisced as it had been fifty-six years since he had been pastor of the church. Rev. Helen Grantham Collins was another pastor who served Ridge Farm Church. She was the wife of Terre Haute singer evangelist Neil Collins. Both are deceased.

There was a new roof put on the church in the thirties. As the years went by older people passed away, younger people went elsewhere. There wasn't enough members to keep it going, resulting in the doors being closed in the mid-thirties. The buildings are no longer standing.

In the eighties the memories of school days and preaching services are only in the memories of a few. As I pass by I remember. *By: Sybil Atkinson Myers*

LOUISE SABENS REMEMBERS

This is an account of the family of James A. Miller, his wife Stella and their two daughters, Eleanor and Louise. The family lived on a rented farm near Paris, Illinois. They decided it was time to buy some farm land of their own, so in the year of 1910, the search began. After looking as far away from Paris, Illinois, as the state of Texas, they came across an advertisement from the Andy Clements Real Estate Agency in Crawfordsville, Indiana. Deciding to pursue the advertisement, Mr. Miller contacted the Agency and through the salesmanship of Mr. Billy Luster, he was shown the 80-acre farm, six miles East of Crawfordsville which was for sale by the Charles Guilliams family. The farm suited Mr. Miller, so the purchase was made in November of 1910.

The Miller family moved to this farm in Montgomery County in March 1911. In addition to household goods, some mature hogs (brood sows) were crated and put on the baggage car of the train and transported from Paris, Illinois to the station at Linnsburg. There neighbors who were contacted in advance, met the Miller family and assisted in hauling the belongings to the farm two miles away. A grandfather drove the three horses and two cows tied behind the wagon overland from Paris. A next door neighbor, William Myers was waiting on the front porch to invite the new arrivals to spend the first night at their home, which was gratefully accepted.

The Miller children, Eleanor, age eight years and Louise, age six years were anxious to get started back to school. At that time, school was only an eight month time, so only three weeks were left. There was transportation to the door in the form of a horse driven hack holding about fifteen children and the driver. So the Miller girls entered the consolidated school of twelve grades at Mace. The first and second grade teacher was Mrs. Ida Wingert. The third and fourth grades were taught by Miss Mable Quigg. Time went by quickly it seemed and with successes as well as some failures, the family carried on the farm activities and were faithful attendants and members of the Mace Methodist Church. Mr. Miller had two brothers who were ordained Methodist Ministers, so an interest in Religion was a part of their life. Daughter Louise showed a talent for music at an early age. In fact, from age four, she was fascinated with the lovely large square grand Emmerson piano in the grandparents' home, and had literally to be bodily carried away from it. When Louise was age ten, the parents bought a parlor organ, thus began her musical education. It was not long until the organ did not suffice for the type of instrumental music Louise had progressed to, so a new piano from the Claypool Music Store in Crawfordsville was purchased. One of Louise's piano teachers was Eliza Harmon, who was well-known in Crawfordsville. Louise became the school pianist and played for morning exercises each day at school as well as for other entertainment and school activities. A talented music teacher by name, Miss Belle Roger of Mace High School conducted some very excellent musical reviews almost to the point of professional. One number in particular stands out in memory. It is now a recording by the Mills Brothers, titled "Shine Little Glow Worm Glimmer." In the performance of this number at Mace H.S. all lights were off and flashlights used by the performers to imitate the glowworms. It was spectacular. Another talented music teacher was Martha Barnhill. When Louise was in seventh grade in 1918, the English class was studying and reading Lew Wallace's book, *Ben Hur*. At that same time, a stage play originating in New York was travelling the U.S. with the live performance of that book. It was widely publicized and a very unusual and spectacular performance. Showing the storm and destruction of the ship in which Ben Hur was a galley slave and also the celebrated chariot race between the proud Roman, Masella and Ben Hur the Christian and Believer in Christ. The stage was revolving and the two chariots with Ben Hur driving the black horses and Masella the two white horses live and racing before your eyes on the stage.

The point here is that the English teacher of the seventh grade at Mace school decided to take members of the class who would go to Indianapolis to see the play live. Louise went as well as two other girl classmates, Mary Ward and Helen Hayes, also others and the teacher as chaperone. The group went from school to the interurban station at Linnsburg bound for Indianapolis.

The play was on stage at the English Theatre on the Circle. It was the most prestigious theatre in the capitol city. Near by was White's Cafeteria, a popular place to eat for the theatre goers. The Mace group ate dinner there, which was of course quite a treat, for most had not been to such an elegant place. After the theatre, the group came back to Linnsburg, arriving about midnight. Since those were horse and buggy days, parents had to make plans for their children staying overnight. Louise and Helen Hayes were to stay at the Mr. and Mrs. Jay Harris home, which was at least a quarter mile from the station. The two girls, thirteen or fourteen years old walked alone to the Harris home at midnight very frightened and imagining big black bears or worse, a kidnapper to carry them away lurking behind every tree or bush. But they arrived safely and were well taken care of by Aunt Lide Harris as she was called by all her friends. She provided school lunch for the next day. Louise remembers the whole event as one of the great experiences of her life. There were many interesting events in Montgomery County, the annual County Fair being a highlight. For the Miller family, especially the two young girls, Eleanor and Louise it was something to be long remembered. At that time, about 1916, the County fair was far more outstanding to them than the State Fair several years later. There were the stands selling cotton candy, hot dogs, souvenirs and trinkets. Of course money was limited. But the merry-go-round was a must, the Ferris Wheel interesting, but too frightening for the young girls. There was horse racing and many local businesses advertising, especially the Claypool piano display, with a player piano in operation almost continuously. That was where Louise could usually be found. Another highlight of living in Montgomery County was the weekly trip to Crawfordsville to shop on Saturday, and to meet other friends there. The big Louis Bischoff store was like magic to go into. Especially on the second floor with beautiful dresses for ladies, and coats and furs. The Graham Department store on North Washington Street was very interesting as well. Also, Woolworth's ten cent store with the soda fountain counter. Another interesting place to be remembered was the Greek Kandy Kitchen on Main Street. Here, dating couples always went for ice cream treats after the movies or just from gadding around.

As the Miller girls, Eleanor and Louise grew-up, boy friends entered the picture. After graduating from Mace High School, Eleanor was married to William McMullen in the Miller farm home, the minister performing the wedding ceremony being Reverend Thomas Stovall, who was at that time, pastor at Mace Church. Rev. Stovall later became District Superintendent of Crawfordsville District of the Methodist Church and passed away recently at 90 plus years of age. Next door neighbor to the Miller family were Mr. and Mrs. Lawrence Foster. Mrs. Foster, Jess, as she was known was a Purdue extension worker and was speaker for groups known as Farmers Institute, which meetings were held around the state and in Montgomery County. She organized the Mace Home Economic Club and helped to get the Home Economic idea for local women in the county.

Mr. Miller worked hard on the farm, though not a rugged man. In 1924, at age 47, he passed away.

Louise was graduated from Mace High School in 1922. At that time, the Mace and New Ross High School classes, both in Walnut Township combined for the graduating service. On February 6, 1924, Louise was married to Frank Sabens. After settling Mr. Miller's financial affairs, Louise and husband Frank became owners of the home farm. Eleanor and husband purchased farm land near Roachdale. Mrs. Miller (Stella) eventually moved to Linnsburg, owning a house there, where she lived until her death in 1951.

In March, 1913, there was an almost disastrous flood in Montgomery County. It rained for days. The Red Cross helped many. Bridges washed out and water was very high. Then of course, the memory of the big fire in Crawfordsville when it seemed the whole town would burn down. Then one misses the Old Crawford Hotel which was quite elegant at one time.

Louise Sabens is now 84, still a musician playing piano at Mace Church and for Crawfordsville Sunshine Chorus. Eleanor McMullen also lives now in Crawfordsville. *Submitted by Louise Sabens*

SQUARE DANCING

Square Dancing has always been part of America's history. In colonial times, settlers often gathered together for husking bees, quilting frolics and barn raisings, and once the work was done they turned to dancing. Often there would be no special reason for the calling of a dance just the desire for a good social get-together, called a junket. An impromptu square dance might be announced by a loud-voiced citizen shouting, "junket - junket".

In the early 1800 the quadrilles were still popular. Toward the latter half of the century the young people wanting dances of a more personal and strenuous nature rebelled against this type of dance. In 1925 square dancing was given a new push. About 1940 the square dance field began to emerge as a big business. Spurred by the tremendous participation at the New York's Worlds Fair in 1940. By 1950 the square dance boom was in full stride. The proliferation of square dancing around the country during the years since 1950 has been phenomenal. It is estimated that there are 6 million people who square dance today.

A partial genealogical chart of square dancing: Square Dancing started with the Morris Dance of England plus the Quadrille of France to become the Singing Quadriles. Then came the Appalachian Mountain Dance and the New England Country Dance to become Western Square Dance and Eastern Square Dance. These two joined together to become today's Square Dance.

There are many square dance clubs in the United States today. The local square dance club is the Sugar Creek Squares. The Sugar Creek Squares was formed October 1973 when two clubs, the Square Busters and Mates & Dates, joined together as one club. Royal blue and white were selected as club colors.

The Sugar Creek Squares were formed to provide a place where dancers may enjoy dancing together in a spirit of friendliness and cooperation.

Membership is open, limited only by facilities. A member must complete a set of square dance lessons.

The club dances twice a month except July, August and November. The dances are held the 2nd and Last Saturday 8 p.m. - 10:30 p.m. at the 4-H Building Crawfordsville, Indiana. *Submitted by: Janet Fields*

STONEWALL JACKSON CAMP #1, LADOGA

In the mid-1890's, a group of Montgomery County men, all former Confederate soldiers, decided to form a camp of the United Confederate Veterans. The United Confederate Veterans was formed after the Civil War in the south. This veteran's organization was made up of former Confederate soldiers and sailors.

It was decided that the newly organized camp should be in Ladoga, Indiana, due partly to the large number of former Confederates in the area and a friendly atmosphere toward the south.

The original charter had 11 members. Their names were: Jonas T. Gish, William P. Camden, John Mangus, Thomas Terry, Isaac Sperry, William Luster, Madison Linkinhoker, Thomas Luster, Jacob Wingert, William Ashwell, and Lewellyn Coppage. William P. Camden was elected Camp Commander and Jacob Wingert was the Chaplain. The camp was named Stonewall Jackson Camp #1, in honor of General Stonewall Jackson. This camp was the only United Confederate Veteran's camp in Indiana, and one of very few north of the Mason-Dixon Line.

During the next 10 years several more members were added. They were: David

Kennedy, Braxton Cash, William "Billy" Mitchell, William Zimmerman, Alex Sheets, and Joseph Moody.

Stonewall Jackson Camp #1 was in existence until about 1920. The last member was William "Billy" Mitchell of Jamestown, who died in 1930. *Submitted by: Andrew Keith Houk, Jr., Jamestown, Indiana; Jay Wilson Jr., Oolitic, Indiana*

UNION CHAPEL CHURCH 1866-1965

Settlers who came to Montgomery County, Indiana, and established homes about eight miles southwest of Crawfordsville, were of strong Christian beliefs, and of religious persuasion. Family prayer was held in many homes, and groups met in an abandoned school house for public worship.

Their united thoughts were "let us hold steadfast without wavering and assembling of ourselves together."

Feeling a need for a church building, four men in 1866, with George Surface as a moderator and Samuel Demoret, Samuel Demoret, Jr. and John Busenbark, organized the construction of Union Chapel United Brethren Church on one half acre of land in Section 29, Township 18, Range 5 West.

The one room wooden structure was rectangular with three windows on each side. One door was in the north end, and two in the south end. A belfry was located on the roof, holding an iron bell, which called the people to worship and was tolled slowly before a funeral.

There was no foundation under the outside sills, except a stone at each corner, and one midway along each side. These rectangular stones were from the quarry of my great grandfathers, Alexander Weir's stone quarry. Similar stones were used as door steps.

Long pews were along each outside wall, and pews in the center floor, with aisles between. Heating was with two round iron stoves which had stove pipes reaching upward to chimneys located above. Light was from kerosene, bracket and hanging lamps, and music was played on a reed pump organ, until a piano replaced it.

In 1866, Rev. Samuel Zwek was the first minister and dedicated the building. Ano Gunkle of Crawfordsville was the first convert.

The building was completely remodeled by E.L. Eckerley in 1927.

Ministers who have served the church are George Surface, Samuel Zwek, William Peters, T.M. Hamelton, Joseph Nye, Ira Mater, Elmer Mater, George Wiley, C.L. Hunt, S. Garrigues, C.I. Rousch, Abe Surface, E.J. Rankins, T.J. Elder, A.D. Williams, W.B. Taylor, John R. Servies, Glen Sponsler, Joseph Abbey, Mrs. Alva Roberts, Rev. Hill, L.W. Simmons, E.L. Eckerley, Ernest Lewallan, J.A. Shaw, A.F. Agnew, Helen Collins, Neil Collins, James Turnbull, Heedlie Cobb, Rev. VanDyke and Henry Karg.

For many years, the church was active and progressive, but with modern transportation, the membership list was small, that in about 1965, the building and land deed reverted to the land owner, from which it came. But, not without leaving behind the memories of a glorious past. *By Mabel Weir Grimes*

UNION HILL PRESBYTERIAN CHURCH

In the records of this church was the following, "On Saturday, August 30, 1834, in a little log school house, near John Porters, a meeting was held by Presbyterians in the neighborhood, for the purpose of having a church organized, at which Rev. James Thomson presided, the following persons gave their names, expressing thereby, a wish to be associated together as a church, was: Joseph Henderson and wife Hannah and daughters, Elizabeth and Matilda; Rebecca Porter; John H. Pogue and Jane, his wife, with their daughters Hannah and Cynthia Ann; Delilah Shanklin; Joshua McDaniel; Williem Youel and Jane, his wife; John Porter and Rachel, his wife; Silas Pogue and Elizabeth, his wife; David D. Berry and Elizabeth B., his wife; Mary Ann Porter; Margaret Crawford; Margaret Evans; William G. McCutcheon; and William Zimmerman".

On motion it was resolved to proceed to the election of three ruling elders, and after the votes were taken it appeared the following persons were duly elected, Joseph Henderson, John H. Pogue, and William Youel.

They had all been Presbyterian before they came to Walnut Township, Montgomery County. Rev. James Thompson, from Wabash College helped them to establish a new church.

The log school where they had their meeting was used as a church for seven or eight years, because on May 25, 1841, church was in the school building. In June, 1842, they spoke of a meeting house, so they may have built a small place. They established a graveyard on the ground where they intended to build a church, and this first meeting house may have been built by June 29, 1848, or the graveyard was already there.

This structure was about 30 feet by 40 feet, with 2 doors at the north end. Men used one door, women the other door. The pulpit was on the north end between the doors, then it was moved to the South end of the room. This church was known as Union Hill, on land donated by John Porter. In 1889 James Mills Martin donated more land on the west, and the church was moved there and remodeled, and services were held in the remodeled building. The church was moved 1896. Sabbath school was organized 1836.

They had many members join the church from 1834-1925. They had elders, deacons, and clerks named, but the list is too long. In 1887 when Rev. Ackman was minister,

Union Chapel U.B. Church

there were 70 new members added.

Members were families of Airharts, Berrys, Brattons, Chambers, Crawfords, Dices, Evans, Lockridges, Loops, Pogues, Porters, Sellers, Smileys, Spohrs, Youels, Walkups, and others from Virginia. Members from Ohio were Johnsons, Linns, Martins, Petersons, Wards. From other areas were Abbotts, Buchanans, Conners, Coulters, Dices, Dukes, Ensmingers, Fosters, Galeys, Harrises, Hanleys, Pattersons, Remleys, Shanklins, Sherveys, Smiths, Thompsons, Wards, Watsons, and Wrights, plus many other families.

In its day, Union Hill Presbyterian Church was well attended. It was between Mace and New Ross, and only the graveyard remains. *By C. Pauline Walters*

WABASH COLLEGE'S RENEWED INTEREST IN LOCAL HISTORY

Over the years those affiliated with the College have taken a keen interest in Crawfordsville and Montgomery County. One need only recall the names of Richard Banta, Theodore Groenert, Robert Harvey and Donald Thompson, to mention a few. In recent years, however, there has been a salutary trend toward involving students as well. What follows is a brief summary of those courses and independent study projects which have focused on our local surroundings and heritage.

Greatly facilitating such exploration is what the College calls its Freshman tutorial program. Each freshman must sign up for one of a variety of topics ranging from international relations and world literature to Indiana legal tradition and Crawfordsville history. Faculty who teach these tutorials, in groups of about a dozen students each, may choose what the content of their inquiries will contain, and almost every year produces something of local or regional interest.

Thus it was that a few years ago Professors John Fischer and Frederick Enenbach directed their students to an historic survey of the inter-urban railroad. Being railway buffs, these two teachers took every opportunity to survey the surviving relics of a once great train network which criss-crossed our county. More recently, there has been considerable fascination with local buildings. Stanley Malinowski set some of his students to pondering which structures were worthy of preservation and what were the peculiar problems involved in restoring a house to its original character. Local buildings were also of concern to some of George Davis' freshmen, as they probed the rationale and justification for preserving one thing and not another.

As some inhabitants of Montgomery County may have had occasion to know there was recently a survey of those structures deemed worthy of listing for historic or architectural reasons. Commissioned by the Historic Landmarks Foundation of Indiana, this inventory of Sites and Structures was carried out by Mr. Marsh Davis, and was one of the first such county surveys to be completed. Helping to support this project financially were certain local individuals as well as Wabash College.

Freshmen are not the only beneficiaries of local study at Wabash College. George Davis and James Barnes particularly enjoy turning their Senior History majors loose on similar research topics. Davis has his students take different Indiana law cases which eventually were appealed to the United States Supreme Court and trace the background of these cases and the points of law in dispute. For several years running, Barnes had his seminar class reconstruct the lives of over 300 Wabash students who served in the Civil War. "For such students," he observed, "this is genuine and original research, for often no one else has tried to piece together the biographies of these long-forgotten veterans."

More recently Davis has asked his seniors to research the origins of the Republican Party in Montgomery and nearby counties. Barnes continues to fill in gaps in the Civil War project, but has also had his students branch out to include research on early college alumni who did not serve in the war. In either case they are much assisted by the College's archivist, Johanna Herring, and by the staff of the Crawfordsville District Public Library. In this respect it is a real community effort, including occasional interviews with surviving descendants of early alumni.

WAVELAND MURAL

Many good things have started because of conversation over a good cup of coffee; and that is where the idea of our mural started.

A Sesquicentennial celebration was planned for June 1985. A group of industrious ladies met at the Waveland Cafe to discuss what they could do to brighten up the town. Thoughts turned to painting a picture for everyone to enjoy as they came to Waveland. They all chose the subjects to use, the location, and hunted people with some talent to get the work done. Several hometown artists were found who were willing to get their paint brushes busy. Old churches, the school building, depot and the foot bridge just off of Old Ford Road were points of interest to be included in the display. Local artists working on this project were Mark Launer, Delores Farley, Rose Collins, Peggy Starnes, Mary Jane Watson, Janet Fagan and Berniece Myers: there were also several sidewalk superintendents.

This mural was used by Channel 6 when they interviewed the Sesquicentennial committee and is a favorite subject for photographers as they travel south on State Road 59.

The mural is located on the north wall of Lost Treasures; a used furniture store owned by Mr. & Mrs. Don Gillogly and Berniece Myers. The owners of the store furnished the paint and equipment for the project. *Submitted by: Berniece Myers*

WAVELAND TELEPHONE EXCHANGE

In 1886, after much deliberation, the town board granted J.W. Cuppy the privilege of erecting a telephone exchange in the town of Waveland. In 1887, when all was ready, the rates were $2.50 a month. Many people were doubtful about this service. So, the company offered installation and a month's service for $1.00 with the promise that the telephone be removed if it was not liked. Few were removed. In 1900, the exchange and lines were overhauled and a new two position switch board was installed. James W. Robertson operated the company for twenty years. The Detcheon Company bought the company in 1928 and it was moved from over the bank where it had been for many years to the William Jarvis house on West Main Street. In August, 1932, the Harry W. Evernham family was transferred from Burnettsville, in White County to Waveland to operate the exchange; Harry as plant manager of Waveland and Russellville and his wife as agent. Many school girls learned to operate the switch board and were paid ten cents an hour for their efforts.

The Evernhams retired in 1955 when the Detcheon Company sold the company to Indiana Bell.

Waveland Mural

The above photo, taken in 1942 shows the home for the Evernhams for 23 years. The right entrance was to the exchange, which included a pay station telephone, office and terminal room. The house was (1960) later purchased by Charles Nixon and moved about a half block West on Main Street. The former lot was purchased by the government and a new Post Office was erected in 1961.

WHITESVILLE SCHOOL

The first school building in Whitesville was a frame building, built 1870, and it lasted until March 1903, when the school was moved to land donated by Frank Wren, on the south side of Whitesville and was used as a community building, or town hall. Many fine plays, suppers, meetings, etc., were held here. In early 1920's Henry Smith, who lived across from this building, was burning trash, and sparks flew across the road and ignited the town hall, and it burned to the ground.

In 1830/40 several settlers near Whitesville, the Eversons, Thompsons, Guntles, Davidsons, Nicols, Manns and Byers decided that schools outside of Whitesville weren't good, and they needed a school in Whitesville. George Everson, Sr., lived in a log cabin, and he built a new house, donating the cabin for a school in Whitesville, in 1852. This was west of the railroad. The first teacher was Sarah Harrison. In 1853/54 a one room frame building was built, east of railroad, across the road northwest from church. Ground was bought from L.J. Cahoon. In 1870, as stated earlier, the 1853/54 room was moved and a two room frame building was built. This building had cloak rooms, and a sliding blackboard partition. Younger pupils on one side, older pupils on the other side. This was the building moved to Frank Wren's property in 1899. First teacher in the new school was Fanny Hall Davis. In 1903 they built a two story brick building, with basement. It had a 3 year high school course and started in 1907. The 1903 building had 4 rooms. The high school courses were soon abandoned, and they had to go to another school. In 1883 Whitesville graduated its first 8th grade students. There were only 13 graduates in the entire county, and Whitesville had 3; they held the graduation for all 13 at Whitesville on April 14, 1883. County Superintendent, John C. Overton, presented the diplomas. In next 40 years 200 pupils graduated here and 90 teachers had taught here. Teachers were Sarah Harrison, Lizzie Wood, Phronia Ensminger, Sallie Stonecipher, Lizzie Barr, Ella Wright, Lizzie Hyatt, Mary Harrison, Laura Funk, Emma Barnett, Rose Cahoon, Nell Bruner, ?? Stover, Maggie Carroll, James Buchanan, James Belch, Mrs. Jennie Hall Porter, Clara Ward, Sadie Blake, Vorhees Brookshire, Julia Martin, Morrie Harney, Charles McClure, Salem G. Patterson, Daniel Gilkey, W.W. Ewing, Mrs. Tillie Goff Ewing, Clara Sanders, Frankie Imel, Myrtle Smith, Joseph Davis, Mrs. Fannie Hallie Davis, Roberts Weeks, Fannie Kelly Wingert, Josephine Imel, Stella Blanch Kelsey, Allie McMahan, Mrs. W.T. Sharp, Howard Griest, George Hultz, Maud Hall, Sarah Hornbaker, May Talbott, Will White, Bertha Peterson, Lela Ghormley, Clara Minnick, Ethel Wasson, Vane Brumbaugh, Earl Kelly, Bruce Haines, Earl Jones, Charles Shanks, Mary Hollowell, Lester Hulse, Lawrence Lookabill, Joe E. Kennedy, Clara Belle Hall, Opal McCullough, C.W. Jack, Mrs. C.W. Jack, taught here 14 years, Ina Phillips, Frances Lambert, Mary A. Hall, Ernest Stout, Eunice Rose, Stella McGee, Ralph Shirly, Edgar Toney, Grace Smith, Lulu Grantham, Clara Corns, Eulalia Hornell, Jennie Tapp, James B. Tharp, Hallie Tapp, Harry Powers, Hallie Sidener, Francis Wilson, Charles A. Terry, And Estella Boaz. These were teachers all before 1923. The following were the teachers after that, Oakel Hesler, Beulah Wingert,f Oral Adamson, Roy Buser, Ruth Morgan Joiner Thomas, Mary G. Servies, Carl Smith, Mrs. Emma Linderman, Josephine Imel, Lucille Manges and Esther Manges, Ruby Davidson Cornell Allen, Pauline McClelland (Swindler) Long, Martha VanCleave (Cowan) Williams, Evelyn Terry Connelly, Tommy Harper, Juanita Graham, ?? Ellis, Mabel Bushong Glover, Margaret Cox Edwards, Charles Switzer. These aren't in order of their teaching.

The Whitesville school closed in 1954, and it was torn down, and the parsonage for the church was built on the land.

C. Pauline Walters

WHITESVILLE COMMUNITY BUILDING

The Whitesville Community Building is remembered for activities held there. Constructed in 1926 it was dedicated on January 7, 1927, by Rev. McCallum, Pastor of the Whitesville Christian Church.

The HALL used before burned down; it was off Elm Street on the Frank Wren lot.

Plays, Square Dances, Box and Penny Suppers, Minstrels, Musicals, School Programs, Traveling Entertainers, Magicians and Meetings were held there.

The loss of the HALL was the main discussion at the next class party held by the Loyal Helpers Class of the Christian Church. They mulled and pondered, then Chester Himes enthusiastically took the lead in the direction of rebuilding.

He, with friends, William White, Forest Corn and several others, scouted the neighborhood for ideas and help. With everyone anxious for a new building, the response was fantastic.

Chester Himes was selected to draw a blueprint. It met with the approval of Directors, Ed Rhoades, Clayton Ward, Edgar Manges, Ralph Himes, and John Tapp.

A lot was bought from William and Nettie Caster on October 4, 1926. It lay south of the dirt road directly across from the red brick school. Casters bought it in 1922 from the Universalist Conference representatives. The Universalist Church used to be there. It burned when struck by lightning June 28, 1912.

Due to his neatness, it kind of fell to Chester Himes to do considerably all of the cement block work. Others worked like the dickens too, sifting sand, unloading blocks and moving lumber supplies.

Everything was done by manual labor with willing hands and strong backs. If a family lived in the Whitesville area then, quite likely they were helping!

The building cost $2,000 with a surplus left over. Families donated as they wished.

The Christian Church Circle Ladies provided many Penny Supper needs also cooking stoves, dishes and various items were donated.

The stage provided a dressing room on the east and a west stage door opened to Sycamore Street. The first play presented in the building was "MUCH ADO ABOUT BETTY" on February 12, 1927. The Loyal Helpers Sunday School Class sponsored it. A rolled up canvas curtain revealed a roomy stage with three dividers on either side. The building always was full when PLAYS were given.

Years brought changes. Lewis Fellows and Chester Himes removed the stage; modernized the kitchen providing cabinets and plumbing for the sink and rest room. Kenneth Ward cemented new steps and front walk.

It is the mpossible to name all who worked through the years. When it was built many were involved and such it has been through the years. A labor of love.

Richard Davidson was treasurer many years, the last directors were Warner Davidson, Wayne Kessler, Carol Terry, Lyle Hulbert, and Lewis Fellows.

Though the enthusiasm for this fine building has waned and is no longer used the MAGICAL MEMORIES still remain.

WHO GOT THE BIG ONE?

"Who got the big one?" is the question which comes to mind while gazing upon the above picture! Most would agree it is the type on the end — Garrie L. Dillman, age four. In the late 1800's and until 1904, many businessmen of the Waveland area owned cottages on Sugar Creek on what is now the Shades property. On the North side of the creek was Pleasant View Feed Mill (owned by a man named Myers). On the South side of the creek were several cottages, used in the summer for get-away homes. The wives and children stayed in the cottages all summer and most of the men drove back and forth for weekend enjoyment. In 1904 or so, there was forest fire on the property and all the cottages burnt. The picture was taken in 1900 and shows the catch of the day! Pictured: (left to right, facing picture) Fred Stubbins (drug store), Charles Johnson (banker), George T. Dillman (hardware), Bill Harshburger (brick yard), Kent K. Straughan (Doctor) and young Garrie, the father of Norman Dillman to whom the large and lovely fishy picture belongs! The picture was taken at the back of the Dillman Cottage.

The Whitesville Community Building

Who Got The Big One? L. to R. Fred Stubbins, Charles Johnson, Geo T. Dillman, Bill Harshburger, Dr. Kent Schraughn, Garie L. Dillman-age 4, around 1900

NEW ROSS SCHOOL

In 1871, a new school was built in New Ross. It was a two story - two department building. This school was used until 1899. It had 2 rooms and was 24 ft. x 36 ft. In 1881 there were 192 students over 6, and under 21 going to this school. Total cost was $9,000.00. Prof. Tilghman Brown was the principal. His wife, Thalia Walters Brown, taught here. This building was sold to George Sperry for $70.00 in June 1899. Another building nearby sold to Isaac Galloday for $85.00, and the lot where the school stood for $125.00. Furniture was reserved by the trustee. This building has 6 windows on each side, one above the other, and two windows on front over the two doors.

In 1899, the trustee, Charles Minnick let the contract for a new school for $5,698 to W.W. Carr of Crawfordsville the building to have four rooms. In February 1899, Mr. Minnick bought 3-1/2 acres from Ed Inlow for $500, between Big Four Railroad and State Street. Hankins did the brick work on the building and the building was dedicated October 20, 1899. The address was delivered by R. Riley. They had a 3 year non-commissioned high school, and Dora Linn Randal graduated here in 1906, after going 3 years to the non-commissioned school. It became a commissioned school in 1910/11, and had an 8 month school term. It may have been remodeled before, but in 1930, they did extensive remodeling to the building, and a building to be used for a gymnasium was built on the west side. They started a school lunch program in the 1940's. This school was closed in 1967, when they consolidated schools and built new schools to serve the pupils. *By C. Pauline Walters*

Marker placed Saturday May 13, 1989; see story on page 36, Quakers in Montgomery County.

Big Four Depot, Crawfordsville, Ind.

Post Office, Crawfordsville, Ind.

CHURCH HISTORY

First Church of the Nazarene Mission on North Grant

FIRST UNITED METHODIST CHURCH

Methodism arrived in the frontier village of Crawfordsville in the summer of 1825 when a Circuit Rider, the Rev. James Armstrong rode into town. Moved by his firey sermon, delivered from a tree stump, five women volunteered to establish a class with the hopes that residents would join them and build a church. Four years later a 40 by 40-foot frame structure was erected on the south boundary of the village. Here Wabash Road and Water street crossed. It was also the point of intersection for two Indian trails.

Membership grew rapidly. By 1835 the congregation was able to support a resident preacher, Rev. J. Miller. Eight years later the men of the church lengthened the frame building by adding 20 foot on the south end. But 1855 brought discussion for construction of a two-story brick edifice. Members raised money for the project by sponsoring oyster-ice cream suppers and lectures by prominent speakers. The county fair also offered opportunity for fund raising when the men and women set up kitchen and dining room facilities in a tent and served meals from 5 o'clock in the morning on throughout the day. The new church was finished by 1857 and its debt retired by the outbreak of the Civil War.

The War revealed a congregation divided in its loyalties. When Rev. William Graham became the pastor in 1862, he found so much divisive feeling that repairs to the parsonage were ignored and the worship services were tense with animosity. Mr. Graham noted that members only behaved courteously when Gen. Wallace and Senator Lane chanced to be home.

Mr. Graham's journal speaks of a Copperhead scare in 1863. The rebels, mainly centered in Montgomery County, were plotting to over-throw Gov. Oliver P. Morton's administration. News of the plot leaked and Gov. Morton dispatched the State Militia to this town. When they detrained and marched to the courthouse square they found a hot, bountiful breakfast prepared by the members of the Methodist Episcopal church. When the Copperheads rode into town, they saw the Militia and fled. From that point on, the Copperheads' threat was reduced and the crisis erased.

With the War over, organizational activity multiplied. To the active Ladies' Aid Society and the men's Foreign Missionary Society was added the Women's Foreign Missionary Society (1871). The Home Missionary Society came later. It was not until 1940 that all three of these women's groups merged to create the Women's Society of Christian Service. The WSCS became known as the United Methodist Women in 1967.

The name of the church also changed. When organized in 1825 all Methodist churches in the U.S. and England were called Methodist Episcopal. Not until 1939 was "Episcopal" deleted from the title by action of the General Conference. Thirty years later Methodist and Evangelical United Brethern sects merged to create United Methodists. The congregation at 212 East Wabash voted to adopt the name "First United Methodist" for this church. Two other local Methodist churches became "The Trinity United Methodist" and "The Christ United Methodist."

The physical plant had changed also—first in 1856 and again in 1886. Increased membership and activity among all age groups made larger facilities a necessity in both eras.

The brick Gothic Revival built in 1856 was razed to be replaced by a brick Romanesque of 1886. All four churches built in 1829, 1856, 1886, and 1976 have stood on the same site, and all have faced south except the Gothic of 1856 which faced east.

The first parsonage date is unknown, but the picture of the 1856 church reveals a two-story frame house had been built just west of the church. It was apparently moved around the corner onto the east side of Green street when a fine brick house went up about 1902 at the old site. In 1924 this parsonage was joined to the Romanesque church of 1886 and labelled the "Parish Hall." At the same time the pastoral family moved into a new brick bungalow next door to the west.

By the late 1950's this above expansion proved inadequate. The congregation chose to pull down the "parish hall" and built a three story educational complex. It was finished early in the 1960's. Then a new parsonage was purchased in the Sycamore Hills addition. Property was added gradually in the half-block area, and the construction of the Georgian Colonial Church began by 1976. Dedication of this edifice was accomplished in 1986.

In a brief history many important events must be omitted, but one of national significance occurred in 1911 when this church initiated the "Every Member Canvas". Inspired by the Rev. Hixon and Frank Evans the plan was successfully executed, and is still duplicated every year. Many churches of all faiths have adopted the plan.

Other decisions which have had worldwide impact stem from the congregation's spiritual and financial support of H.V. Lacey, missionary in 1907 to Pusan, China; Hildegarde Schlemmer's mission work beginning in 1924 in Raipur India; and, Clara Cook's social work in Kentucky. After World War II the Rev. A.J. Coble led this church in a rehabilitation project to assist churches in devastated areas of Europe. More recently evangelical outreach has been done in summer work camps, in children's homes and Indian schools in this country.

Since its founding the church school program has played a major role in the total work. Thousands have received their religious training in classes taught by generous leaders. Within recent years the laic ministry has been reinforced by associate pastors whose professional training brought added dimension to this aspect of development. Since 1988 two full time pastors guide the congregation's spiritual education in the classroom and sanctuary.

Nor has the musical ministry been neglected. In the early years, only congregational singing was raised in worship. Then the harmonium was added—but not until in the 1870's! When the people met in December of 1886 to have the first worship service (and as it turned out—to dedicate that building free of debt at the same time) an orchestra played to accompany the young peoples choir. It was 1890 before the first pipe organ was installed and used until the George Durham's gift of a new pipe organ in 1940, a fine instrument still in use. The sanctuary choir as well as the children's choir have been visible features in the worship service for many years.

With technological changes the church has been able to adopt a televised worship service. Every Sunday since 1981 the service is telecast live to local residents and shut-ins in hospitals and nursing homes.

Another program implemented by volunteers in 1959 is the Thrift Shop. The FISH organization, initiated by Rev. Frank E. Little and the local ministerial association has also provided aid to needy families.

Since the establishment of a Methodist class in 1825 because of the inspiration of those valiant "Women of Israel" (as the historical record calls them), the church's heritage has had great influence. The Centennial year brought a reproduction of the church's founding with a pageant staged on the lawn at Lane Place. The booklet which records for us today what they portrayed on Sept. 16, 1925 owed its creation to the excellent history researched and written by Julia Davidson Waugh; a treasure of information.

Both 125th and 150th anniversary celebrations were held at the church. Thus, few members are unaware of their spiritual ancestry. In fact, with the laying of the cornerstone in this present building, the congregation prepared for its Bicentennial anniversary in 2025. They invested money and records of faith to be inherited by the future church in its work of glorifying the God of their fathers.

Roll of Ministers
Crawfordsville Methodist Church
1825-1989

Circuit Riders
1825-26 Hackaliah Vreedenburg with Rev. James Armstrong, Presiding Elder
1826-27 Henry Buel
1827-28 Eli P. Farmer
1828-29 Stephen R. Beggs
1829-30 James Armstrong
1830-31 Sam'l S. Cooper
1831-32 Richard Hargrave
1832-33 Lorenzo D. Smith
1833-34 John A. Brouse
1834-35 Amasa Johnson

Resident Ministers
1835 J. Miller
1836 Amasa Johnson
1837 Benjamin Barnes
1838 Richard Robinson
1840 Ebenezer Patrick
1841 Sam'l. Brenton
1843 Richard Hargrave
1844 Walter Huffman
1845 Thomas Sinex
1847 Henry B. Beers
1848 Milton Mahan
1850 George Beeswick
1851 Wm. I. Wheeler
1853 George W. Stafford
1854 Hezekiah Smith
1856 A.A. Gee
1857 G.W. Crawfords
1858 Griffith Morgan
1860 Clark Skinner
1862 Wm. Graham
1864 Louis Nedeker
1866 T.L. Webb
1869 A.A. Gee
1872 Sam'l. Beck
1874 L.C. Buckles
1877 James W. Greene
1880 J.W. Harris
1882 S.P. Colvin
1883 Salem B. Town
1885 Alfred Kummer
1887 George W. Switzer
1892 H.A. Ticker
1895 S.V. Leech
1897 E.H. Brumbaugh
1899 S.W. Goss
1902 Paul Curnick
1906 E.D. Smith
1910 Fred W. Hixon
1913 Blaine E. Kirkpatrick
1916 G.F. Craig
1918 J. H. Appleby
1923 Guy O. Carpenter
1930 J.S. Ward
1933 Paul Bendict
1940 Allen B. Rice
1943 C. Howard Taylor
1945 C.M. McClure
1947 Roy W. Michel
1947 Almon J. Coble
1951 Buel E. Horn
1952 Donald F. McMahan
1957 Ralph W. Graham
1959 Hilton H. Whitaker
1962 W. Goddard Sherman
1964 Ralph M. Jones
1967 Frank E. Little
1980 Dale Miller
1985 Lawrence Richert

ALAMO CHRISTIAN CHURCH

The little town of Alamo was plotted by Samuel Truax and William A. Boise in the year of 1837. These men must have had a great foresight as they donated some land for a Seminary or School and some land for a meeting house as they called it. Several denominations used the first house for their church meetings. The original deed of the First Church United was made December 20, 1848, from John Fishero and wife Mary, to the trustees of the Christian meeting house in the town of Alamo. The trustees were Samuel McKinsey, Henderson Harvey and Noah W. Grimes.

Finally, one denomination known as the Alamo Christian Church used the building. At that time the building consisted of only what is the main auditorium now, with no entrance room, no cloak room and no basement. There were two front doors which were located on the south side of the church where the two diamond-shaped windows are at the present time. The pulpit was on the north side of the church, with two aisles leading from the two doors to the pulpit. The building was heated by two large stoves with one located on each side.

In the years 1883-1887 William Wallace McClure lived in the house just east of the church. He conducted a furniture and undertaking business in a building just north of his home. He was a very active member of the church. At one time the church was having financial difficulties, and the roof was so bad that it was nearly impossible to hold meetings on a rainy day. Mr. McClure went to his farm, cut logs and had sheathing and shingles sawed from the logs and did much of the work himself in repairing the roof.

An interesting item in the church records of the 1800's showed that church members had to live a very strict religious life or they would be expelled from the church, and then would have to be readmitted to the church.

Rev. Ewing was the first minister to serve under the Christian Church name in 1889. Some of the other ministers who have served the church are: Rev. Spray, Rev. Brown, Rev. Freed, Rev. Smith, Rev. Higgins, Rev. Penny, Rev. Frank Hole, Rev. Henry Alfred, Rev. Harry Davis, Rev. Paul Eddingfield, Rev. Henry Bell, Rev. John Servies (who served for nearly 25 years), Rev. Forrest Graves, Rev. Noble Carothers, Rev. Morris Finch, Jr., Rev. Hugh Dooley,

Rev. Randy Whitehead, Rev. Terry Phillips, Rev. Glen Kailer. The present minister is Rev. Jim Daniel.

The church is located on the corner of West and Madison Streets, and the first remodeling was done in 1928. It was dedicated on September 30, and the cost was $2077.12. Ed Etter loaned the church the money for the project and didn't charge any interest, although it took 9 years to repay the loan. It was voted at the dedication to have a family night each year, as near that date as possible, for a social event and a business report on all church activities during the previous year.

The second addition and remodeling took place in 1950-51. Material costs were paid for by the church and the work was donated labor.

The third and last addition was made in the summer and fall of 1963 with donated labor by members of the church and community. *This early history written by Myrtle Luzader - 1965.*

Church Improvements Since 1963

In 1964 the Walters brothers donated the lot south-east of the church for a parking lot.

In 1965 the Utterback heirs donated the memorial church directory that is located on the south-west corner of the church lawn.

In the late 60's a new piano and a new organ were purchased.

In 1974 new aluminum siding was put on the church, and a new roof was put on the east portion of the church.

In 1977 new grass carpeting was placed on the front steps, the entryway and the basement steps. A portion of the sidewalk was replaced in front of the church. Also, a new gas stove was purchased for the kitchen.

In 1978 the church pews were upholstered.

In 1979 a portable baptistry was added. More insulation was added to the attic. The well which had been drilled in 1961 was drilled 30 feet deeper. New linoleum was placed in the restrooms. A flood light was put on the front of the church. Also a new drain for the church basement was put in.

In 1980 new carpeting was added to the entire auditorium, and a new P.A. system was purchased. The interior of the church and the basement were repainted. Also, Mrs. Mendenhall donated a new clock for the north wall of the auditorium.

In 1981 a new roof was put on the west portion of the church. Also, the two windows on the east side of the church were stained by Mr. and Mrs. Bob Binford and Mary Fischer.

The cost of these improvements was paid for by the church treasury, the Ladies Aid Society and personal donations. Several of the projects were completed by donated labor.

BETHEL PRESBYTERIAN CHURCH OF SHANNONDALE

Bethel Presbyterian church of Shannondale was organized by Rev. Clairborne Young. He was born on a farm near Thorntown.

In 1831, a group of people met in the home of William Young to form a church which they named Bethel. At this time Mr. Young lived one mile north of Shannondale.

In the early days of the church the services were held in the home or in the school house on the Shaver farm. On this farm two miles west of Shannondale is a group of large rocks. One of them was used as a pulpit when the weather was suitable. In 1967 a plaque was attached to the rock commemorating the site, founder, and the charter members. During the Centennial Celebration, Rev. W. Edward Stokesberry, retired moderator, delivered his address from this Rock.

In 1833, Bethel church held a business meeting at the home of James A. Thomson and made plans for erecting a house of worship. James Scott gave one acre of ground on which to build the church.

The building was erected, covered, and used during the summer of 1835. The windows were not yet in, the doors unhung, and the floor not laid. Flattened logs were used for sleepers, which also served as seats for one year. The church was located across the road, southwest of the present site of Bethel Church, and northwest of the site of the old Shannondale school (now raised).

The second building, the present house of worship, was completed and dedicated in the autumn of 1856.

In the ensuing years there arose a need for facilities to house a pastor. The problem was solved when the Ladies Aid Society set forth to earn money to be put into a Manse Fund. Only one professional carpenter was hired and other labor was donated by the congregation. The building was dedicated in June, 1949. The manse was sold in 1984.

The church underwent extensive redecorating in 1981. This was made possible by the hard work of members and friends who worked at a food tent at the Farm Progress Show near Crawfordsville in 1979.

The Sesquicentennial (150 years) was celebrated March 1981. Rev. Charles A. Hammond, Moderator of General Assembly gave the address along with Rev. Roger Fisk, church pastor.

Rev. Wallace McDonald of Crawfordsville filled the pulpit and served as our moderator for years.

This year, 1989, Carl Crawford celebrated his retirement after 34 years as Sunday School Superintendent, with a reception held in the church basement.

The church pulpit has been filled through the years by 49 pastors or ministers. The most recent is Roger Fisk who came in 1979 and remains until the present time. We are now sharing Rev. Fisk with the Presbyterian church of Thorntown, Indiana.

The church basement is being refurbished at this time.

BROWNS VALLEY CHRISTIAN CHURCH

In the spring of 1898 a group of Christian believers felt the need to establish a Christian Church in Browns Valley, Indiana. With this as a goal, they invited W.H. Brown, who then was a pastor at New Market Christian Church, to come and teach them about the doctrine of the Christian Church.

On June 6, 1898 the church was organized in the school house which was located just east of the home that was occupied by the last living charter member, Mrs. Mollie Carrington and her sister Sally Galey.

The original twenty-eight charter members were:

Sallie Swindler
William J. Swindler
Bettie Carrington
America Wasson
W.T. Williams
L.W. Reynolds
Mollie Carrington
Fannie Williams
Warren Williams
John C. Allen
Lillian E. Allen
Mary L. Reynolds
E.F. Oglesbee
Ida Oglesbee
Theodore R. Wasson
Charles T. Spaulding
Mary Spaulding
Flossa Spaulding
Nannie Davis
George S. Davis
Jennie Davis
John H. Foster
Lela Foster
Elisha Layne
Josephine Layne
J.L. Carrington
George A. Spaulding

On August 13, 1898 a committee was set up to purchase ground for the new church. Even though they had no church building to meet in, services were held in the old drug store owned by Victor McCan on Monday and Tuesday nights. The first minister, W.H. Brown was paid $2.50 per sermon and served until October 1902.

The original building burned down and plans were made to build their first church located across from John Bayless' garage. By the end of 1900 the members were enjoying their new church building and ready to worship and conduct business in an orderly manner.

The logs for the frame came from the George Davis farm and were hauled to the sawmill on mud boats in the snow.

Charles Hybarger sawed the logs at about where the Farm Bureau Elevator used to be.

After many years of worshipping in their church building, they decided to buy the Methodist Church building. On May 14, 1922 the trustees were given authority to look into the matter. On November 6, 1922 the congregation voted 23-0 to buy the Methodist Church and to sell their present building to the primitive Baptist.

The Methodist Church, which is now the Browns Valley Christian Church, was purchased for $2000.00. The Ladies Aid paid $1000.00 down on the church and the Jolly Juniors, a young people's class gave $155.00. The seats out of the old building were sold to the Methodist Church at Waveland for $350.00. Improvements came to $639.42. Pledges were taken to help pay the remainder.

Dedication services for the new Browns Valley Christian Church were held Sunday, April 29, 1923 at 1:30 after a noon basket dinner. Gale Grimes sang a solo. Mr. H.A. Davis was the speaker.

May 8, 1923, the Primitive Baptist congregation bought the old church for $750.00. The bell stayed with the old building.

Moving ahead many years found the church growing and doing well. Many souls were added to God's family. Due to growth space was needed only to provide a place for more classrooms. June 7, 1950 plans were underway to enlarge and remodel the basement. Then June 26, 1960 two classrooms, two restrooms and a baptistry were added. New pulpit furniture was purchased April 26, 1969.

A parsonage had been rented for several years for the ministers and the church was looking for a permanent home that could be bought. November 17, 1973 Ed Stanley offered his home, (directly across the street), to the church for the purchase price of $5000.00. The church quickly accepted his generous offer.

In June 1977, a $10,000.00 scholarship trust fund was set up in memory of Claude and Frances Lydick to help college costs for our young people.

Bob and John Cornell have gone on to Bible College. Bob is now serving a congregation in Illinois. Layton Sparks was ordained into the ministry October 30, 1988 and is now ministering to the Wesley Chapel west of Crawfordsville.

In 1986 new carpeting and pews were installed in the church auditorium. Then in 1988 some remodeling of the basement was done, which included new restrooms, cabinets and painting.

The church has had 34 different ministers since its start. It is interesting to note that the first and the present one have the last name of Brown.

Thanks to the many who started the church so that others can hear the "Good News." Work is still continuing for the Lord in Browns Valley. *Submitted by: Leonard R. Sewell, Clerk of Browns Valley Christian Church*

BROWNS VALLEY MISSIONARY BAPTIST CHURCH

The First Baptist Church in this area was organized four miles north of Waveland in 1826, under the name of Old Union. A few missionary-minded members from this congregation organized the Freedom Baptist Church in 1834. The people of the Browns Valley Community, attending the Freedom Church, received permission to build the Missionary Baptist Church at Browns Valley in 1874 with sixty-six charter members. This church building was destroyed by fire and rebuilt in 1876. It was remodeled, with belfry added, in 1900.

The basement project of installing new furnaces and kitchen facilities was completed in 1956-1959. The sanctuary was redecorated in 1963. The electric organ was purchased in 1965 and replaced in 1986. The restrooms were installed in 1967.

We were in a "yoke field" with the First Baptist Church of New Market from 1969-1972 to help each congregation through a difficult era.

The church adopted a constitution in 1974 and celebrated the centennial year of the church organization. Our Sunday School attendance averaged seventy-five with a membership of one hundred and thirty.

Dee Rice, a member bequeathed the church her estate in 1980, which was used to repair the roof and redecorate the sanctuary.

The church was blessed again by two dear members, Walter and Ruth Taylor Penn, with a huge sum of money. The church has helped several young people to attend seminary, Salvation Army, Edna Martin Christian Center at Indianapolis, local charity, purchased a new pulpit, side chair, a new piano in 1985 and 1987. The pastor's study was refurbished in 1988.

The dedication of the pastor's study was held March 12, 1989, with Rev. Robert Shipley giving the dedicatory message.

Our congregation is small but dedicated. The Missionary Society is active. We have church services at 9:30 A.M. and Sunday School at 10:15 A.M. Everyone is welcome to attend our church.

This history was compiled from the original records of the Browns Valley Baptist Church on March 20, 1989. *Submitted by: Mrs. Franklin Johnson*

THE CHURCH OF JESUS CHRIST OF LATTER-DAY SAINTS (THE MORMONS)

Crowning the top of Covington Hill at the intersection with the Oak Hill Road northwest of Crawfordsville is located the church building of one of Montgomery County's newest congregations. Known by most as The Mormons, The Church of Jesus Christ of Latter-day Saints proclaims the message of the restoration of primitive Christianity here in America. This event transpired in up-state New York in 1823 when God, The Father, and His Son, Jesus Christ, personally visited the young man, Joseph Smith resulting in a new record of scripture, The Book of Mormon, in 1830. This, another testament of Jesus Christ, is a record kept by the early inhabitants of the Americas and attests to the personal visit of the resurrected Christ on this continent.

Although cottage meetings had been held previously, it was in October of 1967 that serious efforts began to get underway to establish a branch of the church in Montgomery County. The original families were those of Rex and Sandy Seipert, Stephen and Ruthanne Thompson, and Steve and Carol Hansen, and the missionaries in those days were Elders Stone and Affleck. By January 1968 regular Sunday meetings were being held in the Little House on the Lew Wallace Study Grounds in Crawfordsville.

Over the years more than one hundred families have participated including, from the Darlington area: Rex and Sandy Seipert, Chris and Myrtilda McDaniel, Ole R and Bud and Carol VanGilder, Jim and Chizeko VanGilder, Donna Smith; From the Linden/New Richmond area: James and Carol McCloud, Wilson and Robbie McArthur, Lisa Kirk, Jon and Karen Lee, Shawn and Melissa O'Gwynn; From the Wingate area: Nellie and Frank and Kathy Jewell, Fred and Sophia Stockdale, Pauline Miller, Linda Shultz, Arlie and Thelma Baity, Sylvia Rehling, Harold and Ruth Covey; From the Waynetown area: Charles and Chere Humphreys, Dee Ann and Nancy Cabell, Bob Olsen; From the Waveland area: Chip Ramsay, Brock Lynch, Steve and Candy Bell, Clayton and Mary Killingsworth, Janet Thomas, Patty Doan, Elsie Adams; From the New Market area: Gene McClure, Emma and Lloyd and Elva Wignall, Eva Eardley, Nancy Dickerson, Rebecca Graham, Freddie and Anita Lewis, Harold and Patsy Bowan; Louise Rouse; From the Ladoga area: Alvin and Hazel Ray, Oscar Williams, Mary Dillon, Lydia Cheshire, Joyce Wilhite, Ralph and Joannie Breedlove, Linda Buckner, Chet and Edythe Kenton Dickerson, Drew and Kim Dickerson, Cecil and Nancy Turpin, Dawn Klein, and Jill Young, Susan Huber, Alfred Smith, Robert and Mary Breedlove; From the New Ross area: Gary and Marilyn Allen, Becky McKinney Graham, Sharon Sills, Fernando and Elena Mirelez, Nancy Dice, Tom and Barbara Swinford; From the immediate Crawfordsville area: Ruth Thomas, Tom and Pia Savoldi, Stephen and Ruthanne Thompson, Helen and Marcia Eubank, Malcomb and Lois Patton, Cleo Swarat, Ellen Hitch, Steve and Carol Hansen, Judy McClure, Jo Ann Paxton, Walter and Martha Largent, David and Danny Aldrich, Russell Kline, Randy and Mary Conkright, David and Carmen Hunter, Kent and Theresa Priebe, Gail and Tony Blackwell, Jim and Ruth Leaming, Frank and Jean Fry, Cindy Delano, Charles Jones, Art King, Betty Gunderman, Harold and Grace Rhoads, Martha and Beckie Willis, Marsha Stout, Grace Swank, Dick and Carol Stone, Tim and Bonnie VanHook, John Redmon, Mike and Sandy Watson, Bill and Yolanda Query, Pat Miller, Curtis and Jorene Watson, Mary Beth Keim, Joe and Beverly Johnson, Carl VanGilder, John and Beulah Wright, Gayle and Mat Hatke, Richard and Beverly Waltman.

Leaders of the Crawfordsville congregation have included: Rex Seipert, Thomas Savoldi, Thomas Swinford, and Freddie Lewis.

Others who have served in a significant measure include those who have planned, prepared, saved, and served a two-year mission from the Montgomery County congregation unto other parts of the world. They have been: Mike Patton to France; Chris McDaniel to Uraguay, South America; Arlie and Thelma Baity to Washington, D.C.; Eric Savoldi to Munich, Germany; Mark Savoldi to Italy; Marcia Eubank to Las Vegas, Nevada; Kenneth (Chip) Ramsay to Seattle, Washington; Todd Thompson to Belgium/Netherlands; Charles Humphreys to Spain; and David Thompson to Brasilia, Brazil, South America; as well as over 100 missionaries from other areas who have labored in Montgomery County.

Unique beliefs of the Mormon people include: continuous revelation through latter-day prophets and apostles and therefore new scripture; priesthood authority and temple ordinances leading to eternal families; no paid ministry; and an attitude of self-responsibility therefore personal growth and development.

Today, the same testimony that Joseph Smith bore to his neighbors in up-state New York may be heard in scores of languages, declaring that God lives, that Jesus is the Christ, that His ancient Gospel has been restored to the earth, and that The Church of Jesus Christ is again available to all mankind.

CHURCH OF CHRIST AT HAW CREEK

According to the civil and church records, on the Second Sunday of this coming November, the Church of Christ on Haw Creek will be 153 years old. The congregation was formed on the second Sunday of November, 1835. Those who constituted the church at that date were as follows: G.T. Harney, Mr. and Mrs. William Rogers, Mr. and Mrs. Joseph W. Pruitt, and Mr. and Mrs. William Kyle. Early church records contain the following information: "On January 21, 1837 this indenture was made and entered into betwixt Lettice Ashby of the County of Montgomery, State of Indiana of the one part and James Daugherty, Thompson Ashby and A.D. Billingsly, Committee in Trust for the Church of Christ on Haw Creek and their successors in trust, of the second part witnesseth for and consideration of the premises, I, Lettice Ashby, have given unto said Committee and their successors forever with all appurtenances on which they shall build or cause to be built a house which shall be exclusively as a house of Religious Worship on the Lords Day."

In the early part of this century the church had pews that were divided by a partition. In the early 1950's the partitions were taken out and made into one continuous pew. These have since been taken out and replaced with beautiful natural oak pews. In the early 1970's a baptistry was added to the back of the building. Being the first minister to baptize an addition into the church in this baptistry, brother Cletis Ellett can testify to how cold the water was. In 1980 the front entrance was remodeled with the addition of restrooms. For many years in the summer the congregation would have a two week meeting with a homecoming on the second Sunday which included a basket dinner on the church grounds and singing in the afternoon.

No church record could be found from January 21, 1837 until the following was recorded on December 11, 1938: "We also find at this date that the names of members attached hereto do constitute those who are now members of the Church of Christ on Haw Creek. Some of the old family names at Haw Creek include Payne, Keller, Scott, Zimmerman, Gill, Glover, Bymaster, Himes, Cunningham, Blaydes, Shackelford, Hobson, Wallace, Long as well as many others not recalled at this time."

The following men have served as elders since the 1930's: Forest Shackelford, William Hobson, Offie Scott, Lawrence Brewer, Everett Wallace and Wilburn Long.

The Church meets each Sunday for worship at 10:30 in the morning and 6:00 on Sunday evening. *John R. Whitley, Secretary*

CHRIST EVANGELICAL LUTHERAN CHURCH

Christ Lutheran Church began as the "United Lutheran Worship Group" in March, 1955. The group met variously at the Old American Legion Building, Simondes Court and Wabash College Chapel (5 years). The congregation organized on September 23, 1956, at Wabash College Chapel, with 71 adults and 41 baptized children.

Organized by Rev. John Frank, Christ Lutheran Church was led by Rev. Richard Kraus for three years and then by Rev. Richard Graef for three years. Rev. John C. Stacy was called as pastor in mid-October, 1961. The congregation entered its newly built facility at 300 W. South Boulevard, on November 4, 1961. All this time it was part of a two-church parish with Phanuel Lutheran Church, Wallace. In mid-1963 it became part of a three-church parish with St. James Lutheran Church of Darlington. Three intern pastors served over the next three years (David Kostka, David Barnett, Howard Marken) to mid-1966. The Darlington congregation dissolved in September, 1966, requesting pastoral care for its members from Christ Lutheran Church. A monument at St. James Lutheran Cemetery, three miles east of Darlington, commemorates the life of this congregation which began in 1837. Phanuel Lutheran Church, Wallace, realigned with First Lutheran Church, Attica, in mid-1968, at which time Christ Lutheran Church called Pastor Stacy on a one-church, one-pastor basis.

In 1969 through 1971 Pastor Stacy was much involved in Community Ministry in Crawfordsville, helping to organize three community ministries: CHRISTIAN NURSING SERVICE (working with Rev. Charlotte (Chris) Hotopp Zachary and a Board, developing the Well Baby Clinic, Meals on Wheels, TeleCheck, Visiting Nurse Service, Senior Clinic and Children's Camp—which he led for 20 years)...FISH (working with Rev. Frank Little and a Board, developing the food pantry, clothing depot, linen closet, appliance center)...HOSPITAL CHAPLAINCY (working with Chris Zachary and Rev. Jack Frick to develop a plan for each new patient at Culver Hospital to receive a chaplain's visit). At this writing, all programs continue.

In 1973 Christ Lutheran Church began involvement in the BETHEL SERIES adult Christian Education Bible study program. Starting that year the church paid the pastor a housing allowance so Pastor could buy his own home, so the church could use the parsonage for Sunday School classes. The parsonage was renamed "Luther House" and served as Sunday School space through Spring, 1979. Then it was used by the "Children's School" for 5 years. It was dismantled in 1987.

Because the congregation outgrew its building, in 1976 the congregation began planning to expand its facilities. Lutheran Laymen's Movement Fund-Raising Counselling Service was contracted and helped us raise a three year pledge of $82,000 in the Spring of 1978. The building pictured here was completed and dedicated on May 6, 1979. It was first used on Easter, 1979, when we also first used the newly published LUTHERAN BOOK OF WORSHIP and worshipped "in the round" (because everything in the worship room is moveable). We also began paying Elston Bank on our $194,000 mortgage at 9-1/4% interest.

In 1984 Christ Lutheran Church became a STEPHEN MINISTRY congregation, with a special training program for lay caring ministry.

In October, 1987, the congregation celebrated Pastor Stacy's 25th anniversary as a Pastor.

Organized as part of the United Lutheran Church in America, Christ Church became a congregation of the Lutheran Church in America on January 1, 1963. On January 1, 1988, Christ Lutheran Church became part of the Evangelical Lutheran Church in America, the fourth largest protestant denomination in North America.

During 1988, one lot bordering South Grant Avenue was sold to a dentist and an optometrist as a location for a Medical Arts building. From the $20,000 received, $15,000 was paid on the mortgage and the remainder paid closing costs and formed a Capital Improvement Fund. Capital Improvement money was invested in repainting and recarpeting the east wing of the church building. The mortgage was renegotiated, with Union Federal Savings and Loan Association, for 15 years at 10% interest.

At the end of 1988, Christ Lutheran Church counted 376 Baptized Members, 287 Confirmed Members, 200 Confirmed, Communing, Contributing members, with an average Sunday attendance of 98.

FIRST BAPTIST CHURCH

Historic Highlights 1838-1988

In the mid-1830's the missionary zeal of New England Baptists sent a number of young missionaries to the frontier state of Indiana. One of these was 22-year-old William M. Pratt, who in 1838 with twelve members, organized the First Baptist Church of Crawfordsville. A year later the church joined Tippecanoe Baptist Association and reported 39 members. Growth was slow, but by 1866 the number had increased to 173.

Financial troubles plagued the church for nearly a century. Pastors moved frequently, often with part of their salary due. For a few years the church received part-time service, sharing the pastor with another congregation.

To maintain a high level of Christian conduct, church discipline held an important place following the Civil War. Charges of non-attendance, neglect of duty, "unchristian conduct", dancing and drunkenness often brought dismissal.

In 1884 the minutes record that members were appointed to aid the pastor in contacting unaffiliated Baptists in the community.

Organizations undoubtedly existed within the church earlier, but it is not until this period that their activities were felt in the life of the whole congregation. Women assumed increasingly important roles. Miss Anna Shue was the first woman to be clerk.

The Baptist Young People's Union, which had been launched as a state movement in 1891, was launched locally in 1897. The Sabbath School, already in existence, was formally organized in September 1899. The desire of the men for an organization of their own was first expressed by Mr. W.T. Whittington at the Annual roll call meeting, November 7, 1906.

Complaints of low spirituality are frequently found in the records and evangelistic meetings brought renewal and conversions, but many pages are devoted to listing the names of those who had lost interest and were dropped.

In 1922 Waneta Deere Hobart and husband, Kenneth, volunteered for Foreign Mission Service. They were commissioned by the Northern Baptist Convention, (now known as American Baptist Churches, U.S.A.) and assigned to Swatow, China.

During the late 20's and early 30's many young people felt God's call to the Christian Ministry or church related vocations. Eleven young men were ordained between 1930 - 1934, six were graduated from Wabash College, Augusta Hartung was sent in 1933 to the Congo as a missionary of the church.

The 1930's and 1940's were years of controversy and tension with a threat to leave the denomination. The issue was resolved in 1954 by a vote of the congregation to continue the historic relationship with the Indiana and American Baptist Conventions.

In 1953 the church began to broadcast its Sunday morning worship services over the local radio station. When the station became defunct, the pastor encouraged the church to purchase the radio transmitter and equipment. After much labor over many months with an outlay of nearly $7,000, the first broadcast from the church occurred on August 13, 1953. Running a radio station was arduous work by the volunteers involved in the operation of WBBS-FM, 106.3 megacycles. The station continued on the air until 1964.

The church has long been known for its emphasis upon evangelism, missions and a co-operative relationship with other churches. There has been a strong music ministry, involving persons in all age groups. Encouraged by the church, many young people have entered various forms of full-time Christian service.

The congregation has worshipped in four buildings. The first was a frame structure erected in 1843 on donated land at the corner of Pike and Walnut Streets. Fifty years later, a brick building was erected on the same site, and was found to be too small by the time the mortgage was burned. The building was razed and a third one begun in 1917, but financial difficulties caused construction to stop at the basement level. This was used for services until the superstructure was completed in 1925.

By the 1960's this building had become crowded, and after years of study, endless discussion and the raising of funds, the congregation united in a vote to leave the corner where they had worshipped for 132 years and relocate to the present site. Moving day was February 2, and Dedication Sunday, June 8, 1975.

In 1988 Pastor James Ranard observed his fourteenth anniversary with the church and became the pastor with the longest continuous tenure in its history. He is known for his pastoral care especially in illness or crisis.

With the burning of the mortgage in 1986, the church approached its one hundred and fiftieth anniversary free of debt. 1988 was spent in commemorating this milestone in the history of Crawfordsville First Baptist Church, 1838 - 1988.

FIRST CHRISTIAN CHURCH

One hundred and seventy years ago, Montgomery County was a vast jungle of forests and streams and not until 1821 was it settled by any white man. Among those early settlers of the county was a young minister of the Christian Church, Michael Combs (born in Tennessee, February 17, 1800), who with his wife and children, settled on eighty acres of land about four miles southwest of Crawfordsville on June 10, 1826. Owing to the fact that there was no organized church and no church building, they met in their humble log cabin homes for prayer and praise to God. Elder Combs, usually led out in those meetings and later offered his services, as minister, to them.

From its humble beginnings in the log cabin, the Christian Church began changing by moving to town in 1833, where a more imposing edifice forty by sixty feet was built. Trustees of the church had made application to the Montgomery County Board of Commissioners for the lot numbered 40 on the original plat of the town of Crawfordsville and this was conveyed by means of a warranty deed to the church trustees.

In 1855 it became apparent that the frame church building was not adequate to care for the increasing membership and plans were drawn up for a new one. Elder J.P. Ewing was called as pastor and it was largely through his efforts and influence that the present building was erected. It was completed and dedicated in the summer of 1889.

In 1903 more space was needed and the present chapel area was added as a Sunday School room. Later, basement rooms were developed by the expanding Sunday School and remodeling in the 1920's completed the educational facilities. During the 1903 renovation, a new pipe organ was dedicated. This was a gift from Mr. and Mrs. James K. Everson in memory of their daughter, Sadie, and was said to be one of the finest instruments in any church in the area. It had the unique property of being powered by water flow. The new addition was dedicated on April 27, 1903. The minister of that time was Rev. Wallace Tharp, one of the most energetic and enthusiastic pastors of his time. He was able to hold the congregation during the ten months of the building program and raised the $10,000 required so that the church was debt-free at the time of dedication.

The ministry of James H. Wilson ushered in the second century of First Christian Church and the centennial year saw a reawakening of enthusiasm. A great pageant was prepared which depicted the history of the church from its founding to 1926. It was directed and casted by members of the congregation and was presented to a pleased audience at the high school auditorium on November 19, 1926. Much of the material was gleaned from the Kerr history. Rev. Wilson remained as minister for ten years, and resigned in 1937.

Rev. Paul E. Million was then called. Some of the most momentous events in world history transpired during the ministry of Rev. Million, which extended through an almost unbelievable span of twenty-five years! He ended his years as pastor in July 1962, when he retired.

In July 1963, Rev. Howard F. Miller was called to serve as minister. His enthusiasm was contagious and soon things began to happen. He felt that a minister of education was essential to a growing church and in February, 1964, Mrs. Olive Hoke joined him in the capacity of minister of education. Through their combined efforts and with complete cooperation of the church board and the congregation, plans were laid for the educational building. The old church parsonage at 211 S. Walnut St. had been used as a church office and for classrooms, but it was razed to make way for the present building. Rev. Miller retired during our Anniversary Year in 1976, after a long and successful ministry. In May 1976, the Rev. John Glosser came, serving until August 1978. In June 1979, the Rev. Glenn Brigman, Jr., our current minister began his call.

In 1981 a long-range planning committee was formed and plans were made to renovate the existing buildings. In October 1984, ground was broken to begin the plans of connecting the sanctuary building to the educational building, creating a narthex, a multipurpose room, installing an elevator and general redecorating. Restrooms were added to the main floor and basement, and were remodeled for handicapped access. The total project came to over $500,000, which was paid for as of two years ago.

This has been a challenging, but exciting time in our church's history. We are in our 163rd year now with our thoughts on our past, but fully realizing that we look to the future of worship and service in Christ's name with a prayer for God's guidance and blessing. *Robert L. Snyder, Church Historian*

THE FIRST CHURCH OF THE NAZARENE

This church was organized July 5, 1920.

In June of 1920, Brother and Sister Guy McHenry came to town and started a prayer band which grew into a tent meeting. A tent was set up on East Market Street at Garfield Street and the first tent service was held on June 11, 1920. The Hooker Sisters sang and Rev. McHenry brought the message. The tent meeting continued with good results and on July 5th the church was organized with 34 charter members. There are still 3 charter members of the Carver family living. Rev. Mertie Hooker was appointed pastor. They moved to the mission hall at 310 North Grant Avenue in September of 1920 and worshipped there until 1922.

They prayed for a church building and they were able to purchase the Presbyterian Church on the corner of Pike and Water Streets for $10,000.00. The congregation worshipped there until 1931. In 1927, the District Assembly of the Northern District of which they were a member, was held in this church.

Due to financial circumstances, the church was sold to the city; this location became the City Building, and has remained the same to this day. They moved back to their initial place on North Grant Avenue in 1931. During a revival at this place, on January 28, 1934 they had 542 in Sunday School. They gave away a ton of coal as first prize for bringing the most to Sunday School. This was during the depression years and John McKinley was the pastor.

Pastors up to this time were: Rev. Mertie Hooker, B.F. Wininger, Guy McHenry, Joe Tyson, D. Johnstone, L.P. Mingledorf, and John McKinley.

In November of 1934 Grant M. Barton came to the city as pastor. He remodeled the building on North Grant and they outgrew this location. The Lord gave Rev. Barton a vision to build a new church uptown. They bought a lot on West Wabash Avenue and built a church. The men came after work to help and the women fixed supper and brought it in. Sometimes they would stay until 11-12 o'clock at night. This was done joyously and with enthusiasm for the Lord supplied the strength. As the Bible says: "The people had a mind to work." They only had $1.41 in the treasury when they started. The church was dedicated on November 25, 1938. Crowds increased, souls were saved, members were added, and the church continued to flourish. The record Sunday School attendance here was 518.

Rev. Barton pastored for 15 years and left in 1949, at which time William Eckel came to town. He remodeled the basement and purchased the house next door for a future annex and educational wing. He was here until 1952; then L.D. Lockwood became pastor and was here for 4 years.

In 1957 Robert Griffin came as the pastor. Under his leadership, they started remodeling the sanctuary. He left in 1959 and Darrell Luther became pastor. He finished the annex. The 45th anniversary was celebrated in 1965 under Rev. Luther.

In 1966 William Muir became the pastor and the building program was concluded and the dedication was held in May, 1967. Melvin Thompson came in 1970 until 1973.

Stanley Gerboth came as pastor in 1973 and was here for 7 years. A property was bought for a parking lot on Walnut Street. After a few months, the parking lot was fenced in. In 1980, the 60th Anniversary was celebrated.

In 1981, Gerald Painter was called to be the pastor and he is still here as of this date. (1989). During 1988, new carpeting was added and ceiling fans installed, a new roof put on, and painting done.

The church has owned 8 parsonages for the pastors and their families. Early 1989, they purchased a parsonage on Walnut Street close to the church.

The church has many arms in which to work. The Sunday School, the World Mission Department, and the Youth Organization. Up to 1989, the General Church has had 81 mission countries, and around 650 missionaries.

EACH PASTOR HAS LEFT THEIR MARK ON THE CHURCH AND WE PAY TRIBUTE TO EACH ONE.

The church will be celebrating the 70th anniversary in 1990. At the present time, there are approximately 200 members. (1989)

The General Church of the Nazarene was founded in 1908, at Pilot Point, Texas, by Dr. Phineas Bresee, with HOLINESS OF HEART as their theme, and their goal is that of winning souls.

Dr. Bresee said we are to have UNITY in essentials, LIBERTY in non-essentials, and CHARITY in all things!

FREEDOM CHURCH

Freedom Church received its name from a statement made by a charter member, Elizabeth Hanna, when she said, "Now we have Freedom."

Freedom Baptist Church is located in Brown Township, five miles north of Waveland, on the corner of State Road 234 W and County Road 650. Across the road is the Freedom Cemetery, the resting place of many former members. The church was first organized in 1835.

November 14, 1835, thirteen members of the Union Baptist Church met in the home of John McIntire. Union Baptist Church was located southwest of Freedom. The thirteen were Elder Jacob Kirkendall, John McIntire, James Galey, Mary Galey, America Galey, Nancy Hanna, Elizabeth Wasson, Eliza Jane Gott, James Hanna, Ezekiel Layne, Jane McIntire, Margaret Hanna, and Mary R. Kirkendall. These people were dissatisfied with the doctrine of the Union Baptist Church. They agreed that no Articles of Faith was necessary and that all of the Disciples of Christ should meet on November 21, 1835. They met again December 26, 1835 in the home of James Galey. At this time, officers were elected and a membership roll was established. It was also agreed that December 26 would be the official birthday of the Church.

The third Saturday in December, 1837 the church approved plans for a permanent "Meeting House." It would be a log cabin 24' x 36' with 10' ceilings and a dirt floor. In May, 1838, a lot was chosen on the Caleb Conner land, which is north of the present Freedom Cemetery.

The church grew in membership; by January 1842 there were 78 members on the roll. By December 1850, a total of 169 were on the church roll.

In the early church at every meeting an inquiry was made about the peace of the church, also to "making grievance known." Quite frequently there were grievances and it became the duty of the Moderator to resolve any quarrel dispute with any member. The church was also concerned about the members' morality and social activities.

In February 1882, a committee reported that a building 34' x 54' was wanted by the church at an estimated cost of $2,500. In June of the same year, a motion was made to start immediately with the building project. The new church was dedicated in August 1883. This was a great improvement over the log cabin.

It was financially difficult constructing and furnishing a new church building. A committee was appointed to ask members to pledge money, produce, animals, grain, fruit or anything else of marketable value.

The new building was heated with two wood burning stoves at a cost of $33. There were two doors for the entrance, one to be used by the men and one for the women. In 1884, cost of belfry and bell tower was estimated at $30. A dozen song books were purchased in 1888 at the cost of $2.40; also the same year the church purchased an organ for $75.

A new gasoline lighting system was installed in October, 1907 at the price of $46. An extensive remodeling was done to the church in 1921. A basement, seats, and furnace added to the total of $5,064.60. William J. Miles, better known as "Uncle Billy Miles," gave a major portion of the finance needed to successfully complete this project. He also made a trip across Illinois over muddy roads in the interest of seats for the church.

"Uncle Billy" was looked upon as a "pillar" of the church. He became a member in February 1865. He held many offices in the church, was ordained a deacon in 1870, to which he served until his death.

Other remodeling that took place in later years was, three Sunday School rooms were added to the east end of the church in 1952. On September 8, 1963, the church dedicated a parsonage which they had purchased in Waveland. Stained glass windows were installed in 1969. A new 24' x 32' addition was added to the west end in 1983.

Freedom Church has often been referred to as the mother church of the Freedom Association. In April 1874, the Browns Valley Baptist Church was granted permission to start a church. Members from Freedom also helped establish a Baptist Church in Waveland. None are existing at the present time.

Numerous licensed and ordained ministers, church pastors, evangelists and missionaries have come from Freedom members.

Freedom has always been concerned and interested in the young people. In May 1848, Sunday School was organized. The church had its first Vacation Bible School in 1961. There has always been an active B.Y.F. (Baptist Youth Fellowship).

Through the years Freedom has been made up of devoted, faithful, and God fearing people. It has always been referred to as "The Light House on the Corner."

GARFIELD CHRISTIAN CHURCH

The Garfield Christian Church was organized on February 1, 1878 by a group of neighbors interested in the Christian religions; originally named the New Union Church with elders E.D. Simmons and L.W. Hutts. The following names were placed on the rolls: 1. Henry Binford, Mary Payne Binford, wife. 2. Elijah Cox, Catherine Cox, wife. 3. David Binford, Georgetta Payne Binford, wife. 4. Ella Vangundy. Twenty-four more names were added in the month of February. No record of where the meetings were held, but it is presumed that it was in the school building. At that time the Vandalia Railroad passed through the country and had a stop-over at Binford station. There was a post office and country store there for many years.

On August 22, 1882, Fred Imel and his wife, Martha deeded 1/2-acre of land to Calvin Long, David Binford, and Henry Binford, trustees of New Union Church, and their successor in office, for the sum of $1.00 with the name of Western Indiana Conference. Also included was the stipulation that should services ever cease to be held, the land would revert back to their heirs.

The present church building was erected in 1883 and dedication services were held December 1, 1883. Business meetings were held on Saturday afternoon before the second Sunday and consisted mostly of collecting conference funds, minister's salary and plans for cutting wood. The women of the congregation served dinner. All meetings closed in peace and fellowship with prayer.

It is not known for sure how or why Binford Station changed its name to Garfield, nor is it known when the church changed its name to Garfield Christian Church, but it has been that way since they had Garfield School in the early 1900s.

In 1946 plans for the annex to be built for Sunday school and social functions were started and were completed in 1948 at a cost of $4,896. In the early 1960s the church was in need of repair as the ceiling was about to fall in. After the death of Maybelle Vannice in 1967, (she left a sizeable bequest to the church), a new furnace was added and the adults started to remodel the Church. AAA Church builders were hired and the sanctuary was stripped to the walls and new lights, walls, ceilings, carpet, and padded pews were added. On the end behind the pulpit was built a cross. The youth group purchased new pulpit furniture, communion table and piano. Water was added to the church shortly afterward. In 1973, a fellowship hall was built across the entire back side of the church, along with restrooms and a kitchen. A portable baptistry was uniquely designed and built by Joe and John Rose. In 1986 vinyl siding was added. In 1987 the members took on the job of reroofing the church and working together until the entire church was done. Everyone pitched in. Men and youth worked on the roof, while the ladies fixed dinner and lunches for everyone.

Today, as it has been for the last 110 years, all the members work together for the church and glory of God.

LINDEN-KIRKPATRICK UNITED METHODIST CHURCH

The first settlers of Madison Township started Methodism services in log homes near the present site of Linden in 1829. The Ebenezer Methodist Episcopal Church was erected in the 1830's one mile west of the present site of Linden at what is now known as "Wilkin's Corner". This log building was replaced in 1855 by a larger frame building which served consecutively as a part of the Crawfordsville, Covington, Newton, and Romney circuits for about 30 years.

Meanwhile, the town of Linden was platted in 1850-51 and church services were being held in the homes of residents. In 1867, the Ebenezer Church building was moved to its present site in Linden. At that time the name was changed to the Linden Methodist Episcopal Church.

In 1892, that building was removed from the church grounds and the original part of the present structure was built. As the years passed, a full basement was excavated and additions were built on the north and west.

In time, as transportation and communication progressed, the separation between the communities of Linden and Kirkpatrick was erased. The Kirkpatrick school was closed in 1928 and children transferred to Linden. The Ladies Aid and Missionary Societies merged in 1941 to form the present United Methodist Women's Organization. In 1949, the Kirkpatrick and Linden Methodist Churches merged into the Linden-Kirkpatrick Methodist Church, meeting at Linden.

An extensive modernization program provided a new education unit on the south and west sides of the church in 1954. The basement was enlarged and kitchen facilities improved.

In 1955, the men formed the present United Methodist Men's Organization.

After the Evangelical United Breathern and the Methodist Churches merged in 1968, the local church changed its name to the Linden-Kirkpatrick United Methodist Church. It became a part of the Indiana West District of the South Indiana Conference in 1976.

Our present pastor is Rev. Richard C. Rhoads. The membership of the church is 229. Attendance is on the rise and this is a direct result of increased excitement and optimism among the laity. In November 1988, the sanctuary was remodeled and this also has added to the increased attendance.

We have a very active Sunday School program with 7 classes for our children and 4 adult classes. We also have two Bible Studies, Short term classes, a Chancel Choir, U.M.Y.F. group, United Methodist Men's & Women's group, and 4-M's (Mission Minded Merry Matrons).

The church promotes numerous outreach and social programs for the entire community and is presently the meeting place for Girl Scouts, 4-H, First Responders, and an exercise class. We feel the future is bright and exciting.

MACE UNITED METHODIST CHURCH

Our forefathers came to this area 1838-1840 from Pennsylvania, Virginia, Ohio and other eastern states. Fredericksburg, now Mace, was named from Frederick Long, who laid off the town, after building cabins and settling, their thoughts turned toward their duty to God and church.

They met in their homes for Worship, ministered to by the circuit riders. 1840's the first church was a log cabin built by the men in the area.

In 1854 a modest chapel was built on the side of the present church. The ground was donated by John Linn. Revivals were held in 1857-1858, 100 new members, 1875-1876, 130 new members. The first Sunday School classes organized were held on Sunday afternoon.

1893, the church was moved one half block westward south and used as a town hall and the present church was built at the cost of $3,000. Much of the timber and materials were donated.

Epworth League was organized in 1894, for the youth group.

1918, the town hall was moved back and incorporated to the present church, with a stage, used for a Sunday School class, church programs and community plays.

1927, the Junior Department of the Sunday School was reorganized under the direction of Mrs. Lida Ward Fletcher. The Ladies Aid was reorganized in 1941 known as Womens Society of Christian Service (WSCS). At present called United Methodist Women (UMW).

First Vacation Bible School was in 1942, under the direction of Reverant Carl Reppert, and has continued each summer.

The improvement committee was organized in 1954 to help with the needs in the church and parsonage with the agreement of the church trustees and administrative board.

The annex was remodeled in 1958 and the stage replaced by a fully equipped kitchen.

1987; the Youth Group met with the New Ross Methodist and are called Godsquad.

We have had many faithful Ministers each contributing to our church and community.

With the many gifts and memorials given to the church, the spiritual gifts of prayer, with the present membership of 173, talent, service and study, may our church "by the side of the road" always be a shining light in the community.

Pastors of the Mace Methodist Church

1840 Circuit riders, pioneer Ministers: Rev. Wilote, Rev. Thomas Brown and Rev. Hargreaves.
1854 John Harrison
1855 James B. Grey
1856 Jesse Hill
1857 Frances Cox
1859 Abram Utter
1860-61 James Parcells
1862 Samuel M. Hayes
1863 Ferris Pierce
1864-65 William M. Fraley
1866-68 George W. Stafford
1869 James Spinks
1870 Franklin Nickols
1871 Jesse Hill
1872-73 John E. Wright
1874-75 Isaac P. Patch
1876 Thomas Bartlett
1877 Jeptha Boicourt
1878-79 Ellijah R. Johnson
1880-82 John Harrison
1883-84 Jonathan B. Coombs
1885 Andrew J. Cliffton
1886-87 C.J. Vaught
1887-88 John M. Stafford
1889 S.A. Ross
1890 William P. Bowman
1891-93 Joseph G. Stephens
1894-95 S.B. Grimes
1896-99 Henry C. Riley
1900-02 Thomas J. Reeder
1903 Richard H. Crowder
1904-05 Henry C. Weston
1906-07 W.A. Mathews
1907-09 Alonzo A. Dunlavey
1910-12 James G. Greenway
1912-13 Frank F. Hargrave
1913-15 Lewis S. Smith
1915-16 Roy J. Hicks
1917-19 Thomas L. Stovall
1920-21 Frank Beal
1922-23 Henry M. Braum
1924-26 John F. Clearwater
1927-30 George L. Hartz
1930-36 James A. Gardner
1936-41 J.P. Alford
1941-47 Carl Reppert
1947-50 Ralph G. Gwin
1950-52 Carl Cogan
1952-56 Ernest F. Prevo
1956-Oct. 58 William Strunce
Nov. 1958-May 59 Max Tudor
Jun. 1959-60 Harold Boaz, Jr.
1960-Oct. 62 Dean V. Stuckey
Feb. 1962-Mar. 64 Del Saxon
Jun. 1964-66 Robert Greeley
1966-68 Mrs. Jo Blan LaRue
1968-71 Jack Frick
1971-77 Victor Link
1977-79 Jewell Dewees
1979-83 Kenneth Wooden
1983-Dec. 86 Jerry Rairdon
1987-Jan. 19, 89 Tim McGee
March 5, 1989 Jeff Barnes

NEW MARKET UNITED METHODIST CHURCH

The New Market United Methodist Church proudly stands today with a history that spans over a century of Methodism and spiritual leadership in the New Market community.

In the spring of 1872, local Methodists and the remaining members of the Old Finley Chapel Church, northeast of New Market, united to organize the original New Market United Methodist Episcopal Church. Services, or classes, as they were called, were first held in a small building on West Main street on the property now owned by Mr. and Mrs. Robert Servies. Reverend Jesse Green of the Ladoga Charge was the minister and Samuel Godfrey, the Presiding Elder.

At the fourth session of the Quarterly Conference of the Ladoga Circuit, August 31, 1872, the following trustees of the Methodist Episcopal Church at New Market were elected: Joseph White, Levi Byrd, W.T. Hicks, William White, A.J. Shular, Joseph Wilson and John White. These trustees made up the Building Committee for the construction of the first House of Worship in New Market.

A plot of land, in the center of the town in the northwestern corner of Scott Township, was donated as a building site by Circuit Rider, Joseph White and wife—with the provision the ground be used for no other purpose.

The building contract was let to S.F. Buchanan and ground-breaking took place in September, 1872. The new edifice was completed and dedicated the last Sunday of September, 1873, by Dr. Andrus, President of Indiana Asbury University (DePauw).

To serve the growing congregation, the first major remodeling was launched under the pastorate of Rev. Andrew Yount in 1897. The sanctuary floor was elevated, a basement and furnace added, tower erected, and new pews, pulpit furniture and Cathedral window installed. This project, at a cost of $2,000, was accomplished by the generous donations and untiring efforts of the church's 121 members, with $800 contributed at the Dedication Services conducted by Rev. G.W. Switzer, February 19, 1899.

In 1915, a five-week Union revival was held by the three New Market Churches in a tent pitched on the Methodist lawn. There were 126 conversions, an impact never equalled in the community.

To keep abreast with the increased church population and its needs in the 1960's, education facilities were expanded. A ground breaking ceremony took place east of the church, September 2, 1962, for the construction of a two-story educational unit, 32'x40', with auditorium, six classrooms and restroom. The new Fellowship Hall was completed the last of December, 1962, at a cost of $14,500. After the building indebtedness was cleared, Dedication Services were conducted June 6, 1965, by Walter L. Porter, Pastor, and Ralph Steele, Superintendent of the Terre Haute District.

A fourth dedication, held October 10, 1971, was that of the modernized sanctuary. Rev. Dale Payne was the pastor and guest speakers were, District Superintendent Sam Phillips and Dr. Burleigh Matthews of Indianapolis. The cost of this remodeling project completed in August, 1971, was $8,997.61.

In October of 1973, the Church observed its 100th Anniversary with special services.

Throughout the century countless contributions, in varying forms—monetary, gift, or labor—have made the Church the attractive Worship Center it is today.

In the 1976 redistricting, the New Market Church became a part of the Indianapolis West District of the South Indiana Conference and was placed on a charge with Waveland Convenant United Methodist Church.

Near the end of November, 1979, the Mary Circle of the United Methodist Women, deeply concerned about the 52 American Hostages held in Iran, put their faith into action. Each day at noon a church representative for a period of one year and two and one-half months broadcast from the Church Tower sound system patriotic or sacred music that could be heard over the town until the hostages were released.

In 1983, under the ministry of Rev. Scott Johnson, a brick house, one-half mile North of New Market was purchased from Mrs. Doris Bazzani for a parsonage. At the Open House, June 24, 1984, dedication and burning of the mortgage was conducted on the lawn. Immediate Past District Superintendent, Charles Ballard and Loren Maxwell from the South Indiana Conference made dedication remarks.

Organizations playing an important role in the church today are: UMW, UMM, Adult Choir, Christian Builders, Future Builders, Alpha Beta Kappa, Youth and Children's Classes, and Evangelism Task Force Committee.

Special Strengths include an active membership, prayer chain, Advent Devotion Books, Newsletters, Church Camp Scholarships, Cub Scout program, Nightcrawlers program, Children's Church, Choir and UMW serving meals for Senior Citizens and families of deceased members.

See: *A CENTURY OF PROGRESS, NEW MARKET, INDIANA 1872-1972* (Crawfordsville Public Library) for a list of ministers during that period. Additional pastors include: Glen Bates, 1976-79; William Patterson, 1979-83; Scott Johnson, 1983-85; Jay Morrison, 1986-88. Today, the New Market United Methodist Church is well-organized according to the Discipline and functions under the current pastor, Michael Gore.

NEW RICHMOND UNITED METHODIST CHURCH

The New Richmond United Methodist Church had its beginning west of New Richmond, on what is now known as the Reuben Swank farm. In 1830 a class was formed and met here in the home of Absolam Kirkpatrick. In 1835 on his farm a 26 x 40 foot building was erected at a cost of $900. It was called "Old Brick Church."

Preaching services were held every four to eight weeks by a traveling circuit preacher. This church served until 1853, when a frame church was built in New Richmond just back of the K of P building, facing what is now Washington Street. It was a single room...men and boys entered through one door and all sat on one side of the church. The women and girls entered through the other door and sat on the opposite side of the church. There was a school building just south of the church. It was later remodeled into a dwelling and was the residence of Dr. D.M. Washburn for many years.

A frame church was erected on the present site in 1888 at a cost of $3400. Rev. James Loder was the pastor, and the church was built by Samuel R. Tribby and dedicated by Rev. George W. Switzer. At that time it was considered to be one of the most beautiful churches in the district.

Soon after this, the Ladies Aid was organized, and has continued as the Missionary Society, Women's Society for Christian Service (WSCS) and now as United Methodist Women or UMW. This group has always been active in missionary work and in early 1900's, sent Jessie Tribby Shelly, Etta Tribby Archey and Ruth Tribby as teachers to a Mission School in Chili, South America.

In 1915 a movement was started to remodel the church, seeking pledges and donations. The building Committee consisted of: Charles Kirkpatrick, Rev. H.E. Moore, Mrs. Nettie Alexander, Mrs. Susan Alexander, Mrs. Lena Hollin, William Inskeep, John G. Utterback and W.O. McBeth.

The architect was Mr. Mann of Chicago, and a Chicago firm did the building at an approximate cost of $10,000. It was completed in 1918. At this time the brick was added to the exterior of the building, and it was dedicated on March 24, 1918 by Rev. Madian Appleby.

In the busy years during World War I and the beginning of World War II several organizations were formed and later disbanded, such as the Loyal Workers Class. Some of the active people giving time and effort to promoting the work of the church were Emma Mason, Mrs. Nelle Nesbitt, Mrs. Fanny Andrews and Mr. J.C. Burgess.

Rev. John Sayre went to the service of his country as a chaplain in 1944. Rev. Arthur Schenck came to replace him and stayed six years.

In 1953 a new Hammond Organ was purchased for the church with Mary Pierce serving as organist for more than 25 years. In the late 1950's the sanctuary was re-decorated, floors refinished, storm sash installed over the stained glass windows. Members served in concession stands at Purdue University football games to earn money for these projects.

In 1973 the "I Am A Methodist" stamp was designed by Pat Payne, who was a member of our church at that time.

In 1975, a community bridge was crossed. Summer Vacation Bible School and Easter Sunrise Services were held jointly with the New Richmond Christian Church, with a yearly alternation of host church. This custom continues today.

Mission work has been done by many of our members some of whom are: 1967-1969 Russell and Frances Miller went as volunteers to the Congo to install telephone systems serving Piper Memorial Hospital, Springer Institute, a Catholic Mission and build a telephone line for David Tshombe, the chief of the Lunda Tribe to government headquarters.

In 1971, Roy Meharry and Rev. Dale Seslar went to Honduras with UMCOR to complete one and build another church. Mr. Meharry returned here in 1974 to help build a church parsonage.

1973 - Rev. Tom True and wife Sharon worked in McCurdy Mission in Espanola, New Mexico. Also in this year our people joined work crews in Monticello, Indiana after their tornado.

1976, 1977 and 1978 Roy again joined UMCOR (United Methodist Overseas Relief) to help in the mission field.

Under our present minister, Rev. Mike Manning in 1988, we are once again working on the building; redoing sills, foundation, cement work, and some roofing.

We are also still supporting local and foreign missions, such as Red Bird Mission in Kentucky, the McCurdy School in New Mexico, and Lena Eschtruth's work with women and children in Africa.

Our membership is holding steady at a little over 100 and we are sharing a pastorate with the Waynetown United Methodist Church.

We are very proud of our church and its accomplishments, as we strive to do the work of the Lord as he commands us to do. We invite you to come and worship with us.

NEW ROSS CHRISTIAN CHURCH

Earliest records in possession of the Christian Church at New Ross are dated 1865. In September 1870, a notice appeared advertising a meeting to be in the Harshbarger schoolhouse south of town on October 1. The purpose of the meeting was to elect trustees so a church could be constructed. The Concord Church would then be known as Church of Christ at Valley City.

Portions of the present building are more than 100 years old. The original church was dedicated in February 1872, the year that Valley City was renamed New Ross. A total of 85 names was added to the roll that day. By 1875, there were 139 names on the roll of the Christian Church of New Ross.

In 1883, the Christian Church had a church bell installed. The bells calling people to church services made a very pleasant sound on a beautiful Sunday morning. Jess Rains tolled the bell.

May 27, 1907, the trustees and other officials met at the church and agreed to rebuild the church. The Sunday School rooms on the east were removed and the main building turned a quarter turn. A room 18'x30' and two vestibules were added on the west and at the rear three rooms were added, one containing the baptistry. The basement contained a furnace and an acetylene light plant. There had been one entrance on the front of the old building; now we have two, one on each side of the front with vestibules and steps.

The Ladies Aid Society met regularly at the church every Friday afternoon for many years. They contributed $500.00 to the building fund and purchased new carpet, which with the inclined floor and circular pews added to the appearance of the sanctuary.

Bro. Earle Wilfley of Crawfordsville was the dedication speaker on Feb. 2, 1908. He directed a pledge service raising $300.00 which was more than the amount needed to complete payment for the building.

During the time since 1908, electric lights have replaced the old gas lights, painting and redecorating and repair work have been done. The furnace has been converted to oil, a restroom was installed, complete kitchen was put in, folding tables and chairs have been purchased, also blinds and drapes were added.

The Church building was repaired and improved from time to time. The sum of $6,200.00 pledged by the fourth Sunday in March 1955, was for the purpose of building an annex on the east side of the main structure. There are classrooms which can be opened into a large auditorium or dining room. A modern kitchen was provided. In 1965 a new baptistry was installed behind the pulpit area of the sanctuary with a beautiful painting providing an appropriate setting for the rite of baptism. Many gifts and purchases added to the religious atmosphere of the rooms. Many of the gifts were given by families and individuals as memorials for their loved ones.

In 1975, the floor was newly carpeted, the ceilings lowered and new lighting was installed. Many improvements such as two furnaces, sound speakers, new song books, copy machine, padding of the church pews, a painting of the "LORDS SUPPER" that was painted by Karl Rhoads. A complete redecorating of the sanctuary was done in 1988.

Last Homecoming was observed October 30, 1988. Speaker was Bro. Kenneth Arnold, a former minister. Special music by Woodsmen Quartet from C'ville.

In 1944 property was purchased to be used as a parsonage. The home was owned by Ernest Linn. It was sold July 10, 1978 to Dawson Feather.

In 1975, the lot south of the church was purchased. A house was torn down and the lot used for parking area.

Church has had many members go into the ministry and mission work. They were Oscar Kelley, Forrest Graves, Paul Eddingfield, Edward Bamish, Floyd Rhoads Jr., George Markey, Robert Sparks and Jean Poland.

Up to the present time there have been 42 ministers serve this congregation. William Schalk is the present minister. Chairman of the church board is Paul Turner, assistant Raymond Linn, secretary is Leo Thompson, and Betty Kinnett is treasurer. Church trustees are Richard Shelton, Raymond Linn, and Leo Thompson. Elders: Raymond Linn, Richard Shelton, and Paul Turner. Deacons: Bradley Thompson, Leo Thompson, Mark Money, David Spohr, James Bradley and Bob O'Kelley. Organist Betty Kinnett, pianist Marjorie Ebaugh, and their assistant Nina Spohr. Song leader Bob O'Kelley and Missions Phyllis Linn. Bradley Thompson is superintendent of Sunday School, assistant Raymond Linn and Richard Shelton is secretary. Teachers are: Betty Kinnett, Mary Lea Schalk, Marjorie Ebaugh, Martha Janssen and William Schalk. Childrens song leader is Martha Janssen. *Prepared by Phyllis Linn, May 1989*

NEW ROSS UNITED METHODIST CHURCH

"Brown's Chapel - 1878" is inscribed in stone above the entry to the New Ross United Methodist located at the northeast corner of State and Green Streets. It refers to a place where a little band of early pioneers first worshipped in 1830 — a log cabin in a clearing one and one-quarter miles east of the settlement first known as Valley City in 1855 and as New Ross in 1875.

Credit is given to Mrs. Nina Dorsey Evans, 1874-1958, for her account of the early history of the church. Rev. Thomas J. Brown and his wife, Susannah, came from Lee County, Virginia, and entered land in Boone County, just over the line from Montgomery County, in 1830. A Methodist, services were first held in his home; then he gave land on which a log church was built—school was also taught there. In 1832, Rev. Brown was appointed to Brown's Chapel in the Whitelick Circuit, which included Jamestown, and Lizton. He organized the Lizton Church in 1832.

The log church building was replaced with a frame structure under the pastorate of Joseph White in 1859. Rev. Brown died in 1860. Susannah buried him in the churchyard, erecting a stone monument, enclosing the area with an iron fence and gate. Later, she, too, was buried there, and a similar shaft marked her grave. The graves were neglected after the turn of the century. However, in 1983, with mutual agreement and a respect for their churches' founder, the congregations at New Ross, Jamestown and Lizton had the Browns' remains exhumed and reinterred in the Montgomery Cemetery at Lizton where another of Brown's churches had stood and other pioneers are buried. The monuments, cleaned and repaired, again mark the graves, and the same iron fence encloses them.

By 1870 the congregation was growing, and more people were moving into the Valley City village. Some parishioners thought it was too far to walk to worship at Brown's Chapel, so when Rev. W.P. McKinsey was appointed to the charge in 1873, he began preaching some in town. They decided to build, and a plot was given by Squire Jessee where the present church now stands. A stone foundation was laid, and bricks were fired on the site, but the Panic of 1873 halted the work. In 1877 Rev. David Handley held a protracted meeting in Adkins Hall. The crowd was so great they moved, by invitation, to continue at the Christian Church, and there were fifty conversions. The time was right, and the new brick building was erected on the "firm foundation" already in place at a cost of $3000.00. It was dedicated in 1880 by Dr. Samuel Godfrey and the pastor, Wesley F. Clark. The Trustees were J.J. Wren, Benjamin Walkup, Dr. Adkins, and Squire Jessee.

The building has withstood the "strain of time" with no major structural changes except for the replacing of the windows in 1910. Rev. George F. Francis was the pastor. Ten beautiful arched, stained-glass memorial panes bear dates and the names of Jennie Peterson, Geo. T. Dorsey, Docia A. Dorsey, Nancy E. Imel, Hannah Lewis, Benjamin Walkup, James A. Jessee, Nancy B. Jessee, Warren Brooks, Robert L. Evans, Henry M. Miller, and Jane Conner Walkup. Trustees were W.P. Peterson, John Brown, Robert Evans, Charles Bratton, and Lewis W. Tipton, the grandfather of a present member, Lewis T. Clark. At that same time, a basement was dug, and a furnace was installed.

Rev. Ernest Prevo was pastor in 1954 when the Annex was added at the northeast corner of the brick edifice to provide classrooms and a kitchen. Much labor was donated, and it was built at a cost of $6000.00. In 1968 the sanctuary's chancel was widened and divided, new railing, pulpit, lectern, altar, and carpet installed. Additional improvements were realized in 1988 when belfry and entry repairs were made, wood paneling installed on the walls at a height of four feet above the baseboard, and a wood cornice was placed at the top of the walls. The woodwork, floors, walls and ceiling were beautifully painted in colors in keeping with the Victorian era. The original bell still peals forth from its lofty tower!

Rev. Jeffrey G. Barnes was appointed to serve the Mace-New Ross Charge in March, this year (1989). He and his wife, Janna, and daughter "Maggie" reside in the parsonage at Mace. The present membership is ninety. There is a strong loyalty and dedication on the part of those who attend, and it is a CARING church. There are classes for all ages, a unit of United Methodist Women, an active youth fellowship called "Godsquad", and the Pollyanna Class. Mrs. Evangeline Inskeep directed the music program until her retirement.

The congregation is proud that one of its former members, Laurence L. Stewart, is a pastor at First United Methodist Church, Vincennes.

The following persons were elected for leadership to serve the church in 1989: Diann Arthur, Irene Bratton, Charles and Helen Bronaugh, Gayle Canada, Lewis and Helen Clark, Helen Evans, Sue Evans, Barbara Falconbury, Denver and Marcella Feltner, Lou Feltner, Martha Feltner, Ruth Fisher, Elizabeth Glim, Brad and Deborah Hackleman, Dorman Harris, Elsie Houchin, Ralph Jarvis, Joed and Joan Linn, Shirley McClaine, Julie Michael, Allen Norris, Mark and Janelle Quasebarth, Delores Radford, Michael Snyder, Alan and Jessie Stewart, Elizabeth Thomas, Andrea Thompson, Chris Thompson, Gene and Waltraut Turner, Louise Walters, David and Mary Lou Wilson, and Marjorie Wright. *This History of The New Ross United Methodist Church has been written and submitted by Marcella Feltner*

TRINITY METHODIST EPISCOPAL CHURCH

Ninety-five years ago in 1894 Rev. George Stafford, pastor of the Methodist Episcopal Church at Jamestown but living in the western part of Crawfordsville, became aware of the need for a place of worship for the growing west part of Crawfordsville. In May of 1894 a meeting of four clergy and eight laymen was called at the home of Andrew Yount. Those present were Rev. H. Middleton (presiding Elder), Rev. J. Green, Dr. H. Tucker (pastor of First Methodist Episcopal Church), Rev. J. Stephens, E. Nutt, T. Myers, Leroy Miller, J. Zuck, F. Nichols, D. Gerard and George Scaggs. Much interest was manifested and it was decided to have another meeting and many other meetings followed. A committee was appointed to select a location for the new church. A lot at the northeast corner of West Pike and Blair Streets was selected. At the session of Northwest Indiana Conference in September 1894, Rev. Joseph Stephens was appointed as minister of the new church.

Interest grew and the election of a Board of Trustees was made and the completion of building plans, so it was possible to lay the corner stone in November of that year. A brick structure was decided on and in February 1895 a revival service was held and the first members of Trinity Church were enrolled. In September 1895 the Northwest Indiana Conference recognized Trinity as a local church. Services during the winter of 1894-95 were held in the church basement; the upper story was completed in the spring of 1895, the devotion and sacrifice of the members made the completion possible and the church was dedicated Sunday, June 9, 1895. The cost of the complete structure was $7,500. The financing of the building was no small project, once each month a social was held with tickets selling at 15 cents, an exceptionally good profit was $28.00. Every Tuesday afternoon a group of women met at the church and made quilts which were sold at the "socials". The church had its 50th anniversary program in May 1944, while the late Rev. Homer Ivey was minister. Then Governor Henry F. Schricker was the speaker.

It was recognized in the middle 1950's that a new building was needed and a 17 member committee was appointed to launch a crusade to obtain pledges and raise funds for the building. Some of these here today were present at our first building project congregational meeting in December 1954. It was a dinner meeting at Pike Street Recreational Center to present the Building Committee's plans to raise $100,000. in 1955-1956-1957. This fund was to build the first unit of the new church.

Trinity United Methodist Church - Crawfordsville, Indiana

After several investigations of possible building sites it was decided by the congregation that the new church should be built on our present property since we already owned the lot and to preserve the concept of our being a "neighborhood" church. We continued to use the original church while our working fund for a new church was accumulating.

A nine man regular building committee was chosen and hired; John Walters, a local engineer was the architect who drew up plans for the entire church. In early spring of 1958 a contract was let to Williams, Beck and Hess, a local construction company to build the first unit. In the spring of 1958 ground was broken and construction started on the educational unit. The cornerstone was laid in the fall of 1958. The educational unit was completed and dedication was in February 1959. We conducted our worship services in the basement in what was then our first Fellowship Hall, and the pews were folding chairs. We continued to pay off the debt incurred to build it, and it was paid off completely three and one half years ahead of schedule in the spring of 1966. The mortgage was burned with appropriate ceremonies in the worship service on May 2, 1966.

The old church building was removed early in 1963 having housed Trinity's services for over 68 years. This cleared the way for the second unit, sanctuary and fellowship hall to be built in 1967. Bishop Richard Raines presided at consecration services on January 14, 1968. In 1968 Trinity became Trinity United Methodist Church.

Today members are continuing the ministry to the west side of Crawfordsville. Many are involved in community programs of Christian service and witness in the church supports area, national and world missionary outreach. The present minister is the Rev. Norris A. Keirn.

During the 95 years, thousands have worshipped here, children have been dedicated to the Lord in holy baptism. The history of Trinity cannot be written on a few pages of a church bulletin, the intellectual, moral and religious influences are all beyond human calculation.

WAVELAND CHRISTIAN CHURCH

Until the founding of The Waveland Christian Church in November of 1867 there were two churches in the neighborhood—The Bank Springs Church, two miles west of town and the Antioch Church, two miles east.

There were forty members in the consolidation of these two churches. Fourth, fifth and sixth generations of some of these members are still in the church.

The Antioch Church was torn down and materials used to erect a new building on West Main Street. This building was used until 1890 at which time the present brick building was erected at a cost of $5,000.00.

On the first Sunday of December 1890 the church house was formally dedicated to the service of Almighty God and has been used for that purpose for nearly a century.

There are two prerequisite for membership in this congregation; confession of faith in "Jesus the Christ, the Son of the Living God" and water baptism "in the name of Jesus for the remission of sins".

In 1950 a new kitchen was built on the north side. Two Sunday School rooms north of the kitchen was added in 1961 at a cost of $2,200.00.

A church library was started in 1965 and a bookcase was donated by the McCarty Family, in memory of Mother Amelia in 1967.

The church withdrew from The Disciples of Christ in 1968. A new roof was replaced on the south side of the church in 1970 at a cost of $2,377.00.

In 1973 it was decided to have church full-time rather than twice a month.

A new parking lot was added on the west side of the church in 1978.

As more room was required an addition consisting of a kitchen, fellowship hall, a half bath and a Ministers Study was constructed in 1981; most of the work being done by the members of the congregation.

The padding of the pews was started with a donation in memory of Clay Williams and Mother Nina Williams and finished in 1983. The brick on the outside of the church was cleaned and a new belfry installed with a donation from Cordelia Harbison's estate in 1987 and a new sound system installed in 1989.

Some of the Pastors who have faithfully served this church were; Rev. C.G. Bartholomew, William Holt, James Conner, T.D. Marris, T.J. Pearcy, Edward Bowers, T.J. Shuey, James C. Barkhardt, C.E. Moorman, Daniel G. Cole, Shelby D. Watts, O.E. Kelly, I.N. Grisso, C.E. Shultz, T.J. Freed, H.C. Burkhardt, M. Smith, R.C. Smith, T.F. Graves, R.D. Thomas, Bro. Hartling, Bro. Grocelose, J.C. Nelson, Sophia Franklin, F.C. Franklin, Bro. DeMoore, R.L. Bond, Paul Osborn, Grover DeNeal, Lester Niles, Michael Golforth, Herbert Swearingen, Dorman Winger, Glen McFarland, Larry Miller and David Finney.

WAVELAND COVENANT UNITED METHODIST CHURCH

The Waveland Covenant Methodist Church was formed in September, 1965 under the leadership of Rev. Walter Porter. It was a result of the merger of the Methodist and Presbyterian Churches of Waveland. An agreement was reached by the two congregations whereby we became a Methodist congregation using the Presbyterian building.

Both of the churches had long histories of being active and very vital parts of the community. There had been many union meetings and good fellowship between the two groups during the years so this made the decision to become one church a very logical one.

In 1968, the Evangelical United Brethern and Methodist Churches around the world merged and so at that time, the church became known as the Waveland Covenant United Methodist Church.

The Waveland Presbyterian Church had been organized November 28, 1828. Rev. James Thompson, who was president of the corporation that founded Wabash College, was chairman of the organizing committee. The church was first named "Providence" but was later changed to the Waveland Presbyterian Church.

The first building was built three-quarters of a mile northeast of Waveland on the banks of Little Raccoon Creek on land owned by William Moore and William Kinder. It was built of hewed logs with benches made of yellow poplar. They were said to be comfortable enough to sit on through a 60-minute sermon! Two years later, a second house of worship was built in the northeast corner of the Presbyterian Cemetery.

In the early days, discipline was very strict. Several members were charged with the sins of slander, profanity, dancing, card playing, horse racing and drinking intoxicants to excess.

In 1848, the congregation built the Waveland Academy which became famous for its educational advantages. The present brick building was erected in 1859 and completed in 1861. In 1923, the main entrance was changed to a Greek porch with massive pillars.

In 1953, an electrical storm caused damage so severe that it was necessary to rebuild the bell tower. During the time of rebuilding and redecorating, the congregation worshiped with the members of the Methodist Church.

At this time, the membership of the church was 100. The elders were Alonzo Deere, Dewey Hazlett, Clarence Milligan, Elton Milligan, Harry Evernham, Forrest Coleman and William McCampbell. Rev. Richard Huddleston was the pastor and Mrs. Kenneth Coleman was choir director and Mrs. Forrest Coleman served as organist.

The first Methodist Society had been organized in the Waveland area at the home of Mrs. Preston McCormick though a circuit rider had preached in the Brown Township area in 1825. The first church building was erected on land deeded by John and Lucinda Milligan in 1842. It was a rough wood structure which was replaced by a brick building begun in 1867 and completed in 1869. The first pastor of the church was Samuel Hayes.

The first parsonage for the pastor was presented to the church in 1878 by Andrew McCormick and a new parsonage was built in 1912.

An annex was built onto the church in 1925 from bricks bought from the old Baptist Church when it was torn down. The sanctuary was remodeled in 1949 but it was damaged by fire and had to be restored in 1951.

The first Sunday School was conducted in the home of John Brush in 1830. It was probably the first Sunday School in Brown Township and in 1832 a Sabbath School in connection with the Presbyterian Church was begun. Classes in the Methodist Church itself were started in 1842.

An Epworth League for Youth was started in 1890; a Ladies Aid in 1896; and a Home Missionary Society in 1924.

Not long after the merger of the two churches, it was decided to add an educational building for extra Sunday School rooms and office space. The Methodist parsonage was sold and the minister lived in the Presbyterian Manse just East of the Church.

For a number of years, the church had its own minister, but in the late 1970's it was decided that it would be more practical to share a minister with the New Market United Methodist Church as had been done previously. In the mid-1980's, New Market bought a newer parsonage so the district officials decided the minister should live there as it was more modern and more easily maintained. Since then, the Waveland parsonage has served as rental property.

Shortly after Jay Morrison became pastor in 1986, the church received a generous gift from the Dr. and Mrs. B.M. Harbeson estate. This money was used to purchase new stained glass windows for the sanctuary, a new furnace, an air-conditioner and a new organ.

Early in 1989, the church remains a vital part of the community with Rev. Michael Gore as pastor.

WAYNETOWN CHRISTIAN UNION CHURCH

On December 30, 1867, a meeting was held at Wesley, for the purpose of perfecting a Christian Organization to be known as the Christian Union Church. The William E. Osborn farm was chosen for the location, and on the first sabbath in June 1874, a house of worship was dedicated. The church is on Road 600 W., one mile south of State Road 136.

Principles essential to the fellowship are -

1. The Oneness of the Church of Christ
2. Christ the Only Head
3. The Bible the Only Rule of Faith and Practice
4. Good Fruits the Only Condition of Fellowship
5. Christian Union Without Controversy
6. Each Local Church Governs itself
7. Partisan Political Preaching Discountenanced

Later in 1938, under the direction of Oliver Schenck, Edgar Henthorn and Carroll Barnett, the men constructed a basement with furnace, kitchen and class rooms.

The 1944 church Service Flag contained ten names - Clarence Ball, Francis Ball, Harry Kinney, Eddie Schenck, Merle Larew, Charles Larew, Bob Larew, Billie Larew, Donald Wilkinson and Richard Wilkinson, who lost his life in a plane mission over Germany. In 1951 the Service Flag contained four - Lowell Barnett, Curtis Calder, Gene Anderson and Gleyre Switzer.

Several years ago the coal furnace was changed to oil. In 1951 the building was renovated with a new roof, wallpaper, storm windows and insulation. The pews and floors were also refinished. During the 1960's the sanctuary ceiling was lowered, and paneling and carpet installed. Also, rest rooms were placed in the basement with carpet covering on the floors. Recently replacement windows and vinyl siding have been added.

Vintage Dress was the highlight of a celebration in October 1967, with previous pastors and many 50 year members attending. June 2, 1974 Centennial of the building was in charge of Rev. Dorman Winger. Viola Schenck reviewed the history and recognized many of the older members.

Our pastors have been men or women called to serve our Lord, but have had other occupations. Those who were or are Montgomery County residents include - Everett Nixon, Merle Sparger, Esther Anderson, John R. Servies, Ralph Watson, Dorman Winger, Brian Rice and Wesley Ehrie, who is our present pastor.

The Church supports home and foreign missions. The Sunday School offerings on the first and third Sundays are used to aid missionaries. Members of the Ladies Aid Society serve willingly within the church and community. The congregation hosts the annual State Council every seven years - there are six sister churches in Indiana. Two ordinances - Baptism and the Lords Supper are observed. Holy communion is observed the first Sunday of each month. Each Sunday morning is Class Bible study and Message with music. The financing is unique in that no offering plates are passed. Any offering is deposited freewill, in a box at the back of the church. A brick bulletin base near the front door holds the original bell.

At the present time Brent Vance and Una Larew are pianists and Cherise Vance is organist. Irene Nixon served as organist from 1962 until her death in 1987. Current elders are Melvin Vance, Leslie Terry, Robert R., Larew and Morris Finch. Serving as trustees are Leslie Terry, Morris Finch, Willis Schenck, Wesley Ehrie and Billie Larew.

A few descendents of the early congregation remain active, but many have left the rural atmosphere to continue their faith in our Christ in many states.

In the spring of 1988 three maple trees were planted near the "Church by the Side of the Road." We are trusting we will continue to give spiritual guidance, and strengthen each other in Christian Love.

"LORD STRENGTHEN OUR FAITH AS WE LOOK FORWARD WITH HOPE TO THAT ETERNAL REWARD NOT MEASURED BY YEARS."

WOODLAND HEIGHTS CHRISTIAN CHURCH

Interest in establishing a New Testament Church was being voiced in the Crawfordsville and surrounding area. A meeting was called on Feb. 11, 1964, and attended by people from 15 churches and New Church Evangelizing Fellowship representatives. At this meeting, a committee was named to find an evangelist for a new church.

Another meeting was called on Feb. 17, 1964, to plan a "Kick-off Rally." The people met in the home of Lyle Shultz and elected officers. Jack Harrison was elected chairman; Sandra Reichard, church secretary, and Kenneth Hershman, treasurer.

On May 1, the rally was held in the Armory at Crawfordsville. The charter was opened for membership and 25 people responded to an invitation for commitment and transferred their membership from various churches to this new church family. The charter was closed on Dec. 31, 1964, with 106 members on the rolls.

While the new congregation searched for a minister, ministers from area churches preached and their elders and deacons provided communion. Services were held in the afternoon in the Armory when possible or shifted to the Municipal Clubhouse or Christ Lutheran Church.

Evangelist Don Sharp of Hoopeston, Ill., was called to serve as the minister in May. He drove from Hoopston each Sunday during May, and he and his family moved to Crawfordsville on June 6. Weekly Bible studies were being held in private homes. It was a daily walk in faith as God opened doors for this new congregation.

The new church looked to the future with excitement, intending that the power of God be heard, seen and felt through its witness of word and life.

An office was opened in downtown Crawfordsville to handle church business. A committee was named to study possible building sites for a new church. Membership continued to grow as did the dedication. The growth was far beyond the fondest dreams of those who dared to hope and plan for such an endeavor.

Members agreed to purchase 21 acres on Indiana 32, east of Crawfordsville. The new church building was to be built on top of the hill in a wooded area. In August, the church adopted the formal name of Woodland Heights Christian Church. Shortly after the land purchase, 14 acres on the back section were sold.

The Christian Education Committee established a graded Sunday School program. It was also agreed to give at least 10 percent of the church's income to missionary causes.

Just one year from the date of organization, ground was broken for a new church building. Nearly 200 attended the ceremonies. The church was designed for a seating capacity of 500. At that time, May 1965, church membership had grown to 128.

By the last of September construction was far enough along that services were being held in the new church. The first congregational meeting was on Oct. 28, 1965. Dedication of the church was on Dec. 26 that year.

Don Sharp resigned as minister in early October 1970. Lucian Robinson accepted the pastorate in early December.

On May 19, 1974, the congregation broke ground for a new addition to the church. It was completed by the end of the year and dedicated the following May.

Robinson resigned in December 1975. Jack Austin of Salem, Ohio was called to be senior minister. He preached his first sermon on Feb. 15, 1976.

The first full-time associate minister, Ralph Swarthout, was named in 1971 to work with youth and Christian Education. He resigned in February 1974. Mark Matthews was associate minister/youth from February 1979 to June 1987. David Church served as associate minister/Christian Education from October 1982 to August 1985. Jon Sullivan is currently serving as associate minister/youth, and started in June 1988.

Del Donaldson started his work at Woodland Heights as pastoral counselor on March 27, 1978 and continues in that position. Carolyn Fischer has served as church secretary since Jan. 3, 1970. In June 1986, Sharon Sitler was named director of Christian Education and Music. She resigned in August 1988.

After completing a ministry of 11 years, Jack Austin resigned, effective April 19, 1987. In June, Mark Matthews assumed the position of senior minister. He resigned on Sept. 11, 1988.

After a long search, Ben Wilson of Carterville, Ill. was called as senior minister in March 1989. The church now has an active membership of 443.

In looking to the future for Woodland Heights, Ben Wilson said, "In our 25-year history, Woodland Heights has seen some very good times. Like all churches, we have also seen some troubled times. Now, we look to the future with renewed hope and big dreams. We dream of starting at least two other congregations to help us reach the unchurched in Crawfordsville. We dream of helping start churches in other areas, where churches are few and the need is great. We dream of more building space here, of leadership training and international outreach. Some would accuse us of dreaming too big, but we have a great God, and no dream for Him is unreachable."

YOUNTSVILLE COMMUNITY CHURCH

The church was founded on two acres of land just west of Yountsville in 1832. Four years later, it was included in the Methodist Coal Creek Mission. The Society of Yountsville was organized in 1842 as a result of a revival meeting in the old log church.

Records show that our present church building was moved to this spot shortly after the land was deeded on April 24, 1843. In 1888, a parsonage was deeded to the 'Trustees' and it still stands just east of the church. Hard times hit in 1930 and the parsonage had to be sold. It was not until 1939 that the basement was put under the church by the men who worshipped there.

During the 1940's and 1950's, the church struggled to keep going, using retired ministers and student ministers. Services were sometimes held only every other Sunday. Our Loving Lord blessed a revival meeting in 1953 which saw many of the congregation receive Jesus Christ as Saviour. This was truly a needed lift which kept the church going at a struggling pace for some years.

In January of 1968, the Yountsville Community Church was organized when the Methodist Synod wanted nothing more to do with Yountsville. Another building project was taken on in 1970 when a Sunday School/Church Annex, on both levels, was placed on the west side of the church which included restrooms inside! Previously, the outdoor type was used.

A most important step was taken by our church in 1973 when they formed a relationship with Village Missions to furnish spiritual leadership. This step has helped make our church what it is today! The present parsonage across the road from the church was built in 1976 and dedicated on February 20, 1977.

The current pastor, James Ireland and wife Dawn have served the church for six years.

In 1988, the men of the church added an enclosed addition to the front of the church which included steps and ramps up the sanctuary and down to the basement. This was dedicated March 26, 1989.

This brief history does not permit the listing of all the remodeling, repairs and improvements made over the years to keep the physical church in good condition. There were many, involving many people and many hours.

We close with an excerpt from the Crawfordsville Journal that appeared about 85 years ago, "Now that new life has been given to the organization through the grace of God, it is impossible for men to foretell the powers for good of the Old Yountsville Church."

Plans are now being made to observe the 150th Anniversary of the Yountsville Church in 1992.

LADOGA PRESBYTERIAN CHURCH

A group of Montgomery County citizens signed a petition to organize the Ladoga Presbyterian Church on October 17, 1873. The Presbytery appointed Reverend R.F. Caldwell and ruling Elder David Fulenwider to visit Ladoga and begin a church. Twenty-nine members were taken into the church as charter members. For six years worship was held in the Methodist Church. In the Spring of 1880 members signed a pledge for the building of a new church. In July of 1880 the ground was purchased and Syl Sharp put up the foundation of the building at 300 North Washington. On July 3, 1881 the new church bell rang and members came to worship.

On March 14, 1874 the following children were baptized: Mary Ann Scott, Robert Carl Scott, Theadore Snodgrass and Augusta Snodgrass. The first wedding was on June 20, 1883. The bride was Lizzie Huntington and the groom was J.F. Warfel.

The church was remodeled in 1891 and Dr. Tuttle, President of Wabash College officiated at the service. The membership was more than 100. The new church addition and furniture had cost six thousand dollars. The church tower and the south window had been donated by Isabel Durham. An east window was a gift from Mrs. Ella Ashby. The pews were from Harry Daugherty. In recent years, a lighted Celtic Cross was donated by Mr. and Mrs. Joe Genung and two front stained glass windows were from Madonna Liebtag in memory of her parents, Mr. and Mrs. Franz O. Myer.

The church records are detailed concerning the 50th Anniversary celebration which took place on October 11, 1931. "An especially pleasing feature of this service was the music rendered by a quartet, Mrs. Grant Rose, Mrs. Cline Graybill, Dr. C.B. Werts and Donald Henry. Mrs. C.W. Clore was the pianist. Wallace Ashby was the chairman. A trio of three boys, Billy Carman, James Barnard, and Paul Lawson, sang, and did well. An historical sketch was prepared by Mrs. Sallie Harney Foster."

LIBERTY CHAPEL CHURCH

Liberty Christian Church was organized on April 25, 1835 by a small band of people who realized the need for Christian fellowship. For the first five years the group met in the Edwin Quick log barn. The first church building was erected on what is now the cemetery ground and was used until 1880 when the present building was erected across the road from the cemetery. In 1900 the vestibule was built and in 1906 the basement was added. Those who ascribed their names to the covenant in 1835 were: Elder Samuel Low, Sarah Low, Edwin Quick, Abigail Quick, Elder Adam Thomas, James Vail, Samuel Potts, and Elizabeth Potts.

Roberts Chapel came into existence about 1842. The name was in honor of Bishop Roberts, a prominent man in early Methodism. The first trustees were Richard Breaks, William Hund and William Lowe. First members were Ezekiel Everett, Ezra Thomas, Elijah Brown and their wives, James and Andrew Shanklin, John Walton, Richard Fox, Mary Tine and Hannah Groendyke.

In 1854 Clarks Chapel Church was built on the New Richmond Road. They decided to disband in 1866 and unite with the Roberts Chapel congregation. Their church building was moved to the site donated by Richard Breaks. The white frame building was used until 1899 when the new building was constructed. The building committee was: Richard Harrison, Calvin and Alvin Breaks, sons of Richard Breaks, Sr. and John and Peter Cowan. In 1949 arrangements were made for Roberts Chapel to join the Liberty Congregation.

The dedication of the newly organized church under the name of Liberty Chapel was celebrated on Sunday, May 15,

1949. Following the regular morning service a basket dinner and fellowship hour was enjoyed in the newly remodeled church. Rev. William Whear, Methodist District Superintendant gave the dedicatory address. The New Richmond robed chorus provided music and a solo by Mrs. Margaret Campbell completed the program. Services are still held in this beautiful rural church.

On April 17, 1967, the trustees received a letter of release from the Methodist Conference. Marian Cowan had the document recorded in the Montgomery County Court House.

In 1970, the sanctuary of the church was remodeled. Extensive work in the kitchen and dining room was done in 1972.

Indianapolis Seminary students were supplied as part time ministers.

In the fall of 1982, the Village Missions of Kansas City, Missouri were invited to supply the church with a full-time minister. Volunteer help remodeled a rented house for the Alan Sparks family.

Our membership is 110, and with new families, Liberty Chapel is on the move. We welcome everyone!

LINDEN BAPTIST CHURCH

The Linden Baptist Church had its origin in the spiritual awakening in West Central Indiana during the 1930's. Under the able leadership of such men as Bro. Barney Antrobus and Dr. Homer Elmore, a host of young men moved about the country side, preaching in long slumbering churches.

In September, 1936, one of these men, Carlyle "Scotty" Scott, came to Linden, his boyhood home, and was used of God in a spiritual awakening which continues today as the Linden Baptist Church.

The church was first organized the New Testament Church, January 10, 1940, after having functioned as the Christian Church under the able ministry of Bro. Austin Elmore.

The church rented a hall on Main Street for several years. Then it purchased the property across from the Town Hall, on Walnut Street, which for many years housed the sanctuary, Sunday School and parsonage.

On January 8, 1947, the church voted to become the Linden New Testament Baptist Church. A parsonage was purchased in the early 1950's to make room for the growing church. On October 23, 1984, the church voted to become the Linden Baptist Church, which it is today.

Under the pastorate of Bro. David Williams the church acquired property from the Indiana Christian Conference and the adjoining property from a private party. The building had fallen into disrepair and was remodeled by the members.

Bro. Carlyle "Scotty" Scott was speaker at the dedication service in 1967, thirty-one years after the memorable awakening in 1936.

Under the leadership of Bro. Hershel Bryant the educational facility was completed.

During its existence, the church had emphasized evangelism and missions. From its midst have gone young men and women to the farthest reaches of the world with the saving Gospel message of Christ.

Its present goal is to be true to the message of Christ, to win the lost to the Redeemer and influence every area of society for the Lord through the application of His Word to every aspect of life.

MILLIGAN MEMORIAL PRESBYTERIAN

A joint gift by General and Mrs. Lew Wallace and Mr. and Mrs. A.B. Blair was used to purchase the land where Milligan Memorial Presbyterian Church now stands. Mrs. Joseph Milligan made a most generous monetary gift to erect the $3,000.00 building in memory of her daughter, Anna. Mrs. Milligan also raised funds from friends. The interest for a church in the east end of Crawfordsville had started in 1888 during a revival at First Presbyterian Church located at the corner of Pike and Water Streets. A group from First Presbyterian and several Wabash College students began to hold prayer meetings, setting a goal of organizing a church within two years. However, it was not until 1894 that the first Sunday School began to meet. The first class had 13 teachers and 7 pupils. But through perseverance the church was finally built. Free of debt, the Chapel, was dedicated on September 27, 1896. The building was octagonal in shape and had a central auditorium. On February 8, 1898 the Chapel was renamed The Presbyterian Memorial Chapel and had 100 members. A church bell was donated by the Parks brothers. The first Bible was a gift from the President of Wabash College, Dr. William P. Kane. The communion set was a gift of Mrs. Munns and was later replaced by a new set, gift from Dr. Maude Arthur, a staff doctor for the State Board of Health. In 1923, because of her numerous gifts to the church, and because of her friendship, the congregation requested that the name of their church be changed honoring Harriet Milligan (Mrs. Joseph) to Milligan Memorial.

In the 90 years, the church has been remodeled four times. A large extension was added in 1918 just after a complete basement had been finished.

Throughout the years these persons have left the church to become ministers: Will Davis, Hugh Brower, Clyde Myers, Rev. Harris, Louis Bean, Thomas Keefe, and Bob Taylor. Over the past several years, the church has been well known in the community because it houses the Christian Nursing Service, A Well Baby Clinic, Home Nursing, Telecheck, The Clothing Room, Pre-Natal and Adult Health Clinic.

ST. BERNARD CATHOLIC CHURCH

Father Edward O'Flaherty, 1st Resident Pastor

1859—1st church built of Virgin timber from area (Corner of Walnut & North Street)

1864—School Established

1872—Land Purchased for Calvary Cemetery

1876—New Church of Red Brick/Stone (Corner Pike & Washington)

1944—8-grade school established

1857—present location under Father Henry Ward

1970—School closed

1985—Present Church construction (Father David Clifford)

Masses held: 5:30 Saturday, 8, 10:30 Sundays

WABASH AVENUE PRESBYTERIAN CHURCH

The Presbyterian Church of Crawfordsville was organized on June 20, 1824 by Isaac Reed, a Presbyterian missionary from the East. The organizing members were Williamson and Miriam Dunn, Hugh and Mary Linn, James Miller, John Cowan, and Drusilla Kerr. In 1827 James Thomson became the first minister and in 1829, Dunn donated a lot on the northeast corner of Pike and Water Streets which was the sight of the first church building. In 1838 a difference in doctrine caused the church to divide and James Thomson left the First Presbyterian Church with about half of the congregation and formed the Center Presbyterian Church, which located on the northwest corner of Pike and Washington Streets. Center Church enjoyed a close relationship with Wabash College; in fact several of their ministers were also presidents of the College. On April 20, 1921, the two congregations united and Wabash Avenue Presbyterian Church was born.

Catholic Church and St. Charles Academy, Crawfordsville, Ind.

FAMILY HISTORY

The Carter Car, front seat is Lucile and Edith Manges. Backseat ids Nellie Manges on the lap is Ethel, on the seat is Edna, on the bike is Cline Manges and Edgar with horse & colt. Photo Courtesy of Edith Kistler

CARL J. ABENDROTH

Carl(ton) J(ohn) Abendroth, son of Elmer T. and Clara (Strassburger) Abendroth; was born at West De Pere, Brown Co., WI, May 12, 1915.

Elmer T. Abendroth, son of John and Helen (Streich) Abendroth, was born at Appleton, Outagamie Co., WI, May 10, 1886. He attended public schools and business college, after which he became a machinist. In 1908 he organized at De Pere, WI, the Western Steel & Iron Works, which he sold in 1930 to the Hudson Manufacturing Co. On June 16, 1930, in partnership with W.A. Zaloudek, he purchased the controlling interest in the Oakes Manufacturing Co., of which he is vice-president. The company operates plants in Tipton and Crawfordsville, IN, and a foreign office in Chicago, IL. Mr. Abendroth resides in Tipton, IN, with his wife, Clara (Strassburger) Abendroth, who was born at Appleton, WI. Her parents, William and Henrietta (Wehrman) Strassburger, are deceased. William Strassburger was a machinist at Appleton, WI. Elmer T. and Clara (Strassburger) Abendroth are the parents of two children: (1) Myron E., who was graduated from Purdue University, after which he became identified with the Oakes Manufacturing Co. (2) Carlton John.

John Abendroth, father of Elmer T., was born in Germany, and later emigrated to America, settling in Wisconsin. He was a farmer. His wife, Helen (Streich) Abendroth, whom he married in Wisconsin, also was born in Germany.

Carl J. Abendroth, the subject of this sketch, was graduated from the International Business College, in Ft. Wayne, IN, following which he was employed as a commercial traveler by the Oaks Manufacturing Co., two years. Since 1937 he has been manager of the Crawfordsville (IN) plant of the Oakes Manufacturing Co. The firm manufactures sheet metal farm equipment, including hog feeders, fountains, and tanks. Products are sold internationally. Mr. Abendroth, who is a Republican, is a member of the following: Elks Lodge; Montgomery County Chapter, Citizens Historical Assn.; and Presbyterian Church. His favorite recreation is golf.

On Nov. 25, 1938, Carl J. Abendroth married Marian Smith, daughter of Harry D. and Nina (Dooley) Smith. Harry D. Smith engages in farming near Tipton, IN. Mrs. Abendroth was born in Tipton.

NORMAN F. ABSTON

Norman F. Abston was born in 1930 near Fayette in Boone Co., IN. In 1942, he moved to Walnut Township north of New Ross and graduated from New Ross High School in 1948.

Parents were Floyd C. and Alice L. (Dodson) Abston. Brothers are Clyde A., Marvin W. and Howard E. Abston. The family lived on farms north of New Ross and later north of Darlington.

Norman F. Abston Family

In 1951, he married Mary M. Herron, daughter of Earl and Cora (Coon) Herron of the Crawfordsville-Waynetown area. Mary's sisters and brothers are Ruby Ralston, Helen Rutledge, William S. Herron, Charles A. Herron, Jack L. Herron and Jane Whipple.

Norman and Mary both worked at R.R. Donnelley and Sons Co. in Crawfordsville. Their children born in Crawfordsville are: Sharon Wingert, Willard, OH; Susan McCumber, Galion, OH; and Steven who married Sue Spicer and lives at Plymouth, OH. Grandchildren are Linda and Lori Courtright, daughters of Sharon and students in the Willard High School.

Norman's grandparents were John J. and Zinetta (Phillips) Abston. John often told of moving from Kentucky to Illinois, then to Indiana, during the Civil War. He was five years old during the first move. They moved by horse and ox teams which swam the Ohio River with loaded wagons in tow. One ox team spooked and started swimming downstream. An older brother jumped in the river and swam to another wagon. They last saw the ox team and wagon going downstream. They left their 400 acre farm to gain safety because of their unwillingness to take sides in the Civil War making them the enemy of both. John was a school teacher and farmer in Boone Co., IN. He lived in the New Ross and Darlington communities in his later years where he died in 1952 at the age of 93.

Maternal grandparents were George W. and Lillie (Parks) Dodson. George was a Baptist Minister and farmer near Danville, IL. Norman's grand (x9) father was John Dodson who arrived as a colonist with Captain John Smith and helped to found Jamestown, VA in 1607.

Norman and family were transferred to Willard Ohio in 1960 by Donnelley where they remain today. Steven works for Donnelley as a Rolltender on a printing press.

Norman and Mary live in rural Willard. They have a small collection of antique automobiles. They remain active in local and national antique auto clubs, having frequently participated in the Classic Car Club's Grand Classic and the Hoosier Auto Shows in Indianapolis.

BARBARA JEAN TITUS ADAMS

The first daughter and second child of Mildred and Raymond Titus, Barbara Jean entered the world on Apr. 14, 1930. She joined older brother Richard.

After her graduation from Crawfordsville High School, Barbara was employed at the Goodman's Department Store in downtown Crawfordsville. From there she went to work as a secretary for the R.R. Donnelley and Sons Company in Crawfordsville and the Kirby Risk Company in Lafayette. From that city, she transferred to Gary, IN to work for Western Union. Here she met and married a steelworker, Harry Adams, son of Delmar and Clara Adams, in 1961. His siblings are: Paul, Calvin, James, Thomas, Billy, Donald, Dorris, Mildred and Shirley. Barbara and Harry have two daughters, Susan Darlene, born May 24, 1963 and Juliene Jean, born Feb. 22, 1968.

After graduation, Susan attended Baylor University in Waco, TX, where she earned a degree in elementary education. She teaches kindergarten at Bells Hills elementary in Waco. She met her husband, Kevin Ross Dyer, a painter, when he was doing some painting for the school. His father and grandfather are also in the painting business.

Juliene enrolled in Commonwealth Business College in Merrillville after her graduation from high school. In addition to attending college, she is employed by Dietrich Industries in Hammond, IN. She is engaged to be married June 10, 1989 to William (Billy) James Costakis, son of Mr. and Mrs. George Costakis.

GENE AND PEGGY AKERS

In March 1952 Gene and Peggy Akers and three young sons moved to "Blackberry Hill" farm, 850N 150W, Coal Creek Township. The 160 acre farm would be home for many years. Earl Eugene (born July 17, 1916 Georgetown, IL) and Margaret Kendall (born May 30, 1917 Indianapolis, IN) met in Washington, D.C. in 1941 where both were working in the F.B.I. During WWII Gene was employed by the Secret Intelligence Service outside the continental United States. Married Nov. 30, 1943 in Indianapolis, they lived in D.C., San Diego, and Portland, OR, before returning to Midwest.

In 1952 the small farm house had electricity but no water or phone. Gene's first move was to pipe in sweet well water. Many improvements followed, and today the farm house is large and convenient.

Anthony, Gene, Peggy and Jonathan Akers

Oldest son: Anthony Eugene (born June 13, 1945 Portland, OR) in 1963 was valedictorian at Coal Creek High School; 1967 B.S. Electrical Engineering, Purdue University; 1966-1971 U.S. Naval Reserves, one year in Vietnam; 1972 M.S., Purdue; 1972-1976 graduate studies, Purdue. Employment: Research and development engineer, Motorola, Schaumburg, IL, division of cellular telephone, auto and hand held. On June 11, 1967 Chicago Heights, IL, married Josephine Cipriani (born Feb. 27, 1945 Chicago Heights), B.S. 1967, Purdue. Children: Joseph Anthony (born Apr. 25, 1968), Anthony Eugene 2nd (born Mar. 6, 1972), Jonathan Perri (born Feb. 26, 1981). The family resides Glenview, IL. Josephine has a jewelry business with her sister.

Second son: Marshall Kendall (born Oct. 7, 1950 Georgetown, IL) 1969 salutatorian Coal Creek High School; 1973 B.A. Wabash College; 1974 B.S. Interdisciplinary Engineering, Purdue; 1975 M.I.A. Krannert Graduate School. Employment: 1975-1987 Air Products, Trexlertown, PA; presently Great Lakes Chemical, West Lafayette, IN. Married May 25, 1974 in Richmond, IN, Martha Jane Baxter (born June 16, 1952 Marion, IN) graduate DePauw School of Nursing 1974. Children: Sarah Alvord (born Oct. 16, 1977), William Kendall (born Jan. 4, 1980), Paul Baxter (born Oct. 19, 1983); all born Allentown, PA. The family now resides Oswego, IL.

Third son: Ralph Charles (born Oct. 25, 1951 Georgetown, IL), Coal Creek High School Class of 1970, attended Ball State University, died May 2,

1973 after two-and-a-half year illness. November 28, 1971 married Jean Kaye Turner (born Nov. 16, 1952 Portland, IN). No children.

Gene worked for Alcoa Aluminum, Lafayette, 1952-1978. In 1969 he taught vocational courses at Alcoa subsidiary in Mexico City. Peggy spent three months there, Marshall and Ralph six weeks each.

Peggy taught English at Tuttle Junior High School, Crawfordsville, 1962-1978. A graduate of Butler University, Class of 1938, she also attended Purdue.

Ethel Eugenia Alvord Akers, Gene's mother, made her home on the Montgomery County farm from 1968 until her death in 1984 at the age of 99.

After retirement, Gene and Peggy traveled via fifth-wheel and spent several winters in Arizona and Texas. In 1987 they purchased a house in Sequim, WA, and now spend part of the year there. As a youth Gene lived in Thurston Co., WA, graduated from Olympia High School and attended Washington State College.

The Akers farm is operated by Betty Stonebraker.

All the family plays tennis, occasionally competing in tournaments. Gene is an active ham radio operator. Tony and Marshall sail and ski.

FRANK F. AND SARAH ANN ALLEN

Frank Fine Allen was born Jan. 8, 1891 near Wallace, IN, a son of Hiram D. and Emma (Myers) Allen. His oldest known ancestor was Isaac C. Allen, a Revolutionary War soldier with George Rogers Clark at Vincennes, buried in Wolfcreek Cemetery south of Wallace. Mr. Allen graduated from Wabash College and Indiana University and was a High School Principal and teacher. Prior to World War II, he taught at New Market and later was Principal at New Richmond. His career included serving as Principal at Jamestown, Otterbein, and Wallace High School many years. His brothers and sisters were Ivan, Edith (Mrs. Homer Krout), Byron, Bernard, Wilbur (Emmett), and Ruby (Mrs. Clifford Spragg).

On Dec. 27, 1920 he married Sarah Ann Foster, daughter of Buel T. and Mattie (LeMay) Foster, buried in Waynetown Masonic Cemetery. Her oldest known ancestor was Rev. John Foster, a Methodist Circuit Rider and Revolutionary War soldier, buried in Pike Co., OH. She was born Apr. 17, 1901 near Armstrong, IL. Prior to marriage she lived with her parents in Wingate and taught school one year at Yountsville. She had one brother, Woodford Foster, a retired printer living in Michigan City.

Frank F. died Jan. 30, 1988 and Sarah died Aug. 30, 1957, both buried in the Waynetown Masonic Cemetery. Their retirement years were spent in Indianapolis.

They had two sons, Gordon M., born Dec. 10, 1921, and Donald F., born May 20, 1923 near Wallace, IN.

Gordon is a self-employed Certified Public Accountant and lives at 9342 Crestview Drive in Indianapolis. He married Betty Jean Cox, a daughter of Orville and Elfleda (Emery) Cox, farmers in the New Richmond community. Her brothers and sisters are Ruthanna (Mrs. Garland Oppy), Howard, Paul, Alice, James, and Margaret (Mrs. Harold Gilmour). Gordon and Betty's children are Stephen J., married to Marilyn Logue of Union County, living in Indianapolis, and Warren L., living in Carmel.

Gordon was an aerial Navigator in World War II on B-17 bombers. He was shot down over Germany, was a P.O.W. at Stalag Luft I, located about 120 miles north of Berlin near the town of Barth, rescued by Russian army near end of war.

Donald married Norma Jean Sullivan, a native of Washington County. He died Aug. 25, 1972 and is buried at Salem. His career was mostly in sales with Indiana Farm Bureau with locations in Indianapolis, Monticello, and Valparaiso where he last resided. His children were Phillip, residing in California, and Jyl, married to Walter Mattes, residing in New Haven, IN near Ft. Wayne. His grandchildren are Joseph Mattes, Julia Allen and Heather Allen. Donald served in World War II and participated in the great invasion of France where he sustained some injuries which probably shortened his life.

JAMES AND ELIZABETH ALLEN

James Allen and Elizabeth Logan were married in Rockbridge Co., VA, on Sept. 1, 1801. The same year they migrated via the Ohio River to near Louisville and proceeded overland to Shelby Co., KY, where they joined friends and relatives who arrived by land.

They were over 50 years of age when they migrated to Montgomery County about 1830 with several of their younger children. **Crawfordsville, IN, Land Entries 1820-1830** shows that James Allen entered on land (at the present site of Waveland) Oct. 7, 1830.

Eleven children were born while they resided in Shelby County. A grandchild told a researcher in the 1930's that Elizabeth returned to Virginia to visit her parents. Elizabeth put two small children on one horse, and she mounted another horse and proceeded overland (probably through the Cumberland Gap) to the Lexington, VA area. When she returned to Shelby County some months later, Elizabeth had two children on one horse, and she was on another horse with a papoose strapped to her back.

Their children: (underlined)

Lavinia married Eleazor Fullenwider and Narcissa married Isaac Rice in Shelby County. Both couples migrated to Montgomery County before 1828. The Fullenwiders had 11 children, and the Rices had eight. Descendants live in the area.

The Waveland Presbyterian Church was organized Nov. 28, 1828, and Narcissa Allen Rice was one of the founders.

James and Elizabeth believed in educating their children, particularly their sons. From the Indiana frontier, they sent four sons named for Presbyterian ministers (John Newton, William Graham, Archibald Cameron and Robert Welsh) to the seminary at Princeton University. A fifth son (James Logan) attended medical school at the University of Pennsylvania and practiced in Rockville. Married Caroline Foote; had one child.

John Newton was teaching in Shelby County at age 16. When Abraham Lincoln crossed the Wabash River at Vincennes to Illinois in 1831, John Newton was a teaching assistant at the Vincennes Academy. While attending Princeton Seminary, his health failed. Was licensed and served as a tutor for a wealthy New Orleans family and died there at age 27, unmarried. William Graham attended Miami University (Ohio) and graduated from Princeton and also graduated from Princeton Seminary. Ordained in 1842 at Henderson, KY. Married Ann Green of Henderson (1844) and had six children with two surviving to adulthood.

In 1838, Archibald Cameron was the first graduate of Wabash College. He attended Princeton Seminary and served several churches and as a chaplain during the Civil War. He married Elizabeth Affleck (1841) in Hickory, PA, and they had nine children.

Robert Welsh attended Wabash College and Princeton Seminary. He married Margaret Ann Maxwell (1846) at Frankfort. They had six children.

Hannah Irwin married 1) John Crawford and 2) Sam Taylor, both Presbyterian ministers. There were no children. Hannah spent her later years with relatives at Milligan Place in Crawfordsville.

Malinda died at age one (1804). Twins, Joseph and Jane, died at age six (1817).

James Allen served as postmaster at Waveland. James and Elizabeth are buried on the Fullenwider lot in the Presbyterian Cemetery at Waveland.
Submitted by James Allen Smith, Champaign, IL

FRANKLIN AND REGINA ALLHANDS

Franklin and Regina Allhands were born in Montgomery County and were descendants of early pioneers. Their ancestors came from Wales, Germany, Scotland and Ireland.

Franklin Delahunt Allhands was born Nov. 7, 1910, the fourth child of Doctor Frank Dallas Allhands. Doctor Allhands, after receiving his degree from the University of Louisville, arrived in Montgomery County, via horse and buggy, in 1898 from Clark County. He married Georgia Goodwin, also from Clark County. They lived in Wingate over 40 years raising four children. Franklin Delahunt graduated from Wingate High School in 1928. He enrolled in several spring terms at Indiana State Teacher's College where he excelled in track, earning three letters during the years 1929, 1931, and 1932. In 1933 he received his B.A. degree from Arizona State College at Flagstaff, AZ. From 1933 to 1937 he coached track and taught social studies at New Richmond High School.

Regina Herron was born Apr. 24, 1907 the second child of Joseph Croy Herron and Mary Belle Armantrout Herron. Her father "Joe" was a successful grocer and involved in the shale brick production north of Crawfordsville. She graduated from Crawfordsville High School in 1925. She attended Depauw University at Greencastle, IN where she was affiliated with the Alpha Phi Sorority. She later transferred to Purdue University and graduated in 1931 with a degree of B.S.HE. She taught five years in the Montgomery County schools before her marriage to Franklin Allhands on Aug. 15, 1936.

August of 1937, seeking greener pastures, they with their young baby, Franklin Dallas, born May 15, 1937, headed west for Florence, AZ. There Franklin taught, coached, and became principal of the Florence Elementary Schools.

During this period Philip Herron Allhands was born July 15, 1938. Anita Joyce Allhands was born June 22, 1939. All were born at Culver Hospital, Crawfordsville. Carolyn Jane was born Mar. 7, 1942 in St. Mary's Hospital, Tucson, AZ.

After ten years, they returned to Montgomery County to live on and manage their farm, south of New Richmond. Franklin was again employed in the Coal Creek Schools teaching Social Studies and coaching basketball and track. He retired in 1971.

In 1956 Regina returned to teaching Home Economics. She retired in 1971.

The family were members of the Presbyterian Church in Florence, AZ as well as in Crawfordsville, IN.

In 1959 Franklin Dallas married Jacqueline Rose Winkler of Morenci, AZ. They have three daughters - Jerri Lynn, Kristi Joyce, and Cindi Jane. They live in LaHabra, CA.

In 1962 Philip Herron married Laura Smith of Salem, OR. They are the parents of two children - Dana Marie and Mark Cawthorn. Their home is in West Linn, OR.

In 1969 Joyce married James Paul Riser of Tucson, AZ. They have two sons - James Paul II and Matthew Joseph. Their home is in Tucson, AZ.

In 1968 Carolyn married Walter Patrick Haney of Crawfordsville, IN. They are divorced. Their children are Jason Nathaniel and Kenyon Colleen. They reside in Tulsa, OK.

GEORGE ALLHANDS

George Allhands was born in Butler Co., OH in about 1820. He was the son of Daniel Allhands, born about 1777, and Patience Saddler, born in Maryland about 1784, who were married Jan. 5, 1803 in Jefferson Co., KY.

The parents of the subject lived in Butler Co., OH for a number of years, and all but one of their children were born there. Daniel was a justice of the peace of that county.

In 1830, the family came to Coal Creek Township. The father purchased land and served as a constable. Besides George, their children and some of their spouses were: Andrew - Margaret Swank; Patsey - Chancellor Livingston; Thomas - Rebecca Oxley; (Thomas died in Butler Co., OH in 1835) Daniel Jr. - 1. Sarah _____, 2. Betsy Ann Herr, 3. Martha Bulker, 4. Elizabeth _____; Elizabeth - Edward Bennett; Nancy - Michael Swank, son of Jacob Swank, who also came to Montgomery County from Butler Co., OH; Katherine - Samuel Oppy; William J. - Catherine Hixon.

The tradition of an old family bible that was written in German indicates that the name Allhands was originally Alhance. The family was said to have been of Pennsylvania German extraction. Doctor Frank D. Allhands, who tended the health of many Montgomery County residents for many years, was a descendant of John Allhands, a brother of the above mentioned Daniel Senior.

George Allhands was married to Julia Ann Alexander on Dec. 21, 1840. Her parents were Richard Alexander, a native of Pennsylvania, and his wife Susannah who was born in Virginia. Richard farmed land in Coal Creek Township which he purchased in 1829.

To this couple was born two children. The eldest, Patience Elizabeth, was born Jan. 16, 1842 and Susan was born on Nov. 4, 1843. The former married Francis Marion Bagby, and the latter became the wife of President Hall Swank.

Julia Ann died Nov. 3, 1847, at the tender age of 23, and is buried in Park Cemetery. George remarried on Apr. 20, 1848 to Esther Killen.

They were the parents of the following children, with some of their spouses: Franklin Pierce - Mary Ann Smith, daughter of William; Olive (probably Mahala Olive); Hellen; Caroline; and William T. George and Esther lived for a time in Fountain County, but later returned to Montgomery County.

George Allhands was a farmer and was a soldier during the Civil War. He died in 1876, and is buried in Oakland Cemetery beneath a simple military stone marked: ALLHANDS, GEO. Co. K 96th IND. INF. *Submitted by Charles M. Cook, Houma, LA*

ROBERT AND MAE ALLHANDS

Robert Love Allhands was born in Charleston, IN Dec. 11, 1875. He was the 9th child of George and Sara Delahunt Allhands. He had 11 brothers and sisters, John Milton, Frank D., Margaret, Luetta, Naomi, Elizabeth, Anna, Ruth, Pleg, Ada and Grace.

Robert (Bob) married Eva Mae Cutrell Nov. 22, 1902. The daughter of Edward and Sara Hollingsworth Cutrell of the Farmers Institute area.

They moved to Wingate in 1902. They lived in town for a few years. Later they lived at the edge of town, later moving to the county line on 80 acres.

Robert Allhands; Ruth Allhands Rice

Shortly after coming to Wingate they started the Allhands Dairy. They were in business for over 40 years. The milk was delivered in glass bottles twice a day in the summertime, one time in winter. They also sold milk through Marmaduke's, Gardner's and Miller's Grocery Stores.

The parents of six children, they had lots of help. The children were Raymond, married Helen Hays, Jeanette married Elden Neal, three children, Vernon (Bud), Eleanor married Ray Scheib, five children. Dorothy married Roy Shoaf, two children and Ruth married Garnet Rice, seven children.

Bob's three brother came to Montgomery County around the time Bob came in the early 1900's.

Frank D. was the Doctor for Wingate for many years. John was a teacher for a while then a Doctor. He moved to Clifside, NC. Pleg taught school then moved to Attica, IN.

The early history of the Allhands family dates back to the 1790's. The name was spelled Allhanse from Ohio Co., VA now West Virginia. The family migrated to Jefferson Co., KY, then on to Clark Co., IN.

Mae passed away Jan. 3, 1952. Bob passed away June 25, 1960. Eleanor passed away Apr. 27, 1965. Bud (Vernon) passed away Nov. 3, 1988.

Bob, Mae and Bud were buried in the Wingate Greenlawn Cemetery. Eleanor is buried in Reading, PA.

FRANCES AND EVERETT ANDERSON

Frances and Everett Anderson moved from Russellville to Crawfordsville, IN in 1986.

Frances (Handy) Anderson was born Jan. 24, 1920 at Bainbridge, IN to Alga and Bertha (Goff) Handy. She married Aug. 4, 1948 to Everett Anderson.

They have one child, Kent Anderson, born Oct. 23, 1949. Kent has a master degree in Electrical Engineering from Rose Hulman and is employed by General Electric Aero Space Research and Development Laboratories at Princeton, NJ.

Alga Handy, father of Mrs. Anderson was born in Vigo Co., IN Jan. 14, 1876, the son of Charles and Mary (Bailey) Handy. He attended the Vigo County Schools and Terre Haute Business College. In 1898, he enlisted in the Spanish-American War and served in the Philippine Island during the Philippine Insurrection. He died at Russellville Oct. 11, 1960. He married Jan. 14, 1914 to Bertha Goff, daughter of George W. and Josephine (Wilson) Goff. She was born Mar. 17, 1879 in Brown Township, Montgomery County and died at Russellville Mar. 23, 1948.

Frances Anderson belongs to the Woodland Heights Christian Church, the Hugenot Society of Indiana and Dorothy Q. Chapter, Daughters of the American Revolution. She descends from seven Revolutionary soldiers, namely: Taunis Dolson, Thomas Handy, James Oliver, George Oliver, John Lemmon, Captain John Lopp and John Hughs.

Everett Anderson was born in Putnam Co., IN on Oct. 22, 1916, the son of James and Rena Whitted Anderson. He is a retired carpenter and cabinet maker. Everett served in World War II from 1941 to 1945 overseas in North Africa and Europe.

James Anderson was born Sept. 9, 1892, son of Martin and Eliza (Myers) Anderson. He is living in Crawfordsville, aged 96 years.

Rena Whitted Anderson was born June 20, 1893, the daughter of John and Lydia (Mahan) Whitted. She died June 16, 1956.

Everett descends from two Revolutionary Soldiers: Joshua Reed and Lt. Col. John McClelland. *Submitted by Frances Anderson*

JAMES M. ANDERSON

James M. Anderson was born in Tennessee in 1843. In the fall of 1861, he enlisted in the Confederate Tennessee Militia for six months. He was captured during the battle of Fort Donelson, TN in February of 1862. He was taken north as a prisoner of war in early March of 1862. While being taken to the prison camp at Camp Tippecanoe in Lafayette, IN, he became sick and died on Mar. 21, 1862. He had died on the prisoner of war train near Crawfordsville, IN. His body was left at Camp Lane in Crawfordsville and his remains were taken to the Old Town Cemetery in Crawfordsville for burial. His gravesite is unmarked.

James M. Anderson and John Bush, another Confederate P.O.W. who is buried in the Old Thorntown Cemetery in Thorntown, IN, were among many southern soldiers who died while prisoners of war on Hoosier soil. *Submitted by: Andrew Keith Houk, Jr.*

RAYMOND ANDERSON

Raymond Anderson, son of Ray and Bessie VanHook Anderson, was born Aug. 25, 1912 on a farm near Shannondale. The family moved to Sugar Creek Township where Raymond attended Bowers School, graduating in 1930.

In 1925 Ray Anderson, Raymond's father, purchased one-half interest in a livestock trucking business that became Gray and Anderson.

Raymond described the first trucks as large cumbersome solid-tired International trucks that pulled similar trailers. Driver comfort was obviously not a consideration in the building of the early trucks; emphasis had to be on dependability and sturdy construction that could withstand the extremely poor road conditions of the era. However for a young farm boy it was his passport to seeing the world. Since driver's licenses and their requirements, as we know them now, were not yet in effect Raymond recalled that several local businessmen got together and signed a permit for him to drive his father's truck. Three of those gentlemen were John Lynch, Bert Brainard and Charles Marshall. All had businesses that necessitated receiving goods from Indianapolis wholesale houses to supply their Darlington stores. These supplies had only been available by mail shipment-this proving to be much too slow and uncertain for efficient business operations. Imagine the excitement of a young teenage farm boy making frequent trips to Indianapolis (which took eight hours) hauling livestock to market and bringing back supplies to local business houses.

In 1928 Frank Gray sold his interest in the trucks to Ray Linn and the business became known as Anderson and Linn which soon expanded into the hardware line, later becoming Anderson Hardware, located in the building which is now occupied by Tri-County Monument.

In 1930 Raymond Anderson became owner and operator of the trucking business, which continued to grow, the services included hauling twine, fertilizer, tomatoes, furniture moving and hauling coal from Indiana mines to customers in the county.

On Nov. 2, 1935 Raymond married Inell Tribbett, born Dec. 10, 1914, the daughter of Lynn and Stella Caldwell Tribbett. They became the parents of Betty Jean, born in 1937 and Katherine Alice, born in 1939. Betty married Tom Cain, a former county resident, and they are the parents of Randy, Cathy and Lisa. Katherine married Charles Scott and has step-sons, Patrick and Kelly.

In 1943, during World War II, gasoline and tires were rationed and it was almost impossible to get the necessary supply of anything, including man power. The trucks were sold to Norman Booher, a native son, who operated out of Shannondale.

After the sale of his trucks Raymond devoted his entire time to his large farming operation and extensive livestock feeding program both in Franklin and Sugar Creek townships. His interests were world affairs, auto racing and flying. He earned his pilot's license and was a member of the Flying Farmers of America.

With the exception of a short time, Raymond and his family resided in Darlington, where he was a member of the United Methodist Church.

The subject of this history, Raymond Anderson, passed away May 11, 1987. *Submitted by Mrs. Raymond Anderson*

WILLIAM L. ANDERSON

William L. Anderson (1847-1924), son of Madison Britts and Salome Harshbarger Anderson, was molded by a rapidly changing frontier world, Ladoga schools, and a family deeply concerned with religion. Stubbornly independent, he broke early from the family Dunkard faith, joined the Disciples of Christ, and took his Divinity Degree at the Unitarian Seminary in Meadville, PA. He then served as pastor in a number of small churches in Ohio and Indiana. Disappointed with the rewards of the ministry, he returned (1880) to take over the family farm just north of Ladoga. Religion remained, however, a central thread of his life as he lectured, wrote, and served as an elder in the local church for 45 years.

Anderson's farming was marked by unconventional originality, as he specialized in raising fruit and vegetables and experimented with unusual crops and procedures. Without loss of dignity, for more than 30 years, he was a familiar sight on the streets of Ladoga as he made his regular rounds peddling produce from a spring wagon.

Perhaps Anderson's most tangible contribution to his community and history are two published writings: a history of Ladoga and one of the Harshbargers. His 64-page *Early History of Ladoga* (1911) is a unique contribution to local history. Factual and direct, it has the quality of source material, since Anderson was intimately involved with the events, scenes, and people about which he wrote.

For Anderson, history and family were inseparable. His maternal grandparents were Jacob and Salome Harshbarger, who in 1831, were among the first settlers. His father came a bit later, but soon Andersons were numerous in the area. In 1879 William married Ora Johnson, daughter of Henry and Margaret Stover Johnson and thereby entered another family of pioneers. By descent, marriage, and friendship he and Ora belonged to a community of inter-related families that came from Virginia and Kentucky, beginning in the 1830's.

Children of William and Ora were: Anna (1875-1966), a missionary teacher in Mississippi; Alice (1877-1961), who had a stenographic and printing business in Indianapolis; Angie (1880-1965), who, with her husband, William Lee, took over the Anderson farm; Edgar, who died in infancy; Harry W. (1885-1971), plant pathologist and professor at the University of Illinois; Paul J. (1884-1971), also a plant pathologist, who directed an agricultural experiment station in Connecticut. The couple's descendants include 11 grandchildren, among them Philip Anderson, a co-recipient of the Nobel prize in physics, and a host of widely scattered great grandchildren.

From 1887 through 1905, Anderson was the very active Secretary of the Harshbarger Association, and, during that period researched and wrote a *History of the Descendants of Jacob and Marie Eva Harshbarger* (1909), a book of character, quality, and significance similar to his *Early History of Ladoga*.

Though Anderson was neither notable as a politician, a joiner, or an achiever in the material world, he was a respected citizen who left a noteworthy heritage for this community and many extended families. *Submitted by Guy Lee*

SHIRLEY DELLINGER ARAM

Shirley Kathleen DELLINGER ARAM was born in Tipton Co., IN, on Apr. 30, 1919. She moved to Montgomery Co., IN about 1921 with her parents, Shirl Blaine Dellinger and Rebecca Heacock Baynes Dellinger.

Shirley attended elementary Wilson School, graduated from Crawfordsville High School, 1936, and entered Purdue University, 1937. In 1939-1942, Shirley worked at Donnelley's in Crawfordsville.

Shirley served in the Women's Army Corp, 1942-1944, mostly as a Lieutenant in recruiting.

Shirley married Nathan Walter ARAM in 1944. Nathan was born in Moline, IL, 1916, and is an Electrical Engineering graduate of Purdue University. Nathan and Shirley have four children, all born in Chicago, IL: Robert Lee, 1946; Stephen Paul, 1950; Alan Walter, 1952; and Richard Bruce, 1954.

Shirley's family lived near Chicago, 1944-1980, where Nathan practiced his profession. The couple, now retired, live near Springfield, MO.

Son Robert graduated from Purdue, 1969 with a BS in Electrical Engineering. He married Nancy Ellen Kitch, 1967. Nancy was born in Breman, IN, 1943, and graduated from Purdue, 1967, with a BA in Pharmacy. They have a daughter, Kathleen Sue, born at Indianapolis, 1973. Robert practices his profession in Indianapolis, IN.

Nathan W. and Shirley Dellinger Aram

Son Stephen graduated from Wheaton College and has a Masters of Divinity from Gordon-Conwell. He married Kathye Jean Hamback in New Delhi, India, 1973. Kathye was born in Milwaukee, WI, 1943, and has an MA from the University of Wisconsin. They have four children: Elizabeth Ann, born at Milwaukee, 1974; Luke Jonathan, born at Katmandu, Nepal, 1977; Justin Paul, born at Epe, Netherlands, 1979; and Joel Stephen, born at Beverly, MA, 1981. The family lives in Winthrop Harbor, IL, where Stephen is a pastor.

Son Alan graduated from Wheaton College with a BA, and completed an MS from Geo. Williams College. He completed a Phy. D. in Psychology, 1988, at Rosemead School of Psychology. He married Roberta Ellen Johns, 1975. Roberta was born in Peoria, IL, 1953, and has a BS in Biology from Wheaton College and an MA in Education from the University of N. Colorado. They have three children: Rachel Ellen, born at Gillette, Wyoming, 1981; Jessica Alice, born at Gillette, 1984; and Jonathan Walter, born at Whittier, CA, 1987. They now live in Springfield, MO.

Son Richard graduated from Wheaton College with a BS in Geology and completed an MS in Geology from Montana State University. He married Sarah Louise Sandahl in 1976. Sarah was born in Geneva, IL, 1954, and has an A.A. degree from College of DuPage. They have three children: Christopher Ryan, born in Houston, TX, 1980; Randall Joseph, born in Billings, MT, 1982; and Sharyl Anne, born in Aurora, CO, 1985. Richard works in Bartlesville, OK. *Authored by Shirley Kathleen Dellinger Aram*

ARBEGUST FAMILY

The Arbegust Family came to America in the 1700's, probably from England. George Arbegust was born Mar. 1, 1770 in what was then listed as Moyamensing-Passyunk Township, Philadelphia Co., PA. He was the son of George and Mary Arbegust. George, Senior lived to be 95 years old (died Jan. 15, 1801). His wife according to newspapers lived to be 104 years of age (died Oct. 22, 1820).

George Arbegust, Junior, married June 24, 1794 to Christianna Matzinger, born Jan. 14, 1778 probably Moyamensing-Passyunk Township. The families lived next door on the census in 1790, 1800 and 1810. Christianna Matzinger's father's name is thought to be George. George and Christianna's children were: William, George, Elizabeth, John,

Christianna, Sarah, Mary, Benjamin, Samuel, Margaret, Charles, another Sarah and Emiline. The first ten were born in Philadelphia County. The rest were born in Hamilton Co., OH.

George and Christianna went to Hamilton County (Cincinnati) about 1816 as they bought land Oct. 1, 1816 from Harman and Elizabeth Brickerhoff (recorded in Book Q, pages 68-69 — southeast corner Section 11, Twp. 3, 2nd fractional range). This places the land in Mill Creek Township which does not exist now (part of Cincinnati).

George died May 29, 1829 in Cincinnati. After his death, Christianna married William Clarkson. He died June 15, 1849. They had no children. Christianna died Jan. 14, 1854 at her home on the Reading Road 1-1/2 miles from the Center of Cincinnati. They are buried in Spring Grove Cemetery in Cincinnati, but were first buried in the Methodist-Protestant Cemetery. The church sold the land that the cemetery was on and the bodies were moved on May 27, 1891 to Spring Grove.

George and Christianna's second son, George was born Mar. 7, 1797 in Philadelphia County. He married Hester Ready (born in Tennessee, daughter of William and Mary?). This couple moved to Sugar Creek Township, Montgomery Co., IN about 1862.

All seven children of George and Hester were born in Hamilton Co., OH, namely: Benjamin F., William, Matilda, Mary Ellen, George W., Samuel P. and Harriet.

Benjamin Franklin Arbegust died May 21, 1871, Lauramie Township, Tippecanoe Co., IN. His wife was Rose Anna Lindsey, who died a few months before (January 2). Buried Monroe Cem. Two daughters: Salome and Mary Ellen. Salome married John K. Wright and Mary Ellen married Abner Fowler Johnson.

Little is known of William and Matilda, above.

Mary Ellen, daughter of George and Hester was born Oct. 12, 1840 in Hamilton Co., OH, died Feb. 2, 1895 Lauramie Township, Tippecanoe Co., IN. She married John I. Davis, son of John and Catherine (Stookey) Davis. Both buried Union cemetery. One daughter, Laura May, born Oct. 15, 1866 married Robert Taylor Clark.

George W. Arbegust died Apr. 19, 1908 Lafayette. He married Dec. 15, 1872 Tippecanoe County to Rose Ann Penrod (born Jan. 5, 1853). She married second Charles Marquard. Buried Union Cem. Samuel P. Arbegust, sixth child of George and Hester died July 27, 1928 Clarks Hill and married Harriett McIntire. Union Cemetery.

Harriet (Hattie) Arbegust, born May 14, 1850, died Feb. 8, 1923. She married Elon Davis Feb. 27, 1868 in Montgomery Co., IN (see Bush history).
Submitted by Phyllis Davis Moore

DON AND JANET NEWKIRK ARMBRUSTER

Don Armbruster and Janet Newkirk were both teaching at Crawfordsville High School in 1969. They married in 1971. Don still teaches industrial arts at Crawfordsville and for several years taught adult night classes in woodworking. In 1987 he received the Indiana Industrial Technology Education Association's Meritorious Teacher Award. Janet taught business classes through 1971 when their daughter, Tina Marie (Dec. 15, 1971), was born. She taught the spring semester of 1973 at Southmont High School. On Nov. 16, 1974 Barry Jay was born. He is named after his paternal grandmother, Nellie (Barry) Armbruster. Janet then temporarily retired from teaching to raise her family and on Aug. 18, 1980 their last child, Lori Jean was born. All three children were born at Culver Hospital, Crawfordsville.

Donald Leo Armbruster was born Mar. 20, 1946 in Good Samaritan Hospital, Cincinnati, OH. He is the son of Joseph Anthony and Nellie (Barry) Armbruster. He attended school through the eighth grade at St. Lawrence Catholic Church and then went to Lawrenceburg High School. After graduating in 1964 he went to Purdue University and received an AAS in Industrial Illustration, a B.S. in education, and later his M.S. at Indiana State University. His great grandfather, Louis Ludwig Armbruster, came here from Fautenbach, Amt Achern, Baden, Germany with his three brothers in the late 1800s.

Janet Melvina (Newkirk) Armbruster was born on May 17, 1947 at Witham Memorial Hospital in Lebanon. Her parents are Lloyd Martin and Helen Marie (Walker) Newkirk. She went to school in Advance for two years and then attended Granville Wells from the third grade until her graduation in 1965. She then earned her B.S. and M.S. in education from ISU.

Janet has a host of interesting ancestors. At least three were Civil War Soldiers. John Shipley Long, her great grandfather, was with the 116th Indiana Volunteer Infantry. He also served as sergeant of the 139th, and he was a member of G.A.R. He died on Sept. 14, 1927 at the age of 82. Janet's great great grandfather, Samuel Dine, was born Nov. 29, 1831 in Johnson Co., IN. According to his Civil War papers he stood 5'11" tall, had light hair, light eyes, and a light complexion. He was paid $341.35 when he was mustered out on July 14, 1865. It was said that he always conducted himself honorably during the following battles: Stone River, Tullahoma, Missionary Ridge, Buzzard Ridge, and Ressaca; all in Tennessee. He also participated in Sherman's March to the Sea. Janet's great great grandfather, Henry Adams, enlisted as a Union soldier in Company F, Ninth Kentucky Calvary on Aug. 11, 1862. That same month he was in the two day fight at Richmond, KY. His horse was shot from under him and he was hit by a piece of shell in the right side which crushed his ribs. He was placed on a horse and taken 185 miles to Louisville where he was unconscious of his condition or his actions until he recovered his senses one month later.

Her oldest American ancestor was Christopher Avery, born about 1590 in England, came to America with his son, James, in 1630 or 1631.

Don has served as New Market PTO president and he is currently active in the Crawfordsville Education Association. He enjoys woodworking in his spare time. Janet is a member of the Dubble Duzzen Home Extension Club. Don is a member of St. Bernard's Church and Janet is a member of the Church of Christ.

Tina is a senior at Southmont High School, where she is active in Royal Ambassadors, Sr. National Honor Society, Academic Team, Key Club, and many other organizations. Barry is a freshman at Southmont and Lori is a third grader at New Market Elementary. The Armbrusters live on Apple Tree Lane in Old Orchard Estates. *Submitted by Tina Armbruster*

THOMAS AND MARTHA ARNETT

Thomas and Martha McFerron Arnett came to Montgomery County in 1834. He helped plat the town of Parkersburg and they are buried in the cemetery there.

Thomas, born about 1766, was the son of Thomas Arnett, Sr. The family lived in Botetourt Co., VA from 1771 to 1792, then moving to Clark Co., KY. In 1807, Thomas Sr. died in Clark County and his will is recorded there. It lists Thomas Jr. and his siblings, giving the estate to his brother Jacob, who was deaf. Thomas and Martha lived in Clark, Montgomery, and Bath counties in Kentucky before selling their holdings and heading for Indiana.

Thomas and Martha were preceded to the area by their son Abijah. Jacob Arnett, another early landowner in the county, was perhaps also a son. Thomas and Martha bought their land at Parkersburg in 1834 and in 1837 sold it to their son David Arnett. Across the road, (all this land is now the Priebe farm), their daughter Nancy Arnett lived with her husband Thomas Coshow. Nancy and David were both deaf. David had been educated at the Kentucky School for the Deaf at the expense of $100 per year. He married Isabel Painter, daughter of Solomon Painter, in Bath Co., KY in 1837, just before coming to assume the farm from his father.

David and Isabel had four children, Mary E. Arnett, David Solomon Arnett, Samuel Newton Stranghan Arnett, and this writer's ancestor, Jacob Washington Eldridge Arnett, born 1857.

Mary and Samuel Newton, both deaf, were educated at the school in Indianapolis. In 1864, Mary married James Wilcox, a deaf carpenter from Ohio. Family legend is that they left the area for Missouri, going on to Washington state.

An interesting historical twist occurred with Samuel's second middle name; 'Stranghan'. A physician, Dr. J.W. Straughan, lived around the corner from David and Isabel at the time of Samuel's birth. The family believes he was named after this doctor. Probate files revealed bills with the doctors signature that show the 'u' and 'n' were identical in his hurried script. His father David could write but not hear and his mother Isabel was able to hear but not write.

David died in 1865 and Isabel in 1866. The three minor boys were placed in the guardianship of Ambrose Armstrong. Before long (mid 1870's) the three of them had gone off to Cass Co., MO in a mule cart. Some of the Arnett descendants now live in nearby Louisburg, KS.

Family lore also told the fate of their slaves. At the end of the civil war, land was deeded and a cabin built for the black family that had come from Virginia with them, Clarissa Higgins and her son Blair. Old plat maps of the area show a small bit of land recorded for Clarissa Higgins.

The Arnetts were also related to Coshow, Stamper, Knox, Evans, Painter, Hamilton and Hughes families. This writer welcomes inquiries or information. Write Marjorie Fox c/o Irma Arnett Ervin, Rt. 1 Box 70, Louisburg, KY 66053.

DANIEL ARNOLD

Daniel Arnold, born near Finn Castle, VA, Dec. 12, 1808 married Nancy Myers in October, 1830. She was the daughter of John Myers, Sr., born 1770 at Lancaster Co., PA and Catherine (Hautz) Myers who were married in 1791. They moved soon after their marriage to Botetourt Co., VA. Nancy was born in Virginia.

Daniel lived with his parents in Virginia until he was 23. After his marriage to Nancy he farmed with his father-in-law, John Sr., in Botetourt County, for one year. Then rented a farm one year.

Nancy's brother John, Jr. came to Montgomery Co., IN and soon after, Nancy and Daniel came in 1832 settling in Clark Township. Nancy's father bought them a farm of 194 acres. This Daniel partly improved, living on it eight years: then selling out buying 320 acres in Scott Township two miles northwest of Ladoga. Meanwhile, John, Sr., had arrived in Montgomery County with his wife Catherine in a big wagon in 1833.

The family lived as those others in the early days, they grew flax, sheared sheep and made the cloth cut and making homespun clothes for the family.

Daniel and Nancy (Myers) Arnold's children were David, Henry, and a son William, who was killed in Virginia during the War. Also Mary, the wife of Samuel F. Graybill. (see index Graybill) Nancy Arnold died Aug. 18, 1845. Daniel married Frances Peffley, their children were Samuel, George R. and John B. Frances the second wife died and Daniel married Margaret Maltby.

Daniel Arnold died Nov. 21, 1893.

Nancy's maternal ancestors came from Hasslock, Germany. Her Great grandfather, Philip Lorentz Hautz, born Sept. 10, 1713, came to America on Ship Friendship from Rotterdam. Arrived in Philadelphia, Sept. 20, 1738. He died Oct. 22, 1788 and is buried in Klopps Churchyard, Hamlin, PA. He married Eva Anna Walborn. Their son Christian and Barbara (Emmert) Hautz were Catherine Hautz parents. They left Berks Co., PA about 1790 and settled in Botetourt Co., VA.

WILLIAM B. ASHWELL

William B. Ashwell was born on June 17, 1827 in Bedford Co., VA, the son of Meredith and Sarah Ellis Ashwell. He was married on Dec. 19, 1855 in Bedford Co., VA to Elvira Hackworth. She was born on Aug. 9, 1837 in Bedford Co., VA, the daughter of Wesley and Jane Hackworth.

When the Civil War started, William B. Ashwell enlisted in the Confederate Army. He served in Captain Thomas Leftwich's Company of Riflemen (Bedford Rifle Greys) of the 14th Regiment Virginia Volunteers. This unit later became Company B, 14th Regiment Virginia Infantry C.S.A. He mustered in on Apr. 24, 1861 in Richmond, VA. His unit was attached to General Robert E. Lee's Army of Northern Virginia. William B. Ashwell fought at the following battles: second battle of Winchester, VA, March, 1862; Cedar Mountain, VA, Aug. 9, 1862; Antietam, MD, Sept. 17, 1862; Chancellorsville, VA, May 1, 1863; Battle of Gettysburg, July 1-3, 1863; Battle of the Wilderness, May, 1864; and Petersburg, VA, September, 1864.

At the Battle of Gettysburg, his unit was attached to Brigadier General L.A. Armistead, Brigade of Major General George E. Pickett's Division. On the afternoon of July 3, 1863, at approximately 3 p.m., the eight brigades attached to Pickett's Division attacked Union Army positions. Pickett's Division attacked with about 10,500 men. The Union forces consisted of 27 regiments and 103 cannons. The battle raged for three hours and was often hand-to-hand combat. The cannons fired canister and grape. When the battle ended, Pickett's Charge had lost over 6,000 men killed and wounded, 792 taken prisoner and 329 missing. William B. Ashwell received a minor bullet wound in the leg. His brigade received 73 percent casualties. William B. Ashwell was present on Apr. 9, 1865 at Appomattox Court House, VA when General Robert E. Lee surrendered.

William B. Ashwell returned home and he moved his family to Clark Township, Montgomery Co., IN in March, 1867. He owned a farm northeast of Ladoga. In the late 1870's they moved northeast of New Ross. In the early 1880's they again moved to just west of Advance in Boone Co., IN.

William B. Ashwell died at his home on Sept. 3, 1907 and is buried in the I.O.O.F. Cemetery in Jamestown. Elvira Hackworth Ashwell died at her daughter's home in Advance on Aug. 27, 1915, and she is buried next to her husband. The Ashwell's were members of the Mt. Zion Methodist Church in Jackson Township, Boone County.

Their children were:

James E., born in 1859, died in 1944, and his wife Martha, 1868-1928. Both are buried in the Jamestown I.O.O.F. Cemetery.

Nancy "Nannie", born in 1866, died in 1936, and her husband Alfred Fletcher Whorley, 1853-1933. Both are buried in the Jamestown I.O.O.F. Cemetery. *Submitted by Andrew Keith Houk, Jr.*

FREDDIE BALES

For many years, the cheery smile, quick wit and readiness to help out in a pinch were enjoyed by co-workers of Freddie Bales. For many years, the humorous observations on the shortcomings and foibles of his fellow men were enjoyed by the faithful readers of Freddie's newspaper columns, "Howdy Cousins" and its predecessor, "The Antique Dealer."

Frederic W. Bales was born Oct. 29, 1901 in Monticello, IL but spent all but a few years in Montgomery Co., IN, growing to manhood on a farm near Garfield. He graduated from Crawfordsville High School in 1920 and Wabash College in 1924. Freddie joined the staff of *The Review* in 1923 where he worked until 1928. He then went to Little Rock, AR to work for *The Democrat*. Missing Indiana, he returned in 1935.

Fred was one of five sons born to Frank and Louise (Jones) Bales. His brothers were: Carl J., Robert, Harold and James Y. (who lost his life while serving as a bombadier during WWII). Fred's wife was Juanita Ames and they had one daughter, Beverly Ann.

Fred and Juanita were members of the First Methodist Church and Freddie remained interested in the Wabash Chapter of the Delta Tau Delta Fraternity until a heart attack claimed his life at the young age of 45.

Freddie's fans and Freddie's friends missed him and his column and will long be remembered for years to come!

Information obtained from articles in the Journal-Review at the time of his death and articles he had written!

CHARLES BANNON

Charles Bannon was born Dec. 17, 1863 at Russell Mills in Parke Co., IN. He was the son of James Clark Bannon and Elizabeth Fulwider. Charles married Mary Melinda (Mollie) Lane daughter of Abraham and Prudence Moore Lane. Mary Melinda was born near Wingate Sept. 1, 1870. They were the parents of five children. Ernest, Eldo, Lenna, Iva and Evan twins, one child died in infancy. Charles died on Apr. 12, 1935 and Mollie passed away Nov. 21, 1924. Charles farmed in the Elmdale, Young's Chapel and Waveland areas.

James' father was Michael. He was a Blacksmith and a Gunsmith who made guns for the Indians and the white people. It was said he was the first Blacksmith in Cincinnati and served in the War of 1812.

Mollie and Charles Bannon

One of Michael's sons was Lewis born in 1818 in Warren Co., OH near Cincinnati who was said to have been a New Light Minister and a Circuit Rider and was one of the founders of Center and Liberty Churches, both near Elmdale.

Genealogical authorities say the Bannon's were chiefs of Ui Dechi situated in the north of Tipperary, Ireland.

James Clark Bannon was born Dec. 6, 1830 near Greenville, OH. He came to Randolph Co., IN. Most of his life was spent in Parke County and Montgomery County.

All five children of Charles and Mollie Bannon are now deceased. There are several grandchildren living in this area.

Ernest and Delta Ballew Bannon had one son Lyle who passed away in 1944.

Eldo and Wanetah Monroe Bannon had two children Virginia Bannon Kelsey and Max Bannon.

Lenna married Alva Smith and they were the parents of Charles, Russell, Jack, and Eileen.

Iva married Cecil Walker and their children were Mary Katherine and Viola May.

Evan married Vera Crane and they were the parents of Richard Lee who was killed in a train accident in 1947.

Clela and Evelyn were his daughters.

BANTA-SHARPE

For many years, Thomas W. Banta lived and farmed in the Linden-New Richmond area. He and his wife, Florence Baxter Banta, were the parents of four sons: Theron S., George, Basle and Perry. The oldest son, Theron, was a life-time resident of Montgomery County. He was born in 1891. He was a graduate of New Richmond High School, Indiana State Normal College (Terre Haute) and Zaner College of Penmanship in Columbus, OH. He married Delia Etta Marcrum in 1914. Her family came to Montgomery County from Kentucky. They lived six miles north of Crawfordsville near Liberty Chapel.

Mr. Banta taught school for several years at

Center, Kirkpatrick, Linden and Waveland. For 25 years, he was assistant cashier of the Waveland State Bank. For many years, he owned and operated a jewelry shop at his home in Waveland. He was made a certified watchmaker by the American Watchmaker's Institute and was a past-president and life member of the Indiana Watchmakers Association. For over 50 years, he hand-embossed the Wabash College diplomas. In 1964, he was presented the Honorary Alumnus Award by Wabash.

Mr. and Mrs. Banta were the parents of two children: Virginia Ruth and J. Myron Banta. Myron followed his father in the watchmakers business. For several years, he worked in a jewelry store in Crawfordsville and later worked with his father. After the death of his father, he opened a jewelry shop in his own home in Waveland. He and his first wife, Myrtle Pope, were the parents of a daughter, Judith Kay Banta. After the death of his first wife, he was married to Jean Sabolick of Terre Haute. Her son and daughter-in-law, Richard and Donna and their son, Kelly, also became residents of Waveland. Judith Kay was married to James Blakeslee of New Market and they became parents of two daughters, Janice and Jodi. At present, they live in Muskego, WI.

Virginia Banta married Wilmer T. Sharpe, the son of Ray and India Perkins Sharpe of Waveland. Ray was a druggist who for many years worked with Frank Burrin in the Burrin Drug Store in Waveland. Later, Ray opened his own store there. Ray and India had two sons, Floyd and Wilmer. Floyd also became a druggist and worked in Indianapolis. He and wife, Elinor had a daughter, Brenda, who was born after Floyd was called into the Army. He was sent to England and then to France where he was killed in a train wreck. His daughter, Brenda, married Michael Kress. They have two sons and live in Martinsville.

Wilmer Sharpe worked with his father in the drug store and upon his father's death, he remodeled the store and continued to operate it until his death in 1969. His wife, Virginia, worked for many years as an assistant librarian in the Waveland Public Library. She was trained in librarianship by Mrs. T.E. Huston, for many years the Waveland Librarian. Later Virginia was employed by the Crawfordsville Radio Station, WCVL. She worked there for ten years, later retiring to Plainfield, IN. She and Wilmer were the parents of a daughter, Pamela Ann Sharpe. She married David L. Bloomer of Indianapolis. They are the parents of two children, John David and Kimberly Ann of Plainfield.
Submitted by: Virginia Banta Sharpe

RALPH L. AND HELEN M. (CUNNINGHAM) BARKER

Ralph and Helen were married Oct. 12, 1940 and have lived in Crawfordsville the past 26 years. Ralph worked in Crawfordsville since 1952 for Beatrice Foods Company, Meadow Gold Dairy Division. He retired from the Teamster Union in 1974. He then worked for the City of Crawfordsville on the golf course for almost ten years. Ralph served in the Philippine Islands during World War II.

Ralph and Helen have four daughters; Patricia married Larry Gene Bowman Apr. 17, 1959. They have four children. Randal Joe married Mary Ellison Apr. 12, 1982. They have a daughter Cassie Lynn. Nedra Sue married Mark Gunn Aug. 18, 1984. They have twin daughters; Andrea Nicole and Ashley Renae. Neil Preston married Lindsie Naylor Nov. 7, 1987. Eric Ray is single. Patricia married second Boyd Sharp. Ralph and Helen's second daughter Linda Lou married Earl Amel Taylor June 22, 1963. They have two daughters: Angela Rene and Teresa Ann. The Barker's third daughter, Debra Kay married Richard Allen Fendley Oct. 9, 1972. They have two children, Pamela Sue and Edward Max. The fourth daughter is Donna Rae who married Robert Matthew Ralston Sept. 27, 1980. Their three children are Amanda Marie, Jamie Ilene, and Nathan Francis Crawford.

Ralph and Helen Barker

Ralph was born in Putnam Co., IN to Grover Cleveland and Bessie Helen (Bymaster) Barker. They were married Apr. 24, 1906 and had 12 children. Lorna Pearl, Lola Mae, Loyd Franklin, Lawrence Russell, Wain Lodell, Ralph Lester, Leatha Marie, Edna Katherine, Kenneth Dwight, Freda Louise, Carl Delbert, and Benjamin Lewis. Ralph's grandparents were David Hogan and Charlotte Emaline (McFall) Barker. Great grandparents were Oliver Perry and Mary (Stewart) Barker. Great-great grandparents were David H. and Lavina (Nelson) Barker. David was born in Monongalia Co., WV in 1804. He migrated to Decatur Co., IN; then to Putnam Co., IN about 1850.

Bessie Helen (Bymaster) Barker's parents were Benjamin Franklin and Isadora (Robbins) Bymaster. Her grandparents were Jonathan and Jane (Boling) Robbins. Jane was a descendant of Pocahontas. On the other side were David Lewis Jr. and Sidney Jane (Clark) Bymaster. Bessie's great great grandparents were David Lewis and Anna (Barry) Bymaster. David Lewis and Anna immigrated from Germany and settled in Montgomery Co., IN around 1850.

Helen (Cunningham) Barker was born in Vigo Co., IN to Raymond and Claudia (Akers) Cunningham. Helen has two sisters. Alberta Ellen married Chester Spencer. Enola Louise was married to James Clodfelter. Helen's grandparents were Samuel Alexander and Zella (Porter) Cunningham. Great grandparents were Francis Pringle and Margaret Elizabeth (McIntire) Cunningham. Great great great grandparents were John Alexander and Susanna (Spencer) Cunningham.

JAMES J. BARNES AND PATIENCE P. BARNES JENNIFER CHASE BARNES, GEOFFREY PRESCOTT BARNES

Patience and Jim Barnes came to Crawfordsville in 1962 when Jim began teaching at Wabash College as an Assistant Professor of History. They came from Amherst, MA, where Jim had taught for three years at his **alma mater**, Amherst College. Jennifer and Geoffrey were both born in Boston, MA, before coming to Montgomery County.

Jim's parents were midwesterners. His father, Harry George Barnes, was born in Campbell, MN: and his mother, Bertha Blaul Barnes, was born in Burlington, IA. They had three sons, Harry Jr., Louis Byington, and James John. Jim grew up in St. Paul, MN, and went to St. Paul Academy before entering Amherst College in 1950 where he received a B.A. **magna cum laude** in 1954. He was elected a Rhodes Scholar in 1954 and completed a B.A. with Honours in History at New College, Oxford, in 1956. He earned a PhD. from Harvard University in Cambridge, MA, in 1960. Wooster College in Ohio bestowed an honorary D.H.L. on him in 1972 in recognition for his excellence in teaching.

Patience Plummer Barnes was born and brought up in Mount Vernon, NY, the daughter of Elinor Keaney Plummer, a native of Cambridge, MA, and Charles Sumner Plummer Jr., the eldest son of a colonial family in Newport, RI. Patience graduated with a B.A. in Government from Smith College in Northampton, MA, in 1954. Her first career was in advertising, with J. Walter Thompson Agency in New York City. Since then she has been a free lance writer and co-author and researcher with her husband. They have collaborated on numerous journal articles and four books.

Barnes Family: G.P., P.P., J.C., and J.J.

Jennifer Chase Barnes grew up in Crawfordsville, attending Hoover, Tuttle, and Crawfordsville High School. She spent one term at St. Felix School in Southwold, England, before entering Smith College in 1978. After graduating from Smith in 1982 she studied singing in London, England, and was admitted to the Opera School of the Royal College of Music in London in 1986. Currently she is studying for an M.Mus. degree at the Royal College. In 1988 she married Richard Philip Edgar Wilson, an Englishman who is also a singer.

Geoffrey Prescott Barnes also spent his youth in Crawfordsville, attending the same schools as Jennifer. He then went to Amherst College from which he graduated **magna cum laude** in 1984. Indiana history is a hobby, and he has had an article published in *Montgomery County Magazine*. For three years he worked at S.O.M.E. (So Others Might Eat) in Washington, D.C. He continues to work with people in poverty at the Good Shepherd Mission, a part of Jubilee Ministries located in the nation's capital.

JAMES AND ANNA ENOCH BARNETT

James and Anna Enoch Barnett came from Washington Co., PA to Butler Co., OH then to Montgomery Co., IN in 1832 with two of their sons. John Barnett, son of James and Anna Barnett married Jane Creason in Preble Co., OH on Aug. 19, 1832 and they bought the farm near Maple Grove School in 1831, northeast of Ladoga. John was in the Indiana Legislature 1841-42. He died 1884. Jane Creason Barnett died 1862. A daughter, Elizabeth died in 1862. They are buried in the Harshbarger Cemetery. In June of 1970, a new stone was put up in the cemetery for Jane 108 years after the first stone by a descendant, Mrs. H.H. Culbertson from California. John and Jane had 13 children, Martha born 1834 married Willis Ellis; Hanna born 1835 married William V. Linn; Mary born 1836; James A. born 1837; according to census, but Mrs. Culbertson had his birthday as Feb. 3, 1833, thus he'd be their first child. He died in Kansas 1915, going there in 1868. He married Sarah Rebecca Harrison in Ladoga, 1863 and had ten children. Nancy Barnett born 1838, married John Berry; Sarah J. born 1844 sent to an asylum, married Samuel Parkhurst; Caroline born 1842; Elizabeth A. born 1846 and died 1862; Amanda born 1844; another child name not known.

John Barnett married his second wife, Rebecca Watkins Gregg on June 18, 1863. She was the daughter of George Watkins and they had three children; Thomas married Laura Mann; Wallace Barnett and Nietta Barnett married James Damewood.

William Barnett the other son of James and Hannah Enoch Barnett, was a Methodist Minister, died in California Gold Rush in 1849. He married Mary Jane Ellis born 1814 in North Carolina to John and Sarah James Ellis (they later lived in the Maple Grove area). Mary Jane Ellis Barnett died July 28, 1907. William and Mary Jane had the following: Lewis Wesley, born 1837, Ladoga married Mary Elizabeth McIntire; served in the Civil War, died Aug. 23, 1922. Dr. Enoch Edward Barnett born 1839, lived northeast of Ladoga, was a Captain in the Civil War. While he was in Libby Prison, Richmond, VA, he began to study medicine and was in with Dr. James S. McClelland. He and Dr. Griffith were classmates in Medical School. He had tuberculosis and he died in Maryville, CA where he is buried in an unmarked grave. He never married. He taught in a one-room school at Greenwood School two miles west of New Ross.

Elizabeth born 1843; James born May 28, 1845, went to Owen Co., IN. I suppose his father was preaching there at the time; he married Margaret McIntire, on Sept. 23, 1871. He died Jan. 25, 1906. The two McIntire girls were the daughters of Jacob and Mary Jane Gray McIntire. Sarah Jane Barnett born 1848 and Elizabeth born 1851 incorrect date for her father died in 1849 and he wasn't in 1850 census. This Barnett family has many descendants in Montgomery County.

MARY ISABELLE BARNETT SMITH

Solomon Ray Barnett and Emma Belle Parvis Barnett Family.

My brother, Voris Maxwell Barnett, and I were born on a farm near Kirkpatrick in 1908 and 1910. When I was one year old, we moved to our grandparents, George W. and Susan Peterson Barnetts' farm near Linden. While there mother's brothers and nephew built us a lovely new house and barn.

Max and I began our education in first grade at Linden.

My father objected to the loamy soil. So when I was nine years old we moved to a 317 acre farm near Young's Chapel purchased by grandfather, dad and Uncle Sam Barnett.

We graduated from the 8th grade at Young's Chapel School, high school at Crawfordsville and Max from Wabash College. Max also attended Indiana State in Terre Haute. I attended college at Indiana State in Terre Haute, also Butler and Purdue.

Max was married to Hilda Garriott in 1939. They both taught many years in Montgomery County and Crawfordsville schools. They have one son, Dr. William Ray Barnett who is a Professor of Religion and Philosophy at Le Moyne College in Syracuse, NY. He has a wife, Terri, and a daughter, Denise.

I began teaching in elementary grades in 1929 in a two-room school near Terre Haute. Later I taught at Young's Chapel, Linden, a suburb of Denver, CO, and West Point near Lafayette, IN making a total of 39 years.

My future husband was introduced to me when we were chosen to participate in a three act Farm Bureau play titled, "Here Comes Charlie." In 1941 at the Young's Chapel home I married Leonard Wert Smith son of Fritz and Effie Wert Smith. Leonard graduated from Crawfordsville High School. He has degrees from Wabash College and Purdue, and attended Indiana State and the University of Colorado in Boulder.

Leonard was teaching at New Market when he was called to service in the U.S. Army Air Corps and spent 3-1/2 years at Lowry Field in Denver, CO. From there he taught again at New Market High School.

In 1946 he accepted a position in the Lafayette School System and worked his way to the top as Superintendent of the Lafayette School Corporation. He retired in 1978.

We have both enjoyed our retirement years and since we have no children of our own we have happy memories of all the students we have had the privilege of working with. *By Mary Isabelle (Barnett) Smith*

THE BATTREALL FAMILY

The Battreall Family (also spelled Batterall) were some of the early settlers of Montgomery County. Andrew, John, and William Battreall left Virginia or Kentucky in the early 1800's and travelled through Miami Co., OH, in 1830; Delaware Co., IN, in 1840; and Andrew Battreall settled in Coal Creek Township of Montgomery Co., IN, about 1845. He was born in 1798, in Virginia, and died on Oct. 30, 1875, in Montgomery County. He was buried in the Greenlawn Cemetery, in Wingate.

On June 28, 1823, Andrew Battreall married Dorinda Thomas, born in 1805, in Kentucky, and died Aug. 15, 1882, in Montgomery Co., IN. She was buried beside her husband. To this union was born nine children: Michael (married Violetta Smith), two infant daughters who died, Mary Malinda (married William Wilson), Susan M., Polly, James A. (married Maria Rhodehamel), William Wayman (married Florence E. Alexander Miles), and Silas A. (married Laura Pasely).

Michael Battreall was born in February of 1827, in Miami Co., OH. He travelled to Montgomery Co., IN, with his parents where he married Violetta Smith on Feb. 25, 1847. To this union was born eight children: Hester Ann (married Joseph H. Price), Andrew, Mary Margaret "Maggie" (married Marion Insley), an infant son who died, Emaline, Malinda E. "Minnie" (married 1st - Cyrus S. Young, 2nd - Rev. David W. Hughes, 3rd - Charles E. Drake), Gilford, and Lilbus "Lillie". Michael was a farmer until the time of his death on Feb. 4, 1894.

Mary Malinda Battreall was born on May 20, 1834, and married William Wilson on Jan. 13, 1857, in Montgomery County. She died on Oct. 16, 1887, in Montgomery County, and is buried in the Masonic Cemetery in Waynetown.

Susan M. and Polly Battreall were born in 1841 and 1843, respectively, in Montgomery Co., IN.

James A. Battreall was born in 1844 in Montgomery Co., IN, and died in 1907, buried in the Pleasant Hill Cemetery in Wingate. He married Maria Rhodehamel, and to this union was born at least two children, Henry and Icy.

William Wayman Battreall was born in August of 1848, in Montgomery Co., IN, and died Feb. 26, 1915, in Crawfordsville. He was buried in the Oak Hill Cemetery in Union Township, Montgomery County. He married Florence E. Alexander Miles on Sept. 13, 1883. To this union was born three children: Lena, Bertha, and Jay T.

Silas A. Battreall married Laura Pasely on July 17, 1870.

BAUER FAMILY

The Bauer Family (Bauer, Power, Powers, Bowers) emigrated from Germany in 1732 arriving through Philadelphia. Valentine's father, Michael, returned to Germany, married, and returned with his wife and first son, Michael, Jr. in August 1739. Valentine was born near Middletown, PA, Sept. 17, 1739. In 1750 the family moved to what is now Petersburg, WV. Their brother, John Martin (Dec. 27, 1741) had two sons, Martin (Oct. 20, 1770) and Abraham (Dec. 28, 1786) who moved to Ross Co., OH in 1804, and on to Indiana in 1829. (Re: Montgomery County History 1881; Volume I, Volume II, Bowen Books 1913) Valentine and John Martin used the names 'Power' and 'Powers' instead of the 'Bauer' German form. Martin and Abraham used 'Bowers' which is familiar here. Valentine and John Martin Bauer supplied beef for prisoners to Winchester Barracks during the Revolutionary War and were patriots. All descendants are eligible for DAR and S.A.R.

Abraham Bowers homesteaded 800 acres in Tippecanoe County in January 1829 while his brother Martin took 1000 acres across the road in Montgomery County. Abraham's brother-in-law, William Bryant, homesteaded 6400 acres adjacent to Martin on the west. Lewis Dunbar took 160 acres 1/2 mile east of Martin in 1830, then acquired more than 400 acres in his lifetime. These lands, wilderness when they came, have all been divided and sold according to inheritance provisos. They cleared and drained the land, built churches, schools, mills and roads, and raised their families. They were prolific in Sugar Creek Township. Lewis and Mary Powers Dunbar had sixteen children: William, Silas, Eliza, John Adam, Susan, Robert, Catherine, Elias, Lewis M., Simon, Marion, Daniel, Elizabeth, Mary, Taylor and an infant who died at birth along with her mother. Lewis remarried and had eight more children.

Abraham's son Abner purchased 160 acres from James Creson in 1842 and that farm at Bowers is where Esther, her son Elias Peter Dunbar and his children were born. Esther was the great granddaughter of John Martin Power.

Abner helped survey the land from Darlington to Frankfort when the railroad was built in the late 1800s and gave the corner of his farm for a warehouse and station which became Bowers, IN. He and his wife received lifetime passes on the railroad for his services. S*ubmitted by Jean Dunbar Socolowski*

DONALD WAYNE AND SHARON LEE WILLIAMS BAYLESS

Spring 1956 Graduation, Alamo High School (the largest class to graduate 18). Two of those Seniors were Donald Wayne Bayless and Sharon Lee Williams.

Donald was born Mar. 7, 1938 the oldest son of the three boys born to Oakel Grant Bayless and Thelma Lucille Cornell Bayless. The other two boys were Edwin Eugene Bayless and Carl Richard Bayless (deceased). The Grant in his dad's name has been traced back on his Grandmother Myers side of Ulysses S. Grant, President of the United States. Don attended Alamo all of his 12 school years and was very active in sports, taking part in basketball, baseball, and track.

Left to right top row: Darrell, Don, Daniel, Sandy, Sharon and Sheryl Bayless

Sharon Lee Williams was born June 29, 1938 the oldest of the three children of Glenn Williams and Dorothy May Walker Williams of Indianapolis, IN. The three children being Sharon Lee, Glenda Rae, and Glenn III. A move to Alamo after the end of World War II when all the service men came home from the War and found a housing shortage; this was to be a temporary move and Sharon's Dad continued to commute to Indianapolis daily, this kept up until just ten years ago when he retired and moved back to Indianapolis after the death of Sharon's Mom and married Mercellia Humel.

Don and Sharon started dating Oct. 9, 1952 as Freshmen and dated for six years before being married Mar. 9, 1958 at Alamo Christian Church. They moved next to the family farm of his parents and started farming. Of this union were born four children Sandra Lee (Sandy) (1959), Darrell Wayne (1961), Daniel Wayne (Boone) (1965), and Sheryl Lee (1979). They have two daughter-in-laws Marianne Ward Bayless and soon to be Jennifer Griffith Bayless. They have three grandchildren Brooke, Danielle, and Ryan. Don farms and works at R.R. Donnelley & Sons and has been on the Alamo Fire Dept. since its beginning over 30 years ago.

Besides farming with her husband, Sharon works at County Market.

Both are members of the Alamo Christian Church, Alamo Masonic Lodge and Aux., Eagles, and American Legion. They enjoy dancing as a hobby and following their children and grandchildren.

FRED BAYLESS

Fred Bayless has many memories of his childhood. Fred walked to Freedom school with his sisters and brothers and back home again one-quarter mile for lunch. Very few trips were made to Waveland or Browns Valley after provisions, because a huckster wagon filled with supplies went right by the Bayless farm. Fred, along with brothers Nelson and Lloyd, loved to hunt and fish which supplemented the family larder. The family also had eggs, cream and meat from their animals. Fred remembers that in the Spring, the Bayless property looked like a big flower garden when the first trees bloomed. Fred and his brother Lloyd never bothered opening a gate on the Bayless farm — they were both good jumpers and did just that! Fred once started driving his car into a ballgame when he was about 16. He got hung-up in a snowdrift and wanted to get to that game so bad, that he walked the 4-1/2 miles into Waveland — to find out that the game had been cancelled. So, he had to stay with his sister, Rose Glascock. Besides plenty of food and good times, there was also a lot of love and guidance for all the Bayless children.

Waneta, Fred, Ed, Fred P. and Thomas Bayless

Fred was born Jan. 25, 1907, the son of Luna and Elizabeth (Priebe) Bayless (see biography). One day, a friend, George Reynolds took Fred to meet a girl — Waneta Brasfield — they played miniature golf and he was fascinated by her left-handed scorekeeping. Later, on May 23, 1931, Fred married his left-handed gal in the home of Rev. H.H. Elmore, north of Crawfordsville. Her parents were: Ola and Ruby (Caldwell) Brasfield. Ola worked for the tomato canning factory. Waneta's siblings are: Ola Eugene "Bud"; Pauline Bayless; Margaret Thomas and Mary Kathryn Crispin. Waneta graduated from New Market in 1931.

Three boys were born to Fred and Waneta. Fred Paul born Jan. 25, 1932, Eddie Dale born June 27, 1936 and Thomas Glen "Tom" born June 10, 1938. All three boys are Crawfordsville High School graduates.

Freddie Paul is an Eagle Scout. One day, at about age 11, he and Fred went squirrel hunting on Fred's father's property. They got three squirrels, one was in a tree and Fred shot it just as a plane went over. Later, it was discovered that there had been three convicts hiding out in the same woods — just feet away from where the Bayless's had been hunting. It came out in the paper the next day that the convicts had shot at the plane — Fred and Freddie Paul know the "rest of the story". Freddie Paul graduated from Purdue and earned his masters at Butler. He is now working on his doctorate degree. While at Purdue, he was in the ROTC and became a 1st Lt. in the Marine Air Corps. As a teenager, he received an award from President Truman for saving a boy's life at the Sportsman Club. During high school, he was in golf, football and wrestling. He now lives at Morgan Hills, CA, where he works for IBM. He married Barbara Johnson and they have three children: Kristie (Aug. 27, 1954, a Purdue graduate; works at IBM in Portland, OR); Kirk (Mar. 17, 1956, an IU graduate — an Army Captain, stationed in Korea) and Robert (Dec. 27, 1957 — part-owner of a Sound System Company, San Francisco).

Eddie Dale is also an Eagle Scout. He received an award for serving 20 years as an adult Scout leader (Webelo Leader, Scoutmaster, Troop committeeman, Assistant District Commissioner, District Training chairman), as well. In high school, Ed was state wrestling champ in 1954 (139#) and was on the State Champion Golf Team. Ed is an IU graduate and was in the Navy ROTC. He married Janis Ewoldt and they are parents of: Edward Randall (Randy, born Feb. 5, 1961). Randy is working on his doctorate degree. He married Susan Beer and they are the proud parents of Nathan. Laura Kay, Randy's sister was born Oct. 3, 1962 and is a Purdue graduate.

Tom works at the state office building. He attended Purdue one year. Tom also does farming and lives next to his parents on State Road 234. The Bayless homeplace (Luna's) burnt down and Tom built the new home — all but the electric wiring and plastering. He also built a rocket with a look-out tower for his children. Tom married Barbara Combs and had Jeff (Nov. 27, 1961) and Thomas Allen (July 9, 1963). Both Allen and Jeff attended Ivy Tech — Allen received a degree in electronics. Tom married a second time to Jamie Taylor Burns and her daughter, Shannon is attending Indiana State University.

Fred and Waneta are both retired — he from Donnelley's and she from the *Journal-Review*. They celebrated their 50th wedding anniversary in 1981 and look forward to #60 just two years away.

Fred stays close to his "roots" and childhood as he is the proud owner of the Bayless "Homeplace" property from whence he took those walks to school and back home again for lunch! *Submitted by Fred Bayless*

IRVIN AND MARY BAYLESS

Irvin Samuel Bayless first saw Mary Hutchison in 1934. He pointed to her and told his cousin, "Someday, I'm going to marry that girl." In the fall of the next year, he finally "officially" met her at a carnival held in the Montgomery County Fair Grounds. But, not until June 24th in 1939 did Irvin finally accomplish his statement.

Irvin was born Dec. 3, 1909 in Montgomery County, the son of Elmer and Pearl (Demoret) Bayless, the next to oldest of five children. He attended school at Browns Valley and New Market. His father farmed.

Sam, Irvin and Mary Bayless

Mary was born June 10, 1916, north of Waynetown, the daughter of Walter Irvin and Millie Catherine (Whitaker) Hutchison. The Hutchisons had six boys and another girl besides Mary. Walter farmed and was also a male nurse. Her mother, Millie also nursed and they kept people in their home to care for. Mary is a Wingate graduate, one of 11 from the year 1934.

Mary worked at R.R. Donnelley's (bindery) for several years while Irvin owned and drove a stock truck. In 1942, they decided upon farming as their livelihood and rented farm land, then eventually purchased acreage in Scott Township where Irvin farmed until his retirement in 1975. He also worked for the county highway (1967-75) and drove a school bus for New Market from 1963-67. Mary worked at JC Penney's from 1968-79.

Mary helped deliver several of her nieces and nephews, so when it came to her own pregnancy she was quite confident in decisions. One, even though avid sports fans, it was mutually agreed that they would not attend the county tourney. They did, however, purchase a radio to listen. Even though Irvin was nervous, Mary refused to go until after the game was over. She was right — it wasn't until 9:12 a.m. (at Culver Hospital) on Jan. 16, 1949 that Irvin and Mary's son, Samuel Wayne Bayless arrived.

Sam graduated from New Market High School in 1967. He married Cheryl Trimble (daughter of Robert and Martha (Shannon) Trimble) May 21, 1972. Two children were born to them: Kimberly Michelle, born Sept. 18, 1974 and Robert Samuel born Apr. 21, 1978. Sam attended Indiana State University and graduated in 1971 where he was inducted into the Industrial Arts Honorary Fraternity. Sam is a carpenter and owns Bayless Specialties where he does silk screening and dye cutting. He is living on the Scott Township farm and is now married to Susan Cook Sylvester.

Irvin died Dec. 3, 1983 and is buried at Waynetown Masonic cemetery. Mary continued living on the farm for awhile but now lives (at the Durham Home) in Crawfordsville where she enjoys travelling with the Senior Citizens. *Submitted by Mary Bayless*

LUNA HARRISON BAYLESS

Luna Harrison Bayless was born near Alamo on July 11, 1862. His sister and brothers were: Laura, died in infancy and George, William, Lemeul and Grant. These children were descendants of fine stock, as their grandmother, Elizabeth Grant was a sister of President Ulysseus S. Grant and their father, John, affectionately referred to as "Uncle Johnny" was a cook in Co. F., of the Army during the Civil War. John Bayless was born May 25, 1828, the son of the above Elizabeth Grant and William Bayless. His wife was Mary Myers, born Jan. 15, 1827. They were married May 3, 1850 and began a succession of long marriages in the Bayless family. They were married 51 years at the time of his death (Mar. 29, 1902). She died five years later.

L to R The Bayless Family: F.R. Lloyd, Elizabeth, Luna and Fred. B.R. Nelson, Mae, Lula, Hazel, Lottie and Rose

Luna had much excitement in his young life, going to Missouri with his family and friends by covered wagon when he was just 14 years old. One day, a long rider galloped up to their wagons, said he was tired and asked to take a nap. He tied his horse to the back of one wagon, crawled inside and slept for quite sometime as they travelled along. Upon awakening, he mounted his horse and silently rode into the forest. Afterwards it was learned that the man was Jesse James, who had just robbed a bank, and that was his method of eluding his captors. The family stayed one winter in Missouri, but as it was not to their liking, they returned to Indiana and settled in Montgomery County.

Luna was first married to Elizabeth Conner Stover, a close relative of the Caleb Conner Prairie Settlement family. They were married Feb. 20, 1884. They had two children: Lottie who married Homer Robison (children: Margaret, Gordon, Gerald, Willard and Namoi) and Lula who married Milton Bryant (children: Ralph, Ronald, Edith, Ruby, Milton, Jr., Robert and Betty). Elizabeth died of Tuberculosis Nov. 20, 1891, leaving Luna, Lottie and Lula in sorrow. A few years later, Nov. 21, 1895 Luna remarried (Elizabeth Priebe). In 1902, the Bayless family proudly moved their family to their 80-acre farm a mile northwest of Freedom Church. Their children were: Mae married Elza Bollman (children: Lael, Jerry and Pat); Hazel married Glen Newkirk (no children); Nelson married Margaret Deer (no children); Fred (see biography) and Lloyd married Genice Patton (one son, Larry).

All eight Bayless children watched Luna and Elizabeth "dance the anniversary waltz" at their 50th anniversary Open House held in the Bayless Home Nov. 18, 1945.

Like their parents and their parents before them, the eight Bayless children celebrated many anniversaries and totalled over 400 years of married life and their children and grandchildren own healthy marriages as well.

Luna died Oct. 13, 1954 proud of his Bayless heritage. Elizabeth died a few months later on Apr. 13, 1955. They, like his parents are buried at Freedom Cemetery. *Submitted by Fred Bayless*

THOMAS BAYNES FAMILY HISTORY

Thomas Priestman Baynes and his wife, Rebecca Roberts Powell Baynes, moved to Montgomery Co., IN, in 1919, from Washington Co., IN. The Baynes couple had retired from a full life of farming and raising their children and wanted a quiet life in their golden years near Rebecca's church, the Christ Scientist.

Thomas was born near Philadelphia, PA, in 1853, one of ten children of a Quaker family. His father was Beezon Baynes. His mother was Lowry Humphreys Baynes, born 1816 in Pennsylvania, died 1896, in Washington Co., IN. In 1855 Thomas moved with his parents from Pennsylvania to Washington Co., IN.

Rebecca was born in Pennsylvania in 1851, also of Quaker heritage. Her father was Joseph B. Powell, who died in Pennsylvania in 1892; her mother was Margaret Roberts Heacock, who died in Pennsylvania in 1889.

In 1877 Thomas and Rebecca were married in Pennsylvania and established their home in Washington Co., IN. There, they were farmers and raised their six biological children; Walter Powell, Helen M., Joseph Powell, Thomas Beezon, Margaret Lowry, and Rebecca Heacock; one adopted child, Theodore; and at least one foster child, John Bicknell.

Thomas and Rebecca Baynes

One of the children, Rebecca Heacock Baynes, married Shirl Blaine Dellinger, and resided many years in Montgomery County, as described elsewhere in this book.

Thomas and Rebecca resided at 1413 East Main St. in Crawfordsville. Rebecca died in 1935 at age 84 and Thomas died in 1938 at age 85. Internments were in Oak Hill Cemetery in Crawfordsville.

Daughter Margaret, who had some disablement caused by a childhood illness, never married and lived with her parents until her mother Rebecca's death.

Theodore Baynes also lived in Crawfordsville, and worked at the Louis & Sheppard plant. Theodore died in 1962; in 1988, his widow, Mary Asher Baynes, still lived in Crawfordsville.

The Baynes ancestral-line surname can be traced over several generations to before leaving England. The Baynes ancestors that figure in American history are:

-James Baynes: born in Yorkshire, England in 1775. He married Elizabeth Priestman. This couple, with their children and two sheep dogs, sailed for America in 1822, aboard the ship "Indian Chief". James died in 1856 near Philadelphia.

-Beezon Baynes; was born at Woodhall Park, Woodhall, Yorkshire, England, in 1818. He traveled to America with his parents. He married Lowry Humphreys, and moved from Pennsylvania in 1855, to Washington Co., IN. He ran a farm, also called Woodhall, near Salem. Beezon died in 1896. and

-Thomas Priestman Baynes; who is the subject of this history. *Authored by Thomas Baynes Dellinger*

FRED BAZZANI

"Neither snow, nor rain nor heat, nor gloom of night stays these couriers from the swift completion of their appointed route." Thus reads the mail carrier's creed. Fred Bazzani was the Waveland rural mail carrier from 1951 through 1976 and always followed the above code. He was born Aug. 26, 1920 in Universal, IN, the son of Italian immigrants, Antonio and Carolina (Berti) Bazzani. Fred graduated from Clinton High School in 1938, then went to the CCC at Shades State Park. He served on the foreign front in World War II as a medic and Chaplain's assistant. After his discharge, he married (Apr. 20, 1946 in Terre Haute) Kathryn Geneva Smith, born July 8, 1920 in Parke Co., IN to Leland "Carl" and Sarah "Hazel" Morgan Smith. Kate graduated from Waveland High School in 1938. After their marriage, Fred attended Rose Poly. Besides his postal job, Fred also worked for Goodman's, Machledt and Servies and operated a private floor covering business. Kate worked as a telephone operator in Waveland and Mallory's in Indianapolis before marrying. Later, she was a secretary/reporter for *Tri-County News*. Kate died Nov. 11, 1982. Fred is now married to the former Doris Simpson of Waveland.

Kate, Larry, Karen, Garry and Fred Bazzani

The Bazzani's had twin sons, Larry and Garry, born Dec. 21, 1946 in Terre Haute and a daughter, Karen, born Dec. 15, 1949 in Crawfordsville.

Larry married Linda Kay Weaver, born June 15, 1948 the daughter of Charles and Marie (Parish) Weaver. Larry won the Purple Heart during the Vietnam conflict. He is employed at R.R. Donnelleys. His son, Robby (born May 15, 1969) also works there. Their daughter, Nikki (born June 4, 1968) is majoring in Elementary Education at Ball State.

Garry married Arlene Layne, born Sept. 22, 1948, the daughter of Harold and Gloria (Nicholson) Layne. Garry is a graduate of Wabash College and is a Supervising Manager at Raybestos. They have two daughters, both born in Crawfordsville, Amy Suzanne (born Nov. 22, 1971) and Heather Lynn (born Mar. 20, 1973). The girls are students at Southmont.

Karen married James William "Jim" Zach, see Zach history. Karen is a 1985 graduate of ISU in School Media and received her Master's of Library Science in 1988 from Indiana University. She is the Children's Librarian at the Crawfordsville District Public Library. She is affiliated with many historical societies, including Dorothy Q Chapter, DAR, where she is currently Regent. Also, the Montgomery and Fountain County Historical Societies, Indiana State Historical Society, Indiana Genealogy Society, Society of Indiana Pioneers and Genealogy Section of the MCHS. She also belongs to work-related organizations, such as: Association of Indiana Media, Indiana Library Association, American Library Association and Stories, Inc. A major love for Karen is writing "Family Roots" in *Montgomery Magazine* where she often features the Bazzani klan. *Submitted by Karen Bazzani Zach*

HENRY BECK

Henry Beck was one of 11 children born to John Martin and Maria Catherina Beck. He was born on the 15th of September 1776 somewhere in North Carolina.

Presumedly, Henry, between 1795 and 1802, farmed on his father's 90 acres and perhaps he gave his brother William a hand too. Henry is listed on the 1802 tax roll but, owned no land. On Wednesday 7, September, Henry, along with Charles Dalton and Abraham Rand were appointed "patrollers" in Captain Bennett's District, which was just north of Salem. Saturday, Sept. 1, 1804, Henry married Sarah (Sally) Jean in Stokes County. His younger brother, Abraham, and a T. Armstrong served as official witnesses.

On Mar. 26, 1804, the U.S. Congress reduced the minimum amount of public land that could be purchased from 460 acres to a minimum of 160 acres. This must have had an effect on the Beck boys and they were "caught up", as were many others in the quest for land and adventure in the "west". In 1806, Solomon, Henry's brother, reportedly went west and purchased a quarter section in what was to become Union Co., IN. Solomon must have painted a rosy picture for when Solomon went west a second time Henry went with him. Solomon and Henry both purchased additional property in Union County.

In about the year 1820, the Henry Beck family pioneered into Union County. They lived in makeshift tents until a crude log cabin or hut was constructed, cleared the land, and began farming their property. They were pioneers in the real sense of the word.

On Sept. 17, 1826, Sarah died giving birth to their son, Josiah Congo, and was buried in the Silver Creek Christian Church Cemetery near their five year old daughter, Martha, who died in 1821. The children of Henry and Sarah were: William W., Henry F., John W., Charity M., Mary, Martha, Elizabeth, Eliza, Lucinda and Josiah C.

Two years later, Henry married Elizabeth Burroughs in Wayne Co., IN, and they moved on to Montgomery County to land they purchased in March of 1831. Henry lived out his days on earth in Montgomery County.

Henry's wife, Elizabeth, died on June 21, 1862 and Henry nearly three years later on Apr. 20, 1865. Both are buried in the Shannondale Cemetery. Henry's last years were feeble and he often wished that "his time would come." His granddaughter, Angeline Crain and her husband, John, lived with him during this time. Angeline, told of Henry's death in this way, "The last thing he noticed was our little girl (Effie Elizabeth Crain) about three years old which he thought a great deal of. The evening before he kissed her and shut his eyes to wake no more." *By Stanley C. Beck, condensed by permission of Roger G. Spurgeon, Sr.*

JOHN MARTIN BECK

John Martin Beck was born Aug. 17, 1740 and is believed to have come from Westerwald, Germany. Sketchy evidence also state that he arrived in Philadelphia in 1752 with his parents. The first real documentation of John in America is on the tax role of Stokes Co., NC in 1796. He was living in the county at this time and remained in the county until his death. John and his family had settled in the Maravian tract called Wachovia. This land was comprised of 100,000 acres and encompassed Forsyth and Stokes Counties. Moravian Bishop, Zinzendorf purchased this land about 1744, and resold sections of it to settlers.

John married a girl named Maria Catharine and her maiden name was possibly Tribles (or Cribles). They were the parents of 11 children though nine of these children are all that genealogists have identified. In the third U.S. Census two of John's sons were listed as tanners. Solomon completed 250 hides valued at $125.00 and Henry completed 80 hides valued at $40.50.

John Martin died Sept. 12, 1819 in Stokes County and a very significant write up on his death was recorded in diaries written by clergy of the Moravian Church, which were published in two volumes by Adelaide L' Fries and entitled "Records of the Moravians in North Carolina". Entries dated September 13 are as follows:

"About three miles from Bethabara Br. Strohle preached the funeral sermon for a married man 80 years old, Johann Martin Beck, whom he had often visited during his illness pointing him to Jesus, The Friend of sinners, and apparently with good effect and...About three miles from here, in a family burying ground, Br. Strohle held the funeral of a man, Johann Martin Beck, nearly 80 years old. He had suffered for a long time from dropsy, with complications. He was born in Germany. Br. Strohle visited him often during his illness..." Five years later, John's wife, Maria Catherine, died and was recorded in the same diary: Dec. 25, 1824. "The festal preaching service was largely attended. Soon after, Br. Strohle went to the home of our neighbor, Mr. William Beck. He had been asked to hold the funeral of Mr. Beck's mother, who fell asleep yesterday at an age of nearly 82 years old. We have known her for many years as a true child of God. Her husband died five years ago. She had 11 children, about 50 grandchildren and a number of great-grandchildren." *By Stanley C. Beck, condensed by permission of Roger G. Spurgeon, Sr.*

WARREN G. AND ELIZABETH MILLER BELL

Warren G. Bell was born Dec. 27, 1920, at Alamo, IN, in Montgomery County. His father was Alonzo Earl Bell, son of Charles Edward and Florence Deets Bell. Charles E. Bell's father, Stephen Bell, moved his family to the Alamo area around 1868 from Harrison Co., OH. Warren's mother was Martha Hatt Bell, daughter of Salina Elizabeth Butcher and William V. Hatt. Warren graduated from Alamo High School in 1939. He was a Hand Compositor at R.R. Donnelley, from 1940 until he retired in 1982. He is a member of the First Baptist Church at Crawfordsville, IN, and Masonic Lodge #50. He served in the Navy during World War II.

Warren married Elizabeth (Betty) Miller on Oct. 17, 1941, at Crawfordsville, IN. Elizabeth was born Nov. 14, 1920, in a house built by her maternal grandfather located at 407 Union Street, in Crawfordsville. Elizabeth's parents were Benjamin Harrison Miller, son of Marion and Clara Caroline Eller Miller, and Mary Elizabeth Wray, daughter of Ruth Burk and Jerome B. Wray. Elizabeth Bell graduated from Crawfordsville High School in 1938. She is also a member of the First Baptist Church in Crawfordsville.

Warren G. holding Gregory W., Elizabeth M., Mariana, Gerald W. and Marilyn Bell

Warren and Elizabeth had four children. Mariana was born Oct. 18, 1945, while her father was in Guam. Guam is in the Mariana Island chain. That's where her father got her name. Their second daughter, Marilyn was born Mar. 20, 1948. Gerald (Jerry) Wayne Bell was born Sept. 1, 1949. Gregory Wray Bell was born Aug. 20, 1950.

Elizabeth worked at R.R. Donnelley before her marriage. Warren and Elizabeth have lived at 608 S. Washington Street in Crawfordsville since 1953.

Mariana married Freddie Gene Threlkeld on Aug. 30, 1975. Fred was born May 1, 1938. He is the son of Joseph and Helen Fernandez Threlkeld. Fred had four children during his first marriage, Darla Threlkeld White, Lorrie, Jeff, and Heath. Mariana and Fred have one son, Christian Warren Joseph Threlkeld, born Jan. 29, 1978, during the blizzard of '78. He is a student at Hoover School. He also plays basketball at the Boys Club in Crawfordsville.

Marilyn attended Purdue University. She is employed by R.R. Donnelley. She has one daughter, Kathleen Kim Bell, born Jan. 18, 1986.

Gerald (Jerry) married Barbara Stonecipher on June 16, 1973. Barbara was born Apr. 11, 1950. She is the daughter of Cecil and Annabel Baird Stonecipher, of Crawfordsville. Jerry has degrees from Ball State University, University of Arizona, Ohio State University, and Brigham Young University. He is an Assistant Professor of Kinesiology, and Director of Sports Injuries Research, University of Illinois, Urbana-Champaign. Barbara is a high school Spanish teacher. They have two children, born in Sacramento, CA, Jason Gerald, born Sept. 7, 1976, and Erin Elizabeth, born Sept. 1, 1978.

Gregory married Martha Townsend McClain, Aug. 16, 1981. She was born Nov. 30, 1944, to Paul and Mildred McCauley Townsend of Newtown. Greg works at R.R. Donnelley and Martha is a first grade teacher at Fountain Central Elementary. Martha has two daughters, Laura McClain Webb, and Amy McClain.

JOHN AND DIANA BENNETT

Diana Herr and John Bennett were married at the Wabash Avenue Presbyterian Church on Dec. 23, 1960.

Diana is the daughter of Eleanor Hostetter and the late Remley Herr and was graduated from Crawfordsville High School and the DePauw University School of Nursing. Her sorority was Delta Zeta.

John was the son of Ruth McCarthy Pinkston and the late William Bennett. He is a graduate of Crawfordsville High School as well as Oakland City College. John taught English and speech at Fountain Central High School and Crawfordsville High School before becoming a sales representative for MidStates Steel and Wire Company. At present he is the owner of the Crawfordsville Burial Vault Company.

Front L to R: Carrie, Diana, John. Back: Michael, Stacey, Jeff and Amy Bennett

Diana began her career as a visiting nurse at Evansville, IN. She has worked as Christian Education Director for the Wabash Avenue Presbyterian Church, a visiting nurse for Lafayette Visiting Nurse Service and at Indiana Home Health Care. Presently she is Program Chair for the Medical Assistant Department at Ivy Tech in Indianapolis. Her memberships include the Art League and an inactive member of Tri Kappa.

John and Diana are the parents of four children. Jeffrey Todd is a recent graduate of Indiana University Law School and is employed at McHale, Cook and Welsh Law Firm in Indianapolis. He was graduated from DePauw University where he belonged to Lambda Chi fraternity.

Stacey Lynn is married to Michael Anderson. They have a son Logan Michael. Stacey and Michael are students at Purdue University.

Amy Diane is a student at Indiana State University. Carrie Ann is a student at Tuttle Junior High School.

The family are active members of the Wabash Avenue Presbyterian Church.

FREDERIC E. BIBLE

Frederic E. Bible was born in Coal Creek Township, Montgomery Co., IN to Richard Montgomery and Mary Frazer Bible December 1885. He attended a nearby grade school. After the death of his father in 1893 he worked with his brothers and his mother on their farm place.

In September 1911 he married Mabel Tomlinson Vincent, daughter of Milo and Miranda Belle McClamroch Tomlinson. Mabel was born October 1892. She graduated from the Linden High School. They lived on Fred's home place west of New Richmond, IN.

A daughter, Kathleen Belle was born Jan. 6, 1915 and a son, Richard was born June 21, 1918 (see Richard Bible and Kathleen Bible Meyer).

Frederic E. and Mabel V. (Tomlinson) Bible

Fred and Mabel joined other farm couples west of New Richmond to form a company to furnish electricity to their homes. The electric line was completed in 1920.

They were members of the New Richmond Church. Fred was on the committee to plan a new church building and Mabel was chairman of the Ladies Aid group who prepared, donated and served noon meals to threshing rings to earn money to pay toward the church mortgage.

After their house burned in 1928 they moved into New Richmond, then to Linden where they opened a real estate office in their home.

Mabel was a member of the Linden American Legion, the Federated Women's Club and the Oriental Chapter 244 of the Order of Eastern Star. She was active in the Home Economics club and she was elected the first president of the Montgomery County Home Economics.

Despite financial reverses in the 1930's, Fred and Mabel's priorities in their 52 years of marriage were their belief in Christian faith, their love of family life in rural areas and their volunteer activities.

Mabel died in September 1963 and Fred died in April of 1965.

GEORGE (BIBEL) BIBLE
1805-1897

Already 23 years old, with farming skills and a pioneer spirit, George Bibel came to the northern fraction of Section Five of Coal Creek Twp. He and his parents Lewis and Mary Bibel and sister Sarah came from Adams Co., OH. Evidenced by the land patent, they were here in October of 1828. They also entered land in Jackson Twp. of Tippecanoe County. The homeplace was established along the county line.

Brother John Bible and his wife, Elizabeth (Satterfield) Bible and four children followed some time near 1836.

Mary Bible Whitlatch, our subject's sister, and her husband, Noah Whitlatch came to Montgomery County about the same time with seven children. Three more were born in Indiana. The Whitlatch family moved on to Iowa.

Wm. Edward Bible; John C. Bible

The pioneer family that settled in the Coal Creek and Jackson Township area stayed in the same area acquiring land as their families matured. Many of the family members were buried in the Sugar Grove Cemetery.

The proud Sugar Grove Community prospered, a school called the Sugar Grove Academy, a church, a scale house, and a blacksmith shop added to their progress.

George married Sealy Calhoon, daughter of John and Sary Calhoon Apr. 5, 1841. They became the parents of nine children. Two children died in early infancy and childhood.

John Calhoon Bible, the eldest of the Bible children was born in 1842. Others were Mary G. in 1846, Lewis 1848, Phillip 1850, Susan S. 1858, Emma 1861, and William Edward in 1863.

John Calhoon Bible served three years in the Civil War. He was a part of the 72nd Infantry Regiment from 1862 until 1865. When he returned home, he married Sarah Louisa Hamilton of the same township.

Mary G. married James G. Clarkson, the son of another early settler. James Clarkson's parents and grandparents came here around 1830 from New Jersey. They were neighbors to the Bibles. Three daughters and two sons were born to this union.

Lewis Bible married Sarah Wilson Oct. 26, 1870. Other marriages were between Phillip Bible and Mary L. Bennett October 1872. Emma Bible married Ashley Paxton Aug. 8, 1888. Two children were born to this marriage: one son, Everett and one daughter Lura. Emma died ten days after Lura's birth. Lura was raised by her Uncle Phillip and Aunt Mary.

George Bible died at his home Jan. 18, 1879 at the age of 74 years, 6 months, 14 days. His wife Sealy died Nov. 28, 1877, at the age of 54 years and 17 days. Their graves are well marked in the Sugar Grove Cemetery.

William Edward who was 17 at the time of his father's death, lived on in the family home and married Hattie Lewis in 1894. William and Hattie lived on there until 1897 when they moved to northern Indiana.

The land is now a part of the Nesbitt Farms. The changes over the past 160 years have been remarkable, changing from the wilderness to open rich farmland with many modern conveniences available.

Our brave dedicated ancestors give us the resolution to face the problems of today's world with much courage.

LEWIS BIBLE

Lewis was the original owner of 134 acres of sections 5 and 8, Twp. 20, Range 5, in 1828. Also 65 acres in section 6 in 1834. His land grant papers have remained in the family, in good condition. They carry Andrew Jackson's signature.

Lewis was raised in Rockingham Co., VA. His father Hans Adam Bible was born 1732 in Germany. He arrived in Port Philadelphia, PA on Nov. 30, 1750, on the ship Sandwich. Adam married Eva Ryan and they had nine children; Lewis, Adam Jr., Christian, Philip, John, George and three daughters. Adam died in Rockingham County Feb. 23, 1795. After his death Eva went to Tennessee with Christian. According to Christian's family records, Eva lived to be 114 years old. She's buried in the Battle Creek Cem., Marion Co., TN.

Our subject married Mary Shoemaker in 1795 and they purchased property in Brooks Gap, Rockingham Co., VA, from Morgan Bryan in 1797; only to have the court award it back to William Bryan who claimed his brother was insane at the time of the sale. He won his case.

Lewis with his wife and three children left Virginia for Adams Co., OH. They homesteaded and farmed the land in Tiffin Twp. where one of the first schools was built on Lewis's property in 1802. Altho' it was beautiful land with rolling hills, it was not productive. So Lewis and Mary with four of their six children came to Montgomery County. He cleared the land and built a homestead for the third time in his life. His children were:

Elizabeth born 1796, Virginia, married Robert Johnston in 1818 and had six children. They remained in Adams Co., OH. Elizabeth died in 1882.

Eva born 1797, Virginia, married Noah Whitlatch in 1816, and came to Montgomery County in 1834. Their daughter married C.J. Oppy. Eva and Noah left Indiana and settled in Marion Co., IA. Eva died in 1889.

John born 1800, Virginia, married Eliza Satterfield in 1826 Ohio. They entered Montgomery County in 1834. They had five children. After Eliza's death John married Mary May in 1840, and they had ten children. John and his family settled in and around Crawfordsville.

George born 1804, Ohio, came here with his father. Married Celia Calhoun in 1841, Tippecanoe County.

Mary Ann born 1817, Ohio, married Andrew Hemphill in 1829, Ohio. They came here in 1834. There's a good account of their family in the White Co., IN History Book. Mary Ann died in 1904.

Sarah born 1817, Ohio, married David McDaniel in 1842, Tippecanoe County.

Lewis wrote his will in 1833, leaving Five Hundred Dollars to each of his children, and the homestead and 40 acres, in the southern tip of Tippecanoe County to George. George and Sarah took care of their father in his later years.

Lewis, his wife, Mary and family members are buried in the Sugar Grove Cem. in Tippecanoe County, Jackson Township. Lewis's tombstone reads; died Dec. 24, 1863, aged 107 years, eight months, 24 days.

RICHARD E. AND EDITH C. BIBLE

Richard Errington Bible married Edith Rachel Collins in Tallahassee, FL on Dec. 23, 1947. They moved to Crawfordsville and later to Linden, IN where they live today.

Richard was born to Fred E. Bible and Mabel Vincent Bible on a farm west of New Richmond. After moving from the farm in 1929, Fred and Mabel were in the Real Estate business in Linden for 35 years. Fred's father was long time Montgomery County resident Richard Montgomery Bible and Mabel was the daughter of Belle McClamroch Vincent of Montgomery County.

Richard E. and Edith C. Bible

Graduating from New Richmond High School in 1936, Richard played basketball, baseball and ran track. He went to Butler University in Indianapolis, graduating in 1940 with a B.S. in Physical Education and Business.

He served in Army Air Corps for four years and was stationed on Iwo Jima. He attained the rank of Captain.

In 1950, Richard received his Master of Science degree from Butler University. He was a member of Lambda Chi Alpha Fraternity.

Richard taught Business Education and coached three sports in several high schools in the area for ten years. He also worked at Alcoa, Brick Yard and National Homes.

After he retired, he developed a sub-division on the east side of Linden. He is a member of American Legion, #697 Linden Lodge F. & A.M. and the Christian Church in New Richmond.

Edith was born in Tallahassee, FL to Moseley Cary Collins and Gladys Porter Collins. Moseley was in the furniture business in Tallahassee for 40 years. He was a great grandson of William Dunn Moseley, the first governor of Florida. Also ex-governor Leroy Collins was his first cousin.

Gladys Collins was born and raised in Boston, MA and graduated from Childrens Hospital. She was a registered nurse in Tallahassee.

Graduating from Leon High School, Tallahassee, FL in 1941, Edith went on to Florida State University and received a B.S. degree in Foods and Nutrition in 1945. She was a member of Kappa Delta Sorority. She spent a year at Shadyside Hospital in Pittsburgh, PA as a Student Dietitian and later worked as Dietitian at Duke Hospital in Durham, NC.

Richard and Edith are parents of two daughters, Mary Edith Bible Carnes and Alice Mayme Bible. Mary Edith graduated from Linden High School in 1967 and from Purdue University in 1971. She is married to Michael W. Carnes, an Indiana University graduate and a banker in North Vernon, IN. They have three children, Allison, Amanda and Ryan.

Mary Edith is an Assistant Director at Muscatatuck State Hospital at Butlerville, IN.

Alice graduated from North Montgomery High School in 1979. In 1983 she received her B.S. degree in Elementary Education from Indiana State University at Terre Haute, IN. While in school, she was a member of Alpha Chi Omega Sorority.

She received her Masters Degree in Special Education from Ball State University, Muncie, IN in 1988.

Alice taught Special Education at Hartsville, SC and Sunman, IN.

She is now teaching at Shelbyville, IN.

JERRY L. AND CAROL HENRY BIGGS

Jerry L. Biggs came to Montgomery County in 1943. He was born Jan. 18, 1929 in Spartanburg, SC, the first child of William Eugene and Ruby Mason Biggs. He has two brothers, Robert Dean who lives near North Salem, Joseph Michael and a sister Shirley Ann (VanHook) of Russellville. His mother was born Aug. 18, 1911 in Spartanburg, SC, she died Dec. 14, 1971. His father was born in Gadsden, AL July 4, 1906, he now lives in Russellville, IN.

Jerry's great grandfather James Madison Biggs was born in England May 2, 1851. He came to the United States at the age of 14 and settled in Georgia, later moving to Gadsden, AL.

Jerry L. and Carol (Henry) Biggs

Carol was born Oct. 15, 1929 in Montgomery County to Carl I. and Pearl Whitecotton Henry. Carl was born Feb. 25, 1899 in Coal Creek Twp. and Pearl was born June 26, 1904 in Union Twp. Carol was the youngest of four children. Minnie Elizabeth (Ausetts) lives in Parma, OH, Ruth Marie (Shillings) lives near Mace and Virginia Avanelle (Bowen) lives in Danville, IN. Pearl died Aug. 22, 1935. Carol was reared in her maternal grandparents home, Mr. and Mrs. William Whitecotton. (See Whitecotton family elsewhere.) Her father died Aug. 31, 1982.

Jerry and Carol both graduated from New Market High School in 1947, they went to work at R.R. Donnelley's that summer and they both operated Linotype machines for 35 years. They were married Nov. 8, 1947. They have one son, Stephen L. Biggs born July 9, 1950 at Culver Hospital. They lived in Crawfordsville until 1963 when they bought and moved to a farm in Franklin Twp. where they still live. They retired from R.R. Donnelley's when they were 55 years old.

Steve married Debbie Dee Douglas, June 8, 1973. Debbie was born Mar. 2, 1955, the daughter of Harold and Evelyn (Blacketer) Douglas. Steve is a development engineer at Crawford Industries in Crawfordsville. They have three children. Brian Douglas born Mar. 2, 1976 at Home Hospital in Lafayette, Tracy Leigh born June 7, 1978 at Culver Hospital and Cristy Ann born Oct. 16, 1987 at Culver Hospital. They have lived in Darlington since 1977. Steve served on the Darlington Town Board for five years. He is past master of the Masonic Lodge #50. Brian and Tracy are active in Scouts and 4-H. Brian is in the Northridge Middle School Band.

THE BINFORDS

Peter Binford was the first Binford to come to Montgomery County. He came to Walnut Township in 1830. His older brother, John, came to Boone County in 1821, but both came from Virginia, where earlier generations had lived. Peter owned sections of land south of Garfield, IN.

Peter was born Aug. 19, 1807, and died Dec. 2, 1873. He married Mariah Whitacre, and they had ten children.

One of Peter's children was David Binford, who was born July 12, 1840 and died in 1930. David married Georgetta Payn, Mar. 10, 1869. Georgetta was born Sept. 17, 1851, and died Mar. 2, 1923. They bought a farm at Garfield, north of the Peter Binford land. Peter left his land to his sons. Peter and several of his brothers are buried in a small cemetery west of Garfield. Bernard Binford, a grandson of David, bought his farm in 1941. The old house burned, then Bernard and his wife, Ida, built a new house. This farm was owned by Binfords until 1951.

James, John, Thomas, and Peter Binford (of earlier generations) in 1781, gave cattle, corn, oats, furniture and bedding for supplying the army during the Revolutionary War. The Binfords, who were all Quakers, did not believe in fighting, so helped by giving of their material things. This gives most of the Binford women a right to become a member of the Daughters of the American Revolution.

David and Georgetta Binford's children were: Luella, born Feb. 5, 1870, died Dec. 27, 1937, and married Aaron Edwin Wilkinson Dec. 19, 1893. Myrtie, born June 12, 1872, died April 1947, and married Byron Cox Sept. 20, 1893. Willard, born Aug. 17, 1874, died Apr. 8, 1952, and married first, Maude Johnson Aug. 26, 1896 (she died 1893), and married second Minnie McLaughlin. Clyde, born Oct. 1, 1876, died Mar. 21, 1950, and married Cora Long Dec. 28, 1898. Grace, born Apr. 14, 1879, died May 11, 1965, and married Oscar Hole, Apr. 30, 1899. Harry, born Oct. 27, 1881, died Sept. 21, 1970, and married Grace Shewmaker Aug. 30, 1910. Owen, born Nov. 15, 1889, died May 18, 1963, and married Ruth White, Aug. 24, 1915.

All of David's children, but Willard, lived all of their lives in Montgomery County. Harry operated a general store at Garfield most of his life, while the rest were farmers.

David owned a threshing machine outfit, and threshed for many people in the surrounding areas. His sons, Clyde and Willard, helped him, then eventually took it over. Later, Clyde and his son, Charles, operated the threshing outfit for years, after Willard moved away.

The farmers formed what was known as "threshing rings". It took several weeks to thresh for all. The women would go to each others homes to help cook for the threshers. The tables were always laden with good home-cooked food. There were lots of good cooks in those days, with them doing everything the hard way, cooking on wood or coal ranges in hot weather, and carrying their water from pitcher pumps. In spite of the hard work, it was always a time of good fellowship.

David and Georgetta have many grandchildren, plus both great, and great-great grandchildren still living here in Montgomery County. To list them all would fill another book. *Compiled and submitted by Zelah Binford Crull*

CLETIS E. AND WILMA R. (DICKSON) BIRGE

Wilma was born Aug. 26, 1931 at Mace. She was the youngest child of Waldo and Anna Dickson. She attended school at Mace, New Richmond and Linden. She graduated from high school in 1949, and began work at Purdue University in May of that year.

On Oct. 1, 1949, she and Cletis were married. He was born in Thomkinsville, KY and moved to Romney with his parents, James Thomas and Chloe Irene (Basil) Birge, when he was a child.

Their first home was in Linden, and on July 14, 1950 their first child, Judy Kay, was born. On Aug. 11, 1954 Cletis and Wilma had another child, Deborah Lynn, that died only six days later, on August the 17th.

Cletis worked with the Monon and L&N Railroads most of his life and was a foreman and then a Roadmaster when he retired. About 1960, Cletis and Wilma bought a restaurant in partnership with friends, but sold their share to the co-owners when Wilma became ill. Again, in 1974, they bought another restaurant in Romney and sold it for a profit about a year later. Wilma worked several jobs, but always returned to Purdue University where she is presently employed as secretary to the Assistant to the Department Head of Computer Science.

In 1986, Cletis and Wilma were divorced.

Wilma visits often with her daughter and grandchildren who live across town. Glen and Julia are regular overnight guests at their Grandma Wilma's, and Wilma looks forward to their visits. *By Roger G. Spurgeon*

GENERAL JOHN CHARLES BLACK

John C. Black was born Jan. 27, 1839 in Mississippi, the son of Reverend John Black and his wife, Josephine L. Culbertson. Reverend Black was born July 12, 1809 in Westmoreland Co., PA. He became a Presbyterian minister and after his marriage, the family moved to Mississippi where the couple's four children were born. In 1846, the family moved to Alleghany City, PA where on Feb. 13, 1847 Reverend John Black died. After his death, his wife Josephine moved the family to Danville, IL. Josephine married Dr. William Fithian in Danville. She died in 1887 at the age of 74 years. She is buried next to her second husband in Danville's Springhill Cemetery.

John C. Black received his early education in Danville, IL. In the fall of 1858, he entered Wabash College in Crawfordsville, IN. On Apr. 12, 1861, while in his junior year at Wabash, he enlisted as a private in the "Montgomery Guards." This company was mustered into the 11th Indiana Infantry Zouaves for a period of three months, and became Company I under the command of Colonel Lewis Wallace. John C. Black became the sergeant of his company. He was mustered out in August of 1861. He returned to Danville, IL where he recruited a company for three years service. The company was mustered into service as Company K, 37th Illinois Infantry. John C. Black was made a major in the regiment. The regiment was attached to Colonel Julius White's Brigade. The Brigade was part of General Curtis' Army. On Mar. 7 and 8, 1862, this force engaged General Price's Confederate Army at the battle of Pea Ridge, AR. The Union force numbered 15,000 men and the Confederate force numbered 35,000 men. The battle raged for two days and ended with the Confederate forces retreating south. John C. Black was awarded the Congressional Medal of Honor for gallantry during the battle. His brother, Captain William P. Black of Company I, 37th Illinois, was also awarded the Congressional Medal of Honor for heroism during the battle of Pea Ridge. He was a graduate of Wabash College in Crawfordsville.

John C. Black was promoted to Lt. Colonel in June of 1862. He fought in the battles of Vicksburg, Mississippi, Port Hudson, Brownsville, TX and Fort Blakely, AL. He was promoted to Colonel and on Mar. 13, 1865, he was promoted to Brevet Brigadier General of Volunteers by President Abraham Lincoln.

After the war, John C. Black returned to Danville, IL where he became a lawyer. In 1871, he married Adaline L. Griggs, daughter of Clark R. and Livona Griggs of Urbana, IL. General Black was elected to Congress for one term and later became the U.S. District Attorney for Northern Illinois. He became very active in the G.A.R. and became Illinois' Department Commander in 1898. He was elected National Commander in Chief of the G.A.R. in 1903.

General Black and his family resided in Chicago, IL for many years. General Black died in Chicago on Aug. 17, 1915. He was buried with full G.A.R. honors in Springhill Cemetery in Danville, IL. His wife, Adaline, died on Aug. 25, 1945 in Philadelphia, PA. She was buried next to her husband.

Their children were:

1. Grace, 1870-1911, married Frank Vrooman.
2. John Donald, born 1872, married Margaret Potter, he became a prominent Chicago lawyer.
3. Josephine L., 1880-1885.

Submitted by Andrew Keith Houk, Jr.

ARIEL AND ERMA WESTFALL BLACKFORD

On Feb. 27, 1906, 19-year-old Ariel (Waxie) Blackford took 15-year-old Erma Westfall as his bride.

Ariel Blackford's ancestors had come to Wayne Township in Montgomery County in the early 1820's. His parents were Charles Albert and Emma

Brown Blackford. Although Ariel had seven siblings, only three lived to adulthood. Each of Ariel's two sisters had one son.

Erma Westfall's ancestors likewise came to Wayne Township in the 1820's. Erma's grandmother, Mary Ann Grenard Bratton, told her granddaughter of coming by ox-cart from Kentucky, sometimes riding, sometimes walking. William Bratton, a member of the Lewis and Clark Expedition, was Erma's great-uncle.

Erma's parents were Vezey and Barbara Ann Bratton Westfall. Erma was an only child born to parents nearly 40 years old. Her mother died when Erma was four. Her father's second wife was abusive to Erma. Her childhood was mostly deprived and unhappy except for a few years spent in Kansas with her maternal grandmother, until her grandmother's death.

Ariel Floyd Blackford, William Vezy, Nina Erma Westfall Blackford and Vivian Clark Blackford

In 1906 the Blackfords were poor, but honest and hard-working. Ariel worked as a painter and wallpaper hanger. Erma took in washings and put out a big garden to can from each year. Money was scarce, but Erma still shared what they had with any who came to their door in need. She helped out many people in times of sickness.

The Blackford family increased with the births of Charles in 1908, V.C. in 1914, William in 1916, and Ruth in 1930. Charles and V.C. were both nicknamed "Waxie." The two younger sons served in World War II. By then Charles was working at Bell Telephone, which would later employ William. Ariel had started his own business as Waynetown's ice man, hauling coal in winter.

Charles married Mary Craft, and they had two sons, Charles Wayne and Donald, both of whom now work for Indiana Bell. V.C. married June DeMoss in 1937. William married Maxine Brewer, and they had a daughter, Anita Louise. They divorced, and William later married Vivian Harlan Richardson.

Ariel Blackford died of heart disease Jan. 17, 1946. Thus he missed seeing some of his grandchildren. V.C. and June Blackford added Robert and Ann to their family, while daughter Ruth married Robert Donnelly in 1949 and had a daughter, Linn, in 1951 and son, William, in 1958. The Donnelly family raised a foster daughter, Denise Cox, from age 12.

The Donnellys moved to Oklahoma in 1971, and Erma thenceforth spent summers in Waynetown and winters in warmer Oklahoma. Erma taught in the Baptist Sunday School until age 87. She was honored as queen of the Waynetown Sesquicentennial Celebration in 1980. Erma enjoyed the 14 great-grandchildren and one great-great-grandson who were born before her death on Mar. 22, 1981. Two sons, Charles and William, and a great-grandson had preceded her in death. Five more great-grandchildren and six great-great-grandchildren have increased the family since 1981.

JENNIE JOHNSON BLAIR

Jennie Johnson Blair was born in 1833 in Madison, IN, the daughter of Rev. James H. Johnson, a Presbyterian Minister, who brought his family to Crawfordsville in 1843.

She was the first Crawfordsville girl to go away to school. She attended a female academy in Cincinnati, OH. On Mar. 29, 1855 she married Robert Blair in Crawfordsville. Four children were born to this union. Lillian Blair born 1862 and died in 1937, was the dean of women instructors at Crawfordsville High School. Rev. John Allen Blair was living in Philadelphia and Charles Blair was living in Geneva, IL at the time of their Mother's death in May 1926. A son William Noble Blair born 1870 and died Apr. 10, 1891. Mr. Robert Blair died many years before his wife.

Jennie was the only woman member of a men's College Fraternity. She was initiated into the Wabash Chapter of Beta Theta Pi in 1867 in appreciation for her kindness to members of the fraternity and for keeping the ritual and chapter records of the Wabash Chapter during the Civil War. Mrs. Blair, up until the time of her death, had worn the badge of Beta Theta Pi, of which fraternity her son, Rev. John Allen Blair, was one of the vice-presidents.

At the time of her death she was living at 314 West Wabash Avenue and was one of the oldest residents of Crawfordsville. She was 93 years of age and was also the oldest member of the Presbyterian Church. *Submitted by Barbara House Taylor, Past President of Beta Mother's Club*

PAUL JR. AND RUTH EBERT BLAKESLEE

Paul and Ruth Blakeslee were married Apr. 9, 1942, in Urbana, IL. They came to Montgomery County in 1945, after World War II. Ruth's parents had moved to a farm in Indiana, and Ruth wanted to be near them. They built a house south of Crawfordsville, on the Ladoga Road. Paul worked at Mid-States Steel & Wire for 35 years. They had five children: Jeanne, born in 1943; James, born in 1946; Patti, born in 1949; Paula, born in 1953; and John, born in 1954.

Paul was active in the PTA of the schools of Whitesville, East Union, and New Market, and was a Boy Scout Leader of Troop 348 at New Market. Both Paul and Ruth were active in church work. Ruth took a three-year correspondence course in creative writing and was published in numerous publications, including *Montgomery Magazine*.

Paul W. and Ruth (Ebert) Blakeslee

Paul was born May 18, 1918, in Davenport, IA, and attended grade school in Peoria, IL, graduating from Keokuk, IA. His parents were Paul and Della Blakeslee. Paul, Sr. was born in 1890 in Montrose, IA, to Mary (Welshimer) and John Blakeslee. Della was born in 1894, in Plymouth, IL, to Edith (Frakes) and (?) Matheney. Paul and Della were married Nov. 11, 1911, and raised six children. Paul, Sr. was in World War I, serving in France. He farmed north of Keokuk.

Ruth was born Feb. 1, 1922, and graduated from Urbana High School. Her father, Ora Ebert, born in 1890 in Ogden, IL, owned Ebert's Grocery. At the same time, he worked at the University of Illinois full time, as a stock clerk, and farmed their six-acre truck farm. Ruth's mother, Daisy, was born in 1898 in Clinton Co., KY, to Ephraim and Desona Neal, who later moved to Urbana, IL. She and Ora were married May 1, 1915, and had ten children. After 1960, Daisy made her home with the Blakeslees, in a trailer. At 91 she still travels extensively, by plane, and drives her car.

Paul, Jr. joined the 106th Cavalry of the National Guard in 1939, and trained in Camp Livingston, LA. The couple lived in Alexandria, LA. He transferred to the 959th Air Base Security Battalion at Camp Campbell, KY, and they lived in Hopkinsville, where Jeanne was born. He served two years in Iceland, as a Master Sergeant.

Two of the Blakeslee offspring remained in Montgomery County: Jeanne (married Fred Deck Jan. 24, 1960) is a sales executive for Nucor Steel, and Patti (married Jim Pearson Feb. 19, 1971) teaches first grade a New Market. James, who was a Lieutenant in the Vietnam War, is a personnel manager at McGraw Edison in Milwaukee, WI (married Judy Banta June 11, 1967); Paula (married Gary Livesay Apr. 28, 1973) is staying home with her children in Colorado; and John (married Vivian Bonham Sept. 1, 1979) is head chemist for Defiance, OH.

The Blakeslees have 16 grandchildren and ten great-grandchildren.

CHARLES AND JEAN BLOCK

Rose Jean Spencer was born July 15, 1922, in Indianapolis. Her family returned to Montgomery County in 1924 and lived there until 1955 when they moved to Florida. Jean met Charles Block at Indiana University. They were married June 9, 1946, in the First Christian Church in Crawfordsville. Jean has carried on the Spencer and McCormick tradition of closeness and devotion to her family. Charles was born May 27, 1922, in Fort Branch, IN. He is a banker and active in civic affairs. In the 1970's he founded Community Banks of Florida, a bank holding company which grew to include 24 banks. Jean and Charles enjoy world travel and have visited over 120 countries, including Antarctica, Tibet, and China. In 1987 they took their children and grandchildren on a picture taking safari in Africa. Jean and Charles have two children, both born in Crawfordsville. Shirley Joan Block was born Apr. 9, 1948. She married Kenneth P. Gould June 17, 1972. Shirley's commitment to family has evolved into her hobby of genealogy. Kenneth is an electrical engineer. They have three children, Chad, Ryan and Jennifer. Roger Earl Block was born Sept. 26, 1952. He married Victoria Mohn Sept. 9, 1972. In 1981 they organized Travel Agents International Inc., a travel franchise with 350 agencies. They have two children, Jason and Jamey. The entire family currently resides in Pinellas Co., FL.

Jean is the only child of Earl Ellis Spencer (Dec. 18, 1887, Parke Co., IN - Apr. 7, 1973, Pinellas Co.,

Charles and Jean Block

FL) and "B" Shirley McCormick (June 21, 1889 near Waveland - Aug. 11, 1942, Crawfordsville). Both Earl and "B" are descended from early Indiana settlers. Earl and "B" married Sept. 12, 1912. Both graduated from Waveland High School, where Earl was captain of the football team, and from Indiana University. "B" devoted her time to her family, church and to helping others. Earl was a businessman and banker in Crawfordsville. He was a family man and was admired for his personal integrity. After the death of "B", Earl married Ethella Barringer (1903-1984) on Jan. 19, 1944. Ethella was a much loved elementary school teacher in Crawfordsville.

Jean's ancestors came to this country in the early 1700's and migrated from the colonies to Kentucky. Jean's great great grandfather, John McCormick, died in 1817 in Kentucky. His wife, Jane Todd McCormick, brought the children to Montgomery Co., IN in the early 1820's. She purchased land north of Waveland. This land has been in the McCormick family ever since. John and Jane's son, Preston McCormick (1807-1864) married Mary Ann Brush (1817-1897). They had ten children, one of whom was Shelby Willis McCormick (1852-1935). Shelby married Margaret Spencer (1859-1909) of Putnam Co., IN on Sept. 19, 1883. They had two daughters, Mary Drew and "B", the mother of our subject. Shelby was a tall gentleman who was stern yet kind. He managed the family farm and owned a hardware store in Waveland.

DAVID C. BOLLMAN

David C. Bollman was born in Ohio in 1843. On Jan. 25, 1876 he married Jennette Busenbark in Montgomery Co., IN. In 1886, David and Jennette moved 6-1/2 miles S.W. of Crawfordsville. They were members of the United Brethren Church.

David had two brothers, Freeman, who had a wooden leg and Joseph E. Bollman who was in the Civil War; he died Jan. 28, 1864 in Natches, MS.

David C. Bollman passed away on Mar. 31, 1912 of heart trouble. Jennette Bollman was born May 19, 1959 in Illinois to John and Sarah Demoret Busenbark and died in 1942 after an illness of 14 months.

Children of David and Jennette were: Minnie, Ada, Roy, Milo, Frank and Jerry.

December 24, 1890, daughter, Minnie married B.F. Vores in the home of her parents. To this union four children were born: Marie, Myrtle, Ray and Leonard, who was a preacher.

Ada Bollman married James (Elby) Emmert in August 1906. This union had one son, Paul.

Roy Bollman married Bertha Deck on July 31, 1915. They had three children: John D., born Feb. 1, 1916; Harold, born Mar. 11, 1917 and Goldie Marie, born Feb. 28, 1918 and died Dec. 4, 1918.

Milo H. Bollman married Eula Emmert (sister of James Emmert) on Dec. 19, 1906. They had one child, Pauline, who married James Wright.

Jerry Bollman married Hannah Miller (Rutan), Apr. 21, 1898; they had one son, Eliza; he married Mae Bayless on Apr. 28, 1917.

Frank C. Bollman was born in Kankakee, IL in April 1883.

He married Clara May Pittman in August 1906 in Montgomery County. Children: Vernida, Wanetta and Frances.

Vernida first married Orville McCormick and had five children: Dorothy, Harry, Phyllis, Paul and Geraldine. Vernida also had a son, Robert Max. Her second marriage was to Elbert Durham and they had no children. Wanetta married a man named Gray and was divorced in the late 40's. Frances married Harry Thompson and they had one son, John and John married and had four children.

There are several descendants of David C. and Jennette Bollman still living in Montgomery County.

CLARENCE BOYD AND JAN MARLENE (MOORE) BONIFACIUS

Clarence Boyd and Jan Marlene (Moore) Bonifacius were married Sept. 3, 1961 at her parents home in Raccoon, IN.

Clarence is the son of Clarence Breeze Bonifacius and Letha (Abbott) Bonifacius. He was born Feb. 5, 1938 in Eubank, KY. Jan Marlene, was born July 14, 1943 in Montgomery Co., IN the daughter of William and Ruth Pauline (Himes) Moore.

Clarence's parents moved their family from Kentucky to the Linden area. They farmed four miles west of Linden. Clarence Breeze worked at the Cherry Grove Elevator, also.

Clarence Boyd and Jan Marlene (Moore) Bonifacius

Clarence Boyd started to school at Linden, IN. Jan Marlene started to school in the large two story red brick school house at Whitesville, IN. She later attended the East Union School north east of Crawfordsville. Her parents lived five miles south of Crawfordsville on a large farm until they bought a farm in Putnam County in the 1950's and moved there. Jan Marlene then graduated from the Roachdale, IN school.

Clarence's parents moved to Roachdale area where his parents also farmed. This is where the subjects of this memoir met - at Roachdale, IN high school ball game.

They lived in Roachdale after their marriage moving to Indianapolis for a few years where he worked. They moved to Mt. Vernon, IL and own the Accurate Automotive Manufacturing Company in that city. Clarence is a member of the Mt. Vernon Chamber of Commerce and the Lions Club and is active in community functions. He is a motorcycle enthusiast.

Jan is a bookkeeper for their business and also works for a Fame Implement Dealer. They both enjoy photography. They belong to the Southwest Church of Christ at Mt. Vernon, IL. Their children are Deborah Jean, born Apr. 7, 1963 at Crawfordsville, IN, Ruby Lynn, born July 1964 at Greencastle and Diana Bonifacius, born Dec. 21, 1972 at Mt. Vernon, IL — died Dec. 22, 1972. She is buried at the Roachdale, IN Cemetery by Clarence Breeze Bonifacius, who died Oct. 4, 1972. Also, two sons of Clarence Boyd by a previous marriage. Kevin Boyd, born Aug. 26, 1957 and Kim Lee Feb. 13, 1959.

Kevin Bonifacius married Connie Miller June 3, 1978, their sons are Clayton Boyd, born Mar. 24, 1981 and Cole Bradley Bonifacius, born July 20, 1985.

Kim Lee married Barbara Moore on Apr. 18, 1986 and Justin Lee was born July 6, 1987. Kim Lee has two children from previous marriages. April Dawn born July 24, 1978 and Joshua Ray born Dec. 31, 1982. Deborah Jean Bonifacius married Jimmie Lockwood (div.) their sons are James Boyd Lockwood, born Feb. 7, 1982 and William Blaine Lockwood born Aug. 4, 1983.

Jan Marlene Bonifacius graduated from Rend Lake College with Honors and Associate in Arts Degree on June 2, 1974, attending college after they moved to Mt. Vernon.

Their residence is on their farm in Mt. Vernon Township northeast of Mt. Vernon, IL. Rural Route #7. (Jan is a descendant of many Montgomery County settlers.)

BONWELL FAMILY

James Bonwell was a soldier in the Revolutionary War from February 1776 to February 1778. He was a corporal and sergeant in the 9th Virginia Regiment. His surname has been spelled both Bonwell and Bonewell. James was born in Scotland and emigrated to the American Colonies where he settled in Virginia. Married Mary Robin in 1769; died in Brown Co., OH in 1820. Fathered three children; Arthur, Mary, and Borden.

Robert Allen Bonwell, Linda Jane (Malsbury) Bonwell, Earl J. Bonwell, Elizabeth Opal (Bonwell) Sayler

John Bonwell was born in Virginia in 1799 and died near Clarksville, IA. He was married three times and fathered 11 children. His first wife was Elizabeth Stafford of North Carolina. She died in 1848 in Shawnee, IN. In 1850, he married Rebecca Combs in Montgomery Co., IN. His third wife was Elizabeth McKee. They were married in Highland Co., OH, in 1855.

James Addison, son of John and Elizabeth was born Sept. 1, 1822 and died in Boswell, IN Dec. 31, 1895. He married Elizabeth Sayers Aug. 3, 1848. Elizabeth was born Feb. 28, 1829 in Taswell Co., VA. They had two children, Elizabeth M. and

Robert Allen. Robert Allen was born July 28, 1853. On Mar. 30, 1882, he married Linda Jane, or Jennie, Malsbury. Jennie was born Apr. 3, 1859. They had two children; Earl J. and Elizabeth Opal. Earl J. was born Mar. 14, 1884. Elizabeth Opal, or Opal as she preferred, was born Jan. 20, 1888. At the time, they lived on a farm in Tippecanoe County, located six miles north of New Richmond, IN.

In 1906, Robert and Linda bought a farm in Montgomery County located one mile south and one mile east of New Market. They moved their family from Tippecanoe County to the farm located on the north side of the road across from Fairview School on what is now 700 south and US 231. He lived there for several years before moving to Crawfordsville, IN in 1922. He was elected Montgomery County Road Superintendent and served in that position for many years. It should be noted that they believed in helping their fellow man and opened up their farm home to two homeless children in addition to their own growing family. A young girl, May, who married Park White lived in the Waveland area, and Frank Martz. They were provided shelter until they were able to be on their own.

Being faithful members of the New Market Methodist Church, they made the journey from Crawfordsville for the Sunday services on a regular basis. While at Sunday services on Oct. 8, 1933, Linda Bonwell was stricken with a sudden illness and died during the worship service. Robert died a few months later at the country home of his son Earl J. where Robert and Linda had started their farm in Montgomery County. Both are buried in Sugar Grove Cemetery.

Earl J. married Ruth Hoss Feb. 16, 1910. They had two children; Robert Paul and David Earl. Elizabeth Opal married Walter L. Sayler Oct. 23, 1912. They had five children; Robert Francis, Lois Esther, Charles Bayard, Ralph Addison and Barbara Jane.

The farm is still in the Bonwell name as of this writing.

BOOE FAMILY

The name Booe was derived from those who came from Rotterdam Holland as Bühe. The Indiana Booe's mostly settled in the Scotts Prairie Community, Fountain County. John Austin Booe (1840-1924) son of Lorenzo Dow Booe and Ellen Matilda Moffet came to Crawfordsville in the late 1870's as a partner of a relative Moffet who had a drug store on Main Street. He married Eva May (1854-1937) whose father was "the father of the Crawfordsville Medical fraternity" — Willis Lafayette May who started practice in 1847. To them were born John Austin Booe, Jr. and Lee May Booe. John Austin Booe, Jr. (1885-1927) married Lily Beth Miller (1893-1981) in 1916. The Miller family lived on West Wabash Avenue where the parking lot of R.R. Donnelleys is now. Two wonderful houses were once there; the homes of the Millers and the Gerard families. To John Austin Booe and Lily Beth Miller was born one daughter, Barbara Lee Booe, Sept. 4, 1918.

John Austin Booe, Jr. had come home from the west coast to take over his father's place in the Nye-Booe Drug Company. Eva May Booe's sister, Harriet had married Marshall Nye. Marshall Nye and John Austin Booe, Sr. had started a drug store in the building that Dr. May owned. He practiced medicine upstairs — the drug store was downstairs.

Barbara Lee Booe grew-up in the house she now lives in — 219 East College — the house Dr. May had built for his daughter Eva and her husband. Next door lived Harriet and Marshall Nye. Nye-Booe on the corner and Nye-Booe down town.

Barbara went to Willson school and graduated from Crawfordsville High School. She attended Transylvania University for three years and transferred to Indiana State Teachers College in 1939 and graduated in 1940. Barbara's father died in 1927; her mother remarried in 1935 to Joseph A. Gremelspacher, band director in Crawfordsville from 1929 to 1939. Beth and Joe operated the "Dobe Inn," a restaurant which occupied the space now known as the Union Federal Savings & Loan.

After graduation from college, Barbara taught two years and then married Jack Bushong. After returning to Crawfordsville, she taught school at "Old Tuttle," Hoover School, and Tuttle Junior High School for 25 years — happy years.

Now retired, Barbara is active in community affairs.

John, son of Jack and Barbara (Booe) Bushong was born Jan. 29, 1944. He graduated from Crawfordsville High School in 1961, received his A.B. from Denison University in Granville, OH, and his M.D. from Indiana University. His speciality is Emergency Medicine which he practices with 12 partners. They are attached to Tri-City Hospital in Oceanside, CA. He and his first wife, Alayne Ginsberg, are parents of two children, Aaron who is a freshman at the University of California, Riverside, and Aimee, a sophomore in high school at Aurora, CO. His second wife, Nancy Lowman, has a son who is a senior in high school and will enter the University of California at Riverside in September. They have a little son, Ian, who is three years old. *Submitted by Barbara Bushong*

THE BOOHER-HAMPTON FAMILIES

Prior to the year of 1800, two closely related intermarried families, the Boohers and Hamptons, lived in the mountains of Sullivan Co., TN.

Seeking a new and better life in the then unsettled fertile farmland of Indiana, Gurdianias and Mahala Hampton Booher and their children, Rhoda E., Jacob, Catherine and Mary (Polly), (twins) and John M. left Tennessee Sept. 23, 1830, arriving in Montgomery Co., IN, Oct. 23, 1830. They settled in northeast Franklin Township, entering land there from the government in 1832.

In October 1834, 37 members of the two families, with their entire belongings loaded in wagons, started for Indiana. They stopped near the little town of Crawfordsville, where the land office was then located. There the majority of them entered land in northeast Franklin Township at a cost of $1.25 per acre. Making the journey were Jacob and Elizabeth Barnett Booher and children, Elizabeth, John M., Jonathan, Jacob Jr., Ambrose, Lucinda, Benjamin, and Leander. (Jacob's first wife, Catherine Barnett, deceased, was a sister to his second wife, Elizabeth); William and Rhoda Hampton Booher and daughters, Elzira and Elizabeth; John and Margaret Zimmerlie Booher and children, Benjamin, John Jacob, William K., Nathaniel, Mary, Nathan, Margaret, Isaac, Elkanah, Susannah Catherine and Jonathan A.; Samuel and Catherine Booher and son, Irenus (Hink); Michael and Catherine Booher Hampton and children, Sarah Ann, Selina, Margaret Jane, Samuel and James (Michael's first wife, Mary Booher, deceased, the mother of Sarah Ann, Selina, Margaret Jane and Samuel, was a half-sister to his second wife, Catherine.) Jesse Baird made the trip with them.

The land was an unbroken forest so there was plenty of hard work. There was the cabin to build, the land to clear and crops to plant among the stumps. There was game in abundance for meat, so that everything was more plentiful than money. Tradition says that Michael Hampton secured a contract from the government to carry mail from Crawfordsville to Kirklin, a distance of 40 miles. He mounted his son Samuel, then in his 12th year, on a good strong horse and once a week, the boy made the trip each way, winding his way through the unbroken wilderness, fording rough frozen streams, regardless of the weather, thus adding his mite to the family income.

Several changes occurred in the two families in the succeeding years. Gurdianias and Mahala Hampton Booher became parents of William, Rhoda, Ward Hampton, Cyrus, Samuel, Lydia, Ira, Elihu and Ephraim R. After the death of Mahala, Gurdianias married Narcessa Boots. After the death of Rhoda Hampton Booher, William married Lydia Kenworthy Cox. They were the parents of Rhoda K., Martha C., Albert W., and Mary Catherine. Sylvanus W. Booher was born to John and Margaret Zimmerlie Booher. Michael and Catherine Booher Hampton became parents of Martin, Elizabeth, Mahala, John, Morgan, Joseph N. and Martha E.

The Boohers and Hamptons contributed much to the farming interest in the township. They were influential in the organization of the Saint James Lutheran Church, a religious faith to which they were dedicated and where the men continued to serve in official capacities throughout their lives.

The writer and many other direct descendants of these hardy mountaineers still live in Montgomery County. *Submitted by Mary Hampton Price*

AMOS BOONE

The Boone family came to Montgomery County in the early 1930's from Kentucky. Amos Boone moved from Mt. Sterling, KY to Indiana with his wife Lena in 1906. There were three children in the family when they settled in the county. Joe, the oldest son, married Mamie Lee Morrison and settled in Darlington. They had two sons David and Alan who both graduated from Wabash College. The second child was Cora Vivian Boone who lived most of her life in California. The youngest of the Boone family was George who married Bertha Peffley of the pioneer Peffley family of Clark Township. George and Bert had two sons, Daniel born in 1935 and Bill, born in 1938. The Boone family lived in Ladoga from 1934 until Bert's death in 1971. The eldest son Dan married Mary Ann Riley of Indianapolis. They had eight children: Steve, Beth, Cheryl, Mark, David John, Mary Pat and Connie. The youngest son, Bill married a New Ross girl, Doris Frederick in 1956. The couple had four children: Kathy, Scott, Chris and Cindy.

Bill graduated from Ladoga High School in 1945 and Wabash College in 1960. The family then moved to Covington where he taught for five years before going to Purdue University to do graduate work in guidance and counseling. He then taught at Fountain Central High School for 17 years before taking a teaching job in Crawfordsville High School where he now teaches. All four Boone children graduated from Fountain Central. Kathy graduated in 1975 and is presently finishing a degree in Physical Education at Indiana State University. She is married to Steve Apple, a 1972 graduate

The Boone Family seated L to R: Dan, Bertha, George and Bill. Taken in 1952.

of Darlington. They have three children: Jennifer, 13, Jessica, six and Janessa, four. Steve is the assistant manager of the Mike Madrid Company of Lafayette. Scott Boone graduated from high school in 1977 starring in football, basketball and baseball before going on to Wabash College and continuing to be a standout in the same three sports. Scott graduated from Wabash in 1981 and is now coaching football and baseball at his alma mater. He is married to the former Jacci Vaught. The couple has one daughter, Bryana. The third child, Chris Anne graduated in 1978 after participating in basketball there. She then graduated from Indiana State University in 1982 and taught at Covington, Coal Creek Central and North Montgomery before returning to ISU to teach freshman writing. She is married to Dale Grubbs, a prominent Hillsboro farmer who raises registered black angus cattle and is known nation-wide for his championship stock. The Grubb's have one child, Kayla Jo who is nearly three. The fourth Boone is Cynthia Jo who was in the first cosmetology class at Fountain Central High School. She attended ISU for one semester and now works for a local oral surgeon, Dr. Richard Walker. She is married to Brad Hesler who is employed by R.R. Donnelley Co. They have one son, Christopher, eight, who lives with them on Main Street in Hillsboro.

The Montgomery County Boones are descended from Edward Boone, the younger brother of Daniel Boone, the famous wilderness scout, explorer and Indian fighter. Edward was killed by the Indians while on a scouting party with his brother in 1780.

THE BOOTS FAMILY

The earliest records of the Boots family go back to Germany (some say Holland) with Adam Stiefel's (the German word for Boot) marriage to Eve _____.

From this marriage came Adam Stiefel II b. 1767. He married Elizabeth Ketterman. They had a son Jacob b. Apr. 17, 1788, d. Oct. 27, 1851 in Darlington.

We have to assume that the Stiefels emigrated to the United States in the latter part of the 18th century or in the early 1800's. The name was changed to Boots ca. 1812. They settled in what was called "Old Virginia" near the Petersons and Haglers.

The Petersons moved into Ohio and wrote back for the other two families to join them in Ohio. The Boots and Haglers bought adjoining farms near Xenia, OH. The Petersons came to Indiana in 1834 settling in Sugar Creek Township in Montgomery County. Census records show the Boots also came during the decade 1830-1840.

Jacob had married Anna Hagler, Dec. 12, 1813. Anna was born June 30, 1792, the daughter of Mary Susanna (Peterson) Hagler. She died Apr. 9, 1838 in Darlington. Their son Eli, b. January 1815 in Green Co., OH d. Sept. 22, 1876 in Darlington.

Eli married Martha Cunningham, b. Jan. 31, 1816 (or 11) in Rockbridge Co., VA d. Feb. 6, 1866 in Darlington. Their children were James F., William H., Samuel, Jacob (died in the Civil War), Ike, presumably Isaac, and a daughter. By his second wife, Margaret, he had Clara and Robert.

Eli's brother Asa had a daughter who married Nate Turnipseed and her father bought her the farm on the corner. This crossroad about five miles north of Darlington still goes by the name of "Turnipseed's Corner". The old brick Boots schoolhouse still stands nearby.

In earlier times this area was known as Bootsville and were all of the Presbyterian denomination. The land was bought from the government and has never been sold outside the Boots families.

Asa bought land on the south side of the east-west road and Eli bought 500 acres on the north side.

Eli's son William H., b. Jan. 7, 1840, d. Oct. 21, 1914 in Darlington, married Martha Hughes in March of 1860. She was b. Aug. 6, 1846 and d. Dec. 24, 1918 in Darlington. Their children were Eli Gilmore, Newton, Wesley, Florence, Emma (Pet) and Virginia (Jenny). Martha (Mattie) besides raising her own six children, also raised her daughter's three little girls since Emma died at a relatively young age. Her daughter Jenny, who married Al Cornell also died young and left three small sons, Floyd, Homer and Lowell Cornell. For a few years she also raised Robert Boots whose mother died when he was about seven days old.

William H. Boots told his grandchildren that during the Civil War he would fill two market baskets full of one dollar bills, worth only 3¢ on the dollar and ride horseback into Darlington to buy staples.

William's son, Eli Gilmore Boots, married Sarah Elizabeth Grimes, the daughter of David Grimes and Phebe Armstrong and granddaughter of John and Sarah Marten Armstrong. Elizabeth, b. Apr. 3, 1873 was confirmed into Saint James Lutheran Church on Feb. 7, 1886. *Submitted by Joyce T. Boots*

THE FAMILY OF ELI AND MARTHA BOOTS

Eli Boots, Sr. was born on Jan. 11, 1815, to Jacob and Anna Boots in Greene Co., OH. He married Martha Lackey, date and place of birth unknown, in Greene Co., OH on Apr. 17, 1834.

All of the children of Eli and Martha were born in Montgomery County. This means they were established in the county before 1836. They built a log cabin at first. Then in 1849 they built the home pictured below. It was built almost completely of walnut timber taken from the family farm. In later years this house was called the "weaning house" since it was used by their off spring as a first home. The picture below was taken in 1955.

Eli, Sr., died on Aug. 22, 1876, in Montgomery County. Martha, age unknown, died in 1866, in Montgomery County.

Children: James Franklin Boots, July 4, 1836; Isica Gillmor Boots, Jan. 3, 1838; William Harrison Boots, Jan. 7, 1840; Samuel Boots, Dec. 19, 1842 - named for uncle who died the year before; Isabella Boots, June 25, 1845; Jacob Boots, born Apr. 17, 1849; and Elvina June Boots, born July 22, 1852.

All births took place in Sugar Creek Township, Montgomery County.

FAMILY OF JACOB AND ANNA BOOTS

Jacob Boots was born Apr. 7, 1788; the name of his parents and place of birth are unknown. According to the records of the German Society of Pennsylvania a Jacob Boots landed at Philadelphia during 1788, with the country of origin being listed as Germany.

The surname Boots is found in southern Holland. The easiest route to a seaport from this part of Holland would have been across the border into the then Holy Roman Empire. At this time the various free cities were referred to as Germany. This was in contrast to the several German kingdoms of Bavaria, Prussia, Hanover, and so on.

The Boots who landed at Philadelphia in 1788 could have been either Jacob's father, or the date given in the family Bible could have been the date he arrived in the United States.

On Dec. 12, 1813, Jacob married Anna Hagler, who was born on Dec. 12, 1792. The place of their marriage is unknown. They settled in Greene Co., OH, near Xenia, sometime before 1815.

Jacob moved to Montgomery Co., IN, during 1838. He joined his sons on land purchased earlier north of Darlington in Sugar Creek Township.

Jacob died on Oct. 25, 1851, in Montgomery County. Anna died on Sept. 9, 1838, the location was not given.

Children: Eli Boots, Sr., Jan. 11, 1815; Mary Ann Boots, Dec. 4, 1816; Ashel Boots, May 10, 1820; Phebe Boots, Feb. 17, 1819; and Samuel Boots, Dec. 21, 1821 - died during 1841.

All births occurred in Greene Co., OH.

LAWRENCE GRIMES BOOTS

Lawrence was the son of Eli Gilmore and Sarah Elizabeth (Grimes) Boots. He was born Dec. 22, 1908. He graduated from Darlington High School and Purdue University, School of Electrical Engineering in 1932. While in college he was a member of the American Institute of Electrical Engineers (AIEE) and after college was a loyal and long standing member of the John Purdue Club. He was a member of the Darlington United Methodist Church and his hobbies were reading and following the Purdue football team. He was able to see Purdue win the Rosebowl in 1967. While in California, he visited his sister, Pearl Hoffman.

His siblings were Mrs. Clyde (Nevah) Misner, Mrs. Lawrence (Juanita) Lockhart, Mrs. Donald (Beatrice) Davidson, Mrs. Gayle (Lois) Cohee, and Mrs. Charles (Viola Pearl) Hoffman.

On Oct. 14, 1933, Lawrence married Joyce Alma Thompson in the Presbyterian Church in Dayton, IN. Joyce was the daughter of Everard and Nona (Dryer) Thompson. David Gregory, a great uncle, named the town of Dayton in Tippecanoe County for Dayton, OH from whence he emigrated. The

Boots Home

farm where she was born was a governmental grant from President Thomas Jefferson. Joyce is a member of the Tippecanoe County Historical Society, the American Daffodil Society, a charter member of the Indiana Daffodil Society, a retired National Judge of Daffodils and a member of Dorothy Q Chapter of DAR.

Their one daughter, Diantha Naylor Boots, is married to Walter T. Martin, Jr. formerly of Brownsburg and who is Purchasing Superintendent of General Motors in Flint, MI. He graduated from Purdue in 1965. Diantha graduated from Darlington High School in 1960 and from Purdue in 1964, majoring in plant pathology. She is now employed as Naturalist for Genessee County in Flint. They have two children, Cyd (Martin) Sturba, a secretary, and Adam Dryer Martin, a sophomore at the University of Michigan.

Joyce graduated from Dayton High School in 1926 and attended Purdue University. She still lives in the house in Darlington which she and Lawrence purchased in 1939.

Lawrence was employed at R.R. Donnelley and Sons for 35 years and at the time of his death on Oct. 25, 1970, he was a supervisor of Department C.M. He was preceded in death by a son, David Lawrence, who died in infancy on Aug. 24, 1937.
Submitted by Joyce T. Boots

FAMILY OF LAWRENCE AND STELLA BOOTS

Lawrence Chayce Boots was born on Nov. 26, 1928, to Wallace and Merl Boots in Montgomery County. He was educated at the Youngs Chapel and Crawfordsville schools. Lawrence served in the Indiana National Guard, 139th Field Artillery between 1949 and 1952.

Lawrence married Stella Bell Jan. 21, 1950, at Alamo. She was born on Jan. 7, 1930 to Alonzo Earl and Martha (Hatt) Bell at Linnsburg, Montgomery County.

Lawrence worked at R.R. Donnelly as a press operator until 1952. At that time he joined with his brother, Samuel, in a Shell Oil jobbership, which later became Boots Brothers Shell Oil Company.

During most of their married life Lawrence and Stella lived in and near New Market. He was active in the New Market Volunteer Fire Department for 25 years. Both were members of the New Market Christian Church. Lawrence was a member of the Masonic Lodge, and Stella the Eastern Star. In the late 1970's Lawrence served as precinct committeeman for the Republican Party from Brown Township Precinct #5.

Lawrence died in April 1981, at St. Elizabeth Hospital, Lafayette, IN, after a long illness with cancer.

Children: Robert Chayce Boots, born Aug. 17, 1952 and Michael Logan Boots, born May 4, 1955.

All births occurred in Montgomery County.

ROBERT AND PHYLLIS BOOTS

Robert and Phyllis Boots reside in Sugar Creek township, Montgomery County. Robert is engaged in grain farming and works as a security guard in the fall and winter months.

Robert was born in 1927 about a mile north of where he presently lives. He is the second of three children born to Paul and Alta Reeder Boots. He attended Bowers School, then served 18 months in the Air Force. After the service, he returned to help his father farm. In 1948 he married Phyllis Bradshaw in Colfax, IN, and started farming on his own, always living in Sugar Creek township.

Two daughters, Joanna Kuchler, also of Sugar Creek township, and Roberta Fulk, of Dayton, IN, were born to this couple. They have four grandchildren.

Robert's father Paul was born in 1900 in the homestead where Robert currently lives. He was the fifth of nine children born to George and Anna Dykes Boots. In 1920 Paul married Alta Reeder, who was born in 1900 at Antwerp, OH. The family moved to Indiana when she was a small child. Her parents were Frank and Lorena Munson Reeder. The other children of Paul and Alta were a son Jack, born in 1921, and died in 1986; and a daughter Rosann Carter, born in 1931, now living in Port Charlotte, FL. Paul died in 1958 and Alta in 1975.

Phyllis was born in 1928 at Colfax, IN, to Addison S. and Mary S. Parks Bradshaw. She is the 12th of 15 children. She graduated from Colfax High School in 1946, and was employed as a secretary before her marriage.

Phyllis' father Addison S. Bradshaw was born in Boone Co., IN, in 1882 and died in 1951. He worked as a carpenter and a general contractor. In 1905 he married Mary S. Parks, also of Boone Co., IN. She was born in 1888 and died in 1964. In 1906 they moved to Colfax, IN, where they lived a few years, then moved to the country where they raised their 15 children; nine of whom are still living at this writing.

The farmstead of Robert and Phyllis has been in the Boots family for many generations. Jacob Boots and his family moved to this place in 1833, from Montgomery Co., OH. His son Asachel married and remained to farm and raise a family of three; Martha Boots Turnipseed, Ellen Boots, and George Boots.

George was next in line to live on the farm. Upon his death and that of his wife Anna, their son Paul and his family lived there. After her husband's death, Alta remained on the farm for nine years. She moved into Colfax, IN, in 1967, at which time our subjects moved to the farm.

ROBERT AND SUSAN BOOTS

Robert Chayce Boots was born on Aug. 17, 1952, to Lawrence and Stella Boots in Montgomery County. He graduated from New Market High School in 1970.

Robert married Susan Lynn Branstetter on Aug. 12, 1972, at the New Market Christian Church. She was born on June 23, 1954, to John Ward and Charlotte Ann (Ewbank) Branstetter in Montgomery County. Susan graduated from South Montgomery High School in 1972.

Susan, Robert and Kristin Boots

Robert received a Bachelor of Science degree from Indiana State University in 1975, and a Master of Arts from the Pennsylvania State University in 1983. He served on active duty in the U.S. Army from 1977 to 1981. Afterwards he served as the first audiovisual archivist for the U.S. Army Military History Institute from 1981 to 1984, at Carlisle Barracks, PA. He then became assistant state archivist for the State of Indiana from 1984 to 1985. A short period was served as historian for the Air Force Wright Aeronautical Laboratories, Wright-Patterson AFB, Dayton, OH, during 1985-86. Robert is currently working for H-C Industries, Crawfordsville, IN.

Susan attended Indiana State University from 1975 to 1977. She graduated with an Associate of Arts Degree from Harrisburg Area Community College in 1980. She attended the Indiana Vocational and Technical Training College in 1986. Susan earned an Associate in Science - Nursing from the University of the State of New York in 1987. Susan is currently a registered nurse at Methodist Hospital of Indiana.

They reside at 201 North Franklin Street, Ladoga, IN.

Children: Kristin Sue Boots, born May 2, 1979, at Carlisle, PA.

SAMUEL BOOTS FAMILY

Samuel Boots was born to Eli and Martha Lackey Boots Dec. 19, 1842, in Sugar Creek Township, Montgomery County. He served in the Civil War with Co. G, 11th Reg. of Indiana Volunteers. Samuel was mustered into the military service of the United States at Indianapolis, by LTC Wood, on Aug. 31, 1861, for a period of three years service. His age was listed as 19, complexion - dark, height - 5'6", occupation - farmer. His father, Eli, did not want him to serve and for a short time disinherited him. During the Battle of Champion Hills, Vicksburg Campaign, May 16, 1863, Samuel was wounded in the leg by canister shot. He recovered in an army hospital and was mustered from service Aug. 30, 1864, at Harpers Ferry, VA.

Samuel was married three times, wives are as follows.

Samuel Boots Family

First: Martha Bowers, born May 8, 1848, in Montgomery County. Date of marriage is unknown, but between 1863 and 1865. Martha died on June 25, 1877, during child birth.

Children: Mary Bell Boots, Jan. 2, 1866; Nella Grant Boots, Feb. 15, 1867; Charles Ellsworth Boots, Sept. 23, 1867; Willard Samuel Boots, Aug. 8, 1871; Annettie Josephine Boots, June 25, 1873; and Martha Laurena Boots, June 25, 1877.

Second: Mary Dunbar, date of birth unknown. Date of marriage unknown. She took her own life Aug. 7, 1883.

Children: Roy Garfield Boots, Dec. 17, 1879.

Third: Ellen Logan Forthner, born on Mar. 23, 1853, in Putnam County. They were married on June 12, 1890, at Lebanon, IN. The above photo was taken in 1898.

Children: Wallace Logan Boots, Apr. 10, 1891.

Samuel died on Dec. 18, 1919, in Montgomery County. He is buried in the Bowers Cemetery north of Darlington. Ellen died on Apr. 24, 1945, at the Indiana Soldiers Home, Lafayette, IN.

WALLACE AND MERL BOOTS

Wallace Logan Boots was born to Samuel and Ellen Boots on Apr. 10, 1891, in Montgomery County. He married Merl V. Buskirk on Dec. 3, 1907. She was born on May 14, 1890, in White County, near Ashland.

Wallace attended Bowers School and worked afterward as a farmer and carpenter. He and Merl resided with Samuel Boots on the Maple Lane Farm, R.F.D. #30, Box #60, Clarks Hill until the late 1920's. This farm was lost in the economic slump of the period. The family moved to Smartsburg, New Market, and Darlington until moving to 801 South John Street Crawfordsville in 1944.

Wallace and Merl Boots

Wallace was active in the Montgomery County Farm Bureau, Farmer's Co-Op Creamery, and the Republican Party during various periods of his life. He was active in the Masonic Lodge and served as master of the Miller Lodge #268, at Clarks Hill in 1923. He was raised to the degree of Master Mason at Darlington Lodge #186 on Apr. 9, 1919.

Wallace and Merl celebrated their 50th wedding anniversary on Dec. 2, 1957, at the Crawfordsville Municipal Clubhouse. All family members were present. The above photograph was taken for that occasion.

Wallace died on Mar. 2, 1965, at his home after a long illness. Merl died on Apr. 30, 1974, at Culver Union Hospital of heart failure. Both are buried in the Bowers Cemetery north of Darlington.

Children: Samuel Lavaun Boots, Dec. 1, 1911; Lois May Boots, Apr. 18, 1917; and Lawrence Chayce Boots, Nov. 26, 1928.

All births occurred in Sugar Creek Township, Montgomery County.

JOHN A. BOWERMAN

The Bowerman family's Montgomery County History dates back to 1834. John's personal history began in the small community of Alamo when he was born Sept. 27, 1921, joining sisters Ida and Estel and big brother Tom. His parents were John H. and Myrtle Iva (Roberts) Bowerman. John grew up on the family farm and graduated from the high school there (1939), then Wabash College in 1943. He began his career, teaching for one year at Darlington High School. He loved sports, so began the coaching portion of his career the next year at Covington. In 1945, he coached and taught at Bowers High School and later became principal there. He earned his Master's Degree from Indiana State University. While at Bowers, John met Marjorie Hungate, the daughter of Ray and Florence Scott Hungate.

John Bowerman

They were married July 12, 1946 in Crawfordsville. John and Marjorie would become the parents of two fine sons, Dick (now a Cardiologist in Tampa, FL) and Brian (a teacher/coach at Southmont). Laura, Dick's daughter and Ryan, Brian's son were John's pride! John was also principal of Darlington and in 1957 became County Superintendent of Schools. In 1960, he switched careers — assistant trust officer 1st National Bank (now Bank 1); the next year becoming Senior Trust Officer (until 1985 when he retired). He also served as Vice President. Even though John's career was now banking, he never waivered from his educational interests — he was a charter member of the adult chapter of Fellowship of Christian Athletes, a 12-year member and Past President of the Crawfordsville School Board, a spectator of a multitude of county (as well as Wabash) games and at his death, was serving on a finding committee for a new organization — the Montgomery County Education Foundation. Besides these organizations, John also belonged to the Alamo Mason (and Eastern Star), Kiwanis, Ouiatenon, Lew Wallace Advisor, Red Cross, Oak Hill Cemetery investment advisor, board member of Friends of the Library, City Plan Commission and treasurer of Boys Club.

John was the recipient of a great number of awards; Rotary Club's Paul Harris Fellow, Christian Nursing Service award, Harmony Award from the Barber Shop Quartet, Wabash Alumni Merit, and in 1968, John received the Sagamore of the Wabash from Governor Robert Orr.

John also served as elder in First Christian Church.

There were other interests in John's life — a major one being history! John held the position of County Historian at the time of his death. He was past president of the Montgomery County Historical Society and was author of "Profiles of Inspiration," (his monthly column in *Montgomery County Magazine*), where he paid tribute to some of the most wonderful people who ever lived in our county. Typical of John, it was requested that contributions be sent to 1) athletic department at Southmont 2) Local History Room of the Crawfordsville District Public Library upon his death (which occurred Nov. 1, 1988).

Words can not express the sorrow felt by any one who knew John Bowerman upon the knowledge of his passing away. In this history book, let it be known that we all must feel a great happiness to have even known such a "Profile of Inspiration!"

Information obtained from article in *Journal-Review* at the time of his death and December 1988 *Montgomery County Magazine*. Written by Karen Zach (with permission of Marjorie, John's devoted wife of 42 plus years!)

THOMAS AND HAZEL BOWERMAN

Tom Bowerman is a native of Ripley Township. He was born son of John and Iva Bowerman on Oct. 16, 1913. His great grandfather came from Butler Co., OH in 1834 and purchased 80 acres of land in Ripley Township on which Tom now resides.

Tom graduated from Alamo H.S. and Wabash College and has a Masters Degree from Indiana State University. He was a teacher and coach in Montgomery County for 37 years. Coaching at Alamo for 22 years and Waynetown for five years, he continued teaching at Waynetown for ten years until his retirement in 1976. He taught Sunday School classes at the Alamo Christian Church for many years and presently serves there as elder.

Hazel (Melvin) Bowerman was born in Kansas City, KS in 1908 and graduated from Baldwin H.S. in Kansas City. She came to Indiana in 1927. She was active in the Alamo Christian Church, teaching the Women's Bible Class for many years and working in the Ladies Aid. She was also active in Home Economics Club, Order of Eastern Star and Rainbow for Girls.

Tom, Hazel, Judith, Charles and Patricia Bowerman

Tom and Hazel were married in Chicago Temple in Chicago on Dec. 26, 1935. They were married for 52 years before Hazel passed away on Mar. 27, 1988. Three children were born of this union - Charles Leo, Patricia Ethel and Judith Lynn.

Charles graduated from Alamo H.S. and Wabash College where he was an outstanding basketball player. After graduating from Wabash in 1961, he played basketball with the Phillips Oilers AAU team. That team won the national AAU tourney in 1962, traveled to Russia, the Middle East and South America playing several games in these areas of the world. He retired from basketball after four years but remained with the company presently holding the position of Senior Vice-President of Marketing. Charles married Coralea Weir in 1960 and they have three children; Cynthia, Cristina and Candice.

Patricia graduated from Waynetown H.S. and Purdue University. In 1967 she married Ronald Bryant, also a graduate of Waynetown and Purdue University. After graduation from Purdue, they both started teaching at Waynetown H.S. In 1971 they both transferred to the new North Montgomery H.S. Pat coached basketball one year at N.M., then Pat and Ron both served as volleyball and gymnastics coaches from 1972-1980. They took volleyball teams to the state tournament in 1977 and 1979 and had some state winners in gymnastics during that time. Pat and Ron have a daughter Sara who attends New Market Elementary School.

Judith graduated from Waynetown H.S. and Indiana University. In 1969 she married Joseph Bratton, a graduate of Waynetown H.S. and Wabash College. Immediately after their marriage, they served one year in the Peace Corps in Sierra Leone, Africa. After their return, Judy continued her studies in Medical School and received her degree from Ohio State. She presently serves as a doctor in Mount Carmel Hospital in Columbus but plans to go into private practice in the next year in Lancaster, OH. Joe is employed by Hewlett Packard Computer Co. The Brattons have two children, Matthew and Abby and live on a 140 acre farm south of Columbus, OH.

KARLE STEELE BOYER

Karle Steele Boyer was born June 22, 1896 in Lafayette, IN to Charles Alonzo Boyer and Mary Alice "Mayme" Steele. Her story appears elsewhere in this book. His ties to Montgomery County go back to his great-great grandparents, David Wray and his wife Martha Passmore, who migrated here in 1824 from Butler Co., OH, and his great-great-great grandfather, Nathan Britton, who came in 1829, also from Butler County. Martha Passmore Wray's family history in the United States goes back to her ancestor John Sharples(s) who left Chester County, England because of persecution for his belief in the Quaker religion. He purchased 1000 acres of land in Chester Co. (now Delaware Co.), PA from William Penn and arrived in this country in August 1682, two months before Mr. Penn.

Karle moved to Chicago, IL as a small child and then moved on to Denver, CO, and, subsequently, back to Chicago. As a youth in Denver, he became interested in softball and played in a league. He maintained a life-long interest in baseball as a result. He organized, and was the first president of, the Peoria Booster Club for the Chicago Cubs. He held an honorary life membership in the Peoria Oldtimers Baseball Club. He was a life member of the Masonic Order, having joined in 1923 at Chicago, IL. He served in the infantry from Illinois during World War I in Boshenen, France.

He was married on Nov. 24, 1920 in Chicago to Elsie Fraser, a Chicago native, daughter of Scottish immigrants William Fraser and Elspeth MacDonald. They had four children: Lois Karel, Marel Catherine, William Elsworth and Wanda Ruth.

Lois, born in Chicago currently lives in Peoria, IL, where she was married in 1945 to John Frank Lipka, born in Elizabeth, NJ. They have two children: Robert John and Mary Anne, both born in Peoria. Bob works for the Bendix Corp. in North Carolina where he lives with his wife, the former Rebecca Lorene Dodge, and their daughters Stephanie, Theresa and Sarah. Mary Anne is a freelance writer in the Chicago area and is married to Daniel Scott Pell, a commercial airline pilot.

Marel, also born in Chicago, is a published author, currently residing in New York where she is employed by a major publishing firm. She was married in New Jersey on Apr. 12, 1948 to John Harayda, Jr. of New Jersey, who is now deceased. Their children are: Janice Carole, also a published author, working in Cleveland, OH; William Gantner of New York; and John III. "Jack" married Lucy Caro of South America and they have Pamela, Lynn and Julliann.

William was born in Indianapolis, IN and married in 1949 in Peoria to Evelyn Mae Phillips of East Peoria. They presently live in Florida as do their children: William Edward who married Rita Schaumburg, Kevin Craig, and Toni Rene who married Eugene Morris.

Wanda was born in Mishawaka, IN. She was married in 1950 in Peoria to Paul William Carey, Jr. who was born in Peoria. They had Rebecca Annette of Peoria, Margaret Evans of Chicago and Linda Joanne of Washington, IL. Linda was married in 1988 to Keith Henderson. She had three children by previous marriages: J.W. Thomas, Brett and Ashley Barton. Wanda died in Peoria in 1977 and Paul in Peoria in 1979. They are buried in his family plot in Peoria's Springdale Cemetery.

As a result of his employment as a manager for Brink's, the armored car company, Karle was transferred to various cities in Illinois, Indiana, and Michigan. He located in Peoria, IL in 1934. In 1941 he began employment with the Caterpillar Tractor Company and retired from there 20 years later.

Karle and Elsie were divorced and each remarried. He was married in Peoria on Feb. 21, 1959 to Mary Marguerite Flanders, born in Danville, IL to Augustus L. Flanders and Julia Proctor. "Maggie" died in Peoria on May 18, 1963 and is buried with her family in Danville. Karle died in Peoria on June 20, 1982, two days before his 86th birthday, and is buried in Springdale Cemetery's Mausoleum. *Submitted by Lois Lipka*

BOZE AND RELATED FAMILIES

Henry Farley was a cooper. He came from Virginia around 1830, married Sarra Carrell Jan. 6, 1837 in Montgomery Co., IN. Sarra was born in Ohio. They owned land east of Pleasant Hill and had four children: William, Mary Elizabeth, Eliza and Sarah C. Mary Elizabeth born May 7, 1844 Montgomery County married James Shelby Ross July 16, 1865 in Montgomery County. James was born Apr. 28, 1838 in Montgomery County to Philip and Cynthia Crouch Ross; who came overland from Ross Co., OH. Philip was murdered Dec. 16, 1838 at Yountsville, IN.

James Ross, a farmer and soldier, fought in the Civil War with the 72nd Indiana Volunteers in Company E (three years). On his return, he married Mary E. Farley and settled in Coal Creek Township. They removed to White Co., IN a short period of time, then returned to their log-cabin near Bristle Ridge. Their children: Boswell, Henry James, Rena, Cynthia Ann, Stephen, Amanda Jane, Margaret Ellen and Mary Elizabeth. Mary E. Farley Ross died Feb. 19, 1912. James died July 8, 1913, both buried in Oakland Cemetery.

Cecil O. and Oakie Leah (Willhite) Boze

Cynthia Ann Ross married George Adam Boze, May 14, 1889, in Montgomery County. They had Raymond O., Feb. 6, 1890 and Cecil O. June 10, 1891.

Cecil married Oakie Leah Willhite and was blest with eight children: Cecil Clare, Donald Grover, Fern Dallas, Virginia May, George Hall, Betty Lou, Willett Anne and Marilyn Jo. They lived at the end of Grace Avenue and East Elmore Street in Crawfordsville, over 40 years. She died 1957 and he in 1965.

His grandpa Ross told him many Civil War stories; how he carried his sweethearts tin-type and returned to marry her. His grandparents lived a stones-throw over the hill from him, so, he and his brother were often with them, they bounced on the big-fat feather-bed and spent endless hours with the old-folks. They were down at the milk-house for fresh milk, worked the old wooden-pump, filling the trough for old Boxer (the horse) who had a stable near-by. He and Ray climbed the apple trees, picked grapes from the purple and white grape vines. They tasted many a home-made bread and jelly or jam sandwich. There were canned apples, vegetables, cured meats, potatoes and so forth from the larder which was always filled to the brim.

Cecil and Ray attended Center School near-by, where Wes Dazey was the teacher. They went to Center Christian Church.

The parents of George Adam Boze were: William Washington and Margaret Collins Boze. They farmed in Liberty Township, White Co., IN. William was a veteran of the Civil War, serving in the 46th Indiana Volunteer Infantry and acted as a Marine on the flotilla to open up the Mississippi River. He and Margaret had: Clara Harrison and George, she died, then he married Laura Blades. They had: Sarah, William, James and Stephen.

Cecil's great grandpa, George Boze, born in Western Ohio, came to White Co., IN. He married Sarah Conwell, who bore him ten children.

These are the memories of Cecil O. Boze, my father. *Submitted by Virginia Boze Scott*

JOSHUA BRADLEY

According to Botetourt Co., VA census of 1810, Joshua Bradley had two sons and one daughter. Leroy Bradley was the youngest child. He was born in 1808 and died July 27, 1881. He married Hannah Graybill, born 1804 died July 17, 1884. Their children were: Mary, born 1826, Daniel, born 1832, George born Jan. 3, 1835 died Feb. 25, 1911 buried in Harshbarger Cemetery, William F. born May 7, 1839 died Dec. 7, 1845, buried in Harshbarger Cemetery and David Josiah, born Oct. 3, 1843 died Apr. 4, 1917.

50th Wedding Anniversary of David J. and Sarah Bradley taken in front of their home 4-1/2 N.E. of Ladoga

Leroy and Hannah Bradley came to Montgomery Co., IN in 1844. They are buried in Harshbarger Cemetery.

David Josiah Bradley married Sarah Jane Otterman June 7, 1864 daughter of Lewis Otterman Jr. and Esther (Hettie) Pefley. Sarah Jane was born Jan. 20, 1841 and died Mar. 17, 1923. She and David Josiah are buried in New Ross Cemetery. Their children were: Rosa born Apr. 16, 1865 died June 15, 1941 buried in Masonic Cemetery, Fanny born May 13, 1866 died Aug. 19, 1955 buried New Ross Cemetery, Ida born Aug. 23, 1867 died Oct. 5, 1938 buried Inlow Cemetery, George Lodi born Apr. 30, 1869 died Jan. 18, 1902 buried New Ross Cemetery, Charles Winton born 1870 died Mar. 24, 1942 buried New Ross Cemetery, James Monroe born Dec. 13, 1873 died Oct. 22, 1962 buried New Ross Cemetery, Lewis Cass born Mar. 25, 1880 died Jan. 26, 1968 buried New Ross Cemetery, Ray L. born Mar. 25, 1884 died July 30, 1963 buried Ladoga Cemetery.

Rosa Bradley married McKinley Tapp, children were: Harry, Hallie, Jennie, Ruth, and John. Fanny married James Tharp, children were: Zena, Iva, Glen, Ray and Sherman. Ida married Charles Myers, no children. George Lodi married Nancy Ellen Myers, child Lila Ruth. Charles Winton married Myrtle Stark, children were: Clara, Hazel, Clyde and Dorothy. James married Bertha Byrd, children were: Luther, Russell and Paul. Lewis married Vinnie Hostetter, child Betty. Ray married Lela Long, no children.

On Oct. 12, 1899, James Monroe Bradley married Bertha Leona Byrd, born Aug. 27, 1879 and died Jan. 24, 1960, buried New Ross Cemetery. She was the daughter of James Henry and Josephine (Shackelford) Byrd. Their children were: Luther Voris, born June 18, 1901, died Nov. 4, 1978, buried New Ross Cemetery. George Russell born Dec. 18, 1904 and Paul James born June 14, 1911, died July 27, 1970, buried New Ross Cemetery.

Luther Bradley married Geneva Clark, Mar. 15, 1924, daughter of John and Fannie (Brown) Clark. She was born June 15, 1901 and died Jan. 16, 1938, buried New Ross Cemetery. They had one daughter Ladonna Berniece, born Jan. 14, 1928. Luther's second marriage on Aug. 10, 1939 was to Harriet Roberta Bastian, born July 23, 1913, daughter of Edgar H. and Lora (Casad) Bastian. Their children were: William Luther born Mar. 3, 1941 and James Edgar born June 28, 1949.

George Russell Bradley was married on May 6, 1926 to Myrtle Mary Jones born Nov. 11, 1904, daughter of Charles E. and Mary Louisa (Henry) Jones. Their children were: George Russell Jr. born June 22, 1933, Richard Edgar born June 9, 1938 died June 13, 1938 buried in Lafayette Cemetery, Robert Edmund born July 2, 1940.

Paul James Bradley married Wilma Mae Buchanan, Sept. 22, 1935. She was born Sept. 29, 1915 daughter of Andrew Fulton and Hazel Florence (Sosbe) Buchanan. Their children were: Michael James born May 12, 1938 died Apr. 6, 1965, buried New Ross Cemetery, Paul David born Sept. 23, 1939, Gary Delmas born Jan. 19, 1941 and Stephen Earl born Aug. 18, 1944. *Submitted by Mrs. Paul (Wilma) Bradley*

ADDISON JUNIOR AND EDITH CLEO BRADSHAW

Addison and Cleo have lived in Montgomery County since 1975. He was employed as a building contractor all his life, born in Colfax, IN in 1920 and died in 1978.

Addison's parents were Addison, Sr., and Mary S. Bradshaw, and he was one of 15 children. In 1941 he married Edith Cleo Smith, of Clinton County. He spent four and one-half years in the army during World War II, serving in Okinawa for a period of time. He returned to Colfax where he remained in business until 1972, when he and Cleo moved to Wickenburg, AZ. They lived there until 1975 when they returned to Indiana, to the Darlington and Garfield area.

Edith Cleo was born in eastern Clinton County to Thomas and Edith Goodnight Smith, being the eighth of nine children. Mr. and Mrs. Smith were married in 1910.

Addison and Edith had three children namely, James (Jim) born in 1945; Judith born in 1947; and Janice born in 1951.

James married Sandra Kelsey, formerly of Shannondale, and they live in Garfield, Montgomery County. James has worked at Donnelly's for 25 years. Donna and David are their children. David is at home, Donna married William Walters of West Lafayette, in 1988 and they now live in Peoria, IL. They have a daughter, Megan, born Feb. 13, 1989.

Judith Bradshaw married Hal Stephen Miller of Cincinnati, OH, and have traveled considerably, since Hal serves in the U.S. Navy. They have two children, Denise and Bradly.

Janice married David L. Crouch of Thorntown, IN. David is employed at Donnelly's in Crawfordsville. They have one daughter, Jennifer.

Edith Cleo now lives in Garfield, North Union Township in Montgomery County, having moved there after the death of her husband.

RUTH MARIAH GRAHAM BRANSTETTER

Ruth Mariah Graham was born in Montgomery Co., IN on Aug. 16, 1900, the youngest daughter of John L. and Mary Mariah King. On Nov. 7, 1922 she married George H. Branstetter and they had three children. Their son, George Lyle Branstetter was born Aug. 11, 1923 and married Louise Ramsey in February 1951. They had two daughters, Ellen Susan Branstetter, and Phyllis Arlene Branstetter who married William Morin in 1943. To this union was born five children: William Jeffrey born in 1943 and married Joan Hurt. They had Kimberly Jo Morin born Jan. 6, 1966. He died in July 1969. James Morin born December 1944 married Valerie Wallace in October 1973, one daughter, Carrie Rae born Jan. 18, 1977. Candice Morin married Charles Thomas on Oct. 11, 1969. No children. John Michael Morin was born Oct. 3, 1949 and married Claudia Ashman in June 1976. They have a daughter, Andrea born Apr. 6, 1977. Mark Christopher Morin was born Nov. 26, 1958.

WELBY PRESTON BRANSTETTER
1892-1969

Welby Preston Branstetter (Web) was one of 12 children born to Matthew Preston and Mary Jane Branstetter. He was born in a small log house southeast of Summer Shade, KY on Aug. 12, 1892. By 1909, when he was 17, he went by train to Linden, IN. The "Mart" McBee home was his abode for the next five years.

Web met Alma McNorton in 1911 and he courted her for quite some time. They were married Oct. 3, 1917.

He made arrangements to farm a farm owned by James and Alice (Ollie) Hart southeast of Linden. They moved to the farm only to have him drafted into the Army, so Alma had to move back to her home. He was a "mule skinner" in the infantry. In his early years at the McBee's he had learned to love livestock, thus his assignment to take care of the mules.

After the war, he returned to the Linden area and farmed on a crop-share basis for Newt Everson, who owned a 180-acre farm. By 1923 Web decided to leave the Everson farm and moved to a 240-acre farm owned by Charles and Goldy Williamson. This farm was three miles southeast of Darlington and the move was made with horses and wagons.

He worked hard and was reasonably successful, not only providing for Alma and their first son, James, but also Alma's father and mother. For a period of two or three years he furnished a place for Alma's sister and her children to live.

By 1931 even with the depression, Web purchased the McDaniel farm one-quarter mile east and south of McClaskey's corner. The purchase price was $5,000.00 for 160 acres. It was financed with a federal land bank loan.

The 30's were tough years. Alma had appendicitis while expecting their second son, Robert Barton, who was born in 1932 and David Wayne had pneumonia soon after he was born in 1934. Web persisted and with a large dairy, hogs, and sheep he was able to pay for the farm in the early 40s.

By the late 30s, Web had phased out all his grade cows and had a registered herd of guernsey cows which he was proud of. In 1939 he was able to buy a new car, the first new car since 1927.

During the 40s he sold breeding stock to farmers as far away as Kentucky. He cleared some of the woods and ditched some of the new fields. He was also busy with 4-H work, advisory board, and all the activities that go with raising three boys.

In 1945 James graduated from high school and was drafted and spent a year in Japan. Barton graduated in 1950 and enrolled in Wabash College and after college served in the Army in Germany. In 1952 Wayne graduated from high school and joined the Navy and later graduated from Indiana University.

In 1952 Web bought 80 acres of the A.D. Peebles estate and James and family moved there.

Web had a heart attack in the early 50s and had to sell a large portion of his cow herd. He kept a few cows and calves so his grandchildren would have some 4-H calves. He also had a few ponies to entertain those kids and others.

He had a fatal heart attack Mar. 4, 1969 in Bowling Green, KY on his way home from a Florida vacation.

At this writing, Alma, now 94 years old, resides in the Lane Health Care Center. James and his wife, Kathryn, live on a farm southeast of Darlington. Barton and his wife, Doyne, own the home place and reside in Milwaukee, WI. Wayne and his wife, Sandy, and family live in Crawfordsville. *Submitted by James P. Branstetter, son*

BRATTONS OF WALNUT TOWNSHIP

In W. Arthur Porter's blue booklet, "A History of Union Presbyterian Church, Walnut Township, Montgomery Co., IN 1834-1934," he states that, "All of the Brattons from Walnut Township are descendants of Capt. James Bratton, who lived and died in Augusta Co., VA. He was the oldest son of Capt. Robert Bratton, who came to Virginia 200 years ago. This Robert Bratton, who was of Scotch-Irish descent, was a Captain of the Augusta Militia in the French and Indian Wars in 1755-57. He married Ann Dunlap, widow of Alexander Dunlap, whose maiden name was McFarland. Their oldest son, Capt. James Bratton (Captain of Augusta Militia, Battle of Guilford Court House, North Carolina Aug. 15, 1781). His wife's name was Rebeca Hogshead, sometimes spelled Hogsett. "Soon after the death of Capt. James Bratton in 1828, two of his sons, William and John, one of his three daughters, Margaret Crawford, and his son-in-law, John Porter moved to Indiana. It is from these two brothers, William (Old Uncle Billy) and John Bratton that all of the Walnut Township Brattons descend.

Front row: Rachel Caldwell, Martha Elvina Crane. Back row: Charles Bruce, John Newton, Benjamin A., and Robert Logan Bratton, sons and daughters of James and Phoebe Bratton — picture taken between 1915-1920.

William Bratton (1782-1862) married Mary G. Berry (1789 - ?). "They moved to Indiana in a four-horse wagon in 1832." With them were their five children, James (1813-1881), David Berry (1815-1895), Abel Washington (1817-1842), Rebecca Ann (1821-1834) and Charles Lewis (1823?-?).

James married Phoebe Allen (1814-1885) from Parke Co., IN. It is said that she had a brother that was a minister and another that ran for the governorship of Illinois on the Democratic ticket. James and Phoebe are buried in Union Hill Cemetery about three miles East of Mace, IN on State Road 136. Eleven children were born to this marriage and all survived through their first marriages and, so far as is recorded, there were no divorces and no separations except by death. Children of James and Phoebe Bratton:

William Harrison (1836-1911) married Nancy Ann Evans (1841-1925).

Margaret J. (1838-1861), married William Walkup.

Mary A. (1840-), married John Chambers.

Francis A. (1842-), married William A. Lewis.

Benjamin A. (1844-) married Mariah Stoner.

Rachel S. (1846-1939), married Jeremiah Columbus Caldwell (?-1917).

George W. (1848-1930) married Dell Rider.

Robert Logan (1850-1932), married Sarah Hannah Davis (1852-1908).

John Newton (1853-1936), married Emma Flannigan.

Martha Elvina (Pine) (1856-), married Henry Crane.

Charles Bruce (1858-1945), married Henryetta Anna Baily (1861-1942).

Presumably, all of these children were either born in or reared in a two-story log house of which part of the foundation logs and stones and chimney bricks still remain on what is believed to be on or close to the original site of the quarter section (160 acres) that William (Old Uncle Billy) and his son, James pioneered in 1832-34.

Upon the death of Phoebe, who had outlived her husband James, her sons, Robert Logan and Charles Bruce purchased the land shares of their living brothers and sisters. A few years later, Robert Logan bought his brother, Charles Bruce's share. Thus Robert L. Bratton became the owner and operator of the pioneer 160 acres. He was a good farmer for his times.

In the late 1800's and early 1900's, he bred and showed pedigreed Poland China hogs and Rhode Island Red chickens. He won many ribbons and silver plated cups at the country fairs and special exhibitions.

Robert Logan married Sarah Hannah Davis. They had two sons, William Franklin (1876-1959) and Walter Virgil (1882-1977). William Franklin married Rutha E. Morrison (1878-1953) and they had a son, James Sherman (1903-1927) and a daughter, Zola Rose (1898-1973). Zola married Charles Byron Smiley (1895-1973), and they had one son, Robert Allen Smiley (1920-1982) who married Margaret Dean Everson (1922-1956). They had one son, Robert Allen Smiley, Jr. (1942-), a Doctor of Veterinary Medicine. He married Janet Kay Steele (1947-). They have two children: Jennifer Hayes and Jason Andrew Smiley.

Walter Virgil Bratton married Borton N. Dorsey (1881-1905). They had one daughter, who died shortly after birth, along with the mother. Walter Virgil then married Nellie Grace Webster (1878-1957). Three children were born to this marriage; Donald Bratton (1912), who died at birth; Robert Webster (1913-), who never married and Ruth Elizabeth (1914-) who married Bernard Lewis Glim (1910-1955). Two children were born to this marriage: Pamela Elizabeth (1948) and Bernard Robert (1949). Bernard Robert Glim married Diane Marie Kormos (1954). They are, as of this writing, expecting their first child.

Walter V. Bratton was an early breeder of Holstein cattle in Montgomery County, as well as a member of the cow-testing association. He also raised harness-horses, and raced the pacer, Elizabeth Direct, 2:06, at local county fairs and at Indianapolis and Springfield, IL Grand Circuit races.

The oldest living descendant of James and Phoebe Bratton, known to this writer, is Marie Merele Bratton (1896-) who married Earl Hill Roberts (1892-1978). Marie was the daughter of Charles Bruce Bratton and Henryetta Baily. She was a member of the first class of graduating nurses in 1917, from the Indiana University School of Nursing. She had one son, John Kenyon (1930) who married Velma Jean Demoret (1930). They have grandchildren, the most recent being Kendi (1987) the daughter of Jill Louise Roberts (1959) and William Mark Butler (1957). Kendi is therefore, the eighth generation removed from Captain Robert Bratton.

Jennifer Hayes Smiley (1972) and Jason Andrew Smiley (1976) are of the ninth generation from Capt. Bratton.

The undersigned takes full responsibility for all errors in spelling of names, dates, and other information contained in the above paragraphs. *Submitted by Robert Webster Bratton*

Info. taken from: Descendants of Peter Porter; History of Union Presbyterian Church, History of William H. Bratton, History of New Ross, deeds and other documents.

JOHN BRATTON

John Bratton and his wife Polly Gambriel Berry came to Indiana from Staunton, VA in 1839. At that time their son Charles was six months old and Margaret was 14 years old. There were ten children. They settled two miles northeast of Mace, IN.

John was born on Apr. 7, 1793 in Virginia son of James and Rebecca (Hogshead) Bratton. He married Polly Berry on Sept. 17, 1818. She was the daughter of Doak Berry.

John and Polly had ten children:
1. James born 1819; 2. John 1821 married Almeda Brockman; 3. Rebecca 1823 married John Cowan; 4. Margaret 1825 married James M. Martin; 5. Robert 1827 married Mary Youell; 6. Nancy 1829 married Alfred Hill; 7. Mary C. married Jackson Quick; 8. Adaline 1833 married Robert Brockman; 9. William 1836 married Elizabeth Kelly; 10. Charles 1840 married Hannah Quick.

The Brattons came from Antrim Ireland and settled in Lancaster Co., PA. John's grandfather Robert Bratton was born May 20, 1712 in Ireland. He was Capt. Major of the Augusta Militia in the French and Indian Wars in 1755-57. He was a member of the Council of War for protection of Virginia Frontier in 1756. He had left Ireland to escape religious persecution. *Compiled by Edith Manges Kistler*

RALPH AND BESSIE FAYE LINN BRATTON

Ralph Bratton, born Nov. 14, 1887 and Bessie Faye Linn, born Dec. 6, 1891 were married June 17, 1909 at the home of her parents William and Ella Linn east of Whitesville, IN. Ralph's parents were Orpheus W. and Ida (Schenck) Bratton.

The subjects of this memoir were both descendants of Montgomery County Pioneer settlers. Bessie's, ancestors were James Washington and Mahala (Cassel) Linn. (refer to index)

Ralph's ancestor was Charles L. Bratton, born June 19, 1819 and Catherine (Dice) Bratton born Nov. 9, 1824. Charles L. Bratton was born in Augusta Co., VA. When 14 years old he accompanied his parents, William and Mary G. Bratton, in a four-horse wagon to Montgomery County. They reached here Oct. 12, 1832. William Bratton was a soldier in the War of 1812. Both William Bratton's grandfathers were in the Revolutionary War.

Ralph and Bessie Faye (Linn) Bratton

Charles L. and Catherine Bratton were married on Jan. 11, 1844 and lived on their farm in Union Township. Ten children were born to them including Orpheus W. Bratton.

Orpheus W. and Ida Schenck Bratton were married January 1887. Four children were born to them, Ralph, Sherman, Raymond, and Ruliff.

Ralph and Bessie Bratton started farming in Walnut township, close to his parents. When Ralph became employed at Bridgeport Brass Co. at Indianapolis they chose to move there. He worked there until he retired in 1960. They had two children: Frances and Byron L.

Frances Lorene married Ed Findell: they had two sons, William Lee and Thomas Ralph. When Ed Findell died Frances married a Mr. Shelbourne.

Byron Bratton served in World War II. He married Martha Miller (div.). Byron played a saxophone in a band when he was young; belonged to the Boy Scouts advancing properly in it according to his efforts and age. He had a quiet type personality yet expressing pleasant humor with friends. He married 2nd Pauline (____) and they moved to Miamisburg, OH.

Bessie Faye was a skilled seamstress and did professional sewing in her home. She was a member of the Christian Church at Indianapolis; also belonged to the Order of Eastern Star and was organist at both for many years. Bessie Linn Bratton had four brothers, Forest M., Charles A., Warner E. and Harry I., and two sisters, Ruby Ann and Ethel May. Ethel May and Harry I., died in infancy.

Bessie died suddenly at her home on Sept. 5, 1961. Ralph continued to live in their home on North Tibbs until his death on June 22, 1969. Both are buried at the Mace Knights of Pythias Cemetery.

WILLIAM LANDEN BRIDGE AND ELIZABETH MAXINE KUNKEL

William Landen ("Bill") Bridge was born July 17, 1917 in Buck Creek, Tippecanoe Co., IN, the sixth of 11 children born to James Franklin Bridge (1884-1967) and Hazel Harrington (1887-1981). James Franklin Bridge was the son of Ira Landen Bridge and Zenith Ann Etter, the grandson of Joseph Bridge and Elizabeth Bennett, and the great-grandson of John Townsend Bridge and Mary Harper.

John Townsend Bridge was born in Boston about 1778 and will be best remembered for the fact that he died by hanging in 1825 for his part in a massacre of nine Indians in Madison County near Pendleton.

William Landen and Elizabeth Maxine (Kunkel) Bridge

Bill graduated from Lafayette's Jefferson High School in 1938 and went to work as a machinist for Alcoa Aluminum. In 1941 he met and married Elizabeth Maxine Kunkel, daughter of Fowler Ezra Kunkel and Elizabeth Bernice Vail of New Richmond. Maxine was born in 1923 at Cherry Grove and spent most of her childhood in New Richmond, where she graduated from high school in 1941.

Bill and Maxine spent the first two years of their married life in Lafayette, then moved to Montgomery County and bought a house in New Richmond next door to her parents. Twin daughters—Carolyn Sue and Marilyn Lou—were born Jan. 9, 1943 in Crawfordsville. Their son Michael William was born Jan. 10, 1946, also in Crawfordsville.

In 1951 Bill went to work as a machinist for the Fairfield Manufacturing Company in Lafayette, where he remained until his retirement in 1979. After 21 years of residence in New Richmond, Bill and Maxine moved back to Lafayette in 1964.

All three of Bill and Maxine's children graduated from Coal Creek Central School, the twins in 1961 and Mike in 1964. Carolyn attended Indiana University. In 1971 in Pensacola, FL, she married Raymond Frederick Haseltine, an officer in the U.S. Navy. In 1983 she married her second husband, Bill K. Dennis, who died in 1986. Carolyn now teaches at a business college in Oklahoma City.

Marilyn graduated from Purdue University in 1966. She spent 15 years in California, working as a development officer for the San Diego Museum of Art and the University of Southern California in Los Angeles. She now resides in Arkansas with her husband Lonnie Cole Brown.

Mike attended Purdue University, then joined the U.S. Army in 1965. He served in Vietnam in 1966-67 and was awarded a Purple Heart for a shrapnel wound received while on duty in Cu Chi. On July 5, 1969 Mike married Catharine Joan Hamilton of Crawfordsville. Their daughter Michele JoAnne was born Feb. 5, 1973. He married his second wife, Mabel Irene Knox-Evans, on May 7, 1981. Mike joined the Crawfordsville Police Department in 1974 and was made Assistant Chief of Police in 1988.

Bill and Maxine, as well as their children, are genealogists, actively engaged in researching their family history.

WALTER C. BRIDGEWATER

Walter came to Montgomery County in 1956 to attend Wabash College and has been a permanent resident, leaving only temporarily for professional study and certain job positions. He was born Mar. 11, 1938 in Scottsburg, IN to Walter S. and Clarice White Bridgewater.

Walter graduated from Scottsburg High School in 1956. He received the B.A. degree from Wabash in 1960 and the M.A. from Indiana University-Bloomington in 1961. He then pursued the Ph.D. at Purdue University and became an alumnus in 1969, having only the dissertation to complete.

Walter C. Bridgewater

Walter is an educator and was employed as an English teacher, reading specialist and career counselor by the Crawfordsville Community Schools from 1961-77. He has also been a reading specialist for the University School, Bloomington, an instructor in the Department of English Education at Purdue, a reading specialist for the Indianapolis Public Schools and Administrative Assistant to the Superintendent for the Scott County Public Schools. He is presently an academic instructor/advisor at the college level.

Our subject also worked regular part-time for Montgomery Ward in the Boulevard Mall, Crawfordsville from 1970-77 as a sales associate and more recently for Wards in their new store in the Lafayette Square Mall, Indianapolis.

Walter is a member of several professional organizations and was initiated in the education honorary fraternity Phi Delta Kappa in 1961. He is a life member and belongs to the Lafayette Chapter. He has served as president of the Crawfordsville Education Association and the Crawfordsville Area Reading Council.

He has supported a variety of community organizations including FISH and gave 25 years of service to scouting. In 1967 he became a member of the Masonic lodge in Crawfordsville. He is a life member of the Montgomery County Historical Society and the Society of Indiana Pioneers. He is also a member of the John Hay Chapter, Sons of the American Revolution and served the State Society as treasurer. Walter was an active member of the Crawfordsville First United Methodist Church from 1961-78, having served as a church school teacher, member and secretary of the Administrative Board. Since 1978 he has been a member of the Linden-Kirkpatrick United Methodist Church, having served on the Administrative Board and being active in United Methodist Men, receiving a life membership in 1982. He was a regular lay assistant until 1987 and became a Certified Lay Speaker in the United Methodist Church in 1973.

He purchased land on Plank Road in North Union Township in 1964 and moved into a house he designed during a very cold January day in 1966 where he lived until 1987 when he moved back into Crawfordsville. Interesting features of Knollwood included one of the largest private libraries in the county, an extensive model railroad layout and a weather/communications center. An elaborate tree house was built in a large ash tree in the back yard. Walter was told that a log cabin with a brick chimney once stood at the location and that Abraham Lincoln had once spent the night there. Bricks embedded under the surface were found when the basement was dug.

NATHAN BRITTON

The early history of Nathan Britton, farmer, is unknown. His first record appears in 1826 as a resident of Hanover Township in Butler Co., OH.

In March 1829 he purchased 72.66 acres near present-day New Market in Union Township of Montgomery Co., IN. In June 1829 he purchased the adjacent 73.22 acres. Rattlesnake Creek and, later, the Logansport and Crawfordsville Railroad crossed on his property. Apparently, he migrated there about that time with his wife Rachel and eight children. It is not certain if Rachel was the mother of the children.

The children, all born in Ohio, were Matilda, Thomas P., Maria, Nathan Jr., Nancy, Elizabeth, Harriet and Ann. The last four girls were minors at the time of their father's death in late December 1833 or the first day or two of January, 1834. No record is found of Rachel after she paid 73¢, the "full share of state, county and poor tax for year 1835".

Matilda was born about 1803. She was married May 9, 1822 in Butler Co., OH to William Mahan. He died in 1848 in Marion Co., IN. The family lived in Montgomery County in 1850 and were members that year of the Mt. Pleasant Christian Church of Linden. Their children were Amanda, born about 1824 in Ohio, who married 1845 in Montgomery Co., IN to Joseph R. Weston; Malinda, born about 1829 in Ohio and married July 1851 in Montgomery County to George N. Pickett; James, born about 1832; Mary born about 1834 who married Edward Rusk; Elizabeth Ann, born about 1839 who married June 1856 in Montgomery County to John L. Burk; Thomas Miller born about 1843; Lucetta Jane, born about 1846; and David who died before his father.

Thomas' history is found elsewhere in this book.

Maria was born about 1807 and married Benjamin Bishop. Their son, John, a tailor, was born Apr. 22, 1832 in Montgomery County, married June 23, 1852 to Elizabeth M. Galey. Their children were James M., George W., Henry C., and Edwin S. John served in both the Mexican and Civil Wars. In May 1879 he was elected to serve for two years on the Crawfordsville City Council. He is buried in Oak Hill Cemetery.

Nathan, Jr., was born about 1809 and married Jan. 19, 1832 in Montgomery County to Charity Welliver. Their known children were John R., Nancy J., William, Amanda, Joseph, Catherine, Robert and Elizabeth. Nothing further is known of this family.

Nancy was born about 1816 and married Thomas Redenbaugh on Feb. 11, 1836 in Montgomery County. The family later moved to Kansas. Nancy died on the way and is buried near Altmont, MO. Their children, all born in Indiana, were: John, Francis Marion, Milton, Maria, Albert and Nancy Emma.

Elizabeth was married Oct. 4, 1836 to William M. Welshares in Montgomery County. She was also a minor at her father's death, and, from the date of her inheritance, it appears that she was born about 1818.

Harriet was married June 13, 1839 in Montgomery County to William Remley. She, also, was a minor when her father died. From the date on which she received her inheritance, it appears that she was born about 1820.

From the date of her inheritance, it appears that Ann was born about 1822. There is some thought that she may have been married Feb. 18, 1845 in Montgomery County to Hiram Smith. Submitted by Lois Lipka.

THOMAS P. BRITTON

Thomas P. Britton was born February 1805 in Ohio to Nathan Britton. His mother is unknown. He was married in Butler Co., OH on Dec. 21, 1826 to Frances "Fanny" Farnsworth. She was born about 1806 in New Jersey and came with her family in 1820 to Butler County. Their oldest child, Samantha was born in Ohio. They migrated to Montgomery County in 1829 with the rest of Thomas' family. Their other children were all born here. They are: Mary Ann, John F., Nancy J., Sarah Elizabeth, William Farnsworth, Jasper "Jap" Nathan, Lydia M., and Thomas H.

Samantha was born Aug. 27, 1827 and married Feb. 12, 1847 to James C. Wray. He was the son of Carson Wray and Cynthia Craig. Their children were: Sarah J., died July 7, 1851, buried Finley Chapel Cemetery; Edna J. born about 1856, married Jan. 1, 1880 to James B. Mullikin; Emelda J.A. born about 1858, died Dec. 30, 1860 and buried in Finley Chapel Cemetery; William Carson born about 1860, died Apr. 26, 1919, married Feb. 20, 1884 to Ida Hampton; Lena Linn born about 1863, died about 1932, married Apr. 3, 1884 to Lafayette Penn; Francis Louisa born about 1848, died about 1910, married Oct. 16, 1866 to John M. Wilkinson; Wilda James "Bud" born about 1866, died Oct. 3, 1915, married Apr. 5, 1891 to Carrie Lida Bowers; Anna J. born about 1869, died about 1955, married Mar. 25, 1891 to Alias Mack Smith; Everett E. born about 1869, died Apr. 19, 1870 and buried Finley Chapel Cemetery; and Edward, also died young and buried in Finley Chapel Cemetery. Samantha died Aug. 20, 1882 and James on Mar. 23, 1872. Both are buried with their small children and other members of her family in the Finley Chapel Cemetery.

Mary Ann's story is found with her husband's, John P. Wray.

John F. was born Jan. 12, 1833 and died May 26, 1850. He is buried in Finley Chapel Cemetery.

Nancy J. was born about 1835 and died Mar. 7, 1856. She is buried with her infant in Finley Chapel Cemetery. She was married Nov. 8, 1851 to Daniel J. Busenbark.

Sarah Elizabeth was born about 1837 and died before November 1875, leaving two children, Thomas F. and Jane S. Seaman, and her husband Joseph S. Seaman, whom she had married Nov. 18, 1854.

William Farnsworth was born Sept. 18, 1840 and died Mar. 15, 1913. He is buried in Maplewood Cemetery in Anderson, IN. He was a Civil War veteran. He was married Nov. 16, 1867 to Keziah Elizabeth Skelton. Their children were: Alvin Wallace, Thomas Allen, Clara Edith, Mary Cordelia, Lida Belle, Freddie Lamont, Bertie Rynan, and Emma Ann.

Jasper "Jap" Nathan, farmer, was born Apr. 8, 1842 and died Dec. 17, 1915. He is buried with others of his family in Crawfordsville's Masonic Cemetery. He was married Jan. 20, 1869 to Ella Childers. Their children were: Ira C., Loren P., Margaret, and John Franklin.

Lydia M. was born about 1846 and married Mar. 10, 1864 to James W. Bennett. Nothing further known of her.

Thomas H. was born about 1847 and died Feb. 6, 1915 in Covington. He was married Nov. 25, 1868 to Abigail Coffin in Montgomery County. They had five children: Fanny, Frank, Minnie, Lena, and Maggie May.

Thomas P. died Aug. 14, 1851 and is buried in the Finley Chapel Cemetery. Frances died November or December 1873 in Montgomery County. Her burial place is unknown. Submitted by Lois Lipka.

BRITTS/MITCHELTREE

Adam Britts was born in Germany in 1742. Because of political turmoil, his family came to America in 1750. His father died soon after landing and was buried at Philadelphia, PA. The Britts family settled in Franklin Co., PA. Adam Britts died in Botetourt Co., VA, October, 1832. This Britts family was German-Swiss, and was the first Britts family to emigrate to the United States. Adam married Margaret Stover in 1768, a sister of Dr. George Stover, who belonged, to the first and only Stover family to emigrate to the United States. They came in 1752. Adam and Margaret Stover Britts had eight children. Also, a brother, George Britts, accompanied Adam to the United States and was buried in Franklin Co., PA between 1773-1787. Adam served in the Revolutionary War as a private in 1779, with Capt. Samuel Rogers 4th or 5th Co. of the 1st Battalion of the Cumberland County Militia. Margaret Stover Britts died at Botetourt Co., VA in 1820. (Dwight D. Eisenhower is also a descendant of this Stover family.)

Top: Laura Mitcheltree, Letha Mitcheltree, Bessie Mitcheltree Fee. Bottom: Iris Mitcheltree McClaine, David M. Fee, Irene Mitcheltree Garner, Robert Garner, Mary Pruitt Mitcheltree Richard McClaine, James McClaine, Eloise McClaine, David T. Mitcheltree

Rebecca Ann (known as Becky) Britts was born in Botetourt Co., VA Apr. 9, 1827. Her parents lived between Fincastle and Salem, VA on a farm. Rebecca was one of the real pioneers of Montgomery Co., IN. The family came to Montgomery County in the fall of 1831 via covered wagon—each taking his or her turn walking. They traveled for six weeks. They settled four miles southwest of Ladoga, IN on Raccoon Creek. There were few settlers in that part of the county. Her parents were Samuel and Catherine Ground Britts. Samuel was born on May 27, 1799, in Botetourt Co., VA and died July 20, 1857 in Ladoga, IN and was buried in the old part of the Ladoga Cemetery. He was married Dec. 13, 1821, in Botetourt Co., VA to Catherine Ground who was also born in Botetourt County on June 18, 1802, and died at Ladoga, IN on Aug. 24, 1871. They had 11 children.

When the Britts family came to Montgomery County it was sparsely settled. The land was covered with dense forest and the Cornstalk Indian tribe was in evidence. Rebecca experienced all of the hardships and deprivations of the early settlers. She was the third child of Samuel and Catherine Ground Britts. Rebecca married George W. Mitcheltree on Feb. 8, 1848, in Montgomery Co., IN. Mr. Mitcheltree was born May 1, 1817, in Mercer Co., PA. He went to school in Pittsburgh. He first settled in Parkersburg, when he came to Indiana. He was an expert cabinet maker of Scotch-Irish ancestry. After marrying Rebecca, they made their home in Crawfordsville, IN where he engaged in the furniture and undertaking business. He is said to have driven the first hearse to a funeral in Crawfordsville. In 1850, they moved to Ladoga where he engaged in the same business. In 1865, they moved to the homestead farm 1-1/2 miles southeast of New Ross. They had two boys and four girls. George died Dec. 26, 1889, and was buried in the Ladoga Cemetery. Rebecca died Feb. 28, 1910, and was also buried in Ladoga. She was a member of the Methodist Episcopal Church, joining in 1856.

Their first child was Louisiana Florence born June 12, 1850 and died Dec. 20, 1874. She was never married, and was buried at Ladoga. She was a teacher, an artist, a dressmaker, and a writer. She wrote articles for the *Atlantic Monthly* magazine.

The second daughter Laura Elizabeth Catherine was the first licensed teacher in Montgomery Co., IN. She was born May 1, 1853, and died Sept. 10, 1894, and was buried in the New Ross Cemetery. She was married to Wilson Tipton from New Ross, May 24, 1877. They had two girls, Esther and Effie.

Esther was born May 2, 1879. She married Dennis Clark on Dec. 18, 1906. They moved to Lake Ann, MI, where on Feb. 23, 1909, their son Lewis Tipton Clark was born. Lewis married Helen Chaffin on June 14, 1930. They had two sons—Paul Merrill Clark born May 16, 1932, now living in Louisville, KY, and Carl Raymond Clark born May 6, 1934. Carl married Dorothy Himes at Whitesville, IN and had four children: Bruce, Chris, Jerrold, and Lynn. Helen an Lewis Clark still live on a farm near New Ross as does their son Carl and his wife. The second Tipton daughter, Effie, married Arthur McLaughlin on July 25, 1901. They had two children Everett Wayne and Madonna.

Georgia Anna Mitcheltree was born May 4, 1857, and died Nov. 22, 1887. She was married to Christian Loop on Oct. 26, 1876. Christian was born on Aug. 17, 1849, and died Feb. 13, 1887. Georgia taught in subscription schools and wrote articles in the *Atlantic Monthly* as her sister Florence had done. Georgia and Christian had two children. Carl Raymond Loop was born Sept. 9, 1877, and died July 23, 1923, in Sicily. He was U.S. Vice Deputy Consul General of London. He married Ethel Roberts of Indianapolis, IN, on Sept. 26, 1901. Ethel was born Aug. 11, 1878 and died 1965, and was buried in New York. Carl and Ethel had one daughter, Mary, born Feb. 25, 1907, who in turn had two boys. She married Prof. Karl Michael. Their two boys were Robert and David. She later married Guy Sleeper and died while living in Florida, but was buried in Pelham Manor, NY. The second child of Georgia Mitcheltree and Christian Loop was Verna born Aug. 28, 1884. She was married to Charles H. Thompson on Dec. 10, 1902. They had two daughters. Kathryn was born May 5, 1909. She was a teacher and married Dr. Richard Swan. They had two daughters Sharon Cook and Sue Pennington living in Ohio. Dr. Swan died very suddenly in 1962. Kathryn then married Herman Riggs and they now live at Anderson, IN. Verna's second daughter Margaret Zona married William Karr in Lebanon, IN on Feb. 27, 1935. Margaret and William had two children—Carol born Sept. 1, 1950, who married Raymond Owens and had a son, John Calvin Owens, born Sept. 6, 1976 and George Karr born Oct. 9, 1954, who married Gwendolyn Diana Halpin on Sept. 6, 1980, and have two children. George and family live in Decatur, IL. Verna Loop Thompson died Mar. 12, 1976, and is buried at Lebanon, IN. Georgia, Christian, and Carl Loop are all buried in Providence Cemetery north of New Ross. Margaret Zona Karr passed on Feb. 20, 1989 and was buried at Henderson, KY on Feb. 22, 1989.

The fourth daughter, Margaret Virginia was born Apr. 8, 1859, and died June 14, 1863. She was buried in the Ladoga Cemetery.

The fifth child, David Thomas Mitcheltree was born Mar. 9, 1861, in Montgomery County. His first marriage was to Mary Elizabeth Peffley on Mar. 6, 1884. She died on Apr. 2, 1891. David and Mary Peffley Mitcheltree had three daughters. Their first daughter, Bessie Lena was born Dec. 14, 1884. She married William I. Fee in Ft. Pierce, FL on Sept. 6, 1911. William Fee was born Apr. 14, 1873 and died Nov. 13, 1958. They had one son, David Mitcheltree Fee, born Dec. 16, 1913. David married Mary Jane Lochrie on Mar. 1, 1938. David and Mary Jane had four children. David Jr. born Aug. 19, 1939, married Ann Danford on Feb. 6, 1962. They had a boy, David III who died shortly after birth in May 1964, and two girls Kimberly and Patty. Letha Jane Fee was born June 7, 1941, and married William Gary Fowler on Apr. 12, 1958. Letha and William had three children, Joan, Jane, and Gary Fowler. Bonnie Kathleen Fee was born June 20, 1944, married Noah Worth Ludlum Jr. on Dec. 4, 1962 and had two children, Kelly Jean and Timothy. Susan Ann Fee was born Oct. 10, 1949, and married Michael Wolz on May 3, 1973. They have no children. David M. Fee, Sr. died Aug. 29, 1976 and is buried at Ft. Pierce, FL.

The second daughter of David and Mary Peffley Mitcheltree was Letha Alice born Aug. 4, 1886 and died May 18, 1904, at 18 years of age. She was buried in the New Ross Cemetery.

Elsie Claire Mitcheltree, the third daughter of David and Mary, was born on Nov. 4, 1888 and died May 18, 1900, also buried at New Ross.

After the death of his first wife David Mitcheltree married Mary Anne Pruitt on Mar. 4, 1903 at Chicago. Mary Anne was born May 20, 1876 in Missouri and died Aug. 21, 1964 at Crawfordsville. She too is buried at New Ross. They had three daughters. The first daughter, Claire Irene, was born Dec. 16, 1903. She married Sherman R. Garner on Apr. 27, 1930 in Boone County. They lived in Crawfordsville where they had one son, Robert Allen Garner on Feb. 24, 1931. Robert married Virginia Shillings on Dec. 23, 1962, and now lives in Indianapolis, IN. Sherman died Dec. 29, 1969. Claire Irene, a school teacher, taught at New Ross, Linden, Alamo, Mt. Zion, and East Union schools. She served as principal of the Young's Chapel School. Formerly of New Ross, she attended the New Ross Methodist Church, where she played the piano and taught all the Sunday School classes except the men's class. She was a graduate of New Ross High School, Butler University and Indiana State University. She held memberships in Trinity United Methodist Church at Crawfordsville, American War Mothers, Indiana Retired Teachers Association, International Travel Study Club, Dorothy Q Chapter DAR., Alpha Delta Kappa Sorority, and the Montgomery County Historical Society. She died Apr. 1, 1989 and was buried in the New Ross Cemetery.

The second daughter of David and Mary Pruitt Mitcheltree was Ruth Florence born Oct. 6, 1905 and died Jan. 28, 1906, buried at New Ross.

Iris Opal Mitcheltree was the third daughter born Feb. 24, 1906, and died Dec. 28, 1932. She married Ezra McClaine on Oct. 26, 1927. Ezra was born Apr. 27, 1906 and died Dec. 21, 1987. They had three children. James David McClaine was born Aug. 28, 1928 and married Alma Joyce Frye of Cisco, TX, on Aug. 6, 1955. James and Joyce had three children—Stephen James born Aug. 29, 1957 and married to Jena Mullein, has two children Christopher born August, 1983 and Lindsay born Dec. 29, 1987; they live in Michigan. James and Joyce's second son, Brian Keith, born Nov. 23, 1959 married Elizabeth Lee on June 13, 1987, and has one son Matthew Scott born July 1, 1988. They live in Midland, TX. James and Joyce McClaine's daughter, Brenda Kay born Mar. 30, 1961 married Cary Carrens on Aug. 24, 1984 and live in Denver, CO. The second son of Iris and Ezra McClaine was Richard Kent McClaine born Mar. 26, 1931. He married Shirley Richardson on Aug. 9, 1953. Shirley was born Dec. 23, 1936. Richard and Shirley had two daughters. Kathy McClaine was born June 13, 1955 and married John Evans on May 4, 1974. They have one daughter, Tiffany born Dec. 28, 1983, and live in St. Louis, MO. The second daughter, Kimberly born Mar. 28, 1959 formerly married to Jeff Servies. Kim and her daughter, Krista born Nov. 29, 1982, live in Crawfordsville, IN. Eloise McClaine was the third child of Iris and Ezra McClaine. She was born Dec. 7, 1932 and died on Aug. 12, 1943. Iris, Ezra, and Eloise are all buried in the New Ross Cemetery.

David Thomas Mitcheltree spent 74 years on the Mitcheltree homestead. He was one of the oldest members of the New Ross Methodist Church and had served 20 years on the Clark Township Advisory Board at the time of his death. He was one of the organizers of the New Ross Bank and his name appeared on the cornerstone of the old Ladoga School building. He was a member of one of the pioneer families of this region, Ladoga having been named by his great grandfather, John Britt, after a lake on the Russo-Finnish border. Mr. Mitcheltree's most vivid memory of the Civil War was the time the Michigan soldiers on a freight train stopped in Ladoga on their way home to eat their supper and refuel the train with wood. The civilian population of that small town fed the soldiers in their homes. A captain who ate in the Mitcheltree home was attracted to the boy, David, because he reminded him of his own four year old son at home. The stories of the war told by the captain impressed David very much. David T. Mitcheltree died on Nov. 29, 1947, of injuries resulting from an automobile accident. He died in his home in Ladoga and was buried in the New Ross Cemetery.

The sixth child of George W. and Rebecca Britts Mitcheltree was James Wesley Mitcheltree born on the Mitcheltree homestead farm on Oct. 27, 1864. He went to California for his health and settled in Redlands. There he met and married Belle Meek. Belle was born May 10, 1871 and died Apr. 23, 1951. They had one daughter, Bertha, who was a violinist born Jan. 7, 1895. Bertha was married at least twice—first to William Bullock, and later, Oct. 17, 1927 to a Frank Fassler in Los Angeles. Her last known address was San Francisco. James Mitcheltree died Dec. 7, 1905. The following is a poem he composed after leaving the old homestead in Indiana:

THE OLD HOMESTEAD

The old homestead; for years it has stood
Like a mother to nourish the generation's babyhood
With its bountiful productions that unceasingly flowed
From it along the old State road;
And its moss covered surface still triumphantly looms,
With a history hidden in cobwebs and gloom,
Like a great silent sphinx, with a future in view,
That spans the old times and the new.

O, the old homestead! How the years whirl round,
As I see it once more my life is unwound,
With all cares of life aside, and I seem
To be again in the sweet, happy dream
Of a child, watching with innocent glee,
The squirrels and the birds that talked there with me,
While the trees were great giants and I but a midge,
As I carelessly rolled on the blue grass at the old homestead.

O, the old homestead! How I wondered and feared,
As far, far away from it for health I peered,

And fancied it led me to the end of the world,
Or in a distant western country whirled;
But I paused at the parting and gazed sighing, down
At the south gate of velvety brown;
And I lingered till-terror of time made me fly,
And with tears, bid my dear mother and the old homestead goodbye.
—James Mitcheltree, Redlands, CA

It might be well to note that this old homestead has remained in the family since 1865. Part of it was owned by Claire Irene Mitcheltree Garner until her death and the remainder is owned by her two nephews James and Richard McClaine. Richard and his wife Shirley live on a part of the original homestead.

DAVID H. BRITTS

David H. Britts, son of Samuel and Catherine Grounds Britts, was born on the farm entered by his father three and one half miles southeast of Ladoga, on June 21, 1841.

He was of a family of 11 children, eight sons and three daughters. The children in order of their births are as follows: George L. born Jan. 7, 1823 and died Dec. 19, 1894; Elizabeth born Feb. 12, 1825 and died Oct. 15, 1910. She married William Byrd and after his death she married Lige Pinnell; Rebecca born Apr. 9, 1827 and died Feb. 28, 1910. She married George Mitcheltree; John C. born July 18, 1929. He was run down by a train in Florida Aug. 5, 1884; Lewis H. born Aug. 29, 1832 and died Oct. 1, 1834; Daniel H. born Aug. 22, 1834 and died Nov. 9, 1838; Henry R. born Jan. 22, 1837 and died June 22, 1860; James A. born June 25, 1839 and died Mar. 20, 1927; David H., our subject born June 21, 1841 and died May 23, 1930; William T. born Aug. 12, 1843 and died July 11, 1845; Sarah C. born Feb. 26, 1847 and died Apr. 3, 1853.

David H. was the last surviving member of the family. He grew to manhood in the community where he was born, acquiring such education as the community and times offered.

He shared the joys and hardships of those pioneer days helping to subdue the primeval forest and cultivating the soil from which most of their living was obtained.

After attaining manhood he set about to establish a home of his own. In this endeavor he chose Miss Colgeth Goodpaster to be his helpmate to whom he was married on Feb. 1, 1866. They went to housekeeping in the Britts homestead.

To this union were born three sons; Samuel born 1867 and died in the year 1873; William H. was born Sept. 10, 1868 and died July 24, 1912; Thomas D.

Colgeth Goodpaster Britts died Dec. 18, 1919. After her death and the death of his son, William Britts, David made his home with his daughter-in-law, Mrs. Emma Britts until her death in March 1929. Uncle Dave, as he was known, spent most of his married life on the farm, which he purchased from his brother, James and was later owned by David's son Thomas, with whom he was living at the time of his death.

Uncle Dave loved to have his friends visit him and talk over the memories of the pioneer days which he did with much pleasure. He was a thrifty and industrious pioneer in his early days. In business, strictly honest. He united with the Christian Church at Ladoga in 1901 under the ministry of W.T. Brooks. His faith in God and in Jesus Christ as his Savior and his hope of a future life comforted him in the end. *Submitted by Robert Garner*

NOAH MONROE BROCK

Noah Monroe Brock, Montgomery County's last Confederate Civil War veteran, was born on Aug. 14, 1836 in Farmington, NC. He was the son of William and Frances Brock.

When the Civil War started, Noah Brock joined the Confederate Army. He served in Company B, 10th Virginia Cavalry. This regiment was also called the "Marse Roberts" Cavalry. Noah Brock was wounded at the Battle of Fredericksburg, VA. He served with the 10th Virginia until the end of the war, being the only man in his company to be present when the regiment was mustered out. Noah Brock had two brothers who served in the Confederate Army and one brother who served in the Union Army during the Civil War.

Noah Brock was married to Emma "Emily" Evaline Church on Apr. 10, 1866 in North Carolina. She was the daughter of Richard and Salena Church and was born on Dec. 31, 1847 in North Carolina. They came to Johnson Co., IN in 1871 where they bought a farm. In 1896 the Brock's moved to a farm three miles northeast of Darlington, IN. Noah Brock was a successful farmer and was noted for growing excellent corn crops on his 117-acre farm.

The children of Noah and Emily Brock were William Lee, 1867-1908; Francis Richard, 1870-1917; Sally Brock Painter and Belle. Their daughter-in-law, Edith Brock, 1878-1966, moved into their home after the death of her husband, William Lee, in 1908.

Emily Church Brock died on Jan. 25, 1936 at the family farm. She was buried in the I.O.O.F. cemetery in Darlington, IN. Noah and Emily would have been married 70 years on Apr. 10, 1936. She was a long-time member of the Potato Creek Methodist Church.

Noah Brock died at his home on June 10, 1942 at the advanced age of 105. He was one of the last surviving Confederate veterans in Indiana at the time of his death. His passing left Dr. Edward Howard Cowan of Crawfordsville as Montgomery County's last Civil War veteran. Noah Brock was buried beside his wife in Darlington's I.O.O.F. cemetery.

During the 1936 Darlington Centennial, Noah Brock was honored as the town's leading citizen. *Submitted by Andrew Keith Houk, Jr. and Jay Wilson, Jr.*

ANDREW AND AMELIA BROCKMAN

The story of the Brockman family begins with Henry Brockman who arrived in St. Marys Co., MD, from Barbados in 1674. His son Samuel was an early settler in Orange Co., VA, where his children and grandchildren married with the other early families of the "western counties". William, one of Samuel's grandsons, served in the Virginia Militia during the Revolution. He married his first cousin, Elizabeth Brockman and they were the parents of ten children, including a daughter named Amelia "Milly". In 1793, Milly married her cousin, Andrew Brockman. (Andrew is thought to have been the son of William's brother, Samuel, who was also a Revolutionary War soldier.) When William and Elizabeth moved to Boone Co., KY, in 1806, Andrew and Milly went with them.

In 1825, Andrew and Milly migrated to Montgomery Co., IN, where Andrew patented 160 acres in Union Township. Andrew died in 1837 and was buried at Shiloh Cemetery, located on the land which he had patented. Milly thereafter lived with her daughter Betsy and died sometime after 1850.

Andrew and Milly had eight children: 1. William died before 1829 leaving an infant daughter named Jane. 2. Mary "Polly" was born in 1795. She married Hiram Leak (son of Robert and Susannah (Leak) Leak of Bracken Co., KY) in 1817 and later settled in Union Township near Andrew and Milly. Polly died in 1829 and is buried at Shiloh Cemetery. 3. Tandy was born about 1797. He married Katherine "Kitty" Leake (daughter of Walter and Susannah (Jones) Leake of Mason Co., KY) in 1819. They migrated to Union Township, then in 1842 they moved to Springville, IA. Their children were Walter, Andrew, Benjamin, Mary, Chesley, James, Luretta, Josiah and Mason. 4. James married Sarah "Sallie" Leake (Kitty's sister) in 1816. After Sallie's death in Kentucky, James came to Indiana where he married Sallie's cousin Frances "Fanny" Leak (Hiram's sister) in 1835. 5. Elizabeth "Betsy" was born in 1802. She married Elisha Leak (Hiram and Fanny's brother) on Christmas Day 1820. They came to Union Township with her parents where Elisha patented land adjoining Andrew's. Betsy died in 1872, probably in Iowa. 6. John was born in 1805. He patented land south of his father's in 1825. In 1827, he married Elizabeth Craig (daughter of Robert and Ann (Newell) Craig of Montgomery County). They had five children: Permelia Ann died young; Almeda Cirtley married John Bratton; Jane Craig married Christopher Dice; Robert Andrew married twice to Adaline Bratton and Susan Thompson; and Elizabeth. In 1837, John married his second wife, Eleanor Buchanon. John died in 1856. He, both wives, some children and grandchildren are buried at Shiloh Cemetery. 7. Lucy was born in 1808. In 1828, she married Hugh Newell Craig (Elizabeth's brother). Their children were Marshall, Robert, Mary, Elizabeth, and two sons who died in infancy. 8. Sally married Aaron Stewart in 1827.

CHARLES NEWTON AND HELEN LOUISE VICE BRONAUGH

Charles is the son of Claude Duncan and Sylvia Opal Wall Bronaugh, born June 15, 1925 on their farm Northwest of New Ross. He has a sister, Nettie Evelyn; she married Robert McCullough, and a brother, John William that married Ruth Frederick. Claude served in the U.S. Navy during World War I and was active in the American Legion. He was owner of the New Ross Limestone Quarry 1939-1947. Claude was born July 7, 1892 and died Jan. 26, 1965. Opal was born Dec. 14, 1893; she died Nov. 24, 1986 and both are buried in the New Ross Cemetery.

Grandparents were George Taylor Bronaugh and Nettie Vaughn Bronaugh of Baker, OR; Newton A. Wall and Evelyn Campbell Wall. Newt was owner of the New Ross Grain Company 1910-1919.

Helen is the daughter of Winfred L. and Anita Robbins Vice, born in Ladoga, IN May 22, 1926. She is one of 11 children and graduated from Ladoga High School in 1944. She attended IUPUI in Indianapolis and was employed as Secretary-Bookkeeper for Custom Farm Services in New Ross.

Charles is a 1944 graduate of New Ross High School and they met at the Free Street Movies in New Ross. They were married in a double cere-

40th Anniversary Sept. 15, 1984. Seated: Helen and Charles Bronaugh. Standing: Jeff, Cheryl, Dave and Eric McClaskey

mony with Norman Rodgers and Martha B. Hicks at New Ross, Sept. 15, 1944.

They have one daughter, Cheryl Lynn; born Nov. 26, 1945. Cheryl graduated from New Ross High School in 1963, and Approved Beauty College, Indianapolis, IN in 1964. She married David McClaskey of Darlington, IN on Aug. 27, 1967 and resides at R.R.#1, New Ross. They have two sons, Jeffrey Alan born Nov. 21, 1968 and Eric Wade born Dec. 22, 1970. Both boys are graduates of Southmont High School and were active in school sports and 4-H.

In 1949 Charles and Helen purchased the Earl Freeman Farm on US 136, two miles Northwest of New Ross, and still live there. Charles has been active in farming, trucking, and owner-operator of Bronaugh Custom (EAR) Corn Shelling. That business spanned a 50 mile radius; he employed numerous youth and shelled a total of 7.5 million bushels of corn. He has also driven a school bus in the South Montgomery Corporation for 22 years.

Charles is a great nephew of Dr. Charles T. Bronaugh, born in 1854; Uncle of Claude and Keifer Bronaugh (cousin of Claude). Dr. Bronaugh graduated from the Indiana College of Medicine, Indianapolis, IN in 1884. He then came to New Ross and started a practice that continued until his death, July 23, 1936. He was widely known in the Medical Profession and County Politics; serving as County Coroner 1890-1894.

From 1837 to 1857, Charles and Helen's home was known as the Dorsey House Inn, and they have tried to keep it in the original spirit of the times. A sign in the front yard designates it as a Montgomery County Historical Site. George Dorsey, grandfather of Keifer Bronaugh became the Postmaster in 1836 when the Governor made the Inn a U.S. post office. It was the first post office in Walnut Township, and Mr. Dorsey named it New Ross. In 1857 it was moved to Valley City, two miles east and because there were two towns by that name in Indiana, the people petitioned to have their name changed to New Ross.

Story and fact tell us when silver and gold was shipped from the Crawfordsville Land Office to Cincinnati, the drivers stopped for rest, food, and entertainment. The wagons were left unguarded and nothing was ever disturbed.

Charles and Helen have been collectors of Antiques for 40 years. One of their prized possessions is the 1939 Chevrolet Team School Bus, still in good running condition; used in the movie "Hoosiers" filmed in Montgomery County in 1986.

We are proud to be a part of Montgomery County History. *Submitted by Charles and Helen Bronaugh*

CHARLIE E. BROOKS FAMILY

Charlie E. Brooks was born on Jan. 6, 1870, to Elias and Phoebe Brooks, at Litchfield, IL. He had one brother, Tom, three sisters, Frances, Phoebe, and Nancy.

He married Cora Edna Whiting, daughter of Franklin and Mary Whiting on Oct. 29, 1893. Cora was born at Greenville, MI. Her mother died when Cora was three years old. Soon after, her father and his little three year old girl went to Missouri, traveling in a covered wagon, pulled by one horse. They settled near Licking, MO. Fate must have had a hand in all of this, as Charlie Brooks family had moved to the same area. And that is where they met and married. Nine children were born to that union.

Charlie was a shoe cobbler by trade, though worked at many other jobs as well.

The family moved to Indiana around 1908. He worked as a farm hand, was custodian at the school at Stone Bluff, IN; was Postmaster, along with the oldest daughter, also at Stone Bluff.

He also worked at the C&E L Car Yards at Danville, IL.

In October 1929, the family moved to Waveland, IN. There Charlie bought the shoe repair business from Ira Sharp and continued doing shoe repair the rest of the time. He was also Town Marshall of Waveland for several years. He died Nov. 25, 1955.

The nine children were: Elmer Franklin (Barney) - Jan. 6, 1895-1972; James Lawrence (Speck) - Oct. 22, 1897-1974; Sadie Alta May - Feb. 10, 1900-1902; Nettie - Oct. 7, 1902-1973; Bertha Francis - Mar. 5, 1905 -; Clyde Edward - Dec. 22, 1907-1974; Goldie Bell - Sept. 14, 1910-; Eulah Faye - June 23, 1913-; and Eva Lena - Mar. 13, 1917-. *Submitted by Eulah Faye Brooks Stockwell*

JOEL BROOKSHIRE

The Brookshire family came from England and first settled in Randolph Co., NC. They were included in the 1790 census. Joel was born in 1782.

In 1830 Joel and wife, Sarah Slack, Drake, Swan and Jane migrated to Indiana and settled in Montgomery County. Drake married Sarah Graves and had ten children. Swan married Sarah Harrison and homesteaded a section of land in Scott Township. They had seven children. Jane married James Bell and had four children. Joel, Drake and Jane settled in Clark Township. Sarah (Sally) Harrison, Swan's wife was a distant cousin of President Benjamin Harrison. Swan did well and prospered and served a term in the state legislature. Drake was a very large man and had to have his clothes tailor made. In fact before his death, he arranged for a tailor made casket. One of his sons, Voris, was an U.S. Congressman.

Swan and Harry Brookshire, John Smalley and James Wm. Brookshire.

Robert, a son of Swan, was considered a character. He never married but wandered over the southwest area of the county sculpturing tombstones. Many old courthouses bore some of his stone work. He is supposed to have found Carlsbad Caverns but did not have the money to develop them. Someone else did and put their name on them. He once joined a posse hunting Billy the Kid. Evidence of his beautiful sculpture work on tombstones can be found in Ladoga Cemetery.

John Allen, another son of Swan, married Rosalie "Rose" Jane Frankenberger and settled in Scott Township on the family farm. They had three children, Charles Allen, Sarah Rachel, and James William. Charles Allen married Amelia Amunson and settled in South Dakota raising three children, Winifred, James, and Betty. Sarah Rachel married Charles Wilson and settled in Topeka, KS and had one child, Jack. James William married Neva Radford and had three children, John Thomas, Jennie Marie, and June Ellen. When John Allen died the farm was divided among the heirs. James William and his wife and children lived on the home place. His grandmother, Sarah, lived with them until her death. James William was Scott Township Trustee in 1913 in addition to being a farmer.

John Thomas married Goldia Wingert of Whitesville and settled down on a farm west of the homeplace. They had two daughters, Kathleen Dell and Martha Ellen.

Jennie Marie married Georga Frantz and eventually settled down on the family farm northeast of Ladoga. This farm was designated one of the centennial farms in Montgomery County. They had no children.

June Ellen moved to Indianapolis and married Marrice Cragun. They had no children.

John Thomas developed hay fever and asthma at an early age forcing him to go by himself to Traverse City, MI every year during the hay fever season. He supported himself by hiring on as deck hand to boats operating out of there.

Since no sons were born to this branch of the family, the Brookshire name stopped when John Thomas died.

WILLIAM L. AND PATRICIA (DAVIS) BROSHEARS

Bill and Pat Broshears came to Montgomery County in December of 1954, where Bill soon began working at Plastene in the Accounting Department. Pat had been a grade school teacher in Terre Haute and Clinton prior to the move. She then stayed home to care for their month-old son (William Davis "Davy" born October 24th).

Bill was born in Sullivan, IN on May 13, 1925, the son of William Lee and Anna (Houston) Broshears. William was a coal miner and one of 11 children, the son of William Logan and Rena (Crabtree) Broshears. Bill's father was born in Ayrshire, IN. Anna Houston came through Ellis Island about 1912 from Galston, Ayrshire, Scotland, the daughter of Hugh and Jessie (Greene) Houston.

Bill graduated from Sullivan High School in 1943. He joined the Air Force where he was a radar operator and bombardier in the Pacific. He went to I.U. in 1946 (where enrollment jumped from 4-10,000 after the War) and graduated from there in 1949 in the School of Business.

Pat was born Oct. 7, 1927, the daughter of Roy E. and Lucille (Rodriguez) Davis, residents of Lafayette. Roy and his father, Tom were both engineers on the Monon Railroad. Pat's great, great grandfather, Josef Felix Rodriguez was born in Cuba. His son, Josef was in the Civil War. Pat graduated from Lafayette Jeff in 1945 and I.U. in 1949, majoring in History.

Bill and Pat met in 1946 in Spanish class. After graduating, Bill went to work in Evansville and Pat taught school at Oakland in Lafayette. They were married in Lafayette in 1951 and moved to Terre Haute where Bill worked at Terre Haute Malleable Foundry office.

Bill and Pat are the parents of Davy, (above) and Betsy Lee born July 24, 1958, "Our Crawfordsville Connection." Davy graduated from Franklin College in 1976 (Economics), met and married Vickie Lynn Rainey in 1976 and remains in Franklin to this day where he is a price analyst at Kawneer. Betsy was in the 100th graduating class of Crawfordsville High School and in 1980, graduated with a Home Ec degree from I.U. She married Michael Swisher in 1982. They are living in Lancaster, PA where Betsy is a Sales Representative for MCI Telephone Company and Mike works at Donnelleys.

Bill and Pat have one grandson, William Christopher (Chris) Broshears, born Feb. 16, 1980, the day after Pat, her mother and daughter became members of Dorothy Q Chapter DAR. Pat's maternal grandmother, Ella Bee was a Virden and her Revolutionary War soldier was John Hopkins from Delaware.

Bill's interests include: golf and the Elk's Club. He is retired and enjoys beachcombing. Pat works part-time in the Montgomery County Recorders office and both Bill and Pat are active members of First United Methodist Church. Pat is also in Delta Theta Tau Sorority and enjoys playing bridge. Submitted by Pat Broshears

CARCIE LEROY BROWN

Carcie Leroy Brown married Mary Elizabeth Eggers on Nov. 16, 1934. To this union, Donald Leroy, Larry Dean and Sharon Kay (Mrs. Jon Foster) were born.

Larry Dean Brown lost his life in the blizzard of 1978.

They have three grandchildren, Sherry Lee and Mary Virginia Foster of Crawfordsville, David Leroy Brown of Otterbein, IN.

Carcie, born June 13, 1913 was the son of William Johnson Brown and Hazel Leola Zachary Brown.

William J. Brown was born Jan. 14, 1888, in Rock Castle Co., KY, the son of Jonas and Pauline Sowders Brown.

Hazel Leola born Aug. 12, 1891, was the daughter of Ephraim and Nancy Watson Zachary. Carcie had five sisters, Geneva, Ivanelle, Nyoda, Bonnie and Nijol, and one brother, William Guy.

Mary E. Brown born February 1917 was the daughter of Glenn and Hallie Ima Moore Eggers. Her paternal grandparents were Turman and Bertha Carter Eggers. Bertha's parents were Sanford and Mary Caroline Carter.

Maternal grandparents were Allen W. Moore and Estella M. Grimes (born near Shannondale). They were former residents of Alamo and Crawfordsville. Their home near Alamo was a large two-story log house. It had a fireplace. There was upstairs rooms but you had to go outside to go up the stairs. After they moved to Crawfordsville, it was a lot of fun to go spend the day at the log house and often cook dinner over the fireplace. They later moved to Mishawaka for health reasons.

Allen Moore's father, Allen Washington Moore served in the Civil War. He came home on leave. When he went back he got black measles and died. They had three sons, George, Kale and Allen. Mrs. Moore later married a Lewellen. They had two daughters, Dora and Oma and one son.

Mary had three sisters, Ruby, Ivall Dean and Wilma, and one brother, Benton Gordon.

Carcie "Bud" as he was known, served with the Infantry Replacement Regiment and was awarded the purple heart and good conduct medal for injuries received while in action in France.

Carcie died in an auto accident near Lafayette on Jan. 18, 1951.

On June 11, 1967, Mary E. Brown married Keith W. Martin, originally from Richmond, IN. They both were employees of Sommer Metalcraft.

Keith had four children, David of Delaware, OH; Russell, Mearil and Shirley Shanklin, all of Crawfordsville. Submitted by Mary E. Martin

MOLLIE K. BROWN

Mollie K. Brown, as her friends in New Ross came to know her, came to Montgomery County on Sept. 10, 1912. She arrived with her family Kathleen, Thomas Leo, Pauline and Walter via the Midland Railroad from Denver, CO.

Her husband, Thomas J. Brown, road master for the Union Pacific Railroad, had received an appointment to Salt Lake City, UT to continue his work. Thomas, the third of five sons, was born near Yountsville of Irish immigrant parents. His parents had died of malaria about 1885.

Having been born in Boone County and raised in New Ross, Mollie decided to come to Indiana for a visit before moving to Utah. It seemed an opportune time for a visit with relatives and friends.

After marriage, Mollie and Thomas lived in Crawfordsville and New Ross. Kathleen was born in Indiana in 1898. The family then moved to Wells, NV in 1900 where Leo was born in 1901.

Among other places, the railroad work took them to Brinkley, AR and Burlington Junction, MO. Burlington Junction was the birthplace of Pauline in 1905. The family also lived in Moreland, KS; Jules Berg, CO and Omaha, NE. They lived in Omaha for five years and it was here that Walter was born in 1907. They then lived in Denver from 1910 to 1912.

Plans to move to Utah were brought to a sudden change when on Oct. 19, 1912 a message was received that Thomas Brown, husband and father, had died of a sudden attack of meningitis.

Mollie kept the family together and for the first year made her home with an aunt, Lucinda Lewis.

Through the years she worked for Carl Kratz, a German baker and restaurant owner. She did clerking for Billie Wall, Owen Lasley and others. Later she was New Ross Postmaster for about 12 years and managed the New Ross Telephone exchange for 13 years.

Kathleen married Ward Gray in 1919. In 1927, a son was born and died in infancy. Kathleen passed away following goiter surgery in 1929.

Leo attended Wabash and became a teacher and barber. He taught in New Ross and Waveland. He lived in Indianapolis and died following an automobile accident in 1955.

Pauline became a teacher and married Marvin Zimmerman. They live on a farm near North Salem. They had three daughters, Molly Ann, Sharon and Kay. Molly Ann died in 1950. Sharon married Paul Richardson and lives in Pennsylvania. Kay married Larry Michael and lives in Columbus, IN.

Walter graduated from Wabash and taught in New Ross and Pinnell schools. He retired from Indiana Public Service. He and his wife, Mary Catherine live in West Lafayette. Their two sons are Samuel W. Brown and Dr. Walter C. Brown, II, DDS of Kokomo, IN.

Four great grandchildren are Jeffrey Lee and Paula Kay Richardson and Walter C. Brown, III and Mary Elizabeth Brown.

Mollie always felt that it was only with the generous help of the community that she was able to keep the family together.

Mollie retired from the telephone company in 1947. She continued to live in her home in New Ross until her death on July 21, 1966. She is buried in the family plot in New Ross Cemetery. *Prepared by Pauline Zimmerman*

RUSSELL LEE BROWN

Russell Lee Brown was born Sept. 4, 1946 at Culver Union Hospital, Crawfordsville, IN; the first child born to Donald Floyd and Vera Beth (Wilson) Brown. Spending his early childhood living with his parents on a farm near Young's Chapel, the family later moved to a farm east of Parkersburg on Corn Stalk Creek. Here his two sisters were born, Rebecca Ann (Mrs. Douglas White) and Betty Lou (Mrs. Darrel Simpson).

After graduation from New Market High School in 1964 he became employed at the Indiana Printing Co.

June 3, 1966 he was married to Barbara Joan Fry in the Parkersburg Christian Church, where they were both members. They established their home at 407 Louise Ave., Crawfordsville.

Barbara, a graduate of New Market High School, lived from February 1953 to January 1964 with her parents, Noble Cassell and Edith Eileen (Nichols) Fry on a farm located on U.S. 231 North of Parkersburg. Her two brothers, Ralph Cassell and Phillip Lynn were born at Culver Union Hospital.

Barbara and Russell became the parents of Angela Sue born Mar. 3, 1967 and Bradley Lee born Dec. 12, 1969.

Barbara was employed as a nurse aid at the Ben Hur Home prior to her marriage. Later she was employed at the new Culver Union Hospital and Houston House.

May 21, 1968 Russell was sworn in as a member of the Crawfordsville City Police Dept. where he still serves.

Russell and his family became active members of the Woodland Heights Christian Church. He helped organize the Woodsman Quartet in February 1979. He continues to sing with this quartet providing gospel music to churches and area events. He is an employee of Ray Risner, B&D Fire Extinguisher Service.

Angela Sue and Bradley Lee attended John Beard School and graduated from Crawfordsville High School.

Russell's father, Donald Floyd Brown, born Nov. 28, 1917 was one of four children born to Jess and Easter (Sparger) Brown in Montgomery County. His brothers Albert, Robert and sister Eleanor (Mrs. Byron Hamm) lived in Montgomery County.

Donald spent his life as a farmer except a time in the military service during World War II.

Russell's parents established their retirement home on West Main, Crawfordsville. Russell's mother, Vera Beth (Wilson) Brown was born Sept. 4, 1922 in Montgomery County to Clayton and Edith (Keller) Wilson. He was a farmer and a butcher working in a slaughter house in the county.

Barbara was born at the Putnam County Hospital on July 6, 1944 living her early years on dairy farms near Greencastle and Roachdale. She attended Roachdale Grade School before going to New Market. Her mother and father were born in Putnam County. Her father Noble spent most of his early life in Montgomery County, going to school at Wilson and Crawfordsville High. Noble and his parents, Clifford H. and Jessie Leona (Clary) Fry, his brother Gregory Clifford and sister, Mary Elizabeth Fry (Mrs. George Dawson) lived on farms in the county. Barbara's paternal great grandparents, Hiram and Ann Elizabeth (Dennis) Fry lived most of their lives in Champaign Co., IL but spent a few years living on East Main in Crawfordsville in the early 1900's.

Angela Sue Brown was married to Phillip Daniel Knarr on Aug. 15, 1987 in the Woodland Heights Christian Church. They met while attending Cincinnati Bible College, Cincinnati, OH. *Compiled by permission Edith E. Fry*

WILLIAM A. BROWN

William A. Brown came with his parents to Montgomery County in 1828, where his father died one month after their arrival. He was the first person buried in the Davis Cemetery, which is on the farm in the Northeast corner of Clark Township.

William A. and Elizabeth Gose Brown had four sons and one daughter. The sons were: Earl, Tillman, Jay and John.

John married Maude Musser, Christmas Eve, 1899. Their only son, Walter A. Brown (Chub) was a 1919 graduate of New Ross High School. His father died at an early age leaving Walter and his mother to run the farm. He attended Purdue and came home to a long life of farming. He married Clair Maguire June 25, 1925, at the Methodist Church in Crawfordsville. They lived all their married life in the home place near New Ross.

Great grandchildren of Walter and Clair Brown: Samantha Mahorney, Cassidy Mahorney, Scott McKinney, Christy McKinney; Amy Lee McKinney, not pictured

Clair Maguire Bratton Brown attended Mace School. She had strong ties with the Linnsburg community and many people who grew up there. She and her sister Larue (Mrs. John Gray) were raised by their grandparents, Harvey B. and Sudie Bratton.

Walter, Clair and Maude Brown were very active in the New Ross Methodist Church as long as their health allowed. He was a director and President of Farmers State Bank of New Ross until his death at the age of 71.

Chub and Clair have two daughters: Mary Catherine and Marilyn Jean. Mary Catherine married Samuel M. Mahorney of Ladoga. Their children: Jeanne C. Daniel and Patrick. Jeanne married Dave Hamernik. She graduated from Indiana State University and Indiana University. She is an elementary teacher at Greenwood, IN. Their home is in Zionsville, IN.

Daniel J.B. served in the Army one year in Germany and one year in Vietnam. He lives near Ladoga. Patrick "Pat", a graduate of Danville Junior college, Danville, IL is employed in hog farming. Pat married Carol Morris of New Ross. They have two children: Cassidy Owen, four and one-half and Samantha Ann two and one half year old.

Marilyn, a graduate of Indiana State University with a degree in Elementary Education, married Dorman Rogers a graduate of Purdue in agriculture and Education Administration. Dorman is a native of Montgomery County, Clark township, being the youngest of three sons of Harmon and Mae Rogers of Clark township.

Marilyn and Dorman are the parents of Geof and Karen who attended Tipton schools. Dr. Geoffrey Rogers, a graduate of Purdue and IU School of Medicine, and his wife, Dr. Lisa Rogers practice medicine in Danville and Champaign, IL.

Karen McKinney, who graduated from Ball State with a degree in education and her husband Tom, who graduated from Purdue with a degree in agriculture, are farmers at Kempton, IN. They have three children: Scott five, Christy three, and Amy Lee three months.

The homeplace remains in our family since being homesteaded so many years ago by the brave people who traveled so far in such hard times.

This is written in memory of our Father and Mother, Walter A. Brown (Chub), born Feb. 22, 1901 died Nov. 7, 1972 and Clair Brown born Dec. 10, 1904 died May 22, 1989. *Submitted by The Mahorneys and Rogers*

ANDREW L. BROWNING

Andrew L. Browning, long-time manager of the Strand Theatre, was transferred to Crawfordsville in January of 1941 to manage the Strand and Vanity theatres, by Harry and Nova Vonderschmitt, the owners at the time.

Andy was born in Greencastle, IN on Mar. 17, 1913 to Robert L. and Elizabeth (Butler) Browning. He was educated in the Greencastle schools graduating from high school in 1931.

He was married to Elizabeth Jean Woolley in Greencastle on Nov. 1, 1936. Jean was the daughter of Samuel H. and Margaret (McInnes) Woolley and was born in Sullivan Co., IN. She passed away Sept. 11, 1987. Andy and Jean celebrated their 50th wedding anniversary in 1986. They drove to Greencastle to dinner and to a MOVIE!

Andy started his career at the Voncastle Theatre in Greencastle in the Spring of 1928, as the Saturday night balcony usher to maintain law and order! Eight years later he was appointed manager of the Voncastle and Granada Theatres until he was transferred to Crawfordsville, to the Strand and Vanity. He served in the U.S. Army Combat Engineers from 1943 to 1946. His service was in the European Theatre of operations in France and Germany. Andy and Jean purchased the Strand from the Vonderschmitt estate in 1977 and remodeled it into the Strand Cinemas I and II in 1979. They sold the Strand in 1985 and he retired after 44 years as manager and owner/manager.

Andy was active in community affairs. He was president of Downtown Crawfordsville in 1985 and served on the board continuously from its organization. He joined the Rotary Club in Greencastle in 1937 and transferred to the Crawfordsville Club in 1941. After returning from the service he rejoined the club, serving as its president, secretary and treasurer and several committees, including Bulletin Editor. He was made a PAUL HARRIS FELLOW by the club.

Andy joined Post 72 of the American Legion in 1946 and was elected Commander in 1952. He served as Adjutant, Finance Officer and many years as Chaplain. He was made an Honorary Lifetime Member in 1969, this being a most prized award.

Service with the Montgomery County Chapter of the American Red Cross became a very satisfying activity. He served as Chairman of the Board of Directors for two years, made a lifetime member of the board and served many years as Chairman of the Service to Military families. He was chairman of the Housing Committee when the Chapter House at 113 S. Water Street was purchased. He was awarded a 35-year certificate of appreciation in 1988.

Andy's political activity included running for City Councilman and in the Democratic primary in 1964 for mayor losing to his friend, Beecher Young. He served on the Plan Commission and was chairman of the Board of Appeals. Andy held the office of Treasurer of the Montgomery County Democratic Central Committee. At the time of this writing, 1989, Andy was serving his third year as a member of the Local Alcoholic Beverage Board.

Andy always said movies are your best entertainment and all movies are good movies; some are just better than others! *Submitted by Andy Browning*

STEVEN AND DORA (SMITH) BRUCE

The Bruce family descends from Robert Bruce or Brix from Scotland. Family members came to America and settled in the state of Virginia, before moving on to Montgomery Co., IN. Steven Bruce and Dora (Smith) Bruce were the parents of five children; Earl, James Cecil, Elsie, Leslie and Arthur.

Earl married and spent his entire life in Kentucky and had no children. Elsie married Jake Roberts of Indianapolis and had two children, James and Jane. James Cecil married Dorothy Redenbaugh and lives south of Crawfordsville. Arthur married Etta Craig and lived in New Ross. They had one daughter, Linda, who married Don Bayless and lives in Lafayette with their two daughters, Stacey and Amy. Leslie married Fredericka Bappert and had two sons, Ernest James and Donald William. Leslie worked for the Montgomery County Farm Bureau for 25 years and retired in 1964 as Manager of the Elevator on East Market Street near downtown Crawfordsville. Leslie died 23 days after retirement. He was also a Veteran of WWI. Fredericka still lives in Crawfordsville.

Ernest James (E.J.) married Judith Witt of Roachdale and have two children; Paula Denise who married Jeff Chastain and David still at home. Ernest is retired from Alcoa Aluminum Plant in Lafayette and Judy is a Registered Nurse at Culver Hospital.

Donald William married Marilyn Weber and has one daughter, Melinda Jo. Donald worked at the Indianapolis Airport for several years before moving to Illinois as a Bakery Distributor. He is now a car salesman and lives with his wife in Rantoul, IL. Melinda is married to John David Galbreath who both live and work in Champaign, IL. *Submitted by Marilyn Bruce*

MICHAEL BRUCH II

Michael Bruch, II, married Rachel Winter born 1815, died Oct. 3, 1883, daughter of John and Elizabeth Pfrimmer Winter, and they lived one forth a mile north of New Ross. Their children were Michael III married Melissa Golliday first in 1879, then married the widow Gott; Elizabeth Bruch, Minnie Bricks, Phillip Bruch, never married and Sarah Bruch married Michael Whoel, had Michael Whoel, Jr. who married Mary Zenor and had Ray and Ethel Whoel, and Anna Whoel. Phillip Bruch owned land west of Greenwood School for many years. His sister Sarah Bruch Whoel lived south of Greenwood School on land they owned. The farm that Phillip owned many people lived on it; James W. Linn and family lived there eight years, then their daughter Dora Evaline Linn Randel and her family lived there ten years. The house has been torn down in the last few years. The Bruch's home north of New Ross, was situated in a beautiful grove of trees and bushes, and was very hard to see from the road.

RICHARD BRUNER FAMILY

Richard Bruner was born in Sterling, Fountain Co., IN, to Ray and Ical Bruner on Feb. 9, 1929. When he was a few months old, the family moved to Alamo, IN. He graduated from Alamo in 1947. He attended Indiana State Teachers College, graduating in 1951. He served in the United States Navy from 1951-55. He is now a teacher at Southmont Junior-Senior High School. He also taught and coached in Fountain and Montgomery counties.

Richard married Betty Hoagland, (born May 31, 1932, daughter of George and Mary Hoagland) formerly of New Richmond, IN. They are parents of three sons: Ron, Alan and Jeff. Ron was active in basketball and baseball in Montgomery County. He graduated with high honors from Waveland in 1971; the last graduating class from Waveland before consolidation. He attended Indianapolis University, formerly Indiana Central. He now lives at Indianapolis and teaches at Beech Grove. He and his wife, Rita are parents of two boys: Jonathan, 11 and Jeremy, eight.

Alan, the second boy also played baseball and basketball in the county. He attended Waveland and graduated with high honors in 1972 from Southmont; the first class to graduate after consolidation. He attended Indiana State. He is now employed at Impex in Crawfordsville. He married Jackie Harvey in 1981. They have no children. He is an avid bird watcher. He works on the bird counts at Shades State Park and Turkey Run State Park. He also belongs to the National Audubon Society.

Jeff, the youngest son was also active in baseball. He graduated from Southmont in the upper part of his class in 1978. He also attended Indiana State University. He is now employed at Encore at Lebanon.

Richard's father, Ray, was born in Fountain County to Harry and Lulu (Howard) Bruner. Ray was a barber most of his adult life in Montgomery County. Ray married Ical Pickett of Wallace. Ray graduated from Wallace.

Ray's parents had two other children. Thelma married Lloyd Smith of Veedersburg. They had one child, Keith. Keith and wife, Lee have two sons, Larry and Rich. They all reside in Baltimore, MD. Lois Bruner married Clyde Lightle. They had two children, Gary and Marylou. Gary and his wife, Betty have three or four children. Marylou married Jim Woods and they have three children. They all reside in Veedersburg. Harry's parents were William Jasper and Sarah (Keller) Bruner. They had four children: Harry, John, Daisy and Gertrude. John and his wife had two children, Alva and Vera. Alva married Mary Cook. Vera married Burl Fruits of Alamo. Neither had children. Daisy married Charles Lowe. They had one child (died young). Gertrude married Harry Lowe (brother of Charles Lowe). They had two children, Wandaline Alward and Max.

Richard's great, great, grandfather, Jacob Bruner was as far back as ever recorded. There is nothing on him only that he moved in to Fountain County. *Submitted by Betty Bruner*

JOHN BUCK

John Buck was called "Daddy" by every man, woman and child in New Richmond. Daddy was a gardener and raised vegetables to sell in the area. Sadly, little details are known about Daddy — his death record says he was a widower; however, the 1910 Census lists him as divorced. Also, according to the death record, both his parents are "Unknown." In a small bleep under the New Richmond News items (Crawfordsville paper) a few days after his death (which occurred Feb. 10, 1918), it states he was 86 and was born and raised in Attica.

John "Daddy" Buck

In the same census as above, it says Daddy was born in Ohio and both parents were born in Pennsylvania. There is a John Buck, age 48 in the 1850 Davis (Attica area) Township, Fountain Co., IN census who was born in Pennsylvania — his wife Christina, age 41 was also born in that state and their son John was born in Ohio — probably Daddy's family.

Although little was/is known about John Buck, one fact was sure — every man, woman and child missed seeing the scraggly-bearded, long-fingered, smiling old man carrying his basket full of veggies for many years after he was gone! *Picture compliment of Joan Oppy, story by Karen Zach*

BUNNELL

The following is the family history of Albert Jerome and Minnie Bunnell and their descendants:

Rome, as he was known to his family and friends, was a grandson of Ephrian Bunnell who was born in Kentucky in 1797 where he married Martha (Patti) Biddle. They moved to Montgomery County and raised five children. Elizabeth, Harriet, Veasey, Ephrian and Martha.

Veasey was married three times. He had five children by his second wife Mary Hays. They were William, Eliza, Charles, Albert Jerome (Rome) and James.

In 1888, Rome married Minnie M. Rider. Minnie was born in 1870 in the Wesley Community to William Rider and Margaret Fields Rider. William Rider was a prominent merchant in Waynetown, a trustee of Union Township for many years and was founder and first President of the Waynetown State Bank, a position he still held at the time of his death in 1921. According to *Beckwith's History of Montgomery Co., IN*, published in 1881, he was a Mason, an Odd Fellow and a Democrat.

Minnie and Rome spent their entire married lives in a home Minnie's father had built for them next door to his home in Waynetown.

Rome and his brothers were carpenters. Rome did the finish work and painting and paper hanging. He was what we would today call an interior decorator.

Minnie was a very gracious and generous lady who could never refuse help to anyone in need. Many young people called the "Bunnell house" their home.

Minnie's love of antiques was not only a hobby with her, but became a business in her later years. After traveling far and wide for many years collecting antiques she finally had room for no more so she opened a shop in her home. After her death an auction sale was held that lasted three days and it was estimated the crowd was in the thousands.

Rome and Minnie had two children, Clifford Rider Bunnell and Mary M. Bunnell. Mary was married to George Gravett. They had two sons, Richard and George Jr. Both of Mary's sons are now deceased, but they are survived by several children and grandchildren.

Clifford Rider Bunnell married Ruby Fern Butts. Clifford died in 1973. Ruby is now 92 and still lives in Waynetown. They had three children. They are William, Helen and Emery.

William is married to Helen Gentry. They reside in Crawfordsville. William has three children, Freddie, Judi and Rex. Freddie has three sons, Freddie Jr., David and Robert. Freddie Jr. has three children Trey, Evan and Kalyin. David has one son, Brian, and Robert has one son, Aaron. Judi has four children, Todd, Tami, Tonda and Trudy. She has eight grandchildren. Rex has four children. Fawn, Eli, Clay and Star.

Helen is married to Milford S. Milligan, Jr. They have three children, James Drake, Charles Milligan and Marie Nanette Kentner. Marie Nanette has one child, Jennifer.

Emery married Tillie Purdy and they are the parents of Cheryl Church and Deborah Bunnell.

Those left at this time to perpetuate this branch of Bunnells are Fred and his three sons and four grandsons, and Rex and his two sons; none of whom reside in this vicinity.

This history spans almost 200 years and seven generations. *Submitted by Helen Milligan*

WILLIAM BURBRIDGE "OUR FIRST JUDGE"

William Burbridge and James Stitt were commissioned by Governor Hendricks Sept. 1, 1823 as the first two associate judges in newly formed Montgomery County to sit with, or in lieu of the presiding judge of the First Judicial Circuit. The commissions were for seven years. A plain farmer and a good blacksmith, also, Mr. Burbridge was "wholly without legal knowledge, except such as is usually acquired by observing persons without the aid of law books. Yet the record does not show that any ... rulings were excepted to or that a new trial was asked on account of any blunder of the court."

He probably was born in Fayette Co. (or Montgomery Co., now Bath) KY on Sept. 8, c.

1789-90. He was the son of Rowland Burbridge (c. 1745-1842), a veteran of the Revolution and Jane Wells Burbridge. Their other children and approximate birth dates were: Jesse, Robert 1779, Thomas 1783, James 1785, Benjamin 1787, Mary (Polly) Jackson 1791, Elizabeth (Betsy) Underwood 1794, John 1796, Martha (Patsy) Mitts 1798 and Joseph Howe 1802.

In about 1786, his family moved from Greenbrier Co., VA to Montgomery Co., KY. Later, as a young man, he removed north, as did his brothers Robert and James, to the new areas in Ohio. While in 1819 he explored the wilderness westward as far as the Wabash River in Indiana, by 1812 he had settled near Chillicothe, OH.

He was married to Margaret Graham (c. 1794-Sept. 2, 1832, buried Wilson-Gwyn Cemetery). She was the daughter of Forgus Graham. Their children and approximate dates of birth were: Forgus Graham 1812, Eliza 1815, Morgan 1816-17, Rowland 1819, Mary Ann 1821, Margaret 1823, James 1826, William 1827, Matilda 1829-30, Nancy 1830, Ann and Jane. On Feb. 15, 1836, Mr. Burbridge married Isabella Steele (1803-1847).

As a volunteer in a company of Kentucky mounted riflemen, the young husband and father served in the War of 1812 as, reportedly, did three of his brothers.

After some years in Ohio, he returned to Indiana, bought land to farm southwest of Crawfordsville on July 13, 1822 (160 Acres Sec. 11, South Union Township, close to William Offield, the first settler of Montgomery County) and moved his family west to Indiana. He added to his holdings over the years.

In 1827, he built the first brick house in Montgomery County, his children assisting in carrying the brick.

Ever sensitive to the peril of Indian attack along the frontier, when news of the Sauk chief Black Hawk's rebellion reached them in 1832, the settlers of Montgomery County assembled all their militia companies to parade in Crawfordsville. From among those homespun-clad 100 Infantry and 50 Cavalry volunteers were promptly provisioned and sent west to assist the Illinois troops. Judge Burbridge commanded that Cavalry. For the farmer-militia, that quick, bloodless campaign was the last war-call ever sounded in the Wabash Valley.

In 1837, he was chosen as one of three Trustees of Montgomery County to select and buy land and build the first County Seminary for educating the young men and women of the area. Earlier, in 1835, when the highly desirable land for the permanent location of Wabash College was purchased, the seller required personal security as well as a mortgage on the quarter section. Two men endorsed the Notes of the College for over $6,000, without any security for themselves, Andrew Shanklin and William Burbridge.

When he died (Jan. 13, 1867), at the home of his son, the *Weekly Review* noted that "in every relations of life, Judge Burbridge maintained a high character for probity, honesty and goodness of heart; he possessed in an eminent degree every virtue that turns and enobles human nature." He had won the "esteem and hearty approbation" of his neighbors; while at least three of his brothers, in affection, had named sons, "William."

As a measure of the long shadow of that esteem: when his own son, William, Jr., died 16 years later, himself a respected Crawfordsville merchant and public servant, *The Saturday Evening Journal*, describing him as "somewhat reserved and diffident," noted that William, Jr. had inherited "many of the excellent qualities of his father, whose name is yet revered and remembered by those who knew him." *Compiled from biographies sent by Ed Bartlett and Frank Brew*

GEORGE WASHINGTON AND MARY HANNA (DOUGLAS) BURK

George Washington Burk was born in Montgomery County on June 9, 1859. He was the son of John Franklin and Martha Rebecca (Reath) Burk. His father was killed in the Civil War near Kingston, GA in May of 1864, leaving him and his three surviving siblings to the care of their mother and the support of their father's Civil War pension.

"Wash," as his friends called him, grew up without the benefit of formal education, making his mark on the world through a strong Hoosier work ethic. He was a quiet man who was what was known as a tenant farmer, working different land around the area.

He married Mary Hanna Douglas, daughter of Jeremiah and Martha Jane (Mitchell) Douglas, in Montgomery County on Sept. 3, 1884. From 1885 to 1906, "Wash" and Mary Hanna brought 11 children into the world. They were Clara, John, Amanda, Martha, Pearl, Alice, Jerry, George, Cora, Bertha, and Bill. All were born in Brown Township, with the exception of Bill Burk, who came along during the family's brief stay in Russellville in Putnam County. His arrival, on Oct. 9, 1906, happened at a difficult time. Shortly before that day, his father, and sister, Martha, both came down with typhoid fever. "Wash" survived, but 16-year-old Martha did not. She died on Oct. 1, 1906, just eight days before the family welcomed the new baby.

Mary Hanna (Douglas) Burk was born on the dirt floor of her parents' log cabin in the area of Whitesville on May 12, 1864. Stories passed down paint a classic picture of an uneducated, hard-working, and warm-hearted product of the 19th Century.

Following the death of her husband "Wash" in Alamo on Dec. 21, 1939, she could often be found tending her garden at home, barefooted and in long sleeves and bonnet to prevent sunburn. She had a knack for children. A crying baby would stop fussing almost immediately in Mary Hanna's caring arms. Her home was loaded with antiques, including a pump organ and an old Victrola crank-type record player.

In her old age, she wore false teeth, which she abhorred, and took **out** whenever she ate! She was fond of sweet potatoes and enjoyed making blackberry and raspberry jam. She loved bacon, too, and was sure to drain the grease from every batch, then soak it up with a big piece of bread and eat it.

Despite her lack of education, she loved reading...mostly newspapers and the Bible. Grandchildren often saw her stooped over the scriptures, magnifying glass in hand, sounding out the larger words in her high-pitched voice. She stayed close to her beloved descendants by often staying in the homes of her children for up to six weeks at a time.

When she died on Feb. 12, 1953, the first grandsons through each of her children acted as pallbearers at her funeral in Wingate. Mary Hanna's life had spanned the administrations of 18 Presidents, from Lincoln to Eisenhower.

JERRY AND MARY (STOUT) BURK

His given name was Jeremiah, but folks just called him "Jerry", or "Jake." Born Aug. 19, 1896 in Brown Township, Jeremiah Caleb Burk was the seventh of the 11 children of George Washington and Mary Hanna (Douglas) Burk.

Jerry quit school after the third grade and left home to work in New Market, IN on the farm of his brother-in-law, Fred Wray.

In 1916, he landed a job with the Pennsylvania Railroad, starting out as a section hand, tamping ties for $1.75 a day. From 1915 to 1917, he also worked as a guard at the Indianapolis 500.

Around 1915, Jerry attended a Stout family reunion. There, he met his future wife, Mary Hazel Stout, daughter of William Everett and Eva (Michaels) Stout. They dated for 12 or 13 years before marrying on Dec. 26, 1931 at the United Brethren Church in Crawfordsville.

Jeremiah Caleb Burk and Mary Hazel Stout Burk

The Depression had cut into Jerry's hours with the railroad, so soon after the wedding they headed to New Market to take on additional work. Jerry found it with a local funeral home, preparing bodies. Further income came from lighting all the gas lights in New Market each evening. They returned to Crawfordsville in late 1934.

During World War II, Jerry was often away in Illinois, cleaning up accidents and keeping the rails clear to Chicago, the rail hub of the nation.

Mary was born in Montgomery County on Apr. 11, 1897. She attended Breaks School as a young girl, about seven miles northwest of Crawfordsville and would be picked up each morning in a horse drawn "hack." Her schooling ended after the eighth grade.

Mary enjoyed playing piano, with the bulk of her repertoire coming from her church hymnal. While Jerry was a Baptist, Mary served in the United Brethren Ladies' Aid at her church, Mount Zion, where her daughter, Jerrine, later married Gordon "Gary" Witt.

Both parents were entirely devoted to their children, Jerrine and Bob. Mary died on Nov. 7, 1960.

The following month, on Dec. 23, 1960, Jerry was nearly killed when his Crawfordsville home at 210 High Street burned to the ground with him inside.

Burn treatment was a rough way to begin retirement for Jerry, who had labored 45 years for the Pennsylvania Railroad without missing a day of work. A new house was built on the site of the old one, and in time his greatest joys came from his growing lot of grandchildren. Jerrine and her husband Gordon "Gary" Witt gave him four: Terry; Cindy, who married Randy Arnold; Julieann, who married W. Scott Fisher; and Susan, who married Edward Steele. Bob and Jackie (Craig) Burke had two: Jayne and "B.J."

Jerry passed away on July 24, 1984 in Crawfordsville. Nine great-grandchildren now claim him as an ancestor: Allison, Eric, and Michelle Fisher of Fruit Heights, UT; Sydney, Stephen, and Mallory Steele of West Palm Beach, FL; and Bambi, Rebecca, and Benjamin Arnold of Marathon, FL.

JOHN FRANKLIN AND MARTHA REBECCA (REATH) BURK

John Franklin Burk, who came to Montgomery County in the late 1850s, was born in 1831 in Philadelphia, PA. He was one of the oldest in the large family of Jesse Burk, a stone mason, and his wife, Elizabeth.

They left for New Jersey between 1836 and 1837, and then on to Red Lion, DE between 1837 and 1840. In 1842 they hopped over the border into Port Deposit, Cecil Co., MD, where they remained for a time.

George Washington Burk; Mary Hanna Douglas Burk

In the spring of 1854, John Franklin Burk and Martha Rebecca Reath, daughter of William and Catherine (McKee) Reath, eloped. It is said she tied several bedsheets together to steal away into the night with John. They made their way to Chester Co., PA where they were married on May 3, 1854.

Martha was born on Mar. 14, 1836, in Maryland. John and she had six children, the first two dying as infants. They were William C. Burk, John Albert Burk, Joseph Nathaniel Burk, George Washington Burk, Samuel Smith Burk, and Mary Elizabeth Burk.

Sometime in the late 1850s, the Burks located in Montgomery County, where John worked the land. Their home was about four and a half miles from Crawfordsville. It was a "staked homestead," consisting of a three-room house of simple construction, on one or two acres of land. They had beds in the kitchen, living room, and "front room," as they called it.

On Dec. 28, 1863, at the height of the Civil War, John signed up with Company "B" of the 120th Regiment of the Indiana Volunteers in Crawfordsville. He was mustered into the service in Lafayette on Jan. 30, 1864.

Less than four months later, John Franklin Burk was dead. According to his company captain, Charles W. Elmore, on Sunday, May 24, 1864, Private Burk "was driving a team in the supply train which was in the rear of Sherman's Army when the train was attacked by rebels and he was killed." The action took place "at or near" Kingston, GA. His failure to return from the war created much confusion, as a neighbor named Galey claimed that John Burk had been in the Confederates' Libby Prison with him. It was four years before Captain Elmore's sworn statement, and a similar one signed by five of John's comrades, cleared up the matter. The testimonies were necessary so that Martha could claim her husband's pension for her family.

Martha raised the four Burk children on her own following John's disappearance. She never remarried. The oldest child, Joseph Nathaniel Burk, and the youngest, Mary Elizabeth Burk, remained single. George Washington Burk, wed Mary Hanna Douglas, while Samuel Smith Burk exchanged vows with Martha "Mattie" Etta.

Martha (Reath) Burk died on Aug. 23, 1909, at age 73.

WILLIAM H. BUSER

The first record of William H. Buser in Montgomery County (Ladoga), is the 1860 census. He was born Dec. 19, 1836 near Xenia, OH. He died Sept. 30, 1925 New Market, IN. He was the seventh of ten children of John and Susannah Haines Buser. His brothers and sisters were: Ann Marie (James Schooley & ? Hopwood); John Hanson (Margaret Demoss); Belle, single; Susan (Hiram Oglesbee); Mary Catherine (Benjamin T. Farber); Joshua Peter (Susan English); Daniel T. (Harriett Fall); Elizabeth L. (George Richardson); Atlee M. (Cynthis E. Messenger).

While in Ladoga he as a cabinet maker, was called upon to fashion coffins. He was ahead of his time because he made some ahead in assorted sizes and this upset the folks around him and they stopped ordering coffins. He left there for New Market where he became a farmer and on Dec. 24, 1863 he married Sara Allen. She was one of six children of Stephen and Ascha Davis Allen. She was born May 22, 1840 and died Sept. 23, 1917 in New Market. They are buried at Freedom Cemetery, Montgomery County. Her brothers and sisters were: Nancy E. (John W. Harrison and ? Hanna); William Warren; Martha J.; Mary Anna; Matilda E. (H.A. Foster).

They had nine children: Gertrude "Todie" died at age ten; Mary Louise "Lou" (Marcus Beckner) one son; William H. Jr. (Emma Miles) six children; John (Etta Follick) two children; Eva N. (Charles W. Easley) six children; Roy (Ethel ? and Clevia Hill); Fannie (Gilbert Rakestraw and Charles Shurr and William Fenstemaker); five children; Stephen Ard (Manna Blanch Simpson and Alice Thomas) six children. *Submitted by I. Jo Summers*

BUSH FAMILY

The earliest members of the Bush family came to America on the Ship, Princess Augusta, Sept. 16, 1736 from Rotterdam last from Cowes, England.

Lewis Bush was born about 1720 as he was supposed to be 16 years of age when he came with his father, John. Lewis Bush served in the Revolutionary War from Rockingham Co., VA and died after 1794. He and wife Eve had: Michael, Sarah, Leonard and John Bush.

Michael, born Jan. 10, 1750 Frederick Co., VA, died Aug. 10, 1825 Concord Township Ross Co., OH. And he and wife, Magdalene (born Aug. 15, 1752, died May 5, 1821) are buried in the Strader Hill Cemetery, Concord Township. Michael Bush also served in the Revolution (Phyllis Jean Davis Moore is in the DAR under Michael). Sarah Bush, born May 16, 1753 in Virginia, died Apr. 2, 1850 Ross Co., OH and married Adam Mallow. Leonard Bush, born Mar. 5, 1755 Hampshire Co., VA died July 6, 1832 Fayette Co., OH, married Virginia Catherine Stingley. Both buried Bush Cemetery, Fayette County. Little is known about John Bush, last child of Lewis.

The above Michael Bush had the first grist mill/distillery and store in Concord Township, Ross Co., OH about 1798.

Children of Michael and Magdalene Bush: John, born Nov. 22, 1772 Hardy Co. (W.) VA died June 23, 1863, married Apr. 14, 1795 Virginia to Mary Wise (Nov. 25, 1776-Oct. 1, 1821). They had nine children: John married second, Feb. 1, 1825 Ross County to Kezia Scofield (Dec. 7, 1801-Dec. 2, 1835). John married third, Nov. 23, 1837 Elizabeth Ross. John and his wives are buried Strader Hill Cemetery.

Elizabeth, second child of Michael and Magdalene Bush, was born Nov. 24, 1776 and married Abram Power.

Michael Bush, Jr., born Nov. 12, 1779 died Tippecanoe Co., IN. Married Dec. 6, 1804 Hardy Co., VA Susannah Power, a sister of Abram.

Eve Bush, born Oct. 31, 1782 Hardy County, died Mar. 3, 1860. She married June 3, 1803 Ross County to Abraham Stookey, born June 4, 1772 South branch of the Potomac Pendelton Co., VA (now WV). He died June 28, 1858 Concord Twp., both buried Strader Hill.

Abraham and Eve Bush Stookey had: Catherine, Delilah, Amy, Mahalah, Isaac and Magdalene all born in Ross Co., OH.

Catherine Stookey, born Sept. 1, 1805 died Feb. 27, 1863 on R.R. Colfax, IN. She married Nov. 27, 1823 Ross Co., OH to John Davis who was born June 3, 1800 Albermarle Co., VA, son of William and Elizabeth Davis. John died May 4, 1868. Both buried Union Cemetery, Lauramie Township, Tippecanoe County. Ten children: William, Joel, Abraham, Lurena, Oze, Avelina, Isaac, John I., Elon, and Mary Davis. All lived in Tippecanoe and Clinton Cos., IN.

Two of their children have Montgomery County connections. Elon was born Sept. 27, 1842 in Perry Township, Clinton County and died there Aug. 20, 1929. On Feb. 23, 1868 in Sugar Creek Township, Montgomery County he married Harriett Arbegust at the Arbegust home. She was born Mar. 14, 1850 and died Feb. 8, 1923 at home R.R. Colfax. (See Arbegust history). They have seven children: Edward, Elvina, Nellie, Maude, Anna, Bessie and May Davis.

Mary, youngest child of Catherine Stookey and John Davis was born May 4, 1846 Perry Township, Clinton Co., IN, died Nov. 8, 1899 in White County. Married Job Joseph H. Ermentrout born Jan. 1, 1840 in Kirkpatrick. He died Nov. 30, 1917 White Co., IN. Both buried I.O.O.F. Cemetery, Brookston. They had three children: Clara Catherine, Charles A. and Lurena A. Ermentrout. The Crawfordsville Public Library has an extensive Davis History written by Phyllis Davis Moore. *Submitted by Phyllis Davis Moore*

JOHN H. AND BARBARA (BOOE) BUSHONG

The name Bushong originally stems from Jean Beauchamp (French) and later Hans Bosehung (German) and finally John Bushong. John H. Bushong's parents were Milo (1888-1941) and Rose Marie Meyer (1886-1956). Milo grew-up on the family farm in Parke County and another farm to which the family moved near Wallace, IN. He taught school in a one-room schoolhouse called "Old Hickory." He attended Wabash College and the Indiana School of Dentistry in Indianapolis and graduated in 1915. While in dental school, he met and married Rose Marie Meyer. The Meyer family originally came from Germany and settled in a German settlement near Cincinnati. Milo enlisted in the army during World War I in 1917 and served in France and Germany as a Captain of the Medical Corps for 18 months. Their son John (Jack) was born while he was overseas.

John H. and Barbara (Booe) Bushong

Upon his return, Milo opened a dental office in Wallace. In 1920 he opened his dental office in Crawfordsville above the First National Bank which was then located on the southwest corner of Washington and Main Streets. This was the office left vacant by the death of the dentist Dr. William R. Kirtley. "Doc," as he was affectionately called, and his wife Rose were active in community affairs. He became Commander and Service Officer of the American Legion, a member of the local Armory Board, and a Major in the Army Reserve. Rose worked side-by-side in these interests and also the Eastern Star where she attained the highest position as Worthy Matron. The respect shown Milo Bushong at his death July 4, 1941 was stated in the Crawfordsville *Journal*: "World War Veterans of Montgomery County gathered at the First Christian Church where they attended funeral services for Dr. Milo Bushong, popular Crawfordsville dentist and former American Legion Commander...burial was made at the Waynetown Masonic Cemetery where a military tribute was accorded the deceased by a Legion firing squad, color guard, and bugler."

John (Jack) Bushong went to Mills School and graduated from Crawfordsville High School in 1936. He attended Wabash College where he was a member of the Kappa Sigma fraternity. After two years at Wabash he transferred to Indiana University as a pre-med student. Interested in flying, he was accepted as a cadet at the Naval Air Station in Pensacola, FL in 1940, received his wings in the Spring of 1941, and then was an instructor in Corpus Christi, TX. After the bombing of Pearl Harbor, he was assigned to the Naval Air Station at Terminal Island, CA. On May 12, 1943, he married Barbara Booe. They lived in Long Beach, CA where their son John Allen was born in 1944. After duty in the Pacific flying into China, Japan, the Philippines and various Pacific Islands, Jack entered I.U. Dental School. Upon completion, the family moved back to Crawfordsville where Jack practiced dentistry in the Ben Hur Building until his retirement in 1978. For 20 years he was the head of the Aviation Board. He is a Commander in the Naval Reserves and the Blue and Gold Officer for this district for the Naval Academy in Annapolis. *Submitted by Barbara Bushong*

MAHLON BUTLER

Mahlon Butler was born in Dinwiddie Co., VA, Jan. 27, 1821, son of Lemuel and Jane Butler. He came to Wayne County near Richmond when six months old. His family came to Montgomery County in 1834 where his father acquired 500 acres of land six miles east of Crawfordsville. This farm now known as Gravelly Run is now owned by Mrs. Aben Abbott, a granddaughter of Mahlon. The Friends Church called Gravelly Run was a part of this farm.

Mahlon Butler obtained education beyond most men of his day, having attended a Seminary near Richmond, and taught school in Rush County. It was here he met Eunice Lacey, daughter of Peirson Lacey, a prominent Rush County citizen. They were married in 1850 and came at once to Montgomery County where he had already built a home, making the trip in easy stages. He was one of the pioneer settlers of Montgomery County coming while the country was almost an unbroken wilderness. "He was widely known as an industrious, hard working, self-reliant man of excellent judgement and above all of eminent piety". It was said "he had no enemies".

Mahlon and Eunice were members of the Society of Friends and maintained fervent interest in that religion all their lives. They never missed a Wednesday evening meeting. Mahlon served as an Elder for 50 years.

To this union were born five children: Emeline, Emily, Jane, Lindley, and Charles. Three of the children preceded their parents in death. Charles Butler became a prominent Republican citizen in Crawfordsville. He later married Hallie Mount, daughter of Gov. James A. Mount. He was one of the early Montgomery County Fair Board Presidents, as well as Board President of the Indiana School for the Blind, an interest developed because two of his sisters were sight impaired. Mrs. Butler mastered Braille so she could communicate with them. Charles was a member of the State Republican Committee.

Mahlon, whose wife died two years prior, was stricken with paralysis March 1st and passed away March 5th at the age of 83 years. He left a heritage of kindness, forbearance and charity in addition to his material assets of over half a section of fine improved land in Montgomery County. *Submitted by Louise Butler Kuonen*

FRED MILAM AND LOUISE DEE (SINGER) BUZZAIRD

Fred Milam Buzzaird was born Apr. 23, 1910 in Bloomington, IN, youngest of the six children of Elmer Sherman Buzzaird and Margaret Katherine Kirby. Elmer was born Sept. 30, 1866 in Owen County to John B. and Mary Ann (Milam) Buzzaird and died July 19, 1936 in Montgomery County. On Mar. 21, 1889 he married Katie, daughter of William M.A. and Nancy (Bunger) Kirby, who was born May 1, 1867 in Monroe County and died Nov. 15, 1951 in Montgomery County.

His siblings were: Frankie M., b. and d. 1890 at five mo., 16 da.; Earl Kirby, b. Mar. 21, 1892, d. 1959; Cecile Mae, b. Jan. 10, 1895, d. 1969, m. Fred B. Jackson, 1921; Ruby, b. Oct. 19, 1896, m. _____ Saunders; and Catherine Virginia, b. Aug. 2, 1905, m. Jay Anderson.

On Nov. 14, 1931, Fred married Louise Dee Singer, born Apr. 19, 1907, the only child of Hugh Franklin and Dottie Margaret (Stephens) Singer, whose biographies are listed elsewhere in this volume. After their marriage, Fred and Louise lived at 804 East College Street.

Fred graduated from Bloomington High School in 1925 at the age of 15, and joined the family farm. He moved to Montgomery County about 1928 and became an assistant manager at Woolworth's. According to his marriage license application in 1931, he was then a livestock dealer, and later worked for Ward Dairy. During the mid- to late-1930s, he managed a concrete block shop for Frank Singer, his father-in-law. In 1941, he was the third person in Indiana to become a certified livestock artificial insemination technician. That year, he and Louise began Dairyman's Artificial Insemination Service, a small bull stud located on the Ladoga Road next to the Saddle Club. In 1946 the business and family were moved to a home on Sugar Creek, five miles northeast of Crawfordsville. The family lived there until 1954, when they moved to Orlando, FL.

Fred Milam and Louise Dee (Singer) Buzzaird. Children Dottie L., Frankie A. and Fred M. Jr.

Louise graduated from Crawfordsville High School in 1925 and attended business school for one year. She worked as a bookkeeper for Burch and Burch Machine Shop until her marriage. After the death of her husband, she returned to work in a doctor's office.

Fred and Louise were the parents of three children: Fred M., Jr., b. Feb. 12, 1933, m. Grace W. Jones Aug. 14, 1954, now living in Oviedo, FL; Dottie Louise, b. Sept. 30, 1937, m. Raymond Carl Davis (b. 1937, d. 1964) Aug. 4, 1957, m. William Howard, May 5, 1967, now living in Oviedo, FL, and Frankie Anita, b. Sept. 16, 1940, m. Alfred L. Hammond, Jr. Jan. 31, 1959, now living in Alachua, FL.

Fred died Feb. 21, 1961, and Louise died Dec. 4, 1973, both in Orange Co., FL. They are buried in Drawdy Cemetery.

BYMASTER HISTORY

We have traced the Bymasters back to the 19th century in Central Europe. At this time a young boy and his cousin left their home in Germany, having no money they signed onto a ship as hands for seven years. David Lewis Byermiester, born July 12, 1796, was one of the boys (he was my great-great-great-grandfather). Upon arriving in America the captain of the ship sold their services to the highest bidder, that being the custom in order to pay their passage and not needing any extra hands. The two cousins went to work in a shipyard on the Atlantic coast. After working the seven years in the shipyard and being free of his debt, David Lewis Bymaster (he dropped the extra letters in his last name when he arrived in America) now moved around to anywhere he could find work. During this time in his life he met and married Anna Berry in Pennsylvania. After their marriage they moved around settling in Montgomery Co., IN, and started farming in the southeast part of the county known as Scott Township near Ladoga. They had six children, John, Lucy, David Lewis, Will, Julia, and Mary.

David Lewis Bymaster, born May 10, 1829, in Pennsylvania, moved with his parents to Ohio then settled in Indiana (this was my great-great-grandfather). David met Sidney Jane Clark; whose family lived about two miles east on the same road. They had seven sons and seven daughters, ten lived to adulthood. Their names were Sarah, Benjamin, Emma, Jefferson, Marinda, Danial Webster, Lucinda, James, Pearl, and Ada.

Daniel and Lillie (Burk) Bymaster

Danial Webster (my great-grandfather) married Lillie Burk. They lived and farmed the same place as his father and grandfather did before him. David and Lillie had seven children, Eva, Lela, Roy, Hallie, Naomi, Ruby Glen, and Manny.

Roy Bymaster born Dec. 19, 1900 (my grandfather) grew up on the same land that he would farm and raise his family on. Roy attended Ford school further east on Haw Creek Road. Roy also drove a school-hack pulled by a team of horses and later a schoolbus. To help pay taxes, as many farmers did then, Roy hauled gravel and graded the road. Roy married Neva McFerran, and had four children, two lived to adulthood, Marjorie, and Glen William. Glen (my father) born Apr. 1, 1925 graduated from Ladoga High School and married Rosemary Goettling. They started farming in Scott Township but moved to Coal Creek Township in 1945, where they later bought a farm on the New Richmond-Linden Blacktop. Glen and Rosemary have three children, Gary, Sherry, and Rick. Even though the Bymasters no longer live on the homestead farm in Scott Township, we are still farming. Rick is currently farming the original homestead farm in Scott Township, owed by Neva Bymaster Zimmerman. The Bymaster family was one of the earlier settlers of Montgomery County and we are still proud to live and farm the land of Montgomery County today. *By Sherry Bymaster Coon*

CANINES OF MONTGOMERY COUNTY

Ralph and Margaret Canine, progenitors of the Canines in Montgomery County, came here in early 1826 from Shelby Co., KY where his father Peter Carnine had been granted 1,000 acres of land for Revolutionary War Service. They settled on a farm north of Waveland where they reared nine children, most of them staying in the county. In September, 1826 the Union Primitive Baptist Church was organized in the Canine home. The church is no longer there, but in Union Cemetery, close to the old family home and still maintained, many of the family lay buried. Two of his grandsons, George and Lemuel Jackson remained in Brown Township and reared families in the Freedom Baptist Church community. Many of them were active in the church there and are buried in the Freedom Cemetery.

George had four children. Lena married Ed Myers and they lived north of Freedom Church until their deaths. Mantie married William Cason. Kittie married Paul Welchel and lived south of Freedom Church on the Charlie Canine farm. Ben lived in Waveland and operated a garage there for many years.

Lemuel Jackson had seven children; one only lived a year. Maude married Roy Martin and lived in Montgomery County. Joe who married Nellie Galey became a chiropractor in Washington D.C. Nannie married Will Wright who died in 1927. She then married Howard Munns and lived in Crawfordsville. Ola married Cinderella Miller and they lived on the Country Club Road in Crawfordsville. L.G. (Tude) married Mertie Miles and lived near Browns Valley. Robert, the oldest son, married Alice Stilwell who was his teacher at the old Freedom School. During the first few years of their marriage they lived near Deers Mill. After their youngest son, David, was born they moved into the Freedom community where they lived the rest of their lives. They were both very active in the Freedom Baptist Church. Robert was a deacon for over 50 years and Alice was a Sunday School teacher. They had two daughters and two sons, one who died in infancy.

Thelma, their older daughter, following in her mother's footsteps, became a teacher. Later she married Ernest Smith who preceded her in death by 28 years. They had no children. They lived in the Smith homestead in Brown Township on a farm bordering Sugar Creek and rented Smith Cabins and Campgrounds for several years. Thelma continued living there until her death in May 1986.

Mary married Everett Brown from Newtown. They lived on the old Canine homestead north of Waveland for a while, then bought a farm west of Parkersburg. They had two daughters. Mary Elizabeth married Lieutenant Oscar Jones of Blanchester, OH. They live in Attica and have two daughters, Susan and Sarah and a son Stephen. Martha Lou married Reverend Donald Tyler from Waynetown. They live in Brownsburg where he pastors the Bethesda Baptist Church and is the administrator of the Bethesda Baptist Schools. They have two daughters, Debbie and Joanna. *Submitted by Margaret Canine*

DAVID G. CANINE FAMILY

David G. Canine, son of Robert and Alice (Stilwell) Canine was born Oct. 2, 1915 near the Shades. He was a sickly child, suffering from asthma and tonsilitis until he and his mother rode the train to Indianapolis to have his tonsils out when he was seven. He also stuttered and was teased by other children. His parents prayed that he could speak so people could understand him, never dreaming he would be able to preach. He graduated from Waveland High School in 1934 where he starred in basketball. He was saved in the summer of 1934 and entered Wabash College in the fall. While a student there he felt the call to become a minister and was called to the Baptist Chapel to be their pastor. In his junior year he married Margaret Priebe. He graduated from Wabash in 1938 and organized East Side Baptist Church that October. He had other very successful ministries in Blanchester, OH; Hazel Park, MI and Highland, IN. There are many young people in the ministry today because of his influence in their lives.

David and Margaret had four children. Patricia, their oldest, married Warren Allem, a graduate of Moody Bible Institute of Chicago and Cedarville College in Cedarville, OH. They had five children; Mike, (Dayton, OH); Cherry (Whittier, CA); Cindy married to Terry Fuestel and living in Hammond, IN; Cathy, a Mary Kay Cosmetic Director in Munster, IN and Candy, a senior at Liberty University in Lynchburg, VA. Warren and Pat currently live in Munster where he is pastor of the Faith Baptist Church and she is an Executive Senior Director with Mary Kay.

Sam the older son, after graduating from Cedarville College, went to Dallas Theological Seminary, where he obtained a Master of Theology Degree. He then pastored for 11 years in Lima, OH. While there he earned a Master of Communication and a Doctor of Philosophy at Bowling Green (Ohio) University. He currently is a professor at the Dallas Seminary. He married June Golden of Stanton, MI. She is a private music teacher and is organist at Grace Bible Church in Dallas. They have one daughter, Michelle.

John, the younger son starred in basketball for Ohio University and was drafted by the Phoenix Suns, but was later cut. The New York Nets wanted to pick him up, but he decided professional basketball was not for him. He taught school in Ferndale, MI and later went into evangelistic work. He earned his Masters and Doctors degrees in Education at Wayne State University, Detroit, MI. He is currently director of Maximum Living with offices in Birmingham, Grand Rapids, and Flint, MI. He is married to Patricia Webb and they have three sons, David, Daniel, and Derek. They live in Bloomfield Hills, MI.

Rebecca, the youngest child, is a graduate of Cedarville College, Cedarville, OH and is currently working toward her Masters Degree at Purdue University. She teaches at Willson School in Crawfordsville. She married Steven Overholt from Royal Oak, MI who is a graduate of Cedarville College and has his Masters from Dallas Theological Seminary. He is currently associate pastor of East Side Baptist Church in Crawfordsville, the church his father-in-law organized in October of 1938. They have three children, Joshua, Joanna, and Jodie.

The history of the Canine family is available in the Crawfordsville Public Library. It was compiled by Edwin Canine, in 1935. He was a professor at Indiana State College (Terre Haute) for many years. *Submitted by Margaret Canine*

CARLILE-CARLISLE

Our story began in the mid 1800's with I. Thomas and Cassandra Carlile in Marion Co., KY.

II. Their son Nathaniel born in 1846 married Martha Ferris and had five children. Nathaniel was shot in the general store in 1888 by someone cleaning a gun; after serving in the 34th Army Regiment at Louisville during the Civil War.

Jean, Esther, Marvin, Kenneth and Berniece Carlile

III. John Taylor was born in 1871 and married Lavone Ella Nelson in 1894. They were a farming family, belonged to the Baptist Church and John was a Mason. They had eight children when Lavone became sick and passed away in 1912. John Taylor loaded up all the children and moved to Indiana just east of Wallace in 1913.

Their children IV. Hattie Kathryn and Thomas Taylor remained at home. Flora Ethel married Zearn Miles in 1927 and are presently still living in Crawfordsville.

IV. Vernest Redmond married Anna Mae Donlouie in 1937. They had one daughter Marilyn.

IV. Ora Esther married Roy Maudlin in 1927 and had three children. V. Shirley married Robert Cox in 1948, James married Mary Wolf in 1953, and Richard married Rosalyn Kelley in 1955. VI. They have ten grandchildren: Cheryl Ann, Caryl Ann and Patricia Cox, Tab R., Tod R., Tonya, Mark, Matt, Brett and Bart Maudlin. VII. There are now 12 great grandchildren: Dillon, Michael and Sara Cox, James Johnson Barnes, Dana and Kevin Sweet, Matt, Melissa, Nathan, Cody and Andrew Maudlin.

IV. Lottie Gertrude married Maurice "Doc" Bratton in 1930. Their children V. Jack married Nancy Polk in 1953, Connie married John Horner in 1958. They have five grandchildren: VI. Jack Chi, Deborah and Jeanine Bratton, Julie and Sam Horner.

IV. Charles Raymond married Evelyn Everson in 1937. Evelyn still remains in Crawfordsville.

IV. Marvin William settled in 1914 just north of Alamo on the Mooney Farm. Marvin married Elizabeth Ann Newkirk in 1917 and they settled on 140 acres in Jackson Twp., Sec. 19 just east of Wallace. They gave birth to five children: V. Leonard who died at birth.

V. Esther Geraldine married Maurice Bryant in 1938 and settled in Waynetown where they gave birth to three sons: VI. Richard Lee, Ronald Maurice and Edwin Eugene. VII. They have three grandchildren: Rodney Lee, Sara Beth and Justin Richard.

V. Kenneth Jerome married Nancy Ann Dawson in 1958 and gave birth to four children: VI. Lindsay Jerome, Suzanne Elizabeth, Judith Lynne and Kevin Jerome. VII. They have two grandchildren: Mason Jerome Carlile and Jessica Lynne Dennis.

V. Barbara Jean married Paul Keith Keller in 1953 and had two daughters: VI. Barbara Ann and Lisa Michelle. They also have three grandchildren: VII. Darrell, Alexia and Jay Grubbs.

V. Berniece Lucille married Eston Myers in 1938 and had six children: VI. Jerry Dean, Sandra Kay, Linda Dianne, Brenda Lucille, Byron Carlisle and Carol Jean. They have 15 grandchildren: VII. Lucinda Joan Calloway, Jerry Dean Myers Jr., Donna Reed, Lawrence and Christa Gillogly, Brian and Dama Mendenhall, Sabrina, Bobbi and Kathy Sommerville, Michael, Ian and Eston Myers, Mandee and Stacey Poole. There are four great grandchildren: VIII. Jeremy and Jonathon Calloway, Jakota Reed and Corey Gillogly. *Submitted by Berniece L. Myers*

CARRINGTON-CLEMENTS

Flora Carrington Wells' parents were Frank T. Carrington and Henrietta Clements Carrington. They married in Browns Valley, IN on Apr. 26, 1903. Frank and Henrietta lived in Browns Valley when their daughter Flora was born on Apr. 10, 1904. It was in 1907 that they moved to Crawfordsville where in 1913 another daughter, Martha, was born. Frank went to work for the Johnson Acetylene Gas Company and later became superintendent.

Frank Carrington was the son of Alexander and Martha Wilson Carrington, who reared a very large family on a farm near Russellville.

Henrietta's parents were James J. Clements and Flora Spaulding Clements (who died in 1901). The Spaulding family lived in Frankfort, IN.

Flora Carrington 1922

Flora Spaulding Clements' father was William Spaulding, a veteran of the Civil War. He fought with the Union Army at Lookout Mountain and was with "Sherman's March to the Sea". William Spaulding's grandfather was Captain John Cook, of Virginia, who fought in the Revolutionary War. Alexander Carrington's great grandfather, Samaul Carrington was with Captain John Hanson's Company, of the 12th Battalion from Charles Co., MD, fought in the Revolutionary War.

James Clements (Flora's grandfather) owned the general store in Browns Valley where he sold everything from needles to farm machinery. He moved to Crawfordsville about 1912, where he owned the J.J. Clements' Coal Company on West Pike street, between Washington and Walnut streets. He lived to be 85 years old. His youngest daughter, Hazel (sister of Henrietta), and her husband, Ben Myers, assumed management of the coal company when James suffered a stroke.

Before, during and after World War I, Saturday was the most important day in Crawfordsville. The stores were open until 9:00 P.M. and most everyone was downtown at that time. It usually took Henrietta Carrington from 6:30 until 9:00 to walk from Bischoff's store on Main street, to Graham's store on Washington street, while she visited with friends and relatives.

Frank Carrington died in April 1923 and Henrietta Carrington died in 1924. Their youngest daughter, Martha, went to California to live with her Aunt, Mabel Clements Cary, wife of Dr. N. Austen Cary.

Martha married Kenneth Means, and reared three children. She passed away in 1987.

Flora graduated from Crawfordsville High School in 1922. The next year, 1923, she married Theodore N. Wells and moved to Indianapolis where she has lived since that time. Theodore died in 1985. Flora, soon to be 85 years old, has 39 direct descendents thus far.

The years Flora Carrington Wells spent in Crawfordsville, were some of the happiest of her life. She visits there often with old friends from her high school days. She still calls Crawfordsville home.

It is a pleasure for her to visit downtown Crawfordsville. The beautiful, old Courthouse still looks the same. Main and Washington streets, except for the names of the stores, is almost the same as it was in the early 1900s. Crawfordsville was, and still is, a great place to grow up!

HOUSTON D. CARSON

Houston D. Carson, a cabinetmaker, was born in Highland Co., OH in December 1821, the son of James and Jane Carson. It is not certain what year he settled in Franklin Township, Montgomery Co., IN. It is known that on Dec. 31, 1843 he married Mary Lane in Montgomery County. She was the daughter of Elisha Lane, a native of Fluvanna Co., VA and Elizabeth Layne, a native of Goochland Co., VA. Mary died in May 1864. Houston later married Cordelia A. Lowman. They had one daughter Martha. Cordelia died on Oct. 1, 1903. Houston died on Jan. 5, 1904.

Houston and Mary Carson were the parents of five children, three of whom grew to adulthood. Eliza Jane was born in 1844 and died in 1912. She married Lewis P. Carson. Frank was born in 1851. Jesse Edgar was born in 1858 and died in 1918. He married Grizzellah Jane Scannel.

Lewis P. and Eliza Jane Carson were the parents of four children-George, Frank, Mary Effie, and Antonia. Mary Effie married Samuel P. Milner. Antonia married James Oliver Jackman on Nov. 26, 1892 in Montgomery County.

James and Antonia Jackman were the parents of a son Glen who was born Oct. 17, 1893. Glen was raised and adopted by his Uncle Jesse Edgar Carson and his wife Grizzellah Jane. Glen thereafter went by the name Carson. On Sept. 23, 1914 he married Florence Avenel Locke, daughter of William A. and Ruth M. (Gibson) Locke. Glen was for many years a barber in Darlington. Florence served as the substitute piano player at the local silent film movie house. She also played organ at the Congregational Christian Church for 45 years. Glen Carson died on Apr. 27, 1955 and Florence Carson died on June 2, 1986.

Glen and Florence Carson were the parents of two sons-William Edgar and Glen Harold. William married Claribel Zenor. They are residents of Lebanon, IN. William was for many years credit manager for Winkler-US Machine. He retired from the Indiana Gas Company in Lebanon, having been employed as Commercial Manager. William and Claribel are the parents of two children-Ronald Alan Carson and Karen Kay Carson Ewing. Ronald and his wife Ute reside in Galveston, TX with their three daughters, Caitlin Maria, Claudia Aenne, and Cecile Florence. Karen and her husband Joe reside in Evansville, IN with their children, Monty Joe, Mark Alan, Matt Ryan, and Megan Elizabeth.

Glen Harold Carson married Norma Ruth Chaney, a native of Greene Co., IN. They have four children-Mary Ann Carson Carpenter, Robert Paul Carson, Richard Lee Carson, and Bette Jane Carson. Robert has one daughter, Emily Suzanne. Richard has two daughters, Kelly Dee and Kimberly Allison. Glen Harold served in the Army Air Force in England and France during World War II. He worked as a buyer for Commercial Filters in Lebanon, IN for over 36 years. He died May 7, 1987 at his home in Crawfordsville.

THE CASTERS OF MONTGOMERY COUNTY

John Caster and Elizabeth Robbins Beck were the founders of the Caster family in Montgomery County. John came to Indiana from Virginia by way of Kentucky and land-granted in 1816. Elizabeth and her family migrated through Ohio from Pennsylvania. They were married in 1840 and began farming on their 160 acre plot eight miles east of Crawfordsville, which would remain in the Caster family for 170 years.

Three sons and two daughters were born of their marriage: Abraham, Isaac, Jacob, Sarah, and Charity. The eldest, Abraham (referred to as "A.B."), was born in 1841. During the Civil War, all three sons served their country honorably.

Jesse and Ione Caster

While the others took up farming around the county, Abraham remained on the original family farm. He was first married to Abbie Sutton, who died, leaving one son, Fred. Later, he married Emma L. Shaver, daughter of Daniel and Sarah Shaver, another old Montgomery County family. This union was blessed with a son, Jesse, born in 1884, and two daughters, Mellie and Ursula.

Due to his father's age, Jesse took over the family farm at the age of 15. He had finished eight grades at Kingsley Chapel, a one-room school located just a few miles down the road, beside a church of the same name. Jesse started what was to be a long life of hard work by serving as janitor of this little church, for the "sum" of five dollars per year. Additional schooling was not available, since the interurban tracks had not yet been laid, and there was no way for young Jesse to get to Crawfordsville High School. Jesse did not let the lack of formal education deter him from living a long and successful life.

In 1911, Jesse married Ione Tribbett, who was a daughter of Albert G. and Adella Mount Tribbett. Her parents were also old-line Montgomery County families, as the Tribbetts and Mounts had deep roots here. Through this union came three daughters and a son: Carolyn, Martha Jean, Elizabeth, and another Abraham, named for his grandfather. Ione had not had the opportunity for a higher education herself, but because of her love of reading and of writing poetry, she hoped to see all of the children attend college.

While their family was growing up, Jesse increased the size of the farm from 160 to 640 acres— a square mile. Grain acreage and animal production combined to make a highly successful enterprise. Jesse also operated a maple sugar camp in his "big north woods," producing hundreds of gallons of delicious syrup for eager customers in Crawfordsville. For his own family he kept a large stand of bees. This was indeed the "sweet" aspect of his farming!

A proud event in this dedicated farmer's life was the hosting of the 1963 National Farm Progress Show.

Jesse was not "just a farmer," but was involved in numerous projects around the county. With friends, he strung the lines and poles for the Shanondale Telephone Co. He was a charter member and a 40-year director of the Montgomery County Sales Pavilion; and he served three terms as a county commissioner. Jesse Caster was a life-long Republican, and at the age of 90, at their annual dinner, he was introduced as "Mr. Republican."

As all good things must come to an end, so, too, did the life of this devoted father and dedicated farmer. At the age of 94, he left this county a much better place than when he entered. It was the end of an era! *Submitted by Elizabeth Caster Backe*

JOHN AND MARY POLLY (MOSIER) CEDARS

John Cedars was born Sept. 1, 1820, in Trenton, NJ. His father came from England, and is thought to have been named John. Young John was with his father who was drowned while swimming a horse in the Fox River of Virginia. His mother, a sister, and he somehow met the Mosier family from Maryland who was enroute to Oregon and joined them. Mary Polly Mosier was born Apr. 6, 1820, somewhere in Maryland. John and she were married in Indiana on Feb. 14, 1838, and continued on their way to Oregon. However, they, his mother and Mary Polly's brothers, John and Will Mosier, returned from Illinois, and settled near Newtown, IN. Some of the family made it to Oregon, though, as there is a town named Mosier. John's mother remarried and was called "Grandma Fowler," living and dying at Attica. Her daughter became John Shield's wife, and mother of Em Westfall.

Standing: Burton (Burt) Cedars, Charles, Oscar Y. and Goldie May, children of George W. and Margaret Singer Cedars

John and Mary Polly Mosier Cedars bought a farm four miles southeast of Waynetown, paying for it with gold. So they called it the "Gold Farm." Here they celebrated their Golden Wedding, Feb. 14, 1888. Their five children were Mary Jane, Thomas Jefferson, Sarah, William Franklin and George Washington Cedars. Mary Polly was left-handed, she died Oct. 14, 1904. John was a farmer and a Democrat; also a member of the Predestinarian Baptist Church at Elmdale. He died in his home Dec. 25, 1909.

Jane married a Shafer and had seven children: Wal (Wallace or Walter), Harry, Howard, Ella, Sarah, Rhoda, and Florence.

Thomas married Jemima Whitaker and had three children — John, Robert and Mary.

Sarah married a Smith and lived at Armstrong, IL. She had a daughter, Mellanie.

Frank married (1st) Sarah _____, and had Albert and _____. 2nd Edna _____ and had Verne.

George lived on with his parents until they died. He married Margaret Emza Singer and had five children. The four that lived were Burt, Charles, Oscar and Goldie. *Submitted by Mary Elizabeth Cedars*

SIMEON CHAPMAN AND SONS

During the 1830s Simeon Chapman, wife Lura (Bingham) Chapman, and many of their seven children resided in Montgomery Co., IN. They were farmers, and loyal family members. The account of their stay in Montgomery County is one of families supporting families, and honoring parents.

Simeon Chapman was a veteran of the Revolutionary War and was of pioneering and Christian stock. About ten years after his birth on May 21, 1764 at Norwich, CT, his father, Uriah Chapman and family settled with about 30 other families upon hostile lands in eastern Pennsylvania known as the Wallenpaupack. Simeon remained there after his marriage in about 1790 until 1825-6, when he moved to Darke Co., OH to join his second eldest son, Marvin, and his young family. In 1830-1, Simeon, Marvin and their families removed to Indiana.

Lura Chapman, Simeon's wife, was blind for the last 40 years of her life. Her sons and their families generally lived near their parents, and each other, during her lifetime and after. In about 1832 Thomas B. Chapman and younger brother Lyman J. Chapman moved to Indiana; Thomas to Tippecanoe County and Lyman to Montgomery County. When Simeon B. Chapman, Simeon Sr.'s youngest son, married in 1833, he and his wife continued as residents of Montgomery County for about five years. By 1840, when all of the Chapmans but Marvin had relocated to nearby Jackson Township, Tippecanoe County, parents Simeon and Lura Chapman were living there with son Simeon B. Even after leaving Indiana in 1840 to eventually relocate in Franklin Co., MO, the four married Chapman brothers, Thomas B., Marvin, Lyman J., and Simeon B., stayed close to each other and their parents. Their blind mother and aged father were remembered and cared for until their deaths in approximately 1845.

While residing in Montgomery County, three of Simeon Chapman's children intermarried with members of the Mitchell family, who hailed from Kentucky. In July, 1832 Lyman J. Chapman married Margery Mitchell. In January 1833 Lura Chapman (twin sister to Simeon B.) married Samuel G. Mitchell. In December 1833 Simeon B. Chapman married Jane Mitchell. For an unknown reason, Lyman's wife Margery died in 1833-4. He remarried a woman of French ancestry named Catherine about 1834.

In counting the grandchildren of Simeon and Lura Chapman, which number at least 51, 12 appear to have been born in Montgomery Co., IN. Like so many other pioneer families, they left their mark in the lives they touched and the families they raised.

BOB AND SUE CHEATHAM

The Cheatham family arrived in Crawfordsville in 1965 with mixed emotions. Bob originated from Monroe County — Sue from Barren Co., KY, and in those regions, friendliness reigned! It was quite different here, but now, after 24 years in Montgomery Co., IN, it feels like home and people seem to have more "Hoosier Hospitality."

Robert "Bob" Darrell Cheatham was delivered Oct. 25, 1946 at his parent's home (by a lady doctor) in Mud Lick, KY. He was a blue baby. Bob's parents are: Robert Albert and Alma Ruth (Houchins) Cheatham. Bob was raised by his grandparents,

Napoleon Bonaparte (Bony) and Annie Mae (Cheatham) Cheatham. Bob has three sisters, Betty, Sondra and Wanda.

Sue Mae Harrison was born May 26, 1947, the first girl and first of seven born in a hospital. Her siblings are: Jerry, Larry, Robert, Danny, Nancy and Michael. There is exactly 21 years to the day between Jerry, the oldest and Michael, the youngest. Sue's parents are: Theron Dale and Ruth (Matthews) Harrison.

Robert Darrell and Sue M. (Harrison) Cheatham, Phillip Darrell and Troy Wayne

Bob's first few years in grade school were spent in a one-room school. He graduated from Gamaliel High School in 1965; Sue from Temple Hill the same year. After graduation, Bob came to Montgomery County to find employment. He started work at Ingress in June and H-C Industries in September. He began as a hopper at H-C and is now a foreman. Sue worked her way through high school (her father didn't think it was necessary for a girl to have a diploma) as a Nurse's Aid at T.J. Sampson Community Hospital in Glasgow. Bob returned to Kentucky on a bus (his car was broken down) to marry Sue on Aug. 17, 1965 in Gainesville, TN by a Justice of the Peace in a tiny courthouse room (yes, they eloped) with the witnesses peering through the door.

Two sons were born to Bob and Sue, both at Culver Hospital. Phillip Darrell on Nov. 29, 1967 and Troy Wayne on Nov. 24, 1970. Both boys were active in Boy Scouts, FFA and band. Both are graduates from Southmont High School, where Troy served as President of the band his Junior year and Drum Major his Senior year. Phil is a student at Indiana State University, studying geology.

The family are members of Woodland Heights Christian Church where the boys are active in the Youth Group and Bob is Elder. Bob's interests include hunting, fishing and camping. Sue also enjoys camping. Sue's real love, however, is people, which is part of the reason she attended Lafayette Beauty Academy. She worked at Donnelley's, Steel Industries and New Ross Steak House prior to the Academy. Her beauty shop is Sue's Southern Shears (located in her home on Traction Road) and her job and their church work helped the family realize that Crawfordsville, Montgomery Co., IN is truly "HOME!"

CHRISTOPHER SANTFORD CHRITTON

Christopher Santford Chritton was born in 1793 in Virginia. His wife, Eura Eaton Drake, was born in 1798 in New Jersey. They were married in Brown Co., OH and moved to Montgomery Co., IN about 1828. Christopher was a skilled and reliable stone and brick mason. He burned the first brick made in the county and put up the first brick chimney in Montgomery County. He assisted in the erection of many important buildings in Crawfordsville, including the courthouse and some of the churches. Christopher was a Democrat and they were members of the Baptist Church. He died in January 1850.

Eura was a devout Christian whose business ability was a definite asset after the death of her husband. In September of 1852, she moved with her younger children to Livingston Co., IL. Besides rearing her own children, she mothered three grandchildren who had lost their mothers. Christopher and Eura Chritton had 17 children; two of whom, Eura and Johnnie, died as small children.

Isaac, the eldest, married Matilda Zucck and they continued to live in Montgomery County where he was a millwright. He is buried near Waynetown. Enoch married Salome Snyder. He was a miller but later homesteaded in Nebraska. Joseph married Nancy Derrickson. Their older children were born in Indiana before they moved to Tennessee. Cary Alexander married Lewisa Henderson. In 1842, Azuba Lucinda married James F. Compton, a plough stocker. Lucinda died when the children were quite small. Catherine married Martin Stine, then a Mr. Kincaid and later married Henry D. Peed. William Washburn Chritton was a wheelwright. He married Loriann Rector who died in 1854. She left a baby, George, who was one of those raised by his grandmother, Eura Chritton. Rachel Ann married Stacey Bell in 1854. In 1866, with their eight children, they moved to Illinois. After Stacey's death, Rachel married Samuel Bowersock. Robert B. Chritton married Elizabeth Scott. Rebecca "Jane" married Jacob Spencer. Charles Santford married Matilda Peed. Three small children survived at Matilda's early death. He later married Pleasant Shepherd. Mary Minerva "Molly" Chritton married Dave Runyon. Christopher Santford (Jr.) married Marry E. Masters. James Chritton, a soldier, died in the Civil War. America Ellen married Rozell Fenner. Seven of these marriages took place in Montgomery Co., IN.

As members of the family married, some migrated westward to other mid-west states. Later generations continued the westward movement to the far west. In 1987, a descendant, Esther Tombaugh Spreen, published a book entitled *THE CHRITTON FAMILY* in which she traced as many of the descendents as she could, as well as the ancestors of the family.

The descendents of Eura and Christopher Chritton are now engaged in a great many kinds of work. Unique among them is Clyde W. Tombaugh, an astronomer, who is credited with the discovery of the planet, Pluto, in 1930. As with all families, many of the boys and a few of the girls have represented our nation in military service. *Submitted by Esther T. Spreen*

CLAMPITT-KUHNS

Ezekiel Clampitt was born in Stokes Co., NC on Nov. 8, 1801, the youngest son of Richard and Elizabeth Masten Clampitt. Richard was born in Kent Co., DE on Jan. 20, 1748. Ezekiel married Ruth Warren in December, 1829. In 1832, they immigrated to Indiana from Stokes County with their small son, John Wesley to near Sheridan, IN. From the *Indianapolis Star Magazine*, we learn this about Ezekiel:

"Ezechiel Clampitt must have had at least a touch of serendipity, that wondrous gift of finding worthwhile things you aren't looking for. Clampitt is credited with 'bringing in' the first natural gas well in Indiana, in 1832 on his farm near Sheridan in Hamilton County. He didn't plan it that way: he was looking for water at the time, so he dug another well. The gas well was 'lit off' (the escaping gas ignited) and for weeks Clampitt's pillar of fire was the talk of the countryside. People came in droves to see it."

Back Row L to R: Nelson, Kenneth. Bottom: Wilbur and Juanita

Ezekial's son, John Wesley was born in 1831. His wife was Delvina Jane Harold. Their third son, Albert Clampitt married Nancy Harshman and had Guy, born July 6, 1890 in Clinton Co., IN.

Guy married Della Kuhns Jan. 24, 1912 in Mulberry, IN. Della was the daughter of Solomon and Dora DeVoss Kuhns and was born on Nov. 22, 1893 near Dayton. There was 11 children in the family. Her father, Solomon, when a small child, immigrated with his mother, Sara Kuhns and her parents, Mr. and Mrs. James McDowell (early 1860's) from Western Pennsylvania to near Dayton. Sara's husband, Ruben Kuhns while serving in the Civil War, died and is buried at Arlington Cemetery.

After residing in Clinton County a few years, Guy and Della moved (1917) to Franklin Township, near Darlington, IN.

Mr. Clampitt was a farmer all his life and they lived at three different locations near Darlington. When he retired in 1945, they purchased a farm in Boone County north of Thorntown, where they lived until their death.

Guy and Della Kuhns Clampitt had five children: Hazel Pauline (died young); Kenneth Harold, a World War II veteran, lives on the family farm in Boone County; Nelson Charles lives on R.R. 7, Crawfordsville; Wilbur K., a World War II veteran, resides in Lafayette and Juanita L. (Mrs. James R. Baker) a member of Dorothy Q Chapter, DAR lives near Ladoga, IN. *Submitted by Juanita L. Baker*

FRED AND INA CLARK

Willis and Hannah Jones Clark moved from Putnam Co., IN to Clark Township, Montgomery Co., IN and had several children. One of their children was James Clark born 1824 died 1901 and married Polly Ann Stark and they had eight children. One of their children was Benjamin F. Clark born 1860, died 1947 and wife Mary Pennington Clark born 1888 died 1943. They lived south of New Ross, east of Ladoga, in Clark Township. They had five sons, Claude married Grace Shaver; Clarence married Effie Morgan, one daughter Maxine; William; Charles married Nora Conner, one son Russell; and Fred Clark born 1882-1956 married Ina Miller.

Fred and Ina had acquired an estate worth $775,000, and they made their wills, leaving some to relatives, friends, but their largest bequest for over $500,000 trust fund for scholarships to deserv-

115

ing students in Montgomery County. They had no children of their own, and this was a great gift for the students who were deserving of scholarships. The Clark Scholarship Committee, made up now of the principals of the three Montgomery County School units. Administered by Bank One, Crawfordsville. The Scholarships are about $50,000 a year, and renewal grants are given when needed for those who have had a scholarship before. In 1979, they gave 133 scholarships, for whatever amount was needed. A student had to carry a full load as required by their school, and had to have a "C" average. The Committee decides what amount each student gets. This was a wonderful gift for students, giving them a chance for further education.

WILLIS CLARK

Willis Clark born Sept. 26, 1796 to William and Winfred Nicholas Clark, died Aug. 7, 1870 married Hannah Jones in 1817. In 1834 they lived in Putnam County, near Brick Chapel, then to Montgomery County, along upper Haw Creek, where Willis died. They had 17 children; Joseph J. born Dec. 30, 1818; William T. born 1820, Kentucky married Mary Ann Allen on Apr. 16, 1840, great grandparents of James W. Clark, of Abilene, TX, source of this Clark Family; Milton Clark; Nathan went to Iowa; James M. Clark born Dec. 21, 1824 and died May 7, 1901 married Polly Ann Stark Nov. 8, 1846 and had eight children, one of their sons Arthur, owned 30 acres, later owned by C. Pauline Walters, near Whitesville, other children were Willis, William, Ella Jane Hooermale, Susan Davidson, Mollie Hardesty, Benjamin F. Clark 1860-1947 married Mary Jane Pennington 1858-1943 they had five sons; Claud 1880-1966 married Grace Shaver; Fred 1882-1956 married Ina Miller, Fred and Ina left their money for scholarships to college bound high school seniors. They had no children, so they did a wonderful thing, approximately 100 Montgomery County students receive this scholarship each year. Fred and Ina are buried in Ladaga Cemetery and a large monument for them is at the front gate.

Clarence Clark, 1884 died several years ago married Effie ? and had daughter Maxine. William 1886-1975; Charlie 1890 died ? married Nora Conner, they had Russell. He married the second time to Clemmie ?.

Other children of Willis, Benjamin F. Clark 1826-1899 married Susan Stark 1829-1896 in 1847, no children born to this union, but adopted 15; Winifred Clark; Oliver Clark married Ann Frankenberger on Dec. 22, 1859; John D. Clark died Mar. 20, 1899 here; Francis died age 19 Putnam County; Lucinda married John Baker June 12, 1851; lived near New Ross; Sidney J. Clark; Susan born Mar. 30, 1837 married John Harshbarger had son Samuel and daughter Elizabeth Myers Harshbarger; Alexander C. Clark married Nancy Ely Dec. 11, 1853; Mary Clark Mar. 6, 1846 died August 1893 married George Morris Sept. 10, 1891; Fannie died 1895. These Clarks were all active in Bethel Christian and Wesley Chapel Church.

John Harshbarger and wife Susan Clark Harshbarger had Claud who married Clara Frame, when she died he married Ruth Conner. In April 1962, a miracle happened as Claud had been blind, but he could see! In 1947, he began having problems with his eyes. He had an operation for glaucoma. Again in 1956 he had another operation and in 1958 he had a cataract removed, but he was left totally blind. On Jan. 10, 1962, he had an operation on his right eye, on the third day when the bandages were removed he could see. He had made cement products in Ladoga for 52 years and retired in 1955.

CLARKSON FAMILY OF COAL CREEK TOWNSHIP

The year of 1830 was an eventful one for 48 year old David Clarkson and his wife Mary. They had come from New Jersey to seek the rich farm land of Coal Creek Twp. Their son, Lewis, came also. He later married Charlotte Gregory.

They settled a large portion of land along the Coal Creek in Sections 6 and 12. The men were wise farmers as the land stayed for many years in the same families.

To Lewis and Charlotte were born four children, McClain in 1832, Joseph in 1836, James G. in 1840 and Peter Clarkson in 1843.

McClain died at the age of 28.

Joseph and his wife Amanda were the parents of Lewis Clarkson who married Ida DeHaven, and Charlotte (Jenny) who married Millard Buxton. Lewis and Ida had no living children but loved and took as their own, Fred Parmon, who still owns the same property at this writing along with his wife, Vera.

James G. married a near neighbor, Mary Bible, daughter of George and Sealy Bible. They lived on the property on the north of the Joseph Clarkson family. James and Mary accumulated considerable land holdings during their productive years. To this union was born three daughters and two sons.

The eldest daughter, Luella, married Alfred Sarver. They were blessed with four sons, Clifford who married Bina Thompson, Luther whose wife's name was Flossie Green, Earl who married Eva Keller, and Hobert who married Ruby Keller.

Next came Anetta (Nettie) who married David Whipple of Linden, originally from Dearborn Co., IN.

Seven children blessed this marriage, however two died in infancy. Raymond, the eldest was the father of a son Kenneth Whipple, Raymond's wife was Minnie Tinsley.

Elga Whipple remained unmarried.

Stella married Gordon Harriman. She bore a daughter, Rita and a son, Gail.

Elsie married Fred Holt of Knox Co., IN; Delbert, Phyllis, and John are children of this marriage. Fred died at the age of 38 in a tragic farm accident near New Richmond.

Virgil Whipple and Reatha Baker Whipple are the parents of Ronald and Joanne.

The third daughter of James and Mary Clarkson was Celia. She married Lloyd Jolley. Mable and Merle were their daughters.

Charles Clarkson, James and Mary's son married Jesse Mitchell. Their daughter was Beatrice. Everett Suitors was her husband.

Edward Clarkson son of James and Mary died at the age of 27.

One other son of Lewis and Charlotte also inherited land adjoining the lands of Joseph and James Clarkson. Peter, the youngest and his wife Susan were the parents of five children at the time of his death. Four names are known at this time, Walter, William, Eudella, and Malissa. The lands they farmed were rolling and along the Coal Creek.

David and Mary are buried in the MeHarry Cemetery, likely some of the earliest graves. Lewis, Charlotte, and son McClain are buried in the Old Turkey Run Cemetery, south of Wingate, near the historic marker of the old church.

Although the family name has faded, the hopes and aspirations of this dear family still grows under other acquired names.

RALPH AND MARY CLARKSON

Ralph Norris Clarkson arrived in Montgomery County with his family early in 1905. He was nine months old. He was born Apr. 16, 1904 in Big Springs, KY. Ralph's parents were James Reuben Clarkson and Anna Jane Norris. James and Anna had seven children: Lorena, Allen, Eva, Ralph, Harry, John, and James Lee.

Ralph's family lived in three different locations before settling on RR 2 near his future bride. Consequently Ralph attended several schools: Youngs Chapel, Breaks school, Mount Tabor school and Crawfordsville High School. Ralph's main occupation throughout his life has been farming. However, he has also: worked in a furniture factory, driven a school bus for four years, worked as a Farm Bureau insurance agent, and worked for Farm Bureau Coop where he was branch manager for 11 years. Ralph has also worked for several auctioneers - most recently John Sayler.

Richard Clarkson, Ralph and Mary Clarkson, Margaret Clarkson Mullen

Mary Elizabeth Jurgensmeyer was born on Mar. 30, 1905 in Homer, IL. Her parents were Alexander Edward Jurgensmeyer and Dora Ethel Wheeler. Mary was an only child. Mary and her parents moved to Montgomery County in 1910 to the farm outside of Crawfordsville where she and Ralph later raised their family.

Mary attended Mount Tabor school for grades one through eight. She graduated from Crawfordsville High School in 1923 - the school and building from which both her children and three of her grandchildren also graduated. While in high school Mary was on the honor roll and was never late or missed a day of school. She worked in the office for the principal. During high school her neighbor and future husband, Ralph, would crank her Model-T Ford for her and then get a ride to school.

Ralph and Mary were married on Nov. 29, 1923. They farmed on Mary's father's farm until 1945 when they moved to Crawfordsville. In 1956 they returned to the farm, acquired more land and lived there until they moved back to Crawfordsville in 1970. The Clarkson farm was well-known in the farming community for its registered polled hereford cattle. Several of their calves went on to become 4-H champions.

Ralph and Mary were both active in the community. Ralph was a member of the Crawfordsville Lion's Club and was secretary of the Montgomery County Farm Bureau. Mary was president of the Mount Tabor Parent Teacher's Association while her children were in school and cooked at the 4-H club camps they attended in the summer. She organized the Mount Tabor Get-Together Club which met in neighbor's homes. She was a member of the Flower Lover's Club, the Crawfordsville Home Economics Club and was the first president of the South Union Extension Homemakers Club. She helped to write the constitution for the Highland Social Club and was also the social and educational leader for the South Union Farm Bureau.

Ralph and Mary were both quite active in the First Christian Church in Crawfordsville. Ralph was an elder from 1954 to 1969. He was superintendent of the Sunday school, president of the Everyman's Bible Class, and chairman of the Board of Elders. Mary was a Sunday school teacher, co-superintendent of the young people's department, helped write the by-laws of the Christian Women's Fellowship and was also a deaconess.

Mary and Ralph have two children: Margaret Jean Mullen who resides in Montgomery County and is employed at Kirby Risk and Richard Clarkson who lives in Sonora, CA and is retired from Sandia. They have five grandchildren: Michael Mayfield, Sandra Steele, Karen Mullen and Craig and Ryan Clarkson. They have also been blessed with five great-grandchildren: Melissa and Elizabeth Steele, Michelle and Mary Mayfield and Matthew Clarkson. Ralph and Mary recently celebrated their 65th wedding anniversary. They currently reside at 1202 South Washington Street in Crawfordsville.

JOHN CLEMENTS

John Clements, son of Mary Hamilton and Henry Clements, married Agnes Fanny Ransdell June 15, 1898.

Mary attended a one-room school at the current intersection of Darlington Ave. and Market Street. Darlington Ave. was then an Indian trace. One day several Indian men came into the school. Mary was scared to pieces. They stared at the teacher and students. Not a word was spoken. The men turned and left, mounted their horses and rode on west.

Henry Clements immigrated from County Armagh, Northern Ireland in 1866, to weave at the woolen mill at Yountsville. Then he sent for his brothers and sisters one by one until most were here.

Later Henry and his sons had a road building crew. Jack Clements was their dynamite man, but the concussion was so great he would have to lie down and sleep off the headache after a blast. Many of the roads in the area and quite a few streets were constructed by these men.

Elizabeth, Pauline and Raymond Clements children of John H. and Agnes Randell Clements

In the 1930s Jack became active in politics and was appointed City Street Commissioner.

Agnes was the youngest of 11 children of Thomas B. and Mary Hendrickson (Henderson). She called her father Pap.

Thomas lost his arm and leg in coupling a train car.

Mary Hendrickson kept the family going by taking in washing. She had the children deliver the finished wash in a little pull wagon.

Aggie's favorite memory of her mother was of her standing in the yard one day with the apple trees in bloom behind her, the grass very green. Mary always wore white. That day her long black hair was blowing loose to dry. She was boiling wash in a large black iron pot.

Aggie and Jack had four children: Pauline Clements Swank; Raymond Green Clements or Bud; Elizabeth Clements Dinwiddie; and John William who died as a toddler.

Pauline married Paul J. Swank from near Wingate. He graduated from Wabash College and served as a Lt. in France in WWI. They had a son John (Jack) who is deaf. Paul became county superintendent of schools in Boone County. Pauline owned a hat shoppe.

Bud (Raymond) married Nelda Warren from near Darlington. They had one son, Warren Roe who graduated from Butler University and married Marilyn Gibson of Indianapolis. They had no children.

Elizabeth married Robert R. Dinwiddie of Crawfordsville. They had one child, Carol Lynn. Elizabeth paid for her own education at Madame Blakers in Indianapolis and taught 35 years in the lower elementary grades. She was a superior reading teacher, but always said she could not teach any one to count higher than ten! Bob graduated from Wabash College just in time for the stock market crash in 1929. He was a city policeman for nine years and retired as store manager for B.F. Goodrich. Carol married Robert J. Bennett, Mar. 15, 1957. They had three children: John R.; Beth Ann; and Patrick Kevin. *Submitted by Carol Bennett*

"PAT" CLINE

In December 1971, Pat Cline moved to Montgomery County from Tipton County where she had lived 40 years. She started her new journalism job as civic affairs editor at the *Journal Review*. It wasn't long before she became intrigued with the rich heritage of the county and started researching its history.

That research led to the founding of *Montgomery Magazine* in January 1976. Pat served as publisher and editor of the publication until 1982, when she sold the monthly historic magazine to the *JOURNAL*. Today she continues as its editor. The magazine has received numerous state and national awards during its existence. Pat has also published two *Montgomery County Almanacs and Area Tour Guides* (1978-79) and *Agriculture: The Heartbeat of Montgomery County (1980)*. Her writings also appear in a number of magazines and books. In 1988, she edited and compiled *Montgomery County; Legend and Lore*, published by the Montgomery County Historical Society.

Throughout her journalism career, Pat has been the recipient of many state and national writing awards and recognitions. She has been active in both community and state organizations, and served as president of Indiana Woman's Press Club in 1985-87. She was named "Woman of Achievement in Indiana", and was awarded the Kate Milner Rabb Award for excellence in journalism plus awards from the Indiana Hospital Association for medical reporting.

Pat Cline

It was in the beginning of the Depression that Pat's father, Paul E. Guilkey moved his family to Indiana from Akron, OH. He and his wife, Kathryn Maddox Guilkey, were both natives of Hamilton Co., IN. They were the parents of three daughters, Thelma, Peggy and Pat. Pat was born Apr. 3, 1929, at Akron. Her legal name is Rose A., but she has always used "Pat" as a pen name. The family settled in Tipton County where Paul Guilkey owned and operated a burial vault industry. After graduating from Tipton High School in 1947, Pat attended St. Vincent's School of Nursing and worked part-time as a nurse for nearly 20 years.

She married Ralph Cline and they were the parents of three sons, Michael, James and Phillip. Michael and James now live in Memphis, TN. Phillip drowned in a scuba diving accident in Hawaii in 1974. Pat changed careers in 1967, and started in journalism at the *Tipton Daily Tribune*. She was managing editor there prior to coming to Crawfordsville. Her marriage to Ralph ended in 1970.

Her mother, Kathryn, died when Pat was still a small child. Later her father married Mary Ann Cole. Paul died in 1980, and Mary, in 1987. Both are buried in Tipton Cemetery. Her sister, Thelma, lives in Miami, FL; and Peggy lives in Colorado Springs, CO.

Pat says the highlight of her career was in 1972 when the *Journal* sent her to Vietnam as a correspondent. Before returning to the states, she visited in seven other countries. Although she no longer has any family living in Indiana, Pat doubts that she will ever leave Montgomery County, a place she has come to love deeply. *Submitted by Pat Cline*

VERN AND GEORGIANA FULWIDER CLORE

Georgiana Fulwider was born Dec. 9, 1906, near Wingate, in Montgomery Co., IN, the oldest daughter of Walter and Eva May Gravett Fulwider. Her grandfather, Jacob Fulwider, had come to Indiana from Virginia, in the 1850's with his parents, Joseph and Sarah Houff Fulwider and eight brothers and sisters.

Vern and Georgia Clore

Georgiana (Georgia) grew-up on the family farm near Wingate. When she was 14, her family moved to a farm in Brown Township near the Shades. She attended school at Waveland.

Vern Clore was born in Parke County, May 13, 1897, on his father's farm in the northeast corner of Howard Township. He was the son of Erastus and Elvie Keeling Clore, grandson of Berriman and Mary Rice Clore and of Dexter and Mary Lowe Keeling. His great grandparents, Israel and Frances Deer Clore, came to Indiana in 1831, where Israel obtained a patent deed at the land office at Crawfordsville for land in Howard Township, Parke County.

Vern and Georgia were married in 1925 and lived with his family for two years. In 1927, they moved to Byron, where they owned and operated the Byron Store. They sold the store in the 1930s to Forrest and Betty Coleman.

In 1932, their daughter, Carol Jean, was born. Georgia's brothers and sisters, Gaynell, Bud, Joe, Fred and Bettie and other family members lived with them at various times. Their home was a gathering place for family, friends, and neighbors.

Vern and his daughter, Carol, both loved horses and participated at the local fairs and horse shows in the 1930s and 1940s.

In 1941, they moved to a small farm at the east edge of Waveland in Montgomery County.

Vern was a farmer, trucker, logger, livestock trader, and had a horse and mule breeding business.

Georgia was known for her cooking and gracious hospitality. She was always there to help family, friends, and neighbors.

Vern died May 9, 1972, just four days before his 75th birthday.

After Vern's death, Georgia babysat for Carl and Jane Steiner for 11 years, helping to raise their three daughters—Amy, Ann and Alice. She considered them a part of her family. She died Mar. 27, 1984.

Their daughter, Carol, married Ronald Rivers in 1950. They have three grown children: Ronna, Bret, and Curtis. Bret married Peggy Kowalski. They have a daughter, Ruth Anna. Curt married Allison Purvis, and they have two sons: Mitchel Curtis and Matthew Clinton.

Ron and Carol live in Kokomo, IN, where Ron is a senior research associate with Haynes International, Inc. Carol is a retired abstractor. S*ubmitted by Carol Rivers*

HENRY FRANCIS CLOUSER

Henry Francis Clouser was born August 1911 to Charles and Martha Clouser in Franklin Township, Montgomery County. He attended St. Michael School in Plymouth, IN for six years. He graduated from Darlington High School in 1928.

He married Elizabeth Bradshaw, daughter of Addison and Mary (Parks) Bradshaw in September 1936. They have 14 children. Henry and Elizabeth moved to Sugar Creek Township in 1946. The children attended Bowers School, the oldest boy graduated in the last class of 1955. Five daughters graduated from St. Joseph Academy, Tipton, IN.

The children are; Thomas, who married Judith Cornell of Darlington, and now live in Crawfordsville. Martha, Randolph Air Force Base, Texas, who married Joseph Porter. Mary married Jerry Cheek of Wingate, they live in Sugar Creek Township. Phyllis married Randall Foye (deceased) of Crawfordsville and she lives in Mace. Philip lives in Fort Wayne, IN. Susanne married Richard Vida of South Bend. They live in Elwood, IN. Marjorie lives at San Antonio, TX: Bill in Cincinnati, OH. Virginia married Calvin Hayes of Indianapolis; they live at Bristol, IN. Gerry married Marilyn Campbell of Crawfordsville. They live in Ft. Wayne, IN. Kevin married Lynn Harbison of Crawfordsville and they live in Indianapolis. Karen married Morris Critchlow of Davies County; they live in Auburn, KY. Tim lives in Lafayette, IN. Ruth married Dann Lowe; they live in Indianapolis.

Mr. Clouser passed away Sept. 29, 1987. *Submitted by Mrs. Henry Clouser*

JOHN CLOUSER FAMILY

The first Clouser to settle in Montgomery County was John Clouser. He was born in the early 1770s in Pennsylvania, where he married Christina Cripps. Six children were born to them in the 1790s and early 1800s: Elizabeth, Joseph, John, David, George, and Catherine.

After he and Christina moved to Ross Co., OH, in about 1800, he served in the 1st Regiment Ohio Militia during the War of 1812 as a Drum Major. It was in 1829 in Ohio that Christina died, at which time John decided to relocate to Montgomery County.

Clouser Mill

On Aug. 25, 1829, John Clouser is listed as an original entrant of land in northeastern Montgomery County, near what is now Darlington. According to family folklore, this first Clouser property was purchased from the local Indians with a sack of silver dollars. Additional land was purchased a month later from John and Nancy Taylor. These properties later became the site of the Clouser Mill, the first mill in Sugar Creek Township, erected in 1830, on the south bank of Sugar Creek.

In about 1830 John Clouser married Jane Goodenough. In 1838, John then sold his property, including the mill, to his son, John. At about this time, the elder John Clouser and his wife moved to Missouri, and the younger John Clouser came to Montgomery County, to take over the family mill.

The younger John Clouser had married Margaret Orick in Ohio, and they had four children: Mary, Alfred, Henry, and Daniel, who they brought to Indiana with them. Margaret, however, refused to move here until John built her a suitable home, as comfortable as she had in Ohio; this home is still standing in the northeast part of the county, near Darlington.

John continued to operate the mill until about 1850, when the original mill was replaced with a newer mill (picture) on the north bank of Sugar Creek, which the family operated for many years thereafter. John and Margaret, and their children, lived in Montgomery County the remainder of their lives, thus firmly establishing the Clouser family in the area. *Submitted by Jo Clouser*

JOHN CLOUSER

John Clouser, eldest son of Simon and Margaret Clouser, was born in Pennsylvania in 1770. Simon served in the Cumberland County Militia during the Revolution.

John married Christina Cripps in 1789 and moved his family to Ross Co., OH in 1800. Christina died in 1829, and John sold his property and moved west. John was one of the original land holders in Montgomery County and bought 80 acres in Sugar Creek Township on Aug. 25, 1829.

A grandchild, child of Everett Young Bowen and Catherine Clouser Bowen was the first to be buried in the Clouser Cemetery. The child may have died on the covered wagon trip, or shortly after.

John Clouser built a grist mill on Sugar Creek, with the aid of Indian neighbors. He began farming and milling. In February 1830 he rode a horse to Crawfordsville and brought back a new bride, Jane Goodenaeu Clouser.

In 1838 he sold his property to his son, John Clouser, Jr., who had come from Ohio. He then moved to Buchanan Co., MO, where he operated a mill. He died in 1846 and was buried in Missouri.

John Clouser, Jr., and his wife, Margarete Orrick Clouser, took over the operation of the Clouser Mill and built a new mill down stream. The second mill was reworked in the 1850's with the help of John's sons, Alfred, Daniel, and Henry. John also had a daughter, Mary, who married James A. Strain in 1841. She died quite young. John Clouser, Jr., built a magnificent house along County Road 950 north of Sugar Creek. It is still in use today and is owned by a descendant. John was quite industrious and at the time of his death in 1866 owned about 720 acres and the Clouser Mill. Margaret died in 1872.

John's eldest son, Alfred, was born in 1826 and took over the operation of the mill. Alfred was married first to Melinda Cory, and later to Mariah Huber. Melinda had two sons, Simon and George. She died in 1853. Alfred and Mariah were married in 1866 and had six children. Their eldest son, Martin, was educated at Valparaiso University and later started the telephone company in Thorntown, IN. Most of Alfred's sons were farmers and at least one of his great grandsons still farms in Montgomery County today.

John Clouser, Jr.'s second son was Henry. He became a farmer and married Rebecca Deck in 1856. Both died in 1895 and were survived by one daughter, Martha.

John and Margaret's youngest child was Daniel, born 1833. He took over the Mill operation and started the Clouser Post Office there. He was the first Postmaster. He married Mahala Hampton in 1859 and they had eight children. Among them was a son, Ira Clouser, who served as State Senator in 1933 and was later Postmaster at Crawfordsville. Several of Daniel's sons also started the Clouser Band, a brass band which played in the area. *Submitted by Julia Clouser*

HOMER W. AND RUTH E. COATS

A quick decision to move can many times be upsetting and disappointing. When Homer W. and Ruth E. Coats moved to a farm in Ripley Township, Montgomery County, early in 1951, it brought new and interesting challenges. There were lean years, better years, but the land was good, the people and communities great.

Bill was born Dec. 24, 1914 to Joseph William and Vereta June Stockdale Coats, near Steam Corner. His brother, Francis, lives at Waynetown.

Brothers George and Eugene are deceased. During the depression years he remained at home to help support the family. Later he attended Lafayette Business College and worked at Lyman Coal Company until he was drafted into the Air Corps in August, 1941. He was stationed at Sheppard Field, TX, then at Aquadulce and Howard Field, Panama Canal Zone, being discharged as a Technical Sergeant in November 1945.

Homer W. and Ruth E. Coats

Ruth was born to William A. and Ruth Edna Smith Price, Dec. 29, 1918 at Covington. Her sister is Winifred L. Stockdale (Mrs. James R.) of Winter Haven, FL. The family moved to a farm southeast of Hillsboro in 1927. After high school Ruth worked in Indianapolis for several years.

On Dec. 21, 1941, Bill and Ruth were married at the First Christian Church in Wichita Falls, TX, remaining two and a half years. Following his discharge, they returned to Fountain County where Bill started farming and continued for 43 years. After moving to Montgomery County this involved miles of shifting machinery; but farming has great appeal, so great, he has no plans to retire. During 1961-73, Bill also worked as a bookkeeper for Mellott Co-op and Scott's Prairie elevators. They both worked as tax preparers for many years. They are members of Scott's Prairie Christian Church and attend Alamo Christian Church.

Their son, David W. was born Oct. 17, 1946. Kathleen L. (deceased) was born Sept. 25, 1948 and Joan E. was born May 4, 1950. Dave graduated from Alamo High School, attended Vincennes University to study retail merchandising. On Apr. 9, 1966 he married Nancye L. Wise of Vincennes. He served two years in the army including a year in Vietnam. They now live in Indianapolis where Dave is self-employed, making various cabinets and other woodcraft products. Their son, Jeffrey W. was born Jan. 6, 1974.

After graduating from Fountain Central High School, Joan received a degree in Mathematics from Indiana State University and has an associate degree in Computer Technology from IUPUI. She married David W. Philpott of Fountain County, Jan. 24, 1969. They have one son, Matthew A. born Dec. 4, 1978. David works at Kokomo Aviation, Joan for Direct Air Commuter Flight, Kokomo and live at Galveston, IN.

Farming is not easy work, but is the only way of life for many. So there are no regrets—Montgomery County is one of the best places to live and to farm.

ERNEST RAY AND AGNES INEZ MYERS COFFING FAMILY

In February 1957 Ernest Ray Coffing and wife Agnes Inez Myers Coffing moved to a farm south of Darlington, IN known as the Lynch Farm. Dr. and Mrs. Robert Pollom owned the Lynch farm. The Coffings previously farmed the Samuel Glascock farm on State Road 32 in Fountain County. Ernest and Agnes were the parents of two children: Rhoda Marie and Ralph Emerson.

Ernest was born Oct. 23, 1926 to Gail McNeal and Mary Marie Hickman Coffing in Fountain County. He lived on a farm and farmed for himself until 1970. He served in the army during W.W.II in the South Pacific. Before he left for the service he married Agnes Myers Apr. 9, 1944. Agnes was born Dec. 18, 1925 in Vermillion Co., IL and lived in and around Fairmount, IL until 1940 when her parents Conard and Ruby Rhoda Loeffler Myers bought and moved to a farm at Veedersburg, IN.

Ernest Ray and Agnes Inez (Myers) Coffing

Rhoda Marie was born Aug. 3, 1945 in Vermillion Co., IL. She married Richard Charles Ames of Brazil, IN Sept. 20, 1964. Richard was born July 22, 1942 to Charles and Helen Ames. They have two daughters, April Lynn born Aug. 18, 1967 and Kimberly Kay born Mar. 11, 1970.

Ralph Emerson was born Dec. 18, 1948 in Montgomery County. He married Delanda Cheryl Peabody Feb. 14, 1970. She was born Mar. 15, 1950 the daughter of John Peabody and Rovene Coons Bunnell. They have two daughters, Kelly Jo born July 11, 1973 and Beth Renee born Apr. 30, 1976.

April Lynn Ames married Ronald Dean Brown Aug. 24, 1985. Ronald born Sept. 17, 1963 the son of Dean Brown and Lou Endicott in Galax, VA. April and Ronald are the parents of Crystal René born July 15, 1986.

If all goes as planned Kimberly Kay will wed Brian Scott Higgins Mar. 4, 1989. Brian is the son of Ed Higgins and Ms. Nancy Simpson and born Apr. 7, 1968.

Ernest Coffing after 1970 did construction work, owned the Coffing Hardware and Dar-Ray Battery works at Darlington, IN. On a Sunday evening in January 1986 the Coffing Hardware burnt. The building was built 1887 by Ira Booher for a harness shop, hardware and buggy shop.

Ralph Coffing graduated from Darlington High School 1966 then went to an Auto-Diesel school in Nashville, TN in 1966-1967. After graduation he worked in garages but decided he preferred carpenter work. Rhoda Ames graduated from Darlington High 1963. She is an Avon District Sales Manager. Richard Ames and Ronald Brown work for R.R. Donnelley and Sons at Crawfordsville, IN.

Agnes' ancestors, Loeffler and Waggnor came from the Black Forest of Germany. The Myers came up from Virginia to Owingsville, KY, Bath County to Homer, IL.

The Coffin came from England to Nantucket. Andrew Coffing put the "G" on Coffin. He was born in Warren Co., OH in 1803 died 1858 in Fountain Co., IN.

COLE FAMILY

Thomas A. Cole, born Jan. 6, 1936, son of Samuel J. Cole of Canonsburg, PA, and Pearl M. Fritts, of Marion (Repton), KY, came to Crawfordsville in 1954 from Harrisburg, IL, where he grew up, to attend Wabash College. While at Wabash, Mr. Cole was a member of the Delta Tau Delta fraternity and majored in zoology. Upon his graduation in 1958, he travelled to Pasadena, CA to attend graduate school at the California Institute of Technology. Mr. Cole received his Doctorate in biochemistry in 1962. Dr. Cole then returned to Wabash College and began teaching Biology there in the same year. He became the Norman E. Treves Professor of Biology (the position previously being held by Dr. Willis H. Johnson, of Crawfordsville) in 1976 and has published over a dozen papers and co-authored six textbooks of biology as well as being president twice of the Indiana College Biology Teachers Association and a member of several state and national committees to further education. Dr. Cole was married in 1967 to Lynda Ryan of Indianapolis and had two children, Thomas J. Cole, born Apr. 2, 1969 and Jennifer R. Cole, born Apr. 17, 1971. The younger Tom grew up in Crawfordsville and was very active in theater at CHS and in the Sugar Creek Players. Tom was very motivated academically and upon his graduation from CHS in 1987, he moved to Cambridge, MA to study Mechanical Engineering at the Massachusetts Institute of Technology. While at MIT, Tom was very active in student life, becoming a member of the Delta Upsilon fraternity and was elected to co-captain the 1989-90 MIT Men's Varsity Heavyweight Crew Team. Jennifer grew up in Columbus, OH and attended Dublin High School. Jennifer is a member of the Class of 1989 and will attend Ohio State University to study business.

The Coles lived at 1000 South Grant Street from 1967 on. They first lived in the farm house which was previously owned by the Leavenworths since the 1920s. In 1972, they built a new house behind the farm house to house their growing family.
Submitted by Thomas J. Cole

COLTRAIN FAMILY

The first known Coltrain in Montgomery County was Solomon, born in 1801 in Guilford Co., NC. He was one of eight children.

Solomon and his wife Esther Andrews (1799) had three children: Linden P., Sarah, and Peninah before coming from Greensboro, NC to Indiana. Two others—Rachel and Mary J. were born in Indiana.

Listed are some of the places mentioned along the route to Indiana. Bruces Cross Roads, Wilkins Store, Courthouse of Henry County, Widow Martin's, Black Water, Amsterdam, Fincastle, Red Sulphur, Sewel's Mountain, Hawk's Nest, Charlestown, Point Pleasant on the Ohio River, Gallipolis, Eaton, Dayton, Richmond, IN, and Economy.

A brother Lindsey, came from North Carolina to Indiana to visit Solomon and on his return home wrote saying it took 12 days to reach the Ohio River and 14 more days to get home.

Some interesting prices in 1853 were—Corn $4.50 per barrel; Bacon, $10.00 per hundred lbs.; Oats, 40 cents per bu.; and $1 for eight hours work in the Copper Mine.

Solomon Coltrain entered several hundred acres of land in eastern Montgomery and western Boone Counties from the Federal Gov't. in 1832-1835. He later sold part of it for $2 per acre.

Little more is known about Solomon until his death on Oct. 10, 1882.

Linden P. (1826), Solomon's only son, was married to Martha A. (?) (1831) to whom were born eight children: Sarah, Rebecca, Emma, John D., Thomas, Melissa, William, and Mary.

Linden, a farmer, left all his family at home to go to the Civil War. Many of the letters sent home to his father and his family are in the possession of the one who submitted this history. In one he stated that he had saved $50.00 and that he would give it to someone to come and take his place. In another he told his father what crops to plant, so that would be done when he got home.

The writer of this history has Linden's death notice, sent to his father, in May, 1863. He was buried in Stones River National Cemetery at Murfreesboro, TN.

John D. (1858-1926) married Sarah E. Hampton. Their children were Roy, Claude, and Zola.

He was a prominent farmer; owned the Hazel Creek Stock Farm east of Darlington. This farm is still in Coltrain ownership.

Roy O. (1886-1972) married Nevah Tribbett. They had two sons Norman F. and John D.

Roy was a breeder of Poland China hogs and Angus cattle.

Norman F. married Lois Parker in 1939. They are parents of two daughters, Sharon Sue and Robyn Ann.

Norman graduated from Darlington High School (1934). He farmed all his life until retiring in 1986. He was a Past Master of Darlington Masonic Lodge and is affiliated with the Methodist church.

Sharon Sue died in infancy. Robyn Ann graduated from Darlington High School (1968) and Ball State University (1972). She is married to George Rauch and has two sons Colin and Erin.

John D. (1929) married Mary Jo Barber. They had three children: Tamara, Douglas, and Gale.

John (Johnny, as many knew him) graduated from Darlington High School in 1947, spent two years at Purdue University, then graduated from Ohio State University in 1953.

He was a well-known veterinarian and practiced in the Darlington and Thorntown areas until his death in 1978. *Submitted by Norman F. Coltrain*

W.A. COLLINGS

W(illiam) A(sbury) Collings, son of William Z. and Mary E. (Andrews) Collings; born at Cicero, Hamilton Co., IN, July 18, 1874.

William Z. Collings, son of Dr. Isaac and Caroline (Hanna) Collings, was born in Clay Co., IN, in 1849. He received his early education in the schools of Hamilton Co., IN, after which he entered the drug business in Cicero, IN, in association with Dr. F.M. Warford. William Z. Collings continued to engage in the drug business until his death, which occurred in 1919. He was a Republican, and was a member of the I.O.O.F., K. of P., and M.E. Church. His wife, Mary E. (Andrews) Collings, who was born near Ft. Wayne, IN, in 1853, died Feb. 21, 1934. Her father, the Rev. William Andrews, who was a Methodist minister, was a circuit rider. The Andrews family is of English descent. William Z. and Mary E. (Andrews) Collings were the parents of five children: (1) William Asbury, (2) Nina F., who graduated from Madam Blaker's School (now a part of Butler University), of Indianapolis. She resides in Indianapolis. (3) Roy T., who graduated from Purdue University in mechanical engineering. (4 and 5) Twins: Harry A. and Clara. Harry A. resides in Indianapolis, and Clara resides in Vincennes, IN, with her husband, Lamont Meek, who is a salesman.

Dr. Isaac Collings, father of William Z., and son of William, was born in Indiana. He attended district schools, and graduated from a medical college in Des Moines, IA, with an M.D. degree about 1857. He then practiced medicine at Boxley, Hamilton Co., IN, until 1862, at which time he enlisted in the 57th Regt., Ind. Vol. Inf., for service in the Civil War. He served as regimental surgeon. In 1865 he was sent with his regiment to serve in the region of the Rio Grande River in Texas. He died on the prairies of Texas, and was given a Masonic funeral by the Masons in his regiment. His wife, Caroline (Hanna) Collings, was a descendant of Gen. Hanna, who served in the Rev. War.

William Collings, father of Dr. Isaac Collings, was born in Kentucky. In the 1820s he moved to Clay Co., IN, where he built a log house near New Maysville. He there engaged in farming. He later moved to Putnam Co., IN, where he died. Other members of the Collings family came to Indiana in territorial days.

W.A. Collings, the subject of this sketch, graduated from DePauw University, A.B., in 1900, and from Columbia University, LL. B., in 1907. After graduating from DePauw University, he taught school four years, becoming superintendent of the Ward H. Watson School at Charlestown, IN. He was admitted to the bar in Marion Co., IN, in 1907, following which he was a clerk in the law office of the Hon. Ward H. Watson, judge of the Appellate Court, two years. During that time Mr. Collings was admitted to practice before all State and Federal courts. In 1909 he became attorney for Evans, DeVore & Co., a real estate business, of Crawfordsville, IN, in which capacity he continued ten years. In 1919 he was made cashier of the First National Bank*, of Crawfordsville, and since 1935 has been president of the bank, of which he is also a director. Mr. Collings, who is a Republican, served as chairman of the County Council two terms. He is vice-president and a director of the Crawfordsville Trust Co., and is chairman of the board of trustees of the Montgomery County Culver Hospital. He served as president of the Indiana Bankers Association from June 1931, to June 1933, being the only man who ever has held this office two terms. Mr. Collings is a member of the following: Montgomery Lodge No. 50, F. and A.M (past worshipful master), Chapter Council, and Commandery (K.T.); Rotary Club (past president); Crawfordsville Country Club; Montgomery County C. of C. (a past director); Montgomery County Chapter, Citizens Historical Association; and First M.E. Church. His favorite recreations are golf, and fishing.

In 1913, W.A. Collings married Elizabeth Schalk, a native of Charlestown, IN. Her parents, Mr. and Mrs. Charles Schalk, are deceased. Charles Schalk was a contractor. Mr. and Mrs. Collings have no children. *Citizens Historical Association Sketch, 1940*

*For a history of the First National Bank, see *History of Montgomery County, Indiana* (A.W. Bowen & Co., Indianapolis, IN, 1913), vol. 1, p. 368.

CAROL JO (GRIMES) COOK

Carol Jo Grimes Cook, second daughter to Richard Lodge and Norma Maxine Farnsworth Grimes born Dec. 15, 1956 in Montgomery Co., IN married Oct. 1, 1976 to Dennis Roy Cook. Dennis and Carol Grimes Cook own and operate Cook Heating and Air Conditioning Co.

Richard Lodge Grimes, third son to Forrest Earl and Tessie Amanda Elliott Grimes born Mar. 10, 1918, married Dec. 29, 1951 to Norma Maxine Farnsworth. Owned Crawfordsville Concrete Septic Tank Co. with father until 1966, retired from Allisons, Indianapolis, IN.

Tessie Amanda Elliott Grimes, fourth child, second daughter to Joseph C. and Ann Cumberland Lodge Elliott born Nov. 5, 1890 married Apr. 28, 1909 to Forrest Earl Grimes in Sidney, OH, died Nov. 20, 1987. Settled in Crawfordsville, Montgomery Co., IN in 1909. Bought and restored the "White Hall" residence on Water St. Bought Yount's Woolen Mill in Yountsville, lost mill during the Depression. Repurchased mill in the 1950's and restored.

Ann Cumberland Lodge Elliott, third child, second daughter of Nelson James and Mary H. McClellan Julien Lodge born June 14, 1862 married Nov. 19, 1883 to Joseph C. Elliott, died 1930s.

Nelson James Lodge, sixth child, fifth son of Jacob and Ann Cumberland Newman Lodge born Jan. 3, 1832, married Apr. 12, 1857 to Mary H. McClellan Julien, died Oct. 15, 1873.

Jacob Lodge, third child, second son of Jacob and Rosanna Hanks Lodge born July 22, 1794 in Loudoun Co., VA married (1) Apr. 10, 1820 to Nancy North, (2) Feb. 27, 1831 to Ann Cumberland Newman, daughter of William and Naomi Cox Newman, (3) Sept. 10, 1835 to Elizabeth Caslin Newman (sister of Ann). Jacob, the father of 15 children, went West with James Ensley in 1818 to Montgomery Co., OH. Purchased small farm. Ten years after first wife's death, sold farm and bought a larger farm on the National Rd. Here, married Ann Cumberland Newman. (Named after her birth on the Cumberland River while her family moved from Tennessee to Ohio in 1804.)

Jacob Lodge, fourth child, second son of Jozabad and Catherine Strange Lodge born May 31, 1759 in Chester Co., PA married Feb. 9, 1786 to Rosanna Hanks (daughter of Wm. Hanks). Leased land in Shelborne Parish, Loudoun Co., VA from Lord Fairfax in 1787. In 1803, he removed to Pennsylvania. In 1804, he purchased 500 acres in Brush Creek Valley, Bedford Co. (now Fulton Co.), PA died May 9, 1851. Rosanna Hanks Lodge, a remarkable woman. Diligent study acquired extensive knowledge of Medicine. Only physician within 20 miles. Remarkable success in treating diseases of women and children. The "tayloress" of Community, cut and made the fine "Camlet" Cloaks. First person buried in McKandree Churchyard.

Jozabad Lodge, sixth child, fifth son to Robert and Elizabeth Lodge born Oct. 19, 1721 in Chester Co., PA married Mar. 22, 1751 to Catherine Strange, died Aug. 19, 1808 in Loudoun Co., VA. After the Revolution, Jozabad removed to Loudoun County where he leased a large tract of land from a McIlhenny.

Robert Lodge, third son to Sir Thomas and Lady Anna Laxton Lodge born 1558, married Elizabeth?. Immigrated to America in 1682. Little is known about their lives except that they were English Quakers. March 3, 1682, Robert and Elizabeth Lodge purchased 500 acres in Chester Co., PA from William Penn.

Sir Thomas Lodge was the High Sheriff of London in 1558 and the Lord Mayor of London in 1562. He was descended from Edward Di Logis,

Baron of Wighton in Cumberland in the 12th Century. Ancestors came originally from France. His wife, Lady Anna Laxton, daughter of Sir Wm. Laxton, former Lord Mayor of London. *Submitted by Carol Jo Grimes Cook, 10th generation of Lodges*

MABEL MARIE GRAHAM COOK

Mabel Marie Graham born May 2, 1898 in Montgomery Co., IN, the daughter of John L. Graham and Mary Mariah King. She married Laymon Henry Cook on June 12, 1918. He died suddenly on Mar. 17, 1978. Their children are: Justus Raymond Cook who married Ruby Surface in July 1939 and their first son was born and with his mother, Ruby died in 1940. Justus then married Vivian Morris and they had a son William Raymond Cook born on Nov. 18, 1944. Justus later married a third time to Ruth Statts and adopted her daughter Georgianna who married Thomas Cleo Smith and they have two sons and one daughter; Cline Devon Cook married Martha Jean Stevens on June 9, 1946 and son, Jack Raymond who married Rebecca Hessler. Jack Raymond Cook, Jr. was born Sept. 2, 1966. Jack married a second time, to Rebecca Batty and they have Kelly Jo Cook born Apr. 12, 1971 and Nicolas Grant Cook born Jan. 25, 1979; Rex Alan Cook born June 4, 1948 and married Judy Lowe, separated and have no children; Gregory Eldon Cook born Dec. 9, 1949 and married Pam Wethington. They have Misty Monee born July 18, 1968; and twins, Brad and Brian born Jan. 15, 1972. Greg was killed in an auto accident on May 14, 1972; Joe Devon Cook was born Aug. 30, 1954 and is not married. All of Cline's family lives in the Lebanon area. Julia Bee Cook born May 1, 1925 married Lloyd Miller on Feb. 27, 1946 and had Sheral Kay Miller born June 8, 1947. She married Dennis Curry on Nov. 6, 1965, no children. Ross Alan Miller born Mar. 28, 1950 is not married. He lives in Coal City, IL and works in a nuclear plant. On Sept. 12, 1977 Julia died. Richard Wayne Cook born Dec. 24, 1927 and was killed in an auto-truck accident on June 21, 1962.

Mabel Marie Graham Cook will be 91 on May 2, 1989 and is living in her own home in Darlington. She was a member of the Potato Creek Methodist Church where she was active in the W.C.S. She is a former member of the Potato Creek Home Economics Club and the Violet Flower Club in Indianapolis.

MAUDE AND OSCAR COOK

Under the "Waveland Items" in the July 19, 1916 Crawfordsville paper, we read the following:

"Word has been received by relatives here announcing the marriage of Miss Maude Straughan, of this place, to Oscar L. Cook, of Indianapolis, a former Waveland boy. Mrs. Cook is the daughter of Dr. and Mrs. K.K. Straughan and left home last week, presumably to visit her cousin, Mrs. Georgia Coshow, at Indianapolis. Their friends extend best wishes."

Just as in love after 50 years of marriage, Maude and Oscar could often be seen strolling hand-in-hand down Green Street of Waveland.

Maude India Straughan, born Dec. 20, 1883 at Browns Valley was the daughter of Kent K. and Lucy (Bridges) Straughan. See page 350-51 of the *History of Montgomery Co., IN* by A.W. Bowen for an interesting tale on Maude's family. Maude graduated from Waveland High School and attended Madame Blaker's School in Indianapolis. She was an accomplished musician and artist (charter member of the Indianapolis Art League) and an active member of the Christian Church and Department Club at Waveland. Before her marriage, Maude taught music and art in Fowler and Waveland schools. Living quite near Mr. N.R. Walker, long-time music teacher at Waveland, strands of Bach and Beethoven could often be heard in stereo by the neighbors.

Oscar L. Cook was born Oct. 19, 1882 near North Salem, the son of William M. and Rosa (Bymaster) Cook. He attended Eel River School there, as well as Waveland. For many years, he worked at Allisons in Indianapolis. In 1945, Maude and Oscar moved back to Waveland where he owned and operated an impressive antique store in the downtown area.

Oscar was an elder in the Christian Church, member of Waveland Lions Club and a 50-year Mason.

The couple had no children of their own, but many Waveland youngsters ate warm cookies from Maude's oven and visited Oscar in the store.

Maude died Aug. 13, 1968 and Oscar followed her almost two years later on June 9, 1970.

Close in life, close in death, they are buried side by side in Maple Ridge Cemetery. *Submitted by Karen Zach, their neighbor*

HAZEL AND ARTHUR COOKSEY

Arthur and Hazel Cooksey moved from Clarks Hill to Waveland in 1953. Arthur was born Nov. 3, 1905 in Owen County near Spencer, IN the son of Elza and Rosa Keller Cooksey. As a young man Arthur worked around Linden.

Hazel Hulvey Cooksey was born July 31, 1912 and grew up north of Darlington. Her parents were Floren and Laura Kirk Hulvey. She was a 1930 graduate of Bowers High School and a member of the old Bowers E.U.B. Church and was baptized in Sugar Creek near the Wm. Wilson home northwest of Thorntown when she was 13 years old.

Arthur and Hazel Cooksey

Besides Arthur and Hazel's love for farming and animals, their concern and care for children was shown in their parenting of foster children. One of their foster sons, Alan Franklin, was known in high school for his quiet, polite manners. Alan is now living in Lancaster, MA and is working for the Auditor of the state. Alan's wife, Miriam Wetherbee Franklin is a nurse in the hospital there. Alan and Miriam have three sons: Scott, David and Michael.

The Cooksey farm is located one mile northeast of Waveland. Although the Cookseys now live in Crawfordsville Arthur continues to be seen around their farm in Waveland. While driving around the community one can always see Arthur's ever present fiesty dog, Stubby, peeking out of the truck window.

When Arthur moved to the farm in 1953 he had an old John Deere tractor. He farmed their 80 acres until he was 82 years old. In 1988 he rented the farm ground.

The old Model A John Deere is still on the farm and is still running. Arthur's easy wit and humor was known in the neighborhood.

COON

The farm now owned by Robert Clifton Coon, has been in the Coon family since the mid-1800s. The farm is located on the Montgomery-Fountain County line about three miles southwest of Wingate. The story of the farm house (three in all) is quite interesting, the first house destroyed by dynamite and the second home was destroyed by fire. The story of the first house built back on the hill behind the present home was blown to pieces by the explosion of dynamite. As the story goes, in the late 1800s, William Coon, his sons, and John Carrington (who lived in the house with his wife and baby) were clearing the pasture behind the house of tree stumps and big rocks so they could farm the ground. It was winter and very cold; John was in charge of the dynamite and found some to be wet. Before going to the field to work that morning, John placed the wet dynamite on the floor near the wood stove in the kitchen. That was a very common practice of drying wet dynamite at that time.

Coon Family: "Dynamite, Fire Destroys Two Homes" Left to Right: Eugene, Francis, Clifton, Mary, Claude--Pearl in front

Mrs. Carrington was in the kitchen ironing with a flat iron, it is believed that when she placed the iron back on the stove to reheat she must have jarred the dynamite causing it to explode. The men working in the pasture had heard the explosion and looked up in time to see the clothing, furniture, Mrs. Carrington, and the baby blown into the air as the house exploded all around them. The men were helpless to do anything to save the mother and the child.

The second house was built by William Stephens Coon for his son Christopher John, his wife Florence Pearl, and their four sons and one daughter. This house was built closer to the road and burned to the ground in 1945, just two days before Christmas, leaving the family homeless. Pearl, Mary, Eugene, and Francis then moved in with Clyde (Buck) Coon, Christopher's brother, who lived on a nearby farm a mile west of Wingate. In 1946, they started building the third house on the same location as the house that burned down. Since Christopher died in 1929, his sons Claude, Clifton, Eugene, and Clay Francis helped their mother build the new house. The family moved into their new home in August of 1947. Later in 1959, Clifton John Coon, now farming the land, bought the farm from his mother, brothers, and sister. Pearl continued living in the house until her death in 1965. In 1967, Clifton's son Robert got married in December, and moved into the house, they still live there today. In 1973, Robert bought the farm from his parents. Today Robert now in his 26th year of farming, lives and farms the land with his wife Sherry and their children Loren, Jason, and Tonya.

We hope that the third time is a charm, and that there will be no more destructible events with the homes on this farm. But then we never know what the future holds for us, do we? *By Sherry Coon*

COONS-SHOCKEY

George W. Coons, born 1797 Jefferson Co., TN, married Julia Ferree, born 1804-1808 Virginia moved in 1829 to Montgomery Co., IN and bought land in Union Township. They had six children: John R., Sarah W., James Madison, and Robert L. born in Tennessee and William J. and Harvey P. born in Montgomery County. James Madison Coons was great-grandfather of Attorney Harold M. Coons, New Albany, IN.

Robert L. Coons, born ca. 1829 Overton Co., TN, married 1852 Montgomery County to Nancy J. VanCleave, born 1827 Kentucky, died 1884, buried at Old Hickory Cemetery, daughter of Levi and Matilda VanCleave. They had three children: Francis C., Theodore D., and Alvora E. born in Montgomery County.

Theodore D. "Fred" Coons, born June 14, 1853, died Nov. 4, 1917 Crawfordsville, married June 17, 1877 Montgomery County to Nora Shockey, born Nov. 7, 1857, died Apr. 11, 1928 both buried at Indian Creek Cemetery in Brown Township. They resided near Browns Valley where "Fred" was a farmer. Nora was the only known child of Francis M. and Mary (Seybold) Shockey of Browns Valley. Mary, born Mar. 16, 1835 Parke Co., IN, died Jan. 6, 1917 Crawfordsville, buried at Indian Creek, married Mar. 27, 1856 Francis M. Shockey, born June 1, 1830, died Apr. 10, 1890 son of Jacob and Mary (Davis) Shockey who came 1822-24 from Fleming Co., KY to Parke Co., IN where they died and are buried at Davis Cemetery in Greene Township. Jacob was eldest child of John Aaron and Priscilla (Crabb) Shockey who moved from Berkeley Co., VA 1801-02 to Kentucky and settled in Fleming County. John was son of John Aaron Christopher Shockey and wife Barbara who moved from Pennsylvania to Cumberland Co., MD. In 1769 he recorded a deed of 132 acres in Frederick Co., MD. In mid-1770's they moved to Berkeley Co., VA where John had received from Lord Thomas Fairfax a grant to 262 acres. John A. C. was third of nine children of John Christopher Shockey, nee Johann Christoffel Schacke, and wife Barbara. John C., born ca. 1715 in Germany came to America through Amsterdam, Holland on the ship "Snow-Molly" that arrived in Philadelphia Sept. 10, 1737. He pledged allegiance to the English Crown and anglicized his name. In 1740 he took up a survey of 100 acres in Medford Township, Bucks Co., PA now part of Pike County.

Mary (Seybold) Shockey was the eldest of nine children of Parke Co., IN pioneers James Sr. and Anna (Harlan) Seybold. James came from Kentucky with parents John and Mary (Reed) Seybold in 1822. Anna came from South Carolina to Union Co., IN 1815-20 then to Parke Co., IN 1821 with parents Aaron and Juliet V. (Jackson) Harlan. Mary (Seybold) Shockey was the Aunt of Frank Seybold of Waveland and Maurice Seybold of Browns Valley sons of her brother Jackson Seybold.

Theodore D. and Nora had eight children: an infant, born and died ca. 1878; Francis E., born 1880, died 1919, married 1902 Hattie E. Easley, born 1876, died 1922 both buried at Indian Creek Cemetery; Harry A., born 1883, died 1954, married 1905 Dorpha S. Caldwell, born 1881, died 1964 both buried at Freedom Cemetery north of Waveland; an infant; Roy Clifford, born 1889, married Lena Thompson; Elmer L.; Carl E., born 1895, died 1967 and wife Mary; and Fern, born 1901, married 1919 Glenn Straub.

Elmer L. Coons, born 1892, died 1971, married 1911 all in Montgomery County, to Flossie F. Parks, born 1893, died 1976 both buried at Masonic Cemetery Crawfordsville. They had three children: Lois E., Louise, and Loraine who married 1940 Paul Hayes. *By Judy L. Harvey Includes research by Ralph and Marie Shockey and Attorney Harold M. Coons*

C.O. AND GEORGIA KRUG COOPER

Casper Owen Cooper was born in Mellott, IN, the son of Charles M. (1869-1971) and Rosa (McAlister) Cooper (1870-1951), on Aug. 5, 1897. He was the fifth child born to this couple, 11 of which grew to adulthood, nine boys and two girls. Three of the boys were to become a part of Montgomery County History.

He attended schools in Mellott, graduating from that school and also from Marion College.

Since all of his grandparents remained in Fountain County, they will not be entered in this sketch. Information on them can be found in the 1983 Fountain County History.

On July 3, 1919, at Mellott, "Cap," as he was more commonly known, was united in marriage with Georgia Faye Krug, who was born in Fountain County, Dec. 7, 1900, the daughter of John Coon and Stella Ellen (Berry) Krug.

They came to Montgomery County in 1919, settling in Wingate where Cap was manager of the Wingate elevator. They remained there until 1946.

He was a member of Mercer Masonic Lodge 633 (32nd degree) of Wingate; also Scottish Rite. They were both members of the Trinity Church in Crawfordsville. He also became active in the Senior Citizens Organization of Crawfordsville.

In 1970 they moved to Tabb, IN to manage an elevator there. He retired from there and they returned to Crawfordsville, where they remained until their deaths.

In 1969 they celebrated their Golden Wedding Anniversary. This in itself was not too unusual, but what made it so was that his father attended this occasion at the age of 100 years.

They were the parents of two children, both born while they lived in Wingate: Ellen Laverne Cooper, born Mar. 19, 1920 and on July 12, 1941, married William Lodell Burkett, born Feb. 12, 1916 in Montgomery County; they were the parents of one son, William L. Burkett, Jr., born July 8, 1948 at Lafayette, IN. On June 9, 1973, at Crown Point, IN, Bill, Jr. married Danielle Gail Hrnjak, born Dec. 19, 1948 at Gary, IN. They reside in Torrence, CA and are the parents of twin sons: Jeffrey Daniel and David William, born Apr. 28, 1976. Ellen passed away Nov. 22, 1980 and is buried close to her parents at Greenlawn Cemetery at Wingate.

John William Cooper was born Sept. 11, 1922 and attended school in Wingate, as did his sister. He also served in W.W. II and on Feb. 11, 1943, on Staten Island, NY, he was married to Alice E. (Betty) Miller, born Feb. 12, 1924, the daughter of Vaughn and Maude (Lashbrook) Miller. Betty passed away Jan. 6, 1987 and is also buried at Wingate.

John and Betty were the parents of three children: William Dean Cooper, born Aug. 8, 1943 at Lafayette, married Oct. 29, 1970 to Judith Fredericks. They have two children: Lori Ann, born December 1978 and Jeanie Cooper, born January 1981. They live in Culver City, CA; Carolyn Jean, born Apr. 30, 1945, married Wallace Rosen and they are the parents of Tracy Allen, born July 5, 1966 and Trevor Allen Rosen, born Apr. 8, 1971. They are divorced and at this time Carolyn lives with her father and is Postmistress at Pine Village, IN; Teresa Lynn, born Aug. 8, 1958 and on June 29, 1973, was united in marriage with Max Whittington; one child Frayne F. Whittington, born Sept. 22, 1973.

Cap died Feb. 2, 1987 and Georgia on Nov. 7, 1973 and are buried at Wingate. *Submitted by Gwen Frees*

DOWIE T. COOPER

Dowie Theodore Cooper, the third son of Charles and Rosa (McAlister) Cooper to become a part of the history of Montgomery Co., IN was born in Mellott, Fountain County on June 19, 1910.

He attended school in Mellott and graduated from Mellott High School. He later went to Indianapolis, where he worked for the Curtiss Wright Company. This was before the United States entered W.W. II. At this time, he enlisted in the U.S. Navy, serving aboard the U.S.S. Thomas Jefferson which was the Presidential ship, but was converted during the war to a transport ship. He was discharged before the end of the War for medical reasons. It was at this time that he came to Montgomery County.

While on leave from the Navy, he met and married Violet Cunningham, born Apr. 18, 1917 in Montgomery County. She was the daughter of Buford and Hazel (Songer) Cunningham. Dowie and Violet were married Nov. 11, 1942. They had many happy years together, but there was no issue. She passed away May 28, 1972 and was laid to rest in Masonic Cemetery at Waynetown, IN.

He is a member of the American Legion and a 31 year member of the Eagles Lodge in Crawfordsville.

He was employed by Hoosier Crown Corporation for 32 years and at the time of his retirement had more years of employment than any other employee.

On Nov. 15, 1975 he was married to Ruby Ward, daughter of Thomas and Ella (South) Ward of Wallace, IN. She was born Sept. 21, 1914. She is a member of both the American Legion and Eagles' Auxiliary.

He had three step children: Barbara Staggs, born Nov. 24, 1931, married Russell Miller; one child, Brian Miller, born Mar. 29, 1958; Charlotte Staggs, born Sept. 29, 1937, married Raymond Holmes; one child, Amy Holmes who married Staci Shirar and they are the parents of one daughter, Eliza Jane Shirar, born Nov. 22, 1988. The third child is Earl Lee Staggs, born Mar. 18, 1944 who married Sandra Nicholson and they are the parents of three children, Angela Sue age 16, Eric Wayne, age 12 and Ryan Matthew age seven. All of this family reside in the Crawfordsville area.

MARION H. COOPER

Marion Harold Cooper, was the second of the

three sons of Charles M. and Rosa (McAlister) Cooper to become a part of the history of Montgomery County.

This is not to say that there were only three children. They were the parents of 16 children, all born in Mellott, IN (Fountain County), five of whom died in infancy and are all buried at Waynetown Masonic Cemetery. There were nine boys and two girls that grew to adulthood.

He was born Jan. 18, 1904 and resided there until he entered the Military in 1942. He attended school in Mellott and graduated from that school. Upon graduation he was employed at Harrison Steel in Attica, worked on a farm for Lee Thorne and also helped his Father, who was a ditcher by trade. His Father always commented that he had walked more miles backward than most had walked forward. He came to Crawfordsville and was employed at R.R. Donnelley Co., before entering the service.

During the time he served in the Army he was stationed at Ft. Benning, GA as a Medic. He was released before the end of the war because of his age. Upon his return to Montgomery County he worked for a time at Curtiss Wright in Indianapolis and then returned to Donnelley's, and remained until his retirement in 1969.

On May 12, 1945 he was united in marriage with Mollie Elmore, born May 9, 1921 in Freedom, KY. She was the daughter of Alfred V. "Bun" (May 3, 1893-Feb. 2, 1973) and Maggie Richey Elmore (July 7, 1904-Oct. 20, 1927). "Bun" is buried at Waynetown and her Mother in Kentucky.

Mollie is very active in Milligan Memorial Church, where they are both members. She is on the board of the Church, also the Christian Nursing Service and handles the clothing for the "Fish Program". She and Marion answer the Fish phone from 8:00 a.m. to 2:00 p.m. She also is President of the Auxiliary of W.W. I Barracks, a Military Organization. She has been a Crossing Guard for the City of Crawfordsville for 33 years. She also handles the "Tele-Check" program, in which she calls several elderly people every day to make sure they are alright. These are all elderly people who live alone and have no family in the area.

Marion is very crippled with Arthritis, but he manages to keep busy. He has made many latchhook pieces and has also made at least two quilts, sewing them all by hand. Most of this work is then sold at the "Church Rummage Sale", held once a year and the proceeds go to the church. He, too served as a Crossing Guard for several years, until his health made it impossible.

They reside on Elmore St. in Crawfordsville. There were no children.

CORD FAMILY

Evidently the Cords migrated to the United States from France in the early 1600's. They settled in Maryland. The following is the direct line of ancestry: Thomas Cord - Hannah Mathews (married 1698); Thomas Cord Jr. - Mary Williams; Amos Cord - Susanne Kimble; Aquille Cord - Milcha Browing; William B. Cord - Elizabeth Caywood; William J. Cord - Susan Phillips; Oliver J. Cord - Mattie Courtney; Claude C. Cord.

The Cords migrated from Maryland to Fleming Co., KY. Amos Cord was probably the first to come to Kentucky.

William J. Cord, the grandfather of the writer had three sons and two daughters: namely Robert L. Cord, John H. Cord, Oliver J. Cord, Cora Cord Fouts and Mary Cord Campbell. Robert L. Cord had one daughter - Genevieve Cord Tracy. John H. Cord had one son and two daughters; Marion Cord (died at 15), Crystal Cord Bonar and Catherine Cord Lockwood. Cora Cord Fouts had three sons and one daughter - Charles, Claude, Roscoe and Ilah Fouts Pearson. Mary Cord Campbell had three daughters and one son - Sarah, Virginia, Mary Lou and Bertram.

Mattie, Oliver J., Claude C., Robert L., Caps (Dog), Wm. Clyde Cord.

Oliver J. Cord and Mattie Courtney Cord who are featured in this article had three sons: William Clyde, Claude C. and Robert L., all three sons served their Country in World War II and William Clyde also in the Korean War. Robert L. gave his life for his country near St. Lo France, Aug. 3, 1944. William Clyde Cord married Kathleen Quillin and had one son and one daughter; Thomas J. married Jan Birr (no children); Anne Q., married Richard Novak they had one son Paul Robert and one daughter, Kathleen Elizabeth Rose.

William Clyde Cord, and Claude C. Cord both attended DePauw University. Claude C. graduated with high distinction and Phi Beta Kappa honors in 1932. Claude C. received an MS degree from Indiana University in 1946. William Clyde Cord spent most of his life in the military and working at Wright-Patterson Air Force Base. He died Jan. 31, 1976.

Claude C. Cord taught school for 36 years and served as a principal for 23 years. He was principal of Alamo High School for 21 years. He is now retired and living in Waynetown, IN.

William J. Cord, father of Oliver J. Cord needs to be especially recognized. He came to Wayne Township, Montgomery County from Fleming Co., KY. Around 1850 he married Susan Phillips, a member of the well-known Phillips family.

William J. was a pioneer teacher in the one room schools of Wayne Township. He taught during the years 1845-1896. Sixteen of the years he taught were in the Maxwell School. He also served as Justice of the Peace for Wayne Township 1870-1886 and he was trustee of Wayne Township 1886-1890. In the entire United States the Cord Family is quite rare and there are very few Cords left in Montgomery County as of 1989.

WILLIAMS CORN

Williams Corn born Feb. 16, 1800 in Kentucky and died Nov. 11, 1859 in Clark Township, IN, was the son of George and Jane Williams Corn. In Shelby Co., KY, on Mar. 16, 1823 he married Sarah Allen born Aug. 16, 1899 in Kentucky, the daughter of Joseph and Rhoda Allen, and died here on May 14, 1874. They came to Parke Co., IN in 1827, then on to Montgomery County in 1830, northeast of Ladoga. He first built a cabin, then in four or five years a larger home. Their children were Rhoda Jane Foxworthy, born in Kentucky in 1824; Albert born in 1825 in Kentucky and married Rachel Randel, daughter of Asa and Margaret Sutton Randel; Elizabeth born 1827 in Kentucky and married Jeremiah Redenbaugh. They then had nine more children born in Indiana; Nancy born 1829 and married Isaac N. Miller; Mary Ann born in 1831; Margaret D. Corn born 1833 and married Noah Castle Linn; Sarah Eliza Corn born 1835 and married William Henry Redenbaugh; John W. Corn born 1839; George Corn born 1841 married Hulda Williams and lived on the homeplace; then their daughter Vinletta Corn married William Frantz and lived there and then their son George Frantz and his wife Jennie Brookshire lived there. Sarah Allen Corn did spinning and weaving making their own clothes. After Williams died Sarah continued living with her son, George, who had bought out the other heirs. The house that stands on the property now was built in 1880 by George Corn. Williams and Sarah Allen Corn's children Rhoda Jane Foxworthy lived near Ladoga; Albert lived near Whitesville; Elizabeth Redenbaugh lived near New Ross; Nancy Miller lived west of New Ross; Margaret D. Corn lived northwest of New Ross; Julia Ann Wright lived near New Market; Sarah Eliza Redenbaugh lived near New Ross.

CORYS OF WALLACE

The Cory families of Montgomery County trace their ancestry back through Fountain Co., IN; through Warren and Butler counties of Ohio; through Washington Co., PA and Union Co., NJ; back to Scotland.

Joseph Edward Cory, Mary Ann (Levingstone) Cory

Joseph Edward Cory, born 1855 in Fountain Co., IN, is the son of David W.B. Cory and Ann Eliza Stiner. Ann Eliza Stiner died at age 26. David Cory, born 1831 in Fountain Co., IN, is the son of James Cory and Nancy Ann Highland. Nancy Highland was born about 1805 in Butler Co., OH. James Cory, born 1805 in Warren Co., OH, is the son of Jeremiah Cory and Mary Bishop.

Jeremiah Cory served as a private in the Morris Co., NJ Militia during the Revolutionary War hauling for the Forage Dept. at Rahway. Jeremiah lived for a while in Washington Co., PA, and then farmed 160 acres in Warren Co., OH, where he died in 1805, the year his son James was born. At his death, the Court of Common Pleas appointed his sons, Daniel and Noah, to administer his estate. Moses and Mary Cory, children of the deceased chose Joseph Lamb their guardian; Jeremiah Cory, a son of the deceased, chose Silas Hurin as his guardian and later names his son Silas Hurin Cory and moved to Fountain Co., IN; the court appoints Joseph Lamb and Mary Cory (soon to marry Stephanos

Clark) as guardians for the minor heirs, Elnathan, Usual, and James.

Jeremiah Cory, born 1741 in Elizabethtown, Union Co., NJ, is the son of Elnathan Cory and Sarah Simpson. Sarah Simpson was born in 1704 in Kings Co., NY. Elnathan Cory, born 1702 in Union Co., NJ, is the son of John Cory III and Priscilla Osborn. John Cory III, born 1674 in Huntington, Long Island, NY, is the son of John Cory II and Mary Cornish. John Cory II, born in England, is the son of John Cory I, who was born 1611 in Norwich, Norfolk Co., England. John Cory I's father was knighted by King Charles I of England. John Cory I, a weaver and Puritan, brought to America in 1636 "The Grate Booke", and became a man of considerable means on Long Island. The Grate Booke has on its front cover the following inscription: "This book given to John Cory by his mother to carry with him to America", was printed in Scotland in 1610, and contains 500 leaves of heavy English parchment. The book is a treatise on the Holy Bible and contains family records on its flyleaves. A case was made for it from the wood from four different places: Cherry - from Elizabethtown, NJ, home of John Cory III, Oak - from a tree on Long island farm of John Cory I, Rosewood - from the farm of William Smith Cory, 1930 heir and Yule - from the Cory farm in Scotland. The first letters of these words spells the name CORY. The Grate Booke can be found in New Galilee, PA in the Cory family.

KENNETH AND CHARLOTTE COSBY

Kenneth E. and Charlotte E. Oliver Cosby are lifelong residents of Montgomery County. Kenny Cosby was born in Browns Valley on Nov. 10, 1916, the second child of Lando H. and Effie M. Friend Cosby. His siblings are Leonard, Lyle, Virginia and Lando Cosby, Jr.

Kenny's parents were married at Crawfordsville on Oct. 22, 1913. His father, Lando, was born Sept. 29, 1891 near Colfax, a son of Oliver M. and Anna A. Martz Cosby. Lando was a successful farmer, as was his father before him. Kenny's mother, Effie, was born Apr. 19, 1893 near Ladoga, the second child of Theodore M. and Fannie W. Myers Friend. Her parents lived in Kentucky before moving to Montgomery County in 1892.

Kenny began farming the Glenn Fullenwider farm at the Pine Grove Crossing between Waveland and Browns Valley in 1936, a year after his graduation from Waveland High School. Special features of the farm were its huge pines, large maples, and rolling hills.

Kenneth and Charlotte Cosby 1941 Wedding Picture

On June 14, 1941, Kenny married Miss Charlotte Emily Oliver. Charlotte was born Aug. 16, 1914 near Whitesville, the second child of Charles A. and Amanda C. Himes Oliver. Charlotte's elder sister, Mary E. Oliver Mueller, resides in Columbus, OH. Her younger brother, Charles E. Oliver, died in 1952.

Charlotte's parents were married at Ladoga on Dec. 25, 1907 and were lifetime residents of Montgomery County. Her father, Charles A., was born Jan. 26, 1866 in Union Township, a son of Jackson and Emily Wilson Oliver. Charles was an industrious farmer. Charlotte's mother, Amanda, was born July 5, 1878 near Ladoga to Abraham and Mary Ann Lemon Himes.

Charlotte graduated from Crawfordsville High School in 1933, then earned her elementary teaching license from Central Normal College in 1936. She taught several years in the Waveland and New Market schools before retiring.

Kenny has been an active member of Browns Valley Christian Church since birth. Charlotte became a member after their marriage and is also a long-time member of the church's Loyal Circle, the Waveland O.E.S., and the Country Ladies.

Kenny and Charlotte are the parents of two children: Elaine Ann Cosby Norman of rural Waveland and Terry Alan Cosby of Crawfordsville. Both are lifetime residents of Montgomery County. Elaine is married to K. Dean Norman and Terry's spouse is Elisabeth Eschenbach Cosby. Kenny and Charlotte are also the proud grandparents of Christopher, Timothy, Erika and Ronda Norman and Colleen and Cary Cosby.

Kenny and Charlotte still live on the farm on which they set up housekeeping 48 years ago. Their house was a novelty when it was erected in 1941. At that time, their landlord worked for the Weyerhauser Company in Washington State. He sent a prefabricated frame house by rail to Browns Valley. From there, Kenny hauled the parts to the farm. Spectators came to watch as the house was being constructed. Later, in 1956, Kenny and Charlotte bought their farm and the years since have been devoted to farming and their family. *Submitted by Elaine Cosby Norman*

LANDO AND EFFIE COSBY

Lando H. Cosby was born Sept. 29, 1891 to Oliver H. and Anna Martz Cosby at Colfax, IN. His grandparents were Oliver C. and Maria Crison Cosby and John and Mary Fouts Martz. Lando was the second child. Others were Bernie, Douglas, Lee, Harley and Evah. The latter two died young.

As a young man, Lando went to Michigan and worked for awhile, but came back to Montgomery County and found work as a farm hand. When he worked for Theodore Friend near Ladoga, he was attracted to their quiet, pretty daughter, Effie May. His brown eyes, dark hair and jovial nature along with being a hard worker led to romance and later marriage. They were married Oct. 22, 1913 and went to housekeeping on a farm in Brown Twp.

Left to right: Lyle, Lando, Effie, Leonard and Kenneth, Virginia and Jr.

Effie was born Apr. 19, 1893 to Theodore and Fannie Myers Friend on a farm near Ladoga. Her parents had moved here from Kentucky in 1892. Other children were Ellis, Ethel, Pauline, Opal, Nellie, Buford, twins Eva and Everett, Arthur, Edna and Waneta. The latter two died as small children. Her grandparents were Manford and Mary Ann Friend, Estill Co., KY and Henry and Tabetha Ann Miller, Mt. Sterling, KY. Great grandparents were Francis and Agnes Walker Myers, Howard Mills, KY. Great great grandparents were Henry Myers Sr. and Hannah Boyles Myers, Mt. Sterling, KY. He was German Dunkard; a Revolutionary war veteran.

The Lord blessed Lando and Effie with Leonard, Kenneth, Lyle, Virginia and Junior. Theirs was a happy Christian home and in 1948 after many years of working and saving they bought a farm west of Parkersburg. Lando enjoyed farming and raising shorthorn cattle. Effie liked her white rock chickens. She was an excellent cook so there were many family dinners, reunions, and picnics. Effie and Lando were devoted Christian parents and were faithful life time members of the Browns Valley Christian Church.

Leonard married Lorene Jenkins; Lando Jr. married Marie Gerlack. They live in Parke County. Kenneth married Charlotte Oliver; Lyle married Estelline Shaffer. They live in Montgomery County. Virginia married Glenn Crosby. They live in Ft. Myers, FL.

The grandchildren had fun when they visited grandma and grandpa and they really enjoyed them too.

Effie had a talent for writing poetry and many friends received cards, notes and letters of encouragement from her.

Effie died Oct. 28, 1961. Although Lando had been afflicted with asthma all his life he lived alone for nine years after her death. He died suddenly in his home July 8, 1970.

TERRY A. AND ELISABETH A. ESCHENBACH COSBY

Terry and Lisa Cosby have lived in Crawfordsville since their marriage on Jan. 18, 1974. They reside at 1408 E. Main, the home they purchased in 1982.

Terry, a Montgomery County native, was born at Culver Hospital on Jan. 21, 1951 to Kenneth E. and Charlotte E. Oliver Cosby of Waveland. Terry was a ten year member of 4-H and was active in baseball, basketball and track. He held the Montgomery County high jump record and graduated from Waveland High School in 1969. In 1973, he received his B.S. degree in agriculture from Purdue where he was a member of Alpha Chi Rho Fraternity. Currently, Terry is farming with his father on Pine Grove Farm in Waveland and spends his spare time doing antique restoration. He also has a growing collection of antique toy soldiers.

Terry's parents are also lifelong residents of Montgomery County. His mother, Charlotte, was born on Aug. 16, 1914 in Whitesville to Amanda C. Himes and Charles A. Oliver. She graduated from Crawfordsville High School and attended Central Normal College. She taught for seven years and is currently a homemaker. Terry's father, Kenneth, was born on Nov. 10, 1916 in Browns Valley, to Effie May Friend and Lando H. Cosby. He attended Browns Valley School through the early grades and graduated from Waveland High School. In 1936 he began farming Pine Grove Farm and purchased it in 1945. Currently he is semi-retired but still farming!

Terry, Lisa, Colleen, and Cary Cosby

Lisa, grew up in Munster in Lake Co., IN and was born at St. Margaret's Hospital on Apr. 4, 1951 in Hammond. She is the daughter of Robert L. and Virginia R. Schuchmann Eschenbach of Dyer, IN. Lisa graduated from Bishop Noll Institute, currently known as Hammond Noll. In 1973, she received her B.A. degree from Purdue University where she was a member of Phi Mu Sorority and the Purduettes. She also received her M.A. from Purdue. Lisa is employed by the North Montgomery School Corp. as an art teacher. She taught art and music at Linden for 15 years and is currently teaching at Pleasant Hill and Sommer Elementaries. She is past president of Tri Kappa Sorority, and a member of Dorothy Q Chapter, DAR, Sugar Creek Players, and Art League.

Lisa's mother, Virginia was born on Oct. 13, 1927, in Chicago to Andrew H. and Rose Anne Weiland Schuchmann. She graduated from George Rogers Clark High School and MacMurray College in central Illinois. She taught school for over ten years, wrote copy for an Indiana radio station and currently is a professional genealogist and antique dealer.

Lisa's father, Robert was born on Sept. 4, 1925, in Chicago to Walter F. and Theresa R. McElroy Eschenbach. He graduated from Whiting High School and attended Indiana University. He was a building contractor and cabinet maker for many years and is currently an antique dealer specializing in clock repair and furniture restoration.

Terry and Lisa have two children, Colleen Erin and Cary Andrew who were born at the original Culver Union Hospital. Colleen was born on Mar. 4, 1978 and is going into the 6th grade. Cary was born on June 21, 1980 and will be entering the 3rd grade. The children participate in many activities including baseball, basketball, soccer, gymnastics, drama, dance and are very interested in art. Colleen is currently taking voice, violin and tap dancing lessons. They attend John Beard Elementary and Tuttle Junior High. *Submitted by Terry and Lisa Cosby*

DR. EDWARD HOWARD COWAN

Dr. Edward Howard Cowan, Montgomery County's last Civil War veteran, was born on Dec. 21, 1846 in Frankfort, IN. He was the eldest son of John Maxwell Cowan and his wife Harriet Doubleday Janney of Frankfort, IN. His grandparents were John Cowan and his wife Anna Maxwell, and Abel Janney and Margaret Porter. See John Maxwell Cowan family.

Dr. Cowan was raised in the Frankfort area and received excellent schooling during childhood. In September of 1862, Edward Howard Cowan entered Wabash College in Crawfordsville, IN. In April, 1864, Indiana Governor Oliver P. Morton called for volunteers to serve 100 days of military service. On May 23, 1864, Edward Howard Cowan, along with many other Wabash students, joined the 135th Regiment Indiana Volunteers. Dr. Cowan was assigned to Company H, as a private. He served in Tennessee. He was discharged on Sept. 29, 1864. He returned to Wabash College in 1865 and graduated in 1867.

In the fall of 1868, Dr. Cowan began the study of medicine under the tutelage of Dr. Moses Baker of Stockwell, a noted physician and surgeon. In 1872 and 1873, Dr. Cowan attended Miami Medical College in Cincinnati, OH. After he graduated he began his practice in Crawfordsville on Apr. 1, 1873 and he continued his active practice for over 55 years. In 1882, Dr. Cowan became Crawfordsville's first health officer.

On Nov. 13, 1877, Dr. Cowan was united in marriage to Lucy L. Ayars of Louisville, KY. His parents were married on the same day 32 years before in Stockwell, IN. Lucy Ayars Cowan was born on Oct. 27, 1855. She was the daughter of Robert and Elizabeth Hicks Ayars of Louisville, KY. Robert Ayars married Elizabeth J. Hicks on June 14, 1832 in Kentucky. Robert was the son of John Gillman Ayars (1764-1838) and his wife Mary Sparks (1768-1821). He was the grandson of Burgin Ayars (1726-1807) and his wife Susannah Gilman. Robert Ayars was born on May 20, 1804 and died on Feb. 11, 1882 in Louisville, KY.

Lucy Cowan was a great niece of Major Ambrose Whitlock who laid out and named Crawfordsville. She was active in the Wabash Avenue Presbyterian Church and Women's Relief Corps. She died on Nov. 10, 1924 in Methodist Hospital in Indianapolis, IN. She is buried in Oak Hill Cemetery.

Dr. Cowan was active in the Grand Army of the Republic. He served as post commander several terms and served as national surgeon general of the G.A.R. During the 75th Reunion of the Battle of Gettysburg, Pennsylvania, Dr. Cowan led the Indiana delegation. Dr. Cowan died at his daughter's home in Dallas, TX on Aug. 1, 1942. He was buried with full military honors next to his wife.

Their children were John Ayars, born Aug. 11, 1880, died Sept. 27, 1891, and is buried next to his parents; and Elizabeth Louise, born June 21, 1884. She married Lewis Ferguson and they are buried in Dallas, TX. *Submitted by Andrew Keith Houk, Jr.*

JOHN COWAN

John Cowan was born Dec. 14, 1768 in Rockbridge Co., VA. He was married May 10, 1796 to Margaret Weir in Rockbridge County. She died after 1805.

John Cowan moved to Blount Co., TN at a young age and later moved to Kentucky, and finally, to Jefferson Co., IN where he married second Anna Maxwell on Dec. 30, 1819. He served in Captain James Bigger's Company of Mounted Rangers from May, 1812 to May, 1814 during the War of 1812. He also served as a mounted ranger at the Battle of Tippecanoe on Nov. 7, 1811. John and Anna Maxwell Cowan moved to Indianapolis in 1821 and came to Montgomery Co., IN in 1822. John Cowan died Aug. 17, 1832 in Frankfort, IN while there on business. He is buried in Frankfort's Old Town Cemetery.

Anna Maxwell Cowan was born Dec. 11, 1781 in Virginia. She was the daughter of Bezaleel and Margaret Anderson Maxwell. Bezaleel Maxwell was born Dec. 20, 1751 in Albemarle Co., VA. His parents were Captain John and Fannie Garner Maxwell. Captain John served in the Colonial and Revolutionary Wars. Bezaleel was married Feb. 6, 1775 to Margaret Anderson, the daughter of Colonel John Anderson. She was born Sept. 4, 1755.

Bezaleel Maxwell served during the Lord Dunmore War in 1774. He enlisted on June 3, 1774 as a private under General Andrew Lewis. On Oct. 10, 1774 General Lewis and his army fought the Battle of Point Pleasant. During the Revolutionary War, Bezaleel Maxwell served with the Virginia Militia. After the war, he and his father John moved their families to Kentucky. Bezaleel bought a farm in Garrard Co., KY. He later moved his family to Jefferson Co., IN. Bezaleel Maxwell died Jan. 9, 1828 and his wife, Margaret, died Mar. 16, 1834. They are both buried in the old Hanover Cemetery in Jefferson Co., IN.

Anna Maxwell Cowan died in Frankfort, IN Jan. 9, 1854 and was buried next to her husband.

The children of John and Anna Weir Cowan were:

1. James Weir, born June 30, 1797, married Isabell Hunter.
2. Mary Ann, born Apr. 18, 1799, died Aug. 9, 1819.
3. Samuel Walker, born Dec. 2, 1801, died Aug. 30, 1834 in Vicksburg, MS.
4. Sarah Tilford, born Oct. 30, 1805, died Jan. 1, 1856. She married Samuel Dunn Maxwell (son of John and Sarah Dunn Maxwell and grandson of Bezaleel and Margaret Maxwell and Samuel and Eleanor Brewster Dunn). Samuel Dunn Maxwell was mayor of Indianapolis 1860-1864.

The children of John and Anna Maxwell Cowan were:

1. John Maxwell, born Dec. 6, 1821 in Indianapolis, IN (see John Maxwell Cowan family). *Submitted by Andrew Keith Houk, Jr.*

JOHN MAXWELL COWAN

John Maxwell Cowan was born on Dec. 6, 1821 in Indianapolis, IN, being the first white child born in that city. His parents were John and Anna Maxwell Cowan. See John Cowan family.

John M. Cowan came to Crawfordsville with his parents in 1822. The family home was located in the south part of Crawfordsville. John M. received his early schooling in the local schools and at home. In 1836, he entered the preparatory school of Wabash College and he graduated from Wabash College in 1842. He received his law degree from Indiana University in 1845. He opened a law firm with James F. Suit in Frankfort, IN. He served two terms as judge of the Eighth Judicial Circuit Court. He moved his family to Crawfordsville in 1864 and in 1870, he opened a law firm in Crawfordsville with Thomas M. Patterson, who later served as U.S. Senator from Colorado. John M. became the assistant cashier and lawyer for the First National Bank of Crawfordsville. He was a trustee of Wabash College for many years. In May of 1881, John M. Cowan moved his family to Springfield, MO, where he purchased a large farm. He later built a home in Springfield.

Judge Cowan cast his first presidential vote for Henry Clay of Kentucky. He had heard Henry Clay speak in Indianapolis, and rode with Mr. Clay on the first train in Indiana, going from Indianapolis to Madison. Judge Cowan was present in Illinois during the famous debate between Stephen A.

Douglas and Abraham Lincoln, and became friends with both men. When Abraham Lincoln visited with Henry Lane in early 1860, Judge Cowan and his son Edward H. called on the Lincolns.

John M. Cowan was married on Nov. 13, 1845 to Harriet Doubleday Janney in Stockwell, IN. She was born July 29, 1826 near Stockwell to Abel Janney and his wife Margaret Porter (daughter of James Porter). Her parents came from Wayne Co., IN in 1823 and were of Quaker descent. Harriet Janney Cowan died on June 28, 1905 in Springfield, MO and is buried in Oak Hill Cemetery in Crawfordsville.

Judge Cowan continued to live in Springfield after his wife's death. Judge Cowan died in his home on June 3, 1920. He was laid to rest next to his wife in Oak Hill Cemetery.

The children of John Maxwell and Harriet Janney Cowan were:

Edward Howard (see Dr. Edward Howard Cowan article).

James Porter Ellis, born Oct. 29, 1848, died Mar. 8, 1927 in Jamaica, NY. He is buried in Oak Hill Cemetery, Crawfordsville. He was married three times.

Laura Anna, born Mar. 14, 1851, died July 12, 1948 in Jamaica, NY. She is buried in Oak Hill Cemetery. She married Allen T. Blaine (1846-1880). He was in Company K, 74th Indiana Infantry.

John William, born Oct. 3, 1853, died Jan. 22, 1922 in Springfield, MO. He is buried in Oak Hill Cemetery. *Submitted by Andrew Keith Houk, Jr.*

ABIJAH FRANKLIN AND ALDEZERA (MORRIS) COX

One county history says of a Cox: "A full history of this family is impossible without giving the history of the whole neighborhood."

The Cox homestead, adjacent to the Abe Caster farm, Road 32, was in the Kingsley Chapel neighborhood. Here Franklin was born, 1852, son of Abijah and Edna Cox. Three siblings reached maturity: Elijah died in war; Kiziah married Clint Tribbett; Eliza, William Dixon.

After attending Mooresville Quaker Academy; Franklin married Aldezera (Allie) Morris, 1873, daughter of Owen David and Delilah (Cory) Morris. Children: Wallace, 1874; Estella Abigail, 1877; Beulah Mae, 1890.

Stella's autograph book shows one year of Windfield, KS, schoolmates, then a return to schoolmates at Kingsley Chapel, near the present Trout picnic shelter. Of its 34 pupils ten were Coxes; eight, were children of Amy Ann (Cox) Hall. Otis became County Superintendent of Schools, helped start 4-H; Oakel attended Boston Seminary, became minister and professor.

Wally married schoolmate, Rosa Cricky, 1895. Their daughter, Alta, married Harold Vannice 1915, farmed near Linden. Wally was proud of his two granddaughters. Marian Louise I.U. '38, teacher, married Harvey Neal 1945, home Lafayette. Wally would point out his great granddaughters: Karen, Rowanna, Marina, Jeannine, the last one (Michelle) he'd stop, "I don't know her name". Betty Dahr M.S.I.U. teacher, married Richard Hayworth 1949, home, Columbia City. Children: William, Robert, Diane (all Purdue). Neal girls, I.U. Purdue, Ball State.

After Allie died, 1901, Franklin moved to Darlington. On Sunday Stella would join Will McClaskey as he walked to church. They were married December, 1903 - Franklin's gift, two horses. Stella enjoyed music and photography. On their newly-purchased farm, she was raising chickens, ducks, a little girl Alice (1905), a little boy Eb (1907).

Franklin and Beulah moved to Crawfordsville. Ed Williamson would take the interurban to call on Beulah.

In 1911 Stella contracted malaria, developed pneumonia, died in September. Franklin died in November.

Alice, DePauw '28, taught in Darlington schools, married, Aug. 27, 1945, a Highview schoolmate, Erving Weesner. School's end, 1946, she left teaching to care for Bob, born June 26, 1946 and John, Jan. 10, 1949.

Ed married a class-mate, Marihelen Paddack, daughter of Ben and Daisy (Hunt) Paddack, Oct. 17, 1928. They began farming on land now theirs. Children: Marilyn (1929), Joan (1931), Dave (1944).

Beulah married Ed Williamson November 1912. They farmed the Frank Buchanan place where Helen Mae was born Apr. 15, 1915. Now they moved to Spry's Hill. Ed farmed, drove a school bus, had a milk route. Back from the city, Beulah and Helen Mae would bring carnations instead of candy.

In Helen Mae's class there was one Floyd Hampton whom she married June, 1941. War came. Ed died 1943.

Service over in the Aleutians, Floyd and Helen Mae returned to the Dan Hampton farm. Young Dan was born in 1947, Dave, in 1953.

Beulah was of the Darlington class of 1909. Her knowledge of family connections, past or present was invaluable. To church, over ice-slick walks, she would wave her supporting dust mop at passersby.

Susan Harper, asked whether hats would be worn to her wedding, said, "Oh, no." then "Correction, there will be one hat." Beulah always wore a hat to dress-up occasions. Sam Stewart's 70th birthday, July 24, 1977 was her last party. She died August 22.

Bulldozer and plow have removed landmarks of the Cox homestead.

BYRON COX AND BERTHA COX GALLANT SON AND GOLD STAR MOTHER

Byron Clark Cox, third child of Denton and Bertha Cox, was born Dec. 5, 1899, at Rossville, IN, and moved with his family to Garfield in 1908. He graduated from Darlington High School in 1916, and that summer attended State Normal at Terre Haute. Then in the fall, Byron, not yet 17, was hired as principal of Shannondale School, where he was younger than some of his pupils.

The U.S. declared war on Germany Apr. 6, 1917. Ten days later Byron enlisted in the army. The dutiful son now became the dutiful soldier. June 28, 1917, he was sent to France with the First Division.

Byron was injured by poison gas May 4, 1918, but recovered sufficiently after three weeks in the hospital to return to the front May 28.

By early June, German troops were threatening Paris, and the Allies, including the First Division, fought fiercely from July 16-August 6 to turn the Germans back. This offensive, known as the Second Battle of the Marne, was the turning point of the war. And when it was over, the dreaded news reached Darlington: Byron Cox had been killed on July 21, 1918, and had been buried in far-away France. He was 18 years old.

Byron and Bertha Cox

Theodore Roosevelt, whose son Quentin died in the same battle, sent this telegram to the Denton Cox family: "Accept my deep sympathy in the death of your gallant son."

Eleven years went by. Then Mar. 2, 1929, Congress passed the remarkable Gold Star Mothers Pilgrimage Act. This statute enabled "mothers of deceased soldiers interred in the cemeteries of Europe to make a pilgrimage to those cemeteries" at government expense.

Bertha Cox was issued a special red passport and an official identity card for the 9,000-mile month-long journey. And in August, 1930, her husband, children, and grandchildren gathered at the Darlington railroad depot to see her off. Her daughter Evelyn remembers, "We were not a kissing family, but everyone got a kiss from Mom that day!"

Later, back home again, Bertha gave public talks about her trip. Her handwritten notes indicate she talked about French towns, French foods, and ancient French cathedrals. She showed a postcard picture of the S.S. Republic, the ship that took her to Cherbourg, and told of being seated at the captain's table for dinner on her birthday. And she kept a birthday card presented to her and signed by several of the ship's crew and passengers.

She showed pictures of the Hotel Ambassador where she stayed in Paris, and of the Compiegne Monument dedicated to the war dead by a grateful French nation. She told of standing on the very battlefield where Byron had fought and died, and finally, of visiting his grave in the nearby cemetery at Oise-Aisne.

These treasured mementos of Bertha Cox's pilgrimage were found among her belongings at the time of her death in 1959.

Byron Cox was the first Montgomery County soldier to die in World War I, and the American Legion Post in Crawfordsville is named in his honor. *Submitted by Julia Perkins*

COX CAFE

The Cox Cafe was started in September 1930 when Cecil and Kenneth Cox leased the restaurant in Darlington from Jim Brooks. The lease expired the following year allowing them to move their restaurant to the Chambers building. When Ken left the business another brother, Keith, took his place staying until the early '40's. At this time Cece and wife Mabel ran the restaurant until January, 1951, when they sold it to Clarence and Bertha Greatbatch.

In the early 30s hotdog and hamburger sandwiches were 5¢ each, ham and pork sandwiches were 10¢ as were French fries. A dinner consisting of meat, potato, a vegetable, side dish and drink was

35¢. Pie (homemade of course) raised the price to 40¢. In the evening short orders were served. You could order a T-bone steak with French fries, salad and drink for 35¢. Many people, to this day, miss Cece's baked ham and roast pork sandwiches.

Alec, Cece Cox in 1932 - Cox Cafe Darlington

The WWII years were good to the restaurant as the town folk stayed in town (due to gas rationing) and could often be found at the restaurant enjoying something from the soda fountain or the good home cooked food.

The most unforgettable times were after the high school basketball games. Everyone showed up. In those days, it was the norm for the school to pay the tab for each ballplayer's, cheerleader's and student manager's refreshment up to 35¢. Alec Cox, another brother, was the coach at Linden and always brought his team in after they had played at Darlington.

Another fun and unusual thing was the big dining table toward the back of the restaurant. It often became a ping pong table with some rather hotly contested games.

The neat old juke box that a lot of kids danced to, the tables with the initials carved in them, and the phone number — 5-7, are all just memories with the rest of it now. *Submitted by Marta Cox Jeffries*

DENTON THORNBURG AND BERTHA CLARK COX

(1) Kenneth Cox, born 1895 died 1944, served in World War I, the National Guard, and World War II as Lt. Colonel in the Air Corps. (a) Married Virgie Carson, died 1936; daughter Nancy married Jim Wright, daughters Beth and Sarah. Nancy teaches in Richmond, KY where they own a pottery business. (b) Married Mae Hunt, teacher, died 1986.

(2) Pauline Cox Marshall (see index)

(3) Byron Clark Cox (see index)

(4) Cecil B. Cox (see index)

(5) Etelka Cox, born 1903 died 1941, married Oliver McLoed, children Richard and Carolyn. Richard married Evelyn Poe; children Larry, Marty, Tom, Doug, Janet, Terri. Richard at age 18 was in World War II on the front line during the advance on Berlin. He graduated from the University of Chicago, Aeronautical Engineering, and is retired from Allison Mfg. Co. in Brownsburg, IN. Carolyn married Raymond Simmons, daughters Pamela and Jane, both married and living in New Jersey. Carolyn was associated with Union Federal Savings and Loan for several years.

(6) Keith Cox (see index)

(7) Alexander Denton Cox, born 1907 died 1977, married Mamie Fletcher. After graduating from Wabash College Alec taught and coached at Francisville, Bowers, Darlington, and Linden. After retiring from teaching he owned and operated Cox Standard Service Station and Used Car Business in Darlington. Mamie taught high schools a total of 26 years at Francisville, New Ross, and Darlington. They have two children, Joe and Julia. Joe, Professor of Nuclear Physics at Atlantic University at Boca Raton, FL, married Joan Allendorf a C.P.A. They have three children, Laurell, Brian, and Jeff. Julia married William Perkins, Professor of Engineering at Illinois University. They have three children, Elizabeth, Susan, and Jim.

(8) Margaret Cox, born 1910, married Paul Edwards, one son John. Margaret, an Indiana State graduate, taught school at Garfield, Darlington, New Market, and Linden, retiring after 44 years of teaching. She is well remembered by her pupils, and held in high esteem by former pupils and fellow teachers. John lives in Dallas, TX, is a computer analyst, and has devised several systems now in use all over the States. He married Becky Alexander; children Dawn, John Jr., Lyric, and Wendy. He is presently married to Carla Pylant; son Seth.

(9) Evelyn Cox born 1913, married Lewis Francis, died 1950; three children Phillip, Patricia, and Penelope. They farmed east of Crawfordsville several years. Evelyn moved to town and worked at Impex as Treasurer/Controller for 24 years. In 1952 she married Donald H. Wingert. Phillip married Sharon McClain; children Debbie, Sally, Mike, Randy, Jeff, Chris, Pam, Jan, Scott, Amy, and David. Phil is presently married to Carol Fitzwater; children Kimberly, and Keri. They own and live on a farm south of Crawfordsville. Phil is Plant Manager at Mid-States. Patty lives in Alexandria, VA and teaches in Fairfax County. She married Frank G. Barnes who became a Major General in the Air Force; three children, Beth, Susan, and Hank. General Barnes served in Europe, Korea, and Vietnam. While stationed at Wright-Patterson A.F.B. in Ohio he died in 1977. Patty is now married to Charles A. Kelly, a prominent Chicago lawyer. Penny taught school at Evanston, IL and St. Paul, MN. She married Thomas W. Osborn; children Edward, Nick, Ben, and Gillian. They lived in Stamford, CT when Penny died in 1979.

DWIGHT AND MARY COX FAMILY

Dwight L. Cox, a native of Montgomery County since 1932, lived on a farm north of Crawfordsville with his parents, Roy E. and Myrl (Cook) Cox. He graduated from Crawfordsville in 1951, started working at R.R. Donnelley Printing and in 1953, he served in the Army (during Korea). After the service, he went back to Donnelley's, and started farming on the side.

He married Mary K. Hougland Sept. 15, 1957 at Salem Methodist Church in Covington. She was born Apr. 23, 1937 and raised in Fountain County, the daughter of Kenneth A. and Hildreth (Stonecipher) Hougland, who were life residents of Fountain County. She graduated in 1955 from Covington and started working at Donnelley's where she met her husband. In 1961, they moved North of Crawfordsville on 231 to a house they had built.

A delightful blessing came on Sept. 19, 1961 — a daughter, Camilla Lynn. She graduated from North Montgomery in 1979 where she was very active in school activities, including plays, Pom Pom girls, and band. In the summer, she was in 4-H (ten year member). During her Senior year, the Cox family had an exchange student from Lund, Sweden. After graduating, she went to work at Purdue as a Secretary where she met her husband, Dr. David Sawick from New York, who is a graduate of Purdue. They were married Sept. 15, 1984. They have a daughter, Annalisa Marie and live in Wildwood, IL, where they both work at Abbott Company. She is a member of the First Baptist Church.

Dwight and Mary Cox, Camilla, Connie and Carla Cox

In 1962, the Cox family bought 60 acres from Dwight's Uncle, Roy Cook, South of Darlington and later bought 40 more acres across the road. They continue to farm and raise hogs on confinement while still working at Donnelley's.

Daughter, Connie Leona was born 1963 and was also active in school activities, including band, cheerleader, gymnastic and was in 4-H for ten years. She graduated from North Montgomery 1981 and worked part-time while going to beauty school. On Oct. 8, 1983, she married Ken Lee of Mulberry. They live on the Cox home place that was purchased from Dwight's Uncle. They have two daughters, Christina Renee five years old and Kendra Elizabeth 18 months. She is a member of the Congregational Christian Church.

Carla Lea, the third daughter was born Mar. 17, 1965, which was a sad beginning, as Mary K.'s father died when Carla was four days old. The three girls, though, brought much joy to Dwight and Mary. Carla also graduated from North Montgomery to keep up with her sisters. She was a cheerleader for four years and went to summer camp. She also was in gymnastics, and went to the State Finals in 1981. She, too, was a ten-year member of 4-H. In 1985, she graduated from Vincennes University with an Associate Degree in Commercial Art. She is presently employed in the Art Department at R.R. Donnelley's. She is a member of the Congregational Christian Church.

As of now, 1989, the Coxes sold the farm in 1983 and bought six apartments North of Crawfordsville. Dwight will retire from Donnelley's in five years. Both belong to the Congregational Christian Church and enjoy their granddaughters very much. *Submitted by Dwight and Mary Cox*

HOMER AND MARIE (STEVENS) COX

Homer Cox and Marie Stevens were married at Waveland in 1946 by the late Rev. McBrayer. They have resided in the same home for over 42 years.

Homer, son of the late Lauevecia Hutson and Homer Merle Cox, was born at Rockville. He was inducted into the Army in January, 1943 and discharged in March, 1946. He was in 607 Pack Artillery stationed at Ft. Carson, CO and later was transferred to 233 General Hospital serving in Hawaii and South Pacific. He remained active in the reserves after being discharged. For over 40 years he was employed on the highway as a heavy machine operator. On his retirement in 1987 he received a citation from Governor Orr for his public service appreciation. Homer remains active in the Raymond Todd Post 323 American Legion. Homer and Marie are very active with the Friendship Senior Citizen group and have taken care of the nutrition site the past winter.

Homer and Marie (Stevens) Cox

Marie is the daughter of the late Raymond and Doris Swank Stevens of Yountsville. Marion Stevens who lives near Yountsville is her brother. He is a school bus driver for Southmont. Marie attended the old Yountsville grade school for eight years and graduated from Alamo High School in 1942. She worked at Donnelleys and Sommer's Metalcraft in Crawfordsville and at Winklers at Lebanon before she was married. She worked for the Tri-Co Newspaper here in Waveland for several years. She is a news correspondent for the Journal Review.

Tresha Ann Meadows of near Alamo is their daughter. She is married to Darrell Meadows, manager of Brandex Farm, and the mother of two children. Melissa, a graduate of Southmont, is a student at IVY Tech at Lafayette, studying to be a respiratory therapist. She also attended Ball State for two years. Mike is also a graduate of Southmont and is serving on the USS Theodore Roosevelt in the Navy.

Son, Homer Ray Cox is married to the former Terri Bennett and is the father of two daughters. He is also employed for the highway department. Daughter, Christy is a Junior at Southmont and will attend Hoosier Girl State this summer, 1989. Little Carri was born on Sept. 19, 1988. Homer Ray is active in the Waveland Masonic Lodge and Eastern Star.

MARY MEHALA DOZIER COX

James Madison Dozier and his wife Elizabeth Taylor (Harris) came to Indiana in 1917, leaving Knox Co., KY where they were born and where their families had lived for five generations before them.

After their marriage in 1900, they acquired considerable acreage on land which had belonged to Jim Matt's great-great grandfather, built a home and sugar cane mill which was "just across the holler" from his parents. Here they farmed for many years, but being very mountainous, only about 30% of the land was tillable which prompted them to seek more level land where they could utilize all the acreage without the thought of "falling out of the field" while plowing the corn crop.

They settled first in Hendricks County but later moved to Montgomery County where they spent the remainder of their lives. Jim Matt died in 1932 and Elizabeth died in 1955.

Their children were Jos. S. Dozier and James Edgar, sons of a first marriage to Addie Peavler, and Etta Pearl Harris, Elizabeth's daughter by her first marriage to Frank Harris, William Dozier died in infancy, Dora Belle, died age ten, Flora Mae born 1905, Rachel Esta born 1907, Frances Ethel born 1909, Mary Mehala born 1912 and Herschell Charles born 1916.

Mary Mehala Dozier married Lee Cox in 1929 and they had three children: Charles L. born 1930, died 1932, Flora Marlene born 1932 married Jack Moore and had six children, Janice Lee married first Dale Curtis, second Larry Fairfield, no children; Barbara Jean born 1952, married first Glen Conkright, second Mark Addler, no children; Melinda Joy born 1954, married Robert Criblez and has children Robert Aaron and Linda Michelle, lives Illinois; Jackie Lee born 1955, married Julie Criblez and has daughters Amanda Kay and Karen Sue, lives Illinois; Roger David born 1956, unmarried; Mark Kevin born 1959 married first Anne Meyer and had daughter Jessica Ann and married second Wilma ____ and has daughter Tami Marie. Marlene Cox Moore married second Robert Cave, no issue.

Gladyne Sue Cox born 1938 married first Franklin Maxwell, second Henry Thompson and has five children: Carla Kay born 1955, married Terry Watt and has sons Robert Lewis and Joshua Henry; Jimmy Lee born 1958 has daughter Misty, married Cecilia Thompson (no relation) and has daughter Melina, lives Georgia; Dorinda Lynn born 1961, married Richard Wilhite and has children Craig Allen and Tonya Reneé; Charles Wayne born 1965, in Marine Corp stationed in North Carolina, married Kristin Smock and has son Kyle Lee, Diana Reneé born 1966 married William Hampton.

Lee and Mary Cox lived most of their married life in Montgomery County where Lee operated a feed store, a service station and drove a school bus in Waveland. After coming to Crawfordsville he operated a service station and Mary managed a grocery store until their retirement. Lee Cox died in 1983 and Mary Cox lives in Crawfordsville, is a member of St. Bernard's Catholic Church, Dorothy Q Chapter DAR and enjoys tending her flowers and babysitting her great grandchildren. *Submitted by Mary Cox*

ROBERT L. AND SHIRLEY COX

Shirley and Robert L. Cox are lifelong residents of Montgomery County except for four years that they spent in the United States Air Force in Texas, Illinois and Alaska.

Bob was born Mar. 12, 1928 to Leona Long Cox and Jasper E. Cox who were also lifetime residents of this county. Jasper Cox was an electrician at Mid-States and had his own business. They had three children - Jasper Cox, Jr., Robert, and Elizabeth Shoaf.

Shirley was born Feb. 17, 1930 at what was called the Pear Orchard home to Ora Carlile Maudlin (See Carlile history) and Roy H. Maudlin. Roy Maudlin worked at R.R. Donnelley & Sons Co. for many years before moving to Oregon. Roy and Ora had three children - Shirley, Richard, and James.

Shirley and Bob were married at the First Christian Church at Crawfordsville on Easter, Mar. 28, 1948. Both are graduates of Crawfordsville High School. After graduation, Shirley worked at Donnelleys as a secretary and later for the U.S. Air Force. She retired to raise her family.

Robert served an apprenticeship at Donnelleys and made a career in the bindery and personnel departments. In 1951 he was called to duty by Uncle Sam. He spent four years in the Air Force, eight years in the National Guard and was recalled to active duty for one year during the Cuban Missile Crisis.

Robert L. and Shirley Cox

Bob always had an interest in farming and in 1959 decided to sell their home in Crawfordsville and move to a farm adjacent to the Shades State Park. Bob did his own farming for 20 years while working at Donnelleys, but later had a tenant farmer. However, on speculating on what he would do after retirement from Donnelleys he decided to buy equipment and return to farming.

Shirley and Bob had three daughters.

Cheryl Ann Cox (Nov. 20, 1953) married Tom Cox of Wabash, IN on Dec. 24, 1972. Tom is an Assistant Controller at Sommer Metalcraft and has his own computer business. They both work hard with the Montgomery County Youth Soccer Association. They have three children, Dillon Thomas (Sept. 29, 1974), Eric Michael (May 15, 1979), and Sara Alicia (Jan. 3, 1985). They attend the North Montgomery Schools.

Caryl Ann Cox (Feb. 24, 1956) married James Barnes of Rockville (Oct. 27, 1979). They have one son, Jason Johnson (Dec. 20, 1974). Jim is an electrical engineering technician, and Caryl is a Regional Director of Health Facilities for Houston Companies. They reside in New Market.

Patricia Gay Cox (July 5, 1957) married Dan Sweet of Joplin, MO July 7, 1985. She had been employed as an executive secretary for Coast-to-Coast. They now own a Coast-to-Coast store at California, MO. They have two children - Dana LeeAnn (Sept. 27, 1986) and Kevin Daniel (June 28, 1988).

Shirley returned to work in the Recorder's Office at the Montgomery County courthouse in 1984. They are members of the Freedom Baptist Church. Their interests are in their family, traveling, and vacationing in Florida and Oregon where Shirley's brothers now reside.

WILLIAM COX

The Cox Ancestry has been traced to William Cox who came to America in 1610 on the Godspeed. Replicas of the Godspeed, Susan Constant, and Discovery are at Hampton, VA, with the names of all the people who came on them to America. William was born in England in 1598 and died in 1656.

Old William's great, great grandson, also named William, who lived in Randolph Co., NC, objecting to slavery, sent his son Elijah to Indiana to look over the land. Elijah came on horseback to Indiana in 1828 when he was 21 years old. He settled in Union Township near Garfield. He wrote his father of the beauty of Indiana, and of the creek that ran through the land, namely Sugar Creek. In 1830 William moved to Indiana, bringing with him three more children and leaving three married children in

North Carolina. He bought 500 acres of land from a Thomas Brown who had come to Indiana from Ohio.

Ed Cox Farm located 425 E: right side of picture shows original two rooms and two rooms up, built in 1834

Meanwhile, Elijah had married Thomas Brown's daughter Nancy. They built a cabin on the Cox land on the bank of Sugar Creek. The cabin, as yet, had no door, only a heavy blanket hung there. One day Elijah had gone to Lafayette, the nearest store in the area, for supplies. Nancy was alone in the one room cabin when a band of Indians rode in to water their horses. One left his horse, came to the cabin and pulled back the blanket. Nancy related to her grandchildren how very frightened she was. Having no place to hide, she began to offer them food. They took all their potatoes, turnips and corn and then left peacefully.

The children of Elijah and Nancy Brown Cox were: Mary Ann born 1833 married Andrew Mote, Elizabeth born 1835 married Ebenezer McClaskey, Esias born 1837 married Jennie Lee, Gutielma born 1840 married Cyrus Cunningham, Keziah born 1843 married Ben McKee, Miriam born 1846 married Al Booher, and Abijah born 1849 married Kate Mong.

Many descendants of this group are now living in Montgomery County. Capt. Eb McClaskey, Esias Cox, and Al Booher served in the Civil War. This group of men helped operate the underground railroad. Esias Cox would take a negro from the station at Garfield to the next station at Thorntown. Always traveling in a closed carriage at night, he delivered his charge and was back home before daybreak. Esias and Jennie Lee Cox stayed on the Cox farm until they moved to Darlington. Others became merchants and all were instrumental in the establishment of Darlington in 1836.

The family of Esias and Jennie Lee Cox were: Siloam born 1864 married Willard Craig, Arizona born 1866 married Stillwell Imel, George born 1868 died in infancy, Byron born 1870 married Myrtle Binford, Denton born 1873 married Bertha Clark, Royal born 1875 married Georgia Peterson, Pearl born 1877 married first Doc Hiatt, second Oscar Brugh, Madge born 1880 married Walter Burgin.

In this group, and their children, are many school teachers, college professors, bankers and merchants mostly in the Darlington area, and men serving in World Wars I and II.

The William Cox who came to Montgomery County in 1830 brought with him his daughter Eliza. She married an Abel Cox who could not read or write. William was appalled! He disowned Eliza, leaving her only a feather bed, saying "she had made her bed, she could lie in it". William's will was recorded in Montgomery County on Nov. 4, 1954, witnessed by Jacob Pickerell and Micajah Griest. His death occurred Jan. 7, 1855. William would have been surprised to learn that two of his great, great grandsons became perhaps the most famous of the Cox educators, namely Otis and Oakel Hall, twin sons of Amy Ann Cox Hall.

Byron Cox, first son of Esias and Jennie stayed on the Cox farm. He lived in the original house built by Elijah and his father William. That house is still standing, remodeled, and after Byron, his son Graydon lived there, and now it is owned and the farm operated by Graydon's son, Ed Cox and family.

WILLIAM COX

William Cox was born in Randolph Co., NC in 1782. He was a fourth generation Cox in America, having descended from John Cox (b. 1688) who immigrated to Pennsylvania with his brothers, from England, to purchase land in the Colony of Pennsylvania, which had been established by the Quaker, William Penn.

Because of religious difficulties in England, many Quakers followed William Penn to America, and purchased land from him which he had obtained in a grant from Charles II of England in payment of money owed to William Penn by Charles II. Three Cox brothers immigrated to York Co., PA, from England in the very early 1700's. There they were able to bring their families and to practice their Quaker faith.

John Cox and his wife, Mary Garretson, had ten children—all born in Pennsylvania. One of their children was Benjamin Cox (1728-1817) who married Martha Garretson (a niece of Mary (Garretson) Cox) in 1751.

Benjamin and Martha Cox emigrated to North Carolina, and settled in Randolph County in that state, and raised seven children. Their fifth child was Joseph Cox (1759-1828), who married Dinah Rich (b. 1759) in 1781. Joseph and Dinah had nine children, all born in North Carolina—the oldest child was William Cox.

In 1816 Joseph and Dinah Cox emigrated from Randolph Co., NC, to Indiana, and settled, with some of their younger children, in Wayne Co., IN. Joseph Cox died in 1828, in Indiana. Dinah must have preceded him in death, because there is no mention of her in Joseph's will.

William Cox stayed in Randolph Co., NC, where, in 1804 he had married Keziah Rhoads (b. 1780), the daughter of William Rhoads and Anna Moffitt. William and Keziah Cox were the parents of five children (all born in North Carolina). They were: Nancy (1806-1869) married Thomas Moffitt (four children); Elijah (1807-1886) married Nancy Brown (nine children); Abijah (1809-1872) married 1. Edna, (Abijah and Edna had nine children) 2. Phebe Kimler; Rosanna (1815-1886) married Joshua Cox (six children); and Eliza (1821-1898) married Abel M. Cox (two children).

In the early 1830s William Cox and his son, Elijah, rode to Indiana to look for land. It is said that William's cousin, Jeremiah Cox accompanied them. Available land was found in Montgomery Co., IN, and in 1833 William Cox purchased 160 acres in Darlington, Montgomery Co., IN, from Thomas and Mary Brown (the parents of Elijah's wife, Nancy Brown). To this property William brought his entire family, excepting his oldest daughter, Nancy, who stayed in North Carolina with her husband Thomas Moffitt and her children.

A Quaker Meeting had been established in Darlington, and all of the Coxes attended Meeting. William died in 1855, and his wife died soon afterward. They are buried in the Quaker section of Greenlawn Cemetery. There are still many descendants of this couple living in Montgomery County.
Submitted by Jeanne Hall Johnson

ROBERT AND WILLIAM CRAIG

Beginning in 1794 the Craigs of York Co., SC, migrated to Harrison Co., KY. The father, James Craig, had been killed in the Revolutionary War at the Battle of Hanging Rock, SC. His widow, Hannah McCoy Craig and her children: John, Robert, James McCoy, Jane and William settled on Mill Creek and Gray's Run in Kentucky. The fate of the daughter Martha is not known.

On Jan. 1, 1801 Robert Craig married Ann Newell, daughter of Hugh Newell, a horse breeder who had gone to the bluegrass country from Pennsylvania. On Nov. 21, 1805 William Craig married Margaret "Peggy" Givens, daughter of Samuel Givens in Bourbon Co., KY.

John Craig, who with his brother Robert, fought in the Revolutionary War after their father was killed, married Mary _____, James McCoy Craig married Sarah McNutt and Jane Craig married William Gray.

Robert S. Craig Family, L. to R: Mary E. Lame Craig, Myrtle O., Clyde M., and Robert S. Craig ca. 1882

By 1825 Robert, tired of trying to get a clear title to his land in Harrison Co., KY, moved to Franklin Twp., Montgomery Co., IN, with his wife and children: James; Elizabeth (married John Brockman); Hugh Newell (married Lucy Brockman); William; Hannah M. (married Peter Vannice); John Y. (married Elizabeth Peeples); Samuel N. (married Charity Grater); and Robert Campbell (married Mary Elizabeth Downing in Linn Co., IA).

When Robert died the winter of 1838-39 his home farm was NE 1/4 of Sect. 32, T19N, R3W. He divided his library of books between his children as his father had done in his will back in South Carolina.

In 1827 William Craig and his wife and family followed Robert and settled in Union Twp. on 160 acres, T19N, R4W. William died July-August 1828 leaving this very young family; Elizabeth (had died); Jane (married Samuel Scott Lowery in Kentucky); Samuel Givens (married Catharine McCree and Rebecca Gilbert); James (married Elizabeth Green and Ann Watson); Martha Hannah (married John Barlow and John Widner); Isabella; Margaret A. (married Pleasant Butler); Mary Esther (married Joseph W. Wilson); Elvira (married Joseph F. Butler); and William Decatur (married Clara Reeves).

The youngest child of Robert Craig, Robert Campbell Craig, married his bride in Iowa, but returned to Franklin Twp. where they raised a family. They had nine children, but only four lived to adulthood: Robert S.; Armenia (married William Hutchings); Franklin Pierce (married Annie Coombs); and Henry A. (married Abby Kendall).

Robert S. Craig, "Campbell" Craig's oldest child, married Mary Elizabeth Lame, daughter of Abel and Frances B. Cox Lame in Boone Co., IN, Aug. 23, 1868. They had two daughters, Clyde Minnie who married Jess McCain and lived in Carroll Co., IN, and Myrtle O. who married Homer "Dot" Larsh and lived in Lebanon and Indianapolis, IN. Clyde had three McCain children: Margaret, Mary and John, all living. Myrtle had two Larsh children, Homer and Leah, both deceased. The Robert S. Craig family is pictured.

Many Craigs throughout the United States can trace their roots to these Craigs of Montgomery Co., IN.

NORMAN LEWIS AND MARY FRANCES CRAMER

Norman was born June 2, 1942 to Herman Ray and Mary Catherine Bilsland Cramer at Culver Union Hospital in Crawfordsville. Herman Ray was born June 26, 1914 to Harry Albert and Della Frances Martin Cramer in Montgomery County. Herman graduated from Waynetown High School and went to work after school at the Waynetown Tile Company for a few years and then went to work at R.R. Donnelley and Sons where he retired after 32 years. His main hobby was his love of Citizen Band Radios and was known to many as "Early Bird". He was a member of the Free Masons Waynetown Lodge. Herman's father, Harry was a house painter in the Waynetown and Crawfordsville area. He was a teller of tall tales and hung around the blacksmith shop playing euchre. Harry was born Sept. 14, 1873 to Henry Thornton and Mary Katherine Pennington Cramer in Boone Co., IN.

Norman Lewis and Mary Frances Cramer

Norman's mother, Mary Catherine was born Nov. 24, 1918 to James Newton and Amanda Luella Moore Bilsland in Cain Township, Fountain Co., IN. James was born Mar. 22, 1866 to James and Eliza Catherine Bastion Bilsland in Troy Township, Fountain County. He was a feed grinder by trade and traveled from farm to farm working for the farmers. In later years he worked for the State Highway and helped construct the first cement highways. A few years before retirement he worked at R.R. Donnelley and Sons as a painter. Amanda Luella was born Oct. 12, 1880 to James Madison and Mary Etta Myer Moore in Cain Township, Fountain Co., IN. James was a farmer in the Yountsville area for many years and then moved to Cain Township, Fountain Co., IN. Mary Catherine worked in the drugstore at Waynetown for several years and then started her own ceramic business. She is a member of the Rebeka Lodge and the Eastern Star.

Mary Catherine and Herman Ray were married Feb. 23, 1935 in Lebanon, Boone Co., IN. Their family includes Marilyn Joan born July 10, 1935, married Walter Eugene Sheets and now lives in Tucson, AZ. They are the parents of four children, Dwayne Lee, Lewis Ray, Ronald and Catherine Sue. Carolyn Sue born Oct. 6, 1937, married Robert Clyde Byers and they are the parents of three children, Carla Jean, Connie Sue and Christopher Jay.

Norman graduated from Waynetown High School and after school went to work at R.R. Donnelley for a few years. After Donnelleys he worked at Montgomery Wards and then to Thomas Funeral Home in Waynetown. In the fall of 1975 he enrolled in Vincennes University for Funeral Service and graduated in 1977 and worked as an intern in Bedford, IN and in 1979 came to Hunt and Sons Funeral Home as director-embalmer. He is a member of the Waynetown Masonic Lodge #302, Eastern Star, Scottish Rite, Valley of Indianapolis and Byron Cox Post #72 American Legion. His hobbies are fishing, sports and woodworking.

On Mar. 30, 1963 Norman married Mary Frances Cress at Waynetown Christian Church. Mary is a member of the Waynetown Order of the Eastern Star No. 435. She served as Worthy Matron in 1974, 1985, 1986, 1987 and 1989. She currently works at Stecks Weathervane. They are the parents of two daughters, Kimberly Ann and Debra Sue.

On June 1, 1989 Norman will be associated with Thomas Funeral Home once again. Norman and Mary will be living in the funeral home, as well as working there!

WALTER AND PEARL MARIE CRESS

Walter Cress was born July 25, 1903 at Indianapolis, IN to Lucien Ernest and Ella Phillips Cress. Lucien, the son of John B. and Mary A. Huker Cress, was born in Indianapolis on Sept. 10, 1868. He had seven sisters and brothers; Millard F., Henry C., Ora B., Willie R., Lulie A., Emma D. and Jennie. Ella was born in 1872 in Greensburg, IN to Jesse and Anna Evens Phillips. Lucien and Ella were married May 19, 1897 in Indianapolis. Their family also included John, Mary and Raymond who died in infancy. Ella died shortly after the birth of Walter (Walt).

When Walt was 12 years of age he left the home of his father and went out on his own. He lived with cousins and spent the years of the depression working at the County Market in Indianapolis and Wassons Department Store. For 39 years he worked for the New York Central Railroad which eventually became the Penn Central. He worked out of Champaign, IL and then in 1948 moved to Crawfordsville. He was a car inspector on the Covington to Indianapolis route. During the reorganization of the railroad in the late 50's he was forced to take early retirement because the railroad abolished the job of car inspector. He worked for short periods at Mid-States Steel and Wire and C'Ville Lanes Bowling Alley. He then became the night inn-keeper and auditor at the Holiday Inn where he worked for 12 years. He also prepared tax returns for many of his friends and associates for many years. Walt was an avid bowler and billiard player. He was inducted into the Champaign County Bowling Hall of Fame in 1965 and traveled to many cities during his lifetime to participate in bowling tournaments. He is remembered by many local citizens for his morning "job" of shooting billiards at the Bank Cigar Store. He collected coins during most of his life and was often read in the editorials in the local newspapers mostly on the merits of women drivers. On Jan. 24, 1943 he married Pearl Marie Stephens Neideffer.

Pearl was born Aug. 30, 1906 at Newman, IL to Cincinatus and Elnora Chapin Stephens. Cincinatus "Natt" was the seventh child of J.B. and Ellen Henry Stephens. His siblings included Mary E., Sarah E., Joseph, John W., Virginia G., Ella, Eliza D., Fanny H. and Arabella R. Elnora Chapin was one of twins born to David O. and Eliza Jane Hopper Chapin at Newport, IL. Her family included her twin, Lenora, Ida Amanda, Charles, Carrie Alice, Jasper, Austin, MayBelle, and Estella C. Natt married Elnora on Nov. 29, 1888 and besides Pearl their family included David Marion, LeRoy, Edith Faye, Lou Estell, Alice Mae, Olive Virgil and Charles Montell. Pearl first married Arthur Earl Neideffer and they had one son, Warren Gary.

Walt and Pearl are the parents of Mary Frances born July 14, 1943 at Champaign, IL. Mary graduated from Crawfordsville High School. She married Norman Cramer Mar. 30, 1963 at Waynetown Christian Church. They are the parents of two daughters, Kimberly Ann born May 1, 1964 and Debra Sue born May 26, 1968 both born at Culver Union Hospital in Crawfordsville. Both daughters graduated from Crawfordsville High School. Kim graduated from Vincennes University and now works in Indianapolis with the mentally and physically handicapped. Debbie is a Junior at Indiana State University at Terre Haute and is majoring in Sociology.

IRVIN J. CROSS

Andrew Bruce Cross came from Pennsylvania and settled in Ladoga. He married Nancy Zimmerman, daughter of Jacob and Adeline Ashwell Zimmerman. Their children were Ethel, Hazel, Irvin, Juanita, and Russell. Ethel never married. Hazel married John Bair, had one son, William. Juanita married John McNulty, had Kenneth, John, Mary, Ethel, James, Martha, and William. Russell married Alta Smith, had James and Nancy. Irvin married Carolyn Peffley, daughter of Chester and Beulah Overman Peffley. The Overman's had a department store in Ladoga in 1917-1919. Irvin and Carolyn's children are Judith, Russell, and Donald. Irvin and Carolyn met while working for John Stanley Telephone Company. They also worked for Detchon Telephone Company, and later Irvin worked for Bell Telephone Co. He then worked for the town of Ladoga and later was town marshall. Carolyn is the librarian at the Ladoga-Clark Township Public Library. *Submitted by Carolyn Cross*

CROW

"What we have heard and know, what our fathers have told us, we will not hide them from their **children: We will tell the next generation...** Psalm 78 vs. 3 & 4

To the descendants of John P. Crow and Amanda Lee Boler this ancestral lineage is written and dedicated.

David, and Honor Dooley Crow were from Illinois, and later moved to the Ladoga-New Market area. They were the parents of: John P. Crow married Amanda Lee Boler. They had six children: Delia Crow married Matt Jones. They had one son, Albert Willie Crow - was never married. John and

Amanda were the parents of the following: **Minnie Mae Crow** - died in infancy.

Charles Patterson Crow married Bessie Lenora Delaney. They had one daughter, May Lucille Crow who married William Redden. They were the parents of Maxine who married Wayne Carmichael; Donald Eugene Redden who married Shirley Elmore; William Redden who married Georgia Switzer; Joyce Redden who married Harland Flint and Fern Marie Redden.

Frank Crow married Julia Mangus. They were the parents of: Ernest Crow who married Mary Zachary. They are the parents of: Sandra Crow who married Ralph Stenson and Rose Marie Crow who married Larry Snodgrass.

Crow Reunion 1988

Mildred Crow married Henry Hester then William Price. Their children are: Virginia Hester, Judith Hester, James Hester, Thomas Hester, William Price, and Eva Janette Price.

Irene Hester married Albert Hester, parents of Albert Dale Hester who married Nelda Bentley; and Russell Hester who married Sally Simpson.

Frank Crow married Mary Ellen Jones parents of: Frank Alan Crow who married Becky Roe and Beverly Crow who married John Erenberger. One child, Robin Crow died in infancy.

Julia Crow later married William Hart. They had one son, Hugh LaVern Hart who married Wilma Jean Rice. They have one daughter, Judith Hart married William Byers.

Floy Crow married Clarence Smith and had one son, Kenneth Lee Smith who married Irene Carroll. They had six children: Billy Smith who married Jo Anne Taylor parents of Linda Smith who married Gerry Garver, Sam Smith who married Sheila Crawley and Sandy Smith who married Dennis Jones; Lorraine Smith who married Clyde Brady, Jr. parents of Rebecca Brady who married Robert Shelton, Cathy Brady who married Dean Lewis then Ray DeGuard, Clyde Brady who married Janice Mann; Dennis Brady, and Dawn Brady who married Steve Wimmer; Harold David Smith who married Joy Stephens, parents of David Smith who married Lisa Craig and Robin Smith; Gerald Smith married Patricia Hybarger, parents of Jannette Smithm who married Ricardo Castro, Gerald Eugene Smith married Rhonda Bush and Geoffry Smith, Larry Wayne Smith married Karol Meese and Karen Lou Smith.

Nellie Crow married William Jones. They had no children.

Fred Crow married Orpha Stewart. Their three daughters are: Lillian Gail Crow married Olin Swinney; parents of David Swinney married Delores Ruschenberg. They have one daughter, Eva Marie. Phyllis Joan Swinney married Carl Cook; parents of Carla Jo Cook married Hans VanEyk, Curtis Cook and Cheri Cook, and Christa Cook. Themla Aileen Crow married Henry Karg parents of Susan Marie Karg and Karen Ann Karg. Norma Jean Crow married Donald Jean Linn; parents of Diana Linn married Ron Mitchum; Judith Ann Linn married Larry Gayloer and Debra Jo Linn married Steven Sladek.

Most are continuing to live in Montgomery County, but a few have moved to other cities and states. *Submitted by Aileen Crow Karg*

THELMA AILEEN CROW

A Teacher, Poet and Writer, who used the pen name of Tackarg. Thelma Aileen Crow, was born in Montgomery Co., IN on June 30, 1918 to Fred and Orpha Fern Crow. She received her early education in the Crawfordsville Schools; received her BS at Taylor University; and MS from Indiana State University. She also attended Miami University in Oxford, OH and Oregon State.

She taught school in Portland, OR, Crawfordsville, IN, Harrison, OH; Perrysville, and Shelbyville, IN.

On Aug. 18, 1944 Thelma married Henry Herbert Karg born Jan. 28, 1920 Westerville, OH, the son of Rollin Orestes and Margaret Dot Warner Karg. He attended Westerville, OH high school, Ohio State; AB at Taylor University, and received BD from Western Evangelical Seminary in Portland, OR. He was a cook during the Battle of the Bulge in World War II. He was Minister-first charge Mt. Zion E.U.B. church 1955-62. The conference sent him to Terre Haute, Rockdale, Perrysville, and Shelby County. He passed away June 3, 1982 exactly 30 years after his graduation from Taylor University in 1952.

Henry and Aileen Karg

To this union was born two daughters: Susan Marie who has her own Karg Marketing advertising business in Indianapolis; and Karen who works at the Indianapolis Childrens' Museum.

Our subject received a school ring in Jr. High for an essay on Washington awarded by the DAR the year the cornerstone was laid for the then new city building in Crawfordsville. Received the National Library of Poetry pin, Golden Poet Awards at Reno and Las Vegas. She was one of many employees of Allison General Motors who received a flag from them during WWII.

Her hobbies are Violin (played in the old Wabash Community Orchestra five years which dissolved when our director, Walter Fertig, left to enter service during WWII) and other orchestras. Writing and attending writers' conferences. Published in books and magazines. Served several hours as a nurses aid at our local hospital during WWII.

Thelma has two sisters, Mrs. Gail Swinney whose husband was an educator and Mrs. Jean Linn whose husband is retired from our local R.R. Donnelley and Sons Company as a pressman. During WWII while at Fort Harrison the two men were stationed together, Donald Linn introduced his sister-in-law and her husband, "The Reverend and Mrs. Karg."

Rev. Karg was an avid stamp collector and had articles published on stamp collecting.

Mrs. Karg is a member of the Christ United Methodist Church, Christian Writers' Group and AAUW Writers, Retired Teachers' Association of Montgomery County.

DAVID MILTON CROWDER

David Milton Crowder, respected citizen and Civil war veteran, was born in Botetourt Co., Fincastle, VA, on Apr. 15, 1846. His parents were James Madison and Jane Crush Crowder.

He was called to serve in the Civil war at the age of 17. He served in the cavalry division, under General Fitzen Lee. His stories and anecdotes, the hunger and fear, and how they determined which soldier would be chosen to go to the nearest chicken roost to steal the old fat rooster. These are stories he told and which are remembered by his many grandchildren.

At the close of the war he came to Indiana, riding a horse all the way, staying four years. He then returned to Virginia and entered the milling business.

Annie Jane Carper, born Mar. 24, 1855 and David Crowder were married May 1, 1872. She was the daughter of William and Jane Carper. Annie was a hard working, God fearing, and Bible reading Methodist. She started reading her Bible at the beginning of each year, and at the year she had completed it. In later years, when her eyesight failed, she had read the Bible from cover to cover 55 years or 55 times.

David and Annie were the parents of six children, all born in Botetourt Co., VA. In the spring of 1887, all the family came west to settle in Franklin township, in Indiana. Later, he purchased a farm in the southeast corner of Madison Township, where he engaged in farming.

Their children were:

Lydia May, born May 4, 1873. Died July 22, 1900.

Carper Godwin, born Feb. 12, 1875.

Seth Wilmer, born Jan. 12, 1877.

Emmett David, born July 6, 1879.

Melvin Benjamin, born Sept. 30, 1881.

Minnie, born 1884, died 1884.

Carper G. Crowder came to Indiana at the age of 12. In 1896 he married Louisa Elmore, who died in 1913. He then married Jessie Pearl Peterson in 1921. Two daughters from these marriages are living today. They are Mrs. Joe (Louise) Booher and Mrs. Andy (Evelyn) Edwards. Carper operated a grocery store, hardware store, and filling station. He died Jan. 30, 1939.

Seth Wilmer, the second son, had a partnership in a grocery store with brother Carper, and owned Riverside Park, west of Darlington. He was a farmer at the time of his death in 1953. He married Mabel Lillian Brown in 1909. Their children are Norman Carper, Arthur Brown, and Lois Maxine.

Emmett David was eight years old when he came to Indiana. He made his living farming and driving school buses. Emmett drove a horse-drawn school hack to Kirkpatrick school four years. He was married twice, first to Harriet Maguire, and to Mabel Hopkins. He leaves three daughters, Jeanette Coltrain, Hilma Mahoy, and Celia Welshimer. He died in 1929.

Melvin Benjamin, the fourth son, was a grocery store operator, filling station operator, and insurance salesman. On June 24, 1902, he married Rose Eskew. They had two children, Zillah Beatrice, born 1904, and Creighton, born 1908. Melvin died in 1948, and is buried in the Shannondale Cemetery.

Lydia was never married. She died July 22, 1900 near Darlington.

David and Annie retired to Darlington in their later years. He suffered a stroke and died on Feb. 9, 1930. She lived on until July 5, 1937. They are both buried in the cemetery in Mace, IN. *By Hilma Mahoy*

MR. AND MRS. WILEY C. CROWDER

Wiley Charles and Lillie Florence Crowder moved from Fountain Co., IN to a 200-acre farm, located north of Yountsville, in 1928. They later purchased the farm in 1934.

W.C. was the second son of John Samuel and Emma Rebecca Crowder Crowder. He was born Mar. 24, 1886 and died May 24, 1968. His brothers were Elijah and Grover.

Lillie was the seventh child of James and Caroline Grimes Keeling. She was born Sept. 25, 1880 and died Oct. 18, 1973. Her brothers included Alfred, Austin and Charles Keeling and her sisters were Viola and Bertha Wildman, Molly Davidson and Flora Quick.

W.C. and Lillie Crowder

W.C. was a farmer and after retirement worked in circulation sales for the *Journal Review*. Lillie was a homemaker and shared her musical talents in the Yountsville Methodist Church where the couple held membership.

They reared four children - Gordon Douglas, Paul Jay, Margaret Rebecca and Mary Kathryn, who were all graduates of Waynetown High School.

The eldest, Gordon (Mar. 18, 1912) married Mary Miller of Hillsboro. They lived on the family farm after his parents' retirement in 1943. They reared five children - Mrs. David (Alberta Jo) White, Mrs. J. Russell (Marilyn Lou) Harris, Mrs. Lawrence (Margaret Sue) Harvey, Mrs. Jerry (Norma Jean) Addler and Robert Wiley. Gordon also boasts 11 grandchildren and one great-granddaughter.

Paul (May 6, 1913) married Emma Gohman of the Barcus Orchard neighborhood. His family has resided at Los Angeles, CA for 45 years. His children are Ronald Paul, Nancy Florence, Michael Keith and Mrs. Roy (Janet Sue) Lant. Paul retired as a bakery supervisor. He has eight grandchildren.

Margaret (Apr. 27, 1915) married William Groves of rural Crawfordsville. They had three children - Billy Joe, Donald Lee (deceased) and Mrs. Fred (Carol Ann) Edwards. They were farmers in the Smartsburg community and Margaret retired as manager of Rapps Clothing Store at Crawfordsville. After her husband's death, she moved to Washington Manor Apartments. She has three grandchildren and one great-granddaughter.

Kathryn (Nov. 21, 1922) married Lawrence Kelsey of New Ross. He is a World War II Army veteran. They reside in the Pleasant Hill neighborhood. He retired as an electrician from Mid-States. They have four sons - Larry Elvin, Damon Edward, Charles Wayne and Rex Eugene and ten grandchildren.

Grandsons, Robert Crowder, Don Groves and Larry and Damon Kelsey were Army veterans, while Ronald Crowder served with the U.S. Marines.

W.C. and Lillie are remembered as honest, hardworking, fun-loving Christian people. They instilled these qualities in their own family along with a sense of pride in their heritage.

They lived in Yountsville and Waynetown after retirement. They were laid to rest in the Waynetown Masonic Cemetery.

A majority of their descendants still reside locally; however, only two carry on the Crowder name in Montgomery County - Gordon and Robert. Robert also purchased and farms 80-acres of the family farm. *Submitted by Alberta White*

FLORENCE AMERICA KEENEY CUNNINGHAM

Florence America Keeney Cunningham was born Oct. 4, 1857. Her parents were William and Lettishia Coolman Keeney. She had a half sister, Mrs. William Layson and a half brother, Walter Coolman. She married James Madison Cunningham, who died in 1917.

He was a blacksmith. It's been said that he made a set of horseshoes that won first prize in 1876 Worlds Fair. Bob Jolley, a grandson, has the horseshoes. They had five children, Dr. B.L. Cunningham, Lettisia, Burford, he was a twin she died at infancy, and Helen. They lived in the house I do now. I remember staying all night at Great Grandmother's many times. She smoked a corn cob pipe. They moved her to Vancleave's nursing home in the early 1940's. She died there in January 1950.

Florence America Keeney Cunningham

Burford, 1887-1954, my grandfather, married Hazel Vae Songer, 1888-1964, from Veedersburg. They had nine children: James Madison, Nema, Mary, Violet, Helen, Burford Jr., Bertha, Lettisia and Rosa Vae. He was a blacksmith too. The blacksmith shop still stands on the property next to mine.

Nema, 1910-1951, my mother, married Allen Butler Myers Mar. 7, 1931. He was born in Winchester, KY Feb. 9, 1908 to Henry Breckenridge Myers, 1882-1936, and Julia Anna Noland, 1881-1950. Both of them were born in Mt. Sterling, KY. (It's recorded Julia's family came to America from Ireland, landed at Annapolis Harbor 1677.) They moved to Roachdale, IN, then to Crawfordsville. Henry was a painter by profession. He helped paint the Crawfordsville courthouse.

Allen "Bud", my father, and my mother lived in the house I do now. They had three children. Lettisia Ann, Rita Jane and Allen "Buddy" Jr. He was a baker. He worked all the bakeries in town, mainly the A-loaf which adjoins our property. He was in World War II. After the bakeries closed he went to work and retired from Midstates. He married Velma Myers in 1958. She had two sons, Bill and Ron Cummings. Dad died June 19, 1981.

I was born Lettisia Ann Myers Dec. 23, 1931. I graduated from Crawfordsville High School in 1949. I married Howard Lee Thompson Nov. 10, 1951. He was born Oct. 3, 1930 to John James and Thelma Marie Courtney Thompson.

We had four girls: Ginger Marie, Larita Ann, Betty Ruth and Violet Louise. Violet died Dec. 25, 1966 when she was six.

Howard was a brick mason. Everybody knew him better as "Bones". Somehow that name got pinned on him as a kid. It went to his grave with him. Howard L. "Bones" Thompson died June 6, 1987.

All our children were born at the Montgomery County Hospital. They live in Crawfordsville with their families. All went to Crawfordsville High School, grandchildren will too. Kimberlee Ruthann Hughes, Howard Allen Hughes, Christina Lynn Long, Terrence Lee Long (stillborn) and Angela Marie Rutledge.

I work at Raybestos and have been there for 22 years. I still live in the house where my Great Grandmother raised most of her family; my mother, all of hers and me, mine.

Lots of changes have been made over the years. With lots of hardships and lots of love, we have been content here and never wanted to move. In fact, if someone would ask Bones where he lived, he would say jokingly, 810 South Heaven.

MARY FRANCES MENEFEE CUNNINGHAM

The subject of this sketch is Mary Frances Menefee Cunningham.

Her maternal grandparents were Nelson and Mary Angles Hartsock! Both from Kentucky. Nelson had a brother Daniel who built The American House on lot No. 2 in 1839 in Waynetown, this house was considered the finest hotel in this part of Indiana. Daniel and his wife Elizabeth ran this hotel until 1851.

E.R. Menefee, Mary Frances Menefee with son Guy Cunningham and Mabel C. Patton

Her mother Mary Hartsock Menefee was married to Edward Rennels Menefee on Aug. 26, 1865. Edward and Mary had lived in Walnut Twp. Section 33 Montgomery County. Her father Edward was the son of Dr. William Menefee of Kentucky. Edward also had a son Dr. William N. Menefee who practiced ENT medicine in New Ross and Crawfordsville. Our subject Mary Frances Menefee Cunningham married Oscar Cunningham on Nov. 10, 1885 in Warren Co., IN. Oscar was the son of Ambrose Franklin Cunningham and Mary A. (Polly) Lockhart. They (Oscar and Mary) had children Lawrence, Art, Mable C., Guy, Helen, Lucille, Walter, and Ruth. Only two children survive today, Mable and Walter. Mable is the oldest born Nov. 19, 1891. Her family was husband Cecil Hugh Patton of Warren County. She has great great grandchildren. Walter Dean born June 18, 1903 lives in Danville, IL. He and his wife Madeline also have great grandchildren.

Nelson Hartsock was a farmer by occupation, he owned land in Monroe, Hendricks and Montgomery County. He died in California in September 1850. His wife Mary Jane Angles lived in Waynetown and died there. She was buried in "Pioneers Cemetery" in Waynetown, Montgomery County. Edward R. Menefee and his wife Mary Hartsock are buried at the Masonic Cemetery State Line, Warren County.

Mary Frances Menefee Cunningham and her husband Oscar are buried at Walnut Corners Cemetery, Vermillion Co., IL. *Submitted by Donald L. Patton*

LEO WAYNE JR. AND LINDA CURRENT

Leo and Linda came to Indiana in September 1966. They have resided in Waynetown since that time. Leo works for Alcoa in Lafayette, Linda works for Hook's Drugs in Crawfordsville.

Leo was born in Maquoketa, IA on May 11, 1939 to Leo Wayne Current Sr. and Elizabeth Bronson Current. Leo Sr. was born on Mar. 19, 1919 in Clinton Co., IA to Orpheus and Zana Poole Current. On Sept. 23, 1938 he married Elizabeth Bronson in Dubuque, IA. Elizabeth was born on July 6, 1921 to William and Anna Montford Bronson. Leo Jr. attended schools in Jackson Co., IA and graduated from Monmouth High School in Monmouth, IA on May 23, 1957. After graduating from high school, Leo worked at Clinton Engines in Maquoketa until 1963 at which time he enlisted in the U.S. Army at Ft. Ord, CA. After basic training he went to paratrooper school at Ft. Benning, GA and then was stationed with the 101st Air Borne Division at Ft. Campbell, KY. Leo served in Vietnam in 1965 and was discharged on Jan. 7, 1966.

Leo Wayne Jr. and Linda Current

Linda was born in Jackson Co., IA on Sept. 18, 1940 to Carl D. Pence and Ernestine Hamilton Pence. Carl was born Aug. 28, 1905 in Appanoose Co., IA to John Delphos Pence and Mabel Gertrude Caster. On July 6, 1938 he married Ernestine Hamilton in Sidney, NE. Ernestine was born in Jackson Co., IA on May 6, 1915 to Ernest Ross Hamilton and Millie Rebecca Brady. Shortly after Linda's birth her parents moved to Cheyenne, WY where they lived until 1956. In November 1956 her family moved back to Iowa where she graduated from Monmouth High School May 16, 1958.

Leo and Linda were married Feb. 7, 1959 in the Little Brown Church in the Vale at Nashua, IA. They are the parents of three children, Tammy, Tim and Lisa.

Tammy is married to Perry Clyde Trinkle, son of Clyde Trinkle and Ida Louise Frost Trinkle. They have one son, Jeremiah James Trinkle (born Nov. 22, 1977). Tammy graduated from North Montgomery High School May 1977 and P.C.I. in Indianapolis on Mar. 29, 1985. She is a Medical Assistant for Dr. Lawrence Reitz in Indianapolis. Perry graduated from North Montgomery High School in 1976 and is employed at R.R. Donnelley & Sons. Perry and Tammy reside in Ladoga where Jeremiah is a fifth grader.

Tim graduated from North Montgomery High School on May 23, 1982. After graduation Tim served five years in the U.S. Navy as a Cryptologic Technician. He was stationed aboard the USS Milwaukee and the USS Spruance. During his last year of service he also attended the University of Mississippi. He was discharged May 22, 1987. Tim is now attending Purdue University where he is a sophomore.

Lisa attends school at North Montgomery High School where she is a sophomore.

CUSTER-AMES

Robert (Custard) Custer was born Cynthiana, Harrison Co., KY, Mar. 18, 1814, left fatherless lived with an Uncle until he came to Indiana at the age of 14 with his mother.

He later settled in Walnut Township, Montgomery County and then married Jane Watkins in 1837, she being the daughter of George and Rebecca Kelly Watkins of Scott Township. They farmed and their home was always open to pioneer preachers and they were members of the Methodist Church. Here they had eight children: George N. born 1839 and died 1856; William Harve born 1841; Aaron R. born 1843; Montgomery Terry born 1846; Sarah born 1852; James C. born 1853; Franklin born 1856 and Eliza Ida born 1859 and died 1862.

Robert and Jane moved to Thorntown about 1871, where Jane died Apr. 2, 1895. Robert then came to live with his son William Harve, in Sugar Creek Township. Robert died there in 1896 and was buried beside Jane in I.O.O.F. cemetery, Darlington, IN.

William Harve 1841-1916 married Rachel Cox 1844-1901; they were farmers. He enlisted in 1861 in the 10th Indiana Volunteer Infantry, where he saw much hard and trying service for three years. They raised three children: Charles B. born Apr. 3, 1869; Laura born Oct. 12, 1871 and died May 3, 1924; and Franklin A. born July 3, 1876. William Harve retired and spent sometime engaged in Grocery and Hardware while living in Darlington.

Charles B. married Isabel Maguire born 1870 and died 1925, daughter of a neighbor, Charles and Harriett Maguire in Sugar Creek Township and lived on a farm adjacent to his Father's farm. Here he farmed until his death on Feb. 2, 1941. He and Isabel are buried in Greenlawn cemetery, Darlington. They had two daughters: Irene Beatrice born July 26, 1895 and Helen Maguire born May 4, 1900 and died Nov. 17, 1896 in San Diego, CA.

Franklin A. married Elinore Turnipseed and lived on his father's farm, where they had one daughter, Truth. Elinore died January 1918 and Franklin then married Iva Hiatt who died 1961, of Darlington.

Irene Beatrice married Floyd Emerson Ames, both graduates of Crawfordsville in 1915. Floyd born Feb. 1, 1895 and died Mar. 1, 1955 was the son of John and Ida Mae McClamrock Ames of North Union Township. They lived and farmed most of their lives on a Custer Farm in Sugar Creek Township and raised two children: Celista Belle born June 20, 1918 and John Custer born Jan. 28, 1922. They built a home in Darlington and left the farm in July 1954 at which time their son John continued with the farm. John married Barbara Thompson born May 19, 1923, died Feb. 12, 1983 she the daughter of Norman and Marie Peterson Thompson. They had four children: John Jeffrey born December 1946, single and lives in Bloomington, IN.

Sallie Ann born June 1948 married Edward Pierce and they have Stacey Ann, Stephanie Jo and Ryan Edward and live at Prairieton, IN.

Steven Bruce born November 1950 married Penny Brown and lives in Crawfordsville, being a factory worker. They have Bridgitte Renee and Steven Tyler.

Curtis Thompson born September 1953 and married Caren Morris and had two sons, Jonathon Dean and Benjamin Andrew. Curtis Thompson Ames' second marriage was to Patti J. Stadler of Ladoga. He is a carpenter and they live in Ladoga.

Later in life John Custer Ames sold insurance and drove a school bus for 16 years. He still owns and lives on a part of his Grandfather's farm and Celista Belle owns a part of it, however, she lives in Crawfordsville, IN.

MAYNARD CARVER DARNALL

Maynard Carver Darnall came to Crawfordsville, IN in 1928 as Principal of Crawfordsville High School. His wife was Edna Hunt Darnall, and his children were Maynard C. Darnall Jr., Marietta Darnall, Martha Darnall, Dorothy Darnall, and Edward C. Darnall.

Maynard Darnall was a descendent of Edward Darnall who came to Maryland in 1714 from Durham, England. Maynard Darnall was born Dec. 31, 1887 in Danville, IN, the son of Milton Thornton and Marietta Carver Darnall. He married Edna Hunt on June 10, 1914, at Dana, IN. He was a graduate of Greencastle High School, and received his Bachelor and Master's degrees from Indiana University.

Maynard Darnall became Superintendent of the Crawfordsville school system in 1931, a position he held until he resigned in 1945. During his tenure Tuttle elementary school was remodeled, and eight classrooms and a gymnasium were built as an addition to Crawfordsville High School in 1938. Crawfordsville had the first public school kindergartens in the state of Indiana because of Maynard Darnall's interest in this area. His educational philosophy was family oriented—he strongly believed school activities should be held on weekends only so that families could maintain a close relationship.

Maynard Darnall was a member of the First Methodist Church, where he served on the Board of Trustees and taught church school. He also served on the library board in Crawfordsville.

Maynard Darnall's legacy to his children was

their education, an intangible with which they could do whatever they liked. Maynard Jr. married Maida Belle Child and lived in Oakland, CA. Marietta married E. William Schilling and lived in Lafayette, IN. Martha married Ralph R. Bozell, Jr. and lived in Bloomfield Hills, MI. Dorothy married Marsh H. Jones, Jr. and lives in Crawfordsville. Edward married Christina Trevino and lives in Edinburg, TX.

Maynard Darnall died Feb. 18, 1949. His many contributions to the youth of this community included a strong music program (band and orchestra) introduction of a mobile dental clinic, from the I.U. Dental School, and introduction of wrestling at the high school.

FRED NEWTON DAUGHERTY, PHYSICIAN

Fred Newton Daugherty, born in Princeton, Gibson Co., IN, Nov. 22, 1896; son of William Edward and Minnie Viola (Selby) Daugherty.

William Edward Daugherty, born in Princeton, IN; son of Hugh and Mary Jane (Waddell) Daugherty. Hugh Daugherty was born in Belfast, Ireland, and later emigrated to America. He was a cabinet-maker by trade. He died in 1877. His wife, Mary Jane (Waddell) Daugherty, was born at New Harmony, Posey Co., IN. William Edward Daugherty, who is a retired contractor, resides in Princeton, IN. His wife, Minnie Viola (Selby) Daugherty, was born at Petersburg, Pike Co., IN. She died in 1939. Her parents, Abner and _____ (Stucky) Selby, were born at Petersburg. Four children were born to William Edward and Minnie Viola (Selby) Daugherty, Fred Newton being the second in order of birth.

Fred Newton Daugherty, the subject of this sketch, graduated from Wabash College, A.B., in 1920, and from Indiana University School of Medicine, M.D., in 1926. He served an internship at St. Elizabeth Hospital, of Lafayette, IN, and since 1927, has conducted a medical practice in Crawfordsville, IN. Dr. Daugherty serves as county physician, and as city health officer. In April 1918, he enlisted as a private, for service in the World War, and was stationed at Camp Zachary Taylor, at Louisville, KY. He was honorably discharged in January 1919. Dr. Daugherty, who is a Republican, is a member of the following: Masonic Lodge (Commandery, K.T.); American Medical Assn.; Indiana State Medical Assn.; Montgomery County Medical Society; Elks lodge; Phi Delta Theta, and Phi Rho Sigma; American Legion; Country Club; Montgomery County Chapter, Citizens Historical Assn.; and Presbyterian Church. His favorite recreation is golf.

In 1926, Fred Newton Daugherty married Elizabeth Clark, who was born in Crawfordsville, IN. Her parents, John B. and Mary (Murphy) Clark, also were born in Crawfordsville. Their parents came to America from Ireland. Dr. and Mrs. Daugherty have no children. *Written in 1940 by the Citizens Historical Association*

LETITIA JANE DAVIDSON

Letitia Jane Davidson was born Oct. 9, 1883 near Wareham, Ospry Township, Ontario, Canada to Robert and Martha Mills Davidson. She was their second daughter. Her siblings being: William Thomas, Robert James, Martha Victoria, Christina Carolyn, Elizabeth and Richard Newton.

Letitia Jane (known as Jenny) came to Indiana in 1892 with her parents. She attended school in New Richmond. On Oct. 28, 1906 she married Grover Williams, a farm hand. This was a brief marriage. Later she went to live with her brother, Robert James Davidson.

Letitia Jane Davidson

Jenny attended the Christian Church in New Richmond and was a highly respected citizen of the community. On July 10, 1919 Jenny passed away at age 35 and is buried in the New Richmond Cemetery next to her parents.

MARTHA VICTORIA DAVIDSON

Martha Victoria Davidson was born May 24, 1881 near Wareham, Ospry Township, Ontario, Canada to Robert and Martha Mills Davidson. She was their first daughter. Her siblings beings: William Thomas, Robert James, Letitia Jane, Christina Carolyn, Elizabeth and Richard Newton. Martha was named after her mother and her middle name for Queen Victoria on whose birthday Martha was born. She was called Mattie.

Otto and Martha Jones

Mattie came to Indiana in 1892 with her parents from Canada. She married Otto Jones who was born in 1876. This marriage was blessed with three children: Mervyn, Ruth Victoria, and Robert F. Otto and Mattie farmed in the area. Later the couple moved to New Richmond where they lived at several addresses.

Otto passed away in 1957 at age 81. Mattie continued to live in New Richmond, visiting her son in Arizona during the winter months. It was on one of these visits that Mattie passed away in 1968 at age 87. She is buried in New Richmond Cemetery next to her husband Otto.

ROBERT DAVIDSON

Robert Davidson came to Coal Creek Township in 1892 from Wareham, Ospry Township, Ontario, Canada. He was born Mar. 18, 1842 in Armagh Co., Ireland. He was the first child of William and Eliza (Ronncha or Ranncha) Davidson. His siblings being: William J.D., Margaret Ann, Elizabeth, and Richard. Robert had a half-brother John and a half-sister Jane from an earlier marriage of William and Margaret (Jackson) Davidson.

Wm. Thomas Davidson, Martha Victoria Davidson, Robert James Davidson. Seated: Christina Carolyn Davidson, Martha Mills Davidson, Letitia Jane Davidson, Robert Davidson.

In 1872 Robert married Miss Martha Mills who was born Feb. 13, 1849 at Toronto, Ontario, Canada. She died at the family farm in Coal Creek Township on June 13, 1925. This union was blessed with seven children: William Thomas, Robert James, Martha Victoria, Letitia Jane, Christina Carolyn, Elizabeth, and Richard Newton.

The Atlantic crossing from Ireland to Canada in 1845-1846 was hard. Robert lost his grandmother on the six week journey. After a few years his father purchased a farm near Wareham, Ontario, Canada where Robert's youngest brother Richard was born. Richard was the first white child to be born in that area.

In 1891 Robert sent his son William to Coal Creek Township to find a piece of farming property for the family to purchase. William stayed with the sons of Levi and Elizabeth Davidson Thomas. Elizabeth Davidson Thomas was a cousin of Robert. The family moved from Canada and settled near New Richmond in 1892.

Robert farmed on his property east of New Richmond until his death on Apr. 28, 1904. He is buried in the New Richmond Cemetery. His obituary stated: "Mr. Davidson was a prominent Mason and Democrat and highly respected in Madison Township." His granddaughter still lives on part of the family farm.

ROBERT JAMES DAVIDSON

Robert James Davidson was born on Nov. 1, 1874, near Wareham, Ospry Township Ontario, Canada to Robert and Martha Mills Davidson. He was their second son. His siblings being: William Thomas, Martha Victoria, Letitia Jane, Christina Carolyn, Elizabeth and Richard Newton.

Mattie and Otto Jones, Carrie and Jim Fouts, Essie and Bob Davidson

Robert James was first married to Lillie Franklin who died in 1919. He then married Essie Armfield on Nov. 28, 1919, a union which lasted 25 years until Essie passed away in 1944. Robert James had a foster daughter, Mrs. Guy Shubert.

Robert James came to Indiana in 1892 with his father and was a farmer in the Elmdale community for 25 years after which he owned and operated a grocery store in Elmdale for two years. The last 12 years Uncle Bob (as he was known) lived with his sister Mattie (Martha Victoria Davidson Jones). He was a member of the New Richmond Methodist Church. Robert passed away Jan. 11, 1958 at age 84 and is buried at the New Richmond Cemetery.

WILLIAM T. DAVIDSON

William Thomas Davidson was born Jan. 26, 1873 near Wareham, Ontario, Canada. He was the eldest child of Robert and Martha Mills Davidson. Other children to survive were Robert James, Martha Victoria, Letitia Jane, and Christina Carolyn. William came to Coal Creek Township in 1891 to find available land. His family followed the next year.

William T. Davidson

William married Mary Elizabeth Meek, daughter of George and Elizabeth Bowen Meek on Mar. 14, 1900. Mary was born in Montgomery County on Dec. 30, 1877. Her brothers and sisters were: George, Albert, Perry, Stephen, Sarah, Cynthia, Susan, Iva, and Amanda.

Six children were born to William and Mary Meek Davidson. The five who survived were Melvin, Mildred, Maude, Olive and Edna.

William or "Billy" as he was known farmed all of his life. He was known for his excellent crops. He raised a lot of fruits and vegetables as well as the usual farm crops. During the 20s the family ran a dairy operation. This meant that the children had to get up before 4:00 A.M. to help milk the cows and get the milk ready for delivery. Milk was bottled and delivered to customers in New Richmond before the children went to school. On one occasion, after delivering the milk, "Billy" Davidson's vehicle was hit by a train near a grain elevator in New Richmond. Witnesses to the accident believed that "Billy" would not survive. He not only survived but was not hurt. He walked away from the accident angry that his milk bottles had been broken.

William lived in Coal Creek Township most of his adult life. He died Nov. 8, 1943. Mary died Apr. 15, 1966. Both are buried in the New Richmond Cemetery. Many of their descendants still live in Montgomery County.

DAVIS FAMILY

William and Elizabeth Davis were the parents of at least five children, one of which was John, born June 3, 1800 in Albermarle Co., VA. When he was about 21 years old, he went to Ross Co., OH where he married Nov. 27, 1823 Catherine (born Sept. 9, 1805), daughter of Abraham and Eve (Bush) Stookey. John first purchased land near Stockwell, IN. Then ca. 1830 in Clinton Co., IN. He died May 4, 1868. Catherine died Feb. 27, 1863 - buried Union Cemetery. Children of John and Catherine were: William, Joel, Lurena, Abraham, Oze, Avelina, Isaac, John I., Elon and Mary Davis.

Elon Davis was born Sept. 27, 1842, Perry Township, Clinton County (died Aug. 20, 1929). He married Harriett, daughter of George and Hester (Ready) Arbegust in Montgomery County Feb. 23, 1868. Their oldest son, Edward B. was born Feb. 8, 1869 in Perry Township. He was a farmer and lived near Colfax. He married Ida May (born Oct. 1, 1870), daughter of Joseph Thomas and Mary Ellen (Anderson) Carson. Two sons Byron Carson and Ernest Lester Davis. She died Apr. 17, 1903 Rural Route, Colfax. Edward married #2 Emma Terrall. They moved to Fulton County, later to Lexington, TN where they live in a log cabin. He died Sept. 4, 1940 and is buried there in the Independence Cemetery.

Ernest Lester Davis, second son of Edward and Ida May was born July 24, 1900 about two miles northwest of Colfax. He was in the Army during WWI. He met Ruby Edna (who was selling tickets at a movie theater), daughter of George and Dora (Locke) Harriman when visiting his brother Byron in Concord, NH. They were married Sept. 14, 1926 at the home of George and Cora Osgood (who had raised Ruby after the young deaths of her parents). After a time in Palm Beach, FL, where Ernest helped build a large hotel, they went to Brownsville, TX, then back to Colfax about 1929 when they served as managers of the Clarks Hill-Lauramie Township, Tippecanoe County Telephone Company. Daughter Phyllis Jean was born July 22, 1930. See below. Son, James Ray was born Mar. 31, 1932. James Ray married June Darlene Phillips on Oct. 25, 1951 Delphi Methodist Church. He is a broker and realtor as well as in the construction business in Delphi. No children.

About 1934, Ernest got a job with the Royal Garment Cleaners (Frankfort) where they cleaned a lot of circus costumes for Ringling Brothers. Son, Richard Lee was born Apr. 20, 1935. Richard married May 16, 1954 (Delphi Methodist Church) Wilma Jean Pattengale. He served in the National Guard at Delphi for eight years, worked for Lahr Ford Garage for 20 years and is now Head Custodian of Hersey School, Tippecanoe County. Their children: Richard Gene, Leetta Darlene, Michael Dean and Robert Lee.

In 1938, Ernest and Ruby started Carroll Cleaners (Delphi) and he owned it until 1953. In 1942, Ernest and Ruby divorced. In August, 1943, he married Velma Scowden in Missouri. Their son, Kenneth Paul was born Dec. 29, 1944 at Rennselaer. Daughter, Lana Lee was born July 7, 1948 in Logansport and Cheryl Susan was born Oct. 17, 1953 in Lafayette. Ernest and Velma moved to Deerfield Beach, FL where he began making fishing lures (Davis Lures) and they are still being sold. He died June 2, 1972 at Boca Raton — buried IOOF Cemetery, Pittsburg, IN. Ruby Harriman Davis remarried Nov. 10, 1947 Fort Wayne to Floyd Addison Sigman — no children. She died Nov. 17, 1984 - Delphi, buried Morning Heights Cemetery at Delphi.

Phyllis Jean Davis, daughter of Ernest and Ruby married June 18, 1947 (Presbyterian Manse, Rossville) Don Robert Moore (born Mar. 8, 1926 Carroll County, son of Henry Newton and Mayme Ellen (Riggle) Moore). Phyllis Jean attended schools in Frankfort, Delphi and Monticello.

Children of Don and Phyllis Moore are: Don Robert II, Jackie Dean and Gary Gene, all born Memorial Hospital, Logansport.

Don Robert II born Oct. 13, 1947 married Connie Lynn Christianson June 18, 1966. He worked as a carpenter for his Uncle James R. Davis for several years but is now a Union Plumber-Pipe Fitter. Don and Connie have Robert Lee, born July 29, 1967 who is also a Union Plumber (Lox Equipment, Delphi); Darrell Dean, born Nov. 27, 1968 and Crystal Renee, born Oct. 14, 1972.

Jackie Dean born Dec. 14, 1948 went to the Army as a Medic in 1968 and was in Vietnam four and one half years. He married Darlene Scott Wakeland September 1974. No children. Divorced in November 1975 after Jack had an auto accident (February 1975) and did not remember Darlene.

Gary Gene was born Jan. 18, 1951. He, too, was in the Army, serving in Germany. He married Debra Kay Hughes June 30, 1973. They lived in Austin, TX while Gary was in the construction business. He now lives in East Haven, CT and is in the building and remodeling business. Children of Gary and Debra: Cody Lane, born Mar. 8, 1976, Kinzie Dawn, born Sept. 26, 1977, Chase Jay born July 28, 1979 and Cassandra Lynn, born Dec. 9, 1981. They divorced in 1982.

From 1966, Phyllis Jean Davis Moore has served as the Curator of the Carroll County Museum, Delphi. Her husband, Don has worked most of his married life for Garrison International transport and Truck Sales, Delphi.

GEORGE E. DAVIS

George E. Davis (1862-1946) was the last descendant in his family to both farm and occupy this homestead located four miles south of Crawfordsville on State Road 47. He and his wife, Amelia Seaman, lived and celebrated their 60th wedding anniversary in this historic landmark home.

George's grandfather, Randolph Davis, settled here when only two other families occupied the site of Crawfordsville. His father, John L. Davis, continued under pioneer conditions until he amassed his fortune and built the above residence considered the finest country home in Montgomery County. This structure burned to the ground in later years.

Davis farm house

John L. had one daughter, Sarah. She married Dr. J.L. Beatty, who practiced locally for over 50 years. They had two daughters, Ruth Fyffe, deceased, and Naomi Beck, a resident of the Franklin Indiana Masonic Home. There are no other descendants in this branch of the family.

While Randolph and John L. Davis were both keen businessmen, George's interests were in the arts. He was a student of the classics, and was an accomplished vocalist and violinist, as well as an equestrian. He was an avid horticulturist, winning many ribbons for his beloved gladiolus.

George married Amelia Seaman, a local school teacher. Amelia, known as Mellie, was one of the four charter members of the Crawfordsville Home Economics Club, and became prominent in numerous civic and cultural activities. She stayed abreast of local and national news, as well as foreign affairs. Always interested in politics, she made numerous trips to Washington, D.C., to attend opening sessions of the Senate. By setting herself as an example she did much to advance the position of the farm woman to one of dignity and prestige. Mellie Davis was a remarkable woman who surely was a forerunner of our present day women's movement.

George and Mellie had two daughters; Lael Corya, who became a Christian Science Practitioner, and Pauline Durham, both deceased. Lael's daughter, Patricia Langston, is deceased and her son, David Langston, lives in England with his children James and Jennifer. Another daughter, Penelope Schuler of Stamford, CT is the mother of Wendy Simmons Taylor and the grandmother of Forrest Taylor. She also has a son, Frederick Siebelts of Greenwich, CT. Penelope has continued an interest in dancing and has taught at many levels. She also has remained active in the Christian Science Church.

Betty Steele is the only child of Pauline Durham. She has pursued a life-long interest in antiques and for many years owned a successful antique business in Westport, CT. She is now retired and living in Scottsdale, AZ. Her daughter, Elizabeth Steele, lives in Grants Pass, OR.

Betty Steel continues to operate the remaining acreage of the original Davis farm.

GEORGE SAMUEL DAVIS

George Samuel Davis, born Mar. 22, 1818 in Kentucky, and his 19 year old bride, Nancy Booher Ellis, also from Kentucky, came to Montgomery Co., IN on horseback in 1847.

They lived first on the Frank Coon's farm three and one-half miles west of New Market. George spent the remainder of his life in the New Market area. He owned several hundred acres of land near what is now Indian Creek Cemetery. He donated the land for the cemetery and was buried there following his death in Oct. 16, 1890.

Nancy Davis died at the home of a daughter in Crawfordsville Oct. 29, 1926 at the age of 98. Her great, great grandfather, Robert Poage, came from Ireland to the colonies in 1739.

George and Nancy had five children. They were Tilghman Thomas; William Warren (died in Infancy); Martha, who married Rice Bennett; Mary Jane who married Rollo Crist; and Ida who married Lewis Haverkamp. All lived in the New Market-Crawfordsville area.

Tilghman Thomas Davis, born May 23, 1848, married Sarah Jane Todd on Oct. 5, 1870. Their children were Walter G. who married Clara Hedrick; Minnie, who married Frank Brachett; Harry Todd, who married Mary Glenn Easley; Pearl who married Jacob Sayler; and Fred. All stayed in the county except Walter and Fred who spent most of their lives in Florida.

Harry Todd Davis, born Apr. 22, 1876 and Mary Glenn Easley (another 19 year old bride) were married Oct. 17, 1897. They lived most of their lives on the Benjamin Easley farm in Brown Township west of New Market. Harry T. Davis was one of the founders of the Indiana Farm Bureau and was a member and President of the Indiana Wool Growers Association. He was also a Director of the Farm Bureau Insurance Company when it started and was active in Democratic politics.

Harry and Mary Davis had four children: They were Alva Glenn who married (1) Rachael Poynts and (2) Naomi McClure; Louise, who married Orville Demoret; Benjamin Harold, who married Dorothy Bond; and Walter Glenn who married Mary DeAth.

Alva Glenn Davis died in 1988, Mrs. Louise Demoret lives in Crawfordsville, Benjamin Harold and his wife have retired and moved from New Jersey to Florida. Walter Glenn Davis and his wife live in Gainesville, GA.

Harry and Mary Davis were descended from Montgomery County branches of the Van Cleave, Whittington, Easley and Todd families who were pioneer settlers of the County. Actually, they were fifth cousins, their common ancestor having been Benjamin Van Cleave (1775-1833).

In 1989 no male descendants of George Samuel Davis remain in Montgomery County, but there are four in Florida, two in New Jersey and one in Maryland. *Submitted by Benjamin Harold Davis*

THOMAS LEE AND SUSAN JANE (NEE HOFFMANN) DAY

A Crawfordsville District Public Library Reference Services Head vacancy lured Tom from being NIALSA Assistant Administrator in Merrillville during May, 1986, just before his becoming La Porte Chess Champ. Renting widow Gladys Bronaugh's 504 S. Green apartment, Tom made weekend conjugal visits to 208 E. Street in La Porte. Upon Susie's La Porte Hospital's C.O.T.A. resignation the old Galey House at 611 E. Wabash received them and their three dogs (Wriggily, Panda and Bear). An anonymous note on moving day warned that proper authorities would be approached unless the dogs' obnoxious barking ceased.

Susie was born Feb. 4, 1947 in Cincinnati to John R. (Salesman) and Hilda (nee Mitchell) Hoffmann. Upon completing a C.O.T.A. program in Columbus Susie was lured to Boston by Cambridge's D'Youville Hospital. During a United Parish in Brookline coffeehour she met Tom. They were wedded June 17, 1978.

The firstborn of Maurice Graham and Bernadine Juanita (Erickson) Day in Ypsilanti, MI on Friday, Aug. 16, 1940, Tom was reared in Willis. A Big Rapids orphan, Bernie had arrived in Willis in 1932.

Legally blind since birth due to a variously diagnosed chronic corneal disease, Susie has obeyed physicians' advice to remain childless. A 1950 polio victim, Tom graduated on time thanks to Kiwanis and Methodist church group provision of a Michigan Bell intercom connecting his bedside to Ypsi Lincoln classrooms. He participated in Wolverine Boys' State. In 1958 Lincoln Librarian Ray W. Binns drove Tom and four schoolchums to Washington, D.C. during cherry blossom time.

Susie is past president of Crawfordsville Newcomers. The short shrift accorded occupational therapy has necessitated Susie's being transported to health care facilities served through the auspices of Rick Weber's Healthmark, Inc. to the Carmel Clay Opportunity School in Noblesville, and now to sites in Montgomery and neighboring counties served by the West Central Indiana Special Education Cooperative. Susie sings soprano with the Wabash Avenue Presbyterian Choir and the local Community Chorus.

Tom is a Presbyterian Deacon, local Lion Tamer, and Montgomery County Educational Foundation Secretary. In Brookline he attained popularity as a carillonneur. A Past-Worshipful Master of Bethhoron Lodge A.F. & A.M., he intends to become a Shriner in 1989. He recently finished donating a 13th gallon of blood.

Their Crawfordsville household has received five Japanese fellows so far. Bon (Osaka) and Yoshiaki Mizukami (Tokyo) were Lions International sponsored. Masato Suzuki (Osaka) and Souichiro Nomura (and his twin Shingiro from Knox College) (Tokyo) have been Wabash College Students.

Is Tom related to Crawfordsville Days? A thoroughgoing mixed DAY/PEPPIATT family genealogy mentions that Tom's great-grandfather Jessie's close relative Shadrach Peppiatt immigrated to the Willis site from the Peppiatt ancestral home at Pitstone (Pightlestone), Buckinghamshire, England in 1866. Shadrach's dog had illegally caught a rabbit and the Game Warden summoned Shadrach. Should Crawfordsville police strictly enforce the dog barking ordinance Tom might feel obliged to flee overseas. Ha!Ha!

FRED N. AND CHARLOTTE DEAN

Fred Nelson Dean was born Mar. 18, 1907, in Sullivan Co., IN. His parents, Charles S. and Rebecca Jane Davis Dean had three children: Mabel E. born in 1889, Melvin S. born in 1892 and Fred N. Fred attended the public schools in Sullivan until the spring of 1918. At that time both parents died within two weeks of each other during the "Great Influenza Epidemic". He spent the next ten years with his older brother, Melvin, at Carlisle, IN, and completed his education in the public schools there.

Charlotte D. Dildine was born Aug. 15, 1910 the first of six children born to Charles Ernest and Mary Dorrough Dildine at Riley, IN. Within that year they purchased property at route one, Oaktown, IN, and spent the rest of their lives at that address.

Following Charlotte came a brother Clarence W. born in 1912, after him came Harold C. born in 1914. Then came Helen Ruth born in 1916 followed by George W. in 1918. Last was Frances E. born in 1920. Helen and Harold both died close together in 1918, the same tragic year that took the parents of Fred Dean.

Like many a romance ours began by meeting at ball games, an occasional movie and most importantly, we came to attend the Oaktown Methodist Church together. It was here that religion made a lasting impression on both, and Fred felt the call to the ministry. Our romance grew and finally led to our marriage on Jan. 21, 1929.

In the interest of briefness, we will simply say that we worked on the farm during those early years. As the Bible would say, "the depression was sore in the land". It was a bleak and barren time in our lives. During the years 1936, 1937, 1938, we obtained government loans that led to our move to route one, Decker, IN. We arrived Feb. 10, 1938 and started life anew on land purchased by the Resettlement Administration. We became a part of a social experiment that the government soon abandoned and sold our farm to us in 1944.

In the late 1940's Fred studied and passed a

correspondence course and was licensed to preach in the Methodist Church.

It was in July of 1957 that we left the farm and moved into the parsonage at Fairview Park Church at Clinton, IN. After serving there for three years we were asked to take the Waveland-New Market charge here in Montgomery County. That was our introduction to this lovely county. While serving here our daughter Melba, graduated from the Waveland High School in 1963.

Following is a list of the Fred and Charlotte "Begats": Mary Jane born Dec. 22, 1929; Ruth Ann born Aug. 16, 1932 died Apr. 22, 1952; Stanley Alan born Jan. 2, 1935; Carolyn June born Mar. 11, 1939; Melba Frances born June 30, 1945; Joyce Elaine born Apr. 27, 1947.

At the June Conference of the United Methodist Church in 1972, we took the retired status and moved back to the farm. Fred was 65 and Charlotte was 62 in August. But there was a need for ministers and so we continued for eight more years on a part time status. By 1980 we could tell we were both ready for a second retirement. We sold the farm and bought our present home at 708 West Main St., Waveland, IN. The last four years we have maintained a winter home at Dundee, FL, which we have enjoyed very much. But wherever we may wander, I know there is no place we would rather be than here in central Indiana in October. *Submitted by Fred Dean*

CARL AND EUNICE DeBARD

Carl O. DeBard (1904-1984) first came to Montgomery County to attend Wabash College where he lettered for three years on the varsity football team and graduated as a history major in 1927. He was the third child of William and Amie (Broshar) DeBard who farmed in Boone County near Advance. His siblings were Basil, Earl and Mary Catherine. Carl's paternal grandparents, Martin and Elizabeth (Davis) DeBard first came to Montgomery County to live in 1870.

Eunice C. Baringer (1905-) and Carl were married in 1928. Eunice was an elementary teacher who taught in Hendricks, Fountain, Boone and Montgomery County. She was the second child of Harry, a tinner and plumber, and Ethel (Heady) Baringer who resided in Jamestown, IN. Her siblings were Ethella and Marion. Ethella Baringer Spencer taught in the elementary schools of Crawfordsville for many years.

Carl and Eunice DeBard

The couple moved to Crawfordsville in 1930 where Carl taught history and was the football coach at Crawfordsville High School from 1930-37. Two children were born to them, Robert in 1929 and Harriett in 1933. Robert was to have three children, Dan DeBard (a graduate of Wabash), Sarah Cooper and Laura Pratt. Harriett had one daughter, Christine Drilling Gianna.

DeBard joined the Indiana National Guard unit in Crawfordsville as a private in 1930. In January of 1941 the Guard was called into active duty prior to World War II while he was teaching at Central High School in Evansville. The 38th Division was sent to the Pacific and Carl served 42 months of overseas duty in Hawaii, New Guinea and the Philippines.

Lt. Colonel DeBard was Battalion Commander of the 139th Field Artillery when this unit made an amphibious landing in the Philippines and fired the first round of artillery ammunition in the 38th Division attack on Bataan. DeBard was awarded the Bronze Star Medal for leadership and valor during combat in the Philippines.

Eunice returned to Crawfordsville where Robert and Harriett attended local schools while her husband was overseas. During this period she served numerous hours as a volunteer Red Cross nurses' aide at Culver Hospital.

After the war Carl was personnel director for Southern Indiana Gas and Electric Company in Evansville, taught at North Central High School in Indianapolis and was engaged in farming near Grandview and Pittsboro, IN.

In 1950 DeBard was appointed to the rank of Brigadier General and was promoted to the rank of Major General in 1954. He was Commanding General of the 38th Indiana National Guard Division from 1953 until his retirement from military duty in 1959. DeBard Hall was named in his honor in the National Guard Armory built at Madison in 1979.

Carl and Eunice returned to Crawfordsville in 1973 where they resided until they moved to Florida in 1978. Carl died in 1984 (age 79) and he was returned for the last time to Crawfordsville where he was interred in the mausoleum at Oak Hill Cemetery.

CHARLES AND IMOGENE DeBUSK

Charles Thomas DeBusk, of French descent, was born Aug. 31, 1913, in Hartsville, Bartholomew Co., IN, the eldest of eight children born to Charles Tilden and Dora Elizabeth (Johnston) DeBusk. He graduated from Hope High School in 1932 with a basketball scholarship and attended Central Normal College, Danville, IN, where he completed a two-year elementary teaching degree in 1934.

That fall, he came to Montgomery County to start his teaching and coaching career in the New Market Joint School. Here he met Imogene Reddish, a hometown veteran teacher of six years. She was the only child of John Fuson and Ruth Hazel (Reeves) Reddish, born Feb. 26, 1910 in Parke County near the Shades State Park where her father was a farmer and stock raiser. When two years of age, her family moved to Montgomery County. Imogene graduated from New Market High School in 1927 and received her two-year elementary teaching degree from Indiana State Normal. At the age of 18, she began her teaching career at Browns Valley where she had received her grade school education. After two years, she went to New Market where she and Charles completed 40 years each in the field of education, retiring in 1975. They both received their B.S. degrees (in 1953) and Charles his masters at Indiana State.

Charles and Imogene were married May 2, 1935 at Lafayette, IN, by Rev. C.B. Stanforth, former New Market Methodist minister, who had also married Imogene's parents in 1908. The young couple lived the first year with her parents on the Clay and Lena (Noble) Reeves homestead (three and one-half miles southwest of New Market), Imogene's grandparents' place, which is still in the family today.

Imogene and Charles DeBusk

They had two sons, both born in Montgomery County: John C. (Jack) born Feb. 23, 1936 and Thomas Noble, born Aug. 28, 1939. Jack married Glenda "Kay" Dove Aug. 5, 1956, in the New Market Methodist Church (where the family has held membership for many years). Jack and Kay have two children: Stacy who married Terry Brown — one child, Jacob Lewis Brown; and Stanley who married Deanna Smith. Jack, in his 34th year at the R.R. Donnelley Printing Company, is currently production control planner in the Hi-Tech area. Kay operates the Dari-King on State Road 47 South. Jack was in partnership with his father in the DeBusk & Sons Polled Shorthorn Cattle business for several years and today maintains his own herd.

Thomas Noble DeBusk married Gilda Jean Gray May 15, 1962. Their children are: Christine who married Gary Pittman; Thomas Jr. (Coast Guards in Florida) and Brett (sophomore at Indiana State). For 26 years, Tom worked at Cummins Engines Company and Gilda still works there. Tom is now representative of an investment company.

Both Jack and Tom graduated from New Market High School. Jack attended Purdue and Tom attended Indiana State and served in the Armed Forces for two years.

As previously stated, besides Charles' teaching (math and history), coaching, athletic director, and referee positions, as well as being assistant elementary principal, he also farmed in Scott and Brown Township and was in the Polled Shorthorn Cattle business, most of his life, starting this endeavor in the 1940's and selling out in 1983. Jack and Tom were very active in 4-H as boys, showing cattle they helped raise on the farm. In 1968, Charles was honored by the state Polled Shorthorn breeders for promotion of the breed — and in 1977, he was one of seven breeders cited as National Shorthorn "Builder of the Breed" award and was featured in the American Shorthorn Association's official magazine in that year. Charles also established a real estate firm in New Market and was a Franklin Life Insurance representative. He was a member of Waveland Masonic Lodge, active in Scottish Rite and Shrine (Indianapolis), State Retired Teacher Association, Montgomery County Retired Teachers and Montgomery County Retired Coaches, as well as other business-related associations. In 1977, he received the Montgomery County Fellowship of Christian Athletes Merit Award of which he was quite proud.

Imogene, a Kappa Delta Pi at Indiana State

College, a member of Iota Chapter of the Delta Kappa Gamma Society, New Market Woman's Club, 50-year member of OES, and Montgomery County Retired Teachers. She also served as Historian for the New Market Centennial (author of *A Century of Progress, New Market, Indiana 1872-1972*), has written New Market Methodist church histories, and served as church music director (and pianist) for more than 40 years. In 1956, her New Market sixth grade class tied for first place in the nation for her creative reading activities and teaching techniques used in the classroom. She and Charles were quite proud of the DeBusk award that the New Market School gives each year for mental attitude in honor of both DeBusk's many years of service. Imogene remains faithful to her church and is in several community organizations.

Charles and Imogene celebrated their Golden Wedding Anniversary in 1985 with an open house at their church (given by their family). Charles died July 8, 1988, and is buried in Masonic (North) Cemetery in Crawfordsville. Imogene continues to live in the same house in New Market that she and Charles had built in 1954. *Submitted by Karen Zach (via information obtained from Imogene DeBusk)*

RICHARD AND MARIAN MARCIEL (HIMES) DECKARD

Richard E. Deckard and Marian Marciel (Himes) Deckard were married Jan. 29, 1937. Both were graduates of the Crawfordsville High School. Marian played violin in the orchestra, was a skilled pianist playing the "Mikado" program and belonged to the Glee Club.

Marian, born Apr. 1, 1917 was the daughter of Chester and Ruby (Linn) Himes and grew up on her parents farm east of Whitesville, IN with her sister Pauline.

Richard E. born Oct. 1, 1913 was the only son of William McKinley and Katie Bethel (Barnhart) Deckard.

Children of Richard and Marian were Jill Lynn, born July 26, 1942, Jack Mitchell born Sept. 16, 1943 and Cheryl Lynn born Jan. 14, 1950.

Marian had the ability to make and keep loyal and lasting friends. She was a member of the Crawfordsville, IN MU chapter of the Sigma Chi Sorority serving as President in 1972 and Treasurer in 1974. Also a former member of the Crawfordsville Athens Chapter No. 97 of Eastern Star. She also worked in the office of Dr. Wesley Shannon.

Richard was a member of the Montgomery Lodge 50 F. & A.M. Order of Eastern Star and Ancient Accepted Scottish Rite Valley of Indianapolis. He enjoyed fishing and bowling.

Richard and Marian Marciel (Himes) Deckard

They were members of the Trinity United Methodist Church.

First of their family to marry was Jill Lynn in 1960 to Harry Lindsey. (Divorced). Their children were Philip, born July 30, 1961 and Kathleen Ann, born Nov. 11, 1963. Jill's subsequent marriage to Lee Salberg took them to California where Samuel was born Oct. 19, 1970. (Divorced).

Cheryl married Kevin Clark and lived at Indianapolis. Following their divorce she moved to Arizona marrying John O'Donnell on Apr. 29, 1982. They live at Apache Junction, AZ.

Jack Mitchell and Alice (Carroll) Deckard, (daughter of Frank and Mary (Fielden) Carroll) were married Mar. 11, 1962 (divorced). Their lovely daughters are Michelle Lea, born Nov. 25, 1964 and Lucinda Jo born July 24, 1968.

Jack Deckard's lineage continues with Jack Mitchell II. Then Mark Allen, his adoptive son on Oct. 14, 1979 following marriage to Darlene Ferguson (divorced).

Richard began his career at Donnelley's in the apprentice program retiring after 39 years in 1976. They resided on Ardmore St.

Marian's health and Richard's former heart attack moved them to seek a drier climate. They moved to Mesa, AZ into a new home at 8001 E. Broadway.

Marian now painted several scenic pictures of Arizona, also one of the remembered "Yountsville Covered Bridge" near Crawfordsville, IN. Richard died June 5, 1978 in their home. He was buried June 9, at the Crawfordsville Masonic Cemetery.

Alone four years, Marian Marciel met Joseph Hepburn. Their warm and loving personalities blended beautifully. They married on Mar. 3, 1982 and resided at the Fountain of the Sun, Arizona address.

Marian looked forward to a first great grandchild. She was Kayla Danielle, born Nov. 4, 1986, daughter of Lucinda Jo, six months old when Marian and Joe returned to attend Michelle's wedding. This occurred June 20, 1987 at the Crawfordsville Woodland Heights Christian Church. Michelle Lea and John Fisher were married.

Marian died Apr. 14, 1988. Masonic Cemetery.

JOEL DEER SR.

Joel Deer Sr. founder of Deers Mill was born Feb. 7, 1789 in Culpepper Co., VA. When he was 22 years old he enlisted in the Army for the War of 1812. He married Sarah Garnet on May 15, 1817; she was born July 18, 1792. After they were married they moved to Boone Co., KY. Five children were born to this marriage: Samantha, Sophia, John, Edmond, and Joel G. When Joel G. was six months old his parents migrated to Montgomery County, his mother riding (horseback) bore the baby in her lap all the way to Montgomery County. Joel Sr.'s wife Sarah died when Joel G. was about 15 years old. Later Joel Sr. married Susan Mallory. The Deer family was one of the early settlers of Montgomery County and their names are enrolled on the list of pioneers of the state. Joel Sr.'s parents came to this country from Germany.

Joel Sr. made his family comfortable in a log cabin he built on a government section of timberland on Sugar Creek. His foresight and business ability suggested the necessity of a Grist Mill and a Sawmill in his neighborhood which he built in 1829.

Joel G. and his brother Edmond purchased the mill from their father. Deers Mill was known as the oldest of its kind in the state of Indiana. Samantha the oldest daughter born July 31, 1818 married Alfred Mitchell born Dec. 18, 1815, they were married in Montgomery County Feb. 14, 1838 and to this union nine children were born: Sarah, Sareptha, Benjamin, Sophia, Mary Annie, Harriet, Theresa Jane, Martha and Valore.

Theresa Jane (Jenny) was born June 29, 1855, married Gilbert Blake from Parke County. He was born June 6, 1852. They were married December 1881. She died Mar. 5, 1942 and he died Feb. 14, 1930. They were the parents of a son who died in infancy and a daughter Jessie who married Zura Monroe. They had two daughters Helen Wanetah and Naomi. Helen Wanetah married Eldo Bannon and they were the parents of Virginia Bannon Kelsey and Max Monroe Bannon. Naomi married Cyril Cox and they had a son Donald Dean Cox. Max and Virginia live near Parkersburg and Don lives in Lafayette and they are the great, great, great grandchildren of Joel Sr.

EUGENE DELLINGER

Eugene Spangler Dellinger was born in Tipton Co., IN on Dec. 26, 1914. He moved to Montgomery Co., IN, about 1921 with his parents, Shirl Blaine Dellinger and Rebecca Heacock Baynes Dellinger. He was the oldest of eight children; his siblings were: Rebecca Powell, Hartley C., Shirley Kathleen, Robert Lowell, Thomas Baynes, George Paul, and Ruthanna. After about 1923, the Dellinger family lived on a 23-acre farm located on the Big-4 Arch Road one-half mile outside the southwest city limits of Crawfordsville.

Eugene attended elementary grades in Crawfordsville, and at Wilson School, located five miles southwest of Crawfordsville. He graduated from Crawfordsville High School in 1934.

Eugene and Valverta Dellinger

Eugene married Valverta Williams on June 19, 1938, in Wallace, IN. Valverta graduated from the Wallace High School in 1938. They lived in Crawfordsville. There were no children born of this union.

After High School, Eugene worked as a farm hired hand for a while. He attended a special course at Purdue University with reference to the care of dairy cattle. He worked for several years as a welder at the Lewis and Sheppard plant in Crawfordsville.

Eugene served in the Indiana National Guard for about five years. He participated in strike duty in Terre Haute in 1934. In 1937, he was one of those called to patrol Evansville during the flood on the Ohio River.

Eugene died of Hodgkins Disease on Sept. 6, 1941, an incurable disease at the time of his death. He is buried at Oak Hill Cemetery in Crawfordsville. *Authored by Thomas Baynes Dellinger*

GEORGE PAUL DELLINGER

George was born in Montgomery Co., IN, Mar. 24, 1928, the seventh of eight children of Shirl Blaine Dellinger and Rebecca Heacock Baynes Dellinger. The family lived on a 23-acre farm located on the Big-4 Arch Road. He attended Wilson and Mt. Zion elementary schools and Crawfordsville High School, graduating in 1945. He served in the U.S. Army Air Force in 1946 and 1947 on bases in Colorado and Florida. He graduated from Purdue University in 1951 with a BS Degree in Forestry and Agriculture. He obtained an MA Degree in Wildlife Management in 1954 from the University of Missouri, in Columbia.

He married Barbara Jean Handy Apr. 7, 1951 in Crawfordsville. Barbara was born in Crawfordsville Aug. 4, 1932. She attended Mt. Zion and Tuttle elementary schools and Crawfordsville High School. They have two children: Carla Jean, born at Columbia, MO Mar. 1, 1954; and Virginia Lee, born in Springfield, MO Dec. 21, 1959. They have lived in Columbia, Willow Springs, West Plains, Jefferson City and Holts Summit in Missouri.

George P., Barbara, Carla and Virginia Dellinger

George has spent his professional career after 1954 as a wildlife biologist working for the Missouri Department of Conservation. He is an avid outdoorsman and has traveled, hunted and fished in many states and Canada. He has been active in numerous service organizations including American Legion, Fraternal Order of Eagles, Rotary International, the Wildlife Society, National Wildlife Federation, Wilderness Society, Missouri Conservation Federation, and Lake Mykee City Council.

Daughter Carla Jean graduated from Jefferson City High School in 1972, and obtained a degree in Special Education from Central Missouri State University in 1976 and, subsequently, advanced training in Drug and Alcohol Abuse Counseling at the Naval Training School in Ft. Lyon, CO. She married Jerry Jones Feb. 3, 1982. Jerry was born in Jefferson City, MO Jan. 17, 1954 and graduated from Jefferson City High School in 1972. They have two adopted children; Melissa, born Apr. 28, 1984 in Missouri; and Wade Tate, born Mar. 31, 1987 in New Mexico. Carla's family lives in Columbia, MO, where Jerry manages his highway construction business.

Daughter Virginia graduated from Jefferson City High School in 1976 and attended a School of Cosmetology in Columbia, MO. She married Hossein Hosseini Sept. 22, 1978 in Columbia, MO. Hossein was born in Tehran, Iran Mar. 22, 1957. Hossein obtained a BS Degree in Computer Science from Central Missouri State University in 1982. They have one child, Sheerein, born in West Covina, CA Mar. 26, 1983. Virginia's family lives in San Diego, CA, where Hossein manages his auto repair and service station business. Both daughters are expecting additions to their families during 1989. *Authored by George P. Dellinger*

HARTLEY DELLINGER

Hartley C. Dellinger was the third of the eight children of Shirl Blaine Dellinger and Rebecca Heacock Baynes Dellinger. He was born in Tipton Co., IN on May 11, 1918, and moved to Montgomery Co., IN, about 1921 with his parents. The Dellinger family lived on a farm on the Big-4 Arch Road, southwest of Crawfordsville.

Hartley attended elementary grades at Wilson School, and graduated from Crawfordsville High School in 1936. In 1940 he graduated from Purdue University with a Chemical Engineering degree and went to work for Union Carbide in Indianapolis.

Hartley entered the U.S. Army in 1942, and served as a radar officer in the South Pacific until the end of hostilities. He saw service in Australia, New Guinea, the Philippines, and several Pacific islands. He was mustered out as a Major in 1945.

Hartley and Margaret Dellinger

Hartley married Margaret Lou Shigley in 1946. Margaret was born in Bloomington, IN, in 1925. She graduated from High School in Rush County in 1942 and attended Indiana Business College. Hartley and Margaret have four children, all born in Indianapolis: Judith Ann, born in 1948; Ted Hartley, born in 1951; Glenn Carl, born in 1956; and Roger Alan, born in 1958.

Hartley worked in his profession in Indianapolis until 1959; in Tonawanda, NY, until 1973; when they returned to Indianapolis. He retired in 1983, and they live in Indianapolis.

Daughter Judith completed an associate degree at Erie County Technical Institute in Buffalo, NY. She married Doil "Shorty" Powell in 1970. Doil was born in Logan Co., KY in 1923. They have two sons, both born in Bowling Green, KY: Jerry Wayne, born in 1972; and James Ray, born in 1973. The family lives in Alvaton, KY.

Son Ted has a BA degree in Journalism from Purdue University. He married Margaret Frick Watt in 1979. Margaret was born in Neptune, NJ, in 1944. She has a BA degree in English from Monmouth College. They have a daughter, Dallas Margaret, born in 1981 in Long Branch, NJ. Ted works with computers and lives in Oakhurst, NJ.

Son Glenn obtained a BS degree in Botany and Chemistry in 1979, and an MBA in 1980, all from Indiana University. He married Sue Gruver in 1980. Sue was born in Akron, OH in 1958. She obtained a BA degree in Business from Indiana University in 1980. They have a son; Matthew Mead, born in 1987 in Indianapolis. Glenn and Sue live in Indianapolis where he works as an Investment Counselor.

Son Roger graduated from High School in Indianapolis and has an Associate Degree in Electronic Technology. He works at his profession in Indianapolis. *Authored by Hartley C. Dellinger*

PETER PAUL DELLINGER

Peter Paul Dellinger lived in Montgomery Co., IN, in the late 1920s and the early 1930s in his widowed, and retired latter years. He was born in Freeport, IL, on Oct. 7, 1859, and died in Elwood, IN, on Dec. 1, 1934. He worked all his life as a laborer.

Peter Paul Dellinger married Charlotte Hartley, a first cousin, on Feb. 13, 1882, in Arcadia, IN. Peter Paul and Charlotte spent their married lives near Tipton, Arcadia and Elwood, IN. They had five children: Leroy, born Apr. 14, 1883; Alta May, born Nov. 16, 1885; Orpha, born Sept. 1, 1889; Shirl Blaine, born Nov. 4, 1892; and Elsie Irene, born Sept. 2, 1895.

Charlotte Hartley was born in Arcadia, IN, on Aug. 17, 1855, and died Sept. 4, 1918, in Arcadia.

Peter Paul Dellinger

Son Leroy married Lydia McGowan and lived in Indiana. Daughter Alta May married Oscar Johnson from the state of Oregon. Daughter Orpha married William C. Idle and lived in Elwood. Son Shirl Blaine married Rebecca Heacock Baynes and lived 50 years in Montgomery County.

Daughter Elsie Irene died of meningitis, while in her teens, on Feb. 16, 1912. She and her parents, Peter Paul, and Charlotte, are buried in the Dunkard Church of Brethren Cemetery in Arcadia.

The Dellinger surname can be traced back over several generations to the ancestor entering America from Germany. The known lineage to Peter Paul is as follows:

-JACOB I; born in 1700 in the Palatinate area of Germany. He and his wife, Maria Barbara, and their first child, arrived in America in 1733 on the ship "Elizabeth". They settled in York Co., PA, as farmers.

-JACOB II; was born in York Co., PA in 1751 and worked as a farmer. He served as a soldier in the American Revolution. He married Christina Schaffer. He died in 1824 in Pennsylvania.

-DANIEL; born in York Co., PA in 1793. He married Christina Keller in 1813. He died in 1829.

-PETER; born in York Co., PA, in 1817. He married Charlotte Spangler in 1846. In 1857 he was working as a mason in Freeport, IL. Charlotte died in 1884 and is buried in Freeport. Peter died in York Co., PA in 1896.

and

-PETER PAUL; who is the subject of this history. *Authored by Thomas Baynes Dellinger*

ROBERT DELLINGER FAMILY

Robert Lowell Dellinger was born in Tipton Co.,

IN, on Oct. 13, 1920. He moved to Montgomery Co., IN about 1921 with his parents, Shirl Blaine Dellinger and Rebecca Heacock Baynes Dellinger. From about 1923 until 1942, Robert lived on the Dellinger family farm on the Big-4 Arch Road, southwest of Crawfordsville.

Robert attended elementary grades at Wilson School, located five miles southwest of Crawfordsville. He graduated from Crawfordsville High School in 1939. While in High School, he played on the football team.

Robert and Marie Dellinger

Robert worked for R.R. Donnelley's in Crawfordsville and for Allison's in Speedway until 1942 when he entered the U.S. Navy.

In the Navy Robert trained at Bunker Hill Naval Air Station and at Fort Pierce, FL. He served in Hawaii and on Samar Island, Philippines, during the hostilities. After the cessation of hostilities, he served in Japan evacuating U.S. prisoners of war. He returned to the U.S. mainland via a round-the-world excursion visiting Singapore, India, South Africa, and landing at Norfolk, VA. He was mustered out of the Navy in December 1945.

Robert married Marie Poynter in 1943. Marie was born in Somerset, KY on Apr. 20, 1918 and graduated from High School at Ladoga, IN. Their two sons, John Robert and David L. were born in Crawfordsville in 1954 and 1957, respectively. Marie died in 1962 and is buried in Ladoga. Robert married June May Sarver Snelling in 1972. June was born in Yountsville, IN, in 1923 and she worked as a Cosmetologist. They now live south of Crawfordsville.

For a couple of years after returning from the Navy, Robert worked in his own barber shop in Ladoga. For several years he farmed near Crawfordsville and also near Ladoga. In 1960, he started work at the Mid-States wiremill in Crawfordsville where he advanced to Foreman. He retired from the mill in 1983.

Robert's two sons graduated from Southmont High School, at Crawfordsville. David graduated from Ball State University in Muncie, IN.

Son John married Sharon M. Reath of Crawfordsville in 1976. Sharon was born in Crawfordsville in 1957 and graduated from Crawfordsville High School. They have two children, Aimee Marie, born at Lafayette, IN in 1983; and Michael Scott, born at Lafayette in 1987. John works at Mid-States Steel & Wire in Crawfordsville.

Son David married Lori Lea Douglas in 1984. Lori was born in Marshall, IL in 1958 and graduated from Marshall High School and Indiana State University at Terre Haute, IN. They have one child, McKenzie Elizabeth, born in Cincinnati, OH, in 1987. David manages a Kinney shoe store in Cincinnati. *Authored by Robert Lowell Dellinger*

SHIRL DELLINGER

The Dellinger family moved to Montgomery County about 1921 from Tipton Co., IN. The arriving family consisted of Shirl Blaine Dellinger; his wife, Rebecca Heacock Baynes Dellinger; and five children: Eugene Spangler, Rebecca Powell, Hartley C., Shirley Kathleen, and Robert Lowell. About 1923, the family moved to a 23-acre farm located on the Big-4 Arch Road one-half mile southwest of Crawfordsville. There, three more children were born: Thomas Baynes, George Paul, and Ruthanna.

Shirl was born in Hamilton Co., IN, 1892, the son of Peter Paul Dellinger and Charlotte Hartley. His ancestors were mainly Lutheran and of German descent.

Mother Rebecca was born in Washington Co., IN, 1888, the daughter of Thomas Priestman Baynes and Rebecca Roberts Powell. Her ancestors were mainly Quaker and English descent.

Shirl and Rebecca Dellinger

Both sets of ancestors had migrated to Indiana through Pennsylvania. Shirl and Rebecca were married in Salem, IN, 1913.

Shirl farmed his own acreage and rented or share-cropped farming land in the area. The homeplace had an 110-tree orchard which provided apples and cider for eating and sale. There were dairy cattle with milk sales. In the 1930s, Shirl raised cattle and hogs for slaughter with meat sales direct to the customer. Truck crops were raised and sold. Gravel was hauled and sold from the gravel pit on the farm. Shirl did custom hay baling and trucking. Mother Rebecca, even though busy with the eight children, found time to raise rabbits and poultry to sell for ever-needed extra money.

The family home expanded over the years. It started out as a single-story, four-room house. In the late 1930s, Shirl bought two houses being removed for a Donnelley plant expansion, dismantled them, and used the salvaged lumber to increase the size of the family home. A second story, a wing for a kitchen, a porch, a full basement, and inside plumbing were added.

Seven children attended elementary grades in rural Wilson School; three attended Mt. Zion. All eight graduated from Crawfordsville High School. Seven went on to Purdue University or other colleges; three graduated with Bachelor degrees. Two obtained three advanced degrees, two Masters and one Ph.D.

Five children served in the Armed Forces; two were in combat in the south Pacific in World War II.

All eight children married and produced 24 grandchildren. In January 1989, there were seven living children, 23 grandchildren, 31 great-grandchildren, and one great-great-grandchild.

Son Eugene died in 1941 at age 27; mother Rebecca died in 1957 at 69, and Shirl died in 1971 at 79. Internments were in Oak Hill Cemetery.

The family farm was sold in 1973, after 50 years of Dellinger ownership. *Authored by Thomas Baynes Dellinger*

THOMAS DELLINGER

Thomas Baynes Dellinger was born in Montgomery Co., IN, on Jan. 31, 1926, the son of Shirl Blaine Dellinger and Rebecca Heacock Baynes Dellinger. The Dellinger family lived southwest of Crawfordsville.

Thomas attended Wilson and Mt. Zion Schools. He graduated from Crawfordsville High School, 1943, and from Purdue University, 1948, with a BS in Chemical Engineering. He obtained an engineering MS, 1961, and a Ph.D., 1970, from Tulsa University.

During 1944-1945 Thomas served in the Army Air Corp, stationed in Texas, Kansas, and Oklahoma.

Tom and Maria Dellinger

Thomas married Maria de la Garza, 1949, in Brownsville, TX. Maria was born in Brownsville, 1928. She has a BA from Our Lady of the Lake College, 1949, San Antonio, TX, and two MA degrees, one from Tulsa University, 1970, and one from University of Texas, Arlington, 1980.

Thomas and Maria have four children: Thomas Thaddeus, born in Caripito, Venezuela, 1950; Rebecca Maria, born in Brownsville, 1953; Margaret Mary, born in Maracaibo, Venezuela, 1956; and Joseph Anthony, born in Tulsa, OK, 1961. Another child, Carl Eugene, born in 1952 in Venezuela, died at 12 days, and is buried in Crawfordsville.

While working as an engineer for oil companies, Thomas and his family lived in Venezuela, Oklahoma, and Texas. He also worked internationally in Europe, Asia, and the Mideast as a consultant from the home offices. Thomas retired in 1988 and devotes more time to his hobbies, genealogy, and bird-banding studies on Purple Martins. Thomas and Maria have lived in Duncanville, TX, since 1970.

Son Thomas (Tad) obtained a BA degree in Business from the University of Tulsa, 1972. Tad married Donna Lynn Bryson in McKeesport, PA, 1979. Donna was born in McKeesport, 1954; she was a Captain in the Air Force as a registered nurse. Tad and Donna have two children: Justin Thomas, born at Sedalia, MO, 1981; and Christopher Michael, born in San Francisco, CA, 1984. Tad is an Air Force Major stationed at Ft. Douglas, UT.

Daughter Rebecca earned a BA from University of Dallas, TX, 1976, and a Masters from University of Texas, Arlington, 1979, both in Biology. Rebecca was a school teacher in Texas and California. She works for the Dallas Zoo's Bird Department.

Daughter Margaret (Meg) obtained a BS degree in Biochemistry from the University of Dallas,

1978. She attended graduate school at the University of Texas, Arlington. She married James Paul Fiegenschue, 1980, in Duncanville. James, born in Dallas, TX, 1953, has a BS in mathematics. Both Meg and James work as computer consultants in the Dallas area.

Son Joseph obtained two BS degrees, in Math and in Geophysics, 1983, from Texas A&M. Joseph has a Masters, 1986, and is finishing a Ph.D. degree in Geophysics, at Stanford University, CA. *Authored by Thomas Baynes Dellinger*

JAMES FRANKLIN DEMORET 1857-1931

James Franklin Demoret was born near Whitesville in Montgomery Co., IN, in 1857. He was a descendant of Nicholas Demoret, born in New Jersey (France) in 1760. Nicholas' parents were said to be French Huguenots who had escaped from France because of religious persecution. They settled in New Jersey where a number of French Huguenots had gone. Nicholas migrated to Pennsylvania, then to the Cincinnati area of Ohio. He and his wife, Lydia Bennett - also from New Jersey, are both buried in Butler Co., OH. He died in 1826 and she in 1867.

Their second child was Samuel Bennett Demoret (James Franklin's grandfather), who was born in Ohio in 1798. In 1819 he married Rebecca Balser, daughter of George and Rebecca (Honnell) Balser. As a Justice of the Peace, he performed the marriage ceremony in 1834 for his younger brother, Bartholomew, to Rebecca's younger sister, Elizabeth Balser. Samuel was a farmer. He and his family left Ohio and moved to Montgomery Co., IN, in the mid-1840's, where his wife died in 1867 and he in 1887.

James F. Demoret, Clara A. Sayler - Their Wedding Day Nov. 27, 1879

Bartholomew was the seventh child of Samuel and Rebecca. He was born in Ohio in 1831 (1832) and moved to Indiana with his family when a teenager. In 1856 he married Mary Ann Whitenack and they had four children, the first of whom was James Franklin (above). After his wife's untimely death in 1865 he married Phoebe Eliza Clouse and they had several children. In the 1880's they moved to Franklin, KS, where he died in 1906 and she in 1923. He too was a farmer.

James Franklin Demoret, born in 1857, married Clara Ann Sayler, daughter of William T. and Malinda (Clodfelter) Sayler on Nov. 27, 1879. (see picture) Two children were born in Indiana before the family moved to Coffee Co., KS where three more were born. He was a farmer. Times were hard and in 1899 the family returned to Indiana and settled in New Market, where they were devoted members of the Methodist Church. Clara died in 1927 and James F. in 1931.

Their five children were: Grace M., who married Thomas Servies; Myrtle B., who married William Gott; Roy H., who married Edith Grenard; Mary Alice, who married Otis E. Hall; and Hazel C., who married Byron Busenbark. Four of these couples settled in Indiana and raised their families there. However, one of them, Mary and Otis E. Hall, who was superintendent of schools in Montgomery County, left Crawfordsville in 1914 and moved to Manhattan, KS for a few years, then to Springfield, MA. Otis died in 1936 and Mary Demoret Hall in 1975. *Submitted by Naomi Hall Talmadge (third daughter of Mary D. and Otis E. Hall; granddaughter of James F.)*

DR. ELLIOTT DETCHON

Dr. Elliott Detchon was born Mar. 15, 1828 in Portage Co., OH. He was a member of a large family of which the father died at a young age. It is not known whether his Mother re-married or not.

He graduated from Linnean Academy in northern Ohio in 1846 and was very proficient in Math and the sciences. He graduated from Medical College in Cleveland, OH.

In 1848 he came, with his brother-in-law, Dr. John Simison, down the Ohio from Cleveland to Toledo, then down the Canal (Wabash to Lafayette, IN). Dr. Simpson remained and set up practice, which Dr. Detchon went on to Parke Co., IN, where he taught school for sometime. It is said that in his youth he worked side by side with John D. Rockefeller in the hay fields of Ohio.

On July 4, 1848, in Rockville, he was joined in marriage with Martha Jane Agnew, born Dec. 20, 1828 in Rockville, the daughter of Mr. and Mrs. Gibson Agnew. They were members of the Cumberland Presbyterian Church in Rockville.

He evidently settled first in Montgomery County, near New Richmond, where he became the typical "Country Dr.", being called out all hours of the day and night. He also doctored in Wingate, Newtown and Crawfordsville, as well as New Richmond.

He and Martha Jane were to become the parents of seven children, all born in Montgomery County: one child was born and died in infancy and is buried in New Richmond Cemetery; Erwin Agnew, (1850-1928) married Annabelle (Lee) June 16, 1892, (1857-1959); Emma, (1857-1907), m. William R. Garver, Oct. 20, 1880; Mattie, (1869-1938), m., William M. White (1863-1931), on May 4, 1892; Seymour Gibson, (1863-1938), m., Alice Williams (1873-1962); Ada M. (1869-1955), m., Frank Gonzales Oct. 28, 1896; Harriet (1871-1951) m., Oct. 28, 1902 Charles Frye McIntire (1864-1919).

Dr. Detchon upon moving to Crawfordsville, built a beautiful home on the corner of Wabash and Green St. where "Walt's Mobile Station" now stands. It was a very large and stately mansion. According to his Grandson Lee, when asked how many rooms it had, his comment was "he didn't really know but he wanted to make sure there was a room for everyone", so as you can see from the size of his family it had to be quite large. I would like to have inserted a picture of it, but his Grandson was afraid of losing it and I can't say that I blame him, but the best I remember it resembled a great deal the home of Lee on East Wabash, which is now owned by Mr. and Mrs. Jack Frees.

Dr. Detchon passed away Dec. 29, 1905 and his wife June 7, 1908. His family is all buried in the Family Burial Plot in Oak Hill Cemetery, Section 8.

LEE DETCHON

Lee Detchon, well known artist of Crawfordsville was born there, July 13, 1900. He was the son of Irwin Agnew and Annabelle (Lee) Detchon.

His parents were married in a beautiful ceremony at the home of his Grandmother, Mrs. Sallie Lee on West College St. According to the accounting of the wedding, the house was decorated with different types and colors of roses in each room. It was held at 8:00 P.M. and the music was provided by The Music Hall Orchestra. A large reception was held in the dining room of that home.

There was just one other child born to this couple, Esther Detchon who later became Mrs. Arch Olds and they, too lived on East Wabash Ave.

Lee Detchon

Lee, the subject of this sketch attended school in Crawfordsville and graduated from Crawfordsville High School. He then entered Wabash College and graduated from there in 1923. While attending Wabash he was a member of Beta Theta Pi, was a member of the Wabash Glee Club and also had his own orchestra while there.

He was a very creative child and studied, privately, here with Fritz Schlemmer. He has Fritz's painting easel, which sits in front of the big window in his home, however he has sold this home and it is not known whether he sold the easel with it or not. I was told, when I talked to him, to gain information for this story that "the people that bought the house have kept his studio as it was and have no plans to change it, only that they would like to obtain some of his paintings for it."

In May of 1947 he was united in marriage with Mary Hannah Peterson, daughter of James and Jessie Peterson. She was born in 1907 and passed away in 1963.

Some of his activities are: President of the Art League, Indiana Artists Club and is a member of the First Methodist Church.

He has had numerous showings, but could not recall but two of them at the time. They were with the New York Historical Society and the Museum in Washington, D.C.

Since selling his big house on East Wabash, he now resides in the home of his sister and her husband, which he inherited upon their deaths. It is a very beautiful home, decorated in the period of the structure, however his paintings have been added. His favorite painting hangs above the davenport in the Family Room. It is a painting of his convertible, which I assume was his first car. His first painting that he did (a large vase of Peonies) hangs on the wall in the living room. The upstairs in the home is almost like a gallery and was very pleasant to visit. *Written by Gwen Frees*

CHARLES L. DeVORE FAMILY

Keith and Esther DeVore bought the old Ben Evans farm north of Crawfordsville on U.S. 231 in 1957. His son Charles L. DeVore and his young family moved from Macon, IL in February of 1958 to the farm in Union Township. Charles had farmed in Illinois and continued to work the land in Montgomery County.

Charles, fourth child of Keith and Esther Merris DeVore, graduated from Lovington High School. He married Lois E. Cummins, daughter of Max and Helen Cummins, in 1947 Lovington, IL. Charles' parents farmed and raised cattle in Illinois and Lois' parents ran a gas station in Lovington. After their marriage they lived near La Place, IL, then moved to a farm near Macon.

Front - Charles, Lois. Back - Howard, Mike, Dee Ann (DeVore) Cabell and Ted DeVore

In Montgomery County, Charles has been an active supporter of 4-H, and has served on the board of directors for the Montgomery County Co-op for many years. Charles and Lois are members of the First United Methodist Church in Crawfordsville. Lois has served as Sunday school teacher, in the church women's society and for many years has worked at the Wesley Thrift Shop.

They have four children: Dee Ann DeVore Cabell, born in 1948; Ted DeVore, born in 1950; Howard DeVore, born in 1959 and Michael DeVore, born in 1960. Dee Ann and Ted graduated from Crawfordsville High School; Howard and Mike graduated from North Montgomery High School.

Dee Ann graduated from Purdue in 1971 in Vocational Home Economics education and married Bruce Cabell, son of John and Norma Cabell of Corydon, IN. Bruce graduated from the Capitol Page School in Washington D.C. and from Purdue in Ag Econ. They have settled in Montgomery County and farm on the Logan farm in Wayne Township. They have three children: Nancy, born in 1968, a student at Purdue; Karen, born in 1971, a senior at North Montgomery; and Mark, born in 1975, an eighth grader at Northridge Middle School.

Ted married Brenda Gorman, daughter of Harold and Louise Gorman in 1970. Ted and Brenda farm on 700 N. and raise hogs and sheep and grains. They have two children: Laura, born in 1972, a junior at North Montgomery, and LuAnn, born in 1975, a seventh grader at Northridge.

Howard moved from Indiana to Arizona in 1978 and married Cindy Weirick in 1981. They have one child Ashley, born in 1987. Howard is a mechanic and has gotten advanced training with Chevrolet and is a drive-ability specialist. He currently lives in Flagstaff, AZ.

Mike lives north of Crawfordsville in the old farmhouse and also farms. He married Vonica Elmore, daughter of Ed and Sue Elmore of Darlington. They have twins Brian and Tiffany, born in 1981. Mike's second marriage is to Diana Cooper.
Submitted by Dee Ann Cabell

LAWRENCE E. AND MABEL (KELSEY) DeVORE

Many Crawfordsville residents will remember Lawrence and Mabel DeVore and their influence on our County. Mr. DeVore was a prominent business man for over a half-century here and his wife was quite active in the community.

Lawrence E. DeVore was born in Greencastle May 31, 1887, the son of Henry V. and Allie Evans DeVore. Sadness due to death entered his life at an early age — his father died when he was four. The family moved to Crawfordsville where he graduated from high school in 1907. He then earned a degree from Wabash College. He was a founder of the Tau Kappa Alpha honorary oratorical fraternity while there.

Upon graduation, Mr. DeVore became a member of the Evans-DeVore farm loan company and was made branch manager (1936) for Mutual Benefit.

On Jan. 13, 1953, Mr. DeVore was elected President of the First National Bank — served three years. He also served as Chairman of the Board.

Mr. DeVore served as President of the Chamber of Commerce and during his term the first boulevard lights were installed in the city and the paved road from Crawfordsville to Indianapolis was approved and constructed.

His love for Wabash never waned. He was trustee for 18 years and was Chairman of the building committee when Waugh Hall, the Student Center, and Morris and Wolcott dorms were built. The Crawfordsville Country Club was also dear to his heart as he served for 36 years as a director. He was also a member of Rotary.

Mabel was the daughter of John P. and Ada (Drake) Kelsey. She was born in Linden on Dec. 16, 1889. She graduated from CHS in her future husband's class. She graduated with high honors from Vassar in 1911.

Returning to Montgomery County, Mabel married Lawrence in Linden on June 26, 1912.

Mabel was active in Needleworkers, Current Events, Art League, Delta Kappa Gamma, Dorothy Q Chapter, DAR, Republic Women, Red Cross, Girl Scouts and Flower Lovers.

Death continued to follow Lawrence, as the couple lost all three of their children; leaving no descendants. Davy (David Kelsey) died in 1921 at age eight, Margaret Evans DeVore (June 2, 1916 - Nov. 22, 1958) and Margaret's twin sister (died at birth). Lawrence was found dead in his attic (403 E. Wabash) at noon on Monday, Apr. 8, 1963. His widow died June 26, 1970 in Wesley Manor (Frankfort).

The DeVores were active members of the Methodist Church and their influence in the community was indeed great!

MICHAEL WILLIAM DeVOTO

Michael William DeVoto, born in Parke Co., IN Aug. 9, 1890, moved to Montgomery County in the early 1920's. He was the seventh child of Louis Arthur and Jane Magnant DeVoto, who moved to Mansfield, IN in 1888 from Chicago where Louis Arthur had been employed as a stone cutter by Chicago and Indiana Brownstone Company.

Michael "Mike" began his career working in the Mansfield flour mill owned by Rohm Brothers. From Mansfield he moved to Marshall, IN, where he also operated a mill.

He was married to Grace Tague, daughter of Thomas Morton and Eva Wade Tague, on Dec. 19, 1912. To them were born in Marshall Arthur M. DeVoto Sept. 13, 1913, and Mildred Evelyn July 22, 1914 d. Jan. 22, 1915.

Grace Tague, Arthur M. DeVoto and Michael Wm.

During World War I, the subject moved to Philadelphia where he worked in the shipyards. Returning to Crawfordsville after the war, he worked for Mid-States Steel & Wire, various construction firms, and the City of Crawfordsville as an electrician.

Three more children were born to Mike and Grace: Donald Edwin Feb. 27, 1918, Lois Ellen June 4, 1923, and Doris J. Mar. 12, 1932.

Arthur M. DeVoto, who died Aug. 1, 1985, was an electrical engineer employed by Sverdrup and Parcel, Architects. He was engineer on such projects as the Cyclatron in Chicago; subway in Washington, D.C.; the New Orleans Stadium, the power plant in Madison, IN; and was loaned to the copper mines in Arizona as a consulting engineer. He was also Resident Engineer on the construction of the Busch Stadium in St. Louis. He was married to Marjorie Bolinger June 4, 1938, and they were parents of John Wayne b. Jan. 6, 1944 d. Aug. 18, 1944; Jachalyn Joyce b. June 16, 1946 and David Harold b. Aug. 25, 1947.

Donald Edwin received his degree from Wabash College, where his honors included Phi Beta Kappa membership, First Rank in Comprehensives, and General Honors. He taught at Wabash 1939-41 and left that position for employment with R.R. Donnelley, where he remained until 1957. In 1959 he established his own counselling firm which was titled DeVoto & Barry Partners, Ltd., Riverside Plaza, Chicago. Donald married Madonna Warner Sept. 26, 1942, and to them were born two sons: Donald Eric Apr. 22, 1948 and Craig W. Apr. 6, 1955. Don, now retired, and Madonna now reside in Oak Brook, IL and Naples, FL.

Lois Ellen received a Bachelor of Science degree in Business Administration from Indiana University and was employed variously by Plastene Corporation, Ladoga Federal Savings and Loan, and in later years as Business Manager and Treasurer of Brazil Public Library. She married Robert E. Myers Apr. 13, 1946, and they are the parents of Mark b. Oct. 14, 1955 and Matthew b. May 26, 1958. Lois and her husband Robert, a retired pharmacist, currently live in Brazil, IN.

Doris Jane, presently employed by Impex Corporation, married Donald E. Bishop, a Production Manager for R.R. Donnelley, on Sept. 26, 1950, and they have two sons: Michael b. Sept. 25, 1951 and Robert H. b. Sept. 8, 1952.

Michael William DeVoto died May 17, 1953 in Crawfordsville, and his wife, Grace, died Aug. 12, 1965. Prepared by Lois Myers

KARL ANTHONY "KNOBBY" DICKERSON

Karl Anthony "Knobby" Dickerson was born in Bloomington, IN Dec. 18, 1905 the son of George W. Dickerson Jr., and Opal Snyder Dickerson. The family moved to Crawfordsville within the next year. His mother died 1918. He lived at 200 W. Market Street the home of his Dickerson grandparents. He attended Mills school and graduated from Crawfordsville High School 1925. He was an All State high school basketball player. He refereed high school and college basketball games for 25 years. He was a player and manager of Crawfordsville Merchants Baseball team. He enjoyed golf, and played with his son in many tournaments. He was elected to the Indiana Basketball Hall of Fame. He was a member of Wabash Avenue Presbyterian Church, and the Elks Lodge.

Mary Jeannette Herron was born in Crawfordsville, May 16, 1906 the daughter of Joseph Croy Herron and Mary Armantrout Herron. She lived at 519 E. Wabash Avenue. She attended Willson school and graduated from Crawfordsville High School 1925. She was active in school organizations, attended DePauw University. She is a member of Art League, Current Events and Tri Kappa. She is a member of Montgomery County Mental Health and volunteers each month at Logansport State Hospital. Serves on the board of Montgomery County Cultural Foundation. An active member of the Wabash Avenue Presbyterian Church. Former President of Church Women United in Indiana. She was 1987 Jefferson Award winner.

Karl A. Dickerson and Mary Jeannette Herron were married March 1930. They have one son, Karl Joseph Dickerson who lives in Indianapolis. Karl was a graduate of Wabash College, Masters Degree from Michigan University. Served in the United States Army two years. He has a Real Estate business in Indianapolis. Karl and Mary Jeannette have four grandchildren, Julia Reim, Janet King, Jeanette Dickerson and Karl A. Dickerson, one great-grandson Lucas K. King.

Karl had business interests in Crawfordsville. He drew the plans for his home at 1015 W. Pike Street. He was employed at Elston Bank 18 years. He was Cashier at the Farmers State Bank, New Ross, IN for 25 years. He retired in 1970. He died 1976.

Karl's grandparents were George W. Dickerson Sr., and Mary Coyle Dickerson. Mr. Dickerson owned a grocery store. Samuel Clark Snyder and Frances Catherin Cope Snyder. Mr. Snyder was a farmer. Karl had one sister Mary Virginia Burke, brothers Earl and Ralph Dickerson deceased. Philip, Edward, and Paul of Crawfordsville.

Mary Jeannette's grandparents were Eli Frederick Armantrout and Mary Catherine Davidson Armantrout. Eli was a farmer. Also Post Master and Justice of Peace in North Union, IN South of Crawfordsville. Howard Franklin Herron and Jennettie Croy Herron owned horses and kept a livery stable on E. Pike Street. All descendents of early settlers in Montgomery.

Mary Jeannette has a sister Regina Allhands, brothers Howard Eli and Joseph D. Herron deceased. Her mother died 1920. Later her father married Elma Conn Quillen, they had one son Winton Conn Herron, her half-brother.

My father transmitted to me a sound heredity on his own side, and he gave me a good mother. *By Alice Stone Blackwell*

ARTHUR AND ELIZABETH (BECK) DICKSON

Elizabeth Beck, the seventh youngster of Henry and Sarah Beck, was born in North Carolina Aug. 27, 1820. Elizabeth was eight when her father remarried and 12 when her father and family moved from Union County to Montgomery Co., IN.

On Sept. 20, 1838 she married Arthur Dickson in Fayette Co., IN. Elizabeth may have met Arthur when visiting her sister, Charity McMahan, who lived in the area where they were married.

Arthur worked in agriculture in Fayette County, when the 1840 census was taken, and in 1852 moved to Knightstown, in Henry County. Here, they purchased a seven room house with intentions of turning it into a night-house, tavern combination. Two years later, they sold this house and bought 120 acres in Montgomery County.

Arthur and Betsy's first five children included James, Henry, William, Sarepta and Josiah. Charles Albert was born Aug. 24, 1855, Fletcher Mar. 15, 1857 and Oliver in October of 1860. On May 11, 1860, their only girl, Sarepta, died and was buried in Shannondale Cemetery. But in the spring of 1863 another little girl, Rosella, was born, much to the delight of Arthur and Betsy. This event was announced by Elizabeth's sister, Eliza Buchanan in a letter, "Betsy has a fine daughter and is saucy of it and Arthur almost had to take his bed over it."

In November of 1868, Eliza Buchanan expressed interest that Arthur and Betsy's boys were not married as yet. The boys answered by stating that they would get around to it "one of these days." And they did! At 28, James Madison married Mary Ann Booher on Mar. 19, 1870. William R. married Elizabeth Jane Cox on Feb. 28, 1872. Josiah married Arminda Rhoads Feb. 28, 1879. Fletcher and Rosella married a brother and sister, Mary E. and Willis L. Hart, and Oliver married Mary Logan. Charles Albert married at least twice.

Betsy died on May 8, 1890 at age 69 and Arthur died Feb. 12, 1904 at age 86. Both are buried in Pisgah Cemetery in Montgomery County near Beckville. Their grave site is marked by a beautiful large stone. *By Stanley C. Beck, condensed by permission by Roger G. Spurgeon Sr.*

JAMES MADISON AND MARY ANN (BOOHER) DICKSON

James Madison Dickson was the son of Arthur and Elizabeth (Beck) Dickson. He was born in Fayette Co., IN on July 24, 1841 and was the eldest of nine children.

On Mar. 10, 1870 at the age of 28, he married Mary Ann Booher. It is not known at this writing all the places that he lived, but in his later years he farmed property between Darlington and Shannondale. After he quit farming, he moved to Beckville. Both, James and Mary, stayed with their children in their old age, rotating between them. Their children were: Quency, Omer, Artie, Rena, Cena, Waldo, Edgar and Ella.

James died at his eldest son, Quency's home when he was about 89 years old. Quency lived in the first house east of the old grocery store in Shannondale. Mary Ann died at her daughter, Ella's home in Thorntown. Both were buried in the Lutheran Cemetery, located between Darlington and Shannondale. By *Roger G. Spurgeon, Sr.*

WALDO FERMAN AND ANNA JANE (JOSEPH) DICKSON

Waldo Ferman Dickson was the son of James Madison and Mary Ann (Booher) Dickson. He was born Aug. 23, 1885 southeast of Darlington on a farm in the Shannondale area. When he was growing up, wrestling and foot races were common sport among the young people, and Waldo could compete well in both. During his latter years, stories he told confirmed his interest and participation in these events. Also, he attended church functions, regularly, which were the main social events of the time. Waldo once stated that the best place to meet a girl was at church. In one of these church meetings, the daughter of the traveling evangelist, Anna Jane Joseph, noticed this fun loving, social minded gentleman, and whispered to her sister that he was the one she would marry. Had Waldo known her plans for him, he might have put off his straight forward way of introducing himself until a later time. After church services, he walked up to Anna, grabbed her and planted a kiss squarely on her lips. His fate was sealed, for on July 5, 1911, Rev. George S. Joseph walked his daughter down the church aisle and gave Anna in marriage to Waldo.

Anna was the daughter of Rev. George S. and Rachel M. (Mason) Joseph. Rachel's parents were Jesse M. and Anna (Marley) Mason, and both came to Indiana from North Carolina. George preached for several community churches. The Pisgah Church near Beckville was one of his churches. George never accepted a salary, but accepted gifts from the members as payment. Besides being a Baptist preacher, he was a full time farmer as well.

Waldo and Anna made their first home near Mace. Waldo rented 40 acres of woods from his father-in-law, built a three room house, cleared the land and farmed it. He later bought this land. Their first child, Alma, was born premature and died after her birth in 1912. Doris D. was born in 1915, Leah L. in 1917, Paul E. in 1925 and Wilma R. in 1931. As well as raising four children in this small house, Waldo took his turn keeping his aging widowed mother.

In 1941, Waldo sold this farm and moved to another farm northeast of New Richmond, IN. This was a welcome move for the family, since the newly boughten house had seven rooms. Then in 1948, Waldo moved his family for the last time to the town of Linden. Here, he ran a slaughter house and during the summer, built fences. He invented a tool that stretched fences and had a patent on it. Waldo and Anna also started a greenhouse business and, Waldo made lawn ornaments, among other items, in his workshop behind their house. By 1949, their children had married and started families of their own. Doris was married to George W. Bottom, Leah to Orville Whitehead and then Carl T. Rohr, Paul to Edith Swank and Wilma to Cletis Birge.

Waldo and Anna never really retired as they grew older but, kept busy with their greenhouse business and garden. Waldo was always tinkering in his workshop. Waldo and Anna always expected their family over for Thanksgiving and Christmas dinners or any other time. For them, it was always convenient to have family and friends visit them. They were blessed by seeing all their grandchildren grow to adulthood and saw many of their great-grandchildren as well. Anna died in their home at Linden on Aug. 11, 1971, and Waldo died in the Ben

Hur nursing home Oct. 11, 1974, in Crawfordsville, IN. All who knew these two liked their company and loved them both. *By Roger G. Spurgeon, Sr.*

GEORGE THEODORE DILLMAN

George Theodore Dillman, the son of John and Ellen Dillman, was born in Newburgh, IN Oct. 2, 1864 and died Dec. 12, 1929.

He first came to Montgomery County in the 1880's, to be employed by the Mahorney Bros. Hardware and Tinning Co. of Crawfordsville.

In 1890 he came to Waveland with a one horse wagon, $19.00 and his tinning tools.

He established a tinning business and a harness making and harness repair shop. As time went on the hardware business and the livery business were incorporated in the enterprise.

December 28, 1892 he married Atha Putnam of Glenwood, IN. To this union were born three children, Garrie L., Maxwell C. and his twin sister Mabel.

The business continued as a family partnership through the years of World War I.

In 1914 Garrie married Mabel Lough, daughter of Henry Harrison "Tip" Lough and Sarah Jane Lough. Max served in the U.S. Marines during World War I.

Garrie continued to work in the business and also was holding a job as night fireman on the Central Indiana R.R. "Owl Run". A railrun of Central Indiana coal to the city of Anderson, IN.

Early in the 1920s a contract was signed with The John Deere Plow Co. and also the International Harvester Co., and the firm entered the Farm Implement business. At this time all of the business was conducted from the "John Fisher Building" and the Livery Building across from the Waveland Library.

Atha Dillman passed away in 1927 and George in 1929.

The partnership was dissolved and Garrie became sole owner of the business.

Max and Mabel and their families moved to Los Angeles, CA.

Max married Margaret McNutt and Mabel married Phillip Seibert.

Max and Margaret raised two children, Dick and Diana. Phil and Mabel had one daughter, Suzanne.

In 1928 the cement block building was constructed, where the business was maintained until it was sold to Phil Hunsicker.

In 1935 the Geo. W. Deere Hardware at 127 N. Washington St. in Crawfordsville was purchased by the Dillman family.

Garrie and Robert ran that store and Norman ran the Waveland store.

During these years the farm land of Wm. Mitchell, Robert Canine, Wm. Glenn and Von Timmons was acquired as their estates were settled by Garrie. Later the Graham and Kritz land on the Russellville Road was acquired.

In 1938 the Company purchased the Ladoga Hardware. This store was later sold to Charles Travis, who had managed it for some time.

Garrie and Mabel Dillman raised four children, Norman, Martha, Robert and Harriett. Norman managed the Waveland store until his entry into the Service. He served in the U.S. Marine Corps during World War II and after the war came back to Crawfordsville, where he and Garrie operated the John Deere Implement business. During this period Garrie was appointed as a Director of the Elston Bank and Trust Co., a position he cherished for the remainder of his life.

The John Deere Implement business was sold to Montgomery County Implement Co. in 1964.

Norman was employed by the McDaniel Freight Lines of Crawfordsville. He later served as Montgomery County Commissioner. He and his wife, Ruby, are now retired and live in Crawfordsville.

Martha was employed in both the Hardware and Implement business. She and her husband, Hubert Massing are now retired in Crawfordsville.

Robert managed the Hardware until it was taken over by Maurine Armstrong Dillman, who is the present owner. Robert passed away in 1986. His wife Betty and stepdaughter Becky are now living in Crawfordsville.

Harriett now resides with her husband Woodrow Harshman in Sebring, FL. Harriett has three children: Anne Scott of Napoleon, IN, Jane Gross of Charlotte, NC and Phil Coon who lives in Teffner, IL. Norman's son, Malcolm Curtis, lives on Crawfordsville R.R. His three daughters Jackie, Jodie, and Janie represent five generations of Montgomery County Dillmans. *Submitted by Norman Dillman*

MARY EMMA FULLENWIDER DOOLEY

Note: Mary Emma Fullenwider was born in Montgomery Co., IN, Oct. 27, 1899 to Samuel "Winter" and Mary Elizabeth (Rice) Fullenwider.

My roots run deep in the history of Montgomery County, as my great grandparents came to Montgomery County in 1822 with a wagon train to the Court House (then a log building housing the Land Office). There were government-authorized men who showed people around to available government land for sale. When you made your selection you returned to the Court House to make application for a Deed which was sent to Washington, D.C. There, the Deed was printed (white sheepskin) and signed by the President (Andrew Jackson at that time). I have seen this deed.

Grandfather David Fullenwider bought land on the Montgomery/Parke County line just west of Waveland, where I grew-up.

My parents were born in Montgomery and Parke counties of pioneer stock and educated in the Waveland schools (graduated from Waveland Presbyterian Academy). Mother was a successful school teacher while being active in church and community affairs. Father remained on the family farm with his parents (David and Elizabeth Moxley Fullenwider). All this while, Father and Mother were good friends, and in 1896, they were married and made their home on his family's farm. Father was a farmer, a friendly person and a student of agriculture. He was an avid reader. He had the first grain binder (McCormick-Deering reaper) in the area; also the first riding plows. He sent away for a new hay seed called alfalfa. Many neighbors and strangers came to see this new crop. Good horses were his pride for they were the pulling power on the farms in those days. I was brought up a farm girl. My faithful pony brought the cows from pasture at milking time in the evening. Mother raised lots of chickens and they were to be fed and watered. Eggs were to be gathered often to keep them fresh. Then there were meals to help prepare and dishes to wash. The farm was a busy place, but fun!

In 1921, I married Owen R. Dooley. I had met him at a party in a relative's home months before. He was a Marine who had returned from France having served his country for 18 months during WWI. We lived on the Fullenwider farm, worked hard and enjoyed life and friends.

To this union was born two sons, James and Robert. The boys helped on the farm and were interested in their church and school. They had 4-H projects in livestock and grain and won their share of Blue Ribbons. Jim went to college in North Carolina, then Denver, CO. Both boys served their country (Air Force). Returning home from the military service, Jim met and married school teacher, Pat Hays. Their son, David and wife, Judy, have three daughters, Sheri and twins, Michelle and Melinda. They live at the Fullenwider Homestead. Jim's daughter, Mary Ann has a son, James and lives in Las Vegas, NV where she works with computers in the Court House.

Robert Dooley and wife, Donna have three grown children: Sgt. Timothy Dooley is with the Military Service in Germany. Jonathan teaches in a government school in Ganado, AZ. Jennifer just graduated from College where she majored in Art.

In 1979, Owen and I retired from the farm and moved to Waveland, where I now live. Owen died Jan. 16, 1985. I layed him to rest in the Bethany Cemetery east of Marshall, his home community that he loved.

I live in a friendly, nice neighborhood, near the stores and post office. My sons and their families are so dear and care for me. I am truly fortunate — May God Bless You All! W*ritten by Mary Emma Dooley, almost 90!*

JEREMIAH DOUGLAS

Jeremiah Douglas, son of Jeremiah I and Anna Asbridge Douglas (born February or May 1, 1767 in England) in the War of 1812 in Ohio died Oct. 15, 1837 in Madison, Jefferson Co., IN. He had married Jane Huthert. She came to Montgomery Co., IN after his death, and in 1850 census she was living with her daughter and her son-in-law, Henry and Mary Douglas Redenbaugh, age 83. 1830 census of Jefferson Co., IN gave Jeremiah as between 60 and 70 years of age.

Their children were Annie Douglas married William Wells; Eliza Douglas married James Fisher; Mary 1799 Liverpool England, died Nov. 15, 1890 and married Henry Redenbaugh born 1800 and died here Sept. 11, 1856, son of Frederick and Margaret Haney Redenbaugh. Mariah Douglas married James Phillips; William Willoby Douglas married Katherine Sheaver; Jane Douglas married ? Rose; Jeremiah III born 1803/9 married Mary Catherine Redenbaugh on Mar. 21, 1825 in Jefferson Co., IN, daughter of Frederick and Margaret Haney Redenbaugh and she died Nov. 22, 1876 in Montgomery County. He married a second time to Elizabeth Redenbaugh born 1805 Hamilton Co., OH. I couldn't find his marriage license to Elizabeth, but his wife in 1880 census was Elizabeth. Their children were Jane Douglas born 1826 died between 1857 and 1859, for she had a child born in 1857, and her husband, Benjamin Hardin Elrod (married Aug. 10, 1847) remarried. Samuel Douglas born Aug. 21, 1827 married Hannah Surface; Jeremiah IV born 1832 married Martha Mitchell Mar. 11, 1856; John Douglas born 1833 married Amelia Mitchell on Dec. 6, 1860 and went to Kansas, then to California. Margaret Ann Douglas born Aug. 19, 1835 married Edward McMullen on Jan. 23, 1853; William H. Douglas born 1837 married Elizabeth McCain on Sept. 5, 1861; Henry Douglas born July 19, 1839 married Matilda Faust on Nov. 5, 1858; he married a second time to Melissa Alice Labaw French on Jan. 30, 1881; Edwin Douglas born 1842 married Mary Thompson on Aug. 7, 1860. All of these marriages in Montgomery Co., IN. Alonzo Douglas born in 1847; James Douglas born in 1846. *Submitted by Pauline Walters*

JEREMIAH AND MARTHA (MITCHELL) DOUGLAS

Jeremiah Douglas was born in Montgomery Co., IN, May 28, 1832, the third of the ten children of Jeremiah Douglas, a basketmaker, and Mary Catherine (Redenbaugh) Douglas. His grandfather, also named Jeremiah Douglas, lost an arm in the War of 1812. The family had come to the area in the early years of Montgomery County from Scotland via Hinton, KY and Madison, IN. Jeremiah married Martha Jane Mitchell, daughter of Gabriel and Ruth (Van Cleave) Mitchell, in Montgomery County on Mar. 11, 1856. They brought four children into the world. They were James Lewis Douglas (b. 1857-d. 1889) who married his cousin, Levina Catherine Douglas, Amanda Jane Douglas, who died unmarried at age 20 in 1878, Mary Hanna Douglas (b. 1864-d. 1953) who became the wife of George Washington Burk, and Mariah Louella Douglas (b. 1872-d. 1914) who married John J. Cox.

Back row: Mary Hanna Douglas and James Lewis Douglas. Front row: Martha Jane (Mitchell) Douglas, Mariah Louella Douglas and Jeremiah Douglas

Jeremiah was a farmer well-known in early Montgomery County. Like his father he owned land a mile and a half east of Whitesville. This land was sold in 1873, when Jeremiah, his wife, children, and parents relocated northwest of New Market.

He passed away on June 28, 1907, at the age of 75 of stomach trouble and heart disease after having been confined to his bed for six weeks prior to his death. We get an interesting insight into the family history from a line in his obituary. It reads, "For years the deceased lived in the hope that he would share in a large fortune which was coming to the Douglas family from Scotland." No doubt this referred to the family legend that Jeremiah's great-grandfather Douglas had been murdered the night he was to take over his inheritance...a family estate in Scotland.

Martha Jane's death came on Feb. 10, 1914. Interestingly, her daughter, Mariah "Louella," who was living at the same home at the time, died the very next day at the age of 42. Martha was just two weeks short of 82 at the time of her passing.

GEORGE WILSON AND JULIA ANN HARDEE DOWDEN

George Wilson Dowden born Mar. 26, 1845 Brown Township, Montgomery Co., IN. Died Jan. 29, 1928 Montgomery County, married Julia Ann Hardee Sept. 13, 1868. He attended college at Greencastle, IN. He loved nature and his last residence was on the banks of Sugar Creek at Bluff Mills (Deers Mill). She was born July 14, 1851 near Offield Creek in Montgomery Co., IN. (The daughter of Joseph H. Hardee and Mary Jane Weir, granddaughter of John Michael Joseph Hardee Revolutionary War Soldier buried in Michael Cemetery this county). Their children were: Lillie Theadocia married Sylvester Keller had Lottie Miles, Charles, Blanch Bowman, Earl, Maude Mitchell, Lon, Ralph, Berniece Heavilin and Roy; Alaska; Bert had Mary Ann, Gertrude Sering and Frank; Pearl Long had Ruby Tague, Kathleen Cochran, Ora, Julia Morrow, Joseph, George and Rosemary Delano; Joseph had Audrey Morrell Rabideux, Louise Miller Scott, Myrtle Spindler, Mary Lytle and Vernon; Eva; Walter had Bernice Henry; Elzie; and Josephine Scott had Byron, Garnal and Eunice Richardson.

His father, Nathaniel, was born Aug. 20, 1821 in Shelby Co., KY married Oct. 21, 1841 Montgomery Co., IN to Theadocia Ann Bayless born Jan. 17, 1823 Butler Co., OH to William and Elizabeth Grant Bayless from New Jersey.

His grandfather, James Dowden born in Virginia died 1831 in Kentucky, married Jan. 6, 1821 Shelby Co., KY to Roxannah Layne. She remarried Aug. 19, 1832 Shelby County to Jacob Hall. Due to encouragement from her brother, William Layne, they moved to Montgomery County with their children: Nathaniel, James and Martha Dowden; Mary Hall and William Hall. She is buried in Masonic Cemetery North at Crawfordsville.

Nathaniel and Theadocia bought acreage from William Conner in Brown Township in 1847, where they raised their children. She died July 16, 1876 and he Oct. 22, 1904 both buried at Freedom Cemetery in this county. Their children were: James, George, Abijah, Sarah Smith, Martha and John.

Great grandfather, Nathaniel Dowden married Agnes McClain 1787 in Mercer Co., KY. He died 1846 in Shelby Co., KY. His will was recorded in the same county. He bought land in 1814 at Clear Creek, KY. Their children were: Ashford, James, Catherine Knight, Nancy Knight, Susan Ransdall, Nathaniel Jr., Mary Freeman, George, Joshua, John, Mahala Underwood, Willis and Elizabeth Hall.

His great grandfather, Tarleton Layne, was born in Virginia, married Tabitha Minter. He was the son of Ayres and Mary Woodson Layne. Tabitha, the daughter of Anthony and Elizabeth Minter. She died 1845 in Montgomery Co., IN. Many of these names are recognized among this county's prominent early residents.

Julia A. Hardee's sister, Lucinda Hardee Nelson, was the grandmother of Fred Nelson Vance, one of Crawfordsville's prominent early artists. He was the son of George and Josephine Nelson Vance. His father was also a local artist. By *Garnal Lee Scott*

WILLARD PARKER DUNBAR AND IRMA CLAIRE (DYKES) DUNBAR

Willard and Irma were born and raised in Sugar Creek Township. Willard (Bill) was born Apr. 1, 1896, fifth child of Elias Peter and Emma Coe (Parker) Dunbar in the Abner Bowers homestead at Bowers, IN. His siblings were Mae, Lillian, Joseph, Austin, Harvey, Roscoe and Theodore.

Their mother, Emma Coe Parker, came from Delaware in 1887 to visit Parker relatives and stayed to marry. Their father, Elias Peter, was also born in the home of Abner Bowers, his grandfather, Feb. 14, 1861, two days after his own father Elias Dunbar died of typhoid fever. His mother, Esther Bowers, died when he was five, so he was raised by his grandfather, bought the farm from the heirs and farmed until retirement to Colfax in 1920.

L to R: Irma Claire (Dykes) Dunbar, Willard Parker Dunbar, Jr., Peter Bauer Dunbar, Jean Claire Dunbar, Samuel Dykes Dunbar, Willard Parker Dunbar 1949

Elias was born two miles west of Colfax in Sugar Creek Township on Aug. 27, 1835, to Lewis and Mary Powers Dunbar. Lewis was born near Hummelstown, PA, on Nov. 12, 1803 to Robert and Magdalena Bretz Dunbar. He married Mary Powers in Ohio in 1822 and settled in Ross Co., OH. In 1830 they moved to Sugar Creek Township. Dunbars descend from William Dunbar who arrived at Northumberland on the Rappahanock River, Virginia in May 1650. Mary was a granddaughter of Valentine Powers (See Bauer Family story).

Irma was born northeast of Bowers on the James Dykes homestead to James Edward (Ed) and Estella (Olinger) Dykes, July 5, 1902. Her sister and brother were Gladys and Clarence (Pat). Their mother died five days after Irma was born. Ed's brother, Samuel Adam, and his wife, Anna (Maguire) Dykes, adopted her and raised her as their own.

James Dykes, Irma's grandfather, was from Georgia. A Confederate, he was captured and imprisoned at Fort Delaware during the Civil War. After the war, he settled near Bowers and married Louisa Smith (Reference: *Montgomery County History* by Bowen). When their son Ed married Estella Olinger, she was a young teacher from near Browns Valley. Her father, David Olinger, a Confederate captured at Cumberland Gap and imprisoned at Camp Douglas near Chicago, came from Tennessee after the Civil War and was one of Montgomery County's earliest doctors. Her mother was Frances Caroline Coons, a direct descendant of Ralph Griffin who fought in the Revolutionary battles at Rocky Mount, Hanging Rock and Kings Mountain. All descendants are eligible for DAR and S.A.R.

Both Bill and Irma attended Bowers School. He was graduated in April, 1916, then transferred to Crawfordsville High School where he was graduated with another diploma six weeks later. She transferred to Crawfordsville after tenth grade and was graduated in 1920.

Bill attended Blue Ridge College, New Windsor, MD two years, served 14 months in the Army Medical Corps in WWI, six months at Camp Taylor, KY, during the flu epidemic of 1918, and completed his college studies at Manchester College, North Manchester, IN in 1921. He taught mathematics and athletics at Kokomo High School one year, then secured a teaching and coaching position at Culver Military Academy. While at Culver, he earned a U.S. Army Reserve commission and rose to the rank of Captain. In 1923 and 1929, he won the State Rifle Championships with the Springfield rifle. He also earned the Distinguished Rifleman rating in the National Matches held at Camp Perry, OH. He was a "Distinguished Marksman" and won appointment to the DEWAR and FIDAC teams, and "the President's Hundred." He was an amateur boxer in the Indiana AAU Championship competition, did graduate study at the University of Chicago, held membership in the Masonic Lodge and served as Post Commander (1929) of the William Alexander Fleet Post #103, American Legion. He served as a Special Deputy Sheriff, Marshall Co., IN from 1925-1931, and was a Life Member of the National Rifle Association. He was a member of Church of the Brethren at White Church, Sugar Creek Township.

Irma attended Oxford College, Oxford, OH one year, transferred to Butler University at Indianapolis, was a member of Pi Beta Phi sorority, a "Butler Beauty", active with the Butler Dramatic Club, and was graduated in 1924. She was active in "The Little Theatre Society of Indiana" (Civic Theatre), Culver Military theatricals, as a dramatic reader, and as a private teacher of dramatic art. She was a member of Potato Creek Methodist Church, Sugar Creek Township.

November 29, 1925, Willard and Irma eloped, were married in North Manchester before the congregation of a minister friend, and settled in Culver. While they lived there, three children were born: Jean Claire, Willard Parker, Jr. and Samuel Dykes.

As a result of the Great Depression, the family moved back to Bowers in 1931. Bill managed to save the Bowers homestead from foreclosure and purchased 80 acres of the Silas Dunbar (his father's uncle) estate in 1933. He later bought an adjoining 80 acres to the north. Their children were raised in the old Silas Dunbar home, a fine Italianate brick house built in 1877 of bricks baked of clay in the field across the road. In the early 1900s, Silas sold that field as part of a 40 acre parcel to Irma's father. It is still part of the Dykes estate.

Bill was recalled to active duty with the Army in 1935 to serve in the Civilian Conservation Corps. He was CCC Camp Commander at Medaryville, IN for six months, then returned home to build a registered, classified Holstein-Friesian dairy herd. Irma managed the farms and cared for the children during his absence. Their fourth child, Peter Bauer, was born in 1936.

They were active in subscribing Sugar Creek Township residents for REMC which brought electricity in 1938 and they founded the Bowers area 4-H Club. They were active members of Farm Bureau.

Irma continued to teach dramatics and gave popular dramatic reading programs for various organizations until her retirement. In later years she served as president of the township Home Economics Club and the Bowers School PTA, was state Recommendations Chairman for Pi Beta Phi, and a member of Book Lovers Club, Darlington, and Dorothy Q. Chapter (Crawfordsville) National Society Daughters of the American Revolution. Bill became noted for his fine herd of Holsteins and his progressive farming and conservation methods. The family became members of the Thorntown Presbyterian Church.

All the children attended Bowers School through tenth grade and were graduated from Crawfordsville High School: Jean, 1945; Bill Jr., 1947; Sam, 1949; Pete, 1954. The three boys returned to Culver Military Academy for Woodcraft summer camp. Jean was graduated from Indiana University, 1949. Bill, Jr. attended Wabash College two years and Purdue University one year before serving four years as a pilot in the United States Air Force; he was graduated from Purdue, January 1958. Sam went one semester to Purdue, joined the United States Air Force and spent three years in England, returned to Purdue and was graduated June 1958; he earned a Master's degree in Business Administration from Auburn University August 1970. Pete was graduated from Harvard College June 1958, served with the United States Naval Air Forces in Japan four years, and earned his Master's degree from the Krannert School of Management at Purdue August 1965.

Bill died Mar. 8, 1960, leaving their 320 acres of land to Irma. She continued living in the Silas Dunbar home and running the business until April 1988. She presently resides in a retirement home in Carmel, IN. *Submitted by Jean Socolowski*

WILLARD PARKER DUNBAR JR.

Willard (Bill) was born Dec. 27, 1929 in Epworth Memorial Hospital, South Bend, IN, the second child of Willard and Irma Dunbar (see history in this book). He lived in Culver, IN till 1931 when the family moved back to Sugar Creek Township and lived with Samuel and Anna Dykes (see S.A. Dykes Vol. II *Montgomery County History*, 1913). In March 1933, they moved to the Silas Dunbar homestead northeast of Bowers.

Bill attended Bowers School through tenth grade and graduated from Crawfordsville High School in 1947. He participated in 4-H Club for ten years and played basketball on the Bowers Junior High and High School teams while helping with the family dairy farming. The summers of 1942, 43, 44 were spent in Woodcraft Camp at Culver Military Academy where he was Battalion Adjutant in 1944. After high school, he attended Wabash College two years and Purdue one year. During this time, he served with the Indiana National Guard at Darlington in Service Battery, 139th Field Artillery Battalion.

Willard P. Dunbar Jr.

In November 1950, Bill enlisted in the U.S. Air Force Aviation Cadet Program and graduated in December 1951 flying P-51 fighters. Early in 1952, he completed Jet Transition at Williams AFB, Arizona and went to Nellis AFB, Nevada to fly F-80's and F-86's in Combat Crew Training. Bill spent the summer of 1952 flying 100 missions in Sabre Jets from Kimpo AFB, Korea, earning the Distinguished Flying Cross and damaging a Russian Mig-15. He was based at Tyndall AFB, FL from December 1952 till December 1954 teaching aerial gunnery and all-weather jet interception.

Bill returned to Purdue in February 1955 and joined the Indiana Air Guard at Hulman Field, IN. In May 1956, he became Base Operations Supervisor, 113th Fighter Interceptor Squadron and served till February 1957 when he again returned to Purdue and graduated in January 1958 with a Bachelor of Science degree in Air Transportation.

Bill farmed the family farms from 1958 to 1965 with ten months out in 1961 and 1962 for Air Force service during the Berlin Crisis. He retired from the Air Guard in October 1964 after serving as Squadron Commander his last two years. He continued Air Force Reserve participation until 1976 when he retired with the rank of Lt. Colonel having flown T-6's, P-51's, T-33's, F-80's, F-86's, and F-84's.

American Airlines hired Bill in May 1965 and he will retire Dec. 27, 1989 after almost 25 years of airline flying. With American, he has flown the DC-6 and 7, B-707 and 720, B-727, and DC-10.

March 15, 1961, Bill married Joan Loretta Peabody (Lake Central Airlines Stewardess) from Skokie, IL and they have made their home in Walnut Fork Addition on S.R. 32 East of Crawfordsville. They have three children, Willard III, June 20, 1962, and Valerie Ann, Oct. 19, 1963, were born in Lebanon at Witham Hospital and Bryant Bauer was born in Highland Park, IL Nov. 4, 1969. Bill III attended Oakaton Community College and Valerie graduated from Purdue in 1984. Bryant is a freshman at the University of Texas at El Paso.

Bill and Joan have made their home in Northbrook, IL since November 1968, but still maintains an active interest in the farms at Bowers. Bill is a member of the Masonic Lodge at Colfax and the American Legion Post at Darlington, also maintaining membership in the Reserve Officers Association of America, Illinois State Rifle Association, Allied Pilots Association, American Airlines Grey Eagles Association, Sabre Pilots Association, and life memberships in the National Rifle Association, and Kappa Sigma Fraternity. He plans to continue flying in Corporate Aviation after retirement from American. *Submitted by Willard Parker Dunbar Jr.*

ROBERT AND ROSEMARY (PLUNKETT) DUNCAN

The Robert T. and Rosemary Plunkett Duncan family includes three children. Bob and Rosemary were married June 15, 1940. He graduated from New Market High School in 1936. He was a star basketball player and distance runner, holding the county record for the mile until 1956. Bob was the son of Bailey and Artie Duncan and was born Mar. 20, 1918. Rosemary is the daughter of John and Iva (Johns) Plunkett and was born Mar. 25, 1920. Bob died Dec. 5, 1984.

Bob attended Wabash College and Purdue University before his marriage. He first worked for Mid-States Steel & Wire before spending about two years with the FBI in Washington, D.C., where his wife and first child, Marlis Gaildene (born Aug. 7, 1941) joined him in Arlington, VA.

He then returned to Mid-States before going into the Army during World War II.

Rosemary graduated from Ladoga High School in 1938. She has been secretary-treasurer of Ladoga Elementary School since 1959.

While Bob was serving in the Army the couple's second child, Robert Steven, was born Oct. 3, 1944.

Upon Bob's discharge from the Army in 1945, he returned to Ladoga to join his family.

A third child, David Brent, was born Nov. 8, 1947.

All three Duncan children graduated from Ladoga High School. Gaildene attended Purdue University for two years before joining the advertising staff at the Journal Review in the fall of 1961. Two years later, she was promoted to women's editor, then to city editor in 1976. In 1981, she was named editor of the newspaper.

She is married to Stanley D. Hamilton. They live at Ladoga and have one daughter, Danielle Denise, born Sept. 12, 1970. She is a 1988 graduate of Southmont High School and is now (1989) a freshman at Indiana State University majoring in geology and palentology. She is a member of Delta Gamma.

Stanley has two other daughters, Debra and Dianne. Debra is married to Clifford Washington. They have two children, Christopher and Megan. Dianne is married to Joe McCullough and has two children, Jennifer Edmiston and Toby McCullough.

Robert Steven is married to the former Evelyn Zachary (daughter of Joe and Esther Zachary of Ladoga). They have two children, Susan (Mrs. James) Keller who is employed by Elston Bank & Trust Company, and Allen, a junior at Purdue, majoring in engineering. He is a member of Theta Chi fraternity.

Steve and Evelyn are employed by R.R. Donnelley & Sons Co. and live at Ladoga.

David is married to the former Melanie Kessler (daughter of Warner and Mary Kessler). They have two sons, Joshua and Jason, both students at Ladoga Elementary School.

David, an ISU graduate, is an industrial arts teacher and coach at Southmont High School. Melanie, a Ball State graduate, is a child psychologist with the North Putnam School District.

The family lives northeast of Ladoga. Submitted by Gaildene (Duncan) Hamilton

CECIL AND PHYLLIS WEIR DUNLAP

The Dunlaps are residents of Ripley Township, living one mile north of Alamo, in an older home that was once a station on the "Underground Railroad".

Cecil was born in Champaign Co., IL, Aug. 14, 1932 to John Wesley and Bessie Blevins Dunlap. He is the youngest of four children. Cecil and his parents moved to Montgomery Co., IN in 1950 where they were farmers.

Cecil graduated from Mahomet High School and took some courses at Purdue University in agriculture. He served in the Army as a cook from 1954 to 1956. In March 1956 he married Phyllis Ann Weir at the Alamo Christian Church. They have one daughter, Janet Sue born on Oct. 28, 1961. She married Tony Johnson on Mar. 7, 1980 in the Alamo Christian Church. They have one daughter, Jaclyn Diane born on Dec. 17, 1984.

Cecil's parents were both born near Maryville, TN, which is close to the Great Smokie Mountains. When they married in 1923 they moved to Illinois to farm.

Phyllis was born on Aug. 12, 1935 in Ripley Township to Granville and Ethel Newkirk Weir. She has one brother, Lawrence of Smartsburg, IN. She graduated from Alamo High School in 1953 and then was employed at R.R. Donnelly's until the birth of their daughter.

Phyllis' father was born Dec. 5, 1893 to John and Bessie Smith Weir. He had one sister, Agnes Gray. His mother died when he was five years old. He was a farmer most of his life. He died Apr. 24, 1969 and is buried at Alamo Cemetery.

Her mother was born in Fountain Co., IN May 18, 1897 to Charles J. and Addie Sophranie Etter Newkirk. She was the eldest of five children. Fern Hudson Pointer, Russell "Docy" Newkirk, Pauline "Polly" Hamm and Leslie Newkirk were her brothers and sisters. She died Mar. 2, 1985 and is, also, buried in Alamo Cemetery.

GEORGE TARKINGTON DURHAM

The subject, George Tarkington Durham, my grandfather and the son of J.Y. Durham and Martha Tarkington Durham was brought to Montgomery County in 1850. His Father's picture below was entered into an Indiana State Fair Photography Contest in the early 1900's and won first prize. One of the reasons was the clarity of the newsprint shown in his hand. They lived north of Waveland on land that was claimed by John Durham around 1822. Booth Tarkington, a first cousin, was often present at family gatherings. The present owners and residents are Gordon and Margaret Moody Moser.

Capt. J.Y. Durham

George Durham purchased the farm that lies one mile directly west of Byron, IN. He built the house that still stands on the corner of the road. This house cost $600 to build. He cut the trees from the farm and had the lumber made from them for the house. Then George went back to Kentucky and claimed a lovely bride by the name of Betty Elliot North. Betty was the daughter of Colonel John North. She was loved and admired by all who knew her. Five children blessed this union and they were: Julia Belle, Rosalie Tarkington, Roscoe Conklin, Henry North, and Betty, who died in infancy. George cleared the land and often placed cedar saplings in the gullies and washes to prevent further land erosion. He was a hard working industrious man that earned the respect of the community. The community responded by electing him trustee of Howard township. The lazy worthless shirkers remembered well the wrath this man could call forth with his deep resonant voice. The children all attended Byron public school.

In early 1900 George traded for a farm that lies two miles east of Waveland. This land lies just west of Pine Grove Crossing. With considerable hard work the family established a fine home.

Julia Belle married Homer H. Elmore. He practiced medicine in Browns Valley for several years before going into the Baptist Ministry. They lived in Browns Valley and his first church was the Browns Valley Baptist Church. Later he became the pastor of the First Baptist Church at Crawfordsville. His last ministry was the Waveland Baptist Church where he was serving when he died. This family was blessed with two sons; Ulysses (now deceased) and Austin who resides in Cedarville, OH.

Rosalie Tarkington married Henry Newton Fullenwider and they had three children: Robert Elliot, W. Terry, and this writer, Betty L. Banner, who resides in Milwaukee, WI. Robert and Terry presently reside in Waveland.

Roscoe Conklin graduated from a business school in Crawfordsville and was employed by the Royal Typewriter Company for years. He was sent by his company to service a typewriter system for the Teddy Roosevelt Presidential Campaign of 1912. Roosevelt insisted that each campaign letter be individually typed and the Royal Company produced a system of one master machine driving ten slave typewriters via vacuum hoses and it was this system that Roscoe maintained for the entire campaign. Roscoe married Tillie Von Talge a Waveland School teacher. She died in the early 1930's and in the middle 1940's he married Rose Steffel of Huntington, IN. Rose still lives in Franklin, NC.

Henry North farmed with his father and before enlisting in the Army he married Pauline Davis of New Market. They had one daughter, Betty Ellyn Steele who is presently living in Scottsdale, AZ. At one time Henry owned the Willard Car Battery distributorship in Hammond, IN and after selling this business he bought a Parking garage in Jackson Park area of Chicago. In the middle 1940's he returned to Waveland and managed my Father's farm that lies south of Pine Grove Crossing. Henry was quite active in the local Raymond Todd American Legion Post and was adored for his sincere friendliness; this was shown in his outgoing interest in his fellow man.

George T. was a zealous farmer who used all the latest methods to improve the land. He was a 32nd degree Mason and a member of the ME church in Waveland. In 1920 George sold his farm and purchased the Rhoads property on the south side of Waveland. George and Betty lived out their lives here and are buried in Freedom cemetery.

JOHN DURHAM

The old Durham estate was located approximately four miles northwest of Waveland. The property was owned by the Durham family as early as 1822, when John Durham, Boyle Co., KY was granted a patent for 160 acres in southwest Montgomery County. Kept in the family for over 155 years, it was a working farm until around 1970.

John Durham willed the land to four of his ten children in 1853; Phoebe, Jeremiah, Brisco, John and Jessie Y.

In Jessie's obituary in 1907, it stated that he came to Indiana after his marriage to Martha Tarkington in 1843. "He shipped his goods by flatboat down the Ohio and up the Wabash to Montezuma." From there he came to the farm by wagon. It also says that except for a very few acres, the farm was in a perfectly wild condition. "He was one of the pioneers, hewing his farm out of virgin forest." In 1871, he was chosen as Representative to the General Assembly. He was "a staunch Democrat and his vote always in the favor of temperance."

Jessie and Martha had eight children; Cornelius, Julia, George, Governor, Laura, Joseph, Bell and William Y.

William Y. Durham died in 1957 at the age of 93. His obituary says he was born in a two-story log house northwest of Waveland in 1863. He and his brother Bell were in the business of horses and were known for trotting colts.

A brother to Jessie Y. was John. He was born in Kentucky in 1808, but came to Indiana between 1834 and 1836. He and his first wife, Mary Fields, lived on the 160 acres his father owned, near Waveland. In 1846 Mary died; the couple had five children. John remarried in 1847 to Sarah Ann Stubbins. She and John had eight children; Samuel Wakefield, Harry, Nancy Belle, Martha Jane, Celia H., Sarah Dorcas, Emma Josephine and Charles Stubbins.

Charles lived on the Durham estate after his marriage to Lizzie Belle Reddish in 1881. She died in 1882. Charles remarried in 1882 to Henrietta "Etta" Owen Norcross. They had eight children between 1885 and 1905; Guy Wakefield, Claude, John Thomas, Margaret Mary, Fred Norcross, Lucy V, Ruth and Bonnie.

The writer's grandmother, Bonnie, married Homer W. Weaver in 1912. They had eight children; Robert, Charles, Mary, John Russell, (the writer's father), Melford "Buck" Durham, Bonnie Jean, Patricia Ruth and Max Dale. Bonnie died in 1935. The writer's father, John R. Weaver died in 1981.

In 1937, Margaret M. Durham Demaree was living on the Durham farm. She married John V. Demaree in 1911. Living with them were her brother Fred Durham, and their Aunt and Uncle; Nancy and Samuel Wakefield Durham. Nancy died in 1937 and Samuel in 1942. His obituary states he died in the house where he was born, on the farm that had been entered from the government by his great grandfather. Margaret and John Demaree stayed on the farm and kept it running until around 1970. Ill health forced them to slowly phase out most of their farming activities. She died in 1972, and he in 1979. The writer's great Uncle Fred Durham lived with relatives until his death in 1981. The farm was sold after over 155 years and no longer belongs to any member of the Durham family. *Submitted by Kathy Weaver*

ROBERT PAUL AND OPAL BURNETA (FRUITS) EARLY

Robert Paul Early was born in 1906 in Indianapolis, the son of Richard and Mae (Matthews) Early. Richard was a shop teacher at Arsenal Technical High School. The family had four children. Robert was afflicted with polio in the epidemic of 1908. In that year a daughter died, and in 1910 Mae died after the birth of a son, Richard. Richard Early soon moved to Detroit, MI, where he helped design the shop department in Detroit's new Manual Technical High School. He took Mary and Robert with him, leaving the baby to be raised by Daniel and Mauree Early in Indianapolis.

Robert attended Purdue and then transferred to Wabash College in Crawfordsville, where he met Opal Fruits. Opal was born in Waynetown in 1910, the daughter of Ollie G. and Delpha (Payne) Fruits. The family moved to Crawfordsville and Opal was graduated in 1928 from CHS. Opal and Robert were married on Mar. 24, 1928, in Jamestown, a birthday elopement. They honeymooned in Florida, while Opal's graduating class marched without her. They lived in Atlanta where Opal learned the intricacies of southern cooking, and developed a lifelong taste for grits, hushpuppies, and rice. Robert was the owner and indifferent manager of a parking lot.

In 1929, Opal and Robert returned to Crawfordsville, where, in November, their daughter Mary was born. Robert began work at the new R.R. Donnelley printing company, where he began training as a proofreader, an occupation he pursued all of his working life. Another daughter, Ann, was born in May of 1931. In the early 30s the family moved to a house at 312 West Pike Street which had earlier been occupied by Opal's grandparents, Jonathan and Rozella. Opal's family, Ollie and Delph (Patsy) lived next door with Opal's sister Martha, at 310. This close arrangement was a grandchild's dream, and Mary remembers often eating an early supper at 310, and another at 312.

Robert Paul Early; Opal (Fruits) Early

The children attended Mills school. Opal sang in the First Presbyterian Church choir under Countess Tinsley, a colorful figure in the music world of Crawfordsville. Opal had a beautiful soprano voice, and was a member of the Music Club and Morning Musicale. Opal and Robert were participants in local theater and other community and college cultural efforts. Church life was very important and due to the proximity of the families, the girls took part in many First Baptist activities as well as First Presbyterian ones.

In the late 30s, Robert began construction of a house on the Camp Rotary Road. Framed by William Keller, an elderly neighbor, the house was built bit by bit by Robert alone, with big job help from friends, and the daily assistance of Opal and, sometimes grudgingly, the girls.

In 1947, the year Mary went to Hanover, the family moved to Kingsport, TN. Opal became a journeyman proofreader, and they enjoyed a full life. Mary married Allen Johnson in 1949, and Ann married Floyd Powers. Robert and Opal purchased a house on the Withlacootchee River in Dunnellon, FL, where they enjoyed several years of retirement, pursuing fishing, music, and the books they both loved. Opal became chief fundraiser and first Librarian of Dunnellon's new library. Robert died in 1961, and Opal in 1974. Both are buried in Dunnellon, in a quiet place where Spanish moss blows. *Submitted by Mary Early Johnson*

CHARLES WOODSON EASLEY

Charles Woodson Easley son of Daniel Woodson and Rebecca Davis Easley, was born Apr. 19, 1869 and died Jan. 13, 1923 in New Market, IN.

He was married Mar. 5, 1890 in New Market to Nancy Eveline "Eve N." Buser. She was a daughter of William Hirum and Sarah Allen Buser. She was born July 17, 1872 in New Market, IN and died Sept. 12, 1940 in Ohio. Both Charley and she are buried at Indian Creek Hill Cemetery, New Market.

Charley was a carpenter and interior decorator. About 1911 he broke his hip in a buggy accident and was crippled the rest of his life. He was town Marshall in New Market for a number of years after his accident.

Charles W. and Eva N. Easley

Eva N. worked at helping in confinement cases and later ran a restaurant in New Market in 1918-1919. She also helped in the delivery of all their seven grandchildren.

New electric lights were installed first in their home as the man, J.C. Saidla, doing the installation roomed at their house. Their six children were born in New Market, IN. J. Lloyd born and died Feb. 26, 1891; J.C. born March 29, died Jan. 3, 1895 of diphtheria; Carette Blanch (Paul Everson); Mary Catherine (Howard Earl Cowdin); Velma Geraldine (Walter Caswell Tague) and Mildred Lenora (John Collyn D. Saidla).

Carette Blanch was born Dec. 24, 1895 and died Aug. 5, 1967 in Montgomery Co., IN. She married Paul Thomas Everson a son of John and Laura Luster Everson. He was born Mar. 12, 1893 west of Ladoga, IN and died Dec. 8, 1961 Crawfordsville, IN. He was a farmer then later worked for R.R. Donnelley & Sons Co. from August 1942 until June 1959. He worked at the Crawfordsville Public Library at the time of his death by a fall from a tall ladder while washing windows on the outside.

They had three daughters born in Montgomery County: Evelyn J. (Charles Carlile); Mariam Geraldine (William Surface) and Margaret Gerdaldine (Robert Smiley).

Evelyn was born May 1, 1915 her husband Charles Carlile son of John Carlile was born Sept. 29, 1911 and died Feb. 18, 1948 in Crawfordsville. He is buried at the Masonic Cemetery there. He was a US Marine in WWII. They had no children. Evelyn lives in Crawfordsville at this time.

Mariam was born Sept. 13, 1917 her husband was William Surface son of Abe and Eve Ellis Surface. He was born Oct. 6, 1918 and died Oct. 23, 1978. He was in the U.S. Navy in WWII. After the war he was a carpenter and contractor to build houses. They had two daughters: Carolyn Ann (Robert Snyder) and Marilyn Sue (Mike Goforth), and four grandchildren. She lives in Crawfordsville at this time.

Margaret was born July 31, 1922 and died Sept. 15, 1956 of leukemia in Crawfordsville. She was married to Robert Smiley a son of Charles Byron and Zola Bratton Smiley. He was born June 1920 and died January 1982. He was in the U.S. Army in WWII. He was a farmer then later worked at Donnelley's. They are buried at the Masonic Cemetery there.

They had one son Robert A. Smiley, Jr. He is a Vet with his own Animal Clinic in Crawfordsville. He is married to Janet Kay Steele and has two children. *Submitted by I. Jo Summers*

DANIEL AND NANCY DEATHERAGE EASLEY

Daniel was the second son of 13 children of Joseph and Mary Catherine Deatherage Easley. Joseph was the sixth son of nine children of Warhan and Ann Woodson Easley. Warhan was the third son of five sons of John and Mary Benskin Easley. John was the first son of six children of Robert and Ann Parker Easley of Henrico Co., VA.

In 1811 Joseph moved all his family of 13 children and their children from Stokes Co., NC to Harrisonville, Shelby Co., KY.

Daniel was born Apr. 20, 1792 in Stokes Co., NC. He died Sept. 18, 1870 in Wapello Co., IA. He married Nancy Deatherage Nov. 6, 1815. In 1824 he moved his family of Sally and Joseph Woodson "JW" to Montgomery Co., IN. In 1850 he followed his daughters to Wapello Co., IA.

He was a farmer as were all his fathers before him.

In the Montgomery Co., IN *Original Entrybook 1821-1836,* Township 17 Range 5 on page 87 Daniel Easley put a patent on three sections of land totalling 224.62 acres dated November 1826.

He is also in *Early Marriage and Will Records Montgomery Co., IN.* On page 45 he is witness for John Vancleave of Brown Twp. Also on page 47 he is witness for Peter Smith of Union Twp.

His children were William, died young; Sarah (Tarleton James W. Layne); Joseph Woodson "JW"; Daniel; Catherine (James Lafollette); Frances (Jacob Wash Layne); Nancy (George Washington Deatherage); Isaac Milford; Angeline (John H. Lafollette). *Submitted by I. Jo Summers*

DANIEL W. EASLEY

Daniel W. Easley was a son of J.W. Easley. He was born Sept. 22, 1848 in New Market, IN. He died Oct. 21, 1917 Montgomery Co., IN. He married July 1868 to Rebecca Davis a daughter of James and Elizabeth Davis Davis. She was born June 16, 1846 and died May 9, 1871. Daniel was a farmer, his name on a 1878 map of Brown Township, Montgomery Co., IN. His children by Rebecca were: Charles Woodson and James B. born Apr. 3, 1871, infant.

He remarried Apr. 3, 1875 to Eveline H. Glenn "Eva H." born Sept. 27, 1847, died Nov. 30, 1927, Knoxville, TN. She was the daughter of Thomas and Martha ? Glenn. She and Daniel W. are buried at Masonic Cemetery, Waynetown, IN.

Daniel W. Easley, Charles W. Easley, Joseph W. Easley and baby J.C. Easley

Their names are in the *New Market Centennial* book page 74 as charter members of the First Baptist Church.

Their children were: Grace "Todie"; Walter F. and Emma Blanche.

Todie died Feb. 4, 1896 at age 30.

Walter F. was born May 23, 1879 Waynetown, IN and died Feb. 17, 1959 Greensburg, IN. He married Aug. 12, 1902 to Velva Gertrude Hood. She was born 1887 and died 1941. They are buried in South Park Cemetery Greensburg, IN. Their children were: Wilber Daniel and Max Glenn Easley.

Walter moved his family from Rushville, IN to Greensbury, IN in 1924. He was a theater owner and civic leader. His second wife was Mildred Emmert.

Wilber Daniel was born June 17, 1909, married to Elizabeth "Billie" Hill. He was in the U.S. Navy for many years. Their children were: Walter Daniel Jr. of Indianapolis and Billie Ann (James Coates) of Cockeysville, MD.

Emma Blanche born Nov. 11, 1880 New Market, IN. She married July 12, 1910 to Bert Long; he was a shoe cobbler. They had four children: Evelyn Elizabeth; Mary Margaret; James Daniel and Robert Lee Long. They moved to Knoxville, TN after 1917.

Max Glenn was born Dec. 20, 1913 Rushville, IN. He was legally blind from childhood. He worked at Mirtz Engineering during WWII in Indianapolis then Charles H. Johnson Corp. till 1976 in Greensburg, IN. He married Esther Mariam Gommelm daughter of Olin and Jessie Forement Gommelm; she was born Aug. 29, 1915 near New Point, IN. She died May 13, 1982 and Max died Apr. 14, 1987. They are buried in South Park Cemetery Greensburg, IN. Their four children were born in Greensburg, IN: Jerry Madison (Barbara) born June 11, 1938, he has two children; Lucinda Rose (Dailey) born Sept. 1942 she has five children; John Michael (Charrie) born July 5, 1945 had two children; Melinda Jane (Dan Kennedy) born Dec. 11, 1947, has one son Patrick. *Submitted by I. Jo Summers*

JOSEPH WOODSON EASLEY "JW"

Joseph Woodson "J.W." was born Sept. 16, 1823 in Woodford Co., KY. He died Feb. 7, 1908 in New Market, IN. He was the second son of nine children of Daniel and Nancy Deatherage Easley. He was brought to Montgomery Co., IN as a year old baby in 1824 from Kentucky.

He was married Mar. 5, 1846 in New Market, IN to Lucinda Jane Vancleave. She was the daughter of Benjamin and Mary (Polly) Brown Vancleave. She was born Aug. 4, 1826 and died Sept. 2, 1893. Both she and J.W. are buried at Indian Creek Hill cemetery, New Market, IN.

L to R: Tilghman, Francis (Mrs. Nelson Rice), Benjamin, Mary (Mrs. Wm. Miles), Daniel, Kate (Mrs. Simeon Rice)

Their children were Mary (William J. Miles); Daniel; Benjamin; Tilghman; Nancy Ann (Thomas F. Miles); Sarah Katharin, "Kate" (Simeon Rice); Emma Jane (unmarried); infant son; Lucinda Frances, "Frany" (Nelson Rice).

J.W. was a farmer as were all his fathers before him. He is in the U.S. census of 1850, 1860, and 1870 in Brown Twp. Montgomery Co., IN.

After Lucinda died he remarried Oct. 24, 1895 to Hannah Voros. They lived in New Market on Pine Street.

As his children married he gave them each 80 acres to farm. Most of their names are on the 1878 land map of Brown Township Range 3, 4 and 5. The homestead was in Range 4 and is still held by Daniel and Opal Tracy Rice, one of the great grandsons of Frany Rice. Their son Dennis Lee Rice is Sheriff of Montgomery Co., IN. *Submitted by I. Jo Summers*

MARY AND VELMA AND MILDRED EASLEY

Mary Catherine daughter of Charley and Eve N. Easley was born May 15, 1899 in New Market, IN and died Nov. 24, 1977 in No. Las Vegas, NV. She was married to Howard Earl Cowdin son of Parker Howard and Edith Caterlin Cowdin. He was born June 18, 1895 in Frankfort, IN and died Jan. 6, 1970 in No. Las Vegas, NV. They both worked for the Nickel Plate RR when they met. They lived most of their lives in Cleveland, OH. They had one daughter, Norma Catherine.

Paul and Coretta Everson, Mary and Earl Cowdin, Velma and Walter Tague, Mildred and John C. Saidla

Norma was born Oct. 12, 1919 in New Market, IN. She was married May 24, 1943 in Houston, TX to Alex Montrose son of Frank Montrose, originally Lichtblau. Al was born Jan. 27, 1918 in Cleveland, OH. He spent 22 years in U.S. Air Force, retired. Then worked as photographer and project manager for Pan American Airways, retired in January 1980. He died June 18, 1983 in No. Las Vegas, NV. They had two children: Nancy (Richard Carson, George Frame) and Jerry. Also three grandchildren and one great grandchild, two step-grandchildren.

Mary and Earl moved to No. Las Vegas to be near their daughter and family. They are buried at Woodlawn Cemetery there.

Velma Geraldine Easley daughter of Charley and Eve N. Easley was born Mar. 15, 1902 New Market, IN. She was married to Walter Caswell Tague. He was the son of Thomas Morton and Lavina Walters Tague, born July 16, 1901. He died June 12, 1971 in Indianapolis, IN and is buried at the Masonic Cemetery Crawfordsville.

He was a restauranteer after they married. Then before WWII he worked for Hayes Trucking; they sent them all around Illinois, Indiana, and western Ohio. In 1942 they returned to Indianapolis where he operated a cafeteria in the former Continental Optical Building.

They owned and operated two package liquor

stores in Indianapolis for many years, retiring in 1967.

He was a member of New Market Christian Church, past master of Pentalpha Masonic Lodge, past patron of Queen Esther Chapter of Eastern Star, Scottish Rite, Murat Shrine, Gatling Gun Club, Past Patrons Association of Marion County, Modern Woodmen of America and Traffic Club and past president of the Indiana State Package Store Association.

They had no children.

She lives in Crawfordsville at this time.

Mildred Lenora Easley daughter of Charley and Eve N. Easley. Her information will be with John Collyn Saidla. *Submitted by I. Jo Summers*

JOHN JAMISON EDDINGFIELD

John Jamison Eddingfield was born Feb. 12, 1815 in Butler Co., OH to John Eddingfield who was born in Fayette Co., PA and wife, Hannah Thompson Eddingfield. John J. married Sarah Williamson, daughter of George Williamson and Margaret Morrison Williamson on Dec. 14, 1842. John J. had made a land entry here in 1837, two and a half miles west of New Ross. They had these children, Dr. George Eddingfield, a doctor at Mace, IN; James Carey Eddingfield, Postmaster at New Ross; William Thompson Eddingfield teacher at one room Greenwood School; Mary A. Eddingfield married James H. Linn, son of James Washington and Mahala Castle Linn; and Oscar Eddingfield born 1853 and died 1933 married Nancy Redenbaugh born 1857 daughter of Jeremiah and Elizabeth Corn Redenbaugh (a sister of Margaret Corn Linn, wife of Noah Castle Linn, son of James Washington Linn and Mahala Castle Linn). Oscar's children were Emma married George Layne and had three children, lived in Indianapolis; Iva married Frank Rice, had two daughters and lived in Indianapolis; twin sons, Ray married Temple Rettinger had Geraldine and Ronald; and Ernest married Ethel Hale and had a son Maurice died in 1988 in Florida. After Ray's death, Temple married Ray's brother-in-law, George Layne. Ray and Ernest had both moved to Indianapolis in their later years. After Ethel died, Ernest married Isabelle Shoemaker, had one son, Francis.

James Carey Eddingfield, brother to Oscar, was postmaster of New Ross and editor of a New Ross paper. He had his poems printed in Crawfordsville papers. He always rode a bicycle. James Carey died in 1933. He married Aretta Huffington. They had two children, Lucile died 1895 age two and Rev. Paul Eddingfield, Indianapolis. This information partly came from him. He was born in 1890 in New Ross. *Submitted by Pauline Waters*

EDMONDS FAMILY

Keith Edmonds and Ruth Bartley (deceased December 1958) had seven children, the second child being Robert Keith Edmonds, born Sept. 11, 1917 in Vermillion Co., IN.

Robert "Bob" K. Edmonds graduated from Perrysville High School in the class of 1936. He married Mildred Kathleen "Kate" Coleman Apr. 1, 1939 at Covington, IN. Kate was born Dec. 10, 1921 to Charles and Emma (Logan) Coleman in Fountain County; however, her grandparents, John and Alcy (Brown) Logan lived in Montgomery County as did Alcy's parents, William and Nancy (Routh) Brown.

Bob and Kate had: Robert Josiah Keith Edmonds, born Dec. 23, 1939 in Vermillion County.

Robert, Kathleen and Bobby Joe Edmonds

In the Spring of 1948, the family moved to Montgomery County to Robert's parents Thunder Valley Farm where they managed the Dairy Farm for nine years, then moved to their current home on 500 West. Robert K. worked at Farm Bureau Co-op until his retirement in 1982.

Robert J.K. graduated from Alamo High School in 1957. He served in the Marine Corps and has worked at Donnelley's for 28 years. Robert J.K. married Mary Patricia "Pat" McKeown on Jan. 19, 1963. They have two children: Marilyn Theresa, born Nov. 4, 1963 and Michelle Elizabeth, born May 6, 1965. Marilyn married Harold Brown. Michelle married James Hardaway and have two sons: Kevin Drew and Charles Edward.

Bob enjoys gardening, raising birds (dove, quail, chickens, turkeys) and rabbits. Kate likes cooking and her more than 50 varieties of cacti.

This year, 1989, Bob and Kate celebrate their 50th wedding anniversary. *Submitted by Kate Edmonds*

CURTIS D. AND REBECCA (CLARK) EDWARDS

Curtis David Edwards was born Aug. 23, 1851 in Butler Co., OH to Seth and Mary Ann (Galbreath) Edwards. They moved to Montgomery County in 1852. Seth and Mary are buried at Shiloh Cemetery.

Charles Edwards, father of Seth, was born Mar. 4, 1777 in New Jersey and died Apr. 16, 1859. He was married to Sara Corra Mar. 5, 1805. She was born in 1789 and died Sept. 23, 1851. Both are buried in Finley Cemetery, Montgomery County.

David Edwards, father of Charles, was born in England in 1743 and died in New Jersey in 1789. He married Deborah Thompson in 1772. David was a Lieutenant in Captain Willett's Company at the battle of Germantown — later was made Captain. Four children were born to this union: Sarah, David, Charles and Curtis.

Back Row, Left to Right: Charles Edwards, wife Mary, May Edwards Sidener, husband Walter; Curtis, Rebecca Edwards, Hattie Edwards Patton, husband Arlie. Front Row, Left to Right: Dog; Ralph Edwards, Cuba Edwards Aso; Andrew Jackson Clark; Edward Patton

On Sept. 27, 1877 Curtis married Rebecca Elizabeth Clark, born Nov. 25, 1857 at McLean Co., IL and died Mar. 22, 1955. She was the daughter of Andrew Jackson and Mary (Reardon) Clark. To this union, six children were born: Mary, Mae, Hattie, Charles, Ralph and Cuba.

Rebecca's grandfather Clark was born in Ireland and came to Pennsylvania when 15 months old. Her father, Andrew, was born Mar. 29, 1829 in Washington Co., PA. He was married Mar. 14, 1850 to Mary Reardon. Five children were born to this Union: Maliessa, Amanda, Kate, Rebecca and Charles. Andrew and Mary are buried at Oak Hill Cemetery.

Rebecca was known to friends as "Becca." She grew to womanhood on a farm south of Smartsburg. She was a member of the Shiloh U.B. Church and later became a charter member of the U.B. Church in Crawfordsville.

Becca was called "Gom" by her grandchildren and the name was kept current by the great-grandchildren. She lived to be 97 and 65 years was spent on the family farm north of Crawfordsville.

Curtis lived in Montgomery County for 69 years. Thirty-seven years of that time was spent on his farm north of Crawfordsville. This is where he learned to drive and when he wanted to stop he could be heard yelling "Whoa! Whoa!" He died on the farm Aug. 5, 1922. He and Becca are buried at Oak Hill Cemetery.

Curt and Becca are survived by one daughter, Cuba Brin-Aso and eight grandchildren: Edward Patton, Forest Patton, Mildred Patton Martin, Curtis Edwards, May Jane Edwards Steen, William Sidener, Andrew Edwards and C. Elizabeth Edwards Olin. All live in Montgomery County with the exception of May Jane Steen and William Sidener. Grandson Andrew now lives in the family home. *Submitted by Clara Elizabeth Edwards Olin*

ELLIS-STINSON

Joe Ellis was born Jan. 15, 1938 at Newport, IN. Joe is the second of three children born to Jonathan and Vera (Armstrong) Ellis. Joe has two sisters: Beverly Jean and Joyce. Beverly married Joseph Livingston and had Jonathan, David and Susan. Joyce married Robert Downs and had Cindy, Larry, Dale and Jay.

Carolyn, Joe, Jon and Kim Ellis

Joe's paternal grandparents were William and Elmira (Asbury) Ellis. His maternal grandparents were Oscar and Nora (Lewis) Armstrong.

Joe grew up on a farm in Fountain County (on the county line road between Fountain and Montgomery Counties). In 1955, Joe moved with his parents to their new home at 103 North Davis Street in Crawfordsville. He attended Crawfordsville High School his senior year and graduated in 1956.

On June 3, 1961, Joe was married to Carolyn Stinson of Indianapolis, IN. Carolyn was born Jan. 31, 1942 in Indianapolis, IN, the oldest of three children born to Herston and Vester (Overton) Stinson. The second oldest is Donald and the youngest is Ronald. Donald married Teresa Bledsoe and had one daughter, Kendra.

Joe and Carolyn reside in Ripley Township, about one-half mile south of Yountsville. They have two children: Kimberly Jo born June 30, 1962 and Jonathan Elwood born Jan. 7, 1965. They were both born in Montgomery County and graduates of Southmont High School. Kim works at Hi-Tek Lighting Company and Jonathan works at R.R. Donnelley & Sons Co.

Joe's paternal great-great-great grandparents were Jonathan and Lydia (Woodrow) Ellis who are buried at Elwood Friends cemetery near Georgetown, IL. Joe's maternal great-great grandfather Alexander P. Armstrong born Dec. 23, 1821 in Tennessee. Alexander came to Indiana about 1843 and married Charlotte Biggs in Parke County.

There is an interesting story about Charlotte's maternal grandfather, William E. Collings. William, known as "Long Knife" by the Indians, was a survivor of the Pigeon Roost Indian massacre which took place Sept. 1, 1812 about five miles south of Scottsburg, IN. William E. Collings, his two children, John and Lydia and Captain Norris were trapped in his house by the Indians. They planned their escape after darkness came, Lydia went first, then her brother John followed by Norris and lastly "Long Knife". He raised his gun to return fire and found that the lock of his gun was broken. When the Indians came close, he would raise his gun and pretend that he was about to fire. By this way he reached the corn-field under cover and escaped.

Carolyn's paternal great-great-great-great grandfather was Hezekiah Blankenship, a Revolutionary war soldier of Virginia. Hezekiah is buried in Haysville Cemetery in Macon Co., TN.

Carolyn's maternal great-great-great-great grandfather was Westberry Overton born in Amelia Co., VA. Westberry resided in Smith Co., TN and in Gibson Co., IN.

Joe enjoys spectator sports, especially IU basketball. Carolyn is a member of the Montgomery County Genealogical society and enjoys doing crafts.

ABIJAH ELMORE

Abijah Elmore settled in Montgomery County, seven miles east of Crawfordsville, IN coming from South Carolina at age 44. He married Keziah and she was 37 when they arrived in Indiana. Born to this union was Absalom, also a farmer, Sarah J. and Abba A. and lastly David E. Elmore. He was born Mar. 22, 1853. He married Alice Lemon, Nov. 7, 1877.

Absalom, the oldest son of Abijah was born Nov. 20, 1833 and died June 14, 1910. David E. Elmore was born in a log cabin located on the farm on the Lebanon Road and died there Dec. 30, 1927. His wife Alice, died Dec. 29, 1936.

The children born to David E. Elmore and Alice Lemon were Homer Hubert Elmore born Aug. 28, 1876 and Elsie his sister who died at the age of 21. Homer H. Elmore graduated from Indiana School of Medicine 1903 and married Julia Belle Durham in 1904. To this union was born two sons, Ulysses H. Elmore 1905 and Austin D. Elmore, Mar. 22, 1910. Ulysses had two daughters, Phyllis Jane and Mary Julia. Austin D. Elmore married Marabeth Shelton in 1935 having graduated from Wabash College in 1932. He was ordained to the gospel ministry June of 1934. Two children were born to this union, David Edward Elmore and Beth Sharon Elmore Warfield. Homer Elmore died in November 1952 at age 76.

JAMES ALVA ELMORE - MARLENE MAE SCOTT ELMORE

James Alva Elmore and Marlene Mae Scott Elmore moved to Crawfordsville in June, 1957. James was born Aug. 24, 1929 and Marlene, Feb. 15, 1932. Both were born in Anderson, in Madison County. They were married July 8, 1956 in Madison County, near Anderson. James is the oldest son of James Henry and Ruby Marie Fishero Elmore; Ruby, being a former resident of Alamo and James H. being reared near Mecca, IN. Their parents were Alva and Jennie McJunkins Fishero of Montgomery County and Harry and Cora Carlin Elmore, of Parke County. Marlene's parents were Wesley Gilbert and Muriel May Batty Scott of Madison County. Their parents were Sanford and Martha Chambers Scott and George and Leanah Lemon Batty of Madison County. George Batty's parents, John Peter and Bashia Batty, came from France in the early 1800's, and settled in Darke Co., OH.

James Alva has one brother, Jerry K., a resident of Catlin, IL. Marlene has two living sisters: Nondas Wollam, and Madge Scott, both of Madison Co., IN. She has a brother, George and a sister, Ellen, deceased.

James and Marlene have two daughters: Leanah Mae, a secretary, born Sept. 9, 1957. She married Mark Alan Brown, an accountant, and a native of Indianapolis, July 8, 1978. They have three children: Nicole Mae, age eight; James Alan, age five; and Mark Leon, age one. They reside in Montgomery County. Their youngest daughter, Joanna Lee Elmore, a registered nurse, married Theodore Joseph Commons, a registered pharmacist, Apr. 12, 1986. They reside in Bedford, IN, Lawrence County.

James and Marlene enjoy their work in the Order of Eastern Star and are past matron and past patron of Athens Chapter No. 97. Marlene is past deputy of District 9. They are active members of the First Christian Church where they both taught Sunday School for many years. James is a former deacon and elder and past Chairman of the Official Board. Marlene is serving as a deacon at the present time.

James is a member, and past Worshipful Master, of Montgomery Lodge No. 50 F. & A.M., the Scottish Rite, and American Legion, having served with the U.S. Marines in Korea during the Korean War. He is a 39 year employee of R.R. Donnelley & Sons Co. Marlene worked as a medical secretary before moving to Crawfordsville. She became a full time homemaker upon the arrival of their first child, and re-entered the working field in 1977, being employed in the cafeteria at Tuttle Middle School since that time.

JAMES BUCHANAN AND MARY ANN (MURRAY) ELMORE

James Buchanan Elmore achieved nationwide recognition in the "Gay Nineties" as the Bard of Alamo and for several years thereafter delighted Hoosiers with his rustic poems. Pastoral scenes, with which he was familiar, inspired most of his poems such as "Sugar Making," "When the Pawpaws Are Ripe," and "The Old Sawmill." However, he also wrote about local people, places, Wabash College and events.

James Buchanan and Mary Ann Murray Elmore

Two poems in particular caught the public's fancy: "The Monon Wreck" based on a railroad tragedy that occurred near Crawfordsville typifies Elmore's style. In part, it goes:

And yonder in the wreck I see
A man that's pinioned down by knee
And hear him moaning and to say
"Cut, Oh, cut my leg away"

But James hastens to add that:

A jackscrew from the mail caboose
Is now applied and lets him loose.

As for the poem, "Sassafras," it concludes with these lines:

Sassafras, Oh sassafras!
Thou art the stuff for me!
And in the Spring I love to sing
Sweet sassafras, of thee!

He gave lectures locally, Indianapolis, and Chicago. He had fan clubs in many states. His poems were printed in newspapers throughout the country.

Wabash College honored him with a James Buchanan Elmore Day in the fall of the year by reading his poetry at noon under the flag pole and giving the students the day off to enjoy nature in the surrounding countryside. Some visited Elmore's grave in the Alamo cemetery.

"I didn't get a publisher because the best I could do was to get ten per cent and you bet I'm not going to give the children of my phenomenal fancy to the world for the fun of it." So saying, he published and sold his books himself. He published four books of prose and verse: *Love Among The Mistletoe*, *Lover in Cuba*, *Twenty Five Years in Jackville*, and *Autum Roses*.

Mr. Elmore attended the Old Alamo Academy where he studied with a large class which included William Humphrey, future member of Congress from Washington State, Oswald Humphrey, a future President of Cornell University and also Eva Ballard, novelist.

He taught school for 20 years. He was a shrewd business man and spent his later years managing his 900-acre farm. James was a member of the Alamo Christian Church and a life-long Democrat.

James Buchanan Elmore was born Jan. 25, 1857, the son of Matthias Elmore III and his wife, Mary Ann Willis, who were among the first settlers in Ripley Township. James was the grandson of Jacob and Mary McKensey Elmore, great grandson of Revolutionary War Veteran Matthias II and Elizabeth Appleton Elmore of Newberry Co., SC, great great grandson of Steven and Sarah Allen Elmore and great great great grandson of Matthias I and Charity Elmore.

At age 23, James married Mary Ann Murray,

daughter of James and Mary Templeton Murray of Nevada City, MO. They had five children: Maud, Roscoe, Grace, Nora and Albert.

Not long before his death in 1942, he wrote: "To her I am indebted for the sweets of this life. She has been to me what the sunshine is to the flowers." *Submitted by Helen Rush*

JAMES BYRON ELMORE

James Byron Elmore was born in 1910 to Albert and Lula Seits Elmore, at the family home near Alamo. He graduated from Wabash College in 1932 with a Bachelor's degree in Science. Later he earned his Master's from Purdue University. In 1934, James married Eva Philpott, daughter of Glenn and Ava Philpott, from Fountain County. They have two children, Phyllis Ann, born in 1936, and Robert Lee, born 1937.

After farming for a few years, James accepted a teaching position in Atwood (Kosciusko County). While living there Phyllis started first grade at Mentone, IN. At the close of the second school year, they moved back to the farm in Montgomery County.

In August 1943 James started teaching in Pine Village High School. Robert started first grade and Phyllis entered second that fall. Both graduated from Pine Village School and later attended Purdue University.

In 1955 Phyllis was married to Norman Dean Butler of Boswell. They had two children: Gayla Rae born in 1956 and Brett Elmore born 1961. Phyllis' second marriage was to Marian (Bill) Miller of Indianapolis in 1966. They have one son, James (Rusty) Miller, born in 1967. Rusty Miller graduated from Springfield College, Springfield, MA in 1989. Brett Elmore Butler is working in the family business at Avon, MA. The family resides in Boston.

Gayla Rae Butler graduated from Purdue in 1978 with a degree in accounting. Later in 1978 she was married to Bryan Neal Wesner, son of James and Alfreda Wesner of Chalmers, IN. They have two children, Michael Bryan born in 1981 and Brianne Michelle born in 1984. They live in Cedar Rapids, IA.

Robert married Janet Landon, daughter of Clarence and Myrna Landon in 1957. He worked at Attica and then moved to Crawfordsville in 1958. They live on the family farm near Alamo. Robert and Janet have three children, two sons and a daughter. The oldest, James Bion was born in 1958, John Clarence in 1959 and Brenda Lee in 1961. All graduated from Southmont High School. After graduation, James Bion served four years in the army. While in service, he married Lorena Stephens, daughter of Walter and Lureaine Stephens, of Crawfordsville. James was stationed in Germany the last two years of his service. When he had completed his four years of service, he enrolled in college. In 1983, he graduated from Ball State University. They are the parents of two sons, Lee Stephens born in 1982 and Jon Patrick born in 1986. They live near Zionsville, IN.

John Clarence has lived all of his life in Montgomery County. In 1984, he married Kelli McCallister, daughter of Roland and Betty McCallister. They have one son, Edward Mathias, born in 1984. They live in Crawfordsville.

Brenda Lee married Dave Simpson, son of James and Mildred Simpson in 1981. They have one son, Isaiah David, born in 1984. They are living in Linden, IN. *Submitted by James B. Elmore Family*

MATTHIAS AND MARY ANN WILLIS ELMORE

Matthias Elmore III came from Warren Co., OH, to Montgomery Co., IN with his parents, Jacob and Mary McKinsey Elmore in 1825 just five years after the first settlement by William Offield. They spent the first winter across the creek from Offield's place. They had a hard time at first. For six weeks once they had nothing to eat but potatoes and an occasional half-starved rabbit. They could have had corn meal, but the creeks were frozen so they couldn't grind. Jacob entered 160 acres from the government Mar. 14, 1826.

Matthias and Mary Ann (Willis) Elmore

Jacob was born Mar. 2, 1784 and died May 22, 1849. He was the son of Matthias II, (Revolutionary War Veteran) and Elizabeth Appleton Elmore; grandson of Steven and Sarah Allen Elmore.

Mary was born Feb. 20, 1790 and died May 22, 1849. She was the daughter of George and Sarah Thomas McKinsey. Jacob and Mary are both buried in Bunkerhill Cemetery. They both came from Palmetto Branch, north of Bush River, Newberry Co., SC to Warren Co., OH. Jacob came in 1805; Mary came later. They had four children: Matthias III, born Sept. 26, 1809 at Waynesville, Warren Co., OH, and died Sept. 19, 1901, and is buried in Alamo Cemetery, Alamo, Indiana; Sarah married Mercer McKinsey; Thomas married Ruth Palmer; Appleton married Irene Brown.

Matthias III helped to build the first road from what is now Yountsville to Crawfordsville. He was also a carpenter by trade and helped build the First Methodist Church in Crawfordsville, however, farming was his chief life's work. He worked for 25 cents a day until he saved enough to buy his first land from the government on Mar. 18, 1837 in Ripley Township, Montgomery Co., IN. He was a member of the Alamo Christian Church and a Democrat.

Matthias III's first marriage was Feb. 12, 1838 to Kezia Jane English from Fountain Co., IN. They had six children: Martha Ann married James Kennedy; Mary Ann married Spencer Smith; Elizabeth Jane married Barney Green; Taylor W. married Samantha Stonebraker; Jacob Win married Maria Bruner; Henry Clay married Ellen Nolen.

Matthias III's second marriage on July 6, 1852 at Montgomery Co., IN, was to Mary Ann Willis Whitaker (born Oct. 5, 1826-died June 30, 1894), a widow with one son, Frances M. Whitaker. She was the daughter of Abner and Eve Butt Willis. To this marriage was born these children: Andrew Matthias; James Buchanan married Mary Ann Murray; America Alice married Peter McMurtrey; Sarah Amanda married Martin Miller; Fannie Ellen married Will Erwin; Annie Mariah married Charles H. McMurtrey; Mary Almeda.

In 1989 the descendants of son James B., the poet, still owned and were living on the first land Matthias III bought in 1837.

ROSCOE MATTHIAS AND L. MYRTLE LATTIMORE ELMORE

Roscoe and Myrtle both started teaching school after high school graduation. Roscoe graduated from Alamo High School, attended Wabash College, Purdue University and Indiana State Normal, now known as Indiana State University at Terre Haute. Here he met Myrtle Lattimore, a fellow student and teacher. They were married Aug. 28, 1909 in the bride's home near Franklin, IN.

Roscoe was a high school and grade school principal, teaching many different subjects. He taught in Montgomery, Clinton, and Newton Counties in Indiana. He was remembered as a strict disciplinarian and for his beautiful penmanship. He was also a farmer owning 875 acres. He was a member of the Alamo Christian Church, Montgomery County Farm Bureau and was a Republican. His residence was 3/4 mile northeast of Alamo.

Dean C. Rush, Roscoe N. Rush and Myrtle Elmore, Roscoe Elmore

Roscoe was born two miles northwest of Alamo, IN (Oct. 2, 1882, died Aug. 28, 1958) to James Buchanan Elmore, the poet (born Jan. 25, 1857-died Mar. 12, 1942, son of Matthias Elmore III and Mary Ann Willis) and Mary Ann (Polly) Murray (born May 22, 1863-died Feb. 2, 1943) the daughter of James and Mary Templeton Murray. He was the second of five children.

Myrtle was born near Franklin (Sept. 5, 1884, died Aug. 21, 1972) the eldest of five children. Her father, William Dupree Lattimore, was the son of William Morton and Laura Dole Arrington Lattimore. Her mother was Sarah Harbourt, the daughter of Henry H. and Sarah Jane Townsend Harbourt. Her grandparents were Paul and Margaret Harbourt and Major and Phoebe Biggs Townsend, who was a survivor of the Pigeon Roost Massacre.

Myrtle was a grade school principal and teacher. She taught in Johnson, Montgomery and Clinton counties. She was a member of the Alamo Christian Church, Christian Church Ladies Aid and the Alamo Extension Homemakers Club. She did research on the Elmore and Lattimore family histories, loved flowers and gardening and did beautiful hand work; such as quilts, crochet, and embroidery.

Roscoe and Myrtle had two children: Helen Marie, a teacher (born Mar. 9, 1910, 2.5 miles south of Alamo), married on July 11, 1937 Doyne Rush, a farmer (born Dec. 4, 1908-died July 6, 1981). Norman Matthias, (born Nov. 30, 1914 near Bowers Station, Sugar Creek Township, Montgomery Co., IN, - died Nov. 11, 1973), married July 4, 1942 Doris Marie Reihl, a chemist (born Apr. 12, 1914).

He was a graduate of Crawfordsville High School, Wabash College and had a Masters Degree from Purdue University in chemistry. He spent 25 years with the Creol Petroleum Corp. in Venezuela, S.A. After retirement, he returned to Crawfordsville and then to Boca Raton, FL.

Roscoe and Myrtle and their son Norman are buried in the Alamo Cemetery at Alamo, IN.

BENJAMIN ELROD

Benjamin Elrod born Oct. 16, 1790 Rowan Co., NC, son of Robert and Elizabeth Douthit Elrod, grandson of Christopher and Aalje Soelle (Sell) Elrod. John and Mary Scott Douthit and Stephen and Elizabeth Douthit Riddle. Robert and Elizabeth died in Orange Co., IN where they came from North Carolina. Benjamin married first Polly Carver on Aug. 15, 1851 in Stokes Co., NC. She was Harold Walter's ancestor. Benjamin then married Sarah Redenbaugh on Oct. 9, 1826 in Jefferson Co., IN. Her parents were Frederick and Margaret Haney Redenbaugh lived in Jefferson Co., IN, then came to live east of New Market, IN. Benjamin and Sarah came here and lived west of New Market. Benjamin died 1856 or 1855. After Sarah died Benjamin had married a third time to Margaret Shelton on Dec. 17, 1844. His heirs were Benjamin H. Elrod, his wife Jane; Joseph McMullen, his wife Mary Susan Elrod McMullen; Samuel K. Elrod, his wife Sarah Ann; John Elrod, his wife Sarah Tilley; Charles Elrod, his wife Mary Jane Tilley. They were all living in Montgomery County when Benjamin's will was read on Jan. 15, 1856, except Samuel K. was living in Orange Co., IN. Martha Elrod married Esaac Kelsey; daughter Hulda must have died, and James B. Elrod.

Benjamin and Polly Carver Elrod had Benjamin Harden Elrod (Harden) Apr. 2, 1821 in Orange Co., IN, died Aug. 21, 1880 in Lyons Co., KS. He married Jane Douglas on June 10, 1847 in Montgomery Co., IN. They had James married Rose Watkins, Thomas married Jennie Ayres and second married ? Cooper; Jeremiah born Aug. 30, 1857 married Martha Ellen Roby Utley, Margaret Jane born 1853 and died July 18, 1950 married Charles Kennedy here in 1870, Martha Hannah and Margaret Jane lived with their Douglas grandparents. Martha Hannah died around 1874, married Alfred Thomas Scott on May 25, 1871. They had infant son, Benjamin who died and Rose Jane Scott Walters who was one year old when her Mother died and she was born in 1872.

When Benjamin H. Elrod died in Lyons Co., KS he named Rose Jane Scott, living in Indiana; Jane Douglas Elrod had a child in 1857 and she must have died, for Benjamin H. Elrod married his second wife Sarah Elizabeth VanCleave McMullen on July 13, 1859 here. She had Benjamin McMullen twin brother of Joseph who married Benjamin H.'s sister Mary Jane. Elizabeth born here Mar. 29, 1825 and died Mar. 15, 1908 in Kansas, daughter of Samuel and Rachel VanCleave. She had five children by her first marriage and he had five children from his marriage with Jane Douglas Elrod. They left here in 1860 and their first child was born in Iowa, four more born in Colorado and Kansas. Benjamin's sister Mary Susan born 1823 in Orange Co., IN and died in 1880's married Joseph McMullen on Sept. 5, 1844, and had 11 children. After she died he married Lucinda Hardee Williams, daughter of John Michael Hardee born 1761 and died June 2, 1839 a Private in Virginia. She was the youngest of his ten children. Lucinda died 1913/14.

Joseph and Mary Susan's children were Lindsay J. married Flora Meharry; Jesse, never married; Henry married first an Elrod and second Mamie Abbott; Emily married William Smith; Martha married John Smith (their son Joseph called Jody, a very wealthy man in Montgomery County); Lydia Margaret married William E. Haun; Louann married Wiley Surface; Mollie married Dave Ray; Sarah married Joseph Douglas. They all lived here. *Submitted by Pauline Walters*

ISAAC COMPTON ELSTON, JR.

Isaac Compton Elston, Jr. a descendant of one of the early settlers of Crawfordsville was born in Crawfordsville on Nov. 13, 1873, the son of Col. Isaac C. and Sarah Mills Elston. He attended Wabash College in 1890-91 and Marietta College in 1891-1893.

At the age of 24 he served as second, and then first lieutenant in Company M., 158th Regiment Indiana Volunteer Infantry in the Spanish American War.

After the war he began his business career in Chicago in association with the Dawes family in the field of public utilities. In 1912 he became an investment banker with the founding of Elston & Co. In 1916 he organized the brokerage firm of Paul H. Davis & Co., which later merged with Hornblower and Weeks. He became a partner in that firm in 1953.

In 1935 Mr. Elston restored the Elston Homestead, built by his grandfather in 1835, and used it as his summer home. In 1940 he became chairman of the board of Elston Bank & Trust Co., also founded by his grandfather. In 1952 he bought the controlling interest of the Citizens National Bank which merged with the Elston Bank.

He was vitally interested in Wabash College, serving on the board of trustees, giving over 11 million dollars to the college over the years, and leaving the Elston Homestead to the College for a president's mansion.

Mr. Elston was married twice. In 1902 he married Pearl Campbell of La Harpe, IL. In 1958 he married Florence Woefel of Chicago.

He was a member of the Wabash Avenue Presbyterian Church, several clubs in Chicago, the Columbia Club in Indianapolis, and the Elks and Country Club of Crawfordsville.

He died Apr. 11, 1964 in Delray Beach, FL. It is possible he was Montgomery County's last Spanish War Veteran. *Submitted by Jean Thompson*

NELSON CHRISTIAN EULER

John Euler (father of Nelson Christian) was born near Wetzler in the Kingdom of Prussia, Germany on Dec. 25, 1845. He came to America with his mother, five sisters and one brother when he was seven years old. He lived in Indianapolis until moving to Jennings County in 1860. He and his brother established a shoe business in North Vernon and for 48 years was prominently identified with the business life of the city. He retired in 1911.

On Feb. 20, 1873 he was married to Mary H. Held of Vernon and they had six children: Harry, Anna, Nelson C., Carrie, Marie and Aaron. Mary Held was born May 19, 1854 in New York.

John Euler was a member of the German Lutheran Church and belonged to the Odd Fellows and Red Men. He was well-known throughout Indiana as a member of the Democratic party having served as Chairman of the Democratic County Committee for Jennings County for 24 years. His wife died in 1905. He died in 1926. Both are buried in Old Vernon Cemetery.

Rear: Faye Sherman; Nelson C., Delores, Inez M. and Nelson F. Euler

Their son, Nelson Christian Euler and Inez Marie Smith of Caldwell, OH were married on Dec. 6, 1903. They were both employed in *The Standard* Office at Greensburg; he in the capacity of foreman and she as a compositor. After moving to Crawfordsville, IN he was a Linotype Operator and she was a Proofreader for *The Journal*.

Both were members of the Wabash Avenue Presbyterian Church in Crawfordsville. Nelson Christian died in 1944. Inez Marie died at Culver Hospital on May 27, 1968.

Children: Nelson Fred Euler was born on Dec. 12, 1905. In 1908, when the family moved to Crawfordsville, young Euler entered the Wilson school in January 1912; then followed periods in the Mills and Tuttle schools and at the end of two years in Jr. High he was allowed to take Latin in 8A because he had attained a percentage of better than 90 in English. He entered Crawfordsville High School in January 1919 and graduated in June 1922. The following September he entered Wabash College and graduated in 1925. He was 19-1/2. He completed the college course of study in a short period of only three years. The family resided at 315 Binford Street.

During his attendance in the Jr. High School, he carried a route for *The Journal* and worked during all the time he was in High School and College. He formed Euler's Entertainers which played at many dances during the last two years of college. After graduation, Nelson put in a couple of years teaching school in Mattoon, IL and Cannon Falls, MN before going to New York City.

Nelson Fred Euler died on Sept. 29, 1987 at age 81 at his home in Toms River, NJ. He served as an Administrator for the Department of Social Services in New York City and retired in July 1970. He is survived by his wife, Margita.

Palma Delores born Aug. 21, 1907 attended Butler University. She married Elbert A. Roberts (Wabash graduate) on July 19, 1928 in Danville, IL. He was a science teacher. She was employed as District Manager for World Book Encyclopedia. She died July 15, 1987.

Sherman Faye was born July 27, 1910. He married Lucille of Crawfordsville. At the time of his mother's death he was with the U.S. Embassy in Tokyo. No further data available.

DALE V. AND MILDRED C. EVANS

Dale and Mildred Evans moved to the John Oldshue farm in Brown Township, a mile and a quarter north of Waveland, on Dec. 18, 1943. They had previously lived on a farm southwest of

153

Russellville, IN, where they had moved after their marriage on Feb. 18, 1939.

Dale was born in Parke County on June 21, 1915 to Earl and Gladys Long Evans. He had one sister, Dorothy Kandrac, now an Indianapolis resident, and one brother, Ronald Richard, who was also a Brown Township resident at the time of his death in 1976.

The family moved to Montgomery County, southeast of Browns Valley where Dale started to school in 1921 and then they moved to Green Township School. He also attended Purdue University for a time where he took a short course in agriculture.

Mildred was born in Montezuma, IN on July 30, 1915, the only child of D.A. and Mary Barr McGaughey who was born and raised in Waveland, the daughter of James W. and Emma Sharp Barr. Mildred attended school in Newport, IN and Russellville, IN from where she was graduated in 1932. She also attended Indiana State University for a short time.

Dale V. and Mildred C. Evans

They had two sons, Dr. Kent Evans, now a school administrator in northern Indiana and Don G. Evans who was killed in a construction accident in 1966, following the completion of his sophomore year at Wabash College. They also had three grandchildren, Lisa Gail, Traci Lynn and Eric Scott.

They were active members of the Methodist Church and later of the Covenant United Methodist Church, after the merger of the Methodist and Presbyterian churches. Dale served in many capacities in the church as did Mildred, who was organist in the church for many years. He was also a member of the Russellville Masonic Lodge and the Montgomery County Farm Bureau and she worked as assistant librarian at the Waveland Brown Township Public Library. They were also honorary members of the Waveland Alumni Association.

Dale was an active farmer until the time of his death, an occupation which he thoroughly enjoyed. He was considered an expert on feeding cattle and was also a grain farmer.

He died Feb. 29, 1988 as the result of a farm accident involved with a feed grinder.

After his death his wife, Mildred, moved to Waveland where she is still active in church and library work, and looks after her almost 98 year old mother. *Submitted by Mildred Evans*

GARY LEE EVANS

Born in Putnam Co., IN on Feb. 7, 1950, Gary Lee Evans grew-up in Fillmore and has recently become a Crawfordsville citizen. Gary is the son of Thomas and Mildred Gladys "Hop" Kelly Evans. Hop was born (1916) in Henderson, KY. She died of a heart attack in 1981 but is remembered by her family and friends as a kind, generous and loving person. Tom was born in 1914, the oldest of three boys. Although Tom only finished third grade, he was a smart man and worked as a farm machinist, radio/TV repairman and draftsman. He also served as the town marshal of Fillmore.

Gary attended school in Fillmore and disliked the idea of only living two houses away from there. He graduated in 1968 from that high school. He attended Indiana State University for three years and received an associate degree in Computer Programming from Clark College, Indianapolis. Gary worked for Bowes Seal Fast (made auto equipment), Grain Dealers Insurance (Indianapolis), and was assistant house manager at the Indianapolis Repertory Theater.

Gary enjoys reading, keeping-up on current events, watching television and crafts. He takes life as it comes and holds a positive attitude. *Submitted by Gary Evans*

EVERHART-EBERHARD

From German history we know the Everhart name was listed as early as A.D. 1081; and this name at that date was listed as living in Wurttemberg, Germany. In researching their movements, the first settler listed was in Pennsylvania, then onto Virginia, the Shenandoah Valley; finally moving to the countryside of Davidson Co., NC.

The first man to assume the spelling of the name as Everhart was in A.D. 1136. They are listed as of the Royal lineage of the Province of Wurttemberg. At early dates, the name was Eberhard, showing they were of symbolic strength, endurance, and solidity. They worked very hard in Germany and prospered.

Everhart Family Members

In September 1764, Christian Eberhard, and his wife, Maria Savilla Guier emigrated to the British colonies in America on the Brittania.

We have been successful in tracing our family of Everharts to 710 years, and for 22 generations.

The first Eberhards to come as American settlers were Michael and Jacob Eberhard. They settled in what is now Lehigh Co., PA. Later other families joined them in 1727.

In September 1764, Christian changed his name to Everhart as a symbol of his freedom from his German ancestors. They lived in Dillinersville, PA.

Peter Eberhard, born Aug. 29, 1757, was the first born son of Christian and Maria Everhart in Philadelphia.

By 1762, we have tax listings of Christian on record in Davidson Co., NC. At this time, he had a son and daughter.

All texts and documents have shown the original name as being Eberhard from the royal family of the province of Wurttemberg, Germany. Other variations of spelling have developed since Eberhards became Americans. The eight other spellings found in the materials are: Everhart, Everheardt, Everhardt, Everheart, Aerhart, Averhart, Aerrhart and Eberhart.

As a general observation of phone books, mailing lists and personal contacts, the Everhart and Eberhart spellings of the name are the most common in the southern part of the United States. Eberhart, Eberhardt and Everhardt are more common in the northern part of the U.S. Everhart, Eberhart and Everhardt are used with the same frequency throughout other parts of the U.S.

The first Everhart to settle in Montgomery County, near Ladoga, was Grandfather John Tillman, son of Alfred and Mary (Warner) Everhart.

Grandfather migrated to Indiana in 1867, and later met and married Theresa Harris. They became parents of ten children: Howard, Frank, Elmer, Ernest, Ralph, Ruth, Cassie, Mary, Doris, and one who died in infancy.

August 7, 1988, a reunion was held at Fair Grove United Methodist Church in Thomasville, NC — the area where our ancestors settled years ago. Many relatives gathered for this special occasion.

The accompanying picture shows only the family members of Grandfather John Tillman and twin brother Frank Edward Everhart. Many others were present to fellowship and reminisce of by-gone days.

Needless to say, we left Davidson Co., NC with memories to last a lifetime! *Submitted by Norma Everhart Mitchell*

HOWARD AND MABEL EVERHART

Howard Mangus Everhart was born in Montgomery County on Sept. 4, 1887, one of ten children of John Tillman and Theresa Harris Everhart. His brothers were Frank, Elmer, Ernest and Ralph. Sisters were Cassie, Ruth, Mary, Doris and one who died in infancy.

Origin of the Everhart name, with its diversified spellings, goes back in history to Würtenburg, Germany. Everharts migrated to Pennsylvania, then the Shenandoah Valley, and finally to Davidson Co., NC. In 1867 grandfather John left North Carolina and his family and settled near Ladoga, IN.

January 12, 1912 Howard married Mabel Bymaster, daughter of Miller and Polyanna Porter Bymaster. They became parents of three children: Reva Irene, Norma Jean and Earl Lawrence.

They lived on a farm about five miles southwest of Ladoga in what is known as Cornstalk Indian Country. On May 12, 1925 at the age of 37 Howard died from blood poisoning caused from injury sustained while repairing the corn planter.

Howard and Mabel Everhart (Graduation Picture)

Norma's memories of her father are few. He worked hard, saved and planned to buy a farm in the near future. They had a new Model T and the family was proud of it. It was black and had a little light outside on a back fender, that could be switched on and off. In the back seat of the car they would take eggs every week to buy groceries. The road had been 'washed out' near their home, but after being repaired, was still very rough. Her father would ask them to be careful and not break the eggs as they hit the bumps. One of Norma's memories - well, she just wasn't careful enough!

Mabel was left with three small children which we're sure was not an easy task. There was no financial help from any source in those days. The money he had was placed in a trust fund for us and although life wasn't easy, each of us graduated from college and have many things for which to be thankful.

Earl married Helen Ping of Waynetown on July 6, 1941. Gary, their son, was born Oct. 26, 1948. Earl and his family live east of Indianapolis, but he continues to operate his power brakes business in downtown Indy.

Reva married Milton Peacock of Crawfordsville Aug. 29, 1942. She was an elementary teacher for 45 years before retirement. She passed away July 3, 1984.

Norma married Bernard Mitchell, son of Robert and Wanetah Mitchell, of near Waveland, June 8, 1946. She retired from the teaching profession having taught 42 years in South Montgomery Schools. They are the parents of Michael who married Rhonda Dooley of Marshall, IN on July 16, 1972. Both are graduates of Purdue. They have two sons - Clint born Aug. 27, 1974 and Matthew born July 6, 1976.

Mabel lived in Ladoga most of her life until her death June 1, 1965.

Norma and Bernard attended a reunion of the Everhart Clan August 1988 in Thomasville, NC from where Grandfather Everhart migrated in youth. We met many relatives for the first time. How rewarding to share that togetherness if only for a weekend! *Submitted by Norma E. Mitchell*

HARRY W. AND EDITH EVERNHAM

Harry and Edith Coonrod, both natives of White County, were married Jan. 14, 1911. Together they operated the Burnettsville, IN telephone exchange; she as agent and Harry as lineman, for almost 20 years.

In 1901, when Harry was 16 years old, he got his first regular job as driver of a team and wagon which hauled a telephone line crew around the countryside, in White County and Burnettsville. In a short time he began working as a lineman for the exchange and received $1.25 a day for his services. He attended and graduated from high school at Monticello. During his high school years he played football. Following high school he tried other jobs, but always returned to the telephone work.

In August 1932 Harry and Edith, with their family, moved to Waveland where Mrs. Evernham served as agent until her retirement July 1957. Harry retired March 1956. He had served as plant man for the Coal Creek Telephone Corporation, with responsibility of keeping in order the lines for both Waveland and Russellville exchanges.

Harry was the son of William and Mary Wilson Evernham, born at Francesville, IN in 1885 and died at Waveland in 1957.

Edith was the daughter of Ruth and David Coonrod, born in White County and died at Waveland in 1978.

Four children were born to this union: Richard, who married Dorothy Barnes and lives in Evansville, IN; Rosemary, living in Indianapolis; Roberta, who married Harold Gilliland, living in Waveland and Byron David who died when very young. Richard had two sons, James and Thomas W.; Roberta had two sons, Jay D. living in England and Brad living in Crawfordsville.

The Evernhams were members of the Waveland Presbyterian Church. Harry was a member of the Masonic Lodge and Waveland Lions Club. With nearly a century of telephone service between them, along with the close confinement which is characteristic of their type of work, the Evernhams had little opportunity to develop hobbies, travel or form interests outside the realm of their employment, but were always interested in the community. *Submitted by Roberta Evernham Gilliland*

JOHN MELVILLE EWBANK

John Melville "Mel" Ewbank was born to John Howard and Ruby (Caplinger) Ewbank at Ladoga, IN, on Feb. 6, 1906. At that time the senior Ewbank was teaching at the Ladoga school. He would later serve as principal at the Cayuga school and serve as a part-time civil engineer in the building of U.S. Highway 41.

John was educated at the New Market and Cayuga schools. He graduated in 1924 from Cayuga. After graduating from high school he worked as a farm hand near Ida, KS. From 1926 to 1928 John worked on the New York Division of the Erie Rail Road out of Jersey City, NJ. During the summer of 1928 he worked in a threshing ring on the Western Wheat Harvest.

In 1929 John went to work for R.R. Donnelly and Sons, Crawfordsville, IN. He started as a time keeper. He met and married Garnet Allee of Marshall, IN, that year. They resided in New Market. On July 14, 1933, a daughter, Charlotte Ann was born. At that time they lived on North Third Street next to the old community building.

In 1930 John was commissioned a second lieutenant in the U.S. Army Reserve through the R.O.T.C. program at Purdue University. He remained in the reserve program until called to active duty during the 1941 mobilization. John participated in the 1942 Louisiana Maneuvers. He was stationed throughout the south until being sent to the Pacific Theater with the 133rd Infantry Regiment in 1944. He served with the U.S. Army occupation forces on Japan from the end of the war to 1946. He continued in the reserve program until 1960, when he retired as a lieutenant colonel.

After the war John returned to Crawfordsville, and R.R. Donnelly where he worked as a production supervisor until retirement in 1968. His wife Garnet passed away suddenly of a heart attack in 1956. He married Mary Bronaugh in 1957.

John passed away at his home of a heart attack on Sept. 15, 1987. He was a member of the New Market Christian Church, the Alamo Masonic Lodge #144, and the Scottish Rite.

JOHN PETER FAUST

John Peter Faust was born near New Market Sept. 6, 1854 to Reuben and Cynthia Faust. He married Ella Anna Armantrout Sept. 28, 1881. Ella was born June 15, 1861 daughter of Joseph and Martha Armantrout. To this union were born three children. Ora Warren Aug. 3, 1882; Mattie E. Apr. 27, 1884 and Ethel L. Mar. 22, 1886.

In early life John Peter united with St. James Lutheran Church near Darlington. Later he and his wife united with the First Christian Church of Linden. He was a deacon and a faithful and active member of the church. He made friends and kept them. He was a devoted husband and father. He was a lover of music and his last words were "Blessed are those who die in the Lord for they rest from their labor and their works do follow them."

John Peter and Ella Armantrout, Ethel, Mattie and Ora Warren Faust

He was a farmer and his death Oct. 3, 1917 was the result of a farm accident when a team of horses ran away with the wagon that he was driving. He was only 62 years old. Ella Armantrout died Apr. 29, 1926.

Ethel L. married Frank Massing Feb. 20, 1912 and died June 8, 1912.

Mattie E. married Fred Rhoads Nov. 8, 1934 and she died Mar. 5, 1960.

Ora Warren and Verna Cecil Pierce were married Aug. 5, 1911 at New Richmond. Ora was a true farmer as his ancestors had been. The day after his wedding he was thrashing. He farmed until he was 92 when he still drove a tractor. Verna was a seamstress. They were members and attended the Linden Methodist Church regularly.

Ora died Nov. 26, 1976 and Verna Cecil died Jan. 8, 1978 at Linden. They lived near Linden in Montgomery County most of their lives.

To this marriage was born four children. Leland Woodrow Apr. 11, 1913; Robert Wray Sept. 28, 1914; Edna Lorene June 21, 1918 and Lloyd Wendell Dec. 15, 1921.

Leland was married to Jean Marie Applegate June 16, 1946. Jean Marie was born Jan. 10, 1920 in Brazil, IN. Her parents were Marion and Essie Marie Shattuck Applegate. Jean was a school teacher in Parke, Putnam, Benton and Montgomery Counties. Leland also followed his ancestors by farming in the Linden area. They both were active in the Linden Methodist Church. Leland was a Trustee and Secretary for many years. They both attend regularly and Leland since ten years old. To this marriage were born three children.

Thomas Eugene Faust born Nov. 21, 1954; Sue Ellen born Nov. 10, 1955 and David Lee born Oct. 1, 1961. They are all graduates of North Montgomery High School and Ball State University and accountants with C.P.A. License.

Thomas lives in Lafayette. He married Judith Irene Molina Nov. 20, 1976 in Linden Methodist Church. Judith is a supervisor at St. Elizabeth Hospital. Their children are Brianne Lauren Aug. 24, 1980; Jonathan Thomas, Mar. 13, 1982 and Brittney Meredith Dec. 21, 1988.

Sue Ellen married Jan Robert Chenoweth June 25, 1988 in their new home in Indianapolis. Jan has accountant and law degrees.

David Lee married Shana Lyn Morrison May 29, 1982 in the Linden Methodist Church. Shana is a first grade teacher at Greencastle where they live. They have a daughter Kyler Nichole born Nov. 3, 1985.

More information on this family is given in the Ora Warren Faust family. *Submitted by Leland Faust*

ORA WARREN FAUST

Ora Warren Faust born Aug. 3, 1882, to John Peter Faust and Ella Anna Armantrout. He married Verna Cecil Pierce July 5, 1911.

Their children were Leland Woodrow Apr. 11, 1913; Robert Wray Sept. 28, 1914; Edna Lorene June 21, 1918 and Lloyd Wendell Dec. 15, 1921.

Robert Wray was also a farmer and served in World War II including D-Day. He married Flora Josephine Franklin, a business teacher at Cascade High School, Mar. 28, 1974. They lived in the Mooresville area. He died Aug. 2, 1967.

Edna Lorene married Henry Robert Elliott Apr. 9, 1939. Edna was a beautician in Ladoga and was a member of Ladoga Christian Church where she and her daughter played the organ and piano together. Robert was the owner and operator of a Marathon Service station. To this union was born one daughter.

Connie Lorene born Nov. 27, 1942. Connie was a bank teller. She married William Luther Bradley Aug. 26, 1962. Bill is a farmer. They have two sons Brad Lee June 22, 1966 who works at R.R. Donnelley Co. and Greg Elliott Aug. 15, 1971 a graduate of Southmont High School where he was a member of the swim team and won many honors.

Ora Warren Faust and Verna Cecil Faust

Lloyd Wendell married Ellen Sabens Nov. 25, 1945, in the Linden Methodist Church. Both were born in Montgomery County and lived in Linden where they raised their family. Lloyd was employed by the Linden State Bank for 46 years, retiring as President. Ellen worked as secretary-treasurer for North Montgomery School Corporation for 22 years. Both are members of the Linden Methodist Church having served in various capacities and have been active in many community activities. Lloyd has been very active in the Masonic Body and Order of the Eastern Star, holding a state office in the latter. To this marriage was born three daughters.

Karen Arlene married Dr. Thomas Maxwell Jamison Apr. 4, 1970. They have a son, Chadwick Maxwell Apr. 12, 1974 and a daughter Courtney Marie Aug. 1, 1977. After graduating from Indiana University they moved to Williamsburg, AL, where Tom is a practicing Radiologist and Karen is a Dental Hygienist.

Linda Kay married Gilbert Ray Smith in the Linden Methodist Church Aug. 22, 1970. They have a daughter Amy Elizabeth Jan. 19, 1976. Both graduated from Indiana State University with a degree in Elementary Education. "Gil" is superintendent of transportation in the New Albany School System and Linda is an elementary teacher for the Floyd Central School system.

Gayle married Richard L. Massa July 19, 1980 in the Linden Methodist Church. Gayle is a graduate of the Woods Dental Assistant School and is employed at the Indiana University School of Dentistry as Supervisor of the Orthodontic Department. Dick is self-employed in an Auto Mechanics Garage in Beech Grove.

For more additional information of this family see The History of John Peter Faust. *Submitted by Edna Elliott*

DENVER D. AND MARCELLA NEES FELTNER

Denver Doyal Feltner, school principal, teacher and farmer, was born near London, Laurel Co., KY, on Nov. 28, 1911, to Moses Whitson and Mary Magdalene "Maggie" Cornett Feltner. He was the third-born of their nine children. The family moved to Indiana in 1922, settling on a farm near Brownsburg, Hendricks County. "Mose" was a farmer and blacksmith. The family moved to New Ross, Montgomery County, in 1929. Denver graduated from New Ross High School in 1930 and worked for Walter Whitecotton at the New Ross Grain and Lumber Company before enrolling at Central Normal College at Danville. He graduated in 1936 and began his teaching career at Mace School, Montgomery County, where he served as sixth grade teacher and principal 25 years. In 1963 the new Walnut Township Elementary School was built, and Denver continued teaching there and was named principal again in 1972. He retired in 1977, having invested 41 years in education in Walnut Township Schools. During those years he combined his teaching with farming.

L. to R.: Richard, Nancy, Marcia and Ruth Ann, Denver and Marcella Feltner

Denver married Marcella Turner Nees, Mar. 19, 1937, in the Methodist Parsonage at Linden, IN. It was the home of her sister, Sara, and her husband, Rev. H. Merrill Ivey. Marcella was born Feb. 9, 1913, at Crawfordsville to Milton Leonidas Nees (born Owen Co., IN, 1873) and Lulu Turner Nees (born New Ross, 1880). Marcella had two sisters, Ruth and Sara, and one brother, David Milton, now deceased. Milton Nees served five terms as Montgomery County Surveyor, and he was the first cashier of the New Ross Farmers State Bank. Lulu was the bank's bookkeeper. Marcella graduated from New Ross High School in 1931 and from Indiana Central Business College. She was employed by the Federal Government in the Resettlement Administration in New Mexico before her marriage.

Denver and Marcella Feltner became the parents of four children—all were born in Culver Hospital at Crawfordsville, and all graduated from New Ross High School. Their son, Richard Lee, born Oct. 16, 1938, married (1) Karen Sommer, Sept. 11, 1959, Wauwatosa, WI. Their children, Richard A., born Jan. 14, 1962, Raleigh, North Carolina, and Susan S., born Aug. 8, 1965, Lansing, MI. Susan married Steven McElwain, June 13, 1987, Louisville, KY. Richard Lee married (2) Janet Croucher Goetz, May 30, 1982, Louisville. She had son, Kevin, born Aug. 31, 1966, and daughter, Kimberly, born May 24, 1967 in Kentucky. Richard L. has B.S. and M.S. Purdue University and PH.D. North Carolina State University, and he is now Dean, Bellarmine College's School of Business, Louisville. Dr. Feltner had the distinction of serving in United States Department of Agriculture as Assistant Secretary with Hon. Earl L. Butz during the Nixon-Ford Administration.

Their daughter, Ruth Ann, born June 5, 1941, married Leonard L. Croteau Apr. 6, 1968, at New Ross. She is a graduate of New Mexico State University and has been an elementary teacher in New Mexico 26 years. They have owned a moving and storage business in Los Alamos and are retiring this year to Truth or Consequences, NM.

Their second daughter, Marcia Claire, born June 24, 1945, married William K. Frazier, June 27, 1965, at New Ross. Both are graduates of Indiana University, and she has taught 20 years in Adams Elementary School, Fort Wayne. They have three sons: Jeffrey A., born Apr. 4, 1967, at Franklin, Keith N., born Jan. 20, 1971, at Fort Wayne, and Christopher P., born Apr. 18, 1975, Fort Wayne.

Their third daughter, Nancy Elizabeth, born Mar. 14, 1948, married Michael P. Hartley, Dec. 27, 1970, at New Ross. Both are graduates of Indiana University, and they have three sons: Michael P., Jr., born Apr. 18, 1974 at Indianapolis, Steven M., born June 21, 1977, Peoria, IL, and Nicholas F. born Aug. 19, 1980, Danville, IN. Nancy is a social worker and school counselor, and they live at Plainfield.

Mr. and Mrs. Feltner have lived all of their married lives south of New Ross on the farm which they purchased from her parents and her mother's estate. Their house was built by Marcella's grandfather, David Milton Turner, in 1878 and has been her home for 71 years. They celebrated 50 years of marriage in 1987 with an Open House hosted by their children in the New Ross United Methodist Church where they are active members. He is a member of the Masonic Lodge and both are members of the Order of Eastern Star at Jamestown. They hold memberships in Indiana Farm Bureau, Retired Teachers' Association, Stated and Local Historical Societies, and she is a 50 year member of the Extension Homemakers Organization. She is also a member of The Pioneers of Indiana. Denver was a director for nearly 40 years of the Crawfordsville Federal Land Bank Association. Marcella was president of the Steering Committee for the New Ross Community Centennial Celebration in 1975.

GLEN AND PATRICIA FERGUSON

Glen Edward Ferguson born Sept. 26, 1926 at Cropsey, IL, is the son of Cecil Ferguson and Ocia Hamilton.

Glen attended school at Waynetown, IN. He served 21 years with the United States Army retiring in 1965 at Fort Knox, KY where he was Chief Warrant Officer W 3. Glen served overseas during W.W. II at Hawaii, Okinawa and Korea. He served in Korea two tours of duty and Germany three tours during peace time. Glen had one brother, Kenneth, who died May 30, 1950.

Glen married Aug. 30, 1947 at Wapella, IL to Patricia Ann Fruits, born Apr. 27, 1931 in New Richmond, IN, daughter of Charles M. and Mary (Smith) Fruits. Pat attended school at New Richmond, IN. Charles Fruits was the son of Noah and Lenora (Lewis) Fruits. Mary is the daughter of John H. and Cinderella (Balser) Smith. Charles and Mary are the parents of eight children: Grace, Herbert, Ralph, Thelma, Marietta, Charles, Pat and Ruth.

Glen and Patricia are the parents of three children: Glenda Ann, Candice Marie and Michael Steven.

Glen and Patricia Ferguson

Glenda Ann born on Feb. 5, 1948 in Crawfordsville, IN. Graduated from Crawfordsville High School and married Feb. 5, 1966 at New Market to Wendall Glenn Smith, son of Russell and Betty Wendall Smith who was born Apr. 2, 1947. They divorced in January 1975. Glenda and her second husband, Lawson Rudd have a son, Bruce Edward Rudd, born July 20, 1978 at Hammond, IN. Glenda is a member of Brownsburg Chapter O.E.S.

Candice Marie was born May 12, 1953 in Trieste, Italy. She graduated from Crawfordsville High School and married Garry Alan Potts on Aug. 7, 1971 at Yountsville, IN. Garry was born July 14, 1952, the son of Wendall Keith and Letha Tucker Potts. They have three children: Tina Marie, born Nov. 19, 1972; Garry Alan, born Nov. 22, 1974; and Amanda LeAnn born Oct. 2, 1976. All were born in Crawfordsville. Garry and Candy are now divorced. Candy works at Hi-Tek Lighting and is a member of New Richmond O.E.S. #377.

Michael Steven born Aug. 2, 1954 in Baumholder, Germany. He graduated from Crawfordsville High School and married Constance Sue VanCleave on Aug. 9, 1974 at Smartsburg, IN. Connie was born Feb. 22, 1956, the daughter of Robert and Mildred (Isenberg) VanCleave. They have two children: Christina Lynn, born Jan. 3, 1975 at Crawfordsville and Christopher Michael, born Apr. 12, 1978 at Crawfordsville. They now live in Dalton, GA. Mike owns M.S. Ferguson Associates. He is an Independent Representative for Crawford Industries of Crawfordsville and Benson International Systems of New York. He is a member of Masonic Lodge No. 50 F.&A.M., Scottish Rite, Yaarab Temple Shrine in Atlanta, Dalton Shrine Club and Dalton Funny Bones Clown unit.

Glen and Pat stay active in the community. He is in Masonic Lodge #50 F.&A.M., Scottish Rite, Murat Shrine, Montgomery County Shrine Club and the Ben Hur Floaters. Also, the New Richmond O.E.S. #377, of which Pat is also a member. She is currently serving is historian of the Genealogy Section of the Montgomery County Historical Society and is a member of the Dorothy Q. Chapter, Daughters of the American Revolution.

WILLIAM H. AND JANET HOUSE FIELDS

William "Bill" Harry Fields is a native of Montgomery County. He was born Dec. 20, 1938 in Waynetown, IN, the second child of William Leslie Fields, born Apr. 28, 1913 Rush Co., IN and Vivian Ruth Cramer, born Feb. 16, 1918, Montgomery Co., IN, and died Jan. 18, 1985 in Montgomery County. His siblings are: Hazel, Jerry, Ruth, Francie, John and Cathy. His paternal grandparents were William Harrison "Harry" Fields, born Nov. 23, 1888, and died July 10, 1933 in Montgomery County, and Jennie Hopkins Fields born Jan. 26, 1893, Tuscola, IL and died Apr. 17, 1973 in Montgomery County. Maternal grandparents were Harry Albert Cramer born Sept. 14, 1873 in Boone County and died Aug. 11, 1953 in Montgomery County, and Della Frances Martin, born Aug. 14, 1881 in Ripley County and died Feb. 25, 1961 in Montgomery Co., IN.

Bill graduated from Waynetown High School and started working at R.R. Donnelley and Sons for 66 cents per hour. He worked there for 16 years before trying the construction business. He now works for Wabash College in the maintenance department. On June 7, 1968 William married Janet Louise House in the Waynetown Methodist Church.

Gayle, Billy, Janet, Bill and Kevin Fields

Janet was born Feb. 16, 1942 in Carroll Co., IN, the eighth child of Lester Merle House, born May 6, 1901 in Warren Co., IN, and died Sept. 7, 1974 in Tippecanoe County, and Myra Louise Redman, born Mar. 15, 1905 in Fountain County, IN.

Her maternal grandparents were John Wesley Redman born Nov. 10, 1975 in Fountain County and Stella May Zimmerman, born June 6, 1883 in Kentucky. Her paternal grandfather was Charles Arnold House, born Apr. 13, 1954 in New York of German and French ancestry, left home at the age of 16 and settled in Warren Co., IN. A contractor, he built most the bridge footings in Warren County. On June 1, 1880 he married Sarah Frances Voltz, born Sept. 3, 1959, daughter of John Jacob Voltz, born July 30, 1833, a native of Wertemberg, Germany, and Elizabeth Catherine Smith, born Jan. 11, 1831 in Ohio, daughter of John and Elizabeth Harmon Smith natives of Virginia. John Jacob left Germany in the fall of 1850 and arrived in America in the following spring. He served in Company D 86th Indiana Infantry in the Civil War. He was a boot and shoemaker; and a farmer.

Janet spent her childhood in Warren County moving to Montgomery County in 1962. She graduated from Williamsport High School in 1960. She has worked as a clerk at the Crawfordsville District Public Library for ten years.

Bill and Janet have four children, Melody Ann (see Robert Roach family) born May 18, 1961 Vermillion Co., IL; Gayle Darlene born Mar. 31, 1963 Montgomery Co., IN; Kevin Wayne July 30, 1965 Tippecanoe County; and William "Billy" Lester born Oct. 13, 1969 in Tippecanoe County. Gayle and Kevin live in Phoenix, AZ. Billy now attends Franklin College. Bill and Janet live in Waynetown. They are active in the Methodist Church, 4-H Club, and the Square Dance Club.

CHAUNCEY AND ESTHER RATCLIFF FINE

On June 3, 1944 Chauncey M. Fine and Esther L. Ratcliff were married by the Rev. Paul Million in the chapel of the 1st Christian Church, Crawfordsville, IN. Chauncey's parents: Jesse David Fine and Susan Atkinson Fine. Esther's parents: Frank P. Ratcliff and Edith L. Thomas Ratcliff. At the time of our marriage Chauncey was serving in the Army Air Force Sept. 22, 1942 to Feb. 14, 1946. Was a flight line inspection and maintenance crew member on P-51's. Mostly stationed at the base in Bartow, FL.

Of this marriage were four children: Gary Steven Nov. 16, 1945. Married Kathryn Buse Oct. 11, 1969. Two adopted children: Angela Sept. 18, 1974 and Eric June 4, 1979. Roger Allen Dec. 31, 1947. Married Beverly Edwards Oct. 29, 1977. One adopted child: Melissa May 16, 1985. Joyce Ellen July 1, 1949. Married William Jeffers Apr. 13, 1969. Two children: Jill June 21, 1973 and Christopher Mar. 26, 1975. Gloria Jeanne Oct. 23, 1952. Married Steven Gangwer Sept. 3, 1972. Two children: Jeremy Sept. 20, 1977 and Aaron Sept. 2, 1980.

Chauncey and Esther (Ratcliff) Fine

Chauncey's employment consisted of being a city letter carrier over 30 years; retiring Apr. 7, 1977. Esther's work was a clerk for Sears Roebuck, 217 E. Main St. leaving there to be in bookkeeping department for Elston Bank, 132 E. Main St. retiring June 30, 1976. Also during this time of 1952-1980 we were in business as Chinchilla Ranchers; raising breeding stock and show animals and Chauncey learning Show Judging kept our family busy and involved.

Places we have lived in Crawfordsville are: in the fall of 1946 rented the west downstairs apartment at 713 W. Pike, owned by Jesse and Susan Fine. After July 1949 purchased property at 619 E. Pike St. The summer of 1953 purchased land from Harold and Elsie Johnson where we moved into our home we had built Oct. 1, 1953. Now 1300 Waynetown

Road. Our retirement years are spent doing part-time business of distribution of pet and home product "SOP-UP" in partnership as our own Corporation.

Our children's occupations are: Gary is staff consultant, CAP Gemini America, Dayton, OH. Lives in Indianapolis at present. Worked for Blue Cross Blue Shield 19 years previous to 1988. Roger's Company, Mid-State Engineering, Indianapolis, does survey and constructing engineering. Beverly a Pharmacist Hooks Drugs at Carmel where they reside. Joyce working with Full Circle Travel Agency, Crawfordsville; husband Bill works with Polk Advertising Company out of Crawfordsville. Was in sales for Western and Southern Insurance 20 years previous. They reside in Crawfordsville. Gloria working as store supervisor for Boise Stage Stop. Steve works as head of maintenance at the same Stop which is Union 76. They live in the country on Black Creek Road, Boise, ID. All the men have served their country's armed forces. We have been active in our church over the last 40+ years at Trinity United Methodist, joining in the summer of 1946. Esther's memberships are United Methodist Women and Dorothy Q Chapter DAR. Chauncey's memberships: United Methodist Men, American Legion, Masonic Lodge, York Rite and Scottish Rite. A yellow box with white ribbon was placed in the St. John's time capsule Nov. 18, 1976.

JOHN AND MARY (CLYMER) FINK

John and Mary Clymer Fink came from New York and Pennsylvania, entering land in Ripley Twp., Montgomery Co., IN, Oct. 11, 1824. John left Mary a widow, before 1835, with Susan, Thomas, Ruben J., Maria, Adeline, and Samuel to raise.

Commodore & Sarah Fink, 1937

Ruben J. married Lucinda Ammerman, 1846. From this union came Isadore, Evan (Ivan), Cyrus, Commodore, Willard, Frances, Ella, Floyd, Addie, Clarence, and Mary.

Commodore married Sarah Lowe, 1880. Sarah was the fourth child of six children born to Michael and Amanda Munns Lowe, and granddaughter of William and Elizabeth Lowe, and John and Jane Fothergill Munns. Commodore and Sarah met at the Yountsville skating rink; he fell over her. They owned land in Union and Franklin Twps.

Otto, Alice, and Mary were their children. Alice, 1888-1979, married J. Leon LePage, 1909. Two daughters came from this marriage, Natalie Ann and Julie Jacqueline.

FLANINGAM FAMILY HISTORY

Archibald Flaningam was born Aug. 14, 1809, in Virginia, the seventh of 11 children of George and Mary Polly (Larrick) Flaningam. He migrated to Franklin Township in 1830, and married Catherine Kashner in 1845.

They began farming, four miles east of Darlington and he and Catherine became the parents of 12 children, nine of whom grew to adulthood.

Their eldest son, Andrew Jackson Flaningam, was the father of James, who owned and operated the Flaningam Hardware in Crawfordsville in the 1920's.

Andrew's grandson, Jack, lived with Uncle Jim and graduated from Crawfordsville High School. He and this contributor met entirely by chance at Martha Ellen Flaningam's art exhibit at Northern Illinois University in 1982.

John Archibald Flaningam, third child of Archibald, married Susan Margaret Clark and they resided at the family homestead, prior to moving into Boone County.

Their son, Edward, operated a dry-goods store in Darlington in the early 1900's.

The sixth child of Archibald was Albert, born in Franklin Township in 1861. He married Sallie Mae Clark, sister to Susan Clark, and they began farming two miles east of Darlington.

One highlight of their courtship was a 15-mile buggy trip to Colfax, then a train ride, via the Vandalia, to the Montgomery County Fair. Dinner was a basket lunch, topped with ice-cold lemonade.

Albert and Sallie were the parents of three children: Forrest, Fred and Nellie.

Forrest returned to Franklin Township and in 1910 married Mary Ellen Woody. They acquired the George Kashner farm, three miles southeast of Darlington. Kashner had built a new barn and a new brick dwelling. Both were built about 1876 and the brick for the house was burnt in a near-by field.

Forrest and Mary were the parents of two sons, Dwight and DeVon, the contributor of this family history.

Nellie married John McCabe of Crawfordsville.

Archibald's youngest son was Samuel. He married Mollie Ward in 1887 and Mollie was able to reach the age of 103. Samuel and his wife lived in Franklin Township, adjacent to the Boone County line. Their oldest son, Walter, married Lola Clark and they became the parents of Norman, Harold, John and Julian.

Their daughter, Alta, married Orville Deck and established their farm home four miles southeast of Darlington. Their children were Edith, Charlotte and Charlene Vernon.

Ruth Flaningam became postmistress at Thorntown and their son, Ward, now lives in Florida. He and Clara Geiger were the parents of Mary Jean Grimes.

Archibald's youngest daughter, Ida Catherine, married Elwood Woody and they lived on their farm near the county line. They were the parents of Raymond, Ralph, Leonard and Ethel Jarrell.

It should be noted that other children of George and Mary Polly Flaningam also came to Franklin Township.

Their eldest son, John, became a pioneer farmer near Darlington in 1825. Two of his grandsons were Ira of Darlington and Homer of Crawfordsville.

The second son of George was Samuel. He married the exuberant Eleanor Abernathy in 1825 at Ross Co., OH, and headed West in a covered wagon for their honeymoon. The trip ended about one mile northeast of Darlington where he obtained five acres of land under the new homestead laws.

Samuel and Eleanor were thrifty and increased their land holdings. They were the parents of 11 children, one of whom was John, who married Rebecca Booher in 1859. They were the parents of Oliver, William, Jasper, Samuel, Luella, and Flora Ford. Within Samuel's family you will find the names of Harris, Needham, Harper, (who became county sheriff), and Lafayette Flaningam, who was the great-uncle of M.L. Flaningam, history professor at Purdue and Ora L. Flaningam, of Midland, MI, the present family historian. He was also the grandfather of Nellie Flaningam Paddack, who celebrated her 90th birthday on May 14, 1988.

The descendants of George and Mary Polly Flaningam made an abundant contribution to the history of Franklin Township, and approximately 80 members of the family are buried at the St. James Lutheran Cemetery, east of Darlington. Most of these descendants were farmers and believed in the principles of the Jacksonian Democratic Party.

NELLIE MAYE FLANINGAM

Nellie Maye Flaningam was born in Franklin Township, Montgomery Co., IN on May 14, 1898, the daughter of Wallace Clinton and Arvella Hopkins Flaningam.

Wallace Clinton Flaningam son of Lafayette and Sarah Meneeley Flaningam was born Feb. 25, 1873 in the Flaningam home one mile east of Darlington, where he spent his boyhood. After his marriage to Arvella Hopkins on Feb. 13, 1895 they established their home a short distance north of his parents' home and they lived there for several years. Wallace came to Darlington as a clerk in a hardware store. He and his half brother, Ellis Booher later established a hardware business of their own. Later he moved to Kirkpatrick and began a Grocery Store which he owned until October 1944. He died Feb. 17, 1946 at Darlington.

Arvella Hopkins was born Jan. 12, 1877 at Chillicothe, OH the daughter of Robert C. and Rebecca Caskey Hopkins; she died Sept. 20, 1963 in Montgomery Co., IN.

Our subject, Nellie May Flaningam married Harley Sylvester Paddack, son of Samuel and Jennie Miller Paddack, on Mar. 14, 1918 in Montgomery Co., IN. Harley a native of Montgomery County was born Jan. 4, 1898. To this union four children were born; W. Royden born Feb. 28, 1921 and married Geneva Fletcher on Dec. 24, 1939, and died July 16, 1982; Barton born Feb. 20, 1929, and married Wilma Moore on Aug. 20, 1950; Patricia born Dec. 23, 1932 and married Gene Hubert Ray on Mar. 16, 1952; Robert born Mar. 6, 1935 and married Shirley Simmons on June 5, 1955.

Harley Sylvester Paddack died Sept. 22, 1958 in Montgomery County. Nellie, who will be 91 years of age on May 14, 1989, is currently residing in Lane Nursing Home in Crawfordsville. *Submitted by Sally Ray*

FOSTER ALEXANDER AND MARY CATHERINE SMITH FLETCHER

Foster Alexander Fletcher was born Apr. 8, 1845 in Unadilla, Otsego Co., NY, the seventh of ten children born to Joseph Alexander Fletcher (born 1805 in Hancock, NH) and his wife Sarah H. Streeter (born 1813 in Chesterfield, NH). Sarah was the daughter of Benjamin and Sarah (Farr) Streeter and a third cousin to John Adams, second President of the United States. Joseph and Sarah both died in Walpole, NH, where several of their children settled.

Family tradition says that Foster walked from

New Hampshire to Indiana at the age of 16, with all his possessions tied up in a red bandana. Foster's brother Charles settled in Montgomery County in 1869 and had land adjacent to him. His brothers Aurelius, Winslow, and Horatio settled in Champaign Co., IL, but Aurelius, owned several farms in Montgomery County, where he still has descendants.

Alexander and Mary Catherine (Smith) Fletcher

Foster became a successful farmer and owned land in Madison, Union and Brown Townships, as well as in southern Indiana and the Dakotas. There is a dry branch running from Black Creek called "Foster Fletcher Ditch." Although Foster was an influential citizen of the area, his grandchildren report that he mistrusted banks and kept his money in tin cans in the barn.

Foster was married Apr. 25, 1875 in Linden to Mary Catherine Smith, who was born Apr. 1, 1852 near Alamo, the daughter of Abigail Smith, and the granddaughter of Catherine Smith. Mary was a fourth generation descendant of Sebastian Stonebraker and Susannah Yeakley. She was raised by Paschal and Margarette Wilhite, who gave her 50 acres of land as a wedding present.

Foster and Mary lived most of their lives on their farm at Cherry Grove near Linden, where they raised 13 children: Lillie Anna, who married William Riley Vail; Mabel A., who died unmarried; Iva J., who died at age 13, and her twin Ida E., who married Ora Busenbark; Charles Robert, who married Mary Elizabeth Ocheltree; Margaret Louise, who married John W. Cox; Paschal Earl, who died at age 8; Walter David, who married Zora Margaret Lehman; Sarah Helen, who married first John Barton, then Emery Luse, and her twin Mary Frances, who married Frederick Dunn; Rasco Russell, who married Marguerite Watts; Ethel, who married Ralph Todd; and Merle Alexander, who married Ruth Naomi Hunt but died soon after.

Once asked how she managed so many children, Mary replied that "They just come along and you make 'em welcome!"

Foster died July 6, 1910, and Mary died Apr. 11, 1939. They are buried in Oak Hill Cemetery, surrounded by the graves of several of their 13 children. Sarah Helen, their last surviving child, died in 1988 at the age of 97.

The farm built by Foster at Cherry Grove was the birthplace of several generations of Fletcher descendants, many of whom still reside in Montgomery County. Although no longer in the Fletcher family, the house and barn still stand, a testament to the enterprising spirit of an earlier generation.

MAX A. FLETCHER

Max Alexander Fletcher lives on a 160 acre farm; 120 acres of which is in Section 13 of Franklin Township. The remaining 40 acres are in Boone County. His parents, Walter David and Zora Margaret (Lehman) Fletcher purchased and moved to this farm early in 1919.

Walter, the eighth child of a family of 13, was the son of Foster A. and Mary (Smith) Fletcher, whose biographical sketch can be found in *History of Montgomery Co., IN* Vol. 1 by A.W. Bowen and Co. Walter was born in Benton Co., IN in 1887. The family soon moved back to Montgomery County. He grew up at their farm home at Cherry Grove. He often recalled the building of the railroad between Crawfordsville and Linden. Walter and Zora were married in 1916 in Crawfordsville, by Rev. Stanforth. Zora was the daughter of John Wesley and Marena Agnes (Kersey) Lehman. She was the fourth child of a family of 12 children. They lived in Montgomery County all of their married life. They were the parents of: Margery Dee born 1919 died 1946, Martha Glee (Mrs. Wesley) Tribbett and Max Alexander.

Zora died Aug. 10, 1969 and Walter died Oct. 7, 1975. They are buried at Oak Hill Cemetery.

Max is married to the former Barbara Karshner, daughter of Mrs. Virginia Karshner of Crawfordsville. They have lived in Montgomery County all of their lives and are the parents of two sons: Gary David Fletcher of Walnut Creek, CA, a Phi Beta Kappa graduate of Depauw University, holds a Doctorate degree from Yale University, and Mark Allen Fletcher of De Pere, MO is a graduate of Purdue University.

JON L. AND SHARON FOSTER

Jon L. and Sharon Foster are life long residents of Montgomery County. They resided on the family farm near Waveland for 25 years.

Jon was born to Henry Lee and Gladys Sharp Foster in January 1936. Jon graduated from Waveland High School in 1954 and served in the U.S. Army for two years in Korea and Japan. In June 1959 he married Sharon Brown at Crawfordsville. They are the parents of two daughters: Mary Virginia, born in 1966, and Sherry Lee born in 1968. Jon farmed for 25 years and drove a school bus for Waveland for 13 years.

Jon's father, Henry Lee, was born in 1902 in Montgomery County to James Thomas and Susan Denman Foster. He had an older sister, Susan Jemima Booher, who spent most of her life in the New Market area. Lee was married to Gladys Sharp and they were the parents of Jon and an older sister, Dorothy Lou Chiros, who lives in Buena Park, CA with her husband and three children. Lee farmed most of his life and worked several years at Whitecotton Hardware and John Deere store at Waveland. He passed away in February 1982.

Jon, Sherry, Mary and Sharon

Jon's mother, Gladys, was born in Wheelers Mill, KY near Elizabeth Town. She later was sent to Indiana where she was adopted from an orphanage by John and Minnie Sharp of Waveland. Gladys was educated at Waveland and was a housewife. She was well-known for her home-made yeast donuts that she sold through out the local area. Gladys passed away at an early age in 1945. Lee later remarried in 1951 to Virginia Moore, who taught school in Montgomery County for 41 years.

Sharon was born in 1941 to Carcie Leroy and Mary Elizabeth Eggers Brown. She graduated from Crawfordsville High School in 1959. Sharon has two brothers: Donald of California, and Larry who passed away in 1978 during the blizzard.

In 1984, the Jon Foster family relocated to Crawfordsville across from Camp Rotary in Old Orchard Estates. Jon is employed by Crawfordsville Electric Light and Power, and Sharon is employed by Hi-Tek Lighting.

DOROTHY LOU FOSTER

The oldest of two children of Lee and Gladys Foster, Dorothy Lou was born in February of 1932. The family lived in the town of Waveland in the home formerly built and resided in by John Conner and later his daughter and husband, Minnie and John Sharp.

After graduation from Waveland High School in 1950, Dorothy Lou attended Indiana State Teachers College in Terre Haute, graduating in 1953. Out-of-state recruiters were common on the college campuses in the 50's and D.L. was offered a teaching job in southern California. She and two of her college roommates traveled to a new adventure — all teaching in an elementary district in Whittier, CA.

Another new teacher to the District in 1953 was Frank Chiros, formerly of Boston, MA who had graduated that year from Whittier College. Frank and Dorothy Lou were married in Crawfordsville, IN in 1954 and returned to Whittier to live. They moved into a new home in 1955 in Buena Park, a rural community with a population of 3,000. One-half mile from their home was a chicken dinner restaurant noted for their boysenberry pie, later to grow into one of the top tourist attractions in the nation — Knotts Berry Farm.

As the years went by the family grew — Louisa Ann born in 1956, Denise Marie in 1957 and Terence Lee in 1963. There are three grandchildren born to Louisa and Chris Adamson, Justin, Jeffrey and Jenna.

Frank retired in 1987 after 34 years in the classroom, but he enjoys subing occasionally and also works part-time at Knotts Berry Farm; Dorothy Lou went back to work after raising the children and is a grants management coordinator for a community college district.

JAMES WILLIAM FOUTS

James William Fouts was born in Montgomery County near Elmdale Nov. 2, 1886, the only child of Joseph and Joanna Morrow Fouts. At the age of 13 months his mother died of Tuberculosis (called Consumption in those days). James went to live with his grandmother on the family farm 1-1/4 miles Northwest of Waynetown. On May 19, 1891 his father remarried Cora Ann Cord and half-siblings arrived soon: Charles Denman, Ilah, Holcy L. (lived one month), Claude Jackson, Roscoe Cord, and Leslie J. (lived 14 months).

James attended school in New Richmond graduating from Elmdale High School where he played on the school's basketball team. He attended Marion Normal School.

On Aug. 6, 1907 James married Miss Christina Davidson in Linden. She died Jan. 16, 1981 at age 94 in Indianapolis. Carrie (as she was called) had been a member of the New Richmond Methodist Church.

James, Letha, Leon and Carrie Fouts

Their union was blessed with two children: Letha Irene and Joseph Leon. The family lived with Martha Davidson one mile east of New Richmond until 1910, when they bought a farm south of New Richmond called "Maple Vale."

Besides farming the 80 acres, Jim (as he was called), made Maple Syrup selling at $2.00 a gallon, sold insurance and became the school trustee for New Richmond. The brick school erected there had his name on the corner stone.

Tragedy struck the household on Dec. 26, 1932 when Jim died at age 46. The farm was sold. Letha and Carrie moved to Crawfordsville and Leon to Bellingham, WA. Carrie worked as a housekeeper in Crawfordsville, then for Mr. Hunter in Indianapolis and then for the state of Indiana until retirement in 1962 at age 75. In October 1963 Carrie and Letha were involved in the explosion at the state fair grounds in Indianapolis. Carrie sustained three broken limbs and her recovery was slow. Carrie continued to live with her daughter Letha and passed away on Jan. 16, 1981. She is buried in the cemetery in New Richmond next to her husband Jim. *Submitted by Karen Moore*

JOSEPH FOUTS

Joseph Fouts was born in Wayne Township Montgomery County on Apr. 21, 1861, the second child of William and Sophia Thompson Fouts. His siblings being: Holcy, Sarah Ellen, John Denman, Rilla J. and Cora M.

On Dec. 30, 1885 Joseph married Miss Joanna Morrow who was born July 10, 1868 near Elmdale and died Dec. 9, 1887. She was the daughter of James Arron and Harriet Elizabeth Rivers Morrow. Their union was blessed with one child: James William Fouts Nov. 2, 1986 named for two grandfathers James Arron Morrow and William Fouts.

Joanna lived a short life as she contracted tuberculosis (or consumption as it was known in those days). The Crawfordsville paper stated in one weekly edition "Mrs. Joseph Fouts is considerable better at this writing." She left a 13 month old son and a husband. As Joseph needed help with his son, he went to live with his mother.

The family lived for a year in Fountain County where Ilah was born and then moved again near Elmdale to a farm where Joanna's parents farmed naming it "Hill Crest Farm". Joseph owned 214 acres and lived there until his death on Dec. 5, 1935 at age 74.

Front: Claude, Roscoe. Seated: Joseph and Cora. Standing: Ilah, Jim, Charlie.

During Joseph's lifetime he was able to see the change from horse and buggy to automobile transportation. He would own nothing but a Ford. Joseph and Cora took two big trips with daughters' family, one to Niagara Falls and last one to visit his brother John in Walla Walla, WA, also stopping to see Cora's relatives in Lewiston, ID.

Cousins Herbert Hoover and his father visited Joseph and Cora. In North Carolina there were over 20 intermarriages between the two families. Joseph was superintendent for the Methodist Church in Elmdale for over 30 years. Cora taught Sunday School. "Get your pants on Ma," Joseph would say, "we're going to town." It was a funny thing to say, as women in those days didn't wear pants.

After Joseph's death Cora remarried Thomas Lewis and went to live in Lewiston, ID on Mar. 18, 1937. They had two good years of marriage, and Cora died on July 27, 1939 at the age of 69. Both Cora and Joseph are buried at Waynetown Masonic Cemetery.

JOSEPH LEON FOUTS

Joseph Leon Fouts was born in Coal Creek Township one mile east of New Richmond on Dec. 26, 1909 on his grandparents' farm. Leon (as he was called) was the second child of James William and Christina Carolyn Davidson Fouts. Like his father, he was named after a grandfather. His sibling was Letha Irene.

Leon attended grade school at Elmdale, graduating from New Richmond High School Apr. 18, 1930. When he talked about his school days, he recounted playing guard on the high school basketball team starting his freshman year, and about a high school teacher who made him retake a test because he "cheated". Leon did better, the second time earning 100%. He was proud of his High School Diploma because it had three Fouts names on it; his name, C.D. Fouts, the principal and his uncle, and James W. Fouts, Trustee, his father.

Margaret holding Jim, Leon, Linda, Gordy and dog Corky Fouts

Leon attended one year of college at Wabash, but the economy being what it was in the 30's he had to drop out. With his father's help, he was able to buy a farm near "Maple Vale," (his father's farm). The farm was sold, along with everything else when Leon's father died.

In 1933 Leon left Indiana and went to Bellingham, WA working as a mechanic. He was joined in marriage to Miss Carol Ina Moore on Oct. 15, 1933, daughter of Jesse and Mabel Echo Edmonds Moore. The couple drove to Indiana, but only to visit. They returned to Walla Walla, WA and lived near his grandfather's brother, John D. Fouts. Leon bought a herd of cows, but they had to be killed because of bangs disease. With nothing left, the couple picked fruit in the Yakima Valley. Later Leon became a guard at the Walla Walla State Penitentiary. The couple was blessed with two children: Linda Lou and Gordon Phillip.

With his cousin's help, Leon was able to hire on with Pacific Northwest Bell in 1940. The couple moved to Seattle. The marriage didn't last and was dissolved in 1948. On Jan. 27, 1950 he remarried Margaret Alice Kerin, daughter of Michael and Mary Kovac Kerin. The couple was blessed with two children: Karen Ann, and James Michael (named for his grandfather).

The couple lived in Seattle, but every few years Leon returned to the state of his birth. He would visit his mother and sister and other Fouts relatives, Roscoe and Claude Fouts. Roscoe's wife Florence was good at putting together Fouts' reunions. There was time also to look at homes of his boyhood, and play Euchre with family.

In Seattle, Leon was called Joe by friends and family. He was involved with his church, Bethany United Presbyterian, first as a deacon and later as an elder; with the Masonic Lodge, and with Cub Scouts with his son Jim. He worked at Pacific Northwest Bell as a PBX installer until his death Oct. 10, 1974 with 33 years of service. Leon is buried on Queen Anne Hill in Seattle, WA. *Submitted by Karen Moore*

LETHA IRENE FOUTS

Letha Irene Fouts was born Mar. 18, 1907, the first child of James William and Christina Carolyn Davidson Fouts, one mile east of New Richmond at her grandparents' farm. She had one brother, Joseph Leon.

She attended grade school at Elmdale and graduated Apr. 27, 1927 from New Richmond High School. She was engaged to Paul Olin but because of a hazing incident at college they didn't marry. Letha completed two years at Ball State studying Home Economics while living with her father's brother, Charles D. Fouts. After her father's death in 1932, she moved to Crawfordsville and worked as a county clerk. She became a member of the Crawfordsville Dramatic Club.

Letha Irene Fouts

On June 1, 1946 Letha married Edward Earl Clark in Indianapolis. They set up housekeeping at the Claypool Hotel and in 1953 bought a three bedroom home in Indianapolis. Their marriage lasted 11 years until Earl (as he was called) died Aug. 10, 1957. Carrie Davidson (Letha's mom) moved in and lived with her until her death. Letha worked for the state of Indiana. Later she took a job with the Brotherhood of Railroad Train Men working there until her retirement in 1972. She was very active in the Indiana Democratic Party and was a delegate at two presidential conventions.

On Mar. 17, 1984 Letha married John Inskeep of Lafayette, a friend of many years. Letha wanted to get married the 17th because they both would be 75. The marriage took place in Ft. Myers, FL at the home of John's son. They took a Caribbean cruise on their honeymoon and set up housekeeping at John's home in Lafayette. Seven months later after entertaining friends, Letha died of a heart attack; she is buried next to her first husband (Earl) in New Richmond.

LEVI FOUTS SR.

Levi Fouts Sr. came to Wayne township before 1830 as he appeared on the 1830 census. He was born in Randalph Co., NC July 2, 1796 the fifth child of Jacob and Eleanor Waymeyer Fouts. The family moved from North Carolina to Ohio and finally to Indiana.

In 1818 Levi Sr. married Miss Sarah Small, born in North Carolina on Apr. 3, 1798, who died on Mar. 29, 1857 at 58 years after 39 years of marriage. This union was blessed with ten children: Eli, Malinda, Nathan, Jehu, Lydia, Jacob, Levi Jr., John, William and Susannah.

Levi Sr. purchased 160 acres in Wayne Township on Oct. 25, 1825 bringing his family there later where the last six of his children were born. In 1834 he became a merchant on Lot No. 2 in Waynetown which is now occupied by the Corner Drug Store. He sold his interest in the store to Simeon Osborne. He farmed until the death of his wife. His youngest son William took over the farm.

In 1857 Levi Sr. went to Ohio and married Amellia King Steward, a widow with two children; Laurie and Margaret. Amellia passed away in 1874 at age 52 after 17 years of marriage, and is buried in Pioneer Cemetery at Waynetown. This union was blessed with three children: George, David and Amos. Levi Sr. lived in Waynetown first as a Hotel Keeper and later had a store in one room of his residence where the Masonic Building now stands. Levi passed away Sept. 29, 1875 at age 79 and is buried at the Pioneer Cemetery in Waynetown.

WILLIAM FOUTS

William Fouts was born in Wayne Township Aug. 24, 1834, the ninth child of Levi Sr. and Sarah Small Fouts. His siblings being: Eli, Malinda, Nathan, Jehu, Lydia, Jacob, Levi Jr., John, and Susannah.

On Dec. 24, 1857 William married Miss Sophia Thompson who was born Mar. 23, 1835 in Indiana and died Fountain County Sept. 15, 1915 at the age of 79 years. She was the daughter of Alexander and Jane Thompson. This union blessed the couple with six children. The first was Holcy born Oct. 14, 1859 and died after 14 months, leaving the couple saddened. Joseph arrived three months later, next came Sarah Ellen, followed by John Denman and Rilla J., who lived only 20 months. Last to arrive was Cora M. to complete the family.

James William Fouts with his grandmother Sophia Fouts

William was a farmer who acquired his father's farm one and a quarter miles northwest of Waynetown after his mother died. His stepbrother Amos came to live with him after Levi Sr. passed away. Brother Levi Jr. farmed next to William.

William watched his children grow and marry. First Sarah married James T. Grey in 1883 and moved to Fountain County. Next Joseph married Joanna Morrow in 1885. William died Apr. 25, 1887 at age 52, leaving Sophia with the farm and two children. John Denman was helpful on the farm. Joanna, Joseph's wife, died after their son's first birthday. Joseph moved back in with his mother and lived with her until he remarried. After Cora M. married, Sophia sold the farm and went to live with Cora. Sarah's husband died and Sophia then moved in with her and lived there until she died. Both William and Sophia are buried at the Masonic Cemetery at Waynetown. *Submitted by Karen Moore*

EDWARD FOWLER FAMILY

Edward R. Fowler was born in Edgar Co., IL on Sept. 1, 1920. He was the third child of seven children born to John Thomas and Florence Todd Fowler. They came to Edgar Co., IL from Woodbury, TN.

Edward Fowler was married in Clinton, IN to Marilyn Collings. She was the fourth child of five children born to Boyd and Fannie Hadley Collings. They lived in Parke Co., IN.

The Fowler family moved to Waveland in 1943. They later moved to a farm in Green Township, Parke Co., IN. In 1946, they purchased a farm at the south edge of Waveland, IN. Mr. Fowler died in August, 1978.

They have one son, Robert Lee Fowler, born Jan. 26, 1953. After graduating from Waveland High School and Purdue University, he joined Elanco Products, the agricultural division of Eli Lilly Co.

He lives in Carmel, IN. He married Janet Berntsen in March, 1979. She is the second of three children born to Walter and Mary Jane Berntsen of Indianapolis, IN. Robert and Janet have two children, a boy, Jason Edward and a girl, Chelsey Leigh Fowler. *Submitted by Marilyn Fowler*

JOHN M. FOXWORTHY

The John M. Foxworthy family moved to Fountain County in March, 1975, after living in Montgomery County the previous years. They now live south of Hillsboro.

Carole is the oldest child born to Lena (Black) and John A. Moody in Crawfordsville on May 6, 1937. She has one sister, Judy, born July 19, 1938, and married Butch Jarvis of New Market and now lives in Terre Haute. Her mother was born in Eldorado, OK, the youngest of four children to Mary (Collins) and John Black. Her father was the second of four children born to Matilda (Eickacker) and John C. Moody in Tilton, IL. The paternal ancestors are German and the maternal, Irish and Scotch. Carole is a 1955 graduate of Crawfordsville and a former employee of Indiana Bell and the Crawfordsville Journal-Review. She is a former member of Sigma Alpha Chi Sorority, Mu Chapter, in Crawfordsville.

John is the oldest of three children born to Ethel (Bryant) and Charles Foxworthy in Darlington on Feb. 18, 1920. His mother was born in Jamestown to Easter (Fletcher) and John Bryant. His father was the son of Viola (Wright) and George Foxworthy and was born in Ladoga. His paternal ancestors were Scotch, Irish, and English.

Carole, Amy and John M. Foxworthy

John had a sister, Mary Joan, born Nov. 30, 1927, and married Donald Grenard of Waynetown. A brother, Stanley, born Feb. 3, 1924, married Gloria Bindhammer, of Ladoga. His sister died Oct. 24, 1984, and his brother Oct. 9, 1988. A 1938 graduate of Ladoga High School, he attended the College of Religion at Butler University in Indianapolis for 2-1/2 years, before being drafted in World War II, and was stationed in India for 2-1/2 years with the 7th Bomb Group. In 1961 he was one of the founders of the Indiana Children's Christian Home in Ladoga, which is supported by the Christian churches. For several years he served as President of the Board of Directors. A printer for R.R. Donnelley & Sons in Crawfordsville for 21 years, he also worked for the *Journal-Review* before starting his own print shop in Waynetown in 1969. In 1962, he began his full-time ministry with Mecca (Parke County) Christian Church. Other churches he has pastored are the New Richmond and Darlington Christian Churches (Interim minister) in Montgomery County and the Wallace and New Liberty Christian churches (Fountain County). John's great-great grandfather, Enoch Foxworthy, was one of the early settlers in Ladoga in 1829. Both sides of his family are from Virginia and they moved to Kentucky before coming to Indiana.

He has been a ham radio operator since 1951, and along with that hobby also enjoys photography.

The couple met while working at the newspaper plant and were married on May 14, 1967, in New Richmond.

They have one daughter, Amy, who was born Feb. 24, 1970 in Crawfordsville. She graduated from Fountain Central High School in 1988 and is a sophomore at Cincinnati Bible College.

John has two sons, Fredric of Crawfordsville and James of Rockville, by a previous marriage, and both were born in Crawfordsville. Seven grandchildren and one great granddaughter complete the family.

FRALEY-MORROW-WEAVER

The family tree of Rebecca Jane 'Becky' Fraley (b. May 10, 1928 m. Joseph Aaron 'Joe' Weaver b. July 4, 1925), branches deep into the history of Indiana and Montgomery County. Some lines reach back to the 1700's.

On Becky's paternal side: Fredrick Fraley's (b. 1742-d. 1825) son, John (b. Sept. 27, 1783-d. Oct. 26, 1855) m. Elizabeth Ann Hackney (b. Aug. 12, 1793-d. Oct. 20, 1846) and had eight children: Caroline, Daniel, William, John, Jacob, Charles, Theodore, and Henry.

Reverend Henry Clay Fraley (b. Apr. 10, 1830-d. Nov. 10, 1882) m. Catharine E. Stanton (b. Feb. 25, 1837-d. Nov. 30, 1895) and had seven children: Arthur, Frank, Henry, Laura, Maud, May, and Elmira. He attended Indiana Asbury, class of 1858. In 1871, poor health forced him from the itinerant ministry and the family settled on his family farm near Linden.

Arthur Stanton and Daisy (Dunkle) Fraley, children Floyd Dunkle and Ruth Fraley Evans

Eldest son, Arthur Stanton Fraley (b. Nov. 18, 1864-d. Dec. 26, 1940) became a civic leader and businessman of the Linden area. After attending DePauw University, he was principal of the local school for 22 years; secretary/treasurer and general manager of The Montgomery Power and Light Company for 27 years; member of the initial Jane M. Stoddard Park board (1917); helped direct the movement to secure a grant from the Carnegie Corporation to build the Linden Public Library (1922) and was a member of its first board; and as a member of the Linden Methodist Episcopal Church he served 50 years in official activities, commencing with election to its official board in 1890.

Arthur m. Daisy Dean Dunkle (b. Nov. 14, 1868-d. Mar. 22, 1959). Daisy was an accomplished musician. When the Linden Christian Church was dedicated in 1899, she played its organ at the ceremony. For 50 years she was the organist of the Linden Methodist Episcopal Church. She was also a charter member of the Linden Order of Eastern Star and was active for 55 years in Oriental Chapter 244. Arthur and Daisy had two children: Floyd and Ruth.

Ruth (b. Dec. 1, 1895-d. Nov. 9, 195) m. Benjamin Crabbs Evans (b. Feb. 16, 1898-d. Sept. 21, 1973) and had two children: Daniel Fraley Evans (b. Feb. 24, 1922) and Benjamin Crabbs Evans, Jr. (b. Mar. 14, 1924-d. Aug. 23, 1987).

Floyd Dunkle Fraley (b. Oct. 26, 1891-d. Apr. 24, 1976) m. Roxie Evangeline 'Van' Morrow (b. Feb. 10, 1898-d. Aug. 9, 1984) and had one child: Rebecca. Floyd, WWI veteran and graduate of DePauw University, was a land owner and farmer in the Linden area all his adult life.

On Becky's maternal side: Thomas Morrow's son, James Aaron Morrow (b. May 15, 1830-d. July 23, 1885) m. Harriet Elizabeth Rivers (b. Sept. 24, 1854-d. Oct. 16, 1892) and had 11 children: William Walles, William Wade, John, Ira, Frank, Ebbert, Joanna, Sarah, James, Harriet, and Simeon.

Ebbert Monroe Morrow (b. Aug. 30-, 1865-d. Feb. 1, 1940) m. Elizabeth Edna 'Lizzie' McClamroch (b. Oct. 11, 1870-d. Nov. 20, 1939) and had nine children: Winnie, Lemuel, Eugenia, Roxie, Ebbert, Harriet, Frank, Ruth, and Mary Ellen.

On Mar. 24, 1920, Roxie Evangeline 'Van' Morrow m. Floyd Dunkle Fraley. Van was a lifelong member of the Linden Women's Club and an active member of the community.

Becky and Joe m. Nov. 6, 1949 and have two children: Bruce and Martha. Bruce Fraley Weaver (b. Feb. 20, 1952) m. Betty Katherin 'Kathy' Roundtree (b. Dec. 7, 1951) and live in Oklahoma City, OK. Martha Jo Weaver (b. May 21, 1955) lives in Linden.

PETE FRANCE

Carlos Washington "Pete" France was born on Mar. 18, 1907, near Mammoth Cave in Park City, KY. He was one of three sons of James Matthew and Carrie (Wilkins) France. His father was a tobacco farmer.

He married Nellie Mae Anderson daughter of Luther Bedford and Bertha (Black) Anderson, of Portland Mills, IN, on Oct. 23, 1941.

Pete was a Naval Veteran of World War II.

Pete and Nellie moved to Waveland in 1945. He started as a welder and worked on Wabash College buildings and R.R. Donnelly's first building. He started his own welding and blacksmith shop in Waveland in 1953, later adding a gas station and auto repair shop.

There they raised seven children, James Russell, Arthur Ray, Robert Earl, David Eugene, Sandra Lee, Terry Joe, and Connie Sue.

Pete's hobby was racing cars at the Waveland race track and at Jungle Park on State road 41.

David Eugene died of a train/truck accident on Jan. 6, 1975, Carlos "Pete" died of a heart attack Sept. 3, 1976 and Nellie died of heart failure July 9, 1978. *Submitted by Sandy France Greene*

WILLIAM T. FRANCIS

William T. Francis was born Nov. 7, 1841 in Bedford, IN. He was the son of Thomas J. and Elizabeth Francis, born in 1814, died July 3, 1894 in Crawfordsville, and is buried in Oak Hill Cemetery.

William T. Francis grew up near Bedford, IN on his parents farm. He received a common education and was raised in the Baptist church.

When the Civil War started, William T. Francis enlisted as a musician in Company K, 14th Regiment Indiana Infantry on June 7, 1861 in Monroe Co., IN. He transferred to Company L, 6th U.S. Cavalry on Oct. 22, 1862. He served until the end of the war. He spent seven months as a prisoner of war and was interred in Libby Prison in Richmond, VA. After the war ended, he returned to Bedford where he became a blacksmith. He later moved to Bloomington, IN. In the early 1870's, the Francis family left Monroe County and moved to Crawfordsville, IN. William T. Francis opened a blacksmith shop on Lafayette Avenue. He became a well-known mechanic and gunsmith. When he retired, he became custodian of the county courthouse and later custodian of the Crawfordsville Country Club.

On Nov. 20, 1879, William T. Francis was united in marriage to Hester S. Collins in Crawfordsville. She was the daughter of James Collins of Montgomery Co., IN.

William T. Francis was a long-time member of McPherson Post #7 G.A.R. in Crawfordsville where he served several terms as vice post commander.

In 1914, William and Hester Francis moved to St. Cloud, FL. They were later joined in St. Cloud by their son, Fred, and his wife Iva.

William T. Francis died of Bright's Disease May 13, 1915 in St. Cloud, FL. His body was returned to Crawfordsville, where he was buried with full G.A.R. honors in Oak Hill Cemetery. The death date of Hester Collins Francis is unknown.

The children of William T. and Hester Collins Francis were:

1. Grace B., married Edgar C. Bean Nov. 12, 1899. They resided in Crawfordsville. 2. Jesse, died at the age of nine months. 3. Bessie, married Henry Charters. They resided in Wheeler, MI. 4. Fred, married Iva M. Hamilton. They resided in St. Cloud, FL. *Submitted by Andrew Keith Houk, Jr.*

MATTHIAS FRANTZ

Matthias Frantz was born Sept. 3, 1808 to Christian Frantz IV and wife Magdaline Houstz. There were three older children. His great, great, great grandfather Christian Frantz I came to America in 1732 from Basle, Switzerland. Matthias' parents died shortly after his birth and his aunt, Catherine Houtz Myers who had a baby about the same time, took him to raise along with her own baby. Her husband, John Myers was a Dunkard minister and in 1833 John Myers moved his family of nine along with Matthias from Virginia to Clark Township, Montgomery County. A son, John Myers Jr. had preceded him to the community.

Matthias married Sallie Graybill, daughter of Daniel and Elizabeth (Kinzer) Graybill. They had five children: Sarah Jane, William H., Elizabeth Ann (m. Thomas Everson), and John Frank. Matthias was a Dunkard minister also.

The son, John Frank, married Elizabeth Myers, daughter of William and Elizabeth (Harshbarger) Myers. They had twin sons and a daughter, all unnamed who died at childbirth, Leona Ellen born Feb. 27, 1861, died Feb. 17, 1868, William M. born June 19, 1864, died Jan. 20, 1954, Sarah Louise and Frank.

George and Jennie Brookshire Frantz

Sarah Louise married Frank Williams and had Opal who married Ed Lafollette, Elizabeth who married John Reed, and Clara who married Richard Peffley. Frank Frantz married Emma Tapp and had May Frantz (Hanna) and Gaynelle.

William M. Frantz married Valletta Corn daughter of George and Hulda (Williams) Corn and lived on the family farm located northeast of Ladoga consisting of 190 acres. In the family there is a beautiful German Bible published in 1763 given to William M. by his grandfather in Aug. 1, 1899. William and Valletta's only son George F. helped his parents on this farm. This farm was later designated as one of the centennial farms in Montgomery County. George married Jennie Marie Brookshire, daughter of James William and Neva (Radford) Brookshire and purchased a house in East Ladoga. When the parents became older, father and son swapped properties and George and Jennie lived on the farm until his mother's death. The farm was rented and George and Jennie purchased property in Ladoga doing extensive remodeling of that house. William suffered a stroke and George and Jennie cared for him until a month before his death. At that time he was in a nursing home in Indianapolis.

George and Jennie were well known and active in the community. George was trustee of Harshbarger Cemetery, deacon for 36 years and trustee for 32 years at Ladoga Christian Church, director of Ladoga State Bank for 26 years, belonged to World War Barricks 1164, 50 year member of Ladoga Masonic Lodge and 22 years in the Order of Eastern Star. He died Nov. 20, 1978.

Jennie belonged to the Order of Eastern Star, Alpha Phi Omega Sorority, Organist and pianist for Ladoga Christian Church 49 years and played organ for the funeral home located directly across the street from their home. She died Jan. 21, 1985.

Having no children, they loved to travel and many people will remember the beautiful slides and interesting talks on their travels which they shared upon their return. *Submitted by Martha Lofland*

FREDERICK FAMILY

The Frederick family emigrated to America from Ireland in the early 1800's. The subjects of this sketch are Oscar and Bertie Frederick who now live in New Ross. Oscar Frederick and Bertie Johnson were married in London, KY in Laurel County, on Jan. 31, 1931. The Fredericks with their two little daughters, Ruth and Corenia rode the Louisville and Nashville railroad from London to Indianapolis for a visit in 1935 and decided to stay. After living in Indianapolis for about seven and a half years, long enough for Bertie to have one garden and another little girl, Doris, born in 1940, the young family again pulled up stakes and moved; this time they moved to Advance in Boone County where Oscar ran a poultry and egg route for several years. While living in Advance, the last child, a son, Charlie, was born.

The Fredericks moved to Montgomery County after buying the grocery store in New Ross in 1946. Frederick's IGA was truly a "Mom and Pop" operation from 1946 to 1951 when Oscar started to work at Allison's in Indianapolis. Bertie continued to operate the grocery store with help from the growing girls and Charlie (he helped with the eggs) until April of 1972.

The Frederick family has always been active in church and community activities. The elder Fredericks are charter members and faithful supporters of the First Assembly of God Church in Crawfordsville and the New Ross Community Club. All four Frederick children were active in school activities as New Ross Bluejays. Ruth graduated from New Ross in 1949 and went to work at the First National Bank in Crawfordsville. She married John Bronaugh, a member of a county pioneer family, in 1951. The Bronaughs have two children, Debbie and Johnny. Both are now married

Oscar and Bertie's Golden Anniversary 1981. Corenia, Ruth, Bertie, Oscar, Doris and Charlie

with families and live on the family farm. Corenia, the second of the Frederick daughters as a high school cheerleader and talented musician who graduated in 1953. She then married James Wright, a descendant of two long-time Montgomery County families, the Wrights and the Jarvises. Jim and Corenia have four children, Terri, Jim, Joe and Mike. The third daughter of the family, Doris, was also active in various clubs at New Ross High School. She graduated in 1957 and married Bill Boone of Ladoga whose Mother was a Peffley, one of the pioneer families in Clark Township. The Boones have four children, Kathy, Scott, Chris, and Cindy. The fourth member of the Frederick family was Charlie, who was an outstanding three sport athlete for the Bluejays, graduating in 1963. He was the County's outstanding athlete in his senior year. Charlie is married to the former Martha Prayor and is the father of two children, Charles and Sarah.

Oscar and Bertie Frederick are still living across from the Bank in New Ross, the same Bank in which Oscar single-handedly prevented a bank robbery in 1983 by grabbing the armed bank robber from behind and scaring him from the Bank. The Fredericks are retired now, Oscar from Allison's in 1980 and Bertie from the grocery store in 1972. Oscar now operates Fred's Bike Shop in the old store building and Bertie oversees three apartments upstairs in the same building. The two oldest daughters Ruth and Corenia live with their husbands in rural New Ross: Doris lives in Veedersburg with her husband, and Charley lives in Indianapolis with his wife and daughter.

GEORGE C. AND GLADYS (REYNOLDS) FREES

George Carthenas Frees came to Montgomery County around 1910. He was born in Terre Haute, IN, June 5, 1892, the son of John Webster and Lydia (Hackett) Frees.

He came here with his mother and step-father, Benjamin Goodin, who was his mother's second husband. It is not known by any of the family what happened to John W., as all of the family that are now living only knew Benjamin and the rest of the family was never discussed, only the fact that George had a sister: Carrie Frees, who married Howard Michaels and they lived in Anderson, IN.

John W. Frees was born in Ohio, the son of Peter, born 1830, and Martha Frees, born in 1833. Both were born in Ohio. He had two brothers and two sisters: Joseph A., b. 1853, Marietta, b. 1857, Jacob, b. 1859 and Samantha, b. 1867, all in Darke Co., OH.

Lydia was born in Pine Village (Warren Co.), IN, the daughter of William Sumers and Ann (Pearson) Hackett; William, b. 1826, New Jersey, Ann, b. 1827 in Ohio. Besides Lydia they had: John G.

Hackett, b. 1847, Daniel W.H., b. 1853, Thomas, b. 1854, George F., b. 1859, Addie, b. ?, and of course Lydia, b. May 25, 1866, d. June 1, 1930.

George was to later meet and marry Gladys Reynolds in Indianapolis, IN on Mar. 25, 1916. She was born Oct. 22, 1898 in Crawfordsville, IN, the daughter of Edwin and Lura Bellus Reynolds.

The house in which she was born stood on Grant Avenue and has long since been torn down, but the log cabin that now stands in the park (Milligan), was a part of that house and was a part of the Underground Railroad in Crawfordsville, during the late 1800's.

Her paternal grandparents were John Henry and Susan (Goble) Reynolds. Her great grandparents were James A. Reynolds of Jefferson Co., NY and Daniel and Elizabeth Goble, both born in Ohio. Her maternal grandparents were, Kate and Leonis Bellus of Vermillion Co., IN, her great grandparents were Peter and Elizabeth Ann (Utter) Glassway, born in Ohio.

Gladys was one of four children born to Edwin and Lura: Susan Ethyl Reynolds, born November 1893, d. September 1978, married John Spivey January 1915; Edwin Roy, b. July 1896 and died February 1960 - married Sylvia Phillips, 1914; Gladys Lavera (the subject of this sketch) b. October 1898, d. June 25, 1963, married George C. Frees, and Paul, b. June 7, 1901 - d. Apr. 29, 1915. George Frees passed away Apr. 22, 1970. All of these children, with the exception of Ethyl Spivey, are buried in Oak Hill Cemetery at Crawfordsville. She is buried at Masonic Cemetery (North).

Gladys and George were the parents of five sons: Carleton Gooden, Dec. 2, 1916-Oct. 11, 1987, married Jesse Joan Swisher; Paul Edgar Frees, b. Feb. 13, 1918, married twice and lives in California; Gale Lamar, b. Apr. 14, 1919, married Mary Krout. She is deceased and he lives in Indianapolis; John Webster, Sept. 15, 1922 - November 1974, married Margaret Kapps, lived and is buried at Gary, IN and Robert James (see sketch).

ROBERT AND GWENDOLYN (BALLAH) FREES

Robert James Frees was born in Crawfordsville, IN Feb. 3, 1924. He was the youngest of five boys born to George C. and Gladys (Reynolds) Frees. His paternal grandparents were John Webster and Lydia (Hackett) Frees; his great grandparents, Peter and Martha (?) Freese of Darke Co., OH, and William S. and Ann (Pearson) Hackett. They were from Warren Co., IN and later returned to Ohio. His maternal grandparents were Edwin and Lura Bellus Reynolds, great grandparents, John Henry and Susan (Goble) Reynolds, Leonis and Kate (Glassway) Bellus. His great great grandparents were: James A. Reynolds of Jefferson Co., NY and Peter and Elizabeth (Utter) Glassway and Edward and Elizabeth Goble, also of Ohio.

"Bob" attended Wilson and Crawfordsville High School where he participated in football, track and wrestling. He also belonged to the Audabon Society and Hi Y. He graduated from there in 1942.

Shortly after graduation he enlisted in the Navy, took his Basic Training at Great Lakes Naval Training Center. After this he was transferred to San Francisco, CA where he became a part of the submarine service, serving on the Sunfish, Sailfish and the Skipjack. When not on the submarines he served on the Subtender, U.S.S. Fulton and saw duty in Guam, Midway, Australia, New Guinea,

Siapan and Tinnian. He was discharged on Christmas Day, 1945 at San Diego.

Shortly after his return to Crawfordsville, he met and married his first wife. They had two daughters: Suzanne and Vada. This marriage ended in divorce in 1951.

On Apr. 12, 1952, he met and married Gwendolyn Ballah who was born in Mellott, IN (Fountain County) Aug. 28, 1930. She is the daughter of Otis Freeman Ballah (Oct. 31, 1892 to Sept. 7, 1959) and is buried at Bonebrake Cemetery, south of Veedersburg, and Elva Irene (Cooper) Davis, born June 14, 1900. She was one of two sets of twins and the only one to survive. She resides in Veedersburg at this time. Gwendolyn is the granddaughter of Melissa Ballah, Charles Marion and Rosa (McAlister) Cooper and great granddaughter of Marion R. and Hannah (Ballah) White Ballah; Cary and Cynthia (Baily) Cartwright Cooper and James A. and Louisa J. (Ray) McAlister, all of Fountain County. Because most all of her family can be found in the 1983 *History of Fountain County*, this is all of the information on her.

She and Robert are both members of the First Christian Church in Crawfordsville. She is a Genealogist and Robert has been active in several organizations: The American Legion (Past Commander), Jaycees, Civil Defense Police, both Local and State (President of State for two years), Boy Scouts, also was a Scout Master for the First Christian Church Troop #342.

They are the parents of one son, James Lee Frees, b. Jan. 21, 1969 who resides at home, does "Creative Writing" in his spare time and is employed at I.P.T.

There is also a granddaughter who has resided in their home since birth: Angela Renee' Frees, b. Oct. 1, 1970. She resides in Crawfordsville at this time and is planning her marriage in April of this year (1989). *Submitted by Gwen Frees*

SUZANNE KAY FREES
VADA LAVONNE FREES

Suzanne Kay Frees was born in Montgomery Co., IN, June 8, 1948, the daughter of Robert J. and Gracie M. Price Frees.

She attended school in Mills and Nicholson Grade schools and also Crawfordsville High School, from which she graduated in 1967.

In later years she attended Ivy Tech, where she became a Physician's assistant and is employed in Indianapolis for a group of Doctors. I believe that they are all Neurologists, but of this I'm not certain.

On June 24, 1967 she married Michael Pritchett, the son of Kenneth and Dorothy (Butler) Pritchett and they became the parents of one daughter, Melissa Dawn Pritchett, born Jan. 28, 1969 in Crawfordsville. Her marriage to Michael ended in divorce and she later married Richard Hedge of Ladoga. This was Sept. 21, 1986. They have just recently completed a new home at Eagle Creek in Indianapolis, as they both are very much the outdoors type of people.

Suzanne and Michael have one granddaughter, Staci Rena Whitlow, born Nov. 9, 1986. Melissa, her husband Terry and Staci reside in Crawfordsville.

Vada Lavonne Frees was born in Crawfordsville, also the daughter of Robert and Gracie M. (Price) Frees. She was born Jan. 20, 1950 and also attended school in the same schools as her sister.

She has one daughter, Angela Renee' Frees, born Oct. 1, 1970. This is the granddaughter mentioned in the sketch of Robert J. and Gwendolyn (Ballah) Frees.

Vada was married on June 15, 1972, at Crawfordsville to Edgar Dale Forrest of Parke County and they were the parents of one son Edgar Dale Forrest Jr., born Sept. 23, 1975 in Florida. They were divorced and she returned to her mother in Charleston, IL where she met and married Larry Oliver. They have one daughter Marie Elaina Oliver, born January 1977 in Effingham, IL where they lived at the time. She now lives in Texas.

Both of these girls were raised by their father and stepmother, from ages of three and four years of age. *Submitted by Gwen Frees*

THE FRENCH FAMILY

The Elmer French family, because of its numerous progeny, is associated with many families in the area, with direct descendants numbering nearly 300 in 1989.

Elmer Edgar French, born Apr. 6, 1876, near Portland Arch in Fountain County died June 9, 1971 at Ladoga, was a son of James and Alice LaBaw French. James was born in 1852, a son of William and Eliza Osborn French. Eliza's father, Daniel Osborn, born in 1791, came to Fountain County in 1824, where he ministered to the communal settlement near Stone Bluff, north of Veedersburg. Daniel's parents, Cyrus and Esther Baldwin Osborn were natives of New Jersey, and later moved to Ohio where they were among the founders of Middletown. Cyrus fought in the Indian Wars in Ohio, and helped bury the dead after St. Clair's defeat. Esther was a true frontierswoman, born in 1763, who grew up in the midst of the Revolution. Cyrus died in 1805, and Esther eventually moved on to Indiana where she died at the age of 90.

Esther's immigrant ancestors included: John Ogden, Governor of East Jersey, William Meeker, a founder of Elizabeth, NJ, William Preston of the New Haven Colony, Cornelis Melyn, Patron of Staten Island, and Ralph Dayton, Thomas Baker and Jacobus Schellinger, all among the founders of East Hampton, Long Island. The Osborns were descendants of Thomas Osborn, village tanner in New Haven and later East Hampton.

Elmer French's mother, Alice LaBaw French, 1858-1936, was a daughter of Benjamin and Elizabeth Smith LaBaw. Benjamin was a descendant of Penelope Van Princin, who was shipwrecked at Sandy Hook off the Jersey coast, later being rescued by friendly Indians and taken to New York where she married Richard Stout and in 1648 returned to Monmouth Co., NJ, as its first settlers.

Elizabeth Smith LaBaw was a descendant of the Martin and Otterbach families, who were among the 13 families from Muesen, Nassau-Siegen, Germany, who emigrated to Fauquier Co., VA, in 1714 — starting the first iron works in the Virginia Colony.

Elmer French was reared by his mother and stepfather, Henry Douglas, near New Market, where he attended school and belonged to the Christian Church. He had three step-brothers: Aaron, Emmons, and Edwin Douglas, a step-sister, Sarah Amanda Gilliland, and three half-brothers, Walter, Homer, and Everett Douglas. A farmer and fence-builder, he first married Mabel Reynolds, 1881-1904, daughter of Lewis and Mary Wright Reynolds of Brown's Valley. Elmer and Mabel had four sons: Earl, Sr. married Mary Gooding, Paul married Juanita Sparks, and twins, Claude married Opal Douglas, and Clyde married Charlotte Roberts. Mabel died when the twins were ten days old and Elmer married secondly, Lillie Kinkead, 1883-1963, daughter of Stephen and Nancy Zimmerman Kinkead of near Ladoga. Stephen was a grandson of Matthew and Sarah Galey Kinkead, who settled in Brown Township in 1829. Elmer and Lillie Kinkead French had eight children: sons, Ernest Sr. married Garnet Gause, Clarence, Ralph married Alleen Morrison, E. Edwin married Eulalia Switzer; daughters: Helen married Howard Webb, Hazel married Howard Hartung, Opal married John McKinstry, and Gladys married John Fletcher. *By Larry J. McKinstry*

FRENCH LINE

I will follow my French Line from Bedford and Berks Counties of Pennsylvania, to Hamilton and Miami Cos., OH to Montgomery Co., IN to Howard County where I now live.

My fourth great grandparents were James and Jane ? French from Pennsylvania and Allegheny Co., MD where James died in 1815. Children: Daniel, Lot (my line below), Jeremiah, Ralph, Benjamin married to Deborah Gist, Elizabeth married "Judge" James Martin, James married to Hannah Dean (whose son Lot and descendents were in Adams and Wells Counties in Indiana) and Mary who married Isaac Lane.

Charlie, Alonza, Lucretia Alice, Edna A., Everette, Elsie, Andrew and Eunice French

My third great grandparents were Lot and Elizabeth Miller French, who came to Montgomery Co., IN from Miami Co., OH in the early 1800's. He owned two farms in Montgomery County, died 1828. Children: Mary "Polly" married James Cowan, Ann married Martin Cumberland and second married Samuel Fisher, Phenamy "Amy" married Henry Applegate, James (see below) Adam Miller French married Mary ?. He was known for naming Lebanon, IN and his daughter Martha became a Doctor; Charolotte married Gabriel Trullinger, Jane married Enoch Richardson, and Sarah married (John Cowan)?

My second great grandparents were James and Abigail McGilliard French of Montgomery Co., IN. Their children: Alfred married Mary Jane Royalty French, Ralph (see below), Susan married Silas S. Baldwin, John, and Ann married James Owen Fisher.

My great grandparents were Ralph first married Amanda McDowell (no children) second married Eliza Ann Fisher. Children were Andrew, Laura, Sylvia married James M. Diller, Alfloretta married Myron Gannon, Alonzo (see below) and Hewitt.

My maternal grandparents were Alonzo Lewis "Lon" French married Alice Lucretia "Lula" Weed. Children: Charles Basil married Mamie E. Gearhart, twins: Evert Thomas French married

Fern Malaby and Elsie Odessa French married Hillery Turner, Myron Andrew "Dick" French married first Neva Gott and second to Gailen Jett (of whom I was named) third wife was Agnes Radcliff and fourth wife was Ruby Henderson Severs, Edna Alforetta French married Fred King DeLon, Sr. and their children were Alice Lorene married Myron Merrick, Gailen Louese DeLon (see below) and Fred King DeLon, Jr. married Joyce Delight Merrell.

I am Gailen Louese DeLon Harris, fourth great granddaughter of James and Jane French, and married to Neil Thomas Harris. Children: Everett Neil, and Thomas Paul. We live at 2528 Walker Ave., Kokomo, IN 46901, phone 1-317-452-3847.

Here are some of the cousins by the dozens that have helped me:

Larry McKinstry fifth great grandson of James and Jane French, now a beautician of Crawfordsville, IN.

Audrey Louise Wisehart Cox Leas, fourth great granddaughter of James and Jane French of Crawfordsville, IN.

Mary Blangy fifth great granddaughter of James and Jane French of R.R., Kokomo, IN.

Jean Fisher Heinmiller, fourth great granddaughter of James and Jane French, now of Meridian, ID.

Ima Joyce McCoppin Smith, fourth great granddaughter of James and Jane French of Carlsbad, CA.

MIKE AND LINDA FRIARS

Mike and Linda (Watson) Friars were married on her 18th birthday, Aug. 29, 1965 at the Roachdale Christian Church, with five (Omer and Florence Adams Henry, Goldie Nichols Galloway, Oral and Nellie Wilson Watson) of their grandparents present. Mike was born Nov. 14, 1944 in Indianapolis, the son of George and Dorothy (Henry) Friars. He has one brother, Jim, born Mar. 28, 1946. Jim married Nancy Rogers of Barnard. They had two sons, James Michael and Anthony Jason. Jim is presently married to Kristy Smith and they are the parents of one son, Bradley Ryan. Jim is a Vice President of Indiana National Bank in Indianapolis. Jim and Mike also have four half-brothers and a half-sister in New Hampshire. Mike is an electrician at R.R. Donnelley's. He is a member of the Sons of the American Legion, Eagles, NRA and Donnelley Club. His interests are guns and computers.

Linda was born in Crawfordsville and graduated from Roachdale in 1965, where she was active in music, FHA, yearbook, 4-H and Job's Daughters. Her interests are collecting owls, bowling and cards. She and her father enjoy woodworking, refinishing antiques and hiking together. She worked for several years with Scouts. Linda and Mike have one son, Matthew Allen Friars, born May 31, 1968 in Greencastle. Matt is a Senior at Butler, studying Public/Corporate Communications and Business. He is a member of the Phi Delta Theta Fraternity, Inter-Fraternal Council, and is an Eagle Scout. He received the Youth Leadership in America Medal.

Linda has two brothers: William "Bill" E. Watson, born Mar. 16, 1945. He married Madonna Grimes Sept. 1, 1963. Children: Pamela Sue, Jeffrey Allen and Janice Lynn (twins) and Ronald Lee Watson. Bill is presently married to Sue Sering. Bill is a machinist at Donnelley's. Linda's other brother is Donald Wayne, born July 26, 1953. He married Denise Hess. Children: Anissa Dawn and Andrea Nicole. Don works in the Corporate Offices of Inland Container.

Linda's father, Richard L. "Dick" Watson drove a truck since he was 13 years old, retiring from Yellow Freight in 1981. He was born Mar. 16, 1920 in Carpentersville. He married Frances Ellen Galloway July 4, 1942 at Mace. Frances' Montgomery County roots are deep. She is the daughter of Charles and Goldie Galloway. Charles owned and operated a Butcher Shop which is still remembered by many Ladoga-area people. Charles' parents were Robert Herron and Martha Ellen (Armstrong) Galloway. Robert H.'s parents were William and Rachel E. (Bailey) Galloway who are buried in Lee Cemetery, Union Township. Martha Ellen Galloway's parents were John Armstrong and Julia Hunt. Julia's parents, Ephraim T. and Esther (Heaton) Hunt moved from Butler Co., OH to Montgomery County in 1830. The first night spent in their cabin was consecrated by reading the Bible. Ephraim T. led the first Methodist Episcopal class at Mace in 1833. At his death (Mar. 23, 1879) his neighbors said, "Uncle Eph is gone. He was truly a good man."

Linda and Mike Friars live on Road 150 South and Linda continues her search for her Montgomery County roots. *Submitted by Linda Watson Friars*

LOWELL AND JANE FRIEND

Lowell E. Friend was born at Browns Valley Apr. 30, 1919, the son of Ellis C. and Etta M. (Hester) Friend and the grandson of Theodore and Fannie (Myers) Friend and John and Ida (Kennedy) Hester. Lowell was the second of five children, having two brothers and two sisters.

His father being a tenant farmer, the family moved around in several different areas; therefore, Lowell attended several different grade schools, but attended Crawfordsville High School all four years, graduating in 1938.

After graduation, he worked at Goodman's Department Store and Gray's Hatchery and Feed Store (the present Enterprise Building on East Market Street) before starting to work at R.R. Donnelley's (Nov. 13, 1939). At Donnelleys he started an apprenticeship as a linotype operator.

Sally, Jane, Dave and Lowell Friend

On Jan. 25, 1941, Lowell married Florence "Jane" Dewey, the daughter of Bert and Elsie (Bennett) Dewey at their home, East of Garfield. Jane was born May 19, 1920 East of New Richmond on the Charles and Ella (Dewey) Zuck farm. Jane had one brother, Robert Lee who passed away in Sherman, TX in May, 1983. Upon graduation, Jane was employed at the F.W. Woolworth Store. In June, 1941, she accepted a job at the A&P Store on West Market.

On Feb. 19, 1942, Lowell entered the Army, being sent to Fort Bragg, NC, where Jane again worked for A&P. The Friends were later sent to Fort Blanding, FL, where Jane was employed by Belk-Linsey in Gainesville. He served approximately four years before being discharged, with the rank of Staff Sergeant on Dec. 23, 1945. Returning home, Lowell completed his apprenticeship at Donnelleys Feb. 21, 1948, along with 30 other returning veterans.

A daughter, Sally Jo, was born Mar. 13, 1947. She grew up in the Friend's present home at New Market across the street from the school where she graduated in 1965. She was active in 4-H, completing ten years of activity. January 9, 1966, Sally married James D. Shelton, the son of Oral and Ethel (Cox) Shelton. They have three children: Angela and Natalie, both Purdue students and Nicholas, a student at North Montgomery. All three were active in 4-H Jr. Leaders and Sports. The family lives on a farm near Garfield where they raise registered Charolis cattle and they also own and operate Shelton Machinery in Indianapolis. Sally works part-time at Crawfordsville Veterinary Clinic. They are members of the Darlington Methodist Church and Cattlemen's Association. James (Jim) graduated from Darlington and attended Purdue University. He is a member of the Linden Masonic Lodge.

March 9, 1949, a son, David Lowell was born. He grew up in New Market graduating from New Market High School in 1967. David participated in sports and was active in 4-H for ten years. He now lives in New Market and has three sons: John, Branden and Matthew. John attends Southmont, belongs to the Key Club, officer in Jr. Leader 4-H Council. Branden also attends South, is in 4-H and sports. Matt attends school in Arizona and is active in sports. Dave is a 20-year employee of AT&T. He is married to Catherine J. "Cathy" Graves, daughter of Phyllis Myers and the late Kelly Graves. Cathy is a graduate of Crawfordsville High School and is employed part-time in Friend's Lamp Shop. David and his family attend New Hope Christian Church. He is a member of Alamo Masonic Lodge, Scottish Rite and Murat Shrine of Indianapolis, S.A.L. of American legion Post No. 72, Telephone Pioneers of America, Director of Montgomery County 4-H, Inc.

After 42 years in the printing business, Lowell retired in 1981 and Jane retired in 1982, after 25 years with the South Montgomery School Corporation Food Service. In 1972, Lowell and Jane started "Friends Lamp Shop" in their home as a hobby which later turned into a thriving specialty small business. Their real specialty was the manufacturing of a miniature hanging lamp with their name in the glass.

Lowell is past president of Sugar Creek Kiwanis Club of Crawfordsville, member of Alamo Masonic Lodge and American Legion Post 72 at Crawfordsville. Jane is a member of S.O.S. Sewing Club and Chi Omega of New Market. The Friends are members of the New Market Christian Church. *Submitted by Lowell Friend*

JOSEPH W. FRISZ

Joseph W. Frisz, was born Mar. 31, 1863, in the neighborhood of St. Ann's and North Vernon, near the Muscatatuck. His youth was spent in a time when men were changing from the use of waterpower, in its simpler forms, to the use of steam. He saw the speeding up of the vast changes that already were making grain fields of the forest. He must have sensed the acceleration of these changes, and it must have affected him, because he became not

165

only the guardian of one of Indiana's most rugged and scientifically interesting and scenic areas, but his interest expanded to the covered bridges and the old-time mills.

Joseph W. Frisz

He became a railroad machinist and grocer at Terre Haute, and he attended night classes at Rose Polytechnic and became proficient as a draftsman. He must have done his own exploring along the western edge of Indiana, for in 1909 he became associated with Morton T. Hidden and Dr. L.J. Willien of Terre Haute in buying 65 acres that included the Devil's Punch Bowl and the falls that spill down toward the level of Sugar Creek. Later he and Dr. Willien bought the Hidden interests, and gradually, in small lots, the holdings were increased — five acres in 1915, 69 acres in 1916, 58 acres in 1917, 66 in 1918 and so on and by 1942 they had 2,112 acres in the property which is known as The Shades. This property is in the corner of three counties: Montgomery, Fountain, and Parke.

Mr. Frisz did not discover The Shades. The Indians found it and were in camp there in 1815.

The Shades had to be financed and had to be made as nearly self-supporting as possible. It was more than a business enterprise for Mr. Frisz. Nature created a real conservationist who loved and preserved the Shades of Death as the Indians called it. In his early work in preserving The Shades his wife, Elizabeth Domenica Kintz, was his secretary, but due to failing health, she could not continue. His daughter Miss Ethel F. Frisz, served as secretary and his sons helped to run The Shades.

Joseph and Elizabeth had the following children: Wilfred P.; F. Leo; Clarence W.; Fabian J.; Paul C.; Helen J. Hauk; Ethel F. and Blanche M. Frisz.

Mr. Frisz, died in 1939. The State of Indiana purchased the area and made it a State park, a credit to Joseph W. Frisz and his family's work, conservation and imagination. *Submitted by Pat Hauk*

CHARLES M. AND MARY (SMITH) FRUITS

Charles M. Fruits was born Apr. 18, 1887 near Alamo, IN. Charles was the son of Noah and Susan (Lewis) Fruits. Charles was a member of the New Richmond Christian Church. He was employed at the New Richmond elevator for 25 years. He also was a carpenter. Charles was active in the Masons, being past master of the New Richmond Lodge No. 604 F&AM, and a past master of the New Richmond Lodge No. 604 F&AM, and a past patron of New Richmond Chapter No. 377 O.E.S.

Charles married Nov. 25, 1908 in Montgomery County Mary Smith, daughter of John H. and Cinderella (Balser) Smith. Mary was born Mar. 23, 1890 in Yountsville. She belonged to the New Richmond Christian Church and New Richmond Chapter #377 O.E.S. in which she was a past matron.

Charles M. and Mary Fruits

Charles and Mary had eight children: they are Grace Juanita married Sept. 24, 1927 to Theodore Mundorff. They had two children: Mary Elizabeth (July 26, 1928 to Jan. 13, 1954) and Donald Ralph. Grace married #2 Samuel Leslie Haire on May 11, 1938. Herbert Merritt. Ralph D. married July 19, 1936 to Leona Louise Lincoln. They have four children: Janice Sue, Donald Roger, Mary Teresa and Sandra Jean. Thelma Lenora. Marietta married Aug. 24, 1940 to Albert Earl Perry. They had six children: Ruth Maureen, Judith Diane (Apr. 10, 1942 to July 9, 1980), Mary Susan, Charles Albert (Sept. 11, 1945 to Feb. 19, 1969), Herbert William and Martha Lynn (Aug. 20, 1952 to Apr. 3, 1989). Charles Ray married May 17, 1945 to Delores Maxine Smith. They have a daughter, Rita Jo. Patricia Ann married Aug. 30, 1947 to Glen Edward Ferguson. Eleanor Ruth married Dec. 27, 1953 Ralph Howard Patrick. They had two girls: Linda Kay and Cynthia Leigh.

Charles and Mary enjoyed making big gardens. He died Jan. 5, 1953 and Mary died Dec. 5, 1968. They are buried in Waynetown Masonic Cemetery. They lived most of their lives in Montgomery County.

DAISY (HENDRICKS) FRUITS

Daisy Fruits of New Richmond will soon be 103 years old. She likes to relate how she wasn't named until she was about six or seven months old because she wasn't expected to live very long! One day, as she was learning to crawl, her father entered the room and said, "Isn't she a Daisy?" — and, so she got her name. In 1986 when New Richmond celebrated its sesquicentennial, Daisy, at 100, rode in the back seat of a convertible at the head of the parade through town. Waving at the crowd, she remarked, "Wouldn't my folks be surprised if they could see me now?"

Daisy, Nellie Lee, Lewis D. and Delmer K. Fruits

She was born July 12, 1886, the youngest of six children of Amanda (Henderson), b. Aug. 28, 1843, d. Sept. 23, 1927 and James Wesley Hendricks, b. July 19, 1838, d. Jan. 1, 1912. Her paternal grandparents were John (b. July 27, 1805, d. Apr. 2, 1874) and Elizabeth, b. Nov. 22, 1808, d. July 17, 1875 Hendricks.

Daisy's parents were married on July 26, 1874. Her father had previously been married to Amanda's older sister, Elizabeth, who died in 1873 after bearing a son, William (b. Aug. 10, 1860, d. Feb. 16, 1912), and a daughter, Charlotte, (b. July 29, 1862, d. June 29, 1863). James Wesley and Amanda's children were: Mary, b. May 19, 1875, d. Sept. 8, 1875; Oscar, b. Mar. 10, 1877, d. Aug. 12, 1887; Eva Bell, b. Nov. 13, 1879, d. Dec. 11, 1972 (married John Higbee July 10, 1904); Alice M., b. Oct. 14, 1881, d. July 26, 1954 (married Joseph Grenard Dec. 24, 1903); Chester b. Feb. 29, 1884, d. July 17, 1962 (m. Dora M. Smith Fe.b 26, 1916); and Daisy.

Daisy was raised on the Hendricks farm on S.R. 25, just south of the Wayne and Ripley Township line. She attended school at Ridgefarm and was baptized at Ridgefarm Church, both of which were just West of SR 25 and 32 Junction, south of her home.

On Nov. 19, 1905, Daisy married Delmer K. Fruits, b. Nov. 26, 1882 and died Sept. 7, 1959. They started housekeeping in a shed Southwest toward Wallace and their daughter, Nellie Lee was born there Oct. 2, 1906. They moved to Daisy's Grandpa Henderson's home where son Lewis D. was born (Sept. 27, 1908). Later they moved to what Daisy called the "Ole Kentucky Home" on SR 25 north of her parents' house and the Wayne-Ripley Township line which is still standing at this time. Delmer ran a restaurant in Waynetown for awhile and they moved to New Richmond about 1926.

Delmer K. Fruits attended Alamo school and his parents were Noah, 1852-1933 and Susan (Lewis), 1856-1928 who were married Feb. 10, 1874. Delmer was raised on the Fruits farm north of Alamo on Co. Rd. 200 S. where his grandfather John settled. His great-grandfather was "Alamo" George Fruits.

Delmer had four brothers and a sister: Charles, b. Apr. 18, 1887, d. Jan. 5, 1953 (married Mary Smith Nov. 25, 1908), lived at New Richmond; Fred, b. Jan. 23, 1881, d. Dec. 11, 1906 (m. Dessie Parker July 16, 1907) lived on the Fruits farm north of Alamo; Merritt, b. Dec. 5, 1878, d. Aug. 2, 1957 (m. Iva McBroom Sept. 25, 1907) lived at Waynetown; Lewis N., b. Feb. 28, 1895, d. Feb. 26, 1908; and Grace, b. June 27, 1885, d. Apr. 5, 1919 (m. Clarence Gilkey July 24, 1903) who moved to Denton, MT. She died there and her descendants live in that area today.

Daisy and Delmer's daughter, Nellie Lee, married Francis Ball (b. Aug. 15, 1904, d. July 23, 1976) on Dec. 11, 1924 and died Jan. 20, 1940. Their son, Lewis D. married Rachel Myers.

Daisy has 14 great grandchildren and 15 great-great grandchildren, soon to be 16. *Submitted by Shirley Fruits*

GEORGE AND CATHARINE FRUITS

George Fruits, Jr. came to Ripley Township in 1821. He was born Jan. 2, 1762 (per tombstone) at Baltimore, MD the second child of George and Margaret Fruits. His siblings being Martin, Margaret, Sarah, Catherine, Jonathan, John, Barbara and David.

On Oct. 29, 1808 George, Jr. married Miss Catharine Stonebraker, born May 6, 1790, in

Mahony Township, Northumberland Co., PA and died Jan. 17, 1880 in this county. She was the daughter of Sabastian and Susan Yeakley Stonebraker. This union was blessed with 13 children: Susan, Elizabeth, Jacob, Sabastian, Margaret, John, George III, Catherine, David, William Jonathan, Michael, and one infant died unnamed.

George and Catharine Fruits Jr.

The grandparents of Catharine Fruits were John Dietrick and Christina Stonebraker. George and Anna Deppen Yeakley were her maternal grandparents. George Yeakley was the son of Benedict and Veronica Ruchti Yeakley.

Our subject died on his farm northeast of Alamo, IN on Aug. 6, 1876. Alamo George received the deed for his land in Ripley Township in 1826. He served in Capt. Kirkwood's Company of Pennsylvania Militia in the Revolutionary War. He was also in the militia under Captain George Miars, joining on Nov. 2, 1781. George enlisted in General Wayne's Army in 1794 and was in the Battle of Maumee where he received a wound in his right thigh. He carried that musketball in his flesh to his grave.

"Alamo" George as he was known was said to have very tough skin allowing him to walk through a brier patch barefoot. He at one time was bald, but later had a fine growth of white hair and cut his third set of teeth.

One of "Alamo" George's greatest disappointments in his life came when he tried to enlist in the Civil War, at the age of 100 years and was refused because of his age.

The Historical Society of Montgomery County had a dedication ceremony at the gravesite of George honoring him as the nation's last survivor of the Revolutionary War.

An American flag was placed beside a tombstone in the quiet county cemetery and serves as a reminder to all of one of Montgomery County's courageous men. Several descendants of George and Catherine Fruits still live in the County.

HERBERT MERRITT FRUITS

Herbert M. Fruits was born Oct. 6, 1911 in Crawfordsville. He was the son of Charles M. and Mary (Smith) Fruits. He graduated from New Richmond High School in 1930. He was married Jan. 1, 1936 to Evangeline Louke, born Aug. 8, 1910, died Mar. 20, 1938. He was employed in Lafayette as a meat cutter before entering the service in 1942. He went overseas in April 1944. Herb was with the 811th Tank Destroyer Unit. He was held prisoner from Dec. 18, 1944 to Apr. 18, 1945. He was confined in Stalag XIII near Nuernburg.

Even though disabled, Herb was a Rural Mail Carrier for 14 years in the New Richmond, Linden and Romney areas. He was also a member of the New Richmond American Legion Post; New Richmond Masonic Lodge 604, F.&A.M., and Rural Mail Carriers Association.

Herbert Merritt Fruits

Herb lived with his mother and cared for her until her death in 1968. Having no children, he looked out after all his nieces and nephews. Herb had five sisters and two brothers: Grace Juanita, 1909-1977; Ralph, born 1911; Thelma, 1916-1924; Marietta, 1918-1987; Charles Ray, 1920-1973; Patricia, born 1931 and Ruth, born 1932.

Herb died Dec. 10, 1974 in Tippecanoe County, at Romney, IN. He is buried at Waynetown Masonic Cemetery. *Submitted by Pat (Fruits) Ferguson*

JOHN S. AND REBECCA (KEYS) ALBERTSON FRUITS

John S. Fruits was born Mar. 11, 1818 in Butler Co., OH. He came to Ripley Township with his parents George Fruits, Jr. and Catherine Stonebraker. John was a farmer and owned land in Ripley Township. On Feb. 11, 1845, John married Rebecca Keys Albertson who was born Feb. 10, 1812. She was the daughter of William Keys and Lydia Thomas. Rebecca was married first to Hiram Albertson.

John and Rebecca had four children: George Keith married Feb. 16, 1888 to Rhoda Shafer. They had five children. Lydia Ann, born Mar. 13, 1848 died Nov. 16, 1859. Charles Fruits married Dec. 28, 1875 to Amanda Brawley. They had two children, Alonzo James and John William. Noah married Oct. 12, 1874 to Susan Lenora Lewis and had six children: Merrit J., Fred E., Delmar K., Grace A., Charles M. and Lewis N. (Feb. 5, 1895-Feb. 26, 1908).

Rebecca died Oct. 29, 1876. She is buried in the Fruits-McCormick Cemetery. On June 29, 1877, John married Rebecca A. Keys born in 1832. She was the daughter of Joseph Keys and Amanda Sparks.

John died Apr. 10, 1894, and is buried in the Fruits-McCormick Cemetery. Rebecca died June 4, 1903 and is buried in the Bunnell Cemetery in Frankfort, IN. *Submitted by Pat (Fruits) Ferguson*

LEWIS AND RACHEL (MYERS) FRUITS

Lewis D. Fruits was a lifelong resident of Montgomery County. Rachel came from Fountain County to live when she was about eight years old when her father died. They were both graduates of Waynetown High School. Rachel attended one year at McMurray College in Jacksonville, IL.

Lewis was born Sept. 27, 1908, the son of Delmer K. and Daisy (Hendricks) Fruits in the farm home of his maternal great grandfather, Henderson - southeast of Waynetown. His maternal grandparents were: James Wesley (July 19, 1838-Jan. 1, 1912) and Amanda (Henderson) (Aug. 28, 1843-Sept. 23, 1927) Hendricks who lived just south of the Wayne-Ripley Township line on what is now State Road 25 on the east side of the road. His paternal grandparents were Noah (1852-1933) and Susan Lenora (Lewis) Fruits who lived north of Alamo on County Road 200 S. He was the great-great grandson of "Alamo" George Fruits, Jr. Lewis had one sister Nellie Lee Fruits (born Oct. 2, 1906) who married Francis Ball (born Aug. 15, 1904) on Dec. 11, 1924, but died Jan. 20, 1940.

Lewis and Rachel (Myers) Fruits

Lewis worked as a mechanic at Danville, IL for a time after high school until he and Rachel were married Oct. 17, 1931. Then, he began farming the Roundtree farm northeast of Alamo where he and Rachel raised their six children. He died there Nov. 20, 1975.

Rachel Fruits was born in Fountain County Apr. 11, 1911 and died Jan. 3, 1973. She was the daughter of Deward O. (1877-1919) and Ada (Catherine) (Lowe) Myers (1888-1984) and had a twin sister, Mary, who died shortly after birth. Her brother, Herman D. Myers (b. 1915) married Doris Gooding and lives near Hillsboro. Rachel's maternal grandparents were Elijah Lowe (1836-1910) and Rachel (Philpott) Lowe (1854-1946) who lived in the Wallace-Waynetown areas. Thru her Philpott ancestors, Rachel was a descendant of Catherine (Stonebraker) Fruits and "Alamo" George. Her paternal grandparents were Noah Ransom Myers (Sept. 9, 1858-Nov. 3, 1929) and Mary Jane (Clore) (Nov. 16, 1851-Nov. 27, 1944) who farmed in Fountain County near the Montgomery line West of Alamo.

Lewis and Rachel were members of the Alamo Christian Church and she was active in Ladies' Aid there and the Alamo Home Demonstration Club. Lewis belonged to the Alamo Masonic Lodge, Indianapolis Scottish Rite, 4-H leader and after retiring, he was an inspector on the interstate highway.

Their children: Russell L. who lives near New Richmond; Verda M. (Mrs. R. Gene) Mills who lives west of Crawfordsville; Dema K. (Mrs. Jay) Delp who lives near Marshall; James L. and Dennis R., who both live at Lake Holiday; and Deanna R. (Mrs. Ron) Waye (twin to Dennis R.) who lives northeast of Alamo on the old "Alamo" George Fruits, Jr. homestead.

There are 14 grandchildren descended from Rachel and Lewis and 15 (soon to be 16) great grandchildren. *Submitted by Shirley D. Fruits*

OLLIE AND DELPHA (PAYNE) FRUITS

In 1909, Ollie G. Fruits, middle son of Jonathan and Rozella (Keys) Fruits and great grandson of

Catherine Stonebraker and George Fruits (this nation's last survivor of the Revolutionary War) was working on a farm outside Waynetown, IN. Delpha Payne, third child of Jeptha, and oldest child of his second wife, Martha (Gentry) Payne came from southern Kentucky to work on this same farm. On May 20th of that year, Ollie (born Oct. 3, 1879) and Delpha (born Apr. 23, 1888) were married. Their first daughter, Opal, was born in Waynetown on Mar. 24, 1910. She married Robert Early, a Wabash student from Detroit, MI in 1928. They had two daughters, Mary (Early) Johnson and Ann (Early) Powers.

Ollie and Delpha (Payne) Fruits.

Ollie and Delpha moved to Crawfordsville where Ollie had a painting and wallpaper hanging business. Delpha was a seamstress and worked at Freedman's Clothing Store. In 1919, they moved to 310 West Pike Street where they lived until their deaths - Delpha, Nov. 16, 1954 and Ollie, July 6, 1956. In this house on West Pike Street their second daughter, Martha Roselyn, was born on Aug. 15, 1923. She graduated from CHS in 1941 and was a proofreader at Donnelleys until 1948. On May 13, 1945, she married Arthur Bryan Lewellen, who was serving in the U.S. Navy. He is the oldest son of Arthur and Frances (Spray) Lewellen. He was born Nov. 23, 1919 and is known as "Bill." He graduated from CHS in 1935, attended Wabash College for two years and began working at Donnelleys Sept. 30, 1937, where he worked until his retirement on his 40th anniversary in 1977. In 1970, he pursued his education by taking night classes and received a degree in Math from Purdue in August 1977. During his retirement he has been a substitute teacher at North Montgomery and involved in the restoration of Lane Place.

Bill and Martha's daughter, Linda Roselyn was born July 10, 1948. She graduated from CHS in 1966 and Kalamazoo College in 1970. She is a French, German and English teacher and taught at Southmont and at Delphi, IN, until she married Byron W. Parker. They purchased a 38-foot sailboat in England and lived on it for three years while they sailed in the Mediterranean, crossed the Atlantic and then sailed in the Caribbean. They now live in Ft. Lauderdale, FL.

Their son, Steven Bryan, was born Dec. 10, 1952. He graduated CHS in 1971 and attended Michigan State and Purdue. After working in Texas and Illinois, he is now studying at Purdue, working for a degree in E.E.

Bill and Martha have lived at 409 Wayne Avenue and are active members of First Baptist Church. *Submitted by Mary Early Johnson*

RUSSELL L. AND SHIRLEY D. (WALP) FRUITS

Russell and Shirley Fruits live near New Richmond on the former Mort Allman farm. Russell was born at Waynetown and grew up northeast of Alamo on the Roundtree farm. Here his parents, Lewis D. and Rachel (Myers) Fruits farmed and raised their six children: Russell L., Verda M., Dema K., James L., and twins Dennis R. and Dianna R. Russell's grandparents are: Delmer K. and Daisy (Hendricks) Fruits, and Deward O. and Ada (Lowe) Myers. He is the third great grandson of "Alamo" George Fruits.

Russell, or "Butch" as he was known in ballplaying days with coach Tom "Pix" Bowerman, graduated from Alamo in 1950. He spent 1951-55 in the Navy, then attended Indiana University from 1956 thru 1959 (B.S. in Business Management). He went to work for Agrico Chemical Co. in Illinois, Tennessee, Michigan and New Jersey until 1968 when the family returned to Indiana. He took over a closed feed mill at Newtown in Fountain County which has grown into the present Newtown Farm Service.

Shirley was born at Indianapolis to Lewis M. and Olive (Marsteller) Walp. In 1941 her family moved to a farm south of Alamo. She graduated in 1951. Siblings: Geneva Mitchell; Robert L.; Doris C. (died 1945); Betty L. (died 1948) and David G. (died 1972). Shirley's maternal grandparents were Hettie (Perry) and George Marsteller who lived first in the New Richmond area then moved to a farm near Russellville. Her great grandfather Nicholas Marsteller sold land in what is now West Lafayette to be used as a campus where Purdue University is situated. A street through that section bears the Marsteller name.

Russell L. and Shirley D. Walp Fruits and family

Shirley and Russ were married in February 1952 in the San Francisco Bay area where he was attending Navy Radar School. They were baptized into the Alamo Christian Church and attend the New Richmond Christian Church. He is a member of Alamo Masonic Lodge, Indianapolis Scottish Rite, Murat Shrine, and Quigle-Palin American Legion Post at Newtown. She is a homemaker and an active booster of 4-H and school activities. She has been active in Girl Scouts locally and the Sycamore Council level, and is bookkeeper for two family businesses.

They have one son and four daughters. Jeffrey L., born at Crawfordsville, graduated from North Montgomery in 1973, where he was active in FFA. He has worked at Newtown Farm Service since then. He is co-manager with his father and is a licensed broker. He and his wife Lee Ann (daughter of Lowell and Jane Rice) were married in 1980. Children: Christopher, Jason and twins Aaron and Ashley.

All four daughters have been active in 4-H and Girl Scouts. Teresa D., born in Crawfordsville, graduated North Montgomery 1975. She and her husband, James A. Wasson, (married 1980) both graduated from Purdue Veterinarian School in 1982. With their sons Jeremy, Zachary, and Ransom, they live near Redkey, IN. Jim is the son of David and Norma Wasson.

Christine G., (born Danville, IL) graduated from North in 1980, Purdue 1984 (B.S. in Horticulture Business Management). She, too, joined the Newtown Family Farm Service. She coaches girl's basketball at Northridge and summer softball at Wingate.

Sandra M., (born Danville, IL) graduated from North in 1981 and earned a B.S. (Computer Science) from Purdue (1986). She was the Goldie Priebe county 4-H award winner in 1982. She lives in Indianapolis and works for Conseco.

Colleen A., (born Crawfordsville) graduated 1988 from North. She is a freshman at Purdue and a talented pianist like her grandmother Walp.

These Fruits daughters and their mother are vocal harmonizers, and with New Richmond Postmaster Wilma Lewellyn, have performed as "JoySing" at several functions over the past few years. *Submitted by Shirley D. Fruits*

DOROTHY (HUGHES) FULFORD

Dorothy (Hughes) Fulford daughter of Merle and Oley Hughes was born in Union Township, Montgomery Co., IN Oct. 21, 1919. After graduating from Crawfordsville High School, Dorothy lived with her parents until after her marriage to Clinton Harris Fulford Oct. 19, 1940. Clint was born Dec. 23, 1917 near Elletsville, IN.

Clint and Dorothy lived about six months in Toledo, OH before they returned to the Hughes farm shortly before Dorothy's father died. Clint and Dorothy were the parents of five children, all born in Union Township.

Lana Lee Fulford born Aug. 16, 1941 married William Joseph Welliever Feb. 26, 1961. William was born July 19, 1940. William and Lana have three children, and live near Crawfordsville.

Yancie Joseph Welliever born Jan. 23, 1962, married Kelli Dee Parker Sept. 10, 1983. Kelli was born Aug. 21, 1964, they live in Hopkinsville, KY. Yancie and Kelli are the parents of Whitney Jo born May 6, 1986 and Cori Keith born Sept. 10, 1988.

Brett Alan Welliever born Aug. 17, 1963 married Ami Jo Cunningham July 16, 1988. Ami was born Nov. 10, 1964. They live in Crawfordsville.

Kalay Ann Welliever born July 31, 1966, married Eric Joseph Karle Sept. 13, 1986. Eric was born Mar. 17, 1964. They were divorced Mar. 17, 1988.

Phyllis Lynn Fulford daughter of Clint and Dorothy Fulford was born Sept. 11, 1943, married Joe Brent Wilson June 30, 1963. Joe was born Dec. 10, 1940, they were parents of three daughters, Mindy Jo born Jan. 31, 1967, Heather Lynn born Feb. 25, 1969, and Tiffany Ann born Mar. 2, 1972. Joe and Phyllis divorced Jan. 17, 1984, Joe lives in Madison Township and Phyllis lives in Crawfordsville. Donna Kay Fulford daughter of Clint and Dorothy (Hughes) Fulford was born Oct. 21, 1944. Donna married William James Milam Nov. 2, 1963, William was born Apr. 20, 1940. They are parents of Brian David Milam, born May 14, 1964 and Alison Melissa Milam, born Apr. 20, 1973, their family lives in Shawnee, KS. Alan Harris Fulford son of Clint and Dorothy was born Nov. 13, 1949 and lives in Albuquerque, NM.

David Clinton Fulford son of Clint and Dorothy Fulford was born July 5, 1956. David married Kathleen Henderson Aug. 29, 1973, Kathleen was born Apr. 6, 1956. David Thomas Fulford, son of David and Kathy was born Sept. 20, 1977.

Clint and Dorothy left their farm in 1964 and in 1975 were living on the Thunder Valley farm. Clint died July 15, 1983 and was buried in Oak Hill Cemetery, Dorothy Fulford moved to her Del-Mar home in Crawfordsville in 1988.

FULLENWIDER

The family can be traced back to the Royal House of Orange of the Netherlands; however, for this history we will confine it to Montgomery County.

Eleazer (fifth of 16 children of Jacob Fullenwider) with his wife Lavinia (daughter of Mr. and Mrs. James Allen) came to Montgomery County in 1830 from Shelby Co., KY. They first settled in Sugar Creek Twp. then moved to a location between Waveland and Browns Valley. This farm is known as the Pine Grove farm, so named on account of the grove of tall pine trees that existed at that time.

Mr. and Mrs. Fullenwider had 11 children of whom two continued to live in Montgomery County. These were James Newton and Chalmers. Each had four children.

The family of Chalmers lived in Crawfordsville, one of whom, J. Newton lived there until his death. The others separated to other states. History of this branch may be found in *Beckwith's Montgomery County History*.

James Newton (son of Eleazer) settled on a farm west of Brownsvalley and raised a family of four children. Robert E., Henry C., James Scott and Lavinia (married Dr. Charles Laughlin). Of these, six children were born.

Henry remained on the farm settled by Eleazer. He and his wife (nee Lorena Glenn) reared two sons. William Glenn and Henry Newton. Both of these played football on the Waveland High School team, at the time of its local glory: WHS 85—Crawfordsville 0, WHS 115—Wiley 0, WHS 135—Russellville 0, called in the third quarter etc. Glenn went west and was employed by the Weyerhauser Lumber Company until retirement. He and his wife, nee Edith McCampbell had one son, Wm., Jr.

Newton married Rosalie Durham (dau. of Geo. T. and Betty North) Durham in 1912. To this union were born three children, Robert E., Wallace "Terry" and Betty Lou.

Robert married Lena Rivers and had four children Betty Wills, Virginia Beach, VA, Roberta Gegner of Crawfordsville, James, Columbus, OH and David of Waveland. Betty has two sons living in Virginia, Douglas and Robert. James has a daughter, Stephanie. Roberta has two daughters, Kristin and Jennifer. David has two sons Mathew and Benjamin, and a daughter Sarah.

Terry has one son Daniel Newton, MSGT USMC, stationed in Hawaii. Daniel has three children, Daniel, Carolann and Digna.

Betty Lou married J.D. Banner and lives in Milwaukee. They have one daughter Cynthia. Cynthia married Fred Ray. They live in Columbus, OH and have two children. A son Christian and a daughter Lauren.

The youngest generation mentioned, is the seventh generation bearing the Fullenwider name and descending from Eleazer, to be living in the county.

When Robert and his wife Lena, sent their oldest son James, off to Vietnam, she was the ninth consecutive woman bearing the name of Fullenwider to have sent a son, brother or husband off to war.
Submitted by Robert E. Fullenwider

JACOB AND MARTHA RHODEHAMEL FULWIDER

Jacob H. Fulwider was born near Colierstown, VA, on Sept. 18, 1849, the son of Joseph H. and Sarah Houff Fulwider. He came with his parents and eight brothers and sisters to Indiana in the early 1850's. They settled in Montgomery County.

Martha Rhodehamel, daughter of John and Sarah Williams Rhodehamel, was born near Pleasant Hill in Posey Co., OH, on Sept. 23, 1851. When she was nine years old, the family moved to Clay Co., IN, where they lived for five years, then moved to Elmdale in Montgomery County.

Jacob and Martha were married Sept. 28, 1869, in Crawfordsville. They lived near Wingate all of their married lives.

They were the parents of nine children—four sons and five daughters. Eljah died in 1881. Mary, Arlie, Sallie and Orville all died of diptheria within a few weeks in late 1893. Another daughter, Maggie, died in 1895, also fo diptheria. Quoting from the *Wingate News* in 1894:

Their own mother prepared them and handed them out the door for burial. It must have been a very black and sorrowful winter. Not only did Jake lose his children, but Mary, his sister, lost several of hers, and many relatives and friends and neighbors lost their children, too.

All of their children had diptheria, except Walter, who was at Merom College that winter. Ben and Leota recovered.

Walter and Ben homesteaded in South Dakota in the late 1890's with some of their cousins, but returned to Montgomery County.

Walter was born Sept. 26, 1871. He married Eva May Gravitt, daughter of Ben and Lydia Razor Gravitt, on Dec. 24, 1904. They had six children: Georgiana, Gaynell, Orville, Joseph, Fred and Bettie.

Benjamin was born Sept. 12, 1876. He married Elsie Bunnell, daughter of Thomas and Mary Bunnell, on Oct. 30, 1897. They had four children: Robert, Glenn, Paul and Mary.

Leota was born Nov. 27, 1877, and married Eldon Bunnell in December, 1895. They had three children: Ethel, Jacob and Iva.

Jacob and Martha were married for 56 years. They were known affectionately in the Wingate community as Uncle Jake and Aunt Matt.

Jake cut down a wild cherry tree on his farm and had a casket made from it at the Crawfordsville Casket Factory several years before his death. He owned a lot of Montgomery County farmland and was known as a hard worker. He died on June 17, 1925, at his home near Wingate and was buried in Liberty Cemetery.

Martha died on May 12, 1936, at the home of her son, Benjamin. She was buried in Liberty Cemetery. Quoting from her obituary:

Most of her life had been lived in one community in Montgomery County where she was known as a devoted wife, mother and grandmother, a kind neighbor and a Christian lady.

Jake and Martha have many descendants living in Montgomery County today.

JOSEPH AND SARAH HOUFF FULWIDER

Joseph Henry Fulwider was born Jan. 19, 1810, in Augusta or Rockbridge Co., VA. He was the son of Jacob and Elizabeth Loman Fulwider, grandson of John and Elsie Hull Fulwider, and great grandson of Ulrich and Margaret Fulwider. Ulrich came to the United States on Aug. 30, 1743 from Switzerland, where he was born Dec. 5, 1723.

Sarah Elizabeth Houff was also born in Augusta or Rockbridge Co., VA, on Sept. 14, 1810.

Joseph and Sarah were married Apr. 6, 1834, and lived in Rockbridge County until sometime in the 1850's. Ten of their 11 children were born there, near Colierstown, VA.

In the early 1850's, they moved to Montgomery Co., IN, with nine children: Elizabeth, James, William Andrew, Benjamin, Margaret, Sarah Jane, Louisa, Joseph and Jacob. John had died at aged 2-1/2 in Virginia. Mary, their 11th child, was born in Indiana.

Elizabeth married James Bannon in 1858 and lived in Montgomery County. James moved to Illinois. William Andrew married Annis Cooley. He died at age 37 from effects of the Civil War. Benjamin married Eliza Thomas and, later, Rachel Morrow. He was a Union soldier in the Civil War. He moved, with his family, to South Dakota. Margaret married Jesse King. They lived in Montgomery County. Sarah Jane married James Groendyke and, later, H. Detchon and lived in Montgomery County. Louisa married General George Coffin and moved to Indianapolis. Joseph died at age 14 in the Civil War. He was a drummer boy, but it is not known on which side he fought. Jacob married Martha Rhodehamel and was a farmer in the Wingate area of Montgomery County. Mary married Lemuel Orwig and moved to Fountain County.

Joseph died on Jan. 19, 1875. Sarah died on May 10, 1890. They are buried in Liberty Cemetery in Montgomery Co., IN.

WALTER A. AND EVA MAE FULWIDER

Walter A. Fulwider was born Sept. 26, 1871 in Coal Creek Twp. He was a hard worker and enjoyed life. He spent the entire 69 years of life in Montgomery County. Walter was the son of Jacob H. and Martha Rhodehamel Fulwider. As a young man he attended Merom College, but had to return home to help his father on the farm. The family purchased land that needed to be cleared of timber with ditching to be done, and Walter did a lot of this work.

Walter and Mae Fulwider (wedding)

Walter married Eva Mae Gravitt Dec. 23, 1904. They were the parents of six children: Georgianna born Dec. 9, 1906; Gaynell born Feb. 2, 1908; Orville (Bud) born Mar. 1, 1910; Joseph, born July 13, 1912; Fredrick, born Mar. 28, 1919 and Bettie I., born Nov. 9, 1924.

The family moved to Brown Twp. in 1921, where they lived on a farm south of the Shades Park.

Walter was a farmer his entire life, having to leave the farm because of poor health in 1935, when they moved to Alamo. They lived in the small town of Alamo, where Walter died Apr. 11, 1940, and his wife, Eva Mae, eight weeks later on June 6.

Georgianna married Vern Clore on Sept. 2, 1925. They had one daughter, Carol Jean, born July 8, 1932.

Gaynell had polio at the age of five years and had a bad curved spine. She was never married; also Orville who drowned at the age of 25, and Fredrick were never married.

Joseph married Rosalie McMullen Aug. 30, 1934. They had three sons, Billy Joe, born June 30, 1935; John Alvin, born Oct. 1940; and George Walter, born Fe.b 17, 1948.

Bettie married Lowell Simpson Apr. 25, 1942. They had two sons, Walter Dale, born Sept. 4, 1943 and Malcom F., born Aug. 14, 1945. Most of the family attended Waveland School and several members of the family still live in Montgomery County at this writing in 1989. *Submitted by Bettie Fulwider Simpson*

SARAH MATILDA GALEY

Sarah Matilda Galey was born Feb. 28, 1907 at 702 South Washington Street, Crawfordsville, IN at the home where she now resides and has lived all her life. She went to Tuttle School and Crawfordsville High School, graduated in 1925. She worked at Donnelleys for two years, and the American Security Company for 38 years under Harrison Young and Clyde Rogers.

February 18, 1940 she married Paul Messmore Stout and to that union one daughter was born July 31, 1941 Lucy Ann Stout.

Sarah's father waS Albert Smith Galey, who was a taylor with a Taylor Shop at 211 South Washington Street. Albert Galey waS born June 28, 1870 in a log cabin a few miles south of Crawfordsville. His father was John Vanice Galey. His grandfather waS Samuel Smith Galey who came from around Shelbyville, KY in the early 1800s. Albert graduated from Wabash College in 1893, and was a 50 year Mason.

Sarah's mother was Felinia Elliott Galey, the daughter of Harvey B. Elliott and Sarah Ann Faust Elliott. She grew up around Crawfordsville. She was born Oct. 26, 1875. She had five sisters. She married Albert Galey June 1, 1904. Her father was a farmer.

Paul Messmore Stout was born Feb. 1, 1907 at Crawfordsville, IN, the son of Harry T. Stout and Anna Beam Stout. Anna Beam Stout's parents were James Beam and Isabelle Williamson Beam. The Stouts were from Waynetown, IN. They had four children: James B. Stout and Dr. Harry T. Stout, deceased. Paul M. Stout and Margaret Stout Vanscoyoc. Anna Beam Stout lived to be over 100 years old. Paul graduated from Crawfordsville High School in 1924 and spent the next 12 years in California, later returned to Crawfordsville. He was a farmer.

Lucy Ann Stout, daughter of Sarah and Paul grew up in Crawfordsville and graduated from high school in 1959. She went two years to Lake Forest College and then married J. Frank Bell, the son of Estel and Marjorie Chadwick Bell. They have two sons, James Rice Bell born Apr. 13, 1968 and Paul Reid Bell born Mar. 29, 1972 and live at Millersburg, OH, where J. Frank is president of Rice-Chadwick Rubber Company at Killbuck, OH. *Submitted by Mary Jeannette Dickerson*

EARL B. AND M. ELIZABETH (PENN) GARDNER

Earl's paternal ancestors came to Putnam Co., IN, from North Carolina in 1826. Earl was born in 1890 to Edward and Cora Anna (Webster) Gardner in Russellville. He had two brothers, Ben and Frank, both deceased, and one sister, Mary Shoaf. Mary lives in Bainbridge. Earl died in 1976.

Elizabeth's paternal grandfather, Joseph Penn, came to Montgomery County in 1857 from Bourbon Co., KY. He was a descendant of William Penn of Pennsylvania. Elizabeth was born in 1895 to Lafayette and Lena (Wray) Penn on their farm southeast of New Market. She had two sisters, Florence and Ruth, and one brother, Ford, who are all deceased. Elizabeth died in 1988.

Earl and Elizabeth Gardner family in 1936 L.to R. Back Row: Wayne Penn, Lorraine, Neal and Earl, Jr. Front Row: Nancy, Jack and Jane

Earl and Elizabeth were married in Crawfordsville in 1915. They started housekeeping in an apartment on South Green Street. They then moved to Kentland, IN. Earl joined the Navy while our country was involved in WWI. Before he was discharged, he was asked to run for sheriff of Newton County on the Republican ticket. Elizabeth campaigned for him until he got home. He won and served one term of office. Two children were born to them in Kentland, Neal in 1916 and Lorraine in 1919.

The family later moved to Ladoga where Earl, Jr. was born in 1923. They then moved to Lapland for a short time, and from there to New Market. Four more children were born in New Market: Wayne Penn in 1926, Jane in 1930, Nancy in 1934 and Jack in 1936. Wayne died in 1944 after a long battle with heart disease caused by rheumatic fever.

Earl worked for Donnelley's for 36 years. He was always active in local politics and served on the New Market town board for many years. He also served as precinct committeeman and Elizabeth was his vice chairman. After retiring from Donnelley's, he served two terms as Republican County chairman.

The six living children are: Neal, who married Mary Lael Martin; they have two sons, Gary and Thomas. Thomas has one daughter, Alyssa. Lorraine, who married Bernard Keim; they have two sons, Mark and Jason. Earl, Jr., who married Phyllis Lewis; they have one daughter, Molly Craft and she has one son, Steven and one daughter, Emily. Jane, who married Robert Ekstrom; they have one son, Dean, and one daughter, Jamie Haddad. Jamie has one son, Roberto, and three daughters, Soladad, and twins, Robin and Jamie. Nancy, who married Robert Rogers; they have two daughters, Robin and Karen. Robin Starnes has two sons, Cameron and Adrian. Karen Breault has a son, Taylor, and a daughter, Kelsey. Jack, who married Patricia Sumner; they have two sons, Roger and Tracy, and one daughter, Jill. Tracy has one son, Mason.

Many of the Gardner family have now scattered to California, Texas, Nevada, Mexico, Ohio, North Carolina and Florida. *Submitted by Nancy Rogers*

GARNER FAMILY

The Garner family is of German-English descent, but came to Indiana from Lexington, KY. William G. Garner bought an 80-acre farm in Montgomery County on June 15, 1831. His son Elias was born in Montgomery County on May 1, 1834, and died Apr. 30, 1890. He married Susan McIntire. Susan was born Oct. 3, 1839 and died July 15, 1930. They are buried at Pisgah Cemetery east of Mace. Their third son John Albert Garner born Sept. 4, 1870 in Boone County and died Feb. 19, 1958, in Crawfordsville. He married Myrtie Lusula Richardson on June 16, 1903, in Boone Co., IN. Myrtie was born Nov. 29, 1873 in Boone County and died Nov. 23, 1958, in Crawfordsville. They are buried in the Jamestown Cemetery. In 1949 they moved from their farm home in Boone County to Crawfordsville where they lived until their death in 1958.

John Albert and Myrtie Richardson Garner had one son, Sherman Ross Garner born May 31, 1904, in Jackson Township in Boone County. On Apr. 4, 1930, he married Claire Irene Mitcheltree, daughter of David T. and Mary Pruitt Mitcheltree. They were married in Boone County but established their home in Crawfordsville, where their son, Robert Allen was born on Feb. 24, 1931. Sherman Garner owned and operated a Regal Grocery store at 210 W. Chestnut St., Crawfordsville, IN from 1935 until 1954. It was in this grocery store that Robert grew. He graduated from Crawfordsville High School in 1949. He graduated from Indiana Business College in 1951 and attended Indiana State and Butler University. He was a corporal in the infantry of the U.S. Army. He was cited for meritorious service in Korea, from March 1952 to June 1953. He also received the combat infantry badge, United Nations badge, commendation ribbon, and three bronze stars. Robert served from Aug. 2, 1951 to July 30, 1953.

On Dec. 23, 1962, Robert Allen Garner married Virginia Shillings, born on Sept. 22, 1932, the daughter of George Russell and Evelyn Lee Donlouie Shillings. Robert and Virginia now live in Indianapolis, IN where Robert is with the Paul Harris, Inc. Stores and Virginia is teacher-librarian with the Brownsburg Community Schools.

Claire Irene Garner was a school teacher and former principal. She died Apr. 1, 1989. Buried New Ross Cemetery. For her family history see Britts/Mitcheltree family in this book.

GARRETT

Richard and Dora Capshaw Garrett moved to Crawfordsville, IN from Veedersburg, IN in December 1974 with their two children, Richard Allen II and Julie Suzette.

Richard and Dora were married Feb. 22, 1969 in the Presbyterian Parsonage in Newtown, IN by Reverend George Phillips.

Richard Allen II was born Aug. 14, 1969 at Home Hospital in Lafayette, IN. Julie Suzette was born Nov. 14, 1971 at Home Hospital in Lafayette.

Rich graduated from Crawfordsville High School in 1988 and works in Waynetown for Miller's Body Shop. Julie is a Junior at Crawfordsville High School. She plans to attend Purdue University and major in Mathematics Education.

Richard Allen I was born Dec. 23, 1944 in Newtown, IN. He was the second of five children of Harry Taylor and Verna Spragg Garrett. He graduated in 1963 from Richland Township High School in Newtown. Upon graduation he worked for Claypool Garage then later worked at Alcoa Corporation in Lafayette. In 1968 he went to work at Ingress Plastines which was sold in 1988 and is now known as Integrated Plastics Technology.

Harry and Verna's other children are William who was born June 27, 1943. He married Sheila Meadows on Nov. 17, 1963. They have one daughter, Lezlie René, who was born Aug. 23, 1967. They now live at Battle Ground, IN.

Carolyn is the only daughter of Harry and Verna. She was born Feb. 14, 1946. She married George Leon Helms on Mar. 21, 1965. They have three children. The first is Cindy who was born Sept. 3, 1967. She married Mark Randolph. Their second child is Marcy who was born Mar. 15, 1973. Their last child is Travis who was born Nov. 16, 1975. They live in Attica, IN.

Harry and Verna's fourth child was Donald who was born Nov. 30, 1948. He married Corliss Ellis on June 21, 1969. They divorced in 1988. They have two sons. Todd was born Dec. 12, 1971. Ryan was born July 29, 1973. They now live in Knoxville, TN.

Wayne was the last child of Harry and Verna. He was born Apr. 17, 1952. He married Janice Hinton on Mar. 20, 1971. They have two children. Jason was born Feb. 20, 1976. Megan was born Feb. 15, 1980. They now live in Lafayette, IN.

Harry Taylor Garrett was born Oct. 8, 1914 in Kentucky. He grew up in the Mellot and Newtown area. He died Dec. 1, 1959. Verna Lucille Spragg was born in Crawfordsville on June 16, 1919. She died Dec. 4, 1974. Both of them are buried in the Wallace Lutheran Cemetery.

Dora Capshaw Garrett was born Apr. 1, 1945 in Indianapolis. She is the third of six children of Ike and Carrie Clark Capshaw. Dora was educated in Indianapolis public schools. In 1955 her family moved to Martinsville, IN where she graduated from Martinsville High School in 1963.

Ike and Carrie have five other children. Ollie was born Oct. 28, 1941. He married Janice Plaskett on June 19, 1965. They have four children. Jeffrey was born Oct. 1, 1966. Christina was born Aug. 20, 1969. Debra was born Dec. 1, 1970. Cynthia was born Apr. 9, 1976. They live in Indianapolis.

Cora was born June 2, 1943. She has one daughter, Deanna, who was born Nov. 23, 1969. They live in Martinsville.

Gloras was born July 14, 1948. She married Dan Traylor on Jan. 16, 1968. They have two children. Tracy was born on Aug. 4, 1968. Andrew was born on Nov. 27, 1984. They live in Crawfordsville.

Linda was born May 5, 1951. She married Gary Cummins on May 14, 1975. They live in Martinsville.

Ike and Carrie's last child is Charley. He was born on Nov. 19, 1954. He lives in Martinsville.

Ike was born June 16, 1912 in Kentucky. Carrie was also born in Kentucky on Sept. 26, 1918. They were married on Apr. 24, 1940 in Kentucky. The now live in Martinsville.

ZANNIE ZARING GARRIOTT
(1886-1979)
DAISY MATNEY GARRIOTT
(1888-1966)

Our family moved into Crawfordsville in 1914 when my father was telegraph operator for the Monon railroad. We later moved to a farm in White County, but in 1917 we moved to the Dr. J.S. Niven farm northwest of Parkersburg.

My brother, Harold, and I attended elementary schools at Swamp College, Browns Valley, and Parkersburg. We attended New Market and Waveland high schools. (The township line was between the two houses on the farm, and we moved from one into the other.)

Harold's wife, Mary Lou Clark Garriott, taught at Roachdale, Ladoga, and Cloverdale, and did her last 20 years of teaching at Greencastle High School.

Harold taught in Roachdale and Cloverdale, served in the Navy, then taught 32 years at DePauw University. He and Mary Lou live in Greencastle. They have a son, Michael, who lives in Roachdale and is supervisor of operations at the Center for Instructional Television of the Indianapolis Public Schools.

Harold and Mary Lou also have twin daughters who live in Albuquerque, NM. Susan is a pediatric intensive care nurse. Sandra is an art therapist serving as a supervisor in the Mental Health Center.

My husband, Maxwell Barnett, began his teaching at Yountsville in 1936, where he taught grades five, six, seven and eight. He was also the principal, coach, and custodian! (Naomi Canine taught grades one, two, three, and four at that time.)

Max and I began teaching in Walnut Township in 1938 and taught there until 1963. In 1964 we moved to Crawfordsville where Max taught mathematics at Tuttle Junior High School until he retired in 1974. I taught at Hoover Elementary School until I retired. We are now living in Punta Gorda, FL.

We have a son, Dr. William R. Barnett, who lives in Manlius, NY and teaches at LeMoyne College in Syracuse. We have a granddaughter, Denise, who is a student at Drake University in Des Moines, IA.

When Harold and I attended Swamp College, we walked two and one half miles to get to school. We lived farthest from it, so the neighborhood children would join us as we passed their homes. There were nine of us walking together by the time we reached the school. In the winter of 1918 the snow was as high as the fences at one time. Later, in our school experiences, we rode in horse-drawn hacks, and finally in buses.

John Bayless was one of our bus drivers. He had a home-made bus mounted on a Model-T chassis. When even his auxiliary transmission couldn't pull through the Brown Township mud, it was understood that all of the larger boys would get out and push.

When he needed to discipline any of the children, he would not say a word, but would suddenly put on the brakes. We would all fall into a heap on the floor, and by the time we could get untangled and back upon the seats, each of us had understood the message he was sending. *By Hilda Garriott Barnett*

JOHN R. GASS

John R. Gass came to Indiana in 1933, and settled in Montgomery County with his family.

John was born Nov. 11, 1911 in Allen Co., KY, to Landon Turnan Gass and Dora E. Edens Gass, the eighth of nine children. John married Nellie I. Link on the 1st of November 1930 in Franklin, KY. Nellie is the daughter of Sanford S. Link and Rhoda A. (Daisy) Choate Link, and was born on July 9, 1915 in Sumner Co., TN.

John did several different jobs before settling in Montgomery County. He worked on several different farms and also helped to build U.S. 40 before being employed in 1945 at Wallace-Murry in Indianapolis, where he was a machinist and worked there until his retirement in 1975, where upon he was asked out of retirement to go to Toronto, Canada to set-up a new machine shop.

John had a lot of friends and enjoyed several hobbies. He also owned and operated a saw sharpening business at his residence. He worked until his death on Sept. 11, 1982.

Nellie worked in several different factories in Crawfordsville before going to work at Culver Union Hospital where she retired after 17 years in 1979.

Nellie after retiring, took care of her home and husband until his death. Nellie enjoys sewing and making quilts. John and Nellie had seven children: (1) James "Pete", who drowned in 1943. (2) Edna who is married to Gerald Newkirk and has two children and four grandchildren. Edna and Gerald live in Montgomery County. (3) Lois, who married Mac Guthrie and had three children and four grandchildren. Lois lives in Texas. (4) Daniel, who lives with his wife Sharon and their daughter and one grandchild in Arizona. (5) Kenneth who with his wife Sylvia live in Montgomery County and has two children and two step-children. (6) Deborah "Susie" who lives in Kansas with her husband Ray and their three children and two step-children and three step-grandchildren. (7) Vickie who lives in Montgomery County with her husband Mike and two sons, Rick and Jeff.

John and Nellie were married for almost 52 years before John's death and four of their children were born in Montgomery County and eight of their grandchildren and two of their great grandchildren were also born in Montgomery County, IN. *Submitted by Vicki Bollman*

GILLOGLY

Our story begins in Ennis Killen Ireland in the mid 1700's when "I" John Gillogly was born, fell in love and married a girl with the last name of Moore. They had a family of which Hugh was our ancestor.

II. Hugh married Hannah and they had ten children. They moved to the U.S. when their son John D., our ancestor, was approximately five years old in 1910 and settled in Green Co., PA.

III. John D. married Mary Ann and had 13 children.

IV. Thomas was born in 1826 in Green County and married Sarah. They had nine children and moved to Newman, IL in 1855 where Sarah became ill and passed away. Thomas then married Bertha and they had ten children.

V. Silas was born in 1851 to Thomas and Sarah, married Julia Moss in 1877 and settled in Illinois. They had five children all in Murdock, IL.

VI. Orville Vane was born in 1878 and married Vada Ethel Smith in 1904. After they had nine children they moved to Judson, IN in 1921. This is the beginning of the present generation.

VII. Two of the children died at birth.

VII. Vera Naomi married Lester Sewell in 1929 and had three children: Leonard, Daniel and Stephen. They have 11 grandchildren: IX. Peggy,

Matthew, Jeffrey, Lisa, Aaron, Dina, Martin, Stephanie, Tracy, Kelly and Scott. X. Ten great grandchildren: Timothy and Benjamin Deaton, Ryan, Kayla and James Gentry, Matthew, Dana and Joshua Sewell, Heather and Brandy Bushman. Vera and Lester moved to Waveland in 1940 where they ran the general store and locker plant until they bought a farm north of town. Vera presently resides in Russellville.

Silas "Wayne" Gillogly

VII. Helen Louise married Harry Branch in 1942 in Terre Haute. They had one son VIII. Harry Dale. IX. They have six grandchildren: Harry Dale Jr., Victor, Tammy, Robert, Don and Brian.

VII. Ruby Irene married Paul Jines in 1942.

VII. Edith Ellen married Virgil Martin in 1936. They had one daughter VIII. Lois who had three children: IX. Terri, Randy and Jayne. X. One great grandson: Gregg McCoy.

VII. Milton "Bill" married Miriam Cramer in 1946 and settled in Waynetown and raised three children: VIII. Robert, Rebecca and Cheryl. They have three grandchildren: IX. Jessica and Nicholas Cripe and Lacey Bowerman. Milton and Miriam still reside in Waynetown.

VII. Robert Morris married Betty Lyons in 1950. They are the parents of two children: VIII. Robert Alan and Bradley. They have one grandchild: IX. Michael. Bob and Betty presently reside south of Russellville.

VII. Silas Wayne married Para Lee Elliott in 1932. They moved to Waveland in 1952. Silas delivered oil for Tidol Oil Co. and Para Lee worked at the telephone office until she purchased the Uptown Cafe in 1956 which she operated until 1966. They are the parents of: VIII. Ronald Wayne and Donald Lee. They have IX. Seven grandchildren: Edward, Rhonda, Bryce, Terri, Donna, Lawrence and Christa. There are also ten great grandchildren: X. Pandi, April, Mealie, Ashley, Rickie, Michael, Jenna, Zachary, Jakota and Corey. *Submitted by Sandy Gillogly*

ROSE GLASCOCK

Rose Glascock was the subject of a great historian's last "Profile of Inspiration." John Bowerman (November 1988 *Montgomery County Magazine*) wrote a "truly great teacher surely is one who goes beyond the textbooks into character-stressing honesty, goodness and making each life count for something." The writer of this sketch can attest to the fact that Rose Mary Bayless Glascock fit into John's category of a truly great teacher! She taught 37 years, 29 in Waveland school. Most of these years was spent with the second grade, which is a crucial time in a life where the teacher needs to go beyond the textbook, stress honesty and goodness and make each life count for something. Rose did just that!

Rose was born on the last day of March, two years after the turn of the century, the daughter of Luna and Elizabeth (Priebe) Bayless (see biography). Rose began school with only one other first grader at the Freedom school where there was about 25 total students in all eight grades. Rose made the exciting trip to Browns Valley for her eighth grade examination and gave the reading "The Last Hymn" at the commencement exercises on June 3, 1915. That fall, she entered Waveland High School, riding to school with a friend in a Klondike pulled by a sorrel horse which was stabled in a livery barn until the end of the school day. In 1919, Rose enrolled in summer term at Normal (Terre Haute). Before she even graduated from High School, though, she was given a teaching position at Liberty School to teach grades 1-4 ($60/month) at the young age of 17.

Jake and Rose Glascock

On Aug. 24, 1921, she married Jake Glasock whom she had first met at a pie supper. Jake was born in Hoopeston, IL on Oct. 11, 1898, the son of Thomas A. and Jane (Roberts) Glasock. He was a 50-year member of Waveland Masons and Waveland Covenant United Methodist Church. Jake worked for Etter Ford in New Market and was assistant engineer for the Indiana State Highway Department. On Aug. 10, 1927, their son, William Dean was born. Bill graduated from Waveland High School in 1945 and Wabash in 1954. He also served in the US Navy during those years and married his hometown sweetheart, Pauline Search on Aug. 10, 1950. They are the parents of Dean, Barry, Todd and Dawn. Bill is retired from Jefferson National Life Insurance and is planning to move to Tucson, AZ soon.

Never one to be lax in the educational department, Rose Glascock continued her education and received her BS degree from Indiana State University the year following her son's graduation (June 1955).

Again quoting John Bowerman's article, Rose's guidelines for teaching should be a "profile of inspiration" to any in the teaching field today: 1) love them 2) build self esteem 3) challenge them 4) listen to them 5) respect them 6) limit them 7) make God a part of their lives 8) develop love of learning 9) think of others 10) let them go! *Submitted by Karen Zach, one of her lucky second graders*

THOMAS GLENN

Thomas Glenn came from Shelby Co., KY to Brown Township in 1826. He was born Oct. 17, 1799 in Woodford Co., KY, the oldest of the three children of Tyre and Nancy Cloak Glenn. Several children of his sister, Frances (1801-1839) and her husband, Littleton Whittington, settled in Brown Township from Shelby County, as did his sister, Elizabeth (1803-1839) and husband, William Hanna.

The grandparents of our subject were Thomas and Elizabeth Craig Glenn and George and Alice Hudnall Cloak. His grandfather, Thomas, was among Harrod's men who established in 1774 what is now Harrodsburg, KY. A land surveyor, he was killed by Indians Sept. 1, 1777 at Fort Henry, site of Wheeling, WV.

Thomas Glenn 1799-1869

Thomas Glenn married, June 9, 1825, in Shelby County, Martha Hanna, born May 12, 1805, Mercer Co., KY and died Mar. 20, 1880 at home. Martha, daughter of James and Martha Poage Hanna, was the granddaughter of James and Martha Hanna and William and Ann Kennedy Poage, among the earliest residents of Fort Harrod, KY. William Poage died in an Indian raid near the Fort, Sept. 3, 1778.

To Thomas and Martha were born 11 children. James Littleton (1826-1898) and America Crowder Whetson, were the parents of Henry Littleton and Lorena Glenn. Margaret Ann (1827-1919) and Samuel Steward were parents of William, Charles, Martha, Mary and Joseph Steward. Parents of Alice, Zenolia and James Hinkle were Rebecca (1831-1919) and William Hinkle. Martha (1833-1854) died in Kentucky. James Davis Jr. was the son of Nancy (1835-1920) and James Davis. After his death Nancy married Francis Watkins. Elizabeth (1840-1864) taught school. Augusta and Marguerite Glenn were the daughters of William Thomas, (1843-1933) and Hattie Edge. Albert and Thomas Rice were the sons of Mary Frances, (1844-1925) and Jonathan Rice. Parents of Viola, Walter and Emma Easley were Evaline Hamblin (1847-1927) and Daniel Easley. Mary Elizabeth (1829-1833) and Tyre (1837-1842) died as children.

Thomas' land grant, signed by John Quincy Adams, was for 160 acres two and one-half miles north of Waveland, known today as "Glennwood". In 1827 he brought his family to a log cabin by a spring near the highest part of his land, the site of a previous Indian encampment. The entire acreage was covered with forest. Later a frame home built in the center of his farm was moved in 1894 nearer the road from Waveland. The descendants of his son, William Thomas, remained on the farm until 1963.

Having been a surveyor in Kentucky, Thomas Glenn surveyed much of the land which had been opened for settlement in Montgomery County. He also was a cabinet maker of some skill; many of his descendants still enjoy and respect the work of his hands. He was Justice of the Peace and Associate Judge. Affectionately known as Uncle Tommy and Aunt Patsy, Thomas and Martha contributed in many ways to the well being of Freedom Church and community. Thomas died at Glennwood Oct. 21, 1869. *Submitted by Mrs. Harriet H. Walters, granddaughter of William Glenn and great granddaughter of Thomas Glenn*

ROBERT JOSEPH GLOVER

Robert Joseph Glover was born in Waveland, IN on July 10, 1851 and died May 29, 1940 in Waveland, IN. He was born, raised, educated and worked in the town of Waveland his entire life. On Aug. 23, 1893 Robert was united in marriage with Miss Eliza "Josephine" Foster of Cincinnati, OH in Indianapolis, IN. To this union their son Robert "Foster" Glover was born Apr. 21, 1896 in Waveland, IN and died May 21, 1971 in Frankfort, IN. Foster married Miss Mary "Virginia" Oldshue (1896-1970) of Waveland, IN Aug. 24, 1919. Their children: Blanche Parker, Martha, Patrica Lee, and Robert Edward Glover.

Robert was the son of Newton J. Glover (1825-1898) who came to Waveland from Orange Co., IN in 1847 as a carriage-maker. In 1853 Newton turned to a mercantile career—the "MILLIGAN-GLOVER" general store on the south-west corner of Cross and Green Street. Remaining in existence for many years by Newton's children Robert, Charles, and John. Newton married Miss Matilda Jane Milligan (1832-1912) of Waveland on Mar. 29, 1849 in Waveland, IN. Matilda's father was John Milligan who platted the original town of Waveland. Newton and Matilda's children were Robert, Alice (Mrs. George Dickey), Mary (Mrs. George Hanna), Charles (m. Emma Allen), John M. (m. Odessa Stanton), and Alexander.

Newton J. Glover's parents were Stephen Glover (1785-1826) and Sarah Kirkham (1787-1875) who came from Kentucky to Orange Co., IN following his father Uriah Glover (1740-1830) who had fought in the American Revolutionary War.

Robert J.'s great-great-great-great-great-grandfather Charles Glover (1610-1665) came to Salem, MA in 1632 from Lincolnshire, England—starting this American "Glover" line. *Submitted by Mrs. Arthur Hayes, Rochester, IN*

JOSEPH AND MINNIE SWANK GOHMAN

Born in Cincinnati, OH, on June 8, 1870, Joseph John Gohman came to Montgomery County via Brown County with his family as a lad. He married Minnie Florence Swank in 1894 and settled on a farm near Crawfordsville on Barcus Road.

Joseph's parents came from German families that had emigrated to The Netherlands.

Minnie's family had lived in Montgomery County for many years. Her father, James Swank (1849-1902), was one of ten children born to Phillip and Polly Ann (Willhite) Swank who farmed near Elmdale in the mid-1800's. Minnie's mother was Margaret Ross (1852-1923), born in Crawfordsville to Harrison and Nancy (Clouse) Ross.

Minnie (1875-1969) was second of nine children born to James and Margaret Swank. They lived near Elmdale; James worked in a factory. The Swanks are buried in the Oakland Cemetery in Elmdale.

Ten children were born to the union of Joseph and Minnie Gohman. Willie, their only son, died at six months from a buggy accident. Their daughters: Clara Belle (1895), Margaret Catherine (1896), Esther Pearl (1900), Dorothy Helen (1902), Ethel Fern (1905), Alma Ruth (1908), Emma Elizabeth (1910), Estella Evelyn Charlotte (1912) and Vera Lucille (1915).

Wedding picture of Minnie Florence Swank and Joseph John Gohman, Dec. 2, 1894. They settled on a farm near Crawfordsville.

Clara's son, Richard, from her first union, was later adopted into the Gohman family and raised on the farm. He attended Wabash College, was successful in the paint industry, married and had four daughters. He lives in Texas with wife, Dorothy. Clara married Homer Bell in 1936. She died in 1979 and is buried in Indianapolis.

Margaret ventured west with Aunt Loretta "Rea" Swank, one of Minnie's sisters. She lived in St. Louis and Salt Lake before settling in Los Angeles, CA, where she met and married Frederick W. Holz, of Graz, Austria. They had three children: Margaret Anne, Betty Jean and Fred, Jr. Both Freds are deceased. Margaret is now 92 years old.

Esther joined Margaret in Salt Lake City, UT, where she met Hilmer Larson, whom she married in Los Angeles in 1922. Esther, widowed, died in Danville in 1985; is buried in Crawfordsville. She had no children.

Dorothy and Ethel graduated from Crawfordsville High School in 1921. Ethel married Ben Bremerman in 1926 and Dorothy married Raymond Main in 1936. Widowed young they enjoyed travels to Hawaii, Europe and the Holy Land. Ethel died in 1986 and Dorothy lives in Indianapolis. Neither had children.

Alma married Basil Reid in 1926 and had two boys, Marlin and Donald; Donald is deceased. Alma divorced and later married Sam Dobbs. Alma, widowed, lives in Plainfield.

Emma married Paul Crowder of Waynetown in 1934, lived in Crawfordsville. Ronald, Nancy and Michael were born before they moved to California where Janet was born. They live in Upland, CA.

Estella married Theodore Hunter in 1936 and they had three children: Teddy Jo, Kenneth and John. Estella, widowed, lives in Plainfield.

Vera married William Hudson in 1937. They had two daughters, Brenda and Joyce. Bill died in 1987; Vera plans to return to Indiana from Florida. *Submitted by Margaret Holz Hostetter*

SONS AND DAUGHTERS OF THEODORE GOHMAN SR. AND CATHERINE BENINGHAUS

Theodore Gohman Sr. and his wife, Catherine Beninghaus Gohman, crossed the Atlantic in an old-fashioned sailing vessel from Amsterdam, Netherlands, to Baltimore, MD, in 1859. They brought with them Theodore Jr. (born 1855), Elizabeth "Lizzie" (1857) and baby Catherine (1859) who died in infancy shortly after the family arrived in America.

Theodore Sr. was born in So. Holland, Netherlands, in 1826 and Catherine was born in Bremen, Germany, in 1820. They were united in marriage in 1853 in Amsterdam, the city where their first three children were born.

These brave immigrants moved west to Ohio and settled in Cincinnati, where five more children were born in the next ten years. Cara or "Carrie" (1863), Anna or "Annie" (1867) and the youngest, Joseph John (1870) survived to join their parents in the next move, to Brown Co., IN. Henry (1861) and Mary (1865) died in infancy.

Back row: Joseph John Gohman, Annie (Gohman) Ham. Front: Carrie (Gohman) Alexander, Lizzie (Gohman) Grosse, Theodore Gohman Jr.

Finally the Gohmans made their home in Montgomery Co., IN, where Theodore Sr. and Catherine lived the rest of their days and found their final resting place in the Catholic Cemetery in Crawfordsville. Theodore preceded his wife in death (1899) and Catherine joined him in 1905.

Theodore Jr. married Sarah "Sally" Reep in Georgetown, IN, in 1879. He farmed near Crawfordsville until he died in 1911. They had nine children: Anna Elizabeth, Henry, Charles, John, Earl, Florence, Walter, Blanche and Cora Belle. The lone living sibling at the time of this writing is Cora Belle Gohman Doss who resides in Redondo Beach, CA. It is interesting to note that Charles Gohman appeared in Bowen's *Montgomery County History*. An epilogue ... Charley lived to be over 100, married three times, had five children by his second wife and two more by his third wife. Theodore Jr. and "Sally" are buried in the Masonic Cemetery in Crawfordsville.

Before the immigrant family left Brown County "Lizzie" met and married (1881) Charles Andrew Grosse. They moved to Iowa in August 1882 where Charles farmed near Finchford until his death in 1899. "Lizzie" and Charles had one son, Walter, and two daughters, Vida May and Maude. "Lizzie" died in Waterloo, IA, in 1947 and was buried in Finchford with Charles.

"Carrie" Gohman married Thomas Alexander in 1883 in Georgetown. Their family home was on a farm south of Ladoga until they moved to Crawfordsville in 1912. They had three children: Frank, Mary and Fred. "Carrie" died in 1952 and is buried in the Masonic Cemetery.

"Annie" Gohman married Isaiah Ham in 1903; they had no children. She was a member of the First Christian Church in Crawfordsville for 60 years. She died in 1946 and was buried in Oak Hill Cemetery.

Joseph Gohman married Minnie Swank in 1894 near New Richmond and farmed near Crawfordsville, where they raised nine daughters: Clara, Margaret, Esther, Dorothy, Ethel, Alma, Emma, Estella, Vera and grandson, Richard. They sold their farm in 1944. Joseph lived until 1952 and Minnie until 1969. They're buried in the Masonic Cemetery.

JOHN MATHEW AND MARY FLO (GLAZE) GOOD

John Mathew "Mike" Good was the great-great-grandson of Rev. John and Susanna (Smeltzer) Good who came to Boone Co., IN 1834 from Washington Co., TN where all but the youngest of their 11 children were born. Like his father their eldest child Rev. Samuel Good was a Lutheran minister. Samuel married Elizabeth Catron and had ten children the eldest being Ireneus who married Margaret Strong and also had ten children: George, married Florida Rogers; Elizabeth, married (1) Squire Blacker, married (2) Henry Zerbe; Ezra, married Sarah McCoy; Martha Jane, married James Elsworth Trout; Thomas Samuel; Alice, d. young; Neva, married Daniel Robertson; Jesse, unmd.; Mary, d. young; and Alva Francis, married (1) Elizabeth A. Dickinson, married (2) Eva Johnson.

Thomas Samuel Good, b. 1867, d. 1897, m. 1891 Boone Co., IN, Elizabeth A. Dickinson and had three children: George E., m. Olus Edna Martin; John Mathew; and Della Frances who m. Ollie Miles, had one son Leonard, and resided in Indianapolis where they owned and operated a motel until retirement in Crawfordsville.

John Mathew Good, b. Feb. 18, 1895 Colfax, Boone Co., IN, m. Nov. 5, 1919 Mary Flo Glaze, b. June 11, 1902 Montgomery County daughter of Yantz and Amanda (Mitchell) Glaze. They lived in Waveland where John was a mechanic and with brother George E. had the first movie house. Later they owned and operated the Good Bros. Bus Line. John and family moved to Sugar Creek Township, Parke Co., IN where John was a woodsman and sawmill operator. He and Mary operated the Cigar Stand Restaurant on Hwy. 41 from about 1937 to 1960 continued by Mary after John died May 11, 1954. John enjoyed woodworking. Mary, m (2) 1960 Robert Earl Payne who was killed by a hit and run car while crossing Hwy. 41 in Nokomis, FL in 1970. Mary, d. June 13, 1981 and she and John were buried at Memory Garden Cemetery in Rockville, IN. They had four children: Evelyn Elizabeth, b. 1921, m. 1940 Morris Rice; John Mathew, Jr., b. 1922, m (1) 1942 Yolanda Guyre who d. 1980; Ora Eugene, b. 1925, d. 1986, m. 1953 Mary Schwab; and Alva Francis, b. 1926, m. Mary Trusler.

Elizabeth Dickinson Bevelheimer Good

John Mathew Good, Jr., a retired carpenter, and his wife the former Reda Blankenbeckler presently reside at the homeplace in Sugar Creek Township, Parke County where Reda has a custom upholstery shop. John was an Army sergeant in WWII in the Pacific Theater. He resided in Westville, IN where he worked with the Boy Scouts and Little League and was a volunteer firechief. His hobby is woodworking. He and Yolanda had five children, Dr. Kenneth John, b. 1944, and Linda Ann (Poterbowski) Good reside in North Mankato, MN where "Ken" is a professor at Mankato State University and has two daughters, Shannon Larissa and Tiffany Ellyn. Linda Louise Good died in infancy. Ron and Jacquelyn Ann (Good, b. 1954) Hermance reside in Michigan City and have a son Christopher James. Terry Lee, b. 1956, and Jaki (Erdoes) Good reside in Bar Harbor, ME and have two children Eden Aurora and John Jeffory. Michael B., "Mickey", b. 1958, and "Debbie" (Gentry) Good reside in Crawfordsville. For several years Mickey worked as an EMT and fireman but is now a real estate and insurance agent. They have three children: Andrea, b. 1980; Craig Michael, b. 1982; and Rebecca, b. 1984. *Submitted by Judy L. Harvey*

THOMAS SAMUEL AND RUBY ROSALIE (TIMBERLAKE) GOOD

Thomas Samuel Good of Waveland is the grandson of Thomas Samuel and Elizabeth A. (Dickinson) Good of Boone Co., IN. Elizabeth A., b. 1870 Boone County, daughter of Civil War Veteran Theodore Dickinson and first wife Emma Bales who m. ca. 1867 and had five children: Alice, m (1) William Lungsford, m (2) Harry Moody, resided in Waveland, and had no children; Elizabeth A.; William, d. young; John, m. Elizabeth Wilson; and Adda, m (1) Courtney Thorne, m (2) Jessie Vermillion. Theodore, m (2) 1886 Julia Larrimore, had infant son; and m (3) 1887 Prudence Harmon and had two daughters: Marilla, m. Leonard Harmon, had five children and resided in Indianapolis; and Nellie, d. unmarried.

Elizabeth A. Dickinson, m. (1) John Bevelheimer (1869-1890) son of Civil War Veteran Reuben Bevelheimer of Ripley and Shelby Cos., IN. They had one daughter, Ethel who m. George Kern. Elizabeth A., m. (2) 1891 Thomas Samuel Good, b. 1867 and d. 1897 Boone County. He was a huckster, a farmer, and deacon of the Lutheran Church. They had three children: George E.; John Mathew, m. Mary Flo Glaze; and Della Frances, m. Ollie Miles, Elizabeth A., m. (3) Alva Francis Good (1877-1945) a brother of Thomas. They resided in Waveland where he was a carpenter. Fall 1930 they moved to Sugar Creek Township, Parke County and lived with Elizabeth's son John Mathew Good. Elizabeth A., d. Dec. 3, 1930 and they are buried at Old Union Cemetery north of Waveland. Alva, m. (2) Eva Johnson and resided in Indianapolis.

Standing L to R: Stella Thomas, Mary Good, Tom Good and Ruby Good. Seated: George Good

George E. Good (1892-1978), m. 1914 Crawfordsville to Olus Edna Martin (1893-1973) they are buried at Old Union Cemetery. She was a great-granddaughter of Rev. War Soldier and Parke County pioneer John Martin, and was a wonderful and meticulous homemaker, mother, and cook. George worked as a fireman for Midland Railroad then was a trucker. From about 1924 to 1938 he and brother John Mathew owned and operated a bus line from Turkey Run Park to Indianapolis. He then leased the Brown Farm west of Waveland and late 1940's bought a farm in Sugar Creek Township, Parke County to where they moved from Waveland. They had two children: Estella Imogene and Thomas Samuel. Estella, b. 1915, m. 1934 Chester Thomas (1907-1976) and had three children: Mrs. Janet Myers, Ms. Judy L. Harvey, and Thomas Clay Thomas named for his WWII veteran uncles, our subject and Raymond Clay Thomas. Estella resides north of Marshall and is owner-breeder of Spice Rack Collie Kennel since 1947.

Thomas Samuel Good, b. 1921, Army Staff Sgt. WWII, served in Europe and soon after trained as a cement finisher. He, m (1) 1946 Joyce Rogers and had a daughter Joy Ann, b. 1949 while they resided in Waveland and later moved to Lafayette. Joy, m. 1973 Carl Frederick Jenks, resides in Crown Point and has a son Joshua Carl, b. 1980. Joy graduated from Purdue and is an elementary teacher. "Tom," as he is called, returned to Waveland, m (2) 1975 Ruby (Timberlake) Newnam, b. 1930 Parke County, daughter of George and "Laura" (Spaun) Timberlake. She has a daughter Donna Elaine (Newnam) Fisher who has three sons: Derrek, Brent, and Cory. Tom retired in 1979 and they reside in Waveland where Ruby is owner-operator of the Narrow Door Liquor Store. Ruby's hobby is crochet. *Submitted by Judy L. Harvey*

GOSHORN FAMILY OF MONTGOMERY COUNTY

The Goshorns of Owen County and more specifically of Clay City, Clay Co., IN established a branch of their family in Montgomery County in 1899 when Ezra Nicholas Goshorn, sixth child of Robert Robison Goshorn (Swiss-German descent) and Julian Sommers, married Lula Mae Harshbarger on Aug. 23, 1899. Lula was the daughter of Lavinia Peffley and Henry Meade Harshbarger. Ezra and Lula started housekeeping in a little house about a mile and a half north of Ladoga on land then owned by Lula's grandfather, Jacob Harshbarger. They later moved up the road into the house where Lavinia and her second husband, Dr. John Calvin Mahorney, lived and where he practiced homeopathic medicine. Lewis J. Goshorn, son of Ezra and Lula, was born there and still lives in this house.

E.N. and Lula (Harshbarger) Goshorn

Ezra N. Goshorn had degrees from Mount Morris College in Illinois and DePauw University in Greencastle, IN. He taught at DePauw a short time before marriage. He was a minister in the Church of the Brethren and was bishop of the Ladoga Brethren Church from 1909 until his death. He was a farmer, a member of the Montgomery County Tax Association, a township director of the Farm Bureau and was greatly respected by the businessmen of the community. Lula Goshorn was for a time on the staff of *The Crawfordsville Journal*.

Ezra N. Goshorn (Jan. 6, 1866-Apr. 15, 1930) and Lula Mae Harshbarger (Aug. 31, 1876-Dec. 18, 1944) had six children: Ramon Riley who died at the age of two, Irene Marie, John Herschel who died in a plane crash near Washington, D.C. in 1974, Roland Henry, Lewis J. and Ruth Elinor. Of these children only Lewis remained in Montgomery County, the others having distinguished careers elsewhere.

Lewis Goshorn married Cynthia Edith Reed (first child of Robert Lawrence Reed and Opal Agnes Davis) on Apr. 16, 1949. Lewis, a graduate of Manchester College, is well known for his collection and knowledge of Montgomery County fossils. His activities have included serving on the board of trustees of the old Culver Union Hospital, being a long-time director of The Ladoga State Bank, and acting as chairman of the Montgomery County School Reorganization Committee. He also served 12 years on the South Montgomery School Board, during which time Southmont High School and Ladoga Elementary School were built. Both Edith and Lewis are very active in the Ladoga Presbyterian Church. Edith worked for Herman Davis at his automobile dealership for many years. She has been treasurer and bookkeeper for several community organizations. Lewis has now retired from farming.

They have one daughter Judith Marie Goshorn, who graduated from Hanover College and attended the University of Nebraska. On May 29, 1977 Judith married David R. Maroney, who has a Doctor's Degree in Geology from the University of Nebraska. They live on and farm the Goshorn acreage and are very active in the Evangelical Orthodox Church. They have three children: Daniel, born Jan. 30, 1982; Joseph, born Mar. 2, 1985; and Benjamin, born Oct. 21, 1987.

GOSS

Fredrick Goss, came with his parents from Switzerland, when he was very small. They settled in Pennsylvania. As time past the Gosses spread into North and South Carolina, 1740, and eventually on into Indiana. It is recorded that Ephriam, the eighth child of Fredrick, slept in a hollow tree in an area of where he and his family settled and began the building of a small town named Gosport, 1817.

Fredrick married Betsy Richards, (Dutch descent) together they had nine children. David, Jacob, Joseph, Daniel, Fredrick Jr., John, George, Ephriam, and Betsy.

Alfred, Dora, Floyd and Frank Goss

Ephriam A. Goss, (of which I am a descendant) married Margaret Minerva Holbert, they also had nine children, Joseph A., George, Thomas H., Elisha, Mary Ann, Benjamin, John C., Margaret M., and Ephriam.

Thomas Holbert Goss married Milda Ann Nichols, they had three children, Alfred Eli, Mary, and Ada.

Alfred Eli Goss (born 1889) married Dora Adaline Pryor, (born 1888) they had four children, Floyd, Frank, Pansy, and Verna.

Ula Frank Goss (1918-1965) married Iva Maxine Barger, they had six children, Frank Jr., Norman Dale, Iva Jane, Mary Susan (I am the writer), Tony Alan, and Alva John.

Mary Susan Goss married Frederick Calvert, we have two daughters, Shenna Sue, and Shawna Lisa. We live in Montgomery County and have since 1970.

Additional information I have at hand is as follows: Ula Frank Goss Jr. married Patricia Ann Nix, they have five children, Timmy Lee, Teresa Ann, Steven Todd, Rhonda Michelle, and Brian Keith. Timmy has a daughter, Brandi Nichol. Teresa has a son, Steven James Jessup.

Norman Dale Goss married Janet Kay Montgomery, they have three children, Lawrance Dale, Norman Eugene, and Jennifer Kay. Lawrance has two children, Lacey Nichol, and Brandon Dale.

Iva Jane Goss married Ronald J. Mitchell, she has two children, William Travis, and Amanda Teresa.

Tony Alan Goss married Debra Kay Brown, they have two daughters, Kristen Marie, and Megan Alyn.

Alva John Goss married Vicki Wilson, they have three children, Jesse Alva, Tiffany Dawn, and Tonya Michael.

This concludes eight generations of the Goss family.

CHARLEY GOTT

Charley Gott, born May 10, 1890 in New Ross, was the son of William and Mary (Stranahan) Gott. He was a barber in early life. Then in 1924 he became ill, and was bedfast and an invalid. But, he laid on a special bed and had a mirror he could look behind him. He could manipulate the bed as invalids now operate a wheel chair. He opened a filling station in New Ross on South Main Street. He was always cheerful, and he made a good living running the filling station, and selling magazine subscriptions. Before he was stricken with paralysis, he was a telephone operator. Several doctors and friends gave him literature to study about radio and he took a test, and received a license to operate a radio. A group of these doctors and friends, and other amateur radio buffs came to his home for his first radio chat. His call letters were W9MX2. He was in contact with people in the area, and also ham operators over the United States and Canada. His bed was close to the gas stations, and he would always converse freely with his customers. He bought a house car, that his bed could be put in, and in 1929, he went to an amateur radio convention in Indianapolis as a delegate. He married Bertha Smith, daughter of Samuel and Florence James Smith. During the 1939 World's Fair, Charley and Bertha, with Carl Walters as driver of their house car went to Chicago to the World's Fair in 1939. He was able to see a lot of the fair from his bed, with his mirror as they traveled over the grounds at the Fair, with Carl seeing that he had special privileges. "Where there's a will there's a way." In 1940, he and Carl went around the countryside selling wool blankets, and they did good at this. Charlie died many years ago. He had a brother Harry Gott, two sisters left here, and a sister Jessie Gott who married Jesse Walters, son of Alva and Nettie Baker Walters, and they had one son Lawrence, who married Louise Paddock. Jessie died and Jesse married Lillian Tofford Baker. He and Jessie Gott had Jessie Lou Walters Stewart and adopted a son James Walters.

GRAY AND McCORMICK FAMILY

I was born Sheilah Jane Gray on July 19, 1955 to Hugh and Emma Gray at Culver Hospital. I have one brother, Michael Hugh born Oct. 12, 1950. I graduated in 1973 from South Montgomery. I was first married Oct. 19, 1974 to William D. Gravens. We had two children, Sandra M. born May 4, 1976 and Jason Wm. born Feb. 17, 1979. I later married Roger "Tedd" Fifer on June 13, 1987 in the front yard of our Homestead Farm. Tedd was formerly from Linden and has two children, Shelly born July 20, 1974 and Tony born Aug. 10, 1977, who still reside in Linden. I currently work at Culver Hospital as a surgery technician and Tedd also works there as a maintenance engineer. My brother Mike, who lives in a trailer next to the house has worked at Sommers Metalcraft for the past ten years. Tedd and I are currently remodeling our 135 year old home. We have 14-1/2 of the once 102-1/2 acre farm that began in 1854. The farm is located two miles east off of 136 on 75 South, which used to be the old road 34.

Hoosier Homestead Award - Robert Orr, Governor of Indiana, Sheila Gray Fifer, Sandy Gravens, John Mutz, Lt. Governor and Jason Gravens

Abigail Hagerman, born in 1796 in New Jersey, married John Line in April 1816 in Butler Co., OH. They had five children: Margaret, Salome, Abigail, Nancy and John. Her husband John died on Dec. 19, 1831, she then married his brother Jaboc and they had one daughter, Ruth Line, born May 14, 1839.

The homestead farm was originally bought by Abigail Line in 1854. She died on Apr. 9, 1875. One of her daughters, Nancy, married Hugh McCormick. He was born on June 24, 1812 in Fermanna Co., Ireland. In 1856 they moved out to the homestead farm where they raised seven children: Abigail, Ellen, Salome Ball, Mary, Maria Line, Nancy Jane and Edith Hagerman. Edith, born Nov. 19, 1866, was married to William Clements Gray who was born Sept. 20, 1887. William's parents, Jasper and Mahala Carr Gray owned most of the land north of 136 East from the Ben Hur Drive-In down Welliver Hill to Walnut Fork on 50 South.

William and Edith had one son, Hugh McCormick Gray, born on Aug. 11, 1889. All of the family up till now and including Hugh had been raised on the same farm. Hugh was first married to

Helen Sayres in 1910. Born to them was Katherine Marthene Gray Grammer Grove, Dallas and Bernard. Hugh's second marriage was to Emma Frame of Ladoga in 1935. Emma was born to Mary Davis and Bertie Frame on Feb. 5, 1914. She was a graduate of Ladoga School. During this time they owned and operated Gray's Dairy and Gray's Grocery on the corner of College and Water Streets and then later at 601 E. Market where Grimes Real Estate now is. Emma owned and operated Gray's Sweeper Shop for 30 years. Hugh died July 23, 1967 and Emma on Feb. 17, 1985.

Also living in Crawfordsville is the great-granddaughter of Maria Line McCormick. Caroline Hutchens Shular was born Dec. 6, 1931 to George Hutchens and Edith Chadwick. She was married to Bob Shular in 1954. They have three children: Richard, Brad and Sara. Caroline is a Music teacher for the North Montgomery Schools.

Also living close is Maxwell Gray who is the grandson of Hugh Gray by his first marriage. Max is a lawyer for the firm of Lowe, Gray, Steele and Hoffman in Indianapolis. Max and his wife Judy have three daughters. *Submitted by Sheila Gray Fifter*

JOHN SANFORD GRAY

John Sanford Gray, born June 14, 1810 in Butler Co., OH, came to Ripley township by wagon in 1838 with his wife, Mary Kemp Gray, born Dec. 24, 1810, also in Butler County. They were married Aug. 2, 1831 in Ohio and brought their four oldest children with them, Annaliza, John Kemp, James Beauchamp and Nancy. Born after the arrival in Montgomery County were John Sanford, Elizabeth, Mary, Santford Peter (Polk), Benjamin Taylor Ristine, Ellis and William Gray.

John Sanford Gray, president of organization to catch horse thieves (see gavel)

The grandparents of John Sanford were John and Elizabeth Johnson Gray. John Gray arrived in Delaware in 1770 from Scotland with his brothers William and Peter. The parents of John Sanford Gray were John and Nancy Beauchamp Gray with John S. being the fourth child. Siblings were Elizabeth, Mary, Abner, William Beauchamp and James Banning Gray. Maternal grandparents were Jesse and Leah Heath Beauchamp of Lexington, KY. Leah Heath was the daughter of William Heath of Somerset Co., MD.

John Sanford Gray was apprenticed in the cabinet making trade as a young boy and as a young man, made coffins during the Cincinnati plague. During this time, he learned the art of winding sheets around the victims and also performed burial services when no one else was available. Over 20 orphans were cared for in his home.

In 1840 John S. Gray purchased a farm two miles east of what is now Waynetown. Some of his land was donated for the Wesley Methodist Church and cemetery. His mother, Nancy Beauchamp Gray was the first person buried in Wesley Cemetery.

"Captain" Gray, as he was known, organized the Wabash Valley Detective Association in the 1840's and 1850's. This was a unit of the National Horse Thieves Detective Association, a vigilante group of men sworn to put a stop to horse thievery which had become so rampant that some of the farmers were unable to till their fields due to the loss of their horses. Captain Gray was in charge at the time of the capture of the famous Redwood gang. In gratitude, the National Horse Thieves Detective Association erected a monument over his grave in Wesley Cemetery. The national organization achieved its greatest strength during the time he was its president.

In 1868 John Sanford Gray supervised the construction of a gravel road from the Montgomery County line to Crawfordsville. It took three years to complete. The workers were paid 37-1/2 cents a day plus whiskey.

Our subject was financially secure and is said to have offered a Morgan horse to anyone naming their child John Sanford. He died Apr. 23, 1895 while his wife died Sept. 20, 1870.

Their son, James Beauchamp Gray, born 1835, married Mary Ann Heath, born 1843, daughter of Abraham and Salome Ball Heath, granddaughter of William Heath of Somerset Co., MD. James Beauchamp was also an excellent carpenter and purchased the farm near Waynetown which is still owned by his two granddaughters, Dorothy and Margaret Gray.

James B. and Mary A. Heath Gray had three children, Polly, Charles Howard and Cooper Gray, born 1876.

Cooper Gray was a genial, well-liked farmer in the Waynetown area who married his second cousin in 1902, Alice May Gray of Linn Co., IA. Three daughters were born to the couple and all three were teachers in the Indiana Public Schools.

SAMUEL CLINE GRAYBILL, JR.

Cline (Samuel Cline Graybill, Jr.) and Helen M. Baldwin Graybill were fourth generation residents of Montgomery County. Their ancestors all came to Montgomery County in about 1827 and bought land in Union, Scott, and Clark Townships. They came from Pennsylvania, some by way of Roanoke, VA, some by way of Ohio, and some by way of Union Co., IN.

Cline was born Apr. 21, 1895 in Scott Township and died Oct. 3, 1978. He married Helen M. Baldwin Aug. 30, 1916. She was born July 6, 1892 in Clark Township. They both graduated from Ladoga High School. He attended Purdue University Agriculture Short Course and she attended Asberry College where she studied Music and Art. They were members of the Ladoga Presbyterian Church, where he served as a trustee, deacon, and elder, and she played the piano and organ, on and off, over a period of 50 years.

Cline owned and operated a farm and trucking business. He served as Democratic Precinct Committeeman in Scott Township and later in Clark Township. He was a member of the Ladoga Town Board, the Ladoga Cemetery Association, and a 50 year member and past Master of the Masonic Lodge.

Helen was a member of the Ladoga Presbyterian Missionary Society, Literary Circle, Music Club, Tri Kappa, Bridge Club, and served as President of the Montgomery County Federation of Clubs.

Cline was the son of Samuel Cline (1850-1933) (m. 1881) and Clara Bell Ward (1859-1937) Graybill. His grandparents were: Samuel (1803-1876) (m. 1834) and Lydia Arnold (1811-1906) Graybill, of Ladoga, Scott Township; and Amzon (1835-1903) (m. 1859) and Phoebe Jane Montgomery (1838-1919) Ward, of Whitesville, Union Township. His great-grandparents were: David Genung (1803-1894) (m. _____) and Elanor Lafuze (1809-1896) Ward; and Will (1803-1864) (m. _____) and Phoebe Fisher (1808-) Montgomery of Union Township, Montgomery County.

Helen was the daughter of Francis Wildey (1853-1927) (m. 1875) and Alice Susan Myers (1857-1926) Baldwin. Her grandparents were: Benjamin Lucas (1828-1909) (m. 1848) and Amelia Brookshire (1829-1880) Baldwin; and Wm. (1816-1909) (m. 1836) and Lydia Harshbarger (1816-1892) Myers. Her great-grandparents were: Lucas (1786-1842) (m. 1809) and Hannah Adams (1787-1865) Baldwin; Joe (1782-1869) (m. 1810) and Sarah Slack (1790-1853) Brookshire; John Sr. (1770-1841) (m. 1791) and Kathern Houts (Hants) (1775-1850) Myers; and Jacob (1792-1866) (m. 1814) Salome Ammen (____-____) Harshbarger. All lived near Ladoga, IN.

John Myers, Sr. financed the founding of Ladoga, buying the cleared land upon which Ladoga was built from Lucas Baldwin.

Cline and Helen had one daughter, Wilda Grace, who was Ladoga Centennial Queen. Wilda married Delbert Theodore Timmerman, and they had two children: Harry Cline and Marilyn Sue. Marilyn Sue married Manfred Werner Fremder and they have three sons, Matthew Philipp, Michael John and Jason Karl.

SAMUEL F. AND MARY C. ARNOLD GRAYBILL

Samuel F. Graybill and Mary C. (Arnold) Graybill was married Sept. 20, 1860. She was born Jan. 19, 1839 in Scott Township to Daniel and Nancy (Myers) Arnold. Nancy was the daughter of John Myers, Sr. and Catherine (Hautz) Myers, who came from Virginia in 1833 to Ladoga (index, Daniel Arnold).

Samuel F. born in Ohio, May 5, 1837 came with his parents Daniel and Elizabeth (Frankebarger) Graybill in 1838 to Ladoga and bought 190 acres of land and raised livestock and farmed, therefore, Samuel was no stranger to hard work as his parents developed and cleared the land. As a pioneer child he assisted in clearing the wilderness. An important step in his life was joining the Regular Baptist Church in 1866. He and Mary conscientiously were devout members. They lived on a farm close to Ladoga and raised four of their children there. Laura born 1869, Alice May, born 1872, Manson, born 1875 and Lucille "Lou" born 1878.

Samuel, with his red hair had sturdy energy and his self denying efforts made it possible for those members of his family to live comfortably.

At some distressful time he suffered the loss of a leg. He was distinguishable by his courtesy and obliging nature and worthy of the trust reposed in him by his neighbors and friends. Mary C. was warm hearted, kind and provided a pleasant home for her family.

When Laura married Jess Oliver and had Verna born 1892 and Letha, born 1894 there was happiness, but Laura died one winter from pneumonia and her small baby passed away not long after.

Samuel F. and Mary C. (Arnold) Graybill

Alice married George Himes and they were so happy with two sons, Lester and Chester, born 1893. Alice died in 1900 soon after Laura's death. Alice was buried at the Harshbarger Cemetery in the same coffin with her stillborn baby. Lou married Roy Gregg and their children were Harry, Dorothy, and Lethe, they lived at a Peluride, CO address, fairly close to Montrose.

Manson, married Effie Otterman and they had Paul, Mabel and Donald. He lived close to his parents' home with his family.

Samuel F. and Mary C. never received public honor in any commercial way, but, they are highly esteemed by their many descendants. (see index, Himes.)

Daniel Graybill died Feb. 13, 1890 and Elizabeth (Frankebarger) Graybill died Feb. 6, 1873. Samuel F. Graybill died Nov. 18, 1898 and is buried in the Harshbarger Cemetery.

GRAYBILL FAMILY

Samuel and Lydia (Arnold) Graybill rode horseback from Virginia to Indiana, after their marriage in Botetourt Co., VA on Apr. 18, 1834. They first came to Putnam County, but, after a few months, settled in Scott Township of Montgomery County, in 1835, and there spent the remainder of their lives. Samuel was a well-read person, owning an unusually large library for that era, and was a successful farmer and business man. He died, aged 73 in 1876, and Lydia lived to the advanced age of 94 years. Both are buried in the Ladoga Cemetery. Their first home was a very simple one—a cabin with a puncheon floor, windows of greased paper, the door hung with large, wooden hinges. In 1859 they erected a two-story brick house on the farm, which became a most attractive and hospitable home for family and friends.

There were eight children born to this couple, five of whom lived to maturity, and became well known citizens in the community: Josephus married Mary Jane Frame and had two children; Mary Magdelena married George E. Lidikay and had seven children; William R. married Armilda Stadler and had three children; Amanda Jane married David Hicks Hostetter and had three children; Samuel Cline married Sarabelle Ward and had three children.

The Graybills of Pennsylvania, Virginia and Indiana are descendants of the German-Swiss exiles, who, being non-conformists, were persecuted because of their religious principles and their refusal to take an oath, or render military service. They took refuge in the Palatinate, where they settled near the town of Mannheim in the fertile and beautiful country beside the Rhine River.

Jakob Krahbiel emigrated to Pennsylvania in 1729, settling in northern Lancaster County, near Manheim. He and his son, Christian, accumulated several hundred acres of land, and built a church near their home which was called White Oak Church, and continued for many years as a place of worship for the Brethren. Christian's wife was Mary Landis, and they had five sons, plus other children. Christian was buried on the farm, his gravestone bearing the name of "Christian Grebil".

The eldest son of Christian was John, born in 1747. John Graybill (planter, Innkeeper, Tunker) married Hannah Borntraeger (daughter of Johann Martin Borntraeger) about 1769. Their children were: Daniel, Solomon, John, Christina, Susannah and Elizabeth. In 1777, the Pennsylvania Legislature made it the duty of every citizen to surrender allegiance, to the King of England, and to take an oath of allegiance to the State of Pennsylvania. Although they were loyal to the state and America, it was against their principles to take an oath. And so John and Hannah, with their family, left Pennsylvania and, with the migration of many other German settlers, went to Botetourt Co., VA. It was several of John Graybill's grandchildren who settled in the Ladoga area in the 1830's. (Many early settlers of Ladoga were from Botetourt Co., VA.)

Some of the Graybills who came to Montgomery County were: Daniel, Jr. and Elizabeth (Frankebarger) Graybill; David and Mary (Graybill) Peffley; LeRoy and Hannah (Graybill) Bradley; Matthias and Sally (Graybill) Frantz; Andrew and Mary (Graybill) Graybill; Benjamin and Elizabeth (Graybill) Kessler; Samuel and Lydia (Arnold) Graybill; Daniel, Jr. and Nancy (Myers) Arnold; and Henry and Hannah (Arnold) Myers. *Submitted by Mrs. Wm. R. Hawley, a great-granddaughter of Samuel and Lydia (Arnold) Graybill*

JUDY GREESON

I met Don and Jean Thompson during the summer of 1975 at a Presbyterian Church event known as "Synod School." We have often said that the Thompsons are responsible for my living in Crawfordsville. At the time of our meeting, Don Thompson was librarian at Wabash College and President of the Planning Commission for the Wabash Valley Area Library Services Authority. Later, in early 1976, Don asked me if I would be interested in the position of Administrator/Reference Librarian for this newly formed library network.

Judy Greeson and Bridgie Brelsford

A few months later, after the usual job interview process, I moved to Crawfordsville. The ALSA became operational on June 1, 1976 - my first day on the job.

The library network began with 16 members with seven counties. Ten years later, when I left Crawfordsville, the network had approximately 70 members within 14 counties. It was very difficult to leave Crawfordsville and all the friendships I had made. However, I felt that it was time to have new geographical and professional experiences in my life. I moved to Clinton, TN in September, 1986 to accept the position of Regional Library Director of the Clinch-Powell Regional Library.

People that know me in Crawfordsville are well aware that I have a passion for auto racing, especially the Indianapolis 500. Growing-up in Indianapolis, I have been attending the 500 every year since 1961. Being a spectator in the grandstand, cheering on my favorite driver like Parnelli Jones or Mario Andretti is an indescribable, exhilarating experience. Being at the Indy 500 each Memorial Day weekend will always be a number one priority in my life.

My family history centers in Indianapolis. I was born Oct. 3, 1946 in that city to George Albert and Irene (Cobb) Greeson. I have two brothers, David and Joe. I attended Emmerick Manual High School in Indianapolis. My B.A. degree is from Indiana Central College (now the University of Indianapolis). I obtained my Masters of Library Science degree at Indiana University in 1970. Before moving to Crawfordsville, I was the library director at Huntington College in Huntington, IN. *Submitted by Judy Greeson*

ROBERT ARNOLD I AND JOY MARCIEL GREGORY

Robert Arnold Gregory I and Joy Marciel (Moore) Gregory were married July 4, 1959. Joy Marciel was born June 7, 1941 at Crawfordsville to William Edward and Ruth Pauline (Himes) Moore. Joy was raised in the Whitesville area and attended the Whitesville School, grades one through six, then grades seventh through first semester of the tenth grade at Crawfordsville Junior and Senior High School.

Her parents bought a farm in 1956 across the Montgomery County line in Putnam County. They moved and Joy Marciel continued with the second semester of the tenth grade at Roachdale High School, graduating in 1959.

Robert Arnold Gregory I, was born Apr. 28, 1940. His parents were John Sherman and Gracie Mae Gregory. They moved to Indiana from Kentucky and resided in Indianapolis where John Sherman worked. Robert Arnold I was born in Indianapolis.

Robert Arnold I and Joy Marciel (Moore) Gregory

In later years their family moved west of Roachdale, IN and lived on a farm.

Robert Arnold I served two years in the Seventh United States Army Division at Regensburg, Germany. While there he was stationed at Fort Skelly.

Joy Marciel joined him and lived at Regensburg.

On Dec. 30, 1960, Liebe Linnett was born at the U.S. Army Hospital located in the Perlacher Forst American Housing Area, Munich, Germany.

In June 1961 Joy Marciel returned with Liebe Linnett to the States. Robert Arnold I was transferred from Germany to Fort Knox, KY. He was stationed there until his discharge June 17, 1962. They moved to Crawfordsville, IN where Robert Arnold I worked at the Raybestos-Manhattan Factory.

During that time their second child Robert Arnold II was born on Apr. 5, 1963. Later moving to the Roachdale area. Five more children blessed their home with their arrival.

Babett Marciel, Dec. 30, 1965, John Edward, born June 2, 1967, Angela Renee on Dec. 27, 1971, (twins) Tina Marlina, and Trina Maria, born Nov. 9, 1975. In August 1976 the Gregory family moved to a farm they bought in Hendericks County in the North Salem area. Joy Chestalina was born Sept. 28, 1978, and Paulina Mae was born Dec. 5, 1981. The latter seven children were born in the Putnam County Hospital at Greencastle.

Liebe Linnett, Babett Marciel and Joy Marciel belong to the Roachdale Order of Eastern Star chapter 247. Liebe and Babett have held stations in the Star. Joy Marciel has held different stations with 1987 and 1988 giving her the Honor of serving the Chapter as Worthy Matron.

Robert Arnold I and his son Robert Arnold II are members of the Masonic Lodge No. 602 of Roachdale. Robert I belongs to the Scottish Rite and Murat Shrine of Indianapolis.

Robert Arnold Gregory I is working at the Allison Gas Turbine Indianapolis Plant. John Edward belongs to the Roachdale No. 602 Demolay and is employed at Phoenix Fabricators and Erectors at Avon, IN.

Robert Arnold II is working in Quality Assurance at Nucor Steel, Whitesville.

Joy Marciel Gregory is a descendant of Montgomery County Settlers. (See index) (Benjamin Kessler, James Washington Linn, Samuel Graybill, Jacob Harshbarger, Daniel H. Himes)

DR. MARTHA E. HUTCHINGS GRIFFITH

Martha E. Hutchings was born Nov. 29, 1842 near Hanover, IN, the eldest of four children and the only girl, to John Work and Elizabeth Cravens Hutchings. Her early girlhood was spent on a farm in Jefferson County. Sometime prior to 1860 the family moved to Vernon in Jennings County in order to have better schools for their children. Martha attended Vernon Academy.

Encouraged by her father, Martha studied medicine with Dr. Nehemiah Richardson of Vernon from 1864 to 1866. She did this secretly, because of the condemnation of the public at the very idea of a woman studying medicine. She entered the Woman's Medical College of Pennsylvania in Philadelphia in 1866. In 1867 she interned in the Woman's Hospital and in 1868 she interned at the New England Hospital for Women and Children in Boston. She returned to the college and graduated in March, 1870. Dr. Hutchings was the first woman in Indiana to receive a diploma from a medical college recognized by the regular profession.

She practiced for 18 months at Madison, IN. She married Dr. Thomas A. Griffith on Oct. 4, 1871. They settled in Darlington. Dr. Martha specialized in obstetrics and worked hard in the field of public health. In the winter of 1887/1888 she went to Philadelphia to take a four-month post-graduate course.

Martha E.H. Griffith M.D.

The Griffiths moved to Crawfordsville in November, 1888 and practiced together, Martha specializing in the diseases of women and children. When the Montgomery County Medical Society was established in 1872, women doctors in the county were not permitted to become members. In 1880 Dr. Martha was admitted to both the Montgomery County and Indiana Medical Societies. In 1895 she served as vice-president of the county society.

Aside from her medical work, Dr. Griffith was active in club work. She was a director of the Indiana Federation of Clubs in 1908, and was the chairwoman of the standing committee on health of the federation in 1909 and 1910.

She was one of the founders of the Community House Association for Women and Girls in Crawfordsville, and was very active in the organization, being on the board of directors until her death. She was one of the organizers of the Crawfordsville Public Library in 1897. She served as a delegate to the state convention of the Woman's Christian Temperance Union in 1892. In addition she was an ardent suffragette. On June 16, 1881 she read a paper at the state convention of the Indiana Woman's Suffrage Association entitled "The Work of Women Physicians in the United States." True to a pledge made at the WCTU convention Dr. Griffith and several other women appeared at the polls in November, 1894, but was not allowed to vote.

In 1912 Dr. Griffith helped organize a branch of the Women's Franchise League in Crawfordsville.

Dr. Griffith wrote a play entitled "Definite: an impromptu charade in four scenes."

The Griffiths had one son, who also became a physician in Crawfordsville, and a daughter who died in childhood.

Dr. Griffith continued practicing until 1923, when she fell and fractured a hip. She never recovered sufficiently to resume her practice. She died on Dec. 28, 1924 at the age of 82. *Submitted by Jean Thompson*

THEODORE GREGORY GRONERT

Prominent educator and distinguished historian, Theodore G. Gronert, head of the department of history of Wabash College, Crawfordsville, IN, is a leader in the cultural affairs of that city. He was born July 28, 1887, in Prairie du Chien, WI, a son of George M. and Anna (Allbright) Gronert.

George M. Gronert was born in 1856 in Crawford County, Wisconsin, a son of Michael and Katherine (Menges) Gronert, natives of Bavaria. The family was originally named Von Gronert, its members being of noble birth. Michael Von Gronert was one who joined the rebels against the monarchy in the constitutional crisis of 1848 and escaped to the United States that year, settling on a farm which he bought near Lynxville, in Crawford Co., WI where he lived for many years. Michael Gronert served three years in a Wisconsin volunteer regiment during the Civil War and was promoted for bravery in action to be sergeant of his company. His wife managed the home farm while he was in service and died in 1865. Michael Gronert lived until 1902.

Anna (Allbright) Gronert, wife of George M. Gronert, was brought to the United States by her parents in her infancy. Seven children were born to Mr. and Mrs. George M. Gronert: (1) Nelda, (2) Theodore G., (3) George, (4) Kathleen, (5) Andrew, who enlisted Apr. 6, 1917, the day war was declared, (6) Edith, (7) Lawrence.

Theodore G. and his two brothers, George and Andrew, served as soldiers in the World War, Lawrence, the remaining brother; being debarred from service by his youth. Theodore G. Gronert enlisted in 1918 and was commissioned Second Lieutenant at Camp Sheridan; he was made adjutant of R.O.T.C. at Center College and was honorably discharged.

Theodore G. Gronert received his preliminary education in the public schools of Prairie du Chien, graduating from the high school in 1904. He was graduated from the University of Wisconsin in 1908 with the degree of Bachelor of Arts, received his Master of Arts degree in 1915 and his Doctor of Philosophy degree in 1917 from that university. He took post-graduate work in the University of Chicago. Mr. Gronert began teaching in the La Crosse (WI) High School. In 1916 he became instructor of history and athletic coach in Center College, Danville, KY, remaining there for three years. He was instructor of history in State College for Women, Denton, TX, 1919-1922, in the University of Arkansas, 1922-1924, and in the latter year came to his present position in Wabash College as professor of history.

Doctor Gronert is co-author with Prof. James I. Osborne of "Wabash College Centennial History, 1832-1932," a work of great merit; he has written articles for Kiwanis Magazine, the *Southwestern Political Science Quarterly, Mississippi Valley Historical Magazine, Indiana Magazine of History* and other publications. He has done and is doing extension work in Texas and Wisconsin. He has assisted in the work of NRA as a speaker in Montgomery County. Doctor Gronert is Independent in his political views. He is a member of the Indiana Historical Society, Mississippi Valley Historical Society, American Historical Association and is curator and secretary of the Montgomery County Historical Society. He is an associate member of the Citizens Historical Association. He is an honorary member of Phi Eta Fraternity and a member of the Kiwanis Club of Crawfordsville. While a student in the University of Wisconsin he was a member of the varsity track team.

Doctor Gronert was married (1918) to Hazel Dessery in Los Angeles, CA, a daughter of Alfred Napoleon and Mary Dessery, both of whom are deceased. Mrs. Gronert is accomplished in music, a graduate of Cincinnati Conservatory of Music, and is a teacher of the violin.

Doctor Gronert's comprehensive knowledge,

his attractive personal qualities and his love of learning and culture have won him many friends. These attributes and his active interest in all progressive undertakings make him a valued citizen of his city and state.

Note: Dr. Gronert died Feb. 3, 1966 in Crawfordsville. Biography written by Citizens Historical Society, 1940

ELIZABETH JANE MILLER HACK

John Winter, son of Christopher and Elizabeth Pfrimmer Winter, came early to New Ross, Walnut Township, Montgomery Co., IN from Corydon, IN. John and Elizabeth, daughter of George and Elizabeth Senn Pfrimmer, had 17 children and he gave each of them 160 acres in Walnut Township area.

One of their daughters was Ann Delilah Winter and married Henry Miller, Jr., son of Henry, Sr. and Catherine Agnes Miller. One of their children was Timothy Miller born 1848 and died 1912. He married Samantha Fillmore Killion born 1850 and died 1928. They had five children and had a pink house in New Ross. Elizabeth Jane, daughter of Timothy and Samantha was born 1878 in New Ross and died August 1961 in Indianapolis. She married Oren Hack and they had five children: John Oren; Elizabeth Virginia; Eleanor; Stephen Ellrod; and Joseph Tinsley Hack.

Elizabeth Jane Miller Hack was a famous lady. A Montgomery County native, and was a novelist. She attended Butler University. When she was 17, she contributed verse and news to the Indianapolis newspapers and to various magazines. *The Yoke*, her first book was published in 1904. Other books were *Saul at Tarsus; The City of Delight; Daybreak; A Story of the Age of Discovery; The Romance of Christopher Columbus;* and *A Love Drama of the Seige and Fall of Jerusalem*. She had began three novels when she died in 1961. Since 1905, she was listed in Who's Who in America.

Her mother was raised by her West grandparents so she dropped Fillmore from her name, and used name S. West Miller. She was a correspondent for many county seat newspapers, and was editor of a trade journal for furniture. Samantha and Timothy both taught school in Montgomery County. So Walnut Township is not without its famous people.

CLOYD O. HAFFNER, O.D.

Dr. Cloyd Owen Haffner moved to Crawfordsville, IN in 1924. He was born in Jay Co., IN on Nov. 12, 1894 and was the oldest child of Susanna Lilly Daugherty and George Elmer Haffner. George farmed all of his life and raised heavy team horses, cattle, swine and grains. Lilly and Elmer Haffner were the parents of seven children.

Through his mother, Cloyd Haffner was a descendant of Revolutionary War Veteran George Emery who was Quarter Master in the Continental Army and wintered at Valley Forge, PA. This ancestor qualified him to be a past member of the Society of Indiana Pioneers.

Cloyd O. Haffner graduated from Muncie Normal Institute (now Ball State University). After this he taught school in North Dakota. This distance was traveled alone on a motorcycle over dirt roads! Later he came back to the Midwest and graduated from Northern Illinois College of Optometry. Dr. Haffner first practiced in New Paris, OH and then Pittsburgh, PA before coming to Crawfordsville.

On Dec. 27, 1915 Cloyd Haffner married Bessie Lee Fisher in Jay Co., IN. They became the parents of six children: Elmer, Maxine, Mildred, Leon, Diane and Phyllis. Both Maxine and Leon later became optometrists.

Bessie Lee and C.O. Haffner O.D.

Elmer Haffner, oldest child of Cloyd and Bessie, died of diphtheria at age four in 1920. Tragedy also struck the family 38 years later when Bessie Haffner died from injuries in an auto accident that took place on May 20, 1958. She was a very efficient, kind and considerate officer manager for her husband.

On Sept. 12, 1959, Cloyd O. Haffner married Minnie Johannsen. He survived his second wife by 13 years.

Many who knew Cloyd O. Haffner relate that he loved people and was a man of faith. He was a member of Crawfordsville's First Christian Church for 60 years and the Gideon Bible Society for 18 years.

Dr. Haffner was a very successful optometrist. His office and optical lens laboratory in the Strand Building at 126 South Green Street was well known throughout the Midwest. He practiced at this location for 55 years and was one of the longest living members of the American Optometric Association. His practice was the last in the state to stop grinding the glass for eyewear.

Cloyd Haffner also became well-known because of his favorite leisure activities, horseshoe pitching. In fact, he was so well-known that in 1937 the Chicago Tribune published a cartoon that depicted Dr. Haffner enthusiastically playing horseshoes in the snow and rain. He was later elected secretary of the Indiana State Horseshoe Association. When he was 76 years old he surprised nearly everyone by winning his last horseshoe trophy against much younger opponents!

He was a personable gentleman and died on July 19, 1983 at the age of 88.

MATHEW HALL

Mathew Hall was born in Ireland in 1735. Many people left Ireland to seek freedom to worship as they pleased. He brought his wife, Agnes Kirk and sons, John, James and Thomas to Frog Level in Newberry Co., SC, where he established a farm. He and his sons served in the Revolutionary War. He is buried in King's Creek Cemetery in South Carolina. In his will he gave 1/10 of the sale of his property to King's Creek Church.

His sons, John, born September 1758, moved to Ohio. Cotton had become very important in the south and slave labor was necessary for its production. People who did not believe in owning slaves moved north. John was buried May 10, 1836 on his farm in Hanover Township, Butler Co., OH. His wife, Elizabeth and three of their 11 children were also buried there. One of his sons, Robert Thomas, born 1797, came to Indiana in 1827 and acquired land in Ripley Township, Montgomery County. In 1977 this land was one of the first farms in the country to receive the honor of being a "Hoosier Homestead Farm" and is still owned by the Hall family in 1989. The first land entry was Nov. 11, 1827, the second entry Oct. 15, 1831. Jane Herron became his wife in 1836. She was the daughter of Thomas Herron. She was born in 1805 and died in 1851. To this union were born six children. Robert died in 1879 and both he and Jane are buried at Yountsville. Only one of their children lived to marry and have a family. Thomas William, born in 1845, married Harriet Brunner in 1873. She was born in 1851 and died in 1928. He died in 1879 and they were buried at Waynetown. They were parents of Johny, Nevada Jane, Thomas Edgar, Charles, Lorena Bell (Lulu), Mary Ann and Zora Elizabeth. Thomas Edgar, born in 1876, married Josephine McMains, born in 1882. She was the daughter of Anderson McMains, a farmer living south of Crawfordsville. Josephine was one of the first nurses to graduate from Culver Hospital. The last two years of her nursing career were spent in the service of her country in World War I. She returned to Crawfordsville and married in December 1919. Thomas Edgar died in 1956 and Josephine in 1963. To this union were born two sons, Robert Thomas in 1921 and Charles Franklin in 1924. Robert was a captain in the Army Air Force in World War II, flying the B1 and B24 bombers. He lost his life flying a P51 fighter plane while stationed in England January 1945. Charles married Nellie Mae Myers, born in 1923, daughter of Carol and Sybil Atkinson Myers on June 24, 1944. They have two children, Vicky Lynn Ridge-Cooney, born Nov. 29, 1945. She is married to Thomas Cooney. They have a son Christopher Thomas, born Jan. 31, 1981. They reside in Seattle, WA. Robert Glen was born Aug. 5, 1951. On Dec. 11, 1971 he married Diana Lynn Rosen, born Oct. 26, 1950. She is the daughter of Robert and Louise Rosen of Wayne Township. Robert (Bob) and his family reside on a farm in Ripley Township. Their two children are Brandon Myers, born July 4, 1974 a student at Southmont High School and Carrie Rene, born Jan. 19, 1978, who attends New Market Elementary.

This historical information was based on many months of research by Lula Hall Barnett, sister of Thomas Edgar Hall.

OAKEL FOWLER HALL 1878-1960

Oakel Fowler Hall was born in Darlington, IN, Dec. 20, 1878, and died in Indianapolis, IN Apr. 15, 1960. Oakel was one of nine children of James Qunicy and Amy Ann (Cox) Hall, both of whom were born in Montgomery County. James Q., born 1850, died 1895, was the son of Joseph and Hannah (Dawson) Hall, and Amy Ann was the daughter of Abel M. and Eliza (Cox) Cox.

The immigrant of this branch of the Hall family was Edward Hall, born in the Parish of Leth-Maclin, County Armaugh, Ireland, in 1723, and "imported to the Colonies at age 11 by James Gilasby, of Philadelphia Port". In 1744 Edward Hall married Eleanor Stuart and settled near Waynesboro, VA, where they raised ten children. The succession of generations, down to Oakel, was as follows: Edward, 1723-1796 Virginia; Thomas, 1754 Virginia - 1836, Kentucky; Thomas, 1776 Virginia - 1840 Indiana; Joseph, 1803 Virginia - 1863 Indiana; James Q. 1850 Indiana - 1895 Indiana; Oakel, 1878 Indiana - 1960 Indiana. Both Edward and Thomas fought in the Revolutionary War. Edward was a corporal and his son Thomas,

179

was a private. Both Oakel's grandfather Joseph and great-grandfather Thomas settled in Montgomery County in the early 1830's.

Oakel and his twin brother, Otis, graduated from Wabash College in 1907, after interrupting their education every other year to work and earn money for tuition and books. During these "off years" from his Wabash studies Oakel taught in country schools in Montgomery and Boone Counties. During his senior year Oakel won a statewide college students oratorical contest and the prize was a years scholarship to a graduate school, and Oakel chose Harvard Divinity School entering in 1907.

Upon his graduation from Harvard Divinity School in 1910 Oakel served as minister to the Winthrop Congregational Church in Charlestown, MA. Oakel wished to return to Indiana so in 1913 he accepted an appointment to the two Methodist churches in Advance and Jamestown, IN. He served these two churches until 1916 when he was appointed student minister for the Methodist church at Purdue University. In 1918 he started teaching sociology classes at Purdue and after a year or two of carrying on both positions gave up the student minister position and taught full time as a member of the Purdue faculty. He maintained his interest in church work by supplying small rural Methodist churches in the Lafayette vicinity who could not afford a regular full time minister. One church, the Stidham Methodist Church in the open country nine miles south-west of Lafayette was served by him for 20 years, 1920 to 1940.

Oakel retired from Purdue in 1947 and served one year as a visiting professor of sociology at Transylvania University, Lexington, KY. After the year at Transylvania he moved to Louisville, KY and for four years supplied small rural churches in Southern Indiana in the vicinity of Louisville. In 1952 Oakel accepted a position as an assistant to the minister of the second Presbyterian Church in Indianapolis that was involved in a relocation program to a new building to be built on North Meridian Street, Indianapolis. His duties included following through on details of the building program and with appearance before groups explaining and gaining support for the church activity. In 1958 his health started to fail and he reluctantly had to give up the church work. He had two years of retirement until his death in 1960 at the age of 82.

On June 30, 1910 Oakel Hall married Edna Arlinda Barker (1891-1975) of Malden, MA, daughter of Nina Rose (Taylor) and John Edward Barker, whose ancestors were ship builders and fishermen of coastal Maine. To this union was born four children - three daughters and one son, all of whom are living. *Submitted by James Edward Hall, son of Oakel F. and Edna A. Hall*

OTIS EARLE HALL 1878-1936

Otis Earle Hall was born in Darlington, IN, Dec. 20, 1878, and died in Springfield, MA, Sept. 29, 1936. Otis was one of nine children of James Quincy and Amy Ann (Cox) Hall, both of whom were born in Montgomery County. James Q., born 1850, died 1895, was the son of Joseph and Hannah (Dawson) Hall, and Amy Ann was the daughter of Abel M. and Eliza (Cox) Cox. Both the grandfather, (Joseph Hall, b. 1803 Virginia, d. 1863 Indiana) and great-grandfather (Thomas Hall, b. 1776 Virginia, d. 1840 Indiana) settled in Montgomery County in the early 1830's.

The immigrant of this branch of the Hall family was Edward Hall, born in the Parish of Leth-Maclin, County Armaugh, Ireland, in 1723, and "imported to the Colonies at age 11 by James Gilasby, of Philadelphia Port". In 1744 Edward Hall married Eleanor Stuart and settled near Waynesboro, VA, where they raised ten children. The succession of generations, down to Otis, was as follows: Edward, 1723-1796 Virginia; Thomas, 1754 Virginia-1836, Kentucky; Thomas, 1776 Virginia-1840 Indiana; Joseph, 1803 Virginia-1863 Indiana; James Q., 1850 Indiana-1895 Indiana; Otis, 1878 Indiana-1936 Massachusetts. Both Edward and Thomas fought in the Revolutionary War. Edward was a corporal and his son, Thomas, was a private.

Otis Earle Hall

Otis and his twin brother, Oakel, graduated from Wabash College in 1907, after interrupting their education nearly every other year to work and earn the money for tuition and books. At one time Otis taught school in Montgomery County, and, from 1904-1905, he was the principal of the New Market High School. After graduation from Wabash, he was the Montgomery County Superintendent of Schools, 1907-1914, where he pioneered in consolidation of Rural Schools and co-authored the book "Better Rural Schools" with Dr. George H. Betts.

Otis was the first State 4-H Club Leader at the State Agriculture College, Manhattan, KS, 1914-1920. While there he authored the 4-H Club Pledge used nationwide to this day. He held the title of Professor of Rural Education at Kansas State Agricultural College. In 1920 he was cited by the United States Food Administration "in appreciation of efficient and patriotic service during the Great War 1917-1918"—with the citation signed by W.P. Innes, Federal Food Administrator of Kansas, and Herbert Hoover, United States Food Administrator.

In 1920 Otis became 4-H Club leader for Hampden Co., West Springfield, MA, holding that position until 1929 when he became Managing Director of the Hampden County Extension Service until his death in 1936. During World War II, when the 4-H Clubs of Kansas were asked to name a Liberty Ship, they chose the name "OTIS E. HALL" in his honor.

On June 25, 1908, Otis Hall married Mary Alice Demoret (1889-1975), daughter of Clara Ann (Sayler) and James Franklin Demoret, of New Market, Montgomery Co., IN, whose ancestors were Indiana pioneers. To this union were born five daughters, all of whom are now living and enjoying their children and grandchildren and one great-grandchild. *Submitted by Lois (Hall) Aseltine, (Mrs. M.L., Jr.) oldest daughter of Otis E. and Mary D. Hall*

ALVA HALLET

Alva Hallett was born on Oct. 6, 1885 on top of Deer's Mill Hill to Elijah Porterfield and Rebecca Newkirk Hallett. He was the youngest of six brothers.

When he was a young boy his father became ill and was hospitalized. Rebecca took her sons to live with her parents near Wallace. Alva helped his grandfather with the farming and attended Gray's School East of Wallace. Because of the time in history that he was born he saw great changes — from walking behind a one-horse plow to farming with a tractor. He went from horse and buggy days to even riding a big jet airplane. On Sept. 2, 1905 he married Stella Hamm and they went to housekeeping in a new home near the grandparent's home. Alva built this small house himself and it cost 200 dollars. Two sons were born to this union: Perry Lee and Paul Leslie.

Alva and Stella Hallett

In 1908 he and Stella moved to a farm they had purchased in Ripley Township, Montgomery County, North and West of Alamo on the county line road. They lived there for 38 years, moving to Alamo in 1946 when Paul Leslie took over the farming after he was married. Alva was a member of the Methodist Church at Alamo. After that church disbanded many years ago, he faithfully attended Alamo Christian Church. He also was a 50 year member of Alamo Masonic Lodge.

Stella died in 1947 at age 60. Alva lived on at Alamo. In 1954 he married Ina Jeffries Elmore. They spent many winters in Venice, FL. She died in 1973. He continued to go to his winter home until his health began to fail. He loved to garden and keep up his yard work and did this until he was in a bad accident at age 92. On July 1, 1977, he was hit by a car while riding his three-wheel bicycle in Alamo. He was seriously injured and never fully recovered. After several weeks in Culver Hospital he went to Lane House Nursing Care Center. He died at age 95 on Jan. 11, 1981 and is buried in Waynetown Masonic Cemetery.

Alva had five grandchildren: William Lee, Jerrell Alva, Stephen Leslie Hallet, Susan Hallet Kauahikaua and Sallie Hallett Thompson. He was a kind and gentle man and had many friends, outliving almost all of them. *Submitted by Ramona Hallett*

JAMES ZENITH HALLETT

James Zenith Hallett was born in Kennebec Co., ME in 1795. He was an early settler (1828) of Montgomery County. At an early age, he served in the War of 1812. He was a Democrat, Baptist and Free Mason. He was buried on his farm near Deer's Mill, dying Aug. 24, 1875. His wife was Cynthia Rinker. Their son, Zenith "Jackson" Hallett was born Apr. 18, 1845 in Brown Township. He married Mary A. Smith (born Oct. 11, 1845 in Rockville, died Feb. 28, 1913, daughter of Reuben and Mary

Helms Smith) in Montgomery County on Aug. 19, 1865. Jackson lived his whole life in the vicinity of Deer's Mill within a three-mile radius of where he was born. In 1914, Jackson married Mrs. Lena Davis of Terre Haute. After an extended illness, Jackson Hallett passed peacefully away on Sept. 14, 1918 at the age of 73 years, four months and 27 days. Mary Smith Hallett's mother had died when she was a young woman and Mary used her motherly instincts to care for her father and raise her five small brothers and sisters, until her marriage to Mr. Hallett. To this union, three boys and three girls were born: Harvey, George, Ellie, Willie, Edna and Susan.

Rick, Ruth and Don Hallett

Their oldest, Harvey Perry Hallett was born May 21, 1866. At age 21, on the first day of the year (1889) he was united in marriage with Druzilla Skimmerhorn. Two of their children died young, Bertha in infancy and Freddie at age seven of St. Vidas Dance. Their other children were Ethel (married Frank Keller), Faye (married Roscoe Keller), Maude (married Wave Beaman), Wandaline (married Forrest Martin), Mary (married Earl Miller) and Bert. Druzilla Hallett was born Sept. 9, 1869 and died Oct. 14, 1948. Harvey P. Hallett passed away May 7, 1914.

Bert Wayne Hallett was born May 16, 1904 at Deer's Mill. He attended Waveland school. He farmed in Brown Township all his life. He married Frances, the daughter of Walter and Nancy (Pollard) Pollitt on Dec. 22, 1925 in Waveland. They were members of Freedom Baptist Church. Joan was their first child, born Aug. 13, 1925. She married Grove Evans and had Susan and John. Don Arvon was born Mar. 30, 1933 in Waveland. Don received his middle name when his mother read it in a newspaper.

Don served four years in the Air Force. He attended Indiana Business College, Indiana University at Indianapolis and Ivy Tech. He held administrative positions with the Indiana State Government, was director of Occupational Development for six counties and is currently manager for Satellite Operations of Ivy Tech. His affiliations include: President of the Montgomery County Council on Aging; Charter Board Member of AARP; Waveland Masonic Lodge and Indiana Scottish Rite. In 1989 was elected Sagamore of the Wabash.

Don married Ruth Hester (see Hester Family). Their son, Richard Wayne (Rick) was born Feb. 15, 1968 in Crawfordsville. Rick is a Senior at Indiana University, studying in Spain at the present. His majors are English and Spanish and he plans to go into International Law. Don, Ruth and Rick are members of the First Baptist Church in Crawfordsville. *Submitted by Don Hallett*

HALSTEAD FAMILY

The Halstead family had its beginning with William Wilson Halstead born in 1844, near Linden, IN. He was married to Rhoda Coyner in Colfax, IN in 1867. They began housekeeping in a three room house, one half mile south of Kirkpatrick and five miles east of Linden in Madison Township. William was a landowner, farmer and stockman. William and Rhoda had eight children, Clyde, Alma, Musetta, William, John, Ruby, Ernest and Josiah. William, Ernest, Ruby and Josiah all graduated from Purdue University. William, John and Josiah (Joe) owned a grain elevator in Kirkpatrick. Later they sold it, William and John moved to Brookston, IN and were in the elevator business there. Josiah farmed with his father. William and Rhoda established a home in Daytona Beach, FL. Rhoda passed away in Florida in 1918 and William died at the homeplace in 1922. The land was divided among the children and Josiah received the homeplace. It still stands with many added rooms.

Josiah married Rena Russell at Brookston in 1980. They had three children, Joe Delwin who attended Indiana University. He farmed with his father. In 1936 he married Fern Wilson of Linden, a school teacher. Her training was at Indiana Teachers College in Terre Haute. Justice Martin attended Purdue. He never married and was a career army man. Doris attended Indiana University and became a teacher in Lafayette. She married George Ray Clayton III of Lafayette in 1940, who had attended Purdue. They had four children, Carol a teacher in LaCrosse, WI. She married James R. Ramsey of Bloomington, IN in 1964. They have two sons, Douglas and David, students in the University of Minnesota. Carol and James are both graduates of Purdue. Preston Ray (deceased 1982) married Nancy Salo of Atlanta, GA in 1965. Both graduated from Purdue. They have two children, Kristen a Junior at Purdue and Greg a freshman at the University of Wisconsin. George R. Clayton IV of Lafayette, attended Purdue and is manager of the truck and van department of Chevrolet. He married Dianne Whitehead of West Point, a school teacher who is a graduate of Ball State University of Muncie, IN. They have two sons, G.R. V and Craig. Both are high school students. Russell Ernst Clayton of Lafayette is co-owner of Deluxe Housing. He married Patricia Cassidy of Lafayette, an air line stewardess. They have three children, Sean, Alicia and Mitchell all in grade and high school.

Doris and George Clayton lived in the homeplace for ten years, then moved to Lafayette. In 1948 Josiah Halstead died. Joe bought the homeplace and farmed. He and his wife Fern, lived across the barnlot in the house his grandfather built for his parents, Josiah and Rena. Joe farmed all his life. He also grew and distributed Genuine Pfister Hybrid Seed Corn, in five counties in Indiana. He was active in community affairs with the Linden Methodist Church and the Linden State Bank. In 1976 Governor Otis Bowen wanted all farmers in Indiana to be honored whose farms had been in the same family for a hundred years or more. After a county dinner with Montgomery farmers, Lt. Governor Robert Orr presented plaques to them. Joe was proud to be a recipient. He passed away in 1978. *Submitted by Fern Halstead*

JOHN HAMILTON

John Hamilton purchased 80 acres of land in Sugar Creek Township, Montgomery County from the U.S. Government in 1831. John, his second wife, Hannah, and most of his family moved to Indiana from Champaign Co., OH. John and Hannah were members of the first Methodist Church in Sugar Creek Township, which met in Roly Kendall's house in 1832. John served as their "class leader". John Hamilton died in 1836. Hannah married Lloyd Wilcoxin in 1837 and moved to Delaware Co., IN.

John Hamilton was born between 1770 and 1775. He married his first wife, Catherine, about 1790. Two sons, Reuben (b. ca. 1792) and James (b. 1797), were born in Pennsylvania. The rest of their children were born in Ohio probably in the Scioto County area: John (b. 1799), Henry (b. ca. 1801), Gabriel (b. 1803), William (b. ca. 1804), and Catherine (b. ca. 1809). (Note: Catherine may have been the daughter of John and his second wife, Hannah). John's wife, Catherine, died between 1808 and 1810 and was buried in Nile Township, Scioto County.

John married his second wife, Hannah, daughter of William and Eleanor Colgan/Colgin, about 1809/1810. Their children were born in the Scioto County and Champaign Co., OH areas: Eleanor (b. ca. 1810), Sarah (b. ca. 1817/1818), Hannah (b. 1819), Nathanial (b. ?), Jesse b. ?), Lavisa (b. 1820), Elizabeth (b. 1824), and Martha Jane (b. ca. 1831).

All of John's children except Reuben moved to Indiana. Additional information about John's sons and their spouses is as follows. Reuben (Elizabeth Cahail/Kahal) lived in Scioto Co., OH and died there in 1852. James (Elizabeth Overpack/Overpeck), John (1st Sarah Weaver, 2nd Mrs. Elizabeth Holloway), Henry (1st Margaret, 2nd Mary), and William (Mary), resided in Clinton Co., IN. James, John and William were buried in the McKendria Cemetery in Clinton County. Gabriel (Elizabeth C. Anderson) resided in Montgomery County and later Black Hawk Co., IA where he died in 1880. Nothing further is known about Nathanial and Jesse.

Five of John's daughters were married in Montgomery County: Catherine (Hiram Clark, 1833), Eleanor (Elihu Brown, 1835), Sarah (Isaac C. Adams, 1836), Hannah (Reuben Stout, 1835), and Lavisa (Abraham Bowers Jr., 1836). Daughters, Elizabeth (William J. Griffin, 1840) and Martha Jane (Horatio Wilcoxon, 1851) were married in Tippecanoe County and Delaware Co., IN respectively.

BERT HAMPTON

Bert Hampton, son of Martin D. and Rebecca Ellen Booher Hampton, was born Oct. 17, 1880 in Franklin Township, Montgomery Co., IN.

October 1834, Hampton and Booher families came by wagon train from Sullivan Co., TN to Franklin Township.

Bert's siblings were Maggie, Alonzo and Daniel. Their mother died Dec. 28, 1889.

April 14, 1892, Martin married Ratie Stalker, a native of North Carolina.

Bert attended Coleman School and worked on his father's farms. January 14, 1909, he married Violet Blanton, born in Hamilton County, June 30, 1885, the daughter of Hiram and Mary Ellen Ward Blanton. Violet attended Hamilton County schools and moved to Montgomery County in 1900. Her siblings were Flora and Theodore (Jack).

Bert and Violet, living on the family farm four miles east of Darlington, became parents of Mary Katherine, born Apr. 9, 1912 and Eugene (Beaner), born Dec. 28, 1919.

181

The family were members of Saint James Lutheran Church, where Bert served in an official capacity many years. Violet transferred to Darlington United Methodist Church.

In 1931 the Hamptons moved to Darlington. Bert continued to supervise his farming operations, co-owned a slaughter house and worked for Anderson and Campbell Hardwares.

Mary K., a graduate of Darlington High School attended DePauw University. September 9, 1939 she married James (Jim) Price. Jim, native of Virginia, graduated from Bowers High School and retired from R.R. Donnelley. He is a member of Elks Lodge. Mary K. was a bookkeeper at Anderson and Campbell Hardwares, office assistant for Production Credit Association and retired from J.C. Penney. She holds membership in Dorothy Q Chapter DAR and American Legion Auxiliary. They live in Darlington where they are active members of the United Methodist Church.

Eugene, a graduate of Darlington High School attended Terre Haute Business College. During World War II he served with Company E 151st Infantry 38th Division. He was seriously wounded Mar. 4, 1945 on Corregidor. October 20, 1951, Eugene married Mary E. Bubeck. While living in Crawfordsville, their children were born: William Barton (Bill), Jan. 6, 1953; Gail Ann, Dec. 18, 1953 and Kurt Alan, Jan. 12, 1957. Later they moved to Darlington. Mary E., a graduate of Marshall, IL high school and Union Hospital Nurse's Training, Terre Haute was a registered nurse at Culver Hospital when she died Mar. 11, 1979. Violet died Apr. 1, 1980.

Eugene married Dolores Hoffa Todd, May 23, 1980. She attended Crawfordsville High School and was co-owner of Golden Rule, Crawfordsville. Eugene was a County Highway clerk, a butcher for West and Rentschler Groceries and from 1961 through 1981 was Postmaster at Darlington. He is a member of American Legion, other service related organizations and Elks Lodge. Dolores is a Lady Elk and a member of American Legion and Eagles Auxiliaries. They reside in Darlington and are members of the United Methodist Church.

Bill graduated from Darlington High School, Notre Dame University and Indiana University Medical School. He interned at Henry Ford Hospital, Detroit, MI. He married Kathleen O'Sullivan, Oct. 4, 1980. Their sons are Geoffrey, Tyler and Kurt. Bill is a Medical Doctor at Sault Ste. Marie, MI.

Gail, a graduate of North Montgomery High School and University of Evansville School of Nursing has a Master's from Indiana University. November 14, 1987 she married Stephen (Steve) Servies. They and Steve's son, Erik live in New York where Gail is a nurse practitioner at the Women's Clinic in Cortland.

Kurt Alan is a graduate of North Montgomery High School and University of Evansville. He holds a Master's in Airport Management. Kurt is a captain in the United States Air Force, stationed at Barksdale Air Force Base, Bossier City, LA.

Bert Hampton, the subject of this history, died July 29, 1961. *Submitted by Mary K. Price*

BERT AND CARRIE HAMPTON

Bert Hampton, born June 10, 1914 to Solomon and Mary Hanna Hampton at New Market, IN. Bert married Carrie Gilland, daughter of Luther and Irene Webb Jackson. Her birthdate Dec. 5, 1910. Bert and Carrie's children; Mary Rose, Anna May and Clarence. Carrie had two children, Earl and Harvey Gilland, by a previous marriage.

Bert's ancestor of his mother's family; namely "Johannes Kesler" came to America from Germany, or a German portion of Switzerland, some time around 1749 - 1751. Probable marriage to Eva Dorothea Leaman, 1755. The earliest documentation of him occurred when his daughter was baptized in 1758. Long wars and heavy taxes prompted many men to leave Germany in the mid-to-late 18th century, but it is not known specifically why Johannes came to America. It is assumed he arrived at the port of Philadelphia, among some 30,000 other immigrants who entered this port.

Their first son was Jacob, born in 1756; a daughter Susanna, who was baptized Oct. 22, 1758, and a son Johannes, baptized Apr. 19, 1761.

Johannes, Sr. farmed in Pennsylvania, but no record of his owning land at this time. However, he took his family to Frederick Co., MD about 1763 and received a patent for 25 acres Feb. 1764, near the present village of Tyrone, near Taneytown. Johannes died March 1823 and his wife, Dorothea, in 1798.

Jacob B. Kessler, son of Johannes and Dorothea, married Elizabeth Shearer and lived in Montgomery Co., PA. They had 12 children. Among them was Benjamin, seventh child, born March 1802. Benjamin first married in Botetourt Co., VA to Eva Mangus and had four children. After her death in 1833 he married Elizabeth Graybill. They had eight children. Benjamin died 1890 and Elizabeth in 1883. Both buried in Dunkard cemetery in Montgomery Co., IN. Around 1848 Benjamin came to Indiana with two covered wagons, one drawn by four horses and the other by three cows and a bull, yoked like oxen. A crate of chickens fastened under the wagon and milk cows following. They had their farming equipment and a still. Good money was to be made in whiskey. They acquired land and built a two story log cabin along Cornstalk Creek, northwest of Ladoga. Benjamin became deaf and was killed by a Monon train near his home, because he did not hear the whistle.

Solomon was the sixth child of Benjamin. He married Hannah Schenck in 1857. After her death in 1863 he married Martha Hannah Pointer. He had four children by the first wife and seven by the second.

Mary Hannah Kessler was the ninth child, born June 1878, married Edward Hampton 1898. Their children: Claude Lyman, born Jan. 31, 1900, died 1978; Opal Marie, born May 24, 1901; Raymond Lee, born June 13, 1904, died February 1974; Manford, born Sept. 22, 1907; Lillie Imogene, born Oct. 28, 1911, died Jan. 24, 1912; Beatrice, born June 10, 1914; Bert born June 10, 1914; Harry Walker, born Oct. 9, 1917.

Mary died Sept. 28, 1965. Edward died Oct. 23, 1944. Both buried in the Masonic Cemetery at Crawfordsville.

Bert and Carrie Hampton are residents of Waveland at this writing, moving there in 1968. *Submitted by Bert Hampton*

ERNEST LLOYD HAMPTON

Mr. Hampton was born in Thorntown, IN on Nov. 29, 1890, the son of Samuel A. and Ida (Walton) Hampton.

Samuel A. was the son of Samuel and Phoebe (Guntle) Hampton. He was born on Feb. 8, 1868 in New Darlington, IN and died on Feb. 2, 1943. On Aug. 8, 1886 he married Ida Walton who was the daughter of Ayre Walton; she died in 1961. To this union two sons were born: Cecil B., born Sept. 25, 1888, died July 25, 1973 and married Flora E. Heffner; also our subject.

Ernest was a plasterer and carpenter most of his life: He also served in WWI where he was gassed in the battle of Argonne. Ernest died in his Crawfordsville home on Oct. 11, 1952.

On Apr. 10, 1919 Ernest married Dorothy Elizabeth Smith, who was born Sept. 28, 1900, the daughter of George Riley and Sarah (Flynn) Smith. Mrs. Hampton died on Nov. 6, 1969. To this union 12 children were born: Eileen (Mert), Helen Gene, Rosemary, Richard, Fredrick (deceased), Sammy (deceased), Donald, Ralph (deceased), Gerald, Shirley, Barbara and Marilyn. Fredrick died at the age of three months of whooping cough. Ralph and Sammy were two and five years of age at their deaths; both died within three days of each other with diphtheria. The rest of the children grew to adulthood and now have families of their own.

Mrs. Hampton remarried before her death to John Scott of this county.

Mr. and Mrs. Hampton rest with their three deceased sons in the St. James Cemetery in Darlington, IN.

THEODORE "DORA" HANKINS

Theodore (called Dora) Hankins, born Mar. 8, 1858 in Hamilton Co., OH to John and Orpha Hancock Hankins. He came to New Ross, IN in 1888. He barbered here until 1890, then he started in the undertaking business. He worked 25 years as a barber, and 12 years of that time he worked also as an undertaker, or embalmer, and he farmed for seven years of that time. He was a very good undertaker or funeral director as they are known now. He had a horse drawn hearse at the funeral of William Joh, June 1916. In 1922 at James W. Linn's funeral he had a motor hearse. He married first Rose Morrison, and they had three children: Harold, Hazel, and Everett. After his first wife died, he married Ida Dorsey, daughter of George and Dosha Jessee Dorsey. George Dorsey had also been an undertaker at the same time as Mr. Hankins. When there was a death, Mr. Hankins would come to the house, embalm the body, then go back and get a casket, or coffin as it was called then and place the embalmed body in the casket, and it was ready for viewing.

At night, a group of friends would bring in food, and sit up all night, watching that nothing happened to the corpse, and giving moral and sympathetic support to the grieving family. Most times funerals were held in the home, sometimes in the church. Nowadays, bodies are whisked away to funeral directors establishments, and no one sees them, until they're ready for viewing. He died in New Ross. *Submitted by Pauline Walters*

BAYLESS WASHINGTON HANNA

Bayless was born Mar. 14, 1828 in Troy, OH to James Jr. and Nancy (Telford) Hanna (see biography) but spent his childhood years and received his education in Crawfordsville. After his junior year at Wabash College, Bayless had to drop-out and move to the south for health reasons. He spent two years in Natchez, MS where he began the study of law with Josiah Winchester. In two years, he passed the bar examination. Upon return to Crawfordsville, Bayless resumed the study of law with future U.S. Senator, Joseph E. McDonald. Bayless was elected and served a term as the prosecuting attorney for

Montgomery County before removing to Terre Haute. While there, Bayless married Sarah Oakalla Read, daughter of the distinguished Dr. Ezra Read. Fourteen children were born (seven lived past infancy): John Telford, Read, Bayless, James Richmond, Oakalla, Mary and Ruth. He also entered into a law practice with Daniel W. Voorhees, who later served three terms as U.S. Senator. Besides being well versed in the law, Bayless was well gifted as a public speaker of national recognition. Thus it was natural for him to enter politics. These were the times preceding the Civil War and the issues of the day were hot. Bayless was an ardent Democrat and spoke against slavery.

Bayless was elected Attorney General of Indiana in 1870, and served with distinction. In 1872, he was delegate to the convention which nominated Horace Greeley. In 1876, he was once again delegate to the convention and managed the forces of Thomas A. Hendricks who eventually was second on the ticket to Mr. Tilden. After his defeat in 1880 for a congressional seat from the 8th District, Bayless moved back to Crawfordsville in 1883 where he owned and edited the Journal Review. After being an elector-at-large (1884 convention which nominated Cleveland/Hendricks), Bayless was first appointed Minister to Persia (which he declined) and then immediately was appointed Minister Resident and Consul General to the Argentine Republic with the Legation at Buenos Ayres. After the Mission was upgraded by Congress through Mr. Hanna's efforts, he was reappointed Envoy Extraordinary and Minister Plenipotentiary in 1887. In June 1889, he was stricken with apoplexy and was compelled by the dangerous condition of his health to come back home (via England), arriving in Crawfordsville August 1890.

Bayless was equally adept and popular as a raconteur at social gatherings. He had a love for the classics, something which he probably inherited from his father. He was also an accomplished writer, and his long-time friend Lew Wallace urged him to write a book. Shortly before the stroke that eventually was his demise, Mr. Hanna was working in that direction, but his earthly efforts ceased before his impending death. He died at home Aug. 2, 1896.

Mr. Hanna, his wife Sarah O., and eldest son John T. are buried in Oak Hill Cemetery in Crawfordsville next to the now unmarked graves of his parents. His two sisters, Martha and Nancy also remained in the Crawfordsville area.

All three sons, Bayless, Read and James R. eventually settled in Chicago.

James Hanna (Speed) Martin, Sr., (son of Mary Craig Hanna Martin, a daughter of Bayless) graduate of Wabash 1926 and lover and sometime resident of Crawfordsville resides in Chicago and has three sons: James Hanna Martin, Jr. (Arlington Heights, IL), Louis Kulp Martin of Gladstone, MI and Hugh Michael Martin of Chicago. All four have spent much time and had many trips to Crawfordsville and Wabash. We no longer reside in Montgomery County, but Montgomery County still resides in our hearts. *Submitted by Hugh M. Martin*

JAMES HANNA, JR.

James Hanna, Jr. born Mar. 31, 1791, died Feb. 18, 1855, was the son of a Scotch-Irish Immigrant. James was born in Washington Co., PA to James and Hannah (Bayless) Hanna. He was raised in Scott Co., KY and then in 1804, the family moved to Dayton, OH (the ultimate resting place of his mother and father).

James, Jr. first came to Crawfordsville in 1833, purchased (in partnership with his brothers Honorable Samuel Hanna of Ft. Wayne and Joseph Hanna and Leroy and Robert C. Gregory) a stock of general merchandise and opened a business in a frame building on the southwest corner of Main and Green Streets. He also purchased a large tract of land in Coal Creek Township 20, Range 5 including parts in Sections 26, 27, 28 and 33 (to date, I have been unable to find out where he resided in Crawfordsville).

In 1835, James' family (including his wife Nancy Telford Hanna, and their children Martha A., Mary Elizabeth, Alexander Little Hannah, and the illustrious Bayless Washington Hanna) also moved to Crawfordsville.

In 1836, the Hanna Building was erected at the Northwest corner of Main and Washington Streets. At the time of this writing, it was still standing. Within recent memory, the building housed G.C. Murphy Store and more recently, the Heathcliff. While Mr. Hanna's means were ample, business and commerce were not the main reason Mr. Hanna moved to Crawfordsville. Mr. Hanna was a devout Christian of the Presbyterian persuasion, and also a self-schooled scholar of the classics. His primary reason for coming to Crawfordsville was to enjoy the facilities at the newly formed Wabash College, at the time a Presbyterian institution. His affection for the College became so singular that his business pursuits ceased, and he became the general traveling agent for the college, soliciting funds for its operation. In the late 1830's, the College burned down. At the same time, Center Presbyterian Church (where he was an elder for many years) had no place to hold services. Thus the Hanna Building was pressed into triple service; the ground floor for the store, the upper floors on weekdays held Wabash College and Sundays, Center Church services!

On Feb. 18, 1855, James Hanna, Jr. died of cholera, while soliciting funds for Wabash College. His body was transported back to Crawfordsville, his final resting place (as well as his wife's) being Oak Hill Cemetery. Their graves had headstones as late as 1983, but have since disappeared. *Submitted by James Hanna Martin, Sr.*

TYRE LITTLETON HANNA

Tyre Littleton Hanna was born in 1834 in Waveland, IN. He was the son of William (1805) and Elisabeth Glenn Hanna who were married in 1829. William was a plantation and slave owner in Mercer Co., KY, but after his marriage, moved to Montgomery Co., IN. Before moving, he freed his slaves, some of whom would not leave him and went to Indiana as free men. He and Elisabeth had three sons: Tyre, William, Jr. and Adam. Elisabeth died in 1839, whereupon William married a second time (1841) to Mary Duncan Watson by whom he had a number of sons and daughters.

Tyre's grandfather was Adam Hanna, born in 1754. He married in 1796 to Nancy Kennedy of Scotch descent in Harrodsburg, KY. He was a farmer and lived in Mercer and then Shelby Co., KY. He served in the War of the Revolution, was wounded in battle, and was a first sergeant in Washington's Army in the winter of 1777-1778 at Valley Forge.

Tyre Hanna served in the Union Army in the War Between the States. In 1880, he married Cornelia Chittenden Kleiser of Swiss descent and 19 years his junior, in Waveland, IN. Although not Catholic, she received part of her education in a convent where she gained considerable of the gentle accomplishments especially in music. At 16 she became a music teacher. One of her brothers was a millwright. She and Tyre had three daughters, Olivia Elisabeth (1882), Cornelia Alberta (1886) and Amy Margaret (1894).

Tyre Littleton Hanna

He was a graduate of Franklin College and became a stock farmer and merchant. He owned a small department store in Waveland, the worn metal plate of which still remains outside the front door of the old building. He was a Montgomery County Commissioner and commissioned among other things, a covered bridge near Waveland. His name, with two other Commissioners, is cut in stone on the front of the "Old Jail" built in 1882 in Crawfordsville and now designated a National Historic Monument.

He was a substantial member of the community and known for his excellent business acumen, kindness to others, especially young people seeking an education. He was highly respected, unpretentious and unostentatious, an excellent and thoughtful provider and a quiet, solid, home-loving Scot. His home still stands in Waveland and now serves as the local mortuary. Word has it that during Tyre's absence, the carpenter building the second story cut all the lumber one foot too short, a lamentable but relatively inconspicuous completion to an otherwise handsome home.

Because of Cornelia's ill health, Tyre and his family moved to the mild climate of southern California in 1910. Their initial move was to Redlands and then to Pasadena where they lived until his death in 1915. Both are buried in the Maple Ridge Cemetery in Waveland, IN.

ELIZABETH MORRISSON BOYNTON HARBERT

Elizabeth Morrisson Boynton, called Lizzie, was born in Crawfordsville on Apr. 15, 1843, the daughter of William and Abbey Sweetser Boynton. She attended a female seminary in Oxford, OH and Terre Haute Female College, a preparatory school in 1862.

In 1869, she joined with other women in a petition to open Wabash College's door to women. They applied for admission and were refused. However, president White granted permission to four young women to attend lectures on chemistry and natural science.

The women took their case to the public, announcing the production of a dramatic sketch entitled *The Coming Women*. Miss Boynton gave a paper on the plight of women in education, which she also sold as an article to the New York *Independent*.

In 1869 a woman's rights convention was held in Crawfordsville. A Woman Suffrage Association for Montgomery County was organized. Lizzie Boynton was elected president. In 1869 she was a speaker at the annual convention of the National Suffrage Association in Cleveland.

Her first book, *The Golden Fleece* was published in 1869. From 1857 to 1872 she wrote poetry and an article on women's rights for the *Wabash*, published by Wabash College.

On Oct. 18, 1870 she married William Soesby Harbert, a former Wabash College student, a Civil War veteran, and a lawyer.

The Harberts lived in Des Moines, IA until 1872 or 1874. While living there, her second book *Out of Her Sphere* was published in 1871. She also took an active part in the suffrage movement as president of the Woman's Suffrage Society of Iowa. She induced the Republican Party of Iowa to put in its state platform a woman's plank.

In 1872 or 1874 they moved to Evanston, IL. Mrs. Harbert edited the women's department, called *Women's Kingdom* for the Chicago InterOcean until 1885. Next she founded *The New Era, a Monthly Magazine Devoted to Philanthropy and Reform*. Between 1870 and 1920 she corresponded with the national leaders of the suffrage and temperance movements. In 1876 she addressed the Democratic National Convention at Cincinnati, OH. She was president of the National Home Economics Association. She was also president of the Social Science Association of Illinois and National Associate Chairwoman of the World Unity League.

She gave many lectures, campaigning for equal suffrage. She published another book, *Amore* in 1892, and contributed articles to magazines, including *The Arena, The Coming Age, Womans Journal*, and *The American Journal of Social Science*.

She had three children, two girls and a boy.

In 1891 she received an honorary PhD from Ohio Wesleyan College, recognizing her for her work on behalf of womanhood.

In 1906, the Harberts moved to Pasadena, CA, where she became vice-president of the Woman's Civic League of Pasadena and vice-president of the Southern California Press Association.

She died on Jan. 19, 1925. Her papers were sold to the Huntington Library in Pasadena in 1969. *Submitted by Jean Thompson*

HARLAN-GREGG-SNYDER-MILLER

I am so fortunate to have the privilege to tell of my honorable ancestors and claim my heritage in Crawfordsville and Montgomery County where they so deeply planted our family roots. This is the place I love most and have the fondest of memories.

My name is Helen Inez Harlan. I was born in Yountsville, Ripley Township Oct. 10, 1901 to George Newton and Carrie Bell (Snyder) Harlan. They were parents of nine children, Charles Merle, he was the City Clerk of Crawfordsville when Mr. Murphy was Mayor, a Democrat Clerk in a Republican town, later Merle joined the Lafayette Police Force and became a detective on the Big-Four railroad. Passed away in Indianapolis in 1944. Paul was a bookkeeper and accountant. Elizabeth A. died at one month. Helen Inez (myself) worked in the bindery department at the Journal Review. Became a book binder retiring in 1967. Doris married and moved to Anderson, IN. Worked at Delco Remy. Ernest worked at Riley Hospital and Wm. H. Block in Indianapolis. Benton worked at Electric Steel. Austin worked at Link Belt. Caretta Louise married and moved on a big farm. Dad spent his last days with her. Merle, Paul, Doris, Ernest and Benton all graduated from Crawfordsville High School. Caretta and I are the only two now living.

Benton Snyder Family

We had a happy life in Crawfordsville and I love it still. "DAD" was foreman of the benchmen in the casket factory. I remember when he made $9.00 a week then $12.00 then $15.00. Working ten then nine then eight hours per day. He raised a family of eight children (one died in infancy) with my mother's help. She was a great seamstress.

My great grandparents George and Ruth (Gregg) Harlan settled in Montgomery County in 1826, both native of Warren Co., OH. The Harlans of English origin have celebrated 300 years in America arriving in 1687. Many of the Harlans became statesman and men of renown. Including James Harlan, senator of Iowa, George Harlan of Warren Co., OH, who left his name in the history of Ohio, my third cousin Mary Eunice Harlan became the wife of Robert Todd Lincoln and my sixth cousin Ida Saxton who became the wife of President William McKinley.

The Gregg family came from Ireland and in 1682 landed in Upland now Chester Co., PA. Ruth Gregg who became the wife of George Harlan was born in Warren Co., OH in 1808. George and Ruth Gregg Harlan were the parents of nine children including my grandfather Marcellus G. Harlan who married Eliza Wray Miller. She died in 1870 and all knowledge of Marcellus was lost. They were parents of three; George Newton Harlan (my father), Charles Miller Harlan, and Clara Alice Harlan Whitely. The Miller grandparents raised the three small children.

My mother, Carrie Bell Snyder, married George Newton Harlan, and her parents Benton and Mary Ellen Miller Snyder were all native of Montgomery County. My great grandfather Andrew Jackson Snyder married Elizabeth Price both native of Maryland. He was a miller and migrated to Ohio. In 1845 he came to Yountsville, Montgomery Co., IN where he purchased the Grain Mill and ground the grain and made fine flour. Their home was a little house near the mill where they raised their brood of four including my grandfather Benton Snyder.

I now live at 2910 Sheffield Drive, Indianapolis, IN where my dearly loved people tenderly care for me.

GEORGE S. HARNEY

George S. Harney was born in Ladoga Dec. 24, 1864, the son of Judge James F. and Louise Harrison Harney. He attended Ladoga Normal School and Wabash College where he was graduated with the class of 1888. He then attended Central Law School in Indianapolis and was admitted to the bar in 1891.

He practiced law with his father until he enlisted in Company M, 158th Indiana Volunteer Infantry during the Spanish American War. He was promoted during the war to the rank of second lieutenant. After his discharge he continued his service in the Indiana National Guard and was promoted to the rank of Captain.

He practiced law in Indianapolis following the war. He joined the Supreme Tribe of Ben Hur as assistant secretary, where he remained for seven years. He became editor of the *Crawfordsville Review*, serving from April 1913 to March 1917 according to the masthead of the Review for those inclusive dates.

When the United States entered World War I, Harney attempted to enlist, but was not accepted because of his age. He worked with the Indiana State Council of Defense in efforts to get war production stepped-up in plants in Indiana.

After working in Greencastle in the personnel department of the American Zinc Mill, Harney returned to Crawfordsville in 1925. He served as secretary of the Montgomery County Chamber of Commerce at least from 1926 to 1928 and perhaps from 1925 to 1929.

After he retired from the Chamber of Commerce, he devoted his time to writing. He had written articles for various magazines and publications. In 1951, he had published a novel entitled *David Lannarck, Midget, a Story of the Circus*.

He was a charter member and first Exalted Ruler of the Crawfordsville Elks Club and was active in that organization over the years. He was also a member of Montgomery County Lodge No. 50, Free and Accepted Masons, the Frank Britton Camp of Spanish American War Veterans of Crawfordsville and a member of the Rotary Club.

He was married Jan. 7, 1908 to Emma Young of Huntington. They had two surviving children, Anna Louise and James Harney.

George S. Harney died Apr. 29, 1952. *Submitted by Jean Thompson*

ANDREW DOUGLAS HARPEL

Andrew Douglas Harpel, born May 24, 1863, in Newton Co., IN to John and Lydia Jennings Harpel, grandson of John and Mary P. Moor Harpel, came to Montgomery Co., IN. He died southeast of Shannondale on May 18, 1961 at age 98. He married Apr. 4, 1894 to Cora Effie Fruits born Mar. 13, 1874, died Mar. 20, 1960, daughter of Ambrose and Jerusha Huff Fruits, granddaughter of George Fruits, III and great granddaughter of George Fruits, Jr., who was born in Maryland Jan. 2, 1762, and died in Alamo, IN Aug. 6, 1876, at the age of 114, a Revolutionary soldier. Cora and Douglas lived on a farm southwest of Shannondale. Their children were John Alfred, born Mar. 3, 1895 and married Fannie Scott. Their children were Mary Lou Bushine, Barbara McClaskey, Dorothy Gratim and one son Donald E. Walter Jennings Harpel born Jan. 4, 1902, married Vivian Lucile Randel, born Dec. 28, 1913, on Nov. 15, 1942, the daughter of Orval and Dora Linn Randel.

Walter had a very modern seed plant in Shannondale. In connection with his business he was twice presented the "Corn King" title.

Walter and Vivian Lucile are both living in a nursing home in Crawfordsville: Leona Faye born Nov. 7, 1903 and married John Cruea on Apr. 27, 1940, had stepchildren; Hazel born 1897 and died

1985, never married; Donald Joseph born Nov. 9, 1918 lives on the farm; Mildred born 1913 and died 1921 on her eighth birthday.

ANDREW JOHNSON (A.J.) HARRIS
1865-1952

A.J. (Jay) Harris was born June 11, 1865 in Botetourt Co., VA, the ninth of ten children born to Robert S. and Mary Elizabeth Rogers Harris. He died at his home in Linnsburg, Jan. 30, 1952.

"Jay" came to New Ross, Walnut Township, Montgomery County in 1879 as a 14 year old boy, with his 15 year old brother "Abe" following the death of their mother. They came to visit their brother "Pete" living near New Ross.

The brothers planned to visit and work for 30 days, make a little money, then move on to Bozeman, MT. Another brother, Henry, lived in Bozeman. "Jay" and "Abe" were hoping to prospect for gold in Montana.

A.J. and Eliza Ann Harris

During his stay near New Ross, "Jay" found a place to work and a good home with a prominent farming family named Sperry. Mrs. Sperry became a very good friend, almost a second mother, as she prepared nourishing meals for him, laundered and mended his clothes. A.J. was so grateful for his new home and friends, that he was uncertain about leaving when he and "Abe" met at the depot to board the train west. He tossed a coin in the air which made his decision to stay.

After working some time for the Sperrys, he went to work for John Lockeridge. This farm is now the Arva Buck farm. He met his wife, Eliza Ann, who lived on a neighboring farm.

Eliza Ann Armstrong, was the daughter of John and Julia Hunt Armstrong. She and A.J. were married Dec. 21, 1890. They engaged in sharecrop farming in the area, later farming her father's farm until after his death. One son, John Ora, was born to them Feb. 16, 1894.

In 1909, A.J. and "Lide" bought 120 acres of unimproved land. Approximately half of this acreage was cleared. The remainder was thicket and swamp. A contract to furnish labor and all materials was let to Harris Brothers, carpenters, in 1910 to build a house and barn. The house was built for $1800 and the barn for $600. A.J. and John cleared and ditched the remainder of the acreage themselves. A.J. and "Lide" farmed there until 1917 when they moved to Linnsburg in semi-retirement. She died in the family home in August, 1947.

John married a neighbor girl, Gertrude Hayes, daughter of prominent farmer William Hayes and his wife Betty Grissom Hayes. They lost a son Kenneth in infancy, and another son, Stanley Hayes, was born to them in 1921. John and Gertrude continued farming until his death in 1950.

Stanley married Alice Clare Munns of the New Market area in 1944. They continued farming operation until his retirement. Stanley and Alice are the parents of three children, Mrs. Larry (Lynn Ellen) Robison, a teacher at Southmont, J. Lamont Harris, an attorney in Crawfordsville, and Mrs. David A. (Sheila Ann) Rhoads. David and Sheila now manage and operate the home farm. Stanley and Alice have five grandchildren, Gail Robison, Ann and Stephen Lamont Harris and Aron Jay and Beth Ann Rhoads.

THOMAS EDMUND HARRIS

Thomas Edmund Harris, farmer, wife and family of Buckingham Co., VA, entered Montgomery County in 1836, settled in Walnut Township, bought 95 acres and built a log cabin. He was elected Justice of Peace and served in the State Legislature. His wife, Rebecca, and five daughters died of consumption and are buried in Pisgah Cemetery.

John Freelan Harris, teacher, farmer, Lutheran, oldest son of Thomas' 11 children, married Caroline Flaningam Casner, Lutheran, settled in Franklin Township, having six children.

His son, Franklin Edmund, farmer, Lutheran, born 1864 married Orrell Ruth Stinette, having four children: Hubert Lee, Hazel May, James Floyd (died age eight months), Cecil Addison.

Hubert Lee, farmer, Lutheran, married Florence De Wein, no heirs.

Hazel Edmiston age 82 1986

Hazel May, teacher, I.U. graduate, Lutheran, married Carl Loland Edmiston, mechanic, Methodist, having three children: John Allen, Jacob Sherman, Jay Paul.

Cecil Addison, WWII, Air Force, Lutheran, Star Mail Route, married Bernice Gregory, having one son, Cecil Anthony Harris, Captain of Phoenix Detective Division, who married Deanna McSpadden, having two children: Deborah Ann, Michael Anthony.

Concerning the children of Hazel May Harris Edmiston, note occupations; no farmer, one teacher.

John Allen, National Guard for 43 years, Warrant Officer four, Methodist, married Betty Louise Davis, receptionist, Methodist, having four children: Jack, Joe, Beth Ann, Bill David.

Jack, Navy, Dental Technician, Methodist, married Melina Ortacio, Lutheran, having two children: Jennifer Lynn, Melissa Joy. Divorced, he married Terri Lee Garrett, having two heirs: Scott Matthew, Megan Nichole.

Joe Edmiston, graduate Ivy Tech, Electronics Field Supervisor, Christian, married Karen Louise Vincent, bank clerk, Christian, having two children: John Dale, Heather Rose.

Beth Ann Edmiston, school bus driver, Christian, married to Duane Shaw, Navy, having one son: Daniel. Divorced, she married James Jordan, EMT.

Bill David Edmiston, Air Force, Bitburg, Germany, Methodist, married Karen Ann Schmidt, having two children: Aerial Nicole, Cody William.

Jacob Serman Edmiston, (Hazel's second son), Army Korean Conflict, 13 months in Germany, engineer, Methodist, married Teresa Ellen Ross, drafting engineer, Catholic, having five children: Susan Jean, Ellen Marie, Mark Blane, Ann Louise, Carla Patricia.

Susan Jean, teacher, graduate Ball State, Catholic, married Robert McKenzie, accountant, graduate Ball State, having three children: Robert Jake, Sean Mathew, Andrew Phillip.

Ellen Marie, bookkeeper, graduate Ivy Tech, Catholic, married Richard Irving Farnham, Wabash graduate, engineer, having two children: Charles Jacob, Rebecca Ellen.

Mark Blane, Navy six years, Fireman Crawfordsville Department, Catholic, married Dianne Hamilton, having one child, Jennifer Leigh. Divorced, he married Cindy Hayes Rusk, legal secretary, having one child Emily Suzanne.

Ann Louise, Purdue graduate, Production Coordinator of Ash Medical Systems, West Lafayette, Catholic.

Carla Patricia a junior at North Montgomery.

Jay Paul Edmiston (Hazel's third son) mechanic, Methodist, married Barbara Ann Buchanan, secretary, Catholic, having three children: Dawn Marie, Stacia Loraine, Christopher Scott.

Dawn Marie, Purdue graduate, computer analyst, Catholic, married Bradley James Knapp, Purdue graduate, doctorate University Wisconsin, industrial chemist, No children.

Christopher Scott, Navy 6 years, Subic Bay, Catholic, married a Filipino girl, Emma. No children. *Submitted by Hazel Harris Edmiston*

HARSHBARGER-MYERS-BALDWIN

The Harshbarger-Myers-Baldwin history is well-known in Montgomery County starting in 1831 when Jacob Harshbarger and family with all his worldly goods came over the mountains, rivers and through the woods from Roanoke, VA to settle in Montgomery County. My mother, Willette Baldwin was part of that family. She was born in 1875, daughter of Susan Alice Myers and Francis Wildey Baldwin, granddaughter of Lydia Harshbarger who came to Indiana in 1831 when she was 15 years old. Since that family's history is well-documented I am going to tell you a little about my father's family.

My grandfather Dr. John Badger Wilson was born in Kentucky in 1830. He was graduated from Rush Medical College of Chicago, and of the College of Physicians and Surgeons of Cincinnati, and held an Honorary Diploma from Indiana Medical College of Indianapolis. In 1860 he married Mary Young, daughter of the first president of Butler College, then called Northwestern Christian College. Of this union were born six children: Gertrude, Lillian, Harvey (my father), Henry, Warren and Allie. In 1870, he moved his family to Ladoga to the big house next to the Opera House on Main Street. In 1879, when my father was 11 years old, his mother who was a singer, rode in an open sleigh dressed in formal clothes wearing a cloak to give a concert in Crawfordsville. She took pneumonia and died at the age of 37. Fortunately for that family, Dr. Wilson married again in 1883 to a wonderful lady — Emma Garrett, a teacher and later principal at

Ladoga Normal, loved by all and especially her step-children. She brought leadership and order into their lives and home.

My mother, Willette Baldwin, a country girl, at age 20 knew who she wanted to marry. He was Harvey Badger Wilson, the doctor's son who had graduated from the Danville Normal, and worked in the grocery and Pharmacy both in which his father held a partnership. He would take the train to New York to see shows. She liked his style! She asked him if he would like to marry her and he said, "Yes." They were married in 1896 and started living in luxury in a beautifully furnished home while the owners were on a six-months vacation. But her life was soon to change. My father bought a five-room house on an acre of land one-half mile west of Ladoga on Road 234. My father had told her he wanted no crying babies in his house. Their union produced seven children: Ronald Baldwin, Chester Harold, Frank Arthur, Pauline, Norma, John Badger and Mary Alice. Dad learned with Ronald that babies only cry when trying to talk, hungry or uncomfortable. We were active in the Presbyterian church and started our education there in Ladoga. Dad bought a grocery store in Crawfordsville and we moved there in 1915.

In 1936, I married Edgar G. Parker of Conneaut, OH. We have one child, Richard Wilson Parker, born in 1943, Cleveland, OH. He is a graduate of Redlands University, Redlands, CA and the University of Northwestern School of Law, Chicago. He is now (1989) General Senior Attorney of the Norfolk-Southern Corporation, Norfolk, VA and lives in Virginia Beach, with his wife (Carol Kratt of Lorain, OH) and their three children: Brian Jeffrey, Lauren Michelle and Lisa Christine. All three children are in independent schools in Virginia Beach. *Submitted by Pauline (Wilson) Parker*

CHARLES AND ANNA (COWAN) HARSHBARGER

Charles Henry Harshbarger and Anna Belle Cowan were raised near 500 North - 400 West, in North Union Township, Montgomery County.

Charles (Aug. 23, 1861 to June 30, 1936) was the son of Abraham (1832-1920) and Lydia Boraker (1831-1864) and his sisters were: Sarah, Ann and Mary Elizabeth and brother Daniel.

Anna Belle (June 27, 1872-Aug. 23, 1950) was the daughter of David Rice and Miranda (Williams) Cowan. Her brothers were Edward and George and sisters Minnie and Della. They both attended common school at 600 North, "Cowan Corner." Anna taught classes at the school located at 360 West - 750 North before her marriage.

They were married Oct. 1, 1891 and lived at the Harshbarger home place. Charles was a farmer and livestock breeder, proud of his Angus stock. Their children were Grover, Lydia Mae (Mrs. Leland Olin), Lloyd, Charles Ralph and Ethel Marie (Mrs. Edward Patton).

The great, great, grandfather Christian Hirschberger was born in Epstein, Bavaria, Germany. A certified taylor, he came to Philadelphia in 1749, married Caroline Funk and lived with his children, Christian II, Daniel, Barbara, Abraham, Henry, Anna, Maria, Elizabeth and Susanna in the Shenandoah Valley, VA before coming to Montgomery County in 1822.

Christian II married Susanna Boraker in 1803; their children were Michael, Barbara, born in Douglas Co., IL and Isaac (Charles' grandfather), Samuel, David, Elizabeth and Christopher, born in Champaign Co., OH. Christian filed for 70 acres of wilderness land in 1823 and brought his family to Wayne Township, north of Sugar Creek in Montgomery County.

Charles and Anna Belle (Cowan) Harshbarger

Isaac (1814-1855) married Sarah Crouch in 1830. They owned 117 acres in northeast Wayne Township. Their children were Christopher, Abraham (Charles' father), James, Elizabeth and Susan.

Isaac's descendents living now on the Harshbarger farms are Helen Olin Langworthy, Mrs. Lloyd Harshbarger and the Roger Harshbarger family.

The Harshbarger history records explains the name as Hirschberger. "Hirsh" means deer, "Berg" means mountain. The people living near the Deermountain in the Alps, at Basle, Switzerland were Hirschbergers.

When they came to America, the colony records spelled it Hershberger then later, in Indiana, it was changed to Harshbarger.

They were preeminently an agricultural family professed Christians. The older members were of Dunkard faith and many came to America as church groups in exile, homeless and penniless.

They had patience and perseverance and in the end more than realized their expectations. *Submitted by Wilberta Olin*

JOHN HART

John Hart was born Mar. 15, 1799 in Pompey, Onondaga Co., NY. He was the son of Deacon Ezra Hart and his wife Polly, and grandson of Joseph Hart, Jr. and his wife Ann Barnes.

John Hart was married on Oct. 12, 1823 to Belinda Brewer. She was born Nov. 8, 1801, the daughter of Jonas Brewer and his wife Belinda Orton of Tyringham, MA, and granddaughter of Colonel Josiah Brewer.

John Hart was an expert mill wright and mill mechanic. While living in upstate New York, he built over 12 water-powered grist mills. In 1832, John Hart moved his family to Newark, OH, where he built a large distillery and a grist mill. In 1835, he moved his family to Dubois Co., IN, where he built a grist mill in Jasper. In 1838, the family moved again and settled in Crawfordsville, Montgomery Co., IN. John constructed a distillery in Crawfordsville and built two water-powered grist mills on Sugar Creek. In the early 1840's, the family moved to Hillsboro, Montgomery Co., IL, and by 1844, the Hart's were living in Washington Co., IA. John Hart died in 1857 in Marion Co., IA, and his wife, Belinda, died in 1882 at her son's home, Jonas D. Hart, in Nodaway, Adams Co., IA.

The children of John and Belinda Brewer Hart were:

1. Jonas Derrell, born Feb. 5, 1827 in Onondaga Co., NY. He went to California in 1849 to pan for gold. On May 9, 1854, he married Lucy Ann Walker in Washington Co., IA. During the Civil War, he served in the 29th Iowa Volunteer Infantry and was later commissioned a Second Lieutenant in Company I, 54th U.S. Cavalry. He owned a large farm near Nodaway, Adams Co., IA. He died June 13, 1813 in Wheatland, WY and is buried in Nodaway, IA. Lucy Ann Walker Hart died in Nodaway, IA Aug. 6, 1906. Jonas D. and his wife Lucy Ann are the 2nd great grandparents of the author of this sketch.

2. Daniel D., born in 1825 in Onondaga Co., NY, married Susan Lelay.

3. Mary Ann, born in 1837 in Dubois Co., IN, married Jacob Koder, Jr.

4. Ezra, born in Montgomery Co., IL, married Emily Fleming Walker. *Submitted by Susan Hart Houk*

F. WALTER AND NELLIE (WILLIAMSON) HARVEY

F. Walter Harvey (b. Jan. 19, 1872, d. Oct. 24, 1931) and Nellie Williamson (b. May 6, 1872, d. Mar. 29, 1971), were married in Waynetown, IN on Mar. 1, 1893. They lived on the family farm, west of Waynetown. He was the son of Joseph Harvey and Sarah Dwiggins Harvey, who homesteaded 240 acres. This land was divided at Joseph's death among his three living sons.

Walter's siblings were, Mary E., who married Thomas Young; Sarah E., who married Faunce Sumner; Martha, who married William Zuck; Albert who died in infancy; Houston, who married Laura Small; Carl Burton, who married Lula Small; Carrie, who married Charles Owen; and Maude, who died at the age of eight.

Walter and Nellie Harvey

Nellie was the daughter of Erusmus and Esther Ball Williamson; granddaughter of Lucinda Welch and Zopher Ball. Zopher's ancestors came from England to Lancaster, VA in the 1600's. Erasmus fought in the Civil War.

Nellie's siblings were Isabelle, who married James Beam; Melissa, who married Rolla Martin; Thomas, who served in the Civil War and died soon after; Asa, who married Mary Livengood; Fannie, who married Nathan Coberly, and Maroah, who married Thomas Hartsock.

Walter and Nellie had five children. Maude E. (b. Dec. 26, 1893, d. Aug. 6, 1989) who married Maurice Riekeberg (d. 1970); Frank L. (b. Sept. 1, 1897), who married Ursa Fowler; they have two children, Margaret Henthorn and Donald Harvey; three grandchildren and eight great grandchildren. Mary S. (b. Feb. 24, 1900), who married Errett Rivers (d. 1972), and have three sons, Charles, Allan, and Jack; nine grandchildren, and eight great grandchildren; Doris (b. Aug. 24, 1903), who married Maurice Horn, and have one daughter, Mary

Lou Delaney; four grandchildren, and three great grandchildren; Alice (b. May 26, 1907), married Warner Chesterson (d. Aug. 4, 1975), and have two children, Rosemary Barrett and Walter Chesterson; 11 grandchildren, and 12 great grandchildren.

Walter's grandfather, Henderson Harvey Jr., married Sarah Rinker. She was the daughter of George Rinker, the youngest of three sons of Jacob and Catherine Rinker. The Rinkers came from Zurich, Switzerland to America in 1725 and are buried in the Rinker Cemetery in Conicville, VA.

The three Rinker sons were officers in the Revolutionary War. George was given a sword by George Washington for his services. This sword has been passed through generations ever since.

Joseph McConnell Harvey, who served in the Civil War, received the sword. George Harvey, son of Burton Harvey, received it after W.W.I. Charles Zuck Jr. is in possession of it now. Charles served in W.W.II, was wounded and a prisoner of war.

Frank Harvey died Feb. 16, 1989.

MARY BANNON HARVEY

Mary Bannon Harvey was the youngest of seven children born to Frank Andrew Bannon and Rose Etta Barker Bannon. She grew up in Parke County near Turkey Run State Park. She married Loyd Harvey of Tangier and they lived in Parke County until 1976. At that time they retired from farming and moved to Crawfordsville. She was widowed in 1984. They have one daughter Sharon Stryker (Mrs. Phillip). Mary is a member of Estabrook Chapter of Daughters of American Revolution, Daughters of War of 1812, and the Daughters of Union Veterans of the Civil War.

Frank Bannon was born 1857 in Randolph Co., IN, the son of John C. and Sarah Bell Bannon. Sara Bell was the daughter of George Bell and Jane Bell. They were believed to have come from central Pennsylvania to Drake Co., OH. Sarah Bannon died in 1861 and is buried in the Bannon family plot near Deerfield in Randolph County along with her mother and father-in-law and an infant child. John C. and his two children joined his brothers in Montgomery County. In 1863 he joined the B Company, 120th Regiment of the Indiana Volunteers at Crawfordsville. He died in service of his country in the Civil War in January 1865. He is buried at Liberty Cemetery. Montgomery County Courts awarded guardianship of Frank and his sister Martha Belle to their uncle, Lewis Bannon, who had moved to Montgomery County in 1845. Reverend Lewis Bannon was a pioneer circuit rider minister and one of the founders of Center Church and Liberty Church in Montgomery County. Reverend Bannon lived to be 101 years old.

John C. and Lewis Bannon were two of 11 children born to Michael and Nancy Clark Bannon. Other children were Jeremiah, Elizabeth, Anna, Rebecca, Nancy, James, Michael, Cora and Will. Early in life they were bricklayers in Darke Co., OH. Both were born in Warren County near Kings Mills, OH.

Michael Bannon was born in Pennsylvania and is believed to be the son of an Irish immigrant from Tipperary Ireland. He had deep religious convictions. An excellent marksman, he often won many shooting contests with both pioneer families and local Indians. He had established a reputation as a talented gunsmith. He was respected as an honest person. Farmers selling livestock in Cincinnati would trust him with their money to keep from losing it to gambling, women, or drinking. He enlisted as a private in Mills Militia from Ohio in the War of 1812 from Warren Co., OH. He served as Chaplain and played the fife during the war. He married Nancy Clark in 1812 at Warren County. Nancy was born in Maryland. Her father was John Clark who served in the 1st Maryland Rifles Division during the Revolutionary War. He moved his family to Ohio where he had a small farm and was a minister near Kings Mills.

HAUK FAMILY

Philip Hauk was born in Holland. He came to America about 1790 with a brother to Pennsylvania. He married Catherine Stonebraker. They were the parents of ten children. Philip II was born Aug. 23, 1807. The family then moved to Butler Co., OH when he was one year old in 1808.

Philip II married Sarah Baldwin, June 25, 1831. He was 24 and she was 17. She was an Aunt to Elias Jackson Baldwin also known as Lucky Baldwin. Lucky Baldwin settled in San Francisco where he began buying property, running a brick yard, bought gold mining stock and became a millionaire. He owned oil developments at Long Beach, founded the towns of Monrovia, Arcadia, Duarte and the town of Baldwin Park named for him. He also founded Santa Anita Race Track. He built the home where "Fantasy Island" the "TV Show" are filmed.

In the spring of 1828 Philip II and nine other men, among them Daniel Vaughn, Adam Miller, John Blankenship, Allen Moore, and five others started westward to look for new homes. They went as far as Chicago, then came back by way of Shawnee Mound, where Indians yet remained. There was much timber there, that being one great thing to look for in those early days for which they could build their cabins and other buildings. They liked it better around Crawfordsville so decided to locate there.

The William Moore family has the old sheepskin patent issued by the U.S. Government and signed by Andrew Jackson.

Philip II and Sarah had six children. Daniel, Absalom, and Katherine were born in Butler Co., OH. Margaret, Marion and Amanda were born in the northeast corner of Wayne Township, Montgomery Co., IN, where the family had moved in February, 1839.

Philip II was a farmer and cabinet maker by trade and also the community casket maker. The story goes that when he saw someone coming down the road carrying a stick, Philip knew someone had died. The stick was the measurement of the body.

Daniel Hauk married Missouri Tracy, Mar. 8, 1859, at Waynetown, IN. Their children were Anna Elizabeth, Absalom Arthur and Sarah Catherine. Anna Elizabeth Hauk married Edward Thurman Broaders. Their children were Claude, Gladys, Irvin, Sarah Ella, Bonnie Marie, Ethel Ann and Carl.

Absalom Arthur Hauk married Emma Josephine Moore. To this union was born Ethel Hauk (Steiner) and Emmett Irl Hauk. Emma died when "Irl" was ten days old. He was reared in the homes of the grandparents and an uncle, William Moore. Absalom then married Elizabeth Watson. To this union was born Martha Ida Hauk and George Hauk.

Emmett Irl Hauk married Cecile Irene Hayes Oct. 27, 1917. To this union was born four children: Herbert Allen Hauk, Lucretia J. Hauk (Himes), Hazel Hauk (Upham), and Viola May Hauk (Wolf).

Herbert married Audrey F. Shouse. Five children were born to this union. Julia Hauk (Morris), Betty Jo Hauk (Townsend), Patricia Hauk (Stultz), John Charles Hauk and Teresa Hauk.

Lucretia J. Hauk married Leonard Himes. To this union was born Mark Irl Himes.

Hazel M. Hauk married John Upham. To this union was born Pamela Upham (Smith) and William Upham.

Viola M. Hauk married Kenneth D. Wolf. To this union was born Richard D. Wolf, Suzanne Marie Wolf (Williams) and Barbara May Wolf (Maxwell). *Submitted by Bill Boone*

MARSHALL AND EDITH (ELMORE) HAUSER

Marshall E. and Edith L. Elmore Hauser have lived in Montgomery County most of their married life. Marshall was born Sept. 13, 1912 at Paris, IL to Clinton W. and Dora E. Tresner Hauser. He has two sisters, Waneita Carrington and Marjorie Reedy. He graduated from Green Township H.S., Parke Co., IN. The earliest information on the Hauser Family is in Colmar, Alsace, France. From there the family moved to Riquewihr, then to England where they came to the United States, landing on Sept. 30, 1727 on the ship "Molly." The ship anchored at Philadelphia, carrying 70 families of the Rhineland. Among them was the Martin Hauser family. From there, Martin and his wife, Maria Margaretha Schaefer Hauser and family moved to North Carolina. From North Carolina some of their descendants moved to southern Indiana. Here Clinton W. Hauser was born on Apr. 2, 1881 to Albert M. and Clara (Holly) Hauser. He married Dora E. Tresner (born Aug. 26, 1886) in Illinois.

Wm., Marshall, Edith, Ernest and Edward Hauser

Edith L. Elmore Hauser (born Mar. 13, 1918) is one of five children born to Albert Murray (born Sept. 20, 1889, died May 13, 1966) and Lula Matilda Seit Elmore (born Apr. 27, 1892, died Aug. 28, 1930). Her brothers and sisters are: James B. (born Sept. 10, 1910), Margaret A. (born June 2, 1913), Lemoyne (born Mar. 29, 1915, died Feb. 2, 1978); Ethel M. (born Mar. 13, 1918) and is the twin to Edith. All the Elmores graduated from Alamo High School.

Edith and Marshall were married on Dec. 3, 1938 in Crawfordsville. They have three sons: William A. (born June 30, 1942) is a graduate of Ladoga High School and is a switching equipment technician for Indiana Bell Telephone Company. He married Louise Hensley (born Dec. 18, 1947). They have two children: Thomas W. (born Oct. 22, 1966) graduated from Southmont High School and Wabash College, receiving an AB degree in Religion. He is currently serving in the U.S. Army. He married (Aug. 10, 1985) Janee Johnson (born Jan. 8, 1965). They have one daughter, Heather Marie (born Jan. 20, 1989) at Columbus, GA. Lisa L., daughter of William and Louise, was born June 10,

1969. She also graduated from Southmont. She is attending PJ's Beauty College at Crawfordsville.

Edward E., second son of Marshall and Edith was born Sept. 21, 1951 and is also a graduate of Ladoga High School. He is an accountant and is self-employed.

Ernest C., third son of Marshall and Edith was born Dec. 5, 1953, graduated from Southmont and received his BS (cum-laude) in Geology from Indiana State University. In 1978, he received his MS degree in geology from the University of Wisconsin, Madison, doing his thesis research on the geology of Spitsburgen, an Island north of Norway. His PhD work was a continuation of his MS thesis. During the winter term of 1981, he was a visiting instructor of geology at Carlton College, Northfield, MN. Currently, he is a post-doctoral Research Assistant at the Department of Geological Science, Cornell University, Ithaca, NY. *Submitted by Edith Elmore Hauser*

HOMER WALTER HAYES

William Washington Hayes born July 19, 1844 in Iredell Co., NC, married Elizabeth Jane Grissom Sept. 29, 1877. Elizabeth born July 21, 1858. She died Jan. 28, 1923. William died Feb. 23, 1937. They were the parents of ten children.

Homer Walter Hayes born Aug. 25, 1881—died Aug. 2, 1951; Perrie Lee Hayes born Apr. 15, 1883—died June 30, 1924; Frances Cordelia Hayes born July 3, 1886—died age three; Versa Olive Hayes born June 30, 1887—died Feb. 19, 1976; Sadie Emma Hayes born Aug. 21, 1890—died Jan. 15, 1984; Estella Mae Hayes born Aug. 13, 1893—died young; Gertrude Augusta Hayes born July 19, 1895—Jan. 10, 1986; Letha Pearl Hayes born July 29, 1899—died Jan. 30, 1933; Johnny Irvin Hayes born and died young; infant boy died.

My father was Homer Walter Hayes. He married Feb. 12, 1908 to Ethel Blanche Peterson. Her parents were Albert K. Peterson and Maud (Martin) Peterson from Darlington, IN. Albert born May 16, 1860—died Oct. 29, 1948. Maud born Dec. 7, 1861—died Jan. 14, 1949.

Paul Hayes, Homer Hayes, Ethel Hayes, Blanche Hayes Helmberger, Frances Hayes Whalin, Harold Hayes, Phyllis Hayes Linn - Dec. 24, 1950

Homer lived on a farm east of Whitesville. He raised hogs, did grain farming, had small dairy herd, livestock hauler, chickens, and misc. trucking.

Five children: 1. Frances Louise Hayes born Nov. 29, 1908, married Thomas Mayborn Whalin Mar. 24, 1934. He was born Jan. 22, 1900—died Nov. 19, 1975. Frances worked at Lilly-Varnish Co. 45 years in Indianapolis before retiring. 2. Paul Robert Hayes born June 10, 1911—died Feb. 4, 1980, married Helen Louise Coons Feb. 17, 1940. Lived on a farm near his parents. Had two children, Robert Coons Hayes born Nov. 18, 1943 and Rebecca Louise born June 16, 1948. Have four grandchildren and two great-grandchildren. 3. Blanche Naomi Hayes born Feb. 10, 1914, married Thomas Calvin Benson Mar. 12, 1932, married Marvin Michael Helmberger May 29, 1948. He was born Oct. 14, 1915—died Jan. 24, 1983. Parents of Calvin Raphiel Benson and Nancy Ellen Helmberger. Have six grandchildren, and three great-grandchildren. Live on farm southeast of Crawfordsville. Grain farm and hogs. 4. Harold Eugene Hayes married Ruby L. Lindamood Dec. 24, 1941. Ruby born Mar. 15, 1924. Parents of three daughters; Jane Susan born Dec. 9, 1946—died Feb. 12, 1949, Marsha Ann born Jan. 14, 1950 and Debra Jeanne born June 19, 1951. Have three grandchildren. Harold worked at RR Donnellys & Sons, retired April 1983. Married Edith Ann Andrews Dec. 10, 1970. Born Apr. 16, 1916. Employed at Donnellys and retired. Now reside in Crawfordsville. 5. Phyllis Irene born Aug. 18, 1928, married Raymond Gene Linn June 5, 1948. Raymond born June 12, 1924. Live on a farm west of New Ross. She graduated from New Ross High School, member of New Ross Christian Church and New Ross Extension Club. Parents of four children, Jeffrey Lee born June 28, 1950, Janis Marie born Sept. 14, 1951, Cheryl Ann born July 14, 1956 and Richard Gene born Feb. 6, 1960. Have eight grandchildren. *Prepared by Phyllis Hayes Linn*

WILLIAM HARRISON HAYS, JR.

William Harrison Hays, Jr. was born in Indianapolis, IN, Dec. 11, 1915 and resided in Sullivan, IN during his childhood. He attended Junior High and High School in Riverdale, the Bronx, NY. Undergraduate work was completed in 1937 at Wabash College, Crawfordsville. He graduated in 1940 from Yale University's Law School. He has resided in Crawfordsville since 1956, where he served as Mayor from 1964 through 1971. Will's father, William Harrison Hays, Sr., was from Sullivan, IN, and never resided in Crawfordsville except as a Wabash College Student (class of 1900). He was born 1879, died 1954. His parents were John T. Hays, born 1845 in Pennsylvania, died 1918, Sullivan, IN; wife, Mary (Cain) Hays, born 1851, died 1918 in Sullivan.

Will's mother, Helen (Thomas) Hays is still remembered by many in Crawfordsville. She was born Oct. 7, 1879 and died Dec. 12, 1957. Her parents were Crawfordsville natives, Albert Duy Thomas (1841-1925) and Ruth (Vance) Thomas (1855-1888).

Will Hays, Sr. and Helen Thomas were married Nov. 18, 1902 in Crawfordsville.

Will, Jr. married Virginia Henderson, originally of Robinson, IL, who was born Mar. 7, 1922. The Hays' children are; Mary Katherine Hays, born Sept. 6, 1943; William Harrison Hays, III, born Oct. 3, 1944 and Amelia Hope Hays, born Aug. 18, 1964.

Much has been written about Will "Bill" Hays, Jr., but Diane Lyons (*Montgomery County Magazine*, December 1985), sums-up his life perfectly: "Bill Hays, Jr. is comfortable with anyone from anywhere. His supreme disposition and compassion for others have made him a favorite friend to those who know him well."

ESTELLE HEETER

Louise "Estelle" Heeter was born Aug. 8, 1903 to Esta Ezra and Donna Gertrude Wachter Heeter in Huntington, IN. Shortly thereafter, Esta received his appointment as a railway mail clerk on the Pennsylvania railway between Pittsburgh and Chicago.

Esta with four brothers and five sisters was reared on a farm within walking distance of Manchester College. His father, Silas Heeter, was a farmer. His mother was Louisa West from Kentucky.

Donna Gertrude Wachter Heeter's parents were Dr. Leander and Elizabeth Anders Wachter from Frederick Co., MD. She had two brothers and three sisters.

In 1901, Bernice Elizabeth Heeter was born to Esta and Donna. Both she and Estelle graduated from Warsaw High School. Bernice majored in language at Otterbein College.

Estella Heeter and Col. Sanders

Estelle attended Manchester College. In 1932, she received a Bachelors degree from Indiana University with majors in math and English. In 1938, she received a Master's degree in math from Columbia University. She received a National Science Foundation Scholarship to study the New Math at Colgate University in the summer sessions of 1960 and 1961.

She taught elementary in Bristol and Wabash, IN, as well as Willson, Mills, Crawfordsville Junior-Senior High School and Tuttle Junior High in Crawfordsville. While on a year leave of absence in 1949, she taught math and English at Bob Jones University.

In 1979, she received the Senior Citizen of the Year Award given by Colonel Sanders. She and her guest, Mary Schlemmer, were the Colonel's guests at the honors luncheon at the Marriot Inn in Indianapolis. They were taken there in a 1978 Cadillac from their homes. A great day!

Her first year in Crawfordsville, Estelle joined the Crawfordsville Branch of the American Association of University Women and its Study Group of Creative Writers. In 1982, she published her original poems in a paperback *Sense and Nonsense*.

In 1987, Earl Elliot, President of the Montgomery Savings and Loan, bought the copyright for copies to sell for the Disabilities Drive. Later that year, she published *Sense and Nonsense, Vol. II*, all new original poems.

She is now chairman of the Creative Writer's Study group.

While in Greenville, SC, she gave a radio broadcast on story writing and one on writing poetry.

She has given programs of her original poems to the Rotarians, Kiwanians, Montgomery County Retired Teachers and Tuttle English students.

Since coming to Crawfordsville in 1932, Estelle has been active in Christ's U.M. Church as teacher of junior boys and adults. She attended Union Theological Seminary for three summer sessions, the last of which was on a Danforth Scholarship.

Estelle highly recommends Crawfordsville as one's hometown! *Submitted by Estelle Heeter*

CHARLES AND CLYDIA HEINEN

Charles and Clydia Heinen moved to Waveland in the summer of 1925 from Indianapolis. He was the seventh of eight children born to Peter and Savilla Marie Baum. Peter was born in Germany and she a Pennsylvania Dutch.

Charles was born Aug. 29, 1886 in Lafayette, where he grew and attended school. He was a tool and die maker by trade, working at Ross Gear.

Clydia Fletcher was born in Russellville, IN, to Henry and Ida McQuowan. He ran a livery stable. Their daughter went to school in Russellville, Waveland and graduated from Ladoga in 1907. She was a clerk in a department store in Lafayette.

Charles and Clydia, Mary Jane, Marjorie, Anita

They were married Feb. 10, 1914, at Lafayette. They moved to Indianapolis where he worked for Pennsylvania Railroad.

There were five children born to this union: Mary Jane, Marjorie (Dude), Anita (Mickey), Robert who lived 11 hrs., and Mildred who died of pneumonia at age 11 months.

In the summer of 1925 they moved to the Andy and Lanilla Miles home north of Waveland. He started a garage in the John Bayless building at Browns Valley. There a few years before moving in with O.K. Galloway in Waveland. O.K. had Plymouth and Dodge dealerships. Few years later he moved to Crawfordsville and Charley moved to Bert Upton building on the corner of N. Cross and Green Street. There was a forge and he had garage and Shell Oil and gas. His daughter Dude helped him.

The girls enrolled in school and Bert Hallett was their school bus driver. All graduated from Waveland High.

Mary Jane married Leonard Cobert who drove Danville-Turkey Run bus. They had two daughters, Virginia (Mrs. Robert Johnston) and Evelyn (Mrs. James Tibbs). They moved to Danville then on to Indianapolis.

Marjorie married Cecil N. Davis from Mecca. He quit school after eighth grade to help support his family in the tile factory, from there he joined C.C.C. and was sent to Bakersfield, CA–to Shades Camp in 1935. He started cooking at Shades Park Inn, then Cleveland Bakery; B & G Cafe in Crawfordsville before starting at Alcoa Aluminum in 1942, retiring in 1972. There were three children born, Charles, Roy and Clydia Mae.

Charles was married, has two children, Melissa Jane (Mrs. Calvin Hubble) and Bryan a senior in high school. Charles works at Russellville Stone Quarry, also has two grandchildren, Megan and Justin.

Roy married Janie Carson of Tangier and has three daughters, Jennifer, Susanne and Cassandra. He is an accountant and lives in Pittsboro.

Clydia Mae married David L. Kennedy of Miami, FL and live in Crawfordsville. They have two sons David N., a student at Ball State and Kristopher a student of Hoover. She works at California Pellett.

Anita married James W. Haskett. He served in World War II and was wounded in Acton, Germany. He died in 1970.

Charley retired after working for Mormon Herrington during World War II at Crawfordsville. She died in 1960, he in 1976.

ALEXANDER HENDERSON

Alexander Henderson who was born in North Carolina Sept. 6, 1815 to Rebecca (Thomas) and James Henderson. There were seven other children: Mary, the oldest, was born in 1813; Zorada was born in 1817; Elizabeth was born in 1819; Gordon was born in 1821; and the names, births and death dates of the others are not known. When Alexander was a small boy, the family moved to Ohio and in 1828, they moved to Indiana to a farm east of Yountsville. In 1830, Rebecca Henderson died and James later married a Miss Roy. To this union, a son Jack was born. The descendants of Alexander and his half brother, Jack are the only known living descendants of James Henderson. James is said to be buried in a cemetery near New Market, but exact whereabouts are unknown.

Alexander, at 14 years, was placed as a "bound boy" in the Edmond Nutt farm home located southeast of Yountsville, where he lived until 21 years old. On Oct. 11, 1838 in Parke County, he married Isabella Chapman, b. Dec. 31, 1819 in Butler Co., OH. At this time he had 120 acres of land, valued at $1.25 per acre and his wife had 80 acres of timberland. They lived in Parke County until 1855 when they sold the above land and bought 160 acres about two miles southeast of Waynetown. They lived on this farm until her death Sept. 9, 1898, which was two months, and two days before their 60th wedding anniversary. They were faithful members of Wesley Methodist Church; he was church steward for more than 20 years; he was also trustee of Wesley Academy when it was purchased by Wayne Township for use as a public school.

Alexander died Mar. 29, 1911 at the age of 95 years, six months and 23 days. They are buried in Wesley Cemetery and were the parents of five girls and five boys; seven of whom taught school: Elizabeth, b. 1839, d. 1973; William, b. 1841, d. 1896; Amanda, b. 1843, d. 1927; James T., b. 1846, d. 1905; Milton, b. 1847, d. 1920; Mary, b. 1849, d. 1943; Alice, b. 1851, d. 1937; Martha, b. 1854, d. 190?; John Chapman, b. 1856, d. 1937 and a son who died in infancy. All were born in Parke County, except John and the infant who died. They also raised a niece, Hannah Florence Chapman, who married Warren Bratton.

There were 36 grandchildren from Alexander and Isabella Henderson. Daisy (Hendricks) Fruits (see biography) and Cousin Floyd Henderson, b. Dec. 12, 1893 of Fargo, ND are the only ones surviving.

CLYDE AND MARTHA HENDRICKSON

Clyde Beaumont Hendrickson and Martha Blanche White were married Aug. 18, 1937 at Centerburg, OH.

They came to Indiana in 1957.

Clyde was born Aug. 13, 1914 at Kansas City, KS, to Clyde Lewis Hendrickson and Anna Pearl Hovey Hendrickson. Martha was born Aug. 20, 1918 at Galeski, OH to John Henry White and Blanche Gertrude Taylor White.

They had nine children: Sylvia, born 1938; Michael, born 1940; Judy, born 1941; Anne, born 1943; Nancy, born 1944; Jack, born 1947; Gaye, born 1950; Pam, born 1955; and Christy, born 1957. Sylvia went to be with the Lord in 1963.

Clyde and Martha have 27 grandchildren and 21 great-grandchildren.

Clyde retired after plastering for 50 years. He also is a veteran of WWII. Martha worked in the Darlington School Cafeteria for four years.

They are members of Darlington Congregational Christian Church.

MILDRED (LOUGH) HENTHORN

Mildred Lough grew up in Waynetown, but spent a few years in Hilltop where her family ran a restaurant. Mildred is the daughter of Wilbur L. and Lola Viola (Wyant) Lough and the fourth of five daughters, all having names beginning with the letter M. Besides Mildred, there was: Mae, Martha, Mary and Mamie.

Mildred's best memory of her six foot, 200 pound brown-haired, blue-eyed father is the time he brought home a huge catch of fish from the Narrows. Wilbur Lough had a hay-baling crew and was also a scrap dealer. He was born Aug. 9, 1880 near Frankfort, the son of Elijah and Harriet (Whittelberry) Lough. He married Lola Viola Wyant Christmas Eve 1907 in Frankfort. Lola, too, was born near Frankfort (in Michigantown) Feb. 9, 1888, the daughter of Abraham and Mary (Earlywine) Wyant. She, too, had brown hair and blue eyes. Soon after their marriage, they moved to the Waynetown area where they lived out the majority of their lives. He died Mar. 5, 1943—Lola died Apr. 15, 1959. They are buried at Waynetown Masonic Cemetery.

Mildred was born Apr. 29, 1917 and graduated from Waynetown High School. Soon after, she married Albert C. Henthorn. She was dressed in her blue silk graduation dress and he in a suit. The ceremony took place at the Tremaine Parsonage June 3, 1935 with friends and relatives attending. The reception consisted of a decorated wedding cake made by her mother and ice cream. They were shivareed by Albert's friends, Willis Schenck and Frank Bunnell. As the newlyweds left Waynetown for a honeymoon to Cincinnati, OH, friends and relatives chased them out of town.

Albert Henthorn was born July 6, 1913 at Waynetown, the son of Edgar L. and Alta (French) Henthorn. He graduated from Waynetown in 1932. He was an auctioneer for 40 years crying sales throughout west central Indiana. He also owned the Albert Henthorn Insurance Agency for more than a quarter of a century. His father, son of William and Lucy Belle (Moore) Henthorn was born Aug. 18, 1887 near Danville, IL. He served as a mail carrier for more than 30 years. He was a 50-year member of Masons at his death on Apr. 23, 1979. Alta French was born Oct. 31, 1894 East of Veedersburg, the daughter of Thomas and Nancy (Redden) French. Edgar and Alta were married Aug. 7, 1912. Both were charter members of the Waynetown Eastern Star. They are also buried in Waynetown Masonic Cemetery, as is Albert, who died May 31,

1980, just two days before he and Mildred would have enjoyed their 45th wedding anniversary.

Mildred and Albert had three children: C. Rex, Thomas J., and Rita (who married Lee Kirkpatrick). Mildred has five grandsons and two granddaughters. Mildred is currently a resident of Williamsburg Health Care where she enjoys visits from relatives and friends and where she takes part in the home's activities. *Submitted by Karen Zach (via information from Mildred Henthorn)*

DR. MILTON HERNDON

Milton Herndon M.D. born in Kentucky at Georgetown Sept. 20, 1801 died here June 3, 1872 and was buried in the I.O.O.F. Cemetery. He married Elizabeth Noble Lindsey Oct. 18, 1826, moved to Montgomery County in 1834. Children: John Lindsey (1827-1858), Richard (infant 1829), Rebecca (Dec. 31, 1829-Sept. 18, 1867), infant (June 11, 1831), Cinchona (Aug. 21, 1832-?), Louisa Indiana (Apr. 1, 1835-Oct. 5, 1839), Joseph Foster (Nov. 12, 1837-Mar. 5, 1843), Louisa Maria (1840-1916), Samuel Henry (1841-1865), Emma ·1844-1873), William (June 7, 1848-May 28, 1851), Pollet or Collet (no date). From another source is found son Daniel born in 1838 also. (The first 11 children were listed in an old family Bible.)

Dr. Milton Herndon Marker

Dr. Milton Herndon was a charter member of the I.O.O.F. lodge here: a noted member, for whom the lodge placed a special memorial stone, still standing, in the I.O.O.F. Cemetery. Tuberculosis hit the family, causing death for many of the family. It is thought that Dr. Milton might be a kinsman of Lincoln's law partner, William H. Herndon, but that relationship has not yet been verified.

As of March 1986, one living descendent of Dr. Herndon was contacted at West Plains, MO; Mr. Hall Thornburgh, a funeral director, born Oct. 13, 1902. Mr. Thornburgh (Dr. Milton's great-grandchild) comes through grandmother Louisa (Mrs. Samuel P. Thompson buried here at Oak Hill. His aunt Lillian Thompson (1880-1953), unmarried, an attorney, is buried, also, at Oak Hill. His mother, Kathrine (Mrs. Eli E. Thornburgh) was a twin to Betty (Thompson) (Green) Breaks—Alvin Breaks—of Crawfordsville—sons by her first husband, John, Joe and Lawrence Green.

Dr. Milton's oldest child, John Lindsey Herndon, was a cadet at the Kentucky Military Institute at Georgetown in 1846-48, a "Merit Roll" cadet. Also, he was a conductor on the Lafayette-Crawfordsville railroad till his death at 30 (T.B.) (I.O.O.F. Cemetery) (Wife, Mary E. Jennison, no issue).

Marriages: Rebecca (Mrs. Henry Sperry) Oct. 3, 1860; Cinchona (Mrs. Isaac N. Schooler) Dec. 31, 1858; Emma Rose (Mrs. William H. Ramey) Feb. 13, 1868. Samuel Henry Herndon, a Civil War corporal, was probably not married; a veteran's stone marks his grave at the I.O.O.F. Cemetery. John Lindsey and Mary E. Jennison were married Apr. 13, 1852. Though the daughters of Dr. Milton Herndon had issue, the name Herndon here passes out of his family. *Researched by Lawrence L. Vaughn Thompson*

ELEANOR AND REMLEY HERR

Remley Herr was born June 18, 1914, at Crawfordsville, IN, and died Dec. 14, 1984, in South Carolina. His parents were Sarah Remley and Shirl Herr who lived at 700 South Water Street, Crawfordsville.

Shirl Herr was born in Boone County, but his father, Benjamin Herr, as a young man owned a saw mill at the intersection of what is now US 231 and State Road 234. While there, he met and married Abigail Davis, a granddaughter of Abigail Hoel Davis who came to the county in the early 1820's.

Sarah Remley's parents were Ambrose and Minerva Shelby Remley. Ambrose's parents John and Sarah McCain Remley were pioneer settlers.

Eleanor and Remley Herr

Remley Herr was a graduate of Crawfordsville High School and Wabash College where he was a member of Kappa Sigma fraternity. He was a farmer most of his life and also worked for the Indiana Department of Revenue. He was active in civic affairs serving on the State PTA Board as Rural Service chairman, President of the Montgomery County Farm Bureau, and County Commissioner. He also represented the Republican party in a bid for the Indiana Senate. As a member of the Montgomery County Historical Board, he served as treasurer and chairman of the Historical Marker committee. Remley wrote many articles for the *Montgomery Magazine* on the Civil War, Indians and his pioneer ancestors.

On Dec. 4, 1937, Remley married Eleanor Hostetter at the home of her parents, Howard and Blanche Miller Hostetter, Bainbridge. In addition to graduating from Bainbridge High School, Eleanor is a graduate of DePauw University where she was a member of Delta Zeta Sorority.

Howard Hostetter's parents, David B. and Hettie Ann Harshbarger Hostetter were both born in southern Montgomery County. Blanche Miller Hostetter's parents, Caroline Crosby and Samuel Miller were descendents of pioneers who settled near Roachdale.

Eleanor taught at Alamo and Crawfordsville High School where she was chairman of the English Department. She is a member of the Art League and Current Events Club. She also belongs to several patriotic societies including Dorothy Q Chapter DAR; Daughters of the American Colonists where she served as State Regent and National Vice President of the Middle West Section; Daughters of Colonial Wars, serving as State Regent; Dames of the Court of Honor; Colonial Dames of the XVII Century and the Huguenot Society. In addition, she was on the original board for the Montgomery County Cultural Foundation.

The Herrs were active members of the Wabash Avenue Presbyterian Church serving in many areas including ruling elder. Their hobbies included traveling, especially to the Caribbean area, and research. Researching the Lincoln Black Hawk Indian War musket took them to Europe, New Orleans and local areas. In 1984 the musket and several relics which had belonged to Sarah Bush and Tom Lincoln were given to the Lincoln Boyhood National Memorial, Lincoln City, IN.

Eleanor and Remley Herr were parents of four daughters: Diana (Mrs. John Bennett), Crawfordsville; Nancy (Mrs. Dale Linvill), Clemson, SC; Sally of Portland, ME; and Cheryl (Mrs. Mark Rains), Alma, MI. They have ten grandchildren and one great grandson.

CHARLES AND JOANN HERRON

Charles Andrew Herron, son of Earl and Cora Coon Herron, was born in Crawfordsville, IN, Apr. 24, 1936. During his high school years at Waynetown he was a "Gladiator." He served in the army for two years after graduation with the rank of sergeant. On Oct. 5, 1957, he married JoAnn Ingalsbe in the Mellott Congregational-Christian Church and they have resided in Waynetown since.

JoAnn is the daughter of Lankford and Mildred Marie Dailey Ingalsbe. She was born in her grandfather Ingalsbe's home in Hope, IL, on Valentine's Day 1941. Her paternal grandparents were Adna and Carrie Ingalsbe; her maternal grandparents were James and Nellie Dailey. Her parents are retired farmers and moved to the Mellott area when JoAnn was in the first grade. She attended Richland Township School. She has worked for North Montgomery School System for 14 years and is food manager in North Ridge kitchen.

Charles Andrew, Jo Ann Ingalsbe Herron, Gary Scott, Brenda Sue, Charles Bradley

Charles was a member of the Waynetown Volunteer Fire Department for 26 years serving as chief for eight years. He also is active in other civic affairs having been on the Pool Board for five years and associated with summer Little League three years. He has been an employee of Boots' Brothers Company for 25 years and is manager of the Fuel and Food Mart at both Waynetown and Waveland.

Charles and JoAnn have three children. The oldest Charles Bradley, born July 28, 1960, graduated from North Montgomery High School; he was on the football and basketball teams. He is a member of Waynetown Volunteer Fire Department and employed with Cherry Grove Farm Bureau. He and Amber Byers, born Aug. 2, 1962, were married Oct.

19, 1985. She works at Crawford's Food Store in Crawfordsville. They live east of Waynetown. As a hobby Brad goes coon hunting.

Gary Scott, born June 8, 1962, graduated from North Montgomery High School; he was on the wrestling, track and football teams. He lives in Lafayette, IN, and works at Lafayette Instrument Company. He has a daughter Tiffany Dawn born July 1, 1985, and a son Jeremy Scott born Apr. 10, 1988. Scott has a great interest in tropical fish.

Brenda Sue, born Oct. 17, 1965, graduated from North Montgomery High School; she was president of the Honor Society, captain of Chargerettes and was a member of Sun Shine Society, Pom Pom Corps and Swing Choir. In 1985 she graduated from the Licensed Practical Nurse Training Program at Vincennes and is now employed at Williamsburg Health Care Center in Crawfordsville. She and Trevor Simpson, born Apr. 16, 1966, were married Sept. 19, 1987. He works at Donnelley's. They reside near Darlington, IN. *Submitted by Ruby Ralston*

JACK AND CAROL HERRON

Jackie Lee Herron was born to Earl and Cora Coon Herron Apr. 14, 1937. As a youth he attended Breaks Grade School in the Roberts Chapel neighborhood as did his father and each of Earl's siblings namely: Zetta married Jacob Bunnell who farmed near Elmdale; Vern married Doris Chesterson - he was a mechanic in Waynetown; twins Lawrence (married Josephine Kincade and both worked at Donnelley's) and Clarence, who also worked at Donnelley's (married Irene Slavens). Jack's family worshipped at Roberts Chapel Church, it also being the church of his father's family. When Roberts Chapel closed, Jack and his family became members of Liberty Chapel Church where his mother was a Sunday School teacher. Jack graduated from Waynetown High School; he was in band and played basketball.

Jack married Edith Ingalsbe and they had two sons. Kevin Lee, born Mar. 16, 1959, graduated from Fountain Central High School in 1977. He moved to Florida and on June 27, 1981, married Debra Coots, born Jan. 16, 1959. Their children are Kristopher Joel born Apr. 8, 1982, and Clarissa Joy born Dec. 1, 1984. In 1987 they moved from Florida locating south of Waynetown. Kevin works at Crawford Industries in Crawfordsville and Debbie at Kroger Company also in Crawfordsville.

Shadrick and Margaret Thompson Herron, Zetta, Vern and Earl

Kurtis Linn, born Nov. 12, 1961, graduated from Osceola High School, Kissimmee, FL in 1980; he was on the wrestling team. He lives in Nashville, TN, where he is studying music at Bellmount College. He has had one song published and recorded.

Jack later married Carol Edwards born Jan. 28, 1937, to Fred Linton and Mary Routh. They have a daughter Jill born Sept. 3, 1973. A student at North Montgomery High School she is active in Winter Guard and Band. While in the eighth grade Jill took first place with a piano solo she performed at Cincinnati Bible College; this earned her a scholarship to the College and a trophy. She has also performed at different area events at DePauw and Butler Universities taking first place in piano and vocal solo. She is a member of the Waynetown Christian Church and Youth Fellowship where her family worships.

Jack and Carol now live on part of the ground once owned by his grandparents, "Shade" and Margaret Herrin. Jack works at Crawford Industries in Crawfordsville and Carol at Donnelley's. Carol's other children are Elizabeth Edwards Vannice, Ralph Edwards, Patti Edwards Wray, Douglas Edwards and Amy Edwards. Amy is a graduate of North Montgomery High School and is attending Ball State University. Carol has seven grandchildren and four step-grandchildren. *Submitted by Ruby Herron Ralston*

WILLIAM AND MARGIE HERRON

William Shadrick Herron, oldest son of Earl "Shorty" and Cora Coon Herron, was born Oct. 21, 1934, at Smartsburg, IN. He graduated from Breaks Grade School and Waynetown High School. Atwood Smith, who taught Bill's father, also taught Bill and all of his siblings at Waynetown. Bill was active in various organizations in high school then graduated from Ball State at Muncie, IN, in 1956. He lived briefly in Downey, CA, where he was a postman then served two years in the Army as a specialist. He has been senior administrative assistant with Morris Plan for 28 years and is now a vice-president of Summit Bank in Indianapolis.

His paternal grandparents were Shadrick Henry and Margaret Frances Thompson Herrin. His paternal great-grandparents were William Andrew and Mary Elizabeth Proctor Herrin; she was the daughter of Willis Green Proctor and Mary Carson Proctor. His maternal grandparents were William Stephens Coon and Mary Catharine Koon Coon; his maternal great-grandparents were Isaac and Ruth Jane Stephens Coon and John Koon III and Mary Temple Koon.

William Shadrick and Margie Maria Ingram Herron

Margie Marie Ingram, born Apr. 16, 1941, also a native of Montgomery County is the daughter of Roy and Mildred Marie Hyten Ingram who farmed near Darlington, IN. Roy's parents were Ova and Minnie Farris Ingram. Mildred's parents were Tillman and Pearl Warbritton Hyten. Margie is controller at Marshall Building Specialties in Indianapolis. Bill and Margie were married in Young's Chapel Church Sept. 6, 1959, and have resided at Greenfield, IN most of their married life. They have two sons and two daughters.

Anthony Shadrick, born Apr. 24, 1960, who graduated from Ball State University where he was a member of Sigma Chi Fraternity, married Ellen Thomas of South Bend on Sept. 29, 1984. They live in Wheaton, IL, and have two children: Jessica Marie, born Oct. 4, 1985, and Thomas Anthony, born Feb. 9, 1988. Ellen is a registered nurse having taken her training at Purdue University. Tony is a Senior Benefit Insurance Consultant at Noble Lowndes in Chicago.

Tina Marie, born Dec. 29, 1961, was Worthy Adviser, Greenfield Assembly No. 16, International Order of Rainbow for Girls in 1980 and dedicated her term of service to her grandmother, Cora Coon Herron. She attended Ball State University, now lives in Indianapolis and has a daughter, Kellin Ann Marie, born Nov. 17, 1987.

Timothy William, born Aug. 3, 1964 served in the Active Marine Reserves, attended Ball State University and now lives in Painesville, OH, where he manages a shoe store.

Kimberlin Ann, born Mar. 3, 1969, graduated from Eastern Hancock High School as did her siblings. She was a member of Model United Nations Club for four years, Model State Legislature Club, Drama Club for four years, High School Credit Cadet Teacher and Office of Education Association. She earned the Outstanding Social Studies Award upon graduation. She is now in her sophomore year at Indiana University and is a member of Tri Sigma Sorority.

LAUREL AND MARY (LYONS) HERSHBERGER

Oasey "Laurel" Hershberger, son of Charles and Alice (Butts) Hershberger, was born Aug. 18, 1892 in Veedersburg, Fountain Co., IN. He attended Nebo School; teacher was Mr. Campbell. Oasey Laurel was a member of the United Brethren Church.

As a teenager, Laurel went with his mother's brother to Kansas to harvest fields. For entertainment, Laurel went to see "Guy Players" at Covington, IN. There he met a young telephone operator, Mary Permela Lyons, born Mar. 24, 1892 to William Joseph and Martha Bell (Miller) Lyons.

Laurel owned a buggy and "Dolly," the driving horse. He was learning the carpenter trade. Laurel and Mary were married June 4, 1912. They lived in a large two-story house in Veedersburg where Fauneil was born Apr. 19, 1913. The house burned July 10, 1913. Only Fauneil was saved by her mother. In the ashes, Laurel found his 13 silver dollars and bone china head to Mary's doll.

Laurel cleared the lot and built a new bungalow with a porch. Their last two children were born here: Luceil Iona on Nov. 20, 1914 and Dale, born Dec. 20, 1915, died Feb. 4, 1916.

Laurel raised Dapple Grey Arabian horses; raised hogs with veterinarian Dr. Warner Overfield and farmed for John Meeker. WWI came and it was decided Laurel should stay at the farm and supply meat. All his help went to serve in the war.

Laurel and Mary moved to Walter J. Haney Farm, west of Wingate, and east of Meharry Cemetery Corner 1959-1974. There was new ground to be cleared and more rental ground available. Fauneil and Luceil were educated at Wingate school; lived there 18 years. Banks were closed and there was a depression that caused starving families until hunger made one feel like stealing anything there was to steal. And, that man had to be admired for trying to save his family!

Laurel and Mary liked everything about New Richmond; they purchased property and land — hired a lot of school-aged boys and men to paint, plant, build and farm. All went to work. Laurel bought feeder cattle and sold them to markets.

Laurel served as President of the Town Board, aided the young school boys with a baseball diamond close to his house and helped the Lions' Club. He organized a riding horse club; set-up a show ring for horse shows; set-up an air-strip where planes could be seen or one could take a plane ride. The little lakes were stocked with fish for sport. There were truck patches to raise extra food. Laurel had a one-acre apple and peach orchard with a grape arbor long as the rows of trees — his pride and joy. He built a shelter house in his park of lakes for meetings and family reunions. Regardless of how bad the day was, Laurel always found something of humor. He loved the sunshine! Laurel and Mary traveled U.S.A., Canada and lived in Florida during winters. From 1959-1974, he fought skin cancer. Laurel and Mary were married 62 years, six months. They are buried in the New Richmond Cemetery, together!

Mary liked being at home for the July 4th celebration. Mary saw fit to let New Richmond have the park for baseball and any use for any special activities You can thank Laurel and Mary only — it was their choice — New Richmond has legal papers of ownership.

The Lyons and Hershberger Families can be found in the *1983 Fountain County History Book. Submitted by Fauneil Hershberger*

ALBERT HOWE HESTER

Albert Howe Hester was born Apr. 8, 1912 to the late William and Susan Branson Hester in Montgomery County. He had three brothers and two sisters. He attended school in Montgomery and Parke Counties.

Virginia Irene Crow was born May 27, 1919 to the late Frank and Julia Mangus Crow. She had one sister and four brothers. She attended school in Montgomery County.

November 4, 1936, Albert and Irene were married. They set up housekeeping on Albert's grandfather Branson's farm. After the farm sold Albert joined his father and two brothers in the carpentry business. They built many homes in Indiana, many still in use today. During W.W. II Albert worked in Lafayette at the Alcoa Plant. In 1947 he began farming again on his Uncle Tom "Linc" Hester's farm. Irene worked as a cook at New Market Schools from 1960-65. They're the parents of two sons.

Albert, Irene, Dale and Russell Hester

The first born, Albert Dale was born Jan. 9, 1939. Dale graduated from New Market High School in 1957. He then joined Albert farming. November 21, 1959, Dale married Nelda Joyce Bentley. Nelda currently serves as Montgomery County Auditor. Dale drives a school bus for South Montgomery School Corp. They're the parents of two children. Gaye Lynn was born Jan. 30, 1961 and graduated from Southmont in 1979. Gaye is employed as a computer programmer in Indianapolis at Resort Condominiums International. Gaye married Mark VanValkenburg Apr. 9, 1983. Mark owns a construction company, and built the home they reside in near Avon. They're expecting their first child July 1989. Timothy Dale was born Feb. 22, 1966 and graduated from Southmont 1984. Tim is employed at Pace Dairy and also frequently helps on the farm. Tim married Corinna Michelle Wolf June 3, 1989. They reside west of Parkersburg.

The second son born to Albert and Irene was Russell Max, born July 11, 1951. Russell graduated from New Market High School in 1969 and from Indiana Business College in 1971. After completing school Russell joined Albert and Dale in the family farming operation. He married Sallie Lou Simpson June 28, 1975. Russell also drives a school bus for South Montgomery School Corp. They're the parents of two sons, Brian Thomas, born Feb. 7, 1980 and Todd Alan, born Jan. 18, 1987.

Albert and Irene are members of the Parkersburg Christian Church where they've been members since 1948. Albert serves as deacon and trustee there. They reside in Lapland in a home built by Albert on the site of Irene's childhood home. Albert also built the homes both sons live in north of Parkersburg. Albert retired from actively farming in 1975 but still enjoys helping his sons farm. He also still enjoys a hammer or saw in his hands whenever possible. Albert and Irene enjoy their four grandchildren and are looking forward to the birth of their first great-grandchild.

DAVID OWEN AND ROSEMARY ANN (MILES) HESTER

David Owen Hester is the grandson of John and Ida (Kennedy) Hester who had 12 children. Their son Clarence and wife Glenna Owens Divers from Virginia lived mostly in Montgomery County, also in Fountain and Putnam Counties where Clarence was a farmer. They had six children: John, m. Betty Eggers, lives north of Wallace, IN, is a farmer and school bus driver, a WWII veteran, and has one son Phil who is a breeder of Siberian Huskies; David Owen; Daniel, m. Shirley Tolan, lives at Richmond, IN, is a computer operator, and has two sons, Bradley Wayne and Scott; Jerry Joseph, m. Dorothy Cline, lives at Columbus, IN where he works for Cummins Engine Co., and has one son, Timothy; Helen, m. Dale Anderson, lives at Crawfordsville where she is a grocery checkout clerk, has one son Greg, who with wife Gayle and daughters Nicole and Jamie resides in Indianapolis; and Beverly, m. Lawrence Rickey a business machines serviceman, lives at Indianapolis and has an adopted daughter, Amanda.

David Owen Hester, b. 1930 at Browns Valley, m. 1953 at Waveland, Rosemary Ann "Rosie" Miles, b. 1934 Waveland, daughter of Harry Victor Miles (1895-1967) and Margaret Marie Trout (1901-1961) who resided in Waveland and are buried at Old Union Cemetery. They had five children: Archie Willard, m. Dorothy Lavely; Ruby Katheryn, m. Garold Echelbarger; John Victor; Rosemary Ann; and Doris Elizabeth, m(1) Leonard Bottomly, m(2) "Kim" Kaemerrlen. Marie was the daughter of James Elsworth Trout, b. 1860 Indiana, and Martha Jane Good, b. 1865 who m. 1883 Boone Co., IN and moved to Waveland in 1911. They had seven children: Rosa, m(2) Ora Stultz; Goldie, m. Perry Stultz a brother to Ora; Roy (1890-1970), m. Ottie Miles a sister of Ollie who m. Della Frances Good; Anna, m. Pete Hendrickson; Omer; Margaret Marie; and Arthur. James Elsworth Trout was the son of James Trout, b. 1824 West Virginia who m. Judy Davidson, b. 1822 Indiana. Martha Jane Good was the daughter of Ireneus Good and Margaret the daughter of William Strong all of Boone County.

David and "Rosie" Hester, marriage photo Aug. 9, 1953

Harry Victor Miles was the grandson of George and Pauline Miles who had 12 children. Their son John (1849-1931) was born in Waveland. He m. 1872 Mary Elizabeth English (1855-1928), daughter of Edward and Melvina, and resided in Waveland where he was a fur trader and operated a coal and grain hauling business. They are buried at the Old Union Cemetery and had 12 children: Leona (1874-78); Lenard (1877-78); Stella (1878-1908), m(1) Ora Bechelhimer, m(2) Steve Frye; Lula (1881-1958), m(1) Quincy Lewis, m(2) Ray Neher; Roy (1883-1939); Henry (1885-1950), m. Goldie Alward; Leslie (1887-1955), m. Helen Wrightsman; Clayton(1890-90); Lewis (1891-1983), m. Katheryn O'Connor; Anna (1892-1937), m. Bert McGaughey; Harry Victor; and Eunice (1897-1973).

David and "Rosie" reside in Waveland where she is a beautician. David is employed with R.R. Donnelley of Crawfordsville. They have two children. Catherine Denise, b. 1956, m. 1977 Brian Utterback who was killed in an auto wreck in 1978. She lives at Waveland. Paul David, b. 1959, m. 1988 Abby (Reasor) Huber whose first husband Tom Huber was killed in a construction accident in 1975. They have a daughter Rebecca Ann Huber, b. 1982, and are expecting in April 1989. They reside in Roachdale. *Submitted by Judy L. Harvey*

DONALD K. AND MARY (RAY) HESTER

Adam and Ann (Vanzant) Hester's last child, James Monroe Hester (see John Hester biography in this book) was born Aug. 13, 1843 and died Mar. 12, 1925. He was a farmer and owned a farm on U.S. 231, one mile north of Parkersburg. He married Lucy Eads in 1875. They had four children: Wallace, Blanche, Stephen "Elmer" and Stella.

Elmer Hester was born July 17, 1880 and died Sept. 28, 1964. He felt so strongly about education that he went to State Normal (Terre Haute) with no aid from his family, even picking walnuts to sell for the purchase price of a top coat to wear to college. He taught for seven years, beginning his career in Walnut Township. In 1906, he married Salome

Kessler, daughter of Nathaniel Graybill and Elizabeth Harshbarger Kessler. The Hesters farmed in southwest Scott Township on the farm purchased from Salome's parents. Elmer served two terms as County Commissioner. He was a meticulous man, both in dress and standards. Elmer and Salome's great grandson, Rick Hallett, wrote: "The most important things parents can give their children are ROOTS and WINGS" and the Hesters and their descendants have tried to follow this advice.

Donald K., Mary K., Mary Beth Keim, Lois Greenlee, Nathan D., Stephen D. Hester, and Ruth E. Hallett

Harold Elmer "Jack" son of Elmer and Salome taught for many years in Ladoga, Darlington, New Market, Southmont and other area schools.

Donald K. Hester was Elmer and Salome's first born (Nov. 11, 1907). He still lives in the home where he was born (the original Kessler homestead?). He graduated from New Market High School in 1925 and has farmed all his life. He and Mary Ray (daughter of Earl and May (Ferris) Ray) who was born Aug. 3, 1914 were married June 8, 1932. They lived with his parents for 14-1/2 years. Mary has devoted her entire life to her husband and five children. Their children are: Mary Beth, born Dec. 5, 1933, married Jason Keim. Children: Stephen, Brian, Jeff and Erik Keim.

Lois Ann, second daughter of Donald and Mary was born Nov. 24, 1935 and married Everett Greenlee. Two sons: Larry and Jon.

See Ruth below.

Nathan David Hester, first son of Donald and Mary was born Oct. 11, 1947 and married Diana Petrey. They have two children: Heather and Micah.

The last child of the Hesters is Donald Stephen, born Sept. 22, 1948. He married Charlotte Nielsen. He has two stepchildren, Melissa and Jason Rush.

Ruth Ellen Hester was born in the Hester home on Feb. 21, 1941. She graduated from New Market High School in 1959. She received a degree in English from Franklin College and her master's from ISU. She taught at Alamo High School for two years and Ladoga for four. When Southmont was built, she received her present room — 120. She married Don Hallett on June 19, 1966 at the First Baptist Church in Crawfordsville. They have one son, Richard W. (Rick). Don and Ruth have built three rental homes, bought three others and remodeled a one-room school (used from 1904-1908) where they now reside. Ruth has owned a bookstore and authored a cookbook.

Longevity runs in the Hester family: John was 78, Adam, 84, James Monroe 81, Stephen Elmer, 84 and Donald K. is now 82. Long marriages are also prominent: John and Mary Hester were married 54-1/2 years, Adam and Anna the same; James Monroe and Lucy 46; Elmer and Salome 58 and Donald K. and Mary 57 so far! *Submitted by Ruth Hester Hallett*

JOHN HESTER

The Hester family arrived in America in 1740 on the ship, Good Brothers. John and Abigail Wright Hester settled in Philadelphia. Abigail was supposedly from a high-bred family and was disinherited when she ran away to marry John, the family gardener.

John Hester, only known son of John and Abigail Wright Hester, was born near now Philadelphia, PA on June 1765 and died on Nov. 21, 1843 in Montgomery Co., IN. He is buried in the LaFollette Cemetery in Russell Township, Putnam County. This is located about two miles from "Parkersville," now known as Parkersburg.

According to records in Kentucky, John Hester and Margaret Gilbert were married on Feb. 3, 1789. To this marriage 13 children were born. The fourth being Adam, born Mar. 1, 1799 of which this history is based.

Adam Hester

After selling their property in Fleming Co., KY in 1835, John and Margaret Hester, with their family, moved to Montgomery Co., IN. Deeds recorded on Sept. 22, 1835 show the purchase of 160 acres in Section 31, Township 17, Range 4 located in the southwest part of Scott Township, Montgomery Co., IN, by John Hester from Charles Nichols.

Records in the Fleming Co., KY Court House show a bond was issued to Adam Hester and Ann VanZant uniting the two in marriage. Ann VanZant was born in Fleming Co., KY on Jan. 16, 1801. She died July 27, 1863 near Parkersburg and is buried in the LaFollette Cemetery southwest of Parkersburg.

Adam Hester settled near Parkersburg in the days of the first settlers back before the days of pike roads and trains. He hauled lime to Crawfordsville and Lebanon with oxen. The lime was used in the building of the court house in Montgomery County. This was the first court house built after the original log court house.

When Adam Hester settled here, the Cornstalk Indians were living along the creek which still bears their name. Adam also broke oxen and sold them to people who came along. He helped chop the first road from the Dr. Straughn property to the Parkersburg Spring.

Adam Hester was a substantial farmer, a Republican in politics, and a Presbyterian in his religious faith. The history of Montgomery County tells of the Presbyterian Church in Scott Township of which John, Margaret and Ann Hester were prominent officers and members.

Adam Hester died Aug. 2, 1882 at the age of 83 years, five months and one day. Evidently from information gathered, he lived a good and prosperous life and did his share of civic work. He is buried in the same LaFollette burial ground along with several of his family and ancestors. Several of his descendants still live in Scott Township and Montgomery County.

RUSSELL MAX HESTER

Russell Max Hester is the second son born to Albert Howe and Virginia Irene Crow Hester on July 11, 1951. He was born in Crawfordsville and raised on the family farm north of Parkersburg. Russell graduated from New Market High School in 1969. He enjoyed track, basketball, band and 4-H while in school. He also graduated from Indiana Business College in 1971. After graduation Russell joined his father and brother, Dale, in the family farming operation.

Sallie Lou Simpson, the first of five children, was born on Mar. 1, 1957 to Austin Merle and Enid Lucille Hockersmith Simpson. She was born at Crawfordsville and raised in New Market. Sallie graduated from Southmont in 1975.

The Hesters - Brian, Sallie, Russell and Tod January 1988

Sallie and Russell were married June 28, 1975 at the Browns Valley Christian Church. They reside in a home built by Russell's father north of Parkersburg, where Russell lived most of his childhood.

Russell was raised in the Parkersburg Christian Church where he and Sallie are still active members. Russell has been deacon for 14 years. He serves as songleader and church treasurer. Sallie plays the piano and organ, teaches Sunday School, and helps with the youth. They enjoy singing together as well.

They are the parents of two sons, Brian Thomas born Feb. 7, 1980 and Todd Alan born Jan. 18, 1987. Brian will be in the fourth grade at New Market the fall of 1989. He enjoys riding his bike, playing with his toy tractors, basketball and helping his dad farm. Todd is an active toddler trying to keep up with is big brother.

Russell continues to farm with his brother. He began driving a school bus for Southmont School Corp. in 1987, after being a substitute for many years. He also is a salesman for Crows Seed Corn Company. Russell enjoys woodworking, golf and ping pong. Sallie enjoys reading and cooking and volunteers at the school. They keep busy with church and school activities. The family also enjoys camping in the woods.

IRA KENWORTHY HIATT

He was a son of Silas and Elzira Booher Hiatt, born Dec. 23, 1850, died Aug. 24, 1914 Darlington. He married Jan. 21, 1873 to Sarah Catherine Mullem, 'Sat', the daughter of William J. and Elizabeth Martz Mullen. Her brother Albert married Ira's sister Clara Hiatt. They had a half sister Rebecca Ellen - died young.

Sat was born June 16, 1853 and died Feb. 13, 1937. Both are buried in IOOF Cemetery Darlington. They owned a grocery store in Darlington.

They had seven children Ethel ('Kip' Henry C. Milner); Iva (Frank A. Custer); Leota (Byrd W. Saidla and Lonie Edwards) one son J.C. Saidla; Mayme (John C. Lynch); Ralph married several times no children; Ada Grace (Emery Moffitt) one son Ned Moffitt; and Hazel (Carl Anderson) two sons Robert and Harry Anderson.

Ira, Ethel, Mayme, Leota Saidla, Ralph. Front Row: Ada, Iva K., Sarah (Mullen) Hiatt, John Collyn Saidla and Hazel.

Leota will be with Byrd W. Saidla. Ada Grace was born Sept. 10, 1888 and died Feb. 10, 1953 in Darlington. She married Mar. 26, 1909 to Emery Leland Moffitt. He was born in 1887 and died Feb. 14, 1944. They are buried in IOOF Cemetery. He owned and operated a garage and filling station in Darlington. They had one son Ned Emery who was born Nov. 3, 1909 and died September 1984 in California. He married Nov. 18, 1933 to Louise Evelyn Tankersley in Colfax, IN. He was an auto mechanic. They moved to California and had three daughters-Sharon Elizabeth (Charles L. Cowen) one son; Judith Ann, single; Mary Catherine (Michael James Golden).

Hazel was born Sept. 5, 1891 Darlington, died Feb. 19, 1979 in Arlington, Tarrant Co., TX. She was married Dec. 24, 1910 Crawfordsville, IN to Carl Oliver Anderson. He was born July 18, 1888 Darlington and died Nov. 1, 1961 Ft. Worth, TX. He worked for an electric company in Fort Worth. They had two sons: Robert Carl born Aug. 29, 1911 died Dec. 21, 1970 in South America. He worked for an oil company and was sent to Venezuela, South America where he married Benedicta Vassquez Bencomo and their four children were: Carlos Hiatt; Hazel Esther; Harry Hiatt and Margo Louise Anderson.

Hazel and Carl's son Harry Hiatt was born Oct. 5, 1916 in Sims, IN and married Feb. 1, 1941 in Fort Worth, TX to Mary Louise Williams. She was born May 12, 1918 Fort Worth, TX. He is a retired accountant from General Dynamic Corp. They have three children: Robert William born Sept. 5, 1943; Judith Lee born Apr. 1, 1946, died Nov. 26, 1964; Carla Hiatt born Sept. 17, 1949. All born and live in and around Fort Worth, TX. *Submitted by I. Jo Summers*

JOHN B. HIATT

John B. was born in Guilford Co., NC in 1791; died Mar. 25, 1851, age 60 years, three months, eight days. He was a son of Jonathan and Rachel Williams Hiatt. Jonathan was a son of John and Sarah Hodgson Hiatt; he was a son of George and Martha Wakefield Hiatt; and he was a son of John and Mary Smith Hiatt of England.

In 1816 John B. married Sarah Kenworthy. She was born in Guilford Co., NC Sept. 12, 1795 and died Feb. 12, 1876 age 83 years, five months, one day. She was a child of Elisha and Mary Cox Kenworthy. They and Sarah's parents all buried in the old Quaker part of Greenlawn Cemetery in Darlington, IN.

He had entered 80 acres of land in 1830 and 80 acres in 1832. They were members of the Quakers - moved their membership in 1826 to White Lick and then to Sugar River in 1830 when it was established near their home. She was a noble and picturesque woman of pioneer life - noted for her obstetrical work, starting in 1836 until a fall disabled her from further practice in 1868. During a period of 42 years she accouched between 400-500 women, with the loss of none. Her heroism as a horsewoman was proverbial and regardless of season, flood or storm, she answered every appeal for help.

Their children were: Iaasc (Mary Elizabeth Tribbett), seven children; Mary J. (Sam Davison) six children; Rachel (John H. Ramey and Asa Dittemore) one son; Silas (Elizabeth Kashner and Elizra Booher) two and seven children; Matilda (William W. McClure) two children; Melinda (William M. Lowman); Sara (John C. Allen) five children: John (Mary A. Lowman) three children.

There is a very good book *Direct lineage and History of John B. and Sarah (Kenworthy) Hiatt and their Descendants of Darlington, IN* written by Marian (Hiatt) Johnson. *Submitted by I. Jo Summers*

SILAS HIATT

Silas was the first white male child born in Montgomery Co., IN, on Aug. 5, 1823. He died May 18, 1901. He was a son of John B. and Sarah Kenworthy Hiatt. He married in 1843 first to Elizabeth Kashner they had two children Eleanor and Ira. She and both children died in 1847. He remarried Aug. 24, 1848 to Elzira Booher a child of William M. and Rhoda Hampton Booher. Her brothers and sisters were: Elizabeth; Rhoda Tribbett; Martha Bowers; Albert; Orfa Warbinton and Mary Cummingham.

She was born Nov. 25, 1824 in Sullivana Co., TN and migrated with her family to Montgomery County in 1833 when she was nine years old. She died Nov. 7, 1900 in Montgomery County. They are buried at IOOF Cemetery Darlington.

He was farmer and stock raiser on his splendid farm of 100 acres which was well improved and in general good shape, the result of his own industry and thrift. He was a member of the I.O.O.F. and Trustee of the Lodge, and in politics was connected with the Republican Party.

They had seven children: Eleanor (Thomas Avery); Ira Kenworthy (Sarah C. Mullen) seven children; Elvira (Jess Bowers); Clara (Albert Mullen) one child; John William (Flora Alice Grimes) five children; Lydia R. single; and Lilly Bell (Rev. John Phillips). *Submitted by I. Jo Summers*

THOMAS HICKS

Thomas Hicks, the first Hicks of whom we have record, was born Dec. 28, 1744, on the south fork of the Potomac River in West Virginia. He married Elizabeth Morrell Jan. 4, 1781. They had seven children: 1. John Hicks; 2. Samuel, born Apr. 17, 1785; 3. William, born Mar. 12, 1788 (who was later a gunsmith at Raccoon); 4. James, born Dec. 2, 1790; 5. Robert, born Dec. 21, 1795, who later disappeared; 6. Jesse, born Apr. 21, 1793; 7. Morrell born Dec. 25, 1798.

1. John Hicks married Elizabeth Sandusky, who later married Mulenburg Proctor. They had five children.

Front Row: Everilla Ann, Desire Catherine Lidick, Sarah Proctor VanCleave, Nancy Elizabeth Carrington, Lucinda Jane. Back Row: Effie May, Nancy Alma, Emily Elizabeth Armstrong, Polina Jane, America Melinda Sayleo, and Laura Alice.

2. Jesse Hicks married Nancy Kinder in Shelby Co., KY, Feb. 4, 1816. They had six children. 1. John Hicks, born Jan. 24, 1816; 2. Martha, who later married Tom Finley; 3. Besty, who never married; 4. Morrell, who later married Cinda Landis (twin sister to Mary Landis, wife of Jim Hicks); 5. Jim, who married Mary Landis (twin sister to Cinda Landis, wife of Morrell Hicks); 6. Sallie, married Criss Acres.

John Hicks married America Proctor Oct. 14, 1841, both are buried in Indian Creek Cemetery, July 10, 1895. They had six children: 1. Sarah Proctor, born July 30, 1842-died Sept. 16, 1923; 2. Nancy Elizabeth, born Dec. 7, 1844-died Jan. 23, 1933; 3. Lauford (Sanford) born May 30, 1847-died Aug. 17, 1850; 4. Lucinda Jane, born Sept. 22, 1849-died February 1935 (unmarried); 5. Everilla Ann, born Feb. 5, 1852-died April 1936 (unmarried); 6. Desire Catherine, born Aug. 28, 1857-died Dec. 4, 1940.

Sarah Proctor Hicks married Edwin VanCleave Dec. 26, 1861. Edwin was born May 2, 1841 and died Oct. 14, 1916. They were members of Indian Creek Primitive Baptist Church on St. Road 234. Both are buried in Indian Creek Cemetery. They made their home from primitive forest about 1862, located two miles southwest of New Market. They had seven children. 1. Emma Elizabeth, born Nov. 17, 1862-died Aug. 22, 1937; 2. American Malinda, born Jan. 13, 1865-died Mar. 19, 1945; 3. John Sanford, born Sept. 19, 1867-died Dec. 15, 1887; 4. Polina (Lina) Jane, born July 15, 1870-died Sept. 2, 1949; 5. Laura Alice, born Mar. 11, 1873-died Apr. 14, 1950; 6. Effie May, born Jan. 17, 1876-died Dec. 7, 1961; 7. Alma Nancy, born Apr. 23, 1879-died Dec. 29, 1974. *Submitted by Robert F. Saylor*

MR. AND MRS. CHESTER C. HILL

Mr. and Mrs. Hill came to Crawfordsville from Lafayette, IN after Mr. Hill had been selected as the first operator of the Crawfordsville Municipal Airport, which opened in 1945. He was one of two sons born to Mr. and Mrs. A.C. Hill in Tippecanoe County, near Dayton, IN, where his father was a farmer. His mother was born in Kansas and came to Indiana as a small child. His brother, Delmer, was a teacher at Dayton High School and later became a farmer in Warren County, specializing in raising Angus Cattle.

Chet graduated from Dayton High School and Purdue University. He was employed in Montgomery County by the Department of Agriculture as

Farm Supervisor for the Farm Security Administration. Later he became a Navy Flight Instructor on the Navy Officers Flight Training Program at Purdue University during World War II.

He married Dorothy Hayes in Lafayette. She was born in Starke Co., IN and grew up in Wabash County. She was one of five children born to Mr. and Mrs. George Hayes, who were born in Illinois. Her father was a farmer and later one of the first automobile dealers in Wabash County. She graduated from North Manchester High School and Manchester College. She worked as Home Management Supervisor for the Farm Security Administration and taught school in LaPorte County, Madison County and Tuttle Junior High School in Crawfordsville.

The Hills have two sons who were born in Crawfordsville and graduated from Crawfordsville High School and Purdue University. Both are airline pilots. John married Catherine Redant who was born in Belgium and grew up in Johannesburg, South Africa. They live in Florence, KY. Bob married Donna Sterling from Fairfield, CA. They live in Marietta, GA.

While at the Airport, Chet soloed many Crawfordsville area residents, and as a private and commercial flight examiner, he issued many certificates in Central Indiana.

After leaving the airport, he became a residential builder in Crawfordsville and surrounding areas, building first on Park Lane, he then developed Hill's First Subdivision on Hillcrest Drive and later developed Hill's Second Subdivision at the Del Mar Addition west of the city off the Country Club Road.

Both Mr. and Mrs. Hill are retired.

EMERT AND EFFIE HILLENBURG

Emert and Effie Hillenburg moved from Monroe Co., IN to Madison Township in 1916. James Emert Hillenburg was born Sept. 29, 1885 in Brown Co., IN. He was the fifth child of Frank and Jane Lucas Hillenburg to survive. Other children of the family were: Oscar, Charles, Alice, and Everett.

Emert and Effie Hillenburg

On Aug. 26, 1903, Emert married Effie Ethel Cain. She was born on Dec. 2, 1887 in Monroe Co., IN, the daughter of William Z. and Laura Grubb Cain. Her brothers and sisters were: Emert, Elmer, Eva, Homer, Mandy, Everett, and Desse Cain. Effie also had a half-sister Martha and half-brothers Don, John, and Glenn Cain from a later marriage of William Z. and Sarah Elkins Cain.

Emert Hillenburg, a farmer and stone quarry worker, brought his family to the Linden area to farm for the Norman family. Emert was a descendent of Daniel Hillenburg of Wythe Co., VA. It is believed that Daniel came to this country as a Hessian soldier. He was captured by the Americans under George Washington at the Battle of Trenton, Dec. 26, 1776. Interned at Lancaster, PA, he later made his way into the Virginia mountains.

Effie Hillenburg's father was a Baptist minister in Monroe County. She grew up with a great interest in education. Emert and Effie had four children: Edith, Vurl, Claude, and Carrell. Both of their daughters became teachers as did two of their granddaughters. Many of Emert and Effie's descendants live in Montgomery County today.

Emert farmed at various locations in Madison and Coal Creek Townships. Later Emert and Effie purchased a farm in Coal Creek Township where they lived for the remainder of their lives. Effie died Sept. 5, 1972. Emert died Apr. 11, 1974. Both are buried in the New Richmond Cemetery.

GARY AND PHYLLIS HILLER

Gary and Phyllis Hiller, accompanied by their one-year old son Scott Allen, moved from Plymouth, IN, to Montgomery County in August, 1969. Dwight David joined their family on November 23 of that same year.

Gary grew up in Ilion, NY, a small town in the central part of the state. He came to Indiana to obtain a college education. He was graduated from Indiana State University in Terre Haute in 1966 with a Bachelors degree in music education. In 1969 he earned his Masters degree in music education. He has taught music classes and has directed bands at the Linden High School, North Montgomery High School, Waynetown School, Darlington School, and Northridge Middle School where he is currently a member of the staff. He also works parttime at the local Dominos Pizza Store. He enjoys playing cribbage and euchre and singing in the Mt. Zion Church Choir in his spare time.

Phyllis was born at Methodist Hospital in Indianapolis even though her parents, Charles and Mildred Query, along with her sister Miriam and her brother David resided in Bloomington. Since she is a "preacher's kid", she has lived in several Indiana towns: Aurora, Boonville, Brookville, and Glenn's Valley. She considers Crawfordsville her home since she has lived here longer than in any other town. She was graduated from Boonville High School in 1962. She attended Indiana State University for three years. She worked at the Plymouth Public Library before her children were born. She is currently employed as a Circulation Clerk at the Crawfordsville Public Library. She is a member of the Calvary Chapel Church. She enjoys writing letters to family and friends, doing cross-stitch embroidery, and collecting recipes.

Scott was graduated from North Montgomery High School in 1987. In the fall of that year he entered Rose Hulman Institute. He is now a sophomore there, majoring in Mechanical Engineering and minoring in Economics. He is the recipient of a Warren Scholarship and also a two-year army ROTC scholarship. He is a member of the Wabash Cadet Battalion, the largest battalion in the United States.

Dwight was graduated from North Montgomery High School in 1988. He participated in various sports while attending school. He has worked as a stock boy and as a meat cutter at the Crawfords Grocery Store on West Market Street. He is presently employed by Crown, Cork, and Seal. He enjoys playing basketball, bowling, and playing softball in his free time. Last summer he played on one of the softball teams that participated in the state softball tournament; even though the team lost, he considered it an honor to play in the final round of the tourney. *Submitted by Phyllis Hiller*

CHESTER AND RUBY LINN HIMES

Wedding vows were solemnized at 8 P.M. Aug. 13, 1916. Chester Himes with a flick of leather reins and a soft "GIDDAP" smartly turned his horse and carriage toward a farm south of New Ross, IN. His beautiful bride Ruby Ann was by his side, daughter of William Asa and Ella (Summers) Linn. Ruby Ann sang soprano solos and was pianist at the Whitesville Christian Church, where she and Chester were members. Ruby's sweet personality drew and kept friends.

Chester was born Dec. 14, 1893 to George and Alice (Graybill) Himes. Ruby was born Nov. 13, 1897. Farming and working together would be happiness.

Year 1919 they moved to the farm they purchased one-half mile east of Whitesville with two-year-old Marian Marciel born 1917. Ruth Pauline was born Feb. 9, 1922. About then, Ruby bobbed her long hair. Surprised Chester! Good naturedly he understood—things were moving faster—he was driving a new Model T Ford!

The depression caused them to double their work. "Himes Poultry and Egg Business" was opened at 212 North Washington Street, Crawfordsville. Provided employment for men also bought fur, hides and wool. Ruby kept the office books and was there each work day.

Chester and Ruby Linn Himes

In May of 1932 Ruby, Marian and Pauline were hospitalized many weeks due to serious injuries from an automobile collision. Christian Faith carried the family through that including hard work and paying close attention to business that helped pay the bills—farmers also favored the Himes Business. It was successful! They weathered the Depression and built a new home in 1938. Marian married Richard Deckard and Ruth Pauline wed William E. Moore. (See Index)

Chester a Charter member of the Farm Bureau also had belonged to the National Horse Thief Detective Association.

In 1945 he received a pilots license from Purdue Airport and allotted a portion of the farm for "Himes Airport". Owning planes and had instructors. Men soloed and hangared planes there. Chester enjoyed thrilling their grandchildren (Joy, Jan, Ruby Moore—Jill, Jack, Cheryl Deckard) with rides.

July 27, 1948, Ruby Ann, Chester's beloved wife for 31 years died. Ensuing months were lonely. Farming, friends and family with the Crawfordsville business helped and then he met the former Mabel White, (widow of Lee Sinclair), with daughter Patricia. They married Sept. 3, 1949. (She was Crawfordsville's City Clerk Treasurer). Supportive of Chester's endeavors. Proved she was the fine wife for him. Chester 56 years old continued to devote his life to agricultural pursuits and stock raising. Other interests were deer hunting and traveling. Chester's heart attack and stroke in the 1970's caused them to seek warmer winter climate. Wintering in their Sun City, AZ condominium and returning by plane to the farm each summer.

After a life of usefulness and honest toil, loved and respected by all, Chester a quiet religious man, Emeritus Elder of the Whitesville Christian Church, died Jan. 31, 1982. Buried at Crawfordsville Masonic Cemetery. Marian died Apr. 14, 1988.

Mabel a member of the Whitesville Christian Church exemplified her Christian faith and encouraging strength to Chester and to his family the 33 years she was at his side. *Submitted by Pauline Himes Moore*

DANIEL AND MARY WRIGHTSMAN HIMES

Daniel Himes, Sr. was born, May 24, 1795 near Bonsacks Station, Roanoke, VA in Botetourt County. He married Mary Wrightsman who was born, July 15, 1796. Their children were: John (1818-1894), David (1820-1865), Susanna (1821-), Daniel H., Jr. (1823-1894), William (1824-), Jacob (1829-1879), Mary Ann (1835-1910), Abraham (1836-), and Sarah Elizabeth (1838-). The first five of their nine children were born in Virginia.

In the year 1826 the Daniel Himes, Sr. family emigrated to Ross Co., OH. The last four children were born in this location. The method of travel to Ohio was by wagon with the probability that some of the family walked. Two dogs accompanied them. While crossing the Ohio river on a ferry boat, one dog jumped off and swam back to the Virginia shore. Arriving in Ross Co., OH, they built a log cabin on a hill top. At Hillsboro, OH the family farmed for 19 years, some sons worked at Rapid Forge, a place where iron products were made and some worked at a distillery nearby. That location is ten miles north east of Hillsboro along Paint Creek.

In the late fall of 1845, Daniel, Sr. and son Daniel walked the entire distance to Montgomery Co., IN. Arriving at William Gish's, their relative's home. Through him a lease was obtained from Samuel Britts to clear some land and build a cabin. Mr. Britts furnished a team and Berniah Hostetter accompanied the two Himes men back to Ohio.

When Mr. Hostetter and the Daniel and Mary (Wrightsman) Himes family arrived at Samuel Britts' home near Ladoga it was cold and a good lot of snow was on the ground. The date was Jan. 5, 1845.

Their home for many years was the cabin built in the fall of 1845. The usual hardships endured by the early settlers fell to the lot of the Himes family making this new home. The entire country was practically unbroken forest and much labor was required in clearing land so a crop could be planted.

John returned to Ohio living his whole life there. Mary Ann died at McCane, KS. Daniel H., Jr. married Mary L. Harshbarger on May 16, 1850, the daughter of Jacob and Saloma Harshbarger. Mary was born Jan. 30, 1833. Jacob Himes married Catherine Linn in 1853; after her death he married Catherine Kessler.

Daniel Himes, Sr. died Feb. 17, 1879 in his 84th year. Mary (Wrightsman) Himes, his wife died Oct. 19, 1866 at the age of 70. Both died at the home of Daniel H. Himes, Jr. which was located one-half mile north of Ladoga.

The Himes family were respected and useful citizens of the Scott Township community and have done their part to make it a worthy place to live. They have lived an honorable and exemplary life. (see index Jacob Himes)

GEORGE AND ALICE MAY GRAYBILL HIMES

George and Alice May (Graybill) Himes were married on Feb. 6, 1890. They had two sons, Lester born Dec. 7, 1890 and Chester, born Dec. 14, 1893.

Alice, the daughter of Samuel F. and Mary Arnold Graybill was born Jan. 3, 1872. She had two sisters and one brother, Ella, Lulu and Manson.

George, born in Montgomery County, May 29, 1865, was the fourth of six sons of Jacob and Catherine (Kessler) Himes. They were John, Benjamin, Meda, Perry, and Samuel. One daughter Emma died in infancy.

George, Lester, Alice and Chester front with white collar

Alice's grandparents, Daniel and Elizabeth (Frankebarger) Graybill came to Montgomery County in September, 1838 and settled in Scott Township. He bought a farm there. Later he built a sawmill and added a gristmill in 1848. Born in Virginia, Nov. 13, 1810, he married Elizabeth on Feb. 9, 1832.

The subject of this sketch, George and Alice lived east of New Market. Alice invested her parents gift of $3,000.00 on the farm they bought and lived on. George with hard labor removed unneeded timber and made improvements. He was successful and enterprising in agricultural pursuits.

He belonged to the Knights of Pythias at New Market and the Horse Thief Detective Association. Alice belonged to the Rathbone Sisters of Dew Drop Temple No. 89 at New Market.

This worthy couple had only ten years together. She and the newborn baby died on Nov. 8, 1900. She, 28 and George 35 years old. Alice with the baby were buried in one casket at the Harshbarger Cemetery north of Ladoga.

George's brother Perry, married just one week was building his wife a new home. Sympathetically they offered to help with the boys. Perry and Mabel (White) Himes moved into the home. Mabel giving her attention to the care of all. When their home was completed Chester and Lester stayed awhile with them attending Eden School. During the summer George took the boys to Alice's sister at Montrose, CO. She and her husband, Greg, owned a ranch there. Returning by train to New Market in the fall and they stayed the winter at Grandmother Catherine's.

April 29, 1903 George married Clara Oliver, born Aug. 16, 1867, an efficient, kind lady. She raised the boys and the two children born to them, Ruth and Merle, and provided a comfortable loving home.

Chester married Ruby Ann Linn from Whitesville on Aug. 23, 1916. Lester and Zola McMullin had been married since Mar. 29, 1913. Ruth and Clyde Johnson were married on Feb. 17, 1924. Merle married Ruby Thompson on Mar. 16, 1929. She was born Mar. 12, 1909 and died Apr. 18, 1950. Merle met and took as his second wife Ruth (Potts) Barth. They were married in Indianapolis on Jan. 19, 1952.

George Himes was a member of the New Market Christian Church and president of the New Market Telephone Company at the time of his death, which occurred on Sunday, Sept. 27, 1936.

Clara Himes died Apr. 24, 1952. Lester died Sept. 16, 1985 and Chester died Jan. 31, 1982.

JACOB AND CATHERINE LINN HIMES

Jacob Himes, born Mar. 25, 1829 and Catherine Linn, born Oct. 10, 1833 were married in 1853 in Montgomery Co., IN. She was a daughter of James Washington and Mahala (Cassell) Linn, who came to Walnut Township, Montgomery Co., IN in 1837. Jacob was the son of Daniel, Sr. and Mary (Wrightsman) Himes.

Jacob and Catherine's daughter Mary Ellen was born Oct. 4, 1853. Catherine (Linn) Himes died March of 1854.

January 11, 1855 Jacob married Catherine Kessler, born Apr. 28, 1834, the daughter of Benjamin and Elizabeth (Graybill) Kessler.

Although farming was his business Jacob was also a skilled carpenter and built their fine home southwest of Whitesville. A long lane gave access to their home that sat back off the road. He constructed barns and other dwellings in the area. Jacob Himes built the original Edgar Manges house - similar to Jacob's and William Asa Linn built the barn. Located on the first road west of Whitesville. Both houses still remain.

Catherine Kessler Himes

Catherine (Kessler) Himes raised Mary Ellen, and the five sons she and Jacob had. Each son married at maturity, they are John (Nov. 6, 1855- died June 14, 1933), married Laurie Zimmerman (1866-1887). She died and John married Lizzie Frame (1858-1936), their son was Mark (May 18, 1892 died April 1945), Nathaniel Benjamin, Oct. 17, 1859 died Sept. 19, 1934, married Elizabeth Thompson in 1883 - she died 1935. Their children were: Gertie (1895-1889) and Ethel (born 1896). Meade (Aug. 2, 1863-died May 1924) married Alice Luster (1866-1942), their children were Ernest (1895-1900), also Ralph, (born Feb. 22, 1899) and Lawrence (born Oct. 30, 1901, his twin sister died in 1902). George (May 29, 1865-died Sept. 27, 1936) married Feb. 6, 1890 Alice Graybill,

(Jan. 3, 1872-died Nov. 8, 1900). Alice and baby were buried together at Harshbarger Cemetery. Their sons were: Lester, (Dec. 7, 1890 died Sept. 16, 1985) married Zola McMullin (October 1894-died 1973) and Chester (Dec. 14, 1893-died Jan. 31, 1982) married Ruby Ann Linn (Nov. 13, 1897-died July 27, 1948). After Alice died George Himes married Clara Oliver (1867-1952) on Apr. 29, 1903. Their children were Ruth born Nov. 29, 1904 and Merle, born Sept. 9, 1906. Perry born Oct. 19, 1873 and died Jan. 23, 1939, married Mabel White (Oct. 31, 1882-Nov. 3, 1938) their children are Norma born June 12, 1904, Audrey born Nov. 5, 1906, Elizabeth born Dec. 26, 1909-died September 1984, Amy born May 28, 1911, Edna born Jan. 19, 1913, and Robert born Nov. 12, 1917.

The first daughter of Jacob Himes, Mary Ellen, married Benjamin Dickerson, they had William born Jan. 24, 1873 also Jane, Alice, John, and George.

Catherine (Kessler) Himes was a Christian in the highest acceptation of the term and she lived this way in her daily life. She was devoted to her family. Her sons engaged in farming and lived useful lives and were respected by all that knew them and their families. Catherine age 82, died Sept. 21, 1916 and was survived by her sons, three brothers, David Kessler, Sol Kessler, Jacob Kessler, and three sisters, Mary Kessler Nees, Ruth Kessler Thompson, and Nancy Kessler Manges. Jacob died May 22, 1870. Both buried at Brethren Cemetery. *Submitted by Pauline Moore*

LESTER HIMES

Lester Himes was born to George and Alice (Graybill) Himes on Dec. 7, 1890. He was married to Zola Lucille McMullen, of Roachdale, IN, Mar. 29, 1913 and went to housekeeping North of Ladoga. Their home was destroyed in 1916 and they moved to the Gott farm West of Parkersburg where they spent the remainder of their lives. Zola died Mar. 29, 1973 on their 60th wedding anniversary. Lester lived to be 94 when he died Sept. 16, 1985. Both are buried in the Masonic Cemetery in Crawfordsville.

They became the parents of five children: Marjorie Fern, Apr. 2, 1915; Herman George, June 18, 1917; Kathryn Louise, Dec. 29, 1919; Hernrty Max, July 23, 1925; Barbara Jean, June 23, 1927.

Marjorie married Rev. Francis McCarty in the depth of the depression, and for more than 50 years devoted her life as a minister's wife serving Baptist churches in Indiana, Massachusetts and Ohio.

Herman joined the U.S. Navy at the beginning of World War II and retired after 25 years with the rank of Captain.

Max became a pilot for the United Air Lines with the rank of Captain at the time of his retirement.

Kathryn's working years were spent as a beautician, during part of the time she owned and managed her own shop.

Barbara was employed for many years as a teller with the Elston Bank and Trust Company.

Lester was a member of the Waveland Masonic Lodge No. 300; both he and Zola were members of Waveland chapter of the Order of Eastern Star No. 539.

NEAL OLDFIELD HINES (1908-)

Neal O. Hines, son of Linnaeus N. Hines (1871-1936) and Bertha Wiggs Hines (1881-1941), was born in Crawfordsville (Nov. 22, 1908), his father then superintendent of schools here, the family home at 8 Mills Place.

Neal lived in Crawfordsville until 1921, when his father, who had served two years as state superintendent, moved on to become president of Indiana State Normal in Terre Haute. A sister, Anne, was born in 1920. Neal was graduated from Indiana University in 1930, then was a news reporter and editor in Huntington, Terre Haute (1930-1941), and took an M.S. in journalism at Northwestern in 1941. After service in the Air Force in WWII (1942-1946), he married Martha Perry, of Terre Haute, and went west with his bride to become a teacher of journalism at the University of California, Berkeley. In 1948, Neal went to the University of Washington, Seattle, as director of publications, later assistant to the president. By 1963 he had moved to Washington, D.C., as director of publications for the National Association of College and University Business Officers, serving there until his return to the Seattle area upon his retirement in 1975. His wife, Martha, a widely-loved participant in community affairs, died in 1986, but Neal, his three daughters—Melissa, Martha, and Nancy—and his sister, Anne, now live in Seattle.

Neal is the author of several books, two of them covering the radiobiological resurveys at Bikini, Eniwetok, and Christmas Island, the nuclear test atolls in the Pacific, where he served three times as a member of the resurvey teams from the University of Washington. He also has covered special aspects of educational and University of Washington history. His writings: ***Proving Ground: An Account of Radiobiological Studies in the Pacific, 1946-1961***, UW Press, 1962; *Atoms, Nature, and Man*, Atomic Energy Commission, 1966; *Fish of Rare Breeding*, Smithsonian Press, 1976; *Denny's Knoll: A History of the Metropolitan Tract of the University of Washington*, UW Press, 1980; *Business Officers in Higher Education*, NACUBO, 1982; and "Bikini," *Encyclopaedia Britannica*, 1976.

BENJAMIN AND SARAH SHAVER HINKLE

Benjamin Hinkle born 1798 in Botetourt Co., VA, son of Rev. John and Magdaline Landis Hinkle, married Sarah Shaver Vineyard, widow of John Vineyard, 1823 in Botetourt Co., VA. She was born 1801 in Virginia and died in Montgomery Co., IN on Mar. 26, 1856. Benjamin died here after 1850. They came to Putnam County via Tennessee, then to Montgomery County in 1833. Sarah was the daughter of Andrew and Ursula Miller Shaver. Their 12 children were: Jeremiah Ledbetter married Angeline Van Cleave. He served in the Mexican War. Their children were Andrew Jefferson Hinkle married Ellen Williams, Elizabeth married 1. John Lafford, and married 2. George Thompson. She had a daughter Lillian Lafford who married 1. Ernest Barker and 2. Jesse Walters; and had four Thompson children: Luna, Opal, died, Rogar Earl, and Herman Thompson. Other children of Jefferson Hinkle were George Hinkle died 1924, Samuel Benjamin died 1924. George and Sam were breeders of fine Duroc hogs, and lived on the farm where their grandfather Benjamin had lived; Simon Hinkle married Rebecca Jane Randel. Susan Hinkle born 1827 in Tennessee married William Randel, brother of Rebecca. They both died in 1866, six weeks apart, here, with dysentery. Their son Andrew Vineyard Randel married Matilda Emaline Linn, daughter of James W. and Mahala Castle Linn. They had William Noah and Myrtie Randel Vannice; Sarah J. Randel married John Henry Starke, John Randel, Mary D. Randel married Isaac Routh, divorced. He was in the Civil War and is buried in Arlington Cemetery; she married 2. John Henry Slaths, widower, George Randel, Clara Ellen Randel married Henry McDaniel, James Goodwin Randel married Sarah Magdaline Wingert, had two sons, Ernest M. and Orval W. Randel married Dora Evaline Linn, had two daughters C. Pauline Walters and V. Lucile Harpel; Elizabeth Hinkle married Jonathan Markey; Amanda married 1. ? Morrison and married 2. Nelson Woods; David Hinkle; Catherine Hinkle Foster; John L. Hinkle; Mary Hinkle Lamson; Benjamin, Jr.; Sarah, and an infant. Sarah Shaver married 1. John Vineyard, had two sons Nicholas and Nathan. He died 1822 then she married Benjamin Hinkle in 1823 in Botetourt Co., VA. *Submitted by Pauline Walters*

JAMES MADISON AND FLORENCE JEANNETTE HODGES

James Madison and Florence Jeannette (Ewbank) Hodges were married on June 7, 1970.

Florence Jeannette was born Mar. 2, 1906 to Wilbur Edward and Alice (Stuck) Ewbank. They lived southwest of Indianapolis and farmed in Perry Township, Marion County.

Florence had three sisters, Ethel Mary, born Mar. 12, 1901, Elsie May, born Sept. 1, 1903, Helen Louise born Aug. 11, 1909, and two brothers Ora Milburn born May 20, 1899 and Herbert, born Aug. 11, 1909 (died February 1910). (Herbert was a twin to Helen Louise).

The Ewbank family purchased 151 acres east of Parkersburg in 1917 in Scott Township, Montgomery County moving to that farm when Florence was 11. On March 2 Wilbur Edward and his son Ora drove the team and wagon with household furnishings to the farm. Alice Ewbank came with her daughters more comfortably, on the train to the Raccoon Train Station.

James Madison and Florence Jeannette Hodges

The Ewbank's attended the Methodist Church in Raccoon where each were members. (Raccoon, located south of the Montgomery-Putnam County Line).

James Madison Hodges was born Nov. 14, 1910. His parents lived close to Romney where his father was employed by the railroad. The family consisted of John Ora and Lora May (Birdge) Hodges and their children, James Madison, Louie Lee, John Wesley, Carl, James Henry, Mac, Chris and Susie, Nettie and Mary. They moved to a farm around Glasgow, KY and raised tobacco.

In 1941 James Madison returned to Montgomery Co., IN and for a while farmed near Waynetown.

James Madison became employed at Crawfordsville's MidStates Steel and Wire Co. and lived at 405 East College St. with his wife Torrie

Ella for 20 years. Their children were Kenneth Edward, Neva Pauline and Robert Lee. Madison's wife died July 7, 1965.

Florence first married Lee Wilson (born Sept. 9, 1900) in August, 1931. He was the son of John C. and Maria Elizabeth (Bugg) Wilson. Lee was associated in the Wilson Brothers Greenhouse at Raccoon until Lee died at age 57 on Aug. 20, 1958. Their family consisted of Raymond Lee and Marjorie Joan.

Through mutual friends James Madison and Florence Jeannette became acquainted. They reside in Raccoon. James Madison retired from MidStates after working there 21 years. Florence worked at Wilson Brothers Greenhouse for 39 years. Those she worked with found her a pleasure to know and both have a host of friends throughout the area and are highly respected. Her hobbies are crocheting and flowers. Their residence is attractive and is always neat with the yard appropriately showing an abundance of beautiful (well-tended) colorful flowers all summer. Florence maintains a happy hospitable home and makes family or friends comfortable with her pleasant manner. Her marvelous sense of humor gained her friends that have remained steadfast through the years.

Madison kept and tended a large garden many years enjoying out-door labor. Both have commendable characteristics and are held in the highest regard by all that know them. Madison is kind and considerate of others, generous and obliging to those he comes in contact with. They are members of the First Assembly of God Church at Crawfordsville. *Submitted by Pauline Moore*

VIRGIL W. AND LUCY FERN (WEIKEL) HOLE

Virgil W. (Wesley) and Lucy Fern (Weikel) Hole were life long residents of Montgomery County and after their marriage on Apr. 16, 1929 in Greencastle, IN lived the rest of their lives on their farm in Coal Creek township. They had three sons: Hurschell David, born May 24, 1930; Lelan Clarence, born May 21, 1932, Floyd Marvin, born Feb. 14, 1935; and two daughters: Zetta Maxine (Mrs. Owen T.) Hanna, born Sept. 13, 1936 and Wilma Rita (Mrs. Fred) Winger born June 14, 1940. All five children were born at home.

Virgil W. Hole was the oldest of the six children of William N. and Lola B. (Hughes) Hole, a prominent farmer in the Youngs Chapel area of Union township. He was born May 15, 1894, at home. He attended Youngs Chapel and Breaks schools. As a young adult he was active in the Youngs Chapel Christian Church. He first married Daisy Henthorn Oct. 6, 1915. They had one son: Lloyd William, born Apr. 17, 1917 and died Jan. 20, 1921. He is buried in the Youngs Chapel cemetery. This marriage ended in divorce.

He secondly married Lucy Fern Weikel a daughter of William Smith and Syntha Dee (Harrision) Weikel of Ripley township, Apr. 16, 1929 in Greencastle, IN.

Virgil started hauling livestock to the Indianapolis Stockyards in 1919 using horse drawn wagons and later switched to a truck. He was very active in livestock trucking in Montgomery County for the rest of his life and was well known by most farmers in the county. He was very skilled at looking at an animal, determining its weight and the price it would bring.

In 1938 when electricity came to the rural area, he wired his own house and barn. Before he completed this job, several neighbors asked if he would wire their homes. What started out as a single job turned into a life-time job as a rural electrician. The requests continued with each additional house and/or barn he wired, thus becoming one of the most prominent rural electricians in this and surrounding counties. In the late 1940's and early 1950's he was active in the Wabash Valley Electric League. After the children were out of high school, his wife, Lucy, started helping him and became very knowledgeable about electrical wiring. They both continued electrical work until about three months before Virgil died on Christmas eve (Dec. 24) 1968.

In February 1969, at age 70, Lucy started a new career as a home/health companion—in her words "just to stay busy". She continued this type of work for nearly 15 years. She died Apr. 5, 1983 two months short of being 85 years of age.

She attended the old Texas school (Ripley Twp.) and graduated from the eighth grade from Ripley Township Public Schools, June 21, 1913 in Alamo.

After eighth grade graduation, at about age 15, Lucy worked several years for Ozias and Laura Hacker in the Youngs Chapel area. Later, she worked for the "Old Glove Factory" in Crawfordsville.

Both Virgil and Lucy are buried in Oak Hill Cemetery, Crawfordsville.

Virgil's paternal grandparents were David C. and Mary Elizebath (Duckett) Hole who came to Montgomery County in the early 1860's. David C. Hole died Apr. 18, 1880 age 42 years, one month, two days and is buried in the Hutton Cemetery on "Old" 47 in Union township. His maternal grandparents were David Wesley and Anna Alberta (Clark) Hughes, both natives of Montgomery County and very prominent farmers.

Lucy Weikel Hole's paternal grandparents were Samuel and Lucy Ann (Smith) Weikel of Ripley Township. At the time of his death Jan. 22, 1916 he had been an active member for nearly 60 years I.O.O.F. He, his wife and four daughters are buried in the I.O.O.F. Cemetery in Crawfordsville.

Lucy's maternal grandparents were Carter and Barbara (Malson) Harrison of South Bethnay, Bartholomew Co., IN. *Submitted by Dr. F. Marvin Hole*

WILLIAM N. HOLE

William N. (Newton) Hole was born on the old Townsly farm near Youngs Chapel, Union township Jan. 16, 1870, the son of David C. and Mary Elizabeth (Duckett) Hole. Shortly after his father died on Apr. 18, 1880 and after the 1880 Census was completed he was taken into the home of Mr. and Mrs. George Clouse where he remained until he was 21 years of age.

On July 23, 1898 he married Lola B. (Belle) Hughes, a native of Montgomery County and whose father, David Wesley Hughes (born Aug. 14, 1848, died Jan. 9, 1932) was a very prominent farmer and citizen in Union township. Her mother was Anna Alberta Clark Hughes (born Dec. 16, 1851, died May 31, 1930).

To this union six children were born: Virgil W. (born May 15, 1894, died Dec. 24, 1968), Flossie Mae Hole Cummins (born Mar. 28, 1896, died Jan. 18, 1965), Bessie Gail Hole Vannette (born Aug. 22, 1897, died July 22, 1965), Lester David (born Aug. 20, 1901, died Apr. 4, 1977), Ruby Alberta (born October 1904, died Dec. 29, 1920), Raymond Kenneth (born Dec. 14, 1912, died June 25, 1988). All were lifelong Montgomery County residents.

A picture of the old William Hole home c. 1903 with left to right at swing, standing: Virgil W., on the swing: Flossie, Lester D. and Bessie, standing at the door are: William N. and Lola B. Hole. To the right of the door standing is Frank Rush.

He was from a family of eight children (five sisters) including Clara (Mrs. Albert) Vail, Emma (Mrs. Rufus) Clevenger and Cynthia Gray.

William and Lola were active members of the Youngs Chapel Christian Church and at the time of his death he was a deacon and trustee. He was also a member of the National Detective Association.

While preparing a grave at Youngs Chapel Cemetery on Jan. 2, 1930 he had a stroke and died on Jan. 31, 1930 without gaining consciousness.

Lola died Nov. 12, 1940 three days after being critically injured while crossing a street in Crawfordsville. She and her husband along with one daughter, Ruby, are buried in the Youngs Chapel Cemetery. *Submitted by F. Marvin Hole*

JOHN D. AND BERTHA MAY HOLLAND

John D. Holland was born in Brown Township, Montgomery Co., IN, a son of Joseph O. and Nancy Elizabeth Smith Holland. The father was born in New York City, and the mother was a native of Indiana. The father came to Indiana in 1864 and settled near Parkersburg, where he was married, later moving near New Market.

John D.'s grandfather, John Holland, came to the United States from England as a stowaway, at the age of 12. He was a sailor by profession. He established his home in New York City and followed the sea until a bale of cotton fell on him in 1860. He died in 1861.

Joseph O. Holland's family consisted of four children, namely; John D.; William Allen, who moved to Oregon; Ira J., who moved to Roachdale and Ida May, who married William Shure of Roachdale and lived there.

John D. and Bertha May Holland

John D. grew up on the home farm in Brown Twp. and received a common school education. In 1900 he married Bertha May Purcell, daughter of James R. Purcell and wife. She was born Sept. 28,

1879. Mrs. Holland died in 1905 at the age of 28, leaving three children; George M. born Dec. 18, 1901, Joseph E. (now James E.) born April 1904 and John "Bert", born April 1905. Upon the death of Mrs. Holland, the grandfather Joseph, came to Waveland to help raise the boys.

Mr. Holland first took up farming, later blacksmithing, then began huckstering and later clerked in a store. When he first came to Waveland he entered the poultry business in 1895, and in 1897 opened a grocery and notion store, later taking up the general mercantile business, carrying a large stock of goods usually found in such stores and enjoying an extensive trade with the surrounding country. Later because of illness he gave up the store and was local Postmaster. He belonged to the F & AM #300 and the Modern Woodmen of America No. 9589 at Waveland and member of the Baptist church.

George married Dorothy Duvall in South Bend, IN Nov. 19, 1932; with two children; Donna and John they later moved to Plano, TX. George died in 1980. Joseph Eldred (now James E.) married Francis Duffy at Crown Point, IN. They later made their home in Appleton, WI. James died in 1985. They have one daughter, Judith.

Bert was always interested in art, and did several oil paintings through the years. He also worked for the railroad and a printing company in Chicago, and later a printing company in California. Waveland was always home to him. He married Geraldine Barker August 1941 in Las Vegas, NV, and after several years they returned to Waveland to make their home there. Bert died in 1978. *Submitted by Geraldine Barker Holland*

HOLLINGSWORTHS

Pinson (1820-1882) and his brother John (1835-1892) whose relative, John Hollingsworth is listed for 160 acres in the original entry land book of Montgomery County, both served in the Civil War. Pinson in the 72nd and later in Wilders Brigade, a calvary unit armed with Spencer repeating rifles. John served with the 11th calvary.

Pinson's first wife gave him; Amos B. 1842, Cueza Jane 1844, and Joseph, 1846. After her death he married Julian Jane Walker (1829-1869) having: Wrsual Gertrude (1850) married Thomas Cox having; George (1871-1880).

Sarah Elizabeth, Lydia Florence, Wrsual Gertrude, Mary Pink and Rosa Pinson

Ethel, (1875) married Harry Justice
Frank (1866) married Neva Martin having Russell
Winona (1878) married Gregg Johnston having Kathleen (1900) Gordon (1902), Marion (1905)
Euratis Frank (1852) believed murdered after the Civil War in the Cherokee strip of the newly opened Oklahoma territory.

Sarah Elizabeth (1855-1936) married Thomas Campbell (1850-1932) having Katherine (1882-1955) who married Bryant Walkup having a son Ben. Zola (1881-1960) unmarried; Laurence; Ruby (1887-1962) married J.L. McElroy.

Lydia Florence (1857) unmarried, owned and operated a dry goods business in Darlington.

Mary Pink (1859-1937) married William Booher having five children; Madge who died as a young adult; Judith who married John Wait and they had but one son, John; Benjamin who was stillborn; Fred and Dale; Lucille unmarried.

Rosa Pinson (1861-1942) married Robert Henry Larrick (1849-1924) and they had three sons: John Walker (1891-1968) unmarried; James Newton (1893-1950) unmarried. Except for the time that Jim served during WWI these two men spent all of their lives in Montgomery County.

Penson Hollingsworth (1901-1975) a banker in the county most of his life. First in Ladoga and then as cashier of the Farmers & Merchants State Bank of Darlington. He married Mary F. Fletcher, (1908-1961) and they had two children: Robert Carl 1936 who married Madonna McMurry and had three sons, John Michael 1957, Bradley Jay, 1959 and Robert Gregory in 1961. Bob is now married to Margaret Bryant of Charles Co., MD, they live in McAllen, TX. The second child was Rebecca L. 1939, who married Tim Dion and living in Rhode Island, Diana L. 1964, married Terry Howell having two sons; Travis Jared 1982 and Seth Adam 1988. The Howells live on part of the "Larrick home place" in Franklin Township. Mary Katherine, 1967, married Geoff Anderson from Lafayette, where they now reside.

The Larrick farm bordered on the north by Sugar Creek, and the creek backs up into a bayou in a 68 acre woods. This spot has been a joy to every generation of this family. Rosa, having three sons of her own, once commented that her house was always full of wet kids and wet clothes; her own kids and at one time or another every kid in Darlington. *Submitted by Mary Anderson*

MARGARET CATHERINE GOHMAN HOLZ

Margaret Catherine Gohman, daughter of Joseph and Minnie Swank Gohman, was born Dec. 27, 1896, on the family farm near Crawfordsville. At 92, Margaret lives in southern California, maintaining her own home, though since 1988, living with her daughter Betty, in Mission Viejo.

Margaret ventured west in the 1920's with sister, Esther and aunt Rea. Their final destination was Los Angeles where all three married.

Margaret married Frederick William Holz (1892-1963), of Graz, Austria, son of Johann von Holzgerlingen and Mary Langer, on Nov. 2, 1927.

Frederick William and Margaret Catherine (Gohman) Holz and baby Margaret Ann

Fred had been orphaned and brought to America by his bachelor uncle, Al Langer. He worked in his uncle's boarding house in Lancaster, PA. Fred left his uncle and traveled, settling in California. He worked at the famous Biltmore Hotel in Los Angeles, across from the historic Pershing Square, until he retired in 1958.

Margaret and Fred enjoyed dancing and outings in his Model T Ford. He built a little house in the El Sereno hills four miles from downtown Los Angeles. The couple had three children: Margaret Anne (1929), Betty Jean (1932) and Frederick William, Jr. (1935). Margaret made many trips back to Indiana on the train and enjoyed reunions on the family farm.

Some of Margaret's early recollections include the terrible buggy accident that took the life of her baby brother, Willie. She recalls sitting between Joseph and Minnie, bouncing over the rocky road when the buggy overturned. Margaret remembers her chores, the kitchen water pump, milking the cows and taking care of younger sisters. She recalls her first date, a buggy ride to a church social with a handsome Hoosier at her side. (This was long before Fred).

Many Swanks and Gohmans settled in the west; more came to visit, only to return to their Indiana home. One memorable visit for Joseph and Minnie Gohman was when, after their 50th wedding anniversary, they were interviewed on the Breakfast Club radio show. Asked how to have an enduring marriage Minnie said, "Never let the sun set on your anger."

Betty Jean married (1952) John M. Prendergast of Brooklyn, NY, whom she met at her Aunt Rea's boarding house. They had three children: John Joseph (1953), Daniel Fred (1955) and Jenny Anne (1963). Daniel married Maureen Quirk: they had three children: Tiffany, Eric and Carley. At the time of writing Jenny was engaged, but brother John was a confirmed bachelor. Betty and John's marriage was dissolved after 26 years; Betty is a department manager in a retail store.

Margaret Anne graduated from Los Angeles State College and earned her Masters degree from UCLA. She enjoyed traveling and taught school for many years, including one year as a Fullbright exchange teacher in Oxford, England. Married (1968), to Donald M. Hostetter, Margaret serves as a school psychologist for LAUSD. They had one daughter, Kathleen Anne (1971).

Fred, Jr. died in 1962 and was buried at Rose Hills in Whittier, CA, one year before his father found his resting place there. *Submitted by Margaret C. Holz*

HOMANN FAMILY

The Homanns settled in Crawfordsville in December of 1977. It was a year of many changes — Kurt finished law school and started his law practice, Carol left her nursing job at I.U. Hospital, they were married, and bought their first home, all in the month of December! Then, the month of January 1978 saw more excitement — the Blizzard of '78 came, Kurt became Deputy Prosecuting Attorney and assisted in his first murder trial, and everyone suffered through the energy crisis. Things were thankfully not as tumultuous for the Homanns before — or since then.

Carol was born and raised in Carmel, IN, one of three children born to Jack and Mary Koss. Her childhood and early adolescence were filled with two interesting activities — swimming and singing.

She achieved great success as a long distance swimmer at the Jordan YMCA, winning state championships in several events, and making one memorable trip to the National AAU Swimming Meet. Singing and music were also important to Carol and she sang the lead in her high school musical "Guys and Dolls."

After graduation from Carmel High School in 1970, Carol enrolled at William Woods College in Fulton, MO. She concentrated on music and played the lead in "A Funny Thing Happened on the Way to the Forum." After two years at William Woods, Carol learned that her first love was nursing, and she transferred to Purdue University, attaining her degree and R.N. license in 1974. She finished her Master's Degree at Purdue in 1981.

Carol, Kurt and Clayton Homann

Kurt grew up on Indianapolis' northeast side, the second of three children born to Charles and Betsy Homann. The family moved to Carmel in 1967 when Kurt was a high school sophomore. He was active in all kinds of music — choral and instrumental, and also got one of his most treasured possessions — a varsity letter in football. He also met someone who would be very important to him a few years later — Carol Koss, the present Mrs. Homann!

Kurt's first introduction to Crawfordsville was when he visited Wabash College as a high school senior. The decision came down to Wabash or Depauw — needless to say, he made the right choice and came to Wabash in 1970. History and Music were his interest areas and he graduated with honors in 1974. From there it was on to I.U. Law School where he finished his degree and passed the Bar Exam in 1977.

Somehow that brings our story back to 1978 when the Homanns "went to housekeeping" in Crawfordsville. Not surprisingly, they quickly became active in theater and music. Carol played the lead in "Annie Get Your Gun" and numerous other roles with the Sugar Creek Players. Kurt also played in several productions and later served the Players as President and Fundraising Chairman of one of the Capital Fund Drives. They have also sung annually with the Community Chorus, often as soloists.

And then came Clayton. July 14, of 1982 the Homann's only child Clayton came into their lives, and what a wonderful time that summer was for the new family of three! It almost seemed like the whole community shared in the Homann's joy.

Well, 11 years have passed since that hurried, harried introduction of the Homanns to Crawfordsville. Carol has been school nurse for ten of those years, and Kurt has continued his law practice, now as a private practitioner in partnership with Bud Groves. This year, 1989, may prove to be as exciting as their first in Crawfordsville because they are moving from their West Main address to the Peter Kennedy homeplace. That will keep them all busy for a few years!

JOHN E. AND GRACE HOPEWELL

John was born near Farmersburg, IN in 1861. He always said that he was Lincoln's first volunteer. He went to live with his aunt and uncle, in Chattanooga, TN when he was 12 years old. He drove a mule-train and hauled lumber down the mountain. He came back home and took a Business Course in Terre Haute. He became a traveling salesman. He called on the Linden Hardware and stopped at the Vyce Hotel in Linden. It was there that he met Grace Wilson, who made her home with Mr. and Mrs. Vyce, and also worked there. They were married Apr. 3, 1901 in Covington. They made their home in Linden, where John bought into a partnership with John McCallum, in the Hardware. In 1905 he became Cashier of the Linden State Bank, which he served for 36 years. He retired from the bank when he was 80 years old.

John E. and Grace Hopewell and three daughters Mary, Ruth and Anna

Grace Wilson was born in 1880 on a farm her mother and father owned, on the Plank Road. She had one brother, Thomas, who lived in Linden all his life. He married Etta Lyons. They had one daughter, Fern Edith who became a school teacher. When Grace's mother died, she went to work at the Vyce Hotel. When the Vyce's retired they took Grace to their home in Covington to live with them. She was an excellent cook and homemaker. She loved her children friends. She and John had three daughters. Ruth is the lone survivor. She and Anna were school teachers. Mary was Postmaster for a while and then had a beauty shop in Linden. Mary married Fred Rosa from Lafayette. Anna married Fay Hunter from Kirklin. They had a son Don who lives in Chester, NJ. He and his wife Susan had two daughters, Cindy and Marci. Ruth married Arthur Coopman in 1934. They had one daughter, Judith Diane and a granddaughter Deborah, who is a senior at Hanover College. Judith is married to Roger Hildebrand.

In the spring of 1915, the Linden Woman's Club began a movement for the Public Library, but delays and discouragement, due to World War I, held up the procedure with the library building, but due to the patience and persistence of John Hopewell, the library became a reality and opened in 1922.

Grace died 1954 and John died in 1947. *Submitted by Ruth Coopman*

RONALD AND MARGARET HORN

In the spring of 1976, Ronald and Margaret Horn purchased the farm which was originally owned by Redden B. Snyder, one of Montgomery County's early settlers. They moved to Montgomery County in September of 1982. Both of them were born in Jackson Township, Tippecanoe County; grew up there and graduated from Southwestern High School.

Ronald Les Horn is the son of Cecil Columbus and Eva Louise (Raub) Horn. He is the youngest of 12 children. Margaret Ann (Meharry) Horn is the youngest of three daughters of Hugh Sayers and Helen Christine (Whitehead) Meharry. Both sets of parents resided in Tippecanoe County and were farmers.

Ron and Margaret Horn; Cheryl and Anita Horn; Shelia and Gene Truncellito; Jeff, Clayton and Dane Horn

Four children were born to the couple; Sheila Jean graduated from McCutcheon High School in 1977 and obtained her degree from DePauw University in 1981. At present, she is the Human Resource Manager for the American Reliance Insurance Company in Lawrenceville, NJ. In 1983 she married Gene Truncellito, son of Fabian Truncellito of Rivervale, NJ; and Madeline Mary (McCormick) Rider of Bourbon, IN. He graduated from North Bergen High School in 1969. Four years later he graduated from Rutgers College and obtained a juris doctor from Seton Hall Law School in 1977. He is employed as the associate senior counsel for the North American Phillips Corporation of Somerset, NJ.

Jeffrey Allen graduated from McCutcheon High School in 1978 and Purdue University in 1983. He holds a bachelor of science degree in Agricultural Mechanization. Currently, he is farmer in Tippecanoe County. He married Cheryl Denise Parent in 1984. She is the oldest daughter of Joseph Malcolm and Linda Marie (Lindley) Parent of Crawfordsville. Cheryl is a 1974 graduate of Crawfordsville High School and is employed by Lithonia Hi-Tek. They are the parents of a son, Jeffrey Clayton, born in 1987.

David Ronald is a 1983 graduate of McCutcheon High School. His degree from Purdue University in 1989 is a bachelor of science degree in Pharmacy. David is presently employed by Hooks, Inc.

Anita Marie graduated from North Montgomery High School in 1986. Currently she is a senior at Rhodes College in Memphis, TN. Her degree will be a bachelor of arts in Political Science, with plans to attend law school after graduation.

A genuine love of the land keeps this couple engaged in the business of farming. They hope to leave their environment better for the next generation, as they too can enjoy a quality life-style. *Submitted by Margaret Horn*

THE HOSTETTER FAMILY

Ulrich Hochstaedter arrived in Philadelphia, with brothers, Christian and Nicklaus, Sept. 15, 1749, on the ship Phoenix. They were German-

Swiss and were Mennonites. One of the characteristics of Mennonites is their instinct for fine lands. They are most thorough and patient farmers. The highly cultivated land, the substantial stone houses and barns, large and excellent orchards and the best of cattle are characteristic. The Hochstaedters settled in that part of Lancaster County that had just been set apart as York Co., PA.

Henry Hostetter, son of Ulrich, born ca 1760, served in the Revolutionary War as a 1st Lt., Pennsylvania Militia, Capt. Andrew Foreman's Co. (Perhaps two dozen descendants have become members of Dorothy Q Chapter, DAR, on his record.) He married Anna Maria Sherman in 1780; they had several children, three of whom, David, Rachael and Henry, all eventually came to Indiana. This family then moved to Rockbridge Co., VA.

David Hostetter, born in Pennsylvania, married Mary Ann Hicks (daughter of Joshua Hicks) in 1808 in Virginia. By way of Montgomery Co., KY, they moved to Pickaway Co., OH. Mary Ann died there in 1824. In 1830 David bought land in Scott Township of Montgomery Co., IN, and in 1831, brought his second wife (Mrs. Mary Boyer) and six children to their new home.

The journey from Ohio was a difficult one. In many places brush had to be cut away, and marshes and streams filled with logs, cross-lain, before they could proceed. It took one week for the trip from Indianapolis to the homesite (just west of the present "Ashby"). There was no Post Office until one was established in Parkersburg in 1834. There were still a few Indians in the area, but the main problem was wild animals which ate or destroyed crops and livestock. Neighborhood drives were organized and, gradually, these problems were conquered. The sacrifices of our ancestors to give us the heritage of productive land should not be forgotten.

David Hostetter's children were Sherman, Jane married George Heckathorn, Beniah, Mary married William Fleming Davidson, Zerelda married Isaac Martin, and David Hicks Hostetter. Lucky and Lewis were born in Indiana.

Rachael Hostetter married John Harvey Goodbar, and was the ancestress of many Montgomery County families. Henry Hostetter settled in northern Indiana, but was the great-grandfather of Date Hostetter, of this county, who was the grandfather of Betty Bradley Swoverland.

David Hicks Hostetter, born in 1822 in Ohio, married Amanda Jane Graybill (see Graybill family) in 1874, and they built a home three miles west of Ladoga. He was a successful farmer, in the Mennonite tradition, and they had a very attractive home, with much hospitality. In 1907 they built, and moved to, a new home in Ladoga, where their granddaughter, Mrs. Wm. R. Hawley, and her husband, now reside. Part of the farm, now owned by Mrs. Hawley, was declared a Century Farm in the Bicentennial year of 1976. David died in 1910, aged 87, and Amanda died in 1935, aged 91. They had three children: Lydia, Samuel and Emma Jane, who married Dr. Harrison Kemper Walterhouse. (See Walterhouse family).

A stone in the yard of his great-great-granddaughter, Druscilla (Hawley) Carroll (Mrs. R.J.), two miles west of Ladoga, on State Road 234, commemorates David Hostetter's coming to Indiana in 1831. *Submitted by Mrs. Wm. R. Hawley*

CATHERINE HARRISON JOHNSON HOSTETTER

Our subject, Catherine Harrison, was born in Ladoga, IN, in 1846, daughter of Sarah Stover (1816-1912) and William Riley Harrison (1812-1871).

Sarah Stover's parents, George and Anna Rader Stover, are buried in the Ladoga Cemetery. They came from Botetourt Co., VA, in 1832 and settled on a tract of 32 acres on Haw Creek, near Ladoga.

William Riley Harrison's parents were Hudson and Elizabeth Beason Harrison. Records show that their farm was adjoining that of Stovers. So W.R. Harrison essentially married the girl next door!

Catherine Harrison Johnson Hostetter

William Riley Harrison was reportedly a third cousin of President William Henry Harrison. A man of ability and education, he was one of the first school teachers of Ladoga. He took his family, including little Catherine Harrison, to Iowa, then ventured to California beckoned by the cry of "Gold" in 1849. In 1858 he returned east to take his family to California.

Catherine Harrison described the journey to Red Bluff, CA, from Waubeek, IA, and her youngest son, Lenus J. Hostetter recorded it: "As they crossed the plains they met with a party of Sioux Indians. Black Bear, the chief, was a Mason, and when Mr. Harrison gave him a sign, the chief embraced him and that night the Indians and Mr. Harrison formed a circle and smoked a pipe of peace. Black Bear gave Mr. Harrison a war club made of a steel ball with a long handle made of rawhide with a buckskin loop to carry it with."

The friendly chief went ahead to pave the way for the emigrant train. The Harrisons were joined by other families headed west. After two encounters with Indians that were not so friendly and provisions were getting scarce, the pioneers were glad that they overtook the 6th Infantry.

The 6th Infantry accompanied the emigrants until they reached Humboldt Valley, NV, where the latter turned off the trail to Honey Lake Valley, Lassen Co., CA, where most of them settled.

Catherine Harrison first married Thomas Benton Johnson in Nov. 13, 1863. He was born in Missouri on Aug. 5, 1842. They had four children: Guy, Sallie E., Samuel T. and Zebnor. The couple ultimately settled in Susanville, CA, in Lassen County.

Catherine's second husband, Francis Marion Hostetter, (1830-1897), son of Abraham and Mary (Burns) Hostetter, also born in Missouri, crossed the plains in 1862, and settled in Lassen County. They were married Jan. 1, 1873, and had five children: Bert, Lela, Milton, Ida and Lenus J.

Francis Marion took unimproved land and turned it into a valuable estate and also owned a sawmill. He sold his ranch and purchased 200 acres.

Catherine Harrison Hostetter died in Lassen County, on Feb. 9, 1929. Her father, William Riley Harrison, was a prominent lawyer and leading Republican in the early days of the west. He was the first judge of Shasta and Tehama Counties and helped to establish Masonic Lodges in Shasta County and Susanville. *Submitted by Donald Marion Hostetter*

ANDREW K. HOUK, JR. FAMILY

Andrew K. Houk, Jr., born Apr. 12, 1950 in Crawfordsville, IN, is the son of Andrew K. Houk, Sr. and Georgia L. Cummings Houk. He attended grade and high school at Granville Wells School and graduated in 1968. He was raised on the family farm located east of New Ross and north of U.S. 136 on the old brick road in Jackson Township, Boone Co., IN. After graduation, he enlisted in the U.S. Navy. He served two tours of duty in the I Corps area in Vietnam and on board the U.S.S. Iwo Jima LPH-2, a helicopter carrier. He was discharged in July, 1972.

Andrew K. Houk, Jr. worked for one year for Cummins Diesel and four years at Witham Hospital, where he was one of the original crew members of the Boone County Ambulance. Among his hobbies are the study of the American Civil War, flower gardening, and the tracing of genealogy. He is a member of the Jamestown Fire Department, Boone County Civil Defense, Jamestown American Legion Post 395, the William Knight Chapter, Greencastle, Sons of the American Revolution, and a deputy of the Boone County Sheriff's Department.

Andrew K. Houk, Jr. was married Oct. 11, 1975, to Susan L. Hart in Martinsville, IN. Susan Hart Houk is the daughter of Leroy E. Hart and Martha J. Lewis Hart, formerly of Martinsville, IN, and now of San Antonio, TX. Susan Hart Houk was born Jan. 26, 1954, in Bedford, IN. She attended schools in Martinsville and graduated from Martinsville High School in 1972. She graduated from Central Business College in Indianapolis in April, 1973. After graduation, she was employed at U.S. Steel's Indianapolis regional office. In April, 1976, she joined the staff of the Lilly Endowment in Indianapolis, where she is currently employed. She works in the Evaluation Section. Among Susan's hobbies are collecting baseball cards, collecting stamps, reading and genealogy. She is a member of the Jamestown American Legion Post 395 Auxiliary, Boone County Civil Defense, the Dorothy Q Chapter, Crawfordsville, Daughters of the American Revolution, and a deputy of the Boone County Sheriff's Department. Both Andrew and Susan are avid genealogists and have written several books on various family genealogies.

In July, 1976, Andrew and Susan purchased their present home at 205 West Main Street in Jamestown. The house sits on the property that Susan's fifth great-grandfather, Jacob Johns, settled in February, 1830. The present house was built in the early 1860's. Jacob Johns and his wife, Rachel, came to Indiana in the 1820's from Clay Co., KY. They were among the first settlers of Jamestown. They are buried in the Johns Cemetery in Jamestown, which is located at 1st Street and Four Winds Drive.

Susan is in the DAR through Colonel Josiah Brewer of Massachusetts. Other Revolutionary War ancestors were Andrew Beaty, Terisha and William Turner, Stephen Hamm and Anthony Fullilove, all from Virginia.

On Apr. 12, 1980, Susan and Andrew opened Jamestown Antiques and Collectibles. They are also owners of the Catcher's Mitt Sports Memorabilia. The Houk's are co-owners, along with Jay Wilson, Jr. and his wife Alice, of Oolitic, IN, of

Historic Lawrence County Press, which is located in Oolitic, Lawrence Co., IN. The Houk's and Wilson's are currently researching information for a book about Montgomery Co., IN Confederate Civil War veterans. They are also in the process of publishing a multiple volume set on Lawrence Co., IN Civil War veterans.

DARRELL AND DEBORAH WRIGHT HOWARD FAMILY

The family roots of Darrell and Deborah began in other counties of Indiana, and not until both Darrell and Deborah finished their college educations did their lives begin here in Montgomery County.

Darrell was born Apr. 27, 1942, in an old farm home on Layton Station Road south of Veedersburg in Wabash Township of Fountain Co., IN. During Darrell's childhood years, family, school, and church were the important aspects of his life. The school years from grade one through grade eight were spent in a four room, red brick building. Rabb School holds many memories of each of his four teachers and his classmates. Grades nine through 12 were spent travelling to and from Perrysville High School which was across the Wabash River in Vermillion County. Church services and youth group services were a regular and integrated part of Darrell's life. Both Rabb School and Cooper's Chapel, the church which he attended, are located on what is now Indiana Highway 32 in Wabash Township of Fountain County. Darrell is the oldest of four children born to Gordon J. and Elizabeth Myrtle Payton Howard. A brother, Jerry, was born in March of 1944; a sister, Vernice, was born November in 1949; and a brother, Dennis, was born in August of 1951. Before coming to Montgomery County, Darrell had lived and/or worked in Minneapolis, MN, and Chicago, IL. He also has served in the United States Armed Forces for two years, with one year being in South Korea.

Deborah was born to Charles Albert and Hazel Marie Neese Wright on Feb. 1, 1947, at St. Anthony Hospital in Vigo County at Terre Haute, IN. Deborah, the youngest of three children, has two brothers. Charles LeRoy, the oldest, was born July 17, 1938, and lives in Terre Haute. Gary, the middle child, was born June 13, 1945, and is living in Oakland City where he teaches music. School, church, music, and family were all important ingredients in Deborah's upbringing, and are a continuing influence in her life. Schools attended during her childhood were Maryland Grade School, Honey Creek Junior/Senior High, Sarah Scott Junior High, and Wiley High School. Many hours were spent with her interests of music in piano and flute. This interest continues still today. While growing up, the family attended church at Zion Evangelical and Reformed Church which later became St. Mark United Church of Christ in Terre Haute. The values of music, education, church, thrift, and self reliance were emphasized by her family.

Both Darrell and Deborah attended and graduated from college at Indiana State University in Terre Haute, but not until they began teaching in Montgomery County did they meet. They met while bowling in a Teacher's Bowling League. She was a second grade teacher at East Union Elementary School of North Montgomery School Corp. - and he, a sixth grade teacher at Laura Hose Elementary School in Crawfordsville. Deborah began her teaching at Granville Wells School in Boone County in January 1969; then moved to East Union School in September 1969 and has been with the North Montgomery School unit to the present teaching second grade. Darrell began his student teaching at Hose School with Don Whitecotten as his supervising teacher. Darrell began his teaching career in 1970 and has taught both sixth and fourth grades. Darrell and Deborah were married at Woodland Heights Christian Church by Rev. Lucian Robinson on July 29, 1972 near Crawfordsville. Their first daughter, Jacque DeAnne, was born on Feb. 5, 1974, at Home Hospital in Lafayette, IN on a cold, crisp winter night with a slight skiff of snow. Jacque is a student at Crawfordsville High School with interests in church, family, school, music, history, reading, travelling, and a very strong interest in genealogy. Sherri Leigh, the second daughter was born on Jan. 24, 1979, on a cold, snowy wintery day at Home Hospital in Lafayette, IN. After a treacherous drive to the hospital, the snow and bad weather caused roads and highways to be closed, so while Deborah was spending the night at the hospital, Darrell was spending the night at the closest Holiday Inn. Sherri is a student at Nicholson Elementary School in Crawfordsville and has interests in music, school, church, nature, family, travelling, history, and Cubs baseball. Jacque and Sherri were christened at Mt. Zion United Methodist Church by Rev. Joe Miller and Rev. Lester Vanest, respectively. Darrell, Deborah, Jacque, and Sherri are members at Woodland Heights Christian Church at Crawfordsville. The Darrell and Deborah Howard family have lived on West Main Street in the Warren Davis addition for the past 13 years.

Darrell and Deborah continue to believe in the strong family values that they have grown up with - whether it be the sounds and sights of nature, the continuing interest in education, church, music or family. These values whether they are formed in Fountain County, Vigo County, or Montgomery County are truly treasured gifts. *Written by Darrell Howard*

AUBREY C. AND EVELYN BLEYTHING HOWELL

Aubrey and Evelyn moved to Montgomery Co., IN in June 1948. They lived three years in Crawfordsville moving in 1952 to the country west of Darlington, IN where they lived for 11 years. In 1963, they moved into the town of Darlington.

Aubrey was employed by David's Plumbing Service. In 1958, he went to work for Raybestos Manhattan and retired from there in 1982. Aubrey was born in Michigantown, IN to Rev. Arthur and Bertha Howell, the second of eight boys. Aubrey spent most of his childhood in Knightsville and Brazil, IN and graduated from Brazil High School. He served four and a half years in the United States Army during World War II in the Southwest Pacific Area: Philippines, Hawaii and New Guinea. Aubrey was in the Division Headquarters of the 38th Division.

Aubrey's father was born in Poseyville, IN to Charles and Katherine N. Howell. Arthur graduated from Poseyville High School and DePauw University at Greencastle, IN. He served the Darlington Methodist Church and other churches in Indiana and Michigan. After he retired from the ministry, he and Bertha lived in Waveland, MI for awhile then moved to Lebanon, IN. After Arthur's death, Bertha moved to the Wesley Manor Retirement Home in Frankfort, IN. Aubrey's mother was born in Knightsville, IN to John and Christina Northway. John was born in England. He and his parents moved to the United States when he was a boy. He was a banker and also did some farming. Bertha worked and helped Arthur in the churches that he served.

Aubrey C. and Evelyn (Bleything) Howell

Evelyn was born in June 1921 in Dearborn, MI to Raymond and Cordelia Rice Bleything. She was the second of three girls. Her parents soon moved to Detroit, MI where she lived for 13 years. In 1934, she, her sisters and mother moved to Indianapolis, IN where she attended Arsenal Technical High School her freshman year. From there, they moved to Brazil, IN. She graduated from Brazil High School.

Evelyn's father was born in 1897 to Ray and Marie Bleything at Rosedale, IN. He worked for Timken Automatic Oil Burners as their chief automotive mechanic for their fleet of trucks. Her mother was born in 1898 to Ulysses Grant and Cora Smith Rice in Bowling Green, IN. In February 1941, Cordelia married Herb Lochridge. After Herb's retirement from Sears Roebuck in Los Angeles, CA, they moved to Yucaipa, CA.

Aubrey and Evelyn were married in December 1941 by Aubrey's father at West Terre Haute, IN. They have two children: Ronald, married to Paula Yenser and they have a daughter, Amber Renee. Christina, married to David LeFevre; they have a son, David C. Both live in Lafayette, IN. *Submitted by Mr. and Mrs. Aubrey Howell*

HUDSON

On Mar. 27, 1822 in Scotland, Lanark County, Gorbals Parish (a suburb of Glasgow), Thomas Hodgson of England and Mary Manson of Midlothian County, Scotland, Leith Parish were joined together in marriage. Thomas was born about 1796 and his occupation was a fisherman. Mary was born July 1, 1789 and died July 12, 1871. She is buried in the Linden Cemetery. Mary was living with her son William in 1869 and in 1870 she is living with a former neighbor, W.C. Devenport. Thomas and Mary had five children: Thomas David, Caroline, John Manson, William J., and James Louis.

On June 7, 1850, in Glasgow, Scotland, Thomas David Hodson and Helen Leechman were married. From the port of Greenock, Scotland Thomas David and Helen sailed on the ship Herald and arrived in New York City July 30, 1850. Thomas David was born in Glasgow, Scotland in 1822 and Helen was born in Scotland about 1820. Their first child, John David was born in Linden, IN, Aug. 4, 1851. Three more children followed: James A., born 1854; Margaret J., born July, 1855 and Louis J., born 1859. All the children were born in Indiana. Thomas and family are all living together in Madison Township in the 1860 Federal Census. Thomas' usual occupation was a Master Joiner (Carpenter).

Hazel J. (Hudson) DeDiemar

Caroline Hudson was born in Glasgow, Scotland about 1828. She married a man named Scott between 1841 and 1851. On the 1860 Federal Census of Indiana, Caroline is living with her older brother Thomas David, along with her three daughters. They are: Jane, Caroline, and Teresa M. Their ages are eight, six, and one, respectively. Caroline's daughters were born in Indiana. Her husband is not listed on the census. Further search for this family has proven unsuccessful.

John Manson Hudson was born in Dunoon, Scotland, about September of 1852. Where he is in the 1860 is unknown. However, in the 1870 Federal Census, John is living in Lafayette, IN. He is married to Margaret, born in Indiana and they have a son, Charles, who is a year old and born in Indiana. John's occupation is a baker. Further search for John after this has proven totally unsuccessful.

William J. Hudson was born in Dunoon, Scotland in the County of Argyll about 1835. William sailed from Greenock, Scotland on the ship Hudson and arrived in New York City Aug. 28, 1851. The Fountain County marriage records show that William Hudson and Anna H. Lupton were united in marriage Oct. 12, 1853. William and Anna had three children: John Manson, born Feb. 1, 1858; Margaret R., born June 1860; and William born Sept. 7, 1862. All of the children were born in Indiana—the latter two being born in Madison township. In the 1870 census John and his brother are living with their Aunt Maria. William, his wife Anna and their daughter Margaret are nowhere to be found. No one alive knows what happened to them. John Manson married Clara Jane Mason on June 13, 1891 in Montgomery County. They had five sons: Thomas W.; Charles Eugene; Clarence Earl; Wilbur (Pete) Francis and Ora H. and two daughters: Hazel Pearl and Mildred Benoid. Charles Eugene and Golda May Whitaker were married on Mar. 23, 1918 in Crawfordsville. They had four children: Lawrence Leroy, Evelyn Louise, Hazel Jewel and Dorothea Darlene. On Mar. 25, 1946 in Crawfordsville, Hazel Jewel Hudson and Robert George De Diemar were married. They had three sons: Robert Steven; Edward Eugene; and David Bryan. Edward Eugene De Diemar and Mary Jane Morales were married on Nov. 8, 1980 in Coral Springs, FL, Broward County and have one son, James Edward born Nov. 5, 1982 in Broward County.

James Louis Hudson was born Feb. 5, 1836 in Dunoon, Scotland in the County of Argyll. He died Sept. 18, 1858 and is buried in Linden Cemetery next to his mother.

Maria Jane, sister of Thomas Hodgson, married John Wyse Aug. 10, 1840 in the County of Argyll, Parish and town of Dunoon. Maria Jane was born Aug. 2, 1817 in the Parish of Barony, Glasgow, Scotland. John Wyse was born about 1814 in Cadder, Scotland in the County of Lanark. John and Maria had three children: Maria, born 1848; John, born 1850 and George born June 21, 1852 in Argyll County, Dunoon. Between 1848 and 1851, John (Maria's husband) and Maria's daughter died. Maria Jane married Peter Foster, born June 30, 1822 in Canada. In the 1860 Federal Census, John and George Wyse are listed, along with a new brother, John A. Foster, five years old, born in Indiana. Maria Jane and Peter Foster are both buried next to each other at the Linden Cemetery. Peter died Dec. 30, 1880 and Maria died Dec. 8, 1886.

BABE AND CHARLOTTE HUDSON - LIFE IN MONTGOMERY COUNTY

Babe D. and Charlotte Gegner Hudson, whose present address is 501 S. Washington Street, Crawfordsville, are the founders of Hudson Machine Tool, Inc. on Elmore Street. Mr. Hudson's parents, whose ancestors were originally from Germany and England eventually settled in Montgomery County via Kentucky around 1900. Thomas Jefferson Hudson and Viola Lucinda Jane Whiteman Hudson reared six children. Babe was born (Jan. 10, 1909) in Crawfordsville. He was reared near Alamo and graduated from Crawfordsville High School in 1927. After a few years of trying various occupations and extensive travel in the western states, he settled into family life marrying Charlotte Leona Gegner (Dec. 3, 1932). Charlotte, whose ancestors were originally from Germany and whose parents, Charles Luce Gegner and Elizabeth Jane Ball Gegner, settled in Montgomery County via Ohio around the 1900's, was born (July 24, 1914) south of Waynetown.

Babe and Charlotte Hudson, Charles, Marilyn K. Sowers, Carolyn Jan Foster, Nancy Servies

Babe and Charlotte have spent most of their married life in Montgomery County except for a year during World War II when they moved to Indianapolis where Mr. Hudson was employed at Allisons. They have worked together throughout the years in such occupations as floor sanding, managing a baseball camp near Alamo during the late 40's when young men ages 13-18 came during the summer months from all over the United States to learn the principles of baseball and take advantage of Mr. Hudson's knowledge of the game. Babe had been an outstanding pitcher and was recruited by a professional baseball team in the early 30's but Charlotte felt that was "a silly way for a grown man to make a living". His expertise in machine tool work led them to the founding of Hudson Machine Tool in 1953. The business began parttime in the family garage on the Waynetown Road and moved when a building was erected on their property. Eventually, the property of Kennedy Alignment was purchased and expanded. The present building on Elmore Street was finished in 1987.

Babe and Charlotte are the parents of four children-three daughters and a son. The oldest daughter resides in Fountain County. Two daughters and a son live in Montgomery County.

The eldest, Marilyn Kay (Dec. 16, 1933), postmaster at Wallace, graduated from Crawfordsville High School in 1952 and attended Indiana University. She married Kedric Leon Sowers of Wallace (May 15, 1955). Ked and Marilyn had four children: Lucinda Lou (Mrs. Gary Ellis), Kedric Lee, David Russell (1962-1983), and Daniel Babe.

Carolyn Jane, the second born, (Dec. 24, 1936), graduated from Crawfordsville High School in 1955, married John Thomas Foster (Dec. 31, 1956), reared four children: Teresa Kay (Mrs. Charles Kriston), John Timothy, Tamara Kim (Mrs. Kevin Bonebrake), and Angela Dawn (Mrs. Todd Stamper). Carolyn graduated from Purdue University in 1969 and works for the Area Four Agency on Aging and Family Service in Montgomery County.

The third child, Nancy Lou (Jan. 16, 1939) graduated from Crawfordsville High School in 1957, married Marlin Burton Harrington (June 14, 1959). They had three children; Marlin Kirk, Kyler Kent, and Stacy Leigh (Mrs. James Haslam). Mr. Harrington died (Apr. 23, 1975). Nancy remarried Max Edward Servies (July 3, 1976). She has three step children: Alis Marie (Mrs. Tim Maloney), Christina Jane (Mrs. Dale Elmore), and Timothy Regan. Nancy graduated in 1972 and received her masters degree in 1980 from Purdue. She teaches speech at Crawfordsville High School.

Charles Thomas (Dec. 17, 1943) married Janice DeBawn, daughter of Howard and Mildred De-Bawn of Waynetown, (May 14, 1966). They have five sons: Brian Charles, Jeffrey Neil, Jason Sean, Joseph Craig and Joshua David. Charles graduated from Crawfordsville High School in 1962 and Indiana State University in 1970. He is presently part owner, president and manager of the family business, Hudson Machine Tool on Elmore Street.

CLARENCE L. HUGHES

Clarence L. Hughes, son of Henry L. and Elsie (Musser) Hughes was born Oct. 21, 1879, and married Romania "Mame" Smith Aug. 1, 1900. Clarence and Mame had three sons; one, Vincent died as an infant. Clarence was a motorman on an interurban and brought the first interurban into Crawfordsville on what was known as the Ben Hur Line. In 1922, Clarence and his family moved to Orlando, FL where they went into the contracting business during the housing boom of the early "Twenties." Clarence L. Hughes died Sept. 3, 1938 and was brought back to Crawfordsville for burial in Oak Hill Cemetery. Romania died Dec. 31, 1964 in Orlando where the family had lived for 42 years. She, too, was brought back to Crawfordsville the area of her birth for burial next to her infant son and husband. Russell Smith Hughes was born on the Henry L. Hughes farm in Union Township on Apr. 19, 1901. Russell married Edith McKinsey Nov. 12, 1923. Edith was born in Clinton Co., IN, Nov. 29, 1901, and died July 5, 1967 at Orlando with burial in Woodlawn Cemetery. Russell married #2 Ruth Maddox Clem on Feb. 28, 1969 in Gainsville, FL. Russell and Edith were the parents of two sons and a daughter: Russell Vincent Hughes was born Aug. 19, 1925 at Orlando. Russell V. married Phyllis Meredith Flake June 2, 1956. Phyllis was born at Cocoa, FL Oct. 28, 1927. Russell V. and Phyllis have two sons, Russell Spencer Hughes born Feb. 13, 1959 at Sarasota and Bradley McKinsey

Hughes born at Sarasota Jan. 17, 1964. Bradley married Cynthia Hester May 24, 1988 at Cordale, GA.

Donald Richard Hughes, son of Russell and Edith was born Mar. 7, 1928 at Orlando, died July 18, 1987 in North Carolina, and buried at Woodlawn Cemetery at Orlando.

Nancy Ann Hughes, daughter of Russell S. and Edith was born at Orlando June 29, 1935. Nancy Ann died Jan. 14, 1956 and is buried in Greenlawn Cemetery.

Harry Hughes, son of Clarence L. and Romania Hughes was born May 21, 1909 in Montgomery Co., IN. Harry married Pauline "Bunny" Hughes May 21, 1935 at Daytona Beach. They were the parents of two sons. Harry died Mar. 26, 1988 at Orlando.

Vincent Smith Hughes, son of Harry and Bunny was born Nov. 17, 1940 at Orlando and married Jacqueline L. Cottrell Dec. 17, 1967. Vincent and Jacqueline have a son Vincent K. Hughes born Apr. 17, 1969 at Orlando and a daughter Magan R. Hughes born May 23, 1973.

David Henry Hughes son of Harry and Bunny was born Dec. 20, 1943 at Orlando and married #1 Rebecca Thomas Wilkins at Orlando July 31, 1965. They are parents of a daughter, Kristin Elizabeth Hughes, born Jan. 30, 1969 at Orlando. David's second marriage was with Linda Naimo Cooper Apr. 26, 1986, and they are parents of a son Patrick Craig Hughes born Sept. 12, 1988 at Orlando. *Submitted by Russell V. Hughes*

HARBOUR H. HUGHES

Harbour H. Hughes was born Mar. 5, 1774 in Gloucester Co., NJ near Estellville. Harbour served in Robert Lucas' New Jersey Militia contingent during the "Whiskey Rebellion" in Pennsylvania. He married Elizabeth Barcus Nov. 15, 1801 in Gloucester County. Harbour was a relative of Ezekiel Hughes who was born Aug. 22, 1767 on a farm called Cromcarnedd Uchaf, Llnbryormair, North Wales where his ancestors lived and farmed for over 200 years. Ezekiel, son of Richard and Mary (Jones) Hughes married Mary Ewing, daughter of Thomas and Mary Ann Ewing, July 16, 1805. Mary Ann was born July 11, 1785. The Ewings and Hughes were related. Harbour and Elizabeth left New Jersey with their children, John, Lydia, Joseph V., William B., Paul, Prudence Jane, and Phebe, and were settled in Coleraine Township, Hamilton Co., OH before 1819. The six of 13 Hughes children, Ogden R., Henry C., Martha Ann, Catherine Ann, Miranda, and Sinderella were born in Ohio. Sinderella died in infancy. An early map and Coleraine Township Business Directory listed "H.H. Hughes...proprietor of Steam Saw and Sorghum Mills and House Joiner, Dunlap P.O." Many homes and buildings were built by Harbour and his sons. Elizabeth Hughes died Jan. 24, 1846 and was buried in the Old Baptist Church cemetery near Dunlap Station in Coleraine Township. Harbour, Ogden's father died Nov. 25, 1847 and was buried where Elizabeth and their infant daughter were buried.

Ogden R. Hughes, son of Harbour and Elizabeth was the eighth child, born Mar. 9, 1819 in Coleraine Township, near Dunlap Station in Hamilton Co., OH. Ogden married Mary Ann Hancock Feb. 21, 1839. His wife, Mary Ann was born in Kentucky June 16, 1820. Their first child, a daughter Mary was born Mar. 10, 1840, (birthplace unknown). Mary Hughes married John Wert and they lived and farmed in Newton Co., IN near the town of Brook. Ogden and Mary Ann were living in Ripley Township on a 120 acre farm located in Sections 10 and 11 when their second child, Henry L. Hughes, was born Mar. 10, 1844. Henry first married Susan Snyder, daughter of Redden and Mrs. Snyder. Susan died Sept. 27, 1877 and was buried in Oak Hill Cemetery at Crawfordsville, (no children by that marriage). Henry L. Hughes married Elsie Musser daughter of Peter and Rebecca (Shippen) Musser Dec. 15, 1878. The Mussers were a pioneer family in Indiana. Elsie was born July 21, 1856 in Ripley Township. Henry and Elsie moved to their farm northwest of Crawfordsville, on the LaGrange road in the Breaks neighborhood near Roberts Chapel Church. In early times the LaGrange road was an Indian trail traveled by the Indians from a camp on Crawfordsville's near north side along Sugar Creek, northwest through Coal Creek township into Tippecanoe County. Henry and Elsie raised three children on this farm and retired in 1915 to their home in Crawfordsville. Henry died Nov. 7, 1922 and Elsie died at the home of her daughter Mrs. Harry Breaks Aug. 11, 1947. Both are buried in Oak Hill Cemetery. Lulu, Henry and Elsie Hughes' daughter, was born in Union Township, Dec. 9, 1881 and married Harry Breaks, son of Alvin and Clara (Messamore) Breaks, Apr. 4, 1904. Harry Breaks was born in the Breaks Homestead, Dec. 10, 1879. A son Alvin H. Breaks was born at the Homestead Apr. 23, 1919 and died unmarried Dec. 12, 1947 with burial in Oak Hill Cemetery. After farming the Homestead all his life, Harry died Mar. 15, 1956 at his home. Lulu died Dec. 22, 1970. Both are buried in Oak Hill Cemetery. Mary Ann (Hughes) Wert and John Wert had a son Emory born in 1856 and died in 1928. Emory had a daughter Jane (Wert) Lipman living in California as late as 1980. Mary Ann Wert died Jan. 23, 1896; she, John and son, Emory are buried at Brook, IN. *Submitted by Harold J. Hughes*

HIRAM HUGHES FAMILY

The earliest record of this branch of the Hughes family, to the best of my recollection, is traced to James B. Hughes who was born Jan. 4, 1819 in Kentucky. There he was married to Lavina Ray who was born Mar. 21, 1825. They migrated to the Young's Chapel area which is in Union Township, Montgomery County, about six miles north of Crawfordsville, IN. There they settled on a farm and in the course of time became parents of ten children; William Sanford, David Wesley, Thomas Jefferson, James Harvey, Nervilla, Ella, Sarah, Emma, John, and Nathaniel.

James B. Hughes died Sept. 22, 1864 at the age of 45. Lavina died Feb. 2, 1892 at the age of 67. Both are buried at the Young's Chapel Cemetery along with at least two of their sons, James Harvey and David Wesley.

Hiram W. and Una M. (Hensley) Hughes

James Harvey Hughes married Laura Belle McIntyre and she bore him four sons; Sanford, Frank, Earl, and Hiram Walter. The first three named all died before they reached the age of 21 and are buried at Young's Chapel.

Hiram Walter Hughes followed in his father's footsteps and became a farmer. The Hughes family was close-knit and several family members owned neighboring farms. The depression forced Hiram to leave the farm and move into Crawfordsville in 1931. There he did day labor for farmers near Crawfordsville, odd jobs, or any other honest work he could find to support his family.

Hiram married Una Mae Hensley Aug. 28, 1913. They had nine children, with three of them dying in infancy; Frank Delmar, Hiram (Junior), and Betty Catherine. The other six children were: Norwood Robert, Ethel Marie, Florence Elva, Rena June, Kenneth Eugene, and Mary Jane.

Hiram was blessed with such a sunny disposition that he was nicknamed "Happy". His booming laugh was so joyous, it was infectious, and you just had to laugh with him. His many, many friends will remember him as both a kind and gentle soul. His honest ways and homespun philosophy left its mark on many of us.

Hiram died Oct. 23, 1957, and his wife Una Mae followed him Aug. 19, 1984. Both are resting peacefully in Young's Chapel Cemetery. *Written by Ethel Marie Hughes Patterson*

JAMES ELBERT HUGHES

James Elbert Hughes, son of Ogden and Mary Ann Hughes was born Sept. 8, 1853 in Ripley Township. Elbert married Nancy J. Ellis Mar. 27, 1872, and they lived on the Ogden Hughes farm after Ogden died. Elbert and Nancy were parents of two sons, also born in Ripley Township. Mary Ann Hughes died Sept. 6, 1872. Later, Ogden married Rebecca (Shippen) Musser, widow of Peter Musser, who were the parents of Elsie Musser, wife of Henry Hughes son of Ogden Hughes. Ogden died on his birthday Mar. 9, 1894, at age 75. Ogden and Mary Ann Hughes are buried in McCormick Cemetery. Ogden's second wife Rebecca Hughes was born in 1829, died in 1898 and was buried in Oak Hill Cemetery.

Charles R. Hughes, born Feb. 19, 1878, married Alta Schenck, who was born Feb. 10, 1882. Charles served in the War of 1898, and later he and Alta lived on the Hughes farm south west of Waynetown until they retired and moved to Crawfordsville. Charles and Alta were parents of a daughter, Beatrice born Jan. 21, 1901 and died Apr. 7, 1934; she never married. Harry E. Hughes, son of Charles and Alta Hughes was born Mar. 23, 1906. Harry married Mary Henry Dec. 23, 1925; Mary was born June 19, 1910. Harry and Mary lived on the Hughes farm after Charles and Alta Hughes moved to Crawfordsville. They raised a son Harry Jr. born Sept. 11, 1937. Harry Jr. married Rosalyn Jean Miller June 19, 1961 at Bluffton, IN. Harry and Jean are the parents of, Bethany Hughes, born Feb. 9, 1970, Lee Ann Hughes born Jan. 24, ____, Mark Hughes born August 1972. Harry Jr. and his family are living in Hannibal, MO.

Geraldine Hughes, daughter of Harry E. and Mary Hughes, was born Dec. 9, 1927. Geraldine married Robert Smith at Mace, IN, Mar. 19, 1971. Robert Smith was born May 28, 1929, they have a son Robert, born Apr. 4, 1947 and a daughter Nona, born July 27, 1949. Robert and Geraldine live in Crawfordsville, IN. Harry E. Hughes died June 24,

1988. This is the first time since 1844, that a member of the family hasn't lived on the farm.

George William Hughes son of James Elbert and Nancy (Ellis) Hughes was born, Feb. 21, 1880. George married Gladys Ammerman born 1884, George and Gladys had a son born in 1922 and died 1923, a daughter Stella Hughes born Feb. 24, 1928, married William Furr. William and Stella have a daughter Dawn (Furr) Welker born May 6, 1957 living in Indianapolis. Dennis Furr, son of William and Stella born May 24, 1958 lives at New Market. Mary Jane Hughes, daughter of George and Gladys Furr born June 7, 1924 married Henry Kyle. *Submitted by Harold Hughes*

MERLE A. HUGHES

Merle A. Hughes son of Henry L. and Elsie (Musser) Hughes was born in Union Township Mar. 2, 1887. He walked about a mile to Hunt School, a one room school, for eight years. In 1902 Breaks Consolidated School was built and absorbed the pupils from Hunt, Quick, and Soap Factory Schools. The new school consisted of grades one through 11. This was probably the first school consolidation in Indiana. The last year of high school was the Class of 1916 and the last year of grade school ended in 1948. Merle pitched semi-pro baseball and also played basketball with the first YMCA teams when basketball was introduced in Montgomery County. Merle married Oley Haines daughter of Joseph William and Florence (Clough) Haines, Dec. 14, 1911. Oley was born Nov. 7, 1886 in Coal Creek Township. After Henry and Elsie moved to Crawfordsville, Merle and Oley lived on the farm, where their children Harold and Dorothy were born. Merle died July 28, 1941 and was buried in Oak Hill Cemetery. Harold continued farming until February 1943, when Oley moved to Crawfordsville. Oley's daughter, Dorothy and son-in-law Clinton Fulford continued farming. Oley worked as a seamstress until retirement in 1969. Oley died Aug. 9, 1969 and was buried in Oak Hill Cemetery. Harold J. Hughes son of Merle and Oley Hughes was born July 20, 1918 in the farm home his grandfather, Henry Hughes built in 1898. After graduation from Crawfordsville High School, Harold farmed with his father until Merle's death. Harold married Ruby Gentry, daughter of the late Elijah Gentry and Leora (Wills) Gentry, Mar. 21, 1943 in St. Petersburgh, FL. During World War II, Harold served with the 15th Air Force in Italy and Africa. Upon his return in 1945 from the service, he and Ruby lived in Lafayette for a year. They are the parents of twin daughters and a son. After returning to the neighborhood where Harold was raised, he and Ruby farmed and he drove a school bus for 16 years. He then with the help of Ruby served four years as Union Township Trustee. Ruby served as Poor-Relief Investigator for 21 years. After Harold's term expired he was employed by the State of Indiana for 16 years. Harold and Ruby Hughes live on the Breaks Farm that was entered by Richard Breaks Dec. 20, 1824. Judy J. Hughes and Julie J. Hughes, daughters of Harold and Ruby (Gentry) Hughes were born Oct. 21, 1946. They graduated from Crawfordsville High School in 1964 and attended Indiana University. Julie married Denny Russell, son of George and Vivian Russell in Vincennes, IN, Feb. 15, 1967. Denny was born July 16, 1948; Denny and Julie were parents of three daughters, all born in Vincennes, IN. Julie and Denny divorced July 31, 1976. Jennifer L. Russell born Sept. 19, 1968, married Daniel Murphy, son of Albert and Susie Murphy June 19, 1987 in Vincennes. Daniel was born Jan. 7, 1963. Daniel and Jennifer have a son Ryan Daniel, born Jan. 9, 1988. Jo Ellen Russell was born Aug. 2, 1970, and Kimberly was born Feb. 5, 1972. Jo Ellen and Kimberly are living with their mother in Palm Bay, FL, where Julie works for The Florida Institute of Technology. Judy married Dr. Manley K. Scheurich, son of Dr. Virgil and Margaret Scheurich, at Crawfordsville Apr. 2, 1967. Manley was born in Oxford, IN Jan. 8, 1941. They had twin daughters Karen Lynn and Kathy Elaine, born Jan. 10, 1969 and a son Michael Joe, born Feb. 4, 1968, in Oxford, IN. Judy and Manley divorced, Jan. 21, 1976 and Judy married Lindell Bice. They live near Lafayette, IN. Judy is a real estate broker in Lafayette.

Jerry J. Hughes, son of Harold and Ruby Hughes, was born Oct. 28, 1952 married Vicky Ellen Rush, Feb. 14, 1975. Vicki, daughter of Charles and Cathy Rush. Vicki was born Nov. 4, 1955. Jerry and Vicki are the parents of three sons, Jeremy Adam, born June 4, 1976, Jason Daniel, born Jan. 2, 1978 and Jonathan Matthew, born Mar. 18, 1972, Jerry and Vicky were divorced Nov. 21, 1986. Jerry lives on the Hughes farm and has his own excavating business. *Submitted by Jerry J. Hughes and sons*

ROSS AND EVIE HUMPHREYS

Ross Humphreys and Evie Higbee were married in the home of her parents, Charles A. and Joanna Phillips Higbee Aug. 17, 1902. They farmed in Wayne Township all their lives. Both were members of the Waynetown Baptist Church where Evie was an active member of the Delta Alpha S.S. class taught by E.A. Fields, a local furniture store merchant.

In 1916, after farming as renters, they built and entire farmstead on land they had purchased a few years earlier. This farm located on Centerville Road is still owned and occupied by members of the family.

The Humphreys had two children: Opal Humphreys-Endicott, who graduated from Waynetown High School, attended Indiana University where she earned A.B. and A.M. degrees in History and taught in Indiana high schools for more than 40 years. A son Harold farmed with his father.

Harold married Eulala Rasor in 1931 and set-up housekeeping on Pearl Lidster's farm, the old Elston Sawyer's homestead now owned by Frank Bunnell, where he (Harold) was born in 1910 and reared to six years of age when he moved with his parents to their new home mentioned above.

Ross and Evie Humphreys "Golden Wedding Anniversary" Aug. 17, 1952

Harold and Eulala bought the Grove Homestead on State Road 25 where Eulala still lives.

Harold and Eulala had a son Charles Edward Humphreys who graduated from Waynetown in 1961 and had a career in the U.S. Air Force from which he retired after more than 20 years with the rank of Master Sergeant.

While in the Air Force, Charles married Cheri Potter of Moultrie, GA. They have three children; Charles Eric, graduate of North Montgomery High School and attended Purdue University. At the time of this writing, he is a missionary in Spain for the Church of Jesus Christ of Latter Day Saints; Carole Lee and Cassandra Marie are students at North.

Opal married Loral Endicott, a Hendricks County farmer who specialized in breeding and sale of Hampshire hogs. Loral died in 1974 and is buried in Jamestown I.O.O.F. cemetery. Loral's daughter, Janet graduated from North Salem High School (1946) and Purdue University (1950). Janet and her husband, Carlisle Morris, a Purdue graduate had four children; Steven, Bradley, Marianne and Mark. All are engineering graduates of Purdue. Janet died in 1975 and is buried in Decatur, IL where she had taught art and operated an arts store.

Ross Humphreys died May 1, 1961; Evie died at the age of 91 Apr. 20, 1975. Both are buried in Waynetown Masonic Cemetery. Harold died May 29, 1985. He, too, is buried in the family plot in Waynetown Masonic Cemetery. *Submitted by Opal Humphreys Endicott*

SAMUEL AND SARAH GRIFFIN HUMPHREYS

Samuel and Sarah Griffin Humphreys came to Section 36 of Coal Creek Township from Vermillion Co., IL in 1893. The family at that time consisted of ten of their 16 children: Jonathan, Frederick, Ross, James, Lee, Wilbur, Alford, Francis Merrian, Asa and Grover. One daughter, Emma died in infancy. Charles, Mary who died in infancy, Zella, Carl and Caroline were born in the white frame house in Coal Creek Township that stood on property where today Donald Prum has a hog operation.

Samuel and Sarah Humphreys

The children attended one room District School located on the southwest corner of the farm and the three room school at Elmdale.

An 80-acre farm belonged to Samuel's father, Thomas B., known to the family as Grandpap, a widower (Rachel Cossort Humphreys had died in 1877) willed this tract to his daughter-in-law, Sarah. The cottage on this tract came to be known as "the Weaner" for several of the sons brought their brides to this cottage to set-up their first home, and farmed as share cropper with their father.

Samuel often drove a team of spotted ponies that he had purchased from gypsies who camped near his farm. When his friends and neighbors began to travel by automobile, Samuel bought a red Cole — at that time considered to be a very fine automobile.

205

Sarah was an excellent homemaker and knew how to delegate chores to any daughter-in-law who happened to stop for an afternoon. These chores varied from helping with cooking, laundry, preserving fruit from the orchards to picking ducks for feather beds and pillows. Each child upon his marriage was given a feather bed, a pair of pillows, comforters and quilts for his new home. There were often bags of dried apples or corn, cans of fruit from the well-stocked cellar, a loaf of warm bread and homemade cookies to take home from a visit to Grandma's. The author of this article remembers receiving a parcel post package containing red plum jelly and homemade sugar cookies when she was a student at Indiana University.

Sarah had dreamed of living in a brick house. In 1923, her dream came true. They sold the farm in Montgomery County and bought one in Parke County southwest of Waveland. The special attraction to this farm seems to have been the brick bungalow and a handsome round barn. It was here that Sarah and Samuel celebrated their 50th wedding anniversary on Jan. 20, 1926 with a family dinner attended by all their 14 living children. Both died in the home — Samuel on Nov. 17, 1927 and Sarah on July 12, 1928. They are buried in Oakland Cemetery north of Elmdale in Montgomery County. *Submitted by Opal Endicott*

DAVID C. HUNTER

David C. Hunter was the son of William B. and Martha Browning Hunter. He was born on Feb. 1, 1843 in Monroe Co., IN. He lived in Bloomington, IN and in Heltonville, Lawrence Co., IN before the Civil War.

David C. Hunter enlisted on Sept. 20, 1861 in Company G, 31st Regiment Indiana Volunteer Infantry at Bloomington, IN. He served as a Corporal. He participated in the battles of Fort Donelson, Fort Henry, Shiloh or Pittsburg Landing, the Atlanta Campaign, Stone River, Chicamauga, battle of Nashville, TN, and the pursuit of General Hood's Army into Alabama. David C. Hunter was promoted to 2nd Lieutenant and transferred to Company H on Oct. 15, 1864. He was promoted to 1st Lieutenant on May 1, 1865. He resigned his commission on May 15, 1865 due to health problems. He returned to Monroe Co., IN in June of 1865.

In 1867 David C. Hunter moved from Bloomington to Crawfordsville, IN. He became a well-known carpenter in Crawfordsville and was noted for his craftsmanship and scrollwork, much of which still graces many of Crawfordsville's older homes.

David C. Hunter was married on Apr. 17, 1890 to Phoebe A. Wallace. They had two sons, John L. and Morton W.

Phoebe A. Wallace Hunter died on Apr. 17, 1910 and is buried in Oak Hill Cemetery in Crawfordsville. After the death of his wife, David C. Hunter moved from his home on West Wabash Avenue to the Duncan Roominghouse where he died on June 22, 1911. He was buried with full G.A.R. honors conducted by McPherson Post #7, Grand Army of the Republic, Crawfordsville. He was buried beside his wife in Oak Hill Cemetery. *Submitted by Andrew Keith Houk, Jr. and Jay Wilson, Jr.*

GEORGE MARSHALL AND SOPHIA EDNA HUNTINGTON

George Marshall and Sophia Edna (Himes) Huntington were lifelong residents of Ladoga, Montgomery Co., IN. He was born Feb. 14, 1867, son of Hiram Samuel and Sarah Louisa (Gregg) Huntington. He died Feb. 16, 1922. He was an eighth generation descendant of Simon, the English immigrant ancestor of the Huntington family in America.

Sophia was born July 9, 1869 near Ladoga, daughter of Daniel H. Himes, Jr., and Mary Louisa (Harshbarger) Himes. She died on Aug. 31, 1945, age 76. They were married on Oct. 21, 1896. Their seven children were Charles Marshall, born Feb. 14, 1898, Earl Gregg who died in infancy, Mary Louisa, born Apr. 12, 1902, Silas Hiram, born May 8, 1905, Daisy Grace who died in infancy, Nellie Ruth, born Aug. 14, 1909, and Eva DeLelia, born Dec. 26, 1911.

George Marshall and Sophia Edna Huntington circa 1896

The Huntington family celebrated every year the coincidence that February 14, Saint Valentine's Day, was the wedding anniversary of George's parents, Sarah and Hiram, and the date of births of George, his brother Harry, and his and Sophia's first born, Charles Marshall.

George was a small man, strong, mild mannered, friendly, a man of high principles, and a devoted father. He was a deacon in the Presbyterian church for many years.

His devoted wife, Sophia, was a strong, genial, tireless, motherly woman, beloved by all who knew her, especially by many of the children in the community who called her "Sophie". Despite many adversities, she retained a bright spirit and a keen sense of humor. Not permitted to accept a college scholarship in her youth, she made sure that her children obtained higher educations.

As junior partner in the firm of Huntington & Son, and later by himself, George was a building contractor in Ladoga for over 30 years. As the active partner, he built many fine houses and other buildings in and near Ladoga, including the Ladoga Grade School, a classic Romanesque Revival style structure. Completed in 1897, that ornate edifice served for 75 years as elementary school for children of the Ladoga community, including all five of his surviving children. Many of the houses built by him remain structurally sound and attractive, with beautiful interior woodwork, and several have been listed in the National Registry of Historic Places. Throughout his career in building, George maintained the high standard of construction established by his father, Hiram Huntington and preceeding partners. By adding to his father's legacy of many excellent structures built in his lifetime, George Huntington was one of the community's notable citizens and a principal contributor to the good development and character of Ladoga.

HIRAM SAMUEL AND SARAH LOUISA HUNTINGTON

Hiram Samuel Huntington was the premier builder of Ladoga, Montgomery Co., IN, from 1866 to 1916. He was born Oct. 19, 1832 in Macidon, NY, near Palmyra, the son of Samuel Dimock and Mary Jane (Howell) Huntington. He was a seventh generation descendant of Simon, the English immigrant ancestor of the Huntingtons in America. Hiram lived in Adrian, MI from 1844 to 1859. He died on May 16, 1923, age 90.

On Feb. 14, 1858, he married Sarah Louisa Gregg of Adrian, who was born July 12, 1930 in Palmyra. Their children were Lizzie Gregg Warfel, born Dec. 8, 1862 in Adrian; George Marshall, born Feb. 14, 1867, and Harry Gregg, born Feb. 14, 1869, both in Ladoga, IN.

Hiram was a tall, quiet, kindly man, of high principles, highly respected in the community. His devoted wife, Sarah, was a small, vivacious, strong-minded woman, active in community affairs. Every year, their family celebrated the coincidence that February 14, Saint Valentine's Day, was the wedding anniversary of Sarah and Hiram, and the date of birth of their sons George and Harry, and George's first born, Charles Marshall Huntington.

Hiram Samuel Huntington circa 1906

The Huntingtons moved in 1859 to New Albany, IN, where he was a trainman on the Monon railroad. From 1861 to 1866, he was a pattern maker in the Union Army arsenal in Nashville, TN, which produced armament for the Union forces during the Civil War.

In 1866, Hiram moved his family to Ladoga, IN, where he operated a planing mill and became the principal building contractor in southeast Montgomery County. In his building and woodworking business, he had a succession of partners, the last being his son George, with whom he built the classic Romanesque Revival style Ladoga Grade School building. Completed in 1897, that ornate edifice served 75 years as the elementary school for children of the Ladoga vicinity, including five of Hiram's and Sarah's grandchildren. Their son-in-law, J. Francis (Frank) Warfel, husband of their daughter, Lizzie, was the first superintendent and a teacher in the Ladoga schools for many years.

During his 50 years as a contractor, Hiram Huntington and partners built many of the buildings in the Ladoga area, including three classic houses now in the National Registry of Historic Places, the Robert L. Ashby Place (1883), southwest of Ladoga, the J.C. Knox house (1895) and the Ed Lidikay house (1895), both in Ladoga. All construction by Huntington and partners was of highest quality. The houses he designed were of the best architectural styles of the era. Hiram, despite poor eyesight, was a skilled mechanic, particularly in fine woodworking. To this day, those houses built by the partnerships and given normal maintenance through the years, are structurally sound and classic in appearance, and the interior woodwork is beautiful.

Hiram Huntington, through his legacy of the many fine houses and other structures he built in his long lifetime, was one of the community's leading citizens and a principal contributor to the development and the character of Ladoga.

JOHN W. AND MARY (LAMB) HURLEY

Mary Lamb, daughter of Simon and Millie Lamb, was born in Vermillion Co., IL on July 13, 1845. She was united in marriage to John W. Hurley on Feb. 23, 1874 in Vermillion Co., IL. She died Sept. 18, 1925 at the age of 80. To their union four children were born; William D., Myrtle D. born Oct. 3, 1882, Pearl, and Alva. When my mother, Myrtle was three years old the family moved to Kimbrell, NE, where she attended school and my grandfather farmed. After 15 years they moved to Montgomery Co., IN on State Road 47, south of Crawfordsville. They also lived on 400S where the airport is now. They moved from there north of Yountsville, IN and later moved to 406 John St. in Crawfordsville, where they both died after 51 years together.

Mary was born and reared in a Christian home and became a Christian in the early years of her life, joining the Methodist church at the Old Asbury Chapel in the old home Community, having finally transferred her membership to the Methodist church in New Market, IN.

J.W. Hurley and Mary (Lamb) Hurley; Left to right front: Mahala Obenchain Pickel, Mary (Lamb) Hurley, Myrtle Dell (Hurley) Pickel, Ida (Pickel) Brown. Back row: J.W. Hurley, Arthur Brown. Sitting: Mary Mahala and Doris Marie Pickel.

As to their children; William D. married Myrtle Brown, no children, lived in Indianapolis. He was a conductor on the Interurban railway from Indianapolis to Crawfordsville.

Pearl married Howard Shanklin. They had three daughters; Gladys, Leonice, and Isabelle. Alva married Anna Woolridge, had one son, Myrl. They lived in Long Beach, CA.

Myrtle D. married Jacob A. Pickel Oct. 4, 1905. She died June 1, 1958 at the age of 75. He died June 1, 1922, at the age of 38, after a farm accident with horses. Their children were Opal Viola, born Feb. 12, 1907. Doris Marie born Sept. 18, 1911, Mary Mahala, born Sept. 27, 1916.

Opal Viola married Laird Glover, no children. Doris Marie married William Hunt, nine living children, one deceased. Mary Mahala married Robert F. Sayler, four living children; John Leslie Sayler, Larry Gene Sayler, Janet Lynn Armstrong, Steven Wayne Sayler. Leslie Allen Sayler died in infancy. They also have four grandchildren; Jeffrey Sayler, Pamala Jo Jeffers, Corey Lynn Bonwell, Kelsie Lynn Sayler.

DAVID C. HUSEMAN AND LYNDA POSTON

David C. Huseman was born Apr. 15, 1946 in Crawfordsville, the third of three children to Juliana (Bauer) and Richard C. Huseman, Sr. His siblings are Richard, Jr., and Flora Wilson.

He is a graduate of Alamo High School and Greenville College, Illinois, and worked on his Masters at the University of Georgia.

He married Lynda Poston Mar. 1, 1975 in Greenville, SC.

Lynda was born Apr. 23, 1948, the second of four children to Grace (Nunn) and Daltrum Poston in Crockett, TX. Her siblings are Karry Sue, Clara Jo and Daltrum Holmes. She is a graduate of Wade Hampton High School, Greenville, SC; Columbia College in South Carolina and was a 1st Lt. in the Air Force.

They own and operate the RD Plastics Company, Inc., in Nashville, TN.

They have one daughter, Rachel Heather, born Nov. 9, 1978 in Nashville.

RICHARD C. HUSEMAN AND CAROLYN E. HANNSMANN

Richard Jr., moved with his family to Montgomery County in 1946, when he was seven. He was born Feb. 16, 1939 in Lafayette, the first of three children to Juliana (Bauer) and Richard C. Huseman, Sr., in Lafayette. His siblings are Flora Wilson and David. He graduated from Alamo High School and Greenville College in Illinois. He received his Masters and Doctorate at the University of Illinois in Champaign.

He married Carolyn E. Hannsman Aug. 26, 1961 in St. Louis.

Carolyn was born Nov. 2, 1941, the third of three daughters to Carolyn (Rudolph) and Walter Hannsman in St. Louis. She's a graduate of Beaumont High School in St. Louis and attended Greenville College, IL. They have two sons.

Douglas Carl, born Nov. 2, 1962 in Champaign, IL. He is a graduate of Cedar Shoals High School and University of Georgia in Athens, GA. He is a 2nd Lt. in the Marines.

Richmond Allyn was born May 3, 1966 in Athens, GA. He is a graduate of Cedar Shoals High School and attended University in Arizona. He works for Sherwin-Williams in Athens.

Dr. Huseman has taught at the University of Georgia since 1964, and since 1976 has served as Chairman of the Department of Management. He has co-authored eight books and many articles and papers for national professional meetings dealing with various aspects of communications and human performance.

RICHARD C. HUSEMAN AND JULIANA S. BAUER

Richard and Juliana Huseman purchased the Runyon property, west of Yountsville, in Ripley Township, Montgomery County late fall of 1945, moving in February 1946. They had opened the Crawfordsville Farm Supply, a Purina franchise, on Main Street, December 1944.

Dick was born Aug. 25, 1911 in St. Louis, the second of four children to Louise (Deibel) and Charles Huseman. His siblings are Rosa Fischer, Charles, Jr., and Lucille Hutson. He graduated from Cleveland High School and Washington University in St. Louis.

Julie was born Apr. 13, 1914 in St. Louis, the first of three children to Flora (Fickeissen) and William Bauer. Her siblings are Flora Schlude and William, Jr. She graduated from Roosevelt High and Hadley Vocational in St. Louis. They were married in St. Louis Mar. 21, 1936 and settled in Lafayette, IN — Dick having been transferred there six months earlier by Ralston Purina.

Wanting to be in business for himself, when a franchise opened in Crawfordsville they decided on a change. Thus the move to Montgomery County. "Thorny Acres" as they named their new home — lots of blackberries on three acres, was different to them — electricity and a path! Lots of remodeling followed. In 1954 they built one of the first caged layer houses in Montgomery County. Their present home now stands on that ground, just west of the original home.

In 1959, when animal feeding changed to elevators, they decided to close the store. For a scant two years they owned and operated a credit agency. June 1961 Dick went to work for Montgomery Savings Association — he really enjoyed working with people. Dick has said "He has been fortunate in always having another job in hand before leaving the present one." He served MSA in many capacities including president and then Chairman of the Board. He retired December 1981 at age 70.

Dick joined Rotary in 1963, being president in 1978; served on Advisory Board in Ripley Township, was chairman of Consolidation Meetings, and treasurer of the Waveland School Building Corporation. He also served with Red Cross, being president in 1989 and worked with Muffy.

Julie kept the books for the store and agency and got involved in volunteer work—June 1963, a Gray Lady in Red Cross; Sheltered Workshop, and since 1966 a Pink Lady in Day Service for Hospital Auxiliary. An extension Homemaker since 1947, first at Alamo and then Yountsville Belles since 1951, she served as president of both clubs and as county president from 1969-1971. She has served on Extension Advisory Board and Muffy; was vice-committee woman for Ripley Township for several years and was a member of the Yountsville Belles Kitchen Band.

The Husemans are active in Yountsville Community church: Dick has taught adult class for 30-plus years and is chairman of the board. Julie, former S.S. teacher, is church organist and on staff of church paper, "The Light." They have three children: Richard, Jr., Flora Wilson and David.

JAMES AND CATHARINE JOHNSON HUTCHISON

James and Catharine Johnson Hutchison emigrated from Kentucky to Ohio.

They had a son, Josiah, born May 15, 1812. When about a year old, he was bound out until of age to Alexander Hamilton. The death of Hamilton released him at about age 11. On Jan. 5, 1832, he married Catharine Hixon. In 1835 they set out for Indiana, arriving at their future abiding place on February 18. They brought two children, Abigail and James, two small horses, an old wagon that cost him $5.00, and $.25 in cash. During the first winter, Josiah made 7,650 rails for Joel Hixon at $.25 per 100, making $1.00 a day, and cleared his first six acres of land at night. They had ten children, James and Abigail, Sarah, Mary, George, John, twin to John, Jasper, Melinda and Irvin.

Josiah died Dec. 27, 1885. Catharine born May 13, 1811, died May 7, 1889.

James never married.

Abigail married Andrew Swank on Apr. 16, 1854.

Sarah married James Wilson and later Jobe Holms.

Mary married James McMullen.

John married Sally Harper.

George married Elizabeth Ann ?

Abigail and Andrew Swank had ten children.

James—never married. He ran the store at Elmdale.

Sarah married Elisha Layne and had Fannie Bunnell, Stella Bunnell, and Abbie Pittman.

Infant son, born and died June 19, 1860.

Abigail married William Swank and had Joseph, Clyde, Benjamin, James, Hettie Humphreys, Ellie Schweitzer, Lula Mason and Elmer.

Nancy married George Biddle and had Lula, Lola Watts, Belinda Fowler, Andrew, Frank, Charles, Julia Branch Ruttkowsky, Eva Bitson and Edna Keller.

Mary married Charles Smith and had three children that died in infancy and Lucretia Peyton, Bertha Cole and Garcie.

Eliza born Feb. 26, 1866, died Nov. 30, 1871.

Josiah married Julia Cox and had Harry, Washington and Abigail.

Belinda never married.

Susan married Joseph Livingston and had Flossie, Gladys Bannon, Myrtle, Dallas, William, and Merle.

Edna Biddle married May 7, 1919 to Floyd Keller, son of John Richardson and Nancy Belle Tate Keller. Edna was born Oct. 25, 1901 and died Dec. 15, 1973. Floyd was born May 2, 1898 and died Aug. 18, 1978.

Floyd worked most of his married life as a building mover. In December 1964, they moved from a farm to Waynetown. They had eight children.

Lawrence married Wilma Jean Linn. They have one son, Larry Michael, who resides in Florida. Lawrence died Dec. 15, 1978. Jean died Jan. 1, 1978.

Mildred married James Laughner. They have five children. Gary married Norma Baker, and have Amy and Emily. Nancy married James Gregg and have Joseph and Aaron. Patricia married Steve Griffin and have Andrew. Susan married Thomas Henthorn and have Libby and Katie. Thomas stillborn.

Helen married Noel Willhite. They have three children. Ronald born Mar. 22, 1948, died Sept. 2, 1949. Gregory married Sharon Humphreys and have Chris Willhite Crissinger. Gregory married Carole Redmon and have Jeff. Pamela married Jimmie Jessie and have Chris. They are divorced.

Robert Keller-stillborn.

Gerold Keller-stillborn.

Harold Keller-four days old.

Grace married Richard Clore and have two children. They reside in Mesa, AZ. Jeff married Roxann Campbell and have Linsey. Julia married Brian Beall.

Infant girl Keller-stillborn.

JOSIAH HUTCHISON

Josiah Hutchison, a farmer and stock raiser from Boston Store, was born in Warren Co., OH on May 15, 1812. His parents, James and Catherine (Johnson) Hutchison, migrated from Kentucky to Ohio, where James Hutchison died in March, 1812 of the cold plague (flu), and his wife lived until her death on Sept. 15, 1847.

Josiah was raised a farmer and received very little education. When about a year old, he was bound out until he was of age to Alex Hamilton of Warren Co., OH. But the death of Mr. Hamilton released him when he was 11 years old. Josiah then lived with his mother, who had remarried.

Catherine Hixon Hutchison

For many years, Josiah Hutchison teamed to Cincinnati. On Jan. 5, 1832, Mr. Hutchison married Catherine Hixon, daughter of James and Abigail Hixon, of Warren Co., OH. Mr. and Mrs. Hutchison lived in Ohio where he farmed and followed huckstering (peddling). In 1835, they set out for Indiana. On Feb. 18, 1835, they arrived at their future abiding-place, which Josiah had spied out a few months before. Grandmother, father and mother had already moved to Indiana a few months ahead. They rented for a short time in Wayne Township. They brought two children, Abigail and James (twins), two small horses, and an old wagon that cost $5.00, which left them with 25 cents.

With such a capital, the man without an education, but with muscles, grit and honesty, began business in the wilds of Montgomery County. He borrowed a little money without giving his note and entered 40 acres. The following year he entered 40 acres more with borrowed money. During the first winter, he made 7,650 rails (wooden poles for fencing) for Joel Hixon at 25 cents per 100 rails. At this price, Josiah earned $1.00 per day, and cleared his first six acres of land by laboring into the night. That six acres he sowed in buckwheat. He raised 300 bushels, hauled it to Chicago, IL by a team of oxen and sold it. While he was busy in the fields, Grandma grew flax, spun thread, and made all their clothes.

Times began to brighten, and Mr. Hutchison added 200 more acres in Coal Creek Township to his farm, and 109 acres in Wayne Township. He also owned a considerable amount of land in Iroquois Co., IL. He dealt largely in young cattle. His credit was always first-class at the bank, and he was a very successful man. He and his wife were members of the Old School Baptist Church. He often fed the multitudes at his own expense when they came to attend the regular Baptist Association. The services were held either at his home or within driving distance.

The children of Josiah and Catherine (Hixon) Hutchison are: Abigail Hutchison (twin to James); James Hutchison (twin to Abigail); Sarah Hutchison; Mary (Aunt Matt) Hutchison (she and her husband were murdered Jan. 7, 1885); Benjamin Hutchison; George Hutchison; John Hutchison (had a twin that died at birth); Jasper Hutchison; Melinda Catherine Hutchison; Irvin Hutchison. *Written by Esther Hutchison Maxwell*

JESSE P. HYMER

Jesse P. Hymer, a farmer and stock raiser was born July 27, 1804 in Fayette Co., KY. On Mar. 16, 1831 he was married to Eliza Gill, also a native of Kentucky, where she was born June 12, 1812. Jesse moved to Putnam County in 1928. There he and Eliza farmed and raised 12 children.

The ninth of their 12 children, James was born May 31, 1849. On Mar. 14, 1893, James married Ella May King, born Apr. 16, 1864, Putnamville, IN. She was the daughter of Andrew and Anna Walter Gump King. This union was blessed with two daughters; Jessie and Mary.

Mary, born Nov. 10, 1900 in Roachdale, IN was married June 16, 1928 to Glen David Hayworth. One of five children, Glen was born Jan. 3, 1896 in Francesville, IN to James and Anna Bledsoe Hayworth. Glen and Mary resided in Mary's family home which she and her family moved into on Mary's 19th birthday. Glen served his country in World War I, and was Superintendent of the Crawfordsville Electric Light and Power Plant. Mary was a 1918 graduate of Crawfordsville High School and attended Oxford College for Women in Oxford, OH. She was an active member of the Dorothy Q. Chapter, Daughters of the American Revolution, and a past president of the Legion Auxiliary, Byron Cox Unit 72. She joined the Wabash Avenue Presbyterian Church on Nov. 12, 1916 in which she was also active.

Virginia King Hayworth, their only daughter was born Aug. 1, 1931 in Crawfordsville. On Oct. 11, 1958 she married David Milton Wilcox in the Wabash Avenue Presbyterian Church. David was born June 20, 1931 to Laban and Lucille Good Wilcox, in Fort Wayne, IN. Laban and Lucille moved to Crawfordsville in the late 50s. Laban was a pharmacist in the Nye-Booe Drugstore, Crawfordsville. Laban also served his country in World War I.

David, a Purdue graduate in Civil Engineering, served in the Korean War. He has worked for the Indiana Department of Highways for over 25 years. Virginia, a graduate of Hanover College, is also an active member in the Daughters of the American Revolution. Together they had two children, Susan born Aug. 7, 1960, and Bruce born July 14, 1965.

Susan married Michael John Grundy, born June 23, 1956 to John and Margaret Ramsey Grundy in Northumberland, Wales. They were married June 21, 1980 in the Wabash Avenue Presbyterian Church. They had two children, Travis Ryan born Nov. 27, 1982, and Sean Michael born Dec. 22, 1985.

Bruce, along with his sister was a member of the Susan E. Wallace Society, Children of the American Revolution when he was younger. He is an Eagle Scout and is still involved with Indian dancing. A current resident of Lafayette, IN, he is a student at Purdue University.

DR. WILLIAM HENRY HYTEN

Dr. Hyten was born Oct. 12, 1823 in Montgomery Co., KY, the son of William Caywood and Eliza Darnell Hyten. This family traveled from Maryland to Indiana in 1833, and settled near Danville, IN. The grandparents, Josiah and Rebecca Caywood Heighton (Hyten) were married in Maryland and lived their lives there. Josiah came from Scotland at a young age.

William Caywood married Eliza Darnell in 1816; she was the daughter of Henry and Sally Turpin Darnell, born in 1801 in Kentucky. This old couple had 12 children.

Dr. William began the study of medicine in Danville, IN under Dr. DePew of that area, and Dr. Hyten started his study and practice in that area. In 1847 Dr. Hyten married Elizabeth Crawford, born 1832 daughter of James and Isabella Robins Crawford. Three children were born to this union; Susan born and died 1849, Safronia born 1850 died 1857, Mary Clay wife of John Goff died 1936.

After the death of Elizabeth in 1857 Dr. William remarried. In 1859 he married Malinda Goodbar daughter of John and Rachel Hostetter Goodbar, who was born 1829 and died in 1905. To this marriage were born eight children; Depew married Florence Goff, John married Jane Adams, Newton married Dora Hostetter, William married Lula Sewell, Effie wife of William Owens, Cora, Bertha, and Tillman who married Pearl Warbritton. All of these children grew to adulthood.

Dr. Hyten continued to practice medicine until his death in 1911. He resided in Parkersburg for 47 years with most of his children around him.

At the time of his death he spoke to his children "Children this is death. I will soon be in better hands and what a glad change that will be for me. The hand of God never tires, nor its movements aimless. In the study of his wonderful event we do well to remember that." *Submitted by Becky Ingram*

PETER IMEL

Peter Imel had a son Samuel born 1799 in Virginia and died in Montgomery County in 1861 coming here from Virginia by way of Preble Co., OH and settling in 1836 just east of Whitesville. On Dec. 20, 1819 he married Susannah Black, in Wayne Co., IN. She was born in North Carolina in 1800. They had land on both sides of the road two miles east of Whitesville. Built a cabin a short distance off the road on the south side of the road. Susannah died Apr. 6, 1870. Their children were Nancy Imel born 1820 and married Miles Corn on Apr. 14, 1842 in Montgomery County; Franklin Imel married Nancy Harris; Frederick Imel married Martha J. Harris; Sarah Imel married Samuel Hamilton; Susan Imel married Samuel Hamilton. These four couples lived near New Ross. Samuel Imel, Jr. married Elizabeth Stone and Stephen Imel born Apr. 20, 1830 and died Sept. 28, 1870 married Rebecca Stone, born Oct. 13, 1838 and died Feb. 23, 1936 the daughter of James H. and Hannah Rettinger Stone on Dec. 11, 1862. Children were Florence Imel born Oct. 4, 1863 and died Dec. 17, 1916 married Robert Hamilton. Children were: Iva; Richard who died at age four; Guy; Tona who married Harry Tapp; and Teron Hamilton. They lived in New Ross; Clara Imel born Dec. 10, 1864 died July 19, 1894; Evelyn Imel born Oct. 17, 1866 died July 29, 1894; Josephine Imel born May 15, 1868 never married, but was engaged to a Whitesville boy Robert Weeks. He died before they were married. She was called Josie and was a schoolteacher. Emory Imel born Dec. 13, 1869. Sarah Imel married Samuel Hamilton in 1873 and after she died Susan married Samuel in 1876.

Samuel Imel, Jr. born Apr. 4, 1832 and died Feb. 2, 1858 married Elizabeth Stone on Apr. 5, 1853. Children were William S. born 1854 died 1875; infant son; Sarah Frances Imel born Oct. 3, 1856 married at Whitesville to Thomas Brooke Luster born Apr. 20, 1864 in Tennessee, A Universalist Minister. Rebecca Ann Imel born Aug. 7, 1858 Whitesville married Francis J. Nickell. Anna wrote poetry and their daughter Faith Elizabeth Nickell wrote poetry too. Faith born Sept. 9, 1888 and died Feb. 3, 1900. In 1900 Anna had a book published of hers and her daughter's poetry.

INGERSOLL FAMILY

Joseph Ingersoll (born New Jersey) removed to Hamilton Co., OH as a young man and married Lydia Barcus. Their son, Van came to Fountain Co., IN (purchased land Oct. 10, 1835). Van and wife Elmira had eight children. Their son, James Knox Polk Ingersoll, born Nov. 9, 1846 married Sally Little Oct. 15, 1874. To this union was born three children: Dessie Brown; Hurley, father of Sarah Simpson of Waynetown and Ellis, father of Martha Fendley.

James, a prominent Montgomery County farmer lived most of his life on a farm near Waynetown. His last 12 years were spent with his son. First memories of Martha Ann Ingersoll Fendley center around her grandfather, James K.P. Ingersoll. He sat on the porch of her parents' home for many hours. He'd often send Marty to fetch apples from the family's cellar. Once she tripped over a brick, ripped a large gash in her head and still carries that scar today.

Marty was born Dec. 7, 1926 and joined her brother Robert Harry. Robert, named after the man who discovered the Ingersoll watch, received one for a gift at his birth. Robert married Velma Surface and had Bob, Bill, David and Janet. He is now deceased.

Ellis John and Harley Ingersoll; Sarah Little and James Knox Polk Ingersoll

Marty was raised on her parents (Ellis John Ingersoll born July 8, 1881 near Waynetown and Mary Della Scott born Nov. 14, 1891 at Meadows of Dan, VA, daughter of A.L. and Princess) farm one and one-half miles South of New Market. Mary put herself through Danville Normal College, taught two years at Ridge Farm School at Waynetown where she roomed with Frank and Harriet Bolser, an aunt to Ellis who always said "thanks to Ellis wanting to get a peak at Mary, there was more wood chopped than ever before!" Ellis and Mary were married Sept. 13, 1913. They honeymooned in Chicago where they rode the SS United States ferry boat around Lake Michigan and purchased hot, homecooked meals for 25¢.

Martha had a happy childhood growing-up on the farm and helping with the poultry business until double tragedy occurred in 1944. At 5:30 Tuesday evening, November 21, Martha went to see why her father had not returned home. When she got to the field, she found him dead. Less than 24 hours after his burial, his wife died on November 25. She was laid to rest in Masonic Cemetery by her husband of 31 years. Sadly, Marty was forced to bear the burden as her brother was serving with the Navy in Australia and could not come home to attend his parents' funerals.

Things began to look-up for Marty, however, as on Feb. 21, 1948, she married Edward Fendley (born May 27, 1924). Three children have blessed this marriage: Debbie Barry (works at the Crawfordsville District Public Library), Richard A. (General Electric Reston, VA) and Scott (RR Donnelley Customer Service).

Ed recently retired from RRD and the Fendleys are now enjoying their leisure time, as well as their four grandchildren, Pamela and Edward Fendley and Shannon and Sara Barry. *Submitted by Martha Ingersoll Fendley*

DAVID ALAN INGRAM

Mr. Ingram was born near Darlington, IN, the son of Roy and Mildred (Hyten) Ingram on Aug. 21, 1951.

David's father, Roy, was born Sept. 1, 1910, the son of Ova and Minnie (Farris) Ingram, whose family was from the Illinois area. Roy was married Apr. 25, 1931, to Mildred Marie Hyten. She was born Oct. 30, 1910, the daughter of Tillman and Rose Pearl (Warbitton) Hyten from Ladoga area. Marie died June 17, 1961 at her home near Darlington on the Ingram family farm. Marie's family was well-known in this and adjacent counties and her grandfather was Dr. William Hyten.

Roy and Marie had six children, namely: Roy Eugene (Gene), Carole Jane who is currently married to Floyd Whitaker; Margie Marie who married William Herron; Ruth Ann who never married, David Alan (our subject) and John Mark.

David was married to Rebecca Hampton on Aug. 27, 1969. She is the daughter of Donald Max and Barbara May (Stevens) Hampton. Mrs. Ingram was born Mar. 11, 1951 in Montgomery County.

Mrs. Ingram's father is the son of Ernest and Dorothy (Smith) Hampton, born May 31, 1935 in Montgomery County. Her mother is the daughter of Russell and Mattie (Parks) Stevens of Yountsville later Crawfordsville. To this union two children were born: Rebecca and Nicholas Lee, who died Mar. 11, 1976 in an auto accident. Nicholas was 22 years young at the time of his death and in the Air Force.

David and Rebecca have two children: Dude Alan born Feb. 23, 1970 and Anna Marie born June 23, 1971; both are students at Southmont High School in this county.

These parents have lived all of their lives in this county. Mr. Ingram is in the Moving Industry where he has 20 years experience. Mrs. Ingram is a factory worker where she has 17 years experience.

HELEN KELSO ISAACS

Helen Kelso Isaacs, daughter of Dr. Reese D. and Victoria Kritz Kelso, was born in Waveland on May 14, 1894. Helen graduated from Waveland High School, attended Northwestern University School of Music where she graduated with a degree in public school music and art. She received a degree in Voice from the Cincinnati Conservatory of Music. She completed graduate work in voice at Bush Conservatory and Chicago Musical College.

Helen taught music and art in the Waveland Public Schools. She then became head of the Voice Department in several Southern Women's Colleges including Womens College at Due West, SC, and Queens College at Charlotte, NC. She returned home and worked as a librarian with the Waveland Brown Township Public Library for 25 years. She was head librarian the last seven years.

She is a member of the Rush Creek Friends Church; Mu Phi Epsilon Music Sorority; National Tri T, Chapter D. of Florida; Waveland Chapter Order of Eastern Star and Honorary English Society at Queens College.

She cared for her mother until her death and then retired in Dunedin, FL. Helen married William P. Isaacs on July 14, 1958. They lived in Dunedin 11 years and then returned to Indiana to live near Rockville.

Helen Kelso and Victoria Kelso Kleiser

Henry S. (1825-1915) and Mary A. (1833-1899) Kritz were the parents of Victoria, Helen's mother. Her siblings were Jessie, Stella, Alice, Nell, Layla, Harry, Francis, Bert, Will and Charles. Francis operated the Postoffice, furniture and undertaking business in Waveland. Charles operated a general store and Bert a men's clothing store in Waveland. Victoria lost her husband, Dr. Reese Davis Kelso (1866-1896) when Helen was two years old. She married Charles Albert Kleiser (1856-1937), a school teacher and farmer. Dr. Arthur J. Kleiser (1862-1942), Charles' brother, had Dr. Reese Kelso as a partner in his medical practice in Waveland. Henry S. Kritz, Victoria's father, taught Greek and Latin at the Wabash College Preparatory school in Crawfordsville. He and a close friend decided to open the Waveland Academy, a private Presbyterian boarding school, that operated until the Waveland Public School was built and operated through taxation. Before his death at 90 years of age, the Waveland Academy students held a school reunion and over 200 students from locations across the United States attended a three day celebration in his honor.

Helen's husband, William, died May 25, 1986. She is still living at home under the care of her stepson, John and step daughter-in-law, Ruth. They are retired teachers from Waveland Elementary and Southmont Schools. Helen is 95, but enjoys good health in spite of arthritis and partial blindness. *Submitted by John Isaacs*

JOHN H. AND RUTH L. ISAACS

John H. and Ruth L. Isaacs are now residents of R.R. 2, Rockville. They were married in Kokomo, IN on Dec. 28, 1947, at the residence of her parents, Mr. and Mrs. Allen J. Lindley. Ruth graduated from West Middleton High School and received her B.S. degree in education from Marion College. After teaching high school English and Latin at West Middleton, Tangier and Kingman, she converted to elementary education and received her M.S. degree with an elementary principal's and supervisor's license from Indiana State University. She retired with 37 years experience from Waveland Elementary School in 1983.

John graduated from Marshall High School in 1940 and received a B.S.A. degree from Purdue University in 1946. He taught Vocational Agriculture and Science in the Tangier, Kingman, Waveland and Southmont schools for 30 years. He took early retirement from teaching and started farming full time in 1976 as a third generation farmer on the home farm, a Hoosier Heritage Farm.

John H. and Ruth L. Isaacs

The Isaacs had two sons: William Allen, born in 1952 and John Carl, born in 1954. W. Allen was deceased in June, 1985, in Sacramento, CA, while working for Deere and Company.

William P. Isaacs, John's father, began farming with the help of the rest of the family at the age of 12-1/2 years. On Mar. 23, 1918, he married Verna E. Johnson, daughter of Henry C. and Minnie Booker Johnson of Montezuma. After serving in World War I, he returned and purchased the home farm from the rest of the family. Two sons, John H. and Gerald W. were born and raised at this location. William served two terms as Howard Township Trustee and six years as Parke County Highway Superintendent. Verna taught int he local high and elementary schools of Parke County for 30 years. She was deceased in 1956. William married Helen Kelso of Dunedin, FL in 1958. They resided there until 1969, when they returned to the farm one mile south of Judson, in Washington Township and built a new home. William died in 1986 at 89 years of age. Helen still lives here at 95 years.

John Carl Isaacs, fourth generation, returned and took over the farming operation in 1987. He had been employed as a research associate and manager of the soybean research station for United Agri-Seeds, Bowling Green, OH. He received a B.S. degree in Agriculture from Purdue in 1976. He married Mary Kay Berberian of West Lafayette in 1985. His mother officiated at the wedding, held at the Rush Creek Friends Church, where Ruth had served as pastor for 14 years of a total of 20 years in the ministry. Mary has a B.S. degree and M.S. degree from Purdue and is a learning disabilities teacher at Crawfordsville High School. *Submitted by John and Ruth Isaacs*

HARVEY JEWELL AND MARTA (COX) JEFFRIES

Because William Cox, born 1598 in England, came to America on the Godspeed in 1610 there are many direct descendants of his living in Montgomery County today.

Cecil B. Cox, a son of Denton and Bertha Clark Cox, born Jan. 2, 1902-died Oct. 16, 1982, was a tenth in line direct descendant of William.

"Cece", a Garfield boy, married Mabel Mullen on Sept. 7, 1929 at Plainfield. She was a daughter of Claud Silas and Grace Hall Mullen of Darlington, born Jan. 18, 1902-died Dec. 11, 1983.

It might be noted here that Claud's maternal grandfather, Silas Hiatt, was the first white child born in Montgomery County. The date was Aug. 6, 1824.

Cece and Mabel had four daughters. Judy, Oct. 11, 1930 - Marta, Jan. 5, 1933 - Jane, Aug. 7, 1934 - Margaret, Apr. 16, 1941. These girls grew up in Darlington when the town and their parent's restaurant, the Cox Cafe, were both very busy places.

Judy married Ray Marquez, lives in Walnut Creek, CA and has two children, Jeff and Marta Jo, and two grandsons, Travis and Matthew.

L to R: Jewell, Joey, Holly, Jon and Jaye Jeffries

Jane lives in Champaign, IL, and has one son, Jim Stewart.

Margaret lives at Darlington, married Allen Wray, has four children, Lisa, Meri, Greg and Sher, and four grandchildren, Alyssa, Samantha, Crystal and Nick.

Harvey Jewell Jeffries, a son of Jewell and Mary Lame Jeffries, was born Apr. 29, 1925 near Ladoga. He served as a nose gunner on a B24 bomber in WWII, flying 43 missions over Europe. After returning home he attended Purdue University. On Mar. 2, 1951 he married Marta at Ladoga.

They have five children: Mullen Jaye - May 26, 1952; Martin Jewell - Apr. 7, 1953; Joseph Kim - Sept. 18, 1954; Holly Joan - Oct. 26, 1955; Jonathan C. - Oct. 6, 1956.

While these children were growing up east of Ladoga the seasons were easily discernable. In spring and summer the entry hall of their home was cluttered with golf clubs, ball gloves and bats. As fall approached a football appeared. No matter what the season, however, a basketball was always in sight.

Sadly, these "signs" began to disappear. Jaye went away to college in Texas. Jewell to Indiana University. Joey later to IUPUI. Holly married, and Jon became a farmer and real estate broker.

Happily, the "signs" are reappearing via grandchildren.

Jaye works for his dad, owner of Roachdale Building Supplies, as a carpenter. He married Susan DeShong. Their children are Bradley 14, Kay 13, students at Southmont; Annie ten, Jon seven, Jamie five attend Ladoga Elementary.

Jewell, a sheep shearer (a dying art) and carpenter for Roachdale Building Supplies, married Nancy MacMillan. They have Andrew four, Nick one and one-half, Daniel, brand new.

Joey, an engineer at Allisons, married Pamela Allen. They have Josie five, Jayne three, and six months old twins, Jerrod and Jaclyn.

Holly married John Corbin, is bookkeeper at Roachdale Building Supplies; they farm and have Jenalee, nearly two.

Jon married Eileen Jones, runs a livestock farm and is busy in real estate.

Time marches on.

LLOYD AND LOUISE JEFFRIES

Pattie "Louise" Smith, born Apr. 28, 1915, the daughter of Ed and Mary Bessie (Branson) Smith, was named for her two grandmothers, Pattie Branson (wife of Enoch) and Louise Thompson (wife of Henry Smith) and married her bus driver, Lloyd Russell Jeffries (born Mar. 9, 1906, son of Charles and Angeline (Brandon) Jeffries) on Nov. 30, 1933. Louise has one sister, Geneva Bayless, living in Buckeye, AZ.

Louise graduated from Waveland High School in April 1933. She first worked as a Clerk-Typist for the State Highway; other jobs include, a secretary for Farm Bureau Insurance, bookkeeper at R.B. Furniture for 20 years. She currently is a Green Thumb worker at the Crawfordsville District Public Library where her main jobs include processing books and inventorying.

Lloyd and Louise Jeffries

Lloyd was a self-employed carpenter and drove the Brown Township school bus for 16 years (1943-59). The Jeffries lived in Brown Township until 1965 when they moved to Crawfordsville. Lloyd died Oct. 16, 1967.

Lloyd and Louise had William "Bill" and Mary Margaret, both born at home in Brown Township and both graduated from Waveland.

Bill married Dorothy Farmer of Indianapolis and they have Keith and Kevin. Bill works on his farm on rural route Rockville. Dorothy is an Institution Teacher at the Department of Corrections, Rockville Training Center. She formally taught music at Russellville and Waveland schools and fourth grade at Bloomingdale. Keith is married to the former Janis Fordice of Russellville. They are the parents of one son, Brian Keith. Jan is an accounting assistant with Telephone and Data Systems at the mid-central regional offices at Roachdale, IN. Keith is a custom farm operator and is employed by Rahn's Farmarket, Inc. at Guion, IN. Kevin is Plant Manager for EES/Water Management Division in Kokomo.

Mary Margaret Jeffries married William Parker of Martinsville and they have one son, Bill and an adopted daughter, Crystal. Bill and Crystal are in Mooresville Schools. Bill Parker is a Public Service employee and works with software. He is a graduate of Indianapolis Business College. Mary Margaret was office manager for Perry Lewis for nine years before her marriage and currently works in Mooresville as a secretary, bookkeeper.

Louise is a member of Pleasant View Baptist Church.

JOH AND HUMBERT

George Joh born 1804 Augusta Co., VA, son of Jacob and Elizabeth Runkle Joh married Anna Wade in Virginia. They came to northwest of New Ross in 1858 after a short time in Preble Co., OH where his parents died. He died June 1, 1888 and Anna died May 28, 1872 in Walnut Township, Montgomery Co., IN. Their children were; William Joh born 1830 and died 1916 near New Ross; Martha Joh Wiseman; Mary Jane Joh born 1835 Staunton Co., VA married in Preble Co., OH on June 18, 1858 to Isaac Humbert, born in 1836 in Darke Co., OH, the son of George and Sarah Henderson Humbert. Mary Jane and Isaac went to Lafayette and he entered the Civil War from there on Aug. 2, 1862. Humberts came from France, then Germany and then to America. Isaac was drowned when ship Sultana blew up, Vicksburg, MS April 1865. He had been captured on July 31, 1864 and taken to infamous Andersonville prison, they were taken from the prison, put on ship Sultana. After his death, Mary Jane Joh Humbert came to her parents, George and Anna Wade Joh, Walnut Township, Montgomery Co., IN.

Her brother William lived with his niece Belle Humbert Linn and her husband James Washington Linn. He had large, gnarled hands. He died in 1916. Their sister Lilly Dora Josephine Humbert married Ulysses P. Harris and Mary Jane Joh Humbert lived her last days with them.

A brother, Henry Humbert disappeared; then the daughter who always said her name was Flora Belle, but on Mary Jane's pension papers it said her name was Letitia Belle, so I presume as her sister had her three names she did have too, and her name was Letitia Flora Belle. She married James Washington Linn II in April 1955. They had four children; Dora Evaline Linn Randel; Earl Joseph Linn, Floyd Isaac Linn; Jennie Flo Linn Robison. Dora Evaline Linn married Orval W. Randel on Feb. 28, 1907. They had two daughters; C. Pauline Randel Walters and V. Lucile Randel Harpel; Earl Joseph Linn married Bonnie June McMullen and they had one son Donald J. Linn who married Jean Crowe. They are the parents of three daughters. Jennie Flo Linn married Roy Robison and has no children.
Submitted by Pauline Walters

DAVID E. JOHNSON

David E. Johnson was born in Clinton Co., IN Apr. 15, 1922 and came to Montgomery County in 1936 with his parents, Harry E. and Lydia Marie (Rude) Johnson. At that time they bought a farm in the northern part of North Union Twp. and his mother still lives there in 1989. David graduated from Linden High School in 1939.

His great grandfather, Robert Greenlief Johnson, was born near Madison, IN in 1837. When he was 19 years old he came north and drove a stagecoach from Lafayette to Indianapolis. He enlisted in the Civil War Nov. 1, 1861 and served in Company A, 46 Ind. Vol.; was mustered out at Indianapolis Jan. 24, 1864. David's grandfather, Harry Johnson, and father, Harry Elsworth Johnson, were both born at Speeds, IN.

His maternal great, great grandparents, Henry and Margaret (?) Rude came by horseback migrating up from Kentucky in the 1840's. It is told that the only possession they brought with them other than the clothes on their backs was an earthenware water jug slung over the horn of their saddle. They settled in Clinton County.

David and Marian Johnson

David served in World War II as a Staff-Sgt. in the XI Corp. Artillery in the Asiatic-Pacific from 1943 to 1946. He married Marian L. Hiatt in 1949. She is the sixth generation of Montgomery County pioneer families. Her parents were Harry L. and Iva (Gant) Hiatt of Darlington, IN. Her great, great grandparents, John B. and Sarah (Kenworthy) Hiatt migrated from Bucks Co., PA to Ohio to Randolph Co., IN and then on to Montgomery County along with Sarah's parents when it opened up in 1823. Sarah Kenworthy Hiatt was a well-known doctor. She was a good horsewoman and regardless of season, flood or storm, answered every call. Sarah's son, Silas Hiatt, is said to be the first male white child born in Montgomery County.

David and Marian are the parents of one son, Mark David Johnson born Apr. 19, 1962. He is a graduate of Wabash College and Indiana University Law School. He is married to Kathryn Burger, daughter of Thomas and Anna Ruth (Foster) Burger of Harrison Co., IN.

David is a member and Past Commander of American Legion Post #72. He served for 15 years as Church School Supt. of the First Christian Church; is a member of the Linden Masonic Lodge #697. He is a lifetime member of the American Polled Hereford Assn. and a lifelong farmer living in North Union Twp. and is retired from the U.S. Postal Service. Marian has had many years of volunteer work and is a Past County President of the Purdue Extension Homemakers Assn.

FRANKLIN BLAIR AND MABLE JEAN WILSHIRE JOHNSON

Franklin Blair Johnson and Mable Jean Wilshire were united in marriage Sept. 18, 1941 by Rev. John Servies. Franklin is the son of Alva and Grace Nichols Johnson, born on Dec. 21, 1917 west of New Market, IN.

Franklin is a 1936 graduate of Crawfordsville High School, attended Purdue University, served in the 82nd Airborne Unit for 33 months in World War II. He was employed as a process engineer with Allison, a division of General Motors for 34 years. He was a partner in the New Market Hardware, served as Montgomery County's weights and measures inspector for ten years, member of the Union Township Advisory Board, county vice chairman and precinct committeeman of the Republican party. He is a member of the Masonic Lodge #50, Veterans of Foreign Wars and of the Browns Valley Baptist Church, where he is a deacon.

Mable is the daughter of Mirt and Melvinia Strode Wilshire. She was born west of Waveland Oct. 20, 1920. She is a 1938 graduate of Waveland

High School and Terre Haute Commercial College. She was employed in Dr. James M. Kirtley and John E. Fraser, DDS office; also a receptionist for Ben Hur Life Insurance and the office of Price of Administration. She is patroness of the Phi Chi Epsilon Sorority, Eastern Star #97, vice chairman of the Montgomery County Republican Central Committee, second vice president of the Republican Women's Club, secretary of the Seventh District Republican Organization, a member, teacher and trustee of the Browns Valley Baptist Church.

Back Row: Ron Johnson, Dennis Provo, Sean and Rodger Samuels, Ken Cleaver, 2nd row: Cindy Johnson, Heather Starks, Peggy Provo, Ada Adamson, Sally Samuels, Michelle Samuels and Nancy Cleaver. 1st row: Errin, Natalie, Frank and Mabel Johnson, Jason Cleaver.

They are parents of four children. Sally is a 1964 graduate of the New Market High School, attended Ball State and Indiana State Universities. She married Rodger Samuels. She is an administrative director for the Ansul Fire Protection Company. They have a daughter, Michelle and a son Sean and reside in Bolingbrook, IL.

Nancy graduated in 1967 from New Market High School and attended Purdue University. She is married to Kenneth Cleaver and has a son Jason. They live in Tustin, CA. She is a management services officer for Beckman Laser Institute and Medical Clinic at the University of California, Irvine, CA.

Peggy is a graduate of New Market High School in the class of 1969 and Indiana State University with a degree in Special Education. She is married to Dennis Provo and has a daughter Heather Starks and they reside in Indianapolis. Peggy is employed with the Northwest Airlines in Indianapolis.

Ronald is a 1973 graduate of Southmont High School and attended Purdue University. His wife is the former Cynthia Wilhite. He is employed as a system analyst for R.R. Donnelley and Sons. Their daughters, Errin and Natalie are students in the Southmont School District. They reside west of New Market on Road 550 S.

MARY EARLY JOHNSON

Mary Early Johnson was born in Crawfordsville, IN in 1929, the oldest daughter of Robert and Opal (Fruits) Early. Her sister, Ann was born in 1931. The Earlys lived at 312 West Pike Street. Robert was a proofreader at R.R. Donnelley, and Opal was active in community life.

Robert worked long hours at Donnelley's and spent much time at home remodelling the house, which had belonged to Opal's grandparents, Jonathan and Rozella Fruits. Later, he built a house on the Camp Rotary Road.

Mary graduated from CHS in 1947, and entered Hanover College. The family moved to Kingsport, TN that year. Ann graduated from Dobyns-Bennett High School in 1949; Mary married Allen W. Johnson of Bellaire, MI, and Annie married Floyd Powers of Crawfordsville. Ann and Floyd had four children: Janet, David (died 1978), Joseph and Elizabeth.

Mary Early Johnson

Mary was married to Al for over 20 years, and five children were born: Allen W., Jr., 1950; Laura Ann, 1953; Nora Jean, 1958; Robert Early, 1962; and Rebecca Louise, 1963. Allen lives in Indianapolis, is married to Li-Yen Koo of Taiwan, and has a daughter, Elizabeth born in 1981. Li-Yen is an assistant principal in Indianapolis, and Allen is a stockbroker in Franklin. Laura, a Herron graduate, is finishing an MFA at the University of Southern Illinois. She is married to Kevin Drake of Waynetown, and they have a daughter, Courtney, born in 1986. Laura designs furniture as sculpture, which she shows regularly in New York, and which has been published in books and magazines. Kevin is also an artist, and is completing a degree in art. Nora is married to Gary Smith of Fort Wayne. They have a son, Jonathan, born in 1985, and are planning another addition to their family. They live in Corvallis, OR, where Gary, or "Duffy," is a realtor, and Nora takes courses at Oregon State toward an eventual degree. Robert lives in Jacksonville, FL. Rob is married to Katherine Pajcic Geiger, and they are the parents of two daughters, Jana Geiger, born in 1979, and Hilary Ann, born in 1983. Kathy is an elementary school teacher, and Robert is regional manager for a builders supply company. He spends time on songwriting, as he has since he was a teenager. Becky lives in New York City, Jackson Heights area, and works at Citibank in Manhattan, economics department. She volunteers with a Girl Scout troop in Manhattan.

In 1974 Mary received a BFA from Indiana University, Herron School of Art. She spent seven years at Wabash College, managing the Theater Gallery doing silk-screened posters and designs, as well as developing a pottery studio for the Wabash Craft Center. In 1979, Mary began work at the Crawfordsville District Public Library. She works in reference, special services, and as display coordinator, schedules art and other exhibits in the Display Hall and other exhibit areas in the Library. Mary is working towards a masters degree in Library and Information Science. She still does a few posters and design commissions and paints watercolors whenever possible, having definite plans to resume oil painting in some easier future schedule.
Submitted by Mary Early Johnson

SAMUEL JOHNSON
EARL LUCIEN JOHNSON
EARL LUCIEN JOHNSON, JR.
HELEN JOHNSON WYNNE

Samuel Johnson (1836-1905) was the first member of his family to live in Montgomery Co., IN. He served as a corporal in the Civil War in Company B, 120th Indiana Infantry. He lived most of his life in Crawfordsville and worked in the post office until his retirement. He married Anna Smith (1856-1939) in 1876. Her family first settled in Brown Co., IN.

They had two children, Earl J. Johnson, Sr. (1882-1951) and Edith Johnson Pierce. Earl L. Johnson graduated in 1900 from Crawfordsville High School. He married Elizabeth Raub of Chalmers, IN in 1913. Earl Sr. became General Manager of the Indiana Match Company in Crawfordsville. He continued in this capacity until 1923 when Indiana Match Company was acquired by Federal Match Company. Later Mr. Johnson became a newspaper broker, negotiating mergers in many cities where two newspapers proved uneconomical and one combined newspaper could be successful. One such merger was that of the *Crawfordsville Journal* and the *Crawfordsville Review*, which Mr. Johnson negotiated. Mr. Alaric Smith, the owner of the *Journal* was the husband of Prairie Smith, the younger sister of Anna, Earl's mother.

In 1934, Mr. Johnson, a Democrat, was elected Montgomery County Treasurer, an office which he performed efficiently and capably for one term before the historic Republican majority returned the Republicans to office.

In 1940, Mr. and Mrs. Johnson moved to Greencastle. In 1951 Mr. Johnson died of injuries sustained in a car accident. His widow, Elizabeth died in 1986.

Earl Johnson Sr. had two children. They were Helen R. Johnson (1915-) and Earl L. Johnson, Jr. (1916-).

Helen graduated from Crawfordsville High School, attended MacMurray College and then worked for Evans & DeVore and then Mutual Benefit Life Insurance Company in Crawfordsville. She married Brooks Wynne in 1939 and they had two children, William Thomas Wynne and Judith Brooks Wynne. After living many years in the Chicago area where Brooks was a corporation lawyer, Helen and Brooks and their children moved to Orlando, FL.

Earl L. Johnson, Jr. graduated from Crawfordsville High School and Wabash College. He entered the United States Army Air Corps, receiving his wings and commission in 1941. He was stationed in the South Pacific in World War II with the 20th Air Force and was a Colonel by the end of the war, leading many bombing missions over Japan. He continued in the Air Force after the war, and commanded several Strategic Air Command Bases in Florida, Puerto Rico and Guam. He was Vice Commander of the 8th Air Force during the Vietnam War and flew many B-52 conventional bombing missions. He retired in 1972 with the rank of Major General.

General Johnson married Peggy Hearn of LaGrange, GA in 1950. They have one daughter, Donna, who is married to Richard Dawson of Redlands, CA. Donna is employed by the Gannett Newspaper Corporation in the promotions department. Gannett Newspapers Corporation prints *USA Today*.

General Johnson and Mrs. Wynne own a residence on Vernon Court in Crawfordsville, thus keeping alive their interest in Montgomery Co., IN.
Submitted by Earl L. Johnson

MARSH HENRY JONES

Marsh Henry Jones was born Aug. 25, 1895, at

the Robbins House on East Main Street in Crawfordsville, the son of Ammon Burkett and Lillie Marsh Jones. His father and grandfather, William Doderick Jones were hotel proprietors, and the Jones family moved to Crawfordsville in 1894 where the family ran the Robbins House, the Ramsey Hotel and the Crawford Hotel.

Marsh Jones was graduated from Crawfordsville High School in 1913 and Wabash College in 1917. He served as a First Lieutenant in the Field Artillery during World War I at Fort Knox and Fort Sill. He returned to Crawfordsville to enter the hotel business with his family. He married Frieda Schelke of Madison, IN on July 3, 1922. Miss Schelke came to Waynetown as a teacher and principal at Waynetown High School. Their children were Marsh H. Jones, Jr. and Margaret Anne Jones.

Marsh Jones devoted his life to public service in the community. He was elected as Republican to serve on the Crawfordsville City Council and also served on the Montgomery County Council. During World War II he was appointed to serve on the Montgomery County Selective Service Board (draft board) where he served five years.

Marsh Jones was member of St. John's Episcopal Church where he served as treasurer and was a member of the vestry.

Margaret Anne Jones was killed in a horse back riding accident Oct. 13, 1945. Marsh H. Jones, Jr. married Dorothy Darnall and lives in Montgomery County.

Marsh Jones died May 11, 1962 in Crawfordsville.

REVEREND WILLIAM HARRISON JORDAN

William Harrison Jordan, a well-known black minister, was born June 4, 1841 in Ohio. He married Rachel Bell, who died in Crawfordsville Oct. 14, 1887 at the age of 43.

William Harrison Jordan enlisted in the Union Army in Indianapolis, IN Jan. 15, 1864 and served as a private in Company D, 28th Regiment, United States Colored Troops. He was discharged Nov. 8, 1865.

In 1867, William Harrison Jordan became a minister in the Afro-Methodist Church for many years. He was also a member of Crawfordsville's black St. Mark's Masonic Lodge #25, Commandery K.T. Both lodges met at 125-1/2 East Main Street. He was also a member of the Order of Owls, Nest #1711 at 130-1/2 East Main Street in Crawfordsville.

William Harrison Jordan died Apr. 8, 1928 at the home of his granddaughter, Mrs. Mary Hyde, at 313 South Oak Street in Crawfordsville. At the time of his death, Reverend Jordan had six grandchildren living and 16 great grandchildren. Reverend Jordan was buried in Section K in Oak Hill Cemetery in Crawfordsville. *Submitted by Andrew Keith Houk, Jr.*

KELLAR - KELLER

According to the family historians, the first KELLER settlers came to the United States from Switzerland where their ancestors lived for centuries. At the time of the great plague in the 14th century the KELLERS, with others such as the Hottels, Rinkers, Fravels, Funkhousers and Sagers, moved down from the mountains and into the Rhine countries to escaped the Black Death. They were related to each other by marriage and religious ties to Europe and came to America together because of these relationships, seeking a peaceful home to the New World.

The first generation included George Keller, b. 1712-d. 1782-83, who married Barbara Ann Hottel, the only daughter of Johannes and Margaret Hottel, was born in Europe before 1730. After her arrival in the United States she married George KELLER.

Harry Everett Kellar and his bride of two months Beatrice Dodson Kellar taken in 1919

The next three generations of KELLERS preceded Alexander and Rachell (Hall) Keller from Shenandoah Co., VA, Green Co., NC, (now Tennessee), Parke Co., IN and then Montgomery Co., IN, Union Township. Alexander KELLER, was the son of Capt. Daniel KELLER and Nancy Krout m. 1833, probably in Rockville, IN. Alexander was born in Parke Co., IN; Rachell was the daughter of John Richardson and Marjory (Van Cleave) Hall, Montgomery Co., IN. Alexander and Rachell are buried in Weir Cemetery, Montgomery County.

One of their children, Robert Newton KELLER, b. 1861-d. 1935, is the writer's grandfather. Robert Newton KELLER and Loretta Potts were married in 1886, in Montgomery County and moved to Anderson, IN, for a brief time, where their son, Harry Everett KELLAR was born. "Newt" and Loretta moved back to Crawfordsville, IN and later to Indianapolis, IN. Loretta died at Methodist Hospital in Indianapolis and her husband died in Springfield, IL, where he was living with his son, Harry (the author's father). Both "Newt" and Loretta are buried in Masonic Cemetery, Crawfordsville.

This KELLAR biography is dedicated to the writer's father, HARRY EVERETT KELLAR, b. Jan. 19, 1897-d. Dec. 10, 1945. He was born in Anderson, but grew up in Crawfordsville. His sister Carrie Ruth, married Ray Clements and lived most of her married life in Hamilton Co., IN. A brother, Archebold Keller, served in WWI, as did Harry, and then lived as a young man in Indianapolis, and in other areas of the United States. Harry Everett married Beatrice Dodson, where he lived and worked in Springfield, OH. Beatrice and Harry were married in Pleasant Township, Clark Co., OH, in 1918. During their married life they lived in Columbus, OH; Lebanon, PA; Boston, MA; Springfield, IL; and Springfield, OH; having raised three children, Harry Everett, Jr., Charles Robert and Edith Ann Kellar Mahaney, the author of this biography.

Although Harry and Beatrice lived in many states, his love and loyalty to Indiana always remained steadfast. His eyes would fill with tears upon hearing, "BACK HOME AGAIN IN INDIANA." Harry, Sr. died in 1945, in Springfield, OH, and is buried there in Ferncliff Cemetery. Beatrice lives in Zionsville, IN, cooking, writing and gardening at the age of 93.

It is fitting that their daughter, Edith Ann, who has lived with her husband, Jack L. Mahaney and their two children, Laurel Ann, b. 1958, and Jackson b. 1960, in Indiana for 29 years, pay tribute to the KELLERS of Montgomery Co., IN. *Submitted by Mrs. Edie Kellar Mahaney*

KELLER

Daniel Keller Sr. married Christina Lamon. They had seven children—Capt. Daniel, Isaac, Philip, Abraham, Sayra, Mary and Elizabeth.

Capt. Daniel was born Apr. 2, 1808 in Tennessee. He married Nancy Krout around 1833-34. Nancy was born Nov. 2, 1816 and died Nov. 24, 1899; daughter of John and Mary McCallister Krout.

Traditions tell us that Daniel and Nancy had to burn gun powder in a shovel to keep wolves from the door when they were building their log cabin in 1838. They had bed clothes hung for doors to keep out the cold. They also built pens to catch the wolves and wild animals and planted vegetables around roots of trees, and thought tomatoes were flowers.

Daniel had a team of oxen named Buck and Bright.

From Dec. 12, 1872 Crawfordsville paper-Captain Keller, while chopping in the woods a short time since, conceived the idea that his hand had offended him in voting the Liberal Ticket and without consideration he applied the ax. He is sitting by the fire now.

They had ten children: Alexander, John, Robert, Mary, Daniel, Rebecca, Marjory, George, Martha and Thomas.

Alexander born Feb. 28, 1835 in Parke Co., IN married Dec. 19, 1861 to Rachell Hall, born Dec. 30, 1842, daughter of John Richardson and Marjory VanCleave Hall. Alexander died Feb. 7, 1911. Rachell died Jan. 8, 1907. Weir Cemetery.

They had 15 children—William, Robert, Johnnie, Margary, Nancy, Henry, George L., Daniel, Joseph, Baby Girl, James, Alvora, Eldora, George A., and Lauranda.

John Richardson born May 31, 1863 Union Township, Montgomery Co., IN died June 4, 1927; married Mar. 6, 1889 to Nancy Belle Tate born June 12, 1864 in Illinois; daughter of Joseph and Elizabeth Krout Tate, died Aug. 2, 1935.

They at one time owned where the Hibernia Mill once stood. The water from Sugar Creek was washing the dirt away from under the Mill, so John moved the mill across the road and took the bottom floor from the mill and made the upper part into a barn to store his machinery and livestock. They had seven children: Eva Sarver, Myrta Swank, Floyd, Raymond, Edna Wilson, Edison, and Ruby Sarver.

Administrators Sale total amount of sale $289.18.

Notice is hereby given that the undersigned administrator of the estate of Daniel Keller (deceased) will sell at Auction on Sat., Dec. 25, 1880.

At the late residents of deceased one mile Northwest of Stump School, the following property—two horses, cattle, about 30 head of hogs, Buggy and harness, farm equipment, wheat in ground and so-forth.

Terms, a credit of 12 months will be given on all sums over $5.00. Under $5.00 cash, the purchaser must give note with approved freehold security. *Submitted by Milton Rush, Administrator, Daniel Keller (deceased)*

NORRIS AND VIRGINIA (BANNON) KELSEY

Norris Kelsey became a resident of Montgomery County in 1930. He is the oldest son of Walter and Nellie Hoffman Kelsey. His father passed away when he was six years old. He came to Crawfordsville to live with his grandmother Maggie Kelsey and later made his home with Ottis and Mary Couger near New Market where now the Crawfordsville Airport is situated. He lived there until he graduated from New Market High School in 1940. In 1942 he married Virginia Bannon at Parkersburg, IN.

Virginia, Rita, Janet, Nancy and Norris Kelsey

They were the parents of three daughters, Janet born in 1943 now deceased; Nancy born in 1947; and Rita born in 1948. Kelsey's parents lived in Michigan where they were married. Kelsey was born in Manistee Co., MI. His father passed away in Montgomery County while visiting his parents in 1927. His mother passed away in 1984 in Pennsylvania. Virginia was born in Scott township, Montgomery County in 1924 to Eldo and Helen Wanetah Monroe Bannon. She is the oldest of two children. She attended Parkersburg grade school for eight years, then attended New Market High School and graduated in 1942.

Virginia's father was born near Elmdale on Oct. 12, 1897 to Charles and Mary Melinda Lane Bannon. He started school at Hickory Corner near Elmdale and attended Breaks High School, north of Crawfordsville. Virginia's brother Max now lives east of Parkersburg on the home place.

Her mother was born near Brownsvalley Mar. 3, 1903 to Zura and Jessie Blake Monroe. Zura was a farmer, Insurance Agent and a schoolbus driver. They lived all their married life in the Freedom community in Brown Township. Kelsey served in the Amphibious Engineers during World War II. He spent several months in Manilla, New Guinea, Philippines and Japan. When he returned home they moved to Freedom community near Waveland and farmed for several years. In 1957 they moved to New Market and lived there until 1988, then moved to her father's farm near Parkersburg. Kelsey retired from Raybestos in 1983, where he had worked for over 20 years. He also was a schoolbus driver for 12 years and worked in construction as a carpenter a few years.

RICHARD SAMUEL KELSEY

Richard Samuel Kelsey married Elizabeth Wilson and farmed for ten years before becoming a self employed livestock hauler of 40 years service to many Montgomery County farmers. They had seven children and lived in Shannondale.

Jeannine Claire Kelsey was born Feb. 15, 1939 and married Gordon Leon Farley, (born July 11, 1936), on June 16, 1957 and were divorced Mar. 9, 1964. They had four children: Twila Kay born Jan. 12, 1958; Terri Jo born Aug. 10, 1959; Thomas Gordon born Feb. 12, 1962; Trent Allen born Apr. 16, 1963.

Then Jeannine married James Eugene Jackman on July 12, 1964. He was born July 2, 1919. Traci Leann was born to them Dec. 4, 1969.

Terri Jo married Donald Everett Sparrow Jr. on Jan. 14, 1978. Don was born Oct. 3, 1957. They have Justin Michael born June 19, 1982 and Beth Renae born June 20, 1988.

Richard Kelsey

Thomas Gordon Farley died Feb. 14, 1962. Twila is unmarried.

Trent Allen married Amy Francis Sulc on May 11, 1985. Amy was born Jan. 29, 1962. They have Brian Allen born on Nov. 12, 1988.

Betheline Kelsey born Sept. 10, 1941 married Carl Richard Gillan (born Aug. 1, 1937) on Jan. 3, 1960. They had two children: Vicki Ann born Dec. 22, 1960 and James Richard born Nov. 6, 1964. Vicki Ann married Gregory Wade Hill on Apr. 30, 1988. Gregg was born on Apr. 15, 1958.

Cora Sue Kelsey born Jan. 25, 1944 and married Bobby Joe Sherfey (born Apr. 22, 1943) on June 9, 1963. They had two children: Deanna Lynne born on Dec. 7, 1964, and Darrin Lee born Feb. 2, 1967.

Sandra Lee Kelsey, born Mar. 30, 1946, married James Lee Bradshaw on Dec. 31, 1964. Jim was born Jan. 25, 1944. They had two children: Donna Jo born July 25, 1965 and David James born Mar. 9, 1968. Donna married William Paul Walters on Feb. 13, 1988. Bill was born Feb. 7, 1964. They are the parents of Megan Rochelle born on Feb. 13, 1989.

Andra Bee born Mar. 30, 1946, twin of Sandra Lee, lived to age of six died on Jan. 15, 1953.

Emily Rose Kelsey born July 15, 1952 and married Thomas James Horn on June 30, 1970. Tom was born Nov. 19, 1952. They had three sons: Mathew Thomas born June 3, 1971; Samuel Lee born Nov. 11, 1972; and Travis James born Apr. 2, 1975.

Robert Wilson Kelsey born Mar. 6, 1956 and married Nancy May Hilt (born Mar. 18, 1956) on Mar. 15, 1975. They became divorced on July 16, 1976.

Bob then married Cheryl Ann Vaught on Dec. 21, 1979. Cheryl was born Sept. 19, 1956. They had two daughters: Sarah Jean born on May 17, 1981 and Allison May born July 11, 1985.

The Kelsey Kids have always found ways to have fun together as a family.

BENJAMIN KESSLER

Benjamin Kessler, 45 years of age and his wife owned 301 acres in Virginia. His brother-in-law in Indiana, said he could do better in Indiana, so he sold his land and they, with nine children left Virginia in two covered wagons for Indiana in 1847.

The family spoke the Dutch-German language and Benjamin could not write. He drove one of the wagons—drawn by four horses. It was filled with furniture and personal belongings. A crate of chickens was underneath the wagon.

Benjamin and Elizabeth Kessler

The eldest son John drove the second wagon which was loaded with farm equipment: a mole board plow, single shovel plow, a double shovel plow for cultivating corn, a one row corn planter, rifle, saws, axes and hoes etc. This wagon was drawn by three cows and a bull yoked like oxen. Milk cows also followed behind.

The family walked or found seats where ever they could. Tradition says that Nathaniel, nine years old sat on the money box which contained $600.00. The youngest child was Anna-six months old.

There were few roads and most of the streams were unbridged. They crossed one railroad on the entire four weeks trip.

The first winter they found a house to live in and 1848 came Benjamin bought 240 acres partly cleared. He built a two story log house. The first floor had three rooms in a row. Walls were all finished except the kitchen. Windows were small and few. A fire place five feet wide was built in the living room. The kitchen also had a fireplace and stove.

The roads at this time were wide paths through the woods.

In 1855 Benjamin built a two story brick house with walnut woodwork and plastered walls.

Benjamin was born in Botetourt Co., VA on Mar. 30, 1802 son of Jacob and Elizabeth Shearer Kessler. He was a member of the Lutheran Church and later joined the Brethern Church in 1843. He gave a piece of his land for the Church of Brethern. It was a huge church and many came for miles to worship there. Sleeping quarters was in the upstairs.

The trees, along the path to the Hopewell School House, where the children went had to be glazed for they were so thick that otherwise the way could have been easily lost.

Benjamin raised flax. When it was large enough, it was pulled up and laid on the ground to bleach. Next it was gathered and scuttched and made into tow. The mother and girls wove it into tablecloths, towels, sheets etc.

Elizabeth Graybill and Benjamin had been married July 25, 1833. Elizabeth died on Apr. 2, 1883 and Benjamin being deaf was killed by a Monon train on July 29, 1890. They are buried in the Brethern Cemetery northwest of Ladoga.

Children: 1. John Kessler; 2. Elizabeth - m. Kenney children of first marriage Eva Mangus; 3. Catherine 1834 m. Jacob Himes; 4. Nathaniel 1836

m. Mary E. Harshbarger; 5. Samuel 1840 m. Josephine Kelsey; 6. Susan 1842 m. Crede Thompson; 7. Mary 1844 m. George Neff; 8. Anna (Nancy) 1847 m. William Manges; 9. Jacob 1849 Belle Northcutt - only one born in Indiana. *Submitted by Edith Kistler*

DAVID L. AND HANNAH CALLAHAN KILEY

David Lawrence Kiley was the oldest son of John and Margaret (Hurley) Kiley. He was born Nov. 26, 1861. His parents emigrated from Ireland in the early 1850's. David and his father were "railroaders". John Kiley worked with a construction team on the Vandalia Railroad. Young David started working for the railroad while in his teens and later became supervisor of the Big Four track. The line ran through Mace Station later changed to Linnsburg. He had two sisters, Ella and Margaret and one brother, John.

David Lawrence Kiley; Hannah Isabel Kiley

David Kiley married Hannah Callahan in Saint Bernard Catholic Church, Crawfordsville, Nov. 9, 1880. Hannah's parents Michael and Bridget (Guiney) Callahan were born in County Cork, Ireland and emigrated to the United States during the "great famine" there in the late 1840's. They were farmers and first settled at Alamo, Ripley Township where Hannah was born Mar. 13, 1863. Her siblings were: Charles, Michael, Margaret, Dora, Mary, Kate and John. Two sisters Dr. Kate Callahan, an osteopath, and Dr. Mary Callahan, an optometrist, had offices in the Ben Hur building in Crawfordsville during the 1930's. The old Callahan home was located on the corner of Wabash and Vine Streets. David and Hannah were the parents of three children: Helena, Walter and Angela. Helena and Angela both died at a young age. Their son, Walter, born Aug. 13, 1888 was a World War I Army veteran. For a short time he attended Notre Dame University but soon became interested in Automotive Mechanics with the emergence of the automobile. He was among the first in the county to own a "horseless carriage". He married Madge M. Long, oldest daughter of Lawrence and Delia Long of Ladoga May 21, 1921. This union was blessed with four children: Mary, Mildred, David and Shirley. Walter worked many years for Capitol Motors Company of Indianapolis. He died Sept. 1, 1961.

"Dave" Kiley was an affable, witty man with twinkling Irish blue eyes. He was always ready to tell an interesting or amusing story. Dave was well known throughout Montgomery County and the state of Indiana. He died Oct. 21, 1925 on his farm north of Whitesville in South Union Township. Hannah died Dec. 26, 1942.

Their grandchildren still own and operate the Kiley farm and many great grandchildren reside in the county. *Submitted by Mildred Leckrone*

KING FAMILY

Henry Benjamin King came to Montgomery County from Shelby Co., OH in about 1839. He was born Aug. 5, 1831 to Henry Newton and Mary King. He died Oct. 24, 1894. On Aug. 16, 1855, he married Rebecca J. Stonebraker, born Nov. 20, 1839, died Jan. 22, 1912. They had ten children. The seventh child was George Henry King, born Feb. 6, 1868 and died May 17, 1930.

On Oct. 15, 1893, George Henry married Clara Conrad, born Jan. 29, 1870 and died Oct. 1, 1959. They had two sons: James Argyl King, born Aug. 2, 1895, died 1969, married Mary Chesterson in 1918. Herbert Benjamin King, born Sept. 19, 1901, died 1970. On Aug. 22, 1923, he married Ruth M. Hinkle, born Apr. 8, 1906. This marriage ended in divorce. Herbert and Ruth had three children:

The eldest of Herbert and Ruth's children was William Henry King, born Jan. 28, 1925. His sibling are: Betty Zachary and Richard King. William joined the Crawfordsville Fire Department in 1952, achieved the rank of Captain, owned and operated an Electric Motor Repair business. He died Dec. 31, 1971 in the line of duty.

On Sept. 12, 1952, he married Joan Jenkins, born Sept. 8, 1926 in Michigantown, IN. She graduated from Methodist Hospital in 1948. William and Joan had two sons. The youngest is John Alan King, born Jan. 19, 1959. He is employed at Impex as a Tool and Die Maker. On Apr. 3, 1982, he married Martha Scott of Noblesville, IN; Martha born Mar. 24, 1960.

Martha and John have one child, Amber Michelle King, born Mar. 18, 1987.

John's brother, David William King, born Aug. 2, 1953, married Deborah Fletcher of Tipton, IN on Mar. 12, 1988. Deborah was born June 28, 1963.

ELIJAH KING, SR.

Elijah King Sr. was born in Bourbon Co., KY Aug. 10, 1803, 13th child in a family of 16 children, to Jesse King and Sitha (Cynthia) Dowell. Jesse and Sitha are buried near Centerville, IN.

On Mar. 18, 1826, he married Eliza Wright Crooks in Kentucky Mar. 28, 1826. She was the daughter of Richard Crooks. Along with other family members they moved to Montgomery Co., IN arriving here in 1827 or 1828. To this union were born nine children: William Edgar King born Apr. 18, 1828 and married Mahersey Bell; Alfred Thompson King born Feb. 20, 1831; John Wallace King born Jan. 14, 1833 married Anna Everett and 2. married Mariah G. Pedric died Sept. 20, 1922 in Montgomery Co., IN; Margaret Jane King born Feb. 1, 1835 in Montgomery Co., IN; James Washington King born Apr. 24, 1837 in Montgomery County; Daniel Newton King born Jan. 23, 1840; Malinda Frances King born Jan. 22, 1842; Joseph Harrison King born Feb. 24, 1844 and married Mary Margaret Fuqua in Clay Co., IN, died Feb. 24, 1892 in Russell Co., KS; Elijah King II born Apr. 14, 1846 married Amanda Ellen Petro, died in Osawatomie, KS.

At age 42 Elijah, Sr. died on Aug. 22, 1845 leaving Eliza with the children to provide for. He is buried in the Breaks' Cemetery, Montgomery Co., IN. She married Richard Breaks in Mar. 27, 1849 in Montgomery County and they had one son Alvin Breaks. Eliza Wright Crooks King Breaks died Aug. 4, 1889 in Montgomery Co., IN and is buried in Oak Hill Cemetery in Crawfordsville, IN. *Submitted by Mabel Graham Cook*

JOHN WALLACE KING

John Wallace King was born in Montgomery Co., IN about six miles north of Crawfordsville on Jan. 14, 1833 and lived all of his life in this area. He was the son of Elijah and Eliza Wright Crooks King both natives of Kentucky. He was a veteran of the Civil War of which he talked very little. He did tell of being so close to the enemy lines that they could not even risk getting food, so the soldiers crawled to where the horses were eating and ate corn with them.

He was married in 1856 to Anna Everet who died in 1864. They had four children namely: Alfred Elijah King died Oct. 9, 1939 age 84; Ezekiel Alonzo "Lon" died on July 3, 1949 age 91; Julia Ann King died Dec. 1, 1935 age 77; and Eliza Frances King.

In 1870 John Wallace married Maria Pedrick died June 18, 1887 and to this union was born Mary Maria King June 4, 1906 age 34 years; Cora King died June 16, 1962 at the age of 88 and married Frank McNorton; Stella King died Dec. 25, 1971 age 95 and had married Alva Clark; Chester who never married, died in Brownsville, TX on Sept. 28, 1928; and Eva Bell married Ernest Williams, second marriage was to John Cooper and later she married Ellis Holmes. She had no children. Eva Bell died in Anderson, IN on Dec. 3, 1952.

John Wallace King was a man of few words, highly respected by adults, but youngsters even his own grandchildren were awed by his sternness. He moved to Darlington after having spent 60 years on his farm which when he bought it was a veritable wilderness. He labored by hand to convert it into one of the best farms north west of Darlington. He died at age 89 on Sept. 20, 1922.

The children from John and Anna Everet settled mostly in the Western States around Kansas and Missouri. They had lived with relatives after the death of their mother except Alonzo who lived with the Breaks family (his grandmother Eliza Wright Crooks King married Richard Breaks after the death of Elijah King) until he married Elizabeth Schleppy of that area. They had three daughters: Ivy who married Wiley Tribbett and they had Walter and Robert Tribbett; Blanch married Homer Cooper and they had five children: Ernest, Helen, Mildred, John and Betty; Anna married Olin Morrison and their children were: Robert, and Margaret Morrison.

Mary Marie King born Nov. 1, 1872 and married John L. Graham on Mar. 22, 1892 in the home of her father John Wallace King. Their first child a son was stillborn. Belva Mae born Jan. 22, 1895 married Jesse Bartley in March 1913 and she died in August 1941. Jesse died July 5, 1967. They had no children. Mabel Marie Graham born May 2, 1898 (see Cook family history). Ruth Mariah Graham born Aug. 16, 1900 (see Branstetter family). *Submitted by Mabel Marie Graham Cook*

JOHN KIRK

John Kirk was born in Athens Co., OH Apr. 13, 1836. He was one of a family of six children, five boys and one girl, who later became Mrs. George Haworth.

In April 1862, at the age of 26, John was married to Louisa Ahle. She was born in Germany, May 10, 1844 and died Jan. 31, 1922 in the home of her daughter, Mrs. Laura Hulvey.

Remembering the boat crossing at an early age, Louisa, along with her parents and siblings, Rosa, William and Richard came to the United States and settled in Ohio. She lived there until her marriage. She was a very industrious wife and mother. Besides her other wifely duties, she knitted socks and mittens for a family of 11 which were born of this union. The eight sons and three daughters born between 1863 and 1882 in the order of their birth were: James, Lewis, Anna Alice, Frank, Alden, Jesse, Alonzo, Laura, Harley, Ray and Ida. Anna Alice and Alonzo died at an early age.

Kirk brothers, John Kirk standing far right.

A member of the Bowers United Brethern Church in which they were instrumental in starting and maintaining, the Kirk home was always open to visiting ministers.

Coming to the Thorntown, Boone County area in the early 60s, our subject built a mill on Sugar Creek that was known as the Old Kirk Mill and together with Mr. George Haworth, his brother-in-law, operated it for several years.

Purchasing a farm in 1895 South West of Bowers Station, Montgomery County, on which the Bowers Tile and Brick Factory was located, Mr. Kirk and his sons operated the factory and were also engaged in farming and thrashing. He and his sons operated more thrashing machines than any other firm in Montgomery County.

Being a swampy area at that time, scores of tiles were needed for ditching and draining. Wagon teams would be lined up North and South for purchases of tile or brick.

In 1877 acreage for the Logansport, Crawfordsville, and South Western Railway was purchased from landowners to run a railroad through Sugar Creek Township. It went directly through what was then the Abner Bowers farm, later to become the John Kirk farm.

Known as the Vandalia line, six passenger trains a day ran between Logansport and Terre Haute. During dry weather, the trains had to be watched closely as the fire boxes often set fires to the adjoining fields.

John Kirk died on his farm July 3, 1903 at the age of 68. At the death of his widow Louisa, 19 years later, the farm was purchased by a son, Harley Kirk who was married to Bertha May Gant, Nov. 29, 1902 at Lafayette, IN. Their children were: Myrl Hole, Mildred Lee and Margaret Flint.

Upon the death of Harley and Bertha, the farm was purchased by Mildred Kirk Lee and husband Robert Lee and was subsequently passed on to Margaret Kirk Flint and daughter Jean Flint.

The farm which will have been in the Kirk family for 100 years in 1995 is being operated by a grandson, William Kirk Hole, the son of Myrl Kirk Hole and husband Lester Hole. Also assisting are great, great grandsons, Gregory and David Hole, the sons of William K. and Alma Newby Hole.

KIRTLEY FAMILY

The advent of the Kirtley family in Montgomery County actually began in 1906 when the young dentist, Dr. William Raymond Kirtley, left his brother's practice in Lebanon and came to Crawfordsville. Dr. Lewis Wallace Kirtley had influenced his younger brother to go to dental school and WRK had graduated from the the Indiana Dental College in Indianapolis (now the Indiana University School of Dentistry) on May 5, 1905.

This branch of the Kirtley family had begun in Johnson Co., IN in 1862 when James Samuel Kirtley and his sister Jessie F. Kirtley moved from Taylor Co., KY, probably to escape the Civil War which was raging in their home state at that time. James Samuel was born in Kentucky in 1842 and his sister in 1845. Once settled in Indiana, each married, Sam to Elsie Clara Records and Jessie to James Harvey Forsythe.

William Raymond and Laurel S. Miller Kirtley

James Samuel Kirtley and Clara E. Records (she transposed the initial) were the parents of three sons and two daughters. Frank Smith b. 1868, Lewis Wallace b. 1870, Jessie Fidelia b. 1872, Elsie Lavinna b. 1875 and William Raymond b. 1884.

Dr. William Raymond Kirtley, known as "Ray" by his family, had a shock of beautiful auburn hair and a pleasing personality. A member of the Christian Church he affiliated with First Christian Church in Crawfordsville where he met Laurel S. Miller. Love soon bloomed and they were married Oct. 7, 1909 at her parents' home, 1101 W. Wabash Ave.

The parents of the bride were Charles Marion Miller, born Dec. 29, 1862 near Beckville and Mamie Lenore Wisehart, born Oct. 25, 1866, also in Montgomery County. To this couple were born Laurel S. Feb. 7, 1887, Lillie Beth, Sept. 7, 1893, and Charles Raymond, Sept. 11, 1898.

Dr. William R. Kirtley and his wife, Laurel S. Kirtley, were the parents of two sons. James Marion (see biography) was born July 23, 1910 in Crawfordsville and William Raymond (Jr.) (see biography) May 30, 1914, also in Crawfordsville. Dr. Kirtley had a busy professional life in dentistry and kept himself current in continuing education. In October 1918, at the height of a world-wide devastating influenza epidemic, he died of that illness at the age of 34.

Laurel S. Miller pursued her primary education in the Smartsburg school and when the family moved to E. Jefferson St., in Crawfordsville, she entered the high school, graduating in 1906. She was a top student and was offered a scholarship to the Western College for Women in Oxford, OH but was unable to accept the honor. Her marriage to the young Dr. Ray Kirtley was a very happy one but tragically short. Widowed at 31 she was determined to see that her two young sons were properly educated and she earned a living by entering the business world as a retail clerk. Later she was persuaded to enter politics and she was elected Crawfordsville's City Clerk, one of the first women locally to gain such an honor. She was re-elected after her first term and then served as deputy to Mabel Himes, the first City Clerk-Treasurer. Subsequently she served as secretary to Dr. Byron N. Lingeman until his retirement. She was a member of the Dorothy Q Chapter DAR, Eastern Star and was twice elected president of the Business and Professional Women's Club. Mrs. Kirtley died May 25, 1970 in Culver Hospital following surgery. She and Dr. Kirtley are buried in the Oak Hill Cemetery.

Dr. William R. Kirtley was a member of the Masonic Lodge and the York Rite bodies in Crawfordsville and the Murat Shrine. He was active in community affairs and was a member of the YMCA board when that edifice was built on Pike St. at Green St. It now serves as Union Township House.

J.M. KIRTLEY

Although they were students in Crawfordsville High School during the same period of time, Dr. J.M. Kirtley and his future wife, Leolia A. Black, knew each other only as fellow students. Leolia (Lee as she later preferred being called) was born in Newtown, IN Nov. 12, 1911 on a day reported to be one of the coldest on record. When the family moved to Montgomery County in 1923 she attended the rural Wilson School and then Crawfordsville High School where she graduated in 1929. She entered the Indiana University School of Nursing and, in spite of a severe illness while a student, she graduated in 1934 with the G.N. degree. While serving as a staff nurse in the Indiana University Hospitals she again became ill but she recovered to marry Dr. Marion Kirtley in Camp Gordon, GA Feb. 14, 1943 where he was on active duty with the rank of Major.

James Marion M.D. and Leolia A. Black Kirtley GN

Lee's parents were Milo N. Black and Gertrude Riffle Black, both natives of Fountain Co., IN. Their family consisted of four girls and one boy. Ramona, the eldest, and Thelma became teachers after their training in Indiana University and taught in Montgomery County as well as several other Indiana places. Geraldine, the third child, graduated from CHS and attended Franklin College. For many years she was a proofreader for the R.R. Donnelley & Sons Co. and for the Indianapolis *Star-News*. William Jennings Black, the only son, was an excellent student at CHS and received the A.B. degree from DePauw University in 1930. Mary, the youngest child, was also a CHS graduate and remained in Crawfordsville for several years, later moving to Anderson, IN.

James Marion Kirtley attended public schools in Crawfordsville, graduating from high school in 1928. He received the A.B. degree from Wabash College in 1932 and the M.D. degree from Indiana University School of Medicine in 1936. After serving an internship and obstetrical residency in the Indiana University Hospitals he returned to Crawfordsville to set up a private practice in 1938. Except for five years on active duty with the U.S. Army during WWII he practiced medicine in Crawfordsville until his retirement in 1982, a 50 year stint.

In politics he was a Democrat and served three terms as a Crawfordsville City Councilman, one four year term as an Indiana State Senator and in 1986 was elected Montgomery County Commissioner.

Honors include the Jefferson Award, presented through the *Indianapolis Star,* two citations as Sagamore of the Wabash, one by Gov. Otis Bowen and the second by Gov. Robert Orr. Wabash College awarded him the honorary degree Doctor of Laws in 1982. He served with the 22nd Infantry Regiment, 4th Infantry Division from 1940-45 and was a D-Day veteran of Utah Beach, Normandy. He received the bronze star with two oak leaf clusters and the combat medical badge while serving as regimental surgeon of the 22nd Infantry.

David James was the first of three sons (see Samuel Kirtley and Raymond Marion Kirtley, biographies) born to James Marion and Lee Kirtley on June 18, 1944 in Methodist Hospital, Indianapolis, while his father was serving with the 4th Infantry Division in Normandy, France. David grew up in Crawfordsville, graduated from CHS and later matriculated in Eureka College in Illinois but then studied at the University of Arizona in Tucson and finally received the B.S. degree from Indiana State University. He never married and has been involved in the audio-visual and teaching professions.

Dr. Kirtley is past president of the Montgomery County Medical Society and the Montgomery County Historical Society. He is a Mason and member of the York and Scottish Rites, as well as the Murat Temple. Lee is past president of the Women's Auxiliary of the Medical Society and member of the Psi Iota Xi Sorority. Both are active in the Christian Church; both served as deacons, he as elder and she as Circle Leader.

The Kirtleys remain as active members of the community today! *Submitted by Dr. J.M. Kirtley*

RAYMOND MARION KIRTLEY

Raymond Marion was the third son born to the J.M. Kirtleys on July 16, 1952 at Coleman Hospital in Indianapolis. He, too, attended the primary and secondary schools in Crawfordsville but decided to pursue his college education at Indiana University in Bloomington. He studied political science and graduated with an A.B. degree. After college he worked in sales and banking in Indianapolis and gained admission to the Indiana University School of Law there and received the J.D. degree from that institution. Another school romance grew to fruition when Ray married Nancy Jane Dahl at the First Methodist Church in Crawfordsville in December 1974. Nancy was the daughter of Donald and Jane Dahl. Donald was a teacher of biology in the Tuttle School and had graduated from Purdue University with a B.S. degree. Jane Tower Dahl received her G.N. degree from the Indiana University School of Nursing and did staff nursing at Culver Hospital, later becoming school nurse for the South Montgomery School Corp.

Nancy Jane (Dahl) and Raymond Marion Kirtley

Nancy Jane Dahl Kirtley graduated from Indiana University with a B.S. degree, having prepared to teach biology. However, she and Ray decided to raise a family and settled in Crawfordsville where Ray began a solo law practice. Politics soon beckoned and in 1984 he was elected Judge of the Montgomery County Court. While residing in Indianapolis during law school days their first child, Kathleen Elizabeth, was born in Methodist Hospital June 13, 1979. Laura Rebecca was born Dec. 11, 1981, also in Methodist Hospital and Sarah Jane arrived on July 19, 1985, delivered by her uncle Dr. Sam Kirtley in Crawfordsville's Culver Union Hospital.

Judge Ray Kirtley and his wife Nancy are members of First Methodist Church. He is a member of the Montgomery County Bar Association and the Indiana State Bar Association. Nancy is an active member of the Psi Iota Xi sorority and she and her husband are active in their support of the Sugar Creek Swimmers in which their three daughters participate. *Submitted by Dr. J.M. Kirtley*

SAMUEL WILLIAM KIRTLEY

Samuel William Kirtley was the second son of James Marion and Lee Kirtley and was born in Coleman Hospital, of the Indiana University Hospitals group in Indianapolis Sept. 9, 1949. He, too, was raised in Crawfordsville, educated there and graduated from Wabash College with the A.B. degree in 1971, stressing pre-medicine. He married Rebecca Louise McCreary, his schoolgirl sweetheart, in August 1971. While Sam studied at Wabash, Becky pursued an occupational therapy degree at Indiana University. After their marriage, they moved to Danville, IN where Sam worked as a medical technician while attending the Indiana University life sciences department and received a M.S. degree in pharmacology. His M.D. degree was granted in 1976 and he embarked on a three year family practice residency at the Methodist Hospital which led to his Diplomate of Family Practice Board achievement.

Along the education way Adam Matthew was born to Sam and Becky Nov. 26, 1972, his paternal grandfather having the high privilege of officiating at his birth in Culver Hospital, Crawfordsville. Other natural children were not to be but Tracy Anne Kirtley, born on July 7, 1978 in Indianapolis became their adopted daughter and became the first female to grace the second generation.

Rebecca Louise McCreary was the daughter of Harold and Norma Jaynes McCreary and was born in Crawfordsville May 23, 1949. Her parents had been married Feb. 14, 1943, the same day that J. Marion and Lee Kirtley were married in far away Georgia. She and Sam were in the same class in high school and were married in the Wabash College chapel.

Samuel William M.D. and Rebecca L. (McCreary) Kirtley

Becky's artistic ability became more manifest in later years when she did research and produced hand-made historically authentic figures of Santa Claus or Saint Nicholas or Father Christmas which have been loved throughout the world. Her mother, Norma McCreary Killian, joined Becky in her project and they have formed a company to meet the demand for their unique products.

Dr. Sam Kirtley practices family medicine with the Greenacres Medical Group, which grew out of his father's private practice. He is active in medical affairs serving as president of the Montgomery County Medical Society and president of the medical staff of the Culver Hospital AMI. In the affairs of the community he is a member of the Tourism Board and he and his wife, Becky, are active in the Methodist Church.

While a student in Wabash College he was a member of the Kappa Sigma fraternity, serving one year as president. His family has been involved in this fraternity, an international men's social college group. His two brothers David and Ray were initiated by the Indiana State University and Indiana University chapters. His father, James M. Kirtley, was a member of the Wabash College chapter and his interest continued through the years and he eventually was elected to the Supreme Executive Committee of the fraternity as Worthy Grand Treasurer. His uncle, Charles Raymond Miller was the beginning of the tradition of Kappa Sigma membership in 1919. C.R. Miller's grandson, Wallace K. Aiken was a Wabash Kappa Sigma and a Kirtley cousin-in-law, Dr. John Bushong, also wore the Star & Crescent. *Submitted by The Kirtley Family*

WILLIAM RAYMOND KIRTLEY, JR.

William Raymond Kirtley followed his older brother, Marion, through the Crawfordsville Schools graduating from CHS in 1932. At Wabash College he earned the A.B. degree in pre-medicine but decided to attend the Northwestern University School of Medicine in Chicago, IL. He received the Bachelor of Medicine degree in 1940 and the M.D. in 1941, after serving an internship in the Indianapolis Methodist Hospital.

While a student in Chicago he met Faye Marie Price of Hillsboro, IL and they were married June 18, 1940 in the University Place Christian Church in Champaign, IL. Bill was called to active duty with the U.S. Army from a residency program in

Indianapolis and was assigned to Camp Grant, IL a medical replacement training facility where he was a faculty member. Toward the end of WWII he was reassigned to the American Division in the South Pacific Theater and served in Japan at war's end.

The first child born to this couple was William Raymond Kirtley III who arrived in the Indianapolis Methodist Hospital Oct. 8, 1948. On Nov. 7, 1953 a sister, Jane Elizabeth was born, also in Indianapolis. Both children grew up in Indianapolis, graduated from the North Central High School and continued their education in college. Bill entered Rose Poly Institute in Terre Haute, now Rose-Hulman, and took electrical engineering. He became an expert in repairs of the huge theater organs and now is retained by the owners of these complicated instruments. A lover of classical music, he now is a staff announcer for an Indianapolis-Danville FM station. He has never married.

Jane Elizabeth received her degree in journalism at Northwestern University in Evanston and later obtained a J.D. degree from the Vanderbilt University Law School in Nashville, TN. She is married to Stephen Cribari, also an attorney, and she serves in Washington, D.C. with a reporters' group interested in defending the freedom of the press amendment to the constitution.

William Raymond Kirtley, the father, served for many years with the Eli Lilly Pharmaceutical Co. in Indianapolis and retired as director of medical research. Faye M. Kirtley died in 1974 of a lung malignancy. In 1976 WRK married Christina Marie Riley who had been born in Liverpool, England. They now reside on Hilton Head Isle, SC where they both enjoy golfing and tennis. Christina has had an enviable record of public service in promoting and working in a school devoted to teaching the children of working parents.

While he was with the Lilly organization, Dr. Kirtley became interested in diabetes and did research on the physiology of the disease. He was a member of the American Diabetes Association and served as secretary for that prestigious group. He was awarded the Banting Medal, named in honor of one of the discoverers of insulin, and presented to scientists who have contributed to the knowledge of diabetes.

EDITH MANGES KISTLER

Edith Manges Kistler started in the 1920's to gather the information about her ancestors and by 1988 she has the names and much information about 125 of them. Nineteen of them lived in Montgomery County. Sixty copies or partial copies have been given to relatives and friends including the Newberry Library and the Crawfordsville Library.

Edith Manges Kistler

In 1939 Edith married William C. Armstrong (who died in 1954) so part of her writings is in the name of Armstrong. She wrote a 48-page booklet of "The Thomas Armstrong Family" including eight generations. The Armstrong family lived at New Richmond and Sugar Grove in Montgomery County but moved west in 1864.

In 1959 Edith married Merton L. Kistler so later writings have the name Kistler.

Edith graduated from Crawfordsville High School and Butler University. She was the daughter of Edgar and Nellie Linn Manges of Whitesville and was born Nov. 3, 1906.

Edith and Pauline Himes Moore compiled a scrapbook of the Whitesville Christian Church including many pictures, clippings and the history. Recently she compiled a scrapbook of 60 pages of the 45 ancestors of Susan Kessler Thompson for her great grandson Ronald Clark of Whitestown, IN.

She has many scrapbooks of travels, families, tombstones of all her ancestors and picturing life of her self and her ancestors, and her teachings. *Submitted by Edith Manges Kistler*

JULIE LeCLERC KNOX

Julie LeClerc Knox, teacher and historian, was born in Vevay, IN, on July 23, 1870. She was the daughter of James Stevenson and Louise LeClerc Knox. She was a direct descendant of the Dufour family that founded Vevay in 1802, and the great granddaughter of Marie Antoinette Dufour Moreland, sister of the Dufour brothers.

Miss Knox was graduated from Vevay High School, taught in the lower grades, then was assistant principal and principal of the high school. Concurrently she attended Indiana University and received the A.B. degree in 1918. She did graduate work at Columbia University and took summer courses at Winona Lake. Her degree was in English with a minor in Latin and French. She became head of the Latin department of the Crawfordsville High School, a position she held for 18 years. She also served as critic Latin teacher at Wabash College. After receiving an inheritance, she resigned her teaching position in 1936.

Miss Knox was active in state educational and historical work. She was president of the classical section of the Indiana State Teachers Association and a member of the state reading circle. She was a member of the state commission on historic markers and served on committees of the Indiana Historical Society. She was president of the Vevay Music Club, Switzerland County Historical Society, and Crawfordsville branch of the American Association of University Women. She traveled extensively in the United States and abroad, and gave lectures on travel, literary, and historical subjects. She was one of the women selected to serve on the board of directors of national Poetry Day on Sept. 14, 1940, at the New York World's Fair.

After returning to Vevay from Crawfordsville, Miss Knox organized a club to encourage creative writing. On several occasions she was president of Julia L. Dumont Club, one of Indiana's oldest literary societies. She was an authority on the French-Swiss people who settled Switzerland County and collected a great deal of material about them.

At an early age Miss Knox had some of her writings published in a newspaper. The *Indiana Magazine of History* printed more than 20 of her articles and she wrote for other magazines. While she was a member of the creative writing group of the Crawfordsville AAUW, she tried writing poetry. Her poems appeared in anthologies and newspapers. She won several prizes for her poetry and was a charter member of Poet's Corner, Inc. She died on Mar. 23, 1965.

Miss Knox was the author of three books: *Some Interesting Pioneer Homesteads In and Around Vevay* (1927); *The Dufour Saga, 1796-1942* (1942); and *Reveries* (1960). *Submitted by Jean Thompson, County Historian*

BETTY JOANN TITUS KORHONEN

The fourth child and second daughter of Raymond and Mildred Cedars Titus, Betty Joann Titus was born on June 27, 1933. She joined siblings Richard, Barbara and Billy. After graduation from Crawfordsville High School, where she was in the top 20% of her class and maintained a B average throughout, she used her business skills at the Abstract and Title Company in Crawfordsville until her move to Seattle, WA in 1956. Here she met and married Darrell Korhonen, (son of Ann and Martin Korhonen), an engineer for U.S. West Communication (formerly Pacific Northwest Bell) on Apr. 5, 1958. Three children were born to this union— Kenneth Martin, Feb. 28, 1959; Mary Ann July 14, 1961 and Susan Jane Mar. 15, 1963. After rearing her children, Betty returned to the work force as a bookkeeper for Dick 'n Dales Inc. of Seattle.

Betty, Darrell, Mary Ann, Kenneth, Susie Korhonen

Kenneth (Kenny) followed in his father's footsteps in joining U.S. West Communication after his high school graduation. Another point of similarity is an interest in antiques. Darrell recently purchased an antique car that is still driveable. Kenny has a whole house full of old radios, etc. Kenny is also a James Dean fan and has just about everything published about the late actor.

Susan (Susie Jane) was united in marriage to Robert Hart, son of Carl and Patricia Hart on Aug. 8, 1981. A daughter, Melissa Lynn was born July 1, 1982. A son, Jonathan Robert was born on July 19, 1983. Susie is presently employed by Boeing Co. where she assembles parts for the 747-400 airplanes.

Mary Ann Korhonen married Jose (Joe) Trujillo, Jr., son of Jose and Mary Jane Trujillo on Feb. 8, 1986. They are expecting a baby in December, 1989. Her husband works for Care Medical Supplies. She works for Kenny Retirement Home.

KROUT FAMILY

The biography of the Krout family beginning with Abraham Krout, an immigrant from Saxony, Germany. He came to America in the early 1700's from Niemberg and settled in Bucks Co., PA. His first son, Jacob, settled in Orangeberg Co., SC about 1770. Jacob Krout was a man well educated and financially secure for those times. Before the Revolutionary War Jacob managed his cotton and indigo plantation. When the state of Georgia was being ravished by the British, under the command of Col. Tarleton at the Battle of the Cowpens, Jacob and his son's fought with Gen. Morgan as Continental soldiers. Jacob Krout's wife, a pious German lady (of Lutheran religion), being forced from their home, hid with her children in the swamp. All she had time to save was the family Bible and Hymn Book. For many years this old family Bible was in the possession of Mary Hanna Krout's family. Inside the back fly leaf was written in faded ink, the name "Kroutewell", which was probably the family name in German.

Jacob Krout was killed at the battle of Briar Creek, Mar. 3, 1779. Under the command of Gen. Ashe, Col. Prevost crossed Briar Creek, 15 miles above Gen. Ashe's position, and with the creek being flooded and not enough time to build a bridge, faced annihilation. The Continentals held for some time but were finally routed. Some were drowned in the swamp but many escaped by swimming or on crowded rafts.

With her possessions destroyed, she and her family travelled to Kentucky and settled in what now is called Campbell County. I found that Michael Krout, one of Jacob's sons, born 1775 Orangeberg County had settled in Campbell County in the year 1800. He purchased 62 acres on the banks of Licking Creek, paid taxes, and worked on the roads. Michael Krout was a private in the Kentucky Militia in the War of 1812, under the command of Cap. William Davis Inf. 71 Reg. May 14, 1814. It is recorded in Campbell Co., KY, that Michael Krout was a farmer, married, and held no slaves. While in Kentucky, he became a life-long friend of Alexander Weir, with whom he soldiered and who married his eldest daughter, Margaret.

In 1828, Michael Krout and Alexander Weir and families came to Montgomery Co., IN in South Union township. Michael settled on Sugar Creek near the Jim Davis Bridge. Alexander Weir settled near where Offields monument now stands. Michael Krout died about 1830. We do not know where he is buried in Weir Cemetery, Montgomery Co., IN. She died May, 1854.

It is from these sturdy ancestors that many of our local families have stemmed. Many generations since have become citizens of Montgomery County endowed with all the qualities our ancestors left us, our faith in God, and ability to live and work with our fellow man without prejudice. *Written by Archie D. Krout, Seventh generation from Michael and Katherine Krout*

CAROLINE VIRGINIA KROUT

Caroline Virginia Krout was born in Crawfordsville Oct. 23, 1852, to Robert K. and Caroline Brown Krout, the second of nine children. Caroline attended the Young Ladies' Seminary of Crawfordsville, and then Crawfordsville High School for a short time. She began teaching in Crawfordsville schools in her 19th year. She taught for five years, until her health failed. She was a "nervous" invalid for several years.

During her illness, Caroline wrote her first story and became a contributor of short stories and feature articles to the *InterOcean, Chicago Daily News, Chicago Journal,* and other papers.

When her health improved, she became an assistant court reporter in Crawfordsville, and later went to Chicago where she was on the staff of the Newberry Library. Her health failed again about 1896, so she returned to the family home in Crawfordsville. Unable to work, she was encouraged by her sister, Mary Hannah and friend, Mrs. Lew Wallace, to write for the periodical market. She wrote about 20 short stories, using her mother's maiden name, Caroline Brown, as a pseudonym. Her first sales were to *St. Nicholas* and *Cosmopolitan.* Next she wrote *Knights in Fustian,* (1900) a story of the Knights of the Colden Circle and the Copperhead insurrection in Indiana in 1863. The background of the story was laid in the southwest part of Montgomery Co., Balhinch. This tale was true to history and to local life, and its literary excellence placed Krout's name high on the roll of Midwestern writers.

Next she wrote *On the We-A Trail* (1903) which dealt with the capture of Vincennes during the Revolutionary War. At the same time, Maurice Thompson was writing *Alice of Old Vincennes* on the same theme. His book was published the same day her manuscript was ready to mail. She offered to not publish her novel, but when Thompson learned of her embarrassment, he exerted all of his kindness to put her at her ease, and encouraged her to publish it. The two novels are not alike, in spite of their common theme. Her book was quite successful. Her third book, *Bold Robin and His Forest Rangers* (1905) consists of six short stories for children.

Her fourth and last novel, *Dionis of the White Veil* (1911) is a romance giving the history of the attempt of priests and nuns to found a Jesuit mission in what was to become Indiana.

Summing up her work Arthur Shumaker says "Caroline Krout is a writer with many faults...but many parts of her narratives move well, her descriptions of nature are skillfully written, and she dug her materials from her native soil. She was so sensitive to criticism and so aware of her own literary faults, that after publishing four books, she gave up writing and lived the last 20 years as a recluse with her sisters in the family home."

She died in her home Oct. 9, 1931. *By Jean Thompson*

MARY HANNAH KROUT

Mary Hannah Krout was born in Crawfordsville Nov. 3, 1851 to Robert and Caroline Krout, the eldest of nine children. Mary Hannah attended the Young Ladies' Seminary at Crawfordsville. When she was 15 her poem "Little Brown Hands" was published in *Our Young Folks.* Its popularity created an immediate demand for her work, and "Little Brown Hands" was incorporated into grade school readers for the next 50 years.

Miss Krout taught school at Bunker Hill when she was 16. She then taught at Crawfordsville for the next 11 years.

In 1869 she joined other young women to petition Wabash College to allow the admission of women. Permission was denied, but she and the others were allowed to attend science classes. These young women organized the Ladies' Reading Association, the true purpose of which was more political than literary.

During the 1870s she wrote two plays "The Widow Selby" and "The Man in the House." The latter was presented on the stage of the English Theater in Indianapolis in 1885.

During this period, Miss Krout was writing columns for the *Crawfordsville Journal* "Topics of the Town" and using the pseudonyms of Mynheer Karl and Ben Offield, she wrote on political affairs in the *Indianapolis Herald.*

Giving up teaching in 1879, she began writing for the *Crawfordsville Journal* and in 1881 she became associate editor of the *Journal.* In 1882 she became editor of the *Terre Haute Express.* She worked 14-hour days, which exhausted her. Mrs. Lew Wallace, who had encouraged her writing, sent money to her and urged her to take a complete rest. In 1888 Miss Krout went to Chicago where she was employed by the newspaper *InterOcean.* She served as a political correspondent during the presidential candidacy of Benjamin Harrison.

For ten years Miss Krout wrote the column "The Woman's Kingdom" for the *InterOcean.* In 1892 she was appointed to the Indiana Board of Women Managers for the Columbian Exposition in Chicago. At this time she was also president of the National Press League.

In 1893 the *InterOcean* sent her to Hawaii, then she went to New Zealand and Australia and then was sent to London as a staff correspondent for the paper for a three year period. Miss Krout also spent a year in China in 1899/1900, staying in Peking for three months and then traveling into the interior almost to the Mongolian frontier.

Always when the opportunity offered, Miss Krout lectured on women's suffrage in the United States, England, New Zealand, China and Hawaii.

During this period she had several books published, *Hawaii and a Revolution* (1898), *A Looker On in London* (1899), *Alice's Visit to the Hawaiian Islands* (1900), *Two Girls in China* (1903).

In 1906 Miss Krout returned to Crawfordsville, and spent her time writing. She completed General Lew Wallace's autobiography with the assistance of his widow, Susan Wallace. She also wrote the *Memoirs of Hon. Bernice Pauahi Bishop* (1908) and *Reminiscences of Mrs. Mary Rice* (1908). *Platters and Pipkins* was published in 1910.

She died May 31, 1927. *Submitted by Jean Thompson*

WILLIAM AUGUSTUS KRUG

William Augustus Krug was born Lancaster, PA, the son of Valentine Krug b. 1754 and died in 1817 Adams Co., PA, and Eva Graff born June 13, 1760 in Lancaster, PA, died there July 12, 1801. Valentine served in the Revolutionary War, and was the son of John Valentine Krug born 1689 in East Germany; died Feb. 18, 1759 in Gebirge Mountains; and Eva Maria Spangler born in 1726 and died Dec. 15, 1802. Their marriage date was Nov. 10, 1743.

William Augustus Krug married Elizabeth Jones and they were blessed with ten children. She died in 1860.

Few men are permitted to live to be 100 years old and perhaps fewer care to but, William Krug, who died at the home of his daughter on West Pike Street on Apr. 17, 1893 would have been 103 years of age on the 17th of September. What he was able to see in all that flight of time would take a whole library to tell. He forgot more of what he had seen and heard before he died than any of us probably will ever know. He was a remarkable old man. Until very recently he retained in a wonderful degree his mental faculties and physically he was as lively as a cricket. His activity was amazing and his joviality not withstanding his wrinkles put many a youth not one fourth as old to shame. He delighted in telling stories and singing old songs that he heard half a century ago. A little time of ten, 15 or 20 years was a small consideration with him. He was a peculiar individual in this city and to find a comparison the oldest inhabitant had to resort to the Bible for Grandpa Krug was on earth long before anything or anybody else was in this locality. His sons who looked old enough to be our grandfather we hear called the boys and we wonder when they will become old men and if they too will live as long as their father.

William Augustus Krug learned to be a saddler in Pennsylvania. He came to this state in 1839 settling at Wingate in this county. He was an Episcopalian in his religious views and an uncompromising Republican politically. He never failed to vote and took a great interest in his party's welfare. The death of his son William who died shortly before him, greatly effected him and he died shortly there after. He made his home with his daughter Louie and his granddaughter Miss Nellie. William J. Krug born June 3, 1814 in York, PA; died Mar. 14, 1893, married Kezia McKean (McCain) born Oct. 22, 1817 Butler Co., OH; died Apr. 14, 1907 Montgomery Co., IN. *By Kathryn Hill Carlstedt*

FOWLER EZRA AND ELIZABETH BERNICE (VAIL) KUNKEL

Fowler Ezra Kunkel (1895-1954) was born in Fountain Co., IN, youngest son of Jacob "Adam" Kunkel (1851-1930) and Nancy Ann Fowler (1853-1935). Adam was born in Adams Co., PA, son of John and Catherine Elizabeth (Schrider) Kunkel. He often told of hearing the first shots of the Battle of Gettysburg while plowing in the fields.

After the Civil War, Adam migrated to Fountain County with his parents. In 1878 he married Nancy Ann Fowler and took up farming near Stone Bluff. After the birth of Fowler, Adam purchased a farm in Montgomery County near Waynetown.

Fowler's mother Nancy was the daughter of Cyrus Moore Fowler (1824-1901) and Charlotte Osborn (1832-1913). Her father Cyrus was the son of Joshua Davis Fowler, a Revolutionary War veteran, and Mary Hall. Her mother Charlotte was the daughter of Oliver and Huldah (Crane) Osborn, who came to Fountain County in 1823 with a religious group called the "Coal Creek Community and Church of God."

Fowler's brothers and sisters were John William (1879-1957) of Waynetown; Emma Charlotte (1881-1906) who married James Edward Vail of Linden; Cyrus "Elmer" (1885-1953) of Washington State; and Nancy Mae (1887-1948) who married Floyd Otis Grenard.

Fowler Ezra and Elizabeth Bernice (Vail) Kunkel

In 1917 Fowler married Elizabeth Bernice Vail, daughter of William Riley Vail and Lillie Anna Fletcher. They settled first on the Kunkel farm near Waynetown, then moved to the Cherry Grove-Linden area, where Fowler took up his life-long profession of carpentry. In 1931 Fowler moved his wife and five children to New Richmond, where he purchased the home in which he and Elizabeth spent the rest of their lives. Elizabeth was assessor for Coal Creek Township, served on the Election Board, and contributed local news to the *Hoosier Graphic* and the Crawfordsville *Journal and Review*.

Their oldest son Donald Riley (1918-1986) served with the U.S. Army during World War II. In 1944 he married Dorotha Maguire, by whom he had two daughters—Sue (Mrs. Philip Mullen of Lafayette) and Betsy (Mrs. Michael Pierce). His widow resides in Linden.

Ralph Fowler, born 1920 on the Kunkel farm near Waynetown, also served with the U.S. Army during World War II. In 1941 he married Lois Lane. He established a plumbing service in New Richmond, where he still resides, as do his son Roger and daughter Janet (Mrs. Bert Brown).

Elizabeth Maxine, born 1923 on the Fletcher farm at Cherry Grove, married William Bridge and had twins Carolyn and Marilyn and son Michael.

Betty June, born 1928 at Cherry Grove, married William Junior Ellis in 1946 and traveled with him throughout his career in the Air Force. They now reside in Alexandria, VA, and have five children—William Jr., John, Melodie, Richard, and Melinda.

Marjorie Ann, born 1930 in Linden, married Howard Cox of Darlington in 1949 and now resides in Romney. Their children are Steven of Lafayette and Vicki (Mrs. William Martin) of New Richmond.

Fowler died in his New Richmond home in 1954. Elizabeth died in Lafayette in 1982. They are buried together in the New Richmond Cemetery. At the time of Elizabeth's death, there were 14 grandchildren and 20 great-grandchildren.

LaFOLLETTE FAMILY

According to the LaFollette family history compiled by John H. LaFollette many years ago, his great grandfather, Joseph LaFollette, was born in France about 1745, came to America with his brothers, George and Charles and their parents. Joseph came to Indiana in 1828.

The most famous of this branch of the family was Robert LaFollette, a Wisconsin Senator, who later ran for President. His son, Robert was also a U.S. Senator.

No attempt will be made to bring forward the records of the entire family. This piece will begin with Francis Marion LaFollette, born Aug. 7, 1848. He married Cornelia E. Shannon. They lived in Lebanon. In addition to three children who died in infancy, they had:

Earl, born Dec. 9, 1879, married Nora Winchester; lived in Darlington, Thorntown and Crawfordsville. They had a daughter, Ellen Jane, born Mar. 19, 1916, who married Montford Mead. Ellen Jane and Monty now live in Denver, CO. Earl died in 1942 and Nora died in 1970.

Carrie, born Dec. 8, 1882, who married Wilbur Rice. They had two sons: (1) Robert who married Violet ?. They had a son, Robert, who lives in Nashville, TN, with his present family and (2) Marion, who is deceased. Wilbur died early and Carrie raised the two boys alone in California. She and Marion then lived in Ohio where she died in 1941.

George Rushton, born Dec. 22, 1885, married Anna Gertrude Payton. They were in business in Crawfordsville for many years. They had two children: (1) William Francis, born Oct. 9, 1913 who married Maxine Vandenburg, and had two children, Robert F. born Sept. 12, 1959, died Feb. 21, 1985 and Lois, born May 18, 1957. William died Dec. 4, 1978. Maxine and Lois live in San Diego, CA.

Alice Virginia, daughter of George Rushton LaFollette was born Apr. 24, 1919. She lives in Orange, CA. She married Donald Emerson Carsrud, now deceased. Two children: Michele JoAnn, born Mar. 25, 1950, living in Beltsville, MD and Robert Steven, born Jan. 28, 1953, who married Jeanette Miller. They live in LaMirada, CA.

Harold, the last child of Francis Marion and Cornelia (Shannon) LaFollette was born Mar. 18, 1890 and married Hazel Perkins. They lived in Eagle Rock, CA. Both are deceased. *Submitted by Alice LaFollette Carsrud*

FRANCIS MARION AND CORNELIA SHANNON LaFOLLETTE FAMILY

Francis Marion (Frank) (1848-1917) Lafayette farmer, cattleman, Lebanon merchant, m. 1878 Cornelia (Neeley) Shannon, Shannondale.

Earle, Carrie, Rushton and Harold. Children of Francis Marion and Cornelia Ellen Shannon LaFollette.

Their children were:

I. Joseph Earle, (1879-1942) banker, in Darlington and Thorntown m. (1904) Nora Lucinda Winchester (1882-1970). One daughter, A. Ellen Jane (1916) teacher, m. (1945) Montford Authur Mead United Way Director, 20 years, retired, Denver, CO.

II. Caroline (Carrie) Belle (1882-19__) m. 1908 to Wilbur Hughes Rice, telegrapher. Two sons: A. Robert (1910-19__) m. Violet. Son: 1. Robert Rice, Nashville, TN. B. Marion (1913-19__) Theatre Organ Musician, California. Upholsterer, Marion, OH.

III. George Rushton (Rush) LaFollette (1885-1945) merchant, Crawfordsville. Farmer, Waveland m. 1912 Anna Gertrude Payton (1893-1959). Two children: A. William Francis (1913-1978) Post Office m. Maxine Yvonne Vandenberg. Two children: 1. Lois Maxine (1957) lives with her mother, San Diego, CA. 2. Robert Francis (1959-1985). B. Alice Virginia Allison (1919) lives Orange, CA m. Donald Carsrud (1913-19__). Two children: 1. Michele JoAnne (1950) single, Washington, D.C. area. 2. Robert Stephen (1953) m. Jeannette Miller, lives LaMirada, CA.

IV. Harold LaFollette (1890-19__) Decorator m. Hazel. No children, California.

V. Paul (1893-1896). *Submitted by Mildred Weliever*

GEORGE WASHINGTON LAFOLLETTE

George Washington and Susannah (Nofsinger)

LaFollette Family. George (1824-1897) m. Susannah (1827-1902) daughter of Joseph and Mary Harshbarger Nofsinger, (Jacob's line), moved from Parkersburg to their farm west of Shannondale on the Overcoat Road, where George had a select herd of shorthorn cattle, and bred fine horses.

George LaFollette Family

This picture of their five remaining (of eight) children was taken 1890, probably. The ones missing are: Robert, b. and d. 1855, Nancy Alice (1857-1876), Carrie b. 1859, m. Crayton Kimler. Died in childbirth, baby also 1880.

From the left: Francis Marion, (Frank), (1848-1917) holding Harold and Cornelia (Neeley) Shannon LaFollette, m. 1878. See history elsewhere.

Joseph (Joe) LaFollette (1851-1929) holding Lee and Alice Buchanon LaFollette, m. 1875. See history elsewhere.

On porch George LaFollette.

Mary Ellen (El), maker of beautiful, meticulously crafted cotton quilts. Never married.

Sussanah, beloved mother and grandmother. Known for her gracious hospitality.

Thomas Wallace (Wal) (1861-1914) farmer and Mary Elizabeth (Minnie) Elmore LaFollette, teacher, m. 1884. Twins: Edith Maye and Edna Maude b. 1885. Mary Hazel, (1887) Twins: Boy, stillborn. Susan (1892-1896). Their farm was north of Shannondale, County Line Road.

James Oliver (Ol) (1865-1935) and Effie Burroughs LaFollette. Ol farmed George's farm. No children. (Active Dorothy Q Chapter D.A.R.).

The grandchildren are on the steps. From left: Bess (Joe's) Rushton, Earle, and Carrie (Frank's), Edna, Edith and Hazel (Wal's).

Wal and Minnie's children:
1. Edith married Clifford Quigg (1912). One daughter (1916) Mildred Maye m. (1939) Richard Weliever. Their children: a. Charles (1941) m. (1963) Roberta (1940) teacher, had: Lauren (1963), Kristine (1967), Brett (1971). b. Robert (1943) farmer, m. (1970) Cathy, had: Denise (1971), Jeremy (1973), Dana (1976). c. Betty Jane (1946) teacher, m. (1965) Sam Moffitt, had: Shane (1971), Travis (1977). d. Mary Lou VMD, (1948) m. Greg Olin, had Tacy (1982), Gabe (1981). e. Donna (1953). f. Nancy (1958) m. Mike Jones had: Kayla (1985). g. Susie (1963) m. 1985, Christopher (Chris) Birdsong.
2. Edna (unmarried). We used her notes on LaFollette Histories.
3. Mary Hazel and Roy Peebles History elsewhere.

George was the youngest of eight sons, tenth of the 12 children of Usual and Nancy Lee LaFollette, grandson of Joseph (1745-1834) and Phoebe Goble LaFollette, b. France, came New Jersey area, America, before the Revolution. Joseph's brothers: Isaac, George and William, came with LaFayette, fought together, all mustered out at Norfolk, VA 1783. Descendants of all are eligible for DAR. Joseph is buried in LaFollette Cemetery, one mile S.W. of Parkersburg. Also, Usual. George: Shannondale.

JOSEPH LaFOLLETTE

Joe (1851-1929) m. 1875 Alice Buchanon, farmed near his father, George LaFollette, 15 years, then opened Hardware Store in Darlington. Their children were:

I. William C. b. 1876, d. 1877.

II. Bess, (1885-1969) m. William Holloway, farmer, merchant, Crawfordsville. Daughter: Alice (1918), m. 1938.

Joe LaFollette

A. Alice (1918) m. (1938) Grant Rhode (1917). Children were: 1. Patricia (1940) m. Donald Stonecipher. Children: a. David (1963), b. Joanne (1965), c. Vicki (1968). 2. Phillip (1941) m. Penny Boyd, 1973.

III. Lee (1888-19__) m. Violet Bundy, had two sons: A. Robert (19__-19__) m. Floss, one daughter: 1. Joan Marie (19__). B. Adrian (19__-19__) m. Betty, sons: 1. William. 2. James.

IV. Lou (1892-1967) m. Merritt Peebles, farmer. One daughter: A. Mary Elizabeth (1917) m. Bernard Hole, see history of Robert W. Peebles Family.

Others: Alice and Joe also raised Cliff Arnold as their own. *Submitted by Mary E. Hole*

JANET SNYDER LAMBERT

Janet Maude Snyder was born in Crawfordsville, IN, on Dec. 17, 1894, the daughter of Francis L. and Mabel Lee Galey Snyder. She graduated from Crawfordsville High School in 1912. As a career, she chose acting first and writing second. She enrolled at Ferry Hall, a junior college in Lake Forest, IL, because it was near Chicago where she could attend plays. She later took lessons with a dramatics teacher and was tutored in French and German. When Walker Whiteside was on tour in Indianapolis in "The Typhoon" he talked with Janet and invited her to join the company. The following fall she had a small part in a New York play. After it closed she joined a stock company in Northhampton, MA, and lived with friends of her family. Here she met Kent Craig Lambert, former Crawfordsville resident and a captain in the army. They were married on Jan. 1, 1918, and three months later Kent left for military duty in France. After the birth of a daughter, Mrs. Lambert quit her acting career.

Janet had an early interest in reading. While growing up in Crawfordsville, she had many contacts with some of the well-known authors of the period. Mary Hannah Krout listened to her youthful poetry and served her tea "in a quaint, pleasant way". Janet said that she sat under the beach tree where Lew Wallace wrote part of *Ben Hur* and watched him paint. She said that Wallace was "quite a talkative old gentleman" but that she had to be very quiet. She was acquainted with Booth Tarkington and George Ade.

All of these contacts gave Mrs. Lambert an interest in literature. About the period before she began to be serious about writing, she remarked: "Because I had decided to write, I constantly tried, but army wife and author rarely go together. It took 19 years, to the point where we were stationed in New York—on Governors Island—before I found myself as a writer." The real foundation of her writing came during the period after World War I when the family spent 20 years around the world in army posts. During this period she told her daughter bedtime stories and provided her with special reading materials that were not available at the posts. She began writing short stories about teenagers that have been lost.

In 1938 Kent Lambert was transferred to Governors Island, NY. While living there, Mrs. Lambert decided to write stories for teenagers. Between 1941 and 1969 she wrote 54 books on a variety of subjects largely of interest to girls. She also wrote articles, poetry, and short stories.

In 1951 Kent Lambert retired from the army and the family moved to their summer home at Long Beach Island, NJ. It was there that Mrs. Lambert died on Mar. 16, 1973. *Submitted by Don Thompson*

THOMAS W. AND DELILAH LAMSON

Thomas W. Lamson was born near Mace, IN, on Sept. 29, 1836, the son of Thomas, Sr. and Anna. Thomas, Sr. (by occupation) was a trader and hailed from New Jersey. Thomas, Jr. married Delilah Burke, born Aug. 25, 1841 (daughter of John) near Rensselaer on Sept. 17, 1855. He died Aug. 31, 1911 and she died Nov. 22, 1915. They are buried in Old Union Cemetery, near Waveland. Tom was in the Civil War, enlisting in 1864 — Co. G., 133 Indiana Infantry. In his obituary, it said he was placed in charge of the first rural route of Waveland "when the roads were not so good and the pay not so high." In the excellent history of Waveland by Virginia Banta Sharpe, it states: "The first mail route was 26 miles long and Thomas Lamson was the first rural mail carrier with his brother as substitute. Mr. Lamson had a new wagon built especially to carry his mail. It came from Delphi, was painted green, enclosed and had glass sides. Its distinctive appearance caused farmers, who eagerly awaited the mail, to recognize it from a distance."

The Lamsons enjoyed 56 years of marriage. Eleven children were born to them:

John E. born Oct. 3, 1857 in Jasper Co., IN, died Sept. 2, 1934; married Sarah Butcher Apr. 9, 1884. He was a farmer. One daughter: Gladys Duncan.

Oleander "Ose" was born Feb. 19, 1859 and died a bachelor. He, too, was a farmer.

Julius, born July 1863, died 1924, married Minnie Carver. Farmer. Children: Ruth, Mary (married Melvin Davidson) and Nell (married Ewing Mason).

Rosa and **Dora** died young.

Martha J. born Mar. 25, 1866, died Feb. 24, 1937, married Hancil Miller. Children: Elsie, never married, Hilda, never married, Calvin, Thomas (went to New Jersey and was a horse trainer) and John.

Charles T. was born Aug. 17, 1869, died Feb. 9, 1946. He ran a threshing ring and was a logger. He married Jennie Hamilton, and had one son, Thomas and a baby girl who died in infancy. Thomas married Esther Myers.

Catherine married Charles Simpson—see their history in this book.

Rollo was born Oct. 28, 1876 and died 1950, a bachelor. He, too, was a farmer.

Harry, born Apr. 5, 1879 died Feb. 8, 1938. He married Susan Seits. Harry followed his brothers— a farmer. Their children: Earl E., died while in the Navy; Glenn, George (McDaniel Freight), Walter (career of service and lived in California) and Vera (Lansing, MI).

Clifford, "Lloyd", born 1881 and died May 25, 1949, a bachelor.

The Lamsons owned a deep belief in God, conducted their lives with honesty and integrity and loved their family and home. *Submitted by Doris Simpson Jeffries Bazzani*

DANIEL AND NANCY McCOLLUM LANDON

Daniel Landon was a colorful citizen that seemed to become a problem to those he lived around in Miami and Montgomery Counties in Ohio in the first 18 years of the 1800's. He is likely the son of William Landon and Experience Cook who lived in Northumberland and Lycoming Counties in Pennsylvania. In the 1930's one of William Landon's descendants spent much time gathering oral testimony from older Landons about the family of William Landon and Experience Cook. She found that they had five sons and three daughters, but the family could only remember the names of three of these children: Elisha Landon who was born in 1772 and married Sarah Herkless and resided in Butler Co., OH; Samuel Landon born in 1786 and married Margaret Sholts and lived in Tioga Co., PA and Daniel Landon, birthdate unknown. Daniel was killed by Indians in 1818 and left a wife and four small children. As the reader will see this description of Daniel Landon matches very closely to the Daniel Landon who caused so much mischief in Miami and Montgomery Counties in Ohio.

Daniel Landon first buys land in Miami Co., OH in 1805, but from 1806-1810 Daniel was postal agent at Fort Wayne, IN and a provisioner to the army. Letters preserved in the Cincinnati Historical Society from him in these years tell of difficulties that he had in supplying the army with food and his contacts with Ohio swindlers.

Daniel Landon marries Nancy McCollum in 1809. Apparently she is the daughter of Hugh McCollum who died in Montgomery, OH in 1817.

From the time of his marriage until the time of his mysterious disappearance or death in 1818 his career seems to have been to get in as much trouble as possible with the courts. There seems to be at least ten court cases in Montgomery and Miami County in which complaints are made against him for such things as damage to property, selling liquor without a license, trespassing, and gaming. In 1818 he disappears and the courts declare him legally dead. His neighbors believed him to be dead. His wife remarried within a year to the man who helped settle his estate, Hugh Scott, in Miami County. In the settlement of the estate it is mentioned that he had at least two heirs, Robert Landon who married a girl named Celina and resided in St. Joseph, IN, and John Landon who married Hanna Bouer and resided in Johnson Co., IA.

JOHN LANDON

John Landon was born in 1794 in Pennsylvania. In the early 1800's the Landons along with several other families with close ties, such as Sheets, Deardorffs, Simmermans, Leslies, and Wilsons appear to have traveled from Pennsylvania to the Montgomery, Preble, Butler, Warren and Hamilton County areas.

In 1813, John Landon enlisted in the War of 1812 at Cincinnati, OH. After the war, and until 1829 he and many of his family lived and farmed in and near Jackson township of Montgomery County.

No one knows who John Landon's parents were. One family tradition is that his mother's name was Rebecca Deardorff and that she was disowned by the family because of her service to the Indians in Carey Mission, MI. Another tradition is that his father was Daniel Landon. From some circumstantial evidence, recent researchers suggest that he might be the son of William Landon of Lycoming Co., PA through his young last wife, Catherine. This would make him the half brother of the Butler County pioneer and long time resident, Elisha Landon.

It is believed that John Landon had younger siblings who also had close ties with Montgomery and surrounding counties: Benjamin who married Mary Deardorff, David who married Ruth Mack, William, Mary who married Samuel Leslie, Affa who married Peter Deardorff, and Rebecca who married Harrison Wilson.

No marriage record has been found for John Landon. Tradition has it that he was married to Elizabeth Porter. However, an 1829 court document in Montgomery County states that he "was" married to one of the daughters of Daniel Sheets and Catherine Hulvah who had moved to the county from Rockingham Co., VA. An 1829 land record does state that John's wife was named Elizabeth. Whether her name was Elisabeth Sheets or whether Miss Sheets had died and he had remarried remains a mystery. What is certain is that Miss Sheets was the mother of at least the first three of John Landon's children. Daniel and Catherine Sheets' children were: Susanah who married Eben Hoopes, Elizabeth, Barbara, Solomon, Hannah, Nancy and Polly.

John Landon's first eight children were apparently born in Montgomery County between 1815-1829. They were Catherine who married Frederick Simmerman, Margaret who married Terrel Hackney, Daniel who married Mary Howell, Solomon who married Elizabeth Parent, Rachel who married Robert Beason, Effie who married Peter Deardorff, David who married Mary Hoffman, and Jonathan who married Isabella Bishop.

Around 1830 John Landon moved to Warren Co., IN with many of his brothers and sisters. Five more children were born to him: Jacob who married Mary Good, Peter who married Elizabeth Lawson, Laban who married Mary Thomson, Sarah who married Thomas Bunce, and John.

John Landon and his family were not unfamiliar with death and its sting nor the rigors of frontier life. It is said their oldest son, Daniel died of questionable circumstances on his way home from the War with Mexico in 1848. Two of their sons died in the Civil War within ten days of each other. John Landon's wife, Elisabeth died after 1850. He remarried to Martha Musgrove. John Landon died between 1860-1870 in Warren Co., IN leaving behind many descendants. Many of these descendants are very interest in learning more about their Landon heritage.

JOANNA ELSTON LANE

Joanna Elston Lane, the daughter of Major Isaac C. and Maria Akin Elston, was born on Sept. 28, 1826, the second of nine children. She went to boarding school at Science Hill in Shelbyville, KY, finishing there in 1844. Joanna married a widower, Henry Smith Lane, when she was 19. Mr. Lane had already bought a six-acre lot with a three-room cottage on it, not far from the Elston mansion. Mrs. Lane supervised the building of six more rooms and the buying of fine furnishings. More additions and changes were made over the years until it became the mansion that it is today.

Mrs. Lane's first public act was to make a speech and to present a flag to a company of Montgomery County volunteers going to the War with Mexico on June 10, 1846. In 1860, Mr. Lane ran for the governorship of Indiana. He was elected, served two days in January, 1861, and then resigned to take a seat in the United States Senate, serving one term from 1861 to 1867. Mrs. Lane took a deep interest in all the important matters to which her husband's life was devoted. She accompanied him to Washington, D.C. She distinguished herself as one of the most gracious and charming hostesses in Washington. According to Admiral George Brown, who was on duty at the Washington Naval Yard, "Mrs. Lane was the only woman in Washington who held what really was a salon. She gathered about her men of every rank, in politics, from the Army and the Navy, the diplomatic corps, and their wives. She was not only a brilliantly intellectual woman, but one whose character and kindliness made friends of all who once met her." She possessed more important information about inside Washington life of the Civil War years and more fascinating gossip than anyone else. She also gave much of her time to the sick, wounded and dying in Washington hospitals.

Upon their return to Crawfordsville in 1867, the Lanes' home was a center of hospitality. After Senator Lane's death in 1881, Lane Place continued to be a meeting place for those who were active and prominent in the life of the state of Indiana. In 1882 Mrs. Lane joined her sister Susan and her husband, Lew Wallace, minister to Turkey for a visit. She accompanied them on a trip to the Holy Land and Egypt. Mrs. Lane continued her interest in politics, attending every Republican Party Convention from 1856 through 1912, two years before her death.

She was very active in community affairs. In November 1896, she edited a special woman's edition of the *Crawfordsville Journal*. She helped in the founding of Culver Union Hospital and gave money to many educational and charitable institutions. She was active in the Methodist Church in Crawfordsville, founded and was the first president of the Woman's Missionary Society of that church in 1871.

Mrs. Lane also did watercolor painting.

According to Rollo Brown, a professor at Wabash College in the early 1900s, Mrs. Lane burned a lot of her old letters, because some of them told of things she did not want to spread further. Inadvertently, she also burned some letters from Abraham Lincoln that she had promised to give Brown.

She died Apr. 6, 1914. On April 9th at a Republican Party Convention at Frankfort, IN, State Chairman Will Hays paid tribute to Mrs. Lane for her role in the Republican Party. *Submitted by Jean Thompson*

GARRET AND BERTHA LAREW

Rev. Charles Postill presided at an Elmdale wedding uniting Garret A. Larew and Bertha Leota Goff on Dec. 24, 1902. G. Abraham, known as Abe, was born Aug. 2, 1881 to Amanda Denny Larew and Garret Larew. His father is subject of a book titled *Civil War Soldier* authored by Karl G. Larew, 1975 Gateway Press, genealogy plus war diary. He had a sister Leora Larew Pierce and half-sister Martha Alice; three half-brothers William, Arthur, and John Henry.

Bertha was born Sept. 18, 1882 to Mary Shelly Goff and Edward Goff. Her brothers were Stillman and Charles, a sister Ida Goff Hayes, a half-brother Ray and half-sister Cora Goff Tingley. She received Common School diploma in Wayne Township and attended another year of classes.

Abe graduated Oakland School and Elmdale High School, Coal Creek Township. Graduated Valparaiso Normal College and began teaching in 1901 at Walnut Grove School (between Linden and New Richmond) later at Oklahoma School just north of Elmdale. They also farmed.

Larew Family 1940

December 1908 found the family moving to Lamar, MO. Teaching school and farming 1909-1911. Returning to Indiana the Missouri farm was traded for 80 acres near Yountsville. This traded for a livery stable and home in Wingate. Abe returned to Missouri harvest season 1912 to operate a threshing ring. He also did threshing in Montgomery County.

Selling the livery stable in 1913 moved to the Hutchison farm. The family lived on many farms before purchasing the Barnett farm in the Christian Union community.

Children were Walter Byron, Lena Larew Sentman, Merle Goff, Mary Larew Diegel, Garret Edward, Charles Stillman, Mildred Larew Horrocks Mellott, Ruth Larew Myers Terry, Robert Ray, Billie Jean and Betty Larew Ping.

Abe drove a horse drawn "hack" to Wingate two years and a Maxwell truck "hack" to Waynetown many years. He contracted school bus route 1935-1955 for Waynetown. The family was active in the Elmdale church and since 1927 the Christian Union church. Abe received his 50 year Masonic award in 1967. Bertha belonged to Waynetown Eastern Star and Wesley Home Demonstration Club.

Older children enjoyed going to grandpa Larew's Boston Store (Elmdale). Abe planted trees but could never cut a live tree. Large gardens were grown, necessary early, but he enjoyed giving produce to others. Their home was open to all—meals and overnight visits. Neighborhood andy-over, baseball, beckon, red-light:greenlight, and yes the shocking machine with cars bumper to bumper.

Some serving in World War II were Walter (career army, also in Korea-retired a Brigadier General), Merle (Navy Seabees), Charles (Navy), Robert (Navy), Billie (Army).

After Bertha's death November 1951, Abe married Pearl Wisehart Reed October 1954. Surviving her death May 1970 to maintain his own home until called to his reward Aug. 11, 1973. Survivors listed ten of the 11 children (Walter died April 1973), 38 grandchildren, and 54 great-grandchildren. Abe's honest understanding life touched thousands. *By Phyllis Larew*

ROBERT AND PHYLLIS LAREW FAMILY

A wedding at Linden Methodist Church Sept. 21, 1946 united Robert Ray Larew and Phyllis Alleen Deckard, Rev. Guy Tremaine officiating. Bob (Dec. 19, 1921) was the son of Garrett Abraham and Bertha Goff Larew. He graduated from Waynetown High School and served U.S. Navy four years in WWII. He was an aviation machinist mate 2nd class and instructed many in the maintenance of fighter and torpedo bomber aircraft.

Phyllis (Apr. 24, 1926) was the daughter of Charley and Bessie Camp Deckard, born in White County, moving to rural Linden March 1931. She graduated from Linden High School and attended both professional and Licensed Practical Nursing schools.

James, Robert R., Richard, Carolyn and Phyllis Larew

Bob owned and operated a Farm Bureau oil truck serving farms and towns in northwest Montgomery County. Full time farming kept them busy 1953-1963 changing to part time farming and Raybestos Manufacturing at Crawfordsville, then became clerk at Waynetown Post Office to complete his working career. Phyllis found pleasure in serving others five years at Waynetown School cafeteria and as LPN at Culver Union Hospital for 18 years before retiring.

Public school for their children was Wallace in Fountain County 1953-1959 moving to and graduating from Waynetown. Daughter Carolyn married Jerry Williams, policeman at Anderson, IN. She graduated Marion County School of Nursing and worked at St. Johns Hospital in Anderson 20 years before moving to Ohio after their divorce. Children were Tammy and Daniel Clayton Williams. Older son James Garrett graduated Indiana University and after Air Force service moved to Atlanta, GA with Bell Telephone. He married Sharon Keesee of Crawfordsville. Their children are Michelle, Jana, and Theodore Garrett. Son Richard Ray graduated from Purdue University, teaching agriculture and science for a short time then into agricultural business. He married Susan Guthrie of Crawfordsville and knew the heartache of deaths of an infant son and daughter and raised a son Jon Jacob. After ten years they divorced.

Following Abe Larew's death in 1973 Bob and Phyllis purchased the farm in Wayne township where the family had lived since February 1927. Both enjoy yard and garden and have continued to grow old fashioned white peaches and red popcorn of previous generations. Many school children have memories of eating popcorn on the Abe Larew schoolbus each Friday.

Both are active in rural Christian Union Church. He is past master of Masonic Lodge #302 and trustee of Waynetown Masonic Cemetery for many years. Phyllis is past matron of Order of Eastern Star #435 and member of Indiana Practical Nurses Association.

LARRICK FAMILY

The original entry record of Montgomery County lists John Tillard as owner of 80 acres in 1830. He was the father of Elizabeth Tillard Holmes Larrick (1822-1888).

Love letters written between Elizabeth and William H. Holmes of Shelby Co., KY are most tender and filled with poetry, but also with the dread that their great love would be short lived. Holmes wrote: "I wonder sometimes if we shall ever enjoy this happiness, what if some unforseen depensation of Providence shall forever blast our hopes?" These words were written to his "Miss Elizabeth" in February of 1837. His fear became a reality when on July 24, 1839, the 22-year old Mr. Holmes did indeed depart this life.

Larrick Brothers picture taken February 1922. Left to right: James Newton, John Walker, Penson Hollingsworth

Isaac Newton Larrick (1819-1877) born in Ross Co., OH of Scotch-Irish extraction, the eldest of five sons: Robert, James, Jacob, and one unnamed. I.N. and Elizabeth Tillard were married Sept. 15, 1842 and began housekeeping near Garfield, then soon moved north of Darlington along Sugar Creek. Her journal of the 1880's tells of the weather, and of the visitors and events of routine farm life of the times. One highlight she always noted was the shipping of hogs to the Indianapolis market, by rail, which they did several times annually.

It was in Franklin Township that I.N. and Elizabeth had seven children: only three of whom survived the "perils of youth". Emma nine and Mary J. seven both died in 1857. Those who carried on were: **John A.** who married Louisa Johnson and had three children: Omer (1886-1962) who married Tessie Davis and had Anita, and a son who died at two years old from burns from a stove. I.N. (1874-1939) never married and William (1873-1912) married Sarah Lawton having Jessie and Marie.

Isaac Newton (1851-1916) was a Darlington

Grocer and Township Trustee. He married Elizabeth Brown and they had two daughters, Maye and Lois.

Robert Henry (1849-1924) a farmer who in 1889 married Rosa Pinson Hollingsworth (1849-1924), the daughter of Pinson and Julian Jane Walker Hollingsworth (1829-1869) of Franklin Township. Robert and Rosa had three sons: John Walker (1891-1968), a farmer never married. James Newton (1893-1950), a farmer and woodsman also never married. Jim and John farmed the home place, raised fine bird dogs and bred and trained harness racing horses. They had a half-mile track laid out in the north corn field. They had some excellent stock—Mary Castle, Ada Rota and from the blood lines of Rip Hanover—Lint and Take. During the first half of this century nearly every County Fair had a race meet. There is very little as exciting as going to the races and hearing the slap of leather harness, the whir of sulky wheels, the pounding of hooves and the snorting of horses giving their all as they make the final turn on a half-mile track coming home on the last stretch. When your horse is leading that thundering pack, the thrill is nearly overwhelming.

Penson Hollingsworth (spelling changed for unknown reason) Larrick was a banker in Montgomery County for many years, first at Ladoga and then as a cashier of Farmers Merchants State Bank at Darlington. He married Mary Fletcher (1908-1961) in 1932. They had two children: Robert Carl (1936) who married Madona McMurry having three sons: John Michael, 1957; Bradley Jay, 1959 and Robert Gregory 1961. Bob is now married to Margaret Bryant from Charles Co., MD; they live in McAllen, TX. Rebecca Louise (1939) married Melvin K. Royer of Linden, having Elizabeth 1959, married Tim Dion and living in Rhode Island; Diana L. 1964 married Terry Howell, having Travis Jared 1982 and Seth Adam 1988. The Howells live on part of the "Larrick Home Place" in Franklin Township. Mary Katherine 1967 married Geoff Anderson from Lafayette, where they reside.

GEORGE M. LAWTON

George M. Lawton was born in Yorkshire, England in 1831 and lived in the woolen mill towns of the West Riding and Manchester, England. He came to America in February 1854 aboard the S.S. Cornelius Grinnell sailing from the port of Liverpool to the port of New York. He married Amelia Warthurst, date and place unknown, and he worked in the woolen mills in Philadelphia, PA. He served with Outfit I of the 45th Pennsylvania Infantry during the Civil War. Family tradition maintains that after he returned from war, he met Daniel Yount who was on a wool buying trip in Pennsylvania. He was offered employment at Yount's Mill in Montgomery Co., IN and George moved with his wife and two small sons to Yountsville in 1866. He worked at Yount's Mill until 1900. He died in December of 1922. He had three sons and one daughter.

William, the oldest son, was born Oct. 31, 1863 in Philadelphia, married Mary E. "Molly" Martz Mar. 25, 1886 at Yountsville and had three sons: Harry born 1887 dying shortly after birth; John E. born June 29, 1889, lived in Crawfordsville all his life, dying May 1960; Gerald E., born May 1893, lived most of his life in Lafayette, dying September 1960. William Lawton died at age 42, Apr. 27, 1905 at Yountsville. He had worked for Younts Mill all of his life except for a short period spent in St. Joseph, MO.

George M. Lawton ca 1890 Family. Enoch, William, John, George m. Sarah (Lawton), Larrick, Amelia (Warthurst) Lawton

Enoch Lawton was born Sept. 21, 1864 in Pennsylvania and came to Yountsville with his parents early in life remaining there except for a brief time in California and Lafayette. He was associated with the Yount's Mill and Snyder grist mill at Yountsville. He married Elizabeth Shanklin Sept. 7, 1886, and had six children, three of whom died in infancy. The surviving children were Mrs. Albert (Grace) Taylor, Mrs. Guy (Ethel) Moore, and Roy Clinton Lawton. Enoch died in an Indianapolis hospital on Mar. 17, 1950.

John Edward Lawton was born at Yountsville on Mar. 16, 1867. He lived most of his life in Yountsville and was a teamster for Yount's Mill. He transported the woolen goods by horse and wagon from the mill to the railroad station in Crawfordsville. He married Jennie Gray on Sept. 14, 1888, and had four children: Mrs. Alonzo (Cecile) Osborn, Mrs. Carl (Minnie) Fugate, Mrs. Roy (Ida) Coombs and George H. Lawton. His wife died in 1899 leaving him with small children who were raised by the Florey and Palin families of Newtown, IN.

He married Lillie G. Gray, a cousin of his first wife, on Nov. 21, 1900 and had two sons: Victor who died at birth and Merle E. Lillie Gray died in 1905 again leaving him with a small son to raise alone. Mr. Lawton died June 5, 1943 at Crawfordsville.

Sarah Lawton was born in 1874 in Yountsville. She married William H. Larrick on June 3, 1896 and had two daughters, Marie in April 1897, and Jesse in October 1899. Except for a few years at Lafayette, she lived all her life in the Crawfordsville area and died there in 1963.

DR. FLORENCE W. LAYNE

Dr. Florence W. Layne, a native of Oil City, PA, the daughter of John W. and Mary E. Webb, was born Dec. 12, 1890. She graduated from Smith College and entered Kirksville College of Osteopathic Medicine in 1919, graduating in May, 1923. In 1920 she married a classmate, Dr. Lloyd Layne of Crawfordsville. She practiced in Crawfordsville with her husband from 1923 until 1947, when she retired. She was a member of St. Bernard's Catholic Church and the American Association of University Women. She had two sons, Dan W. and Donald L., a daughter, Dorothy L. Amastadt, and three grandchildren. She died in February, 1971 at Edinburg, TX and is buried in the Waynetown Masonic Cemetery. *Submitted by Jean Thompson*

JIM AND GLORIA LAYNE

In the Summer of 1938, Gloria Nicholson was walking in the alley behind Producer's Ice Cream on the way home from the Crawfordsville Library. Jim Layne was driving down the same alley and liked what he saw! Gloria fell in love with his blue eyes and he adored her long, dark-brown hair.

James Harold Layne was born in Crawfordsville on May 17, 1919. He weighed 2# at birth, fit into a shoe box and had snow-white hair. Each morning, during childhood, his mother woke him up by calling, "Getty Up, Now, Haddy Wayne Bug." The nickname "Haddy" is sometimes still used today. Jim is the son of James William and Minnie Myrtle (Owens) Layne. James William was a painter, decorator and barber in Crawfordsville. Jim had a brother, Forrest D., deceased and has a sister, Helen Elizabeth Dickerson (Crawfordsville). Jim attended Crawfordsville schools and worked at Sabens' Brothers Service Station for 15 years, then retired from Allison's in 1984. Jim joined the United States Air Force in June 1942 and was discharged Thanksgiving Day, 1945 at Tucson, AZ. He was in the Bombadier and Pilot Training command in Albuquerque, NM.

Arlene Layne Bazzani; Annie Layne France

Jim and Gloria were married in Crawfordsville at the residence of Reverend E.A. Arthur on Aug. 9, 1941. Gloria is the daughter of Donald Winton and Carol Zeta (Krause) Nicholson. Don was employed at Allison's. Gloria also attended Crawfordsville city schools. Gloria's brother, Randolph is deceased and she has one sister, Marilyn Joan Brown (San Diego, CA). Gloria has worked at Hoosier Crown, Allison's, Culver Hospital and Credit Manager at Spiegel.

While Jim was stationed in New Mexico, Carol Ann (Annie) was born Apr. 8, 1945. Annie married Arthur "Ray" France (born Mar. 25, 1944, son of Carlos "Pete" and Nellie (Anderson) France) on Jan. 8, 1966 in Waveland, IN. Ray is a Supervisor at Allison's. He collects Indian arrowheads. Ray and Annie have: Rayan born Mar. 9, 1968, who married Kevin Knott on Dec. 31, 1988 and Layne Matthew born Nov. 28, 1971. He is a Junior at Southmont.

Jim and Gloria's other daughter, Arlene (who has no middle name since they couldn't think of one) was born Sept. 22, 1948 in Crawfordsville. Both she and Annie are Waveland graduates, as well as their husbands. Arlene married Garry Bazzani May 27, 1967 in Waveland. See Bazzani history. Arlene worked at J.C. Penney's and Montgomery Wards. They are the parents of Amy Suzanne and Heather Lynn. The Bazzani's embarked upon a new adventure this year—they are part-owners of the Mountie Market on the East side of New Market.

After his service, Jim and Gloria lived in

Crawfordsville until 1957 when they moved to Waveland. Jim said, "We'll be back in the city within two weeks," but 32 years later, they're still there!

WM. MINTER LAYNE

Between 1830 and 1834 six related families, originally from Goochland Co., VA, but living for about 15 years in Kentucky, moved to Montgomery County. First to arrive in April 1830 was William Minter Layne (1805-1888), his wife Eunice Van Cleave and daughter, Eunice. William cleared land, built a log home, and then built another one ready for the November 1830 arrival of his cousin, Elisha Layne (1777-1860), whose wife Elizabeth Layne Layne (1788-1861), was William's sister. With them were their nine younger children: Eliza, Tarlton, Elisha, Elizabeth, Washington, Miles, William, Preston and Lutitia. The families already in Indiana prepared log homes for the arrival of the others from Kentucky. Arriving in 1832 were Elisha's oldest daughter, Matilda Layne (1808-1847), her husband Thomas Doyel and children, Nancy, James and Thomas. Arriving in 1833 were William and Elizabeth's sister Roxanna Layne (1798-1880), widow of James Dowden, her new husband Jacob Hall, and her Dowden children: Nathaniel, William and Martha. Also in 1833 came another sister Mariah Layne (1810-1906), her husband Jacob Peck and son Romulus. In 1834 there came still another sister, Tabitha Layne (1804-1880), her husband Wilson Gott and children Ferdinand and Mary Jane. Also in 1834 came these people's mother, Tabitha Minter Layne (1768-1845). Widowed in 1819, she was widowed twice more by 1834, and married again in Indiana in 1835 to John Wilson. Also in 1832 came to Putnam County Elisha's deceased brother Sherod Layne's widow Sarah Estes Layne. She joined five of her children living there since 1831: William Layne, Samuel Layne, Sally Hammack, Anna Brown and John Layne with their families.

Dr. Preston Layne and children Will, Minter, Frank and Elizabeth (Mitchell) Layne

Elisha Layne was son of Jacob Layne (1727-1801) and Mary Bradshaw. Siblings were Lucy Martin, Judith Howard, Samuel, John, Molly Busby, Frances, Sherod, Jacob and Ferris. Elizabeth Layne was daughter of Tarlton Layne (1764-1819) and Tabitha Minter. Tarlton Layne was son of Ayres Layne (1724-1795) and Mary Woodson (1740-1829) who was descended through Robert Woodson (1698-1750), Benjamin Woodson (1666-1723), and Col. Robert Woodson (1634-1707) from Dr. John Woodson (1586-1644), who arrived in Virginia in 1619 as surgeon on the ship "George" with Governor Yeardley on board.

Ayres and Jacob Layne were brothers, sons of John Layne (1685-1755) and wife Elizabeth. Other siblings were Charles (who died in 1821, aged 111 years), John, Henry, David, William and Elizabeth Parrish. John Layne, besides farming, taught school and in 1751 wrote an arithmetic manuscript on parchment paper, bound with deerhide which is preserved in the family today. From 1752 to 1847 this book was used to record children's births.

Of Elisha Layne's children: Eliza Galey (1810-1889) left about 1866 for Iowa; Tarlton (1812-1899) left 1849 for Iowa; Elisha (1814-1849) left in 1838 for Tippecanoe County; Elizabeth Long (1816-1875) left 1862 for Iowa; Washington (1819-1879) left about 1850 for Iowa; Miles (1822-1887) left in 1885 for Illinois, but had many descendants in Montgomery County; William (1825-1893) lived in Montgomery County; Preston (1827-1918) was a doctor in Crawfordsville; and Lutitia (1830-1859) died unmarried.

THE LEAK FAMILY

On Dec. 21, 1784, Robert Leak and Susannah Leak were married in Orange Co., VA. Robert had immigrated from England to this country with his father, Dr. Samuel Leake, and brother, William, in 1770. They lived at first in the Valley of Virginia, then settled in Orange and Albemarle Counties. During the Revolution, Samuel and William served in the Virginia Militia. Robert and Susannah were distant cousins, the family connection dating back about four generations in England. Susannah's ancestors, William Leake and Mary Bostick, came to Virginia from England in 1685.

After their marriage, Robert and Susannah lived for some years in Culpeper Co., VA, where their first four children were born: James, Frances "Fanny", Elisha, and Hiram. In 1795, they migrated to Bracken Co., KY, and dropped the final "e" from their name so as to avoid pronunciation as "Leakey". There, Larkin, William, Ann "Nancy", and Lewis were born.

In 1817, Hiram married Mary "Polly" Brockman, daughter of Andrew and Amelia Brockman of Boone Co., KY. On Christmas Day 1820, Elisha married Polly's sister Elizabeth "Betsy". When the Brockman family moved to Union Township, Montgomery Co., IN, in 1825, Elisha and Hiram Leak went with them. Also in the clan was Elisha and Hiram's cousin, Kitty Leake, who was married to Tandy Brockman.

In 1828, Larkin Leak joined his brothers in Union Township. Their mother, Susannah, had died in Kentucky that year and after Robert passed away in 1833, James, Fanny, and William also moved to Indiana, settling in Hendricks County. Only Nancy remained in Kentucky.

Fanny Leak married James Brockman, a widower, in 1835. James had joined the rest of his family in Indiana after the death of his first wife, Sallie Leake (Kitty's sister). When James died, Fanny moved in with the family of her brother Larkin.

Larkin and his wife, Catherine Harris, had two daughters, Martha Ann (Mrs. William McCormich) and Mary. He died in 1876.

Elisha and Betsy Leak lived next door to Betsy's parents. Their children were Robert, Lucy (Mrs. Alexander Hipes), Eliza Ann (Mrs. A.W. Sampson), James, John Lewis (married Evaline Leach), Madeline (Mrs. John Green), Emaline (Mrs. Philip Burch), Andrew Jackson, Sarah (Mrs. George Robertson), and Elizabeth (Mrs. John Halderman). Elisha died in 1845. About eight years later, his family moved to Des Moines, IA.

Hiram and Polly also lived near the Brockmans. They had eight children: Susan (Mrs. Simeon Harrison), Louisa (Mrs. John Stroud), Permelia, Nancy (Mrs. Jerome Rogers), Robert, William (married Nancy Davidson), Mary (Mrs. Jesse Rogers), and Martha (Mrs. Jacob Reepe). Polly died in 1829 and Hiram remarried the following year to Henrietta Harris. Hiram and Henrietta's children were Lewis, Samuel (married 1. Catherine Compton and 2. Hattie Lawrence), Lucretia (Mrs. John Handley), and Charles (married 1. his cousin Virginia Leak, 2. Rebecca Baker and 3. Martha Jones). Hiram died in 1865 and Henrietta died in 1874. Both of them, as well as Polly, are buried at Shiloh Cemetery.

ROBERT A. LEHE FAMILY

Robert Amiel Lehe came to Montgomery County on farmers' moving day, Mar. 1, 1950 to farm the farm owned by Isaac Elston Jr., located in Sugar Creek Township. Robert, better known as Bob, was born Sept. 7, 1921 in White County to Amiel and Mary Hotler Lehe. They were of French ancestry, who had come to this country in 1889.

Bob graduated from Pine Township High School, White County in 1939. He farmed with his father until 1943 when he went to the army, serving in the Philippines theater of operations during World War II.

On Feb. 4, 1948, he married Mardelle Dicus of Swayzee, IN. She had graduated from Montgomery Blair High School in Silver Spring, MD, and Indiana University, class of 1946. Their first son, Robert Tad was born Jan. 30, 1949 in Lafayette, IN. During the three years they lived on the Elston Farm, a second son, James Thomas, was born Sept. 14, 1951.

In March of 1953 Robert had a farm sale and purchased the International Harvester Farm implement dealership in Darlington, IN from Martin and Bill Campbell. He renamed the business Lehe Equipment Sales and remained in business in Darlington for 16 years. He then became licensed as a stock broker, working for the next 16 years for Phil-Mar Investment Co. in Indianapolis, IN. He retired in 1982. An enthusiastic gardener, he was setting out plants in his garden, when he had a massive heart attack on Apr. 13, 1988 and was dead at the scene.

His wife, Mardelle, was a housewife for the first few years of their marriage. In 1961 she began working part time at the Darlington Public Library as the Assistant Librarian, and she remains in that position at the present time.

Both sons graduated from Darlington High School, both were Valedictorians of their respective classes of 1967 and 1969. They both then went on to Wheaton College, Wheaton, IL. Robert Tad studied Philosophy and graduated in 1971. He received a Masters Degree from Northern Illinois University and a Ph.D. from the University of Chicago in 1980. He teaches Philosophy at North Central College in Naperville, IL. On Dec. 15, 1970 he married Marcia Rhea Cravens from Chattanooga, TN whom he met at Wheaton College. She is a candidate for a Ph.D. from Loyola University in Chicago, IL. They are the parents of one son, Jonathan David Lehe, who was born May 1, 1982.

James Thomas Lehe studied Sociology at Wheaton College and worked as a Social Worker on the South side of Chicago for several years. On Mar. 19, 1977 he married Joyce Anita Magee of Dallas, TX. She is a graduate of the University of Texas, and has a Masters Degree in Environmental Sciences also from the University of Texas. They are the parents of two daughters; Katherine Michelle, born Oct. 25, 1980 and Jennifer Elizabeth, born Jan. 29, 1984. *Submitted by Mardelle Lehe*

JULES A. AND ANNIE JANE BLUE LePAGE

Jules A. LePage, 1849-1936, and Annie Jane Blue, 1860-1924, were parents of Jules Leon LePage, 1888-1957. Jules Anthony (naturalized citizen, 1884) came to America a millwright. He worked out of Chicago, and put a mill in many towns in the midwest.

Jules A. and Annie Jane (Blue) LePage

Darlington is one town to receive a new mill. Staying at the boarding house one night, he met a girl waiting on his table. The young girl caught the Frenchman's eye, and soon they were married.

Annie Jane was the daughter of John Wesley, 1832-1909, and Mary J. (Webster) Blue, 1830-1887. The Blues lived in Crawfordsville and Darlington. John Wesley was a cooper.

LEWELLEN FAMILY

According to the *History of Montgomery Co., IN* (published by A.W. Bowen, Indianapolis), the man who caught the largest bass that has been taken from Montgomery County waters was Thomas Lewellen. The bass measured 26 inches long and was 13 inches through the thickest part. This Thomas Lewellen is the grandson of Thomas and Mary Crane Lewellen, and the son of John and Minerva Coon Lewellen.

The first Thomas Lewellen was born on Jan. 11, 1787, in Virginia. After service in the War of 1812, he received two land grants from the federal government in Preble Co., OH. He was married to Mary Crane, Jan. 16, 1816, to which 13 children were born. There were six girls and seven boys. John was born on Jan. 14, 1818, the second child of this union.

John married Minerva Coon on Aug. 10, 1843, to which 12 children were born, seven sons and five daughters.

Thomas Lewellen married Frances Coon on Sept. 29, 1879. To ths union were born six daughters and four sons. One daughter, Goldie survives in 1989 in Crawfordsville. One of their twins, Herbert Gordon is our connection to the next generation although there are many other routes we could take. Herbert married Opal Cruea on July 14, 1921. They had two children: Herbert Galen and Margaret Jane.

Herbert Galen married Hazel Hamilton on Mar. 10, 1946 and there are three children: Herbert Gregory, July 19, 1947, Harold Michael Jan. 1, 1950 and Cynthia Jane, Feb. 5, 1953. There are ten grandchildren currently growing.

John Lewellen, born Preble Co., OH, near Eaton moved his father, Thomas to Ripley Township, Montgomery County in 1838. He located about 7-1/2 miles southwest of Crawfordsville. John and his wife are buried in the Weir Cemetery. At this time, it is not known where his parents are buried, perhaps Weir? Thomas Lewellen was reared on the home farm and assisted with the general work when a boy. He received a meager education, going through the spelling book, and halfway through the school reader when he took up farming. Later, he turned his attention to tile making which he followed for a period of 21 years. He built up an extensive business, there being a great demand for his products owing to their superior quality. He then sold out and purchased the electric light plant at Waynetown.

Thomas and his wife were native to Montgomery County. His wife was daughter of Allen and Louise Stonebraker Moore. Ten children were born to Thomas and Frances, namely: Stella married Fred Wilkinson, Walter married Edith Zachary, Zola married William Smith, Bessie married Frank Ellis, Archie married Katherine Padgett, Goldie married Ralph Maxwell, Edward Orton married Mary West, Herbert Gordon married Opal Cruea, Doris Lucille, unmarried, and Mabel Alice, married Herman Douglas (well-known barber in Monon Hotel in Crawfordsville). Thomas and Frances are buried in the Waynetown Masonic Cemetery.

The fraternal twin syndrome seems to be hereditary in the Lewellen line. Cynthia, daughter of Hazel and Herb Lewellen, Willard, OH has twin boys, Jeremy and Jeffrey. This makes the fourth set of fraternal twins in the family, with Duane Lewellen's sons (who is the son of Walter) in the six generations listed! *Submitted by Herb Lewellen*

WALLACE D. AND EDNA (SHARP) LEWELLYN

Wallace and Edna Lewellyn were married Sept. 25, 1926 at Roachdale, IN.

Wallace was born July 8, 1903 in Chicago to Joseph and Margaret (Morrison) Lewellyn. Other children were: Marie, Guy, and Joseph. The mother died in the WW I flu epidemic when Wallace was 12 yrs. old. The family moved to Logansport and later to Frankfort, IN where he was raised by his grandmother Morrison. At the age of 16 he was on his own, and with his two brothers, traveled and worked throughout the western part of the U.S. When he was a young man he worked for a railroad in Roachdale.

Edna was born July 18, 1907 in Montgomery County to Ross and May (Jeffries) Sharp. Most of her schooling was in Roachdale where the couple met and married.

Wallace D. and Edna Sharp Lewellyn

They lived in Indianapolis from 1926 to 1931. During this time he worked for a steel mill, U.S. Rubber, and Real Silk. They moved to Clark Township for about two years and then returned to Indianapolis where he worked for Zimmer Paper Products.

In 1940 they moved to Ladoga where they lived until 1956. He worked at Allison Div. Gen. Motors during WW II and later at R.R. Donnelly's. For the next seven years they lived in Ft. Myers, FL where he and two sons worked for a paint contractor. In 1963 the returned to Ladoga.

Six children were born to them: Joanne (b. 1927), Joseph Ross (b. 1928-d. 1986), Edna Maye (b. 1931-d. 1979), Wallace (b. 1934), Jack (b. 1937), and Jane (b. 1943).

Joanne married Allen Ray Cummings in Lafayette, IN in 1945. He was an Air Force pilot in WW II and Korea. He was killed in a plane crash in the Philippines in 1950. His rank was Captain. They had a son, Brock Allen (b. May 22, 1948) in Honolulu, T.H. and a daughter, Sarah Diane (b. Oct. 29, 1949) in Tokyo, Japan.

In 1951 Joanne married Derald VanCleave (b. 1926-d. 1978). He was a Sgt. in the Infantry serving in Europe during WW II. They had one daughter, Lori (b. 1957).

Joseph was a Marine Corps. Sgt. serving in Korea. He married Mildred Spencer in Indianapolis in 1964. He had a stepson, Wayne Spencer.

Edna Maye married Roy Gallion in 1954 and they had two daughters, Connie Maye (b. 1956) and Tracy Ellyn (b. 1963), and a son Roy (b. 1958).

Wallace married Shirley Simmons in 1959 and they had a son, Jeffrey Joseph (b. 1960), and a daughter, Jennifer (b. 1963). Wallace served in the Army spending 19 months in Germany. He is presently married to Betty (Crum) Lewellyn. He has a stepson Jim Stone.

Jack married Wilma Ubbinga and they had a daughter, Elizabeth (Libby) (b. 1965), and a son, Christopher (b. 1968).

Jane married Michael Sabens and they had two daughters, Wendy (b. 1967), Christi (b. 1969), and a son, Joshua (b. 1974).

Wallace and Edna had a small antique shop in their home where he refinished antique furniture. Both were members of the Ladoga Christian Church. He was a member of the Masonic Lodge. At this writing, they have 24 living descendants. *Submitted by Joanne VanCleave*

DR. HENRY ADRIN LIDIKAY

Henry Adrin Lidikay, D.V.M. was a younger member of a veterinary partnership that was an institution in itself as it served the Darlington countryside and Montgomery County for half a century. Dr. Henry born Mar. 18, 1907, at Ladoga was the older son of Dr. Milton H. Lidikay, senior partner.

The Lidikay immigrant ancestors, natives of Germany, first settled in Virginia, then migrated through Tennessee and Kentucky into Indiana, with a short residence in Kansas.

Dr. Henry Adrin Lidikay

The elder in the business (Milton) was the sixth son of George E. and Mary Mageline (Graybill) Lidikay of Ladoga. The family had migrated from Jefferson Co., KY to settle in Montgomery County about 1853. Milton born Sept. 13, 1872 was a graduate of Toronto Veterinary College. There exists a family story that young Milton became inspired to prepare for his life's vocation while riding along on calls with Dr. Heighway, a seasoned veterinarian of the Ladoga community. Milton was married to Bertie Lee Foster, daughter of Henry Allen Foster and Matilda Evelyn Allen. They settled in Darlington. To them were born two sons - Henry Adrin, Mar. 18, 1907, and Harry Davis, Apr. 12, 1910.

Our featured subject, Henry Lidikay D.V.M. took his degree from Ohio State University in 1929 and went into practice with his father about 1929. After the retirement of Dr. Milton, Dr. Henry engaged in their chosen profession with other partnerships over a wide field until his retirement in 1971. His service to the community covered 40 years. He is now deceased.

In the early years the problems of brucellosis of cattle, hog cholera and horse and dog ailments opened wider the doors of opportunity to skills to solving many of these problems in veterinary practice today.

Henry married Elda Caldwell, and the two established a home in Darlington. She, an elementary teacher, born Sept. 13, 1907 was the daughter of Frank and Eva (Armstrong) Caldwell of Franklin Township. As a sideline to their veterinary pursuits, the couple enjoyed saddle horses, show ponies and pedigreed Boston Terrier dogs.

Their children are Lyle Myron and Marilee. Lyle, born June 9, 1932, married Betty Joyce Branstetter and they live in Crawfordsville where he is associated with Cork Crown and Seal Co. They have two children - Curtis Lee and Corinne Elaine (Lidikay) Harmon.

Marilee, born July 30, 1935, a music school teacher, is the wife of Reverend Raymond Forrester McCallister of Fulton, MO. Their children are Lynn Ann and Brian Forrester McCallister.

Harry Davis Lidikay, the younger son of Milton H. Lidikay engaged in the installation of high voltage power lines and served in the Navy C.B.'s in Alaska in service in World War II. He and his wife, the former Ethel Hartung, now live in Grand Junction, CO - now retired. They have no issue.

The Lidikay family left upon the Montgomery County community a stamp marked for enterprise, and constructive service. *Submitted by Mrs. Elda Lidikay*

BANDEL LINN, CARTOONIST AND D.J.

Bandel Theodore Linn, one of three famous cartoonists from Montgomery Co., IN, was born in Crawfordsville, Aug. 31, 1911, to Wallace Theodore Linn, D.D.S. and his wife, Hermine Bandel Linn, grandson of Joseph Ray Linn and Mary Ward Linn, and Fred Bandel (Mayor) of Crawfordsville (1880-1892) and wife Lena Steinhauser Bandel.

He began drawing cartoons early in life, and after graduating from Crawfordsville High School in 1928, he entered Wabash College, and he, and Dave Gerard, cartoonist from here, belonged to famed "Sugar Crick" School of Art, and they drew cartoons for the *"Caveman"*, Wabash College's humour magazine. His original cartoons were highly prized by all who had them. William Holeman, the other cartoonist here, said Bandel began drawing cartoons when very young. His cartoons appeared in a host of national magazines, including *Saturday Evening Post, Colliers, Cosmopolitan, The New Yorker, Redbook, King Features Syndicate, Country Gentleman, Successful Farming*, ads for Wheaties, Hilton Hotels, Florida Citrus Commission.

Bandel Linn

He married Winifred Jay from Kokomo in early 1930's. He hitchhiked to New York to get his "foot" into cartooning, in the mid 1930's and became a well known cartoonist then moving his wife and child there. In 1939 moved to Sarasota, FL and cartooned until drafted into the Army Air Force in 1944, becoming a corporal! He became a D.J. at WSPB, after the war ended. Then he moved to St. Joseph, MI in 1958 and continued as a D.J. at station WHFB for 15 years (1958 to 1972). He moved to Pensacola, FL where he did a morning talk and music show on station WCDA, returning in 1985. At WHFB, he was noted for his wry humor, and his taped feminine detractor, "Prunella". The "wackiness" of his cartoons won him the praise of George Burns and Gracie Allen, in a special page dedicated to his work in a syndicated picture magazine *Parade*. He was known as "Pappy" Linn.

Winifred died in Pensacola, FL, February 1973. He married Margaret (Peg) Cummings Finan from Crawfordsville. She's in a nursing home in Pensacola. Bandel and Winifred's children were: Linda, born Aug. 30, 1935 in New York and married Don Edward Priest in Sarasota, FL. Don is in the radio business in Pensacola.

Charles Theodore "Ted" Linn, born June 25, 1943, Sarasota, FL and married Antionette "Toni" Rosalee De Matteo on July 15, 1967 in Benton Harbor, MI. He was in U.S. Air Force 20 years, returning as a Captain in 1983; lives in Tijeras, NM and works as a Civilian for Air Force now at Kirtland, NM. He received his BS degree in Meteorology in University of Oklahoma in 1971; obtained MS degree in Meteorology at Texas A & M University in 1976. Two children: Christopher Theodore born Nov. 17, 1971 Georgia and Courtney Ann born Apr. 10, 1975 in Bryan, TX.

Steven Jay Linn born in Sarasota, FL May 11, 1946 and married Ruth H. Bolt in early 1970 near Benton Harbor, MI. Two children: Christina Michelle born Feb. 26, 1975 and Stephen Jay Linn, Jr. born Mar. 31, 1976 both born in Benton Harbor, MI. They live in St. Joseph, MI.

Bandel Linn died in Pensacola, FL May 7, 1988, buried in Barancas Cemetery in Pensacola. He was 76 and lived a full life of cartooning and radioing. *Submitted by Pauline Walters*

CHARLES A. AND VIRGIE (STARNES) LINN

Charles Asa and Virgie (Starnes) Linn were married on May 15, 1926 and resided at 819 S. Washington St. Crawfordsville, IN. Active members of the Christian Church where Charles served as Deacon and sang in the choir.

Their two sons were William Joseph, born July 14, 1927 and James Richard born Sept. 2, 1934.

Virgie, born Aug. 13, 1899 to Arnett Ivan and Etta (Sampson) Starnes had five sisters, Mary, Ioma, Pauline, Thelma, Eva and one brother Ivan.

Charles A. born Nov. 28, 1893 was the son of William Asa and Ella (Summers) Linn. He had one brother Warner E. and two sisters Bessie and Ruby Ann. Forest M., Ethel May, and Harry I. died in infancy.

Charles was employed at the Robbs Grocery until 1945. He then went to work at the Himes Poultry Company on North Washington St. with Virgie bookkeeper there in 1948. In the 1960's she became a sales clerk at the Fannie Bee Dress Shop and Charles worked at Jones Conoco Service Station.

Virgie was always loving, kind and considerate of those she came in contact with. Especially so to those of her family and close relatives. Christian faith was a part of her being she lived it!

Charles A., William Joseph, Virgie and James Richard Linn

Charles was a pleasant man to meet, genial, obliging and a man of never-failing courtesy.

Charles died Apr. 28, 1966. Virgie died Jan. 9, 1977. Buried at Oak Hill Cemetery.

William Joseph graduated from Crawfordsville High School and Wabash College. Finished graduate work at the University of Rochester in New York in 1953 and has been doing chemical research for over 35 years at the Wilmington Delaware Dupont Company.

William and Ruth Wheatley were married in 1956. They have two sons Steve, born Dec. 12, 1957 and Andy, born Aug. 23, 1959. Ruth, born Oct. 6, 1932 is the daughter of Henry and Frances (Doughten) Wheatley. Steve is a graduate student in biochemistry. He is married to Saundra Knippenburg. Saundra is in the corporate finance department of the Kroger Company.

Andy and Peg Bristow were married June 18, 1988. Her daughter Kate is seven. Andy works at a Printing Firm.

James Richard graduated from Crawfordsville High School and in 1954 from the Cincinnati, OH Co-op College and is employed at the Cincinnati Milacron Machine Tool Company over 37 years.

James Richard and Jean Knisley were married Oct. 15, 1955. Their children are Denise, born Aug. 26, 1957, Cheryl, Nov. 21, 1960 and James born Jan. 9, 1963.

Jean's parents were farmers, (Sherman William Knisley, born Apr. 15, 1896-died 1962—and Ella Mae (Chamblis) Knisley—born Jan. 29, 1904-died 1987).

Denise, a nurse works at Dayton, OH. Her husband Ed Coy is a minister at Brookville, OH. Denise has a beautiful voice and does a lot of singing. Their children are Shawna and Brandon.

Cheryl and Don Bossie were married in 1987 and reside in Cincinnati. She drives a school bus. Don is employed as Foreman at a Bakery. They live in Cincinnati, OH.

James married Annette Pennington. He is in the Auto Body Repair Business and live east of Cincinnati, OH. Their two daughters are Caprice and Courtney Lee. *Submitted by Pauline Moore*

ISAAC AND MARY ANN RANDEL LINN

Isaac and Mary Ann 'Randel' Linn were married on Nov. 20, 1852. She was one of six children born to Asa and Margaret Randel, born July 3, 1836 and died Sept. 28, 1899.

Isaac was a son of James Washington and Mahala 'Cassel' (Castle) Linn. He and his twin brother Noah were born on Nov. 13, 1831. Isaac died Apr. 25, 1870 and Noah died Sept. 10, 1884. (See index)

Isaac and Mary's children were: **Sarah Eliza**, born Mar. 23, 1855, died Oct. 26, 1896. She married John McMullin on Jan. 29, 1877.

Charlie Marten, born Apr. 23, 1847 died Jan. 1, 1893. He married Ida Shelley on Oct. 9, 1890.

Rachel Mahala born Mar. 26, 1861 died Mar. 28, 1883. She married Newt Hostetter on Dec. 30, 1880.

Harry Isaac born Dec. 16, 1888 and died Feb. 17, 1889.

Isaac Linn; Mary Ann Linn

William Asa born Aug. 7, 1857 died Mar. 13, 1916. He married Ella Summers on Dec. 9, 1880.

Isaac and Mary Linn lived on a farm east of Whitesville on the farm his parents bought when they came to Montgomery County in 1837. The farm continues to remain in the Linn family through the years. William was 13 years of age when his father Isaac died. Isaac then shared the responsibility of caring for the home and family. Though Isaac was a member of the Methodist Church, Mary was a Charter Member of the Whitesville Christian Church.

With horses and farm implements of that time the Linn family always kept improving their many acres.

Mary Ann was a skilled seamstress. She had an especially nice lap board that they did neat hand sewing on.

The parents of Mary Ann Linn were Asa Randolph and Margaret Randel (refer to index). *Submitted by Pauline Walters*

JAMES H. LINN FAMILY

James H. Linn born Nov. 28, 1771 in Pennsylvania died in Montgomery County on Apr. 14, 1846. He was the son of Adam, Sr. and Jane Isabelle Dickerson Linn. He came to Butler Co., OH in 1804 and here in 1846. He had married Ella Skyles. She died in 1821. He married again, and she ran through with everything he had. He is buried by his daughter Aunt Betty Chesterson in Finley Chapel cemetery, west of Whitesville. His children were Isabelle Linn, John Linn, Robert Linn, who remained in Ohio, Elizabeth "Betty" Linn Chesterson, Margaret Linn Patterson, William Harrison Linn, Mary Linn, and James Washington Linn born Jan. 7, 1810 and died Apr. 18, 1855 in Montgomery Co., IN. He married Mahala Castle on Mar. 3, 1831 in Warren Co., OH. She must have died 1850 here. He married 2. Lydia Genung. He and Mahala's children were Tobias Linn, Katherine June Himes, William Linn, Mary Elizabeth Epperson, George W., Linn, Eliza Linn, Sarah Ellen Linn Hall, had Perry Hall, Lillie Hall Luster, Ida Hall Wingert, Charles Omer Hall, (died young); John W. Linn, Matilda Emmaline Linn who married Andrew Randel and married 2. Thomas Lytle. Her children were: William N. Randel, Myrtie Randel Vannice, Nellie Lytle Sicks, Charles Lytle, Clarence Lytle and Marion Lytle; Isaac Linn and his twin brother Noah Castle Linn born Nov. 13, 1831 in Butler Co., OH. Noah died Oct. 19, 1884 in Montgomery Co., IN. He married Margaret D. Corn and their children were James Washington Linn, II who married Belle Humbert; Sarah Mahala Vancleave; Nancy Jane Ray, Isaac Linn who married Zula Mote and had Carl, Margaretta and Leslie Linn; Julia Evaline Wright had William Castle Wright; Joseph Andrew Linn born Sept. 6, 1869 and died Oct. 28, 1936 and married Mary Anna Candace Weaver married November 1903 and she died 1960's. Buried Mace Cemetery. They had two children, Mabel Clare Linn born Nov. 17, 1903 - deceased - married Alvis Braxton Myers, son of Alvis Braxton and Leona Brown Myers, Leona born Montgomery Co., IN. They lived in Chicago and Pompano, FL. Had two children, Nylene Myers married Albert Earl Gilbert in 1957. He was a well known nature artist. The National Audubon Society commissioned him to paint four birds pictures for their 150th anniversary. The bald eagle, the cardinal, the blue jay, and the screech owl were the birds he painted for them. He won $1,000,000 in a duck painting contest, had three children, Andrew Earl Gilbert, Kathy Gilbert, Karl Gilbert; Mabel and Braxton's son Lynn Braxton Myers married twice - divorced. Mabel Clare Linn Myers' brother was Lawrence Russell Linn born Aug. 27, 1911 and married Mildred Morrison February 1937. She died in 1977. Their children were Joed Morrison Linn born May 17, 1931 and married 1. Nancy Gray and had three children. Divorced and married 2. Joan ?? He had Jeffrey Lee Linn born 1957 and married in 1977. Robert Lawrence Linn born Sept. 27, 1960, and Donna Marcelle Linn born in 1962. Joed and son Jeffrey live near New Ross.

JAMES WASHINGTON LINN AND MAHALA CASSELL LINN

In 1837 James Washington Linn and Mahala Cassell (Castle, both spellings) came to Indiana to Walnut Township. They were married Mar. 3, 1831 in Warren Co., OH by Benjamin Graves (Record Vol. 2 p. 391).

James W. was born Jan. 7, 1810 to James H. Linn and Ella (Skyles) Linn in Ohio. (refer to Linn in index)

Mahala was the daughter of George V. Cassell born 1782—died 1847, and Catherine (Horine) Cassell born 1789 and died 1878 in Cass Co., IN. He was of Irish ancestry and she Dutch or German and married Frederick Co., MD, Dec. 4, 1805.

George V. Cassell, Mahala's father enlisted in Frederick Co., MD Jan. 14, 1813 and served as a private in Captain James Neals 36th U.S. Infantry War of 1812 from Sept. 15, 1813 until he was discharged Sept. 15, 1814 at Baltimore, MD.

James Washington and Mahala Cassell Linn

James and Mahala Linn bought land located 1-1/2 miles south east of Whitesville, IN on May 22, 1837. (Deed recorded Feb. 1, 1838.)

Their first born were twins, Noah and Isaac. The ten other children were: Tobias, Catherine, William, Mary Elizabeth, George W., Eliza Ann, Sarah Ellen, James H., John W. and Matilda Emmaline. There were ten living children when Mahala died in 1850.

James Washington Linn married Lydia Genung and they had a son, James and an infant that died. When James Washington Linn died on Apr. 18, 1855, the land was heired by his nine living children and his second wife, Lydia. John W. Linn was named administrator of the estate and Isaac Linn bought out each heir.

When the Linn family came into Montgomery County they were engaged in the hardest of labor—clearing the forest land and fencing the clearings with rails they split. James and Mahala chose to locate their home site in the center of the farm.

Isaac having been reared on the home farm was experienced with livestock and anything connected with raising crops. He was 24 years old.

James Washington and Mahala Linn's family were representative of a fine family near Whitesville, IN. Their general surroundings indicated thrift and enterprise. James W. had a natural skill with tools and had passed this on to his sons. Mahala turned her daughters' attention to sewing and cooking skills and other home needs, according to the best methods at that time.

A sketch of Isaac Linn's wife and family appear elsewhere in this book.

Catherine Jane, a sister of Isaac Linn, married Jacob Himes. (refer to index)

JOHN W. LINN

John Linn, son of W. Harrison was active in the days of mud roads-splitting of rails and courting on horseback.

John Linn was born Sept. 4, 1852 in the new home recently built by his parents in Montgomery Co., IN. The means of travel when he was young was by big wagon and horseback, later by spring wagons. He went to see the girls on horseback. The girls rode their own horses when they went anywhere with the fellows.

John W. was married to Mary Anna Martin after

a courtship of two years on Apr. 10, 1873 at the home of the bride's parents James Mills and Margaret Martin. There were no gravel roads at that time and the roads were very muddy that day.

John W. and Anna Linn

Their first home was a log cabin northwest of Mace. A new house with two rooms below and two above was built by them in November. Their oldest son was born here. After the baby came the father put rockers on one of their chairs so the new mother could rock the baby. After three years they bought land east of Mace and lived in a log cabin here until 1881 when they built the house Meredith Manges lives in in 1988. Finally they owned 240 acres in Walnut Township.

In 1906 John W. retired and he and Anna moved to Crawfordsville where they lived the rest of their lives except in 1910 they returned to the farm to build their barn which had been destroyed by fire. John was a very good carpenter. He sold lightning rods for many years. He was never afraid of heights and could climb on any building. After he was 80 years old he made gates from native lumber for his farm.

In 1933 John and Anna spent several days in Chicago and he spent three days at the World's Fair. He was 82 years of age at this time. He was hard of hearing before he was 50 years old. After this misfortune he did not go to public meetings but enjoyed going down town and to the Sales Pavilion and places where he could see. He read a great deal.

With the aid of ear phones he enjoyed the radio. They enjoyed the convenience of a stoker furnace and an electric refrigerator. John like to work with bees so he always had several hives.

John and Anna lacked seven days being married 68 years.

Children: 1. Bertram Linn (Spanish American Veteran); 2. Charles Linn (father of Pearl Shelley); 3. Nellie Linn (Manges); 4. Walter Linn - Attorney at law; 5. Laila Linn (Hartford Livestock Insurance Co.).

Anna did most of her own housework until a year before her death. She died Apr. 3, 1941. John W. died June 15, 1945. He was over 92 years of age. *Submitted by Edith M. Kistler*

JOSEPH RAY LINN

Adam Linn, Jr., born 1785 in Pennsylvania died Mar. 7, 1887 in Montgomery Co., IN, was the son of Adam Linn, Sr. and Jane Isabelle Dickerson Linn; lived in Pennsylvania, came to Butler Co., OH, to Kentucky 1818, and to Montgomery Co., IN in 1846. He is buried in Shiloh Cemetery, no stone there now, his second wife also buried there.

He married 1. Jane Patterson born 1790 in Pennsylvania and she died. He then married Mary Ann Wilson Runyan, widow of Anthony Runyan. Adam and Mary Ann married May 22, 1832 in Butler Co., OH. She had two Runyan children: Susan and Thomas. Mary Ann born Aug. 12, 1801 and died Aug. 8, 1882 here. Adam was in the War of 1812 from Butler Co., OH. He volunteered. They joined the Union Hill Presbyterian Church in Walnut Township in 1850. Adam and Jane had eight children: Adam III; Samuel; William Patterson; Mary; Margaret; Nancy; Jane and Charlotte. Adam and Mary Jane had six children: John Wilson; Sarah E.; Joseph Ray Linn; David Ray; Isabelle; and Abby Marie.

Joseph Ray Linn and grandson Bandel Linn

Joseph Ray Linn born June 16, 1836 in Butler Co., OH and died Apr. 30, 1918 in Montgomery Co., IN. They came here in 1846. He married Mary Ellen Ward, daughter of Uzal and Lydia Lafuse Ward. Mary Ann born Aug. 20, 1857 and died Feb. 1, 1897. He was in Civil War, Private in 86th Indiana Regiment, Company F. Their children were William Joseph Linn, died one year old; Lydia Ann Linn Brown; Uzal Linn married Blanche Peterson; Henry Clifton Linn born 1868 died 1947 married Gertrude Bowman and had three sons; Mark Emerson Linn married Kathryn Shackleford and had four children; Marvin Oakel Linn died age one year; Manson Bruce Linn born Aug. 18, 1908 and died August 1983 Urbana, IL. He married Frances Tharp on Sept. 4, 1932 in Montgomery Co., IN, and they had two daughters. Pegeen Jocelyn and Gretchen Martha. Manson started to school in a one room-eight grade school called Greenwood, two miles west of New Ross. He graduated from New Ross High School. He graduated from Wabash College in 1930, taught there 1930-1932; got a P.H.D. Degree from Cornell University in 1940 and taught there 1932-1942; was professor at University of Illinois 1943 until his retirement in 1974. He was listed in *Indiana Authors;* wrote a book on Vegetable Diseases and many other publications; Fannie Linn Conner; May Linn; Mary Jane, (called Jennie); and Wallace Theodore Linn, a dentist in Crawfordsville, married Hermine (called Minnie) Bandel on Nov. 9, 1903, their child was Bandel Linn, famous cartoonist born in Montgomery Co., IN. He married 1. Winnie Jay and 2. Peg Cummings Finan. He had three children: Linda; Steve; and Charles Theodore, a retired Air Force Captain, lives in New Mexico. Bandel died May 1988 in Sarasota, FL. *Submitted by Pauline Walters*

NOAH CASTLE LINN

Noah Castle Linn was born Nov. 13, 1831 in Butler Co., OH, the son of James Washington and Mahala Castle Linn, grandson of James H. and Ella Skyles Linn and George and Catherine Horine Castle, came to Montgomery Co., IN, 1837. Noah married Margaret D. Corn on June 30, 1855, daughter of Williams and Sarah Allen Corn. Noah died Sept. 10, 1944 west of New Ross, IN. Margaret D. Corn was born May 1, 1833 in Indiana and died Mar. 17, 1909 near New Ross, IN. Their children were Sarah Mahala Linn married Henry Newton Vancleave, had Wallace, Milton and Lilly; Nancy Jane Linn born 1862 and died 1914 married James Ray. After he died in 1887 she married Bud Jones. She had Glen, Ethel Ray Harris, Floyd Ray and Edna Ray (died young). Isaac Linn II born 1863 and died 1909 married Zula Mote on Jan. 21, 1887 (after his death she married Ed Rose). They had Carl, infant died, Margaretta and Leslie Linn; Joseph Andrew Linn born Sept. 6, 1869 and died 1936. He married Anna Candance Weaver and had Mabel Clare Myers, and Lawrence Russell Linn; Julia Evaline Linn born Aug. 23, 1872 and died 1898 and married Wesley Wright. They had infant, died young, and William Castle Wright; James Washington Linn II born Aug. 20, 1861 and died Apr. 11, 1922 and married Letitia Flora Belle Humbert, daughter of Isaac and Mary Joh Humbert born Mar. 4, 1862 in Tippecanoe Co., IN. They married here in April 1885. They lived all their life within a 2-1/2 mile radius of New Ross. They had four children Earl Joseph Linn born June 9, 1888 and died 1967. He married Bonnie June McMullen and had one son Donald J. Linn. Floyd Isaac Linn born Nov. 28, 1891 and died 1973 served in WW I; Jennie Flo born Feb. 24, 1894 and married Roy G. Robison and they had no children; Dora Evaline Linn was born Nov. 7, 1855 near New Ross and died Aug. 6, 1955 at Ladoga, married Orval Wingert Randel on Feb. 28, 1907, son of James G. and Sarah Magdaline Wingert Randel. They had two daughters: Vivian Lucile born Dec. 28, 1913 married Walter J. Harpel, (both in a nursing home) and Crystal Pauline Randel born Dec. 30, 1907 married Harold B. Walters on July 7, 1928. He died on Oct. 6, 1970 and the had one son, Robert Lee Walters born May 11, 1929. He married Mary Alberta Williams on Nov. 29, 1949 and they were divorced in February 1973. He then married Petra ? and they divorced. He then married Marilyn Fairfield Johnson on June 3, 1988. Robert and Mary had five children: Jeffrey Lee born Oct. 2, 1950 and married Brenda Durbin and they have three children: Angela Kristin born Oct. 2, 1974; Jacalyn Suzan, and Ryan Lee; Larry Dean Walters born Nov. 8, 1951 and married Deborah Bronaugh and have two sons: Matthew and Lucas; Connie Kay born Jan. 17, 1954 married Stephen H. Truax and they have four children, Stephanie Nicole, Shannon Camille, Joshua Michael, and Joel Adam Truax. Pamela Sue Walters born Oct. 10, 1955 married Steven Demoret and is divorced. They have two daughters Karmon Leigh, and Kelsey Lochelle Demoret; and Michael Robert Walters born Sept. 15, 1956 married Debra Addler, and they have two children: Heather Michelle and Jacob David Walters. *Submitted by Pauline Walters*

RAYMOND AND PHYLLIS LINN

Raymond Gene Linn born June 12, 1924 in country home near New Ross, IN son of Ernest Edward and Pearl Marie (Clark) Linn. Raymond attended school in New Ross. He served in WW II with 509th Port Battalion in the States, Alaska and India as Corporal. A Gideon and member of Robert Turner Post 427.

After his discharge, he returned to his family farm. He married Phyllis Irene Hayes June 5, 1948, in New Ross Christian Church parsonage by Bro. James Burden. Phyllis was born Aug. 18, 1928, in Culver Hospital to Homer Walter and Ethel Blanche (Peterson) Hayes, who lived on a farm east of Whitesville. She graduated from New Ross High School in 1947. Bought a farm joining his father in 1951. The Linns raise hogs and grain farm and both are active members in New Ross Christian Church. Linns have four children; Jeffrey Lee Linn born June 28, 1950, Janis Marie Sept. 14, 1951, Cheryl Ann July 14, 1956 and Richard Gene Feb. 6, 1960.

Cheryl McMullen, Janis Miethe, Raymond Linn, Phyllis Linn, Jeffrey Linn, Richard Linn

Jeffrey graduated from New Ross High School in 1968, from Indiana Business College in Indianapolis in 1969. He married Karen Denise Johnson Oct. 11, 1969 in Indianapolis. Karen was born June 4, 1950, to Paul and Evelyn Johnson of Indianapolis. They had two daughters, Patricia Ann born in Aurora, CO and Donna Jo born Feb. 23, 1972 in Crawfordsville. Both girls are students at Southmont High School. Jeffrey served as Sgt. in the Air Force from December 1969 to December 1973 in the States, Vietnam and Thailand. He has been employed at Impex in Crawfordsville for 20 years. He married Virginia Marie Sipple Nov. 15, 1986 in Crawfordsville, Virginia was born Mar. 16, 1953 to Harold and Mary Sipple near Clarks Hill. She graduated from Wainwright High School in 1971, Ball State in 1975 and Masters Degree in 1980, now teacher at Southmont Jr. and Sr. High School. Parents of a daughter Kimberly Kay born May 29, 1987.

Janis graduated from New Ross High School in 1969, worked at RR Donnellys and Sons and married Larry Gene Miethe Dec. 12, 1970. He was born Sept. 28, 1951 to Bill and Rosemary Miethe of Ladoga. He graduated from Ladoga High School in 1969. He was employed by Mid-States until Nov. 1, 1981. Parents of three daughters, Shannon Marie born Sept. 16, 1976, Heather Sue born May 5, 1978 and Ashley Linn born Sept. 30, 1980. Family moved to Pamona, CA Nov. 1, 1981. Larry employed by "Davis and Walker" in Irwindale, CA as Plant Manager.

Cheryl graduated from Southmont High School in 1974. Married Kenneth Gene McMullen Aug. 29, 1975. He was born Sept. 21, 1951 to Howard and Frances McMullen. Lived on the family farm west of Ladoga. They lived southeast of New Market and he was employed by Mid-States until September 1984. Parents of two children, Brian Scott born Feb. 19, 1976, Jill Linette born Nov. 19, 1978. Family moved to California, September 1984, now reside in Fontana, CA, employed by Davis and Walker in Irwindale, CA as a foreman.

Richard attended Southmont High School. He lives with his parents and farms with his dad on the farm west of New Ross. *Submitted by Phyllis Linn*

WILLIAM ASA AND ELLA SUMMERS LINN

William Asa and Ella (Summers) Linn were married Dec. 9, 1880. They lived on the farm east of Whitesville that William's grandparents settled on in 1837.

William was the son of Isaac and Mary (Randel) Linn, born Aug. 7, 1857. Ella was the daughter of Harvey and Mary (Bradley) Summers, born Apr. 14, 1862.

Their children were Forest M., born Dec. 20, 1881, died Sept. 10, 1882, Ethel May, born Dec. 24, 1885 died Jan. 9, 1885, Harry Isaac, born Dec. 16, 1888 died Feb. 17, 1889, Warner Earland, born July 25, 1883 died 1975, Bessie Faye, born Dec. 6, 1891 died Sept. 5, 1961, Ruby Ann, born Nov. 13, 1897 died July 27, 1948, Charles Asa, born Nov. 28, 1893 died Apr. 28, 1966. Harry Linn, a nephew lived with them. He was born Sept. 28, 1891 died Feb. 19, 1913, the son of Charles M. and Ida Linn. The nephew, Harry Isaac, was like a brother and son.

William Asa and Ella (Summers) Linn

Ella was a loving mother, friendly to all taking in nephew Harry when his parents died. There was neighborly fellowship at Sunday night suppers in their home and singing around the piano.

When William was 13 his father, Isaac Linn died, leaving him to share the responsibility of caring for the home and family. In early life he became a member of the Christian Church. He was also a member of the Knights of Pythias.

William was a strong man with a love of the land and a good farmer. He had an orchard of Grimes Golden apples, pears and peaches. Built many of the barns around the Whitesville area.

Ella drove the buggy to visit the married children before she died taking some of her baking. Bessie married Ralph Bratton and lived near New Ross. Warner and Stella Myers Linn lived on a farm west of New Ross also. Ella died on Mar. 4, 1911. Only Ruby Ann and brother Charlie at home.

Thirteen year old Ruby took upon herself the home responsibilities, doing the best she could with the help of sister Bessie when she came. However, William Asa married Sarah McGrew on July 15, 1913. Charlie married in 1917. Ruby Ann married Chester Himes on Aug. 13, 1916.

On Mar. 13, 1916 William Asa Linn died. Ruby was a Senior at the Ladoga High School. On the Ecclesia yearbook staff, secretary of the Corinthian Society and the Girls Glee Club. Her nickname was "Dolly".

She was to play the part in a class play on Friday night, Mar. 13, 1916, the day her father William Asa died. Ruby was 17. They were in mourning.

William's estate was left to his children and Sarah McGrew. Charlie and Warner bought Sarah's portion. Warner buying each one's share as the opportunity was provided. The Linn farm remains in the family.

WILLIAM HARRISON LINN

William Harrison Linn was born Nov. 12, 1813, the son of James H. and Ella Skyles Linn in Butler Co., OH. He came to Montgomery County and worked with his brother John Linn who lived in Linnsburg. He returned to Ohio and married Eliza Corrington on Apr. 25, 1836 where he lived for three years.

John went to Ohio and bought a new wagon and brought William Harrison and his wife and child, Mary Ann, along with their possessions in his new wagon to Montgomery County. William Harrison (called Harrison) and his family first lived in a log house. Harrison paid $700 for 80 acres of land east of Mace, IN and later bought 160 more and built a frame house. John W. Linn was the first child born in the new house on Sept. 4, 1852. Harrison died June 6, 1877.

Wm. Harrison Linn; Eliza Linn

Eliza furnished part of the timber for the frame for the Mace Methodist Church which was built in 1893. She also gave $700. Eliza and William Harrison's names are in the stained glass windows of this church.

Eliza was born in Dec. 11, 1818 near Mason, OH the daughter of Samuel and Ruth Dickerson Corrington. Her mother died when she was 14 or 15 years old. Eliza died Dec. 6, 1905.

Children of William Harrison and Eliza are: Mary Ann Linn married William W. Ward; Elizabeth married W.A. Johnson; Nancy married Thomas Hunt; Amanda married Marion Hayes; James Franklin married Nancy Porter; Martha married Thomas Kelsey; Samuel died at age 21; John W. married Anna Martin; and George Washington Linn married Jennie Freeman.

LIVINGSTON FAMILY

William Jasper Livingston (b. 1841) married Polly Anna Vincent (b. 1849) in 1867. Three sons were born to this union - John, Joseph and Charles. They lived in the New Richmond area. John had four daughters and Charles had one daughter. The son, Joseph (b. 1870) married Susan Swank (b. 1875). Three daughters and three sons were born to this union. Flossie (b. 1897), Gladys Bannon (b. 1898), Myrtle (b. 1901), Dallas (b. 1908), William (b. 1910) and Merle (b. 1911). Gladys married Charles Bannon. They lived near Chicago and their three children were Helen Woods (b. 1918), Ida May Fagan (b. 1926), and Richard (b. 1929). Helen had three children-Robert, Carol and Bill. Ida May married Gene Fagan and had two children - Mike and Cathy. Her son Richard married Charlotte and had four children - Joe, Scott, Mancy and Jeff. Richard and his family live in California. Dallas married Mildred McElwee and their children were Joe, who lives in Oklahoma, Janet, Mary and Martha. Most of the family have lived in Montgomery and Fountain Counties and the main occupation has been farming. The last of the six children died in 1988.

William Livingston married Pearl Grimble (b. 1912) in 1933 in Fountain County. He spent his life farming in Fountain and Montgomery Counties, and Pearl did clerical work many years in the same counties. Pearl was the daughter of Albert Grimble (b. 1885) and Ica Primmer Grimble (b. 1888). Pearl's grandfather was George Grimble (b. 1839) and her grandmother was Annie Pickett Grimble (b. 1847). Both came to America from England. Pearl's other grandfather was William Primmer (b. 1867) and the grandmother was Eable Kalfsbeck Primmer (b. 1868) and her family came from Holland. The Grimbles had two sons and the one daughter. Francis (b. 1923) who married Kathleen Schenck (b. 1929) and they had four children-Jack (b. 1950) who married Joyce Smith (b. 1949) and their two children are Justin (b. 1976) and Jana (b. 1978). A daughter Linda (b. 1952) and daughter Bonnie (b. 1953) and son Alan (b. 1956). The other Grimble son was Gene (b. 1929) and married Geneva McFall and they had two sons Randall (dec.) and Robert. They live in the Valpariso area. The daughter, Pearl, was married to William Livingston. They had a daughter and a son. The daughter is Donna (b. 1937) who married Lowell Stockdale (b. 1936). She received her education from Purdue and has spent many years as a teacher and doing substitute teaching. Her husband tills many acres of land and cares for his livestock on their farm south of Hillsboro in Fountain County. They have two children - Cynthia (b. 1962) who received her degree from I.S.U. and now teaching is her profession. She married Scott Ferling (b. 1962) who also farms and their home is in Wayne Township. They have a daughter Sarah Marie (b. 1988). The Stockdale's son is Craig (b. 1966), who received his education from Black Hawk College in Illinois. He lives in Wayne Township also and is interested in farming and raising cattle.

The son is Donald Livingston (b. 1941) who received his degree from Purdue. He spent a few years in the military service before coming back to Indiana. He married Jane Fowler (b. 1941) from Colorado Springs, and they have two children Scott (b. 1971) and Lori (b. 1972). They live in Wayne Township where he is engaged in farming and raising hogs and cattle.

William Livingston died in 1987. The Livingston family has lived in Montgomery County for over 200 years.

JOHN BREAKS AND LELA CLARK LOFLAND

John is a life-long resident of Montgomery County, was born in 1922, oldest son of John Lucas and Clara Breaks Lofland. His siblings are: Luther Lee (1925), Nora Evelyn (1927), Robert Glenn (1929) and James Milton (1933). John is a descendant of two early settlers in Montgomery County. His great-grandfather, Heverlo Lofland, emigrated from Delaware about 1834 and his great-great-grandfather, Richard Breeks (later Breaks), emigrated from Dent, England about 1817 to Indianapolis and then to Montgomery County about 1835, after the death of his first wife, Jane Beard, and became a prominent farmer in the northwest part of Montgomery County. It was Jane's brother, John Beard, who established the first free schools in Indiana. Their son, John Beard Breaks, donated the land on which Breaks School was built (see Breaks School).

John received his elementary education at Youngs Chapel and Breaks Schools and graduated from Waynetown High School in 1940. He served in the army during World War II and Korean Campaign. He worked at R.R. Donnelley for over 46 years, retiring in 1988.

John B. and Lela (Clark) Lofland

Lela was born in 1928 to Leslie Lee and Flossie Butcher Clark in Crawford Co., Robinson, IL, the oldest of four girls. Her sisters are: Hulah Lee, Mary Alice, and Lola Grace. Hulah is married to Charles Odell and resides in Crawfordsville. Lela received her education at Hurricane Grade School and Robinson High School, graduating in 1946. She later earned an associate degree of science in nursing in 1971 and worked as a registered nurse at Culver Union Hospital, retiring in 1988.

John and Lela were married in Crawfordsville in September 1947. To this union were born four children: John Leslie (1949), Miller, IN; Carolyn Mae (Chaney) (1951), Wanamaker, IN; David Edwin (1954), Chicago, IL; and Natalie Fay (Newlon) (1959), Lafayette, IN. John, Carolyn and Natalie graduated from Indiana University and David graduated from Indiana Central (now University of Indianapolis). John Leslie married Debra Schacht from Michigan City in 1975. They have one daughter, Stephanie Michelle. Carolyn married Dan Chaney from Indianapolis in 1981. They have two children, Albert Clifford and Leslie Kathryn. David married Deborah Byster from Chicago, IL in 1983. Natalie married Gary Newlon from Kokomo in 1984.

John and Lela are active members of First Christian Church and have been active with several youth groups with their children; namely, Boy Scouts, Girl Scouts, Campfire for Girls, 4-H and Rainbow for Girls. Both are active members of the Order of Eastern Star. John is now serving as Worshipful Master of Masonic Lodge #50 and as Associate Patron of OES. Lela is a Past Matron of OES, and past president of the Montgomery County Home Extension. They are also members of the Sugar Creekers Camping Club, National Campers and Hikers Association. *Submitted by John Breaks Lofland*

LUTHER LEE AND SANDRA JEAN WHEELER LOFLAND

Luther is a long time resident of Montgomery County, born in 1925, and one of five children of John Lucas and Clara Conard Breaks Lofland. His brothers and sister are: John Breaks, 1922; Nora Evelyn, 1927; Robert Glenn, 1929, and James Milton, 1933.

Heverlo Lofland, a great-grandfather, came from Delaware around 1834. His great-great-grandfather, Richard Breeks, later changed to "Breaks", emigrated to Montgomery County in the early 1800's, from Dent, England. His gravesite is in the Breaks Cemetery in Section 15 in the northwest portion of North Union township. It was his son, John Beard Breaks, who donated the land on which Breaks school was built.

The Luther Lofland Family: L to R Linda, Luther Sr., Luther Jr., Louanne, Sandra and Lisa

Luther received his elementary education at Breaks School and graduated from Waynetown High School in 1943. Upon graduation from high school he served in the U.S. Army Air Corps, Pacific Theatre. After being discharged, he enrolled in Purdue University, School of Agriculture, graduating with a B.S. Degree in 1950. After working in Decatur Co., IN five and one half years, he began working in the trust department of the First National Bank and Trust Company as their farm manager. It has since merged with Bank One.

Sandra (1939) was the daughter of Sherman Morris and Helen Lucille Smith Wheeler, of Gary, IN. Her brother, Harold Sherman Wheeler and his family, reside in Griffith, IN. Sandra graduated from Linden High School in 1957 and in 1981 from St. Mary's of The Woods, in Terre Haute, IN, with a B.S. Degree in Social Sciences. She is presently working in the area of preventing child abuse as a social worker.

Luther and Sandra were married June 1, 1958, in Crawfordsville. Their four children are: Luther Jr. (1959), Louanne Kay (1960), Linda Jane (1966), and Lisa Jean, (1970). Luther Jr. graduated from Indiana State University with a Masters Degree in Education. He married Kristie Brown in 1982. Their family consists of Kari Brown and Luther Lofland III. They reside in West Terre Haute, IN. Louanne attended Taylor University and married Mark I. Cole in 1983. They have a daughter, Lauren Jennifer, born in 1987. They reside in Everett, WA. Linda graduated from North Montgomery High School. She married David M. Gray, in 1985. They reside west of Crawfordsville. Lisa graduated from North Montgomery High School and resides near Crawfordsville.

Luther and Sandra reside in Walnut Fork Addition, just east of Crawfordsville. Luther has served as president of the Indiana Society of Agri-Bankers and has been employed by the bank for over 33 years. He has served as president of the Central Indiana Unit of the WBCCI Airstream Travel Trailer Club. They are both active members at The First Christian Church. *Submitted by Luther Lofland Sr.*

JOHN W. LOGAN

John W. Logan, son of Robert Logan, was born May 7, 1846 Washington Co., IN. He was in the Civil War in Company D, a Pvt, in the Indiana Volunteers. He died Jan. 6, 1938 at Whitesville. He was appointed freight agent at Whitesville in July,

1909 at Monon Depot. He married Alcina Asenath (called Cena) Brown, daughter of William Hugh and Nancy Routh Brown on May 29, 1870. She died 1933. Their children were William Robert born 1871, was killed in an accident in Miami, FL June 1916. He had left here in 1908. He married Cora Ellen Peck and had five children, Eunice; Ida; Wilse; Naomi and Francis (Frank) married Mary Rutan. When she died he married Eve Cole. Frank died 1966.

Josiah Brown Logan (Joe) married Dema Evans and had a son Nelson Eugene Logan who married June _____. They divorced and he married Wilma _____. Eugene and Wilma live at New Whiteland, IN in 1988 and have Jimmie and Sharon. Joe and Dema divorced and he lived in Whitesville with his grandparents. Joe died in 1963.

Grover Logan son of Josiah and Dema lived in Illinois. Emma Logan married Charles Coleman; Della Logan Wood; Ida Josephine Logan married William Noah Randel, son of Andrew and Emmaline Linn Randel. Ida was his second wife. They had Geneva Nellie Rose, Kenneth, and Rose Grace who married John Sherrarad, had ten children, lived in Wyoming; Edna, Ludessa married Fred Rhoades; married Wert Cox.

Cena Logan, even when she was getting old would walk from Whitesville to Ladoga. She always carried a large purse.

GEORGE H. LOMAN

In 1900 George H. and Samatha Susannah Brown "Mantie" Loman and their two children Blanche and George D., Jr. moved to Montgomery Co., IN. They came from Tippecanoe County and purchased a farm in Brown Township near Freedom Baptist Church.

George H. Loman, Sr. was the son of Ephraim (1820-1863) and Eliza Jane Loman (1831-1911) of Tippecanoe County. Ephraim died while serving as a soldier in the Civil War near Vicksburg. He is buried in the Vicksburg Cemetery. Eliza is buried in Asburg Cemetery, Bringhurst, IN. They were parents of two sons George H. (1853-1934) and Dorr F.

Samatha Susannah Brown (1860-1939) was the seventh child of George and Susannah Pugh Brown. George Brown was born Oct. 12, 1818 in Harrison Co., OH and died 1869. Susannah was born Dec. 28, 1823 in Virginia and died in 1914. Both are buried in Pond Grove Cemetery at Otterbein. Other children of the couple were Lafayette, Peter, Cynthia, Mary Jane, Daniel and Sarah.

George H. Sr., George A., Blanche and Samatha Loman

George D. Loman, Jr. and his two sisters were born in Tippecanoe County. George, Jr. was born Aug. 16, 1893 and died May 9, 1975, sister Blanche Loman Dixon born Jan. 10, 1884 and died 1971 and sister Nellie born Dec. 18, 1886 and died Feb. 19, 1887. November 30, 1916 George, Jr. married Mayme Canine. She was born Dec. 18, 1898 to L.G. "Tude" Canine (1878-1970) and Mertie Miles Canine (1878-1943). Mayme died Dec. 26, 1972. Tude Canine was the son of Lemuel Canine (1852-1943) and Lessie Milligan Canine (1855-1922). Mertie Canine was the daughter of Peter and Hannah Miles all of Montgomery County.

Two daughters were born to George, Jr. and Mayme Loman. Helen Jean born Jan. 13, 1918 and Geraldine born Jan. 20, 1920. Helen Jean married John K. Patton (1915-1985) of Browns Valley. Geraldine married Dr. George E. Stouffer of Elkhart.

George, Jr. and Mayme Loman had six grandchildren and 14 great-grandchildren.

Both George, Sr. and George, Jr. were farmers. Five generations have lived on the Loman farms, and attended the Freedom Baptist Church. Living on the Loman farms at the present time are George Jr.'s daughter, Helen Jean Loman Patton and his granddaughter Joan Patton Brenda with her husband William H. Brenda and their daughter Tammy Thomas, who left the farm after high school to attend college.

The following that are mentioned in this article are buried in the Freedom Cemetery: George H. Loman, Sr. Samatha; "Mantie" Brown Loman; George D. Loman, Jr. and Mayme Canine Loman; L.G. "Tude" Canine and Mertie Miles Canine; Lemuel and Lessie Milligan Canine and John K. Patton.

FREDERICK M. AND MARY THOMPSON LONG

Frederick Milburn Long was born in Browns Valley, IN in Montgomery County, Dec. 11, 1848. He was one of nine children born to Henry and Rebecca Holland Long. His father, a blacksmith, was born in 1816 near Richmond, IN. Frederick's paternal grandfather, a Dutch Methodist minister came to Indiana from North Carolina around the year 1800.

Frederick spent his early years in Parke County. He married Mary T. Thompson in Paris, IL, May 21, 1869. They eloped in a farm wagon from her home in Parke County. Mary was the daughter of Thomas L. Thompson and Lydia Sutton Thompson. She was born Oct. 8, 1852. Her parents died when she was very young and she was reared by her paternal grandparents Jesse and Angeline Buckler Thompson.

Frederick M. and Mary (Thompson) Long

Fred and Mary settled on a farm near Bellmore, IN. In 1882 they moved to Ladoga in Montgomery County where Fred worked on the construction of the covered bridge east of town. Later he became the first rural U.S. mail carrier on Rural Route #1, Ladoga, IN. The route ran west of Ladoga, south to Parkersburg Spring, north on Greencastle Road then back east to Ladoga. Sometimes in the winter the mailwagon ran into deep drifted snow making it impossible to open the door. The small stove inside kept him warm until help arrived. After many years of faithful service he retired in 1914.

Frederick Long was a gentle, mild-mannered man. He was Sunday school superintendent of the Methodist Church in Ladoga for many years. In 1919 Fred and Mary celebrated their 50th wedding anniversary quietly with family and close friends. He died at home in Ladoga May 25, 1921. Mary died May 16, 1924. They were the parents of Charlotte (Lottie) and Lawrence Chester. Charlotte, born Aug. 21, 1881, married Clarence Lee Dodd of Ladoga Sept. 12, 1900. Lawrence (Shorty) Long was born Feb. 26, 1871. He was working at Nimons and Bennett Heading Mill in Missouri when he met and married Missouri Cordelia Cook in Malden, MO Feb. 14, 1900. "Delia" was the daughter of James K. and Elizabeth Underhill Cook of Stoddard Co., MO. She was born near Bloomfield, MO Jan. 7, 1879. Lawrence brought "Delia" home to Ladoga where they lived for many years. He died Aug. 15, 1936. This union was blessed with five children: Madge, Madeline, Frederick, Mary and Mamie.

Delia died Jan. 16, 1962. Four of their children are deceased. Mamie Long Sparks resides in Crawfordsville.

In 1984 more than 100 descendents were present at the Long Reunion held in Milligan Park, Crawfordsville.

ARTHUR "PETE" AND WORTH LOOKABILL

Pete and Worth Lookabill were the owners and operators of Pete's Greenhouse on Wayne Avenue for many years. During the last few years they were working in cooperation with Wilson Brothers of Parkersburg which specialized in geraniums, the majority of which were raised with tender loving care by Pete and Worth. Before owning the greenhouse Pete was a refrigeration maintenance man for dairies in the area and he and Worth worked for the High Grade Dairy. Pete was the first auxiliary policeman in Crawfordsville and served for 25 years.

Pete was born Feb. 17, 1894 to William and Lidia Welsh Lookabill in Putnam Co., IN. He attended the Raccoon School and later drove a horse drawn school hack. His family also included a brother, John and a sister, Mae Lookabill Williams. Pete died on Feb. 12, 1973 and is buried in the Russellville Cemetery.

Arthur and Worth Lookabill

Worth was born Oct. 23, 1900 to Thomas and Jessie Obenchain Scott at Parkersburg. Thomas Scott was the son of Thomas Walker and Mary Ann Scott. Jessie was the daughter of George and Nancy Katherine Stultz Obenchain. Thomas's brother Omar married Jessie's sister Mamie and Worth had many double cousins. She had one sister, Hazel who married Charles Williams, and five brothers, Pearl who married Lola White, Offie who married Lucile Shackoford, Russell who married Ina Riddle, Paul who married Ruth Armstrong and Glen who first married Sally Clark, second married Dorothy Hampton and third married Amy Vanhook. On Feb. 10, 1924, Worth married Arthur R. "Pete" Lookabill. Her daughter, Waneta, died in early adulthood. They were very attached to a little girl who grew up next door and during their lives Barbara Karshner (Mrs. Max Fletcher) was a devoted "daughter" and friend. All who knew Worth were touched by her kind and gentle ways and her ability to stay young and adventurous until her death Mar. 13, 1986. She is buried at Russellville Cemetery. *Submitted by Rebecca Neideffer*

THE LOUGH FAMILY

Nicholas Lough, the earliest Lough we have trace of, came from Germany to Virginia when a small boy. He grew up there and married Barbara Miller. To them were born ten children—Jacob, who was the oldest son, settled in Maryland and married Nancie Warner, a cousin of George Washington. They were blessed with 11 children. Some of the family migrated to Kentucky, Ohio, and Indiana. One son, Washington, had three sons—James, William, and George—settled in Parke Co., IN.

Another son, Samuel Lough, born in mid-1840, tells of coming from the Carolinas. He made his way through Kentucky in a covered wagon with an entourage of a cow, chickens and pigs. He finally settled near North Salem, coming about a year later to Montgomery County. He married Charlotte Yelton. Their children were Johnny, Rhufus, Edward, Liza, Hattie, and Avaline. After her death, he married Lucinda Beck. From this union came Clarence, Otto, Ben, Corda, and Orville.

Lough Reunion at the Needhams 1919

Clarence went to California and had four children. Otto married Edna Brown of Thorntown, and her ancestors came from England. Barkers, cousins of Edna, brought the first Berkshire hogs to the U.S. Into this family were born Marion, Donald, Marvin, Nolan, and Marihelen. Donald was a trucker, farmer, and spent 339 days under shell fire during WWII, and has three children—Theresa, Martin, and Gayle. Nolan also served in WWII and married Martha Mahoy to whom a son Larry was born.

Ben Lough married Hattie Farrow of near Jamestown; they are parents of Juanita, Mavis, Julia, and Beverly.

Corda married Walter Stewart, a mail carrier and singer. Their children are Byron, a Wabash College graduate, and former president of Delco-Remey in Anderson; Buren, Beryl, Buford, Beatrice, Evelyn, and William.

Orville, a WWI veteran, married Minnie Farrow, and their children are Martha Jean, Barbara, Howard, Clifford, Max, Audrey, Lucille, and Stanley.

Avaline married Obed Needham. Their two sons are Cecil and Hubert.

Hattie married Fred McCallister, an Indianapolis judge and Wabash College graduate. To this family was born Ralph, who was a contractor who resides near Thorntown.

Clark Woody married Liza, and they are parents of two sons; Richard Woody is a farmer who lives near Darlington.

Donald Lough married Dorothy Martin. Her mother, a teacher, Goldyn Moree Craig, was the daughter of Mr. and Mrs. Frank Craig. Her father was Levi Lawson Martin, a principal and teacher from Jamestown. His father, Charles Francis Martin, was the first recipient of Master Farmer, in 1928, from Hendricks County. He, along with a friend, Granville Wells, organized the Citizens Bank. His son, Herman Wells is the former Chancellor of Indiana University. *Submitted by Mrs. Donald Lough*

CLARENCE ADRIAN AND MAUDE MARGARET CASON LOWE

Clarence Adrian Lowe married Maude Margaret Cason on Nov. 24, 1918 at her parents' house in Crawfordsville, IN. Clarence was born Sept. 6, 1899 in Montgomery County to Fred W. and Frances Lowe.

Maude was born Jan. 13, 1903 at Sterling, IN to William P. and Samatha Cason.

They had 14 children born between 1919 and 1950: Margaret, Martha, Betty, Mary, Jean, Jim, Fred, Patsy, Edward, Wanda, Thomas, Emory, Samuel and Lyda. Thomas died as an infant in 1941.

Clarence and Maude had 50 grandchildren. Two grandchildren died as infants.

Clarence was a graduate of Crawfordsville High School. He worked in the brickyard and spent ten years farming. He also worked as a cement finisher and a carpenter. Clarence was a veteran of World War I, serving in Panama where he was injured.

Maude was a graduate of Waveland School and of Indiana Business College at Indianapolis. Before she was married, she worked as a telephone operator. She also baked pies for local restaurants, the Montgomery County Jail and Culver Union Hospital. Maude's pies were sought after throughout Montgomery County. Some folks would drive 20 miles for a slice of one of her pies.

Maude's paternal grandfather died trying to cross Indian Creek on horseback when the water was high out of its banks. He was a native of France and changed his name from Casone' to Cason upon immigrating to the United States by way of Canada. Maude's maternal grandfather was the Justice of Peace at Waveland in the 1800's.

Maude died Oct. 31, 1979. Clarence died Nov. 8, 1982. *Submitted by The Lowe Family*

EDWARD BRUCE AND NANCY JUNE LOWE

Edward Bruce Lowe married Nancy June Hendrickson on June 17, 1960 at Union Chapel E.U.B. in Bal Hinch.

Edward was born July 30, 1938 at Smartsburg, IN to Clarence A. and Maude M. Cason Lowe.

Nancy was born June 12, 1944 at Centerburg, OH to Clyde B. and Martha B. White Hendrickson.

They have three children: Edward "Scott" born Feb. 25, 1961; Cheryl Denise, born Dec. 23, 1962; and Brooke Janelle, born Dec. 27, 1978.

Scott married Jennifer L. Jess on Feb. 6, 1981 and has three children: Jacob, Lyndsey and Kelley.

Cheryl married Curt A. Jackson on Aug. 25, 1980 and has four children: Matthew, Caleb, Rachel and Nathanael.

Edward has worked as a plasterer for 30 years. The Indianapolis Children's Museum, the Hoosier Dome and the Indianapolis International Airport are only a few projects he has worked on.

Edward also worked for the Crawfordsville Police Reserves for eight years.

Edward and Nancy now reside in Darlington, IN. *Submitted by the Lowe Family*

GEORGE BRUCE LUCKETT

A descendent of Indiana pioneers, G. Bruce Luckett, secretary of The Crawfordsville Shale Brick Company, is one of the prominent industrial leaders of Montgomery Co., IN. Mr. Luckett was born July 18, 1867, in Corydon, IN, a son of Samuel Boone Luckett and Mary Jane (Douglas) Luckett.

Samuel Boone Luckett was born in 1828 in Harrison Co., IN, a son of Hezekiah and Helen (Boone) Luckett. Helen (Boone) Luckett was a daughter of George Boone, nephew of the noted pioneer hunter and scout, Daniel Boone. Hezekiah Luckett was born in Fredericksburg, MD, and came to Booneport, KY, early in the 19th Century. Not long afterward he crossed the Ohio River into Indiana Territory and located on a farm in Harrison County. He served under General Harrison at the Battle of Tippecanoe in 1811 and also served as a soldier in the War of 1812. He was a true pioneer who was ever seeking the rainbow's end on the far frontier. He died at St. Joseph, MO, then a village founded by Joseph Robidoux, the Indian trader.

Samuel Boone Luckett was also of the sturdy breed that sought the heart of the wilderness because the blood of the Boones was in his veins. As a youth of 18 he went to New Mexico in 1846 and served as a teamster conveying ammunition and supplies for the troops of the United States Army during the War with Mexico.

In 1850 he joined the gold seekers on the trail to California, crossing the plains in a covered wagon drawn by oxen. He found a little gold, grew restive and returned to the Middle West by way of the Isthmus of Panama. Presently he bought a farm near Corydon where he lived for a few years, then built a woolen mill in Corydon and was in the manufacturing business there for several years. He was a life long Democrat and a devout Baptist. He was an inventor of ability and manufactured a number of devices now long outgrown and forgotten. In 1881 he moved to Crawfordsville, IN, where he was in the business of manufacturing various devices until he retired a few years prior to his death in 1917. His wife had preceded him in death, passing away in 1907. They were the parents of six children, two of whom reached maturity. They were: Jessie, who died in 1883, and George Bruce, the subject of this record. Mary Jane (Douglas) Luckett was born in 1830 in Shenadoah County, a daughter of Adam and Nancy (Pennybaker) Douglas, of New Market, VA.

G. Bruce Luckett received his preliminary education in the public schools of Crawfordsville and attended Wabash College for two years. He was a traveling salesman for his father's manufacturing firm for nearly 20 years. In 1903 he engaged in a business of his own, manufacturing a line of electrical articles in Crawfordsville. He sold that enterprise in 1908 and was one of the organizers of The Crawfordsville Shale Brick Company which was incorporated in that year. The first officers of the company were: James Evans, president; G. Bruce Luckett, secretary-treasurer. The company manufactures a high quality type of shale brick and also brick granule for roofing. The modern, well-equipped plant is located north of the city near the Lafayette Highway.

Mr. Luckett has been a trustee of Wabash College for the past 17 years. He is past president of the Lane Foundation of Crawfordsville, and of the Johnson Manufacturing Company, a director of the Lafayette Life Insurance Company, and an associate member of the Citizens Historical Association. He was a member of the original board of trustees of the Crawfordsville Municipal Light & Power plant, considered one of the best of the state in a city of its size, a plant which has been operated with great financial success. Mr. Luckett is a Democrat, a member of the Presbyterian Church, and of the Crawfordsville Country Club. He owns two valuable improved farms, one in Montgomery Co., IN, and the other in Parke Co., IN.

George Bruce Luckett was married Aug. 28, 1895, to Carrie Belle Shaver, a daughter of Daniel and Sarah (Himer) Shaver, of Montgomery Co., IN. Both of Mrs. Luckett's parents are now deceased. One daughter, Esther, was born to Mr. and Mrs. Luckett. She was graduated from Northwestern University, Evanston, IL, with the degree of Bachelor of Arts and is now secretary to President Louis B. Hopkins, of Wabash College.

Mr. Luckett is a man of many fine qualities and an attractive personality. He is public-spirited and progressive, always ready to lend his active cooperation in public undertakings for the general benefit. He is a true descendant of heroes who settled the Middle West in early days, and at the same time he is thoroughly a citizen of the modern world.— Citizen Historical Association Biograph -July, 1934

JACOB LUSE FAMILY

Jacob Luse came to Montgomery County in the early 1850's, and bought land in Coal Creek Township, bordering the Fountain and Montgomery County lines. He was born May 16, 1818, and married Charlotte Martin, born July 16, 1821, on Apr. 6, 1845. A log cabin was first built on this acreage, and later a two story house, built in several stages, over the years. They reared ten children. Jacob died June 15, 1893, and Charlotte July 27, 1891. Of the children Esta Ella Luse (Estella) lived on the farm after she married Frank Cottrell on Dec. 16, 1891.

Jacob and Charlotte (Martin) Luse

She was born July 13, 1963 and died Jan. 24, 1907. Frank, born Nov. 12, 1858, died Mar. 3, 1912. They had one daughter, Pearl Genevieve, born July 11, 1898. Genevieve married Raymond Neal, born Nov. 1, 1897, on July 22, 1919. They lived on the family farm for ten years, and two children were born to them during this time; Mary, Apr. 30, 1923, and Margaret, Dec. 3, 1926. They left the farm in 1929 and moved to Greencastle, where they had a third child, a son; Robert, Nov. 7, 1933. Raymond became a successful athletic coach and professor at DePauw University. He retired in 1954 and became postmaster at Greencastle for several years. He died Nov. 25, 1977. Genevieve is now 90 years old and living in a retirement home in Greencastle. Mary married Mark Pickel, born June 17, 1922, on June 17, 1947. They moved to the Luse farm in 1954, with two children, Frank, born Jan. 21, 1949, and Carolyn, born June 22, 1952. They later had two more daughters; Nancy, born May 29, 1955, and Barbara Jean, born June 1, 1958. They remained on the Luse farm until 1978, when they retired from farming and moved to Crawfordsville. Again a tenant family lives on the farm. Who knows, perhaps, in later years a descendant of the original family will again live there. It has been honored as a homestead farm, having been in the same family over 100 years. *Submitted by Mary Pickel*

JOHN DEE AND CHERYL DELENE WHALEN LUZADER

John and Cheryl are residents of South Union Township, Montgomery Co., IN. John is employed by R.R. Donnelley & Sons. He also farms 130 acres in western Ripley Township, Montgomery County and eastern Jackson Township, Fountain Co., IN. Cheryl is employed by Schenck Breeding Farms, Waynetown, IN.

John was born Dec. 14, 1944 to William Dennis and Cora Inez Campbell Luzader while they lived in Jackson Township, Fountain Co., IN. When he was a month old they moved to the Jesse White farm, now the Bill Edwards farm, south of Alamo, Ripley Township. At six years of age the family moved to the north edge of Alamo where he lived until he was married.

Tracey, John, Aaron, Cheryl Luzader

John has two sisters and one brother Martha Kay Swick, Linda Lee Meek and Thomas Jay Luzader.

John attended Alamo School for 12 years graduating in 1962.

Cheryl was born at Crawfordsville, Nov. 11, 1946 to William Keith (1917-1984) and Thelma Claudine Graves Whalen. She has one sister Carol Leeann Kline and one brother William Keith Whalen Jr.

Cheryl graduated from Waynetown High School in 1964. Cheryl's parents both graduated from Crawfordsville High School. Her father was also a graduate of Wabash College of Crawfordsville. He was a teacher in the Montgomery County and Boone County school systems for several years. Cheryl's mother, Claudine still lives in Waynetown.

John and Cheryl were married Aug. 2, 1964 and moved to Crawfordsville. They moved to their present home two miles south of Crawfordsville in May 1971. They have two children, Tracy Marie born Aug. 1, 1966 and John Aaron born June 8, 1971. Tracy is a Senior at Indiana University. Aaron is a Senior at Southmont High School.

John and Cheryl's farm operation contains 40 acres that were purchased by Moses Denman Mar. 4, 1856, great-grandfather of John's grandmother Myrtle Luzader.

Grandparents of John were: William Harry (1894-1981) and Myrtle Blanche Payton (1894-1980) Luzader; Andrew Spinning (1885-1974) and Flo Smith (1890-1965) Campbell Jr.

Cheryl's grandparents were: Walter Willis (1885-1960) and Edna Gertrude McVay (1886-1955) Whalen; Charles Lee (1891-1978) and Ruth Lee Long (1890-1974) Graves.

WILLIAM DENNIS AND CORA INEZ CAMPBELL LUZADER

William Dennis (Bill) Luzader was born Oct. 6, 1920 northeast of Alamo in Ripley Township, Montgomery Co., IN. He is the son of William Harry and Myrtle B. Payton Luzader. He has one brother, Earl Lowell (1916-). He attended schools at Waynetown, Crawfordsville, and Alamo, graduating from Alamo High School in 1939.

Cora Inez Campbell was born Apr. 24, 1921 to Andrew S. and Flo Smith Campbell on a farm northeast of Covington, IN. When she was five they moved to the Boord homestead 1-1/2 miles west of Stone Bluff, IN where she lived until she was married. Inez has two brothers and two sisters. Robert (1913-1981), Ray (1915-), Ruth (1919-), and Louise (1926-). She attended Stone Bluff grade school and graduated from Veedersburg High School in 1938.

Bill and Inez were married Nov. 20, 1941 in Montgomery County and went to housekeeping two miles south of Alamo, IN. In 1943 they moved to the Ruby Owens farm in Fountain Co., IN. January 1945 they moved to the Jesse White Farm 1-1/2 miles south of Alamo. January 1951 they moved to the north edge of Alamo. Bill worked at R.R. Donnelley and Sons, Raybestos, and Indiana Farm Bureau Seed Co. at Crawfordsville. He was a livestock trucker and farmer. They have four children.

1. Martha Kay (Mar. 17, 1943) graduated from Alamo High School in 1961. On Aug. 25, 1963 she married Marvin Lee Swick (Sept. 16, 1942). He is employed at R.R. Donnelley and Sons. She is a teacher's aide at North Montgomery High School. They have five children; Brian Lee (1964), Monica Sue (1966), Dale Andrew (1969), Daryl Wayne (1972), and Joseph Michael (1974). Also four grandchildren; Sarah E. Swick (1986), Amanda R. Swick (1987), Joanie K. Swick (1989), and Barbara N. Swick (1987).

2. John Dee (Dec. 14, 1944), graduated from Alamo High School in 1962 and works at R.R. Donnelley and Sons. August 2, 1964 he married Cheryl Delene Whalen (Nov. 11, 1946). They have two children; Tracy Marie (1966), and John Aaron (1971), and live two miles south of Crawfordsville, IN.

3. Linda Lee (May 24, 1947) graduated from

Alamo High School in 1965 and went to work for Indiana Bell at Crawfordsville and Bloomington, IN. On May 9, 1981 she married Earl Meek (Apr. 17, 1934) an employee of Western Electric, now retired. He has two children; Gayle (1957), and Brian (1959) and one grandson, Joshua Adams (1988).

4. Thomas Jay (Sept. 15, 1956) attended school at Alamo, Waveland and graduated from Southmont Junior and Senior High in 1974. In 1978 he graduated from Purdue University with a B.S. in Industrial Engineering and now works for Eaton/Cutler-Hammer at Lincoln, IL, where he lives. He has one son Matther Thomas (1981) and a step-daughter, Christina Bretney (1979).

Bill and Inez moved in 1975 to a farm two miles south of Alamo that they purchased in 1965.

Bill retired in 1982 and is taking life easy.

WILLIAM HARRY AND MYRTLE BLANCHE PAYTON LUZADER

William Harry Luzader was born Mar. 26, 1894 in Ripley Township, Montgomery County and lived his entire life in Montgomery County. He was the son of Edward Sherman (1865-1940) and Isa Mae McClure Luzader (1873-1960). He was the oldest of four children; the others being Lloyd (1898-1985), Iva (1900-1943), and Paul (1902-1984). Harry married Myrtle Blanche Payton (1894-1980) on Aug. 31, 1913. She was the daughter of Charles E. (1864-1948) and Jemima Angeline Etter Payton (1869-1947). Myrtle had two brothers; Clifford (May 17 - Nov. 7, 1897) and Clarence (1898-1973) and two sisters; Mary A. Selby (1890-1973) and Leona Bushong (1903-1930).

Harry and Myrtle had two sons, Earl Lowell (1916-) and William Dennis (1920-).

Mr. and Mrs. Wm. Harry Luzader taken 1963, 50th wedding anniversary

They resided at Waynetown, Crawfordsville and in 1941 bought and moved to the Payton farm south of Alamo; this farm being in the family since 1856. The farm now belongs to their son, William D. and grandson, John Dee Luzader. Harry and Myrtle continued to live there until her death Sept. 28, 1980. He died Nov. 25, 1981 at the home of his son, Earl. At their death they had two sons, seven grandchildren, 13 great-grandchildren, and one great-great-grandson.

Harry was an active farmer, having served as a director of the Montgomery County Farm Bureau Co-op. They were both members of the Alamo Christian Church and Harry was Past Master and a 50-year member of the Alamo Masonic Lodge, No. 144. Myrtle was a Past Worthy Matron and a 50-year member of the Alamo OES 498. In their later years they spent the winter months in Longwood, FL and the fall months in Manistee, MI.

ROBERT LYON

Robert Lyon born in Scotland, came to live in or near a small village called New Market in Ontario, Canada. I believe he was married after he settled there, to Easter O'Brian. They had six children. John Lyon, Charles Lyon, James Lyon, William Lyon, Robert Lyon and Rebecca Lyon.

Richard Simms was born in Stafford Co., VA of English descent around 1720. He was married to Elizabeth Bridwell, Oct. 15, 1750; to this union was born five children.

Bill Lyon May 1974

Richard Simms Jr., Mar. 13, 1751-death unknown; James Simms, Apr. 16, 1752-1806; Presley Simms, February 1753-1852; Daniel Simms, unknown; and Elizabeth Simms, unknown.

Presley Simms married Nancy Bridwell, date unknown, Presley served five years in the Revolutionary War and two years in the War of 1812. To this union ten children were born. Presley Simms Jr., unknown; Daniel Simms, unknown; Jesse Simms, 1790-unknown; Elizabeth Simms, unknown; Mary Simms, unknown; Langthorn Simms, 1798-unknown; Lucy Simms, 1799-1847; Charles Simms, 1800-1876; Burwell Simms, 1812-unknown; and George Simms, 1814-1903.

George Simms was born in Stafford Co., VA, June 18, 1814. He came to Indiana in 1827. He resided in Montgomery County seven miles northwest of Crawfordsville. George was married to Elizabeth Vester, April 1857. To this union were born seven children. Jacob Simms, Ida Simms, Mary E. Simms, Eliza Simms, Enoch Simms, Lewis Simms and Emma Simms.

William Lyon came to Cherry Grove, IN, June 14, 1871. He married Emma Simms, Apr. 20, 1878. To this union was born four children. Wilbert Lyon, Ora Lyon, Bertha Mabel Lyon and infant daughter.

Ora Lyon was born Nov. 19, 1883, in Coal Creek Township. He married Carrie Conrad, Sept. 9, 1903. To this union was born 12 children. Raymond Lyon - he was a math teacher in Montgomery County, Dorothy, Delbert, Verna - she retired from teaching at Purdue, Harold, Elva, Mabel, Albert, William, Robert, Lawrence and Emily Jane.

William Dan Lyon was born Aug. 22, 1922. He married Francis Lampkin, May 6, 1945. One daughter, Bonita, was born. August 22, 1951, he married his second wife, Juanita Pullen Hall. To this union was born two children. David Rick Lyon, Deborah Kay Lyon and Joy Yvonne Hall (stepdaughter).

Bonita Lyon married Darrel Durnil, Jan. 26, 1963. He died Sept. 25, 1966. To this union one son and one daughter was born. Julie Ann Durnil and Bryan Durnil.

David Rick Lyon married Deborah Wright. To this union two sons were born. Dale Lyon and Brad Lyon.

Deborah K. Lyon married Donald Miller. One son was born, Donald Aaron Jr. Her second marriage was to Ronald Evans, November 1986. One son was born to this union, Nathan Kyle Evans in June of 1988.

Joy Y. Hall married married Price Johnson, Feb. 4, 1966. To this union was born one girl and one boy. Tammy Johnson and Marty Johnson.

Tammy married Kris George, December 1987. One son was born, Reuben James.

Marty Johnson is not married.

Julie Ann Durnil married Bob Palmer. Three children, two girls and a boy. Darrel Durnil, Kristy Palmer and Ashley Palmer.

HARRY C. MACHLEDT

Harry Machledt was a funeral director in Waveland for 38 years. He was the son of John and Ella Machledt, born Dec. 24, 1891 at Montezuma, IN.

He attended school and graduated from Montezuma School, then to the Cincinnati school of embalming. He served his apprenticeship with Hugh Montgomery in Montezuma and Rockville. In 1915 he purchased the funeral director and Furniture business in Waveland from Frank Kritz, where he remained the rest of his life.

Mr. Machledt married Hazel Hendrix, daughter of a prominent Indianapolis family, on June 13, 1913. They had two sons. John H. graduated from Waveland High School and Ohio State University, graduating with high honors. He became a doctor, with his residence at Greenwood, IN. William F. also graduated from Waveland High School, Wabash College and Embalming School in Indianapolis. His last business was in West Lebanon and Williamsport.

Harry was a descendant of Bertram Machledt of Wainer Province, Saxony, who migrated from Dienstad, Germany, travelled across the ocean to America to the port of New Orleans, up the Mississippi River then the Wabash River to Montezuma in 1847. Five generations of the Machledt family made their homes in Montezuma. The first generation to arrive were bridge and canal builders. The second built bridge and railroad builders. The third built brick yards and prospered greatly after the Chicago fire, shipping brick on the nearby railroad to help rebuild the city of Chicago.

Harry's grandfather was a coffin maker at Montezuma, using part of a flat above a business there for making coffins and part as a living quarters.

Harry died Nov. 25, 1948.

DAVID AND VIRGINIA MAHARRY

The Maharry family has lived in Crawfordsville for ten years. Dave teaches Computer Science at Wabash College and Giny has worked as a librarian at the Public Library and is currently employed at Lilly Library at Wabash.

Dave, the third child of John and Eleanor Haley Maharry, was born in Zanesville, OH in 1943. They lived in Youngstown, OH, until John's death in 1959, when David and his mother moved to Oak Park, IL. Dave returned to Ohio for college where he met Ginny.

Ginny, also born in 1943, was raised in North Canton, OH. She is also the youngest of three children, the daughter of Dewey and Alice Kreiling Yonally.

Dave and Ginny were married in the summer of 1965 after graduating from Muskingum College, and soon moved to Lawrence, KS where Dave began graduate work in physics at the University of Kansas, and Ginny began teaching first and second grade in a rural school.

In 1968, John Andrew was born in Lawrence. Ginny became manager of married student housing at KU in order to be at home with the new baby. After three more years of study and research, Dave completed the Ph.D. in theoretical nuclear physics.

After spending all their lives in the midwest, they hoped for a move to either the coast or the mountains, but the best job offer came from Indiana! They settled in Franklin where Dave began teachng at Franklin College in 1971.

1972 brought Jeffrey Scott, a real Hoosier, into the world and the family was complete. They remained in Franklin until 1979 when they moved to 617 East Main Street in Crawfordsville.

In 1981 Ginny completed a Masters Degree from Purdue and began her library career. John will soon graduate from Grinnell College, in Iowa, with a degree in mathematics and Jeff will graduate from CHS with plans to study biology.

The family is active in sports, music, and First Christian Church.

MAHORNEY FAMILY
HOW WE GOT TO MONTGOMERY COUNTY

James B. Mahorney fought in the American Revolution. He served in Col. Buford's regiment in the battles of Camden, Cowpens, Guildord, Eutaw Springs and Ninety Six, where he was wounded. He was discharged at Winchester, VA in 1783.

He married Elizabeth Harris. They had four children, all of whom were born in Shelby Co., KY. One of the off spring was my great-great grandfather, Bennett Mahorney.

Bennett Mahorney married Mary Fisher. They had four children. One was my great-grandfather, Zachariah Fisher Mahorney, who was born in Washington Co., IN Aug. 8, 1818. In 1936 he came to Montgomery Co., IN. In 1840 he married Catherine Harshbarger. They had 11 children. One was my grandfather, Daniel Milton Mahorney.

Daniel went to the local schools. He then went to Toronto University in Toronto, Canada, where he was graduated with a degree in Veterinary Med. He practiced in Liberty, IN before coming back to the homestead to farm and take care of his mother. He married Laura Busenbark in 1896. They had two sons, George Z. Mahorney born Mar. 28, 1897 and Samuel L. Mahorney born Sept. 12, 1898.

My father, George Z. Mahorney attended local schools. He married Orthella Marie Johnson May 2, 1918. They farmed the homestead. They had two children, Alice Marie Mahorney, who was graduated from Butler University with a degree in education and taught Junior High School in Indianapolis, IN for 24 years before retiring in 1985.

I, Samuel Milton Mahorney, graduated from Ladoga High School. I worked in Speedway at Allisons before the war, I served in the USMC in the Infantry and VMTB131 from Southern Central Pacific to Okinawa and then home to farm.

I married Mary Catherine Brown Nov. 22, 1946. We have three children, Jeanne Clair Mahorney Hamernik, Daniel Joseph Bennett Mahorney and Patrick Amond Mahorney. All three graduated from the Ladoga Schools. Jeanne graduated from Indiana State University with a degree in elementary education and attended Indiana University where she got a Masters Degree in Special Education. She teaches in Greenwood, IN. She is married to David Hamernik. She has three stepchildren, Stephanie, Kevin, and Becky Hamernik. Daniel J.B. Mahorney works as a mechanic carpenter, and farmer. He served in the Army one year in Germany and one year at Quang Tri in Vietnam.

Patrick Amond Mahorney attended Danville Jr. College at Danville, IL. He received his Assoc. Degree in Agriculture. He is employed in farming in Montogmery County. He married Carol Morris July 3, 1982. They have two children, Cassidy Owen Mahorney and Samantha Ann Mahorney.

EDGAR C. MANGES

Edgar Manges was a prosperous farmer in the Whitesville community. He had a mechanical mind. In 1901 the Whitesville Cooperative Telephone Co. was formed and Edgar became a stockholder and director. As he was still living at home he put a telephone in his parent's home. At first his mother would not talk over it. He served many years as Secretary and Treas.

Edgar's first automobile was a Carter Car bought in 1909 cost $1850.00. It would run 25 miles per hour. It had acetylene lights. It had no gears but was driven by friction drive. If moisture or dirt got on the wheels, one would have to clean them before going on. This meant these wheels would slip badly on bad roads. There was a law in those early days that if a car met a horse driven vehicle and the horse was afraid the driver of the car had to get out and lead the horse past the car. In 1914 Edgar had this Carter Car made into a truck and he bought a four cylinder Buick.

Edgar and Nellie Manges

Edgar was a 1/4 owner of a threshing machine until combines came into being. For 30 years he was a dealer in fencing, implement business along with help from family he farmed 300 acres of land. He was a Charter member of the Farm Bureau.

His parents were William and Anna Kessler Manges and he was born Sept. 26, 1876 in a log cabin near Whitesville. According to his grade card of Mar. 17, 1885 he had the average grade of 96.

He graduated from grade school at Whitesville on May 28, 1895. Each graduate had to write and deliver an address at their commencement. According to the printed program there were four teachers. Music by the Whitesville Orchestra and ten graduates.

Edgar graduated from the Crawfordsville Business College on Mar. 10, 1899. He roomed on Jefferson Street and while there he met Nellie Linn who was attending Crawfordsville High School. He married Nellie on Oct. 29, 1902 at her parents' home near Mace, IN.

Edgar and Nellie built an eight room house plus pantry, bath with tub only and porches near Whitesville. Most of the lumber for the house was from the timber on the farm. Total cost of the house including carpenter, furnace, ditching, cutting logs and hauling and digging cellar was $2050.79. The barn cost $600.96 and digging a well $185.00. Articles and furniture for housekeeping was $194.99.

They were active members of the Whitesville Church.

They enjoyed several trips to Chicago-International Livestock Show World's Fair visit to Virginia.

Children: Cline b. Oct. 28, 1903 m. Margueritte Loveless-Rachael Peterson; Lucile b. Feb. 3, 1905 m. Dwight Reeves; Edith b. Nov. 3, 1906 m. Merton Kistler; Esther b. Sept. 22, 1908 m. Laurance Rager; Ethel b. July 11, 1910 m. Clayton Terry; Edna b. Feb. 13, 1912 m. Lloyd Gosner; William b. Dec. 3, 1914 m. Betty Taylor; Harold b. May 1, 1917 m. Mary Shephard; Walter b. Dec. 12, 1919 m. Margery Abbott.

Nellie died Feb. 6, 1935 and Edgar died Sept. 22, 1969. They are buried in Oak Hill Cemetery, Crawfordsville, IN. *Submitted by Edith Manges Kistler*

WILLIAM J. MANGES

William Manges' great grandfather John Manges came from Germany to Virginia. William grew up on a farm near Haymakertown, VA. Here he was born on Jan. 23, 1842 to Daniel and Mary Gish Manges. He was born in a small house but later moved with his parents to a large brick home.

He fought in the Civil War as a Confederate soldier and was in the Battle of Gettysburg. His parents were not slave owners so he did not agree with the Confederacy so he escaped as soon as possible and came to Indiana, walking a big part of the way. He told his son that a woman took him in one night and offered him the hospitality of her home. He was a Pvt. Co. 28 VA Inf. (Archives).

William and Anna Manges

He arrived with only 50¢ and worked as a farm hand in Scott Township. He lived with William Frame during the Tornado of 1866. The roof of the Frame brick house was blown off but none were hurt as they all went to the basement when they saw the storm coming. There were three killed in the community.

William Manges helped make the brick that was used in the building of the Bethel Dunkard Church House in 1870 near Ladoga, IN. It is 40 feet x 70 feet and would seat 800 people.

William Manges married Anna Kessler on Dec. 15, 1870 by Rev. R.H. Miller at the home of the bride's parents. Anna was born in Botetourt Co., VA on Mar. 3, 1847. They lived in the Kessler home a few months until William bought 80 acres of land near Whitesville, IN most of which was timber. Whitesville was platted on Sept. 1, 1862.

William first built a log house and later in 1878 a new home was built. William was a prosperous farmer. He died June 18, 1919 and Anna died July 20, 1928.

Children 1. Edgar C. Manges b. Sept. 26, 1876. 2. Minnie Manges Davidson b. June 29, 1879. *Compiled by Edith Manges Kistler*

MARSHALL FAMILY

The Marshall family has played a substantial role in the growth of the town of Darlington. Flavius Marshall and his wife, Sarah Armstrong, moved into their newly purchased home in Darlington in the year 1874. The family from whom they purchased their home was also named Marshall, but it is not known if buyers and sellers were related. Sarah's home had been in Tipton, IN; Flavius' was in Howard Co., IN. Her parentage is known; his is not.

Sarah Armstrong Marshall's father was William Armstrong, born in Northumberland County, Great Britain. He became a naturalized citizen of the U.S. in Ripley County in 1842. On his naturalization document, he swore to "renounce and abjure all allegience and fidelity to every foreign...State and Sovereignty...and particularly to Victoria, the first, the present Queen of Great Britain." He had, by his testimony, arrived in the U.S. "sometime in the year 1832." He was a shoemaker.

The union of Sarah and Flavius produced seven children. Agnus and Mamie died in infancy; Willie, at age 20; and Martha, at age 34 in the flu epidemic in 1917. The other three lived long and productive lives. Charles died at age 79; Minnie, at age 87; Edith, at 89.

Education and artistic expression were emphasized in the Marshall home. The family was very musical. Edith sang beautiful harmony; Martha was a singer highly sought after as a soloist. Charles was a baritone soloist, directed the Methodist Church choir, played cornet in local and state bands, and played the piano by ear. Each of the children had a highly developed sense of humor. The Marshalls had lots of fun. The house usually was full; for at times through the years, Sarah offered room and board to "professionals" such as the local teachers. This supplemented Flavius' income as a salesman. A large edition was added to their house in 1901 to accommodate a large family and roomers.

Minnie, the eldest, was a teacher and educator all of her adult life, teaching in Darlington from 1896 to 1900. She was later a teacher of teachers. She married Adolph Neumannn and had one child, Charlotte. They lived in St. Paul, MN. Charlotte inherited the family musical talent and became a fine pianist. She married Roy Larson, also of St. Paul, and continues to live there after his death. She was an educator like her mother, retiring from teaching only a few years ago.

Edith was a member of the first Darlington High School graduating class in 1899. She also became a teacher and taught in the township and Darlington Schools for 11 years. She married Ernest Weesner and lived with him in Dallas and Denver before returning to settle on the Weesner farm on the edge of Darlington. She became very active in the community and worked as a reporter for the *Darlington Herald* and the *Journal-Review*. She served as editor and compiler of historical information for *Darlington Yesterday and Today* published by her brother, Charles, during the town's centennial celebration in 1936. *Submitted by: Janet Marshall Boeh.*

CHARLES & PAULINE (COX) MARSHALL

Charles, the youngest child of Sarah and Flavius, graduated from Darlington High School in 1903. He had many interests; music, sports, politics (Republican), and a basic curiosity about how things worked. The newspaper business was a perfect career for this man who wanted to make things better. He and Edith purchased *The News*, a local paper, in 1908, published it for a few years, then sold it. Charles then worked on the Darlington *Echo* and a St. Paul newspaper before purchasing the *Echo* and changing its name to *The Darlington Herald*. He was publisher and editor of the *Herald* for 28 years. During this time he was Township Trustee for eight years, served as President of the Town Board for several terms, and spearheaded many town improvements. He was also owner and operator of the Sunshine Theater, Darlington's only moving picture theatre. He opened it during the days of the silent film, hiring a local pianist to improvise appropriately for the action on the screen. He continued to operated the Sunshine until the mid 50s. During this time the interior burned out twice; each time he rebuilt.

A fire also destroyed the *Herald* office building in the late 30s. He relocated and continued to print the paper and do job printing with his new offset press, the newest device on the market at that time. Ill health forced the sale of the newspaper business. Charlie, always an innovator, then installed in the vacated building the newest idea in food preservation, the frozen food locker.

In 1927 Charles married Pauline Cox, also a Darlington native, daughter of Denton and Bertha Cox. She was a graduate of Darlington High School and Indiana University. Their wedding took place in Memphis, TN where she was teaching at LeMoyne College, an all Negro school. In addition to teaching eight years before her marriage, she taught 11 years at Ladoga High School after her children were grown. She wrote articles for and edited the *Herald* for a number of years. Her weekly column, "For The Spirit" was highly regarded. She was very active in the work of the Methodist Church at the local, district, and conference levels. She died in 1988 at the age of 90.

Charles and Pauline's children are Janet and John. Janet graduated from Darlington High School and De Pauw University, earning her Master's Degree in dance from Illinois State University. She taught at Indiana State, Illinois Wesleyan, and Illinois State Universities. Her husband is Jack Boeh, an engineer with General Electric Company in Bloomington, IL. where Janet is now selling real estate. Their children are Sarah, Lisa, and John.

John Armstrong Marshall, who now makes his home in Glendale, CA, is a graduate of Crawfordsville High School and Northwestern University. There, majoring in radio and television, he acquired the professionalism to go on to a career in television with his own children's shows in Palm Beach, FL and Los Angeles. He became successful acting in commercials, later producing commercials in Los Angeles and Phoenix. He is now founder and director of the Right On Program which is dedicated to helping individuals overcome compulsive behavior, particularly, drug abuse. He is also a writer of poetry, television scripts, etc. He is an entrepreneur like his father—in a different place and time. John and his wife, Diane, have four children: Cheri, Cindy, Jennifer, and John.

The Marshall family's tie to Montgomery County, however small, still exists through the ownership of the family home. Janet and John jointly own the 130+ year old house and try to maintain it in near original condition. It remains a personal museum of the Marshall and Cox family roots. *Submitted by Janet Marshall Boeh*

EVI MARTIN

On Feb. 4, 1828 Evi Martin and family moved into the cabin he had built. It was the fifth cabin built in Walnut Township. He made a bedstead of two poles, one post, two auger holes and bed cord brought with him from Cincinnati.

Evi Martin was born Feb. 20, 1796 on Mill Creek, ten miles north of Cincinnati, OH. He was the son of James Martin who married a Miss Wilson.

Evi married Anna Mills on Aug. 19, 1819. Anna was born near Lebanon, OH on Oct. 4, 1799.

Evi and Anna moved to Union Township, Montgomery Co., IN on Nov. 26, 1827. His parents James Martin and wife already lived there. The father is buried at Thorntown, IN.

Evi gave six sons to fight in the Civil War and all were fortunate to return.

In Union Township they toiled ten years without purchasing a nail and got 60¢ a bu. for wheat they raised while butter and eggs had no market price at all.

Evi soon was attacked with a light form of asthma and for three continuous years he was unable to lie down to sleep. During this time they went to Iowa and lived with sons and in 1871 returned to Indiana to make their permanent home with son J.M. Martin.

Children: 1. Margaret Martin; 2. Samuel Martin; 3. James Mills Martin; 4. Abia Martin; 5. Issac Martin; 6. Evi Martin; 7. Marion Martin; 8. William Martin; 9. Frank Martin; 10. Harrison Martin; 11. Jacob Martin.

In later years Evi sold his farm and put the money $3200.00 in a bank and the bank failed. A savings of a life time was lost. In 1830 they had united with the Regular Baptist Church. Worship was held in the Martin Home.

In his prime days Evi supported Whig Principles, but later became a radical Republican. In 1881 Evi and Anna were the oldest couple in Walnut Township and had lived together in happiness for 61 years. They are buried at Union Cemetery, Walnut Township, Montgomery County. Evi died July 15, 1883. Anna Mills Martin died on Sept. 11, 1881. *Compiled by Edith Manges Kistler*

JAMES MILLS MARTIN

In 1889 or 1890 James M. Martin donated ground and the Union Presbyterian Church was moved to this ground near where the cemetery is now. James had joined this church in 1858 when it was located on Porter land.

James M. Martin, Margaret Ann (Bratton) Martin

James M. was born Aug. 28, 1824 in Miami Co., OH. He married Margaret Ann Bratton on Jan. 17, 1849 by Rev. James Settle at the home of her parents, John and Polly Bratton in Walnut Township, Montgomery Co., IN. She joined the Union Church in 1843.

James died of pneumonia on his 43rd wedding anniversary Jan. 17, 1892. Margaret died Nov. 14, 1906 and was 81 years of age. They are buried at Mace, IN.

Children 1. James Martin - died in infancy; 2. Mary Anna Martin - called Anna and married John W. Linn. Great grandmother of the Manges children. 3. Charles Martin (no children but married Mollie ___); 4. Elizabeth Martin (Mears) had children but no grandchildren.; 5. Newton Martin - married but had no children. *Submitted by Edith Kistler*

THOMAS MASON

Thomas MASON was born Dec. 16, 1760, ca Delaware, d. Oct. 4, 1846, Montgomery Co., IN, m. Apr. 17, 1794, Mary Dawson, b. Aug. 17, 1778, d. May 3, 1837, Montgomery Co., IN. Buried in Old Town Cemetery.

SERVICE: Pvt., enlisted under Capt. John Rhoades, Col. Hall's Regt in 1778, Dela Line and served until the Fall of 1782. Revolutionary War.

Bought Lot 40, Tiffon Twp., West Union, OH for $25.00, May 17, 1804 and moved to Montgmery Co., IN to live with or near their son, "as much to gratify my wife as anything else", according to the request to transfer his pension payments from Adams Co., OH to Lafayette, IN., date Dec. 27, 1837. Pension number S 36691.

CHILDREN: John; Priscilla; William D, b. June 10, 1801, d. June 15, 1875, m. Nancy Lambert, b. Jan. 2, 1817, d. Oct. 3, 1895, Montogmery Co., IN; Alice Sarah "Sally", b. May 3, 1803, d. Sept. 20, 1857, m. Robert McGovney, b. Oct. 3, 1802, d. May 15, 1879, Montgomery Co., IN; Eliza, b. July 28, 1807, d. Jan. 15, 1848, Montgomery Co., IN; Thomas Jefferson, b. Dec. 16, 1809, d. Apr. 15, 1875, m. Feb. 8, 1842 Melinda Smith, m. 2nd Apr. 19, 1853 Sarah Cox, b. Nov. 25, 1823, d. Dec. 3, 1878, Montgomery County; Polly (Mary?) b. 1815, m. William W. Sanders who was killed at Nashville Dec. 15, 1864 while with 86th Reg., Co. K, Indiana volunteers; Mahlon Jackson "Jack" b. Mar. 23, 1817, d. Feb. 25, 1884, m. Apr. 2, 1852 Esther Jane Reynolds, b. 1834, d. Dec. 31, 1919, Montgomery Co., IN; Margaret, b. Apr. 30, 1818, d. Dec. 18, 1878, m. James Cook, b. Apr. 6, 1815, d. June 26, 1890, Montgomery Co., IN; Wilson Campbell, b. Jan. 18, 1821, d. Dec. 18, 1879, m. Sept. 2, 1860 Sarah Elizabeth Clossin, b. Oct. 23, 1844. She married second, Levi Martin Aug. 9, 1905. *By Eulalia Mason*

WILSON CAMPBELL MASON

Wilson Campbell Mason, born Jan. 18, 1821 in Adams Co., OH was the youngest of ten children born to Thomas and Mary Dawson Mason. Thomas a Revolutionary War veteran, moved his family to Montgomery Co, IN in 1837.

Wilson served during the Mexican War as Sgt. and Color Bearer in Co. K, 1st Regt., Indiana Volunteers, with Gen. Manson. He was discharged Nov. 15, 1846.

In 1849, he and a friend headed West to strike it rich in the California Gold Rush, but the story handed down says the "friend" took leave with the "find" shortly before they arrived back home.

Before Wilson left for the war, he had fallen in love with Mary Ann Finley, but while he was gone, she married Alexander Clossin Jan. 11, 1844, and their daughter Sarah Elizabeth was born Oct. 23, 1844. Wilson vowed that if couldn't have the mother, he'd wait for the daughter to grow up and he did. They were married Sept. 9, 1860 in Montgomery Co., IN. He was almost 40 and she was 16.

Their children were Perry Wickliff b. 1861, d. Nov. 9, 1950, m. Dec. 24, 1885 Mate (Mata, Mary) Edwards, b. 1870, d. 1925 Montgomery Co., IN; William A., b. 1864, d. 1944, m. Annetta Lowes, b. 1866, d. 1937, Montgomery Co., IN; Mary A. "Molly", b. Nov. 6, 1866, d. Jan. 15, 1909, m. Apr. 26, 1885 in Tippecanoe Co., IN to Milton "Milt" Chesterson, b. May 29, 1854, d. Nov. 11, 1936, Montgomery Co., IN; Findley P., b. July 14, 1869, d. Nov. 13, 1877, Montgomery Co., IN; Walter Overtin, b. Oct 30, 1872 in Tippecanoe Co., IN, just north of New Richmond, d. Aug. 6, 1947 in Montgomery Co., IN, m. Sept. 4, 1894 Estella "Dollie" Warbinton, b. Jan. 28, 1872, d. Mar. 27, 1910. *By Eulalia Mason*

WILLIAM "SAILOR JACK" MATHERS

William Mathers was born on Mar. 1, 1837 in Scotland. He enlisted in the British Navy at the age of 17. He served in the British Navy until 1859. He came to America in 1860. On Sept. 30, 1861, William Mathers enlisted in the U.S. Navy. He was involved with the blockades of Charleston, SC and New Orleans, LA. He was discharged on July 10, 1866. He later re-enlisted in the Navy and served until he was injured in a fall and was discharged.

He came to Crawfordsville in the 1880s. He was a member of McPherson Post #7 G.A.R. in Crawfordsville. He was known around Crawfordsville as "Sailor Jack."

In the 1920s, William "Sailor Jack" Mathers went to live at the Indiana Soldiers and Sailors Home in Lafayette, IN where he died on Feb. 4, 1929. He was buried in the Soldier's Home Cemetery. *Submitted by: Andrew Keith Houk, Jr.*

WILLIAM ZEDECK McBEE

William Zedeck McBee came to Madison Township, Montgomery County by horseback, from West Virginia, in 1852. He was born near Petersburg, Grant Co., WV, Mar. 27, 1830. He was the ninth child of Evans McBee and Sarah Tolbert McBee. His brother, Charles, also came to Madison Township, Montgomery County one year later. William married Mary Elizabeth Shobe, born Mar. 20, 1837 in Ross Co., OH. She came to Montgomery County in 1840 and married William Aug. 23, 1855.

The crossroads four miles east of Linden, on the Linden-Colfax Road is known as McBee corner. William Z. McBee farmed south of McBee corner and his brother Charles, farmed north of McBee corner. One of W.Z. McBee's sons, W.T. McBee, and his wife built a house on the northeast corner of the crossroads. The house is still occupied by one of William Z.'s great-grandsons, Marvin McBee and his wife.

William Z. and his family were active members of the Kirkpatrick Methodist Church. He held an office in the church.

William Z. and Mary had four sons and three daughters. The sons were: Walter Henry, Martin Zedeck, Robert Franklin, and William Thomas. The daughters were: Mary Olive (Ollie), Minnie Lee, and Sarah Melinda (Sallie). Robert Franklin, a fireman on the Nickle Plate railroad, was killed in a horrible train wreck on July 8, 1898.

1905 50th Wedding Anniversary picture William, Mary Elizabeth McBee. Left to right, row one: Isaac C. McBee, Frank (James (Franklin) McBee. Row two: William Joseph McBee (Bill Mac), Deborah McBee-married James Cambell, Verna Lee Scheek married Clyde Leisurre, Minnie Susan McBee, Nancy Elizabeth McBee married Harry (David Harrison) Montgomery, Elsie Lavina McBee married Ralph Parker, Mary Scheek married Johnson, Lena Maud McBee married Walter J. Hoss, Vena Olive McBee married Harold Everson (deceased) - Hal Turnipseed, Mary Josephine McBee married James Irons. Row three: Sarah Melissa (Sally) McBee married Hunter Dain, Olive McBee Hart, Walter Henry McBee, William Z. McBee, Frank Dain, Mary Elizabeth McBee, Martin Zedic McBee, Minnie McBee Scheek Long. Row four: Hunter Dain, Susan Dunbar McBee, James Hart, Mary Emily (Shotts) McBee, Laura Newkirk McBee, David Long, Georgia McBee married George Fox.

William Z. retired from farming and moved to Linden. He and Mary celebrated their 50th Wedding Anniversary there Aug. 23, 1905. They had their children and 13 grandchildren present at the celebration, also many friends.

William died in 1910 and Mary in 1923. They are buried east of McBee corner in the Ermentrout Cemetery.

Grandchildren of W.Z. McBee who have lived in Montgomery County were; Isaac McBee, Nan McBee Montgomery, Maude McBee Hoss, Elsie McBee Parker, and Minnie McBee. Also William J. McBee, Frank McBee, Vena McBee Turnipseed, Josephine McBee Irons and Debbie McBee Campbell.

Many of their children and grandchildren, descendents of William Z and Mary McBee, still reside in Montgomery County.

FRANCIS T. AND MARJORIE F. McCARTY

Francis McCarty was born to George Henry and Amelia Dale McCarty in Waveland, IN, on Sept. 29, 1908. Marjorie was born to Lester and Zola Himes, Apr. 2, 1915, near Ladoga, IN.

At the age of 14 Francis had a strong feeling that he wanted to become a minister. Upon graduating from Waveland High School, he joined the Browns Valley Missionary Baptist Church and entered Franklin College where he completed his freshman year. In 1930 he accepted an invitation to become pastor of the Browns Valley church, and was ordained Mar. 24, 1931.

He and Marjorie were married in the church Aug. 26, 1934 and moved to Franklin to continue his college course. These were difficult Depression years, and because of the financial requirements it was not until 1939 that he could receive his degree from Franklin.

They became the parents of two sons: Richard Francis, b. Aug. 7, 1935, and Ronald Gene, b. Aug. 22, 1940.

At the beginning of World War II they left Indiana and moved to Boston, MA, where he entered Andover Newton Theological School from which he was graduated in 1945. During this time they served the First Baptist Church in Dorchester, in Greater Boston.

A year after the War ended they moved to Ohio where they spent the next 31 years serving American Baptist Churches in Washington Court House, Columbus and Toledo. They worked together as a team in the ministry and their greatest satisfaction was in seeing churches united, happy, caring and growing.

Upon retirement in 1977, they returned to Montgomery County, built their retirement home on Stanley Drive and became active in the First Baptist Church of Crawfordsville.

GEORGE HENRY McCARTY

George Henry McCarty was born at Waveland, IN on Aug. 6, 1885, the son of Susan McCarty. Orphaned at an early age he was reared in the home of John and Effie Alward. He learned the plastering trade from his step-father and many of the houses in Montgomery and surrounding counties were plastered by him and his sons. One of the more notable plastering jobs was the first unit of Turkey Run Inn. He was known for his honesty and fine work.

Henry married Melia Rardin of Parke County on Dec. 26, 1907 in Bloomingdale, IN. They became the parents of seven children: Francis Theron, b. Sept. 29, 1908; Charles LeRoy, b. Oct. 14, 1910, Mildred Lucille, b. Jan. 21, 1913, Mary Catherine, b. Sept. 27, 1914, Dorothy Helen, b. Sept. 11, 1916; d. Mar. 24, 1959, Maxine Marie, b. Oct. 28, 1919, George Henry, Jr., b. Oct. 18, 1925; d. Jan. 3, 1988.

Al three boys learned the plastering trade from their father, but followed it only part-time.

During the Depression Henry worked as the janitor of Waveland High School for 12 years. After World War II he went back to plastering.

Henry died Oct. 9, 1963; Melia (Amelia) was born Sept. 2, 1888 in Parke County, and died Mar. 2, 1967. Both are buried at Indian Creek Hill Cemetery.

RICHARD AND SHIRLEY McCLAINE

Richard Kent McClaine was born Mar. 26, 1931 to Ezra Breckinridge and Iris Opal Mitcheltree McClaine. Ezra was born Apr. 27, 1906 to Omer A. and Daisy E. Hendryx McClaine at Max, IN in Boone County. He farmed all his married life on 500 acres of the family land at New Ross in Montgomery County. On Oct. 26, 1927 he married Iris Opal Mitcheltree, born Feb. 24, 1907, the daughter of David T. and Mary Anna Pruitt Mitcheltree in Montgomery County. Their family also included James David and Eloise. After the death of Iris on Dec. 28, 1932, Ezra on Oct 2, 1936 at LaPlta, MO, married Pauline Cunningham. They had two children Jackie Leon and Gerold Ezra McClaine. Richard graduated from Ladoga High School and farms the family land and a few years ago he became employed by the Montgomery Highway Department. On Aug. 9, 1953, he married Shirley Lois Richardson.

Shirley was born Dec. 23, 1935 at New Market, Montgomery County to Russell Floyd and Esther

Richard McClaine Family

Vivian Hunt Richardson. Her parents were married July 4, 1929 in Montgomery County. Russell was born Sept. 4, 1905 to Elmer and Minnie Gray Richardson in Hendricks County and worked at Detroit Allison in Indianapolis. Esther was born June 14, 1910 to John and Alice Swisher Hunt at Brownsvalley in Montgomery County. Their family also included Max of New Ross, Robert of Kansas, Carolyn Deere of Crawfordsville, Janet Peters of New Mexico and Pat Stemick of Virginia. Shirley graduated from Green Township School in Parke County. She now works as a salesperson and homemaker. Richard and Shirley now live in Mace and they are the parents of Kathy Lynne born June 13, 1955 and Kimberly Ann born Mar. 28, 1959.

On May 4, 1974 Kathy married John Evans, the son of Grove and Joan Evans and they have one daughter, Tiffany Ann born Dec. 28, 1982 and they live in Chesterfield, MO. Kimberly is the mother of one daughter, Krista Lynne born Nov. 29, 1981. Her history appears elsewhere in this volume.

CAPTAIN E.P. McCLASKEY FAMILY

Ebenezer Patrick McClaskey was born May 3, 1834, son of James and Nancy (Poague) McClaskey, Kentucky natives who settled south of Darlington. James was a farmer, teacher, justice of the peace and trustee.

Eb walked through the woods with his father to Morgan School south of Hazel Peeble's corner where his father was teacher. He, too, became a teacher as did his sister, Martha.

The family was active in the First Methodist Church in these parts, Salem, built in 1828, two blocks East and South to Big Run. The cemetery was the family burial ground.

In 1857 Eb married Elizabeth Cox, daughter of Elijah and Nancy (Brown) Cox. She died in 1860 leaving a son John who died of typhoid in Kansas.

In the Civil War, Eb was Captain of Co. B, 120th Indiana Volunteers. He came to be known locally as the Captain.

In 1870, the Captain married Atlanta Harland, daughter of William and Melvina (McCullough) Harland. Children: William Portlock born 1871 and Joseph Harland, born 1872.

While their father was sheriff the boys attended prep school and entered Wabash College. Will graduated 1894. Boys returned to farm to help the Captain; was three terms a member of State Legislature.

January 1909 Joseph married Nettie Mote, daughter of Washington and Mary Ann (Cox) Mote. His parents moved to Darlington leaving homestead to them. 1910 a son Joe Washington arrived. He was only four years old when his father died of appendicitis. Nettie's brother, Elijah came to help with the farm.

Joe married Clara Loveless Feb. 8, 1930, daughter of Adam and Esther (Peterson) Loveless. Richard Wayne was born 1931. Clara died 1984.

At Joe's, Jersey cows were prized possessions. All the children showed them in 4-H.

Richard married a schoolmate, Janet Sue Hampton, daughter of Cecil and Frieda (Conrad) Hampton. The Walter Moffitt farm was added to McClaskey possession and Richard and Janet made it home. Children: Bryan Wayne, born 1953 and Brenda Sue, 1956. Farming, a dairy, school buses kept everyone busy. Janet worked in Darlington bank. Bryan and Brenda carried on 4-H.

In 1981, Bryan married Pamela Joe Ottenger. The Pickering farm was now added to the land. There are in this household, Heather, who bats a mean ball, Amber who wants stars, and Jamie who loves attention. Pam volunteers for community work. Bryan works at Donnelley's but enjoys running a tractor.

Brenda married Jake Dawson of Morocco where he and his father deal in farm products. Brenda can style your hair from her shop at home. There are two daughters, Stacy, who moves fast, Tara with the lovely Irish name.

WILL McCLASKEY FAMILY

In 1903 Will married Stella Cox, daughter of Franklin and Allie (Morris) Cox. They went to their new farm adjacent to the farm home. Stella loved music and photography; her organ came with her. Children: Alice, 1905, Eb 1907.

In 1911 she contracted malaria; pneumonia followed. She died in September. Will's father moved in to help.

The children walked to Highview school with neighbor children.

Will's specialty was Duroc hogs, good ones. A tub of baby pigs was often behind the stove. They were shown at the county fair.

Grandmother died in 1919; the Cap't in 1920. They had given much to others.

Eb married a classmate, Marihelen Paddack Oct. 17, 1928. To carry on Duroc tradition they had bought six good shoats. They died from eating wild cherry shoots.

In November 1929 baby Marilyn arrived. June 9, 1931 their house burned. Until completion of new house baby slept on the porch swing turned to the wall on a table in the well house.

Joan was born, Nov. 23, 1931, in the new house. Dave, Dec. 17, 1944. Will now became "Dappy" to everybody. Eb and Marilyn were good to share the children. There was a beaten path between their house and the one through the woods.

Alice, DePauw 1928 taught school in Darlington. August 27, 1945 she married a Highview schoolmate, Erving Weesner, left teaching at end of school year. Bob Weesner was born June 26, 1946, John Weesner Jan. 10, 1949, Dave now had playmates. In 4-H Dave took Durocs, Weesner sheep were not a success-changed to woodworking and bugs.

Marilyn married classmate, Glen Harper, teacher, coach, Noblesville his home. Children: Alan Wayne, Noblesville fireman. Married Rebecca Holmes. Children: Jaysi, goes to Europe 1989 with children's choir; Abbie, dances. Susan married Ed Mayhall, Purdue, engineer, home Malaysia. Children: George, Kimberly, Sarah. Neal, Ball State, architect married Nancy Agnew, 1982. Home, Dallas, children: Matthew and Beth Ann. Ann, Purdue, teacher, West Lafayette.

Joan married schoolmate, Fred Dunbar, Navy

Pilot, home Alexandria, VA. Children: Karen, Dave, Douglas all graduates of Virginia Tech. Karen, home, Virginia Beach. Dave, engineer, married Jill Morsey, home Pennsylvania children: Candice, Parker. Douglas, landscaper, married Suzannah Creech.

Dave married Cheryl Bronough, New Ross. Busy in farming, school, community, 4-H. Children: Jeff and Eric carry on traditions.

Amma and Appa were always very special to children and grandchildren. Appa died 1978. On Amma's 80th birthday she walked into Dave's quiet house. Suddenly from all sides little voices were singing, "Happy Birthday Amma." A moving moment! All were there except Susan who called.

John Weesner, lend clerk, computer V.A. Indianapolis. Bob Weesner Wabash 1968 IUMD, two years Army Medical Corps, Germany, Cincinnati Medical School married Laine Marshall Phrm.D. Son, Marshall Todd, born 1987.

McClaskey children love to come home!

WALTER ALVA AND MARGARET A. ELMORE McCLURE

Walter Alva's parents were Charles Edward (Feb. 13, 1889 - Nov. 14, 1967) and Sarah O'Rentha Ham (Mar. 20, 1888-Apr. 6, 1953) McClure. To this marriage the following children were born: Walter Alva, Glenn Edward, Robert Bernard, Veda Mae Miller and Harold Lee.

Margaret Angeline Elmore McClure's parents were Albert Murray and Lula M.A. Seits Elmore. There was James Byron who married Eva Philpot; Margaret Angeline who married Walter A. McClure; Rosemary L. who married Carl Snyder; Edith Lillian married Marshall Hauser; Ethel Maxine married Daniel Crooks who passed away, then she married James F. Boyle.

Walter Alva and Margaret A. Elmore McClure married Sept. 11, 1933. They had five sons, James Gilbert who married Alma Jane King of Kokomo. Two sons were born to them: James Montgomery and Eugene Douglas. Carl Richard, married Virginia Ruth Palmer of Tacoma, WA and they had three sons, Cary Walter, Lee Richard and Timmy Dale. Alva Lee married Connie Cruz of California and they had Ivette Marie and Richard Jason. Jack Phillip married Linda Sue Hall of Crawfordsville and they had three sons, Donald Andrew, Stephen Michael and Jeffrey David. Paul Vernon married Evelyn Mante of California and they had one daughter, Jacqulyn Deana. They divorced and he then married Joy Leah Robinson of Costa Mesa, CA.

James Gilbert graduated from Alamo High School. Carl entered the Air Force, got his G.D. there and retired after 20 years service. Alva Lee went to the Air Force and got his G.D. also. He now works for Unisses Computers as field service manager in Charleston, WV. Jack graduated from Crawfordsville High School. He is Senior Instrumentation Engineer with Rockwell in Golden, CO. Paul Vernon went to Riverside Junior College for his degree and is an Associate EMC Engineer with Genisco in Rancho Dominguez, CA.

James Gilbert and Carl Richard were born on the James B. Elmore farm in Ripley Township. Alva was born in Alamo. Jack Phillip and Paul Vernon were born at Culver Union Hospital.

Margaret Elmore McClure worked at the Park & Eat ten years, Tuttle cafeteria and Lane House Nursing Home.

Walter Alva was born in Wayne Township Sept. 13, 1914 and passed away Sept. 23, 1973. He was a cable splicer for Indiana Bell (33 years of service). His son, James Gilbert is retiring after 35 years as a construction supervisor with the same company.

Walter's grandfather, James McClure was in the Civil War — Co. K, 154th Indiana Infantry. His second wife, Mary E. Spohr (1877-1957) was Walter's grandmother. Walter's great grandfather, Moses McClure was born June 26, 1795, died Aug. 24, 1892 and is buried with his wife, Elizabeth (May 17, 1810-July 6, 1883) in Shannondale Cemetery. Moses was a blacksmith.

It is said that the McClure family dates back to three brothers, David, William and John who arrived in America from Scotland about 1650. *Submitted by Margaret McClure*

HISTORY OF McCORMICK FAMILY

Delbert (Del) McCormick rode a bicycle from McCormick's Creek area to Montgomery Co., IN around 1900. He met and married Carrie McCay of Linden. They farmed 500 acres in Jackson Twp. Tippecanoe County, west of Romney for many years. They raised five sons Herbert, Ralph, Ora, Keith, and Harold. Del was a Director of the Romeny Bank, also was a member of the Romney Masonic Lodge for 50 years. He served with his brother-in-law. Dr. Ora McCay, of Romney in the lodge.

Carrie McCormick died in 1938? and Delbert married Anna Murdock Thomas and they continued to reside on the farm for a few years. He sold a Tippecanoe County farm that he and Carrie owned and purchased 120 acres Northwest of Crawfordsville on LaGrange Road. He had a dairy farm there for a few years in partnership with son, Keith, after he returned from service in World War II. Son, Ralph McCormick returned from service in World War II and resumed his position of District Sales Manager with DeKalb Seed Company June 1, 1946. He married Jessie Bass in Rochester, IN on Apr. 20, 1946.

Prudential Insurance Company, Mortgage Loan Division, offered Ralph McCormick a position as Mortgage Loan Appraiser covering 14 counties (the same area he was covering for DeKalb) and he accepted, after much deliberation, on Oct. 1, 1946. He excelled in this work and received much praise and raises in pay because he was a top producer in Farm Mortgage Loans in the United States and Canada. He drove home every night and would dictate his reports to Jessie and she typed reports and he drew diagrams so they could mail reports to the Indianapolis office the next morning. Sons, Patrick Lee and Michael Del were born during this time.

Ralph McCormick suffered a heart attack in May 1951 at Lebanon, IN. While he was in the hospital, his father, Delbert McCormick suffered a heart attack while he was milking a cow. Jessie, Pat and Mike were staying with Del and Annie at the farm and Jessie found Del with his boots on. He always said that was the way he wanted to go. He didn't want to be sick and bedfast.

Ralph was not able to return to work for Prudential Insurance Company due to his health. He started a small business, McCormick Electric Company, but after a few years with unsatisfactory employees decided to close that business and pursue the Mortgage Loan, Real Estate and Insurance Business that he and Jessie could operate themselves.

In 1956 McCormick Agency was established at 1104 West Main Street, Crawfordsville in our home. We represented Prudential Insurance Company, Lafayette Life Insurance Company, Standard Life Insurance Company and others. Companies paid a Finders Fee to Brokers for securing loans for them on Farm Loans, Residential and Business Loans. Ralph McCormick enjoyed this business very much and was very successful in it. He also became a Real Estate Broker and sold the Evans farm north of Crawfordsville to O.S. and Rhoda Ann Johnson. He was their agent and sold the C'ville Lanes to H. B. Layne, also the Holiday Inn to H.B. Layne. O.S. and Rhoda Ann Johnson and Ralph C. McCormick and Jessie McCormick developed the Rodan Addition sub-division (Rodan Addition was named in honor of Rhoda Ann Johnson). The streets in the sub-division, McCormick Drive and Johnson Drive were named for both families.

In 1958 Ralph and Jessie McCormick built a new home and office on Lafayette Road in Rodan Addition. They now had four (4) sons, Patrick, Michael, Timothy and Thomas. Their Mortgage Loan, Real Estate and Insurance business was growing and they began building some spec houses in Rodan Addition also. In 1961 the Carter Insurance Agency at Colfax, IN was purchased and a 2nd office was established there.

Ralph McCormick died in 1962 and Jessie McCormick continued to operate the business. She married Bill Metsker Aug. 11, 1963. He was a farmer and an Air Force Reserve Officer. He had a Farm Sale in 1964 and joined Jessie in the business and changed the name to McCormick-Metsker Agency. Bill suggested we keep both names because some of the boys might want to join the Agency and that did happen.

In 1966 the Enterprise Building was bought because a down town office was needed as business was growing. The Elmer Hughes Insurance Agency in New Richmond was secured and an office was opened there.

In 1981 the Insurance Agency was sold to sons, Michael D. McCormick and Timothy J. McCormick and they operate under McCormick-Metsker Agency, Inc.

Bill Metsker died Aug. 30, 1983. Jessie Metsker continues to operate the McCormick-Metsker Corporation Real Estate Business along with son, Thomas R. McCormick.

Patrick L. McCormick has established his own real estate business, Pat McCormick Realty at 2104 Lafayette Road in Rodan Addition. *Submitted by Jessie Metsker*

HAROLD E. AND RUTH G. McCORMICK

Harold and Ruth McCormick were lifelong residents of Montgomery County with the exception of some 16 years spent in the Hillsboro-Wallace vicinity of Fountain County during the early years of their marriage. The bulk of their adult life was spent earning a livelihood from farming in or near Montgomery County. Their dream of owning their own farm was realized in 1949 with the purchase of a farm located north and west of the village of Yountsville from which they retired to move to 316 Fairlane, Crawfordsville, in 1978.

Harold Earl McCormick was born June 12, 1904 on a farm some two miles north of Alamo, IN, to Herbert Iral and Emma Jane (Stonebraker) McCormick, the third of seven children. He attended Alamo High School graduating with the

Class of 1922, and on Mar. 5, 1924 was married to Ruth.

Ruth Glee Clodfelder was born Apr. 2, 1904 to George and Froney Belle (Keller) Clodfelder in the village of Alamo. Harold and Ruth are the parents of two sons, Francis Eugene and Roy Lee, both born near Hillsboro, IN. They are survived by five grandchildren and two great-grandchildren.

Harold E. and Ruth G. McCormick

As their family responsibilities lessened and time was available, Harold and Ruth were able to devote time to their hobby, genealogy. Although their original interest arose from an interest in researching their own family histories, they gradually compiled a volume of historical information related to families connected to their own, and became quite adept at searching out information from courthouse records, cemetery records, libraries, and all others sources. They spent many hours together, separately, or with interested friends in visiting all conceivable spots where they might locate just that bit of information they needed to confirm an ancestor's place in the family tree. Many vacations were spent traveling to Ohio, North Carolina, Virginia, and Iowa to speak to a distant relative or to search out proof of birth or death from whatever forgotten and musty records they could locate. Needless to say, with the wealth of information they collected and the expertise they developed in conducting their searches, they became known as resource persons for genealogists near and far. At their death in 1988, much of the information which they had collected over many years, but had not placed into organized form, was presented to the local and state libraries and to friends who had helped in gathering it. Harold and Ruth were able to organize family histories for several branches of their families, histories of many schools, churches, and cemeteries of the area into book form, copies of which were given to the local library.

In their books, *"The Family of James McCormick"* and *"The Family of Felix Clodfelder,"* this couple have documented the arrival of their ancestors in Montgomery County. Although unable to document an exact time and place, they were able to set the birth of George McCormick, Harold's great-grandfather in Armagh County, Ireland in 1807. His son James, Harold's grandfather, migrated to America with his father in 1850. After a short stay in New Jersey, and then in Ohio until he reached adulthood, James purchased land in Ripley Township, Montgomery Co., IN on Dec. 25, 1874. Thus was this branch off the McCormick family introduced to Montgomery County.

Ruth and Harold were able to compile an impressive history of the Clodfelder family, tracing back through 12 generations to one Adam Glattfelder of the Swiss canton of Zurich, Switzerland. Record of the marriage of Adam to a Verona Legi on July 29, 1570 was located. It has been documented that a descendent of this marriage, John Peter Glattfelder, his wife and children, and a brother, Casper Glattfelder left Switzerland in 1743 bound for America. John Peter apparently died at sea, but records show his widow and children arrived by ship in Philadelphia on Aug. 30, 1743. Gradual alterations in the spelling of the name from Glattfelder to Glatfelder, to Klodfelter to Clodfelter, and finally to the present Clodfelder, added to the difficulty in establishing relationships. The present spelling apparently derived from an error on the deed to property in Jackson Township, Fountain County, made to Ruth's great grandfather Felix dated Apr. 5, 1837. Felix came to Indiana from North Carolina. This branch of the Clodfelder family was established in Montgomery County in 1901 when Ruth's parents, George and Froney took up residence in the town of Alamo.

Harold and Ruth were members of the Waynetown Baptist Church and of the Montgomery County and Fountain County Historical Societies. They published a number of articles in the Historical Society Journals. Ruth was a member of the Dorothy Q. Chapter Daughters of the American Revolution. Their families and friends are grateful to them for searching out and preserving such a great part of our heritage.

Following their deaths, Harold on Oct. 31, 1988 and Ruth on Dec. 25, 1988 both were buried in the Waynetown Masonic Cemetery. *Submitted by Gene McCormick*

GEORGE AMARQUES LAFAYETTE McCOY

George A. McCoy is a descendent of John McCoy who came from Ireland in the early 1800's. It is said he married an Indian Maiden, but at present time no confirmation of the tribe she belonged is available.

John Sr. fought in the Battle of Tippecanoe and his name is recorded on the Monument that stands at Battleground, IN as a private who gave his life in 1812.

John and the Indian Maiden had two sons Thomas Issac and John Wesley McCoy. John Wesley never married and died at a young age.

Thomas Isaac married Rebecca Elizabeth (Oliver) who gave birth to five children George Amarques born Sept. 5, 1862, John W., Lyde, William and Mary. After the death of Rebecca's parents, Amelia Ann (Lewis) and John W. Oliver, (a Free Will Methodist minister) she divorced Isaac and took Lyde, William and Mary with her. This marriage had been arranged by their parents.

George Amarques Lafayette McCoy

In 1915 Rebecca came to live with George and family until 1917. She had an unusual growth on her arm and had willed her body to science and date of death not known.

Isaac settled in Illinois and married Sue Faucinaugh and had Etta and Nannie. Isaac died in 1923.

George married Addie Mae Gilkey who already had a daughter Maude. Addie lived but six weeks, dying of typhoid fever.

In 1890 George married Addie's sister Gertrude Brown Gilkey daughter of Lydia (Brown) and John R. Gilkey. George had two other marriages, in 1918 to Nora Warrick and divorced in 1920. In the late 1920's he moved to Montgomery County and later married Katie Dittamore. She died about 1942. George died July 1, 1951.

Gertrude was the mother of George's children numbering seven. Edith Rae, Ethel Addie, Lula Leslie, Jennie Frances, Garnet Edward (Bud), Beatrice Fay, and Teddy Parker McCoy. Ethel and Jennie both died at age 12.

Edith married John West and they had 15 children. Helen, James, Mary, John Thomas, George, Gerald, Alfred, Paul, Dale, Donald, Martha, Oscar, twins Max and Maxine, and Robert.

Lula married Merle Fisher, had one daughter, Alberta, who wed Des Stevens and they had three children.

Bud married, Ada Keppe, they had four children. Merrill, Ruth, Fred, and Elizabeth. In 1937 Bud was hit by a train; died three days later.

Bea married George Nichols, they had seven children. Norman, Edwin, Walter, Alice, Oka, and twins Ruth and Naomi. Bea is only living child of the McCoys and resides at Williamsburg Health Care in Crawfordsville. Her age is 88.

Oka, in 1978 had Bea's poems she had written over several years published under the title "Musing by Beatrice".

Ted married Olive Quick and they had four children: Wayne, Gertrude, Larry and Bonnie. Ted moved to Brazil, IN. He was Democrat Mayor for eight consecutive years. This was upsetting to George as he was a staunch Republican.

George McCoy's many descendants are residents of Montgomery County.

D.A. AND MARY BARR McGAUGHEY

Dory Albert and Mary Barr McGaughey moved to Waveland, IN on Aug. 24, 1964 after living on a farm southeast of Russellville, IN since 1931.

He was born in Putnam Co., IN on Nov. 6, 1883, the youngest child of Alfred and Margaret Frank McGaughey. He had one brother, Edward, and three sisters - Stella Russell, Lizzie Zook and Clara Hollingsworth. The family later moved to Vermillion County near Dane, IN and then after a number of years to Greensburg, IN where Dory farmed with his father. However the family still retained their farm in Vermillion County. It was while they were living at Greensburg that Dory was married to Mary Barr in Waveland, on Oct. 11, 1911.

Mary was the daughter of James Wesley and Emma Flora Sharp Barr and was born Feb. 20, 1891. She had one brother Harry L. born May 24, 1886. James and Emma were lifelong residents of Waveland.

James' father was John Wesley Barr, who was a Civil War Veteran. He entered the service on Jan. 1, 1864 and was mustered out on December 21st of the same year as a corporal in Indiana Company H - 40th Regiment Infantry. James' mother was Mary Elizabeth Phillips Barr. John and Mary Elizabeth had six children. James W. born Oct. 21, 1862,

William Charles (Chine), Sarah Barr Brown, Ella Barr Hickman and Molly who died at an early age as the result of goiter surgery.

Emma Sharp Barr was the daughter of Isaac Sharp, son of Samuel Benjamin and Rebecca Crandall Sharp, and Mary Ann Eastlack. Mary Ann was born Feb. 12, 1832 to Samuel Eastlack and Catherine Haines in Woodstown, NJ. When she was three the family moved to Ohio and then on to Indiana when she was 12. She and Isaac were married Sept. 30, 1852. He had always lived in the Waveland area and was a wagonmaker by trade.

They had ten children - Emma being the only girl was born to them on Sept. 12, 1857. The boys were Samuel, William, Theodore, Charles, Frank, Fred, Alva, John and Otho. Emma, as one of the older children, spent many hours caring for her younger brothers and was always a favorite of theirs.

She and James Barr were married Aug. 21, 1885 and had one son Harry in addition to Mary. James died July 28, 1929 and Emma on Aug. 29, 1939.

Mary Barr McGaughey and her husband Dory, moved to the family farm in Vermillion County from Greensburg in the year following their marriage. They lived there until 1931 except for a few months in Montezuma, where their daughter Mildred was born. They then moved to Russellville and lived there before retiring from farming in 1964 and moving to Waveland which was Mary's home town. She had graduated from school there in 1910. She, as well as all of the family, were active members of the Methodist Church except for the years they lived at Russellville where they were members of the Federated Church.

Dory died in 1972, but as of this writing in 1989, Mary still lives alone in her own home in Waveland as she approaches her 98th birthday. *Submitted by Mildred Evans*

CHARLES AND DORIS McINTIRE

Charles Andrew McIntire at the age of 69 is starting a new business. This is the third business that he has started during his lifetime. In 1951, he started the Arrow Electric Company which he owned and operated for 31 years. Then in 1985, he began Maxtron and his new adventure is McIntire Dry Cleaning Incorporated, 306 N. Green Street.

Charles (Charlie) McIntire was born Dec. 29, 1919, in Montgomery County, the fifth and youngest child of Ira and Ida (Weaver) McIntire. He graduated from Crawfordsville High School in 1938.

In June of 1941, he married Doris McCormick in Crawfordsville. She was the only daughter of Howard and Hazel (Hudson) McCormick. Doris was born in Crawfordsville, on Jan. 7, 1922. She graduated from CHS in 1940.

In September of 1941, Charles entered Aero ITI in Los Angeles, CA. By Dec. 29, 1941, Charles was at Great Lakes Naval Training Station as an Apprentice Seaman. He spent the next four years in the service of his country; two and a half years at Pearl Harbor and the next two years at Seattle, WA. He attended Coyne Electrical School in Chicago.

Three children were born to the McIntires. Their first was Michael Andrew, born on Apr. 25, 1945; Mike died at the age of nine on the Mt. Zion school playground. Their daughter, Deborah Dean was born Aug. 2, 1948. Debbi is a graduate of Butler University with a masters in education. She married John Nelson from South Bend, IN on June 13, 1970. They have three children, all born in Indianapolis — Aaron Henry, Kara Dean, Thomas Kilpatrick (T.K.).

Their third child, Mitchel Andrew "Mitch" was born May 13, 1957. He married Jill Spencer on June 7, 1986; they have one child, Danielle Leigh, born Oct. 20, 1988. Mitch is presently working for R.R. Donnelley.

For many years, Charlie was a member of the Lion's club; he also was one of the directors of the civil defense, president of the Mt. Zion PTA, Boy Scouts, American Legion, VFW, and Fourty & Light?

He is a member of the Crawfordsville Masonic Blue Lodge — Scottish Rite — Murat Shrine (president of the Montgomery County Shrine Club 1986) and captain of the local Ben Hur Floaters.

Doris is in American Legion Auxiliary, past member of Beta Sigma Phi, did Girl Scout work for many years and is a board member of AARP.

Doris and Charlie are members of First Christian Church. *Submitted by Doris McIntire*

McKINNEY FAMILY

The McKinney family roots go back to Scotland where five brothers fled the Isle of Skye and came to America in 1734. Daniel, one of the five, had a son, James Collin, who settled in Pennsylvania, and his son Robert, born in 1755, married Esther Layton and moved to New Carlisle, OH. One of his sons was Samuel, born in 1781, who married Sarah Forgey. It was their son, Prestley T. McKinney, born 1809, who came to Indiana in 1834 and bought the farm that has since been the McKinney Homestead. He and his first wife, Sara McClure, had six children, one of them being William, who graduated from Wabash College in 1859, and survived four years of the Civil War, but died a year later as a result of a lung disease contracted in the War.

After Sara's death, P.T. later married Catherine McClure whose grandfather, Christian Bever, founded Pleasant Hill (Wingate). They were the parents of Charles, Frank and Eva.

Miller of Alto, MI. They built a house near Wingate in 1892 that is still the McKinney family home. They had five children: Glenn, Fern, (Rowlett), Hazel, Georgia and Gladys (Mrs. Leigh O. Wright). Georgia was a Presbyterian missionary and served in Iran for 33 years - from 1916 to 1949. She died in 1957.

Glenn was born in 1885 on the farm and graduated from Wabash College in 1909. He married Virginia Pearce of Waveland and returned to the farm. She was the daughter of Rev. Thomas G. Pearce and Ida Ann Beal. Glenn farmed all his life, was an Elder in the Presbyterian Church and served nine years as President of the Fountain County Farm Bureau. They had three children: Lawrence, b. 1912; Ida Lucile (McCord), b. 1913 and Marjory (Mrs. Paul R. Foster), b. 1917.

Glenn died in 1949; Virginia in 1967 and Ida Lucile in 1972. They are buried in the family cemetery (Oak Ridge) on the farm.

Marjory and Paul Foster reside on the Foster family farm near Attica.

Lawrence McKinney graduated from Wabash College in 1934 and married Alice Anderson of Sheffield, PA, in 1936. Her parents, of Swedish descent, were Charles and Anna (Rylander) Anderson. Lawrence and Alice had two children: Anne (Mrs. Jack Huston) born in 1940 who had two children, Glenn and Jill. Pearce, born in 1941, married Charlotte McKinney and they had three children: Noel, Trish and Heather.

Lawrence and Alice returned to the farm in 1938 and continued to farm until retirement in 1978 when they moved to Covington. Pearce continues residing at the Homestead. Alice McKinney served as Fountain-Warren County Public Health Nurse from 1962 until 1975. Members of the McKinney family have all been generous of their time in support of community projects. *Submitted by Lawrence McKinney*

JAMES McMULLEN

James, Joseph and John McMullen, three brothers came from England to the Carolinas in 1775.

James McMullen, Sr. married Jane Robinson, Mar. 14, 1788 and moved to Shelby Co., KY - following trail of Daniel Boone through the "Old Wilderness Pass" to where Louisville now stands.

It was usual for men to go hunting for food, and, on one occasion, a hunting party of which James, Sr., was a member, was attacked and killed by Indians. Their only son, James McMullen, Jr. was born shortly after his father was murdered.

Donna, Bonnie, William, Dode, Everett, Elizabeth and Orval McMullen

James McMullen, Jr. married Martha VanCleave on Oct. 3, 1811 in Kentucky. They came to Indiana locating about two miles south of New Market, IN in 1828. Their children were:

Charles Andrew, Doris Dean, Deborah Dean and Mitchel Andrew McIntire

Alice and Lawrence McKinney

Charles was born in 1857 and married Mary

Anna McMullen married Jesse Vancleave.

Emily McMullen married Benjamin Brown.

John McMullen married Clarise Watkins.

Benjamin McMullen married Sarah E. Vancleave.

Joseph McMullen (twin to Benjamin) married Mary Susan Elrod.

William McMullen married Catherine ?

Lindsay McMullen married Elizabeth Clark.

Marjory Jane McMullen married John Payton.

James Madison McMullen - served in Mexican War. It is believed he was murdered on his way home.

Andrew Jefferson McMullen married Margaret Jane Clark.

Edward Robinson McMullen married Margaret Ann Douglas.

Francis Marion McMullen married Matilda Jane Clark.

Sarah Elizabeth McMullen married Joshua Vancleave.

Lemuel Washington McMullen married Maria Louise Redenbaugh.

It is the lineage of Lemuel Washington that will be continued. They had eight children: Josephus Emmons McMullen (known as "Dode") married Lucinda Elizabeth Graybill. Their children were: Bonnie June McMullen married Earl Joseph Linn. They had one son, Donald J. Linn who married Norma Jean Crow; parents of Diana Mitchum, Judith Gayler, Debra Jo Sladek.

Donna May McMullen who never married.

William McMullen married Eleanor Miller. They had twins, Howard McMullen married Frances Hugelman; parents of Larry McMullen, Kenneth Lee McMullen, and Carmel Sanders. Helena McMullen married Clarence Wilkens. They had one daughter, Jana Wilkens.

Everett McMullen married Fern Swindler and had two daughters: Virginia Lee McMullen married William Vannice parents of Thomas Vannice, Danny Vannice, and Sharyn Sabens. Marilyn McMullen married John Reynolds: parents of Kimberly Burson and Mark Reynolds.

Josephine McMullen married Edmund Conner.

Sarah (Sally) McMullen married George Mangus.

Leonard Franklin McMullen married Ethel Nay. His second marriage was to Versa Hays. Leonard and Versa had two sons. Dwight McMullen and Lowell McMullen married Lois McGinnis: parents of: David McMullen, Dwain McMullen, and Denise Hutchinson.

Fannie McMullen married Arthur Clements.

Margaret McMullen and two children who died in infancy.

In England this family spelled their name "MacMullin but in 1831 it was changed to "McMullen."

LOWELL McMULLEN

Lowell McMullen, a Montgomery County native has lived since the age of four at rural New Ross. After graduation from High School in 1940, he served with the army in the South Pacific during WWII.

Upon completion of the military, he and Lois McGinnis of rural Kingman were married Feb. 28, 1946 at Mace Church.

They began farming by renting his mother's farm where they still reside. Their diversified operation consisted of hogs, chickens, dairy, hay and grain. They shared the family home.

Lowell retired in 1988 and has taken pride in refurbishing antique tractors. He is currently renovating a 1936 Chevrolet coupe. Lois hopes to drive that! Both are members of Montgomery County Pioneer Association. Lowell is a Master Mason, a member of Scottish Rite, American Legion and Mace Methodist Church.

Lois, Denise , David, Dwaine and Lowell McMullen

After Lois graduated from Wallace in 1940, she attended Western Union School. She worked in Anderson as a Teleprinter Operator, also Delco Remy and was a cashier at Krogers in Crawfordsville 11 years. Other memberships include Eastern Star, DAR and Mace Church.

Lowell's father, Leonard Franklin (Oct. 31, 1876) in Boone Co., died Easter morning (Apr. 16, 1933), home near Whitesville. He owned a grocery in Max, IN and worked on the Interurban at Lizton. His mother, Versa (Hayes) McMullen was one of the first graduates from Mace in 1906. She attended the Conservatory of Music in Indianapolis and gave piano lessons. She raised several flocks of turkeys. She died Feb. 19, 1976, age 88.

Lois's parents, Arista Parvin and Bessie (Atkinson) McGinnis of Fountain County, married June 4, 1910. Parvin farmed and was an old time fiddler, playing by ear. He played a fife for local events and loved to coon hunt. Bessie enjoyed quilting. She played a pump organ and banjo.

The McMullen children: David, May 10, 1947, Dwain, Aug. 1, 1948, Denise, Jan. 6, 1952.

David married Cynthia (White) Nuckles of Greenwood June 5, 1976. Cindy had Kimberly Nov. 13, 1969 by a former marriage. They reside in Indianapolis where David is Supervisor of Minnesota Mutual and SSK Financial Services. David graduated from Purdue in 1970 and was in the Army Reserve.

After Dwain's graduation from Purdue in 1970, he joined the Army Reserve and during that time, he and Julianne Morgan of New Ross were married Feb. 20, 1971. Children: Bradley, born Indianapolis Feb. 3, 1976, Kevin, Louisville June 4, 1979, Emily "Hi Mom, Dad, What's Your Hurry, I'm Here!" (born in a car) Huntington, WV, Jan. 26, 1984.

Dwain is Assistant Chief Appraiser of the Army Corps of Engineers in Washington, D.C. They live in Woodbridge, VA. Juli attended Indiana University and is working to get her degree.

Denise graduated from Indiana College of Business and Technology in Indianapolis. She married Steven Hutchinson of Thorntown, Feb. 11, 1978. Children: Brent, born in Michigan Sept. 25, 1980, Jamie Nicole, Gettysburg, July 6, 1982.

Steve is a 1972 Purdue graduate. He worked as Designer in Biglerville, PA, while Denise was employed at Gettysburg College and Rost Jewelers. They presently reside in Rome, GA where Steve is a Designer for Inland.

Lois and Denise have letters in the time capsule in St. John's Church to be opened by descendents in the year 2,076.

EDWIN L. AND PATRICIA L. MCNEIL

Edwin Lee McNeil, youngest son of Boyd O. and Betty Myrtle (Gephart) McNeil, was born July 22, 1933, in the family home East of the New Richmond Methodist Church. His brothers, Boyd Jr. and John, were also born there. His father, Boyd Sr., served in WWI, and later was lineman for the New Richmond Telephone Company, which was owned by his father, John L. McNeil. Boyd Sr. was also a lineman for Montgomery Light & Power Company (forerunner of Tipmont R.E.M.C.). In 1942, he became an electrician for Purdue University, retired in 1960, and died in 1967. Betty was a homemaker and well-known baker, most of New Richmond's children grew-up eating her cookies and angel food cakes. She currently lives in Heritage Healthcare in West Lafayette.

Ed attended New Richmond School, graduated in 1952's class of seven, then attended Purdue. As a young boy, he was active in Boy Scouts, attaining the rank of Life Scout. He camped and served on the staffs at Camp Rotary, serving as assistant camp director in 1953, and visited Philmont Scout Ranch in New Mexico.

In 1953, he moved to Indianapolis as Registrar for the Central Indiana Council, Boy Scouts of America. He also worked briefly for the Indianapolis Star & News, and attended Indiana University Downtown Center. While working with the Council Office, he assisted in organizing the first Mormon Scout Troop in Indianapolis.

He returned to New Richmond in 1956, and joined the staff of Purdue with the Property Accounting Department. In 1962, he was promoted to the Purdue Research Foundation where he is currently Real Estate Manager.

Ed married Patricia Meharry in 1957. Pat was born in Romney in 1934, oldest daughter of Hugh Sayers and Helen (Whitehead) Meharry of Jackson Township, Tippecanoe County. Pat has two sisters, Ada Dean and Margaret Horn. Hugh was a farmer and school bus driver; he died in 1986. Helen is a homemaker and talented seamstress. Pat graduated from Jackson High School and attended Purdue. She worked at Loeb's Department Store in Lafayette, then was cashier at Andrew's Grocery in New Richmond until she and Ed moved to Lafayette in 1961. She worked as Assistant Librarian in Purdue Libraries until their oldest son was born in 1966.

Hugh Michael, born three months premature, weighed 2 lb. 1 oz. and was the smallest male to survive at that time in Lafayette Home Hospital. Mike graduated from Harrison High School and Purdue, and lives in West Lafayette. Their second son, Edwin Lee II, weighing 2 lb. 13 oz. was born in 1968. Lee also graduated from Harrison, north of West Lafayette, and is currently in the Army stationed at Ft. Hood, TX.

Ed and Pat moved East of Lafayette in 1978. Ed is active with the Exchange Club of Lafayette, and is currently its president. In 1982-83, he served as president of the Indiana-Kentucky District Exchange Clubs. *Submitted by Patricia McNeil*

DR. D. ELLA McNICOLL

Dr. D. Ella McNicoll, the daughter of William McNicoll and Lucinda McNicoll Booher, was born in Clinton County, near Frankfort in 1858. She entered the Kirksville College of Osteopathic

Medicine at Kirksville, MO in Oct. 1, 1896 and graduated July 30, 1898. She was the first woman in Indiana to become an osteopathic physician. She practiced most of her life in Frankfort, but did practice in Darlington after she retired to make her home with her half-sister, Mrs. Earl Butler. She died in November, 1943.

Mr. Dan Layne remembers visiting her with his father Dr. Lloyd Lane, perhaps in 1938 to buy a skeleton of a young German woman who died 100 years earlier. The skeleton was named "Gretchen."
By Jean Thompson

CHARLES H. AND RACHEL E. MELVIN HISTORY

Charles Henry and Rachel Emma (Dike) Melvin came to Montgomery County, in August of 1913 settling three miles south of Alamo in Ripley Twp. They brought their family with them.

Charles was born May 18, 1858 in Ohio, died March 1932 at Alamo. The son of Isaac and Electa (Wright) Melvin. Isaac was the son of an only son born: June 1838 died; 1905, buried Fulton, MO. Electa born: Apr. 10, 1838 S.E. Ohio died: 1912 at Eminence, KS. Her father was Henry Wright.

Charles always wanted to be a sheepherder, so after working the mines in Ohio from age 12 to 21 he gathered up his parents and siblings and headed West to Kansas. His siblings: Sim; Frank; Lucy; and twins Maude and Myrtle. They went as far as Illinois when money ran out so they stopped and farmed for a couple years then started again. This time they stopped in Missouri when his father became ill and started a sawmill and were there nearly 11 years. In the meantime Charles went back to Ohio to marry Rachel Emma Dike on Dec. 30, 1883. She was born Dec. 9, 1862, Morgan Co., OH, died Dec. 23, 1942 Veedersburg, IN. Buried Alamo Cemetery. Their children:

Charles H. and Rachel E. Melvin Family

Ernest Sterling born: Sept. 26, 1884 died 1947, married Feb. 14, 1911 to Tessie Martin born 1881 died 1947. Children: Ward; Wilma; Deana. Augusta Ferrin born, Dec. 20, 1886, died February 1927; married Aug. 7, 1906 to Grace Jones born 1881 died 1962. Children: Charles, Hazel, Harold, Ethel, Howard L., Leland Donald (Bill).

Albert Glenn born: Aug. 21, 1890 died February 1961, married 1928 to Iva Etter born 1899 died July 1979. No children.

Chester Clyde born, Oct. 7, 1894, died Nov. 26, 1978; married June 1, 1916 to Beatrice Alma Vancleave born, Aug. 29, 1897. Children: Hobart, Fred, Maxine and Leslie.

Fred Lawrence born 1897 died of flu in WWI 1918 (Navy).

Myrtle Florence born June 1899, died February 1971 married Sept. 2, 1924 to Paul W. Miller born 1897 died February 1977. Children Russell Don, Gene Dale, and LaVera Ellen.

Howard Vaughn born July 14, 1901 1st married Apr. 28, 1920 to Ruth Cheney born 1899 died 1954. Later married Nov. 19, 1956 to Mildred Hean (Anderson) Cawthon born July 19, 1907. No children.

Rachel's parents were Elias Cecil and Elizabeth (Woolman) Dike from Ohio. William Woolman her #4 great-grandfather came to this country from England in 1678 with his son John. They settled in New Jersey. They were of the Quaker Faith. The Dike history goes back a ways too; most of them live in Ohio.

As Charles and Rachel were forging West to Kansas they met people coming back from there. Ask "Where Ya' going'?" They said "To Kansas". Reply, "Ohhhh, DON'T go to Kansas!!!".

CHESTER CLYDE MELVIN

Chester Clyde Melvin came to Ripley Twp., Montgomery County in 1913. He was born Oct. 7, 1894 in Finney Co., KS, the fourth child of Charles Henry and Rachel Emma (Dike) Melvin. His siblings: Ernest (Tex); Agustus (Gus); Glenn (Mose); Fred (Tiny); Myrtle (Sis); and Howard (Judge). Howard survives, living on a cattle ranch near Aguilar, CO. Clyde's nickname (Smalley or Skeet). He graduated Alamo School 1914.

June 1, 1916 Clyde married Beatrice Alma Vancleave born Aug. 29, 1897, Ripley Twp., to Ad and Ida Frances (Denman) Vancleave. She had one sister, Edith Aline, born Oct. 13, 1899, died Dec. 24, 1950; married to Oscar E. Ackerson. They had five children: Marylou; Cedric; Thelma; Ina Mae; Norma.

Clyde and Beatrice children: Hobart Eugene born, Sept. 24, 1917; living in Toledo, OH; Fred Leland, born Apr. 10, 1919 living in Alamo; Mrs. Clarence (Helen Maxine) Elson born, May 13, 1923, living in Mesa, AZ; Leslie Marvin born, Dec. 5, 1927 living on Clyde's farm southwest of Waynetown.

Chester Clyde Melvin Family

Beatrice's grandparents, Moses Hampton and Jemima (Lee) Denman, (daughter of John and Massa (Lucas) Lee); homesteaded property south of Alamo State Road 234, whence Ida F. Vancleave purchased 40 acres from her siblings, now Beatrice's farm.

Clyde's parents migrated from Butler Co., OH to near Eminence, KS where they homesteaded several acres then traded that property to Theodore and Bettie Johnson for the Indiana 465 acre farm. Clyde and his brothers rode the freight train (cattle car) with the family horses from Garden City, KS to Waveland, IN.

Clyde farmed and ran a sawmill on his parents' property for 13 years until purchasing his own farm in 1943 southwest of Waynetown on the county line. He has 80 acres in Fountain County, Jackson Twp., and 47 acres in Montgomery County, Ripley Twp.

Clyde retired from farming in 1951 returning to Beatrice's farm to live. He worked for the State Highway Dept. a few years and in 1956 became Trustee of Ripley Twp., and held office eight years.

Clyde and Beatrice joined Alamo Christian Church and were baptized together shortly before their marriage which took place at the Crawfordsville Orphans Home. Beatrice's parents were Caretakers there.

Clyde taught Sunday School class, was Board Member and Elder at the Church until shortly before his death Nov. 26, 1978; buried in Alamo Cemetery. Clyde was a good citizen, and a loyal Democrat.

Clyde was a very strong man in his youth; the story told was; not long after he came to Alamo he was in the local blacksmith shop, being a newcomer the older townsmen challenged him to lift the blacksmith anvil. Clyde obliged; not only lifted it, but set it on his shoulder. He was a Boy Scout Leader in the '30s and umpired baseball in the '40s.

FRED MELVIN

Fred Melvin was born Apr. 10, 1919 in Crawfordsville the second son of Clyde and Beatrice Melvin. He graduated from Alamo High School in 1937. He enlisted in the military service and served from Jan. 27, 1941 to Nov. 17, 1945.

While stationed in Amarillo, TX he was joined by his fiance, Lois Philpott. They were married July 14, 1943 in Amarillo.

Lois was born in Kingman, IN to Glen and Ava Philpott, May 15, 1921.

Fred and Lois are the parents of three children: Larry Richard born Oct. 16, 1944 in Covington, IN. Elaine Ann Sept. 2, 1948 and Rosalie Ema Dec. 18, 1952. They were born at Crawfordsville.

Larry is an ordained minister and works at the Holidy Inn in Crawfordsville.

Elaine married Gary Hamm from Waynetown. They have two sons, Anthony Wayne born Aug. 3, 1967 and Michael Allen born Jan. 20, 1970. Both were born at Culver Hospital in Crawfordsville. Elaine has been a hairdresser for 22 years.

Rosalie became the bride of Jimmy Ballard of Mooresville on July 8, 1973. They are the parents of Jennifer Ann, born Apr. 8, 1974 in Indianapolis. Joan Elizabeth was born in Valporaiso, IN on Dec. 16, 1980. They currently live in Indianapolis.

Fred is a member of the Alamo Christian Church and Past Master of the Alamo Masonic Lodge. His hobbies include fishing and enjoying his grandchildren.

At present they live on a small farm in the Alamo Community.

HOWARD V. MELVIN

Howard Vaughn Melvin came to Indiana in 1913 with his family to settle three miles south of Alamo, Ripley Twp. Howard the youngest child of Charles Henry and Rachel Emma (Dike) Melvin, was born July 14, 1901 in Finney Co., KS near Eminence. His parents Homestead there and were sheepherders. They traded their land in Kansas for 465 acres south of Alamo. Howard attended school there later married Ruth Cheney born, Dec. 23, 1899, an only child of Harry P. and Estella (Smith) Cheney. Howard owned farms in Montgomery County,

Ripley Twp., and Fountain County, Jackson Twp. He lived 33 years in Alamo area.

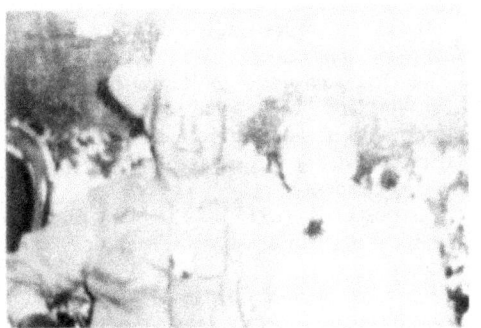

Howard and Mildred Melvin

Due to Ruth's illness they moved to Colorado in 1945. He purchased an old abandoned mining town called Rugby just north of Aguilar, CO where he raises Polled Herford cattle. Ruth died in 1954. Howard then married Nov. 19, 1956 Mildred Jean (Anderson) Cawthon born, July 19, 1907 in Kansas. They still live on the ranch. Mildred's parents were Hugh Hodges (born West Virginia) and Nancy Jane (Johnson) Anderson born in Ohio. Siblings: Mary Adams and Bruce Anderson.

His siblings: Ernest Sterling, born Sept. 26, 1884, died 1947 of heart attack. He was a sheepherder, farmer and worked a sawmill.

Augustus Ferrin, born 1886, died 1927 of congested lungs was a farmer and trucker.

Albert Glenn, born Oct. 21, 1890 died Feb. 10, 1961; massive heart attack. He was a farmer and Lodge member.

Chester Clyde, born Oct. 7, 1894 died Nov. 26, 1978. He worked a sawmill, was a farmer and Trustee of Ripley Twp.

Fred Lawrence, born 1897 died 1918 of Flu in Navy WWI.

Myrtle Florence, born June 1899 died February 1971. She was married to Paul Miller, a homemaker and school teacher.

Howard's parents, siblings and their mates are all buried in Alamo Cemetery.

LESLIE MARVIN MELVIN

Leslie Marvin Melvin born Dec. 5, 1927 in Boone County, near Lebanon, the fourth child of Clyde and Beatrice (Vancleave) Melvin. Siblings: Hobart Eugene "Buck" of Toledo, OH; Fred Leland "Fritz" of Alamo; and Helen Maxine "Dib" Elson of Mesa, AZ.

His parents moved to the "Homeplace" about 1930. It's located three miles southwest of Alamo, Ripley Township. He was raised and roamed the banks of Sugar Creek, near Deers Mill area. Most of his happy days were hunting, fishing, and trips to Sawyer Falls that was on the family property near Shades Park boundary.

Leslie was nicknamed "Sprout" by his grandfather Ad Vancleave and it stuck. Very few people know him by Leslie.

Sprout was President of his Senior class, played basketball, was catcher in baseball; many games umpired by his father Clyde. Graduating from Alamo in 1945, WWII Army veteran, began working at R.R. Donnelley's where he met his wife.

He married Glennadine Melva O'Neal Sept. 4, 1948 at the home of Rev. John Servies.

Melva born June 20, 1928, second child of Jesse Verl and Alpha Morris O'Neal, graduated Covington High 1946. Siblings: Garland Mescal of Florida; Jerald Morris of Covington; Verla Inabel (Peggy) Merryman of Veedersburg; and Donald James of Mellott.

Back Row: Debbie, Melanie. Middle: Connie, Leslie, Melva, Lesley. Front: Kirby, Cynthia Melvin.

Leslie is a grain farmer, also raised cattle and hogs on the family farm four miles northwest of Alamo. A loyal Democrat, he ran for State Representative in 1960, Fountain County.

Their children are:

1. Melanie Dawne, born Oct. 22, 1949, 1st. married on Dec. 30, 1969 to James Robert Garver, born Sept. 22, 1948, died Nov. 29, 1977. Children: Christopher Wayne, born: Oct. 15, 1969; Stacie Dawne, born Feb. 29, 1972, died Dec. 3, 1977. Bad auto wreck. 2nd marriage: James Kenneth Vowels Apr. 17, 1981; born Nov. 5, 1944; stepchildren: Lori Ann Vowels, born May 8, 1967; Jason Tyler Vowels, born Aug. 2, 1971.

2. Debra Lynne, born Dec. 6, 1951 married June 10, 1972 to Thomas E. Norton, born Aug. 30, 1950; divorced 1984. Children: Jason Leo born, Apr. 19, 1974; Brad Leslie, born Apr. 14, 1977; Allison Renae, born Jan. 11, 1986.

3. Connie Maxine, born, Feb. 21, 1954; married Feb. 27, 1972 to David Leroy Noble, born Jan. 9, 1952, divorced 1975. Children: Jessica Page, born July 25, 1972; Jennifer Layla, born Dec. 6, 1974. 2nd marriage to John Dell Miller Sept. 5, 1988, born Jan. 18, 1963.

4. Lesley Diane, born Sept. 18, 1955; married Oct. 13, 1979 to Donald Eugne Baker, born May 14, 1957. Children: Brooke Lynne, born May 6, 1980; Bobbi Jo, born Aug. 9, 1988; Stepchild: Carrie Maureen, born Apr. 3, 1977.

5. Kirby Scott, born May 17, 1957; married July 27, 1979 to Diana Lynn Gooding, born Jan. 16, 1960. Children: Trisha Kyan, born, Apr. 6, 1982; identical twins: Joshua Dale and Jesse Scott, born May 1, 1984; Amber Diane, born Oct. 1, 1986.

6. Cynthia Irene, born Nov. 23, 1959; married Nov. 2, 1979 to Clayton Morgan, born May 20, 1958. Child, Brittany Lynn, born July 24, 1988.

HARVEY GLENN MENNEN

Harvey Glenn Mennen was born Feb. 26, 1925 in Tippecanoe County and was brought to Montgomery County by his parents the following year. He is the youngest son of Herman and Ivy Pearl (Burton) Mennen who were also the parents of Burton, Harold, Mary, Ruth and Hobert, all reared in Montgomery County.

Hobert and Glenn are the only ones still living in Montgomery County.

Glenn graduated from New Richmond High School and completed the short course at Purdue University. He farmed most of his life but is now employed by the Montgomery County Highway Department.

Glenn was married to Doris Bishop of the New Richmond area and was the eighth of ten children of Marvin and Delcie (Mounts) Bishop. Doris was born in Sullivan County and the family moved to Knox County where she attended school until 1947 when her parents moved to Montgomery County. She graduated from New Richmond High School. Glenn and Doris are the parents of two sons, Dennis and Harold.

Dennis was born June 27, 1949 and graduated from Coal Creek Central High School in 1967 and attended Purdue University a short time before he entered the National Guard. He completed the Officers Training School and served six years with the National Guard. He is employed by United Parcel Service. Dennis was married to Teresa Ann Newlin of Mace, IN. She is the daughter of James F. and Jean Huffman Newlin who are also the parents of Kathy Edwards and Linda Harbottle also residents of Montgomery County.

Denny and Teresa are the parents of three children: Jason Dennis born Apr. 9, 1972. Melissa Ann born May 16, 1974 and James Michael born Aug. 17, 1975. The children all attend North Montgomery Schools. Teresa is a secretary at the North Montgomery School Corporation.

Harold graduated from North Montgomery High School in 1972 and attended Butler University. He completed training for heating and air conditioning and later completed the course at Ivy Tech in plumbing. He took the state test and was awarded the contractors license in plumbing for the State of Indiana. Harold was married to Linda Lee Rankin of Wingate, IN in 1975. Linda is the daughter of Robert and Martha (Murdock) Rankin who are also the parents of Sue Ann Hammer.

Harold and Linda are the parents of Ryan Wayne Mennen born Mar. 14, 1977. Ryan attends Northridge Middle School.

In 1988 Harold and Linda purchased Elder Plumbing, Heating and Air Conditioning business in Crawfordsville, IN.

The families of Glenn, Denny and Harold are all members of the Holy Trinity Lutheran Church of Lafayette, IN. Denny and Harold are members of the Masonic Lodge of Wingate, IN. Glenn and Doris appeared as extras in the movie "Hoosiers" filmed in Indiana in 1985.

KATHLEEN BIBLE MEYER

Kathleen Bible Meyer, daughter of Frederic E. and Mabel V. Bible born Jan. 6, 1915 in Coal Creek Township. She graduated from New Richmond High School 1933, Indiana University 1937. She married Meredith Bye Flanigan March 1936 who graduated in 1940 with a Doctor of Medicine degree from Indiana University. Their daughter, Kathleen Luella was born Aug. 10, 1943 in Tucson, AZ while her father was in the United States Air Force. Kathleen and her infant daughter moved back to Linden, IN. Her marriage was dissolved in February 1946. She worked in Real Estate and taught in the West Point and Linden High Schools until 1952.

Kathleen Luella Flanigan attended the Linden grade school and Urbana High School. She graduated from Purdue University in 1965. She married Paul Theodore Carlson Aug. 13, 1966. They attended graduate school. She earned Master's degree in Clothing and Textiles, and he earned a PHD in Metallurgy. They removed to Knoxville, TN. Kathleen attended the University of Tennessee and she is employed as a master teacher in the University of Tennessee Research Laboratory for pre-school children. Paul is employed at Oakridge Laboratory.

Kenneth Lee and Kathleen B. Meyer

Kathleen Bible married Kenneth Lee Meyer, farmer, January 1952. Their daughter, Bette Jane Meyer was born Jan. 14, 1956. She graduated from Urbana High School 1973 and the University of Illinois 1981 with a Doctor of Veterinary degree. She married Robert Edgar Davis who graduated from the University of Illinois with a PH D degree in Chemistry. Their son, Bryan Lee Davis was born in Tuscon, AZ where Robert was employed at the International Business Machine Corporation. Bette practiced in the Desert Small hospital. They moved to Fishkill, NY 1988 and Bette works part time for the Wappinger Falls Animal Hospital.

Kathleen's husband, Lee is retired and he enjoys wordworking projects. She is a member of the Oriental Chapter 244 Order of Eastern Star. She has enjoyed volunteer work as a Sunday School teacher in the Linden First United Methodist Church, Mayview Methodist Church, and Daily Vacation Church School in the Urbana First United Church. Kathleen has been an active member of the Mayview Unit of the Champaign County Homemakers Extension Association.

PHILIP AND JUDY MICHAL

Philip and Judy Michal moved to Wingate in the northwestern part of Montgomery County in May of 1965 after living in Armada, MI the previous nine months. At Armada, Phil worked for Dr. O.C. Krause in a mixed veterinary practice which was primarily dairy.

Judy and Phil met on a blind date in September 1960 while both attended Purdue University. Judy came from rural Clinton County and graduated from Jackson Township High School in 1960. Her parents are William A.T. Price and Kathleen (Cohee) Price.

Phil came from rural Jasper County and graduated from Fair Oaks High School. He is the son of Robert J. and Doris (Yost) Michal. Judy and Phil were married June 9, 1963, at Antioch church just south of Frankfort. Their first son David was born while they were seniors at Purdue and living in the married students apartments. They both graduated from Purdue in June of 1964 just before David's birth on June 23rd.

Phil bought Dr. Raymond Wann's veterinary practice at Wingate which also included a small white frame clinic and a small house located at the corner of Main and McCleur Streets. Judy taught English to grades 8, 9, and 10 at Coal Creek Central the first year (1965-1966) and then interrupted her career to have the second son Richard on Jan. 17, 1967. The family moved to 102 North Davis Street in Crawfordsville in October 1969, and Phil built a new clinic at the Northwest side of the city at the intersection of Old S.R. 55 and U.S. 136. He practiced out of both clinics until 1974 when he sold the Wingate Clinic.

Backrow Chris, Richard. Front Judy, Phil and David Michal

In 1976, Judy returned to Purdue to earn her Master's Degree in Media Science and took a job with the Crawfordsville School system as an elementary librarian at Hoover, Willson, and Beard Schools. After seven years she became a part time facilitator for teachers, helping them to get special materials and speakers for their classes. She still continued to serve as librarian at Hoover and Willson. Phil served on the Crawfordsville City Council from 1981 through 1987 when he was elected Mayor. When he started serving as Mayor in January 1988, he turned over his veterinary practice to Dr. Sharon Odell-Keedy, and they hired an extra veterinarian.

All three sons attended Crawfordsville Schools and entered Purdue University. David graduated in 1986, with a degree in Computer Science and took a job with Intergraph in Huntsville, AL, where he worked for two years. He married Terri Sorrels of Crawfordsville and they have a son Nathaniel. Terri has a daughter Tami who is six, by a previous marriage. Richard Michal is currently a senior at Purdue taking engineering, and will be married to Susan Gran of Indianapolis in December. Susan is a student in elementary education at Purdue. Christopher Michal was born Apr. 12, 1970 at Culver Hospital and he is a freshman at Purdue.

All five members of the family joined the First Christian Church in Crawfordsville and Judy served as an elder and Chairman of Christian Education. Phil has served as Chairman of World Outreach and as an elder in the past. While the family lived at Wingate they were members of the Pleasant Hill United Church of Christ. Both Phil and Judy have belonged to several civic organizations as she belonged to the League of Women Voters, Psi Iota Xi Sorority, and Alpha Delta Kappa Sorority for women educators. She currently is also serving on the Commission for the Status of Women. Phil is a member of Kiwanis and has been active in Church World Service/Crop at the local and state levels. The family has participated in the local Crop Hunger Walk for the past six years.

MILES FAMILY

The Miles Family, a name that was well-known to everyone around Waveland was one of the pioneers of this little town.

George and Paulina settled in the Balhinch area in the early 1800s, due to a sick child who was unable to travel. Death had already taken one child as they journeyed West through Ohio and now death was threatening another in Indiana. George was a well-digger and the town well, located at the corner of the business district in Waveland is one of the first that he dug. It was a popular place both for people and horses.

The George Miles family totalled 12 children, four dying in infancy.

John, the youngest of the 12 was born in 1849 near Waveland. "Uncle John" as he was familiarly known, worked at ditching, cement work and brick laying and later he was engaged in fur buying and the coal business.

Married on Apr. 21, 1872 to Mary Elizabeth English from Armysburg, IN. They, too, had 12 children.

Harry, one of those 12, married Margaret Marie Trout in January of 1915 and started his own family. Five children: Willard, Katheryn, Elizabeth, John and Rosemary completed this Miles family.

War and depression made it difficult to find work so hopping a freight and going over into Illinois was very common. Later, as people recovered from those difficult times, remodelling and new homes gave carpenters work once again. Strawberries, fresh from the patch were picked and delivered by Marie and the youngest daughter. Rosemary came to be known as "The Strawberry Girl."

Carpentry gave Harry the opportunity to go to Florida for the winter of 1952. So, taking his wife and youngest child, he spent the first of many winters in the warm and sunny South.

Graduated from high school and out into the working world, Rosemary married her high school sweetheart, David Hester on Aug. 9, 1953. She and David both became employed at R.R. Donnelleys, a local printing plant. She only worked there prior to starting a family but David has continued to work there for over 35 years.

A daughter, Catherine Denise was born September of 1956 and a son, Paul David was born October of 1959.

The family, after living here and there, settled back in Waveland after purchasing the Alvie Thomas property on East Main Street.

The opportunity to go to beauty school once her own children were in school allowed Rosemary to become a beautician. In October of 1970, Rosie's Beauty Shop was opened for business.

Cathy met and married Brian Utterback in October of 1977. He was killed in an automobile accident on July 7, 1978, a short distance from their home in Fincastel. Cathy presently works at Hook's in the Boulevard Mall and lives at Waveland.

Paul married Abby Huber on May 14, 1988. They have two children; Rebecca and Andrew.

Paul presently works for Larry Cummings Oldsmobile in Crawfordsville and Abby works part-time as a beautician in Greencastle. *Submitted by Rosemary Miles Hester*

BEN AND MAXINE MILLER

Bennet Miller - son of Russell and Frances Miller and Maxine Horn - daughter of Cecil and Eva Horn were married May 31, 1959. Maxine and Ben both graduated from Purdue University. Maxine taught school at Coal Creek Central. Ben went to work for New Richmond Telephone Company which is now Tri-County Telephone Co., Inc. Ben's father, Russell, was ready for the second generation to take over the operating and managing responsibilities of modernizing the company. Ben served in the U.S. Reserves. In the summer of 1960, Maxine went to graduate school at Kansas State University at Manhattan, KS while Ben was finishing his basic training at Fort Riley, KS.

In the fall of 1960, Ben and Maxine returned home where Ben continued to modernize the company. He went to many telephone related schools. A daughter, Melinda Lee was born Mar. 12, 1961. A son, William (Bill) Glen was born on Aug. 20, 1964. Both children went to Coal Creek Central Grade School and North Montgomery High School on which Ben served as a board member. Both also graduated from Purdue University. Both enjoyed sports. Bill especially liked baseball and Melinda liked Volleyball. She also enjoyed her horse and the English shows she participated in.

L to R. Melinda, Maxine, Kim, Bill and Ben Miller. Wedding of son Bill to Kim Kisselback Sept. 10, 1988

As third generation family, they enjoyed working for Tri-County Telephone Company in their spare time.

After college, Melinda went to work at National Exchange Carrier Association (NECA), in Whippany, NJ as a financial analyst. This company was formed as a result of the break-up of AT&T and the Bell Companies. Melinda lives in Morristown, NJ.

After graduating from Purdue, Bill went to work for Tri-County Telephone Company. He married Kim Kisselbach, daughter of Paul and Sue Kisselbach of Auburn, IN, Sept. 10, 1988. Kim works for a dentist in Lafayette.

Ben became quite involved in the telephone industry. In 1981, he received the Pacesetter Award from the Indiana Telephone Association. In 1982, he became the President of the Independent Telephone Pioneers of America (ITPA). On October 1986, he served as Chairman of the United States Telephone Association (USTA). Both required lots of speeches, committee work and traveling. In February of 1987, he received the "Joint Resolution" honor from the Indiana Legislature for his activities in the telephone industry.

Maxine became quite involved in caring for the family and working for our companies. She enjoyed traveling with Ben. Maxine took courses at Purdue and enjoyed her volunteer activities. She served on the board of Purdue Sportswomen Society. Ben and Maxine enjoy their golf activities as well as the sporting activities at Purdue.

Ben is president and Maxine is Secretary-Treasurer of Tri-County Telephone Company and Tri-County Communications Corporation (CATV). They have lived in New Richmond since 1959.

The movie "Hoosiers" was the highlight for our town. Ben, Maxine and son, Bill enjoyed being "Extras" in the movie.

MATHIS MILLER

Mathis Miller was born in Scotland in 1756 and came to America as a young man. He first lived in Pennsylvania, then settled in Virginia. He fought in the Revolutionary War and while fighting in one of the battles was wounded in the head by a bayonet. While living at Pittsburgh, PA he married a girl of German descent by the name of Sarah Price. After the Revolution in 1801, he took his family to Millersville, KY where he died in 1814. There were several children born to this union and William Miller was the first born in 1791 (died in 1872). In 1812 William Miller entered the army and fought several battles in the War of 1812. In 1813 he married Cassandra Ross at Bath Co., KY. Boorn in 1794, died 1869. Cassandra Ross was a direct descendent of George Ross, one of the men who signed the Declaration of Independence. Cassandra Ross was also related to Betsy Ross who made the first American flag. William and Cassandra were the parents of ten children and in 1835 they moved to the south eastern part of Franklin Township in Montgomery Co., IN, where he purchased 160 acres of land for 1000 silver dollars. Being a farmer and a stone mason, William built a house and barn on this land.

Miller Brick House

This Miller homestead has part of that first house still standing today. (1989). At one time after the homestead was settled, William Miller made a trip to Chicago with a team of horses and a wagon load of wheat that he received 55 cents per bushel for the wheat. One of William Millers children was named Samuel Thomas, born in Mar. 27, 1929. Samuel Thomas Miller married Harriet Applegate and to this union ten children were born. They were Wallace, Sylvanis Monroe, Mary Onelia, John Wesly, Rua Cassandra, William Cheever, Ema Elizabeth, Samuel Homer, Otto Lee, and Charles Kincaid. William Cheever born 1867 died 1939 was the 6th child born and raised on the Miller homestead. As a young man William C. worked for Gov. Mount who lived close by. William C. Miller is mentioned in an agricultural book written and published in 1912 that Gov. Mount wrote. William C. Miller married May Miles and started farming on a farm next to where he was born. A few years later their only child was born, her name was Gretchen Lee, born Nov. 1, 1896 died 1968. William C. and his wife purchased a farm 1/4 mile east of Darlington in 1912. On this farm a large brick house was built in 1889, by Issac Cox with brick being made brown clay just east of the house. Gretchen Lee Miller married Alger Budd in 1920 after World War I and farmed just two miles east of the Miller brick house farm. The son of Alger and Gretchen (Miller) Budd, Ralph Budd, born Oct. 30, 1916 now lives with his wife Lucile in Darlington. There were two boys from this marriage, Larry David born Jan. 14, 1942 and Tim Eugene born Aug. 12, 1947. There were two grandsons and one great granddaughter of Ralph and Lucile Budd who prepared this Miller lineage. *Submitted by Ralph Budd*

MICHAEL AND MARY (GASS) MILLER

In 1921 the Miller family decided to honor Aunt Anne Miller, the only child left living of Michael Miller, outliving three brothers and two sisters, John, James, Charles, Mary Ellen, and Jane Miller.

The family decided to have a picnic dinner at the park in Lafayette because Aunt Anne lived in Monon. All enjoyed the day and promised to meet every year from then on.

50th Anniversary of Miller-Gass Reunion

After Aunt Anne passed away they held the reunions in Milligan Park in Crawfordsville. At that time most of the people attending still lived in Montgomery County.

In attendance at the 1921 reunion were, Josephine Kuhn and her husband George. The families of Hannah Bollman, Ezra Bollman, Cinderella Canine, Paul and Myrtle Miller with Mother Arilda, Emma Middlestadt and Otto, Nettie Saylor, Mary McCrea, Carrie Snyder Harlan with husband George, Merle and Paul Harlan and families. Helen, Ernest, Benton, Austin Harlan. Caretta Harlan Sips, and Doris Harlan Merrill. Myrtle and Frank Dodd and children, Austin "Doll" Snyder and George and Bessie Snyder.

Paul and Myrtle Miller were faithful in coming till they died. The only ones in attendance now are the decendants of Carrie Snyder Harlan.

At the last dinner it was decided to call it the Miller - Harlan Reunion. We have our meetings in June at Milligan Park, remembering with love those who started our history. *Submitted by Diana Harlan Wells*

RALPH C. MILLER

Ralph C. Miller was born on a farm in Walnut Township June 1, 1920. This farm had been in the family for four generations. Ralph's parents were Chalmer and Ruth Buser Miller.

Chalmer and his brother Homer were born in a log cabin on this farm to Benjamin Franklin and Flora Buchanan Miller.

Chalmer taught school (Hunt School in Walnut Twp.), farmed, delivered mail, and was Township Trustee. Homer was a Navy Veteran, teacher, and farmer.

Franklin and Flora started housekeeping in the cabin and worked the farm until retirement in 1920. In 1895 they built a new frame house. The logs for this construction were cut on the farm and sawed at Corn's sawmill northeast of Whitesville. The lumber was hauled from the sawmill by team and wagon to the planing mill at New Market and then back home. In 1905 a new barn was built.

Frank Miller's father, Isaac N. Miller, came to Montgomery County from Green Co., OH in 1848. He married Nancy A. Corn in 1849. They were the parents of five sons, George, John, Henry, Franklin, and Albert.

Ralph, Irene and Ruthellen Miller 1977

Nancy Corn Miller's father, William Corn, came to Montgomery County in 1827 from Henry Co., KY. He held an original land grant in Scott Township, Montgomery County, dated Feb. 25, 1830.

Flora Buchanan Miller was the daughter of James and Mary Margaret Myers Buchanan. James' father, David came to Montgomery County from Ohio in 1833. David held two original land grants in Walnut Township, Montgomery County, dated Mar. 12, 1833 and Sept. 17, 1836.

Ruth Buser Miller, Ralph's mother, taught school at Highview in Franklin Twp. before her marriage. She was the daughter of William H. Jr. and Emma Miles Buser. Will Jr. was a farmer and Emma had taught school.

William H. Buser Sr., came to Clark Township, Montgomery County from Green Co., OH in 1855. In his early years he was a cabinet maker but spent most of his life as a farmer in Scott Township. Mr. Buser married Sarah Allen. Her father, Stephen held several original land grants in Brown Twp., Montgomery County, dated 1825 - 1835.

Ruth Buser Miller's maternal grandparents, William H. and Mary Maddox Miles, came to Brown Twp., Montgomery County, from Shelby Co., KY in the 1870s. From 1881 until 1894 they operated the general store and post office in Brownsvalley. The *Crawfordsville Journal*, Sept. 17, 1881 printed the following statement. "Despite its limitations the general store has an important place in the local economy. Such a store is that of William H. Miles of Brownsvalley. Mr. Miles announce that he was selling goods as cheaply as could be purchased anywhere in the county. People should give me a fair trial before going elsewhere. If you want groceries, dry goods, hats, caps, boots, shoes, glassware, tollware, tinware, or anything else usually kept in a first class country store, give me a trial." Mr. Miles also operated a sawmill in that area.

Ralph Miller married Esther Irene Wilson in 1951. They started life together on the Miller farm in the same house where Ralph was born and had always lived. Their farm was designated a "Hoosier Homestead Farm" January 1986.

Ralph, Navy Seebee veteran and farmer, raised Hampshire hogs and served as Walnut Twp. Trustee. Irene retired from Indiana Bell Telephone.

Ralph and Irene have one daughter, Ruthellen, who married Douglas Dawley. Ruthellen is a Biochemist doing post-doctorate work, and Douglas is a science teacher.

RUSSELL AND FRANCES MILLER

Russell Miller came to Montgomery County on July 5, 1933, from Columbus, OH, to take over the ownership and management of the Linden, New Richmond, and Romney Telephone Companies. He was then 27 years of age.

During the summer of 1933 Russell made a service call to repair a telephone at the home of Mr. and Mrs. Frank Demaree in Romney. The telephone was located in a rather dark hallway, and when he was there, Frances passed through. Her mother introduced them, and said that her daughter was just home from "finishing school." What she meant was that she had just finished school, but at any rate Russell came back later to see the "finished product", and they took off from there. They were married in Terre Haute on Aug. 25, 1934.

Russell and Frances moved temporarily to New Richmond in 1935, but have lived there ever since!

Russell and Frances Miller

Russell was a one-man telephone company, and did all of the line-work, installing, and repairing. In fact, the Miller's wedding depended on the weather. If there was a bad thunder-storm, and lines were out and poles were down, Russell had to be on hand to make repairs and couldn't leave to get married. Fortunately, the weather cooperated.

People were still using the old magneto, crank-type phones, with operators to connect one party to another. The operators were paid $50.00 per month and also kept the books. Their living-quarters were provided at the telephone office. Residence rates were $1.50 per month for a telephone.

The Miller's son, Bennet Rhoads Miller, was born July 24, 1937 and their daughter, Mary Edith, arrived on Mar. 18, 1942.

Ben married Maxine Horn on May 30, 1959. They have two children, Melinda and Bill.

Mary Edith married Michael Persson on June 4, 1966, and they have three sons, Michael, Jonathan, and Christopher.

After 30 years of keeping the telephones ringing in their area of Indiana, and seeing many changes made, from magneto to dial phones, no more operators, all automatic equipment, and now sophisticated computers and having their family raised, Russell and Frances decided to see the world. Ben was able to take over the management of the telephone company, which had become the Tri-County Telephone Company in 1959.

In 1967 the Millers installed a small magneto telephone system in a Mission Hospital in Zaire, Africa. They traveled on every continent, and went around the world in 1970.

In 1983 Russell and his brother, Leroy, who had helped Russell start in the telephone business, were honored at an Open-House reception for 50 Years of Telephone Service. This was held at North Montgomery High School, and several hundred people came to congratulate them.

Russell is a 50 year member of the New Richmond Masonic Lodge, and Russell and Francis are also 50 year members of the New Richmond Eastern Star.

They are also 50 year members of the New Richmond United Methodist Church.

THE MILLIGAN FAMILY

It all started in Scotland in the year of 1727 with the birth of Samuel Milligan. In 1754, when he was 27 years old, he moved to Ireland. He married and had a family of eight children. His first wife died and he married his second wife, Sarah Jardine.

In about 1770, he left Ireland and moved to America with Sarah and their eight children. David (born 1776 died 1834) the second son of Samuel and Sarah, married Sarah Margaret Wallace July 1, 1794, and they had ten children. Their fourth and fifth children were twins, James and John, born in 1803 in Swissvale, Perry Co., PA. James died at a young age. John farmed with his father until he was 19 years old, and then went to live with his uncle, Joseph, in Georgetown, District of Columbia. There he attended school until he was 22 years old and then started teaching in 1825. In May 1827, he moved to Ross Co., OH, and again taught school while living with his uncle, Hugh, for 18 months. In 1828, John moved on to Crawfordsville, Montgomery Co., IN, where he started teaching again. At the same time, he started clerking in local stores.

William Moore had started a store in Brown Township on the south bank of Little Raccoon Creek and hired John Milligan to run the store for him. In 1830, Milligan bought the store from Moore and moved it to the corner of Cross and Green Streets in Waveland. This became the first building in Waveland.

Hirom Heddleson laid out the town and entered it into records in 1830. He later sold it to a Mr. Morgan who transferred it to John Milligan in 1834. In 1835, Milligan, with the help of Thomas L. Glenn, surveyor, laid out the town lots. On Christmas Day, 1835, the first lots were sold at auction with the provision that no tavern ever be built within the original town limits.

John Milligan made the following land purchases: 40 acres, Feb. 16, 1837, for $800.00 and 126 acres, Feb. 10, 1837, for $630.00. To make this $1,430.00 purchase in 1837 he may have used his own savings or he may have inherited from his father who died in 1834.

On Jan. 22, 1829, John Milligan married Lucinda Elmore whose family moved to Montgomery County from South Carolina. Of their nine children, the eighth born was James Robert. He was born Jan. 23, 1844, and married Francis Irwin on Nov. 24, 1868. Their union produced six children. Frank Milligan, Mary Lucinda Milligan Taylor, Robert Milligan died three years, Samuel Milligan, Dean Milligan and James Milford Milligan born Aug. 26, 1886 married Ruby A. Strong Feb. 26, 1908 by whom they had six children:

1. J. Kenneth Milligan, born 1908. Married Katherine Boling and had four children: Thomas, Samuel, Elizabeth and Timothy.

2. Richard T. Milligan (twin of Roland), born 1913. Married Donna Rae Black and had five children: James, Caroline, Joe, Cynthia and Jay.

3. Roland D. Milligan (twin of Richard), born 1913. Married Pauline Byrd and had five children: Dean, Allen, Sally, Alex and Jill.

4. Ellen Jane Milligan, born 1915, died 1923.

5. Milford S. Milligan, born 1918. Married Helen Bunnell Drake and had two children: Charles and Marie Nanette.

6. Dale Milligan, born 1925. Married Clara L. Auman and had two children: Nancy and Susan.

Roland D. Milligan and his daughter, Jill Bowman, and her three children (Erin, Sarah and Brian) are the only direct descendants of John Milligan who currenlty live in Waveland.

ROLAND DANIEL MILLIGAN

Roland Daniel Milligan was born Feb. 6, 1913 in Waveland, IN. He was one of the twin sons of James Milford and Ruby Milligan.

Roland spent his childhood and high school years living in Waveland. He and his identical twin brother Dick, spent many of their summers on their grandfather Alexander Strong's farm in Greene Township, Parke County with their Aunt Mayme Lee. Roland graduated from Waveland High School in 1931.

After graduating from high school, Roland attended Indiana Normal College in Terre Haute, IN for one year and then transferred to Wabash College in Crawfordsville, IN. After attending Wabash for one year he withdrew because of illness.

In March of 1935 he married Pauline Byrd of Russellville, IN. They resided in Waveland. Roland worked on the farm in Green Township until they moved to Guion in 1937 to take over the business his brother Dick had been running. Roland ran the Grocery Store and Huckster Wagon and Pauline was the Postmistress.

Around 1939 they left the grocery and Guion and Roland went to work at the Rock Quarry near Waveland.

In 1945 he started a Turkey farm at the edge of Waveland, which he operated until 1948. He was recognized in the *Prairie Farm* magazine for his innovative ideas on raising Turkeys.

In 1948 they moved back to Waveland. Roland and his brothers formed an Allis Chalmers dealership in Crawfordsville. Roland worked at the Milligan Brothers dealership until he retired in 1976.

In the early 1970s Roland bought the farm that had been in the Milligan family for over 100 years.

Roland and his wife Pauline still live in the house they moved to in Waveland in 1948. Roland is operating the chain saw business he started in his home, and farming the small family farm.

Roland and Pauline have five children all born in or near Waveland, IN.

(1) Roland Dean Milligan born 1935.

Married Linda Weatherman and they now reside in Houston, TX. They have four children: Shawn, Amy, Robert, and Suzanne.

(2) Alan Dale Milligan born 1939.

Married Sue Ellen Woodfill and they now reside in Franklin, IN. They have three children: Scott, Kimberly, and Kellie.

(3) Sally Ann Milligan born 1945.

Married Malcolm Simpson and they now reside in Waveland, IN. They have two children: David and Audra.

(4) Alex Byrd Milligan born 1950.

Married Carol Heldeman and they now reside in Rockville, IN. They have three children: Daniel, Emily, and Michael.

(5) Paula Jill Milligan Bowman born 1955.

Now resides in Waveland, IN. She has three children: Erin, Sarah, and Brian. *Submitted by Alex Milligan*

THOMAS KENNETH MILLIGAN

Thomas Kenneth Milligan presently serves as Judge of the 22nd Judicial Circuit of the State of Indiana. Although the circuit has included several of the neighboring counties in the past, presently the circuit includes only Montgomery County and the court is known as the Montgomery Circuit Court. The circuit court was created by the Constitution of the State of Indiana and is the trial wagon court of general jurisdiction for the county (circuit).

Judge Milligan was born Sept. 26, 1941 in Crawfordsville, IN to J. Kenneth Milligan and Katherine Elizabeth Boling Milligan. Judge Milligan was reared in Waveland, IN where his parents resided. He graduated from Waveland High School in the spring of 1959. That fall he enrolled in Wabash College and completed his course of study there graduating in May of 1963.

By the time of college graduation Milligan's application for admittance to the Indiana University School of Law at Bloomington, IN had been accepted. He entered law school in fall of 1963 and graduated in the spring of 1966.

On Aug. 23 1964 Milligan and Martha Suanne Cronkhite were married. Mrs. Milligan is the daughter of Dean Eugene Cronkhite and Susan Jean Myers Cronkhite who moved to Waveland in Montgomery County from the Kingman, Grange Corner, Steam Corner area of Fountain County. Mr. and Mrs. Cronkhite presently live in Crawfordsville.

Mrs. Milligan, having graduated from Indiana State College in 1962, began teaching. During the 1962-1963 and 1963-1964 school years she taught in Crawfordsville at Hoover Elementary School. After her marriage Mrs. Milligan taught two years at Elm Heights Elementary School in Bloomington, IN.

Upon Mr. Milligan's graduation from law school they returned to Montgomery County settling in Crawfordsville. Mrs. Milligan taught another year at Hose Elementary School. Milligan became associated with the law firm of Wernle & Ristine. He soon became a partner and for several years the firm bore the name of Wernle, Ristine & Milligan.

Early in 1974 the Honorable Howard A. Sommer, then judge of the Montgomery Circuit Court, announced his intention to retire after some 30 years on the bench. The position was considered to be an important position which entailed great responsibility and hard work. Judges were notoriously underpaid in comparison to practicing attorneys. The result was that there was no race to the Statehouse to file a declaration of candidacy for election to the position. After considerable soul-searching, discussion with family and friends, and contrary to Mrs. Milligan's preference (although not without her support), Milligan decided to run for the office.

Milligan won the primary election in 1974 and has not been opposed in any election since. He has been reelected twice, first in 1980 and again in 1986, and is presently serving his third term.

Judge and Mrs. Milligan have two children: Katherine Jean Milligan, born Feb. 14, 1968 who is finishing her junior year at Dartmouth College in Hanover, NH; and Benjamin Thomas Milligan, born Dec. 31, 1970, who is preparing to enter Wesleyan University in Middletown, CT. After her year of teaching at Hose Elementary School, Mrs. Miligan retired to devote her energies to homemaking, mothering, church, and volunteer endeavors.

Throughout the years this family has been active in the Crawfordsville community. They have been devoted to Wabash Avenue Presbyterian Church; and they have supported a wide variety of community organizations and activities.

JOHN LEWIS MINNICH

John Lewis Minnich (Sept. 12, 1850; d. Sept. 30, 1927) was 12 years old when his father, Andrew Jackson Minnich, died in the Battle of Seven Pines, near Richmond, VA on June 3, 1862. When he was only 15 years old he left Virginia, tramping through Ohio and on to Indiana. He worked as a farm hand until he had enough money to bring his mother (C. Adeline Mills) and his brother (Charles Austin Minnich) and sister (Francis Susan Minnich) to Indiana, making their abode at Ladoga, IN.

He leased and cleared and drained land north of Ladoga and built a log cabin for the family. This area was called Hog Heaven as it was swampy land.

On Mar. 19, 1876 he was married to Lydia Valentine Himes (b. Feb. 13, 1858; d. July 22, 1944. She was the fourth child of Daniel H. Himes, Jr. and Mary Louise Harshbarger.) They began their married life on a 40 acre lease in the woods of Indiana, from which he cut logs and built a cabin for them to live in. They had five sons, one dying in infancy. The four living sons were Otto Lewis Minnich, Samuel Andrew Minnich, Lee Raymond Minnich and George William McKinley Minnich. These sons have all passed away except for George Minnich who lives in Perris, CA.

In 1910 the family, except the two older sons who had preceded them, came to California, making their home first in LaVerne, later at Chino, Hemet and Pomona.

Most of the descendants of John and Lydia Minnich, now in the fifth generation, live in Southern California.

ALEXANDER MITCHELL

Alexander Mitchell married Sarah Royality and were the parents of eight children: Isom, William, Elizabeth, Maggie, John, Sylvia, Jonathan and Sam.

Isom and wife Rose had Metta, Orville, Edward, Charles, Lee and Hattie.

William married Mary Willhite and had Warren, Leeanise, Elliott, Norman, President Alexander, William and Sarah Ogden.

Elizabeth married Jesse Griffin.

Maggie died at age 12 or 13.

Sylvia—nothing known about her.

John and Sam-nothing known about them.

Jonathan married Nanny Wilson and had eight children: Clara (Harshbarger), Clarence, Dona Applegate Livingston, Mary, died at eight years, Jessie Clarkson, Pearl Lyon, Raymond, and Ali Bunnell.

President Alexander Mitchell, son of William and Mary (Willhite) was born Jan. 8, 1875. He married Margaret Ellen Ross on Feb. 25, 1896. He died May 4, 1912 at age 37. Margaret married John Willhite. Her third marriage was to Charles O. Miller. She passed away Aug. 7, 1968 at age 89.

President Alexander and Margaret had seven children. Margaret and Charles had a son, Robert. Alexander and family lived in Elmdale, where they operated the general store. Their children, Daisy, Virgil, Dallas, Delevon (Jimmy), Eula, and Amaza.

Daisy Laurene was born Oct 17, 1896 and died Oct 22, 1971. She married Edgar Hall Whillite on Feb. 14, 1914. Edgar was born Oct. 10, 1887 and passed away Sept. 7, 1952. They were the parents of eight children, Moyne Argel, John Kenneth, Melba Margaret, Edgar Leon, twins Dale Lloyd and Gale

Floyd, Noel Eugene, and Moyna Arlena. (see Willhite History this book).

Daisy's second marriage was to Roy Brandenburg on Nov. 25, 1959. Virgil was born June 10, 1898 and died Oct. 4 or 5, 1899.

Dallas was born May 30, 1900 and died June 28, 1964. He married Mable Stahlhut and had Nadine and Bonnie. He was employed for many years at Inland Steel Co. of East Chicago.

Elmer was born Aug. 14, 1902. He married Faye Keller, Oct. 27, 1923. They have three children, Helen, Richard, and Berta.

Delevon Donalson "Jimmy" was born Jan. 28, 1905 near Kingman. He was manager of J.C. Penney store in Danville, IL. He married Verna Epperson and adopted Patricia Ann. He died Apr. 6, 1946—age 41.

Eula was born Apr. 11, 1907 and married Frank Haslam on Feb. 13, 1926. They were the parents of Janice, Carolyn, Samuel and Richard. Frank was a railroad operator. He died Apr. 19, 1987.

Amaza was born May 22, 1910. She married Stanley Zimmerman and had Stanley Jr., Donald and Terry. They reside in Sturgis, MI, where they operated a general store.

CHARLES EDWARD MITCHELL

Charles Edward Mitchell: b. Mar. 2, 1922 d. Feb. 22, 1986. He was born on "Bristle Ridge", north of "Boston Store", Coal Creek Twp., the fifth generation buried in Coal Creek Twp. Parents: Raymond Alexander Mitchell and Lula Bell Rodgers. Siblings: 1/2 sister Ernestine Lenora, 1/2 sister Frances Faye Rodgers, Jwanita, twins Claire and Clara, twins Paul and Phillip, Charles, Jonathan Leon, Billy Russell and Max.

Service record: Entered U.S. Army Oct. 8, 1942, assigned to 3416th Ord. MAM Co. Served overseas two years four months 18 days, in Burma, on Stillwell Road, at Tagap, a Motor Pool Camp. Charles set-up buildings with native help and their elephants. One building gave "away" with him on the roof as it fell. Near the end of the war, soldiers complained of the food. Next day Charles became Chief Cook. He traded rice for native chickens, Bar-B-Q'd a tiger over open pit, and at Thanksgiving cooked 32 turkeys, made noodles with tomato juice and powdered eggs, dressing, mashed potatoes and gravy. Repeated at Christmas time.

Charles Edward and Geneva (Walp) Mitchell

Homebound troops left Singapore for Pearl Harbor on the ship Callan and landed at Ft. Lewis Washington, USA. He was honorable discharged Feb. 6, 1946. Rank T 4 Carpenter. Charles had been around the world.

On Oct. 20, 1985, Charles and Geneva M. (Walp b. June 15, 1923, Marion Co., IN) celebrated their 39th Wedding Anniversary. (Her parents Walp-Marsteller, see this book). One stillborn son 1951.

Lee Edward was born Sept. 21, 1952. On Feb. 6, 1983 Lee married Dawn E. Henderson (b. July 4, 1962 Oleath, KS). One daughter April. D. (b. May 19, 1983).

As an "Independent" Contractor, Charles built many farm buildings, remodeled houses and built 19 new homes in Montgomery and nearby counties.

Mitchell Lineage: Wm. b. 1782 d. 1849, Bur. Oakland Cem. Wife: Mary b. 1794 d. 1840.

Alexander b. 1817 KY d. 1858-9 Bur. Oakland Cem. Wife: Sarah A. Royalty b. 1821 KY d. Sept. 12, 1885

Jonathan S. b. Apr. 10, 1848-9 Ind. d. Feb. 10, 1930 Bur. New Richmond Cem. Wife: Nancy M. Wilson b. Feb. 22, 1853 Putnam Co. d. Oct. 17 1925.

Raymond Alexander b. Feb. 4, 1897 Montgomery County d. Oct. 17, 1969 Bur. Oakland Cem. Wife: Lula Belle Rodger b. Dec. 16, 1891 Fountain Co. d. Nov. 12, 1971.

THE FRED J. MITCHELL FAMILY

Fred J. Mitchell, son of Freddie Mitchell and Effie Bever was born Oct. 26, 1921 at Byron, IN. Fred's mother died when he was seven months old. His father then married Lillie Agnes Ward and moved to a farm one mile east of Byron. To this marriage was born three sons; Leonard Orville, Kenneth Warren, and Norman Dale. Fred graduated from Waveland High School. He then entered the Air Force on August 1942 and served until September 1945 in the European Sector.

After returning home, Fred started farming and retired in 1986. Fred's great joy in farming was raising polled hereford cattle.

March 7, 1948, Fred married Naomi Robison, daughter of Homer and Lottie Bayless Robison. They started housekeeping at Byron, IN. At the time Byron had two churches, a store and school. They later moved to Wapaloo and then to a farm east of Marshall.

The Mitchells have Sharon Kay Harris, born Apr. 23, 1951. Sharon is a school teacher in the Crawfordsville schools. Her husband, J. Lamont Harris, is an attorney. Their children are Ann and Stephen.

Rebecca Lou, born July 24, 1953, resides in Indianapolis and is associated with Commonwealth Insurance Company.

Paul David, born Feb. 5, 1957, resides R.R. Kingman and is employed with Nucor Steel Incorporation. He is married to Diane Willhite. Their children are: Amber, Kelly, and Paul Michael.

Fred was always active in the Indiana Crop Improvement Association and the National Polled Hereford Association. He promoted 4-H, being a leader for several years and president of the Fair Board Association. He presently serves as Brown township advisory member and on the Fire Department of Waveland. He has been a member of the Waveland Masonic Lodge since 1945.

Naomi majored in nursing at Indiana University and Ball State. For several years she has worked in vocational rehabilitation serving the disabled. Naomi also was a 4-H leader and county 4-H superintendent. She served Indiana as Worthy Grand Matron, Order of the Eastern Star.

Both have served in the church as teachers, memorial committee, church clerk, and finance committee. They presently belong to the Waveland Covenant Church, and reside at 202 East Green, Waveland.

GABRIEL MITCHELL

Gabriel Mitchell was one of the early settlers of Montgomery County, having arrived in Brown Township in 1826 from Shelby Co., KY.

Of Irish descent, he was the fifth generation of Mitchell in this country, and without question, the fifth generation that could be called "pioneer."

He was born late in 1800 in Shelby Co., KY, the second of five children born to Daniel and Mary (Overstreet) Mitchell. His siblings were Malinda, James, Lucinda, and Paulina.

When Gabriel was not yet six, his father died. His mother remarried in Jefferson Co., KY in October of 1807 to Robert Willson. The family remained in Shelby Co., KY in the proximity of Gabriel's paternal grandparents, Daniel and Judith (Prewitt) Mitchell, though later, several family members, including the Willsons, moved to Iowa. At least four of the five kids were married in Shelby County, with three of them claiming the hands of members of the Van Cleave family.

Gabriel remained in Shelby County and there married Ruth Van Cleave, daughter of John and Margary Jane (Kerns) Van Cleave on Jan. 4, 1821. Gabriel, Ruth, and their young children moved to Brown Township, Montgomery Co., IN in 1826, where they completed their family of about 12 kids. They were Daniel, Samuel, John, Margary, Mary ("Polly"), James, Martha, Sarah, Robert, Nancy, Emily, and Malinda.

A daughter of James and Martha (Van Cleave) McMullen, Marjary Jane, once wrote about their family's brief stay in the home of Gabriel Mitchell as their cabin was being built after their arrival from Shelby Co., KY in 1829:

"The children did not get along together very well...Mama had a sack of peaches she had dried in Kentucky and brought with her. There was no fruit in the new country. The sack of peaches was set under the bed, and Samuel and John, Uncle Gabriel's boys, would...fill their pockets and go out and eat them...Margary, a little girl, but somewhat older than I, had a little stool to sit on. I wanted to sit on the stool, but Margary would not let me....One day, Margary grabbed me by the hair and held on, dragging me about the floor. (Mama) got up from her work and separated us then threw the little stool in the fireplace where it burned to ashes. Aunt Ruth never said a word, neither did Mama." Ruth died sometime in the mid to late 1840s.

In about 1849, Gabriel married his second wife, a widow by the married name of Alice Tucker. They had four more children, David, Joseph, Ruth, and George. Alice was in her mid-30s when she died around 1855/56, possibly the result of childbirth. Gabriel married lastly Margaret James on Sept. 4, 1856 in Montgomery Co., IN. They had no children together.

Gabriel Mitchell's name last appears in the 1870 Census of Montgomery County. Where he went after that, or when and where he died remains a mystery.

ROBERT AND WANETAH MITCHELL

Robert Mitchell was born in the southwestern part of Montgomery County Feb. 20, 1898, son of Jesse and Artie Phipps Mitchell. His mother died when Robert was five and his younger brother, Fred was three years old.

Later Jessie married Ollie Myers and they became parents of a daughter, Mary and a son, Russell.

Robert married Wanetah Tague in 1918, daughter of John and Lizzie Lohman Tague. Wanetah was one of 11 children. The little house in which she was born still stands on the Turkey Run Golf Course. She had learned some very good baking skills from her Aunt Corda Zachary at a very early age.

Robert and Wanetah were the parents of one son, Bernard Fred, born Aug. 2, 1919. For several years the family resided in what is known as Wapalo in Parke County. This community was named for the Indian tribe that once roamed the area. The Fellowship of Christian Athletes Center - National Conference Center Covers several acres of the land today.

Robert and Wanetah Mitchell

Robert and Wanetah were active in the Byron Community nearby, where they attended church and other functions. Bernard attended Byron Grade School and graduated from Marshall High School. Robert served as trustee of Howard Twp. for eight years.

In autumn 1943 the family moved to a farm two miles west of Waveland. Robert was a farmer and livestock dealer as his father Jesse had been.

Wanetah was a homemaker and took pride in her entries in baking contests at the county fairs and often earned the right to go to the Indiana State Fair. She won ribbons several times - actually enough to decorate a pillow, which the family still treasures today. She was also known for being a caring person and was there when her family and friends needed her.

Bernard married Norma Jean Everhart of Ladoga on June 8, 1946. Bernard continued farming with his father. Norma had begun her teaching career at Mace, but taught at Waveland before and after the birth of their son, Robert Michael, who was born Dec. 1, 1949.

Mike attended Waveland School, where he was very active in sports. During the years he had spent a great deal of time on the farm with his grandparents. His love for them and his association with farm life influenced him to enroll in Agriculture Economics at Purdue University. He felt fortunate to be initiated into Farmhouse Fraternity, where he lived for four years, until his graduation from Purdue.

Robert passed away June 3, 1967. Wanetah continued to live in their home place until her death Feb. 25, 1972.

Mike married Rhonda Dooley of Marshall, IN, July 16, 1972. Rhonda also graduated from Purdue and taught school at Walnut Twp. They became parents of Clint Davis, born Aug. 27, 1974 and Matthew Robert, born on July 16, 1976.

Rhonda later attended Depauw University, where she earned her master's degree in the teaching field.

Mike and his family continue to live on his grandparents farm, which borders the Turkey Run Golf Course on the west and overlooks Lake Waveland on the north. *Submitted by Norma Mitchell*

AUSTIN L. AND MARGARET L. UTTERBACK MONEY

Austin Luther and Margaret Leona Money are long-time residents of Montgomery Co., IN. They are both employed at Oak Hill Cemetery Company since April 1955. He is Superintendent and she is in charge of the office, as well as the Secretary/Treasurer of the Cemetery Board.

Austin was born Dec. 2, 1926 at Indianapolis, IN being the eldest of five children of Austin Luther, Sr. and Erma Hazel Courtney Money. His father was born at Pittsboro, IN on Mar. 21, 1879 the son of Aaron Presley and Mary Margaret Surber Money, who were the parents of Austin, Sr., Minnie Pearl, David Roscoe, Irvin Wallace, Ryliss Rosetta, Everett Russell, Lula Fern, Marion Renfro, Rush, Flossie May, Grace, Auburn Alexander and Edith Irene. The family came to Indiana from Kentucky. Austin was educated in the Pittsboro schools and belonged to the Christian Church.

Erma Hazel Courtney was born June 29, 1908 at Muncie, IN. She was the daughter of Elbert Ebert and Lela LaVina Loy Courtney. Her siblings were: Mabel, Dorothy Margaret, Agatha, Clifford and Robert. She was educated in the Muncie schools and in Texas. Erma was a member of First Church of Nazarene.

Austin and Erma were married on Mar. 18, 1926, at McKinney, TX. To this union were born: Austin Luther, Jr., Betty Joan, Donald, Charles Edward and Cheryl Lynn. Austin, Sr. died Feb. 13, 1967. He was a carpenter by trade. Erma passed away June 21, 1984. She was a homemaker. Both are buried at Oak Hill Cemetery, Crawfordsville, IN.

Margaret Leona Money was born Jan. 5, 1929 at Crawfordsville. She is the eldest child of Emmett Andrew and Eva Darlene Fitzwater Utterback. Her siblings are: Lester Newton, Martha Darlene, Donald Eugene and Mary Ann. Martha Darlene passed away at the age of seven weeks and is buried at Masonic Cemetery, Waynetwon, IN. Her father was a brickmaker and horseman by trade. He loved to groom and train horses. He was born at Elmdale. He passed away July 1, 1961. Her mother was a nurse, she always wanting to help someone in need. She was born at New Maysville, IN. She died Mar. 1, 1964. They are both buried at Masonic Cemetery, Waynetown.

Margaret's grandparents were: Lester William and Elva Jaynes Utterback and Newton T. and Mary Margaret Bailes Fitzwater. All are deceased. Utterback's buried at Masonic Cemetery, Waynetown, all Fitzwater's are buried at Mace Cemetery.

Austin and Margaret were married Dec. 2, 1944 at Crawfordsville. To their union were born three lovely children: Marilyn Sue, Linda Lou and Darrell Wayne. They have eight lovely grandchildren, whom they are very proud of being: Angela Michell Allen Hastings, Brian Wayne Allen, Melissa Kay Taylor, Randall Scott Allen, Rebecca Sue Money, Darrell Wayne Money, Jr. and David Wayne Money.

It is at this writing that Austin and Margaret have found love, friendship and many, many hours of enjoyment at their work. They have enjoyed the love of their family, friends and above all the true love and enjoyment of their grandchildren.

Austin and Margaret are avid campers, belonging to the Campers Club of America and Good Sam Club.

ALEXANDER-MONTGOMERY

My ancestor, Alexander Montgomery, was born in Ireland in 1743, and came to this country to serve in the Revolutionary War when he was in his teens. He was an own cousin of General Richard Montgomery, of the British Army, who fell at the seige of Quebec, and who Montgomery County was named after. Alexander came to Bourbon Co., KY after the war, where he farmed. About 1812 he moved to Scott Co., IN, then to Jefferson County. He and his sons and their families came to Montgomery County in 1823. His son, Alexander Montgomery, Jr. (my great, great grandfather) opened a shoe shop in Crawfordsville, but finally purchased a farm nearby, and resumed farming. He served his country in the War of 1812, under General William Henry Harrison, and participated in the battle of Tippecanoe.

His son, Isaac Herrod Montgomery (my great grandfather), was born in 1814 in Jefferson Co., IN. He was educated in the old pioneer subscription schools, and also pursued his studies in the old brick school house in Crawfordsville. When he was a boy of 12 years, he carried the mail from Crawfordsville to Lafayette. This trip was made once a week on horseback, carrying the mail in saddlebags. For this trip he was paid 50¢. He learned the shoemaker's trade at which he worked eight years, but through the greater part of his life carried on farming. He started farming in 1836, after his marriage to Elizabeth Parks. Her father had given them a tract of 40 acres of prairie land in the northern part of Montgomery County, near the boundary line of Tippecanoe County. In early manhood he began to raise and sell cattle, and in this enterprise was quite prosperous. By his good management and practical business methods, he increased his capital and made judicious investments in land. He finally purchased all of his father-in-law's farm and other lands adjoining, until he owned 2000 acres in one body. When he passed away in 1904, the land was given to his eldest son, William H. Montgomery. Upon William's death in 1917, the land was given to his brother (my grandfather, Wallace F. Montgomery), sisters, nieces and nephews. My father, named after his grandfather, Isaac Herrod Montgomery, owned part of this land until his death in 1976. From Biographical History of Tippecanoe County. *Submitted by Martha E. Montgomery*

JOHN AND LENA MOODY

While getting a haircut one day at Fern and Alex's (1937), "John" Anthony Wayne Moody got interested in photography via a talk with his barber, Carl Demaree (who did picture-making on the side). John was working as a linotypist at the *Journal/Review* at the time and asked the night editor, Lloyd McCormick if he could use his camera. John continued working with the newspaper until the mid-1960s when he went into the photography business full-time.

John was born in Tilton, IL on Dec. 22, 1907, the son of John C. and Matilda (Eichacher) Moody. John C. worked on the Big 4 Railroad as a chief dispatcher. Matilda's parents were both German. In 1913, the Moody family moved to Mt. Carmel, IL where John attended school and graduated from Mt. Carmel High in 1927, the year the Aces won the state tourney. John went to work at a commercial shop in Noblesville on April Fool's Day, 1929. In

September, John read an ad for a linotype setter for the Crawfordsville newspaper, hopped on the Interurban and landed the job.

John and Lena Moody

As he sat on the porch in 1935, John noticed a cute gal walking by the Elks' Lodge and liked what he saw. On Nov. 14, 1936, John married his cute gal, Lena Gertrude Black (daughter of John and Mollie (Collins) Black), born May 24, 1913 in Eldorado, OK. She came to Crawfordsville with her mother and sister Annie Wood's family when she was ten years old. Lena graduated from C.H.S. Lena's brother-in-law, Elmer Wood was fire chief here for a few years in the late 1930's.

John and Lena are the parents of two daughters: Carole Anne, born May 6, 1937 and Judith Arlene, born July 19, 1938. Carole Anne weighed three pounds at birth. She married John Foxworthy of Ladoga. John now owns a print shop in Waynetown. John and Carole have a daughter, Amy Jo, a student at Cincinnati Bible College.

Judy married Gene "Butch" Jarvis of New Market. Judy was a beautician for several years in the area. Butch is in Insurance and Real Estate and owns apartments in Terre Haute. Judy and Butch have three children: Pam (married Jeff Sutherland) has two children, P.J. and Tyler. Wayne (married Marie Perez) has one daughter, Brenna Antoinette. Candy (married Jim Bloom) has a daughter, Elizabeth Marie.

John and Lena had a large 40th Anniversary celebration at their church and a family dinner at the Covington Beef House for their 50th.

Lena was affiliated with the Zonta Club. John and Lena are both members of Christ United Methodist Church. The Moodys spend much of their time enjoying their children and grandchildren.

Moody Studio was located at 208 Jennison St. from 1939-42, moving to 303 South Green St. in April of 1942, where it was operated until 1987. As this was written, in April 1989, Moodys are still residing at this address. *Submitted by John Moody*

THOMAS M. MOODY

Thomas M. Moody, oldest son of Sanford and Alice Lough Moody, was born Nov. 30, 1844 in Thompkinsville, KY. He came to Indiana at the age of 12 years. He rode the Monon Railroad to Ladoga, IN, then walked from there to Waveland and Browns Valley area while his father and mother drove a team of oxen with their household goods.

August 25, 1864 Thomas M. married Martha Ellen, daughter of Nathan and Ann Reed Clements of New Albany, IN. Martha was born Sept. 26, 1846.

Thomas served in the Civil War, joining Aug. 13, 1862. He was in the 40th Regiment Infantry, serving with General Sherman on his march to the Sea, and was wounded in the hip at Missionary Ridge.

He was then mustered out June 14, 1865 and arrived in Indianapolis the day Lincoln was shot.

Sanford (Sant) Moody, son of Thomas M. Moody

To Thomas (Pony) and Martha (Matt) were born seven children; Sanford N., Walter, Harry, James, Louisa (Mrs. John Gilliland), Cora Lee and Etha.

Sanford N., born Mar. 29, 1868 at Browns Valley, first married Catherine Theresa Hastaday, daughter of John H. and Margaret Cronin Hastaday, who was born in County Cork, Ireland. She came to America at the age of 16.

The Hastaday siblings were: Henry, Will, Ed, Minnie, Rebecca, Nelle, Abby, Margaret and Catherine.

The children of Sanford (Sant) and Catherine (Katie) were; Owen (died in infancy), Edward, Louis, Clem (Dot), Paul, George (died at age 16), Margaret and Kathryn.

Edward's first marriage was to Mable VanCleave, whose children were Leland and Vivian. His second marriage was to Gladys Murray, they had one daughter, Joan.

Clem (Dot) married Millie Johnston and had two sons, namely; Sanford (Santy) and Thomas (Tommy).

Paul married Helen Lytle. Their daughter was Paula Lynn.

Margaret married Gordon Moser and their two sons were Joseph Gordon and John William. Joseph first married Peggy Sanders, with three children, Katrina, Eric and Kirsten. His second marriage was to Judy Fayhee. John married Karen Dellacca and they had two sons, Jay Todd and Sean Bradley.

Kathryn married Russell Powell. Their children were Phillip R. and Michael (Mike). Phillip married Sue Allman. To this union were born Brock and Lori. Mike married Sue Dellane and they had two daughters; Lisa and Shannon.

Sant's second marriage was to Sabrah Catherine (Katie) Wilhite. Katie had an adopted daughter, Waneta, who came to live with the family. She married Jewell Chaney.

Sant and Katie also raised James T. (Jim) Moody, who was the son of Sant's brother James.

Of Thomas (Posey) and Martha's (Matt) children, Walter died in infancy. Harry married Alice Lunsford. James married Effie Mullimen. Their children were Trent, Bonnie, Dolly, James and Cora Lee.

Louisa (Lou) married John Gilliland, and raised their family at Waveland. Their children were Herman, Grace, Earl, Sherman, Joe, James, John, Martha, Genevieve (Geno), Sue and Harold (Heck).

Cora Lee and Etha died when young. Louisa Gilliland was loved and adored by all that knew her. *Submitted by Margaret Moody Moser*

ALBERT MOORE

Albert Moore was born in Tippecanoe Co., IN, in 1886. He married Amanda C. DeLong, in 1906. They had one child; a son, Ralph F., born in 1909. They were involved in grain and livestock farming. Ralph married Dora M. Brolsma in 1930, at Lafayette, IN.

Dora's parents were John and Jennie Brolsma. They came to the United States from Holland in the 1880s. They came by ship; he at the age of 18, she at the age of five.

Albert, Amanda, Ralph and Dora purchased a farm in Ripley Township, in Montgomery Co., IN, and moved there in 1940. In addition to other livestock, they were in the dairy business, they raised beef cattle and still do.

Ralph was trustee for Ripley Township for four years.

A daughter was born to Dora and Ralph in 1931. Her name is Jean and she married Donald Rhoda. They live at Lafayette. He is employed at Warren Products there. Their children are David, Greg, Sandy and Elaine. Their grandchildren's names are Andrew and Ashley Rhoda.

A son Kenneth was born in 1933. He married Nancy Quisenberry. They live in Ripley Township and are involved in grain and livestock farming. Their children are Michael, Gale and Gary. Their grandchildren's names are Misty and Matthew Carver.

A daughter, Janet, was born in 1941. She married Don Engler. They live at Lansing, MI. He is employed at Schulty, Snyder and Steele Lumber as Vice President and Director of Purchasing. Their children are Cheryl, Lori and Brad.

A son Robert was born in 1943. He married Karen Youngs. They live at Troy, MI. He is General Manager of Automotive Sales and Glass Group of Pittsburg Plate Glass Co., there. Their children are Michelle and Michael.

All the Moore children graduated from Alamo High School.

The Moore's have attended the Alamo Christian Church since the 1940s. Ralph was very active in the Masonic Lodge at Alamo. Ralph and Dora were also active in the Alamo Eastern Star. She still is. She is active in Home Ec., also.

CHARLES M. MOORE

The first job Dad had after working on his father's farm (north of Bellmore, IN) was a depot agent for the C.H. & D. Railroad (now the B&O) at Raccoon, IN.

Dad soon decided this was too confining so he opened his first general store at Portland Mills, IN in 1915, borrowing $800 from an uncle to start the business. When he started in business, some of his loafers were Civil War Veterans, one being his father-in-law, Mr. Alexander, as Dad and Mother were soon married after he opened the store.

Dad would have served in WWI, but he was operated on for ruptured appendix on the kitchen table with the doctor and assistants coming from Indianapolis. The war was over before he was able to serve.

The second General Store he owned was in Milligan, IN, known as Moore and Rambow. While at Milligan, Dad was the Postmaster since the Post Office was in the store. Dad, as Postmaster, was to report the Railway Mail Clerk if he threw the mail off and the railway clerk was to report him if he didn't get the mail sack on the hook, so they had an agreement not to report each other. While in this store, they began to get bakery bread delivered each morning by train from Tuscola, IL. The partners got along alright but Dad sold out to Rambow in the

1930s coming to Waveland during the Great Depression.

This a scene inside Moore's Store. Seated L to Right Rev. C. McBrayer, Ora Porter, Chas. M. Moore and W. West.

He purchased the General Store on the S.W. Corner of Cross (Highway 59) and High St. from S. Love. At this time all the business places in Waveland were full and the town was a busy place with the store staying open at night.

During this time, Dad paid his clerk $6-8 per week and were glad to have work. When WWI started, the stores in the area started closing in the evening at 6:00 p.m. in order to conserve electricity.

Dad always had chairs for loafers (both women and men), so the topics discussed ranged from the national and local news to how the garden and crops were doing, plus fishing and hunting stories thrown in for good measure. He had one standing rule: if a loafer got upset, what was being said was tabled and if he or she got mad they had to leave.

While in business, Dad was head of the Merchants Association. For 20 years, he was president of the Waveland Conservation Club.

Dad was 85 years old when he passed away suddenly on Christmas Eve in 1976 and the trend of the times closed Moore's General Store.

Mother, Hazel Moore, died in 1965. Both are buried in Mt. Moriah Cemetery, north of Hollandsburg, IN.

Charles and Hazel Moore's one son, Clarhud lives at 402 East Green, Waveland, IN, and began working in the store when eight years old, and remained there except for the time spent in the U.S. Engineer Corp. in Japan and Korea.

In all of his stores, Dad gave credit to those who asked for it. Some paid, some didn't — but this was the chance a merchant took. *Submitted by Clarhud Moore*

FREELOVE MOORE

Freelove Groves was born Sept. 5, 1812 near Ewing Station, Fleming Co., KY. Her mother was a Cherokee Indian. While young she moved to Indiana, where Feb. 16, 1837 she married Robert S. Moore, who was also a native of Kentucky. They moved to a farm at the southwest edge of Waveland, where she made her home until 1905. At that time she went to live with her daughter, Mattie Austin at Davenport, IA, where she died Mar. 16, 1906. Mr. Moore, born in 1807, died June 6, 1851.

By her request there was no sermon, but F.N. Johnson read a chapter from the Bible, which she had selected and the choir sang some of her favorite songs. The coffin was borne by six of her grandsons. Another request that she made, was that no hearse be used.

Eight children were born to Freelove and Robert. Lydia Farmer, William Wallace, John T., Mattie Austin, David, George, Dora Hand, and Robert. At the time of her death two of her children were living; Mattie and George. She also left a brother, Benjamin Groves in Union Mills, IA, 28 grandchildren, 36 great grandchildren and three great-great grandchildren. She joined the Christian Church in her early childhood and was always a faithful member.

Freelove Moore

When the Civil War came William Wallace enlisted in the 15th, John T. and David in the 60th, and George in the 4th Regiment.

David married Margaret Mitchell. They had four sons - William H., 1870-1958, Charles M., 1875-1952, Robert, 1880-1902 and Harry.

William H. married Martha Viola Scott, daughter of Archelius and Mary Catherine McMullen Scott. William and Viola had two children, Raymond Howard and Bessie Love.

Raymond married Ava N. Pile, daughter of George and Sarah Jane Pile of Parke County in October 1914. Raymond and Ava had two daughters, Lillian E., who married Edwin Presslor in April 1939, and Vivian, who married Charles W. (Bill) Robison in June 1938.

Bessie married Matthew Daniel Simms and they had one son Robert Dan.

The grandsons of Freelove Moore, namely William Charles and Harry were hard workers in Waveland, helping with the construction of many of the present buildings, such as the Library built in 1914 and the school building in 1912, that was destroyed in 1985 to construct the present building. They also laid the cement sidewalks, built the wells, and cisterns for the town, with the help of the next generation - Raymond Moore, and Ben and Ira Scott (brothers of Viola Scott Moore).

At the funeral of Freelove, her friend F.N. Johnson read a tribute to her: "It has been my fortune to be acquainted with Aunt Freelove for 50 years. Her cheerful, contented disposition was inspiring; her hospitality proverbial; her hand open to the needy, and her heart full of sympathy for the sorrowing. Her manner was unassuming and simplicity itself, but she had the inner adorning of a loving heart. But it is unnecessary for me to enumerate the many sterling qualities of her character for her life was spent among us and was as an open book, known and appreciated by all of her acquaintances."

As a great-great granddaughter of a person such as this, it makes this writer proud to be a descendant of Freelove Moore.

As of this writing in 1989 there are children who are eighth generation of Freelove and Robert S. Moore living at Waveland. *Submitted by Lillian (Moore) Presslor*

JACK THOMAS AND JACQUELINE SUE (LAWTON) MOORE

Jack Thomas and Jacqueline Sue (Lawton) Moore were married June 17, 1961. Their family consists of Micah Shawn, born Aug. 4, 1962 and Kelly Rene, born June 15, 1965. Also Richard William Moore born Apr. 29, 1948 and Jack Edward Franklin Moore, born Feb. 14, 1947.

Jacqueline Sue, born May 1, 1939, daughter of Harry and Mildred B. (Barton) Lawton grew up in Crawfordsville with three brothers, Don, William and Robert. Harry was from Darlington and Mildred from Waveland.

Jack Thomas, born Mar. 10, 1923 was son of Jessee Franklin and Mary Ellen (Stewart) Moore of 109 North Grant Avenue. Jesse Franklin Moore served with the U.S. Army in World War I. He retired from the CRAWFORDSVILLE FIRE DEPARTMENT and was a member of the FIRST - TWO PLATOON SYSTEM that was formed in July, 1922.

Jack, Thomas and Jacqueline Sue Moore

Jack Thomas had a genial obliging nature and worked one year at the HOOSIER CROWN CORPORATION when he was inducted into the U.S. Army. He sailed on the L.S.T. Liberty Ship to Europe and served over 30 months during WORLD WAR II at South Hampton, England — Utah Beach, France and Regensburg, Germany. Returning to United States from Le Harve, France on the S.S. Ward Hunt Ship. He received his discharge Dec. 26, 1946.

Obtaining employment at the Plastene Corporation he operated a press for 16 years and was receiving and shipping clerk for nine years. Ingress-Plastene then honored him with a 25th year award.

In preparation for Crawfordsville's 1965 Centennial, employees of all the Crawfordsville factories (just for fun) formed "BROTHERS OF THE BRUSH" - chapters. Jack Thomas enthusiastically joined the Plastene Chapter called "PLASTENE GOATS." The city side walks sported over 300 distinguished bewhiskered men handsomely dressed for the Centennial. Jack Thomas Moore among them! He belonged to the American Legion and the Veterans of Foreign Wars Post 1431.

Jacqueline Sue is a person of kindly impulses always generous and willing to help others. Her pleasant and marvelous sense of humor gained her friends. Those she worked with at Abney's Meat Market and the Crawfordsville Country Club found her a pleasure to know.

In 1975 the Jack Moore family moved to Sanford, FL.

Jack Edward Franklin Moore and his wife Linda Sue (born Aug. 29, 1948) were married Oct. 21, 1967, they reside in Sanford, FL. Their daughters are Julie Eloise, born July 29, 1968 and Ginger Ellen born Jan. 14, 1974. Todd Allan Scherr, born May 23, 1964 and Julie Eloise were married July 4, 1987. Ginger Ellen attends Lakeview School and plays the Flute in the band.

Micah Shawn married Rosa Mercedes Gonzales on Dec. 28, 1985. Kelly Rene graduated from the Sanford, FL, Oviedo High School in 1984 and works as Desk Receptionist at the Holiday Inn.

Richard William Moore and his wife Sandra (born Sept. 27, 1947) were married July 3, 1970. Their children are Joseph Richard, Shelly Rene and Johnathan Wayne.

Jack Thomas Moore died Nov. 1, 1986 and is buried in the Oaklawn Memorial Park at Lake Mary, FL.

Jacqueline Sue Moore resides at Orlando, FL. (see William Stewart and William E. Moore for more family information).

JAMES ELLA MOORE I

Chas. M. Moore's grandfather, James Ella Moore I was born some where in Texas in March but the year is not known. He was an apprentice to a harness maker and didn't like it so he ran away getting off the train in Judson, IN. He met Catherine Nutgrass, born Apr. 5, 1833 in Kentucky, died July 13, 1914 in Parke County. James Ella Moore I died before their son, James Ella Moore II was born on Jan. 27, 1856. The date of James Ella Moore II death is known, but both are buried in Raccoon Cemetery. James Ella Moore II married Victoria Watson, born on Aug. 5, 1866, dying Mar. 3, 1934, on Mar. 23, 1886 having nine children, with Chas M. Moore being the first son. James Ella Moore II died Apr. 16, 1933, both he and his wife being buried in Mt. Moriah Cemetery.

Mrs. Chas. M. Moore's ancestor, Dr. John Greene, born 1597 died 1659 came to Warwick, RI in 1635 from Salisbury, England. His grandson General Nathaniel Greene during the Revolutionary War. The Greene family was the family, Mary Elizabeth Greene (born 1850, died 1932) was a member. Mary Elizabeth Greene married John S. Alexander, born 1843, died 1923, but no date given when the family came to Indiana. John S. Alexander joined an Indiana Company as a drummer boy at the age of ten years, serving in the Civil War. There were seven children in the family with Mrs. Chas. M. Moore being the youngest. Mr. and Mrs. Alexander are buried in Union Chapel Cemetery.

RAYMOND AND AVA MOORE

Raymond H. Moore, son of William H. and Martha Viola Scott Moore, was born June 4, 1893 and raised in Waveland. Working as a boy at the livery stable, he took people from the railroad station to the Shades Hotel and other duties connected with the business. He attended Waveland School and in high school played on the football team. He and his friends were rather adventurous and when in their late teens took a train to Montana, where they lived in a line shack, using 'buffalo chips' for fuel, and hunting animals for food. Many people came to him to 'witch' for water. He enjoyed the outdoors, and often took his grandchldren to the woods to teach them about nature. Although he had no boys, he helped with Boy Scouts several years, taking them camping and hiking.

Many times he would spend winters in Tulsa, OK working and later St. Petersburg, FL. During World War II he worked in the Kingsbury Ordinance Plant near Knox, IN. After the war he returned to Waveland, and was still working at age 80. He was an active member in the Waveland Christian Church, Lions Club and Masons.

Ava N. Pile Moore was the daughter of George and Sarah (Aunt Sally) Whitaker Pile of Parke County. She was born near Thompkinsville, KY September 1892. Later the family moved to Parke County, IN, where she attended grade school, and attended High School at Waveland, driving each day with horse and buggy.

Raymond and Ava Moore

After their marriage, October 1914, they lived at Milligan, IN for three years, then moved to Waveland, where they kept their residence for the rest of their lives. Ava was always interested in community affairs. She was a member of the Christian Church and Ladies Aid, a member of the Women's Club and Eastern Star. She worked the Parent Teachers Association and was among the mothers who helped organized the first hot lunch at Waveland School, canning the food and preparing the lunches.

Raymond died Aug. 23, 1974 and Ava Dec. 27, 1978.

Raymond and Ava had two daughters; Lillian, born Aug. 2, 1917, and Vivian, born July 9, 1920.

Lillian married Edwin Presslor April 1939. Their children were Linda, Carol and John. Vivian married Charles W. (Bill) Robison in June 1938. Their children were; Beverly, Judith, Margaret Sue and Nancy. *Submitted by Lillian Moore Presslor*

RUBY ELLEN MOORE

Ruby Ellen Moore, born Nov. 15, 1946 is the daughter of William Edward and Ruth Pauline (Himes) Moore. She is a member of the Browns Valley Christian Church.

Ruby started her schooling at the Whitesville, IN school building.

When the surrounding schools consolidated she then went to the East Union School northeast of Crawfordsville. She lived five miles south of Crawfordsville off the Whitesville and Ladoga Road.

Her parents bought a farm in Putnam County and they moved in 1956. Ruby finished her schooling at Roachdale graduating in 1964.

Ruby Ellen Moore

While at Roachdale she was active in chorus for four years, public relations officer for her class her Sophmore and Senior years, editor of the school paper her Junior year and was member of the Future Homemaker's Club of America. Ruby was the class secretary her junior year and took part in the Junior and Senior Plays. She also received the F.H.A. Chapter Degree and the F.H.A. Junior Homemaker's degree.

She enjoyed being involved at the Whitesville Christian Church, where she was a member for many years. Ruby served as song leader, was a kindergarten class teacher and sang religious soprano solos.

The summer of 1963 she worked as nurse aide at the Greencastle Even Tide Nursing Home.

In the Fall of 1964 she moved to Lafayette, IN where she attended the St. Elizabeth School of Nursing.

In 1965 she moved to Johnson City, TN enrolling at the Milligan Bible College.

Ruby has worked at the old Putnam County Hospital at Greencastle two separate times as Nurses Aid.

Ruby Ellen composes religious music and has written several interesting children's stories. One song "Baby Jesus" sung often at Vacation Bible Schools.

Ruby Ellen and Gary Sutton were married June 16, 1967. (Annulled). Her family, besides her parents consists of her sisters and their husbands. Joy Marciel and Robert Gregory; and Jan Marlene and Clarence Bonifacius, also nine nieces, four nephews, one great niece and eight great nephews.

Ruby's daily companion is her Miniature Daschund, she named Gabriel Remo. Having no children she went to choose a pet. This tiny puppy with a wily lift of his front paw and pleading eyes won her heart. Born in July 1973, she brought him home in a shoe box. He is 16 now and the exubrant energy he displayed then has turned to quiet ease and contentment. The joy they have shared is warm and wonderful.

Ruth Ellen Moore lived ten years in Union Township, Montgomery County area and is now residing in the Raccoon, Putnam County area.

She began 4-H work in Montgomery County and resumed it in Putnam. She was a volunteer helper in the Putnam County Mental Health Association and also did volunteer entertainment at the Golden Manor Nursing Home in Ladoga.

WILLIAM AND VIOLA MOORE

William H. Moore, son of David and Margaret Moore, was born June 1870 at Waveland. His brothers were Charles F., born 1875, died 1952; Robert S. born 1880, died 1902, and Harry who died in 1954. They were grandsons of Freelove and Robert S. Moore, who were among the first settlers of Waveland.

William worked hard during his life. An expert brick layer and cement finisher, helping with construction of many of the buildings of Waveland. In 1914 helped construct the Waveland Library, along with his brothers and son, Raymond. He attended school at Waveland where he played football and was also a boxer. He enjoyed outdoor life of hunting and fishing, and was loved by the neighborhood children for his storytelling.

William married Martha Viola Scott, daughter of Archelius and Mary Catherine McMullen Scott. Viola was self taught, having only a third grade education, which was common at that time. She was determined to learn more by reading and studying on her own. She was well read on the Bible and taught a young peoples class at the Waveland Christian Church for many years, where she was a member all her life. She was interested in community affairs and wrote articles for her club and church work. She was a charter member of the American Legion Auxillary. She and William helped raise one of her sister's daughters, and took interest in other young people of their families.

William and Viola Moore at their home on North Cross St. Waveland

To this union were born Raymond H., on June 4, 1893 and Bessie Love on Oct. 16, 1895. Raymond married Ava Pile in October 1914. Their children were Lillian and Vivian.

Lillian married Edwin Presslor in 1939; their children, Linda, who married Jimmy Reed; Carol who married Robert C. Smith, then Rodney Coffman; and John, who married Lana Lieske.

Vivian married Charles W. "Bill" Robinson; their children, Beverly, Judith, Sue and Nancy.

Bessie married Matthew S. (Jim) Simms. Bessie, born Oct. 16, 1895, died Aug. 23, 1955. Matthew, born Mar. 12, 1891, died Dec. 29, 1964. They had one son, Robert Dan, born Feb. 6, 1926 who married Patricia Jean Cook Feb. 16, 1951. Patricia was born Oct. 13, 1927. Robert and Patricia had one son Robert Dan Simms Jr. born June 11, 1956.

Robert Dan Simms Jr. married Dana Bigley June 27, 1987. They had one son Matthew Dan Simms, born Mar. 13, 1988.

Matthew Simms studied law and had a law office in Crawfordsville for some time. He and Bessie moved to Tulsa, OK, where he was also a minister in a large church there. Bessie took great interest in the church also. Later he had a law practice in Tulsa, where he was a criminal lawyer for many years. Robert Dan, his son, followed in the same career and in later years became a Supreme Court Judge at Oklahoma City. *Submitted by Lillian Presslor*

WILLIAM EDWARD AND RUTH PAULINE HIMES MOORE

William Edward Moore and Ruth Pauline (Himes) Moore were married June 16, 1940 in the Whitesville Christian Church by Reverand Barney Stephens. Ruth Pauline is the daughter of Chester and Ruby Ann Linn Himes. She was born Feb. 9, 1922.

William Edward, born Mar. 25, 1920 is the son of Clarence Stephens and Mary Ellen (Stewart) Stephens. (divorced) Mary Ellen married Jesse F. Moore, (William's adoptive father).

Pauline grew up in the Whitesville community and was a member of the Whitesville Christian Church. Following their marriage William was baptized and belonged there.

William chose farming and they lived east of Whitesville amongst friendly neighbors.

Ruby Ellen, Jan Marlene, Joy Marciel, William Edward and Pauline Moore

The children born to them were Joy Marciel on June 7, 1940 — Jan Marlene born July 14, 1943 and Ruby Ellen born Nov. 15, 1946.

World War II brought drastic changes: William worked at the Lafayette Alcoa Aluminum Factory then enlisted in the US Army Air Corp and served two years, returning to farming on his discharge. He farmed 200 acres south of Crawfordsville. He was a Farm Bureau member and Pauline enjoyed the years she was Pet and Hobby Leader. Both are active in Church. Pauline taught a Children's Sunday School Class and William was a Sunday School Superintendent also serving as elder.

They bought a farm in Putnam County. The girls transferred to the Roachdale School. Pauline enrolled at the Milady Beauty Academy, Terre Haute in 1958. Receiving her Diploma in October she operated a Beauty Shop in her home for 20 years. Her other interests are family history, quilting and playing the organ and piano.

William Edward graduated from the Auctioneer School at Decatur, IN being licensed in 1971. During his adult life William was employed at various occupations, beginning upon graduation from Crawfordsville High School in 1938. Those endeavors were bookkeeper-manager of a Fruit Market, Poultry and Egg Business on Walnut Street, Crawfordsville, also Carpenter, Wholesale Retail Milk Delivery, and the Chevrolet Truck Body Plant at Indianapolis. After 18 years at Detroit-Diesel Allison at Indianapolis he retired in 1985.

The subjects of this memoir are members of the Browns Valley Christian Church. They belong to the Montgomery County Historical Society.

Happiest with a hammer in his hand he built a new house on their farm in the 1960s, learning back in 1940, he had a natural skill with carpentering. (see index, Moore, Gregory, Bonifacius, Himes, and Stewart, in regard to their families).

Ruth Pauline is descended from several Montgomery County settlers.

STANLEY AND STELLA SCOTT MORGAN

Although there is no fame or fortune to be recorded from the marriage of Stanley Samuel Morgan and Stella Blanch Scott, there remains enough of their descendants in Montgomery County to make it worth including in this history.

They were married Nov. 6, 1905 in Crawfordsville by the Justice of the Peace. After living a short time in Colorado, they settled in Waveland.

Stanley was born Aug. 21, 1885 to Joseph and Amanda Barker Morgan, who lived on a farm near Byron in Parke County. Stanley's siblings were Courtney, Homer, Cecil and Hazel. Ancestors of Stanley came from Wales. They settled in N. Carolina and Kentucky. Later descendants came to Indiana.

Stella was the daughter of Archelius and Mary Catherine McMullen Scott. She was born Nov. 30, 1885. When her father "Arch" was in the Civil War, his injured and dying friend asked him to take care of his wife and children when the war ended. Arch married her and they had two children. This first wife, Mary McGill died, so he then married Mary C. McMullen. Their children were Viola, Amanda, Laura, William, Ida, Ethel, Ben, Ira (Chase) and Stella, who became Stanley Morgan's wife. Ancestors of Stella came from Scotland to Virginia and on to Montgomery County.

Stanley and Stella were parents of 12 children, namely: Fred, Ruth, Paul, (Jeff), Glenn (Mutt) Maudie, Robert, William (Woody), Raymond, James, Nina Jean, June and Harold.

Woody, Robert and James are residents of Montgomery County, as are some of their descendants and descendants of other of these 12 children. The other surviving children all live in Indiana.

When Stanley was in his teens and early 20s, he traveled with his brother Cecil through the midwest. They took their threshing machine into the Dakotas and Colorado, working with farmers to harvest their grain.

Stanley and Stella worked hard to raise their large family in Waveland during the depression. Stella nurtured her children in a Christian way of life. She raised a large garden and canned vegetables and fruit to feed the family. She cleaned house for the local dentist "Doc" Harbison and his invalid wife. She also "took in laundry."

Stanley hauled coal from a mine near Brazil, IN. Later he became a bookkeeper there. He also worked in his brother Cecil's sawmill. He was a skilled carpenter. On the block at the intersection of John St. and South Boulevard in Crawfordsville, he transformed a cement block garage into a home. Later, in the same block, he constructed two houses. His son, Robert, also built a house there. They all still stand, although they have been altered and added to.

Stella died May 4, 1949 at home on John St. Stanley died Nov. 19, 1954 in Culver Hospital.

Stanley and Stella's family grew. The children married and had their own families. Now there are grandchildren, great grandchildren, great, great grandchildren, nieces, nephews, and their families many of whom are settled in Montgomery County.

If there is any profession that stands out in this family, it is teaching. Daughter Ruth taught school in Montgomery County. Of the grandchildren and their spouses, 11 are school teachers. Four are in the ministry of their own faith. Several are employed at Donnelley's. There are several artists skilled in oil painting.

The hardships of raising this large family brought much love and happiness. Future generations will remember the Morgan history with fondness and fascination. *By June Deener*

EBBERT MONROE MORROW

Ebbert Monroe Morrow was born in Coal Creek Township, Montgomery Co., IN on Aug. 30, 1865. He died on Feb. 1, 1940 at the age of 75. He was the son of James Aaron Morrow and Harriet Rivers Morrow. On Nov. 28, 1889, Ebbert Monroe Morrow married Elizabeth Edna McClamrock, who was born on Oct. 11, 1870 in Montgomery Co., IN. She died on Nov. 20, 1939 at the age of 69. She was the daughter of Lemuel Ball McClamrock and Mary Elizabeth Jones McClamrock. Ebbert and Elizabeth Morrow are both buried in Oak Hill Cemetery in Crawfordsville, IN.

Elizabeth McClamrock, Ebbert Monroe Morrow, Eugenia Morrow, Lemuel James Morrow

Ebbert and Elizabeth Morrow had nine children as follows.

Winnie Dorothea Morrow b. Apr. 1, 1891 d. July 1892, Lemuel James Morrow b. Nov. 3, 1893 d., Eugenia D. Morrow b. July 13, 1895 d. Oct. 29, 1979, Roxy Evangeline Morrow b. Feb. 10, 1898 d. Ebbert Monroe Morrow, Jr. b. Jan. 17, 1901 d. August 1958, Harriet Elizabeth Morrow b. May 14, 1903, Frank Aaron Morrow b. Dec. 3, 1907 d., Ruth May Morrow b. Dec. 3, 1907 d., Mary Ellen Morrow b. Jan. 25, 1914.

Ebbert Monroe Morrow taught nine years in the Montgomery County Schools. He served two terms as Trustee of Coal Creek Township and gained distinction as having awarded the first school bus contract in Indiana while in that office. Interspersed with various farming ventures were his operations of hardware stores in Crawfordsville, Linden, Lebanon, and New Richmond.

Mr. Morrow was of a lovable cheerful nature. Mr. Morrow was the idol of his children. His life was one of tremendous activity and his services to the communities in which he made his home were of untold value. Of particular pride to him was that he was privileged to be one of the charter members of the Masonic Lodge in Wingate and he spent many active years in the interests of that fraternal body. *Submitted by Joan Chaille granddaughter of Ebbert Monroe Morrow*

JAMES AARON MORROW

James Aaron Morrow was born in Coal Creek Township on May 15, 1830, the son of James Morrow "...the first man to enter and claim land in the Coal Creek Township arriving here in September 1823."

On Oct. 12, 1852 James Aaron married Miss Harriet Elizabeth Rivers, who was born Sept. 9, 1833 in Fountain Co., IN. Harriet was the daughter of John Rivers from Kentucky and mother's maiden name was Murray from Virginia. This union was blessed with 11 children: William Walles (lived 22 months), William Wade (lived five years), John R. (lived 17 years), Ira Allen (21 months), James Aaron Jr. (died at birth), Harriet Elizabeth (17 years), Simeon (15 months), Frank Aaron, Ebbert Monroe, Joanna and Sarah E.

The Crawfordsville Weekly wrote the following on Aug. 1, 1885. "James has been in poor health for several years. During his last severe illness he was confined to his bed three or four months. Mr. Morrow had been a resident of this county a long time having lived upon the farm where he died about 28 years. During all those years he had lived an honorable, peaceful life among his neighbors. He became identified with the Christian Church many years ago. As a member he cast his lot with the Center Church which he was a honorable member." James Aaron died July 23, 1885 at age 55 leaving a wife and five children.

James Aaron Morrow, Harriet, Elizabeth (Rivers) Morrow

Harriet remarried Daniel Hawk and lived on the Morrow farm until her death as stated by the Crawfordsville Weekly Journal Oct. 22, 1892. "Mrs. Harriet Hawk died of Consumption at Elmdale on Sunday. She had long been a resident of this vicinity. She was formerly the wife of James Morrow who died some years ago. She raised a family while Mr. Morrow lived. She was a bright, cheerful Christian lady and died lamented by all who know her" on Oct. 16, 1892 at age 92. Both are buried at Pleasant Hill, Wingate.

GEORGE WASHINGTON MOSBARGER

George Washington Mosbarger was born in Ohio, Feb. 5, 1827 to Peter and Nancy Mosbarger, and moved with the family to Montgomery Co., IN. Brothers and sisters were Lucinda, William, Katherine, Nancy, Clarissa, Melvina P., Martha, Jane and Peter.

George Washington and Lettice Van Meter (Ashby) Mosbarger

On Mar. 16, 1848 he was united in marriage to Lettice Van Meter Ashby who was born June 27, 1828 in Montgomery Co., IN, to Milton Ashby, born in Hardin Co., KY in 1801, and Susan Goben Ashby, born Jan. 8, 1803 in Montgomery Co., IN. Susan Goben's sibling's were Melinda, James, Milton, Mary, Susan, Lorenco Dow, Joseph, and Marcellia.

George W. Mosbarger and Lettice Mosbarger bought land in Walnut Twp. in 1855 and sold in 1857. Five children were born in Montgomery Co., Nancy, Jane, Milton, James, Sarah and Marshall. Sometime between 1855 and 1857 they moved to Clarke Co., IA where seven more children were born, Susan, Mary, William, Lucenda, Sherman, George and Ella.

George W. was a shoe cobbler and died at Woodburn, Clark Co., IA Dec. 28, 1900 and Lettice died July 19, 1907 at Oakley, IA.

MOSER

The Moser ancestors came from Germany in 1732, settling in Pennsylvania. Two generations later some Mosers had moved to South Central Ohio. George Moser, born Oct. 23, 1838 married Charlotte Gordon, Dec. 8, 1867. This couple, with their four sons moved to Champaign Co., IL in 1881.

One of those sons, Osmer Gordon, born Apr. 12, 1869 at Chillecothe, OH, married Mary Myrtle Pell, Sept. 4, 1895. The Pells came from England to Illinois by way of Virginia and Kentucky. This couple, with daughter Marian, moved to Indiana 1898 or 1899. Their home was the "Bristle Ridge" farm north of Elmdale, now owned by the Charles Cooley family.

Marian married John D. "Jack" Blacker. Jack played on Wingate's 1913 and 1914 State Champion Basketball teams. Their two sons, Rex and Robert Max, saw much action in the Air Force in Europe during World War II. Robert made the Air Force his career, is retired, living in Lubbock, TX. Rex operates NAPA auto parts stores in northwestern Indiana; lives at Rensselaer, IN.

Two sons were born to O.G. and Mary Moser while living on the "Ridge" farm, Wm. Gordon, Oct. 26, 1902 and Harry Newton, Nov. 20, 1907. This family moved from Wingate to the Reddish-Oglesbee farm east of Waveland in 1917. Mary died Mar. 17, 1942, O.G. July 14, 1949 and are buried in Maple Ridge Cemetery at Waveland.

William Gordon married Margaret Moody and taught school at Rockville and Brazil, IN. Their two sons were born at Brazil, IN; Their sons were born at Brazil; Joseph Gordon and John Wm.

Joseph earned degrees from Rose-Poly (Rose-Hulman) and Purdue University and teaches at West Chester University in Pennsylvania.

John married Karen Dellaca. Their sons are Jay Todd and Sean Bradley. John has degrees from Indiana State and University of Illinois; teaches at North Putnam High School. Karen is librarian at Waveland.

Harry Moser married Naomi Swanay. Their children are Karl Henry, Donn Erwin, and Mary Ann. Harry and Naomi are deceased and buried in Maple Ridge Cemetery.

Karl Moser married John Hunsicker and they have three sons; Kevin, Mark and Eric.

Donn Moser married Anna Jean Fruits. Their sons are Duane and Aaron.

Mary Ann Moser married Clarence Groce. Their children are Brian and Michelle. *Submitted by Wm. Gordon Moser*

MOSSBARGER

I, Billie Klein am proud to add the history of my Mossbarger/Mushbarger family to the Montgomery County family History Book.

The Mossbarger family appeared on the American scene in the late 1700s. Extensive research points to the fact that John Mossbarger, born about 1760, was the immigrant. He most likely came from Bavaria where the records suggest a strong concentration of the surname.

It appears that John settled for a very brief time

in Pennsylvania and Maryland before starting the westward march.

Land, and the privilege of owning it, was a blessing to this family. Various land records show the Mossbarger family acquired their share of it. Records of Greenbrier Co., WV, appears to be the place that John, his wife and 12 children called home for about 15 years.

It was in Greenbrier County that John passed away. His will was executed there on Jan. 29, 1807.

The will is three long pages and is the only known record John left of himself. He made an effort to have his oldest son, Christopher, provide for each child and the mother, Catherine. The last paragraph as taken from the Bunger Family, by Ina Ritchie Sipes, explains his wishes.

"And whereas in the former part of this will, I had directed my son, Christopher, should pay sundry specific legacies, now upon further reflection instead of the legacies aforesaid my will is that he the said Christopher pay unto my sons, John, Joseph, Daniel Peter, Henry and my daughters, Barbara, Lizey, Nancy and Katey, the sum of ten pounds each as soon as they shall attain the age of 21 years, provided that my wife be deceased, otherwise the payments thereof to be deferred until that period, and provided that nothing contained in this last disposition of parts of my estate shall in anywise affect the disposition heretofore made in favor of my wife. My sons, Jacob and John, which are to remain as before."

In the will John mentions a grist mill and a plantation of 278 acres where the family resided.

The land was divided up between his sons. However, it was not long after his death that the various parcels of land were sold as the sons started moving westward.

Peter, John's youngest son, left West Virginia and settled for a time in Gallia Co., OH.

Peter left Gallia about 1826-1827 and purchased land in Montgomery Co., IN.

Peter and his wife, Nancy, had nine children: William H., Lucinda, George Washington, Nancy, Peter, Clarissa, Catherine, Melvina and Martha Jane. The last six children were all born in Montgomery County.

Nancy, wife of Peter, passed away in Clark Township, Montgomery County. Her will was proved Oct. 14, 1850. This will listed the names of her nine children.

George Washington (my great-grandfather) lived in Montgomery County for about 28 years. It was here that he married Letitia Van Meter Ashby.

About 1856, George Washington and his family moved to Clarke Co., IA where he passed away Dec. 28, 1899.

The story of my Mossbarger family exemplifies the American dream. I am proud of my Mossbarger heritage and the part they played in building Montgomery Co., IN. *Submitted by Mrs. Billie Klein*

JAMES A. MOUNT
1834-1901

James Atwell Mount was born Mar. 23, 1843 to Atwell Mount and Lucinda Fulenwider in Montgomery Co., IN. The Mounts came originally from Virginia, the Fulenwilders from Kentucky coming to Montgomery County in 1828. James Atwell was one of 12 children whose mother lived by the Bible which lay on a stand in their living room. The father was an elder in the Presbyterian Church and the mother taught Sunday School. James was taught frugality and hard work, qualities which he brought to the office of Governor of Indiana in his later years. His schooling was meager, sandwiched between farm duties. As a youth of 19 he joined the 72nd Regiment of Indiana and became a member of the renowned Wilder Brigade where he distinguished himself for bravery.

James A. Mount

After the war he entered the Presbyterian Academy in Lebanon, IN. Since his resources were limited he crowded two years of study into one. It was here he met Catharine Boyd, a Lebanon aristocrat, whom he married the following year. They both discovered their love of nature and farm life. They rented a decrepit farm near Shannondale with a run-down house. Three years later they owned the farm and 28 years later owned 500 acres and built a beautiful home. Both were community minded, she lecturing to farm women; he trying various methods of improving agriculture.

Although they preferred to stay on the farm his sense of duty prevailed when he was nominated for State Senator in 1888. He was elected Governor of Indiana in 1897 by the largest plurality ever given a gubernatorial candidate.

His administration saw some sweeping laws adopted. The entire state prison system was remodeled, laws passed regulating child employment, safety facilities in industry, and a medical board was set up to examine applicants to practice medicine. He led the fight for the first compulsory education laws.

Governor Mount, according to his secretary, was "worked to death" and died a few days after retiring from office at the age of 58 years, never realizing his cherished dream of returning to his beloved farm, Willowdale Stock Farm.

The Mounts had three children, Hallie, Helen, and Harry. Hallie Mount Butler had three children, James Everett, Gladys Abbott, and Lois Lippert. The grandson, James Everett, lived on the farm until his death in 1972. It is now owned and farmed by a great-granddaughter, Kathryn Butler Branstetter, and husband, James.

Louise Butler Kuonen and Marion Edward Butler, both of Indianapolis also are children of James Everett. Stanley and Harold Abbott and Margery Manges (a Montgomery County resident) are children of Gladys and the late Aben Abbott.

Lois and the late Kemper Lippert are parents of Marilyn Zimmerman of Loveland, CO and Winston Lippert of Miami, FL.

Governor Mount's long line of descendants serve to prove the truth of the Poem written about him by James Whitcomb Riley titled "A Good Man Never Dies." *Submitted by Louise Butler Kuonen, Kathryn Butler Branstetter great granddaughters.*

KATE BOYD MOUNT

Kate Boyd Mount was born Nov. 10, 1849 in Thorntown, IN to Samuel R. and Rebecca Jane Nesbit Boyd.

In 1854 and the family moved to Lebanon. Kate was raised in the philosophy of responsibility and credibility.

In 1864 Kate enrolled in the Lebanon, Indiana Presbyterian Academy from which she graduated in 1867. At this school she met James Atwell Mount. Following their graduation, they were married in November, 1867.

Because they had little money, they rented a run-down three room house on a farm. They were operating it on a one-half share basis. With hard work they owned their livestock and farm tools and paid cash rent by the end of seven years.

The ideal towards which they worked since the time of their marriage was to have a beautiful and modern home in the country, equipped with such conveniences and helps that should enable them to use their time for general improvement and for the pleasure and advantage of their friends and for the good of humanity as far as their influence could reach.

In 1885 they purchased 500 acres and built a large home on Overcoat Road West of Shannondale. Mrs. Mount was her husband's partner, sharing with him all of his responsibilities and burdens. The Mounts realized that their experiences would be helpful to others. They were both asked to give lectures to farm groups, principally farmers' institutes at various towns in Indiana. Mrs. Mount did not speak of agricultural methods, but of work inside the home. In all her talks the central theme concerned the social and intellectual development of farm families and the improvement of farm homes. Some of her subjects were "How to Better the Intellectual and Social Conditions of Farmers' Families", "The Home and Woman's Place Therein", "Conveniences and Architecture," The Home and its Relation to Christianity," and "The Economy, Its Uses and Abuses." She prompted women to organize their own association of the Indiana Farm Bureau.

In November, 1896 Mrs. Mount contributed an article to the Woman's edition of the **Crawfordsville Journal.** In it Mrs. Mount said "I firmly believe that it lies within the power of every industrious couple who are endowed with reasonable health and the ordinary capabilities of mankind, and who manage their affairs wisely to possess for their latter years the farm home of their dreams. By patient labor self-reliance, good judgment and a strictly temperate life, may such results be gained."

Following her husband's election to the governorship of Indiana in 1897, she performed her duties as First Lady with grace and dignity, making numerous friends in Indianapolis. She was particularly interested in the laws adopted during his term of office, which included the state's first compulsory education law, regulation of child labor, and modification of the prison system.

Governor Mount died in Indianapolis two days after his term ended. Mrs. Mount returned to their Shannondale farm, Willowdale. She died in Indianapolis July 6, 1905. *Submitted by Jean Thompson, County Historian*

CLAUD SILAS MULLEN

Claud Silas Mullen was born Sept. 21, 1878 in Montgomery County to Albert and Clara Hiatt

Mullen. He died at the age of 93 on Aug. 11, 1971 after a very colorful life.

Claud married Grace Hall in 1896. Grace was a fine, gentle woman never having been heard to speak ill of anyone.

Four children were born to the Mullens. Eva was born in 1897. She married Claude Coltrain and died during the flu epidemic in 1918 at age 21. She left no children.

Lester was born in 1898. He married Beatrice Thompson. They had one son who died when he was six months old. Lester died in 1924 at age 26 of tuberculosis.

Claud Silas Mullen and his trotter (Red Check #6 finishing third, by a hoof, at age 84)

Mabel was born in 1903. She married Cecil Cox. She died in 1983, he in 1982. They had four daughters; Judy, Marta, Jane and Margaret, 12 grandchidren and 17 great grandchildren.

Alberta Ruth was born in 1910. She married Herbert Royer. He died in 1980. They had three daughters; Carole, Becky and Cathy, seven grandchildren and seven great-grandchildren.

The patriarch of this big family was a very interesting man. The Darlington area was home to them all. Claud was a successful farmer, trustee of Franklin Township, Sunday School Superintendent of the Darlington Congregational Christian Church for many years and very active in harness horse racing.

Claud drove in his first race on his 30th birthday at Covington. He finished third in each heat and was hooked for life. He toured the county fair circuits in Indiana, Illinois, Ohio and Michigan, doing all his own stable work, training and driving. When he was 85 years old he won a race in grand style at Audubon Park Raceway at Henderson, KY. The fans rose as one to give him a standing ovation.

Claud, and his daughter Alberta, went to New York in the summer of 1966 where he appeared as a contestant on the national television show "What's My Line?". He was 87 years old and the oldest active harness race driver in the United States.

This man was sharp to the end. Always up to date on world affairs, good humored, kind, interested in his family and is very missed. *Submitted by Smarta Jeffries*

MARGARET JEAN MULLEN

Margaret Jean Clarkson Mullen was born Oct. 3, 1926 in Crawfordsville, IN. Her parents are Ralph Norris Clarkson and Mary Elizabeth Jurgensmeyer. She has one brother, Richard Clarkson of Sonora, CA.

Margaret attended school at Mount Tabor school which was across the road from the farm she grew up on. She graduated from Crawfordsville High School May 27, 1943. She received a cost accounting degree from Indiana University.

Margaret Mullen

While in school Margaret was very active in several groups. She belonged to a local 4-H club where she showed cattle, sheep, hogs and also participated in clothing and food projects. She attended 4-H camps during the summer. She also attended band camps and played the alto saxaphone in the high school band. She participated in the Farm Bureau band after high school.

Margaret has worked hard all of her life and held several different positions. Among these are bookkeeping at the Farm Bureau Co-op, Plastene Office, and B and D Lumber. She has also worked at the Gin-Ger-Boo and the Dairy Queen. She worked in the Assessor's Office in 1960. From 1960 to 1975 she worked at Symmes and Williams Electric in downtown Crawfordsville which later became Kostanzer Electric. In 1976 she went to work for Kirby Risk Supply where she is currently employed.

Margaret is quite proud of her children and grandchildren and spends many weekends and summer vacations with them. Michael Richard Mayfield was born Feb. 20, 1949. He graduated from Crawfordsville High School in 1967 and from Ball State University in 1972 with a Masters Degree in Education. He is married to Rita Maxine Robey and they have two daughters, Michelle Rene and Mary Margaret. Mike is a chemistry teacher at Downer's Grove South High School in Downer's Grove, IL where he and his family live.

Sandra Kay Mullen was born May 15, 1954. She graduated from Crawfordsville High School in 1972 and from Ball State University in 1976. She graduated from Purdue University in 1981 with a Master's Degree in Education. She is married to Robert William Steele and they have two daughters, Melissa Kay and Elizabeth Ann. Sandra teaches math at Fountain Central High School. She and her family reside in Attica, IN.

Karen Sue Mullen was born on Sept. 21, 1957. She graduated from Crawfordsville High School in 1975. During high school she began working for Herman Davis Chevrolet in downtown Crawfordsville. She has continued in that line of work. The dealership has since changed to Dave Stetler Chevrolet-Cadillac where Karen is currently employed as the business manager.

WILLIAM J. MULLEN

He was born Aug. 10, 1825 Harrison Co., KY died Apr. 29, 1898 Montgomery Co., IN. He married Jan. 11, 1849 in Montgomery County to Elizabeth Martz a daughter of John M. and Rebecca Martz. She was born Feb. 20, 1831 Ohio, died Sept. 21, 1865 Montgomery County. Both are buried at St. James Cemetery in Franklin Township.

He was a son of William and Sarah Endicott Mullen and grandson of Moses and Martha Hill Endicott of Virginia, - a Private in the Revolutionary War and of Thomas Mullen who was a Captain in American Army, Revolutionary War stationed at Pittsburg, PA. Thomas also spent his earlier years in Old Dominion, removing from Louden Co., VA to Kentucky in 1783. His children were: James, Richard, Nancy, Betsy, Asa, Sally and William.

He was born June 15, 1781 Virginia and died June 5, 1855. He was married to Sarah Endicott in 1806. She was born Aug. 2, 1787 and died Apr. 27, 1827. They were farmers. Their children were Barzilla b. Jan. 7, 1807 (Elizabeth Garnett); Seldon b. June 28, 1809 (Rebecca Mikels); James b. June 30, 1811; Thomas b. Sept. 13, 1813 (Elizabeth Donaldson); Moses b. Dec. 17, 1815 (Sarah A. Swatzer); Martha b. Jan. 18, 1818 (Aaron Miller) and William J. b. Aug. 10, 1825 (Elizabeth Martz).

The children of W.J. and Elizabeth were: Sarah Catherine - she is in Ira Hiatt's writeup; Albert born Aug. 2, 1852 Franklin Township and died Mar. 8, 1905 (Clara Hiatt), one son Claude S. and he had one son and two daughters.

W.J. remarried after Elizabeth died to Sarah J. Lackey and they had one child Rebecca Ellen who died young. *Submitted by I. JO Summers*

LAURA McCUTCHAN MULLER

Laura McCutchan Muller was born July 9, 1903 in Vanderburgh Co., IN to Maggie Ruston and John Allen McCutchan. She was one of six children. She attended Oak Dam High School and taught all eight grades after her high school graduation. She then went to Purdue University for three and one half years in the school of Home Economics. She left to marry Louis R. Muller son of Adeline Russell and Louis H. Muller of Irvington NJ. They moved to Irvington where Rus worked for the Union Carbide Co. Their daughter Jeanne was born Sept. 10, 1928. Rus continued to work for Union Carbide transferring between New Jersey and the Linde Air Plant at Speedway, IN. In 1952 they were living in Brownsburg and Rus was Asst. Superintendant of the plant. On his 50th birthday he quit and retired to a five acre apple orchard and nursery at Lake Manitou, Rochester, IN. Rus died on Feb. 9, 1977.

Laura (McCutchan) Muller

Laura moved to Linden, IN to be near her daughter Jeanne, who married Richard H. Ward of R.R. 6 Crawfordsville on Dec. 2, 1951. Laura has two grandchildren, Richard D. Ward who is operating the family farm and Nancy Ward Reece who married William Reece, Sept. 13, 1980. Nancy is the Aquatics program director at the Bloomington, IN YMCA. She graduated from the University of Evansville with a B.S. in English and Health, and has a Masters in PE from Indiana University. She coached swimming at Ithaca College, Ithaca, NY prior to her marriage. Laura is a member of the Linden Extension Homemakers, The Linden Woman's Club, The 4 M's, and the Methodist Woman's Society. *Submitted by Laura Muller*

JAMES DAVIDSON MURPHY

James Davidson Murphy was born on May 12, 1819, in Ross Co., OH, to William and Priscilla (Ladd) Murphy. The Murphys moved to Tippecanoe Co., IN, in about 1828. On Jan. 29, 1846, James married Anna F. Camby in Tippecanoe County. The daughter of Thomas and Betsy (Fuller) Camby, Anna was born on Feb 5, 1831, probably in Clinton Co., IN. James and Anna moved to Darlington, Montgomery County, in the early 1860s.

James D. Murphy was a master carpenter and did much construction in Darlington. In 1866 James helped in the building of the Darlington Academy and in 1882 he did renovations on the building. He was also involved in the construction of the covered bridge and the Methodist Church.

James Davidson Murphy 1819-1903

James joined the Christian Church at age 30 and was an itinerant lay preacher. He wrote and apparently published an 11 chapter paper on his religious beliefs entitled "An Essay On the Soul of Man, Or, the Science of the Soul."

Anna died on Nov. 13, 1879, aged 48 years and was buried in the I.O.O.F. Cemetery in Darlington. On Feb. 12, 1882, James married Mary Vickery. Mary died on Dec. 6, 1895. James passed away in Darlington on May 26, 1903, aged 84 years. He was buried beside Anna. A few days before his death he was heard to say, "The Lord giveth and the Lord taketh away."

Anna F. Camby and James Davidson Murphy had ten children: Louisa, Joseph, William, Ceora, Eva, Flora, Ulysses, Colfax, James and Ollie.

Louisa F. Murphy (1849-1928) married George W. Benefiel (1854-1904) on June 15, 1871, and lived in Colfax, IN. Louisa moved to Frankfort, IN, in about 1904.

Joseph M. Murphy (1852-1920) was married to Eva R. Largent (c. 1857-?) on July 20, 1879, in Montgomery County. He was employed by Purdue University in West Lafayette.

William H. Murphy (1854-1921) was married on July 7, 1881, to Ada A. Vencil (1858-1906) in Montgomery County. William lived in Darlington and was well known in that section of Indiana as a carpenter and contractor. William was married a second time.

Ceora "Ora" A. Murphy (1857-1941) on Sept. 25, 1879, was married to John Kersey (1852-1925) in Montgomery County. They lived in Darlington until about 1922 when they moved to Indianapolis.

Eva M. Murphy (1860-1913) married James J. Hulet (c. 1852-1912) on Mar. 11, 1880, in Montgomery County. They later lived in Crawfordsville, Michigan City and Minot, ND. Eva taught Indian children in Minot and moved to Frankfort, IN, after her husband's death.

Flora E. Murphy (1862-1940) and George Davis (1862-1945) were married in Darlington on Oct. 7, 1885. They lived in Colfax where they ran a drug store for 57 years.

Ulysses Grant Murphy (1865-1940) married Esther Chenoweth (1868-c. 1967) on Dec. 19, 1886, in Clinton Co., IN. They lived in Colfax where he was a millright and carpenter.

Colfax S. Murphy and James Dolley Murphy both died as infants.

Ollie Myrtle Murphy (1872-1948) and William Aldred Bartholomew (1868-1904) were married on Apr. 14, 1895, in Colfax. Her second husband was Peter Davis (1868-1958) whom she divorced in 1913. Ollie moved from Frankfort to South Bend, IN, in about 1923. *Submitted by Andrew R Likins (great great grandson of Flora Murphy Davis)*

EDGAR LAWRENCE MYERS

Edgar Lawrence Myers, owner of Something Else Pizza in Waveland, is a direct descendant of John George Meier of Germany. John George Meier (wife Sybilla) was born around the turn of the 18th century and immigrated to York/North Co., PA from Germany. His son Christian, and his wife Catherine, moved to Davidson/Rowan County area of Pennsylvania and North Carolina. Spelling of the Meier name was changed, some variations were Meir, Myer, Myers; probably due to limited educational opportunities and retention of the German language through these generations. Their son Peter had nine sons: George (wife Nancy), Joseph (wife Polly), Thomas, Peter, David, Andrew, Jacob, Daniel, and Alexander. Daniel (wife Mary M.) lived in the Wallace area and had 14 children: Emsly, Andrew, Jackson, Jacob, Thomas (died in infancy), Daniel, Phrany, Sarah, Susanne, Catherine, Mary (called Polly), Louise, Eva, Alexander. Alexander and first wife Sally Fisher had five children. He adopted the children of his second wife Elizabeth Roach and they had one child: Frances Marion, Melissa Miller, Mary "Vinnie", Lewis Cass, William George "Butler" (adopted), Margaret Ann Roach, "dr." Joseph Lane, Sarah Sarnetta; Almira V. Alexander was described as speaking broken English. Lewis Cass married Rebecca Lawson and had five children before he was bitten by rabid animal and died at age 44. Rebecca married Milton Taylor Hutts who raised her children: Delia, Henry Lawrence, Columbus Lane, Emma, Emory (who died at age 19 and was buried with his father at Wolfe Creek Cemetery).

Henry Lawrence and wife Wilimina Georgina Bartch (Minnie) lived and farmed in the Wallace/Alamo area as their eldest son started school in Alamo. They moved to Pembrook, IL and farmed raising their ten children.

Carl Cass (named after his real grandfather) Wilfred Elbert, Alfred Monroe, Elizabeth Albertina, Herbert Albert, Milton Taylor (named after his step-grandfather), Hugh Duncan, George Russell (died at 13 months), Hazel Violet, and Omer Marion. Henry and Minnie were buried in St. Anne Cemetery at St. Anne, IL with their two sons and two grandsons.

Hugh Duncan (Dunk) and wife Lenore Violet (Violet) Gilkison were married in Joliet, IL and lived in Harvey, IL until moving to Winamac in 1946. They moved back to the Ladoga area to farm on Bymaster Road in 1949. They had five children: Barbara Jean, Edgar Lawrence (named after his grandfathers), Eleanor Lorraine, Connie Ruth, and Lonnie Leigh (who died at 19 months and was buried with his grandparents at St. Anne Cemetery). Hugh Duncan was buried in Oak Hill Cemetery in Crawfordsville.

Edgar Lawrence and wife Georgia Ann were married in Montgomery County and have three children: Teresa Kay Ginn (by Georgia's first marriage), Denise Yvonne (Georgia's daughter adopted by Edgar), and Duane Jeffery. Edgar lives within 15 miles of the home of his great-great-great-grandfather Daniel. *Submitted by Connie Flick*

ESTON MYERS FAMILY

Eston Lex Myers and Berniece Lucille Carlisle were married on Dec. 17, 1938 in Covington, IN. They went to housekeeping east of Wallace in Fountain County. They moved to a farm south of Veedersburg where their first child, Jerry Dean, was born Dec. 29, 1939. A daughter, Sandra Kay, arrived Dec. 1, 1942. She was born on a farm east of Covington where her father was working for a farmer, Forrest Lease.

Eston was drafted to serve with the United States Navy in World War II. He was a Fireman 1st Class at the time of his discharge. During his absence the family resided on their farm east of Wallace.

On Sept. 7, 1948 Linda Dianne arrived to join the family at Culver Hospital in Montgomery County. Brenda Lucille made her appearance on Jan. 14, 1951. Byron Carlisle was added to the family on Nov. 25, 1953. On Mar. 13, 1958 Carol Jean came to complete this family.

Jerry Dean moved to Florida in 1959 where he married Birdie Lou Allen. They are the parents of Lucinda Joan and Jerry Dean Jr.; they have two grandsons Jeremy Todd and Jonathan Daniel Calloway.

Sandra Kay married Donald Gillogly. They live near Waveland and are the parents of Donna Lynne, Lawrence Vane and Christa Hazell. They also have two grandsons: Jakota Leroy Reed and Corey Lee Gillogly.

Linda Dianne married Allan Mendenhall. They live near Crawfordsville and are the parents of Brian Gene and Dama Dianne.

Brenda Lucille married Richard Sommerville. They are the parents of three girls: Sabrina Lynn, Bobbi Jo and Kathy Jo. They live in Waveland.

Byron Carlisle married Donita Britton. They have three boys: Michael Neil, Ian Craig and Eston Lex. Byron is with the United States Marine Corp now serving in Michigan.

Carol Jean married Maynard Poole and they have two girls Mandee Lynne and Stacey Nicole. Carol now lives in New Ross.

Eston and Berniece moved the family to Waveland in the spring of 1958. At that time Eston worked with his brother, Robert Myers, in the reupholstering shop in Waveland. He later was employed by Wabash College as a security guard. He worked there until the time of his death, Feb. 23, 1977.

Berniece worked for many years at Culver Union Hospital, but is now working for Area IV Council on Aging as site director for the Waveland Nutrition Center. She is a volunteer Emergency Medical Technician with the S.W. Ambulance Service, serving the Waveland community. She is a member of the states "Over 65" EMT Club. Sandra Gillogly also serves the community as a volunteer EMT.

The family members are employed in many fields.

This family is proud of their heritage and proud to have lived in Montgomery County.

You can find the ancestors in the Robert Myers story. *Submitted by Brenda Sommerville*

LEROY AND STELLA MYERS

Leroy Sylvester Myers was born Dec. 19, 1894 near Wallace, IN. His parents were David Sylvester and Mary Ella Etter Myers. They lived in the Wallace and Alamo, IN community. Both are buried in the Alamo Cemetery.

Grandparents John Angerwine Myers of North Carolina and Sarah Palmer Myers of Virginia came to the Alamo community in the late 1830s. Both are buried in the cemetery at Alamo.

Leroy and Stella Myers

Leroy was a graduate of Wallace High School in 1913. He married Stella Isobel Smith at Crawfordsville Apr. 13, 1921. Stella was the daughter of Edison and Elizabeth Bowman Smith of the Alamo Community. Leroy and Stella had two sons; Ray Donald of Waveland and Robert Eugene of Brazil, 11 grandchildren and 23 great grandchildren.

'Roy' farmed around the Alamo area and worked at Sommers Metalcraft at Crawfordsville. He belonged to the Alamo Conservation Club and enjoyed hunting and fishing. He was a member of the Phanuel Evangelical Lutheran Church.

Stella I. Smith Myers was born Mar. 13, 1893 near Alamo. She was a graduate of Alamo High School in 1912, attended Danville Normal Teachers College, Ms Blakers Primary Teachers Classes at Indianapolis, State Teachers College, Terre Haute, IN. She taught 1st to 6th grades at Ripley #7 Ridgefarm School, 2nd grade at Yountsville. She taught two separate times at Alamo Jr. and Sr. High School after 30 years time apart. She was a member of the old Alamo Methodist Church. *Submitted by Roy S. Myers*

RAY DONALD AND BETTIE MYERS

Ray Donald Myers, son of Roy S. and Stella I. Smith Myers, was born Apr. 23, 1926 in Ripley Twp. Montgomery Co., IN. He has one brother, Robert Eugene, living in Brazil, IN.

As a youth attending Alamo grade and high school, he was active in all sports, during the summer he worked for Bud Fruits Sawmill and area farmers. After graduation in 1942 he worked in Buchanan, MI and Jeske Wire Specialty Co. in Crawfordsville.

In November 1943 he was inducted into the U.S. Army, serving in the 80th Infantry Division, in George S. Pattons' 3rd Army. He was in four Battle Campaigns, including the Battle of the Bulge. While in Europe he attended the Weihenstephan Agriculture College, Friezing, Germany. After being discharged from the Army in 1946, he worked for Mid-States Steel and Wire, farmed for several years and retired from the Montgomery County Farm Bureau after 32 years as bookkeeper and branch manager.

Ray Donald and Bettie Myers

On Feb. 26, 1944 he married Bettie Ann Whitecotton of Yountsville. Nine children were born to this union, Judith, Phillip, Kevin, Richard, Jayne, Kyle, twins Jannelle and Jeffrey and Darren. Janelle is deceased. They also have 19 grandchildren.

Bettie was the daughter of Walter and Laura Thompson Whitecotton and was b. Dec. 9, 1926. She was the middle child of five children. Her brothers and sisters; Helen Meadows Coffman, Lee, Bill and Bob, all residing in Indiana. She graduated from New Market High School in 1944 and at this writing has worked for the U.S. Postal Service for 18 years.

Both Don and Bettie are active volunteers, enjoying spectator sports, fishing, hunting and camping. *Submitted by Don and Bettie Myers*

ROBERT MYERS HISTORY

On Sept. 9, 1949 Robert E. Myers and Bessie B. Myers were married. They moved to Waveland, IN into their newly purchased home where they lived for 40 years. Many additions and changes have been necessary due to the birth of their four children.

Robert's ancestors have their roots in Fountain County. His great grandfather and great grandmother were Levi F. Myers Mar. 6, 1841 to Nov. 12, 1864; and Mary Ellen Welsh Myers Jan. 14, 1845 to Apr. 21, 1933. To this union one son was born, Byron F. Myers, after Levi's death, Mary Ellen Myers married Dr. E.E. Fine to this union one son was born Harry N. Fine, who became a lawyer in Crawfordsville.

Byron F. Myers was born 1864 died 1951 was married to Elizabeth Peevler, who was born 1866 died 1958; to this union two sons were born Herman L. and Earl F.; Earl F. married Juanita Schrader, no children were born to this union. Earl was born in 1895 and died 1984; Juanita born 1895 died 1987.

Herman L. was born 1890 died 1977 was married to Hazel Purnell Myers, she was born 1891 and died 1967.

To this union eight children were born: 1917 Elinor Ratcliff Marietta; 1918 Eston, died 1977; 1920 Susan Cronkhite; 1922 Herman Jr.; 1923 Byron, died 1952; 1925 Robert; 1927 Martha Holmes; and in 1930 John, died 1931.

Robert was born in Millcreek Township in Fountain County. After attending school at Steam Corner and Yeddo, he graduated from Kingman High School in 1943. He is a Navy Veteran leaving the service in 1946.

Bessie was born at Hillsboro, IN on Jan. 10, 1928 to Frank and Margaret Gillie Bever. She was the youngest of five children, she attended Hillsboro school and graduated in 1946. She also graduated from Indiana Business College at Indianapolis in 1947.

The Myer's have four children, twin girls Beverly and Betty born July 17, 1951; a son Jeffery born May 30, 1955; and a daughter Joyce born Feb. 17, 1964.

Beverly is married to John Bonsett and lives in Franklin, IN they are the parents of two daughters Anna and Belinda.

Betty is married to Richard Paxson and lives in Jay County near Bryant, IN they are the parents of three children; Mathew, Brenda and Michael.

Jeffery is married to Karen Kelly and lives at Waveland, IN they are the parents of two daughters Nicole and Stacy.

Joyce is still at home.

Robert has operated an Upholstery Business in Waveland for over 40 years, he also served as a substitute rural Letter Carrier and later as regular carrier until his retirement in 1983. *Submitted by Robert E. Myers*

NEES-IVEY

This history pertains to the Nees and Ivey families and to four generations of Methodist ministers, one of whom married a Montgomery County native. Benjamin Franklin Ivey, the first of the subjects, was born in Pickens Co., GA, Mar. 12, 1851, to Elisha F. and Catherine Trimble Ivey, the sixth of their nine children. He was licensed to preach by the Cumberland Presbyterian Church in 1868, the same year he married Emiline Collins, a native of North Carolina. They moved to Indiana in 1874, and he continued preaching and was admitted to the Northwest Indiana Conference of the Methodist Episcopal Church in 1884. He served at New Market and Ladoga as well as at other churches in Putnam and Hendricks Counties. Emiline died in 1895 and is buried at Newtown. "B.F.", as he was affectionately known, continued his ministry and retired in 1910. He married Mary L. Henchman in 1900. She died in 1916. He was associated with St. Paul's Church at Indianapolis until his death Feb. 20, 1928. He is buried in Crown Hill Cemetery, Indianapolis.

The second generation is represented by Homer Pierson Ivey, the seventh-born of Benjamin's and Emiline's seven children. He was born at New Winchester, Aug. 29, 1879. He graduated from Ladoga High School in 1898 and from DePauw University in 1902 with Phi Beta Kappa honors. Homer became a member of the Northwest Indiana Conference of the Methodist Church in 1903. He received his theological degree from Boston University Theological Seminary in 1911. Rev. Ivey was the recipient of an honorary Doctor of Divinity degree conferred by DePauw in 1937. While serving churches in northern Indiana, Homer met and married Zela Tinsley, a native of Tennessee and a school teacher at Union Mills, in 1904. Two sons were born, Homer Merrill and Newell, the latter dying in childhood. Rev. and Mrs. Ivey resided in Crawfordsville, 1931-1937, while he was superintendent of the Crawfordsville District of the Methodist Episcopal Church, and again in 1942 when he returned as pastor at the Trinity Church. He retired in 1946. Mrs. Ivey died in Florida in 1956, and she is buried at Crown Hill Cemetery, Indianapolis. Dr.

Ivey married Mrs. May Gaylor in 1958 in Florida, and she died in 1976. She is buried in Massachusetts. "H.P." spent his remaining years at the Wesley Manor Retirement Home at Frankfort. He died Feb. 11, 1984, after a brief illness, at the age of 104 years. He, too, is interred at Crown Hill. He was the oldest living graduate of Ladoga High School and DePauw University at his death.

H.P. and Sara (Nees) Ivey and their descendants at 100 years—1979

The third minister in this narrative, Homer Merrill Ivey, was born at Walkerton, Nov. 25, 1905, to the above named Homer and Zela Tinsley Ivey. He graduated from Whiting High School in 1923 and from DePauw University in 1927. Admitted to the Northwest Indiana Conference of the Methodist Episcopal Church in 1929, he graduated from Garrett Theological Seminary in 1932. Merrill was appointed to the Linden-Kirkpatrick Charge, Montgomery County, in 1932, to the Knox Church in 1937, and to the Flora Methodist Church in 1941. It was at Flora that he became ill, and he died in the Methodist Hospital at Indianapolis Jan. 24, 1943, at the age of 37 years. A most promising ministry came to an untimely end. While at Linden Merrill met and married a school teacher, Sara Ozella Nees, as his father before him had done. She was born at Crawfordsville July 29, 1907, the daughter of Milton L. and Lulu Turner Nees. The family, consisting of her two sisters, Ruth and Marcella, and a brother, David Milton, moved to the family farm near New Ross in 1918. All the children graduated from New Ross High School; Sara in 1925. She attended Indiana State Normal at Terre Haute, and in 1926 she began a teaching career at Mt. Zion School, Crawfordsville, teaching at New Ross 1927-1931, and at Linden, 1931-1933. Merrill and Sara were united in marriage by his father, H.P. Ivey, in the home of the bride's parents near New Ross on July 29, 1933. Two sons were born, David Merrill, July 26, 1936 at Culver Union Hospital in Crawfordsville, and Daniel Keith, June 6, 1939, at Plymouth.

After her husband's death, Sara and their sons made their home in Las Cruces, NM, together with Ruth Nees, her sister, already a teacher in that city. Sara resumed her teaching career and taught 26 years, retiring in 1969. She had earned her B.S. degree in Education at State Teachers' College, Terre Haute, in 1951. David and Daniel graduated from Las Cruces High School and New Mexico State University. David graduated from the Northwestern University School of Medicine in 1961, having joined the U.S. Air Force his senior year. Colonel Ivey retired in 1980 from the U.S.A.F. and is now an Ophthalmologist at the South Bend Clinic. He married Marietta Coble on June 21, 1958, at South Bend. She was the daughter of Rev. Almon and Betty Coble, former minister at Crawfordsville First Methodist Church. Dr. Coble and Dr. H.P. Ivey officiated at the ceremony. David and Marietta have three children: Sharon, born 1959, Chicago, (she married Michael Seanor, 1983, South Bend, two sons, Dustin, born 1985, Albuquerque, NM, and Ryan, born 1987, Rantoul, IL), David Merrill, Jr., born 1961, Chicago, and Susan, born 1964, Sault Sainte Marie, MI. Dr. and Mrs. Ivey now reside at Mishawaka, and she is secretary at Grace U.M. Church, South Bend.

Daniel, who became the fourth in the Ivey generation to preach, continued his education at Duke University Divinity School, Durham, NC and received his Master of Divinity degree in 1966. The great grandson of "B.F." Ivey, who began his ministry 121 years ago, Dan is proud of his heritage. Admitted to the Virginia Conference in 1963, he has preached 30 years, first supplying the Brazito Methodist Church in New Mexico. Rev. Ivey is now pastor of Arlington Forest U.M. Church, Arlington, VA. He married Dorothy J. Calvert June 24, 1961, at Richmond, VA. The daughter of Rev. Delford and Angeline Calvert, her father and Dr. H.P. Ivey officiated at the wedding ceremony. They are the parents of three children: Keith, born 1964, and Paul, born 1966, both born at Burlington, NC, and Jill, born 1968, at Franklin, VA. Dorothy ("Dot") is Resettlement Counselor in U.S. Office of the United Nations High Commissioner for Refugees in Washington, D.C.

Sara Nees Ivey is a resident of The Hermitage, United Methodist Retirement Home, Alexandria, VA. She is an active member of her church and participates in the affairs of the Home. *Submitted by Marcella N. Feltner and Sara N. Ivey*

MILTON L. AND LULU TURNER NEES

Lulu Inez Turner, born June 25, 1880, at New Ross, died Apr. 17, 1965, Crawfordsville, buried New Ross Cemetery. She was the daughter of David Milton Turner, born Nov. 11, 1844, Clark Co., IN, died June 8, 1897, New Ross, and Osellia Henthorn Turner, born June 8, 1854, Clark County, died Apr. 1, 1890, New Ross. Both buried New Ross Cemetery. D.M. Turner was the son of Williams Turner, Virginia native, born Oct. 7, 1805, died June 16, 1871, buried Hibernia Cemetery, Clark Co., IN, and Sophia H. Flint, born 1811, died Mar. 5, 1850, buried Hibernia Cemetery, Clark County. Osellia Henthorn Turner, daughter of Isaac J. Henthorn, born July 23, 1817, died May 24, 1858, buried New Market, Clark County, and Julia Ann Fordyce, born July 6, 1825, Lawrence County, died Jan. 26, 1911, Crawfordsville, buried New Ross Cemetery. (A teacher, she received some of the first State Public School money.) They were married July 6, 1853, Clark County. Julia married (second) Josiah Wheeler, November 1864.

Lulu Turner Nees had one sister, Julia Myrtle, born Sept. 13, 1877, New Ross, died July 5, 1883, buried New Ross Cemetery; two brothers, Herbert and Eugene, died in infancy, buried Clark County, and a brother, Jewell Stanley, born June 5, 1884, New Ross, died Jan. 2, 1953, buried Mace Cemetery. He married Elsie Mears, born Sept. 15, 1882, daughter of George and Lizzie Mears, at Indianapolis, Sept. 30, 1906. She died Aug. 2, 1938, buried Mace Cemetery. They had no children. Julia Henthorn Wheeler was daughter of Cyrus and Elizabeth Griffy Fordyce. Cyrus was a son of Abraham and Hanna Gard Fordyce.

Milton L. and Lulu T. Nees married June 5, 1901 New Ross, IN

Milton Leonidas Nees married Lulu Turner at New Ross Christian Church June 5, 1901. He was born Mar. 21, 1873, Jordan Village, Owen Co., IN and died July 8, 1946, New Ross, buried New Ross Cemetery. He was the son of David Abner Nees, born Apr. 15, 1843, Poland, Clay County, died May 24, 1883, Independence, KS, and is buried there. He was a Civil War Private with Company "B", 97th Ind. (Inf) and was wounded in the battle of Vicksburg. Milt's mother was Sarah Ann Kennedy Nees, born near Connersville, Fayette County, Feb. 14, 1843, died Jan. 6, 1918, near Jordan Village, buried Olive Hill Cemetery, Owen County. Milt had a brother, Robert, and sisters, Belle Stwalley, Clara Peden and Rose Schoppenhorst. A brother and sister died in early childhood. David Abner Nees was son of William Nees, born 1814, died 1851, buried Poland, and Martha Burchfield Nees, born 1851, died 1901. William was son of Michael and Margaret Freshour Nees, and his wife, Martha, was daughter of Hezekiah and Jane Melton Burchfield. They are buried in Wilkerson Cemetery, Poland, IN.

Sarah Ann Nees was daughter of John B. and Julia Smullen Kennedy, whose parents were Lauden and Elizabeth Ward Smullen, Fayette County. John B. is buried near Williams Creeks, Fayette County, and Julia Ann Kennedy, who died 1884, is buried at Olive Hill Cemetery, Owen County. Their children were: Elizabeth Schroer, James, Eli, Mary Huber Francis, and Sarah Ann Nees.

Milton and Lulu Nees had four children: Ruth Nees, born Sept. 14, 1901, at New Ross, Sara Ozella, born July 29, 1907, Marcella Turner, born Feb. 9, 1913, and David Milton, born Feb. 13, 1916, the latter three all born at Crawfordville. All the children graduated New Ross High School. Ruth received her degree from DePauw University, along with Phi Beta Kappa honors and was a teacher and school administrator 40 years. She taught first in 1921 at the one-room Greenwood School in Walnut Township, and at New Market High School and at Gary before moving to New Mexico in 1932. She was an elementary principal for many years, retiring in 1966. When plans were begun in 1973 for the New Ross Community Centennial Celebration to be held in 1975, Ruth was commissioned by the Steering Committee to write the centennial history. She devoted the following two years to that task, and the History was published in Volumes I and II and was available for the event. Later her health failed, and she has been a resident of Ben Hur and Williamsburg Health Care Homes since 1980.

Sara Nees married Rev. Homer Merrill Ivey, July 29, 1933. (See "Nees-Ivey" this history). Marcella Nees married Denver D. Feltner, Mar. 19, 1937. (See "Feltner-Nees" this history).

David Milton Nees married Evelyn Baker, born Apr. 6, 1913, Martinsville, at the Methodist Parsonage, Knox, IN Feb. 26, 1939. The ceremony was performed by Rev. Merrill Ivey, the groom's brother-in-law. They had two children, Bessie Lou, born Sept. 2, 1941, and David Jerome, born July 27, 1947, both born at Indianapolis. Bessie Lou married Thomas V. Bee, born Jan. 26, 1939, Richland Co., WI, at Bloomington, July 26, 1969. They have John David, born May 14, 1970, Waukegan, IL, and Adrianne Marie, born Nov. 14, 1973, Alexandria, VA. The family lives in Alexandria, VA. Tom is in government work, and Bess, an Indiana University graduate, is with the school there. David M. Nees died Dec. 25, 1982, at Danville, and is buried at West Newton Cemetery.

Both Milton and Lulu Nees taught school before their marriage—he in Owen County and she in Clark Township. He attended Valparaiso University and she the old Terre Haute Normal School. They lived on their farm near New Ross until Milt, a staunch Democrat, was elected Montgomery County Surveyor in 1906. They moved to Crawfordsville, and he served five terms in that office. He was responsible for the building of many bridges, ditches and roads, and he helped to build the first concrete roads in the county. He was also one who helped to route the "Dixie Hiway" through Crawfordsville. Defeated in the 1916 election, the family returned to their farm at New Ross in 1918. In 1920 he was named the first cashier of the newly organized Farmers State Bank, which position he held until his illness in 1945. Lulu became bookkeeper in 1925, and the couple served their community faithfully and well for 25 years. They were active members of the New Ross Christian Church, and he had held membership in the Masonic Lodge and she in the Order of the Eastern Star, and the Home Extension Club. *Submitted by Marcella Nees Feltner*

WARREN GARY AND REBECCA L. NEIDEFFER

Gary and Becky have made their home at 1507 E. Main Street in Crawfordsville for the past 15 years. Gary has been employed for 36 years at R.R. Donnelley & Sons as a trimmer operator. He was born Nov. 11, 1933 in Champaign, IL to Arthur Earl and Pearl Marie Stephens Neideffer. They were divorced shortly after Gary was born and Pearl married Walter Cress. To this union was born Mary Frances Cress who married Norman Cramer. The family moved to Crawfordsville in 1948 and Gary graduated from Crawfordsville High School in 1952. For a short time he worked at the Grab-It-Here. Gary has a son, Randy and a daughter, Kathy both of Crawfordsville. He married Rebecca (Becky) Lynn Spencer on Sept. 28, 1974.

Warren Gary and Rebecca L. Neideffer

Becky was born June 13, 1946 to Clyde Harvey and Cecil Pearl Stewart Spencer from Parke County. She has one brother, Clyde Harvey Jr., and four sisters, Norma Deuece Young, Patricia Marrero, Jane Greil, and Janet Barr. She graduated from Van Buren High School in Clay Co., IN and moved to Crawfordsville in 1964. Becky is the mother of two sons, Charles C. Coltharp, a graduate of the University of Cincinnati School of Architecture and living in Cincinnati and Gary S. Coltharp a graduate of ITT and living in Indianapolis.

Becky is currently the Montgomery County Clerk of Courts, elected to her first term in 1984 and her second in 1988. She is active in the Republican party as a precinct committeewoman and a member of the Republican Women's Club. She is a member of the State and County Historical Society and a member of the Genealogy Section that is compiling this history book. Before entering politics she operated the Cake Pan for ten years.

In 1986, the Visitors and Convention Bureau was formed to promote tourism in Montgomery County and Becky was appointed to the first Tourism Commission. She is currently serving as secretary of the Board of Directors. Her father, Clyde, was a member of the Long Range Planning Commission of Parke County, which helped to form the Covered Bridge Festival and Billie Creek Village.

Becky is also a member of Zonta, a classified service organization for professional women. She is also a Sales Representative for Poltermann Fashions.

Becky and Gary have an Argentine "son", Jose "Pepe" H. Cuadrado. He came to Crawfordsville in 1982 and is married to Dianna Stranger of Roachdale. They are both employed by Raybestos Manhatten and have a daughter, Elizabeth Ann born Nov. 10, 1987 and Michael Edward born Apr. 20, 1989.

ORA AND DOROTHY NEWNUM

Ora and Dorothy Newnum moved to Montgomery County from Fountain County in April of 1941.

When they first came to New Richmond in March of 1941, New Richmond was installing a water system. It was raining, and mud and water covered all the sidewalks. Needless to say, they were discouraged — but time has proved that this was a good place for them to live and raise a family.

Ora was born in Parke County to Roy and Ura Simmons Newnum on Sept. 9, 1912. Dorothy's parents were Claude and Audra Bodine Denton. She was born on Oct. 22, 1918 in Fountain County.

Ora was a graduate of Tangier High School in 1932 and Dorothy from Covington High School in 1936.

Ora and Dorothy settled in New Richmond, where he was associated with the Standard Oil Company of Indiana. He delivered gasoline, diesel fuels, motor oil and heating oils to primarily farmers. As a sideline, Ora refereed baseball, officiated basketball and called square dances.

Ora served in the armed services during World War II, from 1943-45, and is a member of the American Legion. Ora was very active in civic affairs, serving at various times on the Volunteer Fire Department and the Local Town Board. Other memberships for Ora include Masonic Lodge, Elks Lodge, Eastern Star, and for Dorothy her local bridge group, which has been meeting for well over 50 years, and still meets every two weeks, New Richmond Study Club, American Legion Auxiliary and New Richmond Tourism Council, Inc.

Ora and Dorothy Newnum and family

This union was blessed with four children, Roger Wayne, born Apr. 29, 1939, Kenneth Jay born Oct. 10, 1942, Betty Jo born July 23, 1944 and LuAnn born Sept. 14, 1953, who all graduated from Coal Creek Central High School, Roger being enrolled as a freshman in the first year of its existence, and LuAnn graduating with the last Senior class in 1971.

After many years as a housewife, mother and bookkeeper for her husband, Dorothy worked for Tri-County Telephone Company at New Richmond, IN for 20 years.

They have seven grandchildren and one great grandchild. Roger married Ruth Ann McCullough of Wingate on June 24, 1962. They live in Greencastle, IN. They have two children, Jay W. born July 18, 1963 and Julie Ann born June 14, 1965.

After many years in the field of education, Roger is now employed by Kepner Tregoe, a consulting firm.

Kenneth married Ruth Ann Irvin of Rural New Richmond on Aug. 29, 1965 and they have one son, Jay Kenneth born June 24, 1972. They are residents of Crawfordsville, where he is employed by Bank One, and she is with the Crawfordsville School System.

Betty Jo (Jody) married Leo G. Thomas, and with daughter Cynthia Lynne (Cindy) who was born Nov. 12, 1968 live in Battle Creek, MI where he works for State Farm Insurance. However, they will be relocating in Tulsa, OK in the spring of 1989.

LuAnn and Fred W. Stohrer were married Mar. 9, 1979, and with their three children (Emily Louise born Mar. 6, 1977, Andrew William born Nov. 27, 1981 and Michael Denton born Mar. 27, 1984) live in Royal Oak, MI. Fred is employed by Bunzl Co.

When the movie, "Hoosiers" was made in New Richmond (named Hickory) in 1985, Dorothy was very instrumental in starting the annual "Hickory Festival."

Ora was retired from Standard Oil after 30 years in 1971, and Dorothy retired from Tri-County Telephone Company after 20 years in 1981. They are members of the United Methodist Church, where he has served as trustee, and she is still serving as Treasurer.

Ora and Dorothy still live in New Richmond and celebrated their 50th anniversary in 1987.

JAMES ALLEN AND CORA (RIDENGER) NICHOLS

George D. Nichols born Apr. 26, 1827 in Bambury, England married Rachel Williamson from Ohio born 1826. Rachel died in 1861 and George in

1902, and both are buried at Linden, IN Cemetery. George had several marriages. His children were:

William H. born 1856 died 1880 buried at Linden.

Hettie, daughter Myrtle married a Fisher and lived in the New Market area.

James Allen born Dec. 30, 1859 and Cora Emmaline (Ridenger) born Oct. 20, 1867 married Aug. 22, 1886. James died 1934 and Cora 1932.

James' children: Mabel, born 1889, married a Jessie Peters and died in early womanhood.

Grace Ann, born 1895, married Alva Johnson. They ran the Hardware store in New Market during their later years. Ada, Frank and Marvin are their children. Frank has been active politically until his retirement and he is married to Mabel Wilshire.

Alva, born 1902, married Thelma Douglas was working for Horner's when he died in 1961. Daughters, Martha, married Russell Stout and Rebecca, married Thomas Craig.

George, Mabel, Alva, Grace, Cora and Al Nichols

George, born at Linden 1900 and Beatrice McCoy, born 1902, were married in 1921. George, was one of the first group of men hired at R. R. Donnelleys located at the old Match Factory on Elmore St., in May of 1922. Donnelley's employed him until his death in 1952.

George and Bea had seven children including a set of twins. Norman born 1922, Edwin born 1923, Walter born 1926, Alice Nichols Witt born 1928, Oka born 1930, Ruth Nichols Douglas and Naomi Nichols Kinney were born in 1931.

Norman, oldest son, attended Alamo School when they lived at Yountsville, IN. After moving to a farm on the Country Club Road, last known as the Northcutt Gravel Co., he commuted to Alamo in order to graduate with his class of nine in 1940.

In 1942 he was drafted and served 33 months overseas in WWII. In the Philippines he contracted malaria and was sent back to the hospital base alone on foot. He was housed and protected by the Philippic as he journeyed. Because of the malaria he missed the Leyete siege and his life was spared. Upon his return home in 1945 he took employment at R.R. Donnelley's until his death of leukemia, in 1964.

Norman married Alberta Rhodes in 1946 grade school friends. They have been active members of East Side Baptist Church, which Norman spent many hours helping to build on the Traction Road site.

Their children are: Penny born 1947, has been a teacher since 1970 and first taught at Mt. Zion where she acquired her grade school education. Penny married Carl Richardson in 1985 and he had two children.

Pamela, born 1949 married John Majors (a classmate) in 1969 and lives in Louisville, KY, where he is an attorney. They have three boys that include a set of twins.

Phillip born in 1961, is unmarried and at present makes his home with his mother but works in Indianapolis.

CHARLES E. AND MARY (PORTER) NIXON

Charles E. and Mary Nixon, residents of Montgomery Co., IN since 1958. Charles retired from Department of Highways in 1982. He was born on a farm in Illinois, grew to manhood on a farm in Parke County, and farmed there until 1958. His other occupations were: employed at U.S. Army Ammunition Depot, Newport, IN - R.R. Donnelley & Sons and California Pellet Mill Co., both of Crawfordsville, IN.

Charles was born in Douglas Co., IL Aug. 26, 1916 to Everett R. and Celia Jones Nixon. He is the oldest of four children. Charles and his parents moved to Indiana in 1921. His parents farmed in Parke County.

Charles graduated from Greene Twp High School, Parke Co., IN in 1935 and in 1936 he marred Mary L. Porter at Rockville, IN. They have two daughters, Deanna Stevenson of Advance, In, born Mar. 16, 1944 and Rhoda Williams of Greencastle, IN, born July 26, 1949, also two grandsons, Todd Stevenson, Advance, IN and Tom Stevenson, United States Navy.

Charles E. and Mary (Porter) Nixon

Mary was born in Montgomery Co., IN May 11, 1917 to Guy H. and Florence VanCleave Porter; she is the third of eight children. Mary graduated from Waveland High School, Waveland, IN in 1935. She also lived on a farm in Parke County, where her parents were farmers. Besides her duties as a housewife, Mary worked several years at Ben Hur Nursing Home, Crawfordsville, IN until her retirement in 1982.

Charles and Mary still own their farm in Parke County, and the one formerly owned by Charles' parents. They continue living in Waveland, IN. Both belong to the Waveland Christian Church. Charles is a member of Waveland Lodge 300 - F.&A.M., and Mary belongs to Dorothy Q. Chapter of Daughters of the American Revolution.

Mary's father was born in Montgomery County to Benjamin and Barbara Apple Porter, and her mother was also born in Montgomery to Dr. Charles and Dora Yaryan VanCleave.

Genealogy of the antecedents of Mary's grandfather, Charles Van Cleave, M.D., Jan VanCleef is complete to the year 1653, when he migrated from the family town to Cleef in Holland.

Jan Van Cleef settled in Gravesend Township, King's County, Long Island, when it was known as New Netherlands, and was occupied by the English in 1664. Descendants of Jan VanCleef, his grandsons, of which there were many, fought in the American Revolution against the British. One of his grandsons, Aaron Van Cleave and seven of his sons served in the Army of Revolution, - by this time the family had changed their name from Van Cleef to Van Cleave, or English.

Another antecedent married into the Van Der Bilt family, another was the mother of Orville and Wilbur Wright, and one married the brother of Daniel Boone. Squire Boone and his wife are buried in a cave in Harrison Co., IN.

Mary's grandfather, Benjamin Porter was born in Breckenridge, KY to William and Bettie Duncan Porter. Mary's great-grandfather, William Porter enlisted in West Virginia Infantry September 1863, and discharged July 1863. Next he enlisted in Co. I-45th Regiment, Kentucky Mounted Infantry Volunteers, Oct. 8, 1863, and individually mustered out Feb. 21, 1865.

He failed to return to his family at War's end, and the War Dept. records state he survived the War. Another mystery of the Civil War never solved!

MR. AND MRS. FRANK D. NOLAN

Montgomery County was home to Frank and Pearl Nolan. They were born and lived North of Crawfordsville in Union Township their entire lives.

Frank was born to John and Ellen (Davidson) Nolan on June 11, 1876. When he was four, his mother died leaving Frank and a younger brother, Harry. His father married again to Helen Scott. They had four children: Walter, Rose, Mary and John. Frank spent much of his young life with three aunts and an uncle.

He graduated on Mar. 6, 1896 with the first class of the Linden High School.

Pearl Long was born Jan. 17, 1878 to Luther R. and Caroline (Purdum) Long. Other children were Lawrence, Anna (Manson) and Luther L.

Pearl had a common school education, graduating from Eighth Grade in 1894. After a few months training she qualified as a teacher. Before marrying, she taught several years in the Vail and Gobel Schools.

Frank and Pearl were married on June 14, 1899. They set up housekeeping in a new home on their small farm. These buildings still stand across from the south entrance of North Montgomery High School.

Frank and Pearl Nolan

Frank farmed and worked at the Cherry Grove Elevator where the Montgomery County Farm Bureau Plant now stands.

Three daughters were both to them: Ellen, who died in infancy; Edith Miller of Pensacola, FL; and Nola Stowers of Kirklin, IN.

As a newly married couple they were very active in building the new Young Chapel Church, finished in 1905. With some additions and alterations it is still an important part of the community. They remained active and devoted to the Church until Frank's death. He served his Church well in various capacities including an eldership. Pearl also gave time and talent to Church organizations such as Ladies Aid and Missionary Society.

Frank was a Democrat, but valued a man's morality and integrity more than his political affiliations. From a highly Republican County, he was elected to serve in the House of Representatives of the State Legislature for two terms in the 1920's.

He served several years on the Board of Directors of the Producer's Creamery.

Pearl's father died in 1914. Wishing to live closer to Pearl's mother, they bought the Lane farm across from the Long's homestead. When the mother died in 1923, they bought the homeplace and lived there until Frank's death in August 1945. Pearl then moved to Linden to be near her daughter, Edith. She lived there until her death in December 1963.

They were what we call "solid citizens" but enjoyed a real zest for life; being eager to keep up with world affairs and take part in community activities kept them mentally alert. Frank enjoyed music and for several years sang bass in a male quartet. Pearl enjoyed her home and doing beautiful hand-work including quilts and crocheted pieces which have become heirlooms and are still enjoyed. Friends, relatives and their immediate family were all an important part of their lives. They especially enjoyed their grandchildren Wanda (Miller) Millet and Max and Mark Stowers.

Frank and Pearl Nolan were always proud to call Montgomery County home and surely their lives have added a bright page to the county's history.

MORRIS AND ALICE NORMAN

Ralph Morris and Alice Marie (Trusler) Norman came to Montgomery County in 1946. They moved to the farm located on top of Covington Hill north of Crawfordsville just off highway 136 on the site now occupied by the LDS Church. Morris worked at the Hi Tek Brick Co. in addition to farming. In 1948, they moved to the Repp farm located on SR. 234 southwest of New Market. In 1956, they left farming and moved into New Market, purchasing a house on East Main Street. Morris then worked at the California Pellet Mill until his retirement in 1976.

Morris was born on Sept. 22, 1910, near Tangier in Parke, Co., IN, the son of Oscar Hamilton and Mary Martha (Harvey) Norman. He was the fourth of five children. His siblings were, Mable, Foster (who died in infancy), Ward and Buelah. He attended and graduated from Tangier High School in 1929. He was active in church work his entire life. Since 1948, he belonged to the New Market Christian Church where he served many years as Deacon, Elder, and Board Member. He died on Mar. 19, 1983, and is buried in the Indiana Creek Hill Cemetery southwest of New Market on SR47.

Alice, who still resides in New Market, was born at Rockville, Parke, Co., IN, on Jan. 15, 1915. Her parents were John Ralph and Essie Marie (Jackson) Trusler. She was the second of five children. Her siblings were Melvin (Bud), Mildred, John Wallace (Wally), and Mary Catherine. She attended various schools and graduated from Tangier High School in 1933. She was employed by the G C Murphy Store in Crawfordsville and served as a telephone operator for the New Market Telephone System for many years.

Morris and Alice Norman

They have two children, Richard Dale of R3 Crawfordsville, and Kenneth Dean of R1 Waveland. Dale married Leota Jones in 1954, she died in 1977. They have four children, Elsie, Gregory, Luanne and Jeromy. In 1979, Dale married Virginia (Patton) Collins. Dean married Janet Kay (Kelsey) in 1961. She died in an automobile accident in 1971. They had two sons, Christopher Dean and Timothy Lynn. In 1972, Dean married Elaine Ann Cosby who adopted Chris and Tim. Dean and Elaine then had two daughters, Erika Elaine and Ronda Lea.

Morris and Alice also have six great grandchildren, five step grandchildren, and four step great grandchildren. *Submitted by Dean Norman*

WILLIAM OFFIELD

William Offield, first settler was born in North Carolina in 1793, and at the age of 18 years enlisted in the War of 1812.

After leaving the service, he lived for a time in Tennessee, until in 1819 when he immigrated to Morgan Co., IN, with his wife Jane (Laughin) Offield and one child and lived until 1821, when they moved to Montgomery Co., IN.

Here they located, and built a cabin 12 x 15 feet, in Section 16, Township 18, Range 5 West, near a small stream, later called Offield Creek.

From his account book, as one of the four men to serve as County Commissioner, it confirms he was a man of some education.

From local records, Mr. Offield, in July 1822 bought 79.81 acres in Section 4, Township 18, Range 5 West, north of what later is Yountsville, from Merrikin Bond for $100.00. In 1824, the Offields sold this land for $307.50.

Wm. Offield settled here February 1821

Whether from restlessness or adventuresome nature, the family moved to the Ozark Mountains in Missouri and entered a section of land. Later while moving up the Columbia Valley enroute to a new location (later Washington) Jane Offield and one of the sons died of cholera. After proper burial, the other family members moved on where years later, William Offield died and was entered.

In 1881, Peter Kennedy an interested citizen sought to place a marker at the cabin site of Mr. Offield in Section 16. The native gray granite stone, was found in the side yard of Alexander Weir. The upward top smooth side, was used by the Weirs on which to place salt for their cattle. The stone was lettered and placed on the cabin site.

In 1921, Dumont Kennedy and the Historical Society arranged to have the stone marker placed by the roadside to be visible to passersby. It was moved about 200 feet west and 30 feet north of its original position.

On Nov. 21, 1922, many citizens, some officials, and speakers met and had an impressive ceremony of dedication to an honored man. The inscription read, "Wm. Offield Settled Here Feb. 1821." *Information from Historical Records: Written by Mabel Weir Grimes*

JOHN R. AND DIANE (HAFFNER) OILAR

John Ray Oilar moved to Crawfordsville when he married Elizabeth Diane ("Haffner") Melvin on Apr. 14, 1988. Diane has lived in Crawfordsville all of her life. John was born to Kenneth R. and Anna Belle ("Kessinger") Oilar on Jan. 22, 1949, in Lafayette, IN. He has a younger sister Fay. Kenneth is a retired Postal Carrier while Anna Belle presently is employed as a legal secretary in Lafayette.

His ancestors were among the first settlers of the Lafayette, IN area. Colonel Henry Oilar (1800-1868) was a respected military leader. He was also a prominent educator and civic development leader in Chauncey, which later became West Lafayette, and Lafayette. The Oilar family traces its relationship to Abraham Lincoln through Bathsheba McGlamery Oilar, the mother of Colonel Henry Oilar. It has been passed down through generations of the family that Bathsheba Oilar was named after her Aunt Bathsheba who was the grandmother of President Lincoln.

John R. and Diane (Haffner) Oilar

In June of 1967 John graduated from Klondike High School near West Lafayette, IN. Previous to this in 1960 and 1961 he had taken art classes as a Junior High School student from noted artist Sister M. Rufinia, O.S.F. In the summer of 1969 he studied art in Europe. In June of 1971 he graduated with honors from Western New Mexico University in Silver City, NM. While in college he was chosen for membership in honor societies such as Sigma Tau Delta, Pi Gamma Mu and Kappa Delta Pi.

After graduation he taught Junior High School Art for one year. Later John was an artist and a feature writer for two small newspapers in the

Lafayette area. His artwork and research ability have enabled him to be included in publications such as *Men of Achievement* and *Who's Who in the Midwest*.

Diane is the daughter of the late Bessie Lee and Cloyd O. Haffner. Cloyd O. Haffner was a well-known optometrist who practiced in Crawfordsville for 55 years. After graduation from Crawfordsville High School Diane attended Christian College in Columbia, MO where she graduated in 1961. After graduation she was employed as an assistant medical lab. technician in Lafayette. Later she was employed by the R.R. Donnelley Company for 13 years. Diane has lived in the same house in the Elston Grove area in Crawfordsville for the last 25 years. This house at 608 East Wabash Avenue is also the place where she was born and is commonly called "The Wedding Cake House".

John and Diane Oilar are presently employed by Purdue University in West Lafayette, IN.

JAMES EDWARD OLDSHUE

James Edward Oldshue was born on the "old" Oldshue homestead west of Waveland in Parke County Mar. 13, 1858 and died Nov. 11, 1930. On Dec. 26, 1881 James was united in marriage with Miss Emma Blanche Jarvis (1860-1918) the daughter of William and Virginia Switzer Jarvis. To this union three daughters were born; Vivian (Mrs. Leon Guy), Grace (Mrs. Edward Hancock), and Virginia (Mrs. Foster Glover) and four grandchildren: Blanche Glover Parker, Martha Glover Hayes, Patricia Glover Lee and Robert Edward Glover.

James attended the common school and Bloomingdale Academy...then engaged in farming and cattle raising on the farm which he was born, naming it "Limestone Valley Farm". The Oldshue family moved to Waveland in 1914 and became connected with the State Bank of Waveland as Director and President for many years. He was a charter member of Rathbone Lodge, Knights of Pythias.

James' parents were Jacob Oldshue (1816 Pennsylvania - 1897 Indiana) and Mary Barnes (1824 Kentucky - 1909 Indiana). Jacob came to Indiana in 1836 from Ohio with his parents John Oldshue (1790-1861) and Jemima Lincoln (1793-1870). Jacob served in the Mexican War as Quarter-Master Sergeant 5th Regiment Indiana Volunteers returning home to farming and stock raising. His children were Sarah (Mrs. Lawson W. Seybold), Robert (m. Florence Peterman), Martha (Mrs. Jerome B. Dooley), Margaret (Mrs. William Farmer), Amanda (Mrs. Daniel W. Hanna), Willian B. (1856-1856), James Edward m. Emma Blanche Jarvis, John Lincoln (m. Mary W. Canine) whose children were William "Foster" (1903-1984) and Clara May (1905-1980).

James' great great great grandfather John Oldshue (____-1803) started the American "Oldshue" line in York County, PA. *Submitted by Mrs. Arthur Hayes*

DARYL AND WILBERTA QUIGG OLIN

Daryl Leon was born to Leland and Mae (Harshbarger) Olin, Mar. 6, 1921, Charles Harshbarger homeplace, 400 West - 550 North, Union Township.

Wilberta Faye was born to Halfred Lewis and Faye (Conrad) Quigg, Jan. 6, 1922 near Gravelly Run, 500 East - 150 North, Franklin Township.

The Quigg family moved to the New Richmond area in 1928, Daryl and Wilberta attended all 12 grades, graduating with the "1940 class" of 17 members.

Before their marriage in Liberty Chapel, June 8, 1943, Wilberta was employed by J.C. Penney and Hall's Emporium; Daryl, family farm and Farm Bureau Co-op Service Station.

Daryl served 38 months with the U.S. Army Military Police, European Theater from 1944 to 1946.

Daryl and Wilberta (Quigg) Olin and family

They reside at the Olin Farms, 400 West - 650 North, Coal Creek Township, near Daryl's brother Harold and sister Helen Langworthy.

Wilberta's sister, Mrs. Clyde (Wilma) Patton, South on 400 West, younger sister, Mrs. Myron (Winona) Lyon, Sheridan, IN and brother, Francis 500 East - 150 North, Gravelly Run neighborhood where he, Wilma and Wilberta were born.

1. Dennis Jay, Jan. 1, 1947, married Kathleen Campfield, July 9, 1966. Children: Matthew, Luke and Callie Mae. Kathy is school bus driver, organist-pianist of New Richmond Methodist Church, much interest in crafts, spinning and sewing. Dennis and Daryl grain farm, raising Orville Redenbacker popcorn and Dennis drives a school bus. They reside on the Olin Farms.

2. LaDonna, born July 15, 1948, graduate of Community Hospital Nursing School, married Charles G. Howard, July 21, 1973. He is Admission's Director, Rose Hulman Institute of Technology, Terre Haute. Children: Andrew and Emily.

3. LaDonna's twin sister, DeAnna, July 15, 1947, graduated from the University of Evansville School of Nursing, married Edward Block, Aug. 11, 1979. They reside at Fort Branch where he farms and is a mathematics teacher at Tecumseh High School. She works at Deaconess Hospital, Evansville. Children: Brian and Beth.

4. Gregory, Nov. 9, 1950, Raybestos Corporation Production line and inspector since 1969; built his log home at the Olin Farms in 1978-79, married Mary Lou Weliver. Children: Gabriel and Tacy.

5. Marcia, Aug. 20, 1954 married William Hobbs, Oct. 28, 1972. Bill is part-owner of "Intelligent Data System," Noblesville, IN. Marcia is employed at Antique and Unique Shop at Lohman Square. Daughters: Amy and Robyn.

6. Anita, Feb. 26, 1959, Butler University graduate, lives at Fort Collins, CO since 1983, manager of Cuisine, Cuisine, catering and restaurant service.

7. Jo Ella, Mar. 15, 1963, cashier at Thrifty Supply since 1982, married Gerry Haffner Apr. 23, 1983, Inland Container employee, and they live at New Market.

The family has active members of Liberty Chapel Church; Daryl, trustee, Wilberta, Church secretary and Gregory, Superintendent of Sunday School. *Submitted by Wilberta Olin*

DR. LEVERETT AND EFFIE (SWANK) OLIN

Leverett was born in Portage Co., OH (Feb. 12, 1851), son of Ranson and Clara (Clark) Olin. Educated in Buchtel College, Akron, OH, College of Physicians and Surgeons, New York City. Passed his state exams and registered under law of 1885.

He became well-known, when he came to Elmdale in 1876 and people came from some distance for his knowledge.

He married Sarah Ethelyn (Effie) Swank, Sept. 2, 1883, daughter of Benjamin and Ellen (Cowan) Swank. Effie was born Jan. 13, 1863 and died Nov. 24, 1915.

Their oldest son Lester (1884-1965) was a farmer and dedicated teacher at Elmdale, Round Hill, New Richmond and retired from Coal Creek Consolidated School, a respected and beloved teacher and basketball coach. He received his education at Wabash, Valparaiso and Central Normal Colleges. He married Tessie Patton and they had one son, Paul.

Blanche (1886-1928) housewife, married Scott Cowan, farmer, a talented carpenter, lived in North Union with son Byron, Marian and daughters, Margaret and Rebecca.

Great great grandma Rachel Baldwin Cowan, Lester, Blanche, Grace, Leveritt, grandma Effie Olin, Grandpa (Dr.) Olin holding Leland.

Grace (1890-1971) married Virgil Meritt, two sons, Olin, elementary teacher and principal, and Eugene, farmer in Elmdale area.

Leland (1896-1977) married Mae Harshbarger, served in Army, WWI, graduated from Wingate High School in 1915; was member of State Basketball Teams 1913 and 1914. Farm and county highway employee. Sons, Harold and Daryl and daughter Helen Langworthy.

Leverett (1892-1969) married Mary Crowder, elementary school teacher in South Bend schools and Leverett retired from Studebaker Auto plant. One son, Kenneth, elementary teacher and principal.

Ruth, born Apr. 19, 1904 is the only living child, married Ralph Crowder, has one daughter, Alice Jean Donaldson at St. Joseph, MI where Ruth now lives after residing many years at Waukegan, IL. Their son Leon died in 1979.

Reine (1905-1916) was killed in an auto accident at 11 years of age.

Children Edna Ray, Paul Leverne, Marjorie and Leon Noel died in infancy.

This picture of Leverett and Effie's home was at Elmdale, on State Road #55, across from his small office. He practiced there until before his death June 9, 1924. From his office records —

May 21, 1898 — Tom Quillan, attended wife, baby delivered $8.00.

Extracted tooth, Mattie Utterback, 25 cents.

Fractured leg, set, John Nolan, $5.00.

Medicine, John Vancleave, 50 cents.

Lester, Leland and brother-in-laws, Scott Cowan and Virgil Meritt, with Tessie Olin at the piano, formed the "Olin Quartet," that sang at many farm meetings, funerals and church events.

Of the descendants, there are 18 teachers, five nurses, four school bus drivers, one female corporate lawyer, and 15 farm families. They meet each year for reunions at Liberty Chapel Church.

THE OLIVER FAMILY

The Oliver family lived in South Union Township for many years. One member of this family is William Oliver whose offspring has spread into several generations of progeny. William was born ca. 1839 and died ca. 1869. According to the Montgomery County 1860 Census he was listed as a carpenter and the family has said he operated a saw mill. His death at age 30 was due to a crow bar hitting him in the stomach.

William married Nancy E. Thompson (1841-1864) Oct. 19, 1856. They had four children, an infant who died, Ethan A. who died at age five, Florence May and Joseph Milton.

Florence May married John C. Wasson Oct. 9, 1879. They had three children, Ira, Kate and Clara.

Joseph Milton married Anna B. Wasson Apr. 13, 1887. They had four children, William "Willie", Walter, Hazel and Helen.

After Nancy's death, William married her cousin, Lucy Thompson, on Dec. 12, 1864. Lucy was the daughter of William Thompson (1801-1886) and Maria Caldwell (1808-1873). William, Nancy and Lucy are buried in the Findley Cemetery west of Whitesville.

William and Lucy had three children, Charles Thompson, Clara Maria and William Maxwell.

Charles Thompson (1865-1934) married Luella Graham (1861-1943) Aug. 24, 1884 at Parkersburg. Charles farmed at Whitesville and New Richmond. Luella is the daughter of William Graham and Mary Burchman. Seven children were born to Charles and Luella.

Lorena (1885-1979) married Bert Warner of Parkersburg. They farmed in Scott Township. They had five children, Charles, Homer, Mary, Theodore and Oliver.

William Bruce (1887-1972) left Indiana in his early 20's and settled in Ellendale, ND. He served as sheriff and a law enforcement officer for Dickey County and did carpentry in his later years. He married Irma Sizer; they had no children.

Arthur Melton (1889-1975) married Elza McCulley and they had one son, Arthur, Jr. Arthur was an industrial mechanic for the American Steel Foundries in East St. Louis, MO.

Leo Aaron (1892-1963) farmed in the Wingate and Ladoga area. He married Mary Hall and they had seven children, Mildred, Charles, Alfred, Margaret, Leo, Jr., Robert and Evelyn.

Fred Ellworth (1895-1965) lived and farmed in the New Richmond and Wingate area. He married Beatrice Haire and they had two children, David and Joann.

Raymond Maxwell (1898-1987) worked for the U.S. Government railway postal service for 40 years. He married Marie Simmons and they had three children, Delores, Marvin and Dwight Lee who died in infancy.

Clara Maria (1867-1952), the second child born to William and Lucy Oliver, married George Himes who farmed in the New Market community. They had two children, Ruth and Merle.

Ruth married Clyde Johnson, who also farmed in the New Market area, and they had two children, Donald and Phyllis.

Merle married Ruby Thompson and after her death he married Ruth Barth; he had no children.

The third child born to William and Lucy Oliver was William Maxwell (1869-1940). He helped his brother Charles farm; he never married.

CHARLES A. AND AMANDA C. OLIVER

Charles Aaron Oliver was born Jan. 26, 1866 in Montgomery County, near Whitesville. He was the second child of Jackson and Emily Wilson Oliver. His brothers and sisters were James William, Jesse Jackson, Isabell, Franklin V. and Rena.

On Dec. 25, 1907, he married Amanda Catherine Himes, born July 5, 1878. She was the daughter of Abraham and Mary Ann Lemon Himes. To this union three children were born: Mary Elizabeth, who married Ernest R. Mueller of Minnesota in 1930, Charlotte Emily, who married Kenneth Cosby of Waveland in June 1941 and Charles Edward who married Geraldine M. Smith of Crawfordsville in 1937. Charles and Amanda reared their children on their farm west of Whitesville.

Charles A. and Amanda C. Oliver

Mary and Charlotte were very active in 4-H. Both sisters received 4-H scholarships to Purdue University. Mary attended Purdue, but Charlotte chose to go to Central Normal College at Danville, IN to become an elementary teacher. She taught at Youngs Chapel, New Market and Waveland schools. Charles Edward died in 1952, three years after his wife, who died in 1949. After Charles' death, his sisters and her husband, Mary and Ernest Mueller of Columbus, OH, adopted his children, Janet and Robert Larry Oliver.

The grandparents of Charles Aaron were James and Nancy Oliver, who were born in North Carolina and died in Putnam Co., IN and William (Blind Billy) and Susanna Goff Wilson, who also resided in Putnam County and are buried there. Amanda's grandparents were Samuel and Susanna Stoner Lemon, who came from Virginia and settled in the Ladoga area in the 1850's and Daniel and Mary A. Himes, who also lived in Montgomery County at that time.

Charles and Amanda had four grandchildren: Janet Kay and Robert Larry (Oliver) Mueller and Elaine Ann and Terry Alan Cosby.

Amanda attended Maple Grove School in Clark Township. She was the ninth of 11 children — Margaret, Robert, Susan, Ella, Harvey, George, John, Lula, Albert and Ressie Himes. Amanda died Sept. 20, 1961 in Crawfordsville, where she resided after Charles' death.

Charles attended Beech Grove School in south Union Township, which later became his barn. Some of his teachers were Miss Peterson and Nelle Roundtree. All of his life, Charles farmed with horses. He took his cattle about one-half mile to pasture and back every day, rain or shine. Charles died May 21, 1953 at the age of 87. *Submitted by Charlotte Oliver Cosby*

OPPY FAMILY HISTORY

David and Joan Tribby Oppy were both born in Coal Creek Township, as were all four of their parents and several of their grandparents. David's great-grandfather Oppy, also named David, is listed as an early settler of Montgomery County—coming here from Adams Co., OH and settling in Coal Creek Township in 1828. His great-grandmother, Oppy, Elizabeth Edwards, was the daughter of Jesse Edwards, a Revolutionary War veteran. David's paternal grandparents were Christopher John Oppy, born in 1816 in Adam's Co., OH and coming to Montgomery County as a boy; and Margaret Wilson, born in Montgomery County in 1839, whose parents, James and Nicholas Wilson, were both born in Scotland. David's maternal great-grandparents were Thomas M. and Cynthia Jolly Foster—Thomas a native of Mocksville, NC and Cynthia born in Montgomery County; and Irvin and Sarah Groendyke Miller, both born in Montgomery County. Both of his maternal grandparents, Garrett Van Foster, born in 1867, and Mary "Mate" Miller, born in 1870, were born in Coal Creek Twp. His mother, Ruby May Foster, was born in a log house along Coal Creek just south of New Richmond on Sept. 15, 1893. David Miller Oppy was born June 23, 1922 in the same house his father, Edward Templeton Oppy, was born in on Mar. 17, 1875. David was the youngest of four sons, his brothers being: Leland E., born in 1915; Thomas J., born in 1917; and Garland W., born in 1920.

David and Joan Oppy and family August 1987

During World War II he was in the U.S. Army from Mar. 15, 1943 until Jan. 6, 1946 and received three battle stars while serving in the E.T.O. He is a fourth generation farmer in Coal Creek Twp.

Martha "Joan" Tribby was born Aug. 22, 1924 in the same house her father, Gaylord Leander "Trib" Tribby, was born in on Oct. 6, 1898. This house burned in February of 1925. Her mother, Mildred Elizabeth "Punk" Dunn, was born in New Richmond Oct. 4, 1900, the youngest child of Star and Martha Mangold Dunn—both natives of near Zanesville, OH. She has one brother, David Eugene Tribby, born in 1921. Her maternal grandparents were Leander M. "Cap" and Margaret "Maggie" Patton Wilson Tribby. Cap was a native of Northern

Kentucky and moved to Indiana with his parents, William T. and Mahala Myers Tribby, in 1860 when he was 12 years old. Maggie Patton Wilson, daughter of John and Nancy Coons Patton, was born in 1862 south of New Richmond and was the widow of Theodore Alonzo Wilson until she married Cap Tribby in 1896.

David and Joan both graduated from New Richmond High School and were married June 22, 1946 at the New Richmond Methodist Church. They are the parents of four children: Patrick R., born 1947; Starr, born in 1950; Gaylora, born in 1954; and Christopher M., born in 1957. They have four grandchildren: Amanda Sue and Andrew Edward Oppy; and Kennet J. and Andrea Elizabeth DeJesus.

PATRICK R. AND SUSAN KAY SUTHERLIN OPPY HISTORY

Patrick R. "Pat" and Susan Kay "Sue" Sutherlin Oppy were both born at Culver Hospital, Crawfordsville, IN. Pat, oldest child of David M. and M. Joan Tribby Oppy, was born June 10, 1947. He has two sisters, Starr and Gaylora, and a brother, Christopher M. Sue was born Aug. 28, 1951 to Laverne Edward "Vern" and Juanita Irene Taylor Sutherlin and has one brother, Edward Laverne "Ed" born in 1953. Pat and Sue were married Dec. 31, 1971 at the New Market Christian Church. They have two children who were born at Home Hospital, Lafayette IN: Amanda Sue, born Sept. 15, 1974, and Andrew Edward, born Aug. 14, 1981. Pat graduated from Coal Creek Central High School in 1965 and served in the U.S. Army from August 1966 until August 1968. He is now a fifth generation farmer in Coal Creek Township. She is a 1969 graduate of New Market High School and in 1972 received an Associate Degree of Science in Radiologic Technology from Indiana University. She is now employed at the Urgent Care Center of the Arnett Clinic in Lafayette.

Vern, oldest son born to Bertram Beverly "Bert" and Evadna Clouse Sutherlin, was born Apr. 3, 1924. Bert, born in 1901, was one of ten children born to William Henry and Carrie Morris Sutherlin. Evadna was born in 1903 and was the youngest child of Samuel Mack and Polly Ann Brewer Clouse. Both Bert and Evadna were born near Mitchell, IN, as were both Vern and his brother, Robert. The Sutherlins moved from Brookston, IN to a farm south of Crawfordsville in 1948. Bert and Evadna are now residing on East Market Street in Crawfordsville and celebrated their 65th wedding anniversary in 1988.

Juanita Taylor, youngest daughter of four surviving children born to Roy B. and Edna Sowers Taylor, was born Jan. 28, 1928, in Parke County. Roy B. Taylor was born in Parke County in 1895 to Daniel and Nancy Paddock Taylor. Edna Sowers was born at Wheeler, IL in 1901 and was the daughter of Joseph and Ella Foltz Sowers. After her husband's death in 1943 she and her daughters Betty, Dorothy, Genevieve and Juanita moved to Browns Valley and for many years operated a grocery store there. Edna died December 1979 and is buried with other family members in the Bethany Cemetery near Marshall.

Vern and Juanita were married at Browns Valley Dec. 31, 1949. For 28 years Juanita operated Juanita's Beauty Shoppe at her home in New Market. Vern served in the U.S. Army from 1948 until 1950, then was called back to serve in Korea during the war there in 1950 and 1951. Vern is retired from Firestone. *Submitted by Joan Oppy*

CLAY OVERPECK

Many years ago, the seed of the Overpeck Family Tree flourished in the rigorous climate of far away Germany where men were hardy, industrious and brave. These German ancestors, no doubt, heard glowing reports of a new country far to the West where land and opportunities were plentiful and every man free and equal. This report lured the earliest of the Overpecks to migrate in 1745. Two brothers, George and Andrew, came to Buck Co., PA in the early colonial period. That many of our relatives remained on their native soil is evidence by grave markers in German cemeteries which bear the family name, and by frequency with which the name is encountered in prominent writers of classical history and other forms of literature.

Either George Overpeck or his sons, or the descendants of Andrew served with General Washington during those trying days of the Revolutionary War. Tradition tells us that an Overpeck was with Washington when he crossed the ice-filled Delaware River and advanced upon Trenton. In fact, our family history contains no instances of cowardice and all of the members of the family have served well their country when called upon.

The call of the West caused migration by flatboat to the Ohio River to Cincinnati. Still the family name is a common one in the states to the East. Schools and business houses bear the name. It is thought at some early date the mute letters "b" and "p" were confused and the original spelling of Overbeck was discarded for the present form Overpeck.

The descendants of the two brothers who came to Pennsylvania in 1745: George had a son and his children were: Mary or Magdalene, John, Jacob and Isaac. Known descendants of Isaac, whose wife was Margaret Arehart are: John, Sarah, Nancy, Mary, Daniel, George and Valentine.

Andrew Overpeck had a son Andrew. His son Jacob and his wife, Mary, came to Parke County in 1835 and settled south of Mansfield. Jacob's wife Mary was from the line of George Overpeck.

One of Jacob (1774-1839) and wife Mary's ten children was Andrew (1824-1887) whose second wife had one son Elias. Elias married (1875-1948) Mary "Mollie" Miller who was born in Indian Territory (now Oklahoma) when her father was there to stake a claim. It was said that Mrs. Miller taught the Indians our way of cooking. Mr. Miller was active in helping organize Bible Schools in the territory.

Elias and Mollie Overpeck had six children: Norine, Earl, Fred, Marie, Ruth and Clay. Clay (1909-) moved to the Alamo community in 1953 where he farmed, then went into the landscape business where he worked on the atheletic field at the Fellowship of Christian Athletes and the Raccoon Flood Control dams. He was President of the Waveland Lions Club for several years. Mrs. Clay Overpeck (Floy) was active in the Home Demonstration Clubs serving as County President. She was also the last manager of the Shades Inn before it was regrettably torn down. Sons David and John both served in the U.S. Army and daughter, Rosemary was a missionary nurse in Hong Kong for nearly 20 years. *Submitted by the Clay Overpeck Family*

Compiled from family records researched by Marie Overpeck Martin in the 1960's.

CLARENCE REED AND MARY VIOLET McGAUGHEY OVERSTREET

Thomas Overstreet and wife Judith left Bedford, VA, in 1800 and settled at Mitchellsburg, KY. There they farmed 160 acres. They had ten children one of which was James, Clarence Overstreet's ancestor.

James and his wife, Susannah Campbell settled in Casey Co., KY. Their son Aaron Sr. married Catherine Elder. The family moved to Hendricks Co., IN in 1850. Aaron was a blacksmith and farmer. He served in the Civil War. Aaron had six children. One of the children was Aaron S. who is the grandfather of Clarence R. Overstreet. Aaron married Martha Caroline Walter Mar. 4, 1888 in Hendricks County. Their first child was Walter Earl who is Clarence R. Overstreet's father.

Walter Earl worked as a telegrapher for the C.H. & D. railroad. He married Clara Belle Reed, who was a school teacher at Parkersburg, IN. On Mar. 18, 1912, their first son Clarence Reed Overstreet was born.

Clarence Reed attended DePauw University on a Rector Scholarship. In 1932 he transferred to Purdue University, graduating in 1936 with a B.S. in Agriculture and in 1938 received his M.S.

On Aug. 23, 1936 Clarence Reed married Mary Violet McGaughey. She is the daughter of Lafe Vernon McGaughey and Ivyl Pearl Sutherlin McGaughey. Clarence and Mary V. are the parents of two children. A son Walter Keith was born on Oct. 5, 1938 in Ripley Co., IN. A daughter, Mary Dellena was born on Mar. 18, 1943 in Montgomery County.

In 1939 Clarence Reed and Mary Violet moved to Waveland, IN. Clarence was a vocational agriculture teacher at the school. They have resided in Montgomery County ever since. Clarence also taught at Crawfordsville High School. In 1944 he served in the U.S. Navy as a lieutenant and was discharged in April 1946. He was the farm representative for Elston Bank from 1946-48. In 1948 he taught veterans in a farm training program sponsored by the Veterans Administration. Clarence has farmed in Montgomery County since 1940 and still continues in that occupation.

On Mar. 19, 1982, Mary Violet died of cancer. She was laid to rest in Hebron Cemetery, Russellville, IN.

Clarence married Ruth Cheek Campbell in November 1982, in Clay County. She has spent her life in the Brazil area. Clarence and Ruth spend their winters at Dundee, FL. *Submitted by Melba Overstreet*

THE PADDACKS OF DARLINGTON

The Paddacks of Montgomery Co., IN, trace their people back to the Darlington/Linden area. Despite a family tradition about an unusual walking cane that had been passed down from generation to generation which says that the reason it is referred to as the "Nan-Tucket cane" is because although it was to have gone to the first male of each generation, their female ancestor name "Nan", just "tuck it"; research has shown that it was made out of a whale's jawbone and that the family were whalers from Nantucket Island, MA.

Clyda Mary Paddack, born 1869 near Darlington, IN, is the daughter of Josiah Foster Paddack and Caroline Husted. Caroline Husted, born 1843 in Franklin Co., IN, is the daughter of John Husted Jr. and Abigail DuBois. Abigail DuBois, born 1795 in Salem Co., NJ, is the daughter of Josiah DuBois and

Ann Newkirk. John Husted Jr., born 1795 in Cumberland Co., NJ, is the son of John Husted Sr. and Nancy Conner.

Clyda Mary Paddack Todd; Caroline Husted Paddack

Josiah Paddack, born 1845 in Union Co., IN died 1877 of spotted fever with a $3000 life insurance policy and five children under age eight, is the son of Benjamin F. Paddack and Mary Gardner Talbert. This couple were devout Quakers arriving in Montgomery Co., IN, in 1855 from Union Co., IN. Mary Talbert, born 1817, is the daughter of William Talbert and Miriam Gardner. William Talbert, born 1786 in North Carolina, is the son of Richard Bull. Note that all the Quaker Bull families in Guilford Co., NC, had their surname changed to Talbert in 1806. Miriam Gardner, born 1789 in Guilford Co., NC, is the daughter of Eliab Gardner and Sarah Stanton. Eliab Gardner, born 1758 on Nantucket Island, MA, is the son of Richard Gardner and Sarah Macy. Sarah Stanton, born 1762 in Guilford Co., NC is the daughter of William and Phebe Stanton. Benjamin Paddack, born 1816 in Hamilton Co., OH is the son of Samuel Paddack and Deborah Coleman. Deborah Coleman, born 1783 on Nantucket Island, MA, is the daughter of Seth Coleman and Deborah Swain. Samuel Paddack, born 1786 on Nantucket Island, MA, is the son of Benjamin Paddack Jr. and Jemima Coleman. Jemima Coleman, born 1759 on Nantucket Island, MA, is the daughter of William Coleman and Eunice Swain. Benjamin Paddack Jr., born 1762 on Nantucket Island, MA, is the son of Benjamin Paddack Sr. and Elizabeth Stanton. Elizabeth Stanton, born 1737 on Nantucket Island, MA, is the daughter of Samuel Stanton and Sarah Coffin. Benjamin Paddack Sr., born 1734 on Nantucket Island, MA, is the son of Eliphalet Paddack and Naomi Bunker. Naomi Bunker, born 1709 on Nantucket Island, MA, is the daughter of Jabez Bunker and Hannah Gardner. Eliphalet Paddack, born 1705 on Nantucket Island, MA, is the son of Joseph Paddack and Sarah Gardner. Sarah Gardner, born 1672 on Nantucket Island, MA, is the daughter of Joseph Gardner and Bethia Macy. Joseph Paddack, born 1674 in Barnstable Co., MA, called "the first from Cape Cod", is the son of Zachariah Paddack and Deborah Sears. Deborah Sears, born 1639 in Barnstable Co., MA, is the daughter of Richard and Dorothy Sears. Zachariah Paddack, born 1636 at Plymouth, MA, is the son of Robert Paddack.

SAMUEL WESLEY PARKS

Samuel was born May 30, 1875 the son of William and Rebecca Edwards Parks.

The father of our subject William Chambers Parks was first married to Rebecca Deliah Edwards, who was born Apr. 14, 1837 the daughter of William C. Edwards. Rebecca bore ten children before her death in 1906. They were: Nancy wife of George Stevens, Mary, Sade wife of Albert Williams, Mattie wife of Sam Dunwoody, Etta wife of Charles Hughes, Michael, John M. who married Mary Stevens, William, Samuel our subject, Herrald born and died 1904. After Rebecca's death William then married Elizabeth Vonscoyoc and one child was born, Esther born and died 1906. There may have been two more born to this union.

Samuel was married on Apr. 13, 1896 to Mary Stump, who was the daughter of Maryland and Martha Ann Osborn Stump, born July 28, 1875. To this union six children were born; Chester Maryland born 1898 and after suffering a sunstroke as a child of 18 years of age working in the field with his father, died in Logansport Mental Hospital never fully recovering his illness in 1978, Anna Maureen born 1900 died at the age of ten months, Harold Glenn born 1904 died 1922, Opal May born 1908 married Earl Gustin died 1933, Goldie Marie born 1911 died at the age of three and one-half years, Martha Waneta born 1915 married John Russell Stevens.

Of these children Martha is still living in Crawfordsville. This family felt the wrath of heartache and tragedy as did a lot of families of this time. Opal and Anna both died of pneumonia. Goldie met her young death at the hands of diphtheria. Chester lived a long life in the care of others due to the elements of nature. Harold met with a fall from a pair of stilts and as a result had massive internal injuries with complications of tuberculosis and died of the latter.

Mary, a young mother with trampled heart held after watching and nursing her childrens' deaths died one year after her son, Harold. She had contracted tuberculosis.

Samuel doing his best reared the remaining children as best he could and was well-loved and respected for his hardships and heartaches of life.

May God rest all of them for now there is no more pain or heartache. *Submitted by Becky Ingram*

ISAAC AND JANE (HALE) PATTON

The Patton family came to America from Ireland. Isaac Patton and Jane Hale were married in 1820 in Hamilton Co., OH and later moved to Montgomery Co., IN. Isaac died in 1857. His son John (born June 27, 1827) and wife Nancy (Coons) Patton were hardworking, saving people. In the 1850's they bought a farm three miles south of New Richmond. The house rested on a knoll back from the road near the stream, Coal Creek.

In the 1870's a barn was constructed of hand hewn beams and still stands near the road. Near the barn a new, larger home was built in 1870. John died Nov. 29, 1877 at the age of 50. Six months later, his 48 year old wife was killed by a horse. There were eight surviving children from the age of six to 25. The struggle to keep the home together and somehow feed and clothe the family was a story in itself.

John and Nancy Patton's son Charles married Margaret McClamrock (Dec. 5, 1880) and bought land adjoining the home place. Their children were Tessie, Arlie, Ernest and Chelsey. On Aug. 29, 1912 Chelsey (born Feb. 18, 1891) married Edna Deeter (born Aug. 29, 1892). They settled on a farm near Liberty Chapel Church. Their children are Clyde (born Feb. 22, 1920) and Imogene (born Aug. 15, 1929). On Jan. 12, 1940 Clyde married Wilma Quigg (born Feb. 11, 1920) after their graduation from New Richmond High School. They settled on a farm adjoining his parents' farm. Their children are Detra Kay (born Sept. 12, 1944), Marc (born Nov. 24, 1947) and Jerilyn (born Aug. 6, 1952). Detra graduated from Purdue University and spent a year as an exchange teacher in England and is now a teacher in the Goshen school system. She married Edgar Kenny July 15, 1973. They are the parents of Megan Elizabeth (born Aug. 8, 1978). Marc married Laverne Breeding of Nashville, TN on Apr. 20, 1968. They live on a farm near his parents' home. Their son Eric was born Jan. 7, 1973. After graduating from Crawfordsville High School, Jerilyn worked for Indiana Bell before her marriage to Tim Isley on Sept. 21, 1985. They are the parents of Chelsea Jene Isley who was born Jan. 10, 1988.

Imogene graduated from Waynetown High School and Purdue University. She and Donald Creek of Rush County (born Sept. 24, 1929) were married Aug. 26, 1951 after their graduation from Purdue. Their children are Donna Jean (born June 6, 1955) who graduated from Purdue, Sue Ann (born Jan. 1, 1958) who graduated from Indiana University and Daniel (born Apr. 17, 1961) who attended Indiana University. They make their home near Peru where Don is retired from Production Credit Corp.

Imogene Patton Creek, a great granddaughter of John Patton is the present owner of the farm which has been in the Patton family since the 1850's.

ROBERT G. AND LOIS E. (HENDRICKS) PATTON

Robert G. Patton, son of Fern A. and Mary E. (Kemble) Patton was born at New Richmond on Jan. 13, 1919. He graduated from high school there in 1938. After working 35 years at R.R. Donnelley & Co., he retired in 1982. Robert G. had a half-brother, Harlan Locke, and a brother and sister who died in infancy. Harlan Locke married Opal Lee and both are now deceased. Robert has one son, Robert "Bob" Dean Patton who is married to Theresa Walters and lives in Albuquerque, NM. Bob's children are: Mike, Carolyn Ford, Angela, Bobby, Kym and Stacy. Mike and his wife Marcia have one son, Stuart and live in Texas. Carolyn has a son, Paul, Jr., and a daughter, Christina. They live in Arlington, TX.

Robert G. and Lois E (Hendricks) Patton

Robert married Lois E. Hendricks on Mar. 24, 1944. Lois is the daughter of Chester and Dora Smith Hendricks and was born on Oct. 29, 1917 south of Waynetown. Chester was born and lived all his life in the same house, built by his father, James Wesley Hendricks. Lois graduated from Alamo High School in 1935. She had three brothers: Paul, who is married to Doris Servies; Dale who is married to Marjorie Armantrout and Clyde. Clyde's wife, Faye Allen, died and requested her children, Judy and Debbie be raised by Robert and Lois. Judy is married to Harold Smith and has one daughter, Stephanie. Harold works at Cummins. The Smith family lives in Columbus, IN. Debbie married William "Bill" Ritter and has Ryan and Heather. Debbie and Bill live at Lake Holiday. Debbie works at Hi-Tek and Bill at Donnelleys.

After working in banking institutions for 40 years, Lois retired in 1983. Robert and Lois are active in several organizations during their retirement years, namely: Open Door Sunday School Class; First Baptist Church; Athens Chapter No. 97 Order of Eastern Star and Senior Citizen. He is also active in Montgomery County #50 F&AM; Scottish Rite; Shrine; Kiwanis and Low 12 Club. Both Robert and Lois have lived in Montgomery County all their lives.

THE SAM PATTON FAMILY

The Patton Family came to America from England in 1636 and settled in Cambridge, MS. William Patton moved to Ohio and married Elizabeth Grey. They settled on the Miami River between Cincinnati and Hamilton. To this union, a son, Isaac, was born on Feb. 15, 1807. He married Jane Hole in 1820. Her father, Anthony Badgely, was a Revolutionary War soldier. They moved to a farm near Mace in Montgomery County, in the year 1844.

Thomas F. Patton was the youngest of eight children born to Isaac and Jane. His date of birth was Mar. 30, 1844. He was reared in the home of Abigail Davis, after the death of his mother, when he was nine days old.

He received a good education in the Common Schools of the county. At 21 years of age, he married Miss Lucy, a daughter of Josiah and Jane Carson Davis, both of Kentucky. Tom engaged in buying and shipping livestock and farming. To this union were born ten children, Charles, Lora, Eva, James, Dee, Harry, Clyde, Gertrude, Joe, and George, who grew up on a farm in Brown Township, north of Browns Valley.

Joe Patton married Fern Hunt, daughter of Sam and Rosa Doyel Hunt, on Dec. 28, 1912. After teaching in elementary school for five years, Fern joined her husband on the family farm. They became the parents of four children, Sam, Dorothy, Betty, and Don.

Sam Patton was born Dec. 8, 1915. He graduated from Waveland High School in 1933 and from Wabash College in 1937. He began his teaching career in the field of mathematics and science in 1937 at Waveland High School. He married Lael Coons, daughter of Harry and Dorpha Caldwell Coons on Apr. 30, 1939. To this union was born Ronald, Jan. 1, 1947, and Bronna, on Feb. 6, 1955. Donnis, daughter of Don and Marlene Miller Patton, born on Dec. 16, 1960, grew up in the Sam Patton family from the age of six weeks, after the death of her mother. With the exception of two years that Sam served as a Communication Officer in the U.S. Navy in World War II, the family lived on the family farm on SR 234, two miles east of the Shades State Park.

Ron graduated from Waveland High School in 1965 and Wabash College in 1969. He served in the U.S. Army Signal Corps for three years, during the Vietnam War. Ron and Janet Neal Patton are the parents of two daughters, Julie and Sarah. He is Vice President of Regency Electronics in Indianapolis.

Bronna graduated from Southmont High School in 1973 and Ball State University in 1977, with a BS degree in Elementary Education. She received a MA degree from Indiana State University in 1979. She has taught first grade at Hose Elementary School for 12 years.

Donnis graduated from Southmont High School in 1978 and Ball State in 1982, with a BS degree in Biological Science. She did a year of graduate work at Ball State. She graduated from I.U. Medical School in 1987. She will complete her residency at the University of Virginia in 1990, in Internal Medicine.

SAMUEL PAXTON

Samuel and Nancy T. McCorkle Paxton came to Montgomery County in 1832 from Virginia, settling in Union Township near Youngs Chapel. He was born Apr. 19, 1803 in Rockbridge Co., VA the son of Thomas and Martha Steele Paxton. He was the third of nine children. This family lived for many years on 500 acres of land in Virginia which was purchased from Benjamin Borden in 1742, by Samuel's great grandfather, Thomas. His siblings were John Steele, Thomas, William, Martha, Jane, Phoebe, Alexander, and David. His mother came to Indiana about 1840 after the death of his father. She lived with her children who had migrated earlier to Montgomery County, dying Oct. 6, 1846 at the home in the Youngs Chapel neighborhood.

Samuel and Nancy (McCorkle) Paxton

Our subject married Nancy T. McCorkle, Dec. 29, 1825 in Augusta Co., VA. She was born Aug. 16, 1805, the daughter of Alexander and Mary Steele McCorkle. Nancy died June 3, 1879. They were the parents of nine children. These children were Martha, Margaret, James, Mary, David P., Thomas, Elizabeth, Amanda, and Nancy McCorkle. Many descendants remain in Montgomery County.

Samuel enlisted Mar. 4, 1865 in the Civil War and was discharged July 26, 1865. He was a farmer and blacksmith, a hard working, respected citizen of his community. He died Jan. 13, 1879 at his home and is buried at Youngs Chapel Cemetery with his wife Nancy and his mother Martha Steele Paxton. Other members of his immediate family are also buried at Youngs Chapel.

CHARLES AND JEMIMA ANGELINE PAYTON

Charles Enoch Payton was born in Montgomery County May 10, 1864, the son of George Washington Payton (1830-1901) and Mary Ann Aldridge. He had one brother, William T. (1853-1922), and one sister, Margaret Banta (1858-1949). On Sept. 29, 1889, he married Jemima Angeline Etter. She was born July 3, 1869 the daughter of Jefferson Etter (1837-1916) and Elizabeth Ann Denman Etter (1845-1884). She had two brothers and three sisters. William Edward (1863-1941), Mary Ellen Myers (1867-1952), Addie Newkirk (1871-1958), Lawrence Bertram (1874-1946), and Estella Lorraine Elliott (1880-1931).

Charles and Jemima (Tina) Payton

Charlie and "Lina" as she was familiarly and fondly called lived their early married life near Hillsboro, IN. In the late 1890's they purchased part of the Etter Homestead south of Alamo, IN and erected a new house and barn. The farm has been in the family since 1856, a part of which still belongs to a great-grandson John D. Luzader.

To this union was born five children: Mary Ann Shelby, born Sept. 28, 1890, died Oct. 5, 1973; Myrtle Blanch Luzader, born June 21, 1894, died Sept. 28, 1980; Clifford Lucein, born May 15, 1897, died Nov. 7, 1897; Clarence Leslie, born Oct. 25, 1898, died Jan. 28, 1973; Leona Agnes Bushong, born Jan. 23, 1903, died Mar. 23, 1930.

Charlie and "Lina" lived on the farm until 1941 when they sold the farm to Harry and Myrtle Luzader and moved to Alamo, IN. Mr. and Mrs. Payton exemplified The Masters teaching, devoted to their family, home, church and friends. They opened their home to many relatives. Charlie's father and brother William both died at their home.

Lina died suddenly Oct. 7, 1947 after attending a birthday supper at the home of her daughter Myrtle. Charlie passed away May 30, 1948 after an extended illness. They are buried in the Alamo Cemetery.

There are many direct living descendants of Charlie and Lina Payton: two grandsons, 14 great-grandchildren, 26 great-great grandchildren, and nine great-great-great grandchildren.

WILLIAM HARVEY PAYTON

William Harvey Payton was born July 24, 1857 and died Apr. 24, 1940. He married Alice Massa Denman (daughter of Moses H. and Jemima Lee Denman) who was born Apr. 26, 1857 and who died Jan. 26, 1946. They had six children:

(1) Zora Dean, born Apr. 26, 1884, died Oct. 4, 1958. She married Claude Harmless, now deceased. They had one daughter, Mildred Marie, born Dec. 16, 1911. She married Paul Hayworth, now deceased. Mildred lives in Crawfordsville.

(2) Grace Lee, born May 15, 1886, died Dec. 31, 1976. She married Fred Jessup, now deceased, and they had one son, Brooks Melvin, born Apr. 5, 1911, died in February 1932. Grace spent the last several years of her life in California.

(3) Fred Earl, born Nov. 15, 1887, died Sept. 30, 1907.

(4) Ted Gilderoy, born May 6, 1889, died Apr. 19, 1978 in Indianapolis.

(5) Jess Claude, born Aug. 17, 1891, died in September, 1981. He married Elsie Nelson who died in 1947. They moved to Los Angeles, CA, about 1925, and had three children: (a) Beverly Yvonne, born Oct. 27, 1918, who married Richard Higgins and they live in Whittier, CA. The had two girls: Carol, born May 21, 1947, who married Robert Laffranchi. They live in Loleta, CA with

their two girls, Michele and Nicole. Nancy, born July 4, 1950, who married Jerry Heyne. They live in Eureka, CA with their three sons, Jerid Lloyd, Keith Richard and David. (b) Jack, born Oct. 27, 1924, who married Claudean Quinley. They live in Covina, CA. (c) Barbara Jean, born Aug. 3, 1927, died Mar. 7, 1959. She married Chuck Parker and the had one daughter, Pamela, who was seven days old when her mother died.

Will, Grace, Fred, Zora, Alice, Jess, Ted and Gertrude Payton

(6) Anna Gertrude, born Sept. 27, 1893, died July 25, 1959. She married George Rushton LaFollette, born Dec. 22, 1886, died Jan. 25, 1945. They had two children (she moved to California in 1946 and later married Harley Epley, now deceased): (a) William Francis, born Oct. 9, 1913, died Dec. 4, 1978, who married Maxine Vandenberg. They had two children: Robert F., born Sept. 12, 1959, died Feb. 21, 1985, Lois, born May 18, 1957. Maxine and Lois live in San Diego. (b) Alice Virginia, born Apr. 24, 1919, now living in Orange, CA. She married Donald Emerson Carsrud, now deceased, and they had two children: Michele JoAnn, born Mar. 25, 1950, living in Beltsville, MD, and Robert Steven, born Jan. 28, 1953, who married Jeannette Miller. They live in La Mirada, CA. *Submitted by Alice LaFollette Carsrud, who obtained this information from a number of sources, hopes the data is correct, and trusts the readers will be understanding if there are any inaccuracies.*

CECIL AND OMEGA HELMS PEARSON

The farm home of Cecil and Omega Helms Pearson was the scene of the winter wedding of William Leon Sanders and Frances Keeling.

Reverend Ralph Smith performed the ceremony. Guests were: William Keeling, Emma Sanders, Helen Mitchell, Eula Myers, Robert and Hazel Hayes and Theodosia Driver. Also Cecil, Omega and Penny Ann Pearson.

Leon's parents Edward T. Sanders, (July 15, 1882 - May 3, 1950), and Emma Taggart Sanders (Mar. 11, 1884 - Aug. 26, 1967) moved to the Ladoga area from Orange Co., IN about 1915.

Little is known about Edward's parents except his father's name was Jacob. When Edward was quite small his parents died, so he grew up in a relative's home.

Emma's parents were William Taggart and Sarah Baker. She had one sister, Mayme, and two brothers - Elmer and Alvin.

Leon has three sisters - Eula, Lois, and Hazel and one brother Harold.

Lois married Virgil Pearson of New Ross. They were the parents of Carolyn and Phyllis.

Hazel married Robert Hayes of Veedersburg. Their children are Janet and David.

Leon's brother, Harold, gave his life for his country on Mar. 15, 1945 in Europe and is buried in Henri Chapelle Cemetery in Belgium.

Frances' parents were William M. Keeling (Nov. 28, 1886 - Nov. 21, 1959) and Mary E. Payton (June 13, 1888 - Jan. 26, 1941) both of Fountain Co., IN. Grandparents were Milton and Sidney Shipman Keeling also Benjamin and Rebecca McDade Payton. A great, great grandfather Keeling owned large tracts of land which he donated to help establish the town of Veedersburg.

Frances has one brother, Glen, who married Bertha Towel. They had two daughters Sharon and Mary Kay, and one son, Ronald Keeling.

Leon farmed until he was called into the service in June 1941. He served in the Coast Guard Artillery Corps which was stationed at Pearl Harbor when it was bombed by the Japanese on Dec. 7, 1941. He was honorably discharged as Tech. Sergt. in September 1945, after the signing of the Japanese Peace Treaty.

After he returned home he was employed at Donnelley's and later at ALCOA in Lafayette.

Francis is a graduate of Indiana Central College also did post graduate work at Indiana State College. She taught school in Lapel, IN and New Market, IN.

Identical twin daughters Becky Ann and Patsy Jean were born to Leon and Frances on Feb. 24, 1948. They graduated from Ladoga High School and attended Vincennes University.

Becky and Curtis Weir were married in February 1968. Their daughter is Holly Renee.

Patsy became the bride of Michael Fry in June 1967. Their children are Christopher and Jeremy.

BENJAMIN AND LOUISA (WATKINS) PEEBLES FAMILY

Benjamin Peebles, born 1814, came with his parents, Micajah and Mary from Virginia, 1828. He grew up in the Gravelly Run community; married Louisa, daughter of Robert and Agnes Watkins; fathered eight children. (Elsewhere in this book are histories of the two families who stayed in the community.)

Mary Annis Peebles, daughter of Benjamin and Louisa

1. Robert W., history elsewhere.
2. Thaddeus (1840-1865), served in the Civil War. Died in New Bern, NC from a gunshot wound received at Wies's Fork five days earlier.
3. Julietta 1843, married Franklin Moore, widower with infant baby, Emma. They raised five children:

Emma, teacher in Mission School in eastern Tennessee; married Richard Newby who became Superintendent of Western Yearly Meeting of Friends; he served many years.

Wallace (Wallie) merchant, married Myrtie, moved to Noblesville. (Roy and his family would take Aunt Annis in their black "model T" Ford touring-car to visit Wallie's. Sometimes she used the Inter-Urban between Noblesville and Crawfordsville. That necessitated changing cars in Indianapolis.)

Winifred was said to have two boys. No record.

Caroline (Carrie) m. Robert Misner. One son, Robert. (After her husband's death, Carrie and Robert came back to visit Montgomery County relatives.)

Robert Moore died when only 14. He was the special friend of Roy Peebles, father of the writer.

4. Micajah (1845-1923) married Ellenor Parker (1854-1927) had five children, moved to Kansas.

Clarence, born 1879, "married the widow of James Surface, raised her three sons: Ansel, Henry and Ira".

Flora (1883-1943) married Charles Cameron, Aptos, CA had: George, Howard, Vera, Clarence and Vergil.

John, born 1885, wrote this story of his father and mother's family; he told that he had written Esta Fay for all the dates he'd used, as she had the Micajah Peebles Family Bible. He told how he had "crossed-over" in 1906; had "teamed" (that's with horses!) in Edmonton in 1912; had "Homesteaded a quarter" in the "Peace River Country on Dawson Creek". B.C., Canada. (I quote him directly.)

Lelia Mae (1887-1955) married Charles Housley, Oxnard, CA had Frank, Berniece, Crafford and Opal.

Hal Hugh married May. Adopted her three boys; Luther, W.C. and Orville (Chelan, WA). Their children were: Lester (Buster), Francis (Barney), Elizabeth and Beverly.

Esta Fay (1895) married Roy Lackey, had: Vernon, Robert, Jud and Yvonne.

5. Lucinda, b. 1847 married Robert Butler at Gravelly Run Monthly Meeting, moved to Kansas in 1882. They had one child, Myrta, who married Herb Barrington, had Percival, Lester, Marden, Willard and Helen. In 1944 Myrta was interviewed in her own home; then the next week, she sent written verification of all the information she had given: on her family, also on "Uncle Cage and Aunt Ellie's family. (Her notes on Cage's family and John's notes agree.)

6. Walter D. (1850-1920) History given elsewhere.

7. Mary Annis (1855-1944) Teacher: Friends Mission in Alaska. Helped the Friends Missions in Oklahoma; cared for her brother, Walter, after Becky died. Divided her time between Indiana and Kansas relatives. Started Helen Barrington and Helen Peebles writing to each other 1922, pen pals for 30 years. Died while living with Myrta in Wichita, KS.

8. Caroline, (1857-1877) died of tuberculosis, called then "galloping consumption", while living with Walter and Rebeccah. *Submitted by Helen Peebles White*

LEROY AND HAZEL PEEBLES FAMILY

In 1952 Hazel Peebles took her 12 grandchildren to Demaree's Crawfordsville studio for a family photograph. Hazel, (1888-1971) daughter of Wal and Minnie Elmore LaFollette, widow of Leroy Peebles (1886-1933) youngest son of Walter D. and Rebeccah Stephenson Peebles, Top Salesman for the International Agricultural Corporation, Farm Owner and Operator on Overcoat Road-Gravelly Run neighborhood, Musician, International Corn

Show Winner, Breeder of Registered Poland China Hogs and German Shepard Dogs. Roy and Hazel, their four children and ten of 12 grandchildren graduated from Darlington High School.

Wallace, (1910-1974) Grain and Livestock Farmer, m. (1933) Naomi, daughter of Jack and Effie Cooper Reichard.

Lucille, born 1912, Teacher, m. (1936) Keith Cox (1905-1975), son of Denton and Bertha Clark Cox.

Helen, b. 1913, m. Sacramento, CA, 1941, Austin Ford White, P.E. b. Hawaii, to Harry and Ruth Ford White. Retired: Ocean Shores, WA.

Lester, b. 1921, Donnelley's: Plant Engineering and Maintenance Manager, Farm, Breeder of Polled Hereford Cattle. m. (1942) Martha, (1921-1989) daughter of Zoy and Edith Peterson Branstetter.

See text for names

Starting on the left, front row:

Barbara White, R.N., b. 1949, Cook Co., IL, m. (1981) Thomas Oberdieck, Contractor, dau., Meara, b. 1987, Wheaton, IL.

John Peebles, b. 1946, (Wally's) Donnelleys, Pressroom Supervisor m. (1967) Sharon Todd, (1945-1972) mother of two sons: Jason, (1969-1986) Justin, b. 1972. M. (1987) Betty Daugherty, R.N., Darlington.

Janet Sue Cox, b. 1946, Teacher, m. (1971) William Hall, (1934-1979), Children: Jennifer, b. 1972, Heather, b. 1973, William, b. 1977. Cicero, IN.

Mary Jo Cox, b. 1949, Secretary, m. (1970) Steve Harrison, Business Analyst. Children: Mark, b. 1976, Meggan, b. 1978, Sarah, b. 1981. The Woodlands, TX.

Larry Peebles, b. 1946, (Lester's) Rancher, Breeder of Registered Polled Herefords, m. Colorado (1974) Diana Raff. Children: Gary, b. 1974, Triplets: b. 1978: Dinah, Katie, and Roy (d. infant) Rex, 1980. Hotchkiss, CO.

Second row from the left:

Judith Ann White, b. 1947, Cook Co., IL, Teacher, T.H.M.D., M.I.U., Valkenberg, Holland.

David Peebles, b. 1945 (Wally's) Salesman, U.S. Ink Company m. (1968) Margaret Pugh. children: Lance, b. 1970, Erin, b. 1973 Bedford,TX.

Sharon Ann Cox, b. 1943, m. (1961-1982) Dick Shelton, (State Police). Children: 1. Duane, b. 1962, Mechanic, m. (1988) Diane McMurtry. 2. Douglas, b. 1963, (State Police). 3. Debbie, b. 1964, Radio Newscaster, m. (1987) William Calder, son, Chase, b. 1984. Lafayette.

George Cox, b. 1945, Donnelley's Mylar Lineup, m. (1964) Karen Haffner, children: 1. Clark, b. 1964, m. (1986) C.P.A. Christa Barnett, dau. Kayla, b. 1986. 2. Craig, b. 1966, 3. Philip, b. 1973. Darlington.

Back row from left:

Kay Cox, b. 1938, Librarian, m. (1956) Glen Norton, Supervisor, Shumate Printing. Children: 1. Kelly b. 1957, M.S.N., R.N. m. (1982) Geoffrey Buck, Psy D. Boys: Isaac, b. 1983 and Benjamin, b. 1988. 2. Bradley, b. 1959, Machinist. Colfax.

Peggy Peebles, b. 1941, Teacher, m. California, (1971) Royce Foster, Ivy Tech Instructor. His children: Shannon, b. 1965, m. (1987) David Sloan. Scott, b. 1966, Darlington.

Sandra Peebles, b. 1939, Nurse, m. California (1961) Rex Seipert, Electrician, Brigham Young University. Children: 1. Curtis, b. 1961, m. (1983) Stephanie, son, Chris, b. 1985. 2. Blaine, b. 1963, 3. Scott, b. 1967, 4. Mark, b. 1968, 5. Kevin, b. 1971. Orem, UT. *Submitted by Lester Peebles, Compiled by Helen White*

ROBERT W. AND SARAH (ANDERSON) PEEBLES

Robert W. Peebles (1838-1922), eldest son; Benjamin and Louisa (Watkins) Peebles, Quaker, farmer, community leader, m. (1865) Sarah Anderson (1842-1928), daughter: Wright and Mary (Butler) Anderson. When members of the Meeting had come to elder Robert on his choice of a bride from outside of the Meeting, the determined young Man's reply was, "If I must choose between the Meeting and Sally, I choose Sally." Robert and Sarah, their three children and three of their grandchildren lived to celebrate Golden Weddings. Children: I. II. III.

I. Atwell d. Peebles (1865-1949) m. (1889) Hannah Weesner (1867-1951). Children: A,B,C,D.

A. Irene (1890-1984), m. (1907) Carl Needham (1890-1960), son: Archibald and Rachel (Cox) Needham. Children: 1. Kenneth (1908-1915), 2. Charlotte (1912), m. John Dale Weaver M.D. (1911). Children: a. John Dale Jr. (1941), b. Mary Jane. (1944), c. Charotte Ann M.D. (1949). Texas. 3. Marjorie (1917) "rock hound". Took care of her mother, Irene, Omaha, NE.

Robert W. and Sarah (Anderson) Peebles

B. Merritt (1892-1977), farmer, m. (1914) Lou La Follette (1892-1967) daughter: Joseph W. and Alice (Buchanon) La Follette, Child: 1. Mary Elizabeth (1917), m. (1939) Bernard Hole (1914-1975). Children: a. Gerald J. (1942), State Police Detective, m/1 (1960) div. Janet Gick (1942), children: Greg (1961), Brian (1962), Shelly (1964), Alisa Dawn (1972), m/2 (1983) Kathi Thrine (1958), son: Michael Kristopher (1986). b. Robert Allen (1946) m. (1967) div. Libby Cohee (1946), daughter: Norman and Dora (Dale) Cohee. Children: Susannah Lynn (1973), Jennifer Lee (1975), and Amanda Jane (1976). c. Garry Steven (1952), farmer.

C. Agnes (1900-1924), m. (1923) Stephen Perry. Child: 1. Helen Louise. (1924), m. Don Myers, Peru, IN. Children: a. Donna Louisa (1946), b.

Harriet De Lou (1951), c. Darline Kay (1953), d. Dione Sue (1955) e. Donnella May (1959), f. Dawn Gail (1960), Darla Denise (1963), h. Melina Dee (1965), i. Donald James (1967), j. Daniel Walter (1971).

D. Oscar "Punk" (1903-1982), farmer, m. (1930) Ouida Campbell (1911). Children: 1. Linnaeus (1931), heavy equipment operator, m/1 Madge Jarred, div. Children: a. Marcia, b. Mike, c. Janice. 2. Myron (1933), teacher, coach, principal, m/1 Margaret Allie, div. Children: a. Pamela (1960), b. Debbie (1962), c. Douglas M. (1966). Myron m/3 (1985) Deborah Musick.

II. Mabel (1871-1959), m. (1896) Robert Weesner (1873-1956), farmer, (brother of Hannah Weesner). Moved, in 1916, with their four children, to Wisconsin. Children: A.B.C.D.

A. Lowell A. (1899-1968), farmer, m. (1922) Mabel I. Hagen (1899-1983), primary teacher. Children: 1. Kathryn Marie (1924), decorator, m. (1964), div. Robert Kyle. 2. Ruth Ann (1930), has gift shop, m. (1954) Robert Eaton, lawyer, at Graceville, MN. Children: a. Peter. b. John - both married, with children.

B. Erving B. (1904), material control, m. (1945) Alice McClaskey (1905), Darlington teacher. Children: 1. Robert Eliot M.D. (1946), m. (1983) Laine Marshall Pharm. D. (1949), on Bermuda Island. Child: a. Marshall Todd (1987), Ohio. 2. John Philip (1949), office clerk.

C. Marie (1908-1948), flair for Art, Sunday School teacher.

D. Grace (1910), office manager, m. (1980) Elmer Peterson, teacher.

III. Herbert H. (1888-1962), farmer, m. (1910) Blanche Clouser (1890-1971). Everyone knew them as Uncle Herb and Aunt Blanche. The family remembers their annual celebration called "January Birthdays". One of added interest had six babies sleeping on the bed. Maybe few knew the relationship, but all knew "We are family." *Submitted by Erving B. Weesner*

WALTER D. AND REBECCAH (STEPHENSON) PEEBLES FAMILY

Walter (1850-1920) m. Rebeccah, daughter of Archibald and Indiana Chevewoth Stephenson. (They died in measles epidemic. Rebeccah and Josephine were raised by various other Quakers at Gravelly Run.) Their children were:

I. Clifford, (1877) d. infant. T.B. along with his aunt, Caroline Peebles, living at Walter's.

Walter and Rebeccah Stephenson Peebles

II. Orville M. Peebles (1876-1945) Orville, teacher, farmer, m. (1901) Alice, daughter of Henry and Margaret Brown Hitch. Young's Chapel Neighborhood. A. Gladys (1903-1980) teacher, County Attendance Officer m. Adrian Remley, son of Albert J. and Lena Smiley Remley, 1925. Son;

James Adrian Remley, 1935, La Salle, IL m. and d. Sharon, daughter of Estel and Marjorie Chadwick Bell. they had two children: James Chadwick Remley, b. 1960 and Sheila b. 1961. B. Donald (Doc) (1909-1972) County Auditor, farmer m. Mary Anderson, teacher. (Ottowa, IL) Daughter of Asa and Virginia Hamilton Anderson. No children.

III. Archibald E. Peebles (1880-1944) Archie married Mellie, daughter of Frank and Tillie Morris Buchanon. Their first children born: near Darlington: A. Francis (1907-1924); B. Buford Archibald (1908-1957) executive, Bell Telephone. m. Helen Connelly, South Bend. (Daughter of Louis and Elizabeth Hybarger Connelly). Their children: (1) Joan b. 1932, m. 1956. Charles Kubick. Son: Jeffery b. 1958. (2) Kathleen b. 1942. National Air Lines; C. James Manley (1910-1937); D. Marian Louise (1911-1913); E. Robert Owen b. 1916, m. Thelma, daughter of William and Mayme Barcus. Two sons: 1. Jon Manley b. 1938 m. 1962, Sue Grubbs. Children: Melissa (1965) and Molly (1967) Speedway. 2. Mark Owen (1941-1943) Retired, Bradenton, FL. F. Lois Elizabeth b. 1918, Williamsport. m. 1943 John William Milks, son of Lynn H. and Flossie Glen Smith Milks. State Police. Their children were: 1. Kenneth Lee b. 1943 (Md.) m. Janice daughter of Peter and Edith Warner Leuck. Son: Scott Alan b. 1970 2. Ronald Owen b. 1947 (At 27, Chief of Police Lafayette, IN) Married Linda, daughter of Earl and Ester Livengood Hollenbeck. Children: Jeffrey Alan (1968) Brad Michael (1971) Tamara Marie (1972) 3. Richard Alan b. 1952. (writer, composer) m. Melinda, daughter of Donald and Harriett McDowell. Three daughters, b. Ca. Lauren (1982) Dana (1985) and Lindsey (1987). G. William Walter Peebles, b. 1920, Logansport, m. Betty Kraft. (General Telephone Co. Virginia.) Adopted daughter: Beth, 1947. H. Mary Jane Peebles, 1924. (Died: infant) After Mellie's death her sisters took the younger children to raise. Bob lived with Goldie and Charles Williamson, Lois and Bill lived with Mamie and Clyde Loop.

IV. Le Roy Peebles (1886-1933) Roy and Hazel LaFollette Peebles Family. See elsewhere. *Compiled by Helen White, Submitted by Lois Milks*

PEFFLEY FAMILY

From an address written by Joel Peffley, and read on the occasion of the Golden Anniversary of his parents, John and Mary Peffley, May 21, 1878.

"Our company emigrated from Botetourt Co., VA, and was made up of Father's family (five persons) one wagon, and four horses; Jacob Harshbarger's (nine persons) two wagons, six horses; Samuel Britt's (seven persons) one wagon and buggy, five horses; McCormic's (ten persons) one wagon and one horse; J. Fletcher's (three persons) one wagon and one horse; J. Barbour's family (three persons) one wagon and one horse, making a company of 37 persons leagued together for safety and convenience. We travelled nearly 300 miles over the mountains and about the same distance across land where mud and water was about equally distributed. In six weeks and five days we arrived one and one half miles east of Ladoga and occupied an old log cabin. In the spring of 1832, we moved into an old log cabin which still stands on the lot near our home."

Joel Peffley was one of 12 children of John and Mary Magdalene Robinson Peffley. Of the 12, nine survived to adulthood. There were six boys and three girls in the Peffley family who emigrated from Botetourt Co., VA in the 1830's becoming early settlers of Clark Township in Montgomery County. The fourth son, Thomas, born on Mar. 2, 1833, married Melvina Rose in 1857. They had a son, Alfred Wallace Peffley on Mar. 25, 1863. A.W. Peffley married Anna Theodosia Magnus in 1889.

Chester and Beulah Peffley and Grandson Bill Boone taken in 1943

Chester Peffley was the only son of Wal and Annie Peffley. He was born on Feb. 22, 1891. Chet married Beulah Overman of Kokomo. The couple had three daughters, Elizabeth, Bertha and Carolyn. Chet was a farmer and mechanic all his life, living on the family farm east of Ladoga and operating a garage in Ladoga.

The three daughters of Chester and Beulah married local men and raised families in Ladoga. Elizabeth Ann married Lloyd Carmichael in 1932. They had one son, Bill. Bertha married George Boone whose family was descended from Daniel Boone's brother, Edward. The Boone's had two sons, Bill who married Doris Frederick of New Ross and Daniel who now lives in Indianapolis. The youngest Peffley daughter, Carolyn married Irvin Cross. Their three children Judy, Russell and Donald, still reside at Ladoga. The three Peffley daughters, Betty, Bertha and Carolyn have all served as Librarians of the Clark Township-Ladoga Public Library in a building which was at one time the family home of their mother, Beulah Overman.

The ancestors of the Peffley family in America, Nicholas and Barbara Peffley, left Germany with a large group of friends because of religious persecution. Nicholas Peffley was born in Germany about 1700. He married Barbara about 1723. They arrived in Philadelphia on Aug. 19, 1729, founding the Peffley line in America. Much of this information comes from a book entitled *"The Peffley Family in America,"* which is available in the Ladoga Public Library or the Crawfordsville Library.

DAMON AND ELAINE PERSONETT

Damon and Elaine Personett, residents of Montgomery County for most of their lives, presently live on the south edge of Darlington. Damon was born on Dec. 21, 1942 in Montgomery County and Elaine was born on Sept. 20, 1942 in Hiseville, KY. They are 1960 graduates of Darlington High School and they were married Apr. 8, 1962. Damon attended Bailey Technical Institute in St. Louis. He began working for Raybestos in 1965. Elaine, now a homemaker, previously worked as a cook at the Darlington School.

They are the parents of two children, James Eric born Jan. 6, 1964 and Cheryl Renee born Oct. 25, 1967. Eric, a 1982 graduate of North Montgomery High School, is currently employed by Raybestos. December 27, 1986, Eric married Mary Anne Burbrink. She was born Dec. 5, 1964 to Paul and Ginny Burbrink. Eric and Mary Anne have one son, Benjamin Paul, who was born Feb. 24, 1988. They are residents of Darlington. Cheryl also graduated from NMHS in 1985. She lives with her parents and is working for Donnelley's. Cheryl has attended Ball State and Purdue Universities. During the summer of 1988, she worked as a missionary in Mazatlan, Mexico.

Damon's parents, John Robert (Bob) and Opal Jane Anderson Personett spent most of their married lives on a farm on the Montgomery/Boone County line.

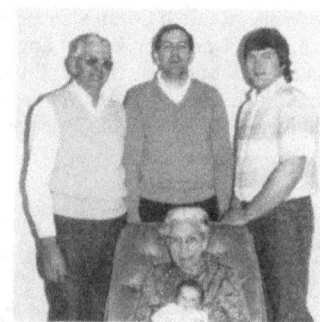

Robert, Damon, Eric, Esther (Hutchins) and Benjamin Paul Personett

Before Bob retired in 1985, he had never lived outside a mile square. Presently they live on a small farm in Smartsburg which was previously owned by Odie Anderson, Opal's father. Damon has two brothers, Allen Ray born Oct. 15, 1946 and Larry Joe born Nov. 29, 1950. Allen served in Vietnam from 1966-1967 when he was injured and transported to Great Lakes Naval Hospital. He was released in 1968 and returned home.

In July of 1969 Allen married Dianna Harwood. They are the parents of Craig Allen born June 30, 1972 and Paula Michelle born July 25, 1974. They reside in Crawfordsville where Allen works for Impex. Larry, currently employed by Hi-Tek, previously worked at Schloot Furniture. In August of 1980, he married Teresa Wilson. They have a daughter, Amanda Jo, who was born Aug. 10, 1981. They too are residents of Crawfordsville.

Damon's grandmother, Esther (Hutchins) Personett settled in Montgomery County in 1901. She moved here from Missouri to live with her uncle. Her second cousin was Paul Hutchins, author of the Sugar Creek Gang Books. In 1916, she married Frank Personett who died in 1987 at the age of 92. Esther currently lives in Crawfordsville. She is the oldest member of the five generations at 93.

Elaine was born to James Orvin and Gladys Marie (Branstetter) Free. The Frees settled here in 1947 from Sumkmer Shade, KY. They first lived in Crawfordsville and then moved to Darlington in 1952. Elaine's father was a farmer and later worked for the County Highway. In 1956, he died in an accident while working for the Highway. Her mother retired in 1986 after serving 24 years as a cook for the Darlington schools. Mrs. Free is still a resident of Darlington.

ALFRED R. PETERSON

Alfred R. Peterson was born on Feb. 6, 1856 in New Ross, the son of James and Hannah Dorsey Peterson, grandson of George and Alice Roller Dorsey and William and Louise Wheat Peterson, all early settlers around New Ross. Alfred married Hattie Hopper on June 8, 1886. Alfred died in 1931 in New Ross. He was not only a good writer, but was a good conversationalist. In 1920 he wrote a history of Union Hall Presbyterian Church, between Mace and New Ross, where his parents had taken him to church in a big wagon. He had two brothers: Emory and John T. and a sister Alice Peterson Morrison.

He told that people visited an hour after church, then someone would invite someone home for dinner, and they'd all have a good time. Alfred was editor of the newspaper the *Darlington Dispatch* for a while. He was called a writer and historian. In his writings he very skillfully portrayed the life and times in a most interesting manner. He was listed in *Indiana Authors and Their Books* by Donald E. Thompson, compiler. He and Hattie had two children, Mildred and Roy Peterson.

NAOMI CLAIR SHANNON PETERSON

Naomi Clair Shannon was born Nov. 19, 1897 the daughter of Charles and Mary Arvilla Shannon. The town of her birth had been named Shannondale in 1851 in honor of her great grandfather David A. Shannon who was the surveyor of Montgomery County for nearly two decades. David was born in York Co., PA on June 26, 1795 and is believed to be the first member of Naomi's lineage to settle in Montgomery Co., IN.

Naomi grew-up with her seven siblings: Carroll, Minnie, Geneva, Palmer Allen, Georgie, Martin and Jack in Shannondale and graduated from Crawfordsville High School in 1915. The following year, she attended Madame Blaker's teacher's school in Indianapolis and began a teaching career in Montgomery County which spanned over 30 years in various towns including Bowers, Ladoga, Linden and Darlington.

Naomi and Husted Peterson

In 1922, Naomi married Husted Peterson, born Apr. 19, 1899 and died Nov. 25, 1969. Husted was an electrician and telephone repairman who together with Naomi built a home in Darlington, IN and had one daughter, Nancy Clair Peterson, born Dec. 30, 1930 and died Jan. 19, 1985. Nancy and her husband, Irv Meitus, had two sons, Gregory Eliott and Robert Shannon. Robert graduated from Wabash college in Crawfordsville, IN in 1988, some 70 years after his grandfather Husted attended college there.

Naomi in known widely for her commitment to education and does not hesitate to tell stories about her early teaching career which reflect the good nature that she brought to the Montgomery County schools throughout her career. Perhaps the most humorous story occurred in 1930 when Naomi was pregnant with Nancy and went to the school trustee to discuss a leave of absence. The school official remarked, "I'm sorry to see you go, Naomi. I sure hope it's nothing I've done." She assured him that it was not his fault.

Naomi is now 91 years old and is an active member of the Dorothy Q. Chapter Daughters of the American Revolution, the Indiana Teachers' Association, and the Darlington Garden and Book Lovers' Clubs. She still resides in the same house built by her and Husted in the early 1920s.

FREDERICK GEORGE PETRY JR.

Frederick George Petry, Jr. was born Apr. 29, 1926 in Vigo Co., IN. He married Wandalene Pickett May 13, 1944 in Montgomery Co., IN. He is the son of Frederick Chalmen Petry and Jessie M. Switzer.

Frederick Chalmen Petry was born Jan. 24, 1905 in Vigo Co., IN. He married Jessie M. Switzer who was born May 1904. He died Apr. 3, 1965 in Montgomery Co., IN. Jessie died Feb. 14, 1953 in Montgomery Co., IN.

Frederick C. Petry's father was George Flave Petry who was born in 1859 in Illinois. He married Fanny Ellen Jackson Oct. 19, 1879. Fanny was born Sept. 8, 1862 in Indiana. They had 13 children eight boys and five girls. Two boys died in childhood. Frederick Chalmen was the last child born.

George Flave Petry's father was William Petry. He was born in 1834. His mother's name was Sabins. They had four children and were living in Clark Co., Parker Township, IL in 1860. They were both born in Pennsylvania.

Jessie M. Switzer was born May 1904. She was the daughter of Jakey A. Switzer and Molly (Mary) Ramsey. They were married Jan. 6, 1896. They had six children, five girls and one boy. Jakey, a native of Fountain Co., IN was born July 30, 1872. He died Jan. 14, 1944 in Parke Co., IN. His father was Andrew Jackson Switzer and his mother was Mary Jane Knout.

Molly Ramsey was originally from Ireland. Her father's given name is unknown. He was the son of Alexander and Mary Ramsey. Molly had one brother and one sister. The sister died in infancy. Molly's father had a sister named Chestine.

WANDALENE PETRY

Wandalene and Fred are residents of Montgomery Co., IN. Both are retired; he from Mid-States Steel & Wire Co., she from Shades State Park.

Wandalene was born in Montgomery County, near Alamo in May 1926. She is the twin sister of Ilene and the third child of Gilbert and Helen Stonebraker Pickett. She has a sister, Mary Evelyn, born in November 1919, and a brother, William Leroy, born in March 1921 and died in February 1984.

Wandalene graduated from Alamo High School in 1944. She married Frederick George Petry Jr. in May 1944. They have three children; Diana Kay born in April 1947, married to Nathan David Hester in December 1966. They have two children, Heather Marie born in April 1971 at Crawfordsville, IN and Micah Nathan born in May 1981 at Lafayette, IN: Janice Sue born in August 1951, married to Douglas Paul Hamilton in October 1970. They have three children, Adrian Scott born in May 1971 at Indianapolis, IN; Rachael Brooke born in November 1978 at Indianapolis, IN; Justin Alexander born in January 1980 at Indianapolis, IN: Richard Lee born in March 1954, married to Sandra Kay Fitzwater in August 1972. They have one daughter Jennifer Brooke born in March 1973 at Terre Haute, IN. They were divorced in 1977 and Richard married Penny Kay King in December 1986.

Wandalene's parents, both born in Montgomery County near Alamo. Her father Henry Gilbert born in June 1895 and died in April 1948, was a farmer and truck driver, the youngest of two children. His father was William born on April 1856 and died July 1940. His mother was Clarissa Ann Ammerman born in June 1857 and died in November 1930. Helen Marie, her mother born in April 1899 and died in May 1965, was a housewife. She was the youngest of three children. Her father was James Stonebraker born in April 1861 and died in January 1940. Her mother, Euphesa Cornelia Tucker born in February 1859 and died in May 1943.

Janice Sue, Richard Lee, Diana Kay, Fred G. and Wandalene Petry

Fred was born in April 1926 at Vigo County, Terre Haute, IN to Fred C. and Jessie Marie (Switzer). He is an only child. He graduated form Alamo High School in 1944, then entered the U.S. Navy in September 1944, where he was stationed on the U.S.S. Dixie in the Pacific area.

Fred's father, born in January 1905 and died in April 1965, was the youngest of 11 children, born to Flavious and Fannie Ellen Jackson at Terre Haute, IN. He was raised in the home of the oldest son, John after his parents died when he was 11 years. He was a farmer and school bus operator.

His mother, born in May 1904 to Jakey and Molly Switzer in Fountain Co., IN died in February 1953. She was the second oldest of six children. She was a housewife.

PETT-FRUITS

Arthur Pett came to the United States, from Kent, England in the late 1890's. Here he met Sue Rinehart from Waterloo, IA. They settled in Montgomery County, and started a Greenhouse and Flower Business in Crawfordsville. This business is still operating today and is known as Minnie Petts Flower Shop.

Arthur and Sue were the parents of nine children, six girls and three boys, June, Mae, Ferne, Autumn, Ruth Harriet. Ray Alvin, Lawrence and Richard. The boys all died at an early age. There are three surviving sisters, June Beatty, of Peoria, IL, Harriet Sellno of Liberty, TX and Ruth Fruits of Crawfordsville.

Ruth married George William Fruits of Alamo, a fourth generation descendant of George Fruits, Jr., a revolutionary soldier, who lived to be 114 years old.

George Fruits, an artist and sign painter, lives in Fort Lauderdale, FL. George and Ruth had four children, Hadley, Sue, Richard and Dan.

Ruth lived several years in the Waynetown area, where Hadley and Sue graduated from Waynetown High School. Ruth later moved to Crawfordsville, where Richard and Dan graduated from Crawfordsville High School.

Hadley is married and living in Nebraska. He is a Sports Writer for his city's newspaper. Hadley has three children, Cathryn, Laura, and Hadley, Jr.

Sue married David Bryan from Ladoga, a Donnelley employee. They live in Crawfordsville and have three children: Rebecca, Brenda and Bradley. Rebecca married Robert Mitchell of Franklin. They had a daughter, Angela Sue. Robert died in an automobile accident in 1980. Rebecca later married Terry Rhoads of Crawfordsville. They live in Kansas City, MO. Terry is the Minister of the Northside Christian Church.

Brenda married Doug Driscoll of California. They live in Columbia City, IN. Doug is manager of the city newspaper. They have two children: Brooke and Andrew.

Brad lives in Hollywood, CA. He graduated form Columbia College. He is now working in Cinematography.

Richard living in Crawfordsville has two children, Kathy Arlene of Indianapolis and Charles Kenneth Woodford of Chicago, IL. Kathy is a hair stylist and Kenneth is a sales representative.

Dan, of Munice, is an artist and teaches art at Ball State University.

Strong family ties are an important part of these families. Holidays and reunions are fun-filled times, when the families get together for dinners, games and fond memories.

JACOB PICKEL

This history begins with the birth of Mary Landis in Virginia in 1789. At the age of 18, she married Joseph Bundurant in Bedford County in Virginia on Nov. 30, 1807. Joseph was 36 years old at the time of their marriage, and was an overseer of a plantation while living in Virginia. Mary and Joseph were the parents of six children: Gabriel, Locky, Emily, Nancy, Mary L., and Joan. Joseph moved his family to Madison County in Iowa where his beloved wife died.

Nancy, the daughter of Joseph and Mary, was born in Campbell County in Virginia on Jan. 16, 1815. She married Jacob Pickel in Virginia around 1832. This marriage produced ten children: Julia Ann, Rachel, Henry, Joseph, Gabriel, Jonas, Nancy II, Mary, Jacob Jr., and Oliver. Jacob and Nancy Pickel settled in Putnam County, along with Nancy's father Joseph Bundurant. Joseph died at the age of 98 and is buried in Pickel Cemetery in Putnam County.

Jacob and Myrtle Pickel

Joseph, the fifth child of Jacob and Nancy Pickel, was born in 1839, He was married to Mahala Obenchain. It was during this time that the Civil War broke out. He served in Company B, 54th Regiment, Indiana Volunteers. After the war, they settled on 86-1/2 acres on road 400S in Montgomery County across from what is now the Crawfordsville Airport. Their children were: Ida, Rachel, Andrew, Flossie, Jacob A., Wilmer, and Otis. Joseph Pickel died in 1920 at the age of 81 and Mahala died in 1925 at the age of 83. Both are buried in Masonic Cemetery at Crawfordsville, IN.

Jacob A., was born Apr. 20, 1884. He married Myrtle Dell Hurley on Oct. 3, 1905. They had three daughters; Opal Viola, Doris Marie, and Mary Mahala. Jacob was a farmer and the family moved to a farm west of New Market owned by Dr. Beatty of New Market. While driving a wagon and team of horses, the horses bolted and ran away with Jacob, overturning and pinning Jacob underneath. Jacob died from his injuries June 1, 1922 at age 38, leaving Myrtle with three young girls to raise. She worked many years at the casket factory in Crawfordsville. On Oct. 4, 1930, she married Howard Lame. Myrtle died on June 1, 1958.

Opal Pickel, born Feb. 12, 1907, married Laird Glover May 29, 1928. He was a prominent auctioneer in Montgomery County. He died Apr. 1, 1988.

Doris Pickel, born Sept. 18, 1911, married William Hunt. They had ten children; Robert, Harry, Ruth, Nancy, David, Connie, Richard, Donald, Peggy, Charles. Doris died Apr. 18, 1967.

Mary Mahala, born Sept. 27, 1916, married Robert Sayler Nov. 25, 1937. They had five children; Leslie Allan, born Mar. 3, 1939; John Leslie, born Nov. 1, 1940; Larry Gene, born Apr. 18, 1944; Janet Lynn, born Mar. 30, 1954; Steven Wayne, born June 2, 1961. Leslie Allan died Mar. 9, 1939. Robert and Mary live in New Market, IN. He is a retired farmer and was Brown Township trustee for 16 years. She was Brown Township clerk. *Submitted by Mary M. (Pickel) Sayler*

JOHN AND SUSANNAH BELL PICKETT

John Pickett came from England in 1860. He moved to this area from Hamilton Co., OH. He was born Jan. 7, 1804 and passed away on Mar. 11, 1895. He married Susannah Bell and made his home in Fountain County, about three miles from Montgomery County. They were blessed with 12 children. Susannah was born Jan. 24, 1811 and died Oct. 29, 1890. They are buried in the Alamo Cemetery along with several of their children.

John and Susannah Bell Picket

Their first born child was Samuel. He was born in Hamilton Co., OH on Sept. 27, 1829 and died Mar. 26, 1863. He married Charlotte Craig and born two sons, William born Apr. 16, 1856, died July 12, 1940. The other is John, born Sept. 8, 1858, died Dec. 28, 1924. Charlotte then married John, a brother of Samuel. A daughter was born to them, Rosa Etta born Dec. 9, 1869 and died July 29, 1930. Rosa married Nelson Rush Sept. 4, 1887.

Rosa and Nelson were blessed with two children, a daughter Myrtle born July 31, 1894 and died December 1972; a son Leslie Doyne, born Dec. 4, 1908 and died July 6, 1981.

ESTHER BELLE KEPPLE PIERSON (KEPPLE-BUNDY-GOTT FAMILIES)

Esther was born Aug. 9, 1897, Darlington, Montgomery Co., IN, second child of Quincy Eli Kepple and Laura Belle Gott. Her siblings were Beatrice (1895-1905), a brother born Mar. 4, 1900. Records of Nobel and Margaret Higer, Colfax, indicate that mother died same date. Esther was placed in a foster home with Alan and Julia Crubaugh in Sugar Creek Township where she spent her childhood. At age 15 she asked the Indiana Court to appoint Crubaughs her legal guardians and request was granted July 5, 1913. Esther attended Thorntown High School and upon graduation she married Pliny Sigfrid Pierson of Chicago. The couple rented the C.L. Crist home, Thorntown, where their son, Robert Allen was born, Oct. 29, 1917. The Piersons divorced and Esther became a registered nurse. Her son stayed with Crubaughs while she attended school. Esther went to Chicago. She met and married George Brannock and moved to Long Beach, CA in 1943. Esther died Oct. 3, 1948 at her home 1529 Sherman Place and services were held at Trinity Baptist Church.

Esther's father, Quincy Kepple, was born Feb. 29, 1872, Darlington. His father was George Kepple who married Esther Bundy Sept. 16, 1869, Marion Co., IN. Esther Bundy's father was Peter and mother Elizabeth Lucas, Peter's first wife. Quincy's siblings were Mallory, John, George and Elizabeth. Quincy joined the 22nd Indiana Infantry Division, Spanish-American War (Philippines), 1898, was widowed in 1900, remarried Dec. 9, 1905, and raised a second family. In his latter years, Quincy was a town barber in Thorntown. He died at Hines Veteran Hospital, near Chicago, Nov. 26, 1942, buried at St. James Lutheran Cemetery, Darlington.

Esther Belle Kepple Pierson, age 20, Robert Allen Pierson, age one, and Pliny Sigfrid Pierson, age 29

Esther's mother, Laura Belle Gott Kepple, was born 1875, Glasgow, KY, second child of Simon H. Gott, a farmer from Bowling Green, KY, and Belle K. Mansfield, daughter of Thomas Mansfield. Laura's siblings were John, Charles, Edward, Morris, Daisy (married George Voltz), Anna May (married Roy Raymond Reagon), Otis, Clifford and Della. Laura married Quincy Kepple June 13, 1894, and died six years later at age 25. No record is available where she died or where she is buried.

Esther's forefathers are her great grandfather, William M. Gott, born May 12, 1833, Bowling Green, KY, married Cordelia Jackson, issue six children: Simon H., M.M. (Montreville), Secilia, Phebe Ann, Sally Jane and James W. Family lived in Indiana and Kentucky. Esther's great great grandfather Richard Gott, born Sept. 29, 1792, North Carolina, married Milly Mannen (1814), issue 11 children. Esther's great great great grandfather was Sutton Gott, born Feb. 17, 1764, married his second wife Mary "Polly" Farmer. Sutton Gott migrated from North Carolina to Warren Co., KY in 1807. At age 15, it is said Sutton ran away from home and was in the Battle of Yorktown. Sutton was a Methodist Minister.

Esther's son, Robert married Carrie Johnson in 1939, Chicago. Two daughters were born, Roberta "Lee" (1943) and Patricia "Lynn" (1950). Lee married James Parker, issue Sherri, Bobby and Troy-Lynn, and Denise. Lynn married James Browning, issue Jeffrey Stuart, Jason Robert, Amanda Lynn and Sara Kimberly. Esther Kepple Pierson's great great great grandchildren are: Destiny Lee, Felisha Denise, Desiree Dawn, Senna Marie and Daryl Lyn Ann, plus a newborn son from Sherri. They all reside in Helper and Price, UT.

This narration is the legacy of Ester to all her descendents.

If anyone wants further and more detailed info, you may contact Robert Pierson, 1216 Hickory Hill Drive, Gautier, MS 39553

KENNETH AND CAROL PITTMAN

Kenneth and Carol Pittman have lived in Montgomery County all of their adult lives.

Kenneth was born in Clay Co., IN Aug. 8, 1939 to John "Harry" and Florence Newport Pittman. He graduated from Brazil High School in 1957 and began working at R.R. Donnelley & Sons in September 1957. At this time Kenneth made his home with his paternal aunt, Dorothy and her husband James "Cecil" Bruce, in the Bal Hinch area.

Kenneth's first marriage was to Patricia Ray Smith of Crawfordsville, in January 1967. One daughter, Angela Renee, was born to them Mar. 21, 1971. Patricia also had two daughters, Cindy and Pam, from her first marriage. They were divorced in 1973.

Angie, Ken, Sam, Carol holding Melinda

On Feb. 12, 1977 Kenneth married Carol Jean Beck. She is the fifth child of Robert E. and Carol Heyer Beck of Indianapolis, and was born there Jan. 3, 1958. At age 12 she moved with her mother to ten acres of land on county road 50 south off of U.S. 136 East. Carol H. Beck built Beckoning Woods Mobile Home Park on this site. Carol J. graduated from Southmont Jr. Sr. High School in 1976.

During a period of time from 1979 to 1984, the Pittman family shared their large home at 512 E. College St., Crawfordsville, with several foster children. In September 1981, one very special child was placed in their home to be adopted. This is their son, Samuel Kenneth Pittman.

On Apr. 1, 1983 Carol became the first female deputy Sheriff in Montgomery County under the merit system, and the first Montgomery County Police Woman to graduate from the Indiana Law Enforcement Academy at Plainfield, IN.

In 1985, Kenneth was hired as the New Market Town Marshal, and the family relocated to 112 E. Main St., New Market.

In July 1987 Carol resigned her position with the Sheriff's Department to stay home with their adopted newborn daughter, Melinda Annette Pittman.

Kenneth served in the United States Army from 1962 to 1965. He served two years stationed in Japan during that time.

VERNON "LEE" AND SHIRLEY PITZER

Down a lane off 234 in Ladoga, shaded by trees, is the home of Vernon "Lee" and Shirley Pitzer.

Lee was born Apr. 17, 1920 to Alva E. and Laura Lucinda. Four brothers and two sisters still survive.

Shirley Jane, only child of George Merle and Ruby Montgomery Newlin, was born Mar. 4, 1924. Lee and Shirley met and married Apr. 25, 1943 in Watseka, Il and on Dec. 2, 1947 Stephanie Lee completed the family.

They moved south of Ladoga in 1951 where Lee dairy farmed for ten years, then moved to their present home in 1961. Lee has worked for the Culvert Company, Crestline Window, the Roachdale Telephone Company, and the Christian Children's Home, where he still works part-time.

Shirley, in addition to being a wife and mother, has worked in the State Vet's office, Crestline, Culvert Company, Tri County Bank, Communications Corp. of Indiana, and as a receptionist at Autumn Care Nursing Home. She, like Lee, is semi-retired, but works part-time at a neighborhood grocery where she visits with friends who come to shop.

Lee and Shirley's daughter, Stephanie, went to school at Ladoga, graduating in 1966. After Ball State, she took a position with Lomas & Nettleton, traveling all over the country to examine and audit documents. When the company moved to Chicago, Stephanie chose not to move, making a career switch to the engineering production office at Prudue University.

Stephanie rode horses and barrel raced at rodeos and horse shows and now is the National Director for the Indiana High School Rodeo Association.

Rodeo has played an important part in their family life. Lee rode bulls when cowboys were paid 50 cents a head, roped calves, and joined Bob McKinley's Wild West Show where he entertained by trick roping. During the summer they would travel to a show or county fair in Indiana, Illinois, Michigan, or Ohio. Horse and equipment were unloaded, and Shirley set up a home in the bed of a truck with a tarp overhead. After Lee finished calf roping, Stephanie would mount his horse, D-Day, and run the barrel race.

In the 1960s, Lee switched over to team roping so the horse could do all the "hard work." Mike Armstrong from Crawfordsville was his regular partner, although Lee was often asked to "head" for others. He would rope and turn the steer for the "heeler" to catch the back feet. Lee say "you have to throw loops and practice until making a loop and tossing it accurately comes as easy as feeding yourself."

Lee and Shirley's home reflects their interests. Shirley paints nature scenes on shovels and tea kettles, homey accents among displays of trophies, china and glassware passed down from families.

Lee buys, raises and trains, setter and pointer dogs for hunting birds. He says clean farming with no fence rows and pesticides have limited the quail and pheasant population, but he sees a return of more and bigger coveys.

A cup of coffee, warmth, hospitality, and talk of horses, dogs, or painting, make a visit to Lee and Shirley Pitzer a real pleasure *Submitted by Lee and Shirley*

DAN POOL

Dan L. Pool was born Mar. 3, 1940 in Olney, IL. He was the first of six children of L.D. "Don" and Pauline Stanley Pool. His parents both worked at the shoe factory in Olney at the time. Dan's father also sold automobiles part time and in May 1940 he opened a Studebaker dealership.

When the war started the family moved to Indianapolis where Mr. Pool worked for Allison's making aircraft engines. The family then moved back to Illinois after the war and Dan entered Silver Street School as a first grader. He was graduated from East Richland High School in 1958 and went to what is now Rose-Hulman in Terre Haute, IN and later transferred to Indiana State University. Dan received a degree in Business Administration in 1963.

Dan met his wife Marty at Indiana State University and they were married in January of 1963. He took a job with General Adjustment Bureau adjusting insurance claims and was assigned to Kokomo, IN. The company then transferred Dan to Crawfordsville in January of 1964. They lived at 310 S. Walnut St. Marty took a job teaching second grade at New Market for two years and then was a guidance counselor at Crawfordsville High School for two years before retiring to have their second son.

Dan and Marty have two boys. Both are graduates of the Crawfordsville school system. The oldest, Barry, is a graduate of Indiana University and Brett is a student at Ball State University.

The company wanted to transfer Dan and his family in 1970. They chose to remain in Crawfordsville and open their own business. In December 1970 the Pool's Bargain Center opened on the south side of Crawfordsville. The business did fairly well and it was expanded in 1973 and 1976 to its present size. They also opened a similar store in Greencastle in 1976.

The Pools also got involved with auto racing in 1973. They purchased half of a race car and ran the United States Auto Club Midget series. Since then the family has traveled all over the United States and part of Canada racing cars. Several Indy 500 competitors have driven the Pool car including Larry Rice from Linden, IN. Others have been A.J. Foyt, Pancho Carter, Johnny Parsons, Tom Bigelow, Lee Kunzman, and Bill Vukovich. The latest driver is Dan's son Brett who started racing in 1988.

The year of 1980 saw another turn in the life of Dan Pool. He became a member of the Crawfordsville City Council. Then in 1982 he was elected to the Indiana General Assembly as a State Representative. Dan has been re-elected three times. He has served as an Assistant Caucus Chairman, Chairman of the Commerce Committee, and Majority Whip for the Indiana House of Representatives. He has also been asked to head up several interim study committees on issues for the General Assembly.

Dan and Marty are members of the Wabash Avenue Presbyterian Church. Dan has served as a coach in the youth baseball program and in the Boys Club biddy basketball program. He also is a past board member of the Montgomery County Boys Club.

E. DENVER AND ESSIE MAE POTTS

Elmer Denver Potts was born Nov. 19, 1899 in Rensselaer, IN. His parents were Ancil and Rebekah Potts. Denver was a farmer in Ripley township, Montgomery Co., IN. He owned two farms, one on State Road 32 West and 600 West — the other at 400 West and Division Road. Denver's siblings were: Ray, Elvin, Herman, Harry and Hazel Potts.

In 1923, Denver married Essie Mae Comer born Feb. 6, 1902 in Jasper County. Her parents were Greely and Maude Comer. Her siblings were: Wayne and Cecil Comer.

Denver and Essie belonged to the Yountsville Church. Essie was a homemaker, and belonged to the Yountsville Bells and other societies of the church.

E. Denver and Essie Mae Potts

Denver and Essie had one son, Wendall Keith Potts born Sept. 18, 1925 and on Apr. 13, 1945 married Letha May Tucker, born Apr. 30, 1927; her parents being Joel and Katie Smith Tucker.

In 1960, Keith became a Minister. Reverend Potts has been the Pastor of churches in Sitkum, Greenacres and Redland, OR — also in Foothills, WA.

They are the parents of three children: Sherman Wayne, born Aug. 8, 1948. He married Alice Kay Henden. They have two children, Vince Allen, born Apr. 24, 1973 and Valerie Suzanne, born Jan. 11, 1978. They live in California. Garry Alan Potts, born July 14, 1952 Montgomery County married Aug. 7, 1972 to Candice Marie Ferguson. They had three children: Tina Marie, Garry Alan, Jr. and Amanda LeAnn. This family can be found in another story in this book. Garry and Candice divorced Aug. 18, 1981. Garry married Apr. 7, 1983 to Elizabeth Cohee Hole. Laura Kay Potts, born Aug. 24, 1963 married Nov. 13, 1982 to Blake Edward McConahy. They have one son, Jared Thomas, born July 10, 1986.

Denver died Aug. 21, 1980 in Washington. Essie died Jan. 30, 1980. Both buried in Oak Hill Cemetery. *Submitted by Amanda LeAnn Potts, age 12*

LESLIE BRYON POWELL

Leslie Bryon Powell was born Mar. 12, 1909, in Montgomery Co., IN. He attended elementary schools near New Market, IN, and Crawfordsville High school.

Martha Evelyn Thomas Powell was born Aug. 11, 1913, in Montgomery Co., IN. She attended Wilson and Tuttle elementary schools and Crawfordsville High School.

Leslie and Martha were married at Crawfordsville on Jan. 19, 1929. They had two children: Thomas Leslie Powell, born Jan. 29, 1930, in Crawfordsville, and William Leonard Powell, born Apr. 1, 1933, in Crawfordsville.

Martha E. Powell

Leslie's parents are Thomas Cecil Powell and Elva S. Linn Powell. Thomas Cecil was born in Boone Co., IN on Feb. 15, 1885; his parents were Newton Powell and Amelia Logan. Elva's parents were Enoch Linn and Juliette Linn. Thomas and Elva spent most of their married life in Montgomery County. Leslie's siblings were Lester Earl, Lyle, and Thomas Clayton.

Martha's parents, Clint Thomas and Blanche Pearl Watson Thomas, were married Sept. 3 or 12, 1900, and moved to Crawfordsville in 1904. Clint was born in Montgomery County on Aug. 18, 1876, and worked as a cabinet maker; he died June 18, 1958. Blanch was born in Fountain Co., IN on Sept. 3, 1881, and died Mar. 5, 1941. Martha's siblings were Kelsey, Mable, Carlton, Opal, Merle, Inetta, Herschel, Kathryne, and Verlin.

Clint Thomas's parents were Frank Thomas born Sept. 27, 1840, and Martha Lowe, born Sept. 7, 1849. Clint was a farmer in Montgomery County and worked as a Superintendent at the Casket Co. in Crawfordsville. Clint married Pearl Shay of Cedar Rapids, IA, in 1944; she died Dec. 17, 1958.

Blanch's parents were George W. Watson and Martha Watson. This Martha was born in Kokomo on Sept. 1 or 7, 1849, moved to Montgomery County "when she was very small". She and her twin sister both died in Crawfordsville at an age of 96 years.

In 1955, Leslie became a member of the Masonic Blue Lodge of Crawfordsville and later became a member of the Scottish Rite Lodge in Indianapolis. Martha joined the Eastern Star in 1957.

Leslie worked as a truck driver for McDaniel Freight Lines in Crawfordsville for 25 years and retired in 1965. Martha worked at the Coats Factory and the Wilson Brothers Shirt Factory in Crawfordsville. During World War II, she made Navy peacoats and Army coats and jackets. During the Korean War, she made Army shirts.

In 1967, Leslie and Martha moved to Sebring, FL; in 1973, they moved to Weatherford, TX where their two sons lived.

Leslie died at Weatherford in 1975, and is buried in the Masonic Cemetery in Waynetown, IN. Martha now lives in Weatherford near her two sons.

Son Thomas married Ruthanna Dellinger in Crawfordsville on July 19, 1952. They have three children and six grandchildren. Thomas and Ruthanna live in Weatherford, TX. Their children and grandchildren live in Weatherford and Granbury, TX.

Son William married Lee Marie Reynolds on Aug. 17, 1957, in Crawfordsville; they have three children. William's family lives in Weatherford. *Submitted by Martha Evelyn Thomas Powell*

RUTHANNA DELLINGER POWELL

Ruthanna Dellinger Powell was born in Montgomery Co., IN on June 12, 1933, the daughter of Shirl Blaine Dellinger and Rebecca Heacock Baynes Dellinger. Ruthanna was the youngest of eight children. Her siblings were Eugene Spangler, Rebecca Powell, Hartley C., Shirley Kathleen, Robert Lowell, Thomas Baynes, and George Paul. The Dellinger family lived on a 23-acre farm located on the Big-4 Arch Road, one-half mile outside the city limits of Crawfordsville.

Ruthanna attended elementary grades at Mt. Zion School, located five miles west of Crawfordsville. She graduated from Crawfordsville High School in 1952 and worked for R.R. Donnelleys for several years. Ruthanna has pursued an associate degree at the junior college in Weatherford, TX.

Thomas and Ruthanna Powell

She married Thomas Leslie Powell in 1952. Thomas was born in Crawfordsville in 1930. He served in the Army in Korea and France in 1950-1953. Thomas and Ruthanna have three children, all born in Crawfordsville: Debra Lynn, born in 1954; Eugene Thomas, born in 1960; and Wayne Lee, born in 1964.

Ruthanna's family lived in Crawfordsville until 1963, when they moved to Lebanon, IN where Thomas worked as a foreman at the Indianapolis Zoo. In 1967, the family moved to Weatherford, TX, where Thomas works as an airplane mechanic with the Department of Army. Ruthanna is a teacher in a Day Care.

Daughter Debra graduated from Weatherford High School in 1972. She married James Larry Bandy at Weatherford in 1975. Larry was born in Granbury, TX in 1949 and graduated from Weatherford High School in 1967. They have four children: Leslie Jean, born at Weatherford in 1975; Blaine Lee, born at San Angelo, TX, in 1978; Kevin Lance, born at Granbury in 1983; and Austin Lynn, born at Granbury in 1984. The Bandy family enjoys playdaying, and riding horses and motorcycles. The Bandys lived in Granbury and Larry works in Ft. Worth as a mechanic.

Son Eugene graduated from Weatherford High School in 1979. He enjoyed riding bulls in rodeos. In 1982 he married Tracye Mathison at Weatherford. Tracye was born in Weatherford in 1964 and graduated from high school there. They have two children: Lorin Nicole, born at Weatherford in 1983; and Bliss Linn, born in Ft. Worth, TX in 1987. Eugene works as a heavy-equipment mechanic.

Son Wayne Lee graduated from Weatherford High school in 1982. He lives in Weatherford and has worked as a heavy-equipment operator. He is now employed by Resdoor Co. that manufactures doors and windows. He likes the outdoors, hunting, and fishing. *Submitted by Ruthanna Dellinger Powell*

HIRAM AUSTIN PRATT

Hiram Austin Pratt wrote, "This is not the style of diary that I ordered. It cost in New York 69 cents and 19 cents postage." This was on a "cloudy" January 1, 1902. Ironically, two days later, his coveted Diary #253 arrived, but since he had began "The Standard Diary," he returned #253. Hiram Pratt was a barber in Waveland. His diary is housed at the Crawfordsville District Public Library. It is wonderful reading, telling interesting facts of the times ($4.20 paid for 40 gallons of oil; $1.80 received on Jan. 20th — "the least I have received on a Monday that I have any recollection of;" $1.25 rent on the shop for a week; five degrees above zero on Feb. 13th and it isn't even a Friday; and on May 9th, "Bob Moore's funeral will be held at two o'clock tomorrow afternoon — Jack Ashley will preach it. The body will be buried in the Old Union Cemetery."

Sadness prevails throughout Hiram Pratt's standard diary, especially every Sunday when "I visited little Willie's grave." Willie was his adopted son (and only child) who died at age 20 on Mar. 12, 1894. On Willie's death anniversary, Wednesday, Mar. 12, 1902 the diary entry reads, "Eight years ago today at 2:40 a.m. My Poor Little Willie died. I was the only person present at his death. He said to me the evening before (Sunday), 'Pa, I don't want you to leave me.'"

Many references are also made to Hiram's first wife, Eliza Franklin Shaw of Vigo County whom Hiram married on Sept. 6, 1866. His second wife was a native Montgomery Countian, Sarah Evaline "Eva" McMains (daughter of Robert, Dec. 7, 1810 — Dec. 18, 1879 and Mary, May 18, 1807 — Apr. 28. 1894) whom he married in this county on Oct. 9, 1888. The McMains were farmers in the Waveland area and came to Indiana from Kentucky in 1826. Eva was born Feb. 28, 1845. Hiram was born Apr. 20, 1840. On that date in his 1902 diary, he notes: "This is my 62nd birthday. I write this without aid of glasses..health is as good as usual." He was born in Parke County on a farm near Milligan and was the son of Erastus and Eliza (Allen) Pratt, both born in Kentucky.

Hiram was quite a man as besides his barber business (1874 *People's Guide Directory of Montgomery County,* p. 268), he also had a sewing machine business, paper agency and laundry service. He was a charter member of Goodwill Lodge #82 of the United Workmen, IOOF, K of P, and Rebekah. Both he and Eva were active in the Waveland Methodist Church and Hiram was a registered Republican. Mr. Pratt was also in the Civil War — Co. B, 36th Regiment of Iowa Volunteers.

Irony shines at the thought of Mr. Pratt dying exactly 27 years after his "sweet little lady." He is buried by her (his first wife) in Farmersburg, IN, his body making its last journey on the Vandalia train to join her. Eva McMains Pratt died May 27, 1917. She is buried in Maple Ridge Cemetery with many of her family members.

Hiram was a truly Christian man — on the last day of the diary, he wrote — "I am truly thankful to the Lord for all his blessings bestowed during the year." *Submitted by Karen Zach*

EDWIN AND LILLIAN PRESSLOR

Edwin Presslor, son of Clayton and Myrtle Keller Presslor, was born in Fountain Co., IN July 15, 1916. He was raised in the Kingman area and attended school there. Helping with farming until 1936 when he started working at Turkey Run Inn as baker. January 1943 he entered the service, serving in Europe with the 274th Infantry Division for 27 months. During a siege at Strasbourg, near the France-Germany border he was injured and received the Purple Heart. He received an honorable discharge as Corporal, Nov. 17, 1945. After working at Allisons at Indianapolis a few years he built his own home in 1946, and he and his father-in-law built two houses in Waveland. He remained in the construction business until his retirement. He was a member of the American Legion Post at Waveland, in which he served as commander and other officer through the years. He was a member and officer of the Carpenters Union. Edwin died Aug. 23, 1984.

Lillian was the daughter of Raymond and Ava Moore, born Aug. 2, 1917 in Parke County, near Milligan, IN. Shortly after the family moved to Waveland, where Raymond was born and raised. Lillian attended schools in Tulsa, OK, Crawfordsville and Waveland; graduating at Waveland in 1934. She was a member of the Waveland Christian Church, a member of the American Legion Auxiliary, holding different offices in this organization, a member of the Woman's Club. After leaving high school she worked as waitress and eventually secretary to the manager. She attended business school in Indianapolis. In 1962 she started working for the USDA, Montgomery County ASCS office where she remained 19 years, retiring in 1982.

Edwin and Lillian Presslor

Edwin and Lillian were married Apr. 4, 1939 at Rockville. They had three children; Linda, born 1943 at Laporte; Carol born 1948 and John Wm., born 1950 at Crawfordsville.

Linda married Jimmy Reed, son of Gilbert and Juanita Reed of Parkersburg. Their children are Denise, Malcolm and Kevin. Denise has three children; Jennifer, Haley and Jesse. Malcolm a son, Jakota. Denises' marriages (1) to Donald Kennedy; (2) Larry White. Malcolm married Donna Gillogly.

Carol's first marriage was to Robert C. Smith, son of Clare and Lala Smith. Their children; Robert C. II, Quentin and Kimberly. Carol's second marriage was to Rodney Coffman, son of Lee and Claudine Coffman. Their children are Yvonne and Michael. Rodney had two girls, Melissa and Lynet by a previous marriage. Robert II (Rob) has two sons, Cody and Sonny. His marriage was to Staci Barker.

John married Lana Lieske of Russellville, her parents were Harold and Flossie Hanks Lieske. Harold was raised in Hendricks County and Flossie in Putnam County. John and Lana's children; John Joe, Brandon Scott and Darrin Cole.

Grandchildren of Linda and Carol; namely, Cody and Sonny Smith, Jennifer Kennedy, Haley and Jess White and Jakota Reed are eighth generation descendants of Freelove Moore, one of the first settlers of Waveland in 1826. *Submitted by Lillian (Moore) Presslor*

PRIEBE FAMILY

August Priebe immigrated to the United States from Prussia, Germany (now East Germany). He married Ottilie Priebe (no relation), also from Germany about the same time (shortly after the Civil War). They settled on about 50 acres of land, north of Freedom Church across Indian Creek. There they built a log cabin and reared eight children, six boys and two girls that were educated at the Freedom School (north and west of Freedom Baptist Church). Two of the boys, Albert and Elmer and one of the daughters, Emma, went to Illinois. Albert became a gardener for the Allerton grounds near Monticello, never married and died after falling out of a tree on the farm. Elmer did not marry until late in life, worked as the manager of Allerton Farms and Emma married and settled in Monticello and had two daughters, Juanita and Pauline Ashby.

The other children stayed in Montgomery County. Paul lived next to the family farm on Indian Creek, never married and died young. Bill married and settled in the New Richmond community on a farm. He and his wife had seven children: Bill, Jr., Dorothy (died in childbirth), Geraldine, Audrey, Lloyd Elmer, Ruth and Norma Jean. Lizzie married Luna Bayless and lived just north of Freedom School until their deaths. Six children; May (married Elza Bollman), Nelson, Rose (married Jake Glascock), Hazel (married Glenn Newkirk), Fred and Lloyd.

Fred married Goldie Bayless and lived on the old Canine homestead north of Waveland, owned then by John Oldshue. They had two son, Fred Herschel, who became a medical doctor on the staff at Methodist Hospital, Indianapolis, and Lincoln, who farms several acres of ground near Parkersburg. Fred later bought a farm near Parkersburg where he lived in the summer and in Sebring, FL in the winter.

Sam was the last one to leave home. He built the country home that stands on top of the hill after crossing Indian Creek north of Freedom Church. The log cabin, the original home, stood several feet back from the new home for many years. Sam married Myrtle Whitecotton and moved to the Nelson Canine farm south of Freedom Church where he farmed 160 acres until he retired and moved back to the homeplace in the fall of 1963. They had nine children. A boy and a girl died in infancy. Margaret, the oldest, married David Canine (see David G. Canine Family). Junior resided at home until his parents' death; now a resident of Ben Hur Nursing Home, Crawfordsville. Charles, a graduate of Wabash College taught school in Montgomery County and was principal of Ladoga and Southmont Schools. He married Bonnie Weaver. Four children: Jeannie, Ed, Danny and Debby. Donald resided in Waveland, but now lives in Crawfordsville. Four children: Chris, Kevin, Bret and Dawn. Mary married Robert Gooding of Waveland. Robert is a graduate of Indiana State Teachers college (Terre Haute) and is currently a teacher at Tuttle Middle School, Crawfordsville. Three children: Roger, Susan and Ray. They live at

Lake Holiday. Martha married Keith Greve of Waveland. They live at Greensburg. Martha is a graduate of Indiana State; Keith of Butler. Three children: Greg, Marsha, and Tom. Marjorie is a graduate of Ball State, Muncie, IN. She is currently an elementary teacher in Butte, MT. Two sons, Chance and Charade Younkin. *Submitted by Margaret Priebe Canine*

FRED HERSCHELL AND MARY LOU PRIEBE

Fred Herschell Priebe was born to Fred and Goldie (Bayless) Priebe, Apr. 24, 1920 near Waveland, IN. After attending schools at Waveland and Parkersburg, he was graduated form New Market High School and Wabash College. He received his MD from University of Cincinnati College of Medicine. In 1941, he married Mary Lou Smith. To this union, four children were born: Stephen Phillip (August 1945), married Betty Grimes - two children, Angela and Jeremy. They now live in Ocala, FL. Stanley Paul, born June 1947 married Jean Dickman - two children, Jessica and Greg - live in Indianapolis. Rebecca Suzanne Priebe married Phillip Thompson - one child, Misha Daun. They live at Lake Holiday. Kent Stuart Priebe married Theresa Ray - two children, Kinsey and Clay. They live in Crawfordsville. Kent is the owner of Powers Funeral Home.

Dr. Priebe practiced in Crawfordsville and Hillsboro. As an internist, he specialized in cardiology and rheumatology. He had the first rheumatology clinic in Indiana. He was on the staff at Wishard General Hospital, Indianapolis and taught at Indiana University Medical School. He did referrals at Culver Hospital and Hendricks County Hospital. Dr. Priebe was a Captain in the U.S. Army during WWII.

Dr. Priebe's activities included Hospital Board at Culver, Eagle Scout (he and Robert Clements (Hillsboro) received their Eagle rank along with five members of their Explorer troop), member of Christian Church, American Heart Association, Arthritis Foundation and AMA. He died at Lilly Research Hospital, Indianapolis, Feb. 15, 1969.

Mary Lou Priebe was born in Indianapolis May 21, 1920. She graduated from New Market School and Central Normal College. She taught school 26-1/2 years, was the wife of a physician 29 years, had four children (see above), grandmother of seven. She has been active in volunteering in Indianapolis hospitals as a Pink Lady, helping to organize Girl Scouts in Hillsboro, All Souls' Hospice, Alpha Delta Kappa, Chi Omega Club, New Market Women's Club and Christian Church.

At present, Mary Lou travels and takes life happily as an active widow. Mary Lou is the daughter of Lois M. (Newhouse) and Artie L. Smith. She lives at 215 W. Main, Crawfordsville. *Submitted by Mary Lou Priebe*

HENRY W. PROFFITT

Henry Washington Proffitt was born Nov. 25, 1864 in West Virginia, probably Mason County. In 1874 he came to Boone Co., IN with his parents Joseph B. (1826-1902) and Elizabeth Meeks Proffitt (1832-1898). The brought 12 children when they came, nine sons and three daughters. Henry married Irena Alice Canada Dec. 23, 1888. For many years he farmed in Boone County, moving to Crawfordsville in 1918 where he entered the mortuary business. They built a new brick home in Crawfordsville in 1923 on Pike Street back of the funeral home. It is presently "The Bungalow Restaurant". She died in 1929, and he in 1945. Henry's second wife was Florence Sandlin (1878-1941).

Henry and "Renie" had five children. Rholla L. (1890-1962) was a baker, marksman, musician, and poet. He married Verna Whitecotton and had a son Max who lives near Brazil, IN, and is a professor (retired) of Indiana State University. He and his wife Martha have a son Edward (1955). Rholla and his second wife, Golda Gibson of North Salem had one son, Paul J. (1925) now married to Arlene Smith (1926) and living near New Ross on the farm Rholla bought, cleared, and built.

Henry W. and Irena Alice (Canada) Proffitt

Asher L. (1893-1973) was the second son of Henry. He married Eula Leinberger (1895-1975) of Greencastle. They had two sons: James Wendell (1925) married Betty Owens (1926) of Greencastle; and Frederick Leinberger (1927) married Velma Phillips (1927). They now live in Westernport, MD. James and Betty have three children: Janet (1950) married Jack Copeland, they live in The Dalles, OR; Jeffrey (1952) married Donna Bowen (1951) and have Brandi (1974) and Derek (1978) — they live in Fountain Valley, CA; Julie (1954) married Jon Jones (1950) and have Jason (1973) and Johnathan (1976) — live at New Richmond. Frederick and Velma have three children: Diane (1956) married Mark Snyder and have Kristie (1977) and Carli (1982); Allen (1957) is single and lives in Dallas; Cynthia (1960) married Donald Schumacker and have Michael (1984). Both Diane and Cynthia live in Maryland.

Ora L. was Henry's third son. His history is elsewhere in this book.

Samuel L. (1897-1917) was the fourth son of Henry and "Renie". He met his death in an automobile accident east of Crawfordsville.

Rosa Victoria (1905) was the only daughter of Henry and "Renie". She married Fred Coulter (1907-1950) and has one son Frederick Proffitt Coulter (1934), a pianist who lives in Miami, FL. He has two children, Fred (1958) and Valerie (1961). Victoria later married Clayton Lanning, and they live in Beulah, MI.

ORA L. PROFFITT

Ora L. Proffitt was born in Boone County Dec. 31, 1894. He grew up on a farm near Whitestown. In 1917 he married Vernita Miller (1897-1974) who was the daughter of John F. and Mary Jane Jones Miller (both teachers). Vernita taught at Jamestown one year before her marriage. In 1918 they moved to Montgomery County where they farmed most of the time until 1943 when they moved back to Boone County (Jamestown). Ora loved to play checkers and was exceptionally good with figures. He died in 1969.

They had six children, two girls and four boys. Margaret Isabelle (1918) married Russell Richardson (1915-1987) who was a Methodist Minister. They had four daughters: Rebecca Carol (1950) married to Merle Miller (1931) of Indianapolis; Betsy Ruth (1953) married to Dennis Borruso (1952) who have sons Adam (1982) and Peter (1984) — the family lives in California; Judith Elaine (1957) married to Joe Stevenson (1962) have a son Luke (1986) and live at Roachdale; and Jill Annette (1959) who lives in Redmond, WA where she works for Pacific Bell Telephone Company.

Ora L. and Vernita (Miller) Proffitt

Margaret was an elementary school teacher through the years until retirement.

Mary Irena (1920) served in the WAC during WWII. She married Joe Pointer (1921) from New Market. He is a retired president of Elston Bank & Trust Company, and she is retired from Indiana Bell Telephone Company.

Henry Miller (1926) married Barbara McBrayer (1927) from Waveland. He preached in the Methodist church for 20 years (various locations). They had four children: Laurel Ann Dieckman (1956), Lisa Lynn Fox (1959), Linda Leigh (1960), and David Charles (1962). Henry and Barbara were divorced in 1970. He now lives in Indianapolis where he is a federal guard.

Ora Merrill (1928) married Betty Libka (1932) and had three children: Charles Stephen (1951, adopted), Leanna Lynn (1953), and Daniel Merrill (1956). Leanna married Sam Mendenhall and has Chad (1973) and Matt (1975). She is now married to David Cochran. Daniel Merrill has one son, Steven Merrill (1983). All Ora Merrill's children now live in the Indianapolis area. Ora lives in New Jersey with his second wife, Nancy Whitaker (1953) from Florida. He is a corporate pilot.

John Meredith (1934) is an accountant at Naples, FL. He married Evelyne Patterson (1933) of Jamestown. They have two daughters: Karen Lynn (1956) married Nevin Hoefert II, and Mary Beth (1968). Karen and Nevin have twin sons Nevin III and John P. born in 1979.

Wayne Eugene (1938) graduated from Purdue University as a pharmacist, after tour of duty in the Navy. He married Linda Crawford (1939) and they have three daughters: Sabrena (1960) a registered nurse at St. Vincents Hospital, Indianapolis; Marena Jo (1965); and Jene Anne (1971). "Gene" is manager of Hooks West in Crawfordsville.

KENNETH AND CAROLYN PUMROY

Carolyn Elizabeth Brown was born Feb. 22, 1923 in Crawfordsville and married Kenneth Pumroy who was born Aug. 28, 1923 in Ottumwa, IA on Aug. 17, 1946. They have three children; Marsha born July 22, 1949, Eric born Jan. 16, 1952 and Anne born Mar. 23, 1955.

Marsha has a Bachelor's Degree and Master's Degree in social work from University of Michigan. She was married Dec. 25, 1969 to Irving B. Remsen III from Ramsey, NJ. They live in Ann Arbor, MI and have one son Matthew Alexander born Aug. 25, 1988.

Eric has a Bachelor's Degree from Earlham College and two Master Degrees, one in history and one in library science from University of Chicago. He married Ann Koopman from Appleton, WI on June 30, 1979. They live in Indianapolis and are the parents of two daughters, Rachel Elizabeth, born Aug. 5, 1982 and Ruth Anne born Apr. 7, 1985.

Anne has a Bachelor of Science Degree in Nursing from University of Southern Alabama and lives in Mobile, AL. On May 23, 1987 she married Victor Birch of Mobile, AL.

Kenneth Pumroy came to Crawfordsville in March, 1944 and was in the Navy V-12 program at Wabash College. He was commissioned an ensign at Notre Dame University during World War II. In 1946 he returned to Wabash College graduating in 1948 with a Bachelor of Arts Degree. He worked at R.R. Donnelley & Sons Company for 37 years.

His parents were Dorothy Fletcher, born Apr. 16, 1895 and Arthur Pumroy born Mar. 18, 1894. Dorothy Fletcher's parents were Alma Schwarm, born May 14, 1875 and Herbert Fletcher. Alma was the daughter of Victoria Roemer and Adam Schwarm. The family came from Germany in the 1830's.

Arthur Pumroy, one of 12 children, was the son of Levi Pumroy and Sarah Pumroy. The Pumroys were descendents of George Pumroy who came to the United States before the American Revolution.

Carolyn Brown Pumroy was the daughter of Grace Nichols born May 17, 1886 and William Newton Brown, born Nov. 2, 1884.

William Brown was the son of Mary Jane Hamilton and Solon Brown born Dec. 6, 1829.

Grace Nichols Brown was the daughter of Mary Jane Crane, born Oct. 7, 1844 in Wisconsin and Francis Nichols, born Nov, 6, 1829. They were married in 1869 and lived in Crawfordsville. Francis was born in Hamilton Co., OH. He was the son of Joseph and Rachel Thompson Nichols.

Francis Nichols first married Martha Mitchell born Aug. 8, 1841 and they had one daughter Ida born Feb. 6, 1859. She was married to John Selby of Alamo.

Mary Jane and Francis Nichols had four children: John Roy, Harry, Everett and Grace.

Mary Jane Crane and her family came from Wisconsin in the 1850's and settled in Montgomery County. Her father was Elihu Crane who was a Baptist preacher, traveling many miles each week by horse-back to preach. Her mother was Ellen Hate Crane and she was a mid-wife in a rural community in Wisconsin. *Submitted by Carolyn Pumroy*

FRANCIS SWAIM AND TACY (JOHNSON) QUIGG

Rev. Francis Quigg was killed in a runaway near Gravelly Run, Aug. 19, 1903 leaving wife, Tacy, and ten children, ages one month to 18 years old.

Francis was born Nov. 26, 1848 near Richmond, IN to Joseph and Lydia (Swaim) Quigg. One of ten children, he came of noble ancestry, Scotch-Irish descendants, County Terry, Ireland.

He came to Darlington area in 1880, farmer and pastor of Darlington, Flat Creek, Gravelly Run Friend's churches. He married Tacy Johnson (July 30, 1850 to Dec. 31, 1935), daughter of Joseph and Jemima (Cox) Johnson on Mar. 15, 1882.

They lived at Johnson farm, 58 acres, next to Gravelly Run Church. They both had common school educations but he excelled in agriculture and horticulture.

Francis Swaim Quigg; Tacy Johnson Quigg

Claude Edward (Apr. 20, 1883 to Feb. 25, 1970) farmer, married Nina Fern Martin, teacher at Breaks School until her marriage. They managed a dairy farm at Smartsburg, and delivered to Crawfordsville daily.

Clifford Albert (Oct. 10, 1885 to May 10, 1975), farmer, and State Farm Insurance Agent, Hobby - Quigg Family History, married Edith Maye LaFollette, daughter Mildred Maye.

Mable Lydia (Feb. 23, 1888 to May 26, 1971) taught at Highview School, where all the Quigg children attended, after she completed eighth grade. She graduated from Earlham College, taught at Darlington and Linden and was one of the first teachers in the state to teach sub-normal Junior High School classes at Shelbyville, IN, later special education students. She was active in Friend's Church quarterly and annual meetings at Sugar Plain, Farmers Institute and Plainfield. She was sent to England in 1915 as a delegate.

Josie Martha (Oct. 11, 1890 to Apr. 22, 1978) married Roy Sorrels, lived at Smartsburg and Crawfordsville. Roy was a livestock truck driver. Son, Dwight, daughter, Bessie.

Rena Ethel (Feb. 25, 1893 to Mar. 18, 1975) lived at home with her Mother, most helpful in keeping the homeplace comfortable for all the family, through the years of her life. She most enjoyed raising and selling fryers and fresh eggs.

Halfred Lewis (Aug. 24, 1895 to Mar. 19, 1973), farmer and swine breeder, served in WWI, married Emma Faye Conrad, elementary teacher at Highview School. He attended Valparaiso and Indiana State College. Children: Wilma Gene, Wilberta, Winona and Francis. Farmed at Darlington, Smartsburg, New Richmond and managed Biddle Stock Farm at Sheridan, IN until his death.

Morris Charles (Feb. 11, 1898 to Nov. 30, 1966), farmer, R.R. Donnelley and County Highway. Married Vera Alice Grimes, after her death, married Ethel Busenbark, New Market High School teacher, now retired.

Curtis Merle (Oct. 22, 1900 to Sept. 27, 1973), farmer and R.R. Donnelley, married Dorothy Faye Crisp, children: Lucille, Lois, Judith, Dorothy and Lyle Wayne.

Bertha Rachel (Mar. 16, 1902 to Jan. 20, 1981) married Orion Oka Hymer, farmer and Wilson Bros. Florists. Children: Wesley Max, Donald and Doris Sue.

Karl Francis (July 18, 1903 to Nov. 14, 1918) was the youngest child and died when he was 15 years old.

Francis and Tacy's legacy was thankfulness through silent prayer, love for each other and many also live that this great universe may be better, having lived in it. *Submitted by Wilberta Olin*

FRANK AND WILLIAM QUISENBERRY FAMILIES

Frank Quisenberry came to Montgomery County from Mount Sterling, KY, in the early 1900's, where he was born in 1888. His first wife was Bessie Payne. Their son, William, was born in 1909 a few miles northeast of Waynetown, IN. Frank's second wife was Edna Cain of Darlington. They were married 51 years, until his death in 1975. They owned several small farms in this county and were engaged in the restaurant business until the late 1960's. Many years ago he owned the Eaglet Cafe on Green Street, and one in the old Ramsey Hotel. For several years they were co-owners of the B&Q Cafe at Market and Green Streets. He was affectionately known as "Quiz". A brother, Thomas Quisenberry, and a sister, Lula Williams, also came to Montgomery County. Mrs. Williams's daughter, Mrs. Paul Canine, still lives here. Edna passed on in 1985 at age 94.

William Quisenberry was married to Mary F. McNutt in Boone County in 1934. They moved to Montgomery County in 1943. Five children were born to them, all of whom were residents of this county until reaching adulthood. The four older children graduated from Alamo High School. Sons James and Morris served two years in U.S. Army, including one year in Vietnam with the Military Advisory Group just prior to the war outbreak.

James received his B.A. degree from Indiana State University, Terre Haute, and M.A. and Ph.D. degrees from Indiana University at Bloomington. At present he is Director of International Students Programs at Southern Illinois University at Carbondale. His wife, Nancy (Forbes), is the Dean of Academic Affairs there. They have a son, James.

Morris is Command Sergeant Major with Indiana National Guard, Indianapolis. He and his wife, Nancy (Kelly), have two children, Debra and Morris W.

Joy (Mrs. Jerry) Bayless, the eldest daughter, and her husband live near Crawfordsville and are employed at Donnelley Printing Company. They have three children, Gregory, Brenda, and Brian, and two grandchildren.

The second daughter, Nancy (Mrs. Kenneth) Moore, and her husband own and operate a large farm in western Montgomery County. They are the parents of three children, Michael, Gale (Carver), and Gary, and two grandchildren.

Third daughter, Janet (Mrs. Homer) Watts, who graduated from Crawfordsville High School, is a district manager for Avon Cosmetics near Cicero, IN. Her husband is a pharmacist. They have three daughters, Christina Branham, Dawn and Dana Watts.

William passed on in June, 1987. Since 1943 he and his wife have owned four farms in this county. They were married 53 years. Besides five years employment at Allison Division of General Motors, Speedway, he worked at the Crawfordsville Post Office 26 years, retiring in 1972. Mary lives near Crawfordsville.

RUBY E. HERRON RALSTON

Earl "Shorty" Herron was born in Montgomery

Co., IN on Leap Year Day, 1904, the son of William Shadrick "Shade" Herrin and Margaret "Maggie" Thompson Herrin. The name was often misspelled "Herron" in records so Shade eventually accepted that spelling. His widow, Maggie, reverted to the original spelling, "Herrin", after his death in 1922.

Shorty's ancestry was Scotch-Irish, German and English, his ancestors living in the Carolinas and later near Quail, Crab Orchard and Bee Lick, KY. His parents came to Montgomery Co., IN, between 1894 and 1898 with his maternal grandparents, James K. and Emily Cable Thompson. They crossed the Ohio River on flatboats and traveled overland in wagons. The families settled northwest of Crawfordsville and near Waynetown.

Shorty worked at Donnelley's in Crawfordsville for over 40 years and also farmed in the Liberty Chapel neighborhood. He loved sports and for many years was a member of the Donnelley bowling team. He also coached the Donnelley women's basketball team.

Donna Rae (Barker), Robert Matthew Ralston, Ruby E. (Herron) Ralston

In 1928 he married Cora Coon of Wingate, the only daughter of William Stephens Coon and Mary Catharine Koon Coon. Cora graduated from Madame Blaker's College, now a part of Butler University, and taught grade school at Wingate and New Richmond prior to her marriage. She was active in Ladies Aid, Home Economics, DAR and Farm Bureau. As Social and Education Leader of the latter, she wrote a column for their newspaper. She was a 50-year member of Waynetown Chapter of the Order of Eastern Star.

Her great-great-grandfather, John Koon I, emigrated from Holland to the United States in about 1738 at age 16. John's grandson, John III, remembered his grandfather's telling him he stood guard at the Battle of Yorktown in the Revolutionary War. John Koon I was then nearly 60 years old.

Her great-great-great grandfather Thomas Selby also served in the Revolutionary War.

Shorty and Cora had seven children: Ruby, of whom more later; Mary, married Norman Abston and lives at Willard, OH; Helen, married Robert Rutledge and lives at Mellott, IN; William, married Margie Ingram and lives near Greenfield, IN; Charles, married JoAnn Ingalsbe and lives at Waynetown, IN; Jack, married first Edith Ingalsbe, then Carol Edwards and lives northwest of Crawfordsville, IN; Ruth Jane, married Kenneth Whipple and lives in Logansport, IN.

Ruby Eileen Herron Ralston, the oldest child, graduated from Home Hospital School of Nursing, Lafayette, IN. She has worked as surgical and obstetrics nurse at Culver Hospital in Crawfordsville, Coleman Hospital in Indianapolis, Good Samaritan Hospital, Portland, OR; has had positions as office nurse in physicians' offices and presently is employed at Ben Hur Nursing Home in Crawfordsville. She enjoys genealogy, tracing her family history, and others. She has one son, Robert Matthew Ralston, chief technician with Cardinal Communications at Peru, IN. He and his wife, Donna, daughter of Ralph and Helen Barker of Crawfordsville, IN, have three children: Amanda Marie, born Sept. 20, 1982; Jamey Eileen, born Mar. 10, 1986; and Nathan Francis Crawford, born June 17, 1988.

JOSEPH RANDEL

Joseph Randel was born May 29, 1765, a native of Union Co., SC, the son of Joseph and Ann Randel. He came to Scott Township, Montgomery County in 1829 and settled on Haw Creek Road on land entered by his nephew William Randel, son of Joseph's brother Thomas Randel of Putnam County. The trail to this county was a long one from South Carolina through Georgia to Barren Co., KY, then to Allen Co., KY, to Scott Township. Joseph was married four times. We do not have the names of his first and third wives. His second wife was Rebecca Roberts whom he married in Union Co., SC and was the mother of his son Asa. His last wife was Cora Rebecca Colquitt, whom he married in Sumner Co., TN. A son Asa Randel was born in Georgia in 1799. He first married Margaret Sulton (Sutton) in Allen Co., KY. He came and they lived North East of Ladoga. After the death of Margaret in 1839, Asa married Sarah Daniels. Asa died in 1870 and he and Margaret are buried in the Inlow Cemetery. William Randel was the son of Asa and Margaret Randel. He was born Mar. 1, 1824 in Kentucky and died Dec. 15, 1865. On Apr. 10, 1845 he was married to Miss Susan Hinkle in Montgomery Co., IN. She was born May 23, 1827 in Tennessee and died in this county on Nov. 3, 1865. The death of William and Susan Hinkle Randel left seven minor children, Andrew V., Sarah J., Mary, John, George, Clara, and James Goodwin Randel, for which Mr. O.B. Wilson was appointed guardian. Andrew V. Randel married Emmaline M. Linn and had Mary Ellen, David Franklin, Myrtie and William Noah Randel who was born 1870 and died 1948. He married Lillian Gertrude Markey on Nov. 21, 1893. She died 1902, and he married Ida Logan on July 14, 1902. She died Apr. 27, 1968. He and his first wife had Bertha 1897-1913; Florence; Ralph and Ida who died in 1902. His second wife had Geneva, died in 1970; Nellie Rose; and Kenneth.

Sarah J. Randel married James Starks. After her death married her sister, Mary Ellen Randel Routh. James and Sarah Starks had Ida, Frank, Letha, Laura Dean, Mertie, Charlotte, and Molly. James and Mary had Goldie, Lela, Lee and Clytie.

John Randel married Lou McDaniel. Clara Randel married Henry McDaniel, brother of Lou McDaniel and had Thomas.

James Goodwin Randel born in Ladoga in June 4, 1858 and married Sarah Magdaline Wingert. They had two sons; Ernest and Orval Randel. Orval Randel married Dora Linn and had two daughters, Crystal Pauline Walters and Vivian Lucille Harpel.

Asa Randel spelled his surname as given in this article, Abraham and Joseph spelled it Randall, and Edward spelled it Randle.

RANDY AND SALLY RAY

Randal Gene Ray was born Oct. 4, 1959 in Montgomery County, the son of Gene Hubert and Patricia Paddack Ray. After graduation from North Montgomery High School in 1977, he began farming with his father on the family farm near Darlington. On Aug. 1, 1981, he married Sally Jo Taylor, born Sept. 26, 1962, the daughter of Richard and Barbara House Taylor.

Sally and Randy have two children Erin Elizabeth Ray born July 18, 1983 in Montgomery Co., IN; and Lindsay Taylor Ray, born Apr. 4, 1986 in Marion Co., IN. They live on a farm south of Darlington. They attended the Congregational Christian Church where Randy serves as a trustee. Sally is a graduate of Southmont High School in 1980; and attended Purdue University in the fall of 1980. She graduated from The House of James Beauty College in 1981. She is owner and operator of The Hair Den beauty shop located in Darlington.

Sally, Randy, Lindsay and Erin Ray

Randy's paternal great grandfather, James R. Ray born 1854 in Jefferson Co., TN, the son of John and Cytha Cheser Ray married Nancy Jane Linn on Sept. 8, 1887 in Montgomery Co., IN. Nancy, born in 1862, was the daughter of Noah Cassell Linn. They had four children. Glen Everett Ray, born May 6, 1892 in Boone Co., IN and died Apr. 25, 1960 in Montgomery Co., IN. On Sept. 4, 1917 he married Lillian Cloe Duncan in Danville, IN and they lived east of Mace on the John Linn farm for 15 years. Cloe was the daughter of Benjamin F. and Olive Boyd Duncan, and died July 9, 1963. Glen and Cloe had three children: Mary Frances born June 1, 1920 and married Mac Dismore. Three children were born to them: Sandy died in infancy; Marsha married Jerry Markey; and Marla Sue. They all live in Texas.

Robert Glen Ray born Aug. 21, 1922, married Thelma Dean Paddack, and have one son, William, born Nov. 20, 1952. William married Peggy Lynn Rice on Dec. 28, 1974 and have daughters: Kelly born Nov. 11, 1977 and Stephanie born Jan. 20, 1980.

Gene Hubert Ray born May 27, 1931 in Montgomery Co., IN and married Patricia May Paddack born Dec. 23, 1932, daughter of Harley and Nellie Flaningam Paddack, on Mar. 16, 1952. Gene and Patricia have three children: Kathy Jo born Apr. 21, 1954 and married Bradley Alan Moore on Jan. 17, 1976. They have one son, Douglas Addington Moore, born Apr. 2, 1981. They live in Crawfordsville. Susan Diane Ray born Dec. 19, 1955 and on July 16, 1977 married Thomas Bowersock. They have two sons: Scott Thomas born Oct. 5, 1979 and Jonnathan Dale born Jan. 1, 1981. Susan and Thomas were divorced in 1988, and she married Joel McCullum on Sept. 2, 1988. They reside in Darlington.

The third child of Gene Hubert Ray is our subject, Randal Gene Ray. Randy enjoys spectator sports, bowling, golf and softball. Sally enjoys crafts, golf and bowling.

FREDERICK REDENBAUGH

Frederick Redenbaugh 1770-1864 Montgomery Co., IN, son of Henry I and Margaret Redenbaugh, Germany to Ohio, married Margaret Haney in Pennsylvania. To this union three children were born in Pennsylvania and nine others in Ohio. They came from Pennsylvania through the Shenandoah Valley to Ohio, then to Jefferson Co., IN and settled in Montgomery County in 1832 and entered land in 1834, number 18562 - book 38 p. 371, for 80 acres. According to the census Margaret was older than Frederick and they lived east of New Market, IN. He was in the War of 1812. Frederick and Margaret Redenbaugh had 12 children: Mary Redenbaugh 1793 Cumberland, PA married Jacob Brandenburg and is buried in Mt. Tabor cemetery; Elizabeth Redenbaugh married Samuel Stucker in Jefferson Co., IN (she may have been the second wife of Jeremiah Douglas); George Redenbaugh 1793 Cumberland, PA married Margaret Stucker; William Redenbaugh 1812, only child living in 1893; Henry Redenbaugh married Mary Douglas Oct. 15, 1823 Jefferson Co., IN; Sarah Redenbaugh married Benjamin Elrod; Susan Redenbaugh died 1887 age 76 married John Ellis on July 1852 here; Samuel 1810 died 1867 in Kansas married Elizabeth Ann Winter here July 25, 1851 and divorced in 1875; Frederick Redenbaugh, Jr. died 1876 married Margaret Boyer and second married Jemima Largent July 20, 1835 Montgomery Co., IN. He married twice more; Thomas Redenbaugh married Nancy Britton Feb. 8, 1836 here. He died Dec. 18, 1878 in Kansas, and Nancy died in St. Joseph, MO on the way to Kansas; Hulda Redenbaugh married William Bailey 1827. He died and she went to Iowa; Mary Catherine Redenbaugh born 1850 died 1876 here married Jeremiah Douglas Mar. 31, 1825 in Jefferson Co., IN. See Douglas family. *By Pauline Walters*

JOHN F. REED FAMILY

In 1764 John F. Reed of Rockbridge Co., VA arrived in Montgomery County, with his wife Levenia Hanger, and four young children, settling in Walnut Twp. near the town of Mace. Although they stayed only a short time in Montgomery County before moving on just across the County line, to Jefferson Twp. in Boone County, many of their children returned to spend their adult lives in Montgomery County.

A daughter Mary Reed, married Oliver Bowman of New Ross, settled near there, raised their family in the New Ross area, and are both buried in Pisgah Cemetery. Daughter Willie B. Reed, married Jesse F. Evans of New Ross, raised their family there, and are both buried in the Union Hill Cemetery, near Mace. Daughter Margaret, died at the age of 18, and was returned to Union Hill Cemetery, Walnut Twp. Montgomery County.

Andrew Baxter Reed the eldest son of John F. Reed, purchased a farm near the family homestead, and remained there his life time, with only a great grandson, Oliver "Sonny" Reed almost becoming a Montgomery County citizen, his home being only a stones throw from the eastern county line, and owning another farm in Walnut Twp., near New Ross.

David Whistel Reed the younger son of John F. Reed, never returned to Montgomery County, his home was next to his father's, in Jefferson Twp. Boone County, however at one time he did own land in Walnut Twp., Montgomery County. Dave's son John Clifford married Lena Marie Slater, their children were Rosemary Reed Carr, and David W. Reed who married Audry Jane Burden, and with them started the return to Montgomery County.

David and Audry had two children, Terrie Dee (Prage) Reed, and John David Reed, husband to Donna Walters. John and Donna married in Ladoga, Montgomery County, and settled in Crawfordsville, having three children, Johan Michelle, Julianne Marie, and Michael David Reed; the last of the John F. Reed Line, and establishing the return to Montgomery County of the Reeds.

JOHN REMLEY

John Remley was born May 21, 1800, near Lebanon, OH. His father, Christian Remley, died when John was 11 years old. His mother, Elizabeth Heck Remley, married Aaron Booram, a short time afterward. This forced John to seek his own way of life. One day as he stood in front of the Golden Lamb Inn in Lebanon he watched a fancy carriage drive away. He looked down and found a green silk bag that held a beautiful purse that contained several gold coins. With these coins he purchased an apprenticeship at a tannery. After learning the trade he walked to Indiana, purchased 80 acres along Sugar Creek west of Crawfordsville, walked back to Ohio and married Sarah McCain at Hamilton. Soon, John returned to his cabin home taking what few things they owned on a flat boat down the Miami and Ohio to the mouth of the Wabash and up to Terre Haute. From there he walked to his new home. Meanwhile his bride, Sarah, came through on horseback accompanied by her uncle and three cousins who walked. Sarah brought eight little peach trees on the horn of her saddle, the first peach trees in Montgomery County.

John built a tannery along Sugar Creek. He and Sarah became the parents of 11 children. Their cabin soon was too small and a new brick house was built, which still stands on the Country Club road.

Their children were:

1. Infant - Oct. 10, 1825 - Oct. 12, 1825. 2. Elizabeth Ann - Nov. 23, 1826 - Feb. 1, 1907. 3. James Christopher - Oct. 9, 1828 - Aug. 15, 1911 m. Mary C. (Byrd). 4. Theodore - Sept. 3, 1830 - Aug. 2, 1831. 5. Ruhannan - Feb. 19, 1832 - July 13, 1862. 6. John McCain Dec. 15, 1833 - Nov. 30, 1904 m. Margaret Gillard. 7. Ambrose - Sept. 25, 1836 - Jan. 18, 1917 m. Minerva Evans Shelby. 8. Malinda - Dec. 28, 1838 - July 29, 1840. 9. Daniel - July 8, 1841 - Feb. 8, 1914 m. Angeline F. Stout. 10. William Frances - Mar. 19, 1843 - Aug. 24, 1905 m. Susan Stout. 11. David Henry - Dec. 21, 1844 - Feb. 7, 1920 m. Elizabeth Busenbark.

Ambrose Remley served three years in the Civil War in the 72nd Regiment in Wilder's Brigade. He served in the mounted infantry and was among those who first used the Spencer repeating rifle. In 1844 he married Minerva Shelby, daughter of Isaac Shelby and Jane Boggs of Shelby Grove in Tippecanoe County. They established their home on road 136 near Wesley Church. Their children were:

1. Isaac Frances - 1868-1869. 2. Fred Shelby - Jan. 10, 1871-Apr. 17, 1953 m. Nellie Adna Brown. 3. Harry C. - June 14, 1873-Oct. 25, 1952 m. Alice L. Brown - June 9, 1878-Oct. 31, 1941. 4. Sarah Jane - Aug. 11, 1878-Sept. 5, 1961 m. Shirl Herr, Apr. 1, 1873-July 1, 1936.

Harry C. and Alice Brown were married Feb. 22, 1899. They lived on his father's section of land at Hoopeston, IL for three years, then returned to Indiana and moved to a farm south of Wesley Church. Their daughter, Mary Helen, was born Mar. 11, 1908.

Mary Helen was educated in the Waynetown Schools and graduated from Cincinnati Conservatory of Music. She received her master's degree from Indiana State University. She was married to David W. Loveless June 6, 1936. Mary Helen taught Music and Art in the Wingate and Waynetown Schools for 42 years. She served as High School Sunshine Sponsor for many years and as State Chairman for two years. She is a charter member of Iota Chapter of Psi Iota Xi, member of Delta Kappa Gamma, Phi Sigma Mu, Dorothy Q Chapter DAR, Daughters of American Colonists, County Historical Society, County Council on Aging, Retired Teachers, Wabash Ave. Presbyterian Church, where she is a member of the choir and chairman of the afternoon circle, and helps with Pre School. *Submitted by Mary Helen Loveless*

MARY HELEN McQUIGG REPP

Mary Helen McQuigg was born Jan. 1, 1900 in Gratiot, OH, the daughter of James William McQuigg and Martha "Matie" Eliza Henslee. Her mother and father were both natives of Ohio and were teachers.

Helen is a graduate of Zanesville, OH high school in 1918 and Ohio University in 1923. She did graduate work at Ohio State University. Her first teaching job was in a one-room, eight grade school and later she taught high school English and History.

Mary Helen McQuigg Repp

On Dec. 7, 1929 she married Edgar Leon Repp. He was born in Tiffin, OH on Sept. 14, 1890, the son of Charles Wesley Repp and Alwilda Belle Rhees natives of Ohio. Mr. Repp was a farmer and they lived on the first farm on the road going west out of Tiffin (known as Hopewell road). After grade school, Edgar attended Heidleburg Academy where he completed his high school in three years. He served overseas in W.W. I and when he returned home he attended Ohio State University graduating in 1926 with a degree in Floriculture.

In June of 1929, Edgar bought the Attica Floral Company from his brother and in December married Helen McQuigg. They settled in Attica, IN and continued to run the flower shop until Oct. 1, 1945. They sold the shop and moved to East Wabash Avenue in Crawfordsville to the house where Helen is presently living.

Edgar bought two farms, one south of Crawfordsville and one north of Crawfordsville, of which he managed. He later purchased three rental properties in Crawfordsville.

Their daughter, Martha Belle was born Nov. 6, 1932. She is a 1950 Crawfordsville High School graduate, and a 1954 graduate of Overland College. She received her masters degree in Merchandising from New York University in 1955. She married Navarre Davis and they have three sons: Bruce Navarre Davis lives in Lake Oswego, OR, and has a Masters Degree in Management from Yale University. Gregory Repp Davis has a degree in Commercial Art from the University of Oregon and lives in Eugene, OR. Marshall Lloyd Davis is a graduate of Oregon University and is living in Hollywood, CA, where he is pursuing a career in acting. Martha and Navarre were divorced in 1979.

On Jan. 3, 1986, Martha married a college classmate from Overland College, Dr. George E. Shambaugh who teaches Endcronology at Northwestern University of Medicine, LaGrange, IL. She has five lovely step-children, four boys and one girl.

Helen is a member of the Methodist Church, Retired Teachers Association, and International Travel Study Club. She is a former member of the A.A.U.W.; W.W. I Auxiliary; and the Home Economics Club.

RETTINGER AND HARRIS FAMILY

David Rettinger and Elizabeth Manges (born Oct. 14, 1824) in Botetourt Co., VA were married on Oct. 24, 1886 in Fincastle, VA and divorced in Virginia. David died soon after the divorce, and Elizabeth came to Whitesville, IN with her children in 1867. Their children were Mary Melissa, George Calvin, David Pierce, Laura Hanks, Jeanette Florence, who married Isaac Childers at Whitesville June 20, 1886; and Keturah Dove Rettinger. Elizabeth Rettinger was a seamstress or a tailor. Her son David Pierce was a Universalist Church Minister. Elizabeth's sister, Catherine Manges married Elijah Ramsay Harris, and had ten children. Cora Belle Harris married Dexter Thomas son of John Lewis and Amanda Doty Thomas, and they had two children. They are Edna Belle Thomas who married Charles Terry and had one daughter, Mildred who died in 1930. Edna Belle Thomas Terry is still living in 1988 and is 102 years of age, but is in a nursing home. George Everett Thomas, Edna's brother, died several years ago, he married Geneva Chambers. Dexter Thomas married his second wife, Theodosia Harris (Docia), who was the sister of Cora Belle Harris. Dexter Thomas lived south of Whitesville.

Elizabeth and Catherine's sister, Rebecca Jane Manges married Thomas Everson.

REYNOLDS FAMILY

William Reynolds, Sr., born Boone Co., KY 1796. Married Mary Miller of Frankfort, KY. Migrated to Indiana 1830. Built grist mill and home northwest of Freedom Church in Brown Township. He fathered eight children: Andrew, Jesse, Napoleon Bonaparte, William Jr., Hannah, Elizabeth, Katherine, and Eliza.

Andrew, born 1824, settled near Old Union Church and had four children. Son Lewis and family settled in Browns Valley.

Jesse worked at Deer's Mill; lived south of mill with wife, Ann Elizabeth Cook.

Napoleon worked at Lusk Mill, was a carpenter and helped build Freedom Church. He married Malinda Crisler, 1849, and settled east of Devil's Backbone. They had five children: Susan Elizabeth, died age ten; Mary Jane 1853-1909; John William 1859-1945; George Wesley 1861-1885; and David Allen 1865-1932.

George Wesley made a pen and ink drawing of Deer's Mill as it was in 1883. George Reynolds of Wayne Lakes, OH has the original.

Reynolds Family Photo: Back L-R: Elva, John, Dorinda, Bertha. Front L-R: George, Bessie, Jess

David Allen whittled out a complete train. The Engine is in a Chicago Museum.

John William in 1895 married Dorinda Sprague, 1874-1956, from Kentucky and lived in Yountsville, IN; was employed as steam engineer at Yount Woolen Mill in 1890. He received serious burns to eyes by steam explosion. The family then moved in with his folks while he recovered.

He moved his family to Browns Valley in 1902. (House was formerly a schoolhouse). Bessie Mae, born in Yountsville 1896-1986; six born in Browns Valley: Clara 1899-1919; Elva 1903-1943; Charles 1907-1909; Bertha 1910; George 1913; and Jesse 1916.

Four are deceased: Bessie, Clara, Elva, and Charles.

He was a painter, carpenter, and rented out his 80 acre farm, northwest of town. The farm purchased previous to his marriage. He cleared the land, put out an orchard, truck patch, and built a barn. Cut all wood used for heating and cooking in home. He sold apples from his orchard, and fruit trees for Stark Bros. Co. He was Director of Browns Valley Bank for years.

Bessie married Lawrence Armstrong, 1914, lived near New Market. Had five children: Virginia Hitch, Homemaker; Maurine Dillman, Owner Dillman's Hdwe.; Royce, Army Service Band, Music Teacher; Forest Lee and Kent, deceased. There are seven grandchildren, three great grandchildren.

Elva married Harley James, worked at Donnelleys in Crawfordsville. Died, 1943 from burns received when age three.

Bertha, worked at Donnelleys until marriage to Ralph Friend, 1940. Resides in Anderson, IN. They have three children: James, Data Processing Mgr.; Joyce Tunnell, Nurse; Sylvia Masters, Dayco employee. There are ten grandchildren, four great grandchildren, one deceased.

George married Mary Whitecotton, 1933; was Linotype Operator at Donnelleys, moved to Dayton, OH 1943. Retired to Wayne Lakes, OH 1976. They have one daughter, Marilyn Sue Liebherr, Professional Artist. There are two grandsons, two great grandsons.

Jesse married Arleen Stanford, Savannah, GA 1945. In W.W. II 1941-1945. Truck driver, retired Millersport, OH 1975. Had three sons: Daryl, CPA; Dennis, Carpenter; both in Vietnam Service; Dale stillborn. There are six grandchildren and one deceased. *Compiled by George Reynolds*

REYNOLDS AND MILES OF WAVELAND

Pearl Dean Reynolds, born 1890 in Waveland, is the daughter of Lewis Washington Reynolds and Mary Luenza Wright. Mary Wright, born 1859 in Lyons, Clinton Co., IA, is the daughter of James Crawford Wright and Caroline Mullen. Caroline Mullen was born in 1834 in Ohio. James Wright, born 1837 in Putnam Co., IN, is the son of Dennis Wright and Lourvanza Crawford. Dennis Wright is from Shelby Co., KY.

Lewis Washington Reynolds and Mary Luenza Wright Reynolds

Lewis Reynolds, born 1856 in Brown Twp., Montgomery Co., IN, is the son of Andrew J. Reynolds and Ellis Miles. Andrew Reynolds, born 1824 in Kentucky, is the son of William Reynolds and Mary Miller. William Reynolds was born in 1796 near Frankfort, KY and is buried in Old Union Cemetery near Waveland.

Ellis Miles, born 1826 in Kentucky, is the daughter of George W. Miles and Paulina Thorne. Paulina was born in 1811 in Kentucky. George Miles, born 1807 in Henry Co., KY, is the son of John F. Miles and Mary Duvall. George died in 1897 and is buried in Old Union Cemetery. Mary Duvall was born in 1766 in Culpepper Co., VA.

John Miles enlisted in Culpepper Co., VA, in 1777 and served as private in Capt. John Gillis' Company of Col. Edward Stephens' Regt. He was in the battle of Monmouth, the storming of Stormy Point, and was discharged in 1781 receiving a pension in 1818 Henry Co., KY. He died in 1828 in Henry Co., KY, and his widow moved to Montgomery Co., IN, received a pension in 1839 here, and lived here until 1851.

John Miles, born 1766 in Culpepper Co., VA, is the son of Charles and Elizabeth Miles. Charles Miles was born in 1727 and Elizabeth was born in 1730, both in Culpepper Co., VA. Charles Miles taught school.

CHARLIE O. AND OLIVE REYNOLDS

Charlie and Olive Reynolds moved to a farm a mile north of Waveland in 1942. The large, brick house on the farm burned shortly thereafter and the family moved into a long tool shed which Charlie made into the family home. Charlie used to say that he was the first in the county with a tri-level house. The tall, red barn, on the farm, was hit by a tornado and the top was lifted off. The rebuilding of the barn increased the width and the Reynolds' farm could be spotted for miles because of the barn.

Charlie Otto Reynolds was the fourth child of eight children born to Branch Long Reynolds and Flora Lucretia Bledsoe from Dubois County. Family roots can be traced back to Hawkins Co., TN. Charlie was born on Aug. 18, 1906 in Dubois County and passed away on Jan. 22, 1984 on the farm at Waveland.

Ida Olive Self married Charlie O. Reynolds on Aug. 16, 1929. Olive was the fifth child of ten children born to George Franklin Self and Cynthia Ellen Wininger from Martin Co., IN. (Although different counties are mentioned, these people were in one area. This area is where Orange, Dubois and Martin Counties all come together. French Lick was the major city at that time). The Self and Wininger families can also be traced back to Hawkins Co., TN. The Civil War seems to have been the cause for many of these families moving north. Ida Olive Self was born on Feb. 16, 1907 in Orange County and she passed away in September of 1988 in a nursing home in Ladoga.

Charlie and Olive Reynolds 50th Anniversary

There were nine children born to Charlie and Olive. They are as follows: Charlotte Faye Cope, Vera Lee, Violet Flo Newell, Bonnie Darlene Miller, Charlie Otto, Ottis, John Adrain, Carol Ann Kaufman, and Darrell Joseph. Although the family has become dispersed, the grandchildren grew up in the area. Faye's children are: Yvonna Dean McGhee, Merrilee Jane Wagner, and Rendy Souter. Vicki's children are: Eddie Joe, Judy Lynn Taylor, Sherry Lee Haun, and Peggy Kay Miller. Bonnie's children are: Brian David, Mark Allen, Rebecca Darlene, and Diane Beth. Otto's children are: Tommy Otto, Timmy Lee, Tony Dale, and Tammy Gail Sward. Ottis' children are: Michael Ottis, and Deborah Jean Estep. John's children are: Cynthia Rene Froedge, Jack Andrew, Joy Lynn Morgan, and Jennifer Sue. Joe's children are: Eddie Joe Barrak, and Josepha Carol Ann.

For many years the family attended the Freedom Baptist Church. Many of the neighbors (such as, Wiatts, Cookseys, and the Hess family) also attended this country church.

Since the death of Charlie Reynolds, his son, John and grandson, Jack, have continued to farm the land. At present, Jack still lives on the farm with his wife, Mary Lou James (also from Waveland) and their two little girls, Candy and Shandra. *Submitted by Carol (Reynolds) Kaufman*

JOHN HENRY REYNOLDS

John Henry Reynolds was the first of this line of Reynolds to come to Montgomery Co., IN coming here from Jefferson Co., NY, where he was born around 1832. He was the son of James A. Reynolds of Ellisburg, NY. His mother is unknown at this time, but there were several children.

His father was a lumberman by trade owning a lumber mill in Jefferson County and he followed in his father's footsteps all his life, working in lumber mills as well as doing carpentry work, as his military record bears out.

He enrolled as a first Sgt. of Co. H 59th Regiment of Indiana Volunteers at Chicago, on Feb. 2, 1862; he was mustered into the military on April 26th for a term of three years. He was promoted to the rank of 2nd Lt., commanding Co. G. since Jan. 8, 1865, (promoted Sept. 18, 1864) and discharged at Washington, D.C., May 31, 1865.

On Feb. 15, 1864, probably while on leave from the Army, he married Susan Goble, born 1847, the daughter of Daniel and Elizabeth Goble. She died around 1884, burial site not known. She was the fifth child of six, born to them. They were born around 1810 and 1812, respectively. Her brothers and sisters were: Martin born around 1838, Hiram, born 1840, Ellen, born 1843, Ann, born 1844 and David born 1850. According to information, they are supposedly all born in Indiana.

John Henry and Susan were the parents of six children: Elizabeth Reynolds was born around 1866 in Montgomery County. On June 10, 1886 she was united in marriage with Edwin Delaney. There were several children. She passed away June 6, 1895 and he later married Ella Servies. Edwin Reynolds, born Aug. 9, 1868 married Lura Bellus. As far as is known, he died in Tell City, IN, but there is no proof of this. Charles E., born May 18, 1870 and on May 17, 1894 married Molly Wilkinson. They later moved to Tennessee where he became a Guard at the Tennessee Prison. Ellen, born 1873 died young. Albert (Shanty), born Feb. 6, 1877, married Laura Emily Harris on Feb. 18, 1899. He passed away May 23, 1959 and is buried in Oak Hill Cemetery with his wife, a daughter and his father on the same lot. John Henry, Jr., was born Aug. 24, 1880 in Montgomery County and married Rosa W. Dowdy who was born Feb. 28, 1882 at Saalsbury, TN. He passed away Feb. 21, 1964 and she in 1961. Both are buried in Slayden, MS. He also lived in Tennessee.

John Henry passed away Sept. 27, 1904.

CHARLES AND BERTHA (LINN) RHOADS

William Rhoads Sr. married Ann Moffitt and had eight children, William Jr. being the first son and fifth child.

William Rhoads Jr. born 1787 died 1860 and his wife Amy (Brewer) had 11 children: John born 1814, William born 1815, Thomas born 1817, James born 1818, Amos born 1820, Naomi born 1821, Jerod born 1823, Margaret (Peggy) born 1825, Jacob born 1827, William Eleander born 1830 and Cyrus born 1834.

William and Amy and family took up residence in Union Township, Montgomery Co., IN in the late 1840's.

Jacob (pictured above) ninth child of William Jr. and Amy Rhoads married Martha Louise Cox in 1850. She was the daughter of William S. and Rachel Cox.

Jacob Rhoads

They had ten children: Rachel Marticia born 1851, married Rufus Nabors, second marriage was to Alvin Vail, Mary Jane born 1852 married Noah Vail, Amy Elizabeth born 1854 married Joe E. Wheeler, Naomi Armilda born 1856 married Josiah Dickson, William Jefferson born 1857 married Florence Idel Beck, Louise Angeline born 1859 died 1860, Thomas Christopher born 1860 married Olive Weesner, Jacob Dosson (Dorsey) born 1863 married Lydia Alice Elkins, Albert Hillary born 1867 married Carrie B. Grimes, Cyrus Willard born September 1870 died November 1870.

A month after the birth of Cyrus, mother Martha died. By the end of the next year Jacob took his second wife Catherine (Goble-Cox) in 1871. She was the widow of James Madison Cox (brother of Martha Louise). James died in 1866 and Catherine was the daughter of Daniel and Matilda Goble.

Jacob and Catherine had one child Charles Wesley born 1876 and he married Bertha Linn, born 1875.

Charles and Bertha married 1901, and four children, Lloyd born August of 1902, infant born and died April 1903, Forest Leona born 1904 married Herman Dicks, they had no children. Russell Leroy born 1907 married Edna Henderson in 1930, and they had no children.

Bertha died in 1940; Charles in 1960; Forest in 1963; Russell in 1970 and Edna in 1988.

Charles married the second time to Julis Ross and she died in 1963.

Russell was a familiar face as he worked in downtown Crawfordsville for many years as did his cousin Lester Powell and the Linn brother cousins.

Edna worked at Allisons and they moved to Speedway, IN for some years then returned to Mace to live their retired years.

No children were born to the children of Bertha and Charley Rhoads; so this leaves no descendents of the Jacob and Catherine (Goble-Cox) Rhoads Line.

JACOB RHOADS

Jacob Rhoads entered Montgomery County in the late 1840's, along with other family members. Engaged in farming in Union Township, he became the progenitor of several generations of Rhoads residents in this area.

Jacob was the seventh son of William, Jr., and Amy (Brewer) Rhoads who migrated from North Carolina, into Ross Co., OH, into Wayne-Randolph Cos., IN, thence to Montgomery County. Jacob and his siblings, numbering 11, all born 1814-1834, Randolph County, were: John, William, Thomas, James, Amos, Naomi, Jared, Peggy, Jacob, William E., and Cyrus.

Two sons of William took brides from Montgomery County: Cyrus, the youngest, married Elizabeth Margaret Vance in 1853, in Montgomery County. The newlyweds, households of other siblings, and the elders made the trek by ox team to Iowa where they homesteaded. Cyrus and Margaret were parents of 12 children whose descendants are today living in Washington and Oregon, as well as the Hawkeye State.

Jacob, our subject, born 1827, died 1890, married first, 1850, in Montgomery County, Martha Louise Cox, daughter of William S. Cox and his wife Rachel — both natives of North Carolina. Children born to them were: Rachel Marticia, Mary Jane, Amy Elizabeth, Naomi Armilda, William Jefferson, Louisa Angeline, Thomas Christopher, Jacob Dosson, Albert Hillary, and Cyrus William.

After the death of his first wife, Jacob married second Mrs. Catherine (Goble) Cox, to whom was born one son, Charles Wesley Rhoads.

Father of this writer was Thomas Christopher Rhoads, born 1860 and grew up in the Kingsley

Chapel neighborhood. He married Olive Weesner, born 1871, daughter of Mahlon and Rachel (Coat) Weesner. The couple reared a family of five while living on the Weesner—Coat family farm adjoining Darlington on the south limits.

General farming, raising chickens, and producing dairy products were means of livelihood. A sound education and habits of industry were foremost goals pursued and achieved by their children. Past their home ran a stretch of concrete pavement later known as Old Indiana 47.

Christopher died 1925; Olive, 1958. Both are buried in Greenlawn Cemetery. They were the parents of Vivian and Carleton—deceased. Three daughters survive: Ramona (Rhoads) Ainsworth, a secondary school teacher living at Darlington, now retired from a long career. She has one daughter, Julia A. Mitchell, also a teacher, living in Pennsylvania, and two grandchildren—Timothy Warren Mitchell and Linda S. (Mitchell) McCain, and two great-grandchildren.

Christine Rhodes, former teacher, married, in 1934, Faye Lavon Parks (Kelly)—both now retired from diversified ranching near Clovis, CA. Of their two sons, Phillip Wayne is deceased. Robert Eugene, a graduate of California State University at Fresno, married 1977, Diana Darlene Kay.

Geneva (Rhoads) Fugate, R.N. from the Indiana University School of Nursing, retired from a long career to Darlington residence.

Of seven generations mentioned, four generations have held residence in Montgomery County. *Submitted by Mrs. Ramona (Rhoads) Ainsworth*

WILLIAM JEFFERSON AND FLORENCE IDELL (BECK) RHOADS

The Rhoads arrived in America from Europe and British Isle in the early 1600's.

Our family Bible records begin with William Rhoads Jr. born 1787, the first son of William Sr. and Anne (Moffett) Rhoads in North Carolina. William Jr. married Amy Brewer in 1812 at Ross Co., OH and migrated to Randolph Co., IN. They took up residence in Union Township, Montgomery Co., IN in the late 1840's.

Back Row: Fred, Grace (Rhoads) Corn, Floyd. Middle Row: Murle, William, Flora, Glenn. Front Row: Lester and Karl Rhoads.

Jacob Rhoads, ninth child of Amy and William, married Martha Louise (Cox) in 1850. They had ten children and by second marriage to Martha's sister-in-law Rachel Cox one child.

William Jefferson, fifth child of Jacob and Martha married Florence Idell Beck in 1884. Their children were (above picture) Murle, Harry (died in infancy), Glenn, Fred, Floyd, Lester, Karl and daughter Grace Rhoads Corn.

Will and Flora farmed in the Tiger Valley, Whitesville, and New Ross neighborhoods. They settled on a 100-acre farm south of New Ross. After Will's death in 1928 Karl farmed until his retirement. He also served two terms as Trustee for Clark Township.

Glenn, their third child, born Mar. 17, 1888 married Faye Wilson born May 9, 1891 daughter of Edwin Davis and Ellen (Faust) Wilson. Two of their six children (Ernest and Raymond died in infancy), Florence, William, Alberta and Rosemary are living.

After several years of farming Glenn and family moved to Crawfordsville and assumed the night-watchman job at Goodmans' Department store in 1929. In 1933 the store burned and at the time of Glenn's death in 1952 he was working for Mid States. After spending two and one-half years in Ben Hur Nursing Home, Faye died at age 95 in 1986.

Florence, born Sept. 23, 1913, married Charles E. Handy of Greencastle in 1931. A girl and boy provided them with four grand children and three great-grandchildren.

William, born Jan. 27, 1917, moved in the 1940's to Lansing, MI. He served in Germany during WW II as MP. He married Elizabeth Foster and they had three girls who have seven children. They raised four foster children and have six other grandchildren.

Alberta, born May 28, 1922, married Norman Nichols in 1946 after his return from WW II. Two girls and a boy provided five grandchildren which includes a set of twin boys. Daughter Penny Nichols Richardson teaches in the North Montgomery School System.

Rosemary, born Dec. 1, 1929 married Rex Howard in 1954 who died from a motorcycle accident May 30, 1959. Their daughter Rosalie Diane Redman lives at New Ross, IN. Rosemary's second marriage was to John R. Peterman in 1969. Rosie and John adopted a son Mark. Janice Peterman one of John's two children lives with them. Petermans have five grandchildren.

Since no male children were born to William, son of Glenn, the line of Rhoads' through Glenn's life is no more.

RICE FAMILY

Jacob Rice was one of four brothers who came from Wales to Hagerstown, MD. With his wife, Anne, Jacob came to Western Pennsylvania about 1770 and established a fort against the Indians. In 1782, when several of the men from Rice's Fort had gone to Hagerstown to exchange pelts and furs for salt, iron, and ammunition, Indians surrounded the fort. When seen, the alarm was given and every man remaining ran for his gun. The Indians commenced firing, but six brave sharpshooters held them off. The Indians called for the people to give up. They amused themselves by shooting the horses, cattle and sheep, and setting fire to an outer barn full of hay. Luckily the night was calm. Finally the Indians retreated, because just as they began to burn the fort itself, rain began falling. The Indians were convinced the "Great Spirit" was angry.

In 1777 Daniel Rice (Jacob's son) married Anna Margaret Leffler. Their son Isaac Rice was born on Christmas Day, 1795, at Rice's Fort. He went to Shelby Co., KY, in 1806. There he married Narcissa Montague Allen in 1821. Before 1828 they migrated to Montgomery Co., IN. Her parents, James and Elizabeth Logan Allen, also moved to Montgomery County (about 1830) and the family lived near Waveland.

Of the nine children born to Isaac and Narcissa, five were born after they lived near Waveland on the Rice farm. The fifth child was Thomas Newton Rice, born June 6, 1829, Montgomery County. Sometime before his death in 1904 in Rockville, he was asked to speak at the Waveland Old Settlers Meeting and presented a speech. In this he described the life of the people, the homes, the terrain, and gives us pride in our ancestor's courage. Narcissa died on the Rice Farm near Waveland in 1845. Isaac died there in 1852. Both are buried in the Waveland Cemetery.

Thomas Newton Rice married Margaret Digby of Mansfield. Her mother had brought her by ship from Belfast, Ireland, after Captain Digby was lost at sea. Thomas and Margaret Rice were the parents of Jane Isabel, born 1857 in Rockville. She married J.S. Nave, an Attica attorney, and her sister, Margaret married Charles Finney, also of Attica.

The daughter of Jane Isabel Rice and J.S. Nave, Margaret Nave Johnson, was born Jan. 10, 1882, in Attica and still resides in the family home 107 years later. A sister, Beatrice Nave Isley, is not living. Mrs. Johnson's husband, Louis Lee Johnson was a noted Attica architect. Their daughter Isabel Johnson Miller also lives in Attica. Her daughter, Winifred Miller Clark lives near Williamsport. Several other descendants live in Indiana, including five great-great-grandchildren of Margaret Nave Johnson. *Submitted by Margaret Nave Johnson and Winifred Miller Clark*

DANIEL E. RICE FAMILY

Daniel E. Rice, son of Elmer J. and Katie Tate Rice, was born July 16, 1932, and resides three miles west of New Market. At age 12, he moved to the adjacent Easley farm homestead. He graduated from New Market School in 1951. On May 2, 1952, he married Opal J. Tracy, daughter of the late Walter and Myrtle Tracy of Crawfordsville. They have three children: Dennis L., born Nov. 4, 1953; Beverly J., born Dec. 22, 1954; and Connie B., born Oct. 21, 1962.

Opal was born Jan. 10, 1933 in Crawfordsville on the day of the big Crawfordsville fire and resided near Ladoga and Waveland. Daniel and Opal reside at the Easley homestead farm. They farm in partnership with Daniel's brother, Arthur.

Dennis graduated from Southmont High School in 1972. He attended Lincoln Technical Institute in Indianapolis where he graduated in 1973. He worked at Etters Ford Garage in New Market until becoming a law enforcement officer. He served with the Indiana State Police from 1975 to 1977, then he became an officer for the Montgomery County Sheriff's Department. Appointed sheriff on Sept. 26, 1983; he was re-elected in November 1986 as Montgomery County sheriff. Married to LuAnne Symmes Douglas, they have one daughter, Rachel Ann; two sons, John and Brian, by LuAnne's previous marriage. LuAnne is an office manager for Cardinal Communications in Crawfordsville.

Beverly graduated from Southmont High School in 1973. Married to Thomas Ray Haniford. They have one daughter, Danielle Jeanette "Jenny". Two sons, Chaddley and Andrew, by Thomas's previous marriage. Thomas is a military technician for the Military Department of Indiana.

Connie graduated from Southmont High School in 1980 and Lafayette Beauty Academy in 1981. She owns and operates Scissor Wizards Styling Salon in New Market. She is married to Jeff Tolin, a welder with his father at New Market Welding. *Submitted by Daniel E. Rice*

DENNIS LEE RICE

Dennis Lee Rice was born Nov. 4, 1953. He is the son of Daniel E. Rice and Opal J. Tracy Rice. He was raised on a farm west of New Market in Brown Township. Dennis attended New Market schools and graduated in the first graduating class of Southmont High School in 1972. After high school Dennis worked for L.G. Etter & Sons in New Market and attended Lincoln Technical Institute. In May, 1975 Dennis began employment with the Indiana State Police in Porter County. During that time he attended and graduated from the Indiana Law Enforcement Academy. On Dec. 1, 1977 Dennis was appointed as a police officer with the Montgomery County Police Department. Dennis worked as patrolman and a detective and also served as the Chief Deputy to Sheriff Charles Stewart. On Aug. 6, 1983 Dennis married LuAnne Symmes Douglas. LuAnne is the daughter of Laura J. Poole Symmes and William L. Symmes of Crawfordsville. LuAnne is the office manager for Cardinal Communications, Inc., Crawfordsville. She is the mother of two sons, John A. Douglas who was born Nov. 26, 1969 and Brian J. Douglas, who was born Sept. 26, 1972. A daughter, Rachel Ann Rice was born to Dennis and LuAnne on Apr. 7, 1983. On Sept. 27, 1983 Dennis was appointed as Sheriff of Montgomery County and is currently serving in that capacity.

ELMER J. RICE FAMILY

William Rice, born July 22, 1840 to Washington and Permelia Deer Rice—was the oldest of six children. Permelia was born in Gallatin Co., KY, to Simeon Deer and Mary Clore Deer on Oct. 1, 1820 and died May 23, 1903. With her parents, she came to Montgomery Co., IN in 1831, and was married to Washington Rice Sept. 12, 1839. Washington, a gunsmith, lived near the Freedom Church and served in the Mexican War. Their other children were (2) Johnathon, father of Thomas, a Montgomery County sheriff in the 1920's, and Albert. (3) Mary E. (Polly) married Jacob Moore, (4) Simeon married Sarah Katherine Easley, (5) James and Martha. William, Johnathon and Simeon spent the most of their lives in Montgomery County as farmers. The others were residents in, and around Mellott, IN, where several of their descendents still reside.

William Rice was first married to Jane Elizabeth, daughter of James Davis who farmed along Sugar Creek, and for whom the old iron bridge on the New Market-Alamo road was named. Nelson Rice was their only surviving son. Jane Elizabeth died in 1864. William's second marriage was to Sarah Jane Davis who bore him nine children. (1) Charles became a veterinarian in Parke County. (2) Amelia married L.B. (Bert) Etter, the original owner of the Etter Ford Agency now owned by two grandsons, John and Bill Etter. (3) Myrtle, (4) William, (5) Stella, (6) Martha, all unmarried; and (7) Otis, (8) Hubert and (9) Nannie. William owned a farm about six miles west of New Market. He was a devout member of the Freedom Baptist Church where he was known for his beautiful singing. He and Sarah Jane retired to New Market where he passed away. Sarah Jane died about 1930. Bill and Stella were good singers, and Myrtle was a piano teacher in New Market.

Nelson married Frances Easly on Dec. 25, 1884. They were farmers owning 100 acres four miles west of New Market. He enjoyed his farming and raised a special breed of chickens called Black Langshangs which he entered in various poultry shows. He prized the silver loving cups he earned. Nelson, also, constructed on the farm, ponds in which he raised fish for market. In one he planted pond lilies which were beautiful.

Standing L to R: David, Daniel E., Arthur W., Alfred, Charles Nelson and Benjamin Rice. Seated: Wilma Rice Hart, Thelma Delano Rice, Sarah Jane Rice Wilbur, Evelyn Rice Reddish, Elizabeth Rice Kelly and Louise Rice Bell.

In their early married years, telephones were a new thing. He is said to have carried the "trunk" line from New Market to Alamo over Sugar Creek by walking on the ice. Nelson died in April 1938, and Frances in 1940. Their two children were Elmer J. and Joseph E. Rice.

Elmer married Goldie Hardee on Dec. 18, 1907. Their children were: (1) Evelyn, married William Reddish with seven children; (2) Joseph, married Stella Coffenberry with one daughter; (3) Katherine died at age 14; (4) Robert, married Thelma Delano with two children; (5) Elizabeth, married O.W. Kelly. In September 1916, Goldie and the three older children were stricken with typhoid fever from which Goldie did not recover. Elmer married Katie Tate Boraker in 1920. They were parents of eight children: Sarah Jane married Elmer Wilbur-seven children; Louise married Archie Bell-five children; Wilma married H. LaVerne Hart-one daughter; Arthur married Luetna McMahan-five children; David married Betty Fordice-two children; Alfred married Ruth McMahan-three sons; Daniel married Opal Tracy-three children; and Benjamin married Jo Ann Teague-four sons. Sanford Boraker, a step-son, married Kate Young. At different times, Elmer was a farmer, auto repairman, owner-operator of a threshing rig and a sawmill. In 1942, he purchased and subsequently farmed his grandfather Easley's homestead farm on which the Old Hickory School was built on. He always lived in Brown township in Montgomery County.

Joseph, the second son of Nelson, married Edith Canine of the Freedom Community. He was a bookkeeper in St. Louis from 1907 to 1916, a farmer with his inlaws to 1923, bookkeeper with White Star Oil Company of Connersville until 1937, and owner of the Rice Hardware and Minneapolis Moline dealership in Waynetown until retirement. Joseph and Edith were active in the Waynetown Baptist Church. They had one son, Charles Nelson, retired in Philadelphia. He married Olive Johnson of Franklin and they had three children—Cecelia, Andrew, and Virginia.

Two of Elmer's sons, Arthur and Daniel, are successful farmers in Brown township. Sarah and Louise are retired farmer's wives. David and Benjamin work in the field of education as did Evelyn. Alfred and Wilma are longtime employees of R.R. Donnelley Company. Elizabeth is retired from Delco Remey. Joseph and Robert are deceased. *Submitted by Evelyn Rice Reddish*

JOSEPH EASLEY RICE

Joseph Easley Rice (July 18, 1889-Apr. 18, 1975), the second son of Nelson and Frances Easley Rice, attended the New Market School and graduated from Business College of Crawfordsville.

Joseph spent about a year in San Juan River Co., UT, with an uncle, and from 1907 to 1917 lived and worked in St. Louis, MO. On July 15, 1914, he married Edith Estelle Canine and from 1917 to 1923 farmed with his father-in-law near Waveland.

In 1923, he became manager of the White Star Oil Company of Connersville, IN. The five divisions of that company were purchased by Socony Vacuum Oil Corporation in 1932; then moved to Indianapolis as their credit manager. In 1937, he bought the Darnell Hardware in Waynetown which operated as Rice Hardware featuring general hardware and appliances as well as maintaining the Minneapolis Moline farm machinery dealership.

Edith and Joseph participated in community activities and served in the Waynetown Baptist Church where Joe was deacon, trustee and choir member. Their son, Charles Nelson, born Mar. 3, 1918, graduated from Shortridge High School in Indianapolis and from Franklin College in Franklin.

Charles married Olive Owen Johnson of Franklin, IN on June 10, 1940. Their three children Andrew, Cecelia, and Virginia live on the west coast and have four grandchildren.

Charles Nelson received a Ph.D. from the University of California at Berkeley, and worked on the Manhattan Project at the Los Alamos, NM Laboratories during World War II. He was assistant professor in chemistry at Purdue University in 1946-47 and worked for Lilly Research Laboratories from 1947 to 1966. From 1966 to 1970 he was with the National Library of Medicine, Bethesda, MD, and retired in 1979 after nine years with Merck and Company of West Point, PA and Rahway, NJ. Charles resides at Fort Washington near Philadelphia, PA. *Submitted by Charles Nelson Rice*

LUTHER V. RICE

Luther V. Rice, a Montgomery County native, built the first Ferris wheel. His grandparents, Jonathan and Sythe Ingram Gill had a daughter Sarah Margaret born in 1839 and died in 1919. She married Jasper Rice on Nov. 24, 1858. Jasper died Aug. 1, 1878 and Sarah Margaret married John Somerville in November 1894. Sarah Margaret and Jasper Rice had two children: Luther V. born Nov. 21, 1861 in Ladoga, IN and Louilla Batman. They had a half sister Kittie Rice from their father's first marriage.

His parents moved to Adell, IA, and farmed until Luther was 18, and they returned to Indiana, near Roachdale, Putnam Co., IN. Kittie married a Reeves and remained in Iowa. Jasper died and Louilla had married James Batman, so they took over the farm, and Luther and his mother returned to Ladoga. Luther attended Cental Indiana Normal College, graduating in Scientific Class of 1882. He taught school for a couple of years, then he wanted to make his dream come true of being an engineer, he attended Cornell University, Ithaca, NY; taking mathematics and engineering courses. He had an excellent education in engineering, and he began spanning rivers with great steel bridges. He built the bridge over the Ohio at Newport, KY.

George Washington Ferris had invented the Ferris Wheel in 1892, and in 1893, Luther built the first Ferris Wheel at the World's Fair in Chicago. That first one has the nameplate and piece of girder in the Science and Industry Museum in Chicago. Part of the Ferris Wheel was used in the bridge over the Kankakee River, Porter Co., IN and the rest of the wheel was destroyed.

Luther had many notable undertakings and achievements of engineering. He lived on the north side of Chicago, with his wife, Jane Neal, from Lebanon. They had a beautiful home. They had a wonderful life together. Then he came down with an incurable disease, and they went everywhere, trying to get his health back, all to no avail. They were in California the last year of his life. He died at 7:30 A.M. on Nov. 19, 1927, ending the life of a wonderful engineer. He died two days before his 66th birthday. His wife and many relatives here survived him.

His funeral was at Ray O. Gills in Ladoga, with Rev. Sam G. Smith officiating. Floral offerings from relatives and friends from far and near filled a room. His cousin Mrs. Minty Rose read his obituary. Mrs. Lee Brookshire and Miss Carrie Robbins, accompanied by Mrs. George Harshbarger sang two duets. Pallbearers were Mark and Forest Shackleford, Richard Rose, Ray Gill, Harry Somerville, and Ward Batman, all of Ladoga.

He lived a full life, his dream was fulfilled in his engineering accomplishments, and Montgomery County can look with pride on his many engineering feats.

The Ladoga people takes the credit for Luther V. Rice getting to construct, Mr. George Washington Gale Ferris' ferris wheel in Chicago World's Fair, and as he did such a good job building it, he was called on to move it to St. Louis for the World's Fair.

The Ladoga people told the man looking for a good engineer to build the Ferris wheel to contact Luther V. Rice, which they did, and he was hired to do the job. And as he done so well with the first one built, St. Louis wanted him to move it to St. Louis World's Fair in 1904, and reconstruct it again, and he did. *By Pauline Walters*

THOMAS W. RICE

Thomas Rice was born to Jonathon and Mary (Glenn) Rice in the Freedom Area, and to this union another son Albert was born.

On Mar. 5, 1899 Thomas was married to Zella Dee Patton. In their early years they lived on a farm on Oak Hill Road. Tom bred and raced fine horses during old county fair years. Later they moved into Crawfordsville. He entered politics and was elected Sheriff for one term, 1928-1932 and lived in what is now known as the Old Jail Museum on North Washington St. He also served as Police Chief two terms after which he was State Parole Officer for several years.

Following retirement form politics he owned and operated the Crawfordsville Bus Co.

Tom and Aunt Dee, by which names they were called by most people who knew them were widely known and respected.

Albert, who married Toadie Stilwell, had one son, Thomas. They were farmers and lived on SR 234 northeast of Browns Valley for many years.
Submitted by Dannie Rice

HOWARD AND FERN RIPPY

Howard Eugene Rippy, Sr. was born June 28, 1926 in Indianapolis to Carlen and Myrtle (Lentz) Rippy. He has one brother, Carl, and one sister, Betty Kasseg.

He was married in Indianapolis on Sept. 1, 1946 to Fern F. Stout, daughter of Edgar N. and Ethel M. (Foltz) Stout. He has three children, Karen, Mary and Howard, Jr.

Howard and Fern Rippy

When the City of Indianapolis purchased Dandy Trail Farms in 1963, where he had lived for 11 years, he came to Montgomery County and bought a farm northeast of Ladoga. The family moved here in August 1965. Karen graduated from Ladoga High and went to Indiana Business College. She married Thomas Carney of Ladoga in 1970. They have three children: Catherine, Cheryl and Allison. Mary was graduated in the first class from Southmont and went on to Indiana State. She is married to H. Craig Bennett, Marietta, GA and they have a son, Cody, born in 1988. Howard, Jr. graduated from Southmont in 1975 and from Purdue in 1979. He is married to Mary Lee Kirkpatrick of Wingate and they have a son, Ryan.

Howard continues to farm in the area with his son. He has been active in various farm organizations and currently is District Five State Director of Indiana Farm Bureau Insurance.

His family was members of St. Paul Evangelical and Reform Church, which later merged with Cong. Christian. A new church was formed in Speedway, St. Luke United Church of Christ. He and Fern were both charter members of that church. In recent years, they have transferred their membership to Ladoga Presbyterian church.

Fern retired in 1987 after nearly 21 years of work at Ladoga Bank.

RIVERS ANCESTORY

John Rivers was one of the organizers of Good Hope Baptist Church in 1796 in Taylor Co., KY. It has been in continuous existence since its organization. It is thought his family moved to Kentucky from Virginia. He was married to Elizabeth ... They had issue: William, Betsy (Mrs. Simeon Hunt), Susannah (Mrs. Laban Hunt), Lucy (Mrs. John Lander), Mary, Martha (Mrs. Thomas McDaniel), Sarah, Isaac, James, John and Richard.

Above William Rivers died in Fountain Co., IN on Feb. 2, 1869. He married Pauline Rhea and had issue: Mary "Mollie" (Mrs. Dr. George Hays), James Riley, Rebecca, Martha, Livonia and Alice Victoria.

James Riley was born Jan. 23, 1802 died July 1, 1879. He married Mary Irene (Polly) Short and had issue: William Franklin, John Campbell, Lutitia Ellen (Mrs. R.E. Nelson), Robert Marion, Joel Peyton, James Madison, Thomas Jefferson, Mary Etta, Joseph Butler, Elizabeth Ann (Mrs. John Patterson), Rebecca Jane (Mrs. John Handley), Nancy Adelene and Henry Waller.

Ray and Lu Re Harbison Rivers

Joseph Butler Rivers was born May 22, 1848 died Dec. 17, 1920; married Emily Hardin Sullivan in 1868 and had issue: Livonia Ellen, Henry Waller, Minnie Grace (Mrs. Edward Davis Suitor), Joseph Hardin, Mary Elizabeth (Mrs. Clyde Smith), Robert Stallard, Nannie Lutitia (Mrs. Sylvester Manson Keller). Joseph Butler Rivers moved to Montgomery Co., IN in 1890.

Henry Waller Rivers was born Nov. 1, 1870 and died January 1941. He married Betty F. Hunt and had issue: Clifford 1893, Roby died in infancy, Bessie 1896 (Mrs. Austin Phillips), Emmett Raymond, Otto James 1899-1988, Patience 1900-1988 (Mrs. Ray Stultz), Roy 1902, Rosie 1908 (Mrs. Raymond Ball, Mrs. John Culver) and Lena 1916 (Mrs. Robert Fullenwider).

Emmett Raymond is our direct lineage. He was born May 20, 1897 died Jan. 17, 1986; buried at Portland Mills Cemetery. He was a trucker and farmer. Had one of the first combines in the area and did custom work. In Oct. 25, 1924 he married Myrtle Lu Re Harbison and had issue: Max Ray July 14, 1926, Reba Ardell Feb. 18, 1930 (Mrs. John Etter) and Billy Joe Jan. 9, 1935.

Max Ray Rivers married Helen Frances Simms (see Simms History) 1944 and had issue: Mary Ann Feb. 10, 1945 (Mrs. Jerry McMindes), Esther Jane July 23, 1948 (Mrs. Tom Fay, divorced), Victor Ray Aug. 24, 1954 married Janet Hohenstein, and Ramona Lea July 23, 1961 (Mrs. Fernando Vazquez). Max and Helen have six grandchildren.
Submitted by Helen Rivers

ROBERT M. AND MELODY ROACH

Robert Michael "Mike" Roach was born Jan. 25, 1956 in Crawfordsville, IN, the fourth child of Robert Roach born Aug. 6, 1921 Montgomery Co., IN and Wilma Cornett Barton Roach born July 31, 1927 in Eubank, KY died Nov. 10, 1978 Montgomery County. Mike's siblings are: Penny Roach Mullens, Charles Barton, Pamela Barton Hood, and Timothy Roach. His paternal grandparents were Archie Roach born June 11, 1879 Montgomery County. He owned and operated Roach's Grocery in Crawfordsville for many years, died July 25, 1951 Montgomery County.

Hattie A. Lewellen Hardaker Roach born July 29, 1881 Montgomery County died Mar. 6, 1940 Montgomery County. Maternal grandparents were Augustus Carlos "Gus" Cornett born Mar. 4, 1890 Ash Co., NC, a farmer in Kentucky until 1940. He then moved to Cincinnati, OH and worked for the city garage 13 years. Moved to Montgomery County in 1957 to live with daughter, Wilma due to failing health, died Oct. 5, 1958 Montgomery County. Sally Rose Allie Roark Cornett born in 1894 Ash Co., NC died in 1939 Eubank, KY.

Robert M. holding Ryan Michael, Meagan Louise, Meloday A. holding Marisa Lynn Roach

Mike is employed at Pace Dairy Foods in Crawfordsville, IN. He enjoys playing guitar and working with his computer in his spare time. On Nov. 1, 1982, Mike married Melody Ann Fields at the Montgomery County Courthouse.

Melody was born May 18, 1961 Vermillion Co., IL, the first child of William Harry Fields born Dec. 20, 1938 Montgomery County and Janet Louise House Fields born Feb. 16, 1942 Carroll Co., IN. Melody's siblings are: Gayle, Kevin and Billy. Her maternal grandparents were, Lester Merle House born May 6, 1901 Warren Co., IN died Sept. 7, 1974. Myra Louise Redman House born Mar. 15, 1905 Fountain Co., IN died Dec. 19, 1981 Marion Co., IN. Her paternal grandparents are William Leslie Fields born Apr. 28, 1913 Rush Co., IN and Vivian Ruth Cramer Fields born Feb. 16, 1918 Montgomery County died Jan. 28, 1985 Montgomery County.

Melody graduated from North Montgomery High School in 1979. She worked as a Nurse's Aide and Physical Therapy Aide at Culver Hospital five years. She is the Assistant Leader of the Montgomery County 4-H Dog Club.

Mike and Melody have three children: Meagan Louise born Jan. 26, 1985, Montgomery County, Marisa Lynn born July 16, 1987, Marion County, and Ryan Michael born Dec. 16, 1988 Montgomery County. They all reside in Crawfordsville, IN.

BERT AND EDNA C. ROBBINS

Bert Robbins, son of Robert Robbins and Martha (Neff) Robbins, was born in 1868 near Ladoga. He married (July, 1890) Edna, daughter of Dr. James Allen Warbington, a Ladoga dentist, and Mary M. Peffley, was born in Ladoga in 1871.

Bert operated a horse drawn dray, hauling mail and shipped goods from the Monon and Midland Railroad stations. Bert died in 1922. A sister of Bert's owned the Carrie Robbins Millinery store in Ladoga for many years and also operated the Opera House Movie Theatre in Ladoga which was above the present bank building until about 1926.

Bert and Edna had ten children, all born in Ladoga:

Anita b. 1891 d. 1982 married to Winfred (Slim) Vice, Ladoga. Eleven children, Ladoga.

Duff George b. 1893 d. 1983 married to Maude Ruff, Romney. Five children, Ladoga.

Hugh W. b. 1894 d. 1970 married to Avis Smith, Bridgeston. Three children, Muncie.

Ruth b. 1896 married to Ralph Kemper, Brook. No children, Crawfordsville.

Lillian b. 1900 d. 1956 married to Richard Cole, Lafayette. Four children, Lafayette.

Carrie b. 1902 married to Albert Norris, Lafayette. Two children, Milwaukee, WI.

Robert J. b. 1904 d. 1972 married to Mary G. Young, Roachdale. One child, Indianapolis.

Mabel b. 1907 married to Rev. Merle Sparger, Crawfordsville. Three children, Crawfordsville.

Wilmer Ira b. 1912 d. 1912.

Donald L. b. 1914 married to Catharine Hudak, Phillips, WI. Seven children, Des Plaines, IL.

At the time of Edna's death at age 83 in 1954, she had 32 grandchildren, 46 great-grandchildren, and eight children living. In 1943, Edna had one son and five grandsons serving in the Armed Forces.

In 1937 the Robbins started holding an annual Robbins Reunion at Milligan Park in Crawfordsville. These have been held each year since with growing numbers. In 1987 we held our 50th Reunion at Ladoga Park with 96 family members and guests present.

Ruth Kemper (oldest living daughter) is 93 yrs. old and lives in Autumn Care Nursing Home in Ladoga. *Submitted by Donald L. Robbins*

DONALD JOE ROBBINS

Donald Joe Robbins, born Apr. 3, 1944, in Crawfordsville, to Orran Ray and Oneta Olive (Smith) Robbins. The middle son of three brothers, Don graduated from Crawfordsville High School in 1962. After graduation he was employed full time with Berry Construction of whom he had served an apprenticeship with since his junior year of high school.

Don married June 17, 1965, to Joyce Ellen Wildman. Joyce, the daughter of Ralph Edward and Betty Marie (Dawson) Wildman, was the eldest of two children. Born July 23, 1946, in Crawfordsville and graduated from C.H.S. in 1964. Joyce started to school at Smartsburg in a two story red brick building, which is no longer standing. It was on the southwest corner of St. Rd. 32 and Branch Smartsburg Road. The only inside plumbing was a small drinking fountain.

Don was going to the army after they were married. After basic training Joyce was to join him. Not knowing, at the time, that the law was, if you were married on or before induction day you were exempt from the draft. Don got his job back and they found residence on Wallace Drive. In 1967 Don built their home on St. Rd. 55.

Their first born was a son, Rodney Martin. Born Nov. 11, 1966, in Crawfordsville. At three months Dr. Kirtley sent him to a bone specialist. He had to wear a series of three casts, for two weeks each, on his right foot and leg, up to his knee. This was to pull the front part of his foot, from being turned in, to being straight. Rodney went to kindergarten at Mt. Zion where his father attended elementary.

On June 18, 1968, their second and last child was born. A daughter, Donna Jo, named after her father. At six months she was diagnosed as acute asthmatic.

In August, 1973, the four of them moved to Brownsburg, Hendricks Co., IN. Don was employed with A.H.M. Graves Construction in Indianapolis. Brownsburg was closer to his work, but not having to live in the big city was their desire.

Rodney played little league football which Don coached. Donna was in Camp Fire's Blue Birds which Joyce was the leader. Both children were very good students. Rodney graduated from B.H.S. in 1985 and Donna in 1986.

When the Robbins family moved to Brownsburg, Don and Joyce brought their church membership from Smartsburg Christian to Brownsburg Christian Church. They both taught Sunday School and raised their children in that church. Rodney and Donna became members in their youth.

January, 1979, Joyce became employed by the Brownsburg School system as custodian in their South Elementary, now named Harris.

Rodney, as of this writing, February, 1989, has gone to Lincoln Technical Inst. while employed by Holiday Inn, at Lebanon, as cook.

Donna Jo is employed by Bank One on the circle in Indianapolis. She is administrative assistant in the trust department. She was married Jan. 14, 1989, to William Joseph Cozzolino III. Donna and Bill are members of Grace Bible Church.

HOMER T. ROBISON

Homer Theophilus Robison was born Aug. 16, 1882, in a log cabin two miles south of Lebanon, IN. In 1900 the family moved west of Alamo on the Heath farm. It was late winter and the temperature did not get above zero any of the four days it took to move. They drove a herd of cattle plus several horses.

Homer graduated from Alamo High School and then furthered his education at Valparaiso University. He then taught school in the Freedom area in Montgomery County. At this time he met a young school teacher, Charlotte (Lottie) Bayless. Lottie received her college education from Danville Normal in Danville, IN. In those times school teachers had to take a test over all subjects taught in the county superintendent's office to qualify for another year of teaching. Lottie and Homer challenged each other and never made a grade below 97.

Homer was the first born to Charles Wesley Robison (descendants of Daniel Boone, Dutch German) and Margaret Cranford Robison, who came from North Carolina. Homer had six sisters and two brothers.

Lottie was born Nov. 14, 1885 to Luna Harrison Bayless and Elizabeth Stever. Luna was a cousin to General Ulysses (Hiram) S. Grant. The Bayless family is Scotch-English. Elizabeth Stever was a niece to the Conner of the Conner Prairie near Noblesville. Lottie was six years old when her mother died from results of the measles. Her father then married Elizabeth Priebe. Lottie has one sister, Lula Bryant, and three half sisters and three half brothers.

In October 1906, Homer and Lottie were married in Danville, IL. They started housekeeping on the John Oldshue farm north of Waveland. They later bought a farm west of Waveland.

Margaret Lottie was born Oct. 30, 1907. Margaret was a nurse, receiving her training at Methodist Hospital. She married Otis Allen and had one child, Dwight, who is a minister in California. Margaret died Dec. 3, 1928.

Gerald Homer was born July 22, 1910. He married Cora Ellen Smith July 7, 1934. They have one child, Dr. Larry Gerald, who resides at Darlington with his wife, Lyn Harris and daughter Gail. Gerald farmed, was a Sunoco delivery man, and was township trustee for eight years. He served on the Waveland Town Board and both he and wife were active in the Waveland Methodist Church. his wife, Cora, was school secretary for 20 years. Gerald died Sept. 18, 1974.

Gordon Bayless was born Nov. 28, 1913. He

married Julianna Johnson, June 4, 1935. They have Theodore Homer, Patricia Whitkowski, Betty Taylo, and Thomas. Gordon graduated from Wabash College and taught chemistry and physics in the Wallace, Sullivan and Michigan City schools in Indiana. Julianna also taught school in the Michigan City schools.

Charles Willard (Bill) was born Apr. 28, 1918, and married Vivian Moore June 26, 1938. Bill has been a salesman all his life selling farm machinery in five states in the west. He has resided in Kansas for over 40 years. His children are Beverly Krantz, Judy Kidney, Sue Biddison, and Nancy Mantel.

Naomi Winifred was born Aug. 5, 1928. She married Fred J. Mitchell, Mar. 7, 1948. Naomi majored in nursing at Indiana University and Ball State University. She has worked in vocational rehabilitation work for several years. They have three children; Sharon Kay Harris, Rebecca Lou, and Paul David.

Homer was always active in community affairs. He served as Brown Township trustee eight years. During this time, Homer supervised the construction of the Waveland gymnasium which still is used in conjunction with the new grade school recently built. Lottie served as township clerk for 16 years.

Homer being a Quaker, and Lottie a Baptist, joined the Methodist church in Waveland. Both were dedicated church workers, serving as teachers and officers. Lottie was member of the Modern Marthas class and Homer as trustee of the church.

Homer died Jan. 13, 1962, and Lottie Oct. 28, 1966. They lived useful and busy lives and left a great heritage of love and service to their family and fellow men. *Submitted by Naomi Mitchell*

ELIJAH ROGERS

About the year 1829, Elijah Rogers came to Indiana with his pioneer parents from Ohio to settle in Sugar Creek township near the little village of Bowers Station. He married Rachel ? who died in 1852. He then married Margaret Venis. From this union came ten children. Two of the children, Mary and David, married a brother and sister, John and Sarah Belle, from the Stull family. All of their children were double cousins. (See STULL, GEORGE WASHINGTON)

The siblings of Elijah and Margaret Venis Rogers were: Mary Rogers, John Rogers, Elizabeth, who married Jesse Coyner; Melissa, who married Jesse Saidla; David Finley, who married Sarah Belle Stull; George who married Isabelle Meek; Mary Adeline, who married John W. Stull; Henry Edwin, Rilla May, who married John Hutchinson; and Nellie May, who married Edwin J. Carr.

John W., Sarah Belle, Mary (Molly) and David F. Rogers

The children of David Finley and Sarah Belle Stull Rogers were: John Franklin, who married Annabelle Mitchell; Claude Chester, who married Rosa Rettinger; Clifford, who married Hazel Clouser; Della, who married Walter Long; Alden, who married Jeanette Zachgo; David, who married Mary Watt; Edward Lee, who married Pauline Engle and Helen Watt; Oakel Hall, who married Charlotte Cones and Mildred Horsley; and Ethel Blanche, who married Raleigh Carr and Leslie Edwards.

The children of Claude and Rosa Rettinger Rogers were: Harley, who married Mary McDonald and Chester Samuel who married Jeanette Bryan and Bette Simmerman.

The children of Clifford and Hazel Clouser Rogers were: Juanita, who died in infancy; Helen, who married Lew Waggoner; and Haven.

The children of Walter and Della Rogers Long were Ellen and Cecil, who married Helen Myers.

The children of Alden and Jeanette Zachgo Rogers were; Robert, who married Rosemary Kelley and Ardith Lindley; and Dorothy, who married Larry Gagnier.

The children of David F. and Mary Watt Rogers were Bonnie Jean, who married Edward Kastl; and Mary Jane, who married William Burkhalter.

The children of Edward Lee and Helen Watt Rogers were: Jack Graham, who married Sharon Rabe and David Lee, who married Hazel Wells.

The children of Oakel and Charlotte Cones Rogers were: Marjorie, who married Earl Bates and Albert Marschke; and Myron Lee, who married Ruth ?. The child of Oakel and Mildred Horsley was Nancy Jane Rogers.

The children of Raleigh and Ethel Blanche Carr were: Laurabelle, who married Glen Reppert; and Lois Mae, who married Leslie Lassiter.

With ten children from John W. and Mary Rogers Stull and ten children from David Finley and Sarah Belle Stull Rogers as double cousins, it was natural that family reunions were frequently held. The first Rogers-Stull family gathering was held at the country home of Walter and Della Rogers in late August, 1921, but did not organize until August, 1924 at Stoddard Park, Linden, IN. The families met for three years at someone's home until 1924 when they went to the park, a central location for all of the families. They then elected officers. As of this date, 1989, the reunion is still being held in Linden, IN. *Submitted by J. Boyd*

DR. HENRY ROGERS

Dr. Henry Rogers was reared in Culpeper Co., VA. He studied medicine in Kentucky. He came to Franklin Township, Montgomery Co., IN where he practiced medicine. He later moved to Clinton Co., MO where his wife died. Dr. Rogers married second Miss Jane Kirkpatrick. They settled on a farm located about two miles west of Parkersburg, IN.

Dr. Henry Rogers served in the War of 1812, fighting with Kentucky troops. He was an Elder in the Christian Church and a member of the Independent Order of Odd Fellows lodge. Jane Rogers was a member of the Presbyterian Church and belonged to the Order of Rebeccas. Dr. Rogers moved his family to Clark Township, Montgomery Co., IN in 1867.

Dr. Henry Rogers died on Nov. 9, 1876, aged 82 years, nine months, and is buried in the Ladoga Cemetery. Jane Rogers died on Nov. 10, 1878, aged 75 years, ten months, 11 days, and is buried next to her husband. Their children were James and Henry Clay (see Dr. Henry Clay Rogers family). *Submitted by Andrew Keith Houk, Jr.*

HENRY CLAY ROGERS, M.D.

In researching the life of Dr. Henry C. Rogers, I was given the name of his granddaughter who lives in Indianapolis. I spent a delightful April afternoon with Helen Rogers. In hearing the stories of her grandfather's life, I was able to picture Dr. Rogers as a man, father, grandfather and as a caring doctor. It is seldom that in doing genealogical research that one is given such insight into the life of a man. I feel mere words cannot do justice to the life of Dr. Henry Clay Rogers.

Dr. Henry Clay Rogers was born Aug. 16, 1844 in Brown Township, Montgomery Co., IN. He was the son of Dr. Henry Rogers and his wife, Jane Points Kirkpatrick.

Dr. Rogers received his early education in one-room schools in the Parkersburg area. He worked on his parent's farm. He enrolled in Wabash College for the fall term in 1864, but never attended due to enlisting in the army. He enlisted in Company I, 135th Indiana Volunteer Infantry, and was mustered in May 25, 1864 with William C. Wilson as Colonel. The regiment marched to Nashville, TN and was assigned to guard the railroad to Chattanooga. The regiment was discharged in late August of 1864.

After his return from the army, Dr. Rogers became a farmer in the Parkersburg and Russellville area.

On Mar. 20, 1866, Henry Clay Rogers was united in marriage with Miss Cintilda Wilson in Russellville. Cintilda's parents were James B. Wilson (1805-1885) and his wife, Susannah Byerly (1808-1889). They are buried in Forgey Cemetery, Putnam Co., IN.

Dr. Rogers decided to follow his father's profession and entered the Russellville (Indiana) College and after graduation, he attended the Indiana Medical College in Indianapolis. He graduated in 1876 and moved his family to Barnard, IN, where he practiced medicine and was postmaster. In 1880, the family moved to Rockville, IN.

Dr. Rogers' specialty was obstetrics. In 1882, he was appointed Health Officer for Parke County and held this office for several terms during his life.

In 1895, Cintilda Rogers died and was buried in the Hebron Cemetery near Russellville.

Dr. Rogers married Eliza M. "Lida" Reid Oct. 7, 1897 in Rockville, IN.

Dr. Rogers was a member of the G.A.R. for 61 years. He belonged to Steele Post #9 in Rockville. He was on the Indiana Soldiers and Sailors Monument Executive Board in Indianapolis, and held several state G.A.R. offices. When Dr. Rogers died Jan. 31, 1946, he was Parke County's last Civil War veteran. He was buried in the Ladoga Cemetery, near Ladoga, IN. Lida Rogers died in 1949 and is buried next to Dr. Rogers.

The children of Dr. and Cintilda Rogers were: James, Anna, Edward and Frank. *Submitted by Andrew Keith Houk, Jr.*

ROBERT ROGERS FAMILY

Robert R. Rogers, 1824-1894, and his wife, Naomi Meloy, 1832-1908, were both born in Warren Co., OH, and came to Montgomery County in the 1870's. His parents were Robert W. Rogers and Catherine LeFevre. Naomi was the daughter of John F. Meloy and Mary Cook. Both the Meloy and LeFevre families were of Huguenot heritage. Isaac LeFevre came to this country in 1708. After revocation of the Edict of Nantes, he escaped from France at the age of 16 with the family Bible which his mother had baked in a loaf of bread. The Meloy family immigrated to America in 1745 through Ireland. The Rogers, LeFevres and Meloys moved westward to Ohio from New Jersey, Pennsylvania, and Maryland.

Charles V., Robert R., Amy, Naomi Meloy and Fred Rogers taken 1870's

Robert and Naomi farmed and raised three children, Charles, 1860-1934, Amy, born 1861, and Fred, 1863-1955. Fred married Bettie Davis, and they owned a farm in Brown Township. His second wife was Minnie Bronaugh. Charles married Nancy Truitt Hole, 1863-1933, from Delaware County. They also farmed in Brown Township and had two sons, Clayton, 1882-1932, and Clyde, 1891-1968. Clyde married Sallie Lee Sparks, 1890-1975, of St. Louis, MO. Her English and Scottish ancestors came to Virginia in the early 1600's. One was Thomas Walker, first explorer of Kentucky.

Clyde and Sallie Lee lived in Crawfordsville. He was County Treasurer from 1924-1928, then managed and later owned the American Security Company. He was graduated from Wabash College in 1914, and his wife was a graduate of Washington University 1913. Their children are Sallie Lee, born 1925, Robert Wallace, born 1929, and Charles Chandler, born 1931.

Sallie is a graduate of Washington University 1947, married James W. Taylor in 1948, and lives in Denver. Their children are Roger William, born 1950, and Nancy Lee, born 1952. Roger married Patricia Weis in 1979, and Nancy married Brent Smith in 1973.

Robert graduated from Wabash College in 1951 and has been associated with the Elston Bank for 35 years. He married Nancy Ann Gardner, born 1934, of New Market in 1955. She is the daughter of Elizabeth Penn, 1895-1988, whose family has been in Montgomery County since the 1870's, and Earl Barton Gardner, 1890-1976. Their children are Robin Ann, born 1956, and Karen Beth, born 1958; both graduates of Ball State University. Robin married Gregory Starnes in 1978, and Karen married Daniel Breault in 1981.

Charles received his Ph.D. in Electrical Engineering from Purdue in 1960. He married Marjorie Andersen in 1954 and lives in Terre Haute. Their children are Kim Charles, born 1955, Cheryl Ann, born 1957, and Sandi Kae, born 1961. Kim married Julie McCarty in 1982, and Sandi married Bradley Gregory in 1984.

The Rogers family has been in Montgomery County for six generations, and Robert R. and Naomi presently have 11 great-great-great-grandchildren.

SAMUEL RONK

Samuel's great grandfather, John Philip Ronc came from Neckerau, Mannheim, Germany, where he married Anna Barbara Schumacker Aug. 21, 1725. They arrived in America on Aug. 19, 1729 aboard the "Martenhouse," and settled in Earl Twp., Lancaster Co., PA. They were given 243 acres adjoining his brother's land on the east. Their children were: Philip, 1731; Michael; Valentine, 1737; George, 1738-40; Anna Eve, 1743; Philip Adam, 1744; Jacob, 1745; Ludwig, 1748; John, 1750; Dorothea and Barbara. John died 1785 and is buried in the family cemetery on a farm near Fetterville, PA.

William and Martha Jane Ronk Heiny children L to R: Arthur, Wilbur, Clara, Annis, Alma, Amy and Edna

George Ranc married Barbara in 1763. Their first child, Catherine, was born Mar. 8, 1768 at Lancaster Co., PA. Before the second child was born they moved to Botetourt Co., VA where Anna Eve, May 2, 1771; John, Jan. 22, 1773; John George, Nov. 4, 1774; Jacob, Oct. 5, 1778; Hannah, 1780-84; Joseph, 1783; Mary, 1785-90; Mary Magdalin, 1792-94; and Barbara were born. George died in 1812 and Barbara May 1, 1815.

John Ronk married Catherine Markey on Dec. 3, 1800. Their children: Samuel, May 5, 1803; Elizabeth; John, 1810; Sarah, 1811; Joseph; Jacob, 1815; and George.

Samuel was born in Botetourt Co., VA and married Nancy S. Feather July 21, 1828. Their first child, Daniel W. was born there also, on Mar. 7, 1830. In September of 1830, Samuel and his family headed for Indiana. Nancy's brother, Adam Feather, was especially fond of Nancy and would not remain in Virginia if she went on the long journey into the western wilds. The trip took six weeks; he and Samuel walked beside the one horse wagon in which rode Nancy and the child and all their earthly possessions. They came together as far as Indianapolis where Adam went on to Bainbridge, IN while Samuel and Nancy settled in Montgomery Co., IN. They had seven more children: Joseph F., May 22, 1833; William P., Oct. 19, 1835; John Thomas, 1839; George H., 1842; Mary M., 1844; James R., 1848; and Jesse D., 1852.

Samuel was a very successful farmer, a Republican and active in the Dunkard religion, known today as "Church of the Brethren". The church was located five miles east of Ladoga on 234 and called the Mount Pleasant Church. Samuel's youngest child, Jesse was a Deacon and later was called to the ministry. The cemetery located across the road from where the church stood, is where Samuel and many other Ronks are buried. Samuel died Nov. 7, 1884 and Nancy Mar. 21, 1867.

According to land records, Samuel bought land in Putnam County on Nov. 29, 1834 and in Montgomery County on Sept. 15, 1837. All in all, he owned several hundred acres and left a farm to each of his children.

William P. Ronk married Mary N. Smith Nov. 13, 1868. Their children: Martha Jane, Sept. 10, 1869; Mattie Ann, Mar. 3, 1871; and George Henry, Aug. 11, 1872. William lived all his life in Montgomery County and died Dec. 11, 1909 and Mary Nov. 27, 1913.

Martha Jane married William W. Heiny of Noblesville, IN on Apr. 4, 1897 and moved there with him. They had seven children: Arthur, Mary Edna, Amy Inis, Alma Ione, Lola Annis, Clara Thelma, and Wilbur Ward. Annis and Clara still reside in Noblesville, the others have died and most are buried at Crownland Cemetery, Noblesville, along with William P. who died Jan. 20, 1935 and Martha on June 1, 1951.

THOMAS E. AND VEDA MAE (JONES) ROSS

Thomas E. Ross was born in Jamestown, IN on Apr. 7, 1930. His father was Chester Ross, died in the Spring of 1968. His mother was the former Cecil P. Shearer. She died Nov. 28, 1988 at the age of 87 years old.

Tom had a brother, Jack A. Ross, two sisters, Barbara and Nancy, and a step-sister Esta Lee Heisel.

He graduated from Crawfordsville High School in 1948. Later he went to work at R.R. Donnelleys at the age of 18. He spent a period of 31 years with that company.

In the year 1949 Tom and I met at the same plant, and began our courtship. Later, we were married Jan. 28, 1950. A period of two years later, Tom went in the Military Service a total of two years, with one year of combat duty with the Engineers in Korea.

My maiden name was Veda Mae Jones, coming from a family of nine children. My father was William A. Jones, died Mar. 1, 1988. My mother was formally Mattie Mae Eaton, died at the age of 84, July 12, 1984. I graduated from New Market High School in 1948. Later, I went to work at R.R. Donnelleys for a period of four years. I started with a hobby of upholstery and in 1969, we opened an upholstery shop to the public. I worked here until Tom quit Donnelleys, then we both became self-employed.

In 1953, we had our first child, Sherry Lynn born April 25 of that year. She graduated from Crawfordsville High School; later became a nurse after her study at Wishard Memorial Hospital. In 1979, she married Victor H. Ruthig, from New Jersey after his study at Purdue. They are now living in Greenwood, IN. They gave us our first grandchild, Eric Mathew, born Nov. 22, 1983.

In 1956, we had a son, Jerry Wayne, born December 19th of that year. He graduated from North Montgomery High School in 1975. He attended Butler University for four years, receiving a degree in Music. He is now doing some music work professionally. In 1986, Nov. 22, he married Rebecca Eve Kesling. They now live near Greenwood, IN. They have their own upholstery business. On Mar. 12, 1989, a son, Adam Jerrison was born.

In 1957, we joined the First Baptist Church in Crawfordsville, which we are still active in today.

On July 18, 1960, our son, Steven Lee was born. He graduated from North Montgomery High School in 1978. He now works for United Parcel. In 1984, on June 23, he married Jamie A. Anderson. They now live in this community as proud parents of a son, Ryan Christopher born Dec. 28, 1987.

On Jan. 28, 1990, we will reach our 40th anniversary. They said it couldn't be done, but we hope to have many more anniversaries giving us a long life together. We still reside in the home we built together on 16 acres 26 years ago. *Submitted by Veda Jones Ross*

FLOYD A. ROUSE

Floyd Rouse came to Montgomery County in 1928. He was born in Vermillion Co., IL May 17, 1921 the sixth child of Rollo and Oral Rouse. His siblings being Opal, Beaulah, Rollo Vern, Mary, Cecil, followed by Lucille and Charles. They settled just west of Turnip Seed Corner where the family farmed about 300 acres. He attended Bowers school.

In 1932 they moved east of New Market where he spent grades five thru 12. In 1935 they moved west of Ladoga in Scott Township. As a teenager he acted as janitor in Punkin Center School for Scott township monthly Farm Bureau meetings. One cold evening as he built the fire in the pot bellied stove, the pipe gave way next to the ceiling. He sent his younger brother Charles to get water from the neighbor's while he held the stove pipe, directing the flames through the ceiling. Charles returned, Floyd was dousing the fire as people arrived for their meeting.

He worked in the Ladoga Canning Factory, stamping cans and placing them on the conveyor belt.

Front Row, 6th Person: Floyd Rouse and sister Lucille (Rouse) Deck to his right - Bowers School about 1928

Floyd returned home with the family one evening to find their barn surrounded by police. They were searching for an escapee. The escapee later turned up at the local jail asking for a night's lodging. The sheriff's wife recognized him, and obliged him by locking the cell. When the sheriff arrived after giving up the search, he learned that his wife had him locked up.

One fall evening while on a break at the canning factory, Floyd went outside and observed a glorious display of Northern Lights. It seemed to light up the whole sky from east to west.

In August of 1942 he was drafted, and served 3-1/2 years in the South Pacific as a mechanic for the 478th Air Service Squadron with the Fifth Air Corps. During his service he was privileged to work on the planes of General Douglas McArthur, General George Marshall, and flying Ace "Major Bond".

After discharge in December 1945 he returned to work on the family farm, where he remained until 1955 when he began working in the tool room at R.R. Donnelley's. In 1958 he returned to farming for his father just east of the canning factory farm. The 12 room house they lived in for 14 years was later bulldozed and buried for the Farm Progress Show. Floyd farmed this farm as well as the home place 3/4 of a mile east until April of 1971 when his father passed away.

He then worked for the State Highway Department for 14 years, then retired in 1986.

He and his wife the former Louise Scott, raised their four children in Montgomery County. They currently enjoy their retirement on R.R. #3 (the New Market - Alamo Road). *Submitted by Louise Rouse*

ROYERS

The Royers of Madison Township are descended from Sebastian DeRoyer, a French Huguenot, born in Lorraine, France in 1680. He with his four sons emigrated to America prior to 1718. Sebastian was a landowner and farmer settling in Lancaster Co., PA. Captain Samuel Royer fought with Washington at Valley Forge in the winter of 1777-78.

As the family increased, members began moving from Pennsylvania: some to Bridgewater, VA, and some to Logan Co., OH. The Ohio branch of the family finally settled in Madison Township, Montgomery Co., IN.

John Morton Winfield Royer (1881-1958) a farmer, married Nellie Shipman (1886-1963) in 1907. This union produced five children: Robert Frances Raper Royer (1907-1973) who married Ruth Evelyn Douglas and they had one daughter; Beverly who married Tyler Nannet of Coal Creek Township, having two sons; Tim and Bryan. Tim married Kay Kiehleauch, and Brian married Karen Freth.

B. Row: Fred, John (father), Bill. F. Row: Bob, Inez, Nellie (mother) and Evelyn Royer

Inez Irene Royer (1909) married Wm. Edgar Scott (1901-1970) and they had six children: William E., Jerry, Jack, Phyllis, Diana and one son died in infancy. Edgar "Bowzer" Scott was an educator and high school basketball coach. Inez now lives in Oxford, IN.

Sadie Evelyn Royer (1910) married Albert Dunbar and they had one daughter, Kenita Jo Evelyn is retired from welfare work and lives in Indianapolis.

William Logan Royer (1912-1963) married Evelyn Nina Storms (1911) of the Concord neighborhood of Tippecanoe County and they had three children: Marilyn June married Howard L. Holt from Bowers Station and they have four children: Lynette married Mark Cox, Clark D. married Rene Wright with a son Jason: Kevin H. married Deanna Dolph having Erin Nichol, Dana Marie and Logan Bradley: Brian W. married Natalie Bennett having Rachel Elizabeth.

All of the Holt family still live in Montgomery County.

Melvin K. Royer married Rebecca Larrick of Darlington and they have three daughters:

Elizabeth L., married Tim Dion of Massachusetts, and they live in Rhode Island. Diana L., married Terry Howell of Crawfordsville and they have two sons: Travis Jared and Seth Adam. They live on the "Larrick" home place in Franklin Township. Mary K., married Geoff Anderson of Lafayette, where they presently reside. Mary is a senior at Purdue University.

Roanne Royer married Lawrence A. Smith having Whitney Rae and Taylor Wade. They live in Coal Creek Township.

The last of John and Nellie's children, Frederick Wayne (1913-1986) married Thelma Clifton who died in 1965 and they had one son, Ronald.

Having three Evelyns in the family was very confusing so in conversation they were referred to as; Evelyn Bill, Evelyn Bob, and Evelyn Dunbar.

Bill and Bob owned and operated the Square Corner Hardware in Linden for many years. Bill was an avid fisherman and ham radio operator; Bob was postmaster for a time and Democratic precinct committeeman. They were influential in bringing the Tipmont REMC facility to Linden. Fred worked for many years at Mid State Steel and Wire Company and lived in Crawfordsville.

CHURCHILL AND HANNAH HAYNES (HAINES) RUSH

Churchill and Hannah Haynes (Haines) Rush and their children settled on a government land grant three miles south of Alamo in Brown Township, Montgomery Co., IN in 1835. Churchill was born May 3, 1792 in Georgia, the son of Jesse and Jane Starnes Rush. He served in the War of 1812 and received a pension which stopped in 1877, at which time it is assumed he died. Churchill and Hannah were married Aug. 15, 1816 in Greene Co., TN by Jon Russell, J.P. We don't know when or where Hannah was born or died. It is believed her father was Abraham Haynes or Haines, and her mother's name was Hannah. They moved to Ohio and stayed there until they came to Indiana and bought land in Brown Township, Montgomery County near Sugar Creek.

Churchill and Hannah's children were: Chester, born ca. 1817 in Tennessee, married Rebecca Blaxom Nov. 28, 1839; Luna, born July 18, 1821 in Tennessee, died June 10, 1908 and married Sarah Jane Bayless July 17, 1844; Jesse P., born ca. 1825 in Ohio and married Mary C. Porter Nov. 9, 1848; Mary L. (Polly) was born Aug. 15, 1827, died September 1884, and married Joseph Smith; Church C. was born ca. 1831 in Ohio; Harriet, born ca. 1838, died Apr. 7, 1911, and never married; Frances (Frankie), Haynes or Haines was born Feb. 16, 1812, died Nov. 6, 1903 and married John Stonebraker July 14, 1850; Andrew K. was born ca. 1834 and died May 27, 1894. He is buried in Davis-Rush Cemetery. He first married Eva Scott. Their two children were: Henry A., born Aug. 11, 1855, died Apr. 12, 1924, and married Sylvia Ann Daley on Dec. 2, 1873. Luna died very young. His second marriage was to Susan Scott, born ca. 1839, sister of Eva. To this marriage was born nine children: Gilbert was born ca. 1861 and never married; Nelson was born July 8, 1862, died Dec. 28, 1939 and married Rosa Etta Pickett Sept. 4, 1887; Sarah (Sally) was born ca. 1864 and died of yellow fever. She never married; Liza was born ca. 1866 and never married; Frances (Franky) was born ca. 1868 and married Edward Weller Dec. 16, 1888; Margaret never married; Charles, born Aug. 31, 1873, died Dec. 18, 1954 and married Blanche Busenbark Caplinger on Jan. 17, 1918; James Rush, born July 1, 1876, died Nov. 24, 1966. He fought in the

Philippines during the Spanish American War. He never married; George died at age two.

DEAN C. AND EDITH J. DUNCAN RUSH

Dean and Edith Rush reside in Ripley Township two miles northwest of Alamo, IN. They own and operate grain and beef cattle farms near Alamo. Dean has been engaged in farming since he was a boy.

Dean was born on Nov. 7, 1938 on a farm at the south edge of Alamo to L. Doyne and Helen Elmore Rush. Dean has one younger brother, Roscoe N.

Dean is a graduate of Alamo High School and received a B.S. Degree in agriculture from Purdue University in 1960. In 1967 he married Edith Jane Duncan. They have two daughters: Julie Deanna, who is a junior at Purdue University majoring in biology; and Kathleen Marie, who is a senior at Southmont High School and will attend Indiana University in the fall of 1989.

Dean, Kathleen, Julie, Edith Rush

Dean has been involved in many community organizations throughout the years. He is a member of the Purdue Agricultural Alumni Association, is a member of the Alamo Christian Church where he has served as deacon, has served in the Army Reserve, is a past patron of the Alamo Order of the Eastern Star, is a member of the Masonic Lodge, and is president of the Alamo Cemetery Association.

Dean's parents have lived in the Alamo area for many years. His father, Doyne, was born Dec. 4, 1908 near Alamo to Nelson and Rosa Etta Pickett Rush and was a farmer until his death July 6, 1981. His mother, Helen, was born Mar. 9, 1910 near Alamo to Roscoe N. and Myrtle Lattimore Elmore. She was a farmwife and teacher. She is still residing in the farmhouse where they began housekeeping.

Edith was born Jan. 31, 1943 at Kingman, IN to Dawson Glenn and Dorothy Jean McCammon Duncan. She is the fourth of five children. After graduating from Kingman High School in 1961, she moved to Steamboat Springs, CO with her Mother, Stepfather, Gerald R. Jones (born Mar. 29, 1909-died Sept. 14, 1978), and younger brother. While living there, she attended Colorado State University in Fort Collins, CO. She is presently a member of the Montgomery County Civic Band, the Evangelical United Brethren Church at Kingman (now the Community Church), the Alamo Ladies Aid, is past Worthy Matron of the Alamo Order of the Eastern Star, and is secretary-treasurer of the Alamo Cemetery Association.

Edith's father was born July 15, 1900 in Jackson Co., IN to Andrew Johnson and Margaret Kirkpatrick Duncan. Glenn started working in coal mines when he was a young man and became Superintendent of Morgan Coal Company near Kingman. He died Jan. 25, 1955.

Her mother was born in Carlisle, IN on Oct. 9, 1910 to Dr. Carl and Faye Brewer McCammon. Dorothy loved music and played piano for silent movies. She still plays piano and organ and resides in Rockville, IN.

JESSE, SR. AND JANE STARNES RUSH

Jesse Rush, Sr. was born Dec. 19, 1776 and died Feb. 27, 1848. He married Jane Starnes in 1790. We do not know Jesse's parents, where he was born, or where he married Jane. In 1789 Jesse witnessed a Franklin Co., GA deed. Next we find Jesse as security for a marriage in Greene Co., TN in 1789 and also listed on Greene County tax lists for a number of years. He was still in Greene County in 1826. On Apr. 20, 1829 there is a land grant in Brown Township, Montgomery Co., IN to Jesse Rush, Sr. All their children came with them except Lewis, who stayed in Greene Co., TN. When they came to Montgomery, we do not know. Sons Churchill, Jeptha, Jesse, Jr. and Leonard took out land grants in Montgomery Co., IN. Most of the Rushes in Montgomery County who were farmers owned their land. Some were carpenters.

Jesse and Jane had 11 children: Churchill was born May 3, 1792 in Georgia and died about 1877. He married Hannah Haynes Aug. 15, 1816 in Greene Co., TN; Thomas was born Sept. 3, 1793 and married Sally Lane Dec. 8, 1813 in Greene Co., TN; Lewis was born Mar. 2, 1795 and married Mary Olinger Feb. 26, 1825 in Greene Co., TN; Margaret was born June 6, 1797 and married Henry Broomer (Bruner) in Greene Co., TN; Rachel was born Dec. 18, 1798, died Apr. 5, 1880, and married David Olinger; Leonard was born Jan. 23, 1801 and died Oct. 29, 1849. He married Margaret Buchanan Mar. 28, 1833 in Montgomery Co., IN; Barbary was born Apr. 5, 1803 and married Mar. 20, 1828 in Montgomery Co., IN; Mary was born May 10, 1804 and married David Stonebraker Oct. 18, 1836 in Montgomery County; Jesse was born Aug. 23, 1806, died Oct. 15, 1844 and married Dorcus Simmons Apr. 2, 1829 in Montgomery Co., IN; Elizabeth was born Feb. 9, 1809 and married John Teterh (Teeters) Jan. 27, 1831 in Montgomery Co., IN; Jeptha was born Mar. 9, 1810 and died Apr. 7, 1863. He married Susannah Stonebraker May 19, 1835 in Montgomery Co., IN.

Jesse's wife, Jane was born Nov. 21, 1772 in North Carolina and died Mar. 24, 1838. She was the daughter of Leonard Starnes (died 1828 in Green Co., TN). He was the son of Joseph Starnes, Sr. (born ca. 1730 and died Apr. 7, 1779 in "Starnes Defeat" at Blue Lick, KY). He was the son of Frederick Starnes, Sr. (born 1700 at Palatinate, Germany, died 1774), the son of John Adam Staring (Starnes) of Germany.

L. DOYNE AND HELEN M. (ELMORE) RUSH

Doyne Rush was a grain and beef farmer. In his early years he also raised horses, sheep, hogs and was a school bus driver for several years. Doyne was active in the community as treasurer of the Alamo Telephone Co., president of Alamo Cemetery Association, deacon and trustee of Alamo Christian Church, member of Masonic Lodge and the Montgomery County Farm Bureau. He was a member of the Alamo Christian Church, and he was a Democrat.

Doyne was born Dec. 4, 1908 one-half mile east of Alamo, the second child of Nelson and Rosa Etta Pickett Rush.

L. Doyne and Helen M. (Elmore) Rush

Nelson Rush was a farmer who lived in Ripley and Brown Townships in Montgomery County. He also lived in Fountain County. He belonged to the Odd Fellows and Rebekah Lodges and was a member of the Horse Thief Detective Association. He was a member of the Christian Church and was a Democrat.

Rosa Etta was the daughter of John and Charlotte Craig Pickett. She was a member of the Christian Church, the Rebekah Lodge and was a Republican.

Doyne's sister, Myrtle Estella, married Earl Stanford, son of David G. and Mary R. Roundtree Stanford. They lived all their lives near Alamo, IN. She graduated from Alamo High School. She was a member of the Christian Church, taught Sunday School for many years, was Past Worthy Matron of Alamo Eastern Star No. 498, Clerk Treasurer of the town of Alamo, Alamo Home Extension Club, and took part in many other community activities.

Doyne was the grandson of Andrew and Susan Scott Rush and John and Charlotte Craig Pickett. Doyne was a graduate of Alamo High School.

On July 11, 1937 Doyne married Helen Marie Elmore at her parent's home northeast of Alamo. They have two sons: Dean Clifton, born Nov. 7, 1938; a graduate of Purdue University; married Edith Jane Duncan Aug. 19, 1967; children, Julie Deanna and Kathleen Marie. Roscoe Nelson, born July 27, 1940; a graduate of Purdue University; married Jacqueline Katherine Cipriani June 10, 1962; children, Roscoe M., Santi A., Robert N., and Nelson J.

Helen was born Mar. 9, 1910 near Alamo to Roscoe M. and Myrtle Lattimore Elmore. Her parents were teachers. Helen graduated from Colfax High School at Colfax, IN and received a Bachelor of Science degree from Indiana State University at Terre Haute. She taught vocational home economics, health and art. She is a member of Alamo Christian Church, Christian Ladies Aid, Order of the Eastern Star, past S. & E. leader of the Ripley Township Farm Bureau, Alamo Home Extension Club and past president of the Montgomery County Home Extension Club. She enjoys painting landscapes and flowers.

At the time of his death on July 6, 1981 they owned 600 acres near Alamo. She still lives in their farm home where she came as a bride 52 years ago.

ROSCOE NELSON AND JACQUELINE K. CIPRIANI RUSH

Roscoe and Jackie are former residents of Montgomery Co., IN. Roscoe is a Senior Vice-President in charge of commercial lending for the First National Bank of Evergreen Park, Evergreen

Park, IL. Jackie is a partner in Fantasy Collections, a jewelry business in Glenview, IL. Roscoe owns a farm in Ripley Township near Alamo and teaches economics at William Rainey Harper College in Palatine, IL.

Roscoe was born at Alamo, IN on July 27, 1940 to Leslie Doyne and Helen Elmore Rush. He is the youngest of two sons. His father was a life-long resident and farmer in Ripley Township near Alamo. His mother was a teacher and still resides in Ripley Township near Alamo.

Robert, Santi, Roscoe M., Nelson, Jackie and Roscoe

Roscoe graduated from Alamo High School in 1958 and Purdue University with a Bachelor of Science Degree in 1962, and a Master of Science Degree in Agricultural Economics in 1967. On June 10, 1962 he married Jacqueline K. Cipriani in Chicago Heights, IL. They have four sons: Roscoe Matthias, born Oct. 18, 1963 in Montgomery County now resides in Dayton, OH; Santi Andrew, born May 27, 1965 in Montgomery County now resides in Ripley Township near Alamo; Robert Nelson, born June 22, 1968 in Nappanee, Elkhart Co., IN currently a student at the University of Illinois; Nelson Jan, born Nov. 4, 1979 in Glenview, Cook Co., IL.

Jackie was born at Chicago Heights, Cook Co., IL on Nov. 13, 1940 to Santi and Elsa Tozzi Cipriani. She is the oldest of three daughters. Her father is a life-long resident of Chicago Heights and owns an Italian food store in Chicago Heights. Her mother was born at Ladd, IL and later moved to Joliet, IL with her family until her marriage. She operated an Italian food store with her husband until her death.

Jackie graduated from Bloom Township High School, Chicago Heights, IL in 1958 and Purdue University with a Bachelor of Science Degree in Bacteriology in 1962. She worked as a bacteriologist at St. James Hospital in Chicago Heights after graduation.

Roscoe and Jackie moved to Ripley Township near Alamo in 1962 where they operated a farm until 1965. In 1965 they moved to West Lafayette, IN where Roscoe was attending graduate school at Purdue University. In 1967 they moved to Nappanee, IN where Roscoe was employed as an Agricultural and commercial loan officer with the First National Bank of Elkhart. In 1973 they moved to Northbrook, IL where Roscoe was employed as a Vice-President in charge of lending with the Evanston Bank, Evanston, IL. In 1974 they moved to Glenview, IL where they currently reside.

Roscoe enlisted in the U.S. Army Reserves in 1961 and served his active duty at Fort Leonardwood, MO. He is currently a member and past president of the Evergreen Park Rotary Club.

DAVID RUSK, SR.

David Rusk, Sr. (1770-1836) was of Scotch origin, exact birthplace unknown. The 1820 Census of Brown Co., OH, lists David, with wife Margaret ____, five females, and seven males. One daughter, Bettsie (Elizabeth) was married to Christopher Mann at the time. Later information was that there were 12 children (listed in the will), six of each. Now, we belive that Robert Rusk was a son, who came to Indiana in 1822 and died in 1823-not a brother. So there probably were 13 children. David Rusk Sr., farmed, bought and sold land. He was of some wealth for that early day. David Sr., and Robert were in the party of settlers who came to Montgomery County in 1822; and Robert Rusk signed for land in the same area that William Heath did, on the same day. It is generally accepted that William Heath was the first settler to sign for land in east Wayne Township. David Rusk, Sr. returned to Ohio to prepare for the move to Indiana. In 1823, Robert Rusk became very ill and called for Jonas and Agnes Mann, old neighbors in Ohio living in Waynetown (Middletown). Robert Rusk died before the will was written, but, the Manns carried his wishes to Crawfordsville. This became the second will recorded in Montgomery County. Robert Rusk willed the land to his brothers, John and William Rusk.

L to R, Back: Squire and Dennis Rusk. Front: Lucetta Burnell, Abigail Grenard and Joanne Biddle children of David Jr. and Martha Ball Rusk

In 1825, John and William entered 160 acres at Middletown north of Coal Creek—the Runyan farm of today. This land has been in the possession of a Rusk family relative for 164 years (1989). In 1829, David Sr. returned to Middletown, and entered 80 acres, joining this land on the north. He also entered 80 acres in Fountain County, which, eventually became the home of Dennis Rusk, his grandson. In 1830, David Rusk, Sr., was living at the end of East Street, in a log cabin. He bought the 160 acres from John and William. The entire family was living in the area by 1830. David helped to build the first house of worship, near the Pioneer Cemetery, a log structure, which later burned.

Christmas Day in 1829, Nancy Rusk and husband, Samuel Mann, donated land for the new frame church, to be built at the east end of the town, near Pioneer Cemetery. There were other donors.

Samuel Mann assisted in platting the town of Waynetown; and sold lots for $20 each.

In the David Rusk, Sr., family, there were twin boys—David Jr., and Jonathon. Jonathon migrated to Missouri, married twice, had a large family. Jonathon spent time in a Confederate prison in the Civil War. Two of his sons fought for the North, and one of them, gave his life at Chickamauga, TN. A third son fought with the Confederates in the Civil War—and later, became a U.S. Marshal. David Rusk, Jr., remained on the homeplace his entire life, and married Martha Ball (a name famous in Colonial History). They were the parents of three boys and three girls. One boy died in youth. David Jr., served as a member of the early school board five years, and was the first single trustee of Wayne Township—making a total of 9-1/2 years service. David Rusk Jr. (1806-1875). Jonathon (1806-1873), David Rusk, Sr., and Jr., are buried in the Pioneer Cemetery. Early family members were Baptists.

DENNIS RUSK

Dennis Rusk was the son of David Rusk, Jr., and Martha Ball. He married Paradine Matilda Maxwell, who lived only six months. Later, he married Margaret Emza Hall, and they established their log cabin home in Fountain County on land his grandfather had bought from the government. Their family was five sons and five daughters. The mother and a daughter died from measles. Another daughter, who was an early school teacher, educated at Ladoga Academy, died from typhoid. Dennis Rusk built a frame house on the Montgomery-Fountain County line. The family moved here in 1866. The last three children were born in the frame house. It is legend that the children were very frightened, when the first train came through on the railroad, about 1867.

Dennis Rusk (1830-1915) was a farmer, owned an elevator at Waynetown, a tile mill was on the farm, and maple syrup camps. Portions of this farm have been in the Rusk family for 160 years. Dennis Rusk furnished the timber used for Snyder's Chapel Church and family members assisted in the construction.

Back Row: Edward, Willard, David, Albert and Berton Rusk. Front Row: Elva Fowler, Delilah Rusk and Mary Parker. Seated: Dennis Rusk

David Rusk (1868-1966), a son of Dennis Rusk and Margaret Emza Hall married Edna Elizabeth Campbell, a daughter of Albert Campbell and Elizabeth Burgner Campbell. Their children were Clarence Orville Rusk, Marguerite Celeste Rusk, and Helen Elizabeth Rusk. Clarence Rusk married Elizabeth Lee Lawson, and their son was Kenneth David Rusk (1928-____). Clarence Rusk (1903-1981). Kenneth Rusk married Barbara Jane Heath and there were three sons.

Dennis Layne (1951-____) married Amber Suzanne Kemble and their daughters were Megan Elisa and Erin Elaine. David Bruce (1953-____) married Cindi Lyn Hayes and their children were Tiffany Shawne and David Heath. (2) Elizabeth (Carty) York, whose daughter was Brandey York. Paul Eugene (1956-____) married Carol Larue Ahl. They operate a Pizza Shop on the same corner in Waynetown where David Rusk, Sr., had his place of business in 1830, as the first merchant in Middletown. What was a large family, is now, a group few in number. To recount the lineage—David Rusk, Sr., David Rusk, Jr., Dennis Rusk, David Rusk, Clarence Rusk, Kenneth David Rusk,—sons Dennis, David and Paul, and the four children mentioned above.

ROBERT AND HELEN HERRON RUTLEDGE

William "Billy" Stephens Coon (Feb. 20, 1856-May 6, 1930) was born near Newtown, IN, the seventh of eight children of Isaac II and Ruth Jane Stephens Coon. Mary Catharine "Cassie" Koon (Sept. 4, 1859-June 30, 1934) was born near Wingate the only daughter of John Koon III and Mary Temple Koon and had one brother, George Washington. William and Mary were married Sept. 4, 1878, and settled on a farm west of Wingate where they would spend the rest of their lives. William's paternal grandparents were Isaac I and Mary Polly Stephens Coon; his maternal grandparents were James Edward and Malinda White Stephens. Mary's paternal grandparents were John Coon II and Susannah Lane Coon; her maternal grandparents were John and Catherine Selby Temple. All the Koon, Coon, Temple and Selby families were settlers of Butler, Montgomery and Warren Counties in Ohio. The farm William and Mary settled on was owned by her father who came from Kentucky and settled in Montgomery Co., IN in 1833. The farm is now owned by two of their granddaughters, Ruby Herron Ralston and Helen Louise Herron Rutledge and her husband, Robert.

L. to R.: Jane, Jack, Charlie, Bill, Helen, Mary, Ruby. Seated: Earl and Cora Herron

There was an old ox road that ran down the lane and curved across the fields to Turkey Run Creek, crossed the Run on a flat wooden bridge and wound on through the fields.

Helen Louise was born Oct. 22, 1931, to Earl Franklin Herron (Feb. 29, 1904-June 3, 1965) and Cora Cleo Coon Herron (Oct. 24, 1901-May 7, 1973). She and Robert Wayne Rutledge were married Apr. 2, 1950, in Liberty Chapel Church. Bob was born Apr. 25, 1931, to Frederic and Muriel Howard Rutledge. Helen and Bob live on a farm west of Mellott and Bob finds pleasure in tilling the ground of his ancestors, the fifth generation to do so. They are active members of Mellott United Church of Christ. They were the parents of four children.

Yvonne Ann, born May 13, 1952, graduated from Fountain Central High School and attended Lincoln Christian College, Lincoln, IL. There she met and married Dale Reed on Aug. 13, 1972. They have two daughters: Carmen Miranda born June 8, 1976, and Melinda Joy born Nov. 14, 1979. Dale was born Mar. 28, 1949, to Ira and Nadene Foster Reed. He graduated from Unity High School in Tolono, IL, then from Lincoln Christian College and is a building contractor. Yvonne is an announcer for W.B.G.L. Radio in Champaign, IL. The family lives in Tolono and are active members of Assembly of God Church in Tuscola where Yvonne is choir director.

John Alvin was born Mar. 9, 1954, and passed away May 1, 1959.

David Earl was born Apr. 4, 1957. He graduated from Fountain Central High School and from I.T.T. Institute, Indianapolis, IN. He has lived in California the past 11 years. He is assistant manager in the parts department of Mercedes-Benz of San Diego. He enjoys surfing as a hobby.

Nadine Sue was born Nov. 27, 1961. She graduated from Fountain Central High School and has earned an Associate Degree in Secretarial Science from Parkland College, Urbana, IL, where she resides. She is office supervisor in the History Department at the University of Illinois. She is a member of the Free Methodist Church and sings in the church choir. She and Yvonne enjoy their music ministry in and around the area; they have performed on television in Decatur, IL.

BYRDELL WILLARD 'BYRD W.' SAIDLA

He was born Oct. 9, 1879, a son of John Henry and Alice M. Thompson Saidla. His brother was John Henry Jr. of Chicago, IL.

In Darlington on Oct. 14, 1900 he married Leota Hiatt. She was born Oct. 12, 1879 and died Aug. 2, 1952 in Darlington. She was a daughter of Ira Kenworth and Sarah Catherine Mullen Hiatt. Her brother and sisters were: Ethel (Kip Milner); Iva (Frank Custer); Mayme (John Lynch); Ralph W.; Ada (Emery Moffett); and Hazel (Carl Anderson). They had one son - John Collyn Delna.

Byrd W. Saidla, Leota (Hiatt) Saidla, John Collyn Saidla

They lived in Lebanon in the early part of their married life, where he worked for the Prudential Insurance Co. They also ran a rooming house next door to the Lebanon Theater for the Performers until about 1912. Then they moved back to Darlington and went into the restaurant business. He was a member of the IOOF Lodge at Lebanon and of the Ku Klux Klan. He died Aug. 25, 1924 of cancer at his home next to the theater on Main Street in Darlington.

Leota remarried Aug. 10, 1930 to Valonia 'Lonie' Edwards, a farmer of Montgomery County. After he retired from the farm they moved back to Leota's house in Darlington. She is buried next to Byrd W. in the IOOF Cemetery and Lonie is buried next to his first wife in Greenlawn in Darlington, IN. *Submitted by I. Jo Summers*

JOHANN ADAM SAIDLA (SEIDLE)

He was born Apr. 7, 1790 in France or Germany. He was married c. 1819 in Germany to Catherine M. Kellar. She was born Nov. 19, 1796 Germany. He died June 10, 1870 and she died Feb. 1, 1870 in Montgomery County, and both buried Union Cemetery, Lauramie Twp., Tippecanoe Co., IN.

They had two sons: Philip Jacob 'PJ' born Oct. 20, 1820 died Feb. 8, 1874 Montgomery County and John Adam Jr. born Nov. 2, 1822, both born in Germany.

They arrived in Baltimore, MD Sept. 30, 1833 from Mochmuhl, Kingdom of Wurttemberg, Germany.

The story always told about him was — He was a Frenchman and a bodyguard of Napoleon Bonaparte. His tour of duty was up while in Germany. He stayed there and married a German girl and they had two boys. The boys were to go into the German Army after the age of 12. So he moved his family to the U.S.A. Darlington, IN. When they came into the U.S. his name was changed from Johann Adam Seidle to John Adam Saidla.

They arrived in Montgomery County Oct. 10, 1833, then in October 1833 he has Patents on four pieces of land in Township 20 Range 3 Sections 14 & 23 for a total of 400 acres. He and his sons are listed as farmers.

PJ's children: Catherine M., Caroline S. 'Carrie' and John Henry.

J. Adam's children: Simon; Abraham; Isaac; Joshua H.; Mary E.; John Adam L.; Jesse A.; Sarah Catherine 'Kate'; Susana N. 'Anna'; Wiliam A.; Lenora Alice 'Allis' and Frank. *Submitted by I. Jo Summers*

JOHN COLLYN 'J.C.' SAIDLA

He was the only child of Byrd W. and Leota Hiatt Saidla; born July 28, 1901 in Darlington, IN and died Sept. 11, 1964, Chesterton, IN. He was married July 12, 1922 in Crawfordsville, IN to Mildred Lenora Easley. She was a daughter of Charles W. and Eva N. Buser Easley. Her brothers and sisters were: L.J. and J.C. infants; Caretta Everson (Paul); Mary Cowdin (Earl) and Velma Tague (Walter). She was born Apr. 5, 1905 New Market, IN and died Feb. 24, 1988 Valparaiso, IN. They both are buried in the IOOF cemetery in Darlington, IN.

They moved to LaPorte, IN two weeks after their marriage where their three children were born. Collyn Jr. Saidla, born July 18, 1923, died Oct. 3, 1942. He was killed from a crash in his airplane in Porter Co., IN.

Ila Joan Saidla, Mildred L. (Easley) Saidla, Collyn Jr. Saidla, John Collyn Saidla, Charles Byrdell Saidla

Ila Joan 'I. Jo' Saidla, born Mar. 9, 1928. She married Oct. 18, 1947, Chesterton, IN to Dallas Burton Summers. He is the only son of Dallas Lester and Ruth Laura Spencer Summers, born Sept. 28, 1926 Chesterton, IN. They have two children: Collyn Burtus Summers and Julie K.

Esgate (E. Edward), Peitrowski (George); and three grandchildren: Sara Esgate; S. Michael W. and Laura Elizabeth Ann Summers.

Charles Byrdell Saidla, born June 8, 1932. He was in the U.S. Air Force and married to Benadine Sieple. They had three children: Judy Ann Watt (Mark); Donald Jay Saidla single; Sharon Marie Cummings (Melvin), and four grandchildren by them: Adrian and Connie Watt; James Saidla and Thomas Cummings. Charles remarried to Rita Defandor; they have a son John Charles Saidla, and he has two children David and Christine Lynn Saidla.

J.C. was self employed most all his working years. He ran the movie projector in the Darlington theater in 1915-17. Beginning in Darlington he helped install electrical wiring in homes then in 1919 went to New Market and wired the homes there. In LaPorte he had an electrical shop then sold it to become the manager of the LaPorte County Power House for the years of 1930-34. After that he started the Atlas Manufacturing Co. When that business outgrew its building he moved it to Chesterton, IN in 1938 buying the old china factory building. By 1940 he had built the Atlas Roller Rink in the upper floor. In 1942 he sold the factory and building and moved the rink to town where the west side of the Ben Franklin store is now. Then in 1946 he built a new building to house his rink and the photography studio and 12 apartments. In 1954 he took schooling and become a noted ceramist along with his Hobby and Craft Shop and Photo Studio.

He was also an amateur radio 'ham' operator for many years starting in his boyhood in Darlington before they had to have call letters. His last call was W9NHA. *Submitted by I. Jo Summers*

JOHN HENRY SAIDLA

He was born June 20, 1856 on the farm of his grandfather - John Adam. He was the son of Philip J. and Lucy A. Kuhnz Saidla. He was married in Darlington on Nov. 28, 1878 to Alice M. Thompson. She was born Aug. 25, 1860 Montgomery County, a daughter of Enoch and Margaret Aldridge Thompson. Her brothers and sisters were: Willard J.; Emily; Frank; Fred and Nellie.

He was a farmer. He was killed Sept. 5, 1880. The obit reads "John A. (should be. H.) Saidla of Sugar Creek Township, in company with a young man he had recently hired, started to the field to cut corn. On the way they stopped to examine a revolver in the hands of the young man. During the examination the weapon was discharged, the contents entering the abdomen of Saidla and so seriously injuring him that he died the next day. Saidla was an industrious young man some 25 years old. A son of Philip Saidla. He leaves a wife and two children."

John Henry Saidla, Alice M. (Thompson) Saidla before 1880

Their children were: Byrdell Willard 'Byrd W.' and John Henry Jr.

Byrd W. was born Oct. 9, 1879 died Aug. 6, 1924 Darlington, IN married Leota Hiatt. They had one son John Collyn Delna Saidla.

John Henry Jr. was born Jan. 15, 1881 Darlington, died Aug. 6, 1969 Chicago, IL. He married Helen 'Lena' Schubert in 1905 in Darlington. They had five children: Bernice Alice b. Mar. 4, 1912 (Arthur M. Green); Lucille 'Lou' b. Dec. 18, 1913 (Charles E. Green); Margaret Louise 'Marge' b. May 5, 1918 (Fred Kirchner Jr.); Norma Jean b. Sept. 26, 1921 (Roy Wilber Erickson); John Ervie 'Bud' b. Sept. 4, 1923 (Ila?) They were all born in Chicago, IL.

After the boys grew up Alice remarried Aug. 22, 1907 in Crawfordsville to Henry D. Beisel. They lived in Frankfort, IN. She died Nov. 30, 1936 there and is buried at the IOOF Cemetery in Darlington with John Henry. *Submitted by I. Jo Summers*

PHILIP JACOB SAIDLA

He was a son of John Adam and Catherine M. Kellar Saidla. He was born in Germany Oct. 20, 1820 and died Feb. 8, 1874 in Montgomery County. He and his brother, J. Adam Jr. were brought to Montgomery County in 1833. In Clinton Co., IN, on Apr. 16, 1848 PJ married Louisianna 'Lucy A' Kuhnz. She was a daughter of Henry and Catherine Zimmerman Kuhnz. Her brothers and sisters were: Charles (Elizabeth); Catherine (Jacob Baer); David; Jonas (Catherine Gushwa); Caroline (William Glauson); Samuel (Susannah Ruch) and infant Stella Ann, Hannah and three more.

She was born Oct. 17, 1828 Lehigh Co., PA, died Apr. 21, 1874 Montgomery County. Both are buried in Union Cemetery Laramie Twp., Tippecanoe Co., IN.

They farmed the land his father John Adam got in 1833. They had three children: Catherine M. b. c. 1849 (George W. Saylor); Caroline S. 'Carrie' b. 1854, d. July 3, 1929, (Joel Goodnight) no children and John Henry (Alice M. Thompson) two sons Byrd W. and John Henry Jr.

When PJ's father died in 1870 he and his brother fought over who would get the homestead farm. A judge in Boone Co., IN ordered it sold and PJ bought it. He didn't get to enjoy it for long as he died two years after he bought it.

The farm was in Sugar Creek Township Montgomery Co., IN. *Submitted by I. Jo Summers*

SANDERS-GORDON FAMILY

In North Carolina, James Gordon born February 1779 married Mary Joh born Dec. 16, 1775. In 1806 they moved to Ohio and then on to Indiana in 1807. Their youngest son, James Smith Gordon was born July 14, 1814 and died Sept. 3, 1911 in Dearborn Co., IN. He came to Franklin Township, Putnam County in 1821. The first home of a white inhabitant was erected by James Gordon. His nephew was the first white child born in Franklin Township. James Gordon married Ann B. Dickerson on Apr. 6, 1842. Samantha Ellen Gordon one of their seven children was born July 12, 1850.

Samantha Gordon married James Alexander Sanders, born June 4, 1845, the son of John and Sarah Gorham Sanders. (Sarah was a triplet). They married in Putnam County in 1868 and their first daughter Clara Florence was born on June 4, 1869. She married Ulysses Grant Ward.

James and Samantha moved to 1-1/2 miles southeast of Whitesville in 1869 and the following year to their farm one mile east of Whitesville. Elva Clyde born Apr. 1, 1878 was their second daughter. Elva married William Friend who had a daughter Mary Florence.

Then on Feb. 26, 1902 Elva Sanders Friend married Jesse Edgar Terry born Aug. 21, 1877. He was the son of Thomas Bowyer Terry born 1848 in Christianburg, VA. He was in the Virginia Mounted Infantry Cavalry, and an officer in the Confederate Army in the Civil War. Thomas Terry married Mary Ellen Teeter, daughter of William and Ellen Fleser Teeter.

Edgar and Elva Terry had a son Donald Norman who died in infancy and a daughter Nelly Merle.

Edgar and Elva were farmers in Whitesville area. Nelly married Lyle Hulbert, son of Orbie and Myrtle Hulbert. They continued farming on the same farm as her parents. Nelly, a Home Economist, taught school in Howard and Montgomery Counties. Kyle has a hobby of photography.

Some of this data from the *Atlas of Putnam County, Indiana, 1879*.

SARVIS TO SERVIES

William Sarvis born between 1776 and 1784 in Shelby Co., KY married Mary (Polly) Shelton before 1798 (probably the daughter of Wilson Shelton).

Nothing is known of his origins. The earliest available record is that he paid taxes in Shelby Co., KY on Aug. 7, 1800. This was an attempt to "reconstruct" the 1800 census of Kentucky after destruction of records by fire.

County records show that William sold 51-1/4 acres of land located near the mouth of Fox Run on Mar. 13, 1824 for $615.00 (There is no record of when the land was acquired.) Neither William or Mary could sign their names to the deed.

Further county records show that William Sarvis bought 109 acres of land on the west side of Fox Run on Oct. 3, 1825.

William died before Nov. 30, 1826. That was the date of an appraisal of his possessions. William's grave has not been found.

The family farm was sold in 1830 to a daughter of the Governor of Kentucky. Widow Sarvis, the remaining children at home, married children and spouses, friends, and neighbors migrated at about the same time to west central Indiana by wagon train, to the area where the eldest son Jonathan Sarvis had acquired land in 1828.

The date and place of death and place of burial of Mary (Polly) Shelton Sarvis is not known. She undoubtedly lived the remainder of her life in Indiana.

To this union 11 children were born, probably all in Kentucky.

Jonathan W. Sarvis born Apr. 11, 1798, Lyda A. Sarvis born Jan. 11, 1800, Nancy G. Sarvis born Sept. 25, 1802, John A. Sarvis born July 22, 1803, Lucinda Sarvis born May 14, 1806, William Anderson Sarvis (later spelled Servies) born Apr. 11, 1808, Samuel H. Sarvis born Apr. 14, 18??, George Waller Sarvis born Dec. 18, 1810, Henry M. Sarvis born Nov. 30, 1812, Juliet E.G. Sarvis born Jan. 17, 1817, and Emily Finetta Sarvis born Dec. 1, 1819.

Of the seven Sarvis children known to have migrated to Indiana, six of them and their families migrated after a short time on to Mahaska Co., IA by wagon train. One remained in the same area near New Market, IN and became the beginning of all the Servies families in Montgomery Co., IN and the whole State of Indiana as research has shown so far.

He was William Anderson Sarvis, who became the only branch of the family to use the spelling of Servies. This spelling is still used by all of William's descendents today and the rest of the family that migrated to Iowa continued to use the spelling of Sarvis. *Submitted by Nina Davidson*

WILLIAM THOMAS SAYLER

William Thomas Sayler was born Feb. 3, 1834 in Russell Township, Putnam Co., IN. According to his own Oral Biography written in 1903 and recorded by his granddaughter, Elva (Sayler) Milligan, he suggests that his forebearers were either Abraham, who arrived in Pennsylvania in 1736 or Peter in 1733. His great grandfather, Godfrey, had five children: William, Godfrey, George, Joseph and Sarah. The family emigrated to Tennessee soon after the Revolutionary War and the father died at the age of 85.

The oldest son of this family was William, who was born in Pennsylvania on Mar. 25, 1789. The rest of the family were born in Tennessee. This William, grandfather of William Thomas Sayler, was at the "Battle of New Orleans," as a Drummer and the family has copies of the official papers citing him for his service to his country in that capacity. William married Catherine Keller before the War of 1812 and they were parents of nine children — all born in Tennessee. The family moved to a very young and, as yet, unsettled Indiana, probably in the mid 1820s. They made their home on the banks of Raccoon Creek in Putnam County.

Their oldest son, Jacob Sayler (born May 31, 1812, died Feb. 27, 1849) and Rebecca McFarlin (1812-1883) were married Dec. 1, 1832. They were the parents of eight children — the oldest of whom was William Thomas Sayler.

Front Row: L to R — Elsie Marie, Francis Milbert, America Melinda and Hubert W. Back row: Walter Leslie, Clarence Lee and Elva Esther Sayler

William Thomas Saylor married Malinda Clodfelter on June 6, 1858. Their eight children were all born in Putnam County. They first lived in Putnam County for 18 years and later moved southwest of New Market, then made their home in New Market. Malinda, born Feb. 18, 1842, died Sept. 25, 1927, was the daughter of Solomon Clodfelter and Sally McGaughey. The children of William and Malinda were: Francis Milbert; Clara Ann, 1861-1927, married 1879 to James Franklin Demoret; Alice Catherine, 1863-1941, married Joseph Clark, a farmer, lumberman and trucker; Alfred Vorhees, 1865-1867; Jackson Purley (twin), 1868-1870; James "Charley" (twin) 1868-1948, well-known auctioneer, married (1) Winnie Spencer in 1893 and #2 Luna Noble; Solomon Jacob 1873-1947, a farmer, married Pearl Davis in 1898; Harvey Bayard 1877-1957, an auctioneer, married 1900, to Ella Brush.

Francis Milbert (above) was born Dec. 31, 1859, married America Malinda Vancleave on his birthday in 1884. They set up housekeeping in a log cabin which stood at southwest corner of Road 700 South and State Road 47. This location was where Walter Leslie was born. They moved south of Browns Valley where the rest of their children were born, namely: Clarence Lee, Elva Esther, Elsie Marie and Hubert W. They moved in 1892 four miles southwest of New Market. At the time of Milbert's death, they had accumulated 960 acres of land raising purebred hogs and cattle. They were faithful members of the Baptist Church of New Market.

Walter Leslie, son of Francis and America, married Elizabeth Opal Bonwell Oct. 23, 1912. They had five children: Robert Francis, born July 11, 1914; Lois Esther, born Sept. 23, 1916, died December 1921; Charles Bayard born Feb. 29, 1922; Ralph Addison born Mar. 24, 1924 and Barbara Jane born Feb. 16, 1927.

Robert Francis married Mary M. Pickel Nov. 25, 1937. Five children were born to this couple: Leslie Allen born Mar. 3, 1939, died Mar. 9, 1939; John Leslie, born Nov. 1, 1940; Larry Gene, born Apr. 18, 1944; Janet Lynn, born Mar. 30, 1954; and Steven Wayne born June 2, 1961.

Charles Bayard, married Betty Scott Curtis July 14, 1957, no children. Ralph Addison married Virginia Vail, three children, two sons and a daughter. Barbara Jane married Grant Jones, three sons. She married Norman Age, had one daughter, then married William Mason.

Clara Ann Sayler, (daughter of our subject, William Thomas Sayler), and husband, James Franklin Demoret had a farm on land that is now Lake Holiday. Soon after their marriage, in 1879, they left Indiana to homestead in Waverly — a town in Coffey Co., KS, on 20 acres of land. They lived there for 15 years and moved back to New Market, IN. Two of their children: Grace (1881-1962) who married Thomas Servies in 1901 and Myrtle Belle (1853-1953) who married William Northcutt Gott in 1904 were born in Indiana. The youngest children, Roy (1886-1966) who married Edith Grenard 1918; Mary Alice (1889-1975) who married Otis E. Hall 1908 and Hazel Clara (1891-1972) who married Guy Byron Busenbark in 1914, were born in Waverly, KS.

Mary Alice Demoret and Otis Earl Hall, above, were married June 25, 1908. They had five daughters: Lois Marie, born Mar. 22, 1910, married Merritt L. Aseltine, Jr. on June 30, 1934. Lois and Merritt have two married sons, six grandchildren and one great granddaughter. Mary Louise, born Sept. 14, 1911, married Kenneth E. Gleason, July 11, 1942, and they are parents of one son and two daughters, and have one grandson. Naomi, born Jan. 14, 1915, married Roger Phelps Talmadge July 11, 1942 and they are parents of a son and a daughter, and have five grandchildren. Waneta, born Oct. 16, 1919, married Charles William Mihle Oct. 26, 1940, and they have two sons and two grandchildren. Jeanne Frances, born Oct. 31, 1921, married Arthur Lloyd Johnson, Feb. 15, 1945, and they are parents of a son and a daughter and have no grandchildren.

Malinda, widow of our subject, William Thomas Sayler, outlived her mate by almost 20 years and was loved and respected by all of her many children, grandchildren and great grandchildren. She delighted in the annual Sayler-Clodfelter reunions, attended by the descendants of her husband William and herself and to each and everyone she gave a strong sense of "family."

The descendants of William Thomas Sayler are fortunate that he, too, had a strong sense of family history and told this story to his granddaughter. *Submitted by Mary Louise Hall Gleason and Robert Francis Sayler*

DR. FAYE O. SCHENCK

Dr. Faye Orr Schenck was born in Crawfordsville on Apr. 12, 1878. His parents were Henry T. and Isabelle Orr Schenck. Henry was born in Crawfordsville on Oct. 31, 1853 (died June 18, 1932), the son of Ruleff and Mary Snook Schenck. Ruleff was born in Ohio and had come to Montgomery Co., IN as a young man. Isabelle Orr was born in Hamilton, OH on Feb. 12, 1856 (died Mar. 20, 1925). She was the daughter of Daniel and Nancy Orr. Dr. Schenck grew up in Crawfordsville, attended public schools, and graduated from high school in 1894. As a young man, he learned the tinners trade from his father, but being interested in medicine, he then graduated from the Indiana Medical School in 1905. He did his internship in Indianapolis. In addition to his private practice, he served as medical examiner for life insurance companies. He is listed as County Physician in 1913.

On Oct. 21, 1908 Dr. Schenck married Anna Winter. Anna was born in Crawfordsville, the daughter of John and Katherine Winter. There were no children from this union.

Dr. Schenck belonged to the Presbyterian Church, was a member of the Modern Woodmen of America, the Tribe of Ben Hur, and the Improved Order of Red Men. He was a director of Union Savings and Loan Association, Oak Hill Cemetery Association and the First National Bank.

He served with the Army Medical Corps in World War I and was a member of the American Legion.

By the 1930s, Dr. Schenck had retired from medical practice and devoted his retirement years to managing a 155-acre farm that he had purchased to the west of the city of Crawfordsville. He had a beautiful home at the intersection of what is now (1989) Schenck Road and the Big-4 Railroad.

Farming neighbors remember Dr. Schenck in his retirement years as a compassionate, kind and friendly individual.

Dr. Schenck died Apr. 6, 1963, at the age of 84. Anna had preceded him in death on Aug. 11, 1953. Both are buried at Oak Hill Cemetery. *Authored in part by Thomas Baynes Dellinger*

JOHN C. AND MARY L. SCHENCK

Roelof Martense Schenck with his three children, Roelof, Jan and Anetj came to New Amsterdam from Amersfoort, Holland on the ship "de ValeKener" June 1650. Our family are descendants of his son, Jan. The Schencks migrated from Long Island to Monmonthe Co., NJ to Warren Co., OH.

Chrineyance Schenck, Sr., born May 6, 1792 in New Jersey, great, great grandson of Jan was a prisoner in the War of 1812 in Ohio. His father William, a Revolutionary soldier came to Ohio early 1800. Chrineyance Sr. bought public land in Wayne Township in 1828 for $1.25 per acre. In 1853 Chrineyance Jr. with his bride, Margaret Hance came to Wayne Township to homestead the 160 acres belonging to his father. He later bought the land from him. They had five children, Sarah Almeda, b. June 23, 1854, married Benjamin F. Ball; Joseph Oscar, b. Mar. 28, 1856, married Nancy E. Westfall; Lydia Belle, b. Nov. 3, 1857; Edgar, b. May 1, 1861, married Lougenia McKinley and Oliver, b. Mar. 7, 1868 married Anna L. Harpel, a school teacher on Dec. 24, 1898. Oliver and Anna had four children, John C., b. Oct. 25, 1899, married Mary L. Moore on June 26, 1919. Kenneth H., b. June 5, 1901, married Ethel V. Switzer. Mabel Viola, b. July 6, 1904. Russell R., b. Sept. 23, 1906, married Gladys V. Keller on Sept. 22, 1928. Both are deceased.

Mary L. and John C. Schenck

John C. Schenck was a farmer and also worked in the loan department (a short time) at Waynetown State Bank of which he was a bank director until his death. His memberships were Christian Union Church, Masonic Lodge, Eastern Star and Low 12 Club. Mary L. Moore, his wife, b. Mar. 10, 1899 was the daughter of Nathaniel and Bessie Moore. Both attended Wayne Township schools and were over 50-year members of their church and Eastern Star. John died July 29, 1979 and Mary died Mar. 8, 1985.

Their daughter, Maxine, b. Mar. 20, 1923 graduated from Waynetown High School in 1941 and St. Elizabeth School of Nursing in Lafayette, IN in 1944. She married David F. Rush in Augusta, GA Aug. 6, 1945. Both are veterans; she serving in the Army Nurse Corps and he in the Air Force in England and France in WWII. They belong to Christian Union Church; Eastern Star and he is a Mason. She is a member of Psi Iota Sorority. Both are retired; she from nursing at Culver Hospital and Ben Hur Surgical Group and he from farming.

David and Maxine have three sons: Gary L., born June 16, 1948; IU graduate, married Joanne McKinney June 30, 1984. He has two children, Melissa, born Jan. 10, 1974 and Jason, born Apr. 2, 1977. Gary is a banker at the Veedersburg State Bank. Warren J., born Nov. 5, 1951; IU graduate, married Jeanne Fulwider (a Lafayette Business College graduate) on Aug. 8, 1971. Their children are Carrie S., born Feb. 25, 1975; Aaron M., born Nov. 27, 1979 and Brandon D., born July 26, 1981. Warren is principal of Roachdale Elementary School. Wayne D., born Nov. 5, 1951, married Vicki Barker on May 20, 1973. Both are Purdue graduates. They have three children: Courtney M., born Mar. 26, 1977; Lindsey S., born Mar. 26, 1980 and Jared W., born May 6, 1982. Wayne is engaged in farming. Vicki is a substitute teacher. *Submitted by Maxine Rush*

ROELOF MARTENSE SCHENCK

Roelof Martense Schenck with his three children, Roelof, Jan and Anetj came to New Amsterdam from Amersfoorth, Holland on the ship "de Valekener" in June 1650. Montgomery County Schencks are descendants of his son, Jan. The Schencks migrated from Long Island to Monmouth Co., NJ on to Warren Co., OH.

Chrineyance Schenck, Sr. (born May 6, 1792 in New Jersey) a great, great great grandson of Jan was a prisoner in the War of 1812 in Ohio. His father, William who came to Ohio early 1800 was a Revolutionary War Soldier. Chrineyance, Sr. bought public land in Wayne Township in 1828 for $1.25 per acre. In 1853 Chrineyance, Jr. with his bride, Margaret Hance came to Indiana to homestead the 160 acres belonging to his father. He later bought the land from him. They had five children, Sarah Almeda (born June 23, 1854) married Benjamin F. Ball; Joseph Oscar (born Mar. 28, 1856) married Nancy E. Westfall; Lydia Belle (born Nov. 3, 1857); Edgar (born May 1, 1861) married Lougenia McKinley and Oliver (born Mar. 7, 1868) married Anna L. Harpel.

J. Oscar (born Mar. 28, 1856, died May 22, 1928) married Mar. 10, 1881 to Nancy Ellen Westfall (born Mar. 5, 1854, died Jan. 18, 1936). They had three children, Alta E. (born Feb. 10, 1882) married Charles Hughes; Era Bell (born Nov. 25, 1885) married Cecil Murphy; Forsest Wilbur (born Mar. 20, 1891) married Opal Berry.

Forest W. was a farmer with memberships in Christian Union Church, Masonic and Eastern Star lodges and Farm Bureau. Opal Berry (born May 8, 1894), his wife, was the daughter of Edward and Mary Elizabeth Berry. Both attended Wayne Township schools. Forest died Oct. 16, 1964 and Opal, died Oct. 10, 1975.

They had five children, Una Leona (born Oct. 9, 1912) married G. Edward Larew; Willis Arnold (born Aug. 19, 1916) married Wilma Busenbark; Horace Wendell (born Oct. 1, 1917) married Margaret Newlin; Elizabeth Alice (born Oct. 12, 1920) married William J. Flocker and Eddie Oscar (born May 14, 1925) married Mary Irene Allen Hannar.

Una L. and G. Edward (born July 2, 1912, died Apr. 9, 1979) were married in their church in 1938 and built a new home on their 110 acre farm in Wayne Township. They have four children: Rosalie Anne (born Mar. 3, 1939, died Mar. 13, 1983) married Charles Robert McMurray (born June 30, 1936). She had four children: David Wayne (born Aug. 9, 1958) married Cynthia Cowan (born Feb. 7, 1954). Cynthia has two girls, Mindi Schull (born June 18, 1975) and Tara Schull (born Sept. 11, 1977). Deanna Kay McMurray (born Sept. 29, 1959) married Ronald Ellingwood (born Dec. 25, 1957). She had Jason Charles, stillborn Sept. 6, 1980 and Ashley Rose, born Feb. 26, 1988. Dale Allen McMurray (born Feb. 11, 1961) married Kelly Renee Sanchez (born May 19, 1963). Her daughter, Leslie Brooke was born May 4, 1988. Daren Jay McMurray (born July 24, 1962) married Terri Light (born Nov. 28, 1961).

Lois Evalyn (born July 14, 1941) an Indiana State graduate married Melvin Vance (born Feb. 3, 1937). She has three children: Angela Dawn (born May 31, 1967), Brent Foster (born June 20, 1969), Cherise Renee (born Feb. 24, 1975).

Sharon Kay (born Dec. 19, 1943) married Philip Comingore (born June 5, 1943). She has two children: June Marie (born Feb. 19, 1969) and Daniel Edward (born June 9, 1972).

Edward Eugene (born Sept. 18, 1946) married Cheryl Bennett (born Feb. 16, 1951). He had three children: Misty Dawn (born Mar. 15, 1973), James Douglas, stillborn Nov. 11, 1974 and Chad Michael (born May 5, 1976). *Submitted by Mrs. Edward Larew*

FRITZ SCHLEMMER: ARTIST

Fritz Schlemmer was and remains Crawfordsville's best-loved, best-remembered artist. He loved to go downtown on Saturday nights and watch the crowds listening to revival speakers emoting on the courthouse steps. His 30s oil painting of the courthouse, commissioned by June Zeller for Bud Zeller (sheriff of Montgomery County in the 50s) shows the leaning of the courthouse tower before anyone noticed its condition. Some of the best paintings were portraits of old men who sat on the courthouse curbing, spitting tobacco—people with plenty of uncommitted time to spend talking and sitting in his downtown studio.

Ftitz Schlemmer

Ferdinand Louis (Fritz) Schlemmer was born in Crawfordsville, IN on Sept. 26, 1892, the son of Otto and Louise Miller Schlemmer. Otto Schlemmer emigrated originally from Aachen, Germany, and became a success in business here, a fact attested to, at least for now, by an interesting building which bears his name across its ornate arched balcony and the year "1899" along its roofpeak.

Otto Schlemmer had two wives and six children, Fritz being a son of the second family which included sisters Hildegarde and Emily.

Fritz attended Crawfordsville High School and spent one year at Wabash College (1910-11), then enrolled in the Chicago Art Institute, where he won a competitive scholarship."

Schlemmer spent six years at the Institute, the last two as a graduate instructor, and he spent three summers during this time at Saugatuck School of Art on Lake Michigan, studying with Walter Marshall Clute. Fritz swam on the Illinois Athletic Club team while living in Chicago.

In 1917, Schlemmer was commissioned 1st Lieutenant in the U.S. Army, serving with the 89th Division in France, at Toul and St. Mihiel. He was then transferred to the Camouflage Corps, and went through the Argonne campaign as Division Camouflage Officer. After the Armistice, Schlemmer studied art in France for a short time, returning to the States in the spring of 1919.

Schlemmer returned to Crawfordsville in 1923.

He established a studio downtown over Ecker's bakery on East Main Street. While at this studio, he taught art classes and began energetically painting the Crawfordsville scene.

Fritz did many commissioned portraits of local people which are treasured today.

On Dec. 23, 1924, Fritz was married to Bernice Deane. They had one daughter Beverly, now Mrs. Ralph Flowers, of Portsmouth, OH. Bernice Schlemmer was the co-owner of the Fannie-Bee dress shop in Crawfordsville. Schlemmer occupied two more studios downtown before going to Wabash College.

In 1939, Schlemmer moved into a studio at Peck Hall and was appointed Wabash College's first Artist-in Residence. His studio was upstairs east in Yandes. The Wabash *Bulletin* describes his studio as "always a place in which to tie a fly, to improve one's pingpong serve, or to argue politics, religion, war or whatnot. Schlemmer's studio, as many a Wabash man has learned, overflows with information on a number of subjects — art included — and entertainment of various sorts."

Fritz died in 1947 of Addison's disease, at 54.
Submitted by Mary Early Johnson

SCHLOOT FAMILY

The Schloot family first arrived in Montgomery County in 1939. Garrett Schloot founded a furniture store in Crawfordsville in 1933. His son, Robert Joseph "Bob" Schloot moved here from Jasonville, IN in 1939. He married Rosanna Harned of Bicknell, IN on Feb. 20, 1938.

They have two children. The first, a daughter, Suzanne, was born on May 24, 1940. She graduated from Crawfordsville High School in 1958 and attended Indiana University. She married Paul Thomas Prince of Crawfordsville on Oct. 1, 1961. Tom Prince graduated from CHS and Wabash College. They have two daughters, Elizabeth Prince born on Aug. 1, 1966 and Kathryn Prince born Sept. 28, 1971. Both girls have graduated from Crawfordsville High School.

Elizabeth married Darrin Clore of Crawfordsville on Nov. 28, 1986. She graduated from PCI as a dental assistant and works in Crawfordsville. "Kathy" will attend Purdue University.

Bob and Rosanna also had a son, Thomas Robert Schloot, born on Mar. 17, 1947. Tom graduated from CHS in 1965 and Indiana State University in 1970. He has worked at Schloot Furniture since he was old enough to work. Tom married Patti Lee O'Heren on Feb. 22, 1975. Patti graduated from North Central High School in Indianapolis and attended Purdue University. Patti and her parents, John and Martha O'Heren originally came to Indiana from Decatur, IL.

Tom and Patti have two daughters, Martha Ann born Dec. 21, 1977 and Amy Jo "A.J." born July 23, 1980.

Rosanna was a charter member of Psi Iotta Xi Sorority. Suzanne was a member, and Patti has served as Chapter President of Psi Iota Xi.

Bob and Tom Schloot are members of Montgomery Lodge #50 and the Scottish Rite Valley of Indianapolis and Murat Shrine. Bob has held several positions in the Church, the First United Methodist.

Patti Schloot is presently a member of the Parrish Council of St. Bernard's Church.

LOREN W. SCHLOOT

Loren W. Schloot came to Crawfordsville, IN in the fall of 1937 and entered Wabash College, having graduated that spring from High School at Jasonville, IN. He graduated from Wabash in June of 1941 and in July married, Norma Jean Smith, his high school sweetheart, who had just finished her second year at DePauw University. In the fall of 1942 he enlisted in the Army Air Force at Patterson Field, OH and served until Dec. 15, 1945, being honorably discharged at Drew Field, Tampa, FL.

Schloot Furniture Company was opened in Crawfordsville in 1933 and by 1939 his brother, Robert, had come to Crawfordsville to manage it. He and their father, Garrett Schloot, had asked Loren to become part of the business upon completion of his army service, and as he had always wanted to make Crawfordsville his home, Norma and he, along with their young daughter, Diann, moved to Crawfordsville in January of 1946.

In 1938 the store moved from the lower floor of the Ben Hur Building to the present location, into what was known as the Graham Department Store building. With this large area to operate in, the store grew with the community, into a store they are proud to call Schloot Furniture Company, Inc.

Another daughter, Joann, came along in 1947 and she along with her sister Diann, graduated from C.H.S. Joann went on to graduate from Purdue and Diann from Butler, both obtaining masters degrees in Education.

In April 1978, Loren retired and sold his interest in the store to Robert, who along with his son, Thomas are running the store and expanding it each year in one of the greatest communities in Indiana.
Submitted by The Schloot family

LYLE AND JUDY SCHMIDT

September 15, 1832, Eber Teter "passed through Crawfordsville,... a promising place". In 1965, his great-great granddaughter, Judith Johnson Schmidt, moved to Crawfordsville. Eber's great-granddaughter, Mildred was born May 31, 1908, the third of five children, to Edith Teter and John Hiatt of Bakers Corner, IN. October 25, 1933, she married James Maurice Johnson, born Oct. 5, 1911, the fourth child of Dessie Phillips and Burgess Johnson. Mildred and Maurice had four children.

Philip Johnson was born June 26, 1934 in Indianapolis; on Nov. 11, 1955, he married Pat Coleman of Frankfort. Pat was born Sept. 8, 1935 to Eleanor Steiger and Charles Coleman. Philip and Pat had four children: Bruce, born Aug. 2, 1956; Aaron, born Nov. 28, 1958; Karen, born Jan. 31, 1962; Rhonda, born Nov. 5, 1968.

Jill, Lucy, Laura, Jim, Lyle and Judy Schmidt

Leah Beth Johnson was born in Sheridan, Nov. 11, 1940 and married Kenneth Merle Bitner, Jr., son of Mavorine Sutton and Kenneth Merle Bitner, Nov. 28, 1958. They had an adopted daughter, Angela, born June 13, 1964.

The youngest child, James Eric Johnson, was born Nov. 1, 1949 in Lebanon, IN; he married Deborah Frey Reeve, daughter of Doris Maxine Beeker and William Frey, June 7, 1986 in Lafayette, IN.

Judith Sharon Johnson was born May 18, 1936 in Indianapolis. She attended Butler University, and received degrees in elementary education and library science from Indiana State University. Judith helped organize "Community Friends", belonged to the Art League, and the Dorothy Q chapter of the Daughters of the American Revolution. Judith married Lyle Schmidt, Sept. 6, 1958 in Sheridan, IN.

Lyle Schmidt was born July 7, 1937 in LaPorte, IN, the son of Eunice Glassman and Norman Schmidt. He had one sibling, Janet, born May 14, 1934; she had four children by Paul Yagelski, and she died Jan. 22, 1985. Norman was born Feb. 16, 1908 in Michigan City, the oldest of four sons. Eunice Glassman, one of two children, was born Aug. 2, 1907 in Chicago. Lyle was a graduate of Indiana State University, was employed by R.R. Donnelley and Sons, helped organize a Ducks Unlimited chapter in 1985, and was on the Sportsman Club board.

Lyle and Judith had four children who began their education in the Crawfordsville and New Market Schools, then completed it in Park Forest, IL. James Norman Schmidt was born Nov. 15, 1959 in Terre Haute and graduated from Illinois State University. He married Joyce Shoub of Portage, IN in Chicago on Apr. 1, 1986. Laura Elizabeth Schmidt was born Feb. 17, 1962 in Indianapolis and graduated from Wheaton College, IL and Rush St. Luke's Presbyterian School of Nursing, magna cum laude. She married Jenerson Coston of North Carolina in 1987 in Chicago. They had a son, Zachary, born May 3, 1987. Lucy Ann Schmidt was born Oct. 15, 1964 in Indianapolis; received a degree in elementary education from Purdue, then married William Black of Glenview, Il in San Jose, CA on June 10, 1988. Jill Susan Schmidt was born Feb. 17, 1966 in Crawfordsville; she graduated from the University of Illinois with a degree in Restaurant-Hotel Management and received a graduate scholarship to attend professional culinary school at Kendall College in Evanston, IL.

CHARLES SCHOEN

Charles Schoen was an early settler in the Darlington and Sugar Creek township area. He was born in 1844 in Germany and emigrated to the United States at the age of 18, having been released from German military conscription due to his short stature.

He was employed by the War Department in Charleston, WV, making boots and shoes for the Union until the close of the war, when he joined his brother in Darlington making shoes. In 1868 he married Elizabeth Ann Huber. They had one son, Walter.

As machine made shoes displaced the bootmaker's trade, Mr. Schoen invested his savings in three farms northeast of Darlington, still owned by his descendants. He was described as being "intensely loyal to American institutions" and was very active in state Republican politics. He died Aug. 4, 1927.

PETER G. SCHREINER
1846-1938

Peter G. Schreiner was born on Sept. 9, 1846 in Nasaw, Kingshofen, Germany. He was the son of John and Mary Martin Schreiner. Along with his parents, at the age of nine, he came to America. His parents settled in the Cincinnati, OH area.

At the age of 11, he began to earn his own way, working in a bristle factory. Bristle shops made brushes from hog bristles. He continued working steadily in this factory until he was 17 years of age.

At 17, he answered the call of Abraham Lincoln for volunteers for service in the Civil War. On Sept.

15, 1863 he enlisted in Co. A, 108th Ohio Volunteer Infantry, joining his regiment at Battle Creek, TN.

Peter G. Schreiner

Mr. Schreiner's was a glorious service as a soldier. From the outset of his career he served in the thick of the fight, taking part in the seige of Chattanooga, the battle of Lookout Mountain and Missionary Ridge. He also endured the hardships of the cold winter of 1863-64 in Rossville, GA.

Again on the fighting line under Sherman at Resaca, Dallas and Kenesaw Mountain, he served as a train guard from Chattanooga, which was the base of supplies, to Atlanta. He was present at the capture of Atlanta, and had the distinction of taking part in Sherman's march from Atlanta to the sea. He was on hand when Savannah was captured on Christmas Day of 1864.

He took part in the sweep through the Carolinas northward, ending in the surrender at Raleigh, NC in April of 1865, and the final surrender of Johnston to Sherman, ending the war.

At the close of the hostilities, Mr. Schriener participated in the Grand Review at Washington, D.C. in May 1865. He received his honorable discharge on July 22, 1865 at Louisville, KY.

At some time later he secured employment as an agent for the bristle factory, traveling for the firm.

On Apr. 28, 1868 he was united in marriage to Miss Mary Eckel in his bride's hometown of Oldenburg, IN. The young couple established their home in Cincinnati, OH, residing there for 25 years. Seven children blessed their home. Two of these children eventually moved to Crawfordsville, one son, Peter G. Schreiner Jr. and one daughter, Mary Magdeline Schreiner Grabman.

Mr. Schreiner served as postmaster at Oldenburg from 1907 to 1913, at which time he retired to private life.

In September 1922, Mr. and Mrs. Schreiner moved to Crawfordsville, IN, to be near their children. They became members of the St. Bernard's Catholic Church. A deeply religious family, their love for God, country, family, and friends was felt by those who knew them.

Mr. Schreiner was a member of the Grand Army of the Republic. Only three Civil War Veterans lived on in Montgomery County after his death.

He was a lifelong Republican, and not only took great pride in this affiliation, but was thoroughly conversant with the political situation in both state and nation and expressed his views freely.

A requiem high mass marked the rites at the church. A military salute was given by the National Guardsmen at the Big Four passenger depot as the funeral party departed for Oldenburg where the burial was made.

Seventy-two descendants were left at the time of his death in 1938. Many others have come to respect this great man who honored his adopted land.

ARCHELIUS SCOTT

Archelius Scott, second son of Edward and Evaline James Scott, born October 1836 at Morton, IN. The parents previously lived near New Ross and Whitesville, IN. Moved to Waveland when "Arch" was young. Edward died at Waveland in 1892.

Arch had nine brothers and sisters; James W., Mary J., John, Barbara, David, Drusella, William F., Alfred and Rebecca. Evaline James Scott, daughter of David and Margaret James, came from Virginia to Kentucky, to Putnam Co., IN then Boone County. She had seven brothers and sisters; James, Terry E., David Jr., Alfred T., Barbara E., Drucilla, who married a Scott, and John B.

Records found on ancestors of Archelius date back to Alexander Caldwell, born 1690, probably Scotland. The Caldwells were scattered after Oliver Cromwell was promoted to Protectorship of England in 1653. Some remained in Ireland, some to Scotland while others crossed the Atlantic. The Ayershire Caldwells from Mount Arid, near Toulon, France went into Scotland during the reign of King Francis I. Alexander and Mary Colwell were married in Wales, but did not have enough money to come to America. They were compelled to bind themselves to ship's captain for as long as it took to pay their fares. It took a year for Alexander to pay off his bondage, then he worked to help Mary pay hers, so they could get started on their own. They were among the first settlers in Westmoreland Co., PA. Alexander and Mary died near Philadelphia. Of this union the son William married Mary McClellan; whose son Robert married Sarah Ann Fryer; whose daughter Elizabeth, married John Scott; whose son, Edward, married Evaline James.

Archelius Scott

When Arch was in the Civil War, his friend who was dying of injuries, asked him to take care of his wife and children when the war was over. When he returned home he married Mary Jane Butcher McGill, the wife of his war buddy. They had two children. When Mary Jane died he married Mary Catherine McMullen, January 1872. They had nine children; Martha Viola, b. October 1873, m. William H. Moore, d. 1947; Sarah Amanda, b. March 1875, m. Robert Adams, d. November 1956; Laura Bell, b. June 1877, m. Fred Cooper, d. 1941; William Edward, b. November 1879, m. Maud Sutton, d. in his 80s; Ida Pearl, b. October 1881, m. Dixon Nicholson, died when young; Ethel May (Dolly) b. March 1884, d. September 1899; Stella Blanche, b. November 1885, m. Stanley Morgan, d. 1949. Benjamin b. June 1888, m. Eva Laurer, d. 1952; Ira Chase, b. May 1891, m. Effie Brown, d. October 1960.

Archelius received a medical discharge from illness contracted in the Army, as a Corporal in Co. B., 43rd Regiment of Indiana Volunteers, in October 1862. He died February 1916, and Mary Catherine died July 1926. Both are buried in Maple Ridge Cemetery in Waveland.

Mary Catherine's ancestors records: John VanCleef born 1628, Amsterdam, Holland; whose son married Jannette Vanderbilt; whose son married Rachel Schenck; whose son married Ruth Muson; whose son married Marjorie Kerns; whose daughter married James McMullen; whose son married Margaret Douglas; whose daughter, Mary Catherine married Archelius Scott. *Submitted by great-granddaughter Lillian (Moore) Presslor*

GARNAL LEE SCOTT

Garnal Lee Scott, long time resident of Montgomery Co., IN was born Oct. 8, 1915 in Parke Co., IN to Loren Franklin Scott born Feb. 19, 1889 in Tipton Co., IN (the son of John Morgan and America Louisa Woolridge Scott.) He married Josephine Dowden Nov. 4, 1912 in Montgomery Co., IN. She was born Dec. 31, 1889 to George and Julia Hardee Dowden in Montgomery County. Garnal's siblings are: Byron, Eunice Richardson and Joseph.

Garnal married Virginia Boze Aug. 12, 1941 in Crawfordsville, IN. She was born Jan. 21, 1920 to Cecil and Oakie Willhite Boze. Their sons are: Byron Clare born Aug. 26, 1942 in Lafayette, IN. He married Iris Elizabeth Swetnam Nov. 23, 1967 (she is a teacher). Their children: Virginia Ellen born Nov. 10, 1969, married David Ward; Claire Elizabeth born Nov. 4, 1970, married Scott Voorhees. We are expecting a Voorhees great grandchild this spring; Janie Katherine born May 4, 1977 is attending Fountain Central Elementary. Byron graduated Crawfordsville High, a Vietnam Marine Veteran.

Garnal Maldon born Aug. 2, 1947 Crawfordsville. He is an Army Engineer Vietnam veteran. He married Ena Gay Jordan Jan. 1, 1968. Children are: Garnal Leon born Nov. 16, 1969, in the U.S. Navy stationed in Japan; John Vincent born Apr. 16, 1971, Southmont senior and signed up for the U.S. Army; Ena Marie born May 19, 1973, a Southmont sophomore; and Byron Curtis born Dec. 29, 1979, student at Walnut Elementary. All born in Crawfordsville.

Garnal Lee and Virginia (Boze) Scott

Gary Curtis born Mar. 15, 1958 Crawfordsville, IN. He married Catherine Anne Olszyks July 4, 1987. He graduated Southmonth, I.T.T. and working for a degree at Purdue University. Cathy is completing her degree at Purdue, plans to be a coach and teacher.

Great-great grandfather, John William Scott married Mary Elizabeth Osborn in Owen Co., KY and had Joseph, Sarah, John and James in Owenton, Owen Co., KY.

Joseph William married Mary Ann Smith, the daughter of Harvey and Celia Chapman Smith. He was born May 2, 1840, married Dec. 16, 1863. She was born Sept. 15, 1847. They had: John, Harvey, Armilda, Wesley, Lucy, Charles, Adaline, Mary, Minnie, Ira, Kathryn, William and Elma. He died Feb. 7, 1922 in Tipton County. She died Mar. 1, 1914 in Benton Co., IN.

John Morgan Scott was born Oct. 23, 1864 in Kentucky, married America Louisa Wooldridge June 10, 1886 in Kentucky and moved to Indiana. She was the daughter of John Edward and Elizabeth Davenport Wooldridge). Their children: Lee, Lenora, Loren Franklin, Lola, John, Della, Maude, Claude, Alma, Dewey, Charles and Susie.

The Scott's believe in Jesus Christ, their church is Baptist. He is a F. & A.M. Past Master, member of Alamo Lodge #144, Scottish Rite Valley of Indianapolis, retired from Mid-States, loves to travel and they are both O.E.S. Alamo #498 members. They reside in the 1856 Shiloh Brick One-Room School which they remodeled to a ranch-type home. This is located on one of the higher elevations in Montgomery County nestled among beautiful trees east of Old Shiloh Cemetery where once stood the historic "United Brethren Church" east of Crawfordsville, IN.

NATHANIEL EDWARD SCOTT

Nathaniel Edward Scott born in 1812 Nicholas Co., KY, died Oct. 10, 1892 Waveland, IN, the son of John and Elizabeth Caldwell Scott, grandson of Jackson Scott, Revolutionary Soldier, who died in Kentucky at the age of 110. Edward married Evelyn James, born 1813 Kentucky, daughter of David and Margaret James. They had come to Putnam Co., IN, then to Walnut Township, Montgomery Co., IN. Their children were: David Scott, drowned in Civil War in Kentucky, John, Archeleus Scott, Druicilla Scott, William, died age 17, Samuel Brenton Scott, infant son, died twin Thomas Alfred Scott born Apr. 7, 1851, Putnam Co., IN and died May 23, 1931. He married 1. Martha Hannah Elrod on May 25, 1871, daughter of Benjamin H. and Jane Douglas Elrod. She died in 1874. They had two children: Benjamin died in infancy and Rose Jane Scott born Feb. 24, 1872 and died May 17, 1947. She married Franklin Albert Walters on Oct. 7, 1888. They had five children, Carl, Opal Walters Smith Shoaf, died age 95, Thalia Walters (1896-1898), Elston Walters (1902-1916) and Harold B. Walters, died Oct. 6, 1970, married C. Pauline Randel, daughter of Orval and Dora Linn Randell on July 7, 1928. They had one son Robert Lee born May 11, 1929. He married Mary A. Williams 1949 divorced in 1973. They had five children: Jeffrey Lee born Oct. 2, 1950 married Brenda Durbin, have three children: Angela Kristy, Joenlyn Suzan, and Ryan Lee; Larry Dean Walters born Nov. 8, 1951 and married Deborah Bronaugh, two sons Matthew Ryan and Lucas Scott; Constance Ray born Jan. 17, 1954 married Stephen Truax have Stephanie Nicole, Shannon Camille, Joshue Michael; and Adam Joel; Pamela Sue born August 1955 married Steven Demoret, divorced, two daughters Karmon Leigh and Kelsey Lachelle; Michael Robert born Sept. 15, 1956 married Debra Addler and have two children, Jacob Daniel and Heather Michelle. Robert Walters married Petra ?. His third marriage is to Marilyn Fairfield Johnson. He is Montgomery County Health Sanitarian.

Thomas Alfred Scott married 2. Maggie Canada on Sept. 30, 1886. They had Dorothy Scott who married 1. John May and married 2. Ora Otenberg; Goldie Scott married Jesse Gregory; Hazel Scott born July 7, 1897 died March 1989 married Jesse Plunkett and had two children: Emma Olive Scott married Norman Burkett and had nine children; and infant son died. Thomas Alfred remained in Walnut Township in Montgomery Co., IN, but his brothers and sisters all lived near Waveland, IN as did his parents.

HENRY ALBERT AND REBECCA (ALWARD) SEITS

Henry Seits was born Dec. 25, 1837 in Ohio and died at Waveland, IN on Dec. 22, 1910. His father, Charles was born in Pennsylvania. Henry was a volunteer in the Civil War in Company C - Thirty-First Regiment of the Indiana Volunteer Infantry. He joined on Aug. 15, 1861 and served three years, being discharged Sept. 15, 1864. On his discharge papers, it is stated he was born in Ohio and was 25 years of age at enlistment. He stood 5'8" tall, and had fair complexion, blue eyes and blonde hair. He participated in battles at Fort Donaldson, Fort Henry, Shiloh, Corinth, Stone River, Chicamauga, and Nashville. The 31st was one of the most active groups from Indiana.

Albert Seits, Lula M.A. (Seits) Elmore, Bill Seits, Mae (Seits) Lampson

Henry's first wife was Lidia Andrus (Apr. 14, 1859 - Apr. 17, 1884). Their children: Francis Marion Seits (Jan. 9, 1861 - Nov. 4, 1861); Clarence Milvin Seits (Sept. 14, 1865 - July 25, 1866); Byran Elijah Seits (Feb. 6, 1871 - May 22, 1898); Effie Esabella Seits (Dec. 12, 1878 - Dec. 4, 1941), married John Alward; Birthie L. Seits (Apr. 4, 1884 - May 10, 1902).

Henry's second wife, Rebecca Alward was born on Jan. 10, 1859 in Illinois. She had two children: James Arista and Jesse Alward. They were married Mar. 22, 1885 and Rebecca's death occurred June 13, 1958.

Henry and Rebecca's children: Charles Henry Albert Seits was born in 1885, died in Terre Haute, married Laura Davis on Mar. 2, 1911. Luella Idella Seits was born Oct. 2, 1890 and died June 14, 1897. Susan Mae Seits was born Sept. 23, 1887, died May 19, 1971 and was married to Harry Lamson. They had five children: Glen, Earl, Walter, Vera, George. Lula Matilda Ann Seits, born Apr. 27, 1893, died Aug. 28, 1930, married Dec. 28, 1909 to Albert M. Elmore. Their children: James B., Margaret, Rose Lemoyne and Ethel and Edith, twins. William Nuton Seits was born May 13, 1897 and died May 25, 1978. He married Ruth Fraizier and served in the U.S. Navy during WWI. Their children: Lee, Leighton and Lawrence. *Submitted by Margaret McClure*

FRED A. AND MARY ANN (PAYTON) SELBY

Fred A. Selby was born Feb. 25, 1887 in Montgomery Co., IN to John Wesley and Ida Nichols Selby. He had one sister, Mrs. Wilfred (Mary) Rush, two brothers, Charles and Scott Selby.

On Dec. 25, 1912 he married Mary Ann Payton (Sept. 28, 1890) of near Alamo. She was the daughter of Charles E. (1869-1948) and Jemima Angeline Etter Payton (1869-1947). She was a graduate of Danville Central Normal Teachers College and taught school in the Alamo Community. Mary had two sisters: Myrtle Blanche (June 21, 1894 - Sept. 28, 1980), Leona Agnes (Jan. 23, 1903-Mar. 23, 1930) and two brothers; Clifford Lucien (May 17, 1897-Nov. 7, 1897), and Clarence Leslie (Oct. 25, 1898-Jan. 28, 1973).

Fred and Mary had one son Homer Chester, born Aug. 3, 1915, who died Oct. 21, 1921 of diptheria.

Fred farmed in his early life and was a partner with his brother, Scott, in a blacksmith shop in Alamo for 35 years. He was stricken with his fatal heart attack while at the blacksmith shop. He died May 8, 1950. He was a member and past master of the Alamo Masonic Lodge No. 144 and the Alamo Christian Church where he was treasurer for many years.

Mary continued to keep her home in Alamo, where she was a member of the Alamo Christian Church and the Alamo Eastern Star, No. 498. She was active in her church and community affairs. She passed away Oct. 5, 1973. They are both buried in the Alamo Cemetery.

CHARLES SENTMAN

My Grandfather tells me the Sentman family migrated from Germany in the late 1600s or early 1700s and settled in Pennsylvania as farmers until the late 1700s when they moved to Greenville, OH. From there they scattered to the four winds.

His Grandfather moved and homesteaded in Veedersburg, IN in Fountain County in the early 1800s as a farmer. Grandad couldn't remember how many children his great grandfather had, but one of them was Amos, a direct descendant of ours, married Nancy Lang and they had nine children: Charles, George, Edgar, Colonel, Elinor, Grace, Emma, Kathleen and Orville.

FOUR FAMILY - FOUR GENERATIONS REPRESENTED; 1st Row: Ron Hartman holding Ronnie Hartman, Jr.; Tim Hartman holding Chris Hartman, Charlees E. Sentman, Sr. and Florence Sentman; Greg Sentman; Rene Sentman holding Kayla Sentman. 2nd Row: Brian Michael; Nanette Hartman Michael; Melissa Hartman holding Kyle Hartman; Rita Sentman Hartman; Beverly Sentman Chaplain; Belinda Chaplain Rivers holding Vanessia Rivers; Sue Sentman and Charles W. Sentman, Jr. 3rd Row: Ray Straw; Cena Chaplain; Monte Chaplain; and Clifford Rivers.

Grandad says his Grandfather Amos was a prominent livestock farmer and buyer in Fountain

County. He would go down the road in his buggy from farm to farm buying livestock till he got the amount he could handle then he would put them in a drove on the road and drive them to the local railroad loading area common all over the county. There they would ship them to livestock market points in Indianapolis, Chicago, etc.

Charles Elmer married Luella Robbins around 1918 and they had five children: Ruby is now a pastor's wife living in Bloomington, IN: Charles Emerson graduated from Veedersburg and moved to Parke County in 1952 where he now runs Turkey Run Canoe Rental, is a licensed plumber, farmer and race car driver; Donald is working and living in Indianapolis; George is retired from a business career in Elwood; Alice is retired from a business career in Goshen, IN.

Grandad, Charles Emerson Sentman, married Florence Olive Briner in 1940 and they had three children: Rita is living in Paris, IL and teaching in the school system there; Beverly is a partner in the Canoe Rental and lives in Parke County; and Charles William owns a Pallet Company, is a well-known auctioneer and a race car driver living in Waveland. They now also have six grandchildren and five great grandchildren.

Charles William married Sue Turner in 1960 and they gave birth to me, Greg Alan Sentman. Dad was a timber buyer and cutter for his sawmill so we moved to Montgomery County in 1964.

I married Rene Bowman, daughter of Idella and the late Reverend Dean Bowman of Marshall, IN in 1986. Our daughter Kayla Rene was born Feb. 4, 1989. I work at the Pallet Company and as an auctioneer. We live in Waveland. *Submitted by Greg Alan Sentman*

FOSTER D. AND CATHERINE TERESA (BLESSING) SERVIES

Foster D. Servies was born in Montgomery County on Aug. 7, 1901 to John William and Mary (Johnson) Servies and was raised in Scott Township. He had one sister and three brothers.

Catherine Teresa Blessing was born in Benton County on Mar. 18, 1905 to Elmer and Mary E. (Maloney) Blessing and was raised in Montgomery County. She had three sisters and nine brothers.

Foster and Catherine were married on Dec. 26, 1923 and celebrated their 50th Wedding Anniversary Dec. 26, 1973. They are the parents of two daughters and five sons.

Mary Alice married Sherman Douglas and they were the parents of six children. Mary now lives with and helps her Mother.

Foster D. and Catherine Teresa (Blessing) Servies and family

Donald Louis married Dorothy Mae Todd and they are the parents of five children. He is a veteran of the Army and served in Germany. He is now retired from R.R. Donnelley & Sons and resides in Crawfordsville.

Lester Max married Norma Jean Dale and they are the parents of four children. He is a veteran of the Army and served in Camp Breckinridge. He is retired from R.R. Donnelley & Sons and is co-owner of U-Rent-It Center and resides in Crawfordsville.

Edward Leo married Ethel Lorraine Britton and they are the parents of four children. He is a veteran of the Army and served in Korea. He has always been a farmer and still farms and resides southwest of Crawfordsville.

Paul Thomas married Phyllis Joan Long and they are the parents of three children. He is a veteran of the Army and served in Germany. He is co-owner of U-Rent-It Center and resides in Crawfordsville.

Charles Willard married Margaret Ann Scott and they are the parents of four children. He is co-owner of U-Rent-It Center and resides in Crawfordsville.

Martha Sue married James Lytle and they are the parents of four children. Sue is remarried to James Becker and is a travel agent and resides in Sarasota, FL.

Being a four generation family there are 29 living grandchildren, one deceased, with all 30 being born in Culver Hospital in Crawfordsville and four step-grandchildren. Also, 40 living great-grandchildren, three deceased, nine step-great grandchildren, with a total of 120 living family members.

Foster and Catherine were married for 58 years, living a good and prosperous life southwest of Crawfordsville on their farm. Foster was a farmer and employed with R.R. Donnelley & Sons for 36 years until he retired in April 1965. He passed away May 5, 1981. Catherine was always a housewife and mother and now resides in Crawfordsville. *Submitted by Ethel Servies*

KIMBERLY ANN McCLAINE SERVIES

Kimberly Ann is the daughter of Richard Kent and Shirley Lois McClaine of Montgomery County. Richard farms and is employed by the Montgomery Highway Department and Shirley is employed by Jr. Concepts and is a homemaker. Kim was born Mar. 28, 1959 at Culver Union Hospital in Crawfordsville and attended Ladoga Elementary and Southmont Junior Senior High School.

Krista Lynne and Kimberly Ann Servies

After high school, Kim was employed by the Elston Bank and Trust and after a short time, went to work at the Montgomery County Clerks office. She married Jeffrey Scott Servies on Oct. 9, 1977 and for a little over a year they lived at Evansville, IN after which they returned to Crawfordsville. On Nov. 29, 1981 they became the parents of Krista Lynne Servies. Kim enjoys gardening, crafts and taking care of her home.

LEONARD RALPH AND DELORES ANN SEWELL

Leonard and Delores Sewell reside at 105 W 150 S in Crawfordsville, IN. Leonard has been employed at R.R. Donnelley and Sons as a pressman for 34 years. Prior to that he was employed by Kroger, the Crawfordsville Casket Company and as farm laborer. Delores is now a housewife. She was employed by R.R. Donnelley for six and one-half years and RMC at Attica.

Both Leonard and Delores and their children are members of the Browns Valley Christian Church. Leonard is presently an elder, teacher and church clerk. Delores is treasurer of the Loyal Circle and has held various teaching positions. Both are members of the choir.

Leonard was born June 12, 1935 at Portland Mills, IN to Lester Floyd and Vera Naomi Gillogly Sewell. The oldest of three boys, he came to Montgomery County in 1939 when his parents moved to Waveland. In 1953 he graduated from Waveland High School.

Delores Ann and Leonard Ralph Sewell

Leonard married Delores Ann Hutson on July 2, 1955 at Waveland by Grover DeNeal. They have two children, Peggy Deanne, born Feb. 24, 1962 and Matthew Scott, born Sept. 7, 1964, and two grandchildren, Timothy Scott born Jan. 7, 1986 and Benjamin Sewell born Feb. 25, 1988. Their children both live in Crawfordsville and Matthew is employed at Plastene.

Leonard's parents operated a grocery store, a huckster wagon in Portland Mills from 1929 to 1939. The huckster wagon covered large areas of Putnam and Parke Counties. They came to Waveland and operated a grocery store until 1944 when they moved to a farm north of Waveland near the Shades State Park.

In 1969 they moved to Russellville, IN. His father then worked at the State Highway Garage in Crawfordsville and at Lake Waveland. He died Aug. 26, 1983 and is buried at Hebron Cemetery at Russellville. His mother taught a class in Sunday School for many years until ill health made her stop. She is still living in Russellville.

Delores was born Mar. 13, 1936 at Wallace, IN to Roy Milton and Lula Mae Elam Hutson. She was the fourth of five children. Her home was south of Wallace and she attended Byron Elementary School and graduated from Waveland High School in 1954.

Delores' father farmed, worked for the State Highway Department, was head chef at Turkey Run State Park for 17 years, was trustee of Howard Township and for the ASCS office in Rockville, IN.

He died Jan. 22, 1970. Her mother was a housewife and she died Oct. 11, 1942. They both are buried in Lutheran Cemetery at Wallace.

RICHARD AND LORETTA SEYBOLD

Jasper Sr. Seybold was born in 1730 at Nurnberg, Bavaria, Germany. He married Rebakah Clendennen born in 1732, on Mar. 1, 1748-49 at London Grove Meeting House, Chester Co., PA. Jasper was a Quaker who furnished beef to the Continental American Army. Their son Jasper Jr. was born Dec. 20, 1757 in Loudoun Co., VA. He married Nancy Carrell (Carroll), on Sept. 13, 1781 at Loudoun County by Parson Thompson. To this union six sons and six daughters were born. Their third child John was born on Apr. 27, 1787, married Mary Reed on Mar. 16, 1809 in Fleming Co., KY. In 1822 John and Mary moved their four sons and three daughters to Parke Co., IN. Both John who died in 1839 and Mary who died in 1845 are buried at Raccoon Cemetery, Green Twp. in Parke County. Their son James Sr. born Nov. 27, 1811 in Fleming Co., KY married Anna Harlan on Sept. 26, 1833 in Parke County. James' occupation was a farmer, also he switched from Quaker to Baptist. They are both buried in the Seybold Cemetery near Guion in Parke County. Their son Jackson A. born May 15, 1844 married Sarah Angeline White. Both are buried in Mount Moriah Cemetery.

Richard and Loretta Seybold

Their son Maurice White born Aug. 21, 1879, married Mary Catherine Allen on Apr. 5, 1905 in Crawfordsville. Maurice was a farmer, both are buried at Indian Creek Hill Cemetery, Browns Valley, IN. The oldest son Warren Hilland, born on Mar. 8, 1906 at Guion, married Bessie Blanche Trump, daughter of Robert Mercer Trump and Eva May Riddell, they had one son Richard Max born Aug. 2, 1931. Richard on Jan. 11, 1951 married Loretta Maxine Newell. Richard like his forefathers before him, is a farmer near Browns Valley, a school bus driver for the South Montgomery School Corporation and a relief rural mail carrier for the postal service. Richard is a Mason and member of York Rite, Scottish Rite and Murat Temple. Both Richard and Loretta are members of the Eastern Star of Waveland and Browns Valley Christian Church.

Loretta was born on Jan. 21, 1932 to Glenn Wesley Newell and Imo Margaret Moody. She is a member of WWC Home Extension Club and the Ladies Loyal Circle at Church. Loretta is a housewife who helps out on the farm. They have four children. The oldest, Regina, born in 1957 is married to Mike Boots; they have two daughters and live in Waveland. Renita born in 1960 is married to Thomas McCormick; she is a member of the Daughters of the American Revolution; they reside in Crawfordsville. Resa born in 1962 married Larry Schick; they have one daughter and also live in Crawfordsville. The youngest son Ryan born in 1964 lives near Browns Valley. *Submitted by Renita McCormick*

SHANKLIN FAMILY

I am Opal Shanklin Smith and have lived in Montgomery County most of my life. My husband, Richard H. (Red) Smith, and I are retired and living in Veedersburg now.

My great, great, great grandfather Andrew Shanklin (1768-1836) was one of the earliest settlers in Montgomery County, purchasing land and entering government land in the western part of the county in 1827. He was born in Augusta (later Rockingham) Co., VA; moved to Montgomery and Bath Counties, KY; married Sarah Crooks; and they were parents of 12 children.

Andrew wanted to acquire more land for his children and came to the frontier country of Montgomery Co., IN. His children, some grown and married, came with him. He was a devout Presbyterian. When Wabash College was established by his church in 1832, co-signed a note guaranteeing payment of money borrowed to build the first buildings.

Four of Andrew's children remained in Montgomery County: William, married Eliza McIntyre; Sarah, married James C. Jackson; Charles, married Martha Austin; and Ann, married George Munns. The others moved farther west.

Andrew and Sarah's son John (1802-1879), married Elizabeth Kiggins, and their children were: Andrew, married Catherine Lowe; John William, Thomas Charlton, married Mary Hayes; James, married Margaret Thomas; Elizabeth, married Francis Sutton; and Susan, married James Sanders.

John and Elizabeth Kiggin's son John William (1829-1913) married Elizabeth Gray in Montgomery County, and their children were; Thomas; Anna, married Clint Thompson; Elizabeth, married Enoch Lawton; Mary Katherine, married William Thomas; George, married Maude Hurley; Howard, married Pearl Hurley; Harry, married (1) Mary Hopping, (2) Mabel Sidener; Willard, married Bessie Smith; Minnie, married Charles Ditamore; and Myrtle, married John Hirst.

John and Elizabeth Gray's son Thomas (1854-1923) married Arminta Leidster, and their children were: Bessie, married James Mitchell; Roy, married Mary Pearson; Lloyd, married Doris Gray; John; June, married Howard Redmon; and Merle, married Lois Slater.

Their son John (1898-1949), my father, married (1) Goldie Dowden and their son was Frank, (2) Edith Charters, and their children were: Leona, married Gene Jackman; Opal (me); Donald, married ?; John, Jr.; Waneta, married John Haworth; Laverne, married Charles Corby; and Helen, married Clarence Crabb. Frank, Leona, Donald, John Jr., (Korean War casualty), and Laverne are deceased.

I was born in 1926, and married (1) James Wyatt and our children are Cecil James, Sharon Kay, (2) Richard H. Smith.

Cecil, born in 1945, married Linda Kinney, and their sons are Tom and Tim. Cecil lost both legs below the knees in the Vietnam conflict, but never gave up and is a national officer of Disabled American Veterans. He lives in Hallowell, ME, and works at Togas VA Hospital.

Andrew and Sarah are buried in Thompson Cemetery north of Yountsville. Thomas, Arminta, Roy, John, June and families, and my Sharon Kay, are buried in Wesley Cemetery.

Richard Crooks, Sarah's father, fought in the Revolutionary War. All her descendants are eligible for membership in Sons or Daughters of the American Revolution.

Old Andrew loved Montgomery County. I'm glad he did.

JOSEPH MARTIN SHANNON

Martin, as he was known, was born June 21, 1902 in Shannondale. He was a son of Charles David and Arvilla Burroughs Shannon. He was a brother to Carroll Burroughs, Palmer Allen, David Eugene, Minnie Lee, Geneva May, Naomi Clair, and Georgie Baird. Only one sister survives at this writing which is Naomi Clair Peterson who will be 92 this year. Martin died Jan. 1, 1985 and is buried at Shannondale.

Martin was educated in Shannondale and graduated from Crawfordsville High School in 1921 where he met and married Mary Margaret White, July 27, 1924. She was born Apr. 17, 1902, died Aug. 21, 1963. They had two daughters, Beverly Jeanne and JoAnne. Beverly was born June 9, 1930 and JoAnne Apr. 4, 1933. Beverly married Robert D. Keeling of Waynetown, she had three children, Lorra Lynn, David Alan and Kimberly Rosanne. She died July 30, 1970 and is buried at Shannondale. JoAnne married Frederick Edmund Butler and they have one son, Frederick Martin Butler. JoAnne and her husband reside in Franklin Township in Montgomery County. Their son resides in California.

Joseph Martin Shannon and daughter JoAnne Shannon Butler age eight months

Martin was the grandson of Joseph Jordan Shannon who was born Feb. 17, 1825 in Woodford Co., KY. He was a doctor and began his practice in Shannondale in 1850 and remained there until his death. Doctor Shannon's father, David Armstrong Shannon surveyed the village of Shannondale and the town was named for David.

Martin was well known in Crawfordsville. He worked 38 years in Freedman's Clothing Store. During the depression, Mr. Freedman lowered his pay from $15.00 a week to $11.00 rather than lay him off. Early on his father and brother Eugene (Jack) all worked at Freedman's store with him. In later years his wife, sister Naomi and her husband Husted Peterson worked several years at the store also.

Music was important to him and his beautiful tenor voice was heard often. He and his family were members of the Wabash Avenue Presbyterian Church, where they all sang in the church choir for many years. He was a charter member of the Lions Club and a life member of the Elks Lodge 483, where he sang in their chorus and barber shop quartet. Many people requested him to sing when their loved ones passed away, at least one person even put that in their will that he should sing at their funeral. They out-lived him. The will was changed.

To write historically of a man you dearly loved is not an easy task. On one hand you could say he never did anything of great importance. On the other hand he was the man who taught us how to ride a two wheeler, made stilts and taught us how to walk on them, taught us fairness, understanding, set a good example for us, was a good husband and a great father. He is survived by four grandchildren who knew him and nine great-grandchildren who will have missed growing up knowing this warm and special man.

JOHN L. SHARP

John L(eon) Sharp, born Westport, Decatur Co., IN, Apr. 24, 1906; son of Walter Marion and Ethel (Curry) Sharp.

Walter Marion Sharp, born at Westport, IN. He later moved to Montgomery Co., IN, where he engaged in farming. His wife, Ethel (Curry) Sharp, was born near Terre Haute, IN. She was the daughter of Harvey Wilson Curry.

John L. Sharp, the subject of this sketch, graduated from Indiana University, B.S. in 1931, and M.D. in 1933. He served his internship at the Indianapolis City Hosp., and since 1934 has practiced his profession in Crawfordsville, IN. Dr. Sharp, who is Independent in politics, is a member of the following: American Medical Association; Indiana State Medical Association; Montgomery County Medical Society; Elks Lodge; Country Club; Montgomery County Chapter, Citizens Historical Association; and Presbyterian Church. His favorite recreations are hunting, fishing, and golf.

On June 28, 1930, Dr. Sharp married Mary Jane Hughes, daughter of William I. and Bell (Creek) Hughes. Mrs. Sharp was born at Alexandria, IN. Dr. and Mrs. Sharp have no children.

ROSS PERRY AND MAY (JEFFRIES) SHARP

Ross and May Sharp, both natives of Clark Township, were married Sept. 26, 1906 and for many years farmed in Montgomery County.

Ross was born July 18, 1886 to Madison and Armine (Ellis) Sharp whose other children are: John, Nina, Lora, Roy, Walter, and Elmer. Three other children died in early childhood.

His paternal grandparents were John and Mary (Clark) Sharp who came from Gibson Co., IN in 1848 and bought land east of Ladoga. Their children were: Sylvester, Perry, Meg, Jane, Ann, and Madison.

May was born June 10, 1887 to James Knox and Mary Etta (Moody) Jeffries. Her brothers and sisters were: Walter, Vince, Arthur (who died in childhood), Harvey, Ethel, Pearl, Mabel, and Paul.

Ross Perry and May (Jeffries) Sharp Family

Her paternal grandparents were Harvey and Malinda (King) Jeffries, pioneers of Putnam County, who came from Henry Co., KY on horseback to settle east of Roachdale.

Her earliest known ancestor was Tillet Jeffries, born 1720 in South Carolina. He and 15 year old son, William, fought in the Revolutionary War. William and Nancy Connell (married 1790) went to Kentucky where they had a long life together. One of their 12 children was Harvey, May's grandfather.

May and Ross had five children: Edna (b. 1907 - d. 1977), a daughter who died at birth, James Madison (b. 1914 - d. 1965), Madonna May (b. 1917 - d. 1987), and Mary Marjorie (b. 1920). They also raised her youngest brother and sister.

The family moved to Roachdale where they operated a dairy for ten years. Edna attended East Haw Creek and Roachdale schools. The three younger children attended school there but were graduated from Ladoga.

James, a graduate of Wabash, attended IU and got his MA in education from Butler. He taught in Shelby County Schools, at Columbus H.S., was assistant principal at Anderson H.S. and principal at Shelbyville H.S. ten years. He was superintendent of Shelby Eastern Schools.

Madonna was a graduate of Indiana Central with her MA from Butler. She taught 38 years in several county schools - 26 being in Speedway.

Marjorie attended University of Maryland, John Hopkins, and Loyola. She taught special education in Maryland.

Edna married Wallace Lewellyn in 1926. Children were: Joanne, Joe, Edna Maye, Wallace, Jack and Jane.

James married Leona Snepp in 1936. Children - Nancy and James.

Madonna married Harold McIlvain in 1940 - daughter Marjorie Ann.

Marjorie married Harry Kelbaugh in 1940. Children - Madonna Sharon and Ross Jeffries.

After farming many years in southern Montgomery County, the Sharps moved to a small farm south of Ladoga. Ross worked for the Montgomery County Soil Conservation before becoming a field man for the Ladoga Canning Co. He died in 1946, and she went to live with daughters. She returned to Ladoga and lived there until her death in 1965.

He was a member of the Masonic Lodge and a deacon in the Ladoga Christian Church. She was also a member there and had belonged to the Ladies Aid and Missionary Societies and was a charter member of the Bethel Community Club. Several descendants live in Montgomery County. *Submitted by Joanne VanCleave*

ANDREW SHAVER

Andrew Shaver born Sept. 6, 1768 son of Andreas (Andrew) and Gertrude Shaver, married Ursula Miller. They moved from Pennsylvania to Virginia. They had ten children, Peter, John G., Catherine, Andrew III, Jonathan born July 10, 1826 and died July 13, 1886 Clark Township, Montgomery Co., IN, married in Virginia to Susan Cook on June 16, 1826 in Virginia. Came here in 1834. He built a Lutheran Church in Ladoga; David Shaver, Mary (Polly); Magdalene Shaver; Elizabeth; Susan and Sarah Shaver born Sept. 12, 1800/01 in Virginia and died Mar. 20, 1856 Walnut Township, Montgomery Co., IN. She married Benjamin Hinkle for her second husband on Aug. 20, 1823 in Virginia. He was the son of John and Magdaline Landis Hinkle. Sarah had married first to John Vineyard on Mar. 21, 1821 in Virginia. He died on November 1822. Benjamin Hinkle was born July 8, 1798 in Virginia and died here Dec. 16, 1861, southwest of New Ross, IN. Jonathan and Susan Cook Shaver had David and Daniel Shaver. David came here with his parents in 1834 and died east of Crawfordsville on Sept. 26, 1878. Daniel Shaver married Sarah Frances Hymer, daughter of Jesse and Eliza Gill Hymer, born Jan. 10, 1832 and died May 8, 1901. Daniel was a very wealthy man, in Franklin Township, Montgomery County and they had the following children: Orlando; James Walson; Emma Lenore married Abraham B. Caster and had Ursula Caster Ward; Jesse Caster; Mellie Elizabeth Saidla; Fred Caster; Samuel Hymer Shaver, Carrie Belle Luckett; other children of Jonathan were Sarah Cedars, Susan Stratton, Jonathan, Jr., John, Francis married Bertha, Martha, Martin Luther, and J.M. Shaver.

Other children who came here were Sarah (Sally) Shaver; Benjamin was the grandson of Jacob and Barbara Teter Hinkle. The Hinkles were Lutherans too. Benjamin and Sarah Hinkle's grandsons, George and Samuel Hinkle lived on the homeplace, southwest of New Ross and the Hinkle reunion was always held there. Benjamin and Sarah are buried in Harshbarger Cemetery. Their children were Nathan and Nicholas Vineyard, by her first marriage, and Jeremiah Leabetter Hinkle, Elizabeth Hinkle Markley, Susan Hinkle born May 2, 1857 in Tennessee and died Nov. 2, 1865 in Montgomery Co., IN. Susan married William Randel born Mar. 1, 1826 Allen Co., KY and died here on Dec. 24, 1865. Their children were; Andrew Vineyard Randel, William Noah Randel, Sarah Randel Starks, John Randel, Mary D. Randel, George Randel, James Goodwin Randel born June 4, 1858 Ladoga married Sarah Magdaline Wingert; they had Orval W. Randel born 1886 and married Dora Evaline Linn (the parents of C. Pauline Walters and V. Lucille Harpel) and Ernest Milford Randel born 1888 and married Clara Ellen Randel McDaniel. *By C. Pauline Walters*

MARY VIRGINIA CRABBS SHAW

On Mar. 19, 1989, a celebration was held for the 90th birthday of Mary Virginia Crabbs Shaw at the Holiday Inn in Crawfordsville. Many of her family and friends attended.

Mary Virginia was born in Crawfordsville on Feb. 15, 1899, the daughter of Tully Carl and Effie Gardner Crabbs. Effie Gardner was born in Putnam Co., IN in 1874 and died in 1966, the daughter of Fred and Mary Allen Gardner. Their homeplace was located south of Russellville in Putnam Co., IN. Later Fred and Mary sold their property and moved to Crawfordsville. Fred was born in 1832 and died in 1908. Mary Ann Allen was born in 1845 and died in 1903. They are buried in the Oak Hill Cemetery in Crawfordsville.

Effie Gardner met and on Nov. 20, 1895 married Tully Carl Crabbs born in 1873 in Ohio and died in Crawfordsville in 1955. They lived in a home at 702 West Main Street. Both Tully and his father, Benjamin F. Crabbs, were involved with the Crabbs, Reynolds, Taylor Company, who were in the seed business. His business associates were Bennett Taylor from Lafayette and Ed Reynolds who lived on the corner of Vernon Court. Effie and Tully were active in the Methodist Church where Tully served on the Board of Directors and was Sunday School Superintendent for many years. He also served on the Board of Directors of the Elston Bank.

Mary Virginia graduated from Crawfordsville High School and went east to Sweet Brier College in Virginia and received her college degree in 1920. In April of 1921, she was invited to visit Lausanne Switzerland as guest of friends of the family. She spent eight months in Europe with her host. While there she studied French. Upon her return she began student teaching in Crawfordsville.

On Feb. 13, 1925, she married Noble Ryan Shaw and they set up housekeeping on Grant Avenue. Noble Ryan Shaw was born Mar. 2, 1895 and died Oct. 22, 1971, the son of William A. Shaw and Mary Ryan Shaw. Mr. Shaw was employed by the Crabbs, Reynolds, Taylor Seed Company. They had three sons: Tully born in 1928, Ryan born in 1931 and Allen born in 1934. They all graduated from Crawfordsville High School and Wabash College.

Tully is married to Trudy McCullough. They have three children: David Shaw lives in Denton, TX; Susan Watson lives in Glendale, AZ; and Sarah Morgan lives in Cleveland, OH. Tully and Trudy live in Bloomington where he is now semi-retired.

Ryan married Virginia and they had no children. Ryan lived in Detroit, MI. In 1985 he slipped on ice and fell causing his death. He is buried in Oak Hill Cemetery in Crawfordsville.

Allen is an Ordained Methodist Minister. He married Lesley Ballantine and they have three children: Fiona, Allison and Andrew. Allen and Lesley live in Edinburgh, Scotland.

Mary Virginia Crabbs Shaw is a member of the Retired Teacher's Association, Montgomery County Historical Society, Dorothy Q. Chapter of the DAR, and a member of the First Methodist Church, where she has attended since she was a child. A life long resident of Crawfordsville she is affectionately known to all as the lady with the ready smile and the flowers in her hair. *Submitted by Barb Taylor with permission of Mary V. Shaw*

JOHN AND CATHERINE SHEETS

Daniel Sheets and his wife, Catherine Hulvey were natives of Rockingham, VA prior to their arrival in Montgomery County, Jackson Township in the first decade of the 1800s. The Sheets, (Sheetz or Schutz) came from the German reformed settlement of the Shenandoah Valley, VA via Cumberland Gap into northern Kentucky, from where they crossed the Ohio River through Hamilton and Butler Counties of Ohio.

Daniel and his wife were married in 1792 at Rockingham Co., VA. They were members of the Friedens German Reformed Church there.

Daniel Sheets is most likely the son of George Sheets of Rockingham, VA. It is believed that prior to his move to Rockingham, VA, George Sheets came from Montgomery Co., PA and were members of the Boeh'm (Blue Church) Evangelical Reformed Church in Whitepan township.

Catherine Hulvey is the daughter of Conrad Hulvey of Rockingham, VA. Conrad was a deacon in the Friedens Reformed Church. His father before him was also named Conrad, and he was the immigrant of the family, having immigrated to the states about 1737. The place of origin of Conrad Hulvey, Sr. is not yet determined.

In the Friedens church record are recorded the following births of children to Daniel and Catherine Sheets between 1792-1802: Susana, (who later married the Montgomery, OH pioneer, Eben Hoopes about 1816), Elizabeth, Barbara, and Solomon. It appears their son, Solomon, became an early Preble County pioneer. One of Daniel and Catherine Sheets' daughters, probably either Barbara or Elizabeth married John Landon, also an early Montgomery County pioneer, around 1815. From early court records of Montgomery County, it appears that John Landon and Catherine Sheets did not like each other very much. From the wording of the court document between John Landon and Catherine Sheets, it seems likely that Daniel Sheets' daughter, Mrs. Landon died before 1829.

It appears that Daniel and Catherine Sheets had other children after their arrival in Montgomery County: Hannah, Nancy, and Polly. Some of these could be nicknames given to the previously stated children rather than additional children, however.

Daniel Sheets died in Montgomery, OH about 1819. Catherine Sheets remained a widow until 1825, when she married again to John Anspach, another Montgomery County pioneer. Together they took John Landon to court to recover land that they felt he did not deserve, because of a broken promise. They recovered the land Catherine Sheets apparently bought with the inheritance left her from her first husband, in Jackson township near the waters of Toms Run. It is said that Catherine Sheets lived to be the ripe old age of 90, thus becoming a long time pioneer of Montgomery County.

LESLIE AND HARRIET SHELTON

Leslie Earl Shelton, second son of Raymond and Ical Goldie Allen Shelton, was born Jan. 25, 1918 in Fountain Co., IN. He attended schools in Fountain County and Crawfordsville and was in the CCC at the Shades in 1935. There he met Harriet. Leslie was later to join the Police Force in Crawfordsville, where he retired as Detective Captain in 1962, after 20 years with the force. He then worked in the Ben Hur Sports Shop for 17 years. In 1960 they moved into the Waveland area in Brown Twp.

Records show that in the middle of the 19th Century an ancestor of Leslie; namely Mary Wilhelm, left her native Germany to come to America and settled in Kentucky. She later met and married George Shelton. Raymond Shelton was the seventh son of this union, born Jan. 2, 1890. Raymond and Ical were married November 1914 at Danville, IL. The family is of Dutch, Irish and German descent. Ical Goldie Allen, youngest of eight children, was the daughter of Cornelius and Harriet Sowers Allen. Cornelius was the son of Isam and Lydia Allen. During the Civil War, Isam and his wife permitted soldiers of both Union and Confederate Armies to stay on the Allen farm as they returned to their homes.

Leslie and Harriet Shelton

Harriet Lorraine Haskett, daughter of Euma and Leonard Haskett, was born Dec. 8, 1918 at the Shades Hotel, northwest of Waveland. She attended and graduated from the Alamo High School. Harriet's ancestors were Abigail Dowden and husband. William Keller, born Mar. 19, 1859, near Wallace, son of George and Deborah Smith Keller, married Mahala Dowden daughter of Abigail. To this union were born seven children, one of whom was Martha Jane Keller. Martha married William Henry Harrison Cotten, son of Isaac and Mary Ann Tyler Cotten, July 9, 1895. William died Feb. 7, 1949 and Martha in March of 1950. Six children were born to this union, among them Euma Rosella Cotten. Euma married Leonard Haskett, son of Caswell and Rebecca Blanton Haskett, Aug. 30, 1916. Euma and Leonard were the parents of seven children, one of whom was Harriet.

Leslie and Harriet were married Dec. 12, 1936 at Crawfordsville. To this union were born; Carolyn, Jan. 7 1938; Larry, Mar. 27, 1939; Robert, Sept. 21, 1940 and Terry, Aug. 13, 1942.

Carolyn's children are Deann, Robert, Sherri and Tim.

Larry's children are Mike and Lori.

Robert's children are Jeff and Steve.

Terry's children are Martoma and Teresa.

THE SHILLINGS FAMILY

George Russell "Slim" Shillings was born Nov. 15, 1911, near Cloverdale, IN in Putnam County, the son of George Ross and Minta Catherine Hartsaw Shillings. Being the oldest of a family of 12 children necessitated that he leave home and begin work at an early age. In 1930, when he was only 19 years old he worked for the Clements and later the Berns Construction Company that built State Road 43 (now U.S. 231) in the Crawfordsville area. It was while working on the road near Cherry Grove that his eye fell upon a young girl, Evelyn Donlouie, living along the way. Evelyn was the youngest daughter of Arch and Mary F. Donlouie who had just moved to Indiana from Wayne Co., KY. On Nov. 21, 1931, the two were married. The following year their only child, Virginia, was born on Sept. 22, 1932.

George or "Slim" as he is affectionately called by his many friends in the area has lived and worked in and around Crawfordsville for 59 years. He is best known by the area farmers for his work on farm implements. Even in his retirement, he still finds time to lend a helping hand to friends in need.

His wife, Evelyn, died on June 18, 1961, and is buried in the Mace Cemetery. He later married Ola Springer from Danville, IN. They continue to reside in the small town of Linnsburg east of Crawfordsville where he has lived since 1955.

The daughter, Virginia, was married on Dec. 23, 1962, to Robert Allen Garner son of Sherman and Claire Irene Garner of Crawfordsville. She and her husband live in Indianapolis where she is a teacher/librarian in the Brownsburg Community Schools.

George has one brother James Ross Shillings living east of Crawfordsville as well as several nieces and nephews in Montgomery County.

LYLE A. AND WILMA W. SHORTZ

Lyle A. and Wilma W. Shortz came to Montgomery County in 1951. They were returning to the area where Lyle's ancestors settled in Indiana, when they came by covered wagon from Virginia in the early 1800s to acquire a farm near Wingate.

Lyle had been employed by R.R. Donnelley & Sons in Chicago and came here as personnel manager of their Crawfordsville plant. He was born in

White County in 1905, grew up in LaPorte County, and graduated from DePauw University in 1927.

Wilma was born in Kansas City in 1910, grew up in Portland, ME, and graduated from Gregg College in Chicago. She worked as a free lance court reporter in Chicago.

Wilma and Lyle played competitive badminton and both won titles in Illinois, Michigan, Ohio, Missouri, Indiana, Chicago, and were ranked nationally. Wilma was Midwest badminton singles champion two years.

Two of their three children were born in Chicago, April in 1943 and Richard in 1945. William was born in Crawfordsville in 1952. All three graduated from Crawfordsville High School and attended Indiana Colleges.

April graduated from Purdue University in the School of Veterinary Science and Medicine, ranked number one in her class, and is practicing veterinary medicine in Michigan.

Richard graduated from Indiana University and Harvard University Law School, and is a senior partner in the law firm of Jones, Day, Reavis and Pogue in California.

William graduated from Indiana University with a degree in Enigmatology in its Independent Learning Program, from the University of Virginia Law School, and is senior editor of Games magazine in New York.

Soon after coming to Montgomery County, Lyle and Wilma purchased 52 acres adjoining the south limits of Crawfordsville and began to raise Arabian horses. Horses became Wilma's interest and she has had published many stories and articles about them.

Lyle has been active in community affairs and served as president of the Chamber of Commerce and Rotary Club.

Wilma was on the board of supervisors of the Montgomery County Soil and Water Conservation District for 15 years, four of them as chairman. She has been active in the League of Women Voters and served as president of that and several other organizations.

Since Lyle's retirement from Donnelley's in 1969, the family still live on their property south of Crawfordsville. They do some winter traveling and continue their activities and interests in their rural environment.

JAMES ARTHUR AND JUANITA HART SHUMAKER

James Arthur and Juanita Ellen (Hart) Shumaker were married Dec. 24, 1935 and began their married life south of Bainbridge, IN. They both were born in Montgomery County.

James was born June 5, 1915 east of Linden, IN and moved when he was just a baby with his parents to a farm two miles north of Whitesville, IN. While the family lived there James and his sister Emma Irene attended the Whitesville school riding in a horsedrawn hack driven by Floyd Hobson. His parents then moved to Putnam County to a farm south of Raccoon. James and Irene walked each school day to Grider School.

James grew to manhood on his parents' farm and learned farming and assisted with the general work during crop seasons. He also learned carpentering.

When he and Juanita married he chose farming as their livelihood. After being married one year they moved to a farm west of Roachdale and raised stock. His fields were well cultivated, fenced and kept neat. He also improved the outbuildings with the residence showing his work. Others observed his efforts begin to seek his skilled wood working services. In connection to farming he began to branch out and built up a carpentering trade. His close application and sound judgement with a steadfast integrity showed him to be skillful. Others ask for him to do improvements on their buildings and his services were in great demand.

James Arthur and Juanita Ellen Shumaker

In 1946 James directed his full attention to carpentering and he and Juanita moved to a home in Raccoon. His work now well known, it was natural that he was kept quite busy. He built many homes in the area, remodeled barnes, sheds or what was needed. His precise work and excellent results so obvious around the neighborhood was an inspiration to all that knew him.

However in the fall of 1966 he was employed at the Crawfordsville Donnelley R.R. & Sons Co. He served as carpenter there until he retired in 1980.

Juanita Ellen, born Feb. 26, 1919 is the daughter of Claude and Ella (Whitt) Hart. She grew up in and around the Ladoga area with three brothers, Claude Junior, Kenneth Dale and Harold Max, a twin to Helen Maxine, Juanita's one sister. During Juanita's childhood she attended her first four school years at Ladoga then her parents moved to a farm southwest of Ladoga and she attended the Parkersburg school. When Juanita was 14 the family moved into Ladoga where she graduated from the Ladoga School.

Juanita is a lady of admirable characteristics and has a wide circle of friends. She is a volunteer at the Autumn Care Home at Ladoga and a member of the Town and Country Extension Homemakers Club in Putnam County. She also worked at the Wilson Brothers Greenhouse at Raccoon many years.

James Arthur is esteemed for his genial and gentlemanly personality, well liked by all that know him.

Both are members of the Parkersburg Christian Church in Scott Township, Montgomery County.

SIMMS FAMILY

Richard Simms was an early settler of Stafford Co., VA. He was born about 1720. He married in 1750 to Elizabeth Bridwell. To this union was born: Richard, Jr., James, Presley, Rhodan, possibly sons David and John, possibly two daughters who married men named Jewel and (possibly) a daughter who married Elijah Harding.

Presley, above, was born February 1753 in Stafford County. He died in Montgomery Co., IN, 1852. At one time, he lived 16 miles below Mount Vernon and six miles from the Potomac River. He fought seven years in the Revolutionary War under General George Washington's command. It is believed he lost two brothers in that war. Presley Simms married Nancy Bridwell. They moved to Kentucky in 1818 and to Montgomery County in 1828. Two of his brothers Rhodan and Richard, Jr. moved on to Clay Co., MO. Presley's name can be found on the monument at the Crawfordsville Court House. Children of Presley and Nancy were: Presley Jr., Daniel, Jesse, Elizabeth (Mrs. Daniel Henderson), Mary (Mrs. Nathaniel Hobson), Langthorn, Lucy (Mrs. David Williams), Charles, Burwell and George.

Augustus B. and Blanche Robison Simms

George was my great grandfather. He was born June 18, 1814 in Virginia and died Mar. 23, 1903. He was married in 1851 to Elizabeth Vester. He had a hand accidentally cut off by one of his brothers as a child. They were using an axe to crack nuts on a stump. George and Elizabeth had issue: Mary Ellen 1852-1939; Lida 1853-1914 (Mrs. Jonathan Everett); Enoch 1854-1939; Louis 1856-1931; Emma 1857-1932 (Mrs. William Lyon); Margaret 1859-1866; Jacob 1861-1919 and Ida 1865-1950 (Mrs. Frank Mills).

Louis was my grandfather. He married Ida Mae Mahan in 1882; lived on the LaGrange Road northwest of Crawfordsville and was a farmer. Louis and Ida Mae had issue: Elizabeth Belle 1884 (Mrs. Fred Bell, Mrs. Roy Trimble, Mrs. Harrison Hibbard); Augustus Belmont Aug. 25, 1886 and Louis Brighty 1889-1929.

Augustus Belmont was my father. He died Aug. 10, 1962 and is buried Oak Hill Cemetery near Crawfordsville. A.B. or Gus Simms as he was known married Lenora Blanche Robison (May 17, 1892 - May 18, 1986) on May 17, 1914. To this union was born: Louis Alma Feb. 13, 1917 died Mar. 4, 1925 of scarlet fever; Charles Augustus Nov. 5, 1921; Marcella Maxine Oct. 21, 1923 died Mar. 23, 1925 of scarlet fever; Helen Frances July 19, 1925 (Mrs. Max Rivers); Lindy Leland Mar. 14, 1928 and Robert Louis Oct. 4, 1930 and three other children who were stillborn. The A.B. Simms family lived northwest of Crawfordsville where the children attended Breaks school. In 1935 moved to Alamo. In 1937 moved to near Waveland and in 1943 moved to West of Ladoga. In 1947, they moved back to the homeplace northwest of C'Ville.

Helen Frances Simms married Max Ray Rivers in 1944 and had issue: Mary Anne Feb. 10, 1945 (Mrs. Jerry McMindes), Esther Jane July 23, 1948 (Mrs. Tom Fay, divorced), Victor Ray Aug. 24, 1954 (married Janet Hohenstien) and Ramona Lea July 23, 1961 (Mrs. Fernando Vazquez). Helen and Max have six grandchildren, namely: Melanie McMindes, Chris McMindes, Erin Hohenstein, Eric and Meggan Rivers and Ray Van Vazquez. Helen and Max are farmers residing northeast of Waveland. *Submitted by Helen Rivers*

FREEMAN L. AND FLORENCE M. SIMMS

Freeman Simms was born in Montgomery County on May 25, 1903, the son of Sherman and Effie Keller Simms. He grew up south of Alamo and married Florence M. Mitchell on Dec. 23, 1921. She was born in Coal Creek Township on Oct. 20, 1905, the daughter of William W. and Sarah J. Kerns Mitchell. William W. was born Dec. 7, 1879 and Sarah Feb. 22, 1882. They were married Nov. 7, 1900 in Montgomery County Sherman was born in Montgomery County, on May 25, 1869 and married Effie on Apr. 21, 1900.

Freeman and Florence Simms

The paternal grandparents of Freeman were George W. and Phoebe J. Johnson Simms. George was born in Tippecanoe County but lived most of his adult life in Montgomery County. He was a Civil War Veteran, having served from 1862 to 1865 with the 30th Btry. Ind. L. Atry. His father Burrell Symmes came from Virginia and married in Montgomery County in 1841 to Elizabeth Hobson. They lived various places in Coal Creek Township and were engaged in farming.

Maternal grandparents of Freeman were William F. and Mahala Dowden Keller. William F. was born on Mar. 19, 1859 near Wallace, IN and married Mahala on Oct. 3, 1878. She was born Dec 13, 1856, south of Crawfordsville. William was the son of George and Deborah Smith Keller. Mahala's parents were James and Abigail Dehaven Dowden.

The paternal grandparents of Florence were William D. and Mary Willhite Mitchell. He was born in 1840, the son of Alexander and Sarah Royalty Mitchell. Mary's parents were President and Sarah Willhite.

Maternal grandparents of Florence were William and Lucinda Stonebraker Kerns.

Freeman and Florence moved away from Montgomery County during the early years of their marriage, living at Newtown, Attica, and eventually Logansport, IN. They had four sons; Hubert, Leo, James and Benny. Florence died in 1984 and is buried at Waynetown. Freeman returned to Montgomery County and presently lives in Wingate. *Submitted by Judith Simms Props, granddaughter*

WAYNE AND TRESSA SIMMS

Wayne Simms, son of William and Lulu Childers Simms was born November 1908, Waynetown, IN. Later the family moved to Waveland. Wayne attended Waveland School and graduated in 1926. He was Master of Lodge F & AM #300 of Waveland in 1946 and Secretary 1971-1987. He retired from the Waveland Post Office May 1971, after 35 years of service.

Wayne and Tressa Surber were married September 1931, and with the exception of a few months, lived in the same house north of Waveland all their married life.

Tressa was the daughter of Edward and Minnie Surber, born August 1910. She attended Waveland School and graduated in 1928. She also worked at the Waveland Post Office for 17 years. Both are members of the Browns Valley Christian Church.

Wayne's ancestor, Richard Simms, was born about 1720 in Stafford Co., VA, and died about 1812, being over 90 when he died. He married in 1750 to Betty Bridwell. After their marriage Betty's father gave them 50 acres of land, which she sold after the death of Richard. Richard and Betty had nine children, one of which was Richard Jr., born 1752 and died in his 99th year. He married Betty Ashby. In 1816 Richard moved to Franklin Co., KY. In 1829 he moved to Clay Co., MO. He was considered a farmer, but taught his son Benjamin the carpenter trade.

Pressley Simms was the third son of Richard and Betty, born about 1753 in Virginia, died 1852 near Crawfordsville, IN. Married Nancy Bridwell, who died 1845. He served in the Revolutionary War and at 61 years served in the War of 1812. His home was destroyed by the British in 1814 and in 1815 he left for Madison Co., KY. Around 1820 he moved to Lawrence Co., IN and around 1828 his name was found in the census records of Montgomery County. He died at age 104.

Pressley and Nancy had ten children, one of which was Charles, being the eighth. Charles was born about 1800 in Virginia and died 1876 in southern Illinois. Married Malinda ___ and they had 12 children. The second child, William H., born 1833 in Sullivan Co., IN and died in 1896 at Waynetown, where he is buried. He was married three times. In all, he had eight children by the three wives.

Charles Edward, first son of his first marriage, married Anna Scott. She was born around Alamo, IN, and died at Waveland. Both are buried at Waynetown. Charles and Anna had two sons. William Allen 1888-1942 and Matthew Scott Simms 1891 - 1966. William married Lulu Childers and had two sons, Wayne and Rowen, and two daughters Aline and Virginia.

Matthew married Bessie Moore and had one son Robert Daniel, who followed his father's profession in law. *Submitted by Wayne Simms*

AUSTIN MERLE SIMPSON

Austin Merle Simpson, born in Fountain County to the late Ray E. and Lillie Grace Peters Simpson, Oct. 4, 1925. In 1927 the family moved to a farm east of Browns Valley where Austin was raised. Austin graduated from Waveland High School in 1944. In 1954 he entered the Army for two years. In September 1956 he began working for IBM in Greencastle, retiring February 1987. He's now working in the spring at Servies Greenhouse in New Market, pursuing his hobby, gardening.

Enid Lucille, daughter of Perry Arthur and Florence Ellen Brown Hockersmith was born, Oct. 11, 1933, in Boone County. In 1940, her family moved to a farm near Freedom Baptist Church. Lucille graduated from New Market High School and from Home Hospital in 1954, a Registered Nurse. She worked full time at Culver Hospital from 1954-57. In 1960, Lucille returned to Culver working part-time as she continues to do.

On Aug. 26, 1956 Austin and Lucille were married at Freedom Baptist Church by her brother, Darrell. Their family of five began with, Sallie Lou, born Mar. 1, 1957. She graduated from Southmont in 1975. Sallie married Russell Max Hester June 28, 1975. They reside on their farm north of Parkersburg. They're members of Parkersburg Christian Church. They've two sons, Brian Thomas, born Feb. 7, 1980 and Todd Alan, born Jan. 18, 1987.

Austin Simpson Family, Front Row: Sallie, Todd, Lucille, Brandon and Austin. 2nd Row: Polly, Peggy, Brook, Brian and Russell. 3rd Row: Larry, Bradley, Brad and Patti

Peggy Sue was born Mar. 16, 1958. She graduated from Southmont in 1976. She married Bradley Lee Grayson July 1, 1978. They're members of East Side Baptist Church. They reside northeast of Darlington with their children, Brook Michelle, born June 26, 1980 and Brandon Lee, born Jan. 19, 1983.

Patti Jean was born Oct. 10, 1959. She graduated from Southmont in 1977. Patti resides in Crawfordsville and is employed at Lew Wallace Inn as a receptionist.

Polly Ann was born Oct. 13, 1963. She graduated from Southmont in 1982. On July 25, 1983, Polly married Larry Wayne Rhoads. They reside in New Market with their daughter, Kayla Ann, born Feb. 29, 1988.

A son, Brad Michael, was born Dec. 10, 1964. Brad graduated from Southmont in 1983. He lives at home and is employed at Moore Building Co. He's the father of, Deborah Jean Hamilton, born July 19, 1987.

The Browns Valley Christian Church has been and still is a vital part of the Simpson family. Austin became a member in his early teens. He served as elder for nearly 30 years. Lucille joined soon after their marriage and has held many positions, also. They also participate in the choir. The three girls were also married there. Patti, Polly, and Brad are members there also. Austin and Lucille enjoy church activities, traveling, and being with their family. *Submitted by Sallie Simpson Hester*

GERALD AND MARGARET (SEAY) SIMPSON

Gerald Lee and Margaret Louise (Seay) Simpson met at Turkey Run State Park in 1942 on a blind date when she was a waitress in the Inn.

Gerald is the son of Ray and Grace (Peters) Simpson (see history in this book). Margaret was born Oct. 29, 1924 in Hillsdale, Vermillion Co., IN, the daughter of Arthur and Mary Elizabeth (Peat) Seay. Both Arthur and Mary were born in Illinois, but began housekeeping West of Waveland on State Road 47 in June of 1910. Margaret's brothers and sisters are now all deceased: Elizabeth Lorene, b. 1911, d. 1953, married Marion Richardson; Irene, b. September 1912, died at age three days; and Arthur "Dean" b. 1916, d. 1978, married Mary

Catherine Muncey. Margaret's parents were farmers and both are buried at Maple Ridge. Margaret attended schools at Hillsdale, Bellmore, Dana, and graduated from Tangier in 1942. She worked at Grab-It-Here Grocery at Kingman for sometime and has always enjoyed being a Housewife and Mother. Margaret likes to crochet, paint and travel.

Gerald attended Browns Valley grade school and graduated in 1942 from Waveland. Gerald drove a truck for Bayless Trucking and has farmed in Sec. 24 Brown Township all his life. Gerald enjoys college ball and traveling.

Gerald and Margaret Simpson Wedding Nov. 25, 1945

Gerald and Margaret were married on Nov. 25, 1945 North of Waveland at his sister's home (Doris and Tom Jeffries) by the Reverend John Servies. They are the parents of five children, all born at Culver Hospital.

Gary Lee, born July 12, 1947 married Karen Chadwick (daughter of Delmas and Rebecca) on Aug. 5, 1967. Gary also farms in Brown Township. He graduated from the Purdue Farm Short Course and was in the Army National Guard. Karen is Secretary at Southmont School Corporation. Their children are: Rodney Lee, born Apr. 13, 1968. He is a Southmont Graduate and is attending ISU, majoring in Elementary Education. Robin Lou born Oct. 8, 1971. She is a student at Southmont.

Larry Joe, born Dec. 19, 1952, married Ruth Larimer (daughter of Paul and Margaret) of Lagrange, IN on Oct. 6, 1973. Larry attended Ball State and is an Associate Manager at Western-Southern Insurance in Lafayette. Children: Amy Renee born Dec. 31, 1976 and Katie Leann born June 14, 1980. Ruth is a seamstress.

Darrell Ray born Sept. 29, 1956 married Betty Lou Brown (daughter of Don and Beth) of Ladoga on Nov. 27, 1976. Darrell farms with his dad. Betty is a homemaker. Children: Darren Ray, born Apr. 13, 1979; Dwayne Michael, born Sept. 4, 1982 and Joanna Lyn, born Sept. 4, 1987.

Karen Sue born May 9, 1959, married Marc McFall (son of David and Pat) from Indianapolis on May 23, 1981. Karen attended Purdue and has taught in Nursery Schools. Marc is a Boy Scout Executive in Hamilton and Tipton Co., IN. One daughter: Tyson Joelle was born Sept. 18, 1986.

Deanna Lou born May 18, 1961, married Brian Rice (son of Alfred and Ruth of New Market) on June 6, 1980. Deanna is a Homemaker and has taught in Pre-Schools. Brian works at Borge-Warner Transmission in Muncie. Children: Brianna Lou, born Jan. 23, 1984.

Gerald and Margaret are members of Browns Valley Christian Church where Gerald is an Elder. Their children are affiliated with churches in their communities. *Submitted by Margaret Simpson*

RAY SIMPSON

Ray Simpson, born June 17, 1891 near Waveland, was the son of Charles and Florence Catherine "Kate" Lamson Simpson. He married Lilly "Grace" Peters on his 18th birthday. She was the daughter of William H. and Nancy (Coons) Peters and was born Feb. 5, 1892. Ray was a farmer in Brown Township and drove a horse-drawn school bus, complete with pot-belly stove to keep the youngsters warm. Ray died from heart trouble at the age of 64 on Sept. 1, 1955. Grace died from a stroke on June 5, 1970 at Culver Hospital. The Simpsons had nine children: Bert (b. Dec. 19, 1909), Doris (b. Aug. 18, 1913), Lowell (b. May 4, 1916), Ruby (b. Sept. 18, 1917), Forrest (b. Aug. 2, 1919), Charles (b. Feb. 22, 1922), Gerald (b. Jan. 7, 1924), Austin (b. Oct. 4, 1925), and Don (b. July 13, 1928). All but Bert (d. Apr. 25, 1981), Lowell (d. Dec. 31, 1986) and Ruby (d. Jan. 23, 1978) now live in Montgomery County.

Top Row. L to R: Don, Forrest, Austin, Gerald, Charles and Lowell. Bottom: Ruby, Grace, Ray, "Kate", Bert and Doris

Bert married Lois Starnes and had: Jeanette, James and Esther Jane. Doris married #1 Tom Jeffries and #2 Fred Bazzani. She had one child, Judy Jeffries Gregg Rivers. Lowell married Betty Fulwider and had: Dale and Malcolm. Ruby married Oscar Moody and had: Dennis, Rita, John and Penny. Forrest served in the Navy during WWII. He married Ethel Sellers and they are the parents of: Max, Michael and Charles E. Charles was an Army man in WWII, married Virginia Jackson and had: Catherine. Gerald served in the Army, married Margaret Seay and had: Gary, Larry, Darrell, Karen and Deanna. Austin was also in the Army, married Lucille Hockersmith and had: Sallie, Peggy, Patti, Polly, and Brad. Don married Lucille's sister, Liz Hockersmith and has no children.

All the Simpson children farmed but Forrest and Austin. Forrest is retired from Allisons and Austin is retired from IBM. Many of the 49 great grandchildren of Ray and Grace (Peters) Simpson live in Montgomery County.

Montgomery County Simpson roots goes back to James H. Sympson and Harriet Harris. James was born July 22, 1844 in Kentucky. He served in the Civil War. He died Jan. 29, 1894. Harriet was born Oct. 19, 1842 and died Oct. 7, 1923. Both are buried in Indiana Creek Cemetery.

Kate Lamson Simpson's parents were: Thomas Lamson (born Sept. 29, 1836 near Mace) and Delilah Burke. Thomas died Aug. 31, 1911. Delilah died Nov. 22, 1915. Both are buried in Union Cemetery, Brown Twp. *Submitted by Doris Simpson Jeffries Bazzani*

HUGH FRANKLIN AND DOTTIE MARGARET (STEPHENS) SINGER

Hugh Franklin Singer was born June 1, 1886 in Wayne Township, the son of William Ellis and Maranda Dee (Baldwin) Singer, whose biographies appear elsewhere in this volume. Frank was the youngest of three children, Lena and John C. being the other two.

About 1905, Frank began work, probably as a laborer, at the Poston Brick Company on Poston Drive in Crawfordsville, and remained with the company for more than 40 years. He retired in the late 1940s as shop superintendent. During the mid-1930s, Frank began a sideline business, a concrete block shop, located in the 800 block of East College Street, just a hundred yards away from the family residence at 805 East College where he and his family had lived since 1921. The block shop operated until about 1950.

Hugh Franklin and Dottie Margaret (Stephens) Singer and daughter Louise D.

On May 30, 1906, he married Dottie Margaret Stephens, born Feb. 10, 1885 in Boone Co., IN. She was one of 11 children born to John T. Stephens, b. Dec. 10, 1843 in Shelby Co., IN, d. Mar. 16, 1906, and Margaret Louise Campbell, b. Apr. 17, 1850 in Knoxville, TN, d. Jan. 21, 1929, both of Irish descent. The family moved from Boone County to Montgomery County about 1886. Dottie's siblings were: Clara, b. Aug. 6, 1878, d. 1961, married Bill Neese Sept. 30, 1905; Minnie E., b. Oct. 8, 1881, d. 1960, married Sylvester Kirby Apr. 1, 1907; Lina, m. Ollie Caldwell; Pansy E., b. Aug. 28, 1887, d. 1960, married Ed B. Middleton Mar. 9, 1905; Will; Ert, married Bess ___; John H., b. Feb. 18, 1890, d. 1977, married Bessie May Sharpe Jan. 23, 1909; Ottis b., Jan. 11, 1888, married Elsie Porter, Oct. 21, 1908; Edward, d. 1904; Fern Alice, b. July 9, 1897, d. Aug. 3, 1970, married John Bryan Sanford Feb. 23, 1916.

Dottie attended beautician's school about the time of her marriage in 1906, and operated a beauty shop out of her home for several years. She apparently was keenly interested in women's issues, and marched in several suffragette parades.

Frank and Dottie had one child, Louise Dee, born Apr. 19, 1907, d. Dec. 4, 1973 in Orlando, FL, married Fred Milam Buzzaird Nov. 14, 1931. Their biographies appear elsewhere in this volume.

Frank died Dec. 28, 1956 and Dottie died May 9, 1962. Both are buried in Oak Hill Cemetery.

WESLEY AND MARY ANN HALL SINGER

J. Wesley Singer was born in Virginia, 1805, his ancestors having come from England. He migrated to Kentucky, and married Lavina Lunsford who died. She had worked her name in the corner of a blue-white bedspread. Wesley then married Mary Ann Hall of Louisville, KY. She was a twin, born in 1818, the daughter of Elijah and Martha Ann Smith Hall. Her twin sister, Naomi, died; also her father.

So her brother, Norman Hall, was her bondsman when she and Wesley Singer were married, Apr. 23, 1839. They came to Montgomery Co., IN, in 1848. The farm where they bought and made their home was just South of Wesley Chapel Methodist Church and School on the East side of the road. Both of them are buried in the churchyard cemetery — he died Mar. 23, 1864, and she on Dec. 4, 1882. Four of their children were born in Kentucky — Jeptha, William Ellis, Hannah and Joseph. Five were born in Montgomery County — Delila, Charles, Margaret Emza (my Grandmother Cedars), John and Sarah. Mary Ann Hall Singer had relatives in 1892 living in Oldham Co., KY, and Pee Wee Valley near Louisville. Their last names were Hall, Arrowsmith, Melone and Ward.

When the Civil War brought tensions, some of the membrs of Wesley Chapel who came from the South, but wanted to be loyal to the North, formed Christian Union Church, a few miles away. There the Singers could remain Democrats. This church is still active as a rural church.

Jeptha Singer taught school and had a Singing School where he used a tuning fork. He enlisted in the Civil War, serving as a Captain in the 5th Cavalry, Co. C (or D?), Indiana. He died after being shot, and is buried at Murfreesboro, TN. His name is memorialized on his parents' tombstone, where the American Legion places a flag each year. *Contributed by Mary Elizabeth Cedars*

WILLIAM ELLIS AND MIRANDA DEE (BALDWIN) SINGER

William Ellis Singer was born Mar. 14, 1843 in Oldham Co., KY, the second of the nine children of J. Wesley Singer, b. 1804 in Virginia, d. Mar. 10, 1863, and Mary Ann Hall, b. 1817 in Kentucky, d. Dec. 15, 1882. Both Wesley and Mary Ann are buried in Wesley Cemetery. The family moved from Kentucky to Wayne Township in 1846.

Ellis's siblings were Jeptha, b. Feb. 5, 1840 in Kentucky, d. Dec. 8, 1863 in Tennessee while serving as a corporal with Company L, 5th Cavalry, 90th Indiana (Thompson's Light Cavalry); Joseph, b. 1846 in Kentucky; Hannah E., b. 1847, d. Mar. 19, 1876; Delila A., b. 1849, married John Bailey Mar. 6, 1879; Charles, b. 1850 married Lottie B. McAllister Oct 28, 1882; Margaret, b. 1853; John, b. 1855, d. 1941, married Mary Thompson, Feb. 15, 1883; and Sarah, b. 1858. The last six children were all born in Montgomery County.

Ellis was a youth of 19 when he joined Thompson's Light Cavalry, the unit of his older brother, on Aug. 22, 1862. He was a private. The unit was posted to the Southern Indiana border during 1862 and 1863, then moved south through Kentucky and Tennessee to later take part in the Battle of Atlanta and Stoneman's Raid in Georgia. He mustered out with the regiment at Murphreesboro, TN, on Sept. 15, 1865 as a corporal.

Ellis returned to Montgomery County after the war and became a carpenter, a craft he pursued the rest of his life. On Mar. 27, 1882, he married Miranda Dee Baldwin at Wesley Station, with Squire Milton Henderson presiding.

Miranda was born Nov. 18, 1860, the seventh child of Elias Jackson Baldwin, b. ca. 1825 in Ohio d. ca 1880, and Mary A. (Polly) Harlow, b. Mar. 20, 1829 in Ohio, d. Sept. 11, 1867, who were married Feb. 12, 1846 in Montgomery County. Miranda's siblings were: William J., b. 1847, d. 1917, m. Eliza Lowe Dec. 27, 1868; David, b. Mar. 15, 1851, d. Jan. 2, 1866; Mary J., b. 1850 m. Charles DeHaven Mar. 30, 1870; Garret, b. 1853, m. Barbara Bucks Dec. 31, 1883; Sarah E., b. 1856, m. Lee Surface Oct. 14, 1888; John P., b. Apr. 20, 1850, d. Oct. 5, 1874; Charles M. (Chad), b. 1862, m. Ida Carver Sept. 25, 1884; George, b. 1865. Polly and several of her children are buried in Wesley Cemetery.

Ellis and Miranda had three children: Lena, b. Feb. 1, 1883, d. 1958; John C., b. Oct. 10, 1884, d. 1948; and Hugh Franklin, b. June 1, 1886, d. Dec. 28, 1956, m. Dottie Margaret Stephens, May 30, 1906. Ellis and Miranda were divorced in 1899.

After the divorce, Ellis left Montgomery County for the soldier's colony at Fitzgerald, GA, where he continued his carpenter's craft. He returned to Montgomery County to live with his youngest son, Frank, a short time before he died on May 8, 1921. He is buried on Oak Hill Cemetery.

Miranda married Samuel Snyder and continued to live in Montgomery County. The Snyders had three duaghters: Doris (Wills), Mary (Grimes), and Margaret (Barker). Miranda died Aug. 8, 1928 and is buried in Wesley Cemetery.

MRS. SARAH ANN MORRIS SKAGGS

John Morris, born in Hamilton Co., OH in 1822 married Ann Holly, born in Bourbon Co., KY, and they came two miles north of New Ross in an early day. They had William Harvey Morris, and Sarah Ann Morris Skaggs, born Apr. 4, 1842 near New Ross. When she was 80 years old in 1922, she told about life in early days. Things she and her brother had to do, but she said others had to do the same thing. She walked three miles to school. She and her brother helped clear land; and they spun yarn to supply their clothing needs. Her parents had a cane mill. They had apple butter boilings, which were a lot of fun. Pulling wax was another past time. They raked wheat after a cradle, and they took grain to Lafayette, the trip taking three days. They would get as far as Wea, along Wea Creek, and camp there, coming and going. They took grain, hay salt, shoe leather, and Orleans sugar to Lafayette. She and her father worked the cane mill until 9 P.M., then would get up the next morning and take wheat to Thorntown, Boone Co., IN, did trading, then returned home by noon, and her mother and brother would be working the cane mill. She said they worked hard chopping wood all day, then would dance all night, not every night though. She joined the Providence Church in September 1878 and taught school at Watkins school, had 40 pupils. She froze her hands milking cows in 1865. From 1902 to 1922 when she wrote the article about her early life, she was a telephone operator at Mace, IN. She married William Skaggs in October 1876; they had no children. Her brother married Mary Jeanette Martin and they had 12; all lived near Mace, IN.

THE JAMES SLATER FAMILY

My family, the James Slater family, lived in Crawfordsville more than 35 years. If my great-grandfather, William Roark, had stayed in the eastern part of Montgomery County near Shannondale, it would have been a different story. But he fell in love with Sarah Hill, a Boone County girl, sold out, and moved there near Dover. He had come from Nicholas Co., KY, with his father John, who entered land in Montgomery County in 1826. William, born in 1812, first bought land in 1832.

My family moved from Jamestown to Crawfordsville in 1917, and my father was in the circulation department of the *Journal-Review* for many years. I was a small girl when the flu epidemic struck in 1918. Schools were closed and while we children were home playing on Nov. 11, 1918, we heard bells ringing and whistles blowing to celebrate the signing of the Armistice and the end of World War I.

My father lived near Sheridan in Hamilton County as a boy and my mother, Sadie Roark, lived in Boone County. They both taught school and my father had studied to be a minister. He was a serious student of the Bible all his life. They were members of the First Baptist Church, Crawfordsville.

I have been so grateful throughout my life for the excellent education I received in the city schools. Some especially good teachers I had were: Jessie Lee, who taught sewing and home furnishings; Julie LeClerc Knox, Latin; Minnie Williams, English literature; H.O. Burgess, world history; and Mary Kinnick, business.

I remember the "fresh air" class at Mills grade school. We students studied with our coats, caps and boots on, with the windows slightly opened, on the theory we would study better in cool temperatures. This was done only one year.

I will never forget the grandeur of Lew Wallace's Ben Hur studio and the white, colonial style home of Henry S. Lane.

Many times I rode the "Yellow Peril," our name for the city street car. Its route was from the west end of Main Street, through the downtown area, and to the east end of Wabash Avenue - then back.

My older brother, Ira, was always interested in radios and electronics and worked with them at P.R. Mallory Company, Indianapolis. I married a classmate, Merle Shanklin, and after he graduated from Wabash College and took a teaching position in Goshen High School, we moved to Goshen, where I now live. After his death at age 51 a city park was named for him. I later married Edward Lange and he died in 1984. My younger brother, John, was killed in a car accident in 1933.

After I retired from Drs. Wellington's office in 1971, I became interested in finding ancestors and am in the Daughters of the American Revolution through a maternal ancestor, and in Colonial Dames of the 17th Century through another maternal ancestor. I hold a county and district office in the General Federation of Women's Clubs.

I am never too busy to forget Crawfordsville. *By Lois Slater Shanklin Lange*

JOHN SMALL

Oldest native born male in Township. And had lived out his life near place of birth (died May 2, 1919).

Township's Oldest Man and Pioneer in clearing the Forests and the Swamps of the community.

John Small was the son of Nathan Small and Louisa Blackford Small and was born Oct. 17, 1835, at the old family homestead, located just west of town (Waynetown, IN) in what is known as the Holman addition, and a short distance east and south where the residence of E.J. Biddle now stands.

The family lineage reaches far back into the past years and across the seas to that historic land of the Scotchman. There in the romantic and picturesque hills of Scotland we get our first acquaintance with our foreparents, John and Sarah Small. Two sons and three daughters were born to this ancestral Scotland home, and in due time the sons, growing to young manhood, in a vision that looked across the broad waters of the Atlantic, saw the beauties and the promises of the new world and came to America.

Nathan, the younger of the brothers was born, May 25, 1767 came to South Carolina, where he located and was married and where the father of the subject of this sketch, Nathan Small was born. A few years later the family came to North Carolina, and then to Wayne County near Richmond, this state, only to finally come to this place, where the senior of the family entered the land just west of town (Waynetown) known as the Elam Small place, and a portion of which is owned by Dr. A.N. Hamilton. (Hamilton land was across from Masonic Cemetery west of Waynetown).

Here the junior Nathan Small, father of our beloved dead, grew to manhood and was married to Louisa Blackford at the old Blackford homestead, near Springboro, OH. To this union were born four daughters and five sons, of which number Uncle John, as we have all known him for so many years, was the third. Born of sturdy pioneer stock, he grew to a vigorous and strong young manhood and did his full share in reclaiming the broad fields west and south of this town from the grip of the forest and the swamps. At about the age of 24, he was united in marriage to Dennis Burch on Dec. 3, 1859. To this union four daughters were born—Verona, Lena, Effie, and Gussie. Verona died in infancy. Then Lena, in the flower of young womanhood, was called in death a few months later to the better land. Once again the dark messenger entered the home, and mother joined the three daughters on the other side. As the years have come and gone, and life's sun for Uncle John has been slowly sinking to rest, the way has been made brighter and happier by the constant and faithful companionship, the care and love of his only daughter, Effie, who now mourns his death. About 20 years ago, Uncle John united with the Christian Church of this place during a meeting conducted by the Rev. Will G. Loucks, and has at all times honored that good confession, given the church and its work a liberal support and living the life of the true Christian man. He was also a member of the Masonic lodge of this place, having become a member many years ago.

Besides the daughter, he is survived by one sister, Mrs. Louisa Williams, the last remaining of this large pioneer family. There are also four nephews, three nieces, four great nephews, and four great nieces and one great, great nephew, Master John William Hendricks, son of Mr. and Mrs. Clinton Hendricks, now of Ligonier.

At the time of his death he was the oldest native born male resident of the township (Wayne). For four score years and more he had lived out his life in this community and had always been faithful to life's highest duties—home and loved ones, and honorable in all his obligations and dealings with his feilowman. Unassuming and quietly he lived, loved and respected in life and honored by all in death. To have known Uncle John Small was to have known a man of sterling character whose influence inspired one to higher thoughts and nobler purposes. The funeral service was held Sunday afternoon at the Christian Church at 2 o'clock and was conducted by Rev. W.H. Kerr of Crawfordsville, an old friend in the family. Rev. Kerr preached a splendid sermon and life the resurrection, paying a touching tribute to the life just closed. The Masonic order had charge and concluded the funeral services, Judge Jerre West giving ritualistic part of service. Buried Waynetown Masonic Cemetery. *Submitted by B. Hamm*

THE SMITH-BAGBY FAMILY

George Henry Smith, son of William and Mary Ann (Wainscott) Smith, was born in Coal Creek Township on May 14, 1862. There he grew into manhood, and as a youth he worked on the farm of Francis Marion Bagby. In time, he and Emma Frances, the daughter of his employer, fell in love. The Bagby family noted, with some amusement, the George no longer treated Emma as a younger sister, to the extent of helping her from the wagon when they went to church. On May 20, 1883, they were wed. The bride, having been born Aug. 28, 1867, was only 16.

Emma's mother was Patience Elizabeth Allhands, a daughter of George and Julia Ann (Alexander) Allhands. Her paternal grandparents were James Bagby and Lucinda Peed who were married in Bracken Co., KY on Feb. 6, 1835. Francis Marion, known as Frank, was born to them Nov. 30, 1838. His siblings, their birth dates, and some of their spouses were: Nancy, ca 1836, - Daniel W. Peed, a cousin; Mary F., ca 1841 - Arron Morrow; John H., ca 1844. All were born in Kentucky.

Sometime after 1843, James Bagby died. In 1846 Lucinda and her siblings signed a document that sold the land of her father Philip Peed Jr. back in Bracken County. He died there in 1831, and her mother Nancy (Brumley) Peed had given consent for Lucinda to marry. However, she signed it as Lucinda Russel, indicating that she had since married to a Russel. Then, apparently again widowed, she married Daniel Ferguson in Montgomery County in 1848. The 1850 census shows the combined family living together, half the children named Bagby, and half Ferguson.

Lucinda's mother Nancy also came to Montgomery, apparently to live with some of her children. Her grave has been found in an unmowed section of the old Waynetown Cemetery. She died in 1841.

Philip Peed Jr. came to Kentucky from King George Co., VA. His mother was Margaret Green, daughter of Richard. This line of Peeds can be accurately traced back to the very early 1700s in Virginia and they probably descend from John Peed who was enumerated among the living and dead, as living after the first Indian massacre of 1623.

Frank Bagby lived to a ripe old age, living in later life with his various Smith grandchildren. He died May 15, 1916, and buried in the Oakland Cemetery.

His grandchildren, the children of George and Emma Smith, and some of their spouses were: Francis Marion (Frank); Charles Earnest - Elsie Wood; Wallis Earl - Gusta Tanner; Edith Mae - Oliver Earl Cook; Richard Foster, died in childhood; Winton Carlyle - Alice Webster. All but Edith who resided in Oklahoma, and Winton who lived in the Rio Grande Valley of Texas, were residents of Indiana.

George Smith died Feb. 21, 1817 of congestive heart failure, and Emma on Feb. 1, 1920 of tuberculosis. They are buried in the Wingate Cemetery (Pleasant Hill). Many descendants of these families are still in the area today. *Submitted by Charles M. Cook*

ARTIE AND LOIS MARGERY SMITH

Artie Lee Smith was one of six children born to William Henry and Emily Jane (McMullen) Smith. He was born Dec. 20, 1892 in Ladoga. He was a veteran of WWI and a member of First Christian Church. Artie died in 1962 and is buried in Masonic Cemetery, Crawfordsville.

On June 8, 1919, he was married to Lois Margery Newhouse. Lois is the daughter of Azariah and Mary Bell (Hunter) Newhouse, Indianapolis. She is a member of First Christian Church, was one of the organizers of Sunshine Chorus—she also was their accompanist—and a Grey Lady for the Red Cross.

To this union were born Mary Louise Priebe (May 1920) and Richard Allen (July, 1923).

There are, in 1989, eight grandchildren, 12 great grandchildren and several step-great-grandchildren. *Submitted by Mary Louise Priebe*

CHARITY FARNSWORTH SMITH

As a widow, Charity Smith was one of the first women to come to the area which was to become Montgomery County, settling there in 1822, only one year after the first settlers arrived. There are many tales describing her as a brave and fearless woman.,

Charity Farnsworth was born in New Jersey in 1776, the daughter of Henry Farnsworth. The family migrated to Washington Co., PA, where she met and married Ephraim Smith. Their oldest children were born in Pennsylvania before they moved to Ohio. Ephraim and Charity decided to investigate government land deals in what was then part of Putnam Co., IN, but Ephraim died before they could leave. Charity decided to go anyway, arriving on Nov. 8, 1822. The next day she went to the land office in Terre Haute and bought 160 acres which were located two miles east of the present site of Crawfordsville. After returning from Terre Haute she settled on the new land and built a one-room cabin. Until this was finished, she and eight children lived in a wagon and a hollowed-out tree trunk. On his travels through the Wabash Valley, Sandford C. Cox remembered seeing "several people who lived east of Crawfordsville including the 'Widow Smith'."

Indians were frequent visitors at the Smith cabin. Charity always shared the family food with them and indicated her friendly intentions by gifts of beads. An Indian legend states that when she made her annual trip to Cincinnati to purchase staples not yet available in Crawfordsville, friendly Indians watched over. After her death, an Indian once told her son Enoch, "She always was a friend to the Indian. She never went to Cincinnati that we did not send a runner with her, although she never knew it."

By 1834 two of Charity's sons had died and all three of her daughters were married but still lived in the county. Her three sons helped clear part of the land in order to plant crops and vegetables. Alvin Ramey remembered that "many of us can recollect with what gladness we would hail 'old Mrs. Smith' and her vegetables, she being for many years the only person who brought green vegetables regularly to market." One of her earliest crops was rye, and with the straw she braided hats which were sold in the market. During the winter she braided them for the following summer. It was said of her that by hard work, continual industry, and leading a frugal life, she was able to give each of her children a farm before she died in 1865.

References

Brelsford, Bridgie Brill. *Indians of Montgomery County, Indiana*. Crawfordsvlle: Montgomery County Historical Society, 1985.

Cantrell, Martha. "Widow Smith was a living legend." *Montgomery Magazine* 10 (June, 1985) pp. 3-4.

Cox, Sandford C. *Recollections of the early settlement of the Wabash Valley.* Lafayette: Courier Steam Book and Job Printing House, 1860. Ramey, Alvin. "Personal reminiscences: the first white inhabitants."
Crawfordsville Journal, June 15, 1871, p. 2.
Submitted by Don and Jean Thompson

CHARLES EDGAR AND MARY BESSIE (BRANSON) SMITH

Charles Edgar (Ed) Smith was born at Whitesville, IN on Dec. 5, 1885. He was the son of Henry R. and Louisa (Thompson) Smith who were married in Montgomery County on Feb. 20, 1879. He had one brother, Earl B. Smith and sister, Carrie (married Dr. Claude F. Peffley), Olive Herrington and Florence McDonald.

Henry R. Smith's parents were: John W. and Harriet.

Ed married Mary Bessie Branson, daughter of Enoch and Pattie (Taylor) Branson at Crawfordsville on Dec. 4, 1912. She had eight brothers and sisters: Thomas, Elbert, Benjamin, Mae, Hugh, Clint, Wilbur and Anna. Mary Bessie Branson was born May 10, 1888 near Russellville.

Ed and Mary Bessie (Branson) Smith resided in Union Township for two years, then moved to Brown Township, where they lived until 1937, finally moving to Putnam Co., IN.

Ed drove a huckster wagon for the Whitesville General Store, owned by Harry Laymon for several years, then went to farming. Ed carried shoes, yard goods, home remedies and groceries, and packed such items in his buggy each morning. One story of Ed's huckster days goes like this, as quoted by his daughter, Louise: "Once he bought a crate of chickens from a family who lived at the bottom of a hill in Bal Hinch. Evidently, the crate wasn't latched tightly, because when Dad got the team of horses to the top of the hill, the chickens were walking back home."

Ed and Mary Bessie had: Pattie Louise who married Lloyd Jeffries and Geneva C. who married Claude Bayless.

The Smiths met while Ed was driving the huckster route. He ate with different customers each day, and the Branson's were his customers.

Mary Branson Smith died May 22, 1927. Ed later married Oakie Mae Whitted (June 23, 1935). He died Aug. 14, 1970. Ed and Mary are buried in the Russellville Cemetery. *Submitted by his daughters*

ENOCH AND ELIZABETH GATTS SMITH

Enoch Smith, Minister and Poet was born in Zionsville, IN on Jan. 27, 1890, the son of Charles T. and Dora Mae Smith. Shortly, after his birth in 1890, the family moved to Crawfordsville.

He attended Willson School and in 1908 graduated from Crawfordsville High School where he had played football and participated in the Shakespeare Club and in 1908 was President of the Polymnian. He was known for his public speaking and took part in the debating and oratorical contests in the area. He received his B.A. Degree from Bethany College in West Virginia and studied at Oberlin School of Theology and the Divinity School of the University of Chicago.

On Mar. 27, 1911 Enoch was ordained to the ministry in the First Christian Church in Crawfordsville.

In 1912 he married Miss Elizabeth Gatts. They had a daughter. He is now retired and living in Lakeland, FL and will be 100 years old on Jan. 27, 1990.

He is well known as a poet. His works include: "Poetic Story of Paul the Apostle", "Columbia's Third, Fourth, and Fifth flights"; "How Beautiful the Trees"; "Apollo-Soyuz"; "The Rising Tide of Divorces, Do We Still Blame"; "The Race is on in America"; and Mt. Helen's Eruption - May 18, 1980".

GEORGE FORREST SMITH

George Forrest Smith of Waynetown, IN Montgomery County was born Dec. 18, 1928 in Evansville, IN to Joseph and Viola Harris Smith of Calhoun, KY. George was the youngest of four children. A brother, Roy Lee and two sisters, Mildred L. and Dorothy. George and Dorothy were Hoosier born and Mildred and Roy were born in Calhoon, KY.

Maternal grandparents, Henry Harris and Sarah Jane McCormick were of Calhoun, KY. Paternal grandparents, Lum Smith and Anna Taylor were also of Calhoun and Rumsey, KY area.

George lived in Evansville until 1955. During this time at age 17 he entered the U.S. Navy, serving honorably for two years then discharged in December of 1947.

On July 25, 1946, he married Joan Jacquelyn Oran of Evansville and remained together until her death on Aug. 8, 1966. Four children were born: Michele Maxine, Linda Diane, Terry Lee and Georgianna. Of these four children, ten grandchildren and two great grandchildren were born.

George and family left Evansville in 1956 as he had entered the ministry in early 50s and was a licensed minister of the Church of God, Cleveland, TN Assembly. Moved to Central Indiana preaching Revivals in Indiana and surrounding states. He was sent to Attica in 1958 to organize a small mission and in early 1961 was sent to Frankfort to organize a Church of God Mission there.

He came to Crawfordsville in 1962 to pastor the Grace Ave. Church and remained active in this church until the death of his wife, Joan in 1966. August 3, 1968, he married Vivian L. Harlan of Waynetown where they have made their home ever since. They are both a member of the Waynetown Christian Church of which George is an elder. George has one step-daughter and two step-grandchildren of this last union.

JOE AND ALLIE (LANG) SMITH

Raymond Busenbark, a Deer's Mill neighbor of Joe Smith's once said, "Old Joe had a cane pole and if there was any fish in Sugar Creek, he'd catch 'em!" Although Joe often fed his large family with the fish, he just as often gave them away — fishing was his relaxation! Timber and gravel pit work was his livelihood.

Joseph Monroe Smith was born near Rockville, IN on Sept. 12, 1851 and died at his Deer's Mill home on Feb. 10, 1926, after a long illness. He was the son of Reuben and Mary (Helm) Smith. It was said that Joe fought hard to live, even wearing felt boots in his bed his last three years due to poor circulation, but when his beloved "Allie" (Almarinda Lang, born Oct. 19, 1854 to Benjamin and Mary (Darst) Lang died on January 31st, he gave up. They are buried side by side in Freedom Cemetery.

Joe and Allie (Lang) Smith

Joe and Allie were married on her 25th birthday in Rockville. She was a devout mother caring for her epileptic son, Guy, with great tenderness for 31 years and her husband for his three-year sickness before their deaths. Joe and Allie's caskets were $100 each; the minister $5; her dress, shoes and hose $31 and his suit, shirt and socks 50¢ more.

To this union, seven children were born: Albertis (Bert); Clarence (Sig); Emily (Pearl); Claude; Ora; Leland "Carl" and Guy.

Bert was born July 20, 1880. He remained a bachelor. At an early age, he left home, settling in Boise, ID in 1916 where he died in December, 1964.

Sig entered life Mar. 4, 1882. He married Jessie Livengood, later her sister, Lela. His children: Betty May died young. Helen married Lloyd Edward Rusk, had Edward Lee, Fred David, Jack Dean and Anna Jean. Edith married Bill Sabens; one child, Mary Sue. Ruth married Robert Smith, had Mark Alan and Phillip Wayne. Ruby married Paul Beach; had Cathy, Sara and Ron. Sig was quite proud of his 50-year Masonic pin (Alamo Lodge), received in 1968.

Pearl liked the name Emily, so gave it to herself. She was born Sept. 20, 1844 and married Marion Crisp, later Lon Woods. Children: Dorothy Faye, married Curtis Quigg and had: Lucille, Lois, Dorothy, Judy and Lyle Wayne. Louis Crisp married Clara Fross - two adopted sons, George Richard and Roger Paul. Pearl's son, Richard Lowell Woods had one daughter, Nancy.

Claude was born Jan. 8, 1887 and married Lulu Banta. Children: Ina May married Floyd Walden, later Joe Gilliland - no children. Frona Lee, married Fred Pollitt, later Bob Chapman - no children. Ruby married Paul Branigan, later Norman Dillman - no children. Claude's son, Hubert, the only one to carry on the Smith name married Jeanette McIntyre. Children: Richard who married Nancy Fink and has Donald Glenn, Dianna Lynn, David Wayne and Dawn Michelle.

Ora, born Aug. 16, 1889 was famous for her pies. She married Walter Myers. Children: Bernard - no children and Celena (married Clark Dinwiddie and had Brenda Lee, Sherry Lou and Mary Sue).

Enoch Smith

Leland "Carl" was a brilliant man, although he only received an eighth grade education. When he took a Civil Service test (Depression time), his score was the highest ever made. His grandchildren remember him in his chair, reading and peeling apples for them to eat. He married Hazel Morgan and had three children: Lois Joyce, Hulda May and Kathryn Geneva Bazzani.

Guy, born Mar. 22, 1895 in Montgomery County was never married.

In conclusion, relax Joe! Many of your descendants also enjoy fishing! *Submitted by Karen Bazzani Zach*

JOHN H. SMITH

John was born Feb. 3, 1830 in Ohio, the son of Robert and Hannah Williamson Smith. John came with his family at the age of six years from Ohio to Yountsville, IN and settled on some farmland there, where the family grew and prospered. John was one of ten children.

The father of our subject, Robert was the son of John Smith who died in Ohio before 1836 and Phebe Smith who is buried in the O'Neal Cemetery with her family. She died in 1846 at the age of 85 years.

Of Robert and Hannah's ten children only seven have been found at this time by this researcher. Those are as follows; Hiram born 1819, Joseph born 1821 who married Martha Goss, Elizabeth born 1823, Ellen who married Levi Wilcox, John our subject, Martha A. and Margaret born 1837 wife of Warren Davis Jr. There are histories elsewhere on most of these children. Robert died June 15, 1865 and Hannah in 1872. Both of these parents were pioneers with true grit each being a helpmate to the other in all lifes hardships of these early times. Our subject, John was married Apr. 3, 1854 to Nancy Logan, who was born June 8, 1833 the daughter of Robert and Margaret Logan.

To John and his wife two children were born; Oscar Douglas born 1854 and married to Elizabeth Mullen, two children were born of this union; Florence May born 1872 wife of Samuel T. Stevens, and Wilbur A. born 1886 and married to Blanche Morrison. The second child of John was Ada J. born 1886.

These were all pioneers in the greatest sense of the word and all raised and nurtured their families in and around Yountsville where they first settled. The family for the most part in death as in life, together, as most are resting in and around Montgomery County. The old home was replaced in the 1960s with a more modern home after being sold after Florence's death. *Submitted by Becky Ingram*

JOHN H. AND CINDERELLA (BALSER) SMITH

John H. Smith born Jan. 20, 1851 in Howard Co., IN came to Ripley Township with his parents. John lived in Ripley Township for 80 years. He was a teamster. The son of Joseph Smith and Mary L. Rush, John's grandparents were: Daniel Smith and Christina Stonebraker. John's siblings were: Harriet married John Switzer; Mary Catherine married Thomas M. Galey; Rachel married George Graham; Emma married Samuel Gilkey; Lista married Joel Lee Patton, #2 Benjamin Galey; Nona J. married Noah Myers; James S. married Mary Susan Alfrey and Alice married Albert Michael.

John H. Smith married Cinderella Balser on Oct. 19, 1878. She was born Feb. 12, 1851 and lived most of her life in Alamo. Her parents were George Balser and Mary Hamm.

Bird, Katie, Mary and Maggie, Grover, John H., Cinderella and Carl Smith

John and Cindy had seven children: Maggie married John Fruits; their children are: Lagora, Gladys who died young, Evelyn and Carol. Bird married Alonzo Fruits and had a son Charles. Grover. Carl married Ola Westfall and had four children: Charles W., Dorman, Robert and Donald. Mary married Charles M. Fruits. Katie married Joel Tucker and three children were born to them: Max, Imogene and Letha. Elsie died young.

John and Cinderella were both members of the Alamo Christian Church. John died July 25, 1934 and Cinderella died Sept. 7, 1944. Both are buried in the Alamo Cemetery.

JOHN HARVEY AND LYDIA JANE SMITH

John Harvey Smith and his wife Lydia Jane Reid Smith with their children Grover, Everett, Edith, Bonnie and William K. left Paint Bank, VA for Indiana on Apr. 10, 1899. Harve drove one team of horses and wagon and nine year old Grover drove a second team and wagon. They settled near Anderson, IN where Harve worked for the railroad. A son, Steve was born the following September. Lydia became homesick for her family in Virginia and they returned to Virginia arriving there Dec. 6, 1900.

Harvey and Lydia Jane Smith Family, Ch. L. to R. Grover, Everett, Bonnie, Wm. K., Steve, Herman and Mildred

Harve soon realized the opportunities for his family were much greater in Indiana and Lydia agreed to come back if they could come on the train. In April of 1902 Lydia's brother, Jake Reid met them at Ladoga. Jake worked on the Kessler Farm and Harve picked up work wherever he could. The children attended Haw Creek School. Another son, Herman was born at Ladoga.

The family then moved to the Coon Farm in the Gravely Run neighborhood and later to the Wisehart Farm west of Smartsburg. They bought the Brothers Farm south of Gravely Run and a daughter, Mildred was born there. Steve later purchased this farm where members of his family still live.

Grover married Marie Lewis of Thorntown. Their children are; Grover O. Jr., Lydia Mae and Marjorie D., Grover O. Jr. and Marjorie (Mrs. Robert F.) Anderson live and farm in the Darlington Community. Lydia (Mrs. Eugene) Johnson lives and farms near Clarks Hill.

Everett married Opal Love of Darlington. Their children are Evelyn, Harvey and Herman. Evelyn and Harvey reside at Crawfordsville and Herman near Rockville.

Edith married Homer Warren of Darlington. Their daughters were Madonna and Catherine Jane.

William K. married Lola Paine of Waveland. Their son is Eugene who lives and farms near Darlington.

Bonnie married William H. Chadwick. Their daughters are Wanda and Betty Lou. Before her marriage she taught school one year in Paint Bank, VA. Bill died in 1934 and Bonnie later married Henry Hartung. Betty Lou (Mrs. Robert) Sosbe lives in Crawfordsville and Wanda (Mrs. Tim) Servies, in Greer, SC.

Steve married Marie LaFollette of Shannondale. Their children are Barbara, Jane, James and John. Jim lives and farms near Garfield. John farms the Harve Smith Farm where his mother resides. Barbara and Jane (Mrs. Ed) Vannice reside in the Crawfordsville area.

Herman was injured as a boy while riding a pony. He used crutches for the rest of his life. He married Iva Taylor of Waynetown. Herman died six weeks before his daughter, Thelma Jean was born. She resides in Crawfordsville.

Mildred married Emerson Linn of Mace. She is the only surviving child of Harve and Lydia and now lives in Florida.

Harve and Lydia were healthy, honest, hard working farmers who loved their family and instilled these values in ther children. All of their children except Mildred, who attended business college, and Herman, who was handicapped, were successful farmers who spent their lives in Montgomery County.

JOHN MARTIN SMITH AND JANE ELIZABETH LEONARD

Valentin Leonhardt and Elizabeth Wallacher came to this country from the Palatinate region on the upper Rhine of Germany shortly before their marriage in Philadelphia in 1748. Their descendants settled in North Carolina, Kentucky, Indiana and Illinois. Jane Elizabeth Leonard belonged to the fifth generation of these immigrants. Little is known of the ancestry of John Martin Smith except that his family came from Delaware.

John M. (1841-1892) and Jane E. (1858-1937) Smith came to Montgomery County in 1892 from Vermilion Co., IL where they had married 19 years earlier. Their six children ranged in age from two to 16 at the time of their relocation from Alvin to a farm east of Waynetown. In the early spring of 1892, Father and the two oldest boys made the trek by foot, driving the cattle and hauling possessions in wagons while Mother and the younger children came by train.

Tragically the father contracted pneumonia and died less than three months after the move, leaving a 32 year old widow with six children to rear. She was a small woman, not much taller than her ten year old son, but despite her diminutive stature, she was a giant of a manager, fieldhand, overseer and teacher to preserve the assets of the family.

Children of John M. and Jane E. Smith Circa 1940; Albert, Laura Patton, Wilbur, Dora Hendricks, Curtis, Sopha Kenyon

The children and grandchildren of this couple were: - Albert (m. Mary Jane Hoover), they had no children: Laura (m. Howard Patton), their children — Clarance, Carrie Ratcliff, Dorris Eggers, and Ruth White; Curtis (m. Jessie Fruits), their children—Edith Snyder, Roy, Ralph, Kenneth, Lester and Edna Legg; Wilbur (m. Elsie Fruits), their children—Cedric, Maybelle Solenberger, Mary Lou O'Sullivan and John; Dora (m. Chester Hendricks), their children—Paul, Lois Patton, Dale and Clyde; Sopha (m. Howard Beam) their son—Merlin (m. Clayton Kenyon) their son—Richard.

When Jane E. moved to town, it was first to a site just east of where the new school was to be located in 1913. She then designed and had built a house one-half block from the downtown area, ideal for a grand old lady living alone and who insisted on doing all her own work. It was situated on a double lot so she would have fruit trees and a huge garden every year. Until not many years before her death at age 79, she did all of her own gardening and yard work.

Jane E. was an active supporter and participant in the Waynetown Baptist Church. Many of the descendants of this couple still live in and around Montgomery County and they continue to be active leaders in their churches and community.

JOSEPH LEE AND REGINA DERDA SMITH

After serving 25 years in the U.S. diplomatic service, Joe and Regina Smith moved to Montgomery County in 1980 when Joe was named Director of Annual Giving at Wabash College. Earlier that year Joe had retired from the Foreign Service as Consul General in Colombia, South America. Joe retired as Director of Alumni Affairs at Wabash in 1987 to begin his own business as a foreign trade consultant.

Joe was born at Shelbyville, IN in 1929, the older son of Omer Joseph and Velda Toon Smith. Both the Smith and Toon families were among the earliest settlers in Franklin Township, Marion Co., IN. Educated in the public schools of Marion and Shelby counties, Joe graduated magna cum laude from Wabash College with Phi Beta Kappa honors in 1951. He subsequently graduated in 1954 with a Doctor of Jurisprudence degree from the Indiana University School of Law. After service in the U.S. Army, Joe was appointed Third Secretary of Embassy in the American Foreign Service and began a career which took him to nine assignments in five countries on three continents.

Joseph Lee and Regina Derda Smith

Joe's parents, who lived most of their lives at Acton in Marion Co., IN, are descended on all sides from ancestors who came to America before 1750. Velda's mother, Maude Thompson, was part of the family which included the well known author and resident of Crawfordsville, Maurice Thompson. Omer, a graduate of Butler University, was a public school teacher and administrator for almost 40 years until he retired and began a second career as general agent for Franklin Life Insurance in central Indiana. He retired again at age 86 when he and Velda moved to Crawfordsville to be near Joe. The elder Smiths spend half the year in Crawfordsville and the other half in Sarasota, FL. Joe's younger brother, James Ross Smith, 1953 graduate of Wabash College, is a professor at Earlham College in Richmond, IN.

Regina and Joe were married in 1969 at Arlington, VA, when both were serving in the U.S. Department of State. Regina was born at Borknenau, East Prussia in 1942 on land that had belonged to her family for more than 300 years. At the end of World War II her region of East Prussia was taken from Germany and given to Poland. She, two sisters, a brother, and her mother remained there until 1957 when they were finally allowed to leave and join their father in the United States. Regina graduated from Hunterdon H.S. in New Jersey and the Institute of Latin American Studies in New York City. After living several years in the United States, Regina's parents, Leo and Lucia Hartiz Derda, returned to Germany where they lived until their deaths in 1976 and 1987. Of their six children, four live in West Germany and two (Regina and a sister) live in the United States.

Joe and Regina are the parents of four children, a son, James, a career naval officer, Nicole, who lives and works in South Carolina, Elizabeth, who lives and works in Indianapolis, and Jessica who also lives and works in Indianapolis.

OMER JOSEPH AND VELDA TOON SMITH

Omer and Velda Smith moved from their home in Acton, IN to Crawfordsville Oct. 31, 1982 to be near their son, Joseph Lee Smith, who was then Director of Alumni Affairs at Wabash College. Omer was born near Fairland in Shelby Co., IN, Dec. 17, 1897, the youngest child of a family of six. His parents were Joseph Moxley Smith and Isabelle Odell Smith. The other children of this marriage were Flora, Dicie, Harry, Grace and Ora. After graduating from Boggstown High School in 1916, followed by a 12 weeks teacher training course at Franklin College, and after passing tests covering all elementary school subjects, Omer was assigned as the teacher in a one room school at Sand Hill in Sugar Creek Township, Shelby County. He remembers the two years teaching 32 pupils in all eight grades at Sand Hill as the most enjoyable of his 38 year teaching career.

Omer Joseph and Velda (Toon) Smith 50th Anniversary Aug. 25, 1975

After the one room school, Omer was successively, the seventh and eighth grade teacher at Boggstown, elementary principal at Bunker Hill in Marion County, and high school social studies and coach of track, baseball and basketball at New Bethel High School at Wanamaker, IN. Then for 25 years, he was high school principal and superintendent at Clark Township, Johnson County, Franklin Township, Marion County, and Moral Township in Shelby County.

Retiring from teaching in 1955, Omer joined Franklin Life Insurance Co. later becoming District Manager with the C.R. Willsey Agency of Indianapolis. He retired from this position in 1985, after completing 30 years in his second career.

Velda, the second daughter of Oral and Maude Thompson Toon, was born in New Bethel (Wanamaker), Marion County on May 22, 1903. Her sisters were Hazel and Harriet. Velda's mother was a first cousin of Maurice Thompson, the well known author.

After graduation from Acton High School in 1921, and a course at Central Business College, Velda became bookkeeper and cashier at the Acton State Bank. In 1925, Velda and Omer were married in the Tuxedo Park Baptist Church in Indianapolis. Following the birth of their two sons, Joseph and James, Velda returned to work as teller and cashier at Wanamaker State Bank. She later worked for the U.S. Internal Revenue Service in Indianapolis, and for the last ten years of her working career, as bookkeeper at the Acton Lumber Co.

In addition to their two sons, Joe, of Crawfordsville, and James R., a professor at Earlham College, Richmond, IN, and their wives, Regina and Natalie, Omer and Velda have seven grandchildren, James, Nicole, Elizabeth and Jessica, and Kimberly, Gregory and Kyrielle.

Both Omer and Velda are 50 year members of the Eastern Star, and Omer is a 50 year member of Pleasant Lodge 134 F. & A.M of Acton, the Murat Shrine and Scottish Rite of Indianapolis. They reside half of the year in Crawfordsville and half in Sarasota, FL.

RALPH C. SMITH FAMILY

Ralph C. Smith, the third child (of six) of Curtis Leroy Smith (Sept. 4, 1880-Mar. 27, 1945) and Jessie Fruits Smith (Sept. 9, 1888 - July 21, 1924), was born Mar. 30, 1914 at Tab, IN. His father worked for the railroad, so the family moved often. After his mother died, Ralph and his brothers and sisters lived with John and Mary Kline at Waynetown. Ralph graduated from Waynetown High School in 1932. He worked at Horner''s after graduation. (Ralph is the great, great grandson of George Fruits, a veteran of the American Revolution.)

Madge Clark, the sixth child (of nine) of Harold Glen Clark (July 27, 1892-May 27, 1965) and Elizabeth Edaline Hurst Clark (July 10, 1889 - Sept. 8, 1970), was born Apr. 29, 1920 on the family farm at Greencastle, IN. She graduated from Fillmore High School in 1938. She worked at the Putnam County Farm and Donnelley's before meeting Ralph. They were married at Crawfordsville May 29, 1941.

Ralph served in the U.S. Army during WWII reaching the rank of first lieutenant. He was based at South Carolina, Georgia, California, Kansas and Texas and went to New Georgia Island in the Pacific before being wounded and sent home. He received the Purple Heart and the Bronze Star. He also sold war bonds. After his four years of active duty, he served six years in the National Guards, earning the rank of captain. He worked at the *Journal Review* and as parts' manager at Horner's, Tippett's Herman Davis, John Deere (Melott and Covington), DeFouw's (Lafayette) and again at Horner's before retiring March 1979.

Madge worked at Woolworth's, RCA (Indianapolis) and as a nurse's aide at Culver Hospital until she retired September 1982.

They lived in Waynetown until the war moved them about, ending in Mineral Wells, TX where their first child was born in 1945, Deatra Maxine. In early 1946 they returned to Indiana and spent four months in Waynetown with the Klines while looking for a home. In June 1946 they moved to R.R. 8, LaGrange Road, where they still reside. Mary Rochelle (1948) and Malcolm Curtis (1951) were born in Crawfordsville.

Deatra graduated from ISU (1967) and taught French at Brownsburg for two years before joining the staff at the public library.

Rochelle married Roger Hoots Oct. 16, 1967. (They divorced Apr. 27, 1973.) She married Robert Dutton (born 1947) on Mar. 8, 1980. Bob adopted Rochelle's two daughters, Anna Michelle (Sept. 5, 1968) and Suzanna Lynne (Mar. 5, 1972), born in Muncie, IN. The Duttons live in Indianapolis. Bob is a policeman. Rochelle is a police dispatcher.

Malcolm married Karen Snyder (born 1952) on June 9, 1973. Their daughters, Sarah Elizabeth (Mar. 6, 1976) and Esther Pauline (Dec. 30, 1977) were born in Indianapolis. Malcolm and Karen graduated from ISU (1974). Malcolm is a policeman. Karen received her Master of Divinity degree from Christian Theological Seminary in 1989. They live in Indianapolis.

ROBERT AND DELORES SMITH

Robert William Smith and Delores Marie Reynolds were married Apr. 16, 1943, at Camp Sutton Army Base near Monroe, NC. Bob served as a lieutenant in the Quartermaster Corps in the CBI Theater of War from July, 1943, to December, 1945. Upon his discharge from the service, the young couple set up housekeeping in their home on Morehouse Gravel Road, West Lafayette, IN. Their eldest son, Mahlon Rhea, was born Dec. 30, 1949. The family moved to Montgomery County in 1952 after purchasing what was known as the Saidla place on State Road 47, 2-1/2 miles east of Darlington which has since been named Weehawk Farm.

Three other children were born to them: Mark Herman on Aug. 22, 1952, Bonnie Mae on Nov. 18, 1954, and Nathan Robert on Mar. 6, 1957. Mahlon and Mark graduated from Darlington High School and Bonnie and Nathan from North Montgomery. At present, Mahlon, his wife Theresa and daughter Ida reside in San Francisco, CA, where he works as a computer programmer and she as a housewife and musician. Mark, a railroad engineer for the Burlington Northern Line, works out of Gillette, WY. Bonnie, Michael, and David Jorgensen live in Huntington, IN, and are both music educators. Nathan, Carla, Bobbie Joe (Hill) and Robby (Hill) reside on the home place with Nathan and Carla dealing in services.

Row 2 Delores Smith, Robby Hill, Carla Smith, Bonnie Jorgensen, and Mahlon Smith. Row 1 Robert, Naan Smith, Michael Jorgensen, Mark Smith and Bobby Hill

Robert (now retired) is a Purdue graduate and has been a watchmaker, a design engineer with Mid States of Crawfordsville, an inventor, and a farmer. Delores (now retired), a graduate of Butler University, taught music and English in the Darlington School for 19 years and private piano students for 25 years. They belong to the Darlington Christian Church where Robert is an elder and trustee and Delores teaches an adult class. She directed the church choir for 30 years as well as directing many of the community cantatas.

Delores' ancestors include the Youngs from England and the (Mac) Duffs from Scotland. Family legend says the Duffs are descendants of Mary Queen of Scots. These families settled in the southwest area of Virginia and were farmers both in Virginia and after moving to Lebanon, IN, in the early 1900s. The Dick and Hermann families from Germany settled in central Illinois, and the Reynolds family from England also settled in Illinois. Seth Thomas Reynolds, Delores' grandfather, was a Baptist minister. Her parents, Herman and Rebecca Reynolds, lived and worked in Lebanon and Lafayette before retiring to a farm on Road 800 E in Montgomery County, adjacent to the Smith Farm.

Bob's people include the Clipp family, the Hancock family whose ancestry can be traced to John Hancock, a signer of the Declaration of Independence, the Rodgers family, and the Smith family. His grandfather, Lemuel R. Rodgers, worked for many years in old Haviland Hall at Purdue University in the model shop, in maintenance, and in security. Bob's parents, Harry O. and Blanche, owned and operated the Lafayette Lumber Company for many years. The Clipps and Hancocks were farmers in the New Albany, IN, area while several of the Smiths were lumbermen and railroaders in Canada and Michigan, while others were merchants in Litchfield, IL. Colorful tales and considerable humor were added to the family by Uncle Frank Hancock who drove a huckster wagon between Louisville and Lafayette. Many of his adventures were recorded by him in unpublished book form. Frank's wife, Ethel, worked for many years in the English Office at Purdue University. Bob and Delores currently live on the Reynolds' farm.

VIVIAN LORENE HARLAN SMITH

Vivian Lorene Harlan Smith was born in Waynetown Montgomery County Mar. 25, 1916 of Clarence J. Harlan and Ella Harper. Clarence (b. 1895) was the eldest son of Elmer and Irena Ingersol Harlan. He had two brothers Vernie J. (b-1898) and Harry C. (b. 1903). The entire family spent most of their lives in Waynetown.

The Harlan family was a family of builders. Elmer, Clarence and Harry contracted and built many of the barns and homes in Waynetown and surrounding communities in the early 1900s. Vernie was connected with the establishment of the telephone lines and in latter life the utility company of Waynetown. The earliest traces of the Harlan family (then spelled Harland) was near Durham England. Later they crossed over into Ireland locating in Donnahlong County Down. Two of the sons George and Michael emigrated to America in 1687 where the "D" was dropped from the last name and became Harlan and remains thus to this day. Locating in Delaware State, the line of Elmer gradually worked its way via Pennsylvania into Indiana. Rush County was first and then to Montgomery County (Waynetown).

The maternal line of Clarence Harlan was Lily Hannah Irena Ingersol who was of the Blackford genealogy line. Starting with a Scot named Benjamin Blackford in Ayrshire-Scotland. The earliest verifiable date comes from Piscatany, NJ in 1676. Irena's great grandmother married Nathaniel Blackford and both great grandparents are buried in the Waynetown Old Town Cemetery.

Vivian married first Howard Franklin Richardson and two children were born.
1. Warren E. Richardson b. Jan. 11, 1937 d. May 5, 1937.
2. Patricia Nadyne Richardson Oct. 21, 1942. Married Russell Hodgkin. Two children. 1. Teresa Dawn Hodgkin; 2. Craig Allen Hodgkin.

After the death of her first husband she then married William V. Blackford - no children and after his death she is now married to George F. Smith, no children but four-stepchildren.

In 1967 she was appointed Acting Postmaster of the Waynetown Post Office where she served until the permanency was appointed. She resides in Waynetown on the Harlan homestead with her husband George Smith.

WILLIE AND EDITH SMITH

William "Willie" Morris Smith was born in Gosport, Owen County, on Mar. 28, 1875 the son of Alfred Gallatin (1844-1896) and Ann Mariah Peterson Smith (1849-1879). After his mother's death, Willie, his brother Samuel, and two first cousins, Earl and Perry Peterson lived with their grandmother, Milly Jane Peterson (1819-1898) on her farm east of Linden. His grandfather, Samuel Peterson (1815-1864), a native of Ohio, came to Montgomery County about 1835. A sister, Arabelle, stayed in Gosport with grandmother, Oradean Smith.

Willie and Sarah Edith Rettinger were married Aug. 15, 1900 at their parents' home northeast of Darlington by Rev. Lute Dunbar. They farmed near

Clarks Hill, Ladoga and New Ross. In 1924 they moved to Veedersburg where they lived the rest of their lives.

Willie, Salome, Edith Smith; Front: Pauline, Clydie and Lloyd Smith 1918

Edith was born July 28, 1873 to John Ephriam (1846-1926) and Saloma "Lomie" Ann Miller Rettinger (1853-1913) in Montgomery County. John was the son of Samuel (1822-1892) and Ruthie McKinzie Rettinger, all of whom were born in Botetourt Co., VA and came to Montgomery County in 1866. Lomie was born July 27, 1853, the daughter of Robert.

Henry (1825-1892) and Sarah Harshbarger Miller (1827-1880). Robert was born in Kentucky and Sarah in Virginia. Robert was a well-known evangelist in the Church of the Brethren. Sarah's great grandfather, Jacob (1725-1792) and wife Maria Eva Petra Hirschberger immigrated to America from Switzerland about 1754, and lived in Lancaster Co., PA. Their descendants moved to the Shenandoah Valley, VA, before coming to Indiana in 1837, settling five miles southwest of Ladoga.

John and Lomie Rettinger had four children: Edith, John, Rosa Rogers and Earl; and 18 grandchildren. They lived in Scott Township.

Willie and Edith Smith had four children: Salome, Lloyd, Pauline, and Clydie, all born in Montgomery County. Salome and Lloyd started school at Whitesville; Pauline started school at Parkersburg, and Clydie at Ford one-room school when they lived on Haw Creek Road.

Salome (1902-1970) graduated from Ladoga High School, attended Vincennes Teachers College, and taught a short time in Ladoga School. She was married to Lee Anderson and they had eight children: John, Sarah, Ruth, Pauline, Bertha, Linda, and two sons who died in infancy. They lived in Boone, Hendricks, Morgan and Marion counties.

Lloyd (1904-1977) graduated from Ladoga High School and married Thelma Bruner. They had one son, Keith. Lloyd was a heavy equipment operator, and operated a gravel pit at his farm on Half-Way Road. Keith is a graduate of Indiana University and a retired Army Major. He and his wife, Lee, have two sons, Larry and Rick, and a granddaughter. They live in Baltimore, MD.

Pauline married Leslie Howard. She was born Aug. 1, 1909, and has operated their Appliance store in Veedersburg since Leslie's death in 1974. They have two children: Margery Ann and William "Bill". Margery married George Keith Smith and they have four children: Jeffrey, Troy, Rhonda and Jonathan, (all graduates of Purdue University) and four grandchildren.

Bill and wife, Gwen, have four children: Anne, Britt Estelle (deceased), Brice, and Grant. Bill is a Superior Court Judge in Port Townsend, WA.

Clydie, born June 28, 1913, married Lawrence Greenburg, and they live on a small farm southeast of Covington. They have three sons: David, Phillip, and Alan. David and wife, Alice, both graduates of Indiana Central College, have two daughters, Kimberly and Jennifer. Phil, a graduate of Purdue and Michigan State, and his wife, Lisa, have two daughters, Terri and Sarah. Alan graduated from Purdue with a PhD in Aeronautical Engineering. He and his wife, Patsy, have three sons: Bradley, Andrew, and Eric.

Willie and Edith Smith were devout members of the Church of the Brethren, Ladoga, also attending and working in other churches wherever they were living. After moving to Veedersburg he worked on the State Highway; and drove Cream routes. He died in 1954. Besides being a homemaker, Edith made and sold lovely quilts. She died in 1961. They are buried in Waynetown Masonic Cemetery.

THE SNYDER FAMILY

In the 1830s, four brothers, from Butler Co., OH, Jacob A., Daniel, David, and Benjamin, settled in Montgomery County, west of Crawfordsville in the Black Creek area. They were sons of Jacob and Saloma Snyder, of Elk Creek, OH, and from a family of 11 children. Of these four brothers, the writer is a direct descendant of Jacob A., who was born Jan. 8, 1785, and died Apr. 30, 1834. He is buried in "Old Town Cemetery in Crawfordsville. He and his wife Sarah, had three sons, Aaron C., John Willard and Jacob.

Aaron C. was born Apr. 22, 1822, in Butler Co., OH and died Jan. 25, 1864. He is buried in the Masonic Cemetery, Crawfordsville. He married Martha Hartman Dec. 17, 1848, and they had six children. They were William J., Martha E., Samuel C., John M., Julia and Mary A.

John M. was born Jan. 14, 1859 and died July 23, 1915. He is buried in Oak Hill Cemetery, Crawfordsville. He married Elizabeth McKeown on Nov. 25, 1881. John M. was a well-driller by trade. John and Elizabeth also raised five orphan children as well as their son, Redden B., my grandfather, who was born May 7, 1883. He married Mary C. Wood, from Kentucky, May 29, 1903. They lived for many years on Crawford St., in a home he built himself. He was maintenance supervisor at Mid States Steel and Wire, where he retired three years past normal retirement age, because his services were in such demand, after working there for 40 years. He was a charter member of the local Eagles fraternity. Mary C., for years, ran an Antique Shop in their home. She spent many hours, weekly, at sales, where she would take me on weekends. Mary C. was born Sept. 28, 1884, in Clay Co., TN. She passed away shortly before Thanksgiving on Nov. 20, 1959. They had two children, Ella G. and Robert Aaron. Redden B. died Jan. 18, 1971.

Robert A. was born May 3, 1911, and survives today. He married Edith C. Meyers, Oct. 5, 1935. He served in the Navy during World War II. They had four children, Robert L., Deanna J., Redden C. and Jerry D.

Robert L. was born Dec. 10, 1938. He served in the U.S. Army from 1959 to 1962. He married Carolyn A. Surface on June 18, 1967. She is the daughter of William A. and Miriam Everson Surface. They have two children, James A. born Jan. 21, 1969 and Susan E., born Aug. 7, 1970. Robert L. spent 23 years in retailing, before changing careers to work as a Prevention Coordinator for Alcohol and other Drug Abuse Prevention, at which he is currently working. Carolyn A. is a nurse, currently working for North Montgomery School Corporation.

Much of the information regarding the early family history was compiled, written and published in 1929, by D.S. Morris, which he gathered from family reunions, which were more of a way of life at the beginning of this century, but have faded away for many families. *Submitted by Robert L. Snyder*

BOBBI JO SOMMERVILLE

My name is Bobbi Jo Sommerville. I am 16 years old and live at 809 W. Main Street, Waveland. I was born at Crawfordsville, IN on Aug. 3, 1972. I am a Junior at Southmont Jr.-Sr. High School.

I have two sisters. Sabrina Lynn, the oldest was born on Jan. 24, 1970. She graduated from Southmont in 1988. She is currently attending Lafayette Beauty Academy. Kathy Jo, the youngest, was born on Sept. 23, 1976. She is a sixth grader at the newly built Waveland Elementary School.

Sommerville Family

My father, Richard Louis, was born in Indianapolis, IN on Oct. 9, 1951. He graduated from Rockville High School in 1969. He worked at RCA in Terre Haute until 1975 when he moved to Waveland and married Brenda Myers Black, my mother. Brenda Myers was born on Jan. 14, 1951. She graduated from Waveland High School in 1968. She later graduated from House of James Beauty School in Crawfordsville. She opened her own Beauty Shop "Brenda's Shear Delight."

My grandparents on my dad's side are Virginia and Louis Sommerville. The family moved to Parke County, Union Township, in August of 1952. They traded their house in town for the 50 acre farm where they still reside. Louis served in the Army in WWII and later was a guard at the correction Center in Putnamville, IN. Virginia was in the Medical Corps and a member of the WAC.

She worked at Putnamville County Hospital as an x-ray technician until recently. Presently, they are both retired. My mother's parents are Eston Lex and Berniece Lucille Myers. They were married in Covington, IN in 1938. Berniece worked as a nurses aid at Culver Hospital. She is currently a volunteer EMT and works for the Council of Aging Area 4 as Site Director. Eston Lex was in the Navy during W.W. II. He worked as Security Guard at Wabash College until he passed away.

My dad's great, great great grandfather immigrated here from Ireland during the religious wars there. He was beaten up and left for dead on a river bank. So he came to America and settled in Kentucky for a while. The family later moved to Scott Co., IN. For further information in my mother's ancestry look under either the Myers or Carlisle family history written about in this same book. *Submitted by Bobbi Jo Sommerville*

DARRELL DAVID SPARKS AND MAMIE SPARKS

Darrell David was born May 22, 1909 in Montgomery County west of New Ross and north of Ladoga, in the area called Hog Heaven, because all the farmers raised a lot of hogs. He was the father of seven children, Darrell Dean, Claude Richard, Bonnie Clair, Phillip Allen, Sandra Lee, Sue Ellen and Judith Ann.

His parents were Charles Richard and Mabel Clair Powell Sparks. Paternal grandparents were Alvin and Lucy Bowen Sparks; they are buried in the New Ross Cemetery. Alvin came to the New Ross area in 1855 from Nichols Co., KY. Great grandparents were George and Catherine Stokes Sparks; they are buried in the Inlow Cemetery. Lucy's parents were Mathew and Catherine Meenach Bowen; they are buried in the Inlow Cemetery.

Darrell David and Mamie Sparks

Maternal grandparents were James William and Sarah Jane Harris Powell. James' parents were John and Elizabeth Welch Powell. John moved to the New Ross area in 1840 from Bath Co., KY.

In 1946 David married Mamie Long at Lebanon, IN; they moved to Crawfordsville where their children were born. He hauled milk from farms to the Creamery on North Washington Street. Later he worked at Allison's Division of General Motors at Indianapolis for 18 years. He retired from there in 1971 and lived on a small farm east of Ladoga, which was part of the Sparks Estate. In 1978 they moved to 201 Waynetown Rd., Crawfordsville, where he died Aug. 20, 1980. He is buried in Ladoga Cemetery.

Mamie was born July 17, 1917 in Ladoga to Lawrence and Missouri Cordelia Cook Long. Her paternal grandparents were Frederick and Mary Thompson Long. Frederick was the first rural mail carrier out of Ladoga; they are buried in the Ladoga Cemetery.

Frederick's parents were Henry and Rebecca Holland Long. Henry's parents were Henry (a Dutch Methodist Minister) and Jamimah Kinon; they came to Indiana before 1812 from North Carolina. Rebecca's parents were Elizah and wife, an English woman, name not available. He was a quaker minister from France.

Mary Long's parents were Thomas and Lydia Sutton, farmers in Parke County. Thomas was the son of Jesse and Angeline Buckler Thompson. They were farmers around Portland Mills and Jesse later bought the grist mill from William Butcher. The Thompson's came to Indiana from Kentucky before 1829.

Maternal grandparents were James Kelly and Mary Elizabeth Underhill Cook from Gravel Hill, MO near Bloomfield.

Mamie worked for Indiana Bell Telephone Co. for 29 years and retired in 1972.

The Sparks and Powell families were active in the New Ross Christian Church. They helped move the church in New Ross from the country south west of New Ross to its present location.

The Long family was active in the Methodist Church at Ladoga. Frederick was Sunday School Superintendent for several years.

David and Mamie and children joined the First Baptist Church of Crawfordsville in April 1963.

C.W. SPENCER

C.W. Spencer purchased the Hardware & Lumber Business from a Mr. Ghormley in 1901. The business was known as C.W. Spencer Hardware and Lumber. C.W. Spencer with his wife, Francis Inge Spencer and his children, Bertha, Fern, Parke, Lowell and Vera then moved to Waveland.

Salesmen (called drummers) at that time traveled to town by train and often spent the night at the local hotel. They were the means of buying merchandise from manufactures and were welcomed by the businessmen.

The Spencer sons, Parke and Lowell worked for their father in the business until they graduated from High School.

Fern married Harry Gillespie the local agent of the Railroad and they made their home in Lebanon, IN. They had a son named Robert.

Vera married Dr. Byron Lingeman, an Eye, Ear and Throat specialist, who had an office in Crawfordsville. They became the parents of two sons, Byron Spencer and Richard.

When World War II was declared, Parke and Lowell served in the Army for two years, returning home following its close.

C.W. was proud of his business and wanted his sons to become a part of it, so he made them partners in 1919, changing the name of the business to C.W. Spencer and Sons. They adopted the slogan of "Service Since 1901" for advertising purposes.

Lowell married Miss Virginia Milligan, a local girl, in 1920, and settled in Waveland. A son Harold was born in 1922.

C.W. Spencer died soon after in 1922. Lowell's wife, Virginia, died in 1923.

Parke married Miss Mae Vandervoir from Terre Haute in 1927 and they became the parents of a son, Charles.

In 1930, Lowell married Miss Zelma Fugate from Terre Haute. They became the parents of two sons, Donn in 1932 and Ray in 1934.

The three sons of Lowell worked in the business with their father until they graduated from High School.

In 1937, Parke was offered a job as Salesman for Fry Roofing Co. in Kansas City, MO. He accepted the job which was offered by a wartime "Buddy" and later became manager of the company.

In 1949, Parke and nephew Robert Gillespie, purchased the Smith and Duckworth Lumber Yard in Crawfordsville, with Robert as manager.

Parke sold his interest in the Waveland business to Lowell at that time. The mother, Francis Inge Spencer, died in 1946. Parke died in Kansas City, MO in 1956.

The Spencer family, over the years, was always active in Community, Church and School Activities, making their equipment available if needed. Spencer's Lumber Truck was a familiar sight in the School yard for a Memorial Day Program or in other places where outdoor stages were needed. In the 1930s during summer months, the truck would be parked under the streetlights at Cross Street on Saturday Night for a concert by the Waveland Band. The Band was composed of any adult or school child who could or would play an instrument. These concerts were really enjoyed by all. People brought their folding chairs and congregated around the bandstand and visited. It would be a "Fun" evening.

Lowell never had any desire to work or live in any place but Waveland, and he didn't.

Due to his failing health, he sold C.W. Spencer & Sons to Larry Servies and Carl Morgan. It then became Servies & Morgan Hardware & Lumber, Mar. 25, 1975.

Lowell Spencer died in Waveland Dec. 10, 1977.

GEORGE McCORMICK SPENCER

Jane Todd McCormick, great-great-grandmother of George McCormick Spencer, sold off her possessions in the winter of 1824-5 and converted them to gold. Accompanied by her four sons and one daughter, the widow traveled the hard trail from her homeland, Shelby, KY to Brown Township, Montgomery County, on horseback. The family settled on a small hill above a spring in the northeast quarter of Section 24, Township 17 North, Range 6 West. By working hard that first wet cold spring they cleared three acres and built a one-room log cabin. In this cabin the original Waveland Methodist Church was later founded. During the spring of 1827, the McCormicks tapped some of the hard sugar maple trees; the syrup was so good that tapping trees came to be done by the widow's descendants for the next 125 years. Bountiful fall crops convinced the family that their choice of land was a good one, so they went to Crawfordsville and "entered" the 160 acres of land on Oct. 30, 1927, receiving a sheepskin parchment deed signed Jan. 3, 1828, by J.Q. Adams, President.

George McCormick and Wilma (Swanay) Spencer

Preston McCormick bought the homestead from his mother Aug. 1, 1832, for $200, later adding another 80 acres. He died Feb. 6, 1864. One of his seven children, Shelby, eventually acquired all of the land, plus other acreage, until at one time he owned some 1500 acres. During the Civil War Shelby built the house in which the present descendants now live.

One of Shelby's two daughters, Drew, inherited part of the land and farmed it with her husband Wilbur A. Spencer. Drew and Wilbur had two children, George McCormick, born Jan. 20, 1911, and Margaret Lee, born five years later. George attended Waveland schools and later became a banker in Russellville. After his parents' death, George bought the land and added 160 adjoining acres. After 40 years with the Russellville Bank, George retired in 1969 and returned to his childhood home, where he and his wife, former Waveland classmate Wilma Swanay, spent many hours clearing and dredging to enlarge the tillable acres, setting out trees, raising chickens and tending a large garden and orchard.

After George's death, Nov. 29, 1983, Wilma moved to Crawfordsville, where their daughter, artist Mary Lee (Mrs. Thomas) Moore also lives. Mary Lee and husband Tom have two sons, Jamie and Drew. Daughter Martha Jo, a former teacher, lives in Delavan, WI with her husband Bill Leyda and three children Edwin, Beth, and Earl. Daughter Margaret Ann Payne, wife of the late Dr. Walter Payne, serves as assistant to the Director of Academic Affairs of the University of the Pacific in Stockton, CA. Son George William Spencer, a former teacher, and his wife Judy now live on and manage the family farm with their three children, George Andrew, and daughters Carrie and Nancy.

MAE SPENCER

Mae Vandevoir Spencer is a gentle gal who says the best decision she ever made in life was getting married. May was born on St. Patrick's Day in 1904. Mae is the daughter of Victor and Nora (Brown) Vandevoir. Victor was the sibling of eight brothers and four sisters. He had black, wavy hair, blue eyes and was an electrician by trade. Nora enjoyed cooking and her home.

Mae married William "Parke" Spencer in 1927. Parke was born in Waveland, July 11, 1895, the son of C.W. Spencer, owner of Spencer Hardware in Waveland. The business was carried on by Parke and his brother, Lowell and later by Lowell and his wife. Parke and Mae also lived in St. Joseph, MI where he was a traveling salesman; Kansas City, MO where he was District Sales Manager for Fry Roofing and Crawfordsville where he was affiliated with Perry Office Supply, as well as a partner with his nephew, Robert Gillespie in the Smith and Duckworth Lumber Company. He was a Mason and Scottish Rite, as well as member of Sigma Pi Fraternity (Ohio Northern University). Parke died June 11, 1956 and is buried in Rose Lawn Cemetery, Terre Haute. The Spencer Family also owned Gould-Spencer Flowers in Crawfordsville.

Mae and Parke adopted a son, Charles. He is a graduate of Waveland High School. Charles works at Hi-Tek. His wife, Carol (Barth) is a QMA (Qualified Medicine Aid) at Williamsburg where she oversees Mae's progress. Charles and Carol have three children: Dorothy Brandenburg, Parke and Charlene Krout.

Mae continues to be happy, keeps up with current events and remains a "Gentle gal." *Submitted by Karen Zach (via information from Mae Spencer)*

MICHAEL AND JOANN BRANSON SPRAGG

Mike and Joann have lived at their present address in Montgomery County since their marriage in 1959 with the exception of three years which Mike spent in military service. He enlisted in the U.S. Army in December 1961 and was trained as a radar computer operator for the firing of Nike-Hercules missiles. A year and a half of that time they spent in Fairbanks, AK. Their only child, Jeffrey Alan, was born at Dyess AFB, Abilene, TX, in 1964. Jeff graduated from Southmont High School in 1982 and Nashville Auto-Diesel College in Nashville, TN, in 1983. He is employed by Fleetwood Travel Trailers of Indiana.

Mike was born in Fountain Co., IN, in 1940, the only child of Paul and Beulah Hutts Spragg. He graduated from Wallace High School in 1958 and is now employed by Coast-to-Coast Stores, Inc. His hobbies include collecting Indian artifacts and restoring old cars. He has completely rebuilt the 1930 Model A Ford pickup he owns.

Mike's father, Paul, was born in Fountain Co., IN, the youngest child of Everett and Emma Shoaf Spragg, and his mother, Beulah, was the youngest of three daughters of Clee and Stella Lambdin Hutts, also of Fountain County. Paul and Beulah were married in 1933 in Bellmore, IN, and lived for a time in Crawfordsville where Paul was working for F.W. Woolworth. They returned to Fountain County before Mike was born, and Paul has been farming since that time. Beulah, who had an early interest in art, decided to renew that interest several years ago and has become an artist.

They both have been very active members of Phanuel Lutheran Church, which was founded by several of Paul's ancestors.

Joann was born in 1941 in Middletown, OH, the only child of William and Ruby Johnson Branson. They moved to Alamo, IN in January of 1946. The town had built a bonfire that night to celebrate their basketball team winning the County tournament. Joann graduated from Alamo High School in 1959, and enjoys doing genealogy research, reading and gardening. She works part-time as leave replacement for the Postmaster at Alamo.

William and Ruby Branson were married in 1940 at Black Water, KY. "Bill" was the youngest of four children of William and Malissie Richardson Branson, of Lee County, KY. He ran a grocery store in Alamo for many years and also drove a school bus. As a young man he served in the CCC near Helena, MT. He passed away in December of 1986 in Bradenton, FL, where he and Ruby had been spending their winters. Ruby was second of five daughters of Hillyard and Isabel Allen Johnson, also of Lee Co., KY. She worked at Wilson Brothers Shirt Factory in Crawfordsville for several years and retired from R.R. Donnelley & Sons after 24 years of employment there. She was married this past summer of 1988 to Bobby D. Gibson, and they make their home in Alamo.

JOSEPH THOMAS AND ERMIL M. (LILLY) SPURGEON

Joseph was the youngest child of William H. and Lauena (Denney) Spurgeon. He was born near Salem, IN on Oct. 24, 1906. He graduated from the DeMotte High School, and rather than farm he chose to work in the Gary steel mills as a craneman. Joe's first wife was Edith Cox, and two children were of this marriage: Charles Roy and Paul Robert. This marriage ended early and tragic by an automobile accident which took the lives of Edith and their youngest son Charles. Soon after, Joe enlisted in the Army as World War II was getting into full swing. Paul was taken care of by Joe's brother John Murray. Joe was stationed in the 489th Ord Evac. Co. in Europe.

Shortly after the war, Joe married Ermil Maryla (Lilly) Spencer. Ermil had lost her first husband in a car-train accident leaving her with three children: Dallas, Essie and Duane. In 1949, Roger Glen was born of their marriage in Lee, IN. He was the only child of this marriage that ended in divorce when Roger was two years old. Ermil moved to Monon with the three children of her first marriage and Roger. She earned a living cleaning houses of several prominent families in Monon. Joe moved to DeMotte with Paul, and had visitation rights with Roger on weekends.

Joe had many talents, he could play several musical instruments and sang as he played. It was said that Joe was the best crane operator in the mill that he worked in, for if a dangerous or difficult crane task was to be done, the supervisors would wait for Joe to do it. In 1961, at the age of 55 Joe died of a heart attack. He was buried in the DeMotte Cemetery, and his funeral was attended by many friends and family. Full Masonic rites were held from the Lodge 642 of Wheatfield.

Ermil, after having raised her children, set up a thrift store in her home. She retired in the late 70s and moved to Linden, IN. She has hobbies of painting, playing the organ and sewing. She presently donates much of her handywork to church and charity. (See "Our Spurgeon Story" in the Crawfordsville, IN library for Lilly and Armstrong lines.) *Submitted by Roger G. Spurgeon, Sr.*

ROGER G. AND JUDY K. (BIRGE) SPURGEON SR.

Roger was born on Aug. 23, 1949, the son of Joseph T. and Ermil M. (Lilly) Spurgeon, on a small farm south of Lee, IN. He grew up in Monon, about four miles east of where he was born. When Roger was 12 years old his father died, and Roger took his father's death very hard. He was strongly attached to his father.

While visiting his sister, Essie Lutes, in Linden, he met Judy K. Birge. He dated her for several years, and they were married in 1968, while he was home on leave from the Marine Corps. Judy was a native of Linden, and some of her ancestors have been in Montgomery County for quite some time. Henry Beck is recorded to have purchased property in the county as early as 1831. Judy's parents are Cletis and Wilma (Dickson) Birge, and they lived in Linden when Judy was born in the Culver Union Hospital in Crawfordsville. Judy graduated from the Linden High School in 1968.

Roger's unit in Vietnam was C Co., 1st Bn., 9th Marines and was based in Quang Tri. His infantry unit worked out of Camp Vandergrif, and was stationed there during his tour of 1969-70. He spent most of his time in the Mountains and Asha Valley.

In 1970, he became a Drill Instructor, and Judy joined him while he served his two year tour at San Diego, CA.

On May 30, 1971, Judy presented Roger with a son and he was named Roger Glen Jr. After his tour on the Drill Field, the family moved to Crawfordsville for about a year, and then moved to their first real home in Wingate. On Dec. 4, 1973 Julie Kay was born in the Culver Union Hospital, and Judy proudly presented her to Roger. In 1984, the family moved to its present home in Linden.

Roger worked at Donnelleys for about five years, then was hired by ALCOA in Lafayette. After working there for about ten months he was promoted to Unit Supervisor and has performed this job in the Extrusion Dept. for about 11 years.

Judy worked off and on during their marriage, and has worked at Purdue, National Homes in Lafayette and at the Target Store in Crawfordsville.

In 1987, Roger enrolled at Purdue University and is presently seeking a Bachelors degree with a major in History and Psychology. Judy enjoys hobbies of sewing and hand-crafts. Roger's hobbies include hunting, fishing, rollerskating and genealogy. He has lineages as far back as 1548 and is a 13th generation descendant of Pocahontas. This and other lineages can be viewed in his compilations and writings in his book prepared for his children. This book entitled "Our Spurgeon Story" and a copy is in the genealogical section of the Crawfordsville library. *Submitted by Roger G. Spurgeon, Sr.*

BILL AND SHIRLEY STEELE

Ralph William Steele (Bill) was born June 10, 1930 in Waynetown, IN. His parents were Clarence Dwight Steele and Lola McClure. Clarence was born in Ohio Apr. 2, 1893 and died Jan. 1, 1965 in Montgomery County. Lola was born Dec. 27, 1894 in Eubanks, KY and died Dec. 6, 1974 in Montgomery County. While in Montgomery County, Clarence and Lola Steele lived in Alamo, Waynetown and Darlington.

Bill was the youngest of five children. His oldest brother James died in infancy. His other siblings, Robert L. Steele, Margaret McKinney and Dorothy Steele all reside in Crawfordsville. Bill was about six when his family moved to a farm west of Darlington.

Bill and Shirley Steele

Shirley Mae Kiley was born Jan. 18, 1934 in Indianapolis, IN. Her parents were John Walter Kiley and Madge Mildred Long. John was born Aug. 13, 1888 and died in 1961. Madge was born Nov. 19, 1900 and she died Jan. 13, 1960. Shirley is also the youngest of five children. She had a sister, Sue Ellen, who died in infancy and has two other sisters, Mary Evelyn McAllister and Mildred Louise Leckrone. She has a brother David Kiley who lives in Crawfordsville.

Bill and Shirley were married on Dec. 23, 1950 at the First United Brethren Church in Crawfordsville. They lived in the Darlington area for six years before buying a house in Crawfordsville in 1956 where Shirley still resides. It was here that Bill and Shirley raised their family.

Bill was a hard worker all of his life. He worked on the farm as a youngster. He later worked at Mid-States Steel and Wire, Ryker Heating and Plumbing and in 1956 went to work for Crawfordsville Electric Power and Light. He worked there for 30 years. Upon his retirement, Bill went to work for Bank One as a custodian.

Bill was also a licensed electrician and spent many hours working throughout the county. Bill was very actively involved in the community in which he lived. He coached and umpired for several years in the summer youth baseball program. From 1964 to 1978 he always took the light company bucket truck out to the football field to tape the games for the local high school. He was always available when any electric work was needed at the park, the ball diamonds, football field, and Strawberry Festival. Bill died Dec. 14, 1986.

Shirley has spent most of her married life raising their four children. Daniel Allen, born May 23, 1951, is married to Lisa Ford and working at Crawfordsville Power and Light. Robert William, born May 22, 1955 is married to Sandra Mullen and working for Public Service in Attica, IN. Douglas Dwight, born June 24, 1956 is residing in Crawfordsville and working at Donnelleys. Mary Louise, born May 14, 1964 is married to Tim Cramer and living in Indianapolis, IN. Shirley and Bill also have two grandchildren, Melissa Kay and Elizabeth Ann Steele living in Attica, IN.

MARY ALICE "MAYME" STEELE

Mary Alice Steele was born June 20, 1878 at Killmore in Clinton Co., IN to George Henry Steele and Laura Priscilla Wray. Her ancestors were early pioneer settlers in Montgomery County. Her great-grandfather, Thomas P. Britton, came with his wife, Frances Farnsworth, and his father, Nathan Britton, from Butler Co., OH to Union Township in 1829. Her grandfather, John P. Wray, came with his parents, David Wray and Martha Passmore, also from Butler County, in 1824.

Mary Alice, known since about age one as Mayme, was married on June 23, 1895 in Lafayette to Charles Alonzo Boyer of Lafayette, the son of Joseph Boyer and Marcella Jane Armstrong. They had one son, Karle Steele, born there June 22, 1896. The family moved to Chicago, IL, shortly after the turn of the century, and a few years later, on to Denver, CO. Mayme and Karle returned to Chicago and she was divorced from Charles there in 1917.

Mary Alice (Mayme) Steele 1878-1938, with her son Karle Steele Boyer 1896-1982, and husband Charles Alonzo Boyer 1873-

She was married on June 19, 1920 in Indianapolis to Lawrence G. Elmore, a member of an old Montgomery County family. He was born in the county on Mar. 20, 1873 to William E. Elmore and Mary Gamble. Lawrence had been previously married to Cora Clements and they had a son Lloyd and a daughter Myrtle Ulala. Lawrence died in 1926 in Indianapolis of lung disease incurred as a result of his employment at a bicycle tire factory. Following his death Mayme worked in the china department of Block's Department Store.

She was married on May 28, 1928 in Frankfort to Alva Elsworth Berry, the son of Louis Berry and Catherine Carter of Clinton County. They made their home in Indianapolis where he owned a tobacco store. Alva died May 31, 1952 in Frankfort and is buried in the family plot in Venemann Cemetery in Clinton County. Mayme died Jan. 21, 1938 in St. Francis Hospital in Beech Grove, IN. After funeral services in Indianapolis, she was buried beside Lawrence in Crawfordsville's Masonic Cemetery in the same plot as her parents, sister Jessie, and Lawrence's daughter Myrtle.

Mayme and her sister Jessie had done home nursing in Indianapolis during the 1920s. After her sister's death in 1926, Mayme opened her home to her young nephew, Elmer White, who remained with her until he was married in the mid-1930s.

During her years of living in Indianapolis, she was very active in the Independent Order of Odd Fellows, the Rebekah Lodge, and the Army War Mothers. Her son Karle had served with the United States Army in France during World War I.

ROBERT STEEL

Robert Steele was born about 1800 in Kentucky. He was married in Bath Co., KY on Apr. 12, 1830 to Mary "Polly" Cassity, the daughter of Jacob Cassity and Rachel Scott. Mary died sometime before 1860.

They had four children: Hiram born about 1831, David born about 1837, Thomas born about 1840 and George Henry born Mar. 14, 1843.

Robert was a farmer and blacksmith in Kentucky. He probably came to Montgomery Co., IN in the 1860s with his son George to be near other relatives who had migrated earlier. In 1870 he lived in Ripley Township and was employed as a toll keeper. George's story is found with his wife's, Laura Priscilla Wray, elsewhere in this book.

Robert died in Montgomery County Mar. 4, 1872. His four sons were still alive at that time. *Submitted by Lois Lipka*

ALLEN R. AND GERRY STEVENS

A.R. Stevens "Steve" was born May 22, 1917 to Orville and Leoma Stevens in Boone Co., IN. Steve was the oldest of eight children. He graduated from Bowers High School in 1935 and soon left the farm and traveled to California where he went to work for North American Aircraft.

When World War II broke out, Steve enlisted in the Army Air Corps, took his basic training in Arizona and was sent, as a Cadet, to Carlsbad Air Corps Base in New Mexico for further training. He was later commissioned a 2nd Lieutenant and kept there as a Bombardier/Navigation instructor. Steve met his wife-to-be, Geraldine Hoose "Gerry", and they were married in the Carlsbad Air Base Chapel on Aug. 29, 1944. Within a few months, Steve was transferred to Ft. Myers, FL to a gunnery school and was about to be sent overseas when the war ended. He received his discharge and returned to Carlsbad where he was employed at the Potash Company of America for three years.

Left to Right: Bill, Pat, A.R. Curtis, Mark, Dick, Dianna, Laura, Grandma Stevens, Jerry and Cindy

Steve and Gerry's three oldest sons, Bill, Dick and Pat, were born in Carlsbad, and in 1948 the family packed and loaded their belongings into a hand-made Montgomery Ward's wagon, hitched it to their old Chevy and headed back to Indiana to farm near Crawfordsville. Steve started farming on a shoe-string but after years of good management and hard work, he was able to purchase more land and, with the help of his sons, was able to provide for and educate the family. Five more children followed, three daughters and two sons. The children attended East Union and St. Bernard's Elementary schools and all graduated from Crawfordsville High School.

Bill, their oldest son, graduated from Purdue University in 1968 with a degree in Engineering. He went to work for Bechtel Corporation in San Francisco, CA. Bill is married to Gabrielle Roome and they live in San Francisco, CA.

Dick attended Indiana Business School in Indianapolis and after graduating, enlisted in the Air Force. Upon his discharge he attended Purdue University and graduated with a degree in Agriculture Economics. He married Janet Stevens of Fort Wayne, IN, and they have a daughter, August Marie, and a son, Andrew. Dick is business manager for Steven's Farms and is also a pilot and flight instructor. Janet operates Stevens Dance Academy in Crawfordsville, IN.

Pat attended Purdue University graduating with a degree in Agriculture Economics. He was married to Linda Federici and they have a daughter, Staci. Pat worked for Production Credit Association for several years, then returned to farming. He eventually moved to Colorado where he is now self-employed.

Dianne graduated from CHS in 1967 and is married to Richard Rule, son of Jewell and Welthea Rule of Crawfordsville. Dick and Dianne are parents of three sons, Ben, Sam and Lee. They live in Fort Collins, CO.

Cynthia graduated from CHS in 1969 and worked at Wabash College where she met Stephen Golliher. They married and are parents of Joseph and Sarah. Steve and Cindy spent four years in Taipei, Taiwan where Steve worked as a purchaser for RCA Corporation. They returned to Indianapolis in 1987 and now live in Carmel, IN.

Laura graduated from CHS in 1971 and is living in Lafayette, IN where she works for Pritsker & Associates.

Mark graduated from CHS in 1972 and attended Indiana State University and Indiana University.

Mark and his brothers, Dick and Curtis, took over the farm operation in 1982 when their father retired due to illness; Steve passed away Feb. 26, 1987 of Lou Gehrig's disease.

Curtis graduated from CHS in 1974. He married Jeannie Budreau of Earl Park, IN and they have two sons, Dustan and Aaron. Jeannie is employed by HC Industries in Crawfordsville.

JOHN RUSSELL STEVENS "STEVIE"

Stevie was born Mar. 19, 1908 in Yountsville to Samuel T. and Florence M. Smith Stevens.

The father of our subject, Samuel was born 1878 in Indiana to Alexander and Laura Harding Stevens.

Florence was the daughter of Oscar D. Smith. Samuel was first married to Elizabeth Hedrick and had one child, Raymond Oliver born 1899 and married Doris Swank both died 1983 after a car accident. Samuel then remarried in 1906 to Florence Smith. To this union three children were born: Mary Elizabeth who married Floyd McCance; three children were born to this union. Mary passed away in 1988. John our subject, and Wilbur who was born 1907 and died the same year. This old couple made life of the land by farming. After Samuel's death in 1942, Florence and her children resided in Yountsville on the old home front. Florence died in 1960.

John was married Jan. 4, 1930 to Martha "Mattie" Parks the daughter of Samuel W. and Mary E. Stump Parks, who was born June 23, 1915 and is still living in Crawfordsville.

To this union two children were born; Mary Lavona born Feb. 10, 1931 and married to James J. Davis, seven children were born to this couple, the second child was Barbara May born May 31, 1935 married first to Donald M. Hampton and had two children. This couple lived in Yountsville until around 1960 then moved to Crawfordsville and indoor plumbing.

Steve and Mattie served most of their lives at the Crawfordsville Country Club, devoting their lives to others by doing all aspects of this social club. Stevie even had a day of his own named "Stevie Day" before his retirement. Stevie was a man of giving and appreciating the smaller gifts of life, land and love. He passed from this life a rich man in friends and family for the love he showered on other in 1986. *Submitted by Becky Ingram*

CHARLES EDWARD "CHARLIE" AND JOSEPHINE "JO" STEWART

Charlie Stewart's life-time dream was to be Montgomery County Sheriff. That dream came true in 1978! Charlie served in different capacities of law enforcement for 28 years before retiring in September 1983. Charlie and Jo Day were married May 25, 1946 in Greencastle, IN. Charlie was born May 28, 1924 in Lizton, the son of Cecil Alonzo and Ida Hood Stewart. Joe was born Aug. 6, 1928 in Parke County, the daughter of Murl and Geneva Lewis Day.

Charles Edward (Charlie) and Josephine (Jo) Stewart

Six children were born to Charlie and Jo: Donna Lee Stewart is married to Robert Shirar. They have three children: Angela, Robert and Jodi. Jo Darlene Stewart is married to Eddie Hamer and has: Rhonda, Tonya and Rodney and a son, Michael is deceased. Nancy Charlene Stewart is married to Rich Jones and has one son, Kent Edward. Charles Michael "Mike" Stewart is married to Karen Billingsley and has one son, Michael. Karen Kay Stewart who was married to Jerry Selby died of cancer Oct. 18, 1971. Peggy Roxanne Stewart who was married to William Leslie has Billy and Karen.

Donna Lee Stewart Shirar is a foreman at Terra Products. Darlene Stewart Hamer is a cashier for Charlie Sentman, auctioneer. Nancy Stewart Jones served as Deputy Surveyor for Montgomery County. Mike Stewart is a construction worker at Nucor.

The Community Drug Awareness Program, 24-hour Deputy Schedule, Law Enforcement Explorer's Post and Detective Division were instigated while Charlie Stewart served as Sheriff.

Charlie Stewart's occupations included: Allison employee, forest guard, owner of S&W Marathon, Stewart House Restaurant and Waveland Drug Store. Charlie also served many years as Waveland Town Marshall and a prison guard at Rockville. Jo Day Stewart worked side by side at most everything her husband decided to do. She raised his children, cooked in his restaurant, did bookkeeping for his filling station and served as Matron for the Sheriff's Department.

Charlie and Jo now live at Oklawaha, FL where they are enjoying their leisure time fishing and refinishing furniture. They make frequent trips to Crawfordsville to enjoy their children and grandchildren. *Submitted by Nancy Stewart Jones*

WILLIAM AND EFFIE MAY (HAMILTON) STEWART

William Stewart, born Dec. 2, 1884 and Effie May 'Hamilton' Stewart, born Sept. 6, 1884 moved to Crawfordsville in 1901. They were married Sept. 28, 1899.

Effie May's grandparents were Samuel Hamilton, born Apr. 8, 1820, died Aug. 28, 1907 and Hannah, born Jan. 26, 1820, died Mar. 6, 1872. They came to Montgomery County from Kentucky with their two sons, Edward Parker T. Hamilton, born Feb. 8, 1850, died Apr. 8, 1928 and Talbert.

March 30, 1869 Edward P. Hamilton married Sarah Ann King, born Mar. 10, 1849, died July 14, 1905. Their children were Herbert, Alma, Lilly, Florence, Josephine and Effie May, wife of William Stewart.

William Stewart's parents, William Stewart and Rebecca 'Poytner' Stewart lived on a farm near Jamestown, IN. Both died while their son William was small. He was reared in the home of Mr. and Mrs. Nathaniel Caldwell.

William Stewart learned carpentering and brick laying and worked at the Brick Yard north of Crawfordsville, IN.

William, Effie May Stewart, Vivian Stewart in white dress. Opposite side Mary Ellen Moore, holding baby Jack Thomas Moore. William Edward Moore, small boy with hands to his face.

William and Effie May Stewart had three daughters, Mary Ellen, born Feb. 24, 1901, Gertrude born July 15, 1908 and Vivian born Dec. 2, 1911.

Mary Ellen married Clarence Stephens, son of Edward E. Stephens and Iva Myrtle 'Kelly' Stephens on Nov. 17, 1917.

Their children were Helen who died shortly after birth and was buried at Finley Cemetery west of Whitesville, IN. Their second child William Edward Stephens was born Mar. 25, 1920. Clarence and Mary E. Stephens divorced.

January 29, 1923 Mary Ellen married Jesse Fran-

317

klin Moore, born June 7, 1891. He was the son of George and Olive Moore who lived at 1104 E. Pike Street, Crawfordsville.

Jack Thomas Moore was born Mar. 10, 1923. Jesse legally adopted William Edward Stephens, changing his name to William Edward Moore.

Jesse Franklin Moore was a fireman with the Crawfordsville Fire Department. He died May 21, 1968.

Mary Ellen died Apr. 9, 1976. Jack Thomas Moore died Nov. 1, 1986.

Gertrude Stewart born July 15, 1908 married Herman Wheat, son of Allen B. Wheat, 1878-1950 and Jenny Susan Wheat, 1880-1956, on Dec. 13, 1924. Their children were Robert Max born Aug. 17, 1925 at Crawfordsville, Marjorie Anne, born May 3, 1931 at Crawfordsville and Susan Lynn, born May 15, 1948 at Frankfort, IN. Gertrude died Oct. 14, 1982.

Vivian Stewart married Donald Brennan on Sept. 26, 1935. He was the son of Thomas and Elizabeth 'Clancy' Brennan, born Jan. 18, 1909. Their sons were William Thomas, born Oct. 1, 1938 at Crawfordsville and David Keith born Jan. 29, 1940, Crawfordsville. Vivian died July 8, 1983.

William Stewart was fondly called "Blackjack Stewart" by his many friends. He'd been a member of the Crawfordsville Eagles Lodge for 27 years when he died May 26, 1935.

Effie May Stewart died 38 years later on Sept. 29, 1973. Both are buried at the Masonic Cemetery.

STOCKDALE FAMILY

The immigrant ancestor, James Stockdale, came to America from Ireland some time between 1784 and 1799. The place of his origin is unknown. He settled in what is now Fleming Co., KY.

His will, which was probated in September 1834 in Fleming County, mentions six children: William, Jennie, Elizabeth, Mary Ann, John and James. Census records show that William, Elizabeth and Mary Ann were born in Ireland and that John was born in Kentucky. The will lists his widow as Mary, but other sources indicate that the mother of John was Sally Curry.

John Francis Stockdale was born May 25, 1799 in Fleming County. He married Cynthia A. McCarty, daughter of Thomas McCarty, May 15, 1820, in the same county. They were the parents of 11 children, all born in Fleming County.

James Francis Stockdale, born Sept. 15, 1826, was the third child of John F. and Cynthia Stockdale. His wife was Emily E. Groves, daughter of Samuel and Mary E. (Sampson) Groves. They were married Feb. 20, 1850, in Fleming County. Two of their nine children were born in Fleming County and the others were born in Parke and Fountain Counties, IN. James and Mary E. Stockdale are buried in Rockfield Cemetery in Fountain County.

George Bishop Stockdale, son of James F. and Emily E. Stockdale, was born Apr. 5, 1860 in Parke Co., IN. His wife, who he married Sept. 29, 1885, was Eleanor "Ella" Booe, daughter of Thomas Jefferson and Mary Ann (Reed) Booe. Their children, Verna, Vereta, James Jefferson, Mary Jane, Charles, Fanny, Guy, Arthur, Rex, Ralph, Paul, and an infant daughter, were all born in Fountain County.

James Jefferson "Jeff" Stockdale was the third child of George B. and Ella Stockdale and was born May 23, 1891. He married Mayme J. Leonard, daughter of Amos and Eleanor "Ella" (Long) Leonard, on Dec. 4, 1912. They were the parents of three children: James, Eleanor and Max, all born in Montgomery County. Jeff Stockdale died May 21, 1951, and Mayme Stockdale died July 29, 1984, in Crawfordsville, IN.

James R. Stockdale was born Oct. 5, 1913, near Alamo, and on Oct. 9, 1937, at Noblesville, IN, he married Winifred L. Price, daughter of William and Ruth Edna (Smith) Price. After he served in the navy during World War II, they lived in Crawfordsville for several years where he operated a refrigeration repair business. They later moved to a farm near Darlington where they raised Southdown sheep. An electrician, he retired from Ross Gear Division of TRW at Lafayette, IN, in 1975. Their last home in Montgomery County was at Lake Holiday. They became residents of Winter Haven, FL, in 1980. Their three children are: Mrs. Roberto (Virginia Kay) Bueno, of near Dayton, IN; Karen Neel, Darlington, IN; John B. Stockdale, Crawfordsville. They have eight grandchildren: J.R., Heather, Robert, and Joseph Bueno; Jason and Todd Neel; Chris and Mark Stockdale. *Submitted by Mrs. James R. Stockdale*

WILLIAM EVERETT AND EVA (MICHAELS) STOUT

William Everett (Bill) Stout was born in Montgomery County Mar. 17, 1861. He was a son of Thomas and Elizabeth (Miller) Stout. Bill was known as a hard-working farmer with a knack for playing piano by ear. His "spread" covered 150 acres along the Waynetown Road on Black Creek.

Wm. Everett and Eva (Michaels) Stout

Bill was married to his first wife, Eva Michaels, on Sept. 9, 1888. Eva was the daughter of James and Laura (White) Michaels of nearby Alamo. She was born in Montgomery County on Mar. 26, 1863. They were members of the United Brethren Church and became the parents of six children: Maude Ruth Stout, who married Alvin Wilbert Cruea; Merle Lee Stout, who married Hazel Maria Joslin; Mary Hazel Stout, who became the wife of Jerry Caleb Burk; John Albert Stout, who wed Della Agnes Kinder; Russell Charles ("Bud") Stout, who married Martha Ann Nichols; and Fred Stout, who was the husband of Edna Mae Lough. Eva died young of chloroform poisoning during an operation, Sept. 14, 1908. She was laid to rest in Oak Hill Cemetery.

Bill remarried on Oct. 9, 1909 to Edna Hayes, by whom he had Clarence Stout, who married Katherine McCarthy, and Virgil LeRoy Stout, who, at age five, was hit and killed by a car. Bill Stout was married a third time to Ida May Mikels, whom he wed around Aug. 22, 1927.

Around 1939, Bill took a terrible fall from a silo and broke his back. Prostate cancer added to his suffering, and on Apr. 20, 1940, William Everett Stout passed away at 79. He was buried alongside his first wife, Eva, in Oak Hill Cemetery.

WILSON AND ESTHER (TURNER) STOUT
THOMAS AND ELIZABETH (MILLER) STOUT

One branch of the Stout family of Montgomery County was established in 1846 with the arrival of Wilson Stout, his wife Julia Esther (Turner) Stout, and children.

Wilson was the 11th of 12 children of Jacomiah and Lydia (Pierce) Stout. He was born July 19, 1807 in Green Co., PA, where Jacomiah's father, Elisha, had taken the family from their native New Jersey.

They later headed west to Oxford, Butler Co., OH where Wilson met and married Julia "Esther" Turner, daughter of Joel Turner, on May 29, 1831. Their first child, Thomas, was born there. Shortly thereafter, they moved on to Alquina, Fayette Co., IN, where children Joel, Mariah, John N., Margaret E., and Susan were born. Following other family members, the Stouts relocated in Montgomery County in 1846. Here, they had three more children: Benjamin F., Sarah Elizabeth, and Mary Ann, for a total of nine children. They lived and farmed on land three miles west of Crawfordsville.

Wilson Stout family - 1880s. Back row: (left to right) Benjamin F. Stout, Elizabeth (Stout) Cowan, Joel Stout, Susan (Stout), Remley, Margaret (Stout) Swank, John Stout. Front row: (left to right) Maria (Stout) Switzer, Wilson Stout, Mary Ann (Stout) Snyder, Julia Esther (Turner) Stout, and Thomas Stout.

Wilson became a Republican when the party was organized to oppose slavery in 1854, and was an active Methodist for 65 years until his passing on Mar. 4, 1892. He was buried in Wesley Chapel Cemetery, where countless other Stouts have been laid to rest, including his mother Lydia, who had lived with Wilson's family in her old age.

Esther was born Oct. 4, 1810 in Genesee Co., NY. The Turner family in the generations before her lived in Connecticut, where her father was born. Her mother died when Esther was around seven, leaving her and two brothers to her father's care. Soon after, she went to live with another family, where she endured unnamed hardships. Later, back with her father, she moved on to Butler Co., OH.

She began her lifetime membership in the Methodist Church in 1841. Her obituary tells us "In the family circle a chapter from (the Bible's) sacred pages read either by herself or her husband and prayer around the family altar were as regular as the evening came." Esther died Oct. 10, 1894. She was buried beside Wilson in Wesley Cemetery.

Wilson and Esther have numerous descendants, including many through son Thomas who, on Nov. 1, 1855, married Elizabeth Miller, daughter of Valentine and Elizabeth (Norman) Miller, of Bartholomew Co., IN.

They spent most of their lives farming in the Black Creek section of Montgomery County, until

Thomas retired. They then moved to Wesley for several years, before their final move to Crawfordsville. Their 11 children included John W., Valentine, James, William Everett, George W., Benjamin Franklin, Minnie Malisa, Charles, and Albert R. Two other children, also named Minnie M. and Albert R., died as babies. Thomas and Elizabeth were members of the United Brethren Church.

Thomas passed away at age 71 in Crawfordsville on July 6, 1903. At nearly 81, Elizabeth followed him on Nov. 30, 1915. Both were buried in Wesley Cemetery.

GEORGE W. STOVER

George W. Stover enlisted on Apr. 22, 1861, at the age of 19, in the 11th Indiana Infantry under then Colonel Lew Wallace. His enlistment was for three months and he was mustered out on August 4. On Sept. 18, 1861, George W. Stover enlisted in Company B, 10th Indiana Infantry in Indianapolis. He was made a corporal. The regimental commander was then Col. Mahlon D. Manson, who later became a Brigadier General. On Sept. 22, 1861 the regiment left Indianapolis for Louisville, KY. On Jan. 19, 1862, the 10th Indiana fought in the battle of Mill Springs, KY. The regiment later fought in the battle of Corinth. When the regiment returned to Nashville, TN, it joined in the pursuit of Confederate General Bragg's Army through Kentucky. On Oct. 8, 1862, while the regiment was engaged in the battle of Chaplin Hills at Perryville, KY, Corporal George W. Stover was killed. He was Montgomery County's first soldier killed in battle during the Civil War. He was first buried in Perryville, KY and later his body was returned to Montgomery County and was interred in the Stover Cemetery northeast of Crawfordsville.

For over 74 years, George W. Stover's body laid in the remote family cemetery. During the 1930s it was decided to remove his body and have re-interred in Oak Hill Cemetery. Dr. Edward H. Cowan, of Crawfordsville, headed the efforts to transfer the soldier's body. On May 27, 1938, George W. Stover's body was removed from the Stover Cemetery and transferred to Oak Hill Cemetery. His casket was made of cast iron and was designed in the manner of an Egyptian sarcophagus. It measured six feet in length and was in an excellent state of preservation.

On May 30, 1938, Dr. Edward H. Cowan, who was Surgeon General of the National Grand Army of the Republic, gave a short dedication at the new grave site of George W. Stover. *Submitted by Andrew Keith Houk, Jr*

MARY STRODE

Mary Elizabeth Strode was born on Oct. 17, 1910, the daughter of William Hulet and Florence Edith (Foster) Strode and grew-up in the New Market area. Her father was born June 13, 1883 in Kentucky. He had three brothers. He died Mar. 27, 1970 of heart disease. He worked for the state highway and R.R. Donnelleys. Mary's mother was born the last day of July in 1888, the daughter of James and Lucinda (Hayes) Foster. Mary remembers her mother as a wonderful cook, donned in a blue dress and apron. Florence died Jan. 9, 1975 of anemia. Both parents are buried Mace K of P. Before his death, Mary and other family members surprised the Strodes with a 65th Anniversary Party.

At 15, Mary was a telephone operator. She later worked for and retired from R.R. Donnelley's. Mary is currently a resident of Williamsburg Health Care and enjoys reading and embroidery work. She serves as resident librarian. *Submitted by Karen Zach (via information from Mary Strode)*

AQUILLA STULL

Aquilla, the brother of George Washington Stull, was born in Montgomery Co., KY. He came to Indiana at the age of 20 and lived most of his life in the vicinity of Waynetown. He was a veteran of the Civil War having served three years in the 63rd Indiana regiment, Company E. He was married to Georgeanna Case. The children of Aquilla and Georgeanna Case Stull were Rachel, who married William Hybarger; Nancy, who married Riley Lindley; Marian Isabelle, who married Charles Gillis; Emily Jane, who married Marion Follick; John W, who married Anna Ross; Bud, Sissy, Lawson, who married Effie Ellis; Lillie who married Bertie Pickett, and Claudia Stull.

The children of William and Rachel Stull Hybarger were: Ora, who married Harry Stone; Grace who married Edgar Coate and James Lowe; Maude, who married Gilbert Bayless; Georgia, who married Raleigh Boyd; Ruby, who married Charles Beetem, and Hazel, who married George Ohm and Don Austin.

Aquilla Stull

The children of Raleigh and Georgia Boyd were Ruby, who died in infancy, Lynn, who married Ethel Jordan and LaVerne Harley; Robert, who married Estel Stringer and Oma Jane Watson; Hazel, who married Thomas Crosley and Lloyd Pickett; Paul who married Elnora Martin; David, who married Ruby Long and Alise Choate; Philip who married Mary Milliner and Patricia Baker; James, who died young; John, who married Dorothy Cartmel; and Joseph, who married Margaret Louise Kraig.

Joseph and Margaret Boyd are the parents of three sons: David, a graduate of Vincennes University is married to Randi Seligman. They have three sons: Nathan, Ryan and Colin. They live in Lafayette, IN. John is a graduate of Indiana University and is married to Bernadette Arden. He lives in Dayton, OH. Robert attended Purdue University. He is married to Christie Ann Toman. They have one son, Kevin. He lives in Indianapolis.

Joseph graduated from Indiana University and Margaret graduated from Purdue University. Both are teachers in the Lafayette School Corporation.

Margaret Kraig Boyd is the granddaughter of Joseph Kraig who served with the Kentucky Militia during the Civil War. He is buried in the Cave Hill Cemetery in Louisville, KY. She is also a direct descendent of John Smith who fought in the Revolutionary War, moved to Tennessee, and then finally settled in Lawrence County, IN where he is buried.

The children of Harry and Ora Hybarger Stone were Virgil and Harry.

The children of Edgar and Grace Hybarger Coate were Lex and Paul. The child of James and Grace Hybarger Lowe was Thelma who married Robert Farmer.

The children of Gilbert and Maude Bayliss were Helen, Lucille, and Velma.

The child of George and Hazel Hybarger Ohm was George William. *Submitted by J. Boyd*

GEORGE WASHINGTON STULL

George Washington Stull was born 1813 in Montgomery Co., KY, about 13 miles from Mt. Sterling on Slade Creek. The house is no longer there and the grist mill operated by his father is only a memory. He moved to Parke Co., IN, and lived near what is now known as the Narrows of Sugar Creek, which is at the East side of Turkey Run State Park. After a few years here, he moved to Fountain County and homesteaded a farm north and west of Yeddo, IN where he spent the remainder of his life. He was a Civil War veteran.

George Washington Stull

George W. Stull and Francis (Fanny) Blevins were blessed with ten children. Charloty died in infancy. Benjamin Franklin married Lydia Burcher. Aquilla died in infancy. John W. married Mary (Mollie) Rogers. John was town marshall of Linden from 1922-1930. George W. Jr. married Alice Burke. Sarah Belle married David Finley Rogers. (John and Sarah Belle Stull married Mary and David Finely Rogers. All of their children were double cousins See ROGERS, ELIJAH) Homer Harry married Mary Herrigodt and Theresa Vanosky. Lucinda married Frank Shipman. Mary Ellen married George Swank and Arthur Sigler. Moses Edward married Rose Belle Riley.

The siblings of John W. Stull and Mary Rogers Stull were: Eva, who married Arthur Vail; Marion Earl, who married Alta May Royer; Harry, who married Lala Kinney; Clara, who married Harry Royer; Forrest (Pat), who married Fay Scott; Virgil (Bode), who married Ethel Harris; and George F. Stull.

Eva Vail was a charter member of the New Testament Baptist Church. Marion Stull was a member of the Crawfordsville Nazarene Church. Harry Royer worked from 1910 to 1953 as a mechanic, blacksmith, and general repair work. He was a member of the Darlington Methodist Church. At the time of her death Clara Royer was a member of the Potato Creek Methodist Church.

The children of Marion E. and Alta Mae Royer Stull were John F., Lucille, Morris, Byron (Penny), Helen, William, James, Margaret, and Mary Mae.

The children of Harry and Lala Kenney Stull were Evelyn and Leon.

The children of Harry and Clara Stull Royer were Mary Mae and Frederick.

The children of Forrest and Fay Scott Stull were Martha, Guy, Wildo, and Max.

The children of Virgil and Ethel Harris Stull were Linda, David, and Stephen. *Submitted by J. Boyd*

RICHARD L. AND ROSEMARY (TROSPER) STULTZ

Richard and Rosemary Stultz have been residents of Montgomery County since 1945. They first settled about 3-1/2 miles southeast of Alamo, IN moving to Waveland in 1949 where they now reside. Richard was employed for 41 years with R.R. Donnelley and Sons at Crawfordsville, retiring from there in 1986. Rosemary also worked for a short time with the same firm. From 1973 to 1986, she worked for Dormeyer Industries at Rockville, retiring in 1986.

Richard was born in 1924 near Fincastle, IN in Putnam County to Arthur R. and Patience Rivers Stultz. He was the oldest of five children. He attended schools in Putnam and Montgomery Counties. Arthur served as a Private during WWI, serving in France. After the war, he married Patience in 1923. Arthur farmed and worked in timber. He passed away in 1973 at the age of 86. Patience was a mother and housewife. She passed away in 1988 at the age of 88. Arthur was from Putnam County and Patience from Montgomery. Richard served WWII with the 8th Air Force. He was a tail gunner on a B-24 aircraft. He served 31 months, some of this time was spent overseas. He came out of the service as a Staff Sergeant with the Purple Heart and air medal with four clusters. In 1943, he married Rosemary Trosper. She was born in 1925 to James A. and Hattie M. Sollars Trosper, at Clinton, IN, in Vermillion County.

Richard and Rosemary Trosper Stultz

Her parents lived most of their life in Clinton. Rosemary was the 11th of 13 children. Her father worked in the coal mines, Newport Powder Plant and Ice House in Clinton. Her father married Hattie M. Sollars in 1902. James passed away in 1954 at the age of 73 and Hattie in 1954, age 68. Their deaths were six weeks apart.

Richard and Rosemary are the parents of five children: Nancy Watson, Richard, Jr., Dianne Livesay, Debbie Metzger, and Kelley Hopkins. They are grandparents to 13 grandchildren: Angie and Vickie Watson, Seth, Casey and Bubba Stultz, Scott, Craig and Darick Livesay, Devin Mitchell, Nicky and Jenny Metzger and Matthew Hopkins. *Submitted by Rosemary Stultz*

GEORGE AND MARTHA TALBOT STUMP

George Stump was born Apr. 23, 1794, in Georgia, and died June 3, 1866, in Union Township, Montgomery Co., IN. His wife was Martha (Patsy) Talbot, born in South Carolina (1805, died Mar. 5, 1892). The name Talbot sometimes Talbert, is French; so perhaps her father's family belonged to the Hugenots. Martha is said to have told her children that she was part Indian, which could have been so, since her mother was in South Carolina. The Talbots emigrated from South Carolina to North Carolina, and on to Kentucky. Somehow, George Stump and Martha met and were married in Campbell County on Aug. 8, 1817? They continued to live in the Blue Grass State and had four children: John who was born in Boone County, Nancy, Robert and Sally. When John was eight years old in 1828, the family moved to Rush Co., IN, for one and a half years. Then they came to Montgomery County, where they are listed in the 1830 Census. At the Land Grant Office in Crawfordsville they entered 120 acres from the United States Government in Union Township. This became their permanent home. They had Margaret, Martha, Ann, William and Henry in Indiana. An acre of land was set aside for building the Stump Schoolhouse. Today, an electrical sub power station is there.

The descendants of George and Martha Stump are eligible to become members of the Society of Indiana Pioneers. Two of their descendants, Perry and Paul Stump, were mayors of Crawfordsville. Margaret married Levi Whitaker, son of John and Catherine Wright Whitaker. I do not know whom the other children married. *Submitted by Mary Elizabeth Cedars*

HARVEY AND MARY SUMMERS

Harvey Summers, born Nov. 1, 1829 in Crawfords Co., PA, later lived east of Whitesville, IN, south of the Isaac and Mary (Randel) Linn farm. Harvey married the former Mary Bradley, the widow of Samuel Burk. (She was the mother of Dr. Clements.) Their children were Ella, born Apr. 19, 1862 and Emma. Emma married James Nicely and Ella married William Asa Linn. (see index Linn)

Harvey M. was formerly affiliated with the German Baptist Church but in 1893 became a member of the M.E. Church at Mace, IN. He was also a member of the Knights of Pythias Lodge.

Harvey and Mary Summers

Mary died at age 48.

The July 31, 1873 *Crawfordsville Journal Weekly*, page 2 column 6 reports Mary Summers was buried at the Burk graveyard near Crawfordsville, IN.

Following Mary's death Harvey married Ann Clements; they had James, born June 17, 1876 (died Nov. 17, 1946). Robert born Oct. 26, 1883 (died May 25, 1958) and Matthias Frantz, born Mar. 13, 1881 (died Dec. 22, 1952). James married Jane Hale (born June 17, 1883 — died Aug. 29, 1958), Matthias married Della Clossin on Feb. 2, 1903 and Robert married Beulah Myers in 1910.

Harvey moved to the Mt. Tabor area and died Dec. 4, 1896 and was buried by the Knights of Pythias at Oak Hill Cemetery.

JAMES W. AND MARGARET ROSS SWANK

James W. Swank, the sixth child of Philip and Polly Ann Whillhite Swank, was born Nov. 8, 1850. He married Margaret Josephine Ross, daughter of Harrison and Nancy Clouse Ross. Margaret was born Jan. 9, 1852. The couple lived in the Elmdale area all of their married life and had nine children. James W. passed away June 18, 1902 and Margaret died of stomach cancer at the home of her daughter, Minnie Florence Gohman, on Jan. 1, 1923. Both were buried in the Oakland Cemetery in Elmdale.

Their first child, Alfred Marcellus, was born June 10, 1873, and died Dec. 21, 1921, as a result of a farm machine accident. Alfred had ten children by his first wife, May Peak, and one by his second wife, Lola Hall.

Minnie Florence, the second child born to the couple, Dec. 6, 1875, lived almost 94 years. She suffered a broken hip and died from a blood clot on Sept. 14, 1969. Minnie married Joseph John Gohman. They owned a farm near Crawfordsville where they raised their nine daughters and grandson. Their one boy died at six months of age. The couple were buried in the Masonic Cemetery in Crawfordsville near their son.

Margaret gave birth to their third child, Nancy Ann, on Feb. 6, 1877, and lost her to tuberculosis on Feb. 27, 1894. Their fifth child, Harry Harrison, born Sept. 24, 1882, also died of tuberculosis, on Jan. 23, 1899. Both teenagers were buried in the Oakland Cemetery.

Bertha Faye was the fourth child born to James and Margaret, on Aug. 2, 1880. Bertha married David Baumgardner Nelson and to this union were born ten children. Bertha died on Dec. 11, 1972, and was buried in Crown Hill Cemetery in Indianapolis.

George Grover was the sixth child. He was born Mar. 14, 1885, and had six children with his wife, Katie Boraker. George was buried in Elmdale. George died Apr. 13, 1973.

Loretta Ellen, called "Re" in later life, was born Mar. 26, 1887. Loretta migrated west, joined by her nieces, Margaret and Esther Gohman, and lived in St. Louis and Salt Lake City before venturing to southern California where she met her husband, Christopher H. Carpenter. They did not have children. Lee Swank, one of Alfred's sons, and Betty Jean Holz, one of Margaret Gohman's daughters, met their mates at Re and Carp's rooming house on Oak Street in Los Angeles. Loretta died in Sun City on Oct. 21, 1966 and was cremated in Los Angeles.

Emma Lee, born Sept. 11, 1889, was the eighth child of James and Margaret. She married J.B. Strahlendorf and had two children. Emma passed away on Nov. 8, 1972.

Ira Wilson, youngest of the Swanks, was born Apr. 24, 1892. He never had children and died Aug. 29, 1934, killed by a wiring tying machine at the company where he worked in Crawfordsville. He was buried in a small cemetery north of Crawfordsville.

PHILLIP AND POLLIE ANN WILHITE SWANK

Phillip Swank born July 4, 1815, died Jan. 21, 1879, son of Jacob and Catherine. They resided in Pennsylvania. At the time of Phillip's birth they were residing in Ohio (1850 census) Jacob Sr. entered land in Montgomery County, March, 1831 from Kentucky and Fountain County. This land was later transferred to Phillip, Wilson Swank and James Ames. Jacob Sr. died Sept. 15, 1851 and Catherine July 2, 1856. Their burial was in Oakland Cemetery near Elmdale, Montgomery County.

December 31, 1835, Phillip married Pollie Ann Wilhite, born Dec. 1, 1817, died Feb. 3, 1897. Daughter of Ekillis and Mary Hall Wilhite. Ekillis born 1768, died Mar. 4, 1833 near Lexington, KY. Mary Hall Wilhite journeyed to Indiana to live with her son, President Hall Wilhite. Mary Hall Wilhite born 1775 died Aug. 25, 1845. Interment in Oakland for Mary Ann, Pollie Ann and Phillip.

Phillip and Pollie lived near Jeffersonville, IN before locating near Elmdale. Phillip was a leader in the community, being active in politics, church, social life, always ready to aid a neighbor, a farmer, part-time horse doctor and auctioneer. Lover of good horses and hounds, he enjoyed horse racing at the surrounding fairs. He often entered his horse at the last minute, playing the part of a "country jake" in order to inveigle a city smart alec into some ridiculous bet, then easily win the race.

Parents of ten children, Mary E., Jacob and Robert E. died in early childhood.

Benjamin Swank born Nov. 3, 1836 died 1912, married Mary Ellen Cowan, daughter of Robert and Rachel Ann Baldwin Cowan. They had six daughters, four sons. Because of the large number he often referred to them as "the tribe of Benjamin." He was admitted to the bar, practicing law in Montgomery County.

President Hall Swank born Dec. 1, 1838, died Jan. 28, 1924, married Susan Allhands. Parents of three boys and three girls. President farmed near Elmdale. During the winter he spent much time hunting, acquiring a reputation of a crack rifle shot.

Permelia Swank, born Feb. 7, 1843 died Apr. 9, 1924. She married David McDonald, parented one son and four daughters.

Amanda Swank born May 18, 1845, died June 16, 1925 married Charles (Daisey) Dazey, mother of five sons and two daughters, lived near Elmdale where her husband farmed. Her son, Henry Dazey was the father of 16 living children, the largest family in the posterity of Phillip Swank.

James W. Swank, born Nov. 8, 1849, died June 18, 1902, married Margaret Ross, spent his life near Elmdale farming and Crawfordsville working in a factory. He was the father of three sons and four daughters. William Jasper Swank born Dec. 2, 1851, married Anna Vincent. Parents of four sons and two daughters. When young, they moved to Noblesville, IN.

Daniel P. Swank born July 28, 1857 died July 18, 1930, married Mary C. Harmon, born Oct. 6, 1857 died Nov. 21, 1915. Parents of John, Lucy and Rita. Daniel farmed near Elmdale. *Submitted by Lester Olin*

SAMUEL DUNN SYMMES

Perhaps no one agency in all the world has done so much for public progress as the press, and an enterprising, well-edited journal is a most important factor in promoting the welfare and prosperity of any community. Montgomery County was certainly indebted to its wide-awake journals, and one of the men who was a potent factor in the local field of newspaperdom was Samuel Dunn Symmes.

Samuel D. Symmes

Mr. Symmes was born in Pleasant, IN, Oct. 20, 1856. He was a son of Rev. Francis Marion Symmes and Mary Jane (Dunn) Symmes. The father was born on Nov. 18, 1827 near Symmes Corners, OH. He was a son of Daniel T. and Lucinda (Randolph) Symmes. Daniel T. Symmes was born at the same place, as was his son. This family was one of the early settlers of Butler County. Mrs. Lucinda Randolph Symmes was a direct descendant of Pocahontas. Rev. Francis Marion Symmes and Mary Jane Dunn were married in March, 1855. She was living at Crawfordsville. She was a daughter of Nathaniel A. and Sophia (Irvin) Dunn. Her father was one of the first settlers of Montgomery County.

Samuel D. Symmes, of this review, received his education in public school in Lebanon and Wabash College. He learned the printer's trade and worked at that for a period of 20 years, becoming well-known to the trade and highly efficient. He was then elected township trustee in which he served for ten years. He discharged his duties in a manner that reflected much credit upon himself and to the satisfaction of all concerned. He worked out the plan of school consolidation.

Mr. Symmes was active in many organizations in Crawfordsville. He was a member of the Patriotic Order Sons of America - national vice-president and state secretary. He was a member of the Knights of Pythias, Modern Woodmen of America, Masonic Order, and a charter member of the Tribe of Ben Hur. He was a member of the Wabash Avenue Presbyterian Church.

Mr. Symmes was married on Mar. 31, 1883 to Nancy Jane McCaine, a daughter of Vardaman McCaine of Bedford. Her father was a native of Ireland. He purchased the Keeney home on South Elm Street and resided there until his death in 1937.

To Mr. Symmes and wife five children were born, Frank A., Clyde D., William V., Ruth and Aileen. Several descendants of Mr. Symmes live in Montgomery County.

BETTY TAYLOR

Betty was born in Parke County near Byron, IN. She was the oldest of five daughters born to Roy B. and Edna L. Sowers Taylor. She was born Sept. 24, 1921.

Betty graduated from Waveland High School in 1939. After high school she worked in the Coleman's Store at Byron.

In 1943, after the death of her father, she and her mother purchased Mrs. Deere's grocery store in Browns Valley. There, along with her mother, they built up the business. It became well known for their meat products, as well as Mrs. Taylor's minced meat which along with the help of the family was made by the gallons just before the Thanksgiving Holidays. The minced meat was sold in several states.

After 30 years both Betty and her mother began to lose their health. Betty lost the use of both legs due to diabetes. After amputation of both legs she did remarkably well with artificial limbs. She and her mother were able to remain in their home for several years, until Betty lost her eyesight. At that time both of them entered the Ben Hur Nursing Home in Crawfordsville.

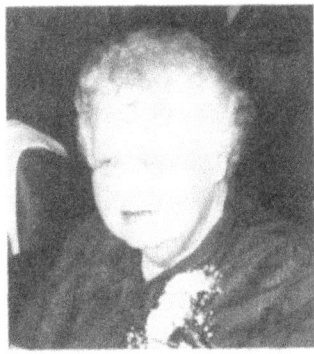

Betty Taylor

Betty was an avid collector of antique dishes and all kinds of cards.

In the nursing home she spent much of her time in therapy, learning Braille, making new friends, and spending many hours learning her way around the home. At this time she became interested in helping other handicapped folks, especially the younger ones. She began to teach a Bible class to them. With a gift of tapes of the Bible from the Browns Valley Christian Church Ladies Aid, her Bible Classes became quite a ritual. She could tell each one of her "Kids" by the footsteps or voice. She also became active in setting up entertainment for recreation night at the home.

Her mother died Dec. 2, 1979. Betty remained at the nursing home, but was able to go out to eat, shop and spend time with each of her three sisters and their families.

She was an avid radio fan as well as listening to her favorite recording stars. Many area ministers made tapes of their sermons that she shared with other residents, as well as her "Kids".

The hi-lites of Betty's life became the friendship she shared with her customers, made while in the grocery store, her Bible School "Kids", and the fellowship with the Browns Valley Christian Church and its members.

She was hospitalized in May with a serious illness, and passed away on July 6, 1986. *Submitted by Mrs. Dorothy Clouser*

DANIEL AND KELLY TAYLOR

Daniel Lyn Taylor born Aug. 21, 1961, Montgomery Co., IN, the son of Richard and Barbara House Taylor both natives of Indiana. He graduated from Wabash College in 1983 with a Bachelor of Arts degree in Political Science and from The Dickinson School of Law in 1986 with a Jurts Doctorate degree.

He is a member of Beta Theta Pi Fraternity and the Delta Theta Phi Law Fraternity. In 1986, he was admitted to practice law in Indiana and joined the law firm of Harding Henthorn & Harris, P.C. in Crawfordsville.

Daniel and Kelly Taylor

On Nov. 25, 1988 he married Kelly Sue Carpenter, born Sept. 5, 1964 in Montgomery County. She is the daughter of Harold and Linda Groves Carpenter. Kelly is a graduate of Indiana State University and is a member of Alpha Chi Omega Sorority. She is a Sales Representative for Public Service of Indiana in Lafayette.

Daniel and Kelly live in Crawfordsville and are active in the community. They attend the First United Methodist Church.

DAVID AND LAURA TAYLOR

David Lee Taylor was born Aug. 21, 1961 in Montgomery Co., IN, the son of Richard and Barbara House Taylor. He graduated from Wabash College in 1983 and the Indiana School of Law in 1986.

David and Laura Taylor

He was admitted to practice law in Indiana and joined the law firm of Carter and Leerkamp in Indianapolis, IN.

On Aug. 16, 1986, he married Laura Kay Price, born Mar. 21, 1964 in Montgomery County, the daughter of Charles and Patricia Coady Price. Laura graduated from Butler University in 1986 and Indiana School of Law in 1989. She is presently employed by the Law firm of Riley Bennett & Egloff in Indianapolis.

David and Laura live in Indianapolis.

RICHARD AND BARBARA TAYLOR

Barbara House born Jan. 14, 1940 in Carroll Co., IN, daughter of Lester Merle House born May 6, 1901 and died Sept. 7, 1974, and Myra Louise Redman, born Mar. 15, 1905 in Fountain Co., IN and died in Marion Co., IN on Dec. 19, 1981. At the age of two years the family moved back to Warren Co., IN the nativity of her father.

On Oct. 16, 1960 she married Richard L. Taylor, born Jan. 28, 1939 in Warren County and they established their new home in Crawfordsville, IN. He was the son of Harold Alfred Taylor born Aug. 11, 1907 in Orange Co., IN and died Oct. 4, 1978 in Warren Co., IN and Weltha Louise Cox born Jan. 30, 1908 Warren Co., IN and died Feb. 1, 1971 in Tippecanoe Co., IN. Harold was a welder by trade.

In 1957 Richard became employed as a machinist with R.R. Donnelley and Sons Printing Company and has continued with the company to the present.

Barbara's maternal grandfather, John Wesley Redman, a farmer, born in Fountain Co., IN on Nov. 10, 1875 and died in Gary, IN on Jan. 7, 1957. Her maternal grandmother, Stella May Zimmerman, born in Casey Co., KY on June 6, 1883 and following the death of her father, William Lewis Zimmerman was placed in the Children's Home of Cincinnati, OH. When she was about 11 years old she was an Orphan Train Rider; a family named Dunklebarger in Fountain County took her in to help with the household chores. She remained with this family until she married John Wesley Redman on Mar. 3, 1901. Stella's mother was Agnes Cordella Carr, daughter of Joseph W. Carr and Rebecca Jane Rairdan natives of Kentucky. The Redman family came to Indiana in the late 1830's from Ross Co., OH. John the son of William Beaman Redman, born in 1842 in Indiana and Margaret Ellen Pearson (Pierson), daughter of William Henry Pearson and Nancy Rector on Oct. 1, 1851 in Fountain County. William was a farmer and they married on Feb. 28, 1875 in Fountain County. William's parents were Peter Redman and Eva Beaman Overly (Oberlin in Germany and changed to Overly when they entered the United States in the 1700's).

Margaret Ellen Pearson's grandfather, Thomas Pearson was born May 1741 in England and died in Warren Co., IN 1833. He served tours of duty in the Revolutionary War and applied for his pension at the age of 92 when he became unable to provide for his own needs. He served with General Thompson in Pennsylvania and was taken prisoner and held for almost a month. He escaped and returned to Philadelphia and returned to his regiment.

The second time he enlisted in 1777 in Capt. Howard's Regiment and was in the battles of Brandywine, Princetown and was with General Washington at Valley Forge.

His third service in the fall of 1799 in Rockingham Co., VA where he served with Capt. Woodson for 18 months at Petersburgh, Charleston. After Charleston he was sent home to Virginia and later moved his family to Stones River, TN. They moved in the early 1830's to Indiana where he was a farmer.

Our subject and her husband live south of Crawfordsville near New Market. Their children are Daniel L. and Kelly Carpenter Taylor; David L. and Laura Price Taylor; Sally and Randal Ray. They have two granddaughters: Erin Elizabeth and Lindsay Taylor Ray.

Barbara is active in the Genealogy Section of the Montgomery County Historical Society, Republican Women's Club, Montgomery County Mother of Twins Club, The National Orphan Train Heritage Society and enjoys crafts, genealogy, reading, bowling and golf. Richard enjoys bowling, golf, woodworking and spectator sports.

WALTER CLARENCE AND MYRTLE ELLEN TAYLOR

Land in Brown Township near Browns Valley has been basic to the Walter and Myrtle Taylor family for more than four generations. Myrtle's mother, Melissa America (Todd) Services, was the daughter of Johnson (1809-1870) and Ruth Ann Todd (1823-1901) who came from Kentucky in 1832 to settle on the land adjacent to the east side of what later became Browns Valley.

Johnson and Ruth Ann Todd had nine children:
John (1841-1931) married Hester Harris 1871, farmed east of Browns Valley about one mile along the old Terre Haute road, now State Road 47. He gave leadership to organize the Browns Valley Bank.

Henry T. (1843-1907) married Mary Griffith 1865. They lived in Browns Valley.

Isaac Shelby (1845-1921) married Delilah Maddox, his first cousin, in 1868 and farmed north of Browns Valley one-half mile.

Walter Clarence and Myrtle Ellen Taylor

George (1847-1939) married Josie Griffith 1871. She died 1878. He married Eva VanCleave 1879 and farmed north-east of Browns Valley across the road from John. A son Raymond, by Eva, was lost in World War I.

Sarah Jane (1851-1938) married Tilghman Davis 1870. They farmed north of Browns Valley and west of New Market.

Pauline (1858-1937) never married.

Johnson (1861-1949) married Julia Smith 1885, moved to Kansas soon after marriage and accumulated a section of prime land in Scott County which was subsequently lost during the dust bowl disaster.

Mary Elizabeth (1866-1959) married George T. Williams 1888. Dr. Williams practiced medicine in Browns Valley for 17 years, moved to Crawfordsville in 1904, served as regimental surgeon in France in World War I, and died in 1944 as Montgomery County's oldest physician.

Melissa America (1856-1927) married William A. Servies 1878. They farmed near Browns Valley for many years and had three children; Orville (1879-1968) married Della Whitington 1898, farmed for years and was for a few years the Village Blacksmith for the Browns Valley community; Blanche (1881-1971) married Frank Wilkinson 1901. They farmed one mile south of Browns Valley most of their working years; Myrtle Ellen (1885-1968) married Walter C. Taylor 1906.

Walter's father was Charles W. Taylor born 1854 in Augusta Co., VA. As a teenager, Charles left his home farm and walked from Virginia over the mountains to Ohio where he worked for a short time and then onto Parke Co., IN where he met and married Mary Ellen Moore 1876.

Mary Ellen Moore's parents were Charles Vincin (1822-1862) and Ruth (Glossin) Moore (1827-1900). Other children in the Moore family were:

Ira (1850-1934) who went to California and was head of the Long Beach "dray" business back in the days of horses.

Elizabeth (1853-1906) married Jabes Wood, a farmer near Bloomingdale. They were grandparents of Wood Carter who was killed by bank robbers in the Bloomingdale Bank in 1936.

Charles (1854-1916) a "house mover" in Ontario, CA.

Martha (1858-1932) married Houston Dooley a farmer near Bloomingdale.

John (1860-1953) a farmer at the west edge of Rockville.

One of John's sons, Foster (called Boots) was an automobile dealer in Terre Haute and owned much of the land that Indiana State University used for its expansion.

Charles W. (1854-1937) and Mary Ellen (Moore) Taylor (1856-1928) had five children:

Bessie (1880-1972) married first to Charles Doyle, then to Harry Glover, a professional carpenter in Crawfordsville.

Henrietta (1883-1981) married Charles Frame and farmed south of Browns Valley and near Jamestown.

Ruth (1885-1982) married Walter E. Penn, a lifetime farmer one mile south of Browns Valley.

Vincent (1893-) married Nancy Cook.

Walter C. Taylor (1878-1941) was born in Parke Co., IN. After a short time, he moved with his parents to New Maysville and later to a farm two miles east of Browns Valley. After graduating from grade school, he worked on neighboring farms until he had saved enough money to buy a team and wagon. Then he started hauling logs to the New Market sawmill. With additional savings he purchased another team and wagon and by hitching the two wagons together and the teams in tandem, he was able to nearly double his capacity for hauling. In 1906, the year he was married, he bought an 80 acre tract of land one and one-half miles east of Browns Valley. There were no buildings and much of the land was still in virgin timber, mostly sugar maple, oak, walnut, beach, hickory and ash. Walter and Myrtle were both active in the Browns Valley Baptist Church. Myrtle taught a Sunday School class and played the piano for church. Walter was the song leader. Both Myrtle and Walter's parents were active deacons in the church. In later years both sets of parents lived in Browns Valley.

Walter and Myrtle had two children. Harold born 1907 and DeElla 1910. Both graduated from Browns Valley grade school and Waveland High School. DeElla trained at Indiana State Normal (now Indiana State University) for a license and taught at Browns Valley school. She married Robert F. Jackson in 1931. He graduated from Purdue University and is retired from the U.S. Corp of Engineers based in Washington, D.C. DeElla owns the tract of land adjacent to Browns Valley that was originally owned and farmed by Johnson and Ruth Ann Todd.

Harold graduated from Purdue University, married Mildred R. Thompson, 1933, and retired after devoting 30 years of service in Agriculture Education to Purdue University and the State Department of Public Instruction. He owns and operates the farm his father cleared and developed and the one originally developed by Shelby Todd. Nearly all of the above families now deceased are buried in Indian Creek Hill Cemetery. Johnson and Ruth Ann Todd are buried in Old Union two miles north of Waveland. *Submitted by Harold B. Taylor*

TERRY

Thomas Winter Terry born Sept. 13, 1805 and his wife, Susan Akers Terry lived in Montgomery Co., VA. Their son, Thomas Bowyer Terry was born Sept. 19, 1848 in Christainburg, VA. He was in the Virginia Mounted Cavalry, and an officer in the Confederate Army of the Civil War. Following the war he came to Montgomery Co., IN to the Ladoga area. He married Mary Ellen Teeter, daughter of William and Ellen Fesler Teeter. They were the parents of 13 children: 1. Tessora Hortense married Walter Goodbar; 2. Lottie Isobell died in infancy; 3. Jesse Edgar married Elva Sanders Friend; 4. Roy Theodore married Edna Anderson; 5. Charles Agustus married Edna Thomas (she still lives in Houston House at age 103); 6. Ada Blanch; 7. Thomas Vorhees married Cora Bunsenbark; 8. Harry Lemuel lived one year; 9. Mary Ellen married Joseph Pattison; 10. Ruth Susan married Bryant O. Hobson; 11. Virginia Ethel; 12. Ralph Waldo married Arta May Tharp; and 13. Ruby Hester.

Jesse Edgar Terry, the third eldest child was born Aug. 21, 1877. He married Elva Sanders Friend born Apr. 1, 1878, the daughter of James Alexander Sanders and Samantha Ellen Sanders. Edgar And Elva were married Feb. 26, 1902. They had a son Donald Norman who died in infancy. They had a daughter Nelly Merle. They lived on a farm in the Whitesville area. The daughter and her husband still live at the same location. Nelly married Lyle Hulbert, son of Orbie and Myrtle Hulbert. Nelly, a Home Economist, taught school in Howard and Montgomery Counties. Lyle has a hobby of photography.

Materials obtained (from Terry History by Mary Lou Garriott and some notes from C. Pauline Walters).

EDNA TERRY (102 YEARS OLD)

Edna Terry is a very extraordinary person. Her courage, determination and mental vigor are outstanding. What makes Edna even more remarkable yet is that she is 102 years old!

Edna Bell Thomas was born on Sept. 11, 1886 in Ladoga, IN. Her father owned a farm in nearby Whitesville. She had a brother 13 years younger.

When Edna was four years old she first saw a telephone at a grocery store in Southern Indiana. The grocer took the receiver down so she could listen to it. He then mentioned there were only six phones anywhere else that he could call. At the age of 15 Edna joined the local Christian Church.

As a young girl Edna well remembers the square dances which were held in the homes of various members in the Ladoga area. When she was 19 years old she married Charlie Terry, then 24, who was a farmer. She remembers that at this time people were paid a dollar a day for wages if they could find work.

Edna Terry, September 1988, 102 years old

A year after Edna and Charlie were married a daughter, Mildred, was born. Unfortunately, 19 days later Edna's mother, who had always been a frail woman, died. Her funeral took place on Christmas Day.

When Mildred Terry was three, a brother named Harmon was born. Harmon passed away at Christmas time at age four. A few years later scarletina spread across Indiana. Edna's second daughter, then three weeks old, died of the disease.

In 1918 Edna and Charlie moved to Crawfordsville where they would live permanently. In Crawfordsville Edna became a close friend of two important women. The first was Martha Williams who founded Houston Healthcare. The second lady was Bessie Haffner, who was the wife of the well-known optometrist C.O. Haffner.

There were only five years that separated the death of Edna's husband Charlie and their daughter Mildred. Still Edna kept going. "You've got to keep on going. I don't care if you can or can't, you've just got to do it," she said recently.

Edna worked in the linen room at Culver Union Hospital for 30 years. She was also strongly involved in volunteer work. She worked as a Red Cross Gray Lady for 12 years and a Pink Lady at the hospital for 19 years. She also enjoyed working for the Crawfordsville Election Board. "Ever since women were allowed to vote I've never missed a vote," she proudly commented.

At 97 she broke her hip at home and had to be admitted to a Crawfordsville nursing home. Edna has outlived six physicians and two lawyers.

When she became 100 Governor Orr called Edna and congratulated her on becoming a member of Indiana's "Century Club." Edna Terry is truly an individual who has been an inspiration to many!

OTIS THAYER

Otis Thayer was Montgomery County Assessor from Jan. 1, 1967 to Dec. 31, 1986. Elected Montgomery Council Jan. 1, 1987. During the 20 years as Assessor he was an officer in the Indiana State Assessors Association for ten years, serving as president for two years. He received the outstanding County Assessors award in 1984 and the Golden Rule award from the Association of Indiana Counties in 1981. He was appointed in 1973 to the Tax Commissioner's Advisory Council by Gov. Otis Bowen, serving for 13 years. He was made a Sagamore of the Wabash by Gov. Robert Orr July 12, 1985.

He was born Sept. 18, 1915 to Otis and Lona Thayer at Crawfordsville. He graduated from Romney High School in 1934.

He served in the Army during World War II in Europe.

In 1942 he married Helen Wagner. They had four children: Marilyn, Gail, Marta and Tim. Marilyn and Tim are deceased, both in 1970. Helen retired November 1987 from Bank One, Crawfordsville after 20 years.

ANSON S. AND JENNIE D. THOMAS

Anson S. Thomas was born Aug. 1, 1889, the son of George A. and Fanny (Driver) Thomas. He was a descendant of pioneer Montgomery County families. Widow Elizabeth Thomas and her eight children, emigrated from Butler County, OH to Montgomery County in 1832. Her son Ezra and his wife Rebecca (Birk) Thomas came with their three children at the same time and settled on Black Creek. Ezra's son Levi, Anson's grandfather, was a County Commissioner at the time the present Jail Museum was built. In 1855 Levi Thomas married

Elizabeth Davidson, the daughter of Richard and Rachael (Webster) Davidson who came from Ireland. Their son George A. Thomas married Fanny Driver, the daughter of George and Mary (Cook) Driver who came from England. Fanny attended Indiana State Normal and taught at the Patton Corner School where she met her future husband. After their marriage in 1886, they settled on their farm in Coal Creek Township. Their children were Anson, Charles and Mary. In 1911 Anson married Jennie Deeter and they took over the farm. His parents moved to Crawfordsville. Anson joined the Indiana State Farm Bureau in 1928 where he served in the Livestock Department and later for 20 years as Director of Tax and Legislative Department.

1956 Children in front L. to R. Alan Metsker, Laine Metsker, Paul Thomas, Couples L. to R. William and Ruth Mt. Metsker, John and Helen F. Ernstes, Anson and Jennie Thomas, Warren and Gale L. Thomas

At this time the family moved to Danville, IN. Anson traveled to all parts of Indiana to discuss legislative matters in many meetings. He was named to the State Tax Study Commission in 1953. He was elected chairman of the Indiana Water Resources Study Commission in 1955. He had a key role in the creation of the Flood Control-Water Resource Commission and later was appointed a member. He had much to do with the law which established the School of Veterinary Medicine at Purdue University. Governor Matthew Welsh bestowed upon him the prestigious Sagamore of the Wabash Award. While they lived in Danville their three children were born: Helen in 1914, Ruth 1917-1962, and Warren 1919, earned degrees from Central Normal College and all taught in Central Indiana high schools. Helen married John Ernstes and lives in Indianapolis. Ruth married William Metsker and taught at Coal Creek Central for several years. They lived on a farm in North Union Township with their sons Laine and Alan. Warren married Gale Lawler and they were the parents of Paul, Steven and Kent. Following Anson's retirement in 1961, he stayed one more year with the Farm Bureau as a consultant. That year Anson and Jennie returned to their home in Crawfordsville. Anson died January 1974 and was buried at Wesley Cemetery where many of his family are buried including his grandparents Levi and Elizabeth Thomas and great-grandparents Ezra and Rebecca Thomas. Anson's widow Jennie, celebrated her 99th birthday in August 1988. She lives in her home in Crawfordsville.

HUBERT THOMAS

In November, 1862, two young men ran away from home in Damascus, VA and joined the Confederate Army. They were the sons of Edward and Mary Widener Thomas. One of those men was Henry Clay Thomas.

While fighting in the Civil War, Henry was captured by the Union Army and brought to a Prisoner Of War Camp in the Lafayette area. When Henry was released, he settled in Guion, IN and married Narcissus Jane Heslar. They are both buried east of Marshall, IN in Bethany Cemetery. They had eight children, one of which was John William Thomas. John William married Stella Ann Abney and they were the parents of nine children, one of which was Hubert Thomas, born at Guion on Nov. 24, 1916.

Hubert attended schools in Parke County and worked at several occupations, including farming north of Waveland on the Ray Rivers farm and the Wilbur Spencer farm. He joined R.R. Donnelley's in 1956 and retired from there in 1981. He has resided in the Waveland area most of his life and is well known throughout the area as a skilled carpenter and woodworker.

Delores, Hubert, Rose Marie, Bill, Steve, Jim, Larry and Terry Thomas

He married Rose Marie Easter on Apr. 24, 1937. She was born Mar. 9, 1919, at Terre Haute, IN, the daughter of Clifford Pleasant and Rose Victoria Dowden Easter. She attended schools in Clay County. A housewife for many years, she joined the staff of Culver Hospital in 1966 as a nurse's aide, retiring from there in 1984. They are the parents of six children, all of whom graduated from Waveland High School, 17 grandchildren and eight great grandchildren.

Their first son, Clifford William "Bill", is employed by R.R. Donnelley's. He married Billie Ann Livesay and they have three children, Darla Sue, Dion Lee and Lori Ann. Darla is married to Steve Morrison. Dion married Jean Wilson and they have two daughters, Sara and Anna. Lori is married to Jay Prosser and they have two daughters, Cassandra and Beth.

Their daughter, Delores Jean, is employed at R.R. Donnelley's. She is married to Gordon Farley and is the mother of two children, Michael Ottis Reynolds and Deborah Jean Estep. Michael is the father of two children, Joshua and Megann. Debbie is married to Billy Estep of Broadway. Virginia and they have two children, Kiana and Kristopher.

Their second son, James Hubert, is employed by Eli Lilly & Co. He married Karen Ann Vance and they have three children, Sheri Lynn, James Darren and Toby Lee.

Their third son, Larry Wayne, is employed by Coast-To-Coast Hardwares. He has three children, Tammy Kay, Jody Wayne and Jeremy Hubert.

Their fourth son, Steven Ray, is employed by Eli Lilly & Co. He is marred to Clida Jane Hux and is the father of two children, Troy Steven, Mathew Ray and two stepchildren, Heather Jill and Wade Matthew.

Hubert and Rose Marie's last child was also a son, Terry Joe. He is employed by R.R. Donnelley's and has two children, Craig Aaron and Timothy Joe.

Hubert and Rose Marie are both members of the Waveland Christian Church.

PRICE JOEL THOMAS

My grandfather, Price Joel Thomas, was five years old, living with his parents, Abrim and Matilda (Hormell) Thomas at the time of the 1850 census of Coal Creek Township, Montgomery Co., IN.

Thomases, Hormells, Cloughs and Westfalls migrated from Miami Co., OH to Indiana.

Abrim and Matilda Thomas married July 23, 1834 in Miami County. Both are buried in Turkey Run Cemetery south of Wingate, IN. Matilda died 1855, age 37; Abrim died 1856.

Price Joel was cared for by his uncle, Dr. John M. Thomas of what was then Pleasant Hill. In 1860, per census, he lived with Ludlow Thomas. Abrim's brother, Michael Thomas, was made guardian of Price and his younger brother William per court records. Price Joel's older brother was killed in the Civil War. He was Cpl. John M. Thomas. His sister Elizabeth married Townsend Bobo. His younger brother William moved to Logan, IA.

Price Joel also enlisted to serve in the Civil War. His enlistment papers give Miami County as his birthplace.

Abrim Thomas was the son of Michael Thomas and Polly Clough (married Harrison Co., KY 1803). Michael Thomas was the son of Abraham Thomas (Revolutionary War) and Susanna Smith of Culpepper Co., VA. Michael served in the War of 1812 and died a few years later. His brother, Adam, was administrator of his estate. At the time of his death Michael still owed money to his brother Samuel. Samuel sued Michael's heirs in Miami Co., OH and this record left a list of Michael's heirs. Michael and his wife are buried near the graves of Abraham and Susanna Thomas in the Thomas Cemetery, Troy, OH.

Price Joel Thomas married Rebecca Meyers in Vigo County in 1871. They had seven daughters and three sons.

One son, Guy, was electrocuted while installing power lines in Iowa in 1920. He had no children.

Another son, John Raymond Thomas, married Marie Cattel in Paris, IL and had three daughters and two sons.

Another son, Leonard Clay Thomas married Laura Lister and lived in Parke Co., IN. They had several children.

The two sons of John Raymond Thomas and Marie were Guy who married late in life (Hazel Orlea) and had no children, and John Joel Thomas who married Ruth Shake and had two daughters, Carolyn and Sherry and one son, John Brian. To the best of our knowledge the Thomas line of Price Joel Thomas is being carried on by John Christopher Thomas, age five, and Matthew James Thomas, age one, of Terre Haute, IN. These are the sons of John Brian Thomas. *Submitted by John Joel Thomas*

RUTH MORGAN JOINER THOMAS

"Oh! That's my name" were the words spoken when television show host, Ralph Edwards, gave Ruth Morgan Joiner her "This Is Your Life" book. Due to the efforts of Ruth's first cousin, Kate Smith Bazzani, many Montgomery County residents viewed Ruth and Her Life on Apr. 11, 1956, Channel WFBM-TV, straight from Hollywood, CA.

At this time, Ruth taught at Mt. Zion school. One

of her pupils, Judith Dye, greeted her and told of their third grade good-bye (a kiss on the cheek from each pupil to the "very best teacher ever!"). Ruth's daughter, Jerry Lou, told of her mother working three jobs (teacher by day, bookkeeper by night and dining room hostess on weekends) to raise her, often helping some of her 11 brothers and sisters at the same time.

Ruth and Jerry Joiner

The reasons Ruth was chosen for "This is Your Life" began in the early hours (2:05 a.m.) of Feb. 6, 1932, when, as night operator at the telephone company in Waveland, she crawled to the switchboard and with a flashlight made calls to the Montgomery County Sheriff (who didn't arrive in time because of a flat tire) and various townspeople who gathered, shot at the bank robbers and chased them out of town.

Her real brush with danger started when she drew the longest straw and won an education trip (she was a Welfare Worker for Montgomery County) to the Indiana State Prison at Michigan City. While there, she was taken hostage and endured a knife poised at her throat for two hours and 20 minutes (as well as a shot in her arm and chest).

Ruth thought she was going to California for an educational workshop with school Superintendent John Ward. Instead, co-welfare worker, Georgia Cole, Alfred Dowd (Prison Warden), Leroy Hunt and Joe Petroski (who helped save Ruth), Theron Banta (Waveland bank cashier) and on a happier note, her brother Bob, sister Maude, Dye, and Ruth's daughter, Jerry were there to help her enjoy "This Is Your Life." She received a 16 mm projector, camera and film; a gold bracelet and a 1956 Mercury Phaeton for sharing her tale.

Ruth Hazel Morgan was born on a farm near Waveland Nov. 6, 1909, the oldest daughter of Stella Blanch (Scott) and Stanley Morgan. See her history. Her middle name stemmed from Sarah "Hazel" Morgan Smith, her aunt and mother of the above mentioned Kate Bazzani. She graduated from Waveland High School and Indiana State Teacher's College. She taught at Whitesville, Union Township schools, Granville Wells (Boone County), as well as the before mentioned Mt. Zion. Often ignoring money, name and prestige, as a social worker, Ruth instead placed babies where they would grow-up with happy lives. She first married Basil Joiner Apr. 27, 1934 in Paris, IL (later married Merle Thomas). One daughter, Jerry Lou Joiner was born Mar. 12, 1936 in Brazil, IN. Jerry is married to Fran Nordmeyer and is the mother of Gregg, Susan, Trent, Kim, Kristjane and Becky. The family lives in Orem, UT where Ruth passed away on May 31, 1987. Ruth was active in the Mormon Church and retirement clubs while in Utah. *Submitted by Jerry Joiner Nordmeyer, Karen Bazzani Zach, and Pauline Walters*

THE THOMPSONS OF WHITESVILLE

The Thompsons and Davidsons of the Whitesville area trace their people back through Butler Co., OH, to Centre and Northumberland counties in Pennsylvania.

Leo Leighton Thompson, born 1887, was the son of David Sylvester Thompson and Nancy Catherine Moore of west of New Market. Nancy, born 1847, was the daughter of James Moore and Margaret Wright. James Moore was born in 1801 in North Carolina. Margaret Wright was born in 1806 in Kentucky. Leo, with his brother Arlie, operated a threshing ring in the Browns Valley area, later farmed, and was co-owner of Haines and Thompson Milling in Crawfordsville.

David Sylvestor Thompson, Nancy Catherine Moore Thompson

David S. Thompson, born 1843 at Whitesville, was the son of Nehemiah Thompson and Nancy Davidson of Whitesville. David, with his brother Johnathon W.P., operated a saw mill west of Ladoga. Nehemiah, born 1803 in Pennsylvania came to this county in 1826 with his bride from Butler Co., OH, and taught school here. His father, Moses Thompson, had entered government land at Whitesville in 1823, having come by way of Ohio and Centre Co., PA from his native state of New Jersey.

Nancy Davidson, born 1800 in Chillaquaque, Northumberland Co., PA, was the daughter of Fleming Davidson and Margaret Lattimore. Fleming Davidson, born 1763 in Pennsylvania, was the son of William Davidson and Sarah Fleming. Margaret Lattimoe was born 1773. William Davidson was born 1725 in Scotland.

BOURBON S. THOMPSON

Bourbon S. Thompson, his wife the former Addie Sophia Shaffer moved to Wingate in 1895 with their children, Charlotte Blanche, George Everett, and Thomas Allen from Clarks Hill, IN. A son Silas died in infancy. Daughter Florence was born in 1896 at Wingate, died in 1909, as did Addie. Bourbon died 1922.

Bourbon was born in 1854, Bourbon Co., KY, the son of Thomas A. and Sarah Smith Thompson, immigrants from England. His other siblings were Mattie, Sam and John.

Addie was born 1857, daughter of Silas and Charlotte (Oyler) Shaffer. Her other siblings were George, Silas, Charles and Harry.

Charlotte Blanche (1882-1968), was married to William Marmaduke (1870-1951), who had one son Rex (1915-). They ran the Corner Grocery in Wingate until 1951.

George Everett (1885-1957), was married to Daisy Viola Abbott (1888-1946), Sept. 24, 1904. Daisy was the daughter of George and Emogene (Bannon) Abbott, half sister to Iona (Jackson) Dooley.

Front Row: Addie, Florence, Bourbon Thompson, Second Row: George, Thomas, Blanche

George Everett was employed as a farmer. In the early '30s operated the Wingate Garage (uptown) and was postmaster from 1932-'36 at Wingate. He was master of the Mercer Lodge F&AM No. 633 in 1935. He also was livestock feed and seed corn salesman.

Their children were Carl Raymond, Maurice Eugene (Bill), Howard Elmer, (1908), Mary Katheryn, (1914) and Kenneth Lee. Howard and Mary died in infancy.

Carl (1905-) was married to Beulah Marie Oswalt (1905-1988). Their children, Everett Eugene, (1926-) and Rosalyn Marie (Coling), (1927-).

Maurice (Bill) (1907-) was married to Ruth Ramona Pogue (1909-1986). Their children, Charles Lee, (1929-), and Charlotte Ann (1931-).

Kenneth Lee (1928-), married to Esther Lucille Ebert (1926-). Their children, Timothy Alan (1950-), Rebecca Sue (1951-), Martha Jane (1955-), and Elizabeth Ann (1957-).

Thomas Allen (1892-1959) was married to Lila Kuskey (1896-). They had one son Roger (1915-1968).

Elizabeth Fulwider, (1836-1875), sister of Jacob Fulwider, stockholder in the Old Brick Yard north of Crawfordsville, was married to James Clark Bannon, (1830-1923). They arrived in Montgomery County in the 1860s. Their children were Emogene, this writer's maternal grandmother, William, Lewis, Charles, Joe, Lena, Sally Arley and Baker.

James Clark Bannon, and brothers William, Lewis and Michael started holding annual family reunions in 1889, and August 13, 1989 will be the 100th continuous gathering, of which the past 60 have been held at Milligan Park, Crawfordsville.

Lewis, (1818-1919), brother of James was a minister in the Christian Church. In 74 years he only missed two conferences. Some of the churches he preached at were Liberty, and Center Christian Church. *Respectfully submitted by Kenneth Thompson*

DONALD T. AND JEAN BEECHER THOMPSON

Donald and Jean Thompson came to Crawfordsville in 1955. Don was librarian at Wabash College until his retirement in 1978. He was born in McCallsburg, IA in 1913 to Andy and Mabel Hanson Thompson. Andy was born in Mitchell Co., IA in 1892 to Chris and Susanna Quitsau Thompson. He graduated from Ellsworth Junior College at Iowa Falls. He was in banking, insurance and farm loans and farm management.

Don's mother was born in McCallsburg, IA to Amos and Louise Lura Hanson.

Jean was born in 1914 at Chicago to William L. and Helen Watson Beecher. William was born in 1870 in Union Co., OH, moved to Chicago in 1892. His parents were Walter and Orinda Sherwood Beecher. William was a graduate of Northwestern Pharmacy School and Northwestern Medical School. He was an allergist. Her mother was born in 1875 to Isaac and Elizabeth Gordon Watson in Norway, KS, grew up in St. Joseph, MO, and moved to Chicago with her family in 1898.

Front row: Kimberly Stuckey, Don and Jean Thompson, Marie Shechan. Back Row: Jeffrey Stuckey, Randall Stuckey, Janet Stuckey Neil, Dave and Karina Thompson and Steven Sheehan

Don graduated from Iowa State College in 1935, from the University of Illinois Library School in 1937, and received an M.A. from Temple University in 1942. He was acting librarian at the University of Alabama during World War II, Director of Libraries at Mississippi State College from 1948 to 1955. Since his retirement Don is active in the Montgomery County Historical Society, has been collecting Lew Wallace's letters for publication, and is a staff writer for *Montgomery Magazine*. He is a member of the Indiana Historical Society, the Kiwanis Club, The American Library Association and the Indiana Library Association, and an elder of the Wabash Avenue Presbyterian Church. He has written several articles and books, including *Indiana Authors and their Books*, 1917-1966, and 1967-1980.

Jean graduated from Northwestern University in 1936 and from the University of Illinois Library School in 1937. She has been on the staff of the Crawfordsville District Public Library since 1957, working with the local history collection. She has been active in the League of Women Voters, AAUW, Current Events Club, the Montgomery County Historical Society, and Church Women United at the state level. She is an elder of the Wabash Avenue Presbyterian Church. She is Montgomery County Historian, by appointment from the Indiana Historical Society.

The Thompsons were married in 1938. They have two children, Neil Bruce. born in 1941 and Janet Louise, born in 1944, both in Tuscaloosa, AL.

Neil graduated from Rutgers University in 1963 and received his masters at San Diego State University in 1975. Neil married Diane Ramsey in 1966 and served in the Navy from 1965 to 1986. They live in Marina, CA.

They have two daughters, Marnie, born in 1967 at New Orleans and Karina, born at Great Lakes, IL in 1970. Marnie married Joseph Sheehan in 1985 and was divorced in 1988. They have one son, Steven, born in 1986. Marnie will marry Thomas J. Butler in September 1989.

Janet graduated from Indiana University in 1966. She married Randall Stuckey from Berne, IN in 1965. They live in Pleasanton, CA. They have a son, Jeffrey David, 20 and Kimberly Ann, 18.

GRIGG MATTHEW THOMPSON

Grigg Matthew Thompson (1811-1888), son of "Elder" Wilson Thompson, and Mary or Polly (Grigg) Thompson, was born in Cape Girardeau Co., MO. His father, a Primitive Baptist preacher had moved there to preach The Gospel. But Grigg and Diantha and their growing family would be all over the wilderness as the years went by — Missouri, Georgia, Indiana, and Kentucky.

Grigg, an eloquent preacher in Georgia (near Calhoun, Gordon County), and a good farmer (no slaves) was, nevertheless, ruined by the Civil War conflict, and followed his two sons (Maurice and Will H.) to Montgomery County, Brown Township, IN shortly after the war (1868).

Tombstone of: Maurice Thompson

He established himself at Union Church with the Canines, only to be criticized over church matters and ostracized by certain ones of the church. He had been a Confederate chaplain during the war — zealous as his two sons, Maurice and Will H., were zealous soldier scouts. He lived, too, awhile (1880) with Maurice and Alice at Sherwood Place here. But not giving up his life's religious mission, he went back to Missouri where he died as a result of a fall from his horse near Ashland. His body was returned to Oak Hill Cemetery here for burial in the family plot.

Diantha Jaegger (Yeager) (1813-1897) and Grigg M. Thompson were married at Connersville, IN, Apr. 7, 1831. Of their 11 children, very little is known except that of Maurice and Will H., the authors, lawyers, archers. Diantha, unusually gifted, came from the Dutch family of culture (New York) and had a good knowledge of several languages and sciences, as well as English literature— a teacher of her children.

Children of Grigg Matthew Thompson: (1) Minerva Caroline (1832— ?) married; (2) Mariah (1839— ?); (3) Mary (1843— ?) died early; (4) Maurice — James Madison— (one U.S. census has his birth 1840, but the memorial stone has 1844) died Feb. 15, 1901; (5) Will Henry (1846-1918) — Will and his wife, Ida Lee (1855-1906), are buried at Lake View Cemetery, Seattle, WA and Ida's mother, Leticia (West) Lee, died at Portland, OR; (6) Thomas Jefferson Thompson (1849—?) married, had offspring; (7) Grigg (1850-1851); (8) Diantha (1854—?) was with her parents here in Brown Township in 1869; (9) Louisa died early; (10) Rebecca, disappointed in love, entered a convent; (11) Anna Belle married.

Members of the Thompson family buried at the Thompson Memorial (Oak Hill) are as follows:

Parents, Grigg Matthew and Diantha; Maurice and wife, Alice Lee (1850-1915); Alice's father, John Lee (1826-1891); Maurice's children— (1) Claude, Lawyer, an 1891 Wabash College graduate; (2) John Grigg (1871-1876) almost five; (3) Agnes (1880-1959) and husband, Austin H. Long (1880-1961).

One of Maurice's daughters, Jessie (1872-1941), Mrs. Alexander Ballard, was buried at Tampa, FL—son J. Lee Ballard, a banker at St. Petersburg.

JOHN W. AND ELVA A. THOMPSON

John W. Thompson was born in Hamilton Co., OH in 1857. His father William operated a ferry across the Ohio River. The family joined other family members in Montgomery County in the 1860's. He made his home and worked for George W. Cook a landowner of 600 acres in Montgomery and Tippecanoe Counties, who settled in Sugar Creek Township in 1834. His grandparents were immigrants from Germany and Ireland. They settled first in Maryland where his father was a farmer and shoemaker. They came on West to Richmond, IN. He married Nancy Corbin and came on to Montgomery County. He had six living children from two marriages. When each of his children married he would give them a start of 80 acres. John W. married his granddaughter Elva Ann, daughter of his eldest son John I. and Nancy (Cox) Cook. John I. had served in the major battles of the Civil War. John and Elva first lived in a log cabin and built a large frame home in Madison Twp. In 1890 they had one son Lloyd I. Thompson. They moved back to Sugar Creek Twp. and bought a farm in the White Church community. Elva was already a member of the Church of the Brethern. In 1910 Lloyd married Zora E. Stover of Colfax; she was born in 1894 to Roy E., and Viola Holt Dunbar Stover. They married in St. Joseph, MI and spent their first months of marriage in Darlington before purchasing the family farm at the north edge of Sugar Creek Township. They had three children, Margaret 1911, John T. 1915 and Marirovene 1924. The family was Methodist and social life was around Potato Creek Church. Margaret graduated from Home Hospital Nurses School in 1932 and worked many years at the Culver Union Hospital. She married Herbert Cox Jarvis in 1938 a farmer in the New Ross area. They had two daughters Doris Ann and Carole Jane. Doris married Peter Keller, they have two daughters and reside in Denton, TX. Carole married Jerry Jaquess in Indianapolis where they reside and they have two daughters. Herbert Jarvis died in 1962 and Margaret married Walter McIntire in 1964; they moved from their farms in New Ross and retired in Darlington.

John I. Thompson was a farmer and mechanic, he married Harriett Louise Driver, they have a daughter Karen Beth Coffenbery. Karen has one daughter and lives at Lake Holiday. Both John and Harriett are deceased.

Marirovene was an office worker and bookkeeper - cashier for 41 years.

The family enjoys many stories from their Mother Zora which were related many times from her early ancestors particularly from her Mother's side the Davis family who arrived here from Virginia. When the Davis family came they bought a farm in Tippecanoe County which is now Purdue University; they suffered so many setbacks from the flooding of the Wabash River and the Indians stealing their livestock, They bought a farm 20 miles away in Clinton County a mile and one half from Colfax.

Her great grandmother Eliabeth (Tharp) Davis watched for the first train that was coming through near their farm and with her children they rode on the flat car into Colfax. The train burnt wood and had to make frequent stops to put in wood and built up steam.

She resided with her grandparents, John Joseph and Mahala (Davis) Holt. Her grandfather was born in New York City of Irish Immigrant parents. His father died of a heat stroke working on a roof, his mother was unable to care for him and he became one of the orphan train children, coming to Jefferson, IN. When he became working age his first job was cutting railroad ties for the Pennsylvania R.R. Later he became a gravel road contractor and built many of the gravel roads in the area.

Her father Roy E. Stove and a bachelor cousin Guy Bailey homesteaded two sections 12 miles from the Canadian North Dakota territory border. He was the first postmaster of the area and also named the County Towner. Her mother later married Morton P. Dunbar a widower with three sons; they owned and operated a very large general store the buildings which now are the famous Miller's Catfish restaurant in Colfax.

Several of her close relatives served in political offices. Those included Charles Davis, assessors in Clinton County, Pete Davis, trustee for Perry Township in Clinton County. Roy A. Holt and Uncle, trustee of Sugar Creek Twp. and Montgomery County Treasurer, also a cousin John Hudson was elected to Democrat Mayor of Lafayette during the Depression years. At that time he was the youngest mayor that had ever been elected to office.
Submitted by Marerovene Thompson

THOMPSONS

Lawrence L. Vaughn Thompson (poet, composer, retired teacher, librarian, genealogist) and Princess (Stone) Thompson (musician, retired teacher, sales person) moved to Crawfordsville in the fall of 1981 at the insistence of son Lee "Squeak" Thompson, who had lived there for several years. (All of their living children, however, have at one time either lived or worked in Crawfordsville.)

Lawrence L. Vaughn and Princess (Stone) Thompson

Mr. Thompson, born at Prairie Creek, IN (Vigo County) on Feb. 25, 1911 to John Carl and Osia (Yeager) Thompson, comes from a long line of pioneer stock (1700's) —Germany, France, England — one line going back to the 1050's (the Polk family) of Abelard and Heloise fame!

Also, his Thompson line includes the authors Maurice and Will H. Thompson (brothers) — cousins to him—and Oscar (son of Will H.) and "Elder" Wilson Thompson, grandfather to Maurice and Will H. Oscar was born here in Crawfordsville. The family lineage comes through a Closs II Thompson (1763-1817) and Rebecca Wilson (1767-1821) of North Carolina.

The father of Closs II married a Jane (Jones) Lee, lineage ancestor of one Lee family line to Crawfordsville. Maurice and Will H. were somewhat related to their wives—to Alice Lee and Ida Lee, daughters of John Lee of railroad work here. Maurice was born James Madison (not Maurice) Thompson; another brother was born Thomas Jefferson Thompson. There were several sisters, too, children of Grigg and Diantha—Grigg, a Baptist minister and possible author (sermons).

Writing and singing seem to have been a special family trait.

Princess Stone, daughter of Sol and Ophelia (Kincaid) Stone, was born Apr. 28, 1918 at St. Helens, KY but was reared at Terre Haute, IN, where she received her B.S. degree (Indiana State) — as did her husband-to-be. Violinist, pianist, organist—Mrs. Thompson has performed at many places over the years: including Turkey Run Inn, Milligan Memorial Church, the late Mr. Al Boone's at the New Richmond museum, and the Holiday Inn here. Mr. and Mrs. Thompson, joint author-composers of several books, non-commercial, (he, with a talent for melody; she, with a talent for harmony) have taught many years—many subjects—in several states.

Present interests: Church—Friendship Baptist (she, associate organist; he, soloist, pianist, now and then); Sunshine Chorus; Historical Society, Genealogy Section; American Association of University Women Writers' Group; Christian Writers' Group; Friends of the Library; Montgomery County Retired Teachers Association (she, a recent president, 1987-88).

Mr. and Mrs. Thompson celebrated their 50th wedding anniversary the afternoon of Dec. 24, 1988 (married at Prairie Creek, IN, on Christmas Night) at the Holiday Inn here. Seven children: (1) Carlton "Rocky:—mechanic, carpenter, Crawfordsville; (2) Lee "Squeak"—roofer, construction worker, Crawfordsville; (3) Joe—State highway worker, Bellmore, IN; (4) Ocie—chef, Lancaster, OH; (5) Larry—factory worker "quality control"-formerly at Bloomingdale, IN, now (1989) living near Columbia, SC: (6 and 7)—Claire and Rebecca—deceased (Claire, gifted child in the book *Come back, Phyllis*).

PHIL AND REBECCA (PRIEBE) THOMPSON

Rebecca Suzanne (Priebe) Thompson was born Nov. 9, 1949. She is the only daughter of Mary Louise (Smith) and Fred Herschell Priebe. She was graduated from New Market High school in 1967. She married Phillip Ray Thompson July 2, 1968. She graduated from IU School of Dentistry in Dental Hygiene, 1970.

Phillip Ray Thompson was born to Clarence Leon and Mildred Jean Thompson July 19, 1949. He graduated from New market. Phil is a Pressman at Donnelley's where he has worked since 1967.

Phil and Becky have one daughter, Misha Daun who was born July 8, 1972. She is a Senior at Southmont Jr-Sr High School. *Submitted by Mary Louise Priebe*

RUSSELL G. AND PHYLLIS M. THOMPSON

Russell G. and Phyllis M. Thompson were married at Grace Lutheran Church in Elkhart, IN on Saturday, Apr. 4, 1953.

Russell Glen has lived in Montgomery County all his life. He was born on the family farm near Alamo on Wednesday, June 11, 1924. His parents were Leo K. and Ivy Myrtle Luzader Thompson. His grandparents were also Montgomery County residents—Arlie and Evaline Layne Thompson and Sherman and Icy McClure Luzader. Russell has one older brother, Ernest Ray Thompson.

Phyllis Marie was born in Elkhart, IN on Oct. 18, 1924. She graduated from Elkhart High School in June 1942, and she attended Elkhart Business College. She is the oldest of seven children born to Kenneth E. and Grace Yeakey Neff.

Russ graduated from Alamo High School in the spring of 1942. Shortly afterward, he entered the Service of his country, serving with the Army Engineers in the South Pacific in World War II. During the Korean conflict he was with the Air Force, stationed at Lawson Air Force Base in Georgia. He was discharged in the fall of 1952. Russell served an apprenticeship at R.R. Donnelleys and was employed there for 37 years until his retirement.

Paul, Russell and Phyllis Thompson - Claudia Neff, Carolyn Holt and Tony

Phyllis and Russell had five children: Claudia Joann, Karl Jeffrey (deceased in 1959), Carolyn Jean, Paul Allen, and Anthony Glen. All of the children graduated from Crawfordsville High School in the classes of '72, '78, '80, and '82.

Claudia (now Mrs. Steven Neff) at the writing, lives in Jeffersonville, IN where she is an audit officer for Indiana National Bank Corp. She graduated from Indiana University campus at South Bend, IN Cum Laude. She and Steve have a son, Curtis.

Carolyn Thompson Holt is now employed by the U.S. Postal Service as a carrier in the West Lafayette Post Office. Prior to that she was employed by Sommer Metalcraft for eight years. She attended Purdue University.

Paul is married to Susan Lyn Warren and he is employed by Inland Container Corp. They are the parents of Kyle Allen an Kristin Marie.

"Tony" for many years was a competitive Sugar Creek AAU swimmer. He is a 1986 DePauw University graduate and at this writing is a graduate student in the chemistry department at the University of Illinois in Champaign-Urbana, IL.

In semi-retirement years Russ works for Crawford Food Stores. Phyllis returned to secretarial work after the children were nearly raised. She worked at Larry Cummings, Inc. for nine years and is now employed part-time in the office of Christ Lutheran Church.

Russell and Phyllis are charter members of Christ Lutheran Church and over the years have been very active. Russ also is a member of the Alamo Lodge. Thru the years, they have enjoyed traveling, camping, gardening, music and theatre.

STEPHEN AND RUTHANNE THOMPSON

Stephen and Ruthanne Thompson have been associated with the establishing of The Mormon Church in Montgomery County from its beginning in the summer of 1967 when they returned from school at Brigham Young University, (see article on The Church of Jesus Christ of Latter-day Saints).

Their children were born (Todd Nelson 1967, David Day, 1969, Rachael Ellen 1970, Andrew Jay 1972, Charitiann 1974, America Jean 1975, and Stephen Corydon 1976) and began to attend Mt. Zion School. Through their elementary years they enjoyed solos in musical production, advanced reading and math, and excellent teachers. At Waynetown School they participated in and enjoyed band, more academics, and some sports. They then attended Northridge and North Montgomery High School, where those that have graduated did so in the top ten of their class. The older three have gone on to Brigham Young University. Their oldest sons have served two-year missions for the Mormon Church: Todd to Belgium/Netherlands and David to Brasilia, Brazil, South America.

Thompson Family - back row: Stephen, Todd, Andrew, David. Front row: Ruthanne, Charitiann, Rachael, Corydon, America.

Ruthanne, who was valedictorian of New Albany High School, has served two terms on the North Montgomery School Board. Stephen, having graduated from Crawfordsville High School, returned to teach physics and mathematics at Crawfordsville for 17 years. He began in 1984 giving computer software seminars.

Ruthanne Day is the daughter of Neil Gilbert Day and Mary Josephine Garver. Neil Day, born 1919 in Huntingburg, IN, is the son of William Harry Day and Frances Rose Hoffman. William H. Day, born 1894 in Warrick Co., IN, is the son of William Travis Day and Sophia Dysee Bruce. Frances Hoffman, born 1896 in Pike Co., IN, is the daughter of Peter Henry Hoffman and Mary Elizabeth Doughty. Mary Josephine Garver, born 1918 Terre Haute, IN, is the daughter of Claude Estee Garver and Maude Daisy Beeson. Claude Garver, born 1888 in Greene Co., IN, is the son of Ira Alvin Garver and Sarah Josephine Motz. Maude Beeson, born 1890 in Clay Co., IN, is the daughter of Jonathan Beeson and Mary Catherine Long. Ruthanne has ancestors from France, Belgium, Germany, and The Netherlands, as well as from the British Isles.

Stephen Jay is the son of David Lewis Thompson and Martha Jean Todd. Jean Todd is the daughter of Carl Summers Todd and Dailie Opal Cory of the Mt. Zion Community. Carl Todd, born 1892 in Carroll Co., IN, is the son of Thomas Corydon Todd and Clyda Mary Paddack and still farms at age 96, (see articles on the Todds of Mt. Zion and the Paddacks of Darlington). Dailie Cory, born 1894 in Wallace, is the daughter of Joseph Edward Cory and Mary Ann Levingston. Mary Levingston is the daughter of James Levingston and Martha Ann Lowe of Fountain Co., IN, (see article on the Corys of Wallace). David L. Thompson is the son of Leo Leighton Thompson and Pearl Dean Reynolds of Crawfordsville. Pearl Reynolds, born 1890, is the daughter of Lewis Washington Reynolds and Mary Luenza Wright. Mary Wright is the daughter of James Crawford Wright of Waveland and Sarah Mullen of Lyons, IA, (see articles on the Thompsons of Whitesville and the Reynolds of Waveland).

JAMES A. THOMSON

In the year 1830, James A. Thomson and his wife Martha came to Indiana from Nicholas Co., KY. James was born May 26, 1799, Martha born Nov. 22, 1804. Their children were: Joseph born Jan. 8, 1825; Mary Oct. 29, 1826; Levi Aug. 28, 1828; Wallace May 12, 1831; Chester May 8, 1833; Martin Dec. 9, 1835; Susan June 5, 1838; Cynthia Aug. 12, 1840; William Apr. 22, 1843. William enlisted with Union Army, was wounded at Battle of Chapion Hill in 1863. He died July 9, 1867. Chester also served in Civil War. He was a Lt. Col. in 72 In. Vol. Mrs. Thomson died May 26, 1866; Mr. Thomson died Dec. 28, 1867. Both are buried in Shannondale Cemetery. Mr. Thomson entered land in 1830. He also served as a judge. They were charter members of the Bethel Presbyterian Church at Shannondale, IN. Mr. Thomson served as clerk of the board for 33 years.

Martin Thomson their son, married Laura Tullis of Attica, IN, on Oct. 24, 1860. After their daughter Lenna was born, Martin entered the Civil War as a Union soldier serving in 72 In. Vol. Regiment. Martin was promoted to Quartermaster Sgt., Mar. 6, 1865, by order of Lt. Col. Chester Thomson, who was his brother. After the war, Martin and family moved from Indiana to Paxton, IL, in 1865. In 1882 he moved to near Centralia, IL. Their children now were; Lenna born Jan. 12, 1862; Flora May 30, 1867 (died in infancy) Everett Dec. 5, 1868; Charles Sept. 14, 1870; Chester July 25, 1874. In 1888 they moved to Girard, KS, and located on a farm in Crawford County. Martin and Laura were members of Presbyterian Church; Martin died Apr. 25, 1894.

Charles Thomson son of Martin and Laura, married Nellie Gemmell of Girard, KS, on Oct. 1, 1897. They were members of the Presbyterian Church. Charles was a farmer and carpenter. Their children were: Merle born Apr. 18, 1899; Anna July 3, 1902; Theodore Sept. 18, 1904; Willis Nov. 15, 1906; Arthur Oct. 11, 1908; Elizabeth Oct. 10, 1910; Paul May 24, 1914. Charles and Nellie spent their married years living near Girard and McCune, KS. Charles passed away Feb. 23, 1933.

Paul Thomson son of Charles and Nellie, married Olive Lanfear of Caldwell, ID., on Aug. 12, 1935. Paul and Olive had gone to McCune, KS High School together and graduated in 1932. Those were the depression years, Olive had gone west with her family in 1933, before her and Paul were married. Their children are: Robert born Dec. 2, 1937; Barbara June 15, 1942. Paul and Olive were involved for many years with Church, school, grange and 4-H club work. They led 4-H for 15 years. Then Paul's health failed and he passed away on Oct. 18, 1984.

Now it is time for our present Thomsons to carry on in the future.

JOSEPH EDMUND TIMMONS

Joseph Edmund Timmons was born in Montgomery County Oct. 4, 1934. His father, Wilbur Edmund Timmons married Helen Marie Sicks on Dec. 24, 1933 in Mt. Zion Church near Crawfordsville. He has two sisters. Nancy Ann married Gerald Martin McBee and has five children; Connie Jo, Mark Allen, James Martin, Mary Ann and William Franklin. Patricia L. married Max Lee Ryker (who died 1987) has three children; Jeffery Allen, Jon Scott, and Marsha Sue.

Joseph Timmons married Eleanor M. Ward on Oct. 2, 1955. Her parents were Clayton Sanders Ward and Helen Hawthorne Rhoades. They have four children. Deborah Lynn, born in 1956 is a teacher in Nashville, TN. Thomas Edmund, born in 1959, married to Magda Miranda of Honduras, lives in New Jersey and is employed by Nabisco. Belinda Leigh born 1960 and employed by Hi-Tek is married to Daniel R. Dickerson a Donnelley employee. They live in Crawfordsville and have two children Jamie Leigh born 1983 and Eric Daniel born 1985. Their youngest daughter is Rebecca Marie, born 1966; is a student at IUPUI in Indianapolis.

Joseph graduated from Darlington High school and Indiana Business college. He has been associated with Union Federal Savings and Loan Association in Crawfordsville since 1954. He became president/manager in 1973. He is a member of First United Methodist Church, Kiwanis and Boy Scouts of America, as well as work related organizations.

His scouting awards include Firecrafter, Order of the Arrow, and Silver Beaver. He served as Scoutmaster of troop #342 sponsored by the First Christian Church from 1970-1987. In 1980 he became the first recipient of the National Eagle Scout Association Scoutmaster Award presented by the Crossroads of America Council.

He had helped 27 boys earn the coveted Eagle award at that time. In 1987 the Commission for Church and Youth Agency Relationship in cooperation with United Methodist Church and Boy Scouts of America presented Joe Timmons with the God and Service recognition award. Today Joe Timmons continues to serve in his community with his work in church and service organizations. He is still involved in scouting and continues to encourage boys to work for their Eagle rank in BSA. *Submitted by Eleanor Ward Timmons, 1989*

ROBERT H. TINSLEY

Robert H(arvey) Tinsley, son of Harvey R. and Elizabeth (Dunn) Tinsley; born in Crawfordsville, Montgomery Co., IN, Feb. 17, 1880.

Harvey R. Tinsley, son of William and Hettie Tinsley, was born in Clonmel, County Tipperary, Ireland. He moved to Crawfordsville, Montgomery Co., IN, in 1866. He subsequently purchased a hardware store which he operated until his death, which occurred in 1926. His wife, Elizabeth (Dunn) Tinsley, was born in Frankfort, IN, daughter of Dr. William P. and Maria (Jones) Dunn. Mrs. Tinsley died in 1894. Mr. and Mrs. Tinsley were the parents of seven children, Robert Harvey having been fourth in order of birth.

Dr. William P. Dunn, father of Elizabeth (Dunn) Tinsley, was born in Madison, IN. His father, Judge

Williamson Dunn, was the son of Samuel and Elinor (Brewster) Dunn. Williamson Dunn, as a soldier in 1813, traversed the whole region of the Wabash Valley on horseback and ten years later, about 1823, he brought his family from Madison, IN, to Crawfordsville, IN, where they settled. Judge Dunn was a strict Presbyterian, and took an active part in the founding of Wabash College. He donated the ground on which the first college stood. This ground was sold and with money procured from the sale, and other donations, the present site was purchased. Judge Williamson Dunn married Miriam Wilson. His mother, Elinor (Brewster) Dunn, was born in Augusta Co., VA, Jan. 25, 1754. She was one of the Brewster Sisters, who gave aid to soldiers of the Revolution. They spun, wove, knit, sewed, and cooked to supply needs of the soldiers. They melted their household utensils of pewter, molding them into bullets, which were sent to the soldiers. Elinor (Brewster) Dunn is buried in the cemetery on Indiana University Campus in Bloomington, IN. A stone marks her grave.

William Tinsley, father of Harvey R., was born in Ireland. He brought his family to America, landing in New York City in 1847. He moved to Cincinnati, OH, where, in his capacity as an architect, he designed and built Fountain Square in Cincinnati and the Ohio State Capitol Building at Columbus, OH, in addition to many other buildings. Prior to the Civil War, he moved to Indianapolis, IN, where he designed and built Christ Episcopal Church and the first Butler University buildings. He later designed the buildings for Wabash College. William Tinsley died in Indianapolis. His wife, Hettie Tinsley, whom he married in Ireland, was a native of that country.

Robert H. Tinsley, the subject of this sketch, was graduated from Wabash College, B.A., in 1903. He was associated with his father in the hardware business until 1931, when he retired for five years. In 1936 he took office as Auditor of Montgomery County and in 1938 was re-elected to the office for a four year term beginning in 1940. Mr. Tinsley, who is a Republican, is a member of the following: Blue Lodge, F. and A.M., Commadery (K.T.), and Shrine; Elks Lodge; Crawfordsville Country Club; Montgomery County Chapter, Citizens Hist. Assn.; and Presbyn. Church. His favorite recreations are golf and fishing.

In 1917, Robert H. Tinsley married Maple Myers, who was born in Danville, IL, daughter of Eader and Lavinia (Tanner) Myers. Eader Myers, who is deceased was in the sporting goods business. His widow resides in Detroit, MI. Mr. and Mrs. Tinsley have no children. *Citizens Historical Association Biography, 1940*

ANNA MARTHENE TITUS

Declared to be "the prettiest baby in Montgomery County" by her proud grandma' Cedars, Anna Marthene Titus made her entrance into the world on Apr. 20, 1942. The fourth daughter and seventh child of Raymond J. and Mildred Cedars Titus joined three sisters, Barbara, Betty and Janice and three brothers, Richard, Billy and Robert.

Anna attended Smartsburg Grade School where she had perfect attendance in third grade. She was awarded a scrapbook from teacher Emma Linderman. Although the country school lacked many things, including indoor restrooms and a cafeteria, it featured two things that she particularly enjoyed - a rotating collection of library books and a music teacher who came once a week. Anna loved to sing and would volunteer to sing solos for her music teacher and class. She also wrote poetry and was asked on one occasion to recite an original poem before a PTA meeting.

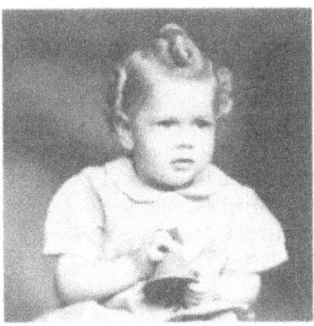

Anna Marthene Titus

One of the most exciting events occurred in second grade. The class read a story from their reader which was aired over the local radio station.

Anna's father liked to garden. One of Anna's delightful memories is running barefoot through the freshly plowed garden on a cool summer night. Anna who also enjoyed growing things planted flower seeds every Spring.

As a child, Anna had an interest in spiritual things. When she heard the church bells ringing, she would beg to go to church. When her Aunt Edna heard of her desire, she arranged for her to be picked-up and taken to Sunday School. It was not, however, until attending a youth camp at the age of 16, that Anna understood the claims of Christ on her life, and made a personal commitment to Christ as Savior.

Upon graduation from Crawfordsville High School in 1960, Anna attended Cedarville College (Ohio) majoring in Elementary Education. After completion of her degree, she taught in Xenia, OH, Indianapolis and Lafayette, IN. She completed a master of science in education degree at Purdue in 1978. While working on her master's degree, Anna was employed at the West Lafayette Public Library. This was to be the beginning of a second career for her. From there, she went to the Purdue libraries where she worked from 1978-1986. She enrolled in library school at Indiana-University in Bloomington, and was awarded her Master of Library Science in August 1987. Upon completion of her degree, she accepted the position of Head of Special Services at the Crawfordsville District Public Library where she is presently employed.

Anna enjoys needlecrafts. While in Lafayette, she worked as a volunteer, teaching art and crafts to the residents of a nursing home. Anna still loves to sing, and finds an outlet to express the joy in her heart through church choir and ministering through music to the residents of nursing homes.

Anna has used her training to work with various children's groups. She enjoys cooking and baking as well as canning and freezing fresh fruits and vegetables. For recreation, she enjoys reading, hiking, biking, bowling and water aerobics. *Submitted by Anna Titus*

JESSE NOBLE TITUS

Jesse Noble Titus, born Aug. 31, 1792, brought his family from Butler Co., OH, to Alamo in Ripley township in the mid-1830s.

In 1843, he laid to rest his wife Sarah VanArsdale in the Bunkerhill Cemetery outside of Alamo. Three years later, he married Catherine Smith, who was born Nov. 25, 1813 in Rockingham, VA, the daughter of Daniel and Christian (Stonebraker) Smith. Jesse and Catherine had two children: Sarah Ellen Stonebraker, born Feb. 10, 1847, died Dec. 28, 1924 in Montgomery County; and Adam Jasper.

The federal census records indicate that throughout Jesse's life, he routinely housed and fed many members of his extended family on his farm east of Alamo. He died on Mar. 7, 1871 and was buried next to his first wife. Catherine also was buried in Bunkerhill Cemetery in 1897.

Adam Jasper Titus, like his father, farmed near Alamo. He was born May 22, 1850 and died on his birthday in 1930. In 1873, he married Julia Hole, born Nov. 8, 1851, the daughter of Isaac and Amanda (Gabriel) Hole. They raised seven children: Estella Mae Garrison, Sarah C., Isaac Guy, Betty E. Johnson, Ernest B., Paul Harold and Ruth E.

Julia died in 1929. She and Adam are buried in Oak Hill Cemetery, Crawfordsville.

Their oldest son, Isaac Guy, was born Mar. 5, 1881. On Nov. 10, 1902, he married Minerva Susan Long, born Nov. 3, 1884, the daughter of Valentine and Mary (Wallace) Long. The couple resided in and around Crawfordsville. He was employed with Johnson Acetylene Co. and R.R. Donnelley and Son, where he was an electrician. They had six children: Gerald Leroy, Raymond Jasper, William Arnold, Isaac Guy Jr., Julia B. Tilford and Eileen Sharp.

Minerva died on Sept. 9, 1945 and Isaac died on Jan. 20, 1948. Both are buried in Oak Hill Cemetery.

Their son Raymond followed in his father's footsteps as a mechanic and electrician. Born July 18, 1906, he married Mildred Cedars on Sept. 24, 1927. She was born May 27, 1905, the daughter of John W. and Nora E. (Stephens) Cedars. They had eight children, Richard, Barbara Adams, William, Betty Korhonen, Robert, Janice Mueller, Anna and Nancy Soards.

Raymond died Mar. 18, 1971 and is buried in Oak Hill Cemetery. His wife still resides in the house he built on the east side of Crawfordsville.

RAYMOND JASPER TITUS

Having a long-standing interest in cars, it was natural that Raymond Jasper (Ray) Titus would go to work (for his uncle, Willard Howie) as an auto mechanic at O'Dell's corner. This was after his marriage to Mildred Cedars which had occurred on Sept. 24, 1927 in Crawfordsville. Mildred worked as a waitress at the Crawford Cafe. It was love at first sight for Mildred when she met Ray on a blind date. His dark eyes and dark curly hair attracted her to him. Being of a rather shy nature, Ray took his brother, Arnold along for moral support. Mildred, however, refused to go out with Ray until he took his brother back home.

While their first born son, Thomas Richard (born Sept. 6, 1928) was a baby, they moved to Anderson, IN where Ray worked for Delco Reme. From there, they moved to Middletown, IN before returning to Crawfordsville. Here he worked for the Perry Lewis Motor Company before opening his own auto repair shop on Pine Street. While Ray kept busy at the shop, Mildred was busy at home. One of her favorite activities was baking spice cakes, which Ray could smell all the way home from the shop. He ran his own shop for seven years, during which time, a daughter Barbara Jean was born (Apr. 14, 1930), a son, William Edward, born Sept. 11, 1931, a daughter Betty Joann, born June 27, 1933 and a son, Robert Joseph, born Nov. 7, 1936 were added to the family. In 1937, he closed his garage and went to work for the Mid-States Steel & Wire Company. He also farmed with his dad on the side, doing custom hay bailing. An exciting year for the Titus family was 1939 as this was when they bought three acres of ground on the East side of town and broke ground for their new home. Ray and his sons helped build the house and Ray and his father did the wiring. A third daughter, Janice Darlene was born during the house building days on July 6, 1939. On Mar. 1, 1942, the family moved into the home. Anna Marthene (born Apr. 20, 1942) joined the family as a house-warming present. A fifth daughter Nancy Ellen was born to the couple Nov. 6, 1945.

After working as a machinist for approximately 20 years, Ray left MidStates to work at the Crawfordsville Light & Power Plant where he was employed from 1958 until his death on Mar. 18, 1971, at age 64.

All the Titus children attended Smartsburg grade school and Crawfordsville High. See separate biographies.

William (Billy) Titus loved farming since childhood. He helped his grandpa and dad by driving the tractor, when his feet could barely reach the pedals. He left school to join his older brother in farming fulltime. He farmed at Thorntown and Royal Center, IN until his untimely death in the farm-related accident in 1952.

Mildred enjoys traveling and collecting salt and pepper shakers from the various states. She also enjoys attending church and especially the singing of hymns.

The question is: will the Titus name continue on? This remains to be seen. Raymond Titus fathered three sons — Richard, Billy, and Robert. Richard had two daughters, but no sons. Billy died at age 20. Robert had twin boys, David and Randy. David has a daughter. Randy is unmarried.

ROBERT JOSEPH TITUS

Robert (Bob) Titus started in 1956 as an assistant operator at the Crawfordsville Power Plant. Having been hired by Mayor Paul Stump, he was dismissed shortly after the 1960 election. With the help of Dr. Burks he secured employment at Raybestos Manhatten, working in a variety of production jobs and layout inspection. He spent the last four years as an electrician. In 1971, he joined Inland Container as a maintenance mechanic, where he is presently employed.

He married Carol Kay Smith, daughter of Earl William and Lilly Smith in 1958. Carol's sisters include: Geraldine, Lorella, Wilma ad Erthie Belle. A brother, Earl William Jr. completes her family.

Twin sons, David Wayne and Randolph Layne were born on Feb. 21, 1959. Finding the task of rearing twins challenging, Carol was instrumental in starting a chapter of Mother of Twins Club in Crawfordsville in 1963, and served as president for several years.

Two daughters, Susan Kay, born Mar. 28, 1960 and Teresa Rae, born July 24, 1962 completed their family.

Upon graduation from Crawfordsville High School, David joined the Marines in 1977, while Randy enrolled in Indiana University's School of Journalism. Upon Randy's graduation in 1981, he first worked as a feature writer at the *Anderson Herald* in Anderson, IN. He left to to St. John's Hospital to work in public relations. After completing his term of service, David married his penpal sweetheart from Japan, Yasuko Noseda, daughter of Mr. and Mrs. Ikuo Noseda on Valentine's day, 1981. They have a daughter, Stephanie Marie, born June 19, 1985. David is presently a member of the Iowa Air National Guard.

Susan married Larry D. Watt, son of Jerry and Minnie Watt. They have three sons, Christopher Duane, born Dec. 31, 1977, Jeremiah Robert, born July 21, 1981 and Drew Lewis born Mar. 13, 1989. Larry works for R.R. Donnelley & Sons. Susan is employed by Pace Dairy.

Teresa married Gordon Ray Anderson, son of Rose and Harold Anderson, on June 9, 1984. A daughter, Whitney Lea was born on her birthday in 1987. Gordon works for Fleetwood trailers. Teresa is employed by Initially.

A graduate of Coal Creek High School, Carol was employed by the Agriculture Department prior to her marriage to Bob. After rearing her family, Carol returned to the work force and is presently employed by Thrifty Supply in the accounting department. Her hobbies include reading, ceramics and needlecraft. Bob enjoys hunting, bicycling and entertaining his grandchildren. *Submitted by Carol Titus*

THE TODDS OF MT. ZION

The Todds of the Mt. Zion community arrived here in March of 1907 from the Gravely Run area of Franklin Twp., Montgomery County, where they had lived for about 14 years. Well-known to this area are the children of Thomas Corydon Todd and Clyda Mary Paddack (see article on the Paddacks of Darlington): Ruth Lucille Todd who married Clarence Mitts and lives near Detroit, MI; Carl Summers Todd, who married Dailie Opal Cory (see article on the Corys of Wallace), and still farms at age 96 in the Mt. Zion community; Frank Husted Todd, who married Ruth Oppy, both of New Richmond deceased; Mabel Clair Todd, who married first Warren William Davis and second William R. Hays, now lives in Bloomington, IN; Oscar Byron Todd, who married first Bernice Elmore and second Helen Marie Mapes, lives in the Mt. Zion community; Mary Thomasine Todd married Everett Clare Plaster both of Lafayette, IN, deceased; and James Foster Todd, who never married and died in 1972.

Oscar Bodillion, America Summers Todd

Thomas Corydon Todd, born 1860 in Carroll Co., IN is the son of Oscar Bodillion Todd and America Summers. Oscar and America are buried in the Attica Riverside Cemetery. America Summers, who was orphaned around age eight with her younger sister Rosetta and brother Gregory, was born in New Albany, IN, in 1830, the daughter of James Summers and Zelima Gregory. James Summers was a school teacher. The Summers children were raised by a Thomas Thompson family in Delphi, IN. Oscar Bodillion Todd, born 1829 in Fayette Co., PA, was the son of Dr. James Caldwell Todd and Nancy Jane Johns. James and Nancy are buried in Zion Cemetery near Flora in Carroll Co., IN. James C. Todd was a pioneer physician in Carroll Co., IN, as well as a Justice of the Peace and early schoolmaster. Nancy Johns, born 1801 in Washington Co., NY, is the daughter of John Jacobs and Rebecca Bowell. Dr. and Mrs. J.C. Todd brought their family to Carroll County in 1837. James C. Todd, born 1795 in Washington Co., NY, is the son of John Todd and Jane Caldwell. John Todd, born 1756 in New Jersey, is the son of the Scotch-Irish Andrew and Mary Todd, who immigrated to America. Jane Caldwell, born 1761 in Washington Co., NY, is the daughter of William Caldwell.

THE TRACY FAMILY

The Tracy family were pioneers in Montgomery County, arriving here in the fall of 1826 from Fleming Co., KY. Three sons of John and Nancy Tracy — Bazle, and two brothers—braved the uninhabited wilds of that time to settle in the area of Wayne Township.

Bazle, who brought his wife, bought 80 acres of land with $100 that took him four years to save, before moving to Indiana. Life was difficult for them and they found work at anything to raise a few cents. He split rails and worked three months in a distillery for three dollars per month. Later, he bought cattle and sold them to new settlers on the prairie for teams. Among his other financial ventures, he shipped goods to New Orleans, sold pork and wheat in Chicago, and continued to buy land.

Saphronia Tracy ca 1890

Although Bazel was illiterate, the 1860 U.S. Census indicated that he was worth $7000 in real estate and $1800 in personal property, substantial sums for the time. He gave each of his children 80 acres of land and had eight farms containing over 200 acres each and had 900 acres in Wayne Township in 1881. He was a Democrat and belonged to the Christian Union Church.

Bazel was born in 1802 in Mason Co., KY but grew up in Fleming Co., KY, where he married Elizabeth Price (born May 8, 1804) on Mar. 14, 1822. They had 11 children, six of whom were dead by 1881: Ann, Thomas, Sarah, Elizabeth, William, Lyddia, Mary, Martha, James, and John.

Less is known about Vezey Tracy, brother of Bazel, who made a land entry in Coal Creek Township in 1827: E 1/2 of NE 1/4 Sec 27. He was born Apr. 9, 1801 in Lexington, KY and it appears that he was married twice and possibly three times. His first marriage is thought to have been to Rachel Hayden, Aug. 14, 1829 in Lewis Co., KY; secondly, to Nancy Grinard Oct. 8, 1839. His children from these marriages and their approximate birthdates included Jonathan (1831), Emily (1834), John H. (1835), Amanda (1838), George (1840), and Francis M. (1841).

Jonathan married Elizabeth Dancer Oct. 3, 1850 in Montgomery County; George married Sarah E. Gilky (born Aug. 15, 1839 in this county) Sept. 1, 1859, and Francis married Mary J. Parker Sept. 2, 1859 in Montgomery County. Mary was the daughter of John Parker and Jane Westfall, both of whom are thought to have been from Virginia.

Only one child of Francis and Mary Tracy is known at this time—Saphrona Ellen Tracy, born May 30, 1860 in Coal Creek township, Montgomery County and died in Riverton, NE of Bright's disease, Aug. 21, 1915. Saphrona married Alfred Newton Waechter, son of Swiss immigrant carpenter, cabinetmaker, and Civil War veteran John Jacob Waechter.

Saphrona was nine when her family settled in Iowa in 1869. There may have been stops in Illinois, since her family does not appear in the 1860 Indiana Census. She married Alfred Waechter Feb. 12, 1880 and had three children: James L. (1881-1924), Arthur T. (1888-1970), and Elsie Viola (1897-1974). Saphrona left five brothers, names unknown, according to her obituary. She and her husband are buried on a hilltop overlooking the Republican River at Riverton, NE. Her descendants continued to move westward, and then eastward again, and are found in Colorado, California, Washington, Ohio, and Maryland.

JAMES TRIBBETT

James Tribbett was born in Maryland, Sept. 18, 1788. In 1816 he posted a marriage bond of $150 to show he was marrying Sarah Gibbons in good faith. They moved west by wagon and settled on a site that would become Darlington, where they purchased 80 acres for $100 from the government. This land grant was signed by President John Quincy Adams. They raised nine children to adulthood. Their third son, John Tribbett, married Anna Cox of Darlington. She was disowned by the Quaker church for the marriage. They owned 400 acres of land and two lots in Darlington, one where the library now stands. They raised eight children to adulthood. Their second son, Franklin, married Orpha Kasher. They lived all of their married life on a farm two miles east of Darlington, where they reared four children. Their second child, Lynn E. Tribbett was a farmer in the Darlington community most of his life. He married Stella Caldwell of Boone County, whom he met when he was doing carpenter work for her father. They were the parents of seven children: Louis W. Tribbett of San Bernardino, CA; Lois Jeanette (died at age three in 1915); Donnis Inell (Mrs. Raymond) Anderson of Darlington; Everett E. Tribbett of Rialto, CA; Frank H. Tribbett (died Apr. 15, 1984); Wesley D. Tribbett of Darlington and Rosemary (Mrs. Paul) Vermillion of Port Lavaca, TX.

Wesley was born near Darlington, Dec. 5, 1921, his birth certificate says, but his mother says it was December 6. A graduate of Darlington High School, he served as a B-29 command pilot, stationed on Saipan, flying 29 combat missions over Japan. All four Tribbett brothers were in the U.S. Air Corp; three of them were pilots. Wesley married Martha G. Fletcher, daughter of Walter and Zora (Lehman) Fletcher of near Darlington. They have lived in Darlington since W.W.II at 303 Madison for the last 35 years. Wesley retired in 1983 after 25 years as superintendent of Darlington Light and Power. He was a 34 year member of the Darlington Volunteer Fire Department. Their children are: Bonnie Sue (Mrs. Steve) Booher of Green Bay, WI. Carolyn Louise of Indianapolis. Lindy Michael of Lafayette and a graduate of Purdue and Dee Ann of Indianapolis, a registered nurse and Purdue graduate. Their two grandchildren are: Michael Steven Booher of Crawfordsville and Karen Sue (Mrs. Steve) Sherwood of West Lafayette, a Purdue graduate. The great-grandchildren are: Sara Sue Booher and Matthew Booher, children of Michael and Tami (Murphy) Booher.

Louis Tribbett has researched and written a history of the Tribbett family, which was the source of much of this material. *Submitted by Mr. and Mrs. Wesley Tribbett*

JOHN TRIBBETT JR.

John Tribbett, Jr. was born May 24, 1921 to John and Helen McDowell Tribbett. He was the eldest of nine children. He married Miss Emma Lou Gregory in their newly furnished home on the Grant McDowell farm in Franklin Township near Shannondale. The grandparents of John Tribbett, Jr. were Grant and Addie Shook McDowell and Charles O. and Della Morris Tribbett.

John Jr. graduated from Dover High School in Boone County. He was the 21st person to be drafted from Montgomery County on July 24, 1942. During World War II, John served three and one-half years in the U.S. Air Force. He was assigned to the Pacific Theatre of Operation for some 31 months. He was stationed at Clark Field in the Philippines at the end of the war. He was a farmer in Franklin for 30 years and was employed for 15 years at the Montgomery County Co-Op in the petroleum department as a route driver. John was a Republican Precinct Committeeman for Franklin Township for 20 years.

John Tribbett family, John Tibbett Jr.

Emma Lou was born Nov. 29, 1926 in Darlington, the daughter of Ollie and Grace Mae Sparks Gregory. Her father was the high school basketball coach and teacher at Darlington High School. Her mother died when Emma Lou was 29 days old and she was raised by her maternal grandparents, Oscar and Emma Beck Sparks. She graduated from Dover High School. Emma Lou was employed in the Montgomery County Treasurers Office for 25 years. She served as Montgomery County Treasurer for two terms-first elected to the office in 1978. She was a Republican Vice-Committeeman for 32 years.

John and Emma Lou are well remembered for the total destruction of their farm, by a tornado, on Palm Sunday in 1965. All buildings and cattle were destroyed, but their three children (ages 15, 12, 11) escaped injury by hovering under a stairway in the basement of the house. John and Emma Lou had purchased the 79 acre Olive Hutton farm on Dec. 23, 1964 so they and their children moved there after the tornado. They have goats and a donkey on their farm.

John and Emma Lou have three children:

John Robert Tribbett, who was born on July 28, 1949. He is a graduate of Darlington High School, Indiana State University and Valparaiso Law School. He is an attorney in Crawfordsville. He married Janice McDonald of Marshfield, MO on Nov. 27, 1982.

Janet Sue Tribbett, who was born on June 11, 1952. She is a graduate of Darlington High School and Indiana College of Business and Technology. She is employed at Raybestos Products Company.

James Allen Tribbett who was born Mar. 28, 1954 is a 1972 graduate of North Montgomery High School where he played basketball. He is a graduate of Florida State University. He is a basketball coach and teacher at Greensboro College at Greensboro, NC.

THE TURNIPSEED FAMILY

Many Montgomery County natives recognize Turnipseed Corner as a familiar landmark of Sugar Creek Township. At the intersection of the Darlington-Stockwell and Linden-Colfax roads, sits the American Gothic style Turnipseed family homestead which was featured in *Montgomery County Remembers*, 1976, and described as, "...an unusual and decidedly lovely vision." The home and farm are still owned by the family heirs.

The first member of the Turnipseed family to come to Sugar Creek Township and occupy this home was Nathan Chaney Turnipseed who came from Highland Co., OH in 1870. He was born Oct. 15, 1855 to Thomas and Mary Jane Chaney Turnipseed.

The home of Nathan and Martha Turnipseed, 1915

On Dec. 2, 1879, he married Martha Boots, the daughter of Asa and Elizabeth Rice Boots. Asa Boots had come to Sugar Creek Township in 1834 with his parents who purchased land there for him and his brother. In 1878 Asa purchased 80 acres adjoining his farm and gave this to Martha. Nathan and Martha Turnipseed expanded this farm to over 200 acres.

Nathan Turnipseed became a prominent farmer and citizen in the northern part of the county. A Republican in politics, he served for several years on the Montgomery County Council. He was also a trustee of the Potato Creek Methodist Episcopal Church.

They had five children, all of whom are now deceased: Clarice who married Will Jobe; Elinore who married Frank Custer; Marie; Walter Asahal who married Vena McBee and lived out his 91 years in the family home; and Thomas B. who married

Hallie Fisher in 1915. The one-room brick schoolhouse that the Turnipseed children attended is still standing just south of the family home.

Thomas and Hallie Turnipseed owned the farm south of the homeplace. They were active members of the Potato Creek Methodist Episcopal Church. Thomas continued Nathan's role as a county leader, also serving on the Montgomery County Council. At the time of his death in 1959 he was chairman of the Council and the following resolution was passed honoring him:

"Thomas B. Turnipseed was well and favorably known by the Citizens of Montgomery County as a successful farmer, family man, and able administrator of the financial affairs of the county.

His long and honorable service in the Council, many years of that service being as president, is worthy of permanent praise. We of the present council shall miss his friendly manner in the conduct of the council affairs, and his gracious treatment and handling of the many citizens of this community who appear before us."

Hallie Fisher Turnipseed's parents were William and Martha Waugh Fisher. The Fishers and Waughs were both pioneer families in Sugar Creek Township. Martha Fisher's father, Milton Byron Waugh, was Captain of the Home Guards during the Civil War. He took a prominent part by helping to raise the quota for his township and caring for the wives and children of the enlisted. One of his sons, James W. Waugh, left his estate to Wabash College to build the science hall known as Waugh Hall.

Thomas and Hallie Turnipseed had one child, Mary Ellen Flaningam, who graduated from Ball State University and worked for many years at the Montgomery County Welfare Department as a caseworker. She has one child, Martha Ellen Flaningam, who graduated Summa Cum Laude from Webster College, Webster Groves, MO, with a degree in Fine Arts. She also received a Master of Fine Arts degree from Northern Illinois University. Both Mary Ellen and Martha Flaningam currently reside in St. Louis.

EMMETT A. AND EVA D. (FITZWATER) UTTERBACK

Emmett Andrew Utterback was born on Jan. 12, 1903 at Elmdale, IN the only child of Lester William and Elva Leona Jaynes Utterback. They were farmers most of their lives near or around Elmdale and Waynetown, IN. He was educated in the Waynetown schools and later moved to Crawfordsville, IN.

Eva Darlene was born Apr. 12, 1906 at New Maysville, IN the seventh child of Newton Tyler and Mary Margaret Bailes Fitzwater. She was educated in the Roachdale schools as well as Kirkpatrick schools.

On Oct. 15, 1926 Emmett Andrew and Eva Darlene were joined in matrimony after a lengthy courtship. To this union five lovely children were born: Margaret Leona, Lester Newton, Martha Darlene, Donald Eugene and Mary Ann. It was on Mar. 5, 1933 little Martha Darlene at the age of seven short weeks passed away. She is buried at Masonic, Waynetown, IN.

Emmett was an avid lover of horses, and gave much of his later years in training and grooming them. He passed away July 1, 1961; is buried at Masonic Cemetery, Waynetown, IN.

It was for the love of people that Eva became interested in nursing. This she carried through until her final days, on Mar. 1, 1964 at the age of 57 years she quietly went to sleep. She is also buried at Masonic Cemetery, Waynetown, IN.

HURSEL AND KATIE BETHEL BARNHART UTTERBACK

Hursel and Katie Bethel Barnhart were married on Nov. 8, 1919 at Greensburg, IN. They resided at 510 Hubbard Street, Crawfordsville, IN.

Katie Bethel Barnhart was married first to William McKinley Deckard and their son, Richard Deckard, was born Oct. 1, 1913.

Hursel Utterback, born Jan. 31, 1891 in Paris, IL was the son of James H. and Margaret Wycoff Utterback. He had two brothers and two sisters and was educated in the Bloomington and Indianapolis schools.

Hursel and Katie Bethel Barnhart Utterback 1968

Katie Bethel was born at Hope, IN on June 2, 1905, the daughter of George and Christena Cummins Barnhart. George was born in Germany and immigrated to the United States. A heavy wood camel back trunk he used to carry his possessions in from Germany, was given proper respect through the years.

Christena was 20 years old and George, a Veteran of the Civil War, 35, 15 years older when they married Aug. 26, 1876 at Hope, IN. They had three sons, George Samuel, Leslie Ervin, William Layden and three daughters, Irene Rose, Gertrude May and Katie Bethel.

Following George's death Christena Barnhart came to Crawfordsville to live in the Hursel and Katie Utterback home for eight years. She was 81 when she died Nov. 9, 1939. Buried in Oak Hill Cemetery.

Hursel was associated with the dry cleaning business. A veteran of World War I he was a charter member of the Crawfordsville Veterans of Foreign Wars Post 1431. He served as commander of the Post in 1928-1941. Also was the Post Quarter Master in the 1950's.

Katie Bethel was a charter member of the Crawfordsville V.F.W. Auxiliary and was an interested active and enthusiastic person devoting considerable time to the Auxiliary.

The Utterback couple were well known in their neighborhood and were respected by all that knew them.

On the night of Jan. 27, 1937 with their families present, Richard Deckard and Marian Marciel Himes were married at the home of Reverend Arthur of Crawfordsville. Marian Marciel was the daughter of Chester and Ruby Linn Himes from Whitesville, (see index Himes and Deckard).

Hursel was a member of the Christian Church of Indianapolis. He retired in 1961. Their home on the east side of Hubbard Street was always neat and the large yard that fronted the house allowed ample room for their grandchildren, Jill, Jack, Cheryl Deckard to play. Richard and Marian lived in the new home nearby.

Hursel and Katie Bethel observed their 50th Wedding Anniversary in an afternoon reception at the Trinity United Methodist Church at 110 S. Blair Street, Crawfordsville on Nov. 9, 1969.

Hursel died July 5, 1970.

Katie Bethel occupied her time more quitely with crocheting and needlepoint work and enjoyed her family and friends. She was the last charter member of the Crawfordsville V.F.W. auxiliary when she died Apr. 11, 1977. Both are buried at the Oak Hill Cemetery.

JOHN G. UTTERBACK

John G (ail) Utterback, son of Albert J. and Elizabeth D. (Gott) Utterback; b. in Wayne Twp., Montgomery Co., IN, Nov. 25, 1877.

Albert J. Utterback, son of Henry and Amy (Blankenship) Utterback, was b. in Wayne Twp., Montgomery Co., IN, Feb. 3, 1850. He was reared on his father's farm and attended rural schools. He later farmed in Wayne township. He died Dec. 30, 1924. He was a Democrat, a member of the Masonic Lodge, and the Methodist Church. Albert J. Utterback was twice married, his first wife being Elizabeth D. (Gott) Utterback, whom he married Nov. 9, 1876. She was born in Brown Twp., Montgomery Co., IN. They were the parents of two children: (1) John Gail. (2) Ernest, who is decd. On Apr. 31, 1893, Albert J. Utterback married Mary Francis, daughter of George and Jane (Bartley) Francis.

Henry Utterback, father of Albert J., was born in Virginia, and in 1840, when a youth, accompanied his parents to Montgomery Co., IN. His father, Thompson Utterback, entered Govt. land in Wayne Township, where he developed a fine farm. He lived there the remainder of his life. Henry Utterback was a farmer. He married Amy Blankenship, a native of Kentucky, and they were the parents of nine children: (1) John B. (2) Albert J. (3) William. (4) Martha. (5) Carrie H. (6) Charles H. (7) Jemima. (8) Harmon. (9) Stella.

John G. Utterback, the subject of this sketch, attended high school in Crawfordsville, IN, and later was a student of Askin's College of Embalming (now the Indiana College of Embalming), at Indianapolis, completing a course embalming and undertaking. In February 1927, Mr. Utterback established a funeral home at Crawfordsville, and since 1929, has operated the establishment with William Lawrence Murphy, as a partnership, the Utterback & Murphy Funeral Home, located at 300 South Grant Avenue. Mr. Utterback, who is a Democrat, is a member of the following: Blue Lodge, F. and A.M., Consistory (32nd deg.); Elks Lodge; Montgomery County C. of C.; Montgomery County Chapter, Citizens Historical Association (an honorary member); and Methodist Church. His favorite recreation is traveling, and he has visited in every state in the Union. Mr. Utterback owns a farm, comprising 288 acres of land, located in Wayne and Union Townships in Montgomery County, where he does general farming.

On Dec. 27, 1899, John G. Utterback married Pearl Bagwood, daughter of Richard and Mary (Frazier) Bagwood. Mrs. Utterback was born in Montgomery Co., IN. There are no children. *Biography by Citizens Historical Association, Aug. 1940*

JAMES AND ESTHER RUSSELL VAIL

James Vail was born in Pennsylvania on Feb. 6, 1792, and died in Union Township, Montgomery Co., IN, on July 7, 1871, being buried in Mt. Pleasant Cemetery, west of Cherry Grove. He married Esther Russell (born Feb. 7, 1803) on Aug. 18, 1821, at Middletown, Butler Co., OH. Her parents were George and Mary (Vail) Russell, who were married at Uniontown, PA, June 5, 1797. Her grandparents were Stephen and Mary Fitz Randolph Vail, from New Jersey, who were the founders of Middletown in 1802. James and Esther Vail had a daughter, Sarah (Sally) born Aug. 14, 1825 in Middletown. Sarah said she was two years old when they moved to Montgomery County. Esther's brother, Isaac Russell, and wife, Mary, settled at Lafayette, Tippecanoe Co., IN. Esther died on July 12, 1834.

Esther Russell Vail

James Vail then married, first, Lavina Lincoln, Oct. 24, 1834, and second, Salina Hampton. Both evidently died, for he married Martha Ann Clevenger White on Apr. 20, 1843 (widow of William Thomas White). She was born Sept. 29, 1816 in Butler Co., OH, and came to Montgomery County with her parents in 1832. James and Martha Vail had seven sons — Alvan, Noah, Peter, Samuel, Shobal, James and Albert — all half-brothers to his daughter, Sarah (Sally).

Sarah Vail married Samuel Williams in December, 1841, and had a son, James and a daughter, Esther. Samuel died in Jasper Co., IN, Mar. 8, 1852. She married Alvarian Osborn at Rensselear on Aug. 21, 1852, and returned to a farm near Montgomery and Fountain County lines Southwest of Waynetown. They had four children — James, Martha, Rhoda and Sarah Elizabeth. Alvarian Osborn was born somewhere in Kentucky in 1827. He enlisted in the Civil War in Grant County, Aug. 21, 1862; but died of typhoid fever, Dec. 27, 1862, and was buried near Munfordsville, KY. James and Rhoda both died. Instead of pursuing a pension, Sarah married Simeon Osborn whose wife had died. On May 16, 1880, Sarah died of a malignancy, and was buried in the Beaver Cemetery. Through Sarah's great grandmother, Mary Randolph Vail, she and her descendants are eligible for many lineage organizations. This include Magna Carta Dames and Descendants of the Knights of the Garter from its Founder, King Edward III of England. Edward Fitz Randolph, the pilgrim, came to Massachusetts in 1631. *Submitted by Mary Elizabeth Cedars*

WILLIAM RILEY AND LILLIE ANNA (FLETCHER) VAIL

William Riley Vail was born Nov. 15, 1870 near Linden in Montgomery Co., IN, the second child of Shobal C. and Nancy (Shelley) Vail. Shobal was the son of James A. Vail and his second wife Martha Ann Clevenger. Nancy was the daughter of David Shelley of Tennessee. Riley Vail had three brothers — Charles, Henry M. of Indianapolis, and James Edward of Linden — and a younger sister Martha.

In 1896 in Montgomery County Riley Vail married Lillie Anna Fletcher, who was born Feb. 15, 1876 in Montgomery County near New Market, the oldest of 13 children born to Foster Alexander Fletcher and his wife Mary Catherine Smith. Lillie Anna had been married first to Charles Pittenger, who died in their first year of marriage.

Wm. Riley and Lillie Ann (Fletcher) Vail Wedding Day Dec. 31, 1896

Five daughters were born to Riley and Lillie Anna—Elizabeth, Mae, Mary, Edith, and Clara.

Elizabeth Bernice Vail, the oldest daughter, was born Feb. 6, 1898 in Linden. In 1917 she married Fowler Ezra Kunkel of Waynetown. Fowler's sister Emma Charlotte had married Elizabeth's uncle, James Edward Vail. Elizabeth and Fowler settled in New Richmond, where they raised five children— Donald Riley, Ralph Fowler, Elizabeth Maxine, Betty June, and Marjorie Ann.

Lala "Mae" Vail, the second daughter of Riley and Lillie Anna, was born Mar. 26, 1901 at Cherry Grove. In 1918 she married Isaac Samuel Fowler, a first cousin of her sister Elizabeth's husband. Mae and "Ike" also settled in New Richmond.

Mary Catherine Vail, the third daughter of Riley and Lillie Anna, was born Dec. 15, 1906. In 1925 she married John V. Rice, who deserted her in St. Louis after she fell ill. She returned home and died in 1927.

Edith Alberta Vail, the fourth daughter of Riley and Lillie Anna, was born Sept. 27, 1909 at Cherry Grove. In 1928 she married Kelsey Leland Thomas of Lafayette, who had a baby son Byron from his first marriage. Edith and Kelsey have five children of their own—Audrey, Robert, Anna, Larry, and Margaret Kay. They celebrated their 60th wedding anniversary in 1988 and still live west of Crawfordsville on State Road 136.

Clara Lucille Vail, youngest daughter of Riley and Lillie Anna, was born Jan. 3, 1914 at Cherry Grove. In 1932 she married Robert Edward Bair, by whom she had four sons—Albert Lee, Ronald, William, and Raymond. Although a long time resident of New Richmond, she now resides in Linden.

Lillie Anna died in 1924, when her youngest daughter was only ten years old. She was buried in Oak Hill Cemetery near her parents. In 1928 Riley married his second wife, Bertha (Hensley) Roach, with whom he spent the last ten years of his life. Remembered as a kind and soft-spoken man who loved to joke, Riley died in 1938 and was buried in Mount Pleasant Cemetery.

VALENTINE FAMILY HISTORY

Dwight and Dorothy Valentine have lived and farmed south of Darlington along County Road 675 E for almost their entire lives. Dwight Dorman Valentine was born Sept. 15, 1906, at Catlin, Vermillion Co., IL, to Russel John and Dottie Belle Cook Valentine. Russel had one brother and five sisters. Dottie had a twin sister, Della Bertha Cook. Russel's parents, Curtis N., and Catherine Martens Valentine, whose father Frederick emigrated from Germany in 1809, moved from near Circleville, OH, to a farm near Catlin.

Dottie's parents, George W. and Eliza Douglass Cook had been residents of Vermillion County since early in the 1800's. In fact, Cyrus Douglass and Ruby Bloss, Dwight's great, great grandparents are recorded in 1826 as the first couple to be married in the newly constituted Vermillion County. Their son, Dorman Bloss Douglas (1827-1915) was said to have found gold during the gold rush of the 1850's. He owned considerable land near Catlin.

Dwight, Dorothy and Marilyn Valentine, 50th Wedding Aug. 15, 1986

In 1913, two Indiana acres could be bought for the price of one Illinois acre. This fact lured Russel and Dottie Valentine from the lush, black soil of the eight mile prairie near Henning, IL, to the infertile, yellow clay of a farm, part of which is in the Lake Holiday development in this county today.

What a challenge this move must have been! The baled hay and farm tools were shipped by railroad boxcar. The household goods and grain were hauled on horse-drawn wagons. Incredible though it seems, the livestock was driven or led the 50 or so miles from northern Vermillion Co., IL, to southwest Montgomery Co., IN. Imagine such a caravan on the roads of the 1980's. The move was accomplished despite the undoubted hardship on man and beast, luckily before and not during the great flood of 1913. Road construction nearby that year saved the day. Four dollars per day was paid for a man and team, and this bridged the financial gap left by poor crops.

In 1914, another move was made to a farm about four miles north as the crow flies. There were 50 acres of fertile creek bottom land, but a big hill to climb and marginal water supply left something to be desired. A 14 mile move was made in 1920 to an 80 acre farm in the Young's Chapel area north of Crawfordsville. Now here was black, level land similar to the prairie land of Vermillion Co., IL. Falling land and farm prices during the "farmer's depression" of the 1920's made it difficult to pay off mortgages requiring an abundance of hard work.

Russel Valentine died Nov. 7, 1929, at the age of 49 of a heart attack. This tragic event required that his son, Dwight, drop out of Purdue in the middle of his third year and become a farmer in his own right. In 1935, Dwight and his mother moved to the

Alamo area to live with her widowed sister, and Dwight continued farming in that area, renting the other land to Lester Hole.

Dwight met Dorothy Esther Christiansen of Alamo at a Sunday School picnic, and they were married Aug. 15, 1936. Their daughter, Marilyn Jane Valentine was born July 4, 1937. The Valentines moved to the Darlington area in 1940.

Dorothy, born May 8, 1915, was the daughter of James Christian Christiansen and Minnie Alice Warbritton. Dorothy has one sister, Gladys Autumn Warbritton Jones who lives in Crawfordsville. Marilyn is a combination of the Scotch, Irish and German ancestry of Dwight and the Danish and another touch of Irish of Dorothy. James came to this country as a teenager on a freighter, returning later to bring the family to Galesburg, Il. James had two sisters, one of whom, along with her entire family, was killed in a train wreck.

Marilyn Jane received a good basic education in the Darlington Public Schools and received her college education from DePauw and Northwestern, graduating in 1959 with a degree in Home Economics. For many years she worked at General Electric Corporation where she met her husband, Robert E. Rollins. Bob is retired while Marilyn is employed by Ott Communications Corporation. Marilyn has one step daughter, Debra Ann.

When Dwight gets into a reflective mood, he finds it almost incredible the number of changes within his lifetime: from horsepower to jet propulsion, from mud roads to paved interstates, and from no electricity or phones to an electronic society. *Submitted by Dwight and Dorothy Valentine*

AD VANCLEAVE FAMILY HISTORY

Ad Vancleave was born Feb. 18, 1865 west of New Market, IN on the family farm just off Route 234.

Ad's ancestor, Jan Van Cleef came to this country about 1653 settling in New Utrecht, Kings Co., Long Island, NY. He was 36 years old. He was born in 1628 coming from the town of Cleef, Holland. He died about 1699.

Through the years the name changed spellings due to poor education and Census Takers spelling as it sounded. Some are Van Clief, Van Clyff, Van Cleave to our Vancleave.

Ad and Ida Vancleave, back row: Edith and Beatrice

Jan VanCleef is listed to have had nine children. His son, our ancestor, Isbrant born about 1678 married Janneke Aertse Vanderbilt who was born Sept. 17, 1682 in New Utrecht. Arron VanCleave, son of Isbrant, born 1711 probably New York, married at Princeton, NJ September 1734 to Rachel Schencks. He was thought to be Captain of a seacoast vessel, from records found. Arron and Rachel had seven sons and one daughter named Jane. She married Squire Boone, brother of Daniel Boone, and she had five of her brothers went to Kentucky with the Boones. She died in 1815 and is buried in a cave in Harrison Co., IN.

Jane's brother Benjamin VanCleave, our ancestor, was born in New Jersey married Ruth Monson, July 11, 1765 in North Carolina. They went with the Boones to Kentucky. They had 13 children. Ralph the sixth child was married to Elizabeth Stibbins Feb. 27, 1805, their first son Johnathan born Dec. 13, 1805 died Mar. 5, 1900 married Elizabeth VanCleave (possibly a cousin) Sept. 6, 1827; she died Apr. 23, 1886. Johnathan came to Indiana with his parents in fall of 1826. After helping clear land to build a cabin he went back to Kentucky for his bride. They lived there all their lives.

Johnathan joined Indian Creek Church of the "Old School" Baptists in May 1842. His wife joined in July same year. Johnathan became an Ordained Minister Nov. 17, 1849. He preached at Indian Creek Church from 1846 to 1899, 53 years.

His son Ransom VanCleave, Ad's father, born Dec. 17, 1838 died Mar. 13, 1923 married Sarah Surface Oct. 28, 1858. She was born Apr. 10, 1837 died Mar. 4, 1906. They had 13 children. Ad was their sixth child. Ransom was a cabinet maker and farmer.

Ad married Ida Frances Denman Sept. 3, 1891. They had two girls. Beatrice Alma born Aug. 29, 1897 married Clyde Melvin June 1, 1916. She survives. Edith Aline born Sept. 21, 1899 died Dec. 23, 1950. She married Oscar E. Ackerson who survives and is soon to be 99 June 1989.

Ad and wife and daughter Edith are buried at Alamo Cemetery. *Submitted by Melva Melvin*

Some of this information was taken from a book compiled by the late Johnny VanCleave who was a junk dealer north of Yountsville, IN. I am the daughter of Ad Vancleave. (Beatrice Melvin)

RALPH VAN CLEAVE

The dates and names written are from the records of Elva Sayler Milligan, written April 1947, and from the Van Cleave Family Record Book.

Ralph Van Cleave born Mar. 18, 1784, married Elizabeth Stubbins, born Feb. 12, 1789. They were married Feb. 29, 1805. They had eight children: Jonathon, born Dec. 13, 1805 - died Mar. 5, 1900; William, born Aug. 23, 1807 - died Sept. 30, 1838; Lucy, born Apr. 1, 1810 - died Apr. 5, 1824; Jane, born Feb. 14, 1812 - died July 13, 1846; Malinda, born May 15, 1814 - died Apr. 7, 1846; Nancy, born Dec. 16, 1817 - death unknown; Cary B., born Sept. 29, 1819 - died Sept. 26, 1823; Emily, born Oct. 4, 1822 - died June 9, 1853.

Ralph and Elizabeth Van Cleave were the great-great grandparents of Elva Sayler Milligan. Ralph Van Cleave died Feb. 2, 1855 and Elizabeth Van Cleave died on Nov. 23, 1848.

Front row: Edwin Van Cleave, Sarah Van Cleave, Walter Sayler - Baby Robert Francis Sayler, Back Row: Francis Milbert Sayler, America Malinda Sayler and Elizabeth Opal Sayler

The great-grandparents of Elva Sayler Milligan were Malinda Van Cleave, and Jonathon Van Cleave, who were first cousins. It was not unusual during those days for cousins to marry. They had five children: Isiah, born Oct. 10, 1836, died Dec. 25, 1907; Emily, born July 4, 1838, died Aug. 24, 1841; Edwin, born May 2, 1841, died Oct. 14, 1916; Marion, born Nov. 10, 1843, death date unknown; Rebecca, born Apr. 3, 1846, died Feb. 18, 1847.

John Van Cleave died Mar. 1, 1846 and Malinda Van Cleave soon followed on Apr. 7, 1846.

Elva's grandparents were Edwin Van Cleave and Sarah Proctor Hicks. Edwin married Sarah on Dec. 26, 1861. Sarah was born on July 30, 1842. They built a log cabin in 1861, the year they were married. It was located on 80 acres one and three-quarter miles southwest of New Market, IN, on County Road 225 West. It is the present location of the Lovold residence. The cabin was a two-story structure with the two rooms above built in 1879. A kitchen and back porch were added in 1894. In 1914 another enclosed porch was added. The original barn was built in 1879.

To this union were born seven children; Emily Elizabeth, born Nov. 17, 1862, died Aug. 22, 1937; America Malinda, born Jan. 3, 1865, died Mar. 19, 1945; John Sanford, born Sept. 19, 1867, died Dec. 15, 1887, Paulina Jane, born July 15, 1870, died Sept. 2, 1949, Laura Alice, born Mar. 11, 1873, died Apr. 14, 1950; Effie May, born Jan. 17, 1876, died Dec. 7, 1961, Nancy Alma born Apr. 23, 1879, died Dec. 29, 1974.

Emily Elizabeth married Albert Armstrong, born July 26, 1865, on Oct. 18, 1891. Albert was killed by a horse on July 30, 1913. Emily died Aug. 22, 1937.

They had four children. Lawrence, born May 5, 1892, died Dec. 2, 1974; Clifford Nelson, born May 14, 1898, died Mar. 22, 1900; Edwin Clay, born Mar. 12, 1901; Mary Lenore, born Sept. 24, 1902, died Apr. 10, 1960.

America Malinda Van Cleave married Francis Milbert Sayler mentioned in the Sayler family history found elsewhere in this publication.

The other four Van Cleave sisters never married.

These dates and notes are from the records of Alma Van Cleave. *Submitted by Larry G. Sayler, a great, great, grandson of Edwin Van Cleave*

WALLACE VANCLEAVE

Wallace Vancleave was born 1881 in Walnut Township, son of Henry Newton and Sarah Mahala Linn Vancleave, and died in 1943 in Darlington, Franklin Township. His mother died in 1884, but he had a good stepmother, Jane (Jennie) Wible Vancleave. His occupation was a paper hanger and decorator but his avocation was anything musical. He was a stubborn person, and when he was 11, his stepmother told him not to go hunting with his father and some other men, but he went, and was shot in the knee, and was always crippled after that. He was known as a ventriloquist and entertainer. He made a one man's band, a great invention of the 20th century. I don't know what year he made the band, but in 1920's he was entertaining all over the county and outside the county. He called his show a musical and ventriloquist show. His one man band was about six feet by four feet by six feet. It was a wooden slot frame and held instruments, operated by pedals. He played the violin, had a harmonica attached around his throat, he could play. He had 18 instruments in the band. He had four guitars, four mandolines, a drum, bells, cymbals, etc. He played perfect time and harmony. He had two dummies one on each end of slots called Henry and Sallie. One time a little four year old boy was listening to him in the Montgomery Ward Store, and he had the dummies talk to the little boy, calling him by name, and the boy was thrilled to pieces. He had a horse head he called Black Diamond, said to have a human mind. Sambo was a little cardboard boy on front of his band, and it danced and kept perfect time. He had pedals to operate all these instruments, and played the violin with his hands and had harmonica attached to his neck, and operated that with his mouth. Took him 20 years to build it. Today his instruments would have been known far and near, and he'd have been on T.V. programs. He had no musical training. He sang too. He had a musical genius for putting together such a wonderful one man band.

He never married until late in life, and he married Nan Pace. He had a brother Milt and sister Lillie, she died young.

REBECCA DELLINGER VAN HORN

Rebecca Powell Dellinger Van Horn was born in Tipton Co., IN, Jan. 18, 1917. She moved to Montgomery Co., IN about 1921 with her parents, Shirl Blaine Dellinger and Rebecca Heacock Baynes Dellinger. After about 1923 the Dellinger family lived on a 23-acre farm located on the Big-4 Arch road one-half mile outside the southwest city limits of Crawfordsville.

Rebecca attended elementary school at Wilson School, graduating from Crawfordsville High School, 1936. In 1937 she entered Purdue University.

Rebecca married John Herman Van Horn, from Greencastle, IN, 1939. John was born, 1915, in Wheatland, IN, and had an AB degree from De Pauw University and a BS degree in electrical engineering from Purdue University. They have four sons: John Michael, born in Chicago, 1942; James Robert, born in Evanston, IL, 1945; Thomas Steven, born in Kansas City, 1948; and William Martin, born in Kansas City, 1955.

John and Rebecca Dellinger Van Horn

Rebecca and John lived near Chicago, IL, until 1946 when they moved to Kansas City. In 1960, they moved to Racine, WI. John worked in his profession as an electrical engineer. In 1978, John retired and the couple now live near Springfield, MO.

Son Michael graduated with honors at Raytown, MO, 1960, and has Bachelor and Masters Degrees in Business. Michael was in the Army, 1966-1968, serving mostly in Germany. He works as a Business Consultant. He is married to Elizabeth Ann McCabe McGirr. Michael and Elizabeth live in San Rafael, CA, with their daughter Rebecca Elizabeth, born in Los Angeles, CA, 1977.

Son James graduated from Racine, WI High School, 1963. James was in the Air Force, 1963-1967, as an airplane mechanic. He has an associate degree in electronics and lives near Colorado Springs, CO, with his wife Shirley Mecklin. James works as a Crew Chief in the Air Force Reserve on a C-130 airplane. James had two sons from a previous marriage: Lee Michael, born in Las Vegas, NE, 1966; and Martin Greg, born in Kansas City, 1969. Grandson Lee married Emmalee Haskisson in 1987 and presented Rebecca a great-grandson, Robert Wesley, born in Kansas City, 1988.

Son Thomas graduated from high school, 1966, in Racine, WI. He has a BA in Art and works as an artist. Thomas was in the Air Force, 1966-1970, mainly with remote duty in Kotchebue, AK in radar surveillance. He married Coleen Garity and their son Thomas Kehl was born, 1978, in Reno, NE. Son Thomas and grandson Kehl now live in Kansas City.

Son William graduated from Racine High School, 1973, and has a BA in Art and a Masters in Fine Arts. He lives in Petaluma, CA, and works as an artist, editor of an art magazine, and a landscaper.
Submitted by Rebecca Powell Dellinger Van Horn

GERRETT VANSWERINGEN

In 1657 Gerrett VanSweringen came to New Amsterdam (now New York City). He was married two times having four sons to carry the name. Some place down the line the Van was dropped, adding the "a" to Swe ingen making it Swearingen. It is not known of any other by this name coming to America.

John Swearingen, the first to arrive in Montgomery County in 1822, came from Butler Co., OH. He was married to Mary Armstrong. He landed on the banks of Sugar Creek above what is known as "Indian Ford". For some time it was questioned if he or Offield arrived first. John and Mary are buried in O'Neal Cemetery, 1844.

Family of Francis Marion Swearingen

Three years later his father, Charles (my great great great grandfather), mother, Nancy Pottenger and brother, Joseph, arrived, settling in Ripley Township. Charles was a farmer and cabinet maker. He made furniture and farming tools for his neighbors and made the first fanning mill in the county. He was successor to the original County commissioners in the 1820's. Charles and Nancy are buried in Yountsville Cemetery.

Joseph (my great great grandfather) followed in his fathers' footsteps, being a cabinet maker. He was a Baptist circuit riding preacher. It was said he could build the casket, prepare the body and preach the funeral. Joseph was married to Rebecca McConnell having nine children.

Francis Marion, a son, (my great grandfather) was born 1830, married Henrietta Gilkey 1852.

They had 16 children, 12 who married: William—Mary Price; Ida—Perry VanCleave; Alice—James Gallaway; Anna—Howard Smith; Jennie—Charles Keys; Margaret—Elmer Steele; Albert—Orpha Edwards; Florence—Walter Yount; James—Myrtle Snyder; Hugh (my grandfather)—Louise Brown; John—Bertha Linn and Harry—Julia Callihan. Infant daughter, died, Laura, Charles and Mary never married. Francis Marion lived on Road 625W just south of St. Rd. 32. Henrietta died in 1878 he in 1908, buried at Waynetown Masonic.

In 1977 there were 397 living descendents from this union. Many of them remaining in and around Montgomery County - the oldest of these is Dean Steel Record Huffman, a resident of Carmen Nursing Home. Frank VanCleave lived to be 104.

An interesting fact abut this family; a brother of Charles, Marmaduke, was captured by the Shawnee Indians in West Virginia. Charles was with him, but Marmaduke persuaded the Indians to let Charles go home if they would take him as a hostage - later Marmaduke was made a Chief of the Shawnee tribe - Chief Blue Jacket. His family settled in Oklahoma. There is a town Blue Jacket, OK. It is believed all Swearingens in America are related.

I would like to name all of our descendents but there is not room for that. There are 11 generations since Gerrett and five of those are buried within 12 miles of each other. I can go to the graves of my father, grandfather, great grandfather, great great grandfather, great great great grandfather in Montgomery County, besides many other descendents. The Swearingen name is the oldest in Montgomery County with living descendents living here. I consider this a history within itself.
Submitted by Dick Swearingen

WINFRED LEE AND ANITA ROBBINS VICE

Winfred (Slim) Vice came to Montgomery County in 1913. He was born Mar. 30, 1892 in Russelville, IN the eighth child of Robert and Louisia Carver Vice. His siblings being: Charley E., Joshua, Myrtle E., Emalie G., John L., Prudence, Harry R., and eight half brothers and sisters by a previous marriage.

Robert Vice, father of Winfred died in his sleep at age 61 in November 1895, and both parents are buried at Russelville. Due to illness and hard times Winfred was placed in an Orphans Home at the age of four in Greencastle and at age seven was transferred to an Orphans Home in Crawfordsville.

Congratulations to Ladoga on Your 150 Years
from
Family of Slim and Anita Vice a Sixth Generation Family of Ladoga
Descendants of Robert and Martha Ann Neff Robbins
Operated the Neff and Robbins Brickyard until early 1900.

Bob Vice, Martha Cornett, Winnie Golladay, Helen Bronaugh, Ruth Ward, Barbara McKenzie, Chet, Kenny, Ike, Virgil, Raymond, and Anita and Slim Vice.

Bob Vice, Martha Cornett, Winnie Golladay, Helen Bronaugh, Ruth Ward, Barbara McKenzie, Chet, Kenny, Ike, Virgil, Raymond, Anita and Slim Vice.

At the age of 12 he ran away from the Home to Michigan looking for his mother. After finding her they both returned to Indiana. He found work west of Ladoga on the Harry Stamp farm, helping train and stable horses.

On Feb. 12, 1915 he married Anita Robbins, born Dec 11, 1891 in Ladoga, the daughter of Bert and Edna Hunt Robbins. She was the granddaughter of Dr. James Allen Warbington Hunt and Mary Magdalene Peffley Hunt. Dr. Hunt was a well known dentist in Ladoga for many years. Paternal grandparents were Robert and Martha Neff Robbins, operators of the Neff-Robbins Brick Yard in Ladoga until early 1900.

Anita attended Ladoga Schools, being in the first grade of the new building, built in 1898. Prior to marriage she worked for her Aunt Carrie Robbins who owned the Carrie Robbins Millinery Shop. In later years she worked at the Ladoga Canning Company and Eva Sidners Department store. Anita was the oldest of ten children; Duff, Hugh, Ruth, Lillian, Carrie, Robert, Mabel, Wilmer, and Donald Robbins.

Winfred and Anita had 11 children, six boys and five girls. All were married; Martha to Loyal Cornett, Robert to Thelma Farmer then to Waltraut Strese, Chester to Dorothy Hicks, Kenneth to Virginia Bennett, Winifred to Samuel Golladay, Harold to Gail Olson, Virgil to Clare Harshbarger, Raymond to Eileen Zackery, Helen to Charles Bronaugh, Ruth to John Ward then to Roy Lee Moore, and Barbara to James McKinzie. Three are deceased, they are; Robert died at age 37, Mar. 28, 1953 while in the U.S. Air Force. Kenneth was owner of Kenny Vice Ford in Ladoga and died July 12, 1985 at the age of 65. Martha died Mar. 9, 1989, at the age of 73. All are buried in the Ladoga Cemetery.

There are 35 grandchildren, 58 great grandchildren, and six great great grandchildren. Two grandchildren and one great grandchild are deceased. John F. Golladay died Dec. 5, 1957 at age 13, Rex Vice died May 4, 1970 at age 27, and Great Grandchild, Kevin Graham died Oct. 27, 1970, at age two and one-half years.

Winfred was a World War I Veteran and very active throughout his life. In 1916 he helped build the Masonic Building in Ladoga and worked in the Veneer Mill. He was employed by the State Highway Department for 15 years. He was Caretaker of the Ladoga Cemetery and also worked for the Town of Ladoga.

Winfred and Anita were active in the American Legion and Auxiliary, having had the following four sons serving in the Armed Forces during World War II.

Tech. Sgt. Robert L. Vice in the Air Force, served in Germany and North Africa from 1946-1953.

Sgt. Virgil E. Vice served in the Army Air Corp in South West Pacific, 1943-1946.

Pvt. Harold L. Vice served in the Anti-Tank Division of Army Stationed at Fort Leonard Wood, MO in 1943.

Pvt. Raymond A. Vice served in the Infantry stationed at Capt Fannen Tyler, TX in 1943.

Pvt. Ronald E. Cornett, a grandson served his Country during the Korean War Army Field Artillery and was stationed at Fort Sill, OK in 1953.

Anita was one of the five Gold Star Mothers in Ladoga. Many will remember Anita for her warm and caring ways. Slim, as he was known stood six foot, three inches tall. They both had a great love for antiques and their home reflected that love.

They resided in Ladoga until their death. Winfred died Feb. 7, 1973 at the age of 80. Anita died June 19, 1982 at the age of 90, and both are buried in the Ladoga Cemetery.

All of the children still reside in Montgomery County with the exception of; Harold in Oregon and Barbara in Florida. *Submitted by: Helen (Vice) Bronaugh and Ruth (Vice) Moore*

JOHN AND ANNA WEAVER WADE

John and Anna Weaver Wade, Augusta Co., VA had nine children, and only two, as far as we know came to Montgomery Co., IN. A son, Isiah Wade, married 1. Susan Troxel in 1833 and married Sarah Jane Troxel in 1855 in Augusta Co., VA, came to New Ross, IN. One of their sons, William Southerd Wade born Dec. 31, 1834 and died Feb. 2, 1879, married Mary Jane Wilson, daughter of Joseph Wilson, had six children, lived in Ladoga, IN; George; Lew; Mary Frances Ronk; Effie Harshbarger; Addie Kellam; and John Lee died. Other children of Isiah was Zeberiah, killed in the Civil War - a Confederate soldier; Rachel Hanger; Mary Ellen Wiseman; Jackson moved to Attica, IN; Ben; and two others, names unknown. Isiah's sister, Anna married George Joh Oct. 17, 1828 in Augusta Co., VA and came to Preble Co., OH, before they settled in Walnut Township, Montgomery Co., IN. George Joh died June 1, 1888 west of New Ross. He and Anna are buried in Union Hill Presbyterian Cemetery, on highway 136 between Mace and New Ross. Their daughter Mary Jane Joh married Isaac Humbert, born 1836 in Darke Co., OH - was killed in Civil War on ship Sultana at Vicksburg, MS in 1865. Their children were: Clyde, Lilly Dora Josephine married Ulysses Harris, had Don, Earl, William, Dorothy Claypool, and Elsie Harris, lived in New Ross. Lutetia Flora Belle Humbert married James W. Linn II, and had Joseph Earl, Floyd Isaac, Jennie Flo Robison, and Dora Evaline Linn who married Orval W. Randel and had two daughters, C. Pauline Walters and V. Lucile Harpel. Lucile has no children.

Pauline born Dec. 30, 1907 married Harold B. Walters, he died Oct. 6, 1970. They had one son, Robert Lee, and he has five children and they have 13 children. All live and have always lived in Montgomery Co., IN.

Pauline is the Author of four area Montgomery County Histories, many family histories, poetry, and has written several stories for the Montgomery Magazine. She also wrote for the Bi-Centennial Issue of the *Journal Review* Newspaper, the Church Histories of Montgomery County, the death records of Montgomery County and her article Doctors of Montgomery County has been in the *Balhinch Gazette*, a Genealogy Newsletter. She was honored for her work in Genealogy by the Genealogy Section of the Montgomery County Historical Society by purchasing and donating a book in her name to the local history room of the Crawfordsville Library. She has been recording the history of Montgomery County for over 40 years. She will be 82 years of age in 1989 and lived in her own home where she keeps active recording Montgomery County's rich history. She is a member of the Whitesville Christian Church, Dorothy Q Chapter DAR, Indiana State Historical Society, and the Montgomery County Historical Society.

ORIE AND FERN WAGNER

Orie and Fern Wagner came to Montgomery Co., IN from Illinois in 1920. They were married on the farm where they resided for 44 years, in Coal Creek Township - two and one-fourth miles North West of New Richmond. Their three children were born there—Roberta Thayer of Lafayette, Helen Thayer of Crawfordsville and William Wagner of Arizona. They retired from the farm in 1975 and moved to Crawfordsville. *Submitted by Helen (Wagner) Thayer*

ISAAC WAINSCOTT

Isaac Wainscott and Hepsey Stringfellow were married in Owen Co., KY in 1823. Isaac was probably Isaac Jr. Hepsey's parents, George Stringfellow, and Milley Jennings, were married in Fauquier Co., VA in 1793. They later settled in Owen County where George died in 1840. Milley died in 1857 in Mahaska Co., IA.

The Kentucky Wainscotts descended from Richard Wainscott who came to Virginia from Surrey England in 1723. He served seven years as a bound servant to pay for his passage. Some of the later generations of Wainscotts came to North Carolina to Kentucky with the Boones.

In about 1832, this couple came to Coal Creek Township where they settled, and raised a large family. Their children, and some of their spouses were: Mary Ann - William Smith; George - Anna Cotrell; Sarah; James W. - Margaret Graves; Rev. Adam W. - Hannah Hutchings; John W. - Peggy Swank; Susannah - David Dasey; Elias (Jake) - Rebecca Oxley; Martha - John Moffet; Francis Marion; Ellen - Henry Rasor; Melvina - Peter House; and Abraham - Susan Utterback.

Isaac was a farmer, and died sometime after 1870. The burial place of this couple has not been located. There are a great many descendants of Isaac and Hepsey still living in the Montgomery County area today. Many girls named Hepsey appeared in the records over the years. Most, if not all, were descended from this Montgomery pioneer. The name came from Hepsabeth of the Bible. *Submitted by Charles M. Cook*

NORMAN R. WALKER

Norman R. Walker (born May 9, 1896 in Orange County) came to Waveland in 1927 with his wife Agnes Hurst Walker (born July 5, 1900 in Harrison County). The Walkers met while students at Indiana Normal in Terre Haute and married on Oct. 16, 1924. Mrs. Walker taught Elementary Education in Montgomery, Putnam and Hendricks Counties for 30 years.

Mr. Walker had a diploma in piano from the National Academy of Music in Chicago at age 21. He received his professional education from Indiana Normal, now known as Indiana State University. He supported himself through six years of college by teaching and performing music on both piano and organ. He took his first full time teaching position in Carrol County and was immediately selected as accompanist for the County Institute. He was also organist for the Baptist Church of Camden.

During Mr. Walker's 37 years as Music and Art teacher he was Montgomery County Music Festival Chairman for four years. He appeared in the *Hammond Times Magazine* and was named to Who's Who in music in 1954. In addition to his public school activities, he taught privately to hundreds of students around Montgomery County. His students remember him for both his professionalism and his keen sense of humor.

Mr. and Mrs. Walker reared three children during their years in Montgomery County. Mrs. Walker passed away Sept. 20, 1975 and Mr. Walker passed away Aug. 4, 1980.

Norman R. Walker

In Montgomery County their daughter, Martha Jo Walker (born Aug. 19, 1930) married Donald E. Cabbage (born Nov. 27, 1929 in Indianapolis) Jan. 1, 1950. Mr. and Mrs. Cabbage continue to reside in Crawfordsville. When added together they have 75 years of service with R.R. Donnelley & Sons Company.

William E. Walker (born Nov. 21, 1931) moved to West Lafayette in 1956 where he made a career with Purdue University and he married Marjorie Bradford of Flemingsburg, KY and reared a son William Bradford Walker (born May 21, 1964) and two daughters Melissa Allen Walker (born Mar. 20, 1966) and Michelle Taylor Walker (born Jan. 26, 1968). William Walker has retired and lives with his wife Michelle Sullivan Walker near Brookston, IN.

John C. Walker (born Nov. 16, 1936) married Diana J. Henriksen (born Jan. 20, 1942) in Billings, MT on Oct. 27, 1968. John Walker is currently living near Milwaukee, WI where they reared two sons, John Norman Walker (born July 19, 1964) currently of Brooklyn, NY and Eric James Walker (born Sept. 12, 1967) living in East Lansing, MI. John C. Walker is an executive with Longview Fibre Company.

The Walkers are well known by their voluntary contribution of musical service to the Waveland Christian Church where Mr. Walker served as organist for 46 years. When he retired as organist he was honored as Organist Emeritus. His daughter Mrs. Martha Jo Cabbage carries on the tradition as a vocalist at the Church of the Nazarene in Crawfordsville. *Submitted by Martha Jo Walker Cabbage*

REBECCA WHITTINGTON WALKER

Rebecca Whittington was the third child of Charles Edgerton Whittington and Sarah Zerelda Armantrout, both born in Montgomery County. She was born on Jan. 24, 1910 in Culver Hospital. The other children were Catharine, Richard, Anna Frances, Sarah Beth and Charlean.

Rebecca graduated from Crawfordsville High School in 1926, and from Indiana University in 1932, with honors, Phi beta Kappa. She was in graduate school one year at Indiana University. In the '30s she worked in Crawfordsville at the township trustee's office and in Terre Haute for the State Welfare Department, and in Crawfordsville as child welfare case worker for the County Public Welfare Department.

While working in Personnel at the Newport dePont plant during WWII, she joined the American Red Cross as a hospital social worker. After six months at the Naval hospital on the Marine base on Parris Island, SC, she was assigned to the Army's 198th General Hospital as Assistant Field Director, heading the Red Cross staff of five. The hospital was sent to the ETO in November, 1944 and set up in Paris in December. It served thousands of U.S. soldiers wounded in action, and released prisoners, both U.S. and Allied. After VE Day the hospital was set up again in Suippes, in eastern France.

While in France she met and married Clyde Lawson Walker, a combat infantry captain from Portland, OR, who had landed on D-day and had been severely wounded in November, 1944. Clyde served from April to November, 1945 as the legal member of the first War Crimes Commission team sent to Germany to gather evidence on the prisons. This was later part of the Nuremberg trails. Clyde was graduated from the University of Oregon and the Northwest School of Law (now part of Lewis and Clark College).

After the war Clyde was in private practice, and an attorney for the Army Corps of Engineers. For years he was head of the Legal Department for the South Pacific Division of the Corps.

The Walkers have two sons, Bruce Whittington Walker, born 1946; Craig Whittington Walker, born 1948; both in Portland. Bruce has an AB and MA from the University of California, Berkeley; Craig has an AB from the University of California, Santa Barbara, and an MA from the University of New Mexico. Bruce is a computer systems analyst in California; Craig works for a construction company in New Mexico.

The Walkers lived in Portland, in Walla Walla, in Atherton, CA and San Francisco. Rebecca and Clyde moved to San Diego in 1981. Clyde has been active in retirement in teaching English and naturalization classes. Rebecca has long been active in the American Association of University Women and the League of Women Voters, for which she served on the California state board. She has written the history of several organizations to which she belonged.

SUSAN ELSTON WALLACE

Susan Arnold Elston was born in Crawfordsville Dec. 25, 1830, daughter of Isaac C. and Maria Akin Elston, the fourth of nine children. Her father was a wealthy merchant, banker, and real estate speculator.

She attended Dr. Gibbon's Friends Boarding School in Poughkeepsie, NY from 1847 to 1849, where she became an accomplished scholar. Her mother encouraged her early literary efforts.

Susan met Lew Wallace shortly after her return from New York. They were married on May 6, 1852. They lived about a year in Covington, where their only son, Henry, was born. In 1853 they moved back to Crawfordsville, where they lived the rest of their lives, except when Lew was in government service.

Mrs. Wallace began writing poetry for publication in 1858. Her most famous poem, The Patter of Little Feet was first published in the *Cincinnati Daily Gazette*, and was reprinted widely.

After the Civil War, Lew Wallace published *The Fair God* in 1873. Although Susan was the better writer, she subordinated her writing to that of her husband, serving as critic and editor, and also handled much of his business affairs with his publishers. However, Mrs. Wallace did continue writing poems and articles for newspapers and magazines, such as *The Atlantic Monthly, Cosmopolitan, Harper's Magazine, The Independent, Ladies' Home Journal,* and others.

When Lew became the Territorial Governor of New Mexico in 1878, Mrs. Wallace wrote articles about that area, later published in book form *The Land of the Pueblos*, in 1888.

While the Wallaces lived in Constantinople when Wallace was minister to Turkey, they took a trip to the Holy Land and Egypt. Their travels were recorded in *The Storied Sea*. The other books, *Repose* in Egypt (1888) and *Along the Bosphorus* (1898) were also collections from articles concerning their experiences in Constantinople and their travels. Susan also wrote *Ginevra*, or, The *Old Oak Chest, A Christmas Story*. Her last book was *City of the King, What Jesus Saw and Heard and Jerusalem as it now Is*, published in 1903.

Mrs. Wallace was a prolific letter writer all of her life, writing as many as four or five letters a day, and she also was a composer of songs. Robert and Katharine Morsberger describe Mrs. Wallace's writing "as romantic as her husband's. She preferred to evoke old myths rather than document modern scenes, making the dead of many centuries rise and walk again. Most of her writing is more poetic meditation than guidebook detail."

Mrs. Wallace also played a prominent role in Crawfordsville's literary circles. She encouraged the literary work of young writers, especially Mary Hannah Krout and her sister's Caroline Virginia Krout.

After Lew Wallace's death in 1905, Mrs. Wallace finished his autobiography with the help of Mary Hannah Krout and saw it through to publication, in spite of her ailing health.

She died Oct. 1, 1907. *Submitted by Jean Thompson, County Historian*

ZERELDA GRAY SANDERS WALLACE

Zerelda Gray Sanders Wallace was born in Millersburg, KY in Aug. 6, 1817, the daughter of Dr. John H. and Polly C. Gray Sanders, the oldest of five daughters. She had some formal schooling, but most of her education came from her father. Her family moved to Indianapolis about 1830. She studied with a Baptist clergyman. She assisted her father in his practice of medicine. In 1836 she married Lieutenant-Governor David Wallace, whose sons she raised, besides six children of her own. When Lew Wallace wrote the novel Ben-Hur, published in 1880, he used her as the model for Ben-Hur's mother.

The Wallaces lived in Crawfordsville for a while, but when Wallace became governor, they moved to Indianapolis. As the governor's wife, she was a skillful hostess and she shared her husband's work. She read law with her stepson and became one of the best-educated women in the midwest. The former governor practiced law. He was not very successful, so that when he died in 1859, he left Zerelda with few assets. She had not only her own children to raise, but also four other children who were making their home with the Wallaces.

Mrs. Wallace opened her house to the Aid Society of the Central Christian Church in Indianapolis. In 1894 at one of these meetings the Woman's Missionary Society of the Christian Church was founded.

Also in 1874, when the Woman's Christian Temperance Union was organized in Cleveland, Mrs. Wallace was elected national vice president and continued in this post for several years.

At the second national convention of the Woman's Christian Temperance Union in 1875, Mrs. Wallace introduced the first woman's suffrage

337

resolution. She also became the first president of the Indiana Woman's Temperance Union in 1874, serving for seven years. In 1875 she headed a body who went to the Indiana Legislature to urge against the repeal of the Baxter law. She addressed the legislature. Most of the men could scarcely conceal their contempt for women in general, and temperance women in particular. Afterwards, a senator said something to the effect that representatives couldn't always vote as they would like, but must represent their constituency, which wanted to repeal the Baxter law. Mrs. Wallace's immediate reaction was why shouldn't she be considered part of his constituency. She told the senator, "You are against our cause, but I'm still grateful to you, because you have made me a woman suffragist."

Coming to the conclusion that the only way to promote temperance legislation was for women to vote, she became a leader in the formation of the Female Equal Suffrage Society in 1878.

In 1880 the Society, together with the Woman Suffrage Association led by Mrs. Wallace, gathered petitions in favor of woman suffrage and presented them to the General Assembly. A resolution to amend the state constitution to delete the word "make" passed, but was defeated in the 1883 session.

Mrs. Wallace gave lectures to temperance groups around the country at age 75. She died on Mar. 19, 1901 at Cataract, IN. *Submitted by Jean Thompson*

STANLEY HOLMES WALLS

Stanley Holmes Walls, born at Riddle, Crawford Co., IN June 6, 1896 was the third of seven children born to Rev. Samuel Lewis and Celia Briner Walls. His early years were spent in southern Indiana where Rev. Walls was a minister of the Church of the United Brethren in Christ.

Mr. Walls enlisted in the United States Navy during WWI and served as Fireman, 3rd class. He was discharged Aug. 23, 1919 at Pittsburgh, PA. In the service he learned to make beautiful belts and purses, using twine and various kinds of knots.

Mr. and Mrs. Stanley Holmes Walls

He loved working in the garden, whether vegetable or flower, and had many hobbies. He started making cement blocks at his home at 700 S. Walnut St. to build a garage, and ended up having enough to build the house, attached garage, and shop at 1606 E. Wabash Ave., where he moved, and started Walls Mum Garden in the 1950s.

A printer by trade, he retired in 1961 after 33 years at the Crawfordsville, IN *Journal-Review*, where he had been a typesetter, compositor, and night foreman. He and Mrs. Walls moved to Paradise Bay Trailer Park, Bradenton, FL and lived there until 1979. While at Bradenton he made lovely lamps using cracked marbles for the shades, and shell pictures and plaques and a variety of other things.

On Jan. 15, 1921 he married Mary Edith Oliver, at Greenfield, Hancock Co., IN, the fourth of five children of Justus Wright "Tus" (or "Pop") and Caroline "Carrie" Brodhecker Oliver of Crawfordsville, formerly of Jackson Co., IN. "Tus" was a farmer and custodian at the Interurban Station.

Mrs. Walls was born at 815 W. Wabash Ave., Crawfordsville Nov. 5, 1894, attended Indiana Business College and worked in the Montgomery County Auditor's Office and Treasurer's Office. She was a great crossword puzzle fan. She was a lovely Christian lady, loved by all who knew her, and a wonderful wife and mother.

He died July 3, 1982. She died Aug. 22, 1987. Buried at Oak Hill.

Their children are Mary Eleanor Edwards of Danville, KY and Eulalia Jean Mason (Mrs. John R.) of Crawfordsville, IN.

LEWIS AND OLIVE (MARSTELLER) WALP

Lewis and Olive (Marsteller) Walp have lived in Montgomery County 50 years. Children: Geneva Mitchell (b. 1923), of Wingate, Betty (b. 1925 d. 1948), Doris (b. 1927 d. 1945), Shirley (b. 1933) of New Richmond, David George (b. 1936 d. 1972). Robert Lewis (b. 1939), of Gosport, IN. There are 12 grandchildren and 12 great-grandchildren.

Lewis' paternal grandparents: Wm. buried Carbon Co., PA; Mary, buried Glassboro, NJ. His father, David Walp (b. 1834) came to Indiana 1880 from Pennsylvania with two young sons, William H. b. 1867 and Alfred F. b. May 1868 in Prince William, Carroll Co., PA (sons of David and Sarah (Smale) Walp). In Jefferson Co., IN S. Lavina Spicer Stout, (b. 1856) was a widow with four children: Bill, Lizzie, Dode and Ora Stout. David and Lavina were married. Their children: Bertha Mae b. March 1891 d. January 1964, Fredrick Robert b. June 1894 d. 1964, Lewis Monroe b. June 14, 1896 d. Mar. 12, 1989, David d. April 1908, and Lavina d. March 1937 and are buried Jefferson County.

Lewis and Olive (Marsteller) Walp married in 1919

At age 13 Lewis Walp came to Montgomery County to work on the Chris Martin farm west of New Richmond. He returned to Jefferson County to care for his widowed mother. He entered WWI in 1918. He returned a handsome soldier to work on his sister Mae Phillips' farm in Putnam County. A nearby farm belonged to the parents of pretty Olive Marsteller.

Olive's paternal grandparents: Nickolas and Elizabeth (Emerson) Marsteller came from Ohio and are buried at Lafayette. In 1850, they sold land to John Purdue for a college campus. A street there carried the Marsteller name. Olive's parents: George E. (b. 1862 d. December 1938) and Hettie (Perry) b. Sept. 19, 1875 d. November 1937 Marsteller. Hettie worked as a maid in the Marsteller home before she married George in 1892. Olive was born Mar. 13, 1902, one mile southeast of New Richmond on the old "Corduroy" road, one of nine children. A brother, Paul and sister, Yvette Clodfelter are living in Lafayette.

Olive's parents moved to Putnam County in 1905. When she was nine, her father had a new "Kurtzman Piano" delivered from Indianapolis. She took summertime lessons for two years from a school teacher then attended the Indianapolis Conservatory of Music for three years. When she was 16, Olive played piano during intermissions and film changes at the Russellville Movie Theater, earning $10 per night. On Sept. 20, 1919, Lewis and Olive eloped to Danville, IN. They lived 13 years in Indianapolis where he earned a "Master Mechanic" license from Chevrolet Co. and had his own garage at 4200 West Washington St. Two of their children started IPS #14. After the "Depression" the family moved to Waynetown, IN in 1939. Then in 1941 they bought a farm, south of Alamo and lived there 33 years before retiring to New Richmond, IN.

WALTERHOUSE FAMILY

Dr. Harrison Kemper Walterhouse, son of Major Thomas S. and Sarah (Kemper) Walterhouse, was born in Muncie, IN May 24, 1879. His father was a prominent Attorney in Muncie until his death in 1882. He had served in the Union Cavalry during the Civil War. Sarah Kemper was a descendant of Johannes Kemper, one of a group of 12 skilled iron workers brought to this country from Nassau-Siegen, Germany, in 1714 by Governor Spottswood of Virginia to build an iron furnace—the first in America. The Kemper home was Muesen, Germany. The Shlomann Sieman Company, at Muesen, developed the new, sophisticated machinery which is being installed in the Nucor plant here in Montgomery County. Many improvements in the iron and steel industry have been developed at Muesen.

Dr. Walterhouse received his education in the Indianapolis High School, Indiana Medical College and John Hopkins Medical School. He practiced medicine in Ladoga for 33 years prior to his death in 1947, as a result of an automobile accident. He was a well-read person who was particularly knowledgeable concerning history. In 1911 he married Emma Jane Hostetter, the daughter of David Hicks and Amanda (Graybill) Hostetter. The Walterhouse home west of Ladoga was a happy and hospitable one. Their children were David Kemper and Jane.

David Walterhouse died of bulbar polio in Japan in 1950 while serving in the Consular Service during the occupation of that country. As a result of his death, and the efforts of his mother and sister, Mitsuya Goto, an interpreter for David in Japan, came to Wabash College in 1951, graduated Magna cum laude, and he is now well-known throughout Japan, Europe and the United States.

Jane Walterhouse became a public school teacher, and later a private secretary in the George S. Olive Co., CPA's. In 1942 she married William R. Hawley, son of Karl and Marion (Pattison) Hawley of South Bend. He served for four years in the Air Force during WWII (26 months in India), completing that service as a Major. He then taught Physics at Arsenal Technical High School in Indianapolis for 22 years, and was a Realtor there for 20 years. In 1967 they moved to the family home in Ladoga. For two years both Mr. and Mrs. Hawley taught in Cono Christian School at Walker, IA. Returning to Ladoga, Mr. Hawley taught at North Putnam High School for nine years before retiring.

Four children were born to the Hawleys: John Harrison, born 1945, a member of the U.S. Marine Corps, died in Vietnam in April, 1967; David Pattison, born 1947, married Claire Stewart, daughter of George and Marie (Kerr) Stewart of Lookout Mountain, TN. David is an Attorney in Chattanooga and he and his wife and two sons (Patrick Bryant and Samuel Stewart) live on Lookout Mountain.

Druscilla Jane, born 1951, graduated from Covenant College at Lookout Mountain, TN, and there met Randy J. Carroll, son of Eugene and Virginia (Miller) Carroll, of Colorado Springs, CO. He is now a dentist in Roachdale, and they live in the former home of her grandparents west of Ladoga. William Walterhouse Hawley, born 1953, spent several years in Colorado in the construction business, and there married Victoria Lauler, daughter of Luis and Lorraine (Thorson) Lauler, of Surrey, England. He studied Engineering at Purdue University and is currently a Field Engineer at Nucor. He built a home two and one-half miles west of Ladoga.
Submitted by Jane Hawley

WILLIAM WALTERS

William Walters born 1827 Fairfield Co., OH died January 1899 New Ross, son of Jacob and Catherine Lamb Walters, married Julia Fritter, died 1910 New Ross, daughter of Enoch and Catherine Fritter on August 1856. William wounded in Civil War, was a blacksmith at New Ross. He and Julia came to New Ross 1868 with six children; Thalia born 1857 married Tilghman Brown; Illinois (Illa) Catherine married Till Rice; Alva Walters born 1860 died 1932 married Nettie Baker; Charles Walters died 1904 married Eva Shepherd; Jennie born 1867 and died New Ross; Pochontas born 1869 New Ross and died 1886; Franklin Albert Walters born July 8, 1866 and died west of New Market, IN on Mar. 31, 1939. He married Rose Jane Scott, daughter of Alfred Thomas and Martha Hannah Elrod Scott, granddaughter of Nathaniel Edward and Evaline James Scott, on Oct. 7, 1888. Rose Jane Scott Walters born Feb. 24, 1872 and died May 17, 1947. Frank and Rose lived in New Ross until 1925, when they bought a farm six miles west of New Ross and 3/4 mile south. In 1936 they bought a larger farm one mile west of New Market. Five children were born to them; Carl born May 27, 1889 and died 1941 married two times; Opal born Aug. 6, 1891 married William Owen Smith. After his death in 1951 she married Carl Shoaf and he died in 1957. She had no children. Thalia born 1896 and died 1897; Elston Virgil born Feb. 9, 1902 and died Oct. 1, 1916 New Ross; Harold Buford Walters born Aug. 12, 1909 New Ross and died Oct. 10, 1970 six miles West of New Ross, 3/4 miles south. He married Crystal Pauline Randel born Dec. 30, 1907, daughter of Orval W. and Dora E. Linn Randel, on July 7, 1928. He farmed, a dairyman, was at Home For Aged for seven years, became Milk Inspector 1950, then Health Sanitarian until his death. He received first award they gave for Outstanding Health Sanitarian in Indiana for 1962. They had one son, Robert Lee born May 11, 1929 married first Mary Alberta Williams on Nov. 20, 1949, daughter of Earl Milton and Nellie Hadley Williams. Five children were born to this union; Jeffrey Lee born Oct. 2, 1950 married Brenda Jean Durbin on Oct. 10, 1971 and has three children, Angela Kristy, Jacalyn Suzan and Ryan Lee; Larry Dean Walters born Nov. 8, 1951 married Deborah Ann Bronaugh on Nov. 13, 1971 and has two children, Matthew Ryan and Lucas Scott; Constance Kay born Jan. 17, 1954 married Stephen Truax on July 29, 1973 and has four children, Stephanie Nicole, Shannon Camille, Joshua Michael, and Joel Adam; Pamela Sue born Oct. 10, 1955 married Steven Demoret 1976 and divorced has two children, Karmon Leigh and Kesley Lachelle; Michael Robert born Sept. 15, 1956 married Debra Addler on Sept. 16, 197? and has two children Heather Michelle and Jacob Daniel Walters. The three boys, Jeffrey, Larry, and Michael live near New Ross and the girls, Constance and Pamela live in Crawfordsville.

Robert Lee Walters was a farmer, dairyman, trustee of Walnut Township, listed in 1965 edition of Jaycees Outstanding Young Men in America and active in church, and since 1970 has been Health Sanitarian of Montgomery Co., IN.

AMAZON WARD FAMILY

Amazon Ward, born Apr. 25, 1831 in Union Co., IN and the son of David and Eleanor Lafuse Ward, married Phoebe Jane Montgomery on Jan. 24, 1859. She was the daughter of James and Phoebe Fisher Montgomery who came to Montgomery County in 1832. The father David, son Amazon and others in their family had come to the Mace, IN area but Amazon only lived there about two years, then he moved to a farm northwest of Whitesville Jan. 1, 1866. In 1874 he erected a nice frame house but on Feb. 21, 1897 it burned to the ground. In March 1881 he began to build his barn. He then erected a two story house 46 x 52 made from bricks made on the farm. The house, on the Ladoga road, four miles south of Crawfordsville is still standing.

Amazon and Phoebe had four children all born in Montgomery County. Clara Belle Ward married Samuel Graybill. Camella May Ward married Thomas Wilkins. Henry Alva never married. Ulysses Grant Ward, born in 1867 married Clara Florence Sanders born 1869 in Putnam County.

Grant and Clara Ward lived in the brick house after a few years of living west of Whitesville near Lapland on state road 43. They had five children. Nora married Leroy Groendyke and had three children James, Nancy and Jean. Clayton Sanders, born 1896, married Helen Hawthorne Rhoades and had two children Edwin Grant and Eleanor Mae. Hazel Marie a twin of Clayton never married. Kenneth Amazon married Velma Christine Linn and had three daughters, Donas, Martha Ellen who married Donald Morrison, and Evelyn Lynn. Their youngest son Gordon Montgomery married Ruth White and had two children Thomas and Connie. Gordon and Ruth Ward lived in the brick house until his death in 1976. The Amazon Ward family history has been taken mostly from the *History of Whitesville and Community Montgomery County, Indiana 1970* by Crystal Pauline Randel Walters with some additions by Eleanor W. Timmons the great granddaughter of Amazon Ward.

HOMER B. AND MYRTLE EVERSON WARD

Homer Bratton Ward was born in Boone County, near Thorntown, IN on Jan. 1, 1892 and was the third child of Joseph Williamson Ward, born July 9, 1850, died Apr. 17, 1942 and Martha Ellen Bratton Ward, born Sept. 26, 1853, died Aug. 31, 1912. His sisters were Lola and Opal. Homer lived in the Whitesville area, educated in Montgomery County schools, graduated from Mace High School and served in World War I.

On June 1, 1918 he married Miss Myrtle Frost Everson, born Apr. 6, 1896 in Walnut township in Montgomery Co., IN. She was the daughter of Albert Newton Everson, born Sept. 21, 1870, died Nov. 27, 1926 and Minnie Belle Gray Everson, born Oct. 11, 1873, died July 22, 1948. Her brothers were Harold Knox Everson who died at age 24 from influenza, Camp Sherman, Chillicothe, OH in World War I. Her younger brother, Clyde Loraine Everson, veterinarian was associated with the extension service at the University of Maryland, died at age 49, July, 1955.

Homer Bratton Ward, Myrtle Everson Ward, Richard H. Ward, Mary I. Ward

Mrs. Ward's great great grandfather was William Miller, the first settler of Crawfordsville, who built the first log cabin in the area and who was one of the seven founders of the Presbyterian Church in the town. Excerpts from material found in the Crawfordsville Library contain a description of the first Court ever held in Montgomery County, which was at the home of William Miller on May 29, 1823, details of when Court convened for the second time, when William Miller sat on the First Grand Jury, and of how it continued to hold its sessions at Miller's house until the growth of litigation and population made it necessary to erect the first regular Court House.

Mrs. Ward attended Tiger Valley School, two years at Mace High School, Hughes High School in Cincinnati, OH for one year and graduated from Crawfordsville High School and then studied vocal music and Art in Cincinnati.

Mr. and Mrs. Ward started their business of farming the year of their marriage and settled on the Everson farm (her parents') near Linden, Madison township in 1921 and farmed there for 40 years. Mr. Ward was one of the most outstanding farmers in the state of Indiana hosting the 22nd Annual Indiana Farm Management Association Tour. Since he attended many extension and agricultural meetings, he was widely known throughout the county. During his farming career, he saw many technological advancements in hybrid seed and machinery. They both traveled extensively and in 1960 spent two months touring Europe.

Their children were Richard (Dick) Harold Ward, living on the home place, Mary Isabel Ward Wilkins, R.R.#1, Linden and Helen Louise who was born June 23, 1926 and died seven months later.

As a family they attended Potato Creek Methodist Church (Sugar Creek Township) and later transferred membership to the Linden Methodist Church.

Mrs. Ward moved to Crawfordsville two years after the death of her husband, June 6, 1961. Her ancestry made her eligible for membership in the DAR. She was a member of the Crawfordsville Athenian, Art League, Music Club, Antique Study Club, Crawfordsville unit of the Indiana State Symphony Society, Indiana and Montgomery County Historical Societies, past president of the Linden Home Demonstration Club, Linden Woman's Club, Montgomery County Federation of Clubs. She was a member of the First United Methodist Church and was active in the Women's Society of Christian Service. She was a cultural leader in the community until her death on Aug. 1, 1985. *Submitted by Mary Wilkins*

RICHARD D. WARD

Richard D. Ward (Rick) was born Sept. 30, 1958, the son of Richard H. Ward and Jeanne M. Ward. His grandparents are Homer B. Ward and Myrtle F. Ward and Louis R. Muller and Laura M. Muller. He has one sister, Nancy Ward Reece (Mrs. Wm.). He is a graduate of N. Montgomery High School and Purdue University where he received a B.S. in Agricultural Economics.

Richard D. Ward

He is a member of Alpha Gamma Rho Fraternity. Rick has been a director of the Montgomery County Soil and Water Association since 1982, serving as treasurer for three years. He is a past President of the Montgomery County Pork Producers, Past President of the Montgomery County Purdue Ag. Alumni Association and a member of the Linden-Kirkpatrick United Methodist Church. In 1987 and 1988 he served as exhibit chairman for the State Pork Producers Convention in Indianapolis, and in 1989 he served as a member of the Exhibit Committee for the World Pork Exp. Rick is farming 1100 acres of land, and raising 6000 head of hogs, and feeding 400 head of cattle each year. *Submitted by Richard D. Ward*

RICHARD H. AND JEANNE M. WARD

Richard H. Ward (Dick) and Jeanne M. Ward live on Edgewood Farms. Dick is a direct descendant of Jacob Miller, the first white settler in Montgomery County. His parents were Homer B. and Myrtle F. Everson Ward. He moved to the farm at the corner of 900 N and 350 E. when he was one year old. He is a graduate of Linden High School and Purdue University where he received his B.S. degree in Ag. Econ. He served in the U.S. Navy during World War II. He is a past president of the Montgomery County Historical Society '62-'63, the Purdue Agricultural Alumni Association '65-'67, the State Farm Management Assoc. '56 and the Montgomery County Extension Board. He was declared a Master Farmer in 1971 by Prairie Farmer. He has served as President of the Purdue Agricultural Trust Fund for 17 years. He has been a lay leader, Sunday School Supt., trustee, and youth leader at the Linden Methodist Church. He was a Cub Scout leader and Boy Scout Advisor for nine years. Dick was appointed to the legislative committee by Gov. Whitcomb, and was a member of Gov. Bowen's Welfare task force. The Ward's hosted the State Farm Management Tour in 1959 and again in 1972. Jeanne and Dick were honored to be invited by President Richard Nixon to be dinner guests at the White House for the Salute to Agriculture Dinner on May 7, 1971.

Jeanne Muller Ward is the daughter of Louis R. and Laura M. Muller. She was born Sept. 10, 1928 in Newark, NJ. She graduated from Irvington High School in New Jersey and has a B.S. in H.E. from Purdue U. She served as Extension Agent H.E. in Carroll County prior to marrying Dick in 1951. Jeanne is past president of the Montgomery County Extension Homemakers, the Linden Woman's Club, the Linden Extension Homemakers, and the MNO Extension Homemakers.

Richard H. and Jeanne Ward

She has served as organizer for the Mission Minded Merry Matrons at Linden for eight years. She was a Girl Scout Leader for 11 years and was awarded the Mary Patterson Award for outstanding service to Girl Scouts in 1971. She has been on the board of directors of the Sycamore Valley Girl Scout Council and the Montgomery County Mental Health Assoc. At present she is serving as Vice-chairman of the Region 4 Board of Trustees for Ivy Tech, to which she was appointed in 1986. She has served on the Linden Library Board since 1979 and as its President for the last five years. She has been a Sunday School teacher, Membership Chairman, Education chairman and Mission Chairman at the Linden Methodist Church. Jeanne and Dick are the parents of two children, Richard D. Ward and Nancy Ward Reece (Mrs. Wm.).

JACOB FRANCIS AND LIZZIE GREGG WARFEL

Jacob F. (Frank) Warfel was the foremost educator in the history of Ladoga, Mongtomery County, and one of the most distinguished early elementary school educators in Indiana. He was a teacher, superintendent of schools, instructor of teachers, newspaper editor and publisher, and civic leader. His distinguished career extended over 50 active years.

He was born on May 1, 1857 near Clermont, IN, son of Martin B. and Indiana (McClellan) Warfel, descendants of Pennsylvania Dutch and Scotch ancestry. He died on Dec. 20, 1942 at age 85.

Frank Warfel moved to Ladoga in 1876, at the age of 19, and attended the Ladoga Normal School for two years. Upon graduating, he became a teacher, and later, president of the Normal. In 1887, he was awarded a life teachers' certificate by the State of Indiana and was appointed principal of Ladoga schools. Later, he taught in schools in Indianapolis and Frankfort, IN, becoming superintendent in Frankfort. In 1897, he returned to Ladoga to be superintendent of schools, initiating instruction in the newly built Ladoga Grade School, a classic Romanesque style building, shown in he background of the above photograph. This distinctive structure, built by Professor Warfel's brother-in-law, George Marshall Huntington, served for 75 years as the elementary school.

J. Frank Warfel

Professor Warfel served as superintendent until 1909 and returned later as science teacher in the high school for several years. For 11 years, he was an instructor in teachers' institutes in Indiana, instructing teachers from 42 counties of the State.

In 1882, Mr. Warfel married Lizzie Gregg Huntington, daughter of Hiram Samuel and Louisa (Gregg) Huntington of Ladoga. She was born in Adrian, MI, Dec. 8, 1862. She died on Dec. 4, 1944. Mrs. Warfel was a talented and gracious lady, active in cultural and social life in the community. Their children were: George Huntington, born Mar. 28, 1884, Charles Martin, who lived from May 5, 1887 to Mar. 23, 1894, Louisa, born Dec. 3, 1889 and died in infancy, Herbert, born Dec. 1, 1890, and Nellie Grace Pefley, born Feb. 10, 1894.

Professor Warfel was a senior officer in the Masonic Order, the Knights Templar, and the Knights of Pythias Lodge.

On Dec. 1, 1890, Professor Warfel acquired the *Ladoga Leader* weekly newspaper, which he published for 18 years while with the Ladoga schools, and continued to publish thereafter until 1916. The preserved editions of the Leader remain a treasured source of history of the community. In later years, he was assistant editor of the *Crawfordsville Review*.

Frank Warfel was a man of extraordinary capabilities, energy and accomplishment. He was personable and genial, and while he was a stern disciplinarian in school, he possessed an exceptional sense of humor. Through his legacy of outstanding educational service and leadership, he was a profound influence on four generations of children in the community and the state. He was one of the outstanding citizens in the history of Ladoga, contributing greatly to the cultural development and character of the community, Montgomery County and Indiana.

THE BERT WARNER FAMILY

Bert Warner lived all of his life and farmed in

Scott Township. He was born Sept. 17, 1884 near Parkersburg to Emanuel (1847-1933) and Rebekah Peffley Warner (1852-1890); he was the sixth of nine children. He married Lorena Oliver on Mar. 4, 1911. Lorena's family were long-time residents of South Union Township. She was born near Whitesville on June 14, 1885 the daughter of Charles T. (1865-1934) and Luella Graham Oliver (1861-1943).

Bert died Dec. 5, 1967 and Lorena died Oct. 28, 1979. They are buried in the Ladoga Cemetery.

There were five children born to Bert and Lorena Warner; all being born in Scott Township and graduating from Ladoga High School except Charles and Homer who graduated from New Market High School.

Charles Emanuel (Jan. 22, 1912) has lived his entire life in Ladoga. He attended Indiana Central Business College, Indianapolis and was employed by R.R. Donnelley & Sons for 25 years. He married Joyce Bryan of Ladoga on Oct. 23, 1937. They had two children, Martha (1940-1981) and Joe (1946).

Homer Eugene (Feb. 14, 1913) earned his B.S. and M.S. degree from Purdue University. He served in World War II in the First Army command by Gen. Hodges, 8th Division, 121st Regiment as Staff Sergeant. He taught school for many years and was Principal and Dean of Boys at Decatur Central High School in Marion County. He married Nellie Caldwell of Ladoga on May 10, 1941 and they had two daughters, Carol (1944) and Phyllis (1957).

Mary Luella (Nov. 23, 1915) attended Indiana Central College (now known as Indianapolis University) earning a two-year teaching certificate and received her B.S. degree from Butler University. She married Kenneth Fletcher of Ladoga on Aug. 29, 1937. They had two children, Nancy (1943) and John (1946). She and her husband both retired from the Indianapolis School System.

Theodore Maxwell (May 1, 1917) attended Indiana Central Business College. He served in World War II with the Seventh, Third, Ninth and British Armies, 103rd and 79th Divisions. He received a battlefield commission as 2nd Lieutenant with the 79th Division. Upon his return from the service he managed Indianapolis Spring Corporation. He established his own spring company in 1976 which is known as Warner Spring, Brake and Alignment Corporation. He married Helen Giddings from Franklin, IN, June 19, 1942 in Baltimore, MD. They have four sons, Theodore Maxwell II "Max" (1944), Robert (1948), James (1952) and John (1960).

Oliver Leslie (Dec. 26, 1921) received his B.S. degree from Purdue University and M.S. degree from Butler University. He served During World War II as a forward observer, rank 1st Lieutenant, in the 80th Infantry Division, 313th F.A., Third Army command by Gen. George S. Patton. He married Berniece Robbins of Ladoga, June 20, 1944 in Indianapolis. They had five children, Allen (1947), Elaine (1949), Eloise (1951), Ellen (1954), and David "Ted" (1956). Oliver spent his entire career in education at Zionsville, Boone County, serving as teacher for ten years, principal for 23 years and retiring as assistant superintendent in 1987.

CHARLES EMANUEL WARNER

My grandparents were Emanuel Warner and Rebecca Peffley and Charles Thompson Oliver and Luella Graham. My grandfather Warner had five sons and three daughters. My grandfather Oliver had six sons and one daughter. Therefore, there were many cousins. My parents were Bert and Rena Oliver Warner. There are four brothers and one sister in my family: Charles, Homer, Mary, Theodore, and Oliver.

Charles married Joyce Bryan - two children.
Homer married Nellie Caldwell - two children.
Mary married Kenneth Fletcher - two children.
Theodore married Helen Giddings - four children.
Oliver married Berniece Robbins - five children.
We all live within a distance of 50 miles.

Vern and Hazel Bryan and their four oldest children - Joseph, Jeanette, Joyce and Vern, Jr. moved to Ladoga in 1919. They lived in Lebanon and Whitestown in Boone County. Vern worked for the Ladoga Telephone Co. as a lineman. Benjamin, Samuel and David were born in Ladoga. John Stanley owned the Telephone Company. Joseph was a registered Pharmacist. Jeanette and Joyce worked for the Telephone Company. Benjamin and son owned the Ladoga Tire Shop. Samuel and wife and two children live in Port Deposit, MD. He is retired from the Navy. David was in the Navy and worked for Indiana Bell. Joseph, Vern, Jr., a Navy retiree, and Jeanette have passed away.

David and wife Sue live on R.R. 5, Crawfordsville. They have three children. Joyce and Charles Warner and son Joe live in Ladoga. They lost their daughter, Martha Barkow in 1981. Jeanette has a daughter, Linda Busby in Winnsboro, TX. *Submitted by Mrs. Charles Warner*

EMANUEL WARNER

Emanuel Warner came to Montgomery County in 1868 from Davidson Co., NC, and can trace his ancestry back to North Carolina, Virginia, and England. He was born Apr. 14, 1847 to Brittian (1806-1888) and Elizabeth Shoaf Warner (ca. 1810-1847). He was the youngest of five children and due to the death of his mother was raised by his sister, "Polly". The oldest child born to Brittian and Elizabeth Warner was Susannah (1831-1866) who married Alfred Everhart. Emanuel came to Indiana with their son, his nephew, John Everhart, who had settled near Ladoga. The other children were Mary "Polly" (1833-1919), Hubbard (1838-1922) and Ellen (1841-1871). The progeny of these families still live in Davidson Co., Thomasville, NC.

Emanuel settled and farmed around the Parkersburg area. He met Rebekah Peffley, born Mar. 9, 1852, and they were married Feb. 14, 1873 in Putnam County. Rebekah was the daughter of Abraham Peffley (1827-1897), a farmer in Putnam County, and Mara Ann Crodian (1825-1886).

Early in Emanuel's married life he became a member of the Dunkard Church. As his deep religious nature shaped itself he became an ardent and diligent student of the Bible.

After Rebekah's death, Apr. 28, 1890, Emanuel married Nancy Miller of Ladoga in 1891 who survived him. They had no children. Emanuel died Nov. 11, 1933 and he, his wife Rebekah, and Nancy are buried at the Blakesburg cemetery near Fincastle.

There were nine children born to Emanuel and Rebekah Warner.

Charles Franklin (1875-1957) spent most of his life in Hobart, IN, and was employed by U.S. Steel Company. He served in the Spanish American War. Charles married Pearl Hunter and they had three children, John, Louisa, and Estelle.

Robert Hyten (1877-1948) was an accountant for the Oliver Implement Company in Omaha, NE. He married Nora Hatfield; they had no children.

Omar William died in infancy.

Emanuel and Rebekah (Peffley) Warner

Mary Ethel (1881-1963) taught school and spent most of her teaching career in the Chicago schools. She married William Greene; they had no children.

Henry Earl (1882-1951) settled in Akron, OH and worked for one of the tire companies and farmed at one time. He married Pearl Cruthers and they had three children, Eldon, Harry, and Roberta.

Bert Abraham (1884-1968) farmed in Scott Township, Ladoga. He married Lorena Oliver, who was also born and raised in Mongtomery County. They had five children, Charles, Homer, Mary, Theodore, and Oliver.

Edgar Leslie (1886-1956) owned a Ford dealership for many years in Ladoga. Because of the death of his mother he was raised by Billy Goodbar. He married Jennie Wilhite of Ladoga and they had three children, Maureen, Madonna, and Leslie, Jr.

Daisey Lee (1888-1985) was raised by her aunt, Sarah Jane Peffley Stackhouse who lived in Minneapolis, MN. She married William English and they had two children, Helen and Lloyd. She was Emanuel's longest living child.

Rebecca Mae (1890-1944) was raised by her grandfather Peffley and her step-grandmother, Amanda. Mae's mother died four days after her birth. She married Jesse Byrd who farmed in Scot Township, Ladoga. They had five children, Josephine, William, Wayne, Imogene, and James.

Bert, Leslie, and Rebecca Mae's children all graduated from Ladoga High School except two of Bert's children, namely Charles and Homer who graduated from New Market High School.

The Warner families have served in the Revolutionary War, Civil War, Spanish American War, World War II, and the Vietnam War.

MAURINE DALLAS WATKINS

Maurine Dallas Watkins was born in Louisville, KY, on July 27, 1896 (in another source this is Lexington in 1901), the daughter of George W. and Georgia M. Long Watkins. The family moved to Crawfordsville, IN, where she graduated from high school in 1914. While in high school she acted in several plays and received some awards for her writing. Her first play, *"Hearts of Gold"*, was presented in 1912 under the auspices of the Ladies Aid Society of the Christian Church, and the financial returns were given to foreign missions.

Miss Watkins attended Hamilton College and Transylvania University for three years. During that time she wrote short stories and plays, and was on the staff of college publications. She transferred to Butler University where she received the A.B. degree in 1919. She then took courses at Radcliffe

College to study playwriting and had one of her plays performed.

In 1923 Miss Watkins spent some time in the advertising department of the Standard Oil Company of Indiana. After working as a crime reporter for the *Chicago Tribune,* she became an associate editor with the Macmillan Company. In 1925 and 1926 she was listed as theater and movie critic for the *American Yearbook.* She wrote long summaries of what had happened in the theater and motion pictures. In the late 1920's she began writing stories and adapting plays for motion pictures.

Miss Watkins was best known for her play "Chicago" which was published in 1927. It played on Broadway and was made into a movie with Phyllis Haver, Victor Varconi, and Eugene Palette. It was reissued in 1942 as "Roxie Hart" with a cast of Ginger Rogers, Adolphe Menjou, George Montgomery, Nigel Bruce, and Phil Silvers.

Miss Watkins was the author of several other plays, some of which were made into movies. "Up the River", made into a movie in 1930, starred Spencer Tracy, Claire Luce, and Humphrey Bogart. Loretta Young, Norman Foster, Guy Kibbee, and Winnie Lightener appeared in "Play Girl". Later in 1932 the play "Tinsel Girl" was adapted into the movie "The Strange Love of Molly Louvain" with a cast of Ann Dvorak, Richard Cromwell, Guy Kibbee, Frank McHugh, and Lee Tracy. Other plays that were made into movies include "Professional Sweetheart" with Ginger Rogers, Norman Foster, Zasu Pitts, Frank McHugh, Allen Jenkins, and Gregory Ratoff; a later version of "Up the River" with Preston Foster, Tony Martin, Phyllis Brooks, Arthur Treacher, and Bill Robinson; "I Love You Again" with Myrna Loy, William Powell, Frank McHugh. and Edmund Lowe; "Libeled Lady" with Jean Harlow, William Powell, Myrna Loy, and Spencer Tracy; (reissue of "Libeled Lady") with Van Johnson, Esther Williams, Lucille Ball, Keenan Wynn, and Ben Blue; and "Search for Beauty" with Buster Crabbe and Ida Lupino.

During the last two decades of her life, Miss Watkins lived in Indianapolis and Jacksonville, FL, where she died on Aug. 10, 1969. She was a classical Greek scholar. Her will provided funds to nearly 20 libraries and institutions for the purchase of classical books. *Submitted by Don Thompson*

DARREL ROBERT AND MARY JANE WATSON

Darrel Robert Watson and Mary Jane Flint were married Nov. 29, 1942 in Fountain Co., IN. Darrel was the only child of Ralph Arnold Watson and Nancy Pearl Furr Watson. He was born Aug. 18, 1923. Darrel's father was a minister and farmer. Darrel was born in Montgomery County.

Mary Jane was one of eight children born to Joe Flint a farmer, and Teenza Margaret Hurley Flint. She was born in Warren County Sept. 24, 1924. Darrel graduated from Crawfordsville High School in 1941. Mary Jane graduated from Hillsboro High School in 1942.

They are the parents of four children and six grandchildren. Richard Allen was born Sept. 11, 1944 married to Nancy Louise Stultz. They have two daughters, Angela Marie and Victoria Kay. Robert Lee was born Aug. 7, 1946, married to Betty Jane Simpson, they have three children, Hope Ann, Jacob Michael, and John David. Edward Michael was born Aug. 1, 1951. Lori Lynn was born Jan. 13, 1961 married Clarence Alvin Brown. They have one son Anthony. Robert served in the Marines for four years and in Vietnam for one year.

Darrel Robert and Mary Jane (Flint) Watson the year they married 1942

Darrel's grandparents were Norris Welby Watson and Bessie Zuck Watson and John Erreet Furr and Leta Jane Myers Furr.

Mary Jane's grandparents were James Flint and Mary Hannah Evans and George Washington Hurley and Nancy Jane Hines Hurley.

Darrel has lived in Montgomery County and farmed here all his life. He has given 30 years of service driving children to school in South Montgomery. He has driven two generations in some families. He drove the same route for 28 years. He also sharpens saws, blades and etc.

Mary Jane is a housewife and an amateur artist who does oil paintings. She was the leader of a puppet team.

They belong to the Browns Valley Christian Church and the Montgomery County Farm Bureau.

Darrel's great grandparents were Marion Watson and Rosanna Liter Watson. His great, great grandparents were Samuel Watson and Mary Stonebraker Watson who purchased land in Montgomery County in 1824 near Alamo. It was purchased from the government and the deed was written on sheep skin. Elmer Wilbur now owns the land. *Submitted by Mrs. Darrel R. Watson*

SAMUEL HENRY WATSON

Samuel Henry Watson, better known to friends in Crawfordsville as "S.H.," or "Sammy," was born Sept. 14, 1871, in Alamo, IN. He was the oldest of five sons born to Marion Watson, a farmer, and Roseanna Liter.

His grandparents, Samuel Watson and Mary Ann Stonebraker, migrated from Butler Co., OH, soon after they were married in 1821. Neighbors were hired to clear his original entry land and he built a log cabin on it in 1827. He was a wheelwright and woodworker as well as a farmer. As a community leader he served as school trustee, township trustee, and township treasurer, and helped to organize Ripley Township's first school.

His mother, Roseanna Liter, descended from the Liter, Ruffner, and Sidener families who were early settlers from Kentucky.

Samuel Henry took both his high school and college education at Wabash College, receiving his degree in 1893. The curriculum at that time was primarily Greek, Latin, and mathematics, and he studied those subjects for eight years at Wabash.

His first teaching position was in a one-room school located in Balhinch. As was the custom, only part of his salary was paid in cash. Parents of pupils welcomed him into their homes, offering room and board in lieu of salary. Apparently families competed to set the best table, as Samuel commented during his lifetime that he never ate as well as when he was boarding with these families.

Samuel Henry Watson, 1952

Later, he was to become principal of the high school in Colfax, IN. In addition to the administrative duties, the teaching of Latin, algebra, and geometry was his responsibility. Finding it difficult to support a growing family on a teacher's salary, he left the position at Colfax and moved to Vincennes. There he served as a revenue officer, inspecting the river boats. Upon the repeal of Prohibition he returned to Crawfordsville, found work at the Match Factory, and subsequently was a warehouse man and shipper for 24 years at R.R. Donnelley and Sons, retiring at age 81.

Samuel married Lettie May Servies, of New Market, Sept. 4, 1898, and they had one son, Herman Darwin Watson. Lettie died in 1907 and Samuel married Charlotte Mary Venis, of Colfax, on Apr. 24, 1910. There were four children from this marriage: Maurice Marion, Samuel David, Mary Louise, and Laura Mae.

Older citizens of Crawfordsville may remember that "Sammy" was six feet tall, a relatively uncommon height for the time in which he lived. He never owned a car and could be seen walking the three miles to and from his home to the Donnelley warehouse daily, even in inclement weather. He was an avid reader, well-known to the local librarian. When that new invention, the radio, was too expensive to buy, he assembled one from pages of instructions and parts which covered the dining room table.

After retirement he continued to live in Crawfordsville. Death came on Oct. 12, 1959, and he was buried at Oak Hill Cemetery. *Submitted by Mary Louise Puailoa*

MARION EDWARD AND MARY ELLEN MIKELS WATTS

Marion Edward Watts and Mary Ellen Mikels Watts were born and lived their entire lives in Montgomery County. Their marriage Nov. 13, 1888 joined together the strands of many families which had been part of early western migrations to the mid-west.

Marion Edward Watts was born July 29, 1867 in Crawfordsville, second of five children of William A. and Hannah Matthews Watts. William Watts, born in Knox Co., OH Dec. 18, 1833, came to Montgomery County in 1856, where he worked as a drayman. On Sept. 14, 1864 he was married to Hannah Matthews, born in England in 1848. From 1868 until 1872 William served as town Marshall, during which time he lost his right arm from being knifed by a prisoner he was taking down Washington St. to the jail. Hannah Watts died Aug. 26, 1887; William died Nov. 7, 1907.

Absent Anthony A. Watts away in service WWI. Back Row: Jeremy Hubble, Maud Watts Hubble, Marguerite Watts Fletcher, Russell Fletcher. Front Row: Woodrow Hubble, Marion Watts, Edward Hubble, Mary Ellen Mikels Watts, and Marguerite Ellen Fletcher

Mary Ellen Mikels was born June 28, 1861, three miles east of Darlington, second child of William P. and Susan Sutton Mikels. Her grandparents, Joel and Mary Pickrell Mikels, purchased Indian land in Franklin Township in August 1832. Mary Ellen's great-grandmother, Sylvia Hudspeth Mikels, born in Surry Co., NC in 1773, came with her husband, John Mikels, through the Cumberland Gap to Washington Co., KY in 1796, then to Montgomery County with her family in 1832; she died in Franklin Twp. in 1839.

Marion Edward Watts worked at many occupations, starting as a drayman with his father and later for the Vaughan & Casey Bottling Co. He worked for many years for the Crawfordsville Casket Co.

Marion and Mary Ellen Watts had five children, only three of whom lived to maturity. Maude Ellen Watts, born Feb. 16, 1889, was married to Jeremy Hubble Feb. 27, 1910, and had two sons; Woodrow Leondrus, born Feb. 18, 1916, killed in a train accident in 1934; and Marion Edward Hubble, born Dec. 12, 1910, married to Bernice Stephens in 1942. Maude Watts Hubble died in February 1977 and her son Marion Edward Hubble died in December, 1985, leaving no descendants.

Anthony Aurelius Watts, born July 17, 1899 was a prominent attorney in Montgomery County. He was married to Mary Falen Mar. 22, 1920; their one child died in infancy.

In World War I, he served with the 150th Field Artillery of the famous Rainbow Division, participating in five of its major battles. He was a past commander of the American Legion Post in Hartford City, IN, past commander of the VFW Post in Crawfordsville and a charter member of the VFW in Indianapolis. He was a 32nd Degree Mason, a member of the Scottish Rite in Indianapolis and belonged to the Woodman and Moose Lodges in Crawfordsville.

Anthony graduated from the LaSalle Law School in Chicago. He served as state legal adviser for the Fraternal Order of Eagles and as a Selective Service Officer for Montgomery County. He was a member of the Montgomery County Bar Association, served two terms as county prosecutor, and served as Union Township Justice of the Peace. He died Mar. 27, 1961.

Marguerite Elizabeth Temperance Watts, born Jan. 12, 1895, was married to Russell R. Fletcher Feb. 8, 1916 by the minister of the Crawfordsville First Christian Church. Russell was the son of Foster A. Fletcher (1845-1910) and Mary Catherine Smith (1852-1939). Foster Fletcher had come from Keene, NH to Montgomery County in 1876. His wife's great-grandfather was Sebastian Stonebraker (1755-1833), who had brought his family to Ripley Twp. in 1828.

Russell and Marguerite Watts Fletcher had one daughter, Marguerite Ellen Fletcher, born Apr. 18, 1918 at Cherry Grove. The mother died Mar. 20, 1923, and she was raised by her grandparents, Marion Edward and Mary Ellen Watts.

Marguerite Ellen Fletcher attended Mills School, graduated from CHS in 1935, attended Butler University. She was employed in the Montgomery County Welfare Dept. working for Mrs. Nine Jones, until her marriage to Frank Hyde Cassell, Mar. 24, 1940. He was born in Chicago, Oct. 12, 1916, son of Frank and Alicia (Robinson) Seymour. He graduated from Wabash College in 1939 and did post-graduate work at the University of Chicago. He was an executive with the Inland Steel Co., 1948 to 1968, Director of the United States Employment Service, 1966 to 1969, and since then Professor of Industrial Relations, Graduate School of Management, Northwestern University.

Frank H. and Marguerite Fletcher Cassell have three sons: Frank Allen, born Feb. 23, 1941, graduated from Wabash College in 1963, received his Phd. in History from Northwestern University. He and Elizabeth Weber were married Apr. 1, 1961 and have two sons, David Cassell, born Nov. 5, 1962 and Jonathan Cassell, born Oct. 7, 1965. David graduated from the University of Minnesota in 1986 and Jonathan from the University of Wisconsin-Milwaukee in 1988. Frank Allen is Professor of Chair of the History Department, University of Wisconsin-Milwaukee.

The second son, Thomas Watts Cassell, also graduated from Wabash College - in 1967. Born Sept. 25, 1945, he was married to Sandra Coe Feb. 14, 1984 in Manama, Bahrain. They have one son, Michael Thomas, born Dec. 16, 1984 in Westchester, IL. Thomas has a Master's Degree in Near East Studies from the University of California - Berkeley, and an MBA from American University, Washington, D.C. He works as a consultant with U.S. companies, both foreign and domestic.

Christopher Bernard Cassell was born Jan. 7, 1952 and graduated from the University of Wisconsin-Milwaukee in 1976. He is a self-employed, audio-systems designer.

The present descendants of Marion Edward and Mary Ellen Watts are a grand-daughter, three great-grandsons and three great-great-grandsons. *Submitted by Marguerite Fletcher Cassell*

MILO WAUGH

Milo Waugh and wife, Elizabeth Kious were early settlers of Sugar Creek Township of Montgomery County. Family tradition says that Milo and Elizabeth rode on horseback to Montgomery County from their home in Buckskin Township of Ross Co., OH, in 1831.

Milo was born in Ross County Jan. 23, 1804, son of Joseph and Mary (Hopkins) Waugh. Married in Fayette Co., OH, Jan. 22, 1829 to Elizabeth Kious, born Feb. 14, 1811 in Fayette Co., OH, daughter of Adam and Margaret (Hidy) Kious. Their oldest child Martha was born in Ross County and so made the trip to Indiana as a small child. Also, coming to Montgomery County about that time were Elizabeth's brothers—Nathan and Absalom Kious. Absalom had married Milo's sister, Mary Waugh. Absalom and Mary lived in Sugar Creek Township before going on to White Co., IN, in 1858. Ten of their 11 children were born in Montgomery County.

Milo and Elizabeth were members of the first church in the township a Methodist Episcopal Church which met at the home of Roley Kendall until they erected a building in 1835. It was a log building with a huge fire-place, puncheon floor and seats. It was in section 13 and was named "Bethel".

This couple lived and reared their children along the Potato Creek. Milo died May 27, 1859 at age 55 years and Elizabeth died May 18, 1864 at age 53. Both are buried in the McKendree Cemetery one mile west of Colfax in Clinton County. Their children:

Martha, b. Aug. 27, 1829, married June 21, 1846 in Montgomery County to William Dunbar and died soon after on Aug. 6, 1847.

Joseph, born Jan. 29, 1832 in Sugar Creek Township, married 1853 to Nancy Angeline Laughlin and moved with their eldest son to Worth Co., MO in the fall of 1855. Joseph remained in North County until his death Aug. 7, 1923. They had nine children.

Harvey, born Apr. 10, 1834, married Aug. 7, 1853 to Nancy Bishop, daughter of John R. Bishop and Susan Dunbar and step-daughter of Nathan Kious. Harvey was the first of Milo's children to leave Sugar Creek Township going in October 1854 to Ringgold Co., IA. Harvey died Jan. 9, 1895 and is buried at Middle Fork Cemetery in Ringgold County. They had 12 children.

Milton Byron, born Feb. 11, 1837 and married, Aug. 13, 1857 to Sarah Elizabeth Saulsberry. Milton B. remained on the family farm and was a life-long resident of Montgomery County. After his wife's death in 1892 he married Oct. 18, 1894 to Margaret Herron. Milton B. died Dec. 20, 1904 in Crawfordsville and is buried at Oak Hill Cemetery. Milton B. and Sarah had seven children.

John Wesley, born Dec. 13, 1839, married July 19, 1860 to Mary E. Henderson, daughter of Alexander and Mahala (Bowers) Henderson. She died June 28, 1864, leaving two children William B. and Martha E. John W. married (2) Apr. 20, 1865 to Julia Ann Hamilton, daughter of John Hamilton and Ann Hamilton. John W. took his family to Henry County, MO in 1886 where he acquired and farmed a large farm which he called Shady Hill Stock Farm. The children of the second marriage were James Henry, Edward Royston, Richard H., Mary Elizabeth, Emma E., Walter Scott, Jennie Mae, John Milo and Minnie Agnes. John W. died Aug. 14, 1910, buried in Carpenter Cemetery.

Margaret Elizabeth, born Feb. 17, 1841, married Oct. 22, 1859 to Alexander Marion Butcher and went to Henry Co., MO in 1866 where their farm adjoined that of her brother John W. Margaret died Oct. 11, 1915, buried Carpenter Cemetery. She had nine children.

Miletus Asbury, born Mar. 13, 1845, married Sept. 2, 1866 to Martha Ann Raper. They came to Henry Co., MO, in 1868 where their five children were born. They moved to Ringgold Co., IA about 1876. He died at Redding, IA Apr. 24, 1909, buried in Middle Fork Cemetery.

Mary Jane, born Apr. 16, 1848 married Dec. 14, 1865 at Colfax, IN to William Nathan Bowers. They moved to a farm near Urbana, Champaign Co., IL in 1874. She died Oct. 20, 1878, leaving five children.

Melissa Ann, born Apr. 14, 1850, married Jan. 24, 1867 to Lafayette Ward and went to Henry Co., MO in 1869. Lafayette died Mar. 4, 1882. She married Jan. 28, 1891 to Abraham Crites. She had six sons by her first marriage. Melissa died Jan. 3, 1932, buried in Carpenter Cemetery.

William Wilson, born Jan. 13, 1853, married Mar. 12, 1876 in Worth Co., MO to Sarah Elizabeth Hathaway. He was a farmer in Worth County and died there May 25, 1924, buried at Middle Fork Cemetery in Ringgold Co., IA. He had eight children.

Sarah Alice, born Sept. 14, 1856, married Dec. 24, 1873 at the home of Milton B. Waugh to Albert G. Furman. They moved to DeWitt Co., IL where he was a farmer and preacher in the Christian Church. Sarah died July 24, 1928 at Clinton, IL. She had six children.

Emma Orevy, born and died Dec. 18, 1858.

It has been 158 years since Milo began his family in Sugar Creek Township of Montgomery County and many descendants can find their roots there. James B. Waugh of Kansas City, KS is a great-great grandson of Milo and Elizabeth through their son John Wesley Waugh. *Submitted by Mrs. James B. Waugh*

WEBER FAMILY

The Weber Family consisting of Koncar (Conrad), Paul, and John and their families with sister Josepha came to Fountain County in 1854 by way of Cincinnati, OH and Louisville, KY, probably up the Ohio River and Wabash River to Attica, IN.

Paul and John Weber made their homes in Attica and Conrad and his family came to Covington. His wife, Theresia Eha, died there in 1863, leaving children Josephine, Leopodine, Maria, Sofia, Englebert, and Conrad Jr. A child Henry Paul was born of his second marriage.

The Webers had been stone cutters and carpenters as Schomberg was a city noted for its stone quarries. It was hard work because it was all done by hand. Because the soil was so stony, little farming was done in that area.

The Webers cut the stones for the first stone Court House in Fountain County, and laid the stones to resemble a castle as in Schomberg, Germany. The Court House was built in the 1860's. Conrad died in 1867. He was also the master carpenter who was the overseer of the first covered bridge built across the Wabash River at Covington, IN.

Weber Family 1949. Gordon Dice Weber, Dorothy June Fine Weber, Marilyn Ruth, Gordon Leon and Delores June Weber.

The History of Schomberg goes back to the year 768. At that time it was only a village. In 1255 it became a town. The ruins of the old castle can still be seen on the Hill Oberhohenberg. There are three Schombergs in Germany. The one the Weber family came from is a little medieval town in the western part at the foot of the Alps near the Black Forest. It is beautiful country not far from Switzerland. Old members remember the elders telling of the migration to the "Amerika".

The Weber Family history is recorded in the Schomberg Catholic Church as far back as 1600, but no written records are in existence earlier.

Conrad Jr. married Clorinda Pink Ella Dice of Fountain Co., IN. They had five children: Lena, Ralph, Susan, Ruby, and Gordon.

Gordon Dice Weber married Dorothy June Fine of Hillsboro, IN in 1929. They had three children: Gordon Leon, Delores June and Marilyn Ruth. The family moved to the Waynetown, IN area in 1937 where Marilyn was born.

Gordon was a farmer and while farming North of the Waynetown area became a partner in the farm management firm of Jackson and Weber, and moved to Crawfordsville. Gordon was killed in a car accident in June of 1959. Dorothy was a retired bookkeeper for the firm and died in March of 1987 while a resident of the Ben Hur Home.

Leon became a partner and later full owner of the firm, but retained the name of Jackson and Weber Farm Management. He resides in New Market, IN and still operates the business. Leon married Betty Joan Canada Hooley who had two sons Mark Alan Hooley and Roger Lee Hooley. Mark is married to Nancy Jeanne Ellis and has two children from a previous marriage. They are Jennifer and Anthony Hooley. Mark is an executive with the railroad system in New Jersey where they reside and Nancy is a Nurse. Roger is married to Cindy Daniel and they have two sons: Aaron and Michael. Roger works for a heating and air conditioning company in Indianapolis and Cindy is a dental assistant. They live in Greenwood, IN.

Delores June is married to Thomas Crews and lives in Silver Spring, MD. They have a son Randall Wesley and a daughter Diane. Thomas is retired from the Government and Delores is a retired nurse.

Marilyn Ruth married Donald William Bruce and they have one daughter, Melinda Jo. Donald worked at the Indianapolis Airport for several years and Marilyn worked for Aetna Casualty Insurance Company. Donald then bought a franchised bakery route in Indianapolis and later Champaign, IL before becoming a car salesman in 1983. They now live in Rantoul, IL. Their daughter Melinda is married to John David Galbreath and they live in Champaign, IL. Melinda is a cellular phone representative and David is manager of a family owned Print Shop in Champaign, IL.

WEESNER-COAT

Among early residents of Franklin Township, were the Weesner and Coat families, who left a positive and wholesome stamp upon their community. Mahlon Weesner and his wife, Rachel (Coat) Weesner, lived just south of the corporate limits of Darlington for many years. They were married 1860 in old Center Friends Meeting which stood where Greenlawn Cemetery now lies.

Mahlon, born 1837 in Wayne Co., IN, died 1878, Darlington, was the son of Michael Weesner of Henry County, who married Hannah Barker, daughter of Isaac and Mary (Cox) Barker.

Rachel Coat, born 1842, West Milton, OH, died 1927, Darlington, was the oldest daughter of Henry and Sarah (Fellow) Coat who migrated from Miami Co., OH. Henry was a grandson of the legendary Marmaduke Coat of Ohio, a Revolutionary War Patriot from South Carolina.

History records that Henry was prominent in the milling trade in Hendricks Co., IN, where he helped lay out the town of Coatesville. Upon removal to Montgomery County in the 1850's, Henry continued his trade while associated with the Silas Kenworthy mill on Sugar Creek west of Darlington. He acquired productive land south of the town, which he later bequeathed to his married daughters.

Henry and Sally Coat were devout members of the Sugar River Monthly Meeting of the Friends Society, genteel folk whose interests were genuinely humanitarian. They were plain in dress and spoke the quaint language of their religious faith. At the close of their lives, well-advanced in years, they were laid to rest in the Quaker burial ground, now a part of Greenlawn Cemetery.

Mahlon and Rachel, having settled into the extended family situation of the Weesner-Coat household, pursued farming, assumed civic duties and the responsibilities of rearing a large family. The early death of her husband, 1878, imposed added burdens upon Rachel's responsibilities as farm manager and parent. A quest for learning in the young Weesners became a family legacy. Teachers, nurses, a missionary, secretaries, homemakers, a doctor, as well as farmers, appear on the family charts.

Children born to Mahlon and Rachel (Coat) Weesner, nine, were: William H., Albanus H., Theodore M., Hannah, Walter, Margaret, Olive, Robert, and Ernest.

Margaret Weesner, the second daughter, born 1870, died 1951, became a professional school person for many years. She was a graduate of Terre Haute State Normal and of Indiana University with the class of 1906. She was a teacher of English, administrator and educator at both the elementary and secondary levels in Montgomery County and elsewhere in Indiana. Miss Weesner always encouraged young people to strive for worthy goals and exerted positive influence in the community.

Although several descendants are widely scattered, locally today, one family only bears the name Weesner: Erving B. Weesner, born 1904, Montgomery County, son of Robert and Mabel (Peebles) Weesner, lives a few miles south of Darlington. In 1945 he married Alice (McClaskey) a former school teacher and granddaughter of Captain E.P. McClaskey. Mr. Weesner is now retired from farming and industry. The couple are known as avid gardeners and avid readers. Mr. Weesner continues active participation in the Indiana Friends Yearly Meeting.

They are parents of two sons—Robert Eliot, M.D. of Cincinnati and John Philip, and have one grandson, Marshall Todd Weesner. *Submitted by Geneva R. Fugate*

ROBERT AND MARGARET MORROW WEIR

In Europe in the 16th 17th century, civil and political liberties and religious freedom were very widely in evidence. In places, certain religions were mandated, and people were persecuted for their belief! The situation was noted in the biography of President Andrew Jackson.

Among the many families who came to the United States, and landed in the New England Colonies was the Robert and Margaret Marrow Weir family from Ireland. Their new residence was located at Breesh Valley, now Blairsville, PA where with some cattle, and farming operations he bought and sold land.

When the Northwest Territory was ceded by England, there was quite a migration of people who left the colonies to locate elsewhere, especially in Georgia, the Carolinas, Kentucky and Indiana.

Three sons of Robert and Margaret Weir were among those who went to Kentucky in the late 17th century. One of the sons, Alexander, who was the founder of the Weir family in Montgomery Co., IN, met and in 1809 married Margaret Krout, the daughter of Michael and Katherine Krout. Alexander worked with his father-in-law, near Licking Creek, on the Ohio River, with keel boats and river transportation.

Public land sales opened in Montgomery Co., IN Dec. 14, 1824, priced at $1.25 an acre and many prosperous forward looking people bought land. Alexander Weir had severance pay for service in the War of 1812, and was given a land grant of 80 acres, southwest of Crawfordsville, in Section 21.

In the summer of 1828, he with his son Robert then 18 years old came and built a comfortable log house on a plateau overlooking acres of sandy bottom land. They returned to Kentucky and brought the wife and family to Indiana. They loved the rugged hills and clear running streams and because of the similarity to their native land called it "my beloved Balhinch." Alexander Weir had a dynamic energetic nature, and ambition to improve life in general. The education of his children was uppermost in his plans. He deeded land on which to build a school house and with help from other parents a school was built.

Alexander Weir was dedicated to God's teachings and prayer and worship service was observed in the home. During his fatal illness he walked in pain in the flower garden of plants they had brought with them years ago.

Family members were given land, a portion of which remains as a heritage, after 180 years. A family reunion is held there each year. A Weir Cemetery was measured off, and there the mortal bodies of Alexander and Margaret are interred. They left to us a legacy, a vast store of knowledge to invent and use, and capabilities to advance with the times.

This biography of the Weir family is written by Mabel Weir Grimes, a great-granddaughter of the first Weir settler in Montgomery Co., IN.

CLYDE AND MARILYN WELSH

Clyde and Marilyn Welsh are life long residents of Montgomery County living at 105 N. Grace Avenue in Crawfordsville nearly 30 years.

They were married Sept. 15, 1956 in the First Christian Church by Rev. Paul Million.

They are the parents of three daughters. Delene, born Apr. 16, 1958; Charna, born Apr. 5, 1962; Jerilyn, born June 3, 1964.

All members of the family are members of Christ United Methodist Church and all are graduates of Crawfordsville High School, including Clyde's father Benjamin. All the daughters attended Ball State University.

Clyde was born Jan. 4, 1933 to Benjamin and Geraldine Welsh. At that time the Welshs were owners of a restaurant in Thorntown, IN. A few months later they moved to Crawfordsville where Benjamin joined his brother Herschel in the Crawford Hotel Cafe.

In 1937 Benjamin became an agent for Prudential Insurance Company, retiring in 1965. Benjamin died Feb. 22, 1979 at the age of 79. Geraldine managed the Val-U Dress Shop, ladies apparel store, during the late 1940's and early 1950's. She died Oct. 21, 1983 at the age of 76.

Clyde and Marilyn Welsh

Clyde has worked in the advertising department of the *Journal Review* for over 30 years. He was also a representative for Prudential Insurance Company for seven years. He was a member of the U.S. Army and Indiana Army National Guard for over 34 years retiring in July 1985 as the Command Sergeant Major of the 38th Infantry Division Artillery. He was a member of the Crawfordsville Jaycees for 14 years and was local President of the organization in 1965.

Marilyn was born Jan. 15, 1936 to Jewell and Myrtle Black. She has five sisters; Phyllis, Rosalie, Margaret, Marcia, Mary and two brothers; Bill and John. Bill died Jan. 16, 1987.

Marilyn worked for Indiana Bell Telephone Company from 1954 to 1958. At that time she retired to raise a family and became a full-time home maker.

Jewell was born in Denton, TX Nov. 11, 1898. He played semi-pro baseball when living in Texas and Oklahoma. He came to Crawfordsville from Oklahoma as a young man and continued playing baseball with the Crawfordsville Merchants. He worked at R.R. Donnelley as a pressman for many years, later going to Raybestos Company and retiring from there. He was a very able singer and sang baritone with the "Athens City Four" quartet. He married Myrtle Todd Mar. 17, 1935. She died Sept. 25, 1974 at the age of 65. Jewell died Sept. 23, 1979 at the age of 80.

DON AND EMMA LOU WELIEVER

Don and Emma Lou Weliever have lived in Montgomery County for most of their lives. They both graduated from Darlington High School in 1938 and 1946 respectively.

Donald Harry, born May 8, 1920, third of four children, to Gladys Cox (1896-1966) and Harry Manual Weliever (1891-1982), is a retired farmer and bookkeeper. He was in the Darlington unit of the National Guard when they were called to duty in 1941. He served in Co. 3, 151st Infantry for five years.

Don and Emma Lou Weliever and family

He attended Terre Haute Business College and worked as a bookkeeper for nine years at the Farmers Feed and Grain Company. He then farmed and served as Township Trustee and school board member from 1960-1970. He retired in 1982.

Emma Lou Vannice was born Feb. 10, 1928, youngest of three children to Fern Young (1891-1956) and John Maurice Vannice (1895-1972). After attending Indiana University, she married Don Aug. 1, 1948. She has served as the local librarian for 20 years.

They reside on her family farm. Her mother's father, Albert A. Young (1861-1923) cleared much of the timber when he bought it in 1890's. He and Almira Martin Young came here from Brown Co., IN.

Emma Lou and Don have four children: Steven J., postmaster at Hillsboro, IN; Stanley C. assistant director program planning at Bath, ME Ironworks; Sabra Ann, a deputy Attorney General in Indianapolis; and Stuart K., an attorney in Fort Wayne, IN.

Steve has two children Anthony Wade (1969) and Thommi JoLee (1977). Stan has two children, Wade Alan (1978) and Garrett Blake (1984).

MARTIN V. WERT

Martin V. Wert was born on a Fountain Co., IN farm on July 17, 1841, the son of Henry and Isabella Wert. He was graduated from the Fountain County High School in 1860. On Oct. 1, 1861 he enlisted in Company B, Tenth Regiment, Indiana Volunteer Infantry. He took part in numerous important campaigns and battles, Rich Mountain, VA, Mill Springs, KY, Corinth, MS, Mission Ridge, TN, Resaca, VA, Kenesaw Mountain, GA, Peachtree Creek, GA, and Atlanta, GA. His rank was recruit. On Sept. 5, 1864 he was transferred to Company B, 58th Indiana Volunteer Infantry. He was honorably discharged on Nov. 1, 1864.

When he returned home he learned the carpentry trade, and in 1870 he came to Crawfordsville to engage in the contracting business. He built many buildings here and also in other states, including Peoria, IL and West Point, VA.

Wert was always interested in military affairs. He was first lieutenant of Company D, first regiment Indiana National Guard from 1890 to 1893. Then he transferred to the second regiment, Company I, and he was elected to captain of Company M.

There is a discrepancy in the record of his Spanish American War service. In Bowen's *History of Montgomery County* Company I started to the front, but the regiment was discharged on Apr. 26, 1898. Wert's obituary stated he was commissioned Captain of Company M, 158th Regiment, Indiana National Guard and left Crawfordsville for Camp Mount Apr. 26, 1898. He is not listed at all on the roster of Montgomery County soldiers. Perhaps he did both. This latter company was discharged October, 1898 without getting into action.

He was elected to the Crawfordsville City Council for two terms and was elected mayor, serving from 1910 to 1914, as a reform mayor through the efforts of citizens who were concerned about the enforcement of anti-liquor laws. He was one of the leading advocates of a sanitary sewerage system for the city and also for the paving of streets.

He was an active member of the G.A.R. and of the First Methodist Church.

Captain Wert was married to Adaline Aston of Cincinnati, OH. They had three sons, Albert E., an architect and Arthur B., a contractor in

Crawfordsville, and another son who died in infancy.

He died Jan. 29, 1928.

Sources: Obituary, *Crawfordsville Journal, Jan. 30, 1928.* Gronert, Ted. *Sugar Creek Saga, 1958.* Bowen, A.C. *History of Montgomery County 1913.*

THOMAS J. WEST

Thomas J. West was born in Logansport, IN on Feb. 21, 1948.

He is the son of Francis and Mildred Baumann West.

Tom has four brothers: James, David, Joseph and Edward and a sister, Linda.

He graduated from Logansport High School. He enjoyed canoeing. After school, he would mow lawns, rake leaves and shovel snow in the neighborhood.

He attended Indiana University and received his B.A. in Psychology and Sociology and a Master of Library Science in 1973.

After graduation, he began work at the Logansport-Cass County Public Library as a Reference Assistant. Tom served as Head of the Reference Department and later as Assistant Director.

In August 1986, he became Director of the Crawfordsville District Public Library.

Tom serves on several state library committees and is a member of library-related organizations. He enjoys classical music, art, reading biographies and the daily newspaper and hiking. *Submitted by Thomas J. West.*

BOB AND MAUDE WHEELER

"Twelve children? How did your folks ever feed, clothe, and educate such a big family?", was the question asked many times of the Wheeler offspring.

Robert Earl Wheeler was born Feb. 24, 1902 in Fairfield, IL to Cordelia May Sanders, born in 1876 and Robert Earl Wheeler. On Sept. 6, 1924 he married Dora Maude Burnam. She was born Aug. 27, 1905 in Osman, IL to Thompson Ernest Burnam, born 1876 and Laura Frances Anderson, born 1880.

In March 1931 Robert (Bob) and Maude, five children, Cordelia, (who made her home with her son) and the Burnams, moved to Montgomery County to farms near Waveland. In March 1932 a farm near the Shades became home. The men at the nearby CCC camp soon approached Maude to do mending and laundry. The extra income helped feed and clothe a family that by 1937 would increase to nine, the last being twins. The delightful aroma of freshly baked bread served with churned butter in Maude's kitchen will never be forgotten. "Boughten" bread was available several years before Maude's tri-weekly routine stopped. Besides caring for a large family she later worked at the shirt factory and R.R. Donnelley's in Crawfordsville and commuted for ten years to Allison's General Motors in Indianapolis.

Bob attended school in Fairfield, IL. He farmed, drove a school bus, hauled coal and ice and worked at the lumber yard, all in the New Market area. He served as recreation director for the WPA and retired after 23 years from Allison's General Motors in 1965. Golf, baseball (White Sox), and Waveland basketball occupied his spare time. From October 1937 through April 1946 the family moved to the New Market area where three more children were born. Tragedy hit the family on Nov. 26, 1942 as their second child, Thomas Earl, born 1926, was killed in an automobile accident within 300 feet of home.

Front Row: Jeanne, June, Sandi, Darlene. Back: Frances, Jack, Jane, Jim, Maude, Bob, Sue, Robert and Bill Wheeler

Frances May, (born 1925) married Gareld Livengood, (born 1921) on Oct. 5, 1946.

Virginia Jeanne, (born 1927) married Christopher Cornett, (born 1924) on Oct. 10, 1948. Children: Thomas Wayne, 1950, and Susan Lynn, 1954.

Dorothy Darlene, (born 1928) married Pearl Brooks, (born 1920) on Dec. 24, 1947. Children: Dennis Lee, 1950 and Janis Lynn, 1953.

Darlene and Frances graduated from New Market School.

Robert Burnam, (born 1930) married Ruth Maxine Oswalt (born 1931) on Nov. 19, 1949. Children: Steven Kent, 1951, Randy Dean, 1954, David Alan, 1956, Daniel Wayne, 1960, and Beverly Ann, 1963.

William Ernest, (born 1933) married Delores Steele in 1956. One child, William Scott, 1957. Divorced and married Emily Wilson, (born 1938) on Dec. 26, 1959. Children: Michael Dean, 1961, and Gerald Allen, 1962.

Mary Jane, (born 1935) married Bobby Starnes, (born 1927) on June 13, 1953. Children: Gregory Dean, 1954, James Robert, 1955, Linda Dianne, 1957, Brian Lee, 1958, and Paula Kay, 1964.

Twins, Jack Allen and June Ellen were born in 1937. Jack married Winifred Fletcher in 1959. Children: Scott Allen, 1961, Todd Wayne, 1962, and Lisa Lynn, 1965. Divorced and married Anna May Sharp, (born 1945) on Oct. 7, 1977. June married James West, (born 1937) on Dec. 11, 1982. James Frederick, (born 1939) married Deanna Burkhart in 1963. Children: Robert Jeffrey, 1963, James Frederick, 1965, and Laura Michelle, 1968. Divorced and married Nancy Masten, (born 1942) on Dec. 21, 1979.

Carolyn Sue, (born 1940) married Rex Sutherlin, (born 1940) in April 1960. Children: Timothy Wayne, 1960, Tamara Sue, 1962, Terri Roxanne, 1966, Trent, 1972 (deceased), Tory Brandon, 1977.

Sandra Kay, (born 1942) married Jimmy Byers, (born 1936) on Apr. 7, 1979.

Bob and Maude bought a home in Waveland in 1946 and through 1960 eight children graduated from Waveland School. Bob died in 1974 and Maude is in ill health. Currently the family has grown to 28 grandchildren and 24 great-grandchildren. *Submitted by Mrs. Robert Wheeler*

JANE AND KENNETH WHIPPLE

Ruth Jane Herron, youngest child of Earl "Shorty" and Cora Coon Herron, was named for her great grandmother, Ruth Jane Stephens Coon. She was born Aug. 1, 1940, in Crawfordsville, IN. She graduated from Waynetown High School in 1958: during high school she was Homecoming Queen in 1958, president of the Sunshine Society, active in Future Homemakers of America and Band.

She worked at Donnelley's prior to her marriage. She has been a cook at family restaurants in Logansport, IN, and is now cook at 4-County Mental Health Center in Logansport; this center serves Cass, Fulton, Miami, Pulaski Counties. Her hobbies are reading, sewing, crocheting.

Jane married Kenneth Leo Whipple in St. Bernard's Church in Crawfordsville, IN, Feb. 15, 1960. They have lived in Logansport since their marriage. Kenneth is the son of Dale and Christina McLochlin Whipple and was born at Winamac, IN, in 1935. He graduated from Star City High School in 1953. He is a pipefitter and has worked occasionally in other states but mostly in Indiana. He was business agent for Local 172, Pipefitters' Union, South Bend, from 1978-1981. He enjoys fishing.

Jane and Kenneth Whipple

Kenneth and Jane have four children. Jean Ann graduated from Logansport High School a member of the Honor Society. She worked for several years at Camelot Center for Children in Logansport. She bakes wedding cakes and other specialty cakes to order. Jean and Sheldon Lee Kemper were married at the Baptist Temple in Logansport Oct. 3, 1981. Sheldon has worked for Wilson Brothers Meat Packing Company at Logansport for 15 years. They have three children: Jennifer Leigh, Kenneth Sheldon and Denise Allison.

Anna Marie graduated from Logansport High School and married John Elpers Feb. 14, 1981, in the Christian Church at Logansport, IN. She enjoys painting and interior decorating. John has worked at Elco Company in Logansport for five years. He enjoys all sports and competes in marathon races. They have three children: Melinda Sue, John Eugene II and Erika Lynn.

Cheryl Lynn graduated from Logansport High School. She has worked as billing clerk and in computer departments. She married Jeffery Carlson at St. Bridget's Catholic Church, Logansport, IN, Oct. 26, 1985. They now live in Indianapolis where Jeff is a salesman with Marshall Building Specialties. Jeff enjoys golf; Cheryl enjoys bicycling. Jeffery graduated from Indiana Central College (now University of Indianapolis) in 1985. They have one daughter, Heather Nicole.

Keith Allen is a senior at Logansport High School. He plays tackle on the football team and is on the track team, competing in discus throw, and shot-put. He was chosen for the All Loganland Football Team two years and received Honorable Mention for the State Football Team 1988-1989 season. His group of the Office Education Association won the District and State Award in 1988.

WHITAKER FAMILY

Robert Albert Whitaker was born, raised, lived

and died in Montgomery County. Born in Union Township on Mar. 13, 1852, Robert was the second son and fifth child of Levi and Margaret Anna Stump. Robert's grandfather and grandmother, John and Catharine Wright Whitaker left Cumberland Co., KY and came to Union Township where they purchased 40 acres of land on June 3, 1835.

According to family lore, John Whitaker was a bellmaker, but, John died suddenly in 1838 and is buried somewhere in Balhinch. John and Catharine were married Jan. 20, 1817 in Cumberland Co., KY by David Wells, Justice of the Peace. John and Catharine had 11 children: Levi, Anna, Esau, Isaac, John, Catharine, William, Luther, Rachel, Margaret, and Noah. Except for Levi and Anna (John and Esau were dead), the family moved first to Illinois and then to Iowa in the 1850's. During the Civil War, William and Noah both fought for the Union Army. Noah died of the measles in Keokuk, IA, Jan. 5, 1862. William was medically discharged for Retinitis Dec. 23, 1863. Because Noah was the sole supporter of Catharine, Catharine received a mother's pension of $8.00 per month.

Back L to R: Albert Wm., Mary (Whitaker) Barricklow, James, Ada (Whitaker) Swank and Millie (Whitaker) Hutchinson. 2nd: Robert Albert Whitaker, Sadie (Whitaker) Switzer, Amanda (Whitaker) Humes, Nettie (Whitaker) Murray, and Esther Lavina (Williams) Whitaker. Front: Golda May (Whitaker) Felton, Hudson and Belle (Whitaker) Broadick.

Levi and Margaret were married Nov. 1, 1842. During their 47 years of marriage, they had 11 children: Jemima J., Martha Jane, William (Big Bill), Catharine, Robert Albert, Mary E., Aaron Buchanan, Margaret Anna, Joseph H., Thomas J. and Henry W. Levi was born in Cumberland Co., KY Jan. 20, 1818 and died Oct. 18, 1891. Levi is buried in Bever Cemetery and has a tombstone the shape of a tree trunk. Margaret was born in Montgomery County July 25, 1828 and died Oct. 5, 1890. Margaret is buried in Weir Cemetery.

An interesting family story places Levi and Margaret in Missouri during the mid-1870's. They had their wagon fully loaded and ready to come back to Montgomery County. Levi and Joseph got into such a heated argument that Joseph shot his father. Levi had to remain behind so Margaret took the family back to Indiana. Later on Levi came back to Indiana. When Levi walked through the front door, Joseph walked out the back door and nobody really ever saw him again. However, in the early 1920's, a man came to Robert and Esther's home looking for chores to do. The man stayed for a while, keeping to himself. Then suddenly the man left. After the man left, Robert commented that the man might have been his brother, Joseph.

Esther Lavina Williams, daughter of Samuel A. Williams and Sarah Vail (both of Ohio) was born Jan. 31, 1850 in Waynetown. Esther had one brother, James Vail, seven years her senior. Their father, Samuel, died Mar. 8, 1852. Esther and Robert were married in Fountain County Sept. 3, 1873. They remained married 54 years until Esther died June 23, 1928. They had one son and eight daughters: James B., Sarah Margaret, Mary Ann, Nettie G., Amanda Elizabeth, Adath Bertha, Millie Catharine, Belle B. and Golda May. Robert died Aug. 22, 1930 at the home of his daughter, Mary Ann Barricklow in Waynetown. Services were held at the Baptist Church and Robert was laid to rest next to Esther at Waynetown Masonic Cemetery.

On Mar. 23, 1918 in Montgomery County, Golda May and Charles Eugene Hudson were joined in marriage. They had one son Lawrence Leroy and three daughters: Evelyn Louise, Hazel Jewel and Dorothy Darlene. Hazel Jewel and Robert George De Diemar were married in Montgomery County Mar. 23, 1946. They moved to Dayton, OH and had three sons: Robert Steven, Edward Eugene and David Bryan. On Nov. 8, 1980 in Coral Springs, FL Edward Eugene De Diemar and Mary Jane Morales were joined in marriage and are the parents of one child: James Edward born Nov. 5, 1982.

FRED WHITECOTTON FAMILY

The Whitecottons who now live in Montgomery County have a common ancestor in Moses Whitecotton I (born in Virginia in 1777). He was the father of Moses II, who was born in Ohio, 1810 and moved to Boone Co., IN circa 1825. Moses II had six children, one of whom was Harrison (born Indiana 1838). Harrison, along with his only child, William, moved to Montgomery County circa 1896. From that date to this, many of the ancestors of Harrison have lived in the Southwest quadrant of Montgomery County.

Harrison lived to be approximately 93 years old. In the later years, his eyesight failed and stories are told of him wandering the woods, feeling of the trees to find the specific White Oak that could be stripped to make baskets. He would dye the strips with other items from the woods before he would weave them into their final forms. One of his baskets still remains in the Whitecotton family.

Mr. and Mrs. Fred Whitecotton

Harrison's only son, William (1868-1951), married Elizabeth Plunkett (1873-1965) and from this union, eight children were born. William was a blacksmith, barn builder, carpenter, house mover, farmer and a general jack of all trades. He was a hard-working man with a quick wit and a lively humor. He did drive an automobile earlier in his life, but a near accident caused him to rethink the need of such a convenience. For the last several years of his life, he made his two or so trips per year to Browns Valley, with a horse pulling a buckboard.

Of William and Elizabeth's children, six were girls and three boys.

Opal 1895-1968, (Ferrell Gilbert) lived most of her life in Crawfordsville. Children: Kenneth, Martha (Homer Hancock), Kate (Lawrence Grimes).

Walter 1897-1962 retired from Mid-States Steel and Wire. He was married to Laura (Thompson) and they had five children: Helen (Meadows/Coffman), Betty (Myers), Lee - owner and operator of The College Street Pharmacy in Crawfordsville, Bill - an insurance agent in Connersville, IN and Bob who is self-employed in Crawfordsville.

Myrtle 1899-1985, (Sam Priebe), lived near Freedom Church. See Priebe Family.

Pearl 1904-1935 (Carl Henry), lived near Freedom Church. Children: Beth (Tony Austts), Ruth (Jim Shillings), Avanell (Forest Bowen) and Carol (Jerry Biggs).

Jenny 1907, twin sister of Fred - died at birth. See Fred below.

Ethel 1910-1933 lived with William and Elizabeth near Freedom Church until her early death.

Mary 1914- (George Reynolds), lived in Ohio for the last several years. One child, Lynn (Bob Liebhere).

John 1918-1985, a farmer near Waveland, married Mary Thompson. Two children: Lois Morgan and Max, who continues to farm on the homeplace.

Fred, twin of Jenny, pictured above with his wife of 60 years, Velma Moody. Fred was in the hardware and John-Deere Implement business in Waveland from 1947 to 1984. He also served as Brown Township Trustee from 1947-1954. Fred and Velma had four children: Joyce (Wayne Surface), Joan (Glenn Livesay), Don who presently serves as Principal of Hoover School in Crawfordsville and Ted (1945-1975) who was involved in the family business until approximately two years prior to his death from cancer. *Submitted by Don Whitecotton*

TYRE GLENN WHITTINGTON

In April 1849, the subject rode horseback with his wife Julia Ann Beatty Whittington to Montgomery County from Shelby Co., KY. He was born Oct. 6, 1820 in Woodford Co., KY, the first of seven children of Littleton and Frances Glenn Whittington, both natives of Kentucky. Two sisters, Lucy Ann and Elizabeth, and a brother, James Henry, died early in life. His oldest brother, William, whose wife was Rebecca J. Davis, lived for a time near the old family farm in Brown Township, later moving to Crawfordsville. Southy Thomas, his second brother, married Nancy Ellen Hutchison. Southy was first a carpenter and later a dentist at Waveland. The third and youngest brother was Joshua Littleton who married Cynthia Elizabeth Alexander. They lived near Cayuga, IN. Littleton Whittington, his father, was the eldest of 15 children, all of whom reached years of maturity. His grandparents were natives of Maryland and were known as descendants of old English Colonial families. Southy, Littleton, and Glenn are family names carried down through many generations.

After receiving a good common-school education he learned the trade of cabinetmaker. Much of is fine furniture still exists.

On Dec. 15, 1842 in Shelby Co., KY he married Julia Ann Beatty who was born Oct. 18, 1822, the daughter of William and Sarah Crosby Beatty. Tyre and Julia's first two sons, William Hanna and James Littleton, were carried by them on two horses as the family came to Indiana. John Thomas, Sarah

Frances, Reese Davis, George Washington, Lucy Ellen and Sherman Grant were born on the family farm, a few miles west of New Market in Brown Township.

Seated left to right: Southy Thomas Whittington, Tyre Glenn Whittington, Joshua Littleton Whittington. Standing: William Whittington

Mr. Whittington first purchased 132 acres of land where he lived and died. A part of this land was given for the site of Old Dowden School where his grandchildren were students. He later bought another 116 acres which he farmed.

In his early years our subject was a member of the Old Whig party, but later was a staunch Republican. He was First Worshipful Master of the Moreland Order of Masons, a position he held for seven years, during which time he brought and initiated three of his sons into the brotherhood.

Mr. Whittington died Sept. 16, 1911 at the family home, surviving his wife Julia Ann, who died Apr. 5, 1901. They are buried at Indian Hill Creek Cemetery in Brown Township. He and his family were active members of the Freedom Baptist Church. Descendants and collateral families still live in Montgomery County.

WANETTA WIATT

Visiting Wanetta was always a treat. After going up the long lane that lead to the Wiatt home on the farm, visitors were greeted by the large collie dogs and often cute puppies toddled under foot. The beautiful collies, flowers and chickens were all part of the memories of the Wiatt farm.

Wanetta Wiatt was born Apr. 14, 1909 in Montgomery Co., IN to Willie and Mabel (Rice) Wiatt. Willie was born Oct. 18, 1885 in Putnam County, the son of Edward and Julia (Slavens) Wiatt. Mabel was born Apr. 14, 1885 in Fountain County to Isaac and Florence (Parrent) Rice.

Wanetta had four brothers. The eldest, Leland was born Feb. 26, 1908, he died in infancy. The youngest member of the family, David was born Aug. 12, 1917. He served in the military from March, 1942 to May, 1945. He lost his health while in the service and was never able to do another days work. David passed away on Mar. 4, 1985. Wanetta's two living brothers are Leo and Isaac. Leo was born Mar. 14, 1910 in Montgomery County; he and his wife, Freeda (Grimes) Wiatt live in Waveland. Isaac was born Jan. 29, 1915 in Parke County; he and his wife, Zoe (McGaughey) Wiatt live in Russellville.

Wanetta graduated from Waveland High School in 1928; neither she nor her brother, David ever married. However, she had three nieces and three nephews, Norma Jean Spencer, Eleanor Pitcock, Debbie Gant, Larry Wiatt, Glenn Wiatt and Darrell Wiatt. They were all close to their "Auntie" as they called her.

Decoration Day 1954 (45 years) Wanetta Wiatt

Wanetta's father died on Apr. 5, 1949 and her mother on Mar. 20, 1955. In July, 1963 Wanetta and brother, David moved from the family farm into Waveland, where they lived until their deaths. Wanetta passed away Oct. 15, 1988.

Wanetta's home was a craft lover's delight; there were crepe paper flowers, button pictures, hooked rugs and handmade quilts throughout. Her handmade quilts were sought by many. She was a collector and lover of antiques. She owned and operated the "Wiatt Cafe" in Waveland for several years. She was a musician, as were her mother and her brothers. She served as pianist and taught a Sunday School Class at Freedom Baptist Church for 31 years. Her brother, Isaac was the choir leader there for about as many. The youth choir at Freedom always looked forward to choir practice nights.

Devotion to her beliefs and her services in church work was exemplary. Her most noted service among the young people of the church was her willingness to be a taxi service for every young person who didn't have a ride.

For those who truly knew Wanetta, she was an artist. She not only left the handwork of her artistic legacy; she left sketches on the lives of many of the young people she served who, in their hearts, could also call her "Auntie". *Submitted by Carol Ann (Reynolds) Kaufman*

RALPH AND BETTY WILDMAN

Married Dec. 23, 1943 at Sioux City, IA where Ralph was stationed in the Air Force. Betty was born at Smartsburg in Montgomery County, four miles east of Crawfordsville, the daughter of Harry and Ethel Mae Earl Dawson. Betty excelled in bookkeeping in school. Graduating in 1941 she did the accounting and bookkeeping for her and her husband when they had their Purina franchise at New Richmond, also, later she did 20 years accounting and bookkeeping for Russell Dawson Inc. Betty's family originated from Dublin, Ireland where her grandfather was born. She has three brothers, George, Russell, and Harry Jr. She has six sisters, Mary Jane Swank, Dortha Parks (deceased), Ruth Johnson, Midge Iverson (deceased), Ruby Cline, Marjorie Randolph.

Ralph and Betty Wildman Dec. 23, 1943

Ralph was born on a farm south of Newtown in Fountain County to Fenton and Pauline Greve Wildman on July 30, 1923. He graduated from Newtown High School in 1941. He took machinist schooling and worked as a tool die maker for Alcoa in Lafayette. He enlisted in the Air Force in December 1942. He served as an engineer and top turret gunner on a B-17 Flying Fortress with the 8th Air Force. After 22 missions over Germany was shot down and had to ditch in the North Sea while trying to get back to base in England. His first mission was the first daylite mission over Berlin and the raid that he was shot down on was the big raid of Apr. 29, 1944 on Berlin. He spent one year as a German P.O.W. where the last six months were the march from Poland.

The Wildman family originated from Kent Co., England, with Ralph's 7th great grandfather being born at Bethersden England in 1613. The Greve family was from Schleswig, Germany. Both families settled in the Atwood-Garrett, IL area. Ralph has four brothers, Jim (deceased), Charles, Bill, and Thomas Philo. He has six sisters, Margie West, Viola Weigle, Rena (deceased), Mary Klutzke, Ethel Holland, and Catherine Hampton. Ralph and Betty have two children, Joyce Ellen Robbins and Frederick Karl. Joyce has two children, Donna Jo Cozillino and Rodney. Fred has three children with his first wife and one by his second wife Kim. They are Janelle Bowling who has one child now. His other three children are Bruce, Jill, and Krystal.

Ralph served an apprenticeship as an offset plate maker at the R.R. Donnelley Printing Company. He was also a feeding advisor with Ralston Purina for seven years. He and Betty also had their own dealership with Ralston Purina at one time. Later spent several years in remodeling and new home construction. Ralph and Betty built their own home from the ground up including the construction, heating, wiring, and plumbing. Betty was as good a carpenter as Ralph when they got done. They remodeled several houses and moved a lot. They met several new friends that way which made it all worth it.

CHARLES O. WILHITE

Charles O. Wilhite was born Oct. 26, 1866, the son of Isaac S. and Isabelle Carnine Wilhite.

He attended Wabash College as a member of the class of 1890. He later studied stenography, and worked for the law firm of Ballard and Ballard. He was secretary to United States Senator Albert J. Beveridge in Washington, D.C. for several years.

He served in the National Guard in the 1890s and was captain of Company M in the 158th Regiment of Indiana Volunteer Infantry during the Spanish American War.

He served as a government secretary in Manila, the Philippines for three years during the Taft Administration.

When he came back to the United States he worked for the United States Forestry Service at Missoula, MT until his retirement in about 1932.

He was a member of Washington Camp No. 6, Patriotic Order Sons of America and of the Frank Britton Camp of Spanish War Veterans of Crawfordsville.

Mr. Wilhite never married.

He died in Missoula, Aug. 24, 1949 and is buried in Oak Hill Cemetery. *Sources:* Obituary *Crawfordsville Journal Review*, Aug. 26, 1949 and Bowen, A.C. *History of Montgomery County 1913*.

DR. MARY HOLLOWAY WILHITE

Dr. Mary Holloway Wilhite, daughter of Washington and Elizabeth Holloway, was born on a farm south of Crawfordsville on Feb. 3, 1831.

Mary supported herself for four years by teaching and dressmaking, before she went to medical school. There was considerable opposition in the community to her studying medicine. Mary studied independently to meet the requirements to enter the Pennsylvania Medical College in 1854. Dr. Holloway became the second Indiana woman to become a physician who had graduated from a medical school. She graduated in June, 1856.

She then returned to Crawfordsville and opened an office at the northwest corner of Grant and Wabash Avenues. In 1862 Dr. Holloway married Eleazer Wilhite, a Crawfordsville tailor. They had seven children, three of whom died in infancy.

Dr. Wilhite met with resentment from most of the male doctors in the county, who regarded her as an intruder and refused to counsel with her. She practiced medicine for 36 years, her patients being mostly women and children. She also worked with the mentally ill.

Dr. Mary H. Wilhite 1831-1892

Dr. Wilhite headed a movement in 1880 to establish a Montgomery County Orphans' Home, which was accomplished on Dec. 10, 1880.

In 1869 a few women in Crawfordsville felt strongly about women's rights. Dr. Wilhite was the chair of the committee on permanent organization of the Montgomery County Woman Suffrage Association. Dr. Wilhite was elected corresponding secretary. Subsequently Dr. Wilhite became a leading spirit in arranging meetings in the cause of the advancement of women. On Apr. 27-28, 1880, the Indiana Equal Suffrage Association State Convention was held at Crawfordsville. Dr. Wilhite was the organizer of the meeting and held the position of vice-president of the Association.

On Dec. 11, 1880 Dr. Wilhite gave an address to the Crawfordsville Equal Suffrage Society, and was also elected vice-president of the Social Science Association of Indiana that year.

Dr. Wilhite wrote articles on various subjects for the Crawfordsville *Saturday Evening Journal* and for Indianapolis papers. Some of her titles were "The Curse and the Cure, How Whisky and Tobacco Produce Poverty and Misery," "God's Poor," "Pretended Poverty," "Dissipation and Poverty," "Finding Homes for Homeless Children," "Woman's Rights," "Where There's a Will, There's a Way."

She died Feb. 8, 1892 from pneumonia contracted while making a house call one below-zero night when she was already ill with a cold.

In a final tribute to her, after her death, a meeting of Montgomery County physicians adopted a resolution which said in part: "We feel that her life has been a sacrifice for the organized good of others. No one was ever too poor to obtain her services. No night was too dark, no storm too hard for her not to respond to calls where humanity demanded the services of a physician. ... That by her labors as a physician and a humanitarian she has built a monument more lasting than could be carved on a marble slab, and hundreds of poor people who have been the recipients of her charity will revere her name."
Submitted by Jean Thompson, County Historian

CLINT KELLY AND MARY ISABEL WARD WILKINS

Clint Kelly Wilkins, lifetime resident and farmer was born in St. Elizabeth Hospital, Lafayette, IN, on Feb. 12, 1923. He is the only child of Harold Ward Wilkins and Eleanor Mae Kelly Wilkins.

Clint married lifetime resident, Mary Isabel Ward, on Aug. 9, 1947, in the St. Bernard's Catholic Church parsonage in Crawfordsville. A reception was held afterwards in the home of her parents, Homer Bratton Ward and Myrtle Frost Everson Ward, near Linden. Mary Isabel was born Apr. 26, 1923, in the family's homestead. She has one brother, Richard Ward, who farms on the home place, and one sister, Helen Louise, who died at seven months.

Clint and Mary both graduated from Linden High School in 1941. He entered Notre Dame University in 1941 and left in February 1943, after being called to serve in the Army Air Corps. Piloting a B-24 bomber, he was stationed in the South Pacific Theater with the 380th Bomb Group, the "Flying Circus", during World War II. After being honorably discharged as a First Lieutenant in 1946, he returned to Linden where he started his lifelong vocation of raising crops and livestock on the family farm with his father. He was elected to the Board of Directors of the Linden State Bank in 1963 and is still serving in that capacity today.

Clint and Mary, Belinda, Ward and C.K. Wilkins

Mary Isabel was an accomplished 4-H'er in school with many county and state sewing honors. After graduation she worked at Fort Benjamin Harrison in Indianapolis for one year. From there, she went to Ward-Belmont College in Nashville, TN, and graduated with a degree in Home Economics in 1945. While attending Ward-Belmont, she entered a two-piece suit in a campus sewing competition—winning first place and advancing to the national finals at the Waldorf-Astoria Hotel in New York City where she won Honorable Mention in 1945.

After their marriage, Clint and Mary gave the Wilkins family homestead the name of "Bel-Dame Farm" derived from the colleges they attended. In October, 1976, Bel-Dame Farm was honored as a Hoosier Homestead Farm (in the same family for over 100 years).

In 1981, Mary attained a certification in Library Science from Purdue University. She presently is head librarian at Linden Public Library. She is also a member of the Linden-Kirkpatrick United Methodist Church and a member of the Linden Women's Club since 1951, member of the Crawfordsville Art League and the Indiana Library Association.

Clint and Mary have three children: Belinda Mae, born July 4, 1949, in Culver Hospital; Ward Kelly, born Oct. 12, 1950, in Culver Hospital; and Clint Kelly Wilkins II, born Jan. 19, 1964, in St. Elizabeth Hospital, Lafayette, IN.

Belinda graduated from Linden High School in 1967. She has participated in a variety of activities, particularly canoeing. She was Indiana State Champion in 1967 in mixed-couples with her partner, and husband-to-be, Bruce Runnels, from Darlington, IN. Together they won the national Downriver Canoeing Championship in 1968. She graduated from William Woods College, Fulton, MO, in 1971, with a degree in Art Education. On May 22, 1971, she married Bruce. After teaching art for several years in Columbus, IN, she earned her Masters Degree from Indiana University (Bloomington campus) in 1979. While in Columbus, she became a certified member of the national Ski Patrol. Belinda and Bruce have one daughter, Hannah Lee, born, Oct. 17, 1985, in Our Lady of Lourdes Hospital, Camden, NJ. At present they live in Frenchtown, NJ.

Ward graduated from Linden High School in 1968. He was a member of the National Honor Society and earned his Eagle Scout Award in 1967. Ward was Junior Men's State Champion in canoeing and won the national Junior men's Downriver Canoeing Championship in 1968. In 1972, he was Alternate to the U.S. Olympic Team in canoeing. He graduated from Purdue University in 1972 with a degree in Agricultural Science. In 1975 he received his Aeronautical Maintenance Degree and presently is living in Ft. Collins, CO where he owns and operates an aviation business.

C.K. attended Linden Elementary School, Coal Creek Middle School and graduated from North Montgomery High School in 1982. He was active in the Future Farmer's of America. He held the office of Treasurer and represented his F.F.A. Chapter in Kansas City at the national convention. Having chosen to stay on the farm and work with his father, the Wilkins family farming tradition now spans five generations. *Submitted by Belinda Runnels*

HAROLD WARD AND ELEANOR MAE KELLY WILKINS

Harold Ward Wilkins, third generation of Wilkins farmers in Montgomery County, was born Aug. 23, 1894, died Oct. 30, 1983. Referred to as "Ward" all of his life, he was raised at the Wilkins family homestead one mile west of Linden. The family home was built in 1904 with bricks shipped in from Ohio in barrels on the old Nickel Plate Railroad that ran along the north edge of the farm. He had one sister, Lala Wilkins Martin. Ward attended Linden High School and graduated from Culver Military Academy in 1912. He served in the U.S. Army, 152nd Infantry, during World War I.

Eleanor Mae Kelly was born May 8, 1896, and died Dec. 29, 1981. Eleanor's parents, Edward and Margaret A. Higgins Kelly lived in Flushing, NY. Eleanor had two sisters and one brother; Margaret, Jeanne, and Edward. Eleanor served in the Army Nurses Corps from 1918 to 1919. She was stationed aboard the hospital ship "General Robert M.

O'Riley" and Camp Mills, Long Island, NY. During this service she met and tended Harold Ward Wilkins, who was in an Army hospital recuperating from an attack of appendicitis suffered while on duty with the U.S. Army.

Eleanor and Harold were married Apr. 22, 1920 in Indianapolis, IN. In 1920, they built the brick bungalow across the road from the large family homestead. Their marriage was blessed with one son, Clint Kelly Wilkins.

Harold Ward Wilkins' mother, Camella Ward Wilkins, born 1862, died 1942, married Thomas Wilkins on June 20, 1883. She was the daughter of Amazon and Phoebe Ward who are buried in Oak Hill Cemetery in Crawfordsville.

Harold Ward Wilkins' father, Thomas Wilkins, born 1861, died 1947 is buried in Linden Cemetery. Thomas attended Valparaiso College and graduated from Wabash College in 1883. He was a member of the Phi Delta Theta Fraternity. His father, Clinton Wilkins, born June 23, 1830 died Jan. 22, 1897, came to Montgomery County from Brown Co., OH, near the town of Ripley and lived there until the winter of 1851 and 1852 when he came to this part of Indiana.

Clinton's parents, with five other children of the family, had preceded him by a few months, while he stayed in Ohio to honor a contract that he had entered into with another person. The family remained for a short time in the northern part of Madison township on what was then known as the Beasley farm and from there located in Tippecanoe County near Romney.

Clinton's wife was Charlotte Ward, born July 27, 1832, died Dec. 15, 1897. Clinton and Charlotte were married on July 4, 1884. Her parents were Thomas and Elizabeth Ward, Sr. She had one brother, Thomas Ward, Jr., born June 17, 1830, died Feb. 24, 1891. He never married. As rumor has it, he was shot and found dead in an area gravel pit. He is buried in New Richmond, IN.

Thomas and Elizabeth Ward, Sr., were born in Leicestershier, England, where they farmed. They chose to sell all of their possessions in a two-day farm sale on the pretext of high taxation in England. They came to Montgomery County via the Maumee and Wabash Rivers by canoe where they were robbed by Indians. *Submitted by Belinda Wilkins Runnels*

WILKINSON FAMILY

Icabod and Anna Taylor Wilkinson lived in New Milford, CT when their son, Murwine was born in 1796. A son, Abram was born to Rachael Barnes and Murwine in Hamilton Co., OH on Nov. 30, 1836. As a boy, Abram and his family moved to a farm near Wallace, IN.

Abram married Elizabeth Caroline Bruner in 1860. They lived on a farm northwest of Wallace where Ira, Clinton, Benton, Earl, Edgar, Arvilla and Uma were born. Ira married Ida Philpott. They had Eston who married Bessie Wert and Jewell who married James Steinbaugh. Their daughter was Sarah. Ira taught school for awhile then he and Clint opened a General Store in Wallace.

Clinton and Jennie Philpott were the parents of Lex. He and his wife Zelpha had two sons.

Benton and wife, Nancy, had one daughter, Grace, who married Karl VanDevanter. They were parents of Virginia, Faith, Juliet and Christine. Bent farmed near Wallace.

Earl and his wife, Lillie, had no children. He practiced law in Crawfordsville.

Edgar died at the age of 19.

A daughter, Arvilla, married DeWitt Shoaf. They had a son, Pearl, who died young and a daughter, Ura, who married Ted Swartz. When Ura was a senior in high school, she was chosen by the Indianapolis Star as the most beautiful woman in Indiana. She was an accomplished musician.

Another daughter, Uma, attended Central Normal School at Danville and Madam Blakers at Indianapolis. She began teaching at Wallace. After her mother died, Uma and Abram moved to Waynetown where she taught primary grades. Abram married Mary Barnes from Hamilton Co., OH. On Apr. 12, 1908, Uma married Hugh Ernest Zuck who owned and operated a general store in Waynetown. Soon after their daughter, Beulah Ernestine, was born in 1910, they sold the store and moved to the old homestead farm near Wallace where Ernest farmed until he retired. A son, Gerald W., was born here on Feb. 1, 1915.

Beulah received her B.S. degree from Indiana State Teacher's College and her M.S. degree from Butler University. She taught school in Davis Township and Wallace in Fountain County. Uma died in 1938. Beulah and Ernest moved to Crawfordsville where she taught first grade at Mills School. On Oct. 20, 1951, she married Charles Curtis Edwards, owner and manager of an appliance store on Road 231 North of Crawfordsville. Curt and Beulah built a home near the store where they continue to reside.

Gerald received a B.S. degree in engineering from Purdue University. He married Genevive Schnelle on Dec. 29, 1941. He served in Germany during WWII. After the war, he joined the U.S. Corps of Engineers and moved to Louisville, KY then to Omaha, NE. He and Genevive have one daughter, Catherine Suzanne who married Richard D. Smith, Jr. They have three children. Catherine Theresa married Michael Darby in 1987. They have one son, Justin. Tricia and Richard D. Smith, III are living at home in Omaha. *Contributed by Beulah Z. Edwards*

WILHEIT (WILLHITE) FAMILY

Matthias Wilheit married Mary Margaret Blankenbaker. They had a son, John, born in 1745 in Orange Co., VA. John married Lucy Stapp. John and Lucy were the parents of 13 children, Archilles, John, Jennie, Catharine, Margret, Jesse, Tobias, Lewis, Joshua, Mourning, Barbara, Martissa and Katie.

Archilles Willheite (spelling changed) was born in 1768. He married Mary Hall on May 1, 1794. He was a Cooper-Barrel Maker. Archilles died Mar. 4, 1833 in Kentucky. Mary died Aug. 25, 1845 and is buried at Oakland Cemetery. They were the parents of seven children, John, Lucinda, Catharine, George, Patsy, President Hall, Mary (Polly) Ann.

President Hall Willhite (spelling changed again) was born Oct. 3, 1809 in Shelby Co., KY and died Dec. 20, 1882. He married Sarah Plunkitt on Feb. 22, 1831. She was born Feb. 6, 1805 and passed away Feb. 26, 1887. They came to Indiana in 1831, owning land Section 29, Twn. 18. They were blessed with 11 children, namely, Patsy, Rillinta, Rebecca, Mary, James, Henry, Sarah, Harvey, William, Mahala, and John.

John was born Mar. 29, 1856 and died Feb. 17, 1924. He married Mary Fowler on Dec. 24, 1879. He married Margaret Ross Mitchell on Aug. 10, 1915. John and Mary had Effie, Alta, Jessie, Edgar, Matie, Elmer, Oakie, and Lou.

Effie born Aug. 31, 1881, died Aug. 22, 1965, married Fremen McBride, who was born Aug. 3, 1881 and died Nov. 29, 1962.

Alta was born Mar. 25, 1883 and died May 12, 1925. She married Lenard Brimberry, born in 1884 and died Mar. 1, 1946. They had nine children.

Jessie was born Nov. 25 or 26, 1885 and died July 12, 1908.

Edgar was born Oct. 10, 1887 and died Sept. 7, 1952. He married Daisy Mitchell on Feb. 14, 1914. She was born Oct. 17, 1896 and died Oct. 22, 1971. They had eight children, Moyne Argel born Oct. 15, 1914 and died Oct. 15, 1914. John Kenneth, born Aug. 22, 1915, died July 12, 1977. He married Erma Parker. They had two children, Marla and Terry. He then married Geraldine Shumaker. They had two children, Sharon (Williams) and Loren.

Melba born July 31, 1917, died Oct. 26, 1980. She married Raymond Zeigler. They had Ann (Huek), Kenton, John, Jane (Lear) and Julie.

Edgar Leon was born Sept. 5, 1919. He married Edna Meyer. They have Tom and Duane.

Twins, Dale Lloyd and Gale Floyd born Feb. 23, 1922. Dale died Apr. 29, 1923. Gale died Mar. 29, 1973. Gale married Barbara Ottinger on Aug. 18, 1944. They had Larry, David, Melvin and Barbara Laurene (Miller).

Noel Eugene was born July 7, 1924. He married Helen Keller on Apr. 15, 1945. Helen was born May 27, 1924. They have Ronald, Gregory and Pamela (Jessie).

Moyna Arlene born Nov. 16, 1926 and died Nov. 26, 1926, ten days old.

Matie was born Oct. 12, 1889 and died Jan. 4, 1946. She married Everette Harper, born Mar. 21, 1887 and died Aug. 9, 1956. They had seven children, John, Leota (Cline), Jean (Ballard), Berniece (Moore), Jessie (Hite), Louise (Connell) (Byrd), and Dorothy (Powell).

Elmer was born Jan. 21, 1892 and died Mar. 13, 1907.

Oakie born Aug. 25, 1895 and died Nov. 13, 1957. She married Cecil Boze on Sept. 19, 1912. He was born June 10, 1891 and died Dec. 23, 1965. They had eight children, Cecil, Donald, Virginia (Scott), George, Betty (Thompson), Anne (Loveless), Fern, and Marilyn (Howell).

Lou was born Feb. 9, 1899 and died Jan. 16, 1953. She married Clark Hershberger Sr. and had Clark Jr. and Jerry. Clark Sr. was born Sept. 6, 1893 and died Feb. 24, 1945. Lou then married Roy Brandenburg on Apr. 8, 1950.

PRESIDENT HALL WILLHITE

President Hall Willhite was born Oct. 3, 1809 to Archilles and Mary Hall Willhite in Shelby Co., KY. February 22, 1831 married Sarah Plunkett, Jefferson Co., IN. She was born Feb. 6, 1815, Shelby Co., KY to William Plunkett. They came to Montgomery Co., IN in 1831. President died Dec. 20, 1882, Sarah died Feb. 26, 1887. They are both buried in Willhite Cemetery near Wingate, IN. Their children: Patsy, Rillinta, Rebecca Plunket, Mary Mitchell, James, Henry, Sarah, Harvey, William, Mahala and John.

John Hall was born Mar. 29, 1856, died Feb. 18, 1929. He married Mary Emily Fowler Dec. 24, 1879; daughter of Jesse and Margaret Parker Fowler; born June 3, 1856 in Montgomery County. She died Nov. 5, 1908, both buried in Willhite Cemetery. Their children: Effie May born Aug. 31, 1881, married Freeman McBride. She died Aug. 22, 1965; Alta Arnetta born Mar. 25, 1883, died May

12, 1926, married Leonard Brimberry. Their children: Lloyd, Mary Thompson, Mabel Cole, Ezra, William, Leah and Samuel; Jesse President born Nov. 26, 1885 drown July 12, 1908; Edgar Hall born Oct. 10, 1887 died Sept. 7, 1952, married Daisy Mitchell. Children: Kenneth, Melba Ziegler, Leon, Gale, Dale, Noel and Moyna; Matie Evelyn born Oct. 12, 1889 died Jan. 4, 1946, married Everett Harper. Their children: Dorthy Powell, Bernice Moore, Louise Byrd, Jessie Hite, John, Jean Ballard and Arnetta Cline; Elmer Lloyd born Jan. 21, 1892 died Mar. 13, 1907; Oakie Leah born Aug. 25, 1895 Fountain Co., IN, died Nov. 13, 1957 married Cecil Boze. Their children: Clare born Apr. 27, 1914 died Oct. 25, 1936, Donald born July 14, 1915 died Feb. 25, 1982, Fern born Mar. 27, 1917 died Dec. 9, 1978 married Ruth Hundley. Their children: Fernandre (Andy) and Mona Tzur; Virginia born Jan. 21, 1920 married Garnal Scott. Their children: Byron, Garnal, and Gary; George born May 5, 1924, married Elnora Cotner. Their children: Cecil and George Jr.; Betty born Nov. 2, 1928, married Leo Thompson. Their children: Bradley, Eric and Martin; Anne born Aug. 11, 1931 married Byron Loveless. Their children: Maryann Vores and Cynthia Goodnight; Marilyn born Aug. 2, 1936, married Richard Howell. Their children: Michael and Malinda.

Lou Ellen born Feb. 9, 1899 Fountain Co., IN, died Jan. 16, 1953, married Clark William Hershberger. Their children: Clark William born Apr. 1, 1921, married Marnell Lauterbur. Their children: Jane Carlson and Jill Hacker; Jerry born Sept. 2, 1930 died Dec. 22, 1956.

President's great-great-grandfather, John Michael Wilhoit, a German protestant, emigrated to America with his wife, Mary Blankenbaker and sons (Tobias, John and Adam). Eva, Matthias, and Philip were born in Spotsylvania Co., VA. In 1728, he owned 289 acres of land in Virginia. In 1746, his will was probated in Orange Co., VA.

His great grandparents were Matthias and Mary Ballenger. His grandfather, John, was a soldier of the American Revolution, born 1745 died 1835 in Kentucky. Married Luch Stapp, their children were: Achilles, John, Jennie, Catherine, Margaret Gutherie, Jesse, Tobias, Lewis, Joshua, Mourning Collins, Barbara Hamilton and Marther Ryker.

All Montgomery County Wilhite-Willhite ancestorage can be traced back to Michael, the emigrant.

DWIGHT AND DORIS WILLIAMS

Dwight Williams was born Aug. 29, 1908 in Crawfordsville, IN to Clinton and Letitia Williams. His father was Superintendent of Mails in Crawfordsville from 1920 until his retirement in 1933. Dwight graduated from Wabash College in 1930 and worked for his brother, Faye Williams, owner of Symmes Williams Electric until he opened the first Sears Roebuck store in Crawfordsville at 215 East Main Street in 1936. He operated this retail store until World War II when he enlisted in the Navy.

Dwight married Doris Dean Carver June 1, 1941. She was the daughter of Grean and Mattie Carver and grew up three miles east of Crawfordsville on U.S. 136 in a 12-room house built by her father from materials acquired by tearing down the Mt. Tabor Church. Her maternal grandparents, Thomas and Cynthia Van Cleave, operated the toll house located at Grant Ave. and Road 32 East at the turn of the century when Perrysville Road was a toll road. Prior to their marriage, Doris worked for Selective Service, during the war she worked at Culver Hospital and later as a receptionist for Ben Hur Life Insurance.

Dwight and Doris Williams

Dwight returned from the war in 1945 and invested in Symmes Williams Electric, Inc. He and his wife Doris were active in the business until 1967 when the business was sold to Raymond Kostanzer. Economics and investments had long been a subject of deep study for Dwight. He began attending international meetings sponsored by hard money advocates. His studies and research resulted in him becoming one of the leading advocates of monetary reform. He helped organize, and was a charter member of, the National Committee to Legalize gold. This powerful committee was successful in persuading Congress to act, and in 1974 it became legal for American citizens to hold and own gold. Dwight has already made a significant contribution to our civilization by his successful efforts to legalize gold and his continuing efforts to return our currency to metal standard, if successful, could well be the greatest legacy any man can give.

Doris has contributed to a better community through her volunteer work as a Pink Lady at Culver hospital, The Symphony Committee, Flower Lovers and American Legion Auxiliary, and has supported children continuously for over 30 years through the Christian Children's Fund.

Doris and Dwight are members of The First Baptist Church.

GEORGE THOMAS WILLIAMS, PHYSICIAN

George Thomas Williams, son of Henry and Nancy J. (Gott) Williams; born in Brown Twp., Montgomery Co., IN, June 8, 1865.

Henry Williams, son of the Rev. Elder Garland and Harriet (Mitchell) Williams, was born in Shelby Co., KY, Oct. 14, 1836. He attended the district schools of his native county. In 1861, he located in Crawfordsville, IN, where he became a prominent citizen. By trade he was a carpenter, contractor and cabinetmaker. He was a Democrat, a member of the K. of P. Lodge, and the Baptist Church, having served many years, as a deacon in his church. He died May 21, 1926. On Nov. 27, 1863, he married Nancy J. Gott, who was born at Browns Valley, Montgomery Co., IN, Dec. 23, 1845. She died in 1895. Her parents, Thomas and Elizabeth (Van Cleve) Gott, were natives of Kentucky, and came to Indiana in 1823. Henry and Nancy J. (Gott) Williams were the parents of four children: (1) Lillian E., who married J.C. Allen. Mrs. Allen is deceased. (2) Charles G., who was a cabinetmaker by trade. He is deceased. (3) Mary L. She died in October 1900. (4) George Thomas.

Rev. Elder Garland Williams, father of Henry, and son of Joseph and Julia Williams, was born in Kentucky. He was an ordained minister of the Baptist Church, and in early days was a preacher in Montgomery Co., IN, where he also farmed. He later became the minister of a church in Crawfordsville. His wife, Harriet (Mitchell) Williams, was a native of Kentucky. Both died in that state.

Joseph Williams, father of the Rev. Elder Garland Williams, was born in Virginia, and moved to Kentucky about 1740, settling in Shelby County. His brother served in the War of 1812, under the command of General Andrew Jackson.

George Thomas Williams, the subject of this sketch, attended the public schools of Montgomery Co., IN. He began the study of medicine in 1882, and graduated from Indiana University with an M.D. degree, in 1887. He took graduate work at the Post-Graduate School of the University of New York. In 1887 Dr. Williams entered the practice of medicine at Russiaville, IN, but remained there only three months, at the end of which time he moved to Browns Valley, IN, where he practiced until 1904 (17 years). Since that time he has maintained a medical practice in Crawfordsville. Dr. Williams, who is a Democrat, is a member of the following: American Medical Assn.; Indiana State Medical Assn.; Montgomery County Medical Society; Montgomery County Chapter, Citizens Historical Assn.; and Baptist Church. Dr. Williams' hobby is collecting books.

On Oct. 17, 1888, George Thomas Williams married Mary E. Todd, daughter of Johnson and Ruth A. (Van Cleve) Todd, both of whom are deceased. Johnson Todd was a prominent farmer of Brown Twp., in Montgomery County. Mrs. Williams was born in Brown Township, May 2, 1866. There are no children. *Citizens Historical Association Biography, Aug. 10, 1940*

HAROLD AND MARY WILLIAMS

Harold and Mary Williams are lifelong residents of Walnut Township in Montgomery County. They were married June 2, 1946, after Harold returned from serving with the 107th Ordnance Corps on Detached Service in Germany. During the "Battle of the Bulge" he escaped after three days behind German lines and was returned to an English hospital to recover. He later returned to duty and was with American troops as they entered Buchenwald, a well-known concentration camp. Both graduated from New Ross High School. Harold received additional schooling from Chicago University, and Mary attended Jordan Conservatory of Music.

In 1946 both returned to and bought the W.C. Loop family farm, which became a Hoosier Century Farm in 1975. They were blessed with five children, Robert, Joanne, Jeanne, Ruth, and Thomas. Robert (Bob) married Eileen Seal on Oct. 3, 1969. They are parents of three children, Heidi, born in Germany, Joshua, and Daniel. Bob is employed at Eli Lilly Clinton Laboratory. Joanne married Larry Stephens on Aug. 30, 1970. They have one child, Jennifer. Larry is also employed at Eli Lilly Clinton Laboratory. Joanne is employed by Child-Adult Resource Center in Rockville.

Jeanne married Larry Plumb on June 4, 1972. They live in Virginia and are the parents of Andrew and expect a daughter in March 1989. Larry is with Bell Atlantic as a Public Relations Manager, and Jeanne is a consultant in Personnel. Ruth married Kevin Roth on Nov. 29, 1985. They have a daughter, Casey. Both are teachers in southern

Indiana, where Kevin was chosen as Outstanding Teacher for 1988. Thomas (Tom) married Judyth Snell on May 14, 1977. They live in Michigan, where he is employed as a Logistics Manager for Miesel-Sysco Food Service. Judyth is a project engineer of Saturn Corporation, a division of General Motors.

Harold and Mary Williams Family

Some interesting facts concerning ancestors and relating to the land and home of Harold and Mary include the following: Christopher Loop, born in 1788 in Pennsylvania, moved from Virginia to Indiana in 1834. One of his sons, Andrew Loop, born Mar. 24, 1816, married Elizabeth Airheart, a girl who came with her family and the Loop family at the same time. Elizabeth and three of her sisters walked the distance of 600 miles. Andrew was known throughout Montgomery County as "Grandfather Loop." He held many offices, including Constable, Justice of the Peace, Trustee, and Notary Public. He was twice lieutenant of the home militia. He lived until age 91, and on his 90th birthday liked to tell about "old times" — the log rollings, building of old log schoolhouses and roads, and how he killed deer and wild turkeys. One of Andrew's and Elizabeth's seven children was William C. Loop, who lived on the same land and built the house now occupied by his descendents, Harold and Mary Williams. He was a Director of Culver Union Hospital, and a Director of Crawfordsville State Bank and Indiana Farmers Mutual Insurance Company. He spent his remaining years in a large home on Wabash Avenue in Crawfordsville.

OTIS AND BLANCHE WILLIAMS

Nathan Otis "Ote" and Blanche May (Ellis) Williams had sad times. Their third child, Sidney Louisa "Lida" was born Aug. 4, 1909 and joined a brother, Russell (Feb. 23, 1901) and sister, Opal (Sept. 24, 1904). All three children died of the same disease (tuberculosis) within one year of each other. Lida died June 16, 1927; Opal the day after Christmas of that year and Russell June 2, 1928. Blanche cared for all the sick ones with great care, as well as diligently raising her only grandchild, Mary Louise Taylor. Lida married Homer M. Taylor and had Mary Louise, born on the farm (which she still owns), southwest of Waynetown on Apr. 1, 1925. After the death of Lida, Homer moved to Chicago and worked for the postal service. Mary Louise married Robert O. Olsen in Chicago on Oct. 16, 1948.

They had three children: Diane Marie (born Apr. 8, 1952 married Roy Archer, and second marriage to John Rentschler). She has three children: Kevin, Mark and Craig. James Max was born Sept. 17, 1956. He is handicapped with Cerebral Palsy and lives at New Hope at Indianapolis. Linda Denise was born May 26, 1959. Linda married Steve Lemon and has Ryan. Mary Louise raised Bob's two children from a previous marriage: Geraldine "Geri", born July 17, 1941 married Don Holman and has Brenda and Brian. Robert Olsen, Jr. was born July 27, 1944 married Alfreda Loggins and has Michele and Jennifer.

July 1946 Golden Wedding Anniversary Blanche Ellis and Otis Williams in center

Mary retired from R.R. Donnelley after 29 years in April of this year (1989).

Otis Williams' parents were: Isaac and Louisa (Small) Williams. For more information on the Small family, see 1881 *Beckwith History of Montgomery County*. Otis was born Feb. 11, 1874 in Fountain County and Blanche was born Oct. 3, 1877 in Fountain County, the oldest child of Marion and Sidney Jane (Blackford) Ellis. Otis and Blanche were married July 22, 1896 and the above picture was taken on their Golden Wedding Day. *Submitted by Mary Louise Taylor Olsen*

STEPHEN WILLIAMS

Stephen Williams and wife Elizabeth Ellis Williams came from North Carolina. Elizabeth Ellis was the daughter of John and Margaret Bryant Ellis, born Feb. 5, 1786 Rowan Co., NC and married in 1813. She died Apr. 23, 1869. Stephen died 1875 and is buried in Harshbarger Cemetery. They came to Wayne Co., IN first, then to Walnut Township, Montgomery Co., IN having the second cabin there and later they moved to Whitesville. Their children were: Bryant Williams born Dec. 17, 1813 North Carolina and died Sept. 9, 1893 here, married Elizabeth Castle born Sept. 7, 1821 and died Sept. 25, 1894. She was the daughter of George and Catherine Horine Castle. Her sister, Mahala Castle married James Washington Linn in Warren Co., OH. She lived in Walnut Township across from her sister, Elizabeth who lived in Union Township. Their brother, Thomas Castle lived in this area three or four years, then moved away. Byran's children were Hulda born 1839 married George Corn II, brother to Margaret Corn who had married Noah Castle Linn. They had Vallie Corn married William Frantz, and they had one son George Frantz who married Jennie Brookshire; Isham Williams born 1843; Charles Williams married Lavenda Schenck; Benjamin Williams; Stephen, Jr. born 1845; William Williams died at age 50; Milton Williams; Mary Ellen Williams born 1851 died 1915 married Andrew Jefferson Hinkle, grandson of Benjamin and Sarah Shaver Hinkle; Kate Williams married Nat Sullivan and had a grocery in Whitesville; George (Dr.) married Molly Stevens; John L. Williams born 1849.

Other children of Stephen and Elizabeth Ellis Williams besides Byran were Jonathan born 1815; Jane born 1817 married Richard Graves lived near New Ross; William Williams; John Ellis Williams married Mary Cross on Dec. 11, 1845; Mary Williams never married, born 1823 and died Mar. 12, 1901 New Ross; Martha born 1825 and died Jan. 12, 1870; George Williams born here. Stephen and Elizabeth had 400 acres of land east of Whitesville.

ANNA WILLSON

Anna Willson was born in Crawfordsville, IN, May 27, 1869, the oldest of three daughters of Levi and Sarah Webster Willson. She attended Crawfordsville public schools, graduating from high school in 1886. She was offered a scholarship to Indiana University but could not accept because she was financially unable to attend. In 1887 she started teaching in the grade schools of Crawfordsville. In 1897 she was appointed principal of Crawfordsville High School.

Anna attended Boston, Chicago, and Harvard Universities, but received the B.S. degree from Purdue in 1912. She continued as principal until 1919 when she was offered the position of dean of girls at Arsenal Technical High School (Indianapolis). When the news of her acceptance was published in the newspaper, she was deluged with requests that she stay in Crawfordsville, so she decided to remain. Six months later the Board of School Trustees notified her that her services were no longer required. Her dismissal caused a storm of protest. Public mass meetings were held and petitions were addressed to the Board of School Trustees. The affair became a national issue as is noted from an editorial in a national education magazine: "The stupidest autocracy we have known in a quarter of a century of educational observation has been achieved by the board of education of Crawfordsville, IN...Anna Willson has been the genius and master of the high school situation."

The Board remained firm and Miss Willson was fired. She went to New York where she attended Columbia University, receiving a master's degree from Teachers College in 1921. Returning to Crawfordsville, she was appointed superintendent of schools on July 1, 1921. She was forced to resign on Feb. 6, 1923, and died on July 6, 1923.

Miss Willson was a dedicated teacher and educator. Under her leadership the high school attained a standard recognized by the best institutions. Her ability to induce more students to continue their work in high school and college was outstanding. The enrollment increased from a class of 22 in 1897, her first class, to a class which was the largest high school graduating class in a city of this size that year in the United States.

Miss Willson was responsible for the founding of the Sunshine Society. The local society, which was the first in what was to become a statewide organization, raises money every Christmas for needy families. She believed in the value of extracurricular activities. Among other things, she organized the Clionian and Polymnian literary societies, the first school orchestra, and directed plays and operettas.

All of Miss Willson's activities were not local. She served on several important committees of the National Education Association, and appeared on its programs several times. She was a member of the National Council of Education, and was the second woman president of the Indiana State Teachers Association.

Miss Willson was loved by all of her students and was affectionally known as Miss Anna. *Submitted by Don Thompson*

WILSON

Irene Wilson was born in Montgomery County, Apr. 30, 1928 to Earl and Lelia G. Zachary Wilson. Earl was born July 15, 1886 in Montgomery County. Lelia Zachary Wilson was born May 3, 1897. They were married Sept. 13, 1913, and spent their honeymoon in Lafayette where they attended a stage play of "Uncle Tom's Cabin."

Earl was a farmer early in his life but spent 40 years in greenhouse work growing flowers and vegetables. Much of this time was spent at the Lettuce Farm on the Country Club Road. Earl and Lelia had three children, a son Carroll L., and two daughters Helen Frances deceased, and Irene (Mrs. Ralph C. Miller).

Earl's father Emerson Bennett Wilson was born Mar. 31, 1858 in Walnut Twp. His wife Harriett Ann (Hattie) Miller was born Oct. 26, 1860. They were married in 1880. Emerson and Hattie farmed in Franklin, Wayne, and Union townships. They raised six children, Edna who married Floyd Ball, Raymond married Edith Moody, Alvin married Edith Carroll, Earl married Lelia Zachary, Ralph married Julia Davis, and Ruth never married.

Emerson's parents Lewis and Elizabeth (Betsy) Morris were born in Ohio and arrived in Walnut Twp. before 1850. They are both buried in Parsons Cemetery north of Mace. Lewis's headstone was taken from the Cemetery and was used as a stepping stone in Crawfordsville until a few years ago when it was returned to the cemetery by the DAR.

Elizabeth Morris Wilson was the daughter of Owen Morris and Abigail Wilson Morris (2nd cousin). They are buried in the old Lostcreek Cemetery in Miami Co., OH. This cemetery is located on the old John Wilson, Sr. farm.

Harriet Wilson's father, Marian Harrison Miller, came to Montgomery County from Bath Co., KY with his parents William and Cosandra Ross Miller in 1835. William purchased 160 acres in Wayne Twp. with $1000.00 in silver. Harriett's mother was Nancy Garvey, daughter of John and Lucy Ramey Garvey. John and Lucy were married June 26, 1826 in Montgomery County.

Lewis Wilson's parents were John Jr. and Letitia Mills Wilson. Letitia Mills's parents were Thomas and Martha Phillips Mills. Thomas was a Revolutionary War soldier.

Several of John Jr. and Letitia Wilson's children migrated to Montgomery County from Miami Co., OH. Matilda Wilson married Jeremiah West, Lydia married Jehil Crane, Lucinda married David Sutton, Thomas J. married Hannah Counts, and of course Lewis who married Elizabeth Morris (Emerson's parents).

John Jr. Wilson served 15 years as Associate Judge of Miami Co., OH, and also served as a State Representative for Miami, Allen and Drake Cos., OH, starting in 1835. He was elected Associate Judge November 1819. John Jr. was the first clerk of the Lostcreek Baptist Church, oldest religious body in Lostcreek Twp., Miami Co., OH. While visiting their Montgomery County children, Letitia died in 1858 and is buried in Parson's Cemetery north of Mace. John Jr. returned to Miami Co., OH and died 1866.

John Wilson, Sr. was born Mar. 30, 1739 in New Jersey, and his wife Lydia (Amy) Thatcher was born 1740 on the Isle of Jersey, Channel Islands. John Wilson, Sr. was a Revolutionary War soldier in the Pennsylvania Militia and also served with Gen. George Rogers Clark in Kentucky in 1782. John Sr. was a member of the first Constitutional Convention for Ohio in 1802 (from *Ohio Statement and Annal of Progress*, by William Taylor, Vol. 1, p.22).

Irene married Ralph C. Miller, Feb. 11, 1951, at the First Baptist Church in Crawfordsville, which is still their church home. They have one daughter, Ruthellen, who is a Biochemist doing post-doctorate work in conjunction with the St. Louis University Medical School and Jefferson Barracks in St. Louis. Ruthellen married Douglas Dawley, a science teacher.

EDWIN DAVIS AND ELIZABETH ELLEN (FAUST) WILSON

The Wilson's came from England and the Thatchers from Wales. John Sr. and Lydia Thatcher Wilson were natives of New Jersey. John Jr. born 1782, married Letitia Mills and lived in Miami Co., OH where he served in the State Legislature, also Justice of the Peace. They had 12 children and in 1849 gave up farming. Two of the children who moved to Montgomery Co., IN were Matilda Wilson West, wife of Judge Jeremiah West and her brother Thomas Jefferson Wilson.

Thomas Jefferson Wilson, born 1824, came to Walnut Township, Montgomery Co., IN in 1850. He married Hanna Hane Counts in Ohio and they had six children. Sallie, born 1849, married Manoah Brown, Edwin Davis, born 1851, married Elizabeth Ellen Faust. Canazada, born 1854, married John Campbell, Nevada, born 1853 died in infancy, Sylvester born 1857, never married and Gilbert, born 1866, married Belle Robbins.

Edwin Davis Wilson and Elizabeth Ellen Faust (born 1851) married in 1873 and she was the daughter of George and Mary Ann (Armantrout) Faust. A few years before Ellen's death in 1909, they moved to the Charles Martin farm east of Providence Church. They had five children, Bernard born 1881, died in infancy, Walter born 1884, Raleigh born 1886, twins George Faust, born 1891, died in infancy and Clara Faye, born 1891.

Glen and Faye (Wilson) Rhoads Davis, Walter and Raleigh Wilson and dog

Walter, married Alpha McIntire and was a mail carrier for the New Ross area until his death in 1927. They had two daughters, Helen, married Clyne Clark and Martha, married George "Bus" Feltner.

Raleigh, married Hazel Myers; had Doris, who married Kenneth Anderson. Elizabeth married Richard Kelsey and Edwin married Betty Ward. Raleigh farmed the Martin farm which he inherited. From grief of Hazel's death, (by car accident), and his upcoming operation, Raleigh took his life. Edwin bought the girl's part of the estate and lives on the farm. Edwin and his son John are the only known male Wilson descendents of John Wilson Sr. living, through the Thomas Jefferson line.

Faye Wilson married Glenn Rhoads and kept house for her father and brothers until her father's marriage to Mary Jane Marker of Plainfield. Glenn and Faye's children were Ernest and Raymond who died in infancy. Florence married Ed Handy, William married Elizabeth Foster and lives in Michigan, Alberta married Norman Nichols, and Rosemary married Rex Howard then John Peterman in 1969.

Davis fell and broke his hip, which didn't mend, and had to walk with crutches. Unable to maintain his home they made their home with Faye and family. Jennie, the only grandmother of the children remember, died in 1931 and Davis in 1937.

Many happy times are remembered of the stories Grandpa told as he chewed tobacco while he twirled his pocket knife between his thumb and forefinger; wearing a hole through the bone handle and into the blade. Great granddaughter Penny Richardson has this momento of David Wilson.

Faye spent two and a half years in a nursing home of a broken hip and died at the age of 95 in 1986.

JAMES L. JR. AND FLORA L. (HUSEMAN) WILSON

Flora L. and James L. Wilson, Jr., purchased the Gill property east of Crawfordsville, in Union Township, Montgomery County and moved there October 1972.

Flora was born May 2, 1941 in Lafayette, IN, the second of three children to Juliana (Bauer) and Richard Huseman. Her siblings are Richard Jr., and David. She moved with her family to Montgomery County in 1946. She graduated from Alamo High School and attended Greenville College in Illinois.

James L. Wilson, Jr., was born May 10, 1938 in Howesville, IN, the first of two sons to Oletha (Griffith) and James L. Wilson, Sr. His brother is William. James graduated from Switz City High School and Greenville College, Illinois and received his Masters from University of Georgia. He teaches Junior High Science, first year in Arthur, IL and since then in Tippecanoe County. At present he is at Wainwright Junior High.

Flora and James were married at the Yountsville Church June 30, 1962. Three daughters were born to this union.

Jacqueline was born June 20, 1965 in Lafayette. She is a graduate of North Montgomery High School and IVTC in Lafayette; married David Surber Mar. 23, 1985. He was born Sept. 16, 1963, the first of two sons to Wanda (Holt) Harrison and David Surber in Crawfordsville. His brother is Scott. He is a graduate of Crawfordsville High School, Mt. Vernon College and Indiana Law Enforcement Academy. He is presently a Law Enforcement Conservation Officer with the Department of Natural Resources in Posey Co., IN where they now reside.

Janet, born May 8, 1967 in Lafayette is a graduate of North Montgomery High School and Trevecca Nazarene College in Nashville, TN. She is working on her Masters Degree there and will be teaching at the elementary level.

Joan was born Sept. 27, 1970 in Lafayette. She graduated from North Montgomery High School and is attending Ball State University.

RALEIGH LEWIS WILSON

Raleigh Lewis Wilson, son of Edwin Davis and Elizabeth Ellen Faust Wilson was born Feb. 19, 1886 and was married to Hazel Gertrude Myers (born Aug. 3, 1892) Mar. 15, 1916. Hazel's parents were William and Cora Gray Myers.

Raleigh was a farmer. They lived west of New Ross a few years then moved east of Beckville in 1924. Hazel was killed in an auto accident, and Raleigh received a broken leg in the same accident. Grief and a coming operation caused him to take his own life. They had three children: Doris Claire, Elizabeth May and Edwin Myers Wilson.

Doris Claire Wilson born June 19, 1916 married Kenneth Herschel Anderson on Aug. 25, 1934. He was born on Dec. 17, 1910, son of Harvey and Ethel James Anderson. They have two children: twins, Eva Kaye and Neva Faye born Aug. 17, 1945. They were married 11 years before the twins were born.

They farmed several years then bought a resort in Wisconsin. He came back to Crawfordsville and did carpenter work. He worked for B&D Lumber and Dawson Construction. They bought a cottage in Minnesota and he did small carpenter jobs there. They have ten grandchildren and one great-grandchild. Kenneth passed away on Jan. 21, 1989.

Elizabeth May Wilson born Sept. 19, 1917, married Richard Samuel Kelsey. Richard was born Nov. 26, 1914 to Emery Elvon and Emma Anna Reagan Kelsey. Richard farmed ten years in Boone and Montgomery Counties. He then moved to Shannondale and ran a livestock-hauling business for 40 years. They had seven children: Jeannine Claire born Feb. 15, 1939; Betheline born Sept. 10, 1941; Cora Sue born Jan. 25, 1944; Sandra Lee and Andra Bee born Mar. 30, 1946; Emily Rose born July 15, 1952, and Robert Wilson born Mar. 6, 1956. Andra died on Jan. 15, 1953. They have 15 grandchildren and four great-grandchildren. One grandchild is deceased.

Edwin Myers Wilson born Jan. 22, 1922, married Betty Jane Ward on Mar. 23, 1946. Betty was born Dec. 20, 1922. Edwin is a farmer. He bought his sisters' shares in the family farm east of Beckville. He also retired from Raymark. He served in Germany in World War II and received the Purple Heart. They have two children: Janet Luanne born Dec. 21, 1950 and John Edwin born Feb. 28, 1957. They have two grandchildren: Brian Dean Bridwell and Laura Lea Bridwell.

Raleigh's ancestors fought in the Revolution. They migrated from New Jersey, to Virginia, to Kentucky, to Ohio and settled in Montgomery Co., IN in 1850.

His father, Edwin Davis Wilson's father, Thomas Jefferson and Hannah Jane Counts both born in the year 1824 married in Ohio and are buried in the old Pisgah Cemetery east of Mace. John Wilson Jr. born 1782 and Lettitia Mills born 1783 were the parents of Thomas Jefferson, of which he was one of 12 children. John Wilson Sr. and Lydia Thatcher both born in the year 1739 were the great-great-grandparents of Raleigh and his brothers Walter, Bernard, and Aaron Faust Wilson and Aaron's twin sister Clara Faye Wilson.

HENRY WINGERT

Henry Wingert, son of Joseph and Katrina Hoover Wingert grandson of Martin and Anna Gingrich Wenger, was born Jan. 25, 1800. He added T to the name. He married Magadaline Frantz born Jan. 19, 1798, daughter of Michael III and Maria Elizabeth Frantz, on Oct. 5, 1822 in Virginia. Henry, Magadaline and their son Christopherr came east of Ladoga in 1866. Henry died Aug. 16, 1881 and Magadaline died Jan. 8, 1880 at Ladoga. They belonged to the Brethern Church and are buried in the Brethern Cemetery northwest of Ladoga. Henry was a woolen machinist and their children were: Joseph died age 11 in Virginia; Elizabeth Ayers died in Virginia; Susanna Haupt died in Pennsylvania; Henry, Jr., Jacob; Christopher; Magadaline; Brown; Katherine Gayhart died in Ladoga; John Wingert married Molly Hicks, they went to Eldorado, KS where he was superintendent of school, but they came back to Ladoga and he died in Crawfordsville on Mar. 19, 1894 and is buried in Ladoga. Molly then married William Brown or Downs. Christopher married Sarah Ayers, he was one of the 70 who voted in the first election after Ladoga had been incorporated. He died in Bloomington, IN, but is buried in Ladoga.

Jacob Wingert, son of Henry and Magdaline Frantz Wingert, was born Nov. 14, 1829 in Salem, VA and died in Montgomery Co., IN on July 7, 1898. In Bedford Co., VA he married Miss Julian Matilda Ashwell on Dec. 16, 1856. She was born in Bedford County on Dec. 6, 1831 and died in Montgomery County on July 3, 1920.

In the spring of 1867, (after Jacob had served in the Civil War as a Confederate Soldier and had been a prisoner for many months) they came by train to Ladoga. In 1868, he bought the Samuel Guntle farm which had a tile and brick factory on the west end which he ran until he retired in Crawfordsville in 1897. He became a member of the Whitesville Church in 1872 and served as an elder and trustee. He donated the first organ to the church. Jacob's children: Joseph, John and Lulu Jane attended Ladoga Normal School. Joseph and Bailey first lived in Ladoga, and later in Crawfordsville. John lived on the homeplace in Whitesville.

The Wingert name was originally Wenger and some of Jacob's cousins spelled it Winger. Jacob and Julian Wingert had 12 children, the first seven being born in Virginia and the last five in Indiana. They are Henry Tompkins b. 1857, died 1858; Jacob Bailey b. 1858, died 1935; John Marion b. 1859, died 1938; Magdaline b. Apr. 11, 1861, died 1948 and married James G. Randel and her second marriage was to Jerre Long; Joseph James b. 1862, die 1951, William Peter b. 1864, died 1937; Anna Belle b. 1866, died 1937; Charles born 1867, died 1942; Daniel Christopher b. 1870, died 1935 in Canada; Andrew David b. 1872, died in infancy; Lulu Jane b. 1875; Elvina "Ella" Susan b. 1877 and died 1959.

Jacob Bailey married Laura Robinson; John Marion married first to Dell Smith and second to Sarah Elizabeth Byrd; Joseph James married Fannie Kelley; William Peter married Ida Kelley; Anna Belle married James Everson; Charles married Maria Follick on Sept. 1, 1889; Lulu Jane married first Lee Chadwick and second Edwin Headley.

JACOB AND JULIAN ASHWELL WINGERT

The Wingert family has its roots in Switzerland, although the name was spelled Wengen, Wenger, Wanger, etc. Because of religious persecution many people were forced to leave the country and Hans Wenger, Jr. came to Philadelphia in 1748. Martin Wenger, his seventh child served in the Revolutionary War. Martin's son, Joseph, spelled his name Winger and later Joseph's son Henry added a "t" to the name.

Henry and Magdaline Frantz Wingert came to Montgomery Co., IN from Bedford Co., VA in 1866 and settled on a farm east of Ladoga. Henry was a woolen merchant, harness maker and a farmer. They lived in the Ladoga area until their deaths. Magdaline died in 1880 and Henry in 1881. They are buried in the Brethren Cemetery northwest of Ladoga.

Their son, Jacob, served in the Confederate Army in Company A, 28th Regiment from Virginia. He was taken prisoner in August, 1864 and was released May 14, 1865, after taking the oath of allegiance to the U.S. He was a northern sympathizer so this was no problem.

In 1867, Jacob, his wife Julian Ashwell Wingert, and their six children came from Virginia and joined Henry and Magdaline on their farm. The six children born in Virginia were Jacob Bailey, John Marion, Sarah Magdaline, Joseph James, William Peter, and Anna Belle. Charles Wingert was born soon after they came to Ladoga. In March, 1868, Jacob and his family moved to a farm one quarter mile east of Whitesville, which they had purchased from Samuel Gunkle. A small four-room frame house stood on the land and here four children were born: Daniel, Andrew David (died in infancy), Lulu Jane and Elvina Susan. More rooms were added and in 1978 with a change of ownership the house was remodeled with two of the original rooms still intact.

Jacob began making bricks for sale and when this proved profitable he bought a "tile mill." He and his sons, with extra help, operated the tile mill for several years. They also cut wood and hauled it to the railroad where it was used in the wood-burning engines.

Julian had brought her spinning wheel with her and made clothes for the family. Later she bought one of the first sewing machines used in the area. She and the girls raised geese and when each of the children married they were supplied with two pillows and a large featherbed.

Jacob and Julian helped organize the Whitesville Church in 1870 and Jacob was an elder and trustee for many years.

Jacob, his wife and daughter Ella moved to Crawfordsville in 1897. Jacob died Aug. 7, 1898, and Julian and daughter moved back to Whitesville. Julian died July 3, 1920, and Ella died June 28, 1958. They are buried in the Harshbarger Cemetery.

Fred, son of William and Ida Kelly Wingert; Leslie and Leland, sons of James and Anna Everson; Ernest, son of James and Sarah Randel; and Harold, son of Bailey and Laura Wingert served in World War I. Harold was killed in the battle of Chateau Thierry. After the war his body was returned to Crawfordsville and buried in Oak Hill Cemetery. *Submitted by Beulah Wingert*

JAMES HAROLD WINGERT'S MILITARY FUNERAL

The first military funeral held in Crawfordsville according to the *Crawfordsville Journal*, August 1919, was for James Harold Wingert, born Nov. 30, 1889 at Ladoga, son of Jacob Bailey and Laura Robinson Wingert, grandson of Jacob and Juliann Ashwell Wingert, and great grandson of Henry and Magdaline Frantz Wingert. They moved to Crawfordsville in 1907, and he graduated from Crawfordsville High School. He enlisted in W.W.I on Mar. 29, 1918 and was assigned to the 112th Infantry of the 38th Division. He only had four weeks training in the U.S., then was sent overseas. He was injured at the Battle of Chateau Thierry on Aug. 10, 1918 and died Aug. 11, 1918. First soldier killed from Crawfordsville. Byron Cox was the first soldier killed from Montgomery County. Harold's body remained in France until August 1919, then it was shipped to New York, then to Crawfordsville. He was buried Aug. 10, 1919. Rev. John Robertson McMahan of the Wabash Avenue Presbyterian Church, where his funeral was held, paid a great tribute to the American Expeditionary Force, who made the great sacrifice for their country. He paid special tribute to James Harold. At the cemetery, the Byron Cox Post of War Mothers stood on each side of the cartege, near the grave, through which the pallbearers carried the casket, draped in an American Flag, and topped with two beautiful floral pieces. A United States Liberty Truck, with a large American Flag, used as a canopy, and a black draped field artillery caisson carrying the body was silhouetted against the sky, and lent a martial note to the background. A fresh wind made the two flags float in the breeze, a beautiful scene. Commander Schulds of Byron Cox Post 72, had charge of the full military honor ceremonies, at the graveside, in Oak Hill Cemetery on a slight knoll. The Crawfordsville City Band led the cortege to the cemetery, playing a funeral march as they moved to the cemetery. Chaplain O.J. Cohee with the rank of Captain, of the U.S. Army Post of Ft. Knox, KY officiated at the grave. After the band took its position north of the grave, Captain Robert Vaughn's squad took its position. Lt. Harry Michael, acting Commander of Byron Cox Post told briefly of James Harold Wingert's life, and paid eloquent tribute to him while he was in the service. Chaplain Cohee gave a short prayer, then the command, "Salute the dead - ready, aim, fire." Thus the first military funeral held in Crawfordsville for the first soldier killed from Crawfordsville, James Harold Wingert, was a very poignant, sad, beautiful service, a wonderful tribute.

JOHN MARION WINGERT FAMILY

John Marion, son of Jacob and Julian (Ashwell) Wingert, married Ola Dell Smith of Boone County in 1892. They had one daughter, Goldia, who married John Brookshire. They had two daughters: Kathleen Devitt and Martha Lofland. Ola died in 1894 and is buried at Jamestown. In 1897, John married Sarah Elizabeth (Betty) Byrd, daughter of Elza and Minerva Davis Byrd.

Elza Byrd served in the Union Army in the Civil War. He was in Company H, 33rd Indiana Infantry. He was born in 1834 and died in 1894. He and his wife were buried in Harshbarger Cemetery.

John (born Nov. 2, 1859) bought the homeplace in 1904 and lived there until his death Feb. 24, 1938. He and Sarah had four children: Opal, Marion, Beulah and Donald. Sarah (Betty) born June 8, 1874, died Apr. 24, 1968. Marion bought the farm and lived there until his death Sept. 27, 1978. He and sister, Opal (died May 21, 1982) are buried in the Masonic Cemetery, Crawfordsville. John and Sarah are buried at Jamestown.

In 1976, the farm was designated a Centennial farm having been owned by one family for 100 years.

Goldia Brookshire operated a hatchery and worked for R.R. Donnelleys for several years. She died Aug. 23, 1984 and is buried in Oak Hill Cemetery.

Kathleen Dell Brookshire married Charles Devitt, Jr. in 1942. They have one son, Charles Michael.

Martha Ellen Brookshire married Robert Glenn Lofland in 1951. They have four children: Karen Suzanne, Robert Lucas, Richard Alan and Lori Ellen. One daughter died in infancy.

Beulah Wingert graduated from Indiana and Ohio Universities. She taught in Ohio and Montgomery Co., IN.

Donald Wingert, a graduate of Wabash College, was a combat crew member in a Troop Carrier Squadron based in China and India during World War II. He was awarded the Distinguished Flying Cross with two clusters for making 51 round trips over the "Hump," and for participating in the supply dropping operations of the northern Burma Campaign.

Donald married Evelyn Cox Francis in 1952, and is retired from R.R. Donnelley Printing Company. He has two step-children: Phillip Francis, Patricia Francis Harrison and one step-child, Penny Francis Osborn who died in 1979. *Submitted by Beulah Wingert*

HAROLD WOLVERTON

Harold Wolverton was born in Parke County to Andrew J. (b. 1884 Parke County) and Elizabeth (Coleman) (born 1886 Parke County) on Feb. 11, 1905. Harold was a farmer and worked for the County Highway Department. He was educated in the Parke County Schools. He served from 1920-28 in the U.S. Navy as a Carpenter's Mate. He was affiliated with Masons and K of P (served as Chancellor Commander three years). Harold died in 1982.

Harold married Nora Pittman (born Apr. 15, 1913) at Brazil and was educated in the Brazil and Crawfordsville schools. Nora enjoys genealogy and her membership in Pythian Sisters. She served as President of April Stars.

The Wolvertons had three children:

Shirley Ann (infant, deceased).

John F., born June 15, 1938 at Brazil. He married Phyllis Sutherlin (born Mar. 2, 1939) at Cloverdale. One child, Eric Lee born Aug. 18, 1963 at Crawfordsville. Eric married Joyce (Hatt) Dowell, born Mar. 15, 1958. (One child, Tonya Dowell). All four work at R.R. Donnelley and Sons.

William Robert, born June 30, 1945 at Crawfordsville. He like his father works for the Highway Department. He married Laverne (Roche) Corwin (born July 30, 1927) at Indianapolis. He has three stepchildren: Stephen, George and Rosie Corwin.

Both Harold and Nora's roots go way back in America as can be seen with the following. Harold's Wolverton lineage is:

Isaac (b. 1856 Parke County) m. Susan Rigdon.

Samuel (b. Jan. 30, 1828 Parke County) m. Nancy Crafton.

Cyrus (b. July 17, 1804 Ohio) m. Jane Bonnell Frazzee.

John (b. 1745 New Jersey) m. Mary Bell.

Joel (b. 1715 New Jersey) m. Elizabeth _____.

Charles, b. England, m. Mary Chadwick.

Mary Chadwick's parents were: John b. 1638 Darby, PA and Elizabeth Light, whose parents were Charles, b. 1597 in England and Elizabeth.

Nora Pittman Wolverton's lineage is as follows:

John B. Pittman (b. 1888 Pulaski Co., KY) m. Ella Boettger.

Thomas (b. 1857 Pulaski County) m. Josephine Pence.

Steven (b. 1829 Lincoln Co., KY) m. Elizabeth Delaney.

Moses (b. 1795) Rowan Co., NC m. Margaret Mize.

Micajah (b. 1750) Revolutionary War Soldier from North Carolina m. Lydia Morgan.

Benjamin.

Lydia Morgan's parents were: William Avery Morgan and Lydia Smith. *Submitted by Nora Wolverton*

JOHN E. WOODWARD

John E. Woodward was born Mar. 17, 1928 in Danville, IL, the fifth of seven children of James LeRoy and Elsie Rosamond Woodward. Their family includes Kenneth and Katherine, twins, Muriel, Bernadine, Donald and Marjorie. John graduated from Danville High School and attended the University of Illinois. On Oct. 17, 1954 he married Shirley Ann Trimell of Oakwood, IL. On June 1, 1956, John became the manager of Nichols Loan Corporation, a consumer financial company in Crawfordsville and with his wife moved to Montgomery County. They are the parents of four children all born at Crawfordsville, IN and all graduated from North Montgomery High School. Mark Alan born February 1957 and graduated from Ball State University with a B.A. in Business. Mark married Phyllis Ann Urbanski on July 27, 1985 and they are expecting their first child in July of 1989. Diane Lynn born September 1959 and graduated from Purdue University in 1981 with a B.A. in Business Management. Diane married Joseph Martin on Aug. 8, 1981 and they are the parents of Kimberly Ann, Joe Jr. and David. Jill Andrea born September 1963 and graduated from Purdue University with a B.A. in Psychology and in May 1989 received her Masters Degree from Ball State University. Jill married Richard Maxwell of Darlington in Reno, NV on Dec. 19, 1988. Michael Andrew born April 1965 and graduated from Ball State University with a B.A. in business in 1987. Michael married Julie Mitchell of Waynetown on Sept. 24, 1983 and they are the parents of Joshua and Tyler and are currently living in Terre Haute, IN.

In February of 1959, John purchased the Credit Bureau, a business that collects and assembles credit information on individual consumers. He added the collection agency in order to collect bad debts owed to medical, retail and commercial clients on a contingent fee basis.

John, the Republican County Chairman, first became interested in Republican politics in 1966 and was a candidate for State Representative. He was defeated in the Primary and in June of 1966 was appointed by then County Chairman, Carl Henthorn, as the Republican member of the County Election Board and continues to serve in that capacity. He was elected as County Chairman on Feb. 1, 1971 to fill the unexpired term of Carl Henthorn who retired. He has served continuously as Chairman since 1976 and under the current term will serve until Mar. 1, 1993.

In 1974, John purchased Nichols Loan and renamed it the Heritage Loan Corporation which he operated until 1978 at which time he sold the business to Avco Financial Services and from 1979 to June 30, 1988 he operated the County License Bureau.

John served in World War II in the United States Navy. He received an honorable discharge in 1948 with the rank of Electronic Technician 3rd Class.

WOODY FAMILY

At 4:30 a.m. on the morning of Friday, Apr. 12, 1861, the Confederate forces of Gen. Beauregard fired upon Fort Sumpter and the Civil War had begun.

Tensions were mounting as Nathan and Ruth

355

(Hadley) Woody gathered their children into their covered wagon and with the breakfast dishes remaining on the table, they left their Wake Co., NC home (near Raleigh) and headed for Indiana.

Their long journey ended in the Walnut Grove area of Boone County. Three of their children, Thomas, James and Mary (Woody) Beesley remained in Boone County. Hugh later moved to Compton, CA. However, a grandson of Thomas, Richard Woody, married Margaret Esther Smith and they now reside three miles northwest of Darlington. Richard is the present treasurer of the Darlington Methodist Church.

Four sons of Nathan Woody: Robert, Alfred, Gurney and Elwood, came to Franklin Twp. around the 1870's to establish their homes. All four brothers were born near Raleigh, NC.

Robert Woody, born 1846, married Cynthia Ann Cook in 1872 and they were the parents of Aletha Miller, Cecile Swazze, Leona Foscett, and Edna, who was able to attain her 101st birthday.

Alfred H. Woody, born 1850, married Sophia Jane Hewitt, daughter of J. Roth Hewitt. They established their farm home three miles east of Darlington and Alfred also served as trustee of the Methodist Episcopal Church when the present sanctuary was built in 1904.

They became the parents of John, Clara, Mary and Walter, all of whom attended DePauw University.

John M. Woody was a merchant and banker in Darlington and the father of Lois Snyder and Mabel Pattee.

Clara Mae Woody was a teacher of English and Latin in the Crawfordsville and Indianapolis schools.

Mary Ellen married Forrest C. Flaningam in 1910 and resided at their farm home three miles southeast of Darlington for 55 years. They were the parents of Dwight and DeVon, a former Superintendent of the Darlington Methodist Sunday School and the contributor of this family history.

Walter E. Woody, after serving in Europe in WWI, married Maude Williamson, and they spent most of their lives in Indianapolis.

Gurney Woody, born 1855, married Mary M. Tribbett in 1879 and served as minister of the Christian Church, near Kirklin, for 25 years. The Rev. Woody and his wife were the parents of the Rev. Orville Woody and Earl Woody, who served as trustee of Franklin Twp. in the 1920's. Orville married Opal Rayle and Earl married Fern Weliever.

Elwood Woody, born 1859, was 16 months of age when his family came to Indiana. He married Ida Catherine Flaningam in 1885 and lived on their family farm near Boone County. They were the parents of Raymond, Ralph, Leonard and Ethel Jarrell.

Other members of the Woody family also came to Franklin Township. William C. Woody, born 1850, south of Raleigh, was the son of Hugh and Matilda Woody. Hugh, a minister in the Friends Church, was a cousin of Nathan. William was a farmer, residing three miles northeast of Darlington, and was appointed postmaster at Darlington in 1900.

Robert, Gurney and Alfred were buried at Greenlawn Cemetery at Darlington, and Elwood, at St. James Lutheran Cemetery.

Nathan and Ruth Woody believed in the new Republican Party, the Abolitionist Cause, and loyalty to the Union. Their descendants continued to live by these principles.

RICHARD AND MARGARET WOODY

Richard and Margaret Smith Woody reside on a farm at Route 6, Crawfordsville, four miles northwest of Darlington. Margaret's paternal grandfather, Solomon W. Peterson born 1835 was one of the early residents of Sugar Creek Township. Solomon was married to Jane Dain. Margaret's maternal grandparents were Hiram and Matilda Smith. Richard and Margaret are parents of three children.

Robert born 1949 is a graduate of Darlington High School, and Indiana State University. He and his wife Margaret reside at Stockwell and are the parents of four sons. Robert is employed by Wabash National Trailer at Lafayette.

James born 1953 is a graduate of Darlington High School and Purdue University. He and his wife Debbie, and son reside at Greencastle, IN. He is employed at United Tractor Service at New Market.

Kristen born 1961 is a graduate of North Montgomery and Purdue. She is a Consulting Engineer with Roy F. Weston Inc. Engineering Firm and resides in Houston, TX.

Richard and Margaret have resided at this location since 1962. Margaret was born at this location and attended Potato Creek Methodist Church as a youngster. They are active members of the Darlington United Methodist Church and have held various offices in the Church. They have just completed their second building mission with the West Indianapolis District of the United Methodist Church. The first in 1988 was to McAllen, TX, the second to Carlsbad, NM.

Margaret, one of four daughters of Harry and Mabel Peterson Smith was born 1925. She attended Bowers School, graduated from Thorntown High School, and Purdue University with a B.S. degree in Home Economics. She was a teacher and dietician at Clinton Prairie High School near Frankfort, IN. for 31-1/2 years before retiring in 1986. She is a member of Darlington Book Lovers Club and M.N.O. Homemakers Extension Club.

Richard born in 1924 in Sugar Creek Township, Boone County, graduated from Thorntown High School and attended Purdue University. His parents were Clark and Lois Long Woody. His great-grandparents, Nathan and Ruth Hadley Woody came from North Carolina in 1861. Richard has been active in various organizations. He served on Montgomery County 4-H Inc. Board, Montgomery County Cattlemen's Association and is currently serving as a board member of Montgomery County Farm Bureau Inc. and has been Secretary-Treasurer for 18 years. He also serves as Secretary-Treasurer of District V Farm Bureau, Inc. He served three years on the Montgomery-Tippecanoe Farmers Home Committee. *Submitted by Richard and Margaret Woody*

DAVID WRAY

Records of other Wrays in Montgomery Co., IN who were related to him indicate that David was probably born in Pennsylvania in the late 1700s. His mother's name is unknown. His father, James Wray, appeared on a list of males over 21 in Hanover Township of Butler Co., OH, in 1807, and he died there in 1814. He left the following children, several of whom later moved to Montgomery Co., IN: David married Dec. 14, 1820 in Butler County to Martha Passmore; Richard; Samuel; William married Aug. 28, 1817 in Butler County to Martha's sister, Abigail Passmore; Lettice "Lettie" married Aug. 28, 1817 in Butler County to Reily Harney; Jane married Feb. 5, 1817 Butler County to Joseph Scott; Carson; Mary; Isabella; and Henry.

In April 1824, David came to Montgomery County and purchased from the government land office in Crawfordsville 80 acres in township 18, section 28 of Union Township, near the Finley Chapel. In June 1830 he sold 20 of those acres to a Henry Wray.

David died in 1830. A Samuel Wray was administrator of his estate. His death left Martha with five small children: Phebe born about 1821, John P. born Nov. 27, 1822, Lavina born Mar. 21, 1825, Cynthian born about 1828, and Susan J. born about 1831. The first two were born in Butler Co., OH and the last three in Montgomery Co., IN. All five married in Montgomery County. John P. was indentured to Samuel Gilliland until his majority.

Phebe was married Jan. 13, 1840 to John Morgan. Their known children were Elizabeth born about 1845 and Cornelia J. born about 1848.

John was first married Dec. 27, 1843 to Julia Ann Busenbark who died six months after their marriage. He married secondly on Mar. 7, 1849 to Mary Ann Britton. More of him later.

Lavina was married first on Apr. 18, 1842 to James Hughes and they had David Wesley, Thomas J., James F., Emma, Lavina, Ellen, Sarah J., Nervilla, Melissa, Anna. She remarried on Apr. 4, 1875 to Samuel Buck. She died Feb. 2, 1893 at her home six miles north of Crawfordsville. She is buried in Young's Chapel Cemetery, Union Township.

Cynthian was married Apr. 5, 1849 to Joseph Jones. She died Feb. 3, 1911 in Coal Creek Township and is buried in Mt. Pleasant Cemetery. They had Samuel, Henry, Martha, Margaret, Emma, Laura E. and Ida.

Susan J. was married Sept. 16, 1853 to James Hall.

JOHN P. WRAY

John P. Wray was born Nov. 27, 1822 in Butler Co., OH, the only son of David Wray and Martha Passmore. His parents migrated in 1824 to Montgomery Co., IN. His father died when John was eight years old and he was indentured to Samuel Gilliland until he reached his majority.

He was married Dec. 27, 1843 in Montgomery County to Julia Ann Busenbark. She died six months later.

He was married Mar. 7, 1849, also in Montgomery County, to Mary Ann Britton, the daughter of Thomas P. Britton and Frances Farnsworth.

Their children were all born in Montgomery County. They were Laura Priscilla, Leanna "Annie" J., Martha Frances, William J., Clara E., and John M.

Mary Ann Britton Wray wife of John P. Wray

Laura Priscilla was born May 6, 1851. She was

married Nov. 25, 1869 to George Henry Steele. Their family story is found elsewhere in this book.

Leanna J. was born Feb. 8, 1854. She was married in Montgomery County on Dec. 30, 1874 to James V. Finley. In 1880 they were residents of Clinton County, living near her sister and brother-in-law, Laura and George Steele. Their children were Frank H., a Crawfordsville baker; Harry, Ola E., Blanche, John and Nora. Leanna died Feb. 5, 1929 at the home of her daughter Blanche in Wabash and is buried in Crawfordsville's Masonic Cemetery.

Martha Frances, named for both her grandmothers, was born Oct. 27, 1855 and died July 8, 1863.

William J. "Billy" was born Dec. 13, 1856. He lived near Linden most of his life. He is thought to have never been married. He died Jan. 22, 1930 at the home of his niece Blanche Finley Schroeder in Marion, IN. He was buried in Crawfordsville's Masonic Cemetery in the family plot.

Clara E. was born Dec. 6, 1860. She was married Jan. 19, 1882 in Montgomery County to Robert A. Fendley and they had a daughter Ruby. Ruby married Frank Reyburn and was living in rural Lafayette in 1930. Clara married secondly on Dec. 27, 1898 in Montgomery County to George E. Jordan. She died May 15, 1923 in Indianapolis and is buried in the family plot in the Masonic Cemetery in Crawfordsville. She had been a member of the Mt. Pleasant Christian Church in Linden.

John M. was born September 1863. On Aug. 24, 1890 in Montgomery County, he married Alfaretta Jackson. Their known children were John N., Ana L., Austin, Charles and William. He is listed in the probate of his brother William J.'s estate in 1930 as Dr. John M. Wray of Route 2, Wolcott, IN.

John P. Wray died suddenly and unexpectedly on Jan. 1, 1867 of typhoid fever and is buried with his wife Mary Ann, who died in 1889, and children, William J. and Clara E. Jordan, in the family plot in Crawfordsville's Masonic Cemetery. He was a farmer who raised timothy, wheat, oats, corn, potatoes, apples, bees, hogs, sheep, cattle and horses. At the time of his death he had just built, or was in the process of building, a sizeable home. A bill for $10,764 for the lumber is included in the probate of his estate. He had already paid $5,000 and the balance was paid by the administrator. He donated half the land for school #5, of which he was a director, in section 13 township 19 of the northern part of Union Township, a few miles northwest of Crawfordsville.

LAURA PRISCILLA WRAY

Laura Priscilla Wray was born May 6, 1851 in Union Township of Montgomery County to John P. Wray and Mary Ann Britton, the oldest of six children. She was married there by Reverend Abraham Utter of the Methodist Episcopal Church on Nov. 25, 1869 to George Henry Steele. George was born Mar. 14, 1843 in Bath Co., KY to Robert Steele and Mary "Polly" Cassity.

After their marriage, George and Laura helped her widowed mother with her farm and the care of her small brothers and sisters. About 1875 the Steeles moved to a farm in Clinton Co., IN. They had seven children, four of whom lived to maturity. They were Mary Alice "Mayme", whose story appears elsewhere in this book, Wray Morgan, Van Orman and Jessie N. Shortly after Jessie's birth the family moved to Lafayette in Tippecanoe County.

George was a very fine carpenter and cabinet maker. In Lafayette he fell from a ladder while repairing an outdoor sign over a jeweler's doorway. He landed on his feet, breaking both legs. He was put into a wagon and taken home. He refused to be carried into the house and crawled up the slight incline on his hands and knees. He was laid up for about two years and was eventually able to walk again. But he was unable to resume his carpentry work. He became a shoemaker as it was something he could do without being on his feet.

Wray Morgan was born Jan. 13, 1884 in Geetingsville in Clinton County. He was married in Lafayette on Jan. 22, 1906 to Bertha Werner of Lafayette, the daughter of John Werner and Amelia Koehler. He was a wall paper hanger. They had no children. Wray died in that city on Apr. 7, 1946 and is buried there in the Springvale Cemetery with Bertha who died in 1957.

Van Orman was born Aug. 9, 1886 in Geetingsville. He was a house painter in Lafayette and for several years was secretary of the painter's union there. He later was a merchant patrolman for ten years until retiring in 1953. He was married in Lafayette on Aug. 9, 1912 to Hazel Rebecca Crites, the daughter of George W. Crites and Effie G. Jinks. Their son, Van Orman, Junior, "Buddy", was born there in May 1917 and was living in 1986 in Flora. Hazel died in September 1918. Van, Senior, was married May 27, 1926 to Sylvia Blanche Taylor. He died July 2, 1959 and Blanche on June 5, 1968. They are buried together in Springvale Cemetery in Lafayette.

Jessie N. was born Sept. 21, 1888 in Frankfort in Clinton County. She was married in Tippecanoe County on Oct. 24, 1902 to William Stone, son of Solomon Stone and Clarissa Bennett. Jessie was married secondly to William White who died Aug. 20, 1918 in Lafayette. They had sons Ralph Waldo and Elmer Hamilton. Jessie died Aug. 17, 1926 in Indianapolis and is buried with her parents and sister Mayme in the Masonic Cemetery in Crawfordsville.

George died Oct. 27, 1917 in Lafayette and was buried in the Springvale Cemetery there. Laura died Mar. 31, 1929 at the Lafayette home of her son Wray. She was buried in the Masonic Cemetery in Crawfordsville and George was moved there to lie beside her.

MARTHA PASSMORE WRAY

Martha Passmore Wray was born Feb. 10, 1804 in Hamilton Co., OH, the ninth of 11 children of Henry Passmore, Sr. and Martha Busel. Henry and Martha had migrated to Crosby Township there from Chester Co., PA around 1797. A street in New Haven, OH still bears his name. Many descendants are living in that area in 1989. Henry's grandfather, John Passmore, was a Quaker who emigrated from Hurst, Berks Co., England, with his wife Mary Buxcey, in 1713 to Chester Co., PA. Henry died in 1836 and Martha in 1842. Both are buried in the Old Baptist Cemetery near Harrison, OH.

Martha's siblings were Mary, Henry Jr., Hannah, Ann, Rebecca, John, Abigail, Phebe, Elizabeth and Margaret.

Martha married David Wray Dec. 14, 1820 in Butler Co., OH. He died in 1830 in Montgomery Co., IN. An account of their family appears in his story in this book. She was married Nov. 24, 1838 to William K. (some records state R.) Miller. On Mar. 9, 1839 they sold their four acres in Catterlin's Addition in Crawfordsville and nothing further is known of them.

LLOYD OWEN WRIGHT

Lloyd Owen Wright was born Dec. 7, 1930, to Robert Owen and Elva May (Huffman) Wright in Dana, IN. Owen worked as a farmer and carpenter. In 1942, he moved his family to a farm south of Waveland, later in 1965 they moved into Waveland.

Owen, along with his six brothers and three sisters were reared near Clinton, IN. His brother, Merle Wright married Rose Peer, no children. Emmett Wright married Martha Chambers; six children, Paul, David, John, Richard, Barbara Sturgeon and Jane Myers. Roscoe married Mary Cannon; four children, Imogene Long, Phyllis (1) Neslar (2) Edwards, Ladonna Riggen and an infant son. Later Roscoe married Mildred Batner, one son, Carl. Versa Wright married Leo Huffman, seven children: Gladys Nesbit, Ray, Earl, Carolyn, Cheryl, Robert and Wretha Shull. Chloral Wright married George Merritt, four children: Neil, Mayne, Tommy Joe and June. Harry Wright married Opal Allen, four children: Mike, Larry, Janet Higgenbotham and Beverly Higgenbotham. Eva Ellen Wright married Jim Long, two children: Ronald and Dennia. Delbert Wright married Virginia Fears, three children: Sharon, Gerald and Marvin.

The Wright Family, taken 1971 left to right, front row: Melvin, James, Dollie, Roy. Back Row: Lloyd, Marjorie, Roger, John

Elva May (Huffman) Wright's parents were James and Susan Sarene Stone from Universal. Elva had one brother, Marion Huffman who married Mabel Pollock, two children, Richard and Edith. Elva had one sister, Phoebe who married George Jones, six children: Emma Jean Coverstone, Darla Layton, Davene Harmon, LaDonna Fox, Georgia Rose Taylor and George Jones, Jr.

Owen's children were: Herbert, Lloyd, Francis, Velma, Virginia and Waunita.

Herbert Leon Wright married Donna Sue Heslar, two daughters: Nancy married Dennis Canada (one daughter, Linette) and Linda married Keith Axsom (two children, Jason and April).

Lloyd Owen Wright married Marjorie Newport in 1951, six children: Roger, John, Melvin, Jim, Dollie and Roy. John is married to Michelle Carpenter (three children, Amber, Brandon and Kendra). Melvin is married to Brenda Long (two sons, Joshua and Matthew).

Lloyd attended Green Township School. He spent two years in the Marines, stationed in North Carolina. He has worked as a mechanic most of his life. He is co-owner and manager of Wright's Alignment Shop at Ladoga since 1976.

Marjorie Newport's parents were William Sherman and Dallie Gertrude McNary Newport from Marshall, IL. Marjorie has one sister, Edith who married Virgil Wallace, Jr., three children: Martha,

Virgil and John. Marjorie attended Marshall, IL High School and Terre Haute Commercial College. She has worked for South Montgomery School Corp. as a Custodian since 1979.

Francis Wright married Barbara Hughes (one son, Darrell). Francis later married Margaret Black Flick.

Velma Wright married Grover Wethington, three children: Stanley, Russell, Diana. Stanley married Kathy Gross (three children, Kristie, Stacy, Scott). He later married Lee Ann Fulwider. Russell Wethington married Drinda Dice (two children, Randall and Kimberly). Diana Wethington married Bryan Matricia (two children, Carey and Monica Kay).

Waunita Wright married Charles Reisinger of Brazil, four children: Jerry, Rodney, Max, Jo Vinn. Max married Lynn Chamness. Jo Vinn married Dale Dickey. *Submitted by Marjorie Wright*

JOHN WYATT

John Wyatt was born in London, England, on June 4, 1748. He died in Milroy, IN, June 17, 1833. His life encompassed one of the most important periods in the history of this country, and it seems fitting that we should remember him now with this monument. His background is of English nobility which we can trace far back into English history. His father was a mariner. Although born in England, he resided prior to the Revolutionary War in Botetourt Co., VA.

He served almost three years in the Continental Army, enlisting in 1778 in his home county in Virginia. He made a deposition before three judges of the Rush Circuit Court in April, 1833, shortly before his death, in which he was asking for a pension for his services. In this he gave a history of his Revolutionary services. After enlisting, he marched to Petersburg, VA, then they joined with other troops and marched to Valley Forge, where they joined the main army under General George Washington. After a short time they marched to New Jersey, where he was in the battle of Monmouth. In December he re-enlisted, and was given a furlough at home. In 1779 they marched to Charleston, SC, where the siege of Charleston lasted six weeks. The Americans lost the battle to the British General Clinton, and Wyatt was taken prisoner. He was a prisoner about six months, when he purchased the protection of a Tory named Joseph Seal, who had enlisted with the British.

October 1986 Tombstone - Milroy, IN. John B. Wyatt of Crawfordsville descendant of John Wyatt 1748 England

By posing under the name of Joseph Seal and using his papers Wyatt was able to get through the British lines and reached his own officers. After they interviewed him, they prevailed upon him to go back as a spy among the Tories. He went back under an old captain's commission. With the help of his papers and some newspapers he had obtained at Charleston he was received by the British and entertained by them. He learned of British plans to attack at New River. He even obtained a written list of their force. Finding that he could not reach the American lines in time to give them this urgent information, he persuaded the Tories to delay because British troops would be arriving in a short time to re-enforce them. They agreed, and again he went through the lines to his officers and communicated his information to them. They raised the militia and marched back to win and took many prisoners. In the summer of 1781 he volunteered again, served two months at Yorktown, and was mustered out about two months after the surrender of Cornwallis at Yorktown.

John Wyatt was married to Susan (Susanna) Summit in 1770 or 1772, probably. Some records give the place of marriage as Virginia, and some as Kentucky. Names and dates are given for 13 children born from 1775 to 1800. There are many descendants of the couple, and a number of them are still in this area. George C. Wyatt, who founded the Wyatt Mortuary was a son of James Summit Wyatt, the youngest son. Frank Wyatt Moore was a descendant of this branch. Mary Wyatt was born in 1784. She married Nathan Tompkins, who was one of the founders of Milroy. Among her descendants are Ellendore Lampton, who is the only member of DAR in Rushville currently who went in under the name of John Wyatt. The late Charles (Cy) Tompkins was also from this branch. There are many others whose background I can give upon request.

For me there are two personal touches I felt in all the material I have received about this man. When he wrote his last Will he asked that when he died his pension should be received by his daughter, Mary, "for her kindness and attention to me in my old age and during my sickness." Also in an article concerning the Wyatts of Virginia in Stella Pickett Hardy's *Colonial Families of the Southern States* she says: "He was remembered by his grandchildren, as an old English gentleman, with powdered hair, knee britches, silver knee and shoe buckles, and silk stockings."

Jean Tompkins, with much help from many sources, primarily those of Virginia Weathers of Colorado and old papers of Mr. George C. Wyatt.

John and Marabeth Wyatt, children of John L. Wyatt.

John L. Wyatt, Philip Wyatt and Connie Wyatt Price, children of John B. Wyatt.

John B. Wyatt, Martha Davis, Mary Louise Wiles and Kathrena Perkins, children of Warder H. Wyatt.

Warder H. Wyatt (and five sisters and brother) children of George C. Wyatt.

George C. Wyatt, son of James Wyatt.

James Wyatt, (and 12 brothers and sisters) son of John Wyatt born 1748.

John Wyatt (born (1748).

Michael P., Christopher J. children of Philip.

John C., Marabeth, Adam and Mason are children of (Jack) and (Connie), grandchildren of John B. Wyatt, great-grandchildren of Warder H. Wyatt, great-great-grandchildren of George C. Wyatt, great-great-great-grandchildren of James Wyatt, great-great-great-great-grandchildren of John Wyatt.

THEODORE GLENN AND BONNIE SUE YAHRAUS

Theodore Glenn and Bonnie Sue Yahraus came to Crawfordsville in 1976 from Hendersonville, NC where their children, Tami Lynne and Anthony Glenn had been born.

Ted was born in Cleveland, OH Aug. 26, 1946 to Edward W. Yahraus and Florentina Pacileo Yahraus. Edward was the son of Theodore Leopold (a Blacksmith) and Aurelia Keifer Jahraus of Leopoldshafen, Germany and Austria-Hungary respectively. Florentina, born in Naples, Italy to Genarro and Camelia Fasula Pacileo, was the youngest of five daughters in a family of six children. The Reverend Pacileo came to Cleveland as a Baptist pastor/missionary to the Italian immigrants in that area. A very talented man, he also painted, built miniature furniture, and drew-up early plans for Cleveland's Hopkins Field Airport. Camelia, a well-educated woman, spoke five languages, had been awarded a medal of honor by the French cavalry commending her courage in breaking a wild horse, played the piano beautifully and served as a librarian and aid to her husband in his ministry.

Bonnie was born in Fort Wayne, IN, Oct. 11, 1947 to Lloyd Beal Antonides and Helena Katherine Ward. The Antonides family first arrived on Long Island, NY in 1693. The Reverend Vincentius Antonides van der Goes came from Holland to pastor a church in Flatbush. Buried under the current church structure, a plague and stained glass window bear testimony of his contribution in the early Dutch Reformed Church. The Beal family were early arrivals to America; Lloyd's grandfather being a builder of flour mills throughout the Southwest. Helena's mother's family were Italian immigrants to Fort Wayne where her grandfather, Vincent Moritz "Morie" operated a fruit market. Little is known of Helena's father's family, except that her grandfather operated a plaster supply business in Ohio. Bonnie's grandmother, Jane K. Moritz Ward was a hardworking, independent woman who purchased, renovated, and operated a rooming house in a beautiful old Victorian townhouse. From this endeavor, she made a living for herself and her daughter.

Both Ted and Bonnie's parents stressed the value of faith, honesty, education and hard work. To set and achieve their goals in life, both graduated from Purdue; Ted as a mechanical engineer, Bonnie as a computer systems engineer. In Crawfordsville, both were employed by Hi-Tek recently. Ted is currently Vice President of Engineering at Indy Lighting. Bonnie is currently renovating an older home in which she hopes to operate a Bed & Breakfast. Together, they have refurbished the O'Neal home at 600 E. Main Street.

They are members of Woodland Heights Christian Church and have supported the school system especially in the development of the A&E program. Both participated in a lighting technology exchange program to China and Ted has published several articles on lighting and developed several patent ideas.

The younger Yahrauses are excellent students, participating also in church youth groups and sports. They have delivered the *Indianapolis Star* for five years. Tami hopes to study bio-chemistry after graduation and Tony is considering engineering or airline piloting. *Submitted by Bonnie Yahraus*

LYN ALLISON (ANTROBUS) YEAGER

Lyn Allison Antrobus was born at midnight, and Dr. George T. Williams, not sure of the exact moment, asked, "Mrs. Antrobus, do you wish the baby's birth date to be the tenth or the eleventh?"

Augusta Antrobus replied, "Let's say the tenth so that if something really fine ever comes to her it will be one day sooner." So, the date was June 10, 1915, Crawfordsville, IN.

Lyn Allison's parents were sincere, dedicated Christians. Rev. Barnabas (Barney) Edward Antrobus was pastor of the Crawfordsville First Baptist Church 1911-1916 and 1927-1939. During his time of service, a dozen young men dedicated themselves to the ministry and one young woman to missionary service in Africa.

Lyn Allison (Antrobus) Yeager

Allison graduated from Crawfordsville High School in the upper quarter of her class in 1933 and received a scholarship to DePauw University. She sang in the college choir for four years, in one of which she supplied in the Faculty Quartet. She graduated in 1937 with a Bachelor of Music degree and membership in two honor societies, Mu Phi Epsilon and Pi Kappa Lambda. Years later she attended Oklahoma College for Women, Texas Tech., Western Kentucky University, Central Missouri State College and received a Master of Science in Education from Henderson State in Arkadelphia, AR. Her teaching career included a Baptist seminary in New York, public schools in Oklahoma and Missouri, Wayland Baptist College, Ouachita College and 15 years at Whiteman Air Force Base. She has been a choir director and/or organist for churches of four denominations in six states for more than 40 years. In 1989 she was in her third year employed as choir director in the United Methodist Church in Smithton, MO.

One week after graduation from DePauw University Allison married Randolph Orville Yeager, a Baptist minister, one of the "boy preachers" of the Baptist Church, June 24, 1937, in the First Baptist Church in Crawfordsville. They had two sons: Gaylen Antrobus Yeager, born in Crawfordsville in 1939 and Rodney Alan Yeager, born in Princeton in 1942. Gaylen became a civil engineer employed by Howard-Needles in Kansas City and Rodney became a full Colonel in the U.S. Air Force and retired in 1989. There are four grandchildren and one great grandchild. Randy and Allison were divorced in 1979.

Randy O. Yeager graduated from Syracuse University, cum laude, and earned a Ph.D. in history from Oklahoma University. He became a professor and taught at Oklahoma University, Wayland, Ouachita, Western Kentucky University, and in 1988-89 at Averett College in Virginia.

In 1986 Allison became a member of the Daughters of the American Revolution and in 1989 became the director of the Helen G. Steele Music Club Chorus in Sedalia, MO. She has had two books published: *Barney*, 1974, and *Log Structures of Warren County, Kentucky,* 1977, plus over 200 magazine articles in history, folk lore and devotionals.

CYRUS S. YOUNG

Cyrus S. Young came to Montgomery County about 1872. He was born in 1851, in Pennsylvania. He worked as a carpenter. He died in 1892.

On June 8, 1873, he married Malinda E. "Minnie" Battreal (also spelled Batterall). She was born July 22, 1856, in Wingate, the daughter of Michael and Violetta Smith Battreall. She died Mar. 16, 1939, in Indianapolis, and was buried in the Masonic Cemetery in Crawfordsville.

To this union was born five children: John M. (married Nettie Armstrong), Guy M. (married Rose M. Nolan), Effie Elizabeth (married David Monroe Harris), Lavanche (married 1st - Montgomery C. Burk, 2nd - John Wise), and Harrison (married Marguerite Stonebraker).

John M. Young was born in 1874 in Newton, and died Jan. 26, 1950, in Indianapolis. He is buried in the Masonic Cemetery in Waynetown. He was a charter member of the Crawfordsville chapter of the Eagles Lodge. He was the father of one son, Lloyd.

Guy M. Young was born in 1877 in Newtown, and later lived in Indianapolis.

Effie Elizabeth Young Harris was born Oct. 1, 1879, in Richland Township, Fountain County. She died at the young age of 34 at the Presbyterian Hospital of Chicago on Nov. 16, 1913. She was the mother of three children: two sons, Ralph, and James Montgomery; and a daughter, Martha Ellen.

Lavanche Young Burk Wise was born in 1883, and later moved to Miami, FL.

Harrison Young was born Sept. 30, 1886, in Newtown, and died Apr. 25, 1951, in Crawfordsville. He is buried in the Masonic Cemetery there. Harrison was the only citizen to serve as chief of both the police and fire departments of Crawfordsville. Harrison first became associated with the Crawfordsville fire department in 1907, serving until 1914. Before joining the fire department, he had driven a horse drawn cab for the McFarland Cab Company. For a number of years he was associated with the Cummings Auto Company and later as manager for the American Security Company's loan office on South Green Street. Prominent in Republican politics in Crawfordsville for many years, Harrison was city chairman during the campaign in 1928 when Dr. Thomas L. Cooksey first was elected mayor. Following the election, Harrison was appointed chief of police, a position he held for four and one-half years. Later during the campaign of Dr. Bertrand E. May for mayor of the city, Mr. Young also served as city chairman for the Republican Party. Following Dr. May's election, Harrison was appointed chief of the fire department in 1935. He continued with the Crawfordsville fire department until his death in 1951. He was the father of only one child, a son, Edgar.

Following the death of Cyrus Young, Malinda married two other times, to Rev. David W. Hughes, and to Charles E. Drake, who both predeceased her.

YOUNT FAMILY

The Yount name was originally spelled Jundt. Hans George and Anna Maria Jundt and four children came from a village on the Rhine, in Alsace, arriving at Philadelphia, PA, on the ship "Brittania", 1731. Upon arriving in this country, they adopted the Anglicized spelling Yount.

Dan and Allen Yount, descendants of this family, migrated to Montgomery County, in 1840. The two brothers proceeded to build a mill on Spring Creek about 200 hundred yards northwest of the brick building that was later erected on Sugar Creek.

Along with the development of the business, came quite a prosperous village. A petition for a post office was granted. The office was named Yountsville, thus "Yountsville".

In 1849 a large wooden mill was built including looms, starting the first spinning and weaving in the area. In 1864 a three story brick structure was built and is standing today. In this building, during the Civil War, cloth was woven for Union Army uniforms.

A boarding house was built to serve the employees of the mill. John and Pat Hardwick are currently renovating the boarding house, now known as Yount's Mill Inn, for use as a bed and breakfast.

Descendants of Allen Yount include: William Price Yount, b. July 19, 1833, married to Sarah Ann Walter, b. July 7, 1834. A son, Walter Vick Yount, b. Oct. 10, 1869, married Florence Swearingen, b. June 5, 1866. To this union were born six children: Harry, Lura, Ernest, Charles, William and Sarah. Harry and Ernest being life time residents and business men of Montgomery County.

Harry married Marye Ann Groll May 10, 1916. In 1917 they moved to Darlington where they operated a grocery and meat market until 1946. In 1949 Harry purchased the Farmer's Feed and Grain Co., from which he retired, leaving its operation to sons Allen and George. Harry and Marye were the parents of five children: Walter (deceased), Allen, Virginia, Kathleen and George. Allen married Nancy Eads in 1953. They are the parents of: Tamara Bronaugh (sons Jason and Joshua), Terry Yount m. Renita Dinius (children Kisha Yount, Heather, Nathan and Joshua Dinius), and Glenda Yount. Virginia married Leonard Holt in 1947. They are the parents of Jill Dale (m. Bill Dale). Kathleen married Perle Bridges in 1950. Three daughters were born to Kathleen and Perle: Candace (m. Richard Royer sons Aaron and Brian), Mitzi Bridges and (Belinda, deceased). George married Ann Grimes in 1951, they have two children: Dennis and Donna (m. Garth Hughes).

Ernest married Laura French Aug. 22, 1922. Ernest and Laura lived in New Market where Ernest was employed by the Farmers State Bank for 45 years. Two children, Irene (deceased), and Don were born to them. In 1956 Don married Virginia Hay. Four children were born of that marriage. Don, Steven (m. Corrine McGure) Tamsen (m. Joseph Impicciche, children Andrea and Christopher), and Kathryn (m. Sam Shelton, daughter Samantha).

Records show the Yount family were active members of the Church as are their descendants.

JAMES W. YOUNT

James W. Yount was born in Kentucky on Dec. 9, 1823. He came to Indiana with three daughters - Matilda, Mary J. and Sophine.

Married Mary Cathrine Shelly on May 14, 1861. Mary was born in Parke County Apr. 18, 1838.

Mary owned land in Parke County, with her brothers. Mary and James sold interest to her brothers. They then bought land in Waveland (about three acres) - West side of the road approaching Waveland on the North.

James enlisted in Civil War July 10, 1863, discharged July 15, 1863.

1880 Census records show James 46 years,

Teameast by trade, Mary 45 yrs., George Morton 17 yrs., Sarah 12 yrs., Tom 10 yrs, John 8 years, Carrie 5 years and Francis 2 years. George Morton was grandfather of Helen Yount Weaver.

Mary C. Yount born April 18, 1838

James died Dec. 16, 1889. After his death Mary started selling off the land. She also gave easement to the railroad to crow her land. Sale of land: to James Canine $75.00, Nov. 16, 1892; John Fisher and Francis Kritz, $3750, Apr. 25, 1893; Tom Moody $75.00, Dec. 18, 1895; John Fisher and Francis Kritz, $100.00, Mar. 9, 1896; Tom Moody, $75.00, Sept. 22, 1899.

Mary died at her daughter's home (Mrs. S.T. White) in Parkersburg on Feb. 15, 1916. At the time of her death she had 31 grandchildren, and 27 great-grandchildren. James and Mary are buried at Maple Ridge Cemetery at Waveland.

Matilda married James Birch. Mary J. married James Webb. Sophine married O. Seward. Lavine married William McKinnes, - when he died she married Joe Nicholson. Sarah married Sam Staggs. Carrie married S.T. White. No trace of Francis. Tom married Emma Birch. John married Irene Ritter. George Morton married Sarah Nickolson Collins.

Tom and Emma had two sons. Everett married; no children; died Apr. 18, 1966. Clarence, unmarried; died Sept. 26, 1957.

Tom died in 1904. Emma remarried and moved to Oregon.

John and Irene had one son Earl. Earl married and had two daughters, G. Morton and Sarah. Children: Clara married Harve Barton, Bessie married Omer Trout, Nettie married three times, Harry married Charlotte Britton.

Harry and Charlotte children: Eugene - died as baby; Sherman died as baby; Joe married Geneva Thompson; Helen married John Weaver; Ruth - married Albert Beasy; Alice Merl married Henry Jester. Joe and Geneva, one daughter; Joe died September 1985.

WILLIAM A. ZACH FAMILY

William A. "Bill" and Mary "Joan" Kritz Zach are relative newcomers to the Montgomery County scene, having arrived in Crawfordsville in 1955. The Zach's came to the area under unusual circumstances. For a number of years, both worked at Michiana Products in Michigan City. When the firm was closed down, Bill began to realize a lack of college education was holding him back in his quest for advancement. Therefore, he decided to begin a college career. However, he had a wife and three small children to support. When the couple discovered two drive-in food stands for sale, they looked into purchasing them since Crawfordsville was within driving distance of Purdue.

Many coney dogs later, on the couple's 14th wedding anniversary (May 31, 1959) and soon after his 38th birthday, Bill's wife and children watched him receive his diploma as a graduate in mechanical engineering.

Barb, Becky, Jim, Joan and Bill Zach

Bill was born Apr. 14, 1921 in LaPorte, the son of Herbert and Helen (Marschke) Zach. He graduated from Isaac C. Elston High School 20 years prior to receiving his college diploma. He is past president of Lions.

Joan was born Nov. 23, 1921 in Mishawaka, the daughter of James William and Sarah "Alice" Thompson Kritz. She graduated from St. Mary's High School in 1939 and South Bend College of Commerce. Joan is past Regent of Dorothy Q DAR, past president of Garden Club, Antique Study Club and other organizations.

Their children were all born in Michigan City: James William (Jim); Rebecca Ann (Becky); and Barbara Joan (Barb).

Jim, born Jan. 17, 1949, is a graduate of C.H.S. and Purdue in Restaurant Management. He served seven years in the Army National Guard where he earned numerous awards in both riflery and cookery. Jim is a member of NRA and William Knight Chapter, S.A.R. He is owner of Zach's Family Restaurant on Greencastle Road. Jim married Karen Bazzani (see Bazzani history) in St. Joseph, MI on Jan. 13, 1968. They have two children, both born in Lafayette, James William "Jay", born Oct. 17, 1969 and Sarah Suzette "Suzie," born Feb. 15, 1972. Jay is past State President of the Children of the American Revolution, Boys' State Alternate, Eagle Scout, attended Congressional Youth Council in Washington, and is a Junior at Wabash College where he is a member of Delta Tau Delta Fraternity. He is majoring in Political Science. Suzie, a Senior at Southmont, is in Royal Ambassadors, language clubs and student council. Jim's family hosted Ruth Vanderschoot, an exchange student from Belgium the 1988-89 school year.

Becky married Brad Hurt on July 5, 1969 at St. Bernard's Church. She is active in Delta Theta Tau Sorority and is Manager at Steck's Attic. Brad is with Browning Investment in Indianapolis. They have two sons, Jacob Fletcher born May 28, 1972 and Aaron Christopher born June 11, 1976. Both are students at Crawfordsville and active in sports.

Barb married Terry Jackson on Dec. 29, 1973. Terry graduated from Wabash and both are Purdue graduates. Terry teaches art at Lafayette Jeff; Barb teaches art at Southwestern.

Bill and Joan are recently retired after 33 years in the restaurant business and enjoy their family, bridge, fishing and following the Boilermakers and Cubs. *Submitted by Karen Bazzani Zach*

ZACHARY

Lelia G. Zachary, born May 3, 1897 in Montgomery County, married Earl Wilson, born July 15, 1886. They were married Sept. 13, 1913, and had three children: a son Carroll L. and two daughters, Helen Frances deceased, and Irene, wife of Ralph C. Miller.

Lelia's parents were Samuel Marion, born Nov. 15, 1870, and Sarah (Sallie) E. Brown Zachary, born Mar. 19, 1871. They were married May 12, 1894. Samuel farmed, operated a grocery, did custom farm work, carpentry, and were great neighbors. Samuel and Sarah raised five girls, Lelia married Earl Wilson, Mary Kate married Fred Dykhuzen, Zuba Olive married Bernard Layton, Emeline Inez married Carl Kennell, and Doris married Harold DeBoy. They had two boys, Lawrence W. married Dora Knott, Alvin Dewey married Margaret Parrott. Lawrence was a Veteran of World War I. Alvin was a Veterinarian, first practiced in Alamo, and later in Indianapolis.

Sarah Brown's parents were William Harvey Brown, born June 21, 1851, and wife Mary E. Huff, born Aug. 13, 1845, both born in Montgomery County. They were married Dec. 31, 1868. William Harvey served as Justice of the Peace, publisher; jeweler, and was in charge of the first Telephone office in New Market. William Harvey and Mary Huff's children were Sarah E. (Sallie) married Samuel M. Zachary, Milton Arthur never married, William Riley married Minnie Zachary, Martha (Mattie) married Joseph Gillis, and Winnie Ellen died at three days.

William Harvey's father, William Armfield Brown, came to Montgomery County from North Carolina before April 1829. He married Dorcus Summy Rush, a widow, Apr. 27, 1848. They had just one child, William Harvey.

Dorcus's father Peter Summy held an original land grant in Brown Twp., dated Nov. 17, 1824, signed by John Quincy Adams. Peter Summy's wife is said to be a Cherokee Indian born in Maryland. Peter was born in Germany.

Mary E. Huff's parents were Arthur and Martha Hall Huff, married June 1, 1844. Arthur died shortly after Mary's birth. She is the only grandchild mentioned in her grandfather Jacob Huff's will, probated Apr. 17, 1867. Jacob Huff came to Brown Twp., Montgomery County from Kentucky before 1844.

Martha Hall Huff's parents were Benjamin and Anna VanCleave Hall. Benjamin Hall held an original land grant in South Union Twp., dated May 3, 1826.

Samuel M. Zachary's parents were John Peter Zachary, born in Montgomery County Mar. 30, 1837, and wife Nancy Ann Eaken, born June 15, 1835 in Montgomery County. They were married July 8, 1858.

Nancy Ann's parents were Andrew and Mildred Bohanon Eaken. They came from Sullivan Co., TN and held an original land grant in North Union Twp. dated Aug. 31, 1823.

John Peter and Nancy Zachary's children were John Westly married Miranda Ferguson, William married Celia Cline, James married Anna Spore, George married Mary Eleate, Eva married Frank Brocies, Samuel M. married Sarah (Sallie) Brown, Charley never married, Lena Belle died before marriage, but was engaged to Pearice Payton, Minnie Ann married William R. Brown.

John Peter Zachary's parents Elijah, born in 1805, and Elizabeth Black Zachary born in 1808 came to Montgomery County in 1828 from Grainger Co., TN, and settled in Union Twp. south of

Crawfordsville. Elijah and Elizabeth had 17 children. Martha married Jimison Wilhite, James married first Elizabeth Mitchell, 2nd to Elizabeth Faries, William married Kesiah McMurry, Elijah Jr. married Margaret Baldwin, John Peter married Nancy Eaken, Catherine married Robert Baldwin, Enoch married Sarah B. Wilhite, Milton Hezekiah married Elizabeth McMurry, Alvin married Isaphema Hatch, Ellen died young, Samuel married Mary Ellen Misner, Jimison married Melcena Brinkey, Redden married Alice McMurry, Margaret married Oliver Jeffrey, Polly and twin girls died young.

FRED AND PATTI ZIMMERMAN

"Ho! Ho! Ho!" is heard around the Zimmerman house every December as Fred dons his red costume and delights a multitude of Montgomery County children when he plays the role of Jolly Old St. Nicholas. Fred was born May 20, 1944 the son of Owen Allen and Beulah F. (Haase) Zimmerman. His father was born May 23, 1908 and died July 11, 1961. His mother born Dec. 24, 1913 died Mar. 20, 1989. He has one brother, Tom of Ladoga and two sisters, Betty Porter and Delma Torrison. Fred's Montgomery County Zimmerman roots go back to Botetourt Co., VA where his grandfather, Benjamin Thomas Zimmerman was born May 1, 1850 (died in Ladoga July 22, 1930), the son of George and Rebecca (Boling) Zimmerman. Benjamin's wife was Harriet Morrison, daughter of Allen and Elvia (Routh) Morrison. Benjamin was a plasterer and continued in his work in the Ladoga area into his 70s. Fred graduated from Ladoga High School in 1964 and has worked at Allison's Gas Turbine (Indianapolis) for 23 years. He was also in the Army National Guard for nine years. Fred has been active in his children's activities, especially ball and 4-H.

Bruce, Fred, Patti and Tami Zimmerman

On Sept. 6, 1964, Fred married Patricia Gail Morris in the New Market Baptist Church. The wedding was performed by her uncle, John Morris. Fred and Patti are looking forward to celebrating their 25th Anniversary this year in September, 1989.

Patti was born Mar. 29, 1945 in Charleston, SC (while her father was in the service) the daughter of Bruce Clayton (born July 21, 1921) and Francis Louise Bryant (born Jan. 14, 1922). Patti has two sisters, Betty Lou Deck and Judy Arlene Brewster, both of Montgomery County.

Patti graduated in 1963 from New Market High School. Her Montgomery County roots are deep in several respects. Among her revered county ancestors are: Daniel Morris, Sr., born June 8, 1781 in New Jersey died Dec. 4, 1859 (wife Elizabeth Evans - both buried Pisgah Cemetery). Daniel Morris received a land grant here Sept. 8, 1829. Also, James H. Linn (a soldier of the War of 1812 whose father was in the Revolution), and Robert Lytle who owned land on the Southeast corner of the crossroads, two miles West of New Ross and gave one acre of this land for Greenwood school.

Patti and Fred lived in Crawfordsville for some years, but on the last day of August 1978, moved to the heart of Linnsburg, the nucleus of Patti's family.

Both children born to Patti and Fred were delivered at Culver Hospital — Bruce Allen born Sept. 27, 1968 and Tami Gailene, born Apr. 22, 1973. Bruce graduated from Southmont High School, where he was active in sports and FFA. Sister Tami is active in sports, also and is a Junior at the school. Bruce also attended Olivet University and Danville Community College.

The Zimmerman family are members of the New Market Baptist Church, but often attend Mace Methodist.

They are active in many community projects. Fred is now Ho, Ho, Ho-ing his second generation of Montgomery County youth and looks forward to #3!

ZUCK FAMILY

John Zuck lived on a farm near Wesley in Montgomery County in the early 1800s. He married Emeline Stout. Their son, Jasper Newton, was born in Montgomery County on Sept. 13, 1846. He married Catherine Eve Shoemaker (born Sept. 17, 1850) of Newberry, IN on Oct. 5, 1875. They lived all their lives in Waynetown and Crawfordsville. Newt was a poultry dealer in both Waynetown and Crawfordsville. They had three children: John Frederick was born Aug. 7, 1876 and died Apr. 4, 1880. Anna Bessie was born July 27, 1878. Hugh Ernest was born Sept. 14, 1881.

Bessie married Norris Welby Watson. They had one son, Ralph, who married Pearl Furr. They had one son, Darrel, who married Mary Jane Flint on Nov. 29, 1942. They had four children, Richard, Robert, Edward and Lori. Richard and his wife, Nancy, have two daughters, Angela and Victoria. Robert and his wife, Betty, have three children, Hope, Jacob, and John. Edward has not married. Lori married Clarence Brown on Mar. 18, 1989 and now lives in Phoenix where she teaches music in the schools.

Ernest became owner and manager of a grocery and dry-goods store in Waynetown. On Apr. 12, 1908, he married Uma Wilkinson, a primary teacher in the Waynetown School. They built a home on South Vine Street. Their daughter, Beulah Ernestine was born there on June 26, 1910. Soon after that, they sold the store and moved to the Wilkinson homestead near Wallace where Ernest farmed until he retired. Their son, Gerald W. was born there on Feb. 1, 1915.

Both children were educated in the Wallace School. Both were active in 4-H work. Beulah helped pay for her college education by selling part of her 4-H Guernseys.

Beulah earned her B.S. degree at Indiana State Teacher's College, Terre Haute and her M.S. degree from Butler University. She taught school at Wallace and Davis Township in Fountain County. After Uma died in 1938, Ernest and Beulah moved to Crawfordsville where Beulah taught at Mills School. On Oct. 20, 1951, she married Charles Curtis Edwards, owner and manager of an appliance store near Manchester. They built a home near the store where they continue to reside.

Gerald graduated from Purdue University with a B.S. degree in civil engineering. He married Genevive Schnelle from Newport, KY on Dec. 29, 1941. He served in the field artillery in Germany during WWII. After the war, he joined the U.S. Corps of Engineers with offices in Louisville, KY, then in Omaha, NE. They built a home in Omaha where they now live in retirement.

Suzanne Catherine Zuck was born Aug. 14, 1946. She married Richard D. Smith, Jr. in 1965. They have three children: Catherine Theresa, born Mar. 26, 1967, married Michael Darby in 1987. They have a son, Justin. Tricia, born Jan. 30, 1970 and Richard D. Smith, III (born Oct. 31, 1971) live with their parents in Omaha. *Submitted by Beulah Edwards*

The old Blacksmith shop Alamo, Indiana

FAMILY TREE

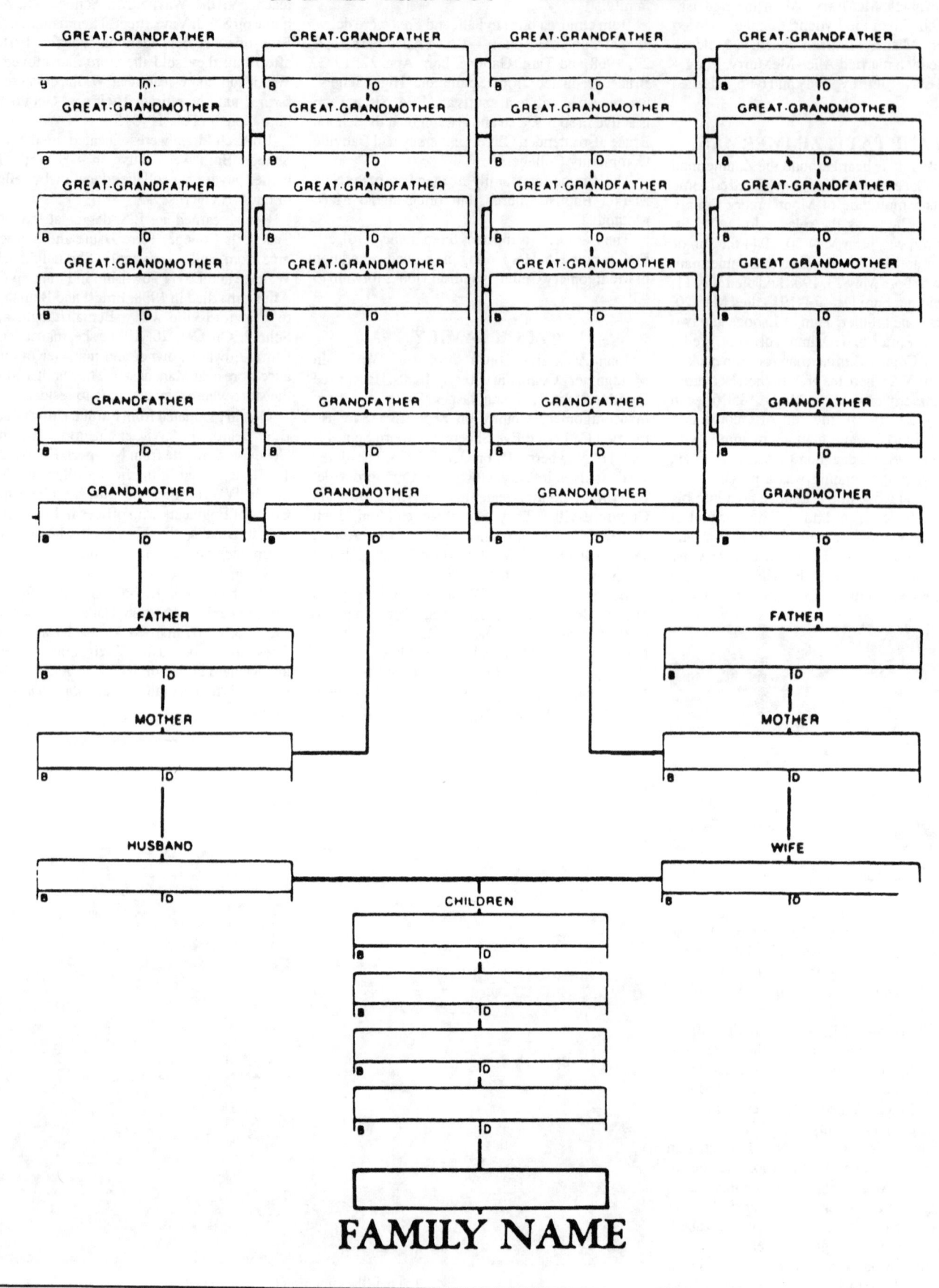

FAMILY NAME

CLUB HISTORY

Waveland Lodge #300 F. & A.M.

MASONIC TEMPLE

The Fraternity of Free and Accepted Masons is the oldest, largest, and most widely known fraternal organization in the world. Though religious in character, Masonry is not a religion nor a substitute for one. Its principles are steadfastly acclaimed as Brotherly Love, Relief and Truth. Believing in charity for all mankind and practice of the Golden Rule, Freemasonry is a way of life.

Five Masonic bodies now use the Temple for their various activities. They are: Montgomery Lodge #50, chartered May 27, 1844; Crawfordsville Chapter #40 Royal Arch Masons, chartered May 20, 1858; Montgomery Council #34 Royal and Select Masters, chartered October 20, 1869; Crawfordsville Commandery #25 Knights Templar, chartered April 28, 1875; and Athens Chapter #97 Order of the Eastern Star, chartered April 23, 1890.

The first home of the Lodge was a frame building on the southeast corner of Washington and Market Streets. An early morning fire in August 1858 destroyed the quarter block containing the lodge building. Quarters were then established on the third floor of 123-125 East Main Street.

In January 1900 the lot for the present Temple was purchased and on October 31, 1901 the cornerstone was laid. The Temple was completed in 1904 at a total cost of approximately $50,000.00. The York Rite Bodies furnished 65% of the cost. All indebtedness was paid in the fall of 1907.

Over the years various improvements were made to the Temple. Most notable were: in 1912 a Hinners pipe organ was added in the gallery of the Lodge room; in 1915 the adjacent lot to the north was purchased and a wing constructed at the rear, providing a modern kitchen for the banquet room on the first floor and a stage and dressing rooms for the Little Theater on the second floor.

The Masonic Temple has proved of inestimable value in the social life of the community as well as serving the various Masonic bodies. The banquet hall and parlors have been ideal places for holding banquets, receptions and various social functions of the city, high school and Wabash College. For many years the Little Theater served various Theatrical groups and the parlors have even served as a funeral home for many lodge members and families.

The five Masonic bodies that currently use the Masonic Temple work both separately and in conjunction with the other bodies, in promulgating brotherly love, truth and charity. The largest project is helping maintain the Indiana Masonic Home at Franklin, IN. This home is available, upon qualification, to all Master Masons and the wives, daughters, mothers, widows and sisters of Master Masons.

For many years the Order of The Eastern Star has served banquets for various organizations and have contributed greatly to many improvements to the Temple as well as the Masonic Home. Both the Lodge and Eastern Star sponsor scholarships for students.

The Royal Arch Masons, Royal and Select Masters and the Knights Templar are part of the York Rite. Besides the aforementioned charitable projects, each of these bodies have their own project. The Royal Arch Masons have as their philanthropy the Royal Arch Research Assistance doing research and helping people with hearing problems. The Royal and Select Masters support the study at Indiana University and other colleges the problems of aging and arteriosclerosis. The Knights Templar help to send ministers to the Holy Land each year but their biggest project is the eye foundation. The Knights Templar Grand Encampment has spent over twenty-five million dollars in helping people of all ages, creeds and races with eye surgery. Two million dollars has been spent on eye research. The Grand Commandery of Indiana has an educational loaning program of over $260,000.00 for loans to students on scholarships.

The Lodge sponsors the Order of DeMolay for boys and the Order of Eastern Star sponsors The Order of Rainbow for girls.

The Masonic Temple is administered and maintained by the Masonic Temple Association which consists of three members from each of the five bodies. The Association has started a restoration fund for the purpose of restoring the Temple in time for its centennial year of 2001. *Submitted by John Breaks Lofland, Worshipful Master, Montgomery Lodge #50*

LINDEN-MADISON TOWNSHIP HISTORICAL SOCIETY

In June 1984, a group of citizens met to form an organization to preserve the history of Linden-Madison Township area. This was prompted by the closing of the Linden Railroad Depot with the possibility of it being abandoned and eventually destroyed. The L-shaped depot is unique in its design having once served the intersection of the Nickel Plate & Monon railroads. The depot is featured in the June 1975 issue of the *Model Railroader* magazine. The organization plans to make the depot into a museum.

The Historical Society received their charter as a non-profit organization in August 1985.

In April 1986 CSX Railroad & Norfolk Southern Railroad donated the depot to the Historical Society with the stipulation that it be moved from its present location.

The land on which the depot is located was purchased from Norfolk & Southern in May 1988, with the requirements that it be moved from both railroad right-of-way.

In April 1989, Norfolk & Southern abandoned their railroad line from Cowden IL. to Frankfort, IN. This included the Linden line. Currently the Historical Society is negotiating with Norfolk & Southern to acquire their right-of-way on the north side of the depot. This would allow the depot to stay in its present location while providing space for parking and the display of a railroad car. CSX has granted us an easement to allow the building in its present location if we install a fence on the west side between their track and the building.

The Society consists of the following 9 board members: Linda Burkle-President, David Layton-V. President, Joe Weaver-Treasurer, Martha Irvin-Secretary, Harry Hailman-Director, Robert Straw-Director, Linda Mussche-Director, William Lyons-Director, and Ron Kirby-Director. Our present membership is 60 with 21 Lifetime members. Meetings are held on the third Tuesday of each month in the basement of the Linden Public Library.

Our purpose is not only to preserve railroad history in our community, but the history of our township once called "Quinine" Township.

WAVELAND LODGE #300 F.&A.M.

The history of Waveland Lodge began in the village of Waveland in 1863 when the Grand Lodge of F.&A.M. with John B. Travel as Grand Master helped the men of Waveland organize and get men trained to work as Officers during the dispensation in the year of 1863. The officers for the ensuing year were as follows: Thomas Kelso W.M., S.T. Whittington S.W., Frank Belton J.W., C. Connor Treasurer, N.P. Davis Secretary, P.C. Mullekin S.D., William Kelso J.D. and J.A. Reed Tyler.

Waveland at that time, one hundred and twenty six years ago, was a small village with not many inhabitants and some of the countryside about was still a wilderness. Streets and highways were wagon roads (dirt or mud, of course). Some of the homes were log cabins in structure, lighting was by candle light and in a few cases kerosene lamps were used. The lodge men traveled either on foot, horseback or buggy and wagon. They spent more time getting to and from lodge than they spent in the meetings. The first Lodge Hall was over John Dietrich's blacksmith shop where Hunt's Television shop is now. This was a two story structure (brick) and was the home of the lodge from 1864 until 1895. A lease was extended from T.L. Hanna to the trustee's of Waveland Lodge #300 F.&A.M. for a term of 99 years on August 22, 1895. Minutes of April 5, 1895 discussed the building of a new Hall. The committee on Ways and Means reported the probable cost of a new Hall to be built over T.L. Hanna's Store at about $1,650.00. T.L. Hanna would not agree to build a Hall at any price, but would give about $230.00 in material toward erecting a hall over his store room. The lodge moved to accept. T.L. Hanna's proposition. The motion was approved and carried. The committee appointed was K.K. Straughan, J.N. Fullenwider, William A. Dietrich, J.L. Dietrich and John Robertson.

The committee finally secured the help of the Herff Jones Co. of Indianapolis, Indiana. With the help of this company a plaque was devised from solid dark walnut 22 inches by 26 inches with appropriate head line and title. The name and dates were engraved on brass plates two and one half inches by one inch. This plaque hangs in the Tyler's room. The new Hall was dedicated at a special call meeting on June 24, 1903. The dedicatory ceremonies were given in due and ancient form by Deputy Grand Master, George Crimes.

Many changes have been made in the lodge room since its dedication in 1903. The whole room has undergone many changes. Since then a new carpet has been installed, a new gas furnace is now in use, the ceiling has been sprayed with an insulation material and new lights have been installed. A new restroom and water facilities were put in. In May 1989 the lodge at Judson, Indiana #518 joined the Waveland Lodge #300 giving us in excess of 135 members. At the same time the Eastern Star Chapter at Judson joined the Waveland Chapter #539 strengthening both the Lodge and Eastern Star. Our lodge has now been in existence some 126 years and it has been a welcome addition to the town of Waveland, Indiana.

Written by Wayne Simms - Former Secretary.

CHRISTIAN WRITER'S GROUP

Inset: Rosemary Duncan. Front Row L. to R.: Myrtle Whitehead, Freida Holland, Princess Thompson, Louise Rouse. Back Row: Judy Gayler, Ted Whitehead, Willard McCalment, Thelma Aileen Karg, Jordan Yates

The Christian Writer's Group was started in July 1983 by Irma Lewis and T. Aileen Karg. Mr. A.F. Harper, Midwest director, encouraged the organization. Most are published writers and there are three music writers in the group.

DOROTHY Q CHAPTER DAUGHTERS OF THE AMERICAN REVOLUTION

Authorized: January 18, 1898, 8th Indiana Chapter, 14 Charter Members.

First Regent: Josephine Tuttle Thomas

June 1902: Bronze Tablet (lists Revolutionary Soldiers buried in County)

1904: History Month Essay Contest Began

1911: Promoted creation of Montgomery County Historical Society

August 26, 1926: First meeting in Col. Isaac C. Elston Chapter House

1936: DAR Good Citizens Began

1979: Tablet with 12 additional Revolutionary Soldiers

1998: Looking forward to our 100th year.

Real Daughters (daughter of Revolutionary Soldier): Lucinda Hardee McMullen and Elvira Mortimer Layne. Sponsors: Susan E. Wallace Society, Children of the American Revolution

BENEVOLENT AND PROTECTIVE ORDER OF ELKS OF CRAWFORDSVILLE

The Benevolent and Protective Order of Elks was organized in New York City in 1867 but was not nationalized until 1871. Crawfordsville Lodge #483 was chartered in 1899 and the first class of 25 Charter Members was initiated and the Officers installed by Logansport Lodge #66 at the P.O.S. of A. Hall. The first Exalted Ruler was George S. "Cap" Harney of Ladoga.

The original Elks Building was built in 1907 on the SW corner of Pike and Water Sts. The current building, about 2 miles east of Crawfordsville on Highway 32, was built in 1979. The Lodge has a current membership of approximately 635 members.

KAPPA KAPPA KAPPA

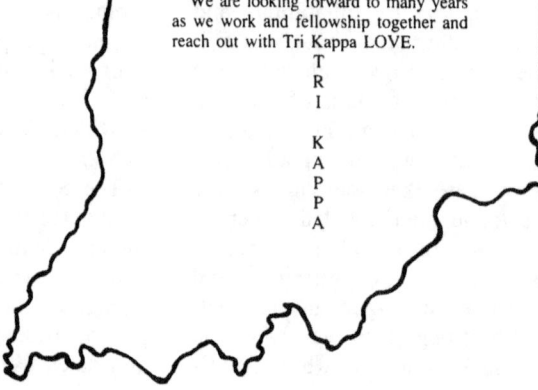

Kappa Kappa Kappa was founded in February, 1901.

Sigma Chapter of Tri Kappa December 16, 1905.

Its objective is to promote culture and education in Indiana. It contributes to the Riley Cheer Guild and to scholarship funds on a State level. Band, choral and college scholarships are presented to Ladoga and Southmont students.

We also contribute to the State and local Mental Health and also collect for the local Cancer Drive.

The making of a quilt, selling nuts and knives and serving Lions Club dinners are our money making projects.

We are looking forward to many years as we work and fellowship together and reach out with Tri Kappa LOVE.

T
R
I

K
A
P
P
A

BUSINESS HISTORY

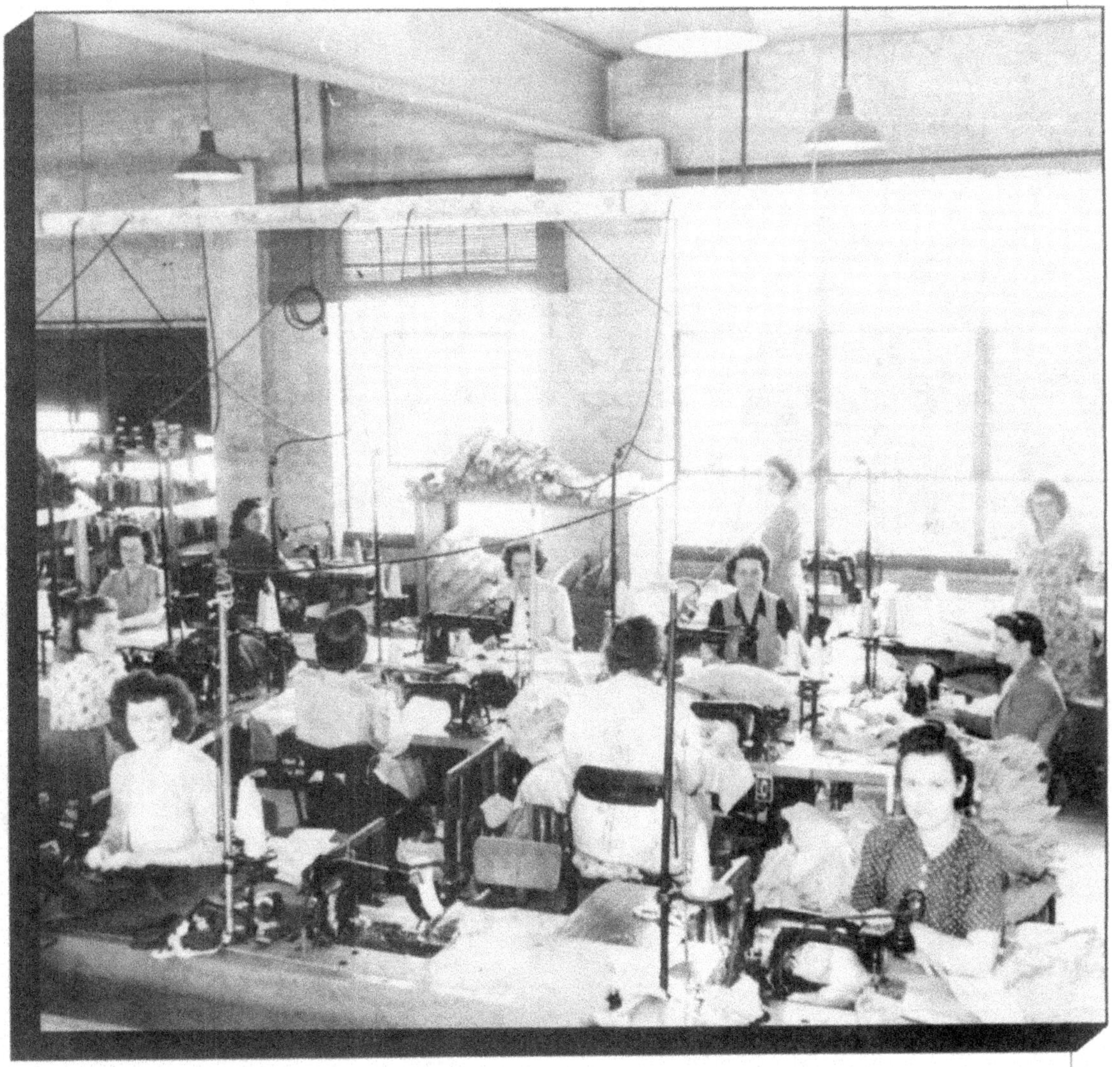

Inside Wilson Brothers Shirt Factory in Crawfordsville 1937-1957 Present-day Lane Nursing Home

ZACH'S FAMILY RESTAURANT

In 1955, two Crawfordsville drive-in restaurants were purchased from Gene Pishaw by a Michigan City couple, Bill and Joan Zach. One was the Toot 'n Tell, located on the point of West Main and Traction Road and the B-K (Greencastle Road - across from the Dairy Queen). Both businesses were operated with few employees at that time and carhops made 35¢/hour. In 1961, the Toot 'n Tell was torn down and a new A&W was built.

1966 was a busy year for the Zach family. Joan and Bill won 150,000 S&H Green Stamps (over 120 books) in an A&W/Reader's Digest Coupon Redemption Drawing. It was also the year the land and buildings of the two previously mentioned drive-ins were sold and a lot across from the Southern-most Mall entrance was purchased to build a drive-in/restaurant combination business. The family decided to terminate the B-K franchise and keep the better-known, nationally-famed A&W one. The original purchase featured a 150' x 200' lot. Construction began in late 1966 but it was not until National Root Beer Week (September 1967) that the new business opened, complete with inside seating for 50 people, electronic ordering for 26 cars, a car canopy for 16, a beautiful black-topped lot, central heating and air-conditioning. At that time, the whole Zach family worked there — Bill (Owner/manager), Joan (bookkeeper), son Jim as assistant manager and daughters, Becky and Barb as counter waitresses. It was the ultimate in A&W restaurants, but many changes were to come.

In July of 1969, Zach's famous coneys sold for 19¢ on Coney Special Day (then Wednesday). That year, with business booming, the Zach's bought a 100' x 200' lot west of the building. In 1969/70, a new addition was added, boosting seating to 90. The North parking area (where houses stood then) was bought in September 1971. In 1971/72, the pagoda roof was added and seating then topped-out at 115 where it presently exists.

The business was incorporated on March 31, 1972. That year, Bill and Joan attended the National A&W Convention

B-K Drive Inn on US 231, 1955

Present building before addition of pagoda roof, 1967

in Disney World where Bill was recognized as President of the Indiana A&W Association.

Changing the image from a drive-in to a restaurant was in full-swing in December of 1973, when the cash register system was computerized which enabled a waitress to accurately price an order in seconds. At the beginning of the Zach's adventure, Joan was sometimes the lone worker — taking, cooking and delivering an order. In 1973, 45 employees tallied hours on the new computer system. Another big plus for Zach's began in 1973 — the serving of breakfast with the specialty, Biscuits and Gravy.

In 1980, due to dissention in the National Company, the family decided to go with a local idea and became Zach's Family Restaurant. Termination of the A&W franchise was accomplished on March 24, 1981 and thanks to our loyal customers, the business continues to grow today.

Several local teams have been sponsored by the restaurant, including the 1981-82 ZFR bowling championship team, with members Jan Bullock, Jan Eppert, Joyce Peterman, Jane Ryan and Mary Weliver.

Several restaurant romances bloomed and blossomed into marriage — many are still nurtured today, but sadly others have been blown to the wind.

February 1988 was the retirement of Bill and Joan after 33 years in the restaurant business. Joan said, "What makes us feel old is that the girls that worked for us in the beginning are now grandmothers!"

A couple of months later, Zach's chicken was declared the best chicken in town via a survey in the *Journal-Review* and Reid Duffy of Channel 6 Duffy's Diner featured Bill, Jim and his wife, Karen on a short segment about Crawfordsville.

Jim purchased the business from his parents at their retirement and along with Jim's son, Jay as manager, daughter Suzie as waitress and long-time assistant manager, Margaret McKinney, Jim is currently in the process of remodelling the building another time. A new air conditioning/heating system, updated kitchen facilities, more office space and a banquet room are the improvements coming this year — 1989!!

BANK ONE, CRAWFORDSVILLE, NA

In 1864 the town of Crawfordsville, Indiana, was a typical county seat town with an assessed valuation of $1,070,915. The businessmen and neighboring farmers, believed the area needed a new and competitive bank. On November 26, 1863, the Crawfordsville JOURNAL carried an announcement of a "bank meeting" to be held December 3, in the court house. The JOURNAL of January 4, 1864, stated that plans for a new bank had been completed. The first formal meeting took place on September 8, 1864.

The first entry in the original minute book, reports that the September 8, 1864, meeting was held for the purpose of electing a permanent organization for a 'National Bank' to be located in Crawfordsville, Montgomery County, Indiana, which would be designated the 'First National Bank of Crawfordsville'.

On November 16, 1864, a CERTIFICATE was received, authorizing the First National Bank of Crawfordsville to commence the business of banking. A room was rented and on the morning of December 2, 1864, the new bank opened for business.

In October, 1950, after a period of negotiation, The First National Bank merged with the Crawfordsville Trust Company. The new organization styled itself, The First National Bank and Trust Company, and continued business in the Trust Company's building on the southeast corner of Washington and Main Streets. Crawfordsville Trust Company had grown out of a partnership formed in May, 1882, as a real estate, loan, and insurance business at 115 South Washington Street.

Early in 1959, a new building was planned for the bank; shortly thereafter several properties at the southeast corner of Washington and Pike Streets, and adjoining, were purchased, and ground was broken in September of the same year. The new bank building at the corner of Washington and Pike Streets was completed in 1960. An addition to the original structure was added in 1972. In December, 1980, the Board of Directors approved a building project to provide space for expansion at the main facility. The initial plan proposed a two story addition onto the southeast corner of the present one story building. The building was completed, and a public open house was held on Sunday, October 9, 1983.

On November 28, 1959, the bank purchased the assets and assumed the liabilities of The Farmers' State Bank of Wingate, Indiana. In June, 1978, the Board decided to proceed with building plans, in Wingate, for a Williamsburg style building with drive-up facilities. The structure was constructed and the move was made into the new facility on January 17, 1980.

On June 5, 1968, an agreement was signed with the Directors of the Ladoga State Bank to merge with the First National Bank and Trust Company. The merger became effective November 30, 1968. Also, at this time the Directors were busy working toward the acquisition of the Farmers' State Bank at New Market. The Farmers' State Bank was dissolved on February 22, 1969, when it became the First National Bank of New Market.

On March 31, 1983, after several months of paperwork and legal processing the structure of the ownership of First National Bank and Trust Company was changed to a one bank holding company. The First Crawfordsville Financial Corporation was formed by the stockholders of the First National Bank and Trust Company of Crawfordsville with all stock in the bank transferred to the ownership of First Crawfordsville Financial Corporation. The first Annual Meeting was held on April 10, 1984.

During the beginning months of 1986, negotiations began with BANC ONE CORPORATION COLUMBUS, OHIO, on the acquisition of the First Crawfordsville Financial Corporation. On November 1, 1986, the acquisition was finalized and The First National Bank and Trust Company of Crawfordsville became BANK ONE, CRAWFORDSVILLE, NA.

Today BANK ONE, CRAWFORDSVILLE, NA, serves their customer base with locations in Crawfordsville, Ladoga, New Market, and Wingate, with 24 hour bank machines located at North Plant R.R. Donnelley, County Market, and the Main Office. At present assets of the bank are 140 million with 80 full-time employees.

PRESIDENTS:

WILLIAM H. DURHAM	1864-1873, 1880-1888, and 1891-1893
ALEXANDER THOMPSON	1873-1880
JOSEPH MILLIGAN	1889-1890
HECTOR S. BRADEN	1894
CAPT. WILLIAM P. HERRON	1895-1927
SOL TANNENBAUM	1927-1935
WILL COLLINGS	1935-1952
LAWRENCE DEVORE	1953-1956
DARNELL MAHORNEY	1957-1965
MARK CARESS	1965-1983
DONALD KITCHENS	1983-1985, and 1986-1988
ROBERT KINCAID	1985-1986

BANK ONE, CRAWFORDSVILLE, NA
Crawfordsville, Indiana   Member FDIC

CALIFORNIA PELLET MILL COMPANY

California Pellet Mill Company traces its origins back to San Francisco, California, where in 1873, two old world artisans from France, Messrs. Toulouse and Delorieux, established a firm bearing their names. They proceeded to manufacture wine presses, grape crushers and stemmers. The company grew and expanded into other needed products such as olive, cider, macaroni, and baling presses and pumps.

In 1880, a mechanical genius, E.T. Meakin, took control of the company and subsequently invented the first continuous wine press.

During the devastating 1906 San Francisco earthquake and fire, the company's property was completely destroyed. Nonetheless, it was back to manufacturing within a few months, utilizing the only asset it possessed, its reputation for quality and honesty.

In 1918, as the passage of the prohibition law became imminent, the wine division of the business was phased out and the name of the company changed to California Press Manufacturing Company. Pioneering in fish reduction, CPM was the first to manufacture continuous fish processing machinery for making fish oil and meal. Also, the company was involved in construction and operation of complete fish reduction plants. Then, in the late 1940's, the industry collapsed when the huge schools of sardines mysteriously disappeared; often attributed to the change in water temperature in their feeding grounds.

The pelleting industry began in 1931 with CPM's sale of the first commercially practical pellet mill to a feed mill in Los Angeles. CPM had not only faced up to the tremendous risk of attempting to market a revolutionary machine during the depths of the depression, but the even more demanding task of orchestrating the establishment of an entirely new industry around the concept of pelleted feed. Mr. Meakin's son, Edgar N. Meakin, was to guide the company's efforts in this direction as pelleting became the main thrust of the business. As the various economic benefits of pelleting became known, the industry grew. California Pellet Mill Company led the way by offering a great variety of mills that satisfied customers needs. Pelleting is a CPM specialty that carries over into many industries; energy, waste processing, chemicals, plastics, and fertilizers.

Realizing that animal feed comprised the giant share of the business, Mr. Meakin sought a centralized, midwest location for an additional plant. On February 12, 1946, CPM bought the factory and site of the W.Q. O'Neall Company, corrugated metal culvert manufacturers, located at 1114 East Wabash Avenue, Crawfordsville, Indiana. The plant was converted into a facility for the manufacture of machinery used in pellet mills. Chester Armstrong was named the first plant manager. The original workforce consisted of twenty people and they began operations on March 8, 1946.

By 1956, the plant of 9,000 square feet had been expanded, after three additions, by 400%. CPM was selling more pellet mills than all other manufacturers combined. The general sales offices were located in Crawfordsville, headed by C.N. Hultberg, Vice President of Sales.

In 1966, the facility was again expanded by 25% including additional production area and an employee lunch room. In 1974, CPM ceased to be a family owned company and became a subsidiary of Ingersoll-Rand, a dynamic and widely recognized worldwide machinery company.

In 1989, CPM is still growing, having added several computerized and robotic machines and innovative heat treating processes. At this time, CPM holds 86% of the market share in the pellet mill industry. There are 105 employees at the Crawfordsville plant.

CPM is indeed a worldwide organization, having plants in Nashua, New Hampshire; Waterloo, Iowa; Amsterdam, Holland; Araaraquara, Brazil; Jurong Town, Singapore; and Wexford, Ireland. Sales office/warehouse facilities are located in Kansas City, Missouri; San Francisco, California; Daventry, England; Malmaison, France; Sydney, Australia; and Wesel, West Germany. *Submitted by Rebecca L. Royer*

CITY OF CRAWFORDSVILLE

ELECTRIC & POWER COMPANY
Daniel T. Arterburn
Karen S. Bell
Carroll M. Borden
Timothy J. Booher
Alice M. Gross
F. Steven Bray
Dale W. Breedlove
William L. Burget
V. Kay Callis
Darlene B. Cass
Steven L. Clark
Joseph L. Coahran
David C. Creech
Terry A. Croy
Fredrick W. Davis
Timothy J. Davis
Webb D. Decker
Frank P. Dickerson III
Richard E. Dyer
Jon L. Foster
Jason L. Gates
Richard A. Gilstrap
Phillip R. Goode
Randall W. Hendrickson
Thomas B. Hoskins
Timothy S. Hutson
Roy E. Kaser
John D. Keller
Kimberlin R. Largent
Alvin K. Leslie
Billy E. Lidester
Robert Scott Lohorn
Myron McAlister
Dennis R. McDonald
Mike McKeown
Mike J. Michael
Jerry D. Mills
Michael W. Mitchell
Dennis L. Morley
Samuel D. Peck
John D. Rady
Timothy W. Rauch
Edward L. Shaw
Carlton E. Shelley
Joseph T. Simpson
James L. Sitler
James G. Smith
Leon R. Smith
Daniel A. Steele
Patsy Storms
Rodney E. Strong
Donald E. Todd
Larry W. Tracy
Raymond L. Waddell
Richard L. Yater

MAYOR'S OFFICE
Philip Q. Michal
Lori J. Hershberger
Mary E. Dawson

CLERK-TREASURER OFFICE
Mary E. Parks
Theresa A. Priebe
Emma Lou Tribbett
Kathy E. Whipple
Norma G. Wilkinson

CITY COUNCIL
Frank E. Gardner
Stephen D. Gentry
Barry L. Gibbs
Joe E. Hinesley
Lawrence L. Houston
Richard Bell
Sharon Remley

JANITORS
James W. Endicott
Carol J. McKinney

ENGINEERING & PLANNING DEPT.
Richard M. Munro
Tami C. Barreto

POLICE DEPARTMENT
Jeffrey C. Largent
Michael W. Bridge
Russell Brown
Arthur E. Chrisman
Mark A. Cox
Lori S. Ford
Rick W. French
David E. Johnson
Kurt Knecht
Neil C. Barclay
Jeffrey W. Line
James M. Lohorn
Candice A. Woodall
Harvey R. Barton
Harry J. McMullen
Richard Shireman
Gary L. Bell
Robert W. Peterman
George A. Plunkett
Michael W. Reath
James R. Rivers
Daniel J. Edwards
Jimmy D. Sessions
Thomas L. Taylor
Hal J. Utterback
Richard Wilson
Stephen W. Yeager

CIVILIAN EMPLOYEES - POLICE DEPT.
Mary T. Brant
Jane E. Brown
Beth A. Houston
Roberta Hall
Janet Armstrong
Beverly A. White
Jody L. Merrill
Rita A. Miller
Lisa C. Steele
Christina L. Wetli

METER MAIDS
Cynthia L. Fields
Sue A. Anderson
Julia K. Morrison

POLICE COMMISSIONERS
Charles S. Fiedler
Carroll R. Black
Charlotte H. Zachary

CROSSING GUARDS
Barbara J. Brown
Nellie Conrad
Mollie Cooper
Sharon K. Crane
William G. Eads
Phyllis M. Gill
Lou Hamilton
Virginia Kirkham
Betty J. Lee
Virginia F. Mahaska
Helen M. Munn
Karen A. Norris
Gloria J. Walters

FIRE & AMBULANCE
Michael Booher
Scott R. Busenbark
Jeffrey L. Davenport
Phillip R. Dossett
Mark B. Edmiston
Kurt A. Flora
James D. Fulwider
Michael T. Garrison
Dave Hampton
Larry D. Harvey
Michael D. Kadinger
Shirley Kadinger
Brian E. Keim
James Barnett
James M. McClure
Todd D. Barton
Brian L. Bechtel
Kurt F. Behme
Jack A. Murphy
William H. Myers
Bradley A. Nichols
Larry D. Patton
Larry C. Remley
James D. Rogers
Eric S. Small
Dana Sowders
David L. Steward
Aaron S. Burber
Dale Taylor
Michael R. Taylor
Dennis R. Weir
Steven E. Wright

STREET & SANITATION
Larry R. Hunt
Jeffrey F. Baker
Oren V. Jones
Donald Kincaid
Carl J. Vangilder
Jerry B. Busse
Charles V. Douglas
Larry E. Fairfield
Larry Dean Haffner
Ross R. Auman
Rodney L. Jenkins
Russell H. Keller
Kirk J. Quinn
Nancy M. Quinn
Robert R. Smith
James H. Tague
Cecil I. Waddell
Ron Whipple
Mary K. Willhite
Robert M. Williams
Joe York
Ronnie Begley

PARK & RECREATION DEPT.
Eugene A. Brooks
Paul R. Clifford
Edward Clifton
Joy L. Cunningham
Margaret Louise Day
Mary W. Decker
Ronald E. Fox
Linda L. Fox
Steven W. Frees
Michael E. Garr
Alice R. Gillilan
Rita M. Hamm
M. Jean Hoffa
Edward M. Kucinski
Bud H. McCandless
Cheryl L. McDonald
Mike J. Michael
Jerry R. Miller
Evelyn Otterman
Larry Riddle
Marylyn J. Showalter
Ed Snively
Joann Spragg
Charles O. Tribbett
Linda L. Wagoner
Barbara J. Burris
Michael D. Weliver
Lottie E. White
Carl Booker
Richard Ora Stark
Fred Carver
Roy Alma
Otis Corett
Sharon L. Eubanks
Anna L. Macy
James N. Hall

SEWER BILLING OFFICE
Genyle N. Webb
Donna L. Clark
Lorna L. Wilshire

SEWER PLANT
Mark D. Evans
Gregg A. Gerold
Philip W. Churchill
Ronald L. Day
Edward M. Flynn
Roy E. Geiger
Boyd C. Jones
Larry L. Kadinger
Bradley J. McAnulty
Troy E. McKinney
Michael E. McKinney
Carla S. Miller
Rusty Lee Miller
Thomas W. Mitchell
Norma J. Richardson
Randall E. Smith
Thomas Terry
Don A. Yount

ELSTON BANK & TRUST COMPANY
1853-1981, BY ROBERT S. HARVEY, 1981

In 1823, a young man named Isaac Elston moved to Crawfordsville with his wife and their entire fortune of 50¢. He began a grocery/hardware store, only the second store for the town of approximately 55 families.

He soon became involved in land development. In 1825 he purchased a large portion of land plotted as a new townsite north of Crawfordsville named Lafayette after the French hero of the Revolutionary War. Elston later donated that land to the city justices. Years later he would develop two other cities, Michigan City, Indiana and Kankakee, Illinois.

In 1835, Elston built a new home in Crawfordsville and moved from his log cabin. Today the Elston House is still a gracious, beautiful structure and the traditional home of the Wabash College President, a gift from the Elston family.

In order to better serve his growing business, Elston formed the Crawfordsville and Wabash Railroad in 1850. At this time there was still no bank in Crawfordsville. Even though the population had grown to 1600, the barter system was still the primary source of payment.

In 1852 the Indiana General Assembly passed the General Banking Act which permitted private banking. Within 9 months Elston had met the state's requirements and The Elston Bank was formed. Montgomery County's first, and for 10 years its only bank, opened for business February 21, 1853.

The new business started operations in a log cabin but soon was moved into a frame building at the Southeast corner of Main and Green Streets. This was the financial center of Montgomery County.

Later in history Elston would bring in his two sons-in-law, Indiana Senator Henry Lane and General Lew Wallace, author of *Ben Hur*, as well as his son Isaac Elston, Jr., who later was named the second president of Elston Bank after his father's death in 1867.

In 1925, the prosperous Elston Bank merged with Farmers & Merchants-Clements Trust Company and the name was legally changed to Elston Bank & Trust Company.

A short time later Elston Bank absorbed Crawfordsville State Bank, which was in financial difficulty. It was at this time, March 21, 1927, that Elston Bank moved to the Crawfordsville State Bank building where the bank is still located.

The name Elston continues to hold a link to the rich heritage and growth of Montgomery County. The many contributions are a direct source of community pride as reflected in the many sites that bear the name Elston, Lane, or Lew Wallace.

Today Elston Bank, with assets of over $136,000,000, employs over 80 people at our six offices and data processing center. We have been an integral part of the growth of Montgomery County now the home of over 35,000 residents. At this time in Montgomery County there are 37 widely diversified manufacturing companies employing 16,350 people. Our newest manufacturing company, Nucor Steel, will begin production in the Summer, 1988 projecting employment of several hundred more.

Excerpted from THE ELSTON

Elston Bank and Trust Company 1926 L. to R. John Hendricks, Ben Flanigan, Wilbur Burnett, Arthur Cordes, May Kline, Frances Blanton, Herbert Morrison, George Leonard, Ernest Ball, Leroy Groendyke, Edgar Taylor

LINDEN STATE BANK

The Linden State Bank was established on December 12, 1899 and located at 101 N. Main Street until 1976 when a new facility was erected at 100 N. Meridian Street.

In 1974 the New Richmond Savings and Loan Association was purchased and a branch established at 5 West Washington Street in New Richmond.

The Linden State Bank survived the depression and also a nighttime and daytime robbery in its earlier days. It has been a center of stability in the community for these 89 years.

Past Directors
J.E. Burke	Leon Little
Chas. Carlson	Leon Little, Jr.
J.L. Cochran	M.Z. McBee
A.B. Coopman	Fielden Morin
J.W. Elliott	Carl Norman
J.P. Halstead	Frank Norman
Bernie Harris	W.O. Parker
John Hopewell	Geo. Rusk
Raymond Hudson	A.D. Snyder
O.A. Irwin	T.H. Vincent
Robert C. King	W.H. Wilson

Present Directors
Lloyd Hudson, Chr.
Clint Wilkins, V. Chr.
Bill Skinner, Secy.
Lloyd W. Faust
C. LaVerne Lutes
Ronald Kerby

Past Presidents
H.C. Shobe   Ward Wilkins
Thos. H. Wilkins   Joe D. Halstead
Howard A. Patton   Lloyd W. Faust

Past Officers
Craig Bailey	Lois Kunkel
Howard L. Davis	Leon Little
J.W. Elliott	Leon Little, Jr.
W.L. Fraley	Ralph W. Little
Esther Hamm	W.H. Montgomery
Brad Hiatt	J.H. White
John E. Hopewell	

Present Officers
C. LaVerne Lutes, Pres. & CEO
Ronald D. Kerby, V. Pres. & T.O.
Richard Brown, Asst. V. Pres.
Lois I. Warren, Cashier

Past Employees
Edna Antle	Lois Norris
Staci Bannon	Ruthanna Oppy
Carolyn Cowden	Sharon Pack
Obed Irwin	Creo Pruett
Mary E. Johnson	Teresa Rogers
Robert C. King	Rebecca L. Royer
Betty Little	Kate Schwidler
Dorothy Little	Alma Van Cleave

Present Employees
Juanita Buckles
Betty Light
Beverly Nannet
Jeanine Oakes Padgett
Linda Perry
Kelly Ryker
Patty Waltz
Nancy White

Linden State Bank about 1907. Pictured in photo is J.H. Whits-Cashier, Thomas Wilkins-President, Thuron Banta-Bookkeeper, Henry Shobe-Vice President.

MONTGOMERY COUNTY GOVERNMENT

CIRCUIT COURT
Thomas K. Milligan, Judge
Marilyn Dossett, Court Reporter
Joyce A. Myers, Secretary

PROBATION DEPARTMENT
Ken T. Kreisher
Brooke A. Earnshaw
Janet E. Campbell
Ruby M. Coon, Secretary

PRE-TRIAL
Joyce I. Carpenter
Pamela Gritten

VICTIM ASSISTANCE
Stacey E. Miller

AUDITOR
Nelda J. Hester, Auditor
Mary Helen Carter, 1st Deputy
Janet Harris
Janet L. McKinney
Patricia A. Kincaid
Pearl Livingston

COUNTY COURT
Raymond M. Kirley, Judge
Julie R. Michael, Court Reporter
Pamela L. Taylor, Secretary

PROSECUTING ATTORNEY
Wayne E. Steele, Prosecutor
Peggy Q. Lohorn, Deputy Prosecutor
Edward B. McClean, Deputy Prosecutor
David P. Meadows, Investigator
Beverly S. Miller
Sarah L. Bradley
Maria McLean
Linda F. Layne
Nancy I. Canada

CLERK OF COURTS
Rebecca Neideffer, Clerk
Teresa L. Davis, Chief Deputy
Beverly J. Eyler, 1st Deputy
Kimberly A. Servies
Janet L. Gilstrap
Donna M. Creech
Becky Remley
Vivian P. Grindley
Mary Krukewitt
Wanda M. Miles, Micrographics
Brenda J. Miller, Micrographics
Wanda Dieterlen, Voter Registration

TREASURER
Carolyn K. Swank, Treasurer
Donna D. Bowling, 1st Deputy
C. Jean Greavu
Lori D. Lanam
Linda M. Parent
Marsha L. Baumgartner

SURVEYOR
Harvey J. Keller, Surveyor
Larry J. Utz, 1st Deputy
Nancy C. Jones
Edna J. Earl, Secretary
Vicki L. Ratcliff

ASSESSOR
Rebecca L. Chadwick, Assessor
Dorothy J. Williams, 1st Deputy
Earlene L. Garrard
Norma J. Wyatt

COMMISSIONERS
Robert M. Thayer
Samuel H. Kessler
James M. Kirtley

RECORDER
Mary A. Gibbs, Recorder
Shirley L. Cox, 1st Deputy
Patricia D. Broshears
Mary E. Bray
Frances B. Thompson

CORONER
Charles L. Burkhart, Coroner
Cecil E. Zachary
Samuel Peck

UNION TOWNSHIP ASSESSOR
Delores J. Corbin, Assessor
Patricia C. Shermer
Peggy L. Hudson
Debra J. Williams

COUNTY COUNCILMEN
Marsh Jones, President
William W. McClamroch
Otis V. Thayer
John L. Wyatt

ATTORNEY
Don C. Schmidt

SHERIFF
Dennis L. Rice, Sheriff
William R. Merchant, Chief Deputy
Ronal E. Newlin
Larry A. Lough
Charles L. Leonard
John G. Dale
Samuel J. Dickerson
Brodie S. Houston
Robert B. Coudret
Luther J. Blanton
James A. Truax
Kathleen Z. Layne
Carole L. Barton
George D. Spurgeon
Richard A. Curtis
Ralph B. Myers
Vicki R. Jackson
Lonnie D. Jones
Laren E. Myers
Catheryn A. Fenters
Catherine Anstett
Sharon K. Fox
Michael Hunley
Dan Penrod

COUNTY HIGHWAY
Gordon Holloway, Supervisor
Doris I. Snellenbarger, Secretary
Joann Hargis
Dick Hargis
Stephen Kinkead
Walter E. Blanton
Alvin D. Rentchler
Ralph K. Swank
Dale A. Conkright
Morris L. Brunton
James R. Miller
Clayton C. Conkright
Richard Manning
Homer R. Cox
Robert L. Beck
Guy T. Franklin
Eugene Vaughn
John C. Goodin
Harold R. Ridge
David A. Caldwell
Raymond N. Snellenbarger
George A. Tyo
Johneadon E. Hendon
William R. Wolverton
Carl Thompson
Austin Trovillo
H. Glenn Mennen
Richard McClaine
David W. Mershon
James D. Rood
Herschell H. Davis

HEALTH DEPARTMENT
Carl B. Howland
Delores M. LaFoe
Robert L. Walters
Hilda S. Jones
Sandy Utterback, Secretary

HEALTH BOARD
Dr. Wesley E. Shannon
Dr. Samuel Kirtley
Carol L. Laursen
Wayne E. Kessler
Thomas D. Martin
Dr. Raymond Halle
Bob J. Tandy

HEALTH MAINTENANCE
Curtis E. McClain

COUNTY HOME
Jerry L. Ward, Supervisor
Constance L. Ward
Terri L. Servies
Jeffrey L. Ward

BUILDING COMMISSIONER
Arthur W. Massing
Clinton M. Parks

SOIL AND WATER
Joseph A. Phelps
Mary K. Barnett

WEIGHTS AND MEASURERS
Charles B. Goff

COUNTY EXTENSION
Virginia A. Servies
William C. Rice
Linda L. Barnett
Dolores A. Epperson

BOARD OF REVIEW
Paul K. Johnson
Wayne Snouwaert

VETERAN
Loran K. Rutledge
Mary J. Rutledge

BROWN TOWNSHIP TRUSTEE
Bettie I. Simpson
Marie Fisher, Deputy

CLARK TOWNSHIP TRUSTEE
J. Donald Rhoads
Keith L. Rhoads, Deputy

COAL CREEK TOWNSHIP TRUSTEE
Edith Fultz
Eunice E. Bishop, Deputy

FRANKLIN TOWNSHIP TRUSTEE
F. Edmund Butler
Jo Anne Butler, Deputy

MADISON TOWNSHIP TRUSTEE
David O. Layton
Freda A. Layton, Deputy

SCOTT TOWNSHIP TRUSTEE
Donald Johnson
Ruth Johnson, Deputy

SUGAR CREEK TOWNSHIP TRUSTEE
Carolyn Maxwell
Donald L. Maxwell, Deputy

UNION TOWNSHIP TRUSTEE
Ramona Hinesley

WALNUT TOWNSHIP TRUSTEE
Meredith Keffer

WAYNE TOWNSHIP TRUSTEE
Elmer J. Edwards
Erika M. Edwards, Deputy
Donis Keffer, Deputy

COURTHOUSE SECURITY GUARD
Robert R. Wethington

MONTGOMERY SAVINGS ASSOCIATION
ORGANIZED IN 1888

In 1888, a group of business leaders gathered to organize a new financial institution - Montgomery Savings Association. Articles of Incorporation and By-Laws had been approved.

The group met on July 18, 1888, in the office of J.W. Cumberland, Justice of the Peace.

William N. Ireland was elected president of the board. Other officers were Cumberland, vice president; A.C. Jennison, secretary; and George Robinson, treasurer. These men also served as directors along with Hume DeBrular, Carl L. Rost and E.G. Wilson. M.W. Bruner was named attorney.

Membership fees were set. Members were assessed 15 cents a share for annual dues, 20 cents per share for weekly dues and 5 cents per share to cover expenses.

The Association started out in fine shape and persons desiring stock could get them from the directors. The Association's objective was to enable as many as possible in saving their surplus earnings so they could secure homes and make other investments.

Montgomery Savings was first located at 113 1/2 N. Washington St. The first loan approved was for $700 at 6 percent per annum.

Ireland resigned as president and director on December 22, 1888. E.G. Wilson became president and John Nicholson replaced Ireland as director. Carl Rost was elected to replace Wilson as vice president.

There were many applications for loans. On June 1889, the board held a special meeting to decide how to handle financing. A three to six month loan was taken out for $2,500 from Citizens Bank at 8 percent interest. This money was applied to the applications on file.

The by-laws were amended in 1891 to strike the 5 cents per share dues. A section was added stating that every member would be entitled to receive $100 per share of stock at maturity.

According to the original minute book, dated from 1888 to 1917, business ran smoothly. The minutes consisted of changing of officers and directors, reports from the treasurer, loans approved and foreclosures.

In 1900 Montgomery Savings capital assets were listed at $1 million, R.E. Bryant was president at the time, and W.W. Morgan was secretary.

Sometime between 1906 and 1912 Montgomery Savings moved from Washington Street to the Crawford Hotel on 202 E. Main Street. (Ref: *Crawfordsville City Directory*)

The county faced many hard economic times during the 1800 and early 1900s. However, none of the local financial institutions collapsed to leave depositors stranded. Other counties were not as fortunate.

Montgomery Savings survived the Depression years and was able to pay dividends to their stockholders.

Among Montgomery Savings early presidents were: William Lee, Judge Jere West, Sol Tannenbaum and William J. Sprow.

From 1940 on, the Association began to make significant changes. One of these was becoming an FSLIC member, which enabled the Association to insure all savings accounts.

Earl Berry, former Crawfordsville mayor, started at the firm in 1909 as bookkeeper. In 1931 he became a director and was elected secretary-treasurer. He succeeded Sprow as president in January 1953. Capital assets had grown to $2 million.

By 1959, Montgomery Savings was the third largest savings institution in the county. On June 29, 1959, Montgomery Savings moved its offices to 122 E. Main St.

Ralph M. Bounnell who had been a director since 1953, was named president in 1965.

Richard C. Huseman joined Montgomery Savings in 1961 as secretary-treasurer. October 1961, he was made a director and in November 1965, he assumed the duties of managing officer. He was elected president in 1973.

Earl F. Elliott joined Montgomery Savings in 1972 and assumed the office of president in January 1982.

In 1985, Montgomery Savings moved to its present location at 119 E. Main St.

THOMAS FUNERAL HOME

The Undertaking Business in Waynetown and its surrounding community was established at the turn of the century with Basil T. Merrellas the local undertaker. At his death in 1921 the business was carried on by John H. Shuler who was a native of Wallace, Indiana. In 1930 Mr. Shuler and Emit Grenard (a Waynetown resident) established a Partnership of Shuler & Grenard Funeral Home. In 1939 Mr. Shuler retired and Darwin & Mary Servies joined her father Emit Grenard in the business.

They established the first Funeral Home in Waynetown in the Rice Kline property on East Washington Street. Prior to this embalming was done at the home by the undertaker, the bodies were left there for viewing and funerals held in the home or the local churches. In 1954 the Servies built the new Funeral Home at 202 State Road #25 South. Mr. Grenard retired in 1956, and 1958 John D. Thomas joined the firm.

In 1968 Mr. & Mrs. Servies retired and John & Maurene Thomas took over the full ownership of the business, which they still hold. Working with them since 1973 is Dan Halford, a licensed director, coming from Columbus, Indiana.

Mr. Thomas is a native of Wallace, Indiana and had lived in that area until attending the Indiana School of Mortu-

Maurene and John Thomas

ary Science in Indianapolis in 1956-57. Mrs. Thomas was born and raised in Beattyville, Kentucky moving to the Rockville community with her parents in 1946. John & Maurene were married Oct. 5, 1952 and lived in the Grange Corner Community 1 yr. where Mr. Thomas' parents still reside. Mr. Thomas is a veteran of the Korean War, serving in Japan & Korea. He is a member of the Waynetown Masonic Lodge #302 F.& A.M. and former secretary; also the Waynetown American Legion, Crawfordsville V.F.W. Post, and the Indiana Funeral Directors Association and the Waynetown merchants association of which he was treasurer for 25 years. Mrs. Thomas is a member of the Wallace O.E.S. Chapter #415. They are members of the Wolf Creek Community Church.

TRI-COUNTY TELEPHONE CO., INC.

The Pyke Telephone System at Romney was the earliest ancestor of the Tri-County Telephone Company. Dr. Albert Pyke started the exchange in early 1890's to establish communications with his patients.

The first switchboard was in the doctor's home and was operated by his wife. When he built an office adjoining his home, the switchboard was moved to his office. This building was used as a telephone office until 1961.

The Central Union Telephone Company purchased the Romney Exchange and in 1914, sold it to Samuel Akers. In 1930, the exchange was bought by Wesley W. Thomas.

The old Pyke exchange served some customers in the New Richmond area in Montgomery County in competition with a co-operative exchange organized by local farmers and owned by Reverend Al Clark. Mr. Chapman acquired the Pyke interests in the New Richmond area and sold them in 1906 to J.L. McNeil, who also purchased the co-operative system and consolidated the two plants into the New Richmond Telephone Company. John Dixon of Lafayette bought the company in 1927. Wesley Thomas purchased it from him in 1927.

Linden was also served by the Pyke exchange, and this plant was acquired by Central Union at the same time it acquired Dr. Pyke's Romney interests. It competed in the Linden area first with a cooperative system and later with the Linden exchange of the Crawfordsville Home Telephone Company. In 1914, Mr. Akers purchased Central Union's Linden exchange and the Crawfordsville Company's competing exchange and combined them. Mr. Thomas acquired this exchange in 1930.

Service in Wingate was first furnished by a co-operative system and in Odell by a system owned by Mr. Harry Lutz. During the 1910's the two exchanges were acquired by Mr. Akers and were later sold to Mr. Dixon.

In 1932 Lee and Mildred Miller met with Wesley Thomas, former owner of Linden, Romney and New Richmond Telephone Companies and agreed on a sale of these companies to Lee and Mildred Miller. Lee's brother, Russell Miller was also a financial partner and was to assume management of the companies.

Russell arrived in Indiana July 5th, 1933 and assumed his position as a working partner. The following year in August he married Frances Demaree and in October he purchased the Kirkpatrick Telephone Company.

On July 24, 1937 Ben was born and March 18, 1942 Mary Edith was born to Russell and Frances Miller. November 1, 1946 Wingate and Odell exchanges were purchased. New Richmond converted to dial in 1956 and the first electronic subscriber carrier system in this area to work on iron wire was installed.

In 1959 Tri-County Telephone Company was incorporated and Ben graduated from Purdue and married Maxine Horn, also a Purdue graduate. Ben went to work for the telephone company and continued the modernization program. In 1960 the Russell Miller family became the sole owner of Tri-County.

All exchanges were converted to dial in 1961 and a daughter, Melinda Lee was born to Ben and Maxine on March 12th. A son, William (Bill) Glen was born on August 20, 1964. Tri-County installed its first computer system primarily for customer billing in 1964.

In 1966 Russell and Frances installed a small telephone system in Africa for the Methodist Mission with retired Tri-County equipment.

In 1971 Colfax Telephone Company was purchased and Extended Area Service was established to all contiguous Tri-County Telephone Company exchanges.

In 1973 Direct Distance Dialing (DDD) was made available to Tri-County customers as was pushbutton service and Tri-County installed the first mobile telephone system in Montgomery County.

Tri-County Telephone Company installed the first Voice Paging System in Montgomery County in 1975.

Tri-County Communications Corporation was formed in 1981 which built the first cable television (CATV) system east of the Mississippi owned by a telephone company.

In 1983 the company filed with the FCC an application to construct and operate a cellular radio mobile telephone system. A joint venture with GTE Mobilnet was later approved. In November of that year the first working fiber optic transmission system in Montgomery and Clinton counties was installed between Linden and Colfax. Also the first digital switch in Montgomery County was installed at Linden.

In 1987 the Paging system was combined with Ameritech Communications in order to provide state wide paging. Bill Miller, graduated from Purdue and began working for Tri-County Telephone Company in 1987. Bill married Kim Kisselbach on September 10, 1988.

In February of 1988 the Colfax office was converted to digital and this was also the year the Tri-County customers could select their long distance provider.

The Company is still family owned with Ben and Maxine having the primary interest. The officers are Ben Miller, President; Harold Widmer, Vice President; Maxine Miller, Secretary-Treasurer; and Russell Miller, Chairman of the Board.

WAVELAND'S NATIONALLY KNOWN AUCTIONEER

Charlie Sentman is one of the most notable residents in all of Waveland. He is recognized for not only living most of his life here but for also being one of the most prominent auctioneers not only in Indiana, but perhaps in all of the United States.

He holds an auctioneer's license in not only Indiana, but in many states throughout the country. They include, Wisconsin, Illinois, Ohio, Tennessee, Kentucky, Alabama, North and South Carolina, Georgia, Minnesota, West Virginia, Virginia and Colorado. Several states do not require an auctioneer's license and Charlie has auctioned in most of them.

Auctioneers have contests and meets much like other professions and in the first year that Indiana ever held a contest, Charlie placed in the top five. Last year he won the Midwest contest held in Kansas City, Missouri and earned a $5000.00 prize which he returned to the Auctioneer's Association to attract and develop new auctioneers.

He is a member of Waveland Masonic Lodge, Indiana Sheriff's Association, Fraternal Order of Eagles and Loyal Order of Moose.

Charlie without doubt is the most traveled resident in all of Waveland. The miles he logs on highways and in air travel to auctions is further extended by the miles he logs on the speedways throughout the Midwest, South and East.

He has a very busy schedule that sees him checking on the Sentman & Sons Pallet Company in Waveland each morning and then is off to Indianapolis where he auctions livestock two to three days a week. He also auctions livestock in Veedersburg, Spencer and other Indiana communities. Charlie auctions not only livestock and race cars, parts and equipment, but is also in great demand for farm, estate, antique, guardianship, bankruptcies, liquidations and heavy equipment.

Even with this busy schedule, he still oversees the building of his three race cars which he races as many as 60 to 70 times in the spring, summer and fall months. In the winter months he conducts auctions of race cars, parts and equipment in major cities in several states. To the racing fraternity, he is Charlie Sentman, The Racing Auctioneer.

Last year he even added driving in a new and popular class of open wheel racing and did it well enough from the

start that he was invited to drive the car in the Florida Speed Weeks competition. He led that series up until the very last night when the car failed him but Charlie literally carried the car and hung on for a second place series finish.

He grew up traveling the Nations fairgrounds speedways when his father was first a driver and later a starter. Charlie has always been a top finisher in the tough late model circuits in which he races and he won the first United States Auto Club Late Model Stock car Championship in 1985.

His grandfather took him to his first auction at a very early age and the more he saw of the excitement, the more determined he became that this was the career he wanted to follow. At first he practiced auctioning while riding a tractor in farm fields. Then he would "auction" the telephone polls as he drove along the highways and today he is the best known of all auctioneers because he is the only auctioneer with experience in so many areas.

The day may come when Charlie and his wife Sue ease out of "life in the fast lane" but together with their son and new granddaughter, feel their "roots" are firmly settled in Waveland the friendly community that has always been home to the greatest auctioneer in America, Charlie Sentman.

For Complete Auction Services:

Charlie Sentman & Assoc.
AUCTIONEER

403 W. MAIN ST.   (317) 435-2646
WAVELAND, IND. 47989

AMI CULVER UNION HOSPITAL

Founded in 1902, Culver Union Hospital has long been recognized for its efforts to bring progressive, high-quality health care to residents of Montgomery and surrounding counties. In 1983, American Medical International (AMI) purchased the hospital and built a new state-of-the-art 120 bed general acute care facility on U.S. 231 near I-74.

Today, AMI Culver Union offers a full range of physician specialties and medical services. Our emergency unit is staffed by a physician 24 hours a day and includes a helipad for the Lifeline air ambulance. A full service laboratory and radiology department, physical and respiratory therapy, intensive and coronary care are all available. A multitude of inpatient and outpatient surgical procedures are performed at AMI Culver Union.

DARLINGTON PUBLIC LIBRARY

The Darlington Public Library was started by the Inter Nos Club and Book Lovers Club in 1914. They applied to the Carnegie Foundation and kept a store front library of donated books for 18 months with each member serving their turn to prove their serious intent of wanting a library. They were granted $10,000 from the fund and with tax money, built and maintained a lovely brick library as designed by local son, Hubert Wilson Peterson.

The first librarian was Nellie Simmons. Faye Miller served from 1916 to 1933. Jessie Delano served from 1933 to 1968. Emma Lou Weliever, present librarian, started in 1969. Mardelle Lehe has served as assistant since 1961.

At present, over 10,000 volumes are held with some 600 records. Just started is an educational video cassette collection. There is a coupon, paperback and pattern exchange.

It is a town-township library and serves Sugar Creek township by contract.

In 1974, a Friends of the Library Fund was started that has enabled the library to maintain its standard of service. It also

enabled the *Darlington Herald's*, 1915-1951, to be microfilmed.

Present Library Board members are: Julia Clouser, Ed Otten and Mary Edie Cox appointed by the North Montgomery School Board; Keith Parker appointed by the Town Board; Patty Ryker appointed by the Township Advisory Board; John "Butch" Dale appointed by the County Commissioners; and Peggy Foster appointed by the County Council.
Submitted by: Emma Lou Weliever

LINDEN PUBLIC LIBRARY

The day the Linden (Carnegie) Public Library opened its doors in May, 1922 with 797 volumes on the shelves was a "fantastic dream come true" due to patience and persistence of members of the Linden Woman's Club and many other interested citizens of the township.

Members of the first library board were J.E. Hopewell, President, Tom Allen, Miss Ethel Browning, Mrs. E. Coleman, A.S. Fraley, Mrs. J.O. Rhea and H.C. Shobe. At the end of the year, 281 borrowers registered and 1,175 books circulated. In 1958 Madison Township and Linden merged under Library Law 1947M.

Today residents and taxpayers of Madison township receive free library service along with several families in surrounding communities who enjoy library service by paying a yearly non-resident fee. There are 12,195 volumes, 586 records, 40 cassettes, 55 videos, paperback exchange and two daily newspapers and 70 magazines are received currently. Today in our 67th year there are 794 borrowers. Reciprocal borrowing is available for users of Indiana public libraries. An interlibrary loan system allows a library user to obtain any book not owned by his/her local library through Wabash Valley ALSA. Gifts of memorial books and pictures, historical newspaper clippings and bequests have enhanced the services. Story hours are sponsored by the Linden Women's Club yearly.

Present board members are: Jeanne M. Ward, president, Marvin R. Oliver, vice-president, David O. Layton, Secretary, Robert W. Prather, Treasurer, Ruth Coopman, Mary J. Harshman and Shirley Crum. Librarians over the years and the year of appointment of each are: Grace T. Vlier, 1921; Minnie McBee, 1926; Charlotte Lucas, 1927; Evelyn Wright, 1933; Fannie Adkisson, 1941; Edith Miller, 1948; Ruth White, 1970; Mary Isabel Wilkins, the present librarian, 1981.

Citizens of Madison township are grateful to the determined citizens who persisted in the early years and they point with pride to their library.

The library, Webster says is "a room or building where a collection of books is kept, an institution in charge of the care and circulation of such a collection; or a collection of books". Linden Library is more than that, it is service—service with a heart. *Written by Mary Wilkins*

SCHLOOT FURNITURE COMPANY
A FULL SERVICE FURNITURE STORE

After visiting and liking future prospects for Crawfordsville, Garrett Schloot opened Schloot Furniture on the first floor of The Ben Hur Building in 1933.

The original Jasonville Hardware and Furniture Company was in Jasonville, Indiana.

Robert J. Schloot, son of Garrett came here in 1939. After attending Wabash College and serving in the Air Force, Loren Schloot also came to Crawfordsville in 1946.

The Business was moved to its present location in 1939. The Store was Incorporated in 1954.

A Budget Store and 2 separate warehouses have been added.

Loren Schloot retired in 1977, at that time Thomas R. Schloot, son of Robert J. Schloot, was added as an officer of the corporation.

BUSENBARK'S

Lawn Equipment & RV Sales & Service
Wilderness Trailers-Starcraft Campers
Simplicity-Snapper-Yazoo

St. Rd. 47 South 5 Miles
Crawfordsville, IN 47933

317-866-0536

GO TO CHURCH SUNDAY

HAPPY HOLLOW FARM FOODS

Martha J. Clough
Ph. 435-2263—106 N Cross, Waveland, IN

MACHLEDT & SERVIES

The Machledt Funeral Home was established in 1915 by Harry C. Machledt. After his death in 1948 the business was operated by his son William F. Machledt. Larry Servies was employed in 1949. In 1956 half interest was purchased from William Machledt. The name was changed to Machledt & Servies Funeral Home. Larry Servies became sole owner in 1962 after the death of William Machledt.

ROLAND D. MILLIGAN
WAVELAND, INDIANA
1961-1989

SAWS   SALES
BRUSH CUTTERS
SERVICE   TRIMMERS

STIHL
— NUMBER ONE WORLDWIDE —

THE NARROW DOOR BOTTLE SHOP

Package
Beer-Liquor-Wine
104 W. Green St., Waveland, Indiana 47989
Ruby Good

Day's Wallpaper

FAMILY RECORD

NAME	BIRTH		DEATH	
	Date	Place	Date	Place

Index

ABBEY, May, 94, Joseph, 41
ABBOTT, Aben 257, Ben, 111, Daisy Viola, 325, George, 325, Gladys, 257, Harold, 257, Harold W., 37, Mamie, 153, Margery, 236, Stanley, 257, 12, 42
ABER, 32
ABERNATHY, Eleanor, 158
ABNER, David, 261
ABNEY, Stella Ann, 324
ABSTON, Alice L. 78, Clyde A., 78, Floyd C., 78, Howard E., 78, John J., 78, Marvin W., 78, Mary, 78, Norman, 78, 280, Norman F., 78 StevenN 78, Zinetta, 78
ACKERSON, Cedric, 244, Ina Mae, 244, Mary Lou, 244, Nora, 244, Oscar E. 244, 334, Thelma, 244
ACKMAN, (REV), 41
ACRES, Criss, 194
ADAMS, Barbara, 329, Billy, 78, Calvin, 78, Clara, 78, Delmar, 78, Donald, 78, Dorris, 78, Elsie, 54, Florence, 165, Hannah, 176, Harry, 78, Henry, 82, Isaac C., 181, J.Q, (Pres.), 314, James, 78, Jane, 209, John, 158, John Quincy, 172, John Quincy (Pres.) 331, Juliene 78, Juliene Jean, 78, Mary 245, Mildred, 78, Paul, 78, Robert, 298, Shirley, 78, Susan, 78, Susan Darlene, 78, Terry, 185, Thomas 78
ADAMS EXPRESS, 12
ADAMSON, Ada, 212, Chris, 159, Jeffrey, 159, Jenna, 159, Justin, 159, Oral, 43
ADDLER, Barbara Jean, 128, Debra, 229, 339, Jerry, 132, Mark, 128, Norma Jean, 132
ADE, George, 221
ADKINS, 67
ADKISSON, Fannie, 381
ADLER, Dorothy H., 366
AFFLECK, Elizabeth, 79, 54
AGE, Norman, 295
AGNEW, A.F., 41, Gibson, 141, Martha Jane, 141, Nancy, 239
AHL, Carol Larue, 292
AHLE, Louisa, 215
AIKEN, Maria, 222, Wallace K., 217
AINSWORTH, Julia A., 284, Ramona, 18, 30, 284
AIRHARTS, 42
AIRHEART, Elizabeth, 352
AKERS, 22, Anthony Eugene, 78, Claudia, 84, Earl Eugene, 78, Ethel Eugenia, 79, Gene, 78, 79, Jean Kaye, 79, Jonathan, 78, Jonathan Perri, 78 Margaret, 78, Marshall, 79, Marshall Kendall 78, Paul Baxter, 78, Peggy, 78, 79, Ralph Charles, 78, Samuel, 378, Sarah Alvord, 78, Susan 323, Tony, 79, William Kendall, 78
AKIN, Maria, 337
ALBERTSON, Hiram, 167, Rebecca, 167,
ALDRICH, Danny, 54, David, 54
ALDRIDGE, Margaret, 294, Mary Ann, 269
ALEXANDER, 252, Becky, 127, Bertha, 313, Carl T., 37, Cynthia Elizabeth, 347, Florence E., 85, Fran, 173, Fred, 173, John, 313, John S., 254, Julia Ann, 80, 308, Lee, 313, Linda, 313, Mary, 31, 173, Nettie, 65, Pauline, 313, Richard, 80, Ruth 313, Sarah 313, Susan 65, Susannah, 80, Ted, 22, Thomas 173, 17
ALEXANDER'SFURNITURE,16
ALFORD, J.P., 63
ALFRED, Henry, 50
ALFREY, Mary Susan, 310
ALIFF, Bob, 15
ALLBRIGHT, Anna, 178
ALLEE, Garnet, 155,
ALLEM, Candy, 112, Cathy, 112, Cherry, 112, Cindy 112, Mike, 112, Pat, 112, Warren, 112
ALLEN, Archibald Cameron, 79, Bernard, 79, Birdie Lou, 259, Brian Wayne, 251, Byron, 79, Cornelius, 303, Donald F. 79, Dwight, 287, Eliza, 277, Emma, 173, Faye, 268, Frank Fine, 79, Gary, 54, Gordon M., 79, Hannah Irwin, 79, Heather, 79, Hiram D., 79, Ical Goldie, 303, Isaac C., 79, Isabel, 315, Isam, 303, Ivan, 79, J.C., 11, 351, James, 79, 169, 284, James Logan 79, Jane, 79, John C., 12, 52, 194, John Newton, 79, Johnny, 12, 13, Joseph, 79, 123, Julia, 79, Lavina, 79, Lavinia, 169, Lillian, 351, Lillian E., 52, Lydia, 303, Malinda, 79, Margaret Lottie, 287, Marilyn, 54, Mary, 302, Mary Ann, 116, Mary Catherine, 301, Mary Irene, 296, Matilda Evelyn, 227, Narcissa, 79, Narcissa Montague, 284, Opal 357, Otis, 287, Pamela, 210, Phoebe, 100, Randall Scott, 251, Rhoda, 123, Richard D., 11, Robert Welsh, 79, Ruby, 43, Sara, 110, Sarah, 123, 148, 151, 152, 229, 248, Stephen, 110, 248, Tom, 381, Wilbert (Emmett), 79, William Graham, 79
ALLENDORF, Joan, 127
ALLERTON, Farms, 277
ALLHANDS, Ada, 80, Andrew, 80, Anita Joyce, 79, Anna, 80, Caroline, 80 Carolyn, 80, Carolyn Jane, 79, Cindi Jane, 80, Dana Marie, 80, Daniel, 80, Daniel, Jr., 80, Dorothy, 80, Elizabeth, 80, Eva Mae, 80, Frank D. 80, Frank Dallan, 79, Frank Dallas, 80, Frankin 79, Franklin Delahunt, 79, Franklin Pierce, 80, George, 80, 308, Grace, 80, Hellen, 80, Jeanette, 80, Jerri Lynn, 80, John, 80, John Milton, 80, Joyce, 80, Katherine, 80, Kristi Joyce, 80, Luetta, 80, Margaret 80, Mark Cawthorn, 80, Nancy, 80, Naomi, 80, Olive, 80, Patience Elizabeth, 80, 308, Patsey, 80, Philip Herron, 79, 80, Pleg, 80, Raymon 80, Regina, 79, 143, Robert Love, 80, Ruth 80, Sara Delahunt, 80, Sarah 80, Susan 80, 321, Thomas, 80, Vernon, 80, William T., 80, William Jr., 80
ALLIE, Margaret, 271
ALLISON, Alice Virginia, 220
ALLMAN, Sue, 252
ALMA, Roy, 372
ALVORD, Ethel Eugenia, 79
ALWARD, Goldie, 192, James Arista, 299, Jesse, 299, John 239, 299, Rebecca, 299, Wandaline, 108
AMASTADT, Dorothy L., 224
AMES, April Lynn, 119, Benjamin Andrew, 133, Bridgitte Renee, 133, Celista Belle, 133, Charles, 119, Curtis Thompson, 133, Helen, 119, James, 321, John, 133, John Custer, 133, John Jeffrey, 133, Jonathon Dean, 133, Juanita, 83, Kimberly Kay,119, Richard Charles, 119, Sallie Ann, 133, Steven Bruce, 133, Steven Tyler, 133
AMMEN, Salome, 176
AMMERMAN, Clarissa Ann, 273, Gladys, 205, Lucinda, 158
AMUNSON, Amelia, 105
ANDERS, Elizabeth, 188, William L., 375
ANDERSEN, Marjorie, 289
ANDERSON, Alice, 81, 242, Angie, 81, Anna, 81, 242, Asa, 272, Bertha, 162, Bessie, 80, Betty, 81, Betty Jean, 81, Bruce, 245, Carl, 293, Carl Oliver, 194, Carla Hiatt, 194, Carlos Hiatt, 194, Charles, 242, Dale, 192, Earl, 14, Edgar, 81, Edna, 323, Elizabeth C., 181, Esther, 71, Eva Kay, 354, Everett, 80, Frances, 80, Gayle, 192, Gene, 71, Geoff, 199, 223, 290, Gordon, 330, Gordon Ray, 330, Greg, 192, Harold, 330, Harry, 194, Harry Hiatt, 194, Harry W., 81, Harvey, 354, Hazel Esther, 194, Hugh Hodges, 245, Jacob, 81, James, 80, James M., 29, 80, Jamie, 192, Jamie A. 289, Jay, 111, John, 125, John Collyn Delna, 293, Judith Lee, 194, Katherine, 81, Katherine Alice, 81, Kenneth, 353, Kenneth Herschel, 354, Kent, 80, King Kone, 15, Laura Frances, 346, Logan Michael, 89, Luther Bedford, 162, Madison Britts, 81, Margaret, 125, Marge Louise, 194, Martin, 80, Mary, 199, 272, Mary Ellen, 135, Mary Katherine, 223, Michael, 89, Mildred Jean, 245, Nellie, 224, Nellie Mae 162, Neva Faye, 354, Nicole, 192, Odie, 272, Opal Jane 272, Paul J. 81, Phillip, 81, Ray, 80, Raymond, 80, 81, Raymond (Mrs.) 331, Robert Carl, 194, Robert F. (Mrs.), 310, Robert William, 194, Rose, 330, Salome, 81, Sarah, 271, Stacey Lynn, 89, Sue A., 372, Teresa, 330, Virginia, 272, Whitney Lea, 330, William L., 81, Wright, 271
ANDERSON HARDWARES, 182
ANDRETTI, Mario, 177
ANDREWS, Edith Ann, 188, Esther, 119, Fanny, 65, Mary E.,120, William Andrews, 120
ANDRUS, (Dr.), 64
ANDRUS, Lidia, 299
ANGLES, Mary, 132,
ANSPACK, John, 303
ANSTETT, Catherine, 375
ANTLE, Edna, 374
ANTONIDES, Lloyd Beal, 358
ANTROBUS, Angusta, 359, Barnabas Edward, 359, Barney, 75, Lyn Allison, 358, 359
APPLE, Barbara, 263, Kathy, 94, Steve, 94
APPLEBY, Madian, 65, 49
APPLEGATE, Dona, 249, Harriet, 247, Henry, 164, Jean Marie, 155, Marion, 155
APPLETON, Elizabeth, 151, 152
ARAM, Alan Walter, 81, Christopher Ryan, 81, Elizabeth Ann, 81, Jessica Alice, 81, Joel Stephen, 81, Jonathan Walter, 81, Justin Paul, 81, Kathleen Sue, 81, Luke Jonathan, 81, Nathan Walter, 81, Rachel Ellen, 81, Randall Joseph, 81, Richard Bruce, 81, Robert Lee, 81, Sharyl Anne, 81, Shirley, 81, Stephen Paul, 81
ARBEGUST, Benjamin, 82, Benjamin F., 82, Benjamin Franklin, 82, Charles, 82, Christianna, 81, 82 Elizabeth, 81, Emiline, 82, George, 81, 82, 135, George Jr., 81, George Sr., 81, George W., 82, Harriet, 82, 110, 135, Hester, 135, John, 81, Margaret, 82, Mary, 81, Mary Ellen, 82, Matilda, 82, Rose Ann 82, Salome, 82, Samuel, 82, Sarah, 82, William 81, 82
ARBENDROTH, Carl, Jr. 78, Carlton John, 78, Clara, 78, Elmer T., 78, John, 78, Marian, 78, Myron E., 78
ARCHER, Diane, 352, Kevin, 352, Roy, 352
ARCHEY, Etta, 65
AREHART, Margaret, 267
ARMANTROUT,Eli Frederick, 143, Ella Anna, 155, 156, Joseph, 155, Marjorie, 268, Martha, 155, Mary, 143, Mary Ann, 353, Mary Belle, 79, Sarah Zerelda, 337,
ARMBRUSTER, Barry, 82, Barry Jay, 82, Don, 82, Donald Leo, 82, Janet, 82, Janet Melvina, 82, Joseph Anthony, 82, Lori, 82, Louis Ludwig, 82, Nellie, 82, Tina, 82, Tina Marie, 82, Lori Jean, 82
ARMFIELD, Essie, 134
ARMISTEAD, L.A. (Brig Gen), 83
ARMSTRONG, 22, Albert, 334, Alexander P., 151, Ambrose, 82, Charlotte, 151, Chester, 371, Clifford Nelson, 334, Ed, 13, Edwin Clay, 334, Eliza Ann, 185, Eva, 227, Forrest Lee, 282, James, 48, 49, Janet, 372, Janet Lynn, 207, John, 95, 165, 185, Kent, 282, Lawrence, 282, 334, Marcella Jane, 316, Martha Ellen, 165, Mary, 335, Mary Lenore, 334, Maurine, 144, Mike, 275, Nettie, 359, Nora, 150, Phebe, 95, Royce, 282, Ruth, 233, Sarah, 95, 237, T., 88, Thomas, 10, 218, Vera, 150, William, 237, William C., 218, Oscar, 150
ARNETT, Abijah, 82, David, 82, David Solomon, 82, Isabel, 82, Jacob, 82, Jacob Washington E., 82, Martha, 82, Mary, 82, Mary E., 82, Nancy, 82, Samuel, 82, Samuel N. Stranghan, 82, Thomas, Jr., 82, Thomas, Sr., 82
ARNOLD, Bambi, 110, Benjamin, 110, Cliff, 221, Daniel, 83, 176, David, 83, Frances, 83, George R., 83, Henry, 83, John R., 83, Kenneth, 66, Lydia, 176, 177, Margaret, 83, Mary, 196, Mary C., 176, 177, Nancy, 82, 83, 176, Randy, 109, Rebecca, 110, Samuel, 83, William, 83, 32
ARNOLDS, Daniel, 82
ARRINGTON, Laura Dale, 152
ARROWSMITH, __307
ARTERBURN, Daniel T., 372
ARTHUR, Diann, 67, Dickson, 143, E.A., 224, Maude, 75
ASBRIDGE, Anna, 144
ASBURY, Elmira, 150
ASELTINE, Lois Marie, 295, Merritt L., Jr., 295
ASHBY, Betty, 305, Edgar, 33, Ella, 74, Emma, 277, Eugene, 33, Juanita, 277, Letitia, 257, Lettice, 55, 256, Milton, 256, Pauline, 277, Robert L., 206, Susan, 256, Thompson, 55, Wallace, 74
ASHE, Gen. 219
ASHER, Mary, 87
ASHER'S PRODUCE, 12, 13
ASHLEY, Jack, 277
ASHMAN, Claudia, 99
ASHWELL, Adeline, 130, James E., 83, Julia Matilda, 354, Julian, 355, Juliann, 354, Martha, 83, Meredith, 83, Nancy "Nannie" 83, William, 40, William B. 29, 83
ASO, Cuba, 150
ASTON, Adaline, 345
ATKINSON, Bessie, 243, Susan, 157 Sybil, 179
AUMAN, Clara L., 249, Ross R., 372
AUSETTS, Minnie Elizabeth, 90
AUSTIN, Jack, 72, Martha, 301, Mattie, 253
AUSTTS, Beth, 347, Tony, 347
AVERY, Christopher, 82, James, 82, Thomas, 194
AXSOM, April, 357, Jason, 357, Keith, 357, Linda, 357
AYARS, Burgin, 125, John Gillman, 125, Lucy L., 125, Robert, 125
AYERS, Sarah, 354
AYRES, Jennie, 153
BABER, Forest, 31
BACHELDER, Clay, 33, Harold, 33, Muter, 33
BADGELY, Anthony, 269
BAER, Jacob, 294
BAGBY, Emma Frances, 308, Francis Marion, 80, 308, James, 308, John H., 308, Mary F., 308, Nancy, 308, Patience Elizabeth, 80
BAGWOOD, Mary, 332, Pearl, 332, Richard, 332
BAILES, Mary Margaret, 251, 332,
BAILEY, Craig, 374, Guy, 327, John, 307, Mary, 80, Rachel E., 165, William, 281
BAILY, Cynthia, 164, Henryetta Anna, 100
BAIR, Albert Lee, 333, John, 130, Raymond, 333, Robert Edward, 333, Ronald, 333, William 130, 333
BAIRD, Annabel, 89, Jesse, 94
BAITY, Arlie, 54, Thelma, 54
BAKER, Bobbi Jo, 245, Brooke Lynne, 245, Carrie Maureen, 245, Donald Eugene, 245, Evelyn, 262, James, 115, Jeffrey F., 372, John, 116, Juanita L., 115, Lillian, 175, Lucinda, 116, Moses (Dr.), 125, Nettie, 175, 339, Nora, 208, Reatha, 116, Rebecca, 225, Sarah, 270, Thomas, 164
BALDWIN, 185, Alice M., 176, Amelia B., 176, Benjamin L., 176, Catherine, 361, Charles M., 307, David, 307, Elias Jackson, 187, 307, Esther, 164, Francis Wildey, 176, 185, Garret, 307, George, 307, Hannah, 176, Helen M., 176, Jamie, 13, John P., 307, Lucas, 176, Lucky, 187, Maranda Dee, 306, Margaret, 361, Mary J., 307, Nig, 13, Rachel Ann, 321, Robert, 360, Sarah, 187, Sarah E., 307, Silas S., 164, Willette, 185, 186, William J., 307
BALES, Beverly Ann, 83, Carl J., 83, Emma, 174, Frank, 83, Freddie, 83, Frederic, 83, Harold, 83, James Y., 83, Juanita, 83, Louise, 83, Robert, 83
BALL, Benjamin, 296, Clarence, 71, Edna, 353, Elizabeth Jane, 203, Ernest, 373, Esther, 186, Floyd, 353, Francis, 71, 166, 167, Lucille, 342, Lucinda Welch, 186, Martha, 292, Raymond, 286, Rosie, 286, Salome, 176, Zopher, 186
BALLAH, Elva Irene, 164, Gwendolyn, 163, 164, Hannah, 164, Marion R., 164, Melissa, 164, Otis Freeman, 164
BALLARD, Alexander, (Mrs.), 326, Charles, 64, Eva, 151, J. Lee, 326, Jean, 350, 351, Jennifer Ann, 244, Jimmy, 244, Joan Elizabeth, 244
BALLENGER, Achilles, 351, Barbara, 351, Catherine, 351, Jennie, 351, Jesse, 351, John, 351, Joshua, 351, Martha, 351, Mary, 351, Matthias, 351, Mourning, 351, Tobias, 351
BALLEW, Delta, 83
BALLUS, Leonis, 163
BALSER, Cinderella, 157, 166, 310, Elizabeth, 141, George, 141, 310, Mary, 310, Rebecca, 141
BAMISH, Beth Baer, 26, Edward, 66
BANDEL, Fred, 227, Hermine (Minnie), 229, Lena, 227
BANDY, Austin Lynn, 276, Blaine Lee, 276, James Larry, 276, Kevin Lance, 276, Leslie Jean, 276,
BANE Building Contractor, 16
BANE Sawmill,16
BANNER, Betty L., 147, Betty Lou, 169, Cynthia, 169, J.D., 169
BANNON, Anna, 187, Baker, 325, Charles, 83, 214, 230, 325, Clela, 83, Cora, 187, Eldo, 83, 138, 214, Elizabeth, 187, Emogene, 325, Ernest, 83, Evan, 83, Evelyn, 83, Frank Andrew, 187, Gladys, 208, 230, Helen, 230, Helen Waneta, 214, Ida May, 230, Iva, 83, James, 169, 187, James Clark, 83, 325, Jeremiah, 187, Joe, 325, John C., 187, Lena, 325, Lenna, 83, Lewis, 83, 325, Lewis (Rev), 187, Lyle, 83, Mary, 187, Mary Melinda, 214, Mary Melinda (Molly), 83, Max, 83, 214, Max Monroe, 138, Michael, 83, 187, 325, Nancy, 187, Rebeca, 187, Richard, 230, Richard Lee, 83, Sally Arley, 325, Staci, 374, Vera, 83, Virginia, 83, 138, 214, Wanetah, 83, Will, 187, William, 325
BANTA, Basle, 83, Delia Etta, 83, Florence, 83, George, 83, J. Myron, 84, Jean, 84, Judith Kay, 84, Judy, 92, Lulu, 309, Margaret, 269, Myrtle, 84, Perry, 83, Richard, 42, Theron, 84, 325, Theron S., 83, Thomas W., 83, Thuron, 374, Virginia, 221, Virginia Ruth, 84
BAPPERT, Fredericka, 107
BARBER, Mary Jo, 120
BARBOUR, J. 272
BARCLAY, Neil C., 372
BARCUS, Elizabeth, 204, Lydia, 209, Mayme, 272, Thelma, 272, William, 272
BARGER, Iva Maxine, 175
BARINGER, Eunice C., 137, Harry, 137, Marion, 137
BARKER, Amanda, 255, Benjamin Lewis, 84, Carl Delbert, 84, David H., 84, David Hogan, 84, Debra Kay, 84, Donna, 280, Donna Rae, 84, Edna Arlinda, 180, Edna Katherine, 84, Ernest, 197, Freda Louise, 84, Geraldine, 199, Grover Cleveland, 84, Hannah, 344, Helen, 280, Helen M., 84, Isaac, 344, John Edward, 180, Kenneth Dwight, 84, Lawrence Russell, 84, Leatha Marie, 84, Linda Lou, 84, Lloyd Franklin, 84, Lola Mae, 84, Lorna Pearl, 84, Margaret, 307, Nina Rose, 180, Oliver Perry, 84, Patricia, 84, Ralph, 4, 280, Ralph L., 84, Ralph Lester, 84, Rose Etta, 187, Stace, 277, Vicki, 296, Wain Lodell, 84
BARKER Excavating, 15
BARKHARDT, James C., 69
BARKOW, Martha, 341
BARLOW, John, 129
BARNARD HOME Comfort Shop, 15
BARNARD, James, 74, **BARNES,** Anna, 186, Benjamin, 49, Bertha Blaul, 84, Beth, 127, Dorothy, 155, Ed, 36, Frank G., 127, Geoffrey, 84, Geoffrey Prescott, 84, Hank, 127, Harry George, 84, Harry Jr., 84, James, 42, 128, James J., 84, James John, 84, James Johnson, 113, Janna, 67, Jason Brandon, 128, Jeff, 63, Jeffrey G., 67, Jennifer Chase, 84, Jim 84, Louise, 84, Maggie, 67, Mary, 265, 350, Patience, 84, Rachel, 350, Susan, 127
BARNES' Crafts, 16
BARNES Grocery, 14
BARNETT, Amanda, 85, Anna, 84, Caroline, 85, Carroll, 71, Cather-

ine, 94, Christa, 271, David, 56, Denise, 85, 171, Elizabeth, 85, 94, Elizabeth A., 85, Emma, 43, Enoch, 31, George W., 85, Hanna, 85, Hilda, 85, 171, James, 31, 84, 85, 372, James E., 85, Jane, 85, John, 84, Linda L., 375, Lowell, 71, Lulu, 179, Martha, 85, Mary, 85, Mary Isabelle, 85, Mary K., 375, Maxwell, 171, Nancy, 36, 85, Nietta, 85, Sam, 85, Sarah J., 85, Susan, 85, Terri, 85, Thomas, 85, Voris Maxwell, 85, Wallace, 85, William 85, William R., 171, William Ray, 85, Lewis Wesley, 85, __, 223
BARNHART, Christena, 332, George, 332, Gertrude May, 332, Irene Rose, 332, Katie, 138, Katie Bethel, 332
BARNHILL, Martha, 39
BARR, Chine, 242, Ella, 242, Emma, 242, Emma Flora, 241, Harry L., 241, James, 242, James W.,154, 241, James Wesley, 241, Janet, 262, Lizzie, 43, Mary, 154, 241, Mary Elizabeth, 241, Molly, 242, Sarah, 242, William Charles, 242
BARRAK, Eddie Joe, 283
BARRETO, Tami C., 372
BARRETT, Rosemary, 187
BARRIGER, John W., 14
BARRINGER, Ethella, 93
BARRINGTON, Helen, 270, Herb, 270, Lester, 270, Marden, 270, Percival, 270, Willard, 270
BARRY, Anna, 84, Debbie, 14, 209, Nellie, 82, Sara, 209, Shannon, 209
BARTCH, Minnie, 259, Wilimina Georgina, 259
BARTH, Carol, 315, Ruth, 196, 266
BARTHOLOMEW, C.G., 69, William Aldred, 259
BARTLETT, Ed, 109, Thomas, 63
BARTLEY, Jane, 332, Jesse, 215, Ruth, 150
BARTON, Ashley, 98, Brett, 98, Carole L., 375, Charles, 286, Grant M. 59, Harve, 360, Harvey R., 372, John, 159, Mildred, 253, Pamela, 286, Todd D., 372, Wilma, 286
BASS, Jessie, 240
BASTIAN, Edgar H., 99, Harriet Roberta, 99, Lora, 99
BASTION, Eliza Catherine, 130
BATES, Earl, 288, Glen, 64
BATMAN, James, 285, Louilla, 285, Ward, 286
BATTREALL, Andrew, 85, Bertha, 85, Emaline, 85, Gilford, 85, Henry, 85, Hester Ann, 85, Icy, 85, Jay T., 85, John, 85, Lena, 85, Lilbus "Lillie", 85, Malinda, 85, Malinda E., 359, Malinda E. "Minnie", 85, Mary, 85, Mary Margaret, 85, Mary Melinda, 85, Michael, 85, 359, Polly, 85, Silas A., 85, Susan M., 85, William, 85, William Wayman, 85
BATTY, Bashia, 151, George, 151, John Peter, 151, Muriel May, 151, Rebecca, 121, John Peter, 151, Leanah, 151
BAUER, Abner, 85, Abraham, 85, John Martin, 85, Juliana, 207, 353, Michael, 85, Michael Jr., 85, Peter, 146, Valentine, 85, William, 207, William Jr., 207, Savilla Marie, 189
BAUMANN, Mildred, 346
BAUMGARTNER, Marsha L., 375
BAXTER, Florence, 83, Martha Jane, 78
BAYLES, Charlotte, 287, W.W., 12, William, 87
BAYLESS, ___, 11, Amy, 107, Boone, 86, Boss, 12, 13, Brenda, 279, Brian, 279, Brooke, 86, Carl Richard, 86, Claude, 309, Daniel, 86, Daniel Wayne, 86, Darrell Wayne, 86, Don, 107, Donald Wayne, 86, Ed, 86, Eddie Dale, 86, Edward Randall, 86, Edwin Eugene, 86, Elizabeth, 86, 87, 172, 287, Elmer, 86, Fred, 86, 277, Fred Paul, 86, Freddie Paul, 86, Geneva, 211, George, 87, Gilbert, 319, Goldie, 277, 278, Grant, 87, Gregory, 279, Hannah, 183, Hazel, 87, 277, Irvin, 86, 87, Irvin Samuel, 86, Jeff, 86, Jennifer, 86, Jerry, 279, John, 13, 52, 87, 171, 189, John W., 12, Joy, 279, Kimberly Michell, 87, Kirk, 86, Kristie, 86, Larry, 87, Laura, 87, Laura Kay, 86, Lemuel, 87, Lester, 12, 13, Lizzie, 277, Lloyd, 86, 87, 277, Lottie, 87, 250, 287, Lula, 87, 287, Luna, 86, 277, Luna Harrison, 87, 287, Lura, 172, Mae, 87, 93, Margaret, 12, 87, Marianne, 86, Mary, 86, 87, 172, May, 277, Nathan, 86, Nelson, 86, 87, 277, Oakel Grant, 86, Pauline, 86, Pearl, 86, Randy, 86, Robert, 86, Robert Samuel, 87, Rose, 86, 277, Roy, 13, Ryan, 86, Sam, 86, 87, Samuel Wayne, 87, Sandra Lee, 86, Sandy, 86, Sarah Jane, 290, Shannon, 86, Sheryl Lee, 86, Stacey, 107, Theeadocia, 145, Thelma Lucille, 86, Thomas Allen, 86, Thomas Glen, 86, Tom, 86, Waneta, 86, Will, 12, William, 87, William W., 11, 12
BAYLISS, Helen, 319, Lucille, 319, Velma, 319
BAYNES, Beezon, 87, Helen M., 87, Joseph Powell, 87, Lowry, 87, Margaret Lowry, 87, Mary Asher, 87, Rebecca, 81, 138, 139, 140, Rebecca Heacock, 276, 335, Theodore, 87, Thomas Beezon, 87, Thomas Priestman, 87, 140, Walter Powell, 87
BAZZANI, Amy Suzanne, 88, 224, Antonio, 87, Arlene, 224, Carolina, 87, Doris, 64, 222, 306, Fred, 87, 88, 306, Garry, 88, 224, Heather Lynn, 88, 224, Karen, 88, 310, 325, 360, Kate, 88, Kate Smith, 325, Kathryn, 87, Kathryn Geneva, 310, Larry, 88, Nikki, 88, Robby, 88
BEACH, Cathy, 309, Paul, 309, Ron, 309, Sara, 309
BEAL, Frank, 63, Ida Ann, 242
BEALL, Brian, 208
BEAM, Anna, 170, Howard, 311, Isabelle, 186, James, 170, 186, Merlin, 311, Richard, 311
BEAMAN, Wave, 181
BEAN, Edgar C., 162, Louis, 75
BEARD, Jane, 231, John, 231
BEARSLEY, Frances, 321
BEASON, Elizabeth, 201, Robert, 222
BEASY, Albert, 360
BEATTY, Dr., 274, J.L., 135, Julia Ann, 347, June, 273, William, 347
BEATY, Andrew, 201
BEAUCHAMP, Jesse, 176, Nancy, 176, Jean, 110
BEAUREGARD, (Gen.), 355
BECHELHIMER, Ora, 192
BECHTEL, Brian L., 372
BECK, Abraham, 88, Anthony, 36, Carol Jean, 275, Charity M., 88, Effie, 31, Eliza, 88, Elizabeth, 36, 88, 113, 143, Emma, 331, Florence Idel, 283, Florence Idell, 284, Henry, 88, 143, 315, Henry F., 88, John Martin, 88, John W., 88, Josiah C., 88, Josiah Congo, 88, Lucinda, 88, 233, Maria Catherina, 88, Martha, 88, Mary, 88, Naomi, 135, Robert E., 275, Robert L., 375, Samuel, 49, Sarah, 143, Solomon, 36, 88, Wesley, 31, William, 31, 88, William W., 88,
BECK, Williams & Hess Cons, 68
BECKER, James, 300
BECKNER, Marcus, 110
BECKWITH, __, 6, H.W., 25
BEE, Adrianne Marie, 262, John David, 262, Julie, 121, Thomas V., 262, Tom, 262
BEECHER, Jean, 325, 326, Walter, 326, William, 326
BEEKER, Doris Maxine, 297
BEER, Susan, 86
BEERS, Henry B., 49
BEESLEY, Mary, 356
BEESON, Carroll, 24, Doc, 12, Jonathan, 328, Mary Catherine, 328, Maude, 328, Maude Daisy, 328
BEESWICK, George, 49
BEETEM, Charles, 319
BEGLEY, Ronnie, 372
BEHME, Kurt F., 372
BEISEL, Henry D., 294
BELCH, James, 43
BELL, Alonzo Earl, 88, 96, Archie, 285, Betty, 88, Candy, 54, Charles Edward, 88, Elizabeth, 88, 89, Elizabeth Belle, 304, Erin Elizabeth, 89, Estel, 170, 272, Florence, 88, Fred, 304, Gary L, 372, George, 187, Gerald, "Jerry" Wayne, 88, 89, Gregory Wray, 88, 89, Henry, 50, Homer, 174, J. Frank, 170, James Rice, 170, Jane, 187, Jason Gerald, 89, Karen S., 372, Kathleen Kim, 89, Louise, 285, Mahersey, 215, Mariana, 88, 89, Marilyn 88, 89, Marjorie, 272, Martha, 88, 187, Mary, 355, Paul Reid, 170, Rachel, 213, Richard, 372, Sarah, 187, Sharon, 272, Stacey, 115, Stella, 96, Stephen, 88, Steve, 54, Susannah, 274, Warren, 88, Warren G., 88, James, 105
BELLUS, Kate Glassway, 163, Lura, 163, 283
BELT, Ruth H., 227
BELTON, Frank, 365
BENCOMO, Benedicta Varsquez, 194
BENDICT, Paul, 49
BENEFIEL, George W., 259
BENGE, Samuel, 26, Samuel E., 37
BENINGHAUS, Catherine, 173
BENNETT, Amy Diane, 89, Beth Ann, 117, Carol, 117, Carrie Ann, 89, Cheryl, 296, Clarissa, 357, Cody, 286, Diana, 89, 190, Edward, 80, Elizabeth, 101, Elsie, 165, H. Craig, 286, James W., 102, Jeffrey Todd, 89, John, 89, 190, John R., 117, Lydia, 141, Martha, 136, Mary, 286, Mary L., 90, Natalie, 290, Patrick Kevin, 117, Rice, 136, Robert J., 117, Stacey Lynn, 89, Terri, 128, Virginia, 336, William, 89
BENOID, Mildred, 203
BENSKIN, Mary, 149
BENSON, Thomas Calvin, 188
BENTLEY, Nelda, 131, Nelda Joyce, 192
BERBERIAN, Mary Kay, 210
BERNTSEN, Jane, 161, Mary, 161
BERRY, Alva Elsworth, 316, Anna, 111, David B., 41, Doak, 100, Earl, 24, 376, Edward, 296, Elizabeth B., 41, John, 85, Louis, 316, Mary Elizabeth, 296, Mary G., 100, Opal, 296, Polly, 100, Stella Ellen, 122, Polly Gambriel, 100, _, 42
BERRY Construction, 287
BERRYS, 14
BERTI, Carolina, 87
BETDORF, Catherine E., 83
BETHEL, Katie, 138
BETTS, George H. (Dr.), 180, Joseph, Sr., 36, Stephen R., 49
BEVELHEIMER, Ethel, 174, John, 174, Reuben, 174
BEVER, Christian, 242, Effie, 250, Frank, 260, Margaret, 260
BEVERIDGE, Albert J., 348
BIAS, Jere, 34, John, 34
BIBEL, George, 89, Lewis, 89, Mary, 89, Sarah, 89
BIBLE, Adam, Jr., 90, Alice Mayme, 90, Christian, 90, Edith C., 90, Elizabeth, 89, 90, Emma, 89, Eva, 90, Fred E., 90, Frederic E., 89, 245, George, 90, 116, Hans Adam, 90, John, 89, 90, John C., 89, Kathleen, 245, Kathleen Belle, 89, Lewis, 89, 90, Mabel, 89, 90, Mabel V., 245, Mary, 89, 90, 116, Mary Ann, 90, Mary Edith, 90, Mary G., 89, Philip, 90, Phillip, 89, Richard, 89, Richard Errington, 90, Richard Montgomery, 89, Sarah, 90, Sealy, 116, Susan S., 89, William Edward 89, 90
BICE, Judy Hughes, 205, Lindell, 205
BICKNELL, John, 87
BIDDISON, Sue, 288
BIDDLE, Andrew, 208, Charles, 208, E.J., 308, Edna, 208, Frank, 208, George, 208, Lula, 208
BIGELOW, Tom, 275
BIGGER, James, 125
BIGGS, Brian Douglas, 91, Carol, 90, 91, 347, Charlotte, 151, Cristy Ann, 91, Debbie Dee, 91, James Madison, 90, Jerry, 91, 347, Jerry L., 90, Joseph Michael, 90, Phoebe, 152, Robert Dean, 90, Ruby, 90, Shirley Ann, 90, Stephen L., 91, Steve, 91, Tracy Leigh, 91, William Eugene, 90
BIGLEY, Dana, 255
BILLINGSLEY, Karen, 317
BILLINGSLY, A.D., 55
BILSLAND, Amanda Luella, 130, Eliza Catherine, 130, James, 130, James Newton, 130, Mary Catherine, 130
BINDHAMMER, Gloria, 161,
BINDHAMMERShoes, 14
BINFORD, Bernard, 91, Bob, 50, Charles, 91, Clyde, 91, David, 61, 91, Georgetta Payne, 61, Grace, 91, Harry, 91, Henry, 61, Ida, 91, James, 91, John, 91, Luella, 91, Mary Payne, 61, Myrtie, 91, Myrtle, 129, Owen, 91, Peter, 91, Thomas, 91, Willard, 91, __, 36
BINGHAM, Lura, 114
BIRCH, Anne, 279, Emma, 360, James, 360, Victor, 279
BIRDGE, Lora May, 197
BIRDSONG, Chris, 221, Christopher, 221, Susie, 221
BIRGE, Cletis, 143, 315, Cletis E., 91, Deborah Lynn, 91, James Thomas, 91, Judy K., 315, Judy Kay, 91, Wilma R., 91
BIRK, Rebecca, 323
BIRR, Jane, 123
BISCHOFF, Louis, 40
BISHOP, Benjamin, 102, Delcie, 245, Donald E., 142, Doris, 245, Edwin S., 102, Elizabeth M., 102, Eunice E., 375, George W., 102, Henry C., 102, Isabella, 222, James M., 102, John, 102, John R., 343, Maria, 102, Marvin, 245, Mary, 123, Michael, 142, Nancy, 343, Robert H., 142
BITNER, Angela, 297, Kenneth Merle, Jr., 297, Kenneth Merle, Sr., 297
BITSON, Eva, 208
BLACK, Bertha, 162, Bill, 345, Brenda, 313, Carroll R., 372, Donna Rae, 248, Elizabeth, 360, Geraldine, 216, Gertrude, 216, Jewell, 345, John, 91, 161, 252, 345, John C., 91, John Charles, 91, John Donald, 91, Josephine, 91, Josephine L., 91, Lena, 161, Lena Gertrude, 252, Leolia, A., 216, Marcia, 345, Margaret, 345, 358, Marilyn, 345, Mary, 161, 345, Milo N., 216, Myrtle, 345, Phyllis, 345, Ramona, 216, Rosalie, 345, Susannah, 209, Thelma, 216, William, 297, William Jennings, 216, William P., 91, Mollie, 252
BLACKER, John, 16, John D., 256, Rex, 256, Robert Max, 256, Squire, 174
BLACKETER, Evelyn, 91
BLACKFORD, Anita Louise, 92, Ann, 92, Ariel, 91, 92, Ariel Floyd, 92, Benjamin, 312, Charles, 92, Charles Albert, 91, Charles Wayne, 92, Donald, 92, Emma, 91, Erma, 91, 92, Louisa, 307, Nathaniel, 312, Nina Erma, 92, Robert, 92, Ruth, 92, Sidney Jane, 352, Vivian, 92, Waxie, 91, 92, William, 92, William V., 312
BLACKWELL, Tony, 54, Gail, 54
BLADES, Laura, 98
BLAINE, Allen T., 126, Laura Anna, 126, Shirl, 81
BLAIR, A.B., 75, Charles, 92, James H., 92, Jennie, 92, John Allen, 92, Lillian, 92, Robert, 92, Tannie, 19, William Noble, 92
BLAKE, Gilbert, 138, Jessie, 138, 214, Sadie, 43
BLAKERS, Madame, 273
BLAKESLEE, Della, 92, James 84, 92, Janice, 84, Jeanne, 92, Jodi, 84, John, 92, Judith Kay, 84, Judy, 92, Mary, 92, Patti, 92, Paul, 92, Paul Sr., 92, Pauls, 92, Ruth 92, Vivian, 92
BLANGY, Mary, 165
BLANKENBAKER, Mary, 351
BLANKENSHIP, Amy, 332, Hezekiah, 151, John, 187
BLANTON, Flora, 181, Frances, 373, Hiram, 181, Luther J., 375, Mary Ellen, 181, Rebecca, 303, Theodore "Jack", 181, Violet, 181, Walter E., 375
BLAUL, Bertha, 84
BLAXOM, Rebecca, 290
BLAYDES Store, 14
BLAYDES, _, 55
BLEDSOE, Anna, 208, Flora Lucretia, 282, Teresa, 151
BLESSING, Catherine Teresa, 300, Elmer, 300, Mary E., 300
BLEVINS, Bessie, 147, Francies, "Fanny", 319
BLEYTHING, Evelyn, 202, Marie, 202, Ray, 202, Raymond, 202
BLOCK, Beth, 265, Brian, 265, Charles, 92, 93, Edward, 265, Jamey, 93, Jason, 93, Jean, 92, 93, Roger Earl, 92, Shirley Joan, 92
BLOOM, Candy, 252, Elizabeth Marie, 252, Jim, 252
BLOOMER, David L., 84, John David, 84, Kimberly Ann, 84, Pamela Ann, 84
BLOSS, Ruby, 334
BLUE, Annie Jane, 226, Ben, 342, John Wesley, 226
BOAZ, Estella, 43, Harold, Jr., 63
BOBO, Townsend, 324
BODINE, Audra, 262
BOEH, Jack, 237, Janet, 237, John, 237, Lisa, 237, Sarah, 237
BOETTGER, Ella, 355
BOGART, Humphrey, 342
BOGER, William H., 29
BOGGS, Jane, 281
BOHANON, Mildred, 360
BOICOURT, Jeptha, 63
BOISE, William A., 50
BOLER, Amanda Lee, 130, 131
BOLING, Jane, 84, Katherine, 248, Katherine Elizabeth, 249
BOLINGER, Marjorie, 142
BOLLMAN, Ada, 93, David C., 93, Eliza, 93, Elza, 87, 277, Ezra, 247, Frances, 93, Frank C., 93, Freeman, 93, Goldie Marie, 93, Hannah, 247, Harold, 93, Jeff, 171, Jerry, 87, 93, John D., 93, Joseph E., 93, Mae, 87, May, 277, Mike, 171, Milo H., 93, Minnie, 93, Pat, 87, Pauline, 93, Rick, 171, Robert Max, 93, Roy, 93, Vernida, 93, Vickie, 171, Wanetta, 93, Lael, 87
BOLSER, Frank, 209, Harriet, 209
BONAPARTE, Napoleon, 293
BONAR, Crystal, 123
BOND, (Major), 290, Dorothy, 136, R.L., 69
BONEBRAKE, Kevin, 203
BONEWELL, __, 93
BONHAM, Vivian, 92
BONIFACIUS, April Dawn, 93, Barbara, 93, Clarence, 254, Clarence Boyd, 93, Clarence Breeze, 93, Clayton Boyd, 93, Cole Bradley, 93, Connie Miller, 93, Deborah Jean, 93, Jan Marlene, 93, Joshua Ray, 93, Kevin Boyd, 93, Kim Lee, 93, Letha Abbott, 93
BONSETT, Anna, 260, Belinda, 260, Beverly, 260
BONWELL, Arthur, 93, Barbara Jean, 94, Borden, 93, Charles Bayard, 94, Corey Lynn, 207, David Earl, 94, Earl J., 93, 94, Elizabeth, 93, Elizabeth M., 93, Elizabeth Opal, 93, 94, 295, James, 93, James Addison, 93, Jennie, 93, 94 John, 93, Linda, 94, Linda Jane, 93, Lois Esther, 94, Mary, 93, Mary Robin, 93, May, 94, Opal, 94, Ralph Addison, 94, Rebecca, 93, Robert, 94, Robert Allen, 93, 94, Robert Francis, 94, Robert Paul, 94, Ruth, 94, Linda Jane, 93
BOOE, Aaron, 94, Aimee, 94, Barbara, 111, Barbara Lee, 94, Eleanor "Ella", 318, Eva May, 94, Ian, 94, John, 94, John Austin, 94, John Austin, Jr., 94, Lee May, 94, Lorenzo Dow, 94, Thomas Jefferson, 318
BOOHER, Isaac, 94, Al, 129, Albert, 194, Albert W., 94, Ambrose, 94, Benjamin, 94, Catherine, 94, Cyrus, 94, Dale, 199, Elihu, 94, Elizabeth, 94, 194, Elizra, 194, Elkannah, 94, Ellis, 158, Elzira, 94, 193, Ephraim R., 94, Fred, 199, Gurdianias, 94, Ira, 94, 119, Irenus, 94, Jacob, 94, Jacob, Jr., 94, Joe, 131, John Jacob, 94, John M., 94, Jonathan A., 94, Judith, 199, Karen Sue, 331, Leander, 94, Louisa, 131, Lucille, 199, Lucinda, 94, 243, Lydia, 94, Madge, 199, Margaret, 94, Margaret Jane, 94, Martha C., 94, Mary, 94, Mary (Polly), 94, Mary Ann, 143, Mary Catherine, 94, Matthew, 331, Michael, 372, Michael Steven, 331, Nancy, 136, Nathan, 94, Nathaniel, 94, Norman, 81, Rebecca, 158, Rebecca Ellen, 181, Rhoda, 94, Rhoda E., 94, Rhoda K., 94, Samuel, 94, Sara Sue, 331, Sarah Jemima, 159, Steve (Mrs.), 331, Susannah Catherine, 94, Sylvanus W., 94, Timothy J., 372, Ward Hampton, 94, William, 94, 199, William K., 94, William M., 194
BOOKER, Carol, 372, John, 29, Minnie, 210
BOONE, Al, 4, Alan, 94, Amos, 94, Bertha, 14, 95, Beth, 94, Bill, 94, 95, 163, 187, 272, Bryana, 95, Cheryl, 94, Chris, 94, 163, Chris Anne, 95, Cindy, 94, 163, Connie, 94, Cora Vivian, 94, Cynthia Jo, 95, Dan, 94, 95, Daniel, 34, 94, 95, 233, 242, 263, 272, 287, 334, David, 94, David John, 94, Doris, 94, Edward, 95, George, 94, 95, 233, 272, Helen, 233, Jacci, 95, Janessa, 95, Jennifer, 95, Jessica, 95, Joe, 94, Kathy, 94, 163, Mamie Lee, 94, Mark, 94, Mary Ann, 94, Mary Pat, 94, Scott, 94, 95, 163, Squire, 263, 334, Steve, 94

BOONE'S Mill, 14
BOORAM, Aaron, 281
BOOTS, __, 22, Anna, 95, Annettie Josephine, 96, Asa, 95, 331, Asachel, 96, Ashel, 95, Beatrice, 95, Charles Ellsworth, 96, Clara, 95, David Lawrence, 96, Diantha Naylor, 95, Eli, 95, 96, Eli Gilmore, 95, Eli, Sr., 95, Elizabeth, 95, Ellen, 96, 97, Elvina June, 95, Emma, 95, Florence, 95, George, 96, Ike, 95, Isaac, 95, Isabella, 95, Isica Gillmore, 95, Jack, 96, Jacob, 95, 96, James F., 95, James Franklin, 95, Jenny, 95, Joyce T., 96, Juanita, 95, Kristin Sue, 96, Lawrence, 96, Lawrence Chayce, 96, 97, Lois, 95, Lois May, 97 Margaret, 95, Martha, 95, 96, 331, Martha Laurena, 96, Mary Ann, 95, Mary Bell, 96, Mattie, 95, Merl, 96, 97, Michael Logan, 96, Mike, 301, Narcessa, 94, Nella Grant, 96, Nevah, 95, Newton, 95, Paul, 96, Pearl, 95, Pet, 95, Phebe, 95, Phyllis, 22, 96, Robert, 95, 96, Robert Chase, 96, Robert Chayce, 96, Roy Garfield, 96, Samuel, 95, 96, 97, Samuel Lavaun, 97, Sarah Elizabeth, 95, Stella, 96, Virginia, 95, Wallace, 96, Wallace Logan, 97, Wesley, 95, Willard Samuel, 96, William H., 95, William Harrison, 95
BORAKER, Kate, 285, Katie, 285, 320, Lydia, 186, Sanford, 285, Susanna, 186
BORDEN, Benjamin, 269, Carroll M., 372
BORNTRAEGER, Hannah, 177, Johann Martin, 177
BORRUSO, Dennis, 278, Peter, 278
BORTZ, Lola (Ward), 31
BORWN, Margaret, 271
BOSEHUNG, Hans, 110
BOSSIE, Cheryl, 228, Don, 228
BOTTOM, George W., 143
BOTTOMLY, Leonard, 192
BOUER, Hanna, 222
BOUNNELL, J.R., 32, Ralph M, 376
BOUSE Pharmacy, 14
BOWAN, Harold, 54, Patsy, 54
BOWELL, Rebecca, 330
BOWEN, (Gov.) 340, A.W., 25, Avanell, 347, Donna, 278, Elizabeth, 135, Everett Young, 118, Forest, 347, Lucy, 314, Mathew, 314, Otis, 217, 323, Otis, (Gov), 181, Virginia, 90
BOWER, Carrie Lida, 102
BOWERMAN, Brian, 97, Candice, 97, Charles, 97, Charles Leo, 97, Christina, 97, Coralea, 97, Cynthia, 97, Dick, 97, Estel, 97, Hazel, 97, Ida, 97, Iva, 97, John, 97, 172, John A., 97, John H., 97, Judith Lynn 97, Judy, 97, Lacey, 172, Laura, 97, Marjorie, 97, Myrtle Iva, 97, Patricia, 97, 98, Patricia Ethel, 97, Ryan, 97, Thomas, 97, Tom, 21, 97, 168
BOWERS, __, 22, Abner, 145, 216, Abraham, Jr., 181, Aubrey, 31, Edward, 69, Esther, 145, Jesse, 194, Mahala, 343, Martha, 194, Mary Jane, 343, Roach, 22, William Nathan, 343
BOWERSOCK, Jonathan Dale, 280, Scott Thomas, 280, Thomas, 280
BOWLING, Donna D., 375
BOWMAN, Blanche, 145, Brian, 249, Cassie Lynn, 84, Dean, 300, Elizabeth, 260, Erin, 249, Floyd, 26, Gertrude, 229, Idella, 300, Jill, 249, Larry Gene, 84, Mary Ellison, 84, Nedra Sue, 84, Oliver, 281, Patricia, 84, Randal Joe, 84, Rene, 300, Sarah, 249, William P., 63, Erin, 249
BOYD, Catherine, 257, J., 288, Kate, 257, Kevin, 319, Raleigh, 319, Rebecca Jane, 257, Samuel R., 257,
BOYER, Charles Alonzo, 98, 316, Joseph, 316, Karle Steele, 98, 316, Kevin Craig, 98, Lois Karel, 98, Marel Catherine, 98, Margaret, 281, Mary, 201, Toni Rene, 98, Wanda Ruth, 98, William Edward, 98, William Elsworth, 98
BOYLAND, __, 13, Jessie, 12, Jessie V., 11, S.N., 11, 13,
BOYLE, James F., 240
BOYLES, Hannah, 124
BOYNTON, Abbey, 183, Elizabeth, 183, Lizzie, 183, 184, William, 183
BOZE, Anne, 350, 351, Betty, 350, 351, Betty Lou, 98, Cecil, 298, 351, Cecil Clare, 98, Cecil O., 98, Clara, 98, Clare, 351, Donald, 351, Donald Glover, 98, Fern Dallas, 98, Fernandre (Andy), 351, George, 98, 350, 351, George Adam, 98, George Hall, 98, George, Jr., 351, James, 98, Marilyn, 350, 351, Marilyn Jo, 98, Mona Tzur, 351, Oakie, 298, Raymond O., 98, Sarah, 98, Stephen, 98, Virginia, 298, 350, 351, Virginia May, 98, Willett Anna, 98, William, 98, William Washington, 98
BOZELL, Ralph R., Jr., 133
BRACE, Charles Loring, 35
BRACKETT, Frank, 136, Minnie, 136
BRADEN, Hector S., 370
BRADFORD, Marjorie, 336
BRADLEY, Bertha, 99, Bertha Leona, 99, Betty, 99, Brad Lee, 156, Charles Winton, 99, Clara, 99, Clyde, 99, Daniel, 98, David J., 98, David Josiah, 98, 99, Dorothy, 99, Fanny, 99, Gary Delmas, 99, Geneva, 99, George, 98, George Lodi, 99, George Russel, Jr., 99, George Russell, 99, Greg Elliott, 156, Hannah, 98, Harriet Roberta, 99, Hazel, 99, Ida, 99, James Edgar, 99, James Monroe, 99, Joshua, 98, Ladonna Berneice, 99, Lela, 99, Leroy, 98, 177, Lewis Cass, 99, Lila Ruth, 99, Luther, 99, Luther Voris, 99, Mary, 98, 230, 320, Michael James, 99, Myrtle Mary, 99, Myrtle Stark, 99, Nancy Ellen, 99, Paul 99, Paul David, 99, Paul James, 99, Ray L., 99, Richard Edgar, 99, Robert Edmund, 99, Rosa, 99, Russell, 99, Sarah, 98, Sarah Jane, 99, Sarah L., 375, Stephen Earl, 99Vinnie, 99, Vinnie (Hostetter), 31, William F., 98, William Luther, 99, 156, Wilma, 99, Wilma Mae, 99
BRADLEY Styles-R-Us,15, **BRADSHAW, Addison, 96, 99, 118, Addison, Sr., 99, Cleo, 99, David, 99, David James, 214, Donna, 99, Do**nna Jo, 214, Elizabeth, 118, James "Jim", 99, James Lee, 214, Janice, 99, Judith, 99, Mary, 118, Mary S., 99, Phyllis, 96, Sandra, 99
BRADY, Cathy, 131, Clyde, 131, Clyde, Jr., 131, Dawn, 131, Dennis, 131, Mollie Rebecca, 133, Rebecca, 131
BRAGGS, (Gen.), 319
BRAINARD, Bert, 81
BRANCH, Brian, 172, Don, 172, Harry, 172, Harry Dale, 172, Harry Dale, Jr., 172, Helen Louise, 172, Julia, 208, Robert, 172, Tammy, 172, Victor, 172
BRANDENBURG, Daisy, 250, Dorothy, 315, Jacob, 281, Roy, 250, 350, Virgil, 250
BRANDON, Angeline, 211
BRANHAM, Christina, 279
BRANIGAN, Paul, 309
BRANSON, Anna, 309, Benjamin, 309, Clint, 309, Elbert, 309, Enoch, 211, 309, Hugh, 309, Joann, 315, Mae, 309, Mary Bessie, 211, 309, Pattie, 211, 309, Susan, 192, Thomas, 309, Wilbur, 309, William, 315
BRANSTETTER, Alma, 99, Betty Joyce, 227, David Wayne, 99, Doyne, 99, Edith, 271, George H., 99, George Lyle, 99, Gladys Marie, 272, James, 99, 257, James P., 99, John Ward, 96, Kathryn, 99, 257, Martha, 271, Mary Jane, 99, Matthew, 99, Robert Barton, 99, Ruth Mariah, 99, Sandy, 99, Susan Lynn, 96, Wayne, 99, Web, 99, Welby Preston, 99, Zoy, 271
BRANT, Mary T., 372
BRASFIELD, Margaret, 86, Mary Kathyrn, 86, Ola, 86, Ola Eugene, 86, Pauline, 86, Ruby, 86, Waneta, 86
BRATTON, Abby, 98, Abel Washington, 100, Adaline, 100, 104, Ann, 100, Barbara Ann, 92, Barton N., 100, Benjamin A., 100, Bessie Faye, 100, 101, 230, Byron, 100, Byron L., 101, Catherine, 100, Charles, 67, 100, Charles Bruce, 100, Charles L., 100, Charles Lewis, 100, Clair, 107, Connie, 113, David Berry, 100, Deborah, 113, Dell, 100, Donald, 100, Emma, 100, Frances, 101, Frances Lorene, 100, Francis A., 100, George W., 100, Harvey, 33, Harvey B., 107, Henryetta Anna, 100, Ida, 100, Irene, 67, Jack, 113, James, 99, 100, 238, James Sherman, 100, Jeanine, 113, John, 100, 104, 238, John Newton, 100, Joseph, 98, Judith, 98, Lottie Gertrude, 113, Margaret, 100, Margaret Ann, 237, Margaret J., 100, Mariah, 100, Marie Merele, 100, Martha, 101, Martha Ellen, 339, Martha Elvina, 100, Mary A. 100, Mary Ann, 92, Mary Anna, 238, Mary C., 100, Mary G., Matthew, 98, 100, Maurice "Doc", 113, Nancy, 100, 113, Nellie Grace, 100, Orph, 30, 31, Orph W., 33, Orpheus W., 100, Pauline, 101, Phoebe, 100, Polly, 238, Rachel S., 100, Ralph, 100, 101, Rebecca, 100, Rebecca Ann, 100, Robert 99, 100, Robert L., 100, Robert Logan, 100, Robert Webster, 100, Ruth Elizabeth, 100, Sarah Hannah, 100, Sudie, 107, Walter V., 100, Walter Virgil, 100, Warren, 189, William, 92, 99, 100, William Franklin, 100, William Harrison, 100, Zola, 148, Zola Rose, 100, __, 42
BRAUM, Henry M., 63
BRAWLEY, Amanda, 167
BRAY, F. Steven, 372, Mary E., 375
BREAKS, Alvin, 74, 190, 215, Alvin H., 204, Betty, 190, Calvin, 74, Clara, 231, Elijah II, 215, Eliza, 215, Harry, 204, Jane Beard, 231, John Beard, 28, Lulu, 204, Richard, 74, 205, 215, 231, Richard, Sr. 74
BREAULT, Daniel, 289, Karen, 170, Karne, 289, Kelsey, 170, Taylor, 170
BREEDING, Laverne, 268
BREEDLOVE, Dale W., 372, Joannie, 54, Mary, 54, Ralph, 54, Robert, 54
BREEKS, Richard, 28, 231
BRELSFORD, Bridgie, 177, 308
BREMERMAN, Ben, 173
BRENDA, Joan, 232, William H., 232
BRENNAN, "Clancy", 318, David Keith, 318, Donald, 318, Elizabeth, 318, Thomas, 318, William Thomas, 318
BRENTON, Samuel, 49
BRETZ, Magdalena, 145
BREW, Frank, 109
BREWER, Amy, 283, 284, Belinda, 186, Faye, 291, Jonas, 186, Josiah, 201, Josiah (Col.), 186, Lawrence, 55, Maxine, 92, Polly Ann, 267
BREWER'S Furniture Store, 15
BREWSTER, Eleanor, 125, Elinor, 329
BRICKERHOFF, Elizabeth, 82, Harman, 82
BRICKS, Minnie, 108
BRIDGE, Bill, 101, Carolyn, 220, Carolyn Sue, 101, Hazel, 101, Ira Landen, 101, James Franklin, 101, John Towsend, 101, Joseph, 101, Marilyn, 220, Marilyn Lou, 101, Maxine, 101, Michael, 220, Michael W., 372, Michael William, 101,Michele Joanne, 101, William, 220, William Landon, 101
BRIDGES, Bartlett, 34, Belinda, 359, Candace, 359, Lucy, 121, Mitzi, 359, Perle, 359
BRIDGEWATER, Clarice, 101, Walter C., 101, Walter S., 101
BRIDWELL, Betty, 305, Brian Dean, 354, Elizabeth, 235, Laura Lea, 354, Nancy, 235, 304, 305
BRIGMAN, Glenn, 58,
BRILL, Bridgie, 308
BRIMBERRY, Ezra, 351, Leah, 351, Leonard, 350, 351, Lloyd, 351, Mabel, 351, Mary, 351, Samuel, 351, William, 351
BRIN-ASO, Cuba, 150
BRINER, Celia, 338, Florence Olive, 300
BRINKLEY, Melcena, 361
BRISTOW, Kate, 227, Peg, 227
BRITON, John F., 102
BRITT, John, 103
BRITTON, Albert, 102, Alvin Wallace, 102, Amanda, 102, Ann, 101, Bertie Rynan, 102, Catherine, 102, Charity, 102, Charlotte, 360, Clara Edith, 102, Donita, 259, Elizabeth, 101, 102, Emma Ann, 102, Ethel Lorraine, 300, Fanny, 102, Frank, 102, 184, 348, Freddie Lamont, 102, Harriet, 101, 102, Jasper "Jap" Nathan, 102, John Franklin, 102, John R., 102, Joseph, 102, Lida Bell, 102, Loren P., 102, Lydia M., 102, Maggie May, 102, Margaret, 102, Maria, 101, 102, Mary Ann, 102, 356, 357, Mary Cordelia, 102, Matilda, 101, Minnie, 102, Nancy, 101, 102, 281, Nancy Emma, 102, Nancy J., 102, Nathan, 98, 101, 102, 316, Nathan Jr., 101, 102, Rachel, 101, Robert, 102, Samantha, 102, Sarah Elizabeth, 102, Thomas, 102, Thomas H., 102, Thomas P., 101, 316, 356, William, 102, William Farnsworth, 102, Ira C., 102, Lena, 102, __, 154
BRITTS, Adam, 102, Becky, 102, Catherine, 102, 104, Colgeth, 104, Daniel, 104, David H., 104, Elizabeth, 104, Emma, 104, George, 102, 104, Henry R., 104, James A., 104, Jennie, 31, John, 104, Lewis, H., 104, Margaret, 102, Rebecca, 103, Rebecca Ann, 102, Samuel, 102, 104, 196, 272, Sarah C., 104, Thoams D., 104, William H., 104, William T., 104
BROADERS, Bonnie Marie, 187, Carl, 187, Claude, 187, Edward Thurman, 187, Ethel Ann, 187, Gladys, 187, Irvin, 187, Sarah Ella, 187
BROCIES, Eva, 360, Frank, 360
BROCK, Belle, 104, Edith, 104, Frances, 104, Francis Richard, 104, Noah Monroe, 29, 104, Sally, 104, William, 104, William Lee, 104
BROCKMAN, Almeda, 100, Almedia Cirtley, 104, Amelia, 225, Amelia "Milly", 104, Andrew, 104, 225, Benjamin, 104, Betsy, 104, Chesley, 104, Elizabeth, 104, Elizabeh "Betsy", 225, Henry, 104, James, 104, 225, Jane, 104, Jane Craig, 104, John, 129, Josiah, 104, Lucy, 129, Luretta, 104, Mary, 104, Mary "Polly", 104, 225, Mason, 104, Permelia Ann, 104, Robert, 100, Robert Andrew, 104, Sally, 204, Samuel, 104, Tandy, 104, 225, Walter, 104, William, 104
BRODHECKER, __, 338
BROLSMA, Dora M., 252, Jennie, 252, John, 252
BRONAUGH, __, 26,Charles, 67, 105, 336, Charles Newton, 104, Charles T., 105, Cheryl, 240, Cheryl Lynn, 105, Claude, 104, 105, Claude Duncan, 104, Debbie, 163, Deborah, 229, 299, Deborah Ann, 339, George Taylor, 104, Helen, 67, 104, 105, 336, Helen Louise, 104, Jason, 359, John, 163, John William, 104, Johnny, 163, Joshua, 359, Keifer, 105, Minnie, 289, Nettie, 104, Nettie Evelyn, 104, Opal, 104, Ruth, 104, Sylvia Opal, 104, Tamara, 359
BRONSON, Elizabeth, 133, William, 133
BROOK, Barney, 12
BROOK'S Cabinet Magician, 15
BROOKS, Barney, 13, 105, Bertha Francis, 105, Charlie E. 105, Clyde Edward, 105, Dennis Lee, 346, Dorothy Darlene, 346, Elias, 105, Elmer Franklin, 105, Eugene A., 372, Eulah Faye, 105, Eva Lena, 105, Frances, 105, Goldie Bell, 105, James Lawrence 105, James Lynn, 346, Jim, 126, Judith, 212, Nancy, 105, Pearl, 346, Phoebe, 105, Phyllis, 342, Sadie Alta May, 105, Speck, 105, Tom, 105, Warren, 67
BROOKSHIRE, Amelia, 176, Betty, 105, Charles Allen, 105, Drake, 105, Hatchery, 14, James, 105, James William, 105, 162, Jane, 105, Jennie, 123, 162, 352, Jennie Marie, 105, 162, Joel, 105, 176, John, 355, John Allen, 105, John Thomas, 105, June Ellen, 105, Kathleen Dell, 105, Lee (Mrs.), 286, Martha Ellen, 105, Neva, 162, Robert, 105, Sarah Rachel, 105, Sarah S., 176, Swan, 105, Voorhees, 43, Voris, 105, Winifred, 105
BROSHAR, Amie, 137
BROSHEARS, Betsy, 106, Betsy Lee, 105, Bill, 105, Chris, 106, Davy, 106, Pat, 105, Patricia D., 375, Vickie Lynn, 106, William Christopher, 106, William Davis "Davy", 105, William Lee, 105, William Logan, 105
BROUSE, John A., 49
BROWER, Hugh, 75
BROWERSOCK, Samuel, 115
BROWN, (Rev), 50, Albert, 106, Alcina Asenath, 232, Alcy, 150, Alice, 281, Angela Sue, 106, 107, Anthony, 342, Barbara, 107, Barbara J., 372, Barbara Joan, 106, Benjamin, 243, Bert, 220, Beth, 306, Betty Lou, 106, 306, Bonnie, 106, Bradley Lee, 106, Caleb, 31, Carcie Leroy, 106, 159, Caroline, 219, Carolyn Elizabeth, 278, Chub, 107, Clair, 107, Clarence, 361, Clarence Alvin, 342, Crystal Rene, 119, Cynthia, 232, Daniel, 232, Dave, 16, David Leroy, 106, Dean, 119, Debra Kay, 175, Don, 306, Donald, 159, Donald Floyd, 106, Donald Leroy, 106, Dorcus Summy, 360, Earl, 107, Easter, 106, Edna, 233, Effie, 298, Eleanor, 106, Elihu, 181, Elijah, 74, Elizabeth, 107, 223, Emma, 91, 92, Everett, 112, Fannie, 99, Florence Ellen, 305, Geneva, 106, George 222, 232, George, G., 30, Grace, 279, Harold, 150, Irene, 152, Ivanelle, 106, Jacob Lewis, 137, James Alan, 151, Jane, 31, Jane E., 372, Jay, 107, Jess, 106, John, 67, 107, John N., 36, Jonas, 106, Kari, 231, Kathleen, 106, Kristie, 231, Lafayette, 232, Larry, 159, Larry Dean, 106, Lonnie Cole, 101, Lori, 361, Louise, 335, Lydia, 241, Lydia Ann (Linn), 229, Mabel Lillian, 131, Magadaline, 354, Manoah, 353, Marilyn, 107, Marilyn Jean, 107, Marilyn Joan, 224, Mark Alan, 151, Mark Leon, 151, Martha (Mattie), 360, Mary, 129, Mary "Polly", 149, Mary Catherine, 107, 236, Mary E., 360, Mary Jane, 232, 279, Maud, 107, Milton Arthur, 360, Minnie Ann, 360, Mollie K., 106, Myrtle, 207, Nancy, 129, 150, 239, Nellie Adna, 281, Nicole Mae, 151, Nijol, 106, Nora, 315, Nyodia, 106, Pauline, 106, Penny, 133, Peter, 232, Rebecca Ann, 106, Richard, 374, Robert, 106, Rollo, 222, Ronald Dean, 119, Russell, 372, Russell Lee, 106, Samantha Susannah, 232, Sarah, 232, Sarah Barr, 242, Sarah E., 360, Sharon, 159, Sharon Kay, 106, Solon, 279, Stacy, 137, Susannah, 67, 232, Terry, 137, Thalia, 45, Thomas, 63, 129, Thomas J., 67, 106, Thomas Leo, 106, Tilgham, 339, Tilghman, 31, 45, Tillman, 107, Vera Beth, 106, W.H., 52, William Guy, 106, Walter, 106, 107, Walter A., 107, William, 150, 354, William A., 107, William Armfield, 360, William Harvey, 360, William Hugh, 232, William J., 106, William Newton, 279, William Riley, 360, Winnie Ellen, 360, __, 17
BROWN Variety Store, 15
BROWNING, Andrew L., 107, Andy, 107, Elizabeth, 107, Ethel, 381, Martha, 206, Milcha, 123, Robert L., 107
BRUBAKER, H.C., 32
BRUCE, Arthur, 107, Cecil, 275, David, 107, Donald William, 107, 344, Dora, 107, Dorothy, 275, Earl, 107, Elsie, 107, James, 275, James Cecil, 107, Linda, 107, Melinda Jo, 107, 344, Nigel, 342, Paula Denise, 107, Robert, 107, Sophia Dysee, 328, Steven, 107, William D., 36
BRUCH, Elizabeth, 108, Melissa, 108, Michael II, 108, Michael III, 108, Philip, 108, Sarah, 108
BRUGH, Oscar, 129
BRUMBAUGH, E.H., 49, Vane, 43
BRUMLY, Nancy, 308
BRUNER, Alan, 108, Alva, 108, Betty, 108, Daisy, 108, Elizabeth Caroline, 350, Gertrude, 108, Harry, 108, Henry Broomer, 291, Ical, 108, Jacob, 108, Jeff, 108, Jeremy, 108, John, 108, Jonathan, 108, Lois, 108, Lulu, 108, M.W., 376, Maria, 152, Nell, 43, Ray, 108, Richard, 108, Rita, 108, Ron, 108, Sarah, 108, Thelma, 108, 313, Vera, 108, William Jasper, 108
BRUNNER, Harriet, 179
BRUNSTMeat, 14
BRUNTON, Morris L., 375
BRUSH, John, 70, Mary Ann, 93
BRYAN, Benjamin, 341, Brad, 274, Bradley, 274, Brenda, 274, David, 274, 341, Hazel, 341, Jeanette,

341, Joseph, 341, Joyce, 341, Morgan, 90, Rebecca, 274, Samuel, 341, Sue, 274, 341, Vern, 341, Vern, Jr., 341, William, 90
BRYAN'S Ladoga Tire Service, 15
BRYANT, Betty, 87, Easter, 161, Edith, 87, Edwin Eugene, 113, Esther Geraldine, 113, Ethel, 161, Hershel, 75, John, 161, Justin Richard, 113, Lula, 287, Margaret, 199, 223, 352, Maurice, 113, Milton, 87, Pat, 97, 98, R.E., 376, Ralph, 87, Richard Lee, 113, Robert, 87, Rodney Lee, 113, Ron, 97, 98, Ronald, 87, 97, 98, Ronald Maurice, 113, Ruby, 87, Sara, 98, Sara Beth, 113, William, 85
BRYSON, Donna, 140
BUBECK, Mary E., 182
BUCHANAN, Andrew Fulton, 99 Barbara Ann, 185, David, 248, Eliza, 143, Flora, 247, Frank, 126, Hazel Florence, 99, James, 43, 248, Margaret, 291, Mary Margaret, 248, S.F., 64, Wilma Mae, 99, __, 42
BUCHANON, Alice, 221, 271, Eleanor, 104, Frank, 272, Mellie, 272, Tillie Morris, 272
BUCK, Arva, 185, Benjamin, 271, Christina, 108, Daddy, 108, Geoffrey, 271, Isaac, 271, John, 108, Kelly, 271, Samuel, 356
BUCKLER, Angeline, 232, 314
BUCKLES, Juanita, 374, L.C., 49
BUCKNER, Linda, 54
BUCKS, Barbara, 307
BUDD, Alger, 247, Larry David, 247, Lucile, 247, Ralph, 247, Tim Eugene, 247
BUDREAU, Jeannie, 317
BUEL, Henry, 49
BUELL, George, 31
BUENO, Heather, 318, J.R., 318, Joseph, 318, Robert, 318
BUFORD, (Col.), 236
BUGG, Maria Elizabeth, 198
BULKER, Martha, 80
BULL, Richard, 268
BULLOCK, Bertha, 103, Jan, 369, William, 103
BUNCE, Thomas, 222
BUNDURANT, Emily, 274, Gabriel, 274, Joan, 274, Joseph, 274, Locky, 274, Mary L., 274, Nancy, 274
BUNDY, Violet, 221
BUNGER, Nancy, 111, __, 257, **BUNKER, Han**nah, 268, Jabez, 268, Naomi, 268
BUNNELL, Aaron, 108, Albert Jerome, 108, Ali, 249, Brian, 108, Charles, 108, Cheryl, 108, Clay, 108, Clifford Rider, 108, David, 108, Deborah, 108, Eldon, 169, Eli, 108, Eliza, 108, Elizabeth, 108, Elsie, 169, Emery, 108, Ephraim, 108, Ephrain, 108, Evan, 108, Fannie, 208, Fawn, 108, Frank, 189, 205, Freddie, 108, Freddie Jr., 108, Harriet, 108, Helen, 108, 248, Iva, 169, Jacob, 169, 191, James, 108, Judi, 108, Kalyin, 108, Martha, 108, Mary, 108, 169, Mary M., 108, Minnie, 108, Patti, 108, Rex, 108, Robert, 108, Rome, 108, Rovene Coons, 119, Ruby, 108, Star, 108, Stella, 208, Thomas, 169, Tillie, 108, Todd, 108, Tonda, 108, Trey, 108, Trudy, 108, Veasey, 108, William, 108, Ethel, 169
BUNNELL Cemetery, 167
BURBER, Aaron S., 372
BURBRIDGE, Ann, 109, Betsy, 109, Eliza, 109, Forgus Graham, 109, Isabella, 109, James, 109, Jane, 109, Jesse, 109, Joseph Howe, 109, Margaret, 109, Martha, 109, Mary Ann, 109, Mary Jackson, 109, Matilda, 109, Morgan, 109, Nancy, 109, Patsy, 109, Polly, 109, Robert, 109, Rowland, 109, Thomas, 109, William 108, 109, 242, William, Jr., 109
BURBRINK, Ginny, 272, Mary Anne, 272, Paul, 272
BURCH, Dennis, 308, Philip, 225
BURCHER, Lydia, 319
BURCHFIELD, Hezekiah, 261, Jane, 261, Martha, 261
BURCHMAN, Mary, 266
BURDEN, Audry Jane, 281, James, 229
BURGER, Kathryn, 211, Thomas, 211
BURGESS, H.O., 307, J.C., 65
BURGET, William L., 372
BURGIN, Walter, 129
BURGNER, Elizabeth, 292
BURK, Alice, 109, Amanda, 109, B.J., 109, Bertha, 109, Bill, 109, Bob, 109, Clara, 109, Cora, 109, Elizabeth, 110, Elizabeth Ann, 102, George, 109, George Washington, 109, 110, 145, Jayne, 109, Jeremiah Caleb, 109, Jerraine, 109, Jerry, 109, Jerry Caleb, 318, Jesse, 110, John, 109, John Albert, 110, John Franklin, 109, 110, John L., 102, Joseph Nathaniel, 110, Lillie, 112, Martha, 109, Martha Etta, 110, Martha Rebecca, 109, Mary Elizabeth, 110, Mary Hanna, 109, Montgomery C., 359, Paul, 36, Pearl, 109, Ruth, 88, Samuel, 320, Samuel Smith, 110, Wash, 109, William C., 110
BURKE, Alice, 319, Delilah, 221, 306, J.E., 374, John, 221, Mary Virginia, 143
BURKETT, Danielle Gail, 122, David William, 122, Ellen Laverne, 122, Jeffrey Daniel, 122, Norman, 36, 299, William Lodell, 122, William Lodell, Jr., 122
BURKHARDT, H.C., 69
BURKHART, Charles L., 375
BURKLE, Linda, 365
BURNAM, Laura Frances, 346, Thompson Ernest, 346
BURNETT, Larry, 15, Wilbur, 373
BURNS, Jamie, 86, Mary, 201, Shannon, 86
BURRIN, Frank, 84
BURRIS, Barbara J., 372
BURROUGHS, Arvilla, 301, Clarence, 31, Effie, 221, Elizabeth, 88
BURRUSO, Adam, 278
BURTON, Ivy Pearl, 245
BUSBY, Linda, 341
BUSE, Kathryn, 157
BUSEL, Martha, 357
BUSENBARK, __, 22, Byron, 141, Daniel J., 102, Elizabeth, 281, Ethel, 279, Guy Byron, 295, Ida E., 159, Jennette, 93, John, 41, 93, Julia Ann, 356, 357, Laura, 236, Raymond, 309, Scott R., 372, Wilma, 296, Ora, 159
BUSENBARK'S, 382
BUSER, Ann Marie, 110, Atlee M., 110, Belle, 110, Daniel T., 110, Elizabeth L., 110, Emma, 248, Ethel, 110, Eva N., 110, 293, Fannie, 110, Gertrude "Todie", 119, John Hanson, 110, Joshua Peter, 110, Mary Catherine, 110, Mary Louise (Lou), 110, Nancy Eveline, 148, Roy, 43, 110, Ruth, 247, Sarah, 248, Stephen A., 110, Susan, 110, William H., 110, William H., Jr., 110, 248, William H., Sr., 248, William Hiram, 148
BUSH, Elizabeth, 110, Ella, 295, Eva, 110, Eve, 135, John, 80, 110, Leonard, 110, Lewis, 110, Magdalene, 110, Michael, 110, Michael, Jr., 110, Sarah, 110, 190
BUSHER, John, 110
BUSHINE, Mary Lou, 184
BUSHMAN, Brandy, 172, Heather, 172
BUSHONG, Barbara, 111, Jack, 94, John, 110, 217, John (Jack), 111, John Allen, 111, John H., 110, Leona, 235, Leona Agnes, 269, Mabel, 43, Milo, 110
BUSKIRK, Merl V., 97
BUSSE, Jerry B., 372
BUTCHER, Alexander Marion, 343, Flossie, 231, Margaret Elizabeth, 343, Salina Elizabeth, 88, Sarah, 221, William, 314
BUTLER, Brett Elmore, 152, Charles, 111, Dorothy, 164, Earl, 244, Elizabeth, 107, Emeline, 111, Emily, 111, Eunice, 111, F. Edmund, 375, Frederick Edmund, 301, Frederick Martin, 301, Gayle Rae, 152, Gladys, 257, Hallie, 111, 257, James Everett, 257, Jane, 111, Jill Louise, 100, JoAnne, 375, Joseph F., 129, Kathryn, 257, Kendi, 100, Lindley, 111, Lois, 257, Louise, 111, 257, Mahlon, 111, Marion, 257, Marion Edward, 257, Mary, 271, Norman Dean, 152, Phyllis, 152, Pleasant, 129, Robert, 270, Thomas J., 326, William George, 259, William Mark, 100
BUTT, Eve, 152
BUTTS, Alice, 191, Ruby Fern, 108
BUTZ, Earl L. (Hon), 156
BUXCEY, Mary, 357
BUXTON, Millard, 116
BUZZAIRD, Catherine Virginia, 111, Cecile Mae, 111, Dottie Louise, 111, Earl Kirby, 111, Elmer Sherman, 111, Frankie Anita, 111, Frankie M., 111, Fred B. Jackson, 111, Fred M., Jr., 111, Fred Milam, 111, 306, John B., 111, Katie, 111, Louise Dee, 111, Ruby, 111
BYERLY, Susannah, 288
BYERMIESTER, David Lewis, 111
BYERS, Amber, 190, Carla Jean, 130, Carolyn Sue, 130, Christopher Jay, 130, Connie Sue, 130, Jimmy, 346, Robert Clyde, 130, Sandra Kay, 346, William, 131, __, 43
BYINGTON, Louise, 84
BYMASTER, Ada, 112, Benjamin, 112, Benjamin Franklin, 84, Bessie Helen, 84, Daniel, 112, Daniel Webster, 112, David Lewis, 84, David Lewis, Jr., 84, Davis, 112, Davis Lewis, 111, Emma, 112, Eva, 112, Gary, 112, Glen, 112, Glen William, 112, Hallie, 112, James, 112, Jefferson, 112, John, 111, Julia, 111, Lela, 112, Lillie (Burk), 112, Lucinda, 112, Lucy, 111, Mabel, 154, Manny, 112, Marinda, 112, Marjorie, 112, Mary, 111, Miller, 155, 154, Naomi, 112, Neva, 112, Pearl, 112, Polyanna, 154, Rick, 112, Road, 259, Rosa, 121, Rosemary, 112, Roy, 112, Ruby Glen, 112, Sarah, 112, Sherry, 112, Will, 111, __, 55
BYRD, Ann, 281, Bertha, 99, Betty, 355, Elizabeth, 104, Elza, 355, Imogene, 341, James, 341, James Henry, 99, Jesse, 341, Josephine, 99, 341, Levi, 64, Louise, 350, 351, Mary C., 281, Pauline, 248, 249, Sarah Elizabeth, 354, 355, Wayne, 341, William, 104, 341
BYRD, Insurance, 15
BYRD'S Pizza, 15
BYRUM, Valentine, 29
BYSTER, Deborah, 231
CABBAGE, Donald E., 336, Martha Jo, 336
CABELL, Bruce, 142, Dee Ann, 54, DeeAnn, 142, John, 142, Karen, 142, Mark, 142, Nancy, 54, 142, Norma, 142
CABLE, Emily, 280
CAHAIL, Elizabeth, 181
CAHOON, L.J., 43, Rose, 43
CAIN, Betty, 81, Cathy, 81, Desse, 195, Edna, 279, Effie Ethel, 195, Elmer, 195, Emert, 195, Eva, 195, Everett, 195, Homer, 195, Lisa, 81, Mandy, 195, Mary, 188, Randy, 81, Tom, 81, William, 195
CALDER, Chase, 271, Curtis, 71, Debbie, 271, William, 271
CALDWELL, Alexander, 298, David A., 378, Dorph S., 122, Dorpha, 269, Elda, 227, Elizabeth, 299, Frank, 227, Jane, 330, Jeremiah Columbus, 100, Maria, 266, Nathaniel, 317, Nathaniel (Mrs.), 317, Nellie, 341, Ollie, 306, R.F., 74, Rachel S., 100, Ruby, 86, Stella, 81, 331, William, 330
CALHOON, John, 89, Sary, 89, Sealy, 89, Celia, 90
CALIFORNIA, Pellet Mill, 371, Press Manufact., 371
CALLAHAN, David, 215, David L., 215, Dora, 215, Hannah, 215, Kate, 215, Margaret, 215, Mary, 215, Michael, 215, Mildred, 215, Shirley, 215
CALLIHAN, Julia, 335
CALLIS, V. Kay, 372
CALLOWAY, Jeremy Todd, 259, Jonathan, 113, Jonathan Daniel, 259, Lucinda Joan, 113, Samuel, 34, Jeremy, 113
CALVERT, Delford, 261, Dorothy J., 261, Frederick, 175, Shawna Lisa, 175, Shenna Sue, 175
CAMBY, Anna F., 259, Thomas, 259
CAMDEN, William, 40, William P., 29, 40
CAMERON, Charles, 270, George, 270, Howard, 270, Vera, 270, Vergil, 270
CAMMON, Carl (Dr.), 291
CAMP, Bessie, 223
CAMPBELL, Albert, 292, Andrew S., 234, Andrew Spinning, Jr., 234, Bertram, 123, Bill, 225, Cora Inez, 234, Debbie, 238, Edna Elizabeth, 292, Elizabeth, 292, Evelyn, 104, Hardwares, 182, Janet E., 375, John, 353, Katherine, 199, Lawrence, 199, Louise, 234, Margaret Louise, 306, Marilyn, 118, Martin, 225, Mary, 123, Mary Lou, 123, Ouida, 271, Pearl, 153, Ray, 234, Robert, 234, Roxanna, 208, Ruby, 199, Ruth Cheek, 267, Sarah, 123, Susannah, 267, Thomas, 199, Virginia, 123, Zola, 199
CAMPFIELD, Kathleen, 265
CANADA, Betty Jean, 344, Dennis, 357, Gayle, 26, 67, Irene Alice, 278, Linette, 357, Nancy I., 375
CANINE, Alice, 112, Ben, 112, Carroll, 26, Charlie, 112, Cinderella, 247, Daniel, 112, David, 112, 277, David T., 112, Derek, 112, Edith, 285, Edith Estelle, 285, Edwin Nelson, 112, George, 112, James C., 360, Joe, 13, 112, John, 112, Kittie, 112, L.G., 112, L.G. "Tude", 232, Lemuel, 232, Lemuel Jackson, 112, Lena, 112, Lessie, 232, Mantie, 112, Margaret, 112, 277, Margaret Priebe, 278, Martha Lou, 112, Mary, 112, Mary Elizabeth, 112, Mary W., 265, Maude, 112, Mayme, 232, Mertie, 232, Michelle, 112, Nannie, 112, Naomi, 171, Nellie, 12, 13, Nelson, 277, Ola, 112, Patricia, 112, Paul, 279, Ralph, 112, Rebecca, 112, Robert, 112, 144, Sam, 112, Thelma, 112, Tude, 12, 112
CANNON, Mary, 357
CANTRELL, Martha, 308
CAPLINGER, Blanche Busenbark, 290, Ruby, 155
CAPSHAW, Carrie, 171, Charley, 171, Christina, 171, Cora, 171, Cynthia, 171, Deanna, 171, Debra, 170, Dora, 170, Gloras, 171, Ike, 171, Janice, 171, Jeffrey, 171, Linda, 171, Ollie, 171
CARESS, Mark, 370
CAREY, Linda Joanne, 98, Paul William, Jr., 98, Rebecca Annette, 98, Margaret Evans, 98
CARLILE, Anna Mae, 113, Barbara Jean, 113, Berniece, 112, Berniece Lucille, 113, Cassandra, 112, Charles, 148, Charles Raymond, 113, Elizabeth Ann, 113, Esther, 112, Esther Geraldine, 113, Evelyn, 113, Flora Ethel, 113, Hattie Kathryn, 113, I. Thomas, 112, James, 113, Jean, 112, John, 148, John Taylor, 113, Judith Lynne, 113, Kenneth, 112, Kenneth Jerome, 113, Kevin Jerome, 113, Levone Ella, 113, Leonard, 113, Lottie Gertrude, 113, Marilyn, 113, Martha, 112, Marvin, 112, Marvin William, 113, Nancy Ann, 113, Nathaniel, 112, Ora Esther, 113, Richard, 113, Suzanne Elizabeth, 113, Thomas, 113, Vernest Redmond, 113, Lindsay Jerome, 113, Mason Jerome, 113
CARLIN, Cora, 151
CARLISLE, Berniece Lucille, 259
CARLSON, Charles, 374, Heather Nicole, 346, Jane, 351, Jeffery, 346, Paul Theodore, 245
CARLSTEDT, Kathryn, 220
CARMAN, Billy, 74
CARMICHAEL, Betty, 14, Bill, 272, Lloyd, 272, Wayne, 131
CARNEGIE, Andrew, 10
CARNES, Allison, 90, Amanda, 90, Mary Edith, 90, Michael W., 90, Ryan, 90
CARNEY, Allison, 286, Catherine, 286, Cheryl, 286, Karen, 286, Quentin, 14, Thomas, 286
CARNEY-STEWART, Ford, 14
CARNINE, Isabelle, 348, Peter, 112
CARO, Lucy, 98
CAROTHERS, Noble, 50
CARPENTER, Austin, 34, Chistopher, H., 320, Guy O., 49, Harold, 322, Joyce I., 375, Kelly Sue, 322, Linda, 322, Mary Ann, 113, Michelle, 357
CARPER, Annie Jane, 131, Godwin, 131, Jane, 131, William, 131
CARR, Joseph W., 322, Mahala, 175, Rebecca Jane, 322, Rosemary, 281, W.W., 45
CARRENS, Brenda Kay, 103, Cary, 103
CARRINGTON, Alexander, 113, Bettie, 52, Eliza, 230, Flora, 113, Frank T., 113, Henrietta, 113, J.L., 52, Jess, 12, 13, John, 121, Martha, 113, Mollie, 52, Samuel, 113, 230, Waneita, 187
CARROLL, Alice, 138, Druscilla, 201, 339, Edith, 353, Eugene, 339, Frank, 138, Irene, 131, Maggie, 43, Nancy, 301, Randy J., 339, Sarra, 98
CARSON, Antonia, 113, Bette Jane, 113, Caitlin Maria, 113, Cecile Florence, 113, Claudia Anne, 113, Eliza Jane, 113, Emily Suzanne, 113, Frank, 113, George, 113, Glen Harold, 113, Houston D., 113, James, 113, Jane, 113, 269, Janie, 189, Jesse Edgar, 113, Joseph Thomas, 135, Karen Kay, 113, Lewis P., 113, Martha Cordelia, 113, Mary, 191, Mary Effie, 113, Mary Ellen, 135, Richard, 149, Richard Lee, 113, Robert Paul, 113, Ronald Alan, 113, Vergie, 127, William Edgar, 113, Ida May, 135, Kimberly Allison, 113
CARSRUD, Alice, 220, Alice Virginia, 220, 270, Donald, 220, Donald Emerson, 220, 270, Jeannette, 220, 270, Michele JoAnn, 270, 220, Robert Stephen, 220, Robert Steven, 270
CARTER, Bertha, 106, Catherine, 316, Mary Caroline, 106, Mary Helen, 375, Poncho, 275, Rosann, 96, Rusty, 26, Sanford, 106
CARTWRIGHT, Cynthia, 164
CARTY, Elizabeth, 292
CARVER, Doris Dean, 351, Fred, 372, Gale, 279, Grean, 351, Ida, 307, Louisa, 335, Marietta, 133, Matthew, 252, Mattie, 351, Minnie, 221, Misty, 252, Polly, 153, __, 59
CARY, Mabel Clements, 113, N. Austen, 113
CASAD, Lora, 99
CASE, Georgeanna, 319
CASH, Braxton, 29, 40
CASKEY, Rebecca, 158
CASLIN, Elizabeth, 120
CASNER, Caroline Flaningam, 185
CASON, Maude, 233, Maude M., 233, Maude Margaret, 233, Samantha, 233, William, 112, William P., 233
CASS, Darlene B., 372
CASSEL, Mahala, 100, 228
CASSELL, Catherine Horine, 228, Christopher Bernard, 343, David, 343, Frank Allen, 343, Frank Hyde, 343, George V., 228, Jonathan, 343, Mahala, 196, Michael Thomas, 343, Thomas Watts, 343
CASSIDY, Patricia, 181
CASSITY, "Polly", 316, Jacob, 316, Mary, 316, Mary "Polly", 357
CASTER, Abe, 126, Abraham, 114, Abraham B., 302, Carolyn, 114, Charity, 114, Elizabeth, 113, 114, Fred, 114, 302, Ione, 114, Isaac, 114, Jacob, 114, Jesse, 114, 302, John, 113, Mabel Gertrude, 133, Martha Jean, 114, Mellie, 114, Sarah, 114, Ursula, 114, 302
CASTLE, Elizabeth, 352, George, 229, 352, Mahala, 150, 197, 228, 229, 352, Thomas, 352
CATERLIN, Edith, 149
CATRON, Elizabeth, 174
CATTEL, Marie, 324
CAVE, Marlene, 128, Robert, 128
CAWTHON, Mildred, 244, Mildred Jean, 245
CAYWOOD, Elizabeth, 123, Rebecca, 208
CEDARS, Albert, 114, Burt, 114, Burton, 114, Charles, 114, Edna, 114, Frank, 114, George W., 114, George Washington, 114, Goldie, 114, Goldie May, 114, Jane, 114, John, 114, 329 Margaret, 114, Mary, 114, Mary Elizabeth, 114, 307, 320, 333, Mary Jane, 114, Mildred, 218, 329, Nora E., 329, Oscar, 114, Oscary Y., 114, Polly, 114, Robert, 114, Sarah, 114, 302, Thomas 114, Thomas Jefferson, 114, Verne, 114, William Franklin, 114
CEDERS, Charley, 39
CHADWICK, Betty Lou, 310, Delmas, 306, Edith, 176, Eugene, 26, John, 355, Karen, 306, Lee, 354, Marjorie, 170, 272, Mary, 355, Rebecca, 306, Rebecca L., 375, Wanda, 310, William H., 310
CHAFFIN, Helen, 103
CHAMBERS, Geneva, 282, Homer, 32, John, 100, Martha, 151, 357, Mary A., 100, __, 42, __, 126
CHAMBLIS, Ella Mae, 227
CHANEY, Albert Clifford, 231, Carolyn Mae, 231, Dan, 231, Jewell, 252, Leslie Kathryn, 231, Mary Jane, 331, Norma Ruth, 113
CHAPIN, Austin, 130, Carrie Alice, 130, Charles, 130, David O., 130, Eliza Jane, 130, Elnora, 130, Estella C., 113, Ida Amanda, 130, Jasper, 130, Lenora, 130, Mary

Belle, 130
CHAPMAN, __, 378, Bob, 309, Celia, 299, Hannah Florence, 189, Isabella, 189, Lura, 114, Lyman 114, Lyman J., 114, Marvin, 114, Simeon, 114, Simeon B., 114, Simeon, Sr., 114, Thomas, 114, Thomas B., 114, Uriah, 114,
CHARLES, King I., 124
CHARTERS, Edith, 301, Henry, 162
CHASTAIN, Jeff, 107
CHEATHAM, Alma Ruth, 114, Annie Mae, 114, Betty, 115, Bob, 114, Napoleon Bonaparte, 115, Phillip Darrell, 115, Robert Albert, 114, Robert Darrell, 114, 115, Sondra, 115, Sue, 114, Sue M., 115, Troy Wayne, 115, Wanda, 115
CHEEK, Jerry, 118, Ruth, 267
CHENEY, Harry P., 244, Ruth, 244
CHENOWETH, Esther, 259, Jan Robert, 155
CHESHIRE, Lydia, 54
CHESTERSON, Alice, 187, "Betty" (Elizabeth), 228, Doris, 191, Mary, 215, Mary A., 238, Milton, 238, Rosemary, 187, Walter, 187, Warner, 187
CHEVEWOTH, Indiana, 271
CHI, Jack, 113
CHILD, Maida Belle, 133
CHILDERS, Ella, 102, Isaac, 282, Lulu, 305
CHIROS, Denise Marie, 159, Dorothy Lou, 159, Frank, 159, Louisa Anna, 159, Terence Lee, 159
CHITTENDEN, Corenlia, 183
CHOATES, Rhonda A., "Daisy", 171
CHRISMAN, Arthur E., 372
CHRISTIAN, Writer's Group, 366
CHRISTIANSEN, Dorothy, 334, James Christian, 334, Minnie Alice, 334, Connie Lynn, 135
CHRITTON, Azuba, 115, Cary Alexander, 115, Catherine, 115, Charles Santford, 115, Christopher Sant. Jr., 115, Christopher Santford, 115, Ellen, 115, Enock, 115, Eura, 115, George, 115, James, 115, Johnnie, 115, Joseph, 115, Mary Minerva "Molly", 115, Rachel Ann, 115, Rebecca "Jane", 115, Robert B., 115, William Washburn, 115, Isaac, 115
CHURCH, Cheryl, 108, Emma Evaline "Emily", 104, Richard, 104, Salena, 104
CHURCHILL, Harmon, 34, Philip W., 372
CIPRIANI, Jacqueline K., 292, Jacqueline Katherine, 291, Josephine, 78, Santi, 292
CLAHAN, Jennie, 31
CLAMPITT, Albert, 115, Della, 115, Delvina Jane, 115, Elizabeth, 115, Ezechiel, 115, Ezekiel, 115, Guy, 115, Hazel Pauline, 115, John Wesley, 115, Juanita, 115, Kenneth Harold, 115, Nancy, 115, Nelson Charles, 115, Richard, 115, Ruth, 115, Wilbur K., 115
CLARK, Al, 378, Alexander C., 116, Alva, 215, Amanda, 150, Andrew, 150, Andrew Jackson, 150, Anna Alberta, 198, Arthur, 116, Benjamin F., 115, 116, Bertha, 129, 210, 271, Bruce, 103, Carl Raymond, 103, Carrie, 171, Charles, 115, 150, Charlie, 116, Chris, 103, Clara, 265, Clarence, 115, 116, Claud, 116, Claude, 115, Clemmie, 116, Clyne, 353, Dennis, 103, Donna L., 372, Dorothy, 103, Earl, 161, Edward Earl, 161, Effie, 116, Elizabeth, 134, 243, Elizabeth Edaline, 312, Ella Jane, 116, Esther, 103, Fannie, 116, Fannie (Brown), 99, Francis, 116, Fred, 115, 116, Geneva, 99, George Rogers, 79, Harold Glen, 312, Helen, 67, 103, Hiram, 181, Hulah Lee, 231, Ina Miller, 116, James, 115, James M., 116, James W., 116, Jerrold, 103, John, 99, 187, John B., 134, John D., 116, Johnathan, 36, Joseph, 295, Joseph J., 116, Kate, 150, Kevin, 138, Lela, 231, Leslie, 231, Lewis, 67, Lewis T., 67, Lewis Tipton, 103, Lola, 158, Lola Grace, 231, Lucinda, 116, Lynn, 103, Madge, 312, Margaret Jane, 243, Mary, 115, 116, 134, 150, 302, Mary Alice, 231, Mary Lou, 171, Matilda Jane, 243, Maxine, 115, 116, Melissa, 150, Milton, 116, Nancy, 187, Nathan, 116, Oliver, 116, Paul Merrill, 103, Pearl Marie, 229, Polly Ann, 116, Rebecca, 150, Rebecca Elizabeth, 150, Robert Taylor, 82, Ronald, 218, Roy, 12, 13, Russell, 115, 116, Sally, 233, Sally Mae, 158, Sidney J., 116, Sidney Jane, 84, 112, Stephanos, 123, Steven L., 372, Susan, 116, Susan Margaret, 158, Vivian, 92, Wesley F., 67, William, 115, 116, William A., 29, William T., 116, Willis, 115, 116, Winfred Nicholas, 116, Winifred, 116, 284, Zella, 12, 13, __, 17, __, 32
CLARK'S, Grocery, 26
CLARKSON, Allen, 116, Amanda, 116, Anna, 116, Annetta (Nettie), 116, Celia, 116, Charles, 116, Christianna, 82, Craig, 117, David, 116, Eudella, 116, Eva, 116, Harry, 116, James G., 89, 116, James Lee, 116, James Reuben, 116, Jessie, 249, John, 116, Joseph, 116, Lewis, 116, Lorena, 116, Luella, 116, Malissa, 116, Margaret Jean, 258, Mary, 116, 117, Matthew, 117, McClain, 116, Peter, 116, Ralph, 116, 117, Ralph Norris, 116, 258, Richard, 117, 258, Ryan, 117, Walter, 116, William, 82, 116
CLARY, Jessie Leona, 107
CLAWSON, William K., 37
CLAY, Henry, 125
CLAYPOOL, Dorothy, 336, **CLAYPOOL Music Store, 39**
CLAYPOOL, Piano Store, 40
CLAYTON, Alicia, 181, Craig, 181, Ernest Russell, 181, G.R.V., 181, George R. IV, 181, George Ray, III, 181, Mitchell, 181, Preston Ray, 181, Sean, 181, Kristen, 181
CLEARWATER, John F., 63
CLEAVER, Jason, 212, Ken, 212, Kenneth, 212, Nancy, 212
CLEM, Ruth, 203
CLEMENTS, (Dr.), 320, Aggie, 117, Agnes, 117, Andy, 39, Bud, 117, Carrie Ruth, 213, Cora, 316, Elizabeth, 117, Hazel, 113, Henrietta, 113, Henry, 117, Jack, 117, James J., 12, 113, John, 117, John William, 117, Mabel, 113, Martha Ellen, 252, Mary, 117, Nathan, 252, Pauline, 117, Ray, 213, Raymond Green, 117, Robert, 278, Warren Roe, 117
CLEMENTS & Moody, 12
CLENDENNEN, Rebekah, 301
CLEVELAND, __, 22, (Pres), 183
CLEVENGER, Emma, 198, Martha Ann, 333, Rufus, 198
CLIFFORD, David, 76, Paul R., 372
CLIFFTON, Andrew J., 63
CLIFTON, Edward, 372, Thelma, 290
CLINE, Arnetta, 351, Benjamin, 34, Cliea, 360, Dorothy, 192, James, 117, Leota, 350, May, 373, Michael, 117, Okel, 26, Pat, 22, 117, Phillip, 117, Ruby, 348, Ralph, 117, Rose A., 117
CLOAK, George, 172, Nancy, 172
CLODFELDER, __, 241
CLODFELTER, Adam, 241, Enola Louise, 84, Felix, 241, Froney Belle, 241, George, 241, James, 84, M.C., 31, Malina, 295, Malinda, 141, Noah J., 32, Solomon, 295, Verona, 241, Yvette, 338
CLORE, Berriman, 118, C.W., 74, Carol Jean, 118, 170, Darrin, 297, Elizabeth, 297, Elvie Keeling, 118, Erastus, 118, Frances Deer, 118, Georgiana, 117, Georgiana Fulwider, 117, Georgianna, 170, Israel, 118, Jeff, 208, Julia, 208, Linsey, 208, Mary, 285, Mary Jane, 167, Mary Rice, 118, Richard, 208, Vern, 117, 118, 170
CLOSSIN, Della, 320, Mary Ann, 238, Sarah Elizabeth, 238
CLOUGH, Florence, 205, Martha J., 382, Polly, 324
CLOUSE, Elizabeth, 118, Evadna, 267, George, 198, Nancy, 174, Nancy, 320, Phoebe Eliza, 141, Polly Ann, 267, Samuel Mack, 267
CLOUSER, Alfred, 118, Bill, 118, Blanche, 271, Catherine, 118, Charles, 118, Christina, 118, Daniel, 118, David, 118, Elizabeth, 118, George, 118, Gerry, 118, Hazel, 288, Henry, 118, Henry Francis, 118, Ira, 118, Jane, 118, John, 118, Julia, 380, Karen, 118, Kevin, 118, Margaret, 118, Marjorie, 118, Martha, 118, Martin, 118, Mary, 118, Philip, 118, Phyllis, 118, Ruth, 118, Simon, 118, Susanne, 118, Thomas, 118, Tim, 118, Virginia, 118
CLUTE, Walter Marshall, 296
CLYATON, Carol, 181
CLYMIR, Mary, 158
COADY, Patricia, 322
COAHRAN, Joseph L., 372
COAT, Henry, 344, Marmaduke, 344, Rachel, 284
COATE, Edgar, 319, Lex, 319, Paul, 319
COATES, James, 149
COATS, Bill, 118, Dana, 119, David, W., 119, Eugene, 119, Francis, 118, George, 119, Homer W., 119, 118, Jeffrey W., 119, Joan E., 119, Joseph William, 118, Kathleen, L., 119, Rachel, 344, Ruth E., 118, 119, Vereta June, 118
COBB, Heedlie, 39, 41, Irene, 177
COBERLY, Fannie, 186, Nathan, 186
COBERT, Mary Jane, 189, Virginia, 189
COBLE, A.J., 49, Almon, 261, Almon J., 49, Betty, 261, Marietta, 261
COCHRAN, David, 278, J.L., 374, Kathleen, 145
COE, Emma, 145, Sandra, 343
COFFENBERRY, Stella, 285, Karen Beth, 326
COFFIN, George (Gen.), 169
COFFING, Andrew, 119, Beth Renee, 119, Ernest Ray, 119, Gail McNeil, 119, Kelly Jo, 119, Ralph Emerson, 119, Rhoda Marie, 119
COFFMAN, Carol, 255, Charlie, 14, Helen, 347, Helen Meadows, 260, Rodney, 255
COGAN, Carl, 63
COHEE, Elizabeth, 276, Gayle, 95, Kathleen, 246, Libby, 271, Lois, 95, Norman, 271, O.J. (Capt.), 355
COLE, Bertha, 208, Daniel G., 69, Eve, 232, Georgia, 325, Jennifer R., 119, Linda, 119, Louanne, 231, Mabel, 351, Mark I, 231, Mary Ann, 117, Pearl, 119, Richard, 287, Samuel J., 119, Thomas A., 119, Thomas J., 119
COLEMAN, Betty, 118, Charles, 150, 232, 297, Deborah, 268, E. (Mrs.), 381, Elizabeth, 355, Emma, 150, Eunice, 268, Forrest, 70, 118, Jemima, 268, Kenneth, 70, Mildred Kathleen "Kate", 150, Pat, 297, Seth, 268, William, 268
COLGAN/COLGIN, Eleanor, 181, Hannah, 181, William, 181
COLING, Rosalyn, Marie, 325
COLLINGS, Boyd, 161, Caroline, 120, Clara, 120, Elizabeth, 120, Fannie, 161, Harry A., 120, Isaac (Dr.), 120, John, 151, Lydia, 151, Marilyn, 161, Mary E., 120, Nina F., 120, Roy T., 120, W.A., 120, Will, 370, William, 33, 120, William Asbury, 120, William E., 151, William Z., 120
COLLINS, Annie, 252, Edith Rachel, 90, Emiline, 260, Gladys Porter, 90, Helen, 39, 41, Hester S., 162, James, 162, Margaret, 98, Mary, 161, Mollie, 252, Moseley Cary, 90, Mourning, 351, Neil, 39, 41, Rose, 42, Sarah, 360, Virginia, 264
COLQUITT, Cora Rebecca, 280
COLTHARP, Charles C., 262, Gary S., 262
COLTRAIN, Claude, 120, 258, Douglas, 120, Emma, 120, Esther, 119, Gale, 120, Jeanette, 131, John D., 120, Linden P., 119, 120, Lindsey, 119, Lois, 120, Martha A., 120, Mary, 120, Mary J., 119, Mary Jo, 120, Melissa, 120, Nevah Tribbett, 120, Norman F., 120, Peninah, 119, Rachel, 119, Rebecca, 120, Robyn Ann, 120, Roy, 120, Roy O., 120, Sarah, 119, 120, Sharon Sue, 120, Tamara, 120, Thomas, 120, Solomon, 119, 120, William, 120, Zola, 120
COLVIN, S.P., 49
COLWELL, Alexander, 298, Mary, 298
COMBS, Barbara, 86, Michael, 58, Rebecca, 93
COMER, Cecil, 276, Essie Mae, 276, Greely, 276, Maude, 276, Wayne, 276
COMINGORE, Daniel Edward, 296, June Marie, 296, Philip, 296, Sharon Kay, 296
COMMONS, Theodore Joseph, 151
COMPTON, Catherine, 225, James F., 115
CONARD, Clara, 231
CONKRIGHT, Barbara Jean, 128, Clayton C., 375, Dale A., 375, Glen, 128, Mary, 54, Randy, 54
CONNELL, Louise, 350, Nancy, 302
CONNELLEY, Terry, 43
CONNELLY, Elizabeth, 272, Helen, 272, Louis, 272
CONNER, (Prairie), 287, Caleb, 87, Edmund, 243, Elizabeth, 87, Fannie (Linn), 229, James, 69, Jane, 67, John, 159, Nora, 115, 116, Ruth, 116, William, 145, __, 42
CONNERS, Smith, 30
CONNOR, C., 365
CONRAD, Clara, 215, Emma Faye, 279, Faye, 265, Freida, 239, Nellie, 372
CONSTANT, Susan, 128
CONWELL, Sarah, 98
COOK, Ann Elizabeth, 282, Brad, 121, Brian, 121, Carla, 131, Carla Jo, 131, Carol Jo, 120, 121, Charles M., 80, Cheri, 131, Christa, 131, Clara, 49, Cleve Devon, 121, Curtis, 131, Cynthia Ann, 356, Della Bertha, 333, Dennis Roy, 120, Dottie Belle, 333, Eliza, 333, Eric Gene, 121, George W., 326, 333, Georgianna, 121, Gregory Eldon, 121, Jack Raymond, Jr., 121, James, 238, James K., 232, James Kelly, 314, Joe Devon, 121, John, 113, Judy, 121, Julie, 121, Justus Raymond, 121, Kelly Jo, 121, Laymon Henry, 121, Mabel Marie, 121, 215, Margaret, 238, Mary, 108, 288, 324, Maude, 121, Missouri Cordelia, 232, 314, Misty, 121, Myrl, 127, Nancy, 323, 326, Nicolas Grant, 121, Oliver Earl, 308, Oscar L., 121, Pam, 121, Patricia Jean, 255, Rex Alan, 121, Richard Wayne, 121, Roy, 127, Ruth, 121, Sharon, 103, Susan, 302, Vivian, 121, William, 34, William Raymond, 121, William W., 121
COOKMAN, Walter, 132
COOKS, Experience, 222
COOKSEY, __, 283, Arthur, 121, Elza, 121, Hazel, 121, Thomas L., 24, Thomas L., (Dr.), 359
COOLEY, Annis, 169, Charles, 256, Maggie, 102
COOLMAN, Lettishia, 132
COOMBS, Annie, 130, Carl, 224, Jonathan B., 63
COON, Christopher John, 121, Clay, 121, Clifton, 121, 122, Clifton John, 121, Claude, 121, Clyde "Buck", 121, Cora, 78, 190, 191, 280, 346, Cora Cleo, 293, Eugene, 121, Florence Pearl, 121, Frances, 226, Francis, 121, Isaac, 191, Isaac I, 293, Isaac II, 293, Jason, 121, John II, 293, Loren, 121, Mary, 121, Minerva, 226, Pearl, 121, Robert, 121, Robert Clifton, 121, Ruby M., 375, Ruth Jane, 346, Sherry, 121, Sherry Bymaster, 112, Tonya, 121, William, 121, William Stephens, 121, 191, 280, 293, __ 17
COONEY, Christopher, 179, Thomas, 179, Vicky Lynn Ridge, 179
COONROD, David, 155, Edith, 155, Ruth, 155
COONS, Alvora E., 122, Carl E., 122, Elmer L., 122, Fern, 122, Frances Caroline, 145, Francie E., 122, Francis C., 122, Frank, 136, Fred, 122, George W., 122, Harold M., 122, Harry, 269, Harry A., 122, Harvey P., 122, Hattie E., 122, Helen Louise, 188, James Madison, 122, John R., 122, Lael, 269, Lois E., 122, Loraine, 122, Louise, 122, Mary, 122, Nancy, 268, 306, Nora, 122, Robert L., 122, Roy Clifford, 122, Sarah W., 122, Theodore D., 122, William J., 122
COOPER, Alice E., "Betty", 122, Betty, 215, C.O., 122, Cap, 122, Carolyn Jean, 122, Cary, 164, Charles, 122, Charles M., 122, 123, Charles Marion, 164, Cynthia, 164, Diana, 142, Dowie Theodore, 122, Effie, 271, Ellen Laverne, 122, Elva Irene, 164, Ernest, 215, Fred, 298, Georgia Faye, 122, Helen, 215, Homer, 215, Jeanie, 122, John, 215, Judith Fredericks, 122, Linda Naimo, 204, Lori Ann, 122, Marion Harold, 122, Mildred, 215, Mollie, 372, Mollie Elmore, 123, Rosa, 122, 123, 164, Rosa McAlister, 122, Samuel S., 49, Sarah, 137, Teresa Lynn, 122, William Dena, 122
COOPER'S, Chapel, 202
COOPMAN, A.B., 374, Arthur, 200, Judith Diane, 200, Ruth, 200, 381
COOTS, Debra, 191
COPE, Charlotte Faye, 283, Frances Catherine, 143
COPELAND, Jack, 278
COPPAGE, Lewellyn, 40, Lewellyn J., 29
COPPER, John William, 122
CORBIN, Delores J., 375, Holly, 211, Jenalee, 211, John, 211, Nancy, 326
CORBY, Charles, 301
CORD, Amos, 123, Anne Q., 123, Aquilla, 123, Catherine, 123, Claude C., 123, Cora, 123, Cora Ann, 159, 160, Crystal, 123, Genevieve, 123, John H., 123, Marion, 123, Mary, 123, Mattie, 123, Oliver J., 123, Robert L., 123, Thomas, 123, Thomas J., 123, Thomas, Jr., 123, Wiliam B., 123, William Clyde, 123, William J., 123
CORDES, Arthur, 373
CORETT, Otis, 372
CORN, Albert, 123, Elizabeth, 123, 150, Forest, 44, George, 123, 162, George II, 352, Grace, 284, Hulda, 162, Julia, 123, Margaret, 150, 352, Margaret D., 228, 229, Margaret Jane, 123, Mary Ann, 123, Miles, 209, Nancy, 123, Nancy A., 247, Rhoda Jane, 123, Sarah Eliza, 123, Valletta, 162, Vallie, 352, Vinletta, 123, Williams, 123, 229, 248
CORNELL, Al, 95, Ben, Sr., 12, Bob, 52, Floyd, 95, Homer, 95, John, 52, Judith, 118, Lowell, 95, Ruby, 43, Thelma Lucille, 86, Augustus Carlos, 286, Christopher, 346, Gus, 286, Loyal, 336, Martha, 336, Mary Magdalene, 156, Ronald E., 336, Sally Rose Allie, 287, Susan Lynn, 346, Thomas Wayne, 346, Virginia Jeanne, 346, Wilma, 286
CORNISH, Mary, 124
CORNS, Clara, 43
CORWIN, George, 355, John J., II, 37, Laverne, (Roche), 355, Rosie, 355, Stephen, 355
CORY, Dailie, 328, Dailie Opal, 123, 328, 330, Daniel, 123, David W.B., 123, Delilah, 126, Elnathan, 124, James, 123, 124, Jeremiah, 123, 124, John I, 124, John II, 124, John III, 124, Joseph Edward, 123, 328, Mary, 123, Mary Ann, 123, 328, Mary Bishop, 123, Melinda, 118, Moses, 123, Nancy Ann, 123, Noah, 123, Silas Hurin, 123, Usual, 124, William Smith, 124
COSBY, Bernie, 124, Cary, 124, Cary Andrew, 125, Charlotte, 124, 266, Charlotte Emily, 124, Colleen, 124, Colleen Erin, 125, Douglas, 124, Effie, 124, Elaine Anne, 124, 264, 266, Evah, 124, Glenn, 124, Harley, 124, Junior, 124, Kenneth, 124, 266, Kenneth E., 124, Lando, 124, Lando H., 124, Lando Jr., 124, Lee, 124, Leonard, 124, Lisa, 125, Lyle, 124, Oliver C., 124, Oliver H., 124, Oliver M., 124, Terry, 124, 125, Terry Alan, 124, 266, Virginia, 124
COSHOW, Georgia, 121, Thomas, 82
COSSORT, Rachel, 205
COSTAKIS, Billy, 78, George, 78, William James, 78
COSTON, Jenerson, 297, Zachary, 297
COTNER, Elnora, 351
COTRELL, Anna, 336, Jacqueline L., 204
COTTEN, Euma Rosella, 303, Isaac, 303, Wm. Henry Harrison, 303
COTTRELL, Frank, 234, Pearl Genevieve, 234
COUDRET, Robert B., 375
COUGER, Mary, 214, Ottis, 214
COULTER, Fred, 278, Frederick Proffitt, 278, Valerie, 278
COULTERS, __, 42
COUNTS, Hannah, 353, 354
COURTNEY, Agatha, 251, Clifford, 251, Dorothy Margaret, 251, Elbert Ebert, 251, Erma Hazel, 251, Mabel, 251, Mattie, 123, Robert, 251, Thelma Marie, 132
COURTRIGHT, Linda, 78, Lori, 78
COVEY, Harold, 54, Ruth, 54
COWAN, Anna Belle, 186, Cynthia,

296, David Rice, 186, Della, 186, Edward, 186, Edward H., 126, Edward H., (Dr.), 319, Edward Howard, 125, 126, Edward Howard (Dr.), 104, Elizabeth Louise, 125, Ellen, 265, George, 186, Harriet Janney, 126, James, 164, James Weir, 125, John, 74, 76, 100, 125, 164, John Ayars, 125, John M., 125, 126, John Maxwell, 125, 126, John William, 126, Laura Anna, 126, Marian, 74, Martha, 28, 43, Mary Ann, 125, Mary Ellen, 321, Minnie, 186, Peter, 74, Rachel Ann, 321, Robert, 321, Samuel Walker, 125, Sarah Tilford, 125, Scott, 266

COWDEN, Carolyn, 374

COWDIN, Earl, 149, Howard Earl, 148, 149, Jerry, 149, Mary, 149, 293, Nancy, 149, Parker Howard, 149

COWEN, Charles L., 194

COX, Abel, 129, Abel M., 129, 179, 180, Abijah, 126, 129, Aldezera, 126, Alec, 127, Alexander Denton, 127, Alice, 79, Allie, 126, 239, Alta, 126, Amy Ann, 126, 129, 179, 180, Anna, 331, Arizona, 129, Audrey Louise, 165, Benjamin, 129, Bertha, 126, 237, 271, Betty Jean, 79, Beulah Mae, 126, Brian, 127, Byron, 91, 129, 354, 355, Byron Clark, 126, 127, Cafe, 126, Camilla Lynn, 127, Carla Lea, 127, Caryl, 128, Caryl Ann, 113, Catherine, 61, Catherine Goble, 283, Cece, 126, 127, Cecil, 126, 258, Cecil B., 127, Charles L., 128, Cheryl Ann, 113, 128, Christy, 128, Clark, 271, Connie Leona, 127, Craig, 271, Cyril, 138, Dave, 126, Denise, 92, Denton, 126, 129, 210, 237, 271, Dillon, 113, Dillon Thomas, 128, Donald Dean, 138, Dwight, 127, Dwight L., 127, Eb, 126, Ed, 129, Edith, 315, Edna, 126, 129, Eileen, 211, Elijah, 61, 126, 128, 129, 239, Eliza, 129, 179, 180, Elizabeth, 129, 239, Elizabeth Jane, 143, Eric Michael, 128, Esias, 129, Estella Abigail, 126, Etelka, 127, Evelyn, 126, 355, Flora Marlene, 128, Frances, 63, Frances B., 130, Franklin, 126, 239, George, 129, 199, 271, Gladyne Sue, 128, Gladys, 345, Graydon, 129, Gutielma, 129, Homer, 127, 128, Homer Merle, 127, Homer R., 375, Howard, 79, 220, Isaac, 247, James, 79, Jane, 258, Janet Sue, 271, Jasper, 128, Jasper, Jr., 128, Jeff, 127, Jemima, 279, Jennie Lee, 129, Jeremiah, 129, Joan, 126, Joe, 127, John, 129, John J., 145, John W., 159, Joseph, 129, Joshua, 129, Judy, 210, 258, Julia, 127, 208, Jyl, 79, Karen, 271, Kay, 271, Kayla, 271, Keith, 126, 271, Ken, 126, Kenneth, 126, 127, Keziah, 126, 129, Lauevecia Hutson, 127, Laurell, 127, Lee, 128, Lucille, 221, 271, Lydia, 94, Mabel, 126, Madge, 129, Margaret, 79, 210, 258, Margaret Louise, 159, Marie, 128, Marie (Stevens), 127, 128, Marilyn, 126, Mark, 290, Mark A., 372, Marta, 127, 258, Martha Louisa, 284, Martha Louise, 283, Mary, 127, 128, 194, 344, Mary Ann, 129, 239, Mary Edie, 380, Mary Jo, 271, Mary K., 127, Mary Mehala, 128, Michael, 113, Miriam, 129, Myrl, 127, Nancy, 127, 129, 239, 326, Naomi, 120, Oakel, 126, Orville, 79, Otis, 126, Patricia, 113, Patricia Gay, 128, Paul, 79, Pauline, 237, Pearl, 129, Philip, 271, Phillip, 79, Rachel, 133, 271, 283, 284, Robert, 113, 128, Robert L., 128, Rosa, 126, Rosanna, 129, Roy E., 127, Royal, 129, Ruth, 165, Ruthanna, 79, Sanford C., 309, Sara, 113, Sara Alicia, 128, Sharon Ann, 271, Shirley, 113, 128, Shirley L., 375, Siloam, 129, Stella, 126, 239, Stephen J., 79, Terri Bennett, 128, Thomas, 199, Tom, 128, Tresha Ann, 128, Variety Store, 15, Wallace, 126, Wally, 126, Warren L., 79, Weltha Louise, 322, Wert, 232, William, 128, 129, William S., 283

COY, Brandon, 228, Denise, 228, Ed, 228, Shawna, 228

COYLE, Mary, 143

COYNER, Jesse, 288, Rhoda, 181

COZILLINO, Donna Jo, 348

COZZOLINO, William Joseph, 287

CRABB, Clarence, 301

CRABBE, Buster, 342

CRABBS, Effie, 302, Mary Virginia, 302, Tully Carl, 302

CRABTREE, Rena, 105

CRAFT, Emily, 170, Mary, 92, Molly, 170, Steven, 170

CRAFTON, Nancy, 355

CRAGUN, Maurice, 105

CRAIG, Abby, 130, Armenia, 130, CampBell, 130, Charlotte, 274, 291, Clyde Minnie, 130, Cynthia, 102, Elizabeth, 104, 129, 172, Elvira, 129, Etta, 107, Frank (M/M), 233, Franklin Pierce, 130, G.F., 49, Goldyn Moree, 233, Hannah M., 129, Henry A., 130, Hugh Newell, 104, 129, Isabella, 129, Jackie, 109, James, 129, James McCoy, 129, Jane, 129, John, 129, John Y., 129, Lesa, 131, Margaret A., 129, Marshall, 104, Martha, 129, Mary, 104, 129, Mary Esther, 129, Myrtle O., 130, Robert, 104, 129, 130, Robert Campbell, 129, Robert S., 129, 130, Samuel Givens, 129, Samuel N., 129, Thomas, 263, Willard, 129, William, 129, William Decatur, 129

CRAIG'S, Flower Shop, 15

CRAIN, Angeline, 88, Effie Elizabeth, 88, John, 88

CRAMER, __, 22, Carolyn Sue, 130, Debbie, 130, Debra Sue, 130, Della Frances, 130, 157, Harry, 130, Harry Albert, 130, 157, Henry Thornton, 130, Herman, 130, Herman Ray, 130, Kim, 130, Kimberly Ann, 130, Marilyn Joan, 130, Mary, 4, 130, Mary Catherine, 130, Mary Frances, 130, 262, Mary Katherine, 130, Miriam, 172, Norm, 4, 26, Norman, 130, 262, Norman Lewis, 130, Tim, 316, Vivian Ruth, 157, 287

CRANDALL, Rebecca, 242

CRANE, Elihu, 279, Ellen, 279, Forest, 16, Henry, 100, Hulda, 220, Jehil, 353, Lydia, 353, Martha Elvina, 100, Mary, 226, Mary Jane, 279, Sharon K., 372, Vera, 83

CRANFORD, Margaret, 287

CRAVENS, Elizabeth, 178, Marcia, 225

CRAWFORD, __, 6, Carl, 51, Elizabeth, 209, G.W., 49, Hotel Cafe, 345, James, 209, John, 79, Lewis, 282, Linda 278, Lourvanza, 282, Margaret, 41, 100, Nathan Francis, 88, Isabella, 209, __, 42

CRAWLEY, Sheila, 131

CREASON, Jane, 84, 85

CREECH, David C., 372, Donna M., 375, Suzannah, 240

CREEK, Bell, 302, Daniel, 268, Donald, 268, Donna Jean, 268, Imogene, 268, Sue Ann, 268

CRESON, James, 85

CRESS, Ella, 130, Emma D., 130, Henry C., 130, Jennie, 130, John, 130, John B., 130, Lucien Ernest, 130, Lulie A., 130, Mary 130, Mary A., 130, Mary Frances, 130, 262, Millard F., 130, Ora B., 130, Pearl, 130, Pearl Marie, 130, 262, Raymond, 130, Walt, 130, Walter, 130, 262, Willie R., 130

CREWS, Diane, 344, Randall Wesley, 344, Thomas, 344

CRIBARI, Jane Elizabeth, 218, Stephen, 218

CRIBLES, Maria Catherine, 88

CRIBLEZ, Julie, 128, Linda Michelle, 128, Melinda Joy, 128, Robert, 128, Robert Aaron, 128

CRICKY, Rosa, 126

CRIPE, Jessica, 172, Nicholas, 172

CRIPPS, Christena, 118, Christina, 118

CRISLER, Malinda, 282

CRISON, Maria, 124

CRISP, Dorothy Faye, 279, 309, Louis, 309, Marion, 309, Richard George, 309, Roger Paul, 309

CRISPIN, Mary Kathryn, 86

CRISSINGER, Chris Willhite, 208

CRIST, Mary Jane, 136, Rollo, 136

CRITCHLOW, Morris, 118

CRITES, Abraham, 343, George, 357, Hazel Rebecca, 357, Melissa Ann, 343

CRODIAN, Mara Ann, 341

CROMWELL, Oliver, 298, Richard, 342

CRONIN, Margaret, 252

CRONKHITE, Dean Eugene, 249, Martha Suanne, 249, Susan, 260, Susan Jean, 249

CROOKS, Daniel, 240, Eliza, 215, Eliza Wright, 215, Richard, 301, Sarah, 301

CROSBY, Caroline, 190, Sarah, 347

CROSS, Andrew Bruce, 130, Carolyn, 14, 15, 29, 130, Donald, 130, 272, Ethel, 130, Hazel, 130, Irvin, 130, 272, James, 130, Juanita, 130, Judith, 130, Judy, 272, Mary, 352, Nancy, 130, Russell, 14, 130, 272

CROTEAU, Leonard L., 156

CROUCH, Cynthia, 98, David L., 99, Janice, 99, Jennifer, 99, Sarah, 186

CROW, Albert Willie, 130, Amanda, 131, Amanda Lee, 130, Beverly, 131, Charles Patterson, 131, David, 130, Delia, 130, Ernest, 131, Floy, 131, Frank, 131, Frank Alan, 131, Fred, 131, Honor, 130, John, 130
John P., 130, Julia, 131, Lillian Gail, 131, May Lucille, 131, Mildred, 131, Minnie Mae, 131, Nellie, 131, Norma Jean, 243, Orpha Fern, 131, Rose Marie, 131, Sandra, 131, Thelma Aileen, 131, Virginia Irene, 192, 193

CROWDER, Alberta Jo, 132, Alice Jean, 265, America, 172, Arthur Brown, 132, C.F., 11, Carper Godwin, 131, Creighton, 132, David Milton, 131, Elijah, 132, Emma, 132, Emma Rebecca, 132, Emmett David, 131, Gordon, 132, Gordon Douglas, 132, Grover, 132, James Madison, 131, Janet, 132, 173, Jeanette, 132, John Samuel, 132, Kathryn, 132, Leon, 265, Lillie Florence, 132, Lois Maxine, 132, Lydia May, 131, Margaret, 132, Margaret Rebecca, 132, Margaret Sue, 132, Marilyn Lou, 132, Mary, 132, 265, Mary Kathryn, 132, Melvin, Benjamin, 132, Michael, 173, Michael Keith, 132, Minnie, 132, Nancy, 173, Nancy Florence, 132, Norma Jean, 132, Norman Carper, 132, Paul, 132, 173, Paul Jay, 132, Ralph, 265, Richard H., 63, Robert, 132, Robert Wiley, 132, Ronald, 132, 173, Ronald Paul, 132, Seth Wilmer, 131, W.C., 132, Wiley Charles, 132, Zillah Beatrice, 132

CROWE, Jean, 211

CROY, Jennette, 143, Terry A., 372

CRUEA, Alvin Wilbert, 318, Donald Joseph, 184, Hazel, 184, John, 184, Leona Faye, 184, Mildred, 184, Opal, 226

CRUM, Betty, 226, Shirley, 381

CRUMM, Damon, 21, 26

CRUSH, Jane, 131

CRUTHERS, Pearl, 341

CRUZ, Connie, 240

CUADRADO, Dianna, 262, Elizabeth Ann, 262, Jose "Pepe" H., 262, Michael Edward, 262

CULBERTSON, H.H. (Mrs.), 85, Josephine L., 91

CULVER, John, 286, Rosie, 286

CUMBERLAND, Ann, 120, J.W., 376, Martin, 164

CUMMINGS, Allen Ray, 226, Bill, 132, Brock Allen, 226, Georgia L., 201, Larry, 246, 327, Margaret, 227, Melvin, 294, Peg, 229, Ron, 132, Sarah Diane, 226 Thomas, 294

CUMMINGS, & Patterson, 14

CUMMINS, Christena, 332, Flossie Mae, 198, Gary, 171, Helen, 142, Linda, 171, Lois E., 142, Max, 142

CUNNINGHAM, Alberta Ellen, 84, Ambrose Franklin, 133, Ami Jo, 168, Art, 132, B.L., (Dr.), 132, Bertha, 132, Buford, 122, Burford, 132, Burford, Jr., 132, Cyrus, 129, Enold Louise, 84, Francis, 84, Guy, 132, Hazel, 122, Helen, 132, 133, Helen M., 84, James Madison, 132, John Alexander, 84, Joy L., 372, Lawrence, 133, Lettisia, 132, Lucille, 133, Mable, C., 132, Martha, 95, Mary, 132, 194, Mary Frances, 132, 133, Nema, 132, Oscar, 132, Pauline, 239, Raymond, 84, Rose Vae, 132, Ruby, 122, Samuel Alexander, 84, Violet, 122, 132, Walter, 133, __, 55, Ruth, 133

CUPPY, J.W., 42

CURNICK, Paul, 49

CURRENT, Leo, 133, Leo Wayne, Sr., 133, Leo, Jr., 133, Linda, 133, Lisa, 133, Orpheus, 133, Tammy, 133, Tim, 133

CURRY, Dennis, 121, Ethel, 302, Harvey Wilson, 302, Sally, 318

CURTIS, (General), 91, Betty Scott, 295, Dale, 128, Janice Lee, 128, Richard A., 375

CUSTARD, Robert, 133

CUSTER, Aaron, R., 133, Charles B., 133, Eliza Ida, 133, Frank, 293, 331, Frank A., 194, Franklin, 133, Franklin, A., 133, George N., 133, Helen, 133, Irene Beatrice, 133, James C., 133, Laura, 133, Montgomery Terry, 133, Robert, 133, Sarah, 133, Truth, 133, William Harve, 133

CUTRELL, Edward, 80, Eva Mae, 80, Sarah 80

DAHL, Donald, 217, Jane, 217, Nancy, 217

DAHR, Betty, 126

DAILEY, James, 190, Lucinda Rose, 149, Michael, 11, Mildred Marie, 190, Nellie, 190

DAIN, Jane, 356

DAISEY, Amanda, 321, Charles, 321, Henry, 321

DAISY, David, 336

DALE, Amelia, 238, Bill, 359, Dora, 271, John "Butch", 380, John G., 375, Norma Jean, 300

DALEY, Sylvia Ann, 290

DALTON, Charles, 88

DAMEWOOD, James, 85

DANCER, Elizabeth, 331

DANFORD, Ann, 103

DANIEL, Cindy, 344, James, 20, Jim, 50

DANIELLE, Kayla, 138

DANIELS, Sarah, 280

DARBY, Catherine Theresa, 350, 361, Justin, 350, 361, Michael, 350, 361

DARNALL, Dorothy, 133, 213, Edna Hunt, 133, Edward, 133, Edward C., 133, Marietta, 133, Marietta Carver, 133, Martha, 133, Maynard, 133, Maynard C., Jr., 133, Maynard Carver, 133, Maynard, Jr., 133

DARNARD, Milton Thornton, 133

DARNELL, Eliza, 108, Henry, 208, Sally, 208

DARST, Mary, 309

DAUGHERTY, Betty, 271, Elizabeth, 134, Fred Newton, 134, Harry, 33, 74, Hugh, 134, James, 55, Mary Jane, 134, Minnie Viola, 134, Susanna Lilly, 179, William Edward, 134

DAVENPORT, Elizabeth, 298, Jeffrey L., 372

DAVIDSON, Beatrice, 95, Bob, 134, Carrie, 160, 161, Christina, 160, Christina Carolyn, 134, 135, 160, Donald, 95, Edna, 135, Elizabeth, 134, 324, Ellen, 263, Essie, 134, Fleming, 325, Jane, 134, John, 134, Judy, 192, Julia, 49, Kenneth, 31, Letitia Jane, 134, 135, Margaret, 325, Margaret Ann, 134, Martha Victoria, 134, 135, Mary Catherine, 143, Mary Lamson, 221, Maude, 135, Melvin, 135, 221, Mildred, 135, Minnie, 237, Molly, 132, Nancy, 225, 325, Nina, 295, Olive, 135, Richard, 44, 134, 324, Richard Newton, 134, Robert, 134, Robert James, 134, 135, Ruby, 43, Sarah, 325, Susan Clark, 116, Thomas Levi, 134, Warner, 44, William, 134, 325, William Fleming, 201, William J.D., 134, William T., 135, William Thomas, 134, 135, __, 43 __, 43

DAVIDSOPN, Elizabeth, 134

DAVIS, Abigail, 190, 269, Abraham, 110, 135, Alva Glenn, 136, Amelia, 135, Anna, 110, Ascha, 110, Avelina, 110, 135, Benjamin Harold, 136, Bessie, 110, Bettie, 289, Betty Louise, 185, Bruce Narvarre, 281, Bryan, 189, Bryan Lee, 246, Byron Carson, 135, Cassandra, 189, Catherine, 82, 135, Cecil N., 189, Charles, 327, Cheryl Susan, 135, Clara, 136, Clifford, 21, 31, Clydia Mae, 189, Dorothy, 136, Edward, 110, Edward B., 135, Elizabeth, 135, 137, 149, 327, Elon, 82, 110, 135, Elva Irene, 164, Elvina, 110, Emma, 135, Ernest, 135, Ernest Lest, 135, Fannie, 43, Fanny, 43, Fred, 136, Fredrick W., 372, George, 42, 52, 136, 259, George E., 135, George S., 52, George Samuel, 136, Gregory Repp, 282, H.A., 52, Harriett, 135, Harry, 50, Harry Todd, 136, Herman, 14, 258, Hershell H., 375, Howard L., 374, Ida, 136, Ida May, 135, Isaac, 110, 135, James, 149, 172, 285, James J., 317, James R., 135, James Ray, 135, James, Jr., 172, Jane Elizabeth, 285, Jennie, 52, Jennifer, 189, Joel, 110, 135, John, 82, 110, John I., 110, 135, 82, John L., 135, 136, Joseph, 43, Josiah, 269, Julia, 353, June Darlene, 135, Kenneth Paul, 135, Lael Corya, 136, Lana Lee, 135, Laura, 299, Laura May, 82, Leeta Darlene, 135, Lena, 181, Louise, 136, Lucille, 105, Lucy, 269, Lurena, 110, 135, Mabel Clair, 330, Mahala, 327, Marjorie, 189, Marsh, 42, Marshall Lloyd, 282, Martha, 136, 358, Martha J., 110, Marvarre, 281, Mary, 110, 122, 135, 136, Mary Ann, 110, Mary Glenn, 136, Mary Jane, 136, Matilda E., 110, Maude, 110, May, 110, Melissa, 189, Mellie, 136, Michael Dean, 135, Minnie, 136, N.P., 365, Nancy E., 110, Nannie, 52, Naomi, 136, 295,Nellie, 110, Opal Agnes, 175, Oze, 110, 135, Patricia, 105, Paul H., 153, Pauline, 147, Pauline Durham, 136, Pearl, 136, Pete, 327, Peter, 259, Phyllis, 82, Phyllis, 82, Phyllis Jean, 110, 135, Rachael, 136, Randolph, 135, 136, Ray, 189, Raymond Carl, 111, Rebecca, 148, 149, Rebecca J., 347, Rebecca Jane, 136, Richard Gene, 135, Richard Lee, 135, Robert Edgar, 246, Robert Lee, 135, Roy E., 105, Ruby, 135, Ruby Edna, 135, Ruby Harriman, 135, Sarah, 135, Sarah Hannah, 100, Sarah Jane, 136, 285, Susanna, 189, T.J., 11, Teresa L., 375, Tessie, 223, Thomas J., 12, Tilghman, 322, Tilghman Thomas, 136, Timothy J., 372, Velma, 135, Walter G., 136, Walter Glenn, 136, Warren William, 330, Warren, Jr., 310, Will, 75, William, 110, 135, William (Capt), 219, William Warren, 110, 136, Wilma Jean, 135

DAVISON, Sam, 194

DAWES, Family, 153

DAWLEY, Douglas, 247, 353, Ruth, 247

DAWSON, Betty, 348, Betty Marie, 287, Brenda, 239, Donna, 212, Dortha, 348, Ethel Mae, 348, George, 107, 348, Hannah, 179, 180, Harry, 348, Harry, Jr., 348, Jake, 239, Marjorie, 348, Mary, 238, Mary E., 372, Mary Elizabeth, 107, Mary Jane, 348, Midge, 348, Nancy Ann, 113, Richard, 212, Ruby, 348, Russell, 348, Ruth, 348

DAY, Frances Rose, 328, Jessie, 136, Jo, 317, Margaret Louise, 372, Mary Josephine, 328, Maurice Graham, 136, Murl, 317, Neil, 328, Neil Gilbert, 328, Ronald L., 372, Ruthanne, 328, Sophia Dysee, 328, Thomas Lee, 136, William Harry, 328, William Travis, 328

DAY'S WALLPAPER, 383

DAYTON, Ralph, 164

DAZEY, Amanda, 321, Charles, 321, Henry, 321, Wes, 98, __, 17

DAZEY'S GARAGE, 16

DEBARD, Basil, 137, Carl O., 137, Dan, 137, Earl, 137, Harriet, 137, Martin, 137, Mary Catherine, 137, Robert, 137, William, 137

DEBAWN, Howard, 203, Janice, 203, Mildred, 203

DEBOY, Doris, 360, Harold, 360

DEBRULAR, Hume, 376

DEBUSK, Brett, 137, Charles, 137, 138, Charles Thomas, 137, Charles Tilden, 137, Christine, 137, Deanna, 137, Dora Elizabeth, 137, Gilda, 137, Glenda Kay, 137, Imogene, 137, 138, Jack, 137, John C., 137, Kay, 137, Stacy, 137, Stanley, 137, Thomas Noble, 137, Thomas, Jr., 137, Tom, 137, Tom, Sr., 137

DEDIEMAR, David Bryan, 203, 347, Edward Eugene, 203, 347, Hazel J., 203, James Edward, 203, 347, Mary Jane, 203, Mary Jane Morales, 347, Robert George, 203, 347, Robert Steven, 103, 347

DEHAVEN, Charles, 307, Ida, 116

DELON, Alice Lorene, 165, Fred King, Jr., 165, Gailen Louese, 165

DELONG, Amanda C., 252
DEMOORE, __, 69
DEMOSS, Margaret, 110
DENEAL, Grover, 69, 300
DEPEW, (Dr.), 209
DEROYER, Sebastian, 290
DESHONG, Susan, 210
DEVORE, Ashley, 142, Brian, 142, Charles L., 142, "Davy" David, 142, Dee Ann, 142, Esther, 142, Henry V., 142, Howard, 142, Keith, 142, Laura, 142, Lawrence, 142, Lois, 142, LuAnn, 142, Mabel, 142, Margaret Evans, 142, Michael, 142, Ted, 142, Tiffany, 142
DEVOSS, Dora, 115
DEVOTO, Arthur M., 142, Craig W., 142, David Harold, 142, Donald Edwin, 142, Donald Eric, 142, Doris J., 142, Grace, 143, Jachalyn Joyce, 142, Jane Magnant, 142, John Wayne, 142, Lois Ellen, 142, Louis Arthur, 142, Michael William, 142, 143, Mildred Evelyn, 142
DEWEIN, Florence, 185
DEAN, Carolyn June, 137, Charles S., 136, Charlotte, 137, Fred, 137, Fred N., 136, Fred Nelson, 136, Hannah, 164, James, 218, Joyce Elaine, 137, Mabel, 136, Mary Jane, 137, Melba, 137, Melba Frances, 137, Melvin S., 136, Rebecca Jane, 136, Ruth Ann, 137, Stanley Alan, 137
DEARDORFF, Mary, 222, Peter, 222, Rebecca, 222
DEATH, Mary, 136
DEATHERAGE, George Washington, 149, Mary Catherine, 149, Nancy, 149
DEATON, Benjamin, 172, Timothy, 172
DECK, Bertha, 93, Charlene Vernon, 158, Charlotte, 158, Edith, 158, Fred, 92, Jeanne, 92, Orville, 158, Rebecca, 118
DECKARD, Alice, 138, Bessie, 223, Charley, 223, Cheryl, 195, 332, Cheryl Lynn, 138, Jack, 195, 332, Jack Mitchell, 138, Jack Mitchell II, 138, Jill, 195, 332, Jill Lynn, 138, Lucinda Jo, 138, Marian Marciel, 138, Mark Allen, 138, Michelle Lea, 138, Phyllis, 223, Phyllis Alleen, 223, Richard, 195, 332, Richard E., 138, William McKinley, 138, 332, Mary W., 372, Webb D., 372
DECKER, Mary W., Webb D., 372
DEENER, June, 255
DEER, __, 6, Edward, 138, Fannie, 12, Frances, 118, Joel, 10, 128, Joel G., 138, Joel, Sr., 138, John, 138, Margaret, 87, Mary, 285, Permelia, 285, Samantha, 138, Simeon, 285, Sophia, 138, Steve, 12, 13
DEERE, Alonzo, 70, Carolyn Richardson, 239, George W., 144, John Implement, 144
DEETER, Edna, 268, Jennie, 324,
DEETS, Florence, 88
DEFANDOR, Rita, 294
DEHAVEN, Abigail, 305
DELAHUNT, Sara, 80
DELANEY, Bessie Lenora, 131, Edwin, 283, Elizabeth, 283, 355, Ella, 283, Lou, 187
DELANO, Cindy, 54, Jessie, 380, Rosemary, 145, Thelma, 285
DELLACA, Karen, 256
DELLANE, Sue, 252
DELLASCA, Karen, 252
DELLINGER, Aimee Marie, 139, Alta May, 139, Carl Eugene, 140, Carla Jean, 139, Christopher Michael, 140, Dallas Margaret, 139, Daniel, 139, David L., 139, Elizabeth, 139, Elsie Irene, 139, Eugene Spangler, 138, 140, 276, George, 139, George Paul, 138, 139, 140, 276, Glenn Carl, 139, Hartley C., 138, 139, 140, 276, Jacob I, 139, Jacob II, 139, John Robert, 139, Joseph, 141, Joseph Anthony, 140, Judith Ann, 139, Justin Thomas, 240, Leroy, 139, Margaret Mary, 140, Maria Barbara, 139, Matthew Mead, 139, McKenzie Elizabeth, 139, Michael Scott, 139, Oraph, 139, Peter Paul, 139, Rebecca, 335, Rebecca Marie, 140, Robert, 140, Robert Lowell, 138, 139, 140, 276, Roger Alan, 139, Ruthanna, 138, 140, 276, Shirl, 81, Shirl Blaine, 87, 138, 139, 140, 276, 335, Shirley, 81, Shirley Kathleen, 138, 140, 276, Ted Hartley, 139, Thomas Baynes, 87, 138, 140, 276, 295, Thomas Thaddeus, 140, Virginia Lee, 139
DELP, Jay, 167, Maud, 13
DEMAREE, Carl, 251, Frances, 248, 378, Frank, 248, John V., 148, Margaret M. Durham, 148
DEMAREE'S PHOTO, 270
DEMORET, Barholomew, 141, Grace, 295, Grace M., 141, Hazel Clara, 295, Hazel C., 141, James Franklin, 141, 180, 295, Karmon Leigh, 229, 299, 339, Kelsey Lachelle, 339, 229, Lachille, 299, Louise, 136, Mary Alice, 141, 180, Mary Alice, 295, Myrtle B., 141, Myrtle Belle, 295, Nicholas, 141, Orville, 136, Pearl, 86, Roy, 295, Roy H., 141, Samuel, 41, Samuel Bennett, 141, Steven, 229, 299, 339, Velma Jean, 100
DENMAN, __, 21, Alice, 269, Charles, 159, Ida Frances, 244, 334, Jemima Lee, 269, Moses, 234, Moses H., 269, Moses Hampton, 244, Susan, 159
DENNEY, Lauena, 315
DENNIS, Ann Elizabeth, 107, Bill K., 101, Jessica Lynne, 113
DENNY, Amanda, 223, __, 32, 33
DENTON, Claude, 262, Dorothy, 262
DEPPEN, Anna, 167
DERDA, Leo, 311, Regina, 311
DERRICKSON, Nancy, 115
DESSERY, Alfred Napoleon, 178, Hazel, 178, Mary, 178
DETCHEON, Company, 42
DETCHON, Ada M., 141 Alice, 141, Annabelle, 141, Company, 14, Elliott (Dr.), 141, Emma, 141, Erwin Agnew, 141, Esther, 141, H., 169, Harriet, 141, Harriett, 141, Irwin Agnew, 141, Lee, 141, Martha Jane, 141, Mary Hannah, 141, Mattie, 141, Seymour Gibson, 141, __, Infant, 141
DEVENPORT, W.C., 202
DEVITT, Charles Michael, 355, Charles, Jr., 355, Kathleen, 355
DEVORE, Lawrence, 370
DEWEES, Jewell, 63
DEWEY, Bert, 165, Ella, 165, Elsie, 165, Florence Jane, 165, Jane, 165, Robert Lee, 165
DIANE, Bernice, 296
DICE, Catherine, 100, Christopher, 104, Clorinda Pink Ella, 344, Mark, 31, Nancy, 54, __, 42, __, 42
DICKERSON, Alice, 197, Ann B., 294, Benjamin, 197, Chet, 54, Daniel R., 328, Drew, 54, Earl, 143, Edward, 143, Edythe Kenton, 54, Eric Daniel, 328, Frank P., III, 372, George, 197, George W., Jr., 143, George W., Sr., 143, Helen Elizabeth, 224, Jamie Leigh, 328, Jane, 197, Jane Isabella, 228, Jane Isabelle, 229, Janet King, 143, Jeanette, 143, John, 197, Julia Reim, 143, Karl, 26, Karl A., 143, Karl Anthony, "Knobby", 143, Karl Joseph, 143, Kim, 54, Mary Ellen, 197, Mary Jeanette, 143, 170, Nancy, 54, Paul, 143, Philip, 143, Ralph, 143, Ruth, 230, Samuel J., 375, William, 197
DICKEY, George, 173
DICKINSON, Elizabeth A., 178, Emma, 174, Theodore, 174
DICKMAN, Jean, 278
DICKS, Herman, 283
DICKSON, Alma, 143, Anna, 36, 91, Arthur, 143, Artie, 143, Cena, 143, Charles Albert, 143, Doris, 143, Edgar, 143, Ella, 143, Fletcher, 143, Henry, 143, James, 143, James Madison, 143, Josiah, 143, 283, Leah, 143, Oliver, 143, Omer, 143, Paul, 143, Quincy, 143, Rena, 143, Rosella, 143, Sarepta, 143, Waldo, 91, 143, William 143, Wilma, 143, 315, Wilma R., 91
DICUS, Mardelle, 225
DIEBEL, Louise, 207
DIECKMAN, Laurel Ann, 278
DIEGEL, Mary, 223
DIETERLEN, Wanda, 375
DIETRICH, J.L., 365, John, 365, William A., 365
DIGBY, (Capt.), 284, Margaret, 284
DIKE, Elias Cecil, 244, Rachel Emma, 244
DILDINE, Charles Ernest, 136, Charlotte D., 136, Clarence W., 136, Frances E., 136, George W., 136, Harold C., 136, Harold Ruth, 136, Mary Dorrough, 136
DILLER, James M., 164
DILLMAN, Betty, 144, Diana, 144, Dick, 144, Ellen, 144, Garrie, 44, Garrie L., 144, George T., 44, George Theodore, 144, Harriett, 144, Jackie, 144, Janie, 144, Jodie, 144, John, 144, Mabel, 144, Malcolm Curtis, 144, Martha, 144, Maurine, 282, Maxwell C., 144, Norman, 144, 309, Robert, 144, Ruby, 144
DILLON, Mary, 54
DINE, Samuel, 82
DINIUS, Heather, 359, Joshua, 359, Kisha, 359, Nathan, 359, Renita, 359
DINWIDDIE, Brenda Lee, 309, Carol Lynn, 117, Clark, 309, Elizabeth, 117, Mary Sue, 309, Robert R., 17, Shery Lou, 309
DION, Elizabeth, 223, Tim, 199, 223, 290
DISMORE, Mac, 280, Marla Sue, 280, Marsha, 280, Sandra, 280
DITAMORE, Charles, 301
DITTAMORE, Katie, 241
DITTEMORE, Asa, 194
DIVERS, Glenna, 192
DIXON, Blanche Loman, 232, Eliza, 126, John, 378, William, 126
DOAN, Patty, 54
DOBBS, Sam, 173
DODD, Clarence Lee, 232
DODDS, Frank, 247, Myrtle, 247
DODGE, Rebecca Lorene, 98
DODSON, Alice L., 78, Beatrice, 213, George W., 78, John, 78, Lillie, 78
DOLPH, Deanna, 290
DOLSON, Taunis, 80
DONALDSON, Alice Jean, 265, Del, 72, Elizabeth, 258
DONLOUIE, Anna Mae, 113, Arch, 303, Evelyn, 303, Evelyn Lee, 170, Mary F., 303
DONNELLEY, R.R., 151
DONNELLY, Linn, 92, Robert, 92, William, 92
DOOLEY, David, 144, Donna, 144, Honor, 130, Hugh, 50, Iona, 325, James, 144, Jennifer, 144, Jerome B., 265, Jim, 144, Jonathan, 144, Judy, 144, Mary Ann, 144, Mary Emma, 144, Melinda, 144, Michelle, 144, Nina, 78, Owen R., 144, Rhonda, 155, 251, Robert, 144, Sheri, 144, Timothy, 144
DOROTHY Q., DAR, 366
DORROUGH, Mary, 136
DORSEY, Barton N., 100, Docia A., 67, Dosha Jessee, 182, George 105, 182, 272, George T., 67, Hannah, 272, Nina, 67, Ida, 182
DOSS, Cora Belle, 173
DOSSETT, Marilyn, 375, Phillip R., 372
DOTY, Amanda, 282
DOUBLEDAY, Harriet, 125, 126
DOUGHTEN, Frances, 227
DOUGHTY, Mary Elizabeth, 328
DOUGLAS, Aaron, 164, Adam, 233, Alonzo, 145, Amanda Jane, 145, Annie, 144, Brian, 284, Brian J., 285, Charles V., 372, Debbie Dee, 91, Edwin, 145, 164, Eliza, 144, Emmons, 164, Evelyn, 91, Everett, 164, Harold, 91, Henry, 144, 164, Herman, 226, Homer, 164, James ,145, James Lewis, 145, Jane, 144, 153, Jane Elrod, 153, Jeremiah, 109, 145, 281, Jeremiah I, 144, Jeremiah III, 144, Jeremiah IV, 144, Jermiah, 144, John, 144, 284, John A., 285, Joseph, 153, Levina Catherine, 145, Lori Lee, 139, LuAnne, 284, 285, Margaret, 298, Margaret Ann, 144, 243, Mariah, 144, Mariah Louella, 145, Martha, 263, Martha Jane, 109, Mary, 144, 145, 281, Mary Hanna, 109, Mary Jane, 233, Nancy, 233, Opal, 164, Rebecca, 263, Ruth, 263, Ruth Evelyn, 290, Samuel, 144, Sherman, 300, Stephen A., 125, Thelma, 263, William H., 144, Walter, 164, William Willoby, 144
DOUGLASS, Cyrus, 334, Dorman Bloss, 334, Eliza, 334, Ruby, 334
DOUTHIT, Elizabeth, 153,John, 153
DOVE, Glenda Kay, 137, Kay, 137, Keturah, 282
DOWD, Alfred, 325
DOWDEN, Abigail, 303, 305, Abijah, 145, Alaska, 145, Ashford, 145, Bert, 145, Catherine, 145, Elizabeth Grant, 145, Elzie, 145, Eva, 145, Frank, 145, George, 145, 298, George Wilson, 145, Gertrude, 145, Goldie, 301, James, 145, 225, 305, John, 145, Joseph, 145, Josephine, 145, 298, Joshua, 145, Julia, 145, 298, Kathleen, 145, Lillie Theadocia, 145, Louise, 145, Mahala, 145, 305, Martha, 145, 225, Mary, 145, Mary Ann, 145, Nancy, 145, Nathaniel, 145, 225, Nathaniel, Jr., 145, Ora, 145, Pearl, 145, Rose Victoria, 324, Ruby, 245, Sarah, 145, Susan, 145, Theadocia, 145, Walter, 145, William, 145, 225
DOWDY, Rosa W., 283
DOWELL, Joyce Hatt, 355, Sitha, 215, Tonya, 355
DOWNING, Mary Elizabeth, 129
DOWNS, Cindy, 150, Dale, 150, Jay, 150, Joyce, 150, Larry, 150, Robert, 150
DOYEL, James, 225, Nancy, 225, Rosa, 269, Thomas, 225
DOYLE, Charles, 323
DOZIER, Addie, 128, Dora Belle, 128, Elizabeth (Taylor), 128, Flora Mae, 128, Frances Ethel, 128, Herschell Charles, 128, James Edgar, 128, James Madison, 128, Jim Matt, 128, Joe S., 128, Mary Mehala, 128, Rachel Esta, 128, William, 128
DRAKE, Ada, 142, Charles E., 85, 359, Courtney, 212, Eura Eaton, 115, Helen, 248, Kevin, 212, Laura, 212
DRILLING, Christine, 137
DRISCOLL, Brenda, 274, Doug, 274
DRIVER, Fanny, 323, George, 324, Harriett Louise, 326, Theodosia, 270
DRYER, Nona, 95
DUBOIS, Abigail, 267, Josiah, 267
DUCKETT, Mary Elizabeth 198
DUFFY, Francis, 199, Reid, 369
DUFOUR, __, 218
DUKE, __, 42
DUMONT, Julia L., 218
DUNBAR, Albert, 290, Austin, 145, Bill, 145, 146, Bill, Jr., 146, Bryant Bauer, 146, Candice, 240, Catherine, 85, Daniel, 85, Dave, 240, Douglas, 240, Elias, 85,145, Elias Peter, 85, 145, Eliza, 85, Elizabeth, 85, Emma Coe, 145, Esther, 85, Fred, 240, Harvey, 145, Irma, 145, 146, Jean, 85, Jean Claire, 146, Jill, 240, Joan, 240, John Adam, 85, Joseph, 145, Karen, 240, Kenita Jo, 290, Lewis, 22, 85, 145, Lewis M., 85, Lillian, 145, Lute (Rev.), 312, Mae, 145, Magdalena, 145, Marion, 85, Martha ,343, Mary, 85,145, Morton P., 327, Parker, 240, Pete, 146, Robert, 85, 145, Roscoe, 145, Sam, 146, Samuel, 146, Silas, 85, 146, Simon, 85, Susan, 85, 343, Suzannah, 240, Taylor, 85, Theodore, 145, Valerie Ann, 146, Viola, 326, Willard, 145, 146, Willard III, 146, Willard Parker, Jr., 146, William, 85, 145, 343
DUNCAN, Allen, 147, Andrew Johnson, 291, Artie, 146, Bailey, 146, Benjamin F., 280, Bettie, 263, Bob, 146, 147, David, 147, David Brent, 147, Dawson Glenn, 291, Edith J., 291, Edith Jane, 291, Evelyn, 147, Gaildene, 147, Gladys, 221, Jason, 147, Joshua, 147, Lillian Cloe, 280, Marlis Gaildene, 146, Mary, 31, Melanie, 147, Olive Boyd, 280, Robert, 146, Robert Steven, 146, 147, Robert T., 146, Rosemary, 14, 146, 366, Steve, 147, Susan, 147
DUNKLE, Daisy Dean, 162
DUNLAP, Alexander, 99, Ann, 99, Bessie, 147, Cecil, 147, Janet Sue, 147, John Wesley, 147, Phyllis, 147
DUNLAVEY, Alonzo, A., 63
DUNN, Elinor, 329, Elizabethh, 328, Frederick, 159, Maria, 328, Mary Jane, 321, Miriam, 76, 329, Nathaniel, A., 321, Samuel, 125, 329, Sarah, 125, William P., (Dr.), 328, Williamson, 76, Williamson (Judge), 329
DUNWOODY, Sam, 268
DURBIN, Brenda, 229, 299, Brenda Jean, 339
DURHAM, Bell, 147, Betty, 147, 169, Brisco, 147, Celia H., 148, Charles Stubbins, 148, Claude, 148, Cornelius, 147, Elbert, 93, Emma Josephine, 148, Fred Norcross, 148, George, 49, 147, George T., 169, George Tarkington, 147, Governor, 147, Guy Wakefield, 148, Harry, 148, Henry North, 47, Home, 87, Isabel, 74, J.Y., 147, Jeremiah, 147, Jessie Y., 147, 148, John, 147, 148, John Thomas, 148, Joseph, 147, Julia, 147, Julia Belle, Jule Belle, 147 151, Laura, 147, Lucy V., 148, Margaret M., 148, Margaret Mary, 148, Martha Jane, 148, Nancy Belle, 148, Pauline, 136, Phoebe, 147, Rosalie, 169, Rosalie Tarkington, 147, Roscoe, Conklin, 147, Ruth, 148, Samuel Wakefield, 148, Sarah Dorcas, 148, William H., 370, William Y., 147, __, 32
DURNIL, Bryan, 235, Darrell, 235, Julie Ann, 235
DUTTON, Anna Michelle, 312, Robert, 312, Suzanne Lynne, 312
DUVALL, Dorothy, 199, Mary, 282
DVORAK, Ann, 342
DWIGGINS, Sarah, 186
DYE, Judith, 325
DYER, Kevin Ross, 78, Richard E., 372, Susan, 78
DYKES, Anna, 96, 145, 146, Clarence, 145, Ed, 145, Estella, 145, Gladys, 145, James, 145, James Edward, 145, Pat, 145, Samuel, 146, Samuel Adam, 145
DYKHUZN, Fred, 360, Mary Kate, 360
EADS, Lucy, 192, Nancy, 359, William G., 372
EAKEN, Andrew, 360, Mildred, 360, Nancy Ann, 360
EARDLEY, Eva, 54
EARL, Edna J., 375, Ethel Mae, 348
EARLY, Ann, 148, 168, 212, Daniel, 148, Mae, 148, Mary, 148, 168, 212, Mauree, 148, Opal, 148, 212, Opal Burnetta, 148, Richard, 148, Robert, 148, 168, 212, Robert Paul, 148
EARNSHAW, Brooke A., 375
EASLEY, Angeline, 149, Barbara, 149, Benjamin, 149, Billie Ann, 149, Carette Blanch, 148, Catherine, 149, Charles, 293, Charles W., 110, Charles Woodson, 148, 149, Charley, 149, 150, Charrie, 149, Daniel, 149, 172, Daniel W., 149, Daniel Woodson, 148, Earl, 293, Emma, 172, Emma Blanche, 149, Emma Jane, 149, Eve N., 149, Frances, 149, 285, Grace "Todie", 149, Hattie E., 122, Isaac Milford, 149, J.C., 293, J. Lloyd, 148, J.C., 148, J.W., 149, James B., 149, Jerry Madison, 149, John, 149, John Michael, 149, Joseph, 149, Joseph Woodson, 149, L.J., 293, Lucinda Rose, 149, Lucinda Frances "Fanny", Mary, 149, Mary Catherine, 148, 149, Mary Glenn, 136, Max Glenn, 149, Melinda Jane, 149, Mildred Lenora, 148, 149, 293, Nancy, 149, Nancy Ann, 149, Paul, 293, Robert, 149, Sally, 149, Sarah, 149, Sarah Katharin "Kate", 149, Sarah Katherine, 285, Tilghman, 149, Velma Geraldine, 148, 149, Viola, 172, Walter, 172, Walter Daniel, Jr., 149, Walter F., 149,Warhan 149, Wilber Daniel, 149, William, 149, __, 136
EASTER, Clifford Pleasant, 324, Rose Marie, 324
EASTERN STAR #539, 365
EASTLACK, Catherine, 242, Mary Anna, 242, Samuel, 242
EATON, Eura, 115, John, 271, Matti Mae, 289, Peter, 271, Robert, 271
EBAUGH, Marjorie, 66
EBERHARD, Christian, 154, Jacob, 154, Michael, 154, Peter, 154
EBERT, Daisy, 92, Esther Lucille, 325, Ora, 92
ECHELBARGER, Garold, 192
ECHO, Mabel, 160
ECKEL, Mary, 298
ECKERLEY, E.L., 41
EDDINGFIELD, Emma, 150, George, (Dr.), 150, James C., 31, James Carey, 150, John, 150, John Jamison, 150, Lucille, 150, Mary A., 150, Maurice, 150, Oscar, 30, 150, Paul, 50, 66, Paul (Rev.), 150, Ray, 150, William T., 31, William Thompson, 150, Iva, 150
EDDINGTON, Ernest, 150, Geraldine, 150, Ronald, 150
EDENS, Dora E., 171
EDGE, Hattie, 172
EDMISTON, Aerial Nicole, 185, Ann Louise, 185, Beth Ann, 185, Bill David, 185, Carl Leland, 185, Carla Patricia, 185, Christopher Scott, 185, Cody William, 185, Dawn Marie, Ellen Marie, 185,

Emily Suzanne, 185, Emma, 185, Heather Rose, 185, Jack, 185, Jacob Sherman, 185, Jay Paul, 185, Jennifer, 147, Jennifer Leigh, 185, Jennifer Lynn, 185, Joan, 185, Joe, 185, John Allen, 185, John Dale, 185, Mark B., 372, Mark Blane, 185, Megan Nichole, 185, Melissa Joy, 185, Scott Matthe, 185, Stacia Loraine, 185, Susan, 185

EDMONDS, Bob, 150, Bobby Joe, 150, Jesse, 160, Kate, 150, Kathleen, 150, Keith, 150, Mabel Echo, 160, Marilyn Theresa, 150, Michelle Elizabeth, 150, Pat, 150, Robert, 150, Robert J.K., 150, Robert Josiah Keith, 150, Robert Keith, 150

EDWARDS, Amy, 191, Andrew, 150, Andy, 131, Becca, 150, Beulah, 350, 361, Beverly, 157, Bill, 234, C. Elizabeth, 150, Carol, 191, 280, Carol Ann, 132, Catherine, 150, Charles, 150, Charles Curtis, 350, 361, Clara Elizabeth, 150, Cuba, 150, Curtis, 30, 150, Curtis David, 150, Daniel J., 372, David, 150, Dawn, 127, Deborah, 150, Don, 25, Douglas, 191, Elizabeth, 191, Elmer J., 375, Erika M., 375, Evelyn, 131, Franklin, 150, Fred, 132, Gom, 150, Hattie, 150, Jean, 25, John, 127, John Jr., 127, Lonia, 194, Lyric, 127, Mae, 150, Margaret Cox, 43, Mary, 150, 238, 338, Mary Ann, 150, Mata, 238, Mate, 238, May Jane, 150, Nancy, 150, Orpha, 335, Patti, 191, Paul, 127, Phyllis, 357, Ralph, 150, Ralph, 191, 325, Rebecca Deliah, 268, Sara Corra, 150, Seth, 127, 150, Valonia "Lonie", 293, Wendy, 127, William C., 268

EGGERS, Benton Gordon, 106, Betty, 192, Dorris, 311, Glenn, 106, Ivall Dean, 106, Mary Elizabeth, 106, 159, Ruby, 106, Turman, 106, Wilma, 106

EHRIE, Wesley, 71

EICHACHER, Matilda, 251, 161

EISENHOWER, Dwight D., 102, __,109

EKERS BAKERY, 296

EKSTROM, Dean, 170, Jamie, 170, Jane, 170, Robert, 170

ELAM, Lula Mae, 300

ELDER, Catherine, 267, Emeritus, 195, T.J., 41

ELKINS, Lydia Alice, 283

ELKS, 366

ELLER, Clara Carolina, 88

ELLETT, Cletis, 55

ELLINGWOOD, Ashley Rose, 296, Deanna Kay, 296, Jason Charles, 296, Ronald, 296

ELLIOT, Letha, 31, __,32

ELLIOTT, Connie Lorene, 156, Earl, 188, Earl F., 376, Edna, 156, Estella Lorraine, 269, Felinia, 170, Harvey B., 170, Henry Robert, 156, J.W., 374, Joseph C., 120, Para Lee, 172, Tessie Amanda, 120

ELLIOTT'S,Marthas Station, 15

ELLIS, Armine, 302, Beverly Jean, 150, Blanche May, 352, Carolyn, 150, 151, Corliss, 171, Effie, 319, Elizabeth, 352, Elmira, 150, Eve, 148, Frank, 226, Gary, 203, James Porter, 126, Joe, 150, 151, John, 85, 220, 281, 352, Jon, 150, Jonathan, 150, 151, Jonathan Elwood, 151, Joyce, 150, Kim, 150, Kimberly Jo, 151, Lydia, 151, Marion, 352, Mary Jane, 85, Melinda, 220, Melodie, 220, Nancy, 136, 205, Nancy J., 204, Nancy Jeanne, 344, Richard, 220, Sarah, 83, Sidney Jane, 352, Vera (Armstrong), 150, William, 150, 220, William, Jr., 220, Willis, 85

ELMORE, Abba A., 151, Abijah, 151, Absalom, 151, Albert, 152, Albert M., 299, Albert Murray, 187, 240, America Alice, 152, Andrew Matthias, 152, Annie Mariah, 152, Appleton, 152, Austin, 75, 147, Austin D., 151, Bernice, 330, Bob, 14, Brenda Lee, 152, Bun, 123, Charity, 151, Charles W., 110, Cora, 151, Dale, 203, David E., 151, David Edward, 151, Ed, 142, Edith, 188, 299 Edith L., 187, Edith Lillian, 240, Edward Mathias, 152, Elizabeth, 151, Elizabeth Jane, 152, Elsie, 151, Ethel, 299, Ethel M., 187, Ethel Maxine, 240, Eva,. 152, Fannie Ellen, 152, Grace, 152, H.H., 13, 86, Harry, 151, Helen, 291, 292, Helen Marie, 152, 291, Henry Clay, 152, Homer, 75, Homer H., 147, Homber Hubert, 151, Ina, 180, Jacob, 151, 152, Jacob Win, 152, James Alva, 151, James B., 152, 187, 240, 299, James Bion, 152, James Buchanan, 151, 152, James Byron, 152, 240, James H., 151, James Henry, 151, Jerry K., 151, Joanna Lee, 151, John Clarence, 152, Jon Patrick, 152, Julia Belle, 147, Keziah, 151, Lawrence G., 316, Leanah Mae, 151, Lee Stephens, 152, Lemoyne, 187, Lloyd, 316, Louisa, 131, Lula, 152, Lula Matilda, 187, Maggie, 123, Margaret, 299, Margaret A., 187, Margaret Angeline, 240, Marlene, 151, Marlene Mae, 151, Martha Ann, 152, Mary, 151, Mary Almeda, 152, Mary Ann, 151, 152, Mary Elizabeth, 221, Mary Julia, 151, Matthis I, 151, Matthias II, 152, Matthias III, 151, 152, Maud, 152, Minnie, 221, 270, Mollie, 123, Myrtle, 152, 153, Myrtle Ulala, 316, Nora, 152, Norman, 153, Norman Matthias, 152, Phyllis Ann, 152, Phyllis Jane, 151, Robert 152, Robert Lee, 152, Roscoe, 152, 153, Roscoe M., 291, Rose Lemoyne, 299, Rosemary L., 240, Ruby, 151, Sarah, 151, 152, Sarah J., 151, Sharon, 151, Shirley, 131, Steven, 151, 152, Sue, 142, Taylor W., 152, Thomas, 152, Ulysses, 147, Ulysses H., 151, Vonica, 142, William E., 316, __, 30

ELPERS, Erika Lynn, 346, John, 346, John Eugene, II, 346, Melinda Sue, 346

ELROD, Benjamin, 153, 281, Benjamin H., 153, 299, Benjamin Harden, 153, 144, Charles, 153, Christopher, 153, Hulda, 153, James 153, James B., 153, Jane, 153, Jane Douglas, 299, Jeremiah, 153, John, 153, Margaret Jane, 153, Martha, 153, Martha Hannah, 153, 299, Mary Susan, 153, 243, Robert, 153, Samuel K., 153, Sarah Ann, 153, Thomas, 153

ELSIE'S PLACE, 16

ELSON, Clarence, 244, Helen Maxine, 245

ELSTON, Bank & Trust Co., 373, Helen, 6, I.C., 32, Isaac, 24, 373, Isaac C., 24, 222, 337, Isaac C., (Col.), 366, 153, Isaac Compton, Jr., 153, Isaac, Jr., 225, 373, Joanna, 222, Maria, 222, 337, Sarah, 153, Susan Arnold, 337

ELY, Nancy, 116

EMERSON, Elizabeth, 338

EMERY, Elfleda, 79, George, 179

EMMERT, Elby, 93, Eula, 93, James, 93, Mildred, 149, Paul, 93

ENDICOTT, James W., 372, Janet, 205, Loral, 205, Lou, 119, Opal, 205, 206, Sarah, 258

ENENBACH, Frederick, 42

ENGLE, Brent, 31, 32

ENGLER, Brad, 252, Cheryl, 252, Don, 252, Lori, 252

ENGLISH, Edward, 192, Helen, 341, Keziah Jane, 152, Lloyd, 341, Mary Elizabeth, 192, 246, Melvina, 192, Suan, 110, William, 341

ENSLEY, James, 120

ENSMINGER, Phronia, 43, __, 42

EPLEY, Harley, 270

EPPERSON, Delores A., 375, Mary Elizabeth, 228, Verna, 250

EPPERT, Jan, 369

ERDOES, Jaki, 174

ERENBERGER, John, 131, Robin Crow, 131

ERICKSON, Bernadine Juanita, 136, Roy Wilber, 294

ERMANCE, Jacquelyn, 174

ERMENTROUT, Charles A., 110, Clara Catherine, 110, Job Joseph H., 110, Lurena, A., 110

ERNEST, James (E.J.), 107

ERNSTES, John, 324

ERWIN, Will, 152

ESHENBACH, Lisa, 125, Robert L., 125, Theresa R., 125, Virginia R., 125, Walter F., 125

ESCHTRUTH, Lena, 65

ESGATE, Julie K. Summers, 293, Sara, 294

ESCHENBACK, Elizabeth, 124

ESKEW, Rose, 132

ESTEP, Deborah Jean, 283, 324, Kiana, 324, Kristopher, 324

ETCHESON, William E. III, 26

ETTER, Addie, 269, Addie Sophraine, 147, Amelia, 285, Bert, 285, Bill, 21, 285, Ed, 50, Estella Lorraine, 269, Ford, 14, 172, Iva, 244, Jemima Angeline, 235, 269, 299, John, 285, 286, L.B., 285, Lawrence Bertram, 269, Mary Ella, 260, Mary Ellen, 269, Reba Ardell, 286, Zenith Ann, 101

EUBANK, Helen, 54, Marcia, 54

EUBANKS, Sharon L., 372

EULER, Aaron, 153, Anna, 153, Carrie, 153, Delores, 153, Harry, 153, Inez, 153, John, 153, Lucille, 153, Margita, 153, Marie, 153, Nelson C., 153, Nelson Christian, 153, Nelson F., 153, Nelson Fred, 153, Palma Delores, 153, Sherman Faye, 153

EVANS, Abbie, 142, Ben, 142, Benjamin Crabbs, 162, Benjamin Crabbs, Jr., 162, Dale, 153, 154, Dale V., 154, Daniel Fraley, 162, Dema, 232, Don G., 154, Earl, 154, Farm, 240, Frank, 49, Gary Lee, 154, Grove, 181, 239, Helen, 31, 67, Helen Hayes, 26, Hop, 154, James, 234, Jesse F., 281, Joan, 181, 239, John, 103, 181, 239, Kathy, 103, Kathy Lynne, 239, Kent (Dr.), 154, Mabel Irene, 101, Margaret, 41, 142, Mark D., 372, Mary Hannah, 342, Mildred, 153, 154, 242, Mildred C., 154, Mildred Gladys, 154, Minerva, 281, Nancy Ann, 100, Nathan Kyle, 235, Nina Dorsey, 67, Robert, 67, Robert L., 67, Ronald, 235, Ronald Richard, 154, Sue, 67, Susan, 181, Thomas, 154, Tiffany, 103, Tiffany Ann, 239, Tom, 154, __, 42, __, 82

EVENS, Anna, 130, 215]

EVERET, Anna, 215

EVERETT, Ezekiel, 74, Jonathan, 304, Lida, 304

EVERHART, Alfred, 154, 341, Cassie, 154, 155, Christian, 154, Doris, 154, 155, Earl, 155, Earl Lawrence, 155, Elmer, 154, 155, Ernest, 154, 155, Frank, 154, 155, Frank Edward, 154, Gary, 155, Helen, 155, Howard, 154, Howard Manges, 155, Howard Mangus, 154, John, 155, 341, John Tillman, 154, 155, Mabel, 154, 155, Mary, 154, 155, Norma Jean, 155, 251, Ralph, 154, 155, Reva, 155, Reva Irene, 155, Ruth, 154, 155, Theresa, 154, Tillman, 154

EVERNHAM, Byron David, 155, Harry, 70, 155, Harry W., 42, James, 155, Richard, 155, Roberta, 155, Rosemary, 155, Thomas W., 155, William, 155

EVERSON, Albert Newton, 339, Anna, 354, Caretta, 149, 293, Clyde Loraine, 339, Evelyn, 113, Evelyn L., 148, George, Sr., 43, Harold Knox, 339, James, 354, James K., 58, John, 148, Leland, 354, Leslie, 354, Margaret Dean, 100, Margaret Geraldine, 148, Mariam, 148, Miriam Geraldine, 313, Myrtle F., 340, Myrtle Frost, 339 Newt, 32, 99, Paul, 149, Paul Thomas, 148, Sadie, 58, Thomas, 282, __, 43

EWBANK, Alice, 197, Charlotte, Ann, 96, 155, Elsie, 197, Ethel Mary, 197, Florence Jeanette, 197, Helen Louise, 197, Herber, 197, John Howard, 155, John Melville, 155, Ora Milburn, 197, Ruby, 155, Wilbur Edward, 197

EWING, (Rev), 50, J.P., 58, Joe, 113, Karen Kay, 113, Mark Alan, 113, Mary Ann, 204, Matt Ryan, 113, Megan Elizabeth, 113, Monty Joe, 113, Thomas, 204, Tillie, 43, W.W., 43

EWOLDT, Janis, 86

EYLER, Beverly J., 375

FAGAN, Cathy, 230, Charlotte, 230, Gene, 230, Ida May, 230, Janet, 42, Jeff, 230, Joe, 230, Mancy, 230, Mike, 230, Scott, 230

FAIRBANK, Crawford, 32

FAIRFAX, Thomas (Lord), 122

FAIRFIELD, Janice Lee, 128, Larry, 128, Larry E., 372, Marilyn, 299

FALCONBURY, Barbara, 67

FALEN, Mary, 343

FALL, Harriett, 110

FARBER, Benjamin T., 110

FARIES, Elizabeth, 361

FARLEY, Brian Allen, 214, Delores, 42, Delores Jean, 324, Eliza, 98, Gordon, 324, Gordon Leon, 214, Henry, 98, Mary Elizabeth, 98, Sarah C., 98, Terri Jo, 214, Thomas Gordon, 214, Trent Allen, 214, Twila Kaye, 214, William, 98

FARMER, Dorothy, 211, Eli P., 49, Lydia, 253, Robert, 319, Thelma, 336, William, 265

FARMER'S SUPPLY CO., 15

FARNHAM, Charles Jacob, 185, Rebecca Ellen, 185, Richard Irving, 185

FARNSWORTH, Charity, 308, Frances, 316, 356, Frances "Fanny", 102

FARNSWORTHY, Norma Maxine, 120

FARR, Sarah, 158

FARRIS, Minnie, 191, 209

FARROW, Hattie, 233, Minnie, 233

FASCULA, Camelia, 358

FASSLER, Bertha, 103, Frank, 103

FATHERGILL, Jane, 158

FAUCINAUGH, Sue, 241

FAUST, Brianne Lauren, 155, Brittney Meredith, 155, Cynthia, 155, Edna Lorene, 155, 156, Elizabeth Ellen, 353, Ellen, 284, Ethel L., 155, Gayle, 156, George, 353, Hazel Gertrude, 354, John Peter, 155, 156, Jonathan Thomas, 155, Karen Arlene, 156, Kyler Nichole, 156, Leland, 156, Leland Woodrow, 155, 156, Leland Woorow, 156, Linda Kay, 156, Lloyd, W., 374, Lloyd Wendell, 155, 156, Matilda, 144, Mattie E., 155, Ora Warren, 155, 156, Reuben, 155, Robert Wray, 155, 156, Sarah Ann, 170, Thomas Eugene, 155

FAY, Esther Jane, 286, 304, Tom, 286, 304

FAYHEE, Judy, 252

FEARS, Virginia, 357

FEATHER, Adam, 289, Dawson, 66, Nancy, 289, Wayne, 26

FEE, Bessie Lena, 103, Bonnie Kathleen, 103, David III, 103, David Jr., 103, David M., 102, David M., Sr., 103, David Mitcheltree, 103, David, Jr., 103, Kimberly, 103, Letha Jane, 103, Mary Jane, 103, Patty, 103, Susan Ann, 103, William I., 103

FELLOW, Sarah, 344

FELLOWS, Lewis, 44

FELTNER, Denver, 67, Denver D., 261, Denver Doyel, 156, George "Bus", 353, Lou, 67, Maggie, 26, Marcella, 67, 156, Marcella N., 26, 261, Marcella Nees, 262, Marcia Claire, 156, Martha, 67, Moses Whitson, 156, Nancy Elizabeth, 156, Richard A., 156, Richard Lee, 156, Ruth Ann, 156, Susan G., 156

FENDERS, Susanna, 32

FENDLEY, Debbie, 209, Debra Kay, 84, Edward, 209, Edward Max, 84, Martha, 209, Pamela, 209, Pamela Sue, 84, Richard A., 209, Richard Allen, 84, Robert A., 357, Ruby, 357, Scott, 209

FENNER, Rozell, 115

FENTERS, Catheryn, 375

FENTSTEMAKER, William, 110

FERGUSON, Candice Marie, 157, 276, Candy, 157, Cecil, 157, Christina Lynn, 157, Christopher Michael, 147, Connie, 157, Daniel, 308, Darlene, 138, Glen, 156, 157, Glen Edward, 156, 166, Glenda Ann, 157, John, 36, Kenneth, 157, Lewis, 125, Mary, 36, Michael Steven, 157, Miranda, 360, Noah, 36, Pat, 4, 21, 157, 167, Patricia, 157, 166

FERLING, Cynthia, 231, Sarah Marie, 231, Scott, 231

FERNANDEZ, Helen, 89

FERREE, Julia, 122

FERRIS, George Wash. Gale, 286, George Washington, 286, Martha, 112, May, 193

FERTIG, Walter, 131

FESLER, Ellen, 323

FICKERSSEN, Flora, 207

FIEDLER, Charles S., 372

FIEGENSCHUE, James, 141, James Paul, 141, Meg, 141

FIELDEN, Mary, 138

FIELDS, Billy, 287, Cathy, 157, Cynthia L., 372, E.A., 205, Francie, 157, Gayle, 287, Gayle Darlene, 157, Harry, 157, Hazel, 157, Janet, 40, Janet Louise, 287, Jennie Hopkins, 157, Jerry, 157, John, 157, Kevin, 287, Kevin Wayne, 157, Lester, 157, Margaret, 108, Mary, 148, Melody Ann, 157, 287, Vivian Ruth, 287, William "Bill" Harry, 157, William "Billy", 157, William Harrison, 157, William Harry, 287, William Leslie, 157, William Lester, 287

FIFER, Roger "Tedd", 175, Sheila, 175, Sheila Gray, 175, 176, Shelly, 175, Tony, 175

FINAN, Peg Cummings, 229

FINCH, John H., 31, Morris, 50, 71

FINDELL, Ed, 101, Frances Lorene, 101, Thomas Ralph, 101, William Lee, 101

FINE, Angela, 157, Beverly, 157, 158, Chauncey, 157, 158, Chauncey M. 157, Dorothy June, 344, E.E., 260, Eric, 157, Esther, 158, Esther L., 157, Esther Ratcliff, 157, Gary, 158, Gary Steven, 157, Glora Jeanne, 157, Harry N., 260, Jesse, 157, Jesse David, 157, Joyce Ellen, 157, Kathryn Buse, 157, Melissa, 157, Roger Allen, 157, Susan, 157

FINK, Addie, 158, Adeline, 158, Alice, 158, Clarence, 158, Commodore, 158, Cyrus, 158, Ella, 158, Evan-Ivan, 158, Floyd, 158, Frances, 158, Isadore, 158, John, 158, Maria, 158, Mary, 158, Nancy, 309, Otto, 158, Ruben J., 158, Samuel, 158, Susan, 158, Thomas, 158, Willard, 158

FINLEY, Blanche, 357, Frank, 357, Harry, 357, James V., 357, John, 357, Mary Ann, 238, Nora, 357, Ola, 357, Tom, 194

FINNEY, Charles, 284, David, 69

FISCHER, John, 42, Mary, 50, Rosa, 207

FISHER, Alberta, 241, Allison, 109, Bessie Lee, 179, Brent, 174, Cory, 174, Derrek, 174, Donna Elaine, 174, Eliza Ann, 164, Eric, 109, Hallie, 332, James, 144, James Owen, 164, Jean, 165, John, 138, 144, 360, Marie, 375, Mary, 236, Merle, 241, Michelle, 109, 110, Myrtle, 263, Phoebe, 176, 339, Ruth, 67, Sally, 259, Samuel, 164, W. Scott, 109, William, 332

FISHERO, Alva, 151, Jennie, 151, John, 50, Mary, 50, Ruby Marie, 151

FISK, Roger, 51

FITHIAN, William, 91

FITZWATER, Carol, 127, Eva Darlene, 251, 332, Newton T., 251, Newton Tyler, 332, Sandra Kay, 273

FLAKE, Phyllis, 203

FLANDERS, Augustus L., 98, Mary Marguerite, 98

FLANIGAN, Ben, 373, Kathleen Luella, 245, Meredith, 245

FLANINGAM, Albert, 158, Alta, 158, Andrew Jackson, 158, Archibald, 158, Caroline, 185, DeVon, 158, Dwight, 158, Edward, 158, Flora, 158, Forrest, 158, Fred, 158, George, 158, Harold, 158, Homer, 158, Ida Catherine, 158, Ira, 158, Jack, 158, James, 158, Jasper, 158, John, 158, John Archibald, 158, Julian, 158, Lafayette, 158, Luella, 158, M.L., 158, Martha Ellen, 158, 332, Mary Ellen, 332, Nellie, 158, 280, Nellie Maye, 158, Norman, 158, Oliver, 158, Ruth, 158, Ora L., 158, Samuel, 158, Wallace Clinton, 158, Walter, 158, Ward, 158, William, 158

FLANINGGAM, DeVon, 357, Dewight, 356, Forrest C., 356, Ida Catherine, 356

FLANNIGAN, Emma, 100

FLESHER, Ellen, 294

FLETCHER, Alexander, 159, Alma, 279, Aurelius, 159, Charles, 159, Charles Robert, 159, Clydia, 189, Deborah, 215, Dorothy, 279, Easter, 161, Emery Luse, 159, Foster, 159, Foster A., 159, 343, Foster Alexander, 158, 333, Gary David, 159, Geneva, 158, Herber, 279, Horatio, 159, Ida E., 159, Iva J., 159, J., 272, John, 164, 341, John, Sr., 32, Joseph Alexander, 158, Kenneth, 341, Lida, 63, Lillie Ann, 220, Lillie Anna, 159, 333, Mabel A., 159, Mamie, 127, Margery Dee, 159, Marguerite Ellen, 343, Marguerite, 159, Mark Allen, 159, Martha G., 331, Martha Glee, 159, Mary, 223, Mary Catherine, 158, 159, 333, Mary F., 199, Mary Frances, 159, Max, 233, Max A., 159, Max Alexander, 159, Merle Alexander, 159, Nancy, 341, Paschal Earl, 159, Rasco Russell, 159, Russell

R., 343, Ruth Naomi, 159, Sarah H., 158, Sarah Helen, 159, Walter, 331, Walter David, 159, Winifred, 346, Winslow, 159
FLICK, Connie, 259, Margaret, 358, Variety Store, 15
FLINT, Harlan, 131, James, 342, Jean, 216, Jo, 342, Margaret, 216, Margaret Kirk, 216, Mary Jane, 342, 361, Sophia H., 261
FLOCKER, William J., 296
FLORA, Kurt A., 372
FLOWERS, Bee, 296, Ralph (Mrs.), 296
FLOYD, Emerson Ames, 133
FLYNN, Edward M., 372, Sarah, 182
FOLLICK, Etta, 110, Maria, 354, Marion, 319
FOLTZ, Ella, 267, Ethel M, 286
FOOTE, Carolina, 79
FORBES, Nancy, 279
FORD, Carolyn, 268, Christina, 268, Flora, 158, Lisa, 316, Lori S., 372, Paul, Jr., 268, Ruth, 271
FORDICE, Betty, 285, David, 285
FORDYCE, Abraham, 261, Cyrus, 261, Elizabeth, 262, Hanna, 261, Julia Ann, 261
FOREMANE, Andrew, (Capt.), 201
FOREMENT, Jessie, 149
FORGEY, Sarah, 242
FORREST, Edgar Dale, 164, Edgar Dale, Jr., 164
FORSYTHE, James Harvey, 216
FOSCETT, Leona, 356
FOSTER, __, 22, Angela Dawn, 203, Anna Ruth, 211, Bertie Lee, 227, Buel T., 79, Catherine, 197, David Sloane, 271, Dorothy Lou, 159, Eliza "Josephine", 173, Elizabeth, 284, 353, Florence Edith, 319, Glayds, 159, H.A., 110, Henry Allen, 227, Henry Lee, 159, James, 319, James Thomas, 159, Jess, 40, John, 12, 30, John, (Rev.) 79, John A., 203, John H., 52, John Thomas, 203, John Timothy, 203, Jon, 106, Jon L., 159, 372, Lawrence, 31, 40, Lee, 159, Lela, 52, Lucinda, 319, Maria Jane, 203, Marjory, 242, Mary Virginia, 106, 159, Nadene, 293, Norman, 342, Paul R., 242, Peggy, 271, 380, Peter, 203, Preston, 342, Royce, 271, Sallie, 74, Sarah Ann, 79, Scott, 271, Shannon, 271, Sherry Lee, 106, 159, Tamara Kim, 203, Teresa Kay, 203, Wesley, 34, Woodford, 79, __, 42
FOSTER'S REPAIR SERVICE, 16
FOUTS, Amos, 161, C.D., 160, Carrie, 134, 160, Charels, 123, Charles D., 160, Charles Denman, 159, 160, Claude, 123, 160, Claude Jackson, 159, 160, Cora, 123, Cora M., 160, 161, David, 161, Eli, 161, Florence, 160, George, 161, Gordon Phillip, 160, Halcy, 160, 161, Halcy L., 160, Holcy L., 159, Ilah, 123, 159, 160, Jacob, 161, James, 160, James Michael, 160, James W., 160, James William, 159, 160, Jehu, 161, Jim, 160, Joanna Morrow, 159, John, 161, John D., 160, John Denman, 160, 161, Joseph, 159, 160, 161, Joseph Leon, 160, 160, Karen Ann, 160, Leon, 160, Leslie J., 159, 160, Letha, 160, Letha Irene, 160, Levi, Jr., 161, Levi, Sr., 161, Linda Lou, 160, Lydia, 161, Malinda, 161, Mary, 124, Nathan, 161, Rilla J., 160, 161, Roscoe, 123, 160, Roscoe Cord, 159, 160, Sarah Ellen, 160, 161, Susannah, 161, William 160, 161
FOWLER, Belinda, 208, Chilsey Leigh, 161, Cyrus Moore, 220, Edward R., 161, Florence Todd, 161, Gary, 103, Grandma', 114, Ike, 333, Isaac Samuel, 333, Jane, 103, 231, Jason Edward, 161, Jesse, 350, Joan, 103, John Thomas, 161, Joshua Davis, 220, Letha Jane, 103, Mae, 333, Mary, 350, Mary Emily, 350, Nancy Ann, 220, Robert Lee, 161, Ursa, 186, William Gary, 103
FOX, Linda L., 372, Lisa Lynn, 278, Marjorie, 82, Richard, 74, Ronald E., 372, Sharon K., 375
FOXWORTHY, Alice (Shaver), 31, Amy, 161, Amy Jo, 252, Carole Anne, 252, Charles, 161, Enoch, 161, Fredric, 161, Gloria, 161, George, 161, James, 161, John, 33, 161, 252, John M., 161, Mary Joan, 161, Rhoda Jane, 123, Stanley, 161, Viola, 161
FOXWORTHY VARIETY STORE, 15
FOYE, Randall, 118
FOYT, A.J., 275
FRAIZIER, Ruth, 299
FRAKES, Edith, 92
FRALEY, A.S., 381, Arthur Stanton, 162, Caroline, 162, Charles, 162, Daniel, 162, Elmira, 162, Floyd Dunkle, 162, Frank, 162, Fredrick, 162, Henry, 162, Henry Clay, (Rev)., 162, Jacob, 162, John, 162, Laura, 162, Maud, 162, May, 162, Rebecca, 162, Rebecca Jane "Becky", 162, Ruth, 162, Theodore, 162, W.L., 374, William, 162, William M., 63
FRAME, __, 22, Charles, 323, Clara, 116, Emma, 176, George, 149, Henrietta, 323, Lizzie, 196, Mary Jane, 177, William, 236
FRANCE, Annie, 224, Arthur Ray, 162, 224, Carlos, 224, Carlos Washington, 162, Carrie, 162, Connie Sue, 162, David Eugene, 162, James Matthew, 162, James Russell, 162, Layne Matthew, 224, Nellie, 224, Pete, 162, 224, Ray, 224, Rayan, 224, Robert Earl, 162, Sandra Lee, 162, Terry Joe, 162
FRANCIS, Bessie, 162, Chris, 127, David, 127, Debbie, 127, Elizabeth, 162, Evelyn Cox, 355, Fred, 162, George, 332, George F., 67, Grace B., 162, Iva, 162, Jan, 127, Jane, 332, Jeff, 127, Jesse, 162, Keri, 127, Kimberly, 127, Lewis, 127, Mary, 261, 332, Mike, 127, Pam, 127, Patricia, 127, 355, Penelope, 127, Penny, 355, Phillip, 127, 355, Randy, 127, Sally, 127, Scott, 127, Thomas J., 162, William T., 162
FRANK, John, 56, Margaaret, 241
FRANKEBARGER, Elizabeth, 176, 177, 196
FRANKEBERGER, Rosalie Jane, "Rose", 105
FRANKLIN, Alan, 121, David, 121, F.C., 69, Flora Josephine, 156, Guy T., 375, Lillie, 134, Michael, 121, Scott, 121, Sophia, 69
FRANTZ, Christian I, 162, Christian IV, 162, Clara, 162, Elizabeth Ann, 162, Frank, 162, George, 105, 123, 162, 352, George F., 162, Jennie Brookshire, 162, John Frank, 162, Leona Ellen, 162, Magadaline, 354, Magdaline, 162, Maria Elizabeth, 354, Matthias, 162, May, 162, Michael III, 354, Sallie, 162, Sarah Jane, 162, Sarah Louise, 162, Valletta, 162, William, 123, 162, 352, William H., 162, William M., 162, 163
FRASER, Elsie, 98, John E., 212, William, 98
FRAVEL, __, 213
FRAZER, Mary, 89
FRAZIER, Christopher P., 156, Jeffrey A., 156, Keith N., 156, Mary, 332, William K., 156
FRAZZEE, Jane Bonnell, 355
FREDERICI, Linda, 317
FREDERICK, Bertie, 163, Charlie, 163, Corenia, 163, Doris, 94, 163, 272, Martha, 163, Oscar, 163, Ruth, 104, 163, Sarah, 163
FREDERICK'S BICYCLE REPAIR, 26
FREDERICKS, Judith, 122
FREE, Elaine, 272, Gladys Marie, 272, James Orvin, 272
FREED, (Rev.), 50, T.J., 69
FREEDMAN, __, 301
FREEMAN, __, 22, Jennie, 230, Mary, 145
FREES, Angela Renee, 164, Bob, 163, Carleton, 163, Carrie, 163, Gale Lamar, 163, George C., 163, George Carthenas, 163, Gladys, 163, Gwen, 141, 164, Gwendolyn, 163, Jack, 141, Jacob, 163, James Lee, 164, Jesse Joan, 163, John Webster, 163, Joseph A., 163, Lydia, 163, Margaret, 163, Marietta, 163, Martha, 163, Mary, 163, Paul Edgar, 163, Peter, 163, Robert J., 163, 164, Robert James, 163, Samantha, 163, Steven W., 372, Suzanne, 164, Suzanne Kay, 164, Vada, 164, Vada Lavonne, 164
FREMDER, Jason K., 176, Manred W., 176, Marilyn S., 176, Matthew P., 176, Michael J., 176
FRENCH, Adam Miller, 164, Alforetta, 164, Alfred, 164, Alonzo Lewis, 164, Alta, 189, Andrew, 164, Ann, 164, Benjamin, 164, Charles Basil, 164, Charlotte, 164, Clarence, 164, Claude, 164, Clyde, 164, Daniel, 164, Dick, 165, E. Edwin, 164, Earl, 12, Earl, Sr., 164, Edna Aloretta, 165, Elizabeth, 164, Elmer Edgar, 164, Elsie Odessa, 165, Ernest, Sr., 164, Evert Thomas, 164, Gladys, 164, Hazel, 164, Helen, 164, Hewitt, 164, James, 164, Jane, 164, Jeremiah, 164, John, 164, Laura, 164, 359, Lot, 164, Martha, 164, Mary, 164, Mary "Polly", 164, Melissa Alice LaBaw, 145, Myron Andrew, 165, Nancy, 189, Opal, 164, Paul, 164, Phenamy "Amy", 164, Ralph, 164, Rick W., 372, Sarah, 164, Susan, 164, Sylvia, 164, Thomas, 189, William, 164
FRESHOUR, Margaret, 261
FRETH, Karen, 290
FREY, William, 297
FRIARS, Anthony Jason, 165, Bradley Ryan, 165, Dorothy, 165, George, 165, James Michael, 165, Jim, 165, Kristy, 165, Linda, 165, Matthew Allen, 165, Mike, 165, Nancy, 165
FRICK, Jack, 56, 63
FRIEND, Arthur, 124, Branden, 165, Buford, 124, Catherine J., 165, Cathy, 165, Dave, 165, David Lowell, 165, Edna, 124, Effie M., 124, Effie May, 124, Ellis, 124, Ellis C., 165, Elva Clyde, 294, Elva Sanders, 323, Ethel, 124, Etta M., 165, Eva, 124, Everett, 124, Fannie, 165, James, 282, John, 165, Lowell E., 165, Manford, 124, Mary Ann, 124, Mary Florence, 294, Nellie, 124, Opal, 124, Pauline, 124, Ralph, 282, Sally Jo, 165, Theodore, 124, 165, Waneta, 124, William, 294
FRISZ, Blanche M., 166, Clarence W., 166, Elizabeth, 166, Ethel F., 166, F. Leo, 166, Fabian J., 166, Helen J., 166, Joseph, 11, 166, Joseph W., 165, 166, Paul C., 166, Wilfred P., 166
FRITTER, Catherine, 339, Enoch, 339, Julia, 339
FRITTS, Pearl M., 119
FRNTZ, Matthias, 177
FROEDGE, Cynthia Rene, 283
FROSS, Clara, 309
FROST, Ida Louise, 133, James Elsworth, 174
FRUITS, "Alamo" George, 166, 168, "Alamo" George, Jr., 167, Aaron, 168, Alonzo, 310, Alonzo James, 167, Ambrose, 184, Anna Jean, 256, Ashley, 168, Barbara, 167, Bud, 260, Burl, 108, Carl, 310, Catherine, 166, 167, Cathryn, 273, Charles, 157, 166, 167, 310, Charles M., 157, 166, 167, 310, Charles Ray, 166, 167, Christine G., 168, Christopher, 168, Colleen, A., 168, Cora Effie, 184, Daisy, 166, 189, Dan, 273, 274, David, 167, Delmar H., 166, Delmar K., 167, 168, Delph, 148, Delpha, 148, Dema K., 167, 168, Denna R., 167, Dennis R., 167, 168, Dianna R., 168, Donald Roger, 166, Elanor Ruth, 166, Elizabeth, 167, Elsie, 311, Evelyn, 310, Fred, 39, 166, Fred E., 167, George, 21, 166, 167, 168, 312, George III, 167, 184, George Jr., 166, 167, 184, 273, George Keith, 167, Geroge William, 273, Gladys, 310, Grace, 157, 166, Grace A., 167, Grace Juanita, 166, 167, Hadley, 273, Hadley, Jr., 273, Herbert, 157, Herbert M., 167, Herbert Merritt, 166, Jacob, 167, James L., 167, 168, Janice Sue, 166, Jason, 168, Jeffrey L., 168, Jerusha Huff, 184, Jessie, 311, John, 166, 167, 310, John S., 167, John William, 167, Jonathan, 148, 167, 212, Kathy Arlene, 274, Lagora, 310, Laura, 273, Lenora, 157, Lewis D., 166, 167, 168, Lewis N., 166, 167, Lydia Ann, 167, Margaret, 167, Marietta, 157, 167, Martha, 148, Martha Roselyn, 168, Martin, 167, Mary, 157, 167, Mary Teresa, 166, McCormick Cemetery, 167, Merrietta, 166, Merrit J., 167, Merritt, 166, Michael, 167, Nellie Lee, 166, 167, Noah, 157, 166, 167, Ollie, 148, Ollie G., 148, 167, 168, Opal, 148, 168, 212, Pat, 157, 167, Patricia, 167, Patricia Ann, 157, 166, Ralph, 157, 167, Ralph D., 166, Rebecca, 167, Richard, 273, 274, Rita Jo, 166, Rozella, 148, 167, 212, Russell L., 167, 168, Ruth, 157, 167, 273, Sabastian, 167, Sandra M., 168, Sarah, 167, Shirley, 166, 168, Shirley D., 167, 168, Sondra Jean, 166, Sue, 273, 274, Susan, 166, 167, Susan Lenora, 167, Teresa D., 168, Thelma, 157, 167, Thelma Lenora, 166, Verda M., 167, 168, William, 167
FRY, Ann Elizabeth, 107, Barbara Joan, 106, Christopher, 270, Clifford H., 107, Edith E., 107, Edith Eileen, 106, Frank, 54, Gregory Clifford, 107, Hiram, 107, Jean, 54, Jeremy, 270, Jessie Leona, 107, Mary Elizabeth, 107, Michael, 270, Noble, 107, Noble Cassell, 106, Phillip Lynn, 106, Ralph Cassell, 106
FRYE, Alma Joyce, 103, John T., 29, Steve, 192
FRYER, Elizabeth, 298, Sarah Ann, 298
FUESTEL, Cathy, 112, Terry, 112
FUGATE, Carl, 224, David Keith, 300, Geneva, 284, Joshua David, 300, Kimberly Ann, 300, Zachary Dane, 300, Zelma, (Miss), 314
FULENWIDER, David, 74, Lucinda, 257
FULFORD, Alan Harris, 168, Clint, 169, Clinton, 205, Clinton Harris, 168, David, 169, David Clinton, 168, David Thomas, 169, Donna Kay, 168, Dorothy, 169, 205, Dorothy Hughes, 168, Kathy, 169, Lana Lee, 168, Phyllis Lynn, 168, Kathleen Henderson, 168
FULK, Roberta, 96
FULLENWINDER, Benjamin, 169, Betty, 169, Betty L., 147, Betty Lou, 169, Carolann, 169, Chalmers, 169, Daniel, 169, Daniel Newton, 169, David, 144, 169, Digna, 169, Douglas, 169, Eleazer, 169, Eleazor, 79, Elizabeth, 144, Glenn, 124, 169, Henry C., 169, Henry Newton, 147, 169, J. Newton, 169, J.N., 365, Jacob, 169, James, 169, James Scott, 169, Lavinia, 169, Lena, 169, 286, Mary Elizabeth, 144, Mary Emma, 144, Mathew, 169, Newton, 169, Robert, 169, 286, Robert E., 169, Robert Elliot, 147, Roberta, 169, Samuel, 144, Sarah, 169, Stephanie, 169, Terry, 147, 169, W. Terry, 147, Wallace "Terry", 169, William, Jr., 169, Winter, 144
FULLER, Betsy, 259
FULLILOVE, Anthony, 201
FULLWIDER, John A., 29
FULTZ, Edith, 375
FULWIDER, Andrew, 169, Arlie, 169, Ben, 169, Benjamin, 169, Bettie, 118, 169, 170, Bettie I., 169, Betty, 306, Billy Joe, 170, Bud 118, Elijah, 169, Elizabeth, 83, 169, Eva May, 117, Fred, 118, 169, Fredrick, 169, 170, Gaynell, 118, 169, 170, George Walter, 170, Georgia, 117, Georgiana, 117, 118, 169, Georgianna, 169, Glenn, 169, Jacob, 117, 169, Jacob H., 169, James, 169, James D., 372, Jeanne, 296, Joe, 118, John, 169, John Alvin, 170, Joseph, 117, 169, 170, Joseph H., 169, Joseph Henry, 169, Lee Ann, 358, Leota, 169, Louisa, 169, Maggie, 169, Margaret, 169, Mary, 169, Orville, 169, Oville 'Bud', 169, 170, Paul, 169, Robert 169, Sallie, 169, Sarah Houff, 117, Sarah Jane, 169, Ulrich, 169, Walter, 170, Walter A., 169, William, 169
FUNK, Caroline, 186, Laura, 43
FUNKHOUSER, __, 213
FUQUA, Mary Margaret, 215
FURMAN, Albert G., 344, Sarah, 344
FURR, Dawn, 205, Dennis, 205, John Erreet, 342, Nancy Pearl, 342, Pearl, 361, Stella, 205, William, 205
FYFFE, Ruth, 135
GABRIEL, Amanda, 329
GALBREATH, John David, 107, 344, Mary Ann, 150
GALEY, __, 22, Albert Smith, 170, America, 60, Benjamin, 310, Eliza, 225, Elizabeth M., 102, Fisher, 13, James, 60, John Vanice, 170, Mabel Lee, 221, Mary, 60, Nellie, 12, 112, Sally, 52, Samuel Smith, 170, Sarah Matilda, 170, Thomas M., 310, __, 42
GALLAWAY, James, 335
GALLION, Connie Maye, 226, Roy, 226, Tracy Ellyn, 226
GALLODAY, Isaac, 45
GALLOWAY, Charles, 14, 165, Frances Ellen, 165, Goldie, 165, Robert Herron, 165, William, 165
GAMBLE, Mary, 316
GANGWER, Aaron, 157, Gloria, 158, Gloria Jeanne, 157, Jeremy, 157, Steve, 158, Steven, 157
GANNON, Myron, 164
GANT, Bertha May, 216, Debbie, 348, Iva, 211
GARD, Hanna, 261
GARDNER, Alyssa, 170, Ben, 170, Bethia, 268, Cora Anna, 170, Earl, 170, Earl Barton, 289, Earl, Jr., 170, Effie, 302, Eliab, 268, Frank, 170, Frank E., 372, Fred, 302, Gary, 170, Hannah, 268, Jack, 170, James A., 63, Jane, 170, Jill, 170, Joseph, 268, Lorraine, 170, M. Elizabeth, 170, Mary, 170, 303, Mason, 170, Miriam, 268, Molly, 170, Nancy Ann, 289, Neal, 170, Phyllis, 170, Roger 170, Sarah, 268, Thomas, 170, Tracy, 170, Wayne, 170, Wayne Penn, 170
GARITY, Coleen, 335
GARLOCK, & Gibson's Hardware, 15
GARNER, Clair Irene, 103, 104, 170, 303, Elais, 170, Fannie, 125, Irene, 103, Iris, 102, John Albert, 170, Myrtie, 170, Robert, 102, 104, Robert Allen, 170, 303, Sherman, 303, Sherman R., 103, Sherman Ross, 170, Virginia, 170, William G., 170
GARNET, Sarah, 138
GARR, Michael E., 372
GARRARD, Earlene L., 375
GARRETSON, Martha, 129, Mary, 129
GARRETT, Carolyn, 171, Corliss, 171, Donald 171, Dora, 170, Emma, 185, Harry, 171, Harry Taylor, 171, Janice, 171, Jason, 171, Julie Suzette, 170, Lezlie Rene, 171, Megan, 171, Richard, 170, Richard Allen I, 171, Richard Allen II, 170, Ryan, 171, Sheila, 171, Terri Lee, 185, Todd, 171, Verna, 171, Wayne, 171, William, 171
GARRIGUES, S., 41
GARRIOTT, Daisy, 171, Harold, 171, Hilda, 85, Mary Lou, 171, 323, Michael, 171, Sandra, 171, Susan, 171, Zannie Zaring, 171
GARRISON, Estella Mae, 329, Michael T., 372
GARVER, Christopher Wayne 245, Claude, 328, Claude Estee, 328, Emma, 141, Ira Alvin, 328, Jerry, 131, Mary Josephine, 328, Maude Daisy, 328, Robert James, 245, Sarah Josephine, 328, Staci Dawne, 245, William R., 141
GARVEY, John, 353, Lucy, 353, Nancy, 353
GARZA, Maria Dela, 140
GASS, Daniel, 171, Deborah "Susie", 171, Edna, 171, James "Pete", 171, John R., 171, Kenneth, 25, 171, Landon Turnan, 171, Mary, 247, Sharon, 171, Sylvia, 171, Tilman, 20, Vickie, 171
GATES, Jason L., 372, Tin Shop, 14
GATTS, Elizabeth, 309
GAUSE, Garnet, 164
GAYHART, Andrew, 29, Katherine, 354
GAYLER, Judith, 243, Judy, 366
GAYLOR, Larry, 131, Mary, 261
GEARHART, Mamie E., 164
GEE, A.A., 49
GEGNER, Charles Luce, 203, Charlotte Leona, 203, Jennifer, 169, Kristin, 169, Roberta, 169
GEIGER, Clara, 158, Jana, 212, Katherine, 212, Roy E., 372
GEMMELL, Nellie, 328
GENTRY, Debbie, 174, Elijah, 205, Helen, 108, James, 172, Kayla, 172, Lorna, 205, Martha, 168, Ruby, 205, Ryan, 172, Stephen D., 372
GENUNG, Joe, 74
GEORGE, Kris, 235, Reuben James, 235
GEPHART, Betty Myrle, 243
GERARD, Dave, 227, David, 24, E., 68, Family, 94
GERBOTH, Stanley, 59
GERLACK, Maria, 124
GEROLD, Gregg A., 372
GHORMLEY, Lela, 43

GIANNA, Christine, 137
GIBBONS, — (Dr), 337, Sarah, 331
GIBBS, Barry L., 372, Mary A., 375
GIBSON, Barber Shop, 14, Bobby D., 315, Golda, 278, Marilyn, 117, Ruth M., 113
GICK, Janet, 271
GIDDINGS, Helen, 341
GILASBY, James, 179, 180
GILBERT, Albert Earl, 228, Andrew Earl, 228, Charley, 30, Ferrell, 347, Karl, 228, Kate, 347, Kathy, 228, Kenneth, 347, Margaret, 193, Martha, 347, Opal, 347, Rebecca, 129
GILKEY, Addie May, 241, Clarence, 166, Daniel, 43, Gertrude Brown, 241, Henrietta, 335, John R., 241, Samuel, 310, Sarah E., 331
GILKEY'S, Mill, 20
GILKISON, Lenore Violet, 259, Violet, 259
GILL, Eliza, 208, 302, Jonathan, 285, Phyllis M., 372, Ray, 286, Sarah Margaret, 285, Sythe Ingram, 285, __, 55
GILLAN, Carl Richard, 214, James Richard, 214, Vicki Ann, 214
GILLAND, Carrie, 182, Earl, 182, Harvey, 182, Margaret, 281
GILLESPIE, Harry 314, Robert, 314, 315
GILLIE, Margaret, 260
GILLILAN, Alice R., 372
GILLILAND, Brad, 155, Earl, 252, Grace, 252, Harold, 155, Harold "Heck", 252, Herman, 252, James, 252, Jay D., 155, Joe, 252, 309, John 252, John (Mrs), 252, Martha, 252, Roberta, 155, Samuel, 356, 357, Sarah Amanda, 164, Sherman, 252, Sue, 252
GILLIS, Charles, 319, John, 282, Joseph, 360, Martha, (Mattie), 360
GILLMORE, Isica, 95
GILLOGLY, April, 172, Bertha, 171, Betty, 172, Bryce, 172, Cheryl, 172, Christa, 113, 172, Christa Hazell, 259, Corey, 113, 172, Corey Lee, 259, Don, 42, Donald, 259, Donald Lee, 172, Donna, 172, 277, Donna Lynne, 259, Edward, 172, Hannah, 171, Helen Louise, 172, Hugh, 171, Jakota, 172, Jenna, 172, John, 171, John D., 171, Lawrence, 113, 172, Lawrence Vane, 259, Mary Ann, 171, Mealie, 172, Michael, 172, Milton "Bill", 172, Miriam, 172, Orville Vane, 171, Pandi, 172, Para Lee, 172, Rebecca, 172, Rhonda, 172, Rickie, 172, Robert, 172, Robert Morris, 172, Ronald Wayne, 172, Ruby Irene, 172, Sandra, 259, Sandy, 172, Sarah, 171, Silas, 171, 172, Silas Wayne, 172, Terri, 172, Thomas, 171, Vera Naomi, 300, Wayne, 172, Zachary, 172
GILLS, Ray O., 286
GILMAN, Susannah, 125
GILMORE, Charles, 22, Harold, 79, Margaret, 79
GILSTRAP, Janet L., 375, Richard A., 372
GINGRICH, Anna, 354
GINN, Teresa Kay, 259
GINSBERG, Alayne, 94
GISH, Jonas T., 29, 40, Mary, 236, William, 196
GIST, Deborah, 164
GIVENS, Margaret "Peggy", 129, Samuel, 129
GLASCOCK, Barry, 172, Bill, 172, Dean, 172, Jake, 172, 277, Jane, 172, Pauline, 172, Rose, 86, 172, 277, Rose Mary, 172, Samuel, 119, Thomas A., 172, Todd, 172, William Dean, 172
GLASOCK, Dawn, 172
GLASSMAN, Eunice, 297
GLASSWAY, Elizabeth Ann, 163, Peter, 163
GLATFELDER, __, 241
GLATTFELDER, Casper, 241, John Peter, 241
GLAWSON, William, 294
GLAZE, Amanda, 174, Mary Flo, 174, Yantz, 174
GLEASON, Kenneth E., 295
GLEN, Flossie, 272
GLENN, Augusta, 172, Elizabeth, 183, 172, Eveline H., 149, Frances, 347, Francis, 172, Henry Littleton, 172, James Littleton, 172, Lorena, 169, 172, Margaret Ann, 172, Marguerite, 172, Martha, 149, Mary, 136, 286, Mary Elizabeth, 172, Mary Frances, 172, Thomas, 149, 172, Thomas L., 248, Tyre, 172 William, 144, William Thomas, 172
GLIM, Bernard Lewis, 100, Bernard Robert, 100, Diane Lee, 100, Elizabeth 67, Pamela Elizabeth, 100, Ruth Elizabeth, 100
GLOSSER, John, 58
GLOSSIN, Ruth, 322
GLOVER, Alexzander, 173, Alice, 173, Blanche, 265, Blanche Parker, 173, Charles, 173, Foster, 265, Harry, 323, John M., 173, Laird, 207, 274, Mabel, 43, Martha, 173, 265, Mary, 173, Newton J., 173, Patrica Lee, 173, Patricia, 265, Robert, 173, Robert "Foster", 173, Robert Edward, 173, 265, Robert Joseph, 173, Stephen, 173, Uriah, 173, __, 32, __, 55
GOBEL, Daniel 283, Matilda, 283
GOBEN, Susan, 256
GOBLE, Ann, 283, Catherine, 283, Daniel, 163, 283, David, 283, Eizabeth, 163, 283, Ellen, 283, Hiram, 283, Martin, 283, Phopebe, 221, Susan, 163, 283
GODFREY, Samuel, 64, 67
GOES, Vander Antonides, 358, Vincentues, 358
GOETLING, Rosemary, 112
GOETZ, Janet Crousher, 156, Kevin, 156, Kimberly, 156
GOFF, Bertha, 80, 223, Bertha Leota, 223, Charles B., 375, Cora, 223, Edward, 223, Florence, 209, George W., 80, Ida, 223, John, 209, Mary 223, Merle, 223, Ray, 223, Robert 12, Stillman, 223, Susanna, 266, Tillie, 43
GOFORTH, Mike, 148
GOHMAN, Alma, 173, Alma Ruth, 173, Ann Elizabeth, 173, Anna, 173, Betty, 199, Blanche, 173, Cara "Carrie", 173, Catherine, 173, Charles, 173, Clara, 173, Clara Belle, 173, Cora Belle, 173, Dorothy, 173, Dorothy Helen, 173, Earl, 173, Elizabeth, 173, Emma, 132, 173, Emma Elizabeth, 173, Estella, 173, Estella Evelyn, 174, Esther, 173, 199, 320, Esther Pearl, 173, Ethel, 173, Ethel Fern, 173, Florence, 173, Henry, 173, John, 173, Joseph, 199, Joseph John, 173, 320, Margaret, 173, 320, Margaret Catherine, 173, 199, Mary, 173, Minnie, 320, Minnie Florence, 320, Rea, 199, Richard, 173, Thodore, Jr., 173, Thodore, Sr., 173, Vera, 173, Vera Lucille, 173, Walter, 173, Willie, 173, 199
GOLDEN, June, 112, Michael James, 194
GOLFORTH, Michael, 69
GOLLADAY, John F., 336, Samuel, 336
GOLLIDAY, Melissa, 108
GOLLIHER, Joseph, 317, Sarah, 317, Stephen, 317
GOMMELM, Esther Mariam, 149, Jessie, 149, Olin, 149
GONZALES, Ada M., 141, Frank, 141, Rosa Mercedes, 254
GOOD, Adda, 174, Alice, 174, Alva Francis, 174, Andrea, 174, Brothers Bus, 14, Craig Michael, 174, Debbie, 174, Della Frances, 174, 192, Eden Aurora, 174, Elizabeth, 174, Elizabeth A., 174, Estella Imogene, 174, Evelyn Elizabeth, 174, Ezra, 174, George, 174, George, E., 174, Ireneus, 174, 192, Jacquelyn Ann, 174, Jaki, 174, Jesse, 174, John (Rev), 174, John Jeffrey, 174, John Mathew, 174, John Mathew, Jr., 174, Joy Ann, 174, Kenneth John (Dr), 174, Linda Ann, 174, Linda Louise, 174, Margaret, 192, Marilla, 174, Martha Jane, 174, 192, Mary, 174, 222, Michael B., 174 Mike, 174, Nellie, 174, Neva, 174, Olus Edna, 174, Ora Eugene, 174, Rebecca, 174, Ron, 174, Ruby, 383, Samuel (Rev), 174, Shannon Larissa, 174, Susanna, 174, Terry Lee, 174, Theodore, 174, Thomas Samuel, 174, Tiffany Ellyn, 174, William 274
GOODBAR, __, 22, Bell, 341, John, 209, John Harvey, 201, Malinda, 209, Rachel, 209, Tessora Hortense, 323, Walter, 323
GOODE, Lucille, 208, Phillip R., 372
GOODENOUGH, Jane, 118
GOODIN, Benjamin, 163, Carleton, 163, Lydia, 163, Tug, 13
GOODING, Diana Lynn, 245, Mary 164, 277, Ray, 277, Robert, 277, Roger, 277, Susan, 277
GOODMAN, Department Store, 78
GOODMAN'S, Dept. Store, 165
GOODNIGHT, Cynthia, 351, Edith, 99, Joel, 294
GOODPASTOR, Colgeth, 104
GOODWIN, Georgia, 79
GORDON, Ann B. Dickeson, 294, Charlotte, 256, Elizabeth, 326, James, 294, James Smith, 294, Mary Joh, 294, Samantha Ellen, 294
GORE, Michael, 64, 70
GORHAM, Sarah, 294
GORMAN, Brenda, 142, Harold, 142, Louise, 142
GORMLEY, Mr., 314
GOSE, Elizabeth, 107
GOSHORN, Edith, 174, Ezra N., 174, Ezra Nicholas, 174, Irene Marie, 175, John Herschel, 175, Judith Marie, 175, Lewis, 21, 175, Lewis J., 174, Louis, 14, Lula, 174, Ramon Riley, 175, Robert Robison, 174, Roland Henry, 175, Ruth Elinor, 175
GOSNER, Lloyd, 236
GOSS, Ada, 175, Alfred Eli, 175, Alva John, 175, Benjamin, 175, Betsy, 175, Daniel, 175, Daivd, 175, Elisha, 175, Ephriam, 175, Ephriam A., 175, Floyd, 175, Fredrick, 175, Fredrick, Jr., 175, George, 175, Iva Jane, 175, Jacob, 175, John, 175, John C., 175, Joseph, 175, Joseph A., 175, Margaret M., 175, Martha, 310, Mary, 175, Mary Ann, 175, Mary Susan, 175, Norman Dale, 175, Pansy, 175, S.W., 49, Steven Todd, 175, Thomas Halbert, 175, Timmy Lee, 175, Tony Alan, 175, Ula Frank, 175, Ula Frank, Jr., 175, Verna, 175
GOTO, Mitsuya, 338
GOTT, Bertha Smith, 175, Charley, 175, Eliza Jane, 60, Elizabeth, 351, Elizabeth D., 332, Ferdinand, 225, Harry 175, Jessie, 175, Mary, 175, Nancy J., 351, Neva, 165, Thomas, 351, Widow, 108, William, 141, 175, William Northcutt, 295, Wilson, 225
GOTTSCHALL, Funeral Home, 14
GOULD, Chad, 92, Jennifer, 92, Kenneth, P., 92, Ryan, 92, Spencer Flowers, 315
GRABMAN, Mary Magdeline, 298
GRAEF, Richard, 56
GRAHAM, Becky McKinney, 54, Belva Mae, 215, Department Store, 40, 297, Forgus, 109, George, 310, John, 215, Juanita, 43, Kevin, 336, Luella, 266, 341, Mabel Marie, 121, 215, Margaret, 109, Ralph W., 49, Rebecca, 54, Ruth Mariah, 99, 215, William, 49, 266, William (Rev), 48, __, 13
GRAMMER, Katherine, 176
GRAN, Susan, 246
GRANT, Elizabeth, 87, Hiram, 287, Ulysses S., 86, 287, 87
GRANTHAM, Helen, 39, Lulu, 43
GRATER, Charity, 129
GRATIM, Dorothy, 184
GRAVENS, Jason, 175, Jason Wiliam, 175, Mike, 175, Sandra M., 175, Sandy, 175, Sheila, 175, William D., 175
GRAVES, Benjamin, 228, Cathy, 165, Charles Lee, 234, Forrest, 50, 66, Jesse, 16, Kelly, 165, Margaret, 336, Richard, 352, Sarah, 105, T.F., 69, Thelma Claudine, 234
GRAVETT, Eva May, 117, George, 108, George, Jr., 108, Mary, 108, Richard, 108
GRAVITT, Ben, 169, Eva Mae, 169, Eva May, 169
GRAY, Abner, 176, Agnes, 147, Alice May, 176, Annaliza, 176, Benj. Taylor Ristine, 176, Charles Howard, 176, Cooper, 176, Cora, 353, Cynthia, 198, David M., 231, Doris, 301, Dorothy, 176, Elizabeth, 176, 301, Ellis, 176, Emma, 175, 176, Flower Shop, 15, Frank, 80, 81, Gilda Jean, 137, Hugh, 175, 176, Hugh McCormick, 176, James Banning, 176, James Beauchamp, 176, Jasper, 175, Jennie, 224, John, 107, 176, John Kemp, 176, John Sanford, 176, Judy, 176, Katherine Marthene, 176, Kathleen, 106, Larue, 107, Lillie G., 224, Linda, 231, Mahala, 175, Margaret, 176, Mary, 176, Maxwell, 176, Michael Hugh, 175, Minnie Bell, 339, Nancy, 176, 228, Peter, 176, Polly, 176, Polly C., 337, Santford Peter (Polk), 176, Sheilah Jane, 175, Ward, 106, William, 129, 176, William Beauchamp, 176, William Clements, 175, Zerelda, 337
GRAY'S, Dairy, 176, Grocery, 176, Hatchery, 165, School, 180, Sweeper Shop, 176
GRAYBILL, Alice, 177, 195, 196, 197, Alice May, 176, 196, Amanda, 338, Amanda Jane, 177, 201, Andrew, 177, Christina, 177, Clara Bell W., 176, Cline, 176, Cline (Mrs), 74, Daniel, 162, 176, 177, 196, Daniel, Jr., 177, Elizabeth, 162, 176, 177, 182, 196, 214, Ella, 196, Hannah, 98, 177, Helen B., 176, John, 177, Josephus, 177, Laura, 176, 177, Lou, 177, Lucille, "Lou", 176, Lucinda Elizabeth, 243, Lulu, 196, Lydia A., 176, Manson, 176, 196, Mary, 83, Mary C., 176, 177, Mary Mageline, 27, Mry Magdelena, 177, Sallie, 162, Sally, 177, Samuel, 176, 177, 178, 339, Samuel Cline, 177, Samuel Cline, Jr., 176, Samuel Cline, Sr., 176, Samuel F., 83, 176, 177, 196, Solomon, 177, Susannah, 177, Truckers, 14, William R., 177
GRAYSON, Bradley Lee, 305, Brandon Lee, 305, Brook Michelle, 305
GREATBATCH, Bertha, 126, Clarence, 126
GREAVU, C. Jean, 375
GREELEY, Horace, 183, Robert, 63
GREEN, Ann, 79, Arthur M., 294, Barney, 152, Betty, 190, Charles E., 294, Elizabeth, 129, Flossie, 116, J., 68, Jesse, 64, Joe, 190, John, 190, 225, Lawrence, 190, Margaret, 308, Richard, 308, Sandy, 162
GREENBURG, Alice, 313, Allen, 313, Andrew, 313, Bradley, 313, David, 313, Eric, 313, Jennifer, 313, Kimberly, 313, Lawrence, 313, Lisa, 313, Patsy, 313, Philip, 313, Sarah, 313, Terri, 313
GREENE, James W., 49, Jessie, 105, John (Dr), 254, Mary Elizabeth, 254, Nathaniel (Gen), 254, William, 341
GREENLEE, Everett, 193, Jon, 193, Larry, 193, Lois, 193
GREENWAY, James G., 63
GREESON, David, 177, George Albert, 177, Irene, 177, Joe, 177, Judy, 177
GREGG, Aaron, 208, Dorothy, 177, Harry, 177, James, 208, Joseph, 208, Judy, 306, Lethe, 177, Lou, 177, Louisa, 340, Rebecca, 85, Roy, 177, Ruth, 184, Sarah Louisa, 206, Sarah Louise, 206
GREGORY, Angela Renee, 178, Babett Marciel, 178, Bernice, 185, Bradley, 289, Charlotte, 116, Emma Lou, 331, Gracie Mae, 177, Jesse, 299, John Sherman, 177, Joy Chestalina, 178, Joy Marciel, 177, 178, Leroy, 183, Liebe Linnett, 178, Ollie, 331, Paulina Mae, 178, Robert, 254, Robert Arnold I, 178, Robert Arnold II, 178, Robert C., 183, Ronald Arnold I, 177, Sandi, 289, Tina Marlina, 178, Trina Maria, 178, Zelema, 330
GREMESPACHER, Joseph A., 94
GRENARD, Donald, 161, Edith, 141, 295, Emit, 377, Floyd Otis, 220, Joseph, 166, Mary, 377, Mary Ann, 92, Mary Joan, 161, __, 17, __, 17
GREVE, Greg, 278, Keith, 278, Marsha, 278, Martha, 278, Pauline, 348, Tom, 278
GREY, Elizabeth, 269, James B., 63, James T., 161
GRIEL, Jane, 262
GRIEST, Howard, 43, Micajah, 129
GRIFFIN, Andrew, 208, Elizabeth, 249, Jesse, 249, Ralph, 145, Robert, 59, Sarah, 205, Steve, 208, William J., 181
GRIFFITH, Jennifer, 86, Josie, 322, Martha E., 178, Mary, 322, Oleta, 353, Thomas A., 178
GRIFFY, Elizabeth, 261
GRIGG, Douglas, 30
GRIGGS, Adaline L., 91, Clark R., 91, Grace, 91, Livonia, 91, Mary "Polly", 326
GRIMBLE, Alan, 231, Albert, 231, Annie Pickett, 231, Bonnie, 231, Francis, 231, Gene, 231, Geneva, 231, George, 231, Ica, 231, Jack, 231, Jana, 231, Joyce, 231, Justin, 231, Kathleen, 231, Linda, 231, Pearl, 231, Randall, 231, Robert, 231
GRIMES, Ann, 359, Betty, 278, Burley, 12, Carol Jo, 120, 121, Caroline, 132, Carrie B., 283, David, 95, Estella, M., 106, Flora Alice, 194, Forrest Earl, 120, Freeda, 348, Gale, 52, George, 365, Joseph, 31, Kate, 347, Lawrence, 347, Mabel, 345, Mabel Weir, 41, Madonna, 165, Mary, 307, Mary Jean, 158, Noah, 20, Noah W., 50, Real Estate, 176, Richard Lodge, 120, S.B., 63, Sarah Elizabeth, 95, Vera Alice, 279
GRINARD, Nancy, 330
GRINDLEY, Vivian P., 375
GRISSO, I.N., 69
GRISSOM, Betty, 185, Elizabeth Jane, 188
GRITTEN, Pamela, 375
GROCE, Clarence, 256
GROCELOSE, __, 69
GROENDYKE, Hannah, 74, James, 169, 339, Jean, 339, Leroy, 339, 373, Nancy, 339
GROENERT, Theodore, 42
GROLL, Marye Ann, 359
GRONERT, Andrew, 178, Anna, 178, Dr., 179, Edith, 178, George, 178, George M., 178, Hazel, 178, Katherine, 178, Kathleen, 178, Lawrence, 178, Michael, 178, Nelda, 178, Theodore G., 178, Theodore Gregory, 178
GROSS, Alice M., 372, Kathy, 358, Lime & Stone Hauling, 16, Jane, 144
GROSSE, Charles Andrew, 173, Maude, 173, Vida May, 173, Walter, 173
GROUND, Catherine, 102
GROUNDS, Catherine, 104
GROVE, Katherine, 176
GROVES, Benjamin, 253, Billy Joe, 132, Bud, 200, Carol Ann, 132, Don, 132, Donald Lee, 132, Emily E., 318, Freelove, 253, Linda, 322, Margaret, 132, Samuel, 318, William, 132
GRUBB, Laura, 195
GRUBBS, Chris Anne, 95, Dale, 95, Jay, 113, Kayla Jo, 95, Sue, 272
GRUNDY, Michael John, 208, Sean Michael, 208, Travis Ryan, 208
GRUVER, Sue, 139
GUIER, Maria Savilla, 154
GUILKEY, Kathryn, 117, Paul, 117, Paul E., 117, Rose A., 117, Thelma, 117
GUILLIAMS, Charles, 39
GUINEY, Bridget, 215
GULWIDER, Walter, 117
GUMP, Anna Walter, 208
GUNDERMAN, Betty, 54
GUNKLE, Ano, 41
GUNN, Andrea Nicole, 84, Ashley Renae, 84, Eric Ray, 84, Mark, 84, Nedra Sue, 84
GUNTLE, Samuel, 354, Phoebe, 182, __, 43
GUSHIVA, Catherine, 294
GUSTIN, Earl, 268
GUTHRIE, Mac, 171, Margaret, 351, Susan, 223
GUY, Leon, 265
GUYRE, Yolanda, 174
GWIN, Ralph G., 63
HAAS, Guy, 12
HAASE, Beulah F., 361, Delbert W., 37
HACK, Eleanor, 179, Elizabeth Virginia, 179, John Oren, 179, Joseph Tinsley, 179, Oren, 179, Stephen Ellrod, 179
HACKER, Jill, 351, Laura, 198, Ozias, 198
HACKETT, Addie, 163, Daniel W.H., 163, George F., 163, John G., 163, Lydia, 163, Thomas, 163
HACKITT, Ann, 163, William Summers, 163
HACKLEMAN, Brad, 67, Deborah, 67
HACKMAN, Gene, 16
HACKNEY, Elizabeth Ann, 162, Terrell, 222
HACKWORTH, Elvira, 83, Jane, 83, Wesley, 83
HADDAD, Jamie, 170, Roberto, 170, Robin, 170, Soladad, 170
HADLEY, Fannie, 161, Nellie, 339, Ruth, 355, 356
HAFFNER, Bessie, 323, Bessie Lee, 265, Cloyd Owen (Dr.), 179, Clyde O., 265, Diane, 179, Elizabeth Diane, 265, Elmer, 179, George Elmer, 179, Gerry, 265, Karen, 271, Larry Dean, 372,

Leon, 179, Maxine, 179, Mildred, 179, Phyllis, 179
HAGEN, Mabel F., 271
HAGERMAN, Abigail, 175
HAGLER, Anna, 95, Mary Susanna, 95
HAILMAN, Harry, 365
HAINES, Abraham, 290, Bruce, 43, Catherine, 242, Florence, 205, Hannah, 290, Joseph William, 205, Oley, 205, Susannah, 110, & Thompson Milling, 325
HAIRE, Beatrice, 266, Samuel Leslie, 166
HALDERMAN, John, 225
HALE, Ethel, 150, Jane, 268, 320
HALEY, Eleanor, 235
HALFORD, Dan, 377
HALL, (Colonel), 238, Amy Ann, 126, 129, 180, Anna, 360, Benjamin, 360, Charles, 179, Charles Franklin, 179, Charles Omer, 228, Clara Bell, 43, DeBard, 137, Edna A., 180, Edna Arlinda, 180, Edward, 179, 180, Elijah, 306, Elizabeth, 145, 179, Fanny, 43, Grace, 210, 258, Hannah, 179, Heather, 271, Hickman, 31, Ida, 228, Jacob, 145, 225, James, 179, 356, James Edward, 180, James N., 372, James Q., 179, James Quincy, 179, 180, Janet Sue, 271, Jeanne Frances, 295, Jennie, 43, Jennie B., 30, Jennifer, 271, John, 179, John Richardson, 213, Johny, 179, Joseph, 179, 180, Joy Y., 235, Juanita Pullen, 235, Lilli, 228, Linda Sue, 240, Lois Marie, 295, Lola, 320, Lorena Bell "Lulu", 179, Lulu, 179, Margaret Emza, 292, Marjory, 213, Martha, 360, Martha Ann, 306, Mary, 145, 220, 266, 321, 350, Mary A., 43, Mary Ann, 179, 306, 307, Mary Louise, 295, Mathew, 179, Maud, 43, Naomi, 141, 295, 306, Nevada Jane, 179, Norman, 307, Oakel, 129, 180, Oakel F., 180, Oakel Fowler, 179, Otis, 129, 180, Otis E., 141, Otis Earle, 180, 295, Perry, 228, Rachell, 213, Robert Glen, 179, Robert Thomas, 179, Roberta, 372, Sarah Ellen, 228, Thomas, 179, 180, Thomas Edgar, 179, Thomas William, 179, Waneta, 295, William, 145, 271, Willis, 145, Zora Elizabeth, 179, Joseph, 180, __, 32
HALLE, Raymond (Dr.), 375
HALLET, Elijah Porterfield, 180, Rebecca, 180
HALLETT, Alva, 180, Bert, 181, Bert Wayne, 181, Bertha, 181, Cynthia, 180, Don, 181, 193, Don Arvon, 181, Druzilla, 181, Edna, 181, Ellie, 181, Ethel, 181, Freddie, 181, George, 181, Harvey, 181, Harvey P., 181, Harvey Perry, 181, Ina, 180, Jackson, 180, 181, James Zenith, 180, Jerrell Alva, 180, Joan, 181, Lena, 181, Mary, 181, Mary A., 180, Maude, 181, Paul Leslie, 180, Perry Lee, 180, Ramona, 180, Richard W., 193, Richard Wayne, 181, Rick, 181, 193, Ruth, 181, Ruth E., 193, Ruth Ellen, 193, Ruth Hester, 193, Sallie, 180, Stella, 180, Stephen Leslie, 180, Susan, 180, 181, Wandaline, 181, William Lee, 180, Willie, 181, Zenith Jackson, 180
HALLIE, Fannie, 43
HALPIN, Gwendolyn Diana, 103
HALSTEAD, Alma, 181, Clyde, 181, Doris, 181, Ernest, 181, Fern, 181, J.P., 374, Joe D., 374, Joe Delwin, 181, John, 181, Josiah, 181, Justice Martin, 181, Musetta, 181, Ruby, 181, William, 181, William Wilson, 181
HAM, Isaiah, 173, Sarah, 240
HAMBACK, Kathye Jean, 81
HAMBLIN, Evaline, 172
HAMELTON, T.M., 41
HAMER, Eddie, 317, Jo Darlene, 317, Michael, 317, Rhoda, 317, Rodney, 317, Tonya, 317
HAMERNIK, Becky, 236, Dave, 107, David, 236, Jeanne, 107, Jeanne Clair, 236, Kevin, 236, Stephanie, 236
HAMILTON, A.N., 308, Adrian Scott, 273, Alex, 208, Alexander, 207, Alma, 317, Ann, 343, Barbara, 351, Catharine Joan, 101, Catherine, 181, Danielle Denise, 147, Deborah Joan, 305, Debra, 147, Dianne, 147, Douglas Paul, 273, Edward Parker T., 317, Effie May, 317, Eleanor, 181, Elizabeth, 181, Ernest Ross, 133, Ernestine, 133, Florence, 317, Gabriel, 181, Gaildene, 147, Guy, 209, Hannah, 181, 317, Hazel, 226, Henry, 181, Herbert, 317, Iva, 209, Iva M., 162, James, 181, Janice Sue, 273, Jennie, 221, Jesse, 181, John, 181, 343, Josephine, 317, Julia Ann, 343, Justin Alexander, 273, Lavisa, 181, Lilly, 317, Lou, 372, Margaret, 181, Martha Jane, 181, Mary, 117, 181, Mary Jane, 279, Nathaniel, 181, Rachael Brooke, 273, Reuben, 181, Richard, 209, Robert, 209, Samuel, 209, 317, Sarah, 181, Sarah Ann, 317, Sarah Louise, 89, Stanley D., 147, Talbert, 317, Teron, 209, Tona, 209, Virginia, 272, William, 181, Ocia, 156, __, 82, Dianne, 185
HAMM, Anthony Wayne, 244, B., 308, Byron, 106, Eleanor, 106, Esther, 374, Gary, 244, Mary, 310, Michael Allen, 244, Pauline, 147, Polly, 147, Rita M., 372, Stella, 180, Stephen, 201
HAMMER, Sue Ann, 245
HAMMOND, Alfred L., Jr., 111, Charles A., 51
HAMPTON, 22, Alonzo, 181, Anna May, 182, Beatrice, 182, Bert, 181, 182, Bill, 182, Catherine, 348, Cecil, 239, Cecil B., 182, Clarence, 182, Claude Lyman, 182, Dan, 126, Daniel, 181, Dave, 126, 372, Diana Renee, 128, Donald, 182, Donald M., 317, Donald Max, 209, Dorothy, 233, Dorothy Elizabeth, 182, Edward, 182, Eileen, 182, Elizabeth, 94, Ernest, 209, Ernest Lloyd, 182, Eugene, 182, Eugene "Beaner", 181, Floyd, 126, Fredrick, 182, Freida, 239, Gail, 182, Gail Ann, 182, Geoffrey, 182, Gerald, 182, Harry Walker, 182, Helen Gene, 182, Helen Mae, 126, Ida, 102, 182, James, 94, Janet Sue, 239, John, 94, Joseph N., 94, Kathleen, 182, Kurt, 182, Kurt Alan, 182, Lillie Imogene, 182, Maggie, 181, Mahala, 94, 118, Manford, 182, Margaret Jane, 94, Marilyn, 182, Martha E., 94, Martin, 94, Martin D., 181, Mary E., 182, Mary Rose, 182, Mert, 182, Michael, 94, Morgan, 94, Nicholas Lee, 209, Opal Marie, 182, Phoebe, 182, Ralph, 182, Ratie, 181, Raymond Lee, 182, Rebecca, 209, Rebecca Ellen, 181, Rhoda, 94, 194, Richard, 182, Rosemary, 182, Sammy, 182, Samuel, 94, 182, Samuel A., 182, Sarah Ann, 94, Sarah E., 120, Selina, 94, Shirley, 182, Solomon, 182, Tyler, 182, Violet, 181, 182, William, 128, William Barton, 182, Barbara, 182, Mary Katherine, 181
HANCE, Margaret, 295, 296
HANCOCK, Edward, 265, Ethel, 312, Frank, 312, Homer, 347, John, 312, Martha, 347, Mary Ann, 204, Orpha, 182
HAND, Dora, 253
HANDLEY, David, 67, John, 225, 286, Rebecca Jane, 286
HANDY, Alga, 80, Charles, 80, Charles E., 284, Ed, 353, Frances, 80, Thomas, 80
HANEY, Carolyn, 80, Jason Nathaniel, 80, Kenyon Colleen, 80, Margaret, 144, 153, 281, W.J., 28, Walter J., 191, Walter Patrick, 80
HANGER, Levenia, 281, Rachel, 336
HANIFORD, Andrew, 284, Beverly Rice, 284, Chaddley, 284, Danielle Jeanette, 284, Thomas Ray, 284, Jenny, 284
HANKINS, John, 182, Orpha, 182, Theodore, 182
HANKS, Flossie, 277, Rosanna, 120, William, 120
HANLEY, __, 42
HANNA, Adam, 183, Alexander Little, 183, Amy Margaret, 183, Bayless, 182, Bayless Washington, 183, Building, 183, Caroline, 120, Cornelia Alberta, 183, Daniel W., 265, Elizabeth, 60, George, 173, Hannah, 183, James, 60, 172, 183, James R., 183, James Richmond, 183, James, Jr., 182, 183, John T., 183, John Telford, 183, Joseph, 183, Margaret, 60, Martha, 172, 183, Martha A., 183, Mary, 109, 145, 182, 183, Mary Elizabeth, 183, May, 162, Nancy, 60, 182, 183, Oakalla, 183, Olivia Elisabeth, 183, Owen T., 198, Read, 183, Ruth, 183, Samuel, 183, Sarah O., 183, T.L., 365, Tyre Littleton, 183, William, 172, 183, Zetta Maxine, 198, __, 110, (Gen.), 120
HANNAH, Martha, 130, 153, Mary, 182
HANNAR, Mary Irene, 296
HANNSMAN, Carolyn E., 207, Walter, 207
HANSEN, Carol, 53, 54, Steve, 54
HANSON, Amos, 326, John, 113, Louise Lura, 326, Mabel, 325, 326
HANTS, Kathern, 176
HAPPY HOLLOW FARM FOODS, 382
HARAYDA, Janice Carole, 98, John III, 98, John, Jr., 98, William Gantner, 98
HARBERT, Elizabeth, 183, William Soesby, 184
HARBESON, B.M., 70
HARBISON, "Doc", 255, Cordelia, 69, Lynn, 118, Myrtle LuRe, 286
HARBOURT, Henry H., 152, Margaret, 152, Paul, 152, Sarah, 152
HARDAKER, Hattie A., 286
HARDAWAY, Charles Edward, 150, James, 150, Kevin Drew, 150
HARDEE, Goldie, John Michael, 145, 153, Joseph, 145, Joseph H., 145, Julia, 298, Julia Ann, 145, Lucinda, 145, 153, Roy, 12
HARDESY, Mollie Clark, 116
HARDIN, Emily, 286
HARDING, Addie, 6, Elijah, 304, Laura, 317
HARDWICK, John, 21, 359, Pat, 359
HARDY, Stella Pickett, 358
HARGIS, Dick, 375, Joann, 375
HARGRAVE, Frank F., 63, Richard, 49
HARGREAVES, (Rev), 63
HARITY, Lucia, 311
HARLAN, Austin, 247, Aaron, 122, Anna, 122, 301, Austin, 184, Benton, 184, 247, Caretta, 247, Carrie Snyder, 247, Charles Merle, 184, Charles Miller, 184, Clara Alice, 184, Clarence, 312, Clarence J., 312, Coretta Louise, 184, Doris, 184, 247, Elizabeth A., 184, Ella, 312, Elmer, 312, Ernest, 184, 247, George, 184, 247, 312, George Newton, 184, Harry, 312, Harry C., 312, Helen, 247, Helen Inez, 184, James, 184, Juliet V., 122, Lily Hannah Irene, 312, Marcellus G., 184, Merle, 247, Michael, 312, Paul, 184, 247, Vernie J., 312, Vivian, 92, Vivian L., 309, Vivian Lorene, 312
HARLAND, Atlanta, 239, George, 312, Melvina, 239, Michael, 312, William, 239
HARLOW, Jean, 342, Mary A., "Polly", 307
HARMLESS, Claude, 269, Mildred Marie, 269, Zora Dean, 269
HARMON, Corrine Elaine, 227, Eliza, 39, Elizabeth, 157, Leonard, 174, Prudence, 174
HARNED, Rosanna, 297
HARNEY, Anna Louise, 184, Cap, 366, G.T., 55, George S., 184, 366, James, 184, James F., 184, Louise, 184, Morrie, 43, Reiley, 356, Sallie, 74
HAROLD, Delvina Jane, 115
HARPEL, Andrew Douglas, 184, Anna, 296, Barbara, 184, Cora Effie, 184, Donald E. Walter, 184, Donald Joseph, 184, Dorothy, 184, Douglas, 184, Fannie, 184, Hazel, 184, John, 184, John Alfred, 184, Leona Faye, 184, Lydia, 184, Mary Lou, 184, Mary P., 184, Mildred, 184, V. Lucile, 197, 211, V. Lucille, 336, Vivian Lucille, 280, Walter J., 229
HARPER, A.F., 366, Abbie, 239, Alan Wayne, 239, Arnetta, 351, Bernice, 351, Dorothy, 351, Ella, 312, Everett, 351, Everette, 350, Glen, 239, Jaysi, 239, Jean, 351, Jessie, 351, John, 350, 351, Louise, 351, Marilyn, 239, Mary, 101, Rebecca, 239, Sally, 208, Susan, 126, 239, Tommy, 43
HARRIMAN, Dora, 135, George, 135, Ruby Edna, 135
HARRINGTON, Hazel, 101, Kyler Kent, 203, Marlin Burton, 203, Marlin Kirk, 203, Stacy Leigh, 203
HARRIS, A.J. (Jay), 185, Abe, 185, Ann, 185, 250, Barnett, 11, Bernie, 374, Catherine, 225, Cecil Addison, 185, Cecil Anthony, 185, Cora Belle, 282, David Monroe, 359, Deborah Ann, 185, Don, 336, Dorman, 26, 67, Earl, 336, Electric, 26, Elijah Ramsay, 282, Eliza Ann, 185, Elizabeth, 236, Elizabeth Taylor, 128, Elsie, 336, Ethel, 319, Ethel Ray, 229, Etta Pearl, 128, Everett Neil, 165, Frank, 128, Franklin Edmund, 185, Gailen DeLon, 165, Grocery, 14, Harriet, 306, Hazel May, 185, Henrietta, 225, Henry, 185, 309, Herbert Lee, 185, Hester, 322, J. Lamont, 185, 250, J. Russell, 132, J.W., 49, James Floyd, 185, James Montgomery, 359, Janet, 375, Jay, 39, Jim, 15, John Freelan, 185, John Ora, 185, Kenneth, 185, Laura Emily, 283, Lide, 40, Lyn, 287, Marilyn, 132, Martha Ellen, 359, Martha J., 209, Michael Anthony, 185, Nancy, 209, Neil Thomas, 165, Paul, 107, Pete, 185, Ralph, 359, Rebecca, 185, Robert S., 185, Sarah Jane, 314, Sharon Kay, 250, 288, Stanley Hayes, 185, Stephen, 250, Stephen Lamont, 185, Theodosia, 282, Theresa, 154, 155, Thomas Edmund, 185, Thomas Paul, 165, Ulysses, 336, Ulysses P., 211, Viola, 309, William, 336, __, 42, (Rev), 75
HARRISON, (General), 233, Benjamin, 105, 219, Carter, 198, Catherine, 201, Clara, 98, Denny, 115, Gravel, 14, Hudson, 201, Jack, 72, Jerry, 115, John, 63, John W., 110, Larry, 115, Louise, 184, Marian, 353, Mark, 271, Mary, 43, Mary Jo, 271, Meggan, 271, Michael, 115, Nancy, 115, Patricia, 355, Richard, 74, Robert, 115, Sarah, 43, 271, Sarah "Sally", 105, Sarah Rebecca, 85, Simeon, 225, Steve, 271, Sue Mae, 115, Syntha Dee, 198, Wanda, 353, William Henry (Gen), 251, William Henry (Pres), 201, William Riley, 201
HARSHBARGER, 185, Abraham, 186, Ann, 186, Anna Belle, 186, Catherine, 236, Cement, 14, Charles, 265, Chalres Henry, 186, Charles Ralph, 186, Clara, 249, Clare, 336, Claud, 116, Daniel, 186, Effie, 336, Elizabeth, 162, 193, Elizabeth Myers, 116, Ethel Marie, 186, Garage, 14, George (Mrs.), 286, Grover, 186, Hattie Ann, 190, Henry Meade, 174, Jacob, 81, 174, 176, 178, 185, 196, 272, John, 116, Lloyd, 186, Lloyd (Mrs.), 186, Lula Mae, 174, Lydia, 176, 185, Lydia Mae, 186, Mae, 265, Marie Eva, 81, Mary, 221, Mary E., 215, Mary Elizabeth, 186, Mary L., 196, Mary Louisa, 206, 249, May, 165, Roger, 186, Saloma, 196, Salome, 81, Salome A., 176, Samuel, 116, Sarah, 186, 313, Susan Clark, 116, __, 66, __, 162
HARSHBURGER, Bill, 44
HARSHMAN, Mary J., 381, Nancy, 115, Woodrow, 144
HART, Carl, 218, Claude, 304, Claude, Jr., 304, Daniel D., 186, Deacon Ezra, 186, Ezra, 186, H. Laverne, 285, Harold Max, 304, Helen Maxine, 304, Hugh LaVern, 131, James, 99, John, 186, Jonas D., 186, Jonas Derrell, 186, Jonathan Robert, 218, Joseph, Jr., 186, Juanita Ellen, 304, Judith, 131, Kenneth Dale, 304, Leroy E., 201, Martha J., 201, Mary Ann, 186, Mary E., 143, Melissa Lynn, 218, Ollie, 99, Patricia, 218, Polly, 186, Robert, 218, Susan, 186, Ssan L., 201, Susie Jane, 218, William, 131, Willis L., 143, Wilma, 285
HARTLEY, Charlotte, 139, 140, Michael P., 156, Michael P., Jr., 156, Nicholas F., 156, Steven M., 156
HARTLING, __, 69
HARTMAN, Elevator, 14, Martha, 313
HARTSAW, Minta Catherine, 303
HARTSOCK, Daniel, 132, Elizabeth, 132, Maroah, 186, Mary, 132, Nelson, 132, Thomas, 186
HARTUNG, Augusta, 57, Ethel, 227, Henry, 310, Howard, 164
HARTZ, George L., 63
HARVEY, Albert, 186, Alice, 187, Burton, 187, Carl Burton, 186, Carrie, 186, Donald, 186, Doris, 186, F. Walter, 186, Frank, 187, Frank L., 186, George, 187, Henderson, 50, Henderson, Jr., 187, Houston, 186, Jackie, 108, Joseph, 186, Joseph McConnell, 187, Judy L., 174, 192, 122, Larry D., 372, Laura, 186, Lawrence, 132, Lloyd, 187, Lula, 186, Margaret, 186, Margaret Sue, 132, Martha, 186, Mary Bannon, 187, Mary E., 186, Mary Martha, 264, Mary S., 186, Maude, 186, Maude E., 186, Nellie, 186, Robert, 42, Robert S., 373, Sarah, 186, 187, Sarah E., 186, Ursa, 186, Walter, 186, Wilson, 302
HARWOOD, Dianna, 272
HASELTINE, Raymond Frederick, 101
HASKETT, Anita Heinen, 189, Caswell, 303, Euma, 303, Harriet Lorraine, 303, James W., 189, Leonard, 303
HASKISSON, Emmalee, 335
HASLAM, Carolyn, 250, Eula, 250, Frank, 250, James, 203, Janice, 250, Richard, 250, Samuel, 250
HASTADAY, Abby, 252, Catherine, 252, Catherine Theresa, 252, Ed, 252, Henry, 252, John H., 252, Margaret, 252, Minnie, 252, Nelle, 252, Rebecca, 252, Will, 252
HASTINGS, Angela Michell Allen, 251
HATCH, Isaphena, 360
HATE, Ellen, 279
HATFIELD, Nora, 341
HATHAWAY, Sarah Elizabeth, 343
HATKE, Sayle, 54, Mat, 54
HATT, John, 297, Joyce, 355, Martha, 88, 96, Mildred, 297, Salina Elizabeth, 88, William V., 88
HAUDER, Dora E., 187
HAUK, Absalom, 187, Absalom Arthur, 187, Amanda, 187, Anna Elizabeth, 187, Betty J., 187, Daniel, 187, Emmett Irl, 187, Ethel, 187, George, 187, Hazel, 187, Helen J., 166, Herbert Allen, 187, John Charles, 187, Julia, 187, Katherine, 187, Lucretia J., 187, Margaret, 187, Marion, 187, Martha Ida, 187, Pat, 166, Patricia, 187, Philip, 187, Philip II, 187, Sarah Catherine, 187, Teresa, 187, Viola May, 187
HAUN, Sherry Lee, 283, William E., 153
HAUPT, Susanna, 354
HAUSER, Albert M., 187, Bill, 21, Clara, 187, Clinton W., 187, Edith, 21, 188, Edith Elmore, 188, Edith L., 187, Edward E., Heather Marie, 187, Janee, 187, Lisa L., 187, Louise, 187, Maria Margaretha, 187, Marshall, 187, 188, 240, Marshall E., 187, Martin, 187, Thomas W., 187, Waneita, 187, William A., 187, William Marshall, 187
HAUTZ, Catherine, 82, 176, Eva Anna, 83, Philip Lorentz, 83
HAVENS, Brothers, 15, George, 33
HAVER, Phyllis, 342
HAVERKAMP, Ida, 136, Lewis, 136
HAWK, Ann, 350, Daniel, 256
HAWLEY, David Pattison, 339, Druscilla, 201, Druscilla Jane, 339, Jane, 339, John Harrison, 339, Karl, 338, Patrick Bryant, 339, Samuel Stewart, 339, William, 201, William R., 338, William Walterhouse, 339
HAWORTH, George, 215, 216, John, 301
HAWTHORNE, Helen, 339
HAY, John, 101, Virginia, 359
HAYDEN, Rachel, 330
HAYES, Arthur, 173, Arthur (Mrs.), 265, Blanche Naomi, 188, Calvin, 118, Cecile Irene, 187, Cyndi Lyn, 292, David, 270, Debra Jeanne, 188, Dorothy, 195, Edna, 318, Estella Mae, 188, Ethel Blanche, 229, Frances Louise, 188, Francis Cordelia, 188, George, 195, Gertrude, 185, Gertrude Augusta, 188, Harold Eugene, 188, Hazel, 270, Helen, 26, 39, Homer Walter, 188, 229, Ida, 223, Jane Susan, 188, Janet, 270, Johnny Irvin, 188, Letha Pearl, 188, Lucinda, 319, Marion, 230, Marsha Ann, 188, Martha, 265, Mary, 301, Paul, 122, Paul Robert, 188, Perrie Lee, 188, Phyllis Irene, 188, 229, Rebecca Louise, 188, Robert, 270, Robert Coons, 188, Sadie Emma, 188, Samuel M., 63, Versa, 243, Versa Olive, 188, William, 185, William Washington,

188
HAYNES, Barbara Jean, 139, Hannah, 290, 291
HAYS, Amelia Hope, 188, Bill, Jr., 188, George, 286, Helen, 31, 80, John T., 188, Mary, 108, 286, Mary Katherine, 188, Mollie, 286, Pat, 144, Will, 24, 222, William Harrison III, 188, William Harrison, Jr., 188, William Harrison, Sr., 188, William R., 330
HAYWORTH, Betty Dahr, 126, Diane, 126, Glen David, 208, James, 208, Mildred Marie, 269, Paul, 269, Richard, 126, Robert, 126, Virginia King, 208, William, 126
HAZLETT, Dewey, 70, Lawrence, 22
HEACOCK, Barbara, 139, Margaret, 87, Rebecca, 81, 138, 139, 140, 276, 335, Shirl, 81
HEADLEY, Edwin, 354
HEADY, Ethel, 137
HEARN, Peggy, 212
HEARTLAND, Co-op, 16
HEATH, Abraham, 176, Barbara Jane, 292, Leah, 176, Mary Ann, 176, William, 176, 292
HEATHCLIFF, __, 183
HEATON, Esther, 165
HEAVILIN, Berniece, 145
HECK, Elizabeth, 281
HECKATHORN, George, 201
HEDDLESON, Hirom, 248
HEDGE, Monuments, 15
HEDRICK, Clara, 136, Elizabeth, 317
HEETER, Bernice Elizabeth, 188, Donna Gertrude, 188, Esta Ezra, 188, Estelle, 188, 189, Louise "Estelle", 188, Silas, 188
HEIGHWAY, (Dr.), 227
HEINEN, Anita, 189, Anita "Mickey", 189, Charles, 189, Clydia, 189, Marjorie "Dude", 189, Mary Jane, 189, Mildred, 189, Peter, 189, Robert, 189, Savilla Marie, 189
HEINMILLER, Jean Fisher, 165
HEINY, Alma Ione, 289, Amy Inis, 289, Arthur, 289, Clara Thelma, 289, Lola Annis, 289, Mary Edna, 289, Wilbur Ward, 289, William W., 289
HEISEL, Esta Lee, 289
HELD, Mary H., 153
HELDERMAN, Carol, 249
HELM, Mary, 309
HELMBERGER, Nancy Ellen, 188
HELMS, Carolyn, 171, Cindy, 171, George Leon, 171, Marcy, 171, Mary, 181, Omega, 270, Travis, 171
HEMPHILL, Andrew, 90, Mary Ann, 90
HENCHMAN, Mary L., 260
HENDEN, Alice Kay, 276
HENDERSON, Alexander, 189, 343, Alice, 189, Amanda, 166, 167, 189, Daniel, 304, Dawn E., 250, Edna, 283, Elizabeth, 41, 166, 189, 304, Floyd, 189, Hannah, 41, Jack, 189, James, 189, James T., 189, John Chapman, 189, Joseph, 41, Kathleen, 168, Martha, 189, Mary, 117, 189, Mary E., 343, Matilda, 41, Milton, 189, Ruby, 165, Sarah, 211, Squire Milton, 307, Virginia, 188, William, 189, Zorada, 189, Keith, 98
HENDON, Johneadon E., 375
HENDRICKS, __, 22, (Governor), 108, Alice M., 166, Charlotte, 166, Chester, 166, 268, 311, Clinton, 308, Clyde, 268, 311, Daisy, 166, 167, 168, 189, Dale, 268, 311, Dora, 268, Doris, 268, Edith (Lindley), 31, Elizabeth, 166, Eva Bell, 166, Faye, 268, James Wesley, 166, 167, 268, John, 166, 373, John William, 308, Lois E., 268, Marjorie, 268, Mary May, 166, Oscar, 166, Paul, 268, 311, Thomas A., 183, William, 166
HENDRICKSON, Anna Pearl, 189, Anne, 189, Christy, 189, Clyde, 189, Clyde Beaumont, 189, Clyde Lewis, 189, Gaye, 189, Jack, 189, Judy, 189, Martha, 189, Martha Blanche, 189, Mary, 117, Michael, 189, Nancy, 189, Nancy June, 233, Pam, 189, Pete, 192, Sylvia, 189, Thomas B., 117, Mary, 117
HENDRIX, Hazel, 235
HENDRYX, Daisey E., 239
HENRIKSEN, Diana J., 336
HENRY, Avanell, 347, Berniece, 145, Beth, 347, Carl, 347, Carl I., 90, Carol, 90, 347, Charles L., 32, Donald, 74, Dorothy, 165, Ellen, 130, Mary, 204, Mary Louisa, 99, Minnie Elizabeth, 90, Omer, 165, Pearl, 90, 347, Ruth, 347, Ruth Marie, 90, Virginia Avanelle, 90
HENSLEE, Martha Eliza, 282
HENSLEY, Bertha, 333, Betty Catherine, 204, Ethel Marie, 204, Florence Elva, 204, Frank Delmar, 204, Hiram, Jr., 204, Hughes, 204, Kenneth Eugene, 204, Louise, 187, Mary Jane, 204, Norwood Robert, 204, Rena June, 204, Una Mae, 204
HENTHORN, Albert, 190, Albert C., 189, Alta, 189, C. Rex, 190, Carl, 355, Daisy, 198, Edgar, 71, 189, Edgar L., 189, Isaac J., 261, Katie, 208, Libby, 208, Lucy Belle, 189, Margaret, 186, Mildred, 189, 190, Osellia, 261, Rita, 190, Thomas, 208, Thomas J., 190, William, 189
HENTHRON, Carl, 24
HEPBURN, Joseph, 138
HERKLESS, Sarah, 222
HERMAN, Davis, 312
HERNDON, Cinchona, 190, Collett, 190, Daniel, 190, Elizabeth, 190, Emma, 190, John Lindsay, 190, Joseph Foster, 190, Louisa Indiana, 190, Louisa Marie, 190, Milton (Dr.), 190, Pollett, 190, Rebecca, 190, Richard, 190, Samuel Henry, 190, William, 190, William H., 190
HERR, Alma, 190, Benjamin, 190, Betsy Ann, 80, Cheryl, 190, Diana, 89, 190, Eleanor, 89, 190, Nancy, 190, Remley, 89, 190, Sally, 190, Sarah, 190, Shirl, 6, 190, 281
HERRIDODT, Mary, 319
HERRIN, Shadrick Henry, 191, William Andrew, 191
HERRING, Johanna, 42
HERRINGTON, Olive, 309
HERRON, Andrew W., 39, Anthony Shadrick, 191, Brad, 191, Brenda Sue, 190, 191, Charles, 280, Charles A., 78, Charles Andrew, 190, Charles Bradley, 190, Clarence, 191, Clarissa Joy, 191, Cora, 78, 190, Earl, 78, 190, 191, 279, 346, Earl Franklin, 293, Frank "Doc", 39, Gary Scott, 190, 191, Helen, 280, 293, Howard Eli, 143, Howard Franklin, 143, Jack, 191, 280, Jack L., 78, Jackie Lee, 191, James D., 38, Jane, 179, 346, Jennette, 143, Jeremy Scott, 191, Jessica Marie, 191, Jill, 191, JoAnn, 190, Joseph Croy, 79, 143, Joseph D., 143, Kevin Lee, 191, Killin Ann Marie, 191, Kimberlin Ann, 191, Kristopher Joel, 191, Kurtis Linn, 191, Lawrence, 191, Margaret, 191, 343, Margie, 191, Mary, 280, Mary Jeanette, 143, Mary M., 78, Ruby, 280, Regina, 79, Ruby, 293, Ruby Eileen, 280, Ruth Jane, 280, Shade, 191, Shadrick, 191, Shorty, 279, 280, Thomas, 179, Thomas Anthony, 191, Tiffany Dawn, 191, Timothy William, 191, Tina Marie, 191, Vern, 191, William, 209, 280, William P. (Capt.), 370, William S., 78, William Shadrick, 191, 280, Winton Conn, 143, Zetta, 191
HERSHBERGER, Alice, 191, Charles, 191, Clark Jr., 350, Clark Sr., 350, Clark William, 351, Dale, 191, Fauneil, 28, 191, 192, Jane, 351, Jerry, 350, 351, Jill, 351, Laurel, 191, 192, Lori J., 372, Luceil Iona, 191, Mary, 28, 192, Oasey, 191, Oasey Laurel, 28
HERSHMAN, Kenneth, 72
HESLAR, Donna Sue, 357, Narcissus Jane, 324
HESLER, Brad, 95, Christopher, 95, Cynthia Jo, 95, Oakel, 43
HESS, __, 283, Denise, 165, Williams, Beck Const., 68
HESSLER, Rebecca, 121
HESTER, Adam, 192, 193, Albert Dale, 131, 192, Albert Howe, 192, 193, Ann, 192, 193, Anna, 193, Beverly, 192, Blanche, 192, Bradley Wayne, 192, Brian, 193, Brian Thomas, 193, 305, Catherine Denise, 192, Charlotte, 193, Clarence, 192, Cynthia, 204, Dale, 192, Daniel, 192, David, 193, 246, David Owen, 192, Diana, 193, 273, Donald K., 192, 193, Elmer, 192, 193, Etta M., 165, Glenna, 192, Harold Elmer, 193, Heather, 193, Heather Marie, 273, Helen, 192, Henry, 131, Ida, 165, 192, Irene, 131, 192, Jack, 193, James, 131, James Monroe, 192, 193, Jerry Joseph, 192, John, 165, 192, 193, Judith, 131, Linc, 192, Lucy, 192, 193, Mary, 192, 193, Mary Beth, 193, Mary K., 193, Mary Ray, 193, Micah, 193, Micah Nathan, 273, Nathan D., 193, Nathan David, 273, Nelda J., 375, Nelda Joyce, 192, Paul David, 192, Phil, 192, Rosemary, 246, Russell, 131, 193, Russell Max, 193, 305, Ruth, 181, Ruth Ellen, 193, Sallie, 193, Salome, 193, Scott, 192, Stella, 192, Stephen "Elmer", 192, Stephen D., 193, Stephen Elmer, 193, Susan, 192, Thomas, 131, Timothy, 192, Todd Alan, 193, 305, Tom, 192, Virginia, 131, Virginia Irene, 193, Wallace, 192, William, 192
HEWITT, J. Roth, 356, Sophia Jane, 356
HEYER, Carol, 275
HEYNE, David, 270, Jerid Lloyd, 270, Jerry, 270, Keith Richard, 270, Nancy, 270
HIATT, Ada, 293, Ada Grace, 194, Brad, 374, Clara, 194, 257, 258, Doc, 129, Eleanor, 194, Elvira, 194, Ethel, 194, 293, Harry L., 211, Hazel, 194, 293, Ira, 194, 258, Ira Kenworth, 293, Ira Kenworthy, 193, 194, Isaac, 194, Iva, 133, 194, 293, John, 194, John B., 194, 211, John William, 194, Jonathan, 194, Leota, 194, 293, 294, Lillie Bell, 194, Lydia R., 194, Marian, 194, Marian L., 211, Mary J., 194, Matilda, 194, Mayme, 194, 293, Melinda, 194, Rachel, 194, Ralph, 194, Ralph W., 293, Sara, 194, Silas, 193, 194, 210, 211
HIBBARD, Elizabeth Belle, 304, Harrison, 304
HICKMAN, Ella, 242, Mary Marie, 119
HICKS, Betsy, 194, Desire Catherine, 194, Dorothy, 336, Elizabeth J., 125, Everilla Ann, 194, James, 194, Jesse, 194, Jim, 194, John, 194, Joshua, 201, Lauford, 194, Lucinda Jane, 194, Martha, 194, Martha B., 105, Mary Ann, 201, Molly, 354, Morrell, 194, Nancy Elizabeth, 194, Roy J., 63, S.T., 11, Sallie, 194, Samuel, 194, Sarah (Proctor), 334, 194, Thomas, 194, W.T., 64, William, 194
HIDDEN, Morton T., 166
HIDY, Margaret, 343
HIGBEE, Charles A., 205, Evie, 205, John, 166
HIGEN, __, 22
HIGGENBOTHAM, Beverly, 357, Janet, 357
HIGGINS, Barbara Jean, 270, Beverly Yvonne, 269, Blair, 82, Brian Scott, 119, Carol, 269, Clarissa, 82, Claudean, 270, Ed, 119, Jack, 270, Margaret A., 349, Nancy, 270, Richard, 269
HIGHLAND, Nancy Ann, 123
HILDEBRAND, Deborah, 200, Roger, 200
HILL, A.C., 194, Alfred, 100, Bert A., 11, Bob, 195, Bobbie Joe, 312, Chester C., 195, Chet, 194, 195, Clevia, 110, Clifton, 29, Delmar, 194, Dorothy, 194, Elizabeth (Billie), 149, Gregory Wade, 214, Jesse, 63, John, 195, Kathryn, 220, Martha, 258, Robby, 312, Sarah, 307, (Rev.), 41
HILLENBURG, Alice, 195, Carrell, 195, Charles, 195, Daniel, 195, Edith, 195, Effie, 195, Emert, 195, Everett, 195, Frank, 195, James Emert, 195, Oscar, 195, Vurl, 195
HILLER, Dwight David, 195, Gary, 195, Phyllis, 195, Scott Allen, 195
HILLIS, Machine Shop, 14
HILT, Nancy May, 214
HIMER, Sarah, 234
HIMES, Abraham, 124, 196, 266, Airport, 195, Albert, 266, Alice, 195, 196, 197, Amanda C., 124, Amanda Catherine, 266, Amy, 197, Audrey, 197, Barbara Jean, 197, Benjamin, 196, Catherine, 196, 197, Catherine Linn, 196, Chester, 44, 138, 177, 195, 196, 197, 255, 332, Clara, 197, Daniel, 249, 266, Daniel H., Jr., 196, 206, Daniel H., 178, Daniel, Sr., 196, David, 196, Dorothy, 103, Edna, 197, Elizabeth, 197, 196, Ella, 195, 266, Emma, 196, Ernest, 196, Ethel, 196, George, 177, 195, 196, 197, 266, Gertie, 196, Harvey, 266, Herman George, 197, Hernsty Max, 197, Jacob, 196, 197, 214, John, 196, 266, Katherine June, 228, Kathryn Louise, 197, Laurie, 196, Lawrence, 196, Leonard, 187, Lester, 177, 196, 197, 238, Lizzie, 196, Louis, 15, Lucretia J., 187, Lula, 266, Lydia Valentine, 249, Mabel, 196, 197, 216, Margaret, 266, Marian, 196, Marian Marciel, 138, 195, Marjorie, 238, Marjorie Fern, 197, Mark, 196, Mark Irl, 187, Mary, 196, Mary A., 266, Mary Ann, 196, Mary Ellen, 196, 197, Mary L., 196, Mary Louisa, 206, May, 196, Meade, 196, Meda, 196, Merle, 196, 197, 266, Nathaniel Benjamin, 196, Norma, 197, Pauline, 138, 218, Perry, 196, 197, Poultry & Eggs, 195, Poultry Co., 227, Ralph, 44, 196, Ressie, 266, Robert, 197, 266, Ruby, 195, Ruby Ann, 195, 197, 230, 255, Ruby Linn, 332, Ruth, 196, 197, 266, Ruth Pauline, 93, Ruth Pauline, 177, 195, 254, 255, Samuel, 196, Sarah, 196, Sophia Edna, 206, Susan, 218, 266, Susanna, 196, Truckers, 14, William, 196, William Asa, 195, Zola, 238, __, 55
HINES, Anne, 197, Bertha, 197, Linnaeus N., 197, Martha, 197, Melissa, 197, Nancy, 197, Nancy Jane, 342, Neal O., 197, Neal Offield, 197
HINESLEY, Joe E., 372, Ramona, 375
HINK, Irenus, 94
HINKLE, Andrew Jefferson, 352, Angeline, 197, Benjamin, 197, 302, 352, Benjamin, Jr., 197, Catherine, 197, David, 197, Elizabeth, 197, 302, Ellen, 197, George, 197, 302, Jacob, 302, James, 172, Jeremiah, 197, John, 302, John (Rev.), 197, John L., 197, Leabetter, 302, Magdalene, 197, Mary, 197, Rebecca, 172, Rebecca Jane, 197, Ruth M., 215, Samuel, 302, Samuel Benjamin, 197, Sarah, 197, Simon, 197, Susan, 197, 280, 302, William, 172, Zenolia, 172
HINTON, Janice, 171
HIPES, Alexander, 225
HIRCHBERGER, Jacob, 313
HIRSCHBERGER, Abraham, 186, Anna, 186, Barbara, 186, Christian, 186, Christian II, 186, Christopher, 186, Daniel, 186, David, 186, Elizabeth, 186, Henry, 186, Isac, 186, James, 186, Maria, 186, Samuel, 186, Susan, 186, Susanna, 186
HIRST, John, 301
HITCH, Ellen, 54, Alice, 271, Henry, 271, Margaret, 271, Virginia, 282
HITE, Jessie, 350, 351
HIXON, (Rev.), 49, Abigail, 208, Catharine, 207, Catherine, 80, 208, Fred W., 49, James, 208, Joel, 207, 208
HOAGLAND, Betty, 108, 36
HOBART, Kenneth, 57, Waneta Deere, 57
HOBBS, Amy, 265, Robyn, 265, William, 265
HOBSON, Bryant O., 323, Elizabeth, 305, Floyd, 304, Frank, 31, Mary, 304, Nathaniel, 304, Ruth Susan, 323, William, 55, __, 55
HOCKER, Harry, 12
HOCKERSMITH, Darrell, 305, Enid Lucille, 193, 305, Liz, 306, Lucille, 306, Perry Arthur, 305
HODGES, (Gen.), 341, Carl, 197, Chris, 197, Flora, 198, Florence Jeanette, 197, James Henry, 197, James Madison, 197, John Ora, 197, John Wesley, 197, Kenneth Edward, 197, Lora May, 197, Louie Lee, 197, Mac, 197, Mary, 197, Nettie, 197, Neva Pauline, 197, Robert Lee, 197, Susie, 197, Torrie Ella, 197
HODGKIN, Craig Allen, 312, Patricia Nodyne, 312, Teresa Dawn, 312
HODGSON, Maria Jane, 203, Mary, 202, Sarah, 194, Thomas, 202, 203, William, 202
HODSON, Caroline, 202, Helen, 202, James Louis, 202, John Manson, 202, Thomas, 202, Thomas David, 202, William J., 202
HOEFERT, John P., 278, Nevin II, 278, Nevin III, 278
HOEL, Abigail, 190
HOFFA, Dolores, 182, M. Jean, 372
HOFFMAN, Charles, 95, Frances, 328, Frances Rose, 328, John R., 136, Mary, 222, Mary Elizabeth, 328, Nellie, 214, Pearl, 95, Peter Henry, 328, Susan Jane, 136, Susie, 136
HOGSET, __, 100
HOGSHEAD, Rebeca, 100
HOHENSTEIN, Erin, 304, Janet, 286, 304
HOKE, Olive, 58
HOLBERT, Margaret, Minerva, 175
HOLE, Alisa Dawn, 271, Alma Newby, 216, Amanda Jane, 271, Bernard, 221, 271, Bessie Gail, 198, Brian, 271, David, 216, David C., 198, Elizabeth, 276, F. Marvin, 198, Flossie Mae, 198, Floyd Marvin, 198, Frank, 50, Garry Steven, 271, Gerald J., 271, Greg, 271, Gregory, 216, Hurschell David, 198, Isaac, 329, Jane, 269, Jennifer Lee, 271, Julia, 329, Lelan Clarence, 198, Lester, 216, 334, Lester David, 198, Lola, 198, Lola B., 198, Lucy, 198, Lucy Fern, 198, Mary E., 221, Mary Elizabeth, 198, Mary Elizabeth, 221, Michael Kristopher, 271, Myrl, 216, Nancy, 289, Oscar, 91, Raymond Kenneth, 198, Robert Allen, 271, Ruby Alberta, 198, Shelly, 271, Susannah Lynn, 271, Virgil W., 198, Virgil Wesley, 198, William K., 216, William Lloyd, 198, William N., 198, William Newton, 198, Wilma Rita, 198, Zetta Maxine, 198
HOLEMAN, William, 227
HOLLAND, Bertha May, 198, Donna, 199, Dorothy, 199, Elizah, 314, Ethel, 348, Francis, 199, Freida, 366, George M., 199, Geraldine, 199, Ida May, 198, Ira J., 198, James E., 199, John, 198, John "Bert", 199, John D., 198, Joseph E., 199, Joseph Eldred, 199, Joseph O., 198, Judith, 199, Nancy Elizabeth, 198, Rebecca, 232, 314, William Shure, 198, William Allen, 198
HOLLENBECK, Earl, 272, Ester Livengood, 272, Linda, 272
HOLLIN, Lena, 65
HOLLINGSWORTH, Euratis Frank, 199, Amos B., 199, Clara, 241, Cueza Jane, 199, Ethel, 199, Frank, 199, John, 199, Joseph, 199, Julian Jane, 223, Lydia Florence, 199, Mary Pink, 199, Pinson, 199, 223, Rosa, 223, Rosa Pink, 199, Russell, 199, Sarah, 80, Sarah Elizabeth, 199, Ursual Gertrude, 199, Winona, 199
HOLLOWAY, Alice, 221, Bess, 221, Elizabeth, 349, Gordon, 375, Mary, 349, Washington, 349, William, 221
HOLLOWELL, Mary, 43
HOLLY, Ann, 307, Clara, 187
HOLMAN, (Addition), 307, Brenda, 352, Brian, 352, Don, 352, Geri, 352
HOLMES, Amy, 122, Charlotte, 122, Elizabeth, 223, Ellis, 215, Martha, 260, Raymond, 122, Rebecca, 239, William H., 223
HOLT, Brian W., 290, Carolyn, 327, Clark D., 290, Delbert, 116, Dennis, 359, Donna, 359, Donna Marie, 290, Erin Nichol, 290, Fred, 116, George, 359, Howard L., 290, Jason, 290, Jill, 359, John, 116, John Joseph, 327, Kathleen, 359, Kevin H., 290, Leonard, 359, Logan Bradley, 290, Lynette, 290, Mahala, 327, Phyllis, 116, Rachel Elizabeth, 290, Roy A., 327, Viola, 326, Wanda, 353, William, 69
HOLZ, Betty Jean, 173, 199, 320, Fred, Jr., 173, Frederick W., 173, Frederick William, 199, Frederick William, Jr., 199, Margaret Anne, 173, 199, Margaret Catherine, 199
HOLZGERLINGER, Johann Von, 199
HOMANN, Betsy, 200, Carol, 199, 200, Charles, 200, Clayton, 200, Kurt, 199, 200
HONNELL, Rebecca, 141
HOOD, Ida, 317, Pamela, 286, Velva Gertrude, 149
HOOERMALE, Ella Jane, 116
HOOKER, Blanche, 12, Mertie, 59, Orrin, 12, __, 59
HOOLEY, Aaron, 344, Anthony, 344, Betty Joan, 344, Jennifer, 344, Mark Alan, 344, Michael,

344, Roger Lee, 344
HOOPES, Eben, 222, 303
HOOSE, Geraldine (Gerry), 316
HOOTS, Roger, 312
HOOVER, Herbert, 160, Katrina, 354, Richard, 311
HOPEWELL, Anna, 200, Grace, 200, J.E., 381, John, 200, 374, John E., 200, 374, Mary, 200, Ruth, 200
HOPEWOOD, __, 110
HOPKINS, Arvella, 158, John, 106, 338, Kelly, 320, Louis B., 234, Mabel, 131, Mary, 343, Matthew, 320, Robert C., 158, Robert T., 34
HOPPER, Eliza Jane, 130, Hattie, 272
HOPPING, Mary, 301
HORINE, Catherine, 229, 352
HORMELL, Matilda, 324
HORN, Anita Marie, 200, Buel E., 49, Cecil, 246, Cecil Columbus, 200, Cheryl Denise, 200, David Ronald, 200, Eva, 246, Eva Louise, 200, Jeffrey Allen, 200, Jeffrey Clayton, 200, Margaret, 200, 243, Matthew Thomas, 214, Maxine, 246, 247, 248, 378, Ronald Les, 200, Samuel Lee, 214, Sheila Jean, 200, Thomas James, 214, Travis James, 214
HORN'S, Photography, 14
HORNBAKER, Sarah, 43
HORNELL, Eulalia, 43
HORNER, Connie, 113, John, 113, Julie, 113, Sam, 113
HORNERS, 312
HORROCKS, Mildred, 223
HORTON'S, New Horizons Greenhs, 16
HOSCHSTAEDTER, Christian, 200, Nicklaus, 200
HORSCHSTARDTER, Ulrich, 200
HOSIER, Martin, 31
HOSKINS, Thomas B., 372
HOSS, Birdie, 12, Maude, 238, Ruth, 94
HOSSEINI, Hossein, 139, Sheerein, 139
HOSTETTER, Abraham, 201, Beniah Mary, 201, Berniah, 196, Bert, 201, Date, 201, David, 201, David B., 190, David Hicks, 177, 201, 338, Donald M., 199, Donald Marion, 201, Dora, 209, Eleanor, 89, 190, Emma Jane, 201, 338, Flower Shop, 15, Francis Marion, 201, Henry, 201, Howard, 190, Ida, 201, Jane, 201, Jean, 31, Kathleen Anne, 199, Lela, 201, Lenus J., 201, Lewis, 201, Lucky, 201, Lydia, 201, Margaret, 173, Milton, 201, Newt, 228, Rachael, 201, Rachel, 209, Samuel, 201, Sherman, 201, Vinnie, 31, 99, Zerelda, 201
HOTLER, Mary, 225
HOTOPP, Chris, 56
HOTSCHIER, Photo, 14
HOTTEL, Barbar Ann, 213, Johannaes, 213, Margaret, 213
HOUCHIN, Elsie, 67
HOUCHINS, Alma Ruth, 114
HOUFF, Sarah, 117, 169, Sarah Elizabeth, 169
HOUGLAND, Hildreth, 127, Kenneth A., 127, Mary K., 127
HOUK, Andrew, 201, Andrew K., Sr., 201, Andrew K., Jr., 201, 202, 206, Keith, 41, Andrew Keith, Jr., 32, 36, 37, 80, 91, 125, 126, 162, 213, 238, 288, 29, 34, Georgia L., 201, Keith, 15, Susan, 202, Susan Hart, 186, 201
HOULEHAN, __, 32
HOUSE, Barbara, 92, 280, 321, 322, Charles Arnold, 157, Janet, 157, Janet Louise, 287, Lester Merle, 157, 287, 322, Myra Louise, 157, 287, 322, Peter, 336, Sarah Frances, 157
HOUSLEY, Berniece, 270, Charles, 270, Clarence, 270, Crafford, 270, Frank, 270, Opal, 270
HOUSTON, Anna, 105, Beth A., 372, Brodie S., 375, Companies, 23, Hugh, 105, Lawrence L., 372
HOUSTZ, Magdaline, 162
HOUTS, Kathern, 176
HOUTZ, Catherine, 162
HOVEY, Anna Pearl, 189
HOWARD, __, 22, (Capt.), 322, Andrew, 265, Charles G., 265, Darrell, 202, Deborah, 202, Dennis, 202, Elizabeth Myrtle, 202, Emily, 265, Gordon J., 202, Jacque DeAnne, 202, Jerry, 202, Leslie, 313, Lulu, 108, Margery Ann, 313, Muriel, 293, Rex, 284, 353, Samuel H., 37, Sherri, 202, Sherri Leigh, 202, Steven, 220, Vernice, 202, Vicki, 220, William, 111, William "Bill", 313
HOWELL, Amber Renee, 202, Arthur (Rev.), 202, Aubrey, 202, Bertha, 202, Charles, 202, Charles A., 29, Christina, 202, Diana L., 223, Evelyn, 202, Katherine N., 202, Malinda, 351, Marilyn, 350, Mary, 222, Mary Jane, 206, Michael, 351, Richard, 351, Ronald, 202, Seth Adam, 199, 223, 290, Terry, 199, 223, 290, Travis Jared, 199, 223, 290
HOWIE, Willard, 329
HOWLAND, Carl B., 375
HRNJAK, Danielle Gail, 122
HUBBLE, Calvin, 189, Jeremy, 343, Justin, 189, Marion Edward, 343, Megan, 189, Melissa, 189, Truckers, 14, Woodrow Leondus, 343
HUBER, Abby, 192, 246, Elizabeth Ann, 297, George, 118, Mariah, 118, Mary, 261, Rebecca Ann, 192, Simon, 118, Susan, 54
HUBERT, Lyla, 294, Myrtle, 294, Nelly Terry, 294, Orbie, 294
HUDAK, Catharine, 287
HUDDLESTON, Richard, 70
HUDNALL, Alice, 172
HUDSON, Anna H., 203, Babe D., 203, Brenda, 173, Brian Charles, 203, Caroline, 203, Caroline Jane, 203, Charles, 203, Charles Eugene, 203, 347, Charles Thomas, 203, Charlotte, 203, Clara Jane, 203, Clarence Earl, 203, Dorothea Darlene, 203, Dorothy Darlene, 347, Evelyn Louise, 203, 347, Fern, 147, Golda May, 203, Hazel, 242, Hazel J., 203, Hazel Jewel, 347, 203, Hazel Pearl, 203, James Louis, 203, Jason Sean, 203, Jeffrey Neil, 203, John, 327, John David, 202, John Manson, 203, Joseph Craig, 203, Joshua David, 203, Joyce, 173, Lawrence Leroy, 203, Lloyd, 374, Louis J., 202, Margaret, 203, Margaret J., 202, Margaret R., 203, Maria, 203, Marilyn Kay, 203, Mildred, 203, Nancy Lou, 203, Ora H., 203, Peggy L., 375, Raymond, 374, Thomas David, 203, Thomas Jefferson, 203, Thomas W., 203, Wilbur "Pete", 203, William, 173, William J., 203, James A., 202
HUDSPETH, Sylvia, 343
HUESTON, Clothing, 14
HUFF, Arthur, 360, Jacob, 360, Jerusha, 184, Martha, 360, Mary E., 360
HUFFINGTON, Aretta, 150
HUFFMAN, Carolyn, 357, Dean Steel Record, 335, Earl, 357, Elva May, 357, Gladys, 357, Jean, 245, Leo, 357, Ray, 357, Robert, 357, Versa, 357, Walter, 49, Wretha, 357
HUGELMAN, Frances, 243
HUGHES, Alta, 204, Anna, 356, Barbara, 358, Beatrice, 204, Bell, 302, Bethany, 204, Bradley, 204, Bradley McKinsey, 203, Catherine Ann, 204, Charles, 268, 296, Charles R., 204, Clarence, 203, Clarence L., 203, 204, Cynthia, 204, David Henry, 204, David W. (Dr.), 359, David W. (Rev.), 85, David Wesley, 198, 204, 356, Debra Kay, 135, Donald Richard, 204, Dorothy, 168, 205, Edith, 204, Edith McKinsey, 203, Elbert, 204, Ella, 204, Ellen, 356, Elmer, 240, Elsie, 204, 205, Emma, 204, 356, Ethel Marie, 204, Ezekiel, 204, Garth, 359, George, 205, George William, 205, Geraldine, 204, Gladys, 205, Harbour H., 204, Harold, 204, 205, Harold J., 205, Harry, 204, Harry E., 204, Harry, Jr., 204, Helen, 31, Henry, 204, Henry C., 204, Henry L., 203, 204, 205, Hiram, 204, Howard Allen, 132, Jacqueline L., 204, James, 356, James B., 204, James Elbert, 204, 205, James F., 356, James Harvey, 204, Jason Daniel, 205, Jeremy Adam, 205, Jerry, 205, Jerry J., 205, John, 80, 204, Jonathan Matthew, 205, Joseph V., 204, Judy, 205, Judy L., 205, Julie J., 205, Kimberlee Ruthana, 132, Kristin Elizabeth, 204, Lavina, 356, Lee Ann, 204, Lola B., 198, Lola Belle, 198, Lulu, 204, Lydia, 204, Magan R., 204, Mame, 203, Mark, 204, Martha, 95, Martha Ann, 204, Mary, 204, Mary Ann, 204, Mary Jane, 205, 302, Melissa, 356, Merle, 168, Merle A., 205, Miranda, 204, Nancy, 205, Nancy Ann, 204, Nancy J., 204, Nathaniel, 204, Nervilla, 204, 356, Ogden, 204, Ogden R., 204, Oley, 168, Oley Haines, 205, Patrik Craig, 204, Paul, 204, Pauline "Bunny", 204, Phebe, 204, Phyllis, Meredith, 203, Prudence Jane, 204, Russell S., 204, Rebecca, 204, Richard, 204, Romania, 203, 204, Rosalyn Jean, 204, Ruby, 205, Russell, 204, Russell Smith, 203, Russell Spencer, 203, Russell V., 204, Ruth, 203, Sarah, 204, Sarah J., 356, Sinderella, 204, Stella, 205, Susan, 204, Thomas J., 356, Thomas Jefferson, 204, Vickey Ellen, 205, Vincent, 203, Vincent K., 204, Vincent Smith, 204, William B., 204, William I., 302, William Sanford, 204, Linda, 204, __, 82
HUKER, Mary A., 130
HULBERT, Lyle, 44, 323, Myrtle, 323, Nelly Marie, 323, Orbie, 323
HULCE, Jo Ellen, 366
HULET, James J., 259
HULL, Elsie, 169
HULSE, __, 22, Lester, 43
HULTBERG, C.N., 371
HULTZ, George, 43
HULVAH, Catherine, 222, 303, Conrad, 303, Conrad, Sr., 303, Floren, 121, Hazel, 121, Laura, 215
HUMBER, George, 211, Isaac, 229
HUMBERT, Belle, 211, Flora Belle, 211, Henry, 211, Isaac, 211, 336, Letilia Flora Belle, 123, Letitia Belle, 211, Letitita Flora Belle, 229, Lilly Dora Josephine, 211, Lutetia Flora Belle, 336
HUMEL, Marcellia, 86
HUMPHREY, Hettie, 208, Oswald, 151, William, 151
HUMPHREYS, Alford, 205, Asa, 205, Carl, 205, Carole Lee, 205, Caroline, 205, Cassandra Marie, 205, Charles, 54, 205, Charles Edward, 205, Charles Eric, 205, Chere, 54, Emma, 205, Francis Merrian, 205, Frederick, 205, Grover, 205, Harold, 205, James, 205, Jonathan, 205, Lee, 205, Lowry, 87, Mary, 205, Opal, 205, Ross, 205, Samuel, 205, Sarah, 205, 206, Sharon, 208, Thomas B., 205, Wilbur, 205, Zella, 205
HUND, William, 74
HUNDLEY, Ruth, 351
HUNLEY, Michael, 375
HUNSICKER, Joan, 256, Phil, 144
HUNT, Alice Swisher, 239, Betsy, 286, Betty F., 286, C.L., 41, Charles, 274, Daisy, 126, David, 274, Donald, 274, Edna, 133, 336, Ephraim T., 165, Esther, 165, Fern, 269, Harry, 274, James Allen, 336, John, 239, Julia, 165, 185, Laban, 286, Larry R., 372, Leroy, 325, Loren "Dutch", 13, Mae, 127, Mary Magdalene, 336, Nancy, 274, Peggy, 274, Richard, 274, Robert, 274, Ruth, 274, Ruth Naomi, 159, Simeon, 286, Susannah, 286, Thomas, 230, William, 207, 274, Connie, 274
HUNTER, __, 160, Carmen, 54, Cindy, 200, David, 54, David C., 206, Don, 200, Fay, 200, Isabell, 125, John, 173, John L., 206, Kenneth, 173, Marci, 200, Mary Bell, 308, Morton W., 206, Pearl, 341, Susan, 200, Teddy Jo, 173, Theodore, 173, William B., 206
HUNTINGTON, Charles Marshall, 206, Earl Gregg, 206, Eva Delelia, 206, George, 206, George Marshall, 206, 340, Harry, 206, Harry Gregg, 206, Hiram, 207, Hiram Samuel, 206, 340, Lizzie, 74, Lizzie Gregg, 340, Louisa, 340, Mary Louise, 206, Nellie Ruth, 206, Samuel Dimock, 206, Sarah Louisa, 206, Sarah Louise, 206, Silas Hiram, 206, Simon, 296, Sophia, 206, Sophia Edna, 206
HUNTS, T.V., 365
HURIN, Silas, 123
HURLEY, Alva, 207, George Washington, 342, John W., 207, Margaret, 215, Mary Lamb, 207, Maude, 301, Myrl, 207, Myrtle D., 207, Myrtle Dell, 274, Pearl, 207, 301, Teenza Margaret, 342, William D., 207
HURST, Agnes, 336, Elizabeth Edaline, 312
HURT, Aaron, 360, Becky, 360, Brad, 360, Jacob, 360, Joan, 99
HUSEMAN, Carolyn L., 207, Charles, 207, Charles, Jr., 207, David, 207, 353, David C., 207, Dick, 207, Douglas Carl, 207, Flora, 207, Flora L., 353, Juliana, 207, 353, Julie, 207, Rachel Heather, 207, Richard, 207, 353, Richard Allyn, 207, Richard C., 376, Ricahrd C., Jr., 207, Richard C., Sr., 207, Richard J., 207
HUSTED, Abigail, 267, Caroline, 267, 268, John, Jr., 267, 268
HUSTON, Anne, 242, Glenn, 242, Jack, 242, Jill, 242, Tom, 10
HUTCHENS, Caroline, 176, George, 176
HUTCHINGS, Armenia, 130, Elizabeth, 178, Hannah, 336, John Work, 178, Martha E., 178, William, 130
HUTCHINS, Esther, 272, Paul, 272
HUTCHINSON, Brent, 243, Jamie Nicole, 243, John, 288, Steven, 243
HUTCHISON, Abigail, 207, 208, Benjamin, 208, Catharine, 207, Catherine, 208, Elizabeth Ann, 208, Esther, 208, George, 208, Irvin, 208, James, 207, 208, Jasper, 208, John, 208, Josiah, 207, 208, Mary, 86, 208, Melinda, 208, Melinda Catherine, 208, Millie, 86, Millie Catherine, 86, Nancy Ellen, 347, Sarah, 208, Walter Irvin, 86
HUTHERT, Jane, 144
HUTSON, Delores Ann, 300, Lauevecia, 127, Lucille, 207, Lula Mae, 300, Roy Milton, 300, Timothy S., 372
HUTTON, Olive, 331
HUTTS, Beulah, 315, Clee, 315, L.W., 61, Milton Taylor, 259
HUX, Clida Jane, 324
HYATT, Lizzie, 43
HYBARGER, Charles, 52, Elizabeth, 272, Georgia, 319, Grace, 319, Maude, 319, Ora, 319, Patricia, 131, Ruby, 319, William, 319
HYDE, Mary, 213
HYMER, Donald, 279, Doris Sue, 279, James, 208, Jesse, 208, 302, Jesse P., 208, Mary, 208, Orion Oka, 279, Sarah Frances, 302, Wesley Max, 279
HYTEN, __, 22, Bertha, 209, Cora, 209, DePew, 209, Effie, 209, Eliza, 208, John, 209, Josiah, 208, Mary Clay, 209, Mildred Marie, 191, 209, Newton, 209, Pearl, 191, Rebecca, 208, Safronia, 209, Susan, 209, Tillman, 191, 209, William, 209, William (Dr.), 209, William Caywood, 208, William Henry, 208
IDLE, William C., 139
IMEL, Clara, 209, Emory, 209, Evelyn, 209, Florence, 209, Frankie, 43, Franklin, 209, Fred, 61, Frederick, 209, Josephine, 31, 43, 209, Martha, 61, Nancy, 209, Nancy E., 67, Peter, 209, Rebecca Ann, 209, Samuel, 209, Samuel, Jr., 209, Sarah, 209, Sarah Frances, 209, Stephen, 209, Stillwell, 129, Susan, 209, William S., 209, __ (Inf. son), 209
IMPICCICHE, Andrea, 359, Christopher, 359, Joseph, 359
INGALSBE, Adna, 190, Carrie, 190, Edith, 191, 280, JoAnn, 190, 280, Lankford, 190, Mildred, 190
INGE, Francis, 314
INGERSOL, Lily Hannah Irene, 312
INGERSOLL, Bill, 209, Bob, 209, David, 209, Dessie, 209, Ellis, 209, Ellis John, 209, Elmira, 209, Hurley, 209, James, 209, James K.P., 209, James Knox Polk, 209, Janet, 209, Joseph, 209, Martha, 209, Martha Ann, 209, Marty, 209, Mary, 209, Mary Della, 209, Robert, 209, Robert Harry, 209, Sarah, 209, Van, 209
INGRAM, Anna Marie, 209, Becky, 209, 317, Carole Jane, 209, David Alan, 209, Dude Alan, 209, John Mark, 209, Margie, 191, 280, Margie Marie, 191, 209, Ova, 191, 209, Roy, 191, 209, Roy Eugene, 209, Ruth Ann, 209, Sythe, 285
INLOW, Ed, 45
INNES, W.P., 180
INSKEEP, John, 161, William, 65
INSLEY, Marion, 85, __, 30
IRELAND, Dawn, 73, James, 73, William N., 376
IRONS, Josephine, 238
IRVIN, Martha, 365, Ruth Ann, 262, Sophia, 321
IRWIN, Francis, 248, Hannah, 79, O.A., 374, Obed, 374
ISAAC, William Allen, 210
ISAACS, Gerald W., 210, Helen, 209, 210, James, 29, John, 210, John Carl, 210, John H., 210, Ruth, 210, Ruth L., 210, William P., 210
ISENBERG, Mildred, 157
ISLEY, Chelsea Jena, 268, Tim, 268
IVERSON, James, 26, Midge, 348
IVEY, B.F., 260, Benjamin Franklin, 260, Catherine, 260, Daniel Keith, 261, David Merrill, 261, David Merrill, Jr., 261, Dorothy, 216, Dot, 261, Elisha F., 260, H. Merrill (Rev.), 156, H.P., 261, Homer, 68, Homer Merrill, 260, 261, Homer Pierson, 260, Jill, 261, Keith, 261, Merrill, 262, Newell, 260, Paul, 261, Sara, 261, Sara N. 261, Sara Nees, 261, Sara Ozella, 261, Sharon, 261, Susan, 261
IVY, Daniel, 261
JACK, C.W., 43
JACKMAN, Gene, 301, Glen, 113, James Eugene, 214, James Oliver, 113, Traci Leann, 214
JACKSON, __, 22, Alfaretta, 357, Andrew, 90, 144, Andrew (Pres.), 344, Barb, 360, Caleb, 233, Cheryl, 233, Curt A., 233, De Ella, 323, Essie Marie, 264, Fannie Ellen, 273, Fanny Ellen, 273, Iona, 325, James C., 301, Juliet V., 122, Luther, 182, Margaret, 134, Matthew, 233, Nathaniel, 233, Rachel, 233, Robert F., 323, Terry, 360, Variety Store, 15, Vicki R., 375, Virginia, 306
JACOBS, John, 330, Rebecca, 330
JAEGGER, Diantha, 326
JAHRAUS, Aurelia, 358, Theodor, 358
JAMES, __, 22, Alfred T., 298, Barbara E., 298, David, 298, 299, David, Jr., 298, Drucilla, 298, Ethel, 354, Evaline, 298, 325, 339, Evelyn, 299, Florence, 175, Harley, 282, Jesse, 87, John B., 298, Margaret, 250, 298, 299, Mary Lou, 283, Sarah, 85, Terry E., 298
JAMISON, Chadwick Maxwell, 156, Courtney Marie, 156, Thomas Maxwell (Dr.), 156
JANNEY, Abel, 125, 126, Harriet, 125, Harriet Doubleday, 126
JANSSEN, Martha, 66
JAQUESS, Jerry, 326
JARDINE, Sarah, 248
JARRED, Madge, 271
JARRELL, Ethel, 158, 356
JARVIS, Brenna Antoinette, 252, Butch, 161, 252, Candy, 252, Carole Jane, 326, Doris Ann, 326, Emma Blanche, 265, Gene, 252, Herbert, 326, Herbert Cox, 326, Judy, 161, Margaret, 326, Marie, 252, Pam, 252, Ralph, 67, Virginia, 265, Wayne, 252, William, 265
JAY, Winnie, 229
JAYNES, Elva, 251, Elva Leona, 332, Norma, 217
JEAN, Sarah, 88
JEFFERS, Bill, 158, Christopher, 157, Jill, 157, Joyce, 158, Joyce Ellen, 157, Pamela Jo, 207, William, 157
JEFFERSON, Thomas, 96
JEFFIRES, Jerrod, 210
JEFFREY, Margaret, 360, Oliver, 360
JEFFRIES, Andrew, 210, Angeline, 211, Annie, 210, Arthur, 302, Bill, 211, Bradley, 210, Brian Keith, 211, Cecil B., 210, Charles, 211, Daniel, 210, Doris, 222, 305, 306, Dorothy, 211, Harvey, 302, Harvey Jewell, 210, Holly, 210, 211, Holly Joan, 210, Ina, 180, Jaclyn, 210, James Knox, 302, Jamie, 210, Jan, 211, Jayne, 210, Jewell, 210, Jon, 210, 211, Jonathan C., 210, Joseph Kim, 210, Josie, 210, Judy, 306, Kay, 210, Keith, 211, Kevin, 211, Lloyd, 309, Lloyd Russell, 211, Louise, 309, Mabel, 302, Marta, 210, 258, Marta Cox, 127, Martin Jewell, 210, Mary Margaret, 211, May, 226, 302, Mullen Jaye, 210, Nick, 210, Paul, 302, Pearl, 302, Tillet, 302, Tom, 305, 306, Vince, 302, Walter, 302, William, 210, 211, 302
JENKINS, Allen, 342, Joan, 215, Lorene, 124, Rodney L., 372

JENKS, Carl Frederick, 174
JENNINGS, Lydia, 184, Milly, 336
JENNISON, A.C., 376, Mary E., 190
JESS, Jennifer, L., 233
JESSE, Nancy B., 67
JESSEE, James A., 67, Squire, 67
JESSIE, Jimmy, 208, Pamela Willhite, 350
JESSUP, Brookes Melvin, 269, Fred, 269, Grace Lee, 269, Steven James, 175
JESTER, Henry, 360
JETT, Gailen, 165
JEWEL, __, 304
JEWELL, Frank, 54, Kathy, 54, Nellie, 54
JINES, Celia, 263, Paul, 172, Ruby Irene, 172
JINKS, Effie G., 357
JOBE, Will, 331
JOH, Clyde, 336, George, 211, 336, Jacob, 211, Lilly Dora Josephine, 336, Martha, 211, Mary, 229, 294, Mary Jane, 211, William, 182, 211
JOHANNSEN, Minnie, 179
JOHNS, Iva, 146, Jacob, 201, Nancy Jane, 330, Rachel, 201, Roberta Ellen, 81
JOHNSON, __, 22, Philip, 297, A.W., 11, 12, Aaron, 297, Abner Fowler, 82, Ada, 263, Al, 212, Allen, 148, 212, Allen W., 212, Allen W., Jr., 212, Alva, 211, 263, Amasa, 49, Arthur Lloyd, 295, Barbara, 86, Becky, 212, Bertie, 163, Betty, 244, Betty E., 329, Beverly, 54, Bruce, 297, Burgess, 297, Catharine, 207, Catherine, 201, 208, Charles, 31, 44, Charles H., 149, Cindy, 212, Clyde, 196, 266, David E., 211, 372, Diana Darlene, 284, Donald, 266, 375, Donna, 212, Earl L., Sr., 212, Earl L. Jr., 212, Earl Lucien, 212, Earl Lucien, Jr., 212, Edith, 212, Elizabeth, 176, 212, Ellijah R., 63, Errin, 212, Eugene (Mrs.), 310, Eva, 174, Evelyn, 230, F.N., 253, Frank, 212, 263, Franklin (Mrs.), 53, Franklin Blair, 211, George, 34, Grace, 211, Guy, 210, Harry, 211, Harry E., 211, Harry Elsworth, 211, Helen R., 212, Henry, 81, Henry C., 210, Hilary Ann, 212, Hillyard, 315, J.J., 30, Jaclyn Diane, 147, James Eric, 297, James H., 92, James Maurice, 297, Jana Geiger, 212, Janee, 187, Jason Brandon, 128, Jemima, 279, Jennie, 92, Joe, 54, Joseph, 279, Judith, Sharon, 297, Julianna, 288, Karen, 297, Karen Denise, 230, Katherine, 212, Kathy, 212, Laura, 212, Laura Ann, 212, Leah Beth, 297, Louis, 284, Louisa, 223, Mabel, 212, Mable Jean, 211, Margaret, 81, Marian, 194, 211, Marilyn, 299, Marilyn Fairfield, 229, Mark David, 211, Marty, 235, Marvin, 263, Mary, 148, 168, 212, 300, Mary E., 374, Mary Early, 297, Maude, 91, Minnie, 210, Nancy, 212, Nancy Jane, 245, Natalie, 212, Nora Jean, 212, O.S., 240, Olive, 285, Olive Owen, 285, Ora, 81, Orthella Marie, 236, Oscar, 139, Paul, 230, Paul K., 375, Peggy, 212, Phoebe J., 305, Phyllis, 266, Price, 235, Rebecca Louise, 212, Rhoda Ann, 240, Rhonda, 297, Rob, 212, Robert Early, 212, Robert Greenlief, 211, Ron, 212, Ronald, 212, Ruby, 315, Ruth, 348, 375, Sallie, 201, Sally, 212, Samuel, 212, Samuel T., 201, Scott, 64, Tacy, 279, Tammy, 235, Theodore, 244, Thomas Benton, 201, Tony, 147, Van, 342, Verna E., 210, W.A., 230, Willis H., 119, Zebnor, 201, __, 42
JOHNSTON, Dora Elizabeth, 138, Gordon, 199, Gregg, 199, Kathleen, 199, Marian, 199, Millie, 252, Robert, 90, 189, Virginia, 90
JOHNSTONE, D., 59
JOINER, Basel, 325, Jerry, 325, Ruth, 43, Ruth Hazel, 324, 325
JOLLEY, Bob, 132, Lloyd, 116, Mable, 116, Merle, 116
JONES, Ammon Burkett, 213, Bob, 188, Boyd C., 372, Bud, 229, Charles, 54, Charles E., 99, Clark, 24, Conoco, 227, Delia Crow, 130, Dennis, 131, Earl, 43, Eileen, 211, Elizabeth, 219, Emma, 356, Georgia, 31, Gerald R., 291, Gladys Autumn, 334, Grace, 244, Grace W., 111, Grant, 295, Hannah, 115, 116, Henry, 356, Herff, 365, Hilda S., 375, Ida, 356, Isaac, 36, Isaac A., 34, Jane, 327, Jason, 278, Jerry, 139, Johnathan, 278, Jon, 278, Joseph, 34, Kent Edward, 317, Laura E., 356, Leota, 264, Lillie, 213, Lonnie D., 375, Louise, 83, Machine Shop, 16, Margaret, 356, Margaret Ann, 213, Maria, 328, Marsh, 375, Marsh H., Jr., 133, 213, Marsh Henry, 212, 213, Martha, 225, 356, Martha Victoria, 134, Mary, 204, Mary Elizabeth, 256, Mary Ellen, 131, Mary Jane, 278, Mary Louisa, 99, Matt, 130, 131, Mattie, 134, Mattie Mae, 289, Melissa, 139, Mervyn, 134, Mike, 221, Myrtle Mary, 99, Nancy, 221, Nancy C., 375, Nancy Charlene, 317, Nina, 343, Oren V., 372, Oscar, 112, Otto, 134, Parnelli, 177, Ralph M., 49, Rick, 317, Robert F., 134, Ruth Victoria, 134, Samuel, 356, Sarah, 112, Stephen, 112, Susan, 112, Susannah, 104, Veda Mae, 289, Wade Tate, 139, William, 131, William A., 289, William Doderick, 213, __, 32
JORDAN, Ena Gay, 298, George E., 357, James, 185, William H., 34, William Harrison, 213
JORGENSEN, David, 312, Michael, 312
JOSEPH, Anna Jane, 143, Elder S., 36, George S., 36, George S. (Rev.), 143
JOSLIN, Hazel Marie, 318
JULIEN, Mary H., 120
JUNDT, Anna Marie, 359, Hans George, 359
JURGENSMEYER, Alexander Edward, 116, Dora Ethel, 116, Mary Elizabeth, 116, 258
JUSTICE, Harry, 199
KADINGER, Larry L., 372, Michael D., 372, Shirley, 372
KAEMERRLEN, Kim, 192
KAHAL, Elizabeth, 181
KAILER, Glen, 50
KALFSBECK, Eable, 231
KANDRAC, Dorothy, 154,
KANE, William P., 75
KAPPA, Kappa Kappa, 366
KAPPS, Margaret, 163
KARG, Aileen Crow, 131, Henry, 41, 131, Henry Herbert (Rev.), 131, Karen Ann, 131, Margaret Dot, 131, Rollin Orestes, 131, Susan Marie, 131, T. Aileen, 366, Thelma, 131, Karen, 131
KARL, Mynheer, 219
KARLE, Eric Joseph, 168
KARR, Carol, 103, George, 103, Gwendolyn, 103, Margaret Zona, 103, William, 103
KARSHNER, Barbara, 159, 233, Virginia, 159
KASER, Roy E., 372
KASHER, Orpha, 331
KASHNER, Catherine, 158, Elizabeth, 194, Goerge, 158
KASSEG, Betty, 286
KAUAHIKAUA, Susan, 180
KAUFMAN, Carol Ann, 283
KEANEY, Elinor, 84
KEEFE, Thomas, 75
KEELING, Alfred, 132, Austin, 132, Bertha, 132, Caroline, 132, Charles, 132, David Alan, 301, Dexter, 118, Elvie, 118, Flora, 132, Frances, 270, Glen, 270, James, 132, Kimberly Rosanne, 301, Lillie, 132, Lorna Lynn, 301, Mary Kay, 270, Mary Lowe, 118, Milton, 270, Molly, 132, Robert D., 301, Ronald, 270, Sharon, 270, Viola, 132, William, 270, William M., 270
KEENE, James Upton, 34
KEENEY, Florence America, 132, William, 132
KEESSEE, Sharon, 223
KEFFER, Donis, 375, Meredith, 30, 31, 375
KEIFER, Aurelia, 358
KEIL, Brothers Oil, 16
KEIM, Adam, 170, Bernard, 170, Brian, 193, Brian E., 372, Erik, 193, Jason, 170, 193, Jeff, 193, Lorraine, 170, Mark, 170, Mary Beth, 54, 193, Shane, 170, Stephen, 193, Timothy, 170, Tony, 170
KEIRN, Norris A., 68
KEITH'S, Blacksmith, 16
KELBAUGH, Harry, 302, Madonna Sharon, 302, Ross Jeffries, 302
KELELR, Sayra, 213
KELLAM, Addie, 336
KELLAR, Archebold, 213, Beatrice, 213, Carrie Ruth, 213, Catherine M., 293, 294, Charles Robert, 213, Edie, 213, Edith Ann, 213, Harry Everett, 213, Harry Everett, Jr., 213
KELLER, Abraham, 213, Alexander, 213, Alexia, 113, Alvora, 213, Barbara Ann, 113, Barbara Jean, 113, Berniece, 145, Blanche, 145, Catherine, 295, Charles, 145, Christina, 139, Daniel, 213, Daniel, Sr., 213, Darrell, 113, Deborah, 305, Doris, 326, Earl, 145, Edison, 213, Edith, 106, Effie, 305, Eldora, 213, Elizabeth, 213, Ethel, 181, Eva, 116, Faye, 181, 250, Floyd, 208, 213, Frank, 181, Froney Belle, 241, George, 213, 303, 305, George A., 213, George L., 213, Gerold, 208, Gladys V., 296, Grace, 208, Harold, 208, Harry Everett, 213, Harvey J., 375, Helen, 208, 350, Henry, 213, Isaac, 213, James, 147, 213, Jay Grubbs, 113, John, 213, John D., 372, John Richardson, 208, 213, Johnnie, 213, Joseph, 213, Larry Michael, 208, Lauranda, 213, Lawrence, 208, Lisa Michelle, 113, Loretta, 213, Lottie, 145, Mahala, 305, Marjory, 213, Martha, 213, Martha Jane, 303, Mary, 213, Maude, 145, Mildred, 208, Myrtle, 277, Nancy, 213, Nancy Belle, 208, Nannie Lutitia, 286, Newt, 213, Paul Keith, 113, Peter, 326, Philip, 213, Rachell, 213, Ralph, 145, Raymond, 213, Rebecca, 213, Robert, 208, Robert Newton, 213, Rosa, 121, Roscoe, 181, Roy, 145, Ruby, 116, Russell H., 372, Sarah, 108, Susan, 147, Sylvester, 145, Sylvester Manson, 286, Thomas, 213, William, 148, 213, 303, William F., 305, __, 55
KELLEY, Fannie, 354, Ida, 354, Oscar, 66, Rosalyn, 113
KELLY, Charles A., 127, Earl, 43, Edward, 349, Eleanor Mae, 349, 350, Elizabeth, 100, 285, Fannie, 43, Hop, 154, Ida, 354, Iva Myrtle, 317, Jeanne, 349, Karen, 260, Margaret, 349, Mildred Gladys, 154, Nancy, 279, O.E., 69, O.W., 285, Rebecca, 133
KELP, Shell, 16
KELSEY, Allison May, 214, Andra Bee, 354, Betheline, 214, Betheline, 354, Charles Wayne, 132, Cora Sue, 214, 354, Damon, 132, Damon Edward, 132, Dick, 214, Emery Elvon, 354, Emily Rose, 214, 354, Essac, 153, Janet Kay, 264, Jeannine Claire, 214, 354, Josephine, 215, Kathryn, 132, Larry, 132, Larry Elvin, 132, Mabel, 142, Madison, 31, Nancy, 214, Norris, 214, Rex Eugene, 132, Richard, 353, Richard Samuel, 214, 354, Rita, 214, Robert Wilson, 214, 354, Sandra, 99, Sandra Lee, 214, 354, Sarah Jean, 214, Stella Blanch, 43, Thomas, 230, Virginia, 83, 138, 214, Walter, 214, John, 142, Lawrence, 132
KELSO, Thomas, 365, Victoria, 209, 210, William, 365
KEMBLE, Amber Suzanne, 292, Mary E., 268
KEMP, Mary, 176
KEMPER, Denise Allison, 346, Jennifer Leigh, 346, Johannes, 338, Kenneth Sheldon, 346, Ralph, 287, Sarah, 338, Lee, 346
KENDALL, Abby, 130, Margaret, 78, Martha Jane, 78, Roley, 343, Roly, 181
KENNEDY, Ann, 172, Charles, 153, Clydia Mae, 189, Dan, 149, David, 40, David A., 29, David L., 189, Donald, 277, Dumont, 6, 24, 264, Eli, 261, Elizabeth, 261, Ida, 165, 192, James, 152, 261, Jennifer, 277, Joe E., 43, John B., 261, Julia Smullen, 261, Mary, 261, Nancy, 183, Patrick, 149, Peter, 6, 264, Peter K., 6, Sarah Ann, 261
KENNELL, Carl, 360, Emeline Inez, 360
KENNY, Edgar, 268
KENTNER, Jennifer, 108, Marie Nanette, 108
KENWORTHY, Lydia, 94, Mary Cox, 194, Sarah, 194, 211
KENYON, Clayton, 311
KEPPE, Ada, 241
KERBY, Ronald, 374, Ronald D., 374
KERIN, Margaret Alice, 160, Michael, 160
KERN, George, 174, Harold, 13
KERNS, Lucinda, 305, Margary Jane, 250, Marjorie, 298, Sarah J., 305, William, 305
KERR, __, 58, Drusilla, 76, Marie, 339, W.H., 308
KERSEY, John, 259, Marena Agnes, 159
KESLER, Johannes, Sr., 182
KESLEY, Andra Bee, 214, Janet, 214, Maggie, 214
KESLING, Rebecca Eve, 289
KESSINGER, Anna Belle, 264
KESSLER, Anna, 236, Anna (Nancy), 215, Benjamin, 177, 178, 182, 196, 214, Catherine, 196, 197, 214, David, 197, Elizabeth, 193, 196, 214, Jacob, 197, 214, Jacob E., 182, John, 214, Mark, 14, Mary, 147, 197, 215, Mary Hannah, 182, Melanie, 147, Nancy, 197, Nathaniel, 214, Nathaniel Graybill, 193, Ruth, 197, Salome, 193, Samuel, 214, Samuel H., 375, Sol, 197, Solomon, 182, Susan, 215, 218, Warner, 21, 147, Wayne, 44, Wayne E., 375
KETTERMAN, Elizabeth, 95
KEYS, Charles, 335, Joseph, 167, Lydia, 167, Rebecca, 167, Rebecca A., 167, Rozella, 167, William, 167
KIBBEE, Guy, 342
KIDNEY, Judy, 288
KIEHLEAUCH, Kay, 290
KIGGINS, Elizabeth, 301
KILEY, Angela, 215, David, 316, David L., 215, David Lawrence, 215, Ella, 215, Hannah, 215, Helen, 215, John, 215, John Walter, 316, Margaret, 215, Mary Evelyn, 316, Mildred Louise, 316, Shirley Mae, 316, Walter, 15, 215
KILLEN, Esther, 80
KILLINGSWORTH, Clayton, 54, Mary, 54
KILLION, Samantha Fillmore, 179
KIMBLE, Susanne, 123
KIMLER, Crayton, 221, Phebe, 129
KINCAID, Donald, 372, Josephine, 191, Ophelia, 327, Patricia A., 375, Robert, 370, __, 115
KINDER, Della Agnes, 318, Nancy, 194, William, 70
KING, Alfred Elijah, 215, Alfred Thompson, 215, Alma Jane, 240, Amanda Ellen, 215, Amber Michelle, 215, Amellia, 161, Andrew, 208, Anna, 215, Anna Everett, 215, Art, 54, Blanch, 215, Chester, 215, Cora, 215, Daniel Newton, 215, David William, 215, Deborah, 215, Edward III, 333, Elijah II, 215, Elijah, Sr., 215, Eliza, 215, Eliza Frances, 215, Ella May, 208, Eva Bell, 215, Ezekiel Alonzo, 215, George Henry, 215, Henry Benjamin, 215, Henry Newton, 215, Herbert Benjamin, 215, Ivy, 215, James Argyl, 215, James Washington, 215, Jesse, 169, 215, Joan, 215, John Alan, 215, John L., 99, John Wallace, 215, Joseph Harrison, 215, Julia Ann, 215, Lon, 215, Lucas K., 143, Malinda, 302, Malinda Frances, 215, Margaret Jane, 215, Maria, 215, Mariah G., 215, Martha, 215, Mary, 215, Mary Margaret, 215, Mary Maria, 215, Mary Mariah, 99, Mehersey Bell, 215, Penny Kay, 273, R.F., 30, Richard, 215, Robert C., 374, Ruth, 215, Sarah Ann, 317, Sitha (Cynthia), 215, Stella, 215, Virginia, 208, William Edgar, 215, William Henry, 215, Charles I, 124
KINKEAD, Lillie, 164, Stephen, 164, 375
KINNETT, Betty, 26, 66
KINNEY, Harry, 71, Lala, 319, Linda, 301, Naomi, 263
KINNICK, Mary, 307
KINON, Jamimah, 314
KINTZ, Elizabeth Domenica, 166
KINZER, Elizabeth, 162
KIOUS, Absalom, 343, Adam, 343, Elizabeth, 343, Margaret, 343, Nathan, 343
KIRBY, Margaret Katherine, 111, Risk Supply, 258, Ron, 365, Sylvester, 306, William M.A., 111
KIRCHNER, Fred, Jr., 294
KIRK, Agnes, 179, Alden, 216, Alice, 216, Alonzo, 216, Anna, 216, Bertha May, 216, Frank, 216, Harley, 216, Ida, 216, James, 216, Jesse, 216, John, 215, Laura, 121, 216, Lewis, 216, Lisa, 54, Louisa, 215, 216, Margaret, 216, Mary, 31, Mildred Lee, 216, Myrl, 216, Ray, 216, Richard, 216, Rosa, 216, William, 216
KIRKENDALL, Jacob, 60, Mary R., 60
KIRKHAM, Sarah, 173, Virginia, 372
KIRKPATRICK, Absalom, 65, Blaine E., 49, Charles, 65, Jane, 288, Jane Points, 288, Lee, 190, Margaret, 291, Mary Lee, 286, Rita, 190
KIRTLEY, (Dr.), 287, Adam Mathew, 217, Becky, 217, Bill, 217, 218, Charles Raymond, 216, Christina, 218, David James, 217, Elsie Lavinna, 216, Faye M., 218, Frank Smith, 216, J.M., 216, 217, James, 217, James M., 212, 375, James Marion, 216, 217, James Samuel, 216, Jane Elizabeth, 218, Jessie F., 216, Jessie Fidelia, 216, Kathleen Elizabeth, 217, Laura Rebecca, 217, Laurel S., 216, Lee, 216, 217, Leolia A. Black, 216, Lewis Wallace, 216, Lillie Beth, 216, Marion, 216, 217, Nancy, 217, Ray, 216, 217, Raymond M., 375, Raymond Marion, 217, Rebecca L., 217, Sam, 217, Samuel, 217, Samuel (Dr.), 375, Samuel William, 217, Tracy Anne, 217, William R., 111, 216, William Raymond, 216, 217, William Raymond III, 218
KISSELBACH, Kim, 247, Paul, 247, Sue, 247, Kim, 378
KISTLER, Edith, 100, 218, 229, 236, 237, 238, Edith M., 215, Merton L., 218
KITCH, Nancy Ellen, 81
KITCHENS, Donald, 370
KLEIN, Billie, 256, 257, Dawn, 54
KLEISER, Arthur J., 210, Charles, 210, Cornelia Chittenden, 183, Victoria, 210
KLINE, Carol Lee Ann, 234, John, 312, Mary, 312, Rice, 377, Russell, 54
KLODFELTER, __, 241
KLUTZKE, Mary, 348
KNAPP, Bradley James, 185
KNARR, Angela Sue, 107, Phillip Daniel, 107
KNECHT, Glenn, 24, Kurt, 372
KNIGHT, Catherine, 145, Nancy, 145
KNIPPENBURG, Saundra, 227
KNISLEY, Ella Mae, 227, Jean, 227, Sherman William, 227
KNOTT, Dora, 360, Kevin, 224, Rayan, 224
KNOX, Emma, 33, Hardware, 14, J.C., 206, James, 33, James Stevenson, 218, Julia, 307, Julie LeClerc, 218, Louise, 218, Mabel Irene, 101, __, 82
KODER, Jacob, Jr. 186
KOEHLER, Amelia, 357
KOON, George Washington, 293, John I, John III, 191, 280, 293, Mary Catharine, 191, 280, Mary Kathearine, 293
KOOPMAN, Ann, 279
KORHONEN, Ann, 218, Betty, 329, Betty Joann, 218, Darrell, 218, Kenneth Martin, 218, Kenny, 218, Martin, 218, Mary Ann, 218, Susan Jane, 218, Susie Jane, 218
KORMOS, Diane Lee, 100
KOSS, Carol, 199, Jack, 199, Mary, 199
KOSTANZER, Electric, 258, Raymond, 351
KOSTKA, David, 56
KOVAC, Mary, 160
KOWALSKI, Peggy, 118
KRAFT, Betty, 272
KRAHBIEL, Christian, 177, Jakob, 177
KRAIG, Joseph, 319
KRANTZ, Beverly, 288
KRATT, Carol, 186
KRATZ, Carl, 106
KRAUS, Richard, 56
KRAUSE, Carol Zeta, 224, O.C., 246
KREILING, Alice, 235
KREISHER, Ken T., 375
KRESS, Michael, 84
KRISTON, Charles, 203
KRITZ, Bert, 210, Charles, 210, Francis, 360, Frank, 235, Harry, 210, Henry S., 210, James William, 360, Jessie, 210, Layla, 210, Mary A., 210, Mary Joan, 360, Nell, 210, Sarah Alice, 360, Stella, 210, Victoria, 209, 210, Will, 210

KROUT, Abraham, 218, Archie D., 219, Caroline, 219, Caroline Virginia, 219, 337, Charlene, 315, Edith, 79, Elizabeth, 213, Homer, 79, Jacob, 218, 219, John, 213, Katherine, 219, 345, Margaret, 219, 345, Mary, 163, Mary Hannah, 6, 219, 221, 337, Mary Jane, 273, Michael, 219, 345, Nancy, 213, Robert, 219, Robert K., 219
KRUG, Elizabeth, 219, Georgie Faye, 122, John Coon, 122, John Valentine, 219, Kezia, 220, Louie, 220, Nellie, 220, Stella Ellen, 122, Valentine, 219, William, 219, 220, William Augustus, 219, 220, William J., 220
KRUKEWITT, Mary, 375
KUBICK, Charles, 272, Jeffrey, 272, Joan, 272
KUCHLER, Joanna, 96
KUCINSKI, Edward M., 372
KUHN, George, 247, Josephine, 247
KUHNS, Charles, 294, David, 294, Della, 115, Dora, 115, Elizabeth, 294, Hannah, 294, Jonas, 294, Louisiana Lucy A., 294, Lucy A., 294, Ruben, 115, Samuel, 294, Sara, 115, Solomon, 115, Stella Ann, 294
KUMMER, Alfred, 49
KUNGMAN, Lee, 275
KUNKEL, Betty June, 333, Donald Riley, 333, Elizabeth Maxine, 333, Emma Charlotte, 333, Fowler Ezra, 333, Lois, 374, Marjorie Ann, 333, Plumbing, 16, Ralph Fowler, 333
KUNKLE, Betsy, 220, Betty June, 220, Cyrus Elmer, 220, Donald Riley, 220, Elizabeth Bernice, 220, Elizabeth Maxine, 220, Emma Charlotte, 220, Fowler Ezra, 101, 220, Jacob Adam, 220, Janet, 220, John, 220, John William, 220, Marjorie Ann, 220, Maxine, 101, Nancy Mae, 220, Ralph Fowler, 220, Roger, 220, Sue, 220
KUNNS, Henry, 294
KUONEN, Louise, 36, 111, 257
KYLE, Henry, 205, Mary Jane, 205, Robert, 271, William, 55
LABAW, Alice, 164, Benjamin, 164, Melissa Alice, 145, __, 12
LAFOE, Delores M., 375
LA FOLLETTE, Adrian, 221, Alice, 221, Alice Virginia, 220, Anna Gertrude, 220, 270, Bess, 221, Betty, 221, Caroline Belle, 220, Carrie, 220, 221, Charles, 220, Cornelia, 220, Cornelia E., 220, Earl, 220, Earle, 221, Edith, 221, Edith Maye, 221, 279, Edna, 221, Edna Maude, 221, Effie, 221, El, 221, Ellen Jane, 220, Floss, 221, Francis Marion, 220, 221, Frank, 220, 221, George, 220, 221, George Rushton, 220, 270, George Washington, 220, 221, Harold, 220, 221, Hazel, 220, 221, 270, 272, Isaac, 221, James, 149, 221, James Oliver, 221, Joan Marie, 221, Joe, 221, John H., 149, 220, Joseph, 220, 221, Joseph Earl, 220, Joseph W. 271, Lee, 221, Lois, 220, 270, Lois Maxine, 220, Lou, 221, 271, Mary Elizabeth, 221, Mary Ellen, 221, Mary Hazel, 221, Mary Lou, 221, Maxine, 220, Maxine Yvonne, 220, Minnie, 221, 270, Nancy Alice, 221, Nancy Lee, 221, Nora, 220, Nora Lucinda, 220, Ol, 221, Paul, 220, Phoebe, 221, Robert, 220, 221, Robert F., 220, 270, Robert Francis, 220, Susan, 221, Susannah, 221, Thomas Wallace, 221, Usual, 221, Violet, 221, Wal, 221, 270, William, 220, 221, William C., 221, William Francis, 220, 270
LARUE, Jo Blan, 63
LAARRICK, Tessie, 223
LACEY, Eunice, 111, H.V., 49, Peirson, 111
LACKEY, Jud, 270, Martha, 95, Robert, 270, Roy, 270, Sarah J., 258, Vern, 270, Yvonne, 270
LADD, Priscilla, 259
LAFFORD, John, 197, Lillian, 197
LAFFRANCHI, Carol, 269, Michele, 270, Nicole, 270, Robert, 269
LAFOLETTE, Usual, 36
LAFOLLETTE, Ed, 162, Opal, 162
LAFUSE, Eleanor, 339, Lydia, 229
LAFUZE, Elanor, 176
LAHR, Ford, 135
LAMB, Catherine, 339, Joseph, 123, Mary, 207, Millie, 207, Simon, 207
LAMBDIN, Stella, 315
LAMBER, Kent Craig, 221
LAMBERT, Frances, 43, Janet, 221, Kent, 221, Nancy, 238
LAME, Abel, 130, Howard, 274, Mary, 210, Mary Elizabeth, 130
LAMON, Christina, 213
LAMPKINS, Francis, 235
LAMPTON, Ellendore, 358
LAMSON, Anna, 221, Catherine, 222, Charles T., 221, Clifford, 222, Delilah, 221, Dora, 221, Earl, 299, Earl E., 222, George, 222, 299, Gladys, 221, Glen, 299, Glenn, 222, Harry, 222, 299, Jennie, 221, John E., 221, Julius, 221, Lloyd, 222, Martha J., 221, Mary, 197, 221, Minnie Carver, 221, Nell, 221, Oleander, 221, Ose, 221, Rollo, 222, Rosa, 221, Ruth, 221, Sarah Butcher, 221, Susan, 222, Thomas, 222, 306, Thomas W., 221, Thomas, Jr., 221, Thomas, Sr., 221, Tom, 221, Vera, 222, 299, Walter, 222, 299
LANDER, John, 286, Lucy, 286
LANDIS, Cinda, 194, Magdalene, 197, 302, Mary, 177, 194, 274
LANDON, Affa, 222, Benjamin, 222, Catherine, 222, Celina, 222, Clarence, 152, Daniel, 222, David, 222, Effie, 222, Elisha, 222, Elizabeth, 222, Jacbo, 222, Janet, 152, John, 222, 303, Jonathan, 222, Laban, 222, Margaret, 222, Mary, 222, Myrna, 152, Nancy, 222, Peter, 222, Rachel, 222, Rebecca, 222, Robert, 222, Samuel, 222, Sarah, 222, Solomon, 222, William, 222
LANE, 240, Abraham, 83, Elisha, 113, Henry, 7, 126, 373, Henry S., 24, 48, 307, Henry Smith, 6, 7, 222, Isaac, 164, James, 11, Joanna, 7, 222, Joanna Elston, 6, Lois, 220, Mary, 113, Mary Malinda, 83, Mary Melinda, 214, Sally, 291, Susannah, 293
LANFEAR, Olive, 328
LANG, Allie, 309, Almarinda, 309, Benjamin, 309, Nancy, 299
LANGE, Edward, 307, Lois, 307
LANGER, Al, 199, Mary, 199
LANGSTON, David, 136, James, 136, Jennifer, 136, Patricia, 136
LANGWORTHY, Helen, 265
LANNARCK, David, 184
LANNING, Clayton, 278
LANT, Janet, 132, Roy, 132
LANUM, Lori D., 375
LAREW, Abe, 223, Amanda, 223, Arthur, 223, Bertha, 223, Betty, 223, Billie, 71, 223, Billie Jean, 223, Bob, 71, 223, Carolyn, 223, Chad Michael, 296, Charles, 71, 223, Charles Stillman, 223, Cheryl, 296, Edward, 296, Edward Eugene, 296, G. Abraham, 223, G. Edward, 296, Garret A., 223, Garret Edward, 223, Garrett, 223, Garrett Abraham, 223, James Douglas, 296, James Garrett, 223, Jana, 223, John Henry, 223, Jon Jacob, 223, Karl G., 223, Lena, 223, Leora, 223, Lois Evelyn, 296, Martha Alice, 223, Mary, 223, Merle, 71, 223, Michelle, 223, Mildred, 223, Misty Dawn, 296, Pearl, 223, Phyllis, 223, Phyllis Alleen, 223, Richard Ray, 223, Robert, 223, Robert R., 71, Robert Ray, 223, Rosalie Anne, 296, Ruth, 223, Sharon Kay, 296, Theodore Garrett, 223, Una Leona, 296, Walter, 223, Walter Byron, 223, William, 223
LARGENT, Eva R., 259, Jeffrey C., 372, Jemima, 281, Kimberlin R., 372, Martha, 54, Walter, 54
LARIMER, Margaret, 306, Paul, 306, Ruth, 306
LARRICK, Anita, 223, Bob, 223, Bradley Jay, 199, 223, Elizabeth, 223, Emma, 223, I.N., 223, Isaac Newton, 223, Jacob, 223, James, 223, James Newton, 199, 223, Jesse, 224, Jessie, 223, Jim, 223, John, 223, John A., 223, John Michael, 199, 223, John Walker, 199, 223, Lois, 223, Louisa, 223, Madonna, 223, Margaret, 223, Marie, 223, 224, Mary Fletcher, 223, Mary J., 223, Mary Polly, 158, Maye, 223, Omer, 223, Penson Hollingsworth, 199, 223, Pinson, 223, Rebecca, 290, Rebecca L., 199, Rebecca Louise, 223, Robert, 223, Robert Carl, 199, 223, Robert Gregory, 199, 223, Robert Henry, 199, 223, Sarah, 223, William, 223, William H., 224
LARRIMORE, Julia, 174
LARRY'S, Taxidermy, 16
LARSH, Homer, 130, Homer "Dot", 130, Leah, 130
LARSON, Hilmer, 173, Roy, 237
LASHBROOK, Maude, 122
LASLEY, Owen, 106
LASSITER, Leslie, 288
LATTIMORE, Margaret, 325, Myrtle, 152, 291, William Dupree, 152, William Morton, 152
LAUGHIN, Jane, 264
LAUGHLIN, Charles, 169, Nancy Angeline, 343
LAUGHNER, Amy, 208, Emily, 208, Gary, 208, James, 208, Nancy, 208, Patricia, 208, Susan, 208, Thomas, 208
LAULER, Luis, 339, Victoria, 339
LAUNER, Mark, 42
LAURER, Eva, 298
LAURSEN, Carol L., 375
LAUTERBUR, Marnell, 351
LAUTHERS, C.L., 30, Charles, 31
LAVERLY, Dorothy, 192
LAWLER, Gale, 324
LAWRENCE, Hattie, 225
LAWSON, Elizabeth, 222, Elizabeth Lee, 292, Gun Shop, 16, Paul, 74, Rebecca, 259
LAWTON, Cecile, 224, Don, 253, Enoch, 24, 301, Ethel, 224, George H., 224, George M., 224, Gerald E., 224, Grace, 224, Harry, 224, 253, Ida, 224, Jacqueline Sue, 253, John E., 224, John W., 224, John Edward, 224, Merle E., 224, Mildred B., 253, Minnie, 224, Robert, 253, Roy Clinton, 224, Sarah, 224, Sarh, 223, William, 224, 253
LAXTON, Lady Anna, 121, William (Sir), 121
LAYMON, Harry, 309
LAYNE, Annie, 224, Arlene, 88, 224, Ayres, 145, Carol Ann, 224, Dan, 244, Dan W., 224, Donald L., 224, Dorothy L., 224, Elisha, 52, 208, 225, Eliza, 225, Elizabeth, 113, 225, Elvira Mortimer, 366, Eunice, 225, Evaline, 327, Ezekiel, 60, Florence W., 224, Forrest D., 224, Francis, 150, George, 150, Gloria, 88, 224, H.B., 240, Harold, 88, 224, Iva, 12, Jacob Wash, 149, James Harold, 224, James William, 224, Jim, 224, 225, Josephine, 52, Kathleen Z., 375, Linda F., 375, Lloyd, 224, 244, Lutitia, 225, Mariah, 225, Mary, 145, Matilda, 225, Miles, 225, Minnie Myrtle, 224, Preston, 12, 225, Roxann, 145, Roxanna, 225, Tabitha, 225, Tarleton, 145, Tarleton James W., 149, Tarlton, 225, Walter, 12, Washington, 225, William, 145, 225, William Minter, 225, Helen, 224
LAYSON, William (Mrs.), 132
LAYTON, Bernard, 360, David, 365, David O., 375, 381, Esther, 242, Freida, 375, Zuba Olive, 360
LECLERC, Julia, 307, Louise, 218
LEFEBRE, David C., 202
LEFEVRE, __, 289, Catherine, 288, David, 202, Isaac, 288
LEMAY, Mattie, 79
LEPAGE, Annie, 226, J. Leon, 158, Jules A., 226, Jules Leon, 226, Julia Jacqueline, 158, Natalie Ann, 158
LEACH, Evaline, 225
LEAK, Andrew Jackson, 225, Ann "Nancy", 225, Charles, 225, Elisha, 104, 225, Eliza Ann, 225, Elizabeth, 225, Emaline, 225, Frances "Fannie", 104, Frances "Fanny", 225, Hiram, 104, 225, James, 225, John Lewis, 225, Katherine "Kitty", 104, Larkin, 225, Lewis, 225, Louisa, 225, Lucretia, 225, Lucy, 225, Madeline, 225, Martha, 225, Martha Ann, 225, Mary, 225, Nancy, 225, Permelia, 225, Robert, 104, 225, Samuel, 225, Sarah, 225, Sarah "Sallie', 104, Susan, 225, Susannah, 104, 225, Virginia, 225, Walter, 104, William, 225
LEAKE, Kitty, 225, Sally, 225, Samuel, 225
LEAMAN, Eva Dorothea, 182, Johannes, 182, Susanna, 182
LEAMING, Jim, 54, Ruth, 54
LEAR, Jane, 350
LEAS, Audrey Louise, 165, James, 22
LEASE, Forrest, 259
LEAVENWORTHS, __, 119
LECKRONE, Mildred, 15, 215, Mildred Louise, 316
LEDBETTER, Jeremiah, 197
LEE, Alice, 327, Annabelle, 141, Betty J., 372, Christina Renee, 127, Connie Leona, 127, Fitzen (Gen.), 132, Guy, 81, Ida, 326, 327, Jane, 327, Jemima, 244, Jessie, 307, John, 244, 326, 327, 336, Jon, 54, Karen, 54, Ken, 127, Kendra Elizabeth, 127, Leticia, 326, Mayme, 249, Mildred, 216, Opal, 268, Patricia, 265, Robert, 216, Robert E., 83, Sallie, 141, William, 81, 376
LEECH, S.V., 49
LEECHMAN, Helen, 202
LEFFLER, Anna Margaret, 284
LEFTWICK, Thomas (Capt.), 83
LEGG, Edna, 311
LEGI, Verona, 241
LEHE, Amiel, 225, Bob, 225, James Thomas, 225, Jennifer Elizabeth, 226, Jonathan David, 225, Joyce, 225, Katherine Michelle, 226, Marcia, 225, Mardelle, 225, 226, 380, Mary, 225, Robert, 225, Robert Amiel, 225, Robert Tad, 225
LEHMAN, John Wesley, 159, Leonard, 16, Zora, 331, Zora Margaret, 159
LEIDSTER, Arminta, 301
LEIGHT, Terri, 296
LEINBERGER, Eula, 278
LELAY, Susan, 186
LEMMON, John, 80
LEMON, Alice, 151, Leanah, 151, Linda, 352, Mary Ann, 124, 266, Ryan, 352, Samuel, 266, Steve, 352
LENTZ, Myrtle, 286
LEONARD, Amos, 318, Charles L., 375, George, 373, Jane Elizabeth, 310, Mayme J., 318
LEONHARDT, Valentine, 310
LESLIE, Alvin K., 372, Billy, 317, Karen, 317, Peggy, 317, Samuel, 222, William, 317
LEUCK, Edith, 272, Janice, 272, Peter, 272
LEVINGSTONE, Mary Ann, 123
LEWALLAN, Ernest, 41
LEWELLEN, Archie, 226, Arthur, 168, Bessie, 226, Betty, 226, Bob, 13, Christopher, 226, Cynthia Jane, 226, Doris, 106, Doris Lucille, 226, Duane, 226, Edna, 226, Edna Maye, 226, Edward Orton, 226, Goldie, 226, Guy, 226, Harold Michael, 226, Hattie A., 286, Herbert Galen, 226, Herbert Gordon, 226, Herbert Gregory, 226, Jack, 226, Jane, 226, Jeffrey Jospeh, 226, Jennifer, 226, Joanne, 226, John, 226, Joseph, 226, Joseph Ross, 226, Libby, 226, Linda Roselyn, 168, Mabel Alice, 226, Margaret Jane, 226, Maria, 226, Oma, 106, Stella, 226, Steven Bryan, 168, Thomas, 226, Wallace, 226, Walter, 226, Zola, 226
LEWELLYN, Edna Maye, 302, Jack, 302, Jane, 302, Joanne, 302, Joe, 302, Wallace, 302, Wilma, 168
LEWIS, Amelia Ann, 241, Andrew, 125, Anita, 54, Dean, 131, Francis A., 100, Freddie, 54, Geneva, 317, Hattie, 90, Irma, 366, Lenora, 157, Lucinda, 106, Marie, 310, Martha J., 201, Nora, 150, Perry, 211, Phyllis, 170, Quincy, 192, Susan, 166, Susan Lenora, 167, Thomas, 160, William A., 100
LEWLLEN, Arthur Bryan, 168
LEYDA, Beth, 315, Bill, 315, Earl, 315, Edwin, 315, Martha Jo, 315
LIBKA, Betty, 278
LIDESTER, Billy E., 372, Horse Training, 16
LIDIKAY, Corrinne Elaine, 227, Curtis Lee, 227, Ed, 206, Elda, 227, George E., 177, 227, Harry Davis, 227, Henry Adrin, 226, 227, Lyle Myron, 227, Marilee, 227, Milton H., 226, 227
LIDSTER, Pearl, 205
LIEBHERE, Bob, 347, Lynn, 347
LIEBHERR, Marilyn Sue, 282
LIEBTAG, Madonna, 74
LIESKA, Harold, 277, Lana, 277
LIESKE, Lana, 255
LIGHT, Betty, 374, Charles, 355, Elizabeth, 355
LIGHTENER, Winnie, 342
LIGHTLE, Betty, 108, Clyde, 108, Gary, 108, Marylou, 108
LIKINS, Andrew, 259
LILLY, Ermil M., 315
LINCOLN, Abraham, 6, 101, 126, 222, 264, 297, Jemmia, 265, Lavina, 333, Leona Louise, 166, Robert Todd, 184, Tom, 190, __, 109
LINDAMOOD, Ruby L., 188
LINDERMAN, Emma, 43, 329
LINDLEY, Allen J., 210, Edith, 31, Linda Marie, 200, Riley, 319
LINDLEY-JOHNSON, Insurance, 16
LINDSEY, Elizabeth, 190, Harry, 138, Kathleen Ann, 138, Philip, 138, Rose Anna, 82
LINE, Abigail, 175, Jaboc, 175, Jeffrey W., 372, John, 175, Margaret, 175, Maria, 176, Nancy, 175, Ruth, 175, Salome, 175
LINGEMAN, Byron (Dr.), 314, Byron N., 216, Byron Spencer, 314, Richard, 314
LINK, Nellie I., 171, Sanford S., 171, Victor, 63
LINKINHOKER, Madison, 29, 40
LINN, "Toni", 227, Abby Marie, 229, Adam III, 229, Adam, Jr., 229, Adam, Sr., 228, 229, Amanda, 230, Andy, 227, Antionette Rosalee, 227, Bandel, 229, Bandel Theodore, 227, Bele Humbert, 228, Bertha, 283, 335, Bessie, 227, Bessie Faye, 100, 230, Betty, 228, Caprice, 227, Carl, 228, 229, Catherine, 196, 228, Charles, 229, Charles A., 101, Charles Asa, 227, 230, Charles F., 33, Charles Theodore, 227, 229, Charlie Marten, 228, Charlotte, 229, Cheryl, 227, 228, Cheryl Ann, 188, 230, Christina Michelle, 227, Courtney, 227, David Ray, 229, Debra Jo, 131, Debra Sladek, 243, Denise, 227, 228, Diana, 131, Diana Mitchum, 243, Donald, 131, Donald J., 211, 229, Donald Jean, 131, Donald Jen, 243, Donna Jo, 230, Donna Marcella, 228, Dora, 280, 299, Dora E., 339, Dora Evaline, 108, 197, 211, 229, 302, 336, Earl Joseph, 211, 229, 243, Eliza, 228, Eliza Ann, 228, Elizabeth, 230, Ella, 100, 195, 227, 228, 230, Ella Skyles, 228, Elva S., 276, Emerson, 310, Emmaline, 232, Emmaline M., 280, Enoch, 276, Ernest, 66, Ernest Edward, 229, Ethel May, 101, 227, 230, Floyd Isaac, 229, 336, Forest M., 101, 227, 230, George W., 228, George Washington, 230, Gretchen Martha, 229, Harry I., 101, 227, Harry Isaac, 228, 230, Henry Clifton, 229, Hermine Bandel, 227, Hugh, 76, Ida, 230, Isaac, 123, 228, 230, 320, Isaac II, 229, Isabelle, 228, 229, James, 227, 228, James Franklin, 230, James H., 150, 228, 229, 230, James Richard, 227, James W., 108, 182, 197, James W., II, 336, James Washington, 100, 123, 150, 178, 196, 211, 228, 229, 352, James Washington II, 228, 229, Jane, 229, Jane Isabelle, 228, Janis Marie, 188, 230, Jean, 131, Jeffrey, 230, Jeffrey Lee, 188, 228, 230, Jennie Flo, 211, 229, Joan, 67, 228, Joed, 67, Joed Morrison, 228, John, 32, 63, 228, 229, 230, 280, John W., 228, 230, 238, John Wilson, 229, Joseph, 123, Joseph A., 31, Joseph Andrew, 228, 229, Joseph Earl, 336, Joseph Ray, 229, Judithf Ann, 131, Judith Gayler, 243, Julia Evaline, 228, 229, Juliette, 276, Katherine June, 228, Kimberly Kay, 230, Laila, 229, Laurence Russell, 228, 229, Leslie, 229, Linda, 227, 229, Lydia Genung, 228, Mabel, 31, Mabel Clore, 228, Mahala, 100, 196, 197, 228, Manson Bruce, 229, Margaret, 228, 229, Margaret "Peg", 227, Margaretta, 229, Mark Emerson, 229, Martha, 230, Marvin Oakel, 229, Mary, 76, 228, 229, 230, Mary Ann, 228, 230, Mary Elizabeth, 228, Mary Jane, 229, Mary Ward, 227, Matilda Emaline, 197, May, 229, Nancy, 123, 228, 229, 230, 280, Nancy Jane, 229, Nellie, 218, 229, 236, Noah, 228, Noah Cassell, 280, Noah Castle, 123, 150, 229, 352, Patricia Ann, 230, Pearl Marie, 229, Pegeen Jocelyn, 229, Phyllis, 66, 188, 230, Rachel Mahala, 228, Ray, 81, Raymond, 66, 230, Raymond Gene, 188, 229, Richard, 230, Ricahrd Gene, 188, 230, Robert, 228, Robert Lawrence, 228, Ruby, 138, 332, Ruby Ann,

227, 101, 196, 197, 230, 255, Ruth, 227, Ruth H., 227, Samuel, 229, 230, Sarah, 230, Sarah E., 229, Sarah Eliza, 228, Sarah Ellen, 228, Sarah Mahala, 229, 334, Stella, 230, Steve, 227, 229, Steve Jay, Jr., 227, Steven Jay, 227, Tobias, 228, Uzal, 229, Velma Christine, 339, Virgie, 227, W. Harrison, 229, Wallace Theodore, 227, 229, Walter, 229, Warner E., 101, Warner Easland, 230, Warren E., 227, William, 100, 228, William Asa, 196, 227, 228, 230, 320, William Harrison, 228, 230, William Joseph, 227, 229, William Patterson, 229, Wilma Jean, 208, Winifred Jay, 227, Zula, 228, Phyllis, 230, __, 42

LINTON, Fred, 191

LINVILLE, Dale, 190

LIPKA, John Frank, 98, Lois, 102, Mary Anne, 98, Robert John, 98, Sarah, 98, Stephanie, 98, Theresa, 98

LIPPERT, Kemper, 257, Lois, 257, Marilyn, 257, Winston, 257

LISTER, Laura, 324

LISTON, D.P., 11

LITER, Rosanna, 342, Roseanna, 342

LITTLE, Betty, 374, Dorothy, 374, Ella, 235, Frank E., 49, Leon, 374, Leon, Jr., 374, Ralph, 374, Sally, 209

LIVENGOOD, Ester, 272, Frances May, 346, Gareld, 346, Jessie, 309, Mary, 186

LIVESAY, Billie Ann, 324, Craig, 320, Darrick, 320, Dianne, 320, Gary, 92, Glenn, 347, Joan, 347, Paula, 92, Scott, 320

LIVINGSTON, Beverly, 150, Chancellor, 80, Charles, 230, Dallas, 208, 230, David, 150, Dona, 249, Donald, 231, Flossie, 208, 230, Gladys, 230, Jane, 231, Janet, 230, Joe, 230, John, 230, Jonathan, 150, Joseph, 150, 208, 230, Linda, 231, Lori, 231, Martha, 230, Mary, 230, Merle, 208, 230, Mildred, 230, Myrtle, 208, 230, Pearl, 231, 375, Polly Anna, 230, Scott, 231, Susan, 150, 230, William, 208, 230, 231, William Jasper, 230

LOCHRIE, Mary Jane, 103

LOCKE, Dora, 135, Florence Avenel, 113, Harlan, 268, William A., 113

LOCKERIDGE, John, 185

LOCKHART, Charles, 31, Juanita, 95, Lawrence, 95, Mary A., 133

LOCKRIDGE, Herb, 202, J.L., 30, __, 42

LOCKWOOD, Catherine, 123, James Boyd, 93, Jimmie, 93, L.D., 59, William Blaine, 93

LODER, James, 65

LODGE, Ann Cumberland, 120, Elizabeth, 120, Jacob, 120, Jozabod, 120, Nelson James, 120, Robert, 120, Rosanna, 120, Thomas (Sir), 120

LOEFFLER, Ruby Rhoda, 119

LOFLAND, Carolyn Mae, 231, Clara, 231, David Edwin, 231, Heverlo, 231, James Milton, 231, John, 231, John Breaks, 36, 231, 364, John Leslie, 231, John Lucas, 231, Karen Suzanne, 355, Kristie, 231, Lauren Jennifer, 231, Lela, 231, Linda, 231, Linda Jane, 231, Lisa, 231, Lisa Jean, 231, Lori Ellen, 355, Louanna Kay, 231, Louanne, 231, Luther, 231, Luther Lee, 231, Luther, III, 231, Luther, Jr., 231, Martha, 162, 355, Natalie Fay, 231, Nora Evelyn, 231, Richard Alan, 355, Robert Glenn, 231, 355, Robert Lucas, 355, Sandra, 231, Stephanie Michelle, 231

LOGAN, Alcy, 150, Amelia, 276, Cena, 232, Della, 232, Elizabeth, 79, 284, Emma, 150, 232, Eunice, 232, Francis (Frank), 232, Grover, 232, Ida, 232, 280, Ida Josephine, 232, Jimmie, 232, John, 150, John W., 231, Josiah Brown, 232, June, 232, Margaret, 310, Mary, 143, Nancy, 310, Naomi, 232, Nelson Eugene, 232, Robert, 231, 310, Sharon, 232, William Robert, 232, Wilma, 232, Wilse, 232

LOGGINS, Alfreda, 352

LOGIS, Edward Di, 120

LOGUE, Marilyn, 79

LOHMAN, Lizzie, 251

LOHORN, James M., 372, Peggy Q., 375, Robert Scott, 372

LOLLIS, William E., 29

LOMAN, Blanche, 232, Eliza Jane, 232, Elizabeth, 169, Ephraim, 232, George D., Jr., 232, George H., Sr., 232, Geraldine, 232, Helen Jean, 232, Nellie, 232

LONG, Austin H., 326, Bert, 149, Branch, 282, Brenda, 357, Calvin, 61, Charlotte "Lottie", 232, Christina Lynn, 132, Cora, 91, Delia, 215, Dennia, 357, Eleanor "Ella", 318, Elizabeth, 225, Eva Ellen, 357, Evelyn Elizabeth, 149, Frederick, 63, 232, 314, Frederick M., 14, Frederick milburn, 232, Georgia M., 341, Gladys, 154, Henry, 232, 314, Imogene, 357, James Daniel, 149, Jerre, 354, Jim, 357, John Shipley, 82, Lawrence, 215, 263, 314, Lawrence Chester, 232, Lela, 99, Leona, 128, Lois, 356, Luther L., 263, Luther R., 263, Madeline, 232, Madge, 215, 232, Madge Mildred, 316, Mamie, 232, 314, Mary, 232, 329, Mary Catherine, 328, Mary Margaret, 149, Minerva, 329, Missouri Cordelia, 314, Pauline, 43, Pearl, 145, 263, Phyllis Joan, 300, Robert Lee, 149, Ronald, 357, Ruth Lee, 234, Terrence Lee, 132, Thomas, 314, Valentine, 329, Walter, 288, Wilburn, 55, __, 55

LONGWORTHY, Helen Olin, 186

LOOKABILL, Arthur, 232, Arthur R., 233, John, 232, Lawrence, 43, Lidia, 232, Mae, 232, Pete, 232, 233, Waneta, 233, William, 232, Worth, 232, 233

LOOP, Andrew, 30, 352, Carl Raymond, 103, Christian, 103, Christopher, 352, Clyde, 31, 272, Elizabeth, 352, Ethel, 103, Georgia Anna, 103, John (Capt.), 80, Mamie, 272, Mary, 103, Verna, 103, W.C., 352, __, 42

LOUCKS, Will G., 308

LOUGH, Alice, 252, Audrey, 233, Avaline, 233, Barbara, 233, Ben, 233, Beverly, 233, Clarence, 233, Clifford, 233, Corda, 233, Donald, 233, Edna Mae, 318, Edward, 233, Elijah, 189, Gale, 233, George, 233, Harriet, 189, Hattie, 233, Henry Harrison "Tip", 144, Howard, 233, Jacob, 233, James, 233, Johnny, 233, Juanita, 233, Julia, 233, Larry A., 375, Liza, 233, Lola Viola, 189, Lucille, 233, Mabel, 144, Marihelen, 233, Marion, 233, Martha, 189, Martha Jean, 233, Martin, 233, Marvin, 233, Mary, 189, Max, 233, May, 189, Mayme, 189, Mildred, 189, Nicholas, 233, Nolan, 233, Orville, 233, Otto, 233, Rhufus, 233, Samuel, 233, Sarah Jane, 144, Stanley, 233, Theresa, 233, Washington, 233, Wilbur, 189, Wilbur L., 189, William, 233, Larry, 233

LOUIS, & Sheppard Plant, 87

LOUKE, Evangeline, 167

LOVE, Bessie, 255, Opal, 310, S., 252

LOVELESS, Adam, 239, Anne, 350, Byron, 351, Clara, 239, Cynthia, 351, David W., 281, Esther, 239, Margueritte, 236, Mary Helen, 281, Maryann, 351

LOW, Jessie, 175, Samuel, 74, Sarah, 74

LOWE, Ada, 168, Ada Catherine, 167, Betty, 233, Brooke Janelle, 233, Catherine, 301, Charles, 108, Cheryl Denis, 233, Clarence, 233, Clarence A., 233, Clarence Adrian, 233, Dann, 118, Edmund, 342, Edward, 233, Edward Bruce, 233, Edward Scott, 233, Elijah, 167, Eliza, 307, Elizabeth, 158, Emory, 233, Frances, 233, Fred, 233, Fred W., 233, Harry, 108, Jacob, 233, James, 319, Jean, 233, Jim, 233, Judy, 121, Kelley, 233, Lyda, 233, Lyndsey, 233, Margaret, 233, Martha, 233, 276, Mary, 118, 233, Maude, 233, Maude M., 233, Maude Margaret, 233, Max, 108, Michael, 158, Nancy, 233, Nancy June, 233, Patsy, 233, Rebecca, 26, Samuel, 233, Sarah, 158, Scott, 233, Thelma, 319, Thomas, 233, Wanda, 233, Wandaline, 108, William, 74, 158

LOWE-GRAY, Steele & Hoff Law, 176

LOWE'S, Frozen Locker, 15, Video, 15

LOWERY, Samuel Scott, 129

LOWMAN, Cordelia A., 113, Mary A., 194, Nancy, 94, William M., 194

LOY, Lela LaVine, 251, Myrna, 342

LUCAS, Charlotte, 381, Jane, 195, Massa, 244, Robert, 204

LUCE, Claire, 342

LUCKETT, Carrie Belle, 234, 302, Esther, 234, G. Bruce, 233, 234, George Bruce, 233, 234, Helen Boone, 233, Hezekiah, 233, Jessie, 233, Mary Jane, 233, Samuel Boone, 233

LUDLOW, Clem, 12

LUDLUM, Kelly Jean, 103, Noah Worth, 103, Timothy, 103

LUNGSFORD, William, 174

LUNSFORD, Alice, 252, Lavina, 306

LUPINO, Ida, 342

LUPTON, Anna H., 203

LUSE, Esta Ella, 234, Estella, 234, Jacob, 234

LUSTER, Alice, 196, Billy, 39, Laura, 148, Lillie, 228, Thomas, 29, 40, Thomas Brooke, 209, William, 29

LUTES, C. LaVerne, 374, Essie, 315

LUTHER, Darrell, 59

LUTZ, Harry, 378

LUZADER, Bill, 234, 235, Cheryl, 234, Earl Lowell, 234, 235, Edward Sherman, 235, Harry, 269, Icy, 327, Inez, 235, Iva, 235, Ivy Myrtle, 327, John, 234, John Aaron, 234, John D., 234, 269, John Dee, 235, Linda Lee, 234, Lloyd, 235, Martha Kay, 234, Matther Thomas, 235, Myrtle, 50, 234, 269, Myrtle Blanch, 269, Paul, 235, Sherman, 327, Thomas Jay, 234, 235, Tracie Marie, 234, Tracy Marie, 234, William Dennis, 234, 235, William Harry, 235

LYDICK, Claude, 52, Frances, 52

LYNCH, Brook, 54, John, 81, 293, John C., 194, Richard E., 37, William R., 29

LYNN, William V., 85

LYON, (Inf. daughter), 235, Albert, 235, Bertha, 235, Bonita, 235, Brad, 235, Charles, 235, Dale, 235, David Rick, 235, Deborah Kay, 235, Delbert, 235, Dorothy, 235, Elva, 235, Emily Jane, 235, Emma, 304, Harold, 235, James, 235, John, 235, Lawrence, 235, Mabel, 235, Myron (Mrs.), 265, Ora, 235, Pearl, 249, Raymond, 235, Rebecca, 235, Robert, 235, Verna, 235, Wilbert, 235, William, 235, 304

LYONS, Betty, 172, Diane, 188, Etta, 200, Joseph, 191, Martha Bell, 191, Mary Permela, 191, Ralph, 28, William, 28, 365

LYTLE, Charles, 228, Clarence, 228, Helen, 252, James, 300, Marion, 228, Mary, 145, Matilda Emmaline, 228, Nellie, 228, Vernon, 145

MACDONALD, Elspeth, 98

MACHLEDT, Bertram, 235, Funeral Home, 382, Harry, 235, Hazel, 235, John, 235, John H., 235, William, 382, William, F., 235, 382

MACK, Ruth, 222

MACMILLAN, Nancy, 210

MACY, Anna L., 372, Bethia, 268

MADDOX, Delilah, 322, Kathryn, 117, Mary, 248, Ruth, 203

MADISON TWP., Historical Society, 365

MADRID, Mike, 95

MAGEE, Joyce Anita, 225

MAGUIRE, Anna, 145, Charles, 133, Clair, 107, Dorotha, 220, Harriet, 131, Harriett, 133, Helen, 133, Isabel, 133, Larue, 107

MAHAN, Amanda, 102, David, 102, Elizabeth Ann, 102, Ida Mae, 304, James, 102, Lucetta Jane, 102, Lydia, 80, Malinda, 102, Mary, 102, Matilda, 101, Milton, 49, Thomas Miller, 102, William, 101

MAHANEY, Edie Kellar, 213, Edith Ann, 213, Jack L., 213, Jackson, 213, Laurel Ann, 213

MAHARRY, Dave, 235, David, 235, Eleanor, 235, Ginny, 235, 236, Jeff, 236, Jeffrey Scott, 236, John, 235, 236, John Andrew, 236, Virginia, 235

MAHASKA, Virginia F., 372

MAHORNEY, Alice Marie, 236, Bennett, 236, Carol, 107, 236, Cassidy Owen, 236, 107, Catherine, 236, Daniel J.B., 107, Daniel Joseph B., 236, Daniel Milton, 236, Darnell, 370, Elizabeth, 236, George Z., 236, James B., 236, Jeanne, 236, Jeanne C., 107, Jeanne Clair, 236, John Calvin, 174, Laura, 236, Mary, 236, Mary Catherine, 107, Orthella Marie, 236, Pat, 107, Patrick, 107, Patrick Amond, 236, Samanatha Ann, 236, Samantha Ann, 107, Samuel L., 236, Samuel M., 107, Samuel Milton, 236, Zachariah Fisher, 236

MAHOY, Hilma, 131, 132, Martha, 233

MAIN, Raymond, 173

MAJORS, John, 263

MALABY, Fern, 165

MALINOWSKI, Stanley, 42

MALLORY, Susan, 138

MALLOW, Adam, 110

MALONEY, Mary E., 300, Tim, 203

MALSBURY, Jennie, 94, Linda Jane, 93, 94

MALSON, Barbara, 198

MALTBY, Margaret, 83

MANGER, William, 29

MANGES, Anna, 237, Catherine, 282, Cline, 236, Daniel, 236, Edgar, 44, 196, 218, 236, Edgar C., 237, Edith, 100, 218, 236, 237, Elizabeth, 282, Esther, 43, Ethel, 236, Harold, 236, John, 236, Lucile, 236, Lucille, 43, Margery, 257, Meredith, 229, Minnie, 237, Nancy, 197, Nellie, 229, Rebecca Jane, 282, Walter, 236, William, 215, 236, 237

MANGUS, Anna Theodosia, 272, Eva, 182, 214, George, 243, John, 29, 40, Julia, 131

MANN, Agnes, 292, Christopher, 292, Janice, 131, Jonas, 292, Laura, 85, Samuel, 292, __, 65

MANNING, Mike, 65, Richard, 375

MANNS, __, 43

MANSON, (General), 238, Anna, 263, Mahlon D. (Col), 319, Mary, 202

MANTE, Evelyn, 240

MANTEL, Nancy, 288

MANTIE, Samantha, 232, Susannah, 232

MAPLES, Helen Marie, 330

MARCUM, Delia Etta, 83

MARKEN, Howard, 56

MARKER, Mary Jane, 353

MARKEY, Catherine, 289, George, 66, Jerry, 280, Jonathan, 197, Lillian Gertrude, 280

MARKLEY, Elizabeth, 302

MARLEY, Anna, 143

MARMADUKE, Charlotte Blanche, 325, Rex, 325, William, 325

MARONEY, Benjamin, 175, Daniel, 175, David R., 175, Joseph, 175

MARQUARD, Charles, 82, Rose Ann, 82

MARQUEZ, Jeff, 210, Marta Jo, 210, Ray, 210

MARRERO, Patricia, 262

MARRIS, T.D., 69

MARROW, Margaret, 344, 345

MARSCHKE, Albert, 288, Helen, 360

MARSDEN, Company, 18

MARSH, Lillie, 213

MARSHALL, Agnus, 237, Charles, 81, 237, Cheri, 237, Cindy, 237, Diane, 237, Edith, 237, Flavius, 237, George (Gen.), 290, Janet, 237, Jennifer, 237, John, 237, John Armstrong, 237, Laine, 271, Mamie, 237, Martha, 237, Minnie, 31, 237, Pauline, 237, Pauline Cox, 127, Sarah, 237, Willie, 237

MARSTELLER, George, 168, George E., 338, Nicholas, 338, Olive, 168, 338, Paul, 338

MARTEN, Sarah, 95

MARTENS, Catherine, 333, Frederick, 333

MARTIN, Abia, 237, Adam Dryer, 96, Almira, 345, Anna, 230, Charles, 238, 353, Charles Francis, 233, Charlotte, 234, Chris, 338, Cyd, 96, David, 106, 355, Della Frances, 130, 157, Diane Lynn, 355, Diantha, 95, Dorothy, 233, Dorsey, 31, Edith Ellen, 172, Edna, 53, Elizabeth, 238, Evi, 237, Forrest, 181, Frank, 237, Harrison, 237, Herman Wells, 233, Hugh M., 183, Hugh Michael, 183, Isaac, 201, 237, Jacob, 237, James, 237, James "Judge", 164, James Hanna, Jr., 183, James Hanna, Sr., 183, James M., 100, 237, James Mills, 229, 237, Jayne, 172, Joe, Jr., 355, John, 174, Jonathan, 30, Joseph, 355, Julia, 43, Keith W., 106, Kimberly Ann, 355, Lala Wilkins, 349, Levi Lawson, 233, Lois, 172, Louis Kulp, 183, Margaret, 229, 237, Margaret Ann, 237, Marie, 267, Marion, 237, Mary, 297, Mary Anna, 228, 229, Mary Jeanette, 307, Mary Lael, 170, Maud, 188, Mearil, 106, Melissa, 186, Mildred, 150, Mollie, 238, Nena Fern, 279, Neva, 199, Newton, 238, Olus Edna, 174, Randy, 172, Rolla, 186, Roy, 112, Russell, 106, Samuel, 237, Shirley, 106, Speed, 183, Terri, 172, Tessie, 244, Thomas D., 375, Virgil, 172, Walter T., Jr., 95, Wandaline, 181, William, 220, 237, __, 42

MARTZ, Anna, 124, Anna A., 124, Elizabeth, 193, 258, Frank, 94, John, 124, John M., 258, Mary E., "Molly", 224, Rebecca, 258

MASON, Alice Sarah, 238, Annetta Lowes, 238, Clara Jane, 203, Dollie, 238, Ed, 28, Eliza, 238, Emma, 65, Estella, 238, Esther Jane, 238, Eulalia, 4, 238, Eulalia J., 338, Ewing, 221, F., 12, Findley P., 238, Frank, 12, Jack, 238, Jesse M., 143, John, 238, John R., 338, Lula, 208, Mahlon Jackson, 238, Margaret, 238, Mary, 238, Mary A., 238, Mata, 238, Mate, 238, Melinda, 238, Molly, 238, Nancy, 238, Nell Lamson, 221, Perry Wickliff, 238, Polly, 238, Priscilla, 238, Rachel M., 143, Ruby, 90, Sally, 238, Sarah Cox, 238, Sarah Elizabeth, 238, Thomas, 238, Thomas Jefferson, 238, Walter Overton, 238, William, 295, William A., 238, William D., 238, Wilson, 238, Wilson Campbell, 238

MASONIC TEMPLE, 364

MASSA, Alice, 269, Richard L., 156

MASSING, Arthur W., 375, Frank, 155, Hubert, 144

MASTEN, Elizabeth, 115, Nancy, 346

MASTERS, Marcy E., 115, Sylvia, 282

MATER, Elmer, 41, Ira, 41

MATHENEY, 92

MATHERS, Sailor Jack, 238, William, 238

MATHEWS, Hannah, 123, W.A., 63

MATHISON, Traceye, 276

MATNEY, Daisy, 171

MATTES, Joseph, 79, Walter

MATTHEWS, Burleigh, 64, Hannah, 342, Mae, 148, Mark, 72

MATZINGER, Christianna, 81, George, 81

MAUDLIN, Andrew, 113, Bart, 113, Brett, 113, Cody, 113, James, 128, Matt, 133, Melissa, 113, Ora Carlile, 128, Ora Esther, 113, Richard, 128, Roy, 113, Roy H., 128, Shirley, 128, Tab R., 113, Tod R., 113, Tonya, 113, Mark, 113

MAXWELL, Anna, 125, Barbara May, 187, Bezaleel, 125, Carolyn, 375, Donald L., 375, Esther, 208, Franklin, 128, Gladyne Sue, 128, Jill Andrea, 355, John, 125, Loren, 64, Margaret Ann, 79, Ralph, 226, Richard, 355, Samuel Dunn, 125, School, 123

MAY, Bert E., 24, Bertrand E., (Dr.), 359, Eva, 94, Harriet, 94, Mary, 90, Willis Lafayette, 94

MAYER, Edna, 350

MAYFIELD, Mary, 117, Mary Margaret, 258, Michael, 117, Michael Richard, 258, Michelle, 117, Michelle Rene, 258, Rita, 258

HALL, Alex A., 11, Ann, 239, Beth Ann, 239, Ed, 239, George, 239, Kimberly, 239, Matthew, 239, Nancy, 239, Neal, 239, Sarah, 239, Susan, 239

McALISTER, James A., 164, Louisa J., 164, Myron, 372, Rosa, 122, 123, 164

McALLISTER, Lottie B., 307, Mary, 15, Mary Evelyn, 316

McANULTY, Bradley J., 372

McARTHUR, Douglas (Gen.), 290, Robbie, 54, Wilson, 54

McBEE, Charles, 238, Connie Jo, 328, Frank, 238, Gerald Martin, 328, Hallie, 20, Ike, 20, Isaac, 238, James Martin, 328, M.Z., 374, Mark Allen, 328, Mart, 99, Martin Zedeck, 238, Marvin, 238, Mary Ann, 328, Mary Olive, 238, Minie, 238, Minnie, 381, Minnie Lee, 238, Robert Franklin, 238, Sarah Melinda, 238, Vena, 331, W.T., 238, Walter Evans, 238, Walter Henry, 238, William Fran-

klin, 328, William J., 238, William Thomas, 238, William Zedeck, 238
McBETH, W.O., 65
McBRAYER, Barbara, 278, C. (Rev.), 253, __, 127
McBRIDE, Freeman, 350
McBRIDGE, Fremon, 350
McBROOM, Iva, 166
McCLURE, Sara, 242
McCABE, Elizabeth Ann, 335, John, 158
McCAIN, Elizabeth, 144, Jess, 130, John, 130, Linda S., 284, Margaret, 130, Mary, 130, Sarah, 190, 281
McCAINE, Nancy Jane, 321, Vardamon, 321
McCALINE, Ezra Beckinridge, 239
McCALLISTER, Betty, 152, Brian Forrester, 227, Fred, 233, Kelli, 152, Lynn Ann, 227, Mary, 213, Ralph, 233, Raymond Forrester, 227, Roland, 152
McCALLUM, John, 200, __, 44
McCALMENT, Willard, 366
McCAMMON, Dorothy Jean, 291
McCAMPBELL, Edith, 169, William, 70
McCAN, Victor, 52
McCANCE, Floyd, 317
McCANDLESS, Bud H., 372
McCARTHY, Katherine, 318, Ruth, 89
McCARTY, Amelia, 69, Amelis, 238, Charles Leroy, 239, Cynthia A., 318, Dorothy Helen, 239, Francis, 197, 238, 239, Francis Theron, 239, George Henry, 238, 239, George Henry, Jr., 239, Julie, 289, Marjorie, 238, 239, Mary Catherine, 239, Maxine Marie, 239, Melia, 239, Mildred Lucille, 239, Richard Francis, 239, Ronald Gene, 239, Susan, 239, Thomas, 318
McCAULEY, Mildred, 89
McCAY, Carrie, 240, Ora, 240
McCLAIN, Agnes, 145, Amy, 89, Curtis E., 375, Laura, 89, Martha, 89, Sharon, 127
McCLAINE, Alma Joyce, 103, Brenda Kay, 103, Brian Keith, 103, Christopher, 103, Daisy E., 239, Elizabeth Lee, 103, Eloise, 102, 103, Ezra, 103, Gerold Ezra, 239, Iris Opal, 103, 239, Jackie Leon, 239, James, 102, 104, James David, 103, Jena Mullien, 103, Kathy, 103, 239, Kathy Lynne, 239, Kimberly Ann, 239, 300, Laura, 102, Lindsay, 103, Lynne, 239, Matthew Scott, 103, Omer A., 239, Pauline, 239, Richard, 102, 104, 375, Richard Kent, 103, 239, 300, Shirley, 67, 103, 104, Shirley Lois, 239, 300, Stephen James, 103
McCLAMROCH, Belle, 90, Edna "Lizzie", 162, Miranda Belle, 89, William W., 375
McCLAMROCK, Elizabeth Edna, 255, Ida Mae, 133, Lemuel Ball, 256, Margaret, 268
McCLASKEY, 99, Alice, 126, 239, 271, 344, Amber, 239, Amma, 240, Appa, 240, Atlanta, 239, Barbara, 184, Brenda Sue, 239, Bryan Wayne, 239, Cheryl, 105, 240, Clara, 239, Dappy, 239, Dave, 240, David, 105, E.P. (Capt.), 344, Eb, 239, Ebenezer, 129, Ebenezer Patrick, 239, Elizabeth, 239, Eric, 240, Eric Wade, 105, Heather, 239, James, 239, Jamie, 239, Janet, 239, Jeff, 240, Jeffrey Alan, 105, Joan, 239, Joe, 239, Joe Washington, 239, John, 239, Joseph, 239, Marilyn, 239, Nancy, 239, Nettie, 239, Pam, 239, Pamela Jane, 239, Richard, 239, Richard Wayne, 239, Stacy, 239, Stella, 126, 239, Tara, 239, Will, 126, 239
McCLEAN, Edward B., 375
McCLELLAN, Indiana, 340, Mary, 298, Mary H., 120, Truckers, 14
McCLELLAND, John (Lt. Col.), 80, Pauline, 43
McCLOUD, Carol, 54, James, 54
McCLURE, Alve Lee, 240, C.M., 49, Carl Richard, 240, Cary Walter, 240, Charles, 43, Charles Edward, 240, David, 240, Donald Andrew, 240, Elizabeth, 240, Eugene Douglas, 240, Gene, 54, Glenn Edward, 240, Grocery, 15, Harold Lee, 240, Icy, 327, Ina Mae, 235, Ivette Merle, 240, Jack Phillip, 240, Jacqulyn Deana, 240, James, 240, James Gilbert, 240, James M., 372, James Montgomery, 240, Jeffrey David, 240, John, 240, Judy, 54, Lee Richard, 240, Lola, 316, Margaret, 240, Margaret Angeline, 240, Margaret Elmore, 240, Moses, 240, Naomi, 136, Paul Vernon, 240, Richard Jason, 240, Robert Bernard, 240, Sarah O'Rentha, 240, Stephen Michael, 240, Timmy Dale, 240, Veda Mae, 240, Walter Alva, 240, William, 240, William W., 194, William Wallace, 50
McCOLLUM, Hugh, 222, Nancy, 222
McCONAHY, Blake Edward, 276, Jared Thomas, 276
McCONNELL, Rebecca, 335
McCOPPIN, Ima Joyce, 165
McCORD, Ida Lucile, 202
McCORKLE, Alexander, 269, Nancy T., 269
McCORMIC, 272
McCORMICK, "B" Shirley, 93, Abigail, 175, Andrew, 70, Annie, 240, Carrie, 240, Cemetery, 204, Del, 240, Delbert, 240, Doris, 242, Dorothy, 93, Edith Hagerman, 175, Ellen, 175, Emma Jane, 240, Francis Eugene, 241, Gene, 241, George, 241, Geraldine, 93, Harold, 21, 38, 240, 241, Harold Earl, 240, Harry, 93, Hazel, 242, Herbert, 240, Herbert Iral, 240, Howard, 242, Hugh, 175, James, 241, Jane, 93, Jessie, 240, John, 93, Keith, 240, Lloyd, 251, Madeline Mary, 200, Maria Line, 175, 176, Mary, 175, Mary Ann, 93, Mary Drew, 93, Michael, 240, Michael D., 240, Michael Del, 240, Mike, 240, Nancy, 175, Nancy Jane, 175, Ora, 240, Orville, 93, Pat, 240, Patrick, 240, Patrick Lee, 240, Paul, 93, Phyllis, 93, Preston, 70, 93, 314, Ralph, 240, Ralph C., 240, Roy Lee, 241, Ruth, 21, 38, 240, 241, Ruth Glee, 241, Salome Ball, 175, Sarah Jane, 309, Shelby Willis, 93, Thomas, 240, 301, Thomas R., 240, Timothy, 240, Timothy J., 240, William, 225
McCOY, Beatrice, 263, Beatrice Fay, 241, Bonnie, 241, Edith Rae, 241, Elizabeth, 241, Ethel Addie, 241, Etta, 241, Fred, 241, Garnet Edward, 241, George A., 241, George Amarques, 241, Gertrude, 241, Gregg, 172, Hannah, 129, Jennie Frances, 241, John, 241, John Wesley, 241, John, Sr., 241, Larry, 241, Lula Leslie, 241, Lyde, 241, Mary, 241, Merrill, 241, Nannie, 241, Ruth, 241, Sarah, 174, Ted, 241, Teddy Parker, 241, Thomas Isaac, 241, Wayne, 241, William, 241
McCREA, Aaron, 34, Mary, 247
McCREARY, Harold, 217, Norma, 217, Rebecca Louise, 217
McCREE, Catherine, 129
McCULLEY, Elza, 266
McCULLOUGH, Dianne, 147, Joe, 147, Melvina, 239, Opal, 43, Robert, 104, Ruth Ann, 262, Toby, 147
McCULLUM, Joe, 280
McCULLY, Trudy, 303
McCUMBER, Susan, 78
McCUTCHAN, John Allen, 258, Laura, 258
McCUTCHEON, William G., 41
McDADE, Rebecca, 270
McDANIEL, Chris, 54, Clara Ellen, 302, David, 90, Henry, 197, 280, Joshua, 41, Lou, 280, Martha, 286, Myrtilda, 54, Sarah, 90, Thomas, 280, 286, __, 99
McDONALD, Cheryl L., 372, David, 321, Dennis R., 372, Florence, 309, Janice, 331, Joseph, 182, Permelia, 321, Wallace, 51
McDOWELL, Donald, 272, Grant, 331, Harriett, 272, Helen, 331, James, 115, Melinda, 272, Sara, 115
McELROY, J.L., 199, Theresa R., 125
McELWAIN, Steven, 156
McELWEE, Mildred, 230
McFALL, Charlotte Emiline, 84, David, 306, Geneva, 231, Marc, 306, Pat, 306, Tyson Joella, 306
McFARLAND, Ann, 99, Glen, 69
McFARLIN, Rebecca, 295
McFERRAN, Neva, 112
McFERRON, Martha, 82
McGAUGHEY, Albert, 241, Bert, 192, Clara, 241, D.A., 154, 241, Dory, 241, 242, Dory Albert, 241, Edward, 241, Ivyl Pearl, 267, Lafe Vernon, 267, Lizzie, 241, Margaret Frank, 241, Mary Barr, 241, 242, Mary Violet, 267, Mildred, 242, Sally, 295, Stella, 241, Zoe, 348
McGEE, Stella, 43, Tim, 63
McGHEE, Yvonna Dean, 283
McGILL, Mary, 255, Mary Jane, 298
McGILLIARD, Abigail, 164
McGINNIS, Arista Parvin, 243, Lois, 243
McGIRR, Elizabeth Ann, 335
McGLAMERY, Bathsheba, 264
McGOVNEY, Robert, 238, Sally, 238
McGOWAN, Lydia, 139
McGRAW, Sarah, 230
McGURE, Corinne, 359
McHENRY, Guy, 59
McHUGH, Frank, 342
McILVAIN, Harold, 302, Marjorie Ann, 302
McINNES, Margaret, 107
McINTIRE, Alpha, 353, Charels Frye, 141, Charles Andrew, 242, Charlie, 242, Danielle Leigh, 242, Debbi, 242, Deborah Dean, 242, Doris, 242, Harriet, 82, 141, Ida, 242, Ira, 242, Jane, 60, Jill, 242, John, 60, Margaret, 326, Margaret Elizabeth, 84, Michael Andrew, 242, Mike, 242, "Mitch", 242, Mitchel Andrew, 242, Susan, 170, Walter, 326
McINTYRE, Earl, 204, Eliza, 301, Frank, 204, Hiram, 204, Hughes, 204, Jeanette, 309, Laura Belle, 204, Sanford, 204
McJUNKINS, Jennie, 151
McKEAN, Kezia, 220
McKEE, Ben, 129, Elizabeth, 93
McKENDREE, __, 343
McKENSEY, Mary, 151
McKENZIE, Andrew Phillip, 185, Richard, 185, Robert Jake, 185, Sean Matthew, 185
McKEOWN, Mary Patricia, 150, Mike, 372, Pat, 150
McKINLEY, Bob, 275, John, 59, Lougenia, 296, William, (Pres.), 184
McKINNEY, Alice, 242, Amy Lee, 107, Anne, 242, Carol J., 372, Charles, 242, Christy, 107, Daniel, 242, Eva, 242, Fern, 242, Frank, 242, Georgia, 242, Gladys, 242, Glenn, 242, Hazel, 242, Ida Lucile, 242, James Collin, 242, Janet L., 375, Karen, 107, Lawrence, 242, Margaret, 316, 369, Marjory, 242, Michael E., 372, Noel, 242, P.T., 242, Pearce, 242, Prestley T., 242, Robert, 242, Samuel, 242, Scott, 107, Tom, 107, Trish, 242, Troy E., 372, William, 242
McKINNIS, Will, 360
McKINSEY, Edith, 203, George, 152, Joanne, 296, Mary, 152, Mercer, 152, Samuel, 50, W.P., 67
McKINSTRY, John, 164, Larry, 165
McKINZIE, Barbara, 336, James, 336, Ruthie, 313
McLAUGHLIN, Arthur, 103, Effie, 103, Everett Wayne, 103, Madonna, 103, Minnie, 91
McLEAN, Maria, 375
McLEOD, __, 12, Leslie, 12
McLOCHLIN, Christina, 346
McLOED, Carolyn, 127, Doug, 127, Janet, 127, Larry, 127, Marty, 127, Oliver, 127, Terri, 127, Tom, 127
McLOWED, Richard, 127
McMAHAN, Allie, 43, Charity, 143, Donald F., 49, John Robertson (Rev.), 355, Luetna, 285, Ruth, 285
McMAINS, Anderson, 179, Josephine, 179, Mary, 277, Robert, 277, Sarah Evaline, 277
McMINDES, Chris, 304, Jerry, 286, 304, Mary Ann, 286, 304, Melanie, 304
McMULLEN, Andrew Jefferson, 243, Anna, 243, Benjamin, 153, 243, Bonnie June, 211, 229, 243, Bradley, 243, Brian Scott, 230, Carmel Sanders, 243, Catherine, 243, Cheryl, 230, David, 243, Denise, 243, Donna May, 243, Dwain, 243, Dwight, 243, Edward, 144, Edward Robison, 243, Eleanor, 40, Emily, 153, 243, Emily, 243, Emily Jane, 308, Everett, 243, Fannie, 243, Francis Marion, 243, Harry J., 372, Helen, 243, Henry, 153, Howard, 243, John, 243, James, 208, 242, 250, 298, James Madison, 243, James, Jr., 242, James, Sr., 242, Jesse, 153, Jull Linette, 230, John, 242, Joseph, 153, 242, 243, Josephine, 243, Josephus Emmons, 243, Kenneth Gene, 230, Kenneth Lee, 243, Kevin, 243, Larry, 243, Lemuel Washington, 243, Leonard Franklin, 243, Lindsay, 243, Lindsay J., 153, Louann, 153, Lowell, 243, Lucinda Hardee, 366, Lydia Margaret, 153, Margaret, 243, Marilyn, 243, Marjory Jane, 243, Mary, 325, Mary Catherine, 253, 254, 255, 298, Mollie, 153, Rosalie, 170, Sarah, 153, Sarah "Sally", 243, Sarah Elizabeth, 153, 243, Virginia Lee, 243, William, 40, 243, Zola, 196, Zola Lucille, 197
McMULLIN, John, 228,
McMURRAY, Charles Robert, 296, Dale Allen, 296, Daren Jay, 296, David Wayne, 296, Deanna Kay, 296, Rosalie, Anne, 296
McMURRY, Alice, 361, Elizabeth, 361, Kesiah, 361, Madona, 223, Madonna, 199
McMURTREY, Charles H., 152, Grocery, 14, Peter, 152
McMURTRY, Diane, 271
McNARY, Dollie Gertrude, 357
McNEAL, Gail, 119
McNEIL, Betty, 243, Boyd O., 243, Boyd, Jr., 243, Ed, 243, Edwin L., 243, Edwin Lee, 243, Edwin Lee II, 243, Hugh Michael, 243, J.L., 378, John, 243, John L., 243, Lee, 243, Pat, 243, Patricia, 243
McNICOLL, D. Ella, 243, Lucinda, 243, William, 243
McNORTON, Alma, 99, Frank, 215
McNULTY, Ethel, 130, James, 130, John, 130, Kenneth, 130, Martha, 130, Mary, 103, William, 130
McNUTT, Margaret, 144, Mary F., 279, Sarah, 129
McQUIGG, James William, 281, Martha "Matie" Eliza, 281
McQUOWAN, Henry, 189, Ida, 189
McSPADDEN, Dan, 20, Deanna, 185
McVAY, Edna Gertrude, 234
MEAD, Ellen Jane, 220, Montford, 220, Montford Arthur, 220, Monty, 220
MEADOWS, Darrell, 128, David P., 375, Helen, 347, Melissa, 128, Mike, 128, Sheila, 171, Tresha Ann, 128
MEAKIN, E.T., 371, Edgar N., 371
MEAN, Kenneth, 113
MEARS, Elizabeth, 238, Elsie, 261, George, 261, Lizzie, 261
MECKLIN, Shirley, 335
MEEK, Albert, 135, Amanda, 135, Belle, 103, Brian, 235, Cynthia, 135, Earl, 235, Earl (Mrs.), 31, Gayle, 235, George, 135, Isabelle, 288, Iva, 135, Joshua Adams, 235, Linda Lou, 234, Mary Elizabeth, 135, Perry, 135, Sarah, 135, Stephen, 135, Susan, 135, Lamont, 120
MEEKER, John, 191, William, 164
MEEKS, Elizabeth, 278
MEESE, Karol, 131
MEHARRY, Ada Dean, 243, Flora, 153, Helen Christina, 200, Hugh Sayers, 200, 243, Patricia, 243, Roy, 65, __, 17
MEHARRY AG. SERVICE, 16
MEIER, Alexander, 259, Andrew, 259, Catherine, 259, Christian, 259, Daniel, 259, David, 259, George, 259, Jacob, 259, John George, 259, Joseph, 259, Mary M., 259, Nancy, 259, Peter, 259, Polly, 259, Sybilla, 259, Thomas, 259
MEITUS, Gregory Eliott, 273, Irv, 273, Robert Shannon, 273
MELLOTT, Mildred, 223
MELONE, 307
MELOY, 289, John F., 288, Mary, 288, Naomi, 288
MELVIN, Albert Glenn, 244, 245, Amber Diane, 245, Augusta, 244, Augusta Ferrin, 245, Austus Ferrin, 244, Beatrice, 244, Charles, 244, Charles Henry, 244, Chester Clyde, 244, 245, Clyde, 244, 245, 334, Connie Maxine, 245, Cynthia Irene, 245, Deana, 244, Debra Lynne, 245, Elaine Ann, 244, Elizabeth Diane, 264, Ernest, 244, Ernest Sterling, 244, 245, Ethel, 244 Frank, 244, Fred, 244, Fred Lawrence, 244, 245, Fred Leland, 244, 245, Glenn, 244, Harold, 244, Hazel, 97, 244, Helen Maxine, 244, 245, Hobart, 244, Hobart Eugene, 244, 245, Howard, 244, 245, Howard L., 244, Howard Vaughn, 244, Isaac, 244, Jesse Scott, 245, Joshua Dale, 245, Kirby Scott, 245, Larry Richard, 244, Leland Donald, 244, Leslie, 244, Leslie Diane, 245, Leslie Marvin, 245, Lois, 244, Lucy, 244, Maude, 244, Maxine, 244, Melanie Dawn, 245, Melva, 245, Mildred, 245, Myrtle, 244, Myrtle Florence, 244, 245, Rosalie E., 244, Sim, 244, Trisha Kyan, 245, Ward, 244, Wilma, 244
MELYN, Cornelis, 164
MENDENHALL, Allan, 259, Brian, 113, Brian Gene 259, Chad, 278, Dama, 113, Dama Dianne, 259, Matt, 278, Sam, 278, __, 50
MENEELEY, Sarah, 158
MENEFEE, Edward R., 133, Edward Rennels, 132, Mary, 132, Mary Frances, 132, William (Dr.), 133, William N. (Dr.), 133
MENGES, Katherine, 178
MENJOU, __, 342, Adolph, 342
MENNACH, Catherine, 314
MENNEN, Burton, 245, Dennis, 245, Doris, 245, H. Glenn, 375, Harold, 245, Harvey Glenn, 245, Herman, 245, Hobert, 245, Ivy Pearl, 245, James Michael, 245, Jason Dennis, 245, Linda Lee, 245, Mary, 245, Melissa, 245, Ruth, 245, Ryan Wayne, 245, Teresa Ann, 245
MERCHANT, William R., 375
MERITT, Auction Service, 16, Eugene, 265, Olin, 265, Virgil, 265, 266
MERRELL, Joyce Delight, 165
MERRELLAS, Basil T., 377
MERRICK, Myron, 165
MERRILL, Doris Harlan, 247, Jody L., 372
MERRIS, Esther, 142
MERRITT, Chloral, 357, George, 357, June, 357, Mayme, 357, Neil, 357, Tommy Joe, 357
MERRYMAN, Verla Isabel, 245
MERSHON, David W., 375
MESSENGER, Cynthis, 110
METSKER, Alan, 324, Bill, 240, Jessie, 240, Laine, 324, William, 324
METZGER, Debbie, 320, Jenny, 320, Nicky, 320
MEYER, Anne, 128, Bette Jane, 246, Kathleen, 89, 245, 246, Kenneth Lee, 246, Rose Marie, 110
MEYERS, Edith C., 313, Rebecca, 324
MIARS, George (Capt.), 167
MICHAEL, Albert, 310, Cemetery, 145, David, 103, Harry (Lt.), 355, Julie, 67, Julie R., 375, Karl, 103, Larry, 106, Mary, 103, Mike J., 372, Robert, 103
MICHAELS, Carrie, 163, Eva, 109, 318, Howard, 163, James, 318
MICHAL, Christopher, 246, Chris, 246, David, 246, Doris, 246, Judy, 246, Nathaniel, 246, Philip, 24, 246, Philip Q., 372, Richard, 246, Robert J., 246, Susan Gran, 246, Terri, 246
MICHEL, Roy W., 49
MIDDLESTADT, Emma, 247
MIDDLETON, Ed B., 306, H., 68
MIETHE, Ashley Linn, 230, Bill, 230, Heather Sue, 230, Janis, 230, Larry Gene, 230, Rosemary, 230, Shannon Marie, 230
MIHLE, Charles William, 295
MIKELS, Ida May, 318, Joel, 342, John, 343, Sylvia, 343, William P., 342, 343
MIKLES, Rebecca, 258
MILAM, Alison Melissa, 168, Brian David, 168, Donna Kay, 168, Mary Ann, 111
MILES, Andrew, 246, Andy, 189, Anna, 192, Archie Willard, 192, Billy, 60, Catherine Denise, 246, Cathy, 246, Charles, 282, Clayton, 192, Doris Elizabeth, 192, Elizabeth, 246, 282, Ellis, 282, Emma, 110, 248, Eunice, 192, Flora Ethel, 113, Florence E., 85, George, 192, 246, 282, Hannah, 232, Harry, 246, Harry Victor, 192, Henry, 192, John, 192, 246, 282, John F., 282, John Victor, 192, Katheryn, 246, Lanilla, 189, Leona, 192, Leonard, 174, 192, Leslie, 192, Lewis, 192, Lottie, 145, Lula, 192, Margaret Marie, 246, 192, Mary, 149, 248, 282, Mary Elizabeth, 246, May, 247, Mertie, 112, 232, Ollie, 174, Ottie,

192, Paul, 246, Paul David, 246, Paulina, 246, Pauline, 192, 282, Peter, 232, Rebecca, 246, Reuben, 12, Rosemary, 192, 246, Rosemary Ann, 192, Rosie, 192, 246, Roy, 192, Ruby Katheryn, 192, Stella, 192, Wanda M., 375, Willard, 246, William H., 248, William J., 60, 149, Zearn, 113

MILKS, Flossie Glen, 272, John William, 272, Lois, 272, Lois Elizabeth, 272, Lynn H., 272

MILLER, 22, Aaron, 258, Adam, 187, Albert, 248, Aletha, 356, Alice E., 122, Anne, 247, Arilda, 247, Barbara, 233, Barbara Laurene, 350, Ben, 246, 247, 378, Benjamin Franklin, 247, Benjamin Harrison, 88, Bennet, 246, Bennett Rhoads, 248, Betty, 122, Beverly S., 375, Bill, 152, 247, 248, 378, Blanche, 190, Bonnie Darlene, 283, Bradly, 99, Brenda J., 375, Brian, 122, Brian David, 283, C.R., 217, Calvin, 221, Carla S., 372, Casandra, 353, Catherine Agnes, 179, Chalmer, 31, 247, Charles, 247, Charles Kincaid, 247, Charles Marion, 216, Charles O., 249, Charles Raymond, 217, Cinderella, 112, Clara Carolina, 88, Connie, 93, Dale, 49, Denise, 99, Diane Beth, 283, Donald, 235, Donald Aaron, Jr., 235, Earl, 181, Edith, 263, 381, Eleanor, 39, 40, 243, Eliza Wray, 184, Elizabeth, 164, 318, Elizabeth "Betty", 88, Elizabeth Jane, 179, Elsie, 221, Ema Elizabeth, 247, Esther Irene, 247, Faye, 380, Flora, 247, Frances, 65, 246, 378, Franklin, 248, Gene Dale, 244, George, 248, Gretchen Lee, 247, Hal Stephen, 99, Hancil, 221, Hannah, 93, Harriett Ann, 353, Hattie, 353, Henry, 124, 248, Henry M., 67, Henry, Jr., 179, Henry, Sr., 179, Hilda, 221, Homer, 31, 247, Howard F., 58, Ina, 115, 116, Irene, 360, Isaac, 30, Isaac N., 123, 247, Isabel, 284, J., 49, J. (Rev.), 48, J.W., 31, Jacob, 340, James, 76, 152, 247, James A., 39, James R., 375, Jane, 247, Jeanette, 220, Jeannette, 270, Jennie, 158, Jerry R., 372, Joe (Rev.), 202, John, 30, 221, 247, 248, John D., 245, John F., 278, John Wesley, 247, Johnnie, 31, Kim, 378, LaVera Ellen, 244, Larry, 69, Laurel S., 216, Lee, 378, Leroy, 68, 248, Lily Beth, 94, Lloyd, 121, Louise, 39, 40, 145, 296, Margaret, 249, Marian, 152, 353, Marion, 88, Mark Allen, 283, Marlene, 269, Martha, 101, Martha Bell, 191, Martha J., 221, Martin, 152, Mary, 132, 181, 242, 247, 267, 282, Mary Edith, 248, 378, Mary Ellen, 184, 247, Mary Onelia, 245, Mathis, 247, Maude, 122, Maxine, 246, 378, Melinda, 247, 248, Melinda Lee, 247, 378, Melissa, 259, Merle, 278, Michael, 247, Mildred, 378, Mollie, 267, Monroe, 247, Myrtle, 247, Nancy, 341, Nancy A., 247, Otto Lee, 247, Pat, 54, Paul, 245, 247, Paul W., 244, Pauline, 54, Peggy Kay, 283, Phyllis, 152, R.H. (Rev.), 236, Ralph, 31, 247, Ralph C., 353, 360, Rebecca Darlene, 283, Rita A., 372, Robert, 249, Robert Henry, 313, Rosalyn Jean, 204, Ross Alan, 121, Rua Cassandra, 247, Russell, 65, 122, 246, 248, 378, Russell Don, 244, Rusty, 152, Rusty Lee, 372, Ruth, 247, Ruth Ellen, 248, 353, S. West, 179, Saloma Ann "Lomie", 313, Samuel, 190, Samuel Homer, 247, Samuel Thomas, 247, Sheral Kay, 121, Stacey E., 375, Stella, 39, 40, Sylvanis, 247, Tabetha Ann, 124, Thomas, 221, Timothy, 179, Ursula, 197, 302, Valentine, 318, Vaughn, 122, Veda Mae, 240, Vernita, 278, Virginia, 339, Wallace, 247, Wanda, 263, William, 247, 339, 353, William Cheever, 247, William Glen, 247, 378, Winifred, 284

MILLER'S, Body Shop, 171, Restaurant, 327

MILLET, Wanda, 263

MILLIGAN, 6, Harriet, 75, Alan Dale, 249, Alex, 248, Alex Byrd, 249, Allen, 248, Amy, 249, Anna, 75, Benjamin Thomas, 249, Broyles, 29, Caroline, 248, Charles, 108, 248, Clara L., 249, Clarence, 70, Cynthia, 248, Dale, 249, Daniel, 249, David, 248, Dean, 248, Dick, 249, Donna Rae, 248, Elizabeth, 248, Ellen Jane, 248, Elton, 70, Elva (Sayler), 334, Elva Sayler, 295, Emily, 249, Francis, 248, Frank, 248, Helen, 108, 248, J. Kenneth, 248, James, 248, James Drake, 108, James Milford, 248, 249, James Robert, 248, Jay, 248, Jill, 248, Joe, 248, John, 11, 70, 248, Joseph, 75, 248, 370, Katherine, 248, Katherine Elizabeth, 249, Katherine Jean, 249, Kellie, 249, Kimberly, 249, Lessie, 232, Lucinda, 70, Marie Nanette, 108, 248, Martha Suanne, 249, Mary Lucinda, 248, Michael, 249, Milford S., 108, 248, Nancy, 249, Paula Jill, 249, Pauline, 248, Richard T., 248, Robert, 248, 249, Roland D., 248, 382, Roland Daniel, 249, Roland Dean, 249, Ruby, 249, Ruby A., 248, S.J., 10, Sally, 248, Sally Ann, 249, Samuel, 248, Sarah Jardine, 248, Sarah Margaret, 248, Scott, 249, Shaw, 249, Susan, 249, Suzanne, 249, Thomas, 248, Thomas K., 375, Thomas Kenneth, 249, Timothy, 248, Virginia (Miss), 314

MILLION, Paul, 157, Paul (Rev.), 345, Paul E., 58

MILLS, Anna, 237, C. Adeline, 249, Frank, 304, Ida, 304, Jerry D., 372, Letitia, 353, Lettitia, 354, Martha, 134, 135, 353, R.G., 167, Sarah, 153, Thomas, 353, Thomas Jefferson, 354, __, 32

MILNER, Ethel, 193, Henry C., 194, Kip, 194, 293, Samuel P., 113

MINNICH, Andrew Jackson, 249, Charles 33, Charles Austin, 249, Frances Susan, 249, Genevieve, 249, George Wm. McKinely, 249, John Lewis, 249, Lee Raymond, 249, Otto Lewis, 249, Romerlus D., 31, Samuel Andrew, 249

MINNICK, Charles, 45, Clara, 43, Frances, 31

MINTER, Anthony, 145, Elizabeth, 145, Tabitha, 145

MIRANDA, Magda, 328

MIRELEZ, Elena, 54, Fernando, 54

MISNER, Clyde, 95, Mary Ellen, 360, Nevah, 95, Robert, 270, Robert, Jr., 270

MITCHELL, Alexander, 249, 250, Alfred, 138, Ali, 249, Amanda, 174, Amanda Teresa, 175, Amaza, 249, 250, Amber, 250, Amelia, 144, Angela Sue, 274, Annabelle, 288, April D., 250, Bernard, 155, Bernard Fred, 251, Berta, 250, Billy, 250, Bonnie, 250, Brandon Dale, 175, Brian Keith, 175, Charles, 249, 250, Charles Edward, 250, Claire, 250, Clara, 249, 250, Clarence, 249, Clint, 155, Clint Davis, 251, Dausy, 249, 350, 351, Daisy Laurene, 249, Dallas, 249, 250, Daniel, 250, David, 250, Delevon, 249, Delevon Donalson, 250, Devin, 320, Dona, 249, Edward, 249, Effie, 250, Elizabeth, 249, 361, Elliott, 249, Elmer, 250, Emily, 250, Ernestine Lenora, 250, Eula, 249, 250, Florence M., 305, Fred, 250, Fred J., 250, 288, Freddie, 250, Gabriel, 145, 250, Geneva, 168, 338, George, 250, Harriet, 138, 351, Hattie, 249, Helen, 250, 270, Hilda, 136, Isom, 249, James, 250, 301, Jane, 114, Jennifer Kay, 175, Jesse, 250, Jesse Alva, 175, Jessie, 249, Jimmy, 249, 250, John, 249, 250, Jonathan, 249, 250, Joseph, 250, Juanita, 250, Julia A., 284, Julie, 355, Kenneth Warren, 250, Kristen Marie, 175, Lacey Nichol, 175, Lawrence Dal, 175, Lee, 249, Lee Edward, 250, Leeanise, 249, Leon, 250, Leonard Orville, 250, Linda S., 284, Lucinda, 250, Maggie, 249, Malinda, 250, Margaret, 249, 253, Margaret Ellen, 249, Margaret Ross, 350, Margary, 250, Margery, 114, Martha, 138, 144, 250, 279, Martha Jane, 109, 145, Mary, 250, 305, 350, Mary "Polly", 250, Mary Annie, 138, Mary Willhite, 249, Matthew, 155, Matthew Robert, 251, Maude, 145, Max, 250, Megan Alyn, 175, Metta, 249, Michael, 155, Michael W., 372, Nadine, 250, Nancy, 250, Nanny, 249, Naomi, 288, Naomi Winifred, 288, Norma, 154, 155, 251, Norma E., 155, Norman, 249, Norman Dale, 250, Norman Eugene, 175, Orville, 249, Patricia Ann, 250, Paul, 250, Paul David, 288, 250, Paul Michael, 250, Paulina, 250, Pearl, 249, Philip, 250, President Alexander, 249, Raymond, 249, Raymond Alexander, 250, Rebecca, 274, Rebecca Lou, 250, 288, Rhonda, 155, 251, Rhonda Michelle, 175, Richard, 250, Robert, 155, 250, 251, 274, Robert Michael, 251, Ronald J., 175, Rose, 249, Russell, 250, Ruth, 250, Sam, 249, Samuel, 250, Samuel G., 114, Sarah, 138, 249, 250, Sarah J., 305, Sarah Ogden, 249, Sareptha, 138, Sharon Kay, 250, 288, Sophia, 138, Cylvia, 249, Thomas W., 372, Tiffany Dawn, 175, Timothy Warren, 284, Tonya Michael, 175, Valore, 138, Verna, 250, Virgil, 249, Wanetah, 155, 251, Warren, 249, William, 144, 249, 250, William "Billy", 29, 40, 41, William D., 305, William Travis, 175, William W., 305, Clint, 155

MITCHELTREE, Belle, 103, Bertha, 103, Bessie Lena, 103, Claire Irene, 103, 170, David, 103, David T., 102, 103, 170, 239, David Thomas, 103, Eloise, 239, Elsie Claire, 103, Florence, 103, George, 104, George W., 102, 103, Georgia, 103, Georgia Anna, 103, Iris, 102, Iris Opal, 103, James, 103, 104, James David, 239, Laura, 102, Laura Elizabeth Cath, 102, Letha Alice, 103, Louisiana Florence, 102, Margaret Virginia, 103, Mary, 102, 103, Mary Anna, 239, Mary Anne, 103, Mary Elizabeth, 103, Opal, 239, Rebecca, 102, 103, Robert Allen, 103, Ruth Florence, 103, Virginia, 103

MITCHUM, Diana, 243, Ron, 131

MITTS, Clarence, 330, Martha, 109, Patsy, 109, Ruth Lucille, 330

MIZE, Margaret, 355

MIZUKAMI, Yoshiaki, 136

MOFFET, Ellen Matilda, 94, John, 336

MOFFETT, Anna, 284, Emery Leland, 194, Emory, 293, Judith Ann, 194, Mary Catherine, 194, Ned Emery, 194, Sharon Elizabeth, 194

MOFFITT, Ann, 283, Anna, 129, Betty Jane, 221, Sam, 221, Shane, 221, Thomas, 129, Travis, 221, Walter, 239

MOHN, Victoria, 92

MOLINA, Judith Irene, 155

MONEE, Misty, 121

MONEY, Auburn Alex., 251, Austin Luther, Jr., 251, Austin Luther, Sr., 251, Betty Joan, 251, Charles Edward, 251, Cheryl Lynn, 251, Darrell Wayne, 251, Darrell Wayne, Jr., 251, David Roscoe, 251, David Wayne, 251, Donald, 251, Edith Irene, 251, Everett Russell, 251, Flossie May, 251, Grace, 251, Irwin Wallace, 251, Linda Lou, 251, Lulu Fern, 251, Marilyn Sue, 251, Marion Renfro, 251, Minnie Pearl, 251, Rush, 251, Ryliss Rosetta, 251

MONG, Kate, 129

MONROE, Helen Wanetah, 138, 214, Lura, 214, Naomi, 138, Wanetah, 83, Zura, 138

MONSON, Ruth, 334

MONTAGUE, Narcissa, 284

MONTFORD, Anna, 133

MONTGOMERY, Alexander, 251, Alexander, Jr., 251, Hugh, 235, Isaac Herrod, 251, James, 339, Janet Kay, 175, Martha E., 251, Nan, 238, Phoebe F., 176, Phoebe Jane, 176, 339, Richard (General), 251, Ruy, 275, Savings, 376, W.H., 374, Wallace F., 251, Will, 176, William H., 251

MONTROSE, Alex, 149, Frank, 149

MOODY, Bonnie, 252, Carole, 161, Carole Anne, 252, Charles W., 12, Charlie, 12, Clem (Dot), 252, Cora Lee, 252, Dennis, 306, Dollie, 252, Edith, 353, Edwqrd, 252, Etha, 252, George, 252, Harry, 174, 252, Imo Margaret, 301, James, 252, James T., 252, Joan, 252, John, 252, 306, John A., 161, John Anthony Wayne, 251, John C., 161, 251, Joseph, 29, 40, Judith Arlene, 252, Judy, 161, 252, Kathryn, 252, Leland, 252, Lena, 252, Louis, 252, Louisa, 252, Margaret, 147, 252, 256, Mary Etta, 302, Matilda, 161, 251, Oscar, 306, Owen, 252, Paul, 252, Paula Lynn, 252, Penny, 306, Rita, 306, Sanford, 252, Sanford N., 252, Santy, 252, Thomas, 252, Thomas M., 252, Tom, 360, Tommy, 252, Trent, 252, Velma, 347, Vivian, 252, Walter, 252, Lena, 161

MOOR, Mary P., 184

MOORE, 21, Albert, 252, Allen, 106, 187, 226, Allen W., 106, Allen Washington, 106, Amanda Kay, 128, Amanda Luella, 130, Anna, 128, Austin, 253, Ava, 255, 277, Barbara, 93, Barbara Jean, 128, Bernice, 351, Berniece, 350, Bessie, 255, 296, 305, Bessie Love, 253, Bob, 277, Boots, 322, Bradley Alan, 280, Carol Ina, 160, Caroline "Carrie", 270, Cassandra Lynn, 135, Charles, 322, Charles F., 254, Charles M., 252, 253, 254, Charles Vincin, 322, Chase Jay, 135, Clarhud, 253, Cody Lane, 135, Connie Lynn, 135, Crystal Renee, 135, Darlene, 135, Darrell Dean, 135, David, 253, 254, Debra, 135, Debra Kay, 135, Don, 135, Don Robert, 135, Don Robert II, 135, Dora, 253, Douglas Addington, 280, Drew, 315, Edward, 255, Elizabeth, 322, Emma Josephine, 187, Flora Marlene, 128, Foster, 322, Frank Wyatt, 358, Franklin, 270, Freelove, 254, Gale, 252, Gary, 135, 252, 279, Gary Gene, 135, George, 106, 253, 318, Ginger Ellen, 253, Guy, 224, H.E., 65, Hallie Ima, 106, Harold, 280, Harry, 253, Hazel, 253, Henry Newton, 135, Jack, 128, 135, 253, Jack Edward, 253, Jack Thomas, 253, 254, 318, Jackie Dean, 135, Jackie Lee, 128, Jacqueline Sue, 253, 254, James, 325, James Ella I, 254, James Ella II, 254, James Madison, 130, Jamie, 315, Jan, 195, Jan Marlene, 93, 254, 255, Janet, 15, 252, Janice Lee, 128, Jean, 252, Jesse, 160, Jesse F., 255, Jesse Franklin, 317, Jessee Franklin, 253, Jessica Ann, 128, John, 322, John T., 253, Johnathan Wayne, 254, Joseph Richard, 254, Joy, 195, Joy Marciel, 177, 254, 255, Julie, 128, Julie Eloise, 253, Kale, 106, Karen, 160, 161, 256, Karen Sue, 128, Kelly Rene, 253, Kenneth, 252, 279, Kinzie Dawn, 135, Lillian, 254, 255, Lillian N., 253, Linda Sue, 253, Lucy Belle, 189, Lydia, 253, Margaret, 254, 325, Mark, 11, Mark Kevin, 128, Martha, 280, 322, Martha Viola, 254, Mary E., 285, Mary Ellen, 253, 322, Mary Etta, 130, Mary L., 296, Mary Lee, 315, Mattie, 253, Mayme Ellen, 135, Melinda Joy, 128, Micah Shawn, 253, 254, Michael, 252, 279, Michelle, 252, Myrtie, 270, Nancy, 279, Nancy Catherine, 325, Nathaniel, 296, Olive, 318, Pauline, 138, 196, 197, 198, 218, Phyllis, 82, 135, Phyllis Jean, 110, Polly, 285, Prudence, 83, Ralph F., 252, Raymond, 254, 277, Raymond H., 255, 254, Raymond Howard, 253, Richard L., 29, Richard William, 253, 254, Robert, 252, 253, Robert Lee, 135, Robert S., 253, 254, Roger David, 128, Rosa, 254, Roy Lee, 336, Ruby Ellen, 254, 255, Ruth, 322, 336, Ruth Pauline, 93, 177, 254, 255, Sandra, 254, Shelly Rene, 254, Tami Marie, 128, Thomas, 253, 315, Viola, 255, Virginia, 159, Vivian, 253, 254, 255, 288, Wallace, 270, William, 70, 93, 187, 248, 254, 255, William Charles, 253, William E., 195, 254, William Edward, 177, 254, 255, William H., 253, 254, 298, William Stewart, 254, William Wallace, 253, Wilma, 128, 158, Winifrd, 270, Phyllis Jean, 135, __, 171

MOORMAN, C.E., 69

MORALES, Mary Jane, 203, 347

MORELAND, Marie Antoinette D., 218

MORGAN, 248, Amanda, 255, Bob, 325, Brittney Lynn, 245, Carl, 314, Cecil, 255, Clayton, 245, Cornelia J., 356, Courtney, 255, Effie, 115, Elizabeth, 356, Fred, 255, General, 219, Glen "Mutt", 255, Griffith, 49, Harold, 255, Hazel, 255, 309, Homer, 255, James, 255, John, 356, Joseph, 255, Joy Lynn, 283, Julianne, 243, June, 255, Lois, 347, Lydia, 355, Maude, 325, Maudie, 255, Nina Jean, 255, Paul "Jeff", 255, Raymond, 255, Robert, 255, Ruth, 43, 255, 325, Ruth Hazel, 325, Sarah, 303, School, 239, Stanley, 298, 325, Stanley Samuel, 255, Stella, 255, Stella Blanche, 325, W.W., 29, 376, William "Woody", 255, William Avery, 355

MORIN, Andrea, 99, Candice, 99, Carrie Rae, 99, Claudia, 99, Fielden, 374, James, 99, Joan, 99, John Michael, 99, Kimberly Jo, 99, Mark Christopher, 99, Valerie, 99, William, 99, William Jeffrey, 99

MORITZ, Vincent, 358

MORLEY, Dennis L., 372

MORRALL, Elizabeth, 194

MORRIS, Allie, 239, Aldezera, 126, Alpha, 245, Bradley, 172, 205, Caren, 133, Carlisle, 205, Carol, 107, 236, Carrie, 267, D.S., 313, Delilah, 126, Della, 331, Elizabeth "Betsy", 353, Eugene, 98, George, 116, John, 307, Julia, 187, Marianne, 205, Mark, 205, Mary Clark, 116, Michael, 172, Owen, 353, Owen David, 126, Robert Alan, 172, Sarah Ann, 307, Steven, 205, Vivian, 121, W. Harney, 32, William Harvey, 307 **MORRISON,** 22, Alice Peterson, 273, Alleen, 164, Blanche, 310, Darla Sue, 324, Donald, 339, Elizabeth, 183, Herbert, 373, Jay, 64, 70, Julia K., 372, Mamie Lee, 94, Margaret, 150, 215, 226, 228, Mildred, 228, Olin, 215, Robert, 215, Rutha E., 100, Shana Lyn, 155, Steve, 324, __, 197

MORROW, Arron, 308, Ebbert, 162, Ebbert Monroe, 162, 255, 256, Eugenia, 162, Eugenia, 162, Eugenia D., 256, Frank, 162, Frank Aaron, 256, Harriet, 162, Harriet Elizabeth, 256, Ira, 162, Ira Allen, 256, James, 162, James Aaron, 160, 162, 255, 256, James Aaron, Jr., 256, Joanna, 159, 160, 161, 162, 256, John, 162, John R., 256, Julia, 145, Lemuel, 162, Lemuel James, 256, Mary Ellen, 162, 256, Rachel, 169, Roxie, 162, Roxie Evangeline, 162, Roxy Evangeline, 256, Ruth, 162, Ruth May, 256, Sarah, 162, Sarah E., 256, Simeon, 162, 256, Thomas, 162, William Wade, 162, 256, William Walles, 162, 256, Winnie, 162

MORSEY, Jill, 240

MORTON, Oliver P., 48, 125

MOSBARGER, Clarissa, 256, George Washington, 256, Jane, 256, Katherine, 256, Lucinda, 256, Martha, 256, Melvina P., 256, Nancy, 256, Peter, 256, Peter, 256, William, 256

MOSER, Aaron, 256, Anna Jean, 256, Brian, 256, Donn Erwin, 256, Duane, 256, Eric, 252, 256, George, 256, Gordon, 147, 252, Harry Newton, 256, Jay Todd, 252, 256, Joan, 256, John William, 252, 256, Joseph Gordon, 252, 256, Karl Henry, 256, Katrina, 252, Kevin, 256, Kirsten, 252, Margaret, 147, 256, Marian, 256, Mark, 256, Mary Ann, 256, Michelle, 256, Osmer Gordon, 256, Sean Bradley, 252, 256, William Gordon, 256

MOSIER, John, 114, Mary, 114, Polly, 114, Will, 114

MOSS, Julia, 171, June, 92, Maud, 31

MOSSBARGER, Barbara, 257, Catherine, 257, Christopher, 257, Clarissa, 257, donald, 257, George Washington, 257, Henry, 257, John, 256, 257, Joseph, 257, Katey, 257, Lizey, 257, Lucinda, 257, Martha Jane, 257, Melvina, 257, Nancy, 257, Peter, 257, William H., 257

MOTE, Andrew, 129, Elijah, 239, Mary Ann, 239, Nettie, 239, Washington, 239, Zula, 229

MOTZ, Sarah Josephine, 328

MOUNT, (Gov.), 247, Adella, 114, Atwell, 257, Catherine, 257, Ed, 31, Elijah, 30, Hallie, 111, 257, Harry, 257, Helen, 257, James A., 111, 257, James Atwell, 257,

Kate, 257, Lucinda, 257
MOUNTS, Delcie, 245
MOXLEY, Elizabeth, 144
MUCK, W.S., 11, William, 12
MUELLER, Ernest R., 266, anet Kay, 266, Janice, 329, Robert Larry, 266
MUIR, William, 59
MULLEKIN, P.C., 365
MULLEM, Sarah Catherine, 193, William J., 193
MULLEN, Albert, 193, 194, 257, 258, Albertha Ruth, 258, Asa, 258, Barzilla, 258, Betsy, 258, Caroline, 282, Clara, 257, 258, Claud Silas, 210, 257, 258, Claude S., 258, Elizabeth, 193, 310, Elizabeth Garnet, 258, Eva, 257, Grace, 258, James, 258, Karen, 117, Karen Sue, 258, Lester, 258, Mabel, 210, 258, Margaret, 116, Margaret Clarkson, 116, Margaret Jean, 117, Margaret Jean, 258, Martha, 258, Mary, 39, Moses, 258, Nancy, 258, Phillip, 220, Rebecca Ellen, 193, 258, Richard, 258, Sally, 258, Sandra, 316, Sandra Kay, 258, Sarah C., 194, Sarah Catherine, 258, 293, Seldon, 258, Susanna, 32, Thomas, 258, William, 258, William J., 258
MULLENS, Penny, 286
MULLER, Jeanne, 258, 340, Laura, 258, 259, Lois H., 258, Louis R., 258, 340, Mary E., 124, Laura M., 340
MULLIEN, Jena, 103
MULLIKEN, James B., 102
MULLIMEN, Effie, 252
MUNCEY, Mary Catherine, 306
MUNDORFF, Donald Ralph, 166, Mary Elizabeth, 166, Theodore, 166
MUNN, Helen M., 372
MUNNS, Alice Clare, 185, Amanda, 158, George, 301, Howard, 112, John, 158, __, 75
MUNRO, Richard M., 372
MUNSON, Lorena, 96, Ruth, 298
MURDOCK, Anna, 240, Martha, 245, McKinley, 16
MURPHY, Albert, 205, Cecil, 296, Clora A., 259, Colfax S., 259, Daniel, 205, Eva M., 259, Flora E., 259, G.C. Store, 183, Jack A., 372, James Davidson, 259, James Dolley, 259, Joseph M., 259, Louisa F., 259, Mary, 134, Ollie Myrtle, 259, Ryan Daniel, 205, Susie, 205, Tami, 331, Ulysses Grant, 259, William, 259, William C., 24, William H., 259, William Lawrence, 332
MURRAY,(Miss), 256, Gladys, 252, James, 152, Mary, 152, Mary Ann, 152, Mary Ann "Polly", 152
MUSGROVE, Martha, 222
MUSSCHE, Linda, 365
MUSSER, Elsie, 203, 204, 205, Maud, 107, Peter, 204, Rebecca, 204
MUTZ, John, 175
MYER, Franz O., 74, Mary Etta, 130
MYERS,185, Agnes Inez, 119, Alexander, 259, Alfred Monroe, 259, Alice Susan, 176, Allen "Bud", Jr., 132, Allen Butler, 132, Almira V., 259, Alvis Braxton, 228, Andrew, 259, Barbara Jean, 259, Bernard, 309, Bernice Lucille, 313, Berniece, 42, Berniece L., 113, Berniece Lucille, 113, Bessie B., 260, Betty, 260, 347, Beulah, 320, Beverly, 260, Brenda Lucille, 113, 259, Butler, 259, Byron, 260, Byron Carlisle, 113, 259, Byron F., 260, Carl Cass, 259, Carol, 39, 179, Carol Jean, 113, 259, Catherine, 82, 162, 176, 259, Celena, 309, Charles, 99, Charley, 39, Clyde, 75, Columbus Lane, 259, Conard, 119, Connie Ruth, 259, Cora, 353, Corner, 38, Daniel, 259, Daniel Walter, 271, Darla Denise, 271, Darline, Kay, 271, Darren, 260, David Sylvester, 260, Dawn Gail, 271, Delia, 259, Denise Yvonne, 259, Deward, 168, Deward O., 167, Sione Sue, 271, Don, 12, 271, Donald James, 271, Donna Louise, 271, Donnella May, 271, Duane Jeffery, 259, Dunk, 259, Eader, 329, Earl F., 260, Ed, 112, Edgar Lawrence, 259, Eleanor Lorraine, 259, Elinor, 260, Elizabeth, 116, 162, 260, Elizabeth Albertina, 259, Emma, 79, 259, Emory, 259, Emsley, 259, Eston, 113, 260, Eston Lex, 259, 313, Eula, 270, Eva, 259, Fannie, 124, 165, Fannie W., 124, Frances Marion, 259, Francis, 124, George Russell, 259, Harriet DeLou, 271, Hazel, 260, 353, Hazel Violet, 259, Henry, 177, 259, Henry Breckenbridge, 132, Henry Lawrence, 259, Henry, Sr., 124, Herbert Albert, 259, Herman L., 260, Herman, Jr., 260, Hugh Duncan, 259, Ian, 113, Ian Craig, 259, Ida, 99, Jackson, 259, Jacob, 259, Jane, 357, Janelle, 260, Janet, 174, Jayne, 260, Jeffery, 260, Jeffrey, 260, Jerry Dean, 113, 259, Jerry Dean, Jr., 113, 259, John, 162, 260, John Angerwine, 260, John, Jr., 83, 162, John, Sr., 82, 176, Joseph Lane, 259, Joyce, 260, Joyce A., 375, Juanita, 260, Judith, 260, Karen, 260, Kevin, 260, Kyle, 260, Laren E., 375, Lavinia, 329, Leona Brown, 228, Leroy Sylvester, 260, Leta Jane, 342, Letissia Ann, 132, Levi F., 260, Lewis Cass, 259, Linda Dianne, 113, 259, Lois E., 142, Lonnie Leigh, 259, Louise, 259, Lucinda Joan, 259, Lydia H., 176, Mabel, 31, Mabel Clore, 229, Maple, 329, Marietta, 260, Mark, 142, Martha, 260, Mary, 87, 167, 259, Mary Ellen, 260, 269, Mary Margaret, 248, Matthew, 142, Melina Dee, 271, Melissa, 259, Michael, 113, Michael Neil, 259, Milton Taylor, 259, Minnie, 259, Mylene, 228, Nancy, 82, 176, 177, Nancy Ellen, 99, Nellie Mae, 179, Nicole, 260, Noah, 310, Noah Ransom, 167, Ollie, 250, Omer Marion, 259, Phillip, 260, Phrany, 259, Phyllis, 165, Polly, 259, Rachel, 166, 167, 168, Ralph G., 375, Ray Donald, 260, Richard, 260, Rita Jane, 132, Robert, 259, 260, Robert E., 142, 260, Robert Eugene, 260, Roy S., 260, Ruth, 223, Sandra Kay, 113, 259, Sarah, 259, Sarah Sarnetta, 259, Stacy, 260, Stella, 38, 230, 260, Susan, 260, Susan Alice, 185, Susan Jean, 249, Susanne, 259, Sybil, 39, Sybil Atkinson, 39, T., 68, Thomas, 259, Velma, 132, Vinnie, 259, Violet, 259, Walter, 309, Wilfred Elbert, 259, William, 39, 162, 176, 353, William George, 259, William H., 372, see also MEIER, 259
MYERS & MYERS LUMBER, 14
NABORS, Rufus, 283
NANNETT, Beverly, 374, Tim, 290, Tyler, 290
NARROW DOOR BOTTLE SHOP, 383
NATION, Carry, 29, 30
NAVE, J.S., 284
NAY, Ethel, 243
NAYLOR, Lindsie, 84
NEAL, Daisy, 92, Desona, 92, Elden, 80, Ephraim, 92, Jane, 269, Jeannine, 126, Karen, 126, Margaret, 234, Marina, 126, Mary, 234, Michelle, 126, Raymond, 234, Robert, 234, Rowanna, 126
NEALS, James, 228
NEDEKER, Louis, 49
NEEDHAM, Archibald, 271, Carl, 271, Cecil, 233, Charlotte, 271, Hubert, 233, Kenneth, 271, Marjorie, 271, Mary Ellen, 26, Obed, 233
NEEL, Jason, 318, Karen, 318, Robert (Mrs.), 318, Todd, 318, Virginia Kay, 318
NEELEY, Cornelia, 220, 221
NEES, 260, Bessie Lou, 262, David Abner, 261, David Jerome, 262, David M., 262, David Milton, 156, 262, Lulu, 262, Lulu T., 261, Marcella, 261, 262, Marcella Turner, 156, Margaret, 261, Martha, 261, Mary, 197, Michael, 261, Milton, 262, Milton L., 26, 261, Milton Leonidas, 156, 261, Robert, 261, Ruth, 26, 31, 156, 261, Sara, 156, 261, Sara Ozella, 261, Sarah Ann, 261
NEESE, Bill, 306, Hazel Marie, 202
NEFF, Claudia, 327, Curtis, 327, George, 215, Grace, 327, Kenneth E., 327, Martha, 287, 336, Phyllis Marie, 327, Steven, 327
NEHER, Ray, 192
NEIDEFFER, Arthur Earl, 130, 262, Becky, 24, 262, Gary, 262, Kathy, 262, Pearl Marie, 130, 262, Randy, 262, Rebecca, 233, 375, Rebecca Lynn, 262, Rebecca L. 262, Warren Gary, 130, 262
NELSON, Aaron Henry, 242, David Baumgarden, 320, Debbi, 242, Elsie, 269, J.C., 69, John, 242, Jodephine, 145, Kara Dean, 242, Lavina, 84, Lavone Ella, 113, Lucinda, 145, Lutita Ellen, 286, R.E., 286, T.K., 242, Thomas Kilpatrick, 242
NESBIT, Gladys, 357, Rebecca Jane, 257
NESBITT, Nelle, 65
NESLAR, Phyllis, 357
NEUMANN, Adolph, 237, Charlotte, 237
NEVITT, 32
NEWBY, Alma, 216, Richard, 270
NEWELL, Ann, 104, 129, Eddie Joe, 283, Glenn Wesley, 301, Hugh, 129, Judy Lynn, 283, Loretta Maxine, 301, Peggy Kay, 283, Sherry Lee, 283, Violet Flo, 283
NEWHOUSE, Azariah, 308, Lois, 308, Margery, 308, Mary Bell, 308
NEWKIRK, Addie, 269, Addie Sophraine, 147, Ann, 268, Charles J., 147, Docy, 147, Elizabeth Ann, 113, Ethel, 147, Gerald, 171, Glen, 87, Glenn, 277, Hazel, 87, 277, Helen Marie, 82, Jackson, 34, Janet, 82, Janet Melvina, 82, Leslie, 147, Lloyd Martin, 82, Rebecca, 180, Russell "Docy", 147
NEWLIN, George Merle, 275, James F., 245, Jean, 245, Margaret, 296, Ronald E., 375, Ruby, 275, Shirley Jane, 275, Teresa Ann, 245
NEWLON, Gary, 231
NEWMAN, Ann, 120, Elizabeth, 120, William, 120
NEWNAM, Donna Elaine, 174, Ruby, 174
NEWNUM, Betty Jo, 262, Jay Kenneth, 262, Jay W., 262, Julie Ann, 262, Kenneth Jay, 262, LuAnn, 262, Ora, 262, Roger Wayne, 262, Roy, 262
NEWPORT, Dollie Gertrude, 357, Edith, 357, Florence, 275, Marjorie, 357, William Sherman, 357
NEWTON, Natalie Fay, 231
NICELY, James, 320
NICHELL, Faith Elizabeth, 209
NICHOL, Brandi, 175
NICHOLS, Alice, 241, 263, Alva, 263, Bradley A., 372, Edith Eileen, 106, Edwin, 241, 263, Everett, 279, F., 68, Francis, 279, George, 241, 263, George D., 262, Goldie, 165, Grace, 211, 279, Grace Ann, 263, Harry, 279, Hettie, 263, Ida, 279, 299, James Allen, 263, John Roy, 279, Joseph, 279, Loan Co., 355, Mable, 263, Martha Ann, 318, Mary Jane, 279, Max, 20, 21, Milda Ann, 175, Myrtle, 263, Naomi, 241, 263, Norman, 241, 263, 284, 353, Oka, 241, 263, Pamela, 263, Penny, 263, 284, Phillip, 263, Rachel, 262, 279, Ruth, 241, 263, Walter, 241, 263, William H., 263
NICHOLSON, Carol Zeta, 224, Dixon, 298, Donald Winton, 224, Gloria, 224, Joe, 360, John, 376, Sandra, 122
NICKELL, Francis J., 209
NICKOLS, Franklin, 63
NICKOLSON, Sarah, 360
NICOLS, 43
NIELSEN, Charlotte, 193
NILES, Lester, 69
NIVEN, J.S., 171
NIX, Patricia Ann, 175
NIXON, Charles, 43, Charles E., 263, Deanna, 263, Everett, 71, Everett R., 263, Irene, 71, Mary, 263, Mary L., 263, Rhoda, 263, Richard (Pres.), 340
NOBLE, David Leroy, 245, Elizabeth, 190, Jennifer Layla, 245, Jessica Page, 245, Lena, 137, Luna, 295
NOFSINGER, Jacob, 221, Joseph, 221, Mary, 221, Susannah, 220
NOLAN, Ellen, 152, 263, Frank 263, 264, Harry, 263, John, 263, 266, Mary, 263, Pearl, 263, 264, Rose, 263, Rose M., 359, Walter, 263
NOLAND, Julia Ann, 132
NORCROSS, Henrietta "Etta" Owen, 148
NORDMEYER, Becky, 325, Francis, 325, Gregg, 325, Jerry Joiner, 325, Kim, 325, Kristjane, 325, Susan, 325, Trent, 325
NORMAN, Alice, 264, Buelah, 264, Carl, 374, Charles, 25, Christopher, 124, Christopher Dean, 264, Elaine, 264, Elaine Ann, 124, Elizabeth, 318, Elsie, 264, Erika, 124, Erika Elaine, 264, Foster, 264, Frank, 374, Fred, 39, Greg, 13, Gregory, 264, Janet, 264, Jeromy, 264, K., Dean, 124, Kenneth Dean, 264, Luanne, 264, Mable, 264, Morris, 264, Oscar Hamilton, 264, Ralph Morris, 264, Richard Dale, 264, Ronda, 124, Ronda Lee, 264, Timothy, 124, Timothy Lynn, 264, Vivian, 25, Vol, 39, Ward, 264
NORRIS, Albert, 287, Allen, 67, Anna Jane, 116, Capt., 151, Carolyn, 26, Karen A., 372, Lois, 374
NORTH, Betty, 169, Betty Elliot, 147, John (Col.), 147, Nancy, 120
NORTHCUTT, Belle, 215
NORTHWAY, Christina, 202, John, 202
NORTON, Allison Renae, 245, Brad Leslie, 245, Bradley, 271, Glen, 271, Jason Lee, 245, Kay, 271, Kelly, 271, Thomas E., 245
NOSEDA, Ikuo, 330, Yosuko, 330
NOVAK, Kathleen Elizabeth R., 123, Paul Robert, 123, Richard, 123
NUCKLES, Cynthia, 243, Kimberly, 243
NUNN, Grace, 207
NUTGRASS, Catherine, 254
NUTT, E., 68, Edmond, 189
NYE, Joseph, 41, Marshall, 94
NYE-BOOE, 94
O'BRIAN, Easter, 235
O'CONNOR, Katheryn, 192
O'DELL, 329
O'DONNELL, John, 138
O'FLAHERTY, Edward, 76
O'GWYNN, Melissa, 54, Shawn, 54
O'HEREN, John, 297, Martha, 297, Patti Lee, 297
O'KELLEY, Bob, 66
O'NEAL, Cemetery, 310, Donald James, 245, Garland M., 245, Glennadine Melva, 245, Jerold Morris, 245, Jesse Verl, 245, Peggy, 245, Verla Isabel, 245
O'SULLIVAN, Kathleen, 182, Mary Lou, 311
OAKES, Jeanine, 374
OBENCHAIN, George, 232, Jessie, 232, Katherine, 232, Mahala, 274, Mamie, 232
OBERDIECK, Barbara, 271, Meara, 271, Thomas, 271
OCHELTREE, Charles Robert, 159, Mary Elizabeth, 159
ODELL, Charles, 231
ODELL-KEEDY, Sharon, 246
OFFIELD, 6, Ben, 219, Jane, 264, William, 109, 264
OGDEN, John, 164
OGLE, E., 28
OGLESBEE, E.F., 52, Hiram, 110, Ida, 52, Will, 137
OHM, George William, 319
OILAR, Bathsheba, 264, Diane, 264, 265, Fay, 264, Henry (Colonel), 264, John, 264, 265, John Ray, 264, Kenneth R., 264
OLDS, Arch, 141, Esther, 141
OLDSHUE, Amanda, 265, Clara May, 265, Foster, 265, Grace, 265, Jacob, 265, James Edward, 265, John, 153, 265, 277, 287, John Lincoln, 265, Margaret, 265, Martha, 265, Mary "Virginia", 173, Robert, 265, Sarah, 265, Virginia, 265, Vivian, 265, William, 265, William B., 265
OLIN, Anita, 265, Blanch, 265, C. Elizabeth, 150, Callie Mae, 265, Clara, 265, Clara Elizabeth, 150, Daryl, 265, Daryl Leon, 265, DeAnna, 265, Dennis Jay, 265, Edna Ray, 265, Gabe, 221, Gabriel, 265, Greg, 221, Gregory, 265, Harold, 265, Helen, 186, 265, JoElla, 265, Kathy, 265, Kenneth, 265, LaDonna, 265, Leland, 16, 265, Leland (Mrs.), 186, Leon Noel, 265, Lester, 265, Leverett, 265, Luke, 265, Marcia, 265, Marjorie, 265, Mary Lou, 221, Matthew, 265, Paul, 160, 265, Paul Laverne, 265, Ranson, 265, Reine, 265, Ruth, 265, Tacy, 221, 265, Tessie, 265, Wilberta Faye, 265
OLINGER, David, 145, 291, David F., 29, Estella, 145, Mary, 291
OLIVER, Alfred, 266, Arthur Milton, 266, Arthur, Jr., 266, Caroline, 338, Carrie, 338, Charles, 266, Charles A., 124, Charles Aaron, 266, Charles E., 124, Charles Edward, 266, Charles T., 341, Charles Thompson, 266, 341, Charlotte, 124, 266, Charlotte Emily, 124, 266, Clara, 196, Clara, 196, Clara Maria, 266, Clara Marie, 266, David, 266, Delores, 266, Dwight Lee, 266, Ethan A., 266, Evelyn, 266, Florence May, 266, Fred Ellworth, 266, George, 80, George S., 338, Hazel, 266, Helen, 266, Isabell, 266, Jackson, 124, 266, James, 80, 266, James William, 266, Janet Kay Mueller, 266, Jess, 176, Jesse Jackson, 266, Joann, 266, John W., 241, Joseph Milton, 266, Justus Wright, 338, Larry, 164, Laura, 176, Leo Aaron, 266, Leo, Jr., 266, Letha, 176, Lorena, 266, 341, Lucy, 266, Luella, 341, Machine Shop, 14, Margaret, 266, Marie Elaina, 164, Marvin, 266, Marvin, R., 381, Mary E., 124, Mary Edith, 338, Mary Elizabeth, 266, Merle, 266, Mildred, 266, Nancy, 266, Pop, 338, Raymond Maxwell, 266, Rebecca Elizabeth, 241, Rena, 266, 341, Robert, 266, Robert Larry, 266, Ruth, 266, Tus, 338, Verna, 176, Walter, 266, William, 266, William Bruce, 266, William Maxwell, 266
OLSEN, Bob, 54, 352, Diane Marie, 352, Geraldine, 352, Geri, 352, James Max, 352, Jennifer, 352, Linda Denise, 352, Mary, 352, Mary Louise, 352, Michele, 352, Robert O., 352, Robert, Jr., 352
OLSON, Gail, 336
OLSZYKS, Catherine Anne, 298
OPPY, Amanda Sue, 267, Andrew Edward, 267, C.J., 90, Christopher M., 267, David M., 267, Garland, 79, Gaylora, 267, Joan, 108, 267, M. Joan, 267, Pat, 267, Patrick R., 267, Ruth, 330, Ruthanna, 79, 374, Samuel, 80, Starr, 267, Sue, 267, Susan Kay, 267, __, 17
ORAN, Joan Jacquelyn, 309
ORICK, Margaret, 118
ORLEA, Hazel, 324
ORR, Daniel, 295, Govenor, 323, Isabelle, 295, Nancy, 295, Robert, 175, 217, 323, Robert, Lt. Gov., 181
ORRICK, Margarete, 118
ORTACIO, Melina, 185
ORTON, Belinda, 186
ORWIG, Lemuel, 169
OSAKA, Bon, 136, Masato Suzuki, 136, Souichiro Nomura, 136
OSBORN, Alonzo, 224, Alvarian, 333, Ben, 127, Charlotte, 220, Cyrus, 164, Daniel, 164, Edward, 127, Eliza, 164, Gillian, 127, James, 333, Martha, 333, Martha Ann, 268, Mary Elizabeth, 298, Nick, 127, Oliver, 220, Paul, 69, Penny, 355, Priscilla, 124, Rhoda, 333, Sarah, 333, Sarah Elizabeth, 333, Simeon, 333, Thomas W., 127, William E., 71
OSBORNE, James I., 178, Simeon, 161
OSGOOD, Cora, 135, George, 135
OSWALT, Beulah Marie, 325
OTENBERG, Ora, 299
OTTEN, Ed, 380
OTTENGER, Pamela Jane, 239
OTTERMAN, Donald, 177, Effie, 177, Evelyn, 372, Mabel, 177, Manson, 177, Paul, 177, Sarah Jane, 99
OTTINGER, Barbara, 350
OVERFIELD, Warner, 191
OVERHOLT, Joanna, 112, Jodie, 112, Joshua, 112, Rebecca, 112, Steven, 112
OVERLY, Eva Beaman, 322
OVERMAN, B.F., 14, Bertha, 14, Beulah, 130, 272
OVERPECK, Aaron S., 268, Aaron, Sr., 267, Andrew, 267, Clarence, 267, Clarence R., 267, Clarence Reed, 267, Clay, 11, 267, Daniel, 267, David, 267, Earl, 267, Elias, 267, Elizabeth, 181, Floy, 267, Fred, 267, George, 267, Isaac, 267, Jacob, 267, James, 267, John, 267, Judith, 267, Magdalene, 267, Marie, 267, Mary, 267, Mary Dellena, 267, Mary V., 267, Mary Violet, 267, Melba, 267, Mollie, 267, Nancy, 267, Norine, 267, Rosemary, 267, Ruth, 267, Sarah, 267, Susannah, 267, Susannah, 267, Thomas, 267, Valentine, 267, Walter Earl, 267, Walter Keith, 267
OVERSTREET, Mary, 250
OVERTON, John C., 43, Vester, 151, Westberry, 151
OWEN, Carrie, 186, Charles, 186

OWENS, Betty, 278, Carol, 103, Glenna, 192, Ida, 11, John Calvin, 103, Minnie Myrtle, 224, Raymond, 103, Ruby, 234, William, 209

OXLEY, Insurance, 16, Rebecca, 80, 336

OYLER, Charlotte, 325

PACE, Nan, 334

PACILEO, Camelia, 358, Florentina, 358, Genarro, 358

PACK, Sharon, 374

PADDACK, Barton, 158, Ben, 126, Benjamin, 268, Benjamin F., 268, Benjamin, Jr., 268, Caroline, 267, 268, Clyda Mae, 330, Clyda Mary, 267, 268, Daisy, 126, Deborah, 268, Don, 25, Eliphalet, 268, Harley, 280, Harley Sylveste, 158, Josiah, 268, Josiah Foster, 267, Louise, 175, Marihelen, 126, 239, Mary Gardner, 268, Naomi, 268, Nellie, 280, Pat, 25, Patricia, 158, Patricia Maye, 280, Robert, 158, 268, Samuel, 158, 268, Thelma Dean, 280, W. Royden, 158, Zachariah, 268, Nellie, 158

PADDOCK, Nancy, 267

PADGETT, Jeanine, 374, Katherine, 226, Remodeling, 16

PAINE, Lola, 310

PAINTER, Gerald, 59, Isabel, 82, Sally, 104, Solomon, 82

PAJCIC, Katherien, 212

PALETTE, Eugene, 342

PALLOM, Robert, 119

PALMER, Ashley, 235, Bob, 235, Darrell, 235, Kristy, 235, Ruth, 152, Sarah, 260, Virginia Ruth, 240

PARCELLS, James, 63

PARENT, Cheryl Denise, 200, Elizabeth, 222, Joseph Malcolm, 200, Linda, 375, Linda Marie, 200

PARISH, Marie, 88

PARKER, Ann, 149, Barbara Jean, 270, Bill, 211, Blanche, 173, 265, Bryon W., 168, Carol, 186, Chuck, 270, Crystal, 211, Dessie, 166, Edgar G., 186, Ellenor, 270, Elsie, 238, Erma, 350, John, 331, Kelli Dee, 168, Lauren Michelle, 186, Lisa Christine, 186, Lois, 120, Margaret, 350, Mary J., 331, Pamela, 270, Pauline, 186, Richard Wilson, 186, W.O., 374, William, 211, Keith, 380

PARKHURST, Samuel, 85

PARKS, Anna Maureen, 268, Brothers, 75, Chester Maryland, 268, Clinton M., 375, Danielle Kay, 284, Deliah, 268, Dortha, 348, Elizabeth, 251, Esther, 268, Etta, 268, Faye Lavon, 284, Flossie F., 122, Goldie Marie, 268, Harold Glenn, 268, Herrald, 268, John M., 268, Keli Kristine, 284, Lillie, 78, Martha, 317, Martha Waneta, 268, Mary, 118, Mary E., 372, Mary S., 96, Mary Sade, 268, Mattie, 209, 268, 317, Michael, 268, Nancy, 268, Opal, 268, Phillip Wayne, 284, Rebecca, 268, Robert Eugene, 284, Samuel, 268, Samuel W., 317, Samuel Wesley, 268, William, 268, William Chambers, 268

PARMON, Fred, 116, Vera, 116

PARNELL, Thelma, 31

PARRENT, Florence, 348

PARRISH, Elizabeth, 225

PARROTT, Margaret, 360

PARSONS, Johnny, 275

PARTON, David, 269

PARVIN, Arista, 243

PASELY, Laura, 85

PASSMORE, Abigail, 356, 357, Ann, 357, Elizabeth, 357, Hannah, 357, Henry, Jr., 357, Henry, Sr., 357, John, 357, Margaret, 357, Martha, 98, 316, 356, 357, Mary, 357, Phebe, 357, Rebecca, 357

PATCH, Isaac P., 63

PATRICK, Cynthia Leigh, 166, Ebenezer, 49, Howard, 166, Linda Kay, 166

PATTEE, Mabel, 356

PATTENGALE, Wilma Jean, 135

PATTERSON, Chevrolet, 14, Elizabeth A., 286, Ethel Marie, 204, Evelyne, 278, James L., 29, James W., 29, Jane, 229, John, 286, Margaret, 228, Mary, 340, Nelson, 34, Pearlie, 31, Salem G., 43, Taylor, 31, Thomas M., 125, William, 64, __, 42

PATTISON, Joe E., 32, Joseph, 323, Marion, 338, Mary Ellen, 323

PATTON, Angela, 268, Arlie, 150, 268, Betty, 269, Bob, 268, Bobby, 268, Bronna, 269, Carolyn, 268, Cecil Hugh, 133, Charles, 268, 269, Chelsey, 268, Clarence, 311, Clyde, 12, 268, 269, Clyde (Mrs.), 265, Debbie, 268, Dee, 269, Detra Kay, 268, Don, 269, Donald L., 133, Donnis, 269, Dorothy, 269, Edward, 150, Edward (Mrs.), 186, Eric, 268, Ernest, 268, Eva, 269, Fern A., 268, Forest, 150, Genice, 87, George, 269, George S. (Gen.), 341, Gertrude, 269, Harry, 269, Hattie, 150, Helen Jean, 232, Howard, 311, Howard A., 374, Imogene, 268, Isaac, 268, 269, J.W., 11, James, 269, James W., 12, Jane, 268, Jerilyn, 268, Jim, 12, Joan, 232, Joe, 269, Joel Lee, 310, John, 268, John K., 232, Judy, 268, Julie, 269, Kym, 268, Lael, 269, Larry D., 372, Lois, 54, 269, 311, Lois E., 268, Lora, 269, Lottie, 12, Lucy, 269, Madeline, 133, Malcomb, 54, Marc, 268, Marcia, 268, Mary E., 268, Mayme, 12, Mike, 54, 268, Mildred, 150, Rebecca, 26, Robert, 269, Robert Dean, 268, Robert G., 268, Ronald, 269, Sam, 269, Sarah, 269, Stacy, 268, Stuart, 268, Tessie, 265, 268, Theresa, 268, Thomas F., 11, 269, Tom, 12, 269, Virginia, 264, Walter Dean, 133, William, 269, Zella Dee, 286, __, 17

PAXON, Brenda, 260, Mathew, 260, Michael, 260, Richard, 260

PAXTON, 22, Alexander, 269, Amanda, 269, Ashley, 90, David P., 269, Elizabeth, 269, Everett, 90, James, 269, Jane, 269, Jo Ann, 54, John Steel, 269, Lura, 89, Margaret, 269, Martha, 269, Mary, 269, Nancy, 269, Phoebe, 269, Samuel, 269, Thomas, 269, Thomas McCorkle, 269, William, 269

PAYN, Georgetta, 91

PAYNE, Bessie, 279, Dale, 64, Delpha, 148, 168, Georgetta, 61, Jeptha, 168, Margaret Ann, 315, Martha, 168, Mary, 61, Pat, 65, Robert Earl, 174, Walter (Dr.), 315, __, 55

PAYTON, Alice, 269, 270, Anna Gertrude, 220, 270, Benjamin, 270, Beverly Yvonne, 269, Charles, 235, Charles E., 299, Charles Enoch, 269, Clarence, 235, Clarence Leslie, 269, 299, Clifford, 235, Clifford Lucein, 269, 299, Elizabeth Myrtle, 202, Elsie, 269, Fred, 270, Fred Earl, 269, George Washington, 269, Gertrude, 270, Grace, 270, Grace Lee, 269, Jemima, 269, Jess, 270, Jess Claude, 269, John, 243, Leona Agnes, 269, 299, Lina, 269, Mary A., 235, Mary Ann, 269, 299, Mary E., 270, Myrtle B., 234, Myrtle Blanch, 269, Myrtle Blanche, 234, 235, 299, Pearice, 360, Ted, 270, Ted Gilderoy, 269, Will, 270, William Harvey, 269, William T., 269, Zora, 270, Zora Dean, 269

PEABODY, Delanda Cheryl, 119, Jean Loretta, 146, John, 119, Milton, 155, Reva, 155

PEAK, May, 320

PEARCE, Thomas, 242, Virginia, 242

PEARCY, T.J., 69

PEARSON, Ann, 163, Carolyn, 270, Cecil, 270, Ilah, 123, Jim, 92, Margaret Ellen, 322, Mary, 301, Nancy, 322, Omega, 270, Penny Ann, 270, Phyllis, 270, Virgil, 270, William Henry, 322

PEAT, Mary Elizabeth, 305

PEAVLER, Addie, 128

PECK, Cora Ellen, 232, Hall, 296, Jacob, 225, Romulus, 225, Samuel, 375, Samuel D., 372

PEDEN, Clara, 261

PEDRIC, Mariah G., 215

PEDRICK, Maria, 215

PEEBLES, A.D., 99, A.W., 272, Agnes, 271, Alfred Wallace, 272, Annie, 272, Archibald, 272, Archie, 272, Atwell D., 271, Barbara, 272, Barney, 270, Benjamin, 270, Benjamin, 271, Bertha, 272, Beth, 272, Betty, 272, Beverly, 270, Bill, 272, Bob, 272, Brad Michael, 272, Buford Archibald, 272, Buster, 270, Caroline, 270, 271, Carolyn, 272, Chester, 272, Clarence, 270, Clifford, 271, Dana, 272, David, 271, Debbie, 271, Diana, 271, Dinah, 271, Douglas M., 271, Elizabeth, 270, 272, Erin, 271, Esta Fay, 270, Flora, 270, Francis, 270, 272, Gary, 271, Gladys, 271, Hal Hugh, 270, Hazel, 239, 270, 272, Helen, 270, 271, 272, Herbert H., 271, Irene, 271, James Manley, 272, Janice, 271, Jason, 271, Jeffrey Alan, 272, Joan, 272, Joel, 272, John, 270, 271, 272, Jon Manley, 272, Julietta, 270, Justin, 271, Kathleen, 272, Katie, 271, Kenneth Lee, 272, Lance, 271, Larry, 271, Lauren, 272, LeRoy, 272, Lelia Mae, 270, Lester, 270, 271, Lindsey, 272, Linnaeus, 271, Lois, 272, Lois Elizabeth, 272, Lou, 221, Louisa, 270, Lucille, 271, Lucinda, 270, Luther, 270, Mabel, 271, Marcia, 271, Margaret, 271, Marian Louise, 272, Mark Owen, 272, Martha, 271, Mary, 270, 272, 344, Mary Annis, 270, Mary Elizabeth, 221, 271, Mary Hazel, 221, Mary Jane, 272, May, 270, Melissa, 272, Mellie, 272, Merritt, 221, 271, Micajah, 270, Mike, 271, Myron, 271, Naomi, 271, Nicolas, 272, Orville, 270, Orville M., 271, Oscar "Punk", 271, Pamela, 271, Peggy, 271, Rebecca, 270, Rebeccah, 270, 271, Rex, 271, Richard Alan, 272, Robert Owen, 272, Robert W., 270, 271, Ronald Owen, 272, Roy, 221, 270, 271, 272, Sandra, 271, Scott Alan, 272, Sue, 272, Tamara Marie, 272, Thaddeus, 270, Thelma, 272, Thomas, 272, W.C., 270, Wallace, 271, Wally, 271, Walter D., 270, 271, William Walter, 272, Molly, 272

PEED, Daniel W., 308, Henry D., 115, John, 308, Lucinda, 308, Matilda, 115, Nancy, 308, Philip Jr., 308

PEEPLES, Elizabeth, 129

PEER, Rose, 357

PEEVLER, Elizabeth, 260

PEFFLEY, Abraham, 341, Amanda, 341, Bertha, 14, 94, Beulah, 130, Carolyn, 130, Carrie, 309, Chester, 14, 130, Clara, 162, Claude (Dr.), 309, David, 177, Family, 14, Frances, 83, Lavina, 174, Mary, 103, Mary Elizabeth, 103, Mary M., 287, Mary Magdalene, 336, Rebecca, 341, Rebekah, 341, Richard, 162, Sarah Jane, 341

PEFLEY, Esther (Hettie), 99, Lewis Otterman, Jr., 99, Nellie Grace, 340

PEITROWSKI, Miss, 294

PELL, Daniel Scott, 98, Mary Myrtle, 256

PENCE, Carl D., 133, John Delphos, 133, Josephine, 355, Linda, 133

PENN, Elizabeth, 170, 289, Florence, 170, Ford, 170, Joseph, 170, Lafayette, 102, 170, Lena, 170, Ruth, 53, 170, 323, Walter, 53, Walter E., 323, William, 120, 129, 170

PENNINGTON, Annette, 228, Mary, 115, Mary Jane, 116, Mary Katherine, 130, Sue, 103

PENNY, (Rev.), 50

PENNYBAKER, Nancy, 233

PENROD, Dan, 375, Rose Ann, 82

PEOPLE'S, Furniture, 14

PEPPIATT,, 136

PEREZ, Marie, 252

PERKINS, Elizabeth, 127, Funeral Home, 14, Hazel, 220, India, 84, Jim, 127, Kathrena, 358, Susan, 127, William, 127

PERRY, Albert Earl, 166, Charles Albert, 166, Hattie, 338, Helen Louise, 271, Herbert William, 166, Judith Diane, 166, Lewis Co., 329, Linda, 374, Martha, 197, Martha Lynn, 166, Ruth Maureen, 166, Stephen, 271, Susan, 166

PERSONETT, Allen, 272, Allen Ray, 272, Amanda Jo, 272, Benjamin Paul, 272, Bob, 272, Cheryl, 272, Cheryl Renee, 272, Craig Allen, 272, Damon, 272, Elaine, 272, Eric, 272, Esther, 272, Frank, 272, James Eric, 272, John Robert, 272, Larry, 272, Larry Joe, 272, Mary Anne, 272, Opal Jane, 272, Paula Michelle, 272

PERSSON, Christopher, 248, Jonathan, 248, Michael, 248

PETE'S, Greenhouse, 232

PETERMAN, Florence, 265, Janice, 284, John, 353, John R., 284, Joyce, 369, Mark, 284, Robert W., 372

PETERS, Grace, 305, Janet, 239, Jesse, 263, Lillie Grace, 305, Lilly "Grace", 306, William, 41, William H., 306

PETERSON, Albert K., 188, Alfred R., 272, Ann Mariah, 312, Bertha, 31, 43, Blanche, 229, Earl, 312, Edith, 271, Elmer, 271, Emory, 273, Esther, 239, Ethel Blanche, 188, 229, Georgia, 129, Harry, 356, Husted, 273, 301, James, 141, 272, Jennie, 67, Jesse, 141, Jessie Pearl, 131, John T., 273, Marie, 133, Mary Hannah, 141, Mary Susanna, 95, Mildred, 273, Milly Jane, 312, Nancy Clair, 273, Naomi Clair, 273, Perry, 312, Rachael, 236, Roy, 273, Samuel, 312, Solomon, 356, Susan, 85, W.P., 67, William, 272, __, 42, __, 95

PETRA, Maria Eva, 313

PETREY, Diana, 193

PETROSKI, Joe, 325

PETRY, Diana Kay, 273, Fannie Ellen, 273, Fanny Ellen, 273, Flavious, 273, Fred, 273, Fred, Sr., 273, Frederick C., 273, Frederick Chalmen, 273, Frederick George, Jr., 273, George Flave, 273, Janice Sue, 273, Jennifer Brooke, 273, Jessie M., 273, John, 273, Richard Lee, 273, Wandalene, 273, William, 273

PETT, Arthur, 273, Autumn, 273, Ferne, 273, June, 273, Lawrence, 273, Mae, 273, Ray Alvin, 273, Richard, 273, Ruth Harriet, 273, Sue, 273

PETTS, Minnie, 273

PETTY, 12

PEYTON, Lucretia, 208

PFRIMMER, Elizabeth, 108, 179, George, 179

PHEBUS, Delbert, 22

PHELPS, Joseph A., 375

PHILLIPS, Anna, 130, Austin, 286, Bessie, 286, Dessie, 297, Ella, 130, Evelyn Mae, 98, George, 170, Ina, 43, James, 144, Jesse, 130, Joanna, 205, John (Rev.), 194, June Darlene, 135, Mae, 338, Martha, 353, Mary Elizabeth, 241, Sam, 64, Susan, 123, Sylvia, 163, Terry, 50, Velma, 278, Zinetta, 78

PHILPOT, Eva, 240

PHILPOTT, Ava, 244, Aver, 152, David W., 119, Eva, 152, Glen, 244, Glenn, 152, Ida, 350, Jennie, 350, Lois, 244, Matthew A., 119, Rachel, 167

PHIPPS, Artie, 250

PICKEL, Andrew, 274, Barbara Jean, 234, Carolyn, 234, Doris Marie, 207, 274, Flossie, 274, Frank, 234, Gabriel, 274, Henry, 274, Ida, 274, Jacob, 274, Jacob A., 207, 274, Jacob, Jr., 274, Jonas, 274, Joseph, 274, Julia Ann, 274, Mark, 234, Mary, 234, 274, Mary M., 295, Mary Mahala, 207, 274, Nancy, 234, Nancy II, 274, Oliver, 274, Opal Viola, 207, 274, Otis, 274, Rachel, 274, Wilmer, 274

PICKERALL, Jacob, 129

PICKERING, Farm, 239

PICKETTAD, George E., 83

PICKETT, Annie, 231, Bertie, 319, Charlotte, 274, George N., 102, Helen, 273, Henry Gilbert, 273, Ical, 108, Ilene, 273, John, 274, 291, Malinda, 102, Mary Evelyn, 273, Rosa Etta, 274, 290, 291, Samuel, 274, Susannah, 274, Wandalene, 273, William, 273, 274, William Leroy, 273

PICKRELL, Mary, 343

PIERCE, Edith, 212, Edward, 133, Ferris, 63, Leora, 223, Lydia, 318, Mary, 65, Michael (Mrs.), 220, Ryan Edward, 133, Stacey Ann, 133, Stephanie Jo, 133, Verna Cecil, 155, 156

PILE, Ava, 255, Ava N., 253, 254, George, 253, 254

PING, Betty, 223, Helen, 155

PINKSTON, Ruth, 89

PINNELL, Elizabeth, 104, Lige, 104

PINSON, Rosa, 223

PIPHER'S, Radiator, 16

PISHAW, Gene, 368

PITCOCK, Eleanor, 348

PITTENGER, Charles, 333

PITTMAN, Abbie, 208, Angela Renee, 275, Benjamin, 355, Carol, 275, Christine, 137, Cindy, 275, Clara May, 93, Gary, 137, Harry, 275, John, 275, John B., 355, Kenneth, 275, Melinda Annette, 275, Micajah, 355, Moses, 355, Nora, 355, Pam, 275, Samuel Kenneth, 275, Steven, 355, Thomas, 355

PITTS, Edgar, 12, 13

PITZER, Alva E., 275, Laura Lucinda, 275, Lee, 275, Shirley, 275, Shirley Jane, 275, Stephanie Lee, 275, Vernon Lee, 275

PLASKETT, Janice, 171

PLUMB, Andrew, 351, Larry, 351

PLUMMER, Charles Sumner Jr., 84, Elinor, 84, Patience, 84

PLUNKETT, Elizabeth, 347, George A., 372, Iva, 146, Jesse, 299, John, 146, Rebecca, 352, Rosemary, 146, Sarah, 350, William, 350

POAGE, Robert, 136, William, 172

POAGUE, John H., 41, Nancy, 239

POE, Evelyn, 127

POGUE, Cynthia Ann, 41, Elizabeth, 41, Hannah, 41, Jane, 41, Ruth Ramona, 325, Silas, 41, __, 42

POINTER, Fern Hudson, 147, Joe, 278, Martha Hannah, 182

POINTS, Jane, 288

POLAND, Jean, 66

POLAR, Ice & Fuel, 15

POLK, Nancy, 113

POLLARD, Nancy, 181

POLLITT, Frances, 181, Fred, 309, Nancy, 181, Walter, 181

POOL, Barry, 275, Brett, 275, Dan, 275, Dan L., 275, Don, 275, Marty, 275, Pauline, 275

POOLE, Laura J., 285, Mandee, 113, Mandee Lynne, 259, Maynard, 259, Stacey, 113, Stacey Nicole, 259, Zana, 133

POPE, Myrtle, 84

PORTER, Benjamin, 263, Elsie, 306Elizabeth, 222, Gladys, 90, Guy H., 263, Insurance, 15, J.F., 30, James, 126, Jennie, 43, John, 41, 100, Joseph, 118, Margaret, 125, 126, Mary Ann, 41, Mary C., 290, Mary L., 263, Nancy, 230, Ora, 253, Peter, 100, Polyanna, 154, 155, Rachel, 41, Rebecca, 41, W. Arthur, 99, Walter L., 64, William, 263, Zella, 84, __, 42

PORTERS, John, 41

POSTILL, Charles, 223

POSTON, Clara Jo, 207, Daltrum, 207, Daltrum Holmes, 207, Karry Sue, 207, Lynda, 207

POTERBOWSKI, Linda Ann, 174

POTTENGER, Nancy, 335

POTTER, Cheri, 205, Margaret, 94

POTTINGER, John, 36, Nancy, 36

POTTS, Amanda LeAnn, 157, 276, Ancil, 276, Candy, 157, E. Denver, 276, Elizabeth, 74, Elmer Denver, 276, Elvin, 276, Essie Mae, 276, Garry Alan, 157, 276, Garry Alan, Jr., 276, Harry, 276, Hazel, 276, Herman, 276, Letha, 157, Loretta, 213, Ray, 276, Rebekah, 276, Ruth, 196, Samuel, 74, Sherman Wayne, 276, Tina Marie, 157, 276, Valerie Suzanne, 276, Vince Allen, 276, Wendall Keith, 157, 276

POWELL, Bliss Linn, 276, Brock, 252, Debra Lynn, 276, Doil "Shorty", 139, Dorothy, 350, 351, Eugene Thomas, 276, G.W., 30, James Ray, 139, James William, 314, Jerry Wayne, 139, John, 314, Joseph B., 87, Leslie Bryon, 276, Lester, 283, Lester Earl, 276, Lisa, 252, Lori, 252, Lorin Nicole, 276, Lyle, 276, Mabel Clair, 314, Michael, 252, Newton, 276, Philip R., 252, Rebecca, 87, 138, 140, 335, Russell, 252, Ruthanna, 276, 277, Shannon, 252, Thomas Cecil, 276, Thomas Clayton, 276, Thomas Leslie, 276, Wayne Lee, 276, William, 342, William Leonard, 276

POWER, 28, Abram, 110, Susannah, 110

POWERS, Ann, 148, 168, 212, David, 212, Elizabeth, 212, Floyd, 148, 212, Funeral Home, 278, Harry, 43, Janet, 212, John Martin, 85, Joseph, 212, Mary, 85, 145, Valentine, 145

POYNTER, Marie, 139, Rebecca, 317

POYNTS, Rachael, 136

PRAGE, Terrie Dee, 281

PRATHER, Robert W., 381

PRATT, Eliza Franklin, 277, Erastus, 277, Eva, 277, Hiram Austin, 277, Laura, 137, Sarah Evaline, 277, William M., 57, Willie, 277

PRAYER, Martha, 163

PREDERGAST, John M., 199

PRENDERGAST, Carley, 199, Daniel Fred, 199, Eric, 199, Jenny Anne, 199, John Joseph, 199, Tiffany, 199
PRESSLOR, Brandon Scott, 277, Carol, 254, 255, 277, Clayton, 277, Darrin Cole, 277, Edwin, 253, 254, 255, 277, John, 254, 255, John Joe, 277, John William, 277, Lillian, 11, 254, 277, Lillina, 253, Linda, 254, 255, 277, Vivian, 255
PRESTON, William, 164
PREVO, Ernest, 67, Ernest F., 63
PREVOST, Colonel, 219
PREWITT, Judith, 250
PRICE, (General), 91, Charles, 322, Connie, 358, Elizabeth, 184, 330, Eva Janette, 131, Faye Marie, 217, Gracie M., 164, James "Jim", 182, Joseph H., 85, Judy, 246, Kathleen, 246, Laura, 322, Mary, 335, Mary K., 182, Patricia, 322, Ruth E., 119, Sarah, 247, William, 131, 318, William A., 119, William A.T., 246, William, Jr., 131, Winifred L., 119, 318
PRIEBE, Albert, 277, Angela, 278, Audrey, 277, August, 277, Bill, 277, Bill, Jr., 277, Bret, 277, Charles, 277, Chris, 277, Danny, 277, Dawn, 277, Debbie, 277, Donald, 277, Dorothy, 277, Ed, 277, Elizabeth, 86, 87, 172, 287, Elmer, 277, Emma, 277, Farm, 82, Fred, 278, Fred Herschel, 277, Fred Herschell, 278, 327, Geraldine, 277, Goldie, 278, Greg, 278, Jeannie, 277, Jeremy, 278, Jessica, 278, Junior, 277, Kent, 54, 278, Kent Stuart, 278, Kevin, 277, Lincoln, 22, 277, Lizzie, 277, Lloyd Elmer, 277, Margaret, 112, 277, Marjorie, 277, Martha, 277, Mary, 277, Mary Lou, 278, Mary Louise, 308, 327, Myrtle, 347, Norma Jean, 277, Otillie, 277, Paul, 277, Rebecca Suzanne, 278, 327, Ruth, 277, Sam, 277, 347, Stanley Paul, 278, Stephen Phillip, 278, Theresa, 54, 278, Theresa A., 372
PRIEST, Dan Edward, 227, Linda Linn, 227
PRIESTMAN, Elizabeth, 87
PRIMMER, Eable, 231, Ica, 231, William, 231
PRINCE, Elizabeth, 297, Kathryn, 297, Kathy, 297, Paul Thomas, 297, Suzanne, 297, Tom, 297
PRINGLE, Francis, 84
PRISCILLA'S, Beauty Salon, 16
PRITCHETT, Dorothy, 164, Melissa Dawn, 164, Michael, 164, Staci Rena Whitlow, 164, Kenneth, 164
PROCTOR, America, 194, Julia, 98, Letha, 31, Mary Elizabeth, 191, Mulenburg, 194, Willis Green, 191
PROFFITT, Allen, 278, Asher L., 278, Brandi, 278, Charles Stephen, 278, Cynthia, 278, Daniel Merrill, 278, David Charles, 278, Diane, 278, Edward, 278, Frederick Leinberger, 278, Henry Miller, 278, Henry Washington, 278, James Wendell, 278, Janet, 278, Jean Ann, 278, Jeffrey, 278, John Meredith, 278, Joseph B., 278, Julie, 278, Karen Lynn, 278, Leanna Lynn, 278, Linda Leigh, 278, Marena Jo, 278, Margaret Isabelle, 278, Martha, 278, Mary Beth, 278, Mary Irena, 278, Max, 278, Ora L., 278, Ora Merrill, 278, Paul J., 278, Rholla L., 278, Rosa Victoria, 278, Sabrena, 278, Samuel L., 278, Steven Merrill, 278, Wayne Eugene, 278
PROPS, Judith, 305
PROSSER, Beth, 324, Cassandra, 324, Jay, 324, Lori Ann, 324
PROSSER'S, Body Shop, 15
PROVO, Dennis, 212, Peggy, 212
PRUETT, Creo, 374
PRUITT, Mary, 102, 170, Mary Anna, 239, Mary Anne, 103
PRUM, Donald, 205
PRYOR, Dora Adaline, 175
PUAILOA, Mary L., 342
PUGH, Margaret, 271, Susannah, 232
PUMROY, Anne, 278, 279, Arthur, 279, Carolyn, 278, 279, Dorothy, 279, Elizabeth, 278, Eric, 278, 279, George, 279, Kenneth, 278, 279, Levi, 279, Marsha, 278, 279, Rachel Elizabeth, 279, Ruth Anne, 279, Sarah, 279
PURCELL, Bertha May, 198, James R., 198
PURDUE, John, 338
PURDUM, Caroline, 263
PURDY, Tillie, 108
PURNELL, Hazel, 260
PURVIS, Allison, 118
PUTNAM, Atha, 144
PYKE, Albert, 378
QUASEBARTH, Janelle, 67, Mark, 67
QUERY, Bill, 54, Charles, 195, Mildred, 195, Miriam, 195, Phyllis, 195, Yolanda, 54
QUICK, Abigail, 74, Edwin, 74, Flora, 132, Hannah, 100, Jackson, 100, Olive, 241
QUIGG, Bertha Rachel, 279, Claude Edward, 279, Clifford, 221, Clifford Albert, 279, Curtis, 309, Curtis Merle, 279, Dorothy, 279, 309, Edith, 221, Francis, 265, Francis, (Rev), 279, Halfred, Lewis, 265, 279, Joseph, 279, Josie Martha, 279, Judith, 279, Judy, 309, Karl Francis, 279, Lois, 309, Lucille, 279, 309, Lyle Wayne, 279, 309, Mable, 39, Mable Lydia, 279, Mildred Maye, 279, Morris Charles, 279, Rena Ethel, 279, Tacy, 279, Wilberta, 279, Wilberta Faye, 265, Wilma, 265, 168, Wilma Jean, 279, Winona, 265, 279
QUILLAN, Tom, 266
QUILLEN, Elma Conn, 143
QUILLIN, Kathleen, 123
QUINLEY, __, 22, Claudean, 270
QUINN, Kirk J., 372, Nancy M., 372
QUIRK, Maureen, 199
QUISENBERRY, Debra, 279, Frank, 279, James, 279, Janet, 279, Joy, 279, Morris, 279, Morris W., 279, Nancy, 252, 279, Thomas, 279, William, 279
QUITSAU, Susanna, 325
RABB, Kate Milner, 117, School, 202
RABIDEUX, Audrey Morrell, 145
RADCLIFF, Agnes, 165
RADER, Anna, 201
RADFORD, Delores, 67, Neva, 105, 162
RADY, John D., 372
RAFF, Diana, 271
RAGSDALE, Henry, 14
RAHN'S, FARM MARKET, 211
RAINES, Richard, 68
RAINEY, Vickie Lynn, 106
RAINIER DRUG STORE, 14
RAINS, Jess, 66, Mark, 190
RAIRDAN, Rebecca Jane, 322
RAIRDON, Jerry, 63
RAKESTRAW, Gilbert, 110
RALSTON, Amanda Marie, 84, 280, Donna Rae, 84, Jamey Eileen, 280, Jamie Ilene, 84, Nathan Francis, 280, Robert Matthew, 84, 280, Ruby, 78, 191, Ruby E., 280, Ruby Eileen, 280, Ruby Herron, 293
RAMEY, Alvin, 309, Emma Rose, 190, John H., 194, William H., 190
RAMSAY, Chip, 54, Kenneth, 54, Alexander, 273, Christine, 273, David, 181, Diane, 326, Douglas, 181, Ellen Susan, 99, James R., 181, Lucy, 353, Margaret, 208, Mary, 273, Molly, 273, Phyllis Arlene, 99
RANARD, James, 57
RAND, Abraham, 88
RANDALL, Abraham, 280
RANDEL, Andrew, 228, 232, Andrew V., 280, Andrew Vineyard, 197, 302, Ann, 280, Asa, 123, 228, 280, Bertha, 280, C. Pauline, 211, Clara, 280, Clara Ellen, 197, Crystal Pauline, 229, 280, 339, David Franklin, 280, Dora, 299, Dora Eveline, 108, Dora Linn, 184, Edna Ludassa, 232, Edward, 280, Ernest, 280, 354, Ernest M., 197, Ernest Milfort, 302, Florence, 280, Geneva, 280, George, 197, 280, Ida, 280, James, 354, James G., 229, 354, James Goodwin, 197, 280, 302, John, 197, Joseph, 280, Kenneth, 232, 280, Margaret, 228, Mary, 280, 320, Mary Ann, 228, Mary D., 197, Mary Ellen, 280, Matilda Emmaline, 228, Myrtie, 197, 228, 280, Nellie Rose, 280, Orval, 184, 280, Orval W., 197, 211, 302, 336, 339, Orval Wingert, 229, Rachel, 123, Ralph, 280, Rebecca Jane, 197, Rose Grace, 232, Sarah 354, Sarah J., 197, 280, Thomas, 280, V. Lucile, 211, Vivian Lucile, 184, 229, 280, William, 197, 280, 302, William N., 228, William Noah, 197, 232, 280, 302, Mary, 230
RANDELL, Orval, 299
RANDOLPH, Cindy, 171, Edward Fitz, 333, Lucinda, 321, Marjorie, 348, Mark, 171, Mary Fitz, 333
RANKIN, Linda Lee, 245, Martha, 245, Robert, 245
RANKINS, E.J., 41
RANSDALL, Susan, 145, Agnes Fanny, 117
RAPER, Martha Ann, 343
RAPP & SONS, 14
RARDIN, Melia, 239
RASOR, Eulala, 205, Henry, 336
RATCLIFF, Carrie, 311, Edith L., 157, Elinor, 260, Esther, 157, Esther L., 157, Frank P., 157, Vickie L., 375
RATOFF, Gregory, 342
RAUB, Elizabeth, 212, Eva Louise, 200
RAUCH, Colin, 120, Erin, 120, George, 120, Robyn Ann, 120, Timothy W., 372
RAY, Alvin, 54, Christian, 169, Cynthia, 169, Dave, 153, Earl, 193, Edna, 229, Floyd, 229, Fred, 169, Gene Hubert, 158, 280, Glen, 229, Glen Everett, 280, Hazel, 54, James, 123, 229, James R., 280, Kathy Jo, 280, Kelly, 280, Lauren, 169, Lavina, 204, Lillian Cloe, 280, Louisa J., 164, Mary, 192, 193, Mary Frances, 280, May, 193, Nancy Jane, 228, Patricia Maye, 280, Randel Gene, 280, Robert Glen, 280, Sallie, 158, Sally, 280, 322, Stephanie, 280, Susan Diane, 280, Thelma Dean, 280, Theresa, 278, William 280
RAYLE, Opal, 356
RAYNER, Frank, 29
RAZOR, Lydia, 169
READ, Ezra, 183, Sarah Oakalla, 183
READY, Hester, 82, 135, Mary, 82, William, 82
REAGAN, Emma Anna, 354
REARDON, Mary, 150
REASOR, Abby, 192
REATCH, Michael W., 372
REATH, Catherine, 110, Elam, 39, Martha Rebecca, 109, 110, Sharon M., 139, William, 110
RECORDS, Elsie Clara, 216
RECTOR, Loriann, 115, Nancy, 322
REDANT, Catherine, 195
REDDEN, Bill, 13, Donald Eugene, 131, Fern Marie, 131, Joyce, 131, Lucille, 13, Maxine, 131, Nancy, 189, William, 131, William, 131
REDDISH, Evelyn, 285, Hazel, 137, Imogene, 137, John Fuson, 137, Lizzie Belle, 148, William, 285
REDENBACKER, Orville, 265
REDENBAUGH, Dorothy, 107, Elizabeth, 144, 281, Francis Marion, 102, Frederick, 144, 153, 281, Frederick, Jr., 281, George, 281, Henry, 144, 281, Henry I, 281, Hulda, 281, Jeremiah, 123, 150, John, 102, Margaret, 281, Maria, 102, Maria Louise, 243, Mary, 281, Mary Catherine, 144, 145, 281, Milton, 12, Nancy, 102, Samuel, 281, Sarah, 153, 281, Susan, 281, Thomas, 102, 281, William, 281, William Henry, 123, Nancy, 150
REDMAN, Eva Beaman, 322, John Wesley, 157, 322, Margart Ellen, 322, Myra Louise, 157, 287, 322, Peter, 322, Rosalie Diane, 284, Stella May, 157, William Beaman, 322
REDMON, Carole, 208, Howard, 301, John, 54
REECE, Nancy Ward, 258, William, 258, 340
REED, Andrew Baxter, 281, Anna, 282, Camen Miranda, 293, Clara Belle, 267, Cynthia Edith, 175, Dale, 293, David W., 281, David Whistel, 281, Denise, 277, Donna, 113, Elizabeth, 162, Gilbert, 277, Haley, 277, Ira, 293, Isaac, 76, J.A., 365, Jakota, 113, 277, Jkota Leroy, 259, Jesse, 277, Jimmy, 255, 277, Johan Michelle, 281, John, 162, John Clifford, 281, John David, 281, John F., 281, Joshua, 80, Juanita, 277, Julianne Marie, 281, Kevin, 277, Margaret, 281, Mary, 122, 281, 301, Mary Ann, 318, Melinda Joy, 293, Michael David, 281, Oliver, 281, Pearl, 223, Robert Lawrence, 175, Rosemary, 281, Sonny, 281, Terrie Dee, 281, Willie B., 281
REEDER, Alta, 96, Frank, 96, Thomas J., 63
REEDY, Marjorie, 187
REEP, Sarah "Sally", 173
REEPE, Jacob, 225
REEVE, Deobrah Frey, 297
REEVES, Clara, 129, Clay, 137, Dwight, 236, Ford, 14, Hazel, 137, Kittie, 285, Lena, 137
REHLING, Sylvia, 54
REICHARD, Effie, 271, Jack 271, Naomi, 271
REID, Basil, 173, Donald, 173, Eliza M., 288, Jake, 310, Lida, 288, Lydia Jane, 310, Marlin, 173
REIHL, Doris Marie, 152
REITZ, Lawrence (Dr.) _, 133
REMLEY, Adrian, 271, Albert J., 271, Ambrose, 190, 281, Becky, 375, Christian, 281, Daniel, 281, David Henry, 281, Donald, 272, Elizabeth, 281, Elizabeth Ann, 281, Fred Shelby, 281, Gladys, 271, Harriet, 102, Harry C., 281, Helen, 6, Isaac Frances, 281, James Adrian, 272, James Chadwick, 272, James Christopher, 281, John, 6, 190, 281, John McCain, 281, Larry C., 372, Lena, 271, Malinda, 281, Margaret, 281, Mary, 272, Mary Helen, 281, Ruhannan, 281, Sarah, 190, Sarah Jane, 281, Sharon, 372, Sheila, 272, Theodore, 281, William, 102, William Frances, 281, __, 42
REMSEN, Irving B. III, 279, Marsha, 279, Matthew Alexander, 279
RENTCHLER, Alvin D., 375, Craig, 352, Diane, 352, John, 352, Mark, 352
REPP, Charles Wesley, 281, Edgar Leon, 281, Helen, 282, Martha Belle, 281, Mary Helen, 281, 282
REPPERT, Carl, 63, Glen, 288
RETTINGER, David, 282, David Pierce, 282, Earl, 313, Edith, 313, George Calvin, 282, Hannah, 209, Jeanette Florence, 282, John, 313, John Ephriam, 313, Keturah Dove, 383, Laura Hanks, 282, Mary Melissa, 282, Rosa, 288, Samuel, 313, Sarah Edith, 312, Temple, 150
REYBURN, Frank, 357
REYNOLDS, Albert, 283, Andrew, 282, Andrew J., 282, Bertha, 282, Bessie Mae, 282, Bonnie Darlene, 283, Branch, 282, Candy, 283, Carol Ann, 283, Charles E., 283, Charlie, 282, 283, Charlie O., 282, Charlie Otto, 282, 283, Charlotte Faye, 283, Clara, 282, Cynthia Rene, 283, Darrell Joseph, 283, David Allen, 282, Deborah Jean, 283, 324, Delores Marie, 312, Ed, 302, Eddie Joe, 283, Edwin, 163, Edwin Roy, 163, Eliza, 282, Elizabeth, 272, 283, Ellen, 283, Ellis, 282, Esther Jane, 238, George, 86, 282, 347, George Wesley, 282, Gladys, 163, Hannah, 282, Herman, 312, Jack Andrew, 283, James A., 163, 283, Jesse, 282, John, 243, John Adrian, 283, John Henry, 163, 283, John Henry, Jr., 283, John William, 282, Josepha Carol Ann, 283, Joshua, 324, Joy Lynn, 283, Katherine, 282, Kimberly Burson, 243, L.W., 52, Laura Emily, 283, Lee Marie, 276, Lewis, 164, 282, Lewis W., 11, Lewis Washington, 282, Lura, 163, Lynn, 347, Mabel, 164, Mark, 243, Mary, 282, 347, Mary Jane, 282, Mary L., 52, Mary Luenza, 282, Megann, 324, Michael Ottis, 283, 324, Molly, 283, Naopleon Bonaparte, 282, Olive, 282, 283, Ottis, 283, Paul, 163, Pearl Dean, 282, Rebecca, 312, Rosa W., 283, Seth Thomas, 312, Shandra, 283, Shanty, 283, Susan, 163, 283, Susan Elizabeth, 282, Susan Ethyl, 163, Sylvia, 163, Tammy Gail, 283, Timmy Lee, 283, Tommy Otto, 283, Vera Lee, 283, Violet Flo, 283, William, 282, William, Jr., 282, William, Sr., 282, Jennifer Sue, 283
RHEA, J.O., 381, Marcia, 225, Pauline, 286
RHEES, Alevilda Belle, 281
RHOADES, Ed, 44, Helen, 339, Helen Hawthorne, 328, John, 238
RHOADS, Albert Hillary, 283, Alberta, 263, 284, Amos, 283, Amy Elizabeth, 283, Arminda, 143, Aron Jay, 185, Beth Ann, 185, Carleton, 284, Charles Wesley, 283, Christine, 284, Cyrus, 283, Cyrus Willard, 283, David A., 185, Donald, 15, Ernest, 284, 353, Florence, 284, Floyd, 284, Floyd, Jr., 66, Forest Leona, 283, Fred, 155, 232, 284, Geneva, 284, Glenn, 284, 353, Grace, 54, 284, Harold, 54, Harry, 284, J. Donald, 375, Jacob, 283, 284, Jacob Dosson, 283, Jerod, 283, John, 283, Kral, 66, 284, Kayla Ann, 305, Keith L., 375, Keziah, 129, Larry Wayne, 305, Lester, 284, Louise Angeline, 283, Margaret "Peggy", 283, Mary Jane, 283, Murle, 284, Maomi Armilda, 283, Opal, 31, Rachel Marticia, 283, Ramona, 284, Raymond, 284, 353, Rebecca, 274, Richard C., 62, Rosemary, 284, Russell Leroy, 283, Sheila Ann, 185, Terry, 274, Thomas, 283, Thomas Christopher, 283, Vivian, 284, William, 32, 129, 283, 284, William Eleander, 283, William Jefferson, 283, 284, William, Jr., 283, 284, William, Sr., 283, 284
RHODA, Andrew, 252, Ashley, 252, David, 252, Donald, 252, Greg, 252,
RHODE, Alice, 221, Grant, 221, Patricia, 221, Penny, 221, Phillip, 221
RHODEHAMEL, John, 169, Maria, 85, Martha, 169
RHONDA, Elaine, 252, Sandy, 252
RICE, Albert, 12, 172, 285, 286, Alfred, 285, 306, Allen B., 49, Amelia, 285, Andrew, 285, Anne, 284, Arthur, 280, 285, Benjamin, 285, Betty, 285, Beverly, 284, Bill, 285, Brian, 71, 306, Brianna Loui, 306, Carrie, 220, Cecelia, 285, Ceclia, 285, Charles, 285, Charles Nelson, 285, Connie, 284, Cordelia, 202, Daniel, 284, 285, Daniel E., 284, 285, David, 285, Dee, 53, Dennis L., 375, Dennis Lee, 285, Elizabeth, 285, 331, Elmer, 285, Elmer J., 284, 285, Evelyn, 285, Francis, 149, Frank, 150, Fred, 12, 13, Garnet, 80, Goldie, 285, Hubert, 285, Isaac, 79, 284, 348, Jacob, 284, James, 285, Jane, 168, Jane Elizabeth, 285, Jane Isabel, 284, Jasper, 285, JoAnn, 285, John V., 333, Johnathan, 285, Jonathan, 172, Joseph, 285, Joseph E., 285, Joseph Easley, 285, Kate, 149, Kate Tate, 284, Katherine, 285, Katie, 285, Kittie, 285, Larry, 275, Lee Ann, 168, Louilla, 285, Louise, 285, Lowell, 168, LuAnne, 284, LuAnne, 285, Luetna, 285, Luther, 286, Luther V., 285, 286, Mabel, 348, Margaret, 284, Marion, 220, Martha, 285, Mary 118, 286, Mary E., 285, Mary Elizabeth, 144, Morris, 174, Myrtle, 285, Nannie, 285, Nelson, 149, 285, Olive, 285, Opal, 285, Opal Tracy, 284, Otis, 285, Peggy Lynn, 280, Permelia, 285, Polly, 285, Rachel Ann, 284, 285, Robert, 220, Robert, 285, Ruth, 80, 306, Sarah, 285, Sarah Jane, 285, Sarah Margaret, 285, Simeon, 149, Simeon, 285, Stella, 285, Thelma, 285, Thomas, 172, 285, 286, Thomas Newton, 37, 284, Thomas W., 286, Till, 339, Tire Service, 26, Toadie Stilwel, 286, Ulysses Grant, 202, Violet, 220, Virginia, 285, Washington, 285, Wilbur, 220, Wilbur Hughes, 220, William, 285, William C., 375, Wilma, 285, Wilma Jean, 131, Zella Dee, 286
RICH, Dinah, 129
RICHARD, Vida, 118
RICHARDS, Betty, 175
RICHARDSON, Betsy Ruth, 278, Carl, 263, Carolyn, 239, Elmer, 239, Enoch, 164, Esther Vivian, 239, Eunice, 145, 298, Franklin, 312, George, 110, Howard, 312, Janet, 239, Jill Annette, 278, Judith Elaine, 278, Malissie, 315, Marion, 305, Max, 239, Minnie Gray, 239, Myrtie Lusula, 170, Nehemiah, 178, Norma J., 372, , Pat, 239, Patricia Nodyne, 312, Paul, 106, Penny, 284, 353, Rebecca Carol, 278, Robert, 239, Russell, 278, Russell Floyd, 239, Shirley, 103, Shirley Lois, 239, Vivian, 92, Warren E., 312
RICHERT, Lawrence, 49
RICHEY, Maggie, 123
RICHY, Abraham, 34
RICKETTS, Tom, 31
RICKEY, Amanda, 192, Lawrence, 192
RIDDELL, Eva May, 301
RIDDLE, Ina, 233, Larry, 372,

Stephen, 153
RIDDLEBARGER, Walter, 14
RIDENGER, Cora Emmaline, 263
RIDER, Dell, 100, Madeline Mary, 200, Margaret, 108, Minnie M., 108, William, 108
RIDGE, Harold R., 375, Vicky Lynn, 179
RIEKENBERG, Maude E., 186, Maurice, 186
RIFFLE, Gertrude, 216
RIGDON, Susan, 355
RIGGINS, Ladonna, 357
RIGGLE, Mayme Ellen, 135
RIGGS, Herman, 103, Kathryn, 103
RILEY, Christina Marie, 218, Henry C., 63, James Whitcomb, 257, Mary Ann, 94, R., 45, Rose Belle, 319
RINEHART, Sue, 273
RINKER, Catherine, 187, Cynthia, 180, George, 187, Jacob, 187, Sarah, 187, __, 213
RIPPY, Betty, 286, Carl, 286, Carlen, 286, Fern, 286, Howard Eugene, Sr., 286, Howard, 286, Howard, Jr., 286, Karen, 286, Mary, 286, Myrtle, 286, Ryan, 286
RISER, James Paul, 80, James Paul II, 80, Joyce, 80, Matthew Joseph, 80
RISNER, Ray, 106
RISTINE, 28, T.H., 6, Theodore H., 6
RITTER, Bill, 269, Debbie, 269, Irene, 360, Wiliam, 260
RIVERS, Alice Victoria, 286, Allan, 186, Bessie, 286, Betsy, 286, Betty F., 286, Billy Joe, 286, Bret, 118, Carol Clore, 118, Charles, 186, Clifford, 286, Curtis, 118, Elizabeth, 286, Elizabeth Ann, 286, Emily, 286, Emmett Raymond, 286, Eric, 304, Errett, 186, Esther Jane, 286, 304, Harriet, 255, Harriet Elizabeth, 160, 162, 256, Harry Waller, 286, Helen, 286, 304, Helen Frances, 304, Henry Waller, 286, Isaac, 286, Jack, 186, James, 286, James Madison, 286, James R., 372, James Riley, 286, Janet, 304, Joel Peyton, 286, John, 256, 286, John Campbell, 286, Joseph Butler, 286, Joseph Harden, 286, Judy, 306, Lena, 169, 286, Livonia, 286, Livonia Ellen, 286, Lucy, 286, Lutitia Ellen, 286, Martha, 286, Mary, 286, Mary Ann, 286, 304, Mary Elizabeth, 286, Mary Etta, 286, Mary Irene, 286, Mary S., 186, Matthew Clinton, 118, Max, 286, 304, Max Ray, 286, 304, Meggan, 304, Minnie Grace, 286, Mitchel Curtis, 118, Mollie, 286, Nancy Adel, 286, Nannie Lutitia, 286, Otto James, 286, Patience, 286, 320, Pauline, 286, Polly, 286, Ramona Lea, 304, 286, Ray, 324, Reba Ardell, 286, Rebecca, 286, Rebecca Jane, 286, Richard, 286, Robert Marion, 286, Robert Stallard, 286, Roby, 286, Ronald, 118, Ronna, 118, Rosie, 286, Roy, 286, Rutha Anna, 118, Sarah, 286, Suannah, 286, Thomas Jefferson, 286, Victor Ray, 286, 304, William, 286, William Franklin, 286
ROACH, Archie, 286, Bertha Hensley, 333, Elizabeth, 259, Hattie A. Lewellen, 286, James R., 375, Margaret Ann, 259, Marisa Lynn, 287, Meagan Louise, 287, Melody, 287, Melody Ann, 157, Mike, 286, 287, Penny, 286, Robert, 157, 286, Robert M., 287, Robert Michael, 286, Ryan Michael, 287, Timothy, 286, Wilma Cornett, 286
ROACH'S, Grocery, 286
ROARK, John, 307, Sadie, 307, Sally Rose, 287, William, 307
ROBB, William Walker, 34
ROBBINS, Anita, 287, 336, Belle, 353, Berniece, 341, Bert, 287, 336, Carrie, 14, 286, 287, 336, Don, 287, Donald, 336, Donald Joe, 287, Donald, K., 287, Donna, 287 Donna Jo, 287, 348, Duff, 336, Duff George, 287, Edna, 336, Elizabeth, 113, Hugh, 336, Hugh W., 287, Isadora, 84, Jonathan, 84, Joyce, 287, 348, Lillian, 287, 336, Luella, 299, Mabel, 287, Mabel, 336, Martha, 287, 336, Oneta Oive, 287, Orran Ray, 287, Robert, 287, 336, 336, Robert J., 287, Rodney, 287, 348, Rodney Martin, 287, Ruth, 287, 336, Wilmer, 336, Wilmer Ira, 287
ROBBS, Grocery, 227
ROBERTS, Alva, 41, Chapel, 74, Charlotte, 164, Earl Hill, 100, Elbert A., 153, Ethel, 103, Jake, 107, James, 107, Jane, 107, 172, Jill Louise, 100, John Kenyon, 100, Margaret, 87, Marie Merele, 100, Rebecca, 87, 140, 280, Velma Jean, 100
ROBERTSON, James, 42, John, 365
ROBEY, Rita Maxine, 258
ROBINS, Isabella, 209
ROBINSON, Alicia, 343, Beverly, 255, Bill, 342, Charles W., 255, George, 376, Jane, 242, Judith, 255, Laura, 343, Lucian, 72, 202, Mary Magdalene, 272, Nancy, 255, Richard, 49, Roy, 211, Sue, 255
ROBISON, Betty, 288, Beverly, 254, 288, Bill, 288, Charles W., 253, 254, Charles Wesley, 287, Charles Willard, 288, Cora, 287, Cora Ellen, 287, Gail, 185, 287, Gerald, 87, Gerlad Homer, 287, Gordon, 87, Gordon Bayless, 287, Homer, 87, 250, 287, 288, Homer T., 287, Homer Theophilus, 287, Jennie FLo, 336, Judith, 254, Judy, 288, Larry, 185, Larry Gerald (Dr.), 287, Lenora Blanche, 304, Lottie, 87, 250, 287, 288, Lyn, 287, Lynn Ellen, 185, Margaret, 87, 287, Margaret Lottie, 287, Margaret Sue, 254, Nancy, 254, 288, Naomi, 87, 250, Naomi Winifred, 288, Patricia, 288, Roy, 229, Sue, 288, Theadore Homer, 288, Thomas, 288, Vivian, 254, 288, Willard, 87
ROBY, Martha Ellen, 153
ROCK, 22
ROCKEFELLER, John D., 141
RODGERS, Francis Faye, 250, Lula Belle, 250, Martha B., 105, Norman, 105
RODRIQUEZ, Josef, 106, Josef Felix, 105, Josef, Jr., 105
ROE, Becky, 131
ROEMER, Victoria, 279
ROGER, Belle, 39, Laurence, 236
ROGER'S, Tree Trimming, 16
ROGERS, Alden, 288, Amy, 289, Anna, 288, Bettie, 289, Catherine, 288, Charles, 289, Charles Chandler, 289, Charles, V., 289, Cheryl Ann, 289, Claude, Chester, 288, Clayton, 289, Clifford, 288, Clyde, 170, 289, David, 288, David Finley, 288, 319, David Lee, 288, Della, 288, Dorman, 107, Edward, 288, Elijah, 288, Elizabeth, 288, Florida, 174, Frank, 288, Fred, 289, Geof, 107, Geoffrey, 107, George, 288, Ginger, 342, Harmon, 107, Helen, 288, Henry (Dr.), 288, Henry C., 288, Henry Clay, 288, Henry Clay (Dr.), 288, Henry Edwin, 288, James, 288, James D., 372, Jane, 288, Jeanette, 341, Jerome, 225, John, 288, John B., 14, Joyce, 174, Julie, 289, Karen, 107, 170, Karen Beth, 289, Kim Charles, 289, Laurabelle, 288, Lemuel R., 312, Lisa, 107, Lois Mae, 288, Mae, 107, Marilyn, 107, Marjorie, 288, 289, Mary, 288, 319, Mary "Mollie", 319, Mary Adelin, 288, Mary Elizabeth, 1285, Melissa, 288, Minnie, 289, Myron Lee, 288, Nancy, 165, 170, 289, Nancy Ann, 289, Nancy Jane, 288, Naomi, 288, 289, Naomi Meloy, 289, Nellie May, 288, Rachel, 288, Rilla May, 288, Robert, 170, 288, 289, Robert R., 288, 289, Robert W., 288, Robert Wallace, 289, Robin, 170, Robin Ann, 289, Rosa, 313, Ruth, 288, Sallie Lee, 289, Sandi Kae, 289, Teresa, 374, William, 55
ROHR, Carl T., 143
ROLLER, Alice, 272
ROLLINGS, Debra Ann, 334
ROLLINS, Bob, 334, Marilyn Jane, 334, Robert E., 344
RONC, Anna Eve, 289, Barbara, 289, Catherine, 289, Dorothea, 289, George, 289, Hannah, 289, Jacob, 289, John, 289, John George, 289, John Philip, 289, Joseph, 289, Mary Magdalin, 289, Michael, 289, Philip, 289, Philip Adam, 289, Valentine, 289
RONK, Daniel W., 289, Elizabeth, 289, George, 289, George H., 289, George Henry, 289, Jacob, 289, James R., 289, Jesse D., 289, John, 289, John Thomas, 289, Joseph, 289, Joseph F., 289, Martha Jane, 289, Mary Etta, 14, Mary Frances, 336, Mary M., 289, Mattie Ann, 289, Paul, 14, Phillip, 289, Samuel, 289, Sarah, 289, Wiliam P., 289
RONNCHSA, Eliza, 134
ROOD, James D., 375
ROOME, Gabriella, 317
ROOSEVELT, Quentin, 126, Teddy, 147, Theodore, 126
ROSA, Fred, 200
ROSE, Ed, 229, Eunice, 43, Grant (Mrs.), 74, Melvina, 272, Minty, 286, Richard, 286, __, 144
ROSEN, Brandon Myers, 179, Carolyn Jean, 122, Carrie Rene, 179, Diana Lynn, 179, Louise, 179, Maggie, 26, Robert, 179, Tracy Allen, 122, Trevor Allen, 122, Wallace, 122
ROSS, Adam Jerrison, 289, Amanda Jane, 98, Anna, 319, Barbara, 289, Betsy, 247, Boswell, 98, Casandra, 353, Cassandra, 247, Chester, 289, Cynthia Ann, 98, Elizabeth, 110, George, 247, Harrison, 174, 320, Henry James, 98, Jack A., 289, James Shelby, 98, Jamie A., 289, Jerry Wayne, 289, Julia, 283, Margaret, 174, 321, Margaret Ellen, 98, 249, Margaret Josephine, 320, Mary Elizabeth, 98, Nancy, 289, 320, Philip, 98, Rebecca Eve, 289, Rena, 98, Ryan Christopher, 289, S.A., 63, Sherry Lynn, 289, Stephen, 98, Steven Lee, 289, Theresa Ellen, 185, Thomas E., 289, Tom, 289, Veda Jones, 290
ROST, Carl, 376, Carl L., 376
ROTH, Casey, 351, Kevin, 351, 352
ROUK, Herman, 12
ROUNDTREE, Mary R., 291
ROUNTREE, Betty Katherin, 162
ROUSCH, C.I., 41
ROUSE, Beaulah, 290, Cecil, 290, Charles, 290, Floyd, 290, Louise, 54, 366, Lucille, 290, Mary, 290, Opal, 290, Oral, 290, Rollo, 290, Rollo Vern, 290
ROUTH, Isaac, 197, Jesse, 30, 36, Mary, 191, Mary Ellen, 280, Nancy, 150, 232
ROWLETT, Fern, 242
ROY, Miss, 189
ROYALITY, Sarah, 249
ROYALTY, Mary Jane, 164, Sarah A., 250
ROYER, Aaron, 359, Alta May, 319, Becky, 258, Beverly, 290, Brian, 359, Carole, 258, Cathy, 258, Diana L., 199, 223, 290, Elizabeth, 223, Elizabeth L., 199, 290, Evelyn Bill, 290, Evelyn Bob, 290, Evelyn Dunbar, 290, Frederick, 320, Frederick, Wayne, 290, Harry, 319, Herbert, 258, Inez Irene, 290, John Morton Winfield, 290, Marilyn June, 290, Mary Katherine, 223, Mary Mae, 320, Melvin K., 199, 223, 290, Rebecca L., 20, 374, Rebecca Louise, 223, Richard, 359, Roanne, 290, Robert Francis Raper, 290, Sadie Evelyn, 290, Samuel (Capt.), 290, Sebastian, 290, William Logan, 290
RUCH, Susannah, 294
RUCHTI, Veronica, 167
RUDD, Bruce Edward, 157, Glenda, 157, Lawson, 157
RUDE, Henry, 211, Lydia Marie, 211, Margaret, 211
RUDOLPH, Carolyn, 207
RUFF, Maude, 287
RUFFNER, __, 342
RUFINIA, Sister M., 264
RUGGS, Charles, 31
RULE, Ben, 317, Jewell, 317, Lee, 317, Richard, 317, Sam, 317, Weltha, 317
RUNKLE, Elizabeth, 211
RUNNELS, Belinda, 349, Bruce, 349
RUNYAN, Anthony, 229, Farm, 292, Mary Ann Wilson, 229, Susan, 229, Thomas, 229
RUNYON, Dave, 115, __, 207
RUSCHENBERG, Delores, 131
RUSH, Aaron M., 296, Andrew, 291, Andrew K., 290, Barbary, 291, Brandon D., 296, Carrie S., 296, Cathy, 205, Charles, 205, 290, Chester, 290, Church C., 290, Churchill, 290, 291, Courtney M., 296, David, 296, David F., 296, Dean C., 152, 291, Dean Clifton, 291, Dorcus, 360, Doyne, 152, 291, Doyne L., 291, Edith, 291, Edith J., 291, Frances "Frankie", 290, Gary L., 296, George, 290, 291, Gilbert, 290, Hannah Haines, 290, Harriett, 290, Helen, 21, 152, 291, 292, Helen M., 291, Henry A., 290, Jackie, 291, 292, James, 290, Jane, 291, Jared W., 296, Jason, 193, 296, Jeptha, 291, Jesse, 290, 291, Jesse P., 290, Jesse, Sr., 291, Jesse, R., 291, Julie Deanna, 291, Kathleen Marie, 291, L. Doyne, 291, Leonard, 291, Leslie DOyne, 274, 292, Lewis, 291, Lindsey S., 296, Liza, 290, Luna, 290, Margaret, 290, 291, Mary, 291, Mary L., 310, Mary L., "Polly", 290, Maxine, 296, Melissa, 193, 296, Milton, 213, Myrtle, 274, Myrtle Estella, 291, Nelson, 274, 290, 291, Nelson J., 291, Nelson Jan, 292, Rachel, 291, Robert N., 291, Robert Nelson, 292, Rosa Etta, 274, Roscoe, 291, 292, Roscoe Matthias, 292, Roscoe N., 152, 291, Roscoe Nelson, 291, Santi A., 291, Santi Andrew, 292, Sarah "Sally", 290, Thomas, 291, Vicki, 296, Vicky Ellen, 205, Warren, 296, Warren J., 296, Wayne, 296, Wayne D., 296
RUSHTON, Bess, 221
RUSK, Anna Jean, 309, Bettsie, 292, Cindy Hayes, 185, Clarence, 293, Clarence Orville, 292, David, 293, David Bruce, 292, David Heath, 292, David, Jr., 292, 293, David, Sr., 292, 293, Dennis, 292, 293, Dennis Layne, 292, Denny, 293, Edward, 102, Edward Lee, 209, Elizabeth, 292, Erin Elaine, 292, Fred David, 309, George, 374, Helen Elizabeth, 292, Jack Dean, 309, John, 292, Jonathan, 292, Kenneth David, 292, 293, Lloyd Edward, 309, Margaret, 292, Marguerite Celeste, 292, May, 102, Megan Elisa, 292, Nancy, 292, Paul, 293, Paul Eugene, 292, Robert, 292, Tiffany Shawne, 292, William, 292
RUSSELL, Adeline, 258, Denny, 205, Esther, 333, George, 205, 333, Isaac, 333, Jennifer L., 205, Jo Ellen, 205, Julie J., 205, Kimberly, 205, Lucinda, 308, Mary, 333, Rena, 181, Stella, 241, Vivian, 205
RUSTAN, Maggie, 258
RUTAN, Hannah, 93, Mary, 232
RUTHIG, Eric Mathew, 289, Sherry Lynn, 289, Victor H., 289
RUTLEDGE, Angela Marie, 132, David Earl, 293, Frederic, 293, Helen, 78, Helen Louise, 293, John Alvin, 293, Loran K., 375, Mary J., 375, Nadine Sue, 293, Robert, 280, 293, Robert Wayne, 293, Yvonne Ann, 293
RUTTKOWSKY, Julia Branch, 208
RYAN, Eva, 90, Jane, 369, Linda, 119
RYKER, Jeffrey Allen, 328, Jon Scott, 328, Kelly, 374, Marsha Sue, 328, Marther, 351, Max Lee, 328, Patty, 380
RYLANDER, Anna, 242,
RYLAND, Carla, 127
SABENS, Bill, 309, Christy, 226, Ellen, 156, Joshua, 226, Louise, 40, Mary Sue, 309, Michael, 226, Sharyn, 243, Wendy, 226
SABENS BROTHERS, 224
SABINS, __, 273
SABOLICK, Donna, 84, Jean, 84, Kelly, 84, Richard, 84
SADDLER, Patience, 80
SAGER, __, 213
SAIDLA, Abraham, 293, Byrd W., 293, Bryd W., 194, Byrd W., 294, Byrdell Willard, 293, 294, Caroline S. "Carrie", 293, 294, Catherine, 294, Catherine M., 293, Charles, 293, Christine Lynn, 293, Collyn, Jr., 293, David, 293, Donald Jay, 293, E. Edward, 293, Frank, 293, George, 293, Ila Joan "I. Jo", 293, Isaac, 293, J. Adam, Jr. 294, J.C., 148, 194, James, 293, Jesse, 288, 293, Johanna Adam, 293, John Adam, 294 John Adam L., 293, John Charles, 293, John Collyn, 150, John Collyn "J.C.", 293, John Collyn D., 148, John Henry, 293, 294, John Henry, Jr., 293, 294, Joshua H., 293, Judy Ann, 293, Kate, 293, Lenoara Alice "Allis", 293, Marge, 294, Mary E., 293, Mellie Elizabeth, 302, Mildred, 150, Philip, 294, Philip J., 294, Philip Jacob "P.J.", 293, Sarah Catherine, 293, Sharon Marie, 293, Simon, 293, Susan N., "Anna", 293, William A., 293, Bernice Alice, 294, John Collyn, 294, John Ervie "Bud", 294, John Henry, Jr., 294, Lucille "Lou", 294, Margaret Louise, 294, Norma Jean, 294
SALBERG, Lee, 138, Samuel, 138
SALENBERGER, Maybelle, 311
SALO, Nancy, 181
SAMPSON, A.W., 225, Etta, 227, Mary E., 318, Michelle, 212, Rodger, 212, Roger, 212, Sally, 212
SANCHEZ, Leslie Brooks, 296, Rene, 296
SANDAHL, Sarah Louise, 81, (Colonel), 188, Becky Ann, 270, Clara, 43, Clara Florence, 339, Cordela May, 346, Edward T., 270, Elva, 323, Elva Clyde Friend, 294, Emma, 270, Eula, 270, Frances, 14, Harold, 270, Hazel, 270, Jacob, 270, 301, James Alexander, 294, 323, John, 294, John H., 337, Lois, 270, Patsy Jean, 270, Peggy, 252, Polly, 238, Polly C., 337, Samantha Ellen, 294, 323, Sarah Gorham, 294, William Leon, 270, William W., 238, Zerelda, 337
SANDUSKY, Bob, 15, Elizabeth, 194
SANFORD, David G., 291, Earl, 291, John Byan, 306
SARVER, Alfred, 116, Bina Thompson, 116, Clifford, 116, Earl, 116, Eva, 213, Flossie, 116, Hobart, 116, June May, 139, Luther, 116, Ruby, 213
SARVIS, see Servies
SATTERFIELD, Eliza, 90, Elizabeth, 89
SAULSBERRY, Sarah Elizabeth, 343
SAUNDERS, Ruby, 111
SAVOLDI, Eric, 54, Mark, 54, Pia, 54, Tom 54
SAWICK, Annalisa Marie, 127, Camilla, 127, David, 127
SAWYER, Elston, 205
SAXON, Ida, 184
SAYERS, Elizabeth, 93
SAYLER, Abraham, 295, Alfred Vorhees, 295, Alice Catherine, 295, Barbara Jane, 295, Charles Bayard, 295, Clara Ann, 141, 180, 295, Clarence Lee, 295, Elizabeth Opal, 93, 94, Elsie Marie, 295, Elva, 334, Elva Esther, 295, Francis Milbert, 295, 334, George, 295, Godfrey, 295, Harvey Bayard, 295, Hubert W., 295, Jackson Purley, 295, Jacob, 136, 295, James "Charley", 295, Janet Lynn, 274, 295, Jeffrey, 207, John, 116, John Leslie, 207, 274, 295, Joseph, 295, Kelsie Lynn, 207, Larry Gene, 207, Larry Gene, 274, 295, Leslie Allan, 274, Leslie Allen, 207, Leslie, Allen, 295, Lois Esther, 295, Pearl, 136, Peter, 295, Ralph Addison, 295, Robert, 274, Robert F., 194, 207, Robert Francis, 295, Sarah, 295, Solomon Jacob, 295, Steven Wayne, 207, 274, 295, Walter L., 94, Walter Leslie, 295, William, 295, William T., 141, William Thomas, 295
SAYLOR, George W., 294, Nettie, 247, Otto, 247
SAYRE, John, 65
SAYRES, Helen, 176
SCAGGS, George, 68
SCHACHT, Debra, 231
SCHAEFER, Maria Margaretha, 187
SCHAFFER, Christina, 139
SCHALK, Charles, 120, Elizabeth, 120, Mary Lea, 66, William, 66
SCHANNEL, Grizzellah Jane, 113
SCHAUMBURG, Rita, 98
SCHEABER, see Shaver
SCHEIB, Eleanor Allhands, 80, Ray, 80
SCHELLINGER, Jacobus, 164
SCHENCK, Alta, 204, Alta E., 296, Anety, 296, Anna, 296, Arthur, 65, Cecil Murphy, 296, Chrienyance, Jr., 296, Chrineyance, Sr., 296, Eddie, 71, Eddie Oscar, 296, Edgar, 296, Elizabeth Alice, 296, Eva Bell, 296, Faye O., (Dr.), 295, Forest William, 296, G. Edward, 296, Hannah, 182, Schenck, Henry T., 295, Horace Wendell, 296, Ida, 100, J. Oliver, 296, John C., 296, Joseph Oscar, 296, Jun, 296, Kathleen, 231, Kenneth H., 296, Lydia Belle, 296,

Mabel Viola, 296, Margaret, 296, Maxine, 296, Oliver, 71, 296, Rachel, 298, Roelof, 295, Roelof Martense, 295, 296, Ruleff, 295, Russell R., 296, Sarah Almeda, 296, Una L., 296, Una Leona, 296, Viola, 71, William, 296, Willis, 71, 189, Willis Arnold, 296, Rachel, 334
SCHERR, Julie Eloise, 253, Todd Allan, 253
SCHEURICK, Judy, 205, Karen Lynn, 205, Kathy Elaine, 205, Manley, K., (Dr.), 205, Margaret, 205, Virgil, 205
SCHICK, Larry, 301
SCHILLING, E. William, 133
SCHLEEPY, Elizabeth, 215
SCHLEMMER, Bernice, 296, Beverly, 296, Diane, 296, Emily, 296, Ferdinand Louis, 296, Fritz, 296, Hildegard, 49, 296, Mary, 188, Otto, 24, 296
SCHLIMMER, Fritz, 141
SCHLOOT, A.J., 297, Amy Jo, 297, Bob, 297, Diann, 297, Elizabeth, 297, Garrett, 297, Joann, 297, Loren, 297, Loren, 381, Loren W., 297, Martha Ann, 297, Norma, 297, Patti Lee, 297, Robert, 297, Robert J., 381, Robert Joseph, 297, Rosanna, 297, Suzanne, 297, Thomas, 297, Thomas R., 297, 381, Thomas Robert, 297, Tom, 297
SCHLUDE, Flora, 207
SCHMIDT, Don C., 375, James Norman, 297, Janet, 297, Jill Susan, 297, Judith Johnson, 297, Judy, 297, Karen Ann, 185, Laura Elizabeth, 297, Lucy Ann, 297, Lyle, 297, Norman, 297
SCHNELLE, Genevieve, 361, Genevive, 350
SCHOEN, Charles, 297, Walter, 297
SCHOOLER, Cinchona, 190, Isaac N., 190
SCHOOLEY, James, 110
SCHOPPENHORST, Rose, 261
SCHRADER, Juanita, 260
SCHREINER, John, 297, Mary Magdeline, 298, Peter G., 297, Peter G., Jr., 298
SCHRICKER, Henry F., 68
SCHRIDER, Catherine Elizabeth, 220
SCHROEDER, Blanche, 357
SCHROER, Elizabeth, 261
SCHUBERT, Helen "Lena", 294
SCHUCHMANN, Andrew H., 125
SCHULDS, (Commander), 355
SCHULER, Penelope, 136
SCHULL, Mindi, 296, Tara, 296
SCHUMACKER, Anna Barbara, 289, Donald, 278, Michael, 278
SCHUMANN, Rose Anne, 125
SCHWAB, Maryl, 74H
SCHWARM, Adam, 279, Alma, 279, Victoria, 279
SCHWEITZER, Ellie, 208
SCHWIDLER, Kate, 374
SCJEPLE, Froeda, 213
SCOFIELD, Kezia, 110
SCOTT, A.L., 209, Adaline, 299, Alex, 33, Alfred, 298, Alfred Thomas, 153, 339, Alma, 299, Amanda, 255, Amy, 233, Ann, 144, Archaleus, 325 Archeleus, 299, Archelius, 153, 254, 255, 299, Armilda, 298, Barbara, 298, Ben, 253, 255, Benjamin, 153, 298, Byron, 145, 298, 351, Byron Clare, 298, Byron Curtis, 298, Carlyle "Scotty", 75, Caroline, 203, Caroline Hudson, 203, Cathy, 298, Charles, 81, 299, Clarie Elizabeth, 298, Claude, 299, Darlene, 135, David, 298, Della, 299, Dewey, 299, Diana, 290, Dorothy, 233, 299, Druicilla, 299, Drusella, 298, Edward, 298, Elizabeth, 115, 299, Ellen, 151, Elma, 299, Emma, 299, Ena Marie, 298, Ethel, 255, Ethel May, 298, Eunice, 145, 298, Eva, 290, Evaline James, 325, Fannie, 184, Fay, 319, Garnal, 145, 351, Garnal Lee, 298, Garnal Leon, 298, Garnal Maldon, 298, Gary, 351, Gary Curtis, 298, George, 151, Glen, 233, Goldie, 299, Harvey, 299, Hazel, 233, 299, Helen, 263, Hugh, 222, Ida, 255, Ida Pearl, 298, Ina, 233, Ira, 253, 255, 299, Ira Chase, 298, Jack, 290, James, 51, 298, James W., 298, Jane, 203, Janie Katherine, 298, Jerry, 290, John, 182, 298, 299, John May, 299, John Morgan, 298, John Vincent, 298, John William, 298, Joseph, 298, 356, Joseph William, 298, Josephine, 145, Katherine, 81, Kathryn, 299, Kelly, 81, Laura, 255, Laura Bell, 298, Lee, 299, Lenora, 299, Lola, 233, 299, Loren Franklin, 298, 299, Louise Miller, 145, Lucile, 233, Lucy, 299, Madge, 151, Maggie Canada, 299, Mamie, 232, Margaret Ann, 300, Marlene Mae, 151, Martha, 151, 215, Martha Hannah, 299, Martha Viola, 253, 254, 298, Mary, 153, 299, Mary Ann, 74, 232, Mary Catherine, 253, 254, 255, Mary Della, 209, Mary J., 298, Mary McMullen, 325, Maude, 299, Minnie, 299, Muriel Mae, 151, Nathan Edward, 325, Nathaniel Edward, 299, Offie, 55, 233, Omar, 232, Patrick, 81, Paul, 233, Pearl, 233, Phyllis, 290, Princess, 209, Rachel, 316, Rebecca, 298, Robert Carl, 74, Rose Jane, 153, 299, 339, Russell, 233, Ruth, 233, Sally, 233, Samuel Brenton, 299, Sanford, 151, Sarah, 298, Sarah Amanda, 298, Stella, 255, Stella Blanch, 255,298, 325, Susan, 290, 291, Susie, 299, Teresa M., 203, Thomas, 232, Thomas Alfred, 299, Thomas Walker, 232, Viola, 255, Virginia, 350, Virginia Ellen, 298, Wesley, 299, Wesley Gilbert, 151, William, 255, 299, William E., 290, William Edgar, 290, William Edward, 298, William F., 298, __, 55
SCOWDEN, Velma, 135
SEAL, Eileen, 351, Joseph, 358
SEALE, Joe, 14
SEAMAN, Amelia, 135, 136, Jane S., 102, Joseph S., 102
SEANOR, Thomas F., 102, Dustin, 261, Michael, 261, Ryan, 261
SEARCH, Pauline, 172
SEARS, Deborah, 268, Dorothy, 268, Richard, 268
SEAY, Arthur, 305, Arthur "Dean", 305, Elizabeth Lorene, 305, Irene, 305, Margaret, 306, Margaret Louise, 305, Mary, 305
SEIBERT, Phillip, 144, Suzanne, 144
SEIPERT, Blaine, 271, Chris, 271, Curtis, 271, Kevin, 271, Mark, 271, Rex, 54, 271, Sandra, 271, Sandy, 54, Scott, 271, Stephanie, 271
SEIT, Lula Matilda, 187
SEITS, Birthie L., 299, Byron Elijah, 299, Charles, 299, Charles Henry Albert, 299, Clarence Melvin, 299, Effie Esabella, 299, Francis Marion, 299, Henry, 299, Lawrence, 299, Lee, 299, Leighton, 299, Luella Idella, 299, Lula, 152, Lula M.A., 240, Rebecca, 299, Susan, 222, Susan Mae, 299, William Nuton, 299
SELBY, Abner, 134, Catherine, 293, Charles, 299, Fred A., 299, Homer Chester, 299, Ida, 279, Jerry, 317, John, 279, John Wesley, 299, Karen Kay, 317, Mary, 299, Mary A., 235, Mary Ann, 269, Minnie Viola, 134, Scott, 20, 299, Thomas, 280
SELF, George Franklin, 282, Ida Olive, 282
SELL, Adalje Soelle, 153
SELLERS, Ethel, 306, __, 42
SELLNO, Harriet, 273
SENN, Elizabeth, 179
SENSABAUGH, George F., 12
SENTMAN & SONS PALLET CO., 379
SENTMAN, Alice, 300, Amos, 299, Beverly, 300, Charles, 299, Charles Elmer, 300, Charles Emerson, 300, VCharles William, 30, Charlie, 317, 379, Colonel, 299, Donald, 300, Edgar, 299, Elinor, 299, Emma, 299, George, 299, Grace, 299, Greg Alan, 300, Kathleen, 299, Kayla Rene, 300, Lena, 223, Orville, 299, Rene, 300, Rita, 300, Ruby, 300, Sue, 379
SERING, Gertrude, 145, Sue, 165
SERVIES, Alisa Marie, 203, Blanche, 322, Catherine Teresa, 300, Charles Willard, 300, Christina Jane, 203, Darwin, 377, Donald Louis, 300, Doris, 268, Edward Leo, 300, Ella, 283, Emily Finetta, 294, Erik, 182, Foster, 300, Foster D., 300, Gail, 182, George Waller, 294, Henry M., 294, Jeff, 103, Jeffrey Scott, 300, John, 50, John (Rev), 245, 306, John A., 294, John P., 33, John R., 41, 71, John William, 300, Jonathan, 294, Jonathan W., 294, Juliet E.G., 294, Kim, 103, Kimberly A., 375, Kimberly Ann, 239, 300, Krista, 103, Krista Lynne, 239, 300, Larry, 314, 382, Lee O., 22, Lester Max, 300, Lettie May, 342, Lucinda, 294, Lyda A., 294, Martha Sue, 300, Mary, 294, 300, 377, Mary Alice, 300, Mary G., 43, Max Edward, 203, Melissa America, 322, Myrtle Ellen, 322, Nancy, 203, Nancy G., 294, O.E., 11, Orville, 322, Orville E., 12, Paul Thomas, 300, Polly, 294, Robert, 64, Samuel H., 294, Stephen "Steve", 182, Terri L., 375, Thomas, 141, Thomas, 295, Tim (Mrs.), 310, Timothy Regan, 203, Virginia A., 375, W.A., 11, William, 294, William A., 12, 322, William Anderson, 294, 295, and Morgan Funeral Home, 15
SERVIS, W.A., 11
SESSIONS, Jimmy D., 372
SEVERS, Ruby Henderson, 165
SEWARD, O., 360
SEWELL, Aaron, 172, Benjamin, 300, Dana, 172, Daniel, 171, Delores, 300, Dina, 172, Jeffrey, 172, Joshua, 172, Kelly, 172, Leonard, 171, 300, Leonard R., 52, Leonard Ralph, 300, Lester, 171, 172, Lester Floyd, 300, Lisa, 172, Lula, 209, Martin, 172, Matthew, 172, 300, Matthew Scott, 300, Peggy, 171, Peggy Deanne, 300, Scott, 172, Stephanie, 172, Stephen, 171, Timothy Scott, 300, Tracy, 172, Vera, 172, Vera Naomi, 171
SEYBOLD, Anna, 122, Frank, 122, Jackson, 122, Jackson A., 301, James, Sr., 122, 301, Jasper, Jr., 301, Jasper, Sr., 301, John, 122, 301, Lawson, 265, Mary, 122, Maurice, 122, Maurice White, 301, Regina, 301, Renita, 301, Resa, 301, Richard Max, 301, Ryan, 301, Warren Hllland, 301
SEYMOUR, Frank, 343
SHACKE, Barbara, 122, Johann Christoffel, 122
SHACKELFORD, Josephine, 99, __, 55, Forest, 55, 286, Kathryn, 229, Mark, 286
SHACKOFORD, Lucile, 233
SHAFER, Ella, 114, Florence, 114, Harry, 114, Howard, 114, Jane, 114, Rhoda, 114, 167, Sarah, 114, Wal, 114, see Shaver
SHAFFER, Addie, 325, Charles, 325, Charlotte, 325, Estelline, 124, Geroge, 325, Harry, 325, Silas, 325
SHAKE, Ruth, 324
SHAMBAUGH, George E. (Dr.), 282
SHAMNESS, Bob, 13
SHANKLIN, Andrew, 74, 109, 301, Ann, 301, Anna, 301, Bessie, 301, Charles, 301, Delilah, 41, Donald, 301, Elizabeth, 224, 301, Frank, 301, George, 301, Gladys, 207, Harry, 301, Helen, 301, Howard, 207, 301, Isabelle, 207, James, 74, 301, John, 301, John William, 301, John, Jr., 301, June, 301, Laverne, 301, Leona, 301, Leonice, 207, Lloyd, 301, Lois, 307, Mary Katherine, 301, Merle, 301, 307, Minnie, 301, Myrtle, 301, Opal, 301, Roy, 301, Sarah, 301, Shirley, 106, Susan, 301, Thomas, 301, Thomas Charlton, 301, Waneta, 301, Willard, 301, William, 301, __, 42
SHANKS, Charles, 43, Marjorie, 13
SHANNON, __, 22, Beverly Jeanne, 301, Carroll, 273, Carroll Burroughs, 301, Charles, 273, Charles David, 301, Cornelia, 220, 221, Cornelia E., 220, David Armstrong, 301, David Eugene, 301, Eugene "Jack", 301, Geneva, 273, Geneva May, 301, Georgia, 31, 273, Georgie Baird, 301, Jack, 273, James Q., 29, Joanne, 301, Joseph Jordan, 301, Martha, 87, Martin, 273, 301, Mary Arvilla, 273, Minnie, 273, Minnie Lee, 301, Naomi Clair, 273, 301, Palmer Allen, 273, 301, Wesley (Dr.), 138, Wesley E., (Dr.), 375
SHARP, Alva, 242, Ann, 302, Anna May, 346, Boyd, 84, Charles, 243, Don, 72, Edna, 226, 302, Elmer, 302, Emma, 154, 242, Emma Flora, 241, Ethel, 302, Frank, 242, Fred, 242, Gladys, 159, Ilene, 329, Ira, 105, Isaac, 242, James, 302, James Madison, 302, Jane, 302, John, 159, 242, 302, John L., 302, Lora, 302, Lucy, 39, Madison, 302, Madonna May, 302, Mary Jane, 302, Mary Marjorie, 302, May, 302, Meg, 302, Minnie, 159, Nancy, 302, Nina, 302, Otho, 242, Perry, 302, Rebecca Crandall, 242, Ross, 302, Ross Perry, 302, Roy, 302, Samuel, 242, Samuel Benjamin, 242, Sylvester, 302, Theodore, 242, W.T., 43, Walter, 302, Walter Marion, 302, William, 242
SHARPE, Bessie May, 306, Brenda, 84, Floyd, 84, India, 84, John, 11, 159, Pamela Ann, 84, Ray, 84, Ross, 226, Virginia, 11, 84, Virginia Banta, 221, Wilmer, 84, Wilmer T., 84
SHARPLESS, John, 98
SHATTUCK, Essie Marie, 155
SHAVER, Alice, 31, Andreas, 302, Andrew, 197, 302, Andrew III, 302, Bertha, 302, Carrie Belle, 234, Catherine, 302, Daniel, 114, 234, 302, David, 302, Elizabeth, 302, Emma L., 114, Emma Lenore, 302, Francis, 302, Gertrude, 302, Grace, 115, 116, J.M., 302, James Walson, 302, John, 302, John G., 302, Jonathan Jr., 302, Martha, 302, Martin Luther, 302, Mary "Polly" Magdale, 302, Orlando, 302, Peter, 302, Sally, 302, Samuel Hymer, 302, Sarah, 114, 197, 234, 302, 352, Susan, 302, Ursula, 197, __, 51
SHAW, Allen, 303, Allison, 303, Andrew, 303, Daniel, 185, David, 303, Duane, 185, Edward L., 372, Eliza Franklin, 277, Frona, 303, J.A., 41, Lesley, 303, Mary Virginia, 302, 303, Noble Ryan, 303, Sarah, 303, Trudy, 303, Tully, 303, Virginia, 303
SHAY, Pearl, 276
SHEARER, Cecil P., 289, Elizabeth, 182, 214
SHEAVER, Katherine, 144
SHEEHAN, Joseph, 326, Steven, 326
SHEET, __, 222
SHEETS, Barbara, 222, 303, Catherine, 303, Catherine Sue, 130, Daniel, 222, 303, Dwayne Lee, 130, Elizabeth, 222, 303, George, 303, Hannah, 222, 303, John, 303, Lewis Ray, 130, Marilyn Joan, 130, Nancy, 222, 303, Polly, 222, 303, Ronald, 130, Solomon, 222, 303 Susana, 303, Susanah, 222, Walter Eugene, 130
SHELBOURNE, __, 101
SHELBY, Drew, 314, Issac, 281, Minerva, 190, Minerva Evans, 281
SHELLEY, Carlton E., 372, David, 333, Ida, 228, Nancy, 333
SHELLY, Jessie, 65, Mary, 223, Mary Catherine, 360
SHELTON, Angela, 165, Carolyn, 303, Deann, 303, Debbie, 271, Dick, 271, Douglas, 271, Duane, 271, Gas Company, 14, George, 303, James D., 165, Jeff, 303, Jim, 165, Larry, 303, Leslie, 303, Lori, 303, Marabeth, 151, Margaret, 153, Martoma, 303, Mary, 294, Mike, 303, Natalie, 165, Nicholas, 165, Oral, 165, Polly, 294, Raymond, 303, Richard, 66, Robert, 131, 303, Ruth (Cox), 165, Sam, 359, Samantha, 359, Sharon Ann, 271, Sherri, 303, Steve, 303, Terry, 303, Tim, 303, Wilson, 294
SHEPARD, Eva, 339
SHEPHARD, Mary, 236
SHEPHERD, Pleasant, 115
SHEPPARD, (& Louis Plant), 87
SHERFEY, Bobbie Joe, 214, Darrin Lee, 214, Deanna Lyne, 214
SHERMAN, Anna Maria, 201, Faye, 153, W. Goddard, 49
SHERMER, Patricia C., 375
SHERRARAD, John, 232
SHERVEY, Harry, 31, William, 31, __, 42
SHERWOOD, Orinda, 326, Steven (Mrs.), 331
SHEWEY, Opal (Rhoads), 31
SHEWMAKER, Grace, 91
SHIELDS, John, 114
SHIGLEY, Margaret Lou, 139
SHILLINGS, Evelyn, 170, George Ross, 303, George Russell, 303, 170, James Ross, 303, Jim, 347, Ruth, 347, Ruth Marie, 90, Slim, 303, Virginia, 103, 170, 303
SHIPLEY, Robert, 53
SHIPMAN, Frank, 319, Nellie, 290, Sidney, 270
SHIPPEN, Rebecca, 204
SHIRAR, Amy (Holmes), 122, Angela, 317, Donna Lee, 317, Eliza Jane, 122, Jodi, 317, Robert, 317, Staci, 122
SHIREMAN, Richard, 372
SHIRLY, Ralph, 43
SHOAF, Arvilla, 350, Carl, 339, De Witt, 350, Elizabeth, 128, 341, Emma, 315, Mary, 170, Opal, 299, Pearl, 350, Roy, 80, Ura, 350
SHOBE, H.C., 374, 381, Henry, 374, Mary Elizabeth, 238
SHOCKEY, Barbara, 122, Francis M., 122, Jacob, 122, John, 122, John Aaron Christ., 122, John Christopher, 122, Marie, 122, Mary, 122, Nora, 122, Ralph, 122
SHOEMAKER, Catherine Eva, 361, Isabelle, 150, Mary, 90
SHOLTS, Margaret, 222
SHOOK, Addie, 331
SHORT, Lyle A., 303, Mary Irene, 286, Polly, 286
SHORTZ, April, 304, Lyle, 303, Richard, 304, William, 304, Wilma, 304, Wilma W., 303
SHOUB, 297
SHOUSE, Audrey F., 187
SHOWALTER, Marilyn J., 372
SHROUDT, Foster, 33
SHUBERT, Guy, 134
SHUCK, __, 22
SHUE, Anna, 57
SHUEY, T.J., 69
SHULAR, A.J., 64, Bob, 176, Brad, 176, Caroline, 176, Edith, 176, Richard, 176, Sara, 176
SHULER, John H., 377
SHULL, Wretha, 357
SHULTZ, C.E., 69, Linda, 54, Lyle, 72
SHUMAKER, Arthur, 219, Emma Irene, 304, Geraldine, 350, James Arthur, 304, Juanita Ellen, 304
SHURR, Charles, 110
SICKS, Helen Marie, 328, Nellie, 228
SIDENER, __, 342, Hallie, 43, Mabel, 301, Variety Store, 15
SIDNER, Eva, 336
SIEPLE, Benadine, 294
SIGLER, Arthur, 319
SIGMAN, Floyd Addison, 135, Ruby, 135
SILLS, Sharon, 54
SILVERS, Phil, 342
SIMISON, John (Dr.), 141
SIMM'S, Garage, 26
SIMMERMAN, Frederick, 222, __, 222
SIMMONS, Darcus, 291, E.D., 61, Jane, 127, L.W., 41, Marie, 266, Nellie, 380, Pamela, 127, Raymond, 127, Shirley, 158, 226, Ura, 262, Wendy, 136
SIMMS, A.B., 304, Aline, 305, Augustus Belmont, 304, Benjamin, 305, Benny, 305, Burwell, 235, 304, Charles, 235, 304, 305, Charles Augustus, 304, Charles Edward, 305, Dana, 255, Daniel, 235, 304, David, 304, Effie, 305, Eliza, 235, Elizabeth, 235, 304, Elizabeth Belle, 304, Emma, 235, 304, Enoch, 235, 304, Freeman, 305, George, 235, 304, 305, George W., 305, Gus, 304, Helen Frances, 304, Hubert, 305, Ida, 235, Ida Mae, 304, Jacob, 235, 304, James 235, 304, 305 Jesse, 235, 304, Jim, 255, John, 304, Judith, 305, Langthorn, 235, 304, Lenora Blanche, 304, Leo, 305, Lewis, 235, Lida, 304, Lindy Leland, 304, Louis, 304, Louis Alma, 304, Louis Brighty, 304, Lucy, 235, 304, Malinda, 305, Marcella Maxine, 304, Margaret, 304, Mary, 235, Mary E., 235, Mary Ellen, 304, Matthew Dan, 255, Matthew Daniel, 253, Matthew S., 255, Matthew Scott, 305, Nancy, 304, Phoebe J., 305, Presley, 235, 304, Presley, Jr., 235, 304, Pressley, 305, Rhoda, 304, Richard, 304, 305, Richard Jr., 235, 304, 305, Robert D., 253, Robert Dan, 255, Robert Dan, Jr., 255, Robert Daniel, 305, Robert Louis, 304, Rowen, 305, Sherman, 305, Tressa, 305, Virginia, 305, Wayne, 305, 365, William, 305, William Allen, 305, William H., 305
SIMPSON, Amy Renee, 306, Audra, 249, Austin, 305, 306, Austin Merle, 305, 193, Bert, 306, Bettie, 170, Bettie I., 375, Betty, 342,

Betty Lou, 106, Brad, 306, Brad Michael, 305, Brenda Lee, 152, Brenda Sue, 191, Catherine, 222, Charles, 222, 306 Charles E., 306, Dale, 306, Darrell, 106, 306, Darrell Ray, 306, Darren Ray, 306, Dave, 152, David, 249, Deanna, 306, Deanna Lou, 306, Don, 306, Doris, 88, 222, 306, Dwayne Michael, 306, Enid Lucille, 193, Esther Jane, 306, Florence Catherine, 306, Forrest, 306, Gary, 306, Gary Lee, 306, Gerald, 306, Gerald Lee, 305, 306, Grace, 305, Isaiah David, 152, James, 152, 306, Jeanette, 306, Joanna Lyn, 306, Joseph, T., 372, Karen, 306, Karen Sue, 306, Katie Leann, 306, Larry, Larry Joe, 306, Lillie Grace, 305, Lowell, 170, 306, Lucille, 305, 306, Malcolm, 249, 306, Malcom F., 170, Manna Blanch, 110, Margaret, 305, Margaret, 306, Max, 306, Michael, 306, Mildred, 152, Nancy, 119, Patti Jean, 305, Patty, 306, Peggy, 306, Peggy Sue, 305, Polly Ann, 305, Ray, 305, 306, Ray E., 305, Robin Lou, 306, Rodney Lee, 306, Ruby, 306, Sallie Lou, 193, 305, Sally, 131, 306, Sarah, 124, 209, Trevor, 191, Virginia, 306, Walter Dale, 170, __, (Dr.), 141

SIMS, Richard, 235

SINCLAIR, Lee, 16, 195; Patricia, 195

SINEX, Thomas, 49

SINGER, Charles, 307, Delila, 307, Delila A., 307, Dottie, 306, Hannah, 307, Hannah E., 307, Hugh Franklin, 111, 306, 306, J. Wesley, 306, 307, Jeptha, 307, John, 307, John C., 306, 307, Joseph, 307, Lena, 306, 307, Louise Dee, 111, Margaret, 307, Margaret Emza, 114, 307, Mary Ann, 307, Sarah, 307, Wesley, 306, 307, William Ellis, 306, 307

SIPES, Ina Ritchie, 257

SIPPLE, Harold, 230, Mary, 230, Virginia Marie, 230

SIPS, Caretta Harlan, 247

SITLER, James L., 372

SIZER, Irma, 266

SKAGGS, Sarah Ann, 307, William, 307

SKELTON, Keziah Elizabeth, 102

SKIMMERHORN, Druzilla, 181

SKINNER, Bill, 374, Clark, 49

SKYLES, Ella, 228, 229, 230

SLACK, Sarah, 105, 176

SLADAK, Steven, 131

SLADEK, Debra Jo, 243

SLATER, Ira, 307, James, 307, John, 307, Lena Marie, 281, Lois, 301, 307

SLATHS, John Henry, 197

SLAVENS, Irene, 191, Julia, 348

SLEEPER, Ethel, 103, Guy, 103

SMALE, Sarah, 338

SMALL, Effie, 308, Elam, 30, Eric S., 372, Gussie, 308, John, 307, Laura, 186, Lena, 308, Louisa, 307, 308, 352, Lula, 186, Nathan, 307, Sarah, 161, 307, Verona, 308

SMELTZER, Susanna, 174

SMILEY, Andrew, 29, Charles Byron, 100, 148, Janet Kay, 100, Jason Andrew, 100, Jennifer Hayes, 100, Lena, 271, Margaret Dean, 100, Robert, 148, Robert A., Jr., 148, Robert Allen, 100, Robert Allen, Jr., 100, Zola, 100, __, 42

SMITH, "Willie", 312, (Rev), 50, Abigail, 159, Ada J., 310, Alaric, 212, Albertis, 309, Alfred, 54, Alfred Gallatin, 312, Alias Mack, 102, Alice, 310, Alta, 130, Alva, 83, Alvin, 310, Amy Elizabeth, 156, Ann Mariah, 312, Anna, 212, 309, Anne, 313, Arabelle, 312, Arlene, 278, Artie, 308, Artie Lee, 308, Atwood, 191, Avis, 287, Barbara, 310, Bert, 309, Bessie, 147, 301, Betty, 157, Betty May, 309, Billy, 131, Bird, 310, Blanche, 312, Bonnie, 310, Bonnie Mae, 312, Brent, 289, Brice, 313, Britt Estelle, 313, Cabins, 112, Carl, 31, 43, 87, 309, 310, Carla, 312, Carol, 330, Carol Kay, 330, Carrie, 309, Catherine, 329, Catherine Suzanne, 350, Catherine Theresa, 361, Cedric, 311, Celia, 298, Charity, 308, Charles, 83, 208, Charles Edgar, 309, Charles Ernest, 308, Charles T., 309, Charles W., 310, Cinderella, 157, Cinderella, 166, Cinderella, 310, Clare, 277, Clarence, 131, Claude, 309, Clyde, 286, Clydie, 313, Cody, 277, Cora, 202, Cora Ellen, 287, Curtis, 311, Curtis Leroy, 311, Daniel, 310, 329, David, 131, David Wayne, 309, Dean Michell, 309, Deanna, 137, Deatra Maxine, 312, Debbie, 268, Deborah, 305, Del, 354, Delores Maxine, 166, Derda, 311, Dianna Lynn, 309, Dicie, 311, Donald, 309, Donals, 310, Donna, 54, Dora, 106, 166, 268, 311, Dora Mae, 309, Dorman, 310, Dorothy, 209, 309, Dorothy Elizabeth, 182, Duckworth Lumber, 315, Duffy, 212, E.D., 49, Earl B., 309, Earl William, 330, Earl William, Jr., 330, Ed, 211, 309, Edison, 260, Edith, 310, 313, Edith Cleo, 99, Edith Mae, 308, Effie, 85, Eileen, 83, Elizabeth, 157, 164, 309, 310, 311, Elizabeth Catherine, 157, Ellen, 310, Elsie, 310, Emily, 309, Emily Jane, 308, Emma, 310, Enoch, 308, 309, Ephraim, 308, Ernest, 112, Erthie Belle, 330, Estella, 244, Ester Pauline, 312, Eugene, 310, Evelyn, 310, Everett, 310, Flo, 234, Flora, 311, Florence, 175, 309, 317, Florence May, 310, Flossie Glen, 272, Franz, 85, Frona Lee, 209, Garcie, 208, Gary, 212, Geneva, 211, Geneva C., 309, George 309, 312, George F., 312, George Forrest, 309, George Henry, 308, George Keith, 313, George Riley, 182, Georgianna, 309, Gerald, 131, Gerald Eugene, 131, Geraldine, 204, 330, Geraldine M., 266, Gilbert Ray, 156, Glenn, 309, Grace, 43, 311, Gracie, 208, Grant, 313, Gregory, 311, Grover, 310, Grover O., 310, Grover O., Jr., 310, Guy, 309, 310, Gwen, 313, Hannah, 310, Harold, 268, Harriett, 309, 310, Harrold David, 131, Harry, 311, Harry D., 78, Harry O., 312, Harvey, 34, 298, 310, Helen, 309, Helen Elston, 6, Helen Lucille, 231, Henry, 43, 211, Henry R., 309, Herman, 310, Hezekiah, 49, Hiram, 102, 310, 356, Hubert, 309, Hulda May, 310, Ida, 312, Ina May, 309, Inez Marie, 153, Isabelle Odell, 311, Jack, 83, James, 310, 311, James G., 372, James R., 311, James Ross, 311, Jane, 310, Jane E., 310, Janette, 131, Jeffrey, 313, Jessica, 311, Jessie, 311, Joan, 309, Joe, 309, 310, 311, John, 157, 310, 311, 319, John (Capt.), 78, John H., 157, 166, 310, John Harvey, 310, John M., 310, John Martin, 310, John W., 309, Jonathan, 212, 313, Joseph, 54, 153, 290, 309, 310, 311, Joseph Lee, 311, Joseph Monroe, 309, Joseph Moxley, 311, Joyce, 231, Julia, 322, Karen Lou, 131, Karol, 131, Kate, 87, Kathryn Geneva, 87, 310, Katie, 276, 310, Keith, 108, 313, Kenneth, 311, Kenneth Lee, 131, Kimberly, 313, Kristy, 165, Kyrielle, 311, Lala, 277, Larry, 108, 313, Larry Wayne, 131, Laura, 80, 311, Lawrence A., 290, Lee, 108, 313, Leland, 309, Leland Carl, 309, Lenna, 83, Leon R., 372, Leonard West, 85, Lester, 311, Lewis S., 63, Lilly, 330, Linda 131, Linda Diane, 309, Lista, 310, Lloyd, 108, 313, Lois Joyce, 309, Lois Margery, 308, Lorella, 330, Lorenzo D., 49, Lorraine, 131, Louisa, 145, 309, Lucy Ann, 198, Lum, 309, Lydia, 355, Lydia Jane, 310, Lydia Mae, 310, M. 69, Maggie, 310, Mahala, 303, Mahlon Rhea, 312, Malcolm Curtis, 312, Mame, 203, Margaret, 356, Margaret Esther, 356, Marion, 78, Marjorie D., 310, Mark Alan, 309, Mark Herman, 312, Martha, 310, Martha Ann, 307, Mary, 157, 166, 167, 175, 180, 194, 309, 310, Mary Louise, 308, Mary A., 159, 180, Mary Ann, 80, 298, Mary Bessie, 211, Mary Catherine, 158, 159, 310, 333, 343, Mary Elizabeth, 286, Mary G., 31, Mary Isabelle, 85, Mary L., 310, Mary Lou, 278, Mary Louise, 327, Mary N., 289, Mary Rochell, 312, Matilda, 356, Melinda, 238, Michele Maxine, 309, Mildred, 310, Mildred L., 309, Myrtle, 43, Nancy, 289, Nancy Elizabeth, 198, Nathan Robert, 312, Nicole, 311, Nina, 78, Nona, 204, Nona J., 310, Nora, 212, Norma Jean, 131, 297, Ola Dell, 355, Olive, 309, Omer, 311, Omer Joseph, 311, Oneta Olive, 287, Opal, 299, 301, 309, 311, Oradean, 312, Oscar, 317, Oscar Douglas, 310, Patricia Ray, 275, Pattie Louise, 211, 309, Pauline, 313, Pearl, 309, Peter, 149, Phebe, 310, Phillip Wayne, 309, Prairie, 212, R.C., 69, Robert, 310, Rachel, 310, Ralph, 311, Ralph, (Rev), 270, Ralph C., 311, Randall E., 372, Regina, 311, Reuben, 180, 309, Rhoda, 313, Rich, 108, Richard, 131, 309, Richard Allen, 308, Richard D. III, 350, 361, Richard D., Jr., 350, 361, Richard Foster, 308, Richard H. "Red", 301, Rick, 313, Robert, 204, 309, 310, Robert C., 255, 277, Robert C. II, 277, Robert R., 372, Robert William, 312, Robin, 131, Romania, 203, Roy, 311, Roy Lee, 309, Ruby, 309, Russell, 83, 157, Ruth Edna, 119, 318, Salome, 313, Sam, 131, Sam G., (Rev), 286, Samuel, 175, 312, Sandy, 131, Sarah, 114, 145, 182, 325, Sarah "Hazel", 88, Sarah Elizabeth, 312, Sarah Hazel, 325, Sig, 309, Sonny, 277, Spencer, 152, Stella, 38, Stella I., 260, Stella Isobel, 260, Stephanie, 268, Steve, 310, Susanna, 324, Suzanne Catherine, 361, Taylor Wade, 290, Terry Lee, 309, Thelma, 112, Thelma Jean, 310, Theresa, 312, Thomas, 99, Thomas Cleo, 121, Tricia, 350, 361, Troy, 313, Vada Ethel, 171, Velda, 311, Viola, 309, Violetta, 85, 359, Vivian Lorene, 312, Wallis Earl, 308, Wendall Glenn, 157, Whitney Rae, 290, Wilbur, 311, Wilbur A., 310, William, 80, 153, 226, 308, 336, William Henry, 308, William K., 310, William Morris, 312, William Owen, 339, Wilma, 330, Winton Carlyle, 308, __, 17, __, 42

SMITH'S WELDING, 26

SMOCK, Kristin, 128

SMULLEN, Elizabeth, 261, Julia, 261, Lauden, 261

SNDER, Myrtle, 335

SNELL, Judyth, 352

SNELLENBARGER, Doris L., 375, Oil Company, 16, Raymond N., 375

SNELLENBARGER'S GARAGE, 16

SNELLING, June May, 139

SNEPP, Leona, 302

SNIVELY, Ed, 372

SNODGRASS, Augusta, 74, Larry, 131, Thadore, 74, William, 29

SNOOK, Mary, 295

SNOUWAERT, Wayne, 375

SNYDER, A.D., 374, Aaron C., 313, Andrew Jackson, 184, Austin "Doll", 247, Benjamin, 313, Benton, 184, Bessie, 247, Carl, 240, Carrie, 247, Carrie Bell, 184, Daniel, 313, David, 313, Deanna J., 313, Drugs, 14, Earli, 278, Edith, 311, Elizabeth, 313, Ella G., 313, Francis L., George, 247, 221, Jacob, 313, Jacob A., 313, James A., 313, Janet Maude, 221, Jerry D., 313, John, 28, 313, John M., 313, John Willard, 313, Julia, 313, Karen, 312, Kristie, 278, Lois, 356, Mabel Lee, 221, Mark, 278, Martha, 313, Martha R., 313, Mary A., 313, Mary C., 313, Michael, 67, Opal, 143, Redden, 204, Redden B., 200, 313, Redden C., 313, Robert, 148, Robert Aaron, 313, Robert L., 58, Robert L., 313, Salome, 115, Salone, 313, Samuel, 307, Samuel C., 313, Samuel Clark, 143, Sarah, 313, Susan, 204, Susan E., 313, William J., 313, Mrs., 204

SOARDS, Nancy, 329

SOCOLOWSKI, Jean, 85, 146

SOCTT, Anna, 305, Edgar Bowzer, 290

SOLLARS, Hattie M., 320

SOMERVILLE, Harry, 286, John, 285, Sarah Margaret, 285

SOMMER, Howard A., 249, __, 128

SOMMERS, Julian, 174, Karen, 156

SOMMERVILLE, Bobbi, 113, Bobbi Jo, 259, 313, Brenda, 259, 260, 313, Kathy, 113, Kathy Jo, 259, 313, Louis, 313, Richard, 259, Richard Lewis, 313, Sabrina, 113, Sabrina Lynn, 259, 313, Virginia, 313

SONGER, Hazel, 122, Hazel Vae, 132

SORRELS, Bessie, 279, Dwight, 279, Roy, 279, Tami, 246, Terri, 246

SOSBE, Hazel Florence, 99, Robert (Mrs.), 310

SOUTER, Rendy, 283

SOUTH, Ella, 122

SOWDERS, Dana, 372, Pauline, 106, Daniel Babe, 203, David Russell, 203, Edna, 267, Edna L., 321, Ella, 267, Harriet, 303, Joseph, 267, Kedric Lee, 203, Kedrie Leon, 203, Lucinda Lou, 203, Marilyn, 203

SPANGLER, Charlotte, 139, Eugene, 140, Eva Maria, 219

SPARGER, Easter, 106, Merle, 71, 287

SPARKS, __, 21, Alan, 74, Alvin, 314, Amanda, 167, Bonnie Clair, 314, Charles Richard, 314, Claude Richard, 314, Darrell David, 314, Darrell Dean, 314, George, 314, Grace Mae, 331, Juanita, 164, Judith Ann, 314, Mamie, 232, Mary, 125, Oscar, 331, Phillip Allen, 314, Robert, 66, Sallie Lee, 289, Sandra Lee, 314, Sue Ellen, 314

SPARROW, Beth Renaae, 214, Donald Everett, Jr., 214, Justin Michael, 214

SPAULDING, Charles T., 52, Flora, 113, Flossa, 52, George A., 52, Mary, 52, William, 113

SPAUN, Laura, 174

SPEED, __, 6

SPENCER, "B", 93, "B" Shirley, 93, Alberta Ellen, 84, Bertha, 314, C.W., 314, 315, Carol, 315, Carrie, 314, Cecil Pearl, 262, Charlene, 315, Charles, 314, 315, Chester, 84, Clyde Harvey, Jr., 262, Clyde Harvey, Sr., 262, Dallas, 315, Donn, 314, Dorothy, 315, Duane, 315, Earl, 93, Earl Ellis, 92, Ermil Maryla, (Lilly), 315, Essie, 315, Ethella (Baringer), 137, Fern, 314, Frances, 314, George Andrew, 314, George McCormick, 314, George William, 314, Harold, 314, Jacob, 115, Jane, 262, 314, Janet, 262, Jean, 31, Jill, 242, Judy, 314, Lowell, 314, 315, Mae, 315, Margaret, 93, Margaret Lee, 314, Martha Jo, 315, Mary Lee, 314, Mildred, 226, Nancy, 314, Norma, 262, Norma Jean, 348, Parke, 314, 315, Patricia, 262, Ray, 314, Rebecca Lynn, 262, Rose Jean, 92, Ruth Laura, 293, Susanna, 84, Vera, 314, Wayne, 226, Wilbur, 324, Wilbur A., 314, William, 315, Wilma, 315, Winnie, 295, __, 92

SPERRY, George, 45, Henry, 190, Isaac, 40, Isaac F., 29, Maud (Moss), 31, Rebecca, 190

SPICER, S. Lavina, 338, Sue, 78

SPINDLER, Myrtle, 145

SPINKS, James, 63

SPIVEY, John, 163, Susan Ethyl, 163

SPOHR, Mary E., 240, Nina, 66, __, 42

SPONSTER, Glen, 41

SPORE, Anna, 360

SPRAGG, Clifford, 79, Everett, 315, Jeffrey, 315, Joann, 315, 372, Lucille, 171, Mike, 315, Paul, 315, Ruby, 79, Verna, 171

SPRAGUE, Dorinda, 282

SPRAY, (Rev), 50, Frances, 168

SPREEN, Esther, 115

SPRINGER, Jean, 31, Ola, 303

SPROW, William J., 376

SPURGEON, Charles Ray, 315, Ermil M., 315, George D., 375, John Murray, 315, Joseph T., 315, Joseph Thomas, 315, Judy K., 36, 315, Julie Kay, 315, Lilly, 315, Paul Robert, 315, Roger, 315, Roger G., 315, Roger G., Sr., 36, 144, 315, Roger Glen, 315, Roger Glen, Jr., 315, William H., 315

STACKHOUSE, Sarah Jane, 341

STACY, John, 56

STADLER, Armilda, 177, James, 36, Patti J., 133

STAFFORD, Elizabeth, 93, George, 68, George W., 49, George W., 63, John M., 63, Odis, 32, William A., 32

STAGGS, Angela Sue, 122, Barbara, 122, Charlotte, 122, Earl Lee, 122, Eric Wayne, 122, Ryan Matthew, 122, Sam, 360, Sandra, 122

STAHLHUT, Mable, 250

STALKER, Ratie, 181

STALNAKER, Leonard A., 37

STAMP, Harry, 336

STAMPER, Todd, 203, __, 82

STANFORD, Arleen, 282, Dale, 282, Daryl, 282, Dennis, 282

STANFORTH, (Rev.), 159, C.B., 137

STANLEY, John, 130, 341, Pauline, 275

STANTON, Catherine E., 162, Elizabeth, 268, Odessa, 173, Phebe, 268, Sarah, 268, William, 268

STAPP, Lucy, 350, 351

STARK, Heather, 212, Myrtle, 99, Polly Ann, 115, Richard Ora, 372

STARKE, John Henry, 197, Charlotte, 280, Clytie, 280, Frank, 280, Goldie, 280, Heather, 212, Ida, 280, James, 280, Laura Dean, 280, Lee, 280, Lela, 280, Letha, 280, Molly, 280

STARNES, Adrian, 170, Arnett Ivan, 227, Bobby, 346, Brian Lee, 346, Cameron, 170, Eldon, 12, Etta, 227, Eva, 227, Frederick, Sr., 291, Gregory, 289, Gregory Dean, 346, Ioma, 227, Ivan, 227, James Robert, 346, Jane, 290, 291, John Adam Staring, 291, Joseph, Sr., 291, Jude, 13, Leonard, 291, Linda Dianne, 346, Mary, 227, Mary Jane, 346, Paula Kay, 346, Pauline, 227, Peggy, 42, Robin, 170, 289, Thelma, 227, Verne, 12, Virgie, 227

STARNS, Lois, 306

STATTLER, Genevieve, 249

STATTS, Ruth, 121

STOCKDALE, Virginia Kay, 318

STEELE, Betty, 136, Betty Ellyn, 147, Clarence Dwight, 316, Daniel A., 372, Daniel Allen, 316, David, 316, Delores, 346, Dorothy, 316, Douglas Dwight, 316, Edward, 109, Elizabeth, 117, 136, Elizabeth Ann, 258, 316, Elmer, 335, George Henry, 316, 357, George Henry, 316, Hiram, 316, Isabelle, 109, J&D Tree Service, 15, James, 316, Janet Kay, 100, 148, Jessie N., 357, Lisa C., 372, Mallory, 110, Margaret, 316, Martha, 269, Mary, 269, Mary Alice, 316, 357, Mary Alice "Mayme", 98, Mary Louise, 316, Mayme, 316, 357, Melissa, 117, Melissa Kay, 258, 316, Ralph, 64, Ralph William "Bill" 316, Robert, 316, 357, Robert L., 316, Robert William, 258, 316, Sandra, 117, Sandra Kay, 258, Shirley Mae, 316, Stephen, 110, Sydney, 110, T.C., 10, Thomas, 316, Van Orman, Jr., 357, Van Orman, Sr., 357, Wayne, E., 375, Wray Morgan, 357

STEEN, May Jane, 150

STEFFEL, Rose, 147

STEIGER, Eleanor, 297

STEINBAUGH, James, 350, Jewell, 350, Sarah, 350

STEINER, Alice, 118, Amy, 118, Ann, 118, Carl, 118, Ethel, 187, Jane, 118

STEINHAUSER, Lena, 227

STEMICK, Pat, 239

STENSON, Ralph, 131

STEPHENS, Alice Mae, 130, Apiaries, 16, Arabella R., 130, Bernice, 343, Bess, 306, Charles Montell, 130, Cincinatus, 130, Clara, 306, Clarence, 255, 317, David Marion, 130, Dottie, 306, Dottie Margaret, 111, 306, 307, Edith Faye, 130, Edward, 282, 306, Edward E., 317, Eliza D., 130, Ella, 130, Ellen, 130, Elnora, 130, Ert, 306, Fanny H., 130, Fern Alice, 306, Helen, 317, Iva Myrtle, 317, J., (Rev.), 68, J.B., 130, James Edward, 293, Jennifer, 351, John H., 306, John T., 306, John W., 130, Joseph, 68, Joseph, 130, Joseph G., 63, Larry, 351, Leroy, 130, Lina, 306, Lorena, 152, Lou Estell, 130, Mary E., 130, Mary Ellen, 255, Mary Polly, 293, Minnie E., 306, Natt, 130, Nora E., 329, Olive Virgil, 130, Ottis, 306, Pansy, E., 306, Pearl, 130, Pearl Marie, 130, 262, Ruth Jane, 191, 293, 346, Sarah E., 130, Virginia G., 130, Walter, 152, Will, 306, William Edward, 317

STEPHENSON, Archibald, 271, Indiana, 271, Rebeccah, 270, 271

STEPHENS, Luriaine, 152

STERLING, Donna, 195
STETLER, Dave, 258
STEVENS, A.R., (Steve), 316, Aaron, 317, Alexander, 317, Andrew, 317, August Marie, 317, Barbara May, 209, 317, Bill, 316, 317, Curtis, 317, Cynthia, 317, Des, 241, Dianna, 317, Dick, 317, Doris Swank, 128, Dustan, 317, George, 268, Gerry, 316, Janet, 317, John Russell, 268, 317, Joy, 131, Laura, 317, Leoma, 316, Marie, 127, Marion, 128, Mark, 317, Martha Jean, 121, Mary, 268, Mary Elizabeth, 317, Mary Lavona, 317, Mattie, 317, Mollie, 352, Orville, 316, Pat, 317, Raymond, 128, Raymond Oliver, 317, Russell, 209, Samuel, 317, Samuel T., 310, Traci, 317, Wilbur, 317
STEVENSON, Deanna, 263, Joe, 278, Luke, 278, Todd, 263, Tom, 263
STEVER, Elizabeth, 287
STEWARD, Amellia, 161, Charles, 172, David L., 372, Joseph, 172, Laurie, 161, Margaret, 161, Martha, 172, Mary, 172, Samuel, 172, William, 172
STEWART, Aaron, 104, Alan, 67, Beatrice, 233, Beryl, 233, Blackjack, 318, Buford, 233, Byron, 233, Cecil Alonzo, 317, Cecil Pearl, 262, Charles, 285, Charles Michael, 317, Charlie, 22, 317, Claire, 339, Donna Lee, 317, Effie May, 317, Evelyn, 233, Fred, 34, George, 339, Gertrude, 317, Jessie, 67, 175, Jim, 210, Jo, 317, Jo Darlene, 317, Karen Kay, 317, Laurence L., 67, Mary, 84, Mary Ellen, 253, 255, 317, Michael, 317, Mike, 317, Nancy Charlene, 317, Orpha, 131, Peggy Roxanne, 317, Rebecca, 317, Sam, 126, Vivian, 317, Walter, 233, William, 233, 317, 318,
STIBBINS, Elizabeth, 334
STIEFEL, Adam, 95, Adam, II, 95, Eve, 95, Jacob, 95
STILWELL, Alice, 112, Andy, 13
STINE, Martin, 115
STINER, Ann Eliza, 123
STINGLEY, Virginia Catherine, 110
STINNETTE, Orrell Ruth, 185
STINSON, Carolyn, 151, Donald, 151, Herston, 151, Kendra, 151, Ronald, 151, Teresa, 151, Vester 151
STITT, James, 108
STOCKDALE, Arthur, 318, Charles, 318, Chris, 318, Craig, 231, Cynthia, 318, Eleanor, 318, Elizabeth, 318, Emily E., 318, Fannie, 318, Fred, 54, George Bishop, 318, Guy, 318, James, 318, James F., 318, James Jefferson, 318, James R., 119, 318, Jennie, 318, John, 318, John B., 318, John F., 318, John Francis, 318, Karen, 318, Mark, 318, Mary, 318, Mary Ann, 318, Mary Jane, 318, Max, 318, Paul, 318, Ralph, 318, Rex, 318, Sophia, 54, Vereta June, 118, Verna, 318, Verta, 118, William, 318, Winifred L., 119
STODDARD, Jane M., 19, 162
STOHRER, Andrew William, 262, Emily Louise, 262, Fred W., 262, Michael Denton, 262
STOKES, Catherine, 314
STOKESBERRY, W. Edward, 51
STONE, Carol, 54, Dick, 54, Elizabeth, 209, Harry, 319, James H., 209, Princess, 327, Rebecca, 209, Sol, 327, Solomon, 357, Virgil, 319, William, 357, __, 54
STONE'S UPHOLSTERY, 16
STONEBRAKER, __, 21, Betty, 79, Catharine, 166, Catherine, 167, 168, 187, Christina, 167, 310, 329, David, 291, Emma Jane, 240, Helen Marie, 273, Homer, 16, James, 273, John, 290, John Dietrick, 167, Louise, 226, Lucinda, 305, Marguerite, 359, Mary, 342, Mary Ann, 342, Rebecca J., 215, Sabastian, 167, 343, Samantha, 152, Sarah Ellen, 329, Sebastian, 159, Susannah, 159, 291
STONECIPHER, Barbara, 89, Cecil, 89, David, 221, Donald, 221, Hildreth, 127, Joanne, 221, Patricia, 221, Sallie, 43, Vicki, 221
STONER, Mariah, 100, Susanna, 266
STOOKEY, Abraham, 110, 135, Amy, 110, Catherine, 82, 110, 135, Delilah, 110, Eve, 135, Isaac, 110, Magdalene, 110, Mahalah, 110
STORMS, Evelyn Nina, 290, Patsy, 372
STOUFFER, George E., 232, Geraldine, 232
STOUT, Albert R., 319, Angeline F., 281, Benjamin, 318, Benjamin Franklin, 319, Bill, 318, 338, Bud, 318, Charles, 319, Clarence, 318, Dode, 338, Edgar N., 286, Elisha, 318, Elizabeth, 318, 319, Emaline, 361, Ernest, 43, Esther, 318, Ethel M., 286, Fern F., 286, Fred, 318, George W., 319, Harry T., 170, Harry T., (Dr), 170, Jacomiah, 318, James, 319, James B., 170, Joel, 318, John Albert, 318, John N., 318, John W., 318, Lizzie, 338, Lucy Ann, 170, Margaret, 170, Margaret E., 318, Mariah, 318, Marsha, 54, Mary Ann, 318, Mary Hazel, 109, 318, Maude Ruth, 318, Merle Lee, 318, Minnie Malisa, 319, Ora, 338, Paul M., 170, Pau messmore, 170, Reuben, 181, Richard, 164, Russell, 263, Russell Charles, 318, S. Lavina, 338, Sarah Elizabeth, 318, Susan, 281, 318, Thomas, 318, 319, Valentine, 318, Virgil Leroy, 318, William Everett, 109, 318, 319, Wilson, 318
STOVALL, Thomas, 40, Thomas L., 63
STOVER, Elizabeth, 87, George, 201, George W., 319, Margaret, 81, 102, Roy, 15, Roy E., 327, Sarah, 201, Viola, 326, Zora E., 326, __, 43
STOWERS, Mark, 263, Max, 263, Nola, 263
STRAFFORD, Odis, 32
STRAHLENDORF, J.B., 320
STRAIN, James A., 118
STRANAHAN, Mary, 175
STRANGE, Catherine, 120
STRANGER, Dianna, 262
STRASSBURGER, Clara, 78, William, 78
STRATTON, Susan, 302
STRAUB, Glenn, 122
STRAUGHAN, J.W., (Dr), 82, K.K., 365, K.K., (Dr.), 121, Kent K., 44, 121, Maude India, 121
STRAW, Robert, 365
STREETER, Benjamin, 158, Sarah, 158, Sarah H., 158
STREICH, Helen, 78
STRESE, Waltraut, 336
STRICKLER, Esther, 33, Ralph, 33
STRINGFELLOW, George, 336, Hepsey, 336
STRODE, Florence Edith, 319, Mary Elizabeth, 319, Melvinia, 211, William Hulet, 319
STRONG, Alexander, 249, Margaret, 174, Rodeny E., 372, Ruby A., 248, William, 192
STROUD, John, 225
STRUNCE, William, 63
STRYKER, Phillip, 187, Sharon, 187
STUART, Eleanor, 179, 180
STUBBINS, Elizabeth, 334, Fred, 44, Sarah Ann, 148
STUCK, Alice, 197
STUCKER, Margaret, 281, Samuel, 281
STUCKEY, David, 326, Dean V., 63, Janet, 326, Jeffrey, 326, Kimberly Ann, 326, Randall, 326
STULL, Aquilla, 319, Benjamin Franklin, 319, Bud, 319, Byron "Penny", 319, Charloty, 319, Clara, 319, Claudia, 319, David, 320, Emily Jane, 319, Eva, 319, Evelyn, 320, Forest "Pat", 319, George W., Jr., 319, George F., 319, George Washington, 319, Guy, 320, Harry, 319, 320, Helen, 319, Homer Harry, 319, James, 319, John F., 319, John W., 288, 319, Lala, 320, Lawson, 319, Leon, 320, Lillie, 319, Linda, 320, Lucile, 319, Lucinda, 319, Margaret, 319, Marian Isabelle, 319, Marion Earl, 319, Martha, 320, Mary Ellen, 319, Mary Mae, 319, Max, 320, Morris, 319, Moses Edward, 319, Nancy, 319, Rachel, 319, Sarah Belle, 288, 319, Sissy, 319, Stephen, 320, Virgil "Bode", 319, Wildo, 320, William, 319
STULL'S BODY SHOP, 15
STULTZ, Arthur R., 320, Bubba, 320, Casey, 320, Debbie, 320, Dianne, 320, Kelley, 320, Nancy, 320, Nancy Louise, 342, Ora, 192, Patricia, 187, Perry, 192, Richard, 320, Richard, Jr., 320, Rosemary, 320, Seth, 320
STULZ, Katherine, 232
STUMP, Ann, 320, George, 320, Henry, 320, John, 320, Margaret, 320, Margaret Anna, 347, Martha, 320, Martha Ann, 268, Mary, 268, Mary E., 317, Maryland, 268, Patsy, 320, Paul, 24, 320, Perry, 320, William, 320
STURBA, Cyd, 95
STURGEON, Barbara, 357
STWALLEY, Belle, 261
SUIT, James F., 125
SUITOR, Edward Davis, 286, Minnie Grace, 286
SUITORS, Everett, 116
SULC, Amy Francis, 214
SULLIVAN, Emily, 286, Michelle, 336, Nat, 352, Norma Jean, 79
SUMMERS, Collyn Burtus, 293, Dallas Burton, 293, Dallas Lester, 293, Ella, 227, 228, 320, Emma, 320, Gregory, 330, Harvey, 230, 320, I. Jo, 149, 150, 194, 258, 294, James, 320, 330, Laura Elizabeth Ann, 294, Mary, 230, Matthias Frantz, 320, Michael W., 294, Oscar, 330, Robert, 320, Rosette, 330, Zelema, 330
SUMMIT, Susan, 358, Susanna, 358
SUMMY, Peter, 360
SUMNER, Faunce, 186, Patricia, 170, Sarah E., 186
SUMMER, Ella, 230
SURBER, David, 353, Edward, 305, Mary M., 251, Minnie, 305, Scott, 353, Tressa, 305
SURFACE, Abe, 41, 148, Ansel, 270, Carolyn A., 313, Carolyn Ann, 148, George, 41, Hannah, 144, Henry, 270, Ira, 270, James, 270, Joyce, 347, Lawrence, 31, Lee, 307, Marilyn Sue, 148, Miriam, 313, Ruby, 121, Sarah, 334, Velma, 209, Wayne, 347, William, 148, William A., 313
SURFICE, Wiley, 153
SUTHERLAND, Jeff, 252, P.J., 252, Pam, 252, Tyler, 252
SUTHERLIN, __, 22, Bert, 267, Bertram Beverly, 267, Carolyn Sue, 346, Carrie, 267, Ed, 267, Edward Laverne, 267, Evadna, 267, Ivyl Pearl, 267, Juanita Irene, 267, Laverne Edward, 267, Phyllis, 355, Rex, 346, Robert, 267, Sue, 267, Susan Kay, 267, Tamara Sue, 346, Terri Roxanne, 346, Timothy Wayne, 346, Timothy Wayne, 346, Tory Brandon, 346, Trent, 346, Vern, 267, William Henry, 267
SUTTON, David, 353, Francis, 301, Gary, 254, Lucinda, 353, Lydia, 232, 314, Margaret, 123, 280, Maud, 298, Mavorine, 297, Susan, 343, Thomas, 314
SWAIM, Deborah, 268, Eunice, 268, Lydia, 279
SWAN, Kathryn, 103, Richard, 103, Sharon, 103, Sue, 103
SWANEY, Naomi, 256, Wilma, 315
SWANK, "Re", 320, Abigail, 208, Alfred Marcellus, 320, Amanda, 321, Andrew, 208, Anna Vincent, 321, Belinda, 208, Benjamin, 208, 265, 321, Bertha Faye, 320, Carolyn K., 375, Catherine, 321, Clyde, 208, Daniel P., 321, Doris, 128, 317, Edith, 143, Effie, 265, Eliza, 208, Elizabeth, 366, Ellen, 265, Elmer, 208, Emma Lee, 320, George, 319, George Grover, 320, Grace, 54, Harry, 208, 320, Ira Wilson, 320, Jack, 117, Jacob, 321, James, 173, 208, 320, James W., 320, 321, John, 117, 321, Joseph, 208, Josiah, 208, Lee, 320, Loretta, 173, Loretta Ellen, 320, Lucy, 321, Margaret, 80, 320, Margaret Ross, 321, Mary, 208, Mary C., 321, Mary E., 321, Mary Ellen, 321, Mary Jane, 348, Michael, 80, Minnie, 173, 199, Minnie Florence, 173, 320, Myrta, 213, Nancy, 208, Nancy Ann, 320, Paul, 16, Paul, Jr., 117, Pauline, 117, Peggy, 336, Permelia, 321, Phillip, 173, 321, Pollie Ann, 321, Polly Ann, 320, President Hall, 80, Ralph K., 375, Reuben, 65, Rita, 321, Robert, 321, Sarah, 208, Sarah Ethelyn, 265, Susan, 80, 208, 230, Susan Allhands, 321, Washington, 208, William, 208, William Jasper, 321, Wilson, 321
SWARAT, Cleo, 54
SWARD, Tammy Gail, 283
SWARTHOUT, Ralph, 72
SWARTZ, Ted, 350, Ura, 350
SWATZER, Sarah A., 258
SWAZZE, Cecile, 356
SWEARINGEN, Albert, 335, Alice, 335, Charles, 335, Florence, 335, 339, Francis Marion, 335, Harry, 335, Herbert, 69, Hugh, 335, Ida, 335, James, 335, Jennie, 335, John, 335, Joseph, 335, Laura, 335, Margaret, 335, Marmaduke, 335, Mary, 335, William, 335
SWEET, Dan, 128, Dana, 113, Dana Lee Ann, 128, Kevin, 113, Kevin Daniel, 128
SWEETZER, Abbey, 183
SWETMAN, Iris Elizabeth, 298
SWICK, Amanda R., 234, Barbara N., 234, Brian Lee, 234, Daryl Wayne, 234, Joanie K., 234, Joseph Michael, 234, Martha Kay, 234, Marvin Lee, 234, Monica Sue, 234, Sarah E., 234
SWINDLER, Fern, 243, Pauline, 43, Sallie, 52, William J., 52
SWINFORD, Barbara, 54, Thomas, 54, Tom, 54
SWINNEY, David, 131, Eva Marie, 131, Gail, 131, Olin, 131, Phyllis Joan, 131
SWISHER, Alice, 239, Betsy, 106, Jesse Joan, 163, Michael, 106
SWITZER, Andrew Jackson, 273, Charles, 43, Ethel V., 296, Eulalia, 164, G.W., 64, George W., 49, 65, Georgia, 131, Gleyre, 71, Jakey, 273, Jakey A., 273, Jessie M., 273, Jessie Marie, 273, John, 310, Mary Jane, 273, Molly, 273, Virginia, 265
SWOVELAND, Betty Bradley, 201
SYMMES AND WILLIAMS ELECTRIC, 258
SYMMES, Aileen, 321, Burrell, 305, Clyde D., 321, Daniel T., 321, Francis Marion (Dr.), 321, Frank A., 321, LuAnne, 284, 285, Ruth, 321, Samuel Dunn, 321, William L., 285, William V., 321
SYMPSON, James H., 306
THOMPSON, Laura, 347
TAGGART, Alvin, 270, Elmer, 270, Emma, 270, Mayme, 270, William, 270
TAGUE, Grace, 142, James H., 372, John, 251, Ruby, 145, Thomas Martin, 142, Thomas Morton, 149, Velma, 149, Walter Caswell, 148, 149, Wanetah, 251
TALBERT, Mary Gardner, 268, Miriam, 268, Richard Bull, 268, William, 268
TALBOT, Martha, 320, Patsy, 320
TALBOTT, May, 43
TALMADGE, Naomi, 141, Roger Phelps, 295
TANDY, Bob, 21, Bob J., 375
TANKERSLEY, Louise Evelyn, 194
TANNENBAUM, Max, 7, Sol, 370, 376
TANNER, Gusta, 308, Lavinia, 329
TAPP, Emma, 162, Hallie, 43, 99, Harry, 99, 209, Jennie, 43, 99, John, 44, 99, McKinley, 99, Rosa Bradley, 99, Ruth, 99
TARKINGTON, Booth, 147, 221, Martha, 147
TARLETON, Col., 219
TATE, Joseph, 213, Kate, 284, Katie, 285, Nancy Belle, 208, 213
TAYLOR, __, 22, Albert, 224, Angela Rene, 84, Anna, 309, 350, Barbara, 4, 92, 280, 303, 321, 322, Barbara (House), 22, Barbara J., 35, Bennett, 302, Bessie, 323, Betty, 12, 236, 267, 288, 321, Blair, 6, Blanche Gertrude, 189, Bob, 75, C. Howard, 49, Charles, 322, 323, Charles W., 322, Dale, 372, Daniel, 267, 322, Daniel L., 322, Daniel Lyn, 321, David L., 322, David Lee, 322, De Ella, 323, Dorothy, 267, Earl Amel, 84, Edgar, 373, Edna, 12, 267, Edna L., 321, Elizabeth, 128, Genevieve, 267, Harold, 12, 323, Harold Alfred, 322, Harold B., 323, Henrietta, 323, Homer M., 352, Iva, 310, James W., 289, Jamie, 86, Joanne, 131, John, 118, Juanita, 267, Juanita Irene, 267, Judy Lynn, 283, Kelly Sue, 321, Laura, 322, Lida, 352, Linda Lou, 84, Mary Ellen, 322, 323, Mary Louise, 352, Mary Lucinda, 248, Melissa Kay, 251, Michael R., 372, Mildred R., 323, Myrtle, 323, Myrtle Ellen, 322, Nancy, 118, 267, 323, Nancy Lee, 289, Nina Rose, 180, Pamela L., 375, Patricia, 289, Pattie, 309, Richard, 280, 321, 322, Roger William, 289, Roy B., 267, 321, Ruth, 53, 323, Sallie, 289, Sally, 322, Sally Jo, 280, Sam, 79, Sylvia Blanche, 357, Theresa Ann, 84, Thomas L., 372, Vincent, 323, W.B., 41, Walter, 323, Walter C., 322, Walter Clarence, 322, Weltha Louise, 322, Wendy, 136, William, 353, William D., 34
TAYLOR'S, Grocery, 13
TEAGUE, JoAnn, 285, Kenneth, 26
TEETER, Ellen Fesler, 323, Ellen Flesher, 294, John, 291, Mary Ellen, 294, William, 294, 323
TELFORD, Nancy, 182, 183
TEMPLE, John, 293, Mary, 191, 293, Shirley, 14
TEMPLETON, Mary, 152
TERRALL, Emma, 135
TERRY, Ada Blanche, 323, Arta May, 323, Carol, 44, Charles, 282, Charles A., 43, Charles Agustus, 323, Charlie, 323, Donald Norman, 323, Edna, 323, Elva Clyde Sanders, 294, Elva Sanders Friend, 323, Harmon, 323, Jesse Edgar, 294, 323, Leslie, 71, Lottie Isabell, 323, Mary Ellen, 323, Mary Ellen Teeter, 294, Mildred, 323, Nelly, 294, Ralph Waldo, 323, Roy Theodore, 323, Ruby Hester, 323, Ruth, 223, Susan, 323, Tessora Hortense, 323, Thomas, 40, 372, Thomas B., 29, Thomas Bowyer, 294, 323, Thomas Vorhees, 323, Thomas Winter, 323, Virginia Ethel, 323
TETER, Barbara, 302, Eber, 297, Edith, 297
TETERH, John, 291
THARP, Arta May, 323, Elizabeth, 327, Fanny, 99, Frances, 229, Glen, 99, Iva, 99, James, 99, James B., 43, Ray, 99, Sherman, 99, Wallace, 58, Zena, 99
THATCHER, Lydia, 354, Lydia "Amy", 353
THAYER, Gail, 323, Helen, 323, 336, Lona, 323, Marilyn, 323, Marta, 323, Otis, 323, Otis V., 375, Robert M., 375, Roberta, 336, Tim, 323
THAYER'S, Service Station, 16
THOMAS, Abraham, 324, Abrim, 324, Adam, 74, Albert D., 188, Alice, 110, Alvie, 246, Anna, 240, 324, 333, Anson, 324, Anson D., 323, Audrey, 333, Byron, 333, Candice, 99, Carlton, 276, Carolyn, 324, Charles, 99, 324, Chester, 174, Clifford William, 324, Clint, 276, Craig Aaron, 324, Cynthia Lynne, 262, Darla Sue, 324, Delores Jean, 324, Dexter, 282, Dion Lee, 324, Dorinda, 85, Edith L., 157, Edna, 323, Edna Bell, 323, Edna Belle, 282, Edward, 324, Eliza, 169, Elizabeth, 67, 323, 324, Ellen, 191, Ezra, 74, 323, Frank, 276, Funeral Home, 130, 377, George A., 323, George Everett, 282, Guy, 324, Heather Jill, 324, Helen, 188, 324, Henry Clay, 324, Herschel, 276, Hubert, 324, Inetta, 276, J.W., 98, James Darren, 324, James Hubert, 324, Janet, 54, Jeremy Hubert, 324, Jessie, 232, Jody Wayne, 324, John, 377, John Brian, 324, John Christopher, 324, John D., 377, John Joel, 324, John Lewis, 282, John M., 324, John Raymond, 324, John William, 324, Josephine, 6, Josephine Tuttle, 366, Kathryne, 276, Kelsey, 276, Kelsey Leland, 333, Kent, 324, Larry, 333, Larry Wayne, 324, Leo G., 262, Leonard Clay, 324, Levi, 324, Lori Ann, 324, Ludlow, 324, Lydia, 167, Mable, 276, Margaret, 86, 301, Margaret Kay, 333, Martha Evelyn, 276, Mary, 324, Matthew James, 324, Maurene, 377, Merle, 276, 325, Michael, 324, Mildred, 282, Mathew Ray, 324, Opal, 276, Paul, 324, Price Joel, 324, R.D., 69, Raymond Clay, 174, Rebecca, 189, Robert, 333, Ruth, 43, 54, 324, 325, Samuel, 324, Sara, 324, Sarah, 152, Sheri Lynn, 324, Sherry, 324, Steven, 324, Steven Ray, 324, Susanna, 324, Tammy, 232, Tammy Kay, 324, Terry Joe, 324, Thomas Clay, 174, Timothy Joe, 324, Toby Lee, 324, Troy Steven, 324, Verlin, 276, Wade Matthew, 324, Warren, 324, Wesley, 378, Wesley W., 378, William, 301, 324
THOMPSON, (General), 322, (Par-

son), 301, Addie, 325, Agnes, 326, Alexander, 161, 370, Alice, 6, 326, Alice M., 293, 294, America Jean, 328, Andrea, 67, Andrew Jay, 328, Andy, 325, Anna Belle, 326, Anthony Glen, 327, Arlie, 327, Barbara, 133, Beatrice, 258, Betty, 190, 350, Betty Ruth, 132, Bill, 325, Bina, 116, Bourbon S., 325, Bradley, 66, 351, Carl, 375, Carl Raymond, 325, Carla Kay, 128, Carlton "Rocky", 327, Carolyn Jean, 327, Cecilia, 128, Charitiann, 328, Charles, 34, Charles H., 103, Charles Lee, 325, Charles Wayne, 128, Charlotte Ann, 325, Charlotte Blanche, 325, Chris, 67, 325, Claire, 327, Clarence Leon, 327, Claude, 6, 326, Claudia Joann, 327, Clint, 301, Closs II, 327, Crede, 215, Daisy Viola, 325, Dave, 326, David, 54, 328, David Day, 328, David Lewis, 328, David S., 325, David Sylvester, 325, Deborah, 150, Diana Renee, 128, Diane, 326, Diantha, 326, Don, 177, 221, 309, 342, 352, Donald, 42, 325, Dorinda Lynn, 128, E., 325, Elizabeth, 196, Elizabeth Ann, 325, Elva, 326, Elva Ann, 326, Emily, 294, Enoch, 294, Eric, 351, Ernest Ray, 327, Esther Lucille, 325, Evaline, 327, Everard, 95, Everett Eugene, 325, Florence, 325, Frances B., 375, Frank, 294, Fred, 294, George, 197, George Everett, 325, Ginger Marie, 132, Gladyne Sue, 128, Grigg, 326, Grigg Matthew, 326, Hannah, 150, Harriett Louise, 326, Harry, 13, 93, Henry, 128, Herman, 197, Howard Elmer, 325, Howard Lee, 132, Ivy Myrtle, 327, J. Walter, 84, James, 70, James K., 280, James Madison, 327, Jane, 161, Janet Louise, 326, Jean, 153, 177, 178, 184, 218, 219, 223, 224, 244, 257, 309, 325, 328, 337, 338, 349, Jesse, 332, 314, Jessie, 326, Jimmy Lee, 128, Joe, 327, John, 93, 325, 326, John Carl, 327, John Grigg, 326, John James, 132, John T., 326, John W., 326, Johnathon W.P., 325, Joyce Alma, 95, Karen Beth, 326, Karina, 326, Karl Jeffrey, 327, Kathryn, 103, Kenneth Lee, 325, Kristin, 128, Kristin Marie, 327, Kyle Allen, 327, Kyle Lee, 128, Larita Ann, 132, Larry, 327, Laura, 260, Lawrence, 366, Lawrence L. Vaughn, 190, 327, Lee "Squeak", 327, Leo, 66, 325, 351, Leo K., 327, Leo Leighton, 325, Lillian, 190, Lloyd, 326, Lloyd T., 326, Louisa, 309, 326, Louise, 211, Lucy, 266, Luna, 197, Mabel, 325, Maggie, 280, Marerovene, 326, Margaret, 326, Margaret Francis, 191, Margaret Zona, 103, Mariah, 326, Marnie, 326, Martha Jane, 325, Martha Jean, 328, Martin, 351, Mary, 145, 307, 314, 326, 347, 351, Mary Katheryn, 325, Mary T., 232, Mathew Grigg, 29, Mattie, 325, Maude, 311, Maurice, 6, 219, 311, 326, 327, Maurice Eugene, 325, Maurice J., 29, Melvin, 59, Mildred, 323, Mildred Jean, 327, Minerva Caroline, 326, Misha Daun, 278, Misha Dawn, 327, Misty, 128, Moses, 325, Nancy, 325, 326, Nancy Catherine, 325, Nancy E., 266, Nehemiah, 325, Neil, 326, Neil Bruce, 326, Nellie, 294, Nona, 95, Norman, 133, Ocie, 327, Opal, 197, Oscar, 327, Paul Allen, 327, Phil, 327, Phillip, 278, Phillip Ray, 327, Phyllis M., 327, Princess, 327, 366, Rachael Ellen, 328, Rachel, 279, Rebecca, 326, 327, Rebecca Sue, 325, Rebecca Suzanne, 278, 327, Roger, 325, Roger Earl, 197, Rosalyn Marie, 325, Ruby, 196, 266, Russ, 327, Russell G., 327, Russell Glen, 327, Ruth, 197, Ruthanne, 54, 328, Sallie, 180, Sam, 325, Samuel P., 190, Sarah, 325, Silas, 325, Sophia, 160, 161, Stephen, 328, Stephen Corydon, 328, Stephen Jay, 328, Steve, 54, Susan, 104, 218, Thomas, 330, Thomas A., 325, Thomas Allen, 325, Thomas Jefferson, 326, 327, Thomas L., 232, Timothy Alan, 325, Todd, 54, 328, Todd Nelson, 328, Tony, 327, Verna, 103, Violet Louise, 132, Will H., 29, 326, 327, Will Henry, 326, Willard J., 294, William, 266, 326, Wilson "Elder", 326, 327, Zora, 326, Lena, 122, Melina, 128, __, 17, __, 42, __, 43

THOMSON, Anna, 328, Arthur, 328, Barbara, 328, Charles, 328, Chester, 328, Cynthia, 328, Elizabeth, 328, Everett, 328, Flora, 328, James, 41, 76, James A., 51, 328, Joseph, 328, Lenna, 328, Levi, 328, Martha, 328, Martin, 328, Mary, 222, 328, Merle, 328, Paul, 328, Robert, 328, Susan, 328, Theodore, 328, Wallace, 328, William, 328, Willis, 328

THOMSPON, Arlie, 325, Maurice James, 326

THORNBURGH, __, 190, Eli E., 190, Katherine, 190

THORNE, Courney, 174, Lee, 16, 123, Pauline, 282

THORSON, Lorraine, 339

THREKELD, George S., 36

THRELKELD, Christian Warren, 89, Darla, 89, Freddie Gene, 89, Heath, 89, Helen, 89, Jeff, 89, Joseph, 89, Lorrie, 89, Mariana, 89

THRINE, Kathi, 271

TIBBS, Evelyn, 189, James, 189

TICKER, H.A., 49

TILDEN, __, 183

TILLARD, Elizabeth, 223, John, 223

TILLEY, Mary Jane, 153, Sarah, 153

TIMBERLAKE, George, 174, Laura, 174, Ruby, 174

TIMMERMAN, Delbert T., 176, Harry C., 176, Marilyn Sue, 176, Wilda G., 176

TIMMONS, Belinda Leight, 328, Deborah Lynn, 328, Joe, 328, Joseph Edmund, 328, Nancy, 328, Patricia L., 328, Rebecca Marie, 328, Thomas Edmund, 328, Von, 144, Wilbur Edmund, 328

TINE, Mary, 74

TINGLEY, Cora, 223

TINSLEY, Countess, 148, Elizabeth, 328, Harvey R., 328, Hettie, 328, 329, Minnie, 116, Robert Harvey, 328, 329, William, 328, 239, Zela, 260, 261

TIPPETTS, __, 312

TIPTON, Effie, 102, 103, Esther, 102, 103, Laura Elizabeth, 102, Lewis W., 67, Wilson, 102

TITUS, Adam Jasper, 329, Anna, 329, Anna Marthene, 329, 330, Arnold, 329, Barbara, 218, 329, Barbara Jean, 78, 329, Betty, 329, Betty E., 329, Betty Joann, 218, 330, Billy, 218, 329, 330, Bob, 330, Carol, 330, David, 330, David Wayne, 330, Edna, 329, Ernest B., 329, Estella Mae, 329, Gerald Leroy, 329, Ilene, 329, Isaac Guy, 329, Isaac Guy, Jr., 329, Janice, 329, Janice Darlene, 330, Jesse Noble, 329, Julia B. Tilford, 329, Mildred, 78, 218, 329, Nancy, 329, Nancy Ellen, 330, Paul Harold, 329, Randy, 330, Ray, 329, Raymond, 78, 218, 330, Raymond J., 329, Raymond Jasper, 329, Richard, 78, 218, 329, 330, Robert, 329, 330, Robert Joseph, 330, Ruth, 329, Sarah C., 329, Stephanie Marie, 330, Susan, 330, Susan Kay, 330, Teresa Rae, 330, Thomas Richard, 329, William, 330, William Arnold, 329, William Edward, 329

TODD, America, 330, Bernice, 330, Carl Summers, 328, 330, Chris, 15, Clyda Mary, 328, Clyda Mary Paddack, 268, Clyda May, 330, Dailie Opal, 328, 330, Dailie Opal Cory, 123, Delilah, 322, Dolores Hoffa, 182, Donald E., 372, Dorothy Mae, 300, Florence, 161, Frank Husted, 330, George, 322, Helen Marie, 330, Henry T., 322, Hester, 322, Isaac Shelby, 322, J.C., 330, J.W., 12, James C., 330, James Caldwell, 330, James Foster, 330, Jane, 93, 314, Jean, 328, John, 322, 330, John W., 12, Johnson, 322, 323, Mabel Clare, 330, Martha Jean, 328, Mary, 13, 322, Mary E., 351, Mary Elizabeth, 322, Mary Thomasine, 330, Melissa America, 322, Myrtle, 345, Nancy Jane, 330, Oscar Bodillion, 330, Oscar Byron, 330, Pauline, 322, Raymond, 11, 127, 147, 322, Ruth, 330, Ruth Ann, 322, 323, Ruth Lucille, 330, Sarah Jane, 136, 322, Sharon, 271, Shelby, 323, Thomas Corydon, 328, 330, __, 136

TOFFORD, Lillian, 175

TOLAN, Shirley, 192

TOLBERT, Sarah, 238

TOLIN, Connie, 284, Jeff, 284

TOMAN, Christie Ann, 319

TOMBAUGH, Clyde W., 115, Ester, 115

TOMLINSON, Mabel, 89, Milo, 89

TOMPKINS, Charles, 358, Cy, 358, Jean, 358, Nathan, 358

TONEY, Edgar, 43

TOON, Maude, 311, Oral, 311, Velda, 311

TOWEL, Bertha, 270

TOWN, Salem B., 49

TOWNSEND, Betty J., 187, Major, 152, Martha, 89, Paul, 89, Sarah Jane, 152

TOZZI, Elsa, 292

TRACY, Amanda, 331, Ann, 330, Bazle, 330, Elizabeth, 330, Emily, 331, Francis M., 331, Genevieve, 123, George, 331, James, 330, John, 330, John H., 331, Jonathan, 331, Larry W., 372, Lee, 342, Lyddia, 330, Martha, 330, Mary, 330, Missouri, 187, Myrtle, 284, Nancy, 330, Opal, 149, 284, 285, Saphrona Ellen, 331, Sarah, 330, Spencer, 342, Thomas, 330, Vezey, 330, Walter, 284, William, 330

TRAVEL, John B., 365

TRAVIS, Charles, 144

TRAYLOR, Andrew, 171, Dan, 171, Gloas, 171

TRAYLOW, Tracy, 171

TREACHER, Arthur, 342

TREMAINE, Guy, 223

TRESNER, Dora E., 187

TREVES, Norman E., 119

TREVINO, Christina, 133

TRI, Kappa, 366

TRI-COUNTY, Telephone, 378

TRIBBETT, Albert G., 114, Bonnie Sue, 331, Carolyn Louise, 331, Charles O., 331, 372, Clint, 126, Dee Ann, 331, Donnis Inell, 331, Emma Lou, 372, Everett E., 331, Frank H., 331, Franklin, 331, Ione, 114, James, 331, James Allen, 331, Janet Sue, 331, John, 331, John Robert, 331, John, Jr., 331, Kiziah, 126, Lindy Micheal, 331, Lloyd, 37, Lois Jeanette, 331, Louis W., 331, Lynn, 81, Lynn E., 331, Mary Elizabeth, 194, Mary M., 356, Nevah, 120, Rhoda, 194, Robert, 215, Rosemary, 331, Walter, 215, Wesley, 159, Wesley D., 331, Wiley, 215

TRIBBY, Etta, 65, Jessie, 65, Ruth, 65, Samuel R., 65

TRIBE, Lunda, 65

TRIBETT, Inell, 81

TRIBLES, Marie Catherine, 88

TRIMBLE, Catherine, 260, Cheryl, 87, Elizabeth Belle, 304, Martha, 87, Robert, 87, Roy, 304

TRIMELL, Shirley Ann, 355

TRINKLE, Clyde, 133, Jeremiah James, 133, Perry Clyde, 133

TROSPER, James A., 320, Rosemary, 320

TROUG, Omer, 192

TROUT, Anna, 192, Arthur, 192, Goldie, 192, James, 192, James Elsworth, 174, 192, Margaret Marie, 192, 246, Omer, 360, Rosa, 192, Roy, 192, __, 126

TROVILLO, Austin, 375

TRUAX, Adam Joel, 299, James A., 375, Joel Adam, 339, Joel Adams, 229, Joshua Michael, 229, 299, 339, Samuel, 50, Shannon Camille, 229, 299, 339, Stephanie Nicole, 229, 299, 339, Stephen, 299, 339, Stephen H., 229

TRUE, Sharon, 65, Tom, 65

TRUITT, Nancy, 289

TRUJILLO, Jose, 218, Mary Jane, 218

TRULLINGER, Gabriel, 164

TRUMP, Bessie Blanche, 301, Robert Mercer, 301

TRUNCELLITO, Gene, 200, Madeline Mary, 200

TRUSLER, Alice Marie, 264, John, 264, John Ralph, 264, Mary, 174, Mary Catherine, 264, Melvin "Bud", 264, Mildred, 264, Wallace, 264

TSHOMBE, David, 65

TTIUS, Randolph Layne, 330

TUCKER, Alice, 250, Ephesa Cornelia, 273, H., 68, Imogene, 310, Joel, 276, 310, Letha, 157, 310, Letha May, 276, Max, 21, 310

TUDOR, Max, 63

TULLIS, Laura, 328

TUNNELL, Joyce, 282

TURNBULL, James, 41

TURNER, D.M., 261, David Milton, 156, 261, Eugene, 261, Gene, 67, Herbert, 261, Hillery, 165, Jean Kaye, 79, Jewell Stanley, 261, Joel, 318, Julia Esther, 318, Julia Myrtle, 261, Lulu, 156, Lulu Inez, 261, Marcella, 261, Osellia, 261, Paul, 66, Robert, 26, Sue, 300, Terisha, 201, Waltraut, 67, William, 201, Williams, 261, __, 12

TURNIPSEED, Clarice, 331, Elinore, 133, 331, Marie, 331, Martha, 96, 331, Nate, 95, Nathan Chaney, 331, Thomas, 331, Thomas B., 331, Vena, 238, Walter Asahal, 331

TURPIN, Cecil, 54, Nancy, 54, Sally, 209

TUTTLE, __, 240, Charles A., 6, Josephine, 6, (Dr.), 74

TYLER, Debbie, 112, Donald, 112, Joanna, 112, Mary Ann, 303

TYO, George A., 375

TYSON, Joe, 59

UBBINGS, Wilma, 226

ULLMAYER, Bakery, 14

UNDERHILL, Elizabeth, 232, Mary Elizabeth, 314

UNDERWOOD, Elizabeth, 109, Mahala, 145

UPHAM, Hazel, 187, John, 187, Pamela, 187, William, 187

UPTON, Bert, 189

URBANSKI, Phyllis, Ann, 355

UTLER, Elizabeth Ann, 163

UTLEY, Martha Ellen, 153

UTTER, Abraham (Reverend), 357, Abram, 63

UTTERBACK, Albert J., 332, Amy, 332, Brian, 192, 246, Carrie, H., 332, Cathy, 246, Charles H., 332, Donald Eugene, 251, Donald Eugene, 332, Elizabeth D., 332, Emmett Andrew, 251, 332, Ernest, 332, Fred, 28, Hal J., 372, Harmon, 332, Henry, 332, Hursel, 332, James H., 332, Jemima, 332, John B., 332, John G, 65, 332, John Gail, 332, Katie Bethel, 332, Lester Newton, 251, 332, Lester William, 251, 332, Margaret, 332, Margaret Leona, 251, 332, Martha, 332, Martha Darlene, 251, 332, Mary, 332, Mary Ann, 251, 332, Mattie, 266, Pearl, 332, Sandy, 375, Stella, 332, Susan, 336, William, 332

UTZ, Larry J., 375

VAIL, Albert, 198, 333, Alvan, 333, Alvin, 283, Arthur, 319, Charles, 333, Clara, 198, 333, Clara Lucille, 333, Ed, 333, Edith, 333, Edith Alberta, 333, Elizabeth, 333, Elizabeth Bernice, 101, 220, 2333, Esther, 333, Esther Russell, 333, Henry M., 333, James, 74, 333, 347, James A., 333, James Edward, 220, 333, Lala Mae, 333, Lillie Anna, 159, Mae, 333, Martha, 333, Martha Ann, 333, Mary, 333, Marty Catherine, 333, Mary Fitz, 333, Nancy 333, Noah, 283, 333, Peter, 333, Riley, 333, Sally, 333, Samuel, 333, Sarah, 333, Schobel C., 333, Shobal, 333, Stephen, 333, Virginia, 295, William Riley, 159, 220, 333

VALENTIME, Dorothy, 333

VALENTINE, Catherine, 333, Curtis N., 333, Dorothy, 334, Dottie, 333, Dottie Belle, 333, Dwight, 333, 334, Dwight Dorman, 333, Marilyn Jane, 334, Russell, 333, Russell John, 333

VAN ARSDALE, Sarah, 329

VAN DEVANTER, Christine, 350, Faith, 350, Grace, 350, Juliet, 350, Karl, 350, Virginia, 350

VANCE, Angela Dawn, 296, Brent Foster, 296, Cherise, 71, Cherise Rene, 296, Elizabeth Margaret, 283, George, 145, Josephine, 145, Karen Ann, 324, Lois, 296, Melvin, 71, 296, Ruth, 188

VANCLEAVE, Aaron, 263, Ad, 244, 245, Alma, 374, Alma Nancy, 194, America Malina, 295, America Malinda, 194, 334, Angeline, 197, Anna, 360, Beatrice, 245, Beatrice Alma, 244, Benjamin, 136, 149, Cary B., 334, Constance Sue, 157, Cynthia, 351, Derald, 226, Edith Aline, 244, Edwin, 194, 334, Effie May, 194, 334, Elizabeth, 334, Emily, 334, Emma Elizabeth, 194, Florence, 263, Henry Newton, 229, 334, Ida F., 244, Isiah, 334, Jane, 334, Jane "Jennie", 334, Jesse, 243, Joanne, 226, 302, John, 149, 250, 266, 334, John Sanford, 194, 334, Jonathon, 334, Joshua, 243, Laura Alice, 194, 334, Levi, 122, Lillie, 335, Lilly, 229, Lori, 226, Lucinda Jane, 149, Lucy, 334, Malinda, 334, Marion, 334, Marjory, 213, Martha, 43, 242, 250, Matilda, 122, Mildred, 157, Milt, 335, Milton, 229, Nan, 335, Nancy, 334, Nancy Alma, 334, Nancy J., 122, Pauline Jane, 334, Perry, 335, Polina Jane, 194, Rachel, 153, Ralph, 334, Rebecca, 334, Robert, 157, Ruth, 145, 250, Samuel, 153, Sarah, 243, Sarah Elizabeth, 153, Sarah Mahala, 123, 228, 334, Thomas, 351, Wallace, 229, 334 William, 334, __, 136

VANCLEAVER, Eunice, 225

VANCLEEF, Isbrant, 334, Jan, 263, 334, John, 298

VANCLEVE, Elizabeth, 351, Ruth A., 351

VANDENBERG, Maxine, 220, 270

VANDERBILT, Jannek Aertse, 334, Jannette, 298

VANDERVOIR, Mae (Miss), 314

VANDEVOIR, Mae, 315, Nora, 315, Victor, 315

VANDYKE, (Rev.), 31

VANEST, Lester (Rev.), 202

VANEYK, Hans, 131

VANGILDER, Bud, 54, Carl, 54, Carl J., 372, Chizeko, 54, Jim, 54, Ole, 54

VANGUNDY, Ella, 61

VANHOOK, Amy, 233, Bessie, 80, Bonnie, 54, Shirley Ann, 90, Tim, 54, Trucking, 16, James Robert, 335, John Herman, 335, John Michael, 335, Lee Michael, 335, Martin Greg, 335, Rebecca, 335, Rebecca Elizabeth, 335, Robert Wesley, 335, Thomas Kehl, 335, Thomas Steven, 335, William Martin, 335

VANHORN, Garrett, 31

VANMETER, Hardware, 14, Letitia, 257, 257, Lettice, 256

VANNETTE, Bessie Gail, 198

VANNICE, Alta, 126, Betty Dahr, 126, Danny, 243, Ed (Mrs.), 310, Elizabeth, 191, Emma Lou, 345, Fern Young, 345, Harold, 126, John Maurice, 345, Marian Louise, 126, Maybelle, 61, Myrtie, Randel, 197, Peter, 129, Thomas, 243, William, 243

VANNORMAN, Nelda, 178

VANOSKY, Theresa, 319

VANPRINCIN, Penelope, 164

VANSCOYCE, Walter D., 31

VANSCOYOC, Margaret, 170

VANSWEARINGEN, see Swearingen, 335

VANSWERINGEN, Garrett, 335

VANZANT, Ann, 192, 193

VARCONI, Victor, 342

VAUGHN, __, 21, Daniel, 187, Eugene, 375, Nettie, 104, Robert (Captain), 355

VAUGHT, C.J., 63, Cheryl Ann, 214, Jacci, 95

VAZQUEZ, Fernando, 286, Fernando Ray, 304, Ramona Lea, 286, Ramonda Lea, 304

VENCIL, Ada L., 259

VENIS, Charlotte Mary, 342, Margaret, 288

VENTRO, Willard, 12

VERGON VARIETY STORE, 15

VERHEY, Erection, Inc., 16

VERMILLION, Jessie, 174, Paul (Mrs.), 331

VESTER, Elizabeth, 235, 304

VICE, Anita, 287, 335, Anita Robbins, 104, Barbara, 336, Charley E., 335, Chester, 336, Chet, 15, Clare, 336, Dorothy, 336, Eileen, 336, Emalie G., 335, Gail, 336, Harold, 336, Harold L, 336, Harry R., 335, Helen, 104, 336, Helen Louise, 104, John L., 335, Joshua, 335, Kenneth, 336, Kenny, 15, Louisa, 335, Martha, 336, Myrtle E., 335, Prudence, 335, Raymond, 336, Raymond A., 336, Rex, 336, Robert, 335, 336, Robert L., 336, Ruth, 336, Slim, 287, 335, 336, Virgil, 336, Virgil E., 336, Virginia, 336, Winfred, 287, 335, 336, Winfred L., 104, Winifred, 336, Monroe, 34

VICKERY, Mary, 259

VINCENT, Anna, 321, Belle, 90, Karen Louise, 185, Mabel, 89, 90, Polly Anna, 230, T.H., 374

VINEYARD, John, 197, 302, Nathan, 302, Nicholas, 302, Sarah Shaver, 197
VIRDEN, Ella Bee, 106
VLIER, Grace T., 381
VOLTZ, Elizabeth Catherine, 157, John Jacob, 157, Sarah Frances, 157
VON TALGE, Tillie, 147
VONGRONERT, Michael, 178
VONCASTLE, Theatre, 107
VONDERSCHMITT, Harry, 107, Nova, 107
VONSCOYOC, Elizabeth, 268
VOORHEES, Scott, 298
VORES, B.F., 93, Leonard, 93, Marie, 93, Myrtle, 93, Ray, 93
VORHEES, Daniel W., 183
VORIS, Mary Ann, 351
VOROS, Hannah, 149
VOWELS, James Kenneth, 245, Jason Tyler, 245, Lori Ann, 245
VREEDENBURG, Hackaliah, 49
VROOMAN, Frank, 91
VUKOVICH, Bill, 275
VYCE, __, 200
WACHTER, Donna Gertrude, 188, Leander (Dr), 188
WADDALL, Mary Jane, 134, Cecil I., 372, Raymond L., 372
WADE, Ann, 211, Anna Weaver, 336, Ben, 336, Eva, 142, George, 336, Isiah, 336, Jackson, 336, John, 336, Lew, 336, Mary Frances, 336, Mary Jane, 336, William Southerd, 336, Zeberiah, 336
WAECHTER, Alfred Newton, 331, Arthur T., 331, Elsie Viola, 331, James, 331, John Jacob, 331
WAGNER, Fern, 336, Helen, 323, 336, Merrilee Jane, 283, Orie, 336, Roberta, 336, William, 336
WAGONER, Linda L., 372
WAINSCOTT, Abraham, 336, Adam W., 336, Elias "Jake", 336, Ellen, 336, Francis Marion, 336, George, 336, Isaac, 336, James W., 336, John W., 336, Martha, 336, Mary Ann, 308, 336, Melvina, 336, Richard, 336, Sarah, 336, Susannah, 336
WAIT, John, 199, John Benjamin, 199
WAKELAND, Darlene, 135
WALBORN, Catherine E., 83, Christian, 83, Eva Anna, 83
WALDEN, Floyd, 309
WALKER, Agnes, 124, Agnes Hurst, 336, Bruce Whittington, 337, Cecil, 83, Clyde Lawson, 337, Craig,Whittington, 337, Dorothy May, 86, Emily Fleming, 186, Eric James, 337, Helen Marie, 82, James M., 29, John C, 337, John Norman, 337, Julian Jane, 199, 223, Lucy Ann, 186, Martha Jo, 337, Mary Katherine, 83, Melissa Allen, 337, Michelle Taylor, 337, N.R., 121, Norman R., 336, Rebecca Whittington, 337, Richard, 95, Thomas, 289, Viola May, 83, William Bradford, 337, William E., 337
WALKUP, Ben, 199, Benjamin, 67, Bryant, 199, Jane Conner, 67, Margaret J., 100, W.B., 31, William, 30, 100, __ 42
WALL, Billie, 106, Evelyn, 104, Newt, 104, Newton A., 104, Sylvia Opal, 104
WALLACE, Cretta, 28, David, 337, Edith, 357, 358, Everett, 55, Henry, 337, James, 28, John, 358, Lew, 6, 7,,23, 24, 39, 48, 54, 75, 219, 221, 222, 307, 337, 373, Lew (Col), 319, Lewis, 91, Martha, 358, Mary, 329, Pheoe A., 206, Sarah Margaret, 248, Susan, 219, 222, 337, Susan E., 366, Valerie, 99, Virgil, 358, Virgil, Jr., 357, Zerelda, 337, __, 55
WALLACHER, Elizabeth, 310
WALLS, Celia, 338, Eulalia Jean, 338, Mary Edith, 338, Mary Eleanor, 338, Samuel Lewis, 338, Stanley Holmes, 338
WALP, Alfred F., 338, Bertha Mae, 338, Betty, 338, Betty L, 168, David, 338, David G., 168, David George, 338, Doris, 338, Doris C., 168, Frederick Robert, 338, Geneva M., 250, Lewis, 338, Lewis M., 168, Lewis Monroe, 338, Mary, 338, Olive, 338, Robert L., 168, Robert Lewis, 338, Shirley, 338, William, 338, William H., 338
WALTER, Anna, 208, C. Pauline, 43, 116, Carl, 299, Martha Caroline, 267, Opal, 299, Sarah Ann, 359, Velma Tague, 293
WALTERHOUSE, David Kemper, 338, Harrison Kemper (Dr), 201, 338, Jane, 338, Thomas S. (Major), 338
WALTERS, Megan, 99, Thalia, 45, Alva, 175, 339, Agngela Kristin, 229, Angela Kristy, 299, 339, Brenda, 299, C. Pauline, 31, 32, 42, 45, 197, 211, 323, 325, 336, Carl, 175, 339, Catherine, 339, Charlie, 339, Connie Kay, 229, Constance Kay, 339, Constance Ray, 299, Crystal Pauline, 280, Deborah, 299, Debra Addler, 299, Donna, 99, 281, Elston, 299, Elston Virgil, 339, Franklin Albert, 339, Gloria J., 372, Harold, 28, 36, 153, Harold B., 229, 299, Harold Buford, 339, Harriet H., 172, Heather Michelle, 229, 299, 339, Jacalyn Suzan, 229, 339, Jacob, 339, Jacob Daniel, 299, 339, Jacob David, 229, James, 175, Jeffrey, 36, Jeffrey Lee, 229, 299, 339, Jennie, 339, Jesse, 175, J97, Jessie, 175, Joenlyn Suzan, 299, Larry, 26, Larry Dean, 229, 299, 339, Lavina, 149, Lawrence, 175, Lillian, 175, Louise, 67, Louise, 175, Lucas, 229, Lucas Scott, 299, 339, Marilyn, 299, Mary, 36, Matthew, 229, Matthew Ryan, 299, 339, Megan Rochelle, 214, Michael Robert, 229, 299, 339, Nettie, 175, Opal, 339, Pamela Sue, 299, 339, Pauline, 28, 29, 31, 32, 33, 36, 145, 150, 182, 197, 228, 229, 286, Petra, 229, 299, Pochontas, 339, Robert, 28, 36, Robert L., 31, 375, Robert Lee, 229, 299, 336, 339, Rose Jane, 153, Ryan Lee, 229, 299, 339, Thalia, 299, 339, Theresa, 268, William, 99, 339, William Paul, 214
WALTMAN, Beverly, 54, Richard, 54
WALTON, Ayre, 182, Ida, 182, John, 74
WALTZ, Patty, 374, Ralph, 19
WALTZ TRUCKING, 16
WANN, Raymond, 246
WARBINGTON, Edna, 287, James Allen, 287
WARBINTON, Dollie, 238, Estella, 238, Orfa, 194
WARBITTON, Rose Pearl, 209
WARBRITTON, Minnie Alice, 334, Pearl, 191, 209
WARD, —, 307, Amazon, 339, 350, Amzon, 176, Betty, 353, Betty Jane, 354, Bonnie, 358, Camella May, 339, Carmella, 350, Charles, 32, Charlotte, 350, Clara, 43, Clara Bell, 176, Clara Belle, 339, Clayton, 44, Clayton Sanders, 328, 339, Connie, 339, Constance L., 375, David, 298, 339, David Genung, 176, Donas, 339, Edwin Grant, 339, Elanor L., 176, Eleanor M., 328, Eleanor Mae, 339, Elizabeth, 261, 350, Ella, 122, Evelyn ILnn, 339, Gordon Montgomery, 339, Hazel Marie, 339, Helen Katherine, 358, Helen Louise, 339, Henry Alva, 339, Homer B., 339, 340, Homer Bratton, 339, J.S., 49, Jane K. Moritz, 358, Jeanne, M., 340, Jeanne,M., 381, Jeffrey L, 375, Jerry L., 375, John, 325, 336, John W., Sr., 31, Joseph Williamson, 339, Kenneth, 44, Kenneth Amazon, 339, Lafayette, 343, Lida, 63, Lola, 31, 339, Marianne, 86, Martha Ellen, 339, Mary, 39, 227, Mary Ellen, 181, 229, Mary Isabel, 339, 349, Melissa Ann, 343, Mollie, 158, Myrtle F., 340, Nancy, 340, Nora, 339, Phoebe, 350, Opal, 339, Phoebe Jane M., 176, Richard D., 258, Richard D. "Rick", 340, Richard H., 258, 340, Richard H. "Dick", 340, Richard Harold, 339, Ruby, 122, Ruth, 336, Sarabelle, 177, Thomas, 122, 339, Thomas Jr., 350, Thomas, Sr., 350, Ulysses Grant, 339, Ursula, 302, Uzal, 229, W.W., 30, William W., 230, __, 42
WARFEL, Charles Martin, 340, Frank, 340, George Huntington, 340, Herbert, 340, Indiana, 340, J. Francis, 206, J.F., 74, Jacob F., 340, Lizzie, 340, Lizzie Gregg, 206, Louisa, 340, Martin B., 340, Nellie Grace, 340
WARFIELD, Sharon, 151
WARFORD, F.M. (Dr), 120
WARNER, Allen, 341, Bert, 266, 340, 341, Bert Abraham, 341, Brittian, 341, Carol, 341, Charles, 266, 341, Charles Emanuel, 341, Charles Franklin, 341, Daisey Lee, 341, David, 341, Edgar Leslie, 341, Edith, 272, Elaine, 341, Eldon, 341, Elizabeth, 341, Ellen, 341, Eloise, 341, Emanuel, 341, Estelle, 341, Harry, 341, Henry Earl, 341, Homer, 266, 341, Homer Eugene, 341, Hubbard, 341, James, 341, Joe, 341, John, 341, Joyce, 341, Leslie, Jr., 341, Louise, 341, Madonna, 142, 341, Mae, 341, Margaret Dot, 131, Martha, 341, Mary, 154, 266, 341, Mary Ethel, 341, Mary Luella, 341, Maureen, 341, Max, 341, Nancie, 233, Oliver, 266, 341, Oliver Leslie, 341, Omar William, 341, Phyllis, 341, Polly, 341, Rebecca Mae, 341, Rebekah, 341, Robert, 341, Robert Hyten, 341, Roberta, 341, Susannah, 341, Ted, 341, Theodore, 266, 341, Theodore Maxwell, 341, Theodore Maxwell II, 341, —, 154,
WARREN, Catherine Jane, 310, Henry, 34, Homer, 310, Lois I., 374, Madonna, 310, Nelda, 117, Ruth, 115, Susan Lyn, 327
WARRICK, Nora, 241
WARTHURST, Amelia, 224
WASHBURN, D.M., 65
WASHINGTON, Megan, 147, (General), 322, Christopher, 147, Clifford, 147, Debra, 147, George, 187, 195, 233, 304, 358
WASSON, __, 22, Anna B., 266, Bettie, 52, Clara, 266, Department Store, 130, Elizabeth, 60, Ethel, 43, Ira, 266, James A., 168, Jeremy, 168, John C., 266, Kate, 266, Ransom, 168, Theodore R., 52, Zachary, 168
WATKINS, Agnes, 270, Clarise, 243, Francis, 172, George, 85, 133, George W., 341, Georgia M., 341, Jane, 133, Louisa, 270, 271, Maurine Dallas, 341, Rebecca, 85, Robert, 270, Rose, 153
WATSON, Andrea Nicole, 165, Angela, 361, Angela Marie, 342, Angie, 320, Anissa Dawn, 165, Ann, 129, Bessie, 361, Betty, 342, 362, Blanche Pearl, 276, Bob, 13, Charlotte, 342, Curtis, 54, Darrel, 361, Darrel Robert, 342, Donald Wayne, 165, Edward, 361, Edward Michael, 342, Elizabeth, 187, 326, George W., 276, Helen, 326, Herman Darwin, 342, Hope, 361, Hope Ann, 342, Isaac, 326, Jacob, 361, Jacob Michael, 342, Janice Lynn, 165, Jeffrey Allen, 165, John, 361, John David, 342, Jorene, 54, Laura Mae, 342, Lettie, 342, Linda, 165, Lori, 361, Lori Lynn, 342, Madonna, 165, Marion, 342, Martha, 276, Mary Ann, 342, Mary Ducan, 183, Mary Jane, 42, 361, Mary Louise, 342, Maurice Marion, 342, Mike, 54, Nancy, 10, 320, 342, 361, Noris Welby, 361, Norris Welby, 342, Oral, 165, Pamela Sue, 165, Pearl, 361, Ralph, 71, 361, Ralph Arnold, 342, Richard, 361, Richard Allen, 342, Richard L., 165, Robert, 361, Robert Lee, 342, Ronald Lee, 165, S.H., 342, Sammy, 342, Samuel, 342, Samuel David, 342, Samuel Henry, 342, Sandy, 54, Sue, 165, Susan, 303, Vicki, 320, Victoria, 254, 361, Victoria Kay, 342, Ward H., 120, Wiliam "Bill" E., 165, —, 42
WATT, Adrian, 294, Carla Kay, 128, Connie, 294, Joshua Henry, 128, Mark, 294, Robert Lewis, 128, Terry, 128
WATTS, Anthony Aurelius, 343, Christopher Duane, 330, Dana, 279, Dawn, 279, Drew Lewis, 330, Hannah, 342, Homer, 279, Janet, 279, Jeremiah Robert, 330, Jerry, 330, John, 36, Larry, 330, Larry D., 330, Lola, 208, Margaret Frick, 139, Marguerite, 159, Marguerite Eliz., 343, Marion Edward, 342, Mary, 288, Mary Ellen, 342, 343, Maude Ellen, 343, Minnie, 330, Ruth, 36, Shelby D., 69, Susan, 330, William A., 342
WAUGH, Edward Royston, 343, Elizabeth, 343, Emma E., 343, Emma Orevy, 344, Harvey, 343, James B., 344, James Henry, 343, James W., 332, Jennie Mae, 343, John Milo, 343, John Wesley, 343, 344, Joseph, 343, Julia, 49, Margaret Elizabeth, 343, Martha, 332, 343, Martha E., 343, Mary, 343, Mary Elizabeth, 343, Mary Jane, 343, Melissa Ann, 343, Miletus Asbury, 343, Milo, 343, Milton B., 343, 344, Milton Byron, 332, 343, Minnie Agnes, 343, Nancy Angeline, 343, Richard H., 343, Sarah, 343, Sarah Alice, 344, Sarah Elizabeth, 343, Walter Scott, 343, William B., 343, William Wilson, 344
WAUGHT, Julia Davidson, 6
WAVELAND, Masonic Lodge, 365
WAYE, Ron, 167
WAYMEYER, Eleanor, 161
WEATHERMAN, Linda, 249
WEAVER, Anna, 336, Anna Candance, 229, Bonnie, 148, 277, Bonnie Jean, 148, Bruce Fraley, 162, Charles, 88, 148, Charlotte Ann, 271, Helen Yount, 360, Homer W., 148, Joe, 365, John, 360, John Dale, 271, John Dale, Jr., 271, John R., 148, John Russell, 148, Joseph Aaron, 162, Kathy, 148, Linda Kay, 88, Marie, 88, Martha Jo, 162, Mary, 148, Mary Anna Cedars, 228, Mary Beth, 271, Max Dale, 148, Melford "Buck" Durham, 148, Nancy, 148, Patricia Ruth, 148, Robert, 148, Ida, 242
WEAVER'S POPCORN RESEARCH, 16
WEBB, Genyle N., 372, Howard, 164, Irene, 182, James, 360, John W., 224, Mary E., 224, Patricia, 112, T.L., 49, Laura, 89,
WEBER, Conrad, 344, Conrad, Jr., 344, Delores June, 344, Elizabeth, 343, Englebert, 344, Gordon Dice, 344, Gordon Leon, 344, Henry Paul, 344, Josepha, 344, Josephine, 344, Koncar, 344, Lena, 344, Leopodine, 344, Maria, 344, Marilyn, 107, Marilyn Ruth, 344, Paul, 344, Ralph, 344, Ruby, 344, Sofia, 344, Susan, 344, Theresia Eha, 344
WEBSTER, Alice, 308, Cora Anna, 170, Mary J., 226, Nellie Grace, 100, Rachael, 324, Sarah, 351
WEED, Alice Lucretia "Lula", 164
WEEKS, Robert, 209, Roberts, 43
WEESNER, Albanus H., 344, Alice, 126, 239, Bob, 126, 239, Dave, 239, Ernest, 237, 344, Ervin, 126, Erving, 239, Erving B., 271, 344, Grace, 271, Hannah, 271, 344, John, 126, 239, John Phillip, 344, John Philip, 271, Kathryn Marie, 271, Lowell A., 271, Mahlon, 284, 344, Margaret, 344, Marie, 271, Marshall Todd, 271, 344, Michael, 344, Olive, 284, 344, Oliver, 283, Robert, 271, 344, Robert Eliot, 271, 344, Ruth Ann, 271, Theodore M., 344, Walter, 344, William H., 344
WEHRMAN, Henrietta, 78
WEIGLE, Viola, 348
WEIKEL, Samuel, 198, William Smith, 198
WEILAND, Rose Anne, 125
WEIR, Alexander, 41, 219, 264, 345, Anna, 125, Bessie, 147, Coralea, 97, Curtis, 270, Dennis R., 372, Ethel, 147, Granville, 147, Holly Renee, 270, John, 147, Mabel, 41, 345, Margaret, 125, Mary Jane, 145, Maxine, 345, Phyllis Ann, 147, Robert, 344, 345
WEIRICK, Cindy, 142
WEIS, Patricia, 289
WEKEL, Lucy Fern, 198
WELCH, —, 22, Benjamin, 345, Charna, 345, Clyde, 345, Delene, 345, Elizabeth, 314, Geraldine, 345, Herschel, 345, Jerilyn, 345, Lucinda, 186, Marilyn, 345, Matthew (Gov.), 324
WELCHEL, Paul, 112
WELIEVER, Anthony Wade, 345, Betty Jane, 221, Brett, 221, Cathy, 221, Charles, 221, Dana, 221, Denise, 221, Don, 345, Donald Harry, 345, Emma Lou, 345, 380, Fern, 356, Garrett Blake, 345, Harry Manual, 345, Jeremy, 221, Kristine, 221, Lauren, 221, Mildred, 220, Mildred Maye, 221, Richard, 221, Roberta, 221, Sabra Ann, 345, Stanley C., 345, Steven J., 345, Stuart K., 345, Thommi Jo Lee, 345, Wade Alan, 345
WELIVER, Donna, 221, Gabe, 221, Mary, 369, Mary Lou, 265, Michael D., 372, Nancy, 221, Susie, 221, Tacy, 221
WELKER, Dawn, 250
WELLER, Edward, 290
WELLIEVER, Ami Jo, 168, Brett Alan, 168, Cori Keith, 168, Kalay Ann, 168, Lana Lee, 168, Whitney Jo, 168, William Joseph, 168, Yancie Joseph, 168
WELLINGTON, —, 307
WELLIVER, Charity, 102, Fred, 32
WELLS, David, 347, Flora Carrington, 113, Hazel, 288, Jane, 109, Theodore N., 113, William, 144
WELSH, Lidia, 232, Mary Ellen, 260
WELSHARES, Elizabeth, 102, William M., 102
WELSHIMER, Celia, 131, Mary, 92
WENDALL, Betty, 157
WENGER, Hans, Jr., 354, Martin, 354
WERNER, Bertha, 357, John, 357
WERT, Albert E., 345, Arthur B., 345, Bessie, 350, Effie, 85, Emery, 204, Henry, 345, Isabella, 345, John, 204, Martin V., 345, Mary Ann, 204
WERTS, C.B., 74, Radio, 15
WESNER, Alfreda, 152, Brianne Michelle, 152, Bryan Neel, 152, James, 152, Michael Bryan, 152
WEST, Alfred, 241, Dale, 241, David, 346, Donald, 241, Edward, 346, Francis, 346, George, 241, Gerald, 241, Helen, 241, James, 241, 346, Jere, 376, Jeremiah, 36, 353, John, 241, John H., 32, John Thomas, 241, Joseph, 346, June, 346, Leticia, 326, Linda, 346, Louisa, 188, Margie, 348, Martha, 241, Mary, 226, 241, Matilda, 353, Max, 241, Maxine, 241, Mildred, 346, Oscar, 241, Paul, 241, Robert, 241, Thomas J., 346, W., 253
WESTFALL, —, 324, Em, 114, Erma, 91, Jane, 331, Nancy Ellen, 296, Nina Erma, 92, Ola, 310, Vezy, 92
WESTON, Amanda, 102, Henry C., 63, Joseph R., 102
WETHERBEE, Miriam, 121
WETHINGTON, All-American Home, 15, Diana, 358, Family Restaurant, 15, Grover, 358, Kristie, 358, Pam, 121, Robert R., 375, Russell, 358, Scott, 358, Stacy, 358, Stanley, 358, Velma, 358
WETLI, Christina L., 372
WHALEN, Cheryl, 234, Cheryl Delene, 234, Walter Willis, 234, William Keith, 234, William Keith, Jr., 234
WHALIN, Thomas Mayborn, 188
WHEAR, William, 74
WHEAT, Allen B., 318, Herman, 318, Jenny Susan, 318, Louise, 272, Marjorie Ann, 318, Robert Max, 318, Susan Lynn, 318
WHEATLY, Frances, 227, Henry, 227, Ruth, 227
WHEELER, Anna May, 346, Beverly Ann, 346, Bob, 346, Carolyn Sue, 346, Cordelia, 346, Cordelia May, 346, Daniel Wayne, 346, Darlene, 346, David Alan, 346, Deanna, 346, Delores, 346, Dora Ethel, 116, Dora Maude, 346, Dorothy Darlene, 346, Emily, 346, Frances, 346, Frances May, 346, Gerald Allen, 346, Harold Sherman, 231, Helen Lucille, 231, Jack, 346, Jack Allen, 346, James Frederick, 346, Jeanne, 346, Jim, 346, Joe E., 283, Josiah, 261, Julia, 261, June, 346, June Ellen, 346, Laura Michelle, 346, Lisa Lynn, 346, Mary Jane, 346, Maude, 346, Michael Dean, 346, Nancy, 346, Randy Dean, 346, Robert Barnum, 346, Robert Earl, 346, Robert Jeffrey, 346, Ruth Maxine, 346, Sandi, 346, Sandra, 231, Sandra Kay, 346, Scott Allen, 346, Sherman Morris, 231, Steven Kent, 346, Sue, 346, Thomas Earl, 346, Todd Wayne, 346, Virginia Jeanne, 346, William Ernest, 346, William I., 49, William Scott, 346, Winifred, 346
WHETSON, America, 172
WHILLITE, Daisy, 250, Dale Lloyd, 249, Edgar Hall, 249, Edgar Leon, 249, Gale FLoyd, 250, John Kenneth, 249, Melba Margaret, 249, Moyna Arlene, 250, Moyne Argel, 249
WHIPPLE, Anna Marie, 346, Cheryl Lynn, 346, Dale, 346, David, 116, Elga, 116, Jane, 78, 346, Jean Ann, 346, Joanne, 116, Kathy E.,

372, Keith Allen, 346, Kenneth, 116, 280, 346, Kenneth Leo, 346, Raymond, 116, Ron, 372, Ronald, 116, Stella, 116, Virgil, 116
WHITAKER, Aaron Buchanan, 347, Adath Bertha, 347, Amanda Elizabeth, 347, Anna, 347, Belle B., 347, Big Bill, 347, Catharine, 347, Catherine, 320, Esau, 347, Esther Lavina, 347, Floyd, 209, Frances M., 152, Golda May, 203, 347, Henry W., 347, Hilton H., 49, Isaac, 347, James B., 347, Jemima, 114, Jemima J., 347, John, 320, John, 347, Joseph H., 347, Levi, 320, 347, Luther, 347, Margaret, 320, 347, Margaret Anna, 347, Mariah, 91, Martha Jane, 347, Mary Ann, 152, Mary E., 347, Millie Catharine, 347, Millie Catherine, 86, Nancy, 278, Nettie G., 347, Noah, 347, Rachel, 347, Robert Albert, 347, Robert Allen, 346, 347, Sarah, 254, Sarah Margaret, 347, Thomas J., 347, William, 347
WHITCOMB, (Gov.), 340
WHITE, 22, (Pres.), 183, Alberta Jo, 132, Austin (Mrs.), 270, Austin Ford, 271, Barbara, 271, Beverly A., 372, Blanche Gertrude, 189, Clarice, 101, Cynthia, 243, Darla, 89, David, 132, Douglas, 106, Elmer, 316, Elmer Hamilton, 357, Haley, 277, Hannah, 164, Helen, 271, Harry, 371, Horace Wallace, 357, J.H., 374, Jess, 277, Jesse, 234, Jessie, 316, John, 64, John Henry, 189, Joseph, 64, 67, Judith Ann, 271, Julius, 91, Larry, 277, Laura, 318, Lola, 233, Lottie, 20, Lottie E., 372, Mabel, 195, 196, 197, Malinda, 293, Martha, 189, Martha Ann, 333, Martha Blanche, 189, Mary Margaret, 301, Mattie (Detchon), 141, May, 94, Nancy, 374, Park, 94, Ralph Waldo, 357, Rebecca Ann, 106, Ruth, 91, 271, 311, 339, 381, Ruth I., 20, S.T., 360, Sarah Angeline, 301, Will, 43, William, 44, 64, William M., 141, William Thomas, 333, Helen, 272
WHITECOTTON, Bettie Ann, 260, Betty, 347, Bill, 260, 347, Bob, 260, 347, Don, 202, 347, Ethel, 347, Fred, 347, Harrison, 347, Helen, 347, Jenny, 347, Joan, 347, John, 347, Joyce, 347, Laura, 347, Lee, 260, 347, Lois, 347, Mary, 282, 347, Max, 347, Moses II, 347, Myrtle, 277, 347, Opal, 347, Pearl, 90, 347, Ted, 347, Velma, 347, Verna, 278, Walter, 260, 347, William, 91, 347
WHITEHEAD, Dianne, 181, Helen, 243, Helen Christine, 200, Myrtle, 366, Orville, 143, Randy, 50, Ted, 366
WHITEMAN, Viola Lucinda Jane, 203
WHITENACK, Mary Ann, 141
WHITESIDE, Walker, 221
WHITING, Cora Edna, 105, Franklin, 105, Mary, 105
WHITINGTON, Della, 322
WHITKOWSKI, Patricia, 288
WHITLATCH, Noah, 89, 90
WHITLEY, John R., 55
WHITLOCK, Ambrose, 125
WHITLOW, Staci Rena, 164
WHITT, Ella, 304
WHITTED, Oakie Mae, 309, Rena, 80
WHITTELBERRY, Harriet, 189
WHITTINGTON, —, 136, Anna Frances, 337, Catherine, 337, Charles, 337, Charles Edgerton, 337, Clifford, 11, Eliszabeth, 347, Frances, 347, Frayne F., 122, George Washington, 348, James Henry, 347, James Littleton, 347, John Thomas, 347, Joshua Littleton, 347, Littleton, 172, 347, Lucy Ann, 347, Lucy Ellen, 348, Rebecca, 337, Reese Davis, 348, Richard, 337, S.T., 365, Sarah Beth, 337, Sarah Frances, 347, 348, Sherman Grant, 348, Southy Thomas, 347, Teresa Lynn, 122, Tyre Glenn, 347, W.T., 57, William, 347, William Hanna, 347
WHOEL, Anna, 108, Ethel, 108, Michael, 108, Michael, Jr., 108, Ray, 108
WHORLEY, Alfred Fletcher, 83
WIATT, —, 283, Darrell, 348, David, 348, Edward, 348, Glenn, 348, Isaac, 348, Larry, 348, Leland, 348, Leo, 348, Wanetta, 348, Willie, 348
WIBLE, Jane, 334, Jennie, 334
WICKLIFFE, Charles, 34
WIDENER, Donnis, 22, Mary, 324
WIDMER, Harold, 378
WIDNER, John, 129
WIGGS, Bertha, 197
WIGNALL, Elva, 54, Emma, 54, Lloyd, 54
WILBUR, Elmer, 285, 342, Sarah Jane, 285
WILCOX, Bruce, 208, David Milton, 208, James, 82, Laban, 208, Levi, 310, Susan, 208
WILCOXIN, Lloyd, 181, Horatio, 181
WILDMAN, Bertha, 132, Betty, 348, Betty Marie, 287, Bill, 348, Bruce, 348, Catherine, 348, Charles, 348, Ethel, 348, Fenton, 348, Fred, 348, Frederick Karl, 348, Jill, 348, Jim, 348, Joyce Ellen, 287, 348, Kim, 348, Krystal, 348, Margie, 348, Mary, 348, Pauline, 348, Ralph, 348, Ralph Edward, 287, Rena, 348, Thomas Philo, 348, Viola, 348
WILES, Mary Louise, 358
WILEY, George, 41
WILFLEY, Earle, 66
WILHEIT, Archilles, 350, Barbara, 350, Catharine, 350, Jennie, 350, Jesse, 350, John, 350, Joshua, 350, Katie, 350, Lewis, 350, Margaret, 350, Martissa, 350, Mourning, 350, Tobias, 350
WILHELM, Mary, 303
WILHITE, Charles O., 348, Craig Allen, 128, Dorinda Lynn, 128, Ekillis, 321, Eleazer, 349, Isaac S., 3498, Jennie, 341, Jimison, 361, Margarette, 159, Martha, 361, Mary, 321, Mary Holloway, 349, Paschal, 159, Pollie Ann, 321, President Hall, 321, Richard, 128, Sabrah Catherine, 252, Sarah B., 360, Tonya Renee, 128, Waneta, 252
WILHOIT, Adam, 351, Eva, 351, John, 351, John Michael, 351, Matthias, 351, Philip, 351, Tobias, 351
WILKENS, Clarence, 243, Jana, 243, Belinda, 349, Carrie, 162, Clint, 374, Clint Kelly, 349, 350, Clint Kelly II, 349, Clinton, 350, Eleanor Mae, 349, Harold Ward, 349, 350, Lala, 349, Mary Isabel, 339, 349, 381, Rebecca Thomas, 204, Thomas, 339, 350, 374, Thomas H., 374, Ward, 349, 374, Ward Kelly, 349
WILKINS', Corner, 62
WILKINSON, Aaron Edwin, 91, Abram, 350, Anna, 350, Arvilla, 350, Bent, 350, Benton, 350, Bessie, 350, Clinton, 350, Donald, 71, Earl, 350, Edgar, 350, Elizabeth Caroline, 350, Eston, 350, Frank, 12, Fred, 226, Grace, 350, Icabod, 350, Ida, 350, Ira, 350, Jennie, 350, Jewell, 350, John M., 102, Lex, 350, Molly, 283, Murwine, 350, Nancy, 350, Norma G., 372, Rachel, 350, Richard, 71, Uma, 350, 361, Zelpha, 350
WILLHEITE, Catharine, 350, George, 350, John, 350, Lucinda, 350, Mary Ann, 350, Polly Ann, 350
WILLHITE, Achilles, 350, Alta, 350, Alta Arnetta, 350, Berniece, 350, Dale, 350, Dale Lloyd, 350, David, 350, Diane, 250, Duane, 350, Edgar, 350, Edgar Hall, 350, Edgar Leon, 350, Effie, 350, Effie May, 350, Elmer, 350, Elmer Lloyd, 350, Fern, 350, Gale, 350, Gale Floyd, 350, Gregory, 208, 350, Harvey, 350, Henry, 350, James, 350, Jef, 208, Jesse President, 350, Jessie, 350, John, 249, 350, John Hall, 350, John Kenneth, 350, Kenneth, 350, Larry, 350, Leon, 350, Leota, 350, Loren, 350, Lou, 350, Lou Ellen, 351, Louise, 350, Mahala, 350, Marla, 350, Mary, 305, 350, Mary K., 372, Matie, 350, Mattie Evelyn, 350, Melba, 350, Melvin, 350, Moyna Arlena, Moyna Arlene, 250, 350, Moyne, 350, Moyne Argel, 350, Noel, 208, 350, Noel Eugene, 350, Oakie, 298, 350, Oakie Leah, 98, 350, Pamela, 208, 350, Patsy, 350, Polly Ann, 174, 320, President Hall, 350, Rebvecca, 350, Rillinta, 350, Ronald, 208, 350, Sharon Williams, 350, Terry, 350, Tom, 350, William, 350
WILLIAMS, A.D., 41, Albert, 268, Alice, 141, Benjamin, 352, Blanche, 352, Bryan, 352, Carolyn, 223, Charles, 11, 233, 352, Charles G., 351, Clay, 69, Clinton, 351, Daniel, 351, Daniel Clayton, 223, David, 75, 304, Debra J., 375, Doris, 351, Dorothy J., 375, Dorothy May, 86, Dwight, 351, Earl Milton, 339, Ellen, 197, Ernest, 215, Esther, 333, 342, Esther Lavina, 347, Fannie, 52, Faye, 351, Frank, 162, G.T., 11, 12, Garland (Rev. Elder), 351, George, 352, George (Dr.), 352, George T., 322, George T. (Dr.), 358, George Thomas, 351, Glen III, 86, Glenda Rae, 86, Glenn, 86, Grover, 134, Harold, 351, Harriet, 351, Hazel, 233, Heidi, 351, Henry, 11, 351, Hulda, 123, 162, 352, Isaac, 352, Isham, 352, James, 123, 333, Jane, 352, Jeanne, 351, Jerry, 223, Joanne, 351, John Ellis, 352, John L., 352, Johnson, 351, Jonathan, 352, Joseph, 351, Joshua, 351, Julia, 351, Kate, 352, Larry, 21, Lavenda, 352, Letitia, 351, Lida, 352, Lillian E., 351, Louisa, 308, 352, Lucinda, 153, Lucy, 304, Lula, 279, Mae, 232, Marcellia, 86, Martha, 28, 43, 323, 352, Mary, 123, 151, 352, Mary A., 299, Mary Alberta, 229, 339, Mary E., 351, Mary Elizabeth, 322, Mary Ellen, 352, Mary L., 351, Mary Louise, 194, Milton, 352, Minnie, 307, Miranda, 186, Nancy J., 351, Nanthan Otis, 352, Nina, 69, Opa, 162, 352, Oscar, 54, Ote, 352, Otis, 352, Rachel, 194, Rhoda, 263, Robert, 351, Robert M., 372, Russell, 352, Ruth, 351, Ruth A., 351, Samuel, 333, 347, Sarah, 169, 333, Sarah Louise, 162, Sarah Vail, 347, Sharon Lee, 86, Sidney Louise, 352, Stephen, 352, Stephen Jr., 352, Suzanne Marie, 187, Tammie, 223, Thomas, 351, 352, Valverta, 138, W.T., 11, 52, Warren, 52, William, 352, Zack, 34, Beck & Hess Construction, 68
WILLIAMSON, Asa, 186, Beulah, 126, Charles, 99, 272, Ed, 126, Erusmus, 186, Esther, 186, Fannie, 186, George, 150, Goldie, 99, 272, Hannah, 310, Helen Mae, 126, Isabelle, 170 186, Maroah, 186, Mary, 186, Maude, 356, Melissa, 186 Nellie, 186, Rachel, 262, Sarah, 150, Thomas, 186,
WILLIEN, L.J., 166
WILLIS, Abner, 152, Beckie, 54, Joe, 21, Martha, 54, Mary Ann, 151, 152
WHILLLHITE, Sarah, 350
WILLS, Betty, 169, Doris, 307, Lorna, 205
WILLSEY, C.R., 311
WILLSON, Robert, 250
WILOTE, — (Rev.), 63
WILSHIRE, Lorna L., 372, Mabel, 263, Mable Jean, 211, Melvinia, 211, Mirt, 211
WILSON, (Miss), 237, Aaron Faust, 354, Abigail, 353, Alberta, 353, Alice, 201, 202, Allie, 185, ALvin, 353, Alvin Dewey, 360, Anna, 352, Ben, 72, Bernard, 353, 354, Blind Billy, 266, Brian Jeffrey, 186, Brothers Greenhouse, 198, 232, Canazada, 353, Carroll, 353, Carroll L., 360, Charles, 105, Chester Harold, 186, Cintilda, 288, Clara Faye, 353, 354, Claude, 13, Clayton, 106, David, 67, Dora, 360, Doris, 353, 360, Doris Claire, 354, E.G., 376, Earl, 353, 360, Edith, 106, Edith Carroll, 353, Edith Moody, 353, Edna, 213, 353, Edwin, 353, Edwin Davis, 284, 353, Edwin Myers, 354, Elizabeth, 174, 214, 353, 354, Elizabeth "Betsy", 353, Elizabeth Ellen, 354, Emeline Inez, 360, Emerson Bennett, 353, Emily, 124, 266, 346, Emma Garrett, 185, Esther Irene, 248, Faye, 284, 353, Fern, 181, Fern Edith, 200, Flora, 207, 353, Flora L., 353, Florence, 198, 353, Florence Jeanette, 198, Francis, 43, Frank Arthur, 186, George Faust, 353, Gertrude, 185, Gilbert, 353, Grace, 200, Hannah, 353, Harrison, 222, Harvey, 185, Harvey Badger, 186, Hazel Gertrude, 353, Heather Lynn, 168, Helen, 353, Helen Frances, 353, 360, Irene, 353, 360, Jack, 105, Jacqueline, 353, James, 208, James B., 288, James H., 58, James L., Jr., 353, James L., Sr., 353, James Madison, 198, Janet, 353, Janet Luanne, 354, Jay, Jr., 29, 41, 201, 202, 206, Jean, 324, Jennifer Chase, 84, Joan 353, Joe Brent, 168, John, 353, John Badger, 185, 186, John C., 198, John Edwin, 354, John, Jr., 353, 354, John, Sr., 353, 354, Joseph, 64, 336, Joseph W., 129, Josephine, 80, Julia Davis, 353, Lawqrence W., 360, Lela G., 360, Lelia G., 353, Letitia, 353, Levi, 352, Lewis, 353, Lillian, 185, Lucinda, 353, Lydia, 353, Lydia "Amy", 353, Margaret, 360, Marjorie Joan, 198, Martha, 113, 353, Mary, 155, Mary Alice, 186, Mary Jane, 336, Mary Kate, 360, Mary Lou, 67, Matilda, 353, Mindy Jo, 168, Miriam, 329, Nancy, 353, Nancy M., 250, Nanny, 249, Nellie, 165, Nevada, 353, Norma, 186, O.B., 280, Oleta, 353, Pauline, 186, Phyllis Lynn, 168, Raleigh, 353, Raleigh Lewis, 353, 354, Ralph, 353, Raymond, 353, Raymond Lee, 198, Rebecca, 327, Richard, 372, Richard Philip Edgar, 84, Ronald Baldwin, 186, Rosemary, 353, Ruth, 353, Sallie, 353, Sarah, 89, 352, Susannah, 288, Sylvester, 353, Teresa, 272, Thomas, 30, 200, Thomas J., 353, Thomas Jefferson, 353, 354, Tiffany Ann, 168, Vera Beth, 106, Vickie, 176, W.H., 374, Walter, 353, 354, Warren, 185, William, 85, 121, 353, William "Blind Billy", 266, Wilson C., 288, Zuba Olive, 360, Henry, 185, Lee, 198
WILSON BROS., Shirt Factory, 367
WILSON'S, Fertilizer, 16, Meat, 15
WILSON-, Gwyn Cem., 109
WIMMER, Steve, 131
WINCHESTER, Josiah, 182, Nora, 220, Nora Lucinda, 220
WINE, Lucille, 36
WINGER, Dorman, 69, 71, Fred, 198, Joseph, 354, Wilmer Rita, 198
WINGERT, Andrew David, 354, Anna Belle, 354, Bailey, 354, Beulah, 31, 43, 355, Charles, 354, Christopher, 354, Daniel, 354, Daniel Christopher, 354, Donald, 355, Donald H., 127, Elizabeth Ayers, 354, Ella, 354, Elvina "Ella" Susan, 354, Fannie, 43, Fred, 354, Goldia, 105, 355, Harold, 354, Henry, 354, Henry Tompkins, 354, Henry, Jr., 354, Ida, 39, 228, Jacob, 29, 40, 354, 355, Jacob Bailey, 354, James Harold, 354, 355, John, 354, John Marion, 354, 355, Joseph, 354, Joseph James, 354, Laura, 354, Lulu Jane, 354, Magadaline, 354, Magdaline, 197, Marion, 355, Opal, 355, Sarah Magaline, 229, Sarah Magdaline, 280, 302, 354, Sharon, 78, Susanna Haupt, 354, William Peter, 354
WININGER, B.F., 59, Cynthia Ellen, 282
WINKLER, Jacqueline Rose, 80, —, 128
WINTER, Ann Delilah, 179, Anna, 295, Christopher, 179, Elizabeth, 108, Elizabeth Ann, 281, John, 108, 179, 295, Katherine, 295
WISE, John, 350, Mary, 110, Nancye L., 119
WISEHART, Audrey Louise, 165, Mamie Lenore, 216
WISEHEART, Pearl, 223
WISEMAN, Martha, 211, Mary Ellen, 337
WITT, Alice, 263, Cindy, 109, Gordon "Gary", 109, Judith, 107, Julieann, 109, Susan, 109, Terry, 109
WOEFEL, Florence, 153
WOELLE, Aalje, 153
WOLF, Barbara May, 187, Kenneth D., 187, Mary, 113, Richard D., 187, Suzanne Marie, 187, Viola May, 187
WOLFE, William H., 29
WOLLAM, Nondas, 151
WOLVERTON, Andrew J., 355, Charles, 355, Cyrus, 355, Eric Lee, 355, Harold, 355, Issac, 355, Joel, 355, John, 355, John F., 355, Samuel, 355, Shirley Ann, 355, Tonya Dowell, 355, William R., 375, William Robert, 355
WOLZ, Michael, 103, Susan Ann, 103
WOOD, Annie, 252, Carter, 322, Della, 232, Elmer, 252, Elsie, 308, Floyd A., 32, Jabes, 322, Jesse, 16, Lizzie, 43, Spencer H., 12
WOODALL, Candice A., 372
WOODEN, Kenneth, 63
WOODFILL, Sue Ellen, 249
WOODFORD, Charles Kenneth, 274
WOODRIDGE, Anna, 207
WOODROW, Lydia, 151
WOODS, Bill, 230, Carol, 230, Helen, 230, Jim, 108, Lon, 309, Marylou, 108, Nancy, 309, Nelson, 197, Richard Lowell, 309, Robert, 230
WOODSON, (Capt.), 322, Ann, 149, Mary, 145
WOODWARD, Bernadine, 355, Diane Lynn, 355, Donald, 355, Elsie Rosamond, 355, James LeRoy, 355, Jill Andrea, 355, John E., 355, Joshua, 355, Julie, 355, Katherine, 355, Kenneth, 355, Marjorie, 355, Mark Alan, 355, Michael Andrew, 355, Muriel, 355, Phyllis Ann, 355, Shirley Ann, 355, Tyler, 355
WOODY, Alfred H., 356, Clara Mae, 356, Clark, 233, 356, Debbie, 356, Earl, 356, Edna, 356, Elwood, 158, 356, Gurney, 356, Hugh, 356, James, 356, John M., 356, Kristen, 356, Leonard, 158, 356, Mary, 356, Marcy C., 313, Mary Ellen, 158, 356, Matilda, 356, Nathan, 355, 356, Orville (Rev.), 356, Ralph, 356, Ralphl, 158, Raymond, 158, 356, Richard, 233, 356, Robert, 356, Thomas, 356, Walter E., 356, William C., 356
WOODRIDGE, America Louisa, 298, Elizabeth, 298, John Edward, 298
WOOLLEY, Elizabeth Jean, 107, Jean, 107, Margaret, 107, Samuel, H., 107
WOOLMAN, Elizabeth, 244, John, 244, William, 244
WRAY, Allen, 210, Alyssa, 210, Ana L., 357, Anna J., 102, Austin, 357, Carson, 102, 356, Charles, 357, Clara E., 356, Crystal, 210, Cynthian, 356, David, 98, 316, 356, 357, Edna J., 102, Edward, 102, Emelda J.A., 102, Everett E., 102, Francis Louisa, 102, Fred, 109, Greg, 210, Henry, 356, Isabella, 356, James, 356, James C., 102, Jane, 356, Jerome, 88, John M., 356, 357, John M. (Dr.), 357, John N., 357, John P., 102, 316, 356, Laura Priscilla, 316, 356, 357, Lavina, 356, Leanna J., 357, Lena, 170, Lena Linn, 102, Lettice, 356, Lisa, 210, Martha Frances, 357, Mary, 356, Mary Elizabeth, 88, Meri, 210, Nick, 210, Patti Edwards, 191, Phebe, 356, Richard, 356, Ruth, 88, Samantha, 210, Samuel, 356, Sarah J., 102, Sher, 210, Susan J., 356, Wilda James "Bud", 102, William, 357, William Carson, 102, William J., 357
WREDE, Mary, 366
WREDE'S, Service Station, 26
WREN, Frank, 43, 44, J.J., 67
WRIGHT, —, 21, Abigail, 193, Amber, 357, Barbara, 357, 358, Beth, 127, Beulah, 54, Beverly, 357, Brandon, 357, Carl, 357, Caroline, 282, Catharine, 347, Catherine, 320, Charles Albert, 202, Charles Leroy, 202, Chloral, 357, Darrell, 358, David, 357, Deborah, 202, 235, Delbert, 357, Dennis, 282, Dollie, 357, Donna Sue, 357, Electa, 244, Eliza, 215, Ella, 43, Elva May, 357, Emmett, 357, Eva Ellen, 357, Evelyn, 381, Francis, 357, 358, Gary, 202, Gerald, 357, Gladys, 242, Harry, 357, Hazel Marie, 202, Henry, 244, Herbert Leon, 357, Hubert, 357, Imogene, 357, James, 163, James Crawford, 282, Jane, 357, Janet, 357, Jim, 127, 163, 357, Joe, 163, John, 54, 357, John E., 63, John, K., 82, Joshua, 357, Julian Ann, 123, Julia Evaline, 228, Kendra, 357, Ladonna, 357, Larry, 357, Leigh O., 242, Linda, 357, Lloyd, 357, Lloyd Owen, 357, Lourvanza, 282, Margaret, 325, Marjorie, 67, 357, 358, Marvin, 357, Mary, 164, 282, Mary Luenza, 282, Matthew, 357, Melvin,

357, Merle, 357, Mike, 163, 357, Nancy, 357, Opal, 357, Orville, 263, Paul, 357, Phyllis, 357, Rene, 290, Richard, 357, Robert Owen, 357, Roger, 357, Roscoe, 357, Roy, 357, Sarah, 127, Sharon, 357, Steven E., 372, Terri, 163, Velma, 357, Versa, 357, Viola, 161, Virginia, 357, Waunita, 357, Wesley, 229, Wilbur, 263, Will, 112, William Castle, 229, James, 93, —, 42
WRIGHT'S, Alignment, 15
WRIGHTSMAN, Helen, 192, Mary, 196
WYANT, Abraham, 189, Lola Viola, 189, Mary, 189
WYATT, Adam, 358, Cecil James, 301, Connie, 358, Elizabeth, 358, George C., 358, Goldie, 358, James, 301, 358, James Summit, 358, John, 358, John B., 358, John L., 358, 375, Kathrena, 358, Marabeth, 358, Martha, 358, Mary, 358, Mary Louise, 358, Mason, 358, Norma J., 375, Philip, 358, Sharon Kay, 301, Susan, 358, Susanna, 358, Tim, 301, Tom, 301, Warder H., 358
WYCOFF, Margaret, 332
WYNN, Keenan, 342
WYNNE, Brooks, 212, Helen, 212, Judith Brooks, 212, William Thomas, 212
WYSE, George, 203, John, 203, Maria, 203, Maria Jane, 203

YAGELSKI, Paul 297
YAHRAUS, Anthony Glenn, 358, Aurelia, 358, Bonnie, 358, Bonnie Sue, 358, Edward W. 358, Florentina, 358, Tami, 358, Ted, 358, Theodor Glenn, 358, Theodor Leopold, 358, Toni, 358
YARYAN, Dora, 263
YATER, Richard L., 372
YATES, Jordan, 366
YEAGER, Diantha, 326, Gaylon Antrobus, 359, Lyn Allison, 358, 359, Osia, 327, Randolph Orville, 359, Rodney Alan, 359, Stephen W., 372
YEAKEY, Grace, 327
YEAKLEY, Benedict, 167, George, 167, Susan, 167, Susannah, 159
YELTON, Charlotte, 233
YENSER, Paula, 202
YONALLY, Alice, 235, Dewey, 235, Ginny, 235
YORK, Brandey, 292, Elizabeth, 292, Joe, 372
YOST, Doris, 246
YOUEL, Jane, 41, Williem, 41, —, 42
YOUELL, James, 30, Mary, 100
YOUNG, Albert A., 345, Allen, 359, Beacher, 107, Charles, 359, Clairborne, 51, Cyrus S., 85, 359, Don, 359, Don A., 372, Effie Elizabeth, 359, Emma, 184, Ernest, 359, George, 359, Glenda, 359, Guy M., 359, Harrison, 170, Harrison, 359, Harry, 359, Irene, 359, Jill, 54, John M., 359, Kate, 285, Kathleen, 359, Kathryn, 359, Kisha, 359, Lavanche, 359, Lloyd, 359, Loretta, 342, Lura, 359, Mary, 185, Mary E., 186, Mary G., 287, Metal Production, 14, Norma Deuece, 262, Sarah, 359, Steven, 359, Tamsen, 359, Terry, 359, Thomas, 186, Virginia, 359, Walter, 335, Walter, 359, Walter Vick, 359, William, 51, 359, William Price, 359
YOUNG BROTHERS MEAT, 14
YOUNGS, Karen, 252
YOUNKIN, Chance, 278
YOUNKIN, Charade, 278
YOUNT, 6, Alice Merle, 360, Andrew, 64, 68, Bessie, 360, Carrie, 360, Clara, 360, Clarence, 360, Dan, 359, Daniel, 224, Eugene, 360, Francis, 360, George Morton, 360, Harry, 360, Helen 360, James W., 359, Joe, 360, John 360, Lavine, 360, Mary J., 359, Matilda, 359, Nettie, 360, Ruth, 360, Sarah, 360, Sherman, 360, Sophine, 359, Tom, 360
ZACH, Barb, 368, Barbara, 360, Becky, 360, 368, Bill, 360, 368, 369, Helen 360, Herbert, 360, James William, 88, 360, Jay, 360, 369, Jim, 88, 360, 368, 369, Joan, 360, 368, 369, Karen, 4, 15, 21, 29, 88, 108, 138, 172, 190, 277, 310, 315, 319, 360, 369, Karen Bazzani, 325, Mary Joan, 360, Rebecca, 360, Sara Suzette, 360, Suzie, 24, 360, 369, William A., 360
ZACH'S FAMILY RESTAURANT, 368
ZACHARY, Alice, 361, Alvin, 361, Anna, 361, Betty, 215, Catherine, 361, Cecil E., 375, Celia, 360, Charley, 361, Charlotte (Chris), 56, Charlotte H., 372, Corda, 251, Edith, 225, Elijah, 360, 361, Elijah, Jr., 361, Elizabeth, 360, 361, Ellen, 361, Enoch, 361, Ephraim, 106, Esther, 147, Eva, 362, Evelyn, 147, George, 361, Hazel Leola, 106, Isaphema, 361, James, 360, 361, Jimison, 361, Joe, 147, John Peter, 360, John Wesley, 360, Kesiah, 361, Lelia G., 353, 3690, Lena Belle, 361, Margaret, 361, Martha, 361, Mary, 131, Mary Eleate, 361, Mary Ellen, 361, Melvina, 361, Milton, Hezekiah, 361, Minnie Ann, 360, Miranda, 360, Nancy Ann, 360, Polly, 361, Redden, 361, Samuel, 361, Samuel Marion, 360, Sarah (Sallie) E., 360, Sarah B., 361, William, 360
ZACHGO, Jeanette, 288
ZACKERY, Eileen, 336
ZALOUDEK, W.A., 78
ZEIGLER, John 350, Julie, 350, Kenten, 350, Raymond, 350
ZELLER, Bud, 296, June, 296
ZENOR, Claribel, 113, Mary, 108
ZERBE, Henry, 174
ZIEGLER, Melba, 351
ZIMERMAN, Delma, 361
ZIMMERLIE, Margaret, 94
ZIMMERMAN, Amaza, 250, Betty, 361, Beulah F., 361, Catherine, 294, Donald, 250, Fred, 361, George Washington, 29, Jacob, 29, 130, John M., 29, Kay, 106, Laurie, 196, Marilyn, 257, Marvin, 106, Mary Lou, 14, Molly Ann, 106, Nancy, 130, 164, Neva Bymaster, 112, Owen Allen, 361, Pattie, 361, Pauline, 106, Sharon, 106, Stanley, 250, Stanley, Jr., 250, Stella May, 157, 322, Terry, 250, Tom, 361, William, 40, William, 41, William H., 29, William Lewis, 322, —, 55
ZOOK, Lizzie, 241
ZUCCK, Matilda, 115
ZUCK, Anna Bessie, 361, Bessie, 342, Beulah Ernestine, 350, 361, Catherine Eva, 361, Catherine Suzanne, 350, Charles, 165, Charles, Jr., 187, Ella, 165, Emaline, 361, Ernest, 350, Ernest, 361, Genevive, 350, Gerald, 350, Gerald, 361, Gerald W., 350, 361, Hugh Ernest, 350, 361, J., 68, Jasper Newton, 361, John, 361, John Frederick, 361, Martha, 186, Suzanne Catherine, 361, Theresa, 350, Uma, 350, Umasie, 361, William, 186, Samuel, 41

NOTES

NOTES

NOTES

NOTES

Waveland School, built 1912

Old Township Road, Ripley Township

Wingate Hotel 1903, left to right-Bourbon Thompson, wife Addie, daughter Florence, unknown, Front Row-Thomas Thompson, unknown, Mr. Stokes, Dave Gardner, unknown, in front, Hary Gardner, Sam Oxley, Front Row-Blanche Thompson, William Marmaduke and Dr. Card

Historical Yount Wollen Mill located 4 miles West of Crawfordsville at Yountsville on Road 32

www.ingramcontent.com/pod-product-compliance
Lightning Source LLC
Chambersburg PA
CBHW081944230426
43669CB00019B/2920